P9-CJF-561

OXFORD

ESSENTIAL
WORLD
ATLAS

The editors are grateful to the following for acting as specialist geography consultants on "The World in Focus" front section:

Professor D. Brunsden, Kings College, University of London, UK
Dr C. Clarke, Oxford University, UK
Dr I. S. Evans, Durham University, UK
Professor P. Haggett, University of Bristol, UK
Professor K. McLachlan, University of London, UK
Professor M. Monmonier, Syracuse University, New York, USA
Professor M-L. Hsu, University of Minnesota, Minnesota, USA
Professor M. J. Tooley, University of St Andrews, UK
Dr T. Unwin, Royal Holloway, University of London, UK

THE WORLD IN FOCUS
Cartography by Philip's

Picture Acknowledgements
Robin Scagell/Galaxy page 3

Illustrations: Stefan Chabluk

WORLD CITIES
Cartography by Philip's

Page 10, Dublin: The town plan of Dublin is based on Ordnance Survey Ireland by permission of the Government Permit Number 8408. © Ordnance Survey Ireland and Government of Ireland.

Page 11, Edinburgh, and page 15, London:
This product includes mapping data licensed from Ordnance Survey® with the permission of the Controller of Her Majesty's Stationery Office. © Crown copyright 2008. All rights reserved. Licence number 100011710.

Vector data courtesy of Gräfe and Unser Verlag GmbH, München, Germany
(city-center maps of Bangkok, Beijing, Cape Town, Jerusalem, Mexico City, Moscow, Singapore, Sydney, Tokyo, and Washington D.C.)
The following city maps utilize base data supplied courtesy of MapQuest.com, Inc. (© MapQuest)
(Las Vegas, New Orleans, Orlando)

All satellite images in this section courtesy of NPA Group, Edenbridge, Kent (www.satmaps.com)

Copyright © 2008 Philip's

Philip's, a division of
Octopus Publishing Group Limited,
2–4 Heron Quays, London E14 4JP
www.octopusbooks.co.uk
An Hachette Livre UK Company
www.hachettelivre.co.uk

Published in North America by
Oxford University Press, Inc.,
198 Madison Avenue,
New York, NY 10016

www.oup.com/us/atlas

OXFORD   Oxford is a registered trademark
UNIVERSITY PRESS   of Oxford University Press

All rights reserved. No part of this publication may be reproduced, stored in a retrieval system, or transmitted, in any form or by any means, electronic, mechanical, photocopying, recording, or otherwise, without the prior permission of the publisher.

Library of Congress Cataloging-in-Publication Data available

ISBN 978-0-19-537386-8

Printing (last digit):
9 8 7 6 5 4 3 2 1

Printed in Hong Kong

OXFORD

ESSENTIAL WORLD ATLAS

FIFTH EDITION

Contents

World Statistics

Countries   vi
Physical Dimensions   vii
User Guide   viii

The World in Focus

Planet Earth   2–3
Restless Earth   4–5
Landforms   6–7
Oceans   8–9
Climate   10–11
Water and Vegetation   12–13
Environment   14–15
Population   16–17
The Human Family   18–19
Wealth   20–21
Quality of Life   22–23
Energy   24–25
Production   26–27
Trade   28–29
Travel and Tourism   30–31

World Cities

Amsterdam   2
Athens   2
Atlanta   3
Baghdad   3
Bangkok   3
Barcelona   4
Beijing   4
Berlin   5
Boston   6
Brussels   6
Budapest   7
Buenos Aires   7
Cairo   7
Cape Town   8
Copenhagen   8
Chicago   9
Delhi   10
Dublin   10
Edinburgh   11
Guangzhou   11
Helsinki   11
Hong Kong   12
Istanbul   12
Jakarta   12
Jerusalem   13
Johannesburg   13
Karachi   13
Kolkata   14
Lagos   14
Las Vegas   14
Lima   14
London   15
Lisbon   16
Los Angeles   16
Madrid   17
Manila   17
Melbourne   18
Mexico City   18
Miami   18
Milan   19
Moscow   19
Montréal   20
Mumbai   20
Munich   21
New Orleans   21
New York   22
Orlando   23
Osaka   23
Oslo   23
Paris   24
Prague   25
Rio de Janeiro   25
Rome   26
San Francisco   26
St Petersburg   27
Santiago   27
São Paulo   27
Seoul   27
Shanghai   28
Singapore   28
Stockholm   29
Sydney   29
Tokyo   30
Tehran   31
Toronto   31
Vienna   32
Warsaw   32
Washington   33
Wellington   33
Index to City Maps   34–39
World Cities Satellite Images   40–48

World Maps

Map Symbols   1

The World: Political
1:95 000 000   2–3

Arctic Ocean
1:35 000 000   4

Antarctica
1:35 000 000   5

Europe

Europe: Physical
1:20 000 000   6

Europe: Political
1:20 000 000   7

Scandinavia 1:6 000 000
Iceland 1:6 000 000
Færoe Islands 1:6 000 000
                                   8–9

Ireland 1:2 000 000
                                   10

Scotland 1:2 000 000
                                   11

England and Wales
1:2 000 000
                                   12–13

British Isles 1:5 000 000
                                   14

Netherlands, Belgium and
Luxembourg 1:2 500 000

                                   15

Central Europe 1:5 000 000

                                   16–17

Eastern Europe and Turkey
1:10 000 000

                                   18–19

France 1:5 000 000
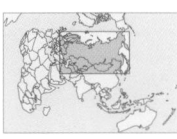
                                   20

Spain and Portugal
1:5 000 000

                                   21

Italy and the Balkan States
1:5 000 000

                                   22–23

The Balearics, the Canaries and
Madeira 1:1 000 000 / 1:2 000 000

                                   24

Malta, Crete, Corfu, Rhodes
and Cyprus
1:1 000 000 / 1:1 300 000

                                   25

Asia

Asia: Physical 1:47 000 000   26

Asia: Political 1:47 000 000   27

Russia and Central Asia
1:20 000 000

                                   28–29

Japan 1:5 000 000
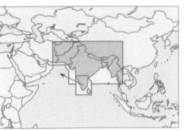
                                   30–31

China and the Far East
1:15 000 000
Hong Kong and Macau 1:1 000 000
                                   32–33

Northern China and Korea
1:6 000 000
                                   34–35

Indonesia and the Philippines
1:12 500 000
Java and Madura 1:7 500 000
Bali 1:2 000 000
                                   36–37

Mainland Southeast Asia
1:6 000 000
Ko Phuket 1:1 000 000
Ko Samui 1:1 000 000
Pinang 1:1 000 000
Singapore 1:1 000 000
                                   38–39

South Asia 1:10 000 000
                                   40–41

Northern India, Pakistan and Nepal
1:6 000 000
Jammu and Kashmir 1:6 000 000

42–43

The Middle East
1:7 000 000

44–45

The Near East 1:2 500 000

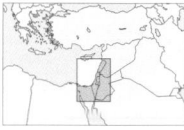

46

Arabia and the Horn of Africa 1:15 000 000

47

Africa

Africa: Physical
1:42 000 000   **48**

Africa: Political
1:42 000 000   **49**

Northern Africa
1:15 000 000
Azores 1:15 000 000
Cape Verde Islands 1:10 000 000

50–51

Central and Southern Africa
1:15 000 000
Seychelles 1:2 500 000
Réunion 1:2 500 000
Mauritius 1:2 500 000
Comoros 1:8 000 000

52–53

East Africa 1:8 000 000

54–55

Southern Africa
1:8 000 000
Madagascar 1:8 000 000

56–57

Australia and Oceania

Australia and Oceania: Physical and Political
1:50 000 000   **58**

New Zealand 1:6 000 000
Samoan Islands 1:6 000 000
Fiji 1:6 000 000
Tonga 1:6 000 000
Tahiti and Moorea 1:1 000 000

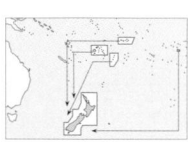

59

Western Australia
1:8 000 000

60–61

Eastern Australia
1:8 000 000
Torres Strait 1:8 000 000
Whitsunday Islands 1:2 500 000
Tasmania 1:8 000 000

62–63

Pacific Ocean
1:51 000 000   **64–65**

North America

North America: Physical
1:35 000 000   **66**

North America: Political
1:35 000 000   **67**

Canada 1:15 000 000

68–69

Western Canada 1:7 000 000

70–71

Eastern Canada 1:7 000 000

72–73

United States 1:15 000 000
Hawai'i 1:15 000 000
Alaska 1:15 000 000

74–75

United States – West
1:6 700 000

76–77

Central and Southern California and Western Washington
1:2 500 000

78–79

United States – Midwest and Northeast
1:6 700 000

00–01

Northeastern United States
1:2 500 000

82–83

United States – South
1:6 700 000

84–85

Mexico 1:8 000 000

86–87

Central America and the West Indies 1:8 000 000
Jamaica 1:3 000 000
Guadeloupe 1:2 000 000
Martinique 1:2 000 000
Puerto Rico 1:3 000 000
Virgin Islands 1:2 000 000
St Lucia 1:2 000 000
Barbados 1:2 000 000

88–89

South America

South America: Physical
1:35 000 000   **90**

South America: Political
1:35 000 000   **91**

South America – North
1:16 000 000
Trinidad and Tobago 1:2 500 000

92–93

Central South America
1:8 000 000

94–95

South America – South
1:16 000 000

96

Index to World Maps
97–176

World Statistics: Countries

This alphabetical list includes the principal countries and territories of the world. If a territory is not completely independent, the country it is associated with is named. The area figures give the total area of land, inland water, and ice. The population figures are 2007 estimates where available. The annual income is the Gross Domestic Product per capita in US dollars. The figures are the latest available, usually 2007 estimates.

Country/Territory	Area km² Thousands	Area miles² Thousands	Population Thousands	Capital	Annual Income US $
Afghanistan	652	252	31,890	Kabul	800
Albania	28.7	11.1	3,601	Tirana	5,500
Algeria	2,382	920	33,333	Algiers	8,100
American Samoa (US)	0.20	0.08	58	Pago Pago	5,800
Andorra	0.47	0.18	72	Andorra La Vella	38,800
Angola	1,247	481	12,264	Luanda	6,500
Anguilla (UK)	0.10	0.04	14	The Valley	8,800
Antigua & Barbuda	0.44	0.17	69	St John's	10,900
Argentina	2,780	1,074	40,302	Buenos Aires	13,000
Armenia	29.8	11.5	2,972	Yerevan	5,700
Aruba (Netherlands)	0.19	0.07	100	Oranjestad	21,800
Australia	7,741	2,989	20,434	Canberra	37,500
Austria	83.9	32.4	8,200	Vienna	39,000
Azerbaijan	86.6	33.4	8,120	Baku	9,000
Azores (Portugal)	2.2	0.86	236	Ponta Delgada	15,000
Bahamas	13.9	5.4	306	Nassau	22,700
Bahrain	0.69	0.27	709	Manama	34,700
Bangladesh	144	55.6	150,448	Dhaka	1,400
Barbados	0.43	0.17	281	Bridgetown	19,700
Belarus	208	80.2	9,725	Minsk	10,200
Belgium	30.5	11.8	10,392	Brussels	36,500
Belize	23.0	8.9	294	Belmopan	7,800
Benin	113	43.5	9,078	Porto-Novo	1,500
Bermuda (UK)	0.05	0.02	66	Hamilton	69,900
Bhutan	47.0	18.1	2,328	Thimphu	1,400
Bolivia	1,099	424	9,119	La Paz/Sucre	4,400
Bosnia-Herzegovina	51.2	19.8	4,552	Sarajevo	6,600
Botswana	582	225	1,816	Gaborone	14,700
Brazil	8,514	3,287	190,011	Brasília	9,700
Brunei	5.8	2.2	375	Bandar Seri Begawan	25,600
Bulgaria	111	42.8	7,323	Sofia	11,800
Burkina Faso	274	106	14,326	Ouagadougou	1,200
Burma (=Myanmar)	677	261	47,374	Rangoon/Naypyidaw	1,900
Burundi	27.8	10.7	8,391	Bujumbura	800
Cambodia	181	69.9	13,996	Phnom Penh	1,800
Cameroon	475	184	18,060	Yaoundé	2,300
Canada	9,971	3,850	33,390	Ottawa	38,200
Canary Is. (Spain)	7.2	2.8	1,682	Las Palmas/Santa Cruz	19,900
Cape Verde Is.	4.0	1.6	424	Praia	7,000
Cayman Is. (UK)	0.26	0.10	47	George Town	43,800
Central African Republic	623	241	4,369	Bangui	700
Chad	1,284	496	9,886	Ndjaména	1,600
Chile	757	292	16,285	Santiago	14,400
China	9,597	3,705	1,321,852	Beijing	5,300
Colombia	1,139	440	44,380	Bogotá	7,200
Comoros	2.2	0.86	711	Moroni	600
Congo	342	132	3,801	Brazzaville	3,700
Congo (Dem. Rep. of the)	2,345	905	65,752	Kinshasa	300
Cook Is. (NZ)	0.24	0.09	22	Avarua	9,100
Costa Rica	51.1	19.7	4,134	San José	13,500
Croatia	56.5	21.8	4,493	Zagreb	15,500
Cuba	111	42.8	11,394	Havana	4,500
Cyprus	9.3	3.6	788	Nicosia	24,600
Czech Republic	78.9	30.5	10,229	Prague	24,400
Denmark	43.1	16.6	5,468	Copenhagen	37,400
Djibouti	23.2	9.0	496	Djibouti	1,000
Dominica	0.75	0.29	72	Roseau	3,800
Dominican Republic	48.5	18.7	9,366	Santo Domingo	9,200
East Timor	14.9	5.7	1,085	Dili	800
Ecuador	284	109	13,756	Quito	7,100
Egypt	1,001	387	80,335	Cairo	5,400
El Salvador	21.0	8.1	6,948	San Salvador	5,200
Equatorial Guinea	28.1	10.8	551	Malabo	4,100
Eritrea	118	45.4	4,907	Asmara	1,000
Estonia	45.1	17.4	1,316	Tallinn	21,800
Ethiopia	1,104	426	76,512	Addis Ababa	700
Faroe Is. (Denmark)	1.4	0.54	48	Tórshavn	31,000
Fiji	18.3	7.1	919	Suva	4,100
Finland	338	131	5,238	Helsinki	35,500
France	552	213	60,876	Paris	33,800
French Guiana (France)	90.0	34.7	200	Cayenne	8,300
French Polynesia (France)	4.0	1.5	279	Papeete	17,500
Gabon	268	103	1,455	Libreville	13,800
Gambia, The	11.3	4.4	1,688	Banjul	800
Gaza Strip (OPT)*	0.36	0.14	1,482	–	1,100
Georgia	69.7	26.9	4,646	Tbilisi	4,200
Germany	357	138	82,401	Berlin	34,400
Ghana	239	92.1	22,931	Accra	1,400
Gibraltar (UK)	0.006	0.002	28	Gibraltar Town	38,200
Greece	132	50.9	10,706	Athens	30,500
Greenland (Denmark)	2,176	840	56	Nuuk	20,000
Grenada	0.34	0.13	90	St George's	3,900
Guadeloupe (France)	1.7	0.66	453	Basse-Terre	7,900
Guam (US)	0.55	0.21	173	Agana	15,000
Guatemala	109	42.0	12,728	Guatemala City	5,400
Guinea	246	94.9	9,948	Conakry	1,000
Guinea-Bissau	36.1	13.9	1,473	Bissau	600
Guyana	215	83.0	769	Georgetown	5,300
Haiti	27.8	10.7	8,706	Port-au-Prince	1,900
Honduras	112	43.3	7,484	Tegucigalpa	3,300
Hungary	93.0	35.9	9,956	Budapest	19,500
Iceland	103	39.8	302	Reykjavik	39,400
India	3,287	1,269	1,129,866	New Delhi	2,700
Indonesia	1,905	735	234,694	Jakarta	3,400
Iran	1,648	636	65,398	Tehran	12,300
Iraq	438	169	27,500	Baghdad	3,600
Ireland	70.3	27.1	4,109	Dublin	45,600
Israel	20.6	8.0	6,427	Jerusalem	28,800
Italy	301	116	58,148	Rome	31,000
Ivory Coast (=Côte d'Ivoire)	322	125	18,013	Yamoussoukro	1,800
Jamaica	11.0	4.2	2,780	Kingston	4,800
Japan	378	146	127,433	Tokyo	33,800
Jordan	89.3	34.5	6,053	Amman	4,700
Kazakhstan	2,725	1,052	15,285	Astana	11,100
Kenya	580	224	36,914	Nairobi	1,600
Kiribati	0.73	0.28	108	Tarawa	1,800
Korea, North	121	46.5	23,302	Pyŏngyang	1,900
Korea, South	99.3	38.3	49,045	Seoul	24,600
Kosovo	10.9	4.2	2,127	Pristina	1,800
Kuwait	17.8	6.9	2,506	Kuwait City	55,300
Kyrgyzstan	200	77.2	5,284	Bishkek	2,000
Laos	237	91.4	6,522	Vientiane	1,900

Country/Territory	Area km² Thousands	Area miles² Thousands	Population Thousands	Capital	Annual Income US $
Latvia	64.6	24.9	2,260	Riga	17,700
Lebanon	10.4	4.0	3,926	Beirut	10,400
Lesotho	30.4	11.7	2,125	Maseru	1,500
Liberia	111	43.0	3,196	Monrovia	500
Libya	1,760	679	6,037	Tripoli	13,100
Liechtenstein	0.16	0.06	34	Vaduz	25,000
Lithuania	65.2	25.2	3,575	Vilnius	16,700
Luxembourg	2.6	1.0	480	Luxembourg	80,800
Macedonia (FYROM)	25.7	9.9	2,056	Skopje	8,400
Madagascar	587	227	19,449	Antananarivo	1,000
Madeira (Portugal)	0.78	0.30	241	Funchal	22,700
Malawi	118	45.7	13,603	Lilongwe	800
Malaysia	330	127	24,821	Kuala Lumpur/Putrajaya	14,400
Maldives	0.30	0.12	369	Malé	3,900
Mali	1,240	479	11,995	Bamako	1,200
Malta	0.32	0.12	402	Valletta	23,700
Marshall Is.	0.18	0.07	62	Majuro	2,900
Martinique (France)	1.1	0.43	436	Fort-de-France	14,400
Mauritania	1,026	396	3,270	Nouakchott	1,800
Mauritius	2.0	0.79	1,251	Port Louis	11,900
Mayotte (France)	0.37	0.14	209	Mamoudzou	4,900
Mexico	1,958	756	108,701	Mexico City	12,500
Micronesia, Fed. States of	0.70	0.27	108	Palikir	2,300
Moldova	33.9	13.1	4,320	Chişinău	2,200
Monaco	0.001	0.0004	33	Monaco	30,000
Mongolia	1,567	605	2,952	Ulan Bator	2,900
Montenegro	14.0	5.4	685	Podgorica	3,800
Morocco	447	172	33,757	Rabat	3,800
Mozambique	802	309	20,906	Maputo	900
Namibia	824	318	2,055	Windhoek	5,200
Nauru	0.02	0.008	14	Yaren District	5,000
Nepal	147	56.8	28,902	Katmandu	1,100
Netherlands	41.5	16.0	16,571	Amsterdam/The Hague	38,600
Netherlands Antilles (Neths)	0.80	0.31	224	Willemstad	16,000
New Caledonia (France)	18.6	7.2	222	Nouméa	15,000
New Zealand	271	104	4,116	Wellington	27,300
Nicaragua	130	50.2	5,675	Managua	3,200
Niger	1,267	489	12,895	Niamey	700
Nigeria	924	357	135,031	Abuja	2,200
Northern Mariana Is. (US)	0.46	0.18	85	Saipan	12,500
Norway	324	125	4,628	Oslo	55,600
Oman	310	119	3,205	Muscat	19,100
Pakistan	796	307	164,742	Islamabad	2,600
Palau	0.46	0.18	21	Melekeok	7,600
Panama	75.5	29.2	3,242	Panamá	9,000
Papua New Guinea	463	179	5,796	Port Moresby	2,900
Paraguay	407	157	6,669	Asunción	4,000
Peru	1,285	496	28,675	Lima	7,600
Philippines	300	116	91,077	Manila	3,300
Poland	323	125	38,518	Warsaw	16,200
Portugal	88.8	34.3	10,643	Lisbon	21,800
Puerto Rico (US)	8.9	3.4	3,944	San Juan	19,600
Qatar	11.0	4.2	907	Doha	29,400
Réunion (France)	2.5	0.97	788	St-Denis	6,200
Romania	238	92.0	22,276	Bucharest	11,100
Russia	17,075	6,593	141,378	Moscow	14,600
Rwanda	26.3	10.2	9,908	Kigali	1,000
St Kitts & Nevis	0.26	0.10	39	Basseterre	8,200
St Lucia	0.54	0.21	171	Castries	4,800
St Vincent & Grenadines	0.39	0.15	118	Kingstown	3,600
Samoa	2.8	1.1	214	Apia	2,100
San Marino	0.06	0.02	30	San Marino	34,100
São Tomé & Príncipe	0.96	0.37	200	São Tomé	1,200
Saudi Arabia	2,150	830	27,601	Riyadh	20,700
Senegal	197	76.0	12,522	Dakar	1,700
Serbia	77.5	29.9	8,024	Belgrade	7,700
Seychelles	0.46	0.18	82	Victoria	18,400
Sierra Leone	71.7	27.7	6,145	Freetown	800
Singapore	0.68	0.26	4,553	Singapore City	48,900
Slovak Republic	49.0	18.9	5,448	Bratislava	19,800
Slovenia	20.3	7.8	2,009	Ljubljana	27,300
Solomon Is.	28.9	11.2	567	Honiara	600
Somalia	638	246	9,119	Mogadishu	600
South Africa	1,221	471	43,998	Cape Town/Pretoria	10,600
Spain	498	192	40,448	Madrid	33,700
Sri Lanka	65.6	25.3	20,926	Colombo	4,100
Sudan	2,506	967	39,379	Khartoum	2,500
Suriname	163	63.0	471	Paramaribo	7,800
Swaziland	17.4	6.7	1,133	Mbabane	4,800
Sweden	450	174	9,031	Stockholm	36,900
Switzerland	41.3	15.9	7,555	Bern	39,800
Syria	185	71.5	19,315	Damascus	4,500
Taiwan	36.0	13.9	22,859	Taipei	29,800
Tajikistan	143	55.3	7,077	Dushanbe	1,600
Tanzania	945	365	39,384	Dodoma	1,100
Thailand	513	198	65,068	Bangkok	8,000
Togo	56.8	21.9	5,702	Lomé	900
Tonga	0.65	0.25	117	Nuku'alofa	2,200
Trinidad & Tobago	5.1	2.0	1,057	Port of Spain	21,700
Tunisia	164	63.2	10,276	Tunis	7,500
Turkey	775	299	71,159	Ankara	9,400
Turkmenistan	488	188	5,097	Ashkhabad	9,200
Turks & Caicos Is. (UK)	0.43	0.17	22	Cockburn Town	11,500
Tuvalu	0.03	0.01	12	Fongafale	1,600
Uganda	241	93.1	30,263	Kampala	1,100
Ukraine	604	233	46,300	Kiev	6,900
United Arab Emirates	83.6	32.3	4,444	Abu Dhabi	55,200
United Kingdom	242	93.4	60,776	London	35,300
United States of America	9,629	3,718	301,140	Washington, DC	46,000
Uruguay	175	67.6	3,461	Montevideo	10,700
Uzbekistan	447	173	27,780	Tashkent	2,200
Vanuatu	12.2	4.7	212	Port-Vila	2,900
Venezuela	912	352	26,024	Caracas	12,800
Vietnam	332	128	85,262	Hanoi	2,600
Virgin Is. (UK)	0.15	0.06	24	Road Town	38,500
Virgin Is. (US)	0.35	0.13	108	Charlotte Amalie	14,500
Wallis & Futuna Is. (France)	0.20	0.08	16	Mata-Utu	3,800
West Bank (OPT)*	5.9	2.3	2,536	–	1,100
Western Sahara	266	103	383	El Aaiún	N/A
Yemen	528	204	22,231	Sana'	2,400
Zambia	753	291	11,477	Lusaka	1,400
Zimbabwe	391	151	12,311	Harare	500

*OPT = Occupied Palestinian Territory N/A = Not available

World Statistics: Physical Dimensions

E ach topic list is divided into continents and within a continent the items are listed in order of size. The bottom part of many of the lists is selective in order to give examples from as many different countries as possible. The order of the continents is the same as in the atlas, beginning with Europe and ending with South America. The figures are rounded as appropriate.

World, Continents, Oceans

	km²	miles²	%
The World	509,450,000	196,672,000	–
Land	149,450,000	57,688,000	29.3
Water	360,000,000	138,984,000	70.7
Asia	44,500,000	17,177,000	29.8
Africa	30,302,000	11,697,000	20.3
North America	24,241,000	9,357,000	16.2
South America	17,793,000	6,868,000	11.9
Antarctica	14,100,000	5,443,000	9.4
Europe	9,957,000	3,843,000	6.7
Australia & Oceania	8,557,000	3,303,000	5.7
Pacific Ocean	155,557,000	60,061,000	46.4
Atlantic Ocean	76,762,000	29,638,000	22.9
Indian Ocean	68,556,000	26,470,000	20.4
Southern Ocean	20,327,000	7,848,000	6.1
Arctic Ocean	14,056,000	5,427,000	4.2

Ocean Depths

Atlantic Ocean	m	ft
Puerto Rico (Milwaukee) Deep	8,605	28,232
Cayman Trench	7,680	25,197
Gulf of Mexico	5,203	17,070
Mediterranean Sea	5,121	16,801
Black Sea	2,211	7,254
North Sea	660	2,165

Indian Ocean	m	ft
Java Trench	7,450	24,442
Red Sea	2,635	8,454

Pacific Ocean	m	ft
Mariana Trench	11,022	36,161
Tonga Trench	10,882	35,702
Japan Trench	10,554	34,626
Kuril Trench	10,542	34,587

Arctic Ocean	m	ft
Molloy Deep	5,608	18,399

Southern Ocean	m	ft
South Sandwich Trench	7,235	23,737

Mountains

Europe		m	ft
Elbrus	Russia	5,642	18,510
Dykh-Tau	Russia	5,205	17,076
Shkhara	Russia/Georgia	5,201	17,064
Koshtan-Tau	Russia	5,152	16,903
Kazbek	Russia/Georgia	5,047	16,558
Pushkin	Russia/Georgia	5,033	16,512
Katyn-Tau	Russia/Georgia	4,979	16,335
Shota Rustaveli	Russia/Georgia	4,860	15,945
Mont Blanc	France/Italy	4,808	15,774
Monte Rosa	Italy/Switzerland	4,634	15,203
Dom	Switzerland	4,545	14,911
Liskamm	Switzerland	4,527	14,852
Weisshorn	Switzerland	4,505	14,780
Taschorn	Switzerland	4,490	14,730
Matterhorn/Cervino	Italy/Switzerland	4,478	14,691
Grossglockner	Austria	3,797	12,457
Mulhacén	Spain	3,478	11,411
Zugspitze	Germany	2,962	9,718
Olympus	Greece	2,917	9,570
Galdhøpiggen	Norway	2,469	8,100
Ben Nevis	UK	1,342	4,403

Asia		m	ft
Everest	China/Nepal	8,850	29,035
K2 (Godwin Austen)	China/Kashmir	8,611	28,251
Kanchenjunga	India/Nepal	8,598	28,208
Lhotse	China/Nepal	8,516	27,939
Makalu	China/Nepal	8,481	27,824
Cho Oyu	China/Nepal	8,201	26,906
Dhaulagiri	Nepal	8,167	26,795
Manaslu	Nepal	8,156	26,760
Nanga Parbat	Kashmir	8,126	26,660
Annapurna	Nepal	8,078	26,502
Gasherbrum	China/Kashmir	8,068	26,469
Broad Peak	China/Kashmir	8,051	26,414
Xixabangma	China	8,012	26,286
Kangbachen	Nepal	7,858	25,781
Trivor	Pakistan	7,720	25,328
Pik Imeni Ismail Samani	Tajikistan	7,495	24,590
Demavend	Iran	5,604	18,386
Ararat	Turkey	5,165	16,945
Gunong Kinabalu	Malaysia (Borneo)	4,101	13,455
Fuji-San	Japan	3,776	12,388

Africa		m	ft
Kilimanjaro	Tanzania	5,895	19,340
Mt Kenya	Kenya	5,199	17,057
Ruwenzori (Margherita)	Ug./Congo (D.R.)	5,109	16,762
Meru	Tanzania	4,565	14,977
Ras Dashen	Ethiopia	4,533	14,872
Karisimbi	Rwanda/Congo (D.R.)	4,507	14,787
Mt Elgon	Kenya/Uganda	4,321	14,176
Batu	Ethiopia	4,307	14,130
Toubkal	Morocco	4,165	13,665
Mt Cameroun	Cameroon	4,070	13,353

Oceania		m	ft
Puncak Jaya	Indonesia	5,029	16,499
Puncak Trikora	Indonesia	4,730	15,518
Puncak Mandala	Indonesia	4,702	15,427
Mt Wilhelm	Papua New Guinea	4,508	14,790
Mauna Kea	USA (Hawai'i)	4,205	13,796
Mauna Loa	USA (Hawai'i)	4,169	13,681
Aoraki Mt Cook	New Zealand	3,753	12,313
Mt Kosciuszko	Australia	2,228	7,310

North America		m	ft
Mt McKinley (Denali)	USA (Alaska)	6,194	20,321
Mt Logan	Canada	5,959	19,551
Pico de Orizaba	Mexico	5,610	18,405
Mt St Elias	USA/Canada	5,489	18,008
Popocatépetl	Mexico	5,452	17,887
Mt Foraker	USA (Alaska)	5,304	17,401
Iztaccihuatl	Mexico	5,286	17,343
Mt Lucania	Canada	5,226	17,146
Mt Steele	Canada	5,073	16,644
Mt Bona	USA (Alaska)	5,005	16,420
Mt Whitney	USA	4,418	14,495
Tajumulco	Guatemala	4,220	13,845
Chirripó Grande	Costa Rica	3,837	12,589
Pico Duarte	Dominican Rep.	3,175	10,417

South America		m	ft
Aconcagua	Argentina	6,962	22,841
Bonete	Argentina	6,872	22,546
Ojos del Salado	Argentina/Chile	6,863	22,516
Pissis	Argentina	6,779	22,241
Mercedario	Argentina/Chile	6,770	22,211
Huascarán	Peru	6,768	22,204
Llullaillaco	Argentina/Chile	6,723	22,057
Nevado de Cachi	Argentina	6,720	22,047
Yerupaja	Peru	6,632	21,758
Sajama	Bolivia	6,520	21,391
Chimborazo	Ecuador	6,267	20,561
Pico Cristóbal Colón	Colombia	5,800	19,029
Pico Bolívar	Venezuela	5,007	16,427

Antarctica	m	ft
Vinson Massif	4,897	16,066
Mt Kirkpatrick	4,528	14,855

Rivers

Europe		km	miles
Volga	Caspian Sea	3,700	2,300
Danube	Black Sea	2,850	1,770
Ural	Caspian Sea	2,535	1,575
Dnepr (Dnipro)	Black Sea	2,285	1,420
Kama	Volga	2,030	1,260
Don	Black Sea	1,990	1,240
Petchora	Arctic Ocean	1,790	1,110
Oka	Volga	1,480	920
Dnister (Dniester)	Black Sea	1,400	870
Vyatka	Kama	1,370	850
Rhine	North Sea	1,320	820
N. Dvina	Arctic Ocean	1,290	800
Elbe	North Sea	1,145	710

Asia		km	miles
Yangtze	Pacific Ocean	6,380	3,960
Yenisey–Angara	Arctic Ocean	5,550	3,445
Huang He	Pacific Ocean	5,464	3,395
Ob–Irtysh	Arctic Ocean	5,410	3,360
Mekong	Pacific Ocean	4,500	2,795
Amur	Pacific Ocean	4,442	2,760
Lena	Arctic Ocean	4,402	2,735
Irtysh	Ob	4,250	2,640
Yenisey	Arctic Ocean	4,090	2,540
Ob	Arctic Ocean	3,680	2,285
Indus	Indian Ocean	3,100	1,925
Brahmaputra	Indian Ocean	2,900	1,800
Syrdarya	Aral Sea	2,860	1,775
Salween	Indian Ocean	2,800	1,740
Euphrates	Indian Ocean	2,700	1,675
Amudarya	Aral Sea	2,540	1,575

Africa		km	miles
Nile	Mediterranean	6,695	4,160
Congo	Atlantic Ocean	4,670	2,900
Niger	Atlantic Ocean	4,180	2,595
Zambezi	Indian Ocean	3,540	2,200
Oubangi/Uele	Congo (D.R.)	2,250	1,400
Kasai	Congo (D.R.)	1,950	1,210
Shabelle	Indian Ocean	1,930	1,200
Orange	Atlantic Ocean	1,860	1,155
Cubango	Okavango Delta	1,800	1,120
Limpopo	Indian Ocean	1,770	1,100
Senegal	Atlantic Ocean	1,640	1,020

Australia		km	miles
Murray–Darling	Southern Ocean	3,750	2,330
Darling	Murray	3,070	1,905
Murray	Southern Ocean	2,575	1,600
Murrumbidgee	Murray	1,690	1,050

North America		km	miles
Mississippi–Missouri	Gulf of Mexico	5,971	3,710
Mackenzie	Arctic Ocean	4,240	2,630
Missouri	Mississippi	4,088	2,540
Mississippi	Gulf of Mexico	3,782	2,350
Yukon	Pacific Ocean	3,185	1,980
Rio Grande	Gulf of Mexico	3,030	1,880
Arkansas	Mississippi	2,340	1,450
Colorado	Pacific Ocean	2,330	1,445
Red	Mississippi	2,040	1,270
Columbia	Pacific Ocean	1,950	1,210
Saskatchewan	Lake Winnipeg	1,940	1,205

South America		km	miles
Amazon	Atlantic Ocean	6,450	4,010
Paraná-Plate	Atlantic Ocean	4,500	2,800
Purus	Amazon	3,350	2,080
Madeira	Amazon	3,200	1,990
São Francisco	Atlantic Ocean	2,900	1,800
Paraná	Plate	2,800	1,740
Tocantins	Atlantic Ocean	2,750	1,710
Orinoco	Atlantic Ocean	2,740	1,700
Paraguay	Paraná	2,550	1,580
Pilcomayo	Paraná	2,500	1,550
Araguaia	Tocantins	2,250	1,400

Lakes

Europe		km²	miles²
Lake Ladoga	Russia	17,700	6,800
Lake Onega	Russia	9,700	3,700
Saimaa system	Finland	8,000	3,100
Vänern	Sweden	5,500	2,100

Asia		km²	miles²
Caspian Sea	Asia	371,000	143,000
Lake Baikal	Russia	30,500	11,780
Tonlé Sap	Cambodia	20,000	7,700
Lake Balqash	Kazakhstan	18,500	7,100
Aral Sea	Kazakhstan/Uzbekistan	17,160	6,625

Africa		km²	miles²
Lake Victoria	East Africa	68,000	26,000
Lake Tanganyika	Central Africa	33,000	13,000
Lake Malawi/Nyasa	East Africa	29,600	11,430
Lake Chad	Central Africa	25,000	9,700
Lake Bangweulu	Zambia	9,840	3,800
Lake Turkana	Ethiopia/Kenya	8,500	3,290

Australia		km²	miles²
Lake Eyre	Australia	8,900	3,400
Lake Torrens	Australia	5,800	2,200
Lake Gairdner	Australia	4,800	1,900

North America		km²	miles²
Lake Superior	Canada/USA	82,350	31,800
Lake Huron	Canada/USA	59,600	23,010
Lake Michigan	USA	58,000	22,400
Great Bear Lake	Canada	31,800	12,280
Great Slave Lake	Canada	28,500	11,000
Lake Erie	Canada/USA	25,700	9,900
Lake Winnipeg	Canada	24,400	9,400
Lake Ontario	Canada/USA	19,500	7,500
Lake Nicaragua	Nicaragua	8,200	3,200

South America		km²	miles²
Lake Titicaca	Bolivia/Peru	8,300	3,200
Lake Poopo	Bolivia	2,800	1,100

Islands

Europe		km²	miles²
Great Britain	UK	229,880	88,700
Iceland	Atlantic Ocean	103,000	39,800
Ireland	Ireland/UK	84,400	32,600
Novaya Zemlya (N.)	Russia	48,200	18,600
Sicily	Italy	25,500	9,800
Corsica	France	8,700	3,400

Asia		km²	miles²
Borneo	Southeast Asia	744,360	287,400
Sumatra	Indonesia	473,600	182,860
Honshu	Japan	230,500	88,980
Sulawesi (Celebes)	Indonesia	189,000	73,000
Java	Indonesia	126,700	48,900
Luzon	Philippines	104,700	40,400
Hokkaido	Japan	78,400	30,300

Africa		km²	miles²
Madagascar	Indian Ocean	587,040	226,660
Socotra	Indian Ocean	3,600	1,400
Réunion	Indian Ocean	2,500	965

Oceania		km²	miles²
New Guinea	Indonesia/Papua NG	821,030	317,000
New Zealand (S.)	Pacific Ocean	150,500	58,100
New Zealand (N.)	Pacific Ocean	114,700	44,300
Tasmania	Australia	67,800	26,200
Hawai'i	Pacific Ocean	10,450	4,000

North America		km²	miles²
Greenland	Atlantic Ocean	2,175,600	839,800
Baffin Is.	Canada	508,000	196,100
Victoria Is.	Canada	212,200	81,900
Ellesmere Is.	Canada	212,000	81,800
Cuba	Caribbean Sea	110,860	42,800
Hispaniola	Dominican Rep./Haiti	76,200	29,400
Jamaica	Caribbean Sea	11,400	4,400
Puerto Rico	Atlantic Ocean	8,900	3,400

South America		km²	miles²
Tierra del Fuego	Argentina/Chile	47,000	18,100
Falkland Is. (E.)	Atlantic Ocean	6,800	2,600

User Guide

The reference maps which form the main body of this atlas have been prepared in accordance with the highest standards of international cartography to provide an accurate and detailed representation of the Earth. The scales and projections used have been carefully chosen to give balanced coverage of the world, while emphasizing the most densely populated and economically significant regions. A hallmark of Philip's mapping is the use of hill shading and relief coloring to create a graphic impression of landforms: this makes the maps exceptionally easy to read. However, knowledge of the key features employed in the construction and presentation of the maps will enable the reader to derive the fullest benefit from the atlas.

Map sequence

The atlas covers the Earth continent by continent: first Europe; then its land neighbor Asia (mapped north before south, in a clockwise sequence), then Africa, Australia and Oceania, North America, and South America. This is the classic arrangement adopted by most cartographers since the 16th century. For each continent, there are maps at a variety of scales. First, physical relief and political maps of the whole continent; then a series of larger-scale maps of the regions within the continent, each followed, where required, by still larger-scale maps of the most important or densely populated areas. The governing principle is that by turning the pages of the atlas, the reader moves steadily from north to south through each continent, with each map overlapping its neighbors.

Map presentation

With very few exceptions (for example, for the Arctic and Antarctica), the maps are drawn with north at the top, regardless of whether they are presented upright or sideways on the page. In the borders will be found the map title; a locator diagram showing the area covered; continuation arrows showing the page numbers for maps of adjacent areas; the scale; the projection used; the degrees of latitude and longitude; and the letters and figures used in the index for locating place names and geographical features. Physical relief maps also have a height reference panel identifying the colors used for each layer of contouring.

Map symbols

Each map contains a vast amount of detail which can only be conveyed clearly and accurately by the use of symbols. Points and circles of varying sizes locate and identify the relative importance of towns and cities; different styles of type are employed for administrative, geographical, and regional place names. A variety of pictorial symbols denote features such as glaciers and marshes, as well as man-made structures including roads, railroads, airports, and canals.

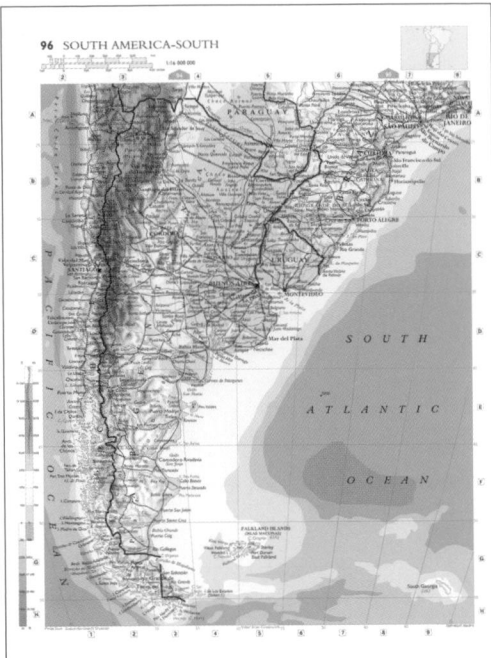

International borders are shown by red lines. Where neighboring countries are in dispute, for example in the Middle East, the maps show the *de facto* boundary between nations, regardless of the legal or historical situation. The symbols are explained on the first page of the World Maps section of the atlas.

Map scales

The scale of each map is given in the numerical form known as the "representative fraction." The first figure is always one, signifying one unit of distance on the map; the second figure, usually in millions, is the number by which the map unit must be multiplied to give the equivalent distance on the Earth's surface. Calculations can easily be made in centimeters and kilometers, by dividing the Earth units figure by 100 000 (i.e. deleting the last five 0s). Thus 1:1 000 000 means 1 cm = 10 km. The calculation for inches and miles is more laborious, but 1 000 000 divided by 63 360 (the number of inches in a mile) shows that the ratio 1:1 000 000 means approximately 1 inch = 16 miles. The table below provides distance equivalents for scales down to 1:50 000 000.

	LARGE SCALE	
1:1 000 000	1 cm = 10 km	1 inch = 16 miles
1:2 500 000	1 cm = 25 km	1 inch = 39.5 miles
1:5 000 000	1 cm = 50 km	1 inch = 79 miles
1:6 000 000	1 cm = 60 km	1 inch = 95 miles
1:8 000 000	1 cm = 80 km	1 inch = 126 miles
1:10 000 000	1 cm = 100 km	1 inch = 158 miles
1:15 000 000	1 cm = 150 km	1 inch = 237 miles
1:20 000 000	1 cm = 200 km	1 inch = 316 miles
1:50 000 000	1 cm = 500 km	1 inch = 790 miles
	SMALL SCALE	

Measuring distances

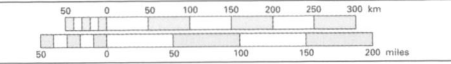

Although each map is accompanied by a scale bar, distances cannot always be measured with confidence because of the distortions involved in portraying the curved surface of the Earth on a flat page. As a general rule, the larger the map scale (i.e. the lower the number of Earth units in the representative fraction), the more accurate and reliable will be the distance measured. On small-scale maps such as those of the world and of entire continents, measurement may only be accurate along the "standard parallels," or central axes, and should not be attempted without considering the map projection.

Latitude and longitude

Accurate positioning of individual points on the Earth's surface is made possible by reference to the geometrical system of latitude and longitude. Latitude *parallels* are drawn west–east around the Earth and numbered by degrees north and south of the Equator, which is designated 0° of latitude. Longitude *meridians* are drawn north–south and numbered by degrees east and west of the *prime meridian*, 0° of longitude, which passes through Greenwich in England. By referring to these coordinates and their subdivisions of minutes ($\frac{1}{60}$th of a degree) and seconds ($\frac{1}{60}$th of a minute), any place on Earth can be located to within a few hundred meters. Latitude and longitude are indicated by blue lines on the maps; they are straight or curved according to the projection employed. Reference to these lines is the easiest way of determining the relative positions of places on different maps, and for plotting compass directions.

Name forms

For ease of reference, both English and local name forms appear in the atlas. Oceans, seas, and countries are shown in English throughout the atlas; country names may be abbreviated to their commonly accepted form (for example, Germany, not The Federal Republic of Germany). Conventional English forms are also used for place names on the smaller-scale maps of the continents. However, local name forms are used on all large-scale and regional maps, with the English form given in brackets only for important cities – the large-scale map of Russia and Central Asia thus shows Moskva (Moscow). For countries which do not use a Roman script, place names have been transcribed according to the systems adopted by the British and US Geographic Names Authorities. For China, the Pin Yin system has been used, with some more widely known forms appearing in brackets, as with Beijing (Peking). Both English and local names appear in the index, the English form being cross-referenced to the local form.

THE
WORLD
IN FOCUS

PLANET EARTH	**2**	WATER & VEGETATION	**12**	QUALITY OF LIFE	**22**
RESTLESS EARTH	**4**	ENVIRONMENT	**14**	ENERGY	**24**
LANDFORMS	**6**	POPULATION	**16**	PRODUCTION	**26**
OCEANS	**8**	THE HUMAN FAMILY	**18**	TRADE	**28**
CLIMATE	**10**	WEALTH	**20**	TRAVEL & TOURISM	**30**

Planet Earth

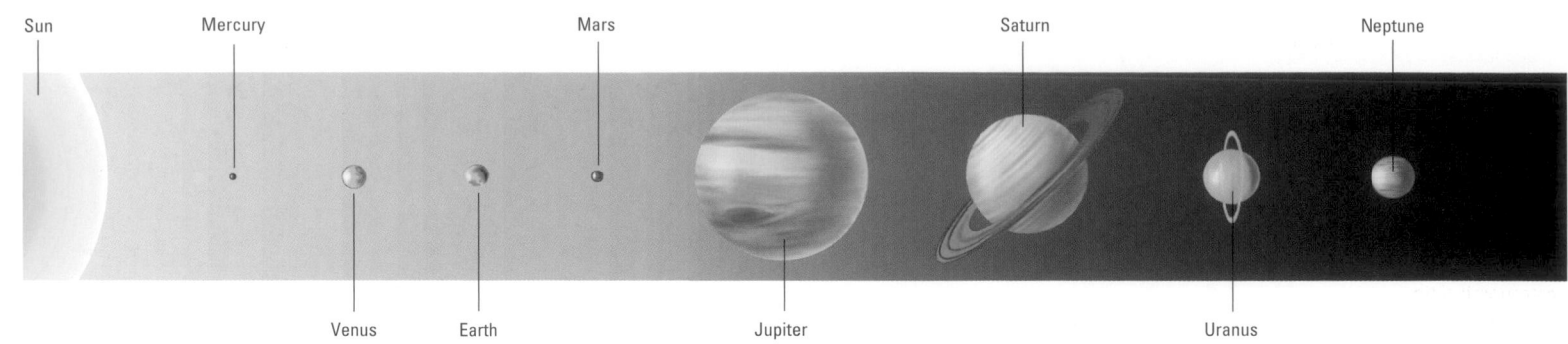

Sun Mercury Mars Saturn Neptune

Venus Earth Jupiter Uranus

The Solar System

A minute part of one of the billions of galaxies (collections of stars) that populate the Universe, the Solar System lies about 26,000 light-years from the center of our own galaxy, the "Milky Way." Thought to be about 5 billion years old, it consists of a central Sun with eight planets and their moons revolving around it, attracted by its gravitational pull. The planets orbit the Sun in the same direction – counterclockwise when viewed from above the Sun's north pole – and almost in the same plane. Their orbital distances, however, vary enormously.

The Sun's diameter is 109 times that of the Earth, and the temperature at its core – caused by continuous thermonuclear fusions of hydrogen into helium – is estimated to be 27 million degrees Fahrenheit. It is the Solar System's only source of light and heat.

Profile of the Planets

	Mean distance from Sun (million miles)	Mass (Earth = 1)	Period of orbit (Earth days/years)	Period of rotation (Earth days)	Equatorial diameter (miles)	Number of known satellites*
Mercury	36.0	0.06	87.97 days	58.65	3,032	0
Venus	67.2	0.82	224.7 days	243.02	7,521	0
Earth	93.0	1.00	365.3 days	1.00	7,926	1
Mars	141.6	0.11	687.0 days	1.029	4,220	2
Jupiter	483.7	317.8	11.86 years	0.411	88,848	63
Saturn	886.6	95.2	29.45 years	0.428	74,900	60
Uranus	1,784	14.5	84.02 years	0.720	31,764	27
Neptune	2,795	17.2	164.8 years	0.673	30,776	13

* Number of known satellites at mid-2008

All planetary orbits are elliptical in form, but only Mercury follows a path that deviates noticeably from a circular one. In 2006, Pluto was demoted from its former status as a planet and is now regarded as a member of the Kuiper Belt of icy bodies at the fringes of the Solar System.

The Seasons

Seasons occur because the Earth's axis is tilted at an angle of approximately 23½°. When the northern hemisphere is tilted to a maximum extent toward the Sun, on June 21, the Sun is overhead at the Tropic of Cancer (latitude 23½° North). This is midsummer, or the summer solstice, in the northern hemisphere.

On September 22 or 23, the Sun is overhead at the equator, and day and night are of equal length throughout the world. This is the autumnal equinox in the northern hemisphere. On December 21 or 22, the Sun is overhead at the Tropic of Capricorn (23½° South), the winter solstice in the northern hemisphere. The overhead Sun then tracks north until, on March 21, it is overhead at the equator. This is the spring (vernal) equinox in the northern hemisphere.

In the southern hemisphere, the seasons are the reverse of those in the north.

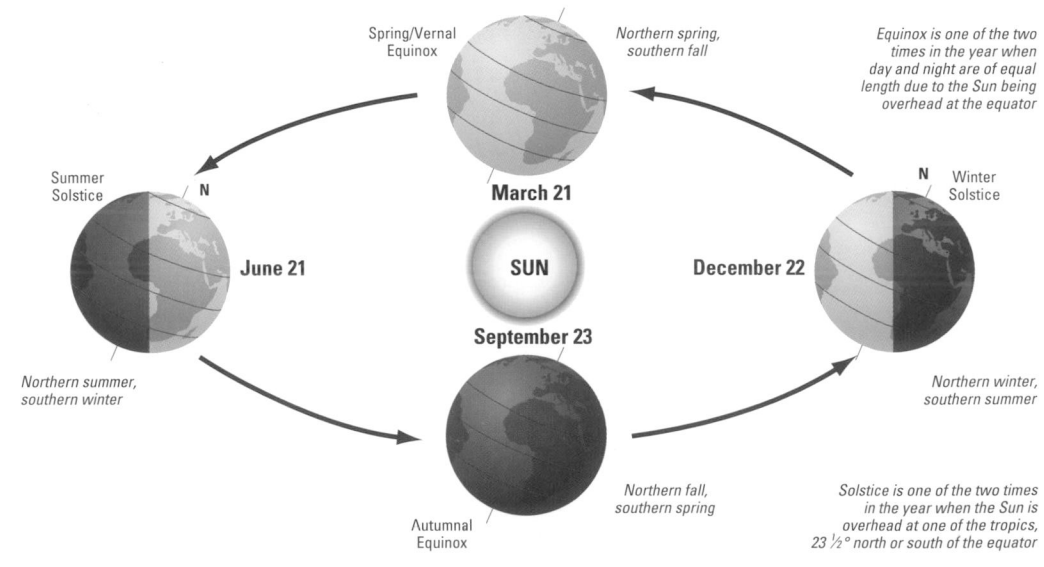

Spring/Vernal Equinox

Northern spring, southern fall

Equinox is one of the two times in the year when day and night are of equal length due to the Sun being overhead at the equator

Summer Solstice

N

Winter Solstice

March 21

June 21

SUN

December 22

September 23

Northern summer, southern winter

Northern winter, southern summer

Northern fall, southern spring

Autumnal Equinox

Solstice is one of the two times in the year when the Sun is overhead at one of the tropics, 23 ½° north or south of the equator

Day and Night

The Sun appears to rise in the east, reach its highest point at noon, and then set in the west, to be followed by night. In reality, it is not the Sun that is moving but the Earth rotating from west to east. The moment when the Sun's upper limb first appears above the horizon is termed sunrise; the moment when the Sun's upper limb disappears below the horizon is sunset.

At the summer solstice in the northern hemisphere (June 21), the Arctic has total daylight and the Antarctic total darkness. The opposite occurs at the winter solstice (December 21 or 22). At the equator, the length of day and night are almost equal all year.

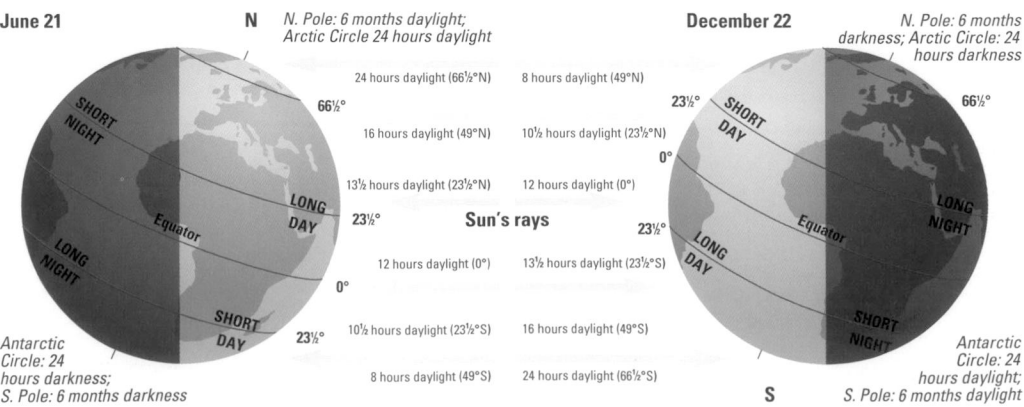

June 21 N N. Pole: 6 months daylight; Arctic Circle 24 hours daylight

24 hours daylight (66½°N) 8 hours daylight (49°N)

66½°

16 hours daylight (49°N) 10½ hours daylight (23½°N)

SHORT NIGHT

13½ hours daylight (23½°N) 12 hours daylight (0°)

LONG DAY

23½° Sun's rays

Equator

12 hours daylight (0°) 13½ hours daylight (23½°S)

LONG NIGHT

0°

SHORT DAY

23½° 10½ hours daylight (23½°S) 16 hours daylight (49°S)

Antarctic Circle: 24 hours darkness; S. Pole: 6 months darkness

8 hours daylight (49°S) 24 hours daylight (66½°S)

December 22 N. Pole: 6 months darkness; Arctic Circle: 24 hours darkness

23½° 66½°

SHORT DAY

0°

LONG NIGHT

23½° Equator

LONG DAY

SHORT NIGHT

Antarctic Circle: 24 hours daylight; S. Pole: 6 months daylight

S

CARTOGRAPHY BY PHILIP'S. COPYRIGHT PHILIP'S

Time

Year: The time taken by the Earth to revolve around the Sun, or 365.24 days.

Leap Year: A calendar year of 366 days, 29 February being the additional day. It offsets the difference between the calendar and the solar year.

Month: The 12 calendar months of the year are approximately equal in length to a lunar month.

Week: An artificial period of 7 days, not based on astronomical time.

Day: The time taken by the Earth to complete one rotation on its axis.

Hour: 24 hours make one day. The day is divided into hours a.m. (ante meridiem or before noon) and p.m. (post meridiem or after noon), although most timetables now use the 24-hour system, from midnight to midnight.

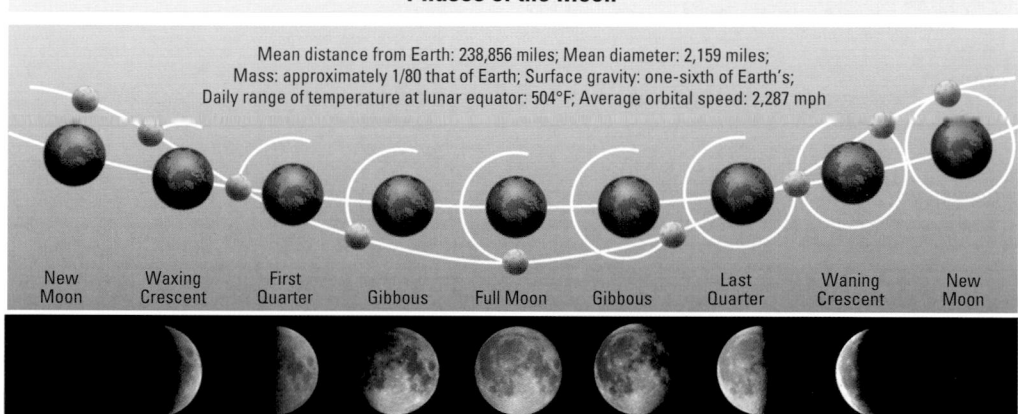

Sunrise

Sunset

The Moon

The Moon rotates more slowly than the Earth, taking just over 27 days to make one complete rotation on its axis. Since this corresponds to the Moon's orbital period around the Earth, the Moon always presents the same hemisphere toward us, and we never see the far side. The interval between one New Moon and the next is 29½ days – this is called a lunation, or lunar month. The Moon shines only by reflected sunlight, and emits no light of its own. During each lunation the Moon displays a complete cycle of phases, caused by the changing angle of illumination from the Sun.

Phases of the Moon

Mean distance from Earth: 238,856 miles; Mean diameter: 2,159 miles;
Mass: approximately 1/80 that of Earth; Surface gravity: one-sixth of Earth's;
Daily range of temperature at lunar equator: 504°F; Average orbital speed: 2,287 mph

New Moon — Waxing Crescent — First Quarter — Gibbous — Full Moon — Gibbous — Last Quarter — Waning Crescent — New Moon

Eclipses

When the Moon passes between the Sun and the Earth, the Sun becomes partially eclipsed (1). A partial eclipse becomes a total eclipse if the Moon proceeds to cover the Sun completely (2) and the dark central part of the lunar shadow touches the Earth. The broad geographical zone covered by the Moon's outer shadow (P), has only a very small central area (often less than 62 miles wide) that experiences totality. Totality can never last for more than 7½ minutes at maximum, but is usually much briefer than this. Lunar eclipses take place when the Moon moves through the shadow of the Earth, and can be partial or total. Any single location on Earth can experience a maximum of four solar and three lunar eclipses in any single year, while a total solar eclipse occurs an average of once every 360 years for any given location.

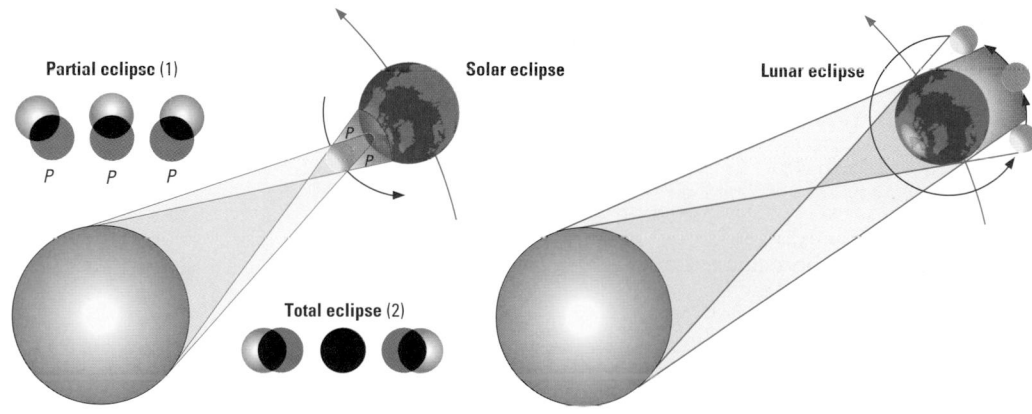

Tides

The daily rise and fall of the ocean's tides are the result of the gravitational pull of the Moon and that of the Sun, though the effect of the latter is not as strong as that of the Moon. This effect is greatest on the hemisphere facing the Moon and causes a tidal "bulge."

Spring tides occur when the Sun, Earth, and Moon are aligned; high tides are at their highest, and low tides fall to their lowest. When the Moon and Sun are furthest out of line (near the Moon's First and Last Quarters), neap tides occur, producing the smallest range between high and low tides.

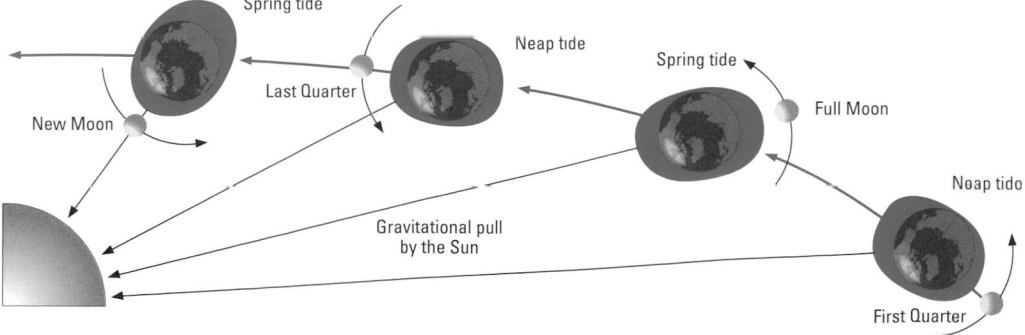

CARTOGRAPHY BY PHILIP'S. COPYRIGHT PHILIP'S

Restless Earth

The Earth's Structure

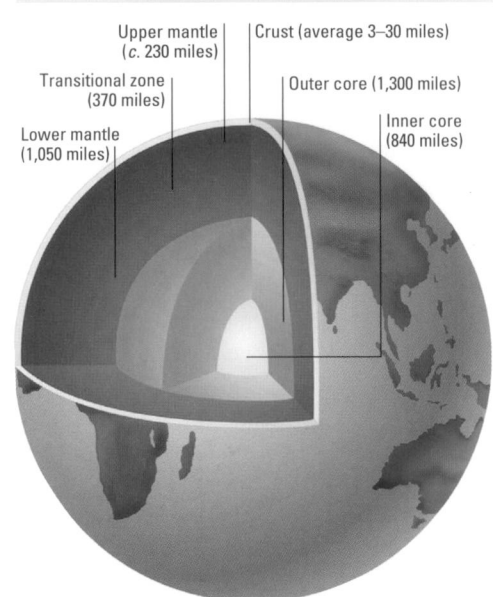

Upper mantle (c. 230 miles)
Crust (average 3–30 miles)
Transitional zone (370 miles)
Outer core (1,300 miles)
Lower mantle (1,050 miles)
Inner core (840 miles)

Continental Drift

About 200 million years ago the original Pangaea land mass began to split into two continental groups, which further separated over time to produce the present-day configuration.

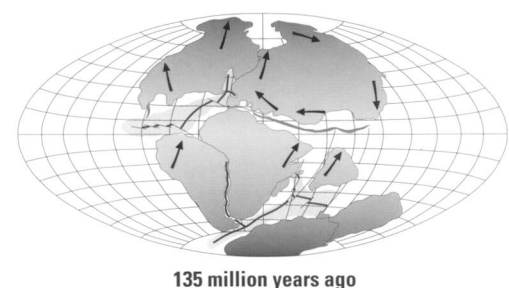

135 million years ago

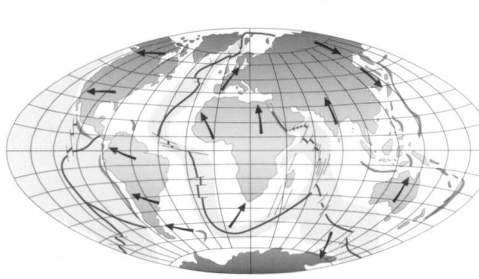

180 million years ago

Laurasia
Tethys Sea
Gondwanaland

— Trench
— Rift
— New ocean floor
— Zones of slippage

Present day

Notable Earthquakes Since 1900

Year	Location	Richter Scale	Deaths
1906	San Francisco, USA	8.3	3,000
1906	Valparaiso, Chile	8.6	22,000
1908	Messina, Italy	7.5	83,000
1915	Avezzano, Italy	7.5	30,000
1920	Gansu (Kansu), China	8.6	180,000
1923	Yokohama, Japan	8.3	143,000
1927	Nan Shan, China	8.3	200,000
1932	Gansu (Kansu), China	7.6	70,000
1933	Sanriku, Japan	8.9	2,990
1934	Bihar, India/Nepal	8.4	10,700
1935	Quetta, India (now Pakistan)	7.5	60,000
1939	Chillan, Chile	8.3	28,000
1939	Erzincan, Turkey	7.9	30,000
1960	S. W. Chile	9.5	2,200
1960	Agadir, Morocco	5.8	12,000
1962	Khorasan, Iran	7.1	12,230
1964	Anchorage, USA	9.2	125
1968	N. E. Iran	7.4	12,000
1970	N. Peru	7.8	70,000
1972	Managua, Nicaragua	6.2	5,000
1974	N. Pakistan	6.3	5,200
1976	Guatemala	7.5	22,500
1976	Tangshan, China	8.2	255,000
1978	Tabas, Iran	7.7	25,000
1980	El Asnam, Algeria	7.3	20,000
1980	S. Italy	7.2	4,800
1985	Mexico City, Mexico	8.1	4,200
1988	N.W. Armenia	6.8	55,000
1990	N. Iran	7.7	36,000
1993	Maharashtra, India	6.4	30,000
1994	Los Angeles, USA	6.6	51
1995	Kobe, Japan	7.2	5,000
1995	Sakhalin Is., Russia	7.5	2,000
1997	N. E. Iran	7.1	2,400
1998	Takhar, Afghanistan	6.1	4,200
1998	Rostaq, Afghanistan	7.0	5,000
1999	Izmit, Turkey	7.4	15,000
1999	Taipei, Taiwan	7.6	1,700
2001	Gujarat, India	7.7	14,000
2002	Baghlan, Afghanistan	6.1	1,000
2003	Boumerdes, Algeria	6.8	2,200
2003	Bam, Iran	6.6	30,000
2004	Sumatra, Indonesia	9.0	250,000
2005	N. Pakistan	7.6	74,000
2006	Java, Indonesia	6.4	6,200
2007	S. Peru	8.0	600
2008	Sichuan, China	7.9	70,000

Earthquakes

Earthquake magnitude is usually rated according to either the Richter or the Modified Mercalli scale, both devised by seismologists in the 1930s. The Richter scale measures absolute earthquake power with mathematical precision: each step upward represents a tenfold increase in shockwave amplitude. Theoretically, there is no upper limit, but most of the largest earthquakes measured have been rated at between 8.8 and 8.9. The 12–point Mercalli scale, based on observed effects, is often more meaningful, ranging from I (earthquakes noticed only by seismographs) to XII (total destruction); intermediate points include V (people awakened at night; unstable objects overturned), VII (collapse of ordinary buildings; chimneys and monuments fall), and IX (conspicuous cracks in ground; serious damage to reservoirs).

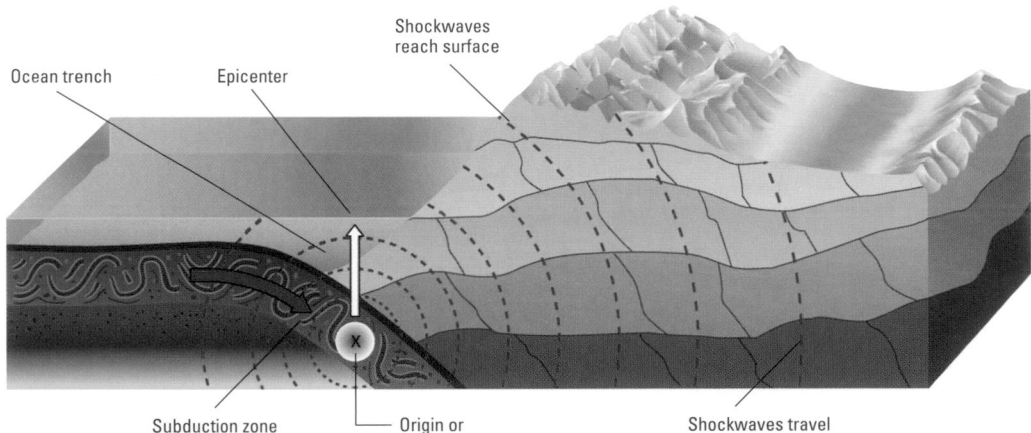

Ocean trench
Epicenter
Shockwaves reach surface
Subduction zone
Origin or focus
Shockwaves travel away from focus

Structure and Earthquakes

Mobile land areas
Submarine zones of mobile land areas
Stable land platforms
Submarine extensions of stable land platforms
Mid-oceanic volcanic ridges
Oceanic platforms

1976 ○ Principal earthquakes and dates (since 1900)

Earthquakes are a series of rapid vibrations originating from the slipping or faulting of parts of the Earth's crust when stresses within build up to breaking point. They usually happen at depths varying from 5 miles to 20 miles. Severe earthquakes cause extensive damage when they take place in populated areas, destroying structures and severing communications. Most initial loss of life occurs due to secondary causes such as falling masonry, fires, and flooding.

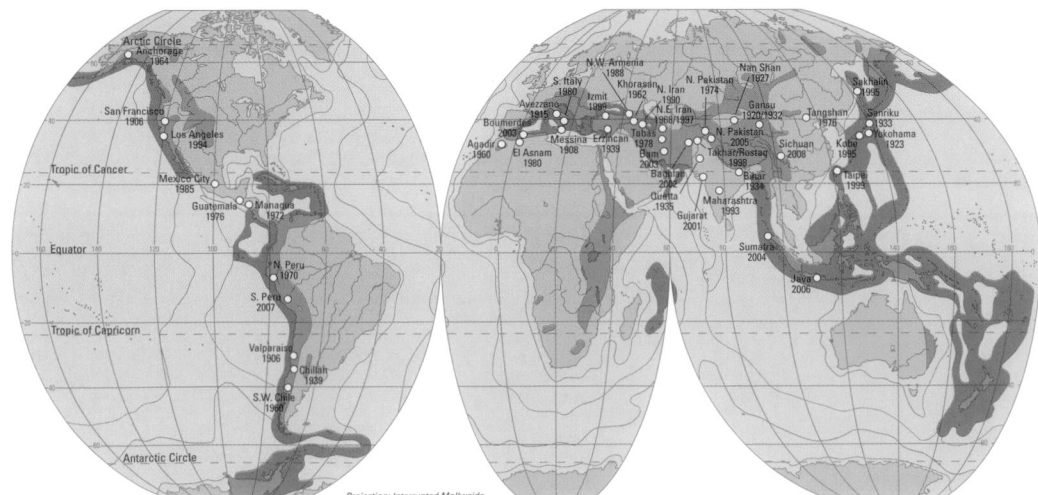

Projection: Interrupted Mollweide

CARTOGRAPHY BY PHILIP'S. COPYRIGHT PHILIP'S

Plate Tectonics

Plate boundaries   PACIFIC   Major plates

➤   Direction of plate movements and rate of movement (cm/year)

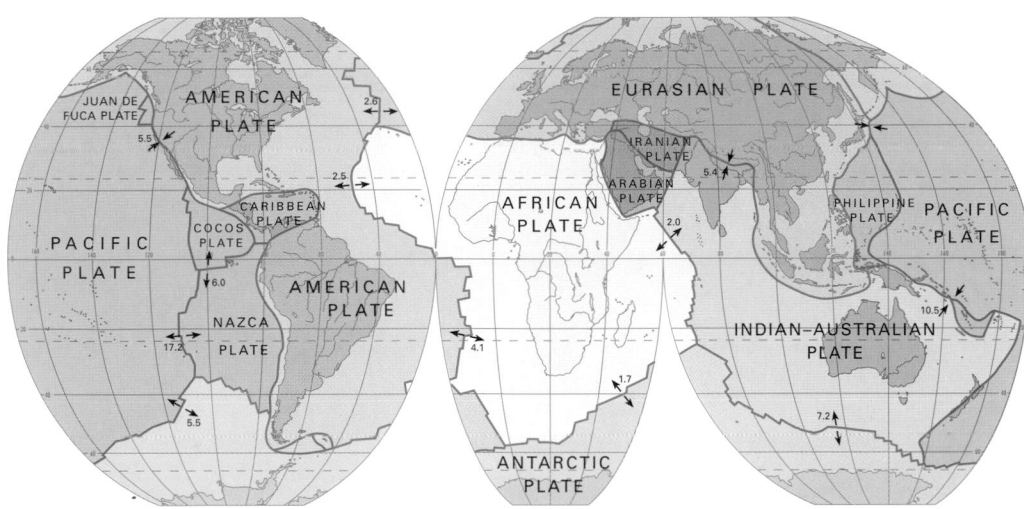

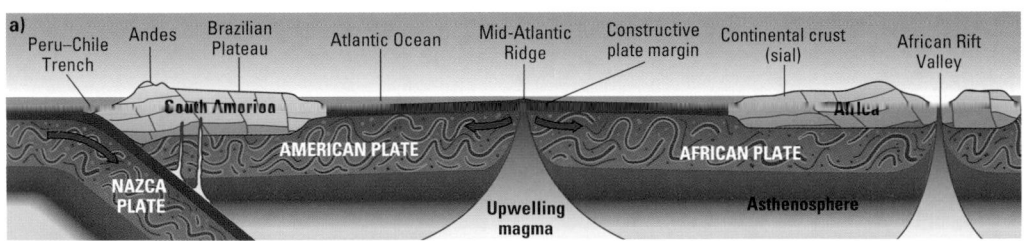

The drifting of the continents is a feature that is unique to Planet Earth. The complementary, almost jigsaw-puzzle fit of the coastlines on each side of the Atlantic Ocean inspired Alfred Wegener's theory of continental drift in 1915. The theory suggested that the ancient super-continent, which Wegener named Pangaea, incorporated all of the Earth's land masses and gradually split up to form today's continents.

The original debate about continental drift was a prelude to a more radical idea: plate tectonics. The basic theory is that the Earth's crust is made up of a series of rigid plates which float on a soft layer of the mantle and are moved about by continental convection currents within the Earth's interior. These plates diverge and converge along margins marked by seismic activity. Plates diverge from mid-ocean ridges where molten lava pushes upward and forces the plates apart at rates of up to 1.6 inches [40 mm] a year.

The three diagrams, left, give some examples of plate boundaries from around the world. Diagram (a) shows sea-floor spreading at the Mid-Atlantic Ridge as the American and African plates slowly diverge. The same thing is happening in (b) where sea-floor spreading at the Mid-Indian Ocean Ridge is forcing the Indian–Australian plate to collide into the Eurasian plate. In (c) oceanic crust (sima) is being subducted beneath lighter continental crust (sial).

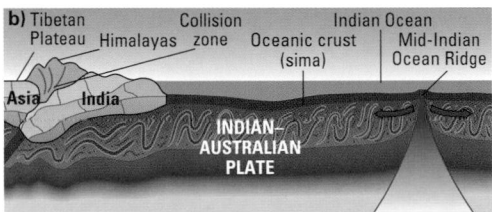

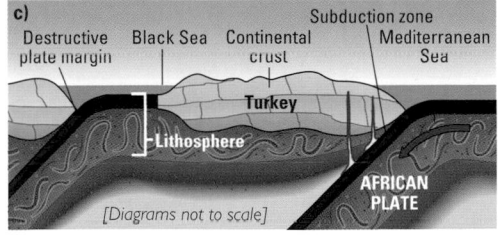

[Diagrams not to scale]

Volcanoes

Volcanoes occur when hot liquefied rock beneath the Earth's crust is pushed up by pressure to the surface as molten lava. Some volcanoes erupt in an explosive way, throwing out rocks and ash, whilst others are effusive and lava flows out of the vent. There are volcanoes which are both, such as Mount Fuji. An accumulation of lava and cinders creates cones of variable size and shape. As a result of many eruptions over centuries, Mount Etna in Sicily has a circumference of more than 75 miles [120 km].

Climatologists believe that volcanic ash, if ejected high into the atmosphere, can influence temperature and weather for several years afterward. The 1991 eruption of Mount Pinatubo in the Philippines ejected more than 20 million tons of dust and ash 20 miles [32 km] into the atmosphere and is believed to have accelerated ozone depletion over a large part of the globe.

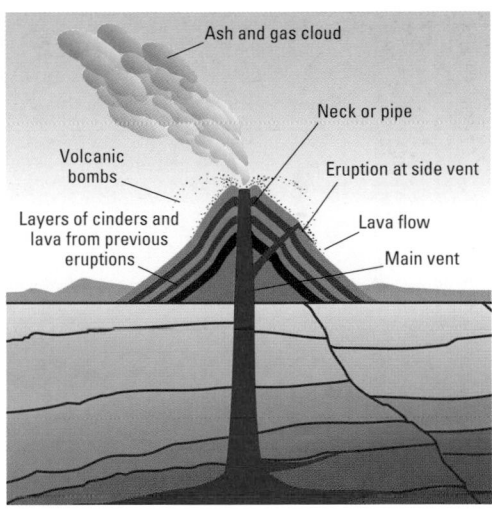

Distribution of Volcanoes

Volcanoes today may be the subject of considerable scientific study but they remain both dramatic and unpredictable: in 1991 Mount Pinatubo, 62 miles [100 km] north of the Philippines capital Manila, suddenly burst into life after lying dormant for more than six centuries. Most of the world's active volcanoes occur in a belt around the Pacific Ocean, on the edge of the Pacific plate, called the "ring of fire." Indonesia has the greatest concentration with 90 volcanoes, 12 of which are active. The most famous, Krakatoa, erupted in 1883 with such force that the resulting tidal wave killed 36,000 people and tremors were felt as far away as Australia.

○   Submarine volcanoes

▲   Land volcanoes active since 1700

—   Boundaries of tectonic plates

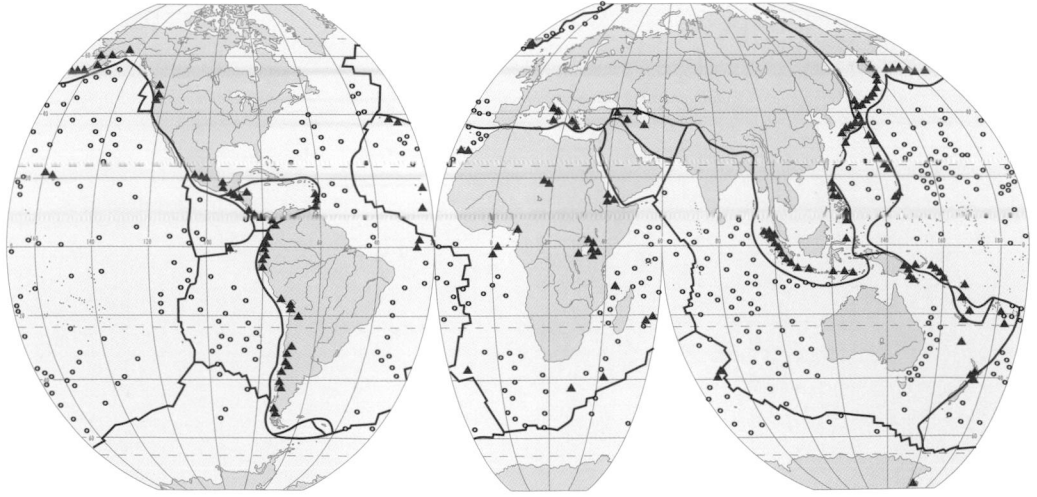

Landforms

The Rock Cycle

James Hutton first proposed the rock cycle in the late 1700s after he observed the slow but steady effects of erosion.

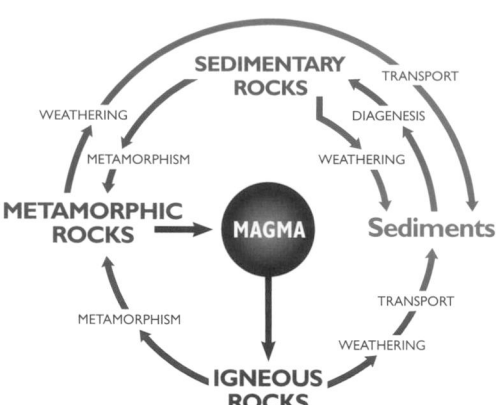

Above and below the surface of the oceans, the features of the Earth's crust are constantly changing. The phenomenal forces generated by convection currents in the molten core of our planet carry the vast segments or "plates" of the crust across the globe in an endless cycle of creation and destruction. A continent may travel little more than 1 inch [25 mm] per year, yet in the vast span of geological time this process throws up giant mountain ranges and creates new land.

Destruction of the landscape, however, begins as soon as it is formed. Wind, water, ice, and sea, the main agents of erosion, mount a constant assault that even the most resistant rocks cannot withstand. Mountain peaks may dwindle by as little as a few fractions of an inch each year, but if they are not uplifted by further movements of the crust they will eventually be reduced to rubble and transported away.

Water is the most powerful agent of erosion – it has been estimated that 100 billion tons of sediment are washed into the oceans every year. Three Asian rivers account for 20% of this total; the Huang He, in China, and the Brahmaputra and Ganges in Bangladesh.

Rivers and glaciers, like the sea itself, generate much of their effect through abrasion – pounding the land with the debris they carry with them. But as well as destroying they also create new landforms, many of them spectacular: vast deltas like those of the Mississippi and the Nile, or the deep fjords cut by glaciers in British Columbia, Norway, and New Zealand.

Geologists once considered that landscapes evolved from "young," newly uplifted mountainous areas, through a "mature" hilly stage, to an "old age" stage when the land was reduced to an almost flat plain, or peneplain. This theory, called the "cycle of erosion," fell into disuse when it became evident that so many factors, including the effects of plate tectonics and climatic change, constantly interrupt the cycle, which takes no account of the highly complex interactions that shape the surface of our planet.

Mountain Building

Mountains are formed when pressures on the Earth's crust caused by continental drift become so intense that the surface buckles or cracks. This happens where oceanic crust is subducted by continental crust or, more dramatically, where two tectonic plates collide: the Rockies, Andes, Alps, Urals, and Himalayas resulted from such impacts. These are all known as fold mountains because they were formed by the compression of the rocks, forcing the surface to bend and fold like a crumpled rug. The Himalayas are formed from the folded former sediments of the Tethys Sea which was trapped in the collision zone between the Indian and Eurasian plates.

The other main mountain-building process occurs when the crust fractures to create faults, allowing rock to be forced upward in large blocks; or when the pressure of magma within the crust forces the surface to bulge into a dome, or erupts to form a volcano. Large mountain ranges may reveal a combination of these features; the Alps, for example, have been compressed so violently that the folds are fragmented by numerous faults and intrusions of molten igneous rock.

Over millions of years, even the greatest mountain ranges can be reduced by the agents of erosion (most notably rivers) to a low rugged landscape known as a peneplain.

Types of faults: Faults occur where the crust is being stretched or compressed so violently that the rock strata break in a horizontal or vertical movement. They are classified by the direction in which the blocks of rock have moved. A normal fault results when a vertical movement causes the surface to break apart; compression causes a reverse fault. Horizontal movement causes shearing, known as a strike-slip fault. When the rock breaks in two places, the central block may be pushed up in a horst fault, or sink (creating a rift valley) in a graben fault.

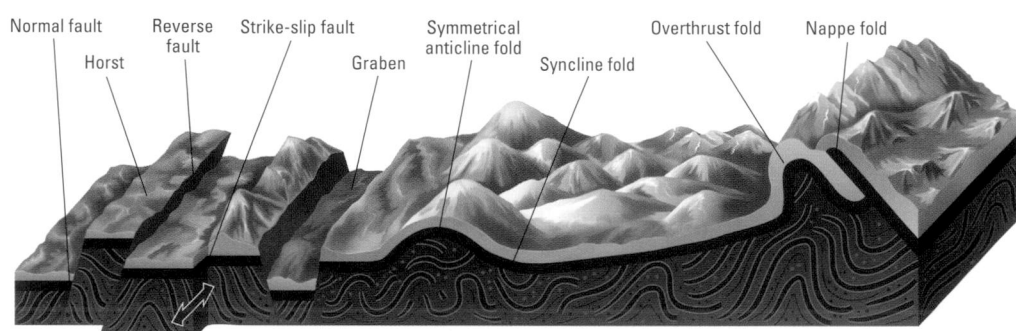

Types of fold: Folds occur when rock strata are squeezed and compressed. They are common, therefore, at destructive plate margins and where plates have collided, forcing the rocks to buckle into mountain ranges. Geographers give different names to the degrees of fold that result from continuing pressure on the rock. A simple fold may be symmetric, with even slopes on either side, but as the pressure builds up, one slope becomes steeper and the fold becomes asymmetric. Later, the ridge or "anticline" at the top of the fold may slide over the lower ground or "syncline" to form a recumbent fold. Eventually, the rock strata may break under the pressure to form an overthrust and finally a nappe fold.

Continental Glaciation

Ice sheets were at their greatest extent about 200,000 years ago. The maximum advance of the last Ice Age was about 18,000 years ago, when ice covered virtually all of Canada and reached as far south as the Bristol Channel in Britain.

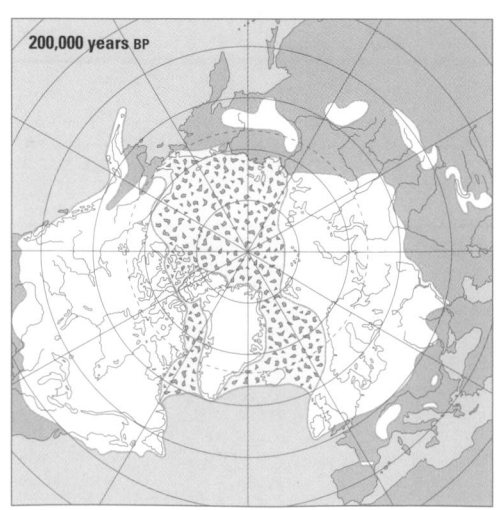

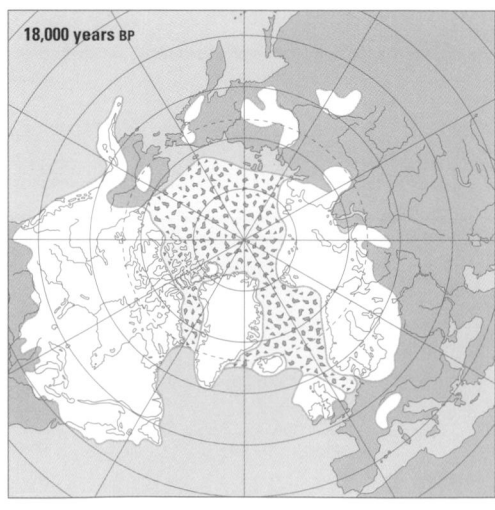

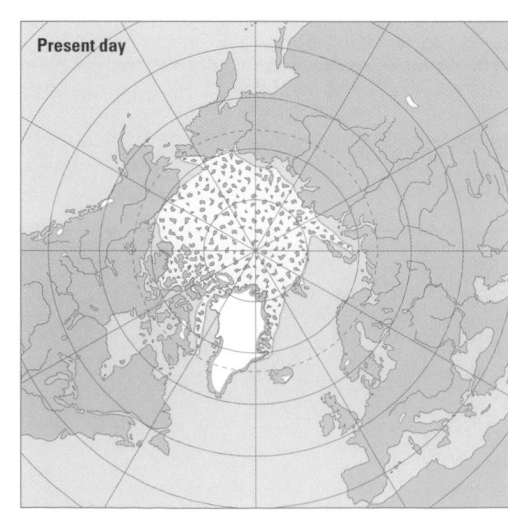

CARTOGRAPHY BY PHILIP'S. COPYRIGHT PHILIP'S

Natural Landforms

A stylized diagram to show a selection of landforms found in the mid-latitudes.

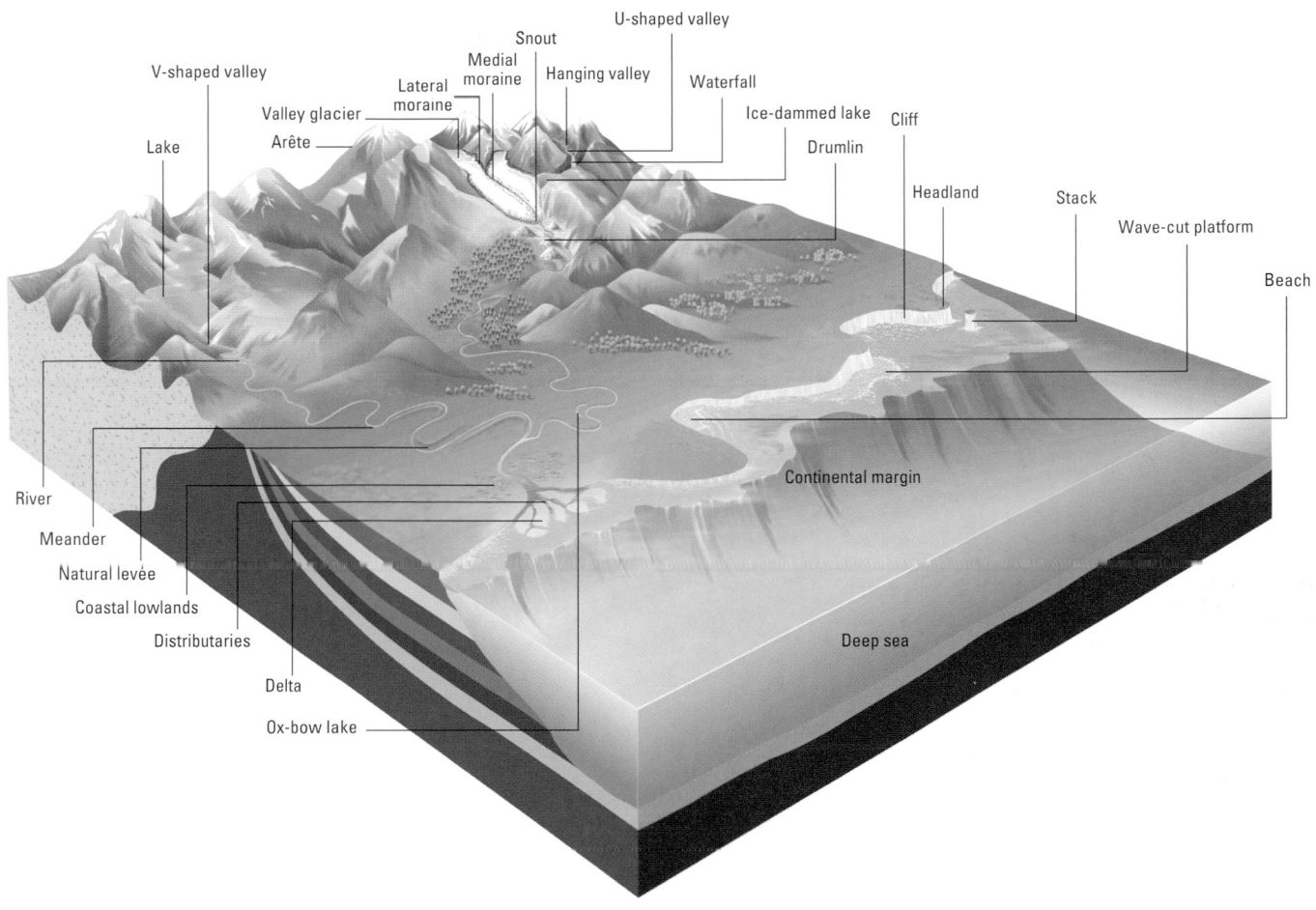

Desert Landscapes

The popular image that deserts are all huge expanses of sand is wrong. Despite harsh conditions, deserts contain some of the most varied and interesting landscapes in the world. They are also one of the most extensive environments – the hot and cold deserts together cover almost 40% of the Earth's surface.

The three types of hot desert are known by their Arabic names: sand desert, called *erg*, covers only about one-fifth of the world's desert; the rest is divided between *hammada* (areas of bare rock) and *reg* (broad plains covered by loose gravel or pebbles).

In areas of *erg*, such as the Namib Desert, the shape of the dunes reflects the character of local winds. Where winds are constant in direction, crescent-shaped *barchan* dunes form. In areas of bare rock, wind-blown sand is a major agent of erosion. The erosion is mainly confined to within 6.5 ft [2 m] of the surface, producing characteristic mushroom-shaped rocks.

Surface Processes

Catastrophic changes to natural landforms are periodically caused by such phenomena as avalanches, landslides, and volcanic eruptions, but most of the processes that shape the Earth's surface operate extremely slowly in human terms. One estimate, based on a study in the United States, suggested that 3 ft [1 m] of land was removed from the entire surface of the country, on average, every 29,500 years. However, the time-scale varies from 1,300 years to 154,200 years depending on the terrain and climate.

In hot, dry climates, mechanical weathering, a result of rapid temperature changes, causes the outer layers of rock to peel away, while in cold mountainous regions, boulders are prised apart when water freezes in cracks in rocks. Chemical weathering, at its greatest in warm, humid regions, is responsible for hollowing out limestone caves and decomposing granites.

The erosion of soil and rock is greatest on sloping land and the steeper the slope, the greater the tendency for mass wasting – the movement of soil and rock downhill under the influence of gravity. The mechanisms of mass wasting (ranging from very slow to very rapid) vary with the type of material, but the presence of water as a lubricant is usually an important factor.

Running water is the world's leading agent of erosion and transportation. The energy of a river depends on several factors, including its velocity and volume, and its erosive power is at its peak when it is in full flood. Sea waves also exert tremendous erosive power during storms when they hurl pebbles against the shore, undercutting cliffs and hollowing out caves.

Glacier ice forms in mountain hollows and spills out to form valley glaciers, which transport rocks shattered by frost action. As glaciers move, rocks embedded into the ice erode steep-sided, U-shaped valleys. Evidence of glaciation in mountain regions includes cirques, knife-edged ridges, or arêtes, and pyramidal peaks.

CARTOGRAPHY BY PHILIP'S. COPYRIGHT PHILIP'S

Oceans

The Great Oceans

Relative sizes of the world's oceans

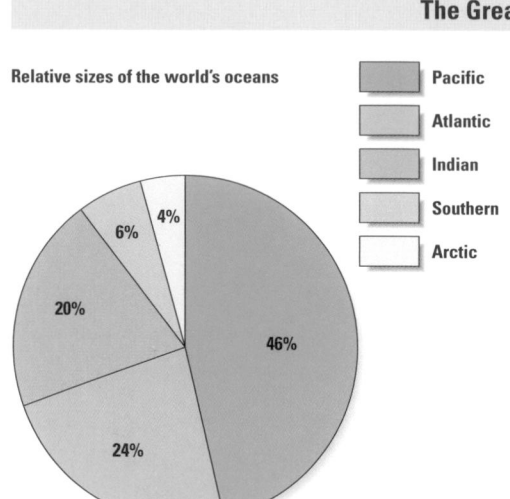

- Pacific
- Atlantic
- Indian
- Southern
- Arctic

From ancient times to about the 15th century, the legendary "Seven Seas" comprised the Red Sea, Mediterranean Sea, Persian Gulf, Black Sea, Adriatic Sea, Caspian Sea, and Indian Sea.

The Earth is a watery planet: more than 70% of its surface – over 140,000,000 sq miles [360,000,000 sq km] – is covered by the oceans and seas. The mighty Pacific alone accounts for nearly 36% of the total, and more than 46% of the sea area. Gravity holds in around 320 million cu. miles [1,400 million cu. km] of water, of which over 97% is saline.

The vast underwater world starts in the shallows of the seaside and plunges to depths of more than 36,000 ft [11,000 m]. The continental shelf, part of the landmass, drops gently to around 650 ft [200 m]; here the seabed falls away suddenly at an angle of 3° to 6° – the continental slope. The third stage, called the continental rise, is more gradual with gradients varying from 1 in 100 to 1 in 700. At an average depth of 16,500 ft [5,000 m] there begins the aptly-named abyssal plain – massive submarine depths where sunlight fails to penetrate and few creatures can survive.

From these plains rise volcanoes which, taken from base to top, rival and even surpass the tallest continental mountains in height. Mauna Kea, on Hawai'i, reaches a total of 33,400 ft [10,203 m], some 4,500 ft [1,355 m] more than Mount Everest, though scarcely 40% is visible above sea level.

In addition, there are underwater mountain chains up to 600 miles [1,000 km] across, whose peaks sometimes appear above sea level as islands, such as Iceland and Tristan da Cunha.

The Ocean Depths

Average and maximum depths of the world's great oceans, in feet

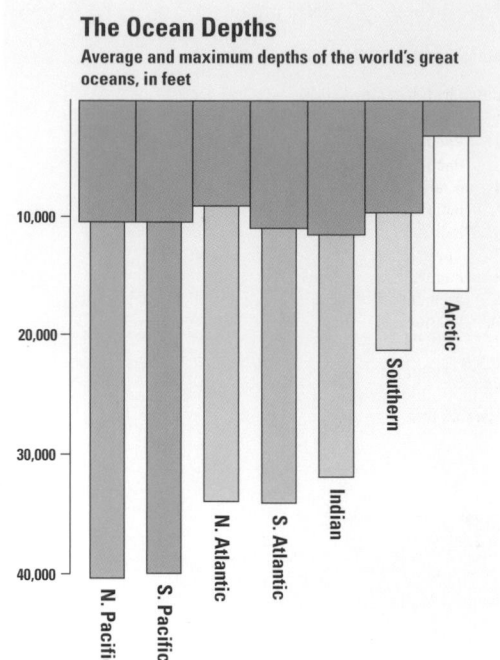

Ocean Currents

January ocean currents

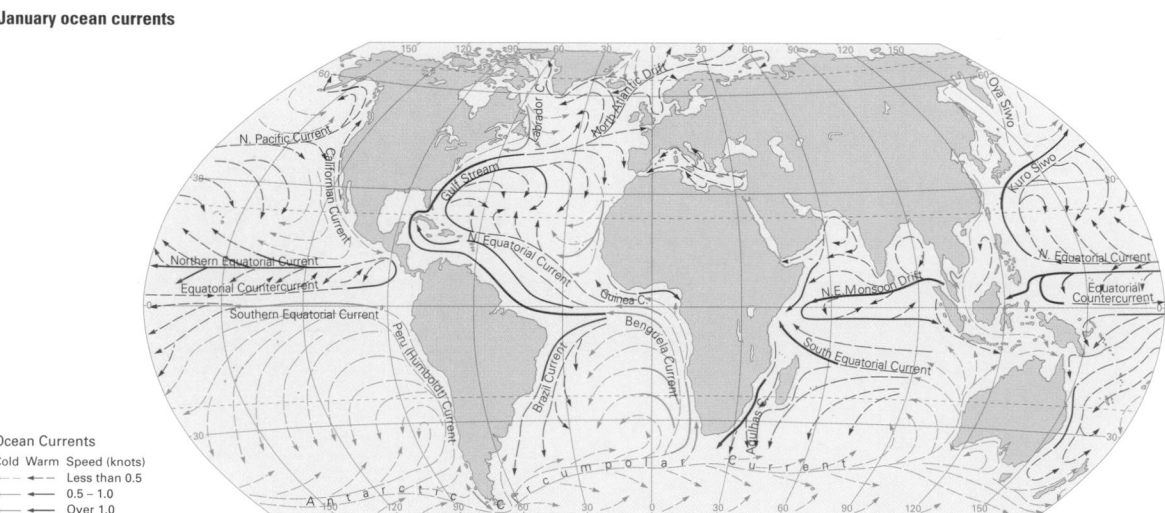

Ocean Currents
Cold Warm Speed (knots)
- Less than 0.5
- 0.5 – 1.0
- Over 1.0

July ocean currents

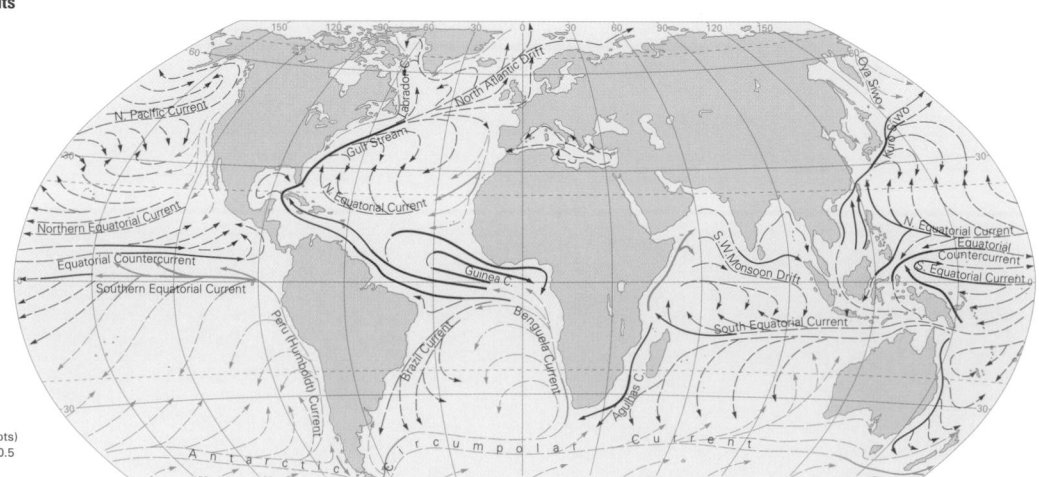

Ocean Currents
Cold Warm Speed (knots)
- Less than 0.5
- 0.5 – 1.0
- Over 1.0

Moving immense quantities of energy as well as billions of tons of water every hour, the ocean currents are a vital part of the great heat engine that drives the Earth's climate. They themselves are produced by a twofold mechanism. At the surface, winds push huge masses of water before them; in the deep ocean, below an abrupt temperature gradient that separates the churning surface waters from the still depths, density variations cause slow vertical movements.

The pattern of circulation of the great surface currents is determined by the displacement known as the Coriolis effect. As the Earth turns beneath a moving object – whether it is a tennis ball or a vast mass of water – it appears to be deflected to one side. The deflection is most obvious near the Equator, where the Earth's surface is spinning eastward at 1,050 mph [1,700 km/h]; currents moving polewards are curved clockwise in the northern hemisphere and counterclockwise in the southern.

The result is a system of spinning circles known as gyres. The Coriolis effect piles up water on the left of each gyre, creating a narrow, fast-moving stream that is matched by a slower, broader returning current on the right. North and south of the Equator, the fastest currents are located in the west and in the east respectively. In each case, warm water moves from the Equator and cold water returns to it. Cold currents often bring an upwelling of nutrients with them, supporting the world's most economically important fisheries.

Depending on the prevailing winds, some currents on or near the Equator may reverse their direction in the course of the year – a seasonal variation on which Asian monsoon rains depend, and whose occasional failure can bring disaster to millions.

CARTOGRAPHY BY PHILIP'S. COPYRIGHT PHILIP'S

World Fishing Areas

Main commercial fishing areas (numbered FAO regions)

Catch by top marine fishing areas, million tons (2005)

1.	Pacific, NW	[61]	21.6	22.7%
2.	Pacific, SE	[87]	15.5	16.3%
3.	Pacific, WC	[71]	11.0	11.6%
4.	Atlantic, NE	[27]	10.0	10.5%
5.	Indian, E	[57]	5.6	5.9%
6.	Indian, W	[51]	4.1	4.3%
7.	Atlantic, EC	[34]	3.4	3.6%
8.	Pacific, NE	[67]	3.1	3.3%
9.	Atlantic, NW	[21]	2.4	2.5%
10.	Atlantic, WC	[31]	2.1	2.2%

Principal fishing areas

Leading fishing nations

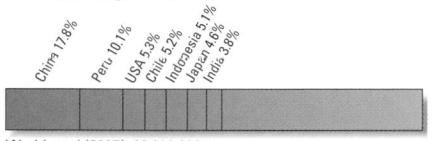

China 17.8% Peru 10.1% USA 5.3% Chile 5.2% Indonesia 5.1% Japan 4.6% India 3.8%

World total (2005): 93,800,000 tons
(Marine catch 89.8% Inland catch 10.2%)

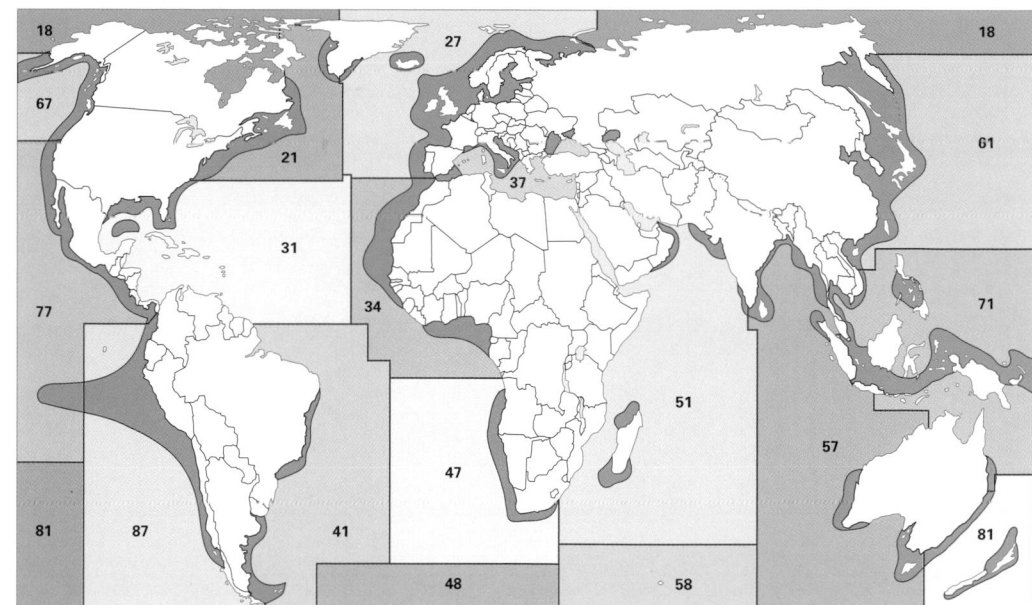

Marine Pollution

Sources of marine oil pollution

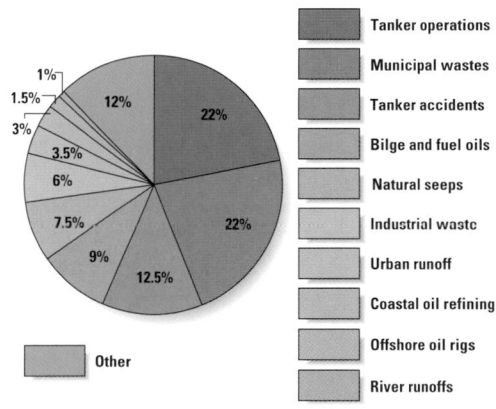

1% / 1.5% / 3% / 3.5% / 6% / 7.5% / 9% / 12.5% / 22% / 22% / 12%

- Tanker operations
- Municipal wastes
- Tanker accidents
- Bilge and fuel oils
- Natural seeps
- Industrial waste
- Urban runoff
- Coastal oil refining
- Offshore oil rigs
- River runoffs

Other

Oil Spills

Major oil spills from tankers and combined carriers

Year	Vessel	Location	Spill (barrels) *	Cause
1979	Atlantic Empress	West Indies	1,890,000	collision
1983	Castillo De Bellver	South Africa	1,760,000	fire
1978	Amoco Cadiz	France	1,628,000	grounding
1991	Haven	Italy	1,029,000	explosion
1988	Odyssey	Canada	1,000,000	fire
1967	Torrey Canyon	UK	909,000	grounding
1972	Sea Star	Gulf of Oman	902,250	collision
1977	Hawaiian Patriot	Hawaiian Is.	742,500	fire
1979	Independenta	Turkey	696,350	collision
1993	Braer	UK	625,000	grounding
1996	Sea Empress	UK	515,000	grounding
2002	Prestige	Spain	463,250	storm

Other sources of major oil spills

Year	Name	Location	Spill (barrels)	Cause
1983	Nowruz oilfield	Persian Gulf	4,250,000†	war
1979	Ixtoc 1 oilwell	Gulf of Mexico	4,200,000	blowout
1991	Kuwait	Persian Gulf	2,500,000†	war

* 1 barrel = 0.136 tons/159 lit./35 Imperial gal./42 US gal. † estimated

River Pollution

Sources of river pollution, USA

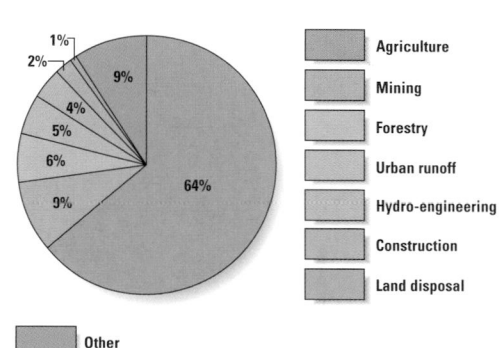

1% / 2% / 9% / 4% / 5% / 6% / 9% / 64%

- Agriculture
- Mining
- Forestry
- Urban runoff
- Hydro-engineering
- Construction
- Land disposal

Other

Water Pollution

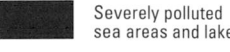

- Severely polluted sea areas and lakes
- Polluted sea areas and lakes
- Areas of frequent oil pollution by shipping
- ◣ Major oil tanker spills
- ▲ Major oil rig blowouts
- ▼ Offshore dumpsites for industrial and municipal waste
- — Severely polluted rivers and estuaries

The most notorious tanker spillage of the 1980s occurred when the *Exxon Valdez* ran aground in Prince William Sound, Alaska, in 1989, spilling 267,000 barrels of crude oil close to shore in a sensitive ecological area. This rates as the world's 28th worst spill in terms of volume.

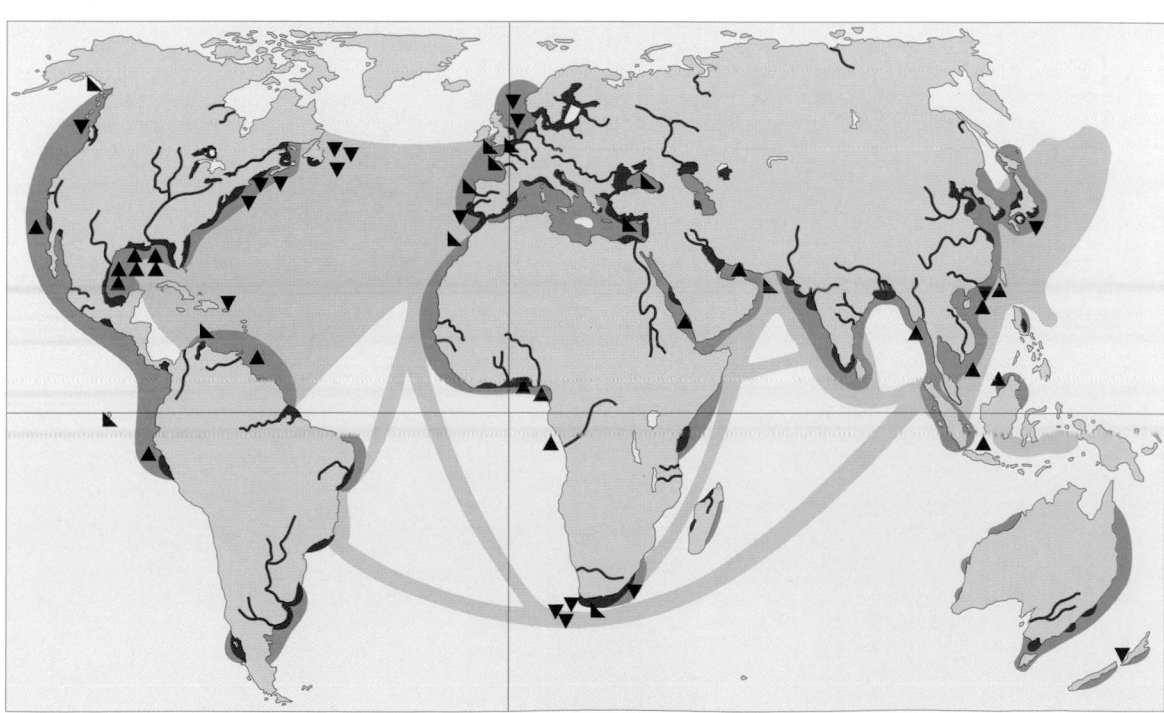

Climate

Climatic Regions

Color of climate region on map · Name of place

SINGAPORE

°C / °F

Average monthly temperature → Average monthly daily maximum temperature · Average monthly daily minimum temperature

Temperature

Average annual precipitation → 2413mm/95in · Precipitation

Average monthly precipitation

Months of the year → J F M A M J J A S O N D · mm / ins

Map labels: Arctic Circle, Eismitte, Edmonton, Krasnoyarsk, Québec, Tropic of Cancer, Bahrain, Ouagadougou, Addis Ababa, Equator, Singapore, Tropic of Capricorn, Buenos Aires, Antarctic Circle

Legend:
- Tropical climate (hot with rain all year)
- Desert climate (hot and very dry)
- Savanna climate (hot with dry season)
- Steppe climate (warm and dry)
- Mild climate (warm and wet)
- Continental climate (wet with cold winter)
- Subarctic climate (very cold winter)
- Polar climate (very cold and dry)
- Mountainous climate (altitude affects climate)

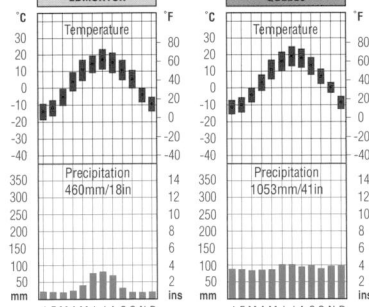
EDMONTON — Precipitation 460mm/18in

QUÉBEC — Precipitation 1053mm/41in

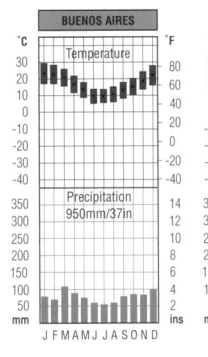
BUENOS AIRES — Precipitation 950mm/37in

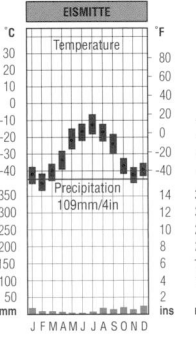
EISMITTE — Precipitation 109mm/4in

OUAGADOUGOU — Precipitation 889mm/35in

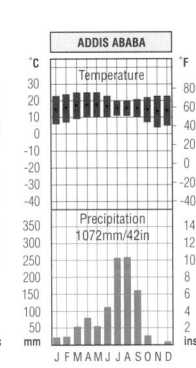
ADDIS ABABA — Precipitation 1072mm/42in

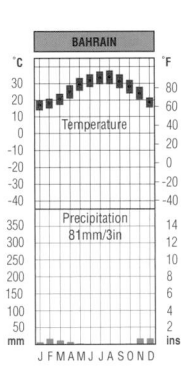
BAHRAIN — Precipitation 81mm/3in

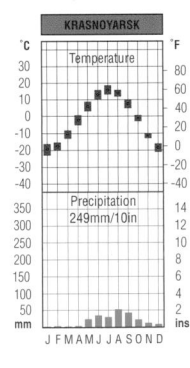
KRASNOYARSK — Precipitation 249mm/10in

Climate Records

Temperature

Highest recorded shade temperature: Al Aziziyah, Libya, 135.9°F [57.7°C], September 13, 1922.

Highest mean annual temperature: Dallol, Ethiopia, 94°F [34.4°C], 1960–66.

Longest heatwave: Marble Bar, W. Australia, 162 days over 100°F [38°C], October 23, 1923 to April 7, 1924.

Lowest recorded temperature (outside poles): Verkhoyansk, Siberia, –93.6°F [–68°C], February 7, 1982.

Lowest mean annual temperature: Polus Nedostupnosti, Pole of Cold, Antarctica, –72°F [–57.8°C].

Precipitation

Driest place: Quillagua, Chile, mean annual rainfall 0.02 inches [0.5 mm], 1964–2001.

Wettest place (12 months): Cherrapunji, Meghalaya, N. E. India, 1,042 inches [26,461 mm], August 1860 to July 1861. Cherrapunji also holds the record for the most rainfall in one month: 115 inches [2,930 mm], July 1861.

Wettest place (average): Mt Wai-ale-ale, Hawai'i, USA, mean annual rainfall 459.8 inches [11,680 mm].

Wettest place (24 hours): Fac Fac, Réunion, Indian Ocean, 71.9 inches [1,825 mm], March 15–16, 1952.

Heaviest hailstones: Gopalganj, Bangladesh, up to 2.25 lb [1.02 kg], April 14, 1986 (killed 92 people).

Heaviest snowfall (continuous): Bessans, Savoie, France, 68 inches [1,730 mm] in 19 hours, April 5–6, 1969.

Heaviest snowfall (season/year): Mt Baker, Washington, USA, 1,140 inches [28,956 mm], June 1998 to June 1999.

Pressure and winds

Highest barometric pressure: Agata, Siberia (at 862 ft [262 m] altitude), 1,083.8 mb, December 31, 1968.

Lowest barometric pressure: Typhoon Tip, Guam, Pacific Ocean, 870 mb, October 12, 1979.

Highest recorded wind speed: Bridge Creek, Oklahoma, USA, 318 mph [512 km/h], May 3, 1999. Measured by Doppler radar monitoring a tornado.

Windiest place: Port Martin, Antarctica, where winds of more than 40 mph [64 km/h] occur for not less than 100 days a year.

Climate

Climate is weather in the long term: the seasonal pattern of hot and cold, wet and dry, averaged over time (usually 30 years). At the simplest level, it is caused by the uneven heating of the Earth. Surplus heat at the Equator passes toward the poles, leveling out the energy differential. Its passage is marked by a ceaseless churning of the atmosphere and the oceans, further agitated by the Earth's diurnal spin and the motion it imparts to moving air and water. The heat's means of transport – by winds and ocean currents, by the continual evaporation and recondensation of water molecules – is the weather itself. There are four basic types of climate, each of which can be further subdivided: tropical, desert (dry), temperate, and polar.

Composition of Dry Air

Nitrogen	78.09%	Sulfur dioxide	trace
Oxygen	20.95%	Nitrogen oxide	trace
Argon	0.93%	Methane	trace
Water vapor	0.2–4.0%	Dust	trace
Carbon dioxide	0.03%	Helium	trace
Ozone	0.00006%	Neon	trace

CARTOGRAPHY BY PHILIP'S. COPYRIGHT PHILIP'S

El Niño

In a normal year, southeasterly trade winds drive surface waters westward off the coast of South America, drawing cold, nutrient-rich water up from below. In an El Niño year (which occurs every 2–7 years), warm water from the west Pacific suppresses upwelling in the east, depriving the region of nutrients. The water is warmed by as much as 12°F [7°C], disturbing the tropical atmospheric circulation. During an intense El Niño, the southeast trade winds change direction and become equatorial westerlies, resulting in climatic extremes in many regions of the world, such as drought in parts of Australia and India, and heavy rainfall in southeastern USA. An intense El Niño occurred in 1997–8, with resultant freak weather conditions across the entire Pacific region.

Normal year

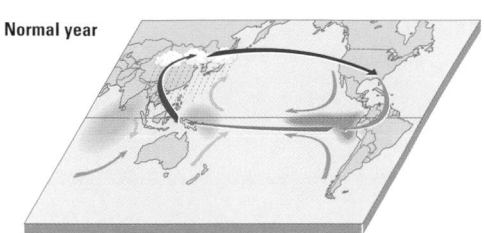

El Niño event

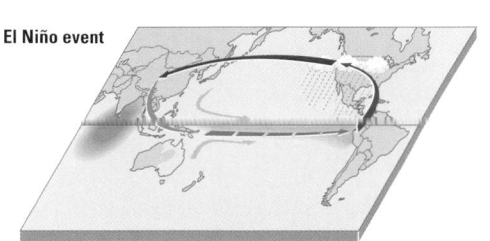

Beaufort Wind Scale

Named after the 19th-century British naval officer who devised it, the Beaufort Scale assesses wind speed according to its effects. It was originally designed as an aid for sailors, but has since been adapted for use on the land.

Scale	Wind speed mph	km/h	Effect
0	0–1	0–1	**Calm** Smoke rises vertically
1	1–3	1–5	**Light air** Wind direction shown only by smoke drift
2	4–7	6–11	**Light breeze** Wind felt on face; leaves rustle; vanes moved by wind
3	8–12	12–19	**Gentle breeze** Leaves and small twigs in constant motion; wind extends small flag
4	13–18	20–28	**Moderate** Raises dust and loose paper; small branches move
5	19–24	29–38	**Fresh** Small trees in leaf sway; wavelets on inland waters
6	25–31	39–49	**Strong** Large branches move; difficult to use umbrellas
7	32–38	50–61	**Near gale** Whole trees in motion; difficult to walk against wind
8	39–46	62–74	**Gale** Twigs break from trees; walking very difficult
9	47–54	75–88	**Strong gale** Slight structural damage
10	55–63	89–102	**Storm** Trees uprooted; serious structural damage
11	64–72	103–117	**Violent storm** Widespread damage
12	73+	118+	**Hurricane**

Conversions

°C = (°F − 32) × 5/9; °F = (°C × 9/5) + 32; 0°C = 32°F
1 in = 25.4 mm; 1 mm = 0.0394 in; 100 mm = 3.94 in

CARTOGRAPHY BY PHILIP'S. COPYRIGHT PHILIP'S

Temperature

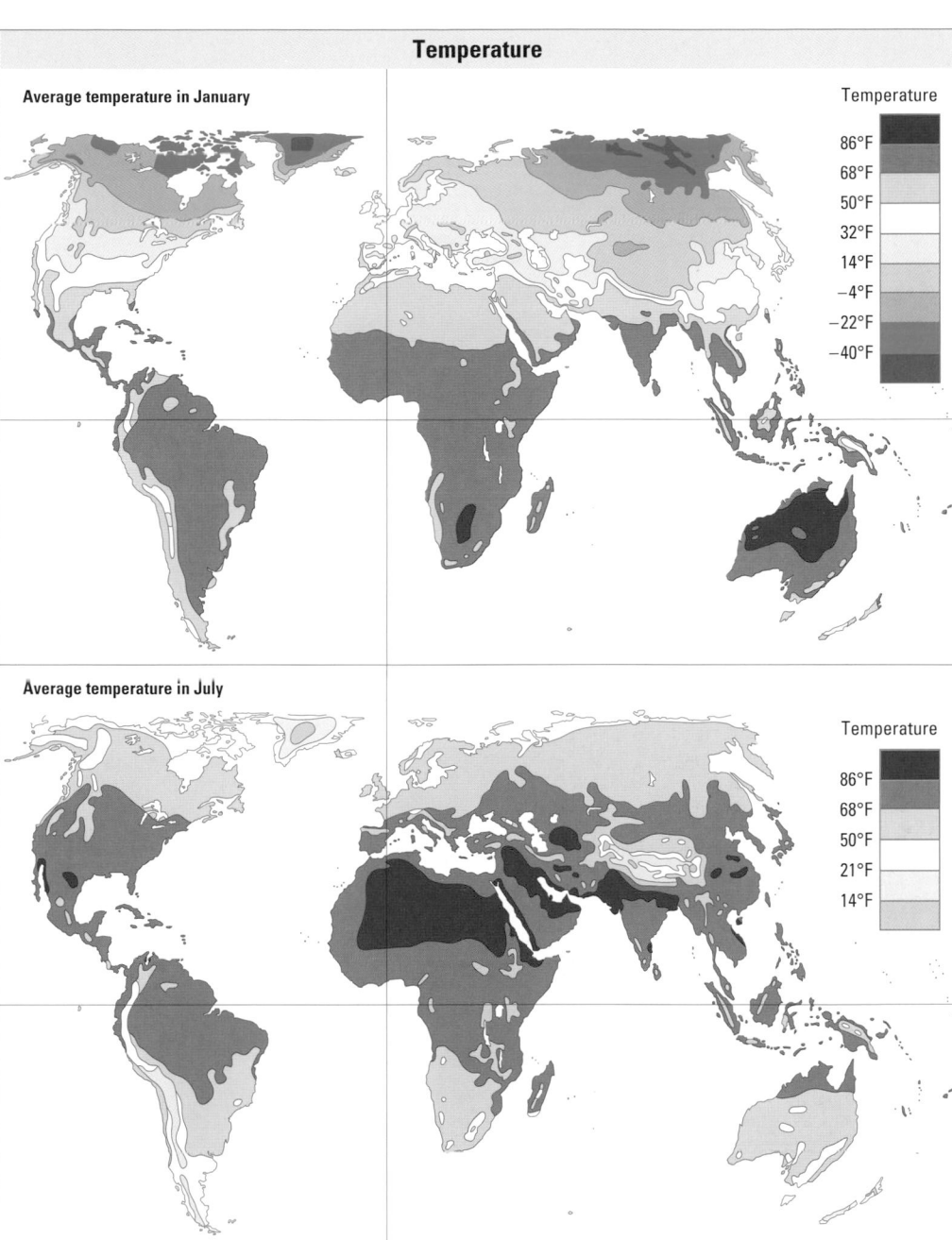

Average temperature in January

Temperature
86°F
68°F
50°F
32°F
14°F
−4°F
−22°F
−40°F

Average temperature in July

Temperature
86°F
68°F
50°F
21°F
14°F

Precipitation

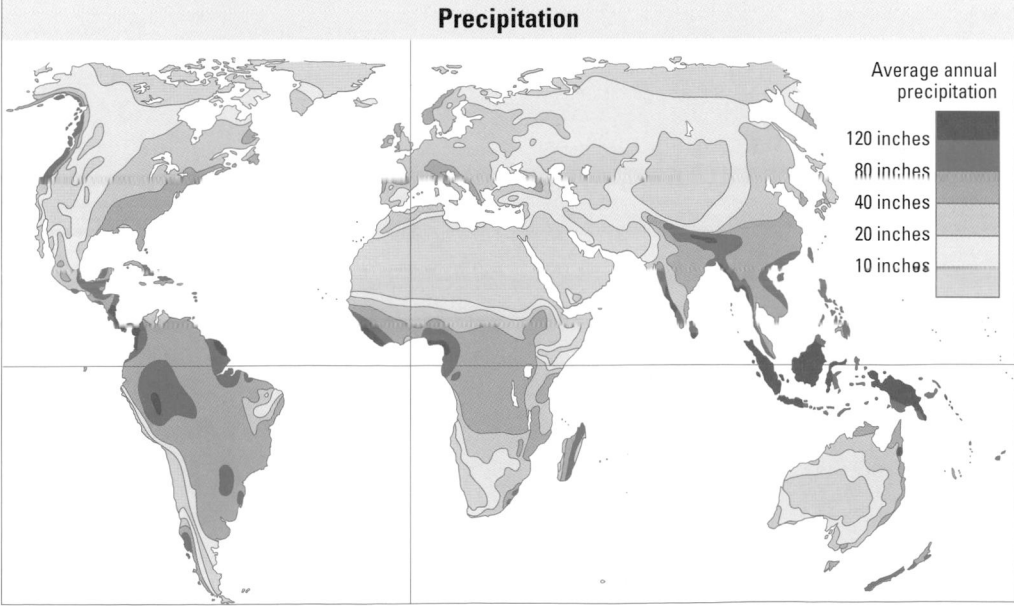

Average annual precipitation
120 inches
80 inches
40 inches
20 inches
10 inches

Water and Vegetation

The Hydrological Cycle

The world's water balance is regulated by the constant recycling of water between the oceans, atmosphere and land. The movement of water between these three reservoirs is known as the hydrological cycle. The oceans play a vital role in the hydrological cycle: 74% of the total precipitation falls over the oceans and 84% of the total evaporation comes from the oceans.

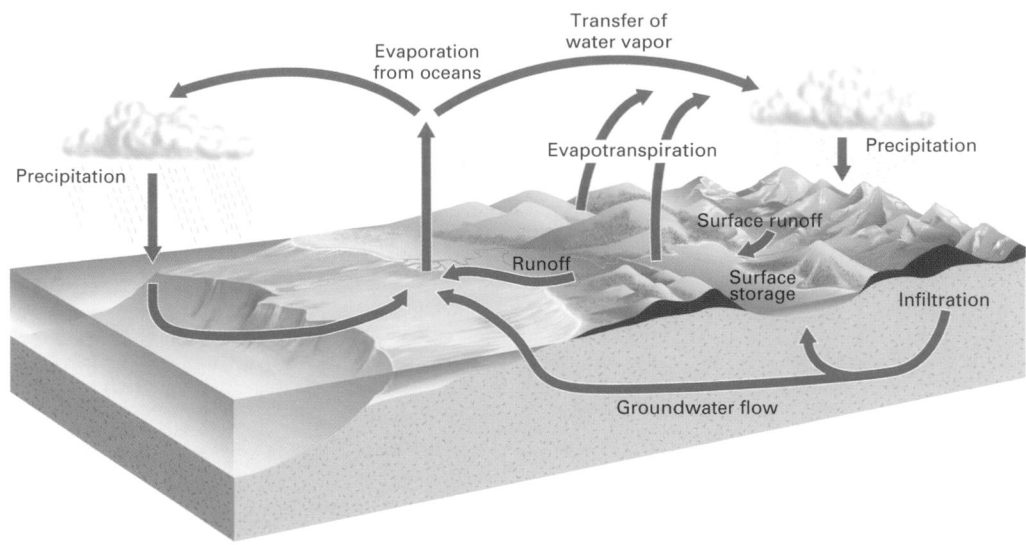

Water Distribution

The distribution of planetary water, by percentage. Oceans and ice caps together account for more than 99% of the total; the breakdown of the remainder is estimated.

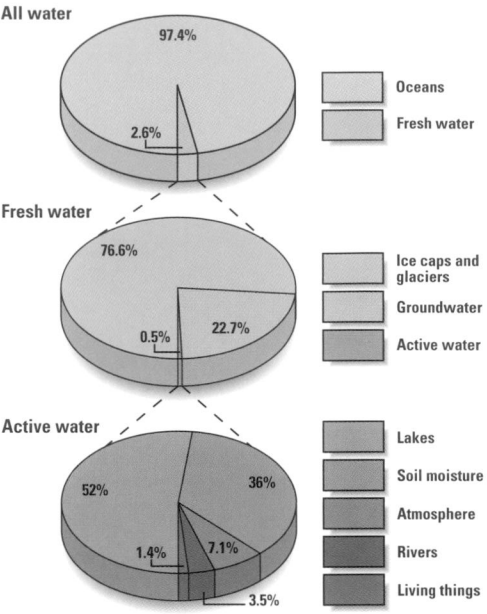

All water
- 97.4% Oceans
- 2.6% Fresh water

Fresh water
- 76.6% Ice caps and glaciers
- 22.7% Groundwater
- 0.5% Active water

Active water
- 52% Lakes
- 36% Soil moisture
- 7.1% Atmosphere
- 3.5% Rivers
- 1.4% Living things

Water Utilization

Domestic | Industrial | Agriculture

The percentage breakdown of water usage by sector, selected countries (2007)

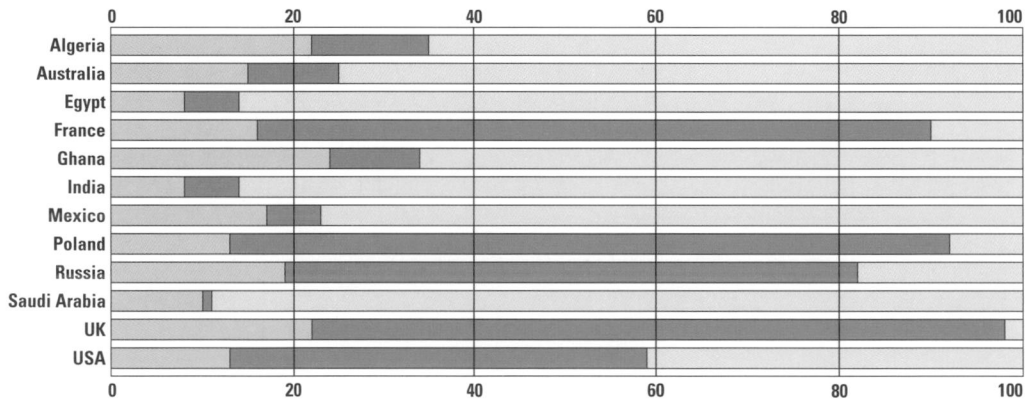

Algeria, Australia, Egypt, France, Ghana, India, Mexico, Poland, Russia, Saudi Arabia, UK, USA

Water Usage

Almost all the world's water is 3,000 million years old, and all of it cycles endlessly through the hydrosphere, though at different rates. Water vapor circulates over days, even hours, deep ocean water circulates over millennia, and ice-cap water remains solid for millions of years.

Fresh water is essential to all terrestrial life. Humans cannot survive more than a few days without it, and even the hardiest desert plants and animals could not exist without some water. Agriculture requires huge quantities of fresh water: without large-scale irrigation most of the world's people would starve. In the USA, agriculture uses 41% and industry 46% of all water withdrawals.

According to the latest figures, the average North American uses 1.3 million liters per year. This is more than six times the average African, who uses just 186,000 liters of water each year. Europeans and Australians use 694,000 liters per year.

Water Supply

Percentage of total population with access to safe drinking water (2005)

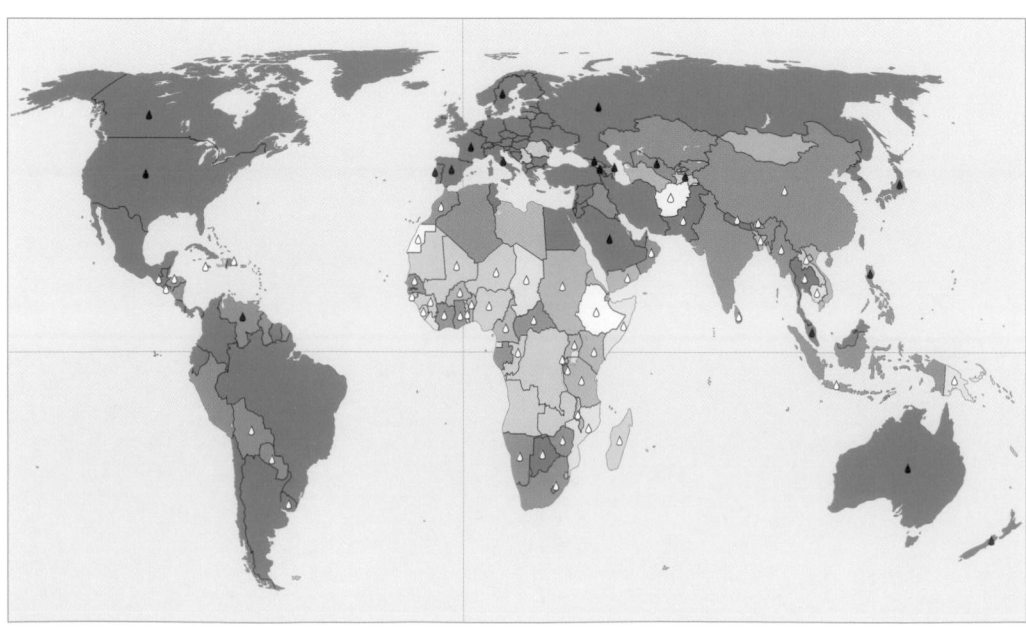

- Over 90% with safe water
- 75 – 90% with safe water
- 60 – 75% with safe water
- 45 – 60% with safe water
- 30 – 45% with safe water
- Under 30% with safe water

⌀ Under 80 liters per person per day domestic water consumption

▲ Over 320 liters per person per day domestic water consumption

NB: 80 liters of water a day is considered necessary for a reasonable quality of life.

Least well-provided countries

Afghanistan	13%	Papua New Guinea	39%
Ethiopia	22%	Cambodia	41%
Western Sahara	26%	Somalia	42%

CARTOGRAPHY BY PHILIP'S. COPYRIGHT PHILIP'S

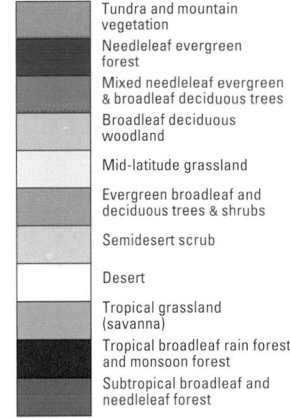

Natural Vegetation

Regional variation in vegetation

- Tundra and mountain vegetation
- Needleleaf evergreen forest
- Mixed needleleaf evergreen & broadleaf deciduous trees
- Broadleaf deciduous woodland
- Mid-latitude grassland
- Evergreen broadleaf and deciduous trees & shrubs
- Semidesert scrub
- Desert
- Tropical grassland (savanna)
- Tropical broadleaf rain forest and monsoon forest
- Subtropical broadleaf and needleleaf forest

The map shows the natural "climax vegetation" of regions, as dictated by climate and topography. In most cases, however, agricultural activity has drastically altered the vegetation pattern. Western Europe, for example, lost most of its broadleaf forest many centuries ago, while irrigation has turned some natural semidesert into productive land.

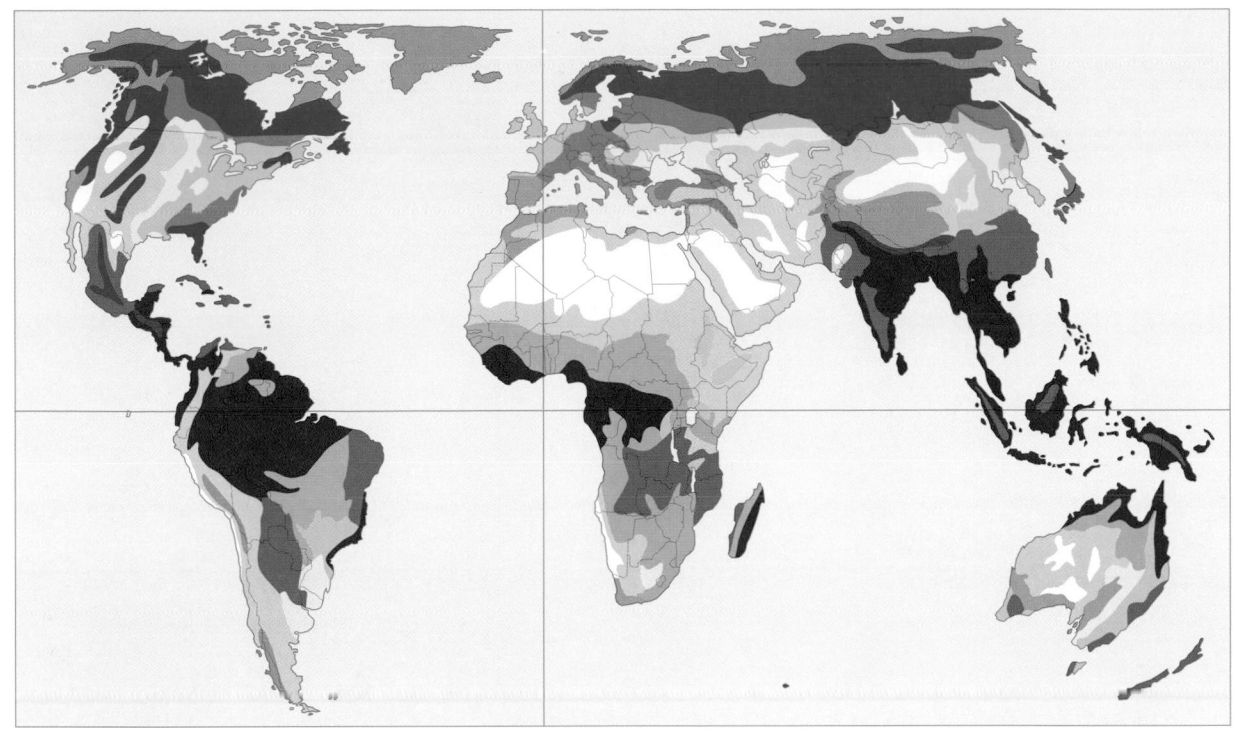

Land Use by Continent (2005)

- Forest
- Permanent pasture
- Permanent crops
- Arable
- Other

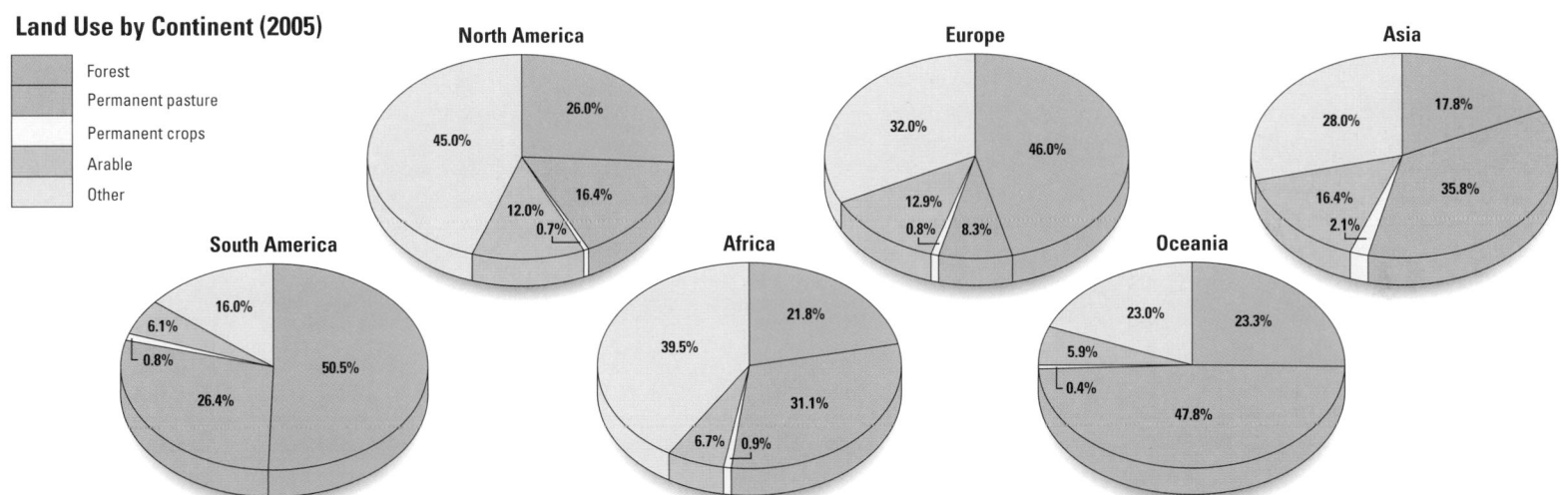

North America
- 26.0%
- 16.4%
- 0.7%
- 12.0%
- 45.0%

Europe
- 46.0%
- 8.3%
- 0.8%
- 12.9%
- 32.0%

Asia
- 17.8%
- 35.8%
- 2.1%
- 16.4%
- 28.0%

South America
- 50.5%
- 26.4%
- 0.8%
- 6.1%
- 16.0%

Africa
- 21.8%
- 31.1%
- 0.9%
- 6.7%
- 39.5%

Oceania
- 23.3%
- 47.8%
- 0.4%
- 5.9%
- 23.0%

Forestry: Production

	Forest and woodland (million hectares)	Annual production (2006, million cubic meters) Fuelwood	Annual production (2006, million cubic meters) Industrial roundwood*
World	*3,869.5*	*1,948.7*	*1762.6*
Europe	1,039.3	152.6	516.7
S. America	885.6	274.6	157.0
Africa	649.9	588.4	66.4
N. & C. America	549.3	131.4	741.9
Asia	517.8	788.9	231.0
Oceania	197.6	12.8	49.6

Paper and Board

Top producers (2006)**		Top exporters (2006)**	
USA	84,317	Canada	14,260
China	57,983	Germany	13,058
Japan	29,473	Finland	12,906
Germany	22,655	Sweden	10,849
Canada	18,176	USA	9,644

* roundwood is timber as it is felled
** in thousand tons

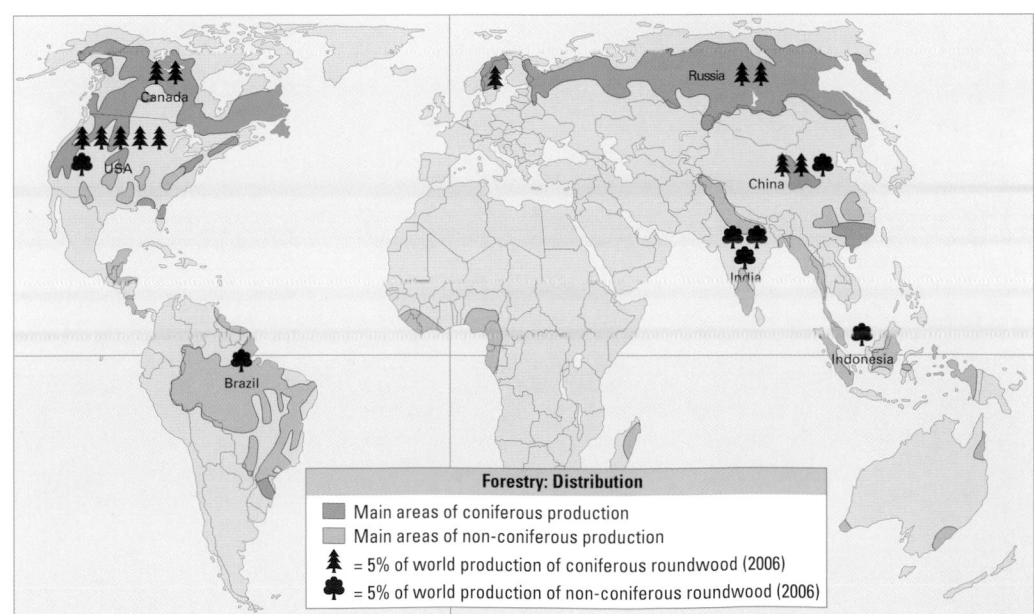

Forestry: Distribution
- Main areas of coniferous production
- Main areas of non-coniferous production
- 🌲 = 5% of world production of coniferous roundwood (2006)
- 🌳 = 5% of world production of non-coniferous roundwood (2006)

CARTOGRAPHY BY PHILIP'S. COPYRIGHT PHILIP'S

Environment

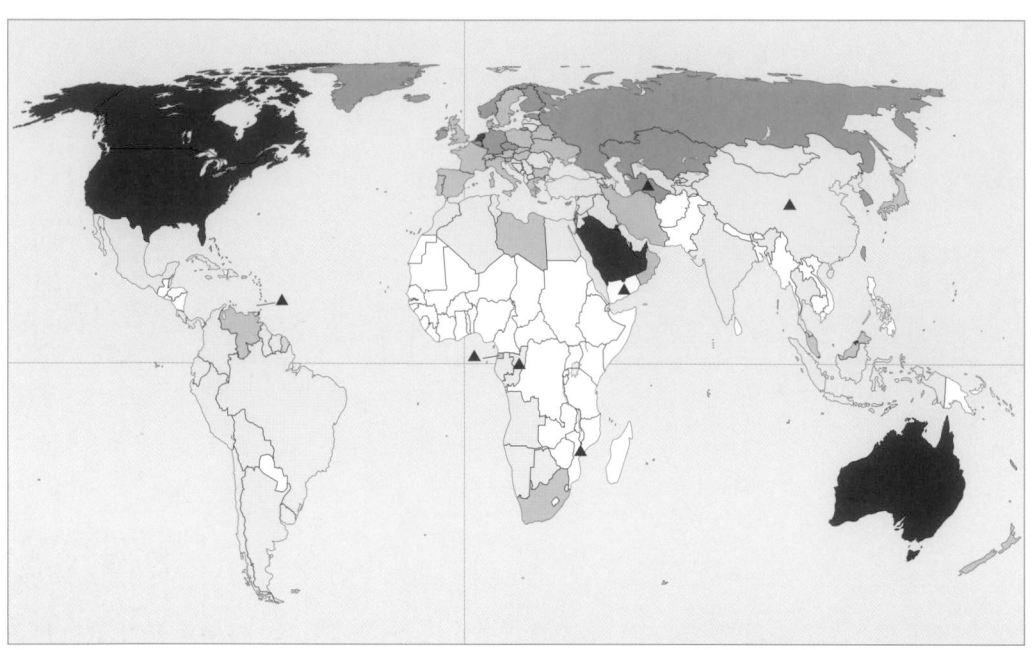

Global Warming

Carbon dioxide emissions in tons per capita (2005)

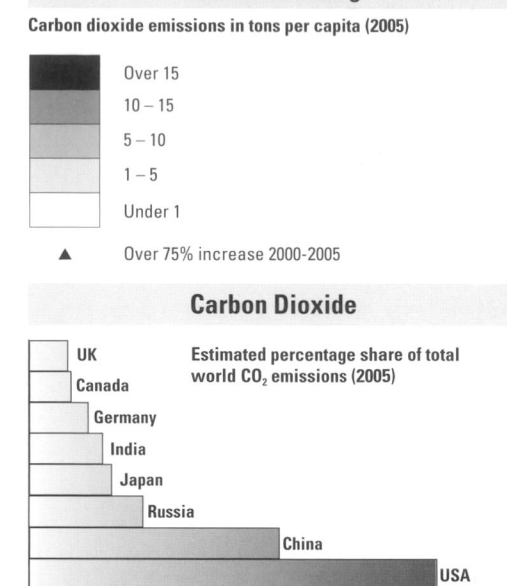

- Over 15
- 10 – 15
- 5 – 10
- 1 – 5
- Under 1

▲   Over 75% increase 2000-2005

Carbon Dioxide

UK
Canada
Germany
India
Japan
Russia
China
USA

Estimated percentage share of total world CO₂ emissions (2005)

$$5\% \quad 10\% \quad 15\% \quad 20\% \quad 25\%$$

Predicted Change in Precipitation

The difference between actual annual average precipitation, 1960-1990, and the predicted annual average precipitation, 2070-2100.
It should be noted that these predicted annual mean changes mask quite significant seasonal detail.

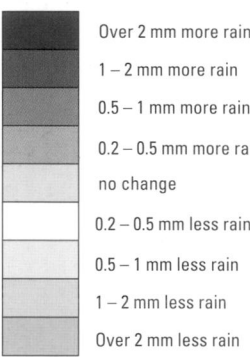

- Over 2 mm more rain
- 1 – 2 mm more rain
- 0.5 – 1 mm more rain
- 0.2 – 0.5 mm more rain
- no change
- 0.2 – 0.5 mm less rain
- 0.5 – 1 mm less rain
- 1 – 2 mm less rain
- Over 2 mm less rain

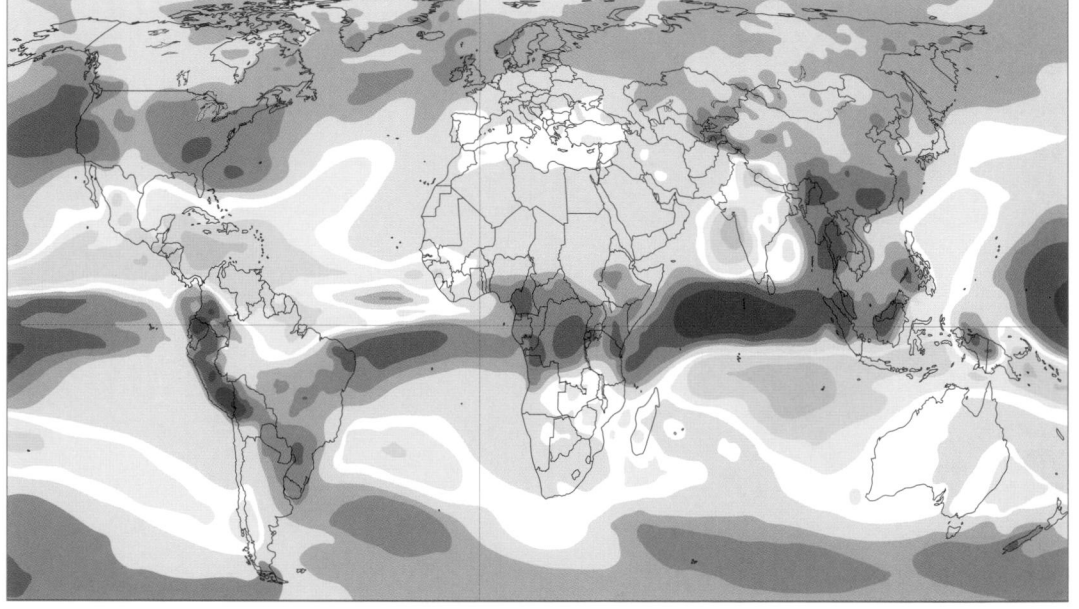

Predicted Change in Temperature

The difference between actual annual average surface air temperature, 1960-1990, and the predicted annual average surface air temperature, 2070-2100.
This map shows the predicted increase, assuming a "medium growth" of global economy and assuming that no measures to combat the emission of greenhouse gases are taken.

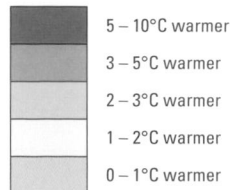

- 5 – 10°C warmer
- 3 – 5°C warmer
- 2 – 3°C warmer
- 1 – 2°C warmer
- 0 – 1°C warmer

Source: The Hadley Centre of Climate Prediction and Research, The Met. Office

CARTOGRAPHY BY PHILIP'S. COPYRIGHT PHILIP'S

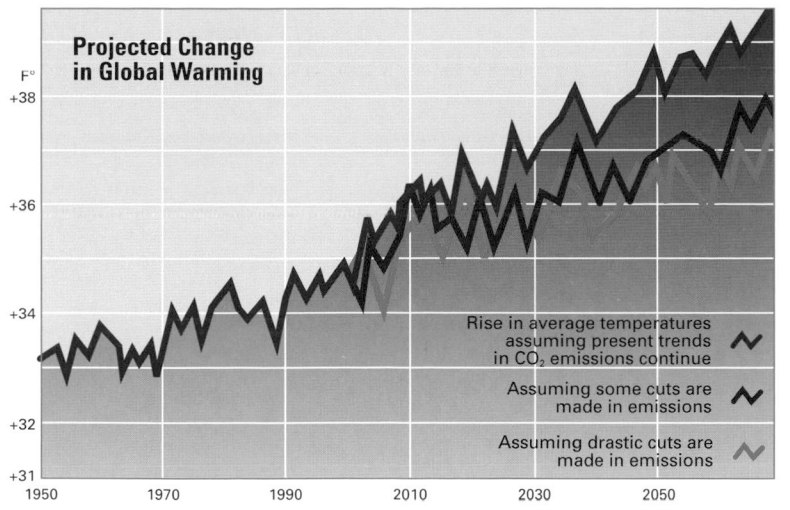

Projected Change in Global Warming

F°
+38
+36
+34
+32
+31

1950   1970   1990   2010   2030   2050

Rise in average temperatures assuming present trends in CO₂ emissions continue

Assuming some cuts are made in emissions

Assuming drastic cuts are made in emissions

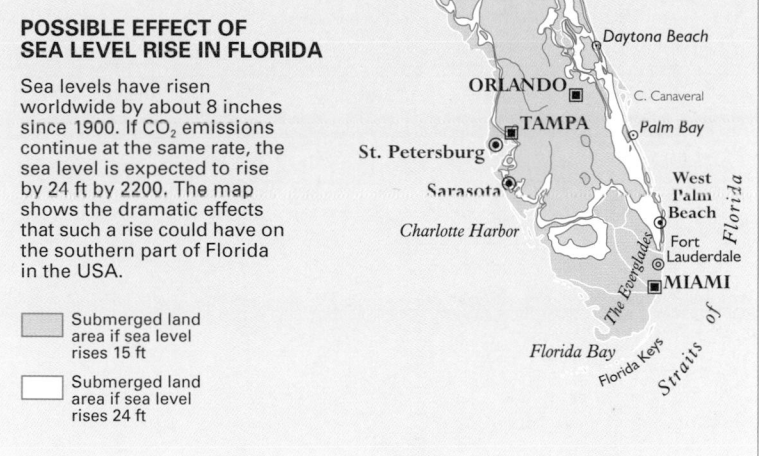

POSSIBLE EFFECT OF SEA LEVEL RISE IN FLORIDA

Sea levels have risen worldwide by about 8 inches since 1900. If CO₂ emissions continue at the same rate, the sea level is expected to rise by 24 ft by 2200. The map shows the dramatic effects that such a rise could have on the southern part of Florida in the USA.

Submerged land area if sea level rises 15 ft

Submerged land area if sea level rises 24 ft

Daytona Beach
ORLANDO
C. Canaveral
TAMPA
Palm Bay
St. Petersburg
Sarasota
West Palm Beach
Charlotte Harbor
Fort Lauderdale
MIAMI
Florida Bay
Florida Keys
Straits of Florida
The Everglades

The Greenhouse Effect

Carbon dioxide is increased by burning fossil fuels and cutting forests

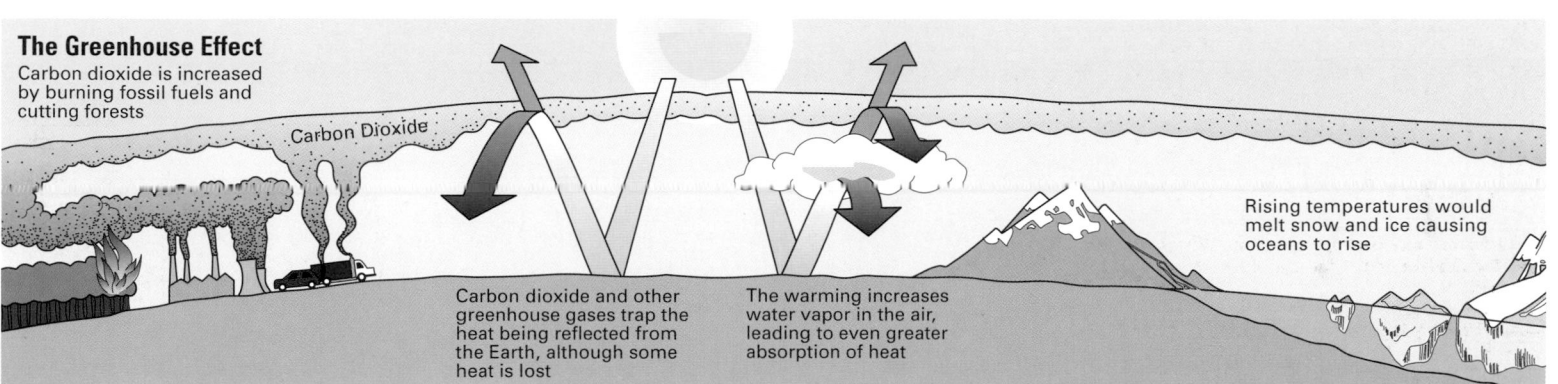

Carbon Dioxide

Carbon dioxide and other greenhouse gases trap the heat being reflected from the Earth, although some heat is lost

The warming increases water vapor in the air, leading to even greater absorption of heat

Rising temperatures would melt snow and ice causing oceans to rise

Desertification

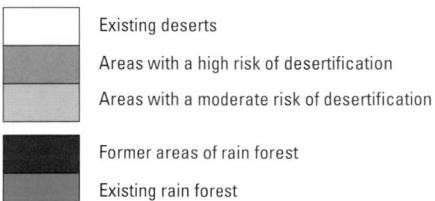

Existing deserts

Areas with a high risk of desertification

Areas with a moderate risk of desertification

Former areas of rain forest

Existing rain forest

Forest Clearance

Thousands of hectares of forest cleared annually, tropical countries surveyed 1980–85, 1990–95 and 2000–05. Loss as a percentage of remaining stocks is shown in figures on each column. Gain is indicated as a minus figure.

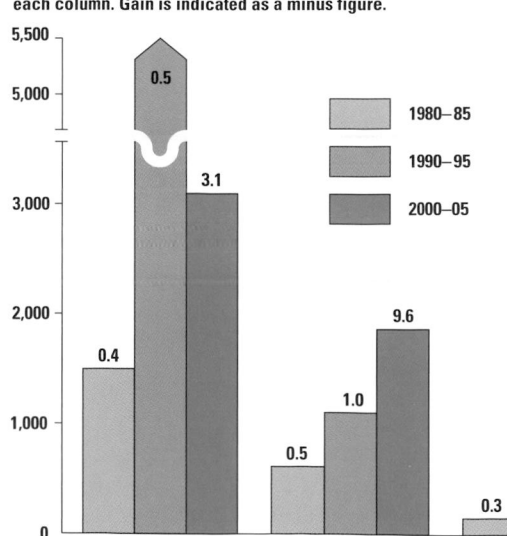

1980–85
1990–95
2000–05

Brazil 0.4 0.5 3.1
Indonesia 0.5 1.0 9.6
India 0.3 0.0 0.7
Burma 0.3 1.4 4.7
Thailand 2.4 2.6 2.0
Vietnam 0.7 1.4 −12.2
Philippines 1.0 3.5 4.2
Costa Rica 4.0 3.0 −0.6

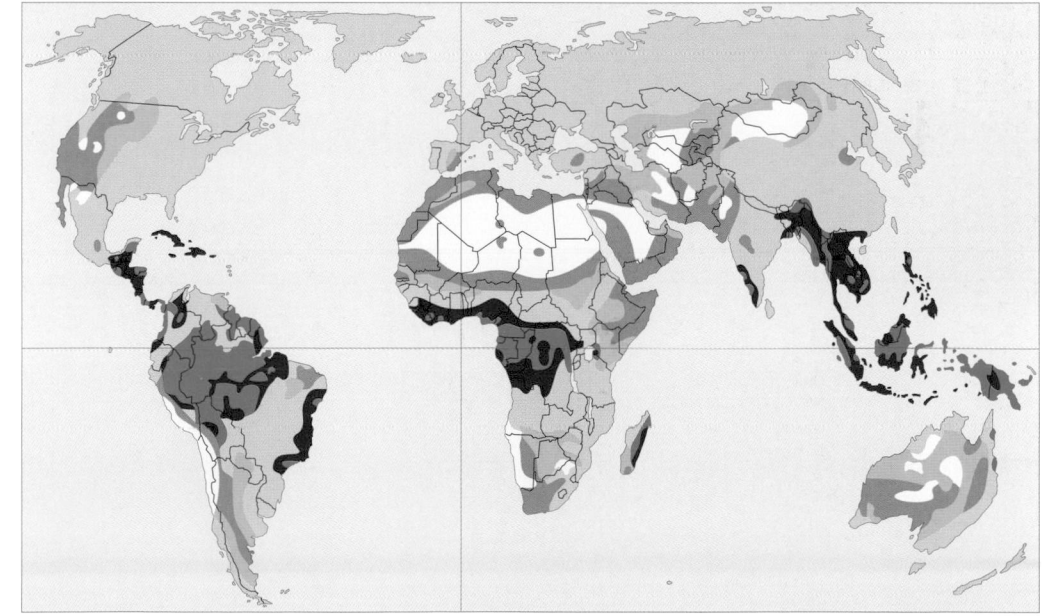

Deforestation

The Earth's remaining forests are under attack from three directions: expanding agriculture, logging, and growing consumption of fuelwood, often in combination. Sometimes deforestation is the direct result of government policy, as in the efforts made to resettle the urban poor in some parts of Brazil; just as often, it comes about despite state attempts at conservation. Loggers, licensed or unlicensed, blaze a trail into virgin forest, often destroying twice as many trees as they harvest. Landless farmers follow, burning away most of what remains to plant their crops, completing the destruction. Some countries such as Vietnam and Costa Rica have successfully implemented reafforestation programs.

CARTOGRAPHY BY PHILIP'S. COPYRIGHT PHILIP'S

Population

Demographic Profiles

Developed nations such as the UK have populations evenly spread across the age groups and, usually, a growing proportion of elderly people. The great majority of the people in developing nations, however, are in the younger age groups, about to enter their most fertile years. In time, these population profiles should resemble the world profile (even Nigeria has made recent progress by reducing its birth rate), but the transition will come about only after a few more generations of rapid population growth.

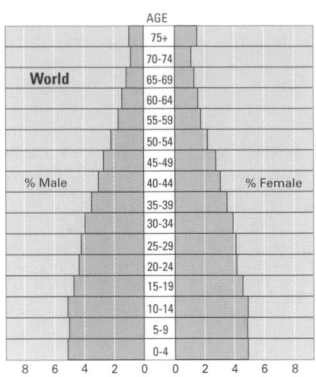

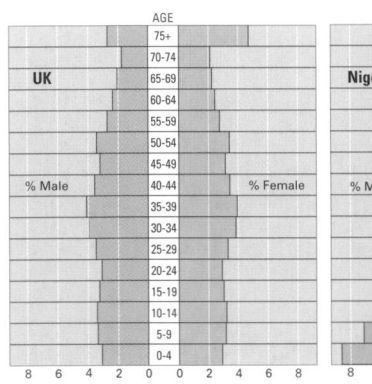

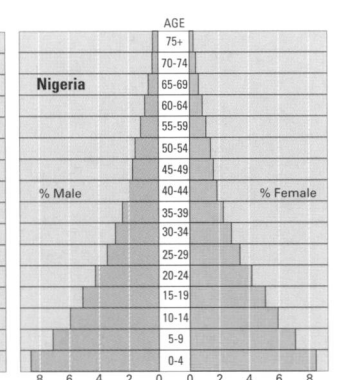

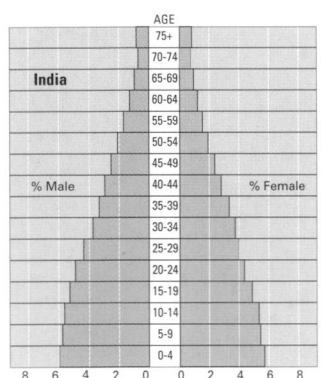

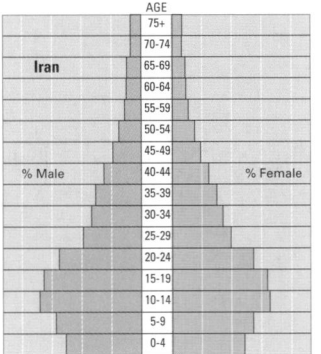

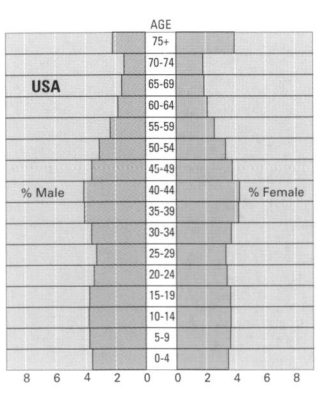

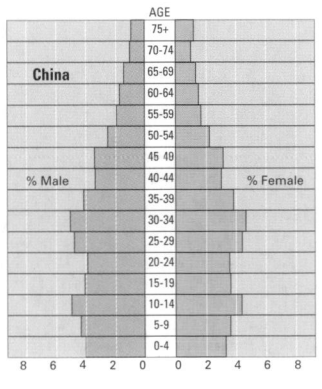

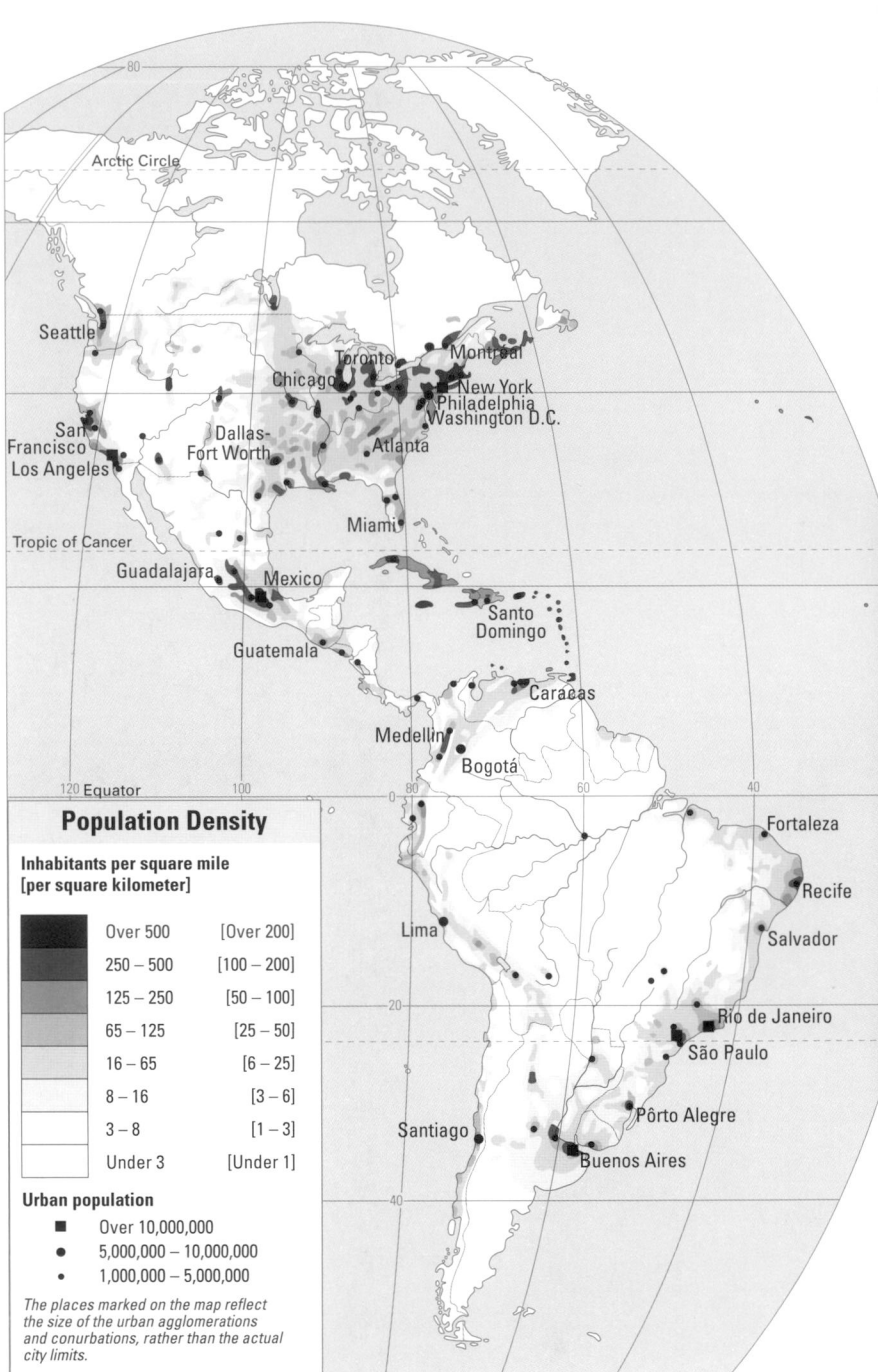

Population Density

Inhabitants per square mile [per square kilometer]

Over 500	[Over 200]
250 – 500	[100 – 200]
125 – 250	[50 – 100]
65 – 125	[25 – 50]
16 – 65	[6 – 25]
8 – 16	[3 – 6]
3 – 8	[1 – 3]
Under 3	[Under 1]

Urban population

■	Over 10,000,000
●	5,000,000 – 10,000,000
•	1,000,000 – 5,000,000

The places marked on the map reflect the size of the urban agglomerations and conurbations, rather than the actual city limits.

Most Populous Nations, in millions (2007 estimates)

1.	China	1,322	9. Nigeria	135	17. Turkey	71
2.	India	1,130	10. Japan	127	18. Congo (Dem. Rep.)	66
3.	USA	301	11. Mexico	109	19. Iran	65
4.	Indonesia	235	12. Philippines	91	20. Thailand	65
5.	Brazil	190	13. Vietnam	85	21. France	61
6.	Pakistan	165	14. Germany	82	22. UK	61
7.	Bangladesh	150	15. Egypt	80	23. Italy	58
8.	Russia	141	16. Ethiopia	77	24. South Korea	49

Continental Comparisons

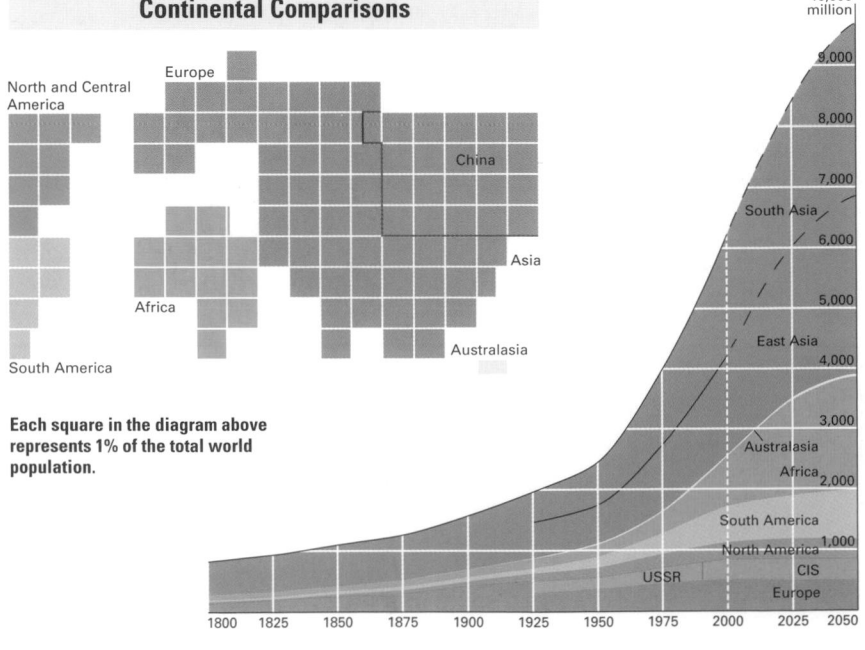

Each square in the diagram above represents 1% of the total world population.

CARTOGRAPHY BY PHILIP'S. COPYRIGHT PHILIP'S

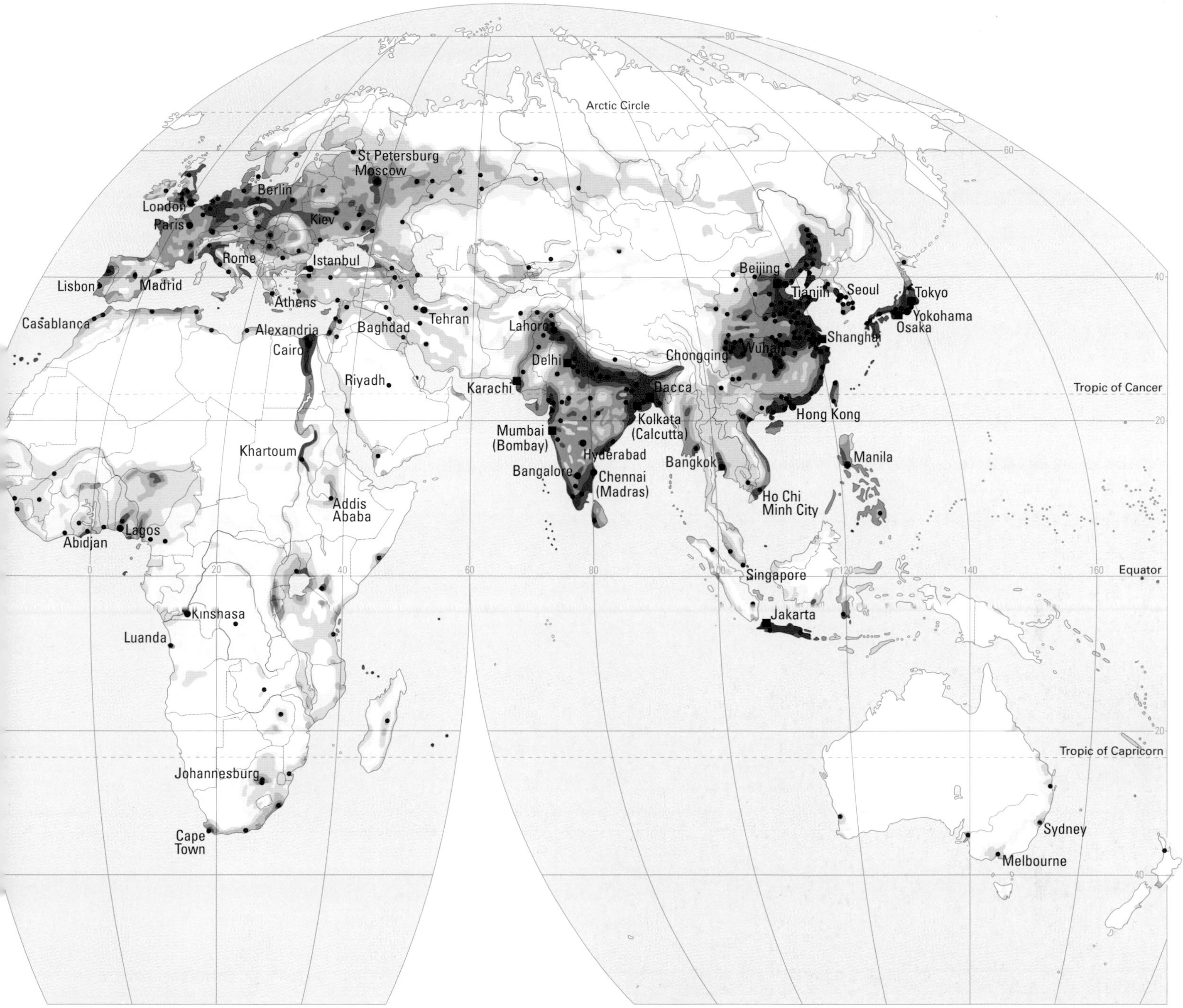

Arctic Circle

St Petersburg
Moscow
Berlin
London
Paris
Kiev
Rome
Istanbul
Lisbon
Madrid
Athens
Casablanca
Alexandria
Baghdad
Tehran
Lahore
Beijing
Tianjin
Seoul
Tokyo
Yokohama
Osaka
Shanghai
Wuhan
Chongqing
Cairo
Riyadh
Delhi
Karachi
Dacca
Kolkata
(Calcutta)
Khartoum
Mumbai
(Bombay)
Hyderabad
Chennai
(Madras)
Bangalore
Bangkok
Hong Kong
Manila
Addis
Ababa
Ho Chi
Minh City
Lagos
Abidjan
Tropic of Cancer
Kinshasa
Singapore
Equator
Luanda
Jakarta
Johannesburg
Tropic of Capricorn
Cape
Town
Sydney
Melbourne

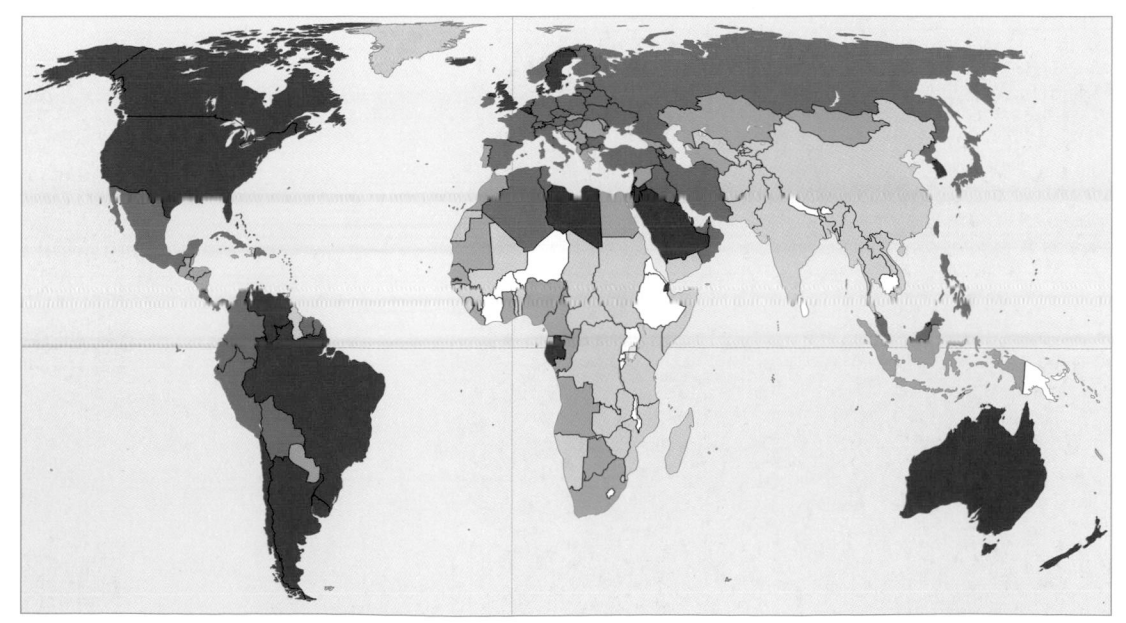
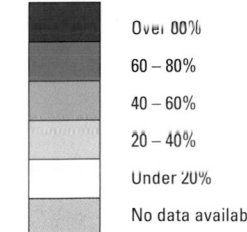

Urban Population

Percentage of total population living in towns and cities (2005)

- Over 80%
- 60 – 80%
- 40 – 60%
- 20 – 40%
- Under 20%
- No data available

Most urbanized		Least urbanized	
Singapore	100%	Burundi	10%
Kuwait	97%	Bhutan	11%
Belgium	97%	Trinidad & Tobago	12%
Bahrain	96%	Uganda	13%
Qatar	95%	Papua New Guinea	13%

CARTOGRAPHY BY PHILIP'S. COPYRIGHT PHILIP'S.

The Human Family

Predominant Languages

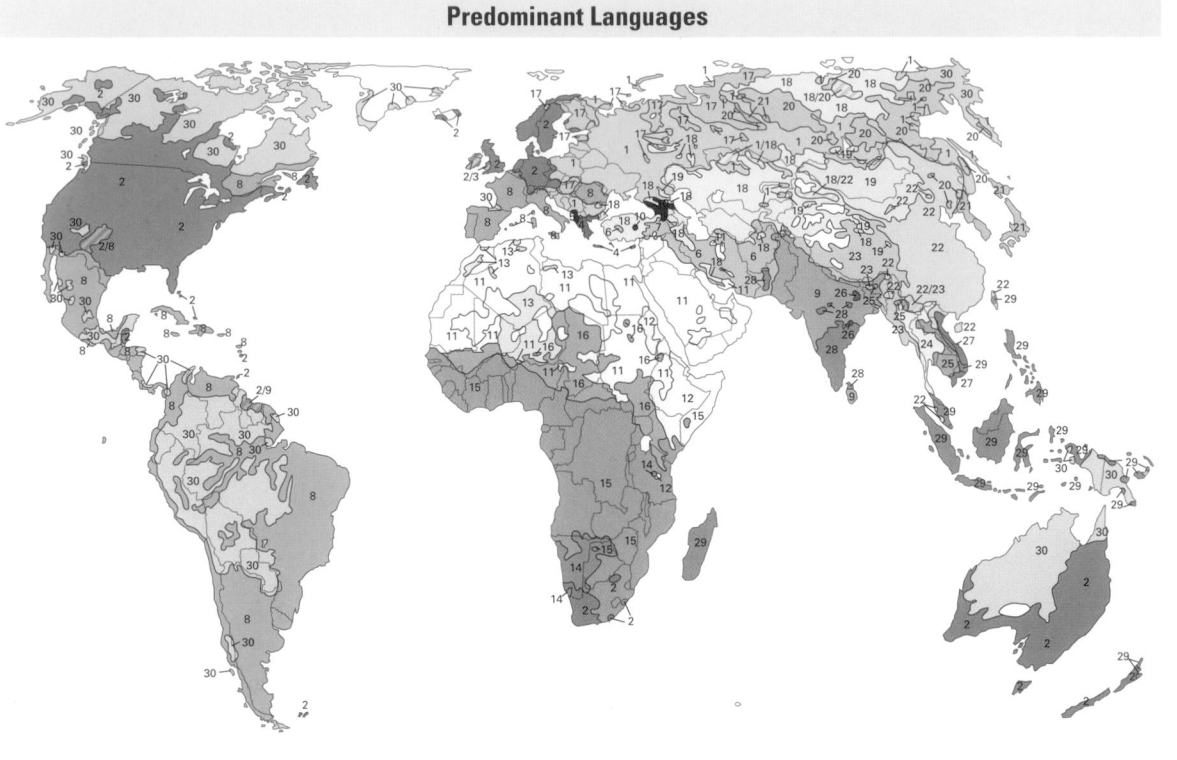

Languages of the World

Language can be classified by ancestry and structure. For example, the Romance and Germanic groups are both derived from an Indo-European language believed to have been spoken 5,000 years ago.

First-language speakers in millions (2005)
Mandarin Chinese 873, Spanish 322, English 309, Portuguese 230, Arabic 206, Hindi 181, Bengali 171, Russian 145, Japanese 122, German 95, Wu Chinese 77, Javanese 75, Telugu 70, Marathi 68, Vietnamese 67, Korean 67, Tamil 65, French 65, Italian 62, Punjabi 60.

Distribution of Living Languages

The figures refer to the number of languages currently in use in the regions shown

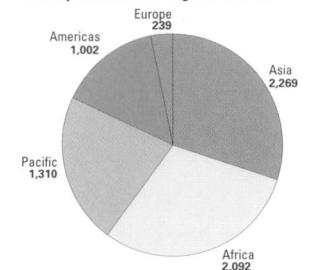

Europe 239
Americas 1,002
Asia 2,269
Pacific 1,310
Africa 2,092

INDO-EUROPEAN FAMILY

1	Balto-Slavic group (incl. Russian, Ukrainian)
2	Germanic group (incl. English, German)
3	Celtic group
4	Greek
5	Albanian
6	Iranian group
7	Armenian
8	Romance group (incl. Spanish, Portuguese, French, Italian)
9	Indo-Aryan group (incl. Hindi, Bengali, Urdu, Punjabi, Marathi)
10	CAUCASIAN FAMILY

AFRO-ASIATIC FAMILY

11	Semitic group (incl. Arabic)
12	Kushitic group
13	Berber group

14	KHOISAN FAMILY
15	NIGER-CONGO FAMILY
16	NILO-SAHARAN FAMILY
17	URALIC FAMILY

ALTAIC FAMILY

18	Turkic group (incl. Turkish)
19	Mongolian group
20	Tungus-Manchu group
21	Japanese and Korean

SINO-TIBETAN FAMILY

| 22 | Sinitic (Chinese) languages (incl. Mandarin, Wu, Yue) |
| 23 | Tibetic-Burmic languages |

| 24 | TAI FAMILY |

AUSTRO-ASIATIC FAMILY

25	Mon-Khmer group
26	Munda group
27	Vietnamese

28	DRAVIDIAN FAMILY (incl. Telugu, Tamil)
29	AUSTRONESIAN FAMILY (incl. Malay-Indonesian, Javanese)
30	OTHER LANGUAGES

Predominant Religions

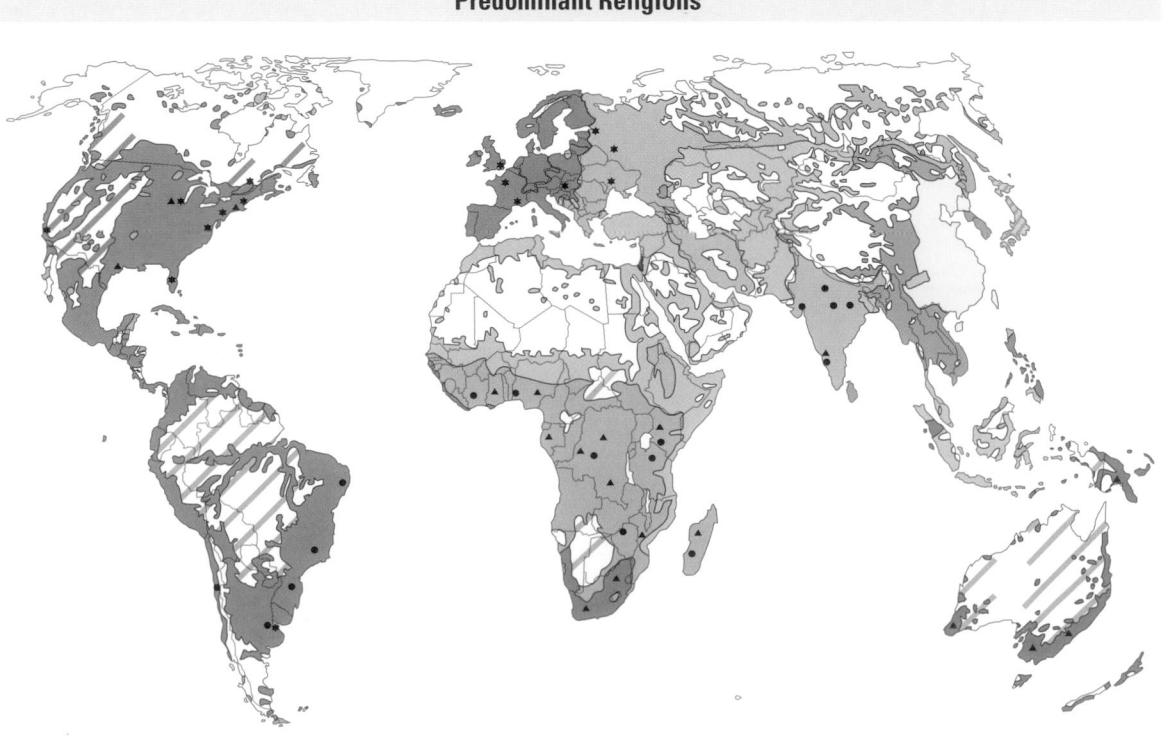

Religious Adherents

Religious adherents in millions (2006)

Christianity	2,100	Hindu	900
Roman Catholic	*1,050*	Chinese folk	394
Protestant	*396*	Buddhism	376
Orthodox	*240*	Ethnic religions	300
Anglican	*73*	New religions	103
Others	*341*	Sikhism	23
Islam	1,070	Spiritism	15
Sunni	*940*	Judaism	14
Shi'ite	*120*	Baha'i	7
Others	*10*	Confucianism	6
Non religious/		Jainism	4
Agnostic/Atheist	1,100	Shintoism	4

- ▲ Roman Catholicism
- Orthodox and other Eastern Churches
- • Protestantism
- Sunni Islam
- Shi'ite Islam
- Buddhism
- Hinduism
- Confucianism
- • Judaism
- Shintoism
- Tribal Religions

CARTOGRAPHY BY PHILIP'S. COPYRIGHT PHILIP'S

United Nations

Created in 1945 to promote peace and cooperation and based in New York, the United Nations is the world's largest international organization, with 192 members and an annual budget of US $2.1 billion (2007). Each member of the General Assembly has one vote, while the five permanent members of the 15-nation Security Council – China, France, Russia, UK, and USA – hold a veto. The Secretariat is the UN's principal administrative arm. The 54 members of the Economic and Social Council are responsible for economic, social, cultural, educational, health, and related matters. The UN has 16 specialized agencies – based in Canada, France, Switzerland, and the USA – which help members in fields such as education (UNESCO), agriculture (FAO), medicine (WHO), and finance (IFC). By the end of 1994, all the original 11 trust territories of the Trusteeship Council had become independent.

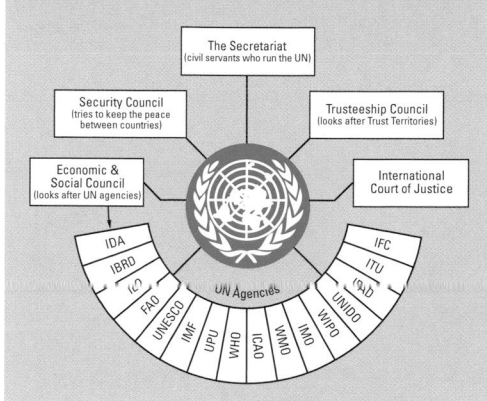

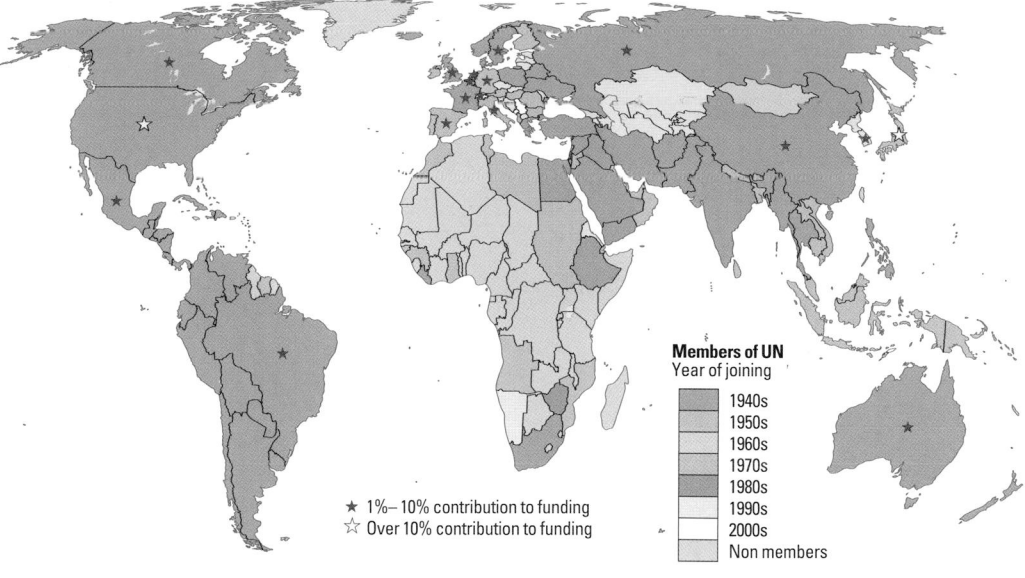

Members of UN
Year of joining
- 1940s
- 1950s
- 1960s
- 1970s
- 1980s
- 1990s
- 2000s
- Non members

★ 1%– 10% contribution to funding
☆ Over 10% contribution to funding

MEMBERSHIP OF THE UN In 1945 there were 51 members; by the end of 2006 membership had increased to 192 following the admission of East Timor, Switzerland, and Montenegro. There are 2 independent states which are not members of the UN – Taiwan and the Vatican City. All the successor states of the former USSR had joined by the end of 1992. The official languages of the UN are Chinese, English, French, Russian, Spanish, and Arabic.

FUNDING The UN regular budget for 2007 was US$ 2.1 billion. Contributions are assessed by the members' ability to pay, with the maximum 24% of the total (USA's share), the minimum 0.01%. The European Union pays over 37% of the budget.

PEACEKEEPING The UN has been involved in 65 peacekeeping operations worldwide since 1948.

International Organizations

ACP African-Caribbean-Pacific (formed in 1963). Members have economic ties with the EU.

APEC Asia-Pacific Economic Cooperation (formed in 1989). It aims to enhance economic growth and prosperity for the region and to strengthen the Asia-Pacific community. APEC is the only intergovernmental grouping in the world operating on the basis of non-binding commitments, open dialogue, and equal respect for the views of all participants. There are 21 member economies.

ARAB LEAGUE (formed in 1945). The League's aim is to promote economic, social, political, and military cooperation. There are 22 member nations.

ASEAN Association of Southeast Asian Nations (formed in 1967). Cambodia joined in 1999.

AU The African Union replaced the Organization of African Unity (formed in 1963) in 2002. Its 53 members represent over 94% of Africa's population. Arabic, French, Portuguese, and English are recognized as working languages.

COLOMBO PLAN (formed in 1951). Its 25 members aim to promote economic and social development in Asia and the Pacific.

COMMONWEALTH The Commonwealth of Nations evolved from the British Empire. Pakistan was suspended in 1999, and Zimbabwe in 2002. In response to its continued suspension, Zimbabwe left the Commonwealth in December 2003. Pakistan was reinstated in 2004, but Fiji Islands was suspended in December 2006 following a military coup. It now comprises 16 Queen's realms, 31 republics and 6 indigenous monarchies, giving a total of 53 member states.

EU European Union (evolved from the European Community in 1993). Cyprus, the Czech Republic, Estonia, Hungary, Latvia, Lithuania, Malta, Poland, the Slovak Republic, and Slovenia joined the EU in May 2004; Bulgaria and Romania joined in January 2007. The other members are Austria, Belgium, Denmark, Finland, France, Germany, Greece, Ireland, Italy, Luxembourg, Netherlands, Portugal, Spain, Sweden, and the UK – together these 27 countries aim to integrate economies, coordinate social developments, and bring about political union.

LAIA Latin American Integration Association (1980). Its aim is to promote freer regional trade.

NATO North Atlantic Treaty Organization (formed in 1949). It continues after 1991 despite the winding up of the Warsaw Pact. Bulgaria, Estonia, Latvia, Lithuania, Romania, the Slovak Republic, and Slovenia became members in 2004.

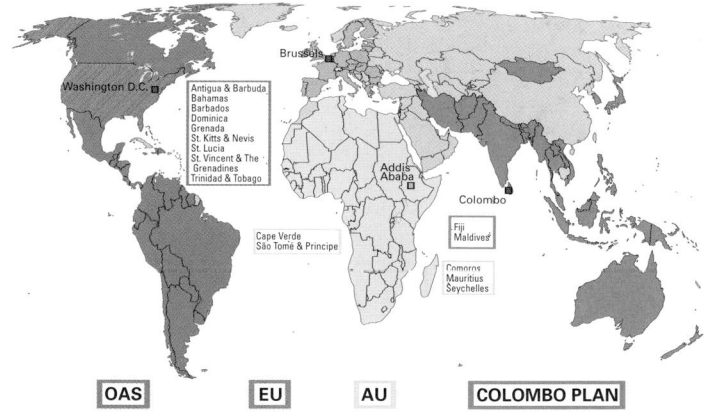

OAS   EU   AU   COLOMBO PLAN

OAS Organization of American States (formed in 1948). It aims to promote social and economic cooperation between developed countries of North America and developing nations of Latin America.

OECD Organization for Economic Cooperation and Development (formed in 1961). It comprises 30 major free-market economies. Poland, Hungary, and South Korea joined in 1996, and the Slovak Republic in 2000. "G8" is its "inner group" of leading industrial nations, comprising Canada, France, Germany, Italy, Japan, Russia, UK, and USA.

OPEC Organization of Petroleum Exporting Countries (formed in 1960). It controls about three-quarters of the world's oil supply. Gabon left the organization in 1996.

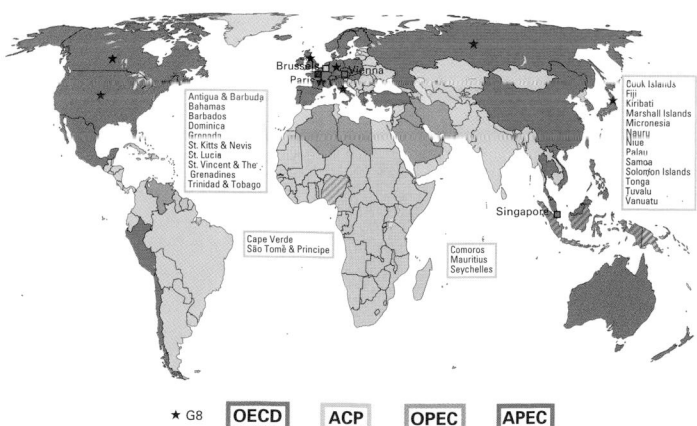

★ G8   OECD   ACP   OPEC   APEC

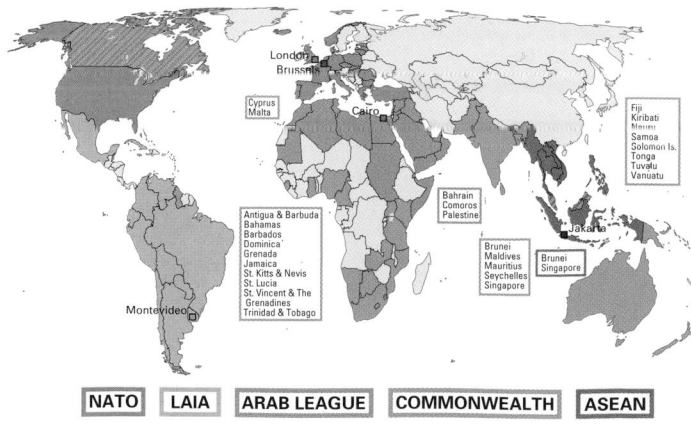

NATO   LAIA   ARAB LEAGUE   COMMONWEALTH   ASEAN

CARTOGRAPHY BY PHILIP'S. COPYRIGHT PHILIP'S

Wealth

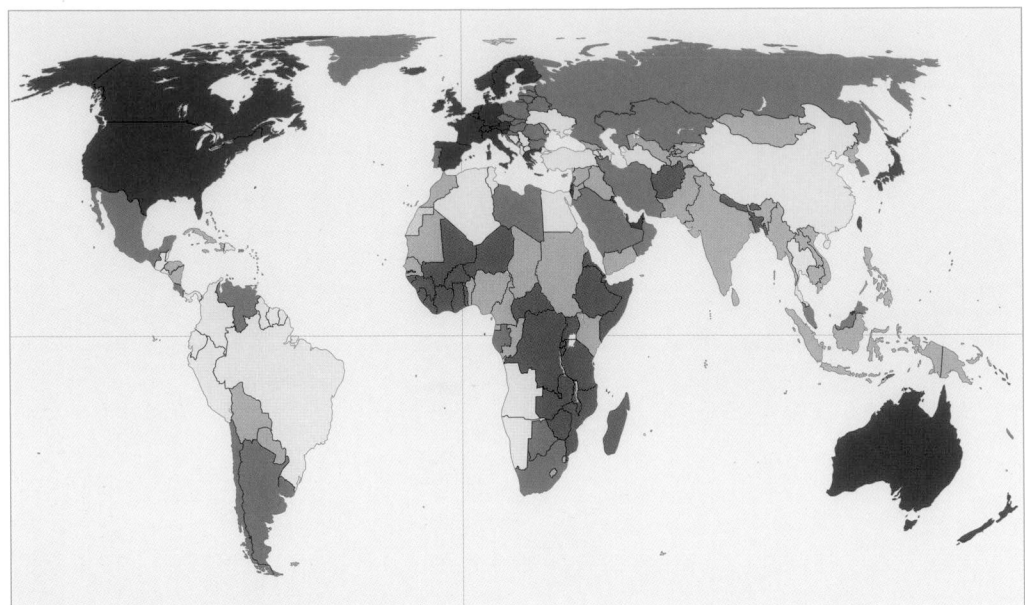

CARTOGRAPHY BY PHILIP'S. COPYRIGHT PHILIP'S

Levels of Income

Gross Domestic Product per capita: the annual value of goods and services divided by the population, using purchasing power parity (PPP) (2007)

- Over 250% of world average
- 100% – 250% of world average

[World average per person US$10,000]

- 50% – 100% of world average
- 15% – 50% of world average
- Under 15% of world average
- No data available

Wealth Creation

The Gross Domestic Product (GDP) of the world's largest economies, US$ million (2007)

1.	USA	13,860,000	23.	Argentina	524,000
2.	China	7,043,000	24.	Thailand	520,000
3.	Japan	4,346,000	25.	South Africa	468,000
4.	India	2,965,000	26.	Pakistan	446,000
5.	Germany	2,833,000	27.	Egypt	432,000
6.	UK	2,147,000	28.	Belgium	379,000
7.	Russia	2,076,000	29.	Malaysia	358,000
8.	France	2,067,000	30.	Venezuela	335,000
9.	Brazil	1,838,000	31.	Sweden	333,000
10.	Italy	1,800,000	32.	Greece	326,000
11.	Spain	1,362,000	33.	Ukraine	321,000
12.	Mexico	1,353,000	34.	Colombia	320,000
13.	Canada	1,274,000	35.	Austria	320,000
14.	South Korea	1,206,000	36.	Switzerland	301,000
15.	Iran	853,000	37.	Philippines	299,000
16.	Indonesia	846,000	38.	Nigeria	295,000
17.	Australia	767,000	39.	Hong Kong	293,000
18.	Taiwan	690,000	40.	Algeria	269,000
19.	Turkey	668,000	41.	Norway	257,000
20.	Netherlands	639,000	42.	Czech Republic	249,000
21.	Poland	624,000	43.	Romania	247,000
22.	Saudi Arabia	572,000	44.	Chile	234,000

The Wealth Gap

The world's richest and poorest countries, by Gross Domestic Product per capita in US $ (2007)

Richest countries			Poorest countries		
1.	Luxembourg	80,800	1.	Congo (Dem. Rep.)	300
2.	Norway	55,600	2.	Liberia	500
3.	Kuwait	55,300	3.	Zimbabwe	500
4.	UAE	55,200	4.	Comoros	600
5.	Singapore	48,900	5.	Guinea-Bissau	600
6.	USA	46,000	6.	Solomon Islands	600
7.	Ireland	45,600	7.	Somalia	600
8.	Hong Kong (China)	42,000	8.	Central African Rep.	700
9.	Switzerland	39,800	9.	Ethiopia	700
10.	Iceland	39,400	10.	Niger	700
11.	Austria	39,000	11.	Afghanistan	800
12.	Andorra	38,800	12.	Burundi	800
13.	Netherlands	38,600	13.	East Timor	800
14.	Canada	38,200	14.	Gambia	800
15.	Australia	37,500	15.	Malawi	800
16.	Denmark	37,400	16.	Sierra Leone	800
17.	Sweden	36,900	17.	Mozambique	900
18.	Belgium	36,500	18.	Togo	900
19.	Finland	35,500	19.	Djibouti	1,000
20.	UK	35,000	20.	Eritrea	1,000
21.	Bahrain	34,700	21.	Guinea	1,000

Continental Shares

Shares of population and of wealth (GNI) by continent

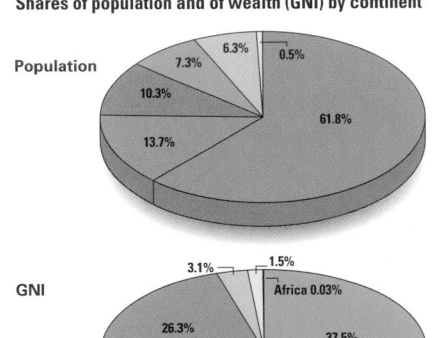

Population

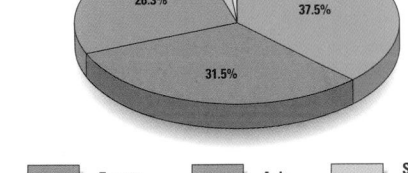

GNI

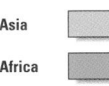

- Europe
- Australia
- Asia
- Africa
- South America
- North America

Inflation

Average annual rate of inflation (2007)

- Over 20%
- 10% – 20%
- 5% – 10%
- 2.5% – 5%
- Under 2.5%
- No data available

Highest inflation		Lowest inflation	
Zimbabwe	.....26,470%	Nauru	..........–3.6%
Burma (Myanmar)	..40%	Vanuatu	.........–1.6%
Venezuela	.........21%	San Marino	......–1.5%
Guinea	............20%	Dominica	........–0.1%
Tajikistan	..........20%	Japan	.............0%

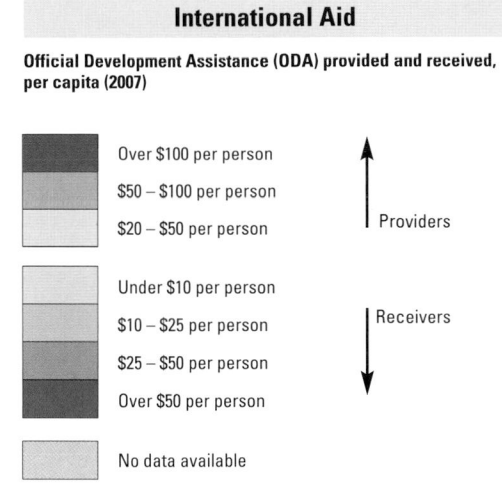

Official Development Assistance (ODA) provided and received, per capita (2007)

Over $100 per person
$50 – $100 per person
$20 – $50 per person — Providers

Under $10 per person
$10 – $25 per person — Receivers
$25 – $50 per person
Over $50 per person

No data available

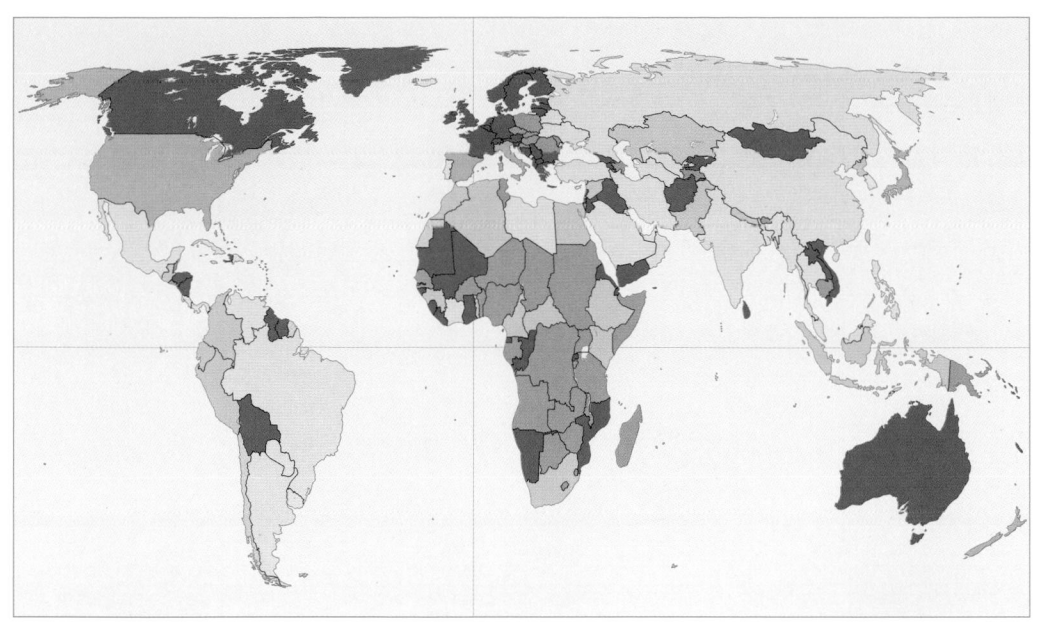

Debt and Aid

International debtors and the aid they receive

Although aid grants make a vital contribution to many of the world's poorer countries, they are usually dwarfed by the burden of debt that the developing economies are expected to repay. It is estimated that the total debt burden of developing countries is US$523 billion.

Debt, US $ per capita (2007)

Aid, US $ per capita (2007)

$13,661
$8,890
$6,137

$3,500
$3,000
$2,500
$2,000
$1,500
$1,000
$500
0

Algeria, Cameroon, Zambia, Papua New Guinea, Syria, Bolivia, Honduras, Ivory Coast, Nicaragua, Angola, Sudan, Mauritania, El Salvador, Peru, Colombia, Ecuador, Kazakhstan, Lebanon, Israel

$40
$80
$120
$160

Jordan, Guyana $177

Distribution of Spending

Percentage share of household spending, selected countries

Food
Medicine & Education
Clothing
Transport
Energy & Housing
Other

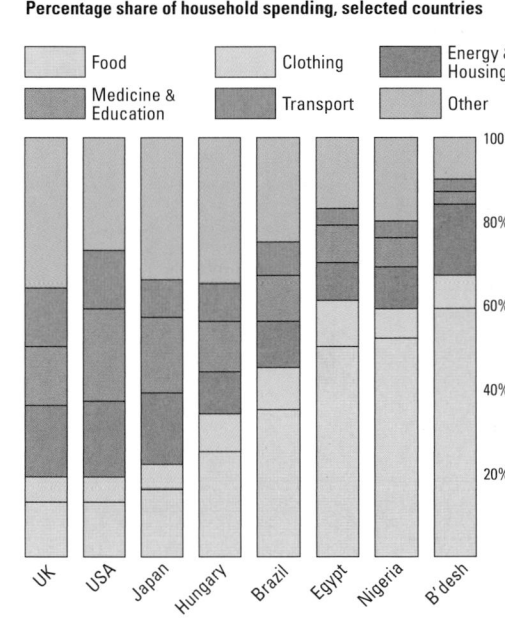

100%
80%
60%
40%
20%

UK, USA, Japan, Hungary, Brazil, Egypt, Nigeria, B'desh

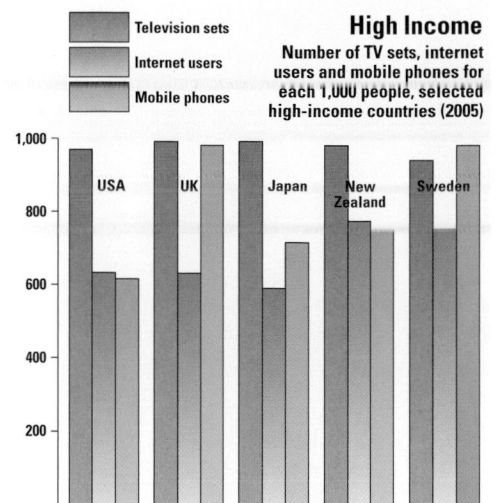

Television sets
Internet users
Mobile phones

High Income

Number of TV sets, internet users and mobile phones for each 1,000 people, selected high-income countries (2005)

1,000
800
600
400
200

USA, UK, Japan, New Zealand, Sweden

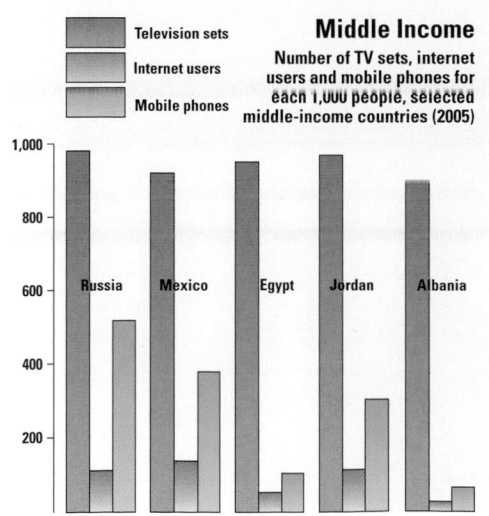

Television sets
Internet users
Mobile phones

Middle Income

Number of TV sets, internet users and mobile phones for each 1,000 people, selected middle-income countries (2005)

1,000
800
600
400
200

Russia, Mexico, Egypt, Jordan, Albania

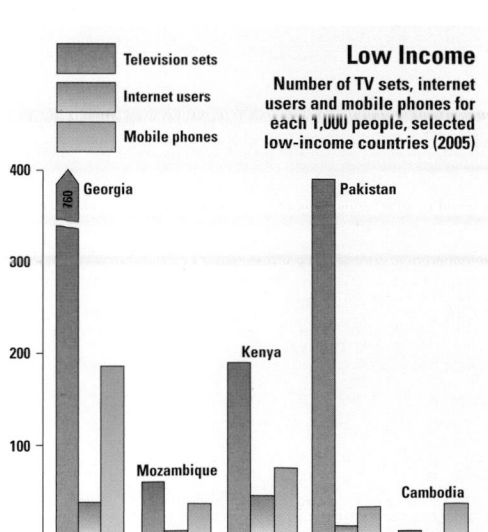

Television sets
Internet users
Mobile phones

Low Income

Number of TV sets, internet users and mobile phones for each 1,000 people, selected low-income countries (2005)

400
300
200
100

760 Georgia, Pakistan, Kenya, Mozambique, Cambodia

Quality of Life

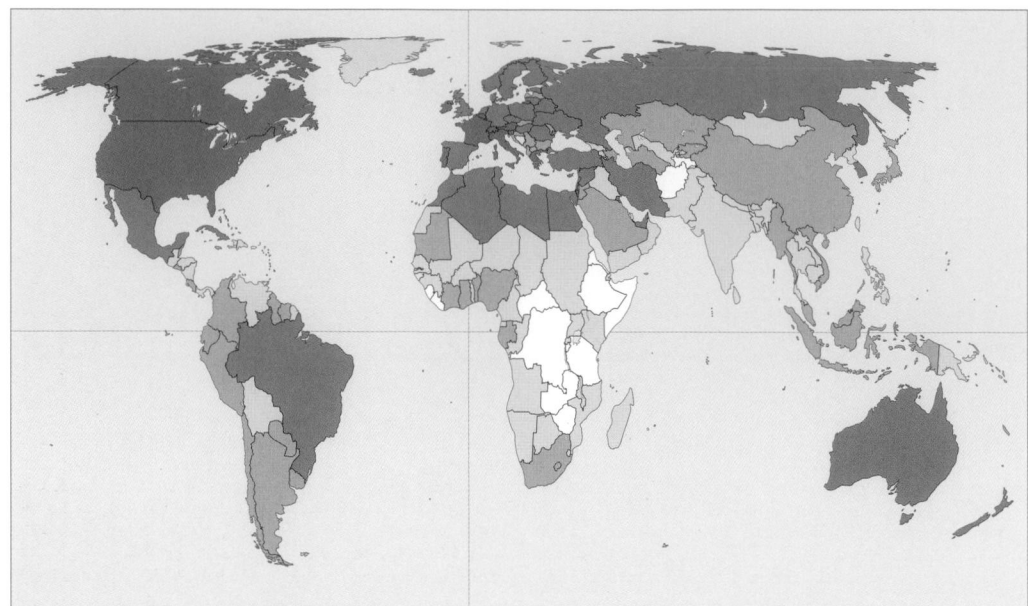

Daily Food Consumption

Average daily food intake in calories per person (2003)

Over 3,500 calories per person

3,000 – 3,500 calories per person

2,500 – 3,000 calories per person

2,000 – 2,500 calories per person

Under 2,000 calories per person

No data available

Hospital Capacity

Hospital beds available for each 1,000 people (2007)

Highest capacity		Lowest capacity	
Japan	14.1	Angola	0.1
Belarus	11.1	Cambodia	0.1
Russia	9.7	Malawi	0.1
Ukraine	8.7	Senegal	0.1
South Korea	8.6	Ethiopia	0.2
Czech Republic	8.4	Nepal	0.2
Germany	8.3	Bangladesh	0.3
Azerbaijan	8.1	Guinea	0.3
Lithuania	8.0	Madagascar	0.3
Hungary	7.9	Mali	0.3
Kazakhstan	7.8	Afghanistan	0.4
Austria	7.6	Chad	0.4
Latvia	7.6	Sierra Leone	0.4
Malta	7.6	Benin	0.5
Iceland	7.5	Nigeria	0.5

Although the ratio of people to hospital beds gives a good approximation of a country's health provision, it is not an absolute indicator. Raw numbers may mask inefficiency and other weaknesses: the high availability of beds in Belarus, for example, has not prevented infant mortality rates over three times as high as in the United Kingdom and the United States.

Life Expectancy

Years of life expectancy at birth, selected countries (2007)

The chart shows combined data for both sexes. On average, women live longer than men worldwide, even in developing countries with high maternal mortality rates. Overall, life expectancy is steadily rising, though the difference between rich and poor nations remains dramatic.

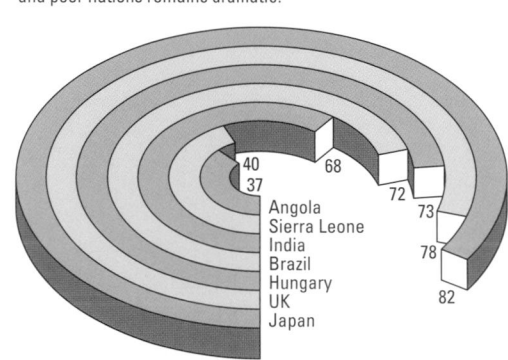

Angola 37
Sierra Leone 40
India 68
Brazil 72
Hungary 73
UK 78
Japan 82

Causes of Death

Causes of death for selected countries by percentage

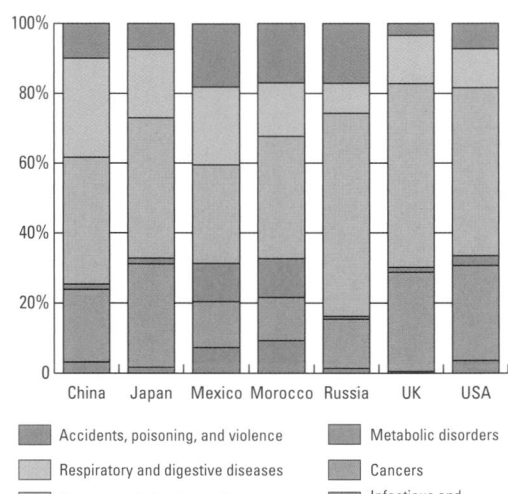

China Japan Mexico Morocco Russia UK USA

- Accidents, poisoning, and violence
- Metabolic disorders
- Respiratory and digestive diseases
- Cancers
- Nervous and circulatory diseases
- Infectious and parasitic diseases

Infant Mortality

Number of babies who died under the age of one, per 1,000 live births (2007)

Over 100 deaths per 1,000 births

50 – 100 deaths per 1,000 births

25 – 50 deaths per 1,000 births

10 – 25 deaths per 1,000 births

Under 10 deaths per 1,000 births

No data available

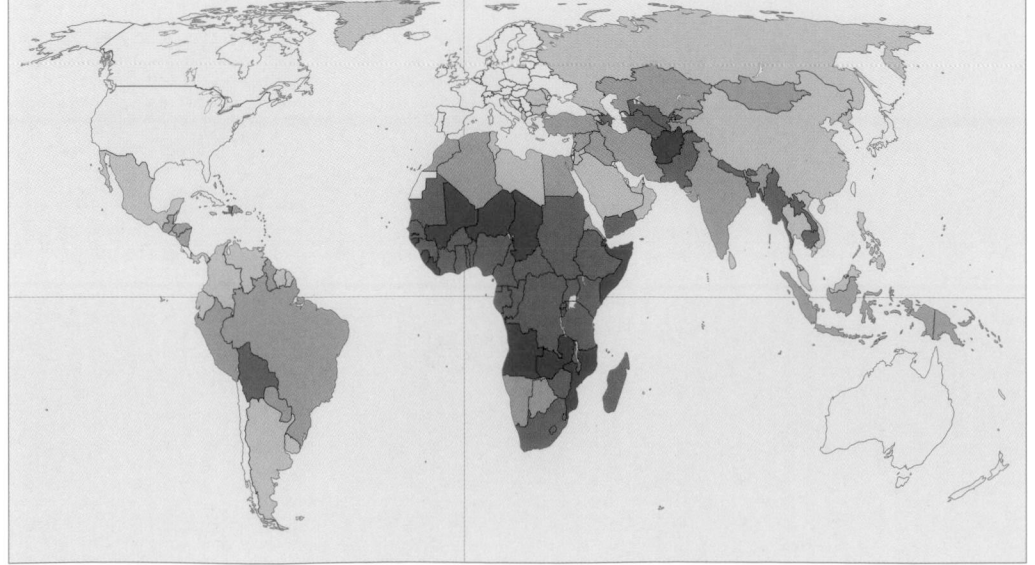

Highest infant mortality		Lowest infant mortality	
Angola	184 deaths	Singapore	2 deaths
Sierra Leone	158 deaths	Sweden	3 deaths
Afghanistan	157 deaths	Hong Kong (China)	3 deaths
Liberia	150 deaths	Japan	3 deaths
Niger	117 deaths	Iceland	3 deaths

CARTOGRAPHY BY PHILIP'S. COPYRIGHT PHILIP'S

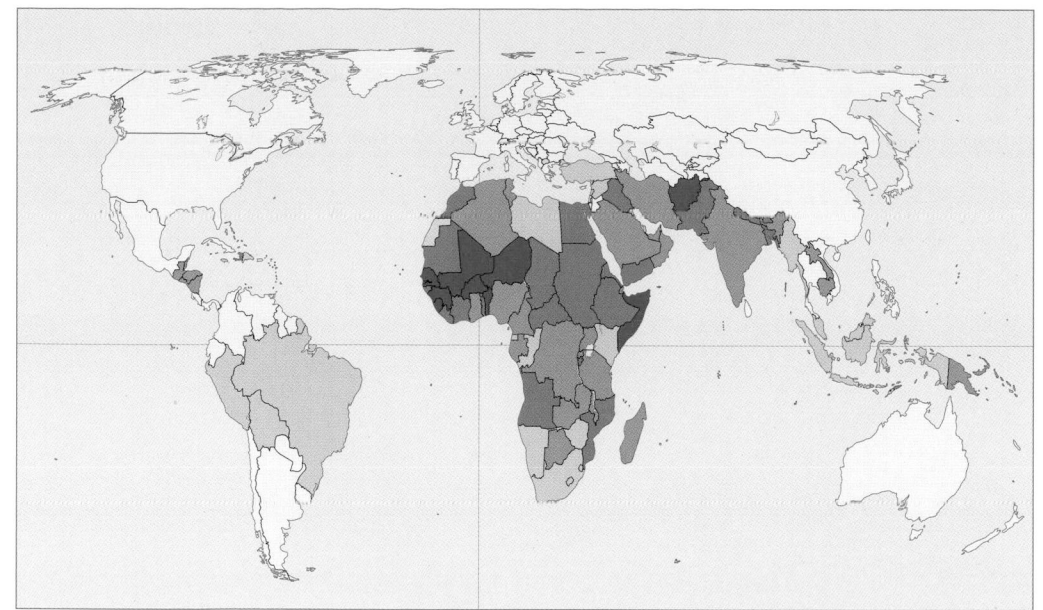

Percentage of the total adult population unable to read or write (2005)

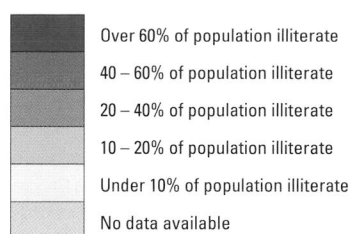

Over 60% of population illiterate

40 – 60% of population illiterate

20 – 40% of population illiterate

10 – 20% of population illiterate

Under 10% of population illiterate

No data available

Countries with the highest and lowest illiteracy rates

Highest		Lowest	
Burkina Faso	87	Australia	0
Niger	83	Denmark	0
Mali	81	Finland	0
Sierra Leone	69	Liechtenstein	0
Guinea	64	Luxembourg	0

Fertility and Education

Fertility rates compared with female education, selected countries (2000–05)

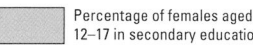 Percentage of females aged 12–17 in secondary education

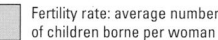 Fertility rate: average number of children borne per woman

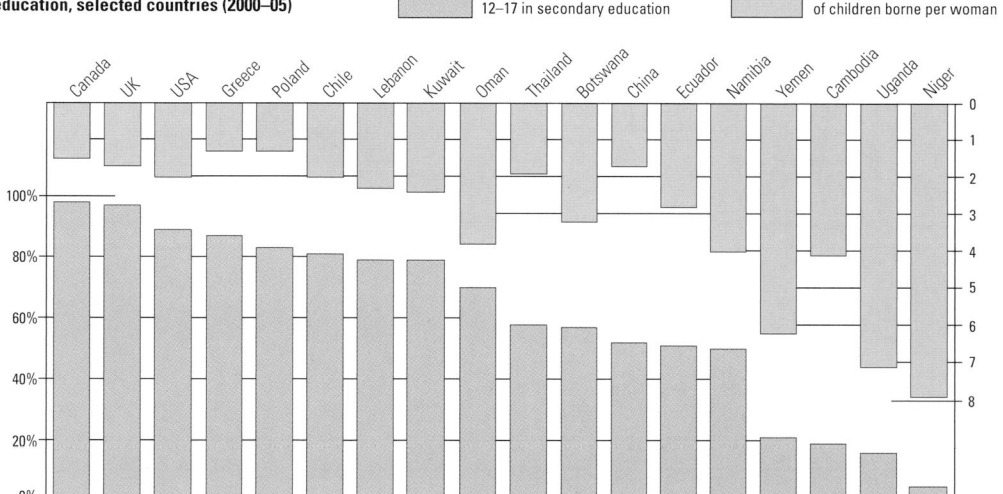

Living Standards

At first sight, most international contrasts in living standards are swamped by differences in wealth. The rich not only have more money, they have more of everything, including years of life. Those with only a little money are obliged to spend most of it on food and clothing, the basic maintenance costs of their existence; air travel and tourism are unlikely to feature on their expenditure lists. However, poverty and wealth are both relative: slum dwellers living on social security payments in an affluent industrial country have far more resources at their disposal than an average African peasant, but feel their own poverty nonetheless. A middle-class Indian lawyer cannot command a fraction of the earnings of a counterpart living in New York, London, or Rome; nevertheless, he rightly sees himself as prosperous.

The rich not only live longer, on average, than the poor, they also die from different causes. Infectious and parasitic diseases, all but eliminated in the developed world, remain a scourge in the developing nations. On the other hand, more than two-thirds of the populations of OECD nations eventually succumb to cancer or circulatory disease.

Human Development Index

The Human Development Index (HDI), calculated by the UN Development Program, gives a value to countries using indicators of life expectancy, education, and standards of living (2005). Higher values show more developed countries.

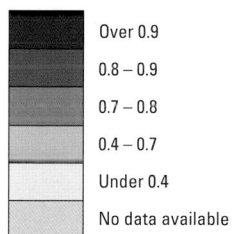

Over 0.9

0.8 – 0.9

0.7 – 0.8

0.4 – 0.7

Under 0.4

No data available

Highest values		Lowest values	
Iceland	0.968	Sierra Leone	0.336
Norway	0.968	Burkina Faso	0.370
Australia	0.962	Guinea-Bissau	0.374
Ireland	0.959	Niger	0.374
Sweden	0.95	Mali	0.380

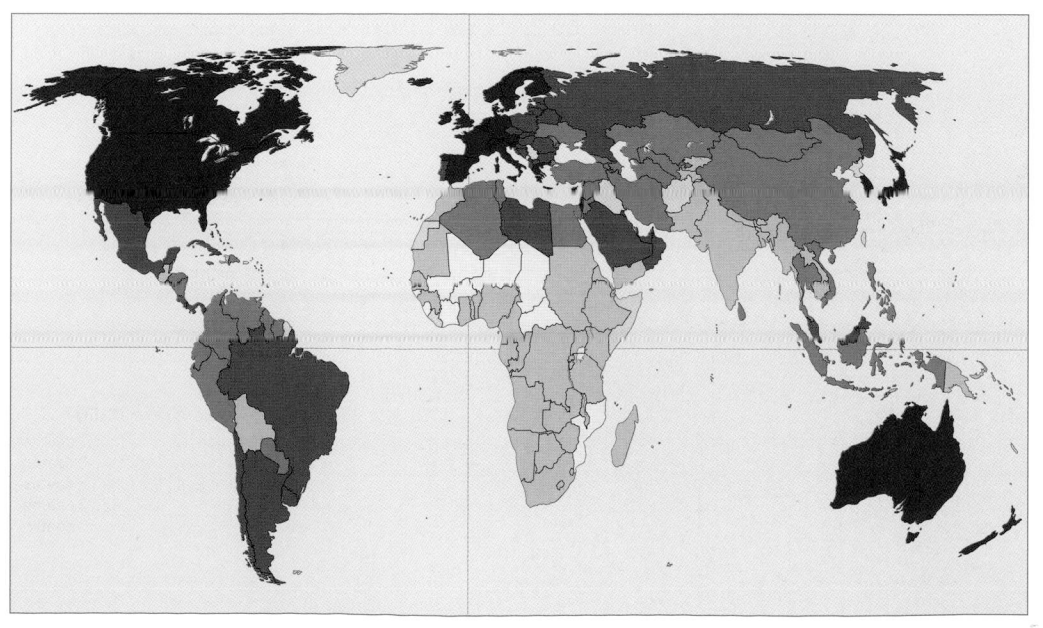

CARTOGRAPHY BY PHILIP'S. COPYRIGHT PHILIP'S

Energy

Production

Each square represents 1% of world energy production (2006)

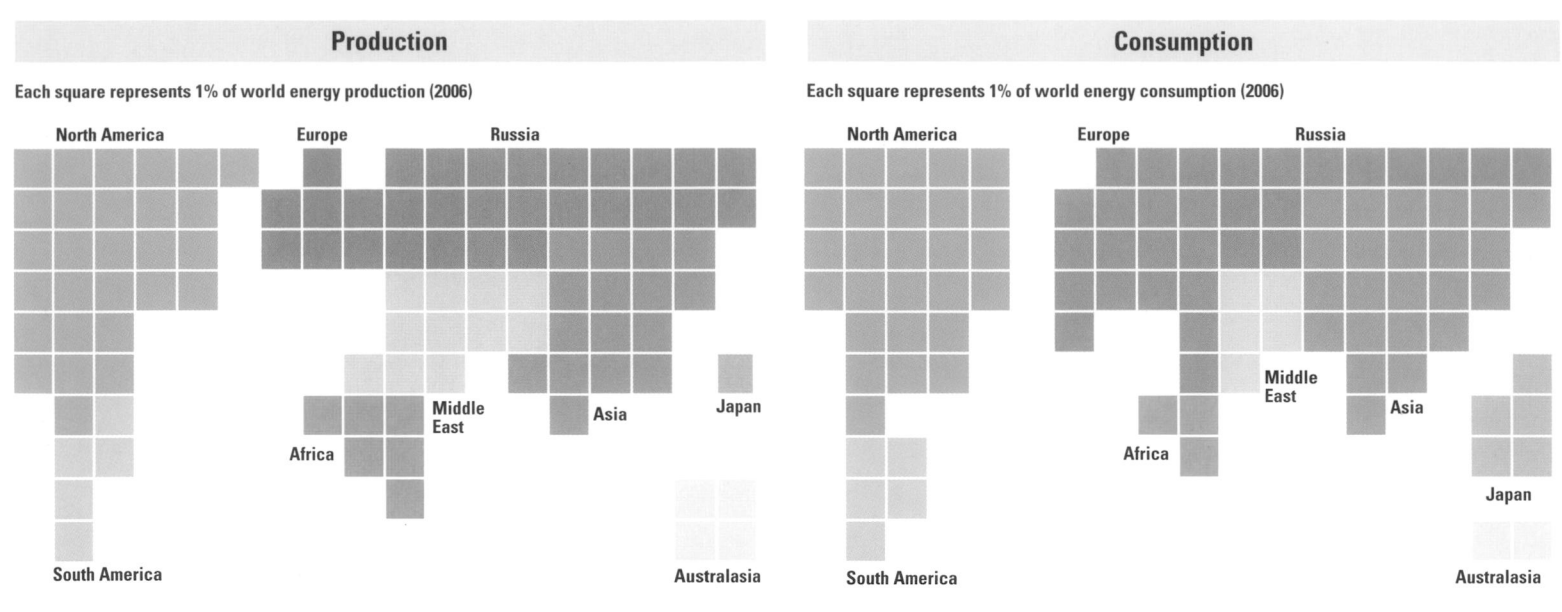

North America Europe Russia

Middle East Asia Japan

Africa

South America Australasia

Consumption

Each square represents 1% of world energy consumption (2006)

North America Europe Russia

Middle East Asia

Africa

South America Japan Australasia

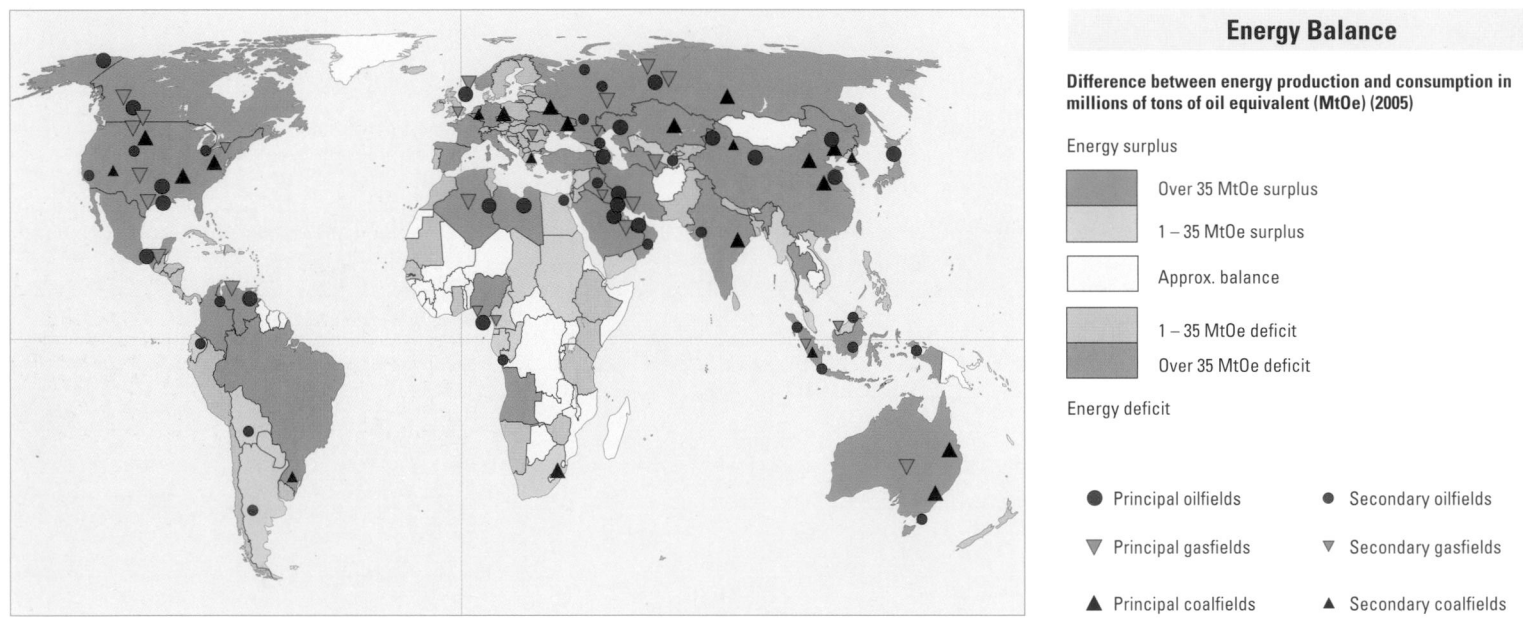

Energy Balance

Difference between energy production and consumption in millions of tons of oil equivalent (MtOe) (2005)

Energy surplus

Over 35 MtOe surplus

1 – 35 MtOe surplus

Approx. balance

1 – 35 MtOe deficit

Over 35 MtOe deficit

Energy deficit

● Principal oilfields   ● Secondary oilfields

▽ Principal gasfields   ▽ Secondary gasfields

▲ Principal coalfields   ▲ Secondary coalfields

World Energy Consumption

Energy consumed by world regions, measured in million tons of oil equivalent in 2006. Total world consumption was 10,878 MtOe. Only energy from oil, gas, coal, nuclear, and hydroelectric sources are included. Excluded are fuels such as wood, peat, animal waste, wind, solar, and geothermal which, though important in some countries, are unreliably documented in terms of consumption statistics.

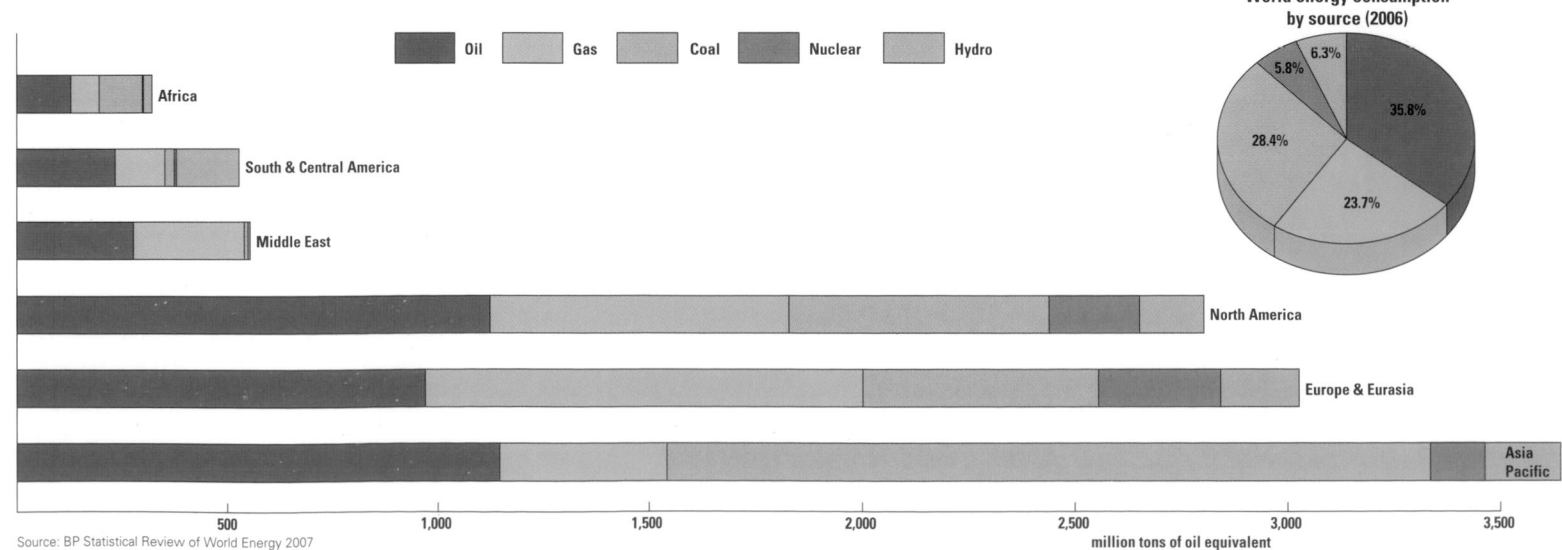

Oil   Gas   Coal   Nuclear   Hydro

Africa

South & Central America

Middle East

North America

Europe & Eurasia

Asia Pacific

500   1,000   1,500   2,000   2,500   3,000   3,500

million tons of oil equivalent

World energy consumption by source (2006)

6.3%
5.8%
28.4%
35.8%
23.7%

Source: BP Statistical Review of World Energy 2007

CARTOGRAPHY BY PHILIP'S. COPYRIGHT PHILIP'S

Energy

Energy is used to keep us warm or cool, fuel our industries and our transport systems, and even feed us; high-intensity agriculture, with its use of fertilizers, pesticides, and machinery, is heavily energy-dependent. Although we live in a high-energy society, there are vast discrepancies between rich and poor; for example, a North American consumes 13 times as much energy as a Chinese person. But even developing nations have more power at their disposal than was imaginable a century ago.

The distribution of energy supplies, most importantly fossil fuels (coal, oil, and natural gas), is very uneven. In addition, the diagrams and map opposite show that the largest producers of energy are not necessarily the largest consumers. The movement of energy supplies around the world is therefore an important component of international trade. In 2006, total world movements in oil amounted to 2,590 million tons.

As the finite reserves of fossil fuels are depleted, renewable energy sources, such as solar, hydro-thermal, wind, tidal, and biomass, will become increasingly important around the world.

Nuclear Power

Major producers by percentage of world total and by percentage of domestic electricity generation (2006)

Country	% of world total production	Country	% of nuclear as proportion of domestic electricity
1. USA	29.6%	1. France	78.7%
2. France	16.1%	2. Lithuania	64.2%
3. Japan	10.9%	3. Slovak Rep.	57.3%
4. Germany	6.0%	4. Belgium	54.7%
5. Russia	5.4%	5. Ukraine	48.4%
6. South Korea	5.3%	6. Switzerland	47.1%
7. Canada	3.4%	7. Bulgaria	43.4%
8. Ukraine	3.2%	8. Sweden	41.5%
9. UK	2.6%	9. Armenia	40.5%
10. Sweden	2.4%	10. South Korea	38.6%

Although the 1980s were a bad time for the nuclear power industry (fears of long-term environmental damage were heavily reinforced by the 1986 disaster at Chernobyl), the industry picked up in the early 1990s. Sixteen countries currently rely on nuclear power to supply over 25% of their electricity requirements. There are over 400 operating nuclear power stations worldwide, with over 100 more planned or under construction.

Hydroelectricity

Major producers by percentage of world total and by percentage of domestic electricity generation (2004)

Country	% of world total production	Country	% of hydroelectric as proportion of domestic electricity
1. Canada	12.2%	1. Bhutan	100%
2. China	11.9%	= Paraguay	100%
3. Brazil	11.6%	= Lesotho	100%
4. USA	9.8%	4. Mozambique	99.8%
5. Russia	6.0%	5. Congo	99.7%
6. Norway	3.9%	= Congo (Dem. Rep.)	99.7%
7. Japan	3.4%	= Uganda	99.7%
8. India	3.0%	8. Nepal	99.6%
9. Sweden	2.3%	9. Zambia	99.5%
10. France	2.2%	10. Norway	98.8%

Countries heavily reliant on hydroelectricity are usually small and non-industrial: a high proportion of hydroelectric power more often reflects a modest energy budget than vast hydroelectric resources. The USA, for instance, produces only 6.7% of its power requirements from hydroelectricity; yet that 6.7% amounts to more than seven times the hydropower generated by most of Africa.

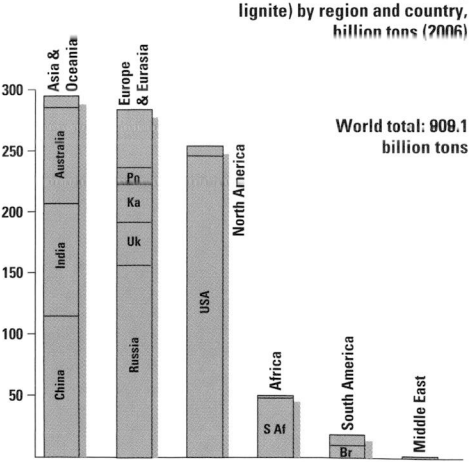

Fuel Exports

Fuels as a percentage of total value of exports (2005)

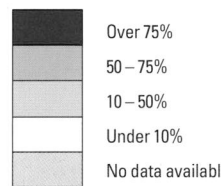

- Over 75%
- 50 – 75%
- 10 – 50%
- Under 10%
- No data available

In the 1970s, oil exports became a political issue when OPEC sought to increase the influence of developing countries in world affairs by raising oil prices and restricting production. But its power was short-lived, following a fall in demand for oil in the 1980s, due to an increase in energy efficiency and development of alternative resources. However, with the heavy energy demands of the Asian economies early in the 21st century, both oil and gas prices have risen sharply.

Conversion Rates

1 barrel = 0.136 tons or 159 liters or 35 Imperial gallons or 42 US gallons

1 ton = 7.33 barrels or 1,185 liters or 256 Imperial gallons or 261 US gallons

1 ton oil = 1.5 tons hard coal or 3.0 tons lignite or 12,000 kWh

1 Imperial gallon = 1.201 US gallons or 4.546 liters or 277.4 cubic inches

Measurements
For historical reasons, oil is traded in "barrels." The weight and volume equivalents (shown right) are all based on average-density "Arabian light" crude oil.

The energy equivalents given for a ton of oil are also somewhat imprecise: oil and coal of different qualities will have varying energy contents, a fact usually reflected in their price on world markets.

World Coal Reserves

World coal reserves (including lignite) by region and country, billion tons (2006)

World total: 909.1 billion tons

World Gas Reserves

World natural gas reserves by region and country, billion tons of oil equivalent (2006)

World total: 166.5 billion tons of oil equivalent

World Oil Reserves

World oil reserves by region and country, billion tons (2006)

World total: 163.6 billion tons

Al: Algeria	**No:** Norway
Au: Australia	**Po:** Poland
Br: Brazil	**Ru:** Russia
Cn: China	**SA:** Saudi Arabia
In: Indonesia	**S Af:** South Africa
Iq: Iraq	**UAE:** United Arab Emirates
Ka: Kazakhstan	**Uk:** Ukraine
Li: Libya	**USA:** United States of America
Ni: Nigeria	**Ve:** Venezuela

Production

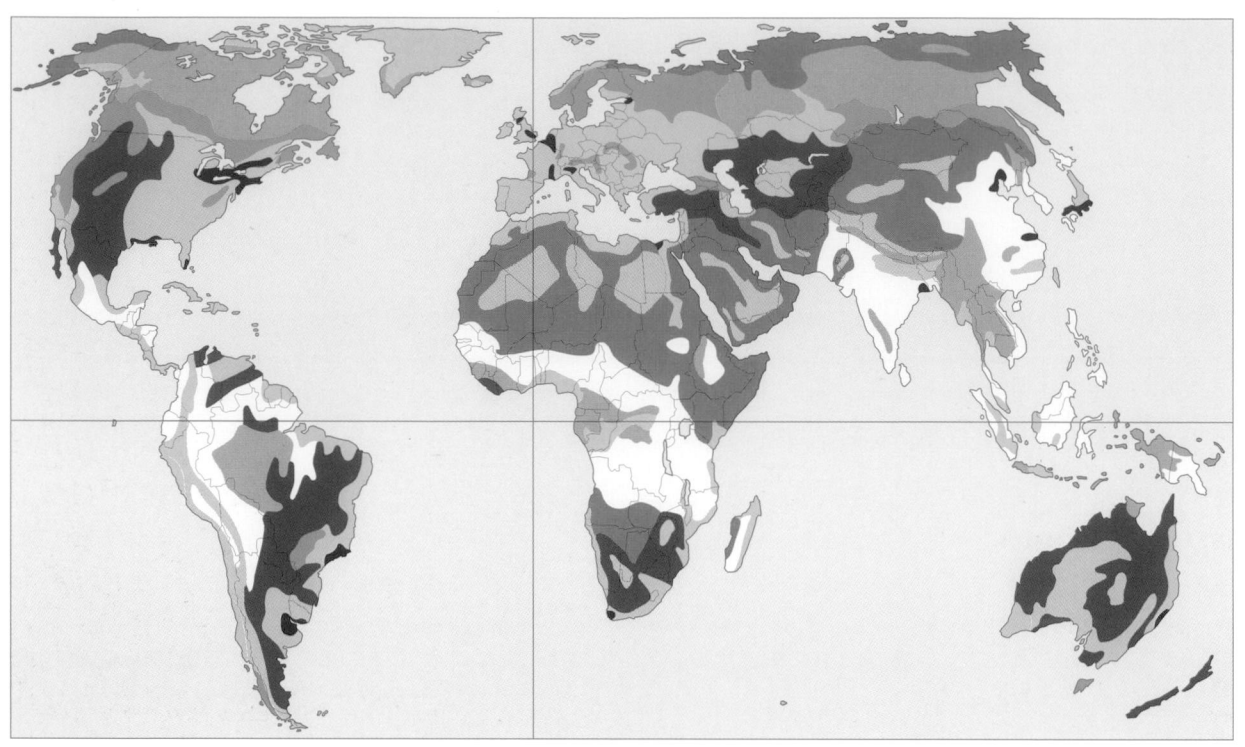

Agriculture

Predominant type of farming or land use

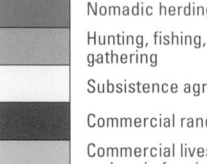

- Nomadic herding
- Hunting, fishing, and gathering
- Subsistence agriculture
- Commercial ranching
- Commercial livestock and grain farming
- Urban areas
- Forestry
- Unproductive land

The development of agriculture has transformed human existence more than any other. The whole business of farming is constantly developing: due mainly to the new varieties of rice and wheat, world grain production has more than doubled since 1965. New machinery and modern agricultural techniques enable relatively few farmers to produce enough food for the world's 6 billion or so people.

Staple Crops

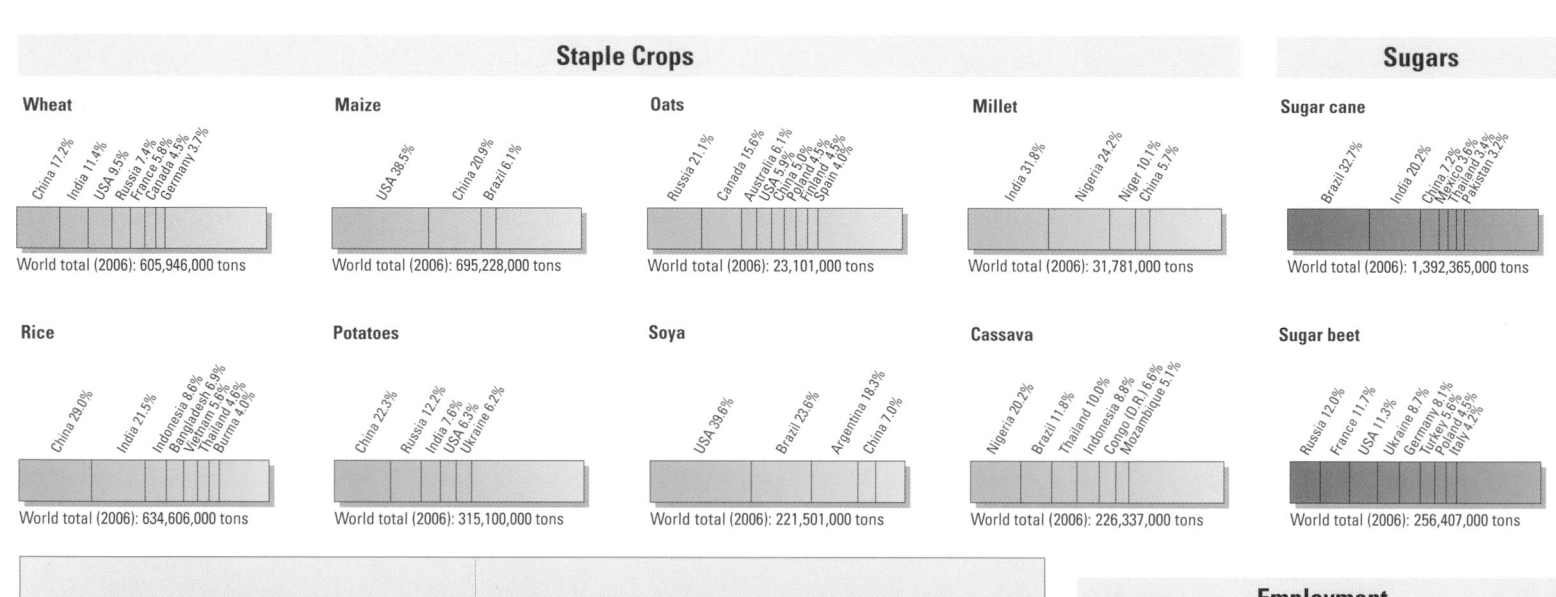

Wheat

China 17.2%
India 11.4%
USA 9.5%
Russia 7.4%
France 5.6%
Canada 4.5%
Germany 3.7%

World total (2006): 605,946,000 tons

Maize

USA 38.5%
China 20.9%
Brazil 6.1%

World total (2006): 695,228,000 tons

Oats

Russia 21.1%
Canada 15.6%
Australia 6.1%
USA 5.9%
China 5.0%
Poland 4.5%
Spain 4.0%

World total (2006): 23,101,000 tons

Millet

India 31.8%
Nigeria 24.2%
Niger 10.1%
China 5.7%

World total (2006): 31,781,000 tons

Rice

China 29.0%
India 21.5%
Indonesia 8.6%
Bangladesh 8.9%
Vietnam 5.6%
Thailand 4.6%
Burma 4.0%

World total (2006): 634,606,000 tons

Potatoes

China 22.3%
Russia 12.2%
India 7.6%
USA 6.3%
Ukraine 6.2%

World total (2006): 315,100,000 tons

Soya

USA 39.6%
Brazil 23.6%
Argentina 18.3%
China 7.0%

World total (2006): 221,501,000 tons

Cassava

Nigeria 20.2%
Brazil 11.8%
Thailand 10.0%
Indonesia 8.8%
Congo (D.R.) 6.6%
Mozambique 5.1%

World total (2006): 226,337,000 tons

Sugars

Sugar cane

Brazil 32.7%
India 20.2%
China 7.2%
Mexico 3.6%
Thailand 3.4%
Pakistan 3.2%

World total (2006): 1,392,365,000 tons

Sugar beet

Russia 12.0%
France 11.7%
USA 11.3%
Ukraine 8.3%
Germany 8.1%
Turkey 5.6%
Poland 4.5%
Italy 4.2%

World total (2006): 256,407,000 tons

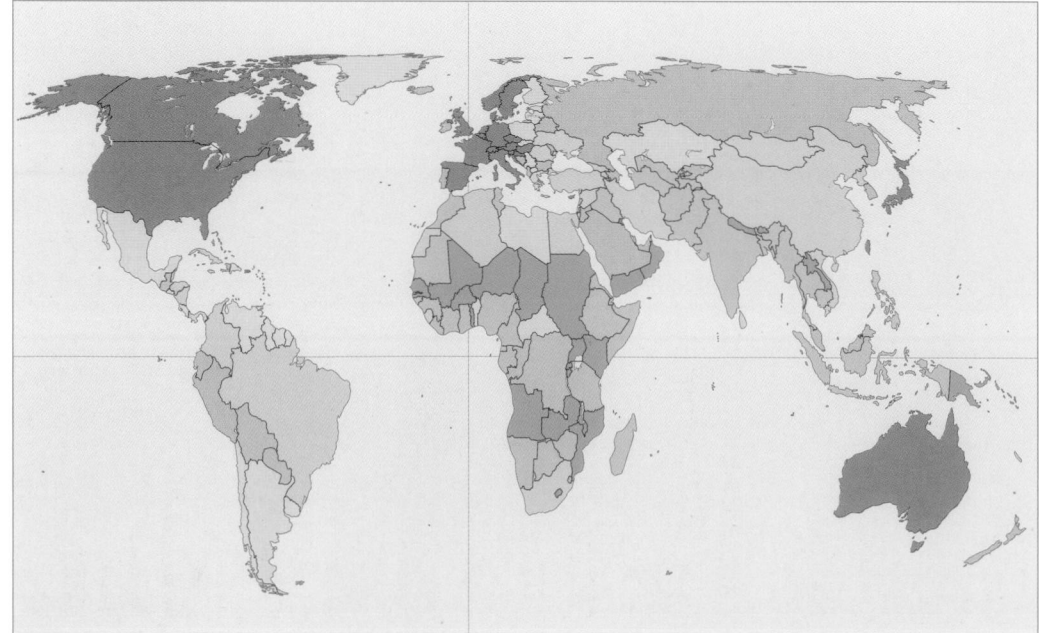

Employment

The number of workers employed in manufacturing for every 100 workers engaged in agriculture (2006)

- Under 10 — Mainly agricultural countries
- 10 – 50
- 50 – 100
- 100 – 200
- 200 – 500 — Mainly industrial countries
- Over 500
- No data available

Countries with the highest and lowest number of workers employed in manufacturing per 100 workers engaged in agriculture (2006)

Highest		Lowest	
Bahrain	7,900	Burundi	2.5
San Marino	4,200	Yemen	5.0
Micronesia	3,822	Oman	5.0
USA	3,271	Rwanda	5.6
Liechtenstein	2,350	Malawi	5.6

CARTOGRAPHY BY PHILIP'S. COPYRIGHT PHILIP'S

Mineral Production

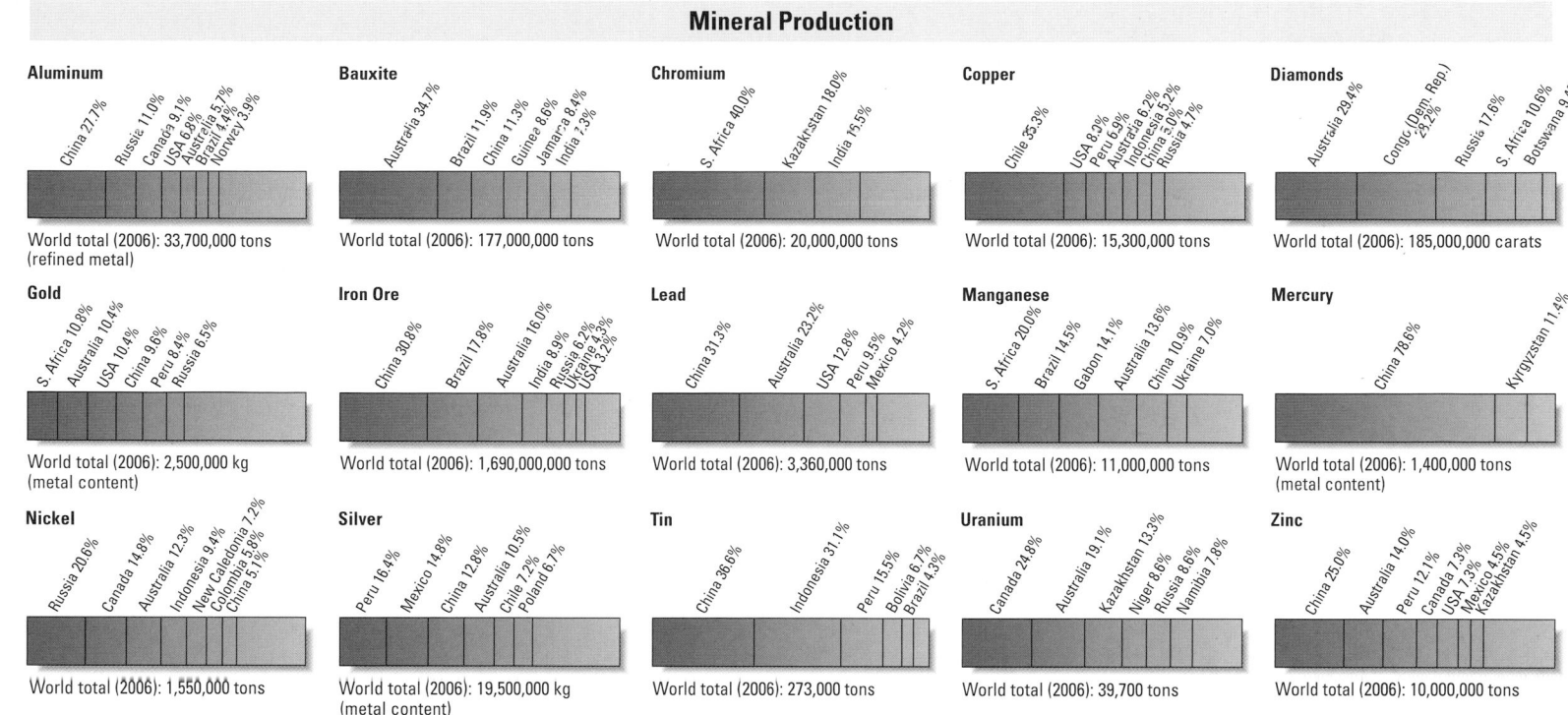

Aluminum
China 27.7% | Russia 11.0% | Canada 9.1% | USA 6.9% | Australia 5.7% | Brazil 4.4% | Norway 3.9%
World total (2006): 33,700,000 tons (refined metal)

Bauxite
Australia 34.7% | Brazil 11.9% | China 11.3% | Guinea 8.6% | Jamaica 8.4% | India 7.3%
World total (2006): 177,000,000 tons

Chromium
S. Africa 40.0% | Kazakstan 18.0% | India 15.5%
World total (2006): 20,000,000 tons

Copper
Chile 35.3% | USA 8.3% | Peru 6.9% | Australia 6.2% | Indonesia 5.52% | Russia 5.0% | Russia 4.7%
World total (2006): 15,300,000 tons

Diamonds
Australia 29.4% | Congo (Dem. Rep.) 23.2% | Russia 17.6% | S. Africa 10.6% | Botswana 9.4%
World total (2006): 185,000,000 carats

Gold
S. Africa 10.8% | Australia 10.4% | USA 10.4% | China 9.6% | Peru 8.4% | Russia 6.5%
World total (2006): 2,500,000 kg (metal content)

Iron Ore
China 30.8% | Brazil 17.8% | Australia 16.0% | India 8.9% | Russia 6.2% | Ukraine 4.3% | USA 3.2%
World total (2006): 1,690,000,000 tons

Lead
China 31.3% | Australia 23.2% | USA 12.8% | Peru 9.5% | Mexico 4.2%
World total (2006): 3,360,000 tons

Manganese
S. Africa 20.0% | Brazil 14.5% | Gabon 14.1% | Australia 13.6% | China 10.9% | Ukraine 7.0%
World total (2006): 11,000,000 tons

Mercury
China 78.6% | Kyrgyzstan 11.4%
World total (2006): 1,400,000 tons (metal content)

Nickel
Russia 20.6% | Canada 14.8% | Australia 12.3% | Indonesia 9.4% | New Caledonia 7.2% | Colombia 5.6% | China 5.1%
World total (2006): 1,550,000 tons

Silver
Peru 16.4% | Mexico 14.8% | China 12.8% | Australia 10.5% | Chile 7.2% | Poland 6.7%
World total (2006): 19,500,000 kg (metal content)

Tin
China 36.6% | Indonesia 31.1% | Peru 15.5% | Bolivia 6.7% | Brazil 4.3%
World total (2006): 273,000 tons

Uranium
Canada 24.8% | Australia 19.1% | Kazakstan 13.3% | Niger 8.6% | Russia 8.6% | Namibia 7.8%
World total (2006): 39,700 tons

Zinc
China 25.0% | Australia 14.0% | Peru 12.1% | Canada 7.3% | USA 7.3% | Mexico 4.5% | Kazakhstan 4.5%
World total (2006): 10,000,000 tons

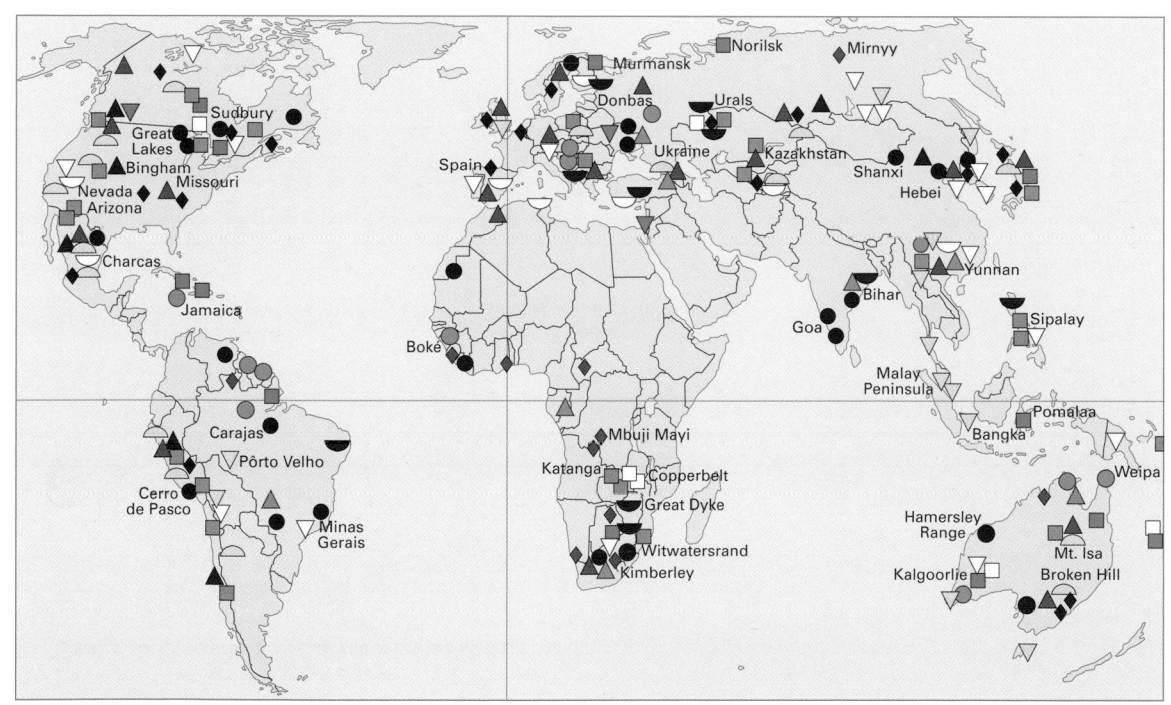

Mineral Distribution

The map shows the richest sources of the most important minerals (major mineral locations are named)

- ⬤ Bauxite
- ◑ Chromium
- ☐ Cobalt
- ▣ Copper
- ◆ Diamonds
- ▽ Gold
- ● Iron ore
- ▲ Lead
- ▲ Manganese
- ▽ Mercury
- ▲ Molybdenum
- ▣ Nickel
- ▽ Potash
- ◗ Silver
- ▽ Tin
- ▽ Tungsten
- ◆ Zinc

The map does not show undersea deposits, most of which are considered inaccessible.

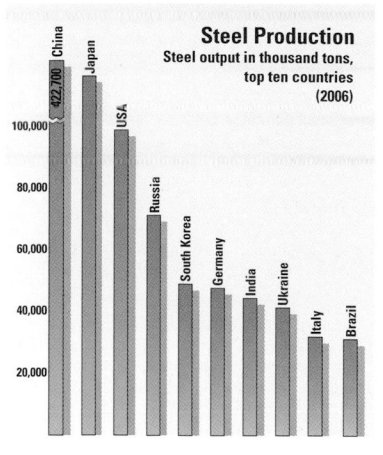

Steel Production
Steel output in thousand tons, top ten countries (2006)

China 422,700 | Japan | USA | Russia | South Korea | Germany | India | Ukraine | Italy | Brazil

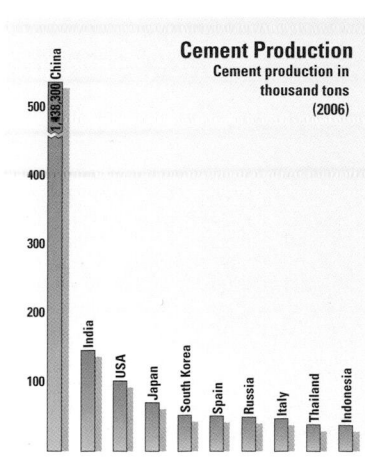

Cement Production
Cement production in thousand tons (2006)

China 1,238,300 | India | USA | Japan | South Korea | Spain | Russia | Italy | Thailand | Indonesia

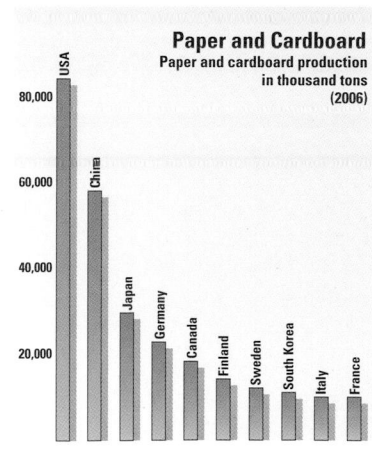

Paper and Cardboard
Paper and cardboard production in thousand tons (2006)

USA | China | Japan | Germany | Canada | Finland | Sweden | South Korea | Italy | France

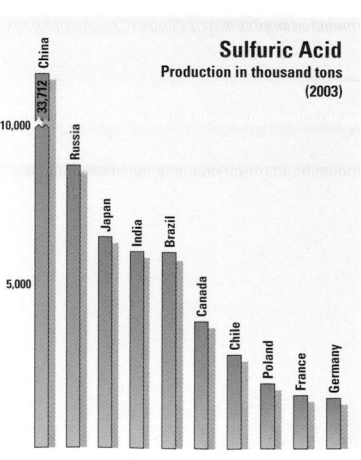

Sulfuric Acid
Production in thousand tons (2003)

China 33,712 | Russia | Japan | India | Brazil | Canada | Chile | Poland | France | Germany

Trade

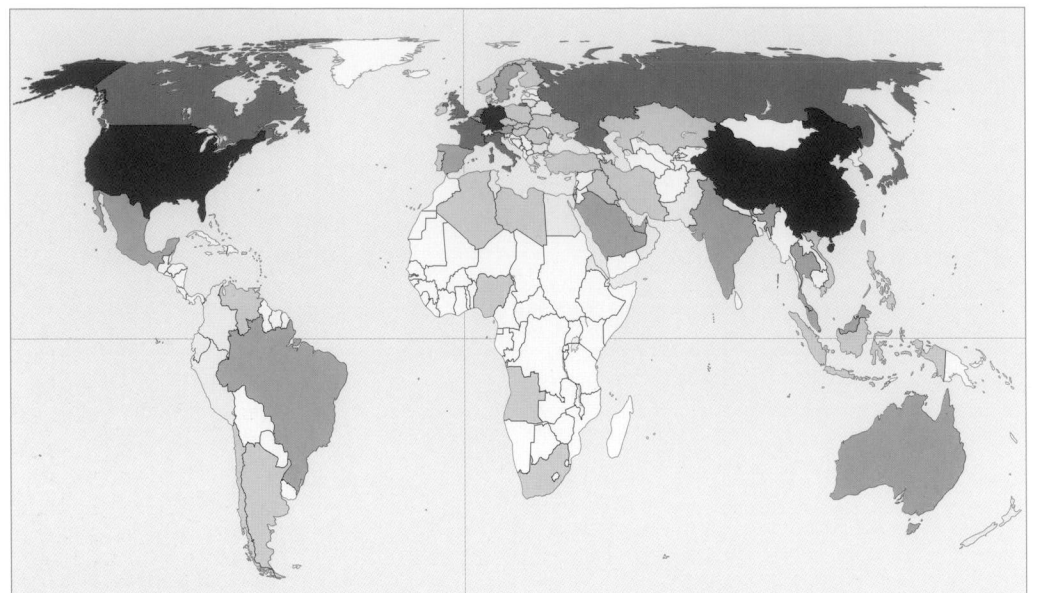

Share of World Trade

Percentage share of total world exports by value (2007)

- Over 5% of world trade
- 2.5 – 5% of world trade
- 1 – 2.5% of world trade
- 0.25 – 1% of world trade
- 0.1 – 0.25% of world trade
- Under 0.1% of world trade

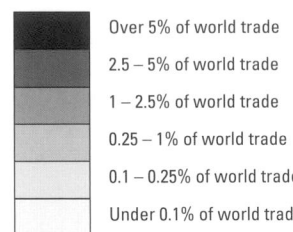

Largest share of world trade		Smallest share of world trade	
Germany	9.8%	East Timor	0.0%
China	8.8%	Eritrea	0.0%
USA	8.2%	Burundi	0.0%
Japan	4.8%	Rwanda	0.0%
France	4.0%	Guinea-Bissau	0.0%

The Main Trading Nations

The imports and exports of the top ten trading nations as a percentage of world trade (2006). Each country's trade in manufactured goods is shown in dark blue

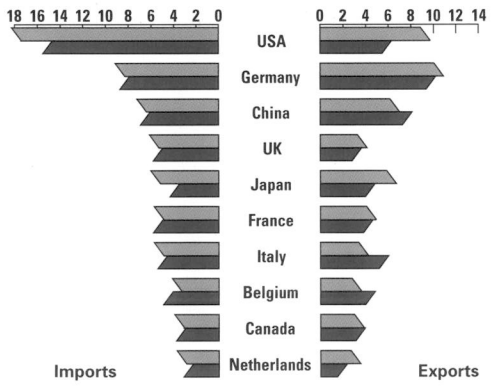

Imports — Exports

USA, Germany, China, UK, Japan, France, Italy, Belgium, Canada, Netherlands

Major exports

Leading manufactured items and their exporters (2007)

Motor Vehicles
World total (2007): US$ 2,706,511 million

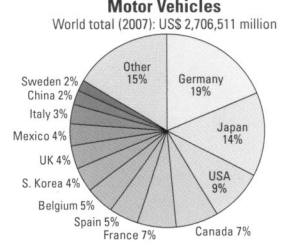

Germany 19%, Japan 14%, USA 9%, Canada 7%, France 7%, Spain 5%, Belgium 5%, S. Korea 4%, UK 4%, Mexico 4%, Italy 3%, China 2%, Sweden 2%, Other 15%

Telecommunications Gear
World total (2007): US$ 577,845 million

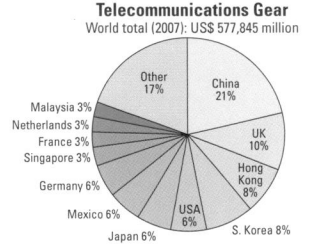

China 21%, UK 10%, Hong Kong 8%, USA 6%, S. Korea 8%, Japan 6%, Mexico 6%, Germany 6%, Singapore 3%, France 3%, Netherlands 3%, Malaysia 3%, Other 17%

Petrol Products
World total (2007): US$ 1,031,202 million

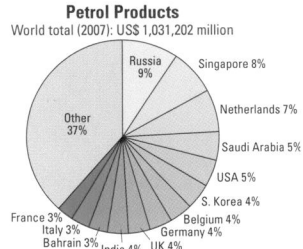

Russia 9%, Singapore 8%, Netherlands 7%, Saudi Arabia 5%, USA 5%, S. Korea 4%, Belgium 4%, Germany 4%, UK 4%, India 4%, Bahrain 3%, Italy 3%, France 3%, Other 37%

Computers
World total (2007): US$ 236,396 million

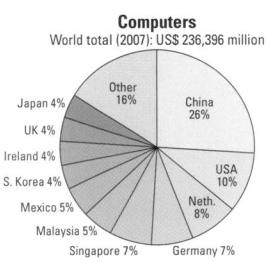

China 26%, USA 10%, Neth. 8%, Germany 7%, Singapore 7%, Malaysia 5%, Mexico 5%, S. Korea 4%, Ireland 4%, UK 4%, Japan 4%, Other 16%

Electrical Components
World total (2007): US$ 4,187,042 million

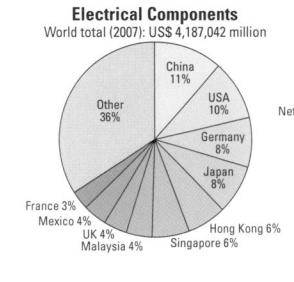

China 11%, USA 10%, Germany 8%, Japan 8%, Hong Kong 6%, Singapore 6%, Malaysia 4%, UK 4%, Mexico 4%, France 3%, Other 36%

Pharmaceuticals
World total (2007): US$ 1,042,778 million

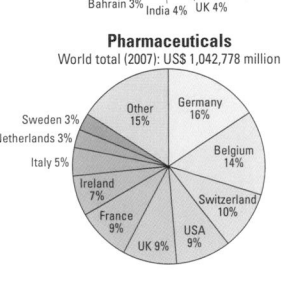

Germany 16%, Belgium 14%, Switzerland 10%, USA 9%, UK 9%, France 9%, Ireland 7%, Italy 5%, Netherlands 3%, Sweden 3%, Other 15%

Balance of Trade

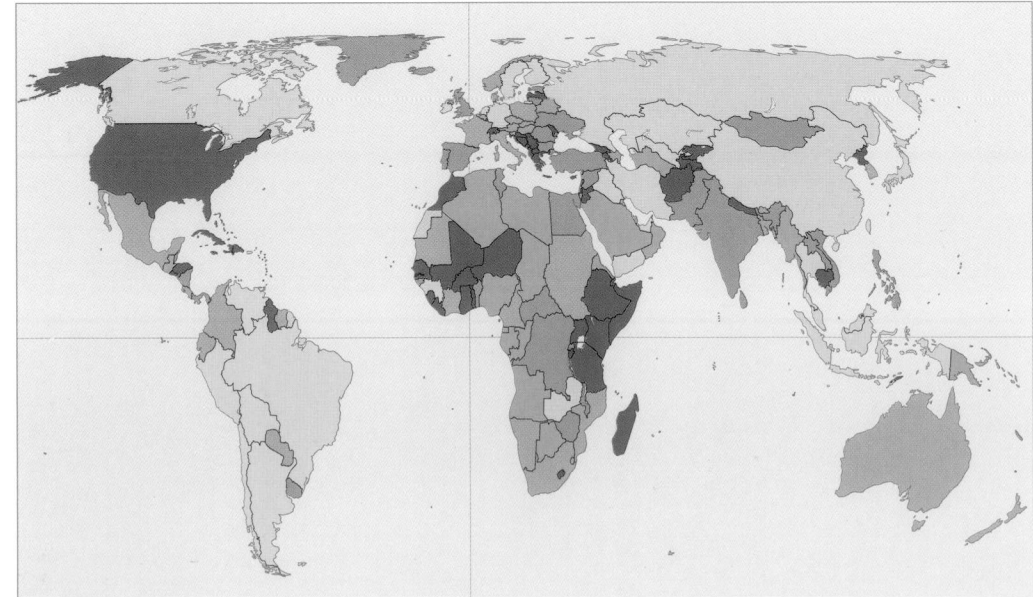

Value of exports in proportion to the value of imports (2007)

Imports exceed exports by:
- More than 40%
- 10 – 40%
- 10% either side
- 10 – 40%
- More than 40%

Exports exceed imports by:

- No data available

The total world trade balance should amount to zero, since exports must equal imports on a global scale. In practice, at least $100 billion in exports go unrecorded, leaving the world with an apparent deficit and many countries in a better position than public accounting reveals. However, a favorable trade balance is not necessarily a sign of prosperity: many poorer countries must maintain a high surplus in order to service debts, and do so by restricting imports below the levels needed to sustain successful economies.

CARTOGRAPHY BY PHILIP'S. COPYRIGHT PHILIP'S

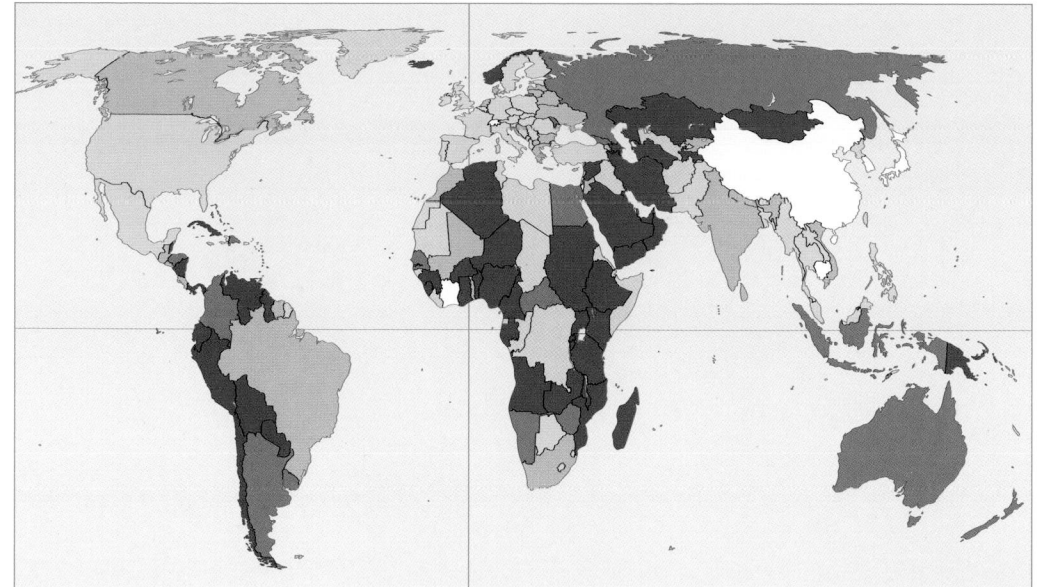

Primary exports as a percentage of total export value (2005)

- Over 75%
- 50 – 75%
- 25 – 50%
- 10 – 25%
- Under 10%
- No data available

Primary exports are raw materials or partly processed products that form the basis for manufacturing. They are the necessary requirements of industries and include agricultural products, minerals, fuels, and timber, as well as many semimanufactured goods such as cotton, which has been spun but not woven, wood pulp, or flour. Many developed countries have few natural resources and rely on imports for the majority of their primary products. The countries of Southeast Asia export hardwoods to the rest of the world, while many South American countries are heavily dependent on coffee exports.

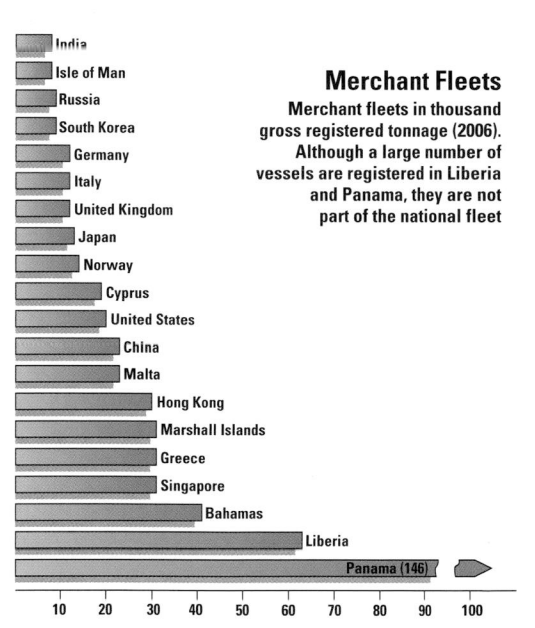

Merchant Fleets

Merchant fleets in thousand gross registered tonnage (2006). Although a large number of vessels are registered in Liberia and Panama, they are not part of the national fleet

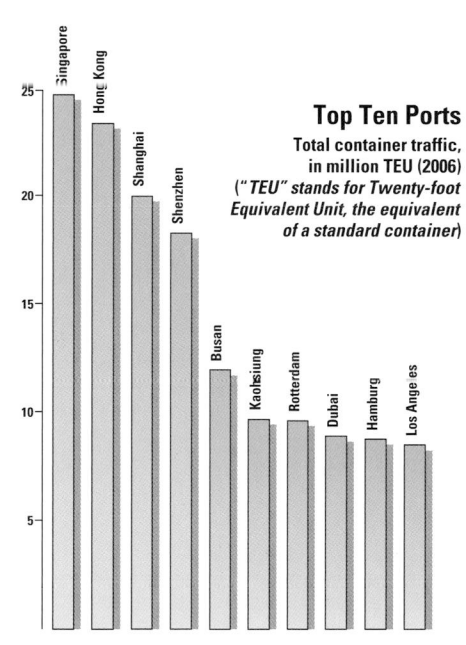

Top Ten Ports

Total container traffic, in million TEU (2006) ("*TEU*" stands for Twenty-foot Equivalent Unit, the equivalent of a standard container)

Types of Vessels
World fleet by type of vessel (2006)

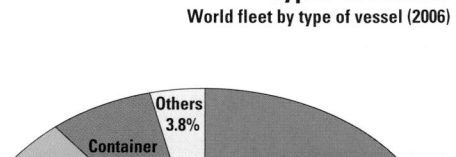

- Others 3.8%
- Container ships 7.4%
- Passenger ships 12.1%
- General cargo ships 38.4%
- Bulk carriers 13.6%
- Oil tankers 24.7%

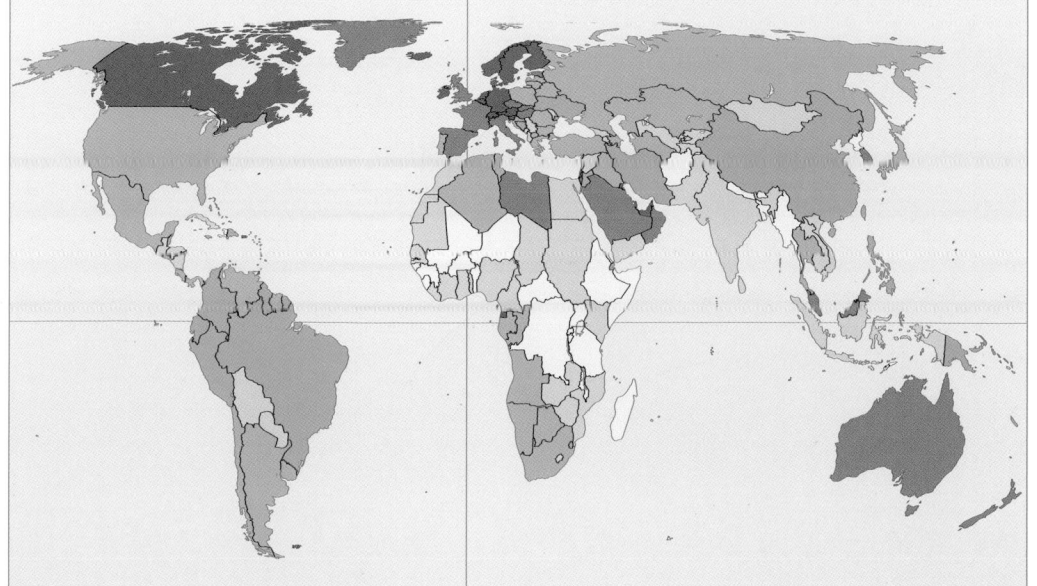

Exports Per Capita

Value of exports in US $, divided by total population (2006)

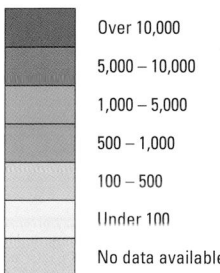

- Over 10,000
- 5,000 – 10,000
- 1,000 – 5,000
- 500 – 1,000
- 100 – 500
- Under 100
- No data available

Highest per capita

Hong Kong	$88,121
Liechtenstein	$72,675
Singapore	$63,132
United Arab Emirates	$52,676
Luxembourg	$41,209

CARTOGRAPHY BY PHILIP'S. COPYRIGHT PHILIP'S

Travel and Tourism

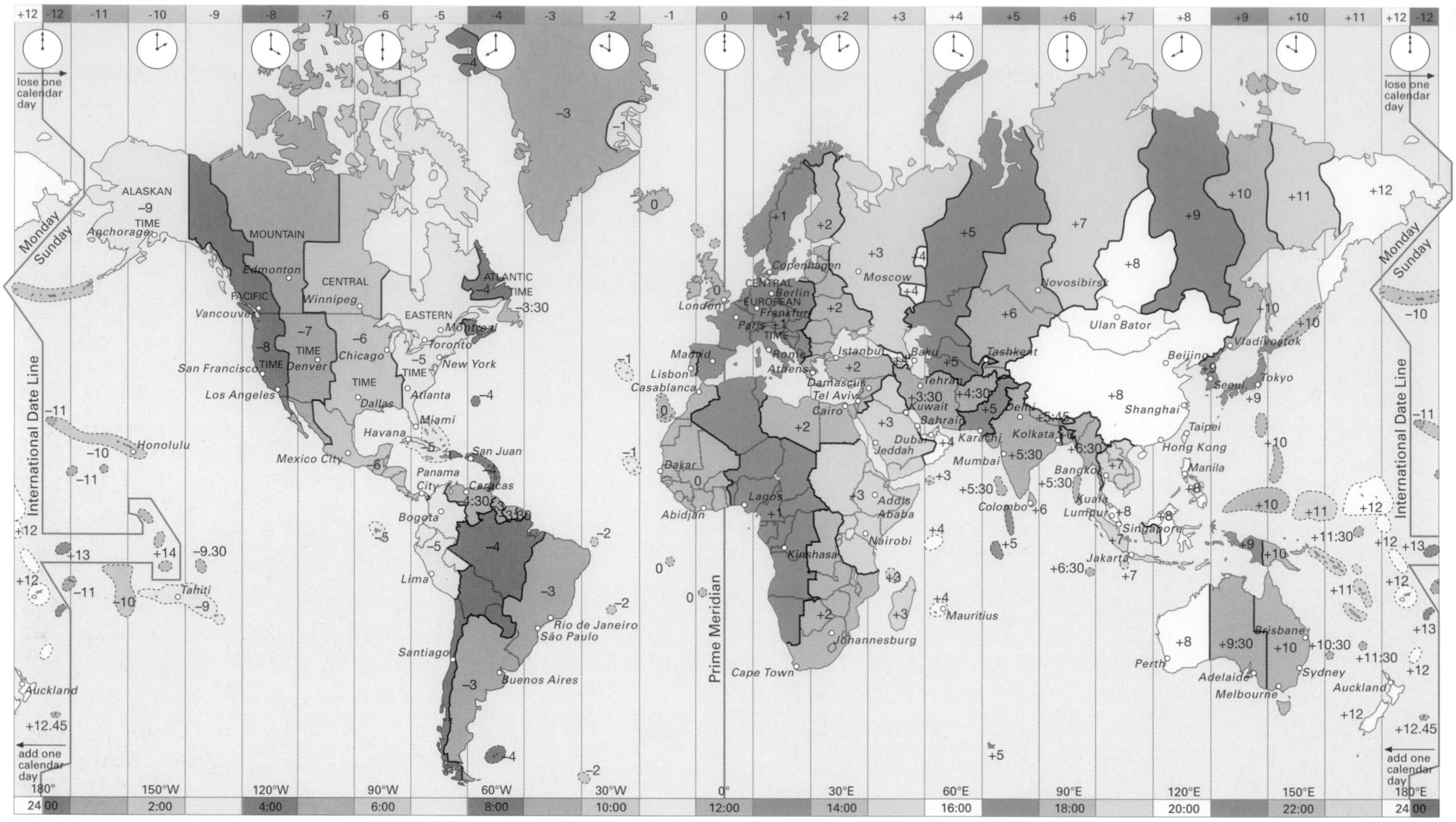

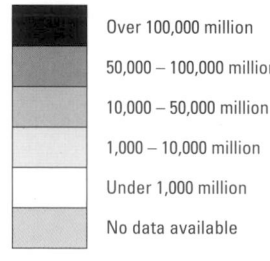

Projection: Mercator

Time Zones

Zones using UT (GMT)	Zones ahead of UT (GMT)	Certain time zones are affected by the incidence of daylight saving time in countries where it is adopted.
Zones behind UT (GMT)	Half-hour zones	
International boundaries	Time-zone boundaries	Actual solar time, when it is noon at Greenwich, is shown along the top of the map.
10 Hours fast or slow of UT or Coordinated Universal Time	International Date Line	

The world is divided into 24 time zones, each centered on meridians at 15° intervals, which is the longitudinal distance the sun travels every hour. The meridian running through Greenwich, London, passes through the middle of the first zone.

Rail and Road: The Leading Nations

Total rail network ('000 km)	Passenger km per head per year	Total road network ('000 km)	Vehicle km per head per year	Number of vehicles per km of roads
1. USA 233.8	Japan 1,891	USA 6,378.3	USA....................12,505	Hong Kong..........287
2. Russia 85.5	Switzerland 1,751	India 3,319.6	Luxembourg 7,989	Qatar....................284
3. Canada 73.2	Belarus...............1,334	China 1,765.2	Kuwait 7,251	UAE.....................232
4. India 63.1	France 1,203	Brazil 1,724.9	France 7,142	Germany 195
5. China 60.5	Ukraine 1,100	Canada............1,408.8	Sweden 6,991	Lebanon 191
6. Germany...............36.1	Russia 1,080	Japan 1,171.4	Germany 6,806	Macau 172
7. Argentina 34.2	Austria...............1,008	France 893.1	Denmark 6,764	Singapore 167
8. France...................29.3	Denmark 999	Australia 811.6	Austria 6,518	South Korea 160
9. Mexico 26.5	Netherlands 855	Spain 664.9	Netherlands 5,984	Kuwait 156
10. South Africa..........22.7	Germany 842	Russia 537.3	UK 5,738	Taiwan 150
11. Brazil.....................22.1	Italy 811	Italy....................479.7	Canada................5,493	Israel 111
12. Ukraine 22.1	Belgium 795	UK 371.9	Italy.....................4,852	Malta 110

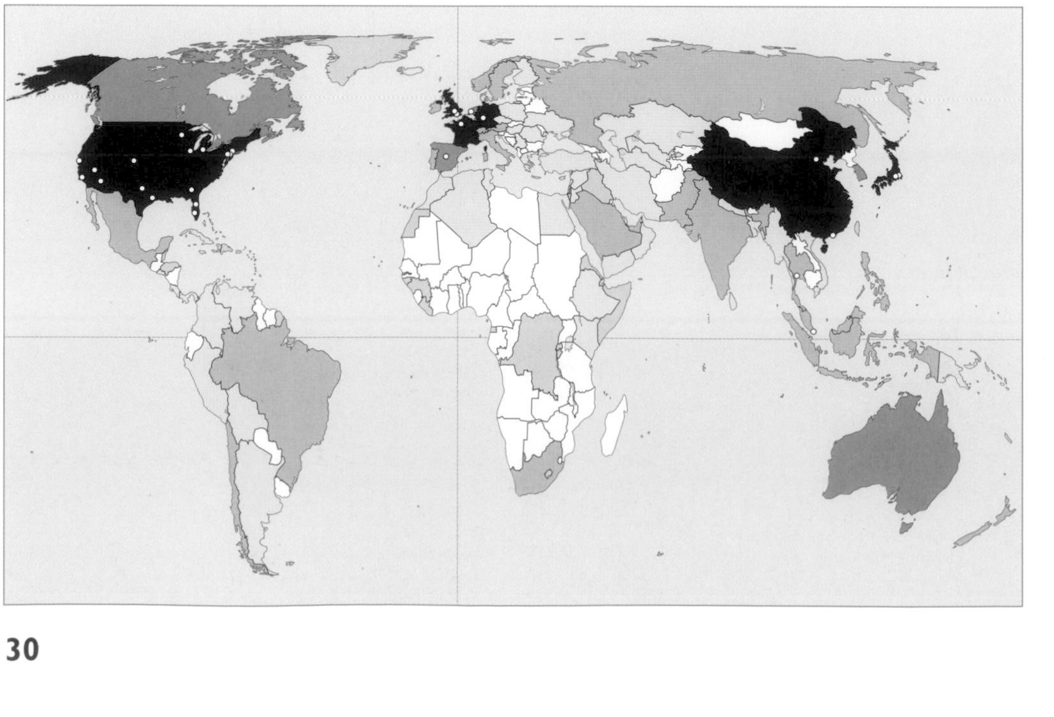

Air Travel

Passenger kilometers flown on scheduled flights (the number of passengers in thousands – international and domestic multiplied by the distance flown from the airport of origin)

	Over 100,000 million
	50,000 – 100,000 million
	10,000 – 50,000 million
	1,000 – 10,000 million
	Under 1,000 million
	No data available
○	Major airports (handling over 30 million passengers)

World's busiest airports (total passengers)		World's busiest airports (international passengers)	
1. Atlanta	(Hartsfield)	1. London	(Heathrow)
2. Chicago	(O'Hare)	2. Paris	(Charles de Gaulle)
3. London	(Heathrow)	3. Amsterdam	(Schipol)
4. Tokyo	(Haneda)	4. Frankfurt	(International)
5. Los Angeles	(International)	5. Hong Kong	(International)

CARTOGRAPHY BY PHILIP'S. COPYRIGHT PHILIP'S

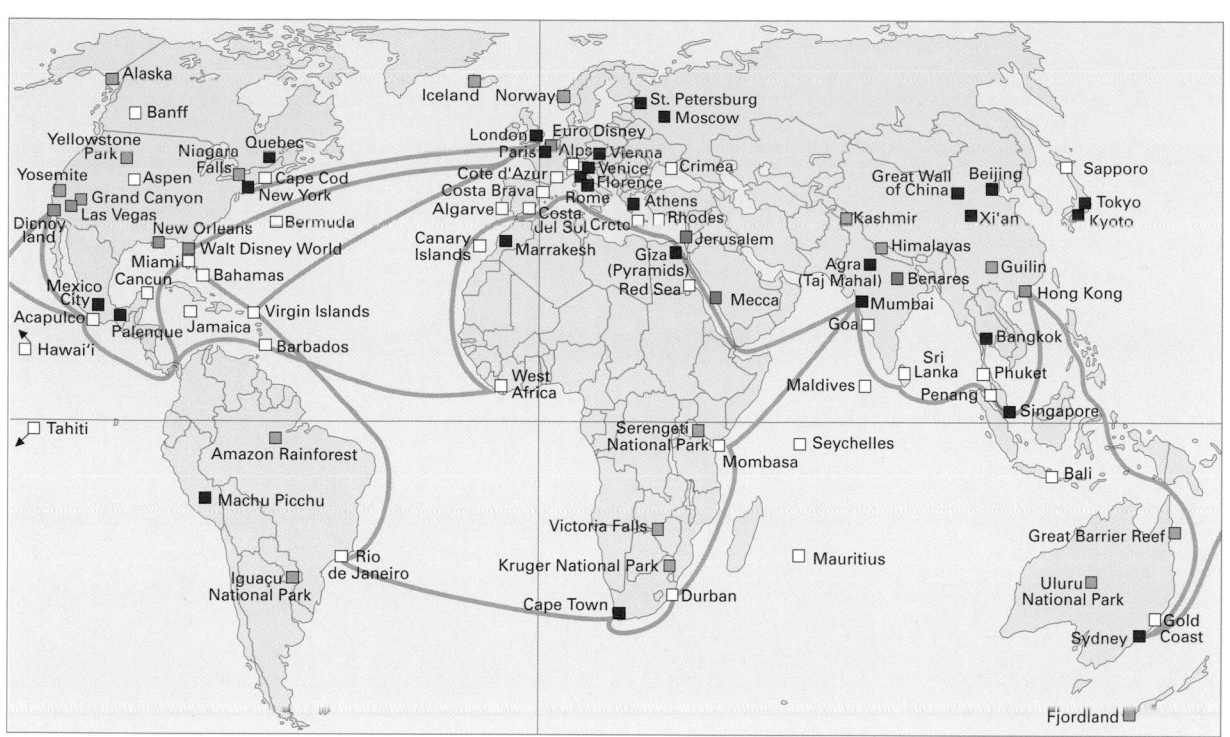

Destinations

- ■ Cultural and historical centers
- □ Coastal resorts
- □ Ski resorts
- ▨ Centres of entertainment
- ▨ Places of pilgrimage
- ▨ Places of great natural beauty
- — Popular holiday cruise routes

Visitors to the USA

Overseas arrivals to the USA, in thousands (2006)

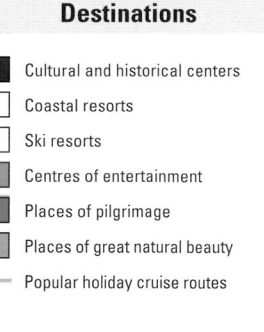

1.	Canada	15,995
2.	Mexico	13,400
3.	UK	4,176
4.	Japan	3,673
5.	Germany	1,386
6.	France	790
7.	South Korea	758
8.	Australia	603
9.	Italy	500
10.	Brazil	525

Tourist Spending

Countries spending the most on overseas tourism, US$ million (2006)

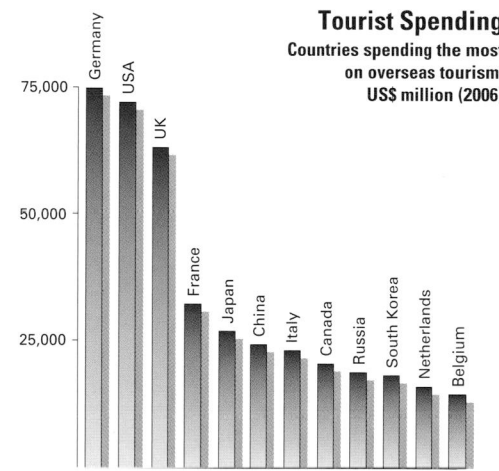

Importance of Tourism

		Arrivals from abroad (2006)	% of world total (2006)
1.	France	76,001,000	9.0%
2.	Spain	55,577,000	6.6%
3.	USA	46,085,000	5.4%
4.	China	41,761,000	4.9%
5.	Italy	36,513,000	4.3%
6.	UK	29,970,000	3.5%
7.	Germany	21,500,000	2.5%
8.	Mexico	20,617,000	2.4%
9.	Turkey	20,273,000	2.4%
10.	Austria	19,952,000	2.4%
11.	Russia	19,940,000	2.4%
12.	Canada	19,152,000	2.3%

The 846 million international arrivals in 2006 represented an additional 43 million over 2005's level – making a new record year for the industry. Growth was common to all regions, but particularly strong in Asia and the Pacific, and in the Middle East.

Tourist Earnings

Countries receiving the most from overseas tourism, US$ million (2006)

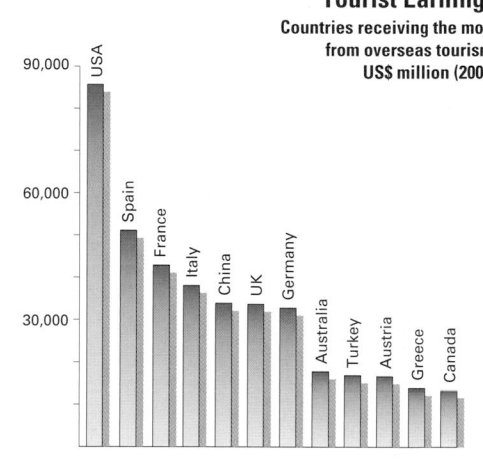

Tourism

Tourism receipts as a percentage of Gross National Income (2005)

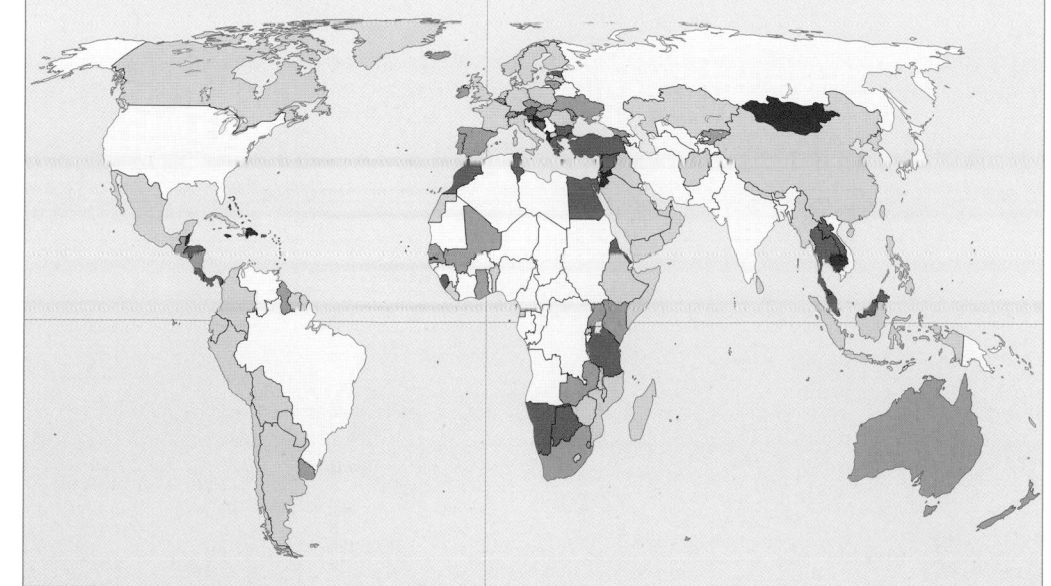

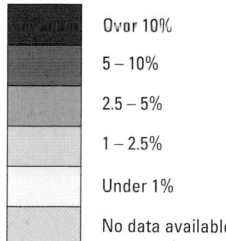

- ■ Over 10%
- ▨ 5 – 10%
- ▨ 2.5 – 5%
- ▨ 1 – 2.5%
- □ Under 1%
- ▨ No data available

Countries most dependent on tourism (highest tourism receipts as a percentage of GNI, 2005)

1.	Palau	63.0%
2.	St Lucia	44.8%
3.	Bahamas	40.2%
4.	Antigua & Barbuda	36.9%
5.	Maldives	36.5%

CARTOGRAPHY BY PHILIP'S. COPYRIGHT PHILIP'S.

– Mt Everest, China/Nepal –

Part of the Himalaya range, Mt Everest – the highest
mountain in the world at 29,035 ft (8,850 m) – lies just
north of center in this image. The two arms of the Rongbuk
glacier flow away from the triangular shaded north wall, with
the Kangshung glacier due east. The international boundary
between China and Nepal bisects the peak, which was
first climbed on May 28, 1953.

WORLD CITIES

Amsterdam	**2**	Hong Kong	**12**	Mumbai	**20**	Tehran	**31**
Athens	**2**	Istanbul	**12**	Munich	**21**	Toronto	**31**
Atlanta	**3**	Jakarta	**12**	New Orleans	**21**	Vienna	**32**
Baghdad	**3**	Jerusalem	**13**	New York	**22**	Warsaw	**32**
Bangkok	**3**	Johannesburg	**13**	Orlando	**23**	Washington	**33**
Barcelona	**4**	Karachi	**13**	Osaka	**23**	Wellington	**33**
Beijing	**4**	Kolkata	**14**	Oslo	**23**		
Berlin	**5**	Lagos	**14**	Paris	**24**	Index	**34–39**
Boston	**6**	Las Vegas	**14**	Prague	**25**		
Brussels	**6**	Lima	**14**	Rio de Janeiro	**25**		
Budapest	**7**	London	**15**	Rome	**26**	WORLD CITIES	
Buenos Aires	**7**	Los Angeles	**16**	San Francisco	**26**	SATELLITE IMAGES	
Cairo	**7**	Lisbon	**16**	St Petersburg	**27**	Cape Town	**40**
Cape Town	**8**	Madrid	**17**	Santiago	**27**	Karachi	**41**
Copenhagen	**8**	Manila	**17**	São Paulo	**27**	London	**42**
Chicago	**9**	Melbourne	**18**	Seoul	**27**	Melbourne	**43**
Delhi	**10**	Mexico City	**18**	Shanghai	**28**	New Orleans	**44**
Dublin	**10**	Miami	**18**	Singapore	**28**	New York	**45**
Edinburgh	**11**	Milan	**19**	Stockholm	**29**	San Francisco	**46**
Guangzhou	**11**	Moscow	**19**	Sydney	**29**	Santiago	**47**
Helsinki	**11**	Montréal	**20**	Tokyo	**30**	Tokyo	**48**

CITY MAPS

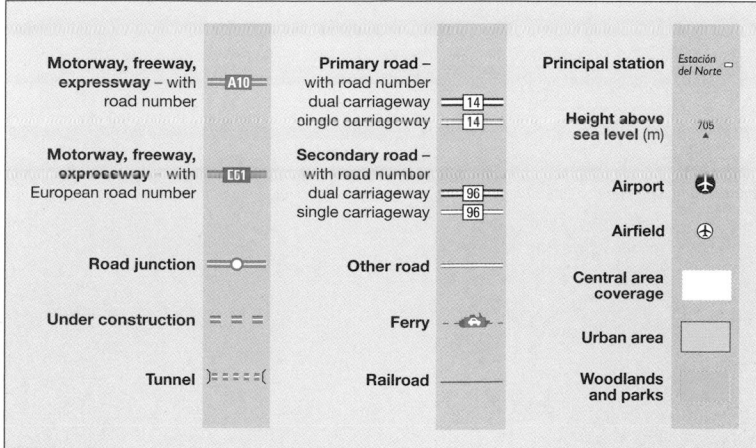

CENTRAL AREA MAPS

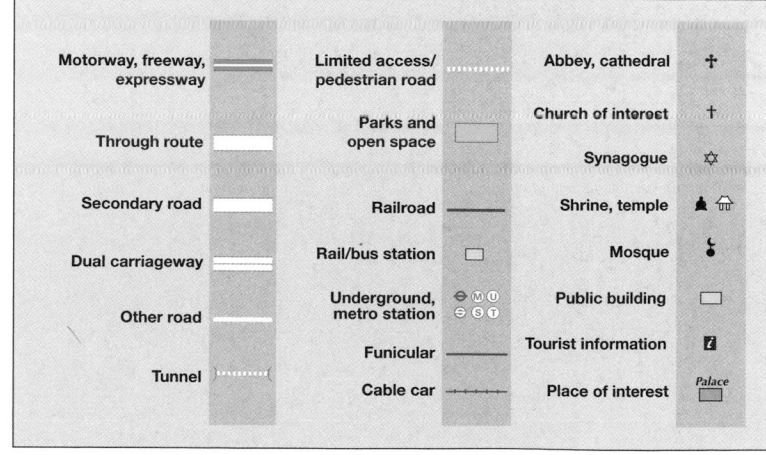

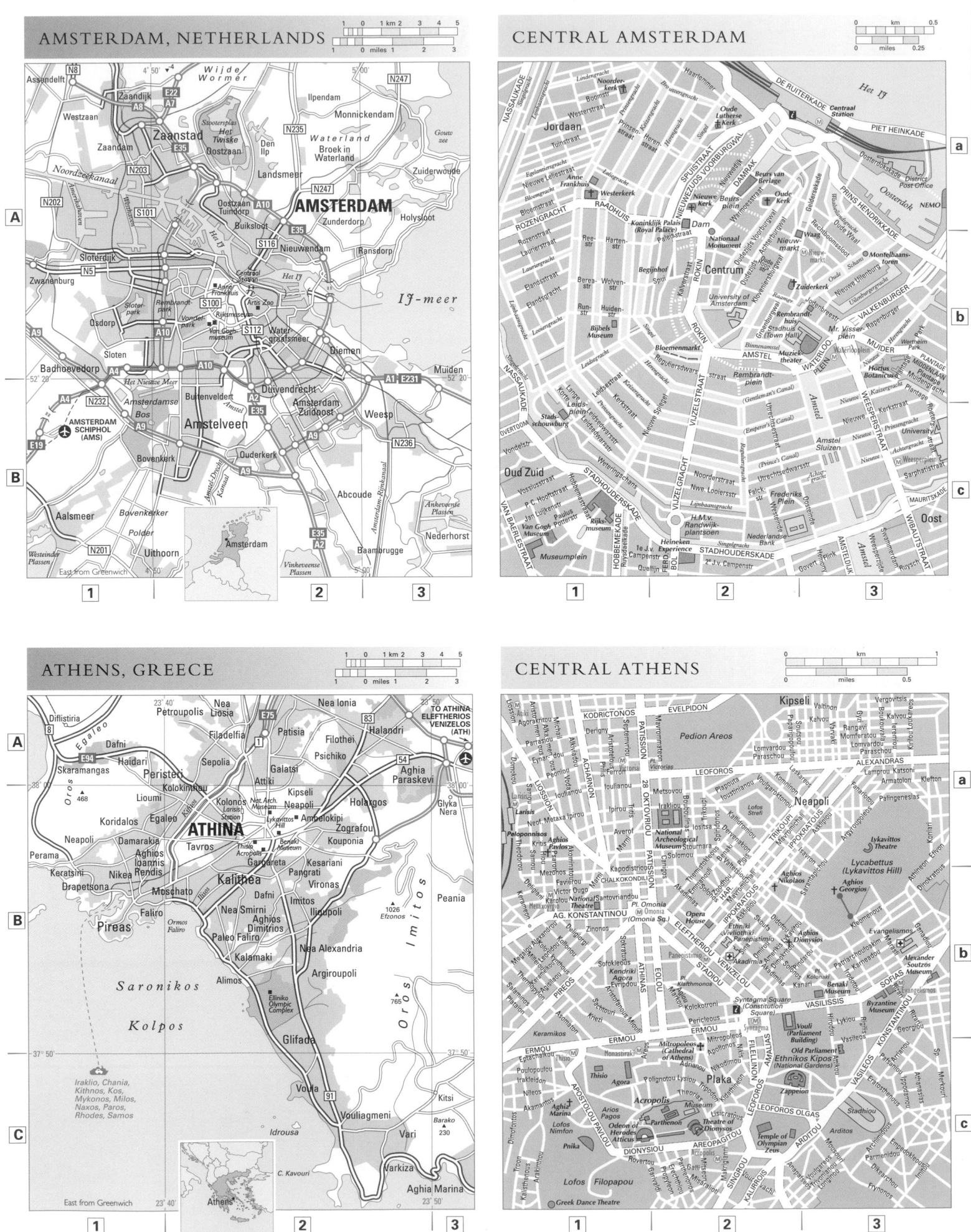

COPYRIGHT PHILIP'S

ATLANTA, GEORGIA

1 0 1 km 2 3 4 5
1 0 miles 1 2 3

85 Interstate route numbers 29 U.S. route numbers 166 State route numbers

BAGHDAD, IRAQ

1 0 1 km 2 3 4 5
1 0 miles 1 2 3

International Zone (Green Zone)

BANGKOK, THAILAND

1 0 1 km 2 3 4 5
1 0 miles 1 2 3

CENTRAL BANGKOK

0 km 1
0 miles 0.5

—S— Skytrain

COPYRIGHT PHILIP'S

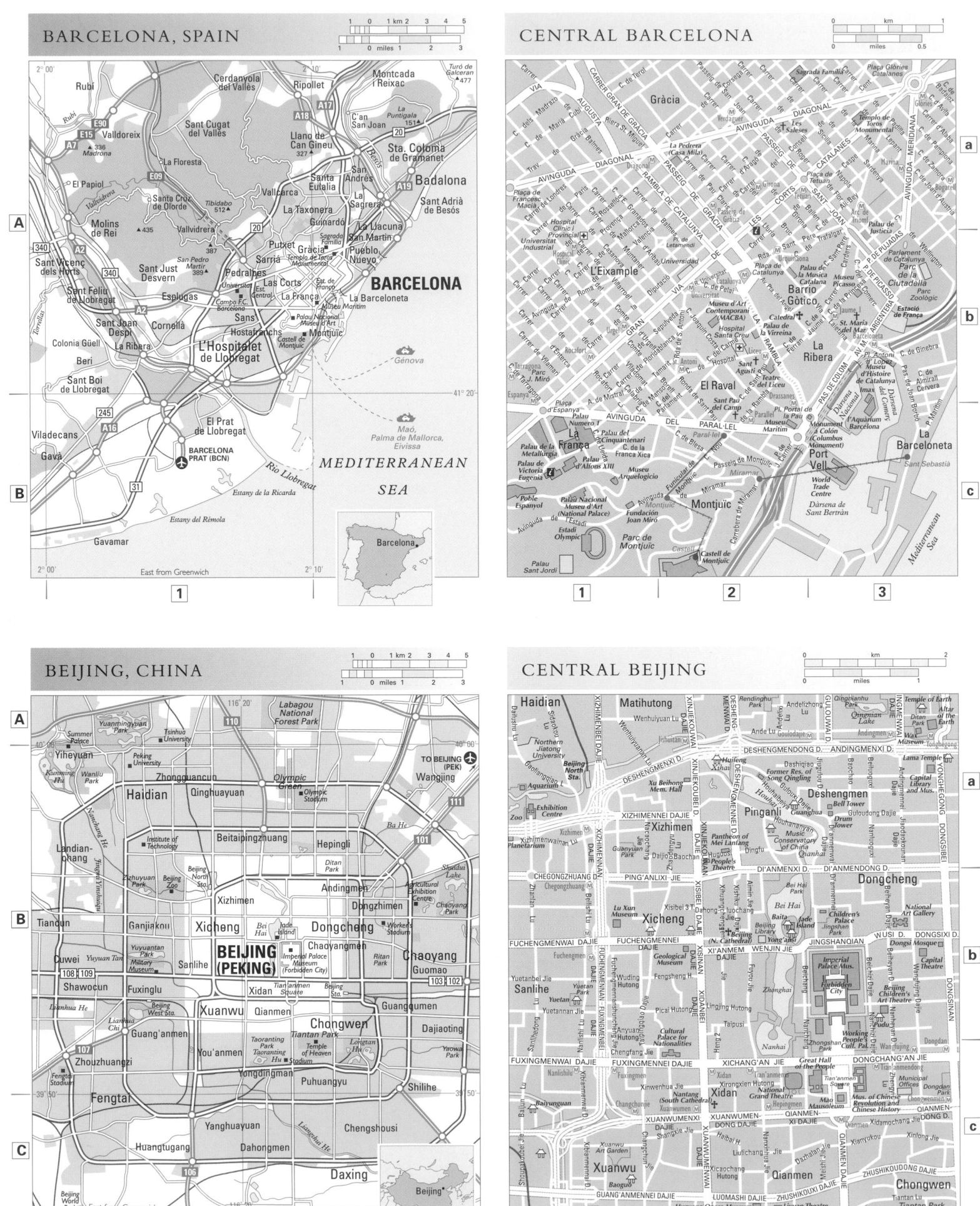

BARCELONA, SPAIN

CENTRAL BARCELONA

BEIJING, CHINA

CENTRAL BEIJING

COPYRIGHT PHILIP'S

BERLIN, GERMANY

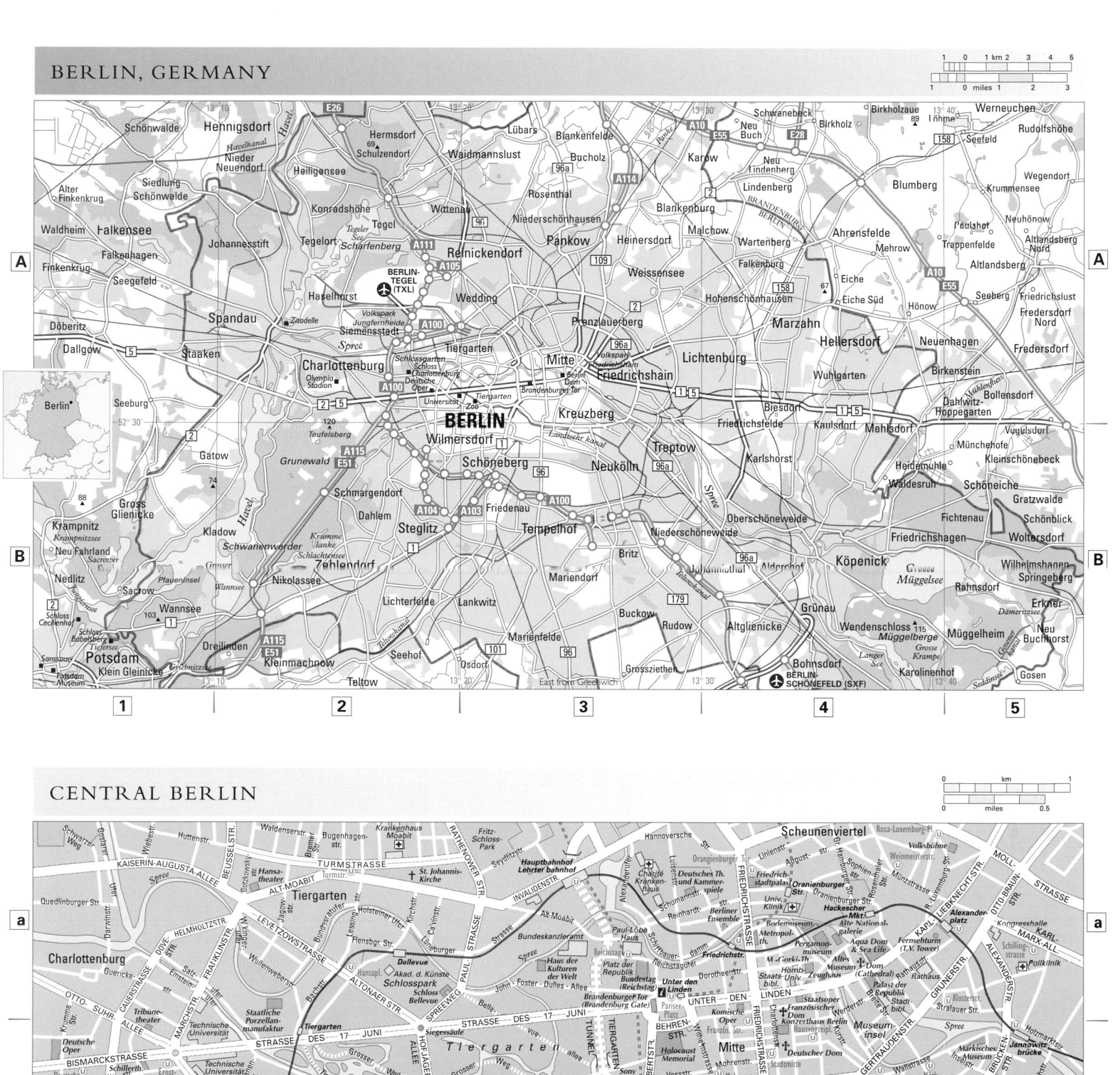

CENTRAL BERLIN

COPYRIGHT PHILIP'S

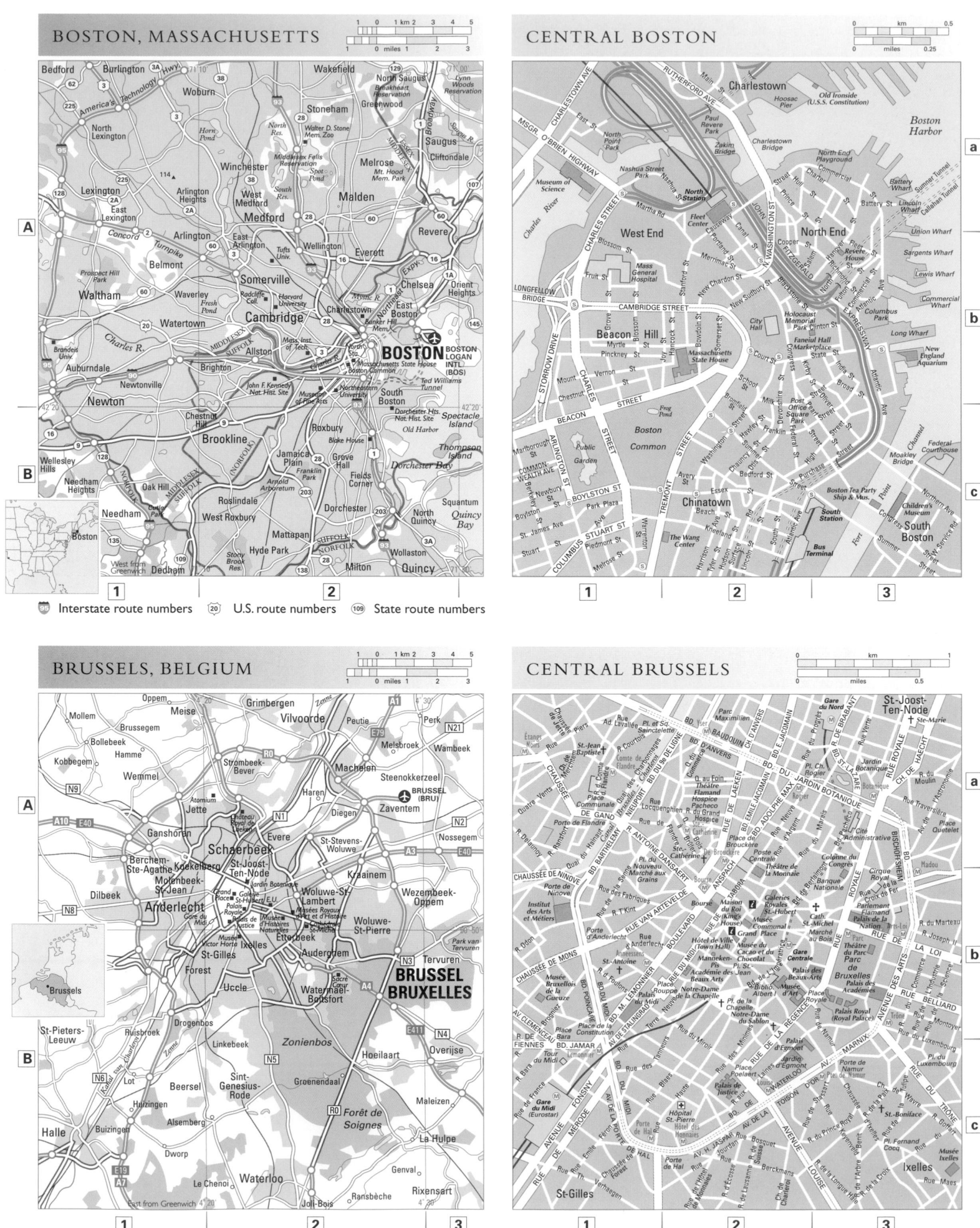

BOSTON, MASSACHUSETTS

Interstate route numbers 20 U.S. route numbers 109 State route numbers

CENTRAL BOSTON

BRUSSELS, BELGIUM

CENTRAL BRUSSELS

COPYRIGHT PHILIP'S

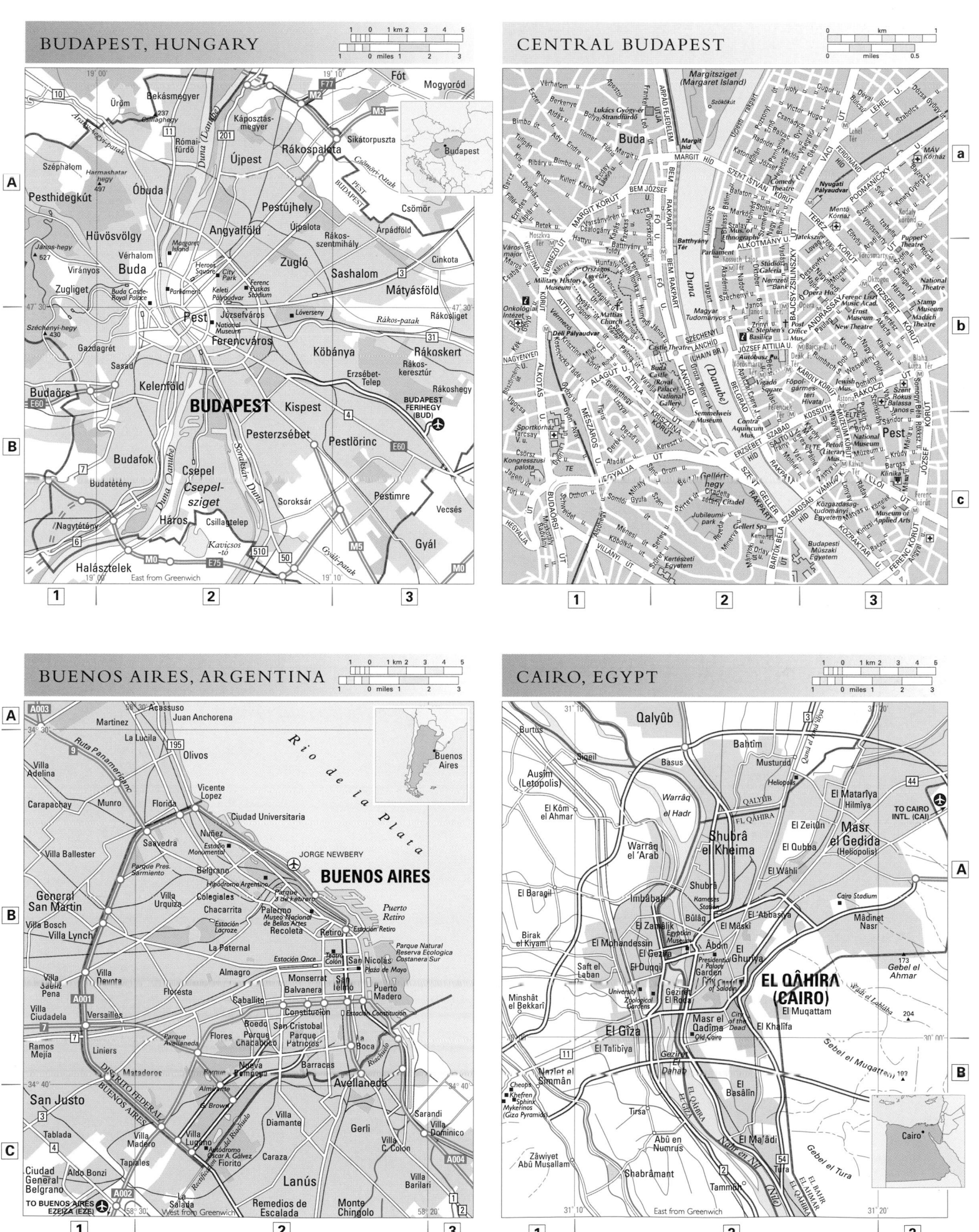

BUDAPEST, HUNGARY

CENTRAL BUDAPEST

BUENOS AIRES, ARGENTINA

CAIRO, EGYPT

COPYRIGHT PHILIP'S

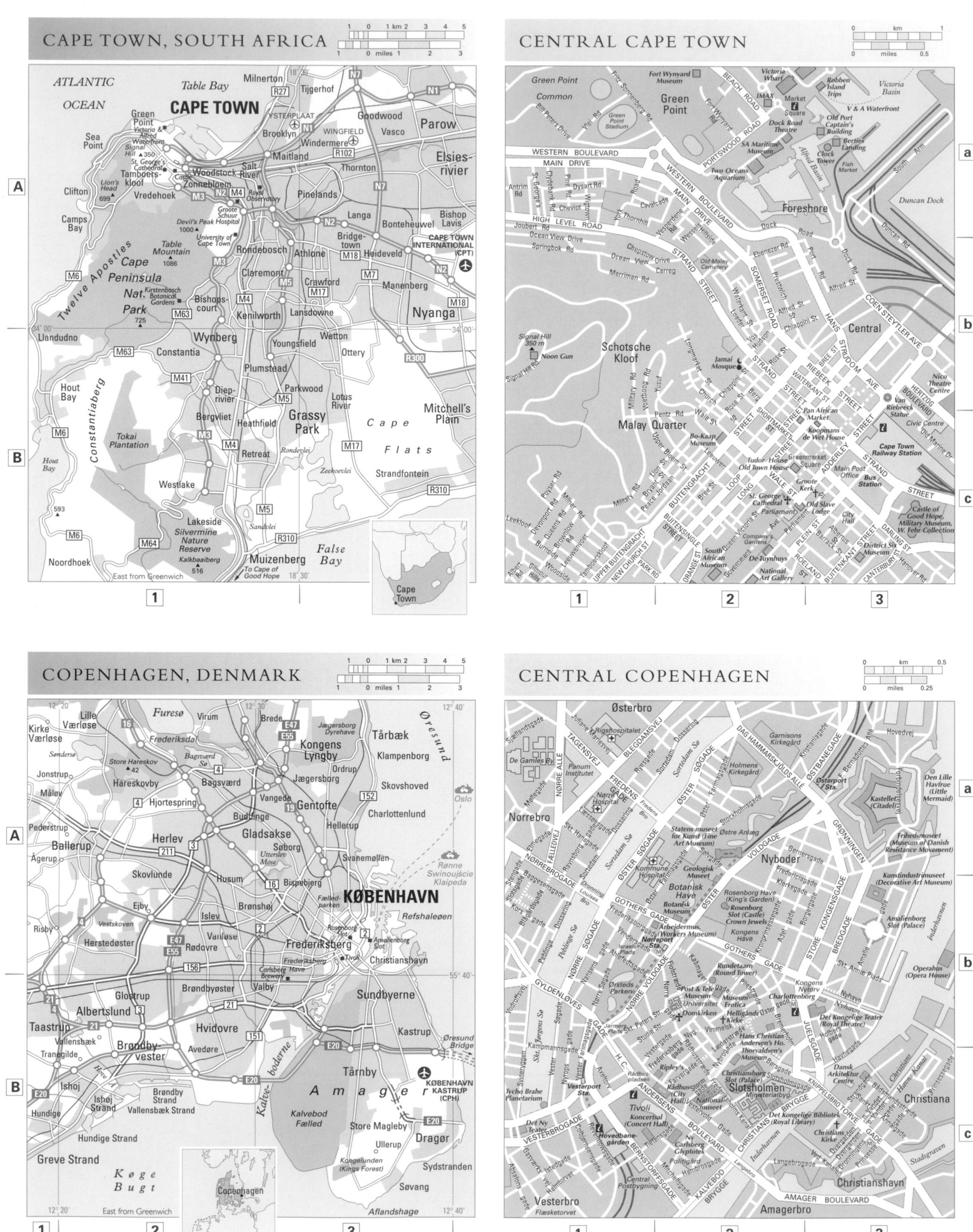

CHICAGO, ILLINOIS

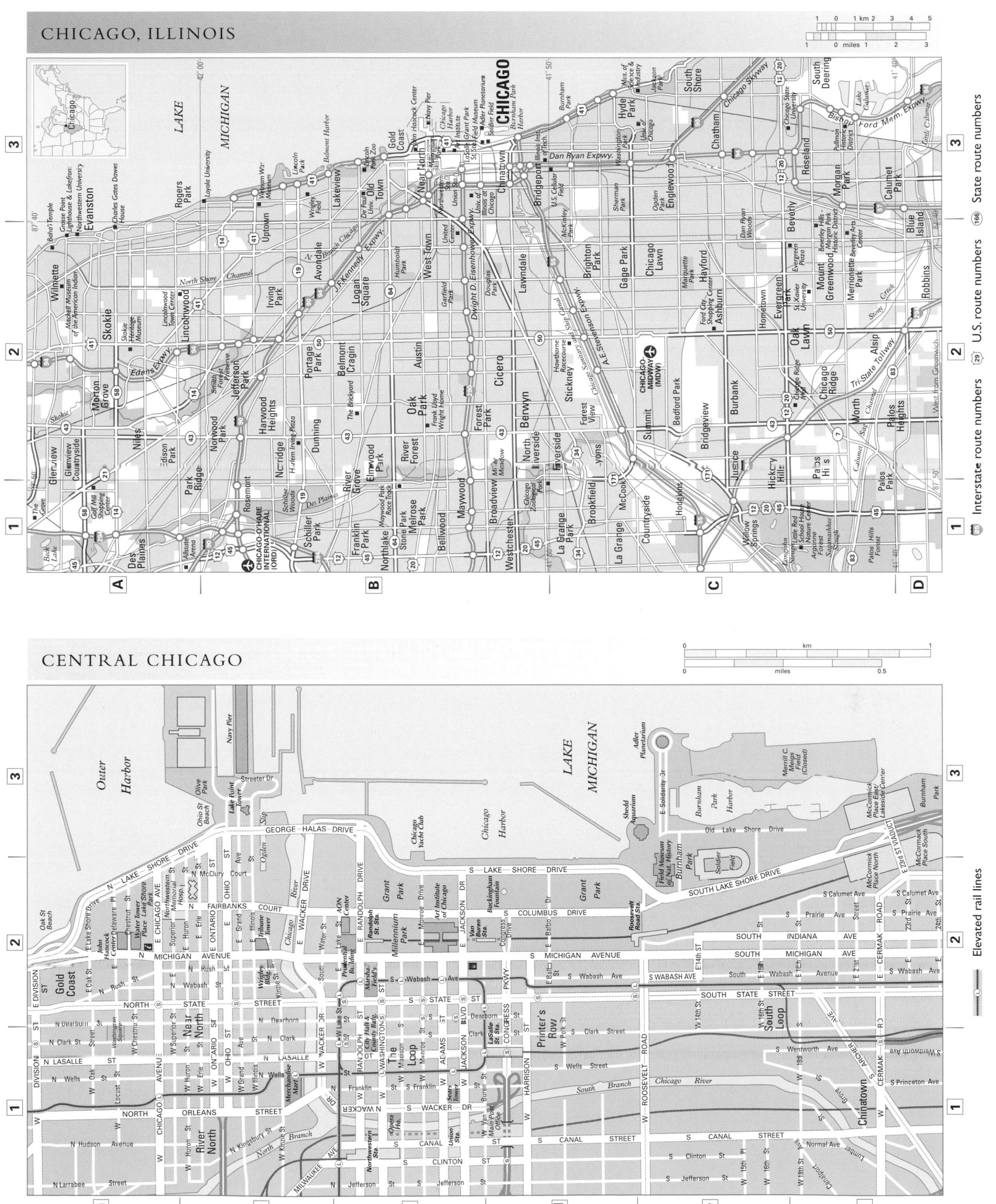

CENTRAL CHICAGO

COPYRIGHT PHILIP'S

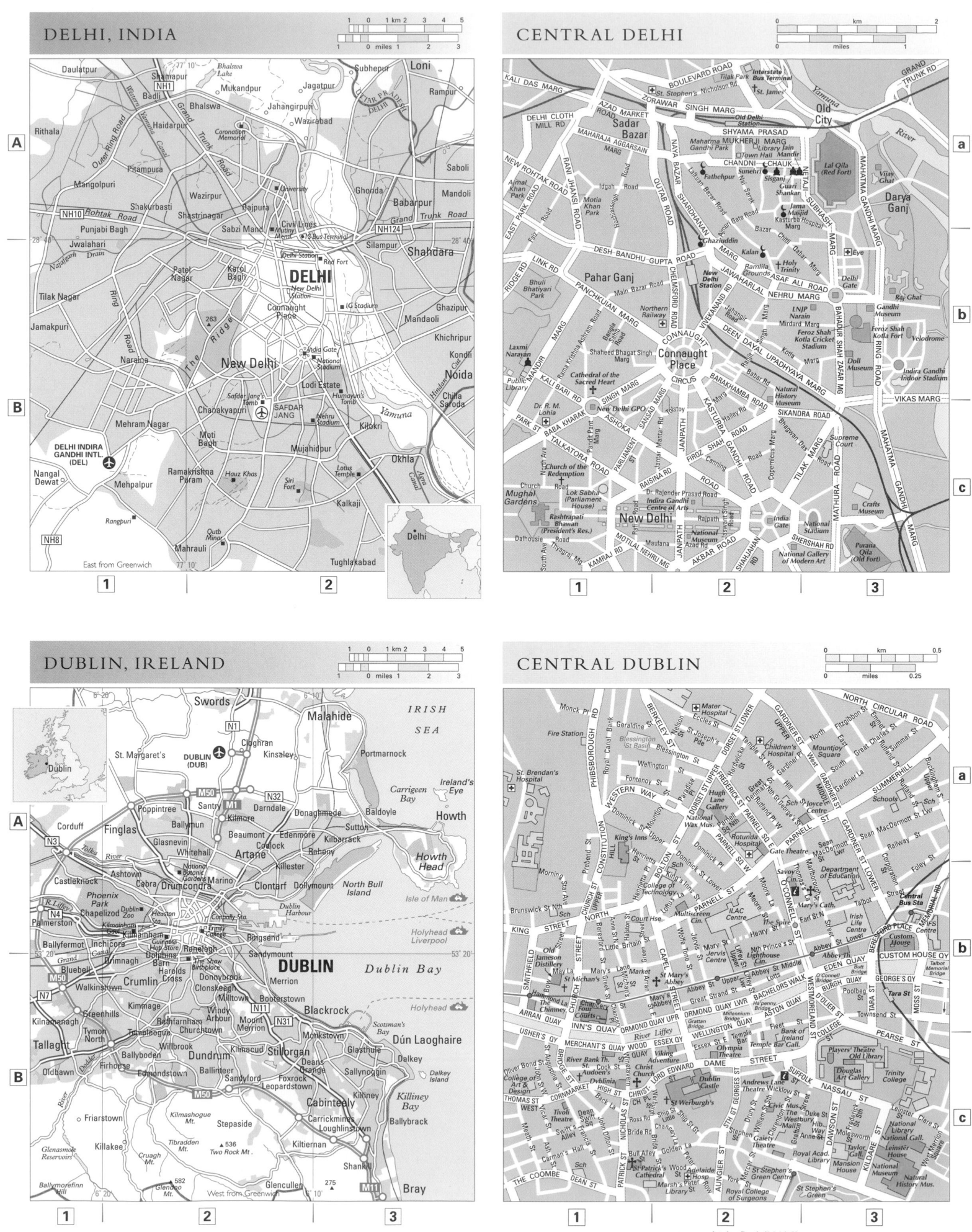

DELHI, INDIA

CENTRAL DELHI

DUBLIN, IRELAND

CENTRAL DUBLIN

Light Rail (LUAS)

COPYRIGHT PHILIP'S

EDINBURGH, U.K.

CENTRAL EDINBURGH

GUANGZHOU, CHINA

HELSINKI, FINLAND

COPYRIGHT PHILIP'S

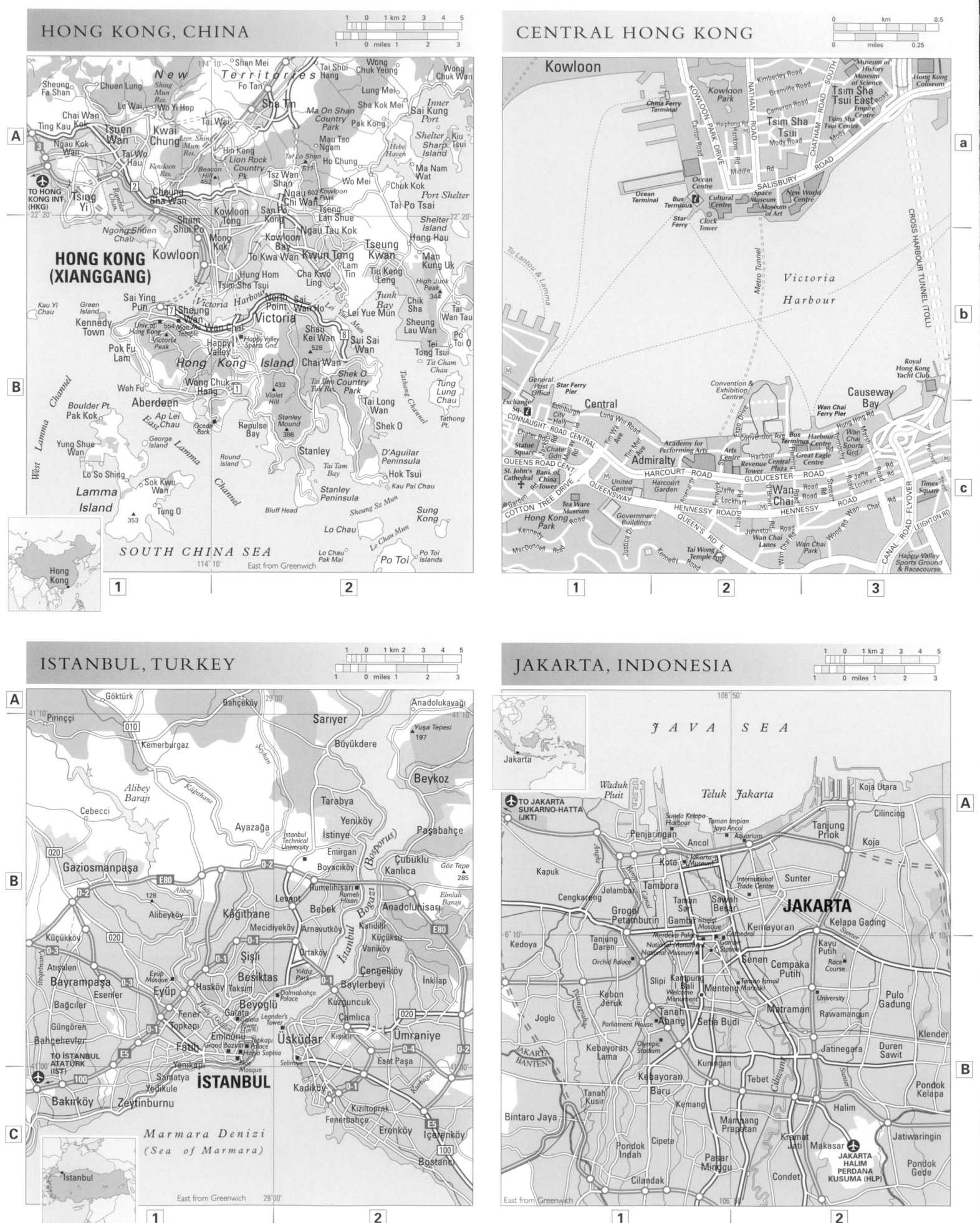

HONG KONG, CHINA

New Territories

Shan Mei · Shing Mun Res · Wo Yi Hop · Tai Wai · Chuen Lung · Sheung Fa Shan · Chai Wan Kok · Ting Kau · Ngau Kok Wan · Tsuen Wan · Kwai Chung · Tsing Yi · Lai Chi Kok · Tai Wo Hau · Lion Rock Country Park · Kowloon Res · Beacon Hill 452 · Sha Tin · Fo Tan · Ma On Shan Country Park · Pak Kong · Lung Mei · Sha Kok Mei · Tai Shui Hang · Wong Chuk Yeung · Inner Sai Kung Port · Shelter Sai Kung Port · Kiu Tsui · Hebe Haven · Shelter Sharp Island · Ma Nam Wat · Chuk Kok · Port Shelter · Tai Po Tsai · Shelter Island · Hang Hau · Man Uk · Tiu Keng Leng · Tseung Kwan

TO HONG KONG INT. (HKG) · Tsing Yi · Cheung Sha Wan · Ngong Shuen Chau · Sham Shui Po · Kowloon Tong · Mong Kok · Kowloon Bay · Ngau Tau Kok · Kwun Tong

Kau Yi Chau · Green Island · Sai Ying Pun · Sheung Wan · Univ. of Hong Kong 554 Mou Tan · Victoria Peak · Kennedy Town · Pok Fu Lam · Happy Valley Sports Gnd · Wan Chai · Victoria · North Point · Sai Wan Ho · Lei Yue Mun · Shau Kei Wan 528 · Sui Sai Wan · Chai Wan · Chik Sha · Sheung Lau Wan · Tai Tau · Po Toi O · Tei Tong Tsui · Tit Cham Chau · Tung Lung Chau

HONG KONG (XIANGGANG) · Kowloon

West Lamma Channel · Boulder Pt · Pak Kok · Ap Lei Chau · East Lamma Channel · George Island · Yung Shue Wan · Lo So Shing · Lamma Island · Sok Kwu Wan · Tung O · 353

Wah Fu · Wong Chuk Hang · Aberdeen · Ocean Park · Repulse Bay · Round Island · Stanley Mound 386 · Stanley · 433 Violet Hill · Shek O Country Park · Tai Long Wan · Shek O · Tai Tam Tuk Res · Tai Tam Bay · Stanley Peninsula · Bluff Head · D'Aguilar Peninsula · Hok Tsui · Kau Pai Chau · Sheung Sz Mun · Sung Kong · Lo Chau Mun · Lo Chau Pak Mai · Lo Chau · Po Toi Islands · Po Toi · Tathong Channel · Tung Lung Chau · Tathong Pt

Hong Kong Island

SOUTH CHINA SEA

114° 10' East from Greenwich

Hong Kong

1   **2**

CENTRAL HONG KONG

Kowloon

China Ferry Terminal · Kowloon Park · Kimberley Road · Granville Road · Cameron Road · Haiphong Rd · Kowloon Park Drive · Nathan Road · Chatham Road South · Mody Road · Middle Rd · Tsim Sha Tsui · Tsim Sha Tsui East · Tsim Sha Tsui Centre · Empire Centre · Museum of History · Museum of Science · Hong Kong Coliseum

Ocean Centre · Ocean Terminal · Bus Terminus · Cultural Centre · Space Museum · Museum of Art · New World Centre · SALISBURY ROAD · Star Ferry · Clock Tower

To Lantau & Lamma · Metro Tunnel · Victoria Harbour · CROSS HARBOUR TUNNEL (TOLL)

General Post Office · Star Ferry Pier · Edinburgh Pl · City Hall · Exchange Sq · CONNAUGHT ROAD CENTRAL · Chater Rd · Chater Gdn · Statue Square · QUEENS ROAD CENT · St John's Cathedral · Bank of China · COTTON TREE DRIVE · Garden Rd · Hong Kong Park · QUEENSWAY · Tea Ware Museum · Government Buildings · Justice Road · MacDonnell Road · Kennedy Road

Central · Admiralty · Lung Wui Road · Tim Mei Ave · Tamar · Academy for Performing Arts · Arts Centre · Convention & Exhibition Centre · Convention Ave · Harbour Centre · Harbour Road · Central Plaza · Great Eagle Centre · HARCOURT ROAD · GLOUCESTER ROAD · HENNESSY ROAD · United Centre · Harcourt Garden · Lockhart Road · Jaffe Road · Johnston Road · Wan Chai · Wan Chai Lanes · Wan Chai Park · Hennessy · Jaffe Road · Lockhart Road · Queen's Rd E · Tai Wong Temple · Happy Valley Sports Ground & Racecourse · Wan Chai Ferry Pier · Causeway Bay · Royal Hong Kong Yacht Club · Hung Hing Rd · Wan Chai Sports Grd · Gloucester Road · Leighton Rd · Canal Road Flyover · Times Square

1   **2**   **3**

ISTANBUL, TURKEY

Göktürk · Bahçeköy · Anadolukavağı · Pirinçci · Sarıyer · Yuşa Tepesi 197 · 010 · Kemerburgaz · Büyükdere · Beykoz · Alibey Barajı · Kâğıthane · Cebeci · Tarabya · Yeniköy · İstinye · Paşabahçe · Ayazağa · İstanbul Technical University · Emirgan · Boyacıköy · Çubuklu · Kanlıca · Göz Tepe 285 · 020 · Gaziosmanpaşa · E80 · Alibey · 128 · Alibeyköy · Levent · Rumelihisarı · Rumeli Hisarı · Bebek · Anadoluhisarı · Elmalı Barajı · Küçükköy · Kâğıthane · Mecidiyeköy · Kandilli · Küçüksu · Vaniköy · E80 · Atışalan · Şişli · Ortaköy · Yıldız Park · Çengelköy · İnkilap · Bayrampaşa · Esenler · Eyüp Mosque · Haskök · Taksim · Beşiktaş · Dolmabahçe Palace · Kuzguncuk · Çamlıca · 020 · Bağcılar · Güngören · Fener · Topkapı · Galata · Beyoğlu · Legender's Tower · Üsküdar · Umraniye · Bahçelievler · Fatih · Topkapı Palace · Eminönü · Grand Bazaar · Kısıklı · Esat Paşa · TO ISTANBUL ATATÜRK (IST) · E5 · 100 · Sanatya · Yenikapı · Haghia Sophia · Mosque · Selimiye · Kadıköy · İSTANBUL · Yedikule · Bakırköy · Zeytinburnu · Kızıltoprak · Fenerbahçe · Erenköy · İçerenköy · 100 · E5 · Bostancı

Marmara Denizi (Sea of Marmara)

İstanbul

East from Greenwich   29° 00'

1   **2**

JAKARTA, INDONESIA

JAVA SEA

106° 50'

Jakarta

Koja Utara · Cilincing · Waduk Pluit · Teluk Jakarta · TO JAKARTA SUKARNO-HATTA (JKT) · Sunda Kelapa Harbour · Teman Impian Jaya Ancol · Aquarium · Tanjung Priok · Koja · Penjaringan · Ancol · Kapuk · Kota · Jakarta Museum · Sunter · Cengkareng · Jelambar · Tambora · Taman Sari · Sawah Besar · International Trade Centre · Kelapa Gading · Grogol Petamburin · Gambir · Istiqlal Mosque · JAKARTA · Kemayoran · Kayu Putih · Kedoya · Tanjung Daren · Merdeka Palace · National Monument · National Museum · Cathedral · Gambir Station · Senen · Cempaka Putih · Race Course · Orchid Palace · Slipi · Kampung Bali Welcome Monument · Menteng · Taman Ismail Marzuki · Matraman · University · Pulo Gadung · Keban Jeruk · Joglo · Parliament House · Tanah Abang · Setia Budi · Kebayoran Lama · Kebayoran Baru · Olympic Stadium · Kuningan · Tebet · Jatinegara · Duren Sawit · Klender · JAKARTA BANTEN · Tanah Kusir · Kemang · Mampang Prapatan · Halim · Pondok Kelapa · Bintaro Jaya · Pondok Indah · Cipete · Kramat Jati Makasar · Pasar Minggu · Cilandak · Condet · JAKARTA HALIM PERDANA KUSUMA (HLP) · Jatiwaringin · Pondok Gede

East from Greenwich   106° 50'

1   **2**

COPYRIGHT PHILIP'S

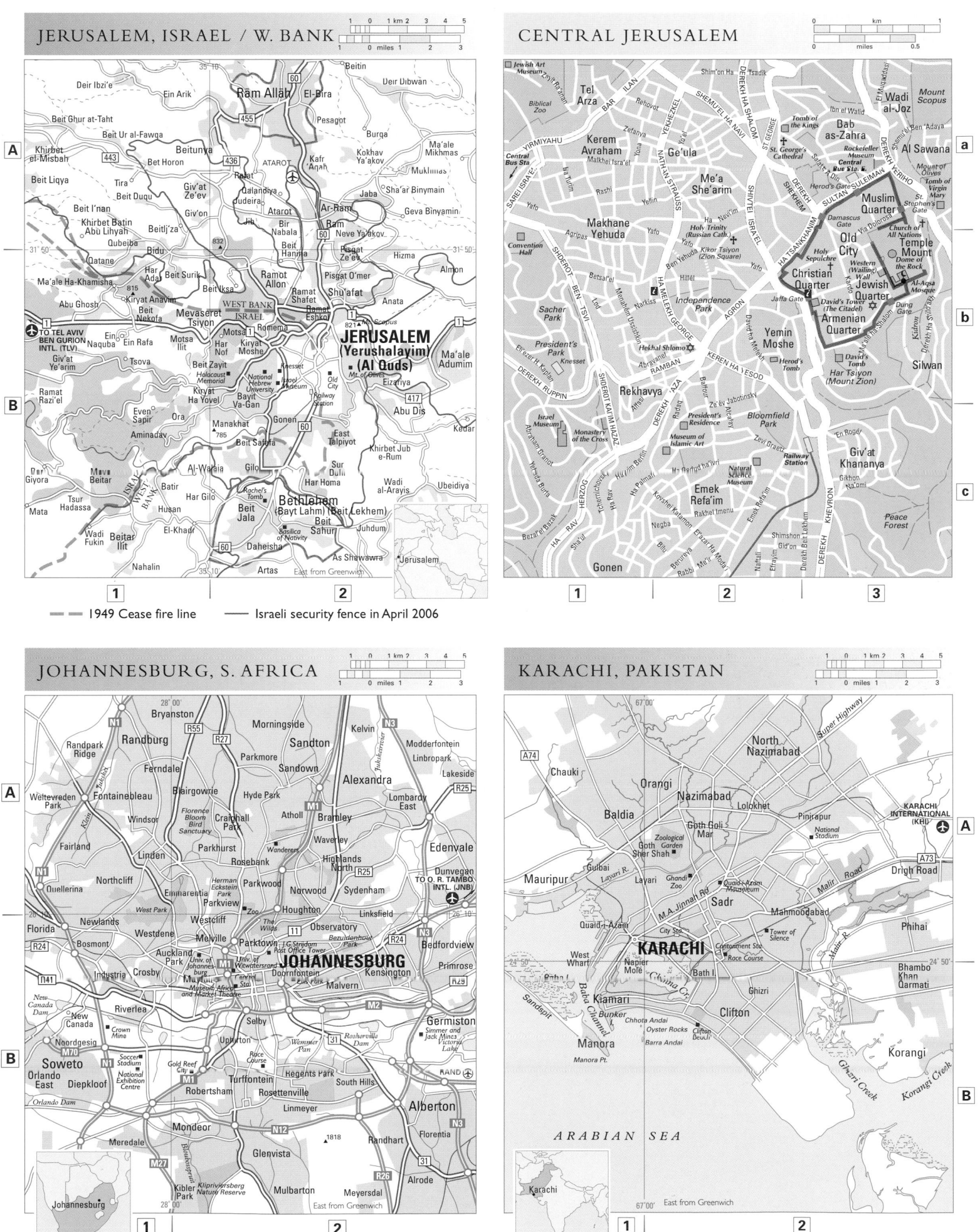

JERUSALEM, ISRAEL / W. BANK

Deir Ibzi'e · Ein Arik · Beitin · Deir Dibwan

Ram Allāh · El-Bira

Beit Ghur at-Taht · Beit Ur al-Fawqa · Pesagot

Beit Liqya · Beitunya · Burqa

Khirbet · 443 · Kokhav · Ma'ale
el-Misbah · 455 · Beit Horon · ATAROT · Ya'akov · Mikhmas

Beit I'nan · Tira · Giv'at · Kafr 'Anah · Muklimas
Ze'ev · 436 · Rafat

Beit Duqu · Qalandiya · Jaba · Geva Binyamin
Beitlj'za · Jib · Giv'on · Bir · Ar-Ram
Qubeiba · Bidu · Nabala · Ram · 60

Ma'ale Ha-Khamisha · Har · Beit Surik · Neve Ya'akov
Adar · Bet Iksa · Pisgat · Hizma · Almon
Kiryat Anavim · 815 · Ze'ev

Abu Ghosh · Beit · Har · Ramot · Pisgat O'mer
Nekofa · Nof · Allon · Shu'afat · Anata

Ein · Motsa · Romema · Ramat · 1
Giv'at · Naquba · Ilit · Har · Shafet
Ye'arim · Ein Rafa · Moshe · 821 · Mt Scopus

JERUSALEM
(Yerushalayim)
Tsova · Beit Zayit · Kiryat · Israel · **(Al Quds)** · Ma'ale
Holocaust · Hebrew · Museum · Eizariya · Adumim
Ramat · Memorial · National · University
Razi'el · Kiryat · Bayit · Old · Railway
Even · Ha Yovel · Va-Gan · City · Station
Sapir · Ora · Manakhat · Gonen · 417
785 · Mt of Olives

Dar · Ma'ale · Beit Safafa · Abu Dis
Giyora · Beitar · Al-Walaja · East · Kedar
Tsur · Husan · Har Homa · Talpiyot · Khirbet Jub
Hadassa · Batir · Har Gilo · Sur · e-Rum
Mata · Rachel's · Baher · Wadi
Tomb · Beit · **Bethlehem** · al-Arayis · Ubeidiya
Wadi · Beitar · Jala · **(Bayt Lahm) (Beit Lekhem)** · Gilo
Fukin · Ilit · El-Khadr · Beit · Beit
Nahalin · Basilica · Sahur · Daheisha · As Shawawra
Daheisha · of Nativity · Juhdum
Artas · East from Greenwich

Jerusalem

1 · **2**

- - - 1949 Cease fire line ——— Israeli security fence in April 2006

CENTRAL JERUSALEM

☐ Jewish Art Museum

Tel Arza · Biblical Zoo · Ge'ula · Shim'on Ha... · Tsadik · Mount Scopus · Wadi al-Joz

Kerem Avraham · Me'a She'arim · Tomb of the Kings · Bab as-Zahra · Al Sawana **a**

Central Bus Sta. · Makhane Yehuda · Rockefeller Museum · Mount of Olives · Tomb of Virgin Mary
Convention Hall · Holy Trinity (Russian Cath.) · Damascus Gate · Muslim Quarter · St Stephen's Gate

Holy Sepulchre · Old City · Church of All Nations · Temple Mount · Dome of the Rock

Sacher Park · Independence Park · Christian Quarter · Western Wailing Wall · Jewish Quarter **b**
President's Park · Hekhal Shlomo · Jaffa Gate · David's Tower (The Citadel) · Armenian Quarter · Dung Gate

Knesset · Yemin Moshe · Herod's Tomb · David's Tomb · Silwan
Rekhavya · Har Tsiyon (Mount Zion)

Israel Museum · Monastery of the Cross · Museum of Islamic Art · Bloomfield Park · En Rogel · Giv'at Khananya **c**

Emek Refa'im · Natural Science Museum · Railway Station · Peace Forest

Gonen

1 · **2** · **3**

JOHANNESBURG, S. AFRICA

Bryanston · Morningside · Kelvin
Randpark Ridge · Randburg · Sandton · Modderfontein
Ferndale · Parkmore · Sandown · Linbropark · Lakeside

Weltevreden Park · Fontainebleau · Blairgowrie · Hyde Park · Alexandra **A**
Fairland · Windsor · Florence Bloom Bird Sanctuary · Craighall Park · Atholl · Bramley · Lombardy East
Linden · Parkhurst · Rosebank · Wanderers · Waverley · Highlands North · Edenvale

Northcliff · Emmarentia · Parkwood · Norwood · Sydenham · Dunvegan
Quellerina · Westcliff · Herman Eckstein Park · Parkview · Houghton · Linksfield

Florida · Newlands · Westdene · The Wilds · Zoo · Observatory · Bedfordview
Bosmont · Melville · Parktown · J G Strijdom Post Office Tower · Bezuidenhout Park
Auckland Park · Univ. of **JOHANNESBURG** · Primrose
Industria · Crosby · Witwatersrand · Doornfontein · Kensington

Riverlea · Museum Africa and Market Theatre · Malvern · Germiston
New Canada Dam · New Canada · Crown Mine · Selby · Wemmer Pan · Rosherville Dam

Soweto · Noordgesig · Soccer Stadium · Gold Reef City · Uptown · Regents Park · South Hills · Alberton **B**
Orlando East · Diepkloof · National Exhibition Centre · Robertsham · Rosettenville · Linmeyer

Mondeor · Turffontein · Randhart · Florentia
Meredale · Glenvista · Mulbarton · Meyersdal
Kibler Park · Alrode · East from Greenwich

Johannesburg

1 · **2**

KARACHI, PAKISTAN

Super Highway
Chauki · North Nazimabad
Orangi · Nazimabad · Lolokhet · KARACHI INTERNATIONAL (KHI)
Baldia · Goth Goli Mar · Pinjrapur · National Stadium **A**
Zoological Garden · Goth Sher Shah · Ghandi Zoo
Mauripur · Gulbai · Layari R. · Quaid-i-Azam Mausoleum · Drigh Road
M.A. Jinnah Rd · Sadr · Mahmoodabad · A73

West Wharf · Quaid-i-Azam · City Sta. · Tower of Silence · Phihai
KARACHI · Cantonment Sta. · Race Course
Napier Mole · Bath I. · Ghizri · Bhambo Khan Qarmati
Kiamari · China Cr. · Clifton
Sandspit · Bunker · Chhota Andai · Oyster Rocks · Clifton Devil
Manora · Oyster Rocks · Barra Andai · Korangi · **B**
Manora Pt. · Ghari Cr. · Ghizri Creek · Korangi Creek

_A R A B I A N   S E A_

Karachi · East from Greenwich

1 · **2**

COPYRIGHT PHILIP'S

KOLKATA, INDIA

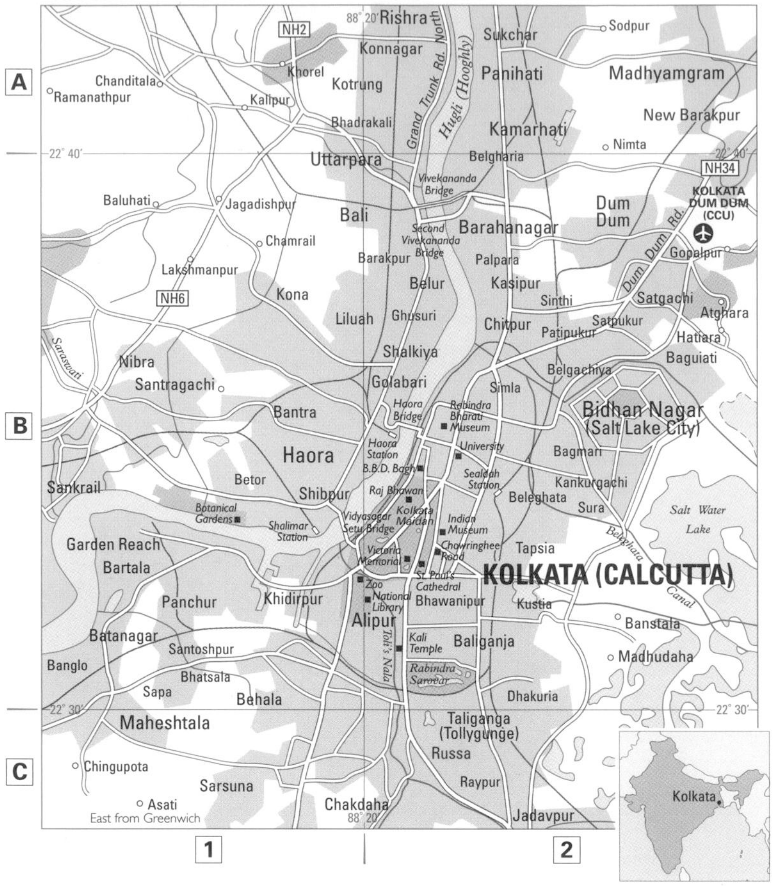

1 0 1 km 2 3 4 5
1 0 miles 1 2 3

NH2
Rishra
Chanditala
Ramanathpur
Khorel
Konnagar
Sodpur
Sukchar
Panihati
Madhyamgram
Kotrung
Kalipur
Bhadrakali
Kamarhati
New Barakpur
Uttarpara
Baluhati
Belgharia
Nimta
Vivekananda Bridge
Jagadishpur
Bali
Barahanagar
Dum Dum
KOLKATA DUM DUM (CCU)
Lakshmanpur
Second Vivekananda Bridge
Palpara
Gopalpur
NH6
Kona
Barakpur
Belur
Kasipur
Sinthi
Satgachi
Atghara
Chamrail
Ghusuri
Chitpur
Patipukur
Satpukur
Hatiara
Baguiati
Liluah
Shalkiya
Simla
Belgachhia
Nibra
Golabari
Bidhan Nagar (Salt Lake City)
Santragachi
Haora Bridge
Rabindra Bharati Museum
Bantra
University
Bagman
Haora
Haora Station
B.B.D. Bagh
Sealdah Station
Kankurgachi
Betor
Raj Bhawan
India Museum
Sura
Shibpur
Beleghata
Vidyasagar Setu Bridge
Kolkata Maidan
Chowringhee Road
Tapsia
Garden Reach
Botanical Gardens
Shalimar Station
Chowringhee Road
Salt Water Lake
Bartala
Victoria Memorial
St. Paul's Cathedral
Panchur
Zoo National Library
Bhawanipur
Kustia
Batanagar
Khidirpur
Alipur
Kali Temple
Baliganja
Banstala
Banglo
Bhatsala
Santoshpur
Rabindra Sarovar
Madhudaha
Sapa
Behala
Dhakuria
Maheshtala
Taliganga (Tollygunge)
Chingupota
Russa
Asati
Sarsuna
Raypur
East from Greenwich
Chakdaha
Jadavpur

KOLKATA (CALCUTTA)

A B C — 22° 40' — 22° 30'
1 2
Kolkata

LAGOS, NIGERIA

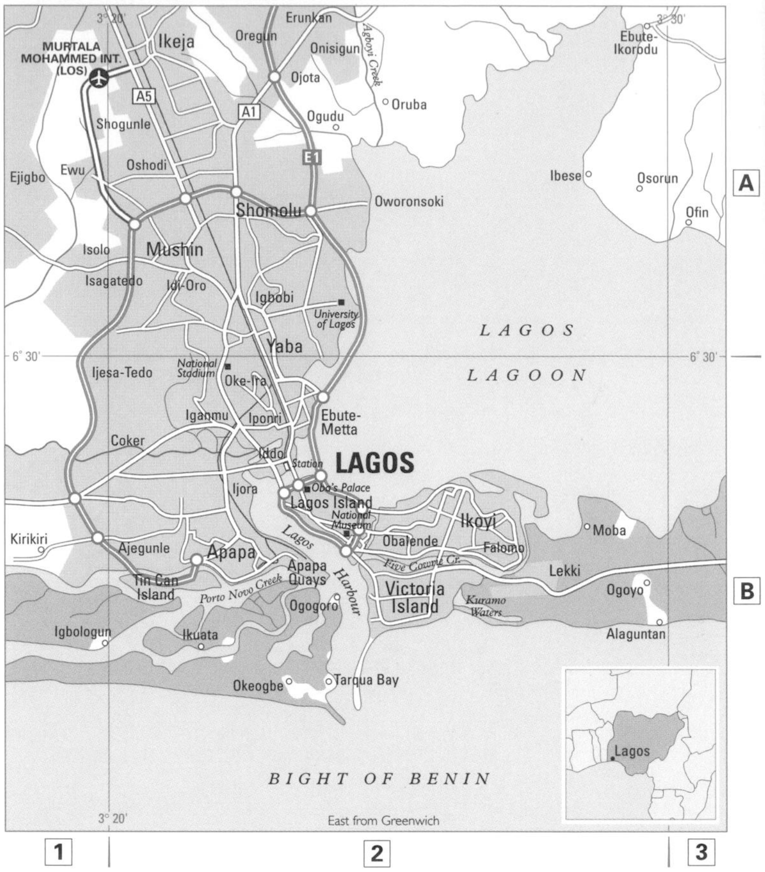

1 0 1 km 2 3 4 5
1 0 miles 1 2 3

MURTALA MOHAMMED INT. (LOS)
Ikeja
Oregun
Erunkan
Ebute-Ikorodu
Shogunle
A5
Ojota
A1
Ogudu
Oruba
Ejigbo
Ewu
Oshodi
E1
Oworonsoki
Ibese
Osorun
Shomolu
Ofin
Isolo
Mushin
Isagatedo
Idi-Oro
Igbobi
University of Lagos
LAGOS LAGOON
Coker
Ijesa-Tedo
National Stadium
Oke-Ira
Iganmu
Iponri
Yaba
Ebute-Metta
Kirikiri
Iddo
Station
Obo's Palace
LAGOS
Ijora
Lagos Island
National Museum
Ikoyi
Moba
Ajegunle
Apapa
Falomo
Tin Can Island
Obalende
Five Cowrie Cr.
Lekki
Apapa Quays
Victoria Island
Kuramo Waters
Ogoyo
Igbologun
Porto Novo Creek
Ogogoro
Alaguntan
Ikuata
Okeogbe
Tarqua Bay

LAGOS

BIGHT OF BENIN
East from Greenwich
Lagos

A B C — 6° 30' — 3° 20'
1 2 3

LAS VEGAS, NEVADA

1 0 1 km 2 3 4 5
1 0 miles 1 2 3

North Las Vegas
15
93
NELLIS AFB
BUS 95
City View Park
574
95
NORTH LAS VEGAS (VGT)
147
Zoological Botanical Park
Las Vegas Natural History Museum
Cashman Field
Nevada State Museum & Historical Society
Sunrise Mountain Natural Area
Las Vegas Art Museum
The Meadows Mall
159
LAS VEGAS
Front Ho.
Sunrise Manor
589
Stratosphere Tower
Sahara
515
Desert Wetlands Park
Fashion Show Mall
Las Vegas Country Club Convention Center
595
596
Treasure Island
The Mirage
Caesars Palace
Venetian
Boulevard Mall
592
Winchester
Whitney (East Las Vegas)
Spring Valley
Bellagio
Monte Carlo
New York New York
Paris
MGM Grand
University of Nevada L.V.
Thomas & Mack
593
Liberace Museum
Sam Boyd Stadium
Luxor
Tropicana
Mandalay Bay
LAS VEGAS
McCARRAN INTL. (LAS)
Paradise
Las Vegas
Galleria at Sunset
Sunset Park
Civic Center
Las Vegas Outlet Center
595
93 95
Enterprise
15
215
Henderson
West from Greenwich

A B — 115° 10' — 36° 10'
1 2

LIMA, PERU

1 0 1 km 2 3 4 5
1 0 miles 1 2 3

Los Olivos
Independencia
Huascar
LIMA CALLAO
Chavatria
San Juan de Lurigancho
755
Cerro San Jeronimo
Bocanegra
Lima
Cerro La Milla
Cerro Observatorio
242
465
LIMA JORGE CHAVEZ (LIM)
San Martin de Porras
Rimac
Rimac
Carmen de La Legua
Palacio de Gobierno
Catedral
El Agustino
Terminal Maritimo
Congreso
Est. Desamparados
482 Cerro El Agustino
Callao
Bellavista
Breña
LIMA
Museo de Arte
La Victoria
Fuerte Real Felipe
La Perla
Campo de Marte
Parque de Reserva
Estadio Nacional
La Punta
Ave. Oscar R. Benavides
Jesús Maria
Universidad Católica
Museo Arqueologia
Parque de las Leyendas
Museo de la Nación
San Luis
San Miguel
Pueblo Libre
Lince
San Borja
Isla San Lorenzo
Magdalena
Avenida Panamericana Sur
Huaca Juliana
San Isidro
Surquillo
Isla Frontón
Miraflores
Santiago de Surco
PACIFIC OCEAN
Estación Atacongo
Vista Alegre
Barranco
La Campiña
Cerro Morro Solar
273
Chorrillos
Punta La Chira
La Encantada

A B C — 12° — 12° 10' — 77° 10'
1 2 3

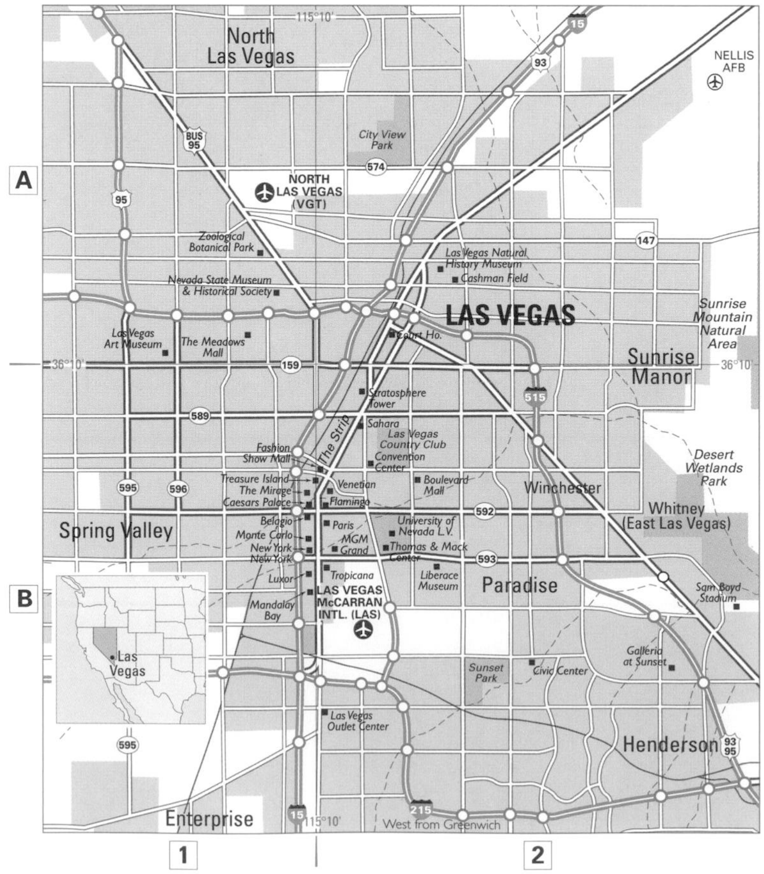

🛡 Interstate route numbers   95 U.S. route numbers   147 State route numbers

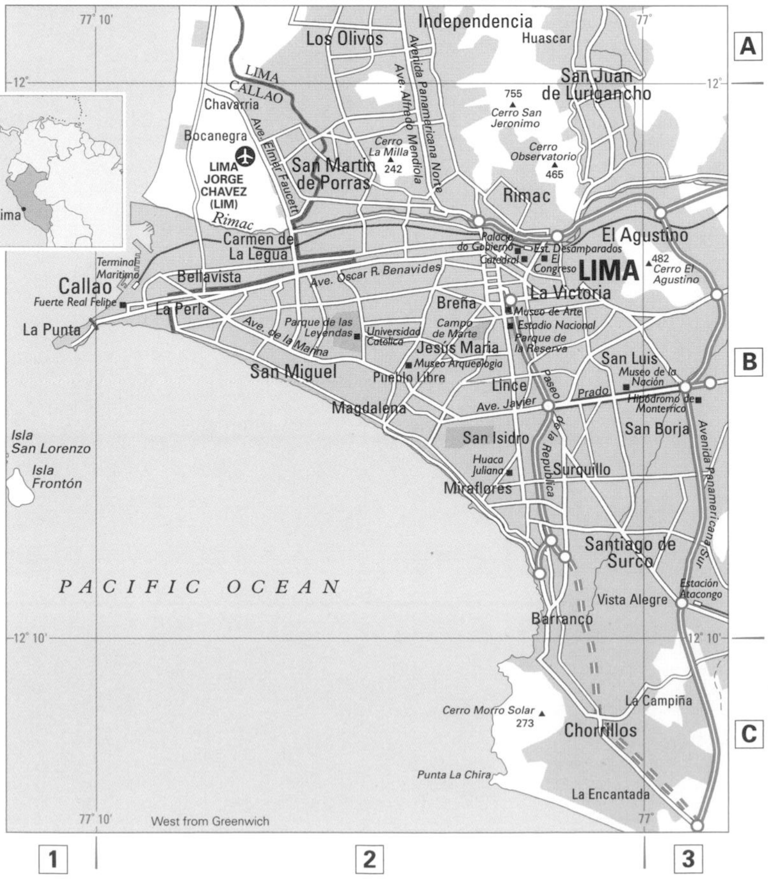

COPYRIGHT PHILIP'S

LONDON, U.K.

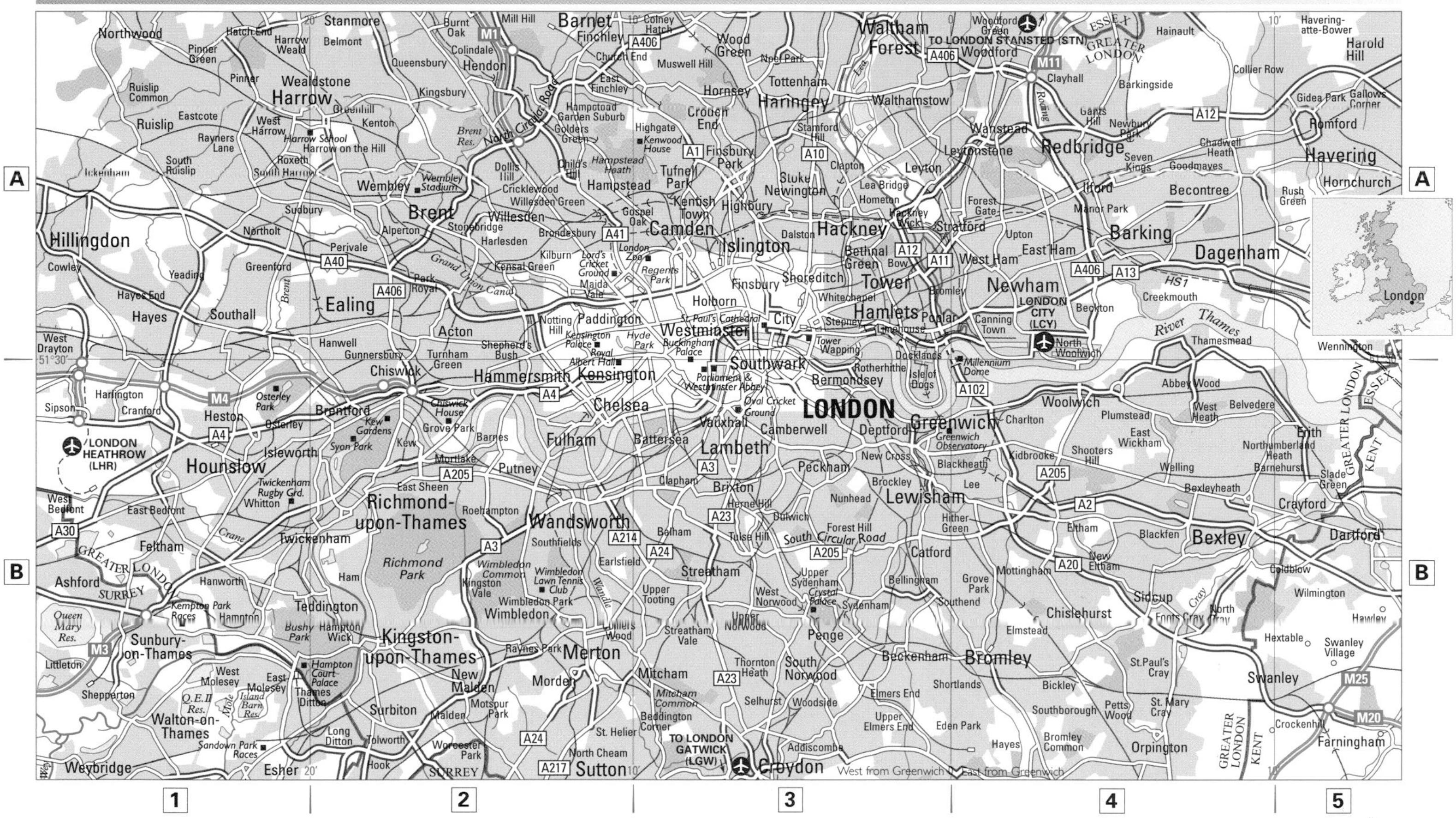

1 0 1 km 2 3 4 5
1 0 miles 1 2 3

Northwood · Stanmore · Barnet · Finchley · Colney Hatch · Wood Green · Waltham Forest · Woodford · Hainault · Havering-atte-Bower · Harold Hill

Pinner Green · Hatch End · Harrow Weald · Belmont · Mill Hill · Burnt Oak · Colindale · Hendon · Muswell Hill · Hornsey · Haringey · Tottenham · Walthamstow · Buckhurst Hill · Barkingside · Collier Row · Romford

Harrow · Wealdstone · Kenton · Kingsbury · East Finchley · Highgate · Crouch End · Finsbury Park · Stamford Hill · Clapton · Leyton · Wanstead · Ilford · Goodmayes · Seven Kings · Gidea Park · Gallows Corner

Hillingdon · Ruislip · Eastcote · Rayners Lane · South Harrow · Wembley · Alperton · Willesden Green · Cricklewood · Hampstead · Kentish Town · Highbury · Stoke Newington · Hackney · Stratford · Newham · East Ham · Barking · Dagenham · Becontree · Rush Green · Hornchurch

Cowley · Northolt · Greenford · Perivale · Brent · Harlesden · Kilburn · Kensal Green · Camden · Islington · Shoreditch · Bethnal Green · Bow · West Ham · Upton · Manor Park · Beckton

Hayes End · Hayes · Southall · Ealing · Acton · Shepherd's Bush · Notting Hill · Paddington · Holborn · City · Whitechapel · Stepney · Limehouse · Poplar · London City (LCY) · North Woolwich · Thamesmead · Wennington

West Drayton · Hanwell · Gunnersbury · Turnham Green · Chiswick · Hammersmith · Kensington · Westminster · Southwark · Bermondsey · Rotherhithe · Isle of Dogs · Millennium Dome · Woolwich · Plumstead · Abbey Wood · Belvedere · Erith

London Heathrow (LHR) · Osterley Park · Brentford · Kew Gardens · Grove Park · Barnes · Fulham · Chelsea · Battersea · Vauxhall · LONDON · Camberwell · Deptford · Greenwich · Charlton · East Wickham · Northumberland Heath · Barnehurst · Slade Green

Hounslow · Isleworth · Twickenham · Syon Park · Mortlake · Putney · Lambeth · Peckham · New Cross · Brockley · Blackheath · Kidbrooke · Shooters Hill · Welling · Bexleyheath · Crayford

Heston · Cranford · Richmond-upon-Thames · Roehampton · Wandsworth · Clapham · Brixton · Herne Hill · Dulwich · Forest Hill · Lewisham · Hither Green · Eltham · Blackfen · Bexley · Dartford

Feltham · East Bedfont · Twickenham · Richmond Park · East Sheen · Wimbledon Park · Wandsworth Common · Balham · Tooting · Streatham · West Norwood · Sydenham · Catford · Grove Park · Mottingham · Sidcup · Wilmington

Ashford · Sunbury-on-Thames · Teddington · Hampton Wick · Kingston-upon-Thames · New Malden · Wimbledon · Mitcham · Thornton Heath · South Norwood · Penge · Beckenham · Bromley · Bickley · Chislehurst · Hextable · Swanley

Shepperton · Walton-on-Thames · Hampton Court Palace · Thames Ditton · Surbiton · Tolworth · Worcester Park · Merton · Morden · Streatham Vale · Norbury · Crystal Palace · Elmstead · St Paul's Cray · St Mary Cray · Swanley Village

Weybridge · Esher · Hook · Chessington · North Cheam · Sutton · Carshalton · Croydon · Addiscombe · Shirley · Eden Park · Hayes · Bromley Common · Orpington · Petts Wood · Crockenhill · Farningham

GREATER LONDON · SURREY · KENT · ESSEX

TO LONDON STANSTED (STN) · TO LONDON GATWICK (LGW) · River Thames · West from Greenwich · East from Greenwich

A1 · A5 · A10 · A12 · A13 · A40 · A406 · A205 · A2 · A20 · A3 · A24 · A23 · A214 · A217 · A30 · A4 · A102 · M1 · M4 · M11 · M25 · M20

1 2 3 4 5
A B

CENTRAL LONDON

0 km 2
0 miles 1

Queen's Park · West Kilburn · Maida Vale · Westbourne Green · Paddington · Bayswater · Notting Hill · Kensington · Holland Park · West Kensington · Hammersmith · Olympia

St John's Wood · Regent's Park · London Zoo · Marylebone · Bloomsbury · King's Cross · St Pancras International · Euston · British Library · Clerkenwell · Hoxton · Shoreditch

Madame Tussaud's · Regent's Park · Baker Street · Marble Arch · Oxford Street · Soho · Holborn · City · Barbican · Moorgate · Liverpool St · Whitechapel

Hyde Park · Kensington Gardens · Mayfair · Piccadilly Circus · Leicester Sq · Covent Garden · Strand · St Paul's · Bank · Tower of London · Tower Bridge · East Smithfield

Knightsbridge · Belgravia · Buckingham Palace · St James · Westminster · Charing Cross · Embankment · Waterloo · Southwark · London Bridge · Bermondsey

Kensington · Brompton · South Kensington · Chelsea · Pimlico · Victoria · Houses of Parliament · Westminster Abbey · Lambeth · Imperial War Mus. · Elephant & Castle · Newington

West Brompton · Chelsea · Pimlico · Vauxhall · The Oval · Kennington · Walworth · Old Kent Road

River Thames · Grand Union Canal · Regent's Canal · Serpentine · Hyde Park

1 2 3 4 5
a b c

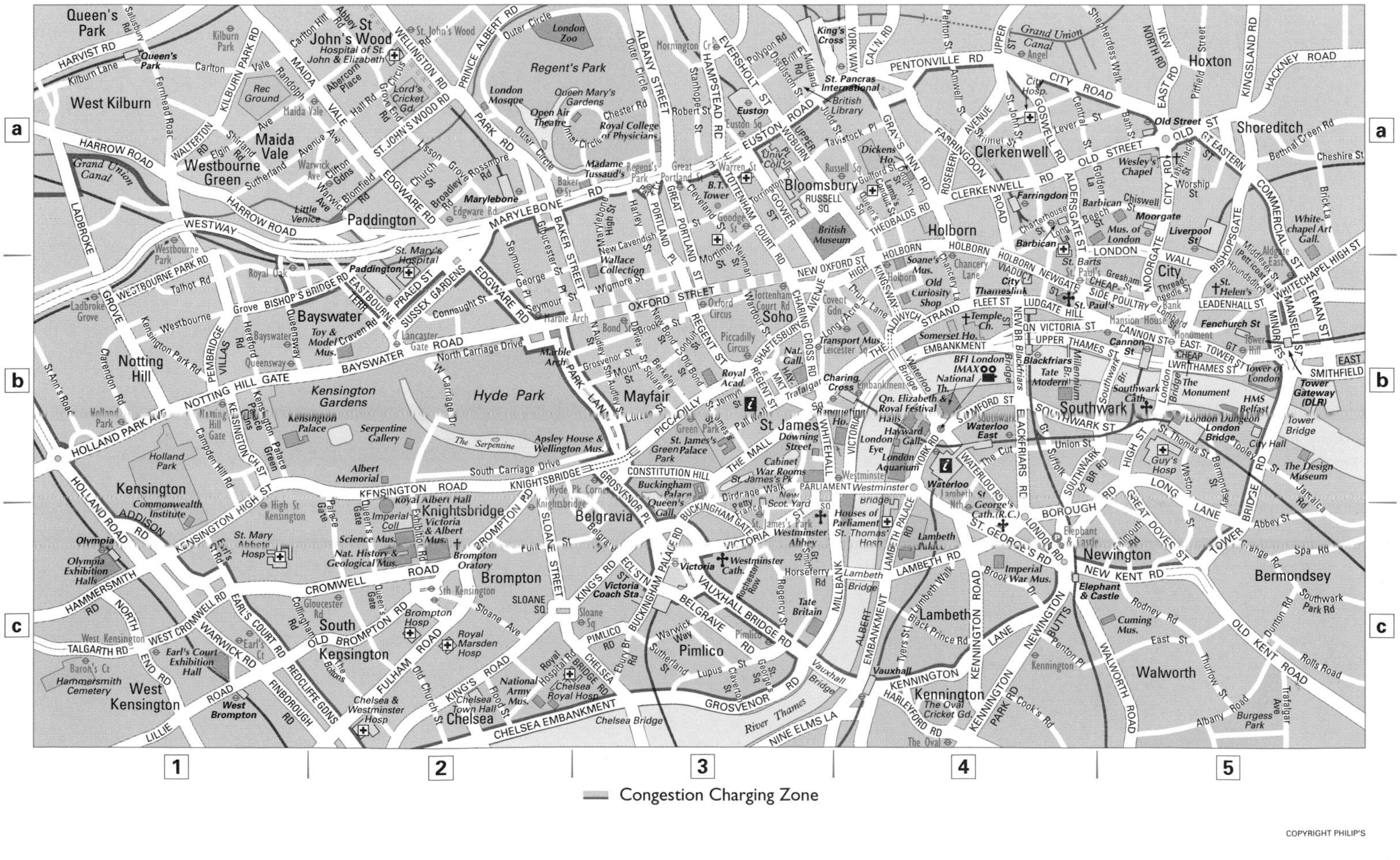

Congestion Charging Zone

COPYRIGHT PHILIP'S

LISBON, PORTUGAL

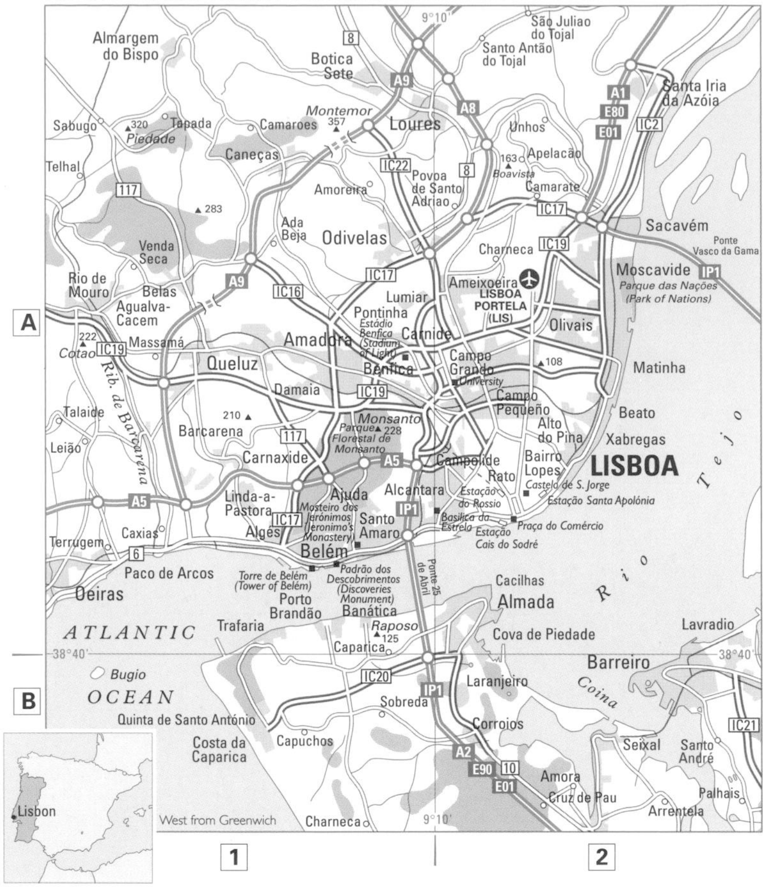

1 km 2 3 4 5
0 miles 1 2 3

Almargem do Bispo
Botica Sete
Santo Antão do Tojal
São Julião do Tojal
Santa Iria da Azóia
Montemor 357
Sabugo
Topada 320 Piedade
Camaroes
Loures
Unhos
Venda Seca
Belas
Agualva-Cacem
Rio de Mouro
Cotão
Massamá
Queluz
Damaia
Barcarena
Leião
Talaide
Terrugem
Caxias
Linda-a-Pastora
Algés
Paço de Arcos
Oeiras
Ada Beja
Odivelas
Caneças
Amoreira
Povoa de Santo Adrião
Apelação
Camarate
Boavista
Charneca
Sacavém
Ponte Vasco da Gama
Moscavide
Parque das Nações (Park of Nations)
Olivais
Matinha
Lumiar
Catnide
Campo Grande
University
Campo Pequeño
Alto do Pina
Beato
Xabregas
Amadora
Benfica
Estádio (Light) Benfica Stadium
Monsanto
Parque Florestal de Monsanto
Campolide
Rato
Bairro Lopes
Castelo de S. Jorge
LISBOA
Ajuda
Mosteiro dos Jerónimos (Jerónimo's Monastery)
Santo Amaro
Belém
Torre de Belém (Tower of Belém)
Padrão dos Descobrimentos (Discoveries Monument)
Banática
Raposo
Alcântara
Estação do Rossio
Basílica do Estrela
Estação Santa Apolónia
Praça do Comércio
Estação Cais do Sodré
Ponte 25 de Abril
Cacilhas
Almada
Cova de Piedade
Lavradio
ATLANTIC OCEAN
Bugio
Quinta de Santo António
Costa da Caparica
Capuchos
Trafaria
Caparica
Sobreda
Corroios
Laranjeiro
Seixal
Santo André
Barreiro
Coina
Amora
Cruz de Pau
Palhais
Arrentela
Charneca
38°40'
West from Greenwich
Lisbon

A5 A8 A9 A1 A2 A7 IC2 IC16 IC17 IC19 IC20 IC21 IC22 IP1 IP7 E01 E80 E90 117 6 8 10

CENTRAL LISBON

km
0 miles 0.5

Palacio de Justiça
Penitenciária
M. S. Sebastião
R. Pinheiro Chagas
Instituto Superior Técnico
Praça Duque Saldanha
Hosp. Infantil
Maternidade
Estefânia
Penha França
Parque Eduardo VII
Praça Marquês de Pombal
Amoreiros
Rato
Anjos
Hospital de Santa Marta
Hospital dos Capuchos
Academia das Ciências
Jardim Botânico
Bairro Lopes
Graça
Palácio de Assembleia Nacional
Instituto de Medicina Legal
Bairro Alto
Elevador da Glória
Restauradores
Theatro Nac. de Dona Maria II
Estação do Rossio
Praça Rossio
Museu do Arqueologia
Castelo de São Jorge (St. George's Castle)
Igreja Sta. Engrácia
Estação Santa Apolónia
Theatro Nac. de São Carlos
Museu de Chiado
Elevador de Santa Justa
Museu de Arte Decorativas
Alfama
Museu Antoniano (St. Anthony Mus.)
Military Museum
Biblioteca Nacional
Sé Cathedral
Baixa
Dom José I
Estação Cais do Sodré
AV. VINTE E QUATRO DE JULHO
RUA DO ARSENAL
R. DA ALFÂNDEGA
AVENIDA INFANTE DOM HENRIQUE
Estação Fluvial
Rio Tejo (Tagus)

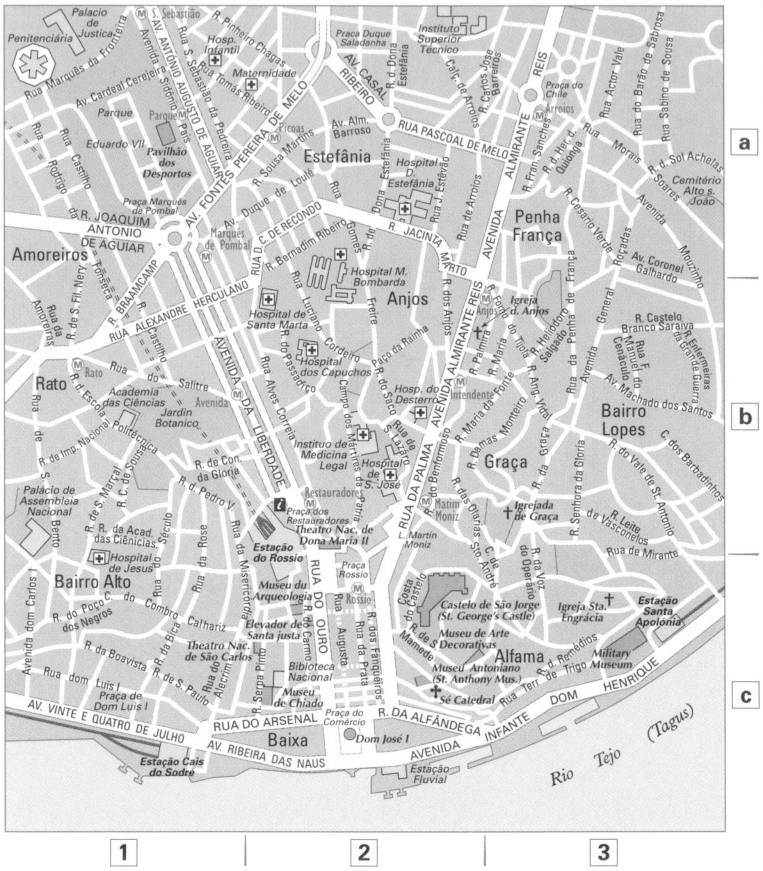

LOS ANGELES, CALIFORNIA

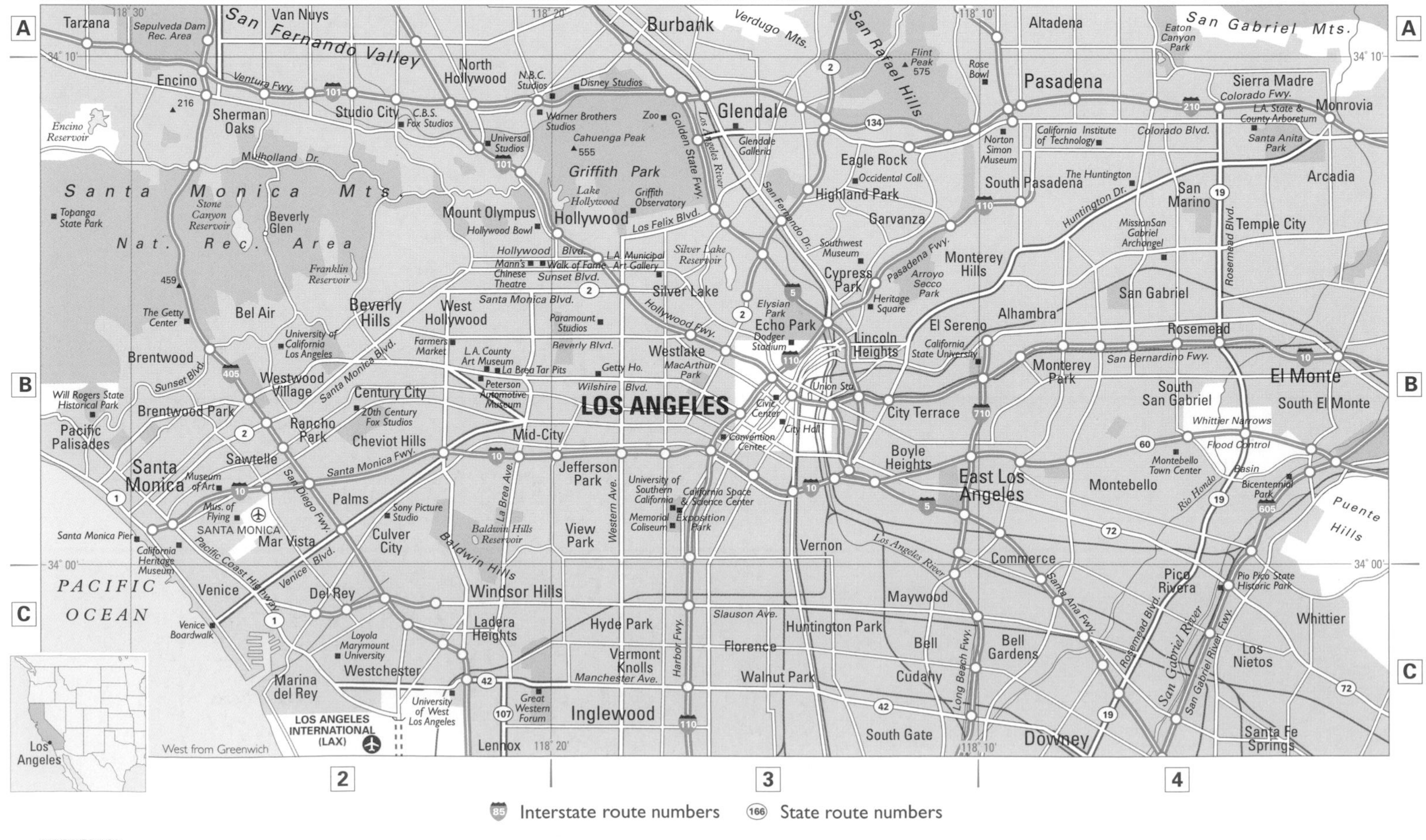

1 km 2 3 4 5
miles 1 2 3

Tarzana
Van Nuys
Burbank
Verdugo Mts.
San Rafael Hills
Altadena
San Gabriel Mts.
Eaton Canyon Park
Sepulveda Dam Rec. Area
San Fernando Valley
Flint Peak 575
Rose Bowl
Encino
Ventura Fwy.
North Hollywood
N.B.C. Studios
Disney Studios
Glendale
Pasadena
Sierra Madre
Monrovia
Encino Reservoir
Sherman Oaks
Studio City
C.B.S.
Fox Studios
Warner Brothers Studios
Zoo
Cahuenga Peak
Glendale Galleria
California Institute of Technology
L.A. State & County Arboretum
Santa Anita Park
Arcadia
Universal Studios
Mulholland Dr.
Griffith Park
Lake Hollywood
Griffith Observatory
Eagle Rock
Occidental Coll.
Norton Simon Museum
The Huntington
Santa Monica Mts.
Topanga State Park
Stone Canyon Reservoir
Beverly Glen
Mount Olympus
Hollywood Bowl
Hollywood
Los Feliz Blvd.
Highland Park
Garvanza
South Pasadena
Huntington Dr.
Mission San Gabriel Archangel
San Marino
Temple City
Nat. Rec. Area
Franklin Reservoir
Hollywood Blvd.
Mann's Chinese Theatre
Walk of Fame
Sunset Blvd.
L.A. Municipal Art Gallery
Silver Lake Reservoir
Southwest Museum
Cypress Park
Monterey Hills
San Gabriel
The Getty Center
Bel Air
Beverly Hills
West Hollywood
Santa Monica Blvd.
Silver Lake
Arroyo Seco Park
Heritage Square
El Sereno
Alhambra
Rosemead
Brentwood
University of California Los Angeles
Paramount Studios
Beverly Blvd.
Getty Ho.
Echo Park
Elysian Park
Dodger Stadium
Lincoln Heights
California State University
Monterey Park
San Bernardino Fwy.
El Monte
Will Rogers State Historical Park
Westwood Village
Century City
20th Century Fox Studios
Farmers Market
L.A. County Art Museum
La Brea Tar Pits
Wilshire Blvd.
Westlake
MacArthur Park
LOS ANGELES
Civic Center
City Hall
Union Sta.
City Terrace
South San Gabriel
El Monte
South El Monte
Pacific Palisades
Brentwood Park
Rancho Park
Cheviot Hills
Mid-City
Museum Automotive
Convention Center
Boyle Heights
East Los Angeles
Montebello Town Center
Whittier Narrows
Flood Control
Santa Monica
Museum of Art
Mus. of Flying
SANTA MONICA
Palms
Sony Picture Studio
Jefferson Park
University of Southern California
California Space & Science Center
Memorial Coliseum
Exposition Park
Vernon
Montebello
Bicentennial Park
Puente Hills
Santa Monica Pier
California Heritage Museum
Mar Vista
Culver City
Baldwin Hills
View Park
Commerce
Pico Rivera
Pio Pico State Historic Park
Venice
Venice Boardwalk
Del Rey
Windsor Hills
Ladera Heights
Hyde Park
Maywood
Huntington Park
Bell
Bell Gardens
Cudahy
Whittier
Los Nietos
Marina del Rey
Loyola Marymount University
Westchester
Vermont Knolls
Manchester Ave.
Florence
Walnut Park
South Gate
Downey
Santa Fe Springs
LOS ANGELES INTERNATIONAL (LAX)
University of West Los Angeles
Great Western Forum
Inglewood
Lennox
PACIFIC OCEAN
West from Greenwich
Los Angeles

Interstate route numbers
State route numbers

COPYRIGHT PHILIP'S

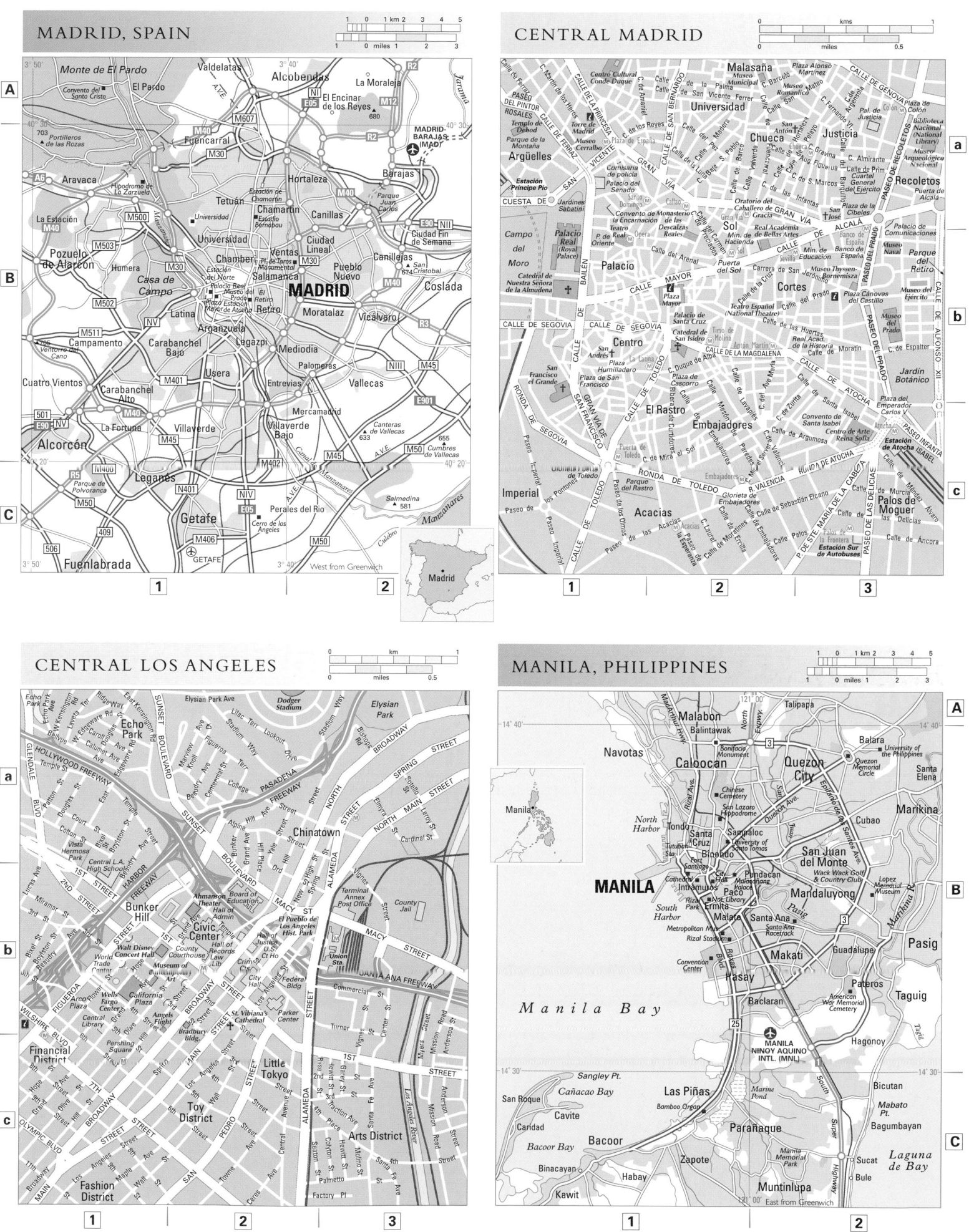

MADRID, SPAIN

Monte de El Pardo · Valdelatas · Alcobendas · La Moraleja
Convento del Santo Cristo · El Pardo · El Encinar de los Reyes · 680
Portilleros de las Rozas · 703 · Fuencarral · Aravaca · Hortaleza · Barajas · MADRID BARAJAS (MAD)
Tetuán · Estación de Chamartín · Canillas · Parque Juan Carlos
La Estación · Universidad · Estadio Bernabéu · Ciudad Lineal · Ciudad Fin de Semana
Pozuelo de Alarcón · Humera · Chamberí · Ventas · Canillejas
Casa de Campo · Salamanca · Pl. de Toros Monumental · Coslada
Latina · Palacio Real · Retiro · Moratalaz · Vicálvaro
Campamento · Carabanchel Bajo · Lagazpi · Mediodía · Palomeras
Cuatro Vientos · Carabanchel Alto · Usera · Entrevías · Vallecas
Alcorcón · La Fortuna · Villaverde · Villaverde Bajo · Mercamadrid · Canteras de Vallecas · Cumbres de Vallecas
Leganés · Salmedina 581
Getafe · Perales del Río · Cerro de los Ángeles
Fuenlabrada · GETAFE · West from Greenwich

Madrid

CENTRAL MADRID

Malasaña · Universidad · Chueca · Justicia · Recoletos
Argüelles · Torre de Madrid · Plaza de España · Sol · Palacio · Cortes
Campo del Moro · Palacio Real (Royal Palace) · Catedral de Nuestra Señora de la Almudena
Centro · El Rastro · Embajadores · Acacias · Imperial

CENTRAL LOS ANGELES

Echo Park · Elysian Park · Dodger Stadium
Chinatown · Bunker Hill · Civic Center · Little Tokyo
Financial District · Toy District · Arts District · Fashion District

MANILA, PHILIPPINES

Malabon · Talipapa · Balintawak · Balara · University of the Philippines
Navotas · Caloocan · Quezon City · Santa Elena
Tondo · Sampaloc · Marikina · Cubao
North Harbor · San Juan del Monte · Wack Wack Golf & Country Club
MANILA · Intramuros · Paco · Mandaluyong · Pasig
South Harbor · Ermita · Malate · Santa Ana · Makati · Guadalupe · Pateros · Taguig
Manila Bay · Pasay · Baclaran · American War Memorial Cemetery
MANILA NINOY AQUINO INTL. (MNL)
Sangley Pt. · Cañacao Bay · Las Piñas · Bicutan · Mabato Pt.
San Roque · Cavite · Bamboo Organ · Parañaque · Bagumbayan
Caridad · Bacoor · Zapote · Manila Memorial Park · Laguna de Bay
Binacayan · Kawit · Habay · Bule · Muntinlupa · Sucat · East from Greenwich

COPYRIGHT PHILIP'S

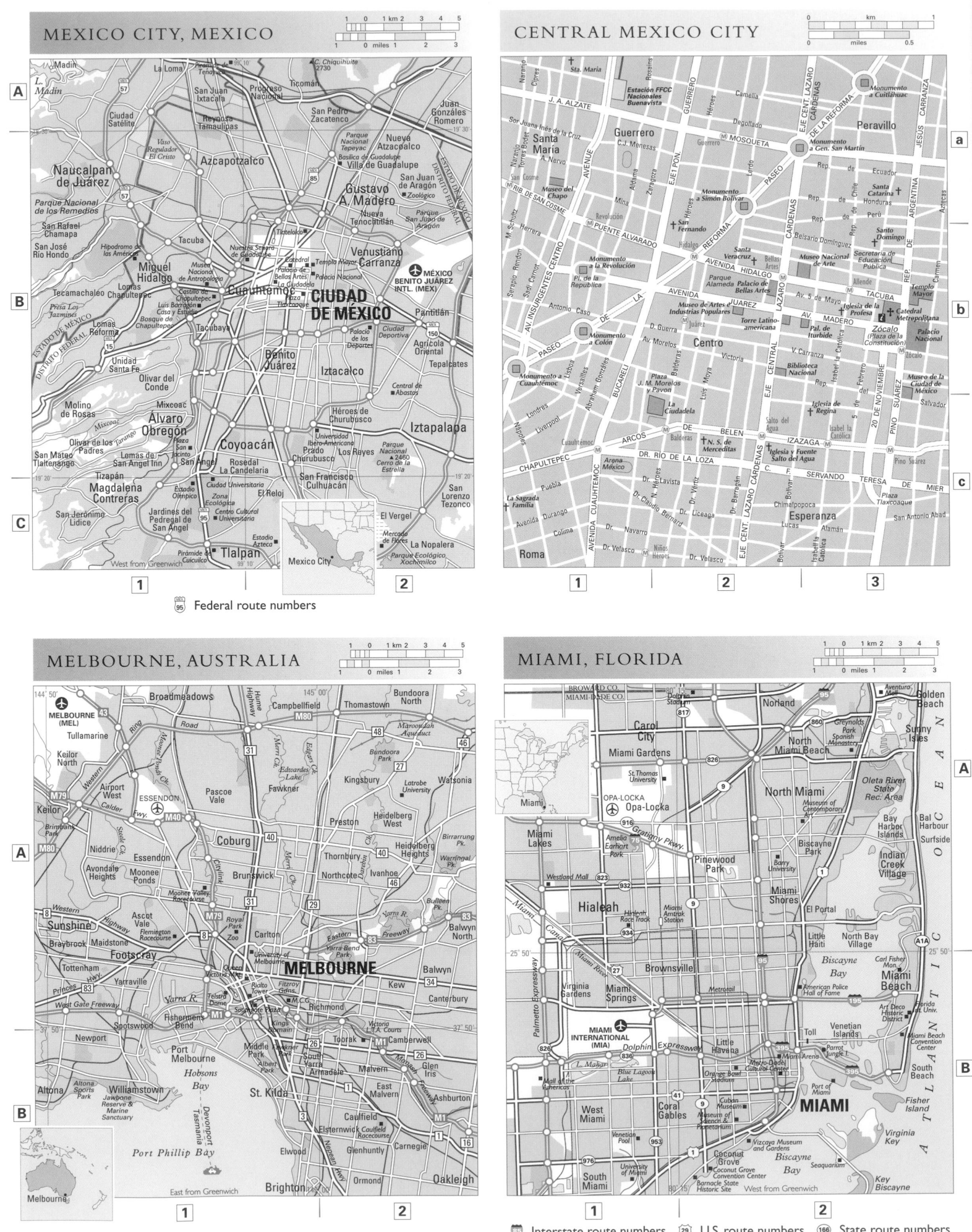

MEXICO CITY, MEXICO

95 Federal route numbers

CENTRAL MEXICO CITY

MELBOURNE, AUSTRALIA

MIAMI, FLORIDA

85 Interstate route numbers   29 U.S. route numbers   166 State route numbers

COPYRIGHT PHILIP'S

MILAN, ITALY

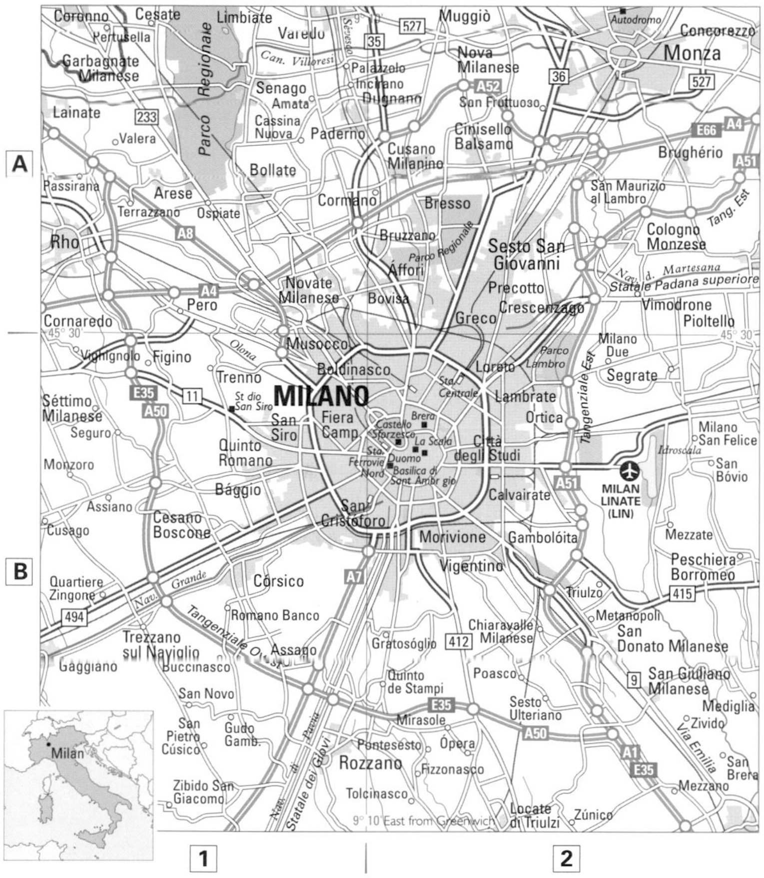

1 0 1 km 2 3 4 5
1 0 miles 1 2 3

Coronno · Cesate · Limbiate · Varedo · Muggiò · Concorezzo · Autodromo
Pertusella · Garbagnate Milanese · Palazzolo Milanese · Nova Milanese · Monza
Senago · Amata · Incirano · Desio · San Fruttuoso
Lainate · Cassina Nuova · Paderno · Cusano Milanino · Brughério
Arese · Bollate · Cormano · Bresso · San Maurizio al Lambro · Cologno Monzese
Rho · Terrazzano · Ospiate · Novate Milanese · Affori · Precotto · Crescenzago · Vimodrone · Pioltello
Passirana · Pero · Bóvisa · Greco
Cornaredo · Figino · Trenno · Baldinasco · Musocco · Loreto · Milano Due · Segrate
Séttimo Milanese · San Siro · **MILANO** · Lambrate · Ortica · Milano San Felice
Vighignolo · Quinto Romano · Fiera Camp · Città degli Studi · San Bóvio
Monzoro · Bággio · Calvairate · Milano Linate (LIN)
Cusago · Assiano · Cesano Boscone · San Cristoforo · Morivione · Gambolóita · Mezzate
Seguro · Quartiere Zingone · Córsico · Vigentino · Triulzo · Peschiera Borromeo
Trezzano sul Naviglio · Romano Banco · Chiaravalle Milanese · Metanopoli · San Donato Milanese
Gággiano · Buccinasco · Assago · Gratosóglio · Poasco · Sesto Ulteriano · Mediglia
San Novo · San Pietro Cúsico · Quinto de Stampi · San Giuliano Milanese · Zivido · San Brera
Mirasole · Rozzano · Fizzonasco · Mezzano
Zibido San Giacomo · Tolcinasco · Opera · Locate di Triulzi · Zúnico

9° 10' East from Greenwich

A1 A2 B1 B2

CENTRAL MOSCOW

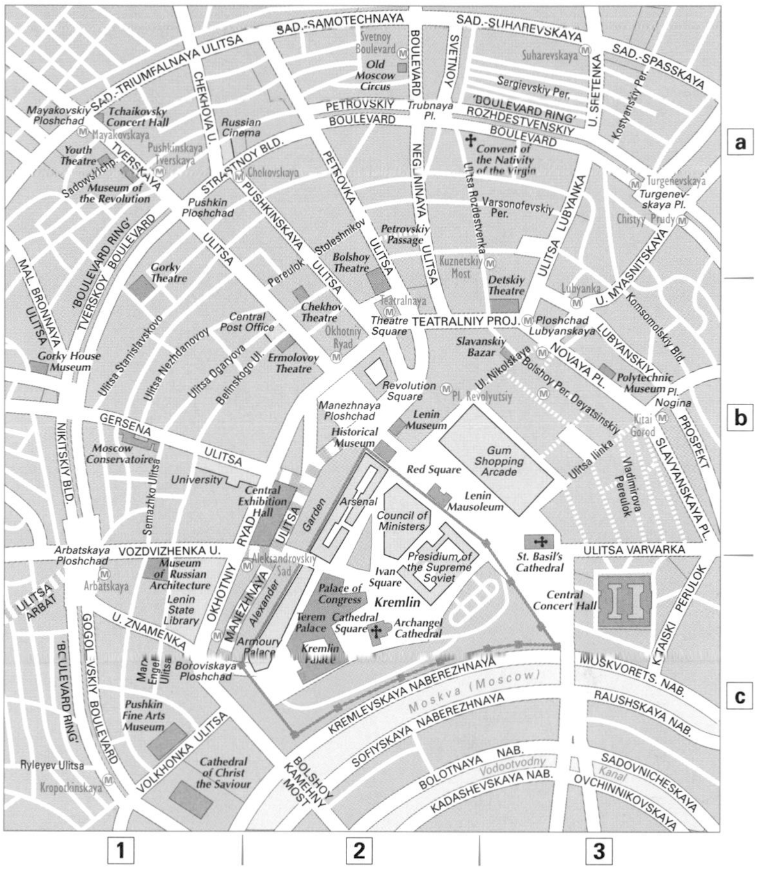

0 km 1
0 miles 0.5

SAD.-SAMOTECHNAYA · SAD.-SUHAREVSKAYA · SAD.-SPASSKAYA
Svetnoy Boulevard · Old Moscow Circus · SVETNOY BOULEVARD
SAD.-TRIUMFALNAYA ULITSA · CHEKHOVA U. · Suharevskaya · U. SRETENKA
Mayakovskaya Ploshchad · Tchaikovsky Concert Hall · Russian Cinema · Trubnaya Pl. · ROZHDESTVENSKY BOULEVARD · Sergievsky Per.
Youth Theatre · TVERSKAYA · Pushkinskaya · PETROVKA · NEG.-NINAYA · Convent of the Nativity of the Virgin
Museum of the Revolution · Pushkin Ploshchad · Petrovskiy Passage · Turgenevskaya Pl.
Gorky Theatre · Bolshoy Theatre · Detskiy Theatre · Chisty Prudy
Chekhov Theatre · Ermolovy Theatre · TEATRALNIY PROJ. · Ploshchad Lubyanskaya · NOVAYA PL.
Central Post Office · Theatre Square · Slavyansky Bazar · Polytechnic Museum · Nogina
Gorky House Museum · Revolution Square · Lenin Museum · Gum Shopping Arcade
Moscow Conservatoire · University · Manezhnaya Ploshchad · Historical Museum · Red Square · Lenin Mausoleum
NIKITSKIY BLVD. · Central Exhibition Hall · Arsenal · Council of Ministers
Arbatskaya Ploshchad · VOZDVIZHENKA U. · Museum of Russian Architecture · Lenin State Library · Presidium of the Supreme Soviet · St. Basil's Cathedral · ULITSA VARVARKA
Palace of Congress · Kremlin · Ivan Square
ULITSA ARBAT · Armoury Palace · Terem Cathedral Palace · Archangel Cathedral · Central Concert Hall
Pushkin Fine Arts Museum · KREMLEVSKAYA NABEREZHNAYA · Moskva (Moscow) · RAUSHSKAYA NAB.
Ryleyev Ulitsa · VOLKHONKA ULITSA · Cathedral of Christ the Saviour · SOFIYSKAYA NABEREZHNAYA · BOLOTNAYA NAB. · SADOVNICHESKAYA · OVCHINNIKOVSKAYA
Kropotkinskaya · BOLSHOY KAMENNIY MOST · BOLOTNAYA · KADASHEVSKAYA NAB.

a b c
1 2 3

MOSCOW, RUSSIA

1 0 1 km 2 3 4 5
1 0 miles 1 2 3

Simferka · Putilkovo · 37° 20' · 37° 30' · 37° 40' · 37° 50' · Medvezhiy Ozyora · Medvezhiy Ozyora
Novonikolyskoye · Mitino · Bratsevo · TO MOSCOW SHEREMETYEVO INTL. (SVO) · Degunino · Vladykino · MOSKVA OBLAST · GOROD MOSKVA · Babushkin
Chernyovo · Penyagino · Tushino · Khimki-Khovrino · Dzerzhinskiy Park · Losiny Ostrov National Park · Pekhra-Pokrovskoye · Almazova
Krasnogorsk · Pavshino · Nikolskiy · Petrovsko-Razumovskoye · Ostankino · Abramtsevo · Vostochnyy · Balashikha
Golyevo · Myakinino · Strogino · Timiryazev Park · Bogorodskoye · Galyanovoo · Novaya
Arkhangelyskoye · Troitse-Lykovo · Pokrovsko-Sresnevo · Petrovskiy Park · Sokolniki Park · Izmaylovo · Gorenki · Pekhra-Yakovievskaya
Zakharkovo · Rublovo · Khorosovo · Frunze · Sokolniki · Izmaylovskiy Park · Vishnyaki · Nikolyskoye · Saltykovka
Razdory · Cherepkovo · Mnevniki · **MOSKVA** · Dzerzhinskiy · Leningrad Station · Bauman · Novogireyevo · Reutov
Barvikha · Krylatskoye · Krasno-Presnenskaya · Bolshoy Theatre · Kursk Station · Perovo · Serebryanka · Kutsino
Romashkovo · Kuntsevo · Fili-Mazilovo · Red Square · Kremlin · St. Basil's Cath. · Lenin Museum · Kuskovo · Plyushchevo · Zheleznodorozhnyy
Poduskino · Nemchinovka · Kiev Station · Zhdanov · Veshnyaki · Fenino
Novoivanovskoye · Davydkovo · Novodevichy Convent · Gorky Park · Pavelet Station · Vykhino · Temnikovo
Lochino · Lomonosov Moscow State University · Fili Sports Centre Lenin Stadium · Moskvoretskiy · Vulyogradskiy Prospekt · Zhulebino · Kozhukhovo · Mikhelysona
Mamonovo · Bakovka · Aminyevo · Leninskiye Gory · Moscow Circus · Tekstilyshchik · Kuzyminki · Marusino
Odintsovo · Zarechye · Ochakovo · Ramenki · Oktyubrskiy · Nogatino · Lyublino · Lyubertsy · Nekrasovka
Meshcherskiy · Yugo-Zarad · Cheryomushki · Dyakovo · Maryino · Kotelyniki · Korenevo
Nikulino · Troparevo · Zyuzino · Volkhonka-Zil · Kuryanovo · Tomilino · Kraskovo
Vnukovo · Choboty · Solntsevo · Belyayevo Bogorodskoye · Bittsevsky Forest Park · Lenino · TO DOMODEDOVO INTL. (DME) · Brateyevo · Kapotnya · Dzerzhinskiy · Chkalova · Malakhovka
Peredelkino · Orlovo · Rasskazovka · Rumyantsevo · Chertanovo · Borisovo · Tokarevo
37° 20' · 37° 30' East from Greenwich · 37° 40' · 37° 50'

A B C
1 2 3 4 5 6

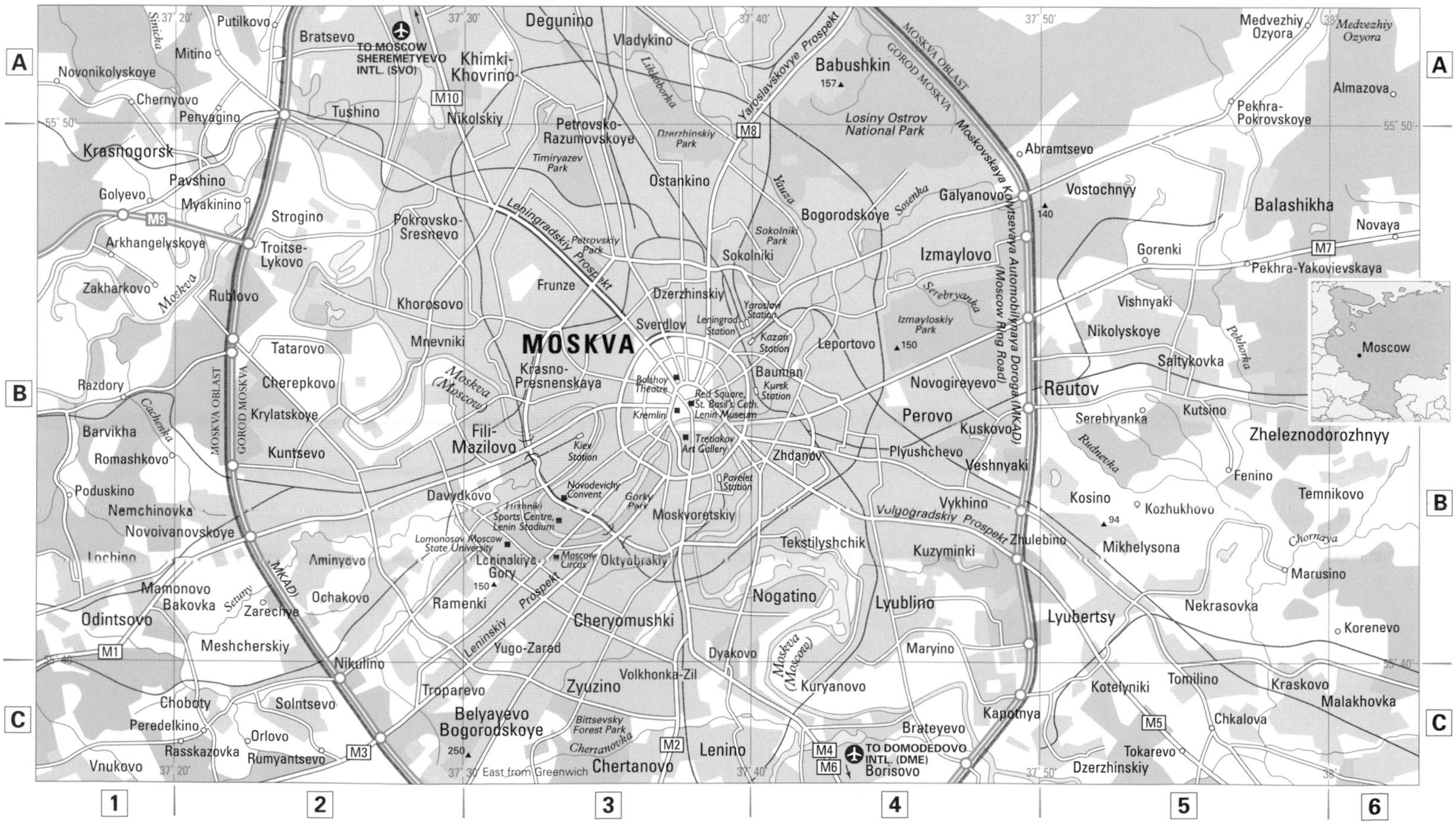

COPYRIGHT PHILIP'S

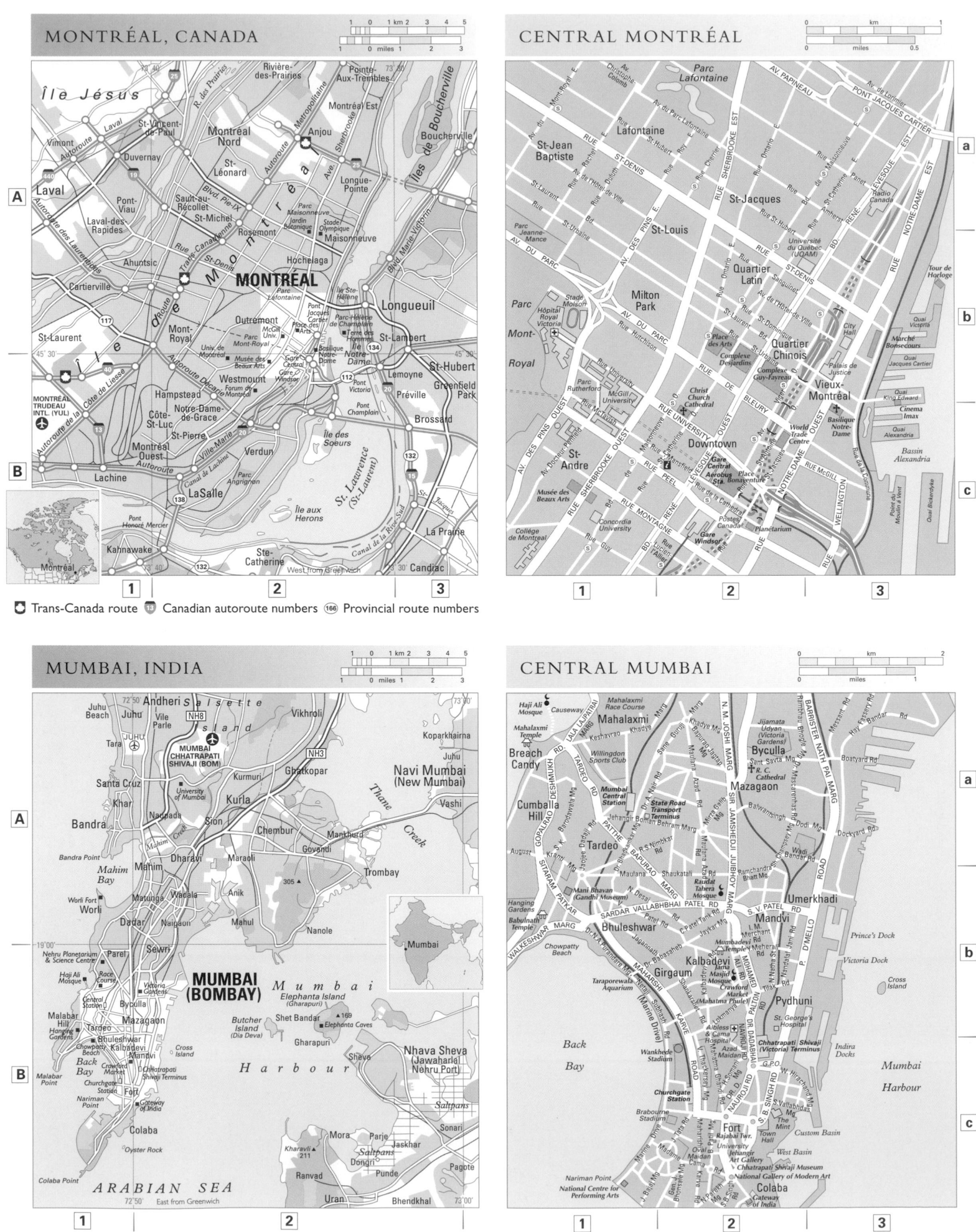

MONTRÉAL, CANADA

1 0 1 km 2 3 4 5
1 0 miles 1 2 3

CENTRAL MONTRÉAL

0 km 1
0 miles 0.5

⬡ Trans-Canada route ▭ Canadian autoroute numbers Ⓛ Provincial route numbers

MUMBAI, INDIA

1 0 1 km 2 3 4 5
1 0 miles 1 2 3

CENTRAL MUMBAI

0 km 2
0 miles 1

COPYRIGHT PHILIP'S

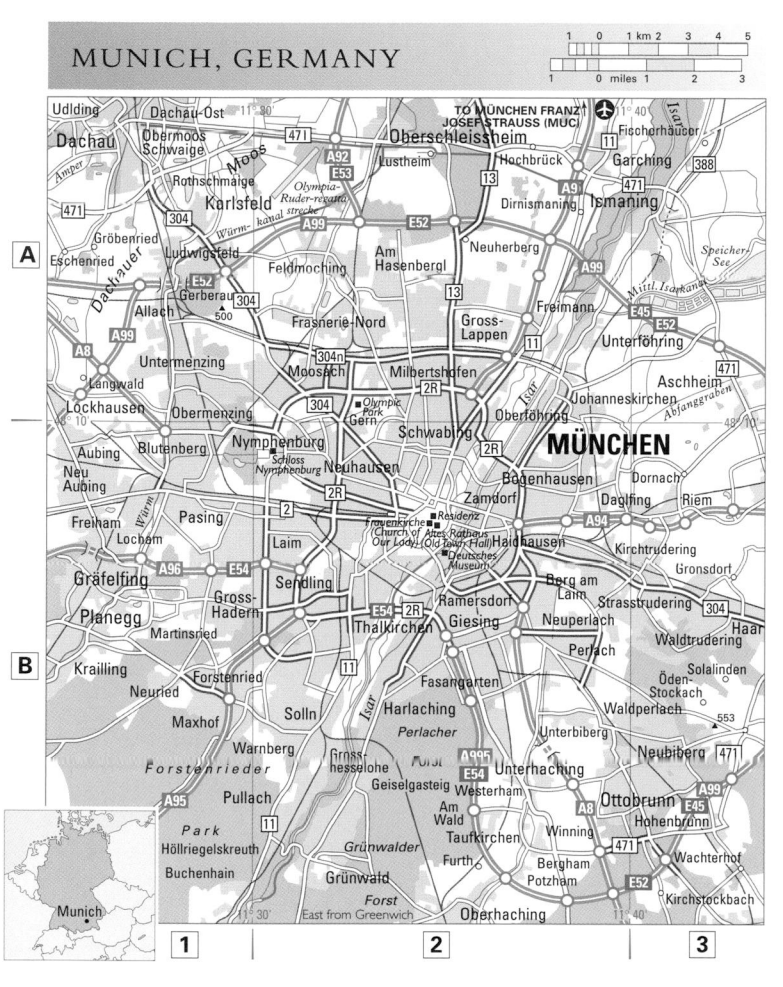

MUNICH, GERMANY

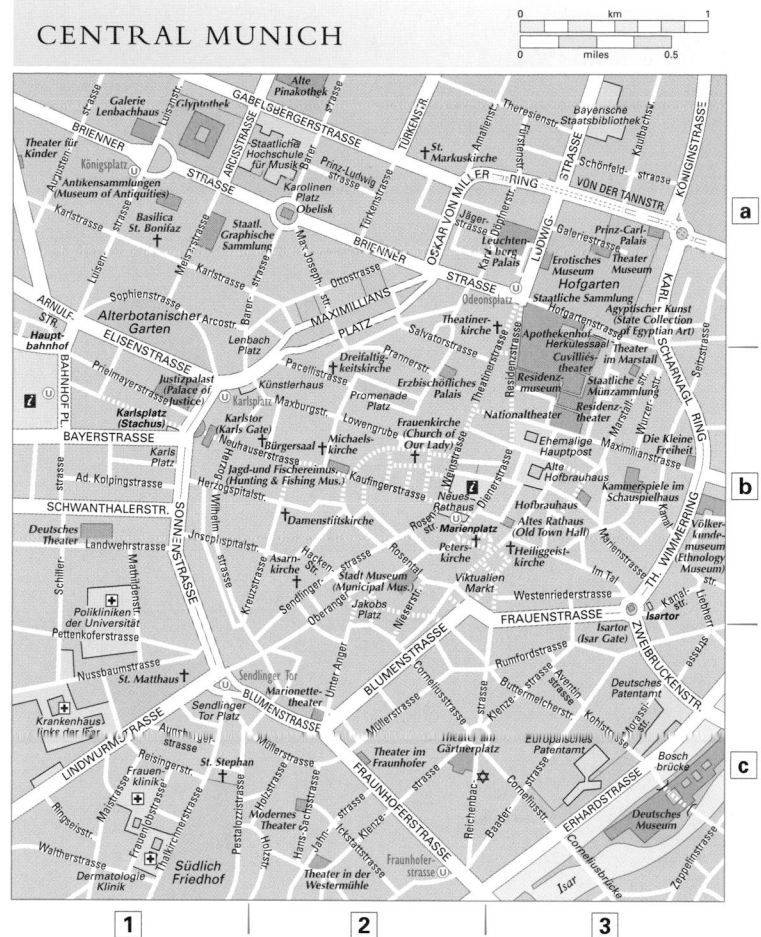

CENTRAL MUNICH

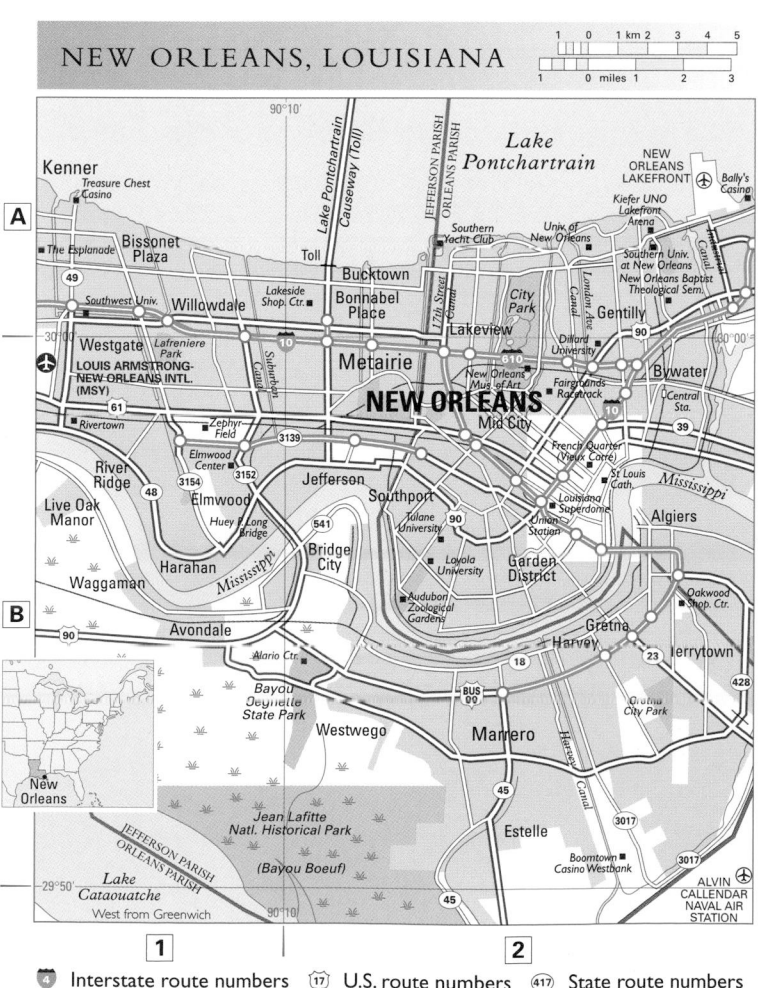

NEW ORLEANS, LOUISIANA

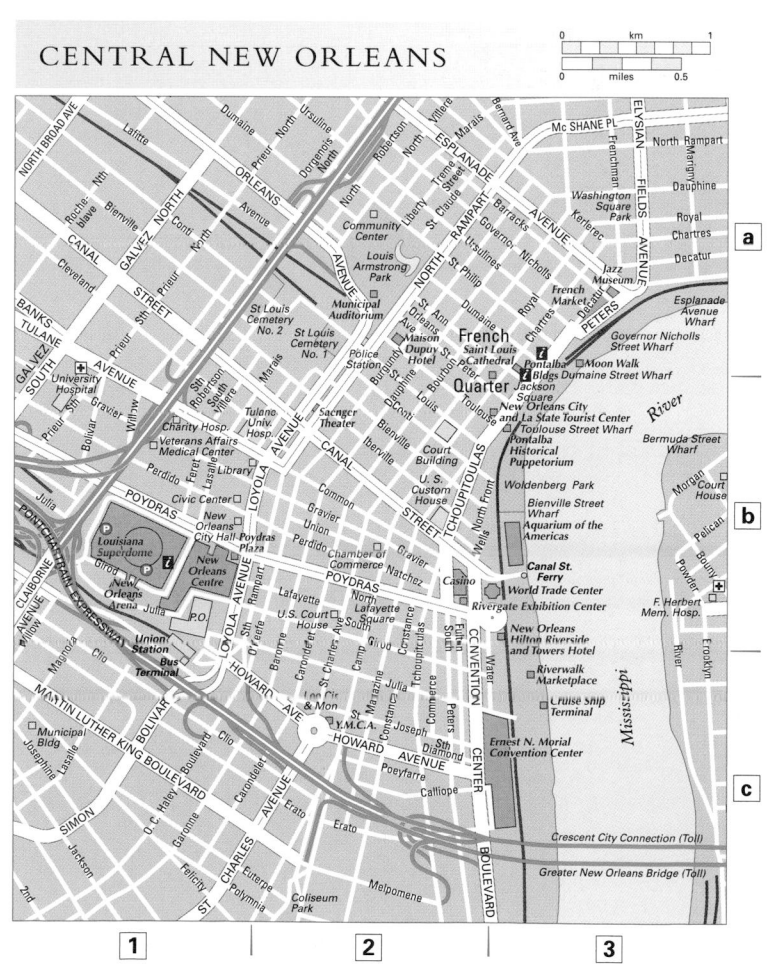

CENTRAL NEW ORLEANS

Interstate route numbers ⑰ U.S. route numbers ④₁₇ State route numbers

COPYRIGHT PHILIP'S

NEW YORK, NEW YORK

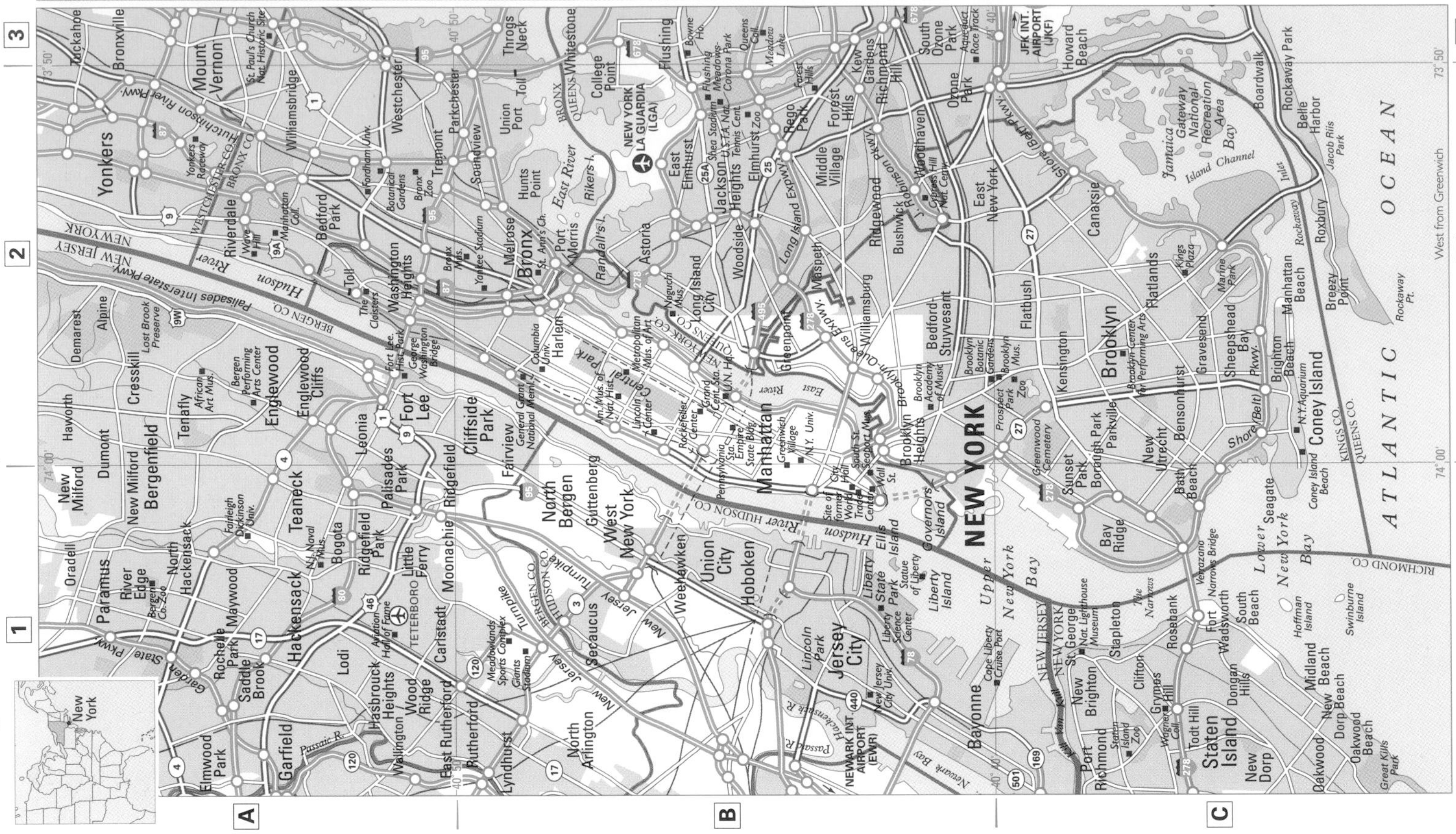

0 1 km 2 3 4 5
0 miles 1 2 3
Interstate route numbers
U.S. route numbers
State route numbers
NEW YORK
ATLANTIC OCEAN

CENTRAL NEW YORK

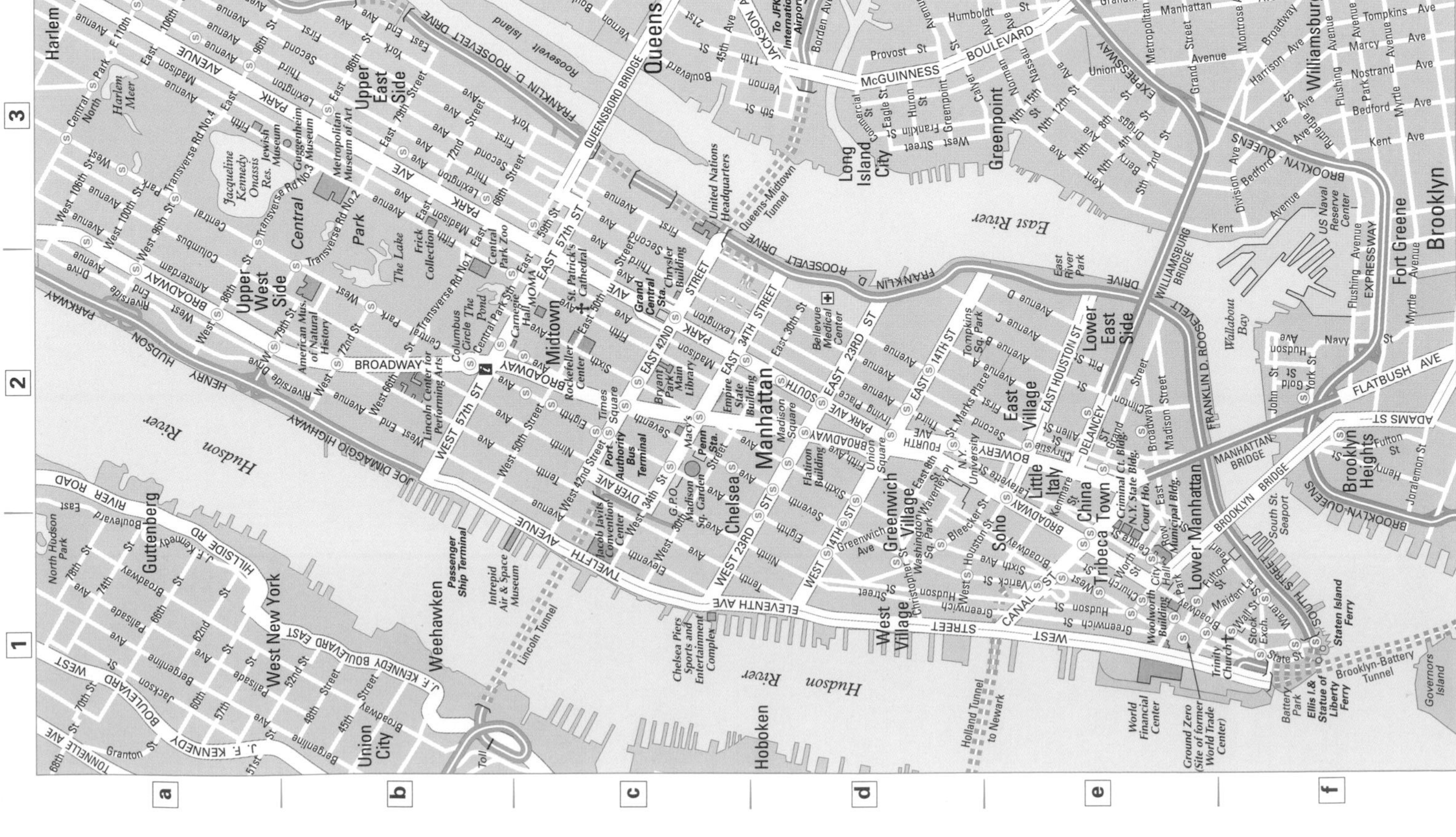

0 km 2
0 miles 1

COPYRIGHT PHILIP'S

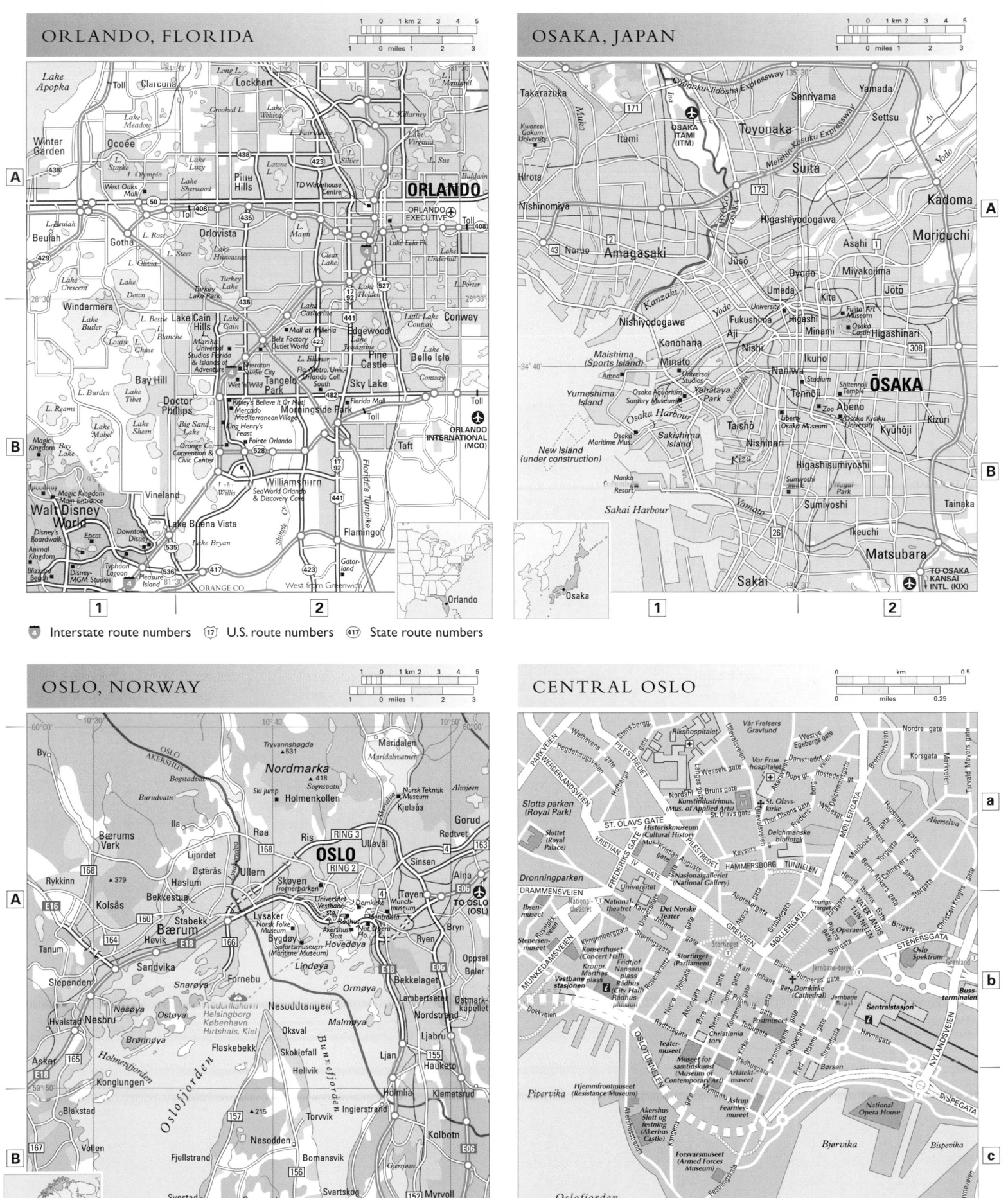

ORLANDO, FLORIDA

1 0 1 km 2 3 4 5
1 0 miles 1 2 3

OSAKA, JAPAN

1 0 1 km 2 3 4 5
1 0 miles 1 2 3

Interstate route numbers   U.S. route numbers   State route numbers

OSLO, NORWAY

1 0 1 km 2 3 4 5
1 0 miles 1 2 3

CENTRAL OSLO

0 km 0.5
0 miles 0.25

COPYRIGHT PHILIP'S

PARIS, FRANCE

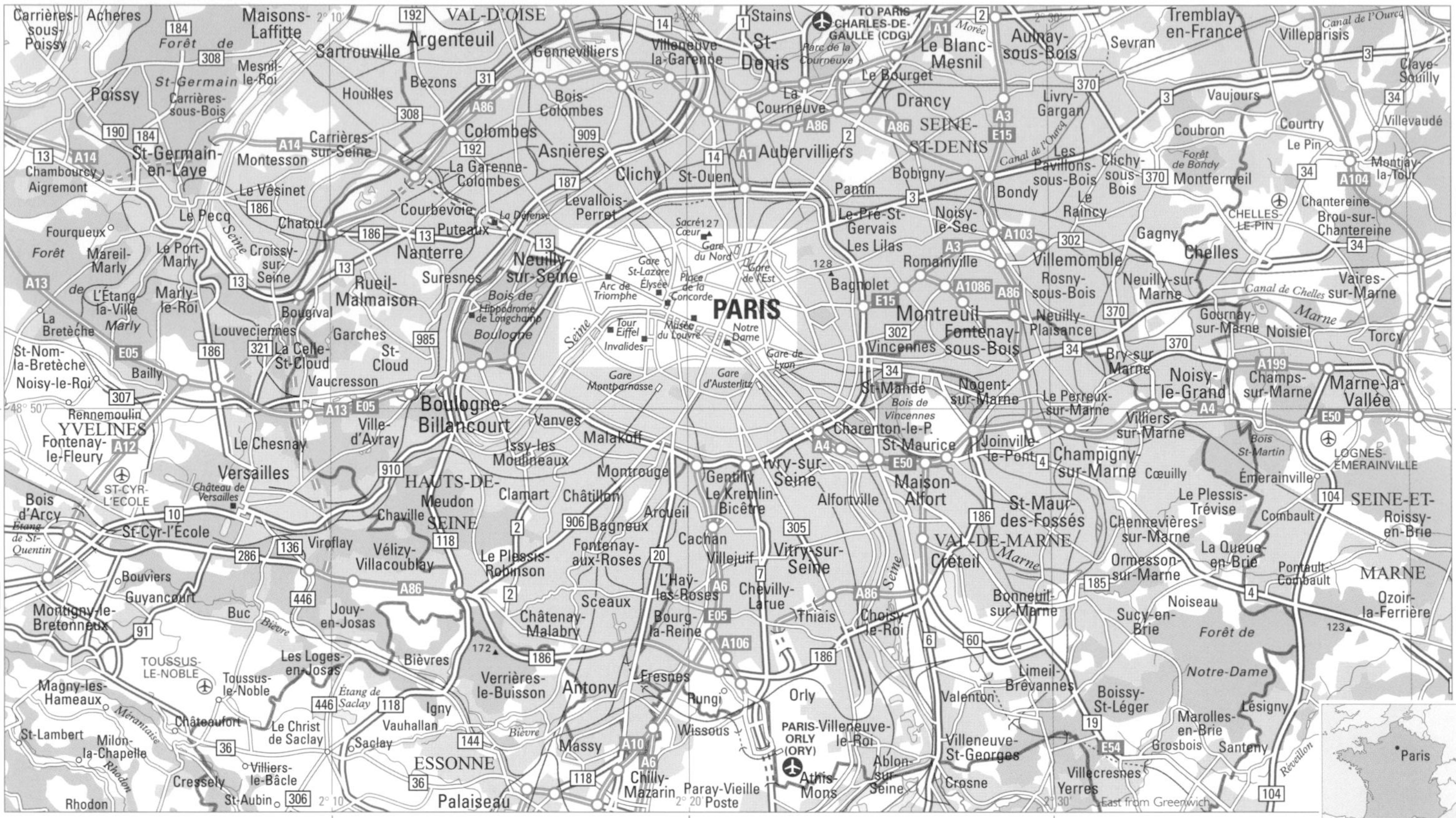

1 0 1 km 2 3 4 5
1 0 miles 1 2 3

Carrières-sous-Poissy · Achères · Maisons-Laffitte · VAL-D'OISE · Stains · St-Denis · TO PARIS CHARLES-DE-GAULLE (CDG) · Le Blanc-Mesnil · Aulnay-sous-Bois · Sevran · Tremblay-en-France · Villeparisis · Claye-Souilly

Forêt de St-Germain · Sartrouville · Argenteuil · Gennevilliers · Villeneuve-la-Garenne · La Courneuve · Le Bourget · Drancy · Livry-Gargan · Vaujours · Courtry

Poissy · Mesnil-le-Roi · Houilles · Bezons · Bois-Colombes · Asnières · SEINE-ST-DENIS · Aubervilliers · Bobigny · Les Pavillons-sous-Bois · Le Raincy · Montfermeil · Le Pin · Montjay-la-Tour

St-Germain-en-Laye · Montesson · Colombes · La Garenne-Colombes · Clichy · St-Ouen · Pantin · Noisy-le-Sec · Romainville · Bondy · CHELLES-LE-PIN · Chanteraine · Brou-sur-Chantereine

A · Chambourcy · Aigremont · Le Vésinet · Chatou · Courbevoie · Puteaux · Levallois-Perret · Neuilly-sur-Seine · Gare St-Lazare · Gare du Nord · Gare de l'Est · Les Lilas · Bagnolet · Rosny-sous-Bois · Villemomble · Gagny · Chelles · Vaires-sur-Marne · Noisiel · Torcy **A**

Fourqueux · Le Pecq · Nanterre · Rueil-Malmaison · Suresnes · Bois de Boulogne · Arc de Triomphe · Sacré-Cœur · **PARIS** · Notre Dame · Montreuil · Fontenay-sous-Bois · Neuilly-Plaisance · Le Perreux-sur-Marne

Mareil-Marly · Le Port-Marly · Marly-le-Roi · Bougival · Garches · St-Cloud · Tour Eiffel · Musée du Louvre · Invalides · Vincennes · St-Mandé · Nogent-sur-Marne · Bry-sur-Marne · Noisy-le-Grand · Champs-sur-Marne · Marne-la-Vallée

L'Étang-la-Ville · Louveciennes · La Celle-St-Cloud · Vaucresson · Gare Montparnasse · Gare de Lyon · Gare d'Austerlitz · Charenton-le-P. · Joinville-le-Pont · Villiers-sur-Marne · Cœuilly · LOGNES-EMERAINVILLE · Émerainville

St-Nom-la-Bretèche · Noisy-le-Roi · Bailly · YVELINES · Fontenay-le-Fleury · Le Chesnay · Boulogne-Billancourt · Vanves · Malakoff · Ivry-sur-Seine · St-Maurice · Champigny-sur-Marne · Le Plessis-Trévise · Combault · SEINE-ET-MARNE · Roissy-en-Brie

Rennemoulin · Versailles · Ville-d'Avray · Issy-les-Moulineaux · Montrouge · Gentilly · Le Kremlin-Bicêtre · Alfortville · Maison-Alfort · St-Maur-des-Fossés · Chennevières-sur-Marne · Ormesson-sur-Marne · La Queue-en-Brie · Pontault-Combault · MARNE

Bois d'Arcy · ST-CYR-L'ÉCOLE · Château de Versailles · St-Cyr-l'École · HAUTS-DE-SEINE · Meudon · Chaville · Clamart · Châtillon · Bagneux · Arcueil · Cachan · Villejuif · Vitry-sur-Seine · Créteil · Bonneuil-sur-Marne · Sucy-en-Brie · Noiseau · Ozoir-la-Ferrière

B · Étang de St-Quentin · Bouviers · Guyancourt · Viroflay · Vélizy-Villacoublay · Le Plessis-Robinson · Fontenay-aux-Roses · Sceaux · L'Haÿ-les-Roses · Bourg-la-Reine · Chevilly-Larue · Thiais · Choisy-le-Roi · VAL-DE-MARNE · Forêt de Notre-Dame **B**

Montigny-le-Bretonneux · Buc · Jouy-en-Josas · Bièvres · Châtenay-Malabry · Antony · Fresnes · Rungis · Orly · Valenton · Boissy-St-Léger · Lésigny · Santeny

Magny-les-Hameaux · TOUSSUS-LE-NOBLE · Toussus-le-Noble · Les Loges-en-Josas · Verrières-le-Buisson · Igny · Bièvre · Choisy · Villeneuve-St-Georges · Limeil-Brévannes · Marolles-en-Brie · Grosbois

St-Lambert · Milon-la-Chapelle · Châteaufort · Le Christ de Saclay · Saclay · Vauhallan · Wissous · PARIS-Villeneuve-ORLY (ORY) · Villeneuve-le-Roi · Ablon-sur-Seine · Crosne · Villecresnes

Rhodon · Cressely · St-Aubin · Villiers-le-Bâcle · ESSONNE · Massy · Chilly-Mazarin · Paray-Vieille-Poste · Athis-Mons · Palaiseau · East from Greenwich

Paris

1 **2** **3** **4**

CENTRAL PARIS

0 km 1
0 miles 0.5

Av. de la Pte. de Champerret · Pte. de Champerret · Montmartre · Sacré Cœur · Bd. Pereire · AV. DE CLICHY

a · Avenue Achille Peretti · Clinique Hartmann · PORTE DE CHAMPERRET · BOULEVARD DE VILLIERS · Moulin Rouge · Musée de l'érotisme · Pigalle · Abbesses · Barbès-Rochechouart · La Chapelle · AV. DE FLANDRE · Canal de St-Martin **a**

Bois de Boulogne · Stade Paul Faber · Les Sablons · Palais des Congrès · Porte Maillot · BD. DE COURCELLES · Monceau · St-Lazare · Gare de l'Est · Gare du Nord · AV. JEAN JAURÈS

PORTE MAILLOT · AV. DE LA GRANDE ARMÉE · Arc de Triomphe · Pl. Charles de Gaulle Étoile · AVENUE FOCH · Pl. du Trône · Belleville

PORTE DAUPHINE · Université Paris IX · Musée Arménien · AVENUE DES CHAMPS ELYSÉES · Palais de l'Élysée · Opéra · Bibliothèque Nationale · Place de la République

b · PORTE DE LA MUETTE · Musée Guimet · Palais Galliera · Th. des Champs Elysées · Grand Palais · Petit Palais · Place de la Concorde · Jardin des Tuileries · Comédie Française · Banque de France · Cons. des Arts et Métiers · Musée Picasso **b**

Musée d'Art Moderne · Palais de Chaillot (Chaillot Palace) · Musée de la Marine · COURS ALBERT 1er · COURS LA REINE · Seine · Quai d'Orsay · Assemblée Nationale · Musée des Arts Décoratifs · Musée du Louvre (Louvre Museum) · Centre Pompidou (Beaubourg) · Archives Nationales · Musée Carnavalet

Musée de l'homme · Tour Eiffel (Eiffel Tower) · l'Université · Min. de l'Éducation · Musée d'Orsay (Orsay Museum) · Palais de Justice · Hôtel de Ville · Le Marais

c · Maison de Radio France · Parc du Champ de Mars · Invalides · Min. de l'Agriculture · Musée Rodin · St-Germain des Prés · Ile de la Cité · Notre Dame · Ile St-Louis · Place de la Bastille · Opéra Bastille **c**

Hôpital Ste. Périne · École Militaire · U.N.E.S.C.O. · Hôpital Laennec · Hôpital Necker · Palais du Luxembourg · Quartier Latin · Sorbonne · Panthéon · Inst. du Monde Arabe · Gare de Lyon · Luxembourg

1 **2** **3** **4** **5**

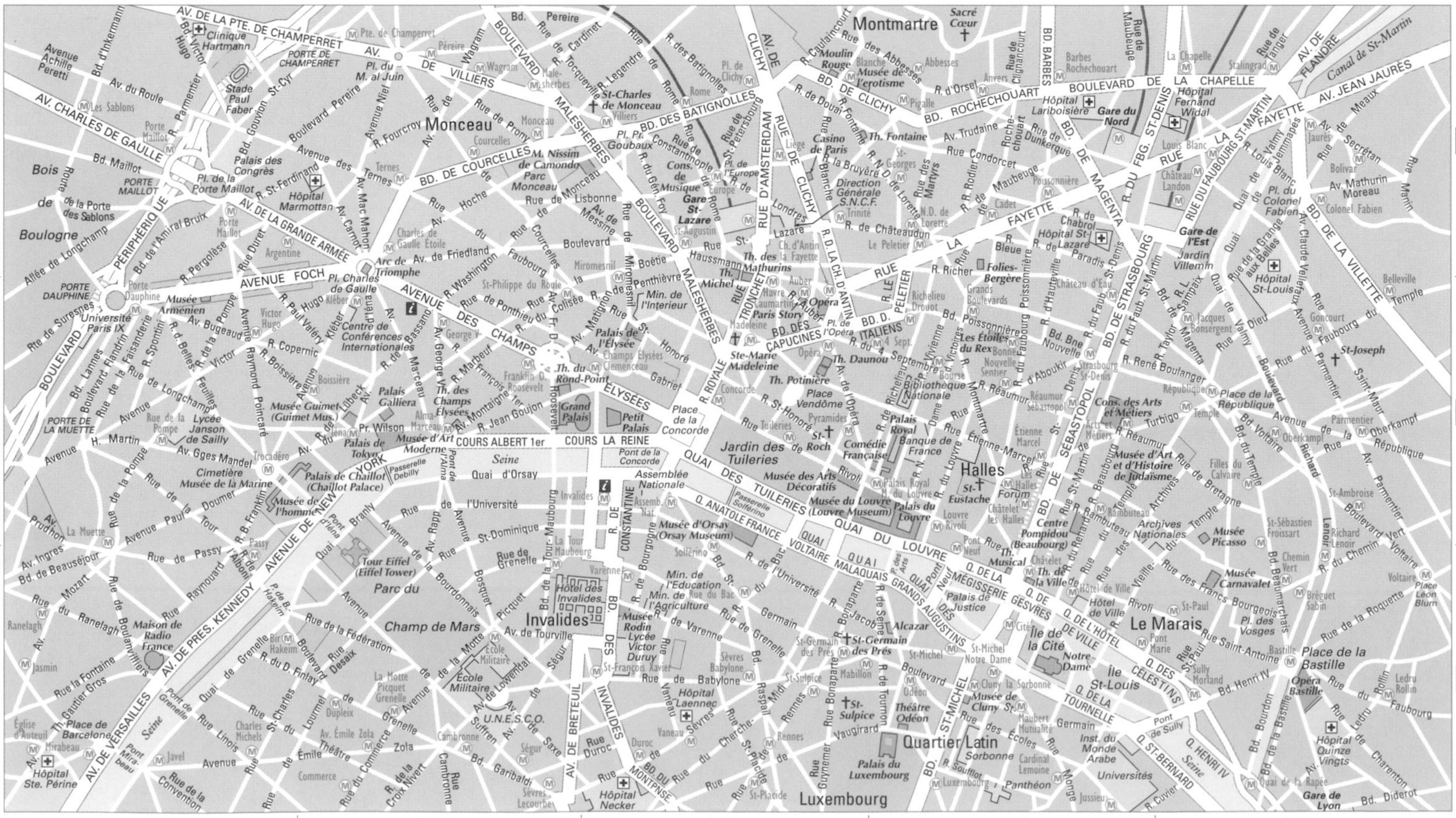

COPYRIGHT PHILIP'S

PRAGUE, CZECH REPUBLIC

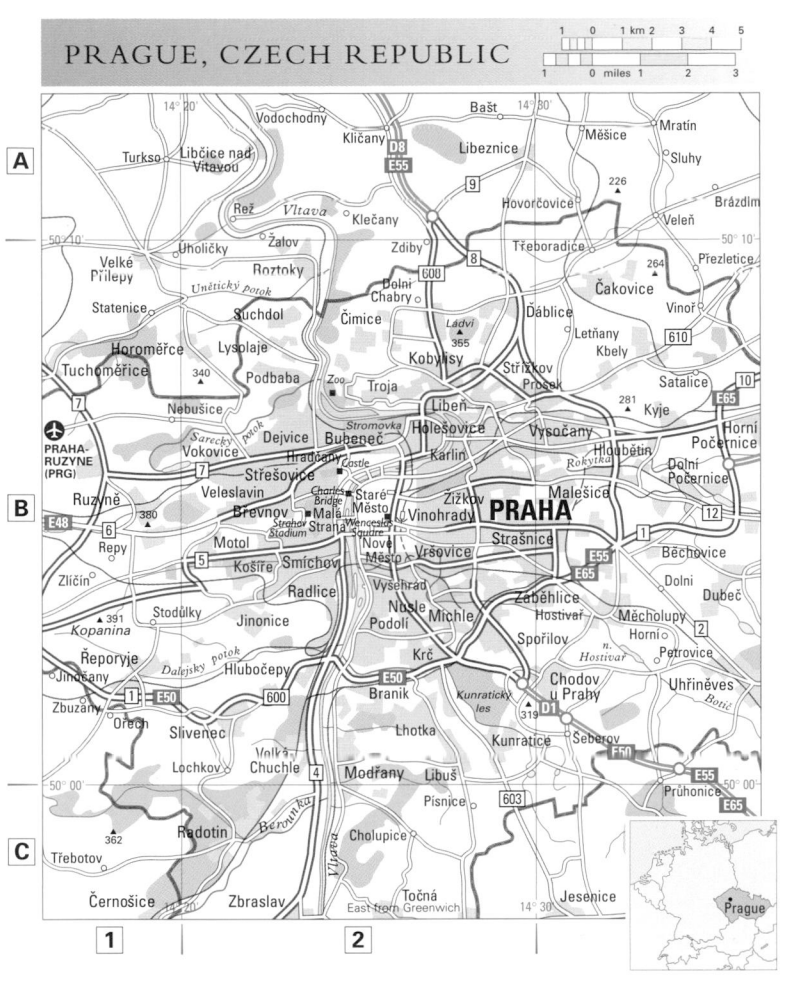

CENTRAL PRAGUE

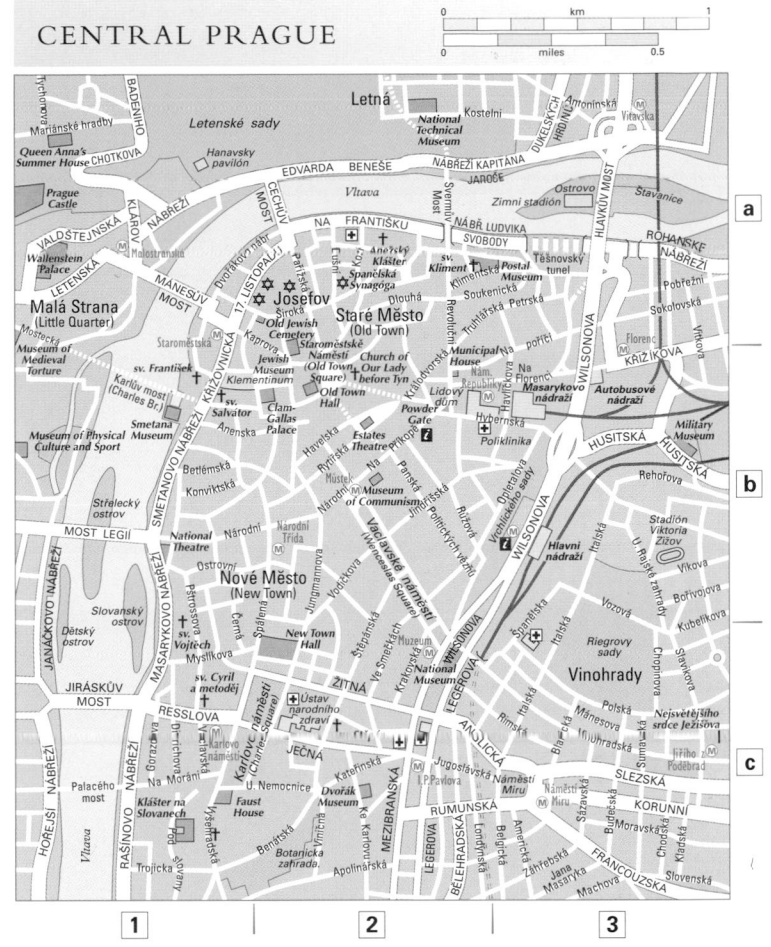

RIO DE JANEIRO, BRAZIL

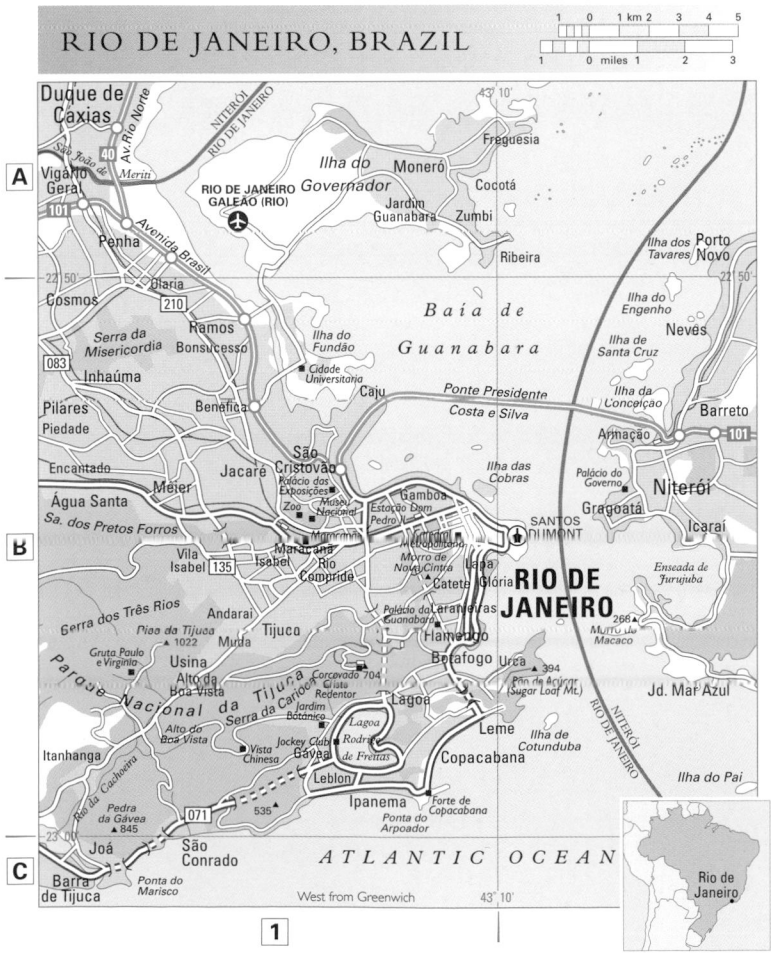

CENTRAL RIO DE JANEIRO

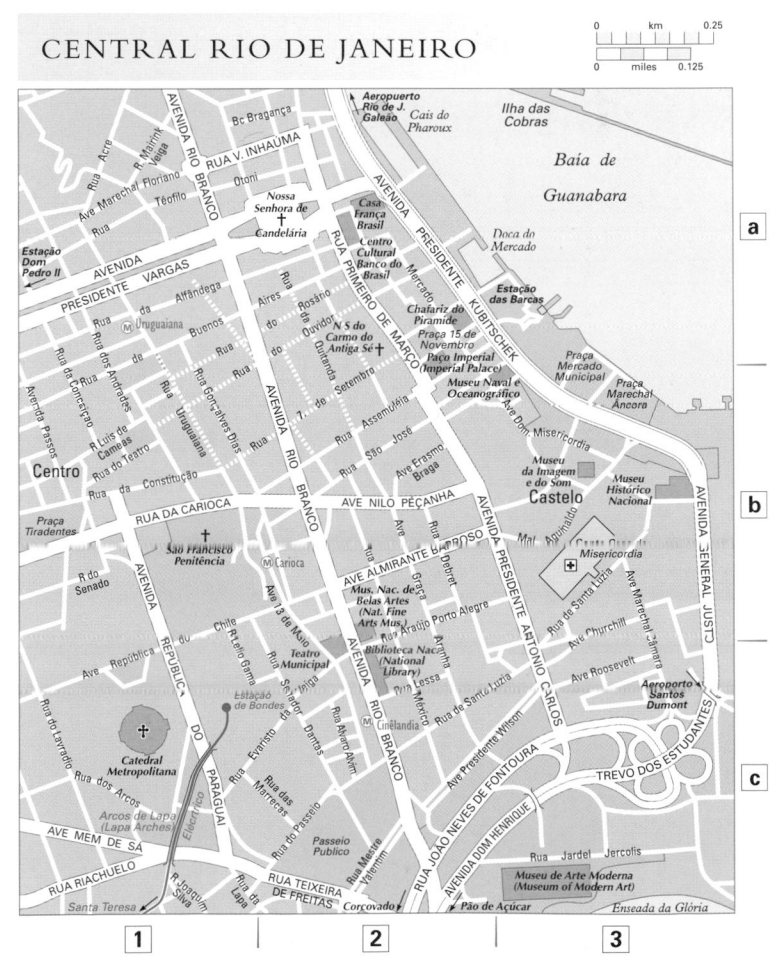

COPYRIGHT PHILIP'S

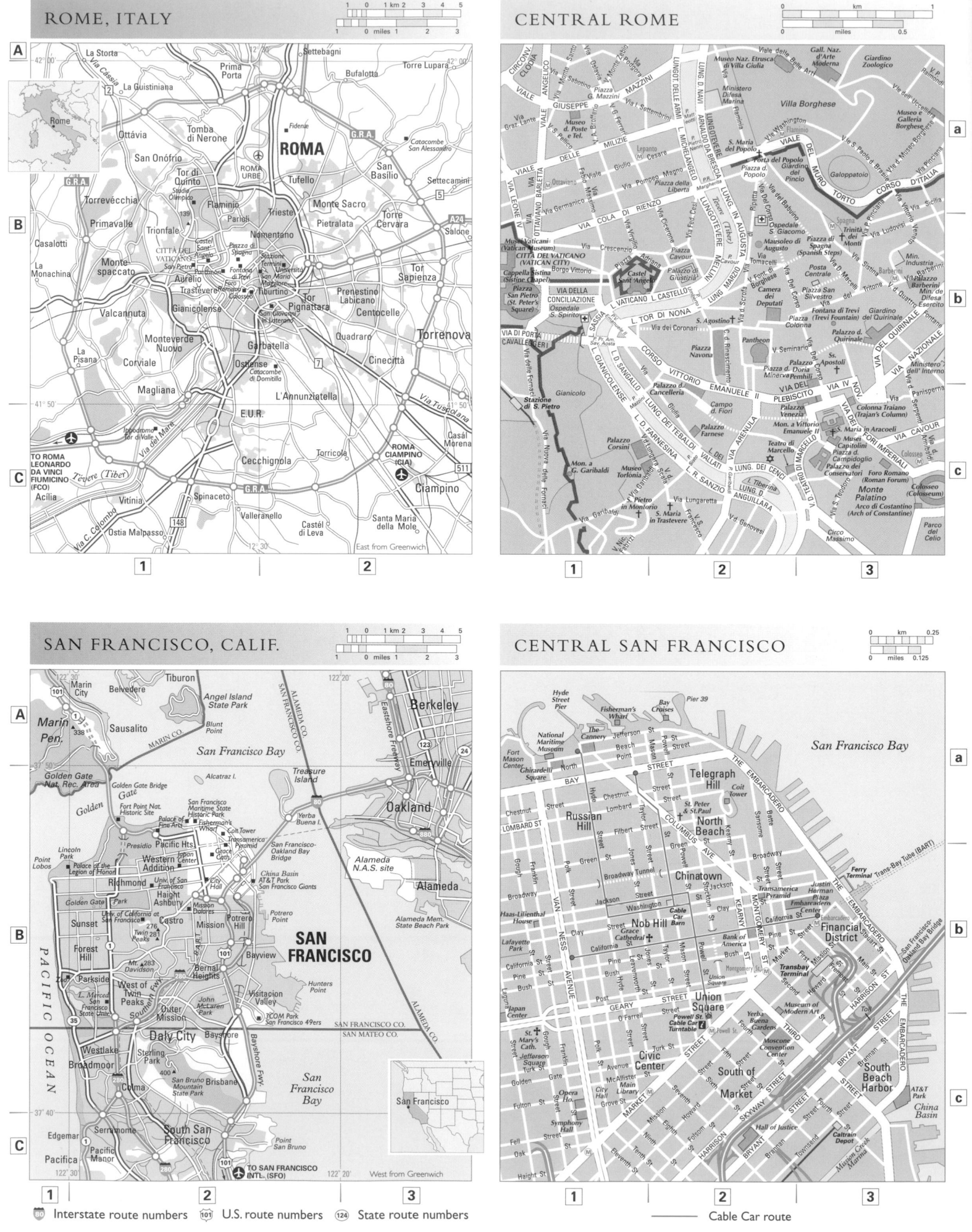

ROME, ITALY

A
42° 00'
La Storta
Via Cassia
Settebagni
Prima Porta
La Giustiniana
Bufalotta
Torre Lupara
42° 00'

Rome

Ottávia
Tomba di Nerone
ROMA

San Onófrio
ROMA URBE
Tufello
San Basílio
Settecamini

Tor di Quinto
Studii Olimpica
Monte Sacro

Torrevécchia
Flaminio
Trieste
Torre Cervara
Salone

B
Primavalle
Trionfale
Parioli
Nomentano
Pietralata

Casalotti
CITTÀ DEL VATICANO
Stazione Termini
Tor Sapienza

Monte-spaccato
San Pietro
Aurelio
Università
Tiburtino

La Monachina
Trastévere
Foro Italico
Prenestino Labicano
Centocelle
Torrenova

Valcannuta
Gianicolense
San Giovanni in Laterano
Tor Pignattara
Quadraro
Cinecittà

Monteverde Nuovo
Garbatella
41° 50'

Corviale
Ostiense
Catacombe di Domitilla
L'Annunziatella

Magliana
E.U.R.
41° 50'

La Pisana

Ippodromo Tor di Valle
Via del Mare
Cecchignola
Torricola
ROMA CIAMPINO (CIA)
511

TO ROMA LEONARDO DA VINCI FIUMICINO (FCO)
Acília
Tévere (Tiber)
Ciampino

C
Vitinia
Spinaceto
G.R.A.
Valleranello
Castél di Leva
Santa Maria della Mole
12° 30'

Via C. Colombo
Ostia Malpasso

East from Greenwich

1   2

CENTRAL ROME

a
Villa Borghese
Gall. Naz. d'Arte Moderna
Giardino Zoologico

S. Maria del Popolo
Porta del Popolo
Museo e Galleria Borghese

CITTÀ DEL VATICANO (VATICAN CITY)
Castel Sant'Angelo
Piazza di Spagna (Spanish Steps)

b
Cappella Sistina (Sistine Chapel)
Piazza San Pietro (St. Peter's Square)
Pantheon
Fontana di Trevi (Trevi Fountain)
Piazza Colonna

Piazza Navona
CORSO VITTORIO EMANUELE II
Palazzo d. Quirinale

c
Mon. a G. Garibaldi
Foro Romano (Roman Forum)
Colosseo (Colosseum)
Monte Palatino
Arco di Costantino (Arch of Constantine)

1   2   3

SAN FRANCISCO, CALIF.

A
122° 30'
Marin City
Tiburon
Belvedere
Angel Island State Park
122° 20'
Berkeley

Marin Pen.
Sausalito
Blunt Point
San Francisco Bay
Emeryville

Golden Gate Nat. Rec. Area
Alcatraz I.
Treasure Island
Oakland

Golden Gate
Fort Point Nat. Historic Site
Fisherman's Wharf
Yerba Buena I.
Alameda N.A.S. site

B
Lincoln Park
Presidio
Pacific Hts.
Transamerica Pyramid
China Basin
AT&T Park
San Francisco Giants
Alameda

Point Lobos
Palace of the Legion of Honor
Western Addition
Japan Center
Grace Cath.
City Hall
Alameda Mem. State Beach Park

Richmond
Univ. of San Francisco
Haight Ashbury
Mission Dolores
Potrero Point

Sunset
Castro
Mission
Potrero Hill
SAN FRANCISCO

Forest Hill
Twin Peaks
Bernal Heights
Bayview
Hunters Point

C
Parkside
West of Twin Peaks
Outer Mission
John McLaren Park
Visitacion Valley
3COM Park San Francisco 49ers
SAN FRANCISCO CO.

Westlake
Broadmoor
Daly City
Bayshore
SAN MATEO CO.
San Francisco Bay

Colma
San Bruno Mountain State Park
Brisbane
San Francisco

37° 40'
Edgemar
Pacifica
South San Francisco
Point San Bruno

TO SAN FRANCISCO INTL. (SFO)
West from Greenwich

1   2   3

80 Interstate route numbers   101 U.S. route numbers   124 State route numbers

CENTRAL SAN FRANCISCO

a
Hyde Street Pier
Fisherman's Wharf
Pier 39
Bay Cruises
San Francisco Bay

National Maritime Museum
The Cannery
Telegraph Hill
Coit Tower

Russian Hill
North Beach

b
Chinatown
Transamerica Pyramid
Ferry Terminal
Trans Bay Tube (BART)

Nob Hill
Grace Cathedral
Financial District

Union Square
Museum of Modern Art
South Beach Harbor

c
Civic Center
South of Market
China Basin
AT&T Park

1   2   3

—— Cable Car route

COPYRIGHT PHILIP'S

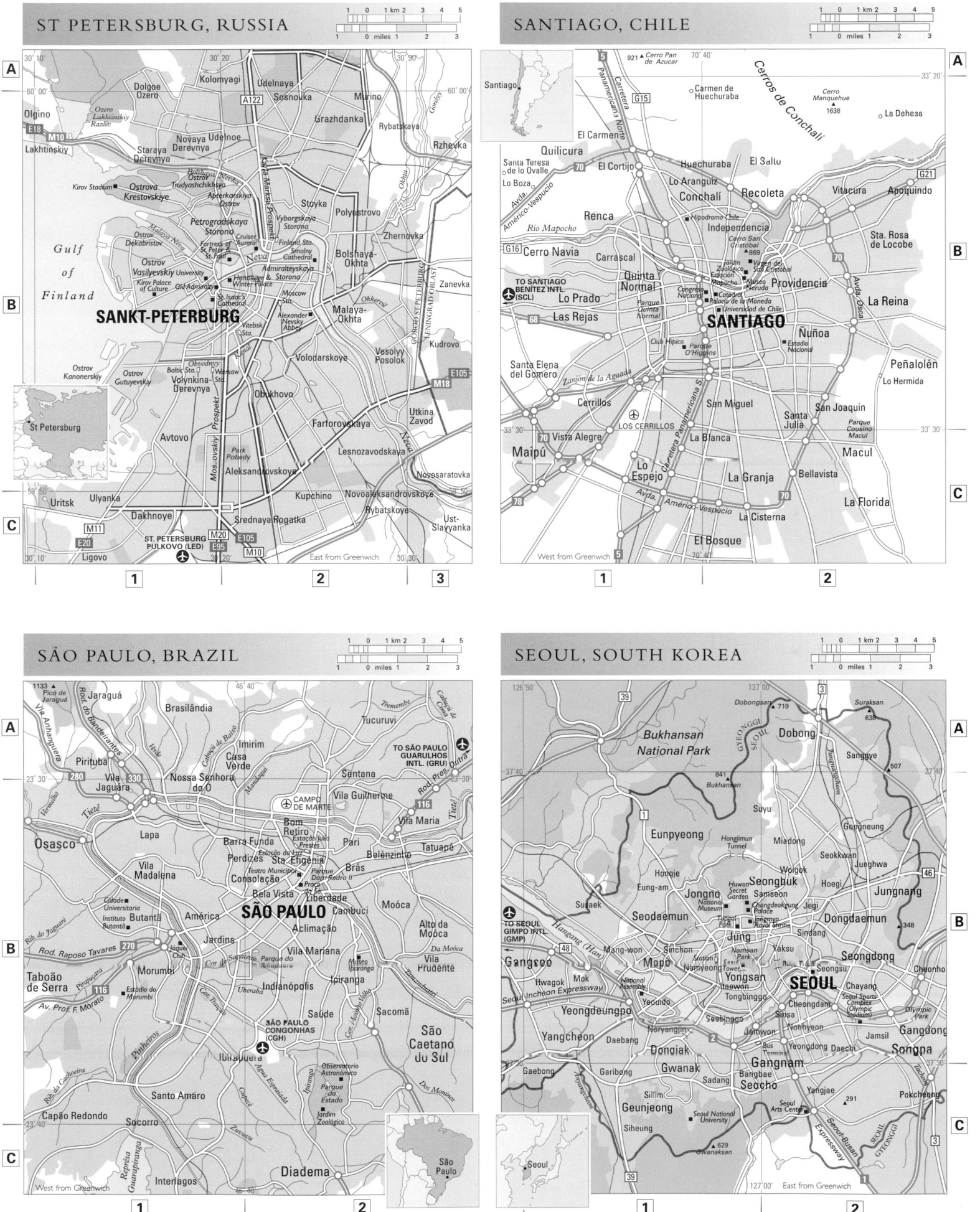

COPYRIGHT PHILIP'S

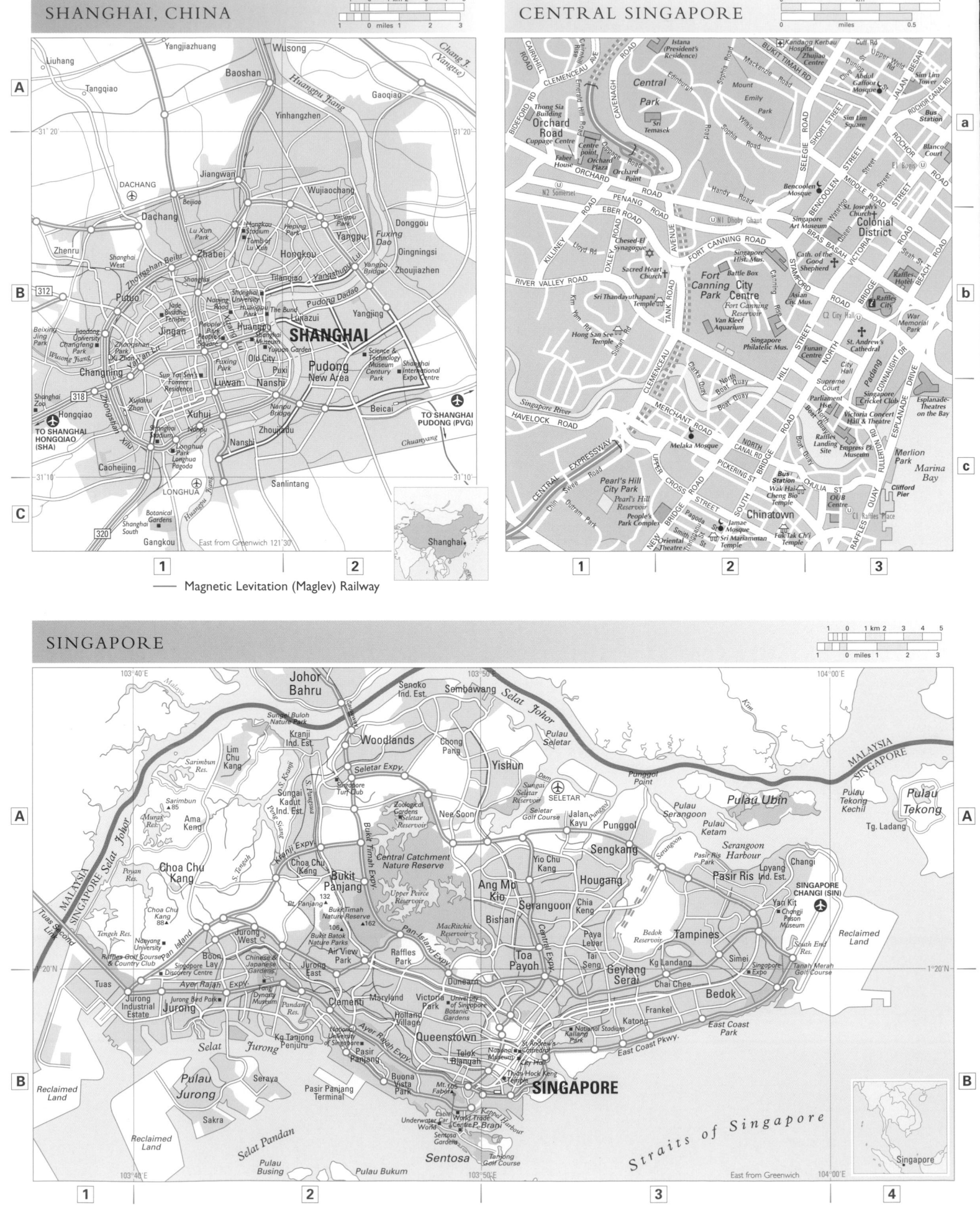

SHANGHAI, CHINA

CENTRAL SINGAPORE

—— Magnetic Levitation (Maglev) Railway

SINGAPORE

COPYRIGHT PHILIP'S

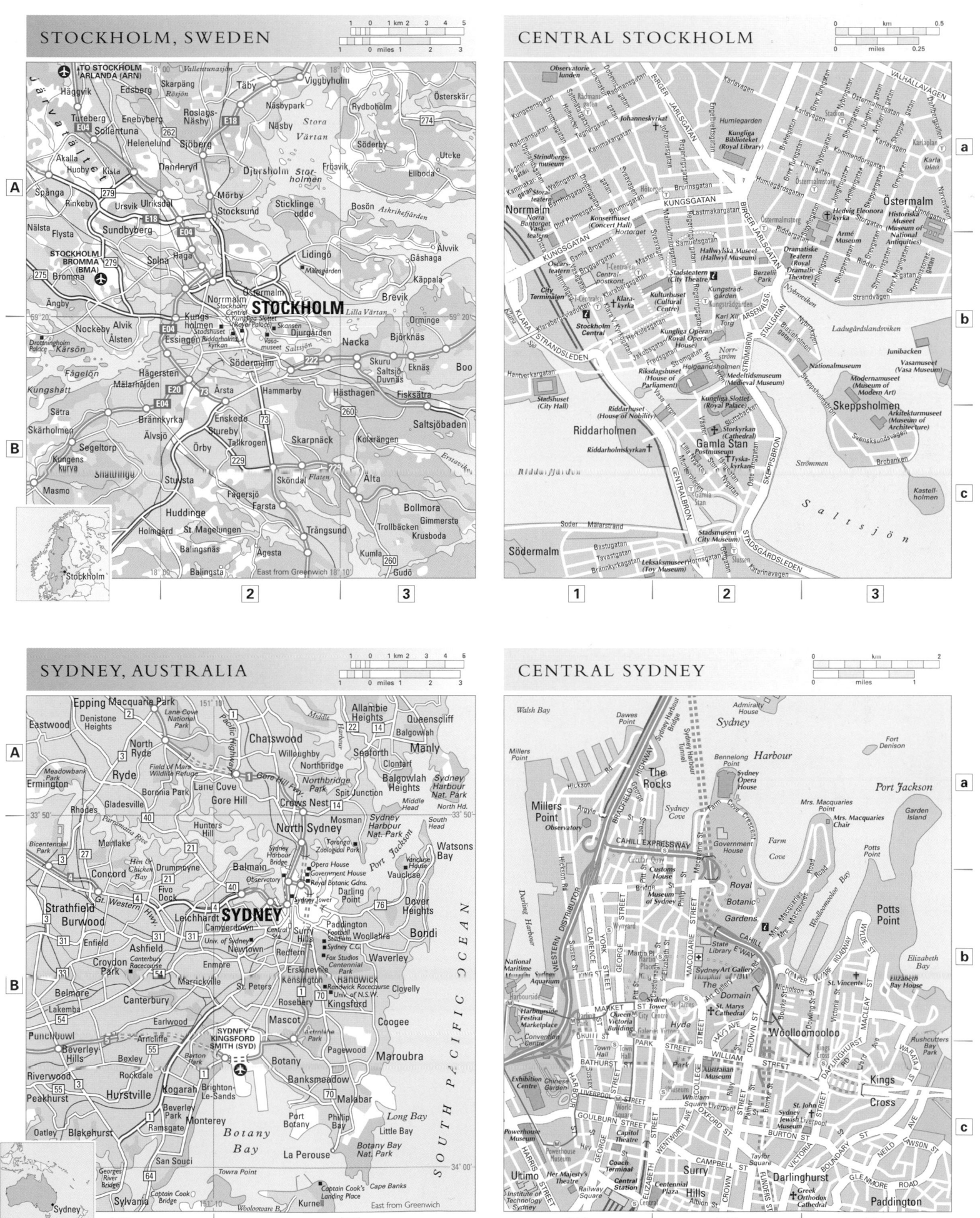

TOKYO, JAPAN

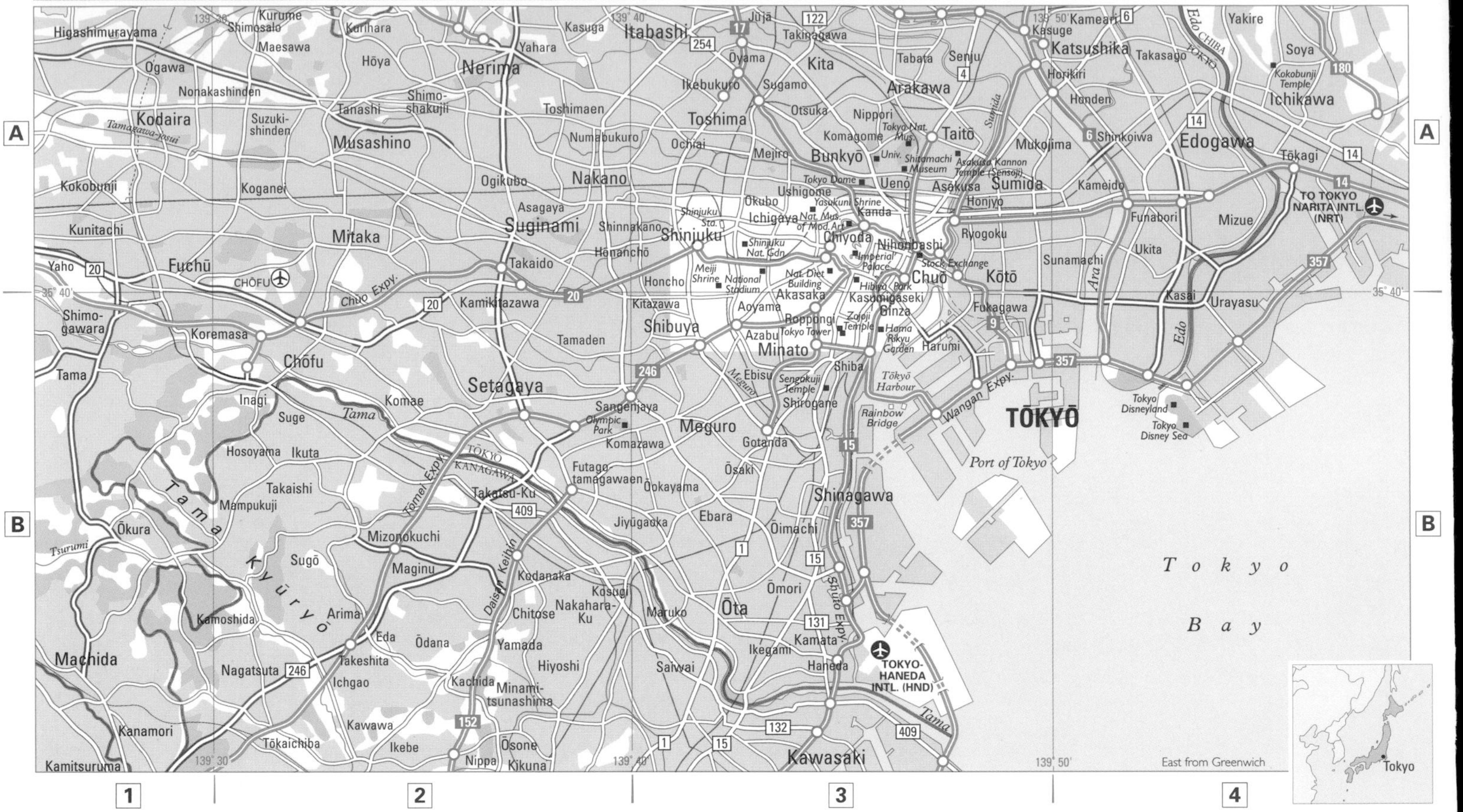

km 0 1 km 2 3 4 5
miles 1 0 miles 1 2 3

Higashimurayama · Kurume · Shimosala · Kurihara · Kasuga · Jūjo · 122 · Takinogawa · Kasuge · Kameari · Yakire · Soya
Shimosala · Maesawa · Hōya · Oyama · Kita · Tabata · Senju · Horikiri · Hunden · Katsushika · Takasago · 180 · Kokubunji Temple · Ichikawa
Kodaira · Nonakashinden · Suzuki-shinden · Tanashi · Shimo-shakujii · Toshimaen · Ikebukuro · Sugamo · Otsuka · Nippori · Mukojima · Shinkoiwa · Edogawa · 14
Kokubunji · Koganei · Musashino · Ogikubo · Nakano · Mejiro · Komagome · Univ. · Shiragmachi Mus. · Asakusa Kannon Temple (Sensoji) · Honjyo · Tōkagi · 14
Kunitachi · Mitaka · Asagaya · Suginami · Ochiai · Okubo · Ushigone · Yasukuni Shrine · Kanda · Ryogoku · Funabori · Mizue · TO TOKYO NARITA INTL (NRT)
Yaho · Fuchū · Takaido · Shinnakano · Homancho · Shinjuku · Ichigaya Nat'l M of Mod Art · Chiyoda · Nihonbashi · Chūō · Kōtō · Sunamachi · Ukita · Urayasu
20 · CHOFU · Chūo Expy. · 20 · Kamikitazawa · Honcho · Kitazawa · Nat. Diet Building · Imperial Palace · Stock Exchange · Fukagawa · 357
Shimo-gawara · Koremasa · Chōfu · Setagaya · Tamaden · Aoyama · Roppongi · Akasaka · Kasogogaseki · Ginza · 9
Tama · Inagi · Suge · Komae · Sangenjaya · Meguro · Ebisu · Azabu · Minato · Tokyo Tower · Shiba · Hama Rikyu Garden · Harumi · TŌKYŌ · Tokyo Disneyland · Tokyo Disney Sea
Olympic Park · Komazawa · Shirogane · Sengakuji Temple · Rainbow Bridge · Port of Tokyo
Takaishi · Mampukuji · Mizonokuchi · Maginu · Futago-tamagaewaen · Gotanda · Ōsaki · Shinagawa · Wangan Expy. · 357
Ōkura · Sugō · Arima · Eda · Ōdana · Kedanaka · Ookayama · Jiyūgaoka · Ebara · Ōimachi · 15 · 357
Kamoshida · Chitose · Nakahara-Ku · Kūsbaji · Matuko · Ōmori · Shūbo Expy · Tokyo Bay
Machida · Takeshita · Yamada · Hiyoshi · Saiwai · Ōta · Kamata · Haneda · TOKYO-HANEDA INTL (HND)
Nagatsuta · 246 · Ichgao · Kachida · Minami-tsunashima · Ikegami · 131
Kanamori · Kawana · Ikebe · 152 · Kikuna · 132 · 409
Kamitsuruma · Tōkaichiba · Nippa · Ōsone · Kawasaki · East from Greenwich · Tokyo

CENTRAL TOKYO

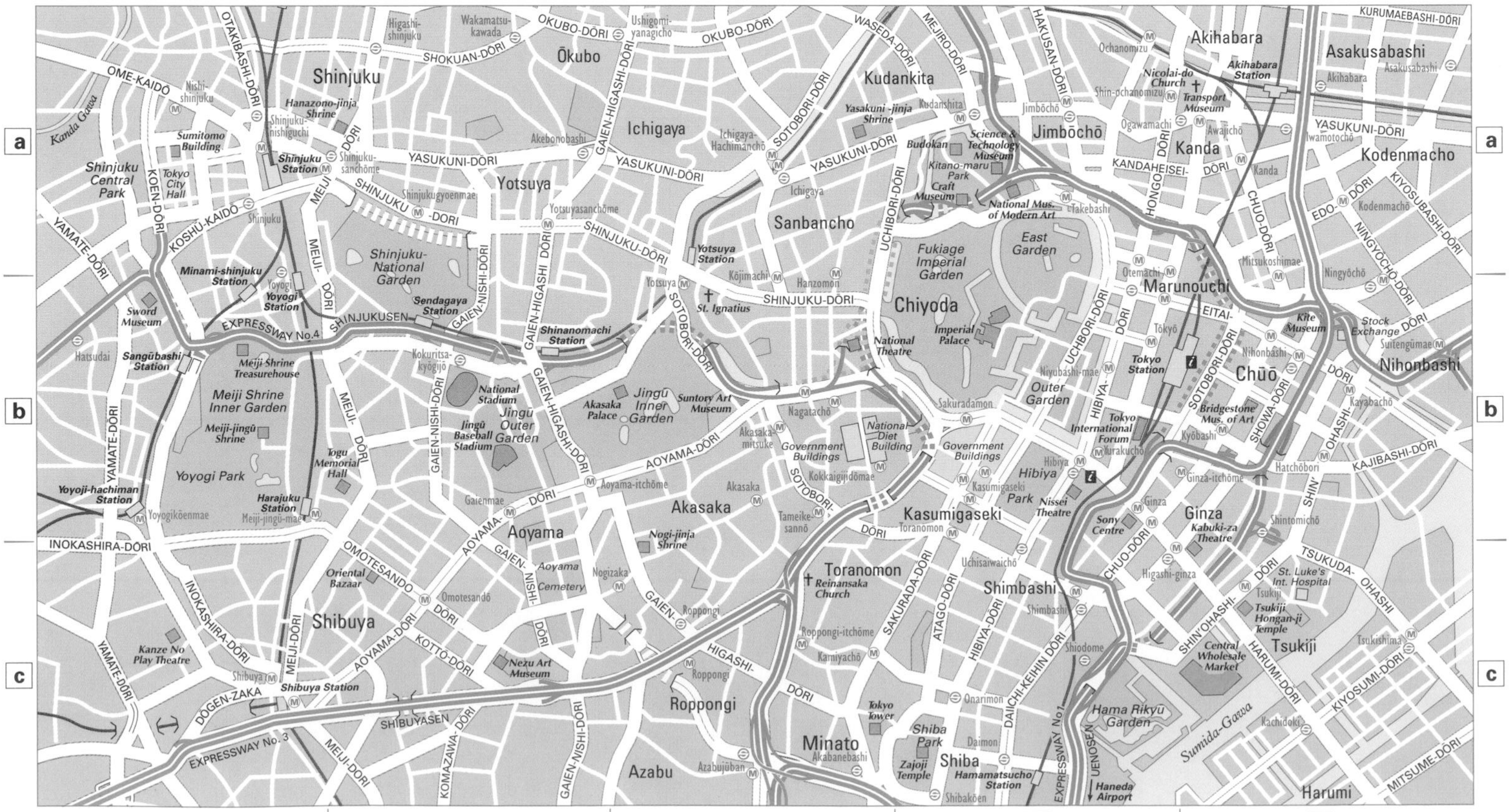

km 0 1
miles 0 0.5

OME-KAIDO · OTAKIBASHI-DORI · Higashi-shinjuku · Wakamatsu-kawada · OKUBO-DORI · Ōkubo · OKUBO-DORI · WASEDA-DORI · KURUMAEBASHI-DORI · Akihabara · Asakusabashi
Nishi-shinjuku · SHOKUAN-DORI · Ushigome-yanagicho · Kudankita · MEJIRO-DORI · HAKUSAN-DORI · Akihabara Station · Asakusabashi
Shinjuku · Hanazono-jinja Shrine · GAIEN-HIGASHI-DORI · Ichigaya · Yasukuni-jinja Shrine · Jimbōcho · Nicolai-do Church · Transport Museum · YASUKUNI-DORI
Kanda Creek · YAMATE-DORI · Sumitomo Building · Shinjuku-nishiguchi · Shinjuku Station · YASUKUNI-DORI · Ichigaya-Hachimancho · Budokan · Science & Technology Museum · Kanda · Kodenmacho
Shinjuku Central Park · Tokyo City Hall · Shinjuku-sanchōme · Yotsuya · Kitano-maru Park · National Mus. of Modern Art · Takebashi · KANDAHEISEI-DORI · CHUO-DORI
KOSHŪ-KAIDO · MEIJI-DORI · SHINJUKU-DORI · Sanbancho · UCHIBORI-DORI · Otemachi · Marunouchi · Stock Exchange · Nihonbashi
Minami-shinjuku Station · Shinjuku-National Garden · Yotsuya Station · Kōjimachi · Fukiage Imperial Garden · East Garden · Tokyo · EITAI
Sword Museum · Yoyogi Station · Sendagaya Station · St. Ignatius · Hanzōmon · Chiyoda · Imperial Palace · Tokyo Station · Chūō · Kite Museum
Sangūbashi Station · Shinanomachi Station · National Theatre · Outer Garden · Tokyo International Forum · Kyobashi · SHOWA-DORI
Meiji Shrine Treasurehouse · National Stadium · Akasaka Palace · Jingū Inner Garden · Suntory Art Museum · Nagatachō · Sakuradamon · Hibiya · Bridgestone Mus. of Art
Meiji Shrine Inner Garden · Jingū Baseball Stadium · Jingū Outer Garden · Nagatachō · National Diet Building · Government Buildings · HIBIYA · Hibiya · Ginza · KAJIBASHI-DORI
Togu Memorial Hall · Meiji-jingū Shrine · Akasaka-mitsuke · Kokkaigijidōmae · Government Buildings · Hibiya Park · Nissei Theatre · Hatchobori
Yoyogi Park · Harajuku Station · Meiji-jingū-mae · AOYAMA-DORI · Akasaka · SOTOBORI-DORI · Kasumigaseki · Nissei Theatre · Ginza-itchōme
INOKASHIRA-DORI · Yoyogi-hachiman Station · Aoyama · Nogi-jinja Shrine · Tameike-sannō · Sony Centre · Kabuki-za Theatre
Oriental Bazaar · OMOTESANDO · Aoyama Cemetery · Toranomon · SAKURADA-DORI · Shimbashi · Shintomichō
Shibuya · Nezu Art Museum · KOTTO-DORI · Omotesando · Reinanzaka Church · Atago Park · HIBIYA-DORI · Tsukiji · St. Luke's Int. Hospital
Kanze No Play Theatre · Nogizaka · Roppongi-itchōme · Kamiyachō · Tsukiji Hongan-ji Temple
Shibuya Station · DOGEN-ZAKA · AOYAMA-DORI · Roppongi · Tokyo Tower · DAICHI-KEIHIN-DORI · Central Wholesale Market · HARUMI-DORI
SHIBUYASEN · KOMAZAWA-DORI · DORI · Minato · Shiba Park · Hama Rikyu Garden · KIYOSUMI-DORI
EXPRESSWAY No.3 · MEIJI-DORI · Azabu · Azabujūban · Zōjōji Temple · Shiba · Hamamatsucho Station · Haneda Airport · Harumi · MITSUME-DORI

Toei Subway · Tokyo Metro

COPYRIGHT PHILIP'S

TEHRAN, IRAN

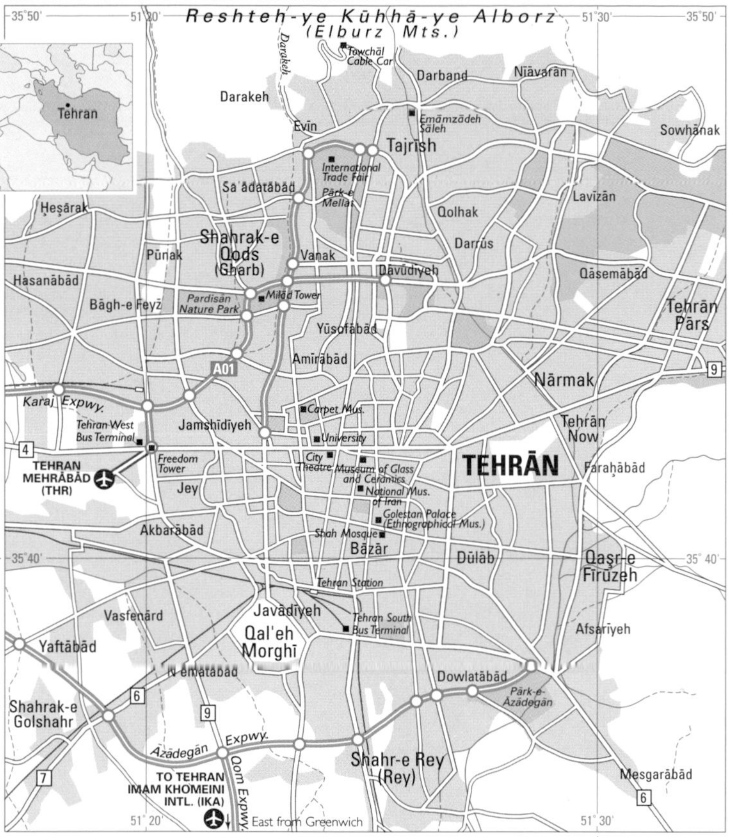

Reshteh-ye Kūhhā-ye Alborz
(Elburz Mts.)

Tehran

Towchāl Cable Car
Darakeh
Darband
Niāvarān
Evīn
Emāmzādeh Sāleh
Sowhānak
Tajrīsh
Sā'ādatābād
Park-e Mellat
International Trade Fair
Qolhak
Lavīzān
Shahrak-e Qods (Gharb)
Vanak
Darūs
Qāsemābād
Pūnak
Dāvūdīyeh
Tehrān Pārs
Hasanābād
Bāgh-e Feyz
Pardīsan Nature Park
Milād Tower
Yūsofābād
Karaj Expwy.
Narmak
Tehran-West Bus Terminal
A01
Amīrābād
Jamshīdīyeh
Carpet Mus.
University
Tehrān Now
TEHRAN MEHRĀBĀD (THR)
Freedom Tower
City Theatre
Museum of Glass and Ceramics
TEHRĀN
Jey
National Mus. of Iran
Farahābād
Akbarābād
Golestan Palace (Ethnographical Mus.)
Shah Mosque
Bāzār
Dūlāb
Qaṣr-e Fīrūzeh
Tehran Station
Vasfenārd
Javādīyeh
Tehran South Bus Terminal
Afsarīyeh
Qal'eh Morghī
N'emátábád
Dowlatābād
Pārk-e Azādegān
Yaftābād
Shahrak-e Golshahr
Āzādegān Expwy.
Qom Expwy.
Shahr-e Rey (Rey)
Mesgarābād
TO TEHRAN IMAM KHOMEINI INTL. (IKA)
East from Greenwich

CENTRAL TORONTO

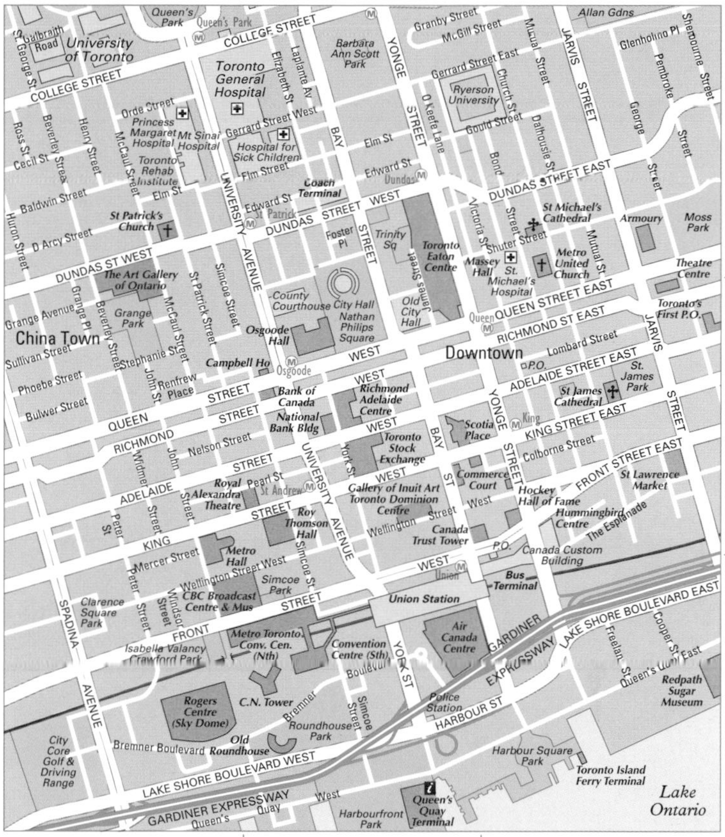

Queen's Park
COLLEGE STREET
University of Toronto
Barbara Ann Scott Park
Granby Street
McGill Street
Toronto General Hospital
Ryerson University
Gerrard Street East
Mutual Street
Jarvis Street
Glenholme Pl
Pembroke
Sherbourne Street
COLLEGE STREET
Orde Street
Princess Margaret Hospital
Mt Sinai Hospital
Gerrard Street West
Hospital for Sick Children
Elm St
Edward St
YONGE STREET
O'Keefe Lane
Bond
St Michael's Cathedral
George
Armoury
Moss Park
Cecil St
Baldwin Street
Toronto Rehab Institute
Film Centre
Coven Terminal
DUNDAS STREET EAST
D'Arcy Street
St Patrick's Church
Edward St
DUNDAS STREET WEST
Foster Pl
Trinty Sq
Toronto Eaton Centre
Massey Hall
St Michael's Hospital
St Michael's Church
Shuter Street
Theatre Centre
DUNDAS ST WEST
The Art Gallery of Ontario
BAY
DUNDAS STREET WEST
Elm St
Massey Hall
United Church
Toronto's First P.O.
China Town
Grange Avenue
County Courthouse
Grange Park
City Hall
Nathan Phillips Square
Old City Hall
QUEEN STREET EAST
RICHMOND ST EAST
St James Park
Sullivan Street
Osgoode Hall
Campbell Ho
Osgoode
Downtown
Lombard Street
St James Cathedral
Phoebe Street
QUEEN
WEST
YONGE
ADELAIDE STREET EAST
Bulwer Street
Renfrew Place
Bank of Canada
National Bank Bldg
Richmond Adelaide Centre
Scotia Place
KING STREET EAST
RICHMOND
STREET
Toronto Stock Exchange
Commerce Court
Colborne Street
ADELAIDE
STREET
Royal Alexandra Theatre
St Andrew
Gallery of Inuit Art
Toronto Dominion Centre
Hockey Hall of Fame
FRONT STREET EAST
KING
Rey Thomson Hall
Canada Trust Tower
Hummingbird Centre
The Esplanade
Mercer Street
Wellington
WEST
P.O.
St Lawrence Market
Metro Hall
Simcoe Park
Canada Custom Building
CBC Broadcast Centre & Mus
Union
Bus Terminal
Clarence Square Park
FRONT
STREET WEST
Union Station
GARDINER
LAKE SHORE BOULEVARD EAST
Isabella Valancy Crawford Park
Metro Toronto Conv. Cen. (Nth)
Convention Centre (Sth)
Air Canada Centre
Queen's Quay East
Rogers Centre (Sky Dome)
C.N. Tower
Bremner Blvd
Police Station
HARBOUR ST
Redpath Sugar Museum
City Core Golf & Driving Range
Bremner Boulevard Roundhouse
Old Roundhouse
Harbour Square Park
Toronto Island Ferry Terminal
LAKE SHORE BOULEVARD WEST
GARDINER EXPRESSWAY
Queen's Quay
Harbourfront Park
Queen's Quay Terminal
Lake Ontario

TORONTO, CANADA

Boyd Conservation Area
407
Metro Toronto Zoo
Little Rouge
Fairport
401
Rouge Hill
27
Humber
East Don
Markham
Brown
Glen Rouge Park
West Rouge
Vaughan
Thornhill
The Promenade
Concord
48
Agincourt
Malvern
401
Highland Creek
2A
Port Union
Pine Grove
Edgeley
Newtonbrook
Willowdale
Morningside Park
407
Fisherville
G. Ross Lord Park
11
East Don Parkland
Fairview Mall
Scarborough Town Centre
Bendale
Woburn
West Hill
Black Creek Pioneer Village
York University
Humber Summit
North York
Northmount
Lansing
404
Highland
Wexford
Eastpoint Park
Beaumonte Heights
Northwood Park
Black Creek
Armour Heights
York Mills
Don Mills
Scarborough
Cliffside
Thistletown
400
Downsview
Lawrence Heights
York Univ.
Wilket Creek Park
Ontario Science Centre
Danforth
Humberwood Park
427
Kipling Heights
Woodbine Centre
Rexdale
Humberlea
401
Yorkdale Shopping Centre
Sunnybrook Health Science Centre
Thorncliffe
Bluffers Park
Malton
Woodbine Race Track
Weston
11A
Forest Hill
Leaside
Dentonia Park
Scarborough Bluffs
27
York
Cedarvale Park
11
Casa Loma
East York
5
Birch Cliff
409
Humber Valley Village
Mount Dennis
Royal Ontario Museum
Don Valley Pkwy
2
Kew Gardens
401
Lambton Mills
Swansea
University of Toronto
Parliament Buildings
Riverdale Park
TORONTO LESTER B. PEARSON INTL. (YYZ)
Old City Hall
& Rogers Centre
Gardiner Expwy
Ashbridge's Bay Park
410
Hanlon
Etobicoke
Islington
Kingsway
High Park
Old Fort York
Parkdale
Union Sta.
TORONTO
Tommy Thompson Park
Markland Wood
427
Humber Bay
Exhibition Place
TORONTO CITY CENTRE (ISLAND)
Toronto Harbour
Burnhamthorpe
Summerville
5
Elizabeth
Humber Bay Park
Ontario Place
Island Park
10
New Toronto
Mimico
Way
Toronto Islands
403
Square One
Dixie Mall
Queen
Humber College
Samuel Smith Park
Gibraltar Point
LAKE   ONTARIO
Toronto
Mississauga
Cooksville
Long Branch
West from Greenwich

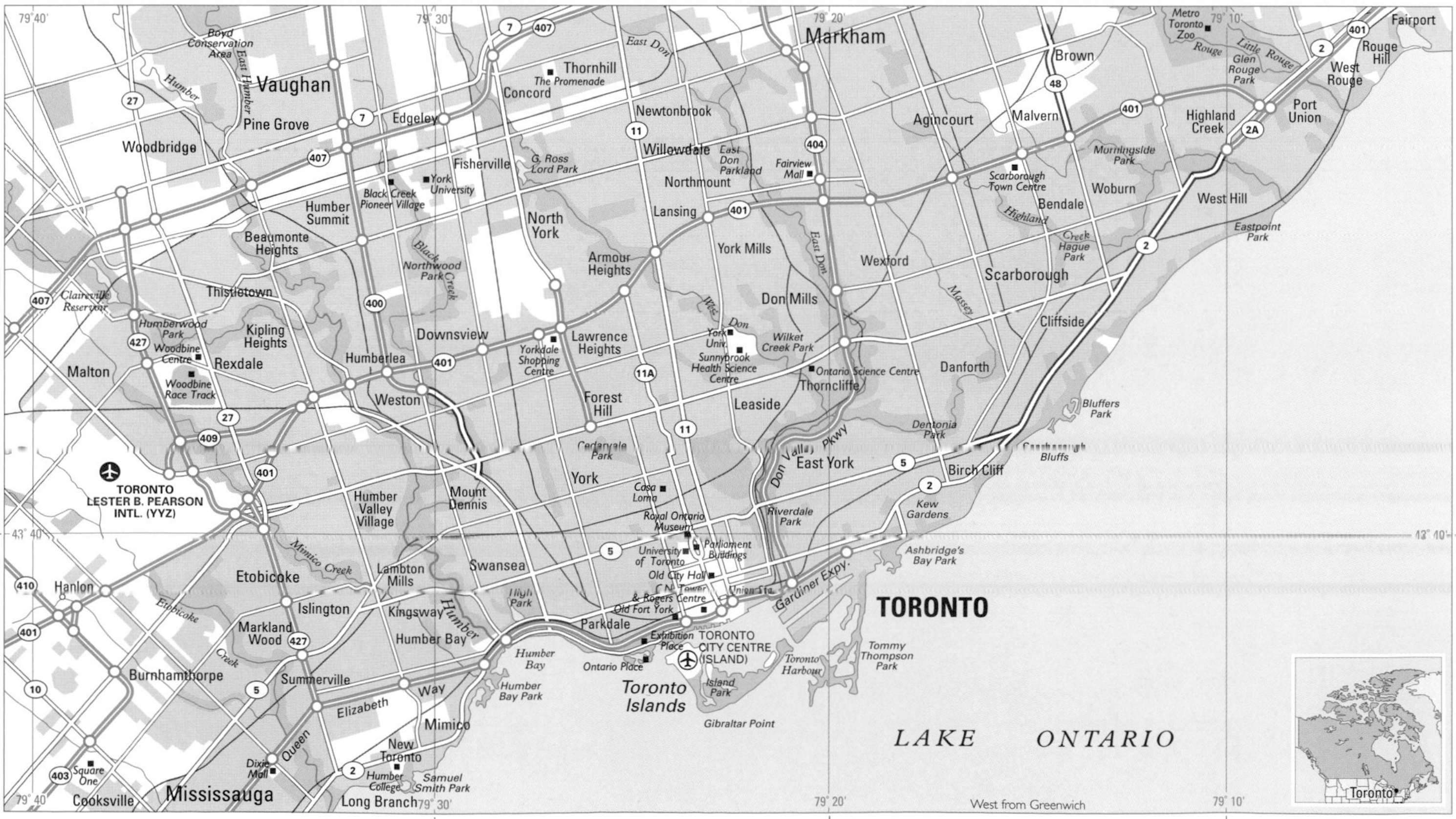

427 Provincial route numbers

COPYRIGHT PHILIP'S

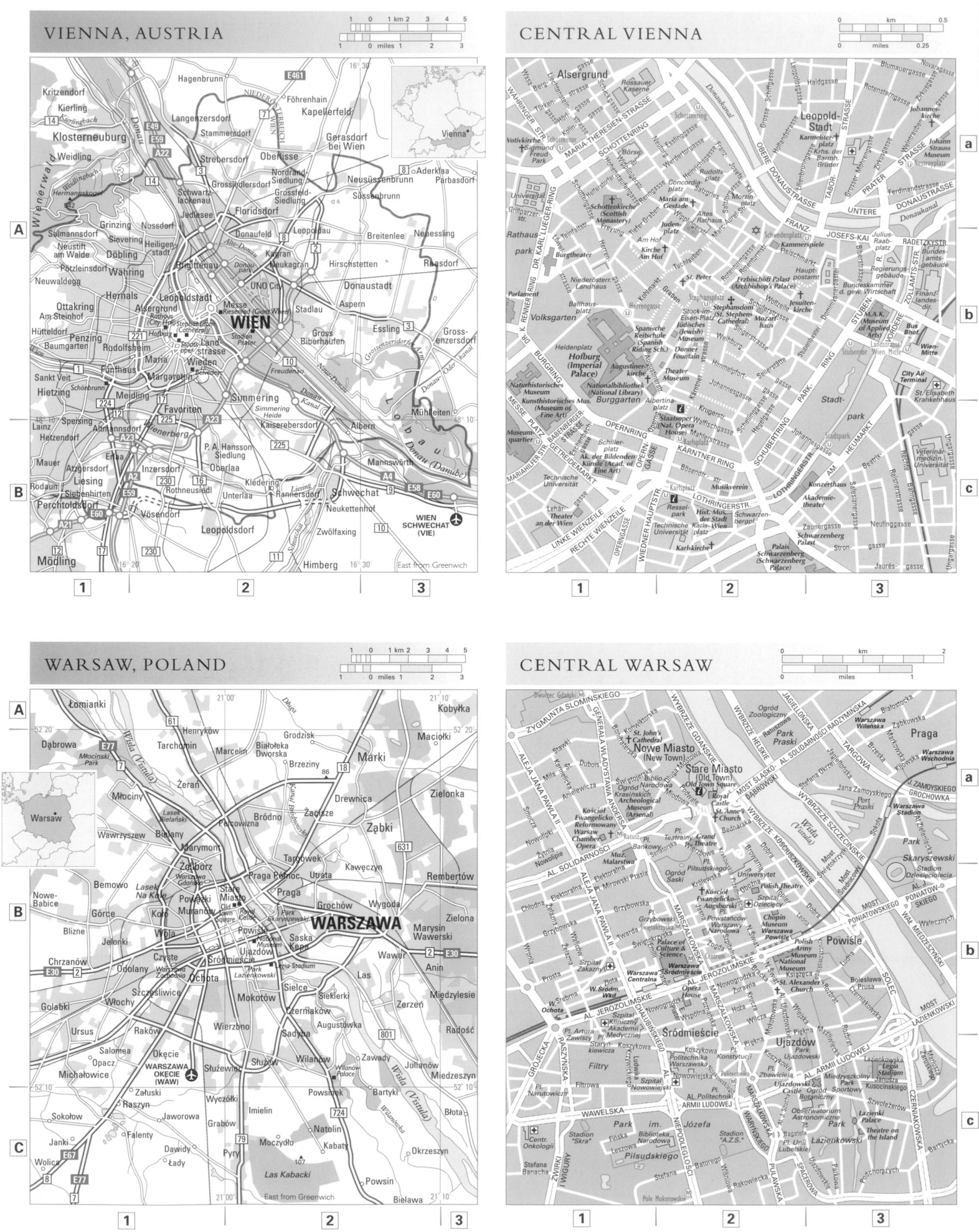

VIENNA, AUSTRIA

CENTRAL VIENNA

WARSAW, POLAND

CENTRAL WARSAW

COPYRIGHT PHILIP'S

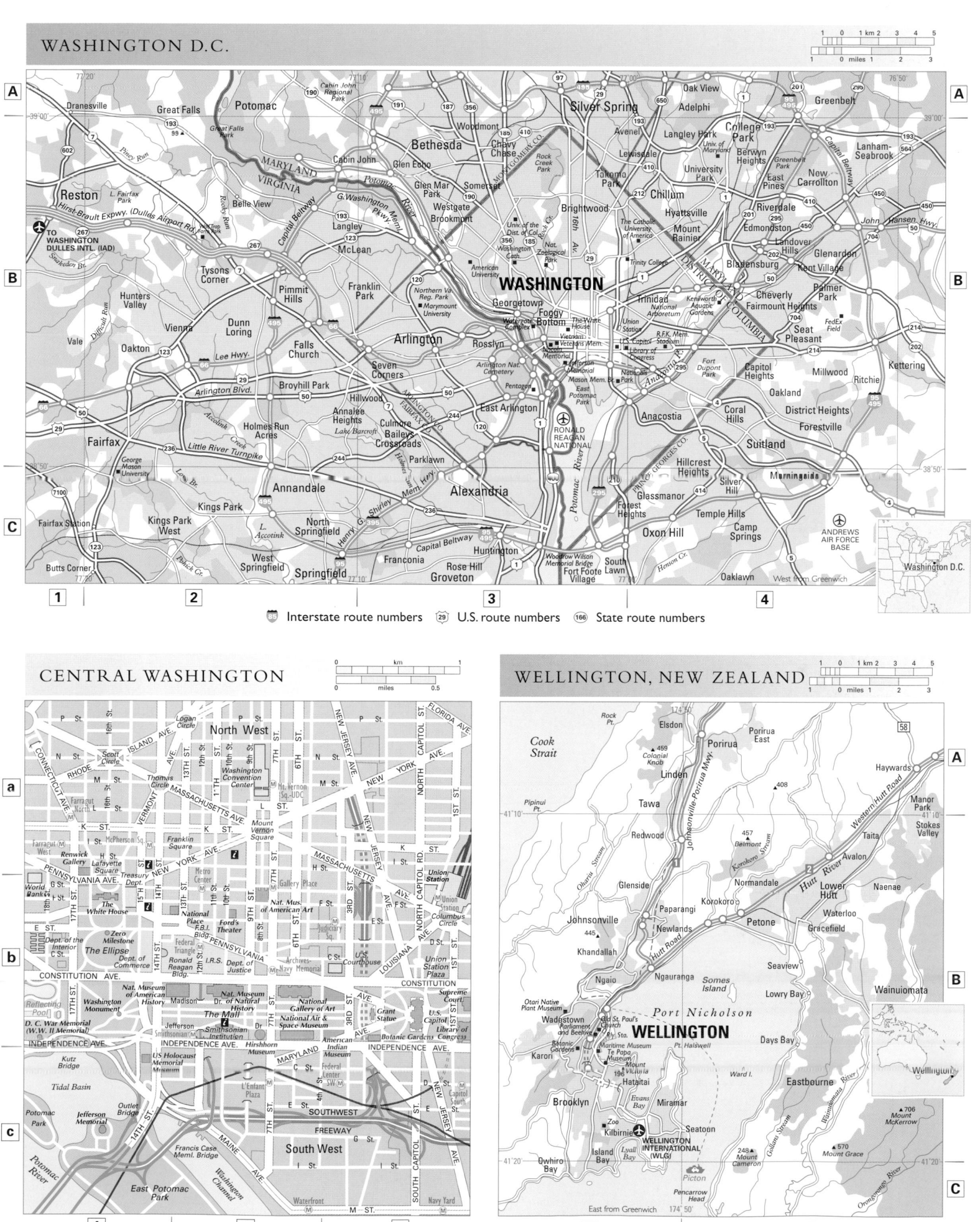

WASHINGTON D.C.

Interstate route numbers • U.S. route numbers • State route numbers

CENTRAL WASHINGTON

WELLINGTON, NEW ZEALAND

COPYRIGHT PHILIP'S

INDEX TO CITY MAPS

The index contains the names of all the principal places and features shown on the City Maps. Each name is followed by an additional entry in italics giving the name of the City Map within which it is located.

The number in bold type which follows each name refers to the number of the City Map page where that feature or place will be found.

The letter and figure which are immediately after the page number give the grid square on the map within which the feature or place is situated.

The letter represents the latitude and the figure the longitude. The full geographic reference is provided in the border of the City Maps.

The location given is the centre of the city, suburb or feature and is not necessarily the name. Rivers, canals and roads are indexed to their name. Rivers carry the symbol → after their name.

An explanation of the alphabetical order rules and a list of the abbreviations used are to be found at the beginning of the World Map Index.

A

Aalām *Baghdad* 3 B2
Aalsmeer *Amsterdam* 2 B1
Abbey Wood *London* 15 B4
Abcoude *Amsterdam* 2 B2
Âbdin *Cairo* 7 A2
Abeno *Osaka* 23 B2
Aberdeen *Hong Kong* 12 B1
Aberdour *Edinburgh* 11 A2
Aberdour Castle *Edinburgh* 11 A2
Abfanggraben → *Munich* 21 A3
Ablon-sur-Seine *Paris* 24 B3
Abramtsevo *Moscow* 19 B3
Abu Dis *Jerusalem* 13 B2
Abû en Numrus *Cairo* 7 B2
Abu Ghosh *Jerusalem* 13 B1
Acassuso *Buenos Aires* 7 A2
Accotink, L. *Washington* 33 C2
Accotink Cr. → *Washington* 33 B2
Achères *Paris* 24 A1
Acília *Rome* 26 C1
Aclimação *São Paulo* 27 B2
Acropolis *Athens* 2 B2
Acton *London* 15 A2
Açúcar, Pão de *Rio de Janeiro* 25 B2
Ada Beja *Lisbon* 16 A1
Adams Park *Atlanta* 3 B2
Addiscombe *London* 15 B3
Adelphi *Washington* 33 A4
Aderklaa *Vienna* 32 A3
Adler Planetarium *Chicago* 9 B3
Admiralteyskaya Storona *St. Petersburg* 27 B2
Åffori *Milan* 19 A2
Aflandshage *Copenhagen* 8 B3
Afsarīyeh *Tehran* 31 B2
Agboyi Cr. → *Lagos* 14 A2
Ågerup *Copenhagen* 8 A1
Ågesta *Stockholm* 29 B2
Aghia Marina *Athens* 2 C3
Aghia Paraskevi *Athens* 2 A2
Aghios Dimitrios *Athens* 2 B2
Aghios Ioannis Rendis *Athens* 2 B1
Agincourt *Toronto* 31 A3
Agra Canal *Delhi* 10 B2
Agricola Oriental *Mexico City* 18 B2
Água Espraiada → *São Paulo* 27 B2
Agualva-Cacem *Lisbon* 16 A1
Ahrensfelde *Berlin* 5 A4
Ahuntsic *Montreal* 20 A1
Ai → *Osaka* 23 A2
Aigremont *Paris* 24 A1
Air View Park *Singapore* 28 A2
Airport West *Melbourne* 18 A1
Ajegunle *Lagos* 14 B2
Aji *Osaka* 23 A1
Ajuda *Lisbon* 16 A1
Akalla *Stockholm* 29 A1
Akasaka *Tokyo* 30 A3
Akbarābād *Tehran* 31 A2
Akershus Slott *Oslo* 23 A3
Al 'Azamīyah *Baghdad* 3 A2
Al Quds = Jerusalem *Jerusalem* 13 B2
Al-Walaja *Jerusalem* 13 B1
Alaguntan *Lagos* 14 B2
Alameda *San Francisco* 26 B3
Alameda Memorial State Beach Park *San Francisco* 26 B3
Albern *Vienna* 32 B2
Albert Park *Melbourne* 18 B1
Alberton *Johannesburg* 13 B2
Albertslund *Copenhagen* 8 B2
Alcantara *Lisbon* 16 A1
Alcatraz I. *San Francisco* 26 B2
Alcobendas *Madrid* 17 A2
Alcorcón *Madrid* 17 B1
Aldershof *Berlin* 5 B4
Aldo Bonzi *Buenos Aires* 7 C1
Aleksandrovskoye *St. Petersburg* 27 B2
Alexander Nevsky Abbey *St. Petersburg* 27 B2
Alexandra *Johannesburg* 13 A2
Alexandra *Singapore* 28 B2
Alexandria *Washington* 33 C3
Alfortville *Paris* 24 B3
Algés *Lisbon* 16 A1
Algiers *New Orleans* 21 B2
Alhambra *Los Angeles* 16 B4
Alibey → *Istanbul* 12 B1
Alibey Barajı *Istanbul* 12 B1
Alibeyköy *Istanbul* 12 B1
Alimos *Athens* 2 B2
Alipur *Kolkata* 14 B1
Allach *Munich* 21 A1
Allambie Heights *Sydney* 29 A2
Allermuir Hill *Edinburgh* 11 B2
Allstate Arena *Chicago* 9 A1
Allston *Boston* 6 A2
Almada *Lisbon* 16 A2
Almagro *Buenos Aires* 7 B2
Almargem do Bispo *Lisbon* 16 A1
Almirante G. Brown, Parque *Buenos Aires* 7 C2
Almon *Jerusalem* 13 B2
Almond → *Edinburgh* 11 B2
Alna *Oslo* 23 A4
Alnsjøen *Oslo* 23 A4
Alperton *London* 15 A2
Alpine *New York* 22 A2
Alrode *Johannesburg* 13 B2
Alsemberg *Brussels* 6 B2
Alsergrund *Vienna* 32 A2
Alsip *Chicago* 9 C2
Älsten *Stockholm* 29 B1
Älta *Stockholm* 29 B3
Altadena *Los Angeles* 16 A4
Alte-Donau → *Vienna* 32 A2
Alter Finkenkrug *Berlin* 5 A1
Altes Rathaus *Munich* 21 B2
Altglienicke *Berlin* 5 B4
Altlandsberg *Berlin* 5 A5
Altlandsberg Nord *Berlin* 5 A5
Altmannsdorf *Vienna* 32 B1
Alto da Boa Vista *Rio de Janeiro* 25 B1
Alto da Moóca *São Paulo* 27 B2
Alto do Pina *Lisbon* 16 A2
Altona *Melbourne* 18 B1
Alvik *Stockholm* 29 B1
Alvin Callendar Naval Air Station *New Orleans* 21 B2
Älvsjo *Stockholm* 29 B2
Älvvik *Stockholm* 29 A3
Am Hasenbergl *Munich* 21 A2
Am Steinhof *Vienna* 32 A1
Am Wald *Munich* 21 B2
Ama Keng *Singapore* 28 A2
Amadora *Lisbon* 16 A1
Amagasaki *Osaka* 23 A1
Amager *Copenhagen* 8 B3
Amāl Qādisiya *Baghdad* 3 B2
Amalienborg Slot *Copenhagen* 8 A3
Amata *Milan* 19 A1
Ambelokipi *Athens* 2 B2
Ameixoeira *Lisbon* 16 A2
América *São Paulo* 27 B1
American Police Hall of Fame *Miami* 18 B2
American Univ. *Washington* 33 B3
Amin *Baghdad* 3 B2
Aminadav *Jerusalem* 13 B1
Amīrābād *Tehran* 31 A2
Amora *Lisbon* 16 B2
Amoreira *Lisbon* 16 A1
Amper → *Munich* 21 A1
Amstel-Drecht-Kanaal *Amsterdam* 2 B2
Amstelveen *Amsterdam* 2 B2
Amsterdam *Amsterdam* 2 A2
Amsterdam ✈ (AMS) *Amsterdam* 2 B1
Amsterdam-Rijnkanaal *Amsterdam* 2 B3
Amsterdam Zuidoost *Amsterdam* 2 B2
Amsterdamse Bos *Amsterdam* 2 B1
Anacosta → *Washington* 33 B4
Anacostia *Washington* 33 B4
Anadoluhisarı *Istanbul* 12 B2
Anadolukavağı *Istanbul* 12 A2
Anata *Jerusalem* 13 B2
Ancol *Jakarta* 12 A1
'Andalus *Baghdad* 3 B1
Andaraí *Rio de Janeiro* 25 B1
Anderlecht *Brussels* 6 A1
Anderson Park *Atlanta* 3 B2
Andingmen *Beijing* 4 B2
Ang Mo Kio *Singapore* 28 A3
Ängby *Stockholm* 29 A1
Angel I. *San Francisco* 26 A2
Angel Island State Park ⌓ *San Francisco* 26 A2
Angke, Kali → *Jakarta* 12 A1
Angyalföld *Budapest* 7 A2
Anik *Mumbai* 20 A2
Anin *Warsaw* 32 B2
Anjou *Montreal* 20 A2
Annalee Heights *Washington* 33 B2
Annandale *Washington* 33 C2
Anne Frankhuis *Amsterdam* 2 A2
Antony *Paris* 24 B2
Aoyama *Tokyo* 30 B3
Ap Lei Chau *Hong Kong* 12 B1
Apapa *Lagos* 14 B2
Apapa Quays *Lagos* 14 B2
Apelacão *Lisbon* 16 A2
Apopka, L. *Orlando* 23 A1
Apoquindo *Santiago* 27 B2
Apterkarskiy Ostrov *St. Petersburg* 27 B2
Ar Kazimiyah *Baghdad* 3 B1
Ar Ram *Jerusalem* 13 A2
Ara → *Tokyo* 30 A4
Arakawa *Tokyo* 30 A3
Arany-hegyi-patak → *Budapest* 7 A2
Aravaca *Madrid* 17 B1
Arbataash *Baghdad* 3 A1
Arc de Triomphe *Paris* 24 A2
Arcadia *Los Angeles* 16 B4
Arcueil *Paris* 24 B2
Arese *Milan* 19 A1
Arganzuela *Madrid* 17 B1
Argenteuil *Paris* 24 A2
Argiroupoli *Athens* 2 B2
Argonne Forest *Chicago* 9 C1
Arima *Tokyo* 30 B2
Arlanda, Stockholm ✈ (ARN) *Stockholm* 29 A1
Arlington *Boston* 6 A1
Arlington *Washington* 33 B3
Arlington Heights *Boston* 6 A1
Arlington Nat. Cemetery *Washington* 33 B3
Armação *Rio de Janeiro* 25 B2
Armadale *Melbourne* 18 B2
Armour Heights *Toronto* 31 A2
Arncliffe *Sydney* 29 B1
Arnold Arboretum *Boston* 6 B2
Árpádföld *Budapest* 7 A3
Arrentela *Lisbon* 16 B2
Arroyo Seco Park *Los Angeles* 16 B3
Årsta *Stockholm* 29 B2
Artane *Dublin* 10 A2
Artas *Jerusalem* 13 B2
Arthur's Seat *Edinburgh* 11 B3
Arts, Place des *Montreal* 20 A2
As Shawawra *Jerusalem* 13 B2
Asagaya *Tokyo* 30 A2
Asahi *Osaka* 23 A2
Asakusa *Tokyo* 30 A3
Asati *Kolkata* 14 C1
Aschheim *Munich* 21 A3
Ascot Vale *Melbourne* 18 A1
Ashbridge's Bay Park *Toronto* 31 B3
Ashburn *Chicago* 9 C2
Ashburton *Melbourne* 18 B2
Ashfield *Sydney* 29 B1
Ashford *London* 15 B1
Ashtown *Dublin* 10 A2
Askisto *Helsinki* 11 B1
Askrikefjärden *Stockholm* 29 A3
Asnières *Paris* 24 A2
Aspern *Vienna* 32 A2
Assago *Milan* 19 B1
Assendelft *Amsterdam* 2 A1
Assiano *Milan* 19 B1
Astoria *New York* 22 B2
Astrolabe Park *Sydney* 29 B2
Atarot *Jerusalem* 13 A2
Atarot ✈ (JRS) *Jerusalem* 13 A2
Atghara *Kolkata* 14 B2
Athens = Athina *Athens* 2 B2
Athina *Athens* 2 B2
Athina ✈ (ATH) *Athens* 2 A3
Athínai = Athina *Athens* 2 B2
Athis-Mons *Paris* 24 B3
Athlone *Cape Town* 8 A2
Atholl *Johannesburg* 13 A2
Atīfiya *Baghdad* 3 A2
Atişalen *Istanbul* 12 B1
Atlanta *Atlanta* 3 B2
Atlanta Hartsfield Int. ✈ (ATL) *Atlanta* 3 C2
Atlanta Zoo *Atlanta* 3 B2
Atomium *Brussels* 6 A2
Attiki *Athens* 2 A2
Atzgersdorf *Vienna* 32 B1
Aubervilliers *Paris* 24 A3
Aubing *Munich* 21 B1
Auburndale *Boston* 6 A1
Auchendinny *Edinburgh* 11 B2
Auckland Park *Johannesburg* 13 B2
Auderghem *Brussels* 6 B2
Augustówka *Warsaw* 32 B2
Aulnay-sous-Bois *Paris* 24 A3
Aurelio *Rome* 26 B1
Ausîm *Cairo* 7 A1
Austerlitz, Gare d' *Paris* 24 A3
Austin *Chicago* 9 B2
Avalon *Wellington* 33 B2
Avedøre *Copenhagen* 8 B2
Avellaneda *Buenos Aires* 7 C2
Avenel *Washington* 33 B4
Avondale *Chicago* 9 B2
Avondale *New Orleans* 21 B1
Avondale Heights *Melbourne* 18 A1
Avtovo *St. Petersburg* 27 B1
Ayazağa *Istanbul* 12 B1
Ayer Chawan, Pulau *Singapore* 28 B2
Ayer Merbau, Pulau *Singapore* 28 B2
Azabu *Tokyo* 30 B3
Azcapotzalco *Mexico City* 18 B1
Azteca, Estadia *Mexico City* 18 C2
Azucar, Cerro Pan de *Santiago* 27 A1

B

Baambrugge *Amsterdam* 2 B2
Baba Channel *Karachi* 13 B1
Baba I. *Karachi* 13 B1
Babarpur *Delhi* 10 A2
Babushkin *Moscow* 19 A3
Back B. *Mumbai* 20 B1
Baclaran *Manila* 17 B2
Bacoor *Manila* 17 C1
Bacoor B. *Manila* 17 C1
Badalona *Barcelona* 4 A2
Badhoevedorp *Amsterdam* 2 A1
Badli *Delhi* 10 A1
Bærum *Oslo* 23 A2
Bağcılar *Istanbul* 12 B1
Bággio *Milan* 19 B1
Bāgh-e-Feyz *Tehran* 31 A1
Baghdād *Baghdad* 3 A2
Baghdād al Muthana ✈ (BGW) *Baghdad* 3 B2
Baghdad Int. ✈ (SDA) *Baghdad* 3 B1
Bagmari *Kolkata* 14 B2
Bagneux *Paris* 24 B2
Bagnolet *Paris* 24 A3
Bagsværd *Copenhagen* 8 A2
Bagsværd Sø *Copenhagen* 8 A2
Baguiati *Kolkata* 14 B2
Bagumbayan *Manila* 17 C2
Baha'i Temple *Chicago* 9 A2
Bahçeköy *Istanbul* 12 A1
Bahçelıevler *Istanbul* 12 B1
Bahtîm *Cairo* 7 A2
Baile Átha Cliath = Dublin *Dublin* 10 A2
Baileys Crossroads *Washington* 33 B3
Bailly *Paris* 24 A1
Bairro Lopes *Lisbon* 16 A2
Baisha *Guangzhou* 11 B2
Baiyun *Guangzhou* 11 A2
Baiyun Hill *Guangzhou* 11 B2
Baiyun Mountain Scenic Area *Guangzhou* 11 A2
Bakırköy *Istanbul* 12 C1
Bal Harbor *Miami* 18 A2
Balara *Manila* 17 B2
Baldia *Karachi* 13 A1
Baldoyle *Dublin* 10 A3
Baldwin, L. *Orlando* 23 A3
Baldwin Hills *Los Angeles* 16 B2
Baldwin Hills Res. *Los Angeles* 16 B2
Balgowlah *Sydney* 29 A2
Balgowlah Heights *Sydney* 29 A2
Balham *London* 15 B3
Bali *Kolkata* 14 B1
Baliganja *Kolkata* 14 B2
Balingsnäs *Stockholm* 29 B2
Balingsta *Stockholm* 29 B2
Balintawak *Manila* 17 B1
Ballerup *Copenhagen* 8 A2
Ballinteer *Dublin* 10 B2
Ballyboden *Dublin* 10 B2
Ballybrack *Dublin* 10 B3
Ballyfermot *Dublin* 10 A1
Ballymorefinn Hill *Dublin* 10 B1
Ballymun *Dublin* 10 A2
Balmain *Sydney* 29 B2
Baluhati *Kolkata* 14 B1
Balvanera *Buenos Aires* 7 B2
Balwyn *Melbourne* 18 A2
Balwyn North *Melbourne* 18 A2
Banática *Lisbon* 16 A1
Bandra *Mumbai* 20 A1
Bandra Pt. *Mumbai* 20 A1
Bang Kapi *Bangkok* 3 B2
Bang Na *Bangkok* 3 B2
Bangbae *Seoul* 27 C1
Bangkhen *Bangkok* 3 A2
Bangkok *Bangkok* 3 B2
Bangkok Don Muang Int. ✈ (BKK) *Bangkok* 3 A2
Bangkok Noi *Bangkok* 3 B1
Bangkok Yai *Bangkok* 3 B1
Banglo *Kolkata* 14 B1
Bangrak *Bangkok* 3 B2
Bangsu *Bangkok* 3 B2
Banks, C. *Sydney* 29 C2
Banksmeadow *Sydney* 29 B2
Banstala *Kolkata* 14 B2
Bantra *Kolkata* 14 B1
Baoshan *Shanghai* 28 A1
Bar Giyora *Jerusalem* 13 B1
Barahanagar *Kolkata* 14 B2
Barajas *Madrid* 17 B2
Barajas, Madrid ✈ (MAD) *Madrid* 17 B2
Barakpur *Kolkata* 14 A2
Barcarena *Lisbon* 16 A1
Barcarena, Rib. de → *Lisbon* 16 A1
Barcelona *Barcelona* 4 A2
Barcelona-Prat ✈ (BCN) *Barcelona* 4 B1
Barcroft, L. *Washington* 33 B3
Barking *London* 15 A4
Barkingside *London* 15 A4
Barnes *London* 15 B2
Barnet *London* 15 A2
Barra Andai *Karachi* 13 B2
Barra Funda *São Paulo* 27 B2
Barracas *Buenos Aires* 7 B2
Barrackpur = Barakpur *Kolkata* 14 A2
Barranco *Lima* 14 B2
Barreiro *Lisbon* 16 B2
Barreto *Rio de Janeiro* 25 B2
Bartala *Kolkata* 14 B1
Barton Park *Sydney* 29 B1
Bartyki *Warsaw* 32 C2
Basus *Cairo* 7 A2
Batanagar *Kolkata* 14 B1
Bath Beach *New York* 22 C1
Bath I. *Karachi* 13 B2
Batir *Jerusalem* 13 B1
Batok, Bukit *Singapore* 28 A2
Battersea *London* 15 B3
Bauman *Moscow* 19 B3
Baumgarten *Vienna* 32 A1
Bay, L. *Orlando* 23 A2
Bay Harbor Islands *Miami* 18 A2
Bay Hill *Orlando* 23 B1
Bay Ridge *New York* 22 C1
Bayit Va-Gan *Jerusalem* 13 B2
Bayonne *New York* 22 B1
Bayou Boeuf *New Orleans* 21 B1
Bayou Segnette State Park ⌓ *New Orleans* 21 B2
Bayrampaşa *Istanbul* 12 B1
Bayshore *San Francisco* 26 B2
Bayt Lahm *Jerusalem* 13 B2
Bayview *San Francisco* 26 B2
Bāzār *Tehran* 31 A2
Beacon Hill *Hong Kong* 12 A2
Beato *Lisbon* 16 A2
Beaumont *Dublin* 10 A2
Beaumonte Heights *Toronto* 31 A1
Bebek *Istanbul* 12 B2
Běchovice *Prague* 25 B3
Beck L. *Chicago* 9 A1
Beckenham *London* 15 B3
Beckton *London* 15 A4
Becontree *London* 15 A4
Beddington Corner *London* 15 B3
Bedford *Boston* 6 A1
Bedford Park *Chicago* 9 C2
Bedford Park *New York* 22 A2
Bedford Stuyvesant *New York* 22 B2
Bedford View *Johannesburg* 13 B2
Bedok *Singapore* 28 B3
Bedok, Res. *Singapore* 28 A3
Beersel *Brussels* 6 B1
Behala *Kolkata* 14 B1
Bei Hai *Beijing* 4 B2
Beicai *Shanghai* 28 B2
Beijing *Beijing* 4 B1
Beit Duqu *Jerusalem* 13 A1
Beit Ghur at-Taht *Jerusalem* 13 A1
Beit Ghur el-Fawqa *Jerusalem* 13 A1
Beit Hanina *Jerusalem* 13 B2
Beit Ij'za *Jerusalem* 13 A1
Beit Iksa *Jerusalem* 13 B2
Beit I'nan *Jerusalem* 13 A1
Beit Jala *Jerusalem* 13 B2
Beit Lekhem = Bayt Lahm *Jerusalem* 13 B2
Beit Liqya *Jerusalem* 13 A1
Beit Nekofa *Jerusalem* 13 B1
Beit Sahur *Jerusalem* 13 B2
Beit Sofafa *Jerusalem* 13 B2
Beit Surik *Jerusalem* 13 B1
Beit Ur al-Fawqa *Jerusalem* 13 A1
Beit Zayit *Jerusalem* 13 B1
Beitaipingzhuan *Beijing* 4 B1
Beitar Ilit *Jerusalem* 13 B1
Beitin *Jerusalem* 13 A2
Beitsun *Guangzhou* 11 B2
Beitunya *Jerusalem* 13 A2
Beixing Jing Park *Shanghai* 28 B1
Békásmegyer *Budapest* 7 A2
Bekkelaget *Oslo* 23 A3
Bekkestua *Oslo* 23 A2
Bel Air *Los Angeles* 16 B2
Bela Vista *São Paulo* 27 B2
Bélanger *Montreal* 20 A1
Belas *Lisbon* 16 A1
Beleghata *Kolkata* 14 B2
Belém *Lisbon* 16 A1
Belém, Torre de *Lisbon* 16 A1
Belènzinho *São Paulo* 27 B2
Belgachiya *Kolkata* 14 B2
Belgharia *Kolkata* 14 B2
Belgrano *Buenos Aires* 7 B2
Bell *Los Angeles* 16 C3
Bell Gardens *Los Angeles* 16 C4
Bellavista *Lima* 14 B2
Bellavista *Santiago* 27 C2
Belle Harbor *New York* 22 C2
Belle Isle *Orlando* 23 B2
Belle View *Washington* 33 B2
Bellingham *London* 15 B3
Bellwood *Chicago* 9 B1
Belmont *Boston* 6 A1
Belmont *London* 15 A2
Belmont, Mt. *Wellington* 33 B2
Belmont Cragin *Chicago* 9 B2
Belmont Harbor *Chicago* 9 B3
Belmore *Sydney* 29 B1
Belur *Kolkata* 14 B2
Belvedere *Atlanta* 3 B3
Belvedere *London* 15 B4
Belvedere *San Francisco* 26 A2
Belyayevo Bogorodskoye *Moscow* 19 C2
Bemowo *Warsaw* 32 B1
Benaki Museum *Athens* 2 B2
Bendale *Toronto* 31 A3
Benefica *Rio de Janeiro* 25 B1
Benfica *Lisbon* 16 A1
Benitez Int. ✈ (SCL) *Santiago* 27 B1
Benito Juárez, Int. ✈ (MEX) *Mexico City* 18 B2
Bensonhurst *New York* 22 C2
Berchem-Ste-Agathe *Brussels* 6 A1
Berg am Laim *Munich* 21 B2
Bergenfield *New York* 22 A2
Bergham *Munich* 21 B2
Bergvliet *Cape Town* 8 B1
Beri *Barcelona* 4 A1
Berkeley *San Francisco* 26 A3
Berlin *Berlin* 5 A3
Berlin Dom *Berlin* 5 A3
Berlin Tegel ✈ (TXL) *Berlin* 5 A2
Bermondsey *London* 15 B3
Bernabeu, Estadio *Madrid* 17 B1
Bernal Heights *San Francisco* 26 B2
Berwyn *Chicago* 9 B2
Berwyn Heights *Washington* 33 B4
Besiktas *Istanbul* 12 B2
Besós → *Barcelona* 4 A2
Bessie, L. *Orlando* 23 B1
Bet Horon *Jerusalem* 13 A1
Bethesda *Washington* 33 B3
Bethlehem = Bayt Lahm *Jerusalem* 13 B2
Bethnal Green *London* 15 A3
Betor *Kolkata* 14 B1
Beulah *Orlando* 23 A1
Beulah, L. *Orlando* 23 A1
Beverley Hills *Sydney* 29 B1
Beverley Park *Sydney* 29 B1
Beverly *Chicago* 9 C3
Beverly Arts Center *Chicago* 9 C2
Beverly Glen *Los Angeles* 16 B2
Beverly Hills *Los Angeles* 16 B2
Beverly Hills -Morgan Park Historic District *Chicago* 9 C2
Bexley *Sydney* 29 B1
Bexley □ *London* 15 B4
Bexleyheath *London* 15 B4
Beykoz *Istanbul* 12 B2
Beylerbeyi *Istanbul* 12 B2
Beyoğlu *Istanbul* 12 B1
Bezons *Paris* 24 A2
Bezuidenhout Park *Johannesburg* 13 B2
Bhadrakali *Kolkata* 14 A2
Bhalswa *Delhi* 10 A2
Bhambo Khan Qarmati *Karachi* 13 B2
Bhatsala *Kolkata* 14 B1
Bhawanipur *Kolkata* 14 B2
Bhendkhal *Mumbai* 20 B2
Bhuleshwar *Mumbai* 20 B1
Białołeka Dworska *Warsaw* 32 B2
Bicentennial Park *Los Angeles* 16 B4
Bicentennial Park *Sydney* 29 B1
Bickley *London* 15 B4
Bicutan *Manila* 17 C2
Bidhan Nagar *Kolkata* 14 B2
Bidu *Jerusalem* 13 B1
Bielany *Warsaw* 32 B1
Bielawa *Warsaw* 32 C2
Biesdorf *Berlin* 5 A4
Bièvre → *Paris* 24 B1
Bièvres *Paris* 24 B2
Big Sand Lake *Orlando* 23 B2
Bilston *Edinburgh* 11 B2
Binacayan *Manila* 17 C1
Binondo *Manila* 17 B1
Bintaro Jaya *Jakarta* 12 B1
Bir Nabala *Jerusalem* 13 A2
Birak el Kiyam *Cairo* 7 A1
Birch Cliff *Toronto* 31 A3
Birkenstein *Berlin* 5 A5
Birkholz *Berlin* 5 A4
Birkholzaue *Berlin* 5 A4
Birrarung Park *Melbourne* 18 A2
Biscayne Park *Miami* 18 A2
Bishop Lavis *Cape Town* 8 A2
Bishopscourt *Cape Town* 8 A1
Bispebjerg *Copenhagen* 8 A3
Bissonet Plaza *New Orleans* 21 A1
Bittsevsky Forest Park *Moscow* 19 C2
Björknas *Stockholm* 29 B3
Black Cr. → *Toronto* 31 A2
Black Creek Pioneer Village *Toronto* 31 A1
Blackfen *London* 15 B4
Blackheath *London* 15 B4
Blackrock *Dublin* 10 B2
Bladensburg *Washington* 33 B4
Blair Village *Atlanta* 3 C2
Blairgowrie *Johannesburg* 13 A2
Blake House *Boston* 6 B2
Blakehurst *Sydney* 29 B1
Blakstad *Oslo* 23 B1
Blanche, L. *Orlando* 23 B1
Blankenburg *Berlin* 5 A3
Blankenfelde *Berlin* 5 A3
Blizne *Warsaw* 32 B1
Błota *Warsaw* 32 C3
Blue Island *Chicago* 9 D2
Blue Mosque = Sultanahme Camil *Istanbul* 12 B1
Bluebell *Dublin* 10 B1
Bluff Hd. *Hong Kong* 12 B2
Bluffers Park *Toronto* 31 A3
Blumberg *Berlin* 5 A4
Blunt Pt. *San Francisco* 26 A2
Blutenberg *Munich* 21 B1
Blylaget *Oslo* 23 B3
Boa Vista, Alto do *Rio de Janeiro* 25 B1
Boardwalk *New York* 22 C3
Boavista *Lisbon* 16 A2
Bobigny *Paris* 24 A3
Bocanegra *Lima* 14 B2
Boedo *Buenos Aires* 7 B2
Bogenhausen *Munich* 21 B2
Bogorodskoye *Moscow* 19 B3
Bogota *New York* 22 A1
Bogstadvatnet *Oslo* 23 A2
Bohnsdorf *Berlin* 5 B4
Bois-Colombes *Paris* 24 A2
Bois-d'Arcy *Paris* 24 B1
Boissy-St-Léger *Paris* 24 B4
Boldinasco *Milan* 19 B1
Bøler *Oslo* 23 A4
Bollate *Milan* 19 A1
Bollebeek *Brussels* 6 A1
Bollensdorf *Berlin* 5 A5
Bollmora *Stockholm* 29 B3
Bolshaya Okhta *St. Petersburg* 27 B2
Bolton *Atlanta* 3 B2
Bom Retiro *São Paulo* 27 B2
Bombay = Mumbai *Mumbai* 20 B2
Bondi *Sydney* 29 B2
Bondy *Paris* 24 A3
Bondy, Forêt de *Paris* 24 A4
Bonifacio Monument *Manila* 17 B1
Bonnabel Place *New Orleans* 21 A2
Bonneuil-sur-Marne *Paris* 24 B4
Bonnington *Edinburgh* 11 B1
Bonnyrigg and Lasswade *Edinburgh* 11 B3
Bonsucesso *Rio de Janeiro* 25 B1
Bonteheuwel *Cape Town* 8 A2
Boo *Stockholm* 29 A3
Booterstown *Dublin* 10 B2
Borisovo *Moscow* 19 C3
Borle *Mumbai* 20 A2
Boronia Park *Sydney* 29 A1
Bosmont *Johannesburg* 13 B1
Bosön *Stockholm* 29 A3
Bosporus = İstanbul Boğazı *Istanbul* 12 B2
Bostancı *Istanbul* 12 C2
Boston *Boston* 6 A2
Boston Common *Boston* 6 A2
Boston Logan Int. ✈ (BOS) *Boston* 6 A2
Botafogo *Rio de Janeiro* 25 B1
Botany *Sydney* 29 B2
Botany B. *Sydney* 29 B2
Botany Bay △ *Sydney* 29 B2
Botič → *Prague* 25 B3
Botica Sete *Lisbon* 16 A1
Boucherville *Montreal* 20 A3
Boucherville, Îs. de *Montreal* 20 A3
Bougival *Paris* 24 A1
Boulder Pt. *Hong Kong* 12 B1
Boulogne, Bois de *Paris* 24 A2
Boulogne-Billancourt *Paris* 24 A2
Bourg-la-Reine *Paris* 24 B2
Bouviers *Paris* 24 B1
Bovenkerk *Amsterdam* 2 B2
Bovenkerker Polder *Amsterdam* 2 B2
Bovisa *Milan* 19 A2
Bow *London* 15 A3
Boyacıköy *Istanbul* 12 B2
Boyd Conservation Area *Toronto* 31 A1
Boyle Heights *Los Angeles* 16 B3
Braepark *Edinburgh* 11 B2
Braid *Edinburgh* 11 B2
Bramley *Johannesburg* 13 A2
Brandeis Univ. *Boston* 6 A1
Brandenburger Tor *Berlin* 5 A3
Brani, Pulau *Singapore* 28 B3
Branik *Prague* 25 B2
Brännkyrka *Stockholm* 29 B2
Brás *São Paulo* 27 B2
Brasilândia *São Paulo* 27 A1
Brateyevo *Moscow* 19 C3
Braybrook *Melbourne* 18 A1
Brázdim *Prague* 25 A3
Breakheart Reservation *Boston* 6 A2
Brede *Copenhagen* 8 A3
Breezy Point *New York* 22 C2
Breitenlee *Vienna* 32 A3
Breña *Lima* 14 B2
Brent □ *London* 15 A2
Brent Res. *London* 15 A2
Brentford *London* 15 B2
Brentwood *Los Angeles* 16 B2
Brentwood Park *Los Angeles* 16 B2
Brera *Milan* 19 B2
Bresso *Milan* 19 A2
Brevik *Stockholm* 29 A3
Břevnov *Prague* 25 B2
Brickyard, The *Chicago* 9 B2
Bridge City *New Orleans* 21 B2
Bridgeport *Chicago* 9 B3
Bridgetown *Cape Town* 8 A2
Bridgeview *Chicago* 9 C2
Brighton *Boston* 6 A2
Brighton *Melbourne* 18 B1
Brighton Beach *New York* 22 C2
Brighton-Le-Sands *Sydney* 29 B1
Brighton Park *Chicago* 9 C2
Brightwood *Washington* 33 B3
Brigittenau *Vienna* 32 A2
Brimbank Park *Melbourne* 18 A1
Brisbane *San Francisco* 26 B2
Britz *Berlin* 5 B3
Brixton *London* 15 B3
Broadmeadows *Melbourne* 18 A1
Broadmoor *San Francisco* 26 B2
Broadview *Chicago* 9 B1
Brockley *London* 15 B3
Bródno *Warsaw* 32 B2
Bródnowski, Kanal *Warsaw* 32 B2
Broek *Amsterdam* 2 A2
Bromley □ *London* 15 B4
Bromley Common *London* 15 B4
Bromma *Stockholm* 29 A1
Bromma ✈ (BMA) *Stockholm* 29 A1
Brøndby Strand *Copenhagen* 8 B2
Brøndbyøster *Copenhagen* 8 B2
Brøndbyvester *Copenhagen* 8 B2
Brondesbury *London* 15 A2
Brønnøya *Oslo* 23 A2
Brønshøj *Copenhagen* 8 A2
Bronxville *New York* 22 A3
Brookfield *Chicago* 9 C1
Brookhaven *Atlanta* 3 A2
Brookline *Boston* 6 B2
Brooklyn *Cape Town* 8 A1
Brooklyn *New York* 22 C2
Brooklyn *Wellington* 33 B1
Brooklyn Heights *New York* 22 B2
Brookmont *Washington* 33 B3
Brossard *Montreal* 20 B3
Brou-sur-Chantereine *Paris* 24 A4
Brown *Toronto* 31 A3
Broyhill Park *Washington* 33 B2
Brughério *Milan* 19 A2
Brunswick *Melbourne* 18 A1
Brussegem *Brussels* 6 A1
Brussel *Brussels* 6 A2
Brussel ✈ (BRU) *Brussels* 6 A2
Brussels = Brussel *Brussels* 6 A2
Bruxelles = Brussel *Brussels* 6 A2
Bruzzano *Milan* 19 A2
Bry-sur-Marne *Paris* 24 A4
Bryan, L. *Orlando* 23 B2
Bryanston *Johannesburg* 13 A1
Bryn *Oslo* 23 A1
Brzeziny *Warsaw* 32 B2
Bubeneč *Prague* 25 B2
Buc *Paris* 24 B1
Buchenhain *Munich* 21 B1
Buchholz *Berlin* 5 A3
Buckhead *Atlanta* 3 A2
Buckingham Palace *London* 15 A3
Buckow *Berlin* 5 B3
Bucktown *New Orleans* 21 A2
Buda *Budapest* 7 A2
Buda Castle = Budaváripalota *Budapest* 7 A2
Budafok *Budapest* 7 B2
Budaörs *Budapest* 7 B1
Budapest *Budapest* 7 B2
Budapest ✈ (BUD) *Budapest* 7 B3
Budatétény *Budapest* 7 B2
Budaváripalota *Budapest* 7 A2
Buddinge *Copenhagen* 8 A3
Buena Vista *San Francisco* 26 B2
Buenos Aires *Buenos Aires* 7 B2
Buenos Aires Ezeiza ✈ (EZE) *Buenos Aires* 7 C1
Bufalotta *Rome* 26 B2
Bugio *Lisbon* 16 B1
Buiksloot *Amsterdam* 2 A2
Buitenveldert *Amsterdam* 2 B2
Buizingen *Brussels* 6 B1
Bukhansan *Seoul* 27 B1
Bukit Panjang Nature Reserve *Singapore* 28 A2
Bukit Timah Nature Reserve *Singapore* 28 A2
Bukum, Pulau *Singapore* 28 B2
Bûlâq *Cairo* 7 A2
Bule *Manila* 17 C2
Bulim *Singapore* 28 A2
Bullen Park *Melbourne* 18 A2
Bund, The *Shanghai* 28 B1
Bundoora North *Melbourne* 18 A2
Bundoora Park *Melbourne* 18 A2
Bunker Hill Memorial *Boston* 6 A2
Bunker I. *Karachi* 13 B1
Bunkyō *Tokyo* 30 A3
Bunnefjorden *Oslo* 23 A3
Buona Vista Park *Singapore* 28 B2
Burbank *Chicago* 9 C2
Burbank *Los Angeles* 16 A3
Burden, L. *Orlando* 23 B1
Burlington *Boston* 6 A1
Burnham Park *Chicago* 9 C3
Burnham Park Harbor *Chicago* 9 B3
Burnhamthorpe *Toronto* 31 B1
Burnt Oak *London* 15 A2
Burntisland *Edinburgh* 11 A2
Burnwynd *Edinburgh* 11 B1
Burqa *Jerusalem* 13 A2
Burtus *Cairo* 7 A1
Burudvatn *Oslo* 23 A2
Burwood *Sydney* 29 B1
Bushwick *New York* 22 B2
Bushy Park *London* 15 B1
Butantã *São Paulo* 27 B1
Butcher I. *Mumbai* 20 B2
Butler, L. *Orlando* 23 B1
Butts Corner *Washington* 33 C2
Büyükdere *Istanbul* 12 B2
Byculla *Mumbai* 20 B2
Bygdøy *Oslo* 23 A3
Bywater *New Orleans* 21 B2

C

C.B.S. Fox Studios *Los Angeles* 16 B2
C.N.N. Center *Atlanta* 3 B2
C.N. Tower *Toronto* 31 B2
Caballito *Buenos Aires* 7 B2
Cabin John *Washington* 33 B2
Cabin John Regional Park ⌓ *Washington* 33 A2
Cabinteely *Dublin* 10 B3
Cabra *Dublin* 10 A2
Cabuçú de Baixo → *São Paulo* 27 A1
Cabuçú de Cima → *São Paulo* 27 A2
Cachan *Paris* 24 B2
Cachoeira, Rib. da → *São Paulo* 27 B1
Cacilhas *Lisbon* 16 A2
Cahuenga Park *Los Angeles* 16 B3
Cain, L. *Orlando* 23 B2
Cairo = El Qâhira *Cairo* 7 A2
Cairo Int. ✈ (CAI) *Cairo* 7 A3
Caju *Rio de Janeiro* 25 B1
Čakovice *Prague* 25 B3
Calcutta = Kolkata *Kolkata* 14 B2
California Inst. of Tech. *Los Angeles* 16 B4
California Los Angeles, Univ. of *Los Angeles* 16 B2
California State Univ. *Los Angeles* 16 B3
Callao *Lima* 14 B2
Caloocan *Manila* 17 B1
Calumet L. *Chicago* 9 C3
Calumet Park *Chicago* 9 C3
Calumet Sag Channel → *Chicago* 9 C2
Calvairate *Milan* 19 B2
Camarate *Lisbon* 16 A2
Camaroes *Lisbon* 16 A1
Camberwell *London* 15 B3
Camberwell *Melbourne* 18 B2
Cambridge *Boston* 6 A2

Cambuci São Paulo 27 B2
Cameron □ London 15 A3
Cameron, Mt. Wellington 33 B2
Çamlıca Istanbul 12 B2
Camp Springs Washington 33 C4
Campamento Madrid 17 B1
Campbellfield Melbourne 18 A1
Camperdown Sydney 29 B2
Campo, Casa de Madrid 17 B1
Campo F.C. Barcelona Barcelona 4 A1
Campo Grande Lisbon 16 A2
Campo Pequeño Lisbon 16 A2
Campolide Lisbon 16 A2
Camps Bay Cape Town 8 A1
C'an San Joan Barcelona 4 A2
Cañacao B. Manila 17 C1
Canarsie New York 22 C2
Candiac Montreal 20 B3
Caneças Lisbon 16 A1
Canillas Madrid 17 B2
Canillejas Madrid 17 B2
Canning Town London 15 A4
Canteras de Vallecas Madrid 17 B2
Canterbury Melbourne 18 A2
Canterbury Sydney 29 B1
Canton = Guangzhou Guangzhou 11 B2
Caoheijing Shanghai 28 B1
Capão Redondo São Paulo 27 B1
Caparica Lisbon 16 A2
Caparica, Costa da Lisbon 16 B1
Cape Flats Cape Town 8 B2
Cape Town Cape Town 8 A1
Cape Town Int. ✕ (CPT) Cape Town 8 A2
Capitol Heights Washington 33 B4
Captain Cook Bridge Sydney 29 C1
Captain Cook Landing Place Park Sydney 29 C2
Capuchos Lisbon 16 B1
Carabanchel Alto Madrid 17 B1
Carabanchel Bajo Madrid 17 B1
Carapachay Buenos Aires 7 B1
Caraza Buenos Aires 7 C2
Carlidad Manila 17 C1
Carioca, Sa. da Rio de Janeiro 25 B1
Carlstadt New York 22 A1
Carlton Melbourne 18 A1
Carmen de Huechuraba Santiago 27 B1
Carmen de la Legua Lima 14 B2
Carnaxide Lisbon 16 A1
Carnegie Melbourne 18 B2
Carnide Lisbon 16 A1
Carol City Miami 18 A1
Carrascal Santiago 27 B1
Carrickmines Dublin 10 B3
Carrières-sous-Bois Paris 24 A1
Carrières-sous-Poissy Paris 24 A1
Carrières-sur-Seine Paris 24 A2
Carrigeen B. Dublin 10 A3
Cartierville Montreal 20 A1
Casa Loma Toronto 31 A2
Casa Verde São Paulo 27 A1
Casál Morena Rome 26 C2
Casalotti Rome 26 B1
Cascade Heights Atlanta 3 B2
Castèl di Leva Rome 26 C2
Castèl Sant'Angelo Rome 26 B1
Castleknock Dublin 10 A1
Castleton Corners New York 22 C1
Cataouatche, L. New Orleans 21 B1
Catete Rio de Janeiro 25 B1
Catford London 15 B3
Catherine, L. Orlando 23 B2
Caulfield Melbourne 18 B2
Cavite Manila 17 C1
Caxias Lisbon 16 A1
Cebeci Istanbul 12 B1
Cecchignola Rome 26 C2
Cecilienhof, Schloss Berlin 5 B1
Cedar Grove Atlanta 3 C3
Cedarvale Park Toronto 31 A2
Cempaka Putih Jakarta 12 B2
Çengelköy Istanbul 12 B2
Cengkareng Jakarta 12 A1
Centennial Olympic Park Atlanta 3 B2
Centennial Park Sydney 29 B2
Center Hill Atlanta 3 B2
Centocelle Rome 26 B2
Central, Gare Montreal 20 B2
Central Park New York 22 B2
Century City Los Angeles 16 B2
Cerdanyola del Vallès Barcelona 4 A1
Cerillos Santiago 27 B1
Cerro de la Estrella △ Mexico City 18 B2
Cerro de los Angeles Madrid 17 C1
Cerro Navia Santiago 27 B1
Cesano Boscone Milan 19 B1
Cesate Milan 19 A1
Cha Kwo Ling Hong Kong 12 B2
Chacarita Buenos Aires 7 B2
Chadwell Heath London 15 A4
Chai Chee Singapore 28 B3
Chai Wan Hong Kong 12 B2
Chai Wan Kok Hong Kong 12 A1
Chakdaha Kolkata 14 C1
Chamartín Madrid 17 B1
Chamberí Madrid 17 B1
Chambourcy Paris 24 A1
Champigny-sur-Marne Paris 24 B4
Champlain, Pont Montreal 20 B2
Champs-sur-Marne Paris 24 A4
Chamrail Kolkata 14 B1
Chanakyapuri Delhi 10 B2
Chanditala Kolkata 14 A1
Changfeng Park Shanghai 28 B1
Changhai = Shanghai Shanghai 28 B2
Changi Singapore 28 A3
Changi, Singapore ✕ (SIN) Singapore 28 A3
Changning Shanghai 28 B1
Chantereine Paris 24 A4
Chantian Guangzhou 11 A2
Chaoyang Beijing 4 B2
Chaoyangmen Beijing 4 B2
Chapelizod Dublin 10 A1
Chapultepec, Bosque de Mexico City 18 B1
Chapultepec, Castillo de Mexico City 18 B1
Charenton-le-Pont Paris 24 B3
Charleroi, Kanal de → Brussels 6 B1
Charles Bridge = Karlův most Prague 25 B2
Charles Gates Dawes House Chicago 9 A2
Charlestown Boston 6 A2
Charlottenburg Berlin 5 A2
Charlottenburg, Schloss Berlin 5 A2
Charlottenlund Copenhagen 8 A3
Charlton London 15 B4
Charneca Lisbon 16 A2
Charneca Lisbon 16 B1
Chase, L. Orlando 23 B1
Châteaufort Paris 24 B1
Châtenay-Malabry Paris 24 B2
Chatham Chicago 9 C3
Châtillon Paris 24 B2
Chatou Paris 24 A1
Chatpur Kolkata 14 B2
Chatswood Sydney 29 A2
Chatuchak Bangkok 3 B2
Chatuchak Park Bangkok 3 B2
Chauki Karachi 13 A1
Chavarria Lima 14 B2
Chaville Paris 24 B2
Chayang Seoul 27 B2
Chelles Paris 24 A4
Chelles, Canal de Paris 24 A4
Chells-le-Pin ✕ Paris 24 A4
Chelsea Boston 6 A2
Chelsea London 15 B2
Chembur Mumbai 20 A2
Chengshousi Beijing 4 C2
Chennevières-sur-Marne Paris 24 B4
Cheongdam Seoul 27 B2
Cheonho Seoul 27 B2
Cheops Cairo 7 B1
Chertanovka → Moscow 19 C2
Chertanovo Moscow 19 C2
Cheryomushki Moscow 19 B2
Chestnut Hill Boston 6 B1
Cheung Sha Wan Hong Kong 12 A1
Cheverly Washington 33 B4
Chevilly-Larue Paris 24 B3
Cheviot Hills Los Angeles 16 B2
Chevy Chase Washington 33 B3
Chhatrapati Shivaji, Mumbai ✕ (BOM) Mumbai 20 A2
Chia Keng Singapore 28 A3
Chiaravalle Milanese Milan 19 B2
Chicago Chicago 9 B3
Chicago, Univ. of Chicago 9 C3
Chicago Harbor Chicago 9 B3
Chicago Lawn Chicago 9 C2
Chicago-Midway ✕ (MDW) Chicago 9 C2
Chicago O'Hare Int. ✕ (ORD) Chicago 9 B1
Chicago Ridge Chicago 9 C2
Chicago River, North Branch → Chicago 9 B2
Chicago Sanitary and Ship Canal Chicago 9 C2
Chicago State Univ. Chicago 9 C3
Chicago Zoo Chicago 9 B1
Chienzui Guangzhou 11 A3
Chik Sha Hong Kong 12 B2
Child's Hill London 15 A2
Chile, Univ. de Santiago 27 B2
Chilla Saroda Delhi 10 B2
Chillum Washington 33 B4
Chilly-Mazarin Paris 24 B2
Chingupota Kolkata 14 C1
Chinna Cr. → Karachi 13 B2
Chiquihuite, Cerro Mexico City 18 A2
Chislehurst London 15 B4
Chiswick London 15 B2
Chiswick House London 15 B2
Chitose Tokyo 30 B2
Chitralada Palace Bangkok 3 B2
Chiyoda Tokyo 30 A3
Choa Chu Kang Singapore 28 A2
Chodov u Prahy Prague 25 B3
Chōfu Tokyo 30 B2
Choisy-le-Roi Paris 24 B3
Cholupice Prague 25 C2
Chom Thong Bangkok 3 B1
Chong Pang Singapore 28 A2
Chongwen Beijing 4 B2
Chorrillos Lima 14 C2
Chowpatty Beach Mumbai 20 B1
Christianshavn Copenhagen 8 A3
Chrzanów Warsaw 32 B1
Chuen Lung Hong Kong 12 A1
Chuk Kok Hong Kong 12 A2
Chulalongkorn Univ. Bangkok 3 B2
Chuō Tokyo 30 A3
Church End London 15 A2
Church of our Lady = Frauenkirche Munich 21 B2
Churchtown Dublin 10 B2
Ciampino Rome 26 C2
Ciampino ✕ (CIA) Rome 26 C2
Cicero Chicago 9 B2
Cilandak Jakarta 12 B1
Cilincing Jakarta 12 A2
Ciliwung → Jakarta 12 B2
Čimice Prague 25 A2
Cinecittà Rome 26 B2
Cinisello Bálsamo Milan 19 A2
Cinkota Budapest 7 A3
Cipete Jakarta 12 B1
Città degli Studi Milan 19 B2
Città del Vaticano = Vatican City ■ Rome 26 B1
City, The London 15 A3
City Hall = Rådhus Oslo 23 A3
City Hall = Stadshuset Stockholm 29 B2
City of the Dead Cairo 7 A2
City Park New Orleans 21 A2
City Terrace Los Angeles 16 B3
Ciudad de México Mexico City 18 B2
Ciudad Deportiva Mexico City 18 B2
Ciudad Fin de Semana Madrid 17 B2
Ciudad General Belgrano Buenos Aires 7 C1
Ciudad Lineál Madrid 17 B2
Ciudad Satélite Mexico City 18 A1
Ciudad Universitaria Buenos Aires 7 B2
Ciudad Universitaria Mexico City 18 C1
Claireville Res. Toronto 31 A1
Clamart Paris 24 B2
Clapham London 15 B3
Clapton London 15 A3
Claremont Cape Town 8 A1
Clayhall London 15 A4
Clear, L. Orlando 23 A2
Clermiston Edinburgh 11 B2
Clichy Paris 24 A2
Clichy-sous-Bois Paris 24 A4
Cliffside Toronto 31 A3
Cliffside Park New York 22 B2
Clifton Cape Town 8 A1
Clifton Karachi 13 B2
Clifton New York 22 C1
Clifton Beach Karachi 13 B2
Cliftondale Boston 6 A2
Cloghran Dublin 10 A2
Clonskeagh Dublin 10 B2
Clontarf Dublin 10 A2
Clontarf Sydney 29 A2
Clovelly Sydney 29 B2
Cobras, I. das Rio de Janeiro 25 B2
Coburg Melbourne 18 A1
Cocotá Rio de Janeiro 25 A1
Cœuilly Paris 24 B4
Coina Lisbon 16 B2
Coker Lagos 14 B2
Colaba Mumbai 20 B1
Colaba Pt. Mumbai 20 B1
Colegiales Buenos Aires 7 B2
Colindale London 15 A2
Colinton Edinburgh 11 B2
College Park Atlanta 3 C2
College Park Washington 33 B4
College Point New York 22 B2
Collégien Paris 24 A4
Collier Row London 15 A4
Colliers Wood London 15 B2
Colma San Francisco 26 B2
Colney Hatch London 15 A3
Cologno Monzese Milan 19 A2
Colombes Paris 24 A2
Colonia Güell Barcelona 4 A1
Colonial Knob Wellington 33 A1
Colosseo Rome 26 B1
Colosseum = Colosseo Rome 26 B1
Combault Paris 24 B4
Comércio, Praça do Lisbon 16 A2
Commerce Los Angeles 16 B4
Conceição, I. da Rio de Janeiro 25 B2
Conchalí Santiago 27 B2
Concord Sydney 29 B1
Concord Toronto 31 A2
Concorde, Place de la Paris 24 A2
Concorezzo Milan 19 A2
Condet Jakarta 12 A2
Coney Island New York 22 C2
Congonhas São Paulo ✕ (CGH) São Paulo 27 B2
Conley → Atlanta 3 C3
Connaught Place Delhi 10 B2
Consolação São Paulo 27 B2
Constantia Cape Town 8 B1
Constitución Buenos Aires 7 B2
Constitution Atlanta 3 B2
Convention Center Los Angeles 16 B3
Conway Orlando 23 B2
Conway, L. Orlando 23 B2
Coogee Sydney 29 B2
Cooksville Toronto 31 B1
Coolock Dublin 10 A2
Copacabana Rio de Janeiro 25 B1
Copenhagen = København Copenhagen 8 A2
Coral Gables Miami 18 B2
Coral Hills Washington 33 B4
Corcovado, Cristo Redentar Rio de Janeiro 25 B1
Corduff Dublin 10 A1
Cormano Milan 19 A2
Cornaredo Milan 19 A1
Córsico Milan 19 B1
Corstorphine Edinburgh 11 B2
Corviale Rome 26 B1
Coslada Madrid 17 B2
Cossigny Paris 24 B4
Cotao Lisbon 16 A1
Côte-St-Luc Montreal 20 B2
Cotunduba, I. de Rio de Janeiro 25 B2
Coubron Paris 24 A4
Countryside Chicago 9 C1
County Art Museum Los Angeles 16 B2
Courbevoie Paris 24 A2
Courtry Paris 24 A4
Cowley London 15 A1
Coyoacán Mexico City 18 B2
Craighall Park Johannesburg 13 A2
Craiglockhart Edinburgh 11 B2
Craigmillar Edinburgh 11 B3
Cramond Edinburgh 11 B2
Cramond Bridge Edinburgh 11 B1
Cramond I. Edinburgh 11 B2
Cranford London 15 B1
Crawford Cape Town 8 A2
Crayford London 15 B5
Creekmouth London 15 A4
Crescent, L. Orlando 23 A1
Crescenzago Milan 19 A2
Cressely Paris 24 B1
Cresskill New York 22 A2
Créteil Paris 24 B3
Cricklewood London 15 A2
Cristo Redentor, Corcovado Rio de Janeiro 25 B1
Crockenhill London 15 B4
Croissy-Beaubourg Paris 24 B4
Croissy-sur-Seine Paris 24 A1
Crosby Johannesburg 13 B1
Crosne Paris 24 B3
Cross I. Mumbai 20 B2
Crouch End London 15 A3
Crown Mine Johannesburg 13 B1
Crows Nest Sydney 29 A2
Croydon London 15 B3
Croydon Park Sydney 29 B1
Cruagh Mt. Dublin 10 B2
Crumlin Dublin 10 B2
Cruz de Pau Lisbon 16 B2
Crystal Palace London 15 B3
Csepel Budapest 7 B2
Csepelsziget Budapest 7 B2
Csillaghegy Budapest 7 A2
Csillagtelep Budapest 7 B2
Csömör Budapest 7 A3
Csömöri-patak → Budapest 7 A3
Cuatro Vientos Madrid 17 B1
Cuauhtémoc Mexico City 18 B2
Cuban Museum Miami 18 B2
Cubao Manila 17 B2
Çubuklu Istanbul 12 B2
Cudahy Los Angeles 16 C3
Cuicuilco, Pirámide de Mexico City 18 C1
Culmore Washington 33 B3
Culver City Los Angeles 16 B2
Cupecé → São Paulo 27 B1
Currie Edinburgh 11 B2
Cusago Milan 19 B1
Cusano Milanino Milan 19 A2
Cutler Park Boston 6 B1
Çuvuşabaşı → Istanbul 12 B1
Cuwei Beijing 4 B1
Cypress Hills New York 22 B2
Cypress Park Los Angeles 16 B3
Czerniaków Warsaw 32 B2
Czyste Warsaw 32 B1

D

Da Moóca → São Paulo 27 B2
Ďáblice Prague 25 B2
Dąbrowa Warsaw 32 B1
Dachang Shanghai 28 B1
Dachang ✕ Shanghai 28 B1
Dachau Munich 21 A1
Dachau-Ost Munich 21 A1
Dachauer Moos Munich 21 A1
Dadar Mumbai 20 A1
Daebang Seoul 27 B1
Daechi Seoul 27 B2
Dafni Athens 2 B2
Dagenham London 15 A4
Daglfing Munich 21 B2
Dahab, Gezîret el Cairo 7 B2
Daheisha Jerusalem 13 B2
Dahlem Berlin 5 B2
Dahlwitz-Hoppegarten Berlin 5 A5
Dahongmen Beijing 4 C2
Dajiaoting Beijing 4 B2
Dakhnoye St. Petersburg 27 C1
Dalejsky potok → Prague 25 B2
Dalgety Bay Edinburgh 11 A1
Dalkeith Edinburgh 11 B3
Dalkey Dublin 10 B3
Dalkey I. Dublin 10 B3
Dallgow Berlin 5 A1
Dalmeny Edinburgh 11 B1
Dalston London 15 A3
Daly City San Francisco 26 B2
Damaia Lisbon 16 A1
Damarakia Athens 2 B1
Dämeritzsee Berlin 5 B5
Dan Ryan Woods Chicago 9 C2
Danderhall Edinburgh 11 B3
Danderyd Stockholm 29 A2
Danforth Toronto 31 A3
Darakeh Tehran 31 A2
Darband Tehran 31 A2
Darling Point Sydney 29 B2
Darndale Dublin 10 A2
Darrūs Tehran 31 A2
Dartford London 15 B5
Dashi Guangzhou 11 B2
Datansha Guangzhou 11 B2
Datun Beijing 4 B2
Daulatpur Delhi 10 A1
Davidson, Mt. San Francisco 26 B2
Davidson's Mains Edinburgh 11 B2
Dāvūdiyeh Tehran 31 A2
Davydkovo Moscow 19 B1
Dawidy Warsaw 32 C1
Daxing Beijing 4 C2
Days Bay Wellington 33 B2
Decatur Atlanta 3 B3
Dedham Boston 6 B1
Degunino Moscow 19 A2
Deir Dibwan Jerusalem 13 A2
Deir Ibzi'e Jerusalem 13 A1
Dejvice Prague 25 B2
Dekabristov, Ostrov St. Petersburg 27 B1
Del Rey Los Angeles 16 C2
Delhi Delhi 10 B2
Delhi Indira Gandhi Int. ✕ (DEL) Delhi 10 B1
Demarest New York 22 A2
Den Ilp Amsterdam 2 A2
Denistone Heights Sydney 29 A1
Dentonia Park Toronto 31 A3
DePaul Univ. Chicago 9 B3
Deptford London 15 B3
Des Plaines Chicago 9 A1
Desert Wetlands Park Las Vegas 14 B2
Deutsche Oper Berlin 5 A2
Deutsches Museum Munich 21 B2
Devil's Peak Cape Town 8 A1
Dhakuria Kolkata 14 B2
Dharavi Mumbai 20 A2
Diadema São Paulo 27 C2
Diegem Brussels 6 A2
Diemen Amsterdam 2 A2
Diepkloof Johannesburg 13 B1
Diepriver Cape Town 8 B1
Difficult Run → Washington 33 B2
Dilbeek Brussels 6 A1
Dilli = Delhi Delhi 10 B2
Dirnismaning Munich 21 A2
Disney-M.G.M. Studios Orlando 23 B1
Disney Studios Los Angeles 16 B3
District Heights Washington 33 B4
Djakarta = Jakarta Jakarta 12 A2
Djursholm Stockholm 29 A2
Döberitz Berlin 5 A1
Döbling Vienna 32 A2
Dobong Seoul 27 B2
Dobongsan Seoul 27 A2
Docklands London 15 A3
Doctor Phillips Orlando 23 B2
Dodder → Dublin 10 B1
Dodger Stadium Los Angeles 16 B3
Dogs, Isle of London 15 B3
Dolgoe Ozero St. Petersburg 27 A1
Dollis Hill London 15 A2
Dollymount Dublin 10 A2
Dolni Prague 25 B3
Dolni Chabry Prague 25 B2
Dolni Počernice Prague 25 B3
Dolphins Barn Dublin 10 B2
Dom Pedro II, Parque São Paulo 27 B2
Don Mills Toronto 31 A2
Don Muang Int. ✕ (BKK) Bangkok 3 A2
Donaghmede Dublin 10 A3
Donau-Oder Kanal Vienna 32 A3
Donaufeld Vienna 32 A2
Donaupark Vienna 32 A2
Donaustadt Vienna 32 A2
Dongan Hills New York 22 C1
Dongcheng Beijing 4 B2
Dongdaemung Seoul 27 B2
Donggou Shanghai 28 B3
Dongjak Seoul 27 B1
Dongjiao Guangzhou 11 B2
Dongri Mumbai 20 B2
Dongshanhu Park Guangzhou 11 B2
Dongzhimen Beijing 4 B2
Donnybrook Dublin 10 B2
Doornfontein Johannesburg 13 B2
Dorchester Boston 6 B2
Dorchester B. Boston 6 B2
Dorchester Heights Nat. Historical Site ⌂ Boston 6 B2
Dornach Munich 21 B3
Dorval Int., Montréal ✕ (YUL) Montreal 20 B1
Dos Moninos → São Paulo 27 C2
Douglas Park Chicago 9 B2
Dover Heights Sydney 29 B2
Dowlatābād Tehran 31 B2
Down, L. Orlando 23 A1
Downey Los Angeles 16 C4
Downsview Toronto 31 A1
Dragør Copenhagen 8 B3
Drancy Paris 24 A3
Dranesville Washington 33 A1
Drapetsona Athens 2 B1
Dreilinden Berlin 5 B2
Drewnica Warsaw 32 B2
Drigh Road Karachi 13 A2
Drimnagh Dublin 10 B2
Drogenbos Brussels 6 B1
Druid Hills Atlanta 3 B2
Drumcondra Dublin 10 A2
Drummoyne Sydney 29 B1
Drylaw Edinburgh 11 B2
Dubeč Prague 25 B3
Dublin Dublin 10 A2
Dublin ✕ (DUB) Dublin 10 A2
Dublin B. Dublin 10 B3
Dublin Harbour Dublin 10 A2
Duddingston Edinburgh 11 B3
Dugnano Milan 19 A2
Duivendrecht Amsterdam 2 B2
Dūlāb Tehran 31 B2
Dulles Int. ✕ (IAD) Washington 33 B1
Dulwich London 15 B3
Dum Dum Kolkata 14 B2
Dum Dum Int. ✕ (CCU) Kolkata 14 B2
Dumont New York 22 A2
Dún Laoghaire Dublin 10 B3
Dundrum Dublin 10 B2
Dunearn Singapore 28 B2
Dúnleary = Dún Laoghaire Dublin 10 B3
Dunn Loring Washington 33 B2
Dunning Chicago 9 B2
Dunvegan Johannesburg 13 A2
Duomo Milan 19 B2
Duque de Caxias Rio de Janeiro 25 A1
Duren Sawit Jakarta 12 A2
Dusit Bangkok 3 B2
Dworp Brussels 6 B1
Dyakovo Moscow 19 B2
Dyker Beach Park New York 22 C1
Dzerzhinskiy Moscow 19 B2
Dzerzhinskiy Park Moscow 19 B2

E

E.U.R. = Esposizione Universale di Roma Rome 26 C1
Eagle Rock Los Angeles 16 B3
Ealing □ London 15 A2
Earlsfield London 15 B2
Earlwood Sydney 29 B1
East Arlington Boston 6 A2
East Arlington Washington 33 B3
East Bedfont London 15 B1
East Boston Boston 6 A2
East Don → Toronto 31 A2
East Don Parkland Toronto 31 A2
East Elmhurst New York 22 B2
East Finchley London 15 A2
East Flatbush New York 22 C2
East Ham London 15 A4
East Humber → Toronto 31 A1
East Lamma Channel Hong Kong 12 B1
East Las Vegas = Whitney Las Vegas 14 B2
East Lexington Boston 6 A1
East Los Angeles Los Angeles 16 B3
East Molesey London 15 B1
East New York New York 22 B2
East Pines Washington 33 B4
East Point Atlanta 3 B2
East Potomac Park Washington 33 B3
East River → New York 22 B2
East Rutherford New York 22 A1
East Sheen London 15 B2
East Talpiyot Jerusalem 13 B2
East Wickham London 15 B4
East York Toronto 31 A2
Eastbourne Wellington 33 B2
Eastcote London 15 A1
Easter Howgate Edinburgh 11 B2
Eastpoint Park Toronto 31 A4
Eastwood Sydney 29 A1
Eaton Canyon Park Los Angeles 16 A4
Ebara Tokyo 30 B3
Ebisu Tokyo 30 B3
Ebute-Ikorodu Lagos 14 A2
Ebute-Metta Lagos 14 B2
Eda Tokyo 30 B2
Edendale Johannesburg 13 A2
Edenmore Dublin 10 A2
Edgars Cr. → Melbourne 18 A1
Edgeley Toronto 31 A1
Edgemar San Francisco 26 C2
Edgewater New York 22 B2
Edgewood Orlando 23 B2
Edinburgh Edinburgh 11 B2
Edinburgh ✕ (EDI) Edinburgh 11 B1
Edinburgh Castle Edinburgh 11 B2
Edison Park Chicago 9 A2
Edmondston Washington 33 B4
Edmondstown Dublin 10 B2
Edo → Tokyo 30 B4
Edogawa Tokyo 30 A4
Edsberg Stockholm 29 A1
Edwards L. Melbourne 18 A1
Efzonos Athens 2 B2
Egaleo Athens 2 B2
Egaleo, Oros Athens 2 B1
Eiche Berlin 5 A4
Eiche Süd Berlin 5 A4
Eiffel, Tour Paris 24 A2
Ein Arik Jerusalem 13 A1
Ein Naquba Jerusalem 13 B1
Ein Rafa Jerusalem 13 B1
Eizariya Jerusalem 13 B2
Ejby Copenhagen 8 A2
Ejigbo Lagos 14 A1
Ekeberg Oslo 23 A3
Eknäs Stockholm 29 B3
El 'Abbasiya Cairo 7 A2
El Agustino Lima 14 B2
El Agustino, Cerro Lima 14 B3
El Baragil Cairo 7 A1
El Basâlîn Cairo 7 B2
El Bira Jerusalem 13 A2
El Bosque Santiago 27 C2
El Carmen Santiago 27 B1
El Cortijo Santiago 27 B1
El Cristo, Vaso Regulador Mexico City 18 B1
El Duqqi Cairo 7 A2
El Encinar de los Reyes Madrid 17 A2
El Gezira Cairo 7 A2
El Ghurîya Cairo 7 A2
El Giza Cairo 7 A2
El Khadr Jerusalem 13 B1
El Khalîfa Cairo 7 A2
El Kôm el Ahmar Cairo 7 A2
El Ma'âdi Cairo 7 B2
El Matariya Cairo 7 A2
El Mohandessin Cairo 7 A2
El Monte Los Angeles 16 B4
El Muqattam Cairo 7 A2
El Mûski Cairo 7 A2
El Pardo Madrid 17 A1
El Portal Miami 18 A2
El Prat de Llobregat Barcelona 4 B1
El Qâhira Cairo 7 A2
El Qubba Cairo 7 A2
El Reloj Mexico City 18 C2
El Retiro Madrid 17 B1
El Salto Santiago 27 B2
El Sereno Los Angeles 16 B3
El Talibîya Cairo 7 B2
El Vergel Mexico City 18 C2
El Wâhli Cairo 7 A2
El Zamâlik Cairo 7 A2
El Zeitûn Cairo 7 A2
Eleftherios Venizelos ✕ (ATH) Athens 2 A3
Elephanta Caves Mumbai 20 B2
Elephanta I. Mumbai 20 B2
Ellboda Stockholm 29 A3
Ellenor, L. Orlando 23 B2
Elliniko Olympic Complex Athens 2 B2
Ellis I. New York 22 B1
Elmers End London 15 B3
Elmhurst New York 22 B2
Elmstead London 15 B4
Elmwood New Orleans 21 B1
Elmwood Park Chicago 9 B2
Elmwood Park New York 22 A1
Elsdon Wellington 33 A1
Elsiesrivier Cape Town 8 A2
Elsternwick Melbourne 18 B2
Eltham London 15 B4
Elwood Melbourne 18 B1
Élysée Paris 24 A2
Elysian Park Los Angeles 16 B3
Emāmzādeh Sāleh Tehran 31 A2
Émerainville Paris 24 B4
Emeryville San Francisco 26 A3
Eminönü Istanbul 12 B1
Emirgan Istanbul 12 B2
Emmarentia Johannesburg 13 A2
Empire State Building New York 22 B2
Encantado Rio de Janeiro 25 B1
Encino Los Angeles 16 B2
Encino Res. Los Angeles 16 B1
Enebyberg Stockholm 29 A1
Enfield Sydney 29 B1
Engenho, I. do Rio de Janeiro 25 B2
Englewood Chicago 9 C3
Englewood New York 22 A2
Englewood Cliffs New York 22 A2
Enmore Sydney 29 B2
Enskede Stockholm 29 B2
Enterprise Las Vegas 14 B1
Entrevias Madrid 17 B1
Epcot Orlando 23 B1
Epping Sydney 29 A1
Erenköy Istanbul 12 C2
Erith London 15 B5
Erlaa Vienna 32 B1
Ermington Sydney 29 A1
Ermita Manila 17 B1
Ershatou Guangzhou 11 B2
Erskineville Sydney 29 B2
Erunkan Lagos 14 A2
Erzsébet-Telep Budapest 7 B3
Eschenried Munich 21 A1
Esenler Istanbul 12 B1
Esher London 15 B1
Eskbank Edinburgh 11 B3
Esplugas Barcelona 4 A1
Esposizione Universale di Roma Rome 26 C1
Essendon Melbourne 18 A1
Essendon ✕ (MEB) Melbourne 18 A1
Essingen Stockholm 29 B1
Essling Vienna 32 A3
Est, Gare de l' Paris 24 A3
Estado, Parque do São Paulo 27 B2
Estelle New Orleans 21 B2
Estrela, Basilica da Lisbon 16 A2
Etobicoke Toronto 31 B1
Etobicoke Cr. → Toronto 31 B1
Etterbeek Brussels 6 B2
Eung-am Seoul 27 B1
Eunpyeong Seoul 27 B1
Evanston Chicago 9 A2
Even Sapir Jerusalem 13 B1
Evere Brussels 6 A2
Everett Boston 6 A2
Evergreen Park Chicago 9 C2
Evīn Tehran 31 A2
Ewu Lagos 14 A1
Exhibition Place Toronto 31 B2
Exposições, Palácio das Rio de Janeiro 25 B1
Eyüp Istanbul 12 B1
Ezeiza ✕ (EZE) Buenos Aires 7 C1

F

Fabour, Mt. Singapore 28 B2
Fælledparken Copenhagen 8 A3
Fågelön Stockholm 29 B1
Fagersjö Stockholm 29 B2
Fairfax Washington 33 B2
Fairfax Station Washington 33 C2
Fairland Johannesburg 13 A1
Fairmilehead Edinburgh 11 B2
Fairmount Heights Washington 33 B4
Fairport Toronto 31 A4
Fairview New York 22 B2
Fairview, L. Orlando 23 A2
Falenty Warsaw 32 C1
Faliro Athens 2 B1
Faliro, Ormos Athens 2 B2
Falkenburg Berlin 5 A4
Falkenhagen Berlin 5 A1
Falkensee Berlin 5 A1
Falls Church Washington 33 B2
Falomo Lagos 14 B2
False Bay Cape Town 8 B2
Fangcun Guangzhou 11 B2
Faraḩābād Tehran 31 A2
Farforovskaya St. Petersburg 27 B2
Farningham London 15 B5
Farsta Stockholm 29 B2
Fasanerie-Nord Munich 21 A2
Fasangarten Munich 21 B2
Fatih Istanbul 12 B1
Favoriten Vienna 32 B2
Fawkner Melbourne 18 A1
Fawkner Park Melbourne 18 B1
FedEx Stadium Washington 33 B4
Feijó Lisbon 16 B2
Feldkirchen Munich 21 B3
Feldmoching Munich 21 A2
Feltham London 15 B1
Fener Istanbul 12 B1
Fenerbahçe Istanbul 12 C2
Fengtai Beijing 4 C1
Fengtai Stadium Beijing 4 B1
Ferencváros Budapest 7 B2
Ferihegy, Budapest ✕ (BUD) Budapest 7 B3
Ferndale Johannesburg 13 A2
Fichtenau Berlin 5 B5
Field Museum of Natural History Chicago 9 B3
Fields Corner Boston 6 B2
Fiera Camp Milan 19 B1
Figino Milan 19 B1
Fijir Baghdad 3 A2
Filadelfia Athens 2 A2
Fili-Mazilovo Moscow 19 B1
Filothei Athens 2 A2
Finchley London 15 A2
Fine Arts, Museum of Boston 6 A2
Finglas Dublin 10 A2
Finsbury London 15 A3
Finsbury Park London 15 A3
Fiorito Buenos Aires 7 C2
Firhouse Dublin 10 B2
Fischerhäuser Munich 21 A3
Fisher Island Miami 18 B2
Fishermans Bend Melbourne 18 A1
Fisherville Toronto 31 A2
Fisksätra Stockholm 29 B3
Fitzroy Gardens Melbourne 18 A1
Five Cowrie Cr. → Lagos 14 B2
Five Dock Sydney 29 B1
Fjellstrand Oslo 23 B2
Flamengo Rio de Janeiro 25 B1
Flamingo Orlando 23 B2
Flaminio Rome 26 B1
Flaskebekk Oslo 23 A2
Flatbush New York 22 C2
Flaten Stockholm 29 B2
Flatlands New York 22 C2
Flemington Racecourse Melbourne 18 A1
Flint Pk. Los Angeles 16 B3
Florence Los Angeles 16 C3
Florence Bloom Bird Sanctuary ⌂ Johannesburg 13 A2
Florentia Johannesburg 13 B2
Flores Buenos Aires 7 B2
Flores, Mercado de Mexico City 18 C2
Floresta Buenos Aires 7 B2
Florida Buenos Aires 7 B2
Florida Johannesburg 13 B1
Floridsdorf Vienna 32 A2
Flushing New York 22 B3
Flushing Meadows Corona Park New York 22 B2
Flysta Stockholm 29 A1
Fo Tan Hong Kong 12 A2
Foggy Bottom Washington 33 B3
Föhrenhain Vienna 32 A2
Fontainebleau Johannesburg 13 A1
Fontenay-aux-Roses Paris 24 B2
Fontenay-le-Fleury Paris 24 B1
Fontenay-sous-Bois Paris 24 A3
Foots Cray London 15 B4
Footscray Melbourne 18 A1
Forbidden City = Imperial Palace Museum Beijing 4 B2
Forest Brussels 6 B1
Forest Gate London 15 A4
Forest Heights Washington 33 C3
Forest Hill London 15 B3
Forest Hill Toronto 31 A2
Forest Hills New York 22 B2
Forest Park Chicago 9 B2
Forest Park New York 22 B2
Forest View Chicago 9 C2
Forestville Washington 33 B4
Fornebu Oslo 23 A2
Foro Romano Rome 26 B1
Forstenried Munich 21 B1
Forstenrieder Park Munich 21 B1
Fort Mumbai 20 B1
Fort Dupont Park Washington 33 B4
Fort Foote Village Washington 33 C3
Fort Lee New York 22 A2
Forth, Firth of Edinburgh 11 A3
Forth Rail Bridge Edinburgh 11 A1
Forth Road Bridge Edinburgh 11 A1
Foshan Guangzhou 11 B2
Fót Budapest 7 A3
Fourqueux Paris 24 A1
Fox Studios Sydney 29 B2
Foxrock Dublin 10 B2
Franconia Washington 33 C3
Frank Lloyd Wright Home Chicago 9 B2
Frankel Singapore 28 B3
Franklin Park Boston 6 B2
Franklin Park Chicago 9 B1
Franklin Park Washington 33 B3
Franklin Res. Los Angeles 16 B2
Franz Josef Strauss ✕ (MUC) Munich 21 A2
Frauenkirche Munich 21 B2
Frederiksberg Copenhagen 8 A3
Frederiksdal Copenhagen 8 A2
Fredersdorf Berlin 5 A5
Freguesia Rio de Janeiro 25 A1
Freidrichshain, Volkspark Berlin 5 A3
Freiham Munich 21 B1
Freimann Munich 21 A2
French Quarter New Orleans 21 B2
Fresh Pond Boston 6 A2
Fresnes Paris 24 B2
Freudenau Vienna 32 A2
Friarstown Dublin 10 B1
Friedenau Berlin 5 B3
Friedrichsfelde Berlin 5 B4
Friedrichshagen Berlin 5 B4
Friedrichshain Berlin 5 A3
Friedrichslust Berlin 5 A5
Friherrs Helsinki 11 B1
Frilufts Museum Helsinki 11 B2
Frontón, I. Lima 14 B1
Frunze Moscow 19 B2
Fuchū Tokyo 30 A1
Fuencarral Madrid 17 B1
Fuenlabrada Madrid 17 C1
Fukagawa Tokyo 30 B3
Fukushima Osaka 23 A1
Fulham London 15 B2
Funabori Tokyo 30 A4
Fundão, I. do Rio de Janeiro 25 B1
Fünfhaus Vienna 32 A2
Füresø Copenhagen 8 A2
Fürth Munich 21 B2
Futago-tamagawaen Tokyo 30 B2
Fuxing Dao Shanghai 28 B2
Fuxing Park Shanghai 28 B1
Fuxinglu Beijing 4 B1

G

G. Ross Lord Park Toronto 31 A2
Gaebong Seoul 27 C1
Gage Park Chicago 9 C2
Gagny Paris 24 A4
Galata Istanbul 12 B1
Galata Tower Istanbul 12 B1
Galatsi Athens 2 A2
Galeão, Int. de ✕ (GIG) Rio de Janeiro 25 A1
Galyanovo Moscow 19 B3
Gambir Jakarta 12 A1
Gamboa Rio de Janeiro 25 B1
Gambolóita Milan 19 B2
Gamlebyen Oslo 23 A3
Gangdong Seoul 27 B2
Gangnam Seoul 27 B1
Gangseo Seoul 27 B1
Gangtou Guangzhou 11 A1
Gangwei Guangzhou 11 B2
Ganjiakou Beijing 4 B1
Ganshoren Brussels 6 A1
Gants Hill London 15 A4
Gaoqiao Shanghai 28 A2
Garbagnate Milanese Milan 19 A1
Garbatella Rome 26 B2
Garches Paris 24 A2
Garching Munich 21 A3
Garden City Cairo 7 A2
Garden Reach Kolkata 14 B1
Garder Oslo 23 B2
Garfield New York 22 A1
Garfield Park Chicago 9 B2
Gargareta Athens 2 B2
Garibong Seoul 27 C1
Garvanza Los Angeles 16 B3
Gåshaga Stockholm 29 A3
Gateway ⌂ New York 22 C2
Gateway of India Mumbai 20 B2
Gatow Berlin 5 B1
Gavà Barcelona 4 B1
Gavamar Barcelona 4 B1
Gávea Rio de Janeiro 25 B1
Gávea, Pedra da Rio de Janeiro 25 B1
Gazdagrét Budapest 7 B1
Gaziosmanpaşa Istanbul 12 B1
Gebel el Ahmar Cairo 7 A3
Gebel el Muqattam Cairo 7 A2
Gebel el Tura Cairo 7 B2
Geiselgasteig Munich 21 B2
General San Martín Buenos Aires 7 B1
Gennevilliers Paris 24 A2
Gentilly New Orleans 21 B2
Gentilly Paris 24 B3
Gentofte Copenhagen 8 A3
Genval Brussels 6 B2
George I. Hong Kong 12 B1
Georges River Bridge Sydney 29 C1
Georgetown Washington 33 B3
Georgia Dome Atlanta 3 B2
Gerasdorf bei Wien Vienna 32 A2
Gerberau Munich 21 A1
Gerli Buenos Aires 7 C2
Germiston Johannesburg 13 B2
Gern Munich 21 B2
Getafe Madrid 17 C1
Getty Center, The Los Angeles 16 B2
Geunjeong Seoul 27 C1
Geva Binyamin Jerusalem 13 A2
Geylang Serai Singapore 28 B3
Gharapuri Mumbai 20 B2
Gharb = Shahrak-e Qods Tehran 31 A2
Ghatkopar Mumbai 20 A2
Ghazipur Delhi 10 B2
Ghizri Karachi 13 B2
Ghizri Cr. → Karachi 13 B2
Ghonda Delhi 10 A2
Ghusuri Kolkata 14 B2
Gianicolense Rome 26 B1
Giant Wheel = Riesenrad Vienna 32 A2
Gibraltar Pt. Toronto 31 B2
Gidea Park London 15 A5
Giesing Munich 21 B2
Gilmerton Edinburgh 11 B3
Gilo Jerusalem 13 B2
Gimmersta Stockholm 29 B3
Ginza Tokyo 30 B3
Giv'at Ram Jerusalem 13 B2
Giv'at Ye'arim Jerusalem 13 B1
Giv'at Ze'ev Jerusalem 13 A2
Giv'on Jerusalem 13 A1
Giza = El Giza Cairo 7 A2
Giza Pyramids Cairo 7 B1
Gjersjøen Oslo 23 B3
Gladesville Sydney 29 B1
Gladsakse Copenhagen 8 A2
Glasnevin Dublin 10 A2
Glassmanor Washington 33 C4
Glasthule Dublin 10 B3
Glen Iris Melbourne 18 B2
Glen Mar Park Washington 33 B3
Glen Rouge Park Toronto 31 A4
Glenarden Washington 33 B4
Glenasmole Reservoirs Dublin 10 B1
Glencorse Res. Edinburgh 11 B2
Glencullen Dublin 10 B2
Glendale Los Angeles 16 B3
Glendoo Mt. Dublin 10 B2
Glenhuntly Melbourne 18 B2
Glenside Wellington 33 B1
Glenview Chicago 9 A2
Glenview Countryside Chicago 9 A2
Glenvista Johannesburg 13 B2
Glifada Athens 2 B2
Glostrup Copenhagen 8 B2
Gogar Edinburgh 11 B2
Göktürk Istanbul 12 A1
Golabari Kolkata 14 B2
Golabki Warsaw 32 B1
Gold Coast Chicago 9 B3
Golden Gate San Francisco 26 B2
Golden Gate ⌂ San Francisco 26 A2
Golden Gate Bridge San Francisco 26 B2
Golden Gate Park San Francisco 26 B2
Golden Horn = Haliç Istanbul 12 B1
Golders Green London 15 A2
Golestan Palace Tehran 31 A2
Gollans Stream → Wellington 33 B2
Gonen Jerusalem 13 B2
Gongneung Seoul 27 B2
Goodmayes London 15 A4
Goodwood Cape Town 8 A2
Gopalpur Kolkata 14 B2
Górce Warsaw 32 B1
Gore Hill Sydney 29 A2
Gorelyy → St. Petersburg 27 A3
Gorgie Edinburgh 11 B2
Gorky Park Moscow 19 B2
Gosen Berlin 5 B5
Gosener kanal Berlin 5 B5
Gospel Oak London 15 A3
Gotanda Tokyo 30 B3
Goth Goli Mar Karachi 13 A2
Goth Sher Shah Karachi 13 A1

Gotha *Orlando* 23 A1
Gournay-sur-Marne *Paris* 24 A4
Governador, I. do *Rio de Janeiro* 25 A1
Governors I. *New York* 22 B1
Grabów *Warsaw* 32 C1
Grace, Mt. *Wellington* 33 B2
Gracefield *Wellington* 33 B2
Gràcia *Barcelona* 4 A2
Gräfelfing *Munich* 21 B1
Gragoatá *Rio de Janeiro* 25 B2
Grand Bazaar = Kapali Carsi *Istanbul* 12 B1
Grand Central Station *New York* 22 B2
Grand Palace *Bangkok* 3 B1
Grande Place *Brussels* 6 A2
Grankulla = Kauniainen *Helsinki* 11 B1
Grant Park *Chicago* 9 B3
Granton *Edinburgh* 11 B2
Grassy Park *Cape Town* 8 B2
Gratosóglio *Milan* 19 B2
Gratzwalde *Berlin* 5 B5
Gravesend *New York* 22 C2
Grazhdanka *St. Petersburg* 27 B2
Great Falls *Washington* 33 B2
Great Falls Park *Washington* 33 B2
Great Western Forum *Los Angeles* 16 C2
Greco *Milan* 19 A2
Green I. *Hong Kong* 12 B1
Green Point *Cape Town* 8 A1
Greenbelt *Washington* 33 A4
Greenbelt Park *Washington* 33 B4
Greenfield Park *Montreal* 20 B3
Greenford *London* 15 A1
Greenhill *London* 15 A2
Greenhills *Dublin* 10 B1
Greenwich □ *London* 15 B3
Greenwich Observatory *London* 15 B3
Greenwich Village *New York* 22 B2
Greenwood *Boston* 6 A2
Grefsen *Oslo* 23 A3
Gresham Park *Atlanta* 3 B2
Gretna *New Orleans* 21 B2
Gretna City Park *New Orleans* 21 B2
Greve Strand *Copenhagen* 8 B1
Griebnitzsee *Berlin* 5 B1
Griffith Park *Los Angeles* 16 B3
Grimbergen *Brussels* 6 A2
Grinzing *Vienna* 32 A2
Gröbenried *Munich* 21 A1
Grochów *Warsaw* 32 B2
Grodzisk *Warsaw* 32 B2
Groenendaal *Brussels* 6 B2
Grogol Petamburin *Jakarta* 12 A1
Gronsdorf *Munich* 21 B3
Grorud *Oslo* 23 A4
Gross-Glienicke *Berlin* 5 B1
Gross-Hadern *Munich* 21 B1
Gross-Lappen *Munich* 21 A2
Grosse Krampe *Berlin* 5 B5
Grosse Müggelsee *Berlin* 5 B4
Grosse Point Lighthouse *Chicago* 9 A2
Grossenzersdorf *Vienna* 32 A3
Grossenzersdorfer Arm → *Vienna* 32 A3
Grosser Biberhaufen *Vienna* 32 A2
Grosser Wannsee *Berlin* 5 B2
Grossfeld-Siedlung *Vienna* 32 A2
Grosshesselohe *Munich* 21 B2
Grossjedlersdorf *Vienna* 32 A2
Grossziethen *Berlin* 5 B3
Ground Zero *New York* 22 B1
Grove, The *Chicago* 9 A1
Grove Hall *Boston* 6 B2
Grove Park *Atlanta* 3 B2
Grove Park *London* 15 B4
Grove Park *London* 15 B2
Groveton *Washington* 33 C3
Grünau *Berlin* 5 B4
Grunewald *Berlin* 5 B2
Grünwald *Munich* 21 B2
Grünwalder Forst *Munich* 21 B2
Grymes Hill *New York* 22 C1
Guadalupe *Manila* 17 B2
Guadalupe, Basílica de *Mexico City* 18 B2
Guanabara, B. de *Rio de Janeiro* 25 B1
Guanabara, Jardim *Rio de Janeiro* 25 A1
Guanabara, Palácio da *Rio de Janeiro* 25 B1
Guang'anmen *Beijing* 4 B1
Guangqumen *Beijing* 4 B2
Guangzhou *Guangzhou* 11 B2
Guanshuo *Guangzhou* 11 B3
Gudö *Stockholm* 29 B3
Güell, Parque de *Barcelona* 4 A2
Guinardó *Barcelona* 4 A2
Gulbai *Karachi* 13 A1
Güngören *Istanbul* 12 B1
Gunnersbury *London* 15 B2
Guomao *Beijing* 4 B2
Gustavo A. Madero *Mexico City* 18 B2
Guttenberg *New York* 22 B1
Gutuyevskiy, Ostrov *St. Petersburg* 27 B1
Guyancourt *Paris* 24 B1
Gwanak *Seoul* 27 C1
Gwanaksan *Seoul* 27 C1
Gyál *Budapest* 7 B3
Gyáli-patak → *Budapest* 7 B2

H

Haaga *Helsinki* 11 B2
Haar *Munich* 21 B3
Habay *Manila* 17 C1
Hackbridge *London* 15 B3
Hackensack *New York* 22 A1
Hackensack → *New York* 22 B1
Hackney □ *London* 15 A3
Hackney Wick *London* 15 A3
Hadr, Warrâq el *Cairo* 7 A2
Haga *Stockholm* 29 A2
Hagenbrunn *Vienna* 32 A2
Hägersten *Stockholm* 29 B1
Häggvik *Stockholm* 29 A1
Hagonoy *Manila* 17 B2
Hague Park *Toronto* 31 A3
Haidari *Athens* 2 A1
Haidarpur *Delhi* 10 A1
Haidhausen *Munich* 21 B2
Haidian *Beijing* 4 B1
Haight-Ashbury *San Francisco* 26 B2
Hainault *London* 15 A4
Haizhou *Guangzhou* 11 B2
Haizhu Guangchang *Guangzhou* 11 B2
Hakunila *Helsinki* 11 B3
Halandri *Athens* 2 A2
Halásztelek *Budapest* 7 B1
Haliç *Istanbul* 12 B1
Halim Perdana Kusuma Int. ✈ (HLP) *Jakarta* 12 B2
Halle *Brussels* 6 B1
Haltiala *Helsinki* 11 B2
Haltiavuori *Helsinki* 11 B2
Ham *London* 15 B2
Hämeenkylä *Helsinki* 11 B1
Hammarby *Stockholm* 29 B2
Hamme *Brussels* 6 A1
Hammersmith *London* 15 B2
Hampstead *London* 15 A2
Hampstead *Montreal* 20 B2
Hampstead Garden Suburb *London* 15 A2
Hampstead Heath *London* 15 A2
Hampton *London* 15 B1
Hampton Court Palace *London* 15 B1
Hampton Wick *London* 15 B2
Hamrā' *Baghdad* 3 B1
Hanala *Helsinki* 11 A3
Haneda *Tokyo* 30 B3
Haneda, Tōkyō ✈ (HND) *Tokyo* 30 B3
Hang Hau *Hong Kong* 12 B2
Hanging Gardens *Mumbai* 20 B1
Hanlon *Toronto* 31 B1
Hanwell *London* 15 A1
Hanworth *London* 15 B1
Haora *Kolkata* 14 B1
Hapeville *Atlanta* 3 C2
Happy Valley *Hong Kong* 12 B2
Har Adar *Jerusalem* 13 B1
Har Gilo *Jerusalem* 13 B2
Har Homa *Jerusalem* 13 B2
Har Nof *Jerusalem* 13 B2
Harahan *New Orleans* 21 B1
Haren *Brussels* 6 A2
Hareskovby *Copenhagen* 8 A2
Haringey □ *London* 15 A3
Harjusuo *Helsinki* 11 B3
Harlaching *Munich* 21 B2
Harlaw Res. *Edinburgh* 11 B2
Harlem *New York* 22 B2
Harlesden *London* 15 A2
Harlington *London* 15 B1
Harmaja *Helsinki* 11 C2
Harmashatar hegy *Budapest* 7 A2
Harolds Cross *Dublin* 10 B2
Háros *Budapest* 7 B2
Harperrig Res. *Edinburgh* 11 B1
Harrow □ *London* 15 A1
Harrow on the Hill *London* 15 A1
Harrow School *London* 15 A1
Harrow Weald *London* 15 A1
Hartsfield-Atlanta Int. ✈ (ATL) *Atlanta* 3 C2
Harumi *Tokyo* 30 B3
Harvard Univ. *Boston* 6 A2
Harvey *New Orleans* 21 B2
Harwood Heights *Chicago* 9 B2
Ḩasanābād *Tehran* 31 B2
Hasbrouck Heights *New York* 22 A1
Haselhorst *Berlin* 5 A2
Hasköy *Istanbul* 12 B1
Hasle *Oslo* 23 B2
Haslum *Oslo* 23 A2
Hästhagen *Stockholm* 29 B2
Hataitai *Wellington* 33 B1
Hatch End *London* 15 A1
Hatiara *Kolkata* 14 B2
Hauketo *Oslo* 23 A3
Hauz Khas *Delhi* 10 B2
Havel → *Berlin* 5 A2
Havelkanal *Berlin* 5 A2
Havering □ *London* 15 A5
Havering-atte-Bower *London* 15 A5
Haworth *New York* 22 A2
Hawthorne Racecourse *Chicago* 9 C2
Hayes *London* 15 B4
Hayes *London* 15 A1
Hayes End *London* 15 A1
Hayford *Chicago* 9 C2
Haywards *Wellington* 33 A2
Heathfield *Cape Town* 8 B1
Heathrow, London ✈ (LHR) *London* 15 B1
Hebe Haven *Hong Kong* 12 A2
Hedong *Guangzhou* 11 B2
Heidelberg Heights *Melbourne* 18 A2
Heidelberg West *Melbourne* 18 A2
Heidemühle *Berlin* 5 B5
Heideveld *Cape Town* 8 A2
Heiligensee *Berlin* 5 A2
Heiligenstadt *Vienna* 32 A2
Heinersdorf *Berlin* 5 A3
Hélène de Champlain, Parc ⌂ *Montreal* 20 A2
Helenelund *Stockholm* 29 A1
Heliopolis = Masr el Gedida *Cairo* 7 A2
Hellersdorf *Berlin* 5 A4
Hellerup *Copenhagen* 8 A3
Helsingfors = Helsinki *Helsinki* 11 B2
Helsinki *Helsinki* 11 B2
Helsinki-Vantaa ✈ (HEL) *Helsinki* 11 B2
Hen and Chicken B. *Sydney* 29 B1
Henderson *Las Vegas* 14 B2
Hendon *London* 15 A2
Hengsha *Guangzhou* 11 B2
Hennigsdorf *Berlin* 5 A2
Henryków *Warsaw* 32 B1
Henson Cr. → *Washington* 33 C4
Henttaa *Helsinki* 11 B1
Heping Park *Shanghai* 28 B2
Hepingli *Beijing* 4 B2
Herlev *Copenhagen* 8 A2
Herman Eckstein Park *Johannesburg* 13 A2
Hermannskogel *Vienna* 32 A1
Hermiston *Edinburgh* 11 B2
Hermitage and Winter Palace *St. Petersburg* 27 B1
Hermsdorf *Berlin* 5 A2
Hernals *Vienna* 32 A2
Herne Hill *London* 15 B3
Héroes de Churubusco *Mexico City* 18 B2
Herons, Î. aux *Montreal* 20 B2
Herstedøster *Copenhagen* 8 A2
Herttoniemi *Helsinki* 11 B3
Ḩeşārak *Tehran* 31 A1
Heston *London* 15 B1
Hetzendorf *Vienna* 32 B1
Hextable *London* 15 B5
Hialeah *Miami* 18 A1
Hiawassa, L. *Orlando* 23 A2
Hickory Hills *Chicago* 9 C2
Hiekkaharju *Helsinki* 11 B3
Hietaniemi *Helsinki* 11 B2
Hietzing *Vienna* 32 A1
Higashi *Osaka* 23 A2
Higashimurayama *Tokyo* 30 A1
Higashinari *Osaka* 23 A2
Higashisumiyoshi *Osaka* 23 B2
Higashiyodogawa *Osaka* 23 A1
High Park *Toronto* 31 B2
Highbury *London* 15 A3
Highgate *London* 15 A3
Highland Cr. → *Toronto* 31 A3
Highland Creek *Toronto* 31 A3
Highland Park *Los Angeles* 16 B3
Highlands North *Johannesburg* 13 A2
Hillcrest Heights *Washington* 33 C4
Hillend *Edinburgh* 11 A1
Hillingdon □ *London* 15 A1
Hillwood *Washington* 33 B3
Hilmīya *Cairo* 7 A2
Hin Keng *Hong Kong* 12 A2
Hirota *Osaka* 23 A1
Hirschstetten *Vienna* 32 A2
History Center *Atlanta* 3 B2
Hither Green *London* 15 B3
Hiyoshi *Tokyo* 30 B2
Hizma *Jerusalem* 13 B2
Hjortekær *Copenhagen* 8 A3
Hjortespring *Copenhagen* 8 A2
Hlubočepy *Prague* 25 B2
Ho Chung *Hong Kong* 12 A2
Hoboken *New York* 22 B1
Hobsons B. *Melbourne* 18 B1
Hochbrück *Munich* 21 A2
Hochelaga *Montreal* 20 A2
Hodgkins *Chicago* 9 C1
Hoegi *Seoul* 27 B2
Hoeilaart *Brussels* 6 B2
Hofburg *Vienna* 32 A2
Hoffman I. *New York* 22 C1
Hohenbrunn *Munich* 21 B3
Hohenschönhausen *Berlin* 5 A4
Holargos *Athens* 2 B2
Holborn *London* 15 A3
Holden, L. *Orlando* 23 B2
Holešovice *Prague* 25 B2
Holland Village *Singapore* 28 B2
Höllriegelskreuth *Munich* 21 B1
Hollywood *Los Angeles* 16 B3
Hollywood Bowl *Los Angeles* 16 B2
Holmenkollen *Oslo* 23 A3
Holmes Run Acres *Washington* 33 B2
Holmgård *Stockholm* 29 B1
Holmlia *Oslo* 23 B3
Holocaust Memorial *Jerusalem* 13 B2
Holyrood House, Palace of *Edinburgh* 11 B3
Holysloot *Amsterdam* 2 A3
Homerton *London* 15 A3
Hometown *Chicago* 9 C2
Hōnanchō *Tokyo* 30 A2
Honcho *Tokyo* 30 A3
Honden *Tokyo* 30 A4
Hondo, Rio → *Los Angeles* 16 B4
Hong Kong *Hong Kong* 12 B1
Hong Kong, Univ. of *Hong Kong* 12 B1
Hong Kong I. *Hong Kong* 12 B2
Hongje *Seoul* 27 B1
Hongjimun Tunnel *Seoul* 27 B1
Hongkou *Shanghai* 28 B1
Hongqiao *Shanghai* 28 B1
Honjyo *Tokyo* 30 A3
Honoré Mercier, Pont *Montreal* 20 B1
Hönow *Berlin* 5 A4
Hook *London* 15 B2
Horikiri *Tokyo* 30 A4
Horn Pond *Boston* 6 A1
Hornchurch *London* 15 A5
Horní *Prague* 25 B3
Horní Počernice *Prague* 25 B3
Hornsey *London* 15 A3
Horoměřice *Prague* 25 B1
Hortaleza *Madrid* 17 B2
Hosoyama *Tokyo* 30 B2
Hostafranchs *Barcelona* 4 A1
Hostivař *Prague* 25 B3
Houbětin *Prague* 25 B3
Houghton *Johannesburg* 13 B2
Houilles *Paris* 24 A2
Hounslow □ *London* 15 B1
Hout Bay *Cape Town* 8 B1
Hove Å → *Copenhagen* 8 B2
Hovedøya *Oslo* 23 A3
Høvik *Oslo* 23 A2
Hovorčovice *Prague* 25 A3
Howard Beach *New York* 22 C2
Howrah = Haora *Kolkata* 14 B1
Howth *Dublin* 10 A3
Howth Hd. *Dublin* 10 A3
Hōya *Tokyo* 30 A2
Hradčany *Prague* 25 B2
Huanghuagang Mausoleum *Guangzhou* 11 B2
Huangpu *Shanghai* 28 B2
Huangpu Jiang → *Shanghai* 28 B1
Huangpu Park *Shanghai* 28 B1
Huangtugang *Beijing* 4 C1
Huascar *Lima* 14 A2
Huay Khwang *Bangkok* 3 B2
Huddinge *Stockholm* 29 B2
Huechuraba *Santiago* 27 B2
Huertas de San Beltran *Barcelona* 4 A1
Huizingen *Brussels* 6 B1
Humayun's Tomb *Delhi* 10 B2
Humber → *Toronto* 31 A1
Humber B. *Toronto* 31 B2
Humber Bay *Toronto* 31 B2
Humber Bay Park *Toronto* 31 B2
Humber College *Toronto* 31 B1
Humber Summit *Toronto* 31 A1
Humber Valley Village *Toronto* 31 A1
Humberlea *Toronto* 31 A1
Humberwood Park *Toronto* 31 A1
Humboldt Park *Chicago* 9 B2
Humera *Madrid* 17 B1
Hunaydī *Baghdad* 3 B2
Hundige *Copenhagen* 8 B2
Hundige Strand *Copenhagen* 8 B2
Hung Hom *Hong Kong* 12 B2
Hunters Hill *Sydney* 29 B1
Hunters Pt. *San Francisco* 26 B2
Hunters Valley *Washington* 33 B2
Huntington *Washington* 33 C3
Huntington Park *Los Angeles* 16 C3
Hurīya *Baghdad* 3 A1
Hurstville *Sydney* 29 B1
Husan *Jerusalem* 13 B1
Husby *Stockholm* 29 A1
Husum *Copenhagen* 8 A2
Hutt → *Wellington* 33 B2
Hütteldorf *Vienna* 32 A1
Hüvösvölgy *Budapest* 7 A2
Huwon Secret Garden *Seoul* 27 B1
Hvalstad *Oslo* 23 A1
Hvalstrand *Oslo* 23 A2
Hvidovre *Copenhagen* 8 B2
Hwagok *Seoul* 27 B1
Hyattsville *Washington* 33 B4
Hyde Park *Boston* 6 B2
Hyde Park *Chicago* 9 C3
Hyde Park *Johannesburg* 13 A2
Hyde Park *London* 15 A2
Hyde Park *Los Angeles* 16 C3
Hyde Park *Sydney* 29 B2

I

Ibese *Lagos* 14 A2
Ibirapuera *São Paulo* 27 B1
Ibirapuera, Parque do *São Paulo* 27 B2
Icarai *Rio de Janeiro* 25 B2
Içerenköy *Istanbul* 12 C2
Ichgao *Tokyo* 30 B2
Ichigaya *Tokyo* 30 A3
Ichikawa *Tokyo* 30 A4
Ickenham *London* 15 A1
Iddo *Lagos* 14 B2
Idi-Oro *Lagos* 14 A2
Iganmu *Lagos* 14 B2
Igbobi *Lagos* 14 A2
Igbologun *Lagos* 14 B1
Igny *Paris* 24 B2
IJ, Het → *Amsterdam* 2 A2
IJ-meer *Amsterdam* 2 A3
Ijesa-Tedo *Lagos* 14 B1
Ijora *Lagos* 14 B2
Ikebe *Tokyo* 30 B2
Ikebukuro *Tokyo* 30 A3
Ikegami *Tokyo* 30 B3
Ikeja *Lagos* 14 A2
Ikeuchi *Osaka* 23 B2
Ikoyi *Lagos* 14 B2
Ikuata *Lagos* 14 B2
Ikuno *Osaka* 23 A2
Ikuta *Tokyo* 30 B2
Ila *Oslo* 23 A2
Ilford *London* 15 A4
Ilioupoli *Athens* 2 B2
Illinois at Chicago, Univ. of *Chicago* 9 B3
Illinois Institute of Technology *Chicago* 9 B3
Ilpendam *Amsterdam* 2 A2
Ilsos → *Athens* 2 B2
Imbâbah *Cairo* 7 A2
Imielin *Warsaw* 32 C2
Imirim *São Paulo* 27 A2
Imitos *Athens* 2 B2
Imitos, Oros *Athens* 2 B2
Imperial Palace Museum *Beijing* 4 B2
Inagi *Tokyo* 30 B2
Inchcolm *Edinburgh* 11 A2
Inchicore *Dublin* 10 A1
Inchkeith *Edinburgh* 11 A3
Inchmickery *Edinburgh* 11 A2
Incirano *Milan* 19 A1
Independencia *Lima* 14 A2
Independencia *Santiago* 27 B2
India Gate *Delhi* 10 B2
Indian Creek Village *Miami* 18 A2
Indianópolis *São Paulo* 27 B2
Indira Gandhi Int. ✈ (DEL) *Delhi* 10 B1
Industria *Johannesburg* 13 B1
Industrial Canal *New Orleans* 21 A2
Ingierstrand *Oslo* 23 B3
Inglewood *Los Angeles* 16 C3
Ingliston *Edinburgh* 11 B1
Inhaúma *Rio de Janeiro* 25 B1
Inner Port Shelter *Hong Kong* 12 A2
Interlagos *São Paulo* 27 C1
Intramuros *Manila* 17 B1
Invalides *Paris* 24 A2
Inverkeithing *Edinburgh* 11 A1
Inzersdorf *Vienna* 32 B2
Ipanema *Rio de Janeiro* 25 B1
Ipiranga *São Paulo* 27 B2
Ipiranga → *São Paulo* 27 B2
Iponri *Lagos* 14 B2
Ireland's Eye *Dublin* 10 A3
Irving Park *Chicago* 9 B2
Isabel *Rio de Janeiro* 25 B1
Isagatedo *Lagos* 14 A1
Isar → *Munich* 21 A3
Ishbīlīya *Baghdad* 3 A2
Ishøj Strand *Copenhagen* 8 B2
Island Bay *Wellington* 33 B1
Island Park *Toronto* 31 B2
Islev *Copenhagen* 8 A2
Isleworth *London* 15 B2
Islington *Toronto* 31 B1
Islington □ *London* 15 A3
Ismaning *Munich* 21 A3
Ismayloskiy Park *Moscow* 19 B3
Isolo *Lagos* 14 A1
Issy-les-Moulineaux *Paris* 24 B2
İstanbul *Istanbul* 12 C1
İstanbul Boğazı *Istanbul* 12 B2
Istinye *Istanbul* 12 B2
Itä Hakkila *Helsinki* 11 B3
Itaewon *Seoul* 27 B1
Itami *Osaka* 23 A1
Itanhanga *Rio de Janeiro* 25 B1
Ivanhoe *Melbourne* 18 A2
Ivry-sur-Seine *Paris* 24 B3
Ixelles *Brussels* 6 B2
Izmaylovo *Moscow* 19 B3
Iztacalco *Mexico City* 18 B2
Iztapalapa *Mexico City* 18 B2

J

Jaba *Jerusalem* 13 A2
Jacaré *Rio de Janeiro* 25 B1
Jackson Heights *New York* 22 B2
Jackson Park *Chicago* 9 C3
Jacques-Cartier *Montreal* 20 A3
Jacques-Cartier, Pont *Montreal* 20 A2
Jadavpur *Kolkata* 14 C2
Jade Buddha Temple *Shanghai* 28 B1
Jægersborg *Copenhagen* 8 A3
Jægersborg Dyrehave *Copenhagen* 8 A3
Jagadishpur *Kolkata* 14 B1
Jagatpur *Delhi* 10 A2
Jaguaré, Rib. do → *São Paulo* 27 B1
Jahangirpur *Delhi* 10 A2
Jakarta *Jakarta* 12 A2
Jakarta, Teluk *Jakarta* 12 A1
Jakarta Halim Perdana Kusuma Int. ✈ (HLP) *Jakarta* 12 B2
Jalan Kayu *Singapore* 28 A3
Jamaica B. *New York* 22 C3
Jamaica Plain *Boston* 6 B2
Jamakpuri *Delhi* 10 B1
Jamshīdīyeh *Tehran* 31 A2
Jamsil *Seoul* 27 B2
Jamwon *Seoul* 27 B2
Janki *Warsaw* 32 C1
Jaraguá *São Paulo* 27 A1
Jaraguá, Pico de *São Paulo* 27 A1
Jardim Paulista *São Paulo* 27 B1
Järvatältet *Stockholm* 29 A1
Jaskhar *Mumbai* 20 B2
Jatinegara *Jakarta* 12 B2
Javādīyeh *Tehran* 31 B2
Jaworowa *Warsaw* 32 C1
Jean Lafitte Nat. Historical Park ⌂ *New Orleans* 21 B1
Jedlesee *Vienna* 32 A2
Jefferson *New Orleans* 21 B2
Jefferson Memorial *Washington* 33 B3
Jefferson Park *Chicago* 9 B2
Jefferson Park *Los Angeles* 16 B3
Jegi *Seoul* 27 B2
Jelambar *Jakarta* 12 A1
Jelonki *Warsaw* 32 B1
Jerónimos, Mosteiro dos *Lisbon* 16 A1
Jersey City *New York* 22 B1
Jerusalem *Jerusalem* 13 B2
Jessamine, L. *Orlando* 23 B2
Jésus, Î. *Montreal* 20 A1
Jesús Maria *Lima* 14 B2
Jette *Brussels* 6 A1
Jey *Tehran* 31 B2
Jianggao *Guangzhou* 11 A2
Jiangwan *Shanghai* 28 B1
Jib *Jerusalem* 13 A2
Jihād *Baghdad* 3 B1
Jingan *Shanghai* 28 B1
Jinočany *Prague* 25 B1
Jinonice *Prague* 25 B2
Jiulong = Kowloon *Hong Kong* 12 B1
Jiyūgaoka *Tokyo* 30 B3
Jizā'ir *Baghdad* 3 B2
Jizīra *Baghdad* 3 B2
Joglo *Jakarta* 12 B1
Johannesburg *Johannesburg* 13 B2
Johannesburg, Univ. of *Johannesburg* 13 B2
Johanneskirchen *Munich* 21 A2
Johannestift *Berlin* 5 A2
Johannisthal *Berlin* 5 B4
John F. Kennedy Nat. Historic Site ⌂ *Boston* 6 A2
John McLaren Park *San Francisco* 26 B2
Johnsonville *Wellington* 33 B1
Joinville-le-Pont *Paris* 24 B3
Joli-Bois *Brussels* 6 B2
Jollas *Helsinki* 11 B3
Jongmyo Royal Shrine *Seoul* 27 B1
Jongno *Seoul* 27 B1
Jonstrup *Copenhagen* 8 A2
Joppa *Edinburgh* 11 B3
Jorge Chavez, Int. ✈ (LIM) *Lima* 14 B2
Jorge Newbery ✈ (AEP) *Buenos Aires* 7 B2
Jósefa Pilsudskiego Park *Warsaw* 32 B1
Jōtō *Osaka* 23 A2
Jouy-en-Josas *Paris* 24 B2
Juan Anchorena *Buenos Aires* 7 A2
Juan González Romero *Mexico City* 18 A2
Juárez Int. ✈ (MEX) *Mexico City* 18 B2
Judeira *Jerusalem* 13 A2
Juhdum *Jerusalem* 13 B2
Juhu *Mumbai* 20 A2
Jūjā *Tokyo* 30 A3
Jukskeirivier → *Johannesburg* 13 A2
Julianów *Warsaw* 32 B2
Jung *Seoul* 27 B1
Jungfernheide, Volkspark *Berlin* 5 A2
Jungfernsee *Berlin* 5 B1
Junghwa *Seoul* 27 B2
Jungnang *Seoul* 27 B2
Jungnangcheon → *Seoul* 27 B1
Juniper Green *Edinburgh* 11 B2
Junk B. *Hong Kong* 12 B2
Jurong *Singapore* 28 B2
Jurong, Selat *Singapore* 28 B2
Jurong Industrial Estate *Singapore* 28 B1
Jurujuba, Enseada de *Rio de Janeiro* 25 B2
Jūsō *Osaka* 23 A1
Justice *Chicago* 9 C2
Jwalahari *Delhi* 10 B1

K

Kaapstad = Cape Town *Cape Town* 8 A1
Kabaty *Warsaw* 32 C2
Kadıköy *Istanbul* 12 C2
Kadoma *Osaka* 23 A2
Kafr 'Aqab *Jerusalem* 13 A2
Kâğıthane *Istanbul* 12 B1
Kâğıthane → *Istanbul* 12 B1
Kagran *Vienna* 32 A2
Kahnawake *Montreal* 20 B1
Kaimes *Edinburgh* 11 B2
Kaiserebersdorf *Vienna* 32 B2
Kaivoksela *Helsinki* 11 B2
Kalamaki *Athens* 2 B2
Kalbadevi *Mumbai* 20 B1
Kalipur *Kolkata* 14 A1
Kalithea *Athens* 2 B2
Kalkaji *Delhi* 10 B2
Kalookan = Caloocan *Manila* 17 B1
Kalvebod Fælled *Copenhagen* 8 B3
Kalveboderne *Copenhagen* 8 B3
Kamarhati *Kolkata* 14 A2
Kamata *Tokyo* 30 B3
Kameari *Tokyo* 30 A4
Kameido *Tokyo* 30 A4
Kami-Itabashi *Tokyo* 30 A3
Kamikitazawa *Tokyo* 30 B2
Kamitsuruma *Tokyo* 30 B1
Kamoshida *Tokyo* 30 B2
Kampong Landang *Singapore* 28 A3
Kampong Tanjong Penjuru *Singapore* 28 B2
Kampung Bali *Jakarta* 12 B1
Kanamori *Tokyo* 30 B1
Kanda *Tokyo* 30 A3
Kandilli *Istanbul* 12 B2
Kankurgachi *Kolkata* 14 B2
Kanlıca *Istanbul* 12 B2
Kanonerskiy, Ostrov *St. Petersburg* 27 B1
Kansai Int. ✈ (KIX) *Osaka* 23 B2
Kanzaki → *Osaka* 23 A1
Kapali Carsi *Istanbul* 12 B1
Kapellerfeld *Vienna* 32 A2
Káposztásmegyer *Budapest* 7 A2
Kapotnya *Moscow* 19 C3
Käppala *Stockholm* 29 A3
Kapuk *Jakarta* 12 A1
Käpylä *Helsinki* 11 B2
Karachi *Karachi* 13 A2
Karachi Int. ✈ (KHI) *Karachi* 13 A2
Karkh *Baghdad* 3 A2
Karlin *Prague* 25 B2
Karlsfeld *Munich* 21 A1
Karlshorst *Berlin* 5 B4
Karlův most *Prague* 25 B2
Karol Bagh *Delhi* 10 B2
Karolinenhof *Berlin* 5 B4
Karori *Wellington* 33 B1
Karow *Berlin* 5 A3
Karrādah *Baghdad* 3 B2
Kärsön *Stockholm* 29 B1
Kasai *Tokyo* 30 B4
Kasipur *Kolkata* 14 B2
Kastrup *Copenhagen* 8 B3
Kastrup, København ✈ (CPH) *Copenhagen* 8 B3
Kasuga *Tokyo* 30 A2
Kasuge *Tokyo* 30 A3
Kasumigaseki *Tokyo* 30 B3
Katong *Singapore* 28 B3
Katsushika *Tokyo* 30 A4
Kau Pai Chau *Hong Kong* 12 B2
Kau Yi Chau *Hong Kong* 12 B1
Kaulsdorf *Berlin* 5 B4
Kauniainen *Helsinki* 11 B1
Kawasaki *Tokyo* 30 B3
Kawawa *Tokyo* 30 B2
Kawęczyn *Warsaw* 32 B2
Kayu Putih *Jakarta* 12 B2
Kbely *Prague* 25 B3
Kebayoran Baru *Jakarta* 12 B1
Kebayoran Lama *Jakarta* 12 B1
Kebon Jeruk *Jakarta* 12 B1
Kedar *Jerusalem* 13 B2
Kedoya *Jakarta* 12 B1
Keilor *Melbourne* 18 A1
Keilor North *Melbourne* 18 A1
Keimola *Helsinki* 11 A1
Kelapa Gading *Jakarta* 12 A2
Kelenföld *Budapest* 7 B2
Kelvin *Johannesburg* 13 A2
Kemang *Jakarta* 12 B1
Kemayoran *Jakarta* 12 B2
Kemerburgaz *Istanbul* 12 B1
Kempton Park Races *London* 15 B1
Kenilworth *Cape Town* 8 A1
Kennedy Town *Hong Kong* 12 B1
Kenner *New Orleans* 21 A1
Kensal Green *London* 15 A2
Kensington *Johannesburg* 13 B2
Kensington *London* 15 B2
Kensington *New York* 22 C2
Kensington *Sydney* 29 B2
Kensington Palace *London* 15 A2
Kent Village *Washington* 33 B4
Kentish Town *London* 15 A3
Kenton *London* 15 A2
Kenwood House *London* 15 A3
Kepa *Warsaw* 32 B2
Keppel Harbour *Singapore* 28 B2
Kesariani *Athens* 2 B2
Kettering *Washington* 33 B5
Kew *London* 15 B2
Kew *Melbourne* 18 A2
Kew Gardens *London* 15 B2
Kew Gardens *Toronto* 31 A3
Key Biscayne *Miami* 18 B2
Khalīj *Baghdad* 3 B2
Khandallah *Wellington* 33 B1
Khansā' *Baghdad* 3 A2
Kharavli *Mumbai* 20 B2
Khefren *Cairo* 7 B1
Khichripur *Delhi* 10 B2
Khidirpur *Kolkata* 14 B1
Khimki-Khovrino *Moscow* 19 A2
Khirbet Batin Abu Lihyah *Jerusalem* 13 A1
Khirbet el-Misbah *Jerusalem* 13 A1
Khirbet Jub e-Rum *Jerusalem* 13 B2
Khlong San *Bangkok* 3 B2
Khlong Toey *Bangkok* 3 B2
Khorel *Kolkata* 14 A1
Khorosovo *Moscow* 19 B1
Kiamari *Karachi* 13 B1
Kierling *Vienna* 32 A1
Kierlingbach → *Vienna* 32 A1
Kifisos → *Athens* 2 B2
Kikuna *Tokyo* 30 B2
Kilbarrack *Dublin* 10 A3
Kilbirnie *Wellington* 33 B1
Kilburn *London* 15 A2
Kilnakee *Dublin* 10 B2
Killester *Dublin* 10 A3
Killiney *Dublin* 10 B3
Killiney B. *Dublin* 10 B3
Kilmacud *Dublin* 10 B2
Kilmainham *Dublin* 10 A2
Kilmainham Gaol *Dublin* 10 A2
Kilmashogue Mt. *Dublin* 10 B2
Kilmore *Dublin* 10 A2
Kilnamanagh *Dublin* 10 B1
Kilo *Helsinki* 11 B1
Kilokri *Delhi* 10 B2
Kiltiernan *Dublin* 10 B2
Kimmage *Dublin* 10 B2
Kindi *Baghdad* 3 B2
Kinghorn *Edinburgh* 11 A2
Kings Domain *Melbourne* 18 A1
Kings Forest = Kongelunden *Copenhagen* 8 B3
Kings Park *Washington* 33 C2
Kings Park West *Washington* 33 C2
Kingsbury *London* 15 A2
Kingsbury *Melbourne* 18 A2
Kingsford *Sydney* 29 B2
Kingsford Smith, Sydney ✈ (SYD) *Sydney* 29 B2
Kingston-upon-Thames □ *London* 15 B2
Kingston Vale *London* 15 B2
Kingsway *Toronto* 31 B1
Kinsaley *Dublin* 10 A2
Kipling Heights *Toronto* 31 A1
Kipseli *Athens* 2 B2
Kirchstockbach *Munich* 21 B3
Kirchtrudering *Munich* 21 B3
Kirikiri *Lagos* 14 B1
Kirke Værløse *Copenhagen* 8 A1
Kirkhill *Edinburgh* 11 B2
Kirkliston *Edinburgh* 11 B1
Kirknewton *Edinburgh* 11 B1
Kirov Palace of Culture *St. Petersburg* 27 B1
Kiryat Anavim *Jerusalem* 13 B1
Kiryat Ha Yovel *Jerusalem* 13 B1
Kısıklı *Istanbul* 12 B2
Kispest *Budapest* 7 B2
Kista *Stockholm* 29 A1
Kita *Osaka* 23 A2
Kita *Tokyo* 30 A3
Kitazawa *Tokyo* 30 B3
Kiu Tsiu *Hong Kong* 12 A2
Kivistö *Helsinki* 11 B2
Kızıltoprak *Istanbul* 12 C2
Kizuri *Osaka* 23 B2
Kjelsås *Oslo* 23 A3
Kladow *Berlin* 5 B1
Klampenborg *Copenhagen* 8 A3
Klecany *Prague* 25 A2
Kledering *Vienna* 32 B2
Klein Jukskei → *Johannesburg* 13 A1
Kleinmachnow *Berlin* 5 B2
Kleinschönebeck *Berlin* 5 B5
Klemetsrud *Oslo* 23 A4
Klender *Jakarta* 12 A2
Kličany *Prague* 25 A2
Kliprivierberg Nature Reserve *Johannesburg* 13 B2
Klosterneuburg *Vienna* 32 A1
Kőbánya *Budapest* 7 B2
Kobbegem *Brussels* 6 A1
København *Copenhagen* 8 A2
København ✈ (CPH) *Copenhagen* 8 B3
Kobylisy *Prague* 25 B2
Kobyłka *Warsaw* 32 A3
Kodaira *Tokyo* 30 A1
Kodanaka *Tokyo* 30 B2
Koekelberg *Brussels* 6 A1
Koganei *Tokyo* 30 A2
Kogarah *Sydney* 29 B1
Koivupää *Helsinki* 11 B2
Koja *Jakarta* 12 A2
Koja Utara *Jakarta* 12 A2
Kokhav Ya'akov *Jerusalem* 13 A2
Kokobunji *Tokyo* 30 A1
Kokobunji-Temple *Tokyo* 30 A4
Kolarängen *Stockholm* 29 B3
Kolbotn *Oslo* 23 B3
Kolkata *Kolkata* 14 B2
Kolkata Dum Dum Int. ✈ (CCU) *Kolkata* 14 B2
Kolkata Maidan *Kolkata* 14 B1
Koło *Warsaw* 32 B1
Kolokinthou *Athens* 2 B2
Kolomyagi *St. Petersburg* 27 A1
Kolonos *Athens* 2 B2
Kolsås *Oslo* 23 A2
Komae *Tokyo* 30 B2
Komagome *Tokyo* 30 A3
Komazawa *Tokyo* 30 B3
Kona *Kolkata* 14 B1
Konala *Helsinki* 11 B2
Kondli *Delhi* 10 B2
Kongelunden *Copenhagen* 8 B3
Kongens Lyngby *Copenhagen* 8 A3
Kongo *Helsinki* 11 A1
Konnagar *Kolkata* 14 A2
Konohana *Osaka* 23 A1
Konradshöhe *Berlin* 5 A2
Kopanina *Prague* 25 B1
Koparkhairna *Mumbai* 20 A2
Köpenick *Berlin* 5 B4
Korangi *Karachi* 13 B2
Koremasa *Tokyo* 30 B1
Koridalos *Athens* 2 B1
Korokoro *Wellington* 33 B2
Korokoro Stream → *Wellington* 33 B2
Kosino *Moscow* 19 B4
Kosugi *Tokyo* 30 B2
Kota *Jakarta* 12 A1
Kōtō *Tokyo* 30 A3
Kotrung *Kolkata* 14 A2
Kouponia *Athens* 2 B2
Kowloon *Hong Kong* 12 B1
Kowloon Peak *Hong Kong* 12 A2
Kowloon Res. *Hong Kong* 12 A1
Kowloon Tong *Hong Kong* 12 A1
Kraainem *Brussels* 6 A2
Krailling *Munich* 21 B1
Krampnitz *Berlin* 5 B1
Krampnitzsee *Berlin* 5 B1
Kranji, Sungei → *Singapore* 28 A2
Kranji Industrial Estate *Singapore* 28 A2
Krasno-Presnenskaya *Moscow* 19 B2
Krč *Prague* 25 B2
Kremlin *Moscow* 19 B2
Krestovskiye, Ostrov *St. Petersburg* 27 B1
Kreuzberg *Berlin* 5 A3
Kritzendorf *Vienna* 32 A1
Krumme Lanke *Berlin* 5 B2
Krummensee *Berlin* 5 A5
Krung Thep = Bangkok *Bangkok* 3 B2
Krusboda *Stockholm* 29 B3
Kuangchou = Guangzhou *Guangzhou* 11 B2
Küçükköy *Istanbul* 12 B1
Küçüksu *Istanbul* 12 B2
Kudrovo *St. Petersburg* 27 B3
Kulosaari *Helsinki* 11 B3
Kumla *Stockholm* 29 B3
Kungens kurva *Stockholm* 29 B1
Kungliga Slottet *Stockholm* 29 B2
Kungshatt *Stockholm* 29 B1
Kungsholmen *Stockholm* 29 A2
Kuningan *Jakarta* 12 B1
Kunitachi *Tokyo* 30 A1
Kunming Hu *Beijing* 4 B1
Kunratice *Prague* 25 B2
Kupchino *St. Petersburg* 27 B2
Kuramo Waters *Lagos* 14 B2
Kurbağalı → *Istanbul* 12 C2
Kurihara *Tokyo* 30 A2
Kurla *Mumbai* 20 A2
Kurmuri *Mumbai* 20 A2
Kurume *Tokyo* 30 A2
Kuryanovo *Moscow* 19 C3
Kuskovo *Moscow* 19 B3
Kustia *Kolkata* 14 B2
Kuzguncuk *Istanbul* 12 B2
Kuzyminki *Moscow* 19 B3
Kwai Chung *Hong Kong* 12 A1
Kwangchow = Guangzhou *Guangzhou* 11 B2
Kwun Tong *Hong Kong* 12 B2
Kyje *Prague* 25 B3
Kyūhōji *Osaka* 23 B2

L

La Barceloneta *Barcelona* 4 A2
La Blanca *Santiago* 27 C2
La Boca *Buenos Aires* 7 B2
La Bretèche *Paris* 24 A1
La Campiña *Lima* 14 C2
La Celle-St-Cloud *Paris* 24 A1
La Cisterna *Santiago* 27 C2
La Courneuve *Paris* 24 A3
La Dehesa *Santiago* 27 B2
La Encantada *Lima* 14 C2
La Estación *Madrid* 17 B1
La Floresta *Barcelona* 4 A1
La Florida *Santiago* 27 C2
La Fortuna *Madrid* 17 B1
La França *Barcelona* 4 A1
La Garenne-Colombes *Paris* 24 A2
La Giustiniana *Rome* 26 B1
La Grange *Chicago* 9 C1
La Grange Park *Chicago* 9 C1
La Granja *Santiago* 27 C2
La Guardia, New York ✈ (LGA) *New York* 22 B2
La Hulpe *Brussels* 6 B2
La Llacuna *Barcelona* 4 A2
La Loma *Mexico City* 18 A1
La Lucila *Buenos Aires* 7 B2
La Maladrerie *Paris* 24 A1
La Milla, Cerro *Lima* 14 B2
La Monachina *Rome* 26 B1
La Moraleja *Madrid* 17 A2
La Nopalera *Mexico City* 18 C2
La Paternal *Buenos Aires* 7 B2
La Perla *Lima* 14 B2
La Perouse *Sydney* 29 B2
La Pisana *Rome* 26 B1
La Prairie *Montreal* 20 B3
La Punta *Lima* 14 B1
La Puntigala *Barcelona* 4 A2
La Queue-en-Brie *Paris* 24 B4
La Reina *Santiago* 27 B2
La Ribera *Barcelona* 4 A1
La Sagrera *Barcelona* 4 A2
La Salada *Buenos Aires* 7 C2
La Scala *Milan* 19 B2
La Storta *Rome* 26 A1
La Taxonera *Barcelona* 4 A2
La Victoria *Lima* 14 B2
Laajalahti *Helsinki* 11 B1
Laajasalo *Helsinki* 11 B3
Laaksolahti *Helsinki* 11 B1
Labagou National Forest *Beijing* 4 A2
Lablāba, W. el → *Cairo* 7 A2
Lachine *Montreal* 20 B1
Lachine, Canal de *Montreal* 20 B2
Lad Phrao *Bangkok* 3 B2
Ladera Heights *Los Angeles* 16 C2
Ládví *Prague* 25 B2
Łady *Warsaw* 32 C1
Lafontaine, Parc *Montreal* 20 A2
Lagoa *Rio de Janeiro* 25 B1
Lagos *Lagos* 14 B2
Lagos Harbour *Lagos* 14 B2
Lagos-Ikeja ✈ (LOS) *Lagos* 14 A1
Lagos Island *Lagos* 14 B2
Lagos Lagoon *Lagos* 14 B2
Laguna de B. *Manila* 17 C2
Laim *Munich* 21 B2
Lainate *Milan* 19 A1
Lainz *Vienna* 32 B1
Lake Buena Vista *Orlando* 23 B1
Lake Cain Hills *Orlando* 23 B2
Lake Fairfax Park *Washington* 33 B2
Lakemba *Sydney* 29 B1
Lakeside *Cape Town* 8 B1
Lakeside *Johannesburg* 13 A2
Lakeview *Chicago* 9 B3
Lakeview *New Orleans* 21 B2
Lakewood Park *Atlanta* 3 B2
Lakhtinskiy *St. Petersburg* 27 B1
Lakhtinskiy Razliv, Oz. *St. Petersburg* 27 B1
Lakshmanpur *Kolkata* 14 B1
Laksi *Bangkok* 3 A2
Lal Qila *Delhi* 10 B2
Lam Tin *Hong Kong* 12 B2
Lambert *Oslo* 23 A3
Lambeth □ *London* 15 B3
Lambrate *Milan* 19 B2
Lambro, Parco *Milan* 19 B2
Lambton Mills *Toronto* 31 B1
Lamma I. *Hong Kong* 12 B1
Landianchang *Beijing* 4 B1
Landover Hills *Washington* 33 B4
Landsmeer *Amsterdam* 2 A2
Landstrasse *Vienna* 32 A2
Landwehr kanal *Berlin* 5 B3
Lane Cove *Sydney* 29 A1
Lane Cove Nat. Park △ *Sydney* 29 A1
Langa *Cape Town* 8 A2
Langenzersdorf *Vienna* 32 A2
Langer See *Berlin* 5 B4
Langley *Washington* 33 B2
Langley Park *Washington* 33 B4
Langwald *Munich* 21 A1
Lanham *Washington* 33 B4
Lankwitz *Berlin* 5 B3
L'Annunziatella *Rome* 26 C2
Lansdowne *Cape Town* 8 A2
Lansing *Toronto* 31 A2
Lanús *Buenos Aires* 7 C2
Lapa *Rio de Janeiro* 25 B1
Laranjeiras *Rio de Janeiro* 25 B1
Las Acacias *Lima* 14 B2
Las Arenas *Lima* 14 B1
Las Corts *Barcelona* 4 A1
Las Kabacki *Warsaw* 32 C2
Las Pinas *Manila* 17 C1
Las Rejas *Santiago* 27 B1
Las Vegas *Las Vegas* 14 A2
Las Vegas McCarran Int. ✈ (LAS) *Las Vegas* 14 B2
LaSalle *Montreal* 20 B2
LaSalle Street Station *Chicago* 9 B3
Lasek Bielański *Warsaw* 32 B1
Lasek Na Kole *Warsaw* 32 B1
Latina *Madrid* 17 B1
Lauttasaari *Helsinki* 11 C2
Laval-des-Rapides *Montreal* 20 A1
Lavīzān *Tehran* 31 A2
Lavradio *Lisbon* 16 A2
Lawndale *Chicago* 9 B2
Lawne L. *Orlando* 23 A2
Lawrence Heights *Toronto* 31 A2
Layari *Karachi* 13 A2
Layari → *Karachi* 13 A1
Łazienkowski Park *Warsaw* 32 B2
Le Blanc-Mesnil *Paris* 24 A3
Le Bourget *Paris* 24 A3
Le Chenoi *Brussels* 6 B2
Le Chesnay *Paris* 24 B1
Le Christ de Saclay *Paris* 24 B2
Le Kremlin-Bicêtre *Paris* 24 B3
Le Mesnil-le-Roi *Paris* 24 A1
Le Pecq *Paris* 24 A1
Le Perreux *Paris* 24 A3
Le Pin *Paris* 24 A4
Le Plessis-Robinson *Paris* 24 B2
Le Plessis-Trévise *Paris* 24 B4
Le Port-Marly *Paris* 24 A1
Le Pré-St-Gervais *Paris* 24 A3
Le Raincy *Paris* 24 A4
Le Vésinet *Paris* 24 A1
Lea Bridge *London* 15 A3
Leaside *Toronto* 31 A2
Leblon *Rio de Janeiro* 25 B1
Lee *London* 15 B4
Leganés *Madrid* 17 C1
Legazpi *Madrid* 17 B1
Lehtisaari *Helsinki* 11 B2
Lei Yue Mun *Hong Kong* 12 B2
Leião *Lisbon* 16 A1
Leichhardt *Sydney* 29 B1
Leith *Edinburgh* 11 B3

Lekki Lagos 14 B2
Leme Rio de Janeiro 25 B1
Lemoyne Montreal 20 B3
Lenin Moscow 19 B2
Lenino Moscow 19 C2
Leninskiye Gory Moscow 19 B2
Lennox Los Angeles 16 C2
Leonia New York 22 A2
Leopardstown Dublin 10 B2
Leopoldau Vienna 32 A2
Leopoldsdorf Vienna 32 B2
Leopoldstadt Vienna 32 A2
Leportovo Moscow 19 B3
Leppävaara Helsinki 11 B1
Les Lilas Paris 24 A3
Les Loges-en-Josas Paris 24 B1
Les Pavillons-sous-Bois Paris 24 A4
Lésigny Paris 24 B4
Lesnozavodskaya St. Petersburg 27 B2
Lester B. Pearson Int., Toronto ✕ (YYZ) Toronto 31 A1
L'Étang-la-Ville Paris 24 A1
Letňany Prague 25 B3
Letopolis = Ausîm Cairo 7 A1
Levallois-Perret Paris 24 A2
Levent Istanbul 12 B2
Lewisdale Washington 33 B4
Lewisham □ London 15 B3
Lexington Boston 6 A1
Leyton London 15 A3
Leytonstone London 15 A4
L'Haÿ-les-Roses Paris 24 B3
L'Hospitalet de Llobregat Barcelona 4 A1
Lhotka Prague 25 B2
Liangshui He → Beijing 4 C2
Lianhua Chi Beijing 4 B1
Lianhua He → Beijing 4 B1
Libčice nad Vitavou Prague 25 A2
Libeň Prague 25 B2
Liberdade São Paulo 27 B2
Liberton Edinburgh 11 B3
Liberty I. New York 22 B1
Liberty Osaka Museum Osaka 23 B1
Liberty State Park ⌂ New York 22 B1
Libeznice Prague 25 A2
Libuš Prague 25 B2
Lichiao Guangzhou 11 B2
Lichtenburg Berlin 5 A4
Lichterfelde Berlin 5 B2
Lidingö Stockholm 29 A2
Lieshi Lingyuan Guangzhou 11 B2
Liesing Vienna 32 B1
Liesing → Vienna 32 B2
Ligovo St. Petersburg 27 C1
Lijordet Oslo 23 A2
Likhoborka → Moscow 19 A2
Lilla Värtan Stockholm 29 A3
Lille Værløse Copenhagen 8 A2
Liluah Kolkata 14 B1
Lim Chu Kang Singapore 28 A2
Lima Lima 14 B2
Lima Jorge Chavez, Int. ✕ (LIM) Lima 14 B2
Limbiate Milan 19 A1
Limehouse London 15 A3
Limeil-Brévannes Paris 24 B3
Linate, Milano ✕ (LIN) Milan 19 B2
Linbropark Johannesburg 13 A2
Lincoln Center for Performing Arts New York 22 B2
Lincoln Heights Los Angeles 16 B3
Lincoln Memorial Washington 33 B3
Lincoln Park Chicago 9 B3
Lincoln Park New York 22 B1
Lincoln Park San Francisco 26 B1
Lincoln Park Zoo Chicago 9 B3
Lincolnwood Chicago 9 A2
Linda-a-Pastora Lisbon 16 A1
Linden Johannesburg 13 A2
Linden Wellington 33 A1
Lindenberg Berlin 5 A4
Lindøya Oslo 23 A3
Liniers Buenos Aires 7 B1
Linkebeek Brussels 6 B2
Linksfield Johannesburg 13 A2
Linmeyer Johannesburg 13 B2
Linna Helsinki 11 A2
Lintuvaara Helsinki 11 B1
Lion Rock Country Park ⌂ Hong Kong 12 A2
Lion's Head Cape Town 8 A1
Lioumi Athens 2 B2
Lisboa Lisbon 16 A2
Lisboa ✕ (LIS) Lisbon 16 A2
Lisbon = Lisboa Lisbon 16 A2
Lishui Guangzhou 11 A1
Little B. Sydney 29 B2
Little Calumet → Chicago 9 D3
Little Ferry New York 22 A1
Little Lake Conway Orlando 23 B2
Little Red School House Nature Center Chicago 9 C1
Little Rouge → Toronto 31 A4
Liuhang Shanghai 28 A1
Liurong Temple Guangzhou 11 B2
Live Oak Manor New Orleans 21 B1
Livry-Gargan Paris 24 A4
Liwan Guangzhou 11 B2
Ljan Oslo 23 A3
Llano de Can Gineu Barcelona 4 A2
Lo Aranguiz Santiago 27 B2
Lo Boza Santiago 27 B1
Lo Chau Hong Kong 12 B2
Lo Chau Pak Mai Hong Kong 12 B2
Lo Espejo Santiago 27 C1
Lo Hermida Santiago 27 B2
Lo Prado Santiago 27 B1
Lo So Shing Hong Kong 12 B1
Lo Wai Hong Kong 12 A1
Loanhead Edinburgh 11 B3
Lobau Vienna 32 A3
Lobos, Pt. San Francisco 26 B1
Locham Munich 21 B1
Lochkov Prague 25 B2
Lockhausen Munich 21 A1
Lodi New York 22 A1
Lodi Estate Delhi 10 B2
Logan Int., Boston ✕ (BOS) Boston 6 A2
Logan Square Chicago 9 B2
Lognes-Émerainville ✕ (XLG) Paris 24 B4
Löhme Berlin 5 A5
Lokolhet Karachi 13 A2
Lomas Chapultepec Mexico City 18 B1
Lomas de San Angel Inn Mexico City 18 B1
Lombardy East Johannesburg 13 A2
Lomianki Warsaw 32 A1
Lomus Reforma Mexico City 18 B1
London London 15 B3
London Avenue Canal New Orleans 21 A2
London City ✕ (LCY) London 15 A4
London Heathrow ✕ (LHR) London 15 B1
London Zoo London 15 A3
Long B. Sydney 29 B2
Long Branch Toronto 31 B1
Long Brook → Washington 33 C2
Long Ditton London 15 B2
Long Island City New York 22 B2
Longchamp, Hippodrome de Paris 24 A2
Longhua Pagoda Shanghai 28 B1
Longhua Park Shanghai 28 B1
Longjohn Slough Chicago 9 C1
Longtan Hu → Beijing 4 B2
Longue-Pointe Montreal 20 A2
Longueuil Montreal 20 A3
Loni Delhi 10 A2
Loop, The Chicago 9 B3
Lord's Cricket Ground London 15 A2
Loreto Milan 19 B2
Los Angeles Los Angeles 16 B3
Los Angeles Int. ✕ (LAX) Los Angeles 16 C2
Los Cerrillos ✕ (ULC) Santiago 27 B1
Los Nietos Los Angeles 16 C4
Los Olivos Lima 14 A2
Los Remedios △ Mexico City 18 B1
Los Reyes Mexico City 18 B2
Losiny Ostrov △ Moscow 19 A3
Lot Brussels 6 B1
Lotus River Cape Town 8 B2
Lotus Temple Delhi 10 B2
Loughlinstown Dublin 10 B3
Louis Armstrong New Orleans Int. ✕ (MSY) New Orleans 21 A1
Louise, L. Orlando 23 B1
Louisiana Superdome New Orleans 21 B2
Loures Lisbon 16 A1
Louveciennes Paris 24 A1
Louvre, Musée du Paris 24 A3
Lower B. New York 22 C1
Lower Hutt Wellington 33 B2
Lower New York B. = Lower B. New York 22 C1
Lower Shing Mun Res. Hong Kong 12 A1
Lowry Bay Wellington 33 B2
Loyola Univ. Chicago 9 B3
Lu Xun, Tomb of Shanghai 28 B1
Lu Xun Park Shanghai 28 B1
Lübars Berlin 5 A3
Lucy, L. Orlando 23 A2
Ludwigsfeld Munich 21 A1
Luhu Guangzhou 11 B2
Lumiar Lisbon 16 A2
Lundtofte Copenhagen 8 A3
Lung Mei Hong Kong 12 A2
Luojiang Guangzhou 11 B2
Lustheim Munich 21 A2
Luwan Shanghai 28 B1
Luzhniki Sports Centre Moscow 19 B2
Lyndhurst New York 22 B1
Lynn Woods Res. Boston 6 A2
Lyon, Gare de Paris 24 A3
Lyons Chicago 9 C2
Lysaker Oslo 23 A2
Lysakerselva → Oslo 23 A2
Lysolaje Prague 25 B2
Lyublino Moscow 19 B3

M

Ma Nam Wat Hong Kong 12 A2
Ma On Shan Country Park ⌂ Hong Kong 12 A2
Ma'ale Adumim Jerusalem 13 B2
Ma'ale Ha Khamisha Jerusalem 13 B1
Ma'ale Mikhmas Jerusalem 13 A2
Maantiekylä Helsinki 11 A3
Maarifa Baghdad 3 B2
Mabato Pt. Manila 17 C2
Mabel, L. Orlando 23 B1
Macaco, Morro do Rio de Janeiro 25 B2
McCarran Int., Las Vegas ✕ (LAS) Las Vegas 14 B2
McCook Chicago 9 C2
McGill Univ. Montreal 20 A2
Machelen Brussels 6 A2
Machida Tokyo 30 B1
Maciołki Warsaw 32 B2
McKerrow, Mt. Wellington 33 B2
McKinley Park Chicago 9 C2
McLean Washington 33 B2
Macupocho → Santiago 27 B1
MacRitchie Res. Singapore 28 A2
Macul Santiago 27 C2
Madhudaha Kolkata 14 B2
Madhyamgram Kolkata 14 A2
Madín Mexico City 18 A1
Madín, L. Mexico City 18 A1
Madīnah Al Manṣūr Baghdad 3 B2
Mâdinet Nasr Cairo 7 A2
Madrid Madrid 17 B1
Madrid Barajas ✕ (MAD) Madrid 17 B2
Madrona Barcelona 4 A1
Maesawa Tokyo 30 A2
Magdalena Lima 14 B2
Magdalena Contreras Mexico City 18 C1
Maghreb Baghdad 3 A2
Maginu Tokyo 30 B2
Magliana Rome 26 B1
Magny-les-Hameaux Paris 24 B1
Maheshtala Kolkata 14 C1
Mahim Mumbai 20 A2
Mahim B. Mumbai 20 A1
Mahlsdorf Berlin 5 A4
Mahmoodabad Karachi 13 A2
Mahrauli Delhi 10 B2
Mahul Mumbai 20 A2
Maida Vale London 15 A2
Maidstone Melbourne 18 A1
Maipú Santiago 27 C1
Maisonneuve, Parc Montreal 20 A2
Maisons-Alfort Paris 24 B3
Maisons-Laffitte Paris 24 A1
Maissoneuve Montreal 20 A2
Maitland Cape Town 8 A1
Makasar Jakarta 12 A2
Makati Manila 17 B2
Mäkiniitty Helsinki 11 A2
Malá Strana Prague 25 B2
Malabar Sydney 29 B2
Malabar Hill Mumbai 20 B1
Malabar Pt. Mumbai 20 B1
Malabon Manila 17 B1
Malacañang Palace Manila 17 B1
Malahide Dublin 10 A3
Malakoff Paris 24 B2
Mälarhöjaen Stockholm 29 B1
Malate Manila 17 B1
Malaya Neva St. Petersburg 27 B1
Malaya Okhta St. Petersburg 27 B2
Malchow Berlin 5 A3
Malden Boston 6 A2
Malden London 15 B2
Maleizen Brussels 6 B3
Malešice Prague 25 B3
Malir → Karachi 13 B2
Malleny Mills Edinburgh 11 B2
Malmi Helsinki 11 B2
Malmøya Oslo 23 A3
Måløv Copenhagen 8 A1
Malton Toronto 31 A1
Malvern Johannesburg 13 B2
Malvern Melbourne 18 B2
Malvern Toronto 31 A3
Mampang Prapatan Jakarta 12 B1
Mampukuji Tokyo 30 B2
Man Budrukh Mumbai 20 A2
Man Khurd Mumbai 20 A2
Manakhat Jerusalem 13 B2
Mandaluyong Manila 17 B2
Mandaoli Delhi 10 B2
Mandaqui → São Paulo 27 A2
Mandoli Delhi 10 A2
Mandvi Mumbai 20 B2
Manenberg Cape Town 8 A2
Mang Kung Uk Hong Kong 12 B2
Mang-won Seoul 27 B1
Mangolpuri Delhi 10 A1
Manguinhos ✕ Rio de Janeiro 25 B1
Manhattan New York 22 B2
Manhattan Beach New York 22 C2
Manila Manila 17 B1
Manila Ninoy Aquino Int. ✕ (MNL) Manila 17 B2
Mankkaa Helsinki 11 B1
Manly Sydney 29 A2
Mann, L. Orlando 23 A2
Mann's Chinese Theatre Los Angeles 16 B2
Mannswörth Vienna 32 B3
Manor Park London 15 A4
Manor Park Wellington 33 A2
Manora Karachi 13 B1
Manora Pt. Karachi 13 B1
Manquehue, Cerro Santiago 27 B2
Manzanares, Canal de Madrid 17 C2
Mapo Seoul 27 B1
Mar Vista Los Angeles 16 B2
Maracanã Rio de Janeiro 25 B1
Maraoli Mumbai 20 A2
Marcelin Warsaw 32 B1
Mareil-Marly Paris 24 A1
Margareten Vienna 32 A2
Maria Vienna 32 A2
Maridalen Oslo 23 A3
Maridalsvatnet Oslo 23 A3
Mariendorf Berlin 5 B3
Marienfelde Berlin 5 B3
Marikina Manila 17 B2
Marikina → Manila 17 B2
Marin City San Francisco 26 A1
Marin Pen. San Francisco 26 A1
Marina del Rey Los Angeles 16 C2
Marino Dublin 10 A2
Marisco, Ponta do Rio de Janeiro 25 C1
Markham Toronto 31 A2
Marki Warsaw 32 A2
Markland Wood Toronto 31 B1
Marly, Forêt de Paris 24 A1
Marly-le-Roi Paris 24 A1
Marne-la-Vallée Paris 24 A4
Marolles-en-Brie Paris 24 B4
Maroubra Sydney 29 B2
Marquette Park Chicago 9 C2
Marrero New Orleans 21 B2
Marrickville Sydney 29 B1
Marsfield Sydney 29 A1
Marsha, L. Orlando 23 B2
Marte, Campo de São Paulo 27 B2
Martesana, Navíglio della Milan 19 A2
Martin Luther King Nat. Historic Site ⌂ Atlanta 3 B2
Martinez Buenos Aires 7 A1
Martinkylä Helsinki 11 B2
Martinsried Munich 21 B1
Maruko Tokyo 30 B3
Maryino Moscow 19 B3
Maryland Singapore 28 B2
Marymont Warsaw 32 B1
Marysin Wawerski Warsaw 32 B2
Marzahn Berlin 5 A4
Mascot Sydney 29 B2
Maomo Stockholm 29 B1
Maspeth New York 22 B2
Masr el Gedida Cairo 7 A2
Masr el Qadīma Cairo 7 A2
Massachusetts Inst. of Tech. Boston 6 A2
Massamá Lisbon 16 A1
Massey → Toronto 31 A3
Massy Paris 24 B2
Mata Jerusalem 13 B1
Matinha Lisbon 16 A2
Matramam Jakarta 12 B2
Matsubara Osaka 23 B2
Mattapan Boston 6 B2
Mátyásföld Budapest 7 A3
Mau Tso Ngam Hong Kong 12 A2
Mauer Vienna 32 B1
Mauripur Karachi 13 A1
Maxhof Munich 21 B1
Mayfair Johannesburg 13 B2
Maywood Chicago 9 B1
Maywood Los Angeles 16 C3
Maywood New York 22 A1
Maywood Park Race Track Chicago 9 B1
Mazagaon Mumbai 20 B2
Meadowbank Park Sydney 29 A1
Měcholupy Prague 25 B3
Měčice Prague 25 A3
Mecidiyeköy Istanbul 12 B2
Medford Boston 6 A2
Mediodia Madrid 17 B2
Meguro Tokyo 30 B3
Meguro → Tokyo 30 B3
Mehpalpur Delhi 10 B1
Mehrābād ✕ (THR) Tehran 31 A1
Mehram Nagar Delhi 10 B1
Mehrow Berlin 5 A4
Meidling Vienna 32 A2
Méier Rio de Janeiro 25 B1
Meiji Shrine Tokyo 30 A3
Meise Brussels 6 A1
Mejiro Tokyo 30 A3
Melbourne Melbourne 18 A1
Melbourne ✕ (MEL) Melbourne 18 A1
Melkki Helsinki 11 C2
Mellunkylä Helsinki 11 B3
Mellunmäki Helsinki 11 B3
Melrose Boston 6 A2
Melrose New York 22 B2
Melrose Park Chicago 9 B1
Melsbroek Brussels 6 A2
Melville Johannesburg 13 B2
Menteng Jakarta 12 B1
Mérantaise → Paris 24 B1
Mercamadrid Madrid 17 B2
Merced, L. San Francisco 26 B2
Meredale Johannesburg 13 B1
Merlimau, Pulau Singapore 28 B2
Merri Cr. → Melbourne 18 A1
Merrion Dublin 10 B2
Merrionette Park Chicago 9 C2
Merton □ London 15 B2
Mesgarābād Tehran 31 B3
Messe Vienna 32 A2
Metairie New Orleans 21 A2
Metanópoli Milan 19 B2
Metro-Dade Cultural Centre Miami 18 B2
Metro Toronto Zoo Toronto 31 A3
Metropolitan Museum of Art New York 22 B2
Meudon Paris 24 B2
Mevaseret Tsiyon Jerusalem 13 B1
Mevo Beitar Jerusalem 13 B1
México Mexico City 18 B2
México, Ciudad de Mexico City 18 B2
Mexico City Int. ✕ (MEX) Mexico City 18 B2
Meyersdal Johannesburg 13 B2
Mezzate Milan 19 B2
Miadong Seoul 27 B2
Miami Miami 18 B2
Miami Beach Miami 18 B2
Miami Canal Miami 18 A1
Miami Int. ✕ (MIA) Miami 18 B1
Miami Shores Miami 18 A2
Miami Springs Miami 18 B1
Miasto Warsaw 32 B2
Michałowice Warsaw 32 B1
Michle Prague 25 B2
Mid-City Los Angeles 16 B2
Mid City New Orleans 21 B2
Middle Harbour Sydney 29 A2
Middle Hd. Sydney 29 A2
Middle Park Melbourne 18 B1
Middle Village New York 22 B2
Middlesex Fells Reservation Boston 6 A2
Midland Beach New York 22 C1
Midwood New York 22 C2
Miedzeszyn Warsaw 32 B3
Międzylesie Warsaw 32 B3
Miessaari Helsinki 11 C1
Miguel Hidalgo Mexico City 18 B1
Milan = Milano Milan 19 B1
Milanese, Parco Regionale ⌂ Milan 19 A1
Milano Milan 19 B1
Milano Due Milan 19 B2
Milano Linate ✕ (LIN) Milan 19 B2
Milano San Felice Milan 19 B2
Milbertshofen Munich 21 A2
Mill Hill London 15 A2
Millennium Dome London 15 A4
Miller Meadow Chicago 9 B2
Millerhill Edinburgh 11 B3
Milltown Dublin 10 B2
Millwood Washington 33 B4
Milnerton Cape Town 8 A1
Milon-la-Chapelle Paris 24 B1
Milton Boston 6 B2
Milton Bridge Edinburgh 11 B2
Mimico Toronto 31 B2
Mimico Creek → Toronto 31 B1
Minami Osaka 23 A2
Minamitsunashima Tokyo 30 B2
Minato Osaka 23 B1
Minato Tokyo 30 B3
Minshât el Bekkarî Cairo 7 A1
Miraflores Lima 14 B2
Miramar Wellington 33 B1
Misericordia, Sa. da Rio de Janeiro 25 B1
Mission San Francisco 26 B2
Mississauga Toronto 31 B1
Mitaka Tokyo 30 A2
Mitcham London 15 B2
Mitcham Common London 15 B3
Mitchell Museum of the American Indian Chicago 9 A2
Mitchell's Plain Cape Town 8 B2
Mitte Berlin 5 A3
Mittel Isarkanal → Munich 21 A3
Mixcoac Mexico City 18 B1
Miyakojima Osaka 23 A2
Mizonokuchi Tokyo 30 B2
Mizue Tokyo 30 A4
Młocinski Park Warsaw 32 B1
Młociny Warsaw 32 B1
Mnevniki Moscow 19 B1
Moba Lagos 14 B2
Moczydło Warsaw 32 C2
Modderfontein Johannesburg 13 A2
Modřany Prague 25 B2
Mogyoród Budapest 7 A3
Moinho Velho, Cor. → São Paulo 27 B2
Mok Seoul 27 B1
Mokotów Warsaw 32 B2
Molenbeek-St-Jean Brussels 6 A1
Molino de Rosas Mexico City 18 B1
Mollem Brussels 6 A1
Mollins de Rey Barcelona 4 A1
Mondeor Johannesburg 13 B2
Moneda, Palacio de la Santiago 27 B2
Moneró Rio de Janeiro 25 A1
Mong Kok Hong Kong 12 B2
Monkstown Dublin 10 B3
Monnickendam Amsterdam 2 A3
Monrovia Los Angeles 16 B4
Monsanto Lisbon 16 A1
Monsanto, Parque Florestal de Lisbon 16 A1
Mont-Royal Montreal 20 A2
Mont-Royal, Parc Montreal 20 A2
Montana de Montjuich Barcelona 4 A1
Montcada i Reixac Barcelona 4 A2
Monte Chingolo Buenos Aires 7 C2
Montebello Los Angeles 16 B4
Montemor Lisbon 16 A1
Monterey Hills Los Angeles 16 B3
Monterey Park Los Angeles 16 B4
Montespaccato Rome 26 B1
Montesson Paris 24 A1
Monteverde Nuovo Rome 26 B1
Montfermeil Paris 24 A4
Montigny-le-Bretonneux Paris 24 B1
Montjay-la-Tour Paris 24 A4
Montjuïc Barcelona 4 A2
Montparnasse, Gare Paris 24 A2
Montréal Montreal 20 A2
Montréal, Î. de Montreal 20 A2
Montréal, Univ. de Montreal 20 B2
Montréal Est Montreal 20 A2
Montréal-Nord Montreal 20 A2
Montréal-Ouest Montreal 20 B1
Montréal Trudeau Int. ✕ (YUL) Montreal 20 B1
Montreuil Paris 24 A3
Montrouge Paris 24 B2
Montserrat Buenos Aires 7 B2
Monza Milan 19 A2
Monzoro Milan 19 B1
Moóca São Paulo 27 B2
Moonachie New York 22 B1
Moonee Ponds Melbourne 18 A1
Moonee Valley Racecourse Melbourne 18 A1
Moosach Munich 21 A2
Mora Mumbai 20 B2
Moratalaz Madrid 17 B2
Mörby Stockholm 29 A2
Morden London 15 B2
Morée → Paris 24 A3
Morgan Park Chicago 9 C3
Moriguchi Osaka 23 A2
Morivione Milan 19 B2
Morningside Edinburgh 11 B2
Morningside Johannesburg 13 A2
Morningside Washington 33 C4
Morningside Park Orlando 23 B2
Morningside Park Toronto 31 A3
Morro Solar, Cerro Lima 14 C2
Mortlake London 15 B2
Mortlake Sydney 29 B1
Morton Grove Chicago 9 A2
Morumbi São Paulo 27 B1
Moscavide Lisbon 16 A2
Moschato Athens 2 B2
Moscow = Moskva Moscow 19 B2
Moskva Moscow 19 B2
Moskvoretskiy Moscow 19 B2
Mosman Sydney 29 B2
Moti Bagh Delhi 10 B2
Motol Prague 25 B2
Motsa Jerusalem 13 B2
Motsa Ilit Jerusalem 13 B1
Motspur Park London 15 B2
Mottingham London 15 B4
Mount Dennis Toronto 31 A2
Mount Greenwood Chicago 9 C2
Mount Hood Memorial Park ⌂ Boston 6 A2
Mount Merrion Dublin 10 B2
Mount Olympus Los Angeles 16 B2
Mount Rainier Washington 33 B4
Mount Vernon New York 22 A3
Müggelberge Berlin 5 B4
Müggelheim Berlin 5 B5
Muggiò Milan 19 A2
Mühleiten Vienna 32 A3
Mühlenfliess → Berlin 5 A5
Muiden Amsterdam 2 A3
Muizenberg Cape Town 8 B1
Mujahidpur Delhi 10 B2
Mukandpur Delhi 10 A2
Mukhmas Jerusalem 13 A2
Muko → Osaka 23 A1
Mukojima Tokyo 30 A3
Mulbarton Johannesburg 13 B2
Mullach Íde = Malahide Dublin 10 A3
Mumbai Mumbai 20 B2
Mumbai Chhatrapati Shivaji Int. ✕ (BOM) Mumbai 20 A2
Mumbai Harbour Mumbai 20 B2
Munch-museum Oslo 23 A3
Münchehofe Berlin 5 B5
München Munich 21 B2
München Franz Josef Strauss Int. ✕ (MUC) Munich 21 A2
Munich = München Munich 21 B2
Munkkiniemi Helsinki 11 B2
Munro Buenos Aires 7 B1
Muntinlupa Manila 17 C2
Murai Res. Singapore 28 A2
Muranów Warsaw 32 B1
Murino St. Petersburg 27 B2
Murrayfield Edinburgh 11 B2
Murtala Mohammed International ✕ (LOS) Lagos 14 A1
Musashino Tokyo 30 A2
Museu Nacional Rio de Janeiro 25 B1
Mushin Lagos 14 A2
Musocco Milan 19 B1
Mustansiriya Baghdad 3 A2
Musturud Cairo 7 A2
Muswell Hill London 15 A3
Mutanabi Baghdad 3 B2
Muthana Baghdad 3 B2
Mykerinos Cairo 7 B1
Myllypuro Helsinki 11 B3
Mystic → Boston 6 A2

N

Nacka Stockholm 29 B3
Naenae Wellington 33 B2
Nærsnes Oslo 23 B1
Nagatsuta Tokyo 30 B2
Nagytétény Budapest 7 B1
Nahalin Jerusalem 13 B1
Najafgarh Drain → Delhi 10 B1
Nakahara Tokyo 30 B2
Nakano Tokyo 30 A2
Namsan Park Seoul 27 B1
Namyeong Seoul 27 B1
Nanbiancun Guangzhou 11 B1
Nanchang He → Beijing 4 B1
Nandang Guangzhou 11 B2
Nangal Dewat Delhi 10 B1
Naniwa Osaka 23 B1
Nanole Mumbai 20 A2
Nanpu Bridge Shanghai 28 B2
Nanshi Shanghai 28 B1
Nanterre Paris 24 A2
Napier Mole Karachi 13 B1
Naraina Delhi 10 B1
Nariman Point Mumbai 20 B1
Nariman Pt. Mumbai 20 B1
Nārmak Tehran 31 A2
Naruo Osaka 23 A1
Näsby Stockholm 29 A2
Näsbypark Stockholm 29 A2
National Arboretum Washington 33 B3
National Zoological Park Washington 33 B3
Nationals Park Washington 33 B3
Nativity, Basilica of Jerusalem 13 B2
Natolin Warsaw 32 C2
Naucalpan de Juárez Mexico City 18 B1
Naupada Mumbai 20 A2
Navi Mumbai Mumbai 20 A2
Navíglio di Pavia Milan 19 B1
Navíglio Grande Milan 19 B1
Navotas Manila 17 B1
Navy Pier Chicago 9 B3
Nazal Hikmat Beg Baghdad 3 A2
Nazimabad Karachi 13 A2
Nazlet el Simmân Cairo 7 B1
Nea Alexandria Athens 2 B2
Nea Ionia Athens 2 A2
Nea Liosia Athens 2 A2
Nea Smirni Athens 2 B2
Neapoli Athens 2 B2
Near North Chicago 9 B3
Nebušice Prague 25 B1
Nederhorst Amsterdam 2 B3
Nedlitz Berlin 5 B1
Nee Soon Singapore 28 A2
Needham Boston 6 B1
Needham Heights Boston 6 B1
Nellis Air Force Base ✕ (LSV) Las Vegas 14 A2
N'ematābād Tehran 31 B2
Nerima Tokyo 30 A3
Nesodden Oslo 23 B3
Nesoddtangen Oslo 23 A3
Nesøya Oslo 23 A2
Neu Aubing Munich 21 B1
Neu Buch Berlin 5 A4
Neu Buchhorst Berlin 5 B5
Neu Fahrland Berlin 5 B1
Neu Lindenberg Berlin 5 A4
Neubiberg Munich 21 B3
Neuenhagen Berlin 5 A4
Neuessling Vienna 32 A3
Neuhausen Munich 21 B2
Neuherberg Munich 21 A2
Neuhönow Berlin 5 A5
Neuilly-Plaisance Paris 24 A4
Neuilly-sur-Marne Paris 24 A4
Neuilly-sur-Seine Paris 24 A2
Neukagran Vienna 32 A2
Neukettenhof Vienna 32 B2
Neukölln Berlin 5 B3
Neuperlach Munich 21 B2
Neuried Munich 21 B1
Neustift am Walde Vienna 32 A1
Neusüssenbrunn Vienna 32 A2
Neuwaldegg Vienna 32 A1
Neve Ya'akov Jerusalem 13 A2
Neves Rio de Janeiro 25 B2
New Baghdād Baghdad 3 B2
New Barakpur Kolkata 14 A2
New Brighton New York 22 C1
New Canada Johannesburg 13 B1
New Canada Dam Johannesburg 13 B1
New Carrollton Washington 33 B4
New Cross London 15 B3
New Delhi Delhi 10 B2
New Dorp New York 22 C1
New Dorp Beach New York 22 C1
New Malden London 15 B2
New Milford New York 22 A1
New Mumbai = Navi Mumbai Mumbai 20 A2
New Orleans New Orleans 21 B2
New Orleans Int. ✕ (MSY) New Orleans 21 A1
New Territories Hong Kong 12 A1
New Toronto Toronto 31 B1
New Utrecht New York 22 C2
New York New York 22 B3
New York La Guardia ✕ (LGA) New York 22 B2
Newark B. New York 22 B1
Newbattle Edinburgh 11 B3
Newbury Park London 15 A4
Newcraighall Edinburgh 11 B3
Newham □ London 15 A4
Newhaven Edinburgh 11 B2
Newington Edinburgh 11 B2
Newlands Johannesburg 13 B1
Newlands Wellington 33 B1
Newport Melbourne 18 B1
Newton Boston 6 B1
Newtonbrook Toronto 31 A2
Newtongrange Edinburgh 11 B3
Newtonville Boston 6 A1
Newtown Sydney 29 B2
Ngaio Wellington 33 B1
Ngau Chi Wan Hong Kong 12 A2
Ngau Tau Kok Hong Kong 12 B2
Ngauranga Wellington 33 B1
Ngong Shuen Chau Hong Kong 12 B1
Ngua Kok Wan Hong Kong 12 A1
Nhava Sheva Mumbai 20 B2
Niāvarān Tehran 31 A2
Nibra Kolkata 14 B1
Nidāl Baghdad 3 B2
Niddrie Edinburgh 11 B3
Niddrie Melbourne 18 A1
Nieder Neuendorf Berlin 5 A2
Niederschöneweide Berlin 5 B3
Niederschönhausen Berlin 5 A3
Niemeyer Rio de Janeiro 25 B1
Nieuwendam Amsterdam 2 A2
Nihonbashi Tokyo 30 A3
Niipperi Helsinki 11 B1
Nikea Athens 2 B1
Nikolassee Berlin 5 B2
Nikolskiy Moscow 19 B1
Niles Chicago 9 A2
Nimta Kolkata 14 A2
Ninoy Aquino Int. ✕ (MNL) Manila 17 B2
Nippa Tokyo 30 B2
Nippori Tokyo 30 A3
Nishi Osaka 23 A1
Nishinari Osaka 23 B1
Nishinomiya Osaka 23 A1
Nishiyodogawa Osaka 23 A1
Niterói Rio de Janeiro 25 B2
Nockeby Stockholm 29 B1
Noel Park London 15 A3
Nogatino Moscow 19 B3
Nogent-sur-Marne Paris 24 A3
Noida Delhi 10 B2
Noiseau Paris 24 B4
Noisiel Paris 24 A4
Noisy-le-Grand Paris 24 A4
Noisy-le-Roi Paris 24 A1
Noisy-le-Sec Paris 24 A3
Nokkala Helsinki 11 C1
Nomentano Rome 26 B2
Nonakashinden Tokyo 30 A2
Nongminyundong Jiangxisuo Guangzhou 11 B2
Nonhyeon Seoul 27 B2
Nonthaburi Bangkok 3 A1
Noordgesig Johannesburg 13 B1
Noordzeekanaal Amsterdam 2 A1
Nord, Gare du Paris 24 A3
Nordmarka Oslo 23 A3
Nordrand-Siedlung Vienna 32 A2
Nordstrand Oslo 23 A3
Normandale Wellington 33 B2
Norridge Chicago 9 B2
Norrmalm Stockholm 29 A2
North Arlington New York 22 B1
North Bay Village Miami 18 A2
North Bergen New York 22 B1
North Bull I. Dublin 10 A3
North Cheam London 15 B2
North Cray London 15 B4
North Decatur Atlanta 3 B3
North Druid Hills Atlanta 3 B3
North Esk → Edinburgh 11 B2
North Gyle Edinburgh 11 B2
North Hackensack New York 22 A1
North Harbor Manila 17 B1
North Hd. Sydney 29 A2
North Hollywood Los Angeles 16 B2
North Las Vegas Las Vegas 14 A1
North Las Vegas ✕ (VGT) Las Vegas 14 A1
North Lexington Boston 6 A1
North Miami Miami 18 A2
North Miami Beach Miami 18 A2
North Nazimabad Karachi 13 A2
North Pt. Hong Kong 12 B2
North Queensferry Edinburgh 11 A1
North Quincy Boston 6 B2
North Res. Boston 6 A2
North Riverside Chicago 9 B2
North Saugus Boston 6 A2
North Shore Channel → Chicago 9 B2
North Springfield Washington 33 C2
North Station Boston 6 A2
North Sydney Sydney 29 B2
North Woolwich London 15 A4
North York Toronto 31 A2
Northbridge Sydney 29 A2
Northbridge Park Sydney 29 A2
Northcliff Johannesburg 13 A1
Northcote Melbourne 18 A2
Northeastern Univ. Boston 6 A2
Northern Virginia Regional Park ⌂ Washington 33 B3
Northlake Chicago 9 B1
Northmount Toronto 31 A2
Northolt London 15 A1
Northumberland Heath London 15 B5
Northwestern Station Chicago 9 B3
Northwestern Univ. Chicago 9 A2
Northwood London 15 A1
Northwood Park Toronto 31 A1
Norwood Johannesburg 13 A2
Norwood Park Chicago 9 B2
Noryangjin Seoul 27 B1
Nossa Senhora do Ó São Paulo 27 B1
Nossegem Brussels 6 A3
Notre-Dame Paris 24 A3
Notre-Dame, Basilique Montreal 20 B2
Notre-Dame, Bois Paris 24 B4
Notre-Dame-de-Grace Montreal 20 B2
Notting Hill London 15 A2
Nova Milanese Milan 19 A2
Novate Milanese Milan 19 A1
Novaya Derevnya St. Petersburg 27 A1
Nové Město Prague 25 B2
Novoaleksandrovskoye St. Petersburg 27 B2
Novodevichy Convent Moscow 19 B2
Novogireyevo Moscow 19 B3
Novosaratovka St. Petersburg 27 B3
Nowe-Babice Warsaw 32 B1
Nöykkiö Helsinki 11 B1
Nueva Atzacoalco Mexico City 18 B2
Nueva Pompeya Buenos Aires 7 C2
Nueva Tenochtitlán Mexico City 18 B2
Nuijala Helsinki 11 B1
Numabukuro Tokyo 30 A2
Nuñez Buenos Aires 7 B2
Nunhead London 15 B3
Ñuñoa Santiago 27 B2
Nusle Prague 25 B2
Nussdorf Vienna 32 A2
Nyanga Cape Town 8 A2
Nymphenburg Munich 21 B2
Nymphenburg, Schloss Munich 21 B2

O

O.R. Tambo Int. ✕ (JNB) Johannesburg 13 A2
Oak Grove Atlanta 3 A3
Oak Hill Boston 6 B1
Oak Lawn Chicago 9 C2
Oak Park Chicago 9 B2
Oak View Washington 33 A4
Oakdale Atlanta 3 A2
Oakland San Francisco 26 B3
Oakland Washington 33 B4
Oaklawn Washington 33 C4
Oakleigh Melbourne 18 B2
Oakton Washington 33 B2
Oakwood Beach New York 22 C1
Oatley Sydney 29 B1
Obalende Lagos 14 B2
Oba's Palace Lagos 14 B2
Oberföhring Munich 21 B2
Oberhaching Munich 21 B2
Oberlaa Vienna 32 B2
Oberlisse Vienna 32 A2
Obermenzing Munich 21 A1
Obermoos Schwaige Munich 21 A1
Oberschleissheim Munich 21 A2
Oberschöneweide Berlin 5 B4
Observatory Johannesburg 13 B2
Óbuda Budapest 7 A2
Obukhovo St. Petersburg 27 B2
Obvodnyy Kanal St. Petersburg 27 B1
Ocean Park Hong Kong 12 B2
Ochota Warsaw 32 B1
Ocoee Orlando 23 A1
Ōdana Tokyo 30 B2
Öden-Stockach Munich 21 B3
Odilampi Helsinki 11 B1
Odivelas Lisbon 16 A1
Odolany Warsaw 32 B1
Oeiras Lisbon 16 A1
Ofin Lagos 14 A3
Ogawa Tokyo 30 A1
Ogden Park Chicago 9 C2
Ogikubo Tokyo 30 A2
Ogogoro Lagos 14 B2
Ogoyo Lagos 14 B2
Ogudu Lagos 14 A2
O'Hare Int., Chicago ✕ (ORD) Chicago 9 B1
Ohariu Stream → Wellington 33 B1
O'Higgins, Parque Santiago 27 B2
Ōimachi Tokyo 30 B3
Ojota Lagos 14 A2
Oke-Ira Lagos 14 A3
Okęcie Warsaw 32 B1
Okęcie, Warszawa ✕ (WAW) Warsaw 32 B1
Okeogbe Lagos 14 B2
Okhla Delhi 10 B2
Okhta → St. Petersburg 27 B2
Okkervil → St. Petersburg 27 B2
Okrzeszyn Warsaw 32 C2
Oksval Oslo 23 A3
Oktyabrskiy Moscow 19 B2
Okubo Tokyo 30 A3
Ōkura Tokyo 30 B1
Olari Helsinki 11 B1
Olaria Rio de Janeiro 25 B1
Old Admiralty St. Petersburg 27 B1
Old City Jerusalem 13 B2
Old City Shanghai 28 B1
Old Fort York Toronto 31 B2
Old Harbor Boston 6 B2
Old Town = Stare Miasto Warsaw 32 B2
Old Town Chicago 9 B3
Old Town Hall = Altes Rathaus Munich 21 B2
Oldbawn Dublin 10 B1
Olgino St. Petersburg 27 A1
Olimpico, Estadio Mexico City 18 C1
Olivais Lisbon 16 A2
Olivar de los Padres Mexico City 18 B1
Olivar del Conde Mexico City 18 B1
Olives, Mt. of Jerusalem 13 B2
Olivia, L. Orlando 23 B1
Olivos Buenos Aires 7 B2
Olona → Milan 19 B1
Olympia, L. Orlando 23 A1
Olympic Green Beijing 4 B2
Olympic Stadium = Turner Field Atlanta 3 B2
Olympic Stadium Beijing 4 B2
Olympic Stadium Helsinki 11 B2
Olympique, Stade Montreal 20 A2
Ōmori Tokyo 30 B3
Onisigun Lagos 14 A2
Ontario Science Centre Toronto 31 A2
Ōokayama Tokyo 30 B3
Oostzaan Tuindorp Amsterdam 2 A2
Opa-Locka Miami 18 A1
Opa-Locka ✕ (OPF) Miami 18 A1
Opacz Warsaw 32 B1
Ophirton Johannesburg 13 B2
Oppegård Oslo 23 B3
Oppem Brussels 6 A1
Oppsal Oslo 23 A4
Ora Jerusalem 13 B1
Oradell New York 22 A1
Oradell Res. New York 22 A1
Orange Bowl Stadium Miami 18 B2
Orangi Karachi 13 A2
Ordrup Copenhagen 8 A3
Orech Prague 25 B1
Oregun Lagos 14 A2
Orient Heights Boston 6 A3
Orlando Orlando 23 A2
Orlando Dam Johannesburg 13 B1
Orlando East Johannesburg 13 B1
Orlando Executive ✕ (ORL) Orlando 23 A2
Orlando Int. ✕ (MCO) Orlando 23 B3
Orlovista Orlando 23 A2
Orly Paris 24 B3
Orly, Paris ✕ (ORY) Paris 24 B3
Ormesson-sur-Marne Paris 24 B4
Ormond Melbourne 18 B2
Ormøya Oslo 23 A3
Orpington London 15 B4
Ortaköy Istanbul 12 B2
Ortica Milan 19 B2
Oruba Lagos 14 A2
Ōsaka Osaka 23 B2
Ōsaka Castle Osaka 23 A2
Ōsaka Harbour Osaka 23 B1
Ōsaka Itami Int. ✕ (ITM) Osaka 23 A1
Ōsaka Kansai Int. ✕ (KIX) Osaka 23 B2
Ōsaki Tokyo 30 B3
Osasco São Paulo 27 B1
Osdorf Berlin 5 B3
Osdorp Amsterdam 2 A1
Oshodi Lagos 14 A2
Oslo Oslo 23 A3
Oslo ✕ (OSL) Oslo 23 A4
Ōsone Tokyo 30 B2
Osorun Lagos 14 A2
Ospiate Milan 19 A1
Ostankino Moscow 19 B2
Osterley London 15 B1
Osterley Park London 15 B1
Östermalm Stockholm 29 A2
Österskär Stockholm 29 A3
Ostia Malpasso Rome 26 C1
Ostiense Rome 26 B1
Østmarkkapellet Oslo 23 A4
Ostøya Oslo 23 A2
Østre Aker Oslo 23 A3
Ōta Tokyo 30 B3
Otaniemi Helsinki 11 B1
Otari Open Air Museum Wellington 33 B1
Otsuka Tokyo 30 A3
Ottakring Vienna 32 A1
Ottávia Rome 26 B1
Ottery Cape Town 8 B2
Ottobrunn Munich 21 B3
Ouderkerk Amsterdam 2 B2
Oulunkylä Helsinki 11 B2
Ourcq, Canal de l' Paris 24 A3
Outer Mission San Francisco 26 B2
Outremont Montreal 20 A2
Overijse Brussels 6 B3
Owhiro Bay Wellington 33 C1
Oworonsoki Lagos 14 A2
Oxgangs Edinburgh 11 B2
Oxon Hill Washington 33 C4
Oyodo Osaka 23 A1
Oyster Rock Mumbai 20 B1
Oyster Rocks Karachi 13 B2
Ozoir-la-Ferrière Paris 24 B4
Ozone Park New York 22 B2

P

Pacific Heights San Francisco 26 B2
Pacific Manor San Francisco 26 C2
Pacific Palisades Los Angeles 16 B1
Pacifica San Francisco 26 C2
Paco Manila 17 B1

Paco de Arcos Lisbon 16 A1
Paddington London 15 A2
Paddington Sydney 29 B2
Paderno Milan 19 A1
Pagewood Sydney 29 B2
Pagote Mumbai 20 B2
Pai, I. do Rio de Janeiro 25 B2
Pak Kok Hong Kong 12 B1
Pak Kong Hong Kong 12 A2
Pakila Helsinki 11 B2
Palacio Real Madrid 17 B1
Palaiseau Paris 24 B2
Palazzolo Milan 19 A1
Paleo Faliro Athens 2 B2
Palermo Buenos Aires 7 B2
Palhais Lisbon 16 B2
Palisades Park New York 22 A1
Palmer Park Washington 33 B4
Palmerston Dublin 10 A1
Palms Los Angeles 16 B2
Paloheinä Helsinki 11 B2
Palomeras Madrid 17 B2
Palos Heights Chicago 9 D2
Palos Hills Chicago 9 C2
Palos Hills Forest Chicago 9 C1
Palos Park Chicago 9 C1
Palpara Kolkata 14 B2
Panchur Kolkata 14 B1
Pandacan Manila 17 B2
Pandan, Selat Singapore 28 B2
Pandan Res. Singapore 28 B2
Pangrati Athens 2 B2
Pangsua, Sungei → Singapore 28 A2
Panihati Kolkata 14 A2
Panjang, Bukit Singapore 28 A2
Panke → Berlin 5 A3
Pankow Berlin 5 A3
Pantheon Rome 26 B1
Panthersville Atlanta 3 B3
Pantin Paris 24 A3
Pantitlán Mexico City 18 B2
Panyu Guangzhou 11 B2
Paparangi Wellington 33 B1
Papiol Barcelona 4 A1
Paradise Las Vegas 14 B2
Paramount Studios Los Angeles 16 B3
Paramus New York 22 A1
Paranaque Manila 17 B1
Paray-Vieille-Poste Paris 24 B3
Pardisān Nature Park Tehran 31 A2
Parel Mumbai 20 B1
Pari São Paulo 27 B2
Parioli Rome 26 B1
Paris Paris 24 A3
Paris Orly ✈ (ORY) Paris 24 B3
Parje Mumbai 20 B2
Pārk-e Āzādegān Tehran 31 B2
Pārk-e Mellat Tehran 31 A2
Park Ridge Chicago 9 A1
Park Royal London 15 A2
Parkchester New York 22 B2
Parkdale Toronto 31 B2
Parkhurst Johannesburg 13 A2
Parklawn Washington 33 B3
Parkmore Johannesburg 13 A2
Parkside San Francisco 26 B2
Parktown Johannesburg 13 B2
Parkview Johannesburg 13 A2
Parkville New York 22 C2
Parkwood Cape Town 8 B1
Parkwood Johannesburg 13 A2
Parow Cape Town 8 A2
Parque Chacabuco Buenos Aires 7 B2
Parque Patricios Buenos Aires 7 B2
Parramatta → Sydney 29 A1
Paşabahçe Istanbul 12 B2
Pasadena Los Angeles 16 B4
Pasar Minggu Jakarta 12 B1
Pasay Manila 17 B1
Pascoe Vale Melbourne 18 A1
Pasig Manila 17 B2
Pasig → Manila 17 B2
Pasila Helsinki 11 B2
Pasing Munich 21 B1
Pasir Panjang Singapore 28 B2
Pasir Ris Singapore 28 A3
Passaic New York 22 A1
Passaic → New York 22 B1
Passirana Milan 19 A1
Patel Nagar Delhi 10 B1
Pateros Manila 17 B2
Pathumwan Bangkok 3 B2
Patipukur Kolkata 14 B2
Patisia Athens 2 A2
Paulo E. Virginia, Gruta Rio de Janeiro 25 B1
Paulshof Berlin 5 A5
Paya Lebar Singapore 28 A3
Peakhurst Sydney 29 B1
Peania Athens 2 B3
Pearson Int. Toronto ✈ (YYZ) Toronto 31 A1
Peckham London 15 B3
Pederstrup Copenhagen 8 A2
Pedralbes Barcelona 4 A1
Pedregal de San Angel, Jardines del Mexico City 18 C1
Peip'ing = Beijing Beijing 4 B1
Peking = Beijing Beijing 4 B1
Pelcowizna Warsaw 32 B2
Peñalolén Santiago 27 B2
Pencarrow Hd. Wellington 33 C2
Peng Siang → Singapore 28 A2
Penge London 15 B3
Penha Rio de Janeiro 25 A1
Penicuik Edinburgh 11 B2
Penjaringan Jakarta 12 A1
Pentagon Washington 33 B3
Penzing Vienna 32 A1
People's Park Shanghai 28 B1
People's Square Shanghai 28 B1
Perales del Rio Madrid 17 C2
Perchtoldsdorf Vienna 32 B1
Perdizes São Paulo 27 B2
Peristeri Athens 2 A2
Perivale London 15 A2
Perk Brussels 6 A2
Perlach Munich 21 B2
Perlacher Forst Munich 21 B2
Pero Milan 19 A1
Peropok, Bukit Singapore 28 A2
Perovo Moscow 19 B3
Pertusella Milan 19 A1
Pesagot Jerusalem 13 A2
Pesanggrahag, Kali → Jakarta 12 B1
Peschiera Borromeo Milan 19 B2
Pesek, Pulau Singapore 28 B2
Pest Budapest 7 B2
Pesterzsébet Budapest 7 B2
Pesthidegkút Budapest 7 A1
Pestimre Budapest 7 B3
Pestlőrinc Budapest 7 B3
Pestújhely Budapest 7 A2
Petas Helsinki 11 B2
Petone Wellington 33 B2
Petrogradskaya Storona St. Petersburg 27 B2
Petroupoli Athens 2 A2
Petrovice Prague 25 B3
Petrovskiy Park Moscow 19 B2
Petrovsko-Razumovskoye Moscow 19 B2
Pettycur Edinburgh 11 A2
Peutie Brussels 6 A2
Pfaueninsel Berlin 5 B1
Phaya Thai Bangkok 3 B2
Phihai Karachi 13 A2
Phillip B. Sydney 29 B2
Phoenix Park Dublin 10 A2
Phra Khanong Bangkok 3 B2
Phra Nakhon Bangkok 3 B2
Phra Pradaeng Bangkok 3 C2
Phranakhon Bangkok 3 B1
Pico Rivera Los Angeles 16 C4
Piedade Lisbon 16 A1
Piedade Rio de Janeiro 25 B1
Piedade, Cova da Lisbon 16 A2
Piedmont Park Atlanta 3 B2
Pierre Elliott Trudeau ✈ (YUL) Montreal 20 B1
Pietralata Rome 26 B2
Pihlajamäki Helsinki 11 B2
Pihlajasaari Helsinki 11 C2
Pilares Rio de Janeiro 25 B1
Pilton Edinburgh 11 B2
Pimmit Hills Washington 33 B2
Pine Castle Orlando 23 B2
Pine Grove Toronto 31 A1
Pine Hills Orlando 23 A2
Pinewood Park Miami 18 A2
Piney Run → Washington 33 B2
Pingzhou Guangzhou 11 B2
Pinheiros → São Paulo 27 B1
Pinjrapur Karachi 13 A2
Pinner London 15 A1
Pinner Green London 15 A1
Pioltello Milan 19 A2
Pipinui Pt. Wellington 33 A1
Piræus = Pireas Athens 2 B1
Piraiévs = Pireas Athens 2 B1
Pirajuçara → São Paulo 27 B1
Pireas Athens 2 B1
Pirinççi Istanbul 12 B1
Pirituba São Paulo 27 A1
Pirkkola Helsinki 11 B2
Pisgat O'mer Jerusalem 13 B2
Pisgat Ze'ev Jerusalem 13 B2
Pisnice Prague 25 C2
Pitampura Delhi 10 A1
Pitkäjärvi Helsinki 11 B1
Planegg Munich 21 B1
Plaza Mayor Madrid 17 B1
Pleasure Island Orlando 23 B1
Plumstead Cape Town 8 B1
Plumstead London 15 B4
Plyushchevo Moscow 19 B3
Po Toi Hong Kong 12 B2
Po Toi O Hong Kong 12 B2
Poasco Milan 19 B2
Podbaba Prague 25 B2
Podoli Prague 25 B2
Pohick Creek → Washington 33 C2
Pointe-Aux-Trembles Montreal 20 A2
Poissy Paris 24 A1
Pok Fu Lam Hong Kong 12 B1
Pokcheong Seoul 27 C2
Polton Edinburgh 11 B3
Polvoranca, Parque de Madrid 17 C1
Polyustrovo St. Petersburg 27 B2
Pomprap Bangkok 3 B2
Pondok Gede Jakarta 12 A2
Pondok Indah Jakarta 12 B1
Pont-Viau Montreal 20 A1
Pontault-Combault Paris 24 B4
Pontinha Lisbon 16 A1
Poplar London 15 A3
Poppintree Dublin 10 A2
Porirua Wellington 33 A2
Porirua East Wellington 33 A2
Port Botany Sydney 29 B2
Port Mearnóg = Portmarnock Dublin 10 A3
Port Melbourne Melbourne 18 B1
Port Nicholson Wellington 33 B2
Port Richmond New York 22 C1
Port Shelter Hong Kong 12 A2
Port Union Toronto 31 A4
Portage Park Chicago 9 B2
Portela, Lisboa ✈ (LIS) Lisbon 16 A2
Porter, L. Orlando 23 A3
Portmarnock Dublin 10 A3
Porto Brandão Lisbon 16 A1
Pôrto Novo Rio de Janeiro 25 A2
Porto Novo Cr. → Lagos 14 B2
Portobello Edinburgh 11 B3
Portrero San Francisco 26 B3
Potomac Washington 33 A2
Potrero Pt. San Francisco 26 B2
Potsdam Berlin 5 B1
Potzham Munich 21 B2
Pötzleinsdorf Vienna 32 A1
Póvoa de Santo Adriao Lisbon 16 A2
Powązki Warsaw 32 B1
Powiśle Warsaw 32 B2
Powsin Warsaw 32 C2
Powsinek Warsaw 32 C2
Poyan Res. Singapore 28 A2
Pozuelo de Alarcón Madrid 17 B1
Prado, Museo del Madrid 17 B1
Prado Churubusco Mexico City 18 B2
Praga Warsaw 32 B2
Prague = Praha Prague 25 B2
Praha Prague 25 B2
Praha ✈ (PRG) Prague 25 B1
Praires, R. des → Montreal 20 A2
Prater Vienna 32 A2
Precotto Milan 19 A2
Prenestino Labicano Rome 26 B2
Prenzlauerberg Berlin 5 A3
Preston Melbourne 18 A1
Pretos Forros, Sa. dos Rio de Janeiro 25 B1
Préville Montreal 20 B3
Přezletice Prague 25 B3
Prima Porta Rome 26 B1
Primavalle Rome 26 B1
Primrose Johannesburg 13 B2
Progreso Nacional Mexico City 18 A2
Prosek Prague 25 B3
Prospect Hill Park Boston 6 A1
Providencia Santiago 27 B2
Průhonice Prague 25 C3
Psichiko Athens 2 A2
Pudong New Area Shanghai 28 B2
Pueblo Libre Lima 14 B2
Pueblo Nuevo Barcelona 4 A2
Pueblo Nuevo Madrid 17 B2
Puerto Madero Buenos Aires 7 B2
Puhuangyu Beijing 4 B2
Puistola Helsinki 11 B3
Pukinmäki Helsinki 11 B2
Pulkovo Int. ✈ (LED) St. Petersburg 27 C1
Pullach Munich 21 B1
Pullman Historic District Chicago 9 C3
Pulo Gadung Jakarta 12 B2
Pūnak Tehran 31 A2
Punchbowl Sydney 29 B1
Punde Mumbai 20 B2
Punggol Singapore 28 A3
Punggol, Sungei → Singapore 28 A3
Punggol Pt. Singapore 28 A3
Punjabi Bagh Delhi 10 A1
Puotila Helsinki 11 B3
Puteaux Paris 24 A2
Putney London 15 B2
Putuo Shanghai 28 B1
Putxet Barcelona 4 A1
Puxi Shanghai 28 B1
Pyramids Cairo 7 B1
Pyry Warsaw 32 C1

Q

Qalandiya Jerusalem 13 A2
Qal'eh Morghī Tehran 31 B2
Qanâ el Ismâ'ilîya Cairo 7 A2
Qāsemābād Tehran 31 A3
Qasr-e Firūzeh Tehran 31 B3
Qatane Jerusalem 13 B1
Qianmen Beijing 4 B2
Qinghuayuan Beijing 4 B1
Qingningsi Shanghai 28 B2
Qolhak Tehran 31 A2
Quadraro Rome 26 B2
Quaid-i-Azam Karachi 13 A1
Quartiere Zingone Milan 19 B1
Qubeiba Jerusalem 13 A1
Quds Baghdad 3 A2
Queen Mary Res. London 15 B1
Queen Victoria Market Melbourne 18 A1
Queensbury London 15 A2
Queenscliffe Sydney 29 A2
Queensferry Edinburgh 11 B1
Queenstown Singapore 28 B2
Quellerina Johannesburg 13 A1
Queluz Lisbon 16 A1
Quezon City Manila 17 B2
Quilicura Santiago 27 B1
Quincy Boston 6 B2
Quincy B. Boston 6 B3
Quinta Normal Santiago 27 B1
Quinto de Stampi Milan 19 B2
Quinto Romano Milan 19 B1
Quirinale Rome 26 B1

R

R.F.K. Memorial Stadium Washington 33 B4
Raasdorf Vienna 32 A3
Radcliffe College Boston 6 A2
Rådhus Oslo 23 A3
Radlice Prague 25 B2
Radość Warsaw 32 B3
Radotin Prague 25 C2
Rafat Jerusalem 13 A2
Raffles Park Singapore 28 B2
Raheny Dublin 10 A3
Rahnsdorf Berlin 5 B5
Rajakylä Helsinki 11 B3
Rajpura Delhi 10 A2
Rákos-patak → Budapest 7 B3
Rákoshegy Budapest 7 B3
Rákoskeresztúr Budapest 7 B3
Rákoskert Budapest 7 B3
Rákosliget Budapest 7 B3
Rákospalota Budapest 7 A2
Rákosszentmihály Budapest 7 A2
Raków Warsaw 32 B1
Ram Jerusalem 13 A2
Râm Allâh Jerusalem 13 A2
Ramadān Baghdad 3 B2
Ramakrishna Puram Delhi 10 B1
Rāmallāh = Râm Allâh Jerusalem 13 A2
Ramanathpur Kolkata 14 A1
Ramat Allon Jerusalem 13 B2
Ramat Eshkol Jerusalem 13 B2
Ramat Razi'el Jerusalem 13 B1
Ramat Shafet Jerusalem 13 B2
Rambler Channel Hong Kong 12 A1
Ramenki Moscow 19 B1
Ramersdorf Munich 21 B2
Rameses Station Cairo 7 A2
Ramos Rio de Janeiro 25 B1
Ramos Mejía Buenos Aires 7 B1
Ramot Jerusalem 13 B2
Rampur Delhi 10 A2
Ramsgate Sydney 29 B1
Rancho Park Los Angeles 16 B2
Rand ✈ (QRA) Johannesburg 13 B2
Randalls I. New York 22 B2
Randburg Johannesburg 13 A1
Randhart Johannesburg 13 B2
Randpark Ridge Johannesburg 13 A1
Randwick Sydney 29 B2
Ranelagh Dublin 10 A2
Rangpuri Delhi 10 B1
Rannersdorf Vienna 32 B2
Ransbèche Brussels 6 B2
Ransdorp Amsterdam 2 A2
Ranvad Mumbai 20 B2
Raposo Lisbon 16 A1
Rastaala Helsinki 11 B1
Rastila Helsinki 11 B3
Raszyn Warsaw 32 C1
Rathfarnham Dublin 10 B2
Ratho Edinburgh 11 B1
Ratho Station Edinburgh 11 B1
Rato Lisbon 16 A2
Ravelston Edinburgh 11 B2
Rawamangun Jakarta 12 B2
Rayners Lane London 15 A1
Raynes Park London 15 B2
Raypur Kolkata 14 C2
Real Felipe, Fuerte Lima 14 B2
Reams, L. Orlando 23 B1
Reclining Buddha = Wat Pho Bangkok 3 B1
Recoleta Buenos Aires 7 B2
Recoleta Santiago 27 B2
Red Fort = Lal Qila Delhi 10 B2
Red Square Moscow 19 B2
Redbridge □ London 15 A4
Redfern Sydney 29 B2
Redwood Wellington 33 B1
Refshaleøen Copenhagen 8 A3
Regents Park Johannesburg 13 B2
Regent's Park London 15 A3
Rego Park New York 22 B2
Reinickendorf Berlin 5 A3
Rekola Helsinki 11 B3
Rembertów Warsaw 32 B2
Rembrandtpark Amsterdam 2 A2
Remedios de Escalada Buenos Aires 7 C2
Rèmola, Estany del Barcelona 4 B1
Renca Santiago 27 B1
Rennemoulin Paris 24 A1
Řeporyje Prague 25 B1
Repulse Bay Hong Kong 12 B2
Repy Prague 25 B1
Residenz Munich 21 B2
Reston Washington 33 B2
Retiro Buenos Aires 7 B2
Retiro Madrid 17 B1
Retiro, Puerto Buenos Aires 7 B2
Retreat Cape Town 8 B1
Reutov Moscow 19 B4
Réveillon → Paris 24 B4
Revere Boston 6 A2
Rexdale Toronto 31 A1
Reynosa Tamaulipas Mexico City 18 A1
Rho Milan 19 A1
Rhodes Sydney 29 A1
Rhodon Paris 24 B1
Rhodon → Paris 24 B1
Rialto Towers Melbourne 18 A1
Ribeira Rio de Janeiro 25 A1
Ricarda, Estany de la Barcelona 4 B1
Richmond Melbourne 18 A2
Richmond San Francisco 26 B2
Richmond Hill New York 22 B2
Richmond Park London 15 B2
Richmond-upon-Thames □ London 15 B2
Ridge, The Delhi 10 B2
Ridgefield New York 22 B1
Ridgefield Park New York 22 A1
Ridgewood New York 22 B2
Riem Munich 21 B3
Riesenrad Vienna 32 A2
Rijksmuseum Amsterdam 2 A2
Rikers I. New York 22 B2
Rimac Lima 14 B2
Ringsend Dublin 10 A2
Rinkeby Stockholm 29 A1
Rio Compride Rio de Janeiro 25 B1
Rio de Janeiro Rio de Janeiro 25 B1
Rio de Janeiro Galeão ✈ (GIG) Rio de Janeiro 25 A1
Rio de Mouro Lisbon 16 A1
Ripollet Barcelona 4 A1
Ris Oslo 23 A3
Risby Copenhagen 8 A1
Rishra Kolkata 14 A2
Ritchie Washington 33 B4
Rithala Delhi 10 A1
Rive Sud, Canal de la Montreal 20 B2
River Edge New York 22 A1
River Forest Chicago 9 B2
River Grove Chicago 9 B1
River Ridge New Orleans 21 B1
Riverdale New York 22 A2
Riverdale Washington 33 B4
Riverdale Park Toronto 31 A2
Riverlea Johannesburg 13 B1
Riverside Chicago 9 C2
Riverwood Sydney 29 B1
Rivière-des-Praires Montreal 20 A2
Rixensart Brussels 6 B3
Riyad Baghdad 3 B2
Rizal Park Manila 17 B1
Rizal Stadium Manila 17 B1
Røa Oslo 23 A2
Robbins Chicago 9 D2
Robertsham Johannesburg 13 B2
Rochelle Park New York 22 A1
Rock Cr. → Washington 33 B3
Rock Creek Park Washington 33 B3
Rock Pt. Wellington 33 A1
Rockaway Beach New York 22 C3
Rockaway Pt. New York 22 C2
Rockdale Sydney 29 B1
Rockefeller Center New York 22 B2
Rocky Run → Washington 33 B2
Roda, Gezîret el Cairo 7 A2
Roda I. = Roda, Gezîret el Cairo 7 A2
Rodaon Vienna 32 B1
Rødovre Copenhagen 8 A2
Rodrigo de Freitas, L. Rio de Janeiro 25 B1
Roehampton London 15 B2
Rogers Park Chicago 9 A3
Roihuvuori Helsinki 11 B3
Roissy-en-Brie Paris 24 B4
Rokytka → Prague 25 B3
Roma Rome 26 B1
Roma Urbe ✈ Rome 26 B2
Római-Fürdő Budapest 7 A2
Romainville Paris 24 A3
Roman Forum = Foro Romano Rome 26 B1
Romano Banco Milan 19 B1
Rome = Roma Rome 26 B1
Romema Jerusalem 13 B2
Romford London 15 A5
Ronald Reagan Nat. Washington ✈ (DCA) Washington 33 B3
Rondebosch Cape Town 8 A1
Roppongi Tokyo 30 B3
Rose, L. Orlando 23 A1
Rose Bowl Los Angeles 16 B4
Rose Hill Washington 33 C3
Rosebank Johannesburg 13 A2
Rosebank New York 22 C1
Rosebery Sydney 29 B2
Rosedal La Candelaria Mexico City 18 B2
Roseland Chicago 9 C3
Rosemead Los Angeles 16 B4
Rosemont Chicago 9 B1
Rosemont Montreal 20 A2
Rosenborg Slot Copenhagen 8 A3
Rosenthal Berlin 5 A3
Rosettenville Johannesburg 13 B2
Rosewell Edinburgh 11 B3
Rosherville Dam Johannesburg 13 B2
Rösjön Stockholm 29 A2
Roslags-Näsby Stockholm 29 A2
Roslin Edinburgh 11 B3
Roslindale Boston 6 B2
Rosny-sous-Bois Paris 24 A4
Rosslyn Washington 33 B3
Rosyth Edinburgh 11 A1
Rotherhithe London 15 B3
Rothneusiedl Vienna 32 B2
Rothschmaige Munich 21 A1
Rouge Hill Toronto 31 A4
Round I. Hong Kong 12 B2
Roxbury Boston 6 B2
Roxeth London 15 A1
Royal Botanic Gardens Edinburgh 11 B2
Royal Observatory Edinburgh 11 B2
Royal Palace = Kungliga Slottet Stockholm 29 B2
Royal Palace = Palacio Real Madrid 17 B1
Royal Park Melbourne 18 A1
Röylä Helsinki 11 B1
Rozas, Portilleros de las Madrid 17 B1
Roztoky Prague 25 B2
Rozzano Milan 19 B1
Rubí → Barcelona 4 A1
Rudolfsheim Vienna 32 A2
Rudolfshöhe Berlin 5 A5
Rudow Berlin 5 B3
Rueil-Malmaison Paris 24 A2
Ruisbroek Brussels 6 B1
Ruislip London 15 A1
Rumelihisarı Istanbul 12 B2
Rungis Paris 24 B3
Rusāfa Baghdad 3 A2
Rush Green London 15 A5
Russa Kolkata 14 C2
Rutherford New York 22 B1
Ruzyně Prague 25 B1
Ruzyne, Praha ✈ (PRG) Prague 25 B1
Rybatskaya St. Petersburg 27 B2
Rydboholm Stockholm 29 A3
Ryde Sydney 29 A1
Ryogoku Tokyo 30 A3
Rzhevka St. Petersburg 27 B3

S

Sa'ādatābād Tehran 31 A2
Saadūn Baghdad 3 B2
Saavedra Buenos Aires 7 B2
Saboli Delhi 10 A2
Sabugo Lisbon 16 A1
Sabzi Mand Delhi 10 A2
Sacavém Lisbon 16 A2
Saclay Paris 24 B2
Saclay, Étang de Paris 24 B1
Sacomã São Paulo 27 B2
Sacré Cœur Paris 24 A3
Sacrow Berlin 5 B1
Sacrower See Berlin 5 B1
Sadang Seoul 27 C1
Saddle → New York 22 A1
Saddle Brook New York 22 A1
Sadr Karachi 13 A2
Sadr City Baghdad 3 A2
Sadyba Warsaw 32 B2
Safdar Jang's Tomb Delhi 10 B2
Saft el Laban Cairo 7 A2
Saganashkee Slough Chicago 9 C1
Sagene Oslo 23 A3
Sagrada Familia, Templo de Barcelona 4 A2
Sahar, Mumbai ✈ (BOM) Mumbai 20 A2
Sai Kung Hong Kong 12 A2
Sai Wan Ho Hong Kong 12 B2
Sai Ying Pun Hong Kong 12 B1
St-Aubin Paris 24 B1
St-Cloud Paris 24 A2
St-Cyr-l'École Paris 24 B1
St-Cyr-l'École ✈ Paris 24 B1
St-Denis Paris 24 A3
St-Germain, Forêt de Paris 24 A1
St-Germain-en-Laye Paris 24 A1
St-Gilles Brussels 6 B2
St. Helier London 15 B2
St-Hubert Montreal 20 B3
St. Hubert, Galeries Royales Brussels 6 A2
St. Isaac's Cathedral St. Petersburg 27 B1
St-Jacques → Montreal 20 B3
St-Joost-Ten-Node Brussels 6 A2
St. Kilda Melbourne 18 B1
St-Lambert Montreal 20 A3
St-Lambert Paris 24 B1
St-Laurent Montreal 20 A1
St-Léonard Montreal 20 A2
St. Magelungen Stockholm 29 B2
St-Mandé Paris 24 A3
St. Margaret's Dublin 10 A2
St-Martin, Bois Paris 24 B4
St. Mary Cray London 15 B4
St-Maur-des-Fossés Paris 24 B3
St-Maurice Paris 24 B3
St-Michel Montreal 20 A2
St. Nikolaus-Kirken Prague 25 B2
St-Ouen Paris 24 A3
St. Paul's Cray London 15 B4
St. Peters Sydney 29 B2
St. Peter's Square = San Pietro, Piazza Rome 26 B1
St. Petersburg = Sankt-Peterburg St. Petersburg 27 B1
St. Petersburg Pulkovo Int. ✈ (LED) St. Petersburg 27 C1
St-Pierre Montreal 20 B2
St-Pieters Leew Brussels 6 B1
St-Quentin, Étang de Paris 24 B1
St. Stephens Cathedral = Stephansdom Vienna 32 A2
St-Stevens-Woluwe Brussels 6 A2
St-Vincent-de-Paul Montreal 20 A2
St. Xavier Univ. Chicago 9 C2
Ste-Catherine Montreal 20 B2
Ste-Hélène, Î. Montreal 20 A2
Saiwai Tokyo 30 B3
Sakai Osaka 23 B1
Sakai Harbour Osaka 23 B1
Sakra, Pulau Singapore 28 B2
Salam Baghdad 3 A2
Salamanca Madrid 17 B1
Sallynoggin Dublin 10 B3
Salmannsdorf Vienna 32 A1
Salmedina Madrid 17 C2
Salomea Warsaw 32 B1
Salsette I. Mumbai 20 A2
Salt Lake City = Bidhan Nagar Kolkata 14 B2
Salt River Cape Town 8 A1
Salt Water L. Kolkata 14 B2
Saltsjö-Duvnäs Stockholm 29 B3
Samatya Istanbul 12 C1
Sampaloc Manila 17 B1
Samphan Thawong Bangkok 3 B2
Samseon Seoul 27 B2
Samuel Smith Park Toronto 31 B1
Samut Prakan Bangkok 3 B2
San Andrés Barcelona 4 A2
San Angel Mexico City 18 B1
San Basilio Rome 26 B2
San Borja Lima 14 B2
San Bóvio Milan 19 B2
San Bruno, Pt. San Francisco 26 C2
San Bruno Mountain State Park ⌂ San Francisco 26 B2
San Cristóbal Buenos Aires 7 B2
San Cristóbal Madrid 17 B2
San Cristóbal, Cerro Santiago 27 B2
San Cristóbal, Virgen del Santiago 27 B2
San Cristoforo Milan 19 B1
San Donato Milanese Milan 19 B2
San Francisco San Francisco 26 B2
San Francisco B. San Francisco 26 B3
San Francisco Culhuacán Mexico City 18 C2
San Fruttuoso Milan 19 A2
San Gabriel Los Angeles 16 B4
San Gabriel → Los Angeles 16 C4
San Giuliano Milanese Milan 19 B2
San Isidro Lima 14 B2
San Jerónimo Lídice Mexico City 18 C1
San Joaquín Santiago 27 B2
San José Río Hondo Mexico City 18 B1
San Juan → Manila 17 B2
San Juan de Aragón Mexico City 18 B2
San Juan de Aragón, Parque Mexico City 18 B2
San Juan de Lurigancho Lima 14 A2
San Juan del Monte Manila 17 B2
San Juan Ixtacala Mexico City 18 A1
San Just Desvern Barcelona 4 A1
San Justo Buenos Aires 7 C1
San Lorenzo Tezonco Mexico City 18 C2
San Luis Lima 14 B2
San Marino Los Angeles 16 B4
San Martín Barcelona 4 A2
San Martín de Porras Lima 14 B2
San Mateo Tlaltenango Mexico City 18 B1
San Miguel Lima 14 B2
San Miguel Santiago 27 B2
San Nicolás Buenos Aires 7 B2
San Onófrio Rome 26 B1
San Pedro Mártir Barcelona 4 A1
San Pedro Zacatenco Mexico City 18 A2
San Pietro, Piazza Rome 26 B1
San Po Kong Hong Kong 12 A2
San Rafael Chamapa Mexico City 18 B1
San Rafael Hills Los Angeles 16 A3
San Roque Manila 17 B2
San Siro Milan 19 B1
San Souci Sydney 29 B1
San Telmo Buenos Aires 7 B2
San Vicenç dels Horts Barcelona 4 A1
Sandown Johannesburg 13 A2
Sandown Park Races London 15 B1
Sandton Johannesburg 13 A2
Sandvika Oslo 23 A2
Sandyford Dublin 10 B2
Sandymount Dublin 10 B2
Sangenjaya Tokyo 30 B2
Sanggye Seoul 27 B2
Sangley Pt. Manila 17 C1
Sankrail Kolkata 14 B1
Sankt-Peterburg St. Petersburg 27 B1
Sankt Veit Vienna 32 A1
Sanlihe Beijing 4 B1
Sanlintang Shanghai 28 C1
Sans Barcelona 4 A1
Sanssouci Berlin 5 B1
Sant Ambrogio, Basilica di Milan 19 B2
Sant Boi de Llobregat Barcelona 4 A1
Sant Cugat Barcelona 4 A1
Sant Feliu de Llobregat Barcelona 4 A1
Sant Joan Despi Barcelona 4 A1
Santa Ana Manila 17 B2
Santa Anita Park Los Angeles 16 B4
Santa Coloma de Gramenet Barcelona 4 A2
Santa Cruz Manila 17 B1
Santa Cruz Mumbai 20 A1
Santa Cruz, I. de Rio de Janeiro 25 B2
Santa Cruz de Olorde Barcelona 4 A1
Santa Efigénia São Paulo 27 B2
Santa Elena Manila 17 B2
Santa Elena del Gomero Santiago 27 B1
Santa Eulalia Barcelona 4 A2
Santa Fe Springs Los Angeles 16 C4
Santa Iria da Azóia Lisbon 16 A2
Santa Julia Santiago 27 C2
Santa Monica Los Angeles 16 B2
Santa Monica Mts. Los Angeles 16 B2
Santa Rosa de Locobe Santiago 27 B2
Santa Teresa de la Ovalle Santiago 27 B2
Santahamina Helsinki 11 C3
Santana São Paulo 27 A2
Santeny Paris 24 B4
Santiago Santiago 27 B2
Santiago Benítez ✈ (SCL) Santiago 27 B1
Santiago de Surco Lima 14 B2
Santo Amaro Lisbon 16 A1
Santo Amaro São Paulo 27 B1
Santo André Lisbon 16 B2
Santo Antão do Tojal Lisbon 16 A2
Santo Antônio, Qta. de Lisbon 16 B1
Santo Tomas, Univ. of Manila 17 B1
Santos Dumont ✈ (SDU) Rio de Janeiro 25 B2
Santoshpur Kolkata 14 B1
Santragachi Kolkata 14 B1
Santry Dublin 10 A2
Sanyuanli Guangzhou 11 B2
São Caetano do Sul São Paulo 27 B2
São Conrado Rio de Janeiro 25 B1
São Cristóvão Rio de Janeiro 25 B1
São Jorge, Castelo de Lisbon 16 A2
São Julião do Tojal Lisbon 16 A2
São Paulo São Paulo 27 B2
São Paulo Congonhas ✈ (CGH) São Paulo 27 B2
Sapa Kolkata 14 B1
Sapateiro, Cor. do → São Paulo 27 B1
Sarandi Buenos Aires 7 C2
Saraswati → Kolkata 14 A1
Sarecky potok → Prague 25 B2
Sarimbun Singapore 28 A2
Sarimbun Res. Singapore 28 A2
Sarjyer Istanbul 12 A2
Sarriá Barcelona 4 A1
Sarsuna Kolkata 14 C1
Sartrouville Paris 24 A2
Sasad Budapest 7 B2
Sashalom Budapest 7 A3
Saska Warsaw 32 B2
Satalice Prague 25 B3
Satgachi Kolkata 14 B2
Satpukur Kolkata 14 B2
Sätra Stockholm 29 B1
Saúde São Paulo 27 B2
Saugus Boston 6 A2
Saugus → Boston 6 A2
Sault-au-Récollet Montreal 20 A2
Sausalito San Francisco 26 A2
Sawah Besar Jakarta 12 A1
Sawtelle Los Angeles 16 B2
Scald Law Edinburgh 11 B2
Scarborough Toronto 31 A3
Scarborough Bluffs Toronto 31 A3
Sceaux Paris 24 B2
Schaerbeek Brussels 6 A2
Scharfenberg Berlin 5 A2
Schiller Park Chicago 9 B1
Schiller Woods Chicago 9 B1
Schiphol, Amsterdam ✈ (AMS) Amsterdam 2 B1
Schlachtensee Berlin 5 B2
Schlossgarten Berlin 5 A2
Schmargendorf Berlin 5 B2
Schönblick Berlin 5 B5
Schönbrunn Vienna 32 A1
Schöneberg Berlin 5 B3
Schönefeld Berlin 5 B4
Schöneiche Berlin 5 B5
Schönwalde Berlin 5 A1
Schulzendorf Berlin 5 A2
Schwabing Munich 21 B2
Schwanebeck Berlin 5 A4
Schwanenwerder Berlin 5 B2
Schwarzlackenau Vienna 32 A2
Schwechat Vienna 32 B2
Schwechat, Wien ✈ (VIE) Vienna 32 B3
Science and Industry, Museum of Chicago 9 C3
Scitrek Museum Atlanta 3 B2
Scopus, Mt. Jerusalem 13 B2
Scottdale Atlanta 3 B3
Scutari = Üsküdar Istanbul 12 B2
Sea Point Cape Town 8 A1
Seabrook Washington 33 B5
Seacliff San Francisco 26 B2
Seaforth Sydney 29 A2
Seagate New York 22 C1
Seat Pleasant Washington 33 B4
Seaview Wellington 33 B2
SeaWorld Orlando 23 B2
Šeberov Prague 25 B3
Secaucus New York 22 B1
Seddinsee Berlin 5 B5
Seeberg Berlin 5 A5
Seeburg Berlin 5 A1
Seefeld Berlin 5 A5
Seegefeld Berlin 5 A1
Seehof Berlin 5 B2
Segeltorp Stockholm 29 B1
Segrate Milan 19 B2
Seguro Milan 19 B1
Seixal Lisbon 16 B2
Selby Johannesburg 13 B2
Seletar, Pulau Singapore 28 A3
Seletar Hills Singapore 28 A3
Seletar Res. Singapore 28 A2
Selhurst London 15 B3
Sembawang Singapore 28 A2
Senago Milan 19 A1
Sendling Munich 21 B2
Senju Tokyo 30 A3
Senriyama Osaka 23 A2
Sentosa Singapore 28 B2
Seobinggo Seoul 27 B1
Seocho Seoul 27 C1
Seodaemun Seoul 27 B1
Seokkwan Seoul 27 B2
Seongbuk Seoul 27 B2
Seongdong Seoul 27 B2
Seongsu Seoul 27 B2
Seoul Seoul 27 B2
Seoul Nat. Univ. Seoul 27 C1
Seoul Tower Seoul 27 B1
Sepolia Athens 2 A2
Sepulveda Dam Rec. Area ⌂ Los Angeles 16 A2
Serangoon Singapore 28 A3
Serangoon, Pulau Singapore 28 A3
Serangoon, Sungei → Singapore 28 A3
Serangoon Harbour Singapore 28 A3
Seraya, Pulau Singapore 28 B2
Serebryanka → Moscow 19 B3
Serramonte San Francisco 26 C2
Sesto San Giovanni Milan 19 A2
Sesto Ulteriano Milan 19 B2
Setagaya Tokyo 30 B2
Seter Oslo 23 A3
Setia Budi Jakarta 12 B1
Settebagni Rome 26 A2
Settecamini Rome 26 B2
Séttimo Milanese Milan 19 B1
Settsu Osaka 23 A2
Seutula Helsinki 11 A2
Seven Corners Washington 33 B3
Seven Kings London 15 A4
Seventeenth Street Canal New Orleans 21 A2
Sévesco → Milan 19 A1
Sevran Paris 24 A4
Sewri Mumbai 20 B2
Sforzesco, Castello Milan 19 B2
Sha Kok Mei Hong Kong 12 A2
Sha Tin Hong Kong 12 A2
Sha'ar Binyamin Jerusalem 13 A2
Shabrâmant Cairo 7 B2
Shah Mosque Tehran 31 A2
Shahdara Delhi 10 A2
Shahe Guangzhou 11 B2
Shahr-e Rey Tehran 31 B2
Shahrak-e Golshahr Tehran 31 A1
Shahrak-e Qods Tehran 31 A2
Shaikh Aomar Baghdad 3 A2
Shakurbasti Delhi 10 A1
Shalkiya Kolkata 14 B2
Sham Shui Po Hong Kong 12 B1
Shamapur Delhi 10 A1
Shamian Guangzhou 11 B2
Shan Mei Hong Kong 12 A2
Shanghai Shanghai 28 B2
Shanghai Hongqiao ✈ (SHA) Shanghai 28 B1
Shanghai Pudong ✈ (PVG) Shanghai 28 B2
Shankill Dublin 10 B3
Sharp I. Hong Kong 12 A2
Shastrinagar Delhi 10 A2
Shau Kei Wan Hong Kong 12 B2
Shawocun Beijing 4 B1
Shayuan Guangzhou 11 B2
Sheen, L. Orlando 23 B1
Sheepshead Bay New York 22 C2
Shek O Hong Kong 12 B2
Shelter I. Hong Kong 12 B2
Shepherds Bush London 15 A2
Shepperton London 15 B1
Sheremetyevo ✈ (SVO) Moscow 19 A2
Sherman Oaks Los Angeles 16 B2
Sherman Park Chicago 9 C2
Sherwood, L. Orlando 23 A2
Shet Bandar Mumbai 20 B2
Sheung Fa Shan Hong Kong 12 A1
Sheung Lau Wan Hong Kong 12 B2
Sheung Wan Hong Kong 12 B1
Sheva Mumbai 20 B2
Sheva Nhava Mumbai 20 B2
Shiba Tokyo 30 B3
Shibpur Kolkata 14 B1
Shibuya Tokyo 30 B3
Shilihe Beijing 4 B2
Shimogawara Tokyo 30 B1
Shimosalo Tokyo 30 A2
Shimoshakujii Tokyo 30 A2
Shinagawa Tokyo 30 B3
Shing Mun Res. Hong Kong 12 A1
Shinjuku Tokyo 30 A3
Shinjuku Nat. Garden Tokyo 30 A3
Shinkoiwa Tokyo 30 A4
Shinnakano Tokyo 30 A3
Shipai Guangzhou 11 B3
Shirinashi → Osaka 23 B1
Shirogane Tokyo 30 B3
Shitennoji Temple Osaka 23 B2
Shiweitang Guangzhou 11 B2
Shogunle Lagos 14 A2
Shomolu Lagos 14 A2
Shooters Hill London 15 B4
Shoreditch London 15 A3
Shortlands London 15 B4
Shu'afat Jerusalem 13 B2
Shubrâ Cairo 7 A2
Shubrâ el Kheima Cairo 7 A2
Shuikou Guangzhou 11 A2
Sidcup London 15 B4
Siebenhirten Vienna 32 B1
Siedlung Berlin 5 A1
Siekierki Warsaw 32 B2
Sielce Warsaw 32 B2
Siemensstadt Berlin 5 A2
Sierra Madre Los Angeles 16 B4
Sievering Vienna 32 A2
Sighthill Edinburgh 11 B2
Signal Hill Cape Town 8 A1
Siheung Seoul 27 C1
Sikátorpuszta Budapest 7 A3
Silampur Delhi 10 B2
Sillim Seoul 27 C1
Silver, L. Orlando 23 A2
Silver Hill Washington 33 C4
Silver Lake Los Angeles 16 B3
Silver Spring Washington 33 A3
Silvermine Nature Reserve Cape Town 8 B1
Silvolantekojärvi Helsinki 11 B2
Simei Singapore 28 A3
Simla Kolkata 14 B2
Simmering Vienna 32 A2
Simmering Heide Vienna 32 A2
Simonkylä Helsinki 11 B3
Sinchon Seoul 27 B1
Sindang Seoul 27 B1
Singapore ■ Singapore 28 B3
Singapore, Univ. of Singapore 28 B2
Singapore Changi ✈ (SIN) Singapore 28 A3
Sinki, Selat Singapore 28 B2
Sinsa Seoul 27 B2
Sint-Genesius-Rode Brussels 6 B2
Sion Mumbai 20 A2
Sipson London 15 B1
Siqeil Cairo 7 A1
Şişli Istanbul 12 B1
Skansen Stockholm 29 B2
Skärholmen Stockholm 29 B1
Skarpäng Stockholm 29 A2
Skarpnäck Stockholm 29 B2
Skaryszewski, Park Warsaw 32 B2
Skokie Chicago 9 A2
Skokie → Chicago 9 A2
Skokie Heritage Museum Chicago 9 A2
Skokloster Oslo 23 A3
Sköndal Stockholm 29 B2
Skovlunde Copenhagen 8 A2
Skovshoved Copenhagen 8 A3
Skuru Stockholm 29 B3
Sky Lake Orlando 23 B2
Skyland Atlanta 3 A3
Slade Green London 15 B5
Slependen Oslo 23 A2
Slipi Jakarta 12 B1
Slivenec Prague 25 B2
Sloten Amsterdam 2 A1
Sloterdijk Amsterdam 2 A1
Sloterpark Amsterdam 2 A1
Sluhy Prague 25 A3
Służew Warsaw 32 B2
Służewiec Warsaw 32 B2
Smíchov Prague 25 B2
Smith Forest Preserve Chicago 9 B2
Smolny St. Petersburg 27 B2
Smolny Cathedral St. Petersburg 27 B2
Snake Creek Canal Miami 18 A2
Snakeden Branch → Washington 33 B1
Snarøya Oslo 23 A2
Snättringe Stockholm 29 B1
Søborg Copenhagen 8 A2
Sobreda Lisbon 16 B1
Söderby Stockholm 29 A3
Södermalm Stockholm 29 B2
Sodpur Kolkata 14 A2
Soeurs, Î. des Montreal 20 B2
Sognsvatn Oslo 23 A3
Soignes, Forêt de Brussels 6 B2
Sok Kwu Wan Hong Kong 12 B1
Sokolniki Moscow 19 B3
Sokolniki Park Moscow 19 B3
Sokołów Warsaw 32 C1
Solalinden Munich 21 B3
Sollentuna Stockholm 29 A1
Solln Munich 21 B2
Solna Stockholm 29 A1
Somerset Washington 33 B3
Somerville Boston 6 A2
Somes I. Wellington 33 B2
Sonari Mumbai 20 B2
Sønderso Copenhagen 8 A2
Songpa Seoul 27 B2
Sony Picture Studio Los Angeles 16 B2
Sord = Swords Dublin 10 A2
Soroksár Budapest 7 B2
Soroksari Duna → Budapest 7 B2
Sosenka → Moscow 19 B3
Sosnovka St. Petersburg 27 B2
Sŏul = Seoul Seoul 27 B2

Soundview *New York* 22 B2
South Beach *Miami* 22 C1
South Bend Park *Atlanta* 3 B2
South Boston *Boston* 6 A2
South Decatur *Atlanta* 3 B3
South Deering *Chicago* 9 C3
South El Monte *Los Angeles* 16 B4
South Gate *Los Angeles* 16 C3
South Harbor *Manila* 17 B1
South Harrow *London* 15 A1
South Hd. *Sydney* 29 B2
South Hills *Johannesburg* 13 B2
South Lawn *Washington* 33 C3
South Miami *Miami* 18 B1
South Norwood *London* 15 B3
South of Market
 San Francisco 26 B2
South Ozone Park
 New York 22 B2
South Pasadena *Los Angeles* 16 B4
South Res. *Boston* 6 A2
South Ruislip *London* 15 A1
South San Francisco
 San Francisco 26 C2
South San Gabriel
 Los Angeles 16 B4
South Shore *Chicago* 9 C3
Southall *London* 15 A1
Southborough *London* 15 B4
Southend *London* 15 B3
Southern California, Univ.
 of *Los Angeles* 16 B3
Southfields *London* 15 B2
Southport *New Orleans* 21 B2
Southwark □ *London* 15 B3
Southwest Museum
 Los Angeles 16 B3
Sevang *Copenhagen* 8 B3
Soweto *Johannesburg* 13 A1
Sowhānak *Tehran* 31 A3
Soya *Tokyo* 30 A4
Spandau *Berlin* 5 A1
Spånga *Stockholm* 29 A1
Spanish Monastery *Miami* 18 A2
Spectacle I. *Boston* 6 A3
Speicher-See *Munich* 21 A3
Speising *Vienna* 32 B1
Sphinx *Cairo* 7 B1
Spinaceto *Rome* 26 C1
Spit Junction *Sydney* 29 A2
Spofilov *Prague* 25 B3
Spot Pond *Boston* 6 A2
Spotswood *Melbourne* 18 B1
Spring Valley *Las Vegas* 14 B1
Springeberg *Berlin* 5 B5
Springfield *Washington* 33 C2
Squantum *Boston* 6 B2
Srednaya Rogatka
 St. Petersburg 27 B2
Sródmieście *Warsaw* 32 B2
Stenkam *Helsinki* 11 C1
Stabekk *Oslo* 23 A2
Stadlau *Vienna* 32 A2
Stadshuset *Stockholm* 29 B2
Stains *Paris* 24 A3
Stamford Hill *London* 15 A3
Stammersdorf *Vienna* 32 A2
Stanley *Hong Kong* 12 B2
Stanley Pen. *Hong Kong* 12 B2
Stanmore *London* 15 A2
Stapleton *New York* 22 C1
Staraya Derevnya
 St. Petersburg 27 A1
Staré Město *Prague* 25 B2
Stare *Miasto* *Warsaw* 32 B2
Starke, L. *Orlando* 23 A1
Staten Island Zoo *New York* 22 C1
Staten Islands Ferry
 Terminal *New York* 22 C1
Statenice *Prague* 25 B1
Stedelijk Museum
 Amsterdam 2 A2
Steele Creek *Melbourne* 18 A1
Steenokkerzeel *Brussels* 6 A2
Steer, L. *Orlando* 23 A2
Steglitz *Berlin* 5 B2
Stepaside *Dublin* 10 B2
Stephansdom *Vienna* 32 A2
Stepney *London* 15 A3
Sterling Park *San Francisco* 26 B2
Sticklinge udde *Stockholm* 29 A2
Stickney *Chicago* 9 C2
Stillorgan *Dublin* 10 B2
Stockholm *Stockholm* 29 B2
Stockholm Arlanda ✈
 (ARN) *Stockholm* 29 A2
Stocksund *Stockholm* 29 A2
Stodůlky *Prague* 25 B1
Stoke Newington *London* 15 A3
Stokes Valley *Wellington* 33 B2
Stone Canyon Res.
 Los Angeles 16 B2
Stone Park *Chicago* 9 B1
Stonebridge *London* 15 A2
Stoneham *Boston* 6 A2
Stony Brook Res. *Boston* 6 B2
Stony Creek ➝ *Chicago* 9 C2
Stora Värtan *Stockholm* 29 A2
Store Hareskov *Copenhagen* 8 A2
Store Magleby *Copenhagen* 8 B3
Storholmen *Stockholm* 29 A2
Stoyka *St. Petersburg* 27 B2
Straiton *Edinburgh* 11 B3
Strandfontein *Cape Town* 8 B2
Strašnice *Prague* 25 B3
Strasstruderíng *Munich* 21 B3
Stratford *London* 15 A4
Strathfield *Sydney* 29 B1
Streatham *London* 15 B3
Streatham Vale *London* 15 B3
Strebersdorf *Vienna* 32 A2
Strešovice *Prague* 25 B2
Strip, The *Las Vegas* 14 B2
Strížkov *Prague* 25 B3
Strombeek-Bever *Brussels* 6 A2
Stromovka *Prague* 25 B2
Studio City *Los Angeles* 16 B2
Stureby *Stockholm* 29 B2
Stuvsta *Stockholm* 29 B2
Subhepur *Delhi* 10 A2
Suburban Canal
 New Orleans 21 B1
Sucat *Manila* 17 C2
Suchdol *Prague* 25 B2
Sucy-en-Brie *Paris* 24 B4
Sue, L. *Orlando* 23 A2
Sugamo *Tokyo* 30 A3
Sugar Loaf Mt. = Açúcar,
 Pão de *Rio de Janeiro* 25 B2
Suge *Tokyo* 30 B2
Suginami *Tokyo* 30 A2
Sugō *Tokyo* 30 B2
Sui Sai Wan *Hong Kong* 12 B2
Suita *Osaka* 23 A1
Sukchar *Kolkata* 14 A2
Sukhumvit Camil *Istanbul* 12 B1
Sumida *Tokyo* 30 A3
Sumida ➝ *Tokyo* 30 A3
Sumiyoshi *Osaka* 23 B2

Sumiyoshi Shrine *Osaka* 23 B1
Summerville *Toronto* 31 B1
Summit *Chicago* 9 C2
Sunamachi *Tokyo* 30 A4
Sunbury-on-Thames
 London 15 B1
Sundbyberg *Stockholm* 29 A1
Sundbyerne *Copenhagen* 8 B3
Sung Kong *Hong Kong* 12 B2
Sungei Kadut Industrial
 Estate *Singapore* 28 A2
Sungei Selatar Res.
 Singapore 28 A3
Sunrise Manor *Las Vegas* 14 A2
Sunrise Mountain Natural
 Area *Las Vegas* 14 A2
Sunset Park *Las Vegas* 14 B2
Sunset Park *New York* 22 C2
Sunter *Jakarta* 12 A2
Sunter, Kali ➝ *Jakarta* 12 B2
Suomenlinna *Helsinki* 11 C2
Sur Bahr *Jerusalem* 13 B2
Sura *Kolkata* 14 B2
Suraksan *Seoul* 27 A2
Surbiton *London* 15 B2
Suresnes *Paris* 24 A2
Surfside *Miami* 18 A2
Surquillo *Lima* 14 B2
Surrey Hills *Sydney* 29 B2
Susaek *Seoul* 27 B1
Süssenbrunn *Vienna* 32 A2
Sutton *Dublin* 10 A3
Sutton *London* 15 B2
Suyu *Seoul* 27 B2
Suzukinshima *Tokyo* 30 A2
Svanemøllen *Copenhagen* 8 A3
Sveaborg = Suomenlinna
 Helsinki 11 C2
Sverdlov *Moscow* 19 B2
Svestad *Oslo* 23 B2
Svinö *Helsinki* 11 C1
Swanley *London* 15 B4
Swansea *Toronto* 31 B2
Swinburne I. *New York* 22 C1
Swords *Dublin* 10 A2
Sydenham *Johannesburg* 13 A2
Sydney *Sydney* 29 B2
Sydney, Univ. of *Sydney* 29 B2
Sydney Harbour △ *Sydney* 29 B2
Sydney Harbour Bridge
 Sydney 29 B2
Sydney Kingsford Smith ✈
 (SYD) *Sydney* 29 B2
Sydstranden *Copenhagen* 8 B3
Sylvania *Sydney* 29 C1
Syon Park *London* 15 B2
Szczęśliwice *Warsaw* 32 B2
Széchenyi-hegy *Budapest* 7 B1
Széphalom *Budapest* 7 A1

T

Taastrup *Copenhagen* 8 B1
Tabata *Tokyo* 30 A3
Tablada *Buenos Aires* 7 C1
Table B. *Cape Town* 8 A1
Table Mountain △
 Cape Town 8 A1
Table Mt. *Cape Town* 8 A1
Taboão da Serra *São Paulo* 27 B1
Täby *Stockholm* 29 A2
Tacuba *Mexico City* 18 B1
Tacubaya *Mexico City* 18 B1
Tafelbaai = Table B.
 Cape Town 8 A1
Taft *Orlando* 23 B2
Tagig ➝ *Manila* 17 B2
Taguig *Manila* 17 B2
Tai Lo Shan *Hong Kong* 12 A2
Tai Po Tsai *Hong Kong* 12 A2
Tai Seng *Singapore* 28 A3
Tai Shui Hang *Hong Kong* 12 A2
Tai Tam B. *Hong Kong* 12 B2
Tai Tam Tuk Res.
 Hong Kong 12 B2
Tai Wai *Hong Kong* 12 A2
Tai Wan Tau *Hong Kong* 12 B2
Tai Wo Hau *Hong Kong* 12 A1
Tainaka *Osaka* 23 B2
Taishō *Osaka* 23 B1
Taita *Wellington* 33 B2
Tajrish *Tehran* 31 A2
Takaido *Tokyo* 30 A2
Takaishi *Tokyo* 30 B2
Takarazuka *Osaka* 23 A1
Takasago *Tokyo* 30 A4
Takatsu *Tokyo* 30 B2
Takeshita *Tokyo* 30 B2
Takinegawa *Tokyo* 30 A3
Takoma Park *Washington* 33 B3
Taksim *Istanbul* 12 B1
Talaide *Lisbon* 16 A1
Taliganga *Kolkata* 14 B2
Talipapa *Manila* 17 A2
Tallaght *Dublin* 10 B1
Tallkrogen *Stockholm* 29 B2
Tama ➝ *Tokyo* 30 B2
Tama Kyūryō *Tokyo* 30 B2
Tamaden *Tokyo* 30 B2
Tamagawa-josui ➝ *Tokyo* 30 A1
Taman Sari *Jakarta* 12 A1
Tamanduateí ➝ *São Paulo* 27 B2
Tamborskkloof *Cape Town* 8 A1
Tambora *Jakarta* 12 A1
Tammisalo *Helsinki* 11 B3
Tammoh *Cairo* 7 B2
Tampines *Singapore* 28 A3
Tanah Abang *Jakarta* 12 A1
Tanah Kusir *Jakarta* 12 B1
Tangelo Park *Orlando* 23 B2
Tanjung Duren *Jakarta* 12 B1
Tanjung Priok *Jakarta* 12 A2
Tanum *Oslo* 23 A1
Tapada *Lisbon* 16 A1
Tapanila *Helsinki* 11 B3
Tapiales *Buenos Aires* 7 C1
Tapiola *Helsinki* 11 B1
Tapsia *Kolkata* 14 B2
Tara *Mumbai* 20 A2
Tarabya *Istanbul* 12 B2
Tårbæk *Copenhagen* 8 A3
Tarchomin *Warsaw* 32 B1
Tardeo *Mumbai* 20 B1
Targówek *Warsaw* 32 B2
Tárnby *Copenhagen* 8 B3
Tarqua Bay *Lagos* 14 B2
Tathong Channel
 Hong Kong 12 B2
Tathong Pt. *Hong Kong* 12 B2
Tatuapé *São Paulo* 27 B2
Taufkirchen *Munich* 21 B2
Tavares, I. dos *Rio de Janeiro* 25 A2
Tavros *Athens* 2 B2
Tawa *Wellington* 33 B1
Te Papa Museum
 Wellington 33 B1
Teaneck *New York* 22 B1
Tebet *Jakarta* 12 B1

Tecamachalco *Mexico City* 18 B1
Ted Williams Tunnel *Boston* 6 A2
Teddington *London* 15 B1
Tegel *Berlin* 5 A2
Tegel, Berlin ✈ (TXL) *Berlin* 5 A2
Tegeler See *Berlin* 5 A2
Tegelort *Berlin* 5 A2
Teheran = Tehrān *Tehran* 31 A2
Tehrān *Tehran* 31 A2
Tehrān Mehrābād ✈
 (THR) *Tehran* 31 A1
Tehrān Pārs *Tehran* 31 A3
Tejo, Rio ➝ *Lisbon* 16 A2
Tekstilyshchik *Moscow* 19 B3
Telhal *Lisbon* 16 A1
Telok Blangah *Singapore* 28 B2
Teltow *Berlin* 5 B2
Teltow kanal *Berlin* 5 B3
Tempelhof *Berlin* 5 B3
Temple City *Los Angeles* 16 B4
Temple Hills *Washington* 33 C4
Temple of Heaven *Beijing* 4 B2
Templeogue *Dublin* 10 B2
Temppeliaukio Church
 Helsinki 11 B2
Tenafly *New York* 22 A1
Tenayuca, Piramide de
 Mexico City 18 A1
Tengah ➝ *Singapore* 28 A2
Tennoji *Osaka* 23 B2
Tepalcates *Mexico City* 18 B2
Tepeyac △ *Mexico City* 18 B2
Terrazzano *Milan* 19 A1
Terre des Hommes *Montreal* 20 A2
Terrugem *Lisbon* 16 A1
Terrytown *New Orleans* 21 B2
Tervuren *Brussels* 6 B3
Tervuren, Park van *Brussels* 6 B3
Tetuán *Madrid* 17 B1
Teufelsberg *Berlin* 5 B2
Thalkirchen *Munich* 21 B2
Thames Ditton *London* 15 B2
Thamesmead *London* 15 A4
Thana Cr. ➝ *Mumbai* 20 A2
Thisio *Athens* 2 B2
Thistletown *Toronto* 31 A1
Thomastown *Melbourne* 18 A2
Thompson I. *Boston* 6 A3
Thon Buri *Bangkok* 3 B1
Thornbury *Melbourne* 18 A2
Thorncliffe *Toronto* 31 A2
Thornhill *Toronto* 31 A2
Thornton *Cape Town* 8 A2
Thornton Heath *London* 15 B3
Threipmuir Res. *Edinburgh* 11 B2
Throgs Neck *New York* 22 B3
Tiancun *Beijing* 4 B1
Tianhe *Guangzhou* 11 B3
Tibati, I. *Rio de Janeiro* 25 D1
Tibidabo *Barcelona* 4 A1
Tibradden Mt. *Dublin* 10 B2
Tiburon *San Francisco* 26 A2
Tiburtino *Rome* 26 B2
Ticomán *Mexico City* 18 A2
Tiefersee *Berlin* 5 B5
Tiergarten *Berlin* 5 A3
Tigerhof *Cape Town* 8 A2
Tijuca *Rio de Janeiro* 25 B1
Tijuca, Pico da *Rio de Janeiro* 25 B1
Tijuca △ *Rio de Janeiro* 25 B1
Tikkurila *Helsinki* 11 B3
Tilak Nagar *Delhi* 10 B1
Tilangiao *Shanghai* 28 B2
Timah, Bukit *Singapore* 28 A2
Timiryazev Park *Moscow* 19 B2
Tin Can I. *Lagos* 14 B2
Ting Kau *Hong Kong* 12 A1
Tira *Jerusalem* 13 A1
Tirsa *Cairo* 7 B2
Tishrīyaa *Baghdad* 3 B2
Tiu Keng Leng *Hong Kong* 12 A2
Tizapán *Mexico City* 18 C1
Tlalnepantla ➝ *Mexico City* 18 A1
Tlalpan *Mexico City* 18 C2
To Kwai Wan *Hong Kong* 12 B2
Toa Payoh *Singapore* 28 A3
Točná *Prague* 25 C2
Toco Hills *Atlanta* 3 B2
Todt Hill *New York* 22 C1
Tōkagi *Tokyo* 30 A4
Tokai Plantation *Cape Town* 8 B1
Tōkaichiba *Tokyo* 30 B2
Tōkyō *Tokyo* 30 A3
Tōkyō B. = Tōkyō-Wan
 Tokyo 30 B3
Tōkyō Disneyland *Tokyo* 30 B4
Tōkyō Haneda ✈ (HND)
 Tokyo 30 B3
Tōkyō Harbour *Tokyo* 30 B3
Tōkyō-Wan *Tokyo* 30 B4
Tolka ➝ *Dublin* 10 A1
Tollygunge = Taliganga
 Kolkata 14 B2
Tolworth *London* 15 B2
Tomba di Nerone *Rome* 26 B1
Tommy Thompson Park
 Toronto 31 B2
Tondo *Manila* 17 B1
Tongbinggo *Seoul* 27 B2
Tongqiao *Shanghai* 28 A1
Toorak *Melbourne* 18 A2
Topanga State Park △
 Los Angeles 16 B1
Topkapı *Istanbul* 12 B1
Topkapı Palaca *Istanbul* 12 B1
Tor di Quinto *Rome* 26 B1
Tor Pignattara *Rome* 26 B2
Tor Sapienza *Rome* 26 B2
Torcy *Paris* 24 A4
Toronto *Toronto* 31 B2
Toronto, Univ. of *Toronto* 31 B2
Toronto City Centre ✈
 (YTZ) *Toronto* 31 B2
Toronto Harbour *Toronto* 31 B2
Toronto I. *Toronto* 31 B2
Toronto Lester B. Pearson
 Int. ✈ (YYZ) *Toronto* 31 A1
Torre Lupara *Rome* 26 B2
Torre Nova *Rome* 26 B2
Torrellas ➝ *Barcelona* 4 A1
Torrevécchia *Rome* 26 B1
Toshima *Tokyo* 30 A3
Toshimaen *Tokyo* 30 A2
Tottenham *London* 15 A3
Tottenham *Melbourne* 18 A1
Toussus-le-Noble *Paris* 24 B1
Toussus-le-Noble ✈ (TNF)
 Paris 24 B1
Towchal Cable Car *Tehran* 31 A2
Tower Hamlets □ *London* 15 A3
Tower of London *London* 15 A3
Towra Pt. *Sydney* 29 C2
Tøyen *Oslo* 23 A4
Toyonaka *Osaka* 23 A1
Trafaria *Lisbon* 16 A1
Traição, Cor. ➝ *São Paulo* 27 B2

Trappenfelde *Berlin* 5 A4
Trastévere *Rome* 26 B1
Treasure I. *San Francisco* 26 B2
Třeboradice *Prague* 25 B3
Třebotov *Prague* 25 C1
Tremblay-en-France *Paris* 24 A4
Tremembe ➝ *São Paulo* 27 A2
Tremont *New York* 22 B2
Trenno *Milan* 19 B1
Treptow *Berlin* 5 B3
Três Rios, Sa. dos
 Rio de Janeiro 25 B3
Trevi, Fontana di *Rome* 26 B1
Trezzano sul Naviglio *Milan* 19 B1
Trieste *Rome* 26 B2
Trinidad *Washington* 33 B4
Trinity *Edinburgh* 11 B2
Trinity College *Dublin* 10 A2
Trionfale *Rome* 26 B1
Triulzo *Milan* 19 B2
Troja *Prague* 25 B2
Trollbäcken *Stockholm* 29 B3
Trombay *Mumbai* 20 A2
Troparevo *Moscow* 19 C1
Trudeau, Montréal ✈
 (YUL) *Montreal* 20 A1
Trudyashchikhsya,
 Ostrov *St. Petersburg* 27 B1
Tryvasshøgda *Oslo* 23 A3
Tseng Lan Shue *Hong Kong* 12 A2
Tseung Kwan *Hong Kong* 12 A2
Tsim Sha Tsui *Hong Kong* 12 B2
Tsing Yi *Hong Kong* 12 A1
Tsova *Jerusalem* 13 B1
Tsuen Wan *Hong Kong* 12 A1
Tsur Hadassa *Jerusalem* 13 B1
Tsurumi ➝ *Tokyo* 30 B3
Tsz Wan Shan *Hong Kong* 12 A2
Tuas *Singapore* 28 B1
Tuchoměřice *Prague* 25 B1
Tuckahoe *New York* 22 A2
Tucuruvi *São Paulo* 27 A2
Tufello *Rome* 26 B2
Tufnell Park *London* 15 A3
Tufts Univ. *Boston* 6 A2
Tughlakabad *Delhi* 10 B2
Tullamarine *Melbourne* 18 A1
Tulse Hill *London* 15 B3
Tung Lung Chau *Hong Kong* 12 B2
Tung O *Hong Kong* 12 B1
Tunis *Baghdad* 3 A2
Tuomarila *Helsinki* 11 B1
Tureberg *Stockholm* 29 A1
Turffontein *Johannesburg* 13 B2
Turkey L. *Orlando* 23 A2
Turkey Lake Park *Orlando* 23 A2
Turner Field *Atlanta* 3 B2
Turnham Green *London* 15 B2
Turnhouse *Edinburgh* 11 B1
Tuscolana, Via *Rome* 26 B2
Twelve Apostles *Cape Town* 8 A1
Twentieth Century Fox
 Studios *Los Angeles* 16 B2
Twickenham *London* 15 B2
Twickenham Rugby
 Ground *London* 15 B2
Twin Peaks *San Francisco* 26 B2
Two Rock Mt. *Dublin* 10 B2
Tymon North *Dublin* 10 B1
Tysons Corner *Washington* 33 B2

U

U.S. Capitol *Washington* 33 B3
U.S. Cellular Field *Chicago* 9 C3
Ubeidiya *Jerusalem* 13 B2
Uberaba ➝ *São Paulo* 27 B2
Ubin, Pulau *Singapore* 28 A3
Uccle *Brussels* 6 B2
Udelnaya *St. Petersburg* 27 A2
Udelnoe *St. Petersburg* 27 B3
U딐ding *Munich* 21 A1
Ueno *Tokyo* 30 A3
Ūholíčky *Prague* 25 B1
Ühřiněves *Prague* 25 B3
Uithoorn *Amsterdam* 2 B1
Ujazdów *Warsaw* 32 B2
Újpalota *Budapest* 7 A2
Ukita *Tokyo* 30 A4
Ullerup *Copenhagen* 8 B3
Ullevål *Oslo* 23 A3
Ulriksdal *Stockholm* 29 A1
Ulyanka *St. Petersburg* 27 B1
Um Al-Khanazir Island
 Baghdad 3 B2
Umeda *Osaka* 23 A1
Ümraniye *Istanbul* 12 B2
Underground Atlanta
 Atlanta 3 B2
Underhill, L. *Orlando* 23 A3
Uneětický potok ➝ *Prague* 25 B2
Unhos *Lisbon* 16 A2
Unidad Santa Fe
 Mexico City 18 B1
Union City *New York* 22 B1
Union Port *New York* 22 B2
Union Station *Toronto* 31 B2
United Center *Chicago* 9 B2
United Nations
 Headquarters *New York* 22 B2
Universal Studios
 Los Angeles 16 B2
Universal Studios *Orlando* 23 B2
Universidad *Madrid* 17 B1
University Park *Washington* 33 B4
Unterberg *Munich* 21 A3
Unterföhring *Munich* 21 A3
Unterhaching *Munich* 21 B2
Unterlaa *Vienna* 32 B2
Untermenzing *Munich* 21 A1
Upper B. *New York* 22 C1
Upper Elmers End *London* 15 B3
Upper New York B. =
 Upper York B. *New York* 22 C1
Upper Norwood *London* 15 B3
Upper Sydenham *London* 15 B3
Upton *London* 15 A4
Uptown *Chicago* 9 B3
Uran *Mumbai* 20 B2
Urayasu *Tokyo* 30 B4
Urbe ✈ *Rome* 26 B2
Urca *Rio de Janeiro* 25 B2
Uritsk *St. Petersburg* 27 B1
Ūröm *Budapest* 7 A2
Ursus *Warsaw* 32 B1
Usera *Madrid* 17 B1
Ushigome *Tokyo* 30 A3
Üsküdar *Istanbul* 12 B1
Ust-Slavyanka
 St. Petersburg 27 C3
Uteke *Stockholm* 29 A2
Utrata *Warsaw* 32 C1
Uttarpara *Kolkata* 14 B1
Uttersløv Mose *Copenhagen* 8 A2

V

Vaclavské náměstí *Prague* 25 B2
Vadaul *Mumbai* 20 A2
Vaires-sur-Marne *Paris* 24 A4
Valby *Copenhagen* 8 B2
Valcannuta *Rome* 26 B1
Valdelatas *Madrid* 17 A1
Valdoreix *Barcelona* 4 A1
Valenton *Paris* 24 B3
Valera *Milan* 19 A1
Vallcarca *Barcelona* 4 A1
Valldoreix *Barcelona* 4 A1
Vallecas *Madrid* 17 B2
Vallecas, Cumbres de
 Madrid 17 B2
Vallensbæk *Copenhagen* 8 B2
Vallensbæk Strand
 Copenhagen 8 B2
Vallentunasjön *Stockholm* 29 A2
Valleranello *Rome* 26 C1
Vallisaari *Helsinki* 11 C3
Vallvidrera *Barcelona* 4 A1
Valvidrera ➝ *Barcelona* 4 A1
Van Gogh Museum
 Amsterdam 2 A2
Vanak *Tehran* 31 A2
Vanda = Vantaa *Helsinki* 11 B2
Vangede *Copenhagen* 8 A3
Vaniköy *Istanbul* 12 B2
Vanlose *Copenhagen* 8 A2
Vantaa *Helsinki* 11 B2
Vantaankoski *Helsinki* 11 B2
Vantaanpuisto *Helsinki* 11 B2
Vanves *Paris* 24 B2
Varedo *Milan* 19 A1
Varkiza *Athens* 2 C2
Vartiokylä *Helsinki* 11 B3
Vartiosaari *Helsinki* 11 B3
Vasamuseet *Stockholm* 29 B2
Vasco *Cape Town* 8 A2
Vasfanārd *Tehran* 31 B2
Vashi *Mumbai* 20 A2
Vasilyevskiy, Ostrov
 St. Petersburg 27 B1
Vatican City ■ *Rome* 26 B1
Vaucluse *Sydney* 29 B2
Vaucluse House *Sydney* 29 B2
Vaucresson *Paris* 24 A1
Vaughan *Toronto* 31 A1
Vauhallan *Paris* 24 B2
Vaujours *Paris* 24 A4
Vauxhall *London* 15 B3
Vecsés *Budapest* 7 B3
Veleň *Prague* 25 B2
Veleslavin *Prague* 25 B2
Vélizy-Villacoublay *Paris* 24 B2
Velka-Chuchle *Prague* 25 C2
Velké Přílepy *Prague* 25 B1
Venda Seca *Lisbon* 16 A1
Venetian Islands *Miami* 18 B2
Venice *Los Angeles* 16 C2
Ventas *Madrid* 17 B1
Ventorro del Cano *Madrid* 17 B1
Venustiano Carranza
 Mexico City 18 B2
Verde ➝ *São Paulo* 27 A1
Verdi *Athens* 2 A2
Verdugo Mts. *Los Angeles* 16 A2
Verdun *Montreal* 20 B2
Vérhalom *Budapest* 7 A2
Vermelho ➝ *São Paulo* 27 B1
Vermont Knolls *Los Angeles* 16 C3
Vernon *Los Angeles* 16 B3
Verrières-le-Buisson *Paris* 24 B2
Versailles *Buenos Aires* 7 B1
Versailles *Paris* 24 B1
Veshnyaki *Moscow* 19 B3
Vesolyy Posolok
 St. Petersburg 27 B2
Vestra *Helsinki* 11 B2
Vestskoven *Copenhagen* 8 B2
Vicálvaro *Madrid* 17 B2
Vicente Lopez *Buenos Aires* 7 B2
Victoria, Mt. *Wellington* 33 B1
Victoria, Pont *Montreal* 20 B2
Victoria and Alfred
 Waterfront *Cape Town* 8 A1
Victoria Gardens *Mumbai* 20 B2
Victoria Island *Lagos* 14 B2
Victoria L. *Johannesburg* 13 B2
Victoria Lawn Tennis
 Courts *Melbourne* 18 B2
Victoria Park *Singapore* 28 B2
Victoria Peak *Hong Kong* 12 B1
Vienna = Wien *Vienna* 32 A2
Vienna *Washington* 33 B2
Vietnam Veterans
 Memorial *Washington* 33 B3
Vietnam War Museum
 Chicago 9 B3
Vieux Carré = French
 Quarter *New Orleans* 21 B2
View Park *Los Angeles* 16 C3
Vigário Geral *Rio de Janeiro* 25 A1
Vigentino *Milan* 19 B2
Viggbyholm *Stockholm* 29 A2
Vighignolo *Milan* 19 B1
Viikki *Helsinki* 11 B3
Vikhroli *Mumbai* 20 A2
Vila Guilherme *São Paulo* 27 B2
Vila Isabel *Rio de Janeiro* 25 B1
Vila Jaguára *São Paulo* 27 B1
Vila Madalena *São Paulo* 27 B1
Vila Maria *São Paulo* 27 B2
Vila Mariana *São Paulo* 27 B2
Vila Prudente *São Paulo* 27 B2
Viladecans *Barcelona* 4 B1
Vile Parle *Mumbai* 20 A2
Villa Adelina *Buenos Aires* 7 B1
Villa Ballester *Buenos Aires* 7 B1
Villa Barilari *Buenos Aires* 7 B1
Villa Bosch *Buenos Aires* 7 B1
Villa C. Colon *Buenos Aires* 7 B1
Villa Ciudadela *Buenos Aires* 7 B1
Villa de Guadalupe
 Mexico City 18 B2
Villa Devoto *Buenos Aires* 7 B1
Villa Diamante *Buenos Aires* 7 C2
Villa Dominico *Buenos Aires* 7 C2
Villa Lugano *Buenos Aires* 7 C1
Villa Luro *Buenos Aires* 7 B1
Villa Madero *Buenos Aires* 7 C1
Villa Pena
 Buenos Aires 7 B1
Vila Urquiza *Buenos Aires* 7 B1
Villaverde *Madrid* 17 B1
Villaverde Bajo *Madrid* 17 B1
Ville-d'Avray *Paris* 24 B2
Villecresnes *Paris* 24 B4
Villejuif *Paris* 24 B3
Villemomble *Paris* 24 A3
Villeneuve-la-Garenne
 Paris 24 A2
Villeneuve-le-Roi *Paris* 24 B3
Villeneuve-St-Georges *Paris* 24 B3
Villeparisis *Paris* 24 A4
Villevaudé *Paris* 24 A4
Villiers-le-Bâcle *Paris* 24 B1

Villiers-sur-Marne *Paris* 24 A4
Villinki *Helsinki* 11 C3
Villoresi, Canale *Milan* 19 A1
Vilvoorde *Brussels* 6 A2
Vimodrone *Milan* 19 B2
Vimont *Montreal* 20 A1
Vincennes *Paris* 24 A3
Vincennes, Bois de *Paris* 24 B3
Vineland *Orlando* 23 B1
Vinings *Atlanta* 3 A1
Vinohrady *Prague* 25 B2
Vinof *São Paulo* 25 B3
Violet Hill *Hong Kong* 12 B2
Virányos *Budapest* 7 A1
Virginia, L. *Orlando* 23 B2
Virginia Gardens *Miami* 18 B1
Virginia Key *Miami* 18 B2
Viroflay *Paris* 24 B2
Vironas *Athens* 2 B2
Virum *Copenhagen* 8 A2
Visitacion Valley
 San Francisco 26 B2
Vista Alegre *Lima* 14 B3
Vista Alegre *Santiago* 27 C1
Vista Grove *Atlanta* 3 A3
Vitacura *Santiago* 27 B2
Vitinia *Rome* 26 C1
Vizcaya Museum and
 Gardens *Miami* 18 B2
Vladykino *Moscow* 19 A2
Vokovice *Prague* 25 B2
Volgelsdorf *Berlin* 5 B5
Volkhonka-Zil *Moscow* 19 C2
Vollen *Oslo* 23 B1
Volodarskoye *St. Petersburg* 27 B2
Volynkina-Derevnya
 St. Petersburg 27 B2
Vondelpark *Amsterdam* 2 A2
Vösendorf *Vienna* 32 B2
Voula *Athens* 2 C2
Vouliagmeni *Athens* 2 C2
Vredehoek *Cape Town* 8 A1
Vršovice *Prague* 25 B2
Vyborgskaya Storona
 St. Petersburg 27 B2
Vykhino *Moscow* 19 B3
Vyšehrad *Prague* 25 B2

W

Wachterhof *Munich* 21 B3
Wadala *Mumbai* 20 A2
Wadestown *Wellington* 33 B1
Wadi al-Arayis *Jerusalem* 13 B2
Wadi Fukin *Jerusalem* 13 B1
Waduk Pluit *Jakarta* 12 A1
Waggaman *New Orleans* 21 B1
Wah Fu *Hong Kong* 12 B1
Wahda *Baghdad* 3 B2
Waidmannslust *Berlin* 5 A3
Wainuiomata *Wellington* 33 B2
Wainuiomata ➝
 Wellington 33 B2
Wakefield *Boston* 6 A2
Waldesruh *Berlin* 5 B4
Waldperlach *Munich* 21 B3
Waldtrudering *Munich* 21 B3
Walkinstown *Dublin* 10 B1
Wall Street *New York* 22 B2
Walt Disney World *Orlando* 23 B1
Walter D. Stone Memorial
 Zoo *Boston* 6 A2
Waltham *Boston* 6 A1
Waltham Forest □ *London* 15 A3
Walthamstow *London* 15 A3
Walton-on-Thames *London* 15 B1
Wambeek *Brussels* 6 A3
Wan Chai *Hong Kong* 12 B2
Wandle ➝ *London* 15 B2
Wandsworth □ *London* 15 B2
Wangjing *Beijing* 4 B2
Wannsee *Berlin* 5 B1
Wansdorf *Berlin* 5 A1
Wanstead *London* 15 A4
Wapping *London* 15 A3
Ward I. *Wellington* 33 B2
Wards I. *New York* 22 B2
Warnberg *Munich* 21 B2
Warner Brothers Studios
 Los Angeles 16 B2
Warrâq el 'Arab *Cairo* 7 A2
Warringal Park *Melbourne* 18 A2
Warriston *Edinburgh* 11 B2
Warsaw = Warszawa
 Warsaw 32 B2
Warszawa *Warsaw* 32 B2
Warszawa ✈ (WAW)
 Warsaw 32 B1
Wartenberg *Berlin* 5 A4
Washington *Washington* 33 B3
Washington Dulles Int. ✈
 (IAD) *Washington* 33 B2
Washington Heights
 New York 22 B2
Washington Park *Chicago* 9 C3
Washington Ronald
 Reagan Nat. ✈ (DCA)
 Washington 33 B3
Wat Pho *Bangkok* 3 B1
Water of Leith ➝ *Edinburgh* 11 B1
Watergraafsmeer *Amsterdam* 2 A2
Waterland *Amsterdam* 2 A2
Waterloo *Brussels* 6 B2
Waterloo *Wellington* 33 B2
Watermael-Boitsfort *Brussels* 6 B2
Watertown *Boston* 6 A1
Watsonia *Melbourne* 18 A2
Waverley *Boston* 6 A1
Waverley *Sydney* 29 B2
Waverley □ *Sydney* 29 B2
Wawer *Warsaw* 32 B2
Wawrzyszew *Warsaw* 32 B1
Wazirabad *Delhi* 10 A2
Wazirabad *Delhi* 10 A2
Wazirpur *Delhi* 10 A2
Wedding *Berlin* 5 A3
Weehawken *New York* 22 B1
Weesp *Amsterdam* 2 B3
Weidling *Vienna* 32 A1
Weidlingbach *Vienna* 32 A1
Weissensee *Berlin* 5 A3
Wellesley Hills *Boston* 6 B1
Welling *London* 15 B4
Wellington *Wellington* 33 B2
Wellington *Wellington* 33 B2
Wellington Int. ✈ (WLE)
 Wellington 33 B2
Weltevreden Park
 Johannesburg 13 B2
Wembley *London* 15 A2
Wemmel *Brussels* 6 A1
Wemmer Pan *Johannesburg* 13 B2
Wenceslas Square =
 Vaclavské náměstí
 Prague 25 B2
Wendenschloss *Berlin* 5 B4
Wenneuchen *Berlin* 5 A5

Worli *Mumbai* 20 B1
Worth *Chicago* 9 C2
Wren's Nest *Atlanta* 3 B2
Wrigley Field *Chicago* 9 B3
Wuhlgarten *Berlin* 5 A5
Wujiaochang *Shanghai* 28 B2
Würm ➝ *Munich* 21 A1
Würm-kanal *Munich* 21 A1
Wusong *Shanghai* 28 A2
Wyczółki *Warsaw* 32 C1
Wygoda *Warsaw* 32 B2
Wynberg *Cape Town* 8 B1

X

Xabregas *Lisbon* 16 A2
Xianggang = Hong Kong
 Hong Kong 12 B1
Xiaogang Park *Guangzhou* 11 B2
Xiaoping *Guangzhou* 11 A1
Xiasha chong *Guangzhou* 11 B1
Xicheng *Guangzhou* 11 B1
Xicheng *Beijing* 4 B2
Xidan *Beijing* 4 B2
Xizhimen *Beijing* 4 B1
Xochimilco, Parque
 Ecológico *Mexico City* 18 C2
Xuanwu *Beijing* 4 B2
Xuhui *Shanghai* 28 B1

Y

Yaba *Lagos* 14 A2
Yaftābād *Tehran* 31 B1
Yahara *Tokyo* 30 A2
Yaho *Tokyo* 30 A1
Yakire *Tokyo* 30 A4
Yaksu *Seoul* 27 B2
Yamada *Osaka* 23 A2
Yamada *Tokyo* 30 B2
Yamato ➝ *Osaka* 23 B2
Yan Kit *Singapore* 28 B2
Yanbu *Guangzhou* 11 B1
Yangcheon *Seoul* 27 B1
Yanghuayuan *Beijing* 4 C1
Yangjae *Seoul* 27 C2
Yangjiazhuang *Shanghai* 28 A1
Yangjing *Shanghai* 28 B2
Yangpu *Shanghai* 28 B2
Yangpu Park *Shanghai* 28 B2
Yannawa *Bangkok* 3 B2
Yarmük *Baghdad* 3 B1
Yarra Bend Park *Melbourne* 18 A2
Yarraville *Melbourne* 18 A1
Yauza ➝ *Moscow* 19 B4
Yeading *London* 15 A1
Yedikule *Istanbul* 12 C1
Yenikapı *Istanbul* 12 B1
Yeniköy *Istanbul* 12 B2
Yeongdeungpo *Seoul* 27 B1
Yeongdong *Seoul* 27 C2
Yeouido *Seoul* 27 B1
Yerba Buena I.
 San Francisco 26 B2
Yerres *Paris* 24 B4
Yerushalayim =
 Jerusalem *Jerusalem* 13 B2
Yiexiu *Guangzhou* 11 B2
Yiheyuan *Beijing* 4 B1
Yin Park *Istanbul* 12 B2
Yindangshen *Shanghai* 28 A2
Yishun *Singapore* 28 A3
Ylästö *Helsinki* 11 B2
Yodo ➝ *Osaka* 23 A2
Yongdingmen *Beijing* 4 B2
Yongfucun *Guangzhou* 11 B2
Yongsan *Seoul* 27 B1
Yonkers *New York* 22 A2
York *Toronto* 31 A2
York Mills *Toronto* 31 A2
York Univ. *Toronto* 31 A1
You'anmen *Beijing* 4 B1
Youngsfield *Cape Town* 8 B1
Yuanmingyuan Park *Beijing* 4 A1
Yuanxiatian *Guangzhou* 11 A2
Yuexiu Park *Guangzhou* 11 B2
Yugo-Zarad *Moscow* 19 B2
Yuhalixqui, Volcan
 Mexico City 18 C2
Yung Shue Wan *Hong Kong* 12 B1
Yūsofābād *Tehran* 31 A2

Z

Zaandam *Amsterdam* 2 A1
Zaandijk *Amsterdam* 2 A1
Zaanstad *Amsterdam* 2 A1
Zábehlice *Prague* 25 B2
Zabki *Warsaw* 32 B2
Zacisze *Warsaw* 32 B2
Zahrā *Baghdad* 3 A1
Žalov *Prague* 25 B1
Zaluski *Warsaw* 32 C1
Zamdorf *Munich* 21 B2
Zanevka *St. Petersburg* 27 B2
Zapote *Manila* 17 C1
Zaventem *Brussels* 6 A2
Zawady *Warsaw* 32 B2
Zāwiyet Abū Musallam
 Cairo 7 B1
Zawrā' Park *Baghdad* 3 B2
Zbraslav *Prague* 25 C2
Zbuzany *Prague* 25 B1
Zdiby *Prague* 25 B2
Zeekoevlei *Cape Town* 8 B2
Zehlendorf *Berlin* 5 B2
Zenne ➝ *Brussels* 6 A2
Zephyr Field *New Orleans* 21 B1
Žerań *Warsaw* 32 B2
Zeytinburnu *Istanbul* 12 C1
Zhabei *Shanghai* 28 B1
Zlatanov *Moscow* 19 B3
Zhernovka *St. Petersburg* 27 B2
Zhicun *Guangzhou* 11 B2
Zhongshan Park *Shanghai* 28 B1
Zhongshan Park *Shanghai* 28 B1
Zhoujiadu *Shanghai* 28 B1
Zhoujiazhen *Shanghai* 28 A2
Zhouzhuangzi *Beijing* 4 B1
Zhulebino *Moscow* 19 B4
Zhushadi *Guangzhou* 11 A3
Zielona *Warsaw* 32 B3
Zielonka *Warsaw* 32 B3
Zizhuyuan Park *Beijing* 4 B1
Žižkov *Prague* 25 B2
Žličín *Prague* 25 B1
Zografou *Athens* 2 B2
Žoliborz *Warsaw* 32 B2
Zonnebloem *Cape Town* 8 A1
Zugliget *Budapest* 7 A2
Zugló *Budapest* 7 A2
Zuiderwoude *Amsterdam* 2 A2
Zumbi *Rio de Janeiro* 25 A1
Zunderdorp *Amsterdam* 2 A1
Zuvuvu ➝ *São Paulo* 27 C1
Zwanenburg *Amsterdam* 2 A1
Zwölfaxing *Vienna* 32 B2

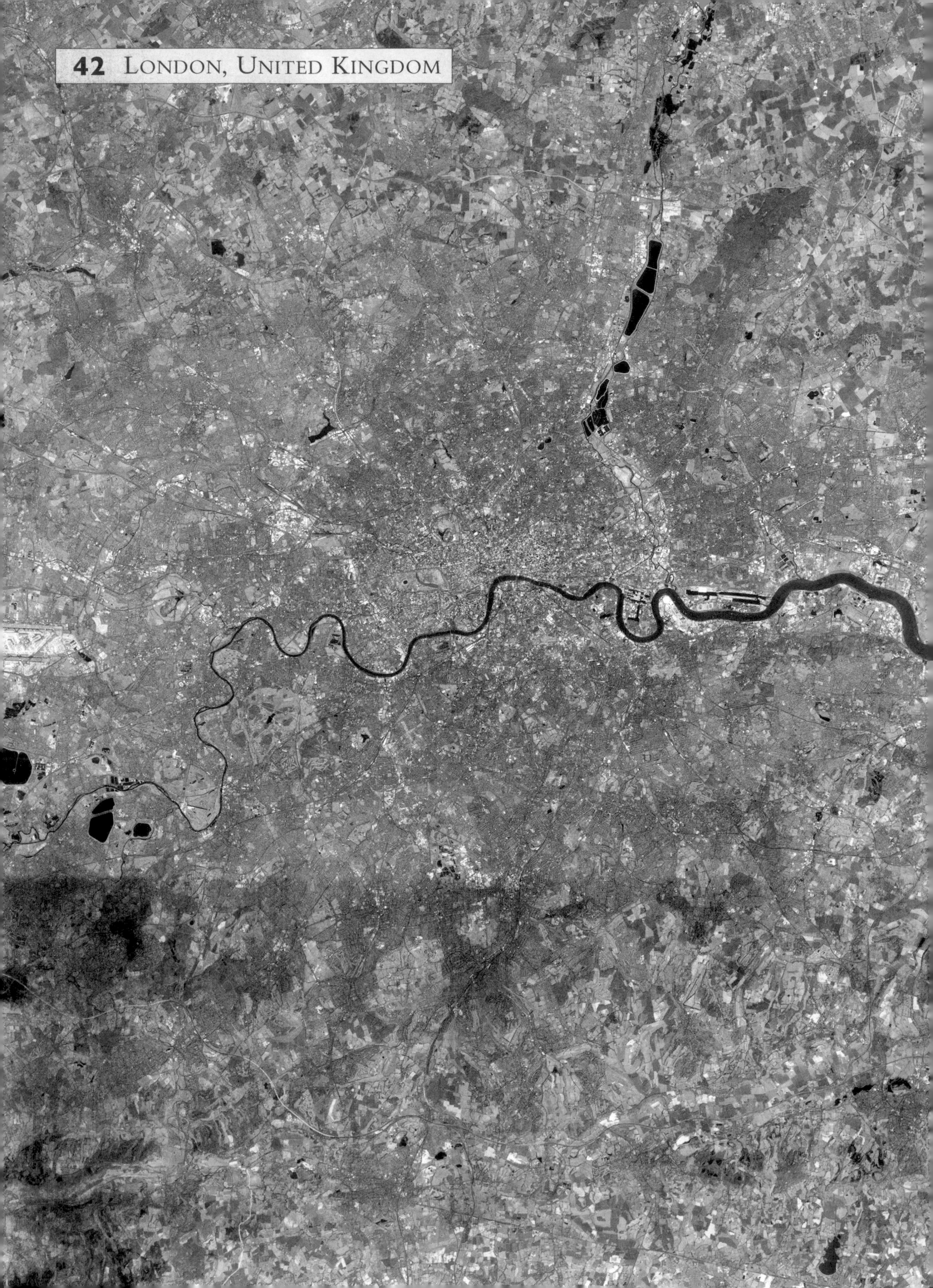

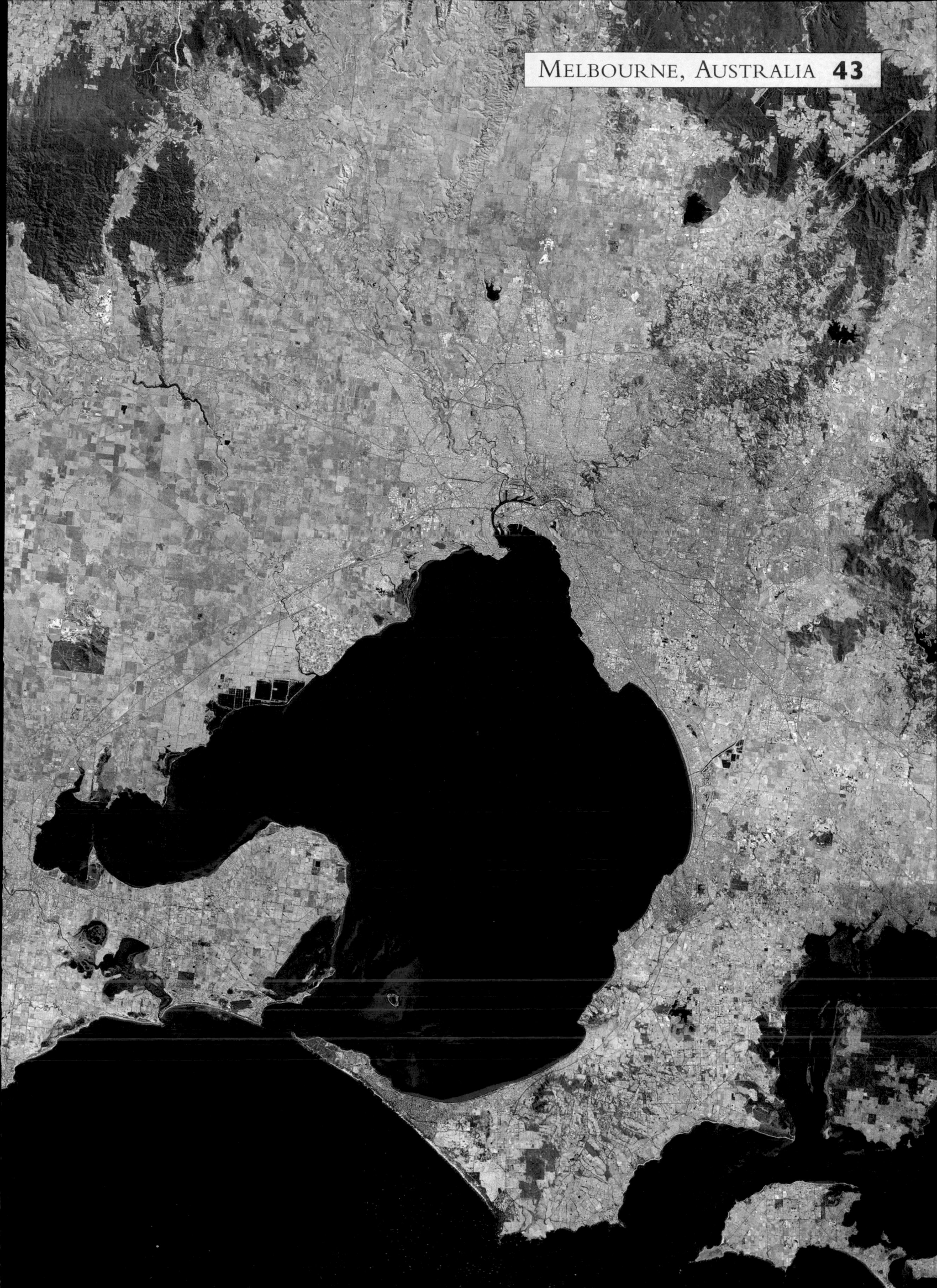

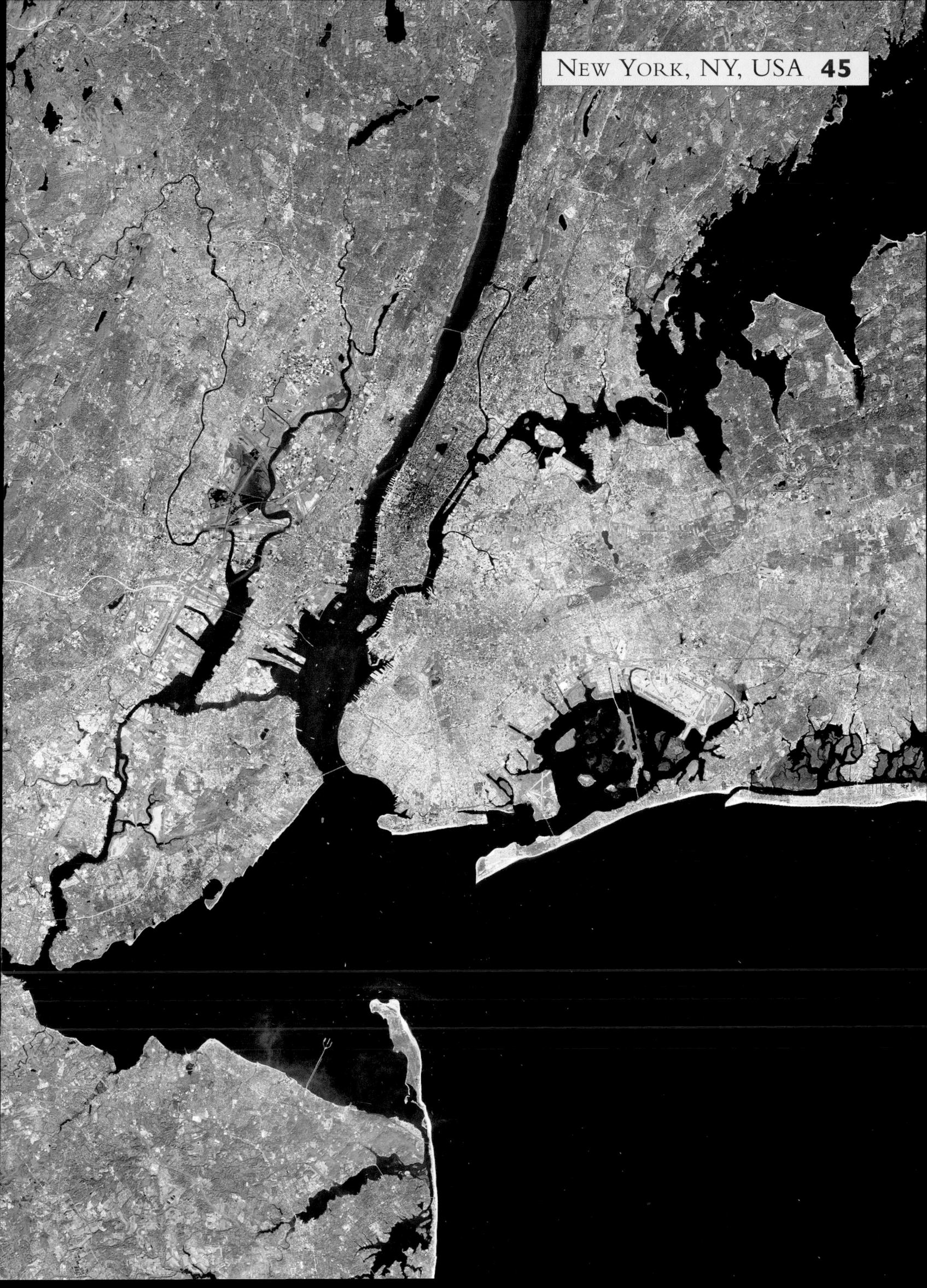

WORLD
MAPS

SETTLEMENTS

■ **PARIS**   ◉ Rotterdam   ◉ Livorno   ◉ Brugge   ◉ Exeter   ○ Torremolinos   ○ Oberammergau   ○ Thira

Settlement symbols and type styles vary according to the scale of each map and indicate the importance
of towns on the map rather than specific population figures

• Vaduz   Capital cities have red infills   ∴   Ruins or archaeological sites

⬠   Urban agglomerations   ⌄   Wells in desert

ADMINISTRATION

────── International boundaries   ·········· Internal boundaries   **PERU**   Country names

─ ─ ─ · International boundaries   ⬡ National parks   KENT   Administrative
(undefined or disputed)   area names

International boundaries show the *de facto* situation where there are rival claims to territory

---

COMMUNICATIONS

══════ Motorways, freeways   ──⌣── Principal railways   ᴸᴴᴿ ✈ Principal airports
and expressways

────── Principal roads   ─ ─ ─ Railways   ⊕   Other airports
under construction

───── Other roads   ──── Other railways   ············· Principal canals

→┄┄⊢ Road tunnels   →┄┄⊢ Railway tunnels   ⤨   Passes

PHYSICAL FEATURES

⌇⌇⌇ Perennial streams   ▧ Intermittent lakes   ▲ 8850 Elevations in metres

─ ─ ─ Intermittent streams   ⁙ Swamps and marshes   ▼ 8500 Sea depths in metres

⬭ Perennial lakes   ▥ Permanent ice   1134 Height of lake surface
and glaciers   above sea level in metres

⬚ Sand deserts

ELEVATION AND DEPTH TINTS

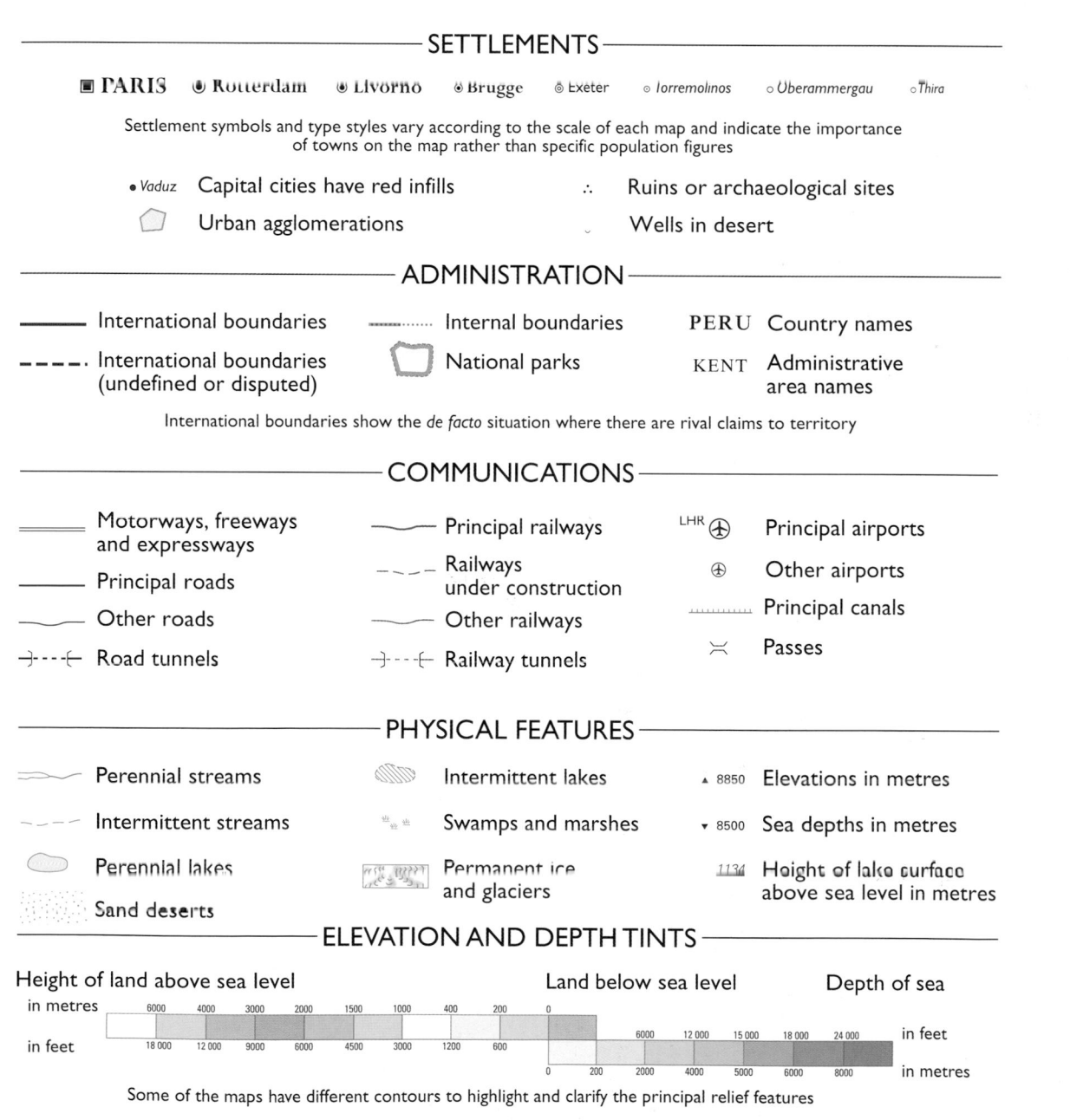

Height of land above sea level   **Land below sea level**   **Depth of sea**

in metres   6000 4000 3000 2000 1500 1000 400 200   0

in feet   18 000 12 000 9000 6000 4500 3000 1200 600

6000 12 000 15 000 18 000 24 000   in feet

0   200   2000   4000   5000   6000   8000   in metres

Some of the maps have different contours to highlight and clarify the principal relief features

Equatorial Scale 1:95 000 000

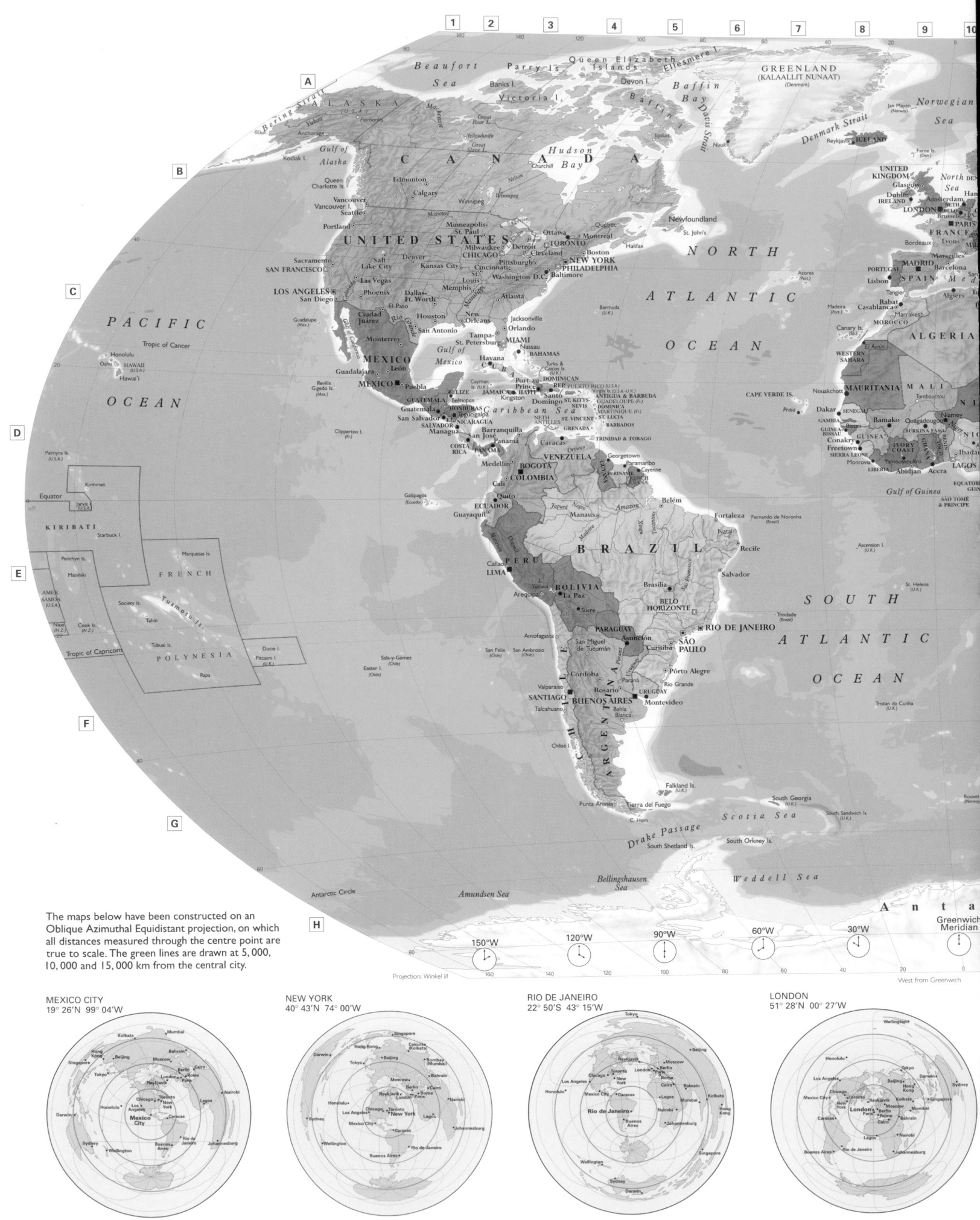

The maps below have been constructed on an Oblique Azimuthal Equidistant projection, on which all distances measured through the centre point are true to scale. The green lines are drawn at 5, 000, 10, 000 and 15, 000 km from the central city.

Projection: Winkel III

West from Greenwich

MEXICO CITY
19° 26'N 99° 04'W

NEW YORK
40° 43'N 74° 00'W

RIO DE JANEIRO
22° 50'S 43° 15'W

LONDON
51° 28'N 00° 27'W

COPYRIGHT PHILIP'S

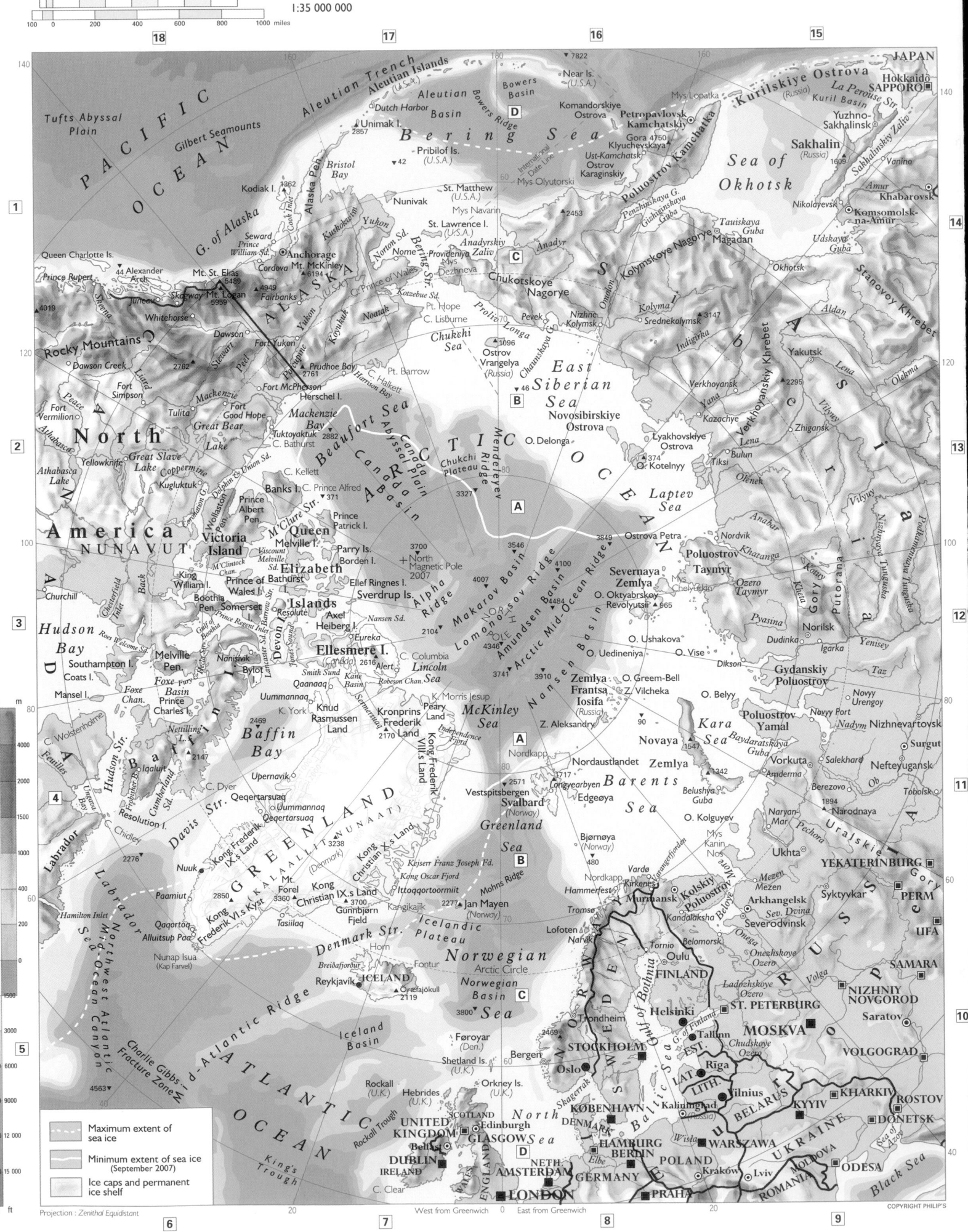

1:35 000 000

100 0   200 400 600 800 1000 1200 1400 km

100   0   200   400   600   800   1000 miles

18   17   16   15

PACIFIC
OCEAN

Tufts Abyssal
Plain

Gilbert Seamounts

Aleutian Trench

Aleutian Islands
(U.S.A.)

Bowers
Basin

Near Is.
(U.S.A.)

7822

JAPAN

Kurilskiye Ostrova
(Russia)

Hokkaidō
SAPPORO

Mys Lopatka

La Perouse Str.

Kuril Basin

Dutch Harbor

Aleutian
Basin

Bowers
Ridge

Komandorskiye
Ostrova

Petropavlovsk-
Kamchatskiy

Gora 4750
Klyuchevskaya

Ust-Kamchatsk
Ostrov
Karaginskiy

Poluostrov Kamchatka

Yuzhno-
Sakhalinsk

Sakhalin
(Russia)

1609

Sakhalinskiy Zaliv

B e r i n g   S e a

Unimak I.
2857

Pribilof Is.
(U.S.A.)

42

International
Date Line

60

Mys Olyutorski

Sea of
Okhotsk

Vanino

St. Matthew
(U.S.A.)

Nunivak

2453

Anadyrskiy
Zaliv

Penzhinskaya G.
Gizhiginskaya
Guba

Tauiskaya
Guba

Amur

Khabarovsk

Komsomolsk-
na-Amur

Kodiak I. 1362

Seward

G. of Alaska

Prince
William Sd.

Anchorage

Cook Inlet

Mt. McKinley
6194

St. Lawrence I.
(U.S.A.)

Nome

Norton Sd.

Provideniya
Mys
Dezhneva

Anadyr

Anadyr

Mys Navarin

Nikolayevsk

Magadan

Kolymskoye Nagorye

Udskaya
Guba

Okhotsk

Mt. St. Elias
5489

Cordova

Mt. Logan
5959

4949

Fairbanks

Kuskokwim

Bering Str.

Chukotskoye
Nagorye

Stanovoy Khrebet

Queen Charlotte Is.

Prince Rupert
44
Alexander
Arch.

Juneau
Skagway

4019

Whitehorse

A L A S K A
(U.S.A.)

Yukon

Prince of Wales I.

Kotzebue Sd.

Pt. Hope
C. Lisburne

Proliv Longa

1096

Pevek

Nizhne-
Kolymsk

Kolyma

Srednekolymsk

3147

Omolon

Indigirka

Verkhoyansk

Yakutsk

Lena

Aldan

Olekma

Rocky Mountains

Dawson Creek

2762

Dawson

Stewart

Fort Yukon

Pelly

Porcupine

Prudhoe Bay
C. Halkett

Pt. Barrow

Harrison Bay

Chaunskaya
G.

46

**E a s t
S i b e r i a n
S e a**

B

Yana

Verkhoyanskiy Khrebet

2295

Zhigansk

120

Fort Good Hope

Peel

Fort McPherson

Herschel I.

Beaufort Sea

Ostrov
Vrangelya
(Russia)

Novosibirskiye
Ostrova

Kazachye

Bulun

Tiksi

120

N o r t h

Fort
Simpson

Tulita

Mackenzie
Bay

Tuktoyaktuk 2882
C. Bathurst

Canada Abyssal Plain

A R C T I C

O. Delonga

Lena

Olenek

Fort
Vermilion

Great Bear
Lake

Canada Basin

Mendeleyev Ridge

Chukchi
Plateau

Lyakhovskiye
Ostrova

Kotelnyy

374

Anabar

Nizhnyaya Tunguska

Peace

Yellowknife

Great Slave
Lake

Coppermine

Kugluktuk

C. Kellett

Banks I.

C. Prince Alfred
371

3327

A

**L a p t e v
S e a**

Ostrova Petra

Nordvik

Khatanga

Khatanga

A m e r i c a

Athabasca
Lake

C A N A D A

Wollaston
Pen.

Dolphin & Union Str.

Victoria
Island

M'Clure Str.

Prince
Albert
Pen.

Melville I.

Prince
Patrick I.

Parry Is.
Borden I.

3700

North
Magnetic Pole
2007

3546

4007

Makarov Basin

4100

3849

Severnaya
Zemlya

Mys
Chelyuskin

Poluostrov
Taymyr

O. Oktyabrskoy
Revolyutsii

965

Ozero
Taymyra

Pyasina

Norilsk

Dudinka

Gorlo

Kheta

Putorana

Yenisey

100

NUNAVUT

King
William I.

Viscount
Melville
Sd.

M'Clintock
Chan.

Prince of
Wales I.

Bathurst
I.

Ellef Ringnes I.

Sverdrup Is.

Alpha
Ridge

NORTH
POLE

Lomonosov Ridge

Amundsen Basin

4484

4346

O. Ushakova

O. Uedineniya

O. Vise

Dikson

Gydanskiy
Poluostrov

Igarka

Taz

100

3

Churchill

Boothia
Pen.

Back

Chesterfield
Inlet

Roes Welcome Sd.

Gulf of Boothia

Prince Regent Inlet

Resolute

Devon I.

Axel
Heiberg I.

Nansen Sd.

Eureka

2104

3741

Arctic Mid-Ocean Ridge

3910

Nansen Basin

4346

O. Greem-Bell
Z. Vilcheka

O. Belyy

Novyy
Urengoy

Norilsk

Novyy Port

80

**H u d s o n
B a y**

Southampton I.

Coats I.

Melville
Pen.

Foxe
Basin

Prince
Charles
I.

2469

Resolute

Lancaster Sound

Jones Sound

Ellesmere I.
(Canada)
2616

Alert

C. Columbia

**Lincoln
Sea**

Robeson Chan.

Smith Sund

Kane Basin

Morris Jesup

Peary
Land

Independence Fjord

**McKinley
Sea**

A

**Zemlya
Frantsa
Iosifa**
(Russia)

Z. Aleksandry

90

**K a r a
S e a**

Novaya

1547

Z e m l y a

Baydaratskaya
Guba

Poluostrov
Yamal

Vorkuta

Salekhard

Amderma

Nadym

Ob

Nizhnevartovsk

Tobolsk

Mansel I.

Foxe
Chan.

Hudson Str.

Melville
Pen.

Nanisivik

Bylot
I.

Qaanaaq

K. York

Uummannaq

Kronprins
Frederik
Land

2170

Kong
Frederik
VIII.s Land

Kong
Frederik
VI.s Land

Nordkapp

Nordaustlandet

2571

1717

1342

Belushya
Guba

Narodnaya
1894

Berezovo

Naryan-
Mar

Pechora

Surgut

Nefteyugansk

4

C. Wolstenholme

Feuilles

2147

Baffin

Ungava
Bay

Hudson Str.

Frobisher Bay

Cumberland Sd.

**Baffin
Bay**

Nettilling
L.

K. Rasmussen
Land

Knud
Rasmussen
Land

Smith Sund

Kong
Frederik
VIII.s Land

**B a r e n t s
S e a**

Edgeøya

Longyearbyen

Vestspitsbergen

Svalbard
(Norway)

Novyy
Urengoy

O. Kolguyev

Mys
Kanin
Nos

YEKATERINBURG

PERM

UFA

ft   m

12 000 4000

**Labrador
Sea**

Iqaluit

Resolution I.

Chidley

Davis Str.

Upernavik

C. Dyer

Qeqertarsuaq

Uummannaq

Qeqertarsuaq

**G R E E N L A N D
(K A L A A L L I T   N U N A A T)**
(Denmark)

3238

Kong
Christian IX.s Land

Kong
Frederik
IX.s Land

Kejser Franz Joseph Fd.

Kong Oscar Fjord

Ittoqqortoormiit

**Greenland
Sea**

Bjørnøya
(Norway)

480

Vardø

Kirkenes

Hammerfest

Tromsø

Vardø

Nordkapp

Hammerfest

Mezen

Megen

Mys
Kanin
Nos

Ukhta

Arkhangelsk

Kolskiy
Poluostrov

Kandalaksha

Severodvinsk

Syktyvkar

6000   2000

4500   1500

1200   400

600   200

0   0

500   1500

Labrador

2276

Nuuk

Paamiut

2850

Mt.
Forel
3360

Kong
Christian IX.s Land

3700

Gunnbjørn
Fjeld

Kangikajik

2277

Jan Mayen
(Norway)

Mohns Ridge

**Icelandic
Plateau**

Bjørnøya
(Norway)

Murmansk

Kola

Kirkenes

Belomorsk

Sev. Dvina

Beloye
More

Belomorsk

Onezhskoye
Ozero

1000 3000

2000 6000

3000 9000

**N O R T H W E S T
A T L A N T I C**

Mid-Ocean Canyon

**Labrador
Sea**

Qaqortoq

Alluitsup Paa

Nunap Isua
(Kap Farvel)

Qaqortoq

Tasiilaq

Breiðafjörður

Horn

Fontur

Øræfajökull
2119

Denmark Str.

2850

Kangikajik

**Icelandic
Plateau**

Arctic Circle

**Norwegian
Sea**

3800

2469

Trondheim

Bergen

Oslo

S W E D E N

N O R W A Y

Gulf of Bothnia

FINLAND

Helsinki

Oulu

Tornio

Ladozhskoye
Ozero

Onezhskoye
Ozero

ST. PETERBURG

NIZHNIY
NOVGOROD

SAMARA

R U S S I A

4000 12 000

5000 15 000

5

Reykjavík

ICELAND

**Iceland
Basin**

Mid-Atlantic Ridge

Charlie Gibbs
Fracture Zone

4563

40

A T L A N T I C

OCEAN

King's
Trough

Rockall Trough

Rockall
(U.K.)

Hebrides
(U.K.)

Orkney Is.
(U.K.)

Shetland Is.
(U.K.)

**North
Sea**

Bergen

STOCKHOLM

OSLO

Skagerrak

Baltic Sea

Tallinn
EST.

Rīga

LAT.

Vilnius

LITH.

G. of Finland

Chudskoye
Ozero

Saratov

VOLGOGRAD

10

40

m   ft

Projection : Zenithal Equidistant

6

20

7

West from Greenwich

0

East from Greenwich

8

20

9

COPYRIGHT PHILIP'S

Maximum extent of
sea ice

Minimum extent of sea ice
(September 2007)

Ice caps and permanent
ice shelf

**UNITED
KINGDOM**

Edinburgh
Glasgow
SCOTLAND

Belfast

DUBLIN

IRELAND

ENGLAND

LONDON

NETH.

AMSTERDAM

GERMANY

HAMBURG
BERLIN

KØBENHAVN

DENMARK

Elbe

HAMBURG
BERLIN

POLAND

WARSZAWA

Kraków

Wisła

Kaliningrad
(Russia)

BELARUS

KYYIV

UKRAINE

Lviv

MOLDOVA

ROMANIA

PRAHA

KHARKIV

DONETSK

ROSTOV

ODESA

Sea of
Azov

Black Sea

C. Clear

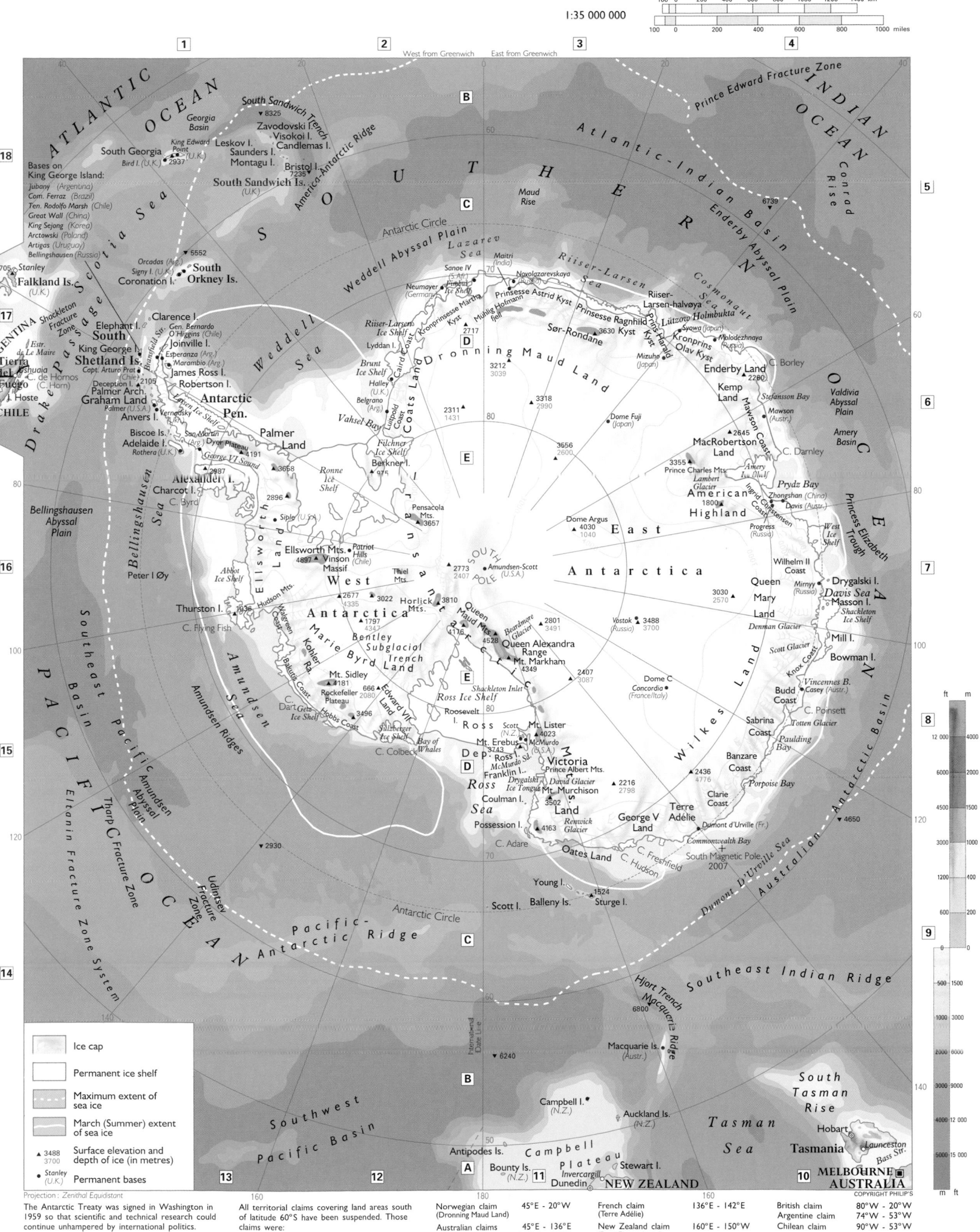

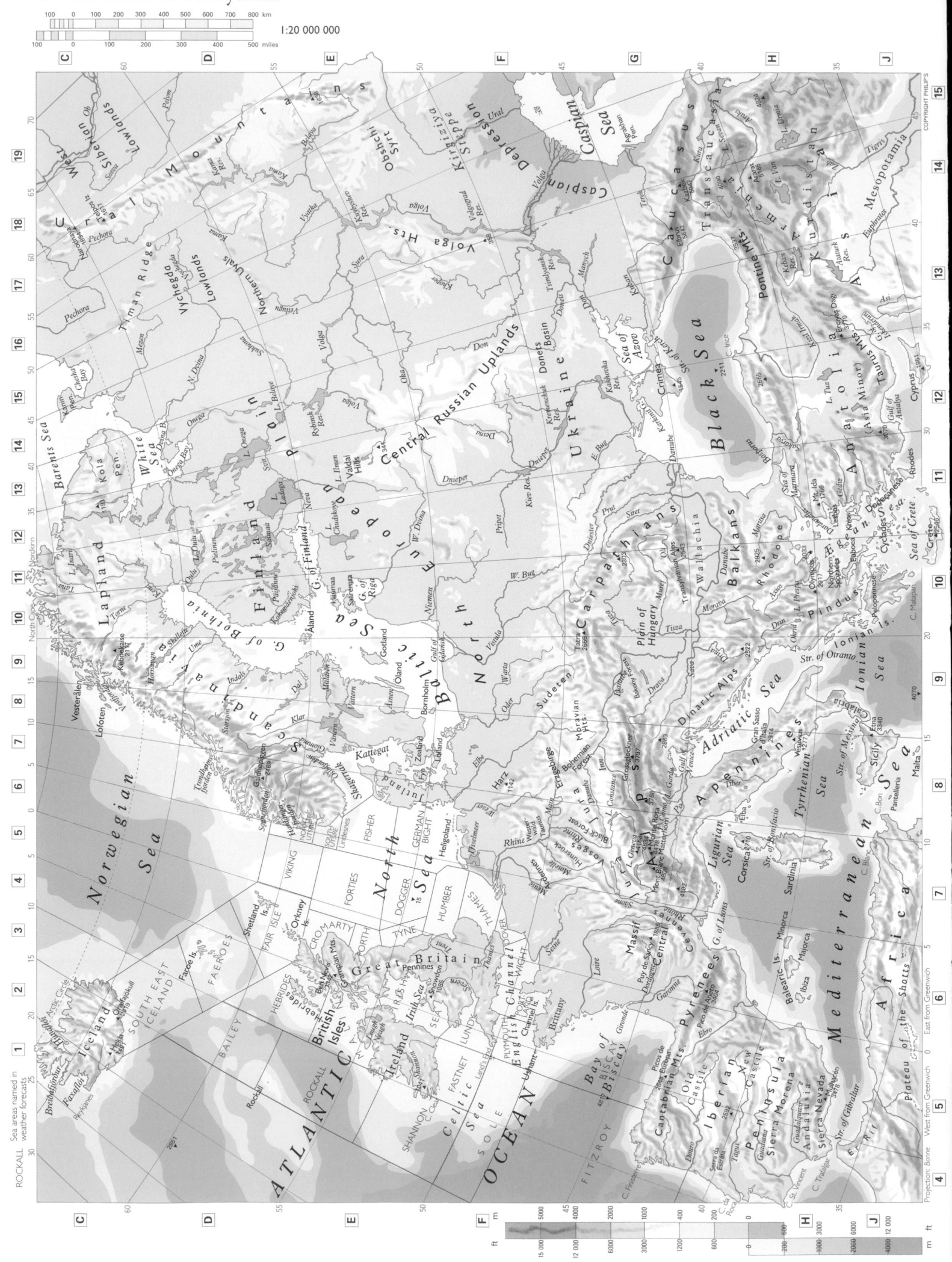

1:20 000 000

COPYRIGHT PHILIP'S

ROCKALL Sea areas named in weather forecasts

Projection: Bonne

1:20 000 000

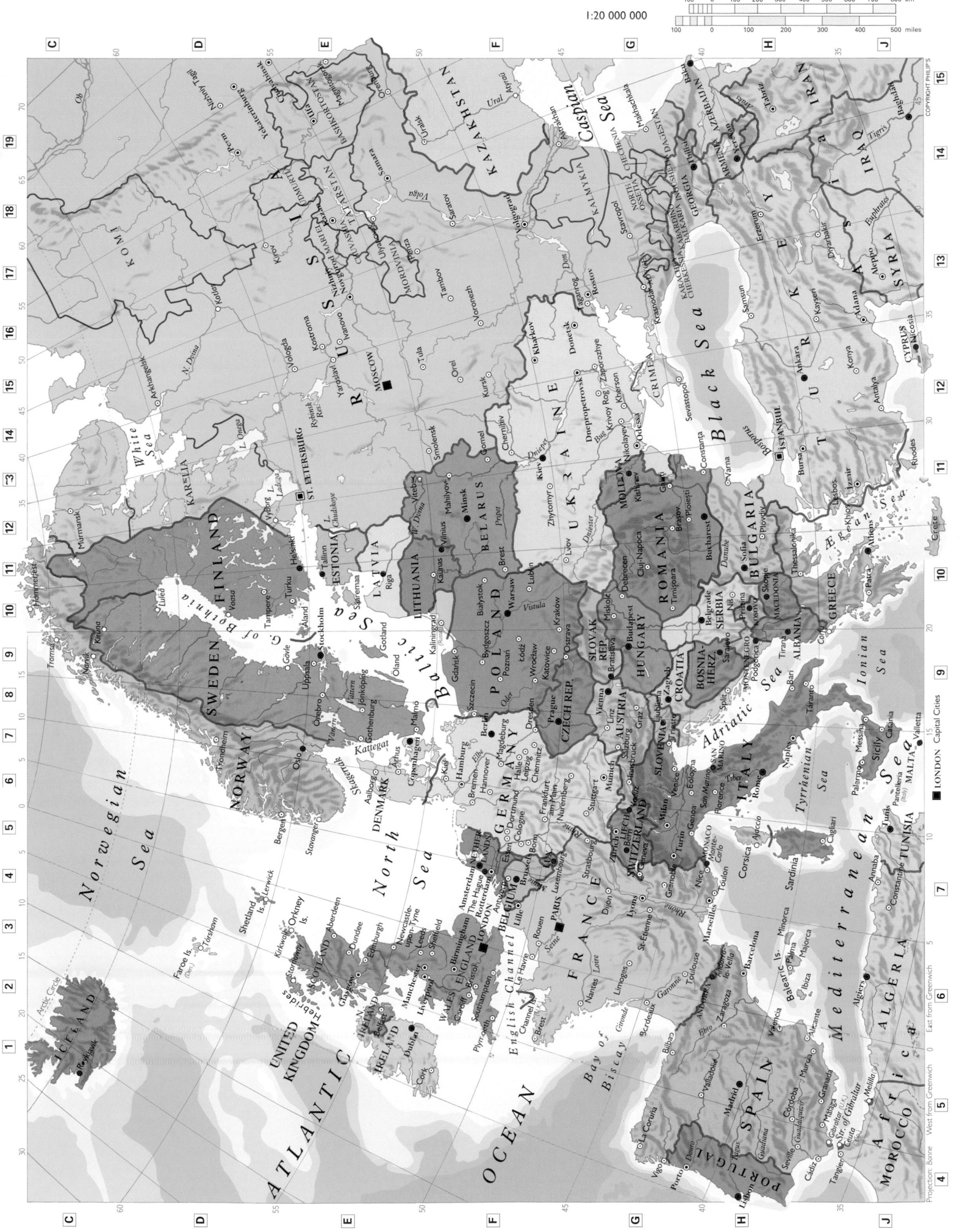

A **B** **C** **D** **E** **F**

BARENTS SEA

RUSSIA

FINLAND

KARELIA

LAPLAND

Lappland

NORGE (NORWAY)

SVERIGE (SWEDEN)

Gulf of Bothnia

ATLANTIC OCEAN

NORWEGIAN SEA

Murmansk · Severomorsk · Kola · Pechenga · Nikel

Varangerhalvøya · Vardø · Vadsø · Kirkenes · Båtsfjord

Nordkapp · Magerøya · Hammerfest · Honningsvåg · Alta · Kautokeino · Karasjok

Tromsø · Narvik · Harstad · Bodø · Saltdalen · Fauske · Mo · Mosjøen

Kiruna · Gällivare · Jokkmokk · Boden · Luleå · Piteå · Skellefteå · Umeå

Oulu · Kemi · Tornio · Haparanda · Rovaniemi · Kemijärvi · Salla

Vaasa · Pori · Tampere · Kuopio · Joensuu · Mikkeli · Kajaani

Östersund · Sundsvall · Sollefteå · Härnösand · Hudiksvall · Söderhamn

Trondheim · Steinkjer · Namsos · Mosjøen · Brønnøysund

Österdalen · Gudbrandsdalen · Dalarna · Jämtland · Härjedalen · Trøndelag

Arctic Circle

18

ICELAND on same scale

ÍSLAND

Reykjavík · Keflavík · Akureyri · Vatnajökull · Hekla · Mýrdalsjökull · Vík · Höfn · Selfoss · Vestmannaeyjar · Surtsey · Heimaey · Húsavík · Grímsey

FÆROE ISLANDS on same scale

Føroyar (Faroe Is.) · Tórshavn · Nordoyar · Streymoy · Eysturoy · Vágar · Sandoy · Suðuroy

Scale 1:6 000 000

50 0 25 50 75 100 125 150 175 km
50 0 25 50 75 100 125 miles

1:2 000 000

10 0 10 20 30 40 50 60 70 80 km
10 0 10 20 30 40 50 miles

A
B
C
D
E

11
13

SCOTLAND
Kintyre
Brodick
Arran
Mull of Oa
Campbeltown
Mull of Kintyre
Ailsa Craig
Firth of Clyde
Cairnryan
Stranraer
Portpatrick
L. Ryan

Trawbreaga B.
Malin Hd.
Inishtrahull
Malin
Glengad Hd.
Tory I.
Sheep Haven
Mulroy B.
Fanad Hd.
Lough Swilly
Inishowen Pen.
Moville
Carndonagh
Buncrana
Giants Causeway
Portstewart
Portrush
Rathlin I.
Ballycastle
Cushendall
GLENARIFF
554
269
Hd.
Horn Hd.
Dunfanaghy
Bloody Foreland
Errigal 752
L. Foyle
Coleraine
Limavady
Ballymoney
Mts. of Antrim
Carncastle
Larne
Inishfree B.
Gweedore
Derryveagh Mts.
Rathmelton
Londonderry
Ballymena
Cushendun
Larne
Aran I.
The Rosses
Dunglow
GLENVEAGH
Letterkenny
LONDONDERRY
601
Crohy Hd.
DONEGAL
Strabane
Sawel Mt. 683
Randalstown
Ballyclare
Carrickfergus
Gweebarra B.
Dawros Hd.
Lifford
Sion Mills
Newtownstewart
Spering Mts.
NORTHERN
Antrim
Belfast L.
Bangor
Ardara
Glenties
Lavagh More 676
TYRONE
Omagh
Moneymore
Cookstown
Lough Neagh
Belfast
Donaghadee
Newtownards
Glencolumbkille
Slieve League 601
Donegal
Ballyshannon
Ulster
Dromore
Irvinestown
Enniskillen
Dungannon
Coalisland
IRELAND
Lisburn
Saintfield
Ards Pen.
St. John's Pt.
Killybegs
Donegal Bay
Ballygawley
Armagh
Craigavon
Lurgan
Portadown
DOWN
Portaferry
Rossan Pt.
Inishmurray I.
Bundoran
Lower L. Erne
Ballinamallard
Monaghan
Middletown
Keady
Banbridge
Downpatrick
St. John's Pt.
Ballyquintin Pt.
Broad Haven
Portacloy
Downpatrick Hd.
Lenadoon Pt.
Killala B.
Manorhamilton
FERMANAGH
Upper L. Erne
Clones
MONAGHAN
577
Castleblaney
Newry
Mourne Mts.
852
Slieve Donard
Dundrum
Newcastle
Dundrum B.
Erris Hd.
Belmullet
Sligo Bay
Sligo
Lackagh Hills
Crossmaglen
Slieve Gullion
Warrenpoint
Kilkeel
Mullet Pen.
Bangor
Bunnyconnellan
Dromore West
544
Colooney
L. Allen
LEITRIM
Annalee
Coothill
Carlingford L.
Greenore
Inishkea North
Inishkea South
Blacksod Bay
380
Killala
Ballina
Crossmolina
Slieve Gamph Range
SLIGO
Ballymote
L. Arrow
L. Key
Leitrim
Carrick-on-Shannon
L. Oughter
Belturbet
CAVAN
Carrickmacross
Dundalk
Dundalk Bay
Achill Hd.
Nephin Beg 806
Nephin 672
Foxford
Charlestown
Boyle
L. Gowna
Cavan
Kingscourt
Ardee
Dunleer
Clogher Hd.
Achill I.
Clare I.
Cortaun Pen.
Castlebar
Swinford
Ballaghaderreen
ROSCOMMON
Castlerea
Strokestown
L. Sheelin
Ceananus Mor (Kells)
LOUTH
Drogheda
Newport
Knock
LONGFORD
Granard
Oldcastle
MEATH
Balbriggan
Westport
Louisburgh
Claremorris
Ballyhaunis
Longford
Roscommon
Castlepollard
Blackwater
An Uaimh (Navan)
Rush
Croagh Patrick 765
Mweelrea 819
Partry Mts.
Ballinrobe
Connacht
Castlebar
IRELAND
Mullingar
Trim
Dunshaughlin
Lambay I.
Killary Harbour
683
Lough Mask
Glennamaddy
Lough Ree
WESTMEATH
Royal Canal
Leinster
Malahide
Inishturk
Inishbofin
Inishshark
Connemara
Lough Corrib
Tuam
Mount Bellew Bridge
Athlone
Moate
Kinnegad
Cloncurry
Maynooth
DUB
Swords
DUBLIN
Slyne Hd.
CONNEMARA
Oughterard
GALWAY
Athenry
Ballinasloe
Clara
Grand Canal
Edenderry
Allen
Liffey
DUBLIN
Clondalkin
Dun Laoghaire
Howth Hd.
Bertraghboy B.
Clifden
Roundstone
Galway
Loughrea
Shannonbridge
Ferbane
Tullamore
Daingean
Rathangan
KILDARE
Droichead Nua
Naas
Clondalkin
Killiney
Bray
123
Galway Bay
Black Hd.
Burren
Kinvarra
Gort
Slieve Aughty
368
Portumna
OFFALY
Birr
Mountmellick
Port Laoise
Kildare
Monasterevin
Athy
Portlaoise Res.
WICKLOW
Greystones
Inishmore
Aran Is.
Inishmaan
Inisheer
Lisdoonvarna
BURREN
345
Crusheen
Feakle
Borrisokane
Slieve Bloom 529
Arderin
Mountrath
Durrow
Carlow
Balinglass
WICKLOW MTS.
Lugnaquilla 926
Wicklow
Wicklow Hd.
Cliffs of Moher
Hags Hd.
Ennistimon
Tulla
Lough Derg
Nenagh
Roscrea
Donaghmore
LAOIS
Castlecomer
Tullow
Shillelagh
Arklow
Liscannor Bay
Mal Bay
Mutton I.
Milltown Malbay
CLARE
Ennis
Killaloe
Silvermine Mts. 694
Keeper Hill
Templemore
Johnstown
Thurles
Kilkenny
Callan
Muine Bheag
Gorey
Ballycanew
Cahore Pt.
Kilkee
Sixmilebridge
Limerick
TIPPERARY
Golden Vale
796
Mt. Leinster
Bunclody
Enniscorthy
Loop Hd.
Kilrush
Shannon Airport
Cashel
Kilkenny
CARLOW
784
Blackstairs Mt.
WEXFORD
Tarbert
Foynes
Glin
LIMERICK
Rathkeale
Tipperary
Slievenamon 722
Carrick-on-Suir
Clonmel
New Ross
Wexford Harbour
Mouth of the Shannon
Ballybunion
Listowel
Newcastle West
Abbeyfeale
Kilfinane
Galtymore 920
Galty Mts.
Caher
Comeragh Mts. 795
Rosslare
Rosslare Harbour
Greenore Pt.
Kerry Hd.
Ballyheige
Ardfert
Feale
Rath Luirc (Charleville)
519
Mitchelstown
Clonmel
Knockmealdown Mts. 792
Waterford
Tramore
Passage East
Wexford
Smerwick Harbour
Tralee B.
Tralee
Slieve Mish
Munster
Newmarket
Kanturk
Buttevant
Mallow
Nagles Mts.
Fermoy
Blackwater
Lismore
Dungarvan
Dunmore East
Tramore B.
Hook Hd.
Saltee Is.
Kilmore Quay
Carnsore Pt.
Brandon B.
953
Brandon Mt.
853
Castlemaine
Maine
Laune
Millstreet
429
Youghal
Youghal B.
Waterford Harbour
Great Blasket I.
Dunmore Hd.
Dingle
Dingle Bay
Glenbeigh
Killorglin
Killarney
Boggeragh Mts. 646
CORK
Midleton
Youghal B.
St. David's Hd.
St. David's
Inishvickillane
Valencia I.
775
Macgillycuddy's Reeks
Carrauntoohil 1041
L. Leane
KILLARNEY
Macroom
Blarney
Cork
Cobh
Cork Harbour
St. Brides Bay
Puffin I.
Cahirciveen
Kenmare
Kilgarvan
707
Lee
Passage West
Crosshaven
115
WALES
Great Skellig
Ballinskelligs B.
Sneem
Caha Mts. 686
Glengarriff
Bandon
Kinsale
Old Head of Kinsale
Dursey I.
Castletown Bearhaven
Bear I.
Bantry
Whiddy I.
Dunmanus B.
Clonakilty
Dursey Hd.
Crow Hd.
Bantry Bay
Skull
Long I.
Baltimore
Sherkin I.
Clear I.
Clonakilty B.
Galley Hd.
Mizen Hd.
C. Clear
Fastnet Rock

A T L A N T I C   O C E A N
I R I S H   S E A
St. George's Channel
North Channel
C E L T I C   S E A

ft m
1500 500
600 200
300 100
0 0
50 150
100 300
200 600
500 1500
1000 3000
2000 6000
m ft

Projection : Lambert's Conformal Conic

West from Greenwich

COPYRIGHT PHILIP'S

Key to Scottish unitary
authorities on map
1 CITY OF ABERDEEN   8 EAST RENFREWSHIRE
2 DUNDEE CITY   9 NORTH LANARKSHIRE
3 WEST DUNBARTONSHIRE   10 FALKIRK
4 EAST DUNBARTONSHIRE   11 CLACKMANNANSHIRE
5 CITY OF GLASGOW   12 WEST LOTHIAN
6 INVERCLYDE   13 CITY OF EDINBURGH
7 RENFREWSHIRE   14 MIDLOTHIAN

ORKNEY IS.
on same scale

ORKNEY

SHETLAND IS.
on same scale

SHETLAND

WESTERN
ISLES

ATLANTIC

OCEAN

SCOTLAND

NORTH

SEA

NORTHERN
IRELAND

ENGLAND
Newcastle-upon-Tyne

Projection : Lambert's Conformal Conic

West from Greenwich

COPYRIGHT PHILIP'S

1:2 000 000

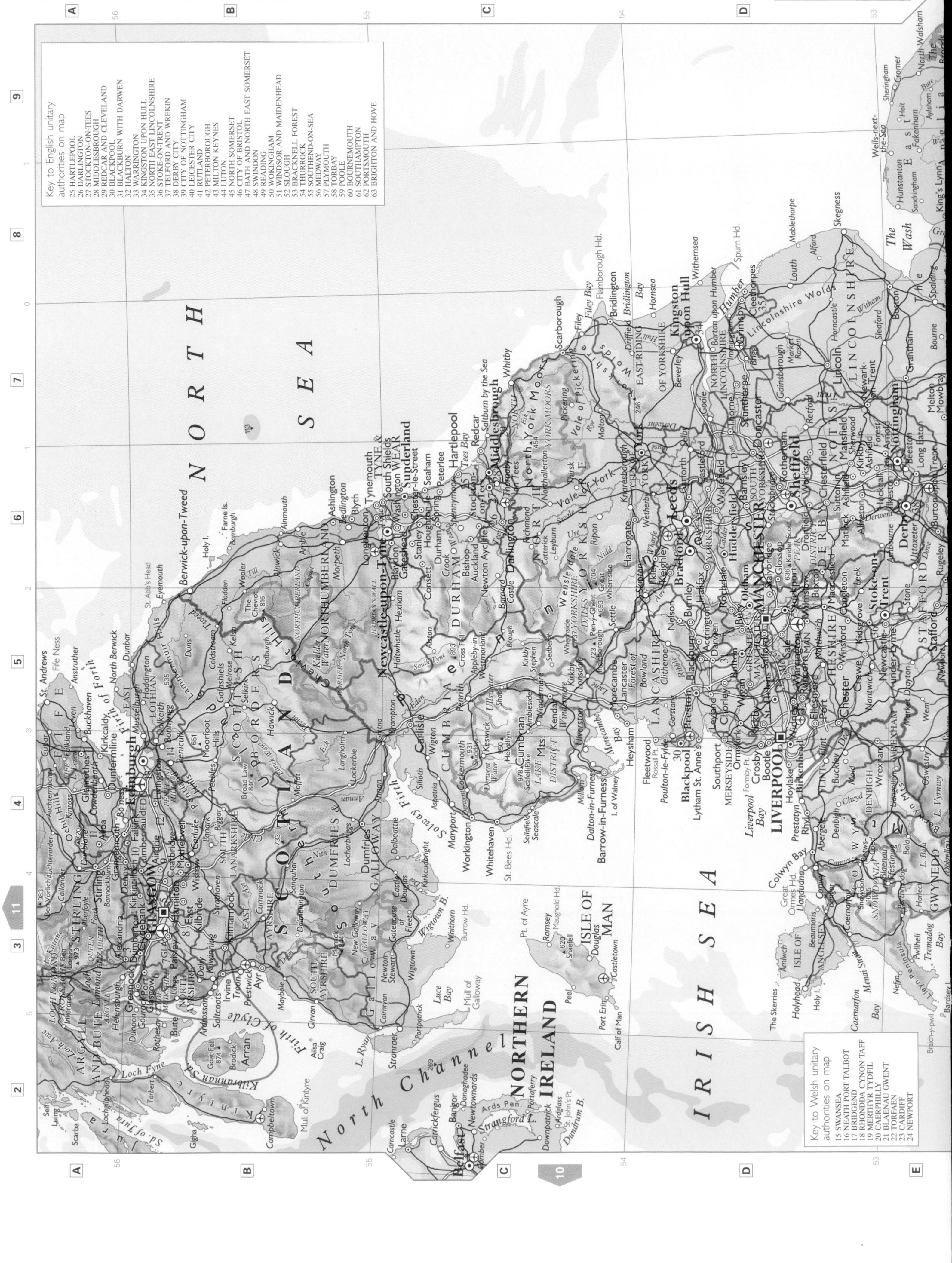

10 0 10 20 30 40 50 60 70 80 km

10 0 10 20 30 40 50 miles

Key to English unitary authorities on map

25 HARTLEPOOL
26 DARLINGTON
27 STOCKTON-ON-TEES
28 MIDDLESBROUGH
29 REDCAR AND CLEVELAND
30 BLACKPOOL
31 BLACKBURN WITH DARWEN
32 HALTON
33 WARRINGTON
34 KINGSTON UPON HULL
35 NORTH EAST LINCOLNSHIRE
36 STOKE-ON-TRENT
37 TELFORD AND WREKIN
38 DERBY CITY
39 CITY OF NOTTINGHAM
40 LEICESTER CITY
41 RUTLAND
42 PETERBOROUGH
43 MILTON KEYNES
44 LUTON
45 NORTH SOMERSET
46 CITY OF BRISTOL
47 BATH AND NORTH EAST SOMERSET
48 SWINDON
49 READING
50 WOKINGHAM
51 WINDSOR AND MAIDENHEAD
52 SLOUGH
53 BRACKNELL FOREST
54 THURROCK
55 SOUTHEND-ON-SEA
56 MEDWAY
57 PLYMOUTH
58 TORBAY
59 POOLE
60 BOURNEMOUTH
61 SOUTHAMPTON
62 PORTSMOUTH
63 BRIGHTON AND HOVE

Key to Welsh unitary authorities on map

15 SWANSEA
16 NEATH PORT TALBOT
17 BRIDGEND
18 RHONDDA CYNON TAFF
19 MERTHYR TYDFIL
20 CAERPHILLY
21 BLAENAU GWENT
22 TORFAEN
23 CARDIFF
24 NEWPORT

NORTH SEA

IRISH SEA

North Channel

SCOTLAND

NORTHUMBERLAND

CUMBRIA

DURHAM

NORTH YORKSHIRE

LANCASHIRE

LINCOLNSHIRE

NORTHERN IRELAND

ISLE OF MAN

NOTTS

STAFFORD

GWYNEDD

Newcastle-upon-Tyne

Sunderland

Hartlepool

Middlesbrough

Scarborough

Kingston upon Hull

Leeds

Bradford

MANCHESTER

LIVERPOOL

Sheffield

Nottingham

Derby

Stoke-on-Trent

Chester

Blackpool

Carlisle

Edinburgh

GLASGOW

Belfast

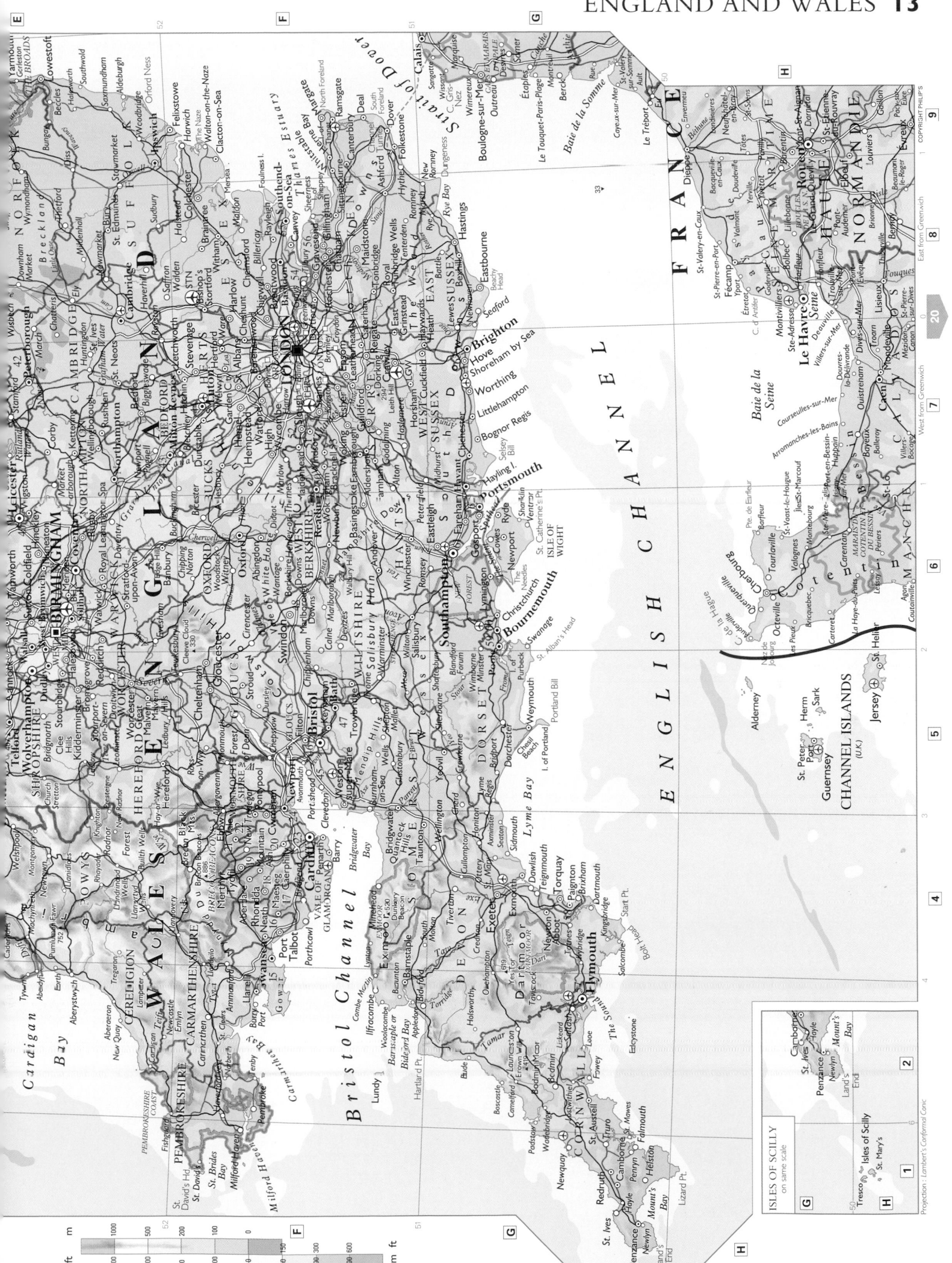

ISLES OF SCILLY
on same scale

1:5 000 000

Projection: Conical with two standard parallels

West from Greenwich

East from Greenwich

COPYRIGHT PHILIP'S

1:2 500 000

NORTH SEA

UNITED KINGDOM

NETHERLAND

BELGIUM

LUXEMBOURG

GERMANY

FRANCE

Projection : Lambert's Conformal Conic

COPYRIGHT PHILIP'S

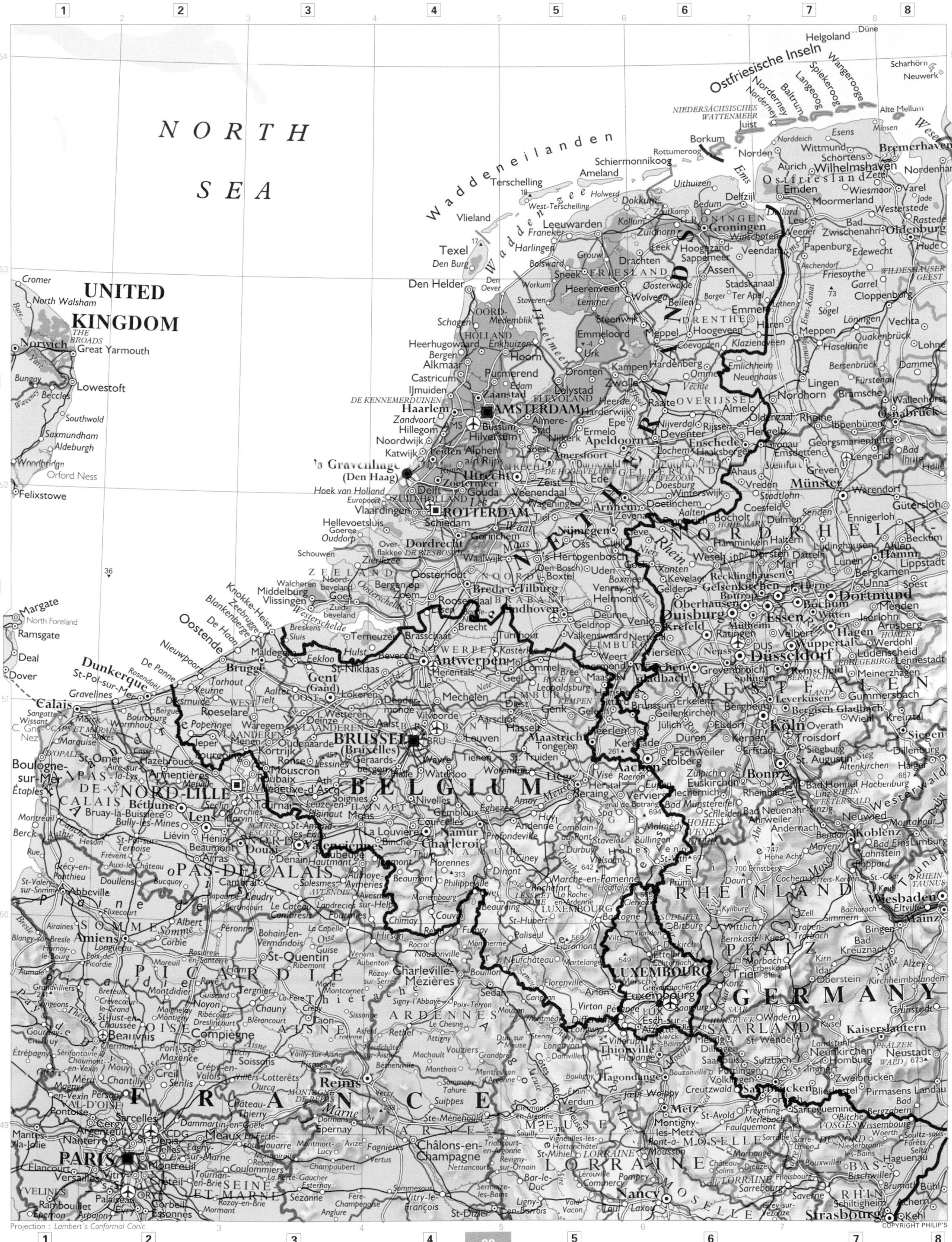

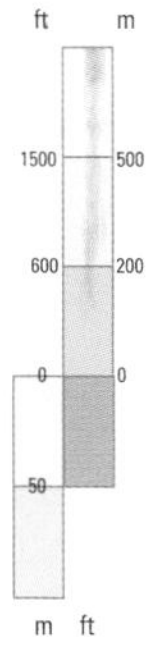

Underlined towns give their name to the administrative area in which they stand.

COPYRIGHT PHILIP'S

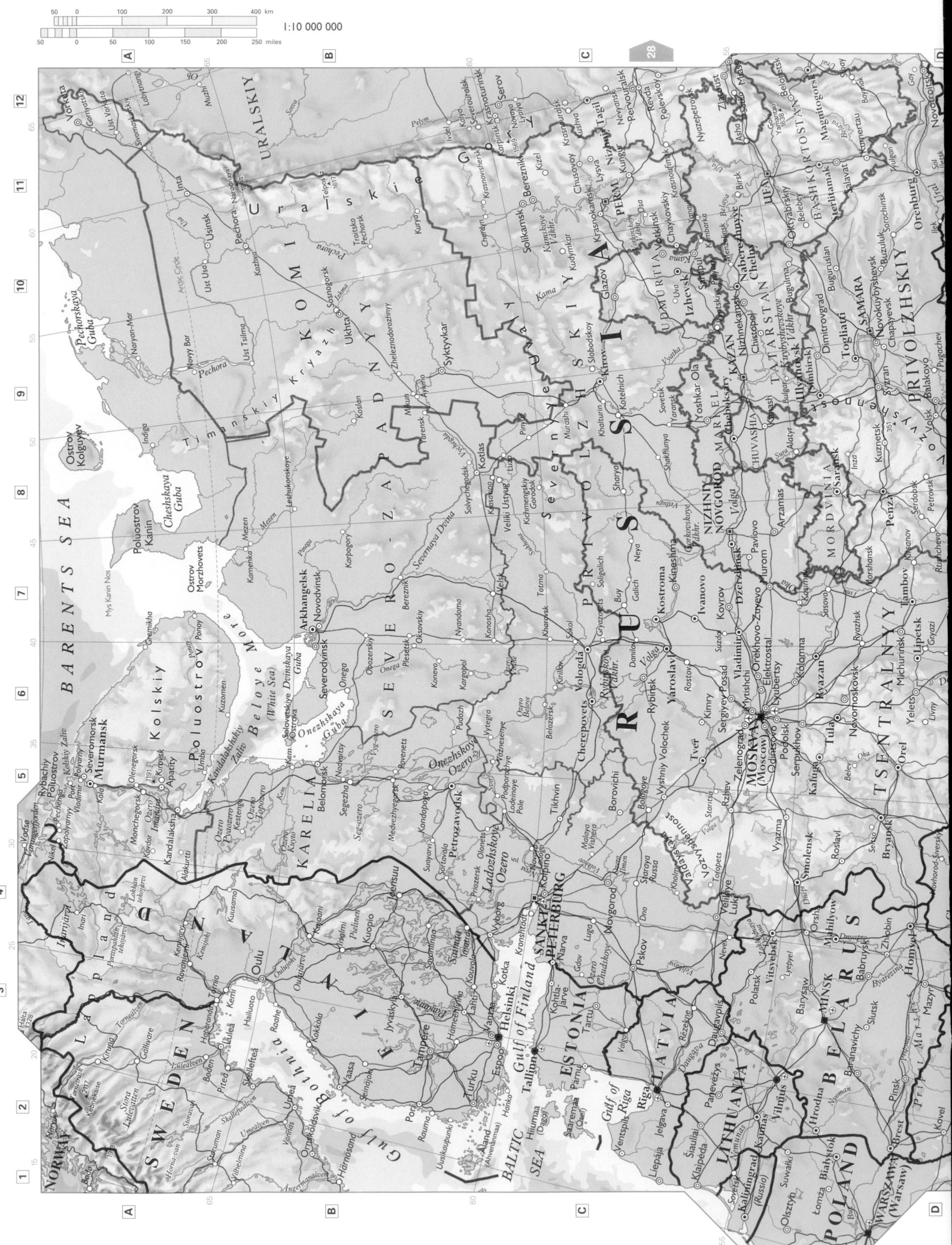

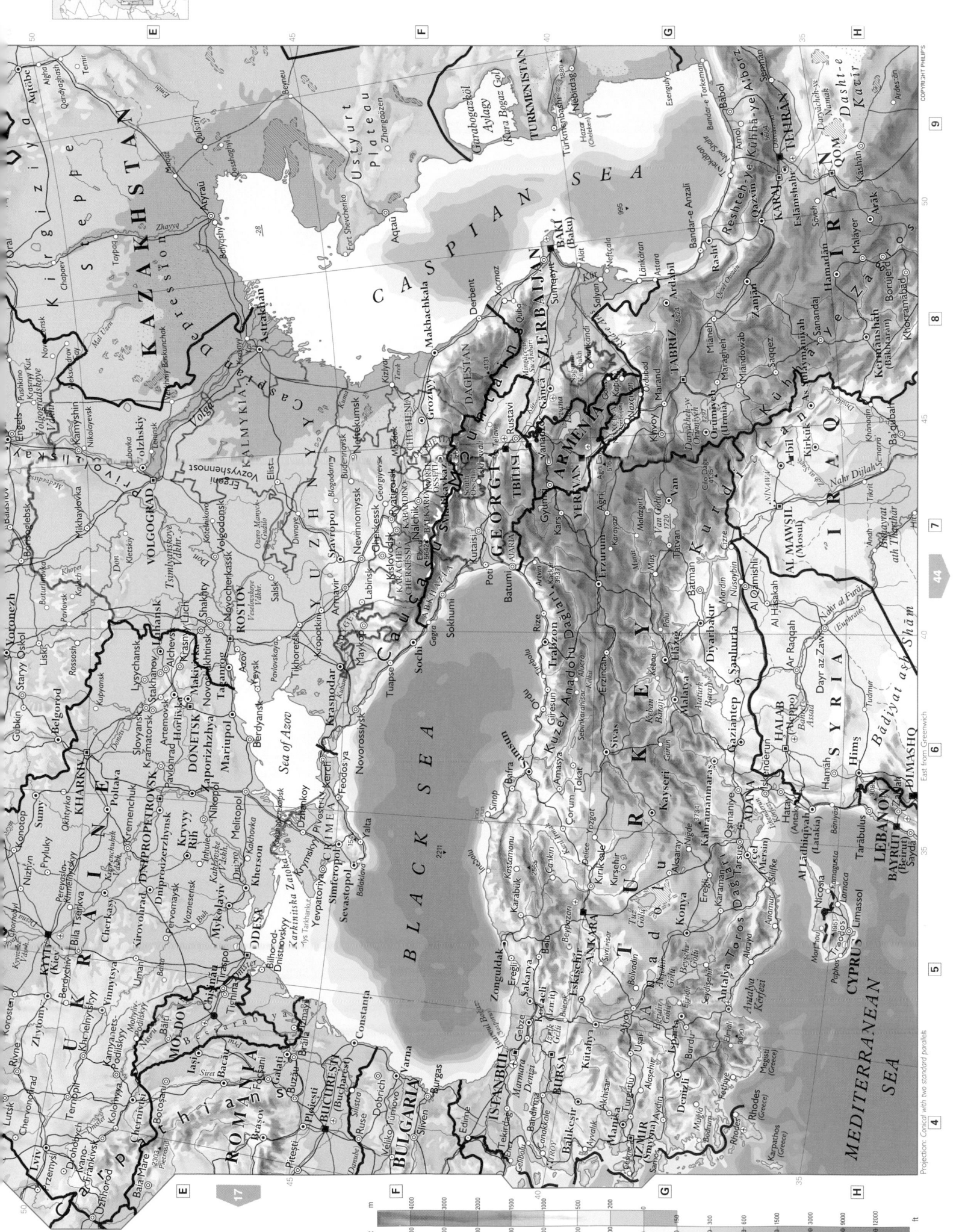

COPYRIGHT PHILIP'S

Projection: Conical with two standard parallels

East from Greenwich

1:5 000 000

50 ... 0 25 50 75 100 125 150 175 km
50 ... 0 25 50 75 100 125 miles

East from Greenwich

West from Greenwich

Projection: Conical with two standard parallels

COPYRIGHT PHILIP'S

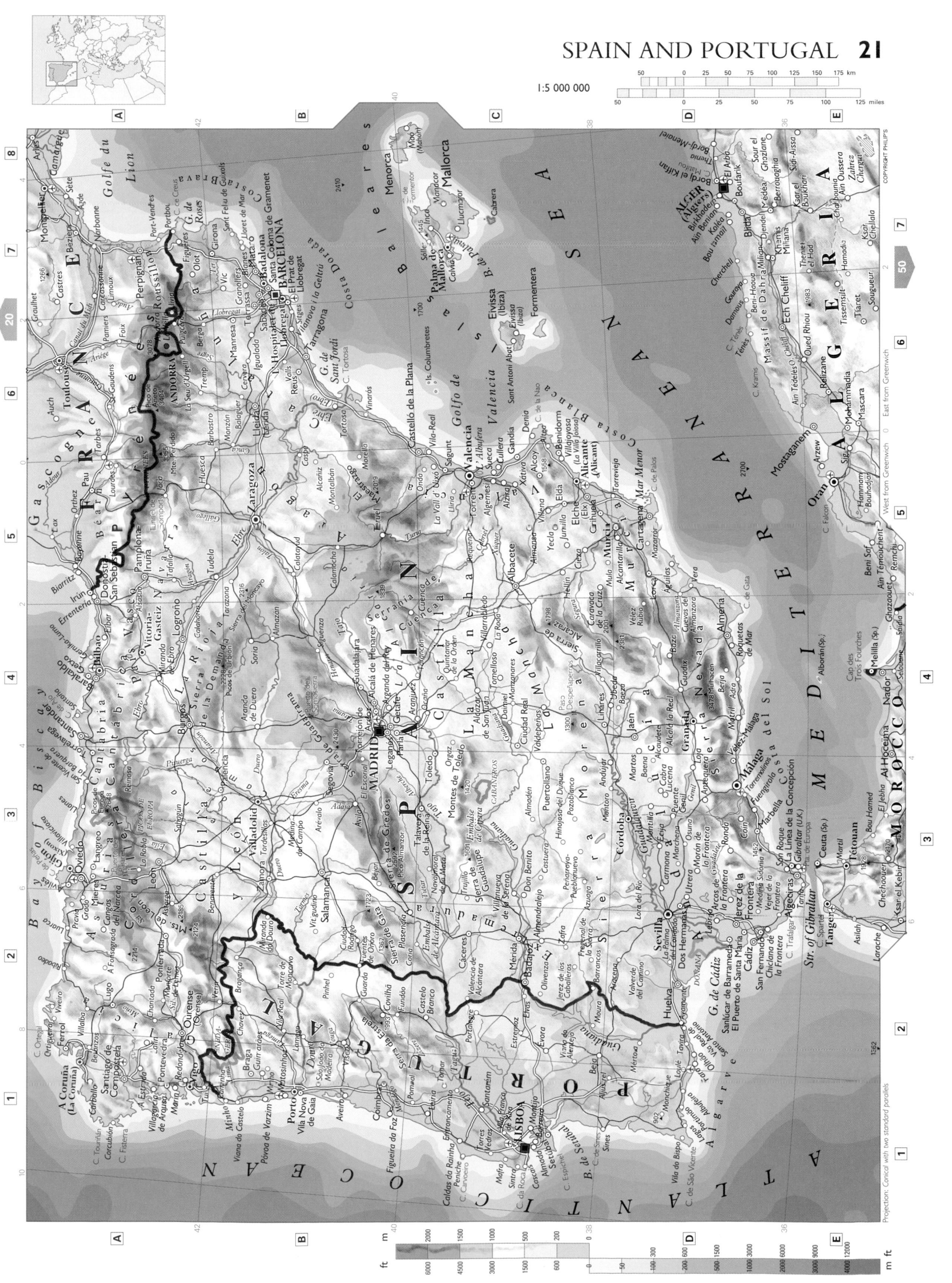

COPYRIGHT PHILIP'S

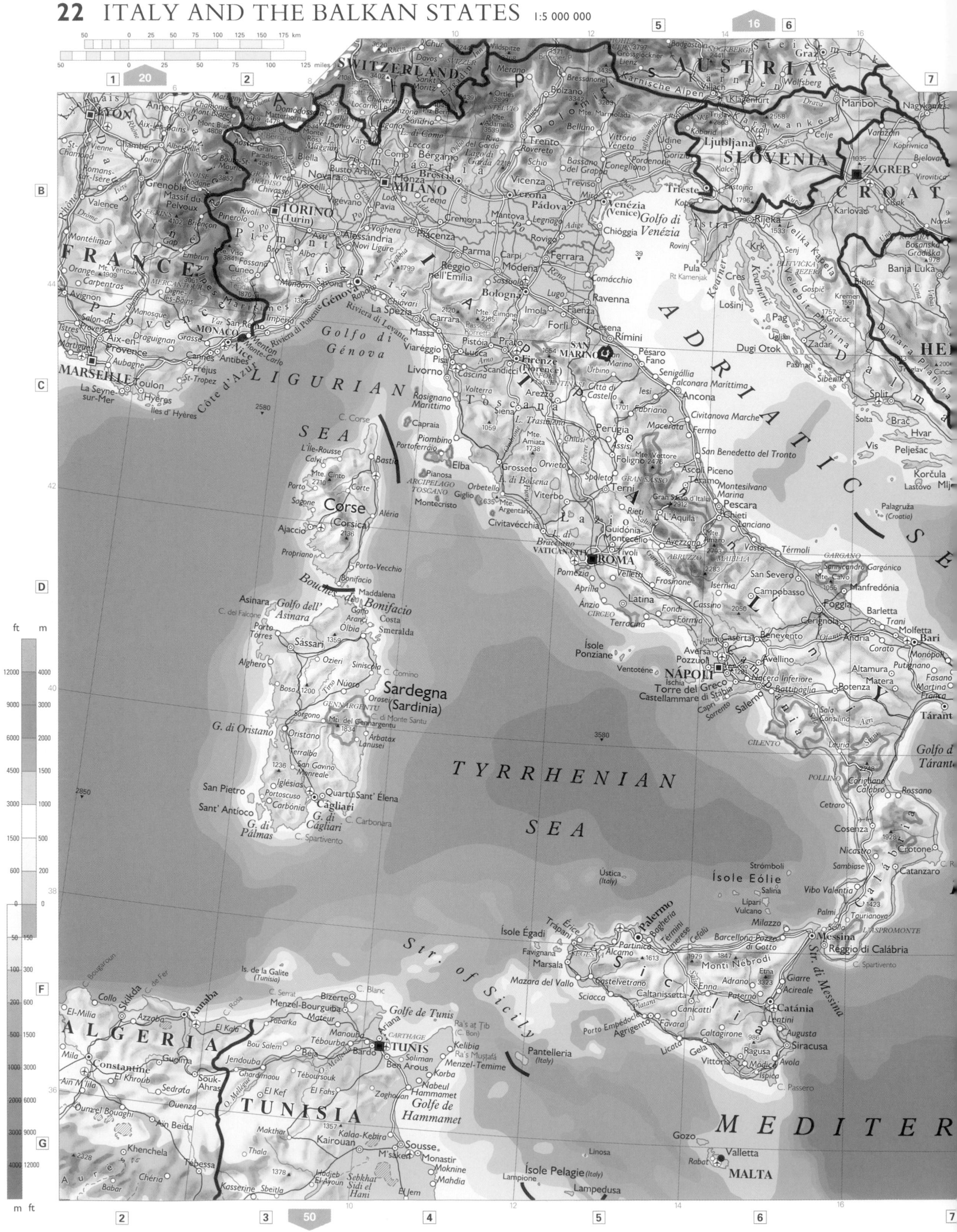

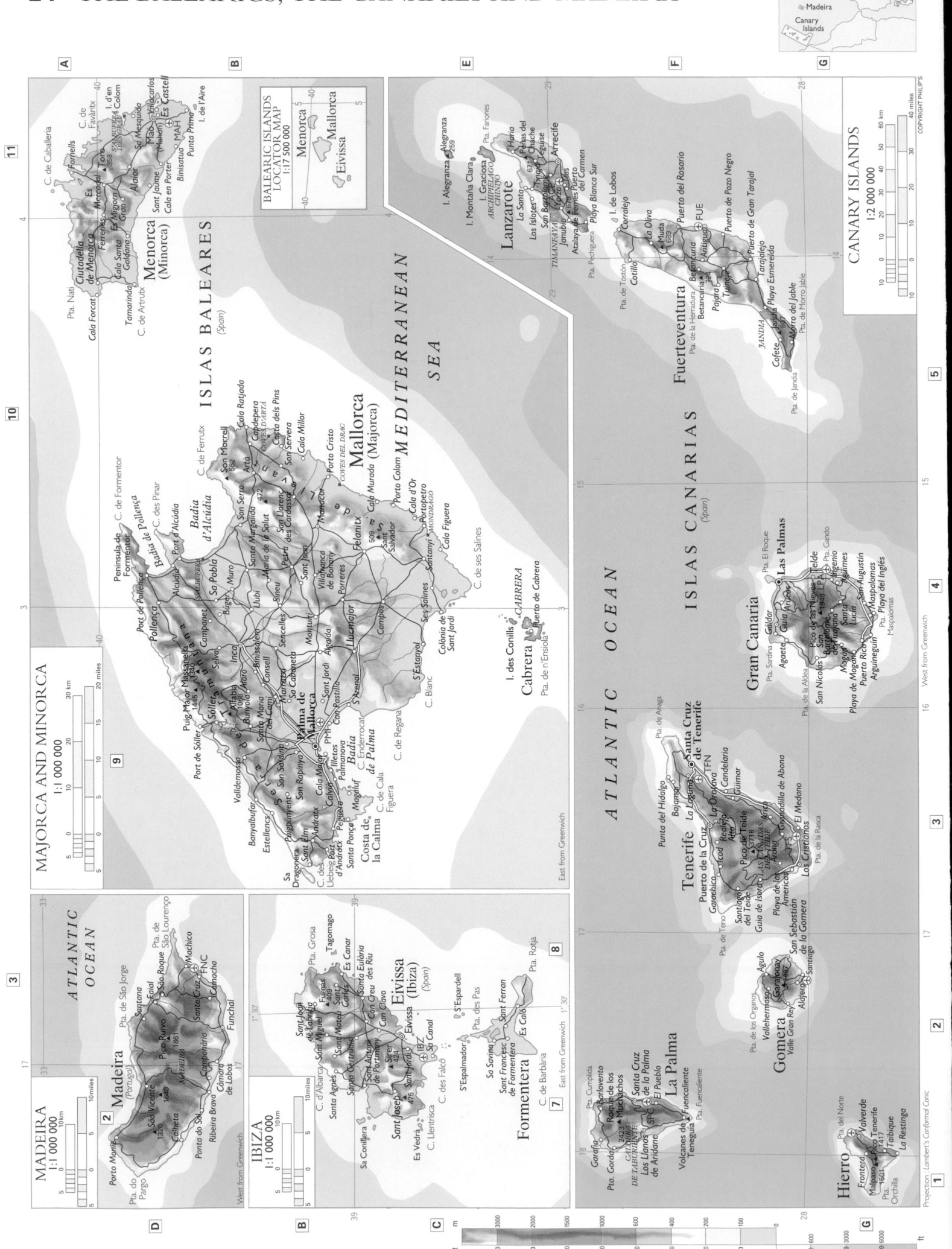

ISLAS BALEARES *(Spain)*

Menorca (Minorca)

Mallorca (Majorca)

MEDITERRANEAN SEA

MAJORCA AND MINORCA
1:1 000 000

BALEARIC ISLANDS LOCATOR MAP
1:17 500 000

Menorca

Mallorca

Eivissa

Cabrera
CABRERA

ATLANTIC OCEAN

MADEIRA
1:1 000 000

Madeira
(Portugal)

IBIZA
1:1 000 000

Eivissa (Ibiza)
(Spain)

Formentera

Lanzarote

Fuerteventura

ATLANTIC OCEAN

ISLAS CANARIAS
(Spain)

Gran Canaria

Tenerife

Gomera

La Palma

Hierro

CANARY ISLANDS
1:2 000 000

COPYRIGHT PHILIP'S

Projection: Lambert's Conformal Conic

Corfu
Malta
Rhodes
Crete
Cyprus

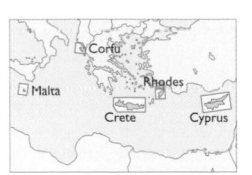

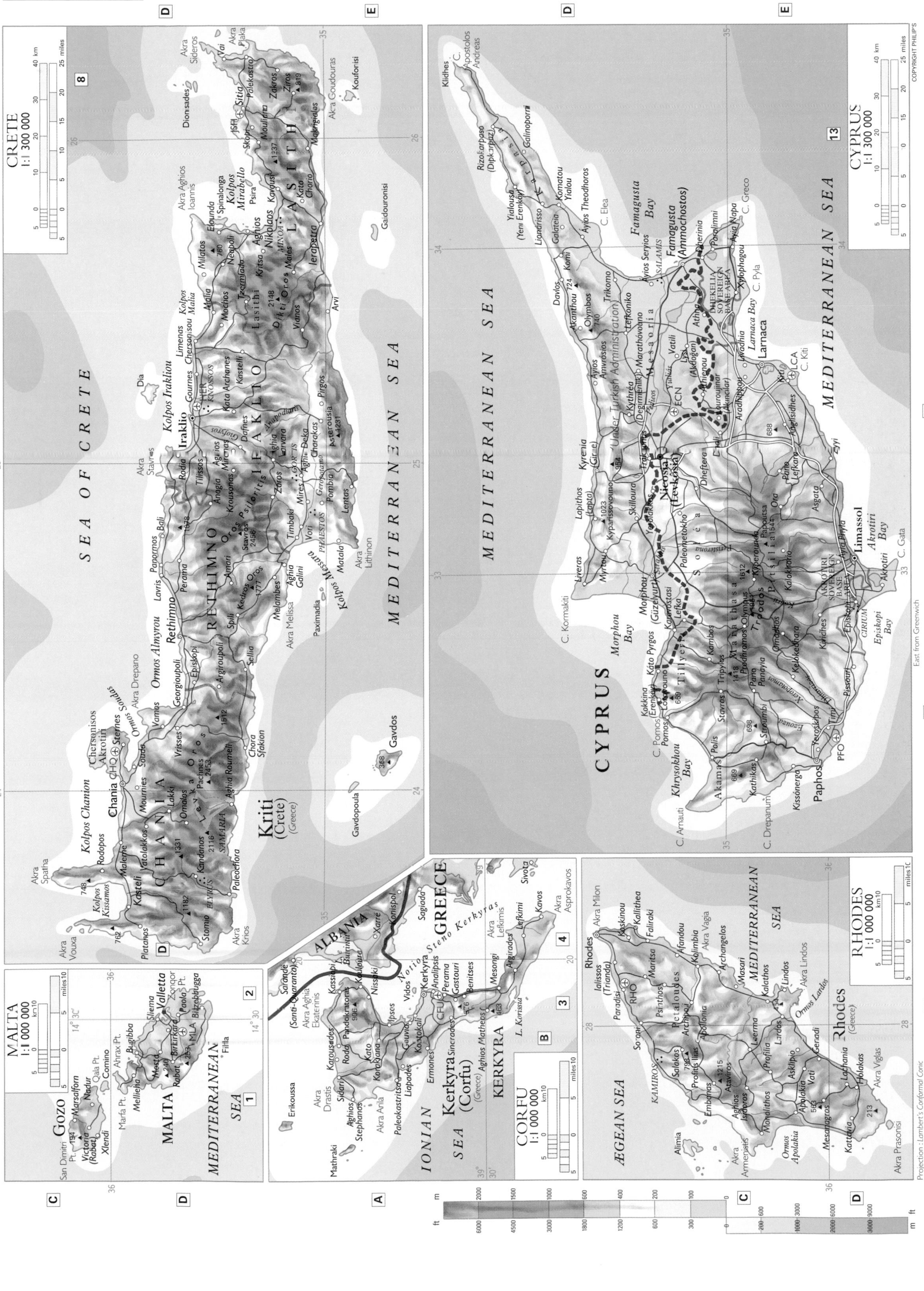
CRETE
1:1 300 000
SEA OF CRETE
MEDITERRANEAN SEA
Kriti
(Crete)
(Greece)
CYPRUS
1:1 300 000
MEDITERRANEAN SEA
CYPRUS
MALTA
1:1 000 000
GOZO
MEDITERRANEAN SEA
CORFU
1:1 000 000
Kerkyra
(Corfu)
(Greece)
IONIAN SEA
ALBANIA
GREECE
RHODES
1:1 000 000
Rhodes
(Greece)
ÆGEAN SEA
MEDITERRANEAN SEA
Projection: Lambert's Conformal Conic
East from Greenwich
COPYRIGHT PHILIP'S

100 0   200   400   600   800   1000 1200 1400 km
100 0   200   400   600   800   1000 miles

1:47 000 000

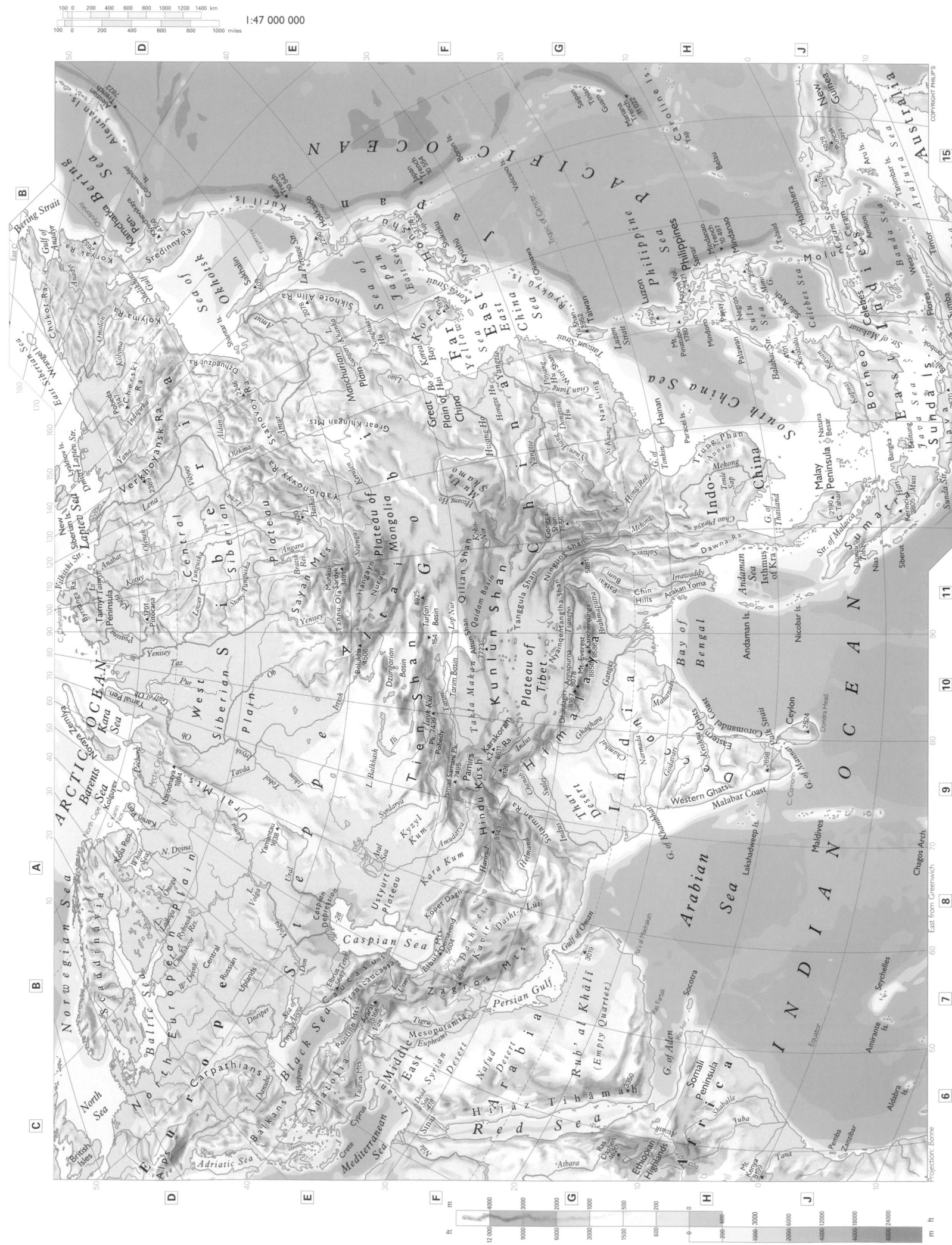

COPYRIGHT PHILIP'S

Projection: Bonne

m 4000   3000   2000   1000   500   200   0
ft 12 000 9000   6000   3000   1500   600   0   200   4000   6000   12000 18000 24000 ft
                                                    0   1000   2000   3000   4000   6000 m

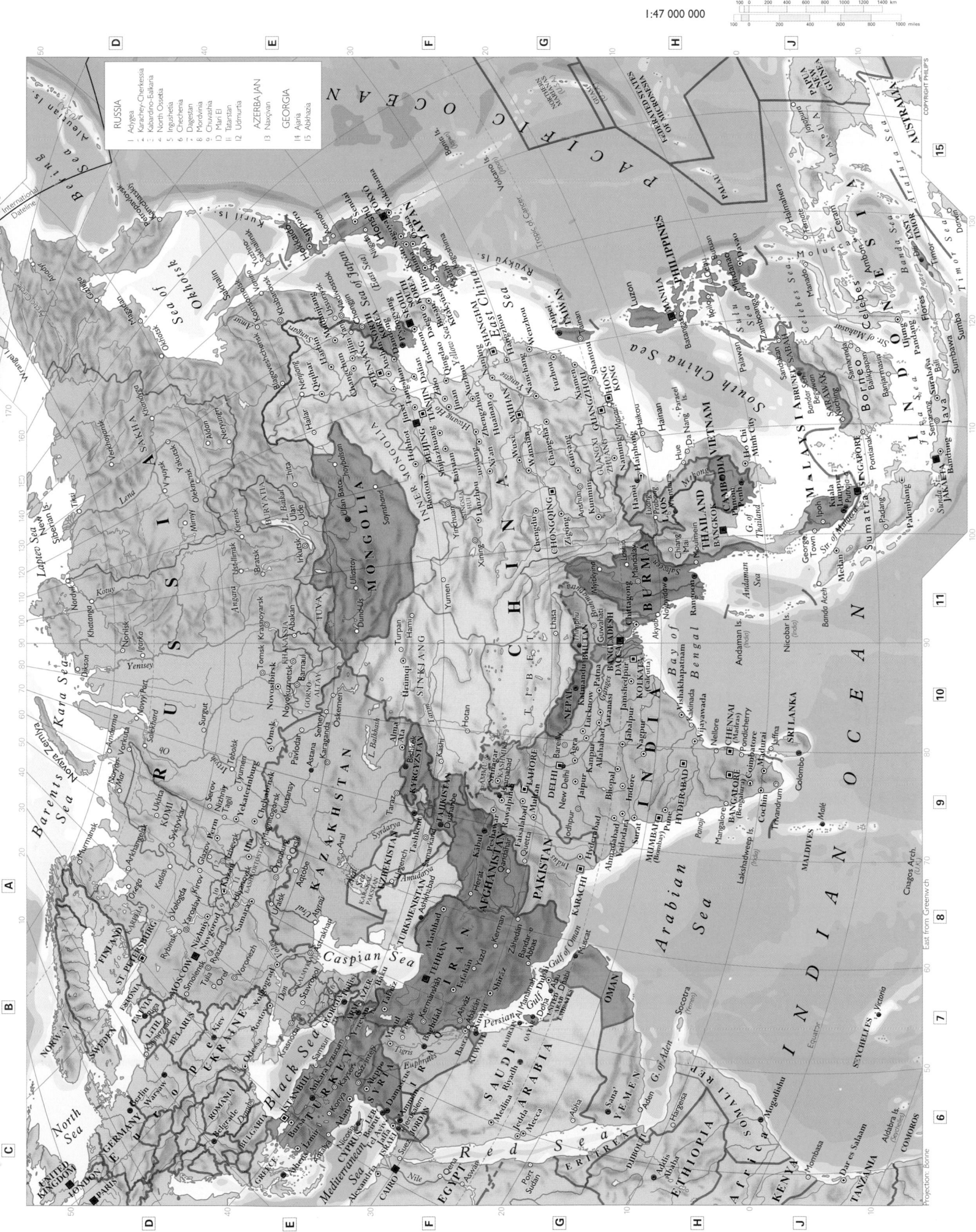

1:47 000 000

COPYRIGHT PHILIPS

RUSSIA
1 Adygea
2 Karachey-Cherkessia
3 Kabardino-Balkaria
4 North Ossetia
5 Ingushetia
6 Chechenia
7 Dagestan
8 Mordvinia
9 Chuvashia
10 Mari El
11 Tatarstan
12 Udmurtia

AZERBAJAN
13 Naxçivan

GEORGIA
14 Ajaria
15 Abkhazia

Projection: Bonne

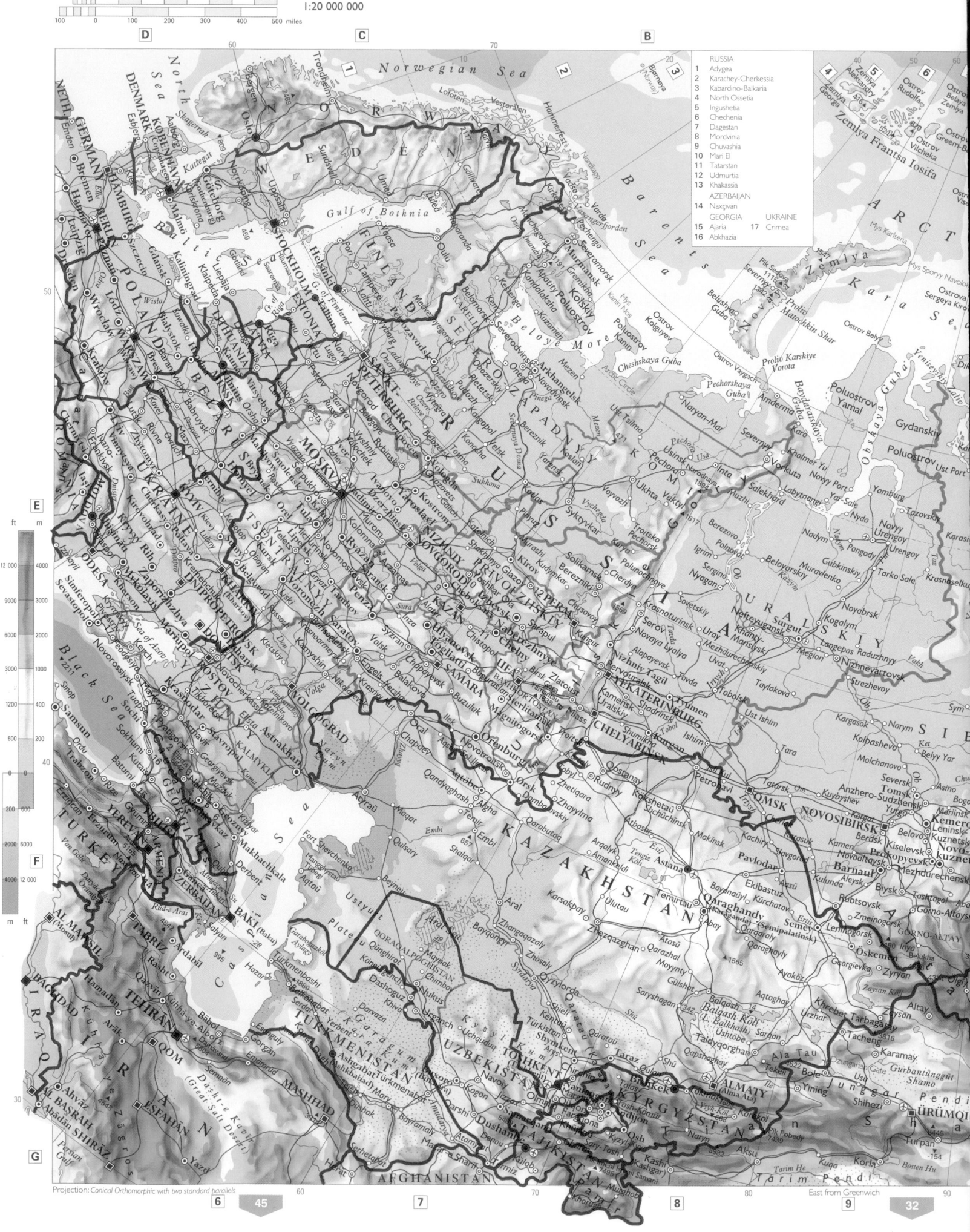

RUSSIA
1 Adygea
2 Karachey-Cherkessia
3 Kabardino-Balkaria
4 North Ossetia
5 Ingushetia
6 Chechenia
7 Dagestan
8 Mordvinia
9 Chuvashia
10 Mari El
11 Tatarstan
12 Udmurtia
13 Khakassia
AZERBAIJAN
14 Naxçivan
GEORGIA   UKRAINE
15 Ajaria   17 Crimea
16 Abkhazia

COPYRIGHT PHILIP'S

1:5 000 000

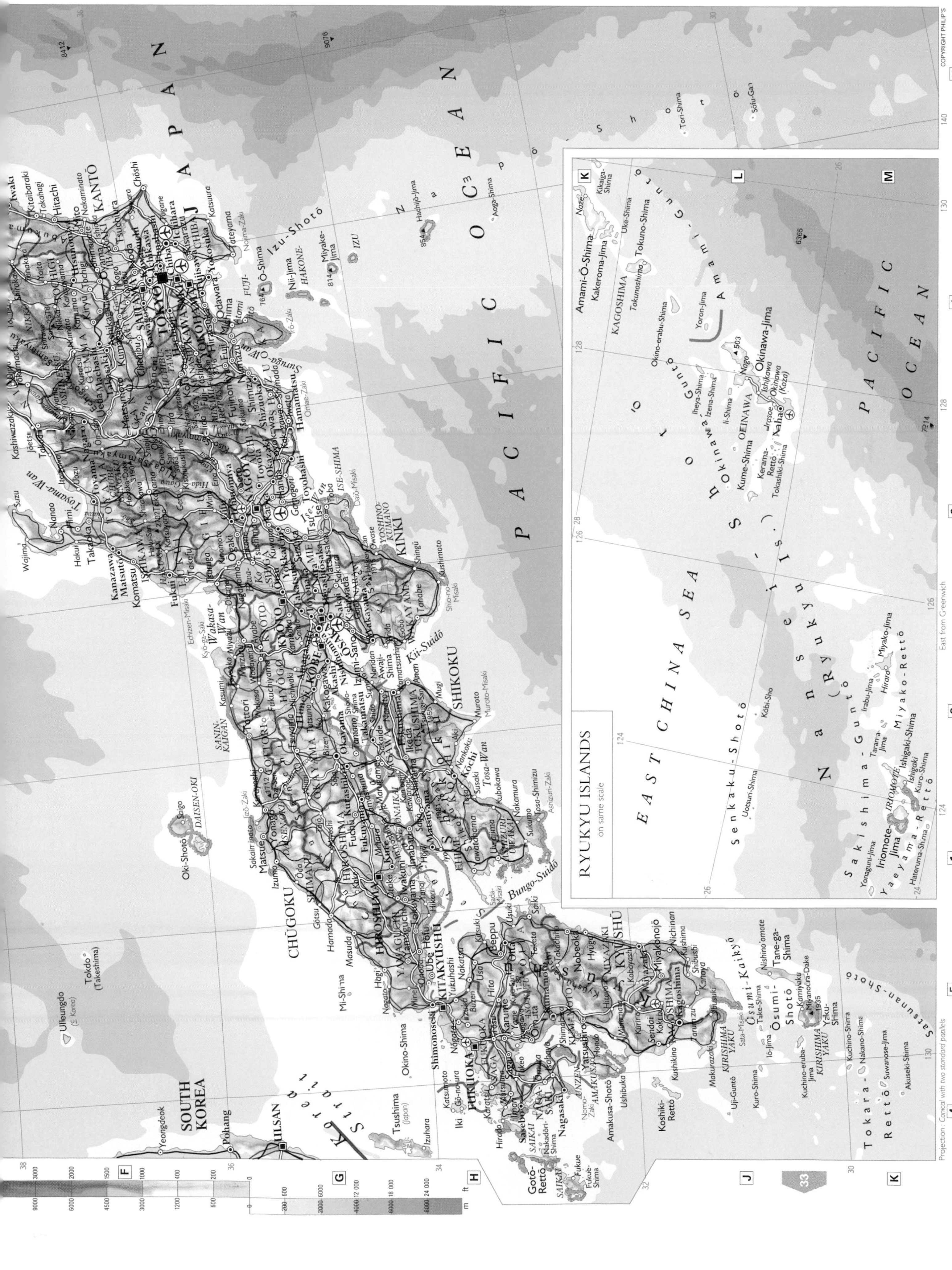

COPYRIGHT PHILIP'S

J A P A N

KANTŌ GUMMA TŌCHIGI IBARAKI SAITAMA TOKYO CHIBA KANAGAWA

P A C I F I C   O C E A N

Izu-Shotō HAKONE FUJI IZU Ō-Shima Nii-Jima Miyake-Jima Hachijō-Jima Aoga-Shima

CHŪBU KINKI KYŌTO KOBE ŌSAKA HYOGO MIE NARA WAKAYAMA

SHIKOKU EHIME KOCHI TOKUSHIMA KAGAWA Tosa-Wan Bungo-Suidō

CHŪGOKU HIROSHIMA YAMAGUCHI SHIMANE TOTTORI OKAYAMA Matsue DAISEN-OKI Oki-Shotō

SAN-IN-KAIGAN Wakasa-Wan Toyama-Wan Noto Kanazawa Matsuto Komatsu Fukui HIDA

SOUTH KOREA Yeongdeok Pohang ULSAN Tsushima (Japan) Iki Izuhara

KYŪSHŪ FUKUOKA NAGASAKI SAGA ŌITA KUMAMOTO MIYAZAKI KAGOSHIMA Beppu Nobeoka

KIRISHIMA YAKU Ōsumi-Kaikyō Tane-ga-Shima Yaku-Shima Ōsumi-Shotō

Tokara-Rettō Nakano-Shima Suwanose-Jima Akuseki-Shima Satsunan-Shotō

Gotō-Rettō SAIKAI Fukue Amakusa-Shotō Koshiki-Rettō

Tokdo (Takeshima) Ulleungdo (S. Korea)

RYUKYU ISLANDS
on same scale

E A S T   C H I N A   S E A

Amami-Ō-Shima Kikaiga-Shima Naze KAGOSHIMA Kakeroma-Jima Tokunoshima Tokuno-Shima Okino-erabu-Shima Yoron-Jima A m a m i - G u n t ō

Iheya-Shima Izena-Shima Ii-Shima Nago Ishikawa Okinawa-Jima OKINAWA Naha Kume-Shima Kerama-Rettō Tokashiki-Shima O k i n a w a - G u n t ō

N a n s e i   (R y u k y u)   I s l a n d s

Senkaku-Shotō Uotsuri-Shima Kōbi-Sho S a k i s h i m a - G u n t ō Tarama-Shima Miyako-Jima Miyako-Rettō Irabu-Jima Hirara

Y a e y a m a - R e t t ō Yonaguni-Jima IRIOMOTE Iriomote-Jima Ishigaki Ishigaki-Shima Kuro-Shima Hateruma-Shima

P A C I F I C   O C E A N

East from Greenwich

Projection : Conical with two standard parallels

ft m
9000 24,000
7500 18,000
6000 12,000
4500 6000
3000 2000
1500 1000
600 400
200 600
0

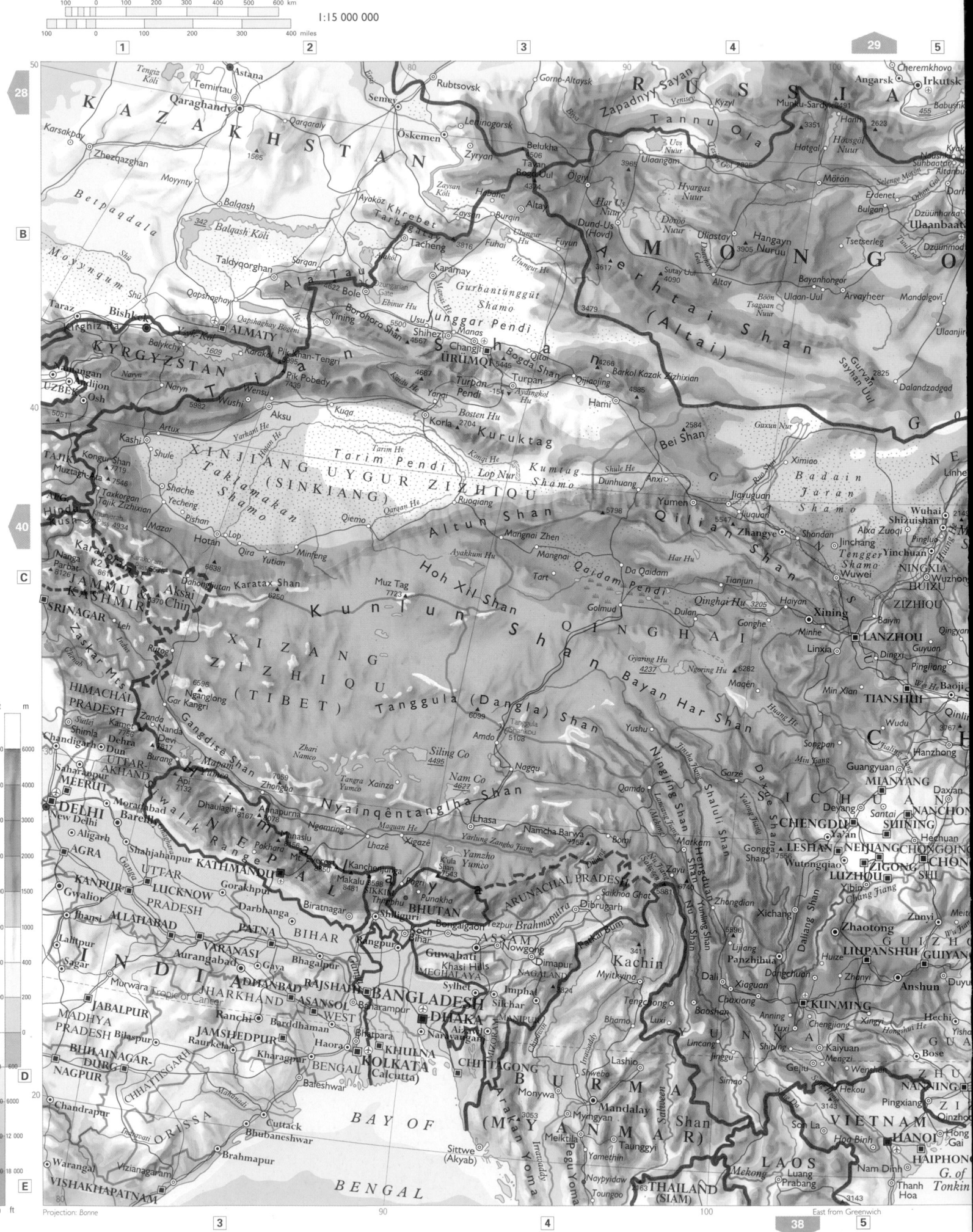

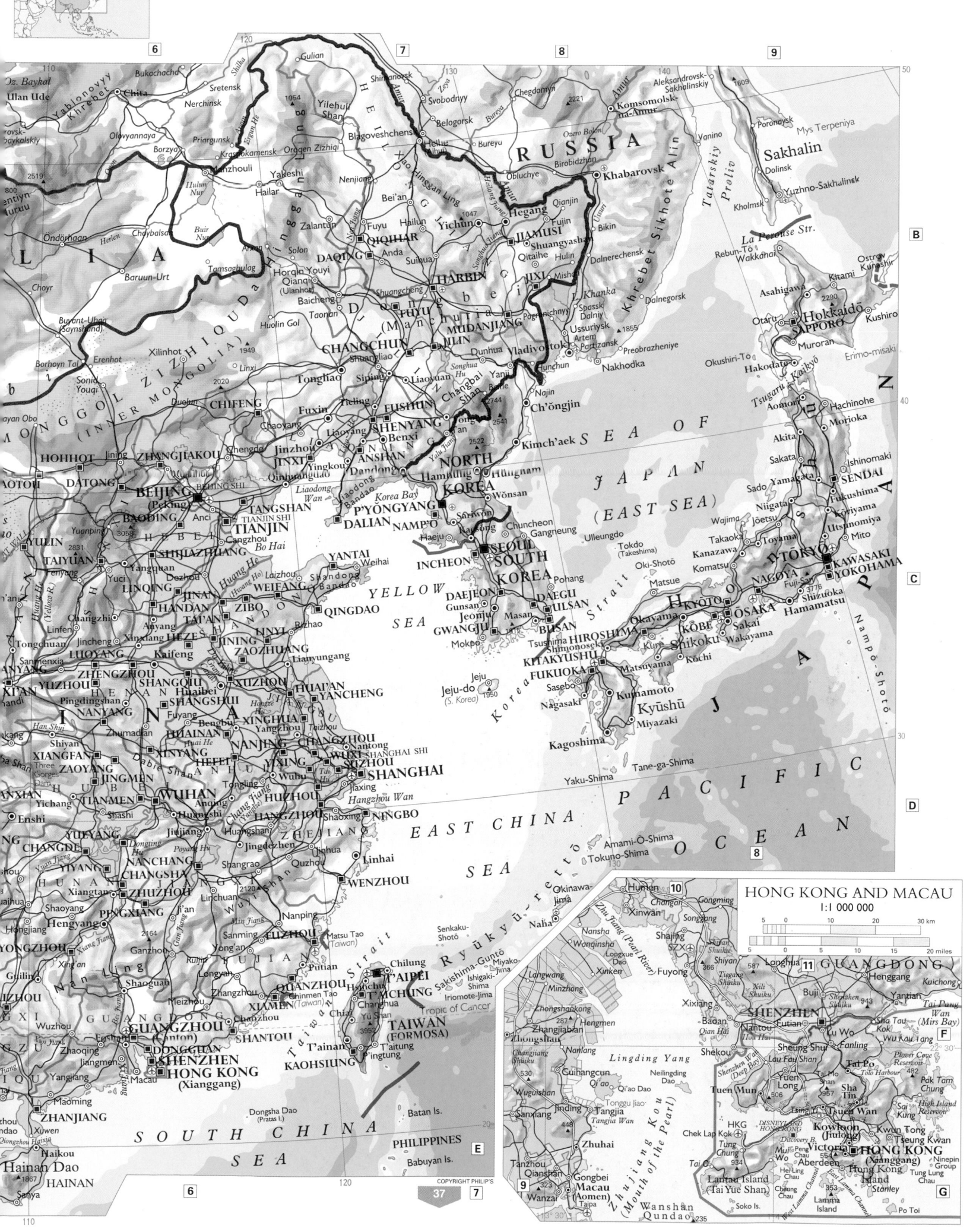

HONG KONG AND MACAU
1:1 000 000

COPYRIGHT PHILIP'S

1:6 000 000

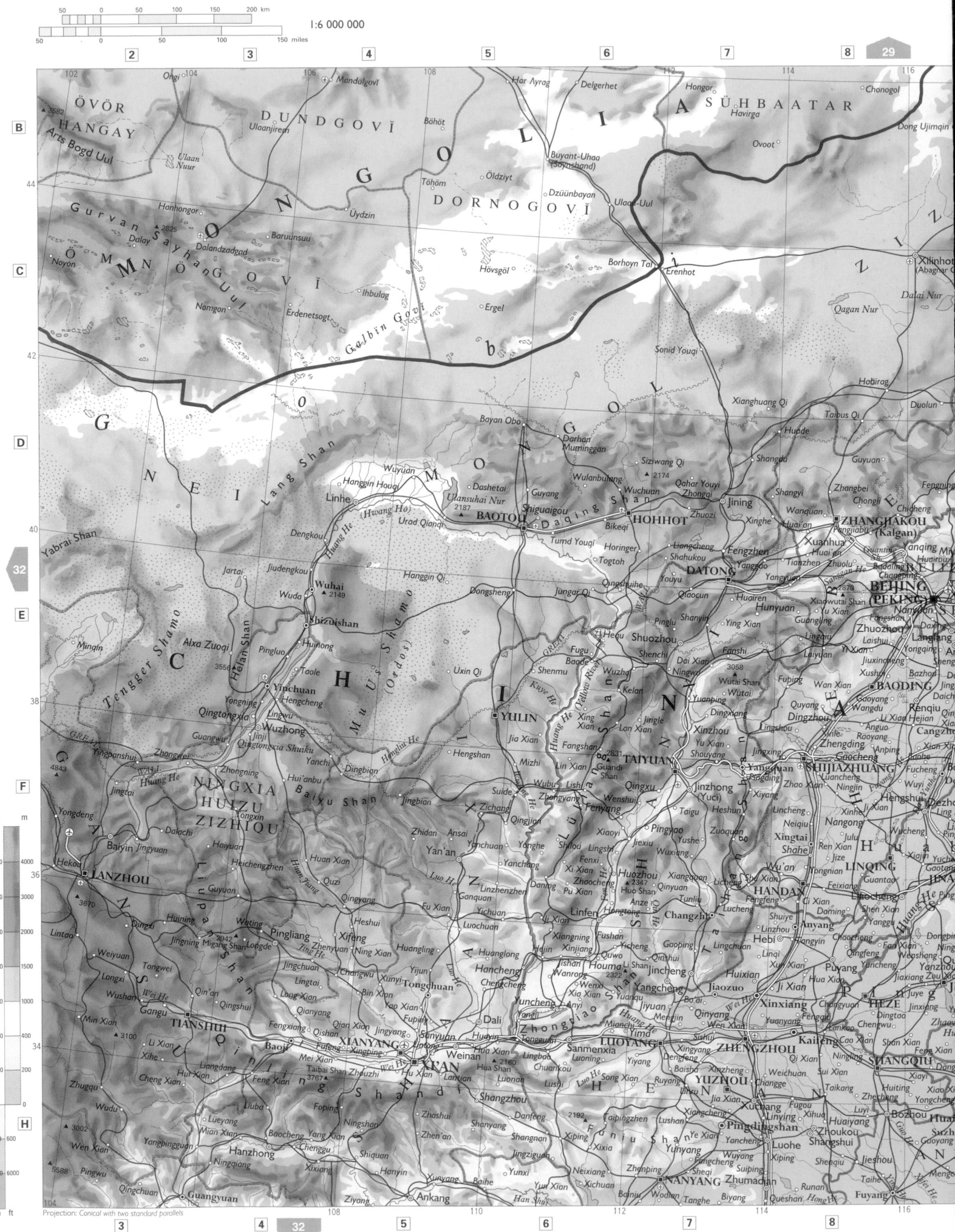

Projection: Conical with two standard parallels

COPYRIGHT PHILIP'S

Projection: Mercator

East from Greenwich

33

JAVA AND MADÚRA
1:7 500 000

50 0 50 100 150 200 250 300 km
50 0 50 100 150 200 miles

BALI
1:2 000 000

10 0 10 20 30 km
10 0 10 20 miles

Major labels:

PHILIPPINES — Luzon, MANILA, Quezon City, San Fernando, Baguio, Tuguegarao, Angeles, Batangas, Lucena, Naga, Legazpi, Mindoro, Calapan, Masbate, Samar, Tacloban, Cebu, Mandaue, Bacolod, Iloilo, Negros, Panay, Bohol, Dumaguete, Puerto Princesa, Zamboanga, Davao, General Santos, Cotabato, Cagayan de Oro, Iligan, Butuan, Surigao, Mindanao

SULU SEA, CELEBES SEA, Visayan Sea, Bohol Sea, Mindanao Trench, Sulu Arch.

JAKARTA, Tangerang, Bekasi, Bogor, BANDUNG, Sukabumi, Cirebon, Tegal, Pekalongan, Semarang, Surakarta, Yogyakarta, Kediri, Malang, SURABAYA, Madura, Sampang, Pamekasan, Sumenep, BANTEN, JAWA BARAT, JAWA TENGAH, JAWA TIMUR, Bali

BALI SEA, Singaraja, Denpasar, Bali, Jawa, Lombok, Mataram, Ampenan, Kuta, Nusa Dua, Nusa Penida, INDIAN OCEAN

PACIFIC OCEAN, Manado, GORONTALO, Tolitoli, Halmahera, Ternate, Tidore, SULAWESI (Celebes), Palu, Kendari, UJUNG PANDANG, Makasar, MOLUCCA SEA, CERAM SEA, Buru, Seram (Ceram), Ambon, MALUKU, BANDA SEA, Buton, Muna, Sorong, IRIAN JAYA, PAPUA BARAT, Pegunungan Maoke, Pegunungan Van Rees, Jayapura, Sentani, PAPUA NEW GUINEA, Biak, Manokwari, FLORES SEA, Flores, Sunda Is., Sumbawa, NUSA TENGGARA TIMUR, Sumba, Kupang, EAST TIMOR, Dili, ARAFURA SEA, Merauke, Kepulauan Tanimbar, Kepulauan Kai, Kepulauan Aru, Equator

62

COPYRIGHT PHILIP'S

50   0   50   100   150   200 km
50   0   50   100   150 miles

1:6 000 000

COPYRIGHT PHILIP'S

1:10 000 000

continuation southwards
on same scale

Projection: Conical with two standard parallels

COPYRIGHT PHILIP'S

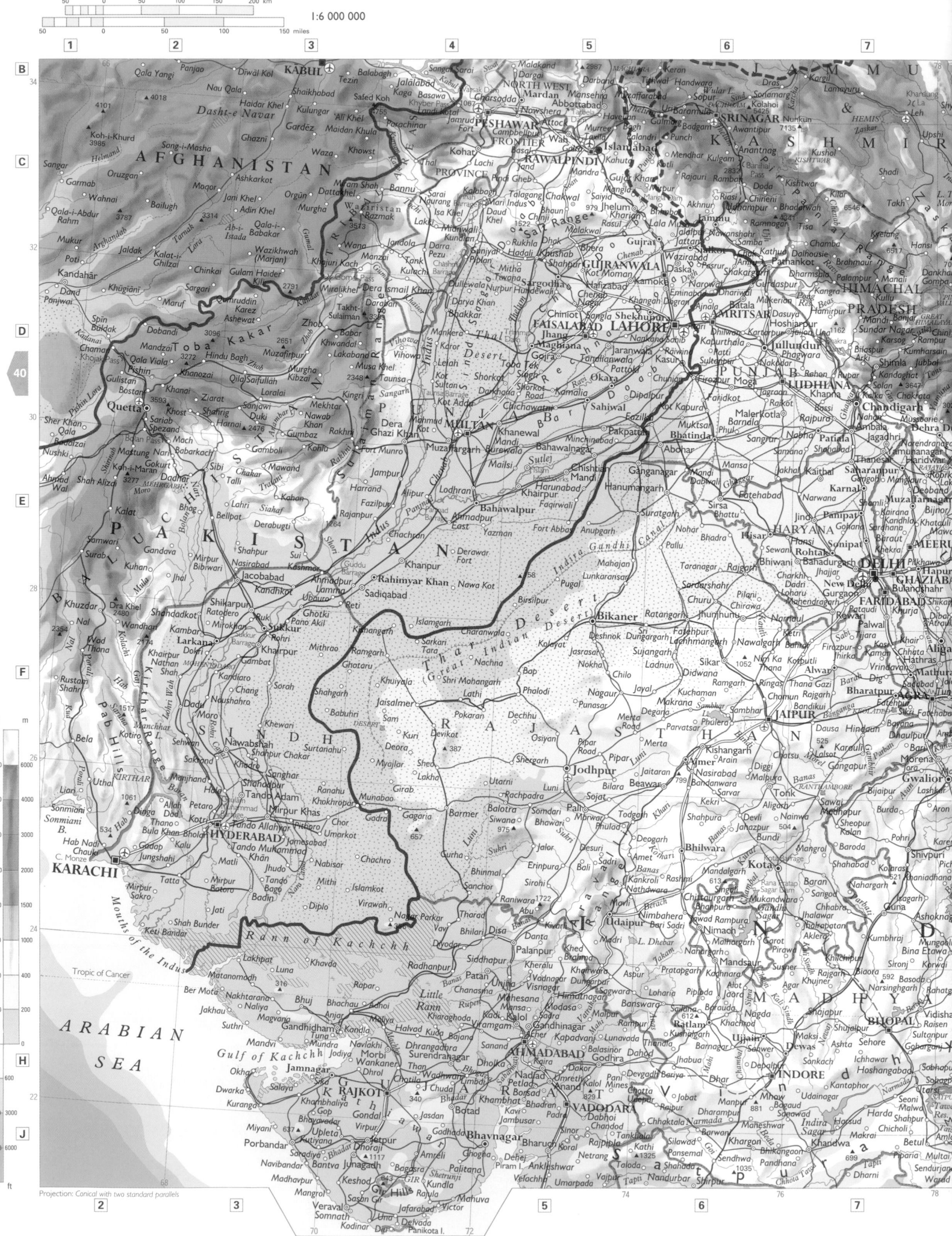

JAMMU AND KASHMIR
on same scale

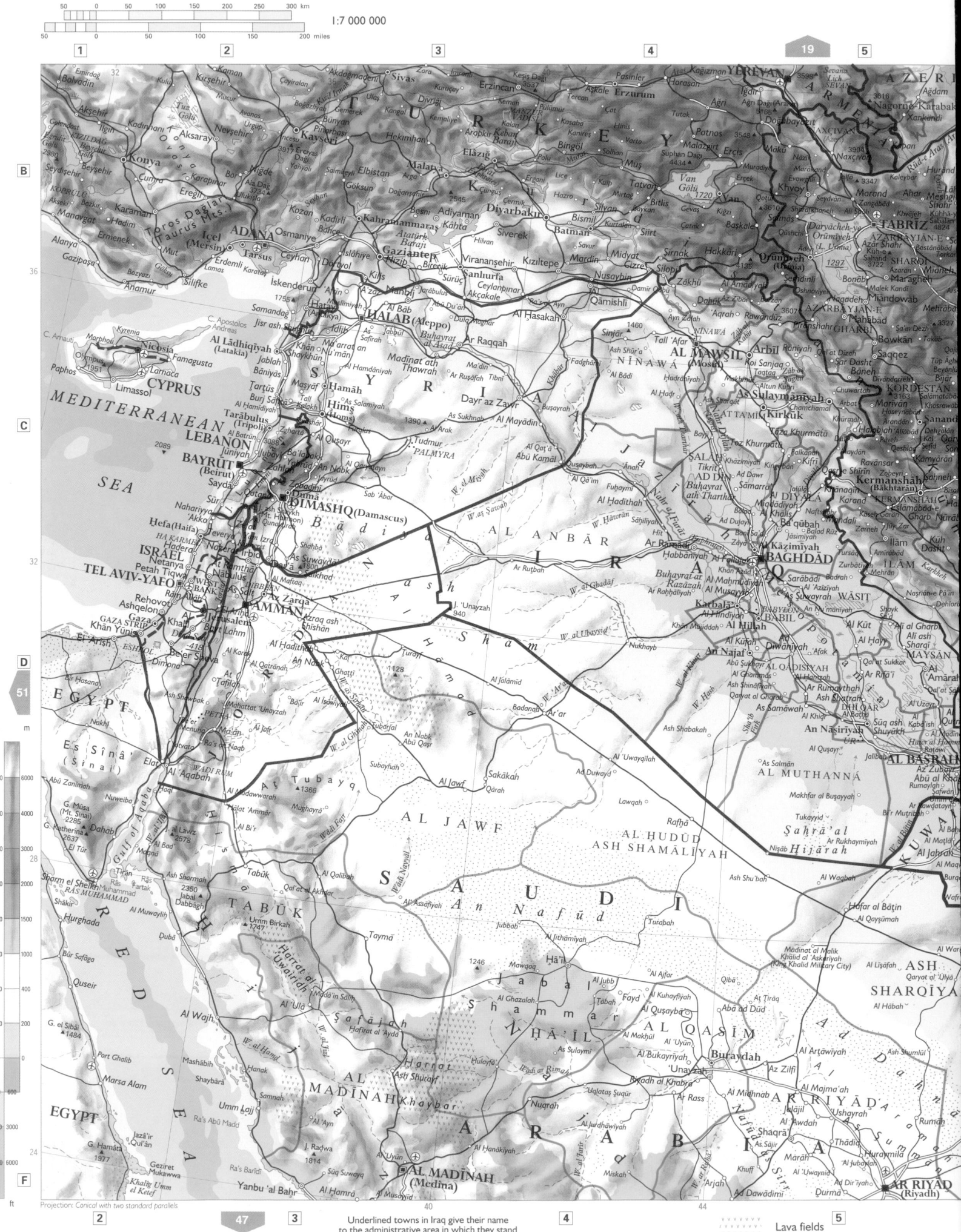

50 0 50 100 150 200 250 300 km

1:7 000 000

50 0 50 100 150 200 miles

Projection: Conical with two standard parallels

Underlined towns in Iraq give their name
to the administrative area in which they stand

Lava fields

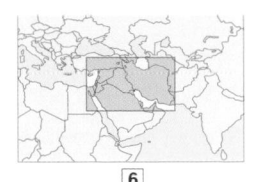

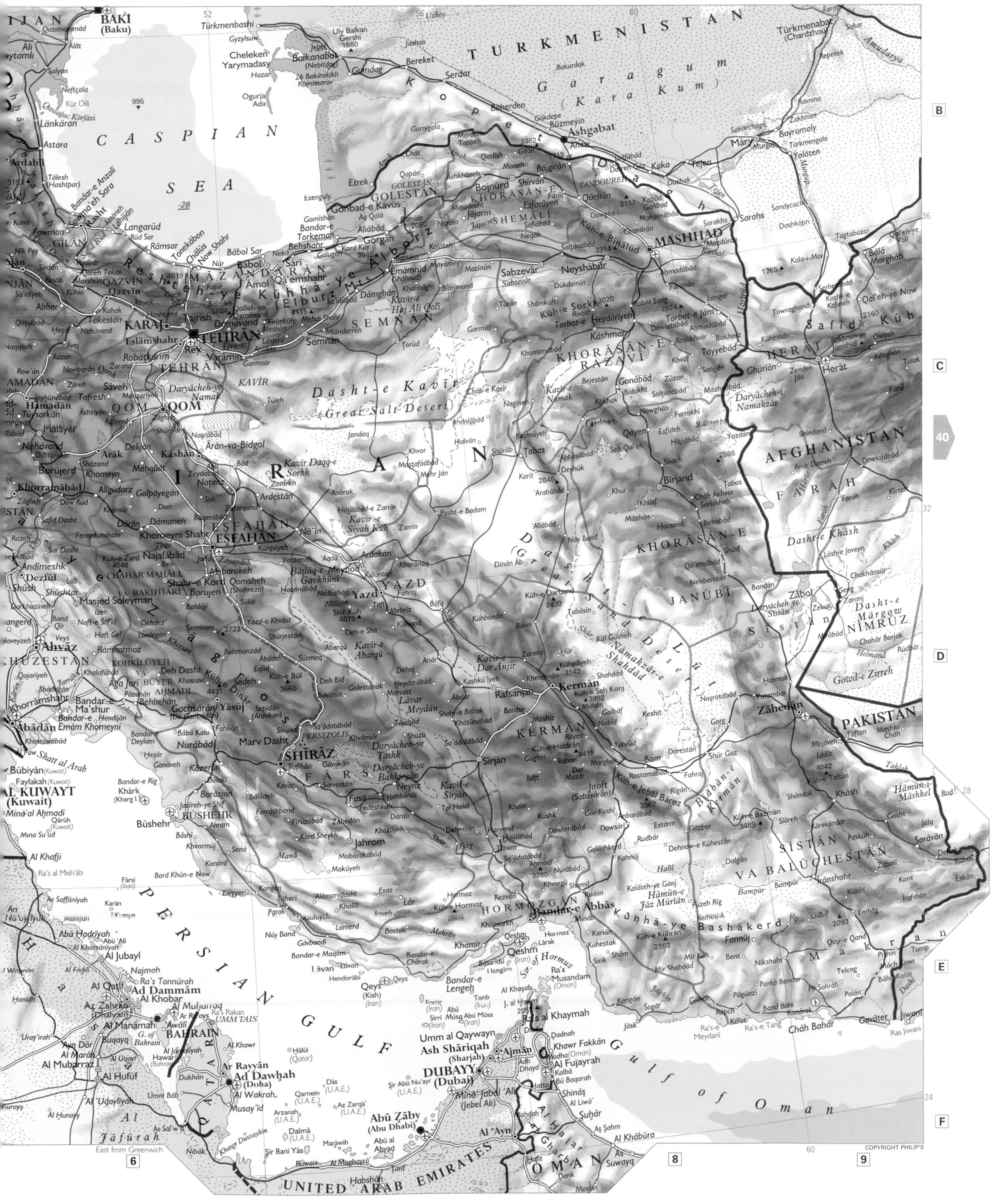

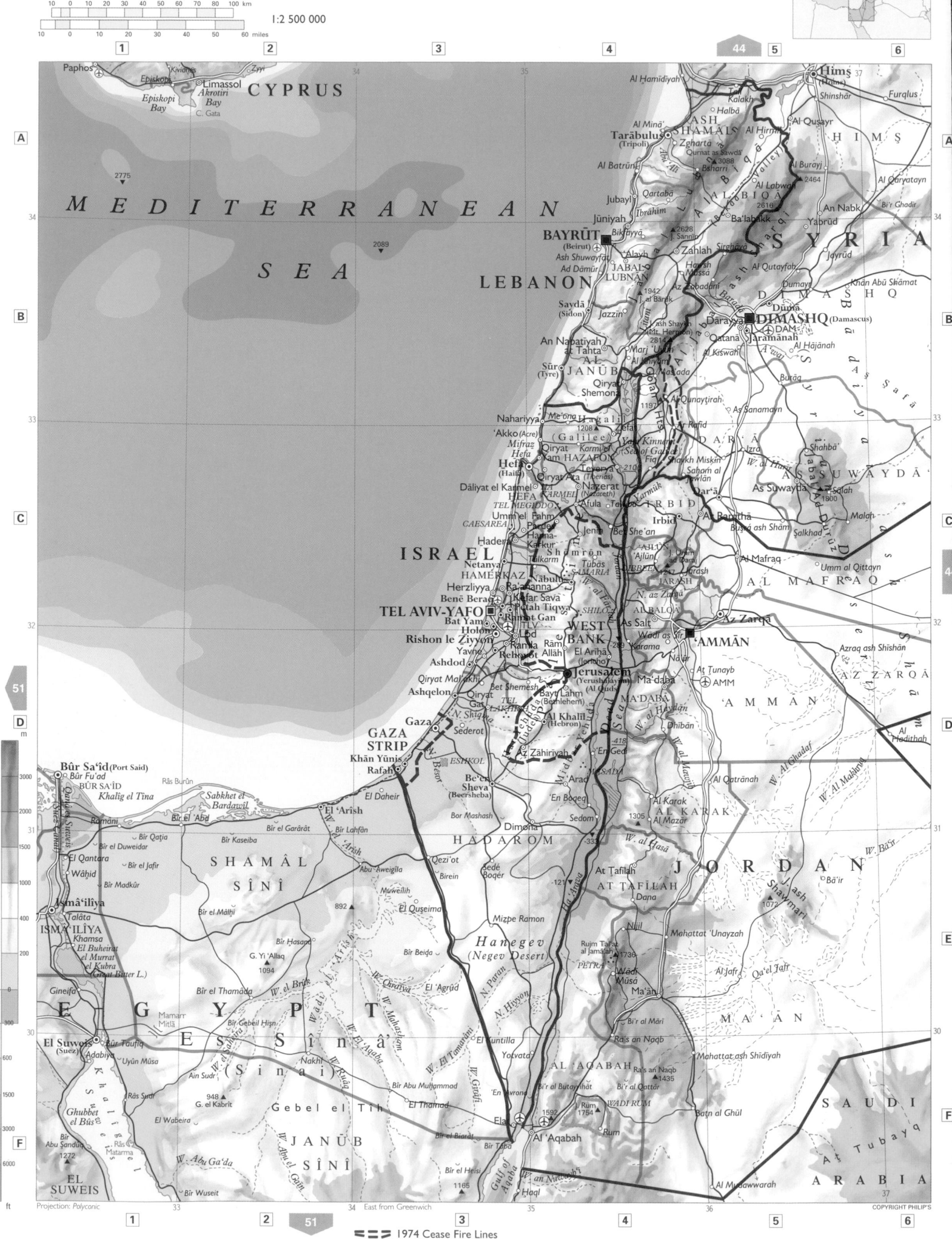

1:2 500 000

1974 Cease Fire Lines

Projection: Polyconic   East from Greenwich   COPYRIGHT PHILIP'S

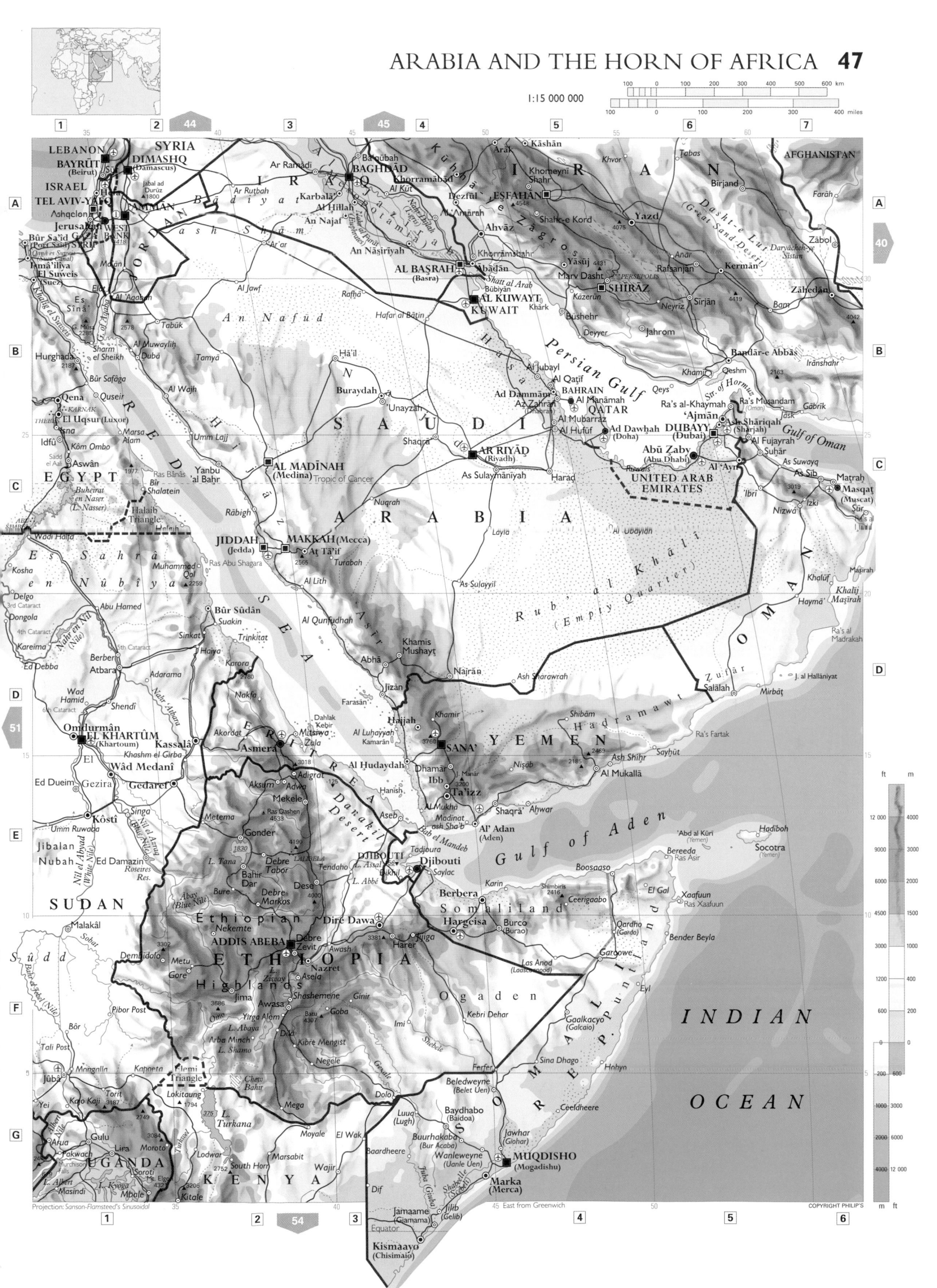

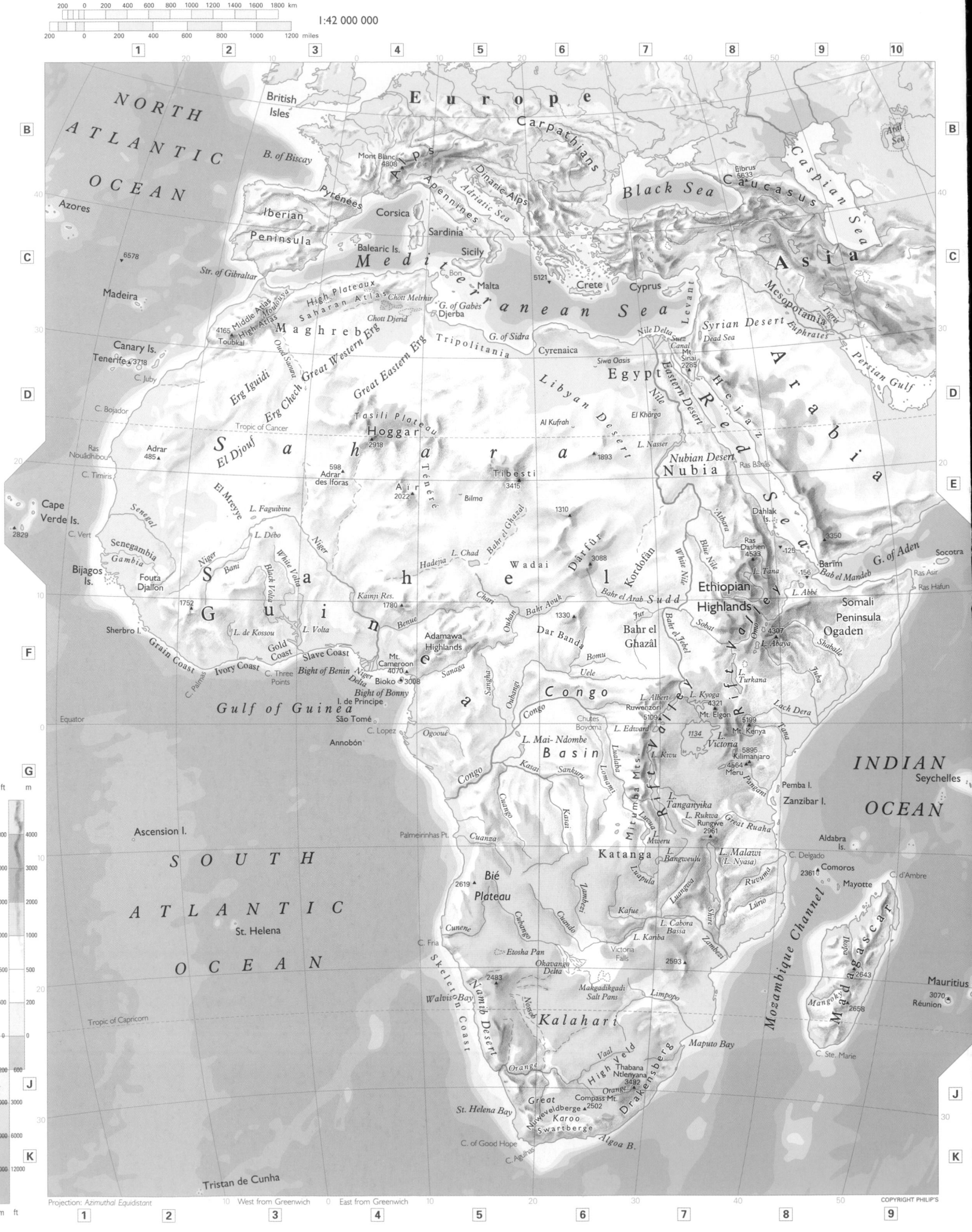

200 0 200 400 600 800 1000 1200 1400 1600 1800 km
1:42 000 000
200 0 200 400 600 800 1000 1200 miles

North Atlantic Ocean
British Isles
B. of Biscay
Mont Blanc 4808
Pyrénées
Alps
Apennines
Dinaric Alps
Adriatic Sea
Carpathians
Europe
Black Sea
Caucasus
Elbrus 5633
Caspian Sea
Aral Sea
Azores
Iberian Peninsula
6578
Str. of Gibraltar
Corsica
Sardinia
Balearic Is.
Sicily
Crete
Cyprus
5121
Mediterranean Sea
Asia
Madeira
C. Bon
Malta
Levant
Mesopotamia
Tigris
Euphrates
Canary Is.
Tenerife 3718
C. Juby
Middle Atlas
High Atlas
Anti Atlas
Saharan Atlas
High Plateaux
Chott Melrhir
Chott Djerid
G. of Gabès
Djerba
G. of Sidra
Maghreb
Tripolitania
Cyrenaica
Egypt
Nile Delta
Suez Canal
Mt. Sinai 2285
Dead Sea
Siwa Oasis
Syrian Desert
Arabia
Hejaz
Red Sea
Persian Gulf
4165
Toubkal
Oued Saoura
Erg Iguidi
Erg Chech
Great Western Erg
Great Eastern Erg
Sahara
Tasili Plateau
Hoggar 2918
Libyan Desert
Al Kufrah
El Kharga
Nile
L. Nasser
Eastern Desert
Nubian Desert
Nubia
Ras Banâs
C. Bojador
Tropic of Cancer
Ras Nouâdhibou
C. Timiris
Adrar 485
El Djouf
Adrar des Iforas
598
Aïr 2022
Ténéré
Bilma
Tibesti 3415
1893
1310
Dahlak Is.
Cape Verde Is.
2829
C. Vert
Senegal
L. Faguibine
L. Débo
El Mreyye
Niger
White Nile
L. Chad
Bahr el Ghazal
Wadai
Darfûr
3088
Kordofan
Blue Nile
Atbara
Ras Dashen 4533
-125
Barím
Bab el Mandeb
G. of Aden
Socotra
Senegambia
Gambia
Bijagos Is.
Fouta Djallon
Bani
Sahel
Hadejia
Chari
Kanji Res. 1780
Benue
L. de Kossou
L. Volta
Black Volta
White Volta
Adamawa Highlands
Sudd
Bahr el Arab
Bahr Auok
1330
Dar Banda
Bahr el Ghazâl
Jur
Sobat
Ethiopian Highlands
4307
L. Tana
L. Abbe
Somali Peninsula
Ogaden
Ras Asir
Ras Hafun
1752
Guinea
Sherbro I.
Grain Coast
Ivory Coast
Gold Coast
Slave Coast
C. Palmes
C. Three Points
Bight of Benin
Niger Delta
Bight of Bonny
Mt. Cameroon 4070
Bioko 3008
I. de Principe
São Tomé
Sanaga
Sangha
Oubangui
Uele
Bomu
Congo
Dar Banda
Shabelle
Juba
Equator
Gulf of Guinea
C. Lopez
Ogooué
Annobón
L. Mai-Ndombe
Congo
Basin
Chutes Boyoma
Lualaba
L. Edward
L. Albert
Ruwenzori 5109
Mt. Elgon 5199
1134
L. Kyoga 4321
Mt. Kenya 5895
L. Victoria
Kilimanjaro 5895
Meru 4564
Mitumba Mts.
L. Kivu
Great Rift Valley
L. Tanganyika
Pemba I.
Zanzibar I.
Pangani
Indian Ocean
Seychelles
Ascension I.
South Atlantic Ocean
St. Helena
Kasai
Kasai
Sankuru
Lomami
Cuanza
Cuango
Palmeirinhas Pt.
Bié Plateau 2619
Katanga
Luapula
L. Mweru
L. Bangweulu
L. Rukwa
Rungwe 2961
Great Ruaha
L. Malawi (L. Nyasa)
Ruvuma
Lúrio
C. Delgado
2361
Comoros
Mayotte
C. d'Ambre
Kafue
Luangwa
Zambezi
Cabango
Cuando
Cunene
Etosha Pan
Okavango Delta
Victoria Falls
L. Cabora Bassa
L. Kariba
Zambezi
2593
Mozambique Channel
Aldabra Is.
Madagascar
Mangoky
2643
3070
Réunion
Mauritius
C. Fria
Skeleton Coast
Walvis Bay
Namib Desert
2483
Nossob
Makgadikgadi Salt Pans
Kalahari
Limpopo
C. Ste. Marie
Tropic of Capricorn
St. Helena Bay
Orange
Vaal
Nieuveldberge
Great Karoo
Swartberge
High Veld
Thabana Ntlenyana 3482
Compass Mt. 2502
Drakensberg
Maputo Bay
C. of Good Hope
C. Agulhas
Algoa B.
Tristan de Cunha

ft   m
12000   4000
9000   3000
6000   2000
3000   1500
1500   500
600   200
0   0
200   600
1000   3000
2000   6000
4000   12000
m   ft

Projection: Azimuthal Equidistant
10 West from Greenwich   0 East from Greenwich   10
COPYRIGHT PHILIP'S

1:42 000 000

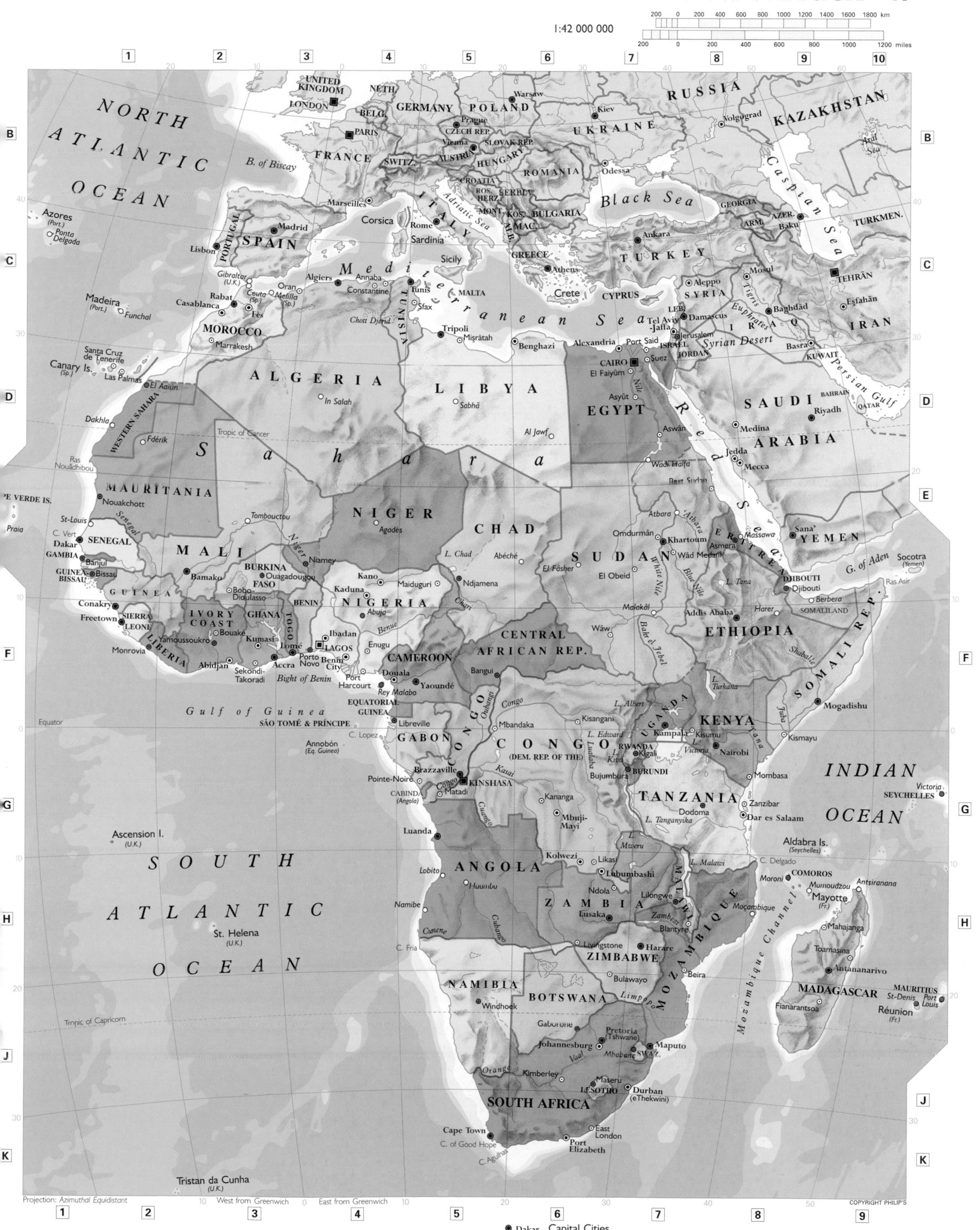

● Dakar Capital Cities

Projection: *Azimuthal Equidistant*   West from Greenwich   East from Greenwich   COPYRIGHT PHILIP'S

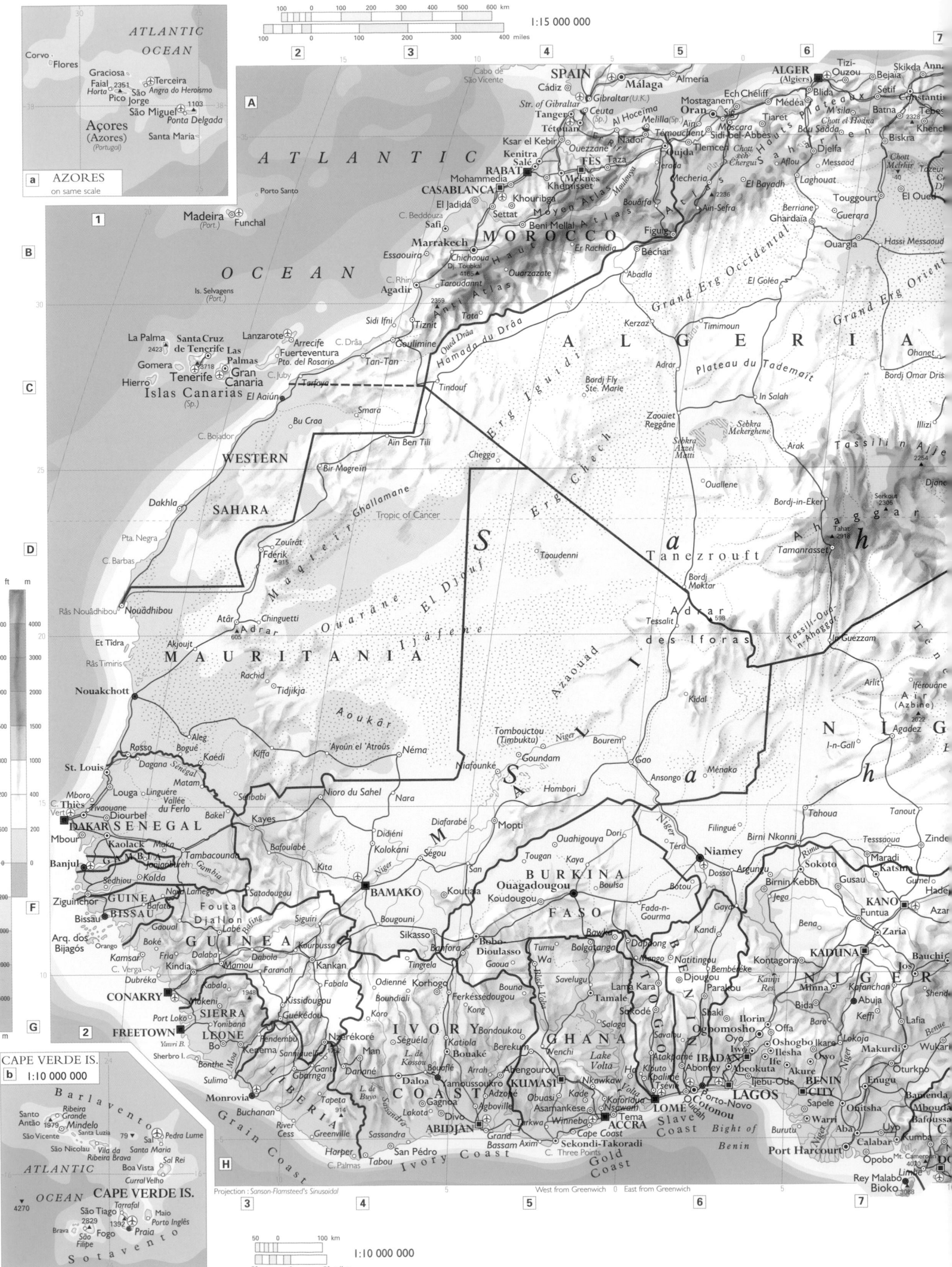

1:15 000 000

ATLANTIC OCEAN

Corvo • Flores
Graciosa
Faial 2351 • Terceira
Horto • São Jorge • Angra do Heroísmo
Pico • Ponta Delgada
São Miguel 1103
Santa Maria
Açores (Azores) (Portugal)

a AZORES on same scale

b CAPE VERDE IS. 1:10 000 000

Barlavento
Santo Antão • Ribeira Grande • Mindelo • Santa Luzia
São Vicente 1979 • São Nicolau • Santa Maria • Pedra Lume 79 • Vila da Ribeira Brava • Sal Rei • Boa Vista
Santa Maria • Maio • Porto Inglês
São Tiago 2829 • Tarrafal 1392
Brava • São Filipe • Praia
Fogo 4270

ATLANTIC OCEAN
Sotavento

CAPE VERDE IS.

1:10 000 000

SPAIN

MOROCCO
ALGERIA
WESTERN SAHARA
MAURITANIA
MALI
SENEGAL
GAMBIA
GUINEA BISSAU
GUINEA
SIERRA LEONE
LIBERIA
IVORY COAST
BURKINA FASO
GHANA
TOGO
BENIN
NIGER
NIGERIA

Projection: Sanson-Flamsteed's Sinusoidal
West from Greenwich 0 East from Greenwich

COPYRIGHT PHILIPS

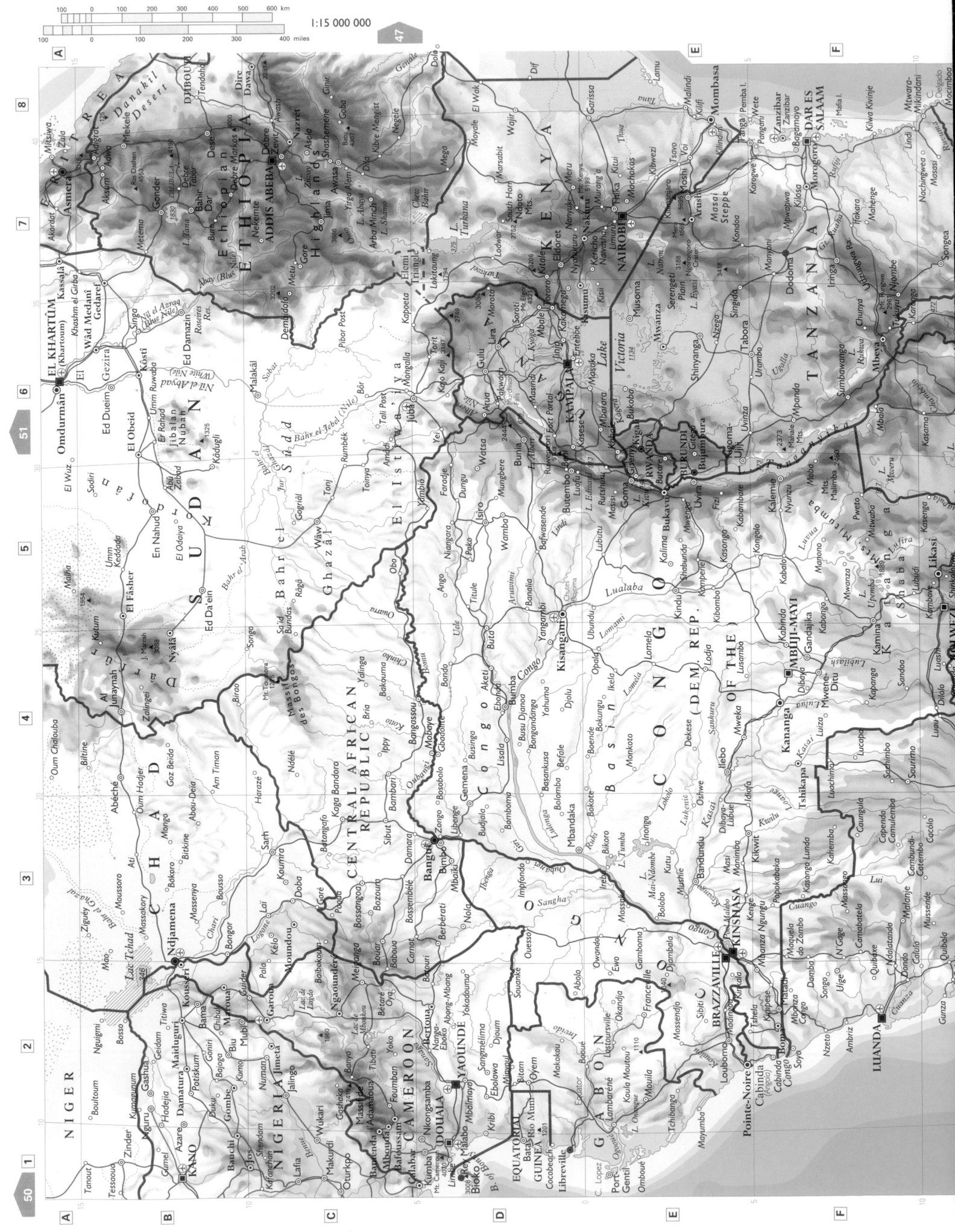

1:15 000 000

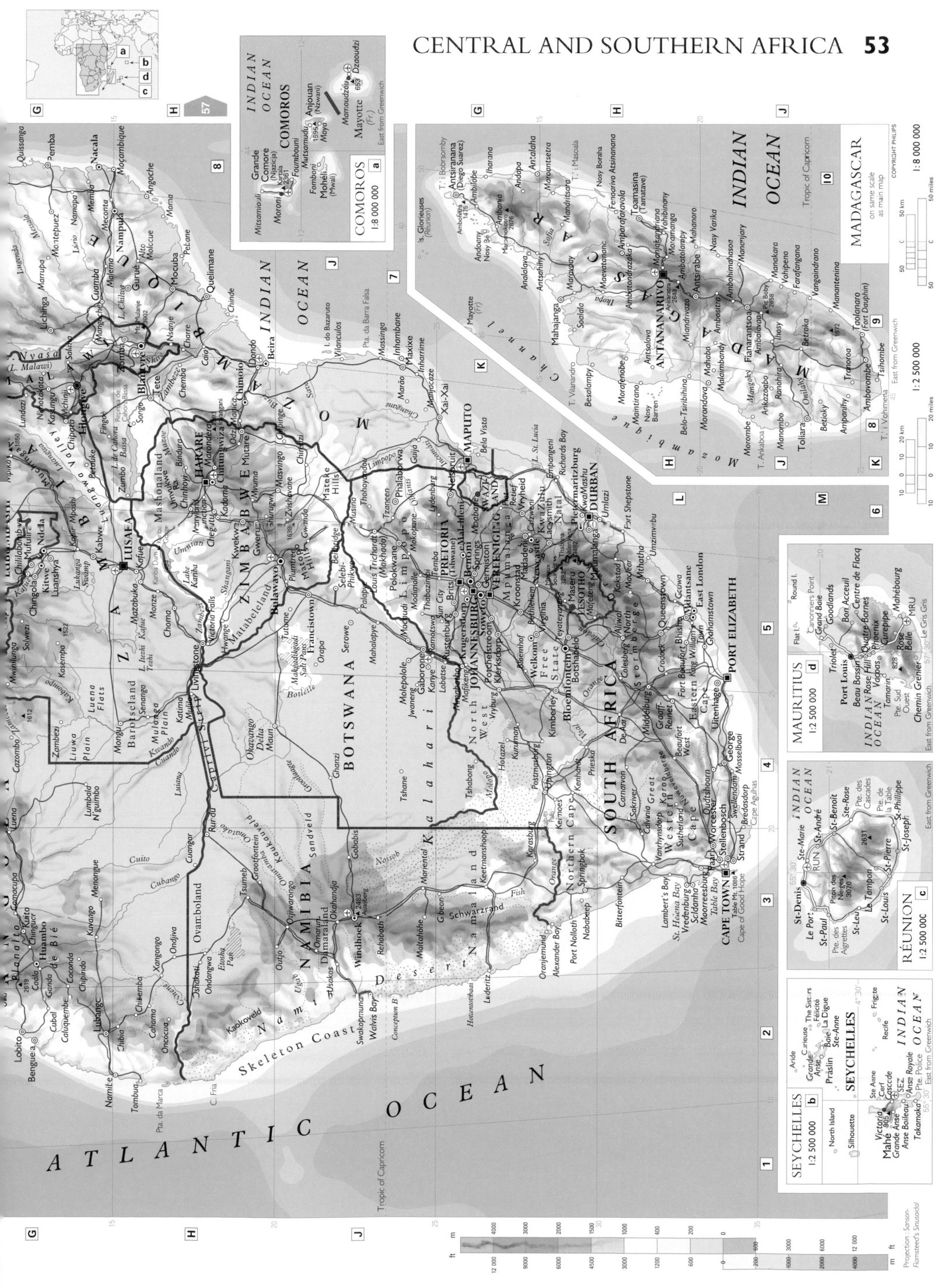

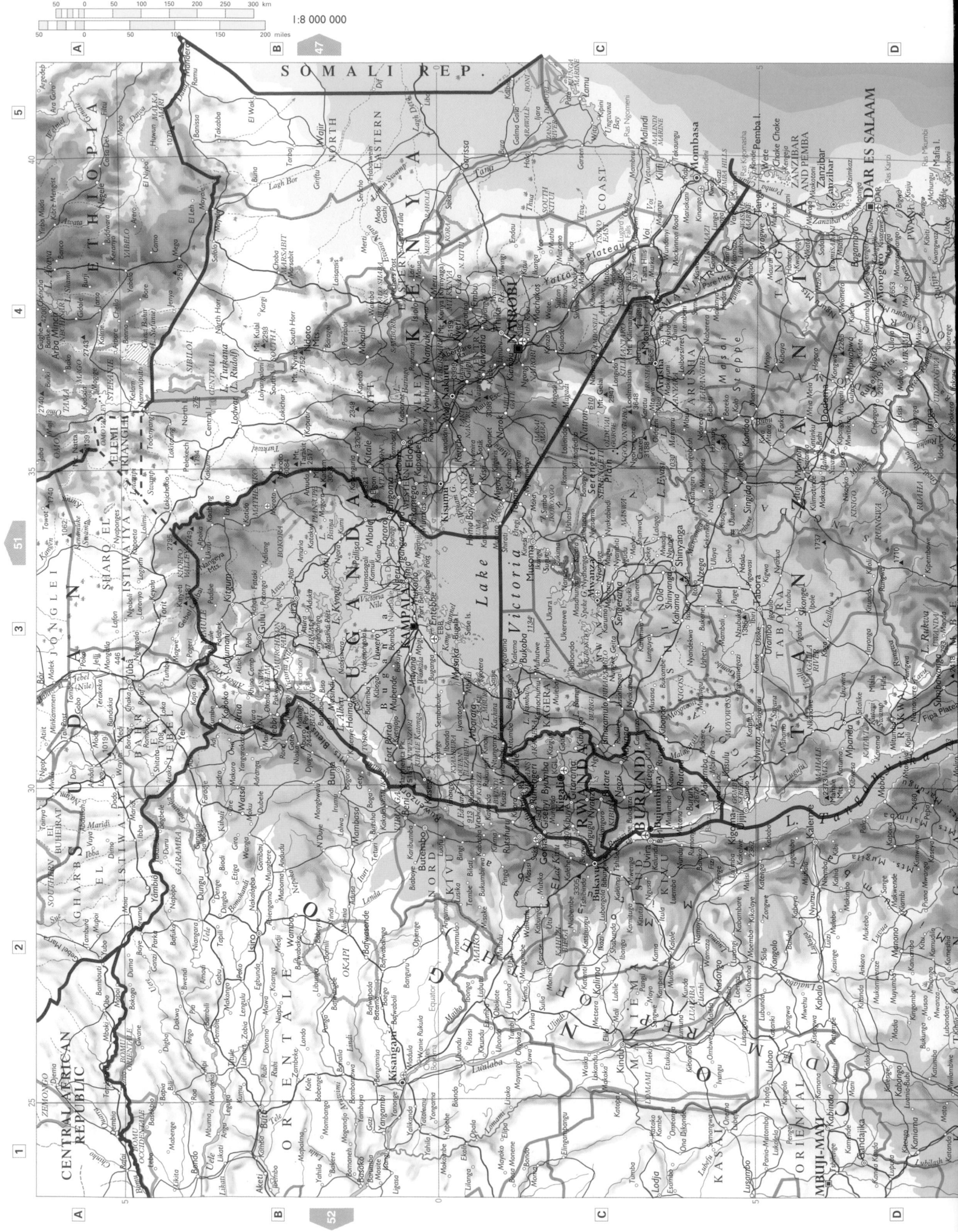

INDIAN OCEAN
ZIMBABWE
BOTSWANA
SOUTH AFRICA
NAMIBIA
ANGOLA
HARARE
LUSAKA
Bulawayo
Beira
Lilongwe
Blantyre
Nampula
Projection: Lambert's Equivalent Azimuthal
COPYRIGHT PHILIP'S

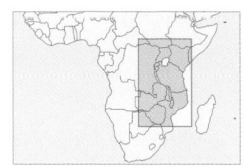

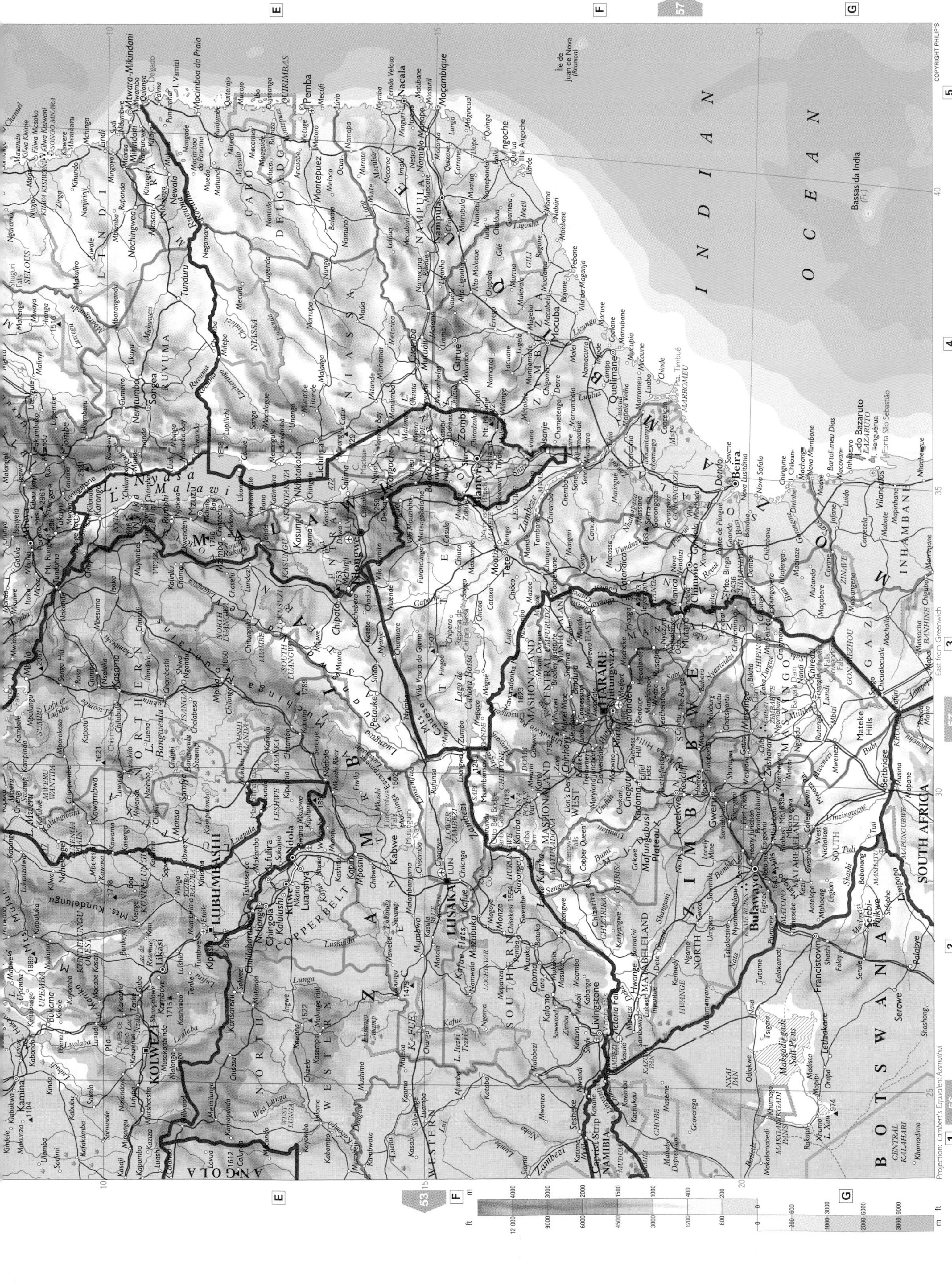

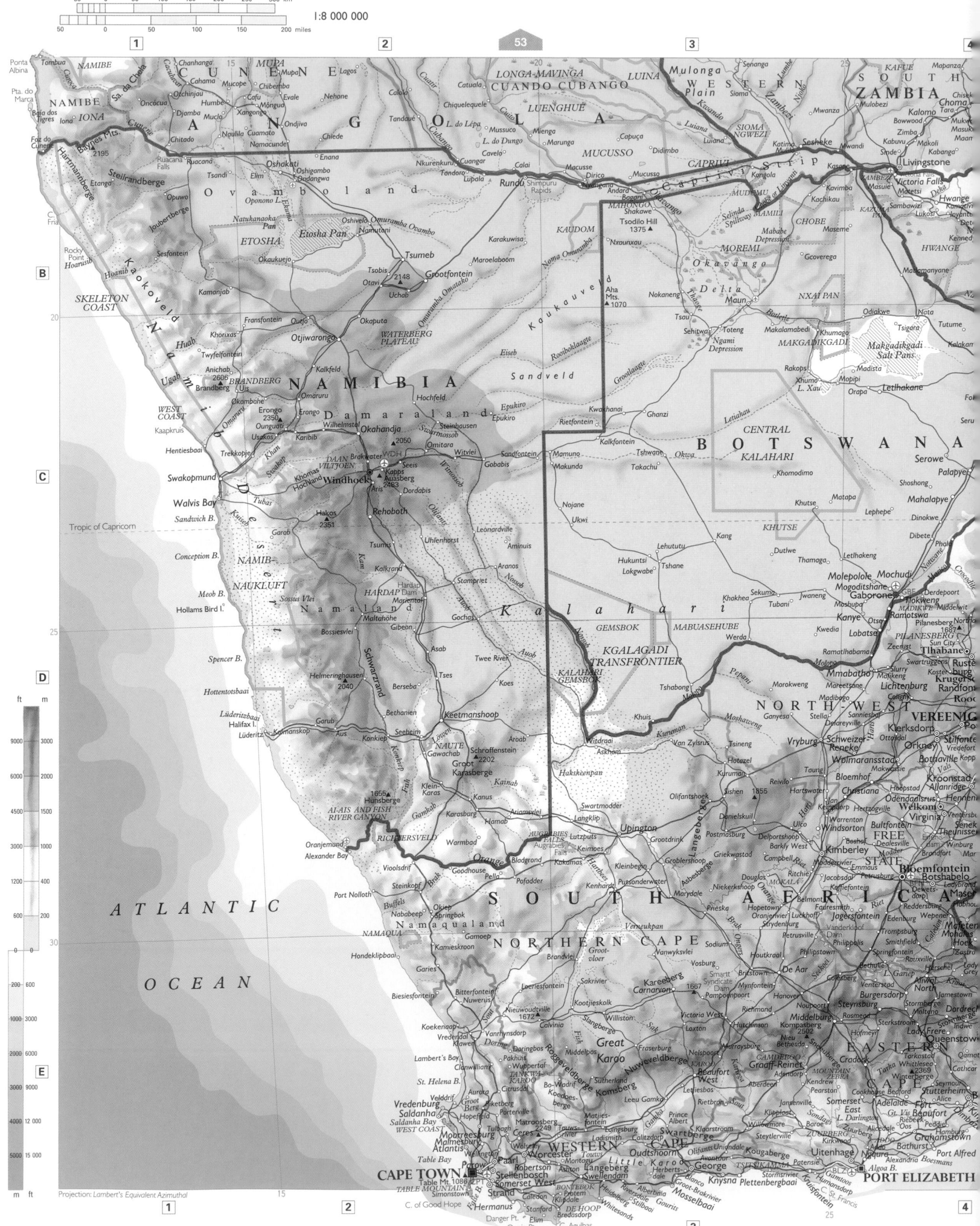

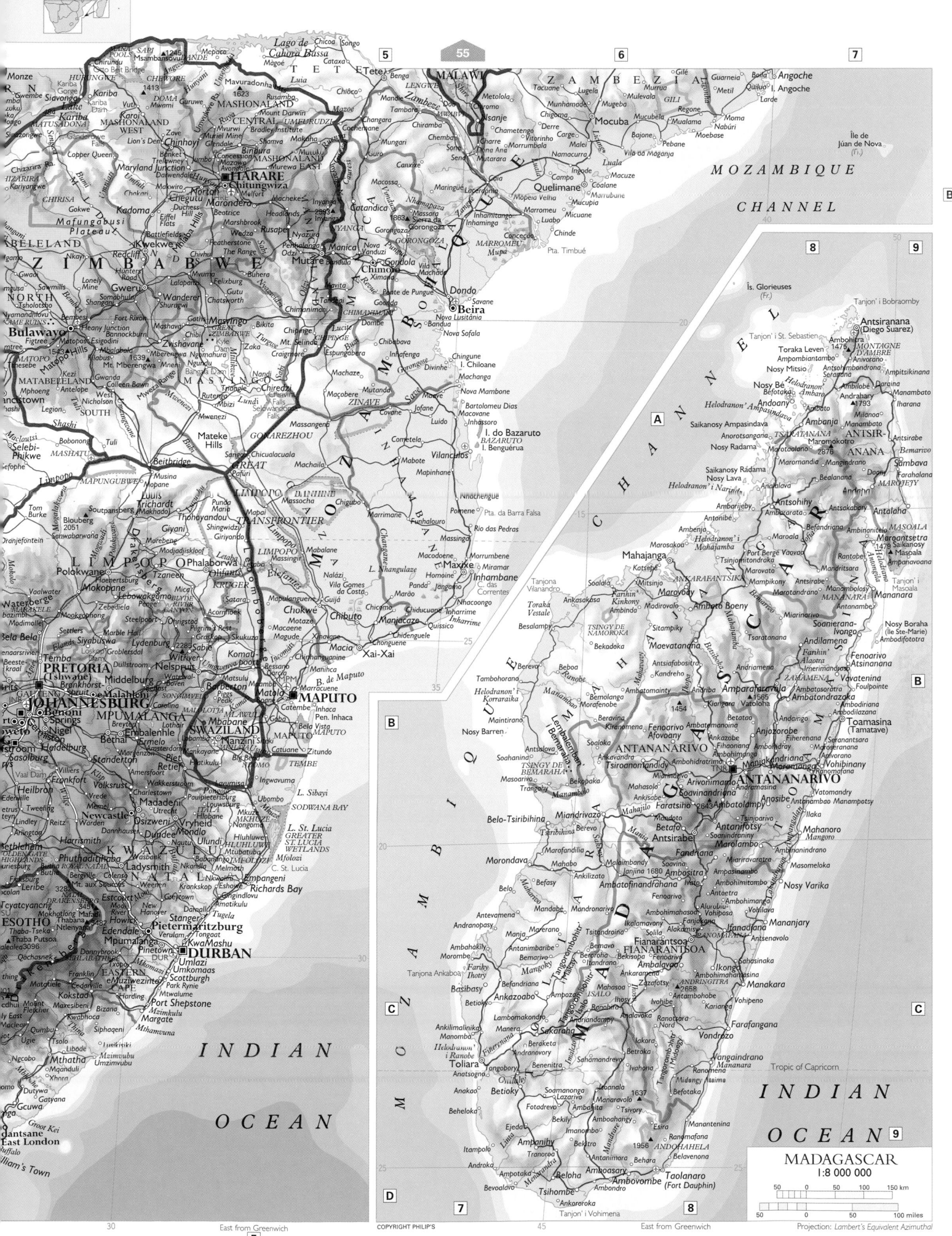

MADAGASCAR
1:8 000 000

INDIAN OCEAN

MOZAMBIQUE CHANNEL

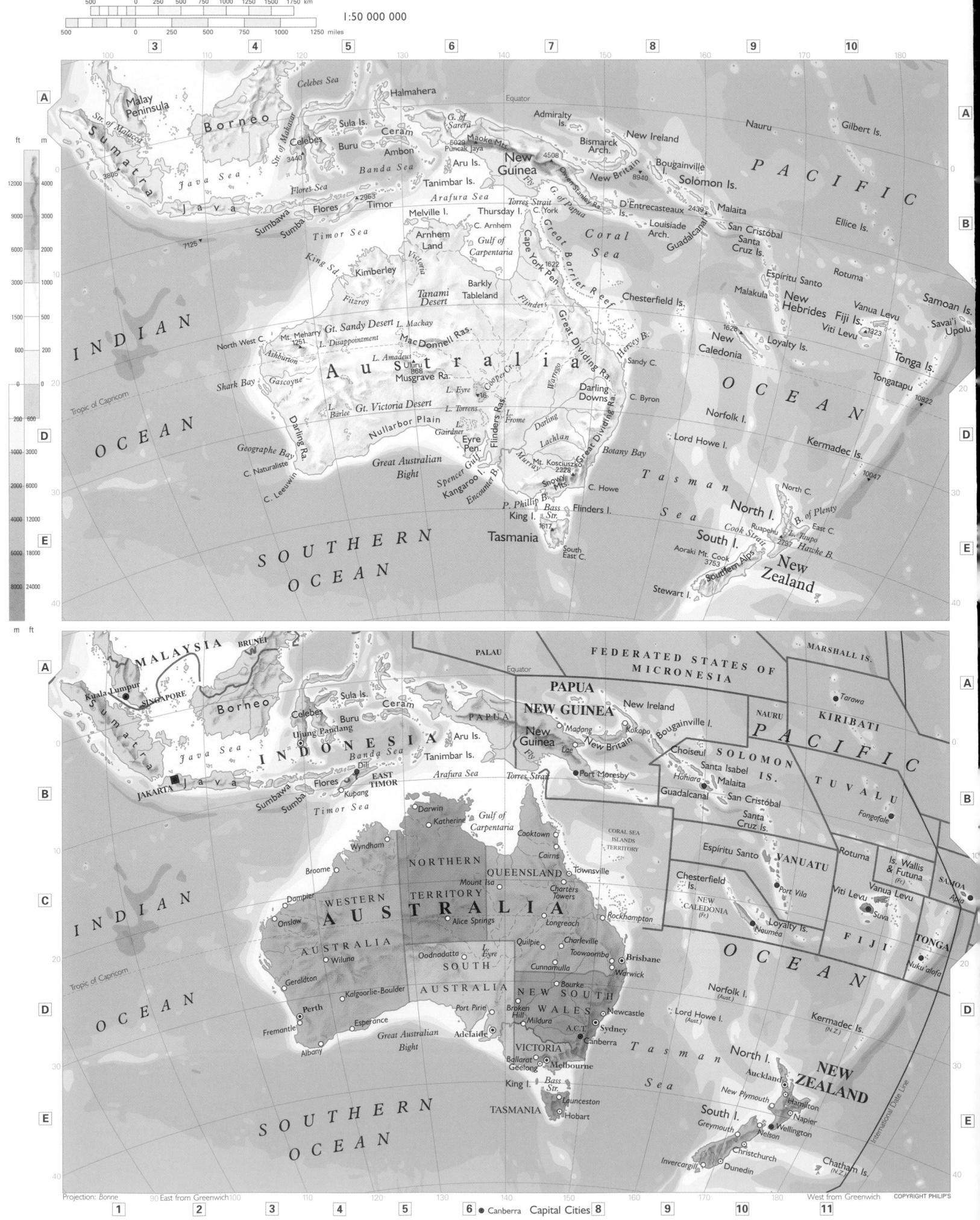

1:50 000 000

● Canberra   Capital Cities

1:6 000 000

50 0 50 100 150 200 km
50 0 50 100 150 miles

FIJI a
on same scale

PACIFIC OCEAN

Great Sea Reef
Kia
Udu Pt.
Ringgold Is.
Labasa
Rabi
Yaqaga
Vanua Levu
Naitaba
Buca
KORO SEA
Yasawa Group
Yasawa
Nacula
Naviti
Waya
Viwa
Mamanuca Group
Malolo
Lautoka
Nadi
Viti Levu
Sigatoka
Korolevu
Navua
Suva
Nausori
Ovalau
Levuka
Wakaya
Makogai
Nairai
Gau
Batiki
Koro
Northern Lau Group
Vanua Balavu
Vatu Vara
Cicia
Nayau
Lakeba Passage
Lakeba
Tubou
Oneata
Moce
Southern Lau Group
Namuka-i-Lau
Yagasa Cluster
Ogea Levu
Kadavu
Kadavu Passage
Ono
Matuku
Totoya
Fulaga
Ogea Driki

East from Greenwich West from Greenwich

SAMOA
Falelima
Asau
Safune
Savai'i
Taga
Mulifanua
Manono
Apia
Falefa
Amaile
Upolu
OLE PUPU PUE
Safata Bay

PACIFIC OCEAN

AMERICAN SAMOA (U.S.A.)
Tutuila
Leone
Pago Pago
Vaitogi
Ofu
Olosega
Ta'ū
Aunu'u
Manu'a Is.

SAMOAN ISLANDS b
on same scale

West from Greenwich

TONGA c
on same scale

PACIFIC OCEAN

Fonualei
Toku
Vava'u
Neiafu
Vava'u Group
Late
Home Reef
Disney Reef
Ofolanga
Ha'ano
Foa
Lifuka
Uiha
Ha'apai Group
Tofua
Kao
Kotu Group
Fonuafo'ou
Nomuka
Mango
Oto Tolu Group
Tonumea
Hunga Ha'apai
Nomuka Group

TONGA
Nuku'alofa
Tongatapu
Tongatapu Group
Eua

West from Greenwich

TASMAN SEA

PACIFIC OCEAN

North Island

C. Reinga
C. Maria van Diemen
North C.
Houhora Heads
Ahipara B.
Mongonui
Kaitaia
Okaihau
B. of Islands
C. Brett
Rawene
Waitangi
Opua
Hokianga Harbour
Kaikohe
Hikurangi
Waipoua Forest
Whangarei
Whangarei Harb.
Dargaville
Bream B.
Bream Hd.
Little Barrier I.
Great Barrier I.
C. Rodney
Cuvier I.
Kaipara Harbour
Warkworth
Helensville
Hauraki Gulf
C. Colville
Coromandel
Whitianga
Takapuna
AUCKLAND
Papakura
Thames
Manukau
Papatoetoe
Pukekohe
Whangamata
Waiuku
Mercer
Whangamata
Mayor I.
Waikato
Huntly
Morrinsville
Waihi
Tauranga Harb.
Whakaari (White I.)
Runaway
Raglan
Hamilton
Cambridge
Te Aroha
Tauranga
Te Puke
Bay of Plenty
Kawhia Harbour
Te Awamutu
Opotiki
East C.
Kawhia
Otorohanga
Rotorua
L. Tarawera
Murupara
Hikurangi 1753
Waitomo Caves
Te Kuiti
Mokai
Wairakei
Rangitaiki Mts.
Waikaremoana
UREWERA
Waipiro
Tolaga Bay
Mokau
New Plymouth
Inglewood
North Taranaki Bight
Mt. Taranaki or Mt. Egmont
C. Egmont
2518
Stratford
Ohakune
WHANGANUI
Taumarunui
Tuiwera
Gisborne
Wairoa
Ormond
Opunake
Eltham
Raetihi
Ruapehu 2797
TONGARIRO
Waiouru
Waikokopu
Mahia Pen.
Hawera
South Taranaki Bight
Waverley
Taihape
Mangaweka
Hawke Bay
Napier
Hastings
Wanganui
Bulls
Halcombe
Feilding
Waipukurau
Dannevirke
Palmerston North
Foxton
Shannon
Levin
Otaki
Masterton
Paraparaumu
Kapiti I.
Upper Hutt
Lower Hutt
Petone
Greytown
Martinborough
Featherston
Wellington
C. Palliser
Cook Strait
C. Turnagain

South Island

C. Farewell
Golden B.
D'Urville I.
ABEL TASMAN
Collingwood
Takaka
Tasman B.
KAHURANGI
Karamea
Motueka
Nelson
Havelock
Picton
Queen Charlotte Sd.
Karamea Bight
Tasman Mts.
Richmond
Wakefield
Blenheim
Seddon
Ward
Seddonville
Lyell
Murchison
NELSON LAKES
Kaikoura
Granity
Inangahua
Rotoroa
Tapuae-o-Uenuku 2885
Westport
Greymouth
Reefton
PAPAROA
Punakaiki
Blackball
Hanmer Springs
Waiau
Runanga
Spenser Mts.
Waiau
Kumara
Stillwater
L. Brunner
Jacksons
ARTHUR'S PASS
Culverden
Amberley
Hokitika
Ross
Waikari
Rangiora
Pegasus Bay
Oxford
Kaiapoi
New Brighton
Whitecliffs
Christchurch
Lyttelton
Banks Pen.
Akaroa
WESTLAND
Aoraki/Mt. Cook 3753
Methven
Springfield
Rakaia
Little River
Ellesmere
Rakaia
Staveley
Ashburton
Canterbury Plains
Pirake
MOUNT COOK
Mount Cook
Fairlie
Temuka
Timaru
MOUNT ASPIRING
Mt. Aspiring 3033
Jackson B.
FIORDLAND
Milford Sd.
Sutherland Falls
Milford Sound
Earnslaw 2819
Wanaka
L. Wanaka
Arrowtown
Cromwell
Kurow
Naseby
Tokarahi
St Andrews
Canterbury Bight
Oamaru
Maheno
Hampden
Secretary I.
Doubtful Sd.
Dunback
Queenstown
Clyde
Alexandra
Roxburgh
Waikouaiti
Port Chalmers
Breaksea Sd.
Resolution I.
Dusky Sd.
Manapouri
L. Te Anau
L. Wakatipu
Lumsden
Kingston
Garston
OTAGO
Lawrence
Milton
Balclutha
Port Chalmers
Dunedin
C. Saunders
Solander I.
Clifden
Tuatapere
Orepuki
Riverton
Invercargill
Bluff
Otautau
Winton
Mataura
Wyndham
Edievale
Waikaia
Gore
Clinton
Kaitangata
Nugget Pt.
Tapanui
Owaka
Stewart I. (Rakiura)
Halfmoon Bay
RAKIURA
Port Pegasus
South West C.

Projection : Conical with two standard parallels

East from Greenwich

TAHITI & MOOREA d
1:1 000 000

Pte. Aroa
Papetoai
B. de Matavai
Pte. Vénus
Mahina
Moorea (France)
Mt. Tohiea 1207
Afareaitu
Papeete
Arue
Papenoo
Tiarei
Pirae
Faaa
Faaone
Punaauia
Mt. Aorai 2060
Mt. Orohena 2241
Hitiaa
Haapiti
Pte. Nuupere
Paea
Mt. Teufera 1757
Vaihiria
Faaone
Tahiti (France)
Papara
Papeari
Tautira
Isthme de Taravao
Afaahiti
Pte. Tautira
Maraa
Atimaono
Mataiea
Vairao
Taravao
Pueu
Mt. Rooniu 1332
Teahupoo
Presqu'île de Taiarapu

PACIFIC OCEAN

10 0 10 km
10 0 10 miles
1:1 000 000

West from Greenwich

COPYRIGHT PHILIP'S

ft / m
9000 / 3000
6000 / 2000
3000 / 1000
1200 / 400
600 / 200
0
600 / 200
6000 / 2000
12 000 / 4000
18 000 / 6000
m / ft

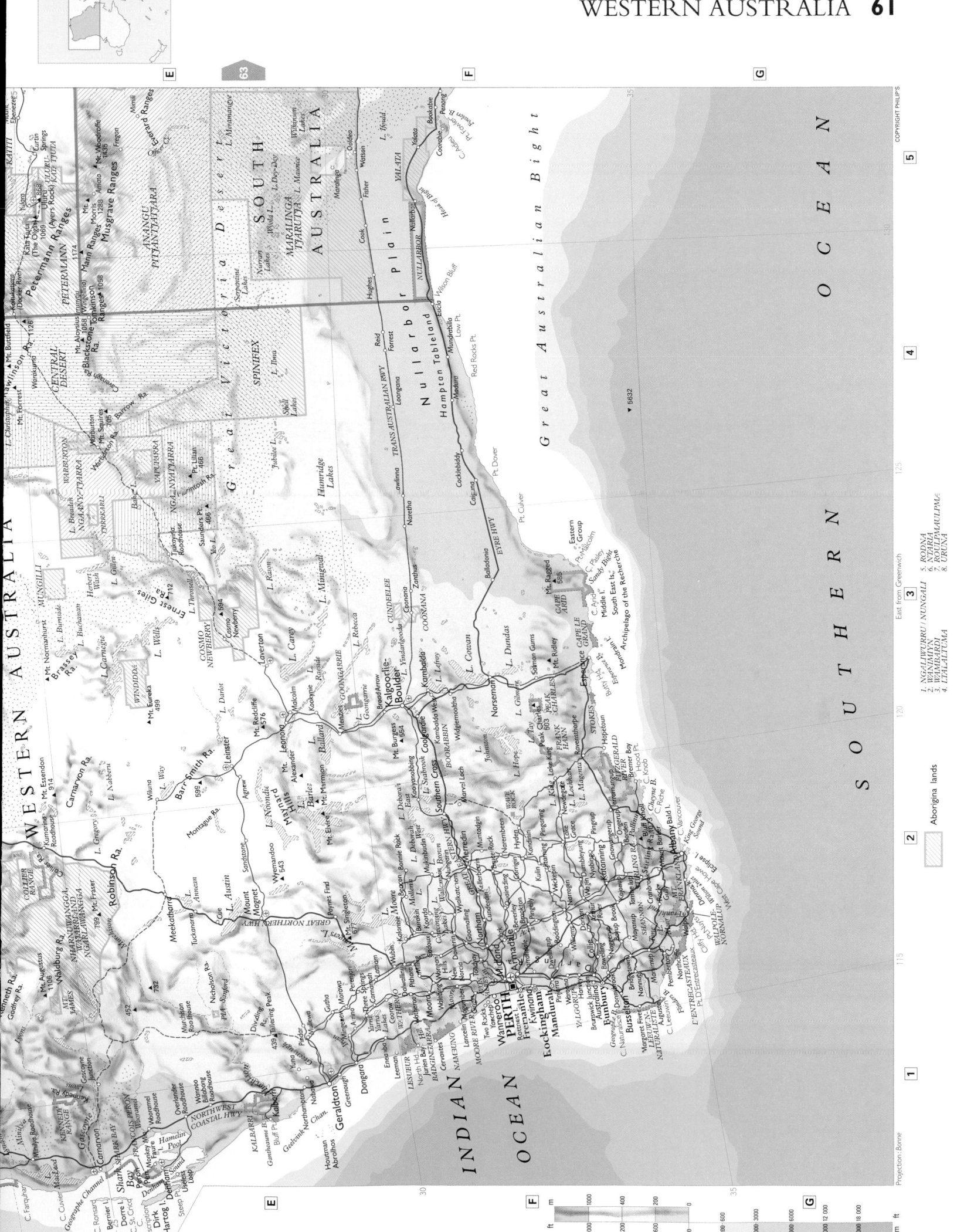

E   F   G

KAITTJ

SOUTH
AUSTRALIA

ANANGU
PITJANTJATJARA

MARALINGA
TJARUTJA   YALATA

Great Victoria Desert

PETERMANN Ranges

Musgrave Ranges

CENTRAL
DESERT

WARBURTON
NGAANYATJARRA

SPINIFEX

NGAANYATJARRA

WINDIDDA

COSMO
NEWBERRY

MUNGILLI

WESTERN AUSTRALIA

Nullarbor Plain

Hampton Tableland

NULLARBOR

Great Australian Bight

SOUTHERN

OCEAN

TRANS AUSTRALIAN HWY

EYRE HWY

Kalgoorlie-
Boulder

GOONGARRIE

COOLGARDIE

Esperance

Archipelago of the Recherche

CAPE LE
GRAND

CAPE ARID

Norseman

STOKES

FITZGERALD

STIRLING RANGE

Albany

PERTH

Fremantle

Mandurah

Bunbury

Busselton

WALPOLE
NORNALUP

INDIAN

OCEAN

GREAT NORTHERN HWY

Geraldton

SHARK BAY

Carnarvon

Aborigina lands

1. NGALIWURRU / NUNGALI   5. RODNA
2. WININMIYN   6. NTARA
3. WAMBARDI   7. ROULPMAULPMA
4. LHALALTUMA   8. URUNA

m
ft
1000
3000
1200
600
0
6000
2000
4000 12 000
6000 18 000

Projection: Bonne   East from Greenwich   COPYRIGHT PHILIP'S

1:8 000 000

50 0 50 100 150 200 250 300 km

50 0 50 100 150 200 miles

PAPUA NEW GUINEA

CORAL SEA

TORRES STRAIT on same scale as main map

a

Gulf of Papua

Torres Strait

Thursday I. Horn I.
Prince of Wales I.
Cape York
Cape York Peninsula

QUEENSLAND
OLD MAPOON

b

CORAL SEA

Hayman I.
Hook I.
WHITSUNDAY
Whitsunday I.
Hamilton I.
Lindeman I.
Shaw I.
Cumberland
Carlisle I.
SMITH ISLANDS
CUMBERLAND ISLANDS
Brampton I.
St. Bees I.
Hillsborough Channel
Slade Point
Mackay

Bowen
Gloucester I.
Mt. McGuire 738
Prosepine
Whitsunday Pass.
Repulse Bay
C. Conway
REPULSE ISLANDS
Midge Point
NEWRY ISLANDS
Seaforth
Yalboroo
Kungari
Bucasia
Farleigh
Walkerston
Balnagowan
Finch Hatton
Netherdale
Broken River
EUNGELLA
Mt. Dalrymple 1259

QUEENSLAND

WHITSUNDAY ISLANDS

1:2 500 000

Abington Reef

Great Barrier Reef

CORAL SEA

Great Barrier Reef

Cairns

Townsville

QUEENSLAND

NORTHERN TERRITORY

Gulf of Carpentaria

Arnhem Land

Mount Isa

Alice Springs

Tropic of Capricorn

Simpson Desert

Great Dividing Range

Rockhampton
Gladstone

Capricorn Coast

COPYRIGHT PHILIP'S

Aboriginal lands

on same scale

Projection: Bonne

East from Greenwich

RUSSIA

Yekaterinburg   Tomsk
Moskva   Novosibirsk
Astana (Aqmola)   Semey   Irkutsk   Chita   Blagoveshchensk
KAZAKHSTAN
Aral Sea   Balqash Köl
Almaty   Ulaanbaatar   MONGOLIA   Harbin   Khabarovsk
Toshkent   Ürümqi   Changchun   Shenyang
KYRGYZSTAN
TAJIKISTAN   Beijing   Tianjin   NORTH KOREA
AFGHANISTAN   Kābul   Srinagar   Kunlun Shan   Taiyuan   Dalian   SOUTH KOREA   Seoul
PAKISTAN   Lahore   CHINA   Lanzhou   Qingdao   Kyōto   Osaka   JAPAN
Delhi   XIZANG   Xi'an   Yellow Sea   Kyūshū   Yokohama
Kanpur   Lhasa   Himalaya   Chongqing   Nanjing   Wuhan   Shanghai
INDIA   Nepal   Changsha   Hangzhou   East China Sea
Kolkata (Calcutta)   Dhaka   BURMA   Mandalay   Kunming   Fuzhou   Okinawa   Ryūkyū-rettō (Japan)
BANGLADESH   Guangzhou   Taipei   TAIWAN
Hyderabad   Macau   Hong Kong
Bay of Bengal   Rangoon   THAILAND   Hanoi   Hainan   C. Engano   Luzon   Philippine Sea
Chennai (Madras)   Bangkok   CAMBODIA   Paracel Is.   Manila   PHILIPPINES
Andaman Is. (India)   Phnom Penh   Mindoro   Samar
Nicobar Is. (India)   Thanh Pho Ho Chi Minh   South China Sea   Palawan
SRI LANKA   Colombo   G. of Thailand   MALAYSIA   Sulu Sea   Mindanao   Davao
Kuala Lumpur   BRUNEI   SABAH   Celebes Sea
Singapore   SARAWAK   Maluku   Halmahera
Palembang   Borneo   Sulawesi   Buru   Seram
INDONESIA   Ujung Pandang   Banda Sea
Jakarta   Java Sea   Surabaya   Flores   Flores Sea   Dili   EAST TIMOR
Java   Bali   Sumbawa   Sumba   Timor

Cocos Is. (Austral.)   Christmas I. (Austral.)   North Australian Basin
INDIAN   Broome
OCEAN   Exmouth Plateau   Darwin   C. Arnhem   Gulf of Carpentaria
Wharton Basin   North West C.   Cairns   Townsville
Geraldton   AUSTRALIA   Mount Isa   Alice Springs   Rockhampton
Perth Basin   Brisbane
Perth   Great Australian Bight   Sydney   Canberra
Naturaliste Plateau   Adelaide   Mt. Kosciuszko 2228
Albany   Murray   Melbourne
South Australian Basin   Bass Str.   Tasmania   Hobart
SOUTHERN   OCEAN

Sea of Okhotsk   Okhotsk   Poluostrov Kamchatka   Aleutian Basin   Bering Sea
Sakhalin   Kurilskiye Ostrova (Russia)   Petropavlovsk-Kamchatskiy   Komandorskiye Ostrova (Russia)   Near Is. (U.S.A.)   Andreanof Is. (U.S.A.)
La Pérouse Str.   Kuril-Kamchatka Trench   Aleutian Trench   7822
Sapporo   Hakodate   10,542   Northwest   Emperor Seamount Chain   Chinook Trough
Sea of Japan   Shatsky Rise   Pacific
Sendai   Fuji-San 3776   Tōkyō   10,554   Japan Trench   Basin   Hawaiian
Nagoya   Shikoku   Midway Is. (U.S.A.)
Iwo-Jima (Japan)   Ogasawara Gunto (Japan)   Minami-Tori-Shima (Japan)   Lisianski I. (U.S.A.)
Kyushu-Palau Ridge   Sitito-Ozima-Ridge   Kazan-Rettō (Japan)   Mid Pacific Mountain
West Mariana Basin   NORTHERN MARIANAS (U.S.A.)   East Mariana Basin   Wake I. (U.S.A.)   PACIFIC
Tinian   Saipan   GUAM (U.S.A.)   MARSHALL IS.
Philippine Basin   Mariana Trench   Challenger 11,022 Deep   Enewetak Atoll   Bikini Atoll   Kwajalein   Majuro
Yap   Caroline Is.   Chuuk   Micronesia   Ralik Chain   Ratak Chain   Jaluit I.
Mindanao Trench   Melekeok   PALAU   FED. STATES OF MICRONESIA   Pohnpei   Palikir   Butaritari
4101   West Caroline Basin   East Caroline Basin   Tarawa   Gilbert Is.   Howland I. (U.S.A.)   Baker I. (U.S.A.)
Eauripik Rise   Solomon Rise   Melanesian Basin   Banaba   Phoenix Is.   Abariringa Enderbury
PAPUA NEW GUINEA   NAURU   Melanesia   KIRIBATI
Puncak Jaya 5029   PAPUA   Admiralty Is.   Bismarck Arch.   New Ireland
New Guinea   4840   Kokopo   Bougainville   SOLOMON IS.   Fongafale   TUVALU   Tokelau (N.Z.)
Lae   New Britain   Honiara   Guadalcanal   Rotuma   Is. Wallis & Futuna (Fr.)   SAMOA   Apia
7440   Port Moresby   Torres Strait   C. York   Louisiade Arch.   Santa Cruz I. 9165   Vanua Levu
Arafura Sea   Coral Sea Basin   Espiritu Santo   VANUATU   Viti Levu   FIJI   Suva
Coral Sea   Is. Chesterfield   Port Vila   West Fiji Basin   7570   Nuku'alofa   TONGA
Great Barrier Reef   NEW CALEDONIA (Fr.)   Nouméa   Is. Loyauté   South Fiji Basin   10,822   Tonga Trench
Great Dividing Ra.   Middleton Reef   Norfolk Ridge   Kermadec Is. (N.Z.)   Kermadec Trench 10,047
Lord Howe I. (Austral.)   Norfolk I. (Austral.)   New Caledonia Trough
Tasman Sea   East Tasman Plateau   Auckland   NEW ZEALAND   Wellington
Aoraki Mt. Cook 3753   Christchurch   Chatham Is. (N.Z.)
South Tasman Rise   Tasman Basin   Dunedin   Bounty Trough   Bounty Is. (N.Z.)
Invercargill   Cook Strait   Antipodes Is. (N.Z.)
Auckland Is. (N.Z.)   Campbell Plateau   Campbell I. (N.Z.)
Macquarie Is. (Austral.)
OCEAN

Ninetyeast Ridge   Sumatera   Sunda Islands   Selat Sunda   Java East Ridge
Nouvelle Amsterdam (Fr.)   I. St. Paul (Fr.)   Mid-Indian Ridge
Is. Crozet (Fr.)   Kerguelen (Fr.)   Heard I. (Austral.)
Broken Ridge

Elevation scale:
ft / m
12 000 / 4000
9000 / 3000
6000 / 2000
3000 / 1000
1500 / 500
600 / 200
0 / 0
600 / 200
3000 / 1000
6000 / 2000
12 000 / 4000
18 000 / 6000
24 000 / 8000

1:35 000 000

1:35 000 000

100 0 200 400 600 800 1000 1200 1400 km
100 0 200 400 600 800 1000 miles

B **A** **B**

C

RUSSIA
Asia
St. Lawrence I.
Bering Strait
Bering Sea

ARCTIC OCEAN

International Date Line

GREENLAND (Denmark)
Denmark Strait
ICELAND
Reykjavík

Baffin Bay
Davis Strait
Nuuk

Beaufort Sea
Queen Elizabeth Is.
Ellesmere I.

Baffin Island

D

ALASKA (U.S.A.)
Yukon
Porcupine
Fairbanks
Anchorage
Gulf of Alaska
Kodiak I.

Victoria I.

NORTHWEST
Arctic Circle
Mackenzie
Great Bear L.
YUKON TERRITORY
Whitehorse
TERRITORIES
Yellowknife
Great Slave L.
Back

NUNAVUT
Iqaluit

Hudson Strait

E

Juneau

BRITISH COLUMBIA
Skeena
Peace
Fraser
Athabasca

CANADA
Athabasca
ALBERTA
Edmonton
Calgary
SASKATCHEWAN
Saskatchewan
Regina

Churchill
MANITOBA

Nelson

Hudson Bay

Eastmain

L. Winnipeg

St. Lawrence
QUÉBEC

LABRADOR

NEWFOUNDLAND
St-Pierre et Miquelon (Fr.)
St. John's

F

Vancouver
Victoria
WASHINGTON
Olympia
Seattle
Portland
Salem
Columbia
OREGON

MONTANA
Helena
Missouri

NORTH DAKOTA
Bismarck
SOUTH DAKOTA

MINNESOTA
Minneapolis-St. Paul
WISCONSIN
Madison

Winnipeg

L. Superior
L. Huron
L. Michigan
MICHIGAN
Lansing
Milwaukee
Detroit

ONTARIO
Ottawa
Montréal
Québec
NEW BRUNSWICK
Fredericton
MAINE
Augusta
NOVA SCOTIA
Halifax
Charlottetown
PRINCE EDWARD I.

TORONTO
Buffalo
NEW YORK
Cleveland
Hartford
Concord
Boston
Providence
MASS.
N.H.
VER.

G

Sacramento
San Francisco
San Jose
CALIFORNIA
Carson City
NEVADA

IDAHO
Boise
Snake

WYOMING
UTAH
Salt Lake City

NEBRASKA
Lincoln

IOWA
Madison

UNITED STATES

ILLINOIS
CHICAGO
INDIANA
Indianapolis
Springfield
OHIO
Columbus
Cincinnati
Toledo

Pittsburgh
PA.
Baltimore
PHILADELPHIA
NEW YORK
Washington D.C.
Richmond
MD.
DEL.
W.V.
VIRGINIA

NORTH ATLANTIC OCEAN
Bermuda (U.K.)

Las Vegas
Los Angeles
San Diego
Tijuana

COLORADO
Denver
KANSAS
Topeka
Kansas City
MISSOURI
St. Louis

KENTUCKY
Nashville
TENNESSEE
Memphis
Raleigh
NORTH CAROLINA
Charlotte

PACIFIC OCEAN

Santa Fe
Albuquerque
ARIZONA
Phoenix
Tucson
NEW MEXICO

OKLAHOMA
Oklahoma City
ARKANSAS
Little Rock

MISSISSIPPI
Birmingham
Jackson
ALABAMA
Montgomery

Columbia
SOUTH CAROLINA
Charleston
Atlanta
GEORGIA

Mexicali
El Paso
Ciudad Juárez
Rio Grande

TEXAS
Dallas
Ft. Worth
Austin
Houston
San Antonio

Baton Rouge
LOUISIANA
New Orleans

Jacksonville
Tallahassee
FLORIDA
Orlando
Tampa-St. Petersburg

Tropic of Cancer

Guadalupe (Mex.)

Hermosillo

MÉXICO

Monterrey
Torreón
Culiacán

Gulf of Mexico

MIAMI
Nassau
BAHAMAS
Turks & Caicos Is. (U.K.)

Florida Str.

H

Revilla Gigedo Is. (Mex.)

León
San Luis Potosí
Guadalajara
MÉXICO
Toluca
Puebla
Acapulco
Mérida

Belmopán
BELIZE

Havana
CUBA
Cayman Is. (U.K.)
JAMAICA
Kingston

HAITI
Port-au-Prince
DOMINICAN REP.
Santo Domingo
San Juan
PUERTO RICO (U.S.A.)

Caribbean Sea

J

GUATEMALA
Guatemala
EL SALVADOR
San Salvador
HONDURAS
Tegucigalpa
NICARAGUA
Managua
L. Nicaragua
COSTA RICA
San José
PANAMA
Panamá

Maracaibo
Barranquilla
VENEZUELA
Medellín
COLOMBIA
South America

Projection: Bonne
7 ■ MÉXICO Capital Cities **8** West from Greenwich **9** **10** **11** **12**
COPYRIGHT PHILIP'S

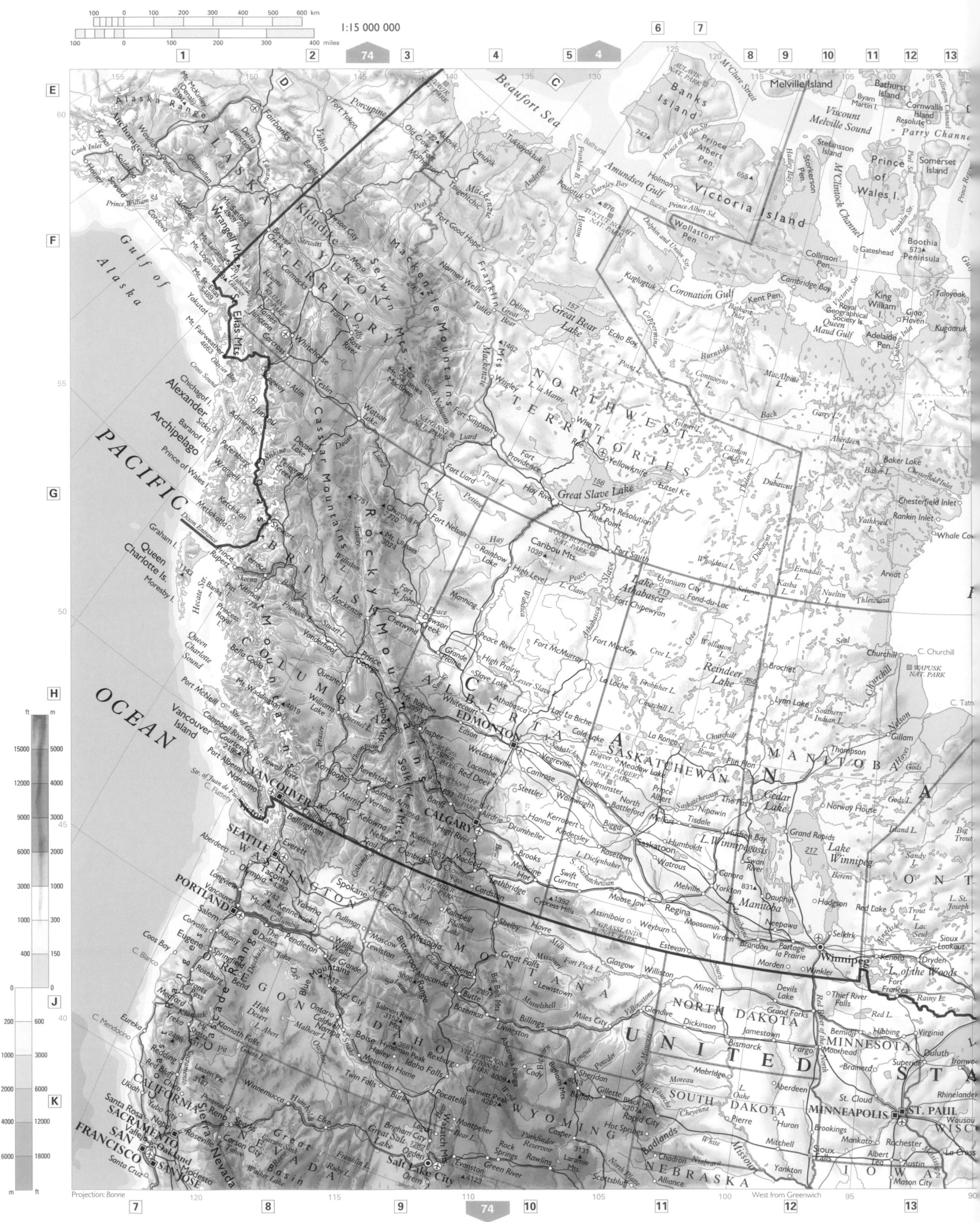

1:15 000 000

Projection: Bonne

West from Greenwich

COPYRIGHT PHILIP'S

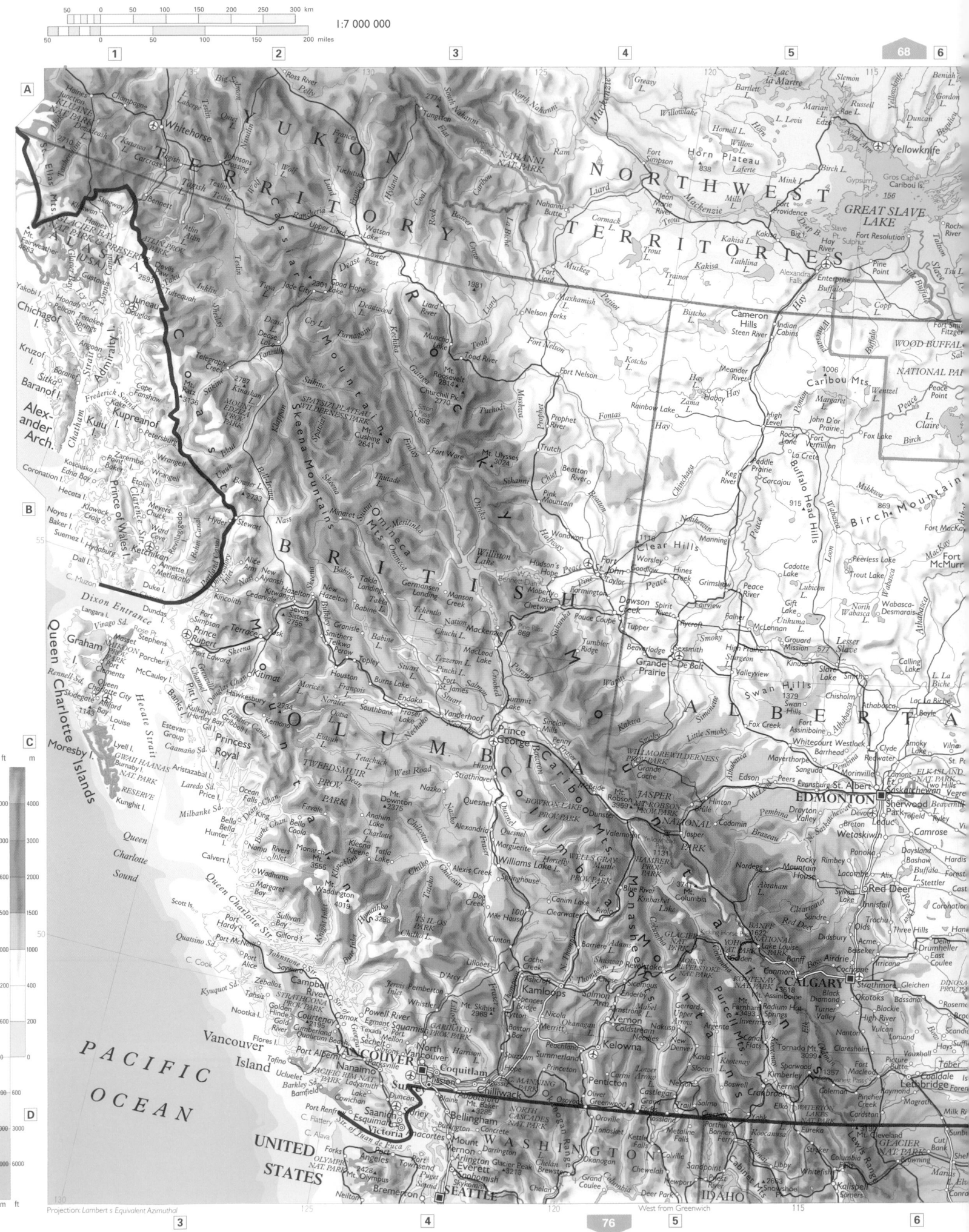

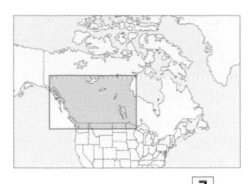

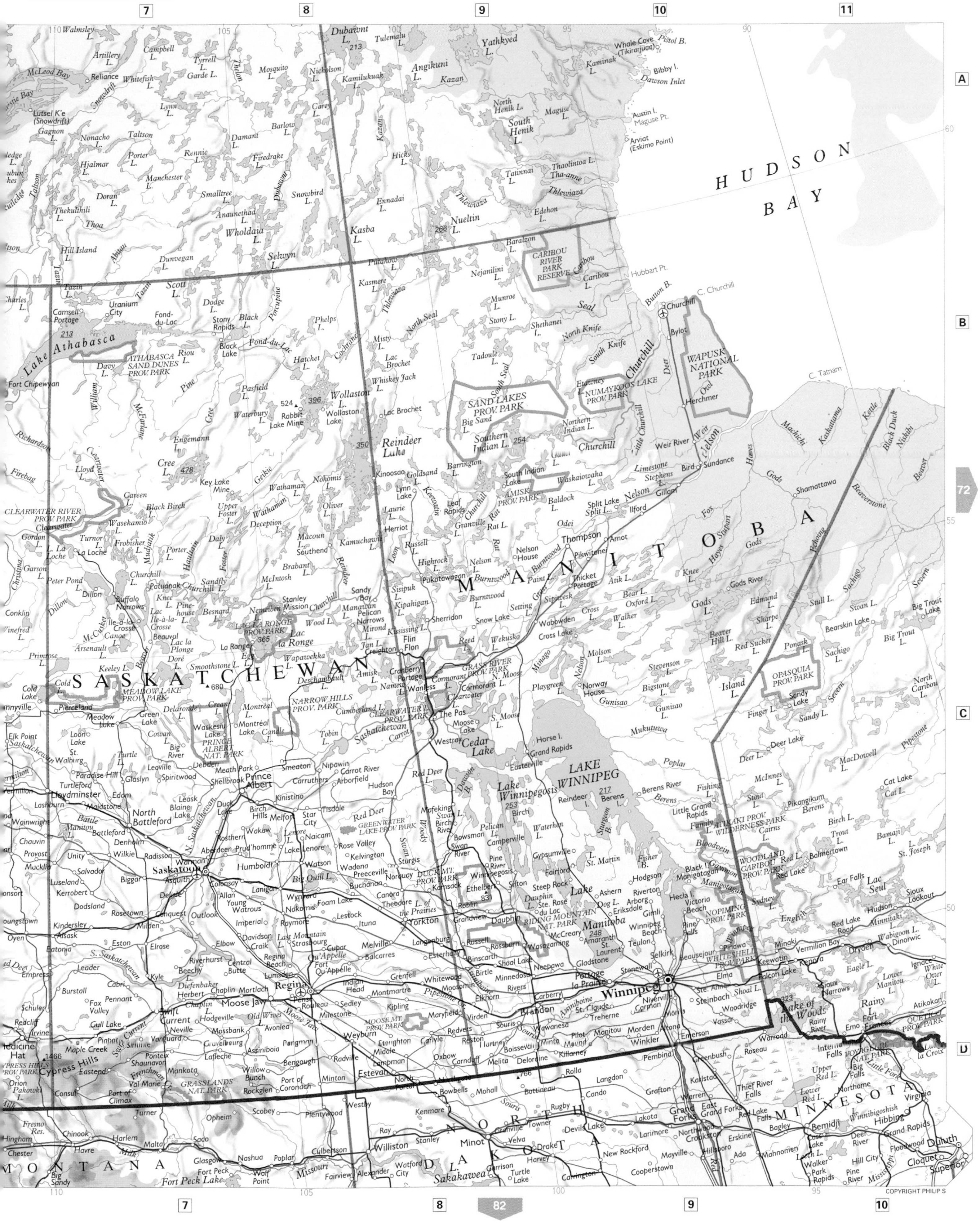
7
8
9
10
11
A
B
C
D
HUDSON BAY
SASKATCHEWAN
MANITOBA
NORTH DAKOTA
MINNESOTA
MONTANA
Lake Athabasca
Reindeer Lake
Wollaston L.
LAKE WINNIPEG
Lake Winnipegosis
Lake Manitoba
Cedar Lake
Lake of the Woods
Nueltin L.
Dubawnt L.
Southern Indian L.
ATHABASCA SAND DUNES PROV. PARK
SAND LAKES PROV. PARK
NUMAYKOOS LAKE PROV. PARK
WAPUSK NATIONAL PARK
CARIBOU RIVER PARK RESERVE
CLEARWATER RIVER PROV. PARK
LAC LA RONGE PROV. PARK
MEADOW LAKE PROV. PARK
NARROW HILLS PROV. PARK
PRINCE ALBERT NAT. PARK
GRASS RIVER PROV. PARK
OPASQUIA PROV. PARK
ATIKAKI PROV. WILDERNESS PARK
WOODLAND CARIBOU PROV. PARK
NOPIMING PROV. PARK
WHITESHELL PROV. PARK
RIDING MOUNTAIN NAT. PARK
DUCK MT. PROV. PARK
MOOSE MT. PROV. PARK
GRASSLANDS NAT. PARK
CYPRESS HILLS PROV. PARK
QUETICO PROV. PARK
VOYAGEURS NAT. PARK
Churchill
Thompson
The Pas
Flin Flon
Prince Albert
Saskatoon
Regina
Moose Jaw
Swift Current
Medicine Hat
Yorkton
Brandon
Winnipeg
Lloydminster
North Battleford
Grand Forks
Minot
Williston
Duluth
Kenora
Dryden
Fort Frances
International Falls
Bemidji
COPYRIGHT PHILIP S

72

82

1:7 000 000

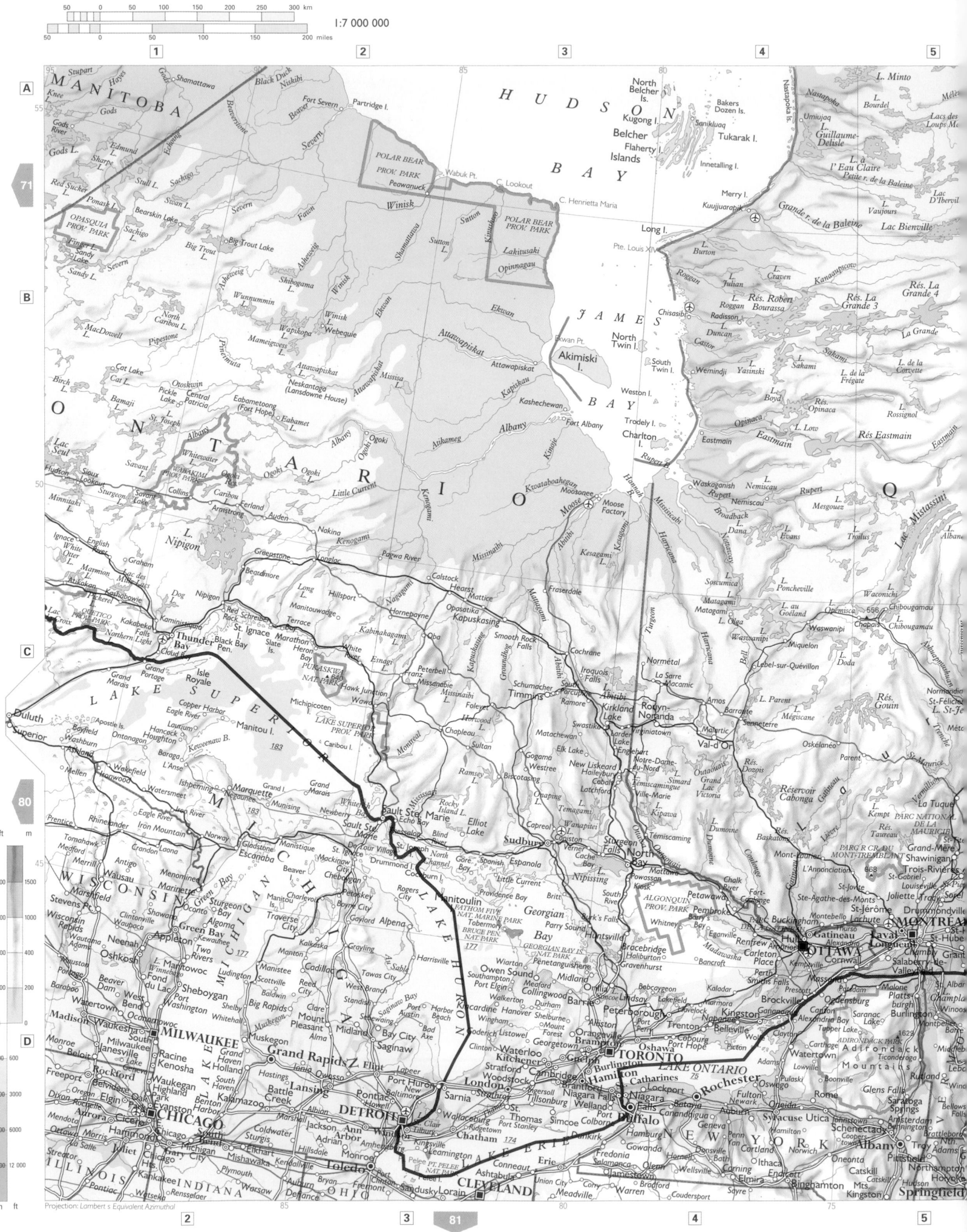

69

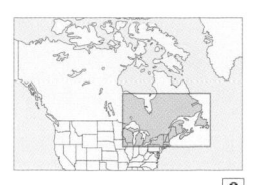

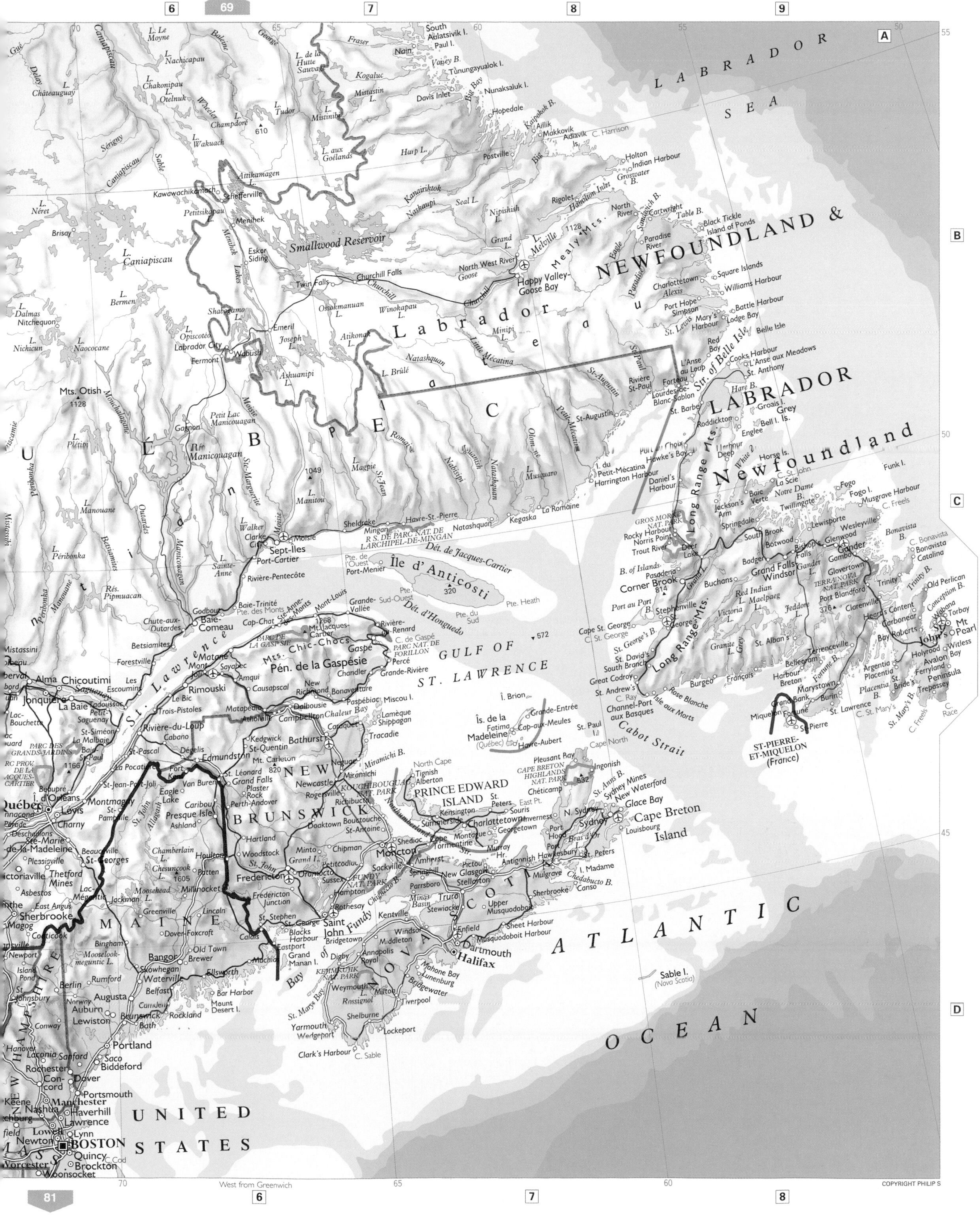
6
7
8
9
A
B
C
D
LABRADOR SEA
NEWFOUNDLAND & LABRADOR
Labrador
Newfoundland
QUÉBEC
Smallwood Reservoir
Churchill Falls
Happy Valley-Goose Bay
Mealy Mts.
Nain
Hopedale
Makkovik
Postville
Cartwright
Labrador City
Fermont
Schefferville
Sept-Îles
Port-Cartier
Baie-Comeau
Île d'Anticosti
GULF OF ST. LAWRENCE
Pén. de la Gaspésie
Gaspé
Rimouski
Rivière-du-Loup
Chicoutimi
Jonquière
Québec
Lévis
Sherbrooke
St. Lawrence
Strait of Belle Isle
Long Range Mts.
Corner Brook
Stephenville
Grand Falls-Windsor
Gander
St. John's
Avalon Peninsula
Channel-Port aux Basques
Cabot Strait
ST-PIERRE-ET-MIQUELON (France)
Îs. de la Madeleine (Québec)
PRINCE EDWARD ISLAND
Charlottetown
Summerside
NEW BRUNSWICK
Fredericton
Moncton
Saint John
Bathurst
Edmundston
NOVA SCOTIA
Halifax
Dartmouth
Truro
Yarmouth
Bay of Fundy
Cape Breton Island
Sydney
Glace Bay
Sable I. (Nova Scotia)
ATLANTIC OCEAN
MAINE
Bangor
Augusta
Portland
Manchester
BOSTON
UNITED STATES
West from Greenwich
70
65
60
55
50
45
COPYRIGHT PHILIP S

81

100 0 100 200 300 400 500 km

1:15 000 000

100 0 50 100 150 200 250 300 350 miles

11 **12** **13** **14** **16** 68 **17**

PACIFIC OCEAN

G

40

Anchorage 3363 miles 5412 km Washington D.C.

2010 miles 3234 km

2438 miles 3923 km

H

2785 miles 4482 km

San Francisco

35

2395 miles 3854 km Honolulu Tropic of Cancer

J

30

K

West from Greenwich

135 130 125 120

ALASKA on same scale

RUSSIA

ARCTIC OCEAN

CHUKCHI SEA

C Koryakskoye Nagor'ye

D Bering Strait

BERING SEA

E

Aleutian Islands

Gulf of Alaska

Projection: Albers' Equal Area with two standard parallels

4 **5** **6** **7** **8** **9** **10** **11** **12**

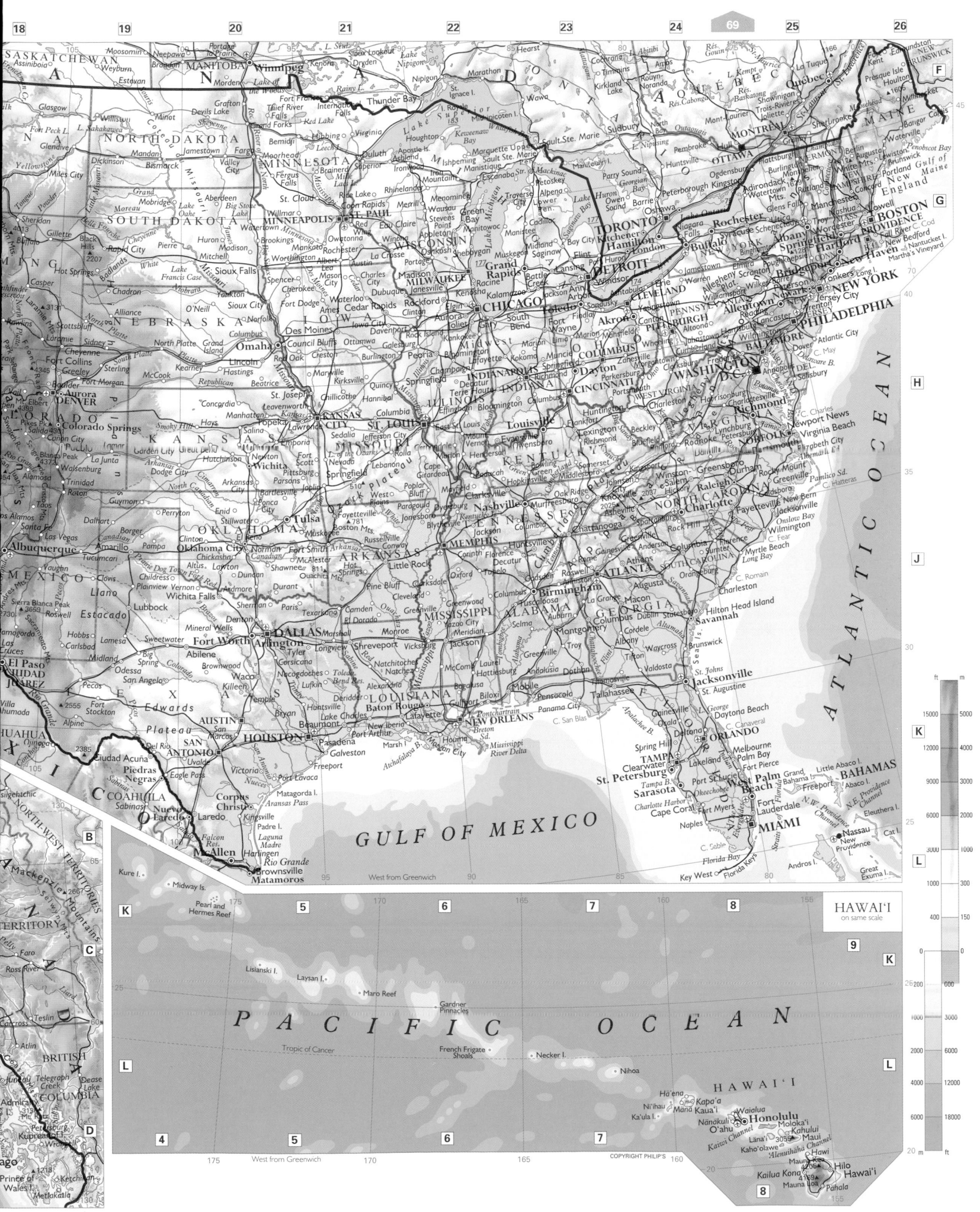

HAWAI'I
on same scale

GULF OF MEXICO

PACIFIC OCEAN

ATLANTIC OCEAN

COPYRIGHT PHILIP'S

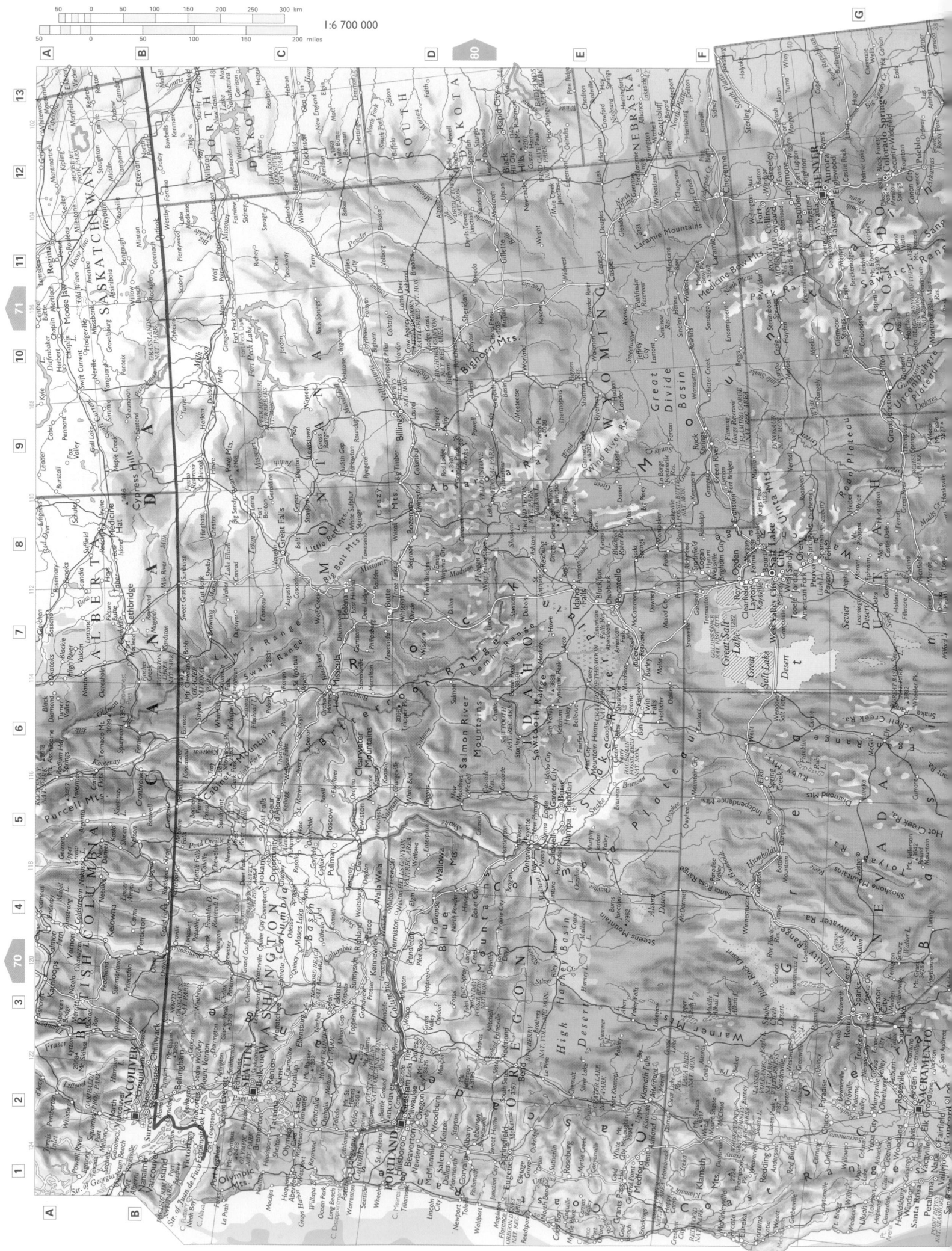

COPYRIGHT PHILIP'S

Lava fields

Projection: Albers' Equal Area with two standard parallels

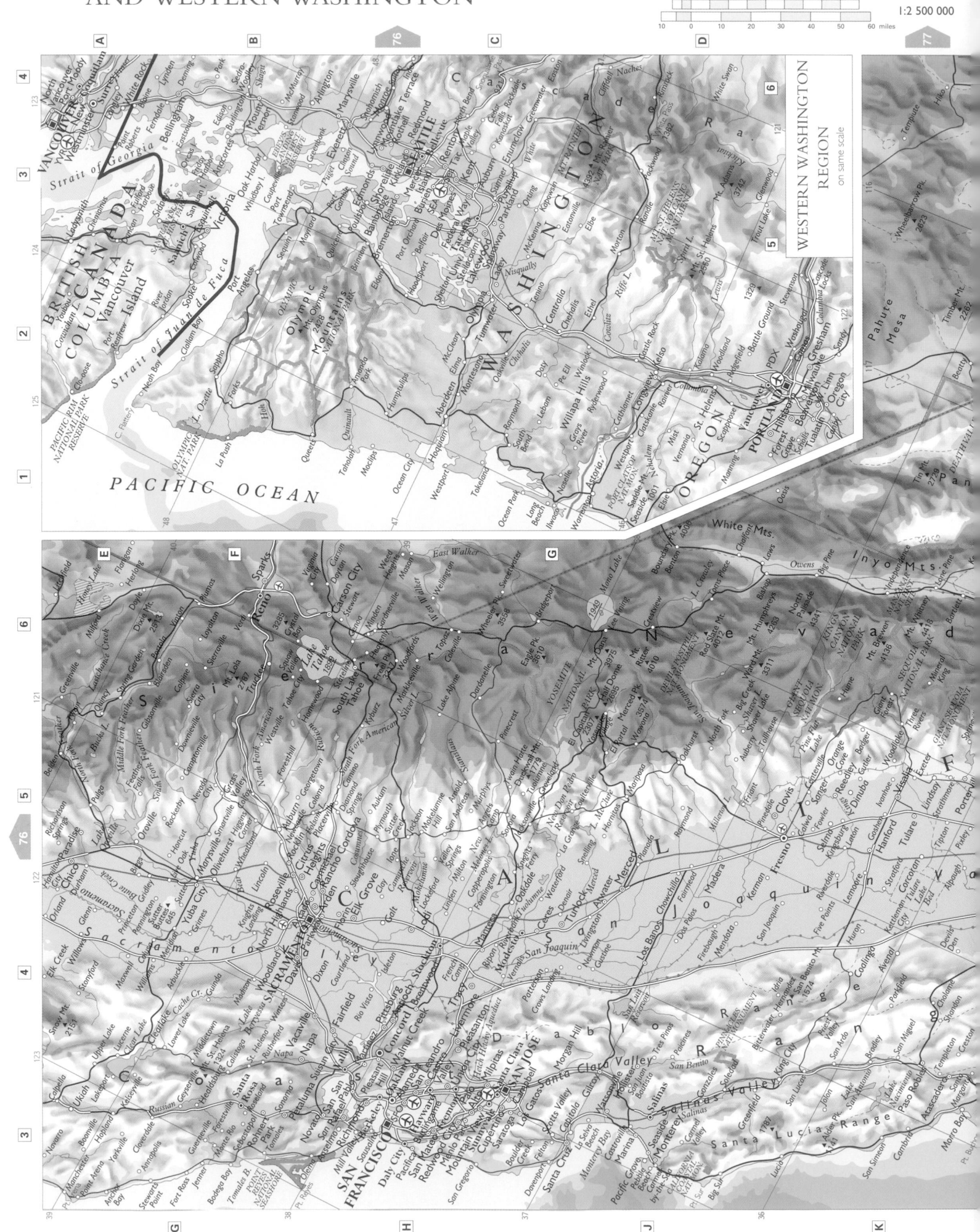

WESTERN WASHINGTON REGION
on same scale

1:2 500 000

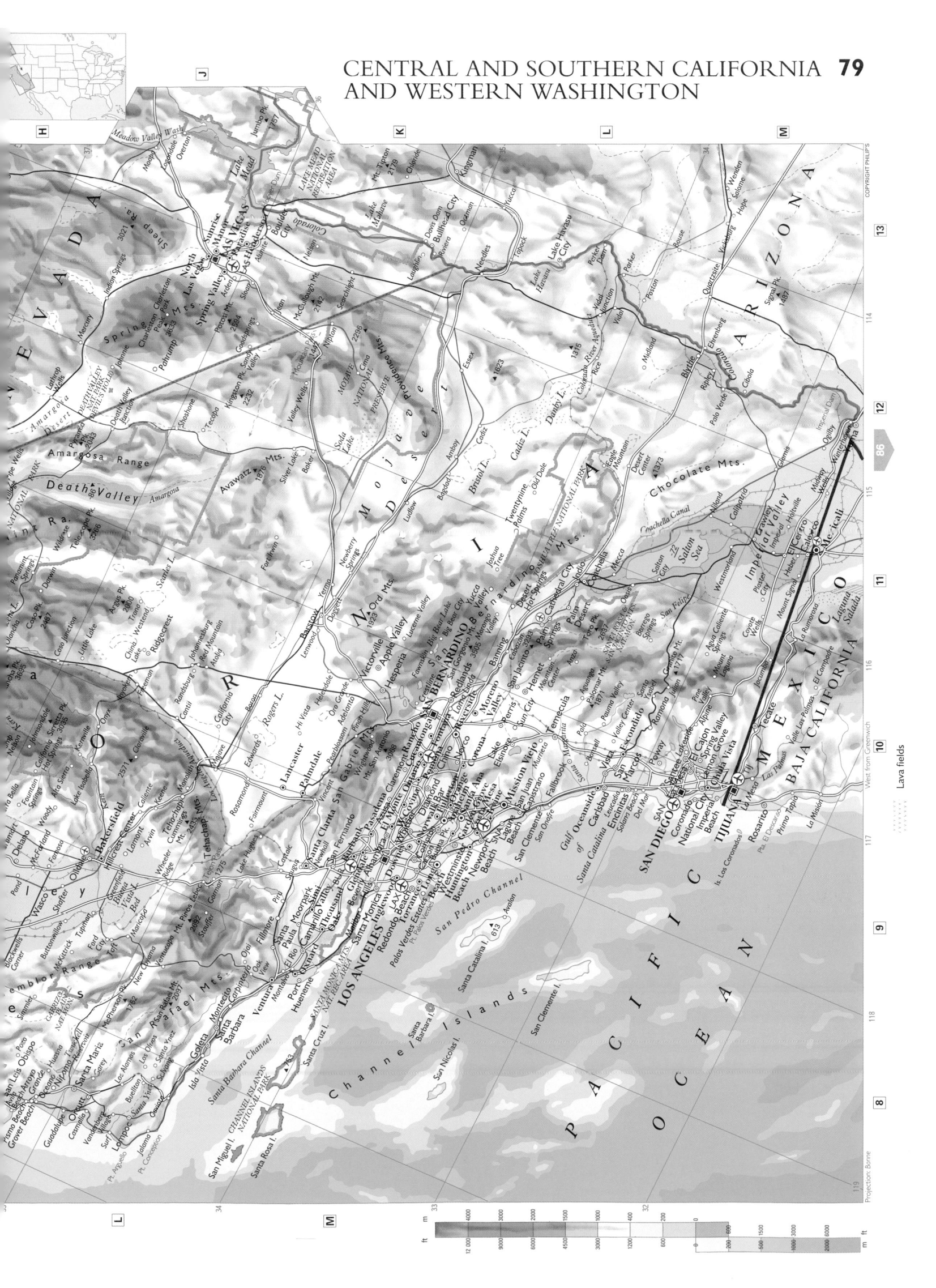

Lava fields

1:6 700 000

Projection: Albers' Equal Area with two standard parallels

West from Greenwich

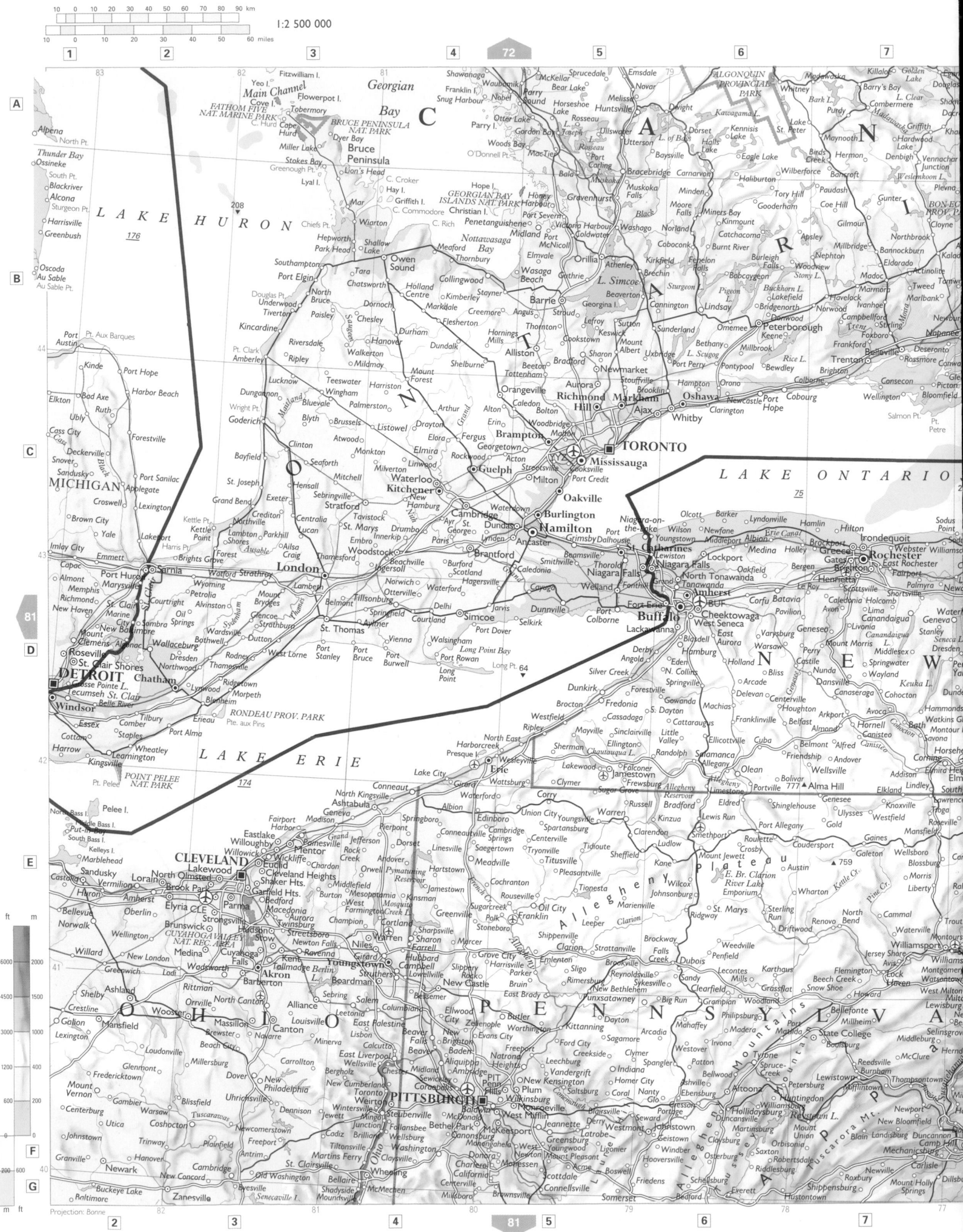

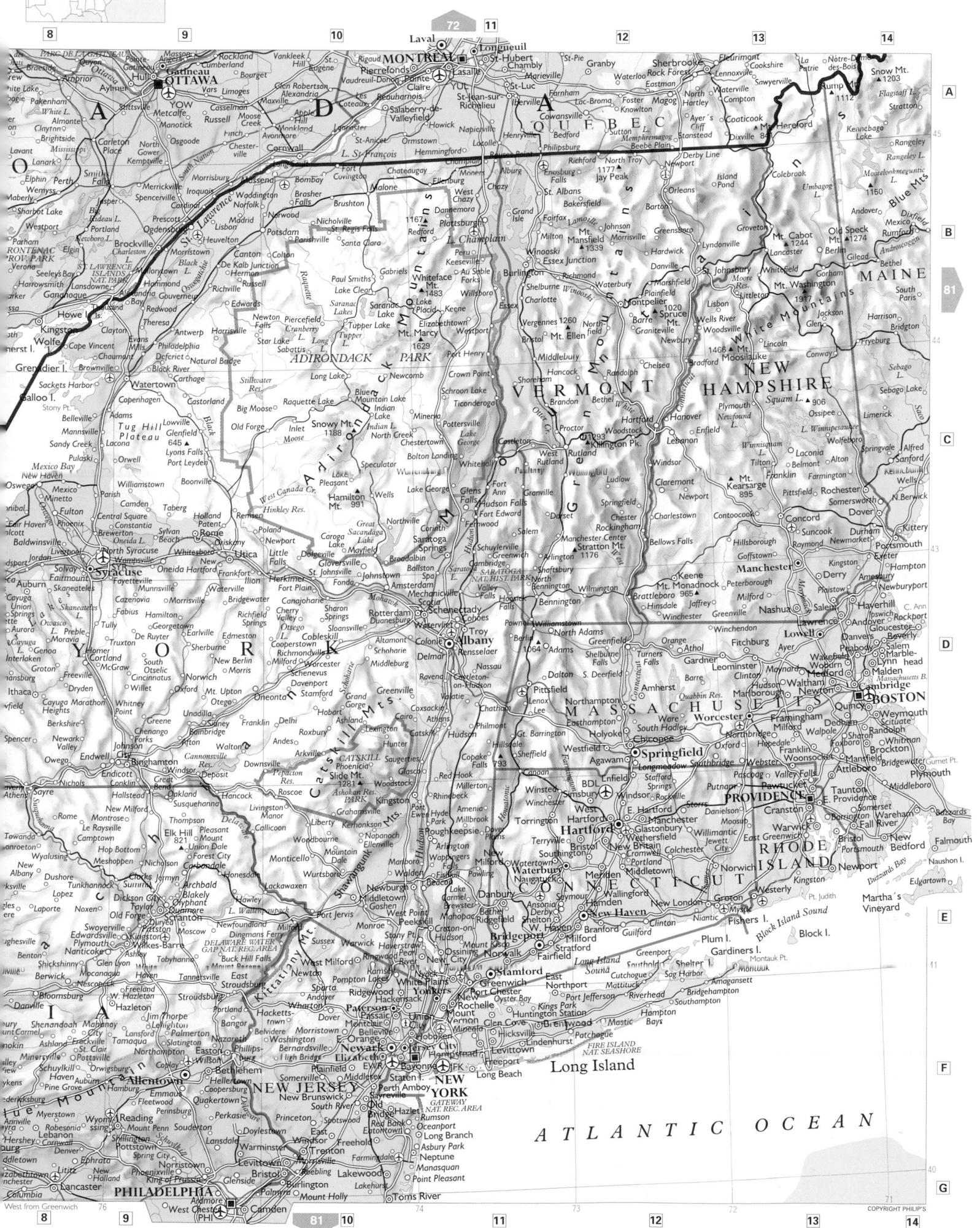

COPYRIGHT PHILIP'S

1:6 700 000

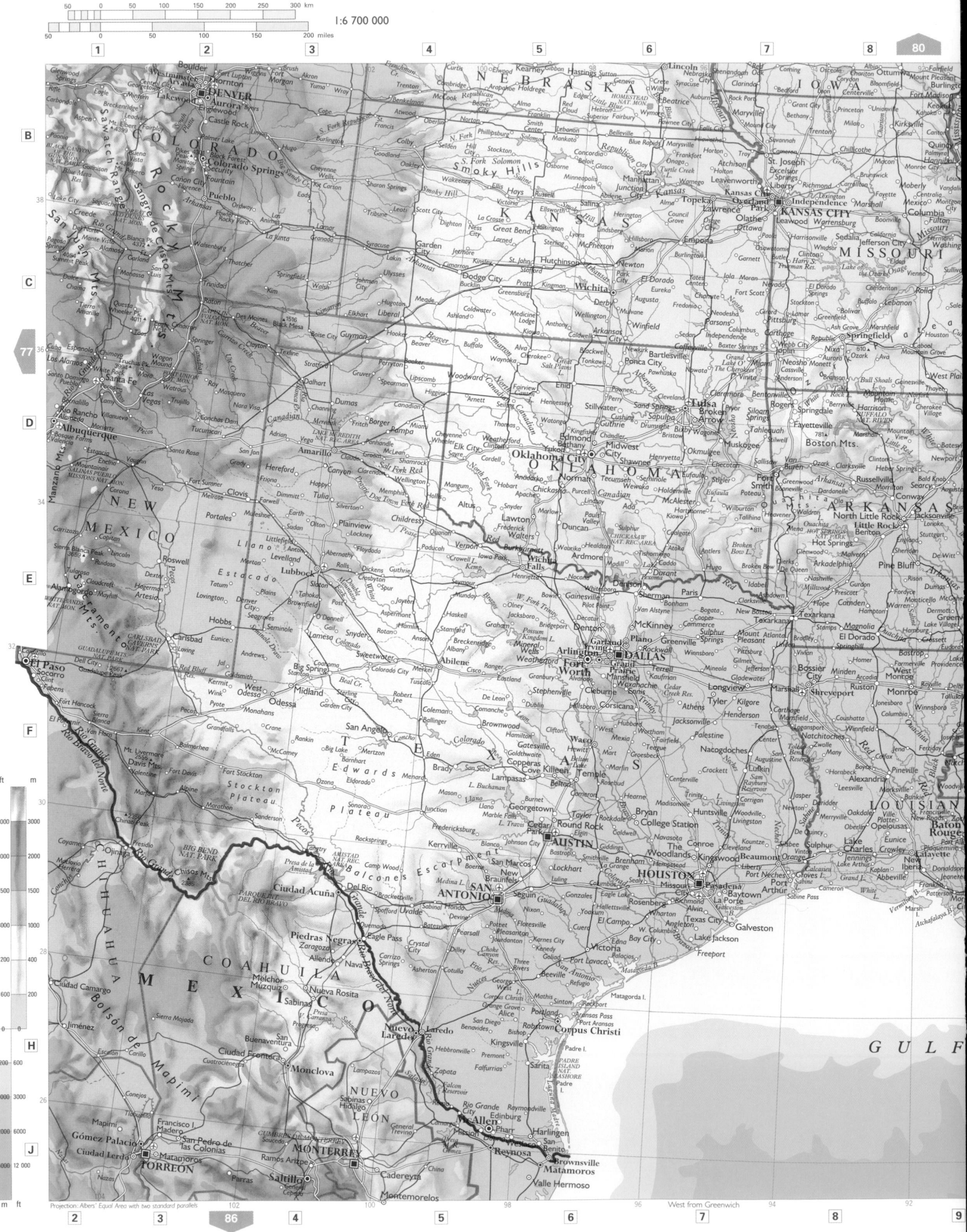

1:8 000 000

State names in Central Mexico

1 DISTRITO FEDERAL   3 GUANAJUATO   5 MÉXICO   7 QUERÉTARO
2 AGUASCALIENTES   4 HIDALGO   6 MORELOS   8 TLAXCALA

Projection: Bi-polar oblique Conical Orthomorphic

West from Greenwich

PUERTO RICO d
1:3 000 000
10   0   10 20 30 40 50 km
10   0   10   20   30 miles

VIRGIN ISLANDS e
1:2 000 000
10   0   10   20   30 km
10   0   10   20 miles

ST. LUCIA f
1:1 000 000
5   0   10 km
5   0   5   10 miles

BARBADOS g
1:1 000 000
5   0   10 km
5   0   5   10 miles

PUERTO RICO (U.S.A.)

ATLANTIC OCEAN
Pta. Aguijereada
Isabela
Aguadilla
Arecibo
Barceloneta
Manatí
Vega Baja
Bayamón
SAN JUAN
SJU
Río Grande
San Sebastián
Utuado
Carolina
Sierra de Luquillo
Dewey
Fajardo
Pta. Puerca
Culebra
Mayagüez
Adjuntas
Caguas
Naguabo
San Germán
Cordillera Central
Mts. de Uroyán
Yauco
Cerro de Punta 1338
Cayey
Humacao
Yabucoa
Esperanza
Vieques
Guánica
Ponce
Coamo
Guayama
Pta. Aguila
I. Caja de Muertos

VIRGIN ISLANDS (U.K.)

Rufling Pt.
The Settlement
Anegada
East Pt.
Great Camanoe
Jost Van Dyke I.
Guana I.
Virgin Gorda
Tortola
Beef I.
Spanish Town
Hans Lollik I.
Road Town
Cruz Bay
Peter I.
Charlotte Amalie
St. John I.
St. Thomas I.
Virgin Is. (U.S.A.)

ST. LUCIA

Cap Point
Pte. Hardy
Esperance Bay
Gros Islet
Marquis
Castries
Girard
Anse la Raye
Dennery
Canaries
Millet
Soufrière
Trou Gras Pt.
Mt. Gimie 950
Soufrière Bay
Petit Piton 750
Micoud
Gros Piton 796
Vierge Pt.
Gros Piton Pt.
Choiseul
ST. LUCIA
Laborie
Vieux Fort
C. Moule à Chique

BARBADOS

ATLANTIC OCEAN
Crab Hill
North Point
Spring Hall
Fustic
Boscobelle
Portland
245 Belleplaine
Speightstown
BARBADOS
Westmoreland
Mt. Hillaby 340
Hillcrest
Alleynes Bay
Martin's Bay
Holetown
Massiah Street
Jackson
Bridgefield
Bridgetown
Six Cross Roads
Black Rock
Ellerton
The Crane
Bridgetown
Edey
St. Martins
Carlisle Bay
Oistins
Oistins Bay
Chancery Lane
Worthing
BGI
South Point

Main map

ATLANTIC OCEAN
BAHAMAS
Arthur's Town
New Bight
Cat I.
San Salvador I.
Conception I.
Rum Cay
Tropic of Cancer
Long I.
Clarence Town
Samana Cay
Crooked I. Passage
Crooked I.
Plana Cays
Albert Town
Acklins I.
Snug Corner
Mayaguana I.
Cay Verde
Mira por vos Cay
Turks & Caicos Is. (U.K.)
Hogsty Reef
Caicos Passage
Caicos Is.
Little Inagua I.
Cockburn Town
Cay Santo Domingo
INAGUA
Lake Rose
Turks Is.
Great Inagua I.
Matthew Town
Mouchoir Bank
Silver Bank
Navidad Bank
Silver Bank Passage
Guantánamo
Puerto Rico Trench
Baracoa
Î. de la Tortue
Cap-Haïtien
Monte Cristi
Milwaukee Deep 9200
Maisí
Port-de-Paix
Puerto Plata
Santiago de los Caballeros
San Francisco de Macorís
GUANTÁNAMO BAY (U.S.A.)
Paso de los Vientos (Windward Passage)
Jean Rabel
Fort Liberté
La Vega
Nagua
Samaná
Cap-à-Foux
Gonaïves
Hinche
La Isabela
Sabana de la Mar
Bayamón
SAN JUAN
Virgin Gorda
Anegada
Jérémie
St.-Marc
Pico Duarte 3175
Hato Mayor
C. Engaño
Aguadilla
Arecibo
Carolina
Virgin Is.
Sombrero (U.K.)
Dame Marie
HAITI
DOMINICAN REP.
San Juan
San Pedro de Macorís
Higüey
Mayagüez
Ponce
Fajardo
St. Thomas
Road Town
Anguilla (U.K.)
Massif de la Hotte
PORT-AU-PRINCE
L. Enriquillo
SANTO DOMINGO
La Romana
Caguas
Charlotte Amalie
St.-Martin (Fr.)
Les Cayes
Aquín
Petit Goâve
Jacmel
Baní
San Cristóbal
Isla Saona
Mona Passage
PUERTO RICO (U.S.A.)
Guayama
Vieques
Virgin Is. (U.S.A.)
St. Maarten
St.-Barthélemy (Fr.)
Pointe-à-Gravois
Î. à Vache
Pedernales
Barahona
Azua de Compostela
Isla Mona
Christiansted
Saba (Neth.)
ANTIGUA & BARBUDA
Hispaniola
Frederiksted
St. Croix (U.S.A.)
St. Eustatius (Neth.)
Mt. Liamuiga 1156
ST. KITTS & NEVIS
St. John's
Antigua
Antilles
Basseterre
Nevis
Redonda (U.K.)
Montserrat
Hills 914
Guadeloupe Passage
Ste.-Rose
Le Moule
La Désirade
Beata Ridge
GUADELOUPE (Fr.)
1467
Pointe-à-Pitre
Marie-Galante (Fr.)
Basse-Terre
Grand-Bourg
Î. des Saintes (Fr.)
Dominica Passage
Venezuelan
Portsmouth 1447
DOMINICA
Roseau
MORNE TROIS PITONS
Basin
Diablotin
Martinique Passage
I. de Aves (Venezuela)
Mt. Pelée 1397
Ste.-Marie
CARIBBEAN SEA
Fort-de-France
Le François
Rivière-Pilote
MARTINIQUE
St. Lucia Channel (Fr.)
Castries
ST. LUCIA
Soufrière
Basin
St. Vincent Passage
Aves Ridge
Soufrière 1234
St. Vincent
Speightstown 340
Kingstown
BARBADOS
Bridgetown
Lesser Antilles
Bequia
ST. VINCENT & THE GRENADINES
ABC Lesser Islands
Canouan
The Grenadines
Pta. Gallinas
Oranjestad
Aruba (Neth.)
Curaçao
Bonaire
Carriacou
Willemstad
NETH. ANTILLES
ARC. LOS ROQUES
St. George's 840
GRENADA
COLOMBIA
Pen. de la Guajira
Pta. Espada
Paraguaná
Is. Las Aves
I. Blanquilla (Ven.)
Tobago
Punto Fijo
Is. Los Roques (Ven.)
I. Orchila (Ven.)
Is. Los Hermanos
Is. Los Testigos (Ven.)
Scarborough
ARRAN-QUILLA
Santa Marta
Ríohacha
Uribia
Golfo de Venezuela
MÉDANOS DE CORO
Puerto Cumarebo
NUEVA ESPARTA
I. de Margarita
Port of Spain
Galera Pt.
Barranoa
GUAJIRA
Punta Cardón
La Vela
CUEVA DE LA QUEBRADA EL TORO
La Asunción
Porlamar
Arima
Trinidad
TAYRONA
SA. NEVADA DE STA. MARTA
San Rafael
FALCÓN
Maracay
La Guaira
CARACAS
VARGAS
I. La Tortuga (Ven.)
Pen. de Paria
Río Claro
ISLA DE SALAMANCA
Cabimas
Mene de Mauroa
Baragua
Puerto Cabello
Güiria
TRINIDAD & TOBAGO
Ciénaga
Sierra Nevada de Santa Marta 5775
MARACAIBO
La Concepción
Altagracia
MIRANDA
Higuerote
Cumaná
Carúpano
G. de Paria
San Fernando
Serpent's Mouth
Fundación
Pta. Rita
LARA
Carora
Puerto La Cruz
SUCRE
Cariaco
MAGDALENA
Ciudad Ojeda
Lago de Maracaibo
BARQUISIMETO
VALENCIA
Villa de Cura
San Juan de los Morros
Barcelona
Maturín
MONAGAS
Valledupar
Agustín Codazzi
ZULIA
Machiques
Mene Grande
YARACUY
CARABOBO
Aragua de Barcelona
Anaco
DELTA
El Carmen
CÉSAR
CIÉNAGAS DEL CATATUMBO
Betijoque
Trujillo
El Tocuyo
San Carlos
Valle de la Pascua
El Tigre
ANZOÁTEGUI
AMACURO
Calamar
Perijá
San Carlos del Zulia
Acarigua
COJEDES
Tucupita
Plato
CATATUMBO-BARI
Valera
Guanare
Portuguesa
GUÁRICO
Calabozo
Santa María de Ipire
Zambrano
PORTUGUESA
El Báúl
Los Barrancos
Mompós
MÉRIDA
Ciudad Bolivia
BARINAS
El Sombrero
Magdalena
Ciudad Guayana
Magangué
SA. NEVADA
Barinas
San Fernando de Apure
Sierra Imataca
El Barco
Libertad
Majagual
SANTANDER
Cord. de Mérida
San Fernando de Atabapo
BOLÍVAR
BARINAS
Ciudad Bolívar
Ocaña
Bruzual
Apure
El Pao
Simití
Cúcuta
TÁCHIRA
VENEZUELA
Achaguas
Caicara
Mapire
Orinoco
El Callao
Tumeremo
Guasipati
Upata
Embalse de Guri

Jamaica Channel
Navassa I. (U.S.A.)
C. Carcasse
Î. de la Gonâve
Antilles
Leeward Islands
Windward Islands

West from Greenwich
COPYRIGHT PHILIP'S

4000 3000 2000 1500 1000 400 200 0
600 6000 12 000 18 000 24 000 ft
12 000 9000 6000 4500 3000 1200 600 0
200 2000 4000 6000 8000 m

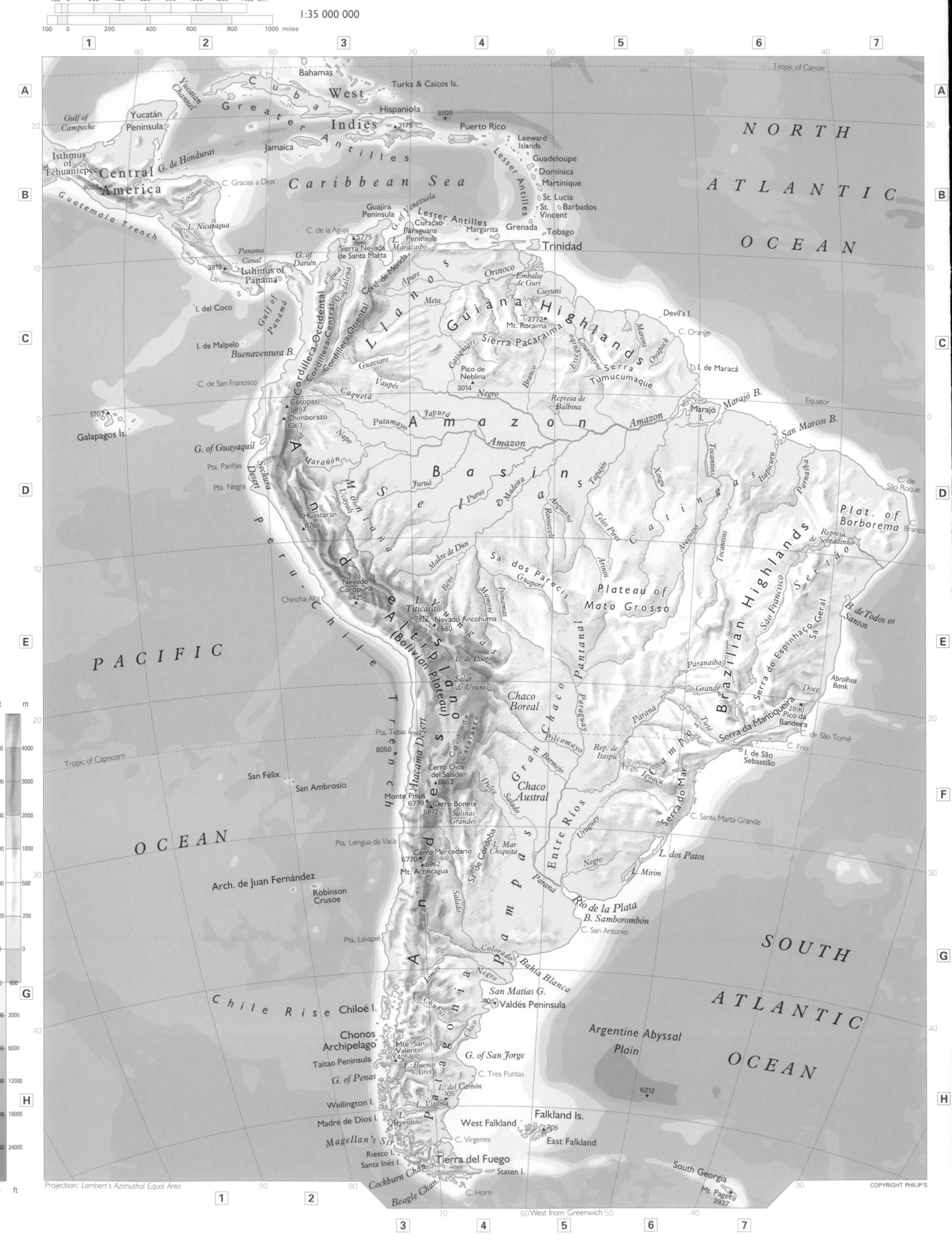

1:35 000 000

100 0 200 400 600 800 1000 1200 1400 km
100 0 200 400 600 800 1000 miles

Projection: Lambert's Azimuthal Equal Area

COPYRIGHT PHILIP'S

1:35 000 000

Projection: Lambert's Azimuthal Equal Area

COPYRIGHT PHILIP'S

■ LIMA Capital Cities

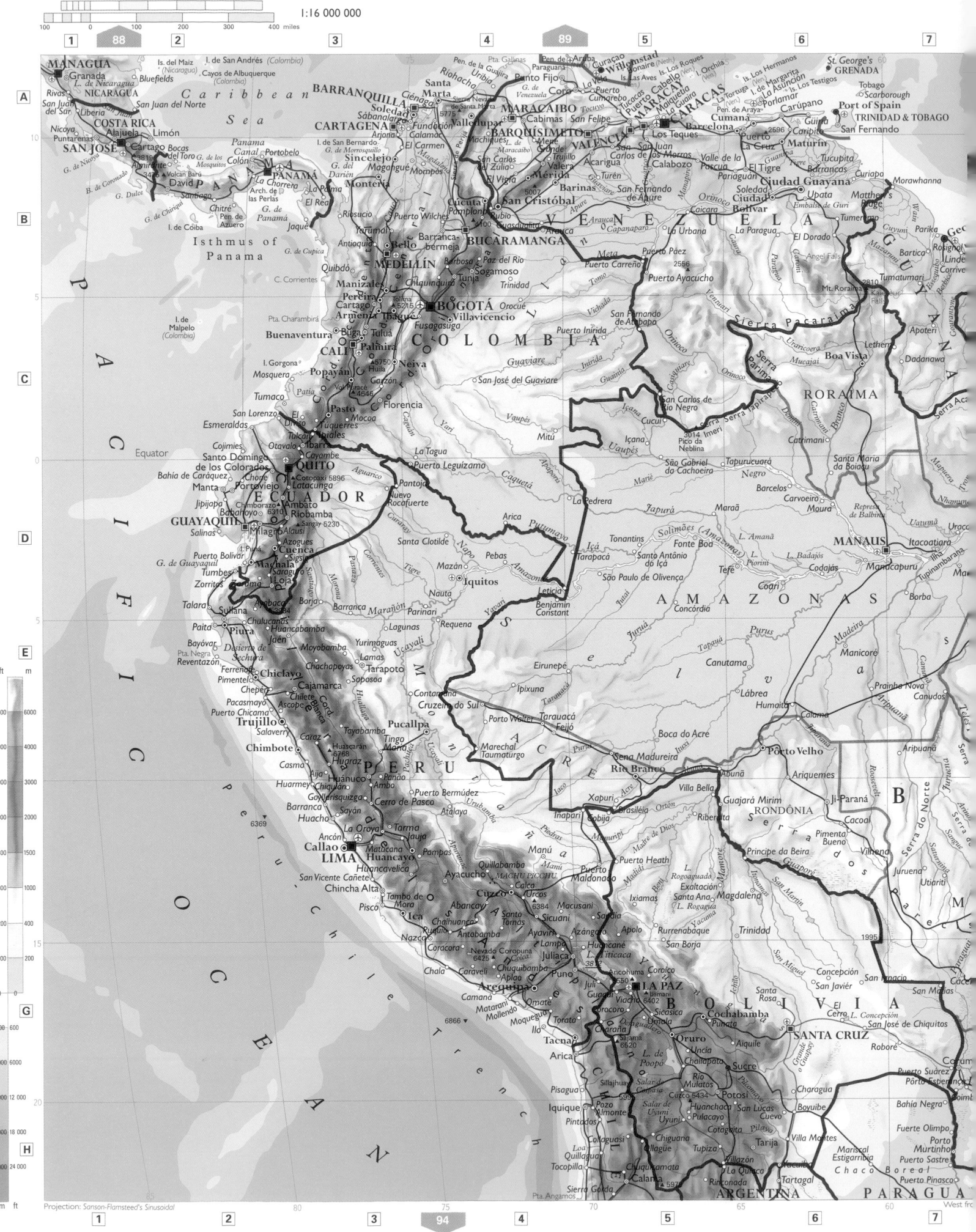

TRINIDAD AND TOBAGO
1:2 500 000

ATLANTIC

OCEAN

Tobago
Charlotteville
Castara 565 Little
Plymouth Main Ridge Tobago Roxborough
Buccoo Reef Scarborough
Crown Pt. Rocky Bay

ATLANTIC OCEAN

North Pt.

VENEZUELA
Pen. de Paria
Macuro
Güiria

Corozal Pt.
Monos Maraval
Port of Spain
San Juan
Chaguanas

Blanchisseuse
La Vache Pt.
Maracas Bay
Village
Chupara Pt.
Sans Souci
Northern Range
936 Tunapuna
Valencia Matura
Arima Bay
Caroni Sangre Grande
Talparo Upper Manzanilla
Couva Narwa Cocos
Swamp Bay
Point Lisas
Otaheite Bay Rio Claro
Gasparillo Guatuaro Pt.
Toco Galera Pt.
Redhead
Salybia

Trinidad

Golfo de Paria

San Fernando
Brighton La Brea
Guapo Bay Pitch
Point Fortin Lake
Cedros Bay Palo Seco
Bonasse Erin Pt.
Icacos Pt.

Princes Town
Penal
Siparia 304 Trinity
La Lune Hills
Moruga

Pierreville
Mayaro Bay
Basse Terre Guayaguayare
Galeota Pt.

Serpent's Mouth Pta. Bombedor

West from Greenwich

VENEZUELA

ATLANTIC

OCEAN

own
Amsterdam
uw Nickerie
Totness Paramaribo Nieuw Amsterdam
akoegron Albina
SURINAME Moengo St-Laurent du Maroni
1230 Sinnamary
FRENCH Kourou
GUIANA Cayenne
Kaw Approuague
St-Georges
Oiapoque
Camopi

Serra Tumucumaque

AMAPÁ
Merirumã
Macapá
Mazagão
I. Caviana
I. Mexiana
C. Maguarinho
Chaves
Afuá Curuçá Salinópolis
I. de Marajó Vigia
Breves BELÉM
Marajó Castanhal Bragança
Viseu

Equator

São Pedro & São Paulo (Braz.)

Óbidos Monte Almeirim
Alenquer Alegre Prainha
Juruti Porto de Moz
Santarém Gurupá
Belterra Breves
Brasília Legal
Altamira
Itaituba

PARÁ
Baião
Cametá
Tucuruí

Represa de Tucuruí

Acailândia
Maraba
São João do Araguaia
Carajás
Tocantinópolis

I. Grande de Gurupá

Abaetetuba
Curralinho

Cururupu
Turiaçu
Pinheiro Viana
Rosário São Luís
Itapecuru-Mirim
Santa Inês
Codó
Pedreiras
Bacabal

Alcântara
Barreirinhas
Luís Correia
Parnaíba
Tutóia
Granja
Camocim
Sobral
Itapipoca
Caucaia
FORTALEZA
Cascavel

Rocas

Fernando de Noronha (Braz.)

Caxias
Campo Maior
Piripiri
Teresina
Senador Pompeu
Crateús
Quixadá
Ipu
Maranguape
Baturité
Russas
Aracati
Areia Branca
Macau
Ceará-Mirim

MARANHÃO
Imperatriz
Barra do Corda
Colinas

CEARÁ

RIO GRANDE
DO NORTE NATAL
Mossoró
Caraúbas

Canguaretama
Mamanguape
Cabedelo

Floriano
Oeiras
Picos
Valença do Piauí
Nova Iorque
Riachão
Carolina
Estreito
Porto Franco

PIAUÍ
Uruçuí
São João do Piauí

Chapada do Araripe
Iguatu
Cajazeiras
Juazeiro do Norte
Crato
Salgueiro
Ouricuri
Paulistana

PARAÍBA
Patos Currais Novos
Campina Grande
João Pessoa
Caruaru
Olinda
RECIFE
Jaboatão

Serra dos Dois Irmãos
São João do Piauí
Remanso
Casa Nova
Juazeiro
Petrolina

PERNAMBUCO
Garanhuns
Palmares
Rio Largo
Rio de Santo Antão

Santa Filomena
Parnaguá
Barra

Palmas
Porto Nacional

TOCANTINS

Caracol
São Francisco
Xique-Xique
Barreiras
Ibotirama
Santa Maria da Vitória
Posse
Carinhanha

Paulo Afonso
Senhor do Bonfim
Jacobina
Mundo Novo
Queimadas
Serrinha

6059

Pesqueira
Arcoverde
Propriá
Penedo
Capela
São Cristóvão
Aracaju
Estância

SERGIPE
ALAGOAS
MACEIÓ
Palmeira dos Indios
Arapiraca

BAHIA
Feira de Santana
Alagoinhas
Santo Amaro
Cachoeira
Castro Alves
Nazaré
Valença
SALVADOR
B. de Todos os Santos

TO GROSSO

Planalto do

MATO GROSSO
Diamantino
Cuiabá Mato Grosso
Santo Antônio
Rondonópolis
Coxim

DO SUL
Aquidauana
Miranda

Campo Grande

Barra do Garças
Aruanã
Niquelândia
1678

Uruaçu
Campos Belos
São Domingos
Carinhanha

Januária
Monte Azul
Salinas
Pirapora

Brumado
Condeúba
Vitória da Conquista
Itapetinga
Itaberaba
Jequié
Ubaitaba
Ilhéus
Canavieiras

Belmonte
Porto Seguro
Prado

Banco dos
Abrolhos

27

Trindade (Braz.)

GOIÁS
Goiás
Anápolis
GOIÂNIA
Jataí
Rio Verde
Itumbiara
Quirinópolis

DIST. FED.
BRASÍLIA
Luziânia
Formosa
Cristalina

Paracatu
Unaí
Patos de Minas

MINAS GERAIS
Montes Claros
Araçuaí
Teófilo Otoni
Nanuque
Mucuri

Conceição da Barra
São Mateus

Paranaíba
Ituiutaba
Uberlândia
Araguari
Patrocínio
Ibiá
Araxá
Uberaba
Frutal
Prata
Ituiutaba

Curvelo
Diamantina
Itabira
Itabira
Governador Valadares
Ipatinga
Colatina
Linhares

ESPÍRITO SANTO

Sabará
BELO HORIZONTE
Ouro Prêto
Cariacica
VITÓRIA
Vila Velha

Campo Grande
Santa Fé do Sul
Três Lagoas
Andradina
Araçatuba
Presidente Prudente
Presidente Epitácio
Penápolis
Marília

Ribeirão Prêto
Franca
Barretos
Poços de Caldas
Guaxupé

São João del Rei
Barbacena
Juiz de Fora
Conselheiro Lafaiete
Divinópolis
Ponte Nova

Cachoeiro de Itapemirim
Campos

Dourados
Ponta Porã
Pedro Juan Caballero

Bauru
Jaú
Piracicaba
Limeira
Botucatu
Assis
São Carlos
Araraquara

SÃO PAULO
CAMPINAS
Volta Redonda
Petrópolis
Nova Friburgo
Três Rios
São Lourenço
Caldas

RIO DE JANEIRO
Niterói
Cabo Frio

55 50 45 40 35 30

COPYRIGHT PHILIP'S

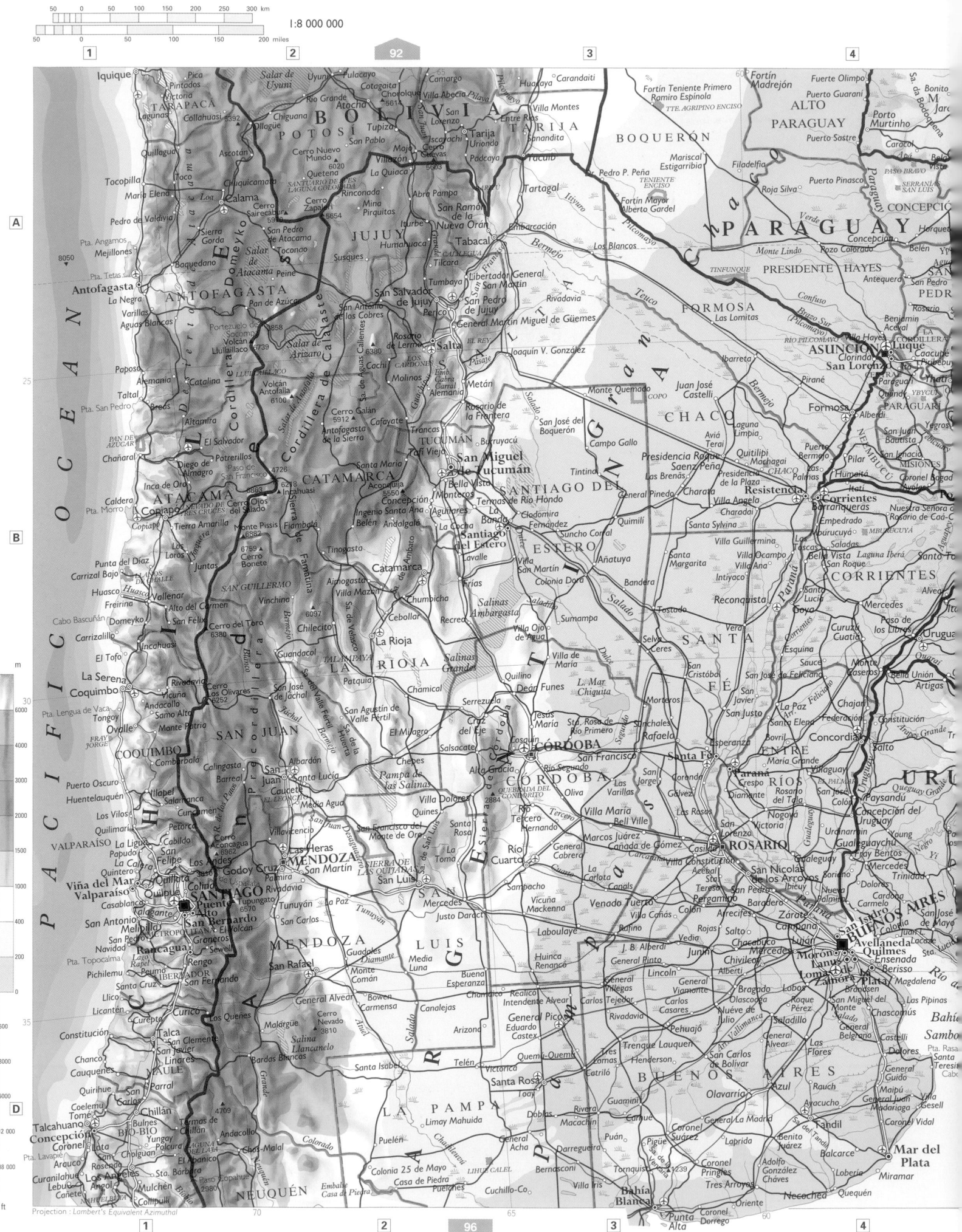

1:8 000 000

Projection : Lambert's Equivalent Azimuthal

1:16 000 000

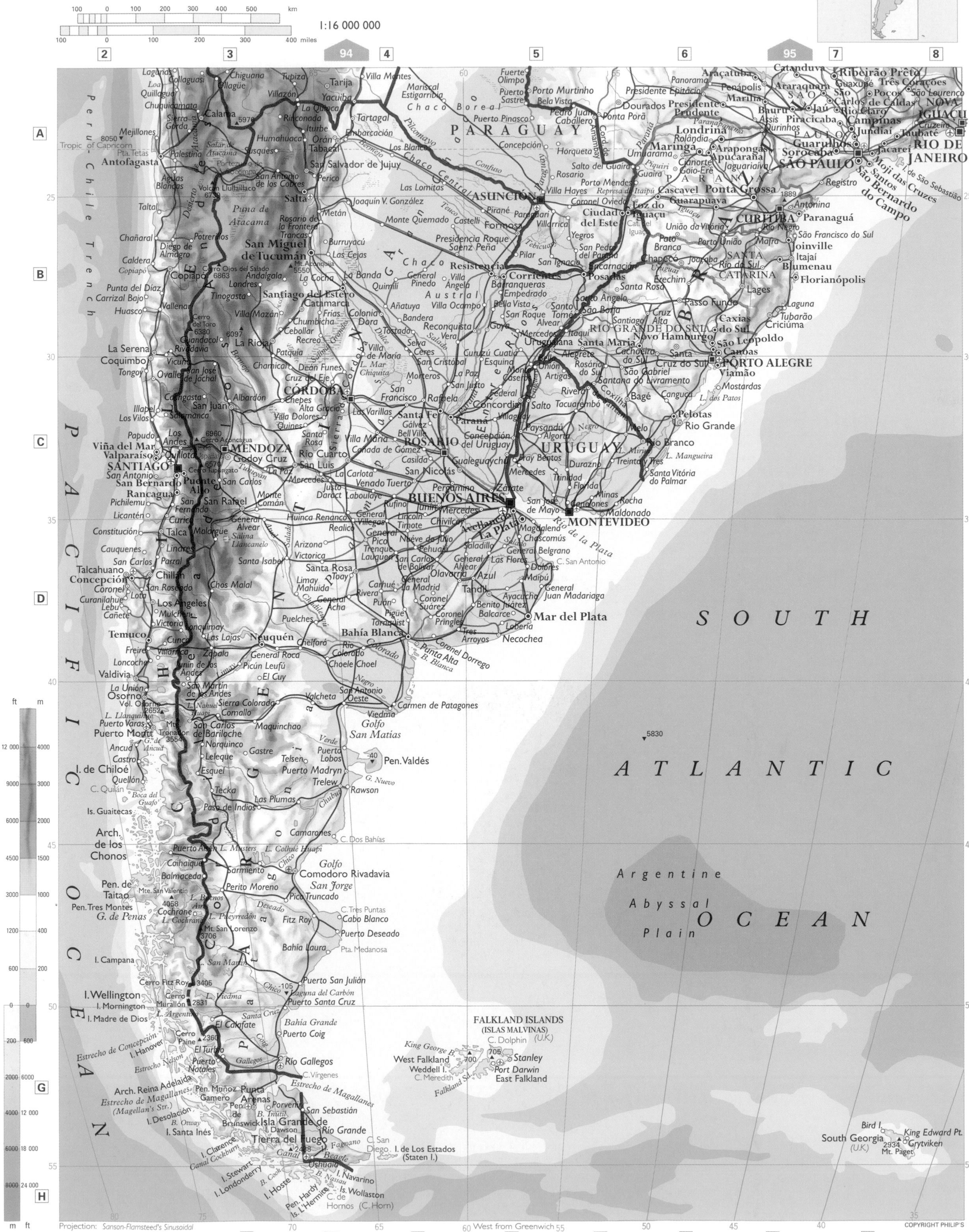

100   0   100   200   300   400   500 km
100   0   100   200   300   400 miles

2   3   94   4   5   6   95   7   8

ft   m
12 000   4000
9000   3000
6000   2000
4500   1500
3000   1000
1200   400
600   200
0   0
600   2000
2000   6000
4000   12 000
6000   18 000
8000   24 000
m   ft

PARAGUAY

Chaco Boreal

Chaco Central

ASUNCIÓN

Antofagasta
Tropic of Capricorn
Calama
Chuquicamata
Mejillones
Taltal
Chañaral
Caldera
Copiapó
Huasco
Vallenar
La Serena
Coquimbo
Ovalle
Illapel
Los Vilos
Valparaíso
Viña del Mar
SANTIAGO
San Antonio
San Bernardo
Rancagua
Talca
Linares
Chillán
Concepción
Talcahuano
Los Ángeles
Temuco
Valdivia
Osorno
Puerto Montt
I. de Chiloé
Castro

San Miguel de Tucumán
Salta
San Salvador de Jujuy
Santiago del Estero
Catamarca
La Rioja
San Juan
CÓRDOBA
MENDOZA
San Luis
Río Cuarto
San Rafael
Neuquén
Santa Rosa
Bahía Blanca

ROSARIO
Santa Fe
Paraná
BUENOS AIRES
La Plata
Mar del Plata

URUGUAY
MONTEVIDEO
Durazno
Melo
Rivera
Paysandú
Salto
Rio Grande
Pelotas

PORTO ALEGRE
Novo Hamburgo
São Leopoldo
Canoas
Viamão
Caxias do Sul
Criciúma
Tubarão
Laguna
Florianópolis
Blumenau
Itajaí
Joinville
CURITIBA
Paranaguá
Ponta Grossa
Foz do Iguaçu
Ciudad del Este
Cascavel
Londrina
Maringá
SÃO PAULO
Campinas
Jundiaí
Santos
São Bernardo do Campo
Sorocaba
RIO DE JANEIRO
Ribeirão Preto
IGUAÇU

RIO GRANDE DO SUL
SANTA CATARINA
PARANÁ

Resistencia
Corrientes
Posadas
Formosa
Concepción

Neuquén
Viedma
Carmen de Patagones
Golfo San Matías
Pen. Valdés
Puerto Madryn
Trelew
Rawson
Golfo San Jorge
Comodoro Rivadavia
Sarmiento
Perito Moreno
Río Gallegos
Puerto Santa Cruz
Puerto San Julián
Puerto Deseado
Fitz Roy
El Calafate
Puerto Natales
Punta Arenas
Porvenir
Río Grande
Ushuaia
Tierra del Fuego
I. de Los Estados (Staten I.)
C. de Hornos (C. Horn)

SOUTH ATLANTIC OCEAN

Argentine Abyssal Plain

FALKLAND ISLANDS
(ISLAS MALVINAS) (U.K.)
West Falkland
East Falkland
Stanley
Port Darwin

South Georgia (U.K.)
Bird I.
King Edward Pt.
Mt. Paget 2934

PACIFIC OCEAN

Peru-Chile Trench

Projection: Sanson-Flamsteed's Sinusoidal
West from Greenwich

1   2   3   4   5   6   7   8   9

COPYRIGHT PHILIP'S

INDEX TO WORLD MAPS

The index contains the names of all the principal places and features shown on the World Maps. Each name is followed by an additional entry in italics giving the country or region within which it is located. The alphabetical order of names composed of two or more words is governed primarily by the first word, then by the second, and then by the country or region name that follows. This is an example of the rule:

Mīr Kūh *Iran*	26°22N 58°55E	**45** E8
Mīr Shahdād *Iran*	26°15N 58°29E	**45** E8
Mira *Italy*	45°26N 12°8E	**22** B5
Mira por vos Cay *Bahamas*	22°9N 74°30W	**89** B5

Physical features composed of a proper name (Erie) and a description (Lake) are positioned alphabetically by the proper name. The description is positioned after the proper name and is usually abbreviated:

Erie, L. *N. Amer.*	42°15N 81°0W	**82** D4

Where a description forms part of a settlement or administrative name, however, it is always written in full and put in its true alphabetical position:

Mount Morris *U.S.A.*	42°44N 77°52W	**82** D7

Names beginning with M' and Mc are indexed as if they were spelled Mac. Names beginning St. are alphabetized under Saint, but Sankt, Sint, Sant', Santa and San are all spelt in full and are alphabetized accordingly. If the same place name occurs two or more times in the index and all are in the same country, each is followed by the name of the administrative subdivision in which it is located.

The geographical co-ordinates which follow each name in the index give the latitude and longitude of each place. The first co-ordinate indicates latitude – the distance north or south of the Equator. The second co-ordinate indicates longitude – the distance east or west of the Greenwich Meridian. Both latitude and longitude are measured in degrees and minutes (there are 60 minutes in a degree).

The latitude is followed by N(orth) or S(outh) and the longitude by E(ast) or W(est).

The number in bold type which follows the geographical co-ordinates refers to the number of the map page where that feature or place will be found. This is usually the largest scale at which the place or feature appears.

The letter and figure that are immediately after the page number give the grid square on the map page, within which the feature is situated. The letter represents the latitude and the figure the longitude. A lower-case letter immediately after the page number refers to an inset map on that page.

In some cases the feature itself may fall within the specified square, while the name is outside. This is usually the case only with features that are larger than a grid square.

Rivers are indexed to their mouths or confluences, and carry the symbol ➥ after their names. The following symbols are also used in the index: ■ country, ☑ overseas territory or dependency, ☐ first-order administrative area, △ national park, ⌂ other park (provincial park, nature reserve or game reserve), ✕ (LHR) principal airport (and location identifier), ✿ Australian aboriginal land

Abbreviations used in the index

A.C.T. – Australian Capital Territory
A.R. – Autonomous Region
Afghan. – Afghanistan
Afr. – Africa
Ala. – Alabama
Alta. – Alberta
Amer. – America(n)
Ant. – Antilles
Arch. – Archipelago
Ariz. – Arizona
Ark. – Arkansas
Atl. Oc. – Atlantic Ocean
B. – Baie, Bahía, Bay, Bucht, Bugt
B.C. – British Columbia
Bangla. – Bangladesh
Barr. – Barrage
Bos.-H. – Bosnia-Herzegovina
C. – Cabo, Cap, Cape, Coast
C.A.R. – Central African Republic
C. Prov. – Cape Province
Calif. – California
Cat. – Catarata
Cent. – Central
Chan. – Channel
Colo. – Colorado
Conn. – Connecticut
Cord. – Cordillera
Cr. – Creek
Czech. – Czech Republic
D.C. – District of Columbia
Del. – Delaware
Dem. – Democratic
Dep. – Dependency
Des. – Desert
Dét. – Détroit
Dist. – District
Dj. – Djebel
Dom. Rep. – Dominican Republic

E. – East
El Salv. – El Salvador
Eq. Guin. – Equatorial Guinea
Est. – Estrecho
Falk. Is. – Falkland Is.
Fd. – Fjord
Fla. – Florida
Fr. – French
G. – Golfe, Golfo, Gulf, Guba, Gebel
Ga. – Georgia
Gt. – Great, Greater
Guinea-Biss. – Guinea-Bissau
H.K. – Hong Kong
H.P. – Himachal Pradesh
Hants. – Hampshire
Harb. – Harbor, Harbour
Hd. – Head
Hts. – Heights
I.(s). – Île, Ilha, Insel, Isla, Island, Isle
Ill. – Illinois
Ind. – Indiana
Ind. Oc. – Indian Ocean
Ivory C. – Ivory Coast
J. – Jabal, Jebel
Jaz. – Jazīrah
Junc. – Junction
K. – Kap, Kapp
Kans. – Kansas
Kep. – Kepulauan
Ky. – Kentucky
L. – Lac, Lacul, Lago, Lagoa, Lake, Limni, Loch, Lough
La. – Louisiana
Ld. – Land
Liech. – Liechtenstein
Lux. – Luxembourg
Mad. P. – Madhya Pradesh
Madag. – Madagascar
Man. – Manitoba
Mass. – Massachusetts

Md. – Maryland
Me. – Maine
Medit. S. – Mediterranean Sea
Mich. – Michigan
Minn. – Minnesota
Miss. – Mississippi
Mo. – Missouri
Mont. – Montana
Mozam. – Mozambique
Mt.(s) – Mont, Montaña, Mountain
Mte. – Monte
Mti. – Monti
N. – Nord, Norte, North, Northern, Nouveau, Nahal, Nahr
N.B. – New Brunswick
N.C. – North Carolina
N. Cal. – New Caledonia
N. Dak. – North Dakota
N.H. – New Hampshire
N.I. – North Island
N.J. – New Jersey
N. Mex. – New Mexico
N.S. – Nova Scotia
N.S.W. – New South Wales
N.W.T. – North West Territory
N.Y. – New York
N.Z. – New Zealand
Nac. – Nacional
Nat. – National
Nebr. – Nebraska
Neths. – Netherlands
Nev. – Nevada
Nfld & L. – Newfoundland and Labrador
Nic. – Nicaragua
O. – Oued, Ouadi
Occ. – Occidentale
Okla. – Oklahoma
Ont. – Ontario
Or. – Orientale

Oreg. – Oregon
Os. – Ostrov
Oz. – Ozero
P. – Pass, Passo, Pasul, Pulau
P.E.I. – Prince Edward Island
Pa. – Pennsylvania
Pac. Oc. – Pacific Ocean
Papua N.G. – Papua New Guinea
Pass. – Passage
Peg. – Pegunungan
Pen. – Peninsula, Péninsule
Phil. – Philippines
Pk. – Peak
Plat. – Plateau
Prov. – Province, Provincial
Pt. – Point
Pta. – Ponta, Punta
Pte. – Pointe
Qué. – Québec
Queens. – Queensland
R. – Rio, River
R.I. – Rhode Island
Ra. – Range
Raj. – Rajasthan
Recr. – Recreational, Récréatif
Reg. – Region
Rep. – Republic
Res. – Reserve, Reservoir
Rhld-Pfz. – Rheinland-Pfalz
S. – South, Southern, Sur
Si. Arabia – Saudi Arabia
S.C. – South Carolina
S. Dak. – South Dakota
S.I. – South Island
S. Leone – Sierra Leone
Sa. – Serra, Sierra
Sask. – Saskatchewan
Scot. – Scotland
Sd. – Sound
Sev. – Severnaya
Sib. – Siberia

Sprs. – Springs
St. – Saint
Sta. – Santa
Ste. – Sainte
Sto. – Santo
Str. – Strait, Stretto
Switz. – Switzerland
Tas. – Tasmania
Tenn. – Tennessee
Terr. – Territory, Territoire
Tex. – Texas
Tg. – Tanjung
Trin. & Tob. – Trinidad & Tobago
U.A.E. – United Arab Emirates
U.K. – United Kingdom
U.S.A. – United States of America
Ut. P. – Uttar Pradesh
Va. – Virginia
Vdkhr. – Vodokhranilishche
Vdskh. – Vodoskhovyshche
Vf. – Vîrful
Vic. – Victoria
Vol. – Volcano
Vt. – Vermont
W. – Wadi, West
W. Va. – West Virginia
Wall. & F. Is. – Wallis and Futuna Is.
Wash. – Washington
Wis. – Wisconsin
Wlkp. – Wielkopolski
Wyo. – Wyoming
Yorks. – Yorkshire

A

A Coruña *Spain* 43°20N 8°25W **21** A1
A Estrada *Spain* 42°43N 8°27W **21** A1
A Fonsagrada *Spain* 43°8N 7°4W **21** A2
Aabenraa *Denmark* 55°3N 9°25E **9** J13
Aachen *Germany* 50°45N 6°6E **16** C4
Aalborg *Denmark* 57°2N 9°54E **9** H13
Aalen *Germany* 48°51N 10°6E **16** D6
Aalst *Belgium* 50°56N 4°2E **15** D4
Aalten *Neths.* 51°56N 6°35E **15** C6
Aalter *Belgium* 51°5N 3°28E **15** C3
Äänekoski *Finland* 62°36N 25°44E **8** E21
Aarau *Switz.* 47°23N 8°4E **20** C8
Aare → *Switz.* 47°33N 8°14E **20** C8
Aarhus = Århus *Denmark* 56°8N 10°11E **9** H14
Aarschot *Belgium* 50°59N 4°49E **15** D4
Aba *Dem. Rep. of the Congo* 3°58N 30°17E **54** B3
Aba *Nigeria* 5°10N 7°19E **50** G7
Abaco I. *Bahamas* 26°25N 77°10W **88** A4
Ābādān *Iran* 30°22N 48°20E **45** D6
Ābādeh *Iran* 31°8N 52°40E **45** D7
Abadla *Algeria* 31°2N 2°45W **50** B5
Abaetetuba *Brazil* 1°40S 48°50W **93** D9
Abagnar Qi = Xilinhot *China* 43°52N 116°2E **34** C9
Abah, Tanjung *Indonesia* 8°46S 115°38E **37** K18
Abai *Paraguay* 25°58S 55°54W **95** B4
Abakan *Russia* 53°40N 91°10E **29** D10
Abancay *Peru* 13°35S 72°55W **92** F4
Abariringa *Kiribati* 2°50S 171°40W **64** H10
Abarqū *Iran* 31°10N 53°20E **45** D7
Abashiri *Japan* 44°0N 144°15E **30** B12
Abashiri-Wan *Japan* 44°0N 144°30E **30** C12
Ābay = Nîl el Azraq → *Sudan* 15°38N 32°31E **51** E12
Abay *Kazakhstan* 49°38N 72°53E **28** E8
Abaya, L. *Ethiopia* 6°30N 37°50E **47** F2
Abaza *Russia* 52°39N 90°6E **28** D9
'Abbāsābād *Iran* 33°34N 58°23E **45** C8
Abbay = Nîl el Azraq → *Sudan* 15°38N 32°31E **51** E12
Abbaye, Pt. *U.S.A.* 46°58N 88°8W **80** B9
Abbé, L. *Ethiopia* 11°8N 41°47E **47** E3
Abbeville *France* 50°6N 1°49E **20** A4
Abbeville *Ala., U.S.A.* 31°34N 85°15W **85** F12
Abbeville *La., U.S.A.* 29°58N 92°8W **84** G8
Abbeville *S.C., U.S.A.* 34°11N 82°23W **85** D13
Abbeyfeale *Ireland* 52°23N 9°18W **10** D2
Abbot Ice Shelf *Antarctica* 73°0S 92°0W **5** D16
Abbotsford *Canada* 49°5N 122°20W **70** D4
Abbottabad *Pakistan* 34°10N 73°15E **42** B5
ABC Islands = Netherlands Antilles ☒ *W. Indies* 12°15N 69°0W **92** A5
Abd al Kūrī *Yemen* 12°5N 52°20E **47** E5
Ābdar *Iran* 30°16N 55°19E **45** D7
'Abdolābād *Iran* 34°12N 56°30E **45** C8
Abdulpur *Bangla.* 24°15N 88°59E **43** G13
Abéché *Chad* 13°50N 20°35E **51** F10
Abel Tasman △ *N.Z.* 40°59S 173°3E **59** D4
Abengourou *Ivory C.* 6°42N 3°27W **50** G5
Åbenrå = Aabenraa *Denmark* 55°3N 9°25E **9** J13
Abeokuta *Nigeria* 7°3N 3°19E **50** G6
Aberaeron *U.K.* 52°15N 4°15W **13** E3
Aberayron = Aberaeron *U.K.* 52°15N 4°15W **13** E3
Aberchirder *U.K.* 57°34N 2°37W **11** D6
Abercorn *Australia* 25°12S 151°5E **63** D5
Aberdare *U.K.* 51°43N 3°27W **13** F4
Aberdare △ *Kenya* 0°22S 36°44E **54** C4
Aberdare Ra. *Kenya* 0°15S 36°50E **54** C4
Aberdeen *Australia* 32°9S 150°56E **63** E5
Aberdeen *Canada* 52°20N 106°8W **71** C7
Aberdeen *China* 22°14N 114°8E **33** G11
Aberdeen *S. Africa* 32°28S 24°2E **56** E3
Aberdeen *U.K.* 57°9N 2°5W **11** D6
Aberdeen *Idaho, U.S.A.* 42°57N 112°50W **76** E7
Aberdeen *Md., U.S.A.* 39°31N 76°10W **81** F15
Aberdeen *Miss., U.S.A.* 33°49N 88°33W **85** E10
Aberdeen *S. Dak., U.S.A.* 45°28N 98°29W **80** C4
Aberdeen *Wash., U.S.A.* 46°59N 123°50W **78** D3
Aberdeen, City of □ *U.K.* 57°10N 2°10W **11** D6
Aberdeen L. *Canada* 64°30N 99°0W **68** E12
Aberdeenshire □ *U.K.* 57°17N 2°36W **11** D6
Aberdovey = Aberdyfi *U.K.* 52°33N 4°3W **13** E3
Aberdyfi *U.K.* 52°33N 4°3W **13** E3
Aberfeldy *U.K.* 56°37N 3°51W **11** E5
Aberfoyle *U.K.* 56°11N 4°23W **11** E4
Abergavenny *U.K.* 51°49N 3°1W **13** F4
Abergele *U.K.* 53°17N 3°35W **12** D4
Abernathy *U.S.A.* 33°50N 101°51W **84** E4
Abert, L. *U.S.A.* 42°38N 120°14W **76** E3
Aberystwyth *U.K.* 52°25N 4°5W **13** E3
Abhā *Si. Arabia* 18°0N 42°34E **47** D3
Abhar *Iran* 36°9N 49°13E **45** B6
Abhayapuri *India* 26°24N 90°38E **43** F14
Abidjan *Ivory C.* 5°26N 3°58W **50** G5
Abilene *Kans., U.S.A.* 38°55N 97°13W **80** F5
Abilene *Tex., U.S.A.* 32°28N 99°43W **84** E5
Abingdon *U.K.* 51°40N 1°17W **13** F6
Abingdon *U.S.A.* 36°43N 81°59W **81** G13
Abington Reef *Australia* 18°0S 149°35E **62** B4
Abitau → *Canada* 59°53N 109°3W **71** B7
Abitibi → *Canada* 51°3N 80°55W **72** B3
Abitibi, L. *Canada* 48°40N 79°40W **72** C4
Abkhaz Republic = Abkhazia □ *Georgia* 43°12N 41°5E **19** F7
Abkhazia □ *Georgia* 43°12N 41°5E **19** F7
Abminga *Australia* 26°8S 134°51E **63** D1
Åbo = Turku *Finland* 60°30N 22°19E **9** F20
Abohar *India* 30°10N 74°10E **42** D6
Abomey *Benin* 7°10N 2°5E **50** G6
Abong-Mbang *Cameroon* 4°0N 13°8E **52** D2
Abou-Deïa *Chad* 11°20N 19°20E **51** F9
Aboyne *U.K.* 57°4N 2°47W **11** D6
Abra Pampa *Argentina* 22°43S 65°42W **94** A2
Abraham L. *Canada* 52°15N 116°35W **70** C5
Abreojos, Pta. *Mexico* 26°50N 113°40W **86** B2
Abrolhos, Banco dos *Brazil* 18°0S 38°0W **93** F11
Abrud *Romania* 46°19N 23°5E **17** E12
Absaroka Range *U.S.A.* 44°45N 109°50W **76** D9
Abu *India* 24°41N 72°50E **42** G5
Abū al Abyad *U.A.E.* 24°11N 53°50E **45** E7
Abū al Khaṣīb *Iraq* 30°25N 48°0E **44** D5
Abū 'Alī *Si. Arabia* 27°20N 49°27E **45** E6
Abū 'Alī → *Lebanon* 34°25N 35°50E **46** A4
Abu Dhabi = Abū Ẓāby *U.A.E.* 24°28N 54°22E **45** E7
Abū Du'ān *Syria* 36°25N 38°15E **44** B3
Abu el Gaīn, W. → *Egypt* 29°35N 33°30E **46** F2
Abu Ga'da, W. → *Egypt* 29°15N 32°53E **46** F1
Abū Ḥadrīyah *Si. Arabia* 27°20N 48°58E **45** E6
Abu Hamed *Sudan* 19°32N 33°13E **51** E12
Abū Kamāl *Syria* 34°30N 41°0E **44** C4
Abū Madd, Ra's *Si. Arabia* 24°50N 37°7E **44** E3
Abū Mūsā *U.A.E.* 25°52N 55°3E **45** E7
Abū Qaṣr *Si. Arabia* 30°21N 38°34E **44** D3
Abu Shagara, Ras *Sudan* 21°4N 37°19E **51** D13
Abu Simbel *Egypt* 22°18N 31°40E **51** D12
Abū Şukhayr *Iraq* 31°54N 44°30E **44** D5
Abu Zabad *Sudan* 12°25N 29°10E **51** F11
Abū Ẓāby *U.A.E.* 24°28N 54°22E **45** E7
Abū Zeydābād *Iran* 33°54N 51°45E **45** C6
Abuja *Nigeria* 9°5N 7°32E **50** G7
Abukuma-Gawa → *Japan* 38°6N 140°52E **30** E10
Abukuma-Sammyaku *Japan* 37°30N 140°45E **30** F10
Abunā *Brazil* 9°40S 65°20W **92** E5
Abunā → *Brazil* 9°41S 65°20W **92** E5
Aburo *Dem. Rep. of the Congo* 2°4N 30°53E **54** B3
Abut Hd. *N.Z.* 43°7S 170°15E **59** E3
Ābyek *Iran* 36°4N 50°33E **45** B6
Acadia △ *U.S.A.* 44°20N 68°13W **81** C19
Açailândia *Brazil* 4°57S 47°0W **93** D9
Acajutla *El Salv.* 13°36N 89°50W **88** D2
Acámbaro *Mexico* 20°2N 100°44W **86** D4
Acaponeta *Mexico* 22°30N 105°22W **86** C3
Acapulco *Mexico* 16°51N 99°55W **87** D5
Acaraí, Serra *Brazil* 1°50N 57°50W **92** C7
Acarigua *Venezuela* 9°33N 69°12W **92** B5
Acatlán *Mexico* 18°12N 98°3W **87** D5
Acayucán *Mexico* 17°57N 94°55W **87** D6
Accomac *U.S.A.* 37°43N 75°40W **81** G16
Accra *Ghana* 5°35N 0°6W **50** G5
Accrington *U.K.* 53°45N 2°22W **12** D5
Acebal *Argentina* 33°20S 60°50W **94** C3
Aceh □ *Indonesia* 4°15N 97°30E **36** D1
Achalpur *India* 21°22N 77°32E **40** J10
Acharnes *Greece* 38°5N 23°44E **23** E10
Acheloos → *Greece* 38°19N 21°7E **23** E9
Acheng *China* 45°30N 126°58E **35** B14
Acher *India* 23°10N 72°32E **42** H5
Achill Hd. *Ireland* 53°58N 10°15W **10** C1
Achill I. *Ireland* 53°58N 10°1W **10** C1
Achinsk *Russia* 56°20N 90°20E **29** D10
Acireale *Italy* 37°37N 15°10E **22** F6
Ackerman *U.S.A.* 33°19N 89°11W **85** E10
Acklins I. *Bahamas* 22°30N 74°0W **89** B5
Acme *Canada* 51°33N 113°30W **70** C6
Acme *U.S.A.* 40°8N 79°26W **82** F5
Aconcagua, Cerro *Argentina* 32°39S 70°0W **94** C2
Aconquija, Mt. *Argentina* 27°0S 66°0W **94** B2
Açores, Is. dos *Atl. Oc.* 38°0N 27°0W **50** a
Acornhoek *S. Africa* 24°37S 31°2E **57** C5
Acraman, L. *Australia* 32°2S 135°23E **63** E2
Acre = 'Akko *Israel* 32°55N 35°4E **46** C4
Acre □ *Brazil* 9°1S 71°0W **92** E4
Acre → *Brazil* 8°45S 67°22W **92** E5
Actinolite *Canada* 44°32N 77°19W **82** B7
Acton *Canada* 43°38N 80°3W **82** C4
Ad Dammām *Si. Arabia* 26°20N 50°5E **45** E6
Ad Dāmūr *Lebanon* 33°43N 35°27E **46** B4
Ad Dawādimī *Si. Arabia* 24°35N 44°15E **44** E5
Ad Dawḥah *Qatar* 25°15N 51°35E **45** E6
Ad Dawr *Iraq* 34°27N 43°47E **44** C4
Ad Dir'īyah *Si. Arabia* 24°44N 46°35E **44** E5
Ad Dīwānīyah *Iraq* 32°0N 45°0E **44** D5
Ad Dujayl *Iraq* 33°51N 44°14E **44** C5
Ad Duwayd *Si. Arabia* 30°15N 42°17E **44** D4
Ada *Minn., U.S.A.* 47°18N 96°31W **80** B5
Ada *Okla., U.S.A.* 34°46N 96°41W **84** D6
Adabiya *Egypt* 29°53N 32°28E **46** F1
Adair, C. *Canada* 71°30N 71°34W **69** C17
Adaja → *Spain* 41°32N 4°52W **21** B3
Adak *U.S.A.* 51°45N 176°45W **74** E4
Adak I. *U.S.A.* 51°45N 176°45W **74** E4
Adamaoua, Massif de l' *Cameroon* 7°20N 12°20E **51** G8
Adamawa Highlands = Adamaoua, Massif de l' *Cameroon* 7°20N 12°20E **51** G8
Adamello, Mte. *Italy* 46°9N 10°30E **20** C9
Adaminaby *Australia* 36°0S 148°45E **63** F4
Adams *Mass., U.S.A.* 42°38N 73°7W **83** D11
Adams *N.Y., U.S.A.* 43°49N 76°1W **83** C8
Adams *Wis., U.S.A.* 43°57N 89°49W **80** D9
Adams, Mt. *U.S.A.* 46°12N 121°30W **78** D5
Adam's Bridge *Sri Lanka* 9°15N 79°40E **40** Q11
Adams L. *Canada* 51°10N 119°40W **70** C5
Adam's Peak *Sri Lanka* 6°48N 80°30E **40** R12
Adana *Turkey* 37°0N 35°16E **44** B2
Adapazarı = Sakarya *Turkey* 40°48N 30°25E **19** F5
Adarama *Sudan* 17°10N 34°52E **51** E12
Adare, C. *Antarctica* 71°0S 171°0E **5** D11
Adaut *Indonesia* 8°8S 131°7E **37** F8
Adavale *Australia* 25°52S 144°32E **63** D3
Adda → *Italy* 45°8N 9°53E **20** D8
Addis Ababa = Addis Abeba *Ethiopia* 9°2N 38°42E **47** F2
Addis Abeba *Ethiopia* 9°2N 38°42E **47** F2
Addison *U.S.A.* 42°1N 77°14W **82** D7
Addo *S. Africa* 33°32S 25°45E **56** E4
Addo △ *S. Africa* 33°30S 25°50E **56** E4
Ādeh *Iran* 37°42N 45°11E **44** B5
Adel *U.S.A.* 31°8N 83°25W **85** F13
Adelaide *Australia* 34°52S 138°30E **63** E2
Adelaide *S. Africa* 32°42S 26°20E **56** E4
Adelaide I. *Antarctica* 67°15S 68°30W **5** C17
Adelaide Pen. *Canada* 68°15N 97°30W **68** D12
Adelaide River *Australia* 13°15S 131°7E **60** B5
Adelaide Village *Bahamas* 25°0N 77°31W **88** A4
Adelanto *U.S.A.* 34°35N 117°22W **79** L9
Adele I. *Australia* 15°32S 123°9E **60** C3
Adélie, Terre *Antarctica* 68°0S 140°0E **5** C10
Adelie Land = Adélie, Terre *Antarctica* 68°0S 140°0E **5** C10
Aden = Al 'Adan *Yemen* 12°45N 45°0E **47** E4
Aden, G. of *Ind. Oc.* 12°30N 47°30E **47** E4
Adendorp *S. Africa* 32°15S 24°30E **56** E3
Adh Dhayd *U.A.E.* 25°17N 55°53E **45** E7
Adhoi *India* 23°26N 70°32E **42** H4
Adi *Indonesia* 4°15S 133°30E **37** E8
Adieu, C. *Australia* 32°0S 132°10E **61** F5
Adieu Pt. *Australia* 15°14S 124°35E **60** C3
Adige → *Italy* 45°9N 12°20E **22** B5
Adigrat *Ethiopia* 14°20N 39°26E **47** E2
Adilabad *India* 19°33N 78°20E **40** K11
Adirondack ⌂ *U.S.A.* 44°0N 74°20W **83** C10
Adirondack Mts. *U.S.A.* 44°0N 74°0W **83** C10
Adis Abeba = Addis Abeba *Ethiopia* 9°2N 38°42E **47** F2
Adjumani *Uganda* 3°20N 31°50E **54** B3
Adjuntas *Puerto Rico* 18°10N 66°43W **89** d
Adlavik Is. *Canada* 55°0N 58°40W **73** B8
Admiralty G. *Australia* 14°20S 125°55E **60** B4
Admiralty Gulf ✪ *Australia* 14°16S 125°52E **60** B4
Admiralty I. *U.S.A.* 57°30N 134°30W **70** B2
Admiralty Inlet *Canada* 72°30N 86°0W **69** C14
Admiralty Is. *Papua N. G.* 2°0S 147°0E **58** B7
Adolfo González Chaves *Argentina* 38°2S 60°5W **94** D3
Adolfo Ruiz Cortines, Presa *Mexico* 27°15N 109°6W **86** B3
Adonara *Indonesia* 8°15S 123°5E **37** F6
Adoni *India* 15°33N 77°18E **40** M10
Adour → *France* 43°32N 1°32W **20** E3
Adra *India* 23°30N 86°42E **43** H12
Adra *Spain* 36°43N 3°3W **21** D4
Adrano *Italy* 37°40N 14°50E **22** F6
Adrar *Algeria* 27°51N 0°11E **50** C6
Adrar *Mauritania* 20°30N 7°30W **50** D3
Adrar des Iforas *Africa* 19°40N 1°40E **50** E6
Adrian *Mich., U.S.A.* 41°54N 84°2W **81** E11
Adrian *Tex., U.S.A.* 35°16N 102°40W **84** D3
Adriatic Sea *Medit. S.* 43°0N 16°0E **22** C6
Adua *Indonesia* 1°45S 129°50E **37** E7
Adwa *Ethiopia* 14°15N 38°52E **47** E2
Adygea □ *Russia* 45°0N 40°0E **19** F7
Adzhar Republic = Ajaria □ *Georgia* 41°30N 42°0E **19** F7
Adzopé *Ivory C.* 6°7N 3°49W **50** G5
Ægean Sea *Medit. S.* 38°30N 25°0E **23** E11
Aerhtai Shan *Mongolia* 46°40N 92°45E **32** B4
Afaahiti *Tahiti* 17°45S 149°17W **59** d
'Afak *Iraq* 32°4N 45°15E **44** C5
Afandou *Greece* 36°18N 28°12E **25** C10
Afareaitu *Moorea* 17°33S 149°47W **59** d
Afghanistan ■ *Asia* 33°0N 65°0E **40** C4
Aflou *Algeria* 34°7N 2°3E **50** B6
Afognak I. *U.S.A.* 58°15N 152°30W **74** D9
Africa 10°0N 20°0E **48** E6
'Afrīn *Syria* 36°32N 36°50E **44** B3
Afton *N.Y., U.S.A.* 42°14N 75°32W **83** D9
Afton *Wyo., U.S.A.* 42°44N 110°56W **76** E8
Afuá *Brazil* 0°15S 50°20W **93** D8
'Afula *Israel* 32°37N 35°17E **46** C4
Afyon *Turkey* 38°45N 30°33E **19** G5
Afyonkarahisar = Afyon *Turkey* 38°45N 30°33E **19** G5
Āgā Jarī *Iran* 30°42N 49°50E **45** D6
Agadés = Agadez *Niger* 16°58N 7°59E **50** E7
Agadez *Niger* 16°58N 7°59E **50** E7
Agadir *Morocco* 30°28N 9°55W **50** B4
Agaete *Canary Is.* 28°6N 15°43W **24** F4
Agalega Is. *Mauritius* 11°0S 57°0E **3** E12
Agar *India* 23°40N 76°2E **42** H7
Agartala *India* 23°50N 91°23E **41** H17
Agassiz *Canada* 49°14N 121°46W **70** D4
Agassiz Icecap *Canada* 80°15N 76°0W **69** A16
Agats *Indonesia* 5°33S 138°0E **37** F9
Agattu I. *U.S.A.* 52°25N 173°35E **74** E2
Agawam *U.S.A.* 42°5N 72°37W **83** D12
Agboville *Ivory C.* 5°55N 4°15W **50** G5
Ağdam *Azerbaijan* 40°0N 46°58E **44** B5
Agde *France* 43°19N 3°28E **20** E5
Agen *France* 44°12N 0°38E **20** D4
Āgh Kand *Iran* 37°15N 48°4E **45** B6
Aghia Deka *Greece* 35°3N 24°58E **25** D6
Aghia Ekaterinis, Akra *Greece* 39°50N 19°50E **25** A3
Aghia Galini *Greece* 35°6N 24°41E **25** D6
Aghia Varvara *Greece* 35°8N 25°1E **25** D7
Aghios Efstratios *Greece* 39°34N 24°58E **23** E11
Aghios Ioannis, Akra *Greece* 35°20N 25°40E **25** D7
Aghios Isidoros *Greece* 36°9N 27°51E **25** C9
Aghios Matheos *Greece* 39°30N 19°47E **25** B3
Aghios Nikolaos *Greece* 35°11N 25°41E **25** D7
Aghios Stephanos *Greece* 39°46N 19°39E **25** A3
Aghiou Orous, Kolpos *Greece* 40°6N 24°0E **23** D11
Aginskoye *Russia* 51°6N 114°32E **29** D12
Agnew *Australia* 28°1S 120°31E **61** E3
Agori *India* 24°33N 82°57E **43** G10
Agra *India* 27°17N 77°58E **42** F7
Ağri *Turkey* 39°44N 43°3E **19** G7
Agri → *Italy* 40°13N 16°44E **22** D7
Ağrı Dağı *Turkey* 39°50N 44°15E **44** B5
Ağri Karakose = Ağri *Turkey* 39°44N 43°3E **19** G7
Agrigento *Italy* 37°19N 13°34E **22** F5
Agrinio *Greece* 38°37N 21°27E **23** E9
Agua Caliente *Mexico* 32°29N 116°59W **79** N10
Agua Caliente Springs *U.S.A.* 32°56N 116°19W **79** N10
Água Clara *Brazil* 20°25S 52°45W **93** H8
Agua Fria ⌂ *U.S.A.* 34°14N 112°0W **77** J8
Agua Hechicera *Mexico* 32°28N 116°15W **79** N10
Agua Prieta *Mexico* 31°18N 109°34W **86** A3
Aguadilla *Puerto Rico* 18°26N 67°10W **89** d
Aguadulce *Panama* 8°15N 80°32W **88** E3
Aguanga *U.S.A.* 33°27N 116°51W **79** M10
Aguanish *Canada* 50°14N 62°2W **73** B7
Aguanish → *Canada* 50°13N 62°5W **73** B7
Aguapey → *Argentina* 29°7S 56°36W **94** B4
Aguaray Guazú → *Paraguay* 24°47S 57°19W **94** A4
Aguarico → *Ecuador* 0°59S 75°11W **92** D3
Aguaro-Guariquito △ *Venezuela* 8°20N 66°35W **89** E6
Aguas Blancas *Chile* 24°15S 69°55W **94** A2
Aguas Calientes, Sierra de *Argentina* 25°26S 66°40W **94** B2
Aguascalientes *Mexico* 21°53N 102°18W **86** C4
Aguascalientes □ *Mexico* 22°0N 102°20W **86** C4
Aguila, Punta *Puerto Rico* 17°57N 67°13W **89** d
Aguilares *Argentina* 27°26S 65°35W **94** B2
Águilas *Spain* 37°23N 1°35W **21** D5
Agüimes *Canary Is.* 27°58N 15°27W **24** G4
Aguja, C. de la *Colombia* 11°18N 74°12W **90** B3
Agujereada, Pta. *Puerto Rico* 18°30N 67°8W **89** d
Agulhas, C. *S. Africa* 34°52S 20°0E **56** E3
Agulo *Canary Is.* 28°11N 17°12W **24** F2
Agung, Gunung *Indonesia* 8°20S 115°28E **37** J18
Agur *Uganda* 2°28N 32°55E **54** B3
Agusan → *Phil.* 9°0N 125°30E **37** C7
Aha Mts. *Botswana* 19°45S 21°0E **56** B3
Ahaggar *Algeria* 23°0N 6°30E **50** D7
Ahar *Iran* 38°35N 47°0E **44** B5
Ahipara B. *N.Z.* 35°5S 173°5E **59** A4
Ahiri *India* 19°30N 80°0E **40** K12
Ahmad Wal *Pakistan* 29°18N 65°58E **42** E1
Ahmadabad *India* 23°0N 72°40E **42** H5
Aḥmadābād *Khorāsān, Iran* 35°3N 60°50E **45** C9
Aḥmadābād *Khorāsān, Iran* 35°49N 59°42E **45** C8
Aḥmadī *Iran* 27°56N 56°42E **45** E8
Ahmadnagar *India* 19°7N 74°46E **40** K9
Ahmadpur East *Pakistan* 29°12N 71°10E **42** E4
Ahmadpur Lamma *Pakistan* 28°19N 70°3E **42** E4
Ahmedabad = Ahmadabad *India* 23°0N 72°40E **42** H5
Ahmednagar = Ahmadnagar *India* 19°7N 74°46E **40** K9
Ahome *Mexico* 25°55N 109°11W **86** B3
Ahoskie *U.S.A.* 36°17N 76°59W **85** C16
Ahram *Iran* 28°52N 51°16E **45** D6
Ahrax Pt. *Malta* 36°0N 14°22E **25** D1
Ahuachapán *El Salv.* 13°54N 89°52W **88** D2
Ahvāz *Iran* 31°20N 48°40E **45** D6
Ahvenanmaa = Åland *Finland* 60°15N 20°0E **9** F19
Aḥwar *Yemen* 13°30N 46°40E **47** E4
Ai → *India* 26°26N 90°44E **43** F14
Ai-Ais *Namibia* 27°54S 17°59E **56** D2
Ai-Ais and Fish River Canyon △ *Namibia* 24°45S 17°15E **56** C2
Aichi □ *Japan* 35°0N 137°15E **31** G8
Aigrettes, Pte. des *Réunion* 21°3S 55°13E **53** c
Aiguá *Uruguay* 34°13S 54°46W **95** C5
Aigues-Mortes *France* 43°35N 4°12E **20** E6
Aihui = Heihe *China* 50°10N 127°30E **33** A7
Aija *Peru* 9°50S 77°45W **92** E3
Aikawa *Japan* 38°2N 138°15E **30** E9
Aiken *U.S.A.* 33°34N 81°43W **85** E14
Aileron *Australia* 22°39S 133°20E **62** C1
Aillik *Canada* 55°11N 59°18W **73** A8
Ailsa Craig *Canada* 43°8N 81°33W **82** C3
Ailsa Craig *U.K.* 55°15N 5°6W **11** F3
Aim *Russia* 59°0N 133°55E **29** D14
Aimere *Indonesia* 8°45S 121°3E **37** F6
Aimogasta *Argentina* 28°33S 66°50W **94** B2
Aïn Ben Tili *Mauritania* 25°59N 9°27W **50** C4
Aïn-Sefra *Algeria* 32°47N 0°37W **50** B5
Ain Sudr *Egypt* 29°50N 33°6E **46** F2
Aïn Témouchent *Algeria* 35°16N 1°8W **50** A5
Ainaži *Latvia* 57°50N 24°24E **9** H21
Ainsworth *U.S.A.* 42°33N 99°52W **80** D4
Aiquile *Bolivia* 18°10S 65°10W **92** G5
Aïr *Niger* 18°30N 8°0E **50** E7
Air Force I. *Canada* 67°58N 74°5W **69** D17
Air Hitam *Malaysia* 1°55N 103°11E **39** M4
Airdrie *Canada* 51°18N 114°2W **70** C6
Airdrie *U.K.* 55°52N 3°57W **11** F5
Aire → *U.K.* 53°43N 0°55W **12** D7
Aire, I. de l' *Spain* 39°48N 4°16E **24** B11
Airlie Beach *Australia* 20°16S 148°43E **62** b
Aisne → *France* 49°26N 2°50E **20** B5
Ait *India* 25°54N 79°14E **43** G8
Aitkin *U.S.A.* 46°32N 93°42W **80** B7
Aitutaki *Cook Is.* 18°52S 159°45W **65** J12
Aiud *Romania* 46°19N 23°44E **17** E12
Aix-en-Provence *France* 43°32N 5°27E **20** E6
Aix-la-Chapelle = Aachen *Germany* 50°45N 6°6E **16** C4
Aix-les-Bains *France* 45°41N 5°53E **20** D6
Aizawl *India* 23°40N 92°44E **41** H18
Aizkraukle *Latvia* 56°36N 25°11E **9** H21
Aizpute *Latvia* 56°43N 21°40E **9** H19
Aizuwakamatsu *Japan* 37°30N 139°56E **30** F9
Ajaccio *France* 41°55N 8°40E **20** F8
Ajai ⌂ *Uganda* 2°52N 31°16E **54** B3
Ajaigarh *India* 24°52N 80°16E **43** G9
Ajalpan *Mexico* 18°22N 97°15W **87** D5
Ajanta Ra. *India* 20°28N 75°50E **40** J9
Ajari Rep. = Ajaria □ *Georgia* 41°30N 42°0E **19** F7
Ajaria □ *Georgia* 41°30N 42°0E **19** F7
Ajax *Canada* 43°50N 79°1W **82** C5
Ajdābiyā *Libya* 30°54N 20°4E **51** B10
Ajka *Hungary* 47°4N 17°31E **17** E9
'Ajlūn *Jordan* 32°18N 35°47E **46** C4
'Ajlūn □ *Jordan* 32°18N 35°47E **46** C4
'Ajmān *U.A.E.* 25°25N 55°30E **45** E7
Ajmer *India* 26°28N 74°37E **42** F6
Ajnala *India* 31°50N 74°48E **42** D6
Ajo *U.S.A.* 32°22N 112°52W **77** K7
Ajo, C. de *Spain* 43°31N 3°35W **21** A4
Akabira *Japan* 43°33N 142°5E **30** C11
Akagera △ *Rwanda* 1°31S 30°33E **54** C3
Akamas *Cyprus* 35°3N 32°18E **25** D11
Akan △ *Japan* 43°20N 144°20E **30** C12
Akanthou *Cyprus* 35°22N 33°45E **25** D12
Akaroa *N.Z.* 43°49S 172°59E **59** E4
Akashi *Japan* 34°45N 134°58E **31** G7
Akbarpur *Bihar, India* 24°39N 83°58E **43** G10
Akbarpur *Ut. P., India* 26°25N 82°32E **43** F10
Akçakale *Turkey* 36°41N 38°56E **44** B3
Akdoğan = Lysi *Cyprus* 35°6N 33°41E **25** D12
Akelamo *Indonesia* 1°35N 129°40E **37** D7
Aketi *Dem. Rep. of the Congo* 2°38N 23°47E **52** D4
Akhisar *Turkey* 38°56N 27°48E **23** E12
Akhnur *India* 32°52N 74°45E **43** C6
Akhtyrka = Okhtyrka *Ukraine* 50°25N 35°0E **19** D5
Aki *Japan* 33°30N 133°54E **31** H6
Akimiski I. *Canada* 52°50N 81°30W **72** B3
Akincilar = Louroujina *Cyprus* 35°0N 33°28E **25** E12
Akita *Japan* 39°45N 140°7E **30** E10
Akita □ *Japan* 39°40N 140°30E **30** E10
Akjoujt *Mauritania* 19°45N 14°15W **50** E3
Akkeshi *Japan* 43°2N 144°51E **30** C12
'Akko *Israel* 32°55N 35°4E **46** C4
Aklavik *Canada* 68°12N 135°0W **68** D4
Aklera *India* 24°26N 76°32E **42** G7
Akō *Japan* 34°45N 134°24E **31** G7
Akola *India* 20°42N 77°2E **40** J10
Akordat *Eritrea* 15°30N 37°40E **47** D2
Akpatok I. *Canada* 60°25N 68°8W **69** E18
Åkrahamn *Norway* 59°15N 5°10E **9** G11
Akranes *Iceland* 64°19N 22°5W **8** D2
Akron *Colo., U.S.A.* 40°10N 103°13W **76** F12
Akron *Ohio, U.S.A.* 41°5N 81°31W **82** E3
Akrotiri *Cyprus* 34°36N 32°57E **25** E11
Akrotiri Bay *Cyprus* 34°35N 33°10E **25** E12
Aksai Chin *China* 35°15N 79°55E **43** B8
Aksaray *Turkey* 38°25N 34°2E **44** B2
Aksay = Aqsay *Kazakhstan* 51°11N 53°0E **19** D9
Akşehir *Turkey* 38°18N 31°30E **44** B1
Akşehir Gölü *Turkey* 38°30N 31°25E **19** G5
Aksu *China* 41°5N 80°10E **32** B3
Aksum *Ethiopia* 14°5N 38°40E **47** E2
Aktsyabrski *Belarus* 52°38N 28°53E **17** B15
Aktyubinsk = Aqtöbe *Kazakhstan* 50°17N 57°10E **19** D10
Akure *Nigeria* 7°15N 5°5E **50** G7
Akureyri *Iceland* 65°40N 18°6W **8** D4
Akuseki-Shima *Japan* 29°27N 129°37E **31** K4
Akyab = Sittwe *Burma* 20°18N 92°45E **41** J18
Al 'Adan *Yemen* 12°45N 45°0E **47** E4
Al Aḥsā = Hasa *Si. Arabia* 25°50N 49°0E **45** E6
Al Ajfar *Si. Arabia* 27°26N 43°0E **44** E4
Al Amādīyah *Iraq* 37°5N 43°30E **44** B4
Al 'Amārah *Iraq* 31°55N 47°15E **44** D5
Al Anbār □ *Iraq* 33°25N 42°0E **44** C4
Al 'Aqabah *Jordan* 29°31N 35°0E **46** F4
Al 'Aqabah □ *Jordan* 29°30N 35°0E **46** F4
Al Arak *Syria* 34°38N 38°35E **44** C3
Al 'Aramah *Si. Arabia* 25°30N 46°0E **44** E5
Al Arṭāwīyah *Si. Arabia* 26°31N 45°20E **44** E5
Al 'Āşimah = 'Ammān □ *Jordan* 31°40N 36°30E **46** D5
Al 'Assāfīyah *Si. Arabia* 28°17N 38°59E **44** D3
Al 'Awdah *Si. Arabia* 25°32N 45°41E **44** E5
Al 'Ayn *Si. Arabia* 25°4N 38°6E **44** E3
Al 'Ayn *U.A.E.* 24°15N 55°45E **45** E7
Al 'Azīzīyah *Iraq* 32°54N 45°4E **44** C5
Al Bāb *Syria* 36°23N 37°29E **44** B3
Al Bad' *Si. Arabia* 28°28N 35°1E **44** D2
Al Bādī *Iraq* 35°56N 41°32E **44** C4
Al Baḥrah *Kuwait* 29°40N 47°52E **44** D5
Al Baḥral Mayyit = Dead Sea *Asia* 31°30N 35°30E **46** D4
Al Balqā' □ *Jordan* 32°5N 35°45E **46** C4
Al Bārūk, J. *Lebanon* 33°39N 35°40E **46** B4
Al Başrah *Iraq* 30°30N 47°50E **44** D5
Al Baṭḥā *Iraq* 31°6N 45°53E **44** D5
Al Batrūn *Lebanon* 34°15N 35°40E **46** A4
Al Bayḍā *Libya* 32°50N 21°44E **51** B10
Al Biqā *Lebanon* 34°10N 36°10E **46** A5
Al Bi'r *Si. Arabia* 28°51N 36°16E **44** D3
Al Bukayrīyah *Si. Arabia* 26°9N 43°40E **44** E4
Al Burayj *Syria* 34°15N 36°46E **46** A5
Al Faḍilī *Si. Arabia* 26°58N 49°10E **45** E6
Al Fallūjah *Iraq* 33°20N 43°55E **44** C4
Al Fāw *Iraq* 30°0N 48°30E **45** D6
Al Fujayrah *U.A.E.* 25°7N 56°18E **45** E8
Al Ghadaf, W. → *Jordan* 31°26N 36°43E **46** D5
Al Ghammās *Iraq* 31°45N 44°37E **44** D5
Al Ghazālah *Si. Arabia* 26°48N 41°19E **44** E4
Al Ḥadīthah *Iraq* 34°0N 41°13E **44** C4
Al Ḥadīthah *Si. Arabia* 31°28N 37°8E **46** D6
Al Ḥaḍr *Iraq* 35°35N 42°44E **44** C4

Al Hājanah *Syria*	33°20N 36°33E	**46** B5
Al Hajar al Gharbī *Oman*	24°10N 56°15E	**45** E8
Al Hāmad *Si. Arabia*	31°30N 39°30E	**44** D3
Al Hamdānīyah *Syria*	35°25N 36°50E	**44** B3
Al Hamīdīyah *Syria*	34°42N 35°57E	**46** A4
Al Hammar *Iraq*	30°57N 46°51E	**44** D5
Al Hamrā' *Si. Arabia*	24°2N 38°55E	**44** E3
Al Hamzah *Iraq*	31°43N 44°58E	**44** D5
Al Hanākīyah *Si. Arabia*	24°51N 40°31E	**44** E4
Al Harūj al Aswad *Libya*	27°0N 17°10E	**51** C9
Al Hasakah *Syria*	36°35N 40°45E	**44** B4
Al Hayy *Iraq*	32°5N 46°5E	**44** C5
Al Hijarah *Asia*	30°0N 44°0E	**44** D4
Al Hillah *Iraq*	32°30N 44°25E	**44** C5
Al Hillah *Si. Arabia*	23°35N 46°50E	**47** B4
Al Hindīyah *Iraq*	32°30N 44°10E	**44** C5
Al Hirmil *Lebanon*	34°26N 36°24E	**46** A5
Al Hoceïma *Morocco*	35°8N 3°58W	**50** A5
Al Hudaydah *Yemen*	14°50N 43°0E	**47** E3
Al Hudūd ash Shamālīyah □		
Si. Arabia	29°10N 42°30E	**44** D4
Al Hufūf *Si. Arabia*	25°25N 49°45E	**45** E6
Al Humaydah *Si. Arabia*	29°14N 34°56E	**44** D2
Al Hunayy *Si. Arabia*	25°58N 48°45E	**45** E6
Al Isāwīyah *Si. Arabia*	30°43N 37°59E	**44** D3
Al Jafr *Jordan*	30°18N 36°14E	**46** E5
Al Jāfūrah *Si. Arabia*	25°0N 50°15E	**45** E7
Al Jaghbūb *Libya*	29°42N 24°38E	**51** C10
Al Jahrah *Kuwait*	29°25N 47°40E	**44** D5
Al Jalāmīd *Si. Arabia*	31°20N 40°6E	**44** D3
Al Jamalīyah *Qatar*	25°37N 51°5E	**45** E6
Al Janūb □ *Lebanon*	33°20N 35°20E	**46** B4
Al Jawf *Libya*	24°10N 23°24E	**51** D10
Al Jawf *Si. Arabia*	29°55N 39°40E	**44** D3
Al Jawf □ *Si. Arabia*	29°30N 39°30E	**44** D3
Al Jazair = Algeria ■		
Africa	28°30N 2°0E	**50** C6
Al Jazirah *Iraq*	33°30N 44°0E	**44** C5
Al Jithāmīyah *Si. Arabia*	27°41N 41°43E	**44** E4
Al Jubayl *Si. Arabia*	27°0N 49°50E	**45** E6
Al Jubaylah *Si. Arabia*	24°55N 46°25E	**44** E5
Al Jubb *Si. Arabia*	27°11N 42°17E	**44** E4
Al Junaynah *Sudan*	13°27N 22°45E	**51** F10
Al Kaba'ish *Iraq*	30°58N 47°0E	**44** D5
Al Karak *Jordan*	31°11N 35°42E	**46** D4
Al Karak □ *Jordan*	31°0N 36°0E	**46** E5
Al Kāzimīyah *Iraq*	33°22N 44°18E	**44** C5
Al Khābūrah *Oman*	23°57N 57°5E	**45** F8
Al Khalīl *Si. Arabia*	28°24N 48°29E	**45** E6
Al Khalīl *West Bank*	31°32N 35°6E	**46** D4
Al Khāliş *Iraq*	33°49N 44°32E	**44** C5
Al Kharsānīyah		
Si. Arabia	27°13N 49°18E	**45** E6
Al Khaşab *Oman*	26°14N 56°15E	**45** E8
Al Khawr *Qatar*	25°41N 51°30E	**45** E6
Al Khidr *Iraq*	31°12N 45°33E	**44** D5
Al Khiyām *Lebanon*	33°20N 35°36E	**46** B4
Al Khobar *Si. Arabia*	26°17N 50°12E	**45** E6
Al Khums *Libya*	32°40N 14°17E	**51** B8
Al Kiswah *Syria*	33°23N 36°14E	**46** B5
Al Kūfah *Iraq*	32°2N 44°24E	**44** C5
Al Kufrah *Libya*	24°17N 23°15E	**51** D10
Al Kuhayfiyah *Si. Arabia*	27°12N 43°3E	**44** E4
Al Kūt *Iraq*	32°30N 46°0E	**44** C5
Al Kuwayt *Kuwait*	29°30N 48°0E	**44** D5
Al Labwah *Lebanon*	34°11N 36°20E	**46** A5
Al Lādhiqīyah *Syria*	35°30N 35°45E	**44** C2
Al Līth *Si. Arabia*	20°9N 40°15E	**47** C3
Al Liwā' *Oman*	24°31N 56°36E	**45** E8
Al Luḩayyah *Yemen*	15°45N 42°40E	**47** D3
Al Madīnah *Iraq*	30°57N 47°16E	**44** D5
Al Madīnah *Si. Arabia*	24°35N 39°52E	**44** E3
Al Mafraq *Jordan*	32°17N 36°14E	**46** C5
Al Mafraq □ *Jordan*	32°17N 36°15E	**46** C5
Al Maghreb = Morocco ■		
N. Afr.	32°0N 5°50W	**50** B4
Al Maḩmūdīyah *Iraq*	33°3N 44°21E	**44** C5
Al Majma'ah *Si. Arabia*	25°57N 45°22E	**44** E5
Al Makhruq, W. →		
Jordan	31°28N 37°0E	**46** D6
Al Makhūl *Si. Arabia*	26°37N 42°39E	**44** E4
Al Manāmah *Bahrain*	26°10N 50°30E	**45** E6
Al Maqwa' *Kuwait*	29°10N 47°59E	**44** D5
Al Marāh *Si. Arabia*	25°35N 49°35E	**45** E6
Al Marj *Libya*	32°25N 20°30E	**51** B10
Al Maţlā *Kuwait*	29°24N 47°40E	**44** D5
Al Mawsil *Iraq*	36°15N 43°5E	**44** B4
Al Mayadin *Syria*	35°1N 40°27E	**44** C4
Al Mazār *Jordan*	31°4N 35°41E	**46** D4
Al Midhnab *Si. Arabia*	25°50N 44°18E	**44** E5
Al Minā' *Lebanon*	34°24N 35°49E	**46** A4
Al Miqdādīyah *Iraq*	34°0N 45°0E	**44** C5
Al Mubarraz *Si. Arabia*	25°30N 49°40E	**45** E6
Al Mudawwarah *Jordan*	29°19N 36°0E	**46** F5
Al Mughayrā' *U.A.E.*	24°5N 53°32E	**45** E7
Al Muḩarraq *Bahrain*	26°15N 50°40E	**45** E6
Al Mukallā *Yemen*	14°33N 49°2E	**47** E4
Al Mukhā *Yemen*	13°18N 43°15E	**47** E3
Al Musayjīd *Si. Arabia*	24°5N 39°5E	**44** E3
Al Musayyib *Iraq*	32°49N 44°20E	**44** C5
Al Muthanná □ *Iraq*	30°30N 45°15E	**44** D5
Al Muwaylih *Si. Arabia*	27°40N 35°30E	**44** E2
Al Qādisīyah □ *Iraq*	32°0N 45°0E	**44** D5
Al Qā'im *Iraq*	34°21N 41°7E	**44** C4
Al Qalībah *Si. Arabia*	28°24N 37°42E	**44** D3
Al Qāmishlī *Syria*	37°2N 41°14E	**44** B4
Al Qaryatayn *Syria*	34°12N 37°13E	**46** A6
Al Qaşīm □ *Si. Arabia*	26°0N 43°0E	**44** E4
Al Qaţ'a *Syria*	34°40N 40°48E	**44** C4
Al Qatīf *Si. Arabia*	26°35N 50°0E	**45** E6
Al Qatrānah *Jordan*	31°12N 36°6E	**46** D5
Al Qatrūn *Libya*	24°56N 15°3E	**51** D9
Al Qayşūmah *Si. Arabia*	28°20N 46°7E	**44** D5
Al Quds = Jerusalem		
Israel/West Bank	31°47N 35°10E	**46** D4
Al Qunayţirah *Syria*	32°55N 35°45E	**46** C4
Al Qunfudhah *Si. Arabia*	19°3N 41°4E	**47** D3
Al Qurnah *Iraq*	31°1N 47°25E	**44** D5
Al Quşayr *Iraq*	30°39N 45°50E	**44** D5
Al Quşayr *Syria*	34°31N 36°34E	**46** A5
Al Qutayfah *Syria*	33°44N 36°36E	**46** B5
Al 'Ubaylah *Si. Arabia*	21°59N 50°57E	**47** C5
Al 'Udaylīyah *Si. Arabia*	25°8N 49°18E	**45** E6
Al 'Ulā *Si. Arabia*	26°35N 38°0E	**44** E3
Al 'Uqayr *Si. Arabia*	25°40N 50°15E	**45** E6
Al 'Uqayr *Si. Arabia*	25°40N 50°15E	**45** E6
Al 'Uwaynid *Si. Arabia*	24°50N 46°0E	**44** E5
Al 'Uwayqīlah *Si. Arabia*	30°30N 42°10E	**44** D4
Al 'Uyūn *Hijāz, Si. Arabia*	24°33N 39°35E	**44** E3
Al 'Uyūn *Najd, Si. Arabia*	26°30N 43°50E	**44** E4
Al 'Uzayr *Iraq*	31°19N 47°25E	**44** D5
Al Wajh *Si. Arabia*	26°10N 36°30E	**44** E3
Al Wakrah *Qatar*	25°10N 51°40E	**45** E6
Al Waqbah *Si. Arabia*	28°48N 45°33E	**44** D5
Al Wari'āh *Si. Arabia*	27°51N 47°25E	**44** E5
Al Yaman = Yemen ■		
Asia	15°0N 44°0E	**47** E3
Ala Dağ *Turkey*	37°44N 35°9E	**44** B2
Ala Tau *Asia*	45°30N 80°40E	**28** E9
Ala Tau Shankou = Dzungarian		
Gate *Asia*	45°10N 82°0E	**32** B3
Alabama □ *U.S.A.*	33°0N 87°0W	**85** E11
Alabama → *U.S.A.*	31°8N 87°57W	**85** F11
Alabaster *U.S.A.*	33°15N 86°49W	**85** E11
Alaçam Dağları *Turkey*	39°18N 28°49E	**23** E13
Alacant = Alicante *Spain*	38°23N 0°30W	**21** C5
Alachua *U.S.A.*	29°47N 82°30W	**85** G13
Alagoa Grande *Brazil*	7°3S 35°35W	**93** E11
Alagoas □ *Brazil*	9°0S 36°0W	**93** E11
Alagoinhas *Brazil*	12°7S 38°20W	**93** F11
Alaior *Spain*	39°57N 4°8E	**24** B11
Alajero *Canary Is.*	28°3N 17°13W	**24** F2
Alajuela *Costa Rica*	10°2N 84°8W	**88** D3
Alakamisy *Madag.*	21°19S 47°14E	**57** C8
Alaknanda → *India*	30°8N 78°36E	**43** D8
Alakurtti *Russia*	66°58N 30°25E	**8** C24
Alamarvdasht *Iran*	27°37N 52°59E	**45** E7
Alameda *Calif., U.S.A.*	37°46N 122°15W	**78** H4
Alameda *N. Mex.*,		
U.S.A.	35°11N 106°37W	**77** J10
Alamo *U.S.A.*	37°22N 115°10W	**79** H11
Alamogordo *U.S.A.*	32°54N 105°57W	**77** K11
Alamos *Mexico*	27°1N 108°56W	**86** B3
Alamosa *U.S.A.*	37°28N 105°52W	**77** H11
Åland *Finland*	60°15N 20°0E	**9** F19
Ålands hav *Europe*	60°0N 19°30E	**9** G18
Alania = North Ossetia □		
Russia	43°30N 44°30E	**19** F7
Alanya *Turkey*	36°38N 32°0E	**44** B1
Alaotra, Farihin' *Madag.*	17°30S 48°30E	**57** B8
Alapayevsk *Russia*	57°52N 61°42E	**28** D7
Alappuzha = Alleppey		
India	9°30N 76°28E	**40** Q10
Alaró *Spain*	39°42N 2°47E	**24** B9
Alarobia-Vohiposa		
Madag.	20°59S 47°9E	**57** C8
Alaşehir *Turkey*	38°23N 28°30E	**23** E13
Alaska □ *U.S.A.*	64°0N 154°0W	**74** C9
Alaska, G. of *Pac. Oc.*	58°0N 145°0W	**68** F3
Alaska Peninsula *U.S.A.*	56°0N 159°0W	**74** D8
Alaska Range *U.S.A.*	62°50N 151°0W	**68** E1
Ālāt *Azerbaijan*	39°58N 49°25E	**45** B6
Alatau Shan = Ala Tau		
Asia	45°30N 80°40E	**28** E9
Alatyr *Russia*	54°55N 46°35E	**18** D8
Alausí *Ecuador*	2°0S 78°50W	**92** D3
Alava, C. *U.S.A.*	48°10N 124°44W	**76** B1
Alavo = Alavus *Finland*	62°35N 23°36E	**8** E20
Alavus *Finland*	62°35N 23°36E	**8** E20
Alawa ♦ *Australia*	15°42S 134°39E	**62** B1
Alawoona *Australia*	34°45S 140°30E	**63** E3
Alayawarra ♦ *Australia*	22°0S 134°30E	**62** C1
'Alayh *Lebanon*	33°46N 35°33E	**46** B4
Alba *Italy*	44°42N 8°2E	**20** D8
Alba-Iulia *Romania*	46°8N 23°39E	**17** E12
Albacete *Spain*	39°0N 1°50W	**21** C5
Albacutya, L. *Australia*	35°45S 141°58E	**63** F3
Albanel, L. *Canada*	50°55N 73°12W	**72** B5
Albania ■ *Europe*	41°0N 20°0E	**23** D9
Albany *Australia*	35°1S 117°58E	**61** G2
Albany *Ga., U.S.A.*	31°35N 84°10W	**85** F12
Albany *N.Y., U.S.A.*	42°39N 73°45W	**83** D11
Albany *Oreg., U.S.A.*	44°38N 123°6W	**76** D2
Albany *Tex., U.S.A.*	32°44N 99°18W	**84** E5
Albany → *Canada*	52°17N 81°31W	**72** B3
Albarca, C. d' *Spain*	39°4N 1°22E	**24** B7
Albardón *Argentina*	31°20S 68°30W	**94** C2
Albatross B. *Australia*	12°45S 141°30E	**62** A3
Albemarle *U.S.A.*	35°21N 80°12W	**85** D14
Albemarle Sd. *U.S.A.*	36°5N 76°0W	**85** C16
Alberche → *Spain*	39°58N 4°46W	**21** C3
Alberdi *Paraguay*	26°14S 58°20W	**94** B4
Albert, L. *Africa*	1°30N 31°0E	**54** B3
Albert, L. *Australia*	35°30S 139°10E	**63** F2
Albert Edward Ra.		
Australia	18°17S 127°57E	**60** C4
Albert Lea *U.S.A.*	43°39N 93°22W	**80** D7
Albert Nile → *Uganda*	3°36N 32°2E	**54** B3
Albert Town *Bahamas*	22°37N 74°33W	**89** B5
Alberta □ *Canada*	54°40N 115°0W	**70** C6
Alberti *Argentina*	35°1S 60°16W	**94** D3
Albertinia *S. Africa*	34°11S 21°34E	**56** E3
Alberton *Canada*	46°50N 64°0W	**73** C7
Albertville *France*	45°40N 6°22E	**20** D7
Albertville *U.S.A.*	34°16N 86°13W	**85** D11
Albi *France*	43°56N 2°9E	**20** E5
Albia *U.S.A.*	41°2N 92°48W	**80** E7
Albina *Suriname*	5°37N 54°15W	**93** B8
Albina, Ponta *Angola*	15°52S 11°44E	**56** B1
Albion *Mich., U.S.A.*	42°15N 84°45W	**81** D11
Albion *Nebr., U.S.A.*	41°42N 98°0W	**80** E4
Albion *Pa., U.S.A.*	41°53N 80°22W	**82** E4
Alborán *Medit. S.*	35°57N 3°0W	**21** E4
Ålborg = Aalborg *Denmark*	57°2N 9°54E	**9** H13
Alborz, Reshteh-ye Kūhhā-ye		
Iran	36°0N 52°0E	**45** C7
Albufeira *Portugal*	37°5N 8°15W	**21** D1
Albuquerque *U.S.A.*	35°5N 106°39W	**77** J10
Albuquerque, Cayos de		
Caribbean	12°10N 81°50W	**88** D3
Alburg *U.S.A.*	44°59N 73°18W	**83** B11
Albury *Australia*	36°3S 146°56E	**63** F4
Alcalá de Henares *Spain*	40°28N 3°22W	**21** B4
Alcalá la Real *Spain*	37°27N 3°57W	**21** D4
Álcamo *Italy*	37°59N 12°55E	**22** F5
Alcañiz *Spain*	41°2N 0°8W	**21** B5
Alcântara *Brazil*	2°20S 44°30W	**93** D10
Alcântara, Embalse de		
Spain	39°44N 6°50W	**21** C2
Alcantarilla *Spain*	37°59N 1°12W	**21** D5
Alcaraz, Sierra de *Spain*	38°40N 2°20W	**21** C4
Alcaudete *Spain*	37°35N 4°5W	**21** D3
Alcázar de San Juan		
Spain	39°24N 3°12W	**21** C4
Alchevsk *Ukraine*	48°30N 38°45E	**19** E6
Alcira = Alzira *Spain*	39°9N 0°30W	**21** C5
Alcova *U.S.A.*	42°34N 106°43W	**76** E10
Alcoy *Spain*	38°43N 0°30W	**21** C5
Alcúdia *Spain*	39°51N 3°7E	**24** B10
Alcúdia, B. d' *Spain*	39°47N 3°15E	**24** B10
Aldabra Is. *Seychelles*	9°22S 46°28E	**49** G8
Aldama *Mexico*	22°55N 98°4W	**87** C5
Aldan *Russia*	58°40N 125°30E	**29** D13
Aldan → *Russia*	63°28N 129°35E	**29** C13
Aldea, Pta. de la		
Canary Is.	28°0N 15°50W	**24** G4
Aldeburgh *U.K.*	52°10N 1°37E	**13** E9
Alder Pk. *U.S.A.*	35°53N 121°22W	**78** K5
Alderney *U.K.*	49°42N 2°11W	**13** H5
Aldershot *U.K.*	51°15N 0°44W	**13** F7
Aledo *U.S.A.*	41°12N 90°45W	**80** E8
Aleg *Mauritania*	17°3N 13°55W	**50** E3
Alegranza *Canary Is.*	29°23N 13°32W	**24** E6
Alegranza, I. *Canary Is.*	29°23N 13°32W	**24** E6
Alegre *Brazil*	20°50S 41°30W	**95** A7
Alegrete *Brazil*	29°40S 56°0W	**95** B4
Aleksandriya = Oleksandriya		
Ukraine	50°37N 26°19E	**17** C14
Aleksandrov Gay *Russia*	50°9N 48°34E	**19** D8
Aleksandrovsk-Sakhalinskiy		
Russia	50°50N 142°20E	**29** D15
Aleksandry, Zemlya		
Russia	80°25N 48°0E	**28** A5
Além Paraíba *Brazil*	21°52S 42°41W	**95** A7
Alemania *Argentina*	25°40S 65°30W	**94** B2
Alemania *Chile*	25°10S 69°55W	**94** B2
Alençon *France*	48°27N 0°4E	**20** B4
Alenquer *Brazil*	1°56S 54°46W	**93** D8
'Alenuihähä Channel		
U.S.A.	20°30N 156°0W	**75** L8
Aleppo = Halab *Syria*	36°10N 37°15E	**44** B3
Aléria *France*	42°5N 9°26E	**20** E9
Alert *Canada*	83°2N 60°0W	**69** A20
Alès *France*	44°9N 4°5E	**20** D6
Alessándria *Italy*	44°54N 8°37E	**20** D8
Ålesund *Norway*	62°28N 6°12E	**8** E12
Aleutian Basin *Pac. Oc.*	57°0N 177°0E	**64** B9
Aleutian Is. *Pac. Oc.*	52°0N 175°0W	**74** E5
Aleutian Range *U.S.A.*	60°0N 154°0W	**74** D9
Aleutian Trench *Pac. Oc.*	48°0N 180°0E	**4** D17
Alexander, Mt.		
Australia	28°58S 120°16E	**61** E3
Alexander Arch. *U.S.A.*	56°0N 136°0W	**68** F4
Alexander Bay *S. Africa*	28°40S 16°30E	**56** D2
Alexander City *U.S.A.*	32°56N 85°58W	**85** E12
Alexander I. *Antarctica*	69°0S 70°0W	**5** C17
Alexandra *Australia*	37°8S 145°40E	**63** F4
Alexandra *N.Z.*	45°14S 169°25E	**59** F2
Alexandra Falls *Canada*	60°29N 116°18W	**70** A5
Alexandria = El Iskandarîya		
Egypt	31°13N 29°58E	**51** B11
Alexandria *B.C.,*		
Canada	52°35N 122°27W	**70** C4
Alexandria *Ont.,*		
Canada	45°19N 74°38W	**83** A10
Alexandria *Romania*	43°57N 25°24E	**17** G13
Alexandria *S. Africa*	33°38S 26°28E	**56** E4
Alexandria *U.K.*	55°59N 4°35W	**11** F4
Alexandria *La., U.S.A.*	31°18N 92°27W	**84** F8
Alexandria *Minn.,*		
U.S.A.	45°53N 95°22W	**80** C6
Alexandria *S. Dak.,*		
U.S.A.	43°39N 97°47W	**80** D5
Alexandria *Va., U.S.A.*	38°49N 77°5W	**81** F15
Alexandria Bay *U.S.A.*	44°20N 75°55W	**83** B9
Alexandrina, L.		
Australia	35°25S 139°10E	**63** F2
Alexandroupoli *Greece*	40°50N 25°54E	**23** D11
Alexis → *Canada*	52°33N 56°8W	**73** B8
Alexis Creek *Canada*	52°10N 123°20W	**70** C4
Aleysk *Russia*	52°40N 83°0E	**28** D9
Alfabia *Spain*	39°44N 2°44E	**24** B9
Alfenas *Brazil*	21°20S 46°10W	**95** A6
Alford *Aberds., U.K.*	57°14N 2°41W	**11** D6
Alford *Lincs., U.K.*	53°15N 0°10E	**12** D8
Alfred *Maine, U.S.A.*	43°29N 70°43W	**83** C14
Alfred *N.Y., U.S.A.*	42°16N 77°48W	**82** D7
Alfreton *U.K.*	53°6N 1°24W	**12** D6
Ålgård *Norway*	58°46N 5°53E	**9** G11
Algarve *Portugal*	36°58N 8°20W	**21** D1
Algeciras *Spain*	36°9N 5°28W	**21** D3
Algemesí *Spain*	39°11N 0°27W	**21** C5
Alger *Algeria*	36°42N 3°8E	**50** A6
Algeria ■ *Africa*	28°30N 2°0E	**50** C6
Alghero *Italy*	40°33N 8°19E	**22** D3
Algiers = Alger *Algeria*	36°42N 3°8E	**50** A6
Algoa B. *S. Africa*	33°50S 25°45E	**56** E4
Algoma *U.S.A.*	44°36N 87°26W	**80** C10
Algona *U.S.A.*	43°4N 94°14W	**80** D6
Algonac *U.S.A.*	42°37N 82°32W	**82** D2
Algonquin □ *Canada*	45°50N 78°30W	**72** C4
Algorta *Uruguay*	32°25S 57°23W	**96** C5
Alhambra *U.S.A.*	34°5N 118°7W	**79** L8
Alhucemas = Al Hoceïma		
Morocco	35°8N 3°58W	**50** A5
'Alī al Gharbī *Iraq*	32°30N 46°45E	**44** C5
'Alī ash Sharqī *Iraq*	32°7N 46°44E	**44** C5
Äli Bayramlı *Azerbaijan*	39°59N 48°52E	**45** B6
'Alī Khēl *Afghan.*	33°57N 69°43E	**42** C3
Alī Shāh *Iran*	38°9N 45°50E	**44** B5
'Alīābād *Golestān, Iran*	36°40N 54°33E	**45** B7
'Alīābād *Khorāsān, Iran*	32°30N 57°30E	**45** C8
'Alīābād *Kordestān, Iran*	35°4N 46°58E	**44** C5
'Alīābād *Yazd, Iran*	31°41N 53°49E	**45** D7
Aliağa *Turkey*	38°47N 26°59E	**23** E12
Aliakmonas → *Greece*	40°30N 22°36E	**23** D10
Alicante *Spain*	38°23N 0°30W	**21** C5
Alice *S. Africa*	32°48S 26°55E	**56** E4
Alice *U.S.A.*	27°45N 98°5W	**84** H5
Alice → *Queens.,*		
Australia	24°2S 144°50E	**62** C3
Alice → *Queens.,*		
Australia	15°35S 142°20E	**62** B3
Alice Arm *Canada*	55°29N 129°31W	**70** B3
Alice Springs *Australia*	23°40S 133°50E	**62** C1
Alicedale *S. Africa*	33°15S 26°4E	**56** E4
Aliceville *U.S.A.*	33°8N 88°9W	**85** E10
Aliganj *India*	27°30N 79°10E	**43** F8
Aligarh *Raj., India*	25°55N 76°15E	**42** G7
Aligarh *Ut. P., India*	27°55N 78°10E	**42** F8
Alīgūdarz *Iran*	33°25N 49°45E	**45** C6
Alimia *Greece*	36°16N 27°43E	**25** C9
Alingsås *Sweden*	57°56N 12°31E	**9** H15
Alipur *Pakistan*	29°25N 70°55E	**42** E4
Alipur Duar *India*	26°30N 89°35E	**41** F16
Aliquippa *U.S.A.*	40°37N 80°15W	**82** F4
Alitus = Alytus *Lithuania*	54°24N 24°3E	**9** J21
Aliwal North *S. Africa*	30°45S 26°45E	**56** E4
Alix *Canada*	52°24N 113°11W	**70** C6
Aljustrel *Portugal*	37°55N 8°10W	**21** D1
Alkmaar *Neths.*	52°37N 4°45E	**15** B4
All American Canal		
U.S.A.	32°45N 115°15W	**77** K6
Allagash → *U.S.A.*	47°5N 69°3W	**81** B19
Allah Dad *Pakistan*	25°38N 67°34E	**42** G2
Allahabad *India*	25°25N 81°58E	**43** G9
Allan *Canada*	51°53N 106°4W	**71** C7
Allanridge *S. Africa*	27°45S 26°40E	**56** D4
Allegany *U.S.A.*	42°6N 78°30W	**82** D6
Allegheny → *U.S.A.*	40°27N 80°1W	**82** F5
Allegheny Mts. *U.S.A.*	38°15N 80°10W	**81** F13
Allegheny Plateau		
U.S.A.	41°30N 78°30W	**81** E14
Allegheny Res. *U.S.A.*	41°50N 79°0W	**82** E6
Allègre, Pte. *Guadeloupe*	16°22N 61°46W	**88** b
Allen, Bog of *Ireland*	53°15N 7°0W	**10** C5
Allen, L. *Ireland*	54°8N 8°4W	**10** B3
Allendale *U.S.A.*	33°1N 81°18W	**85** E14
Allende *Mexico*	28°20N 100°51W	**86** B4
Allentown *U.S.A.*	40°37N 75°29W	**83** F9
Alleppey *India*	9°30N 76°28E	**40** Q10
Aller → *Germany*	52°56N 9°12E	**16** B5
Alleynes B. *Barbados*	13°13N 59°39W	**89** g
Alliance *Nebr., U.S.A.*	42°6N 102°52W	**80** D2
Alliance *Ohio, U.S.A.*	40°55N 81°6W	**82** F3
Allier → *France*	46°57N 3°4E	**20** C5
Alliford Bay *Canada*	53°12N 131°58W	**70** C2
Alligator Pond *Jamaica*	17°52N 77°34W	**88** a
Alliston *Canada*	44°9N 79°52W	**82** B5
Alloa *U.K.*	56°7N 3°47W	**11** E5
Allora *Australia*	28°2S 152°0E	**63** D5
Alluitsup Paa *Greenland*	60°30N 45°35W	**4** C5
Alma *Canada*	48°35N 71°40W	**73** C5
Alma *Ga., U.S.A.*	31°33N 82°28W	**85** F13
Alma *Kans., U.S.A.*	39°1N 96°17W	**80** F5
Alma *Mich., U.S.A.*	43°23N 84°39W	**81** D11
Alma *Nebr., U.S.A.*	40°6N 99°22W	**80** E4
Alma *Wis., U.S.A.*	44°20N 91°55W	**80** C8
Alma Ata = Almaty		
Kazakhstan	43°15N 76°57E	**28** E8
Alma Hill *U.S.A.*	42°2N 78°0W	**82** D7
Almada *Portugal*	38°41N 9°8E	**21** C1
Almaden *Australia*	17°22S 144°40E	**62** B3
Almadén *Spain*	38°49N 4°52W	**21** C3
Almalyk = Olmaliq		
Uzbekistan	40°50N 69°35E	**28** E7
Almanor, L. *U.S.A.*	40°14N 121°9W	**76** F3
Almansa *Spain*	38°51N 1°5W	**21** C5
Almanzor, Pico *Spain*	40°15N 5°18W	**21** B3
Almanzora → *Spain*	37°14N 1°46W	**21** D5
Almaty *Kazakhstan*	43°15N 76°57E	**28** E8
Almazán *Spain*	41°30N 2°30W	**21** B4
Almeirim *Brazil*	1°30S 52°34W	**93** D8
Almelo *Neths.*	52°22N 6°42E	**15** B6
Almendralejo *Spain*	38°41N 6°26W	**21** C2
Almere-Stad *Neths.*	52°20N 5°15E	**15** B5
Almería *Spain*	36°52N 2°27W	**21** D4
Almirante *Panama*	9°10N 82°30W	**88** E3
Almond *U.S.A.*	42°19N 77°44W	**82** D7
Almont *U.S.A.*	42°55N 83°3W	**82** D1
Almonte *Canada*	45°14N 76°12W	**83** A8
Almora *India*	29°38N 79°40E	**43** E8
Almyrou, Órmos *Greece*	35°23N 24°20E	**25** D6
Alness *U.K.*	57°41N 4°16W	**11** D4
Alnmouth *U.K.*	55°24N 1°37W	**12** B6
Alnwick *U.K.*	55°24N 1°42W	**12** B6
Aloi *Uganda*	2°16N 33°10E	**54** B3
Alon *Burma*	22°12N 95°5E	**41** H19
Alor *Indonesia*	8°15S 124°30E	**37** F6
Alor Setar *Malaysia*	6°7N 100°22E	**39** J3
Alot *India*	23°56N 75°40E	**42** H6
Aloysius, Mt. *Australia*	26°0S 128°38E	**61** E4
Alpaugh *U.S.A.*	35°53N 119°29W	**78** K7
Alpena *U.S.A.*	45°4N 83°27W	**81** C12
Alpha *Australia*	23°39S 146°37E	**62** C4
Alpha Ridge *Arctic*	84°0N 118°0W	**4** A2
Alphen aan den Rijn		
Neths.	52°7N 4°40E	**15** B4
Alpine *Ariz., U.S.A.*	33°51N 109°9W	**77** K9
Alpine *Calif., U.S.A.*	32°50N 116°46W	**79** N10
Alpine *Tex., U.S.A.*	30°22N 103°40W	**84** F3
Alps *Europe*	46°30N 9°30E	**20** C8
Alpurrurulam *Australia*	20°59S 137°50E	**62** C2
Alsace □ *France*	48°15N 7°25E	**20** B7
Alsask *Canada*	51°21N 109°59W	**71** C7
Alsasua *Spain*	42°54N 2°10W	**21** A4
Alsek → *U.S.A.*	59°10N 138°12W	**70** B1
Alsta *Norway*	65°58N 12°40E	**8** D15
Alston *U.K.*	54°49N 2°25W	**12** C5
Alta *Norway*	69°57N 23°10E	**8** B20
Alta Gracia *Argentina*	31°40S 64°30W	**94** C3
Alta Sierra *U.S.A.*	35°42N 118°33W	**79** K8
Altaelva → *Norway*	69°54N 23°17E	**8** B20
Altafjorden *Norway*	70°5N 23°5E	**8** A20
Altai = Aerhtai Shan		
Mongolia	46°40N 92°45E	**32** B4
Altai = Gorno-Altay □		
Russia	51°0N 86°0E	**28** D9
Altamaha → *U.S.A.*	31°20N 81°20W	**85** F14
Altamira *Brazil*	3°12S 52°10W	**93** D8
Altamira *Chile*	25°47S 69°51W	**94** B2
Altamira *Mexico*	22°24N 97°55W	**87** C5
Altamont *U.S.A.*	42°42N 74°2W	**83** D10
Altamura *Italy*	40°49N 16°33E	**22** D7
Altanbulag *Mongolia*	50°16N 106°30E	**32** A5
Altar *Mexico*	30°43N 111°44W	**86** A2
Altar, Gran Desierto de		
Mexico	31°50N 114°10W	**86** B2
Altata *Mexico*	24°40N 107°55W	**86** C3
Altavista *U.S.A.*	37°6N 79°17W	**81** G14
Altay *China*	47°48N 88°10E	**32** B3
Altea *Spain*	38°38N 0°2W	**21** C5
Altiplano *Bolivia*	17°0S 68°0W	**92** G5
Alto Araguaia *Brazil*	17°15S 53°20W	**93** G8
Alto Cuchumatanes =		
Cuchumatanes, Sierra de los		
Guatemala	15°35N 91°25W	**88** C1
Alto del Carmen *Chile*	28°46S 70°30W	**94** B1
Alto Ligonha *Mozam.*	15°30S 38°11E	**55** F4
Alto Molocue *Mozam.*	15°50S 37°35E	**55** F4
Alto Paraguai □		
Paraguay	21°0S 58°30W	**94** A4
Alto Paraná □ *Paraguay*	25°30S 54°50W	**95** B5
Alton *Canada*	43°54N 80°5W	**82** C4
Alton *U.K.*	51°9N 0°59W	**13** F7
Alton *Ill., U.S.A.*	38°53N 90°11W	**80** F8
Alton *N.H., U.S.A.*	43°27N 71°13W	**83** C13
Altona *Canada*	49°6N 97°33W	**71** D9
Altoona *U.S.A.*	40°31N 78°24W	**82** F6
Altun Kupri *Iraq*	35°45N 44°9E	**44** C5
Altun Shan *China*	38°30N 88°0E	**32** C3
Alturas *U.S.A.*	41°29N 120°32W	**76** F3
Altus *U.S.A.*	34°38N 99°20W	**84** D5
Alucra *Turkey*	40°22N 38°47E	**19** F6
Alūksne *Latvia*	57°24N 27°3E	**9** H22
Alunite *U.S.A.*	35°59N 114°55W	**79** K12
Alusi *Indonesia*	7°35S 131°40E	**37** F8
Alva *U.S.A.*	36°48N 98°40W	**84** C5
Alvarado *Mexico*	18°46N 95°46W	**87** D5
Alvarado *U.S.A.*	32°24N 97°13W	**84** E6
Alvaro Obregón, Presa		
Mexico	27°52N 109°52W	**86** B3
Alvear *Argentina*	29°5S 56°30W	**94** B4
Alvesta *Sweden*	56°54N 14°35E	**9** H16
Alvin *U.S.A.*	29°26N 95°15W	**84** G7
Alvinston *Canada*	42°49N 81°52W	**82** D3
Älvkarleby *Sweden*	60°34N 17°26E	**9** F17
Alvord Desert *U.S.A.*	42°30N 118°25W	**76** E4
Älvsbyn *Sweden*	65°40N 21°0E	**8** D19
Alwar *India*	27°38N 76°34E	**42** F7
Alxa Zuoqi *China*	38°50N 105°40E	**34** E3
Alyangula *Australia*	13°55S 136°30E	**62** A2
Alyata = Ālāt *Azerbaijan*	39°58N 49°25E	**45** B6
Alyth *U.K.*	56°38N 3°13W	**11** E5
Alytus *Lithuania*	54°24N 24°3E	**9** J21
Alzada *U.S.A.*	45°2N 104°25W	**76** D11
Alzamay *Russia*	55°33N 98°39E	**29** D10
Alzira *Spain*	39°9N 0°30W	**21** C5
Am Timan *Chad*	11°0N 20°10E	**51** F10
Amadi		
Dem. Rep. of the Congo	3°40N 26°40E	**54** B2
Âmâdi *Sudan*	5°29N 30°25E	**51** G12
Amadjuak L. *Canada*	65°0N 71°8W	**69** E17
Amagansett *U.S.A.*	40°59N 72°9W	**83** F12
Amagasaki *Japan*	34°42N 135°23E	**31** G7
Amahai *Indonesia*	3°20S 128°55E	**37** E7
Amaile *Samoa*	13°59S 171°22W	**59** b
Amakusa-Shotō *Japan*	32°15N 130°10E	**31** H5
Åmål *Sweden*	59°3N 12°42E	**9** G15
Amaliada *Greece*	37°47N 21°22E	**23** F9
Amalner *India*	21°5N 75°5E	**40** J9
Amamapare *Indonesia*	4°53S 136°38E	**37** E9
Amambaí *Brazil*	23°5S 55°13W	**95** A4
Amambaí → *Brazil*	23°22S 53°56W	**95** A5
Amambay □ *Paraguay*	23°0S 56°0W	**95** A4
Amambay, Cordillera de		
S. Amer.	23°0S 55°45W	**95** A4
Amami-Guntō *Japan*	27°16N 129°21E	**31** L4
Amami-Ō-Shima *Japan*	28°0N 129°0E	**31** L4
Aman, Pulau *Malaysia*	5°16N 100°24E	**39** c
Amaná, L. *Brazil*	2°35S 64°40W	**92** D6
Amanat → *India*	24°7N 84°4E	**43** G11
Amanda Park *U.S.A.*	47°28N 123°55W	**78** C3
Amankeldi *Kazakhstan*	50°10N 65°10E	**28** D7
Amapá *Brazil*	2°5N 50°50W	**93** C8
Amapá □ *Brazil*	1°40N 52°0W	**93** C8
Amaranth *Canada*	50°36N 98°43W	**71** C9
Amargosa → *U.S.A.*	36°14N 116°51W	**79** J10
Amargosa Desert		
U.S.A.	36°40N 116°30W	**79** J10
Amargosa Range *U.S.A.*	36°20N 116°45W	**79** J10
Amari *Greece*	35°13N 24°40E	**25** D6
Amarillo *U.S.A.*	35°13N 101°50W	**84** D4
Amarkantak *India*	22°40N 81°45E	**43** H9
Amaro, Mte. *Italy*	42°5N 14°5E	**22** C6
Amarpur *India*	25°5N 87°0E	**43** G12
Amarwara *India*	22°18N 79°10E	**43** H8
Amasya *Turkey*	40°40N 35°50E	**19** F5
Amata *Australia*	26°9S 131°9E	**61** E5
Amatikulu *S. Africa*	29°3S 31°33E	**57** D5

Amatitlán Guatemala 14°29N 90°38W 88 D1
Amay Belgium 50°33N 5°19E 15 D5
Amazon = Amazonas →
  S. Amer. 0°5S 50°0W 93 D8
Amazonas □ Brazil 5°0S 65°0W 92 E6
Amazonas → S. Amer. 0°5S 50°0W 93 D8
Ambah India 26°43N 78°13E 42 F8
Ambahikily Madag. 21°36S 43°41E 57 C7
Ambahita Madag. 24°1S 45°16E 57 C8
Ambala India 30°23N 76°56E 42 D7
Ambalavao Madag. 21°50S 46°56E 57 C8
Ambanja Madag. 13°40S 48°27E 57 A8
Ambararata Madag. 15°3S 48°33E 57 B8
Ambarchik Russia 69°40N 162°20E 29 C17
Ambarijeby Madag. 14°56S 47°41E 57 A8
Ambaro, Helodranon'
  Madag. 13°23S 48°38E 57 A8
Ambato Ecuador 1°5S 78°42W 92 D3
Ambato Madag. 13°24S 48°29E 57 A8
Ambato, Sierra de
  Argentina 28°25S 66°10W 94 B2
Ambato Boeny Madag. 16°28S 46°43E 57 B8
Ambatofinandrahana
  Madag. 20°33S 46°48E 57 C8
Ambatolampy Madag. 19°20S 47°35E 57 B8
Ambatomainty Madag. 17°41S 45°40E 57 B8
Ambatomainoina Madag. 18°18S 47°37E 57 B8
Ambatondrazaka
  Madag. 17°55S 48°28E 57 B8
Ambatosoratra Madag. 17°37S 48°31E 57 B8
Ambenja Madag. 15°17S 46°58E 57 B8
Amberg Germany 49°26N 11°52E 16 D6
Ambergris Cay Belize 18°0N 87°55W 87 D7
Amberley Canada 44°2N 81°42W 82 B3
Amberley N.Z. 43°9S 172°44E 59 E4
Ambikapur India 23°15N 83°15E 43 H10
Ambilobé Madag. 13°10S 49°3E 57 A8
Ambinanindrano Madag. 20°5S 48°23E 57 C8
Ambinanitelo Madag. 15°21S 49°35E 57 B8
Ambinda Madag. 16°25S 45°52E 57 B8
Amble U.K. 55°20N 1°36W 12 B6
Ambleside U.K. 54°26N 2°58W 12 C5
Ambo Peru 10°5S 76°10W 92 F3
Amboahangy Madag. 24°15S 46°22E 57 C8
Ambodifototra Madag. 16°59S 49°52E 57 B8
Ambodilazana Madag. 18°6S 49°10E 57 B8
Ambodiriana Madag. 17°55S 49°18E 57 B8
Ambohidratrimo Madag. 18°50S 47°26E 57 B8
Ambohidray Madag. 18°36S 48°18E 57 B8
Ambohimahamasina
  Madag. 21°56S 47°11E 57 C8
Ambohimahasoa Madag. 21°7S 47°13E 57 C8
Ambohimanga Madag. 20°52S 47°36E 57 C8
Ambohimitombo Madag. 20°43S 47°26E 57 C8
Ambohitra Madag. 12°30S 49°10E 57 A8
Amboise France 47°24N 1°2E 20 C4
Ambon Indonesia 3°43S 128°12E 37 E7
Ambondro Madag. 25°13S 45°44E 57 D8
Amboseli, L. Kenya 2°40S 37°10E 54 C4
Amboseli △ Kenya 2°37S 37°13E 54 C4
Ambositra Madag. 20°31S 47°25E 57 C8
Ambovombe Madag. 25°11S 46°5E 57 D8
Amboy U.S.A. 34°33N 115°45W 79 L11
Amboyna Cay
  S. China Sea 7°50N 112°50E 36 C4
Ambridge U.S.A. 40°36N 80°14W 82 F4
Ambriz Angola 7°48S 13°8E 52 F2
Amchitka I. U.S.A. 51°32N 179°0E 74 E3
Amderma Russia 69°45N 61°30E 28 C7
Amdhi India 23°51N 81°27E 43 H9
Ameca Mexico 20°33N 104°2W 86 C4
Ameca → Mexico 20°41N 105°18W 86 C3
Amecameca de Juárez
  Mexico 19°8N 98°46W 87 D5
Ameland Neths. 53°27N 5°45E 15 A5
Amenia U.S.A. 41°51N 73°33W 83 E11
America-Antarctica Ridge
  S. Ocean 59°0S 16°0W 5 B2
American Falls U.S.A. 42°47N 112°51W 76 E7
American Falls Res.
  U.S.A. 42°47N 112°52W 76 E7
American Fork U.S.A. 40°23N 111°48W 76 F8
American Highland
  Antarctica 73°0S 75°0E 5 D6
American Samoa ☑
  Pac. Oc. 14°20S 170°0W 59 b
American Samoa △
  Amer. Samoa 14°15S 170°28W 59 b
Americana Brazil 22°45S 47°20W 95 A6
Americus U.S.A. 32°4N 84°14W 85 E12
Amersfoort Neths. 52°9N 5°23E 15 B5
Amersfoort S. Africa 26°59S 29°53E 57 D4
Amery Basin S. Ocean 68°15S 74°30E 5 C6
Amery Ice Shelf Antarctica 69°30S 72°0E 5 C6
Ames U.S.A. 42°2N 93°37W 80 D7
Amesbury U.S.A. 42°51N 70°56W 83 D14
Amet India 25°18N 73°56E 42 G5
Amga Russia 60°50N 132°0E 29 C14
Amga → Russia 62°38N 134°32E 29 C14
Amgu Russia 45°45N 137°15E 30 B8
Amgun → Russia 52°56N 139°38E 29 D14
Amherst Canada 45°48N 64°8W 73 C7
Amherst Mass., U.S.A. 42°23N 72°31W 83 D12
Amherst N.Y., U.S.A. 42°59N 78°48W 82 D6
Amherst Ohio, U.S.A. 41°24N 82°14W 82 E2
Amherst I. Canada 44°8N 76°43W 83 B8
Amherstburg Canada 42°6N 83°6W 72 D3
Amiata, Mte. Italy 42°53N 11°37E 22 C4
Amidon U.S.A. 46°29N 103°19W 80 B2
Amiens France 49°54N 2°16E 20 B5
Aminuis Namibia 23°43S 19°21E 56 C2
Amīrābād Iran 33°20N 46°16E 44 C5
Amirante Is. Seychelles 6°0S 53°0E 26 J7
Amisk △ Canada 56°43N 98°0W 71 B9
Amisk L. Canada 54°35N 102°15W 71 C8
Amistad, Presa de la
  Mexico 29°26N 101°3W 86 B4
Amistad △ U.S.A. 29°32N 101°12W 84 G4
Amite U.S.A. 30°44N 90°30W 85 F9

Amla India 21°56N 78°7E 42 J8
Amlapura = Karangasem
  Indonesia 8°27S 115°37E 37 J18
Amlia I. U.S.A. 52°4N 173°30W 74 E5
Amlwch U.K. 53°24N 4°20W 12 D3
'Ammān Jordan 31°57N 35°52E 46 D4
'Ammān □ Jordan 31°40N 36°30E 46 D5
'Ammān ✈ (AMM)
  Jordan 31°45N 36°2E 46 D5
Ammanford U.K. 51°48N 3°59W 13 F4
Ammassalik = Tasiilaq
  Greenland 65°40N 37°20W 4 C6
Ammochostos = Famagusta
  Cyprus 35°8N 33°55E 25 D12
Ammon U.S.A. 43°28N 111°58W 76 E8
Amnat Charoen
  Thailand 15°51N 104°38E 38 E5
Amnura Bangla. 24°37N 88°25E 43 G13
Āmol Iran 36°23N 52°20E 45 B7
Amorgos Greece 36°50N 25°57E 23 F11
Amory U.S.A. 33°59N 88°29W 85 E10
Amos Canada 48°35N 78°5W 72 C4
Åmot Norway 59°57N 9°54E 9 G13
Amoy = Xiamen China 24°25N 118°4E 33 D6
Ampanavoana Madag. 15°41S 50°22E 57 B9
Ampang Malaysia 3°8N 101°45E 39 L3
Ampangalana, Lakandranon'
  Madag. 22°48S 47°50E 57 C8
Ampanihy Madag. 24°40S 44°45E 57 C7
Amparafaravola Madag. 17°35S 48°13E 57 B8
Ampasinambo Madag. 20°31S 48°0E 57 C8
Ampasindava, Helodranon'
  Madag. 13°40S 48°15E 57 A8
Ampasindava, Saikanosy
  Madag. 13°42S 47°55E 57 A8
Ampenan Indonesia 8°34S 116°4E 37 K18
Amper → Germany 48°29N 11°55E 16 D6
Amphoe Kathu Thailand 7°55N 98°21E 39 a
Amphoe Thalang Thailand 8°1N 98°20E 39 a
Ampitsikinana Madag. 12°57S 49°49E 57 A8
Ampombiantambo
  Madag. 12°42S 48°57E 57 A8
Ampotaka Madag. 25°3S 44°41E 57 D7
Ampoza Madag. 22°20S 44°44E 57 C7
Amqui Canada 48°28N 67°27W 73 C6
Amravati India 20°55N 77°45E 40 J10
Amreli India 21°35N 71°17E 42 J4
Amritsar India 31°35N 74°57E 42 D6
Amroha India 28°53N 78°30E 43 E8
Amsterdam Neths. 52°23N 4°54E 15 B4
Amsterdam U.S.A. 42°56N 74°11W 83 D10
Amsterdam ✈ (AMS)
  Neths. 52°18N 4°45E 15 B4
Amsterdam, I. = Nouvelle
  Amsterdam, Î. Ind. Oc. 38°30S 77°30E 3 F13
Amstetten Austria 48°7N 14°51E 16 D8
Amudarya → Uzbekistan 43°58N 59°34E 28 E6
Amund Ringnes I.
  Canada 78°20N 96°25W 69 B12
Amundsen Abyssal Plain
  S. Ocean 65°0S 125°0W 5 C14
Amundsen Basin Arctic 87°30N 80°0E 4 A
Amundsen Gulf Canada 71°0N 124°0W 68 C7
Amundsen Ridges
  S. Ocean 69°15S 123°0W 5 C14
Amundsen-Scott Antarctica 90°0S 166°0E 5 E
Amundsen Sea Antarctica 72°0S 115°0W 5 D15
Amuntai Indonesia 2°28S 115°25E 36 E5
Amur → Russia 52°56N 141°10E 29 D15
Amurang Indonesia 1°5N 124°40E 37 D6
Amursk Russia 50°14N 136°54E 29 D14
Amyderya = Amudarya →
  Uzbekistan 43°58N 59°34E 28 E6
An Bien Vietnam 9°45N 105°0E 39 H5
An Cabhán = Cavan
  Ireland 54°0N 7°22W 10 B4
An Cóbh = Cóbh Ireland 51°51N 8°17W 10 E3
An Daingean = Dingle
  Ireland 52°9N 10°17W 10 D1
An Hoa Vietnam 15°40N 108°5E 38 E7
An Longfort = Longford
  Ireland 53°43N 7°49W 10 C4
An Muileann gCearr = Mullingar
  Ireland 53°31N 7°21W 10 C4
An Nabatīyah at Tahta
  Lebanon 33°23N 35°27E 46 B4
An Nabk Si. Arabia 31°20N 37°20E 44 D3
An Nabk Syria 34°2N 36°44E 46 A5
An Nafūd Si. Arabia 28°15N 41°0E 44 D4
An Najaf Iraq 32°3N 44°15E 44 C5
An Nás = Naas Ireland 53°12N 6°40W 10 C5
An Nāṣirīyah Iraq 31°0N 46°15E 44 D5
An Nhon Vietnam 13°55N 109°7E 38 F7
An Nu'ayrīyah Si. Arabia 27°30N 48°30E 45 E6
An Nu'mānīyah Iraq 32°32N 45°25E 44 C5
An Ros = Rush Ireland 53°31N 6°6W 10 C5
An tAonach = Nenagh
  Ireland 52°52N 8°11W 10 D3
An Thoi, Dao Vietnam 9°58N 104°0E 39 H5
An tInbhear Mór = Arklow
  Ireland 52°48N 6°10W 10 D5
An Uaimh Ireland 53°39N 6°41W 10 C5
Anabar → Russia 73°8N 113°36E 29 B12
'Anabtā West Bank 32°19N 35°7E 46 C4
Anaconda U.S.A. 46°8N 112°57W 76 C7
Anacortes U.S.A. 48°30N 122°37W 78 B4
Anadarko U.S.A. 35°4N 98°15W 84 D5
Anadolu Turkey 39°0N 30°0E 19 G5
Anadyr Russia 64°35N 177°20E 29 C18
Anadyr → Russia 64°55N 176°5E 29 C18
Anadyrskiy Zaliv Russia 64°0N 180°0E 29 C19
Anaga, Pta. de Canary Is. 28°34N 16°9W 24 F3
'Ānah Iraq 34°25N 42°0E 44 C4
Anaheim U.S.A. 33°50N 117°55W 79 M9
Anahim Lake Canada 52°28N 125°18W 70 C3
Anakapalle India 17°42N 83°6E 41 L13
Anakie Australia 23°32S 147°45E 62 C4
Analalava Madag. 14°35S 48°0E 57 A8
Analavoka Madag. 22°23S 46°30E 57 C8

Analipsis Greece 39°36N 19°55E 25 A3
Anambar → Pakistan 30°15N 68°50E 42 D3
Anambas, Kepulauan
  Indonesia 3°20N 106°30E 36 D3
Anambas Is. = Anambas,
  Kepulauan Indonesia 3°20N 106°30E 36 D3
Anamosa U.S.A. 42°7N 91°17W 80 D8
Anamur Turkey 36°8N 32°58E 44 B2
Anan Japan 33°54N 134°40E 31 H7
Anand India 22°32N 72°59E 42 H5
Anangu Pitjantjatjara ☉
  Australia 27°0S 132°0E 61 E5
Anantapur India 14°39N 77°42E 40 M10
Anantnag India 33°45N 75°10E 43 C6
Ananyiv Ukraine 47°44N 29°58E 17 E15
Anapodiaris → Greece 34°59N 25°20E 25 E7
Anápolis Brazil 16°15S 48°50W 93 G9
Anapu → Brazil 1°53S 50°53W 93 D8
Anār Iran 30°55N 55°13E 45 D7
Anārak Iran 33°25N 53°40E 45 C7
Anas → India 23°26N 74°0E 42 H5
Anatolia = Anadolu
  Turkey 39°0N 30°0E 19 G5
Anatsogno Madag. 23°33S 43°46E 57 C7
Añatuya Argentina 28°20S 62°50W 94 B3
Anatye ☉ Australia 22°29S 137°3E 62 C2
Anaunethad L. Canada 60°55N 104°25W 71 A8
Anbyŏn N. Korea 39°1N 127°35E 35 E14
Ancaster Canada 43°13N 79°59W 82 C5
Anchor Bay U.S.A. 38°48N 123°34W 78 G3
Anchorage U.S.A. 61°13N 149°54W 68 F2
Anci China 39°20N 116°40E 34 E9
Ancohuma, Nevado
  Bolivia 16°0S 68°50W 92 G5
Ancón Peru 11°50S 77°10W 92 F3
Ancona Italy 43°38N 13°30E 22 C5
Ancud Chile 42°0S 73°50W 96 E2
Ancud, G. de Chile 42°0S 73°0W 96 E2
Anda China 46°24N 125°19E 33 B7
Andacollo Argentina 37°10S 70°42W 94 D1
Andacollo Chile 30°14S 71°6W 94 C1
Andalgalá Argentina 27°40S 66°30W 94 B2
Åndalsnes Norway 62°35N 7°43E 8 E12
Andalucía □ Spain 37°35N 5°0W 21 D3
Andalusia □ = Andalucía □
  Spain 37°35N 5°0W 21 D3
Andalusia U.S.A. 31°18N 86°29W 85 F11
Andaman Is. Ind. Oc. 12°30N 92°45E 27 G11
Andaman Sea Ind. Oc. 13°0N 96°0E 36 B1
Andamooka Australia 30°27S 137°9E 63 E2
Andapa Madag. 14°39S 49°39E 57 A8
Andara Namibia 18°2S 21°9E 56 B3
Andenes Norway 69°19N 16°18E 8 B17
Andenne Belgium 50°28N 5°5E 15 D5
Anderson Alaska,
  U.S.A. 64°25N 149°15W 74 C10
Anderson Calif., U.S.A. 40°27N 122°18W 76 F2
Anderson Ind., U.S.A. 40°10N 85°41W 81 E11
Anderson Mo., U.S.A. 36°39N 94°27W 80 G6
Anderson S.C., U.S.A. 34°31N 82°39W 85 D13
Anderson → Canada 69°42N 129°0W 68 C6
Andes U.S.A. 42°12N 74°47W 83 D10
Andes, Cord. de los
  S. Amer. 20°0S 68°0W 92 H5
Andfjorden Norway 69°10N 16°20E 8 B17
Andhra Pradesh □ India 18°0N 79°0E 40 L11
Andijon Uzbekistan 41°10N 72°15E 28 E8
Andikíthira = Antikythira
  Greece 35°52N 23°15E 23 G10
Andilamena Madag. 17°1S 48°35E 57 B8
Andīmeshk Iran 32°27N 48°21E 45 C6
Andizhan = Andijon
  Uzbekistan 41°10N 72°15E 28 E8
Andoany Madag. 13°25S 48°16E 57 A8
Andoas Peru 2°47S 76°40W 92 D3
Andong S. Korea 36°40N 128°43E 35 F15
Andongwei China 35°6N 119°20E 35 G10
Andorra ■ Europe 42°30N 1°30E 20 E4
Andorra La Vella Andorra 42°31N 1°32E 20 E4
Andover U.K. 51°12N 1°29W 13 F6
Andover Maine, U.S.A. 44°38N 70°45W 83 B14
Andover Mass., U.S.A. 42°40N 71°8W 83 D13
Andover N.J., U.S.A. 40°59N 74°45W 83 F10
Andover N.Y., U.S.A. 42°10N 77°48W 82 D7
Andover Ohio, U.S.A. 41°36N 80°34W 82 E4
Andoya Norway 69°10N 15°50E 8 B16
Andradina Brazil 20°54S 51°23W 93 H8
Andrahary Madag. 13°37S 49°17E 57 A8
Andramasina Madag. 19°11S 47°35E 57 B8
Andranopasy Madag. 21°17S 43°44E 57 C7
Andranovory Madag. 23°8S 44°10E 57 C7
Andratx Spain 39°39N 2°25E 24 B9
Andreanof Is. U.S.A. 51°30N 176°0W 74 E4
Andrews S.C., U.S.A. 33°27N 79°34W 85 E15
Andrews Tex., U.S.A. 32°19N 102°33W 84 E3
Ándria Italy 41°13N 16°17E 22 D7
Andriamena Madag. 17°26S 47°30E 57 B8
Andriandampy Madag. 22°45S 45°41E 57 C8
Andriba Madag. 17°30S 46°58E 57 B8
Andringitra △ Madag. 22°13S 46°58E 57 C8
Androka Madag. 24°58S 46°31E 57 C7
Andros Greece 37°50N 24°57E 23 F11
Andros I. Bahamas 24°30N 78°0W 88 B4
Andros Town Bahamas 24°43N 77°47W 88 B4
Androscoggin →
  U.S.A. 43°58N 69°52W 83 C14
Andselv Norway 69°4N 18°34E 8 B18
Andújar Spain 38°3N 4°5W 21 C3
Andulo Angola 11°25S 16°45E 52 G3
Anegada Br. Virgin Is. 18°45N 64°20W 89 e
Anegada Passage
  W. Indies 18°15N 63°45W 89 C7
Aneto, Pico de Spain 42°37N 0°40E 21 A6
Ang Mo Kio Singapore 1°23N 103°50E 39 d
Ang Thong Thailand 14°35N 100°31E 38 E3
Ang Thong, Ko Thailand 9°37N 99°41E 39 b
Ang Thong △ Thailand 9°40N 99°43E 39 H2
Angamos, Punta Chile 23°1S 70°32W 94 A1

Angara → Russia 58°5N 94°20E 29 D10
Angarsk Russia 52°30N 104°0E 29 D11
Angas Hills Australia 23°0S 127°50E 60 D4
Angaston Australia 34°30S 139°8E 63 E2
Ånge Sweden 62°31N 15°35E 8 E16
Ángel, Salto = Angel Falls
  Venezuela 5°57N 62°30W 92 B6
Ángel de la Guarda, I.
  Mexico 29°20N 113°25W 86 B2
Angel Falls Venezuela 5°57N 62°30W 92 B6
Angeles Phil. 15°9N 120°33E 37 A6
Ängelholm Sweden 56°15N 12°58E 9 H15
Angels Camp U.S.A. 38°4N 120°32W 78 G6
Ångermanälven →
  Sweden 62°40N 18°0E 8 E17
Ångermanland Sweden 63°36N 17°45E 8 E17
Angers Canada 45°31N 75°29W 83 A9
Angers France 47°30N 0°35W 20 C3
Ängesån → Sweden 66°16N 22°47E 8 C20
Angikuni L. Canada 62°12N 99°59W 71 A9
Angkor Cambodia 13°22N 103°50E 38 F4
Angledool Australia 29°5S 147°55E 63 D4
Anglesey U.K. 53°17N 4°20W 12 D3
Anglesey, Isle of □ U.K. 53°16N 4°18W 12 D3
Angleton U.S.A. 29°10N 95°26W 84 G7
Angmagssalik = Tasiilaq
  Greenland 65°40N 37°20W 4 C6
Ango Dem. Rep. of the Congo 4°10N 26°5E 54 B2
Angoche Mozam. 16°8S 39°55E 55 F4
Angoche, I. Mozam. 16°20S 39°50E 55 F4
Angol Chile 37°56S 72°45W 94 D1
Angola Ind., U.S.A. 41°38N 85°0W 81 E11
Angola N.Y., U.S.A. 42°38N 79°2W 82 D5
Angola ■ Africa 12°0S 18°0E 53 G3
Angoulême France 45°39N 0°10E 20 D4
Angoumois France 45°50N 0°25E 20 D3
Angra do Heroismo
  Azores 38°39N 27°13W 50 a
Angra dos Reis Brazil 23°0S 44°10W 95 A7
Angtassom Cambodia 11°1N 104°41E 39 G5
Angu
  Dem. Rep. of the Congo 3°23N 24°30E 54 B1
Anguang China 45°15N 123°45E 35 B12
Anguilla ☑ W. Indies 18°14N 63°5W 89 C7
Anguo China 38°28N 115°15E 34 E8
Angurugu Australia 14°0S 136°25E 62 A2
Angus Canada 44°19N 79°53W 82 B5
Angus □ U.K. 56°46N 2°56W 11 E6
Angwa → Zimbabwe 16°0S 30°23E 57 B5
Anhanduí → Brazil 21°46S 52°9W 95 A5
Anholt Denmark 56°42N 11°33E 9 H14
Anhui □ China 32°0N 117°0E 33 C6
Anhwei = Anhui □ China 32°0N 117°0E 33 C6
Anichab Namibia 21°0S 14°46E 56 C1
Animas → U.S.A. 36°43N 108°13W 77 H9
Anivorano Madag. 18°44S 48°58E 57 B8
Anjalankoski Finland 60°45N 26°51E 8 F22
Anjar India 23°6N 70°10E 42 H4
Anjou France 47°20N 0°15W 20 C3
Anjouan Comoros Is. 12°15S 44°20E 53 a
Anjozorobe Madag. 18°22S 47°52E 57 B8
Anju N. Korea 39°36N 125°40E 35 E13
Ankaboa, Tanjona
  Madag. 21°58S 43°20E 57 C7
Ankang China 32°40N 109°1E 34 H5
Ankara Turkey 39°57N 32°54E 19 G5
Ankarafantsika △ Madag. 16°8S 47°5E 57 B8
Ankaramena Madag. 21°57S 46°39E 57 C8
Ankaratra Madag. 19°25S 47°12E 53 H9
Ankasakasa Madag. 16°21S 44°52E 57 B7
Ankavandra Madag. 18°46S 45°18E 57 B8
Ankazoabo Madag. 22°18S 44°31E 57 C7
Ankazobe Madag. 18°20S 47°10E 57 B8
Ankeny U.S.A. 41°44N 93°36W 80 E7
Ankilimalinika Madag. 22°58S 43°45E 57 C7
Ankilizato Madag. 20°25S 45°1E 57 C8
Ankisabe Madag. 19°17S 46°29E 57 B8
Ankoro
  Dem. Rep. of the Congo 6°45S 26°55E 54 D2
Ankororoka Madag. 25°30S 45°11E 57 D8
Anlong Veng Cambodia 14°14N 104°5E 38 E5
Anmyeondo S. Korea 36°25N 126°25E 35 F14
Ann, C. U.S.A. 42°38N 70°35W 83 D14
Ann Arbor U.S.A. 42°17N 83°45W 81 D12
Anna Russia 37°28N 89°15W 80 G9
Annaba Algeria 36°50N 7°46E 50 A7
Annalee → Ireland 54°2N 7°24W 10 B4
Annam Vietnam 16°0N 108°0E 38 E7
Annamitique, Chaîne
  Asia 17°0N 106°0E 38 D6
Annan U.K. 54°59N 3°16W 11 G5
Annan → U.K. 54°58N 3°16W 11 G5
Annapolis U.S.A. 38°59N 76°30W 81 F15
Annapolis Royal Canada 44°44N 65°32W 73 D6
Annapurna Nepal 28°34N 83°50E 43 E10
Annean, L. Australia 26°54S 118°14E 61 E2
Annecy France 45°55N 6°8E 20 D7
Annette I. U.S.A. 55°9N 131°28W 70 B2
Anning China 24°55N 102°26E 32 D5
Anniston U.S.A. 33°39N 85°50W 85 E11
Annobón Atl. Oc. 1°25S 5°36E 49 G4
Annotto B. Jamaica 18°17N 76°45W 88 a
Annville U.S.A. 40°20N 76°31W 83 F8
Anogia Greece 35°16N 24°52E 25 D6
Anorotsangana Madag. 13°56S 47°55E 57 A8
Anosibe Madag. 19°26S 48°13E 57 B8
Anping Hebei, China 38°15N 115°30E 34 E8
Anping Liaoning, China 41°5N 123°30E 35 D12
Anqing China 30°30N 117°3E 33 C6
Anqiu China 36°25N 119°10E 35 F10
Ansai China 36°50N 109°20E 34 F5
Ansan S. Korea 37°21N 126°52E 35 F14
Ansbach Germany 49°28N 10°34E 16 D6
Anse Boileau Seychelles 4°43S 55°29E 53 b
Anse Royale Seychelles 4°44S 55°31E 53 b
Anshan China 41°5N 122°58E 35 D12
Anshun China 26°18N 105°57E 32 D5
Ansley U.S.A. 41°18N 99°23W 80 E4

Anson U.S.A. 32°45N 99°54W 84 E5
Anson B. Australia 13°20S 130°6E 60 B5
Ansongo Mali 15°25N 0°35E 50 E6
Ansonia U.S.A. 41°21N 73°5W 83 E11
Anstruther U.K. 56°14N 2°41W 11 E6
Ansudu Indonesia 2°11S 139°22E 37 E9
Antabamba Peru 14°40S 73°0W 92 F4
Antakya = Hatay Turkey 36°14N 36°10E 44 B3
Antalaha Madag. 14°57S 50°20E 57 A9
Antalya Turkey 36°52N 30°45E 19 G5
Antalya Körfezi Turkey 36°15N 31°30E 19 G5
Antambohobe Madag. 22°20S 46°47E 57 C8
Antanambao-Manampotsy
  Madag. 19°29S 48°34E 57 B8
Antanambe Madag. 16°26S 49°52E 57 B8
Antananarivo Madag. 18°55S 47°31E 57 B8
Antananarivo □ Madag. 19°0S 47°0E 57 B8
Antanifotsy Madag. 19°39S 47°19E 57 B8
Antanimbaribe Madag. 21°30S 44°48E 57 C7
Antanimora Madag. 24°49S 45°40E 57 C8
Antarctic Pen. Antarctica 67°0S 60°0W 5 C18
Antarctica 90°0S 0°0 5 E
Antelope Zimbabwe 21°2S 28°31E 55 G2
Antequera Paraguay 24°8S 57°7W 94 A4
Antequera Spain 37°5N 4°33W 21 D3
Antero, Mt. U.S.A. 38°41N 106°15W 76 G10
Antevamena Madag. 21°2S 44°8E 57 C7
Anthony Kans., U.S.A. 37°9N 98°2W 80 G4
Anthony N. Mex.,
  U.S.A. 32°0N 106°36W 77 K10
Anti Atlas Morocco 30°0N 8°30W 50 C4
Anti-Lebanon = Sharqi, Al Jabal
  ash Lebanon 33°40N 36°10E 46 B5
Antibes France 43°34N 7°6E 20 E7
Anticosti, Î. d' Canada 49°30N 63°0W 73 C7
Antigo U.S.A. 45°9N 89°9W 80 C9
Antigonish Canada 45°38N 61°58W 73 C7
Antigua Canary Is. 28°24N 14°1W 24 F5
Antigua Guatemala 14°34N 90°41W 88 D1
Antigua W. Indies 17°0N 61°50W 89 C7
Antigua & Barbuda ■
  W. Indies 17°20N 61°48W 89 C7
Antikythira Greece 35°52N 23°15E 23 G10
Antilla Cuba 20°40N 75°50W 88 B4
Antilles = West Indies
  Cent. Amer. 15°0N 65°0W 89 D7
Antioch U.S.A. 38°1N 121°48W 78 G5
Antioquia Colombia 6°40N 75°55W 92 B3
Antipodes Is. Pac. Oc. 49°45S 178°40E 64 M9
Antlers U.S.A. 34°14N 95°37W 84 D7
Antoetra Madag. 20°46S 47°20E 57 C8
Antofagasta Chile 23°50S 70°30W 94 A1
Antofagasta □ Chile 24°0S 69°0W 94 A2
Antofagasta de la Sierra
  Argentina 26°5S 67°20W 94 B2
Antofalla Argentina 25°30S 68°5W 94 B2
Antofalla, Salar de
  Argentina 25°40S 67°45W 94 B2
Anton U.S.A. 33°49N 102°10W 84 E3
Antongila, Helodrano
  Madag. 15°30S 49°50E 57 B8
Antonibé Madag. 15°7S 47°24E 57 B8
Antonibé, Presqu'île d'
  Madag. 14°55S 47°20E 57 A8
Antonina Brazil 25°26S 48°42W 95 B6
Antrim U.K. 54°43N 6°14W 10 B5
Antrim U.S.A. 40°7N 81°21W 82 F3
Antrim □ U.K. 54°56N 6°25W 10 B5
Antrim, Mts. of U.K. 55°3N 6°14W 10 A5
Antrim Plateau Australia 18°8S 128°20E 60 C4
Antsakabary Madag. 15°3S 48°56E 57 B8
Antsalova Madag. 18°40S 44°37E 57 B7
Antsenavolo Madag. 21°24S 48°3E 57 C8
Antsiafabositra Madag. 17°18S 46°57E 57 B8
Antsirabe Antananarivo,
  Madag. 19°55S 47°2E 57 B8
Antsirabe Antsiranana,
  Madag. 14°0S 49°59E 57 A8
Antsirabe Mahajanga,
  Madag. 15°57S 48°58E 57 B8
Antsiranana Madag. 12°25S 49°20E 57 A8
Antsiranana □ Madag. 12°16S 49°17E 57 A8
Antsohihy Madag. 14°50S 47°53E 57 A8
Antsohimbondrona Serana
  Madag. 13°7S 48°48E 57 A8
Antu China 42°30N 128°20E 35 C15
Antwerp = Antwerpen
  Belgium 51°13N 4°25E 15 C4
Antwerp U.S.A. 44°12N 75°37W 83 B9
Antwerpen Belgium 51°13N 4°25E 15 C4
Antwerpen □ Belgium 51°15N 4°40E 15 C4
Anupgarh India 29°10N 73°10E 42 E5
Anuppur India 23°6N 81°41E 43 H9
Anuradhapura Sri Lanka 8°22N 80°28E 40 Q12
Anurrete ☉ Australia 20°50S 135°38E 62 C2
Anveh Iran 27°23N 54°11E 45 E7
Anvers = Antwerpen
  Belgium 51°13N 4°25E 15 C4
Anvers I. Antarctica 64°30S 63°40W 5 C17
Anxi China 40°30N 95°43E 32 B4
Anxious B. Australia 33°24S 134°45E 63 E1
Anyang China 36°5N 114°21E 34 F8
Anyang S. Korea 37°23N 126°55E 35 F14
Anyer Indonesia 6°4S 105°53E 37 G11
Anyi China 35°2N 111°2E 34 G6
Anza U.S.A. 33°35N 116°39W 79 M10
Anze China 36°10N 112°12E 34 F7
Anzhero-Sudzhensk
  Russia 56°10N 86°0E 28 D9
Ánzio Italy 41°27N 12°37E 22 D5
Ao Makham Thailand 7°50N 98°24E 39 a
Ao Phangnga △ Thailand 8°10N 98°32E 39 a
Aoga-Shima Japan 32°28N 139°46E 31 H9
Aoji N. Korea 42°31N 130°23E 35 C16
Aomen = Macau
  China 22°12N 113°33E 33 G10
Aomori Japan 40°45N 140°45E 30 D10
Aomori □ Japan 40°45N 140°40E 30 D10
Aonla India 28°16N 79°11E 43 E8

Aorai, Mt. *Tahiti* 17°34S 149°30W **59 d**
Aoraki Mount Cook
  N.Z. 43°36S 170°9E **59 E3**
Aoral, Phnum *Cambodia* 12°0N 104°15E **39 G5**
Aosta *Italy* 45°45N 7°20E **20 D7**
Aotearoa = New Zealand ■
  Oceania 40°0S 176°0E **59 D6**
Aoukâr *Mauritania* 17°40N 10°0W **50 E4**
Aozou Strip *Chad* 22°0N 19°0E **51 D9**
Apá → *S. Amer.* 22°6S 58°2W **94 A4**
Apache *U.S.A.* 34°54N 98°22W **84 D5**
Apache Junction
  U.S.A. 33°25N 111°33W **77 K8**
Apalachee B. *U.S.A.* 30°0N 84°0W **85 G13**
Apalachicola *U.S.A.* 29°43N 84°59W **85 G12**
Apalachicola →
  U.S.A. 29°43N 84°58W **85 G12**
Apaporis → *Colombia* 1°23S 69°25W **92 D5**
Aparados da Serra △
  Brazil 29°10S 50°8W **95 B5**
Aparri *Phil.* 18°22N 121°38E **37 A6**
Apatity *Russia* 67°34N 33°22E **8 C25**
Apatula = Finke
  Australia 25°34S 134°35E **62 D1**
Apatzingán *Mexico* 19°5N 102°21W **86 D4**
Apeldoorn *Neths.* 52°13N 5°57E **15 B5**
Apennines = Appennini
  Italy 44°30N 10°0E **22 B4**
Api *Nepal* 30°0N 80°57E **32 C3**
Apia *Samoa* 13°50S 171°50W **59 b**
Apiacás, Serra dos *Brazil* 9°50S 57°0W **92 E7**
Apies → *S. Africa* 25°15S 28°8E **57 D4**
Apizaco *Mexico* 19°25N 98°8W **87 D5**
Aplao *Peru* 16°0S 72°40W **92 G4**
Apo, Mt. *Phil.* 6°53N 125°14E **37 C7**
Apolakia *Greece* 36°5N 27°48E **25 C9**
Apolakia, Ormos *Greece* 36°5N 27°45E **25 C9**
Apollonia = Sūsah
  Libya 32°52N 21°59E **51 B10**
Apollonia *Greece* 36°15N 27°58E **25 C9**
Apolo *Bolivia* 14°30S 68°30W **92 F5**
Apopa *El Salv.* 13°48N 89°10W **88 D2**
Aporé → *Brazil* 19°27S 50°57W **93 G8**
Apostle Is. *U.S.A.* 47°0N 90°40W **80 B8**
Apostle Islands △ *U.S.A.* 46°55N 91°0W **80 B8**
Apóstoles *Argentina* 28°0S 56°0W **95 B4**
Apostolos Andreas, C.
  Cyprus 35°42N 34°35E **25 D13**
Apoteri *Guyana* 4°2N 58°32W **92 C7**
Appalachian Mts. *U.S.A.* 38°0N 80°0W **81 G14**
Appennini *Italy* 44°30N 10°0E **22 B4**
Apple Hill *Canada* 45°13N 74°46W **83 A10**
Apple Valley *U.S.A.* 34°32N 117°14W **79 L9**
Appleby-in-Westmorland
  U.K. 54°35N 2°29W **12 C5**
Appledore *U.K.* 51°3N 4°13W **13 F3**
Appleton *U.S.A.* 44°16N 88°25W **80 C9**
Approuague →
  Fr. Guiana 4°30N 51°57W **93 C8**
Aprília *Italy* 41°36N 12°39E **22 D5**
Apsley *Canada* 44°45N 78°6W **82 B6**
Apucarana *Brazil* 23°55S 51°33W **95 A5**
Apure → *Venezuela* 7°37N 66°25W **92 B5**
Apurímac → *Peru* 12°17S 73°56W **92 F4**
Aqaba = Al 'Aqabah
  Jordan 29°31N 35°0E **46 F4**
Aqaba, G. of *Red Sea* 29°0N 34°40E **44 D2**
'Aqabah, Khalīj al = Aqaba, G. of
  Red Sea 29°0N 34°40E **44 D2**
'Aqdā *Iran* 32°26N 53°37E **45 C7**
'Aqrah *Iraq* 36°46N 43°45E **44 B4**
Aqsay *Kazakhstan* 51°11N 53°0E **19 D9**
Aqtaū *Kazakhstan* 43°39N 51°12E **19 F9**
Aqtöbe *Kazakhstan* 50°17N 57°10E **19 D10**
Aqtoghay *Kazakhstan* 46°57N 79°40E **28 E8**
Aquidauana *Brazil* 20°30S 55°50W **93 H7**
Aquila *Mexico* 18°36N 103°30W **86 D4**
Aquiles Serdán *Mexico* 28°36N 105°53W **86 B3**
Aquin *Haiti* 18°16N 73°24W **89 C5**
Aquitain, Bassin *France* 44°0N 0°30W **20 D3**
Ar Rafid *Syria* 32°57N 35°52E **46 C4**
Ar Raḥḥālīyah *Iraq* 32°44N 43°23E **44 C4**
Ar Ramādī *Iraq* 33°25N 43°20E **44 C4**
Ar Ramthā *Jordan* 32°34N 36°0E **46 C5**
Ar Raqqah *Syria* 35°59N 39°8E **44 C3**
Ar Rashidiya = Er Rachidia
  Morocco 31°58N 4°20W **50 B5**
Ar Rass *Si. Arabia* 25°50N 43°40E **44 E4**
Ar Rayyan *Qatar* 25°17N 51°25E **45 E6**
Ar Rifā'ī *Iraq* 31°50N 46°10E **44 D5**
Ar Riyāḍ *Si. Arabia* 24°41N 46°42E **44 E5**
Ar Ru'ays *Qatar* 26°8N 51°12E **45 E6**
Ar Rukhaymīyah *Iraq* 29°22N 45°38E **44 D5**
Ar Rumaythah *Iraq* 31°31N 45°12E **44 D5**
Ar Ruṣāfah *Syria* 35°45N 38°49E **44 C3**
Ar Ruṭbah *Iraq* 33°0N 40°15E **44 C4**
Ara *India* 25°35N 84°32E **43 G11**
'Arab *U.S.A.* 34°19N 86°30W **85 D11**
'Arab, Bahr el → *Sudan* 9°0N 29°30E **51 G11**
'Arab, Shaṭṭ al → *Asia* 29°57N 48°34E **45 D6**
'Arabābād *Iran* 33°2N 57°41E **45 C8**
Arabia *Asia* 25°0N 45°0E **26 F6**
Arabian Desert = Es Sahrâ' Esh
  Sharqîya *Egypt* 27°30N 32°30E **51 C12**
Arabian Gulf = Persian Gulf
  Asia 27°0N 50°0E **45 E6**
Arabian Sea *Ind. Oc.* 16°0N 65°0E **26 G8**
Aracaju *Brazil* 10°55S 37°4W **93 F11**
Aracati *Brazil* 4°30S 37°44W **93 D11**
Araçatuba *Brazil* 21°10S 50°30W **95 A5**
Aracena *Spain* 37°53N 6°38W **21 D2**
Araçuaí *Brazil* 16°52S 42°4W **93 G10**
'Arad *Israel* 31°15N 35°12E **46 D4**
Arad *Romania* 46°10N 21°20E **17 E11**
Arādān *Iran* 35°21N 52°30E **45 C7**
Aradhippou *Cyprus* 34°57N 33°36E **25 E12**
Arafura Sea *E. Indies* 9°0S 135°0E **58 B6**
Aragón □ *Spain* 41°25N 0°40W **21 B5**

Aragón → *Spain* 42°13N 1°44W **21 A5**
Araguacema *Brazil* 8°50S 49°20W **93 E9**
Araguaia → *Brazil* 5°21S 48°41W **93 E9**
Araguaína *Brazil* 7°12S 48°12W **93 E9**
Araguari *Brazil* 18°38S 48°11W **93 G9**
Araguari → *Brazil* 1°15N 49°55W **93 C9**
Araín *India* 26°27N 75°2E **42 F6**
Arak *Algeria* 25°20N 3°45E **50 C6**
Arāk *Iran* 34°0N 49°40E **45 C6**
Arakan Coast *Burma* 19°0N 94°0E **41 K19**
Arakan Yoma *Burma* 20°0N 94°40E **41 K19**
Araks = Aras, Rūd-e →
  Asia 40°5N 48°29E **44 B5**
Aral *Kazakhstan* 46°41N 61°45E **28 E7**
Aral Sea *Asia* 44°30N 60°0E **28 E7**
Aral Tengizi = Aral Sea
  Asia 44°30N 60°0E **28 E7**
Aralsk = Aral *Kazakhstan* 46°41N 61°45E **28 E7**
Aralskoye More = Aral Sea
  Asia 44°30N 60°0E **28 E7**
Aramac *Australia* 22°58S 145°14E **62 C4**
Aran I. *Ireland* 55°0N 8°30W **10 A3**
Aran Is. *Ireland* 53°6N 9°38W **10 C2**
Aranda de Duero *Spain* 41°39N 3°42W **21 B4**
Arandān *Iran* 35°23N 46°55E **44 C5**
Aranjuez *Spain* 40°1N 3°40W **21 B4**
Aranos *Namibia* 24°9S 19°7E **56 C2**
Aransas Pass *U.S.A.* 27°55N 97°9W **84 H6**
Aranyaprathet *Thailand* 13°41N 102°30E **38 F4**
Arapey Grande →
  Uruguay 30°55S 57°49W **94 C4**
Arapgir *Turkey* 39°5N 38°30E **44 B3**
Arapiraca *Brazil* 9°45S 36°39W **93 E11**
Arapongas *Brazil* 23°29S 51°28W **95 A5**
Ar'ar *Si. Arabia* 30°59N 41°2E **44 D4**
Araranguá *Brazil* 29°0S 49°30W **95 B6**
Araraquara *Brazil* 21°50S 48°0W **93 H9**
Araras, Serra das *Brazil* 25°0S 53°10W **95 B5**
Ararat *Australia* 37°16S 142°58E **63 F3**
Ararat, Mt. = Ağrı Dağı
  Turkey 39°50N 44°15E **44 B5**
Araria *India* 26°9N 87°33E **43 F12**
Araripe, Chapada do
  Brazil 7°20S 40°0W **93 E11**
Araruama, L. de *Brazil* 22°53S 42°12W **95 A7**
Aras = Aras, Rūd-e →
  Asia 40°5N 48°29E **44 B5**
Aras, Rūd-e → *Asia* 40°5N 48°29E **44 B5**
Arauca *Colombia* 7°0N 70°40W **92 B4**
Arauca → *Venezuela* 7°24N 66°35W **92 B5**
Arauco *Chile* 37°16S 73°25W **94 D1**
Aravalli Range *India* 25°0N 73°30E **42 G5**
Arawale △ *Kenya* 1°24S 40°9E **54 C5**
Araxá *Brazil* 19°35S 46°55W **93 G9**
Araxes = Aras, Rūd-e →
  Asia 40°5N 48°29E **44 B5**
Araya, Pen. de *Venezuela* 10°40N 64°0W **92 A6**
Araz = Aras, Rūd-e →
  Asia 40°5N 48°29E **44 B5**
Arba Minch *Ethiopia* 6°0N 37°30E **47 F2**
Arbat *Iraq* 35°25N 45°35E **44 C5**
Árbatax *Italy* 39°56N 9°42E **22 E3**
Arbīl *Iraq* 36°15N 44°5E **44 B5**
Arborfield *Canada* 53°6N 103°39W **71 C8**
Arborg *Canada* 50°54N 97°13W **71 C9**
Arbroath *U.K.* 56°34N 2°35W **11 E6**
Arbuckle *U.S.A.* 39°1N 122°3W **78 F4**
Arcachon *France* 44°40N 1°10W **20 D3**
Arcade *U.S.A.* 42°32N 78°25W **82 D6**
Arcadia *Fla., U.S.A.* 27°13N 81°52W **85 H14**
Arcadia *La., U.S.A.* 32°33N 92°55W **84 E8**
Arcadia *Pa., U.S.A.* 40°47N 78°51W **82 F6**
Arcata *U.S.A.* 40°52N 124°5W **76 F1**
Archangel = Arkhangelsk
  Russia 64°38N 40°36E **18 B7**
Archangelos *Greece* 36°13N 28°7E **25 C10**
Archbald *U.S.A.* 41°30N 75°32W **83 E9**
Archer → *Australia* 13°28S 141°41E **62 A3**
Archer B. *Australia* 13°20S 141°30E **62 A3**
Archer Bend = Mungkan
  Kandju △ *Australia* 13°35S 142°52E **62 A3**
Archers Post *Kenya* 0°35N 37°35E **54 B4**
Arches △ *U.S.A.* 38°45N 109°25W **76 G9**
Archipel-de-Mingan △
  Canada 50°13N 63°10W **73 B7**
Archipiélago Chinijo △
  Canary Is. 29°20N 13°30W **24 E6**
Archipiélago Los Roques △
  Venezuela 11°50N 66°44W **89 D6**
Arckaringa Cr. →
  Australia 28°10S 135°22E **63 D2**
Arco *U.S.A.* 43°38N 113°18W **76 E7**
Arcos de la Frontera
  Spain 36°45N 5°49W **21 D3**
Arcot *India* 12°53N 79°20E **40 N11**
Arctic Bay *Canada* 73°1N 85°7W **69 C14**
Arctic Mid-Ocean Ridge
  Arctic 87°0N 90°0E **4 A**
Arctic Ocean *Arctic* 78°0N 160°0W **4 B18**
Arctic Red River = Tsiigehtchic
  Canada 67°15N 134°0W **68 D5**
Arctowski *Antarctica* 62°30S 58°0W **5 C18**
Arda → *Bulgaria* 41°40N 26°30E **23 D12**
Ardabīl *Iran* 38°15N 48°18E **45 B6**
Ardabīl □ *Iran* 38°20N 48°0E **45 B6**
Ardakān = Sepīdān *Iran* 30°20N 52°5E **45 D7**
Ardakān *Iran* 32°19N 53°59E **45 C7**
Ardara *Ireland* 54°46N 8°25W **10 B3**
Ardee *Ireland* 53°52N 6°33W **10 C5**
Arden *Canada* 44°43N 76°56W **82 B8**
Arden *Calif., U.S.A.* 38°36N 121°33W **78 G5**
Arden *Nev., U.S.A.* 36°1N 115°14W **79 J11**
Ardenne *Belgium* 49°50N 5°5E **15 E5**
Ardennes = Ardenne
  Belgium 49°50N 5°5E **15 E5**
Arderin *Ireland* 53°2N 7°39W **10 C4**
Ardestān *Iran* 33°20N 52°25E **45 C7**
Ardfert *Ireland* 52°20N 9°47W **10 D2**

Ardglass *U.K.* 54°17N 5°36W **10 B6**
Ardivachar Pt. *U.K.* 57°23N 7°26W **11 D1**
Ardlethan *Australia* 34°22S 146°53E **63 E4**
Ardmore *Okla., U.S.A.* 34°10N 97°8W **84 D6**
Ardmore *Pa., U.S.A.* 40°2N 75°17W **83 F9**
Ardnamurchan, Pt. of
  U.K. 56°43N 6°14W **11 E2**
Ardnave Pt. *U.K.* 55°53N 6°20W **11 F2**
Ardrossan *Australia* 34°26S 137°53E **63 E2**
Ardrossan *U.K.* 55°39N 4°49W **11 F4**
Ards Pen. *U.K.* 54°33N 5°34W **10 B6**
Arecibo *Puerto Rico* 18°29N 66°43W **89 d**
Areia Branca *Brazil* 5°0S 37°0W **93 E11**
Arena, Pt. *U.S.A.* 38°57N 123°44W **78 G3**
Arenal *Honduras* 15°21N 86°50W **88 C2**
Arendal *Norway* 58°28N 8°46E **9 G13**
Arequipa *Peru* 16°20S 71°30W **92 G4**
Arévalo *Spain* 41°3N 4°43W **21 B3**
Arezzo *Italy* 43°25N 11°53E **22 C4**
Arga *Turkey* 38°21N 37°59E **44 B3**
Arganda del Rey *Spain* 40°19N 3°26W **21 B4**
Argarapa ○ *Australia* 22°20S 134°58E **62 C1**
Argenta *Canada* 50°11N 116°56W **70 C5**
Argentan *France* 48°45N 0°1W **20 B3**
Argentário, Mte. *Italy* 42°24N 11°9E **22 C4**
Argentia *Canada* 47°18N 53°58W **73 C9**
Argentina ■ *S. Amer.* 35°0S 66°0W **96 D3**
Argentine Basin *Atl. Oc.* 45°0S 45°0W **96 H6**
Argentino, L. *Argentina* 50°10S 73°0W **96 G2**
Argeş → *Romania* 44°5N 26°38E **17 F14**
Arghandab → *Afghan.* 31°30N 64°15E **42 D1**
Argirades *Greece* 39°27N 19°58E **25 B3**
Argiroupoli *Greece* 35°17N 24°20E **25 D6**
Argolikos Kolpos *Greece* 37°20N 22°52E **23 F10**
Argos *Greece* 37°40N 22°43E **23 F10**
Argostoli *Greece* 38°11N 20°29E **23 E9**
Arguello, Pt. *U.S.A.* 34°35N 120°39W **79 L6**
Arguineguín *Canary Is.* 27°46N 15°41W **24 G4**
Argun → *Russia* 53°20N 121°28E **29 A13**
Argungu *Nigeria* 12°40N 4°31E **50 F6**
Argus Pk. *U.S.A.* 35°52N 117°26W **79 K9**
Argyle, L. *Australia* 16°20S 128°40E **60 C4**
Argyle *U.S.A.* 44°57N 168°50E **59 F2**
Argyll □ *U.K.* 56°6N 5°0W **11 E4**
Argyll & Bute □ *U.K.* 56°13N 5°28E **11 E3**
Århus *Denmark* 56°8N 10°11E **9 H14**
Ariadnoye *Russia* 45°8N 134°25E **30 B7**
Ariamsvlei *Namibia* 28°9S 19°51E **56 D2**
Ariana *Tunisia* 36°52N 10°12E **51 A8**
Arica *Chile* 18°32S 70°20W **92 G4**
Arica *Colombia* 2°0S 71°50W **92 D4**
Arico *Canary Is.* 28°9N 16°29W **24 F3**
Arid, C. *Australia* 34°1S 123°10E **61 F3**
Arida *Japan* 34°5N 135°8E **31 G7**
Aride *Seychelles* 4°13S 55°40E **53 b**
Ariège → *France* 43°30N 1°25E **20 E4**
Arila, Akra *Greece* 39°43N 19°39E **25 A3**
Arima *Trin. & Tob.* 10°38N 61°17W **93 K15**
Arinos → *Brazil* 10°25S 58°20W **92 F7**
Ario de Rosales *Mexico* 19°12N 101°43W **86 D4**
Aripo, Mt. *Trin. & Tob.* 10°45N 61°15W **93 K15**
Aripuanã *Brazil* 9°25S 60°30W **92 E6**
Aripuanã → *Brazil* 5°7S 60°25W **92 E6**
Ariquemes *Brazil* 9°55S 63°6W **92 E6**
Arisaig *U.K.* 56°55N 5°51W **11 E3**
Aristazabal I. *Canada* 52°40N 129°10W **70 C3**
Arivonimamo *Madag.* 19°1S 47°11E **57 B8**
Arizaro, Salar de
  Argentina 24°40S 67°50W **94 A2**
Arizona *Argentina* 35°45S 65°25W **94 D2**
Arizona □ *U.S.A.* 34°0N 112°0W **77 J8**
Arizpe *Mexico* 30°20N 110°10W **86 A2**
'Arjah *Si. Arabia* 24°43N 44°17E **44 E5**
Arjeplog *Sweden* 66°3N 17°54E **8 C17**
Arjeplouvve = Arjeplog
  Sweden 66°3N 17°54E **8 C17**
Arjona *Colombia* 10°14N 75°22W **92 A3**
Arjuna *Indonesia* 7°49S 112°34E **37 G15**
Arka *Russia* 60°15N 142°0E **29 C15**
Arkadelphia *U.S.A.* 34°7N 93°4W **84 D8**
Arkadhia *Greece* 37°30N 22°20E **23 F10**
Arkalyk = Arqalyk
  Kazakhstan 50°13N 66°50E **28 D7**
Arkansas □ *U.S.A.* 35°0N 92°30W **84 D8**
Arkansas → *U.S.A.* 33°47N 91°4W **84 E9**
Arkansas City *U.S.A.* 37°4N 97°2W **80 G6**
Arkaroola *Australia* 30°20S 139°22E **63 E2**
Arkhangelsk *Russia* 64°38N 40°36E **18 B7**
Arki *India* 31°9N 76°58E **42 D7**
Arklow *Ireland* 52°48N 6°10W **10 D5**
Arkport *U.S.A.* 42°24N 77°42W **82 D7**
Arkticheskiy, Mys
  Russia 81°10N 95°0E **29 A10**
Arkville *U.S.A.* 42°9N 74°37W **83 D10**
Arlanza → *Spain* 42°3N 4°17W **21 A3**
Arlanzón → *Spain* 42°3N 4°17W **21 A3**
Arlbergpass *Austria* 47°9N 10°12E **16 E6**
Arlbergtunnel *Austria* 47°9N 10°12E **16 E6**
Arles *France* 43°41N 4°40E **20 E6**
Arlington *S. Africa* 28°1S 27°53E **57 D4**
Arlington *N.Y., U.S.A.* 41°42N 73°54W **83 E11**
Arlington *Oreg., U.S.A.* 45°43N 120°12W **76 D3**
Arlington *S. Dak., U.S.A.* 44°22N 97°8W **80 C5**
Arlington *Tex., U.S.A.* 32°44N 97°6W **84 E6**
Arlington *Va., U.S.A.* 38°53N 77°7W **81 F15**
Arlington *Vt., U.S.A.* 43°5N 73°9W **83 C11**
Arlington *Wash., U.S.A.* 48°12N 122°8W **78 B4**
Arlington Heights
  U.S.A. 42°5N 87°59W **80 D10**
Arlit *Niger* 19°0N 7°38E **50 E7**
Arlon *Belgium* 49°42N 5°49E **15 E5**
Arlparra *Australia* 22°11S 134°30E **62 C1**
Arltunga *Australia* 23°26S 134°41E **62 C1**
Armadale *Australia* 32°9S 116°0E **61 F2**
Armagh *U.K.* 54°21N 6°39W **10 B5**
Armagh □ *U.K.* 54°18N 6°37W **10 B5**
Armando Bermudez △
  Dom. Rep. 19°3N 71°0W **89 C5**
Armavir *Russia* 45°2N 41°7E **19 E7**
Armenia *Colombia* 4°35N 75°45W **92 C3**
Armenia ■ *Asia* 40°20N 45°0E **19 F7**

Armenistis, Akra *Greece* 36°8N 27°42E **25 C9**
Armidale *Australia* 30°30S 151°40E **63 E5**
Armour *U.S.A.* 43°19N 98°21W **80 D4**
Armstrong *B.C.,*
  Canada 50°25N 119°10W **70 C5**
Armstrong *Ont., Canada* 50°18N 89°4W **72 B2**
Arnarfjörður *Iceland* 65°48N 23°40W **8 D2**
Arnaud → *Canada* 59°59N 69°46W **69 F18**
Arnauti, C. *Cyprus* 35°6N 32°17E **25 D11**
Arnett *U.S.A.* 36°8N 99°46W **84 C5**
Arnhem *Neths.* 51°58N 5°55E **15 C5**
Arnhem, C. *Australia* 12°20S 137°30E **62 A2**
Arnhem B. *Australia* 12°20S 136°10E **62 A2**
Arnhem Land *Australia* 13°10S 134°30E **62 A1**
Arnhem Land ○
  Australia 12°50S 134°50E **62 A1**
Arno → *Italy* 43°41N 10°17E **22 C4**
Arno Bay *Australia* 33°54S 136°34E **63 E2**
Arnold *U.K.* 53°1N 1°7W **12 D6**
Arnold *U.S.A.* 38°15N 120°21W **78 G6**
Arnot *Canada* 55°56N 96°41W **71 B9**
Arnøya *Norway* 70°9N 20°40E **8 A19**
Arnprior *Canada* 45°26N 76°21W **83 A8**
Arnsberg *Germany* 51°24N 8°5E **16 C5**
Aroa, Pte. *Moorea* 17°28S 149°46W **59 d**
Aroab *Namibia* 26°41S 19°39E **56 D2**
Aron *India* 25°57N 77°56E **42 G6**
Arona *Canary Is.* 28°6N 16°40W **24 F3**
Aros → *Mexico* 29°9N 107°57W **86 B3**
Arqalyk *Kazakhstan* 50°13N 66°50E **28 D7**
Arrah = Ara *India* 25°35N 84°32E **43 G11**
Arrah *Ivory C.* 6°40N 3°58W **50 G5**
Arran *U.K.* 55°34N 5°12W **11 F3**
Arras *France* 50°17N 2°46E **20 A5**
Arrecife *Canary Is.* 28°57N 13°37W **24 F6**
Arrecifes *Argentina* 34°6S 60°9W **94 C3**
Arrée, Mts. d' *France* 48°26N 3°55W **20 B2**
Arriaga *Mexico* 16°14N 93°54W **87 D6**
Arrilalah *Australia* 23°43S 143°54E **62 C3**
Arrino *Australia* 29°30S 115°40E **61 E2**
Arrow, L. *Ireland* 54°3N 8°19W **10 B3**
Arrowtown *N.Z.* 44°57S 168°50E **59 F2**
Arroyo Grande *U.S.A.* 35°7N 120°35W **79 K6**
Ars *Iran* 37°9N 47°46E **44 B5**
Arsenault L. *Canada* 55°6N 108°32W **71 B7**
Arsenev *Russia* 44°10N 133°15E **30 B6**
Arta *Greece* 39°8N 21°2E **23 E9**
Artà *Spain* 39°41N 3°21E **24 B10**
Artà, Coves d *Spain* 39°40N 3°24E **24 B10**
Arteaga *Mexico* 18°28N 102°25W **86 D4**
Artem *Russia* 43°22N 132°13E **30 C6**
Artemovsk *Russia* 54°45N 93°35E **29 D10**
Artemovsk *Ukraine* 48°35N 38°0E **19 E6**
Artesia = Mosomane
  Botswana 24°2S 26°19E **56 C4**
Artesia *U.S.A.* 32°51N 104°24W **77 K11**
Arthur *Canada* 43°50N 80°32W **82 C4**
Arthur → *Australia* 41°2S 144°40E **63 G3**
Arthur Cr. → *Australia* 22°30S 136°25E **62 C2**
Arthur Pt. *Australia* 22°7S 150°3E **62 C5**
Arthur River *Australia* 33°20S 117°2E **61 F2**
Arthur's Pass *N.Z.* 42°54S 171°35E **59 E3**
Arthur's Pass △ *N.Z.* 42°56S 171°42E **59 E3**
Arthur's Town *Bahamas* 24°38N 75°42W **89 B4**
Artigas *Antarctica* 62°30S 58°0W **5 C18**
Artigas *Uruguay* 30°20S 56°30W **94 C4**
Artillery L. *Canada* 63°9N 107°52W **71 A7**
Artois *France* 50°20N 2°30E **20 A5**
Artrutx, C. de *Spain* 39°55N 3°49E **24 B10**
Artsyz *Ukraine* 46°4N 29°26E **17 E15**
Artux *China* 39°40N 76°10E **32 C2**
Artvin *Turkey* 41°14N 41°44E **19 F7**
Artyk *Russia* 64°12N 145°6E **29 C15**
Aru, Kepulauan *Indonesia* 6°0S 134°30E **37 F8**
Aru Is. = Aru, Kepulauan
  Indonesia 6°0S 134°30E **37 F8**
Arua *Uganda* 3°1N 30°58E **54 B3**
Aruanã *Brazil* 14°54S 51°10W **93 F8**
Aruba ☑ *W. Indies* 12°30N 70°0W **89 D6**
Arucas *Canary Is.* 28°7N 15°32W **24 F4**
Arué *Tahiti* 17°31S 149°30W **59 d**
Arun → *Nepal* 26°55N 87°10E **43 F12**
Arun → *U.K.* 50°49N 0°33W **13 G7**
Arunachal Pradesh □
  India 28°0N 95°0E **41 F19**
Arusha *Tanzania* 3°20S 36°40E **54 C4**
Arusha □ *Tanzania* 4°0S 36°30E **54 C4**
Arusha △ *Tanzania* 3°16S 36°47E **54 C4**
Arusha Chini *Tanzania* 3°32S 37°20E **54 C4**
Aruwimi →
  Dem. Rep. of the Congo 1°13N 23°36E **54 B1**
Arvada *Colo., U.S.A.* 39°48N 105°5W **76 G11**
Arvada *Wyo., U.S.A.* 44°39N 106°8W **76 D10**
Arvayheer *Mongolia* 46°15N 102°48E **32 B5**
Arvi *Greece* 34°59N 25°28E **25 E7**
Arviat *Canada* 61°6N 93°59W **71 A10**
Arvidsjaur *Sweden* 65°35N 19°10E **8 D18**
Arvika *Sweden* 59°40N 12°36E **9 G15**
Arvin *U.S.A.* 35°12N 118°50W **79 K8**
Arwal *India* 25°15N 84°41E **43 G11**
Arxan *China* 47°11N 119°57E **33 B6**
Arys *Kazakhstan* 42°26N 68°48E **28 E7**
Arzamas *Russia* 55°27N 43°55E **18 C7**
Arzanah *U.A.E.* 24°47N 52°34E **45 E7**
Aş Şafā *Syria* 33°10N 37°0E **46 B6**
As Saffānīyah *Si. Arabia* 28°5N 48°50E **45 E6**
Aş Şafīrah *Syria* 36°5N 37°21E **44 B3**
Aş Şahm *Oman* 24°10N 56°53E **45 E8**
As Sājir *Si. Arabia* 25°11N 44°36E **44 E5**
As Salamīyah *Syria* 35°1N 37°2E **44 C3**
As Salt *Jordan* 32°2N 35°43E **46 C4**
As Sal'w'a *Qatar* 24°23N 50°50E **45 E6**
As Samāwah *Iraq* 31°15N 45°15E **44 D5**
As Sanamayn *Syria* 33°3N 36°10E **46 B5**
As Sohar = Şuḩār *Oman* 24°20N 56°40E **45 E8**
As Sukhnah *Syria* 34°52N 38°52E **44 C3**
As Sulaymānīyah *Iraq* 35°35N 45°29E **44 C5**
As Sulaymī *Si. Arabia* 26°17N 41°21E **44 E4**

As Sulayyil *Si. Arabia* 20°27N 45°34E **47 C4**
As Summān *Si. Arabia* 25°0N 47°0E **44 E5**
As Suwaydā' *Syria* 32°40N 36°30E **46 C5**
As Suwaydā' □ *Syria* 32°45N 36°45E **46 C5**
As Suwayq *Oman* 23°51N 57°26E **45 F8**
Aş Şuwayrah *Iraq* 32°55N 45°0E **44 C5**
Asab *Namibia* 25°30S 18°0E **56 D2**
Asad, Buḩayrat al *Syria* 36°0N 38°15E **44 C3**
Asahi-Gawa → *Japan* 34°36N 133°58E **31 G6**
Asahigawa = Asahikawa
  Japan 43°46N 142°22E **30 C11**
Asaluyeh *Iran* 27°29N 52°37E **45 E7**
Asamankese *Ghana* 5°50N 0°40W **50 G5**
Asan → *India* 26°37N 78°24E **43 F8**
Asansol *India* 23°40N 87°1E **43 H12**
Asau *Samoa* 13°27S 172°33W **59 b**
Asbesberge *S. Africa* 29°0S 23°0E **56 D3**
Asbestos *Canada* 45°47N 71°58W **73 C5**
Asbury Park *U.S.A.* 40°13N 74°1W **83 F10**
Ascensión *Mexico* 31°6N 107°59W **86 A3**
Ascensión, B. de la
  Mexico 19°40N 87°30W **87 D7**
Ascension I. *Atl. Oc.* 7°57S 14°23W **49 G2**
Aschaffenburg *Germany* 49°58N 9°6E **16 D5**
Aschersleben *Germany* 51°45N 11°29E **16 C6**
Áscoli Piceno *Italy* 42°51N 13°34E **22 C5**
Ascope *Peru* 7°46S 79°8W **92 E3**
Ascotán *Chile* 21°45S 68°17W **94 A2**
Aseb *Eritrea* 13°0N 42°40E **47 E3**
Asela *Ethiopia* 8°0N 39°0E **47 F2**
Asenovgrad *Bulgaria* 42°1N 24°51E **23 C11**
Aşgabat = Ashgabat
  Turkmenistan 38°0N 57°50E **45 B8**
Asgata *Cyprus* 34°46N 33°15E **25 E12**
Ash Fork *U.S.A.* 35°13N 112°29W **77 J7**
Ash Grove *U.S.A.* 37°19N 93°35W **80 G7**
Ash Shabakah *Iraq* 30°49N 43°39E **44 D4**
Ash Shamāl □ *Lebanon* 34°25N 36°0E **46 A5**
Ash Shāmīyah *Iraq* 31°55N 44°35E **44 D5**
Ash Shārīqah *U.A.E.* 25°23N 55°26E **45 E7**
Ash Sharmah *Si. Arabia* 28°1N 35°16E **44 D2**
Ash Sharqāt *Iraq* 35°27N 43°16E **44 C4**
Ash Shaṭrah *Iraq* 31°30N 46°10E **44 D5**
Ash Shawbak *Jordan* 30°32N 35°34E **46 E4**
Ash Shiḩr *Yemen* 14°45N 49°36E **47 E4**
Ash Shinafiyah *Iraq* 31°35N 44°39E **44 D5**
Ash Shu'bah *Si. Arabia* 28°54N 44°44E **44 D5**
Ash Shumlūl *Si. Arabia* 26°31N 47°20E **44 E5**
Ash Shūr'ab *Iraq* 35°58N 43°13E **44 C4**
Ash Shurayf *Si. Arabia* 25°43N 39°14E **44 E3**
Ash Shuwayfāt *Lebanon* 33°45N 35°30E **46 B4**
Asha *Russia* 55°0N 57°16E **18 D10**
Ashau *Vietnam* 16°6N 107°22E **38 D6**
Ashbourne *U.K.* 53°2N 1°43W **12 D6**
Ashburn *U.S.A.* 31°43N 83°39W **85 F13**
Ashburton *N.Z.* 43°53S 171°48E **59 E3**
Ashburton → *Australia* 21°40S 114°56E **60 D1**
Ashcroft *Canada* 50°40N 121°20W **70 C4**
Ashdod *Israel* 31°49N 34°35E **46 D3**
Ashdown *U.S.A.* 33°40N 94°8W **84 E7**
Asheboro *U.S.A.* 35°43N 79°49W **85 D15**
Ashern *Canada* 51°11N 98°21W **71 C9**
Asherton *U.S.A.* 28°27N 99°46W **84 G5**
Asheville *U.S.A.* 35°36N 82°33W **85 D13**
Ashewat *Pakistan* 31°22N 68°32E **42 D3**
Asheweig → *Canada* 54°17N 87°12W **72 B2**
Ashford *Australia* 29°15S 151°3E **63 D5**
Ashford *U.K.* 51°8N 0°53E **13 F8**
Ashgabat *Turkmenistan* 38°0N 57°50E **45 B8**
Ashibetsu *Japan* 43°31N 142°11E **30 C11**
Ashikaga *Japan* 36°28N 139°29E **31 F9**
Ashington *U.K.* 55°11N 1°33W **12 B6**
Ashizuri-Uwakai △
  Japan 32°56N 132°32E **31 H6**
Ashizuri-Zaki *Japan* 32°44N 133°0E **31 H6**
Ashkarkot *Afghan.* 33°3N 67°58E **42 C2**
Ashkhabad = Ashgabat
  Turkmenistan 38°0N 57°50E **45 B8**
Ashḵhāneh *Iran* 37°26N 56°55E **45 B8**
Ashland *Kans., U.S.A.* 37°11N 99°46W **80 G4**
Ashland *Ky., U.S.A.* 38°28N 82°38W **81 F12**
Ashland *Maine, U.S.A.* 46°38N 68°24W **81 B19**
Ashland *Mont., U.S.A.* 45°36N 106°16W **76 D10**
Ashland *Ohio, U.S.A.* 40°52N 82°19W **82 F2**
Ashland *Oreg., U.S.A.* 42°12N 122°43W **76 E2**
Ashland *Pa., U.S.A.* 40°45N 76°20W **83 F8**
Ashland *Va., U.S.A.* 37°46N 77°29W **81 G15**
Ashland *Wis., U.S.A.* 46°35N 90°53W **80 B8**
Ashley *N. Dak., U.S.A.* 46°2N 99°22W **80 B4**
Ashley *Pa., U.S.A.* 41°12N 75°55W **83 E9**
Ashmore and Cartier Is.
  Ind. Oc. 12°15S 123°0E **60 B3**
Ashmore Reef *Australia* 12°14S 123°5E **60 B3**
Ashmyany *Belarus* 54°27N 25°52E **17 A13**
Ashokan Res. *U.S.A.* 41°56N 74°13W **83 E10**
Ashoknagar *India* 24°34N 77°43E **42 G7**
Ashqelon *Israel* 31°42N 34°35E **46 D3**
Ashta *India* 23°1N 76°43E **42 H7**
Ashtabula *U.S.A.* 41°52N 80°47W **82 E4**
Āshtiyān *Iran* 34°31N 50°0E **45 C6**
Ashton *S. Africa* 33°50S 20°5E **56 E3**
Ashuanipi, L. *Canada* 52°45N 66°15W **73 B6**
Ashuapmushuan →
  Canada 48°37N 72°20W **72 C5**
Ashville *U.S.A.* 40°34N 78°33W **82 F6**
Asia 45°0N 75°0E **26 E9**
Asia, Kepulauan
  Indonesia 1°0N 131°13E **37 D8**
Asifabad *India* 19°20N 79°24E **40 K11**
Asinara *Italy* 41°4N 8°16E **22 D3**
Asinara, G. dell' *Italy* 41°0N 8°30E **22 D3**
Asino *Russia* 57°0N 86°0E **28 D9**
Asipovichy *Belarus* 53°19N 28°33E **17 B15**
'Asīr *Si. Arabia* 18°40N 42°30E **47 D3**
Asir, Ras *Somali Rep.* 11°55N 51°10E **47 E5**
Askham *S. Africa* 26°59S 20°47E **56 D3**
Askim *Norway* 59°35N 11°10E **9 G14**
Askja *Iceland* 65°3N 16°48W **8 D5**
Asklipio *Greece* 36°4N 27°56E **25 C9**

Askøyna *Norway*   60°29N 5°10E **8 F11**
Asmara = Asmera
  Eritrea   15°19N 38°55E **47 D2**
Asmera *Eritrea*   15°19N 38°55E **47 D2**
Åsnen *Sweden*   56°37N 14°45E **9 H16**
Aso Kuju △ *Japan*   32°53N 131°6E **31 H5**
Aspatria *U.K.*   54°47N 3°19W **12 C4**
Aspen *U.S.A.*   39°11N 106°49W **76 G10**
Aspermont *U.S.A.*   33°8N 100°14W **84 E4**
Aspiring, Mt. *N.Z.*   44°23S 168°46E **59 F2**
Asprokavos, Akra *Greece*   39°21N 20°6E **25 B4**
Aspur *India*   23°58N 74°7E **42 H6**
Asquith *Canada*   52°8N 107°13W **71 C7**
Assab = Aseb *Eritrea*   13°0N 42°40E **47 E3**
Assal, L. *Djibouti*   11°40N 42°26E **47 E3**
Assam □ *India*   26°0N 93°0E **41 G18**
Assateague Island ○
  U.S.A.   38°15N 75°10W **81 F16**
Asse *Belgium*   50°24N 4°10E **15 D4**
Assen *Neths.*   53°0N 6°35E **15 A6**
Assiniboia *Canada*   49°40N 105°59W **71 D7**
Assiniboine ➤ *Canada*   49°53N 97°8W **71 D9**
Assiniboine, Mt.
  Canada   50°52N 115°39W **70 C5**
Assis *Brazil*   22°40S 50°20W **95 A5**
Assisi *Italy*   43°4N 12°37E **22 C5**
Assynt, L. *U.K.*   58°10N 5°3W **11 C3**
Astana *Kazakhstan*   51°10N 71°30E **32 A2**
Āstāneh *Iran*   37°17N 49°59E **45 B6**
Astara *Azerbaijan*   38°30N 48°50E **45 B6**
Astarabad = Gorgān
  Iran   36°55N 54°30E **45 B7**
Asterousia *Greece*   34°59N 25°3E **25 E7**
Asti *Italy*   44°54N 8°12E **20 D8**
Astipalea *Greece*   36°32N 26°22E **23 F12**
Astorga *Spain*   42°29N 6°8W **21 A2**
Astoria *U.S.A.*   46°11N 123°50W **78 D2**
Astrakhan *Russia*   46°25N 48°5E **19 E8**
Astrebla Downs
  Australia   24°12S 140°34E **62 C3**
Asturias □ *Spain*   43°15N 6°0W **21 A3**
Asunción *Paraguay*   25°10S 57°30W **94 B4**
Asunción Nochixtlán
  Mexico   17°28N 97°14W **87 D5**
Aswa ➤ *Uganda*   3°43N 31°55E **54 B3**
Aswa-Lolim ○ *Uganda*   2°43N 31°35E **54 B3**
Aswân *Egypt*   24°4N 32°57E **51 D12**
Aswan High Dam = Sadd el Aali
  Egypt   23°54N 32°54E **51 D12**
Asyût *Egypt*   27°11N 31°4E **51 C12**
At Tafilah *Jordan*   30°45N 35°30E **46 E4**
At Tafilah □ *Jordan*   30°45N 35°30E **46 E4**
At Ta'if *Si. Arabia*   21°5N 40°27E **47 C3**
At Ta'mīm □ *Iraq*   35°30N 44°20E **44 C5**
At Tirâq *Si. Arabia*   27°19N 44°33E **44 E5**
At Tubayq *Si. Arabia*   29°30N 37°0E **44 D3**
At Tunayb *Jordan*   31°48N 35°57E **46 D4**
Atacama □ *Chile*   27°30S 70°0W **94 B2**
Atacama, Desierto de
  Chile   24°0S 69°20W **94 A2**
Atacama, Salar de *Chile*   23°30S 68°20W **94 A2**
Atakeye ○ *Australia*   22°30S 133°45E **60 D5**
Atakpamé *Togo*   7°31N 1°13E **50 G6**
Atalaya *Peru*   10°45S 73°50W **92 F4**
Atalaya de Femes
  Canary Is.   28°56N 13°47W **24 F6**
Atami *Japan*   35°5N 139°4E **31 G9**
Atamyrat *Turkmenistan*   37°50N 65°12E **28 F7**
Atâr *Mauritania*   20°30N 13°5W **50 D3**
Atari *Pakistan*   30°56N 74°2E **42 D6**
Atascadero *U.S.A.*   35°29N 120°40W **78 K6**
Atasū *Kazakhstan*   48°30N 71°0E **28 E8**
Atatürk Barajı *Turkey*   37°28N 38°30E **19 G6**
Atauro *E. Timor*   8°10S 125°30E **37 F7**
Ataviros *Greece*   36°12N 27°50E **25 C9**
Atbara *Sudan*   17°42N 33°59E **51 E12**
'Atbara, Nahr ➤ *Sudan*   17°40N 33°56E **51 E12**
Atbasar *Kazakhstan*   51°48N 68°20E **28 D7**
Atchafalaya B. *U.S.A.*   29°25N 91°25W **84 G9**
Atchison *U.S.A.*   39°34N 95°7W **80 F7**
Āteshān *Iran*   35°35N 52°37E **45 C7**
Ath *Belgium*   50°38N 3°47E **15 D3**
Athabasca *Canada*   54°45N 113°20W **70 C6**
Athabasca ➤ *Canada*   58°40N 110°50W **71 B6**
Athabasca, L. *Canada*   59°15N 109°15W **71 B7**
Athabasca Sand Dunes ○
  Canada   59°4N 108°43W **71 B7**
Athboy *Ireland*   53°37N 6°56W **10 C5**
Athenry *Ireland*   53°18N 8°44W **10 C3**
Athens = Athina *Greece*   37°58N 23°43E **23 F10**
Athens *Ala., U.S.A.*   34°48N 86°58W **85 D11**
Athens *Ga., U.S.A.*   33°57N 83°23W **85 D13**
Athens *N.Y., U.S.A.*   42°16N 73°49W **83 D11**
Athens *Ohio, U.S.A.*   39°20N 82°6W **81 F12**
Athens *Pa., U.S.A.*   41°57N 76°31W **83 E8**
Athens *Tenn., U.S.A.*   35°27N 84°36W **85 D12**
Athens *Tex., U.S.A.*   32°12N 95°51W **84 E7**
Atherley *Canada*   44°37N 79°20W **82 B5**
Atherton *Australia*   17°17S 145°30E **62 B4**
Athi River *Kenya*   1°28S 36°58E **54 C4**
Athienou *Cyprus*   35°3N 33°32E **25 D12**
Athína *Greece*   37°58N 23°43E **23 F10**
Athínai = Athína
  Greece   37°58N 23°43E **23 F10**
Athlone *Ireland*   53°25N 7°56W **10 C4**
Athna *Cyprus*   35°3N 33°47E **25 D12**
Athol *U.S.A.*   42°36N 72°14W **83 D12**
Atholl, Forest of *U.K.*   56°51N 3°50W **11 E5**
Atholville *Canada*   47°59N 66°43W **73 C6**
Athos *Greece*   40°9N 24°22E **23 D11**
Athy *Ireland*   53°0N 7°0W **10 C5**
Ati *Chad*   13°13N 18°20E **51 F9**
Atiak *Uganda*   3°12N 32°2E **54 B3**
Atik L. *Canada*   55°15N 96°0W **71 B9**
Atikaki ○ *Canada*   51°30N 95°31W **71 C9**
Atikameg ➤ *Canada*   52°30N 82°46W **72 B3**
Atikokan *Canada*   48°45N 91°37W **72 C1**
Atikonak L. *Canada*   52°40N 64°32W **73 B7**

Atimaono *Tahiti*   17°46S 149°28W **59 d**
Atitlán △ *Cent. Amer.*   14°38N 91°10W **87 E6**
Atiu *Cook Is.*   20°0S 158°10W **65 J12**
Atka *Russia*   60°50N 151°48E **29 C16**
Atka I. *U.S.A.*   52°7N 174°30W **74 E5**
Atkinson *U.S.A.*   42°32N 98°59W **80 D4**
Atlanta *Ga., U.S.A.*   33°45N 84°23W **85 E12**
Atlanta *Tex., U.S.A.*   33°7N 94°10W **84 E7**
Atlantic *U.S.A.*   41°24N 95°1W **80 E6**
Atlantic City *U.S.A.*   39°21N 74°27W **81 F16**
Atlantic-Indian Basin
  Antarctica   60°0S 30°0E **5 B4**
Atlantic Ocean   0°0 20°0W **2 D8**
Atlas Mts. = Haut Atlas
  Morocco   32°30N 5°0W **50 B4**
Atlin *Canada*   59°31N 133°41W **70 B2**
Atlin, L. *Canada*   59°26N 133°45W **70 B2**
Atlin ○ *Canada*   59°10N 134°30W **70 B2**
Atmore *U.S.A.*   31°2N 87°29W **85 F11**
Atoka *U.S.A.*   34°23N 96°8W **84 D6**
Atolia *U.S.A.*   35°19N 117°37W **79 K9**
Atqasuk *U.S.A.*   70°28N 157°24W **74 A8**
Atrai ➤ *Bangla.*   24°7N 89°22E **43 G13**
Atrak = Atrek ➤
  Turkmenistan   37°35S 53°58E **45 B8**
Atrauli *India*   28°2N 78°20E **42 E8**
Atrek ➤ *Turkmenistan*   37°35N 53°58E **45 B8**
Atsuta *Japan*   43°24N 141°26E **30 C10**
Attalla *U.S.A.*   34°1N 86°6W **85 D11**
Attapu *Laos*   14°48N 106°50E **38 E6**
Attawapiskat *Canada*   52°56N 82°24W **72 B3**
Attawapiskat ➤
  Canada   52°57N 82°18W **72 B3**
Attawapiskat L. *Canada*   52°18N 87°54W **72 B2**
Attica *Ind., U.S.A.*   40°18N 87°15W **80 E10**
Attica *Ohio, U.S.A.*   41°4N 82°53W **82 E2**
Attikamagen L. *Canada*   55°0N 66°30W **73 B6**
Attleboro *U.S.A.*   41°57N 71°17W **83 E13**
Attock *Pakistan*   33°52N 72°20E **42 C5**
Attopeu = Attapu *Laos*   14°48N 106°50E **38 E6**
Attur *India*   11°35N 78°30E **40 P11**
Attu I. *U.S.A.*   52°55N 172°55E **74 E2**
Attur *India*   11°35N 78°30E **40 P11**
Atuel ➤ *Argentina*   36°17S 66°50W **94 D2**
Atura *Uganda*   2°20N 32°20E **54 B3**
Åtvidaberg *Sweden*   58°12N 16°0E **9 G17**
Atwater *U.S.A.*   37°21N 120°37W **78 H6**
Atwood *Canada*   43°40N 81°1W **82 C3**
Atwood *U.S.A.*   39°48N 101°3W **80 F3**
Atyraū *Kazakhstan*   47°5N 52°0E **19 E9**
Au Sable *U.S.A.*   44°25N 83°20W **82 B1**
Au Sable ➤ *U.S.A.*   44°25N 83°20W **82 B1**
Au Sable Forks *U.S.A.*   44°27N 73°41W **83 B11**
Au Sable Pt. *U.S.A.*   44°20N 83°20W **82 B1**
Auas *Honduras*   15°29N 84°20W **88 C3**
Auasberg *Namibia*   22°37S 17°13E **56 C2**
Aubagne *France*   43°17N 5°37E **20 E6**
Aube □ *France*   48°34N 3°43E **20 B5**
Aube ➤ *France*   48°34N 3°43E **20 B5**
Auberry *U.S.A.*   37°7N 119°29W **78 H7**
Auburn *Ala., U.S.A.*   32°36N 85°29W **85 E12**
Auburn *Calif., U.S.A.*   38°54N 121°4W **78 G5**
Auburn *Ind., U.S.A.*   41°22N 85°4W **81 E11**
Auburn *Maine, U.S.A.*   44°6N 70°14W **81 C18**
Auburn *N.Y., U.S.A.*   42°56N 76°34W **83 D8**
Auburn *Nebr., U.S.A.*   40°23N 95°51W **80 E6**
Auburn *Pa., U.S.A.*   40°36N 76°6W **83 F8**
Auburn *Wash., U.S.A.*   47°18N 122°14W **78 C4**
Auburn Ra. *Australia*   25°15S 150°30E **63 D5**
Auburndale *U.S.A.*   28°4N 81°48W **85 G14**
Aubusson *France*   45°57N 2°11E **20 D5**
Auch *France*   43°39N 0°36E **20 E4**
Auchterarder *U.K.*   56°18N 3°41W **11 E5**
Auchtermuchty *U.K.*   56°18N 3°13W **11 E5**
Auckland *N.Z.*   36°52S 174°46E **59 B5**
Auckland Is. *Pac. Oc.*   50°40S 166°5E **64 N8**
Aude □ *France*   43°13N 3°14E **20 E5**
Auden *Canada*   50°14N 87°53W **72 B2**
Audubon *U.S.A.*   41°43N 94°56W **80 E6**
Augathella *Australia*   25°48S 146°35E **63 D4**
Aughnacloy *U.K.*   54°25N 6°59W **10 B5**
Aughrim *Ireland*   53°18N 8°19W **10 C3**
Augrabies Falls *S. Africa*   28°35S 20°20E **56 D3**
Augrabies Falls △
  S. Africa   28°40S 20°22E **56 D3**
Augsburg *Germany*   48°25N 10°52E **16 D6**
Augusta *Australia*   34°19S 115°9E **61 F2**
Augusta *Italy*   37°13N 15°13E **22 F6**
Augusta *Ark., U.S.A.*   35°17N 91°22W **84 D9**
Augusta *Ga., U.S.A.*   33°28N 81°58W **85 E14**
Augusta *Kans., U.S.A.*   37°41N 96°59W **80 C6**
Augusta *Maine, U.S.A.*   44°19N 69°47W **81 C19**
Augusta *Mont., U.S.A.*   47°30N 112°24W **76 C7**
Augustów *Poland*   53°51N 23°0E **17 B12**
Augustus, Mt. *Australia*   24°20S 116°50E **61 D2**
Augustus I. *Australia*   15°20S 124°30E **60 C3**
Aujuittuq = Grise Fiord
  Canada   76°25N 82°57W **69 B15**
Aukštaitija △ *Lithuania*   55°15N 26°0E **9 J22**
Aukum *U.S.A.*   38°34N 120°43W **78 G6**
Auld, L. *Australia*   22°25S 123°50E **60 D3**
Ault *U.S.A.*   40°35N 104°44W **76 F11**
Aunis *France*   46°5N 0°50W **20 C3**
Au, Pulau *Malaysia*   2°35N 104°10E **39 L5**
Auponhia *Indonesia*   1°58S 125°27E **37 E7**
Auraiya *India*   26°28N 79°33E **43 F8**
Aurangabad *Bihar,
  India*   24°45N 84°18E **43 G11**
Aurangabad *Maharashtra,
  India*   19°50N 75°23E **40 K9**
Aurich *Germany*   53°28N 7°28E **16 B4**
Aurillac *France*   44°55N 2°26E **20 D5**
Aurora *Canada*   44°0N 79°28W **82 C5**
Aurora *S. Africa*   32°40S 18°29E **56 E2**
Aurora *Colo., U.S.A.*   39°43N 104°49W **76 G11**
Aurora *Ill., U.S.A.*   41°45N 88°19W **80 E9**
Aurora *Mo., U.S.A.*   36°58N 93°43W **80 G7**
Aurora *N.Y., U.S.A.*   42°45N 76°42W **83 D8**
Aurora *Nebr., U.S.A.*   40°52N 98°0W **80 E5**

Aurora *Ohio, U.S.A.*   41°21N 81°20W **82 E3**
Aurukun *Australia*   13°20S 141°45E **62 A3**
Aurukun ○ *Australia*   13°36S 141°48E **62 A3**
Aus *Namibia*   26°35S 16°12E **56 D2**
Ausable ➤ *Canada*   43°19N 81°46W **82 C3**
Auschwitz = Oświęcim
  Poland   50°2N 19°11E **17 C10**
Auski Roadhouse
  Australia   22°22S 118°41E **60 D2**
Austin *Minn., U.S.A.*   43°40N 92°58W **80 D7**
Austin *Nev., U.S.A.*   39°30N 117°4W **76 G5**
Austin *Pa., U.S.A.*   41°38N 78°6W **82 E6**
Austin *Tex., U.S.A.*   30°17N 97°45W **84 F6**
Austin, L. *Australia*   27°40S 118°0E **61 E2**
Austin I. *Canada*   61°10N 94°0W **71 A10**
Austra *Norway*   65°8N 11°55E **8 D14**
Austral Is. = Tubuaï, Îs.
  French Polynesia   25°0S 150°0W **65 K13**
Austral Seamount Chain
  Pac. Oc.   24°0S 150°0W **65 K13**
Australia ■ *Oceania*   23°0S 135°0E **58 D6**
Australian-Antarctic Basin
  S. Ocean   60°0S 120°0E **5 C9**
Australian Capital Territory □
  Australia   35°30S 149°0E **63 F4**
Australind *Australia*   33°17S 115°42E **61 F2**
Austria ■ *Europe*   47°0N 14°0E **16 E8**
Austvågøya *Norway*   68°20N 14°40E **8 B16**
Autlán de Navarro
  Mexico   19°46N 104°22W **86 D4**
Autun *France*   46°58N 4°17E **20 C6**
Auvergne □ *France*   45°20N 3°15E **20 D5**
Auvergne, Mts. d' *France*   45°20N 2°55E **20 D5**
Auxerre *France*   47°48N 3°32E **20 C5**
Auyuittuq △ *Canada*   67°30N 66°0W **69 D18**
Av-Dovurak *Russia*   51°17N 91°35E **29 D10**
Ava *U.S.A.*   36°57N 92°40W **80 G7**
Avallon *France*   47°30N 3°53E **20 C5**
Avalon *U.S.A.*   33°21N 118°20W **79 M8**
Avalon Pen. *Canada*   47°30N 53°20W **73 C9**
Avanos *Turkey*   38°43N 34°51E **44 B2**
Avaré *Brazil*   23°4S 48°58W **95 A6**
Avawatz Mts. *U.S.A.*   35°40N 116°30W **79 K10**
Aveiro *Brazil*   3°10S 55°5W **93 D7**
Aveiro *Portugal*   40°37N 8°38W **21 B1**
Āvej *Iran*   35°40N 49°15E **45 C6**
Avellaneda *Argentina*   34°50S 58°22W **94 C4**
Avellino *Italy*   40°54N 14°47E **22 D6**
Avenal *U.S.A.*   36°0N 120°8W **78 K6**
Aversa *Italy*   40°58N 14°12E **22 D6**
Avery *U.S.A.*   47°15N 115°49W **76 C6**
Aves, I. de *W. Indies*   15°45N 63°55W **89 C7**
Aves, Is. las *Venezuela*   12°0N 67°30W **89 D6**
Avesta *Sweden*   60°9N 16°10E **9 F17**
Aveyron □ *France*   44°5N 1°16E **20 D4**
Aveyron ➤ *France*   44°5N 1°16E **20 D4**
Aviá Terai *Argentina*   26°45S 60°50W **94 B3**
Aviemore *U.K.*   57°12N 3°50W **11 D5**
Avignon *France*   43°57N 4°50E **20 E6**
Ávila *Spain*   40°39N 4°43W **21 B3**
Avila Beach *U.S.A.*   35°11N 120°44W **79 K6**
Avilés *Spain*   43°35N 5°57W **21 A3**
Avis *U.S.A.*   41°11N 77°19W **82 E7**
Avoca *U.S.A.*   42°25N 77°25W **82 D7**
Avoca ➤ *Australia*   35°40S 143°43E **63 F3**
Avoca ➤ *Ireland*   52°48N 6°10W **10 D5**
Avola *Canada*   51°45N 119°19W **70 C5**
Avola *Italy*   36°56N 15°7E **22 F6**
Avon *U.S.A.*   42°55N 77°45W **82 D7**
Avon ➤ *Australia*   31°40S 116°7E **61 F2**
Avon ➤ *Bristol, U.K.*   51°29N 2°41W **13 F5**
Avon ➤ *Dorset, U.K.*   50°44N 1°46W **13 G6**
Avon ➤ *Warks., U.K.*   52°0N 2°8W **13 E5**
Avon Park *U.S.A.*   27°36N 81°31W **85 H14**
Avondale *Zimbabwe*   17°43S 30°58E **55 F3**
Avonlea *Canada*   50°0N 105°0W **71 D8**
Avonmore *Canada*   45°10N 74°58W **83 A10**
Avonmouth *U.K.*   51°30N 2°42W **13 F5**
Avranches *France*   48°40N 1°20W **20 B3**
Awa-Shima *Japan*   38°27N 139°14E **30 E9**
A'waj ➤ *Syria*   33°23N 36°20E **46 B5**
Awaji-Shima *Japan*   34°30N 134°50E **31 G7**
'Awālī *Bahrain*   26°0N 50°30E **45 E6**
Awantipur *India*   33°55N 75°3E **43 C6**
Awasa *Ethiopia*   7°2N 38°28E **47 F2**
Awash *Ethiopia*   9°1N 40°10E **47 F3**
Awatere ➤ *N.Z.*   41°37S 174°10E **59 D5**
Awbārī *Libya*   26°46N 12°57E **51 C8**
Awbārī, Idehan *Libya*   27°10N 11°30E **51 C8**
Awe, L. *U.K.*   56°17N 5°16W **11 E3**
Awjilah *Libya*   29°8N 21°7E **51 C10**
Axe ➤ *U.K.*   50°42N 3°4W **13 F5**
Axel Heiberg I. *Canada*   80°0N 90°0W **69 B14**
Axim *Ghana*   4°51N 2°15W **50 H5**
Axios ➤ *Greece*   40°57N 22°35E **23 D10**
Axminster *U.K.*   50°46N 3°0W **13 G4**
Ayabaca *Peru*   4°40S 79°53W **92 D3**
Ayabe *Japan*   35°20N 135°20E **31 G7**
Ayacucho *Argentina*   37°5S 58°20W **94 D4**
Ayacucho *Peru*   13°0S 74°0W **92 F4**
Ayaguz = Ayaköz
  Kazakhstan   48°10N 80°10E **32 B3**
Ayaköz *Kazakhstan*   48°10N 80°10E **32 B3**
Ayamonte *Spain*   37°12N 7°24W **21 D2**
Ayan *Russia*   56°30N 138°16E **29 D14**
Ayaviri *Peru*   14°50S 70°35W **92 F4**
Aydın *Turkey*   37°51N 27°51E **23 F12**
Aydıngkol Hu *China*   42°40N 89°15E **32 B3**
Ayer *U.S.A.*   42°34N 71°35W **83 D13**
Ayer Hitam *Malaysia*   5°24N 100°16E **39 c**
Ayers Cliff *Canada*   45°10N 72°3W **83 A12**
Ayers Rock = Uluru
  Australia   25°23S 131°5E **61 E5**
Ayeyarwady = Irrawaddy ➤
  Burma   15°50N 95°6E **41 M19**
Áyia Napa *Cyprus*   34°59N 34°0E **25 E13**
Áyia Phyla *Cyprus*   34°43N 33°1E **25 E12**
Áyios Amvrósios
  Cyprus   35°20N 33°35E **25 D12**

Áyios Seryios *Cyprus*   35°12N 33°53E **25 D12**
Áyios Theodhoros
  Cyprus   35°22N 34°1E **25 D13**
Aykhal *Russia*   66°0N 111°30E **29 C12**
Aykino *Russia*   62°15N 49°56E **18 B8**
Aylesbury *U.K.*   51°49N 0°49W **13 F7**
Aylmer *Canada*   42°46N 80°59W **82 D4**
Aylmer, L. *Canada*   64°5N 108°30W **68 E10**
'Ayn, Wādī al *Oman*   22°15N 55°28E **45 F7**
Ayn Dār *Si. Arabia*   25°55N 49°10E **45 E7**
Ayn Zālah *Iraq*   36°45N 42°35E **44 B4**
Ayolas *Paraguay*   27°10S 56°59W **94 B4**
Ayon, Ostrov *Russia*   69°50N 169°0E **29 C17**
'Ayoûn el 'Atroûs
  Mauritania   16°38N 9°37W **50 E4**
Ayr *Australia*   19°35S 147°25E **62 B4**
Ayr *Canada*   43°17N 80°27W **82 C4**
Ayr *U.K.*   55°28N 4°38W **11 F4**
Ayr ➤ *U.K.*   55°28N 4°38W **11 F4**
Ayre, Pt. of *I. of Man*   54°25N 4°21W **12 C3**
Ayton *Australia*   15°56S 145°22E **62 B4**
Aytos *Bulgaria*   42°42N 27°16E **23 C12**
Ayu, Kepulauan
  Indonesia   0°35N 131°5E **37 D8**
Ayutla *Guatemala*   14°40N 92°10W **88 D1**
Ayutla de los Libres
  Mexico   16°54N 99°13W **87 D5**
Ayvacık *Turkey*   39°36N 26°24E **23 E12**
Ayvalık *Turkey*   39°20N 26°46E **23 E12**
Az Zabadānī *Syria*   33°43N 36°5E **46 B5**
Aẕ Ẕāhirīyah *West Bank*   31°25N 34°58E **46 D3**
Aẕ Ẕahrān *Si. Arabia*   26°10N 50°7E **45 E6**
Az Zarqā *Jordan*   32°5N 36°4E **46 C5**
Az Zarqā ➤ *Jordan*   32°5N 36°4E **46 C5**
Az Zarqā' *U.A.E.*   24°53N 53°4E **45 E7**
Az Zībār *Iraq*   36°52N 44°4E **44 B5**
Az Zilfī *Si. Arabia*   26°12N 44°52E **44 E5**
Az Zubayr *Iraq*   30°26N 47°40E **44 D5**
Azad Kashmir □
  Pakistan   33°50N 73°50E **43 C5**
Azamgarh *India*   26°5N 83°13E **43 F10**
Azángaro *Peru*   14°55S 70°13W **92 F4**
Azaouad *Mali*   19°0N 3°0W **50 E5**
Āzār Shahr *Iran*   37°45N 45°59E **44 B5**
Azarān *Iran*   37°25N 47°16E **44 B5**
Azärbayjan = Azerbaijan ■
  Asia   40°20N 48°0E **19 F8**
Āzarbāyjān-e Gharbī □
  Iran   37°0N 44°30E **44 B5**
Āzarbāyjān-e Sharqī □
  Iran   37°0N 47°0E **44 B5**
Azare *Nigeria*   11°55N 10°10E **50 F8**
A'zāz *Syria*   36°36N 37°4E **44 B3**
Azbine = Aïr *Niger*   18°30N 8°0E **50 E7**
Azerbaijan ■ *Asia*   40°20N 48°0E **19 F8**
Azimganj *India*   24°14N 88°16E **43 G13**
Azogues *Ecuador*   2°35S 78°0W **92 D3**
Azores = Açores, Is. dos
  Atl. Oc.   38°0N 27°0W **50 a**
Azov *Russia*   47°3N 39°25E **19 E6**
Azov, Sea of *Europe*   46°0N 36°30E **19 E6**
Azovskoye More = Azov, Sea of
  Europe   46°0N 36°30E **19 E6**
Azraq ash Shīshān
  Jordan   31°50N 36°49E **46 D5**
Aztec *U.S.A.*   36°49N 107°59W **77 H10**
Azúa de Compostela
  Dom. Rep.   18°25N 70°44W **89 C5**
Azuaga *Spain*   38°16N 5°39W **21 C3**
Azuero, Pen. de *Panama*   7°30N 80°30W **88 E3**
Azul *Argentina*   36°42S 59°43W **94 D4**
Azusa *U.S.A.*   34°8N 117°52W **79 L9**
Azzel Matti, Sebkra
  Algeria   26°10N 0°43E **50 C6**

B

Ba Be △ *Vietnam*   22°25N 105°37E **38 A5**
Ba Don *Vietnam*   17°45N 106°26E **38 D6**
Ba Dong *Vietnam*   9°40N 106°33E **39 H6**
Ba Ngoi = Cam Lam
  Vietnam   11°54N 109°10E **39 G7**
Ba Tri *Vietnam*   10°2N 106°36E **39 G6**
Ba Vì △ *Vietnam*   21°1N 105°22E **38 B5**
Ba Xian = Bazhou *China*   39°8N 116°22E **34 E9**
Baa *Indonesia*   10°50S 123°0E **60 B3**
Baardheere *Somali Rep.*   2°20N 42°27E **47 G3**
Baarle-Nassau *Belgium*   51°27N 4°56E **15 C4**
Bāb el Mandeb *Red Sea*   12°35N 43°25E **47 E3**
Bābā, Koh-i- *Afghan.*   34°30N 67°0E **40 B5**
Baba Burnu *Turkey*   39°29N 26°2E **23 E12**
Bābā Kalū *Iran*   30°7N 50°49E **45 D6**
Babadag *Romania*   44°53N 28°44E **17 F15**
Babaeski *Turkey*   41°26N 27°6E **23 D12**
Babahoyo *Ecuador*   1°40S 79°30W **92 D3**
Babai = Sarju ➤ *India*   27°21N 81°23E **43 F9**
Babar *Indonesia*   8°0S 129°30E **37 F7**
Babarkach *Pakistan*   29°45N 68°0E **42 E3**
Babb *U.S.A.*   48°51N 113°27W **76 B7**
Baberu *India*   25°33N 80°43E **43 G9**
Babi Besar, Pulau
  Malaysia   2°25N 103°59E **39 L4**
Babinda *Australia*   17°20S 145°56E **62 B4**
Babine *Canada*   55°22N 126°37W **70 B3**
Babine ➤ *Canada*   55°45N 127°44W **70 B3**
Babine L. *Canada*   54°48N 126°0W **70 C3**
Babo *Indonesia*   2°30S 133°30E **37 E8**
Baboua *C.A.R.*   5°49N 14°58E **52 C2**
Babruysk *Belarus*   53°10N 29°15E **17 B15**
Babuhri *India*   26°49N 69°43E **42 F3**
Babusar Pass *Pakistan*   35°12N 73°59E **43 B5**
Babuyan Chan. *Phil.*   18°40N 121°30E **37 A6**
Babylon *Iraq*   32°34N 44°22E **44 C5**

Bac Can *Vietnam*   22°8N 105°49E **38 A5**
Bac Giang *Vietnam*   21°16N 106°11E **38 B6**
Bac Lieu *Vietnam*   9°17N 105°43E **39 H5**
Bac Ninh *Vietnam*   21°13N 106°4E **38 B6**
Bac Phan *Vietnam*   22°0N 105°0E **38 B5**
Bac Quang *Vietnam*   22°30N 104°48E **38 A5**
Bacabal *Brazil*   4°15S 44°45W **93 D10**
Bacalar *Mexico*   18°43N 88°27W **87 D7**
Bacan, Kepulauan
  Indonesia   0°35S 127°30E **37 E7**
Bacarra *Phil.*   18°15N 120°37E **37 A6**
Bacău *Romania*   46°35N 26°55E **17 E14**
Bacerac *Mexico*   30°18N 108°50W **86 A3**
Bach Long Vi, Dao
  Vietnam   20°10N 107°40E **38 B6**
Bach Ma △ *Vietnam*   16°11N 107°49E **38 D6**
Bachhwara *India*   25°35N 85°54E **43 G11**
Back ➤ *Canada*   65°10N 104°0W **68 D11**
Bacolod *Phil.*   10°40N 122°57E **37 B6**
Bacuk *Malaysia*   6°4N 102°25E **39 J4**
Bácum *Mexico*   27°33N 110°5W **86 B2**
Bād *Iran*   33°41N 52°1E **45 C7**
Bad ➤ *U.S.A.*   44°21N 100°22W **80 C3**
Bad Axe *U.S.A.*   43°48N 83°0W **82 C2**
Bad Ischl *Austria*   47°44N 13°38E **16 E7**
Bad Kissingen *Germany*   50°11N 10°4E **16 C6**
Bada Barabil *India*   22°7N 85°24E **43 H11**
Badagara *India*   11°35N 75°40E **40 P9**
Badain Jaran Shamo
  China   40°23N 102°0E **32 B5**
Badajós, L. *Brazil*   3°15S 62°50W **92 D6**
Badajoz *Spain*   38°50N 6°59W **21 C2**
Badakhshān □ *Afghan.*   36°30N 71°0E **40 A7**
Badaling *China*   40°21N 116°0E **33 B6**
Badalona *Spain*   41°26N 2°15E **21 B7**
Badalzai *Afghan.*   29°50N 65°35E **42 E1**
Badampahar *India*   22°10N 86°10E **41 H15**
Badanah *Si. Arabia*   30°58N 41°30E **44 D4**
Badarinath *India*   30°45N 79°30E **43 D8**
Badas, Kepulauan
  Indonesia   0°45N 107°5E **36 D3**
Baddo ➤ *Pakistan*   28°0N 64°20E **40 F4**
Bade *Indonesia*   7°10S 139°35E **37 F9**
Baden *Austria*   48°1N 16°13E **16 D9**
Baden *U.S.A.*   38°30N 80°14W **82 F4**
Baden-Baden *Germany*   48°44N 8°13E **16 D5**
Baden-Württemberg □
  Germany   48°20N 8°40E **16 D5**
Badgam *India*   34°1N 74°45E **43 B6**
Badgastein *Austria*   47°7N 13°9E **16 E7**
Badger *Canada*   49°0N 56°4W **73 C8**
Badger *U.S.A.*   36°38N 119°1W **78 J7**
Bādghīs □ *Afghan.*   35°0N 63°0E **40 B3**
Badgingarra △
  Australia   30°23S 115°22E **61 F2**
Badin *Pakistan*   24°38N 68°54E **42 G3**
Badlands *U.S.A.*   43°55N 102°30W **80 D2**
Badlands △ *U.S.A.*   43°38N 102°56W **80 D2**
Badrah *Iraq*   33°6N 45°58E **44 C5**
Badrinath *India*   30°44N 79°29E **43 D8**
Badu *Australia*   10°7S 142°11E **62 a**
Badulla *Sri Lanka*   7°1N 81°7E **40 R12**
Badung, Selat *Indonesia*   8°40S 115°22E **37 K18**
Baena *Spain*   37°37N 4°20W **21 D3**
Baengnyeongdo
  S. Korea   37°57N 124°40E **35 F13**
Baeza *Spain*   37°57N 3°25W **21 D4**
Bafatá *Guinea-Biss.*   12°8N 14°40W **50 F3**
Baffin B. *N. Amer.*   72°0N 64°0W **69 C19**
Baffin I. *Canada*   68°0N 75°0W **69 D17**
Bafing ➤ *Mali*   13°49N 10°50W **50 F3**
Bafliyūn *Syria*   36°37N 36°59E **44 B3**
Bafoulabé *Mali*   13°50N 10°55W **50 F3**
Bafoussam *Cameroon*   5°28N 10°25E **52 C2**
Bāfq *Iran*   31°40N 55°25E **45 D7**
Bafra *Turkey*   41°34N 35°54E **19 F6**
Bāft *Iran*   29°15N 56°38E **45 D8**
Bafwasende
  Dem. Rep. of the Congo   1°3N 27°5E **54 B2**
Bagaha *India*   27°6N 84°5E **43 F11**
Bagamoyo *Tanzania*   6°28S 38°55E **54 D4**
Bagan Datoh *Malaysia*   3°59N 100°47E **39 L3**
Bagan Serai *Malaysia*   5°1N 100°32E **39 K3**
Baganga *Phil.*   7°34N 126°33E **37 C7**
Bagani *Namibia*   18°7S 21°41E **56 B3**
Bagansiapiapi *Indonesia*   2°12N 100°50E **36 D2**
Bagasra *India*   21°30N 71°0E **42 J4**
Bagaud *India*   22°19N 75°53E **42 H6**
Bagdad *U.S.A.*   34°35N 115°53W **79 L11**
Bagdarin *Russia*   54°26N 113°36E **29 D12**
Bagé *Brazil*   31°20S 54°15W **95 C5**
Bagenalstown = Muine Bheag
  Ireland   52°42N 6°58W **10 D5**
Baggs *U.S.A.*   41°2N 107°39W **76 F10**
Bagh *Pakistan*   33°59N 73°45E **43 C5**
Baghain ➤ *India*   25°32N 81°1E **43 G9**
Baghdād *Iraq*   33°20N 44°23E **44 C5**
Bagheria *Italy*   38°5N 13°30E **22 E5**
Baghlān *Afghan.*   32°12N 68°46E **40 A6**
Baghlān □ *Afghan.*   36°0N 68°30E **40 B6**
Bagley *U.S.A.*   47°32N 95°24W **80 B6**
Bago = Pegu *Burma*   17°20N 96°29E **41 L20**
Bagodar *India*   24°5N 85°52E **43 G11**
Bagrationovsk *Russia*   54°23N 20°39E **9 J19**
Baguio *Phil.*   16°26N 120°34E **37 A6**
Bah *India*   26°53N 78°36E **43 F8**
Bahadurganj *India*   26°16N 87°49E **43 F12**
Bahadurgarh *India*   28°42N 76°54E **42 E7**
Bahama, Canal Viejo de
  W. Indies   22°10N 77°30W **88 B4**
Bahamas ■ *N. Amer.*   24°0N 75°0W **89 B5**
Bahār *Iran*   34°54N 48°26E **45 C6**
Baharampur *India*   24°2N 88°27E **43 G13**
Baharu Pandan = Pandan
  Malaysia   1°32N 103°46E **39 d**
Bahawalnagar *Pakistan*   30°0N 73°15E **42 E5**
Bahawalpur *Pakistan*   29°24N 71°40E **42 E4**
Baheri *India*   28°45N 79°34E **43 E8**

Bahgul → India 27°45N 79°36E 43 F8
Bahi Tanzania 5°58S 35°21E 54 D4
Bahi Swamp Tanzania 6°10S 35°0E 54 D4
Bahía = Salvador Brazil 13°0S 38°30W 93 F11
Bahía □ Brazil 12°0S 42°0W 93 F10
Bahía, Is. de la Honduras 16°45N 86°15W 88 C2
Bahía Blanca Argentina 38°35S 62°13W 94 D3
Bahía de Caráquez
  Ecuador 0°40S 80°27W 92 D2
Bahía Kino Mexico 28°47N 111°58W 86 B2
Bahía Laura Argentina 48°10S 66°30W 96 F3
Bahía Negra Paraguay 20°5S 58°5W 92 H7
Bahir Dar Ethiopia 11°37N 37°10E 47 E2
Bahmanzād Iran 31°15N 51°47E 45 D6
Bahraich India 27°38N 81°37E 43 F9
Bahrain ■ Asia 26°0N 50°35E 45 E6
Bahror India 27°51N 76°20E 42 F7
Bāhū Kalāt Iran 25°43N 61°25E 45 E9
Bai Bung, Mui = Ca Mau, Mui
  Vietnam 8°38N 104°44E 39 H5
Bai Duc Vietnam 18°3N 105°49E 38 C5
Bai Thuong Vietnam 19°54N 105°23E 38 C5
Baia Mare Romania 47°40N 23°35E 17 E12
Baia Sprie Romania 47°46N 15°43E 51 G9
Baião Brazil 2°40S 49°40W 93 D9
Baïbokoum Chad 7°46N 15°43E 51 G9
Baicheng China 45°38N 122°42E 35 B12
Baidoa = Baydhabo
  Somali Rep. 3°8N 43°30E 47 G3
Baie-Comeau Canada 49°12N 68°10W 73 C6
Baie-St-Paul Canada 47°28N 70°32W 73 C5
Baie Ste-Anne Seychelles 4°18S 55°45E 53 b
Baie-Trinité Canada 49°25N 67°20W 73 C6
Baie Verte Canada 49°55N 56°12W 73 C8
Baihar India 22°6N 80°33E 43 H9
Baihe China 32°50N 110°5E 34 H6
Ba'iji Iraq 35°0N 43°30E 44 C4
Baijnath India 29°55N 79°37E 43 E8
Baikal, L. = Baykal, Oz.
  Russia 53°0N 108°0E 29 D11
Baikonur = Bayqongyr
  Kazakhstan 45°40N 63°20E 28 E7
Baikunthpur India 23°15N 82°33E 43 H10
Baile Átha Cliath = Dublin
  Ireland 53°21N 6°15W 10 C5
Baile Átha Fhirdhia = Ardee
  Ireland 53°52N 6°33W 10 C5
Baile Átha I = Athy Ireland 53°0N 7°0W 10 C5
Baile Átha Luain = Athlone
  Ireland 53°25N 7°56W 10 C4
Baile Átha Troim = Trim
  Ireland 53°33N 6°48W 10 C5
Baile Brigín = Balbriggan
  Ireland 53°37N 6°11W 10 C5
Băileşti Romania 44°1N 23°20E 17 F12
Bainbridge Ga., U.S.A. 30°55N 84°35W 85 F12
Bainbridge N.Y., U.S.A. 42°18N 75°29W 83 D9
Bainbridge Island
  U.S.A. 47°38N 122°32W 78 C4
Baing Indonesia 10°14S 120°34E 37 F6
Bainiu China 32°50N 112°15E 34 H7
Ba'ir Jordan 30°45N 36°55E 46 E5
Baird Mts. U.S.A. 67°0N 160°0W 74 B8
Bairiki = Tarawa Kiribati 1°30N 173°0E 64 H9
Bairin Youqi China 43°30N 118°35E 35 C10
Bairin Zuoqi China 43°58N 119°15E 35 C10
Bairnsdale Australia 37°48S 147°36E 63 F4
Baisha China 34°20N 112°32E 34 G7
Baitadi Nepal 29°35N 80°25E 43 E9
Baiyin China 36°45N 104°14E 34 F3
Baiyu Shan China 37°15N 107°30E 34 F4
Baj Baj India 22°30N 88°5E 43 H13
Baja Hungary 46°12N 18°59E 17 E9
Baja, Pta. Mexico 29°58N 115°49W 86 B1
Baja California Mexico 31°10N 115°12W 86 A1
Baja California □ Mexico 30°0N 115°0W 86 B2
Baja California Sur □
  Mexico 25°50N 111°50W 86 B2
Bajag India 22°40N 81°21E 43 H9
Bajamar Canary Is. 28°33N 16°20W 24 F3
Bajana India 23°7N 71°49E 42 H4
Bajatrejo Indonesia 8°29S 114°19E 37 J17
Bajera Indonesia 8°31S 115°2E 37 J18
Bäjgīrān Iran 37°36N 58°24E 45 B8
Bajimba, Mt. Australia 29°17S 152°6E 63 D5
Bajo Boquete Panama 8°46N 82°27W 88 E3
Bajo Nuevo Caribbean 15°40N 78°50W 88 C4
Bajoga Nigeria 10°57N 11°20E 51 F8
Bajool Australia 23°40S 150°35E 62 C5
Bakel Senegal 14°56N 12°20W 50 F3
Baker Calif., U.S.A. 35°16N 116°4W 79 K10
Baker Mont., U.S.A. 46°22N 104°17W 76 B2
Baker, L. Canada 64°0N 96°0W 68 E12
Baker, Mt. U.S.A. 48°50N 121°49W 76 B3
Baker City U.S.A. 44°47N 117°50W 76 D5
Baker I. Pac. Oc. 0°10N 176°35W 64 G10
Baker I. U.S.A. 55°20N 133°40W 70 B2
Baker L. Australia 26°54S 126°5E 61 E4
Baker Lake Canada 64°20N 96°3W 68 E12
Bakers Creek Australia 21°13S 149°7E 62 C4
Bakers Dozen Is. Canada 56°45N 78°45W 72 A4
Bakersfield Calif., U.S.A. 35°23N 119°1W 79 K8
Bakersfield Vt., U.S.A. 44°45N 72°48W 83 B12
Bakharden = Bäherden
  Turkmenistan 38°25N 57°26E 45 B8
Bākhtarān = Kermānshāh
  Iran 34°23N 47°0E 44 C5
Bākhtarān = Kermānshāh □
  Iran 34°0N 46°30E 44 C5
Bakı Azerbaijan 40°29N 49°56E 45 A6
Bakkafjörður Iceland 66°2N 14°48W 8 C6
Bakouma C.A.R. 5°40N 22°56E 52 C4
Bakswaho India 24°15N 79°18E 43 G8
Baku = Bakı Azerbaijan 40°29N 49°56E 45 A6
Bakutis Coast Antarctica 74°0S 120°0W 5 D15
Baky = Bakı Azerbaijan 40°29N 49°56E 45 A6
Bala Canada 45°1N 79°37W 82 A5
Bala U.K. 52°54N 3°36W 12 E4
Bala, L. U.K. 52°53N 3°37W 12 E4
Balabac I. Phil. 8°0N 117°0E 36 C5

Balabac Str. E. Indies 7°53N 117°5E 36 C5
Balabagh Afghan. 34°25N 70°12E 42 B4
Ba'labakk Lebanon 34°0N 36°10E 46 B5
Balabalangan, Kepulauan
  Indonesia 2°20S 117°30E 36 E5
Balad Iraq 34°0N 44°9E 44 C5
Balad Rūz Iraq 33°42N 45°5E 44 C5
Bālādeh Fārs, Iran 29°17N 51°56E 45 D6
Bālādeh Māzandaran, Iran 36°12N 51°48E 45 B6
Balaghat India 21°49N 80°12E 40 J12
Balaghat Ra. India 18°50N 76°30E 40 K10
Balaguer Spain 41°50N 0°50E 21 B6
Balaklava Ukraine 44°30N 33°30E 19 F5
Balakovo Russia 52°4N 47°55E 18 D8
Balamau India 27°10N 80°21E 43 F9
Balancán Mexico 17°48N 91°32W 87 D6
Balashov Russia 51°30N 43°10E 19 D7
Balasinor India 22°57N 73°23E 42 H5
Balasore = Baleshwar
  India 21°35N 87°3E 41 J15
Balaton Hungary 46°50N 17°40E 17 E9
Balbina, Represa de Brazil 2°0S 59°30W 92 D7
Balboa Panama 8°57N 79°34W 88 E4
Balbriggan Ireland 53°37N 6°11W 10 C5
Balcarce Argentina 38°0S 58°10W 94 D4
Balcarres Canada 50°50N 103°35W 71 C8
Balchik Bulgaria 43°28N 28°11E 23 C13
Balclutha N.Z. 46°15S 169°45E 59 G2
Balcones Escarpment
  U.S.A. 29°30N 99°15W 84 G5
Bald I. Australia 34°57S 118°27E 61 F2
Bald Knob U.S.A. 35°19N 91°34W 84 D9
Baldock L. Canada 56°33N 97°57W 71 B9
Baldwin Mich., U.S.A. 43°54N 85°51W 81 D11
Baldwin Pa., U.S.A. 40°21N 79°58W 82 F5
Baldwinsville U.S.A. 43°10N 76°20W 83 C8
Baldy Peak U.S.A. 33°54N 109°34W 77 K9
Baleares, Is. Spain 39°30N 3°0E 24 B10
Balearic Is. = Baleares, Is.
  Spain 39°30N 3°0E 24 B10
Baleine → Canada 58°15N 67°40W 73 A6
Baleine, Petite R. de la →
  Canada 56°0N 76°45W 72 A4
Baler Phil. 15°46N 121°34E 37 A6
Baleshare U.K. 57°31N 7°22W 11 D1
Baleshwar India 21°35N 87°3E 41 J15
Baley Russia 51°36N 116°37E 29 D12
Balfate Honduras 15°48N 86°25W 88 C2
Balgo Australia 20°9S 127°58E 60 D4
Bali Greece 35°25N 24°47E 25 D6
Bali India 25°11N 73°17E 42 G5
Bali Indonesia 8°20S 115°0E 37 J18
Bali □ Indonesia 8°20S 115°0E 37 J18
Bali, Selat Indonesia 8°18S 114°25E 37 J17
Bali Sea Indonesia 8°0S 115°0E 37 J17
Baliapal India 21°40N 87°17E 43 J12
Balige Indonesia 2°14N 99°7E 39 L2
Balik Pulau Malaysia 5°21N 100°14E 39 c
Balıkeşir Turkey 39°39N 27°53E 23 E12
Balikpapan Indonesia 1°10S 116°55E 36 E5
Balimbing Phil. 5°5N 119°58E 37 C5
Baling Malaysia 5°41N 100°55E 39 K3
Balkan Mts. = Stara Planina
  Bulgaria 43°15N 23°0E 23 C10
Balkanabat Turkmenistan 39°30N 54°22E 45 B7
Balkhash = Balqash
  Kazakhstan 46°50N 74°50E 28 E8
Balkhash, Ozero = Balqash Köli
  Kazakhstan 46°0N 74°50E 28 E8
Ballachulish U.K. 56°41N 5°8W 11 E3
Balladonia Australia 32°27S 123°51E 61 F3
Ballaghaderreen Ireland 53°55N 8°34W 10 C3
Ballarat Australia 37°33S 143°50E 63 F3
Ballard, L. Australia 29°20S 120°40E 61 E3
Ballater U.K. 57°3N 3°3W 11 D5
Ballenas, Canal de
  Mexico 29°10N 113°29W 86 B2
Balleny Is. Antarctica 66°30S 163°0E 5 C11
Ballia India 25°46N 84°12E 43 G11
Ballina Australia 28°50S 153°31E 63 D5
Ballina Ireland 54°7N 9°9W 10 B2
Ballinasloe Ireland 53°20N 8°13W 10 C3
Ballinger U.S.A. 31°45N 99°57W 84 F5
Ballinrobe Ireland 53°38N 9°13W 10 C2
Ballinskelligs B. Ireland 51°48N 10°13W 10 E1
Ballston Spa U.S.A. 43°0N 73°51W 83 D11
Ballyboghil Ireland 53°32N 6°16W 10 C5
Ballybunion Ireland 52°31N 9°40W 10 D2
Ballycanew Ireland 52°37N 6°19W 10 D5
Ballycastle U.K. 55°12N 6°15W 10 A5
Ballyclare U.K. 54°46N 6°0W 10 B5
Ballydehob Ireland 51°34N 9°28W 10 E2
Ballygawley U.K. 54°27N 7°2W 10 B4
Ballyhaunis Ireland 53°46N 8°46W 10 C3
Ballyheige Ireland 52°23N 9°49W 10 D2
Ballymena U.K. 54°52N 6°17W 10 B5
Ballymoney U.K. 55°5N 6°31W 10 A5
Ballymote Ireland 54°5N 8°31W 10 B3
Ballynahinch U.K. 54°24N 5°54W 10 B6
Ballyquintin Pt. U.K. 54°20N 5°30W 10 B6
Ballyshannon Ireland 54°30N 8°11W 10 B3
Balmaceda Chile 46°0S 71°50W 96 F2
Balmertown Canada 51°4N 93°41W 71 C10
Balmoral Australia 37°15S 141°48E 63 F3
Balmorhea U.S.A. 30°59N 103°45W 84 F3
Balochistan = Baluchistan □
  Pakistan 27°30N 65°0E 40 F4
Balonne → Australia 28°47S 147°56E 63 D4
Balotra India 25°50N 72°14E 42 G5
Balqash Kazakhstan 46°50N 74°50E 28 E8
Balqash Köli Kazakhstan 46°0N 74°50E 28 E8
Balrampur India 27°30N 82°20E 43 F10
Balranald Australia 34°38S 143°33E 63 E3
Balsas → Brazil 7°15S 44°35W 93 E9
Balsas Mexico 17°55N 102°10W 86 D4
Balsas del Norte Mexico 18°0N 99°46W 87 D5
Balta Ukraine 47°56N 29°45E 17 D15
Bălți Moldova 47°48N 27°58E 17 E14
Baltic Sea Europe 57°0N 19°0E 9 H18

Baltimore Ireland 51°29N 9°22W 10 E2
Baltimore Md., U.S.A. 39°17N 76°36W 81 F15
Baltimore Ohio, U.S.A. 39°51N 82°36W 82 G2
Baltinglass Ireland 52°56N 6°43W 10 D5
Baltit Pakistan 36°15N 74°40E 43 A6
Baltiysk Russia 54°41N 19°58E 9 J18
Baluchistan □ Pakistan 27°30N 65°0E 40 F4
Balurghat India 25°15N 88°44E 43 G13
Balvi Latvia 57°8N 27°15E 9 H22
Balya Turkey 39°44N 27°35E 23 E12
Balykchy Kyrgyzstan 42°26N 76°12E 32 B2
Balyqshy Kazakhstan 47°4N 51°52E 19 E9
Bam Iran 29°7N 58°14E 45 D8
Bama Nigeria 11°33N 13°41E 51 F8
Bamaga Australia 10°50S 142°25E 62 A3
Bamaji L. Canada 51°9N 91°25W 72 B1
Bamako Mali 12°34N 7°55W 50 F4
Bambari C.A.R. 5°40N 20°35E 52 C4
Bambaroo Australia 18°50S 146°10E 62 B4
Bamberg Germany 49°54N 10°54E 16 D6
Bamberg U.S.A. 33°18N 81°2W 85 E14
Bambili
  Dem. Rep. of the Congo 3°40N 26°0E 54 B2
Bamburgh U.K. 55°37N 1°43W 12 B6
Bamenda Cameroon 5°57N 10°11E 52 C2
Bamfield Canada 48°45N 125°10W 70 D3
Bāmīān □ Afghan. 35°0N 67°0E 40 B5
Bamiancheng China 43°15N 124°2E 35 C13
Bampūr Iran 27°15N 60°21E 45 E9
Bampūr → Iran 27°24N 59°0E 45 E8
Ban Ao Tu Khun Thailand 8°9N 98°20E 39 a
Ban Ban Laos 19°31N 103°30E 38 C4
Ban Bang Hin Thailand 9°32N 98°35E 39 H2
Ban Bang Khu Thailand 7°57N 98°23E 39 a
Ban Bang Rong Thailand 8°3N 98°25E 39 a
Ban Bo Phut Thailand 9°33N 100°2E 39 b
Ban Chaweng Thailand 9°32N 100°3E 39 b
Ban Chiang Klang
  Thailand 19°25N 100°55E 38 C3
Ban Choho Thailand 15°2N 102°9E 38 E4
Ban Dan Lan Hoi Thailand 17°0N 99°35E 38 D2
Ban Don = Surat Thani
  Thailand 9°6N 99°20E 39 H2
Ban Don Vietnam 12°53N 107°48E 38 F6
Ban Don, Ao → Thailand 9°20N 99°25E 39 H2
Ban Dong Thailand 19°30N 100°59E 38 C3
Ban Hong Thailand 18°18N 98°50E 38 C2
Ban Hua Thanon Thailand 9°26N 100°1E 39 b
Ban Kantang Thailand 7°25N 99°31E 39 J2
Ban Karon Thailand 7°51N 98°18E 39 a
Ban Kata Thailand 7°50N 98°18E 39 a
Ban Keun Laos 18°22N 102°35E 38 C4
Ban Khai Thailand 12°46N 101°18E 38 F3
Ban Kheun Laos 20°13N 101°7E 38 B3
Ban Khlong Khian
  Thailand 8°10N 98°26E 39 a
Ban Khlong Kua Thailand 6°57N 100°8E 39 J3
Ban Khuan Thailand 8°20N 98°25E 39 a
Ban Khuan Mao Thailand 7°50N 99°37E 39 J2
Ban Ko Yai Chim
  Thailand 11°17N 99°26E 39 G2
Ban Laem Thailand 13°13N 99°59E 38 F2
Ban Lamai Thailand 9°28N 100°3E 39 b
Ban Lao Ngam Laos 15°28N 106°10E 38 E6
Ban Le Kathe Thailand 15°49N 98°53E 38 E2
Ban Lo Po Noi Thailand 8°1N 98°34E 39 a
Ban Mae Chedi Thailand 19°11N 99°31E 38 C2
Ban Mae Nam Thailand 9°34N 100°0E 39 b
Ban Mae Sariang
  Thailand 18°10N 97°56E 38 C1
Ban Mê Thuôt = Buon Ma Thuot
  Vietnam 12°40N 108°3E 38 F7
Ban Mi Thailand 15°3N 100°32E 38 E3
Ban Muong Mo Laos 19°4N 103°58E 38 C4
Ban Na Bo Thailand 9°19N 99°41E 39 b
Ban Na Mo Laos 17°7N 105°40E 38 D5
Ban Na San Thailand 8°53N 99°52E 39 H2
Ban Na Tong Laos 20°56N 101°47E 38 B3
Ban Nam Bac Laos 20°38N 102°20E 38 B4
Ban Nam Ma Laos 22°2N 101°37E 38 A3
Ban Ngang Laos 15°59N 106°11E 38 E6
Ban Nong Bok Laos 17°5N 104°48E 38 D5
Ban Nong Boua Laos 15°40N 106°33E 38 E6
Ban Nong Pling
  Thailand 15°40N 100°10E 38 E3
Ban Pak Chan Thailand 10°32N 98°51E 39 G2
Ban Patong Thailand 7°54N 98°18E 39 a
Ban Phai Thailand 16°4N 102°44E 38 D4
Ban Phak Chit Thailand 8°0N 98°24E 39 a
Ban Pong Thailand 13°50N 99°55E 38 F2
Ban Rawai Thailand 7°47N 98°20E 39 a
Ban Ron Phibun Thailand 8°9N 99°51E 39 H2
Ban Sakhu Thailand 8°4N 98°18E 39 a
Ban Sanam Chai
  Thailand 7°33N 100°25E 39 J3
Ban Sangkha Thailand 14°37N 103°52E 38 E4
Ban Tak Thailand 17°2N 99°4E 38 D2
Ban Tako Thailand 14°5N 102°40E 38 E4
Ban Tha Dua Thailand 17°59N 98°39E 38 C2
Ban Tha Nun Thailand 8°12N 98°18E 39 a
Ban Tha Yu Thailand 8°30N 98°21E 39 a
Ban Thahine Laos 14°12N 105°33E 38 E5
Ban Thong Krut Thailand 9°25N 99°57E 39 b
Ban Xien Kok Laos 20°54N 100°39E 38 B3
Ban Yen Nhan Vietnam 20°57N 106°2E 38 B6
Banaba Kiribati 0°45S 169°50E 64 H8
Banalia
  Dem. Rep. of the Congo 1°32N 25°5E 54 B2
Banam Cambodia 11°20N 105°17E 39 G5
Bananal, I. do Brazil 11°30S 50°30W 93 F8
Banaras = Varanasi
  India 25°22N 83°0E 43 G10
Banas → Gujarat, India 23°45N 71°25E 42 H4
Banas → Mad. P., India 24°15N 81°30E 43 G9
Bânâs, Ras Egypt 23°57N 35°59E 51 D13
Banbridge U.K. 54°21N 6°16W 10 B5
Banbury U.K. 52°4N 1°20W 13 E6
Banchory U.K. 57°3N 2°29W 11 D6

Bancroft Canada 45°3N 77°51W 82 A7
Band Bonī Iran 25°30N 59°33E 45 E8
Band Qīr Iran 31°39N 48°53E 45 D6
Banda Mad. P., India 24°3N 78°57E 43 G8
Banda Ut. P., India 25°30N 80°26E 43 G9
Banda, Kepulauan
  Indonesia 4°37S 129°50E 37 E7
Banda Aceh Indonesia 5°35N 95°20E 36 C1
Banda Banda, Mt.
  Australia 31°10S 152°28E 63 E5
Banda Elat Indonesia 5°40S 133°5E 37 F8
Banda Is. = Banda, Kepulauan
  Indonesia 4°37S 129°50E 37 E7
Banda Sea Indonesia 6°0S 130°0E 37 F8
Bandai-Asahi △ Japan 37°38N 140°5E 30 F10
Bandai-San Japan 37°36N 140°4E 30 F10
Bandān Iran 31°23N 60°44E 45 D9
Bandanaira Indonesia 4°32S 129°54E 37 E7
Bandanwara India 26°9N 74°38E 42 F6
Bandar = Machilipatnam
  India 16°12N 81°8E 41 L12
Bandar-e Abbās Iran 27°15N 56°15E 45 E8
Bandar-e Anzalī Iran 37°30N 49°30E 45 B6
Bandar-e Bushehr = Büshehr
  Iran 28°55N 50°55E 45 D6
Bandar-e Chārak Iran 26°45N 54°20E 45 E7
Bandar-e Deylam Iran 30°5N 50°10E 45 D6
Bandar-e Emām Khomeynī
  Iran 30°30N 49°5E 45 D6
Bandar-e Lengeh Iran 26°35N 54°58E 45 E7
Bandar-e Maqām Iran 26°56N 53°29E 45 E7
Bandar-e Ma'shur Iran 30°35N 49°10E 45 D6
Bandar-e Rīg Iran 29°29N 50°38E 45 D6
Bandar-e Torkeman Iran 37°0N 54°10E 45 B7
Bandar Lampung
  Indonesia 5°20S 105°10E 36 F3
Bandar Maharani = Muar
  Malaysia 2°3N 102°34E 39 L4
Bandar Penggaram = Batu Pahat
  Malaysia 1°50N 102°56E 39 M4
Bandar Seri Begawan
  Brunei 4°52N 115°0E 36 D5
Bandar Sri Aman = Sri Aman
  Malaysia 1°15N 111°32E 36 D4
Bandawe Malawi 11°58S 34°5E 55 E3
Bandeira, Pico da Brazil 20°26S 41°47W 95 A7
Bandera Argentina 28°55S 62°20W 94 B3
Banderas, B. de Mexico 20°40N 105°25W 86 C3
Bandhavgarh India 23°40N 81°2E 43 H9
Bandi → India 26°12N 75°47E 42 F6
Bandikui India 27°3N 76°34E 42 F7
Bandırma Turkey 40°20N 28°0E 23 D13
Bandjarmasin = Banjarmasin
  Indonesia 3°20S 114°35E 36 E4
Bandon Ireland 51°44N 8°44W 10 E3
Bandon → Ireland 51°43N 8°37W 10 E3
Bandula Mozam. 19°0S 33°7E 55 F3
Bandundu
  Dem. Rep. of the Congo 3°15S 17°22E 52 E3
Bandung Indonesia 6°54S 107°36E 37 G12
Băneh Iran 35°59N 45°53E 44 C5
Banes Cuba 21°0N 75°42W 89 B4
Banff Canada 51°10N 115°34W 70 C5
Banff U.K. 57°40N 2°33W 11 D6
Banff △ Canada 51°30N 116°15W 70 C5
Bang Fai → Laos 16°57N 104°45E 38 D5
Bang Hieng → Laos 16°10N 105°10E 38 D5
Bang Krathum Thailand 16°34N 100°18E 38 D3
Bang Lamung Thailand 13°3N 100°56E 38 F3
Bang Mun Nak Thailand 16°2N 100°23E 38 D3
Bang Pa In Thailand 14°14N 100°35E 38 E3
Bang Rakam Thailand 16°45N 100°7E 38 D3
Bang Saphan Thailand 11°14N 99°28E 39 G2
Bang Thao Thailand 7°59N 98°18E 39 a
Bangaduni I. India 21°34N 88°52E 43 J13
Bangala Dam Zimbabwe 21°7S 31°25E 55 G3
Bangalore India 12°59N 77°40E 40 N10
Banganga → India 26°55N 81°12E 43 F9
Bangaon India 23°0N 88°47E 43 H13
Bangassou C.A.R. 4°55N 23°7E 52 D4
Banggai Indonesia 1°34S 123°30E 37 E6
Banggai, Kepulauan
  Indonesia 1°40S 123°30E 37 E6
Banggai Arch. = Banggai,
  Kepulauan Indonesia 1°40S 123°30E 37 E6
Banggi, Pulau Malaysia 7°17N 117°12E 36 C5
Banghāzī Libya 32°11N 20°3E 51 B10
Bangka Sulawesi, Indonesia 1°50N 125°5E 37 D7
Bangka Sumatera,
  Indonesia 2°0S 105°50E 36 E3
Bangka, Selat Indonesia 2°30S 105°30E 36 E3
Bangka-Belitung □
  Indonesia 2°30S 107°0E 36 E3
Bangkalan Indonesia 7°2S 112°46E 37 G15
Bangkinang Indonesia 0°18N 101°5E 36 D2
Bangko Indonesia 2°5S 102°9E 36 E2
Bangkok Thailand 13°45N 100°35E 38 F3
Bangla = West Bengal □
  India 23°0N 88°0E 43 H13
Bangli Indonesia 8°27S 115°21E 37 J18
Bangong Co China 33°45N 78°43E 43 C8
Bangor Down, U.K. 54°40N 5°40W 10 B6
Bangor Gwynedd, U.K. 53°14N 4°8W 12 D3
Bangor Maine, U.S.A. 44°48N 68°46W 81 C19
Bangor Pa., U.S.A. 40°52N 75°13W 83 F9
Bangued Phil. 17°40N 120°37E 37 A6
Bangui C.A.R. 4°23N 18°35E 52 D3
Banguru
  Dem. Rep. of the Congo 0°30N 27°10E 54 B2
Bangweulu, L. Zambia 11°0S 30°0E 55 E3
Bangweulu Swamp
  Zambia 11°20S 30°15E 55 E3
Banhine △ Mozam. 22°49S 32°57E 57 C5
Baní Dom. Rep. 18°16N 70°22W 89 C5
Banī Sa'd Iraq 33°34N 44°32E 44 C5
Banihal Pass India 33°30N 75°12E 43 C6
Banissa Kenya 3°55N 40°19E 54 B4
Bāniyās Syria 35°10N 36°0E 44 C3

Banja Luka Bos.-H. 44°49N 17°11E 22 B7
Banjar India 31°38N 77°21E 42 D7
Banjar → India 22°36N 80°22E 43 H9
Banjarmasin Indonesia 3°20S 114°35E 36 E4
Banjul Gambia 13°28N 16°40W 50 F2
Banka India 24°53N 86°55E 43 G12
Banket Zimbabwe 17°27S 30°19E 55 F3
Bankipore India 25°35N 85°10E 41 G14
Banks I. = Moa Australia 10°11S 142°16E 62 a
Banks I. B.C., Canada 53°20N 130°0W 70 C3
Banks I. N.W.T., Canada 73°15N 121°30W 68 C7
Banks Pen. N.Z. 43°45S 173°15E 59 E4
Banks Str. Australia 40°40S 148°10E 63 G4
Bankura India 23°11N 87°18E 43 H12
Banmankhi India 25°53N 87°11E 43 G12
Bann → Armagh, U.K. 54°30N 6°31W 10 B5
Bann → L'derry., U.K. 55°8N 6°41W 10 A5
Bannang Sata Thailand 6°16N 101°16E 39 J3
Banning U.S.A. 33°56N 116°53W 79 M10
Bannockburn Canada 44°39N 77°33W 82 B7
Bannockburn U.K. 56°5N 3°55W 11 E5
Bannockburn Zimbabwe 20°17S 29°48E 55 G2
Bannu Pakistan 33°0N 70°18E 40 C7
Bano India 22°40N 84°55E 43 H11
Bansgaon India 26°33N 83°21E 43 F10
Banská Bystrica
  Slovak Rep. 48°46N 19°14E 17 D10
Banswara India 23°32N 74°24E 42 H6
Bantaeng Indonesia 5°32S 119°56E 37 F5
Banten □ Indonesia 6°30S 106°0E 37 G11
Bantry Ireland 51°41N 9°27W 10 E2
Bantry B. Ireland 51°37N 9°44W 10 E2
Bantul Indonesia 7°55S 110°19E 37 G14
Bantva India 21°29N 70°12E 42 J4
Banyak, Kepulauan
  Indonesia 2°10N 97°10E 36 D1
Banyalbufar Spain 39°42N 2°31E 24 B9
Banyo Cameroon 6°52N 11°45E 52 C2
Banyumas Indonesia 7°32S 109°18E 37 G13
Banyuwangi Indonesia 8°13S 114°21E 37 J17
Banzare Coast Antarctica 68°0S 125°0E 5 C9
Bao Ha Vietnam 22°11N 104°21E 38 A5
Bao Lac Vietnam 22°57N 105°40E 38 A5
Bao Loc Vietnam 11°32N 107°48E 39 G6
Bao'an = Shenzhen
  China 22°32N 114°5E 33 F10
Baocheng China 33°12N 106°56E 34 H4
Baode China 39°1N 111°5E 34 E6
Baodi China 39°38N 117°20E 35 E9
Baoding China 38°50N 115°28E 34 E8
Baoji China 34°20N 107°5E 34 G4
Baoshan China 25°10N 99°5E 32 D4
Baotou China 40°32N 110°2E 34 D6
Baoying China 33°17N 119°20E 35 H10
Baoyou = Ledong China 18°41N 109°5E 38 C7
Bap India 27°23N 72°18E 42 F5
Bapatla India 15°55N 80°30E 41 M12
Bāqerābād Iran 33°2N 51°58E 45 C6
Ba'qūbah Iraq 33°45N 44°50E 44 C5
Baquedano Chile 23°20S 69°52W 94 A2
Bar Montenegro 42°8N 19°6E 23 C8
Bar Ukraine 49°4N 27°40E 17 D14
Bar Bigha India 25°21N 85°47E 43 G11
Bar Harbor U.S.A. 44°23N 68°13W 81 C19
Bar-le-Duc France 48°47N 5°10E 20 B6
Bara India 25°16N 81°43E 43 G9
Bara Banki India 26°55N 81°12E 43 F9
Barabai Indonesia 2°32S 115°34E 36 E5
Baraboo U.S.A. 43°28N 89°45W 80 D9
Baracoa Cuba 20°20N 74°30W 89 B5
Baradā → Syria 33°33N 36°34E 46 B5
Baradero Argentina 33°52S 59°29W 94 C4
Baraga U.S.A. 46°47N 88°30W 80 B9
Barail Range India 25°15N 93°20E 41 G18
Barakaldo Spain 43°18N 2°59W 21 A4
Barakar → India 24°7N 86°14E 43 G12
Barakot India 21°33N 84°59E 43 J11
Barakpur India 22°44N 88°30E 43 H13
Baralaba Australia 24°13S 149°50E 62 C4
Baralzon L. Canada 60°0N 98°3W 71 B9
Baramula India 34°15N 74°20E 43 B6
Baran India 25°9N 76°40E 42 G7
Baran → Pakistan 25°13N 68°17E 42 G3
Baranavichy Belarus 53°10N 26°0E 17 B14
Baranof U.S.A. 57°5N 134°50W 70 B2
Baranof I. U.S.A. 57°0N 135°0W 68 F4
Barapasi Indonesia 2°15S 137°5E 37 E9
Barasat India 22°46N 88°31E 43 H13
Barat Daya, Kepulauan
  Indonesia 7°30S 128°0E 37 F7
Barataria B. U.S.A. 29°20N 89°55W 85 G10
Barauda India 23°33N 75°15E 42 H6
Baraut India 29°13N 77°7E 42 E7
Barbacena Brazil 21°15S 43°56W 95 A7
Barbados ■ W. Indies 13°10N 59°30W 89 g
Barbària, C. de Spain 38°39N 1°24E 24 C7
Barbas, C. W. Sahara 22°20N 16°42W 50 D2
Barbastro Spain 42°2N 0°5E 21 A6
Barbeau Pk. Canada 81°54N 75°1W 69 A16
Barberton S. Africa 25°42S 31°2E 57 D5
Barberton U.S.A. 41°1N 81°39W 82 E3
Barbosa Colombia 5°57N 73°37W 92 B4
Barbourville U.S.A. 36°52N 83°53W 81 G12
Barbuda W. Indies 17°30N 61°40W 89 C7
Barcaldine Australia 23°43S 145°6E 62 C4
Barcellona Pozzo di Gotto
  Italy 38°9N 15°13E 22 E6
Barcelona Spain 41°22N 2°10E 21 B7
Barcelona Venezuela 10°10N 64°40W 92 A6
Barceloneta Puerto Rico 18°27N 66°32W 89 d
Barcelos Brazil 1°0S 63°0W 92 D6
Barcoo → Australia 25°30S 142°50E 62 D3
Bardaï Chad 21°25N 17°0E 51 D9
Bardas Blancas
  Argentina 35°49S 69°45W 94 D2
Bardawîl, Sabkhet el
  Egypt 31°10N 33°15E 46 D2

Barddhaman *India* 23°14N 87°39E **43** H12
Bardejov *Slovak Rep.* 49°18N 21°15E **17** D11
Bardera = Baardheere
 Somali Rep. 2°20N 42°27E **47** G3
Bardīyah *Libya* 31°45N 25°5E **51** B10
Bardsey I. *U.K.* 52°45N 4°47W **12** E3
Bardstown *U.S.A.* 37°49N 85°28W **81** G11
Bareilly *India* 28°22N 79°27E **43** E8
Barela *India* 23°6N 80°3E **43** H9
Barents Sea *Arctic* 73°0N 39°0E **4** B9
Barfleur, Pte. de *France* 49°42N 1°16W **20** B3
Bargara *Australia* 24°50S 152°25E **62** C5
Bargi Dam *India* 22°59N 80°0E **43** H9
Barguzin *Russia* 53°37N 109°37E **29** D11
Barh *India* 25°29N 85°46E **43** G11
Barhaj *India* 26°18N 83°44E **43** F10
Barharwa *India* 24°52N 87°47E **43** G12
Barhi *India* 24°15N 85°25E **43** G11
Bari *India* 26°39N 77°39E **42** F7
Bari *Italy* 41°8N 16°51E **22** D7
Bari Doab *Pakistan* 30°20N 73°0E **42** D5
Bari Sadri *India* 24°28N 74°30E **42** G6
Barīdī, Ra's *Si. Arabia* 24°17N 37°31E **44** E3
Barīm *Yemen* 12°39N 43°25E **47** E8
Barinas *Venezuela* 8°36N 70°15W **92** B4
Baring, C. *Canada* 70°0N 117°30W **68** B8
Baringo, L. *Kenya* 0°47N 36°16E **54** B4
Barisal *Bangla.* 22°45N 90°20E **41** H17
Barisal □ *Bangla.* 22°45N 90°20E **41** H17
Barisan, Pegunungan
 Indonesia 3°30S 102°15E **36** E2
Barito *→ Indonesia* 4°0S 114°50E **36** E4
Baritú △ *Argentina* 23°43S 64°40W **94** A3
Barjūj, Wadi *→ Libya* 25°26N 12°12E **51** C8
Bark L. *Canada* 45°27N 77°51W **82** A7
Barkakana *India* 23°37N 85°29E **43** H11
Barker *U.S.A.* 43°20N 78°33W **82** C6
Barkley, L. *U.S.A.* 37°1N 88°14W **85** C10
Barkley Sound *Canada* 48°50N 125°10W **70** D3
Barkly East *S. Africa* 30°58S 27°33E **56** E4
Barkly Homestead
 Australia 19°52S 135°50E **62** B2
Barkly Tableland
 Australia 17°50S 136°40E **62** B2
Barkly West *S. Africa* 28°5S 24°31E **56** D3
Barkol Kazak Zizhixian
 China 43°37N 93°2E **32** B4
Bârlad *Romania* 46°15N 27°38E **17** E14
Bârlad *→ Romania* 45°38N 27°32E **17** F14
Barlee, L. *Australia* 29°15S 119°30E **61** E2
Barlee, Mt. *Australia* 24°38S 128°13E **61** D4
Barletta *Italy* 41°19N 16°17E **22** D7
Barlovento *Canary Is.* 28°48N 17°48W **24** F2
Barlovento *C. Verde Is.* 17°0N 25°0W **50** b
Barlow L. *Canada* 62°0N 103°0W **71** A8
Barmedman *Australia* 34°9S 147°21E **63** E4
Barmer *India* 25°45N 71°20E **42** G4
Barmera *Australia* 34°15S 140°28E **63** E3
Barmouth *U.K.* 52°44N 4°4W **12** E3
Barna *→ India* 25°21N 83°3E **43** G10
Barnagar *India* 23°7N 75°19E **42** H6
Barnala *India* 30°23N 75°33E **42** D6
Barnard Castle *U.K.* 54°33N 1°55W **12** C6
Barnaul *Russia* 53°20N 83°40E **28** D9
Barnesville *Ga., U.S.A.* 33°3N 84°9W **85** E12
Barnesville *Minn.,*
 U.S.A. 46°43N 96°28W **80** B5
Barnet □ *U.K.* 51°38N 0°9W **13** F7
Barneveld *Neths.* 52°7N 5°36E **15** B5
Barnhart *U.S.A.* 31°8N 101°10W **84** F4
Barnsley *U.K.* 53°34N 1°27W **12** D6
Barnstable *U.S.A.* 41°42N 70°18W **81** E18
Barnstaple *U.K.* 51°5N 4°4W **13** F3
Barnstaple Bay = Bideford Bay
 U.K. 51°5N 4°20W **13** F3
Barnwell *U.S.A.* 33°15N 81°23W **85** E14
Baro *Nigeria* 8°35N 6°18E **50** G7
Baroda = Vadodara
 India 22°20N 73°10E **42** H5
Baroda *India* 25°29N 76°35E **42** G7
Baroe *S. Africa* 33°13S 24°33E **56** E3
Baron Ra. *Australia* 23°30S 127°45E **60** D4
Barotseland *Zambia* 15°0S 24°0E **53** H4
Barpeta *India* 26°20N 91°10E **41** F17
Barqa *Libya* 27°0N 23°0E **51** C10
Barques, Pt. Aux *U.S.A.* 44°4N 82°58W **82** B2
Barquísimeto *Venezuela* 10°4N 69°19W **92** A5
Barr Smith Range
 Australia 27°4S 120°20E **61** E3
Barra *Brazil* 11°5S 43°10W **93** F10
Barra *U.K.* 57°0N 7°29W **11** E1
Barra, Sd. of *U.K.* 57°4N 7°25W **11** E1
Barra de Navidad
 Mexico 19°12N 104°41W **86** D4
Barra do Corda *Brazil* 5°30S 45°10W **93** E9
Barra do Garças *Brazil* 15°54S 52°16W **93** G8
Barra do Piraí *Brazil* 22°30S 43°50W **95** A7
Barra Falsa, Pta. da
 Mozam. 22°58S 35°37E **57** C6
Barra Hd. *U.K.* 56°47N 7°40W **11** E1
Barra Mansa *Brazil* 22°35S 44°12W **95** A7
Barraba *Australia* 30°21S 150°35E **63** E5
Barrackpur = Barakpur
 India 22°47N 88°21E **43** H13
Barraigh = Barra *U.K.* 57°0N 7°29W **11** E1
Barranca *Lima, Peru* 10°45S 77°50W **92** F3
Barranca *Loreto, Peru* 4°50S 76°50W **92** D3
Barranca del Cobre △
 Mexico 27°18N 107°40W **86** B3
Barrancabermeja
 Colombia 7°0N 73°50W **92** B4
Barrancas *Venezuela* 8°55N 62°5W **92** B6
Barrancos *Portugal* 38°10N 6°58E **21** C2
Barranqueras *Argentina* 27°30S 59°0W **94** B4
Barranquilla *Colombia* 11°0N 74°50W **92** A4
Barraute *Canada* 48°26N 77°38W **72** C4
Barre *Mass., U.S.A.* 42°25N 72°6W **83** D12
Barre *Vt., U.S.A.* 44°12N 72°30W **83** B12
Barreal *Argentina* 31°33S 69°28W **94** C2

Barreiras *Brazil* 12°8S 45°0W **93** F10
Barreirinhas *Brazil* 2°30S 42°50W **93** D10
Barreiro *Portugal* 38°39N 9°5W **21** C1
Barretos *Brazil* 20°30S 48°35W **93** H9
Barrhead *Canada* 54°10N 114°24W **70** C6
Barrie *Canada* 44°24N 79°40W **82** B5
Barrier Ra. *Australia* 31°0S 141°30E **63** E3
Barrier Reef *Belize* 17°9N 88°3W **87** D7
Barrington *U.S.A.* 41°44N 71°18W **83** E13
Barrington L. *Canada* 56°55N 100°15W **71** B8
Barrington Tops
 Australia 32°6S 151°28E **63** E5
Barringun *Australia* 29°1S 145°41E **63** D4
Barron *U.S.A.* 45°24N 91°51W **80** C8
Barrow *U.S.A.* 71°18N 156°47W **74** A8
Barrow *→ Ireland* 52°25N 6°58W **10** D5
Barrow, Pt. *U.S.A.* 71°23N 156°29W **74** A8
Barrow Creek *Australia* 21°30S 133°55E **62** C1
Barrow I. *Australia* 20°45S 115°20E **60** D2
Barrow-in-Furness *U.K.* 54°7N 3°14W **12** C4
Barrow Pt. *Australia* 14°20S 144°40E **62** A3
Barrow Ra. *Australia* 26°0S 127°40E **61** E4
Barrow Str. *Canada* 74°20N 95°0W **4** B3
Barry *U.K.* 51°24N 3°16W **13** F4
Barry's Bay *Canada* 45°29N 77°41W **82** A7
Barsat *Pakistan* 36°10N 72°45E **43** A5
Barsi *India* 18°10N 75°50E **40** L9
Barsoi *India* 25°48N 87°57E **41** G15
Barstow *U.S.A.* 34°54N 117°1W **79** L9
Barthélemy, Col *Vietnam* 19°26N 104°6E **38** C5
Bartica *Guyana* 6°25N 58°40W **92** B7
Bartle Frere *Australia* 17°27S 145°50E **62** B4
Bartlesville *U.S.A.* 36°45N 95°59W **84** C7
Bartlett *Calif., U.S.A.* 36°29N 118°2W **78** J8
Bartlett *Tenn., U.S.A.* 35°12N 89°52W **85** D10
Bartlett, L. *Canada* 63°5N 118°20W **70** A5
Bartolomeu Dias *Mozam.* 21°10S 35°8E **55** G4
Barton *U.S.A.* 44°45N 72°11W **83** B12
Barton upon Humber
 U.K. 53°41N 0°25W **12** D7
Bartow *U.S.A.* 27°54N 81°50W **85** H14
Barú, Volcan *Panama* 8°55N 82°35W **88** E3
Barumba
 Dem. Rep. of the Congo 1°3N 23°37E **54** B1
Baruun Urt *Mongolia* 46°46N 113°15E **29** E12
Baruunsuu *Mongolia* 43°43N 105°35E **34** C3
Barwani *India* 22°2N 74°57E **42** H6
Barysaw *Belarus* 54°17N 28°28E **17** A15
Barzān *Iraq* 36°55N 44°3E **44** B5
Bāsa'idū *Iran* 26°35N 55°20E **45** E7
Basal *Pakistan* 33°33N 72°13E **42** C5
Basankusa
 Dem. Rep. of the Congo 1°5N 19°50E **52** D3
Basarabeasca *Moldova* 46°21N 28°58E **17** E15
Basarabia = Bessarabiya
 Moldova 47°0N 28°10E **17** E15
Basawa *Afghan.* 34°15N 70°50E **42** B4
Bascuñán, C. *Chile* 28°52S 71°35W **94** B1
Basel *Switz.* 47°35N 7°35E **20** C7
Bashäkerd, Kühhä-ye
 Iran 26°42N 58°35E **45** E8
Bashaw *Canada* 52°35N 112°58W **70** C6
Bāshī *Iran* 28°41N 51°4E **45** D6
Bashkir Republic =
 Bashkortostan □
 Russia 54°0N 57°0E **18** D10
Bashkortostan □ *Russia* 54°0N 57°0E **18** D10
Basibasy *Madag.* 22°10S 43°40E **57** C7
Basilan *Phil.* 6°35N 122°0E **37** C6
Basilan Str. *Phil.* 6°50N 122°0E **37** C6
Basildon *U.K.* 51°34N 0°28E **13** F8
Basim = Washim *India* 20°3N 77°0E **40** J10
Basin *U.S.A.* 44°23N 108°2W **76** D9
Basingstoke *U.K.* 51°15N 1°5W **13** F6
Baskatong, Rés. *Canada* 46°46N 75°50W **72** C4
Basle = Basel *Switz.* 47°35N 7°35E **20** C7
Basoda *India* 23°52N 77°54E **42** H7
Basoko
 Dem. Rep. of the Congo 1°16N 23°40E **54** B1
Basque Provinces = País Vasco □
 Spain 42°50N 2°45W **21** A4
Basra = Al Başrah *Iraq* 30°30N 47°50E **44** D5
Bass Str. *Australia* 39°15S 146°30E **63** F4
Bassano *Canada* 50°48N 112°20W **70** C6
Bassano del Grappa *Italy* 45°46N 11°44E **22** B4
Bassas da India *Ind. Oc.* 22°0S 39°0E **55** G4
Basse-Pointe *Martinique* 14°52N 61°8W **88** c
Basse-Terre *Guadeloupe* 16°0N 61°44W **88** b
Basse Terre *Trin. & Tob.* 10°7N 61°19W **93** K15
Bassein *Burma* 16°45N 94°30E **41** L19
Basses, Pte. des
 Guadeloupe 15°52N 61°17W **88** b
Basseterre
 St. Kitts & Nevis 17°17N 62°43W **89** C7
Bassett *U.S.A.* 42°35N 99°32W **80** D4
Bassi *India* 30°44N 76°21E **42** D7
Bastak *Iran* 27°15N 54°25E **45** E7
Baştām *Iran* 36°29N 55°4E **45** B7
Bastar *India* 19°15N 81°40E **41** K12
Basti *India* 26°52N 82°55E **43** F10
Bastia *France* 42°40N 9°30E **20** E8
Bastogne *Belgium* 50°1N 5°43E **15** D5
Bastrop *La., U.S.A.* 32°47N 91°55W **84** E9
Bastrop *Tex., U.S.A.* 30°7N 97°19W **84** F6
Basuo = Dongfang
 China 18°50N 108°33E **38** C7
Bat Yam *Israel* 32°2N 34°44E **46** C3
Bata *Eq. Guin.* 1°57N 9°50E **52** D1
Bataan □ *Phil.* 14°40N 120°25E **37** B6
Batabanó *Cuba* 22°41N 82°18W **88** B3
Batabanó, G. de *Cuba* 22°30N 82°30W **88** B3
Batac *Phil.* 18°3N 120°34E **37** A6
Batagai *Russia* 67°38N 134°38E **29** C14
Batala *India* 31°48N 75°12E **42** D6
Batama
 Dem. Rep. of the Congo 0°58N 26°33E **54** B2
Batamay *Russia* 63°30N 129°15E **29** C13

Batang *Indonesia* 6°55S 109°45E **37** G13
Batangafo *C.A.R.* 7°25N 18°20E **52** C3
Batangas *Phil.* 13°35N 121°10E **37** B6
Batanta *Indonesia* 0°55S 130°40E **37** E8
Batatais *Brazil* 20°54S 47°37W **95** A6
Batavia *U.S.A.* 43°0N 78°11W **82** D6
Batchelor *Australia* 13°4S 131°1E **60** B5
Batdambang *Cambodia* 13°7N 103°12E **38** F4
Batemans B. *Australia* 35°40S 150°12E **63** F5
Batemans Bay *Australia* 35°44S 150°11E **63** F5
Batesburg-Leesville
 U.S.A. 33°54N 81°33W **85** E14
Batesville *Ark., U.S.A.* 35°46N 91°39W **84** D9
Batesville *Miss., U.S.A.* 34°19N 89°57W **85** D10
Batesville *Tex., U.S.A.* 28°58N 99°37W **84** G5
Bath *U.K.* 51°23N 2°22W **13** F5
Bath *Maine, U.S.A.* 43°55N 69°49W **81** D19
Bath *N.Y., U.S.A.* 42°20N 77°19W **82** D7
Bath & North East Somerset □
 U.K. 51°21N 2°27W **13** F5
Batheay *Cambodia* 11°59N 104°57E **39** G5
Bathsheba *Barbados* 13°13N 59°32W **89** g
Bathurst *Australia* 33°25S 149°31E **63** E4
Bathurst *Canada* 47°37N 65°43W **73** C6
Bathurst *S. Africa* 33°30S 26°50E **56** E4
Bathurst, C. *Canada* 70°34N 128°0W **68** C6
Bathurst B. *Australia* 14°16S 144°25E **62** A3
Bathurst Harb.
 Australia 43°15S 146°10E **63** G4
Bathurst I. *Australia* 11°30S 130°10E **60** B5
Bathurst I. *Canada* 76°0N 100°30W **69** F11
Bathurst Inlet *Canada* 66°50N 108°1W **68** D10
Batiki *Fiji* 17°48S 179°10E **59** a
Batlow *Australia* 35°31S 148°9E **63** F4
Batman *Turkey* 37°55N 41°5E **44** B4
Baţn al Ghūl *Jordan* 29°36N 35°56E **46** F4
Batna *Algeria* 35°34N 6°15E **50** A7
Batoka *Zambia* 16°45S 27°15E **55** F2
Baton Rouge *U.S.A.* 30°27N 91°11W **84** F9
Batong, Ko *Thailand* 6°32N 99°12E **39** J2
Batopilas *Mexico* 27°1N 107°44W **86** B3
Batouri *Cameroon* 4°30N 14°25E **52** D2
Båtsfjord *Norway* 70°38N 29°39E **8** A23
Battambang = Batdambang
 Cambodia 13°7N 103°12E **38** F4
Batticaloa *Sri Lanka* 7°43N 81°45E **40** R12
Battipáglia *Italy* 40°37N 14°58E **22** D6
Battle *U.K.* 50°55N 0°30E **13** G8
Battle *→ Canada* 52°43N 108°15W **71** C7
Battle Creek *U.S.A.* 42°19N 85°11W **81** D11
Battle Ground *U.S.A.* 45°47N 122°32W **78** E4
Battle Harbour *Canada* 52°16N 55°35W **73** B8
Battle Lake *U.S.A.* 46°17N 95°43W **80** B6
Battle Mountain
 U.S.A. 40°38N 116°56W **76** F5
Battlefields *Zimbabwe* 18°37S 29°47E **55** F2
Battleford *Canada* 52°45N 108°15W **71** C7
Batu *Ethiopia* 6°55N 39°45E **47** F2
Batu *Malaysia* 3°15N 101°40E **39** L3
Batu, Kepulauan
 Indonesia 0°30S 98°25E **36** E1
Batu Ferringhi *Malaysia* 5°28N 100°15E **39** c
Batu Gajah *Malaysia* 4°28N 101°3E **39** K3
Batu Is. = Batu, Kepulauan
 Indonesia 0°30S 98°25E **36** E1
Batu Pahat *Malaysia* 1°50N 102°56E **39** M4
Batuata *Indonesia* 6°12S 122°42E **37** F6
Batugondang, Tanjung
 Indonesia 8°6S 114°29E **37** J17
Batukau, Gunung
 Indonesia 8°20S 115°5E **37** J18
Batumi *Georgia* 41°39N 41°44E **19** F7
Batur *Indonesia* 8°15S 115°20E **37** J18
Batur, Danau *Indonesia* 8°15S 115°24E **37** J18
Batur, Gunung
 Indonesia 8°14S 115°23E **37** J18
Batura Sar *Pakistan* 36°30N 74°31E **43** A6
Baturaja *Indonesia* 4°11S 104°15E **36** E2
Baturité *Brazil* 4°28S 38°45W **93** D11
Baturiti *Indonesia* 8°19S 115°11E **37** J18
Bau *Malaysia* 1°25N 110°9E **36** D4
Baubau *Indonesia* 5°25S 122°38E **37** F6
Baucau *E. Timor* 8°27S 126°27E **37** F7
Bauchi *Nigeria* 10°22N 9°48E **50** F7
Baudette *U.S.A.* 48°43N 94°36W **80** A6
Bauer, C. *Australia* 32°44S 134°4E **63** E1
Bauhinia *Australia* 24°35S 149°18E **62** C4
Baukau = Baucau
 E. Timor 8°27S 126°27E **37** F7
Bauld, C. *Canada* 51°38N 55°26W **69** G20
Bauru *Brazil* 22°10S 49°0W **95** A6
Bausi *India* 24°48N 87°1E **43** G12
Bauska *Latvia* 56°24N 24°15E **9** H21
Bautzen *Germany* 51°10N 14°26E **16** C8
Bavānāt *Iran* 30°28N 53°27E **45** D7
Bavaria = Bayern □
 Germany 48°50N 12°0E **16** D6
Bavispe *→ Mexico* 29°15N 109°11W **86** B3
Bawdwin *Burma* 23°5N 97°20E **41** H20
Bawean *Indonesia* 5°46S 112°35E **36** F4
Bawku *Ghana* 11°3N 0°19W **50** F5
Bawlake *Burma* 19°11N 97°21E **41** K20
Baxley *U.S.A.* 31°47N 82°21W **85** F13
Baxter *U.S.A.* 46°21N 94°17W **80** B6
Baxter Springs *U.S.A.* 37°2N 94°44W **80** G6
Baxter State △ *U.S.A.* 46°5N 68°57W **81** B19
Bay City *Mich., U.S.A.* 43°36N 83°54W **81** D12
Bay City *Tex., U.S.A.* 28°59N 95°58W **84** G7
Bay Minette *U.S.A.* 30°53N 87°46W **85** F11
Bay Roberts *Canada* 47°36N 53°16W **73** C9
Bay St. Louis *U.S.A.* 30°19N 89°20W **85** F10
Bay Springs *U.S.A.* 31°59N 89°17W **85** F10
Bay View *N.Z.* 39°25S 176°50E **59** C6
Baya
 Dem. Rep. of the Congo 11°53S 27°25E **55** E2
Bayamo *Cuba* 20°20N 76°40W **88** B4
Bayamón *Puerto Rico* 18°24N 66°9W **89** d
Bayan Har Shan *China* 34°0N 98°0E **32** C4

Bayan Hot = Alxa Zuoqi
 China 38°50N 105°40E **34** E3
Bayan Lepas *Malaysia* 5°17N 100°16E **39** c
Bayan Obo *China* 41°52N 109°59E **34** D5
Bayan-Ovoo = Erdenetsogt
 Mongolia 42°55N 106°5E **34** C4
Bayana *India* 26°55N 77°18E **42** F7
Bayanaūyl *Kazakhstan* 50°45N 75°45E **28** D8
Bayandalay *Mongolia* 43°30N 103°29E **34** C2
Bayanhongor *Mongolia* 46°8N 102°43E **32** B5
Bayard *N. Mex., U.S.A.* 32°46N 108°8W **77** K9
Bayard *Nebr., U.S.A.* 41°45N 103°20W **80** E2
Baybay *Phil.* 10°40N 124°55E **37** B6
Baydaratskaya Guba
 Russia 69°0N 67°30E **28** C7
Baydhabo *Somali Rep.* 3°8N 43°30E **47** G3
Bayern □ *Germany* 48°50N 12°0E **16** D6
Bayeux *France* 49°17N 0°42W **20** B3
Bayfield *Canada* 43°34N 81°42W **82** C3
Bayfield *U.S.A.* 46°49N 90°49W **80** B8
Bayındır *Turkey* 38°13N 27°39E **23** E12
Baykal, Oz. *Russia* 53°0N 108°0E **29** D11
Baykan *Turkey* 38°7N 41°44E **44** B4
Baymak *Russia* 52°36N 58°19E **18** D10
Baynes Mts. *Namibia* 17°15S 13°0E **56** B1
Bayombong *Phil.* 16°30N 121°10E **37** A6
Bayonne *France* 43°30N 1°28W **20** E3
Bayonne *U.S.A.* 40°40N 74°6W **83** F10
Bayovar *Peru* 5°50S 81°0W **92** E2
Baygongyr *Kazakhstan* 45°40N 63°20E **28** E7
Bayram-Ali = Baýramaly
 Turkmenistan 37°37N 62°10E **45** B9
Baýramaly *Turkmenistan* 37°37N 62°10E **45** B9
Bayramiç *Turkey* 39°48N 26°36E **23** E12
Bayreuth *Germany* 49°56N 11°35E **16** D6
Bayrūt *Lebanon* 33°53N 35°31E **46** B4
Bayt Lahm *West Bank* 31°43N 35°12E **46** D4
Baytown *U.S.A.* 29°43N 94°58W **84** G7
Bayun *Indonesia* 8°11S 115°16E **37** J18
Baza *Spain* 37°30N 2°47W **21** D4
Bazaruto, I. do *Mozam.* 21°40S 35°28E **57** C6
Bazaruto △ *Mozam.* 21°42S 35°26E **57** C6
Bazhou *China* 39°8N 116°22E **34** E9
Bazmān, Küh-e *Iran* 28°4N 60°1E **45** D9
Beach *U.S.A.* 46°58N 104°0W **80** B2
Beach City *U.S.A.* 40°39N 81°35W **82** F3
Beachport *Australia* 37°29S 140°0E **63** F3
Beachville *Canada* 43°5N 80°49W **82** C4
Beachy Hd. *U.K.* 50°44N 0°15E **13** G8
Beacon *Australia* 30°26S 117°52E **61** F2
Beacon *U.S.A.* 41°30N 73°58W **83** E11
Beaconsfield *Australia* 41°11S 146°48E **63** G4
Beagle, Canal *S. Amer.* 55°0S 68°30W **96** H3
Beagle Bay *Australia* 16°58S 122°40E **60** C3
Beagle Bay ◉ *Australia* 16°53S 122°40E **60** C3
Beagle G. *Australia* 12°15S 130°25E **60** B5
Béal an Átha = Ballina
 Ireland 54°7N 9°9W **10** B2
Béal Átha na Sluaighe =
 Ballinasloe *Ireland* 53°20N 8°13W **10** C3
Bealanana *Madag.* 14°33S 48°44E **57** A8
Beals Cr. *→ U.S.A.* 32°10N 100°51W **84** E4
Beamsville *Canada* 43°12N 79°28W **82** C5
Bear *→ Calif., U.S.A.* 38°56N 121°36W **78** G5
Bear *→ Utah, U.S.A.* 41°30N 112°8W **74** G17
Bear I. *Ireland* 51°38N 9°50W **10** E2
Bear L. *Canada* 55°8N 96°0W **71** B9
Bear L. *U.S.A.* 41°59N 111°21W **76** F8
Bear Lake *Canada* 45°27N 79°34W **82** A5
Beardmore *Canada* 49°36N 87°57W **72** C2
Beardmore Glacier
 Antarctica 84°30S 170°0E **5** E11
Beardstown *U.S.A.* 40°1N 90°26W **80** E8
Bearma *→ India* 24°20N 79°51E **43** G8
Béarn *France* 43°20N 0°30W **20** E3
Bearpaw Mts. *U.S.A.* 48°12N 109°30W **76** B9
Bearskin Lake *Canada* 53°58N 91°2W **72** B1
Beas *→ India* 31°10N 74°59E **42** D6
Beata, C. *Dom. Rep.* 17°40N 71°30W **89** C5
Beata, I. *Dom. Rep.* 17°34N 71°31W **89** C5
Beatrice *U.S.A.* 40°16N 96°45W **80** E6
Beatrice *Zimbabwe* 18°15S 30°55E **55** F3
Beatrice, C. *Australia* 14°20S 136°55E **62** A2
Beatton *→ Canada* 56°15N 120°45W **70** B4
Beatton River *Canada* 57°26N 121°20W **70** B4
Beatty *U.S.A.* 36°54N 116°46W **78** J10
Beau Bassin *Mauritius* 20°13S 57°27E **53** d
Beauce, Plaine de la
 France 48°10N 1°45E **20** B4
Beauceville *Canada* 46°13N 70°46W **73** C5
Beaudesert *Australia* 27°59S 153°0E **63** D5
Beaufort *Malaysia* 5°30N 115°40E **36** C5
Beaufort *N.C., U.S.A.* 34°43N 76°40W **85** D16
Beaufort *S.C., U.S.A.* 32°26N 80°40W **85** E14
Beaufort Sea *Arctic* 72°0N 140°0W **66** B5
Beaufort West *S. Africa* 32°18S 22°36E **56** E3
Beauharnois *Canada* 45°20N 73°52W **83** A11
Beaulieu *→ Canada* 62°3N 113°11W **70** A6
Beauly *U.K.* 57°30N 4°28W **11** D4
Beauly *→ U.K.* 57°29N 4°27W **11** D4
Beaumaris *U.K.* 53°16N 4°6W **12** D3
Beaumont *Belgium* 50°15N 4°14E **15** D4
Beaumont *U.S.A.* 30°5N 94°6W **84** F7
Beaune *France* 47°2N 4°50E **20** C6
Beaupré *Canada* 47°3N 70°54W **73** C5
Beauraing *Belgium* 50°7N 4°57E **15** D4
Beausejour *Canada* 50°5N 96°35W **71** C9
Beauvais *France* 49°25N 2°8E **20** B5
Beauval *Canada* 55°9N 107°37W **71** B7
Beaver *Okla., U.S.A.* 36°49N 100°31W **84** C4
Beaver *Pa., U.S.A.* 40°42N 80°19W **82** F4
Beaver *Utah, U.S.A.* 38°17N 112°38W **76** G7
Beaver *→ B.C., Canada* 59°52N 124°20W **70** B4
Beaver *→ Sask., Canada* 55°26N 107°45W **71** B7
Beaver *→ U.S.A.* 36°35N 99°30W **84** C5
Beaver City *U.S.A.* 40°8N 99°50W **80** E4

Beaver Creek *Canada* 63°0N 141°0W **68** E3
Beaver Dam *U.S.A.* 43°28N 88°50W **80** D9
Beaver Falls *U.S.A.* 40°46N 80°20W **82** F4
Beaver Hill L. *Canada* 54°5N 94°50W **71** C10
Beaver I. *U.S.A.* 45°40N 85°33W **81** C11
Beavercreek *U.S.A.* 39°43N 84°11W **81** F11
Beaverhill L. *Canada* 53°27N 112°32W **70** C6
Beaverlodge *Canada* 55°11N 119°29W **70** B5
Beaverstone *→ Canada* 54°59N 89°25W **72** B2
Beaverton *Canada* 44°26N 79°9W **82** B5
Beaverton *U.S.A.* 45°29N 122°48W **78** E4
Beawar *India* 26°3N 74°18E **42** F6
Bebedouro *Brazil* 21°0S 48°25W **95** A6
Bebera, Tanjung
 Indonesia 8°44S 115°51E **37** K18
Becán *Mexico* 18°34N 89°31W **87** D7
Bécancour *Canada* 46°20N 72°26W **81** B17
Beccles *U.K.* 52°27N 1°35E **13** E9
Bečej *Serbia* 45°36N 20°3E **23** B9
Béchar *Algeria* 31°38N 2°18W **50** B5
Becharof L. *U.S.A.* 57°56N 156°23W **74** D8
Beckley *U.S.A.* 37°47N 81°11W **81** G13
Beddouas, C. *Morocco* 32°33N 9°9W **50** B4
Bedford *Canada* 45°7N 72°59W **83** A12
Bedford *S. Africa* 32°40S 26°10E **56** E4
Bedford *U.K.* 52°8N 0°28W **13** E7
Bedford *Ind., U.S.A.* 38°52N 86°29W **80** F10
Bedford *Iowa, U.S.A.* 40°40N 94°44W **80** E6
Bedford *Ohio, U.S.A.* 41°23N 81°32W **82** E3
Bedford *Pa., U.S.A.* 40°1N 78°30W **82** F6
Bedford *Va., U.S.A.* 37°20N 79°31W **81** G14
Bedford, C. *Australia* 15°14S 145°21E **62** B4
Bedfordshire □ *U.K.* 52°4N 0°28E **13** E7
Bedok *Singapore* 1°19N 103°56E **39** d
Bedourie *Australia* 24°30S 139°30E **62** C2
Bedum *Neths.* 53°18N 6°36E **15** A6
Beebe Plain *Canada* 45°1N 72°9W **83** A12
Beech Creek *U.S.A.* 41°5N 77°36W **82** E7
Beechy *Canada* 50°53N 107°24W **71** C7
Beed = Bir *India* 19°4N 75°46E **40** K9
Beef I. *Br. Virgin Is.* 18°26N 64°30W **89** e
Beenleigh *Australia* 27°43S 153°10E **63** D5
Be'er Menuha *Israel* 30°19N 35°8E **44** D2
Be'er Sheva *Israel* 31°15N 34°48E **46** D3
Beersheba = Be'er Sheva
 Israel 31°15N 34°48E **46** D3
Beestekraal *S. Africa* 25°23S 27°38E **57** D4
Beeston *U.K.* 52°56N 1°14W **12** E6
Beeton *Canada* 44°5N 79°47W **82** B5
Beeville *U.S.A.* 28°24N 97°45W **84** G6
Befale
 Dem. Rep. of the Congo 0°25N 20°45E **52** D4
Befandriana *Mahajanga,*
 Madag. 15°16S 48°32E **57** B8
Befandriana *Toliara,*
 Madag. 21°55S 44°0E **57** C7
Befasy *Madag.* 20°33S 44°23E **57** C7
Befotaka *Antsiranana,*
 Madag. 13°15S 48°16E **57** A8
Befotaka *Fianarantsoa,*
 Madag. 23°49S 47°0E **57** C8
Bega *Australia* 36°41S 149°51E **63** F4
Begusarai *India* 25°24N 86°9E **43** G12
Behābād *Iran* 32°24N 59°47E **45** C8
Behala *India* 22°30N 88°18E **43** H13
Behara *Madag.* 24°55S 46°20E **57** C8
Behbehān *Iran* 30°30N 50°15E **45** D6
Behm Canal *U.S.A.* 55°10N 131°0W **70** B2
Behshahr *Iran* 36°45N 53°35E **45** B7
Bei Jiang *→ China* 23°2N 112°58E **33** D6
Bei Shan *China* 41°30N 96°0E **32** B4
Bei'an *China* 48°10N 126°20E **33** B7
Beihai *China* 21°28N 109°6E **33** D5
Beijing *China* 39°53N 116°21E **34** E9
Beijing □ *China* 39°55N 116°20E **34** E9
Beilen *Neths.* 52°52N 6°27E **15** B6
Beilpajah *Australia* 32°54S 143°52E **63** E3
Beinn na Faoghla = Benbecula
 U.K. 57°26N 7°21W **11** D1
Beipiao *China* 41°52N 120°32E **35** D11
Beira *Mozam.* 19°50S 34°52E **55** F3
Beirut = Bayrūt *Lebanon* 33°53N 35°31E **46** B4
Beiseker *Canada* 51°23N 113°32W **70** C6
Beit Lekhem = Bayt Lahm
 West Bank 31°43N 35°12E **46** D4
Beitaolaizhao *China* 44°58N 125°58E **35** B13
Beitbridge *Zimbabwe* 22°12S 30°0E **55** G3
Beizhen = Binzhou
 China 37°20N 118°2E **35** F10
Beizhen *China* 41°38N 121°54E **35** D11
Beizhengzhen *China* 44°31N 123°30E **35** B12
Beja *Portugal* 38°2N 7°53W **21** C2
Béja *Tunisia* 36°43N 9°12E **51** A7
Bejaïa *Algeria* 36°42N 5°2E **50** A7
Béjar *Spain* 40°23N 5°46W **21** B3
Bejestān *Iran* 34°30N 58°5E **45** C8
Bekaa Valley = Al Biqā
 Lebanon 34°10N 36°10E **46** A5
Békéscsaba *Hungary* 46°40N 21°5E **17** E11
Bekily *Madag.* 24°13S 45°19E **57** C8
Bekisopa *Madag.* 21°40S 45°54E **57** C8
Bekitro *Madag.* 24°33S 45°18E **57** C8
Bekodoka *Madag.* 16°58S 45°7E **57** B8
Bekok *Malaysia* 2°20N 103°7E **39** L4
Bekopaka *Madag.* 19°9S 44°48E **57** B7
Bekuli *Indonesia* 8°22S 114°13E **37** J17
Bela *India* 25°50N 82°0E **43** G10
Bela *Pakistan* 26°12N 66°20E **42** F2
Bela Bela *S. Africa* 24°51S 28°19E **57** C4
Bela Crkva *Serbia* 44°55N 21°27E **23** B9
Bela Vista *Brazil* 22°12S 56°20W **94** A4
Bela Vista *Mozam.* 26°10S 32°44E **57** D5
Belan *→ India* 24°2N 81°45E **43** G9
Belarus ■ *Europe* 53°30N 27°0E **17** B14
Belau = Palau ■ *Palau* 7°30N 134°30E **58** A6
Belavenona *Madag.* 24°50S 47°4E **57** C8
Belawan *Indonesia* 3°33N 98°32E **36** D1
Belaya *→ Russia* 54°40N 56°0E **18** D10

Belaya Tserkov = Bila Tserkva
  Ukraine 49°45N 30°10E **17 D16**
Belaya Zemlya, Ostrova
  Russia 81°36N 62°18E **28 A7**
Belcher Is. Canada 56°15N 78°45W **72 A3**
Belden U.S.A. 40°2N 121°17W **78 E5**
Belebey Russia 54°7N 54°7E **18 D9**
Beledweyne Somali Rep. 4°30N 45°5E **47 G4**
Belém Brazil 1°20S 48°30W **93 D9**
Belén Argentina 27°40S 67°5W **94 B2**
Belén Paraguay 23°30S 57°6W **94 A4**
Belen U.S.A. 34°40N 106°46W **77 J10**
Belet Uen = Beledweyne
  Somali Rep. 4°30N 45°5E **47 G4**
Belev Russia 53°50N 36°5E **18 D6**
Belfair U.S.A. 47°27N 122°50W **78 C4**
Belfast S. Africa 25°42S 30°2E **57 D5**
Belfast U.K. 54°37N 5°56W **10 B6**
Belfast Maine, U.S.A. 44°26N 69°1W **81 C19**
Belfast N.Y., U.S.A. 42°21N 78°7W **82 D6**
Belfast I. U.K. 54°40N 5°50W **10 B6**
Belfield U.S.A. 46°53N 103°12W **80 B2**
Belfort France 47°38N 6°50E **20 C7**
Belfry U.S.A. 45°9N 109°1W **76 D9**
Belgaum India 15°55N 74°35E **40 M9**
Belgavi = Belgaum India 15°55N 74°35E **40 M9**
Belgium ■ Europe 50°30N 5°0E **15 D4**
Belgorod Russia 50°35N 36°35E **19 D6**
Belgorod-Dnestrovskiy =
  Bilhorod-Dnistrovskyy
  Ukraine 46°11N 30°23E **19 E5**
Belgrade = Beograd
  Serbia 44°50N 20°37E **23 B9**
Belgrade U.S.A. 45°47N 111°11W **76 D8**
Belgrano Antarctica 77°52S 34°37W **5 D1**
Belhaven U.S.A. 35°33N 76°37W **85 D16**
Beli Drim → Europe 42°6N 20°25E **23 C9**
Belimbing Indonesia 8°24S 115°2E **37 J18**
Belinyu Indonesia 1°35S 105°50E **36 E3**
Beliton Is. = Belitung
  Indonesia 3°10S 107°50E **36 E3**
Belitung Indonesia 3°10S 107°50E **36 E3**
Belize ■ Cent. Amer. 17°0N 88°30W **87 D7**
Belize City Belize 17°25N 88°10W **87 D7**
Belkovskiy, Ostrov
  Russia 75°32N 135°44E **29 B14**
Bell → Canada 49°48N 77°38W **72 C4**
Bell I. Canada 50°46N 55°35W **73 B8**
Bell-Irving → Canada 56°12N 129°5W **70 B3**
Bell Peninsula Canada 63°50N 82°0W **69 E15**
Bell Ville Argentina 32°40S 62°40W **94 C3**
Bella Bella Canada 52°10N 128°10W **70 C3**
Bella Coola Canada 52°25N 126°40W **70 C3**
Bella Unión Uruguay 30°15S 57°40W **94 C4**
Bella Vista Corrientes,
  Argentina 28°33S 59°0W **94 B4**
Bella Vista Tucuman,
  Argentina 27°10S 65°25W **94 B2**
Bellaire U.S.A. 40°1N 80°45W **82 F4**
Bellary India 15°10N 76°56E **40 M10**
Bellata Australia 29°53S 149°46E **63 D4**
Belle Fourche U.S.A. 44°40N 103°51W **80 C2**
Belle Fourche →
  U.S.A. 44°26N 102°18W **75 G19**
Belle Glade U.S.A. 26°41N 80°40W **85 H14**
Belle-Île France 47°20N 3°10W **20 C2**
Belle Isle Canada 51°57N 55°25W **73 B8**
Belle Isle, Str. of Canada 51°30N 56°30W **73 B8**
Belle Plaine U.S.A. 41°54N 92°17W **80 E7**
Belle River Canada 42°18N 82°43W **82 D2**
Bellefontaine U.S.A. 40°22N 83°46W **81 E12**
Bellefonte U.S.A. 40°55N 77°47W **82 F7**
Belleoram Canada 47°31N 55°25W **73 C8**
Belleplaine Barbados 13°15N 59°34W **89 g**
Belleville Canada 44°10N 77°23W **82 B7**
Belleville Ill., U.S.A. 38°31N 89°59W **80 F9**
Belleville Kans., U.S.A. 39°50N 97°38W **80 F5**
Belleville N.J., U.S.A. 40°47N 74°9W **83 F10**
Belleville N.Y., U.S.A. 43°46N 76°10W **83 C8**
Bellevue Idaho, U.S.A. 43°28N 114°16W **76 E6**
Bellevue Nebr., U.S.A. 41°9N 95°54W **80 E6**
Bellevue Ohio, U.S.A. 41°17N 82°51W **82 E2**
Bellevue Wash., U.S.A. 47°37N 122°12W **78 C4**
Bellin = Kangirsuk
  Canada 60°0N 70°0W **69 F18**
Bellingen Australia 30°25S 152°50E **63 E5**
Bellingham U.S.A. 48°46N 122°29W **78 B4**
Bellingshausen Abyssal Plain
  S. Ocean 64°0S 90°0W **5 C16**
Bellingshausen Sea
  Antarctica 66°0S 80°0W **5 C17**
Bellinzona Switz. 46°11N 9°1E **20 C8**
Bello Colombia 6°20N 75°33W **92 B3**
Bellows Falls U.S.A. 43°8N 72°27W **83 C12**
Bellpat Pakistan 29°0N 68°5E **42 E3**
Belluno Italy 46°9N 12°13E **22 A5**
Bellwood U.S.A. 40°36N 78°20W **82 F6**
Belmont Canada 42°53N 81°5W **82 D3**
Belmont S. Africa 29°28S 24°22E **56 D3**
Belmont U.S.A. 42°14N 78°2W **82 D6**
Belmonte Brazil 16°0S 39°0W **93 G11**
Belmopan Belize 17°18N 88°30W **87 D7**
Belmullet Ireland 54°14N 9°58W **10 B2**
Belo Horizonte Brazil 19°55S 43°56W **93 G10**
Belo-sur-Mer Madag. 20°42S 44°0E **57 C7**
Belo-Tsiribihina Madag. 19°40S 44°30E **57 B7**
Belogorsk Russia 51°0N 128°20E **29 D13**
Beloit Kans., U.S.A. 39°28N 98°6W **80 F4**
Beloit Wis., U.S.A. 42°31N 89°2W **80 D9**
Belokorovichi Ukraine 51°7N 28°2E **17 C15**
Belomorsk Russia 64°35N 34°54E **18 B5**
Belonia India 23°15N 91°30E **41 H17**
Beloretsk Russia 53°58N 58°24E **18 D10**
Belorussia = Belarus ■
  Europe 53°30N 27°0E **17 B14**
Belovo Russia 54°30N 86°0E **28 D9**
Beloyarskiy Russia 63°42N 66°40E **28 C7**
Beloye, Ozero Russia 60°10N 37°35E **18 B6**

Beloye More Russia 66°30N 38°0E **8 C25**
Belozersk Russia 60°1N 37°45E **18 B6**
Belpre U.S.A. 39°17N 81°34W **81 F13**
Belrain India 28°23N 80°55E **43 E9**
Belt U.S.A. 47°23N 110°55W **76 C8**
Beltana Australia 30°48S 138°25E **63 E2**
Belterra Brazil 2°45S 55°0W **93 D8**
Belton U.S.A. 31°3N 97°28W **84 F6**
Belton L. U.S.A. 31°6N 97°28W **84 F6**
Beltsy = Bălți Moldova 47°48N 27°58E **17 E14**
Belturbet Ireland 54°6N 7°26W **10 B4**
Belukha Russia 49°50N 86°50E **28 E9**
Beluran Malaysia 5°48N 117°35E **36 C5**
Belushya Guba Russia 71°32N 52°19E **28 B6**
Belvidere Ill., U.S.A. 42°15N 88°50W **80 D9**
Belvidere N.J., U.S.A. 40°50N 75°5W **83 F9**
Belyando → Australia 21°38S 146°50E **62 C4**
Belyando Crossing
  Australia 21°32S 146°51E **62 C4**
Belyuen Australia 12°34S 130°42E **60 B5**
Belyy, Ostrov Russia 73°30N 71°0E **28 B8**
Belyy Yar Russia 58°26N 84°39E **28 D9**
Belzoni U.S.A. 33°11N 90°29W **85 E9**
Bemaraha, Lembalemban' i
  Madag. 18°40S 44°45E **57 B7**
Bemarivo Madag. 21°45S 44°45E **57 C7**
Bemarivo → Antsiranana,
  Madag. 14°9S 50°9E **57 A9**
Bemarivo → Mahajanga,
  Madag. 15°27S 47°40E **57 B8**
Bemavo Madag. 21°33S 45°25E **57 C8**
Bembéréke Benin 10°11N 2°43E **50 F6**
Bembesi Zimbabwe 20°0S 28°58E **55 G2**
Bembesi → Zimbabwe 18°57S 27°47E **55 F2**
Bemetara India 21°42N 81°32E **43 J9**
Bemidji U.S.A. 47°28N 94°53W **80 B6**
Bemolanga Madag. 17°44S 45°6E **57 B8**
Ben Iran 32°32N 50°45E **45 C6**
Ben Cruachan U.K. 56°26N 5°8W **11 E3**
Ben Dearg U.K. 57°47N 4°56W **11 D4**
Ben En △ Vietnam 19°37N 105°30E **38 C5**
Ben Gardane Tunisia 33°11N 11°11E **51 B8**
Ben Hope U.K. 58°25N 4°36W **11 C4**
Ben Lawers U.K. 56°32N 4°14W **11 E4**
Ben Lomond N.S.W.,
  Australia 30°1S 151°43E **63 E5**
Ben Lomond Tas.,
  Australia 41°38S 147°42E **63 G4**
Ben Lomond U.K. 56°11N 4°38W **11 E4**
Ben Lomond △
  Australia 41°33S 147°39E **63 G4**
Ben Luc Vietnam 10°39N 106°29E **39 G6**
Ben Macdhui U.K. 57°4N 3°40W **11 D5**
Ben Mhor U.K. 57°15N 7°18W **11 D1**
Ben More Argyll & Bute,
  U.K. 56°26N 6°1W **11 E2**
Ben More Stirling, U.K. 56°23N 4°32W **11 E4**
Ben More Assynt U.K. 58°8N 4°52W **11 C4**
Ben Nevis U.K. 56°48N 5°1W **11 E3**
Ben Quang Vietnam 17°3N 106°55E **38 D6**
Ben Tre Vietnam 10°14N 106°23E **39 G6**
Ben Vorlich U.K. 56°21N 4°14W **11 E4**
Ben Wyvis U.K. 57°40N 4°35W **11 D4**
Bena Nigeria 11°20N 5°50E **50 F7**
Benalla Australia 36°30S 146°0E **63 F4**
Benares = Varanasi
  India 25°22N 83°0E **43 G10**
Benavente Spain 42°2N 5°43W **21 A3**
Benavides U.S.A. 27°36N 98°25W **84 H5**
Benbecula U.K. 57°26N 7°21W **11 D1**
Benbonyathe Hill
  Australia 30°25S 139°11E **63 E2**
Bend U.S.A. 44°4N 121°19W **76 D3**
Bender Beyla Somali Rep. 9°30N 50°48E **47 F5**
Bendery = Tighina
  Moldova 46°50N 29°30E **17 E15**
Bendigo Australia 36°40S 144°15E **63 F3**
Benē Beraq Israel 32°6N 34°51E **46 C3**
Benenitra Madag. 23°27S 45°5E **57 C8**
Benevento Italy 41°8N 14°45E **22 D6**
Benga Mozam. 16°11S 33°40E **55 F3**
Bengal, Bay of Ind. Oc. 15°0N 90°0E **41 M17**
Bengaluru = Bangalore
  India 12°59N 77°40E **40 N10**
Bengbu China 32°58N 117°20E **35 H9**
Benghazi = Banghāzī
  Libya 32°11N 20°3E **51 B10**
Bengkalis Indonesia 1°30N 102°10E **39 M4**
Bengkulu Indonesia 3°50S 102°12E **36 E2**
Bengkulu □ Indonesia 3°48S 102°16E **36 E2**
Bengough Canada 49°25N 105°10W **71 D7**
Benguela Angola 12°37S 13°25E **53 G2**
Benguérua, I. Mozam. 21°58S 35°28E **57 C6**
Beni Dem. Rep. of the Congo 0°30N 29°27E **54 B2**
Beni → Bolivia 10°23S 65°24W **92 F5**
Beni Mellal Morocco 32°21N 6°21W **50 B4**
Beni Suef Egypt 29°5N 31°6E **51 C12**
Beniah L. Canada 63°23N 112°17W **70 A6**
Benidorm Spain 38°33N 0°9W **21 C5**
Benin ■ Africa 10°0N 2°0E **50 G6**
Benin, Bight of W. Afr. 5°0N 3°0E **50 H5**
Benin City Nigeria 6°20N 5°31E **50 G7**
Benito Juárez Argentina 37°40S 59°43W **94 D4**
Benitses Greece 39°32N 19°55E **25 A3**
Benjamin Aceval
  Paraguay 24°58S 57°34W **94 A4**
Benjamin Constant
  Brazil 4°40S 70°15W **92 D4**
Benjamin Hill Mexico 30°9N 111°7W **86 A2**
Benkelman U.S.A. 40°3N 101°32W **80 E3**
Bennett Canada 59°51N 135°0W **70 B2**
Bennett, L. Australia 22°50S 131°2E **60 D5**
Bennetta, Ostrov
  Russia 76°21N 148°56E **29 B15**
Bennettsville U.S.A. 34°37N 79°41W **85 D15**
Bennington N.H., U.S.A. 43°0N 71°55W **83 D11**
Bennington Vt., U.S.A. 42°53N 73°12W **83 D11**
Benom Malaysia 3°50N 102°6E **39 L4**
Benoni S. Africa 26°11S 28°18E **57 D4**

Benque Viejo Belize 17°5N 89°8W **87 D7**
Benson Ariz., U.S.A. 31°58N 110°18W **77 L8**
Benson Minn., U.S.A. 45°19N 95°36W **80 C6**
Bent Iran 26°20N 59°31E **45 E8**
Benteng Indonesia 6°10S 120°30E **37 F6**
Bentinck I. Australia 17°3S 139°35E **62 B2**
Bentley Subglacial Trench
  Antarctica 80°0S 115°0W **5 E15**
Bento Gonçalves Brazil 29°10S 51°31W **95 B5**
Benton Ark., U.S.A. 34°34N 92°35W **84 D8**
Benton Calif., U.S.A. 37°48N 118°32W **78 H8**
Benton Ill., U.S.A. 38°0N 88°55W **80 G9**
Benton Pa., U.S.A. 41°12N 76°23W **83 E8**
Benton Harbor U.S.A. 42°6N 86°27W **80 D10**
Bentong Malaysia 3°31N 101°55E **39 L3**
Bentonville U.S.A. 36°22N 94°13W **84 C7**
Benue → Nigeria 7°48N 6°46E **50 G7**
Benxi China 41°20N 123°48E **35 D12**
Beo Indonesia 4°25N 126°50E **37 D7**
Beograd Serbia 44°50N 20°37E **23 B9**
Beolgyo S. Korea 34°51N 127°21E **35 G14**
Beppu Japan 33°15N 131°30E **31 H5**
Beqa Fiji 18°23S 178°8E **59 a**
Beqaa Valley = Al Biqâ
  Lebanon 34°10N 36°10E **46 A5**
Ber Mota India 23°27N 68°34E **42 H3**
Bera, Tasik Malaysia 3°5N 102°38E **39 L4**
Berach → India 25°15N 75°2E **42 G6**
Beraketa Madag. 23°7S 44°25E **57 C7**
Berastagi Indonesia 3°1N 98°31E **39 L2**
Berat Albania 40°43N 19°59E **23 D8**
Berau → Tanjungredeb
  Indonesia 2°9N 117°29E **36 D5**
Berau, Teluk Indonesia 2°30S 132°30E **37 E8**
Beravina Madag. 18°10S 45°14E **57 B8**
Berber Sudan 18°0N 34°0E **51 E12**
Berbera Somali Rep. 10°30N 45°2E **47 E4**
Berbérati C.A.R. 4°15N 15°40E **52 D3**
Berbice → Guyana 6°20N 57°32W **92 B7**
Berdichev = Berdychiv
  Ukraine 49°57N 28°30E **17 D15**
Berdsk Russia 54°47N 83°2E **28 D9**
Berdyansk Ukraine 46°45N 36°50E **19 E6**
Berdychiv Ukraine 49°57N 28°30E **17 D15**
Berea U.S.A. 37°34N 84°17W **81 G11**
Berebere Indonesia 2°25N 128°45E **37 D7**
Bereeda Somali Rep. 11°45N 51°0E **47 E5**
Berehove Ukraine 48°15N 22°35E **17 D12**
Bereket Turkmenistan 39°16N 55°32E **45 B7**
Berekum Ghana 7°29N 2°34W **50 G5**
Berens → Canada 52°25N 97°2W **71 C9**
Berens I. Canada 52°18N 97°18W **71 C9**
Berens River Canada 52°25N 97°0W **71 C9**
Beresford U.S.A. 43°5N 96°47W **80 D5**
Berestechko Ukraine 50°22N 25°5E **17 C13**
Berevo Mahajanga,
  Madag. 17°14S 44°17E **57 B7**
Berevo Toliara, Madag. 19°44S 44°58E **57 B7**
Berezhany Ukraine 49°26N 24°58E **17 D13**
Berezina = Byarezina →
  Belarus 52°33N 30°14E **17 B16**
Bereznik Russia 62°51N 42°40E **18 B7**
Berezniki Russia 59°24N 56°46E **18 C10**
Berezovo Russia 64°0N 65°0E **28 C7**
Berga Spain 42°6N 1°48E **21 A6**
Bergama Turkey 39°8N 27°11E **23 E12**
Bérgamo Italy 45°41N 9°43E **20 D8**
Bergen Neths. 52°40N 4°43E **15 B4**
Bergen Norway 60°20N 5°20E **8 F11**
Bergen U.S.A. 43°5N 77°57W **82 C7**
Bergen op Zoom Neths. 51°28N 4°18E **15 C4**
Bergerac France 44°51N 0°30E **20 D4**
Bergholz U.S.A. 40°31N 80°53W **82 F4**
Bergisch Gladbach
  Germany 50°59N 7°8E **15 D7**
Bergville S. Africa 28°52S 29°18E **57 D4**
Berhala, Selat Indonesia 1°0S 104°15E **36 E2**
Berhampore = Baharampur
  India 24°2N 88°27E **43 G13**
Berhampur = Brahmapur
  India 19°15N 84°54E **41 K14**
Bering Glacier U.S.A. 60°20N 143°30W **74 C11**
Bering Sea Pac. Oc. 58°0N 171°0W **66 D1**
Bering Strait Pac. Oc. 65°30N 169°0W **74 B6**
Beringovskiy Russia 63°3N 179°19E **29 C18**
Berisso Argentina 34°56S 57°50W **94 C4**
Berja Spain 36°50N 2°56W **21 D4**
Berkeley U.S.A. 37°51N 122°16W **78 H4**
Berkner I. Antarctica 79°30S 50°0W **5 D18**
Berkshire U.S.A. 42°19N 76°11W **83 D8**
Berkshire Downs U.K. 51°33N 1°29W **13 F6**
Berlin Germany 52°31N 13°23E **16 B7**
Berlin Md., U.S.A. 38°20N 75°13W **81 F16**
Berlin N.H., U.S.A. 44°28N 71°11W **83 B13**
Berlin N.Y., U.S.A. 42°42N 73°23W **83 D11**
Berlin Wis., U.S.A. 43°58N 88°57W **80 D9**
Berlin L. U.S.A. 41°3N 81°0W **82 E4**
Bermejo → Formosa,
  Argentina 26°51S 58°23W **94 B4**
Bermejo → San Juan,
  Argentina 32°30S 67°30W **94 C2**
Bermejo, Paso = Uspallata, P. de
  Argentina 32°37S 69°22W **94 C2**
Bermen, L. Canada 53°35N 68°55W **73 B6**
Bermuda ☑ Atl. Oc. 32°18N 64°45W **67 F13**
Bern Switz. 46°57N 7°28E **20 C7**
Bernalillo U.S.A. 35°18N 106°33W **77 J10**
Bernardo de Irigoyen
  Argentina 26°15S 53°40W **95 B5**
Bernardsville U.S.A. 40°43N 74°34W **83 F10**
Bernasconi Argentina 37°55S 63°44W **94 D3**
Bernburg Germany 51°47N 11°44E **16 C6**
Berne = Bern Switz. 46°57N 7°28E **20 C7**
Berneray U.K. 57°43N 7°11W **11 D1**
Bernier I. Australia 24°50S 113°12E **61 D1**
Bernina, Piz Switz. 46°20N 9°54E **20 C8**
Beroroha Madag. 21°40S 45°10E **57 C8**
Beroun Czech Rep. 49°57N 14°5E **16 D8**
Berri Australia 34°14S 140°35E **63 E3**

Berriane Algeria 32°50N 3°46E **50 B6**
Berry Australia 34°46S 150°43E **63 E5**
Berry France 46°50N 2°0E **20 C5**
Berry Is. Bahamas 25°40N 77°50W **88 A4**
Berryessa, L. U.S.A. 38°31N 122°6W **78 G4**
Berryville U.S.A. 36°22N 93°34W **84 C8**
Berseba Namibia 26°0S 17°46E **56 D2**
Bershad Ukraine 48°22N 29°31E **17 D15**
Berthold U.S.A. 48°19N 101°44W **80 A3**
Berthoud U.S.A. 40°19N 105°5W **76 F11**
Bertoua Cameroon 4°30N 13°45E **52 D2**
Bertraghboy B. Ireland 53°22N 9°54W **10 C2**
Berwick U.S.A. 41°3N 76°14W **83 E8**
Berwick-upon-Tweed
  U.K. 55°46N 2°0W **12 B6**
Berwyn Mts. U.K. 52°54N 3°26W **12 E4**
Besal Pakistan 35°4N 73°56E **43 B5**
Besalampy Madag. 16°43S 44°29E **57 B7**
Besançon France 47°15N 6°2E **20 C7**
Besar Indonesia 2°40S 116°0E **36 E5**
Besnard L. Canada 55°25N 106°0W **71 B7**
Besni Turkey 37°41N 37°52E **44 B3**
Besor, N. → Egypt 31°28N 34°22E **46 D3**
Bessarabiya Moldova 47°0N 28°10E **17 E15**
Bessarabka = Basarabeasca
  Moldova 46°21N 28°58E **17 E15**
Bessemer Ala., U.S.A. 33°24N 86°58W **85 E11**
Bessemer Mich., U.S.A. 46°29N 90°3W **80 B8**
Bessemer Pa., U.S.A. 40°59N 80°30W **82 F4**
Beswick Australia 14°34S 132°53E **60 B5**
Bet She'an Israel 32°30N 35°30E **46 C4**
Bet Shemesh Israel 31°44N 35°0E **46 D4**
Betafo Madag. 19°50S 46°51E **57 B8**
Betancuria Canary Is. 28°25N 14°3W **24 F5**
Betanzos Spain 43°15N 8°12W **21 A1**
Bétaré Oya Cameroon 5°40N 14°5E **52 C2**
Betatao Madag. 18°11S 47°52E **57 B8**
Bethal S. Africa 26°27S 29°28E **57 D4**
Bethanien Namibia 26°31S 17°8E **56 D2**
Bethany Canada 44°11N 78°34W **82 B6**
Bethany Mo., U.S.A. 40°16N 94°2W **80 E6**
Bethany Okla., U.S.A. 35°31N 97°38W **84 D6**
Bethel Alaska, U.S.A. 60°48N 161°45W **74 C7**
Bethel Conn., U.S.A. 41°22N 73°25W **83 E11**
Bethel Maine, U.S.A. 44°25N 70°47W **83 B14**
Bethel Vt., U.S.A. 43°50N 72°38W **83 C12**
Bethel Park U.S.A. 40°19N 80°2W **82 F4**
Bethlehem = Bayt Lahm
  West Bank 31°43N 35°12E **46 D4**
Bethlehem S. Africa 28°14S 28°18E **57 D4**
Bethlehem U.S.A. 40°37N 75°23W **83 F9**
Bethulie S. Africa 30°30S 25°59E **56 E4**
Béthune France 50°30N 2°38E **20 A5**
Betioky Madag. 23°48S 44°20E **57 C7**
Betong Malaysia 1°24N 111°31E **36 D4**
Betong Thailand 5°45N 101°5E **39 K3**
Betoota Australia 25°45S 140°42E **62 D3**
Betpaqdala Kazakhstan 45°45N 70°30E **32 B2**
Betroka Madag. 23°16S 46°0E **57 C8**
Betsiamites Canada 48°56N 68°40W **73 C6**
Betsiamites → Canada 48°56N 68°38W **73 C6**
Betsiboka → Madag. 16°3S 46°36E **57 B8**
Bettendorf U.S.A. 41°32N 90°30W **80 E8**
Bettiah India 26°48N 84°33E **43 F11**
Betul India 21°58N 77°59E **40 J10**
Betws-y-Coed U.K. 53°5N 3°48W **12 D4**
Beulah Mich., U.S.A. 44°38N 86°6W **80 C10**
Beulah N. Dak., U.S.A. 47°16N 101°47W **80 B3**
Beverley Australia 32°9S 116°56E **61 F2**
Beverley U.K. 53°51N 0°26W **12 D7**
Beverly U.S.A. 42°33N 70°53W **83 D14**
Beverly Hills Calif.,
  U.S.A. 34°4N 118°24W **79 L8**
Beverly Hills Fla.,
  U.S.A. 28°55N 82°28W **85 G13**
Bevoalavo Madag. 25°13S 45°26E **57 D7**
Bewas → India 23°59N 79°21E **43 H8**
Bewdley Canada 44°5N 78°19W **82 B6**
Bexhill U.K. 50°51N 0°29E **13 G8**
Beyānlū Iran 36°0N 47°51E **44 C5**
Beyneu Kazakhstan 45°18N 55°9E **19 E10**
Beypazarı Turkey 40°10N 31°56E **19 F5**
Beyşehir Gölü Turkey 37°41N 31°33E **44 B1**
Béziers France 43°20N 3°12E **20 E5**
Bezwada = Vijayawada
  India 16°31N 80°39E **41 L12**
Bhabua India 25°3N 83°37E **43 G10**
Bhachau India 23°20N 70°16E **42 H4**
Bhadar → Gujarat, India 22°17N 72°20E **42 H5**
Bhadar → Gujarat, India 21°27N 69°47E **42 J3**
Bhadarwah India 32°58N 75°46E **43 C6**
Bhadgaon = Bhaktapur
  Nepal 27°38N 85°24E **43 F11**
Bhadohi India 25°25N 82°34E **43 G10**
Bhadra India 29°8N 75°14E **42 E6**
Bhadrakh India 21°10N 86°30E **41 J15**
Bhadran India 22°19N 72°6E **42 H5**
Bhadravati India 13°49N 75°40E **40 N9**
Bhag Pakistan 29°2N 67°49E **42 E2**
Bhagalpur India 25°10N 87°0E **43 G12**
Bhagirathi → Uttarakhand,
  India 30°8N 78°35E **43 D8**
Bhagirathi → W. Bengal,
  India 23°25N 88°23E **43 H13**
Bhakkar Pakistan 31°40N 71°5E **42 D4**
Bhakra Dam India 31°30N 76°45E **42 D7**
Bhaktapur Nepal 27°38N 85°24E **43 F11**
Bhamo Burma 24°15N 97°15E **41 G20**
Bhandara India 21°5N 79°42E **40 J11**
Bhanpura India 24°31N 75°44E **42 G6**
Bhanrer Ra. India 23°40N 79°45E **43 H8**
Bhaptiahi India 26°23N 86°30E **43 F12**
Bharat = India ■ Asia 20°0N 78°0E **40 K11**
Bharatpur Chhattisgarh,
  India 23°44N 81°46E **43 H9**
Bharatpur Nepal 27°34N 84°10E **43 F11**

Bharuch India 21°47N 73°0E **40 J8**
Bhatinda India 30°15N 74°57E **42 D6**
Bhatpara India 22°50N 88°25E **43 H13**
Bhattu India 29°36N 75°19E **42 E6**
Bhaun Pakistan 32°55N 72°40E **42 C5**
Bhaunagar = Bhavnagar
  India 21°45N 72°10E **40 J8**
Bhavnagar India 21°45N 72°10E **40 J8**
Bhawari India 25°42N 73°4E **42 G5**
Bhayavadar India 21°51N 70°15E **42 J4**
Bhera Pakistan 32°29N 72°57E **42 C5**
Bhikangaon India 21°52N 75°57E **42 J6**
Bhilai = Bhilainagar-Durg
  India 21°13N 81°26E **41 J12**
Bhilainagar-Durg India 21°13N 81°26E **41 J12**
Bhilsa = Vidisha India 23°28N 77°53E **42 H7**
Bhilwara India 25°25N 74°38E **42 G6**
Bhima → India 16°25N 77°17E **40 L10**
Bhimbar Pakistan 32°59N 74°3E **43 C6**
Bhind India 26°30N 78°46E **43 F8**
Bhinga India 27°43N 81°56E **43 F9**
Bhinmal India 25°0N 72°15E **42 G5**
Bhisho S. Africa 32°50S 27°23E **57 E4**
Bhiwandi India 19°20N 73°0E **40 K8**
Bhiwani India 28°50N 76°9E **42 E7**
Bhogava → India 22°26N 72°20E **42 H5**
Bhola Bangla. 22°45N 90°35E **41 H17**
Bholari Pakistan 25°19N 68°13E **42 G3**
Bhopal India 23°20N 77°30E **42 H7**
Bhubaneshwar India 20°15N 85°50E **41 J14**
Bhuj India 23°15N 69°49E **42 H3**
Bhumiphol Res. Thailand 17°20N 98°40E **38 D2**
Bhusawal India 21°3N 75°46E **40 J9**
Bhutan ■ Asia 27°25N 90°30E **41 F17**
Biafra, B. of = Bonny, Bight of
  Africa 3°30N 9°20E **52 D1**
Biak Indonesia 1°10S 136°6E **37 E9**
Biała Podlaska Poland 52°4N 23°6E **17 B12**
Białogard Poland 54°2N 15°58E **16 A8**
Białystok Poland 53°10N 23°10E **17 B12**
Biaora India 23°56N 76°56E **42 H7**
Biärjmand Iran 36°6N 55°53E **45 B7**
Biaro Indonesia 2°5N 125°26E **37 D7**
Biarritz France 43°29N 1°33W **20 E3**
Bias Indonesia 8°24S 115°36E **37 J18**
Bibai Japan 43°19N 141°52E **30 C10**
Bibby I. Canada 61°55N 93°0W **71 A10**
Biberach Germany 48°5N 9°47E **16 D5**
Bibungwa
  Dem. Rep. of the Congo 2°40S 28°15E **54 C2**
Bicester U.K. 51°54N 1°9W **13 F6**
Bicheno Australia 41°52S 148°18E **63 G4**
Bichia India 22°27N 80°42E **43 H9**
Bickerton I. Australia 13°45S 136°10E **62 A2**
Bid = Bir India 19°4N 75°46E **40 K9**
Bida Nigeria 9°3N 5°58E **50 G7**
Bidar India 17°55N 77°35E **40 L10**
Biddeford U.S.A. 43°30N 70°28W **81 D18**
Bideford U.K. 51°1N 4°13W **13 F3**
Bideford Bay U.K. 51°5N 4°20W **13 F3**
Bidhuna India 26°49N 79°31E **43 F8**
Bidokht Iran 34°20N 58°46E **45 C8**
Bidor Malaysia 4°6N 101°15E **39 K3**
Bidyadanga Australia 18°45S 121°43E **60 C3**
Bié, Planalto de Angola 12°0S 16°0E **53 G3**
Bieber U.S.A. 41°7N 121°8W **76 F3**
Biel Switz. 47°8N 7°14E **20 C7**
Bielefeld Germany 52°1N 8°33E **16 B5**
Biella Italy 45°34N 8°3E **20 D8**
Bielsk Podlaski Poland 52°47N 23°12E **17 B12**
Bielsko-Biała Poland 49°50N 19°2E **17 D10**
Bien Hoa Vietnam 10°57N 106°49E **39 G6**
Bienne = Biel Switz. 47°8N 7°14E **20 C7**
Bienville, L. Canada 55°5N 72°40W **72 A5**
Biesiesfontein S. Africa 30°57S 17°58E **56 E2**
Big → Canada 54°50N 58°55W **73 B8**
Big B. Canada 55°43N 60°35W **73 A7**
Big Bear City U.S.A. 34°16N 116°51W **79 L10**
Big Bear Lake U.S.A. 34°15N 116°56W **79 L10**
Big Belt Mts. U.S.A. 46°30N 111°25W **76 C8**
Big Bend Swaziland 26°50S 31°58E **57 D5**
Big Bend ∆ U.S.A. 29°20N 103°5W **84 G3**
Big Black → U.S.A. 32°3N 91°4W **85 E9**
Big Blue → U.S.A. 39°35N 96°34W **80 F5**
Big Creek U.S.A. 37°11N 119°14W **78 H7**
Big Cypress △ U.S.A. 26°0N 81°10W **85 H14**
Big Desert Australia 35°45S 141°10E **63 F3**
Big Falls U.S.A. 48°12N 93°48W **80 A7**
Big Fork → U.S.A. 48°31N 93°43W **80 A7**
Big Horn Mts. = Bighorn Mts.
  U.S.A. 44°25N 107°0W **76 D10**
Big I. Canada 61°7N 116°45W **70 A5**
Big Lake U.S.A. 31°12N 101°28W **84 F4**
Big Moose U.S.A. 43°49N 74°58W **83 C10**
Big Muddy Cr. →
  U.S.A. 48°8N 104°36W **76 B11**
Big Pine U.S.A. 37°10N 118°17W **78 H8**
Big Piney U.S.A. 42°32N 110°7W **76 E8**
Big Quill L. Canada 51°55N 104°50W **71 C8**
Big Rapids U.S.A. 43°42N 85°29W **81 D11**
Big Rideau L. Canada 44°40N 76°15W **83 B8**
Big River Canada 53°50N 107°0W **71 C7**
Big Run U.S.A. 40°57N 78°55W **82 F6**
Big Sable Pt. U.S.A. 44°3N 86°1W **80 C10**
Big Salmon → Canada 61°52N 134°55W **70 A2**
Big Sand L. Canada 57°45N 99°45W **71 B9**
Big Sandy U.S.A. 48°11N 110°7W **76 B8**
Big Sandy → U.S.A. 38°25N 82°36W **81 F12**
Big Sandy Cr. = Sandy Cr. →
  U.S.A. 41°51N 109°47W **76 F9**
Big Sandy Cr. →
  U.S.A. 38°7N 102°29W **76 G12**
Big Sioux → U.S.A. 42°29N 96°27W **80 D5**
Big South Fork ∆
  U.S.A. 36°27N 84°47W **85 C12**
Big Stone City U.S.A. 45°18N 96°28W **80 C5**
Big Stone Gap U.S.A. 36°52N 82°47W **81 G12**

Big Stone L. *U.S.A.* 45°18N 96°27W **80** C5
Big Sur *U.S.A.* 36°15N 121°48W **78** J3
Big Timber *U.S.A.* 45°50N 109°57W **76** D9
Big Trout L. *Canada* 53°40N 90°0W **72** B2
Big Trout Lake *Canada* 53°45N 90°0W **72** B2
Biğa *Turkey* 40°13N 27°14E **23** D12
Bigadiç *Turkey* 39°22N 28°7E **23** E13
Biggar *Canada* 52°4N 108°0W **71** C7
Biggar *U.K.* 55°38N 3°32W **11** F5
Bigge I. *Australia* 14°35S 125°10E **60** B4
Biggenden *Australia* 25°31S 152°4E **63** D5
Biggleswade *U.K.* 52°5N 0°14W **13** E7
Biggs *U.S.A.* 39°25N 121°43W **78** F5
Bighorn *U.S.A.* 46°10N 107°27W **76** C10
Bighorn → *U.S.A.* 46°10N 107°28W **76** C10
Bighorn Canyon ⌓ *U.S.A.* 45°10N 108°0W **76** D10
Bighorn L. *U.S.A.* 44°55N 108°15W **76** D9
Bighorn Mts. *U.S.A.* 44°25N 107°0W **76** D10
Bigstone L. *Canada* 53°42N 95°44W **71** C9
Bigwa *Tanzania* 7°10S 39°10E **54** D4
Bihać *Bos.-H.* 44°49N 15°57E **16** F8
Bihar *India* 25°5N 85°40E **43** G11
Bihar □ *India* 25°0N 86°0E **43** G12
Biharamulo *Tanzania* 2°25S 31°25E **54** C3
Biharamulo ⌓ *Tanzania* 2°24S 31°26E **54** C3
Bihariganj *India* 25°44N 86°59E **43** G12
Bihor, Munţii *Romania* 46°29N 22°47E **17** E12
Bijagós, Arquipélago dos *Guinea-Biss.* 11°15N 16°10W **50** F2
Bijaipur *India* 26°2N 77°20E **42** F7
Bijapur *Chhattisgarh, India* 18°50N 80°50E **41** K12
Bijapur *Karnataka, India* 16°50N 75°55E **40** L9
Bījār *Iran* 35°52N 47°35E **44** C5
Bijawar *India* 24°38N 79°30E **43** G8
Bijeljina *Bos.-H.* 44°46N 19°14E **23** B8
Bijnor *India* 29°27N 78°11E **42** E8
Bikaner *India* 28°2N 73°18E **42** E5
Bikapur *India* 26°30N 82°7E **43** F10
Bikeqi *China* 40°43N 111°20E **34** D6
Bikfayyā *Lebanon* 33°55N 35°41E **46** B4
Bikin *Russia* 46°50N 134°20E **30** A7
Bikin → *Russia* 46°51N 134°2E **30** A7
Bikini Atoll *Marshall Is.* 12°0N 167°30E **64** F8
Bikita *Zimbabwe* 20°6S 31°41E **57** C5
Bīkkū Bīttī *Libya* 22°0N 19°12E **51** D9
Bila Tserkva *Ukraine* 49°45N 30°10E **17** D16
Bilara *India* 26°14N 73°53E **42** F5
Bilaspur *Chhattisgarh, India* 22°2N 82°15E **43** H10
Bilaspur *Punjab, India* 31°19N 76°50E **42** D7
Bilauk Taungdan *Thailand* 13°0N 99°0E **38** F2
Bilbao *Spain* 43°16N 2°56W **21** A4
Bilbo = Bilbao *Spain* 43°16N 2°56W **21** A4
Bíldudalur *Iceland* 65°41N 23°36W **8** D2
Bílé Karpaty *Europe* 49°5N 18°0E **17** D9
Bilecik *Turkey* 40°5N 30°5E **19** F5
Bilgram *India* 27°11N 80°2E **43** F9
Bilhaur *India* 26°51N 80°5E **43** F9
Bilhorod-Dnistrovskyy *Ukraine* 46°11N 30°23E **19** E5
Bilibino *Russia* 68°3N 166°20E **29** C17
Bilibiza *Mozam.* 12°30S 40°20E **55** E5
Billiluna *Australia* 19°37S 127°41E **60** C4
Billings *U.S.A.* 45°47N 108°30W **76** D9
Billiton Is. = Belitung *Indonesia* 3°10S 107°50E **36** E3
Bilma *Niger* 18°50N 13°30E **51** E8
Biloela *Australia* 24°24S 150°31E **62** C5
Biloxi *U.S.A.* 30°24N 88°53W **85** F10
Bilpa Morea Claypan *Australia* 25°0S 140°0E **62** D3
Biltine *Chad* 14°40N 20°50E **51** F10
Bima *Indonesia* 8°22S 118°49E **37** F5
Bimbo *C.A.R.* 4°15N 18°33E **52** D3
Bimini Is. *Bahamas* 25°42N 79°25W **88** A4
Bin Xian *Heilongjiang, China* 45°42N 127°32E **35** B14
Bin Xian *Shaanxi, China* 35°2N 108°4E **34** G5
Bina-Etawah *India* 24°13N 78°14E **42** G8
Binalbagan *Phil.* 10°12N 122°50E **37** B6
Binalong *Australia* 34°40S 148°39E **63** E4
Bīnālūd, Kūh-e *Iran* 36°30N 58°30E **45** B8
Binatang = Bintangau *Malaysia* 2°10N 111°40E **36** D4
Binche *Belgium* 50°26N 4°10E **15** D4
Bindki *India* 26°2N 80°36E **43** F9
Bindura *Zimbabwe* 17°18S 31°18E **55** F3
Bingara *Australia* 29°52S 150°36E **63** D5
Bingham *U.S.A.* 45°3N 69°53W **81** C19
Binghamton *U.S.A.* 42°6N 75°55W **83** D9
Bingöl *Turkey* 38°53N 40°29E **44** B4
Binh Dinh = An Nhon *Vietnam* 13°55N 109°7E **38** F7
Binh Khe *Vietnam* 13°57N 108°51E **38** F7
Binh Son *Vietnam* 15°20N 108°40E **38** E7
Binhai *China* 34°2N 119°49E **35** G10
Binisatua *Spain* 39°50N 4°11E **24** B11
Binissalem *Spain* 39°41N 2°50E **24** B9
Binjai *Indonesia* 3°20N 98°30E **36** D3
Binnaway *Australia* 31°28S 149°24E **63** E4
Binongko *Indonesia* 5°57S 124°2E **37** F6
Binscarth *Canada* 50°37N 101°17W **71** C8
Bintan *Indonesia* 1°0N 104°0E **36** D2
Bintangau *Malaysia* 2°10N 111°40E **36** D4
Bintulu *Malaysia* 3°10N 113°0E **36** D4
Bintuni *Indonesia* 2°7S 133°32E **37** E8
Binzert = Bizerte *Tunisia* 37°15N 9°50E **51** A7
Binzhou *China* 37°20N 118°2E **35** F10
Bío Bío □ *Chile* 37°35S 72°0W **94** D1
Bíobío → *Chile* 36°49S 73°10W **94** D1
Bioko *Eq. Guin.* 3°30N 8°40E **52** D1
Bir *India* 19°4N 75°46E **40** K9
Bîr Abu Muḩammad *Egypt* 29°44N 34°14E **46** F3
Bi'r ad Dabbāghāt *Jordan* 30°26N 35°32E **46** E4
Bi'r al Butayyihāt *Jordan* 29°47N 35°20E **46** F4
Bi'r al Mārī *Jordan* 30°4N 35°33E **46** E4
Bi'r al Qaṭṭār *Jordan* 29°47N 35°32E **46** F4
Bir Atrun *Sudan* 18°15N 26°40E **51** E11
Bîr Beiḍa *Egypt* 30°25N 34°29E **46** E3
Bîr el 'Abd *Egypt* 31°2N 33°0E **46** D2
Bîr el Biarât *Egypt* 29°30N 34°43E **46** F3
Bîr el Duweidar *Egypt* 30°56N 32°32E **46** E1
Bîr el Garârât *Egypt* 31°3N 33°34E **46** D2
Bîr el Heisi *Egypt* 29°22N 34°36E **46** F3
Bîr el Jafir *Egypt* 30°50N 32°41E **46** E1
Bîr el Mâlḥi *Egypt* 30°38N 33°19E **46** E2
Bîr el Thamâda *Egypt* 30°12N 33°27E **46** E2
Bîr Gebeil Ḥiṣn *Egypt* 30°2N 33°18E **46** E2
Bi'r Ghadīr *Syria* 34°6N 37°3E **46** A6
Bîr Ḥasana *Egypt* 30°29N 33°46E **46** E2
Bîr Kaseiba *Egypt* 31°0N 33°17E **46** E2
Bîr Lahfân *Egypt* 31°0N 33°51E **46** D2
Bîr Madkûr *Egypt* 30°44N 32°33E **46** E1
Bîr Mogreïn *Mauritania* 25°10N 11°25W **50** C3
Bi'r Muṭribah *Kuwait* 29°54N 47°17E **44** D5
Bîr Qaṭia *Egypt* 30°58N 32°45E **46** E1
Bîr Shalatein *Egypt* 23°5N 35°25E **51** D13
Birāk *Libya* 27°31N 14°20E **51** C8
Biratnagar *Nepal* 26°27N 87°17E **43** F12
Birawa *Dem. Rep. of the Congo* 2°20S 28°48E **54** C2
Birch → *Canada* 58°28N 112°17W **70** B6
Birch Hills *Canada* 52°59N 105°25W **71** C7
Birch I. *Canada* 52°26N 99°54W **71** C9
Birch L. *N.W.T., Canada* 62°4N 116°33W **70** A5
Birch L. *Ont., Canada* 51°23N 92°18W **72** B1
Birch Mts. *Canada* 57°30N 113°10W **70** B6
Birch River *Canada* 52°24N 101°6W **71** C8
Birchip *Australia* 35°56S 142°55E **63** F3
Bird *Canada* 56°30N 94°13W **71** B10
Bird I. = Aves, I. de *W. Indies* 15°45N 63°55W **89** C7
Bird I. *S. Georgia* 54°0S 38°3W **96** G9
Birds Creek *Canada* 45°6N 77°52W **82** A7
Birdsville *Australia* 25°51S 139°20E **62** D2
Birdum Cr. → *Australia* 15°14S 133°0E **60** C5
Birecik *Turkey* 37°2N 38°0E **44** B3
Birein *Israel* 30°50N 34°28E **46** E3
Bireuen *Indonesia* 5°14N 96°39E **36** C1
Birigüi *Brazil* 21°18S 50°16W **95** A5
Bīrjand *Iran* 32°53N 59°13E **45** C8
Birkenhead *U.K.* 53°23N 3°2W **12** D4
Bîrlad = Bârlad *Romania* 46°15N 27°38E **17** E14
Birmingham *U.K.* 52°29N 1°52W **13** E6
Birmingham *U.S.A.* 33°31N 86°48W **85** E11
Birmingham Int. ✈ **(BHX)** *U.K.* 52°26N 1°45W **13** E6
Birmitrapur *India* 22°24N 84°46E **41** H14
Birni Nkonni *Niger* 13°55N 5°15E **50** F7
Birnin Kebbi *Nigeria* 12°32N 4°12E **50** F6
Birobidzhan *Russia* 48°50N 132°50E **29** E14
Birr *Ireland* 53°6N 7°54W **10** C4
Birrie → *Australia* 29°43S 146°37E **63** D4
Birsilpur *India* 28°11N 72°15E **42** E5
Birsk *Russia* 55°25N 55°30E **18** C10
Birtle *Canada* 50°30N 101°5W **71** C8
Birur *India* 13°30N 75°55E **40** N9
Biržai *Lithuania* 56°11N 24°45E **9** H21
Birżebbuġa *Malta* 35°50N 14°32E **25** D2
Bisa *Indonesia* 1°15S 127°28E **37** E7
Bisalpur *India* 28°14N 79°48E **43** E8
Bisbee *U.S.A.* 31°27N 109°55W **77** L9
Biscarrosse *France* 44°22N 1°20W **20** D3
Biscay, B. of *Atl. Oc.* 45°0N 2°0W **20** D1
Biscayne B. *U.S.A.* 25°40N 80°12W **85** J14
Biscoe Is. *Antarctica* 66°0S 67°0W **5** C17
Biscostasing *Canada* 47°18N 82°9W **72** C3
Bishkek *Kyrgyzstan* 42°54N 74°46E **28** E8
Bishnupur *India* 23°8N 87°20E **43** H12
Bisho = Bhisho *S. Africa* 32°50S 27°23E **57** E4
Bishop *Calif., U.S.A.* 37°22N 118°24W **78** H8
Bishop *Tex., U.S.A.* 27°35N 97°48W **84** H6
Bishop Auckland *U.K.* 54°39N 1°40W **12** C6
Bishop's Falls *Canada* 49°2N 55°30W **73** C8
Bishop's Stortford *U.K.* 51°52N 0°10E **13** F8
Bisina, L. *Uganda* 1°38N 33°56E **54** B3
Biskra *Algeria* 34°50N 5°44E **50** B7
Bismarck *U.S.A.* 46°48N 100°47W **80** B3
Bismarck Arch. *Papua N. G.* 2°30S 150°0E **58** B7
Biso *Uganda* 1°44N 31°26E **54** B3
Bison *U.S.A.* 45°31N 102°28W **80** C2
Bīsotūn *Iran* 34°23N 47°26E **44** C5
Bissagos = Bijagós, Arquipélago dos *Guinea-Biss.* 11°15N 16°10W **50** F2
Bissau *Guinea-Biss.* 11°45N 15°45W **50** F2
Bistcho L. *Canada* 59°45N 118°50W **70** B5
Bistriţa *Romania* 47°9N 24°35E **17** E13
Bistriţa → *Romania* 46°30N 26°57E **17** E14
Biswan *India* 27°29N 81°2E **43** F9
Bitam *Gabon* 2°5N 11°25E **52** D2
Bitkine *Chad* 11°59N 18°13E **51** F9
Bitlis *Turkey* 38°20N 42°3E **44** B4
Bitola *Macedonia* 41°1N 21°20E **23** D9
Bitolj = Bitola *Macedonia* 41°1N 21°20E **23** D9
Bitter Creek *U.S.A.* 41°33N 108°33W **76** F9
Bitterfontein *S. Africa* 31°1S 18°32E **56** E2
Bitterroot → *U.S.A.* 46°52N 114°7W **76** C6
Bitterroot Range *U.S.A.* 46°0N 114°20W **76** D6
Bitterwater *U.S.A.* 36°23N 121°0W **78** J6
Biu *Nigeria* 10°40N 12°3E **51** F8
Biwa-Ko *Japan* 35°15N 136°10E **31** G8
Biwabik *U.S.A.* 47°32N 92°21W **80** B7
Bixby *U.S.A.* 35°57N 95°53W **84** D7
Biyang *China* 32°38N 113°21E **34** H7
Biysk *Russia* 52°40N 85°0E **28** D9
Bizana *S. Africa* 30°50S 29°52E **57** E4
Bizen *Japan* 34°43N 134°8E **31** G7
Bizerte *Tunisia* 37°15N 9°50E **51** A7
Bjargtangar *Iceland* 65°30N 24°30W **8** D1
Bjelovar *Croatia* 45°56N 16°49E **22** B7
Björneborg = Pori *Finland* 61°29N 21°48E **8** F19
Bjørnevatn *Norway* 69°40N 30°0E **8** B24
Bjørnøya *Arctic* 74°30N 19°0E **4** B8
Black = Da → *Vietnam* 21°15N 105°20E **38** B5
Black → *Canada* 44°42N 79°19W **82** B5
Black → *Ariz., U.S.A.* 33°44N 110°13W **77** K8
Black → *Ark., U.S.A.* 35°38N 91°20W **84** D9
Black → *La., U.S.A.* 31°16N 91°50W **84** F9
Black → *Mich., U.S.A.* 42°59N 82°27W **82** D2
Black → *N.Y., U.S.A.* 43°59N 76°4W **83** C8
Black → *Wis., U.S.A.* 43°57N 91°22W **80** D8
Black Bay Pen. *Canada* 48°38N 88°21W **72** C2
Black Birch L. *Canada* 56°53N 107°45W **71** B7
Black Canyon of the Gunnison ⌓ *U.S.A.* 38°40N 107°35W **76** G10
Black Diamond *Canada* 50°45N 114°14W **70** C6
Black Duck → *Canada* 56°51N 89°2W **72** A2
Black Forest = Schwarzwald *Germany* 48°30N 8°20E **16** D5
Black Forest *U.S.A.* 39°0N 104°43W **76** G11
Black Hd. *Ireland* 53°9N 9°16W **10** C2
Black Hills *U.S.A.* 44°0N 103°45W **80** D2
Black I. *Canada* 51°12N 96°30W **71** C9
Black L. *Canada* 59°12N 105°15W **71** B7
Black L. *Mich., U.S.A.* 45°28N 84°16W **81** C11
Black L. *N.Y., U.S.A.* 44°31N 75°36W **83** B9
Black Lake *Canada* 59°11N 105°20W **71** B7
Black Mesa *U.S.A.* 36°58N 102°58W **84** C3
Black Mt. = Mynydd Du *U.K.* 51°52N 3°50W **13** F4
Black Mts. *U.K.* 51°55N 3°7W **13** F4
Black Range *U.S.A.* 33°15N 107°50W **77** K10
Black River *Jamaica* 18°0N 77°50W **88** a
Black River *U.S.A.* 44°0N 75°47W **83** C9
Black River Falls *U.S.A.* 44°18N 90°51W **80** C8
Black Rock *Barbados* 13°7N 59°37W **89** g
Black Rock Desert *U.S.A.* 41°10N 118°50W **76** F4
Black Sea *Eurasia* 43°30N 35°0E **19** F6
Black Tickle *Canada* 53°28N 55°45W **73** B8
Black Volta → *Africa* 8°41N 1°33W **50** G5
Black Warrior → *U.S.A.* 32°32N 87°51W **85** E11
Blackall *Australia* 24°25S 145°45E **62** C4
Blackball *N.Z.* 42°22S 171°26E **59** E3
Blackbraes △ *Australia* 19°10S 144°10E **62** B3
Blackbull *Australia* 17°55S 141°45E **62** B3
Blackburn *U.K.* 53°45N 2°29W **12** D5
Blackburn, Mt. *U.S.A.* 61°44N 143°26W **74** C11
Blackburn with Darwen □ *U.K.* 53°45N 2°29W **12** D5
Blackdown Tableland △ *Australia* 23°52S 149°8E **62** C4
Blackfoot *U.S.A.* 43°11N 112°21W **76** E7
Blackfoot → *U.S.A.* 46°52N 113°53W **76** C7
Blackfoot Res. *U.S.A.* 42°55N 111°39W **76** E8
Blackpool *U.K.* 53°49N 3°3W **12** D4
Blackpool □ *U.K.* 53°49N 3°3W **12** D4
Blackriver *U.S.A.* 44°46N 83°17W **82** B1
Blacks Harbour *Canada* 45°3N 66°49W **73** C6
Blacksburg *U.S.A.* 37°14N 80°25W **81** G13
Blacksod B. *Ireland* 54°6N 10°0W **10** B1
Blackstairs Mt. *Ireland* 52°33N 6°48W **10** D5
Blackstone *U.S.A.* 37°5N 78°0W **81** G14
Blackstone Ra. *Australia* 26°0S 128°30E **61** E4
Blackwater = West Road → *Canada* 53°18N 122°53W **70** C4
Blackwater *Australia* 23°35S 148°53E **62** C4
Blackwater → *Meath, Ireland* 53°39N 6°41W **10** C4
Blackwater → *Waterford, Ireland* 52°4N 7°52W **10** D4
Blackwater → *U.K.* 54°31N 6°35W **10** B5
Blackwell *U.S.A.* 36°48N 97°17W **84** C6
Blackwells Corner *U.S.A.* 35°37N 119°47W **79** K7
Bladensburg △ *Australia* 22°30S 142°59E **62** C3
Blaenau Ffestiniog *U.K.* 53°0N 3°56W **12** E4
Blaenau Gwent □ *U.K.* 51°48N 3°12W **13** F4
Blagodarnoye = Blagodarnyy *Russia* 45°7N 43°37E **19** E7
Blagodarnyy *Russia* 45°7N 43°37E **19** E7
Blagoevgrad *Bulgaria* 42°2N 23°5E **23** C10
Blagoveshchensk *Russia* 50°20N 127°30E **29** D13
Blahkiuh *Indonesia* 8°31S 115°12E **37** J18
Blain *U.S.A.* 40°20N 77°31W **82** F7
Blaine *Minn., U.S.A.* 45°10N 93°13W **80** C7
Blaine *Wash., U.S.A.* 48°59N 122°45W **78** B4
Blaine Lake *Canada* 52°51N 106°52W **71** C7
Blair *U.S.A.* 41°33N 96°8W **80** E5
Blair Athol *Australia* 22°42S 147°31E **62** C4
Blair Atholl *U.K.* 56°46N 3°50W **11** E5
Blairgowrie *U.K.* 56°35N 3°21W **11** E5
Blairsden *U.S.A.* 39°47N 120°37W **78** F6
Blairsville *U.S.A.* 40°26N 79°16W **82** F5
Blakang Mati, Pulau *Singapore* 1°15N 103°50E **39** d
Blake Pt. *U.S.A.* 48°11N 88°25W **80** A9
Blakely *Ga., U.S.A.* 31°23N 84°56W **85** F12
Blakely *Pa., U.S.A.* 41°28N 75°37W **83** E9
Blanc, C. *Spain* 39°21N 2°51E **24** B9
Blanc, Mont *Europe* 45°48N 6°50E **20** D7
Blanca, B. *Argentina* 39°10S 61°30W **96** D4
Blanca, Cord. *Peru* 9°10S 77°35W **92** E3
Blanca Peak *U.S.A.* 37°35N 105°29W **77** H11
Blanche, C. *Australia* 33°1S 134°9E **63** E1
Blanche, L. *S. Austral., Australia* 29°15S 139°40E **63** D2
Blanche, L. *W. Austral., Australia* 22°25S 123°17E **60** D3
Blanchisseuse *Trin. & Tob.* 10°48N 61°18W **93** K15
Blanco *S. Africa* 33°55S 22°23E **56** E3
Blanco *U.S.A.* 30°6N 98°25W **84** F5
Blanco → *Argentina* 30°20S 68°42W **94** C2
Blanco, C. *Costa Rica* 9°34N 85°8W **88** E2
Blanco, C. *U.S.A.* 42°51N 124°34W **76** E1
Blanda → *Iceland* 65°37N 20°9W **8** D3
Blandford Forum *U.K.* 50°51N 2°9W **13** G5
Blanding *U.S.A.* 37°37N 109°29W **77** H9
Blanes *Spain* 41°40N 2°48E **21** B7
Blankenberge *Belgium* 51°20N 3°9E **15** C3
Blanquilla *Venezuela* 11°51N 64°37W **89** D7
Blanquillo *Uruguay* 32°53S 55°37W **95** C4
Blantyre *Malawi* 15°45S 35°0E **55** F4
Blarney *Ireland* 51°56N 8°33W **10** E3
Blasdell *U.S.A.* 42°48N 78°50W **82** D6
Blåvands Huk *Denmark* 55°33N 8°4E **9** J13
Blaydon *U.K.* 54°58N 1°42W **12** C6
Blayney *Australia* 33°32S 149°14E **63** E4
Blaze, Pt. *Australia* 12°56S 130°11E **60** B5
Blekinge *Sweden* 56°25N 15°20E **9** H16
Blenheim *Canada* 42°20N 82°0W **82** D3
Blenheim *N.Z.* 41°38S 173°57E **59** D4
Bletchley *U.K.* 51°59N 0°44W **13** F7
Bleus, Monts *Dem. Rep. of the Congo* 1°30N 30°30E **54** B3
Blida *Algeria* 36°30N 2°49E **50** A6
Bligh Sound *N.Z.* 44°47S 167°32E **59** F1
Bligh Water *Fiji* 17°0S 178°0E **59** a
Blind River *Canada* 46°10N 82°58W **72** C3
Bliss *Idaho, U.S.A.* 42°56N 114°57W **76** E6
Bliss *N.Y., U.S.A.* 42°34N 78°15W **82** D6
Blissfield *U.S.A.* 40°24N 81°58W **82** F3
Blitar *Indonesia* 8°5S 112°11E **37** H15
Block I. *U.S.A.* 41°11N 71°35W **83** E13
Block Island Sd. *U.S.A.* 41°15N 71°40W **83** E13
Bloemfontein *S. Africa* 29°6S 26°7E **56** D4
Bloemhof *S. Africa* 27°38S 25°32E **56** D4
Blois *France* 47°35N 1°20E **20** C4
Blönduós *Iceland* 65°40N 20°12W **8** D3
Blongas *Indonesia* 8°53S 116°2E **37** K19
Bloodvein → *Canada* 51°47N 96°43W **71** C9
Bloody Foreland *Ireland* 55°10N 8°17W **10** A3
Bloomer *U.S.A.* 45°6N 91°29W **80** C8
Bloomfield *Canada* 43°59N 77°14W **82** C7
Bloomfield *Iowa, U.S.A.* 40°45N 92°25W **80** E7
Bloomfield *N. Mex., U.S.A.* 36°43N 107°59W **77** H10
Bloomfield *Nebr., U.S.A.* 42°36N 97°39W **80** D5
Bloomington *Ill., U.S.A.* 40°28N 89°0W **80** E9
Bloomington *Ind., U.S.A.* 39°10N 86°32W **80** F10
Bloomington *Minn., U.S.A.* 44°50N 93°17W **80** C7
Bloomsburg *U.S.A.* 41°0N 76°27W **83** F8
Bloomsbury *Australia* 20°48S 148°38E **62** b
Blora *Indonesia* 6°57S 111°25E **37** G14
Blossburg *U.S.A.* 41°41N 77°4W **82** E7
Blouberg *S. Africa* 23°8S 28°59E **57** C4
Blountstown *U.S.A.* 30°27N 85°3W **85** F12
Blue Earth *U.S.A.* 43°38N 94°6W **80** D6
Blue Hole △ *Belize* 17°24N 88°30W **88** C2
Blue Lagoon △ *Zambia* 15°28S 27°26E **55** F2
Blue Mesa Res. *U.S.A.* 38°28N 107°20W **76** G10
Blue Mountain Lake *U.S.A.* 43°51N 74°27W **83** C10
Blue Mountain Pk. *Jamaica* 18°3N 76°36W **88** a
Blue Mt. *U.S.A.* 40°30N 76°30W **83** F8
Blue Mts. *Jamaica* 18°3N 76°36W **88** a
Blue Mts. *Maine, U.S.A.* 44°50N 70°35W **83** B14
Blue Mts. *Oreg., U.S.A.* 45°0N 118°20W **76** D4
Blue Mud B. *Australia* 13°30S 136°0E **62** A2
Blue Mud Bay ✿ *Australia* 13°25S 136°2E **62** A2
Blue Nile = Nîl el Azraq → *Sudan* 15°38N 32°31E **51** E12
Blue Rapids *U.S.A.* 39°41N 96°39W **80** F5
Blue Ridge *U.S.A.* 36°40N 80°50W **81** G13
Blue River *Canada* 52°6N 119°18W **70** C5
Bluefield *U.S.A.* 37°15N 81°17W **81** G13
Bluefields *Nic.* 12°20N 83°50W **88** D3
Bluevale *Canada* 43°51N 81°15W **82** C3
Bluff *Australia* 23°35S 149°4E **62** C4
Bluff *N.Z.* 46°37S 168°20E **59** G2
Bluff *U.S.A.* 37°17N 109°33W **77** H9
Bluff Knoll *Australia* 34°24S 118°15E **61** F2
Bluff Pt. *Australia* 27°50S 114°5E **61** E1
Bluffton *U.S.A.* 40°44N 85°11W **81** E11
Blumenau *Brazil* 27°0S 49°0W **95** B6
Blunt *U.S.A.* 44°31N 99°59W **80** C4
Bly *U.S.A.* 42°24N 121°3W **76** E3
Blyde River Canyon ⌓ *S. Africa* 24°37S 31°2E **57** C5
Blyth *Canada* 43°44N 81°26W **82** C3
Blyth *U.K.* 55°8N 1°31W **12** B6
Blythe *U.S.A.* 33°37N 114°36W **79** M12
Blytheville *U.S.A.* 35°56N 89°55W **85** D10
Bo *S. Leone* 7°55N 11°50W **50** G3
Bo Duc *Vietnam* 11°58N 106°50E **39** G6
Bo Hai *China* 39°0N 119°0E **35** E10
Bo Xian = Bozhou *China* 33°55N 115°41E **34** H8
Boa Vista *Brazil* 2°48N 60°30W **92** C6
Boa Vista *C. Verde Is.* 16°0N 22°49W **50** b
Boaco *Nic.* 12°29N 85°35W **88** D2
Bo'ai *China* 35°10N 113°3E **34** G7
Boalsburg *U.S.A.* 40°47N 77°49W **82** F7
Boane *Mozam.* 26°6S 32°19E **57** D5
Boardman *U.S.A.* 41°2N 80°40W **82** E4
Bobadah *Australia* 32°19S 146°41E **63** E4
Bobbili *India* 18°35N 83°30E **41** K13
Bobcaygeon *Canada* 44°33N 78°33W **82** B6
Bobo-Dioulasso *Burkina Faso* 11°8N 4°13W **50** F5
Bobonong *Botswana* 21°58S 28°20E **55** G2
Bóbr → *Poland* 52°4N 15°4E **16** B8
Bobraomby, Tanjon' i *Madag.* 12°40S 49°10E **57** A8
Bobruysk = Babruysk *Belarus* 53°10N 29°15E **17** B15
Boby, Pic *Madag.* 22°12S 46°55E **53** J9
Boca del Río *Mexico* 19°5N 96°4W **87** D5
Boca do Acre *Brazil* 8°50S 67°27W **92** E5
Boca Raton *U.S.A.* 26°21N 80°5W **85** H14
Bocas del Dragón = Dragon's Mouths *Venezuela* 11°0N 61°50W **93** K15
Bocas del Toro *Panama* 9°15N 82°20W **88** E3
Bochnia *Poland* 49°58N 20°27E **17** D11
Bochum *Germany* 51°28N 7°13E **16** C4
Bocoyna *Mexico* 27°52N 107°35W **86** B3
Bodaybo *Russia* 57°50N 114°0E **29** D12
Boddam *U.K.* 59°56N 1°17W **11** B7
Boddington *Australia* 32°50S 116°30E **61** F2
Bodega Bay *U.S.A.* 38°20N 123°3W **78** G3
Boden *Sweden* 65°50N 21°42E **8** D19
Bodensee *Europe* 47°35N 9°25E **20** C8
Bodhan *India* 18°40N 77°44E **40** K10
Bodmin *U.K.* 50°28N 4°43W **13** G3
Bodmin Moor *U.K.* 50°33N 4°36W **13** G3
Bodø *Norway* 67°17N 14°24E **8** C16
Bodrog → *Hungary* 48°11N 21°22E **17** D11
Bodrum *Turkey* 37°3N 27°30E **23** F12
Boende *Dem. Rep. of the Congo* 0°24S 21°12E **52** E4
Boerne *U.S.A.* 29°47N 98°44W **84** G5
Boesmans → *S. Africa* 33°42S 26°39E **56** E4
Bogalusa *U.S.A.* 30°47N 89°52W **85** F10
Bogan → *Australia* 30°20S 146°55E **63** D4
Bogan Gate *Australia* 33°7S 147°49E **63** E4
Bogantungan *Australia* 23°41S 147°17E **62** C4
Bogata *U.S.A.* 33°28N 95°13W **84** E7
Bogda Shan *China* 43°35N 89°40E **32** B3
Boggabilla *Australia* 28°36S 150°24E **63** D5
Boggabri *Australia* 30°45S 150°5E **63** E5
Boggeragh Mts. *Ireland* 52°2N 8°55W **10** D3
Boglan = Solhan *Turkey* 38°57N 41°3E **44** B4
Bognor Regis *U.K.* 50°47N 0°40W **13** G7
Bogo *Phil.* 11°3N 124°0E **37** B6
Bogong, Mt. *Australia* 36°47S 147°17E **63** F4
Bogor *Indonesia* 6°36S 106°48E **37** G12
Bogotá *Colombia* 4°34N 74°0W **92** C4
Bogotol *Russia* 56°15N 89°50E **28** D9
Bogra *Bangla.* 24°51N 89°22E **41** G16
Boguchany *Russia* 58°40N 97°30E **29** D10
Bogué *Mauritania* 16°45N 14°10W **50** E3
Bohemian Forest = Böhmerwald *Germany* 49°8N 13°14E **16** D7
Böhmerwald *Germany* 49°8N 13°14E **16** D7
Bohol □ *Phil.* 9°50N 124°10E **37** C6
Bohol Sea *Phil.* 9°0N 124°0E **37** C6
Bohorok *Indonesia* 3°30N 98°12E **39** L2
Bohuslän *Sweden* 58°25N 12°0E **9** G15
Boi, Pta. do *Brazil* 23°55S 45°15W **95** A6
Boiaçu *Brazil* 0°27S 61°46W **92** D6
Boigu *Australia* 9°16S 142°13E **62** a
Boileau, C. *Australia* 17°40S 122°7E **60** C3
Boise *U.S.A.* 43°37N 116°13W **76** E5
Boise City *U.S.A.* 36°44N 102°31W **84** C3
Boissevain *Canada* 49°15N 100°5W **71** D8
Bojador, C. *W. Sahara* 26°0N 14°30W **50** C3
Bojana → *Albania* 41°52N 19°22E **23** D8
Bojnūrd *Iran* 37°30N 57°20E **45** B8
Bojonegoro *Indonesia* 7°11S 111°54E **37** G14
Bokaro *India* 23°46N 85°55E **43** H11
Boké *Guinea* 10°56N 14°17W **50** F3
Bokhara → *Australia* 29°55S 146°42E **63** D4
Boknafjorden *Norway* 59°14N 5°40E **9** G11
Bokor △ *Cambodia* 10°50N 104°1E **39** G5
Bokora ⌓ *Uganda* 2°12N 31°32E **54** B3
Bokoro *Chad* 12°25N 17°14E **51** F9
Bokpyin *Burma* 11°18N 98°42E **39** G2
Bokungu *Dem. Rep. of the Congo* 0°35S 22°50E **52** E4
Bolan → *Pakistan* 28°38N 67°42E **42** E2
Bolan Pass *Pakistan* 29°50N 67°20E **40** E5
Bolaños → *Mexico* 21°12N 104°5W **86** C4
Bolbec *France* 49°30N 0°30E **20** B4
Boldājī *Iran* 31°56N 51°3E **45** D6
Bole *China* 45°11N 81°37E **32** B3
Bolekhiv *Ukraine* 49°0N 23°57E **17** D12
Bolesławiec *Poland* 51°17N 15°37E **16** C8
Bolgatanga *Ghana* 10°44N 0°53W **50** F5
Bolgrad = Bolhrad *Ukraine* 45°40N 28°32E **17** F15
Bolhrad *Ukraine* 45°40N 28°32E **17** F15
Bolivar *Mo., U.S.A.* 37°37N 93°25W **80** G7
Bolivar *N.Y., U.S.A.* 42°4N 78°10W **82** D6
Bolivar *Tenn., U.S.A.* 35°12N 89°0W **85** D10
Bolivia ■ *S. Amer.* 17°6S 64°0W **92** G6
Bolivian Plateau = Altiplano *Bolivia* 17°0S 68°0W **92** G5
Bollnäs *Sweden* 61°21N 16°24E **8** F17
Bollon *Australia* 28°2S 147°29E **63** D4
Bolmen *Sweden* 56°55N 13°40E **9** H15
Bolobo *Dem. Rep. of the Congo* 2°6S 16°20E **52** E3
Bologna *Italy* 44°29N 11°20E **22** B4
Bologoye *Russia* 57°55N 34°5E **18** C5
Bolomba *Dem. Rep. of the Congo* 0°35N 19°0E **52** D3
Bolonchén *Mexico* 20°1N 89°45W **87** D7
Boloven, Cao Nguyen *Laos* 15°10N 106°30E **38** E6
Bolpur *India* 23°40N 87°45E **43** H12
Bolsena, L. di *Italy* 42°36N 11°56E **22** C4
Bolshevik, Ostrov *Russia* 78°30N 102°0E **29** B11
Bolshoy Anyuy → *Russia* 68°30N 160°49E **29** C17
Bolshoy Begichev, Ostrov *Russia* 74°20N 112°30E **29** B12
Bolshoy Kamen *Russia* 43°7N 132°19E **30** C6
Bolshoy Kavkas = Caucasus Mountains *Eurasia* 42°50N 44°0E **19** F7
Bolshoy Lyakhovskiy, Ostrov *Russia* 73°35N 142°0E **29** B15
Bolshoy Tyuters, Ostrov *Russia* 59°51N 27°13E **9** G22
Bolsward *Neths.* 53°3N 5°32E **15** A5
Bolt Head *U.K.* 50°12N 3°48W **13** G4
Bolton *Canada* 43°54N 79°45W **82** C5
Bolton *U.K.* 53°35N 2°26W **12** D5
Bolton Landing *U.S.A.* 43°32N 73°35W **83** C11
Bolu *Turkey* 40°45N 31°35E **19** F5
Bolungavík *Iceland* 66°9N 23°15W **8** C2

Bolvadin *Turkey* 38°45N 31°4E **44** B1
Bolzano *Italy* 46°31N 11°22E **22** A4
Bom Jesus da Lapa
 Brazil 13°15S 43°25W **93** F10
Boma *Dem. Rep. of the Congo* 5°50S 13°4E **52** F2
Bombala *Australia* 36°56S 149°15E **63** F4
Bombay = Mumbai
 India 18°56N 72°50E **40** K8
Bombay *U.S.A.* 44°56N 74°34W **83** B10
Bombedor, Pta.
 Venezuela 9°53N 61°37W **93** L15
Bomboma
 Dem. Rep. of the Congo 2°25N 18°55E **52** D3
Bombombwa
 Dem. Rep. of the Congo 1°40N 25°40E **54** B2
Bomili
 Dem. Rep. of the Congo 1°45N 27°5E **54** B2
Bømlo *Norway* 59°37N 5°13E **9** G11
Bomokandi ➤
 Dem. Rep. of the Congo 3°39N 26°8E **54** B2
Bomu ➤ *C.A.R.* 4°40N 22°30E **52** D4
Bon, C. = Ra's aṭ Ṭīb
 Tunisia 37°1N 11°2E **22** F4
Bon Acceuil *Mauritius* 20°10S 57°39E **53** d
Bon Echo △ *Canada* 44°55N 77°16W **82** B7
Bon Sar Pa *Vietnam* 12°24N 107°35E **38** F6
Bonāb *Iran* 36°35N 48°41E **45** B6
Bonaigarh *India* 21°50N 84°57E **43** J11
Bonaire *Neth. Ant.* 12°10N 68°15W **89** D6
Bonampak *Mexico* 16°44N 91°5W **87** D6
Bonang *Australia* 37°11S 148°41E **63** F4
Bonanza *Nic.* 13°54N 84°35W **88** D3
Bonaparte Arch.
 Australia 14°0S 124°30E **60** B3
Bonar Bridge *U.K.* 57°54N 4°20W **11** D4
Bonasse *Trin. & Tob.* 10°5N 61°54W **93** K15
Bonaventure *Canada* 48°5N 65°32W **73** C6
Bonavista *Canada* 48°40N 53°5W **73** C9
Bonavista *Canada* 48°42N 53°5W **73** C9
Bonavista B. *Canada* 48°45N 53°25W **73** C9
Bondo
 Dem. Rep. of the Congo 3°55N 23°53E **54** B1
Bondoukou *Ivory C.* 8°2N 2°47W **50** G5
Bondowoso *Indonesia* 7°55S 113°49E **37** G15
Bone, Teluk *Indonesia* 4°10S 120°50E **37** E6
Bonerate *Indonesia* 7°25S 121°5E **37** F6
Bonerate, Kepulauan
 Indonesia 6°30S 121°10E **37** F6
Bo'ness *U.K.* 56°1N 3°37W **11** E5
Bonete, Cerro *Argentina* 27°55S 68°40W **94** B2
Bong Son = Hoai Nhon
 Vietnam 14°28N 109°1E **38** E7
Bongaigaon *India* 26°28N 90°34E **32** D4
Bongandanga
 Dem. Rep. of the Congo 1°24N 21°3E **52** D4
Bongor *Chad* 10°35N 15°20E **51** F9
Bongos, Massif des *C.A.R.* 8°40N 22°25E **52** C4
Bonham *U.S.A.* 33°35N 96°11W **84** E6
Boni △ *Kenya* 1°35S 41°18E **54** C5
Bonifacio *France* 41°24N 9°10E **20** F8
Bonifacio, Bouches de
 Medit. S. 41°12N 9°15E **22** D3
Bonin Is. = Ogasawara Gunto
 Pac. Oc. 27°0N 142°0E **27** F16
Bonn *Germany* 50°46N 7°6E **16** C4
Bonne Terre *U.S.A.* 37°55N 90°33W **80** G8
Bonners Ferry *U.S.A.* 48°42N 116°19W **76** B5
Bonney, L. *Australia* 37°50S 140°20E **63** F3
Bonnie Rock *Australia* 30°29S 118°22E **61** F2
Bonny, Bight of *Africa* 3°30N 9°20E **52** D1
Bonnyrigg *U.K.* 55°53N 3°6W **11** F5
Bonnyville *Canada* 54°20N 110°45W **71** C6
Bonoi *Indonesia* 1°45S 137°41E **37** E9
Bonsall *U.S.A.* 33°16N 117°14W **79** M9
Bontang *Indonesia* 0°10N 117°30E **36** D5
Bontebok △ *S. Africa* 34°5S 20°28E **56** E3
Bonthe *S. Leone* 7°30N 12°33W **50** G3
Bontoc *Phil.* 17°7N 120°58E **37** A6
Bonython Ra. *Australia* 23°40S 128°45E **60** D4
Boodjamulla △ *Australia* 18°15S 138°6E **62** B2
Bookabie *Australia* 31°50S 132°41E **61** F5
Booker *U.S.A.* 36°27N 100°32W **84** C4
Booligal *Australia* 33°58S 144°53E **63** E3
Böön Tsagaan Nuur
 Mongolia 45°35N 99°9E **32** B4
Boonah *Australia* 27°58S 152°41E **63** D5
Boone *Iowa, U.S.A.* 42°4N 93°53W **80** D7
Boone *N.C., U.S.A.* 36°13N 81°41W **85** C14
Booneville *Ark., U.S.A.* 35°8N 93°55W **84** D8
Booneville *Miss., U.S.A.* 34°39N 88°34W **85** D10
Boonville *Calif., U.S.A.* 39°1N 123°22W **78** F3
Boonville *Ind., U.S.A.* 38°3N 87°16W **80** F10
Boonville *Mo., U.S.A.* 38°58N 92°44W **80** F7
Boonville *N.Y., U.S.A.* 43°29N 75°20W **83** C9
Boorabbin △ *Australia* 31°3S 120°10E **61** F3
Boorindal *Australia* 30°22S 146°11E **63** E4
Boorowa *Australia* 34°28S 148°44E **63** E4
Boosaaso *Somali Rep.* 11°12N 49°18E **47** E4
Boothia, Gulf of *Canada* 71°0N 90°0E **68** C14
Boothia Pen. *Canada* 71°0N 94°0W **68** C13
Bootle *U.K.* 53°28N 3°1W **12** D4
Booué *Gabon* 0°5S 11°55E **52** E2
Boquilla, Presa de la
 Mexico 27°31N 105°30W **86** B3
Boquillas del Carmen
 Mexico 29°11N 102°58W **86** B4
Bor *Serbia* 44°5N 22°7E **23** B10
Bôr *Sudan* 6°10N 31°40E **51** G12
Bor Mashash *Israel* 31°7N 34°50E **46** D3
Bora Bora
 French Polynesia 16°30S 151°45W **65** J12
Borah Peak *U.S.A.* 44°8N 113°47W **76** D7
Borås *Sweden* 57°43N 12°56E **9** H15
Borāzjān *Iran* 29°22N 51°10E **45** D6
Borba *Brazil* 4°12S 59°34W **92** D7
Borborema, Planalto da
 Brazil 7°0S 37°0W **90** D7
Bord Khūn-e Now *Iran* 28°3N 51°28E **45** D6
Borda, C. *Australia* 35°45S 136°34E **63** F2

Bordeaux *France* 44°50N 0°36W **20** D3
Borden *Australia* 34°3S 118°12E **61** F2
Borden-Carleton *Canada* 46°18N 63°47W **73** C7
Borden I. *Canada* 78°30N 111°30W **69** B9
Borden Pen. *Canada* 73°0N 83°0W **69** C15
Border Ranges △
 Australia 28°24S 152°56E **63** D5
Borders = Scottish Borders □
 U.K. 55°35N 2°50W **11** F6
Bordertown *Australia* 36°19S 140°45E **63** F3
Borðeyri *Iceland* 65°12N 21°6W **8** D3
Bordj Fly Ste. Marie
 Algeria 27°19N 2°32W **50** C5
Bordj-in-Eker *Algeria* 24°9N 5°3E **50** D7
Bordj Mokhtar *Algeria* 21°20N 0°56E **50** D6
Bordj Omar Driss *Algeria* 28°10N 6°40E **50** C7
Borehamwood *U.K.* 51°40N 0°15W **13** F7
Borgarfjörður *Iceland* 65°12N 13°45E **8** D15
Borgarnes *Iceland* 64°32N 21°55W **8** D3
Børgefjellet *Norway* 65°20N 13°45E **8** D15
Borger *Neths.* 52°54N 6°44E **15** B6
Borger *U.S.A.* 35°39N 101°24W **84** D4
Borgholm *Sweden* 56°52N 16°39E **9** H17
Borhoyn Tal *Mongolia* 43°50N 111°58E **34** C6
Borikhane *Laos* 18°33N 103°43E **38** C4
Borisoglebsk *Russia* 51°27N 42°5E **19** D7
Borisov = Barysaw
 Belarus 54°17N 28°28E **17** A15
Borja *Peru* 4°20S 77°40W **92** D3
Borkou *Chad* 18°15N 18°50E **51** E9
Borkum *Germany* 53°34N 6°40E **16** B4
Borlänge *Sweden* 60°29N 15°26E **9** F16
Borley, C. *Antarctica* 66°15S 52°30E **5** C5
Borneo *E. Indies* 1°0N 115°0E **36** D5
Bornholm *Denmark* 55°10N 15°0E **9** J16
Borogontsy *Russia* 62°42N 131°8E **29** C14
Borohoro Shan *China* 44°6N 83°10E **32** B3
Boron *U.S.A.* 35°0N 117°39W **79** L9
Borongan *Phil.* 11°37N 125°26E **37** B7
Borovichi *Russia* 58°25N 33°55E **18** C5
Borrego Springs
 U.S.A. 33°15N 116°23W **79** M10
Borrisokane *Ireland* 53°0N 8°7W **10** D3
Borroloola *Australia* 16°4S 136°17E **62** B2
Borşa *Romania* 47°41N 24°50E **17** E13
Borsad *India* 22°25N 72°54E **42** H5
Borth *U.K.* 52°29N 4°2W **13** E3
Borūjerd *Iran* 33°55N 48°50E **45** C6
Boryeong *S. Korea* 36°21N 126°36E **35** F14
Boryslav *Ukraine* 49°18N 23°28E **17** D12
Borzya *Russia* 50°24N 116°31E **29** D12
Bosa *Italy* 40°18N 8°30E **22** D3
Bosanska Gradiška
 Bos.-H. 45°10N 17°15E **22** B7
Boscastle *U.K.* 50°41N 4°42W **13** G3
Boscobelle *Barbados* 13°17N 59°35W **89** g
Bose *China* 23°53N 106°35E **32** D5
Boseong *S. Korea* 34°46N 127°5E **35** G14
Boshan *China* 36°28N 117°49E **35** F9
Boshof *S. Africa* 28°31S 25°13E **56** D4
Boshrūyeh *Iran* 33°50N 57°30E **45** C8
Bosna ➤ *Bos.-H.* 45°4N 18°29E **23** B8
Bosna i Hercegovina = Bosnia-
 Herzegovina ■ *Europe* 44°0N 18°0E **22** B7
Bosnia-Herzegovina ■
 Europe 44°0N 18°0E **22** B7
Bosnik *Indonesia* 1°5S 136°10E **37** E9
Bosobolo
 Dem. Rep. of the Congo 4°15N 19°50E **52** D3
Bosporus = İstanbul Boğazı
 Turkey 41°5N 29°3E **23** D13
Bosque Farms *U.S.A.* 35°51N 106°42W **77** J10
Bossangoa *C.A.R.* 6°35N 17°30E **52** C3
Bossier City *U.S.A.* 32°31N 93°44W **84** E8
Bosso *Niger* 13°43N 13°19E **51** F8
Bostan *Pakistan* 30°26N 67°2E **42** D2
Bostānābād *Iran* 37°50N 46°50E **44** B5
Bosten Hu *China* 41°55N 87°40E **32** B3
Boston *U.K.* 52°59N 0°2W **12** E7
Boston *U.S.A.* 42°22N 71°3W **83** D13
Boston Bar *Canada* 49°52N 121°30W **70** D4
Boston Mts. *U.S.A.* 35°42N 93°15W **84** D8
Boswell *Canada* 49°28N 116°45W **70** D5
Boswell *U.S.A.* 40°10N 79°2W **82** F5
Botad *India* 22°15N 71°40E **42** H4
Botany B. *Australia* 33°58S 151°11E **58** E8
Botene *Laos* 17°35N 101°12E **38** D3
Bothaville *S. Africa* 27°23S 26°34E **56** D4
Bothnia, G. of *Europe* 62°0N 20°0E **8** F19
Bothwell *Australia* 42°20S 147°1E **63** G4
Bothwell *Canada* 42°38N 81°52W **82** D3
Botletle ➤ *Botswana* 20°10S 23°15E **56** C3
Botoşani *Romania* 47°42N 26°41E **17** E14
Botou *Burkina Faso* 12°42N 1°59E **50** F6
Botshabelo *S. Africa* 29°14S 26°44E **56** D4
Botswana ■ *Africa* 22°0S 24°0E **56** C3
Bottineau *U.S.A.* 48°50N 100°27W **80** A3
Bottrop *Germany* 51°31N 6°58E **15** C6
Botucatu *Brazil* 22°55S 48°30W **95** A6
Botum Sakor △
 Cambodia 11°5N 103°15E **39** G4
Botwood *Canada* 49°6N 55°23W **73** C8
Bou Saâda *Algeria* 35°11N 4°9E **50** A6
Bouaflé *Ivory C.* 7°1N 5°47W **50** G4
Bouaké *Ivory C.* 7°40N 5°2W **50** G4
Bouâr *C.A.R.* 6°0N 15°40E **52** C3
Bouârfa *Morocco* 32°32N 1°58W **50** B5
Boucaut B. *Australia* 12°0S 134°25E **62** A1
Bouctouche *Canada* 46°30N 64°45W **73** C7
Bougainville, C. *Australia* 13°57S 126°4E **60** B4
Bougainville I. *Papua N. G.* 6°0S 155°0E **58** B8
Bougainville Reef
 Australia 15°30S 147°5E **62** B4
Bougie = Bejaïa *Algeria* 36°42N 5°2E **50** A7
Bougouni *Mali* 11°30N 7°20W **50** F4
Bouillon *Belgium* 49°44N 5°3E **15** E5
Boulder *Colo., U.S.A.* 40°1N 105°17W **76** F11
Boulder *Mont., U.S.A.* 46°14N 112°7W **76** C7
Boulder City *U.S.A.* 35°58N 114°49W **79** K12

Boulder Creek *U.S.A.* 37°7N 122°7W **78** H4
Boulder Dam = Hoover Dam
 U.S.A. 36°1N 114°44W **79** K12
Boulia *Australia* 22°52S 139°51E **62** C2
Boulogne-sur-Mer *France* 50°42N 1°36E **20** A4
Boulsa *Burkina Faso* 12°39N 0°34W **50** F5
Boultoum *Niger* 14°45N 10°25E **51** F8
Bouma △ *Fiji* 16°50S 179°52E **59** a
Boun Neua *Laos* 21°38N 101°54E **38** B3
Boun Tai *Laos* 21°23N 101°58E **38** B3
Bouna *Ivory C.* 9°10N 3°0W **50** G5
Boundary Peak *U.S.A.* 37°51N 118°21W **78** H8
Boundiali *Ivory C.* 9°30N 6°20W **50** G4
Bountiful *U.S.A.* 40°53N 111°52W **76** F8
Bounty Is. *Pac. Oc.* 48°0S 178°30E **64** M9
Bounty Trough *Pac. Oc.* 46°0S 178°0E **64** M9
Bourbonnais *France* 46°28N 3°0E **20** C5
Bourdel L. *Canada* 56°43N 74°10W **72** A5
Bourem *Mali* 17°0N 0°24W **50** E5
Bourg-en-Bresse *France* 46°13N 5°12E **20** C6
Bourg-St-Maurice *France* 45°35N 6°46E **20** D7
Bourgas = Burgas
 Bulgaria 42°33N 27°29E **23** C12
Bourges *France* 47°9N 2°25E **20** C5
Bourget *Canada* 45°26N 75°9W **83** A9
Bourgogne □ *France* 47°0N 4°50E **20** C6
Bourke *Australia* 30°8S 145°55E **63** E4
Bourne *U.S.A.* 52°47N 0°22W **12** E7
Bournemouth *U.K.* 50°43N 1°52W **13** G6
Bournemouth □ *U.K.* 50°43N 1°52W **13** G6
Bouse *U.S.A.* 33°56N 114°0W **79** M13
Bousso *Chad* 10°34N 16°52E **51** F9
Bouvet I. = Bouvetøya
 Antarctica 54°26S 3°24E **2** G10
Bouvetøya *Antarctica* 54°26S 3°24E **2** G10
Bovill *U.S.A.* 46°51N 116°24W **76** C5
Bovril *Argentina* 31°21S 59°26W **94** C4
Bow ➤ *Canada* 49°57N 111°41W **70** C6
Bow Island *Canada* 49°50N 111°23W **70** D6
Bowbells *U.S.A.* 48°48N 102°15W **80** A2
Bowdle *U.S.A.* 45°27N 99°39W **80** C4
Bowelling *Australia* 33°25S 116°30E **61** F2
Bowen *Argentina* 35°0S 67°31W **94** D2
Bowen *Australia* 20°0S 148°16E **62** J6
Bowen Mts. *Australia* 37°0S 147°50E **63** F4
Bowers Basin *Pac. Oc.* 53°45N 176°0E **4** D16
Bowers Ridge *Pac. Oc.* 54°0N 180°0E **4** D17
Bowie *Ariz., U.S.A.* 32°19N 109°29W **77** K9
Bowie *Tex., U.S.A.* 33°34N 97°51W **84** E6
Bowkān *Iran* 36°31N 46°12E **44** B5
Bowland, Forest of *U.K.* 54°0N 2°30W **12** D5
Bowling Green *Ky.,*
 U.S.A. 36°59N 86°27W **80** G10
Bowling Green *Ohio,*
 U.S.A. 41°23N 83°39W **81** E12
Bowling Green, C.
 Australia 19°19S 147°25E **62** B4
Bowling Green Bay △
 Australia 19°26S 146°57E **62** B4
Bowman *U.S.A.* 46°11N 103°24W **80** B2
Bowman I. *Antarctica* 65°0S 104°0E **5** C8
Bowmanville = Clarington
 Canada 43°55N 78°41W **82** C6
Bowmore *U.K.* 55°45N 6°17W **11** F2
Bowral *Australia* 34°26S 150°27E **63** E5
Bowraville *Australia* 30°37S 152°52E **63** E5
Bowron ➤ *Canada* 54°3N 121°50W **70** C4
Bowron Lake △ *Canada* 53°10N 121°5W **70** C4
Bowser L. *Canada* 56°30N 129°30W **70** B3
Bowsman *Canada* 52°14N 101°12W **71** C8
Bowwood *Zambia* 17°5S 26°20E **55** F2
Box Cr. ➤ *Australia* 34°10S 143°50E **63** E3
Boxmeer *Neths.* 51°38N 5°56E **15** C5
Boxtel *Neths.* 51°36N 5°20E **15** C5
Boyce *U.S.A.* 31°23N 92°40W **84** F8
Boyd L. *Canada* 52°46N 76°42W **72** B4
Boyle *Canada* 54°35N 112°49W **70** C6
Boyle *Ireland* 53°59N 8°18W **10** C3
Boyne ➤ *Ireland* 53°43N 6°15W **10** C5
Boyne City *U.S.A.* 45°13N 85°1W **81** C11
Boynton Beach *U.S.A.* 26°32N 80°4W **85** H14
Boyolali *Indonesia* 7°32S 110°35E **37** G14
Boyoma, Chutes
 Dem. Rep. of the Congo 0°35N 25°23E **54** B2
Boysen Res. *U.S.A.* 43°25N 108°11W **76** E9
Boyuibe *Bolivia* 20°25S 63°17W **92** G6
Boyup Brook *Australia* 33°50S 116°23E **61** F2
Boz Dağları *Turkey* 38°20N 28°0E **23** E13
Bozburun *Turkey* 36°43N 28°4E **23** F13
Bozcaada *Turkey* 39°49N 26°3E **23** E12
Bozdoğan *Turkey* 37°40N 28°17E **23** F13
Bozeman *U.S.A.* 45°41N 111°2W **76** D8
Bozen = Bolzano *Italy* 46°31N 11°22E **22** A4
Bozhou *China* 33°55N 115°41E **34** H8
Bozoum *C.A.R.* 6°25N 16°35E **52** C3
Bozyazı *Turkey* 36°6N 33°0E **44** B2
Bra *Italy* 44°42N 7°51E **20** D7
Brabant □ *Belgium* 50°46N 4°30E **15** D4
Brabant L. *Canada* 55°58N 103°43W **71** B8
Brač *Croatia* 43°20N 16°40E **22** C7
Bracadale, L. *U.K.* 57°20N 6°30W **11** D2
Bracciano, L. di *Italy* 42°7N 12°14E **22** C5
Bracebridge *Canada* 45°2N 79°19W **82** A5
Bräcke *Sweden* 62°45N 15°26E **8** E16
Brackettville *U.S.A.* 29°19N 100°25W **84** G4
Bracknell *U.K.* 51°25N 0°43W **13** F7
Bracknell Forest □ *U.K.* 51°25N 0°44W **13** F7
Brad *Romania* 46°10N 22°50E **17** E12
Bradenton *U.S.A.* 27°30N 82°34W **85** H13
Bradford *Canada* 44°7N 79°34W **82** B5
Bradford *U.K.* 53°47N 1°45W **12** D6
Bradford *Pa., U.S.A.* 41°58N 78°38W **82** E6
Bradford *Vt., U.S.A.* 43°59N 72°9W **83** C12
Bradley *Ark., U.S.A.* 33°6N 93°39W **84** E8
Bradley *Calif., U.S.A.* 35°52N 120°48W **78** K6
Bradley Institute
 Zimbabwe 17°7S 31°25E **55** F3
Brady *U.S.A.* 31°9N 99°20W **84** F5
Braeside *Canada* 45°28N 76°24W **83** A8

Braga *Portugal* 41°35N 8°25W **21** B1
Bragado *Argentina* 35°2S 60°27W **94** D3
Bragança *Brazil* 1°0S 47°2W **93** D9
Bragança *Portugal* 41°48N 6°50W **21** B2
Bragança Paulista
 Brazil 22°55S 46°32W **95** A6
Brahestad = Raahe
 Finland 64°40N 24°28E **8** D21
Brahmanbaria *Bangla.* 23°58N 91°15E **41** H17
Brahmani ➤ *India* 20°39N 86°46E **41** J15
Brahmapur *India* 19°15N 84°54E **41** K14
Brahmaputra ➤ *Asia* 23°40N 90°35E **43** H13
Braich-y-pwll *U.K.* 52°47N 4°46W **12** E3
Braidwood *Australia* 35°27S 149°49E **63** F4
Brăila *Romania* 45°19N 27°59E **17** F14
Brainerd *U.S.A.* 46°22N 94°12W **80** B6
Braintree *U.K.* 51°53N 0°34E **13** F8
Braintree *U.S.A.* 42°13N 71°0E **83** D14
Brak ➤ *S. Africa* 29°35S 22°55E **56** D3
Brakwater *Namibia* 22°28S 17°3E **56** C2
Brampton *Canada* 43°45N 79°45W **82** C5
Brampton *U.K.* 54°57N 2°44W **12** C5
Brampton I. *Australia* 20°49S 149°16E **62** b
Branco ➤ *Brazil* 1°20S 61°50W **92** D6
Brandberg *Namibia* 21°10S 14°33E **56** C1
Brandenburg = Neubrandenburg
 Germany 53°33N 13°15E **16** B7
Brandenburg *Germany* 52°25N 12°33E **16** B7
Brandenburg □ *Germany* 52°50N 13°0E **16** B6
Brandfort *S. Africa* 28°40S 26°30E **56** D4
Brandon *Canada* 49°50N 99°57W **71** D9
Brandon *U.S.A.* 43°48N 73°6W **83** C11
Brandon B. *Ireland* 52°17N 10°8W **10** D1
Brandon Mt. *Ireland* 52°15N 10°15W **10** D1
Brandsen *Argentina* 35°10S 58°15W **94** D4
Brandvlei *S. Africa* 30°25S 20°30E **56** E3
Branford *U.S.A.* 41°17N 72°49W **83** E12
Braniewo *Poland* 54°25N 19°50E **17** A10
Bransfield Str. *Antarctica* 63°0S 59°0W **5** C18
Branson *U.S.A.* 36°39N 93°13W **80** G7
Brantford *Canada* 43°10N 80°15W **82** C4
Bras d'Or L. *Canada* 45°50N 60°50W **73** C7
Brasher Falls *U.S.A.* 44°49N 74°47W **83** B10
Brasil = Brazil ■ *S. Amer.* 12°0S 50°0W **93** F9
Brasil, Planalto *Brazil* 18°0S 46°30W **90** E6
Brasília *Brazil* 15°47S 47°55W **93** G9
Brasília Legal *Brazil* 3°49S 55°36W **93** D7
Braslaw *Belarus* 55°38N 27°0E **9** J22
Braşov *Romania* 45°38N 25°35E **17** F13
Brasschaat *Belgium* 51°19N 4°27E **15** C4
Brassey, Banjaran
 Malaysia 5°0N 117°15E **36** D5
Brassey Ra. *Australia* 25°8S 122°15E **61** E3
Brasstown Bald *U.S.A.* 34°53N 83°49W **85** D13
Brastad *Sweden* 58°23N 11°30E **9** G14
Bratislava *Slovak Rep.* 48°10N 17°7E **17** D9
Bratsk *Russia* 56°10N 101°30E **29** D11
Brattleboro *U.S.A.* 42°51N 72°34W **83** D12
Braunau *Austria* 48°15N 13°3E **16** D7
Braunschweig *Germany* 52°15N 10°31E **16** B6
Braunton *U.K.* 51°7N 4°10W **13** F3
Brava *C. Verde Is.* 15°0N 24°40W **50** b
Bravo del Norte, Rio = Grande,
 Rio ➤ *N. Amer.* 25°58N 97°9W **84** H6
Brawley *U.S.A.* 32°59N 115°31W **79** N11
Bray *Ireland* 53°13N 6°7W **10** C5
Bray, Mt. *Australia* 14°0S 134°30E **62** A1
Bray, Pays de *France* 49°46N 1°26E **20** B4
Brazeau ➤ *Canada* 52°55N 115°14W **70** C5
Brazil *U.S.A.* 39°32N 87°8W **80** F10
Brazil ■ *S. Amer.* 12°0S 50°0W **93** F9
Brazilian Highlands = Brasil,
 Planalto *Brazil* 18°0S 46°30W **90** E6
Brazo Sur ➤ *S. Amer.* 25°21S 57°42W **94** B4
Brazos ➤ *U.S.A.* 28°53N 95°23W **84** G7
Brazzaville *Congo* 4°9S 15°12E **52** E3
Brčko *Bos.-H.* 44°54N 18°46E **23** B8
Bré = Bray *Ireland* 53°13N 6°7W **10** C5
Breaden, L. *Australia* 25°51S 125°28E **61** E4
Breaksea Sd. *N.Z.* 45°35S 166°35E **59** F1
Bream B. *N.Z.* 35°56S 174°28E **59** A5
Bream Hd. *N.Z.* 35°51S 174°36E **59** A5
Breas *Chile* 25°29S 70°24W **94** B1
Brebes *Indonesia* 6°52S 109°3E **37** G13
Brechin *Canada* 44°32N 79°10W **82** B5
Brechin *U.K.* 56°44N 2°39W **11** E6
Brecht *Belgium* 51°21N 4°38E **15** C4
Breckenridge *Colo.,*
 U.S.A. 39°29N 106°3W **76** G10
Breckenridge *Minn.,*
 U.S.A. 46°16N 96°35W **80** B5
Breckenridge *Tex.,*
 U.S.A. 32°45N 98°54W **84** E5
Breckland *U.K.* 52°30N 0°40E **13** E8
Brecon *U.K.* 51°57N 3°23W **13** F4
Brecon Beacons *U.K.* 51°53N 3°26W **13** F4
Brecon Beacons △ *U.K.* 51°50N 3°30W **13** F4
Breda *Neths.* 51°35N 4°45E **15** C4
Bredasdorp *S. Africa* 34°33S 20°2E **56** E3
Bree *Belgium* 51°8N 5°35E **15** C5
Bregenz *Austria* 47°30N 9°45E **16** E5
Breiðafjörður *Iceland* 65°15N 23°15W **8** D2
Brejo *Brazil* 3°41S 42°47W **93** D10
Bremen *Germany* 53°4N 8°47E **16** B5
Bremer Bay *Australia* 34°21S 119°16E **61** F2
Bremer I. *Australia* 12°5S 136°45E **62** A2
Bremerhaven *Germany* 53°33N 8°36E **16** B5
Bremerton *U.S.A.* 47°34N 122°37W **78** C4
Brenham *U.S.A.* 30°10N 96°24W **84** F6
Brennerpass *Austria* 47°2N 11°30E **16** E6
Brent *U.S.A.* 32°56N 87°10W **85** E11
Brentwood *U.K.* 51°37N 0°19E **13** F8
Brentwood *Calif.,*
 U.S.A. 37°56N 121°42W **78** H5
Brentwood *N.Y., U.S.A.* 40°47N 73°15W **83** F11
Bréscia *Italy* 45°33N 10°15E **20** D9
Breskens *Neths.* 51°23N 3°33E **15** C3

Breslau = Wrocław *Poland* 51°5N 17°5E **17** C9
Bressanone *Italy* 46°43N 11°39E **22** A4
Bressay *U.K.* 60°9N 1°0W **11** A7
Brest *Belarus* 52°10N 23°40E **17** B12
Brest *France* 48°24N 4°31W **20** B1
Brest-Litovsk = Brest
 Belarus 52°10N 23°40E **17** B12
Bretagne □ *France* 48°10N 3°0W **20** B2
Breton *Canada* 53°7N 114°28W **70** C6
Breton Sd. *U.S.A.* 29°35N 89°15W **85** G10
Brett, C. *N.Z.* 35°10S 174°20E **59** A5
Brevard *U.S.A.* 35°14N 82°44W **85** D13
Breves *Brazil* 1°40S 50°29W **93** D8
Brewarrina *Australia* 30°0S 146°51E **63** E4
Brewer *U.S.A.* 44°48N 68°46W **81** C19
Brewer, Mt. *U.S.A.* 36°44N 118°28W **78** J8
Brewster *N.Y., U.S.A.* 41°24N 73°36W **83** E11
Brewster *Ohio, U.S.A.* 40°43N 81°36W **82** F3
Brewster *Wash., U.S.A.* 48°6N 119°47W **76** B4
Brewster, Kap = Kangikajik
 Greenland 70°7N 22°0W **4** B6
Brewton *U.S.A.* 31°7N 87°4W **85** F11
Breyten *S. Africa* 26°16S 30°0E **57** D5
Bria *C.A.R.* 6°30N 21°58E **52** C4
Briançon *France* 44°54N 6°39E **20** D7
Bribie I. *Australia* 27°0S 153°10E **63** D5
Bribri *Costa Rica* 9°38N 82°50W **88** E3
Bridgefield *Barbados* 13°9N 59°36W **89** g
Bridgehampton *U.S.A.* 40°56N 72°19W **83** F12
Bridgend *U.K.* 51°30N 3°34W **13** F4
Bridgend □ *U.K.* 51°36N 3°36W **13** F4
Bridgenorth *Canada* 44°23N 78°23W **82** B6
Bridgeport *Calif., U.S.A.* 38°15N 119°14W **78** G7
Bridgeport *Conn.,*
 U.S.A. 41°11N 73°12W **83** E11
Bridgeport *N.Y., U.S.A.* 43°9N 75°58W **83** C9
Bridgeport *Nebr., U.S.A.* 41°40N 103°6W **80** E2
Bridgeport *Tex., U.S.A.* 33°13N 97°45W **84** E6
Bridger *U.S.A.* 45°18N 108°55W **76** D9
Bridgeton *U.S.A.* 39°26N 75°14W **81** F16
Bridgetown *Australia* 33°58S 116°7E **61** F2
Bridgetown *Barbados* 13°6N 59°37W **89** g
Bridgetown *Canada* 44°55N 65°18W **73** D6
Bridgewater *Australia* 42°44S 147°14E **63** G4
Bridgewater *Canada* 44°25N 64°31W **73** D7
Bridgewater *Mass.,*
 U.S.A. 41°59N 70°58W **83** E14
Bridgewater *N.Y.,*
 U.S.A. 42°53N 75°15W **83** D9
Bridgewater, C.
 Australia 38°23S 141°23E **63** F3
Bridgnorth *U.K.* 52°32N 2°25W **13** E5
Bridgton *U.S.A.* 44°3N 70°42W **83** B14
Bridgwater *U.K.* 51°8N 2°59W **13** F5
Bridgwater B. *U.K.* 51°15N 3°15W **13** F4
Bridlington *U.K.* 54°5N 0°12W **12** C7
Bridlington B. *U.K.* 54°4N 0°10W **12** C7
Bridport *Australia* 40°59S 147°23E **63** G4
Bridport *U.K.* 50°44N 2°45W **13** G5
Brig *Switz.* 46°18N 7°59E **20** C7
Brigg *U.K.* 53°34N 0°28W **12** D7
Brigham City *U.S.A.* 41°31N 112°1W **76** F7
Bright *Australia* 36°42S 146°56E **63** F4
Brighton *Australia* 35°5S 138°30E **63** F2
Brighton *Canada* 44°2N 77°44W **82** B7
Brighton *Trin. & Tob.* 10°13N 61°39W **93** K15
Brighton *U.K.* 50°49N 0°7W **13** G7
Brighton *U.S.A.* 43°8N 77°34W **82** C7
Brighton *Colo., U.S.A.* 45°7N 76°29W **83** A8
Brightside *Canada* 40°15N 80°39W **82** F4
Brilliant *U.S.A.* 40°15N 80°39W **82** F4
Bríndisi *Italy* 40°39N 17°55E **23** D7
Brinkley *U.S.A.* 34°53N 91°12W **84** D9
Brinnon *U.S.A.* 47°41N 122°54W **78** C4
Brion, Î. *Canada* 47°46N 61°26W **73** C7
Brisay *Canada* 54°30N 70°31W **73** B5
Brisbane *Australia* 27°25S 153°2E **63** D5
Brisbane ➤ *Australia* 27°24S 153°9E **63** D5
Bristol *Australia* 51°26N 2°35W **13** F5
Bristol *Conn., U.S.A.* 41°40N 72°57W **83** E12
Bristol *Pa., U.S.A.* 40°6N 74°51W **83** F10
Bristol *R.I., U.S.A.* 41°40N 71°16W **83** E13
Bristol *Tenn., U.S.A.* 36°36N 82°11W **85** C13
Bristol *Vt., U.S.A.* 44°8N 73°4W **83** B11
Bristol, City of □ *U.K.* 51°27N 2°36W **13** F5
Bristol B. *U.S.A.* 58°0N 160°0W **74** D8
Bristol Channel *U.K.* 51°18N 4°30W **13** F3
Bristol I. *Antarctica* 58°45S 28°0W **5** B1
Bristow *U.S.A.* 35°50N 96°23W **84** D6
Britain = Great Britain
 Europe 54°0N 2°15W **6** E5
British Columbia □
 Canada 55°0N 125°15W **70** C3
British Indian Ocean Terr. =
 Chagos Arch. ☑ *Ind. Oc.* 6°0S 72°0E **26** J9
British Isles *Europe* 54°0N 4°0W **6** E5
British Mts. *N. Amer.* 68°50N 140°0W **74** B12
British Virgin Is. ☑
 W. Indies 18°30N 64°30W **89** e
Brits *S. Africa* 25°37S 27°48E **57** D4
Britstown *S. Africa* 30°37S 23°30E **56** E3
Britt *Canada* 45°46N 80°34W **82** A4
Brittany = Bretagne □
 France 48°10N 3°0W **20** B2
Britton *U.S.A.* 45°48N 97°45W **80** C5
Brive-la-Gaillarde *France* 45°10N 1°32E **20** D4
Brixen = Bressanone
 Italy 46°43N 11°39E **22** A4
Brixham *U.K.* 50°23N 3°31E **13** G4
Brno *Czech Rep.* 49°10N 16°35E **17** D9
Broach = Bharuch *India* 21°47N 73°0E **40** J8
Broad ➤ *U.S.A.* 34°1N 81°4W **85** D14
Broad Arrow *Australia* 30°23S 121°15E **61** F3
Broad B. *U.K.* 58°14N 6°18W **11** C2
Broad Haven *Ireland* 54°20N 9°55E **10** B2
Broad Law *U.K.* 55°30N 3°21W **11** F5
Broad Pk. = Faichan Kangri
 India 35°48N 76°34E **43** B7
Broad Sd. *Australia* 22°0S 149°45E **62** C4

Broadalbin *U.S.A.* 43°4N 74°12W **83** C10
Broadback → *Canada* 51°21N 78°52W **72** B4
Broadhurst Ra. *Australia* 22°30S 122°30E **60** D3
Broads, The *U.K.* 52°45N 1°30E **12** E9
Broadus *U.S.A.* 45°27N 105°25W **76** D11
Brochet *Canada* 57°53N 101°40W **71** B8
Brochet, L. *Canada* 58°36N 101°35W **71** B8
Brock I. *Canada* 77°52N 114°19W **69** B9
Brocken *Germany* 51°47N 10°37E **16** C6
Brockport *U.S.A.* 43°13N 77°56W **82** C7
Brockton *U.S.A.* 42°5N 71°1W **83** D13
Brockville *Canada* 44°35N 75°41W **83** B9
Brockway *Mont., U.S.A.* 47°18N 105°45W **76** C11
Brockway *Pa., U.S.A.* 41°15N 78°47W **82** E6
Brocton *U.S.A.* 42°23N 79°26W **82** D5
Brodeur Pen. *Canada* 72°30N 88°10W **69** C14
Brodick *U.K.* 55°35N 5°9W **11** F3
Brodnica *Poland* 53°15N 19°25E **17** B10
Brody *Ukraine* 50°5N 25°10E **17** C13
Brogan *U.S.A.* 44°15N 117°31W **76** D5
Broken Arrow *U.S.A.* 36°3N 95°48W **84** C7
Broken Bow *Nebr., U.S.A.* 41°24N 99°38W **80** E4
Broken Bow *Okla., U.S.A.* 34°2N 94°44W **84** D7
Broken Bow Lake *U.S.A.* 34°9N 94°40W **84** D7
Broken Hill *Australia* 31°58S 141°29E **63** E3
Broken Ridge *Ind. Oc.* 30°0S 94°0E **64** L1
Broken River Ra. *Australia* 21°0S 148°22E **62** b
Bromley □ *U.K.* 51°24N 0°2E **13** F8
Bromo *Indonesia* 7°55S 112°55E **37** G15
Bromsgrove *U.K.* 52°21N 2°2W **13** E5
Brønderslev *Denmark* 57°16N 9°57E **9** H13
Bronkhorstspruit *S. Africa* 25°46S 28°45E **57** D4
Brønnøysund *Norway* 65°28N 12°14E **8** D15
Brook Park *U.S.A.* 41°23N 81°48W **82** E4
Brookhaven *U.S.A.* 31°35N 90°26W **85** F9
Brookings *Oreg., U.S.A.* 42°3N 124°17W **76** E1
Brookings *S. Dak., U.S.A.* 44°19N 96°48W **80** C5
Brooklin *Canada* 43°55N 78°55W **82** C6
Brooklyn Park *U.S.A.* 45°6N 93°23W **80** C7
Brooks *Canada* 50°35N 111°55W **70** C6
Brooks Range *U.S.A.* 68°0N 152°0W **74** B9
Brooksville *U.S.A.* 28°33N 82°23W **85** G13
Brookton *Australia* 32°22S 117°0E **61** F2
Brookville *U.S.A.* 41°10N 79°5W **82** E5
Broom, L. *U.K.* 57°55N 5°15W **11** D3
Broome *Australia* 18°0S 122°15E **60** C3
Brora *U.K.* 58°0N 3°52W **11** C5
Brora → *U.K.* 58°0N 3°51W **11** C5
Brosna → *Ireland* 53°14N 7°58W **10** C4
Brothers *U.S.A.* 43°49N 120°36W **76** E3
Brough *U.K.* 54°32N 2°18W **12** C5
Brough Hd. *U.K.* 59°8N 3°20W **11** B5
Broughton Island = Qikiqtarjuaq *Canada* 67°33N 63°0W **69** D19
Brown, L. *Australia* 31°5S 118°15E **61** F2
Brown, Pt. *Australia* 32°32S 133°50E **63** E1
Brown City *U.S.A.* 43°13N 82°59W **82** C2
Brown Willy *U.K.* 50°35N 4°37W **13** G3
Brownfield *U.S.A.* 33°11N 102°17W **84** E3
Browning *U.S.A.* 48°34N 113°1W **76** B7
Brownsville *Oreg., U.S.A.* 44°24N 122°59W **76** D2
Brownsville *Pa., U.S.A.* 40°1N 79°53W **82** F5
Brownsville *Tenn., U.S.A.* 35°36N 89°16W **85** D10
Brownsville *Tex., U.S.A.* 25°54N 97°30W **84** J6
Brownville *U.S.A.* 44°0N 75°59W **83** C9
Brownwood *U.S.A.* 31°43N 98°59W **84** F5
Browse I. *Australia* 14°7S 123°33E **60** B3
Bruas *Malaysia* 4°30N 100°47E **39** K3
Bruay-la-Buissière *France* 50°29N 2°33E **20** A5
Bruce, Mt. *Australia* 22°37S 118°8E **60** D2
Bruce Pen. *Canada* 45°0N 81°30W **82** B3
Bruce Peninsula △ *Canada* 45°14N 81°36W **82** A3
Bruce Rock *Australia* 31°52S 118°8E **61** F2
Bruck an der Leitha *Austria* 48°1N 16°47E **17** D9
Bruck an der Mur *Austria* 47°24N 15°16E **16** E8
Brue → *U.K.* 51°13N 2°59W **13** F5
Bruges = Brugge *Belgium* 51°13N 3°13E **15** C3
Brugge *Belgium* 51°13N 3°13E **15** C3
Bruin *U.S.A.* 41°3N 79°43W **82** E5
Brûk, W. el → *Egypt* 30°15N 33°50E **46** E2
Brûlé *Canada* 53°15N 117°58W **70** C5
Brûlé, L. *Canada* 53°35N 64°4W **73** B7
Brumado *Brazil* 14°14S 41°40W **93** F10
Brumunddal *Norway* 60°53N 10°56E **8** F14
Bruneau *U.S.A.* 42°53N 115°48W **76** E6
Bruneau → *U.S.A.* 42°56N 115°57W **76** E6
Brunei = Bandar Seri Begawan *Brunei* 4°52N 115°0E **36** D5
Brunei ■ *Asia* 4°50N 115°0E **36** D5
Brunner, L. *N.Z.* 42°37S 171°27E **59** E3
Brunssum *Neths.* 50°57N 5°59E **15** D5
Brunswick = Braunschweig *Germany* 52°15N 10°31E **16** B6
Brunswick *Ga., U.S.A.* 31°10N 81°30W **85** F14
Brunswick *Maine, U.S.A.* 43°55N 69°58W **81** D19
Brunswick *Md., U.S.A.* 39°19N 77°38W **81** F15
Brunswick *Mo., U.S.A.* 39°26N 93°8W **80** F7
Brunswick *Ohio, U.S.A.* 41°14N 81°51W **82** E3
Brunswick, Pen. de *Chile* 53°30S 71°30W **96** G2
Brunswick B. *Australia* 15°15S 124°50E **60** C3
Brunswick Junction *Australia* 33°15S 115°50E **61** F2
Brunt Ice Shelf *Antarctica* 75°30S 25°0W **5** D2
Brus Laguna *Honduras* 15°47N 84°35W **88** C3
Brush *U.S.A.* 40°15N 103°37W **76** F12
Brushton *U.S.A.* 44°50N 74°31W **83** B10
Brusque *Brazil* 27°5S 49°0W **95** B6
Brussel *Belgium* 50°51N 4°21E **15** D4
Brussel ✕ **(BRU)** *Belgium* 50°54N 4°29E **15** D5
Brussels = Brussel *Belgium* 50°51N 4°21E **15** D4
Brussels *Canada* 43°44N 81°15W **82** C3
Bruthen *Australia* 37°42S 147°50E **63** F4
Bruxelles = Brussel *Belgium* 50°51N 4°21E **15** D4
Bryan *Ohio, U.S.A.* 41°28N 84°33W **81** E11
Bryan *Tex., U.S.A.* 30°40N 96°22W **84** F6
Bryan, Mt. *Australia* 33°30S 139°5E **63** E2
Bryansk *Russia* 53°13N 34°25E **18** D4
Bryce Canyon △ *U.S.A.* 37°30N 112°10W **77** H7
Bryne *Norway* 58°44N 5°38E **9** G11
Bryson City *U.S.A.* 35°26N 83°27W **85** D13
Bsharri *Lebanon* 34°15N 36°0E **46** A5
Bū Baqarah *U.A.E.* 25°35N 56°25E **45** E8
Bu Craa *W. Sahara* 26°45N 12°50W **50** C3
Bū Ḩasā *U.A.E.* 23°30N 53°20E **45** F7
Bua *Fiji* 16°48S 178°37E **59** a
Bua → *Malaysia* 12°45S 34°16E **55** E3
Bua Yai *Thailand* 15°33N 102°26E **38** E4
Buan *S. Korea* 35°44N 126°44E **35** G14
Buapinang *Indonesia* 4°40S 121°30E **37** E6
Bubanza *Burundi* 3°6S 29°23E **54** C2
Bubi → *Zimbabwe* 22°20S 31°7E **55** G3
Būbiyān *Kuwait* 29°45N 48°15E **45** D6
Buca *Fiji* 16°38S 179°52E **59** a
Bucaramanga *Colombia* 7°0N 73°0W **92** B4
Bucasia *Australia* 21°2S 149°10E **62** b
Buccaneer Arch. *Australia* 16°7S 123°20E **60** C3
Buccoo Reef *Trin. & Tob.* 11°10N 60°51W **93** J16
Buchach *Ukraine* 49°5N 25°25E **17** D13
Buchan *U.K.* 57°32N 2°21W **11** D6
Buchan Ness *U.K.* 57°29N 1°46W **11** D7
Buchanan *Canada* 51°40N 102°45W **71** C8
Buchanan *Liberia* 5°57N 10°2W **50** G3
Buchanan, L. *Queens., Australia* 21°35S 145°52E **62** C4
Buchanan, L. *W. Austral., Australia* 25°33S 123°2E **61** E3
Buchanan, L. *U.S.A.* 30°45N 98°25W **84** F5
Buchanan Cr. → *Australia* 19°13S 136°33E **62** B2
Buchans *Canada* 48°50N 56°52W **73** C8
Bucharest = Bucureşti *Romania* 44°27N 26°10E **17** F14
Bucheon *S. Korea* 37°28N 126°45E **35** F14
Buchon, Pt. *U.S.A.* 35°15N 120°54W **78** K6
Buck Hill Falls *U.S.A.* 41°11N 75°16W **83** E9
Buckeye Lake *U.S.A.* 39°55N 82°29W **82** G2
Buckhannon *U.S.A.* 39°0N 80°8W **81** F13
Buckhaven *U.K.* 56°11N 3°3W **11** E5
Buckhorn L. *Canada* 44°29N 78°23W **82** B6
Buckie *U.K.* 57°41N 2°58W **11** D6
Buckingham *Canada* 45°37N 75°24W **72** C4
Buckingham *U.K.* 51°59N 0°57W **13** F7
Buckingham B. *Australia* 12°10S 135°40E **62** A2
Buckinghamshire □ *U.K.* 51°53N 0°55W **13** F7
Buckle Hd. *Australia* 14°26S 127°52E **60** B4
Buckleboo *Australia* 32°54S 136°12E **63** E2
Buckley *U.K.* 53°10N 3°5W **12** D4
Buckley → *Australia* 20°10S 138°49E **62** C2
Bucklin *U.S.A.* 37°33N 99°38W **80** G4
Bucks L. *U.S.A.* 39°54N 121°12W **78** F5
Bucureşti *Romania* 44°27N 26°10E **17** F14
Bucyrus *U.S.A.* 40°48N 82°59W **81** E12
Budalin *Burma* 22°20N 95°10E **41** H19
Budapest *Hungary* 47°29N 19°3E **17** E10
Budaun *India* 28°5N 79°10E **43** E8
Budd Coast *Antarctica* 68°0S 112°0E **5** C8
Bude *U.K.* 50°49N 4°34W **13** G3
Budennovsk *Russia* 44°50N 44°10E **19** F7
Budge Budge = Baj Baj *India* 22°30N 88°5E **43** H13
Budgewoi *Australia* 33°13S 151°34E **63** E5
Budjala *Dem. Rep. of the Congo* 2°50N 19°40E **52** D3
Buellton *U.S.A.* 34°37N 120°12W **79** L6
Buena Esperanza *Argentina* 34°45S 65°15W **94** C2
Buena Park *U.S.A.* 33°52N 117°59W **79** M9
Buena Vista *Colo., U.S.A.* 38°51N 106°8W **76** G10
Buena Vista *Va., U.S.A.* 37°44N 79°21W **81** G14
Buena Vista Lake Bed *U.S.A.* 35°12N 119°18W **79** K7
Buenaventura *Colombia* 3°53N 77°4W **92** C3
Buenaventura *Mexico* 29°51N 107°29W **86** B3
Buenos Aires *Argentina* 34°36S 58°22W **94** C4
Buenos Aires *Costa Rica* 9°10N 83°20W **88** E3
Buenos Aires □ *Argentina* 36°30S 60°0W **94** D4
Buenos Aires, L. *Argentina* 46°35S 72°30W **96** F2
Buffalo *Mo., U.S.A.* 37°39N 93°6W **80** G7
Buffalo *N.Y., U.S.A.* 42°53N 78°53W **82** D6
Buffalo *Okla., U.S.A.* 36°50N 99°38W **84** C5
Buffalo *S. Dak., U.S.A.* 45°35N 103°33W **80** C2
Buffalo *Wyo., U.S.A.* 44°21N 106°42W **76** D10
Buffalo → *Canada* 60°5N 115°5W **70** A5
Buffalo → *S. Africa* 28°43S 30°37E **57** D5
Buffalo ⌓ *U.S.A.* 36°14N 92°36W **84** C8
Buffalo Head Hills *Canada* 57°25N 115°55W **70** B5
Buffalo L. *Alta., Canada* 52°27N 112°54W **70** C6
Buffalo L. *N.W.T., Canada* 60°12N 115°25W **70** A5
Buffalo Narrows *Canada* 55°51N 108°29W **71** B7
Buffalo Springs ⌓ *Kenya* 0°32N 37°35E **54** B4
Buffels → *S. Africa* 29°36S 17°3E **56** D2
Buford *U.S.A.* 34°10N 84°0W **85** D12
Bug = Buh → *Ukraine* 46°59N 31°58E **19** E5
Bug → *Poland* 52°31N 21°5E **17** B11
Buga *Colombia* 4°0N 76°15W **92** C3
Bugala I. *Uganda* 0°40S 32°20E **54** C3
Buganda *Uganda* 0°0 31°30E **54** C3
Buganga *Uganda* 0°3S 32°0E **54** C3
Bugel, Tanjung *Indonesia* 6°26S 111°3E **37** G14
Búger *Spain* 39°45N 2°59E **24** B9
Bugibba *Malta* 35°57N 14°25E **25** D1
Bugsuk I. *Phil.* 8°12N 117°18E **36** C5
Bugulma *Russia* 54°33N 52°48E **18** D9
Bugungu ⌓ *Uganda* 2°17N 31°50E **54** B3
Buguruslan *Russia* 53°39N 52°26E **18** D9
Buh → *Ukraine* 46°59N 31°58E **19** E5
Buhera *Zimbabwe* 19°18S 31°29E **57** B5
Buhl *U.S.A.* 42°36N 114°46W **76** E6
Builth Wells *U.K.* 52°9N 3°25W **13** E4
Buir Nur *Mongolia* 47°50N 117°42E **33** B6
Buji *China* 22°37N 114°5E **33** F11
Bujumbura *Burundi* 3°16S 29°18E **54** C2
Bukachacha *Russia* 52°55N 116°50E **29** D12
Bukama *Dem. Rep. of the Congo* 9°10S 25°50E **55** D2
Bukavu *Dem. Rep. of the Congo* 2°20S 28°52E **54** C2
Bukene *Tanzania* 4°15S 32°48E **54** C3
Bukhara = Buxoro *Uzbekistan* 39°48N 64°25E **28** F7
Bukhoro = Buxoro *Uzbekistan* 39°48N 64°25E **28** F7
Bukima *Tanzania* 1°50S 33°25E **54** C3
Bukit Badung *Indonesia* 8°49S 115°10E **37** K18
Bukit Kerajaan *Malaysia* 5°25N 100°15E **39** c
Bukit Mertajam *Malaysia* 5°22N 100°28E **39** c
Bukit Ni *Malaysia* 1°22N 104°12E **39** d
Bukit Panjang *Singapore* 1°23N 103°46E **39** d
Bukit Tengah *Malaysia* 5°22N 100°25E **39** c
Bukittinggi *Indonesia* 0°20S 100°20E **36** E2
Bukoba *Tanzania* 1°20S 31°49E **54** C3
Bukum, Pulau *Singapore* 1°14N 103°46E **39** d
Bukuya *Uganda* 0°40N 31°52E **54** B3
Būl, Kuh-e *Iran* 30°48N 52°45E **45** D7
Bula *Indonesia* 3°6S 130°30E **37** E8
Bulahdelah *Australia* 32°23S 152°13E **63** E5
Bulan *Phil.* 12°40N 123°52E **37** B6
Bulandshahr *India* 28°28N 77°51E **42** E7
Bulawayo *Zimbabwe* 20°7S 28°32E **55** G2
Buldan *Turkey* 38°2N 28°50E **23** E13
Buldir I. *U.S.A.* 52°21N 175°56E **74** E3
Bulgan *Mongolia* 48°45N 103°34E **32** B5
Bulgar *Russia* 54°57N 49°4E **18** D8
Bulgaria ■ *Europe* 42°35N 25°30E **23** C11
Buli, Teluk *Indonesia* 0°48N 128°25E **37** D7
Buliluyan, C. *Phil.* 8°20N 117°15E **36** C5
Bulim *Singapore* 1°22N 103°43E **39** d
Bulkley → *Canada* 55°15N 127°40W **70** B3
Bull Shoals L. *U.S.A.* 36°22N 92°35W **84** C8
Bulleringa △ *Australia* 17°39S 143°56E **62** B3
Bullhead City *U.S.A.* 35°8N 114°32W **79** K12
Büllingen *Belgium* 50°25N 6°16E **15** D6
Bullock Creek *Australia* 17°43S 144°31E **62** B3
Bulloo → *Australia* 28°43S 142°30E **63** D3
Bulloo L. *Australia* 28°43S 142°25E **63** D3
Bulls *N.Z.* 40°10S 175°24E **59** D5
Bulman *Australia* 13°39S 134°20E **62** A1
Bulnes *Chile* 36°42S 72°19W **94** D1
Bulsar = Valsad *India* 20°40N 72°58E **40** J8
Bultfontein *S. Africa* 28°18S 26°10E **56** D4
Bulukumba *Indonesia* 5°33S 120°11E **37** F6
Bulun *Russia* 70°37N 127°30E **29** B13
Bumba *Dem. Rep. of the Congo* 2°13N 22°30E **52** D4
Bumbah, Khalīj *Libya* 32°20N 23°15E **51** B10
Bumbiri I. *Tanzania* 1°40S 31°55E **54** C3
Bumhpa Bum *Burma* 26°51N 97°14E **41** F20
Bumi → *Zimbabwe* 17°0S 28°20E **55** F2
Buna *Kenya* 2°58N 39°30E **54** B4
Bunaken *Indonesia* 1°37N 124°46E **37** D6
Bunazi *Tanzania* 1°3S 31°23E **54** C3
Bunbury *Australia* 33°20S 115°35E **61** F2
Bunclody *Ireland* 52°39N 6°40W **10** D5
Buncrana *Ireland* 55°8N 7°27W **10** A4
Bundaberg *Australia* 24°54S 152°22E **63** C5
Bundey → *Australia* 21°46S 135°37E **62** C2
Bundi *India* 25°30N 75°35E **42** G6
Bundjalung △ *Australia* 29°16S 153°21E **63** D5
Bundoran *Ireland* 54°28N 8°16W **10** B3
Bung Kan *Thailand* 18°23N 103°37E **38** C4
Bungay *U.K.* 52°27N 1°28E **13** E9
Bungil Cr. → *Australia* 27°5S 149°5E **63** D4
Bungle Bungle = Purnululu △ *Australia* 17°20S 128°20E **60** C4
Bungo-Suidō *Japan* 33°0N 132°15E **31** H6
Bungoma *Kenya* 0°34N 34°34E **54** B3
Bungotakada *Japan* 33°35N 131°25E **31** H5
Bungu *Tanzania* 7°35S 39°0E **54** D4
Bunia *Dem. Rep. of the Congo* 1°35N 30°20E **54** B3
Bunji *Pakistan* 35°45N 74°40E **43** B6
Bunkie *U.S.A.* 30°57N 92°11W **84** F8
Bunnell *U.S.A.* 29°28N 81°16W **85** G14
Buntok *Indonesia* 1°40S 114°58E **36** E4
Bunya Mts. △ *Australia* 26°51S 151°34E **63** D5
Bunyola *Spain* 39°41N 2°42E **24** B9
Bunyu *Indonesia* 3°35N 117°50E **36** D5
Buol *Indonesia* 1°15N 121°32E **37** D6
Buon Brieng *Vietnam* 13°9N 108°12E **38** F7
Buon Ma Thuot *Vietnam* 12°40N 108°3E **38** F7
Buong Long *Cambodia* 13°44N 106°59E **38** F6
Buorkhaya, Mys *Russia* 71°50N 132°40E **29** B14
Buqayq *Si. Arabia* 26°0N 49°45E **45** E6
Bur Acaba = Buurhakaba *Somali Rep.* 3°12N 44°20E **47** G3
Bûr Safâga *Egypt* 26°43N 33°57E **44** E2
Bûr Sa'îd *Egypt* 31°16N 32°18E **51** B12
Bûr Sûdân *Sudan* 19°32N 37°9E **51** E13
Bura *Kenya* 1°4S 39°58E **54** C4
Burakin *Australia* 30°31S 117°10E **61** F2
Burao = Burco *Somali Rep.* 9°32N 45°32E **47** F4
Burāq *Syria* 33°11N 36°29E **46** B5
Buraydah *Si. Arabia* 26°20N 43°59E **44** E4
Burbank *U.S.A.* 34°12N 118°18W **79** L8
Burco *Somali Rep.* 9°32N 45°32E **47** F4
Burda *India* 25°50N 77°35E **42** G6
Burdekin → *Australia* 19°38S 147°25E **62** B4
Burdur *Turkey* 37°45N 30°17E **19** G5
Burdwan = Barddhaman *India* 23°14N 87°39E **43** H12
Bure *Ethiopia* 10°40N 37°4E **47** E2
Bure → *U.K.* 52°38N 1°43E **12** E9
Bureya → *Russia* 49°27N 129°30E **29** E13
Burford *Canada* 43°7N 80°27W **82** C4
Burgas *Bulgaria* 42°33N 27°29E **23** C12
Burgeo *Canada* 47°37N 57°38W **73** C8
Burgersdorp *S. Africa* 31°0S 26°20E **56** E4
Burgess, Mt. *Australia* 30°50S 121°5E **61** F3
Burghead *U.K.* 57°43N 3°30W **11** D5
Burgos *Spain* 42°21N 3°41W **21** A4
Burgsvik *Sweden* 57°3N 18°19E **9** H18
Burgundy = Bourgogne □ *France* 47°0N 4°50E **20** C6
Burhaniye *Turkey* 39°30N 26°58E **23** E12
Burhanpur *India* 21°18N 76°14E **40** J10
Burhi Gandak → *India* 25°20N 86°37E **43** G12
Burhner → *India* 22°43N 80°31E **43** H9
Burias I. *Phil.* 12°55N 123°5E **37** B6
Burica, Pta. *Costa Rica* 8°3N 82°51W **88** E3
Burien *U.S.A.* 47°28N 122°20W **78** C4
Burigi, L. *Tanzania* 2°2S 31°22E **54** C3
Burigi ⌓ *Tanzania* 2°20S 31°6E **54** C3
Burin *Canada* 47°1N 55°14W **73** C8
Buriram *Thailand* 15°0N 103°0E **38** E4
Burkburnett *U.S.A.* 34°6N 98°34W **84** D5
Burke → *Australia* 23°12S 139°33E **62** C2
Burke Chan. *Canada* 52°10N 127°30W **70** C3
Burketown *Australia* 17°45S 139°33E **62** B2
Burkina Faso ■ *Africa* 12°0N 1°0W **50** F5
Burk's Falls *Canada* 45°37N 79°24W **72** C4
Burleigh Falls *Canada* 44°33N 78°12W **82** B6
Burley *U.S.A.* 42°32N 113°48W **76** E7
Burlingame *U.S.A.* 37°35N 122°21W **78** H4
Burlington *Canada* 43°18N 79°45W **82** C5
Burlington *Colo., U.S.A.* 39°18N 102°16W **76** G12
Burlington *Iowa, U.S.A.* 40°49N 91°14W **80** E8
Burlington *Kans., U.S.A.* 38°12N 95°45W **80** F6
Burlington *N.C., U.S.A.* 36°6N 79°26W **85** C15
Burlington *N.J., U.S.A.* 40°4N 74°51W **83** F10
Burlington *Vt., U.S.A.* 44°29N 73°12W **83** B11
Burlington *Wash., U.S.A.* 48°28N 122°20W **78** B4
Burlington *Wis., U.S.A.* 42°41N 88°17W **80** D9
Burma ■ *Asia* 21°0N 96°30E **41** J20
Burnaby I. *Canada* 52°25N 131°19W **70** C2
Burnet *U.S.A.* 30°45N 98°14W **84** F5
Burney *U.S.A.* 40°53N 121°40W **76** F3
Burnham *U.S.A.* 40°38N 77°34W **82** F7
Burnham-on-Sea *U.K.* 51°14N 3°0W **13** F5
Burnie *Australia* 41°4S 145°56E **63** G4
Burnley *U.K.* 53°47N 2°14W **12** D5
Burns *U.S.A.* 43°35N 119°3W **76** E4
Burns Junction *U.S.A.* 42°47N 117°51W **76** E5
Burns Lake *Canada* 54°14N 125°45W **70** C3
Burnside → *Canada* 66°51N 108°4W **68** D10
Burnside, L. *Australia* 25°22S 123°0E **61** E3
Burnsville *U.S.A.* 44°47N 93°17W **80** C7
Burnt River *Canada* 44°41N 78°42W **82** B6
Burntwood → *Canada* 56°8N 96°34W **71** B9
Burntwood L. *Canada* 55°22N 100°26W **71** B8
Burqān *Kuwait* 29°0N 47°57E **44** D5
Burqin *China* 47°43N 87°0E **32** B3
Burra *Australia* 33°40S 138°55E **63** E2
Burray *U.K.* 58°51N 2°54W **11** C6
Burren *Ireland* 53°9N 9°5W **10** C2
Burren △ *Ireland* 53°1N 8°58W **10** C3
Burren Junction *Australia* 30°7S 148°58E **63** E4
Burrinjuck, L. *Australia* 35°0S 148°36E **63** F4
Burro, Serranías del *Mexico* 28°56N 102°5W **86** B4
Burrow Hd. *U.K.* 54°41N 4°24W **11** G4
Burrum Coast △ *Australia* 25°13S 152°36E **63** D5
Burruyacú *Argentina* 26°30S 64°40W **94** B3
Burry Port *U.K.* 51°41N 4°15W **13** F3
Bursa *Turkey* 40°15N 29°5E **23** D13
Burstall *Canada* 50°39N 109°54W **71** C7
Burton *Ohio, U.S.A.* 41°28N 81°8W **82** E3
Burton *S.C., U.S.A.* 32°26N 80°43W **85** E14
Burton, L. *Canada* 54°45N 78°20W **72** B4
Burton upon Trent *U.K.* 52°48N 1°38W **12** E6
Buru *Indonesia* 3°30S 126°30E **37** E7
Burûn, Râs *Egypt* 31°14N 33°7E **46** D2
Burundi ■ *Africa* 3°15S 30°0E **54** C3
Bururi *Burundi* 3°57S 29°37E **54** C2
Burutu *Nigeria* 5°20N 5°29E **50** G7
Burwell *U.S.A.* 41°47N 99°8W **80** E4
Burwick *U.K.* 58°45N 2°58W **11** C5
Bury *U.K.* 53°35N 2°17W **12** D5
Bury St. Edmunds *U.K.* 52°15N 0°43E **13** E8
Buryatia □ *Russia* 53°0N 110°0E **29** D12
Busan *S. Korea* 35°5N 129°0E **35** G15
Busango Swamp *Zambia* 14°15S 25°45E **55** E2
Busaso = Boosaaso *Somali Rep.* 11°12N 49°18E **47** E4
Buşayrah *Syria* 35°9N 40°26E **44** C4
Būshehr *Iran* 28°55N 50°55E **45** D6
Būshehr □ *Iran* 28°20N 51°45E **45** D6
Bushenyi *Uganda* 0°35S 30°10E **54** C3
Bushire = Būshehr *Iran* 28°55N 50°55E **45** D6
Businga *Dem. Rep. of the Congo* 3°16N 20°59E **52** D4
Buşra ash Shām *Syria* 32°30N 36°25E **46** C5
Busselton *Australia* 33°42S 115°15E **61** F2
Bussum *Neths.* 52°16N 5°10E **15** B5
Busto Arsízio *Italy* 45°37N 8°51E **20** D8
Busu Djanoa *Dem. Rep. of the Congo* 1°43N 21°23E **52** D4
Busuanga I. *Phil.* 12°10N 120°0E **37** B6
Busungbiu *Indonesia* 8°16S 114°58E **37** J17
Buta *Dem. Rep. of the Congo* 2°50N 24°53E **54** B1
Butare *Rwanda* 2°31S 29°52E **54** C2
Butaritari *Kiribati* 3°30N 174°0E **64** G9
Bute *U.K.* 55°48N 5°2W **11** F3
Bute Inlet *Canada* 50°40N 124°53W **70** C4
Butemba *Uganda* 1°9N 31°37E **54** B3
Butembo *Dem. Rep. of the Congo* 0°9N 29°18E **54** B2
Butere *Kenya* 0°13N 34°30E **54** B3
Butha Qi *China* 48°0N 122°32E **33** B7
Butiaba *Uganda* 1°50N 31°20E **54** B3
Butler *Mo., U.S.A.* 38°16N 94°20W **80** F6
Butler *Pa., U.S.A.* 40°52N 79°54W **82** F5
Buton *Indonesia* 5°0S 122°45E **37** F6
Butte *Mont., U.S.A.* 46°0N 112°32W **76** C7
Butte *Nebr., U.S.A.* 42°58N 98°51W **80** D4
Butte Creek → *U.S.A.* 39°12N 121°56W **78** F5
Butterworth = Gcuwa *S. Africa* 32°20S 28°11E **57** E4
Butterworth *Malaysia* 5°24N 100°23E **39** c
Buttevant *Ireland* 52°14N 8°40W **10** D3
Buttfield, Mt. *Australia* 24°45S 128°9E **61** D4
Button B. *Canada* 58°45N 94°23W **71** B10
Buttonwillow *U.S.A.* 35°24N 119°28W **79** K7
Butty Hd. *Australia* 33°54S 121°39E **61** F3
Butuan *Phil.* 8°57N 125°33E **37** C7
Butung = Buton *Indonesia* 5°0S 122°45E **37** F6
Buturlinovka *Russia* 50°50N 40°35E **19** D7
Buurhakaba *Somali Rep.* 3°12N 44°20E **47** G3
Buxa Duar *India* 27°45N 89°35E **43** F13
Buxar *India* 25°34N 83°58E **43** G10
Buxoro *Uzbekistan* 39°48N 64°25E **28** F7
Buxtehude *Germany* 53°28N 9°39E **16** B5
Buxton *U.K.* 53°16N 1°54W **12** D6
Buy *Russia* 58°28N 41°28E **18** C7
Buyant-Uhaa *Mongolia* 44°55N 110°11E **33** B6
Buyo, L. de *Ivory C.* 6°16N 7°10W **50** G4
Büyük Menderes → *Turkey* 37°28N 27°11E **23** F12
Büyükçekmece *Turkey* 41°2N 28°35E **23** D13
Buzău *Romania* 45°10N 26°50E **17** F14
Buzău → *Romania* 45°26N 27°44E **17** F14
Buzen *Japan* 33°35N 131°5E **31** H5
Buzi → *Mozam.* 19°50S 34°43E **55** F3
Büzmeýin *Turkmenistan* 38°3N 58°12E **45** B8
Buzuluk *Russia* 52°48N 52°12E **18** D9
Buzzards Bay *U.S.A.* 41°45N 70°37W **83** E14
Bwana Mkubwe *Dem. Rep. of the Congo* 13°8S 28°38E **55** E2
Bwindi △ *Uganda* 1°2S 29°42E **54** C2
Byam Martin I. *Canada* 75°15N 104°15W **69** B11
Byarezina → *Belarus* 52°33N 30°14E **17** B16
Bydgoszcz *Poland* 53°10N 18°0E **17** B9
Byelorussia = Belarus ■ *Europe* 53°30N 27°0E **17** B14
Byers *U.S.A.* 39°43N 104°14W **76** G11
Byesville *U.S.A.* 39°58N 81°32W **82** G3
Byfield △ *Australia* 22°52S 150°45E **62** C5
Bykhaw *Belarus* 53°31N 30°14E **17** B16
Bykhov = Bykhaw *Belarus* 53°31N 30°14E **17** B16
Bylas *U.S.A.* 33°8N 110°7W **77** K8
Bylot *Canada* 58°25N 94°8W **71** B10
Bylot I. *Canada* 73°13N 78°34W **69** C16
Byrd, C. *Antarctica* 69°38S 76°7W **5** C17
Byrock *Australia* 30°40S 146°27E **63** E4
Byron, C. *Australia* 28°43S 153°38E **63** D5
Byron Bay *Australia* 28°43S 153°37E **63** D5
Byrranga, Gory *Russia* 75°0N 100°0E **29** B11
Byrranga Mts. = Byrranga, Gory *Russia* 75°0N 100°0E **29** B11
Byske *Sweden* 64°57N 21°11E **8** D19
Byskeälven → *Sweden* 64°57N 21°13E **8** D19
Bytom *Poland* 50°25N 18°54E **17** C10
Bytów *Poland* 54°10N 17°30E **17** A9
Byumba *Rwanda* 1°35S 30°4E **54** C3

C

C.W. McConaughy, L. *U.S.A.* 41°14N 101°40W **80** E3
Ca → *Vietnam* 18°45N 105°45E **38** C5
Ca Mau *Vietnam* 9°7N 105°8E **39** H5
Ca Mau, Mui *Vietnam* 8°38N 104°44E **39** H5
Ca Na *Vietnam* 11°20N 108°54E **39** G7
Caacupé *Paraguay* 25°23S 57°5W **94** B4
Caaguazú △ *Paraguay* 26°5S 55°31W **95** B4
Caála *Angola* 12°46S 15°30E **53** G3
Caamaño Sd. *Canada* 52°55N 129°25W **70** C3
Caazapá *Paraguay* 26°8S 56°19W **94** B4
Caazapá □ *Paraguay* 26°10S 56°0W **95** B4
Caballeria, C. de *Spain* 40°5N 4°5E **24** A11
Cabanatuan *Phil.* 15°30N 120°58E **37** A6
Cabano *Canada* 47°40N 68°56W **73** C6
Cabazon *U.S.A.* 33°55N 116°47W **79** M10
Cabedelo *Brazil* 7°0S 34°50W **93** E12
Cabildo *Chile* 32°30S 71°5W **94** C1
Cabimas *Venezuela* 10°23N 71°25W **92** A4
Cabinda *Angola* 5°33S 12°11E **52** F2
Cabinda □ *Angola* 5°0S 12°30E **52** F2
Cabinet Mts. *U.S.A.* 48°10N 115°50W **76** B6
Cabo Blanco *Argentina* 47°15S 65°47W **96** F3
Cabo Frio *Brazil* 22°51S 42°3W **95** A7
Cabo Pantoja *Peru* 1°0S 75°10W **92** D3
Cabo San Lucas *Mexico* 22°53N 109°54W **86** C3
Cabo Verde = Cape Verde Is. ■ *Atl. Oc.* 16°0N 24°0W **50** b
Cabonga, Réservoir *Canada* 47°20N 76°40W **72** C4
Cabool *U.S.A.* 37°7N 92°6W **80** G7
Caboolture *Australia* 27°5S 152°58E **63** D5
Cabora Bassa Dam = Cahora Bassa, Lago de *Mozam.* 15°20S 32°50E **55** F3
Caborca *Mexico* 30°37N 112°6W **86** A2
Cabot, Mt. *U.S.A.* 44°30N 71°25W **83** B13

Cabot Hd. *Canada* 45°14N 81°17W 82 A3
Cabot Str. *Canada* 47°15N 59°40W 73 C8
Cabra *Spain* 37°30N 4°28W 21 D3
Cabrera *Spain* 39°8N 2°57E 24 B9
Cabri *Canada* 50°35N 108°25W 71 C7
Cabriel → *Spain* 39°14N 1°3W 21 C5
Caçador *Brazil* 26°47S 51°0W 95 B5
Čačak *Serbia* 43°54N 20°20E 23 C9
Caçapava do Sul *Brazil* 30°30S 53°30W 95 C5
Cáceres *Brazil* 16°5S 57°40W 92 G7
Cáceres *Spain* 39°26N 6°23W 21 C2
Cache Bay *Canada* 46°22N 80°0W 72 C4
Cache Cr. → *U.S.A.* 38°42N 121°42W 78 G5
Cache Creek *Canada* 50°48N 121°19W 70 C4
Cachi *Argentina* 25°5S 66°10W 94 B2
Cachimbo, Serra do *Brazil* 9°30S 55°30W 93 E7
Cachinal de la Sierra *Chile* 24°58S 69°32W 94 A2
Cachoeira *Brazil* 12°30S 39°0W 93 F11
Cachoeira do Sul *Brazil* 30°3S 52°53W 95 C5
Cachoeiro de Itapemirim *Brazil* 20°51S 41°7W 95 A7
Cacoal *Brazil* 11°32S 61°18W 92 F6
Cacólo *Angola* 10°9S 19°21E 52 G3
Caconda *Angola* 13°48S 15°8E 53 G3
Caddo *U.S.A.* 34°7N 96°16W 84 D6
Cader Idris *U.K.* 52°42N 3°53W 13 E4
Cadereyta de Jiménez *Mexico* 25°36N 100°0W 86 B5
Cadibarrawirracanna, L. *Australia* 28°52S 135°27E 63 D2
Cadillac *U.S.A.* 44°15N 85°24W 81 C11
Cadiz *Phil.* 10°57N 123°15E 37 B6
Cádiz *Spain* 36°30N 6°20W 21 D2
Cadiz *Calif., U.S.A.* 34°30N 115°28W 79 L11
Cadiz *Ohio, U.S.A.* 40°22N 81°0W 82 F4
Cádiz, G. de *Spain* 36°40N 7°0W 21 D2
Cadiz L. *U.S.A.* 34°18N 115°24W 77 J6
Cadney Park *Australia* 27°55S 134°3E 63 D1
Cadomin *Canada* 53°2N 117°20W 70 C5
Cadotte Lake *Canada* 56°26N 116°23W 70 B5
Cadoux *Australia* 30°46S 117°7E 61 F2
Caen *France* 49°10N 0°22W 20 B3
Caernarfon *U.K.* 53°8N 4°16W 12 D3
Caernarfon B. *U.K.* 53°4N 4°40W 12 D3
Caernarvon = Caernarfon *U.K.* 53°8N 4°16W 12 D3
Caerphilly *U.K.* 51°35N 3°13W 13 F4
Caerphilly □ *U.K.* 51°37N 3°12W 13 F4
Caesarea *Israel* 32°30N 34°53E 46 C3
Caetité *Brazil* 13°50S 42°32W 93 F10
Cafayate *Argentina* 26°2S 66°0W 94 B2
Cafu *Angola* 16°30S 15°8E 56 B2
Cagayan de Oro *Phil.* 8°30N 124°40E 37 C6
Cagayan Is. *Phil.* 9°40N 121°16E 37 C5
Cágliari *Italy* 39°13N 9°7E 22 E3
Cágliari, G. di *Italy* 39°8N 9°11E 22 E3
Caguán → *Colombia* 0°8S 74°18W 92 D4
Caguas *Puerto Rico* 18°14N 66°2W 89 d
Caha Mts. *Ireland* 51°45N 9°40W 10 E2
Cahama *Angola* 16°17S 14°19E 56 B1
Caher *Ireland* 52°22N 7°56W 10 D4
Cahersiveen *Ireland* 51°56N 10°14W 10 E1
Cahora Bassa, Lago de *Mozam.* 15°20S 32°50E 55 F3
Cahore Pt. *Ireland* 52°33N 6°12W 10 D5
Cahors *France* 44°27N 1°27E 20 D4
Cahul *Moldova* 45°50N 28°15E 17 F15
Cai Bau, Dao *Vietnam* 21°10N 107°27E 38 B6
Cai Nuoc *Vietnam* 8°56N 105°1E 39 H5
Caia *Mozam.* 17°51S 35°24E 55 F4
Caianda *Angola* 11°2S 23°31E 55 E1
Caibarién *Cuba* 22°30N 79°30W 88 B4
Caicara *Venezuela* 7°38N 66°10W 92 B5
Caicó *Brazil* 6°20S 37°0W 93 E11
Caicos Is. *Turks & Caicos* 21°40N 71°40W 89 B5
Caicos Passage *W. Indies* 22°45N 72°45W 89 B5
Caiguna *Australia* 32°16S 125°29E 61 F4
Caird Coast *Antarctica* 75°0S 25°0W 5 D1
Cairn Gorm *U.K.* 57°7N 3°39W 11 D5
Cairngorm Mts. *U.K.* 57°6N 3°42W 11 D5
Cairngorms △ *U.K.* 57°10N 3°50W 11 D5
Cairnryan *U.K.* 54°59N 5°1W 11 G3
Cairns *Australia* 16°57S 145°45E 62 B4
Cairns L. *Canada* 51°42N 94°30W 71 C10
Cairo = El Qâhira *Egypt* 30°2N 31°13E 51 B12
Cairo *Ga., U.S.A.* 30°52N 84°13W 85 F12
Cairo *Ill., U.S.A.* 37°0N 89°11W 80 G9
Cairo *N.Y., U.S.A.* 42°18N 74°0W 83 D10
Caiseal = Cashel *Ireland* 52°30N 7°53W 10 D4
Caisleán an Bharraigh = Castlebar *Ireland* 53°52N 9°18W 10 C2
Caithness *U.K.* 58°25N 3°35W 11 C5
Caithness, Ord of *U.K.* 58°8N 3°36W 11 C5
Caja de Muertos, I. *Puerto Rico* 17°54N 66°32W 89 d
Cajamarca *Peru* 7°5S 78°28W 92 E3
Cajazeiras *Brazil* 6°52S 38°30W 93 E11
Cala d'Or *Spain* 39°23N 3°14E 24 B10
Cala en Porter *Spain* 39°52N 4°8E 24 B11
Cala Figuera *Spain* 39°20N 3°10E 24 B10
Cala Figuera, C. de *Spain* 39°27N 2°31E 24 B9
Cala Forcat *Spain* 40°0N 3°47E 24 B10
Cala Major *Spain* 39°33N 2°37E 24 B9
Cala Mezquida = Sa Mesquida *Spain* 39°55N 4°16E 24 B11
Cala Millor *Spain* 39°35N 3°22E 24 B10
Cala Murada *Spain* 39°27N 3°17E 24 B10
Cala Ratjada *Spain* 39°43N 3°27E 24 B10
Cala Santa Galdana *Spain* 39°56N 3°58E 24 B10
Calabar *Nigeria* 4°57N 8°20E 50 H7
Calabogie *Canada* 45°18N 76°43W 83 A8
Calabozo *Venezuela* 9°0N 67°28W 92 B5
Calábria □ *Italy* 39°0N 16°30E 22 E7
Calahorra *Spain* 42°18N 1°59W 21 A5
Calais *France* 50°57N 1°56E 20 A4
Calais *U.S.A.* 45°11N 67°17W 81 C20
Calakmul ⌓ *Mexico* 18°14N 89°48W 87 D7
Calalaste, Cord. de *Argentina* 25°0S 67°0W 94 B2
Calama *Brazil* 8°0S 62°50W 92 E6
Calama *Chile* 22°30S 68°55W 94 A2
Calamar *Colombia* 10°15N 74°55W 92 A4
Calamian Group *Phil.* 11°50N 119°55E 37 B5
Calamocha *Spain* 40°50N 1°17W 21 B5
Calang *Indonesia* 4°37N 95°37E 36 D1
Calanscio, Sarīr *Libya* 27°30N 21°30E 51 C10
Calapan *Phil.* 13°25N 121°7E 37 B6
Călăraşi *Romania* 44°12N 27°20E 17 F14
Calatayud *Spain* 41°20N 1°40W 21 B5
Calauag *Phil.* 13°55N 122°15E 37 B6
Calavite, C. *Phil.* 13°26N 120°20E 37 B6
Calbayog *Phil.* 12°4N 124°38E 37 B6
Calca *Peru* 13°22S 72°0W 92 F4
Calcasieu L. *U.S.A.* 29°55N 93°18W 84 G8
Calcium *U.S.A.* 44°1N 75°50W 83 B9
Calcutta = Kolkata *India* 22°34N 88°21E 43 H13
Calcutta *U.S.A.* 40°40N 80°34W 82 F4
Caldas da Rainha *Portugal* 39°24N 9°8W 21 C1
Calder → *U.K.* 53°44N 1°22W 12 D6
Caldera *Chile* 27°5S 70°55W 94 B1
Caldera de Taburiente △ *Canary Is.* 28°43N 17°52W 24 F2
Caldwell *Idaho, U.S.A.* 43°40N 116°41W 76 E5
Caldwell *Kans., U.S.A.* 37°2N 97°37W 80 G5
Caldwell *Tex., U.S.A.* 30°32N 96°42W 84 F6
Caledon *Canada* 43°51N 79°51W 82 C5
Caledon *S. Africa* 34°14S 19°26E 56 E2
Caledon → *S. Africa* 30°31S 26°5E 56 E4
Caledon B. *Australia* 12°45S 137°0E 62 A2
Caledonia *Canada* 43°7N 79°58W 82 C5
Caledonia *U.S.A.* 42°58N 77°51W 82 D7
Calemba *Angola* 16°0S 15°44E 56 B2
Calen *Australia* 20°56S 148°48E 62 b
Caletones *Chile* 34°6S 70°27W 94 C1
Calexico *U.S.A.* 32°40N 115°30W 79 N11
Calf of Man *I. of Man* 54°3N 4°48W 12 C3
Calgary *Canada* 51°0N 114°10W 70 C6
Calheta *Madeira* 32°44N 17°11W 24 D2
Calhoun *U.S.A.* 34°30N 84°57W 85 D12
Cali *Colombia* 3°25N 76°35W 92 C3
Calicut *India* 11°15N 75°43E 40 P9
Caliente *U.S.A.* 37°37N 114°31W 77 H6
California *Mo., U.S.A.* 38°38N 92°34W 80 F7
California *Pa., U.S.A.* 40°4N 79°54W 82 F5
California □ *U.S.A.* 37°30N 119°30W 78 H7
California, Baja, T.N. = Baja California □ *Mexico* 30°0N 115°0W 86 B2
California, Baja, T.S. = Baja California Sur □ *Mexico* 25°50N 111°50W 86 B2
California, G. de *Mexico* 27°0N 111°0W 86 B2
California City *U.S.A.* 35°10N 117°55W 79 K9
California Hot Springs *U.S.A.* 35°51N 118°41W 79 K8
Calilegua △ *Argentina* 25°36S 64°50W 94 B3
Calingasta *Argentina* 31°15S 69°30W 94 C2
Calipatria *U.S.A.* 33°8N 115°31W 79 M11
Calistoga *U.S.A.* 38°35N 122°35W 78 G4
Calitzdorp *S. Africa* 33°33S 21°42E 56 E3
Callabonna, L. *Australia* 29°40S 140°5E 63 D3
Callan *Ireland* 52°32N 7°24W 10 D4
Callander *U.K.* 56°15N 4°13W 11 E4
Callao *Peru* 12°3S 77°8W 92 F3
Callicoon *U.S.A.* 41°46N 75°3W 83 E9
Calling Lake *Canada* 55°15N 113°12W 70 B6
Calliope *Australia* 24°0S 151°16E 62 C5
Calma, Costa de la *Spain* 39°28N 2°26E 24 B9
Calne *U.K.* 51°26N 2°0W 13 F6
Calola *Angola* 16°25S 17°48E 56 B2
Caloundra *Australia* 26°45S 153°10E 63 D5
Calpella *U.S.A.* 39°14N 123°12W 78 F3
Calpine *U.S.A.* 39°40N 120°27W 78 F6
Calstock *Canada* 49°47N 84°9W 72 C3
Caltagirone *Italy* 37°14N 14°31E 22 F6
Caltanissetta *Italy* 37°29N 14°4E 22 F6
Calulo *Angola* 10°1S 14°56E 52 G2
Calvert → *Australia* 16°17S 137°44E 62 B2
Calvert I. *Canada* 51°30N 128°0W 70 C3
Calvert Ra. *Australia* 24°0S 122°30E 60 D3
Calvi *France* 42°34N 8°45E 20 E8
Calvià *Spain* 39°34N 2°31E 24 B9
Calvillo *Mexico* 21°51N 102°43W 86 C4
Calvinia *S. Africa* 31°28S 19°45E 56 E2
Calwa *U.S.A.* 36°42N 119°46W 78 J7
Cam → *U.K.* 52°21N 0°16E 13 E8
Cam Lam *Vietnam* 11°54N 109°10E 39 G7
Cam Pha *Vietnam* 21°7N 107°18E 38 B6
Cam Ranh *Vietnam* 11°54N 109°12E 39 G7
Cam Xuyen *Vietnam* 18°15N 106°0E 38 C6
Camabatela *Angola* 8°20S 15°26E 52 F3
Camacha *Madeira* 32°41N 16°49W 24 D3
Camacupa *Angola* 11°58S 17°22E 53 G3
Camagüey *Cuba* 21°20N 77°55W 88 B4
Camaná *Peru* 16°30S 72°50W 92 G4
Camanche Res. *U.S.A.* 38°14N 121°1W 78 G6
Camaquã *Brazil* 30°51S 51°49W 95 C5
Camaquã → *Brazil* 31°17S 51°47W 95 C5
Câmara de Lobos *Madeira* 32°39N 16°59W 24 D3
Camargo *Mexico* 26°19N 98°50W 87 B5
Camarillo *U.S.A.* 34°13N 119°2W 79 L7
Camarón, C. *Honduras* 16°0N 85°5W 88 C2
Camarones *Argentina* 44°50S 65°40W 96 E3
Camas *U.S.A.* 45°35N 122°24W 78 E4
Camas Valley *U.S.A.* 43°2N 123°40W 76 E2
Camballin *Australia* 17°59S 124°12E 60 C3
Cambará *Brazil* 23°2S 50°5W 95 A5
Cambay = Khambhat *India* 22°23N 72°33E 42 H5
Cambay, G. of = Khambhat, G. of *India* 20°45N 72°30E 40 J8
Cambodia ■ *Asia* 12°15N 105°0E 38 F5
Camborne *U.K.* 50°12N 5°19W 13 G2
Cambrai *France* 50°11N 3°14E 20 A5
Cambria *U.S.A.* 35°34N 121°5W 78 K5
Cambrian Mts. *U.K.* 52°3N 3°57W 13 E4
Cambridge *Canada* 43°23N 80°15W 82 C4
Cambridge *Jamaica* 18°18N 77°54W 88 a
Cambridge *N.Z.* 37°54S 175°29E 59 B5
Cambridge *U.K.* 52°12N 0°8E 13 E8
Cambridge *Mass., U.S.A.* 42°23N 71°7W 83 D13
Cambridge *Minn., U.S.A.* 45°34N 93°13W 80 C7
Cambridge *N.Y., U.S.A.* 43°2N 73°22W 83 C11
Cambridge *Nebr., U.S.A.* 40°17N 100°10W 80 E3
Cambridge *Ohio, U.S.A.* 40°2N 81°35W 82 F3
Cambridge Bay *Canada* 69°10N 105°0W 68 D11
Cambridge G. *Australia* 14°55S 128°15E 60 B4
Cambridge Springs *U.S.A.* 41°48N 80°4W 82 E4
Cambridgeshire □ *U.K.* 52°25N 0°7W 13 E7
Cambuci *Brazil* 21°35S 41°55W 95 A7
Cambundi-Catembo *Angola* 10°10S 17°35E 52 G3
Camden *Australia* 34°1S 150°43E 63 B5
Camden *Ala., U.S.A.* 31°59N 87°17W 85 F11
Camden *Ark., U.S.A.* 33°35N 92°50W 84 E8
Camden *Maine, U.S.A.* 44°13N 69°4W 81 C19
Camden *N.J., U.S.A.* 39°55N 75°7W 83 G9
Camden *N.Y., U.S.A.* 43°20N 75°45W 83 C9
Camden *S.C., U.S.A.* 34°16N 80°36W 85 D14
Camden Sd. *Australia* 15°27S 124°25E 60 C3
Camdenton *U.S.A.* 38°1N 92°45W 80 F7
Camelford *U.K.* 50°37N 4°42W 13 G3
Cameron *Ariz., U.S.A.* 35°53N 111°25W 77 J8
Cameron *La., U.S.A.* 29°48N 93°20W 84 G8
Cameron *Mo., U.S.A.* 39°44N 94°14W 80 F6
Cameron *Tex., U.S.A.* 30°51N 96°59W 84 F6
Cameron Highlands *Malaysia* 4°27N 101°22E 39 K3
Cameron Hills *Canada* 59°48N 118°0W 70 B5
Cameroon ■ *Africa* 6°0N 12°30E 51 G7
Cameroun, Mt. *Cameroon* 4°13N 9°10E 52 D1
Cametá *Brazil* 2°12S 49°30W 93 D9
Camiguin I. *Phil.* 18°56N 121°55E 37 C6
Camilla *U.S.A.* 31°14N 84°12W 85 F12
Caminha *Portugal* 41°50N 8°50W 21 B1
Camino *U.S.A.* 38°44N 120°41W 78 G6
Cammal *U.S.A.* 41°24N 77°28W 82 E7
Camocim *Brazil* 2°55S 40°50W 93 D10
Camooweal *Australia* 19°56S 138°7E 62 B2
Camooweal Caves △ *Australia* 20°1S 138°11E 62 C2
Camopi *Fr. Guiana* 3°12N 52°17W 93 C8
Camp Hill *U.S.A.* 40°14N 76°55W 82 F8
Camp Nelson *U.S.A.* 36°8N 118°39W 79 J8
Camp Pendleton *U.S.A.* 33°13N 117°24W 79 M9
Camp Verde *U.S.A.* 34°34N 111°51W 77 J8
Camp Wood *U.S.A.* 29°40N 100°1W 84 G4
Campana *Argentina* 34°10S 58°55W 94 C4
Campana, I. *Chile* 48°20S 75°20W 96 F1
Campanário *Madeira* 32°39N 17°2W 24 D2
Campanet *Spain* 39°46N 2°58E 24 B9
Campánia □ *Italy* 41°0N 14°30E 22 D6
Campbell *S. Africa* 28°48S 23°44E 56 D3
Campbell *Calif., U.S.A.* 37°17N 121°57W 78 H5
Campbell *Ohio, U.S.A.* 41°5N 80°37W 82 E4
Campbell I. *Pac. Oc.* 52°30S 169°0E 64 N8
Campbell L. *Canada* 63°14N 106°55W 71 A7
Campbell Plateau *S. Ocean* 50°0S 170°0E 5 A11
Campbell River *Canada* 50°5N 125°20W 70 C3
Campbellford *Canada* 44°18N 77°48W 82 B7
Campbellpur *Pakistan* 33°46N 72°26E 42 C5
Campbellsville *U.S.A.* 37°21N 85°20W 81 G11
Campbellton *Canada* 47°57N 66°43W 73 C6
Campbelltown *Australia* 34°4S 150°49E 63 E5
Campbeltown *U.K.* 55°26N 5°36W 11 F3
Campeche *Mexico* 19°51N 90°32W 87 D6
Campeche □ *Mexico* 19°0N 90°30W 87 D6
Campeche, Golfo de *Mexico* 19°30N 93°0W 87 D6
Camperdown *Australia* 38°14S 143°9E 63 F3
Camperville *Canada* 51°59N 100°9W 71 C8
Câmpina *Romania* 45°10N 25°45E 17 F13
Campina Grande *Brazil* 7°20S 35°47W 93 E11
Campinas *Brazil* 22°50S 47°0W 95 A6
Campo Grande *Brazil* 20°25S 54°40W 93 H8
Campo Maior *Brazil* 4°50S 42°12W 93 D10
Campo Mourão *Brazil* 24°3S 52°22W 95 A5
Campobasso *Italy* 41°34N 14°39E 22 D6
Campos *Brazil* 21°50S 41°20W 95 A7
Campos *Spain* 39°26N 3°1E 24 B10
Campos Belos *Brazil* 13°10S 47°3W 93 F9
Campos Novos *Brazil* 27°21S 51°50W 95 B5
Camptonville *U.S.A.* 39°27N 121°3W 78 F5
Camptown *U.S.A.* 41°44N 76°14W 83 E8
Câmpulung *Romania* 45°17N 25°3E 17 F13
Camrose *Canada* 53°0N 112°50W 70 C6
Camsell Portage *Canada* 59°37N 109°15W 71 B7
Çan *Turkey* 40°2N 27°3E 23 D12
Can Clavo *Spain* 38°57N 1°27E 24 C7
Can Creu *Spain* 38°58N 1°28E 24 C7
Can Gio *Vietnam* 10°25N 106°58E 39 G6
Can Pastilla *Spain* 39°32N 2°42E 24 B9
Can Tho *Vietnam* 10°2N 105°46E 39 G5
Canaan *U.S.A.* 42°2N 73°20W 83 D11
Canada ■ *N. Amer.* 60°0N 100°0W 68 G11
Canada Abyssal Plain *Arctic* 80°0N 140°0W 4 B18
Canada Basin *Arctic* 80°0N 145°0W 4 B18
Cañada de Gómez *Argentina* 32°40S 61°30W 94 C3
Canadian *U.S.A.* 35°55N 100°23W 84 D4
Canadian → *U.S.A.* 35°28N 95°3W 84 D7
Canadian Shield *Canada* 53°0N 75°0W 66 D12
Canajoharie *U.S.A.* 42°54N 74°35W 83 D10
Çanakkale *Turkey* 40°8N 26°24E 23 D12
Çanakkale Boğazı *Turkey* 40°17N 26°32E 23 D12
Canal Flats *Canada* 50°10N 115°48W 70 C5
Canalejas *Argentina* 35°15S 66°34W 94 D2
Canals *Argentina* 33°35S 62°53W 94 C3
Canandaigua *U.S.A.* 42°54N 77°17W 82 D7
Canandaigua L. *U.S.A.* 42°47N 77°19W 82 D7
Cananea *Mexico* 31°0N 110°18W 86 A2
Canarias, Is. *Atl. Oc.* 28°30N 16°0W 24 F4
Canaries *St. Lucia* 13°55N 61°4W 89 f
Canarreos, Arch. de los *Cuba* 21°35N 81°40W 88 B3
Canary Is. = Canarias, Is. *Atl. Oc.* 28°30N 16°0W 24 F4
Canaseraga *U.S.A.* 42°27N 77°45W 82 D7
Canatlán *Mexico* 24°31N 104°47W 86 C4
Canaveral, C. *U.S.A.* 28°27N 80°32W 85 G14
Canaveral ⌓ *U.S.A.* 28°28N 80°34W 85 G14
Canavieiras *Brazil* 15°39S 39°0W 93 G11
Canberra *Australia* 35°15S 149°8E 63 F4
Canby *Calif., U.S.A.* 41°27N 120°52W 76 F3
Canby *Minn., U.S.A.* 44°43N 96°16W 80 C5
Canby *Oreg., U.S.A.* 45°16N 122°42W 78 E4
Cancún *Mexico* 21°8N 86°44W 87 C7
Candelaria *Argentina* 27°29S 55°44W 95 B4
Candelaria *Canary Is.* 28°22N 16°22W 24 F3
Candelo *Australia* 36°47S 149°43E 63 F4
Candi Dasa *Indonesia* 8°30S 115°34E 37 J18
Candia = Iraklio *Greece* 35°20N 25°12E 25 D7
Candle L. *Canada* 53°50N 105°18W 71 C7
Candlemas I. *Antarctica* 57°3S 26°40W 5 B1
Cando *U.S.A.* 48°32N 99°12W 80 A4
Canea = Chania *Greece* 35°30N 24°4E 25 D6
Canelones *Uruguay* 34°32S 56°17W 95 C4
Cañete *Chile* 37°50S 73°30W 94 D1
Cangas del Narcea *Spain* 43°10N 6°32W 21 A2
Canguaretama *Brazil* 6°20S 35°5W 93 E11
Canguçu *Brazil* 31°22S 52°43W 95 C5
Canguçu, Serra do *Brazil* 31°20S 52°40W 95 C5
Cangzhou *China* 38°19N 116°52E 34 E9
Caniapiscau → *Canada* 56°40N 69°30W 73 A6
Caniapiscau, L. *Canada* 54°10N 69°55W 73 B6
Canicattì *Italy* 37°21N 13°51E 22 F5
Canim Lake *Canada* 51°47N 120°54W 70 C4
Canindeyu □ *Paraguay* 24°10S 55°0W 95 A5
Canisteo *U.S.A.* 42°16N 77°36W 82 D7
Canisteo → *U.S.A.* 42°7N 77°8W 82 D7
Cañitas de Felipe Pescador *Mexico* 23°36N 102°43W 86 C4
Çankırı *Turkey* 40°40N 33°37E 19 F5
Cankuzo *Burundi* 3°10S 30°31E 54 C3
Canmore *Canada* 51°7N 115°18W 70 C5
Cann River *Australia* 37°35S 149°7E 63 F4
Canna *U.K.* 57°3N 6°33W 11 D2
Cannanore *India* 11°53N 75°27E 40 P9
Cannes *France* 43°32N 7°1E 20 E7
Canning Town = Port Canning *India* 22°23N 88°40E 43 H13
Cannington *Canada* 44°20N 79°2W 82 B5
Cannock *U.K.* 52°41N 2°1W 13 E5
Cannonball → *U.S.A.* 46°26N 100°35W 80 B3
Cannondale Mt. *Australia* 25°13S 148°57E 62 D4
Cannonsville Res. *U.S.A.* 42°4N 75°22W 83 D9
Cannonvale *Australia* 20°17S 148°43E 62 b
Canoas *Brazil* 29°56S 51°11W 95 B5
Canoe L. *Canada* 55°10N 108°15W 71 B7
Cañon City *U.S.A.* 38°27N 105°14W 76 G11
Cañón de Río Blanco △ *Mexico* 18°43N 97°15W 87 D5
Cañón del Sumidero △ *Mexico* 19°22N 96°24W 87 D5
Canonniers Pt. *Mauritius* 20°2S 57°32E 53 d
Canora *Canada* 51°40N 102°30W 71 C8
Canowindra *Australia* 33°35S 148°38E 63 E4
Canso *Canada* 45°20N 61°0W 73 C7
Cantabria □ *Spain* 43°10N 4°0W 21 A4
Cantabrian Mts. = Cantábrica, Cordillera *Spain* 43°0N 5°10W 21 A3
Cantábrica, Cordillera *Spain* 43°0N 5°10W 21 A3
Cantal, Plomb du *France* 45°3N 2°45E 20 D5
Canterbury *Australia* 25°23S 141°53E 62 D3
Canterbury *U.K.* 51°16N 1°6E 13 F9
Canterbury Bight *N.Z.* 44°16S 171°55E 59 F3
Canterbury Plains *N.Z.* 43°55S 171°22E 59 E3
Cantil *U.S.A.* 35°18N 117°58W 79 K9
Canton = Guangzhou *China* 23°6N 113°13E 33 D6
Canton *Ga., U.S.A.* 34°14N 84°29W 85 D12
Canton *Ill., U.S.A.* 40°33N 90°2W 80 E8
Canton *Miss., U.S.A.* 32°37N 90°2W 85 E9
Canton *Mo., U.S.A.* 40°8N 91°32W 80 E8
Canton *N.Y., U.S.A.* 44°36N 75°10W 83 B9
Canton *Ohio, U.S.A.* 40°48N 81°23W 82 F3
Canton *Pa., U.S.A.* 41°39N 76°51W 82 E8
Canton *S. Dak., U.S.A.* 43°18N 96°35W 80 D5
Canton L. *U.S.A.* 36°6N 98°35W 84 C5
Canudos *Brazil* 7°13S 58°5W 92 E7
Canumã → *Brazil* 3°55S 59°10W 92 D7
Canutama *Brazil* 6°30S 64°20W 92 E6
Canutillo *U.S.A.* 31°55N 106°36W 84 F1
Canvey *U.K.* 51°31N 0°37E 13 F8
Canyon *U.S.A.* 34°59N 101°55W 84 D4
Canyon De Chelly ⌓ *U.S.A.* 36°10N 109°20W 77 H9
Canyonlands △ *U.S.A.* 38°15N 110°0W 77 G9
Canyons of the Ancients ⌓ *U.S.A.* 37°30N 108°55W 77 H9
Canyonville *U.S.A.* 42°56N 123°17W 76 E2
Cao Bang *Vietnam* 22°40N 106°15E 38 A6
Cao He → *China* 40°10N 124°32E 35 D13
Cao Lanh *Vietnam* 10°27N 105°38E 39 G5
Cao Xian *China* 34°50N 115°35E 34 G8
Cap-aux-Meules *Canada* 47°23N 61°52W 73 C7
Cap-Chat *Canada* 49°6N 66°40W 73 C6
Cap-de-la-Madeleine *Canada* 46°22N 72°31W 72 C5
Cap-Haïtien *Haiti* 19°40N 72°20W 89 C5
Cap Pt. *St. Lucia* 14°7N 60°57W 89 f
Capac *U.S.A.* 43°1N 82°56W 82 C2
Capanaparo → *Venezuela* 7°1N 67°7W 92 B5
Cape → *Australia* 20°59S 146°51E 62 C4
Cape Arid △ *Australia* 33°58S 123°13E 61 F3
Cape Barren I. *Australia* 40°25S 148°15E 63 G4
Cape Breton Highlands △ *Canada* 46°50N 60°40W 73 C7
Cape Breton I. *Canada* 46°0N 60°30W 73 C7
Cape Charles *U.S.A.* 37°16N 76°1W 81 G15
Cape Coast *Ghana* 5°5N 1°15W 50 G5
Cape Cod ⌓ *U.S.A.* 41°56N 70°6W 81 E18
Cape Coral *U.S.A.* 26°33N 81°57W 85 H14
Cape Crawford *Australia* 16°41S 135°43E 62 B2
Cape Dorset = Kinngait *Canada* 64°14N 76°32W 69 E16
Cape Fear → *U.S.A.* 33°53N 78°1W 85 E15
Cape Girardeau *U.S.A.* 37°19N 89°32W 80 G9
Cape Hatteras ⌓ *U.S.A.* 35°30N 75°28W 85 D17
Cape Hillsborough △ *Australia* 20°54S 149°2E 62 b
Cape Le Grand △ *Australia* 33°54S 122°26E 61 F3
Cape Lookout ⌓ *U.S.A.* 35°45N 76°25W 85 D16
Cape May *U.S.A.* 38°56N 74°56W 81 F16
Cape May Point *U.S.A.* 38°56N 74°58W 81 F16
Cape Melville △ *Australia* 14°26S 144°28E 62 A3
Cape Range △ *Australia* 22°3S 114°0E 60 D1
Cape St. George *Canada* 48°28N 59°14W 73 C8
Cape Tormentine *Canada* 46°8N 63°47W 73 C7
Cape Town *S. Africa* 33°55S 18°22E 56 E2
Cape Upstart △ *Australia* 19°45S 147°48E 62 B4
Cape Verde Is. ■ *Atl. Oc.* 16°0N 24°0W 50 b
Cape Vincent *U.S.A.* 44°8N 76°20W 83 B8
Cape York Peninsula *Australia* 12°0S 142°30E 62 A3
Capela *Brazil* 10°30S 37°0W 93 F11
Capella *Australia* 23°2S 148°1E 62 C4
Capesterre-Belle-Eau *Guadeloupe* 16°4N 61°36W 88 b
Capesterre-de-Marie-Galante *Guadeloupe* 15°53N 61°14W 88 b
Capim → *Brazil* 1°40S 47°47W 93 D9
Capitan *U.S.A.* 33°35N 105°35W 77 K11
Capitán Arturo Prat *Antarctica* 63°0S 61°0W 5 C17
Capitol Reef △ *U.S.A.* 38°15N 111°10W 77 G8
Capitola *U.S.A.* 36°59N 121°57W 78 J5
Capoche → *Mozam.* 15°35S 33°0E 55 F3
Capraia *Italy* 43°2N 9°50E 20 E8
Capreol *Canada* 46°43N 80°56W 72 C3
Capri *Italy* 40°33N 14°14E 22 D6
Capricorn Coast *Australia* 23°16S 150°49E 62 C5
Capricorn Group *Australia* 23°30S 151°55E 62 C5
Capricorn Ra. *Australia* 23°20S 116°50E 60 D2
Caprivi Game △ *Namibia* 17°55S 22°37E 56 B3
Caprivi Strip *Namibia* 18°0S 23°0E 56 B3
Captains Flat *Australia* 35°35S 149°27E 63 F4
Capulin Volcano ⌓ *U.S.A.* 36°47N 103°58W 84 C3
Caquetá → *Colombia* 1°15S 69°15W 92 D5
Caracal *Romania* 44°8N 24°22E 17 F13
Caracas *Venezuela* 10°30N 66°55W 92 A5
Caracol *Belize* 16°45N 89°6W 88 C2
Caracol *Mato Grosso do Sul, Brazil* 22°18S 57°1W 94 A4
Caracol *Piauí, Brazil* 9°15S 43°22W 93 E10
Carajas *Brazil* 6°5S 50°23W 93 E8
Carajás, Serra dos *Brazil* 6°0S 51°30W 93 E8
Carangola *Brazil* 20°44S 42°5W 95 A7
Caransebeş *Romania* 45°28N 22°18E 17 F12
Caraquet *Canada* 47°48N 64°57W 73 C6
Caratasca, L. de *Honduras* 15°20N 83°40W 88 C3
Caratinga *Brazil* 19°50S 42°10W 93 G10
Caraúbas *Brazil* 5°43S 37°33W 93 E11
Caravaca de la Cruz *Spain* 38°8N 1°52W 21 C5
Caravelas *Brazil* 17°45S 39°15W 93 G11
Caraveli *Peru* 15°45S 73°25W 92 G4
Caravelle, Presqu'île de la *Martinique* 14°46N 60°48W 88 c
Caraz *Peru* 9°3S 77°47W 92 E3
Carazinho *Brazil* 28°16S 52°46W 95 B5
Carballo *Spain* 43°13N 8°41W 21 A1
Carberry *Canada* 49°50N 99°25W 71 D9
Carbó *Mexico* 29°42N 110°58W 86 B2
Carbón, L. del *Argentina* 49°35S 68°21W 90 G3
Carbonara, C. *Italy* 39°6N 9°31E 22 E3
Carbondale *Colo., U.S.A.* 39°24N 107°13W 76 G10
Carbondale *Ill., U.S.A.* 37°44N 89°13W 80 G9
Carbondale *Pa., U.S.A.* 41°35N 75°30W 83 E9
Carbonear *Canada* 47°42N 53°13W 73 C9
Carbónia *Italy* 39°10N 8°30E 22 E3
Carcajou *Canada* 57°47N 117°6W 70 B5
Carcarana → *Argentina* 32°27S 60°48W 94 C3
Carcasse, C. *Haiti* 18°30N 74°28W 89 C5
Carcassonne *France* 43°13N 2°20E 20 E5
Carcross *Canada* 60°13N 134°45W 70 A2
Cardamon Hills *India* 9°30N 77°15E 40 Q10
Cardamom Mts. = Kravanh, Chuor Phnum *Cambodia* 12°0N 103°32E 39 G4
Cárdenas *Cuba* 23°0N 81°30W 88 B3
Cárdenas *San Luis Potosí, Mexico* 22°0N 99°38W 87 C5
Cárdenas *Tabasco, Mexico* 17°59N 93°22W 87 D6
Cardiff *U.K.* 51°29N 3°10W 13 F4
Cardiff □ *U.K.* 51°31N 3°12W 13 F4
Cardiff-by-the-Sea *U.S.A.* 33°1N 117°17W 79 M9
Cardigan *U.K.* 52°5N 4°40W 13 E3
Cardigan B. *U.K.* 52°30N 4°30W 13 E3
Cardinal *Canada* 44°47N 75°23W 83 B9
Cardona *Uruguay* 33°53S 57°18W 94 C4

Cardoso, Ilha do *Brazil* 25°8S 47°58W **95** B5
Cardston *Canada* 49°15N 113°20W **70** D6
Cardwell *Australia* 18°14S 146°2E **62** B4
Careen L. *Canada* 57°0N 108°11W **71** B7
Carei *Romania* 47°40N 22°29E **17** E12
Careme = Ciremay
  Indonesia 6°55S 108°27E **37** G13
Carey *U.S.A.* 43°19N 113°57W **76** E7
Carey, L. *Australia* 29°0S 122°15E **61** E3
Carey L. *Canada* 62°12N 102°55W **71** A8
Carhué *Argentina* 37°10S 62°50W **94** D3
Caria *Turkey* 37°20N 28°10E **23** F13
Cariacica *Brazil* 20°16S 40°25W **93** H10
Caribbean Sea *W. Indies* 15°0N 75°0W **89** D5
Cariboo Mts. *Canada* 53°0N 121°0W **70** C4
Caribou *U.S.A.* 46°52N 68°1W **81** B19
Caribou → *Man.,*
  Canada 59°20N 94°44W **71** B10
Caribou → *N.W.T.,*
  Canada 61°27N 125°45W **70** A3
Caribou I. *Canada* 47°22N 85°49W **72** C2
Caribou Is. *Canada* 61°55N 113°15W **70** A6
Caribou L. *Man., Canada* 59°21N 96°10W **71** B9
Caribou L. *Ont., Canada* 50°25N 89°5W **72** B2
Caribou Mts. *Canada* 59°12N 115°40W **70** B5
Caribou River △ *Canada* 59°35N 96°35W **71** B9
Carichíc *Mexico* 27°56N 107°3W **86** B3
Carinda *Australia* 30°28S 147°41E **63** E4
Carinhanha *Brazil* 14°15S 44°46W **93** F10
Carinhanha → *Brazil* 14°20S 43°47W **93** F10
Carinthia = Kärnten □
  Austria 46°52N 13°30E **16** E8
Caripito *Venezuela* 10°8N 63°6W **92** A6
Carleton, Mt. *Canada* 47°23N 66°53W **73** C6
Carleton Place *Canada* 45°8N 76°9W **83** A8
Carletonville *S. Africa* 26°23S 27°22E **56** D4
Carlin *U.S.A.* 40°43N 116°7W **76** F5
Carlingford L. *U.K.* 54°3N 6°9W **10** B5
Carlinville *U.S.A.* 39°17N 89°53W **80** F9
Carlisle *U.K.* 54°54N 2°56W **12** C5
Carlisle *U.S.A.* 40°12N 77°12W **82** F7
Carlisle B. *Barbados* 13°5N 59°37W **89** g
Carlisle I. *Australia* 20°49S 149°18E **62** b
Carlos Casares *Argentina* 35°32S 61°20W **94** D3
Carlos Tejedor *Argentina* 35°25S 62°25W **94** D3
Carlow *Ireland* 52°50N 6°56W **10** D5
Carlow □ *Ireland* 52°43N 6°50W **10** D5
Carlsbad *Calif., U.S.A.* 33°10N 117°21W **79** M9
Carlsbad *N. Mex.,*
  U.S.A. 32°25N 104°14W **77** K11
Carlsbad Caverns △
  U.S.A. 32°10N 104°35W **77** K11
Carluke *U.K.* 55°45N 3°50W **11** F5
Carlyle *Canada* 49°40N 102°20W **71** D8
Carmacks *Canada* 62°5N 136°16W **68** E4
Carman *Canada* 49°30N 98°0W **71** D9
Carmarthen *U.K.* 51°52N 4°19W **13** F3
Carmarthen B. *U.K.* 51°40N 4°30W **13** F3
Carmarthenshire □ *U.K.* 51°55N 4°13W **13** F3
Carmaux *France* 44°3N 2°10E **20** D5
Carmel *U.S.A.* 41°26N 73°41W **83** E11
Carmel-by-the-Sea
  U.S.A. 36°33N 121°55W **78** J5
Carmel Valley *U.S.A.* 36°29N 121°43W **78** J5
Carmelo *Uruguay* 34°0S 58°20W **94** C4
Carmen *Paraguay* 27°13S 56°12W **95** B4
Carmen → *Mexico* 30°42N 106°29W **86** A3
Carmen, I. *Mexico* 25°57N 111°12W **86** B2
Carmen de Patagones
  Argentina 40°50S 63°0W **96** E4
Carmensa *Argentina* 35°15S 67°40W **94** D2
Carmi *Canada* 49°36N 119°8W **70** D5
Carmi *U.S.A.* 38°5N 88°10W **80** F9
Carmichael *U.S.A.* 38°38N 121°19W **78** G5
Carmila *Australia* 21°55S 149°24E **62** C4
Carmona *Costa Rica* 10°0N 85°15W **88** E2
Carmona *Spain* 37°28N 5°42W **21** D3
Carn Ban *U.K.* 57°7N 4°15W **11** D4
Carn Eige *U.K.* 57°17N 5°8W **11** D3
Carnamah *Australia* 29°41S 115°53E **61** E2
Carnarvon *Australia* 24°51S 113°42E **61** D1
Carnarvon *Canada* 45°3N 78°41W **82** A6
Carnarvon *S. Africa* 30°56S 22°8E **56** E3
Carnarvon △ *Australia* 24°54S 148°2E **62** C4
Carnarvon Ra. *Queens.,*
  Australia 25°15S 148°30E **62** D4
Carnarvon Ra. *W. Austral.,*
  Australia 25°20S 120°45E **61** E3
Carnation *U.S.A.* 47°39N 121°55W **78** C5
Carncastle *U.K.* 54°54N 5°53W **10** B6
Carndonagh *Ireland* 55°16N 7°15W **10** A4
Carnduff *Canada* 49°10N 101°50W **71** D8
Carnegie *U.S.A.* 40°24N 80°5W **82** F4
Carnegie, L. *Australia* 26°5S 122°30E **61** E3
Carnegie Ridge *Pac. Oc.* 1°0S 87°0W **65** H19
Carnic Alps = Karnische Alpen
  Europe 46°36N 13°0E **16** E7
Carniche Alpi = Karnische Alpen
  Europe 46°36N 13°0E **16** E7
Carnot *C.A.R.* 4°59N 15°56E **52** D3
Carnot, C. *Australia* 34°57S 135°38E **63** E2
Carnot B. *Australia* 17°20S 122°15E **60** C3
Carnoustie *U.K.* 56°30N 2°42W **11** E6
Carnsore Pt. *Ireland* 52°10N 6°22W **10** D5
Caro *U.S.A.* 43°29N 83°24W **81** D12
Caroga Lake *U.S.A.* 43°8N 74°28W **83** C10
Carol City *U.S.A.* 25°56N 80°14W **85** J14
Carolina *Brazil* 7°10S 47°30W **93** E9
Carolina *Puerto Rico* 18°23N 65°58W **89** d
Carolina *S. Africa* 26°5S 30°6E **57** D5
Caroline I. *Kiribati* 9°58S 150°13W **65** H12
Caroline Is. *Micronesia* 8°0N 150°0E **64** G6
Caroni *Trin. & Tob.* 10°34N 61°23W **93** K15
Caroní → *Venezuela* 8°21N 62°43W **92** B6
Caronie = Nébrodi, Monti
  Italy 37°54N 14°35E **22** F6
Caroona *Australia* 31°24S 150°26E **63** E5
Carpathians *Europe* 49°30N 21°0E **17** D11
Carpați Meridionali
  Romania 45°30N 25°0E **17** F13

Carpentaria, G. of
  Australia 14°0S 139°0E **62** A2
Carpentras *France* 44°3N 5°2E **20** D6
Carpi *Italy* 44°47N 10°53E **22** B4
Carpinteria *U.S.A.* 34°24N 119°31W **79** L7
Carra, L. *Ireland* 53°41N 9°14W **10** C2
Carrabelle *U.S.A.* 29°51N 84°40W **85** G12
Carraig Mhachdire Rois =
  Carrickmacross
  Ireland 53°59N 6°43W **10** C5
Carraig na Siúire = Carrick-on-
  Suir *Ireland* 52°21N 7°24W **10** D4
Carranya ◎ *Australia* 19°13S 127°46E **60** C4
Carranza, Presa V.
  Mexico 27°20N 100°50W **86** B4
Carrara *Italy* 44°5N 10°6E **20** D9
Carrauntoohill *Ireland* 52°0N 9°45W **10** D2
Carrick-on-Shannon
  Ireland 53°57N 8°5W **10** C3
Carrick-on-Suir *Ireland* 52°21N 7°24W **10** D4
Carrickfergus *U.K.* 54°43N 5°49W **10** B6
Carrickmacross *Ireland* 53°59N 6°43W **10** C5
Carrieton *Australia* 32°25S 138°31E **63** E2
Carrillo *Mexico* 26°54N 103°55W **86** B4
Carrington *U.S.A.* 47°27N 99°8W **80** B4
Carrizal Bajo *Chile* 28°5S 71°20W **94** B1
Carrizalillo *Chile* 29°5S 71°30W **94** B1
Carrizo Cr. → *U.S.A.* 36°55N 103°55W **77** H12
Carrizo Plain △ *U.S.A.* 35°11N 119°47W **78** K7
Carrizo Springs *U.S.A.* 28°31N 99°52W **84** G5
Carrizozo *U.S.A.* 33°38N 105°53W **77** K11
Carroll *U.S.A.* 42°4N 94°52W **80** D6
Carrollton *Ga., U.S.A.* 33°35N 85°5W **85** E12
Carrollton *Ill., U.S.A.* 39°18N 90°24W **80** F8
Carrollton *Ky., U.S.A.* 38°41N 85°11W **81** F11
Carrollton *Mo., U.S.A.* 39°22N 93°30W **80** F7
Carrollton *Ohio, U.S.A.* 40°34N 81°5W **82** F3
Carron → *U.K.* 57°53N 4°22W **11** D4
Carron, L. *U.K.* 57°22N 5°35W **11** D3
Carrot → *Canada* 53°50N 101°17W **71** C8
Carrot River *Canada* 53°17N 103°35W **71** C8
Carruthers *Canada* 52°52N 109°16W **71** C7
Carson *Calif., U.S.A.* 33°49N 118°16W **79** M8
Carson *N. Dak., U.S.A.* 46°25N 101°34W **80** B3
Carson → *U.S.A.* 39°45N 118°40W **78** F8
Carson City *U.S.A.* 39°10N 119°46W **78** F7
Carson Sink *U.S.A.* 39°50N 118°25W **76** G4
Cartagena *Colombia* 10°25N 75°33W **92** A3
Cartagena *Spain* 37°38N 0°59W **21** D5
Cartago *Colombia* 4°45N 75°55W **92** C3
Cartago *Costa Rica* 9°50N 83°55W **88** E3
Cartersville *U.S.A.* 34°10N 84°48W **85** D12
Carterton *N.Z.* 41°2S 175°31E **59** D5
Carthage *Tunisia* 36°52N 10°20E **22** F4
Carthage *Ill., U.S.A.* 40°25N 91°8W **80** E8
Carthage *Mo., U.S.A.* 37°11N 94°19W **80** G6
Carthage *N.Y., U.S.A.* 43°59N 75°37W **81** D16
Carthage *Tex., U.S.A.* 32°9N 94°20W **84** E7
Cartier I. *Australia* 12°31S 123°29E **60** B3
Cartwright *Canada* 53°41N 56°58W **73** B8
Caruaru *Brazil* 8°15S 35°55W **93** E11
Carúpano *Venezuela* 10°39N 63°15W **92** A6
Caruthersville *U.S.A.* 36°11N 89°39W **80** G9
Carvoeiro *Brazil* 1°30S 61°59W **92** D6
Carvoeiro, C. *Portugal* 39°21N 9°24W **21** C1
Cary *U.S.A.* 35°47N 78°46W **85** D15
Casa de Piedra *Argentina* 38°55S 67°28W **94** D2
Casa de Piedra, Embalse
  Argentina 38°5S 67°32W **94** D2
Casa Grande *U.S.A.* 32°53N 111°45W **77** K8
Casa Nova *Brazil* 9°25S 41°5W **93** E10
Casablanca *Chile* 33°20S 71°25W **94** C1
Casablanca *Morocco* 33°36N 7°36W **50** B4
Cascada de Basaseachic △
  Mexico 28°9N 108°15W **86** B3
Cascade *Seychelles* 4°39S 55°29E **53** b
Cascade *Idaho, U.S.A.* 44°31N 116°2W **76** D5
Cascade *Mont., U.S.A.* 47°16N 111°42W **76** C8
Cascade Locks *U.S.A.* 45°40N 121°54W **78** E5
Cascade Ra. *U.S.A.* 47°0N 121°30W **78** D5
Cascade Res. *U.S.A.* 44°32N 116°3W **76** D5
Cascades, Pte. des *Réunion* 21°9S 55°51E **53** c
Cascais *Portugal* 38°41N 9°25W **21** C1
Cascavel *Brazil* 24°57S 53°28W **95** A5
Cáscina *Italy* 43°41N 10°33E **22** C4
Casco B. *U.S.A.* 43°45N 70°0W **81** D19
Caserta *Italy* 41°4N 14°20E **22** D6
Casey *Antarctica* 66°0S 76°0E **5** C8
Caseyr, Raas = Asir, Ras
  Somali Rep. 11°55N 51°10E **47** E5
Cashel *Ireland* 52°30N 7°53W **10** D4
Casiguran *Phil.* 16°22N 122°7E **37** A6
Casilda *Argentina* 33°10S 61°10W **94** C3
Casino *Australia* 28°52S 153°3E **63** D5
Casiquiare → *Venezuela* 2°1N 67°7W **92** C5
Casma *Peru* 9°30S 78°20W **92** E3
Casmalia *U.S.A.* 34°50N 120°32W **79** L6
Caspe *Spain* 41°14N 0°1W **21** B5
Casper *U.S.A.* 42°51N 106°19W **76** E10
Caspian Depression
  Eurasia 47°0N 48°0E **19** E8
Caspian Sea *Eurasia* 43°0N 50°0E **19** F9
Cass City *U.S.A.* 43°36N 83°10W **82** C1
Cass Lake *U.S.A.* 47°23N 94°37W **80** B6
Cassadaga *U.S.A.* 42°20N 79°19W **82** D5
Casselman *Canada* 45°19N 75°5W **83** A9
Casselton *U.S.A.* 46°54N 97°13W **80** B5
Cassiar Mts. *Canada* 59°30N 130°30W **70** B2
Cassino *Italy* 41°30N 13°49E **22** D5
Cassville *U.S.A.* 36°41N 93°52W **80** G7
Castaic *U.S.A.* 34°30N 118°38W **79** L8
Castalia *U.S.A.* 41°24N 82°49W **82** E2
Castanhal *Brazil* 1°18S 47°55W **93** D9
Castara *Trin. & Tob.* 11°17N 60°42W **93** J16
Castellammare di Stábia
  Italy 40°42N 14°29E **22** D6
Castelli *Argentina* 36°7S 57°47W **94** D4
Castelló de la Plana *Spain* 39°58N 0°3W **21** C5

Castelo *Brazil* 20°33S 41°14W **95** A7
Castelo Branco *Portugal* 39°50N 7°31W **21** C2
Castelsarrasin *France* 44°2N 1°7E **20** E4
Castelvetrano *Italy* 37°41N 12°47E **22** F5
Casterton *Australia* 37°30S 141°30E **63** F3
Castile *U.S.A.* 42°38N 78°3W **82** D6
Castilla-La Mancha □
  Spain 39°30N 3°30W **21** C4
Castilla y Leon □ *Spain* 42°0N 5°0W **21** B3
Castillos *Uruguay* 34°12S 53°52W **95** C5
Castle Dale *U.S.A.* 39°13N 111°1W **76** G8
Castle Douglas *U.K.* 54°56N 3°56W **11** G5
Castle Rock *Colo.,*
  U.S.A. 39°22N 104°51W **76** G11
Castle Rock *Wash.,*
  U.S.A. 46°17N 122°54W **78** D4
Castlebar *Ireland* 53°52N 9°18W **10** C2
Castlebay *U.K.* 56°57N 7°31W **11** E1
Castleblaney *Ireland* 54°7N 6°44W **10** B5
Castlederg *U.K.* 54°42N 7°35W **10** B4
Castleford *U.K.* 53°43N 1°21W **12** D6
Castlegar *Canada* 49°20N 117°40W **70** D5
Castlemaine *Australia* 37°2S 144°12E **63** F3
Castlemaine *Ireland* 52°10N 9°42W **10** D2
Castlepollard *Ireland* 53°41N 7°19W **10** C4
Castlereagh *Ireland* 53°46N 8°29W **10** C3
Castlereagh → *Australia* 30°12S 147°32E **63** E4
Castlereagh B. *Australia* 12°10S 135°10E **62** A2
Castleton *U.S.A.* 43°37N 73°11W **83** C11
Castleton-on-Hudson
  U.S.A. 42°31N 73°45W **83** D11
Castletown *I. of Man* 54°5N 4°38W **12** C3
Castletown Bearhaven
  Ireland 51°39N 9°55W **10** E2
Castor *Canada* 52°15N 111°50W **70** C6
Castor → *Canada* 53°24N 78°58W **72** B4
Castorland *U.S.A.* 43°53N 75°31W **83** C9
Castres *France* 43°37N 2°13E **20** E5
Castricum *Neths.* 52°33N 4°40E **15** B4
Castries *St. Lucia* 14°2N 60°58W **89** f
Castro *Brazil* 24°45S 50°0W **95** A6
Castro *Chile* 42°30S 73°50W **96** E2
Castro Alves *Brazil* 12°46S 39°33W **93** F11
Castro Valley *U.S.A.* 37°42N 122°5W **78** H4
Castroville *U.S.A.* 36°46N 121°45W **78** J5
Castuera *Spain* 38°43N 5°37W **21** C3
Cat Ba, Dao *Vietnam* 20°50N 107°0E **38** B6
Cat Ba △ *Vietnam* 20°47N 107°3E **38** B6
Cat I. *Bahamas* 24°30N 75°30W **89** B4
Cat L. *Canada* 51°40N 91°50W **72** B1
Cat Lake *Canada* 51°40N 91°50W **72** B1
Cat Tien △ *Vietnam* 11°25N 107°17E **39** G6
Catacamas *Honduras* 14°54N 85°56W **88** D2
Cataguases *Brazil* 21°23S 42°39W **95** A7
Catalão *Brazil* 18°10S 47°57W **93** G9
Çatalca *Turkey* 41°8N 28°27E **23** D13
Catalina *Canada* 48°31N 53°4W **73** C9
Catalina *Chile* 25°13S 69°43W **94** B2
Catalina *U.S.A.* 32°30N 110°50W **77** K8
Catalonia = Cataluña □
  Spain 41°40N 1°15E **21** B6
Cataluña □ *Spain* 41°40N 1°15E **21** B6
Catamarca *Argentina* 28°30S 65°50W **94** B2
Catamarca □ *Argentina* 27°0S 65°50W **94** B2
Catanduanes □ *Phil.* 13°50N 124°20E **37** B6
Catanduva *Brazil* 21°5S 48°58W **95** A6
Catánia *Italy* 37°30N 15°6E **22** F6
Catanzaro *Italy* 38°54N 16°35E **22** E7
Catarman *Phil.* 12°28N 124°35E **37** B6
Catatumbo-Bari △
  Colombia 9°3N 73°12W **89** E5
Catbalogan *Phil.* 11°46N 124°53E **37** B6
Catchacoma *Canada* 44°44N 78°19W **82** B6
Cateel *Phil.* 7°47N 126°24E **37** C7
Catembe *Mozam.* 26°0S 32°33E **57** D5
Caterham *U.K.* 51°15N 0°4W **13** F7
Cathair na Mart = Westport
  Ireland 53°48N 9°31W **10** C2
Cathair Saidhbhín = Cahersiveen
  Ireland 51°56N 10°14W **10** E1
Cathcart *S. Africa* 32°18S 27°10E **56** E4
Cathedral City *U.S.A.* 33°47N 116°28W **79** M10
Cathlamet *U.S.A.* 46°12N 123°23W **78** D3
Catlettsburg *U.S.A.* 38°25N 82°36W **81** F12
Catoche, C. *Mexico* 21°35N 87°5W **87** C7
Catriló *Argentina* 36°26S 63°24W **94** D3
Catrimani *Brazil* 0°27N 61°41W **92** C6
Catrimani → *Brazil* 0°28N 61°44W **92** C6
Catskill *U.S.A.* 42°14N 73°52W **83** D11
Catskill △ *U.S.A.* 42°8N 74°39W **83** D10
Catskill Mts. *U.S.A.* 42°10N 74°25W **83** D10
Catt, Mt. *Australia* 13°49S 134°23E **62** A1
Cattaraugus *U.S.A.* 42°20N 78°52W **82** D6
Catterick *U.K.* 54°23N 1°37W **12** C6
Catuala *Angola* 16°25S 19°2E **56** B2
Catuane *Mozam.* 26°48S 32°18E **57** D5
Catur *Mozam.* 13°45S 35°30E **55** E4
Caubvick, Mt. = Iberville, Mt. d'
  Canada 58°50N 63°50W **69** F19
Cauca → *Colombia* 8°54N 74°28W **92** B4
Caucaia *Brazil* 3°40S 38°35W **93** D11
Caucasus Mountains
  Eurasia 42°50N 44°0E **19** F7
Caucete *Argentina* 31°38S 68°20W **94** C2
Caungula *Angola* 8°26S 18°38E **52** F3
Cauquenes *Chile* 36°0S 72°22W **94** D1
Caura → *Venezuela* 7°38N 64°53W **92** B6
Cauresi → *Mozam.* 17°8S 33°0E **55** F3
Causapscal *Canada* 48°19N 67°12W **73** C6
Cauvery → *India* 11°9N 78°52E **40** P11
Caux, Pays de *France* 49°38N 0°35E **20** B4
Cavalier *U.S.A.* 48°48N 97°37W **80** A5
Cavan *Ireland* 54°0N 7°22W **10** B4
Cavan □ *Ireland* 54°1N 7°16W **10** C4
Cave Creek *U.S.A.* 33°50N 111°57W **77** K8
Cavenagh Ra. *Australia* 26°12S 127°55E **61** E4
Cavendish *Australia* 37°31S 142°2E **63** F3
Caviana, I. *Brazil* 0°10N 50°10W **93** C8

Cavite *Phil.* 14°29N 120°54E **37** B6
Cawndilla L. *Australia* 32°30S 142°15E **63** E3
Cawnpore = Kanpur
  India 26°28N 80°20E **43** F9
Caxias *Brazil* 4°55S 43°20W **93** D10
Caxias do Sul *Brazil* 29°10S 51°10W **95** B5
Cay Sal Bank *Bahamas* 23°45N 80°0W **88** B4
Cayambe *Ecuador* 0°3N 78°8W **92** C3
Cayenne *Fr. Guiana* 5°5N 52°18W **93** B8
Cayey *Puerto Rico* 18°7N 66°10W **89** d
Cayman Brac
  Cayman Is. 19°43N 79°49W **88** C4
Cayman Is. ☑ *W. Indies* 19°40N 80°30W **88** C3
Cayman Trough
  Caribbean 19°0N 81°0W **66** H11
Cayuga *Canada* 42°59N 79°50W **82** D5
Cayuga *U.S.A.* 42°54N 76°44W **83** D8
Cayuga Heights *U.S.A.* 42°27N 76°29W **83** D8
Cayuga L. *U.S.A.* 42°41N 76°41W **83** D8
Cazenovia *U.S.A.* 42°56N 75°51W **83** D9
Cazombo *Angola* 11°54S 22°56E **53** G4
Ceanannus Mor *Ireland* 53°44N 6°53W **10** C5
Ceará = Fortaleza *Brazil* 3°45S 38°35W **93** D11
Ceará □ *Brazil* 5°0S 40°0W **93** E11
Ceará-Mirim *Brazil* 5°38S 35°25W **93** E11
Ceatharlach = Carlow
  Ireland 52°50N 6°56W **10** D5
Cébaco, I. de *Panama* 7°33N 81°9W **88** E3
Cebollar *Argentina* 29°10S 66°35W **94** B2
Cebu *Phil.* 10°18N 123°54E **37** B6
Cecil Plains *Australia* 27°30S 151°11E **63** D5
Cedar → *U.S.A.* 41°17N 91°21W **80** E8
Cedar City *U.S.A.* 37°41N 113°4W **77** H7
Cedar Creek Res. *U.S.A.* 32°11N 96°4W **84** E6
Cedar Falls *Iowa, U.S.A.* 42°32N 92°27W **80** D7
Cedar Falls *Wash.,*
  U.S.A. 47°25N 121°45W **78** C5
Cedar Key *U.S.A.* 29°8N 83°2W **85** G13
Cedar L. *Canada* 53°10N 100°0W **71** C9
Cedar Park *U.S.A.* 30°30N 97°49W **84** F6
Cedar Rapids *U.S.A.* 41°59N 91°40W **80** E8
Cedartown *U.S.A.* 34°1N 85°15W **85** D12
Cedarvale *Canada* 55°1N 128°22W **70** B3
Cedarville *S. Africa* 30°23S 29°3E **57** E4
Cedarville *U.S.A.* 41°32N 120°10W **76** F3
Cedral *Mexico* 23°50N 100°45W **86** C4
Cedro *Brazil* 6°34S 39°3W **93** E11
Cedros, I. *Mexico* 28°12N 115°15W **86** B1
Cedros B. *Trin. & Tob.* 10°16N 61°54W **93** K15
Ceduna *Australia* 32°7S 133°46E **63** E1
Ceel Gaal *Somali Rep.* 10°58N 50°20E **47** E5
Ceel Waaq *Kenya* 2°49N 40°56E **54** B5
Ceeldheere *Somali Rep.* 3°50N 47°8E **47** G4
Ceerigaabo *Somali Rep.* 10°35N 47°20E **47** E4
Cefalù *Italy* 38°2N 14°1E **22** E6
Ceglèd *Hungary* 47°11N 19°47E **17** E10
Cekik *Indonesia* 8°12S 114°27E **37** J17
Celaque △ *Honduras* 14°30N 88°43W **88** D2
Celaya *Mexico* 20°31N 100°37W **86** C4
Celebes = Sulawesi
  Indonesia 2°0S 120°0E **37** E6
Celebes Sea *Indonesia* 3°0N 123°0E **37** D6
Celina *U.S.A.* 40°33N 84°35W **81** E11
Celje *Slovenia* 46°16N 15°18E **16** E8
Celle *Germany* 52°37N 10°4E **16** B6
Celtic Sea *Atl. Oc.* 50°9N 9°34W **14** F2
Cenderwasih, Teluk
  Indonesia 3°0S 135°20E **37** E9
Center *N. Dak., U.S.A.* 47°7N 101°18W **80** B3
Center *Tex., U.S.A.* 31°48N 94°11W **84** F7
Centerburg *U.S.A.* 40°18N 82°42W **82** F2
Centerville *Calif., U.S.A.* 36°44N 119°30W **78** J7
Centerville *Iowa, U.S.A.* 40°44N 92°52W **80** E7
Centerville *Tenn.,*
  U.S.A. 35°47N 87°28W **85** D11
Centerville *Tex., U.S.A.* 31°16N 95°59W **84** F7
Central = Tsentralnyy →
  Russia 52°0N 40°0E **28** D4
Central □ *Kenya* 0°30S 37°30E **54** C4
Central □ *Malawi* 13°30S 33°30E **55** E3
Central □ *Zambia* 14°25S 28°50E **55** E2
Central, Cordillera
  Colombia 5°0N 75°0W **92** C3
Central, Cordillera
  Costa Rica 10°10N 84°5W **88** D3
Central, Cordillera
  Dom. Rep. 19°15N 71°0W **89** C5
Central, Cordillera
  Puerto Rico 18°8N 66°35W **89** d
Central African Rep. ■
  Africa 7°0N 20°0E **51** G9
Central America *America* 12°0N 85°0W **66** H11
Central Australia ◎
  Australia 22°30S 128°30E **60** D4
Central Butte *Canada* 50°48N 106°31W **71** C7
Central City *Colo.,*
  U.S.A. 39°48N 105°31W **76** G11
Central City *Ky., U.S.A.* 37°18N 87°7W **80** G10
Central City *Nebr., U.S.A.* 41°7N 98°0W **80** E4
Central Desert ◎
  Australia 19°56S 130°46E **60** C5
Central I. *Kenya* 3°30N 36°0E **54** B4
Central Island △ *Kenya* 2°33N 36°1E **54** B4
Central Kalahari ◎
  Botswana 22°30S 23°0E **56** C3
Central Makran Range
  Pakistan 26°30N 64°15E **40** F4
Central Pacific Basin
  Pac. Oc. 8°0N 175°0W **64** G10
Central Patricia *Canada* 51°30N 90°9W **72** B1
Central Point *U.S.A.* 42°23N 122°55W **76** E2
Central Russian Uplands
  Europe 54°0N 36°0E **6** E13
Central Siberian Plateau
  Russia 65°0N 105°0E **29** C12
Central Square *U.S.A.* 43°17N 76°9W **83** C8
Centralia *Canada* 43°17N 81°28W **82** C3
Centralia *Ill., U.S.A.* 38°32N 89°8W **80** F9
Centralia *Mo., U.S.A.* 39°13N 92°8W **80** F7

Centralia *Wash., U.S.A.* 46°43N 122°58W **78** D4
Centre de Flacq *Mauritius* 20°12S 57°43E **53** d
Centreville *N.Y., U.S.A.* 42°28N 78°14W **82** D6
Centreville *Pa., U.S.A.* 41°44N 79°45W **82** E5
Cephalonia = Kefalonia
  Greece 38°15N 20°30E **23** E9
Cepu *Indonesia* 7°9S 111°35E **37** G14
Ceram = Seram *Indonesia* 3°10S 129°0E **37** E7
Ceram Sea = Seram Sea
  Indonesia 2°30S 128°30E **37** E7
Ceredigion □ *U.K.* 52°16N 4°15W **13** E3
Ceres *Argentina* 29°55S 61°55W **94** B3
Ceres *S. Africa* 33°21S 19°18E **56** E2
Ceres *U.S.A.* 37°35N 120°57W **78** H6
Cerf *Seychelles* 4°38S 55°9E **53** b
Cerignola *Italy* 41°17N 15°53E **22** D6
Cerigo = Kythira *Greece* 36°8N 23°0E **23** F10
Çerkezköy *Turkey* 41°17N 28°0E **23** D12
Cerralvo, I. *Mexico* 24°15N 109°55W **86** C3
Cerritos *Mexico* 22°25N 100°16W **86** C4
Cerro Chato *Uruguay* 33°6S 55°8W **95** C4
Cerro Cofre de Perote △
  Mexico 19°29N 97°8W **87** D5
Cerro Corá △ *Paraguay* 22°35S 56°2W **95** A4
Cerro de Pasco *Peru* 10°45S 76°10W **92** F3
Cerro el Copey △
  Venezuela 10°59N 63°53W **89** D7
Cerro Hoya △ *Panama* 7°17N 80°45W **88** E3
Cerro Saroche △
  Venezuela 10°8N 69°38W **89** D6
Cerventes *Australia* 30°31S 115°3E **61** F2
Cervera *Spain* 41°40N 1°16E **21** B6
Cesena *Italy* 44°8N 12°15E **22** B5
Cēsis *Latvia* 57°18N 25°15E **9** H21
Česká Rep. = Czech Rep. ■
  Europe 50°0N 15°0E **16** D8
České Budějovice
  Czech Rep. 48°55N 14°25E **16** D8
Českomoravská Vrchovina
  Czech Rep. 49°30N 15°40E **16** D8
Çeşme *Turkey* 38°20N 26°23E **23** E12
Cessnock *Australia* 32°50S 151°21E **63** E5
Cetinje *Montenegro* 42°23N 18°59E **23** C8
Cetraro *Italy* 39°31N 15°55E **22** E6
Ceuta *N. Afr.* 35°52N 5°18W **21** E3
Cévennes *France* 44°10N 3°50E **20** D5
Ceyhan *Turkey* 37°4N 35°47E **44** B2
Ceyhan → *Turkey* 36°38N 35°40E **44** B2
Ceylanpınar *Turkey* 36°50N 40°2E **44** B4
Ceylon = Sri Lanka ■
  Asia 7°30N 80°50E **40** R12
Cha-am *Thailand* 12°48N 99°58E **38** F2
Chacabuco *Argentina* 34°40S 60°27W **94** C3
Chachapoyas *Peru* 6°15S 77°50W **92** E3
Chachoengsao *Thailand* 13°42N 101°5E **38** F3
Chachran *Pakistan* 28°55N 70°30E **42** E4
Chachro *Pakistan* 25°5N 70°15E **42** G4
Chaco □ *Argentina* 26°30S 61°0W **94** B3
Chaco □ *Paraguay* 26°0S 60°0W **94** A4
Chaco → *Argentina* 36°46N 108°39W **77** H9
Chaco △ *Argentina* 27°0S 59°30W **94** B4
Chaco Austral *S. Amer.* 27°0S 61°30W **96** B4
Chaco Boreal *S. Amer.* 22°0S 60°0W **92** H6
Chaco Central *S. Amer.* 24°0S 61°0W **96** A4
Chaco Culture △
  U.S.A. 36°3N 107°58W **77** H10
Chacon, C. *U.S.A.* 54°42N 132°0W **70** C2
Chad ■ *Africa* 15°0N 17°15E **51** F8
Chad, L. = Tchad, L.
  Chad 13°30N 14°30E **51** F8
Chadileuvú → *Argentina* 37°46S 66°0W **94** D2
Chadiza *Zambia* 14°45S 32°27E **55** E3
Chadron *U.S.A.* 42°50N 103°0W **80** D2
Chadyr-Lunga = Ciadâr-Lunga
  Moldova 46°3N 28°51E **17** E15
Chae Hom *Thailand* 18°43N 99°35E **38** C2
Chae Son △ *Thailand* 18°42N 99°38E **38** C2
Chaem → *Thailand* 18°11N 98°38E **38** C2
Chaeryŏng *N. Korea* 38°24N 125°36E **35** E13
Chagai Hills = Chāh Gay Hills
  Afghan. 29°30N 64°0E **40** E3
Chagda *Russia* 58°45N 130°38E **29** D14
Chaghcharān *Afghan.* 34°31N 65°15E **40** B4
Chagos Arch. ☑ *Ind. Oc.* 6°0S 72°0E **26** J9
Chagres → *Panama* 9°33N 79°37W **88** E4
Chaguanas *Trin. & Tob.* 10°30N 61°26W **93** K15
Chāh Ākhvor *Iran* 32°41N 59°40E **45** C8
Chāh Bahar *Iran* 25°20N 60°40E **45** E9
Chāh-e Kavīr *Iran* 34°29N 56°52E **45** C8
Chāh Gay Hills *Afghan.* 29°30N 64°0E **40** E3
Chahār Borjak *Afghan.* 30°17N 62°3E **40** D3
Chahār Mahāll va Bakhtiari □
  Iran 32°0N 49°0E **45** C6
Chai Badan *Thailand* 15°12N 101°8E **38** E3
Chai Wan *China* 22°16N 114°14E **33** G11
Chaibasa *India* 22°42N 85°49E **43** H11
Chainat *Thailand* 15°11N 100°8E **38** E3
Chaiya *Thailand* 9°23N 99°14E **39** H2
Chaiyaphum *Thailand* 15°48N 102°2E **38** E3
Chaj Doab *Pakistan* 32°15N 73°0E **42** C5
Chajari *Argentina* 30°42S 58°0W **94** C4
Chak Amru *Pakistan* 32°22N 75°11E **42** C6
Chakar → *Pakistan* 29°29N 68°2E **42** E3
Chakari *Zimbabwe* 18°5S 29°51E **57** B4
Chake Chake *Tanzania* 5°15S 39°45E **54** D4
Chakhānsūr *Afghan.* 31°10N 62°0E **40** D3
Chakonipau, L. *Canada* 56°18N 68°30W **73** A6
Chakradharpur *India* 22°45N 85°40E **43** H11
Chakrata *India* 30°42N 77°51E **42** D7
Chakwal *Pakistan* 32°56N 72°53E **42** C5
Chala *Peru* 15°48S 74°20W **92** G4
Chalchihuites *Mexico* 23°29N 103°53W **86** C4
Chalcis = Halkida
  Greece 38°27N 23°42E **23** E10
Chalfant *U.S.A.* 37°32N 118°21W **78** H8
Chalhuanca *Peru* 14°15S 73°15W **92** F4
Chalisgaon *India* 20°30N 75°10E **40** J9
Chalk River *Canada* 46°1N 77°27W **72** C4
Chalky Inlet *N.Z.* 46°3S 166°31E **59** G1

Challapata Bolivia 18°53S 66°50W 92 G5
Challenger Deep Pac. Oc. 11°30N 142°0E 64 F6
Challenger Fracture Zone
  Pac. Oc. 35°0S 105°0W 65 L17
Challis U.S.A. 44°30N 114°14W 76 D6
Chalmette U.S.A. 29°56N 89°57W 85 G10
Chalon-sur-Saône France 46°48N 4°50E 20 C6
Chalong Thailand 7°50N 98°22E 39 a
Châlons-en-Champagne
  France 48°58N 4°20E 20 B6
Chálten, Cerro = Fitz Roy, Cerro
  Argentina 49°17S 73°5W 96 F2
Chālūs Iran 36°38N 51°26E 45 B6
Cham, Cu Lao Vietnam 15°57N 108°30E 38 E7
Chama U.S.A. 36°54N 106°35W 77 H10
Chamaicó Argentina 35°3S 64°58W 94 D2
Chaman Pakistan 30°58N 66°25E 40 D5
Chamba India 32°35N 76°10E 42 C7
Chamba Tanzania 11°37S 37°0E 55 E4
Chambal → India 26°29N 79°15E 43 F8
Chamberlain
  Australia 15°30S 127°54E 60 C4
Chamberlain U.S.A. 43°49N 99°20W 80 D4
Chamberlain →
  Australia 15°30S 127°54E 60 C4
Chamberlain L. U.S.A. 46°14N 69°19W 81 B19
Chambers U.S.A. 35°11N 109°26W 77 J9
Chambersburg U.S.A. 39°56N 77°40W 81 F15
Chambéry France 45°34N 5°55E 20 D6
Chambeshi → Zambia 11°53S 29°48E 52 G6
Chambly Canada 45°27N 73°17W 83 A11
Chambord Canada 48°25N 72°6W 73 C5
Chamchamal Iraq 35°32N 44°50E 44 C5
Chamela Mexico 19°32N 105°5W 86 D3
Chamical Argentina 30°22S 66°27W 94 C2
Chamkar Luong
  Cambodia 11°0N 103°45E 39 G4
Chamoli India 30°24N 79°21E 43 D8
Chamonix-Mont Blanc
  France 45°55N 6°51E 20 D7
Chamouchuane =
  Ashuapmushuan →
  Canada 48°37S 72°20W 72 C5
Champa India 22°2N 82°43E 43 H10
Champagne Canada 60°49N 136°30W 70 A1
Champagne France 48°40N 4°20E 20 B6
Champaign U.S.A. 40°7N 88°15W 80 E9
Champassak Laos 14°53N 105°52E 38 E5
Champawat India 29°20N 80°6E 43 E9
Champdoré, L. Canada 55°55N 65°49W 73 A6
Champlain U.S.A. 41°18N 80°31W 82 E4
Champlain U.S.A. 44°59N 73°27W 83 B11
Champlain, L. U.S.A. 44°40N 73°20W 83 B11
Champotón Mexico 19°21N 90°43W 87 D6
Champua India 22°5N 85°40E 43 H11
Chana Thailand 6°55N 100°44E 39 J3
Chañaral Chile 26°23S 70°40W 94 B1
Chanārān Iran 36°39N 59°6E 45 B8
Chanasma India 23°44N 72°5E 42 H5
Chancery Lane Barbados 13°3N 59°30W 89 h
Chanco Chile 35°44S 72°32W 94 D1
Chand India 21°57N 79°7E 43 J8
Chandan India 24°38N 86°40E 43 G12
Chandan Chauki India 28°33N 80°47E 43 E9
Chandannagar India 22°52N 88°24E 43 H13
Chandausi India 28°27N 78°49E 43 E8
Chandeleur Is. U.S.A. 29°55N 88°57W 85 G10
Chandeleur Sd. U.S.A. 29°55N 89°0W 85 G10
Chandigarh India 30°43N 76°47E 42 D7
Chandil India 22°58N 86°3E 43 H12
Chandler Australia 27°0S 133°19E 63 D1
Chandler Canada 48°18N 64°46W 73 C7
Chandler Ariz., U.S.A. 33°18N 111°50W 77 K8
Chandler Okla., U.S.A. 35°42N 96°53W 84 D6
Chandod India 21°59N 73°28E 42 J5
Chandpur Bangla. 23°8N 90°45E 41 H17
Chandrapur India 19°57N 79°25E 40 K11
Chānf Iran 26°38N 60°29E 45 E9
Chang Pakistan 26°59N 68°30E 42 F3
Chang, Ko Thailand 12°0N 102°23E 39 G4
Ch'ang Chiang = Chang Jiang →
  China 31°48N 121°10E 33 C7
Chang Jiang → China 31°48N 121°10E 33 C7
Changa India 33°53N 77°35E 43 C7
Changan China 22°48N 113°48E 33 F10
Changanacheri India 9°25N 76°31E 40 Q10
Changanassery = Changanacheri
  India 9°25N 76°31E 40 Q10
Changane → Mozam. 24°30S 33°30E 57 C5
Changbai China 41°25N 128°5E 35 D15
Changbai Shan China 42°20N 129°0E 35 C15
Changchiak'ou = Zhangjiakou
  China 40°48N 114°55E 34 D8
Ch'angchou = Changzhou
  China 31°47N 119°58E 33 C6
Changchun China 43°57N 125°17E 35 C13
Changchunling China 45°18N 125°27E 35 B13
Changde China 29°4N 111°35E 33 D6
Changdo-ri N. Korea 38°30N 127°40E 35 E14
Changhai = Shanghai
  China 31°15N 121°26E 33 C7
Changhua Taiwan 24°2N 120°30E 33 D7
Changhŭngni
  N. Korea 40°24N 128°19E 35 D15
Changi Singapore 1°23N 103°59E 39 d
Changi, Singapore ✈ (SIN)
  Singapore 1°23N 103°59E 39 M4
Changji China 44°1N 87°19E 32 B3
Changjiang China 19°20N 108°55E 38 C7
Changjiang Shuiku
  China 22°29N 113°27E 33 G10
Changjin N. Korea 40°23N 127°15E 35 D14
Changjin-ho N. Korea 40°30N 127°15E 35 D14
Changli China 39°40N 119°13E 35 E10
Changling China 44°20N 123°58E 35 B12
Changlun Malaysia 6°25N 100°26E 39 J3
Changping China 40°14N 116°12E 34 D9
Changsha China 28°12N 113°0E 33 D6
Changshan Qundao
  China 39°11N 122°32E 35 E12

Changuinola Panama 9°26N 82°31W 88 E3
Changwu China 35°10N 107°45E 34 G4
Changyi China 36°40N 119°30E 35 F10
Changyuan China 35°15N 114°42E 34 G8
Changzhi China 36°10N 113°6E 34 F7
Changzhou China 31°47N 119°58E 33 C6
Chanhanga Angola 16°0S 14°8E 56 B1
Chania Greece 35°30N 24°4E 25 D6
Chania □ Greece 35°30N 24°0E 25 D6
Channapatna India 12°40N 77°15E 40 N10
Channel Is. U.K. 49°19N 2°24W 13 H5
Channel Is. U.S.A. 33°40N 119°15W 79 M7
Channel Islands △
  U.S.A. 34°0N 119°24W 79 L7
Channel-Port aux Basques
  Canada 47°30N 59°9W 73 C8
Channel Tunnel Europe 51°0N 1°30E 13 F9
Chantada Spain 42°36N 7°46W 21 A2
Chanthaburi Thailand 12°38N 102°12E 38 F4
Chantrey Inlet Canada 67°48N 96°20W 68 D12
Chanute U.S.A. 37°41N 95°27W 80 G6
Chao Phraya →
  Thailand 13°40N 100°31E 38 F3
Chao Phraya Lowlands
  Thailand 15°30N 100°0E 38 E3
Chaocheng China 36°4N 115°37E 34 F8
Chaoyang China 41°35N 120°22E 35 D11
Chaozhou China 23°42N 116°32E 33 D6
Chapaev Kazakhstan 50°25N 51°10E 19 D9
Chapais Canada 49°47N 74°51W 72 C5
Chapala Mozam. 15°50S 37°35E 55 F4
Chapala, L. de Mexico 20°15N 103°0W 86 C4
Chapayevsk Russia 53°0N 49°40E 18 D8
Chapecó Brazil 27°14S 52°41W 95 B5
Chapel Hill U.S.A. 35°55N 79°4W 85 D15
Chapleau Canada 47°50N 83°24W 72 C3
Chaplin Canada 50°28N 106°40W 71 C7
Chaplin L. Canada 50°22N 106°36W 71 C7
Chappell U.S.A. 41°6N 102°28W 80 E2
Chapra = Chhapra
  India 25°48N 84°44E 43 G11
Chara Russia 56°54N 118°20E 29 D12
Charadai Argentina 27°35S 59°55W 94 B4
Charagua Bolivia 19°45S 63°10W 92 G6
Charaña Bolivia 17°30S 69°25W 92 G5
Charanwala India 27°51N 72°10E 42 F5
Charata Argentina 27°13S 61°14W 94 B3
Charcas Mexico 23°8N 101°7W 86 C4
Charcot I. Antarctica 70°0S 70°0W 5 C17
Chard U.K. 50°52N 2°58W 13 G5
Chardon U.S.A. 41°35N 81°12W 82 E3
Chardzhou = Türkmenabat
  Turkmenistan 39°6N 63°34E 45 B9
Charente → France 45°57N 1°5W 20 D3
Chari → Chad 12°58N 14°31E 51 F8
Chārīkār Afghan. 35°0N 69°10E 40 B6
Chariton → U.S.A. 41°1N 93°19W 80 E7
Chariton → U.S.A. 39°19N 92°58W 80 F7
Chärjew = Türkmenabat
  Turkmenistan 39°6N 63°34E 45 B9
Charkhari India 25°24N 79°45E 43 G8
Charkhi Dadri India 28°37N 76°17E 42 E7
Charleroi Belgium 50°24N 4°27E 15 D4
Charleroi U.S.A. 40°9N 79°57W 82 F5
Charles, C. U.S.A. 37°7N 75°58W 81 G16
Charles, Peak Australia 32°52S 121°11E 61 F3
Charles City U.S.A. 43°4N 92°41W 80 D7
Charles L. Canada 62°39N 74°15W 69 E17
Charles L. Canada 59°50N 110°33W 71 B6
Charles Town U.S.A. 39°17N 77°52W 81 F15
Charlesbourg Canada 46°51N 71°16W 81 B18
Charleston Ill., U.S.A. 39°30N 88°10W 80 F9
Charleston Miss., U.S.A. 34°1N 90°4W 85 D9
Charleston Mo., U.S.A. 36°55N 89°21W 80 G10
Charleston S.C., U.S.A. 32°46N 79°56W 85 E15
Charleston W. Va.,
  U.S.A. 38°21N 81°38W 81 F13
Charleston L. Canada 44°32N 76°0W 83 B9
Charleston Peak
  U.S.A. 36°16N 115°42W 79 J11
Charlestown Ireland 53°58N 8°48W 10 C3
Charlestown S. Africa 27°26S 29°53E 57 D4
Charlestown Ind.,
  U.S.A. 38°27N 85°40W 81 F11
Charlestown N.H.,
  U.S.A. 43°14N 72°25W 83 C12
Charlestown of Aberlour
  U.K. 57°28N 3°14W 11 D5
Charleville = Rath Luirc
  Ireland 52°21N 8°40W 10 D3
Charleville Australia 26°24S 146°15E 63 D4
Charleville-Mézières
  France 49°44N 4°40E 20 B6
Charlevoix U.S.A. 45°19N 85°16W 81 C11
Charlotte Mich., U.S.A. 42°34N 84°50W 81 D11
Charlotte N.C., U.S.A. 35°13N 80°50W 85 D6
Charlotte Vt., U.S.A. 44°19N 73°16W 83 B11
Charlotte Amalie
  U.S. Virgin Is. 18°21N 64°56W 89 e
Charlotte Harbor U.S.A. 26°57N 82°4W 85 H13
Charlotte L. Canada 52°12N 125°19W 70 C3
Charlottesville U.S.A. 38°2N 78°30W 81 F14
Charlottetown Nfld. & L.,
  Canada 52°46N 56°7W 73 B8
Charlottetown P.E.I.,
  Canada 46°14N 63°8W 73 C7
Charlotteville
  Trin. & Tob. 11°20N 60°33W 93 J16
Charlton Australia 36°16S 143°24E 63 F3
Charlton I. Canada 52°0N 79°20W 72 B4
Charny Canada 46°43N 71°15W 73 C5
Charolles France 46°27N 4°16E 20 C6
Charre Mozam. 17°13S 35°10E 55 F4

Charsadda Pakistan 34°7N 71°45E 42 B4
Charters Towers
  Australia 20°5S 146°13E 62 C4
Chartres France 48°29N 1°30E 20 B4
Chascomús Argentina 35°30S 58°0W 94 D4
Chase Canada 50°50N 119°41W 70 C5
Chasefu Zambia 11°55S 33°8E 55 E3
Chashma Barrage
  Pakistan 32°27N 71°20E 42 C4
Chāt Iran 37°59N 55°16E 45 B7
Châteaubriant France 47°43N 1°23W 20 C3
Chateaugay U.S.A. 44°56N 74°5W 83 B10
Châteauguay, L. Canada 56°26N 70°3W 73 A5
Châteaulin France 48°11N 4°8W 20 B1
Châteauroux France 46°50N 1°40E 20 C4
Châteaux, Pte. des
  Guadeloupe 16°15N 61°10W 88 b
Châtellerault France 46°50N 0°30E 20 C4
Chatham = Miramichi
  Canada 47°2N 65°28W 73 C6
Chatham Canada 42°24N 82°11W 82 D2
Chatham U.K. 51°22N 0°32E 13 F8
Chatham U.S.A. 42°21N 73°36W 83 D11
Chatham Is. Pac. Oc. 44°0S 176°40W 64 M10
Chatham Rise Pac. Oc. 43°0S 180°0E 64 M10
Chatmohar Bangla. 24°15N 89°15E 43 G13
Chatra India 24°12N 84°56E 43 G11
Chatrapur India 19°22N 85°2E 41 K14
Chats, L. des Canada 45°30N 76°20W 83 A8
Chatsu India 26°36N 75°57E 42 F6
Chatsworth Canada 44°27N 80°54W 82 B4
Chatsworth Zimbabwe 19°38S 31°13E 55 F3
Chàttâgâm = Chittagong
  Bangla. 22°19N 91°48E 41 H17
Chattahoochee U.S.A. 30°42N 84°51W 85 F12
Chattahoochee →
  U.S.A. 30°54N 84°57W 85 F12
Chattanooga U.S.A. 35°3N 85°19W 85 D12
Chatteris U.K. 52°28N 0°2E 13 E8
Chatturat Thailand 15°40N 101°51E 38 E3
Chau Doc Vietnam 10°42N 105°7E 39 G5
Chaukan Pass Burma 27°8N 97°10E 41 F20
Chaumont France 48°7N 5°8E 20 B6
Chaunskaya G. Russia 69°0N 169°0E 29 C17
Chautauqua L. U.S.A. 42°10N 79°24W 82 D5
Chauvin Canada 52°45N 110°10W 71 C6
Chaves Portugal 41°45N 7°32W 21 B2
Chawang Thailand 8°25N 99°30E 39 H2
Chaykovskiy Russia 56°47N 54°9E 18 C9
Chazy U.S.A. 44°53N 73°26W 83 B11
Cheb Czech Rep. 50°9N 12°28E 16 C7
Cheboksary Russia 56°8N 47°12E 18 C8
Cheboygan U.S.A. 45°39N 84°29W 81 C11
Chech, Erg Africa 25°0N 2°15W 50 D5
Chechenia □ Russia 43°30N 45°29E 19 F8
Checheno-Ingush Republic =
  Chechenia □
  Russia 43°30N 45°29E 19 F8
Chechnya = Chechenia □
  Russia 43°30N 45°29E 19 F8
Checotah U.S.A. 35°28N 95°31W 84 D7
Chedabucto B. Canada 45°25N 61°8W 73 C7
Cheduba I. Burma 18°45N 93°40E 41 K18
Cheektowaga U.S.A. 42°54N 78°45W 82 D6
Cheepie Australia 26°33S 145°1E 63 D4
Chegdomyn Russia 51°7N 133°1E 29 D14
Chegga Mauritania 25°27N 5°40W 50 C4
Chegutu Zimbabwe 18°10S 30°14E 55 F3
Chehalis U.S.A. 46°40N 122°58W 78 D4
Chehalis → U.S.A. 46°57N 123°50W 78 D3
Cheju = Jeju S. Korea 33°31N 126°32E 35 H14
Cheju-do = Jeju-do
  S. Korea 33°29N 126°34E 35 H14
Chekiang = Zhejiang □
  China 29°0N 120°0E 33 D7
Chela, Sa. da Angola 16°20S 13°20E 56 B1
Chelan U.S.A. 47°51N 120°1W 76 C3
Chelan, L. U.S.A. 48°11N 120°30W 76 B3
Cheleken = Hazar
  Turkmenistan 39°34N 53°16E 19 G9
Cheleken Yarymadasy
  Turkmenistan 39°30N 53°15E 45 B7
Chelforó Argentina 39°0S 66°33W 96 D3
Chelkar = Shalqar
  Kazakhstan 47°48N 59°39E 28 E6
Chelm Poland 51°8N 23°30E 17 C12
Chelmno Poland 53°20N 18°30E 17 B10
Chelmsford U.K. 51°44N 0°29E 13 F8
Chelsea Australia 38°5S 145°8E 63 F4
Chelsea U.S.A. 43°59N 72°27W 83 C12
Cheltenham U.K. 51°54N 2°4W 13 F5
Chelyabinsk Russia 55°10N 61°24E 28 D7
Chelyuskin, C. = Chelyuskin, Mys
  Russia 77°30N 103°0E 29 B11
Chelyuskin, Mys Russia 77°30N 103°0E 29 B11
Chemainus Canada 48°55N 123°42W 78 B3
Chemba Mozam. 17°9S 34°53E 55 H6
Chemin Grenier Mauritius 20°29S 57°28E 53 d
Chemnitz Germany 50°51N 12°54E 16 C7
Chemult U.S.A. 43°14N 121°47W 76 E3
Chen, Gora Russia 65°16N 141°50E 29 C15
Chenab → Pakistan 30°23N 71°2E 42 D4
Chenab Nagar Pakistan 31°45N 72°52E 42 D5
Chenango Forks U.S.A. 42°15N 75°51W 83 D9
Cheney U.S.A. 47°30N 117°35W 76 C5
Cheng Xian China 33°43N 105°42E 34 H3
Chengcheng China 35°8N 109°56E 34 G5
Chengchou = Zhengzhou
  China 34°45N 113°34E 34 G7
Chengde China 40°59N 117°58E 35 D9
Chengdu China 30°38N 104°2E 32 C5
Chenggu China 33°10N 107°21E 34 H4
Chengjiang China 24°39N 103°0E 32 D5
Chengmai China 19°50N 109°58E 38 C7
Ch'engtu = Chengdu
  China 30°38N 104°2E 32 C5
Chengwu China 34°58N 115°50E 34 G8
Chengyang China 36°18N 120°21E 35 F11

Chenjiagang China 34°23N 119°47E 35 G10
Chennai India 13°8N 80°19E 40 N12
Cheò, Eilean a' = Skye
  U.K. 57°15N 6°10W 11 D2
Cheom Ksan Cambodia 14°13N 104°56E 38 E5
Cheonan S. Korea 36°48N 127°9E 35 F14
Cheongdo S. Korea 35°38N 128°42E 35 G15
Cheongju S. Korea 36°39N 127°27E 35 F14
Cheorwon S. Korea 38°15N 127°10E 35 E14
Chepén Peru 7°15S 79°23W 92 E3
Chepes Argentina 31°20S 66°35W 94 C2
Chepo Panama 9°10N 79°6W 88 E4
Chepstow U.K. 51°38N 2°41W 13 F5
Chequamegon B. U.S.A. 46°39N 90°51W 80 B8
Cher → France 47°21N 0°29E 20 C4
Cheraw U.S.A. 34°42N 79°53W 85 D15
Cherbourg France 49°39N 1°40W 20 B3
Cherdyn Russia 60°24N 56°29E 18 B10
Cheremkhovo Russia 53°8N 103°1E 29 D11
Cherepovets Russia 59°5N 37°55E 18 C6
Chergui, Chott ech
  Algeria 34°21N 0°25E 50 B6
Cherikov = Cherykaw
  Belarus 53°32N 31°20E 17 B16
Cherkasy Ukraine 49°27N 32°4E 19 E5
Cherkessk Russia 44°15N 42°5E 19 F7
Cherlak Russia 54°15N 74°55E 28 D8
Chernaya Russia 70°30N 89°10E 29 B9
Chernigov = Chernihiv
  Ukraine 51°28N 31°20E 18 D5
Chernigovka Russia 44°19N 132°34E 30 B6
Chernihiv Ukraine 51°28N 31°20E 18 D5
Chernivtsi Ukraine 48°15N 25°52E 17 D13
Chernobyl = Chornobyl
  Ukraine 51°20N 30°15E 17 C16
Chernogorsk Russia 53°49N 91°18E 29 D10
Chernovtsy = Chernivtsi
  Ukraine 48°15N 25°52E 17 D13
Chernyakhovsk Russia 54°36N 21°48E 9 J19
Chernysheyskiy Russia 63°0N 112°30E 29 C12
Cherokee Iowa, U.S.A. 42°45N 95°33W 80 D6
Cherokee Okla., U.S.A. 36°45N 98°21W 84 C5
Cherokee Village U.S.A. 36°18N 91°31W 84 C9
Cherokees, Grand Lake O' The
  U.S.A. 36°28N 94°55W 84 C7
Cherrapunji India 25°17N 91°47E 41 G17
Cherry Valley U.S.A. 42°48N 74°45W 83 D10
Cherskogo Khrebet
  Russia 65°0N 143°0E 29 C15
Chersonisos Greece 35°18N 25°22E 25 D7
Chersonisos Akrotiri
  Greece 35°30N 24°10E 25 D6
Cherven Belarus 53°45N 28°28E 17 B15
Chervonohrad Ukraine 50°25N 24°10E 17 C13
Cherwell → U.K. 51°44N 1°14W 13 F6
Cherykaw Belarus 53°32N 31°20E 17 B16
Chesapeake U.S.A. 36°49N 76°16W 81 G15
Chesapeake B. U.S.A. 38°0N 76°10W 81 F14
Cheshire □ U.K. 53°14N 2°30W 12 D5
Cheshskaya Guba Russia 67°20N 47°0E 18 A8
Cheshunt U.K. 51°43N 0°1W 13 F7
Chesil Beach U.K. 50°37N 2°33W 13 G5
Chesley Canada 44°17N 81°5W 82 B3
Chester U.K. 53°12N 2°53W 12 D5
Chester Calif., U.S.A. 40°19N 121°14W 76 F3
Chester Ill., U.S.A. 37°55N 89°49W 80 G9
Chester Mont., U.S.A. 48°31N 110°58W 76 B8
Chester Pa., U.S.A. 39°51N 75°22W 81 G16
Chester S.C., U.S.A. 34°43N 81°12W 85 D14
Chester Vt., U.S.A. 43°16N 72°36W 83 C12
Chester W. Va., U.S.A. 40°37N 80°34W 82 F4
Chester-le-Street U.K. 54°51N 1°34W 12 C6
Chesterfield U.K. 53°15N 1°25W 12 D6
Chesterfield, Îs. N. Cal. 19°52S 158°15E 58 C8
Chesterfield Inlet
  Canada 63°30N 90°45W 68 E13
Chesterton Ra.
  Australia 25°30S 147°27E 63 D4
Chesterton Range △
  Australia 26°16S 147°22E 63 D4
Chestertown U.S.A. 43°40N 73°48W 83 C11
Chesterville Canada 45°6N 75°14W 83 A9
Chesuncook L. U.S.A. 46°0N 69°21W 81 C19
Chéticamp Canada 46°37N 60°59W 73 C7
Chetumal Mexico 18°30N 88°20W 87 D7
Chetumal, B. de
  Cent. Amer. 18°40N 88°10W 87 D7
Chetwynd Canada 55°45N 121°36W 70 B4
Cheviot, The U.K. 55°29N 2°9W 12 B5
Cheviot Hills U.K. 55°20N 2°30W 12 B5
Cheviot Ra. Australia 25°20S 143°45E 62 D3
Chew Bahir Ethiopia 4°40N 36°50E 47 G2
Chewelah U.S.A. 48°17N 117°43W 76 B5
Cheyenne Okla., U.S.A. 35°37N 99°40W 84 D5
Cheyenne Wyo., U.S.A. 41°8N 104°49W 76 F11
Cheyenne → U.S.A. 44°41N 101°18W 80 C3
Cheyenne Wells
  U.S.A. 38°49N 102°21W 76 G12
Cheyne B. Australia 34°35S 118°50E 61 F2
Chhabra India 24°40N 76°54E 42 G7
Chhaktala India 22°6N 74°11E 42 H6
Chhapra India 25°48N 84°44E 43 G11
Chhata India 27°42N 77°30E 42 F7
Chhatarpur Jharkhand,
  India 24°23N 84°11E 43 G11
Chhatarpur Mad. P.,
  India 24°55N 79°35E 43 G8
Chhep Cambodia 13°45N 105°24E 38 F5
Chhindwara Mad. P.,
  India 23°3N 79°29E 43 H8
Chhindwara Mad. P.,
  India 22°2N 78°59E 43 H8
Chhlong Cambodia 12°15N 105°58E 38 F5
Chhota Tawa → India 22°14N 76°36E 42 H7
Chhoti Kali Sindh →
  India 24°2N 75°31E 42 G6

Chhuikhadan India 21°32N 80°59E 43 J9
Chhuk Cambodia 10°46N 104°28E 39 G5
Chi → Thailand 15°11N 104°43E 38 E5
Chiai Taiwan 23°29N 120°25E 33 D7
Chiamboni Somali Rep. 1°39S 41°35E 52 E8
Chiang Dao Thailand 19°22N 98°58E 38 C2
Chiang Kham Thailand 19°32N 100°18E 38 C3
Chiang Khan Thailand 17°52N 101°36E 38 D3
Chiang Khong Thailand 20°17N 100°24E 38 B3
Chiang Mai Thailand 18°47N 98°59E 38 C2
Chiang Rai Thailand 19°52N 99°50E 38 C2
Chiang Saen Thailand 20°16N 100°5E 38 B3
Chiapa → Mexico 16°42N 93°0W 87 D6
Chiapa de Corzo Mexico 16°42N 93°0W 87 D6
Chiapas □ Mexico 16°30N 92°30W 87 D6
Chiapas, Sa. Madre de
  Mexico 15°40N 93°0W 87 D6
Chiautla de Tapia
  Mexico 18°18N 98°36W 87 D5
Chiávari Italy 44°19N 9°19E 20 D8
Chiavenna Italy 46°19N 9°24E 20 C8
Chiba Japan 35°30N 140°7E 31 G10
Chiba □ Japan 35°30N 140°20E 31 G10
Chibabava Mozam. 20°17S 33°35E 57 C5
Chibemba Cunene, Angola 15°48S 14°8E 53 H2
Chibemba Huila, Angola 16°20S 15°20E 56 B2
Chibi Zimbabwe 20°18S 30°25E 57 C5
Chibia Angola 15°10S 13°42E 53 H2
Chibougamau Canada 49°56N 74°24W 72 C5
Chibougamau, L.
  Canada 49°50N 74°20W 72 C5
Chibuk Nigeria 10°52N 12°50E 51 F8
Chibuto Mozam. 24°40S 33°33E 57 C5
Chic-Chocs, Mts. Canada 48°55N 66°0W 73 C6
Chicacole = Srikakulam
  India 18°14N 83°58E 41 K13
Chicago U.S.A. 41°52N 87°38W 80 E10
Chicago Heights U.S.A. 41°30N 87°38W 80 E10
Chichagof I. U.S.A. 57°30N 135°30W 68 F4
Chichaoua Morocco 31°32N 8°44W 50 B4
Chichawatni Pakistan 30°32N 72°42E 42 D5
Chichén-Itzá Mexico 20°37N 88°35W 87 C7
Chicheng China 40°55N 115°55E 34 D8
Chichester U.K. 50°50N 0°47W 13 G7
Chichester Ra. Australia 22°12S 119°15E 60 D2
Chichibu Japan 35°59N 139°10E 31 F9
Chichibu-Tama △
  Japan 35°52N 138°42E 31 G9
Ch'ich'ihaerh = Qiqihar
  China 47°26N 124°0E 33 B7
Chicholi India 22°1N 77°40E 42 H8
Chickasaw △ U.S.A. 34°26N 97°0W 84 D6
Chickasha U.S.A. 35°3N 97°58W 84 D6
Chiclana de la Frontera
  Spain 36°26N 6°9W 21 D2
Chiclayo Peru 6°42S 79°50W 92 E3
Chico U.S.A. 39°44N 121°50W 78 F5
Chico → Chubut, Argentina 44°0S 67°0W 96 E3
Chico → Santa Cruz,
  Argentina 50°0S 68°30W 96 G3
Chicoa Mozam. 15°36S 32°20E 55 F3
Chicomo Mozam. 24°31S 34°6E 57 C5
Chicomostoc Mexico 22°28N 102°46W 86 C4
Chicontepec Mexico 20°58N 98°10W 87 C5
Chicopee U.S.A. 42°9N 72°37W 83 D12
Chicoutimi Canada 48°28N 71°5W 73 C5
Chicualacuala Mozam. 22°6N 31°42E 57 C5
Chidambaram India 11°20N 79°45E 40 P11
Chidenguele Mozam. 24°55S 34°11E 57 C5
Chidley, C. Canada 60°23N 64°26W 69 E19
Chiducuane Mozam. 24°35S 34°25E 57 C5
Chiede Angola 17°15S 16°22E 56 B2
Chiefs Pt. Canada 44°41N 81°18W 82 B3
Chiem Hoa Vietnam 22°12N 105°17E 38 A5
Chiemsee Germany 47°53N 12°28E 16 E7
Chiengi Zambia 8°45S 29°10E 55 D2
Chiengmai = Chiang Mai
  Thailand 18°47N 98°59E 38 C2
Chiese → Italy 45°8N 10°25E 20 D9
Chieti Italy 42°21N 14°10E 22 C6
Chifeng China 42°18N 118°58E 35 C10
Chignecto B. Canada 45°30N 64°40W 73 C7
Chiguana Bolivia 21°0S 67°58W 94 A2
Chigwell U.K. 51°37N 0°6E 13 F8
Chihli, G. of = Bo Hai
  China 39°0N 119°0E 35 E10
Chihuahua Mexico 28°38N 106°5W 86 B3
Chihuahua □ Mexico 28°30N 106°0W 86 B3
Chiili = Shieli Kazakhstan 44°20N 66°15E 28 E7
Chik Bollapur India 13°25N 77°45E 40 N10
Chikmagalur India 13°15N 75°45E 40 N9
Chikwawa Malawi 16°2S 34°50E 55 H6
Chilanga Zambia 15°33S 28°16E 55 F2
Chilapa Mexico 17°36N 99°10W 87 D5
Chilas Pakistan 35°25N 74°5E 43 B6
Chilaw Sri Lanka 7°30N 79°50E 40 R11
Chilcotin → Canada 51°44N 122°23W 70 C4
Childers Australia 25°15S 152°17E 63 D5
Childress U.S.A. 34°25N 100°13W 84 D4
Chile ■ S. Amer. 35°0S 72°0W 96 D2
Chile Rise Pac. Oc. 38°0S 92°0W 65 L18
Chilecito Argentina 29°10S 67°30W 94 B2
Chililabombwe Zambia 12°18S 27°43E 55 E2
Chilim Pakistan 35°5N 75°5E 43 B6
Chilin = Jilin China 43°44N 126°30E 35 C14
Chilka L. India 19°40N 85°25E 41 K14
Chilko → Canada 52°0N 123°40W 70 C4
Chilko L. Canada 51°20N 124°10W 70 C4
Chillagoe Australia 17°7S 144°33E 62 B3
Chillán Chile 36°40S 72°10W 94 D1
Chillicothe Ill., U.S.A. 40°55N 89°29W 80 E9
Chillicothe Mo., U.S.A. 39°48N 93°33W 80 F7
Chillicothe Ohio, U.S.A. 39°20N 82°59W 81 F12
Chilliwack Canada 49°10N 121°54W 70 D4
Chilo India 27°25N 73°32E 42 F5
Chiloane, I. Mozam. 20°40S 34°55E 57 C5
Chiloé, I. de Chile 42°30S 73°50W 96 E2
Chilpancingo Mexico 17°33N 99°30W 87 D5

Chiltern Hills U.K. 51°40N 0°53W **13** F7
Chilton U.S.A. 44°2N 88°10W **80** C9
Chilubi Zambia 11°5S 29°58E **55** E2
Chilubula Zambia 10°14S 30°51E **55** E3
Chilumba Malawi 10°28S 34°12E **55** E3
Chilung Taiwan 25°3N 121°45E **33** D7
Chilwa, L. Malawi 15°15S 35°40E **55** F4
Chimaltitán Mexico 21°35N 103°50W **86** C4
Chimán Panama 8°45N 78°40W **88** E4
Chimanimani Zimbabwe 19°48S 32°52E **57** B5
Chimay Belgium 50°3N 4°20E **15** D4
Chimayo U.S.A. 36°0N 105°56W **77** J11
Chimba Zambia 9°54S 31°28E **55** D3
Chimbay Uzbekistan 42°57N 59°47E **28** E6
Chimborazo Ecuador 1°29S 78°55W **92** D3
Chimbote Peru 9°0S 78°35W **92** E3
Chimkent = Shymkent
  Kazakhstan 42°18N 69°36E **28** E7
Chimoio Mozam. 19°4S 33°30E **55** F3
Chimpembe Zambia 9°31S 29°33E **55** D2
Chin □ Burma 22°0N 93°0E **41** J18
Chin Hills Burma 22°30N 93°30E **41** H18
Chin Ling Shan = Qinling Shandi
  China 33°50N 108°10E **34** H5
China Mexico 25°42N 99°14W **87** B5
China ■ Asia 30°0N 110°0E **33** C6
China, Great Plain of
  Asia 35°0N 115°0E **26** E13
China Lake U.S.A. 35°44N 117°37W **79** K9
Chinan = Jinan China 36°38N 117°1E **34** F9
Chinandega Nic. 12°35N 87°12W **88** D2
Chinati Peak U.S.A. 29°57N 104°29W **84** G2
Chincha Alta Peru 13°25S 76°7W **92** F3
Chinchaga ➤ Canada 58°53N 118°20W **70** B5
Chinchilla Australia 26°45S 150°38E **63** D5
Chinchorro, Banco
  Mexico 18°35N 87°22W **87** D7
Chinchou = Jinzhou
  China 41°5N 121°3E **35** D11
Chincoteague U.S.A. 37°56N 75°23W **81** G16
Chinde Mozam. 18°35S 36°30E **55** F4
Chindwin ➤ Burma 21°26N 95°15E **41** J19
Chineni India 33°2N 75°15E **43** C6
Chinga Mozam. 15°13S 38°35E **55** F4
Chingola Zambia 12°31S 27°53E **55** E2
Chingole Malawi 13°4S 34°17E **55** E3
Ch'ingtao = Qingdao
  China 36°5N 120°20E **35** F11
Chinguetti Mauritania 20°25N 12°24W **50** D3
Chingune Mozam. 20°33S 34°58E **57** C5
Chinhanguanine
  Mozam. 25°21S 32°30E **57** D5
Chinhoyi Zimbabwe 17°20S 30°8E **55** F3
Chini India 31°32N 78°15E **42** D8
Chiniot Pakistan 31°45N 73°0E **42** D5
Chínipas Mexico 27°23N 108°32W **86** B3
Chinji Pakistan 32°42N 72°22E **42** C5
Chinju = Jinju S. Korea 35°12N 128°2E **35** G15
Chinko ➤ C.A.R. 4°50N 23°53E **52** D4
Chinle U.S.A. 36°9N 109°33W **77** H9
Chinnampo = Namp'o
  N. Korea 38°52N 125°10E **35** E13
Chino Japan 35°59N 138°9E **31** G9
Chino U.S.A. 34°1N 117°41W **79** L9
Chino Valley U.S.A. 34°45N 112°27W **77** J7
Chinon France 47°10N 0°15E **20** C4
Chinook U.S.A. 48°35N 109°14W **76** B9
Chinook Trough
  Pac. Oc. 44°0N 175°0W **64** C10
Chinsali Zambia 10°30S 32°2E **55** E3
Chinsura = Chunchura
  India 22°53N 88°27E **43** H13
Chióggia Italy 45°13N 12°17E **22** B5
Chíos = Híos Greece 38°27N 26°9E **23** E12
Chipata Zambia 13°38S 32°28E **55** E3
Chipindo Angola 13°49S 15°48E **53** G3
Chipinge Zimbabwe 20°13S 32°28E **55** G3
Chipinge □ Zimbabwe 20°14S 33°0E **55** G3
Chipley U.S.A. 30°47N 85°32W **85** F12
Chipman Canada 46°6N 65°53W **73** C6
Chipoka Malawi 13°57S 34°28E **55** E3
Chippenham U.K. 51°27N 2°6W **13** F5
Chippewa ➤ U.S.A. 44°25N 92°5W **80** C7
Chippewa Falls U.S.A. 44°56N 91°24W **80** C8
Chipping Norton U.K. 51°56N 1°32W **13** F6
Chiputneticook Lakes
  N. Amer. 45°35N 67°35W **81** C20
Chiquián Peru 10°10S 77°0W **92** F3
Chiquibul △ Belize 16°49N 88°52W **88** C2
Chiquimula Guatemala 14°51N 89°37W **88** D2
Chiquinquira Colombia 5°37N 73°50W **92** B4
Chirala India 15°50N 80°26E **40** M12
Chiramba Mozam. 16°55S 34°39E **55** F3
Chirawa India 28°14N 75°42E **42** E6
Chirchiq Uzbekistan 41°29N 69°35E **28** E7
Chiredzi Zimbabwe 21°0S 31°38E **57** C5
Chiricahua △ U.S.A. 32°0N 109°20W **77** K9
Chiricahua Peak
  U.S.A. 31°51N 109°18W **77** L9
Chirikof I. U.S.A. 55°50N 155°40W **74** D8
Chiriquí, G. de Panama 8°0N 82°10W **88** E3
Chiriquí, L. de Panama 9°10N 82°0W **88** E3
Chirisa △ Zimbabwe 17°53S 28°15E **55** F2
Chirivira Falls Zimbabwe 21°10S 32°12E **55** G3
Chirmiri India 23°15N 82°20E **43** H10
Chirripó Grande, Cerro
  Costa Rica 9°29N 83°29W **88** E3
Chirundu Zimbabwe 16°3S 28°50E **57** B4
Chisamba Zambia 14°55S 28°0E **55** E2
Chisapani Nepal 28°37N 81°16E **43** E9
Chisasibi Canada 53°50N 79°0W **72** B4
Chisholm Canada 54°55N 114°10W **70** C6
Chisholm U.S.A. 47°29N 92°53W **80** B7
Chishtian Mandi
  Pakistan 29°50N 72°55E **42** E5
Chisimaio = Kismaayo
  Somali Rep. 0°22S 42°32E **47** H3
Chisimba Falls Zambia 10°12S 30°56E **55** E3
Chişinău Moldova 47°2N 28°50E **17** E15

Chisos Mts. U.S.A. 29°5N 103°15W **84** G3
Chistopol Russia 55°25N 50°38E **18** C9
Chita Russia 52°0N 113°35E **29** D12
Chitipa Malawi 9°41S 33°19E **55** D3
Chitose Japan 42°49N 141°39E **30** C10
Chitral Pakistan 35°50N 71°56E **40** B7
Chitré Panama 7°59N 80°27W **88** E3
Chittagong Bangla. 22°19N 91°48E **41** H17
Chittagong □ Bangla. 24°5N 91°0E **41** G17
Chittaurgarh India 24°52N 74°38E **42** G6
Chittoor India 13°15N 79°5E **40** N11
Chitungwiza Zimbabwe 18°0S 31°6E **55** F3
Chiusi Italy 43°1N 11°57E **22** C4
Chivasso Italy 45°11N 7°53E **20** D7
Chivhu Zimbabwe 19°2S 30°52E **55** F3
Chivilcoy Argentina 34°55S 60°0W **94** C4
Chiwanda Tanzania 11°23S 34°55E **55** E3
Chizera Zimbabwe 17°36S 27°45E **55** F2
Chizarira □ Zimbabwe 17°44S 27°52E **55** F2
Chizela Zambia 13°8S 25°0E **55** E2
Chkalov = Orenburg
  Russia 51°45N 55°6E **18** D10
Chloride U.S.A. 35°25N 114°12W **79** K12
Cho Bo Vietnam 20°46N 105°10E **38** B5
Cho-do N. Korea 38°30N 124°40E **35** E13
Cho Phuoc Hai Vietnam 10°26N 107°18E **39** G6
Choa Chu Kang Singapore 1°22N 103°41E **39** d
Choba Kenya 2°30N 38°5E **54** B4
Chobe △ Botswana 18°37S 24°23E **56** B4
Chocolate Mts.
  U.S.A. 33°15N 115°15W **79** M11
Choctawhatchee ➤
  U.S.A. 30°25N 86°8W **85** F11
Choele Choel Argentina 39°11S 65°40W **96** D3
Choiseul St. Lucia 13°47N 61°3W **89** f
Choiseul Solomon Is. 7°0S 156°40E **58** B8
Choix Mexico 26°43N 108°17W **86** B3
Chojnice Poland 53°42N 17°32E **17** B9
Chōkai-San Japan 39°6N 140°3E **30** E10
Choke Canyon Res.
  U.S.A. 28°30N 98°20W **84** G5
Chokurdakh Russia 70°38N 147°55E **29** B15
Cholame U.S.A. 35°44N 120°18W **78** K6
Cholet France 47°4N 0°52W **20** C3
Cholguan Chile 37°10S 72°3W **94** D1
Choloma Honduras 15°37N 87°57W **88** C2
Choluteca Honduras 13°20N 87°14W **88** D2
Choluteca ➤ Honduras 13°0N 87°20W **88** D2
Chom Bung Thailand 13°37N 99°36E **38** F2
Chom Thong Thailand 18°25N 98°41E **38** C2
Choma Zambia 16°48S 26°59E **55** F2
Chomolungma = Everest, Mt.
  Nepal 28°5N 86°58E **43** E12
Chomun India 27°15N 75°40E **42** F6
Chomutov Czech Rep. 50°28N 13°23E **16** C7
Chon Buri Thailand 13°21N 101°1E **38** F3
Chon Thanh Vietnam 11°24N 106°36E **39** G6
Chone Ecuador 0°40S 80°0W **92** D3
Chong Kai Cambodia 13°57N 103°35E **38** F4
Chong Mek Thailand 15°10N 105°27E **38** E5
Chong Phangan Thailand 9°39N 100°0E **39** b
Chong Samui Thailand 9°21N 99°50E **39** b
Ch'ŏngjin N. Korea 41°47N 129°50E **35** D15
Chŏngju N. Korea 39°40N 125°5E **35** E13
Chŏngli China 40°58N 115°15E **34** D8
Chongqing China 29°35N 106°25E **32** D5
Chongqing Shi □ China 30°0N 108°0E **32** C5
Chonguene Mozam. 25°3S 33°49E **57** C5
Chongwe Zambia 15°21S 28°42E **55** F2
Chonos, Arch. de los Chile 45°0S 75°0W **96** F2
Chop Ukraine 48°26N 22°12E **17** D12
Chopim ➤ Brazil 25°35S 53°5W **95** B5
Chor Pakistan 25°31N 69°46E **42** G3
Chora Sfakion Greece 35°15N 24°9E **25** D6
Chorbat La India 34°42N 76°37E **43** B7
Chorley U.K. 53°39N 2°38W **12** D5
Chornobyl Ukraine 51°20N 30°15E **17** C16
Chorolque, Cerro Bolivia 20°59S 66°5W **94** A2
Chorregon Australia 22°40S 143°32E **62** C3
Chorro el Indio △
  Venezuela 7°43N 72°9W **89** E5
Chortkiv Ukraine 49°2N 25°46E **17** D13
Chorzów Poland 50°18N 18°57E **17** C10
Chos-Malal Argentina 37°20S 70°15W **94** D2
Ch'osan N. Korea 40°50N 125°47E **35** D13
Choszczno Poland 53°7N 15°25E **16** B8
Chota Peru 6°30S 78°30W **92** E3
Chotila India 22°23N 71°15E **42** H4
Chotta Udepur India 22°19N 74°1E **42** H6
Chowchilla U.S.A. 37°7N 120°16W **78** H6
Choybalsan Mongolia 48°4N 114°30E **33** B6
Choyr Mongolia 46°24N 108°30E **34** B6
Christchurch N.Z. 43°33S 172°47E **59** E14
Christchurch U.K. 50°44N 1°47W **13** G6
Christian I. Canada 44°50N 80°12W **82** B4
Christian Sd. U.S.A. 55°56N 134°40W **75** D13
Christiana S. Africa 27°52S 25°8E **56** D4
Christiansted
  U.S. Virgin Is. 17°45N 64°42W **89** C7
Christie B. Canada 62°32N 111°10W **71** A6
Christina ➤ Canada 56°40N 111°3W **71** B6
Christmas Cr. ➤
  Australia 18°29S 125°23E **60** C4
Christmas I. = Kiritimati
  Kiribati 1°58N 157°27W **65** G12
Christmas I. Ind. Oc. 10°30S 105°40E **64** J2
Christopher, L.
  Australia 24°49S 127°42E **61** D4
Chtimba Malawi 10°35S 34°13E **55** E3
Chū = Shū Kazakhstan 43°36N 73°42E **28** E8
Chu ➤ Vietnam 19°53N 105°45E **38** C5
Chu Lai Vietnam 15°28N 108°45E **38** E7
Chuadanga Bangla. 23°38N 88°51E **43** H13
Chuak, Ko Thailand 9°28N 99°41E **39** b
Ch'uanchou = Quanzhou
  China 24°55N 118°34E **33** D6
Chuankou China 34°20N 110°59E **34** G6
Chubbuck U.S.A. 42°55N 112°28W **76** E7

Chūbu □ Japan 36°45N 137°30E **31** F8
Chubu-Sangaku △
  Japan 36°30N 137°40E **31** F8
Chubut ➤ Argentina 43°20S 65°5W **96** E3
Chuchi L. Canada 55°12N 124°30W **70** B4
Chuda India 22°29N 71°41E **42** H4
Chudskoye, Ozero
  Russia 58°13N 27°30E **9** G22
Chugach Mts. U.S.A. 60°45N 147°0W **74** C10
Chūgoku □ Japan 35°0N 133°0E **31** G6
Chūgoku-Sanchi Japan 35°0N 133°0E **31** G6
Chugwater U.S.A. 41°46N 104°50W **76** F11
Chukchi Plateau Arctic 78°0N 165°0W **4** B17
Chukchi Sea Russia 68°0N 175°0W **29** C19
Chukotskiy Mys Russia 64°14N 173°8W **74** C5
Chukotskiy Poluostrov
  Russia 66°0N 174°0W **74** B5
Chukotskoye Nagorye
  Russia 68°0N 175°0E **29** C18
Chula Vista U.S.A. 32°38N 117°5W **79** N9
Chulucanas Peru 5°8S 80°10W **92** E2
Chulym ➤ Russia 57°43N 83°51E **28** D9
Chum Phae Thailand 16°40N 102°6E **38** D4
Chum Saeng Thailand 15°55N 100°15E **38** E3
Chumar India 32°40N 78°35E **43** C8
Chumbicha Argentina 29°0S 66°10W **94** B2
Chumikan Russia 54°40N 135°10W **29** D14
Chumphon Thailand 10°35N 99°14E **39** G2
Chumuare Mozam. 14°31S 31°50E **55** E3
Chuna ➤ Russia 57°47N 94°37E **29** D10
Chuncheon S. Korea 37°58N 127°44E **35** F14
Chunchura India 22°53N 88°27E **43** H13
Chunga Zambia 15°0S 26°2E **55** F2
Chunggang-ŭp
  N. Korea 41°48N 126°48E **35** D14
Chunghwa N. Korea 38°52N 125°47E **35** E13
Chungju S. Korea 36°58N 127°58E **35** F14
Chungking = Chongqing
  China 29°35N 106°25E **32** D5
Chungt'iaoshan = Zhongtiao
  Shan China 35°0N 111°10E **34** G6
Chunian Pakistan 30°57N 74°0E **42** D6
Chunya Tanzania 8°30S 33°27E **55** D3
Chunyang China 43°38N 129°23E **35** C15
Chupara Pt.
  Trin. & Tob. 10°49N 61°22W **93** K15
Chuquibamba Peru 15°47S 72°44W **92** G4
Chuquicamata Chile 22°15S 69°0W **94** A2
Chur Switz. 46°52N 9°32E **20** C8
Churachandpur India 24°20N 93°40E **41** G18
Church Stretton U.K. 52°32N 2°48W **13** E5
Churchill ➤ Man.,
  Canada 58°47N 94°12W **71** B10
Churchill ➤ Nfld. & L.,
  Canada 53°19N 60°10W **73** B7
Churchill, C. Canada 58°46N 93°12W **71** B10
Churchill Falls Canada 53°36N 64°19W **73** B7
Churchill L. Canada 55°55N 108°20W **71** B7
Churchill Pk. Canada 58°10N 125°10W **70** B3
Churki India 23°50N 83°12E **43** H10
Churu India 28°20N 74°50E **42** E6
Churún Merú = Angel Falls
  Venezuela 5°57N 62°30W **92** B6
Chushal India 33°40N 78°40E **43** C8
Chuska Mts. U.S.A. 36°15N 108°50W **77** H9
Chusovoy Russia 58°22N 57°50E **18** C10
Chute-aux-Outardes
  Canada 49°7N 68°24W **73** C6
Chuuk = Truk
  Micronesia 7°25N 151°46E **64** G7
Chuvash Republic = Chuvashia □
  Russia 55°30N 47°0E **18** C8
Chuvashia □ Russia 55°30N 47°0E **18** C8
Chuwārtah Iraq 35°43N 45°34E **44** C5
Chuy Uruguay 33°41S 53°27W **95** C5
Ci Xian China 36°20N 114°25E **34** F8
Ciadâr-Lunga Moldova 46°3N 28°51E **17** E15
Ciamis Indonesia 7°20S 108°21E **37** G13
Cianjur Indonesia 6°49S 107°8E **37** G12
Cianorte Brazil 23°37S 52°37W **95** A5
Cibola U.S.A. 33°17N 114°42W **79** M12
Cicero U.S.A. 41°51N 87°44W **80** E10
Cicia Fiji 17°45S 179°18W **59** a
Ciéagas del Catatumbo △
  Venezuela 9°25N 71°54W **89** E5
Ciechanów Poland 52°52N 20°38E **17** B11
Ciego de Ávila Cuba 21°50N 78°50W **88** B4
Ciénaga Colombia 11°1N 74°15W **92** A4
Cienfuegos Cuba 22°10N 80°30W **88** B3
Cieszyn Poland 49°45N 18°35E **17** D10
Cieza Spain 38°17N 1°23W **21** C5
Cihuatlán Mexico 19°14N 104°35W **86** D4
Cijara, Embalse de Spain 39°18N 4°52W **21** C3
Cijulang Indonesia 7°42S 108°27E **37** G13
Cilacap Indonesia 7°43S 109°0E **37** G13
Cill Airne = Killarney
  Ireland 52°4N 9°30W **10** D2
Cill Chainnigh = Kilkenny
  Ireland 52°39N 7°15W **10** D4
Cill Dara = Kildare Ireland 53°9N 6°55W **10** C5
Cill Mhantáin = Wicklow
  Ireland 52°59N 6°3W **10** D5
Cilo Dağı Turkey 37°28N 43°55E **19** G7
Cimarron Kans., U.S.A. 37°48N 100°21W **80** G3
Cimarron N. Mex.,
  U.S.A. 36°31N 104°55W **77** H11
Cimarron ➤ U.S.A. 36°10N 96°16W **84** C6
Cimișlia Moldova 46°34N 28°44E **17** E15
Cimone, Mte. Italy 44°12N 10°42E **22** B4
Cinca ➤ Spain 41°26N 0°21E **21** B6
Cincar Bos.-H. 43°55N 17°5E **22** C7
Cincinnati U.S.A. 39°9N 84°27W **81** F11
Cincinnatus U.S.A. 42°33N 75°54W **83** D9
Ciney Belgium 50°18N 5°5E **15** D5
Cinto, Mte. France 42°24N 8°54E **20** E8

Circle Alaska, U.S.A. 65°50N 144°4W **74** B11
Circle Mont., U.S.A. 47°25N 105°35W **76** C11
Circleville U.S.A. 39°36N 82°57W **81** F12
Cirebon Indonesia 6°45S 108°32E **37** G13
Ciremay Indonesia 6°55S 108°27E **37** G13
Cirencester U.K. 51°43N 1°57W **13** F6
Cirium Cyprus 34°40N 32°53E **25** E11
Cisco U.S.A. 32°23N 98°59W **84** E5
Citlaltépetl = Orizaba, Pico de
  Mexico 18°58N 97°15W **87** D5
Citrus Heights U.S.A. 38°42N 121°17W **78** G5
Citrusdal S. Africa 32°35S 19°0E **56** E2
Città del Vaticano = Vatican
  City ■ Europe 41°54N 12°27E **22** D5
Città di Castello Italy 43°27N 12°14E **22** C5
Ciudad Acuña Mexico 29°18N 100°55W **86** B4
Ciudad Altamirano
  Mexico 18°20N 100°40W **86** D4
Ciudad Anáhuac
  Mexico 27°14N 100°7W **86** B4
Ciudad Bolívar Venezuela 8°5N 63°36W **92** B6
Ciudad Camargo
  Mexico 27°40N 105°10W **86** B3
Ciudad Cortés Costa Rica 8°55N 84°0W **88** E3
Ciudad de México Mexico 19°24N 99°9W **87** D5
Ciudad de Valles
  Mexico 22°0N 99°0W **87** C5
Ciudad del Carmen
  Mexico 18°38N 91°50W **87** D6
Ciudad del Este Paraguay 25°30S 54°50W **95** B5
Ciudad Delicias = Delicias
  Mexico 28°13N 105°28W **86** B3
Ciudad Frontera
  Mexico 26°56N 101°27W **86** B4
Ciudad Guayana
  Venezuela 8°0N 62°30W **92** B6
Ciudad Guerrero
  Mexico 28°33N 107°30W **86** B3
Ciudad Guzmán
  Mexico 19°41N 103°29W **86** D4
Ciudad Juárez Mexico 31°44N 106°29W **86** A3
Ciudad Lerdo Mexico 25°32N 103°32W **86** B4
Ciudad Madero Mexico 22°19N 97°50W **87** C5
Ciudad Mante Mexico 22°44N 98°59W **87** C5
Ciudad Obregón
  Mexico 27°29N 109°56W **86** B3
Ciudad Real Spain 38°59N 3°55W **21** C4
Ciudad Rodrigo Spain 40°35N 6°32W **21** B2
Ciudad Victoria Mexico 23°44N 99°8W **87** C5
Ciudadela Spain 40°0N 3°50E **24** B10
Civitanova Marche Italy 43°18N 13°44E **22** C5
Civitavécchia Italy 42°6N 11°48E **22** C4
Cizre Turkey 37°19N 42°10E **44** B4
Clackmannanshire □
  U.K. 56°10N 3°43W **11** E5
Clacton-on-Sea U.K. 51°47N 1°11E **13** F9
Claire, L. Canada 58°35N 112°5W **70** B6
Clairton U.S.A. 40°18N 79°53W **82** F5
Clallam Bay U.S.A. 48°15N 124°16W **78** B2
Clanton U.S.A. 32°51N 86°38W **85** E11
Clanwilliam S. Africa 32°11S 18°52E **56** E2
Clara Ireland 53°21N 7°37W **10** C4
Claraville U.S.A. 35°24N 118°20W **79** K8
Clare Australia 33°50S 138°37E **63** E2
Clare U.S.A. 43°49N 84°46W **81** D11
Clare □ Ireland 52°45N 9°0W **10** D3
Clare ➤ Ireland 53°20N 9°2W **10** C2
Clare I. Ireland 53°49N 10°0W **10** C1
Claremont Calif., U.S.A. 34°6N 117°43W **79** L9
Claremont N.H., U.S.A. 43°23N 72°20W **83** C12
Claremont Pt. Australia 14°1S 143°41E **62** A3
Claremore U.S.A. 36°19N 95°36W **84** C7
Claremorris Ireland 53°45N 9°0W **10** C3
Clarence ➤ Australia 29°25S 153°22E **63** D5
Clarence ➤ N.Z. 42°10S 173°56E **59** E4
Clarence, I. Chile 54°0S 72°0W **96** G2
Clarence I. Antarctica 61°10S 54°0W **5** C18
Clarence Str. Australia 12°0S 131°0E **60** B5
Clarence Town Bahamas 23°6N 74°59W **89** B5
Clarendon Pa., U.S.A. 41°47N 79°6W **82** E5
Clarendon Tex., U.S.A. 34°56N 100°53W **84** D4
Clarenville Canada 48°10N 54°1W **73** C9
Claresholm Canada 50°2N 113°33W **70** C6
Clarie Coast Antarctica 68°0S 135°0E **5** C9
Clarinda U.S.A. 40°44N 95°2W **80** E6
Clarington Canada 43°55S 78°41W **82** C6
Clarion Iowa, U.S.A. 42°44N 93°44W **80** D7
Clarion Pa., U.S.A. 41°13N 79°23W **82** E5
Clarion ➤ U.S.A. 41°7N 79°41W **82** E5
Clarion Fracture Zone
  Pac. Oc. 20°0N 120°0W **66** H7
Clark U.S.A. 44°53N 97°44W **80** C5
Clark, Pt. Canada 44°4N 81°45W **82** B3
Clark Fork U.S.A. 48°9N 116°11W **76** B5
Clark Fork ➤ U.S.A. 48°9N 116°15W **76** B5
Clarkdale U.S.A. 34°46N 112°3W **77** J7
Clarke City Canada 50°12N 66°38W **73** B6
Clarke Ra. Australia 40°32S 148°10E **63** G4
Clarke Ra. Australia 20°40S 148°30E **62** b
Clarkesville U.S.A. 34°37N 83°31W **85** D13
Clarksburg U.S.A. 39°17N 80°30W **81** F13
Clarksdale U.S.A. 34°12N 90°35W **85** D9
Clarkston U.S.A. 46°25N 117°3W **76** C5
Clarksville Ark., U.S.A. 35°28N 93°28W **84** D8
Clarksville Tenn.,
  U.S.A. 36°32N 87°21W **85** C11
Clarksville Tex., U.S.A. 33°37N 95°3W **84** E7
Clatskanie U.S.A. 46°6N 123°12W **78** D3
Claude U.S.A. 35°7N 101°22W **84** D4
Claveria Phil. 18°37N 121°4E **37** A6
Clay U.S.A. 38°17N 121°10W **78** G5
Clay Center U.S.A. 39°23N 97°8W **80** F5
Claypool U.S.A. 33°25N 110°51W **77** K8
Claysburg U.S.A. 40°17N 78°27W **82** F6
Claysville U.S.A. 40°7N 80°25W **82** F4

Clayton Canada 45°11N 76°19W **83** A8
Clayton N. Mex.,
  U.S.A. 36°27N 103°11W **77** H12
Clayton N.Y., U.S.A. 44°14N 76°5W **83** B8
Clear, C. Ireland 51°25N 9°32W **10** E2
Clear Hills Canada 56°40N 119°30W **70** B5
Clear I. Ireland 51°26N 9°30W **10** E2
Clear L. U.S.A. 39°2N 122°47W **78** F4
Clear Lake Iowa, U.S.A. 43°8N 93°23W **80** D7
Clear Lake S. Dak.,
  U.S.A. 44°45N 96°41W **80** C5
Clear Lake Res. U.S.A. 41°56N 121°5W **76** F3
Clearfield Pa., U.S.A. 41°2N 78°27W **82** E6
Clearfield Utah, U.S.A. 41°7N 112°2W **76** F7
Clearlake U.S.A. 38°57N 122°38W **78** G4
Clearwater Canada 51°38N 120°2W **70** C4
Clearwater U.S.A. 27°59N 82°48W **85** H13
Clearwater ➤ Alta.,
  Canada 52°22N 114°57W **70** C6
Clearwater ➤ Alta.,
  Canada 56°44N 111°23W **71** B6
Clearwater L. Canada 53°34N 99°49W **71** C9
Clearwater Lake △
  Canada 54°0N 101°0W **71** C8
Clearwater Mts. U.S.A. 46°5N 115°20W **76** C6
Clearwater River △
  Canada 56°55N 109°10W **71** B7
Cleburne U.S.A. 32°21N 97°23W **84** E6
Clee Hills U.K. 52°26N 2°35W **13** E5
Cleethorpes U.K. 53°33N 0°3W **12** D7
Cleeve Cloud U.K. 51°56N 2°0W **13** F6
Clemson U.S.A. 34°41N 82°50W **85** D13
Clerke Reef Australia 17°22S 119°20E **60** C2
Clermont Australia 22°49S 147°39E **62** C4
Clermont U.S.A. 28°33N 81°46W **85** G14
Clermont-Ferrand France 45°46N 3°4E **20** D5
Clervaux Lux. 50°4N 6°2E **15** D6
Clevedon U.K. 51°26N 2°52W **13** F5
Cleveland Miss., U.S.A. 33°45N 90°43W **85** E9
Cleveland Ohio, U.S.A. 41°29N 81°41W **82** E3
Cleveland Okla., U.S.A. 36°19N 96°28W **84** C6
Cleveland Tenn., U.S.A. 35°10N 84°53W **85** D12
Cleveland Tex., U.S.A. 30°21N 95°5W **84** F7
Cleveland, C. Australia 19°11S 147°1E **62** B4
Cleveland, Mt. U.S.A. 48°56N 113°51W **76** B7
Cleveland Heights
  U.S.A. 41°31N 81°33W **82** E3
Cleveländia Brazil 26°24S 52°23W **95** B5
Clew B. Ireland 53°50N 9°49W **10** C2
Clewiston U.S.A. 26°45N 80°56W **85** H14
Clifden Ireland 53°29N 10°1W **10** C1
Clifden N.Z. 46°1S 167°42E **59** G1
Cliffdell U.S.A. 46°56N 121°5W **78** D5
Cliffy Hd. Australia 35°1S 116°29E **61** G2
Clifton Australia 27°59S 151°53E **63** D5
Clifton Ariz., U.S.A. 33°3N 109°18W **77** K9
Clifton Colo., U.S.A. 39°7N 108°25W **76** G9
Clifton Tex., U.S.A. 31°47N 97°35W **84** F6
Clifton Beach Australia 16°46S 145°39E **62** B4
Clinch ➤ U.S.A. 35°53N 84°29W **85** D12
Clingmans Dome
  U.S.A. 35°34N 83°30W **85** D13
Clint U.S.A. 31°35N 106°14W **84** F1
Clinton B.C., Canada 51°6N 121°35W **70** C4
Clinton Ont., Canada 43°37N 81°32W **82** C3
Clinton N.Z. 46°12S 169°23E **59** G2
Clinton Ark., U.S.A. 35°36N 92°28W **84** D8
Clinton Conn., U.S.A. 41°17N 72°32W **83** E12
Clinton Ill., U.S.A. 40°9N 88°57W **80** E9
Clinton Ind., U.S.A. 39°40N 87°24W **80** F10
Clinton Iowa, U.S.A. 41°51N 90°12W **80** E8
Clinton Mass., U.S.A. 42°25N 71°41W **83** D13
Clinton Miss., U.S.A. 32°20N 90°20W **85** E9
Clinton Mo., U.S.A. 38°22N 93°46W **80** F7
Clinton N.C., U.S.A. 35°0N 78°22W **85** D15
Clinton Okla., U.S.A. 35°31N 98°58W **84** D5
Clinton S.C., U.S.A. 34°29N 81°53W **85** D14
Clinton Tenn., U.S.A. 36°6N 84°8W **85** C12
Clinton Wash., U.S.A. 47°59N 122°21W **78** C4
Clinton, C. Australia 22°30S 150°45E **62** C5
Clinton Colden L.
  Canada 63°58N 107°27W **68** E10
Clintonville U.S.A. 44°37N 88°46W **80** C9
Clipperton, I. Pac. Oc. 10°18N 109°13W **65** F17
Clipperton Fracture Zone
  Pac. Oc. 19°0N 122°0W **65** G16
Clisham U.K. 57°58N 6°49W **11** D2
Clitheroe U.K. 53°53N 2°22W **12** D5
Clo-oose Canada 48°39N 124°49W **78** B2
Cloates, Pt. Australia 22°43S 113°40E **60** D1
Clodomira Argentina 27°35S 64°14W **94** B3
Clogher Hd. Ireland 53°48N 6°14W **10** C5
Clonakilty Ireland 51°37N 8°53W **10** E3
Clonakilty B. Ireland 51°35N 8°51W **10** E3
Cloncurry Australia 20°40S 140°28E **62** C3
Cloncurry ➤ Australia 18°37S 140°40E **62** B3
Clondalkin Ireland 53°19N 6°25W **10** C5
Clones Ireland 54°11N 7°15W **10** B4
Clonmel Ireland 52°21N 7°42W **10** D4
Cloquet U.S.A. 46°43N 92°28W **80** B7
Clorinda Argentina 25°16S 57°45W **94** B4
Cloud Bay Canada 48°5N 89°26W **72** C2
Cloud Peak U.S.A. 44°23N 107°11W **76** D10
Cloudcroft U.S.A. 32°58N 105°45W **77** K11
Cloverdale U.S.A. 38°48N 123°1W **78** G4
Clovis Calif., U.S.A. 36°49N 119°42W **78** J7
Clovis N. Mex., U.S.A. 34°24N 103°12W **77** J12
Cloyne Canada 44°49N 77°11W **82** B7
Cluain Meala = Clonmel
  Ireland 52°21N 7°42W **10** D4
Cluj-Napoca Romania 46°47N 23°38E **17** E12
Clunes Australia 37°20S 143°45E **63** F3
Clutha ➤ N.Z. 46°20S 169°49E **59** G2
Clwyd ➤ U.K. 53°19N 3°31W **12** D4
Clyde Canada 54°9N 113°39W **70** C6
Clyde N.Z. 45°12S 169°20E **59** F2

Clyde *U.S.A.*   43°5N 76°52W **82 C8**
Clyde → *U.K.*   55°55N 4°30W **11 F4**
Clyde, Firth of *U.K.*   55°22N 5°1W **11 F3**
Clyde Muirshiel △ *U.K.*   55°50N 4°40W **11 F4**
Clyde River *Canada*   70°30N 68°30W **69 C18**
Clydebank *U.K.*   55°54N 4°23W **11 F4**
Clymer *N.Y., U.S.A.*   42°1N 79°37W **82 D5**
Clymer *Pa., U.S.A.*   40°40N 79°1W **82 D5**
Coachella *U.S.A.*   33°41N 116°10W **79 M10**
Coachella Canal
  U.S.A.   32°43N 114°57W **79 N12**
Coahoma *U.S.A.*   32°18N 101°18W **84 E4**
Coahuayana →
  Mexico   18°41N 103°45W **86 D4**
Coahuila □ *Mexico*   27°20N 102°0W **86 B4**
Coal → *Canada*   59°39N 126°57W **70 B3**
Coalane *Mozam.*   17°48S 37°2E **55 F4**
Coalcomán *Mexico*   18°47N 103°9W **86 D4**
Coaldale *Canada*   49°45N 112°35W **70 D6**
Coalgate *U.S.A.*   34°32N 96°13W **84 D6**
Coalinga *U.S.A.*   36°9N 120°21W **78 J6**
Coalisland *U.K.*   54°33N 6°42W **10 B5**
Coalville *U.K.*   52°44N 1°23W **12 E6**
Coalville *U.S.A.*   40°55N 111°24W **76 F8**
Coamo *Puerto Rico*   18°5N 66°22W **89 d**
Coari *Brazil*   4°8S 63°7W **92 D6**
Coast □ *Kenya*   2°40S 39°45E **54 C4**
Coast Mts. *Canada*   55°0N 129°20W **70 C3**
Coast Ranges *U.S.A.*   39°0N 123°0W **78 G4**
Coatbridge *U.K.*   55°52N 4°6W **11 F4**
Coatepec *Mexico*   19°27N 96°58W **87 D5**
Coatepeque *Guatemala*   14°46N 91°55W **88 D1**
Coatesville *U.S.A.*   39°59N 75°50W **81 F16**
Coaticook *Canada*   45°10N 71°46W **83 A13**
Coats I. *Canada*   62°30N 83°0W **69 E15**
Coats Land *Antarctica*   77°0S 25°0W **5 D1**
Coatzacoalcos *Mexico*   18°7N 94°25W **87 D6**
Cobá *Mexico*   20°31N 87°45W **87 C7**
Cobalt *Canada*   47°25N 79°42W **72 C4**
Cobán *Guatemala*   15°30N 90°21W **88 C1**
Cobar *Australia*   31°27S 145°48E **63 E4**
Cóbh *Ireland*   51°51N 8°17W **10 E3**
Cobija *Bolivia*   11°0S 68°50W **92 F5**
Cobleskill *U.S.A.*   42°41N 74°29W **83 D10**
Coboconk *Canada*   44°39N 78°48W **82 B6**
Cobourg *Canada*   43°58N 78°10W **82 C6**
Cobourg Pen. *Australia*   11°20S 132°15E **60 B5**
Cobram *Australia*   35°54S 145°40E **63 F4**
Cóbué *Mozam.*   12°0S 34°58E **55 E3**
Coburg *Germany*   50°15N 10°58E **16 C6**
Coburg I. *Canada*   75°57N 79°26W **69 B16**
Cocanada = Kakinada
  India   16°57N 82°11E **41 L13**
Cochabamba *Bolivia*   17°26S 66°10W **92 G5**
Cochemane *Mozam.*   17°0S 32°54E **55 F3**
Cochin *India*   9°58N 76°20E **40 Q10**
Cochin China = Nam-Phan
  Vietnam   10°30N 106°0E **39 G6**
Cochran *U.S.A.*   32°23N 83°21W **85 E13**
Cochrane *Alta., Canada*   51°11N 114°30W **70 C6**
Cochrane *Ont., Canada*   49°0N 81°0W **72 C3**
Cochrane *Chile*   47°15S 72°33W **96 F2**
Cochrane → *Canada*   59°0N 103°40W **71 B8**
Cochrane, L. *Chile*   47°10S 72°0W **96 F2**
Cochranton *U.S.A.*   41°31N 80°3W **82 E4**
Cockburn *Australia*   32°5S 141°0E **63 E3**
Cockburn, Canal *Chile*   54°30S 72°0W **96 G2**
Cockburn I. *Canada*   45°55N 83°22W **72 C3**
Cockburn Ra. *Australia*   15°46S 128°0E **60 C4**
Cockermouth *U.K.*   54°40N 3°22W **12 C4**
Cocklebiddy *Australia*   32°0S 126°3E **61 F4**
Cockpit Country, The
  Jamaica   18°15N 77°45W **88 a**
Coco → *Cent. Amer.*   15°0N 83°8W **88 D3**
Coco, I. del *Pac. Oc.*   5°25N 87°55W **65 J19**
Cocoa *U.S.A.*   28°21N 80°44W **85 G14**
Cocobeach *Gabon*   0°59N 9°34E **52 D1**
Cocos B. *Trin. & Tob.*   10°25N 61°2W **93 K15**
Cocos Is. *Ind. Oc.*   12°10S 96°55E **64 J1**
Cocos Ridge *Pac. Oc.*   4°0N 88°0W **65 G19**
Cod, C. *U.S.A.*   42°5N 70°10W **81 D18**
Codajás *Brazil*   3°55S 62°0W **92 D6**
Codó *Brazil*   4°30S 43°55W **93 D10**
Cody *U.S.A.*   44°32N 109°3W **76 D9**
Coe Hill *Canada*   44°52N 77°50W **82 B7**
Coelemu *Chile*   36°30S 72°48W **94 D1**
Coen *Australia*   13°52S 143°12E **62 A3**
Coeur d'Alene *U.S.A.*   47°41N 116°46W **76 C5**
Coeur d'Alene L.
  U.S.A.   47°32N 116°49W **76 C5**
Coevorden *Neths.*   52°40N 6°44E **15 B6**
Cofete *Canary Is.*   28°6N 14°23W **24 F5**
Coffeyville *U.S.A.*   37°2N 95°37W **80 G6**
Coffin B. *Australia*   34°38S 135°28E **63 E2**
Coffin Bay *Australia*   34°37S 135°29E **63 E2**
Coffin Bay △ *Australia*   34°34S 135°19E **63 E2**
Coffin Bay Peninsula
  Australia   34°32S 135°15E **63 E2**
Coffs Harbour *Australia*   30°16S 153°5E **63 E5**
Cognac *France*   45°41N 0°20W **20 D3**
Cohocton *U.S.A.*   42°30N 77°30W **82 D7**
Cohocton → *U.S.A.*   42°9N 77°6W **82 D7**
Cohoes *U.S.A.*   42°46N 73°42W **83 D11**
Cohuna *Australia*   35°45S 144°15E **63 F3**
Coiba, I. de *Panama*   7°30N 81°40W **88 E3**
Coig → *Argentina*   51°0S 69°10W **96 G3**
Coigeach, Rubha *U.K.*   58°6N 5°26W **11 C3**
Coihaique *Chile*   45°30S 71°45W **96 F2**
Coimbatore *India*   11°2N 76°59E **40 P10**
Coimbra *Brazil*   19°55S 57°48W **92 G7**
Coimbra *Portugal*   40°15N 8°27W **21 B1**
Coín *Spain*   36°40N 4°48W **21 D3**
Coipasa, Salar de *Bolivia*   19°26S 68°9W **92 G5**
Cojimies *Ecuador*   0°20N 80°0W **92 C2**
Cojutepeque *El Salv.*   13°41N 88°54W **88 D2**
Cokeville *U.S.A.*   42°5N 110°57W **76 E8**
Colac *Australia*   38°21S 143°35E **63 F3**
Colatina *Brazil*   19°32S 40°37W **93 G10**
Colbeck, C. *Antarctica*   77°6S 157°48W **5 D13**

Colborne *Canada*   44°0N 77°53W **82 C7**
Colby *U.S.A.*   39°24N 101°3W **80 F3**
Colca → *Peru*   15°55S 72°43W **92 G4**
Colchester *U.K.*   51°54N 0°55E **13 F8**
Colchester *U.S.A.*   41°35N 72°20W **83 E12**
Cold L. *Canada*   54°33N 110°5W **71 C7**
Cold Lake *Canada*   54°27N 110°10W **71 C6**
Coldstream *Canada*   50°13N 119°11W **70 C5**
Coldstream *U.K.*   55°39N 2°15W **11 F6**
Coldwater *Canada*   44°42N 79°40W **82 B5**
Coldwater *Kans., U.S.A.*   37°16N 99°20W **80 G4**
Coldwater *Mich., U.S.A.*   41°57N 85°0W **81 E11**
Colebrook *U.S.A.*   44°54N 71°30W **83 B13**
Coleman *Canada*   49°40N 114°30W **70 D6**
Coleman *U.S.A.*   31°50N 99°26W **84 F5**
Coleman → *Australia*   15°6S 141°38E **62 B3**
Colenso *S. Africa*   28°44S 29°50E **57 D4**
Coleraine *Australia*   37°36S 141°40E **63 F3**
Coleraine *U.K.*   55°8N 6°41W **10 A5**
Coleridge, L. *N.Z.*   43°17S 171°30E **59 E3**
Colesberg *S. Africa*   30°45S 25°5E **56 E4**
Coleville *U.S.A.*   38°34N 119°30W **78 G7**
Colfax *Calif., U.S.A.*   39°6N 120°57W **78 F6**
Colfax *La., U.S.A.*   31°31N 92°42W **84 F8**
Colfax *Wash., U.S.A.*   46°53N 117°22W **76 C5**
Colhué Huapi, L.
  Argentina   45°30S 69°0W **96 F3**
Coligny *S. Africa*   26°17S 26°15E **57 D4**
Colima *Mexico*   19°14N 103°43W **86 D4**
Colima □ *Mexico*   19°10N 104°0W **86 D4**
Colima, Nevado de
  Mexico   19°33N 103°38W **86 D4**
Colina *Chile*   33°13S 70°45W **94 C1**
Colinas *Brazil*   6°0S 44°10W **93 E10**
Coll *U.K.*   56°39N 6°34W **11 E2**
Collahuasi *Chile*   21°5S 68°45W **94 A2**
Collarenebri *Australia*   29°33S 148°34E **63 D4**
Colleen Bawn *Zimbabwe*   21°0S 29°12E **55 G2**
College *U.S.A.*   64°52N 147°49W **74 C10**
College Park *U.S.A.*   33°39N 84°27W **85 E12**
College Station *U.S.A.*   30°37N 96°21W **84 F6**
Collie *Australia*   33°22S 116°8E **61 F2**
Collier B. *Australia*   16°10S 124°15E **60 C3**
Collier Ra. *Australia*   24°45S 119°10E **61 D2**
Collier Range △
  Australia   24°39S 119°7E **61 D2**
Collierville *U.S.A.*   35°3N 89°40W **85 D10**
Collina, Passo di *Italy*   44°2N 10°56E **22 B4**
Collingwood *Canada*   44°29N 80°13W **82 B4**
Collingwood *N.Z.*   40°41S 172°40E **59 D4**
Collins *Canada*   50°17N 89°27W **72 B2**
Collins Bay *Canada*   44°14N 76°36W **83 B8**
Collinson Pen. *Canada*   69°58N 101°24W **68 D11**
Collinsville *Australia*   20°30S 147°56E **62 C4**
Collipulli *Chile*   37°55S 72°30W **94 D1**
Collooney *Ireland*   54°11N 8°29W **10 B3**
Colmar *France*   48°5N 7°20E **20 B7**
Colo → *Australia*   33°25S 150°52E **63 E5**
Cologne = Köln *Germany*   50°56N 6°57E **16 C4**
Colom, I. d'en *Spain*   39°58N 4°16E **24 B11**
Coloma *U.S.A.*   38°48N 120°53W **78 G6**
Colomb-Béchar = Béchar
  Algeria   31°38N 2°18W **50 B5**
Colombia ■ *S. Amer.*   3°45N 73°0W **92 C4**
Colombian Basin
  S. Amer.   14°0N 76°0W **66 H12**
Colombo *Sri Lanka*   6°56N 79°58E **40 R11**
Colón *B. Aires, Argentina*   33°53S 61°7W **94 C3**
Colón *Entre Ríos,
  Argentina*   32°12S 58°10W **94 C4**
Colón *Cuba*   22°42N 80°54W **88 B3**
Colón *Panama*   9°20N 79°54W **88 E4**
Colón, Arch. de *Ecuador*   0°0 91°0W **90 D1**
Colònia de Sant Jordi
  Spain   39°19N 2°59E **24 B9**
Colonia del Sacramento
  Uruguay   34°25S 57°50W **94 C4**
Colonia Dora *Argentina*   28°34S 62°59W **94 B3**
Colonial Beach *U.S.A.*   38°15N 76°58W **81 F15**
Colonie *U.S.A.*   42°43N 73°50W **83 D11**
Colonsay *Canada*   51°59N 105°52W **71 C7**
Colonsay *U.K.*   56°5N 6°12W **11 E2**
Colorado □ *U.S.A.*   39°30N 105°30W **76 G11**
Colorado → *Argentina*   39°50S 62°8W **96 D4**
Colorado → *N. Amer.*   31°45N 114°40W **77 L6**
Colorado → *U.S.A.*   28°36N 95°59W **84 G7**
Colorado City *U.S.A.*   32°24N 100°52W **84 E4**
Colorado Plateau *U.S.A.*   37°0N 111°0W **77 H8**
Colorado River Aqueduct
  U.S.A.   33°50N 117°23W **79 L12**
Colorado Springs
  U.S.A.   38°50N 104°49W **76 G11**
Colotlán *Mexico*   22°6N 103°16W **86 C4**
Colstrip *U.S.A.*   45°53N 106°38W **76 D10**
Colton *U.S.A.*   44°33N 74°56W **83 B10**
Columbia *Ky., U.S.A.*   37°6N 85°18W **81 G11**
Columbia *La., U.S.A.*   32°6N 92°5W **84 E8**
Columbia *Miss., U.S.A.*   31°15N 89°50W **85 F10**
Columbia *Mo., U.S.A.*   38°57N 92°20W **80 F7**
Columbia *Pa., U.S.A.*   40°2N 76°30W **83 F8**
Columbia *S.C., U.S.A.*   34°0N 81°2W **85 D14**
Columbia *Tenn., U.S.A.*   35°37N 87°2W **85 D11**
Columbia → *N. Amer.*   46°15N 124°5W **78 D2**
Columbia, C. *Canada*   83°6N 69°57W **69 A18**
Columbia, District of □
  U.S.A.   38°55N 77°0W **81 F15**
Columbia, Mt. *Canada*   52°8N 117°20W **70 C5**
Columbia Basin *U.S.A.*   46°45N 119°5W **76 C4**
Columbia Falls *U.S.A.*   48°23N 114°11W **76 B6**
Columbia Mts. *Canada*   52°0N 119°0W **70 C5**
Columbia Plateau
  U.S.A.   44°0N 117°30W **76 E5**
Columbiana *U.S.A.*   40°53N 80°42W **82 F4**
Columbretes, Is. *Spain*   39°50N 0°50E **21 C6**
Columbus *Ga., U.S.A.*   32°28N 84°59W **85 E12**
Columbus *Ind., U.S.A.*   39°13N 85°55W **81 F11**
Columbus *Kans., U.S.A.*   37°10N 94°50W **80 G6**
Columbus *Miss., U.S.A.*   33°30N 88°25W **85 E10**
Columbus *Mont.,
  U.S.A.*   45°38N 109°15W **76 D9**

Columbus *N. Mex.,
  U.S.A.*   31°50N 107°38W **77 L10**
Columbus *Nebr., U.S.A.*   41°26N 97°22W **80 E5**
Columbus *Ohio, U.S.A.*   39°58N 83°0W **81 F12**
Columbus *Tex., U.S.A.*   29°42N 96°33W **84 G6**
Colusa *U.S.A.*   39°13N 122°1W **78 F4**
Colville *U.S.A.*   48°33N 117°54W **76 B5**
Colville → *U.S.A.*   70°25N 150°30W **74 A9**
Colville, C. *N.Z.*   36°29S 175°21E **59 B5**
Colwood *Canada*   48°26N 123°29W **78 B3**
Colwyn Bay *U.K.*   53°18N 3°44W **12 D4**
Comácchio *Italy*   44°42N 12°11E **22 B5**
Comalcalco *Mexico*   18°16N 93°13W **87 D6**
Comallo *Argentina*   41°0S 70°5W **96 E2**
Comanche *U.S.A.*   31°54N 98°36W **84 F5**
Comandante Ferraz
  Antarctica   62°30S 58°0W **5 C18**
Comayagua *Honduras*   14°25N 87°37W **88 D2**
Combahee → *U.S.A.*   32°30N 80°31W **85 E14**
Combarbalá *Chile*   31°11S 71°2W **94 C1**
Combe Martin *U.K.*   51°12N 4°3W **13 F3**
Comber *Canada*   42°14N 82°33W **82 D2**
Comber *U.K.*   54°33N 5°45W **10 B6**
Combermere *Canada*   45°22N 77°37W **82 A7**
Comblain-au-Pont
  Belgium   50°29N 5°35E **15 D5**
Comeragh Mts. *Ireland*   52°18N 7°34W **10 D4**
Comet *Australia*   23°36S 148°38E **62 C4**
Comilla *Bangla.*   23°28N 91°10E **41 H17**
Comino *Malta*   36°1N 14°20E **25 C1**
Comino, C. *Italy*   40°32N 9°49E **22 D3**
Comitán de Domínguez
  Mexico   16°15N 92°8W **87 D6**
Commerce *Ga., U.S.A.*   34°12N 83°28W **85 D13**
Commerce *Tex., U.S.A.*   33°15N 95°54W **84 E7**
Committee B. *Canada*   68°30N 86°30W **69 D14**
Commodore, C. *Canada*   44°47N 80°54W **82 B4**
Commonwealth B.
  Antarctica   67°0S 144°0E **5 C10**
Commoron Cr. →
  Australia   28°22S 150°8E **63 D5**
Communism Pk. = imeni Ismail
  Samani, Pik *Tajikistan*   39°0N 72°2E **28 F8**
Como *Italy*   45°47N 9°5E **20 D8**
Como, Lago di *Italy*   46°0N 9°11E **20 D8**
Comodoro Rivadavia
  Argentina   45°50S 67°40W **96 F3**
Comorin, C. = Kanniyakumari
  India   8°3N 77°40E **40 Q10**
Comoros ■ *Ind. Oc.*   12°10S 44°15E **53 a**
Comox *Canada*   49°42N 124°55W **70 D4**
Compiègne *France*   49°24N 2°50E **20 B5**
Compostela *Mexico*   21°14N 104°55W **86 C4**
Comprida, I. *Brazil*   24°50S 47°42W **95 A6**
Compton *Canada*   45°14N 71°49W **83 A13**
Compton *U.S.A.*   33°53N 118°13W **79 M8**
Comrat *Moldova*   46°18N 28°40E **17 E15**
Con Cuong *Vietnam*   19°2N 104°54E **38 C5**
Con Dao △ *Vietnam*   8°42N 106°35E **39 H6**
Con Son *Vietnam*   8°41N 106°37E **39 H6**
Conakry *Guinea*   9°29N 13°49W **50 G3**
Conara *Australia*   41°50S 147°26E **63 G4**
Concarneau *France*   47°52N 3°56W **20 C2**
Conceição *Mozam.*   18°47S 36°7E **55 F4**
Conceição da Barra
  Brazil   18°35S 39°45W **93 G11**
Conceição do Araguaia
  Brazil   8°0S 49°2W **93 E9**
Concepción *Argentina*   27°20S 65°35W **94 B2**
Concepción *Bolivia*   16°15S 62°8W **92 G6**
Concepción *Chile*   36°50S 73°0W **94 D1**
Concepción *Mexico*   18°15N 90°5W **87 D6**
Concepción *Paraguay*   23°22S 57°26W **94 A4**
Concepción □ *Chile*   37°0S 72°30W **94 D1**
Concepción → *Mexico*   30°32N 113°2W **86 A2**
Concepción, Est. de
  Chile   50°30S 74°55W **96 G2**
Concepción, L. *Bolivia*   17°20S 61°20W **92 G6**
Concepción, Pta.
  Mexico   26°53N 111°50W **86 B2**
Concepción del Oro
  Mexico   24°38N 101°25W **86 C4**
Concepción del Uruguay
  Argentina   32°35S 58°20W **94 C4**
Conception, Pt. *U.S.A.*   34°27N 120°28W **79 L6**
Conception B. *Canada*   47°45N 53°0W **73 C9**
Conception I. *Bahamas*   23°52N 75°9W **89 B4**
Concession *Zimbabwe*   17°27S 30°56E **55 F3**
Conchas Dam *U.S.A.*   35°22N 104°11W **77 J11**
Concho *U.S.A.*   34°28N 109°36W **77 J9**
Concho → *U.S.A.*   31°34N 99°43W **84 F5**
Conchos → *Chihuahua,
  Mexico*   29°35N 104°25W **86 B4**
Conchos → *Chihuahua,
  Mexico*   27°29N 106°45W **86 B3**
Conchos → *Tamaulipas,
  Mexico*   24°55N 97°38W **87 B5**
Concord *Calif., U.S.A.*   37°59N 122°2W **78 H4**
Concord *N.C., U.S.A.*   35°25N 80°35W **85 D14**
Concord *N.H., U.S.A.*   43°12N 71°32W **83 C13**
Concordia *Antarctica*   75°6S 123°23E **5 D17**
Concordia *Argentina*   31°20S 58°2W **94 C4**
Concórdia *Amazonas,
  Brazil*   4°36S 66°36W **92 D5**
Concórdia *Sta. Catarina,
  Brazil*   27°14S 52°1W **95 B5**
Concordia *Mexico*   23°17N 106°4W **86 C3**
Concordia *U.S.A.*   39°34N 97°40W **80 F5**
Concrete *U.S.A.*   48°32N 121°45W **78 B4**
Condamine *Australia*   26°56S 150°9E **63 D5**
Conde *U.S.A.*   45°9N 98°6W **80 C4**
Condeúba *Brazil*   14°52S 42°0W **93 F10**
Condobolin *Australia*   33°4S 147°6E **63 E4**
Condon *U.S.A.*   45°14N 120°11W **76 D3**
Conegliano *Italy*   45°53N 12°18E **22 B5**
Conejera, I. = Conills, I. des
  Spain   39°11N 2°58E **24 B9**
Conejos *Mexico*   26°14N 103°53W **86 B4**

Conemaugh → *U.S.A.*   40°28N 79°19W **82 F5**
Confuso → *Paraguay*   25°9S 57°34W **94 B4**
Congleton *U.K.*   53°10N 2°13W **12 D5**
Congo (Brazzaville) = Congo
  Africa   1°0S 16°0E **52 E3**
Congo (Kinshasa) = Congo, Dem.
  Rep. of the ■ *Africa*   3°0S 23°0E **52 E4**
Congo ■ *Africa*   1°0S 16°0E **52 E3**
Congo → *Africa*   6°4S 12°24E **52 F2**
Congo, Dem. Rep. of the ■
  Africa   3°0S 23°0E **52 E4**
Congo Basin *Africa*   0°10S 24°30E **52 E4**
Congonhas *Brazil*   20°30S 43°52W **95 A7**
Congress *U.S.A.*   34°9N 112°51W **77 J7**
Conills, I. des *Spain*   39°11N 2°58E **24 B9**
Coniston *Canada*   46°29N 80°51W **72 C3**
Conjeeveram = Kanchipuram
  India   12°52N 79°45E **40 N11**
Conklin *Canada*   55°38N 111°5W **71 B6**
Conklin *U.S.A.*   42°2N 75°49W **83 D9**
Conn, L. *Ireland*   54°3N 9°15W **10 B2**
Connacht □ *Ireland*   53°43N 9°12W **10 C2**
Conneaut *U.S.A.*   41°57N 80°34W **82 E4**
Conneautville *U.S.A.*   41°45N 80°22W **82 E4**
Connecticut □ *U.S.A.*   41°30N 72°45W **83 E12**
Connecticut → *U.S.A.*   41°16N 72°20W **83 E12**
Connell *U.S.A.*   46°40N 118°52W **76 C4**
Connellsville *U.S.A.*   40°1N 79°35W **82 F5**
Connemara *Ireland*   53°29N 9°45W **10 C2**
Connemara △ *Ireland*   53°32N 9°52W **10 C2**
Connersville *U.S.A.*   39°39N 85°8W **81 F11**
Connors Ra. *Australia*   21°40S 149°10E **62 C4**
Conoonee → *Suriname*   5°48N 55°55W **93 B7**
Conquest *Canada*   51°32N 107°14W **71 C7**
Conrad *U.S.A.*   48°10N 111°57W **76 B8**
Conrad Rise *S. Ocean*   53°0S 41°0E **5 B5**
Conran, C. *Australia*   37°49S 148°44E **63 F4**
Conroe *U.S.A.*   30°19N 95°27W **84 F7**
Consecon *Canada*   44°0N 77°31W **82 C7**
Conselheiro Lafaiete
  Brazil   20°40S 43°48W **95 A7**
Consell *Spain*   39°40N 2°49E **24 B9**
Consett *U.K.*   54°51N 1°50W **12 C6**
Consort *Canada*   52°1N 110°46W **71 C6**
Constance = Konstanz
  Germany   47°40N 9°10E **16 E5**
Constance, L. = Bodensee
  Europe   47°35N 9°25E **16 E5**
Constanța *Romania*   44°14N 28°38E **17 F15**
Constantine *Algeria*   36°25N 6°42E **50 A7**
Constitución *Chile*   35°20S 72°30W **94 D1**
Constitución *Uruguay*   31°0S 57°50W **94 C4**
Constitución de 1857 △
  Mexico   32°4N 115°55W **86 A1**
Consul *Canada*   49°20N 109°30W **71 D7**
Contact *U.S.A.*   41°46N 114°45W **76 F6**
Contai *India*   21°54N 87°46E **43 J12**
Contamana *Peru*   7°19S 74°55W **92 E4**
Contas → *Brazil*   14°17S 39°1W **93 F11**
Contoocook *U.S.A.*   43°13N 71°45W **83 C13**
Contra Costa *Mozam.*   25°9S 33°30E **57 D5**
Contwoyto L. *Canada*   65°42N 110°50W **68 D8**
Conway = Conwy *U.K.*   53°17N 3°50W **12 D4**
Conway *Australia*   20°24S 148°41E **62 b**
Conway *Canada*   44°6N 76°54W **82 B8**
Conway *Ark., U.S.A.*   35°5N 92°26W **84 D8**
Conway *N.H., U.S.A.*   43°59N 71°7W **83 C13**
Conway *S.C., U.S.A.*   33°51N 79°3W **85 E15**
Conway, C. *Australia*   20°34S 148°46E **62 b**
Conway, L. *Australia*   28°17S 135°35E **63 D2**
Conwy *U.K.*   53°17N 3°50W **12 D4**
Conwy □ *U.K.*   53°10N 3°44W **12 D4**
Conwy → *U.K.*   53°17N 3°50W **12 D4**
Coober Pedy *Australia*   29°1S 134°43E **63 D1**
Cooch Behar = Koch Bihar
  India   26°22N 89°29E **41 F16**
Cooinda *Australia*   13°15S 130°5E **60 B5**
Cook *Australia*   30°37S 130°25E **61 F5**
Cook *U.S.A.*   47°51N 92°41W **80 B7**
Cook, B. *Chile*   55°10S 70°0W **96 H3**
Cook, C. *Canada*   50°8N 127°55W **70 C3**
Cook, Mt. = Aoraki Mount Cook
  N.Z.   43°36S 170°9E **59 E3**
Cook Inlet *U.S.A.*   60°0N 152°0W **68 F1**
Cook Is. *Pac. Oc.*   17°0S 160°0W **65 J12**
Cook Strait *N.Z.*   41°15S 174°29E **59 D5**
Cookeville *U.S.A.*   36°10N 85°30W **85 D12**
Cookhouse *S. Africa*   32°44S 25°47E **56 E4**
Cooks Harbour *Canada*   51°36N 55°52W **73 B8**
Cookstown *Canada*   44°11N 79°42W **82 B5**
Cookstown *U.K.*   54°39N 6°45W **10 B5**
Cooksville *Canada*   43°35N 79°38W **82 C5**
Cooktown *Australia*   15°30S 145°16E **62 B4**
Coolabah *Australia*   31°1S 146°43E **63 E4**
Cooladdi *Australia*   26°37S 145°23E **63 D4**
Coolah *Australia*   31°48S 149°41E **63 E4**
Coolamon *Australia*   34°46S 147°8E **63 E4**
Coolgardie *Australia*   30°55S 121°8E **61 F3**
Coolidge *U.S.A.*   32°59N 111°31W **77 K8**
Coolidge Dam *U.S.A.*   33°10N 110°32W **77 K8**
Cooma *Australia*   36°12S 149°8E **63 F4**
Coon Rapids *U.S.A.*   45°9N 93°19W **80 C7**
Coonabarabran
  Australia   31°14S 149°18E **63 E4**
Coonamble *Australia*   30°56S 148°27E **63 E4**
Coonana *Australia*   31°0S 123°0E **61 F3**
Coonana △ *Australia*   30°51S 122°53E **61 F3**
Coondapoor *India*   13°42N 74°40E **40 N9**
Coongie *Australia*   26°4S 139°59E **63 D2**
Cooninnie, L. *Australia*   26°4S 139°59E **63 D2**
Cooper *U.S.A.*   33°23N 95°42W **84 E7**
Cooper Cr. → *Australia*   28°29S 137°46E **63 D2**
Cooper Ridge *Pac. Oc.*   10°0N 150°30W **65 G12**
Cooperstown *N. Dak.,
  U.S.A.*   47°27N 98°8W **80 B4**
Cooperstown *N.Y.,
  U.S.A.*   42°42N 74°56W **83 D10**

Coorabie *Australia*   31°54S 132°18E **61 F5**
Coorong, The *Australia*   35°50S 139°20E **63 F2**
Coorow *Australia*   29°53S 116°2E **61 E2**
Cooroy *Australia*   26°22S 152°54E **63 D5**
Coos Bay *U.S.A.*   43°22N 124°13W **76 E1**
Cootamundra *Australia*   34°36S 148°1E **63 E4**
Cootehill *Ireland*   54°4N 7°5W **10 B4**
Copahue Paso *Argentina*   37°49S 71°8W **94 D1**
Copainalá *Mexico*   17°4N 93°9W **87 D6**
Copake *U.S.A.*   42°7N 73°31W **83 D11**
Copán *Honduras*   14°50N 89°9W **88 D2**
Cope *U.S.A.*   39°40N 102°51W **76 G12**
Copenhagen = København
  Denmark   55°40N 12°26E **9 J15**
Copenhagen *U.S.A.*   43°54N 75°41W **83 C9**
Copiapó *Chile*   27°30S 70°20W **94 B1**
Copiapó → *Chile*   27°19S 70°56W **94 B1**
Coplay *U.S.A.*   40°44N 75°29W **83 F9**
Copo △ *Argentina*   25°53S 61°41W **94 B3**
Copp L. *Canada*   60°14N 114°40W **70 A6**
Copper Canyon = Barranca del
  Cobre △ *Mexico*   27°18N 107°40W **86 B3**
Copper Center *U.S.A.*   61°58N 145°18W **74 C10**
Copper Harbor *U.S.A.*   47°28N 87°53W **80 B10**
Copper Queen *Zimbabwe*   17°29S 29°18E **55 F2**
Copperas Cove *U.S.A.*   31°8N 97°54W **84 F6**
Copperbelt □ *Zambia*   13°15S 27°30E **55 E2**
Coppermine = Kugluktuk
  Canada   67°50N 115°5W **68 D8**
Coppermine → *Canada*   67°49N 116°4W **68 D8**
Copperopolis *U.S.A.*   37°58N 120°38W **78 H6**
Coquet → *U.K.*   55°20N 1°32E **12 B6**
Coquille *U.S.A.*   43°11N 124°11W **76 E1**
Coquimbo *Chile*   30°0S 71°20W **94 C1**
Coquimbo □ *Chile*   31°0S 71°0W **94 C1**
Coquitlam *Canada*   49°17N 122°45W **70 D4**
Corabia *Romania*   43°48N 24°30E **17 G13**
Coracora *Peru*   15°5S 73°45W **92 G4**
Coraki *Australia*   28°59S 153°17E **63 D5**
Coral *U.S.A.*   40°29N 79°10W **82 F5**
Coral Bay *Australia*   23°8S 113°46E **60 D1**
Coral Gables *U.S.A.*   25°43N 80°16W **85 J14**
Coral Harbour *Canada*   64°8N 83°10W **69 E15**
Coral Sea *Pac. Oc.*   15°0S 150°0E **58 C8**
Coral Sea Basin *Pac. Oc.*   14°0S 152°0E **64 J7**
Coral Sea Islands Terr. □
  Australia   20°0S 155°0E **38 G8**
Coral Springs *U.S.A.*   26°16N 80°16W **85 H14**
Coraopolis *U.S.A.*   40°31N 80°10W **82 F4**
Corato *Italy*   41°9N 16°25E **22 D7**
Corbett △ *India*   29°20N 79°0E **43 E8**
Corbin *U.S.A.*   36°57N 84°6W **81 G11**
Corby *U.K.*   52°30N 0°41W **13 E7**
Corcaigh = Cork *Ireland*   51°54N 8°29W **10 E3**
Corcoran *U.S.A.*   36°6N 119°33W **78 J7**
Corcovado △ *Costa Rica*   8°33N 83°35W **88 E3**
Corcubión *Spain*   42°56N 9°12W **21 A1**
Cordele *U.S.A.*   31°58N 83°47W **85 F13**
Cordell *U.S.A.*   35°17N 98°59W **84 D5**
Córdoba *Argentina*   31°20S 64°10W **94 C3**
Córdoba *Mexico*   18°53N 96°56W **87 D5**
Córdoba *Spain*   37°50N 4°50W **21 D3**
Córdoba □ *Argentina*   31°22S 64°15W **94 C3**
Córdoba, Sierra de
  Argentina   31°10S 64°25W **94 C3**
Cordova *U.S.A.*   60°33N 145°45W **68 C4**
Corella → *Australia*   19°34S 140°47E **62 B3**
Corfield *Australia*   21°40S 143°21E **62 C3**
Corfu = Kerkyra *Greece*   39°38N 19°50E **25 A3**
Corfu *U.S.A.*   42°57N 78°24W **82 D6**
Corfu, Str. of = Kerkyras, Notio
  Steno *Greece*   39°34N 20°0E **25 A4**
Coria *Spain*   39°58N 6°33W **21 C2**
Coria del Río *Spain*   37°16N 6°3W **21 D2**
Corigliano Cálabro *Italy*   39°36N 16°31E **22 E7**
Coringa Is. *Australia*   16°58S 149°58E **62 B4**
Corinth = Korinthos
  Greece   37°56N 22°55E **23 F10**
Corinth *Miss., U.S.A.*   34°56N 88°31W **85 D10**
Corinth *N.Y., U.S.A.*   43°15N 73°49W **83 C11**
Corinth, G. of = Korinthiakos
  Kolpos *Greece*   38°16N 22°30E **23 E10**
Corinto *Brazil*   18°20S 44°30W **93 G10**
Corinto *Nic.*   12°30N 87°10W **88 D2**
Cork *Ireland*   51°54N 8°29W **10 E3**
Cork □ *Ireland*   51°57N 8°40W **10 E3**
Cork Harbour *Ireland*   51°47N 8°16W **10 E3**
Çorlu *Turkey*   41°11N 27°49E **23 D12**
Cormack L. *Canada*   60°56N 121°37W **70 A4**
Cormorant *Canada*   54°14N 100°35W **71 C8**
Cormorant L. *Canada*   54°15N 100°50W **71 C8**
Corn Is. = Maíz, Is. del
  Nic.   12°15N 83°4W **88 D3**
Cornélio Procópio *Brazil*   23°7S 50°40W **95 A5**
Corner Brook *Canada*   48°57N 57°58W **73 C8**
Cornești *Moldova*   47°21N 28°1E **17 E15**
Corning *Ark., U.S.A.*   36°25N 90°35W **85 C9**
Corning *Calif., U.S.A.*   39°56N 122°11W **76 G2**
Corning *Iowa, U.S.A.*   40°59N 94°44W **80 E6**
Corning *N.Y., U.S.A.*   42°9N 77°3W **82 D7**
Cornwall *Canada*   45°2N 74°44W **83 A10**
Cornwall *U.S.A.*   40°17N 76°25W **83 F8**
Cornwall □ *U.K.*   50°26N 4°40W **13 G3**
Cornwall I. *Canada*   77°37N 94°38W **69 B13**
Cornwallis I. *Canada*   75°8N 95°0W **69 B13**
Corny Pt. *Australia*   34°55S 137°0E **63 E2**
Coro *Venezuela*   11°25N 69°41W **92 A5**
Coroatá *Brazil*   4°8S 44°0W **93 D10**
Corocoro *Bolivia*   17°15S 68°28W **92 G5**
Coroico *Bolivia*   16°0S 67°50W **92 G5**
Coromandel *N.Z.*   36°45S 175°31E **59 B5**
Coromandel Coast *India*   12°30N 81°0E **40 N12**
Corona *Calif., U.S.A.*   33°53N 117°34W **79 M9**
Corona *N. Mex., U.S.A.*   34°15N 105°36W **77 J11**
Coronado *U.S.A.*   32°41N 117°10W **79 N9**
Coronado, B. de *Costa Rica*   9°0N 83°40W **88 E3**
Coronados, Is. Los
  Mexico   32°26N 117°19W **79 N9**
Coronation *Canada*   52°5N 111°27W **70 C6**

Coronation Gulf
Canada 68°25N 110°0W **68** D10
Coronation I. *Antarctica* 60°45S 46°0W **5** C18
Coronation Is. *Australia* 14°57S 124°55E **60** B3
Coronda *Argentina* 31°58S 60°56W **94** C3
Coronel *Chile* 37°0S 73°10W **94** D1
Coronel Bogado
Paraguay 27°11S 56°18W **94** B4
Coronel Dorrego
Argentina 38°40S 61°10W **94** D3
Coronel Oviedo
Paraguay 25°24S 56°30W **94** B4
Coronel Pringles
Argentina 38°0S 61°30W **94** D3
Coronel Suárez
Argentina 37°30S 61°52W **94** D3
Coronel Vidal *Argentina* 37°28S 57°45W **94** D4
Coropuna, Nevado *Peru* 15°30S 72°41W **92** G4
Corowa *Australia* 35°58S 146°21E **63** F4
Corozal □ *Belize* 18°23N 88°23W **87** D7
Corozal Pt. *Trin. & Tob.* 10°45N 61°37W **93** K15
Corpus *Argentina* 27°10S 55°30W **95** B4
Corpus Christi *U.S.A.* 27°47N 97°24W **84** H6
Corpus Christi, L. *U.S.A.* 28°2N 97°52W **84** G6
Corralejo *Canary Is.* 28°43N 13°53W **24** F6
Corraun Pen. *Ireland* 53°54N 9°54W **10** C2
Correntes, C. das *Mozam.* 24°6S 35°34E **57** C6
Corrib, L. *Ireland* 53°27N 9°16W **10** C2
Corrientes *Argentina* 27°30S 58°45W **94** B4
Corrientes □ *Argentina* 28°0S 57°0W **94** B4
Corrientes ➤ *Argentina* 30°42S 59°38W **94** C4
Corrientes ➤ *Peru* 3°43S 74°35W **92** D4
Corrientes, C. *Colombia* 5°30N 77°34W **92** B3
Corrientes, C. *Cuba* 21°43N 84°30W **88** B3
Corrientes, C. *Mexico* 20°25N 105°42W **86** C3
Corrigan *U.S.A.* 31°0N 94°52W **84** F7
Corrigin *Australia* 32°20S 117°53E **61** F2
Corriverton *Guyana* 5°55N 57°20W **92** B7
Corry *U.S.A.* 41°55N 79°39W **82** E5
Corse □ *France* 42°0N 9°0E **20** F8
Corse, C. *France* 43°1N 9°25E **20** E8
Corsica = Corse □ *France* 42°0N 9°0E **20** F8
Corsicana *U.S.A.* 32°6N 96°28W **84** E6
Corte *France* 42°19N 9°11E **20** E8
Cortés, Mar de = California, G. de
Mexico 27°0N 111°0W **86** B2
Cortez *U.S.A.* 37°21N 108°35W **77** H9
Cortland *N.Y., U.S.A.* 42°36N 76°11W **83** D8
Cortland *Ohio, U.S.A.* 41°20N 80°44W **82** E4
Çorum *Turkey* 40°30N 34°57E **19** F5
Corumbá *Brazil* 19°0S 57°30W **92** G7
Corunna = A Coruña
Spain 43°20N 8°25W **21** A1
Corvallis *U.S.A.* 44°34N 123°16W **76** D2
Corvette, L. de la *Canada* 53°25N 74°3W **72** B5
Corvo *Azores* 39°43N 31°8W **50** a
Corydon *U.S.A.* 40°46N 93°19W **80** E7
Cosalá *Mexico* 24°23N 106°41W **86** C3
Cosamaloapan de Carpio
Mexico 18°22N 95°48W **87** D5
Cosenza *Italy* 39°18N 16°15E **22** E7
Coshocton *U.S.A.* 40°16N 81°51W **82** F3
Cosmo Newberry
Australia 28°0S 122°54E **61** E3
Cosmo Newberry ◉
Australia 27°59S 122°53E **61** E3
Cosmonaut Sea *S. Ocean* 66°30S 40°0E **5** C5
Coso Junction *U.S.A.* 36°3N 117°57W **79** J9
Coso Pk. *U.S.A.* 36°13N 117°44W **79** J9
Cosquín *Argentina* 31°15S 64°30W **94** C3
Costa Blanca *Spain* 38°25N 0°10W **21** C5
Costa Brava *Spain* 41°30N 3°0E **21** B7
Costa Daurada *Spain* 41°12N 1°15E **21** B6
Costa del Sol *Spain* 36°30N 4°30W **21** D3
Costa Mesa *U.S.A.* 41°5N 9°35E **22** D3
Costa Rica ■ *Cent. Amer.* 10°0N 84°0W **88** E3
Costa Smeralda *Italy* 41°5N 9°35E **22** D3
Cosumnes ➤ *U.S.A.* 38°16N 121°26W **78** G5
Cotabato *Phil.* 7°14N 124°15E **37** C6
Cotagaita *Bolivia* 20°45S 65°40W **94** A2
Côte d'Azur *France* 43°25N 7°10E **20** E7
Côte-d'Ivoire = Ivory Coast ■
Africa 7°30N 5°0W **50** G4
Coteau des Prairies
U.S.A. 45°20N 97°50W **80** C5
Coteau du Missouri
U.S.A. 47°0N 100°0W **80** B4
Cotentin *France* 49°15N 1°30W **20** B3
Cotillo *Canary Is.* 28°41N 14°1W **24** F5
Cotonou *Benin* 6°20N 2°25E **50** G6
Cotopaxi *Ecuador* 0°40S 78°30W **92** D3
Cotswold Hills *U.K.* 51°42N 2°10W **13** F5
Cottage Grove *U.S.A.* 43°48N 123°3W **76** E2
Cottam *Canada* 42°8N 82°45W **82** D2
Cottbus *Germany* 51°45N 14°20E **16** C8
Cottonwood *U.S.A.* 34°45N 112°1W **77** J7
Cotulla *U.S.A.* 28°26N 99°14W **84** G5
Coudersport *U.S.A.* 41°46N 78°1W **82** E6
Couedic, C. du *Australia* 36°5S 136°40E **63** F2
Coulee City *U.S.A.* 47°37N 119°17W **76** C4
Coulee Dam Nat. Recr. Area =
Lake Roosevelt △
U.S.A. 48°5N 118°14W **76** B4
Coulman I. *Antarctica* 73°35S 170°0E **5** D11
Coulonge ➤ *Canada* 45°52N 76°46W **72** C4
Coulterville *U.S.A.* 37°43N 120°12W **78** H6
Council *Alaska, U.S.A.* 64°53N 163°41W **74** C7
Council *Idaho, U.S.A.* 44°44N 116°26W **76** D5
Council Bluffs *U.S.A.* 41°16N 95°52W **80** E6
Council Grove *U.S.A.* 38°40N 96°29W **80** F5
Coupeville *U.S.A.* 48°13N 122°41W **78** B4
Courantyne ➤ *S. Amer.* 5°55N 57°5W **92** B7
Courcelles *Belgium* 50°28N 4°23E **15** D4
Courtenay *Canada* 49°45N 125°0W **70** D4
Courtland *Canada* 42°51N 80°38W **82** D4
Courtland *U.S.A.* 38°20N 121°34W **78** G5
Courtrai = Kortrijk
Belgium 50°50N 3°17E **15** D3

Courtright *Canada* 42°49N 82°28W **82** D2
Coushatta *U.S.A.* 32°1N 93°21W **84** E8
Coutts Crossing
Australia 29°49S 152°55E **63** D5
Couva *Trin. & Tob.* 10°25N 61°27W **93** K15
Couvin *Belgium* 50°3N 4°29E **15** D4
Cove I. *Canada* 45°17N 81°44W **82** A3
Coventry *U.K.* 52°25N 1°28W **13** E6
Covilhã *Portugal* 40°17N 7°31W **21** B2
Covington *Ga., U.S.A.* 33°36N 83°51W **85** E13
Covington *Ky., U.S.A.* 39°5N 84°30W **81** F11
Covington *Tenn., U.S.A.* 35°34N 89°39W **85** D10
Covington *Va., U.S.A.* 37°47N 79°59W **81** G14
Cowal, L. *Australia* 33°40S 147°25E **63** E4
Cowan, L. *Australia* 31°45S 121°45E **61** F3
Cowan L. *Canada* 54°0N 107°15W **71** C7
Cowangie *Australia* 35°12S 141°26E **63** F3
Cowansville *Canada* 45°14N 72°46W **83** A12
Coward Springs
Australia 29°24S 136°49E **63** D2
Cowcowing Lakes
Australia 30°55S 117°20E **61** F2
Cowdenbeath *U.K.* 56°7N 3°21W **11** E5
Cowell *Australia* 33°39S 136°56E **63** E2
Cowes *U.K.* 50°45N 1°18W **13** G6
Cowichan L. *Canada* 48°53N 124°17W **78** B2
Cowlitz ➤ *U.S.A.* 46°6N 122°55W **78** D4
Cowra *Australia* 33°49S 148°42E **63** E4
Coxilha Grande *Brazil* 28°18S 51°30W **95** B5
Coxim *Brazil* 18°30S 54°55W **93** G8
Cox's Bazar *Bangla.* 21°26N 91°59E **41** J17
Coyote Wells *U.S.A.* 32°44N 115°58W **79** N11
Coyuca de Benitez
Mexico 17°2N 100°4W **87** D4
Coyuca de Catalán
Mexico 18°20N 100°39W **86** D4
Cozad *U.S.A.* 40°52N 99°59W **80** E4
Cozumel *Mexico* 20°31N 86°55W **87** C7
Cozumel, Isla *Mexico* 20°30N 86°40W **87** C7
Crab Hill *Barbados* 13°19N 59°38W **89** g
Cracow = Kraków
Poland 50°4N 19°57E **17** C10
Cracow *Australia* 25°17S 150°17E **63** D5
Cradle Mt.-Lake St. Clair △
Australia 41°49S 147°56E **63** G4
Cradock *Australia* 32°6S 138°31E **63** E2
Cradock *S. Africa* 32°8S 25°36E **56** E4
Craig *U.S.A.* 40°31N 107°33W **76** F10
Craigavon *U.K.* 54°27N 6°23W **10** B5
Craigmore *Zimbabwe* 20°28S 32°50E **55** G3
Craik *Canada* 51°3N 105°49W **71** C7
Crailsheim *Germany* 49°8N 10°5E **16** D6
Craiova *Romania* 44°21N 23°48E **17** F12
Cramsie *Australia* 23°20S 144°15E **62** C3
Cranberry L. *U.S.A.* 44°11N 74°50W **83** B10
Cranberry Portage
Canada 54°35N 101°23W **71** C8
Cranbrook *Australia* 34°18S 117°33E **61** F2
Cranbrook *Canada* 49°30N 115°46W **70** D5
Crandon *U.S.A.* 45°34N 88°54W **80** C9
Crane *Oreg., U.S.A.* 43°25N 118°35W **76** E4
Crane *Tex., U.S.A.* 31°24N 102°21W **84** F3
Crane, The *Barbados* 13°6N 59°27W **89** g
Cranston *U.S.A.* 41°47N 71°26W **83** E13
Crater L. *U.S.A.* 42°56N 122°6W **76** E2
Crater Lake △ *U.S.A.* 42°55N 122°10W **76** E2
Craters of the Moon △
U.S.A. 43°25N 113°30W **76** E7
Crateús *Brazil* 5°10S 40°39W **93** E10
Crato *Brazil* 7°10S 39°25W **93** E11
Craven, L. *Canada* 54°20N 76°56W **72** B4
Crawford *U.S.A.* 42°41N 103°25W **80** D2
Crawfordsville *U.S.A.* 40°2N 86°54W **80** E10
Crawley *U.K.* 51°7N 0°11W **13** F7
Crazy Mts. *U.S.A.* 46°12N 110°20W **76** C8
Crean L. *Canada* 54°5N 106°9W **71** C7
Crediton *Canada* 43°17N 81°33W **82** C3
Crediton *U.K.* 50°47N 3°40W **13** G4
Cree ➤ *Canada* 58°57N 105°47W **71** B7
Cree ➤ *U.K.* 54°55N 4°25W **11** G4
Cree L. *Canada* 57°30N 106°30W **71** B7
Creel *Mexico* 27°45N 107°38W **86** B3
Creemore *Canada* 44°19N 80°6W **82** B4
Creighton *Canada* 54°45N 101°54W **71** C8
Creighton *U.S.A.* 42°28N 97°54W **80** D5
Crema *Italy* 45°22N 9°41E **20** D8
Cremona *Italy* 45°7N 10°2E **20** D9
Cres *Croatia* 44°58N 14°25E **16** F8
Crescent City *U.S.A.* 41°45N 124°12W **76** F1
Crespo *Argentina* 32°2S 60°19W **94** C3
Cresson *U.S.A.* 40°28N 78°36W **82** F6
Crestline *Calif., U.S.A.* 34°14N 117°18W **79** L9
Crestline *Ohio, U.S.A.* 40°47N 82°44W **82** F2
Creston *Canada* 49°10N 116°31W **70** D5
Creston *Calif., U.S.A.* 35°32N 120°33W **78** K6
Creston *Iowa, U.S.A.* 41°4N 94°22W **80** E7
Crestview *Calif., U.S.A.* 37°46N 118°58W **78** H8
Crestview *Fla., U.S.A.* 30°46N 86°34W **85** F11
Crete = Kriti *Greece* 35°15N 25°0E **25** D7
Crete *U.S.A.* 40°38N 96°58W **80** E6
Créteil *France* 48°47N 2°27E **20** B5
Creus, C. de *Spain* 42°20N 3°19E **21** A7
Creuse ➤ *France* 47°0N 0°34E **20** C4
Crewe *U.K.* 53°6N 2°26W **12** D5
Crewkerne *U.K.* 50°53N 2°48W **13** G5
Crianlarich *U.K.* 56°24N 4°37W **11** E4
Criciúma *Brazil* 28°40S 49°23W **95** B6
Crieff *U.K.* 56°22N 3°50W **11** E5
Crimea □ *Ukraine* 45°30N 33°10E **19** E5
Crimean Pen. = Krymskyy
Pivostriv *Ukraine* 45°0N 34°0E **19** F5
Crişul Alb ➤ *Romania* 46°42N 21°17E **17** E11
Crişul Negru ➤
Romania 46°42N 21°16E **17** E11
Crna ➤ *Macedonia* 41°33N 21°59E **23** D9
Crna Gora = Montenegro ■
Europe 42°40N 19°20E **23** C8

Crna Gora *Macedonia* 42°10N 21°30E **23** C9
Crna Reka = Crna ➤
Macedonia 41°33N 21°59E **23** D9
Croagh Patrick *Ireland* 53°46N 9°40W **10** C2
Croatia ■ *Europe* 45°20N 16°0E **16** F9
Crocker, Banjaran
Malaysia 5°40N 116°30E **36** C5
Crockett *U.S.A.* 31°19N 95°27W **84** F7
Crocodile = Umgwenya ➤
Mozam. 25°14S 32°18E **57** D5
Crocodile Is. *Australia* 12°3S 134°58E **62** A1
Crohy Hd. *Ireland* 54°55N 8°26W **10** B3
Croix, L. la *Canada* 48°20N 92°15W **72** C1
Croker, C. *Australia* 10°58S 132°35E **60** B5
Croker, C. *Canada* 44°58N 80°59W **82** B4
Croker I. *Australia* 11°12S 132°32E **60** B5
Croker Islands Seas ◉
Australia 11°20S 132°30E **60** B5
Cromarty *U.K.* 57°40N 4°2W **11** D4
Cromer *U.K.* 52°56N 1°17E **12** E9
Cromwell *N.Z.* 45°3S 169°14E **59** F2
Cromwell *U.S.A.* 41°36N 72°39W **83** E12
Crook *U.K.* 54°43N 1°45W **12** C6
Crooked ➤ *Canada* 54°50N 127°23W **86** C3
Crooked ➤ *U.S.A.* 44°32N 121°16W **76** D3
Crooked I. *Bahamas* 22°50N 74°10W **89** B5
Crooked Island Passage
Bahamas 22°55N 74°35W **89** B5
Crookston *Minn., U.S.A.* 47°47N 96°37W **80** B5
Crookston *Nebr., U.S.A.* 42°56N 100°45W **80** D3
Crookwell *Australia* 34°28S 149°24E **63** E4
Crosby *U.K.* 53°30N 3°3W **12** D4
Crosby *N. Dak., U.S.A.* 48°55N 103°18W **80** A2
Crosby *Pa., U.S.A.* 41°45N 78°23W **82** E6
Crosbyton *U.S.A.* 33°40N 101°14W **84** E4
Cross City *U.S.A.* 29°38N 83°7W **85** G13
Cross Fell *U.K.* 54°43N 2°28W **12** C5
Cross L. *Canada* 54°45N 97°30W **71** C9
Cross Lake *Canada* 54°37N 97°47W **71** C9
Cross Sound *U.S.A.* 58°0N 135°0W **68** F4
Crossett *U.S.A.* 33°8N 91°58W **84** E9
Crosshaven *Ireland* 51°47N 8°17W **10** E3
Crossmaglen *U.K.* 54°5N 6°36W **10** B5
Crossmolina *Ireland* 54°6N 9°20W **10** B2
Crossville *U.S.A.* 35°57N 85°2W **85** D12
Croton-on-Hudson
U.S.A. 41°12N 73°55W **83** E11
Crotone *Italy* 39°5N 17°8E **22** E7
Crow ➤ *Canada* 59°41N 124°20W **70** B4
Crow Agency *U.S.A.* 45°36N 107°28W **76** D10
Crow Hd. *Ireland* 51°35N 10°9W **10** E1
Crowell *U.S.A.* 33°59N 99°43W **84** E5
Crowley *U.S.A.* 30°13N 92°22W **84** F8
Crowley, L. *U.S.A.* 37°35N 118°42W **78** H8
Crown Point *Ind., U.S.A.* 41°25N 87°22W **80** E10
Crown Point *N.Y., U.S.A.* 43°57N 73°26W **83** C11
Crown Pt. *Trin. & Tob.* 11°18N 60°51W **93** J16
Crownpoint *U.S.A.* 35°41N 108°9W **77** J9
Crows Landing *U.S.A.* 37°23N 121°6W **78** H5
Crows Nest *Australia* 27°16S 152°4E **63** D5
Crowsnest Pass *Canada* 49°40N 114°40W **70** D6
Croydon *Australia* 18°13S 142°14E **62** B3
Croydon □ *U.K.* 51°22N 0°5W **13** F7
Crozet, Is. *Ind. Oc.* 46°27S 52°0E **3** G12
Crusheen *Ireland* 52°57N 8°53W **10** D3
Cruz, C. *Cuba* 19°50N 77°50W **88** C4
Cruz Alta *Brazil* 28°45S 53°40W **95** B5
Cruz Bay *U.S. Virgin Is.* 18°20N 64°48W **89** e
Cruz del Eje *Argentina* 30°45S 64°50W **94** C3
Cruzeiro *Brazil* 22°33S 45°0W **95** A7
Cruzeiro do Oeste *Brazil* 23°46S 53°4W **95** A5
Cruzeiro do Sul *Brazil* 7°35S 72°35W **92** E4
Cry L. *Canada* 58°45N 129°0W **70** B3
Crystal Bay *U.S.A.* 39°15N 120°0W **78** F7
Crystal Brook *Australia* 33°21S 138°12E **63** E2
Crystal City *U.S.A.* 28°41N 99°50W **84** G5
Crystal Falls *U.S.A.* 46°5N 88°20W **80** B9
Crystal River *U.S.A.* 28°54N 82°35W **85** G13
Crystal Springs *U.S.A.* 31°59N 90°21W **85** F9
Csongrád *Hungary* 46°43N 20°12E **17** E11
Cu Lao Hon *Vietnam* 10°54N 108°18E **39** G7
Cua Rao *Vietnam* 19°16N 104°27E **38** C5
Cuácua ➤ *Mozam.* 17°54S 37°0E **55** F4
Cuamato *Angola* 17°2S 15°7E **56** B2
Cuamba *Mozam.* 14°45S 36°22E **55** E4
Cuando ➤ *Angola* 17°30S 23°15E **53** H4
Cuando Cubango □
Angola 16°25S 20°0E **56** B3
Cuango = Kwango ➤
Dem. Rep. of the Congo 3°14S 17°22E **52** E3
Cuanza ➤ *Angola* 9°21S 13°9E **52** F2
Cuarto ➤ *Argentina* 33°25S 63°2W **94** C3
Cuatrociénegas *Mexico* 26°59N 102°5W **86** B4
Cuauhtémoc *Mexico* 28°25N 106°52W **86** B3
Cuba *N. Mex., U.S.A.* 36°1N 107°4W **77** H10
Cuba *U.S.A.* 42°13N 78°17W **82** D6
Cuba ■ *W. Indies* 22°0N 79°0W **88** B4
Cuc Phuong △ *Vietnam* 20°17N 105°38E **38** B5
Cuchumatanes, Sierra de los
Guatemala 15°35N 91°25W **88** C1
Cuckfield *U.K.* 51°1N 0°8W **13** F7
Cucuí *Brazil* 1°12N 66°50W **92** C5
Cucurpé *Mexico* 30°20N 110°43W **86** A2
Cúcuta *Colombia* 7°54N 72°31W **92** B4
Cuddalore *India* 11°46N 79°45E **40** P11
Cuddapah *India* 14°30N 78°47E **40** M11
Cuddapan, L. *Australia* 25°45S 141°26E **62** D3
Cue *Australia* 27°25S 117°54E **61** E2
Cuenca *Ecuador* 2°50S 79°9W **92** D3
Cuenca *Spain* 40°5N 2°10W **21** B4
Cuenca, Serranía de
Spain 39°55N 1°50W **21** C5
Cuernavaca *Mexico* 18°55N 99°15W **87** D5
Cuero *U.S.A.* 29°6N 97°17W **84** G6

Cueva de la Quebrada del Toro △
Venezuela 10°46N 69°3W **89** D6
Cuevas del Almanzora
Spain 37°18N 1°58W **21** D5
Cuevo *Bolivia* 20°15S 63°30W **92** H6
Cuiabá *Brazil* 15°30S 56°0W **93** G7
Cuiabá ➤ *Brazil* 17°5S 56°36W **93** G7
Cuihangcun *China* 22°27N 113°32E **33** G10
Cuijk *Neths.* 51°44N 5°50E **15** C5
Cuilco *Guatemala* 15°24N 91°58W **88** C1
Cuillin Hills *U.K.* 57°13N 6°15W **11** D2
Cuillin Sd. *U.K.* 57°4N 6°20W **11** D2
Cuilo = Kwilu ➤
Dem. Rep. of the Congo 3°22S 17°22E **52** E3
Cuito ➤ *Angola* 18°1S 20°48E **56** B3
Cuitzeo, L. de *Mexico* 19°55N 101°5W **86** D4
Cukai *Malaysia* 4°13N 103°25E **39** K4
Culbertson *U.S.A.* 48°9N 104°31W **76** B11
Culcairn *Australia* 35°41S 147°3E **63** F4
Culebra *Puerto Rico* 18°19N 65°18W **89** d
Culgoa ➤ *Australia* 29°56S 146°20E **63** D4
Culgoa Flood Plain △
Australia 28°58S 147°5E **63** D4
Culiacán *Mexico* 24°50N 107°23W **86** C3
Culiacán ➤ *Mexico* 24°30N 107°42W **86** C3
Culik *Indonesia* 8°21S 115°37E **37** J18
Culion *Phil.* 11°54N 119°58E **37** B5
Cullarin Ra. *Australia* 34°30S 149°30E **63** E4
Cullen *U.K.* 57°42N 2°49W **11** D6
Cullen Pt. *Australia* 11°57S 141°54E **62** A3
Cullera *Spain* 39°9N 0°17W **21** C5
Cullman *U.S.A.* 34°11N 86°51W **85** D11
Cullompton *U.K.* 50°51N 3°24W **13** G4
Culpeper *U.S.A.* 38°30N 78°0W **81** F14
Culuene ➤ *Brazil* 12°56S 52°51W **93** F8
Culver, Pt. *Australia* 32°54S 124°43E **61** F3
Culverden *N.Z.* 42°47S 172°49E **59** E4
Cumaná *Venezuela* 10°30N 64°5W **92** A6
Cumberland *B.C., Canada* 49°40N 125°0W **70** D4
Cumberland *Ont., Canada* 45°29N 75°24W **83** A9
Cumberland *U.S.A.* 39°39N 78°46W **81** F14
Cumberland ➤ *U.S.A.* 37°9N 88°25W **80** G9
Cumberland, L. *U.S.A.* 36°52N 85°9W **81** G11
Cumberland Gap △
U.S.A. 36°36N 83°40W **81** G12
Cumberland I. *U.S.A.* 30°50N 81°25W **85** F14
Cumberland Is. *Australia* 20°35S 149°10E **62** b
Cumberland Island △
U.S.A. 30°12N 81°24W **85** F14
Cumberland L. *Canada* 54°3N 102°18W **71** C8
Cumberland Pen. *Canada* 67°0N 64°0W **69** D19
Cumberland Plateau
U.S.A. 36°0N 85°0W **85** D12
Cumberland Sd. *Canada* 65°30N 66°0W **69** D19
Cumbernauld *U.K.* 55°57N 3°58W **11** F5
Cumborah *Australia* 29°40S 147°45E **63** D4
Cumbria □ *U.K.* 54°42N 2°52W **12** C5
Cumbrian Mts. *U.K.* 54°30N 3°0W **12** C5
Cumbum *India* 15°40N 79°10E **40** M11
Cuminá ➤ *Brazil* 1°30S 56°0W **93** D7
Cummings Mt. *U.S.A.* 35°2N 118°34W **79** K8
Cummins *Australia* 34°16S 135°43E **63** E2
Cumnock *Australia* 32°59S 148°46E **63** E4
Cumnock *U.K.* 55°28N 4°17W **11** F4
Cumpas *Mexico* 30°2N 109°48W **86** B3
Cumplida, Pta.
Canary Is. 28°50N 17°48W **24** F2
Cunco *Chile* 38°55S 72°2W **96** D2
Cumcumén *Chile* 31°53S 70°38W **94** C1
Cundeelee ◉ *Australia* 30°43S 123°25E **61** F3
Cunderdin *Australia* 31°37S 117°12E **61** F2
Cunene ➤ *Angola* 17°20S 11°50E **56** B1
Cúneo *Italy* 44°23N 7°32E **20** D7
Çüngüş *Turkey* 38°13N 39°17E **44** B3
Cunillera, I. = Sa Conillera
Spain 38°59N 1°13E **24** C7
Cunnamulla *Australia* 28°2S 145°38E **63** D4
Cupar *Canada* 50°57N 104°10W **71** C8
Cupar *U.K.* 56°19N 3°1W **11** E5
Cupertino *U.S.A.* 37°19N 122°2W **78** H4
Cupica, G. de *Colombia* 6°25N 77°30W **92** B3
Curaçao *Neth. Ant.* 12°10N 69°0W **89** D6
Curanilahue *Chile* 37°29S 73°28W **94** D1
Curaray ➤ *Peru* 2°20S 74°5W **92** D4
Curepipe *Mauritius* 20°19S 57°31E **53** d
Curepto *Chile* 35°8S 72°1W **94** D1
Curiapo *Venezuela* 8°33N 61°5W **92** B6
Curicó *Chile* 34°55S 71°20W **94** C1
Curieuse *Seychelles* 4°15S 55°44E **53** b
Curitiba *Brazil* 25°20S 49°10W **95** B6
Curitibanos *Brazil* 27°18S 50°36W **95** B5
Currabubula *Australia* 31°16S 150°44E **63** E5
Currais Novos *Brazil* 6°13S 36°30W **93** E11
Curral Velho *C. Verde Is.* 16°8S 22°48W **50** b
Curralinho *Brazil* 1°45S 49°46W **93** D9
Currane, L. *Ireland* 51°49N 10°4W **10** E1
Currant *U.S.A.* 38°44N 115°28W **76** G6
Currawinya △ *Australia* 28°55S 144°27E **63** D3
Current ➤ *U.S.A.* 36°15N 90°55W **84** C9
Currie *Australia* 39°56S 143°53E **63** F3
Currie *U.S.A.* 40°16N 114°45W **76** F6
Curtea de Argeş
Romania 45°12N 24°42E **17** F13
Curtin Springs *Australia* 25°20S 131°45E **61** E5
Curtis *U.S.A.* 40°38N 100°31W **80** E3
Curtis Group *Australia* 39°30S 146°37E **63** F4
Curtis I. *Australia* 23°35S 151°10E **62** C5
Curuápanema ➤ *Brazil* 2°25S 55°2W **93** D7
Curuçá *Brazil* 0°43S 47°50W **93** D9
Curuguaty *Paraguay* 24°31S 55°42W **95** A4
Çürüksu Çayı = Büyük
Menderes ➤ *Turkey* 37°28N 27°11E **23** F12
Curup *Indonesia* 4°26S 102°13E **36** E2

Cururupu *Brazil* 1°50S 44°50W **93** D10
Curuzú Cuatiá *Argentina* 29°50S 58°5W **94** B4
Curvelo *Brazil* 18°45S 44°27W **93** G10
Cusco = Cuzco *Peru* 13°32S 72°0W **92** F4
Cushendall *U.K.* 55°5N 6°4W **10** A5
Cushing *U.S.A.* 35°59N 96°46W **84** D6
Cushing, Mt. *Canada* 57°35N 126°57W **70** B3
Cusihuiriáchic *Mexico* 28°14N 106°50W **86** B3
Custer *U.S.A.* 43°46N 103°36W **80** D2
Cut Bank *U.S.A.* 48°38N 112°20W **76** B7
Cutchogue *U.S.A.* 41°1N 72°30W **83** E12
Cuthbert *U.S.A.* 31°46N 84°48W **85** F12
Cutler *U.S.A.* 36°31N 119°17W **78** J7
Cuttaburra ➤ *Australia* 29°43S 144°22E **63** D3
Cuttack *India* 20°25N 85°57E **41** J14
Cuvier, C. *Australia* 23°14S 113°22E **61** D1
Cuvier I. *N.Z.* 36°27S 175°50E **59** B5
Cuxhaven *Germany* 53°51N 8°41E **16** B5
Cuyahoga Falls *U.S.A.* 41°8N 81°29W **82** E3
Cuyahoga Valley △
U.S.A. 41°24N 81°33W **82** E3
Cuyo *Phil.* 10°51N 121°2E **37** B6
Cuyuni ➤ *Guyana* 6°23N 58°41W **92** B7
Cuzco *Bolivia* 20°0S 66°50W **92** H5
Cuzco *Peru* 13°32S 72°0W **92** F4
Cwmbran *U.K.* 51°39N 3°2W **13** F4
Cyangugu *Rwanda* 2°29S 28°54E **54** C2
Cyclades *Greece* 37°0N 24°30E **23** F11
Cygnet *Australia* 43°8S 147°1E **63** G4
Cynthiana *U.S.A.* 38°23N 84°18W **81** F11
Cypress Hills *Canada* 49°40N 109°30W **71** D7
Cypress Hills △ *Canada* 49°40N 109°30W **71** D7
Cyprus ■ *Asia* 35°0N 33°0E **25** E12
Cyrenaica = Barqa *Libya* 27°0N 23°0E **51** C10
Cyrene *Libya* 32°53N 21°52E **51** B10
Czar *Canada* 52°27N 110°50W **71** C6
Czech Rep. ■ *Europe* 50°0N 15°0E **16** D8
Częstochowa *Poland* 50°49N 19°7E **17** C10

D

Da ➤ *Vietnam* 21°15N 105°20E **38** B5
Da Hinggan Ling *China* 48°0N 121°0E **33** B7
Da Lat *Vietnam* 11°56N 108°25E **39** G7
Da Nang *Vietnam* 16°4N 108°13E **38** D7
Da Qaidam *China* 37°50N 95°15E **32** C4
Da Yunhe ➤ *Hopei,*
China 39°10N 117°10E **35** E9
Da Yunhe ➤ *Jiangsu,*
China 34°25N 120°5E **35** G11
Da'an *China* 45°30N 124°7E **35** B13
Daan Viljoen △ *Namibia* 22°2S 16°45E **56** C2
Daba Shan *China* 32°0N 109°0E **33** C5
Dabbagh, Jabal *Si. Arabia* 27°52N 35°45E **44** E2
Dabhoi *India* 22°10N 73°20E **42** H5
Dabo = Pasirkuning
Indonesia 0°30S 104°33E **36** E2
Dabola *Guinea* 10°50N 11°5W **50** F3
Dabung *Malaysia* 5°23N 102°1E **39** K4
Dacca = Dhaka *Bangla.* 23°43N 90°26E **43** H14
Dacca = Dhaka □
Bangla. 24°25N 90°25E **43** G14
Dachau *Germany* 48°15N 11°26E **16** D6
Dachigam △ *India* 34°10N 75°0E **42** B6
Dacre *Canada* 45°22N 76°57W **82** A8
Dadanawa *Guyana* 2°50N 59°30W **92** C7
Dade City *U.S.A.* 28°22N 82°11W **85** G13
Dadhar *Pakistan* 29°28N 67°39E **42** E2
Dadnah *U.A.E.* 25°32N 56°22E **45** E8
Dadra & Nagar Haveli □
India 20°5N 73°0E **40** J8
Dadri = Charkhi Dadri
India 28°37N 76°17E **42** E7
Dadu *Pakistan* 26°45N 67°45E **42** F2
Daegu *S. Korea* 35°50N 128°37E **35** G15
Daejeon *S. Korea* 36°20N 127°28E **35** F14
Daejeong *S. Korea* 33°8N 126°17E **35** H14
Daet *Phil.* 14°2N 122°55E **37** B6
Dafnes *Greece* 35°13N 25°3E **25** D7
Dagana *Senegal* 16°30N 15°35W **50** E2
Dagash *Sudan* 19°19N 33°25E **51** E12
Dagestan □ *Russia* 42°30N 47°0E **19** F8
Daggett *U.S.A.* 34°52N 116°52W **79** L10
Daghestan Republic =
Dagestan □ *Russia* 42°30N 47°0E **19** F8
Dağlıq Qarabağ =
Nagorno-Karabakh □
Azerbaijan 39°55N 46°45E **44** B5
Dagö = Hiiumaa *Estonia* 58°50N 22°45E **9** G20
Dagu *China* 38°59N 117°40E **35** E9
Dagupan *Phil.* 16°3N 120°20E **37** A6
Daguragu *Australia* 17°33S 130°30E **60** C5
Daguragu ◉ *Australia* 17°24S 130°48E **60** C5
Dahab *Egypt* 28°31N 34°31E **44** D2
Dahlak Kebir *Eritrea* 15°50N 40°10E **47** D3
Dahlonega *U.S.A.* 34°32N 83°59W **85** D13
Dahod *India* 22°50N 74°15E **42** H6
Dahongliutan *China* 35°45N 79°20E **43** B8
Dahra *Libya* 29°30N 17°50E **51** C9
Dahūk *Iraq* 36°50N 43°1E **44** B3
Dai Hao *Vietnam* 18°1N 106°25E **38** C6
Dai-Sen *Japan* 35°22N 133°32E **31** G6
Dai Xian *China* 39°4N 112°58E **34** E7
Daicheng *China* 38°42N 116°38E **34** E9
Daikondi = Day Kundī □
Afghan. 34°0N 66°0E **40** C5
Daingean *Ireland* 53°18N 7°17W **10** C4
Daintree *Australia* 16°20S 145°20E **62** B4
Daintree △ *Australia* 16°8S 145°2E **62** B4
Daiō-Misaki *Japan* 34°15N 136°45E **31** G8
Daisen-Oki △ *Japan* 35°23N 133°34E **31** G6
Daisetsu-zan *Japan* 43°30N 142°57E **30** C11
Daisetsu-Zan △ *Japan* 43°40N 142°55E **30** C11
Dajarra *Australia* 21°42S 139°30E **62** C2
Dajiawa *China* 37°9N 119°0E **35** F10
Dak Dam *Cambodia* 12°20N 107°21E **38** F6
Dak Nhe *Vietnam* 15°28N 107°48E **38** E6
Dak Pek *Vietnam* 15°4N 107°44E **38** E6
Dak Song *Vietnam* 12°19N 107°35E **38** F6

Dak Sui *Vietnam* 14°55N 107°43E 38 E6
Dakar *Senegal* 14°34N 17°29W 50 F2
Dakhla *W. Sahara* 23°50N 15°53W 50 D2
Dakhla, El Wâhât el
  Egypt 25°30N 28°50E 51 C11
Dakor *India* 22°45N 73°11E 42 H5
Dakota City *U.S.A.* 42°25N 96°25W 80 D5
Đakovica *Kosovo* 42°22N 20°26E 23 C9
Dalachi *China* 36°48N 105°0E 34 F3
Dalai Nur *China* 43°20N 116°45E 34 C9
Dālakī *Iran* 29°26N 51°17E 45 D6
Dalälven → *Sweden* 60°12N 16°43E 9 F17
Dalaman → *Turkey* 36°41N 28°43E 23 F13
Dalandzadgad *Mongolia* 43°27N 104°30E 34 C3
Dalap-Uliga-Darrit = Majuro
  Marshall Is. 7°9N 171°12E 64 G9
Dalarna *Sweden* 61°0N 14°0E 8 F16
Dālbandīn *Pakistan* 29°0N 64°23E 40 E4
Dalbeattie *U.K.* 54°56N 3°50W 11 G5
Dalbeg *Australia* 20°16S 147°18E 62 C4
Dalby *Australia* 27°10S 151°17E 63 D5
Dale City *U.S.A.* 38°38N 77°19W 81 F15
Dale Hollow L. *U.S.A.* 36°32N 85°27W 85 C12
Dalgān *Iran* 27°31N 59°19E 45 E8
Dalhart *U.S.A.* 36°4N 102°31W 84 C3
Dalhousie *Canada* 48°5N 66°26W 73 C6
Dalhousie *India* 32°38N 75°58E 42 C6
Dali *Shaanxi, China* 34°48N 109°58E 34 G5
Dali *Yunnan, China* 25°40N 100°10E 41 G22
Dalian *China* 38°50N 121°40E 35 F11
Daliang Shan *China* 28°0N 102°45E 32 D5
Daling He → *China* 40°55N 121°40E 35 D11
Dāliyat el Karmel *Israel* 32°43N 35°2E 46 C4
Dalkeith *U.K.* 55°54N 3°4W 11 F5
Dallas *Oreg., U.S.A.* 44°55N 123°19W 76 D2
Dallas *Tex., U.S.A.* 32°47N 96°48W 84 E6
Dalles, The *U.S.A.* 45°36N 121°10W 76 D3
Dalmā *U.A.E.* 24°30N 52°20E 45 E7
Dalmacija *Croatia* 43°20N 17°0E 22 C7
Dalmas, L. *Canada* 53°30N 71°50W 73 B5
Dalmatia = Dalmacija
  Croatia 43°20N 17°0E 22 C7
Dalmau *India* 26°4N 81°2E 43 F9
Dalmellington *U.K.* 55°19N 4°23W 11 F4
Dalnegorsk *Russia* 44°32N 135°33E 30 B7
Dalnerechensk *Russia* 45°50N 133°40E 30 B6
Dalnevostochnyy ☐
  Russia 67°0N 140°0E 29 C15
Daloa *Ivory C.* 7°0N 6°30W 50 G4
Dalry *U.K.* 55°42N 4°43W 11 F4
Dalrymple, L. *Australia* 20°40S 147°0E 62 C4
Dalrymple, Mt. *Australia* 21°1S 148°39E 62 b
Dalsland *Sweden* 58°50N 12°15E 9 G15
Dalton *Ga., U.S.A.* 34°46N 84°58W 85 D12
Dalton *Mass., U.S.A.* 42°28N 73°11W 83 D11
Dalton *Nebr., U.S.A.* 41°25N 102°58W 80 E2
Dalton-in-Furness *U.K.* 54°10N 3°11W 12 C4
Dalvík *Iceland* 65°58N 18°32W 8 D4
Dálvvadis = Jokkmokk
  Sweden 66°35N 19°50E 8 C18
Dalwallinu *Australia* 30°17S 116°40E 61 F2
Daly → *Australia* 13°35S 130°19E 60 B5
Daly City *U.S.A.* 37°42N 122°27W 78 H4
Daly L. *Canada* 56°32N 105°39W 71 B7
Daly River *Australia* 13°46S 130°42E 60 B5
Daly River-Port Keats ◎
  Australia 14°13S 129°36E 60 B4
Daly Waters *Australia* 16°15S 133°24E 62 B1
Dam Doi *Vietnam* 8°50N 105°12E 39 H5
Dam Ha *Vietnam* 21°21N 107°36E 38 B6
Daman *India* 20°25N 72°57E 40 J8
Dāmaneh *Iran* 33°1N 50°29E 45 C6
Damanhûr *Egypt* 31°0N 30°30E 51 B12
Damant L. *Canada* 61°45N 105°5W 71 A7
Damanzhuang *China* 38°5N 116°35E 34 E9
Damar *Indonesia* 7°7S 128°40E 37 F7
Damara *C.A.R.* 4°58N 18°42E 52 D3
Damaraland *Namibia* 20°0S 15°0E 56 C2
Damascus = Dimashq
  Syria 33°30N 36°18E 46 B5
Damaturu *Nigeria* 11°45N 11°55E 52 B2
Damāvand *Iran* 35°47N 52°0E 45 C7
Damāvand, Qolleh-ye
  Iran 35°56N 52°10E 45 C7
Damba *Angola* 6°44S 15°20E 52 F3
Dâmboviţa → *Romania* 44°12N 26°26E 17 F14
Dame Marie *Haiti* 18°36N 74°26W 89 C5
Dāmghān *Iran* 36°10N 54°17E 45 B7
Damiel *Spain* 39°4N 3°37W 21 C4
Damietta = Dumyât
  Egypt 31°24N 31°48E 51 B12
Daming *China* 36°15N 115°6E 34 F8
Damoh *India* 23°50N 79°28E 43 H8
Dampier *Australia* 20°41S 116°42E 60 D2
Dampier, Selat *Indonesia* 0°40S 131°0E 37 E8
Dampier Arch.
  Australia 20°38S 116°32E 60 D2
Damri, Chuor Phnum
  Cambodia 11°30N 103°0E 39 G4
Damyang *S. Korea* 35°19N 126°59E 35 G14
Dana *Indonesia* 11°0S 122°52E 37 F6
Dana *Jordan* 30°41N 35°37E 46 E4
Dana, L. *Canada* 50°53N 77°20W 72 B4
Dana, Mt. *U.S.A.* 37°54N 119°12W 78 H7
Danané *Ivory C.* 7°16N 8°9W 50 G4
Danau Poso *Indonesia* 1°52S 120°35E 37 E6
Danbury *U.S.A.* 41°24N 73°28W 83 E11
Danby L. *U.S.A.* 34°13N 115°5W 79 J6
Dand *Afghan.* 31°28N 65°32E 42 D1
Dande → *Zimbabwe* 15°56S 30°16E 55 F3
Dandeldhura *Nepal* 29°20N 80°35E 43 E9
Dandeli *India* 15°5N 74°30E 40 M9
Dandenong *Australia* 38°0S 145°15E 63 F4

Dandong *China* 40°10N 124°20E 35 D13
Danfeng *China* 33°45N 110°25E 34 H6
Danger Is. = Pukapuka
  Cook Is. 10°53S 165°49W 65 J11
Danger Pt. *S. Africa* 34°40S 19°17E 56 E2
Danginpuri *Indonesia* 8°40S 115°13E 37 K18
Dangla Shan = Tanggula Shan
  China 32°40N 92°10E 32 C4
Dangrek, Mts. = Dangrek, Phnom
  Thailand 14°20N 104°0E 38 E5
Dangrek, Phnom
  Thailand 14°20N 104°0E 38 E5
Dangriga *Belize* 17°0N 88°13W 87 D7
Dangshan *China* 34°27N 116°22E 34 G9
Daniel *U.S.A.* 42°52N 110°4W 76 E8
Daniel's Harbour
  Canada 50°13N 57°35W 73 B8
Danielskuil *S. Africa* 28°11S 23°33E 56 D3
Danielson *U.S.A.* 41°48N 71°53W 83 E13
Danilov *Russia* 58°16N 40°13E 18 C7
Daning *China* 36°28N 110°45E 34 F6
Dank *Oman* 23°33N 56°16E 45 F8
Dankhar Gompa *India* 32°10N 78°10E 42 C8
Danlí *Honduras* 14°4N 86°35W 88 D2
Danmark = Denmark ■
  Europe 55°45N 10°0E 9 J14
Dannemora *U.S.A.* 44°43N 73°44W 83 B11
Dannevirke *N.Z.* 40°12S 176°8E 59 D6
Dannhauser *S. Africa* 28°0S 30°3E 57 D5
Dansville *U.S.A.* 42°34N 77°42W 82 D7
Danta *India* 24°11N 72°46E 42 G5
Dantan *India* 21°57N 87°20E 43 J12
Dante = Xaafuun
  Somali Rep. 10°25N 51°16E 47 E5
Danube = Dunărea →
  Europe 45°20N 29°40E 17 F15
Danvers *U.S.A.* 42°34N 70°56W 83 D14
Danville *Ill., U.S.A.* 40°8N 87°37W 80 E10
Danville *Ky., U.S.A.* 37°39N 84°46W 81 G11
Danville *Pa., U.S.A.* 40°58N 76°37W 83 F8
Danville *Va., U.S.A.* 36°36N 79°23W 81 G14
Danville *Vt., U.S.A.* 44°25N 72°9W 83 B12
Danzhou *China* 19°31N 109°33E 38 C7
Danzig = Gdańsk
  Poland 54°22N 18°40E 17 A10
Dapaong *Togo* 10°55N 0°16E 50 F6
Daqing Shan *China* 40°40N 111°0E 34 D6
Daqq e Dorkh, Kavīr
  Iran 33°45N 52°50E 45 C7
Dar Banda *Africa* 8°0N 23°0E 48 F6
Dar el Beida = Casablanca
  Morocco 33°36N 7°36W 50 B4
Dar es Salaam *Tanzania* 6°50S 39°12E 54 D4
Dar Mazār *Iran* 29°14N 57°20E 45 D8
Dar'ā *Syria* 32°36N 36°7E 46 C5
Dar'ā ☐ *Syria* 32°55N 36°10E 46 C5
Dārāb *Iran* 28°50N 54°30E 45 D7
Daraban *Pakistan* 31°44N 70°20E 42 D4
Daraina *Madag.* 13°12S 49°40E 57 A8
Daraj *Libya* 30°10N 10°28E 51 B8
Dārān *Iran* 32°59N 50°24E 45 C6
Dārayyā *Syria* 33°28N 36°15E 46 B5
Darband *Pakistan* 34°20N 72°50E 42 B5
Darband, Kūh-e *Iran* 31°34N 57°8E 45 D8
Darbhanga *India* 26°15N 85°55E 43 F11
D'Arcy *Canada* 50°33N 122°29W 70 C4
Dardanelle *Ark., U.S.A.* 35°13N 93°9W 84 D8
Dardanelle *Calif., U.S.A.* 38°20N 119°50W 78 G7
Dardanelles = Çanakkale Boğazı
  Turkey 40°17N 26°32E 23 D12
Dārestān *Iran* 29°9N 58°42E 45 D8
Dârfûr *Sudan* 13°40N 24°0E 51 F10
Dargai *Pakistan* 34°25N 71°55E 42 B4
Dargaville *N.Z.* 35°57S 173°52E 59 A4
Darhan *Mongolia* 49°37N 106°21E 32 B5
Darhan Muminggan Lianheqi
  China 41°40N 110°28E 34 D6
Darıca *Turkey* 40°45N 29°23E 23 D13
Darién, G. del *Colombia* 9°0N 77°0W 92 B3
Darién ☐ *Panama* 7°36N 77°57W 88 E4
Dariganga = Ovoot
  Mongolia 45°21N 113°45E 34 B7
Darjeeling = Darjiling
  India 27°3N 88°18E 43 F13
Darjiling *India* 27°3N 88°18E 43 F13
Darkan *Australia* 33°20S 116°43E 61 F2
Darkhana *Pakistan* 30°39N 72°11E 42 D5
Darkhazīneh *Iran* 31°54N 48°39E 45 D6
Darkot Pass *Pakistan* 36°45N 73°26E 43 A5
Darling → *Australia* 34°4S 141°54E 63 E3
Darling Downs
  Australia 27°30S 150°30E 63 D5
Darling Ra. *Australia* 32°30S 116°20E 61 F2
Darlington *U.K.* 54°32N 1°33W 12 C6
Darlington *U.S.A.* 34°18N 79°52W 85 D15
Darlington ☐ *U.K.* 54°32N 1°33W 12 C6
Darlington, L. *S. Africa* 33°10S 25°9E 56 E4
Darlot, L. *Australia* 27°48S 121°35E 61 E3
Darlowo *Poland* 54°25N 16°25E 16 A9
Darmstadt *Germany* 49°51N 8°39E 16 D5
Darnah *Libya* 32°45N 22°45E 51 B10
Darnall *S. Africa* 29°23S 31°18E 57 D5
Darnley *Australia* 9°35S 143°46E 62 a
Darnley, B. *Canada* 69°30N 123°30W 68 B7
Darnley, C. *Antarctica* 68°0S 69°0E 5 C6
Darr → *Australia* 23°39S 143°50E 62 C3
Darra Pezu *Pakistan* 32°19N 70°44E 42 C4
Darregueira *Argentina* 37°42S 63°10W 94 D3
Darrington *U.S.A.* 48°15N 121°36W 76 B3
Dart → *U.K.* 50°24N 3°39W 13 G4
Dart, C. *Antarctica* 73°6S 126°20W 5 D14
Dartford *U.K.* 51°26N 0°13E 13 F8
Dartmoor *U.K.* 50°38N 3°57W 13 G4
Dartmoor △ *U.K.* 50°37N 3°59W 13 G4
Dartmouth *Canada* 44°40N 63°30W 73 D7
Dartmouth *U.K.* 50°21N 3°36W 13 G4
Dartmouth Res.
  Australia 26°4S 145°18E 63 D4

Dartuch, C. = Artrutx, C. de
  Spain 39°55N 3°49E 24 B10
Darvaza *Turkmenistan* 40°11N 58°24E 28 E6
Darvel, Teluk = Lahad Datu,
  Telok *Malaysia* 4°50N 118°20E 37 D5
Darwen *U.K.* 53°42N 2°29W 12 D5
Darwendale *Zimbabwe* 17°41S 30°33E 55 F3
Darwha *India* 20°15N 77°45E 40 J10
Darwin *Australia* 12°25S 130°51E 60 B5
Darwin *U.S.A.* 36°15N 117°35W 79 J9
Darya Khan *Pakistan* 31°48N 71°6E 42 D4
Daryācheh-ye Bakhtegān
  Iran 29°40N 53°50E 45 D7
Daryoi Amu = Amudarya →
  Uzbekistan 43°58N 59°34E 28 E6
Dās *U.A.E.* 25°20N 53°30E 45 E7
Dashen, Ras *Ethiopia* 13°8N 38°26E 47 E2
Dashetai *China* 41°0N 109°5E 34 D5
Dashköpri *Turkmenistan* 36°16N 62°8E 45 B9
Dashoguz *Turkmenistan* 41°49N 59°58E 28 E6
Dasht → *Pakistan* 25°10N 61°40E 40 G2
Daska *Pakistan* 32°20N 74°20E 42 C6
Dasuya *India* 31°49N 75°38E 42 D6
Datça *Turkey* 36°46N 27°40E 23 F12
Datia *India* 25°39N 78°27E 43 G8
Datong *China* 40°6N 113°18E 34 D7
Dattakhel *Pakistan* 32°54N 69°46E 42 C3
Datu, Tanjung *Indonesia* 2°5N 109°39E 36 D3
Datu Piang *Phil.* 7°2N 124°30E 37 C6
Datuk, Tanjong = Datu, Tanjung
  Indonesia 2°5N 109°39E 36 D3
Daud Khel *Pakistan* 32°53N 71°34E 42 C4
Daudnagar *India* 25°2N 84°24E 43 G11
Daugava → *Latvia* 57°4N 24°3E 9 H21
Daugavpils *Latvia* 55°53N 26°32E 9 J22
Daulpur *India* 26°45N 77°59E 42 F7
Dauphin *Canada* 51°9N 100°5W 71 C8
Dauphin *U.S.A.* 40°22N 76°56W 82 F8
Dauphin I. *U.S.A.* 30°15N 88°11W 85 F10
Dauphiné *France* 45°15N 5°25E 20 D6
Dausa *India* 26°52N 76°20E 42 F7
Davangere *India* 14°25N 75°55E 40 M9
Davao *Phil.* 7°0N 125°40E 37 C7
Davao G. *Phil.* 6°30N 125°48E 37 C7
Dāvar Panāh = Sarāvān
  Iran 27°25N 62°15E 45 E9
Davenport *Calif., U.S.A.* 37°1N 122°12W 78 H4
Davenport *Iowa, U.S.A.* 41°32N 90°35W 80 E8
Davenport *Wash., U.S.A.* 47°39N 118°9W 76 C4
Davenport Ra. *Australia* 20°28S 134°0E 62 C1
Davenport Range △
  Australia 20°36S 134°22E 62 C1
Daventry *U.K.* 52°16N 1°10W 13 E6
David *Panama* 8°30N 82°30W 88 E3
David City *U.S.A.* 41°15N 97°8W 80 E5
David Glacier *Antarctica* 75°20S 162°0E 5 D21
David Gorodok = Davyd Haradok
  Belarus 52°4N 27°8E 17 B14
Davidson *Canada* 51°16N 105°59W 71 C7
Davidson Mts. *U.S.A.* 68°41N 142°22W 74 B11
Davis *Antarctica* 68°34S 77°55E 5 C6
Davis *U.S.A.* 38°33N 121°44W 78 G5
Davis Dam *U.S.A.* 35°12N 114°34W 79 K12
Davis Inlet *Canada* 55°50N 60°59W 73 A7
Davis Mts. *U.S.A.* 30°50N 103°55W 84 F3
Davis Sea *Antarctica* 66°0S 92°0E 5 C7
Davis Str. *N. Amer.* 65°0N 58°0W 69 D19
Davlos *Cyprus* 35°25N 33°54E 25 D12
Davos *Switz.* 46°48N 9°49E 20 C8
Davy L. *Canada* 58°53N 108°18W 71 B7
Davyd Haradok *Belarus* 52°4N 27°8E 17 B14
Dawei = Tavoy *Burma* 14°2N 98°12E 38 E2
Dawes Ra. *Australia* 24°40S 150°40E 62 C5
Dawlish *U.K.* 50°35N 3°28W 13 G4
Dawna Ra. *Burma* 16°30N 98°30E 38 D2
Dawros Hd. *Ireland* 54°50N 8°33W 10 B3
Dawson *Canada* 31°46N 84°27W 85 F12
Dawson, B. *Canada* 52°53N 100°49W 71 C8
Dawson, I. *Chile* 53°50S 70°50W 96 G2
Dawson B. *Canada* 52°40N 94°20W 71 C10
Dawson City *Canada* 64°10N 139°30W 68 E4
Dawson Creek *Canada* 55°45N 120°15W 70 B4
Dawson Inlet *Canada* 61°50N 93°25W 71 A10
Dawson Ra. *Australia* 24°30S 149°48E 62 C4

De Smet *U.S.A.* 44°23N 97°33W 80 C5
De Soto *U.S.A.* 38°8N 90°34W 80 F8
De Tour Village *U.S.A.* 46°0N 83°56W 81 B12
De Witt *U.S.A.* 34°18N 91°20W 84 D9
Dead Sea *Asia* 31°30N 35°30E 46 D4
Deadwood *U.S.A.* 44°23N 103°44W 80 C2
Deadwood L. *Canada* 59°10N 128°30W 70 B3
Deal *U.K.* 51°13N 1°25E 13 F9
Deal I. *Australia* 39°30S 147°20E 63 F4
Dealesville *S. Africa* 28°41S 25°44E 56 D4
Dean → *Canada* 52°49N 126°58W 70 C3
Dean, Forest of *U.K.* 51°45N 2°33W 13 F5
Dean Chan. *Canada* 52°30N 127°15W 70 C3
Deán Funes *Argentina* 30°20S 64°20W 94 C3
Dease → *Canada* 59°56N 128°32W 70 B3
Dease L. *Canada* 58°40N 130°5W 70 B2
Dease Lake *Canada* 58°25N 130°6W 70 B2
Death Valley *U.S.A.* 36°15N 116°50W 79 J10
Death Valley △ *U.S.A.* 36°29N 117°6W 79 J9
Death Valley Junction
  U.S.A. 36°20N 116°25W 79 J10
Debagram *India* 23°51N 90°33E 43 H14
Debar *Macedonia* 41°31N 20°30E 23 D9
Debden *Canada* 53°30N 106°50W 71 C7
Dębica *Poland* 50°2N 21°25E 17 C11
DeBolt *Canada* 55°12N 118°1W 70 B5
Deborah East, L.
  Australia 30°45S 119°30E 61 F2
Deborah West, L.
  Australia 30°45S 119°5E 61 F2
Debre Markos *Ethiopia* 10°20N 37°40E 47 E2
Debre Tabor *Ethiopia* 11°50N 38°26E 47 E2
Debre Zebit *Ethiopia* 11°48N 38°30E 47 E2
Debrecen *Hungary* 47°33N 21°42E 17 E11
Decatur *Ala., U.S.A.* 34°36N 86°59W 85 D11
Decatur *Ga., U.S.A.* 33°46N 84°16W 85 E12
Decatur *Ill., U.S.A.* 39°51N 88°57W 80 F9
Decatur *Ind., U.S.A.* 40°50N 84°56W 81 E11
Decatur *Tex., U.S.A.* 33°14N 97°35W 84 E6
Deccan *India* 18°0N 79°0E 40 L11
Deception Bay *Australia* 27°10S 153°5E 63 D5
Deception I. *Antarctica* 63°0S 60°15W 5 C17
Deception L. *Canada* 56°33N 104°13W 71 B8
Dechang *China* 27°25N 102°2E 32 D5
Děčín *Czech Rep.* 50°47N 14°12E 16 C8
Deckerville *U.S.A.* 43°32N 82°44W 82 C2
Dedéagach = Alexandroupoli
  Greece 40°50N 25°54E 23 D11
Dedham *U.S.A.* 42°15N 71°10W 83 D13
Dedza *Malawi* 14°20S 34°20E 55 E3
Dee → *Aberds., U.K.* 57°9N 2°5W 11 D6
Dee → *Dumf. & Gall., U.K.* 54°51N 4°3W 11 G4
Dee → *Wales, U.K.* 53°22N 3°17W 12 D4
Deep B. *China* 22°25N 113°55E 33 G10
Deep Bay = Shenzhen Wan
  China 22°27N 113°55E 33 G10
Deepwater *Australia* 29°25S 151°51E 63 D5
Deer → *Canada* 58°23N 94°13W 71 B10
Deer L. *Canada* 52°40N 94°20W 71 C10
Deer Lake *Nfld. & L.,
  Canada* 49°11N 57°27W 73 C8
Deer Lake *Ont., Canada* 52°36N 94°20W 71 C10
Deer Lodge *U.S.A.* 46°24N 112°44W 76 C7
Deer Park *U.S.A.* 47°57N 117°28W 76 C5
Deer River *U.S.A.* 47°20N 93°48W 80 B7
Deeragun *Australia* 19°16S 146°33E 62 B4
Deerdepoort *S. Africa* 24°37S 26°27E 56 C4
Defiance *U.S.A.* 41°17N 84°22W 81 E11
Degana *India* 26°50N 74°20E 42 F6
Dégelis *Canada* 47°30N 68°35W 73 C6
Deggendorf *Germany* 48°50N 12°57E 16 D7
Degh → *Pakistan* 31°3N 73°21E 42 D5
Degirmenlik = Kythréa
  Cyprus 35°15N 33°29E 25 D12
Deh Bīd *Iran* 30°39N 53°11E 45 D7
Deh Dasht *Iran* 30°47N 50°33E 45 D6
Deh-e Shīr *Iran* 31°29N 53°45E 45 D7
Dehaj *Iran* 30°42N 54°53E 45 D7
Dehak *Iran* 27°11N 62°37E 45 E9
Dehdez *Iran* 31°43N 50°17E 45 D6
Dehej *India* 21°44N 72°40E 42 J5
Dehestān *Iran* 28°30N 55°35E 45 D7
Dehgolān *Iran* 35°17N 47°25E 44 C5
Dehibat *Tunisia* 32°0N 10°47E 51 B8
Dehlorān *Iran* 32°41N 47°16E 44 C5
Dehnow-e Kühestān
  Iran 27°58N 58°32E 45 E8
Dehra Dun *India* 30°20N 78°4E 42 D8
Dehri *India* 24°50N 84°15E 43 G11
Dehui *China* 44°30N 125°40E 35 B13
Deinze *Belgium* 50°59N 3°32E 15 D3
Dej *Romania* 47°10N 23°52E 17 E12
Deka → *Zimbabwe* 18°4S 26°42E 56 B4
DeKalb *U.S.A.* 41°56N 88°46W 80 E9
Dekese
  Dem. Rep. of the Congo 3°24S 21°24E 52 E4
Del Mar *U.S.A.* 32°58N 117°16W 79 N9
Del Norte *U.S.A.* 37°41N 106°21W 77 H10
Del Rio *U.S.A.* 29°22N 100°54W 84 G4
Delambre I. *Australia* 20°26S 117°5E 60 D2
Delano *U.S.A.* 35°46N 119°15W 79 K7
Delano Peak *U.S.A.* 38°22N 112°22W 76 G7
Delareyville *S. Africa* 26°41S 25°26E 56 D4
Delavan *U.S.A.* 42°38N 88°39W 80 D9
Delaware *U.S.A.* 40°18N 83°4W 81 E12
Delaware ☐ *U.S.A.* 39°0N 75°20W 81 F16
Delaware → *U.S.A.* 39°15N 75°20W 81 G16
Delaware B. *U.S.A.* 39°0N 75°10W 81 F16
Delaware Water Gap △
  U.S.A. 41°10N 74°55W 83 F10
Delay → *Canada* 56°56N 71°28W 73 A5
Delegate *Australia* 37°4S 148°56E 63 F4
Delevan *U.S.A.* 42°29N 78°29W 82 D6
Delft *Neths.* 52°1N 4°22E 15 B4
Delfzijl *Neths.* 53°20N 6°55E 15 A6
Delgado, C. *Mozam.* 10°45S 40°40E 55 E5
Delgerhet *Mongolia* 45°50N 110°30E 34 B6

Delgo *Sudan* 20°6N 30°40E 51 D12
Delhi *Canada* 42°51N 80°30W 82 D4
Delhi *India* 28°39N 77°13E 42 E7
Delhi *La., U.S.A.* 32°28N 91°30W 84 E9
Delhi *N.Y., U.S.A.* 42°17N 74°55W 83 D10
Delia *Canada* 51°38N 112°23W 70 C6
Delice *Turkey* 39°54N 34°2E 19 G5
Delicias *Mexico* 28°13N 105°28W 86 B3
Delijān *Iran* 33°59N 50°40E 45 C6
Déline *Canada* 65°11N 123°25W 68 D7
Delisle *Canada* 51°55N 107°8W 71 C7
Deliverance I. *Australia* 9°31S 141°34E 62 a
Dell City *U.S.A.* 31°56N 105°12W 84 F2
Dell Rapids *U.S.A.* 43°50N 96°43W 80 D5
Delmar *U.S.A.* 42°37N 73°47W 83 D11
Delmenhorst *Germany* 53°3N 8°37E 16 B5
Dclonga, Ostrova
  Russia 76°40N 149°20E 29 B15
Deloraine *Australia* 41°30S 146°40E 63 G4
Deloraine *Canada* 49°15N 100°29W 71 D8
Delphi *U.S.A.* 40°36N 86°41W 80 E10
Delphos *U.S.A.* 40°51N 84°21W 81 E11
Delportshoop *S. Africa* 28°22S 24°20E 56 D3
Delray Beach *U.S.A.* 26°28N 80°4W 85 H14
Delta *Colo., U.S.A.* 38°44N 108°4W 76 G9
Delta *Utah, U.S.A.* 39°21N 112°35W 76 G7
Delta Dunărea ☐
  Romania 45°15N 29°25E 17 F15
Delta Junction *U.S.A.* 64°2N 145°44W 68 E2
Deltona *U.S.A.* 28°54N 81°16W 85 G14
Delungra *Australia* 29°39S 150°51E 63 D5
Delvada *India* 20°46N 71°2E 42 J4
Delvinë *Albania* 39°59N 20°6E 23 E9
Demak *Indonesia* 6°53S 110°38E 37 G14
Demanda, Sierra de la
  Spain 42°15N 3°0W 21 A4
Demavend = Damāvand,
  Qolleh-ye *Iran* 35°56N 52°10E 45 C7
Dembia *C.A.R.* 4°58N 23°53E 54 B1
Dembidolo *Ethiopia* 8°34N 34°50E 47 F1
Demchok *India* 32°42N 79°29E 43 C8
Demer → *Belgium* 50°57N 4°42E 15 D4
Deming *N. Mex.,
  U.S.A.* 32°16N 107°46W 77 K10
Deming *Wash., U.S.A.* 48°50N 122°13W 78 B4
Demini → *Brazil* 0°46S 62°56W 92 D6
Demirci *Turkey* 39°2N 28°38E 23 E13
Demirköy *Turkey* 41°49N 27°45E 23 D12
Demopolis *U.S.A.* 32°31N 87°50W 85 E11
Dempo *Indonesia* 4°2S 103°15E 36 E2
Den Bosch = 's-Hertogenbosch
  Neths. 51°42N 5°17E 15 C5
Den Burg *Neths.* 53°3N 4°47E 15 A4
Den Chai *Thailand* 17°59N 100°4E 38 D3
Den Haag = 's-Gravenhage
  Neths. 52°7N 4°17E 15 B4
Den Helder *Neths.* 52°57N 4°45E 15 B4
Den Oever *Neths.* 52°56N 5°2E 15 B5
Denair *U.S.A.* 37°32N 120°48W 78 H6
Denali = McKinley, Mt.
  U.S.A. 63°4N 151°0W 68 E1
Denau *Uzbekistan* 38°16N 67°54E 28 F7
Denbigh *Canada* 45°8N 77°15W 82 A7
Denbigh *U.K.* 53°12N 3°25W 12 D4
Denbighshire ☐ *U.K.* 53°8N 3°22W 12 D4
Dendang *Indonesia* 3°7S 107°56E 36 E3
Dendermonde *Belgium* 51°2N 4°5E 15 C4
Dengfeng *China* 34°25N 113°2E 34 G7
Dengkou *China* 40°18N 106°55E 34 E5
Denham *Australia* 25°56S 113°31E 61 E1
Denham, Mt. *Jamaica* 18°13N 77°32W 88 a
Denham Ra. *Australia* 21°55S 147°46E 62 C4
Denham Sd. *Australia* 25°45S 113°15E 61 E1
Denholm *Canada* 52°39N 108°1W 71 C7
Denia *Spain* 38°49N 0°8E 21 C6
Denial B. *Australia* 32°14S 133°32E 63 E1
Deniliquin *Australia* 35°30S 144°58E 63 F3
Denimoo = Fort Resolution
  Canada 61°10N 113°40W 70 A6
Denison *Iowa, U.S.A.* 42°1N 95°21W 80 D6
Denison *Tex., U.S.A.* 33°45N 96°33W 84 E6
Denison Plains *Australia* 18°35S 128°0E 60 C4
Denizli *Turkey* 37°42N 29°2E 19 G4
Denman Glacier
  Antarctica 66°45S 99°25E 5 C7
Denmark *Australia* 34°59S 117°25E 61 F2
Denmark ■ *Europe* 55°45N 10°0E 9 J14
Denmark Str. *Atl. Oc.* 66°0N 30°0W 66 C17
Dennery *St. Lucia* 13°55N 60°54W 89 f
Dennison *U.S.A.* 40°24N 81°19W 82 F3
Denny *U.K.* 56°1N 3°55W 11 E5
Denpasar *Indonesia* 8°39S 115°13E 37 K18
Denpasar ✈ (DPS)
  Indonesia 8°44S 115°10E 37 K18
Denton *Mont., U.S.A.* 47°19N 109°57W 76 C9
Denton *Tex., U.S.A.* 33°13N 97°8W 84 E6
D'Entrecasteaux, Pt.
  Australia 34°50S 115°57F 61 F2
D'Entrecasteaux △
  Australia 34°20S 115°33E 61 F2
D'Entrecasteaux Is.
  Papua N. G. 9°0S 151°0E 58 B8
Denver *Colo., U.S.A.* 39°42N 104°59W 76 G11
Denver *Pa., U.S.A.* 40°14N 76°8W 83 F8
Denver City *U.S.A.* 32°58N 102°50W 84 E3
Deoband *India* 29°42N 77°43E 42 E7
Deogarh *India* 25°32N 73°54E 42 G5
Deoghar *India* 24°30N 86°42E 43 G12
Deolali *India* 19°58N 73°50E 40 K8
Deoli = Devli *India* 25°50N 75°50E 42 G6
Deora *India* 26°22N 70°55E 42 F4
Deori *India* 23°24N 79°1E 43 H8
Deoria *India* 26°31N 83°48E 43 F10
Deosai Mts. *Pakistan* 35°40N 75°0E 43 B6
Deosri *India* 26°46N 90°29E 43 F14
Depalpur *India* 22°51N 75°33E 42 H6
Deping *China* 37°25N 116°58E 35 F9

Deposit *U.S.A.* 42°4N 75°25W **83** D9
Depuch I. *Australia* 20°37S 117°44E **60** D2
Deputatskiy *Russia* 69°18N 139°54E **29** C14
Dera Ghazi Khan
  Pakistan 30°5N 70°43E **42** D4
Dera Ismail Khan
  Pakistan 31°50N 70°50E **42** D4
Derabugti *Pakistan* 29°2N 69°9E **42** E3
Derawar Fort *Pakistan* 28°46N 71°20E **42** E4
Derbent *Russia* 42°5N 48°15E **19** F8
Derby *Australia* 17°18S 123°38E **60** C3
Derby *U.K.* 52°56N 1°28W **12** E6
Derby Conn., *U.S.A.* 41°19N 73°5W **83** E11
Derby Kans., *U.S.A.* 37°33N 97°16W **80** G5
Derby N.Y., *U.S.A.* 42°41N 78°58W **82** D6
Derby City □ *U.K.* 52°56N 1°28W **12** E6
Derby Line *U.S.A.* 45°0N 72°6W **83** B12
Derbyshire □ *U.K.* 53°11N 1°38W **12** D6
Derdepoort *S. Africa* 24°38S 26°24E **56** C4
Dereham *U.K.* 52°41N 0°57E **13** E8
Derg ➔ *U.K.* 54°44N 7°26W **10** B4
Derg, L. *Ireland* 53°0N 8°20W **10** D3
Deridder *U.S.A.* 30°51N 93°17W **84** F8
Dermott *U.S.A.* 33°32N 91°26W **84** E9
Derry = Londonderry
  U.K. 55°0N 7°20W **10** B4
Derry = Londonderry □
  U.K. 55°0N 7°20W **10** B4
Derry N.H., *U.S.A.* 42°53N 71°19W **83** D13
Derry Pa., *U.S.A.* 40°20N 79°18W **82** F5
Derryveagh Mts. *Ireland* 54°56N 8°11W **10** B3
Derwent ➔ *Cumb., U.K.* 54°39N 3°33W **12** C4
Derwent ➔ *Derby, U.K.* 52°57N 1°28W **12** E6
Derwent ➔ *N. Yorks.,*
  U.K. 53°45N 0°58W **12** D7
Derwent Water *U.K.* 54°35N 3°9W **12** C4
Des Moines *Iowa, U.S.A.* 41°35N 93°37W **80** E7
Des Moines *N. Mex.,*
  U.S.A. 36°46N 103°50W **77** H12
Des Moines *Wash.,*
  U.S.A. 47°24N 122°19W **78** C4
Des Moines ➔ *U.S.A.* 40°23N 91°25W **80** E8
Desaguadero ➔
  Argentina 34°30S 66°46W **94** C2
Desaguadero ➔ *Bolivia* 16°35S 69°5W **92** G5
Desar *Malaysia* 1°31N 104°17E **39** d
Descanso, Pta. *Mexico* 32°21N 117°3W **79** N9
Deschaillons-sur-St-Laurent
  Canada 46°32N 72°7W **73** C5
Deschambault L.
  Canada 54°50N 103°30W **71** C8
Deschutes ➔ *U.S.A.* 45°38N 120°55W **78** D5
Dese *Ethiopia* 11°5N 39°40E **47** E2
Deseado ➔ *Argentina* 47°45S 65°54W **96** F3
Deseronto *Canada* 44°12N 77°3W **82** B7
Desert Center *U.S.A.* 33°43N 115°24W **79** M11
Desert Hot Springs
  U.S.A. 33°58N 116°30W **79** M10
Deshnok *India* 27°48N 73°21E **42** F5
Desierto Central de Baja
  California △ *Mexico* 29°40N 114°50W **86** B2
Desna ➔ *Ukraine* 50°33N 30°32E **17** C16
Desolación, I. *Chile* 53°0S 74°0W **96** G2
Despeñaperros, Paso
  Spain 38°24N 3°30W **21** C4
Dessau *Germany* 51°51N 12°14E **16** C7
Dessye = Dese *Ethiopia* 11°5N 39°40E **47** E2
D'Estrees B. *Australia* 35°55S 137°45E **63** F2
Desuri *India* 25°18N 73°35E **42** G5
Det Udom *Thailand* 14°54N 105°5E **38** E5
Dete *Zimbabwe* 18°38S 26°50E **56** B4
Detmold *Germany* 51°56N 8°52E **16** C5
Detour, Pt. *U.S.A.* 45°40N 86°40W **80** C10
Detroit *U.S.A.* 42°19N 83°12W **82** D1
Detroit Lakes *U.S.A.* 46°49N 95°51W **80** B6
Deua △ *Australia* 35°32S 149°46E **63** F4
Deurne *Neths.* 51°27N 5°49E **15** C5
Deutsche Bucht *Germany* 54°15N 8°0E **16** A5
Deutschland = Germany ■
  Europe 51°0N 10°0E **16** C6
Deva *Romania* 45°53N 22°55E **17** F12
Devakottai *India* 9°55N 78°45E **40** Q11
Devaprayag *India* 30°13N 78°35E **43** D8
Deventer *Neths.* 52°15N 6°10E **15** B6
Deveron ➔ *U.K.* 57°41N 2°32W **11** D6
Devgadh Bariya *India* 22°40N 73°55E **42** H5
Devikot *India* 26°42N 71°12E **42** F4
Devils Den *U.S.A.* 35°46N 119°58W **78** K7
Devils Hole = Death Valley △
  U.S.A. 36°29N 117°6W **79** J9
Devils Lake *U.S.A.* 48°7N 98°52W **80** A4
Devils Paw *Canada* 58°47N 134°0W **70** B2
Devils Postpile △ *U.S.A.* 37°37N 119°5W **78** H7
Devils Tower *U.S.A.* 44°35N 104°42W **76** D11
Devils Tower △
  U.S.A. 44°48N 104°55W **76** D11
Devine *U.S.A.* 29°8N 98°54W **84** G5
Devizes *U.K.* 51°22N 1°58W **13** F6
Devli *India* 25°50N 75°20E **42** G6
Devon *Canada* 53°24N 113°44W **70** C6
Devon □ *U.K.* 50°50N 3°40W **13** G4
Devon I. *Canada* 75°10N 85°0W **69** B15
Devonport *Australia* 41°10S 146°22E **63** G4
Devonport *N.Z.* 36°49S 174°49E **59** B5
Dewas *India* 22°59N 76°3E **42** H7
Dewetsdorp *S. Africa* 29°33S 26°39E **56** D4
Dewey *Puerto Rico* 18°18N 65°18W **89** d
Dexter *Maine, U.S.A.* 45°1N 69°18W **81** C19
Dexter *N. Mex., U.S.A.* 33°12N 104°22W **77** K11
Dey-Dey, L. *Australia* 29°12S 131°4E **61** E5
Deyhūk *Iran* 33°15N 57°30E **45** C8
Deyyer *Iran* 27°55N 51°55E **45** E6
Dez ➔ *Iran* 31°39N 48°52E **45** D6
Dezadeash L. *Canada* 60°28N 136°58W **70** A1
Dezfūl *Iran* 32°20N 48°30E **45** C6
Dezhneva, Mys *Russia* 66°5N 169°40W **29** C19
Dezhou *China* 37°26N 116°18E **34** F9

Dhadhar ➔ *India* 24°56N 85°24E **43** G11
Dhahiriya = Aẓ Ẓāhirīyah
  West Bank 31°25N 34°58E **46** D3
Dhahran = Aẓ Ẓahrān
  Si. Arabia 26°10N 50°7E **45** E6
Dhak *Pakistan* 32°25N 72°33E **42** C5
Dhaka *Bangla.* 23°43N 90°26E **43** H14
Dhaka □ *Bangla.* 24°25N 90°25E **43** G14
Dhali *Cyprus* 35°1N 33°25E **25** D12
Dhamār *Yemen* 14°30N 44°20E **47** E3
Dhampur *India* 29°19N 78°33E **43** E8
Dhamtari *India* 20°42N 81°35E **41** J12
Dhanbad *India* 23°50N 86°30E **43** H12
Dhangarhi *Nepal* 28°55N 80°40E **43** E9
Dhankuta *Nepal* 26°55N 87°40E **43** F12
Dhanpuri *India* 23°13N 81°30E **43** H9
Dhar *India* 22°35N 75°26E **42** H6
Dharampur *India* 22°13N 75°18E **42** H6
Dharamsala = Dharmsala
  India 32°16N 76°23E **42** C7
Dharan *Nepal* 26°49N 87°17E **43** F12
Dhariwal *India* 31°57N 75°19E **42** D6
Dharla ➔ *Bangla.* 25°46N 89°42E **43** G13
Dharmapuri *India* 12°10N 78°10E **40** N11
Dharmjaygarh *India* 22°28N 83°13E **43** H10
Dharmsala *India* 32°16N 76°23E **42** C7
Dharni *India* 21°33N 76°53E **42** J7
Dharwad *India* 15°30N 75°4E **40** M9
Dhasan ➔ *India* 25°48N 79°24E **43** G8
Dhaulagiri *Nepal* 28°39N 83°28E **43** E10
Dhebar, L. *India* 24°10N 74°0E **42** G6
Dheftera *Cyprus* 35°5N 33°16E **25** D12
Dhenkanal *India* 20°45N 85°35E **41** J14
Dherinia *Cyprus* 35°3N 33°57E **25** D12
Dhī Qār □ *Iraq* 31°0N 46°15E **44** D5
Dhiarrizos ➔ *Cyprus* 34°41N 32°34E **25** E11
Dhībān *Jordan* 31°30N 35°46E **46** D4
Dhimarkhera *India* 23°28N 80°22E **43** H9
Dhodhekánisos = Dodecanese
  Greece 36°35N 27°0E **23** F12
Dholka *India* 22°44N 72°29E **42** H5
Dhoraji *India* 21°45N 70°37E **42** J4
Dhrangadhra *India* 22°59N 71°31E **42** H4
Dhrol *India* 22°33N 70°25E **42** H4
Dhuburi *India* 26°2N 89°59E **41** F16
Dhule *India* 20°58N 74°50E **40** J9
Di Linh *Vietnam* 11°35N 108°4E **39** G7
Di Linh, Cao Nguyen
  Vietnam 11°30N 108°0E **39** G7
Dia *Greece* 35°28N 25°14E **25** D7
Diablo Range *U.S.A.* 37°20N 121°25W **78** J5
Diafarabé *Mali* 14°9N 4°57W **50** F5
Diamante *Argentina* 32°5S 60°40W **94** C3
Diamante ➔ *Argentina* 34°30S 66°46W **94** C2
Diamantina *Brazil* 18°17S 43°40W **93** G10
Diamantina ➔
  Australia 26°45S 139°10E **63** D2
Diamantina △ *Australia* 23°33S 141°23E **62** C3
Diamantina *Brazil* 14°30S 56°30W **93** F7
Diamond Bar *U.S.A.* 34°1N 117°48W **79** L9
Diamond Harbour
  India 22°11N 88°14E **43** H13
Diamond Is. *Australia* 17°25S 151°5E **62** B5
Diamond Mts. *U.S.A.* 39°40N 115°50W **76** G6
Diamond Springs
  U.S.A. 38°42N 120°49W **78** G6
Diaoyu Tai = Senkaku-Shotō
  E. China Sea 25°45N 123°30E **31** M1
Dībā *U.A.E.* 25°45N 56°16E **45** E8
Dibai *India* 28°13N 78°15E **42** E8
Dibaya
  Dem. Rep. of the Congo 6°30S 22°57E **52** F4
Dibaya-Lubue
  Dem. Rep. of the Congo 4°12S 19°54E **52** E3
Dibbeen △ *Jordan* 32°20N 35°45E **46** C4
D'Iberville, Lac *Canada* 55°55N 73°15W **72** A5
Dibete *Botswana* 23°45S 26°32E **56** C4
Dibrugarh *India* 27°29N 94°55E **41** F19
Dickens *U.S.A.* 33°37N 100°50W **84** E4
Dickinson *U.S.A.* 46°53N 102°47W **80** B2
Dickson *U.S.A.* 36°5N 87°23W **85** C11
Dickson City *U.S.A.* 41°28N 75°36W **83** E9
Didiéni *Mali* 13°53N 8°6W **50** F4
Didsbury *Canada* 51°35N 114°10W **70** C6
Didwana *India* 27°23N 74°36E **42** F6
Diefenbaker, L. *Canada* 51°0N 106°55W **71** C7
Diego de Almagro *Chile* 26°22S 70°3W **94** B1
Diego Suarez = Antsiranana
  Madag. 12°25S 49°20E **57** A8
Diekirch *Lux.* 49°52N 6°10E **15** E6
Dien Ban *Vietnam* 15°53N 108°16E **38** E7
Dien Bien *Vietnam* 21°20N 103°0E **38** B4
Dien Khanh *Vietnam* 12°15N 109°6E **39** F7
Dieppe *France* 49°54N 1°4E **20** B4
Dierks *U.S.A.* 34°7N 94°1W **84** D7
Diest *Belgium* 50°58N 5°4E **15** D5
Dif *Somali Rep.* 0°59N 40°58E **47** G3
Dig *India* 27°28N 77°20E **42** F7
Digba
  Dem. Rep. of the Congo 4°25N 25°48E **54** B2
Digby *Canada* 44°38N 65°50W **73** D6
Digges Is. *Canada* 62°40N 77°50W **69** E16
Diggi *India* 26°22N 75°26E **42** F6
Dighinala *Bangla.* 23°15N 92°5E **41** H18
Dighton *U.S.A.* 38°29N 100°28W **80** F3
Digne-les-Bains *France* 44°5N 6°12E **20** D7
Digos *Phil.* 6°45N 125°20E **37** C7
Digranes *Iceland* 66°4N 14°44W **8** C6
Digul ➔ *Indonesia* 7°7S 138°42E **37** F9
Dihang = Brahmaputra ➔
  Asia 23°40N 90°35E **43** H13
Dijlah, Nahr ➔ *Asia* 31°0N 47°25E **44** D5
Dijon *France* 47°20N 5°3E **20** C6
Dikhil *Djibouti* 11°8N 42°20E **47** E3
Dikkil = Dikhil *Djibouti* 11°8N 42°20E **47** E3
Diksmuide *Belgium* 51°2N 2°52E **15** C2
Dikson *Russia* 73°40N 80°5E **28** B9

Dikti Oros *Greece* 35°8N 25°30E **25** D7
Dila *Ethiopia* 6°21N 38°22E **47** F2
Dili *E. Timor* 8°39S 125°34E **37** F7
Dilley *U.S.A.* 28°40N 99°10W **84** G5
Dillingham *U.S.A.* 59°3N 158°28W **74** D8
Dillon *Canada* 55°56N 108°35W **71** B7
Dillon *Mont., U.S.A.* 45°13N 112°38W **76** D7
Dillon *S.C., U.S.A.* 34°25N 79°22W **85** D15
Dillon ➔ *Canada* 55°56N 108°56W **71** B7
Dillsburg *U.S.A.* 40°7N 77°2W **82** F7
Dilolo
  Dem. Rep. of the Congo 10°28S 22°18E **52** G4
Dimapur *India* 25°54N 93°45E **32** D4
Dimas *Mexico* 23°43N 106°47W **86** C3
Dimashq *Syria* 33°30N 36°18E **46** B5
Dimashq □ *Syria* 33°30N 36°30E **46** B5
Dimbaza *S. Africa* 32°50S 27°14E **57** E4
Dimboola *Australia* 36°28S 142°7E **63** F3
Dîmbovița = Dâmbovița ➔
  Romania 44°12N 26°26E **17** F14
Dimbulah *Australia* 17°8S 145°4E **62** B4
Dimitrovgrad *Bulgaria* 42°5N 25°35E **23** C11
Dimitrovgrad *Russia* 54°14N 49°39E **18** D8
Dimitrovo = Pernik
  Bulgaria 42°35N 23°2E **23** C10
Dimmitt *U.S.A.* 34°33N 102°19W **84** D3
Dimona *Israel* 31°2N 35°1E **46** D4
Dinagat *Phil.* 10°10N 125°40E **37** B7
Dinajpur *Bangla.* 25°33N 88°43E **41** G16
Dinan *France* 48°28N 2°2W **20** B2
Dīnān Āb *Iran* 32°4N 56°49E **45** C8
Dinant *Belgium* 50°16N 4°55E **15** D4
Dinapur *India* 25°38N 85°5E **43** G11
Dīnar, Kūh-e *Iran* 30°42N 51°46E **45** D6
Dinara Planina *Croatia* 44°0N 16°30E **22** C7
Dinard *France* 48°38N 2°6W **20** B2
Dinaric Alps = Dinara Planina
  Croatia 44°0N 16°30E **22** C7
Dindigul *India* 10°25N 78°0E **40** P11
Dindori *India* 22°57N 81°5E **43** H9
Ding Xian = Dingzhou
  China 38°30N 114°59E **34** E8
Ding'an *China* 19°42N 110°19E **38** C8
Dingbian *China* 37°35N 107°32E **34** F4
Dingin *Belgium* 52°3N 10°2W **10** D1
Dingle *Ireland* 52°9N 10°17W **10** D1
Dingle B. *Ireland* 52°3N 10°20W **10** D1
Dingmans Ferry *U.S.A.* 41°13N 74°55W **83** E10
Dingo *Australia* 23°38S 149°19E **62** C4
Dingtao *China* 35°5N 115°35E **34** G8
Dingwall *U.K.* 57°36N 4°26W **11** D4
Dingxi *China* 35°30N 104°33E **34** G3
Dingxiang *China* 38°30N 112°58E **34** E7
Dingzhou *China* 38°30N 114°59E **34** E8
Dinh, Mui *Vietnam* 11°22N 109°1E **39** G7
Dinh Lap *Vietnam* 21°33N 107°6E **38** B6
Dinin ➔ *Ireland* 52°43N 7°18W **10** D4
Dinira △ *Venezuela* 9°57N 70°6W **89** E6
Dinokwe *Botswana* 23°29S 26°37E **56** C4
Dinorwic *Canada* 49°41N 92°30W **71** D10
Dinosaur □ *Canada* 50°47N 111°30W **70** C6
Dinosaur △ *U.S.A.* 40°30N 108°45W **76** F9
Dinuba *U.S.A.* 36°32N 119°23W **78** J7
Dionísiades *Greece* 35°20N 26°10E **25** D8
Diourbel *Senegal* 14°39N 16°12W **50** F2
Dipalpur *Pakistan* 30°40N 73°39E **42** D5
Dipkarpaz = Rizokarpaso
  Cyprus 35°36N 34°23E **25** D13
Diplo *Pakistan* 24°35N 69°35E **42** G3
Dipolog *Phil.* 8°36N 123°20E **37** C6
Dipperu △ *Australia* 21°56S 148°42E **62** C4
Dir *Pakistan* 35°8N 71°59E **40** B7
Dire Dawa *Ethiopia* 9°35N 41°45E **47** F3
Dirfis Oros *Greece* 38°40N 23°54E **23** E10
Diriamba *Nic.* 11°51N 86°19W **88** D2
Dirk Hartog I. *Australia* 25°50S 113°5E **61** E1
Dirranbandi *Australia* 28°33S 148°17E **63** D4
Disa *India* 24°18N 72°10E **42** G5
Disappointment, C.
  U.S.A. 46°18N 124°5W **76** C1
Disappointment, L.
  Australia 23°20S 122°40E **60** D3
Disaster B. *Australia* 37°15S 149°58E **63** F4
Discovery B. *Australia* 38°10S 140°40E **63** F3
Discovery B. *China* 22°18N 114°1E **33** G11
Disko = Qeqertarsuaq
  Greenland 69°45N 53°30W **66** C14
Disney Reef *Tonga* 19°17S 174°7W **59** c
Diss *U.K.* 52°23N 1°7E **13** E9
Disteghil Sar *Pakistan* 36°20N 75°12E **43** A6
District of Columbia □
  U.S.A. 38°55N 77°0W **81** F15
Distrito Federal □ *Brazil* 15°45S 47°45W **93** G9
Distrito Federal □
  Mexico 19°15N 99°10W **87** D5
Diu *India* 20°45N 70°58E **42** J4
Dīvāndarreh *Iran* 35°55N 47°2E **44** C5
Divide *U.S.A.* 45°45N 112°45W **76** D7
Dividing Ra. *Australia* 27°45S 116°0E **61** E2
Divinópolis *Brazil* 20°10S 44°54W **93** H10
Divnoye *Russia* 45°55N 43°21E **19** E7
Divo *Ivory C.* 5°48N 5°15W **50** G4
Dīwāl Kol *Afghan.* 34°23N 67°52E **42** B2
Dixie Mt. *U.S.A.* 39°55N 120°16W **78** F6
Dixon *Calif., U.S.A.* 38°27N 121°49W **78** G5
Dixon *Ill., U.S.A.* 41°50N 89°29W **80** E9
Dixon Entrance *U.S.A.* 54°30N 132°0W **68** E5
Dixville *Canada* 45°4N 71°46W **83** A13
Diyālā □ *Iraq* 33°45N 44°50E **44** C5
Diyālā ➔ *Iraq* 33°13N 44°30E **44** C5
Diyarbakır *Turkey* 37°55N 40°18E **44** B4
Diyodar *India* 24°8N 71°50E **42** G4
Djakarta = Jakarta
  Indonesia 6°9S 106°52E **37** G12
Djamba *Angola* 16°45S 13°58E **56** B1
Djambala *Congo* 2°32S 14°30E **52** E2
Djanet *Algeria* 24°35N 9°32E **50** D7
Djawa = Jawa *Indonesia* 7°0S 110°0E **36** F3

Djelfa *Algeria* 34°40N 3°15E **50** B6
Djema *C.A.R.* 6°3N 25°15E **54** A2
Djerba, Î. de *Tunisia* 33°50N 10°48E **51** B8
Djerid, Chott *Tunisia* 33°42N 8°30E **50** B7
Djibouti *Djibouti* 11°30N 43°5E **47** E3
Djibouti ■ *Africa* 12°0N 43°0E **47** E3
Djolu *Dem. Rep. of the Congo* 0°35N 22°5E **52** D4
Djougou *Benin* 9°40N 1°45E **50** G6
Djoum *Cameroon* 2°41N 12°35E **52** D2
Djourab, Erg du *Chad* 16°40N 18°50E **51** E9
Djugu
  Dem. Rep. of the Congo 1°55N 30°35E **54** B3
Djukbinj △ *Australia* 12°11S 131°2E **60** B5
Djúpivogur *Iceland* 64°39N 14°17W **8** D6
Dmitriya Lapteva, Proliv
  Russia 73°0N 140°0E **29** B15
Dnepr = Dnipro ➔
  Ukraine 46°30N 32°18E **19** E5
Dneprodzerzhinsk =
  Dniprodzerzhynsk
  Ukraine 48°32N 34°37E **19** E5
Dnepropetrovsk =
  Dnipropetrovsk
  Ukraine 48°30N 35°0E **19** E6
Dnestr = Dnister ➔
  Europe 46°18N 30°17E **17** E16
Dnieper = Dnipro ➔
  Ukraine 46°30N 32°18E **19** E5
Dniester = Dnister ➔
  Europe 46°18N 30°17E **17** E16
Dnipro ➔ *Ukraine* 46°30N 32°18E **19** E5
Dniprodzerzhynsk
  Ukraine 48°32N 34°37E **19** E5
Dnipropetrovsk *Ukraine* 48°30N 35°0E **19** E6
Dnister ➔ *Europe* 46°18N 30°17E **17** E16
Dno *Russia* 57°50N 29°58E **9** H23
Dnyapro = Dnipro ➔
  Ukraine 46°30N 32°18E **19** E5
Do Gonbadān = Gachsārān
  Iran 30°15N 50°45E **45** D6
Doaktown *Canada* 46°33N 66°8W **73** C6
Doan Hung *Vietnam* 21°30N 105°10E **38** B5
Doany *Madag.* 14°21S 49°30E **57** A8
Doba *Chad* 8°40N 16°50E **51** G9
Doba *Pakistan* 26°57N 67°10E **42** G2
Dobandi *Pakistan* 31°13N 66°50E **42** D2
Dobbyn *Australia* 19°44S 140°2E **62** B3
Dobele *Latvia* 56°37N 23°16E **9** H20
Doberai, Jazirah *Indonesia* 1°25S 133°0E **37** E8
Doblas *Argentina* 37°5S 64°0W **94** D3
Dobo *Indonesia* 5°45S 134°15E **37** F8
Doboj *Bos.-H.* 44°46N 18°4E **23** B8
Dobrich *Bulgaria* 43°37N 27°49E **23** C12
Dobruja *Europe* 44°30N 28°15E **17** F15
Dobrush *Belarus* 52°25N 31°22E **17** B16
Doc, Mui *Vietnam* 17°58N 106°30E **38** D6
Docker River = Kaltukatjara
  Australia 24°52S 129°5E **61** D4
Doctor Arroyo *Mexico* 23°40N 100°11W **86** C4
Doctor Pedro P. Peña
  Paraguay 22°27S 62°21W **94** A3
Doda *India* 33°10N 75°34E **43** C6
Doda, L. *Canada* 49°25N 75°13W **72** C4
Dodecanese *Greece* 36°35N 27°0E **23** F12
Dodekanisa = Dodecanese
  Greece 36°35N 27°0E **23** F12
Dodge City *U.S.A.* 37°45N 100°1W **80** G3
Dodge L. *Canada* 59°50N 105°36W **71** B7
Dodgeville *U.S.A.* 42°58N 90°8W **80** D8
Dodoma *Tanzania* 6°8S 35°45E **54** D4
Dodoma □ *Tanzania* 6°0S 36°0E **54** D4
Dodori □ *Kenya* 1°55S 41°7E **54** C5
Dodsland *Canada* 51°50N 108°45W **71** C7
Dodson *U.S.A.* 48°24N 108°15W **76** B9
Doesburg *Neths.* 52°1N 6°9E **15** B6
Doetinchem *Neths.* 51°59N 6°18E **15** C6
Dog Creek *Canada* 51°35N 122°14W **70** C4
Dog L. Man., *Canada* 51°2N 98°31W **71** C9
Dog L. Ont., *Canada* 48°48N 89°30W **72** C2
Dogran *Pakistan* 31°48N 73°35E **42** D5
Doğubayazıt *Turkey* 39°31N 44°5E **44** B5
Doha = Ad Dawḩah
  Qatar 25°15N 51°35E **45** E6
Dohazari *Bangla.* 22°10N 92°5E **41** H18
Dohrighat *India* 26°16N 83°31E **43** F10
Doi *Indonesia* 2°14N 127°49E **37** D7
Doi Inthanon △ *Thailand* 18°33N 98°34E **38** C2
Doi Khuntan △ *Thailand* 18°30N 99°14E **38** C2
Doi Luang *Thailand* 18°30N 101°0E **38** C3
Doi Luang △ *Thailand* 19°22N 99°35E **38** C2
Doi Saket *Thailand* 18°52N 99°9E **38** C2
Doi Suthep △ *Thailand* 18°49N 98°53E **38** C2
Dois Irmãos, Sa. *Brazil* 9°0S 42°30W **93** E10
Dokkum *Neths.* 53°20N 5°59E **15** A5
Dokri *Pakistan* 27°25N 68°7E **42** F3
Dolak, Pulau *Indonesia* 8°0S 138°30E **37** F9
Dolbeau-Mistassini
  Canada 48°53N 72°14W **73** C5
Dole *France* 47°7N 5°31E **20** C6
Dolgellau *U.K.* 52°45N 3°53W **12** E4
Dolgelley = Dolgellau
  U.K. 52°45N 3°53W **12** E4
Dolinsk *Russia* 47°21N 142°48E **29** E15
Dollard *Neths.* 53°20N 7°10E **15** A7
Dolo *Ethiopia* 4°11N 42°3E **47** G3
Dolomites = Dolomiti
  Italy 46°23N 11°51E **22** A4
Dolomiti *Italy* 46°23N 11°51E **22** A4
Dolores *Argentina* 36°20S 57°40W **94** D4
Dolores *Uruguay* 33°34S 58°15W **94** C4
Dolores *U.S.A.* 37°28N 108°30W **77** H9
Dolores ➔ *U.S.A.* 38°49N 108°17W **77** G9
Dolphin, C. *Falk. Is.* 51°10S 59°0W **96** G5
Dolphin and Union Str.
  Canada 69°5N 114°45W **68** D8
Dom Pedrito *Brazil* 31°0S 54°40W **95** C5
Doma *Zimbabwe* 16°15S 30°30E **55** F3
Domariaganj ➔ *India* 26°17N 83°44E **43** F10
Domasi *Malawi* 15°15S 35°22E **55** F4
Dombarovskiy *Russia* 50°46N 59°32E **28** D6

Dombås *Norway* 62°4N 9°8E **8** E13
Dome Argus *Antarctica* 80°50S 76°30E **5** E12
Dome C. *Antarctica* 75°12S 123°37E **5** D17
Dome Fuji *Antarctica* 77°20S 39°45E **5** D5
Domel I. = Letsôk-aw Kyun
  Burma 11°30N 98°25E **39** G2
Domeyko *Chile* 29°0S 71°0W **94** B1
Domeyko, Cordillera
  Chile 24°30S 69°0W **94** A2
Dominador *Chile* 24°21S 69°20W **94** A2
Dominica ■ *W. Indies* 15°20N 61°20W **89** C7
Dominica Passage
  W. Indies 15°10N 61°20W **89** C7
Dominican Rep. ■
  W. Indies 19°0N 70°30W **89** C5
Domodóssola *Italy* 46°7N 8°17E **20** C8
Domville, Mt. *Australia* 28°1S 151°15E **63** D5
Don ➔ *Russia* 47°4N 39°18E **19** E6
Don ➔ *Aberds., U.K.* 57°11N 2°5W **11** D6
Don ➔ *S. Yorks., U.K.* 53°41N 0°52W **12** D7
Don, C. *Australia* 11°18S 131°46E **60** B5
Don Benito *Spain* 38°53N 5°51W **21** C3
Don Figuerero Mts.
  Jamaica 18°5N 77°36W **88** a
Don Sak *Thailand* 9°18N 99°41E **39** b
Dona Ana = Nhamaabué
  Mozam. 17°25S 35°5E **55** F4
Donaghadee *U.K.* 54°39N 5°33W **10** B6
Donaghmore *Ireland* 52°52N 7°36W **10** D4
Donald *Australia* 36°23S 143°0E **63** F3
Donaldsonville *U.S.A.* 30°6N 90°59W **84** G9
Donalsonville *U.S.A.* 31°3N 84°53W **85** F12
Donau = Dunărea ➔
  Europe 45°20N 29°40E **17** F15
Donauwörth *Germany* 48°43N 10°47E **16** D6
Doncaster *U.K.* 53°32N 1°6W **12** D6
Dondo *Angola* 9°45S 14°25E **52** F2
Dondo *Mozam.* 19°33S 34°46E **55** F3
Dondo, Teluk *Indonesia* 0°50N 120°30E **37** D6
Dondra Head *Sri Lanka* 5°55N 80°40E **40** S12
Donegal *Ireland* 54°39N 8°5W **10** B3
Donegal □ *Ireland* 54°53N 8°0W **10** B4
Donegal B. *Ireland* 54°31N 8°49W **10** B3
Donets ➔ *Russia* 47°33N 40°55E **19** E7
Donets Basin *Ukraine* 49°0N 38°0E **6** F13
Donetsk *Ukraine* 48°0N 37°45E **19** E6
Dong Ba Thin *Vietnam* 12°8N 109°13E **39** F7
Dong Dang *Vietnam* 21°54N 106°42E **38** B6
Dong Giam *Vietnam* 19°25N 105°31E **38** C5
Dong Ha *Vietnam* 16°55N 107°8E **38** D6
Dong Hene *Laos* 16°40N 105°18E **38** D5
Dong Hoi *Vietnam* 17°29N 106°36E **38** D6
Dong Khe *Vietnam* 22°26N 106°27E **38** A6
Dong Ujimqin Qi *China* 45°32N 116°55E **34** B9
Dong Van *Vietnam* 23°16N 105°22E **38** A5
Dong Xoai *Vietnam* 11°32N 106°55E **39** G6
Dongara *Australia* 29°14S 114°57E **61** E1
Dongbei *China* 45°0N 125°0E **30** A5
Dongchuan *China* 26°8N 103°1E **32** D5
Dongfang *China* 18°50N 108°33E **38** C7
Dongfeng *China* 42°40N 125°34E **35** C13
Donggala *Indonesia* 0°30S 119°40E **37** E5
Donggang *China* 39°52N 124°10E **35** E13
Dongguan *China* 22°58N 113°44E **33** D6
Dongguang *China* 37°50N 116°30E **34** F9
Donghae *S. Korea* 37°29N 129°7E **35** F15
Dongjingcheng *China* 44°5N 129°10E **35** B15
Dongnae *S. Korea* 35°12N 129°5E **35** G15
Dongning *China* 44°2N 131°5E **35** B16
Dongola *Sudan* 19°9N 30°22E **51** E12
Dongping *China* 35°55N 116°20E **34** G9
Dongsheng *China* 39°50N 110°0E **34** E6
Dongtai *China* 32°51N 120°21E **35** H11
Dongting Hu *China* 29°18N 112°45E **33** D6
Donington, C. *Australia* 34°45S 136°0E **63** E2
Doniphan *U.S.A.* 36°37N 90°50W **80** G8
Dønna *Norway* 66°6N 12°30E **8** C15
Donna *U.S.A.* 26°9N 98°4W **84** H5
Donnacona *Canada* 46°41N 71°41W **73** C5
Donnelly's Crossing
  N.Z. 35°42S 173°38E **59** A4
Donnybrook *Australia* 33°34S 115°48E **61** F2
Donnybrook *S. Africa* 29°59S 29°48E **57** D4
Donora *U.S.A.* 40°11N 79°52W **82** F5
Donostia = Donostia-San
  Sebastián *Spain* 43°17N 1°58W **21** A5
Donostia-San Sebastián
  Spain 43°17N 1°58W **21** A5
Donwood *Canada* 44°19N 78°16W **82** B6
Doomadgee *Australia* 17°56S 138°49E **62** B2
Doomadgee ۞ *Australia* 17°56S 138°49E **62** B2
Doon ➔ *U.K.* 55°27N 4°39W **11** F4
Doon Doon ۞ *Australia* 16°18S 128°14E **60** C4
Dora, L. *Australia* 22°0S 123°0E **60** D3
Dora Báltea ➔ *Italy* 45°11N 8°3E **20** D8
Doran L. *Canada* 61°13N 108°6W **71** A7
Dorchester *U.K.* 50°42N 2°27W **13** G5
Dorchester, C. *Canada* 65°27N 77°27W **69** D16
Dordabis *Namibia* 22°52S 17°38E **56** C2
Dordogne ➔ *France* 45°2N 0°36W **20** D3
Dordrecht *Neths.* 51°48N 4°39E **15** C4
Dordrecht *S. Africa* 31°20S 27°3E **57** E4
Doré L. *Canada* 54°46N 107°17W **71** C7
Dori *Burkina Faso* 14°3N 0°2W **50** F5
Doring ➔ *S. Africa* 31°54S 18°39E **56** E2
Doringbos *S. Africa* 31°59S 19°16E **56** E2
Dorking *U.K.* 51°14N 0°19W **13** F7
Dornbirn *Austria* 47°25N 9°45E **16** E5
Dornie *U.K.* 57°17N 5°31W **11** D3
Dornoch *U.K.* 44°18N 80°51W **82** B4
Dornoch *U.K.* 57°53N 4°2W **11** D4
Dornoch Firth *U.K.* 57°51N 4°4W **11** D4
Dornogovĭ □ *Mongolia* 44°0N 110°0E **34** C6
Doro, Kavo *Greece* 38°9N 24°38E **23** E11
Dorohoi *Romania* 47°56N 26°23E **17** E14
Döröö Nuur *Mongolia* 48°0N 93°0E **32** B4
Dorr *Iran* 33°17N 50°38E **45** C6
Dorre I. *Australia* 25°13S 113°12E **61** E1
Dorrigo *Australia* 30°20S 152°44E **63** E5

Dorris *U.S.A.* 41°58N 121°55W **76** F3
Dorset *Canada* 45°14N 78°54W **82** A6
Dorset *Ohio, U.S.A.* 41°40N 80°40W **82** E4
Dorset □ *U.K.* 50°45N 2°26W **13** G5
Dortmund *Germany* 51°30N 7°28E **16** C4
Dörtyol *Turkey* 36°50N 36°13E **44** B3
Doruma
   Dem. Rep. of the Congo 4°42N 27°33E **54** B2
Dorüneh *Iran* 35°10N 57°18E **45** C8
Dos Bahías, C. *Argentina* 44°58S 65°32W **96** F3
Dos Hermanas *Spain* 37°16N 5°55W **21** D3
Dos Palos *U.S.A.* 36°59N 120°37W **78** J6
Dosso *Niger* 13°0N 3°13E **50** F6
Dothan *U.S.A.* 31°13N 85°24W **85** D12
Doty *U.S.A.* 46°38N 123°17W **78** D3
Douai *France* 50°21N 3°4E **20** A5
Douala *Cameroon* 4°0N 9°45E **52** D1
Douarnenez *France* 48°6N 4°21W **20** B1
Double Island Pt.
   Australia 25°56S 153°11E **63** D5
Double Mountain Fork →
   U.S.A. 33°16N 100°0W **84** E4
Doubs → *France* 46°53N 5°1E **20** C6
Doubtful Sd. *N.Z.* 45°20S 166°49E **59** F1
Doubtless B. *N.Z.* 34°55S 173°26E **59** A4
Douglas *Canada* 45°31N 76°56W **82** A8
Douglas *I. of Man* 54°10N 4°28W **12** C3
Douglas *S. Africa* 29°4S 23°46E **56** D3
Douglas *Ariz., U.S.A.* 31°21N 109°33W **77** L9
Douglas *Ga., U.S.A.* 31°31N 82°51W **85** F13
Douglas *Wyo., U.S.A.* 42°45N 105°24W **76** E11
Douglas Apsley △
   Australia 41°45S 148°11E **63** G4
Douglas Chan. *Canada* 53°40N 129°20W **70** C3
Douglas Pt. *Canada* 44°19N 81°37W **82** B3
Douglasville *U.S.A.* 33°45N 84°45W **85** E12
Dounreay *U.K.* 58°35N 3°44W **11** C5
Dourada, Serra *Brazil* 13°10S 48°45W **93** F9
Dourados *Brazil* 22°9S 54°50W **95** A5
Dourados → *Brazil* 21°58S 54°18W **95** A5
Dourados, Serra dos
   Brazil 23°30S 53°30W **95** A5
Douro → *Europe* 41°8N 8°40W **21** B1
Dove → *U.K.* 52°51N 1°36W **12** E6
Dove Creek *U.S.A.* 37°46N 108°54W **77** H9
Dover *Australia* 43°18S 147°2E **63** G4
Dover *U.K.* 51°7N 1°19E **13** F9
Dover *Del., U.S.A.* 39°10N 75°32W **81** F16
Dover *N.H., U.S.A.* 43°12N 70°56W **83** C14
Dover *N.J., U.S.A.* 40°53N 74°34W **83** F10
Dover *Ohio, U.S.A.* 40°32N 81°29W **82** F3
Dover, Pt. *Australia* 32°32S 125°32E **61** F4
Dover, Str. of *Europe* 51°0N 1°30E **13** G9
Dover-Foxcroft *U.S.A.* 45°11N 69°13W **81** C19
Dover Plains *U.S.A.* 41°43N 73°35W **83** E11
Dovey = Dyfi → *U.K.* 52°32N 4°3W **13** E3
Dovrefjell *Norway* 62°15N 9°33E **8** E13
Dow Rūd *Iran* 33°28N 49°4E **45** C6
Dowa *Malawi* 13°38S 33°58E **55** E3
Dowagiac *U.S.A.* 41°59N 86°6W **80** E10
Dowerin *Australia* 31°12S 117°2E **61** F2
Dowgha'i *Iran* 36°54N 58°32E **45** B8
Dowlatābād *Kermān,*
   Iran 28°20N 56°40E **45** D8
Dowlatābād *Khorāsān,*
   Iran 35°16N 59°29E **45** C8
Down □ *U.K.* 54°23N 6°2W **10** B5
Downey *Calif., U.S.A.* 33°56N 118°9W **79** M8
Downey *Idaho, U.S.A.* 42°26N 112°7W **76** E7
Downham Market *U.K.* 52°37N 0°23E **13** E8
Downieville *U.S.A.* 39°34N 120°50W **78** F6
Downpatrick *U.K.* 54°20N 5°43W **10** B6
Downpatrick Hd. *Ireland* 54°20N 9°21W **10** B2
Downsville *U.S.A.* 42°5N 75°0W **83** D10
Downton, Mt. *Canada* 52°42N 124°52W **70** C4
Dowsārī *Iran* 28°25N 57°59E **45** D8
Doyle *U.S.A.* 40°2N 120°6W **78** E6
Doylestown *U.S.A.* 40°21N 75°10W **83** F9
Dozois, Rés. *Canada* 47°30N 77°5W **72** C4
Dra Khel *Pakistan* 27°58N 66°45E **42** F2
Drâa, C. *Morocco* 28°47N 11°0W **50** C3
Drâa, Hamada du *Algeria* 28°0N 7°0W **50** C4
Drâa, Oued → *Morocco* 28°40N 11°10W **50** C3
Drac → *France* 45°13N 5°41E **20** D6
Drac, Coves del *Spain* 39°31N 3°19E **24** B10
Drachten *Neths.* 53°7N 6°5E **15** A6
Drăgăşani *Romania* 44°39N 24°17E **17** F13
Dragichyn *Belarus* 52°15N 25°8E **17** B13
Dragoman, Prokhod
   Bulgaria 42°58N 22°53E **23** C10
Dragon's Mouths
   Venezuela 11°0N 61°50W **93** K15
Draguignan *France* 43°32N 6°27E **20** E7
Drain *U.S.A.* 43°40N 123°19W **76** E2
Drake *U.S.A.* 47°55N 100°23W **80** B3
Drake Passage *S. Ocean* 58°0S 68°0W **5** B17
Drakensberg *S. Africa* 31°0S 28°0E **57** D4
Drama *Greece* 41°9N 24°10E **23** D11
Drammen *Norway* 59°42N 10°12E **9** G14
Drangajökull *Iceland* 66°9N 22°15W **8** C2
Dras *India* 34°25N 75°48E **43** B6
Drastis, Akra *Greece* 39°48N 19°40E **25** A3
Drau = Drava →
   Croatia 45°33N 18°55E **23** B8
Drava → *Croatia* 45°33N 18°55E **23** B8
Drayton *Canada* 43°46N 80°40W **82** C4
Drayton Valley *Canada* 53°12N 114°58W **70** C6
Drenthe □ *Neths.* 52°52N 6°40E **15** B6
Drepano, Akra *Greece* 39°16N 23°8E **23** E10
Drepanum, C. *Cyprus* 34°54N 32°19E **25** E11
Dresden *Canada* 42°35N 82°11W **82** D2
Dresden *Germany* 51°3N 13°44E **16** C7
Dresden *U.S.A.* 42°41N 76°57W **82** D8
Dreux *France* 48°44N 1°23E **20** B4
Driffield *U.K.* 54°0N 0°26W **12** C7
Driftwood *U.S.A.* 41°20N 78°8W **82** E6
Driggs *U.S.A.* 43°44N 111°6W **76** E8
Drin → *Albania* 42°1N 19°38E **23** C8
Drina → *Bos.-H.* 44°53N 19°21E **23** B8
Drøbak *Norway* 59°39N 10°39E **9** G14

Drobeta-Turnu Severin
   Romania 44°39N 22°41E **17** F12
Drochia *Moldova* 48°2N 27°48E **17** D14
Drogheda *Ireland* 53°43N 6°22W **10** C5
Drogichin = Dragichyn
   Belarus 52°15N 25°8E **17** B13
Drogobych = Drohobych
   Ukraine 49°20N 23°30E **17** D12
Drohobych *Ukraine* 49°20N 23°30E **17** D12
Droichead Atha = Drogheda
   Ireland 53°43N 6°22W **10** C5
Droichead na Bandan = Bandon
   Ireland 51°44N 8°44W **10** E3
Droichead Nua *Ireland* 53°11N 6°48W **10** C5
Droitwich *U.K.* 52°16N 2°8W **13** E5
Drôme → *France* 44°46N 4°46E **20** D6
Dromedary, C. *Australia* 36°17S 150°10E **63** F5
Dromore *U.K.* 54°31N 7°28W **10** B4
Dromore West *Ireland* 54°15N 8°52W **10** B3
Dronfield *U.K.* 53°19N 1°27W **12** D6
Dronning Maud Land
   Antarctica 72°30S 12°0E **5** D3
Dronten *Neths.* 52°32N 5°43E **15** B5
Druk Yul = Bhutan ■
   Asia 27°25N 90°30E **41** F17
Drumbo *Canada* 43°16N 80°35W **82** C4
Drumcliff *Ireland* 54°20N 8°29W **10** B3
Drumheller *Canada* 51°25N 112°40W **70** C6
Drummond *U.S.A.* 46°40N 113°9W **76** C7
Drummond I. *U.S.A.* 46°1N 83°39W **81** B12
Drummond Pt. *Australia* 34°9S 135°16E **63** E2
Drummond Ra.
   Australia 23°45S 147°10E **62** C4
Drummondville *Canada* 45°55N 72°25W **72** C5
Drumright *U.S.A.* 35°59N 96°36W **84** D6
Druskininkai *Lithuania* 54°3N 23°58E **9** J20
Drut → *Belarus* 53°8N 30°5E **17** B16
Druzhina *Russia* 68°14N 145°18E **29** C15
Dry Harbour Mts.
   Jamaica 18°19N 77°24W **88** a
Dry Tortugas *U.S.A.* 24°38N 82°55W **85** F13
Dryander △ *Australia* 20°13S 148°34E **62** b
Dryden *Canada* 49°47N 92°50W **71** D10
Dryden *U.S.A.* 42°30N 76°18W **83** D8
Drygalski I. *Antarctica* 66°0S 92°0E **5** C7
Drygalski Ice Tongue
   Antarctica 75°24S 163°30E **5** D21
Drysdale → *Australia* 13°59S 126°51E **60** B4
Drysdale I. *Australia* 11°41S 136°0E **62** A2
Drysdale River △
   Australia 14°56S 127°2E **60** B4
Du Gué → *Canada* 57°21N 70°45W **72** A5
Du Quoin *U.S.A.* 38°1N 89°14W **80** F9
Duanesburg *U.S.A.* 42°45N 74°11W **83** D10
Duaringa *Australia* 23°42S 149°42E **62** C4
Duarte, Pico *Dom. Rep.* 19°2N 70°59W **89** C5
Dubai = Dubayy *U.A.E.* 25°18N 55°20E **45** E7
Dubāsari Vdkhr.
   Moldova 47°30N 29°0E **17** E15
Dubawnt → *Canada* 64°33N 100°6W **71** A8
Dubawnt L. *Canada* 63°8N 101°28W **71** A8
Dubayy *U.A.E.* 25°18N 55°20E **45** E7
Dubbo *Australia* 32°11S 148°35E **63** E4
Dubele
   Dem. Rep. of the Congo 2°56N 29°35E **54** B2
Dublin *Ireland* 53°21N 6°15W **10** C5
Dublin *Ga., U.S.A.* 32°32N 82°54W **85** E13
Dublin *Tex., U.S.A.* 32°5N 98°21W **84** E5
Dublin □ *Ireland* 53°24N 6°20W **10** C5
Dublin ✈ (DUB) *Ireland* 53°25N 6°20W **10** C5
Dubno *Ukraine* 50°25N 25°45E **17** C13
Dubois *Idaho, U.S.A.* 44°10N 112°14W **76** D7
Du Bois *Pa., U.S.A.* 41°7N 78°46W **82** E6
Dubossary = Dubăsari
   Moldova 47°15N 29°10E **17** E15
Dubossary Vdkhr. = Dubăsari
   Vdkhr. *Moldova* 47°30N 29°0E **17** E15
Dubovka *Russia* 49°5N 44°50E **19** E7
Dubrajpur *India* 23°48N 87°25E **43** H12
Dubréka *Guinea* 9°46N 13°31W **50** G3
Dubrovitsa = Dubrovytsya
   Ukraine 51°31N 26°35E **17** C14
Dubrovnik *Croatia* 42°39N 18°6E **23** C8
Dubrovytsya *Ukraine* 51°31N 26°35E **17** C14
Dubuque *U.S.A.* 42°30N 90°41W **80** D9
Duchesne *U.S.A.* 40°10N 110°24W **76** F8
Duchess *Australia* 21°20S 139°50E **62** C2
Ducie I. *Pac. Oc.* 24°40S 124°48W **65** K15
Duck → *U.S.A.* 36°2N 87°52W **85** C11
Duck Cr. → *Australia* 22°37S 116°53E **60** D2
Duck Lake *Canada* 52°50N 106°16W **71** C7
Duck Mountain △
   Canada 51°45N 101°0W **71** C8
Duckwall, Mt. *U.S.A.* 37°58N 120°7W **78** H6
Dudhi *India* 24°15N 83°10E **43** G10
Dudinka *Russia* 69°30N 86°13E **29** C9
Dudley *U.K.* 52°31N 2°5W **13** E5
Dudwa *India* 28°30N 80°41E **43** E9
Dudwa △ *India* 28°30N 80°40E **43** E9
Duero = Douro → *Europe* 41°8N 8°40W **21** B1
Dufftown *U.K.* 57°27N 3°8W **11** D5
Dugi Otok *Croatia* 44°0N 15°3E **16** G8
Duisburg *Germany* 51°26N 6°45E **16** C4
Duiwelskloof = Modjadjiskloof
   S. Africa 23°42S 30°10E **57** C5
Dükdamīn *Iran* 35°59N 57°43E **45** C8
Dukelský Průsmyk
   Slovak Rep. 49°25N 21°42E **17** D11
Dukhān *Qatar* 25°25N 50°50E **45** E6
Duki *Pakistan* 30°14N 68°25E **40** D6
Duku *Nigeria* 10°43N 10°43E **51** F8
Dulce *U.S.A.* 36°56N 107°0W **77** H10
Dulce → *Argentina* 30°32S 62°33W **94** C3
Dulce, G. *Costa Rica* 8°40N 83°20W **88** E3
Dulf *Iraq* 35°7N 45°51E **44** C5
Duliu *China* 39°2N 116°55E **34** E9
Dullewala *Pakistan* 31°50N 71°25E **42** D4
Dullstroom *S. Africa* 25°27S 30°7E **57** D5
Dulq Maghār *Syria* 36°22N 39°34E **44** B3

Duluth *U.S.A.* 46°47N 92°6W **80** B7
Dum Dum *India* 22°39N 88°26E **43** H13
Dum Duma *India* 27°40N 95°40E **41** F19
Dumaguete *Phil.* 9°17N 123°15E **37** C6
Dumai *Indonesia* 1°35N 101°28E **36** D2
Dumaran *Phil.* 10°33N 119°50E **37** B5
Dumas *Ark., U.S.A.* 33°53N 91°29W **84** E9
Dumas *Tex., U.S.A.* 35°52N 101°58W **84** D4
Dumayr *Syria* 33°39N 36°42E **46** B5
Dumbarton *U.K.* 55°57N 4°33W **11** F4
Dumbleyung *Australia* 33°17S 117°42E **61** F2
Dumfries *U.K.* 55°4N 3°37W **11** F5
Dumfries & Galloway □
   U.K. 55°9N 3°58W **11** F5
Dumka *India* 24°12N 87°15E **43** G12
Dumoine → *Canada* 46°13N 77°51W **72** C4
Dumoine, L. *Canada* 46°55N 77°55W **72** C4
Dumont d'Urville
   Antarctica 67°0S 110°0E **5** C10
Dumont d'Urville Sea
   S. Ocean 63°30S 138°0E **5** C9
Dumraon *India* 25°33N 84°8E **43** G11
Dumyât *Egypt* 31°24N 31°48E **51** B12
Dún Dealgan = Dundalk
   Ireland 54°1N 6°24W **10** B5
Dún Garbhán = Dungarvan
   Ireland 52°5N 7°37W **10** D4
Dún Laoghaire *Ireland* 53°17N 6°8W **10** C5
Duna = Dunărea →
   Europe 45°20N 29°40E **17** F15
Dunagiri *India* 30°31N 79°52E **43** D8
Dunaj = Dunărea →
   Europe 45°20N 29°40E **17** F15
Dunakeszi *Hungary* 47°37N 19°8E **17** E10
Dunărea → *Europe* 45°20N 29°40E **17** F15
Dunaújváros *Hungary* 46°58N 18°57E **17** E10
Dunav = Dunărea →
   Europe 45°20N 29°40E **17** F15
Dunay *Russia* 42°52N 132°22E **30** C6
Dunback *N.Z.* 45°23S 170°36E **59** F3
Dunbar *U.K.* 56°0N 2°31W **11** E6
Dunblane *U.K.* 56°11N 3°58W **11** E5
Duncan *Canada* 48°45N 123°40W **78** B3
Duncan *Ariz., U.S.A.* 32°43N 109°6W **77** K9
Duncan *Okla., U.S.A.* 34°30N 97°57W **84** D6
Duncan, L. *Canada* 53°29N 77°58W **72** B4
Duncan L. *Canada* 62°51N 113°58W **70** A6
Duncan Town *Bahamas* 22°15N 75°45W **88** B4
Duncannon *U.S.A.* 40°23N 77°2W **82** F7
Duncansby Head *U.K.* 58°38N 3°1W **11** C5
Duncansville *U.S.A.* 40°25N 78°26W **82** F6
Dundalk *Canada* 44°10N 80°24W **82** B4
Dundalk *Ireland* 54°1N 6°24W **10** B5
Dundalk *U.S.A.* 39°15N 76°31W **81** F15
Dundalk Bay *Ireland* 53°55N 6°15W **10** C5
Dundas = Uummannaq
   Greenland 77°33N 68°52W **69** B18
Dundas *Canada* 43°17N 79°59W **82** C5
Dundas, L. *Australia* 32°35S 121°50E **61** F3
Dundas I. *Canada* 54°30N 130°50W **70** C2
Dundas Str. *Australia* 11°15S 131°35E **60** B5
Dundee *S. Africa* 28°11S 30°15E **57** D5
Dundee *U.K.* 56°28N 2°59W **11** E6
Dundee *U.S.A.* 42°32N 76°59W **82** D8
Dundee City □ *U.K.* 56°30N 2°58W **11** E6
Dundgovĭ □ *Mongolia* 45°10N 106°0E **34** B4
Dundrum *U.K.* 54°16N 5°52W **10** B6
Dundrum B. *U.K.* 54°13N 5°47W **10** B6
Dunedin *N.Z.* 45°50S 170°33E **59** F3
Dunedin *U.S.A.* 28°1N 82°46W **85** G13
Dunfanaghy *Ireland* 55°11N 7°58W **10** A4
Dunfermline *U.K.* 56°5N 3°27W **11** E5
Dungannon *Canada* 43°51N 81°36W **82** C3
Dungannon *U.K.* 54°31N 6°46W **10** B5
Dungarpur *India* 23°52N 73°45E **42** H5
Dungarvan *Ireland* 52°5N 7°37W **10** D4
Dungarvan Harbour
   Ireland 52°4N 7°35W **10** D4
Dungeness *U.K.* 50°54N 0°59E **13** G8
Dunglow *Ireland* 54°57N 8°21W **10** B3
Dungo, L. do *Angola* 17°15S 19°0E **56** B2
Dungog *Australia* 32°22S 151°46E **63** E5
Dungu
   Dem. Rep. of the Congo 3°40N 28°32E **54** B2
Dungun *Malaysia* 4°45N 103°25E **39** K4
Dunhua *China* 43°20N 128°14E **35** C15
Dunhuang *China* 40°8N 94°36E **32** B4
Dunk I. *Australia* 17°59S 146°29E **62** B4
Dunkeld *Australia* 33°25S 149°29E **63** E4
Dunkeld *U.K.* 56°34N 3°35W **11** E5
Dunkerque *France* 51°2N 2°20E **20** A5
Dunkery Beacon *U.K.* 51°9N 3°36W **13** F4
Dunkirk = Dunkerque
   France 51°2N 2°20E **20** A5
Dunkirk *U.S.A.* 42°29N 79°20W **82** D5
Dúnleary = Dún Laoghaire
   Ireland 53°17N 6°8W **10** C5
Dunleer *Ireland* 53°50N 6°24W **10** C5
Dunmanus B. *Ireland* 51°31N 9°50W **10** E2
Dunmanway *Ireland* 51°43N 9°6W **10** E2
Dunmara *Australia* 16°42S 133°25E **62** B1
Dunmore *U.S.A.* 41°25N 75°38W **83** E9
Dunmore East *Ireland* 52°9N 7°0W **10** D5
Dunmore Hd. *Ireland* 52°10N 10°35W **10** D1
Dunmore Town
   Bahamas 25°30N 76°39W **88** A4
Dunn *U.S.A.* 35°19N 78°37W **85** D15
Dunnellon *U.S.A.* 29°3N 82°28W **85** G13
Dunnet Hd. *U.K.* 58°40N 3°21W **11** C5
Dunning *U.S.A.* 41°50N 100°6W **80** E4
Dunnville *Canada* 42°54N 79°36W **82** D5
Dunolly *Australia* 36°51S 143°44E **63** F3
Dunoon *U.K.* 55°57N 4°56W **11** F4
Dunphy *U.S.A.* 40°42N 116°31W **76** F5
Dunseith *U.S.A.* 48°50N 100°3W **80** A3
Dunshaughlin *Ireland* 53°31N 6°48W **10** C5
Dunsmuir *U.S.A.* 41°13N 122°16W **76** F2
Dunstable *U.K.* 51°53N 0°32W **13** F7
Dunstan Mts. *N.Z.* 44°53S 169°35E **59** F2

Dunster *Canada* 53°8N 119°50W **70** C5
Dunvegan *U.K.* 57°27N 6°35W **11** D2
Dunvegan L. *Canada* 60°8N 107°10W **71** A7
Dupree *U.S.A.* 45°4N 101°35W **80** C3
Dupuyer *U.S.A.* 48°13N 112°30W **76** B7
Duque de Caxias *Brazil* 22°46S 43°18W **95** A7
Durack → *Australia* 15°33S 127°52E **60** C4
Durack Ra. *Australia* 16°50S 127°40E **60** C4
Durack River *Australia* 15°32S 127°39E **60** C4
Durance → *France* 43°55N 4°45E **20** E6
Durand *U.S.A.* 44°38N 91°58W **80** C8
Durango *Mexico* 24°3N 104°39W **86** C4
Durango □ *Mexico* 24°50N 105°20W **86** C4
Durango *U.S.A.* 37°16N 107°53W **77** H10
Durant *Miss., U.S.A.* 33°4N 89°51W **85** E10
Durant *Okla., U.S.A.* 33°59N 96°25W **84** E6
Durazno *Uruguay* 33°25S 56°31W **94** C4
Durazzo = Durrës
   Albania 41°19N 19°28E **23** D8
Durban *S. Africa* 29°49S 31°1E **57** D5
Durbuy *Belgium* 50°21N 5°28E **15** D5
Düren *Germany* 50°48N 6°29E **16** C4
Durg = Bhilainagar-Durg
   India 21°13N 81°26E **41** J12
Durgapur *India* 23°30N 87°20E **43** H12
Durham *Canada* 44°10N 80°49W **82** B4
Durham *U.K.* 54°47N 1°34W **12** C6
Durham *Calif., U.S.A.* 39°39N 121°48W **78** F5
Durham *N.C., U.S.A.* 35°59N 78°54W **85** D15
Durham *N.H., U.S.A.* 43°8N 70°56W **83** C14
Durham □ *U.K.* 54°42N 1°45W **12** C6
Durlas = Thurles *Ireland* 52°41N 7°49W **10** D4
Durmā *Si. Arabia* 24°37N 46°8E **44** E5
Durmitor *Montenegro* 43°10N 19°0E **23** C8
Durness *U.K.* 58°34N 4°45W **11** C4
Durrës *Albania* 41°19N 19°28E **23** D8
Durrow *Ireland* 52°51N 7°24W **10** D4
Dursey I. *Ireland* 51°36N 10°12W **10** E1
Dursley *U.K.* 51°40N 2°21W **13** F5
Dursunbey *Turkey* 39°35N 28°37E **23** E13
Duru
   Dem. Rep. of the Congo 4°14N 28°50E **54** B2
Durūz, Jabal ad *Jordan* 32°35N 36°40E **46** C5
D'Urville, Tanjung
   Indonesia 1°28S 137°54E **37** E9
D'Urville I. *N.Z.* 40°50S 173°55E **59** D4
Duryea *U.S.A.* 41°20N 75°45W **83** E9
Dushak *Turkmenistan* 37°13N 60°1E **45** B9
Dushanbe *Tajikistan* 38°33N 68°48E **28** F7
Dushore *U.S.A.* 41°31N 76°24W **83** E8
Dusky Sd. *N.Z.* 45°47S 166°30E **59** F1
Dussejour, C. *Australia* 14°45S 128°13E **60** B4
Düsseldorf *Germany* 51°14N 6°47E **16** C4
Dutch Harbor *U.S.A.* 53°53N 166°32W **74** E4
Dutlwe *Botswana* 23°58S 23°46E **56** C3
Dutton *Canada* 42°39N 81°30W **82** D3
Dutton → *Australia* 20°44S 143°10E **62** C3
Dutywa *S. Africa* 32°8S 28°18E **57** E4
Duwayhin, Khawr
   U.A.E. 24°20N 51°25E **45** E6
Duyfken Pt. *Australia* 12°33S 141°38E **62** A3
Duyun *China* 26°18N 107°29E **32** D5
Dvina, Severnaya →
   Russia 64°32N 40°30E **18** B7
Dvinsk = Daugavpils
   Latvia 55°53N 26°32E **9** J22
Dvinskaya Guba *Russia* 65°0N 39°0E **18** B6
Dwarka *India* 22°18N 69°8E **42** H3
Dwellingup *Australia* 32°43S 116°4E **61** F2
Dwight *Canada* 45°20N 79°1W **82** A5
Dwight *U.S.A.* 41°5N 88°26W **80** E9
Dyatlovo = Dzyatlava
   Belarus 53°28N 25°28E **17** B13
Dyce *U.K.* 57°13N 2°12W **11** D6
Dyer, C. *Canada* 66°37N 61°16W **69** D19
Dyer Bay *Canada* 45°10N 81°20W **82** A3
Dyer Plateau *Antarctica* 70°45S 65°30W **5** D17
Dyersburg *U.S.A.* 36°3N 89°23W **85** C10
Dyfi → *U.K.* 52°32N 4°3W **13** E3
Dymer *Ukraine* 50°47N 30°18E **17** C16
Dysart *Australia* 22°32S 148°23E **62** C4
Dyfi → *U.K.* 52°32N 4°3W **13** E3
Dzaoudzi *Mayotte* 12°47S 45°16E **53** a
Dzavhan Gol → *Mongolia* 48°54N 93°23E **32** B4
Dzerzhinsk *Russia* 56°14N 43°30E **18** C7
Dzhalinda *Russia* 53°26N 124°0E **29** D13
Dzhambul = Taraz
   Kazakhstan 42°54N 71°22E **28** E8
Dzhankoy *Ukraine* 45°40N 34°20E **19** E5
Dzhezkazgan = Zhezqazghan
   Kazakhstan 47°44N 67°40E **28** E7
Dzhizak = Jizzax
   Uzbekistan 40°6N 67°50E **28** E7
Dzhugdzur, Khrebet
   Russia 57°30N 138°0E **29** D14
Dzhungarskiye Vorota =
   Dzungarian Gate *Asia* 45°10N 82°0E **32** B3
Działdowo *Poland* 53°15N 20°15E **17** B11
Dzibilchaltún *Mexico* 21°10N 89°35W **87** C7
Dzierżoniów *Poland* 50°45N 16°39E **17** C9
Dzilam de Bravo *Mexico* 21°24N 88°53W **87** C7
Dzūkija △ *Lithuania* 54°10N 24°30E **9** J21
Dzungarian Basin = Junggar
   Pendi *China* 44°30N 86°0E **32** B3
Dzungarian Gate *Asia* 45°10N 82°0E **32** B3
Dzüünbayan *Mongolia* 44°52N 106°28E **32** B5
Dzüünmod *Mongolia* 47°45N 106°58E **32** B5
Dzyarzhynsk *Belarus* 53°40N 27°1E **17** B14
Dzyatlava *Belarus* 53°28N 25°28E **17** B13

E

E.C. Manning ○ *Canada* 49°5N 120°45W **70** D4
Eabamet L. *Canada* 51°30N 87°46W **72** B2
Eabametoong *Canada* 51°30N 88°0W **72** B2
Éadan Doire = Edenderry
   Ireland 53°21N 7°4W **10** C4
Eads *U.S.A.* 38°29N 102°47W **76** G12

Eagar *U.S.A.* 34°6N 109°17W **77** J9
Eagle *Alaska, U.S.A.* 64°47N 141°12W **68** E3
Eagle *Colo., U.S.A.* 39°39N 106°50W **76** G10
Eagle → *Canada* 53°36N 57°26W **73** B8
Eagle Butte *U.S.A.* 45°0N 101°10W **80** C3
Eagle Grove *U.S.A.* 42°40N 93°54W **80** D7
Eagle L. *Calif., U.S.A.* 40°39N 120°45W **76** F3
Eagle L. *Maine, U.S.A.* 46°20N 69°22W **81** B19
Eagle Lake *Canada* 45°8N 78°29W **82** A6
Eagle Lake *Maine, U.S.A.* 47°3N 68°36W **81** B19
Eagle Lake *Tex., U.S.A.* 29°35N 96°20W **84** G6
Eagle Mountain
   U.S.A. 33°49N 115°27W **79** M11
Eagle Nest *U.S.A.* 36°33N 105°16W **77** H11
Eagle Pass *U.S.A.* 28°43N 100°30W **84** G4
Eagle Pk. *U.S.A.* 38°10N 119°25W **78** G7
Eagle Pt. *Australia* 16°11S 124°23E **60** C3
Eagle River *Mich., U.S.A.* 47°25N 88°18W **80** B9
Eagle River *Wis., U.S.A.* 45°55N 89°15W **80** C9
Eaglehawk *Australia* 36°44S 144°15E **63** F3
Eagles Mere *U.S.A.* 41°25N 76°33W **83** E8
Ealing □ *U.K.* 51°31N 0°20W **13** F7
Ear Falls *Canada* 50°38N 93°13W **71** C10
Earle *U.S.A.* 35°16N 90°28W **85** D9
Earlimart *U.S.A.* 35°53N 119°16W **79** K7
Earlville *U.S.A.* 42°44N 75°32W **83** D9
Earn → *U.K.* 56°21N 3°18W **11** E5
Earn, L. *U.K.* 56°23N 4°13W **11** E4
Earnslaw, Mt. *N.Z.* 44°32S 168°27E **59** F2
Earth *U.S.A.* 34°14N 102°24W **84** D3
Easley *U.S.A.* 34°50N 82°36W **85** D13
East Anglia *U.K.* 52°30N 1°0E **12** E9
East Angus *Canada* 45°30N 71°40W **73** C5
East Antarctica *Antarctica* 80°0S 90°0E **5** D7
East Aurora *U.S.A.* 42°46N 78°37W **82** D6
East Ayrshire □ *U.K.* 55°26N 4°11W **11** F4
East Bengal *Bangla.* 24°0N 90°0E **41** G17
East Beskids = Vychodné Beskydy
   Europe 49°20N 22°0E **17** D11
East Brady *U.S.A.* 40°59N 79°37W **82** F5
East Branch Clarion River L.
   U.S.A. 41°35N 78°35W **82** E6
East C. = Dezhneva, Mys
   Russia 66°5N 169°40W **29** C19
East C. *N.Z.* 37°42S 178°35E **59** B7
East Caroline Basin
   Pac. Oc. 4°0N 146°45E **64** G6
East Chicago *U.S.A.* 41°38N 87°27W **80** E10
East China Sea *Asia* 30°0N 126°0E **33** D7
East Coulee *Canada* 51°23N 112°27W **70** C6
East Dereham = Dereham
   U.K. 52°41N 0°57E **13** E8
East Dunbartonshire □
   U.K. 55°57N 4°13W **11** F4
East Falkland *Falk. Is.* 51°30S 58°30W **96** G5
East Grand Forks *U.S.A.* 47°56N 97°1W **80** B5
East Greenwich *U.S.A.* 41°40N 71°27W **83** E13
East Grinstead *U.K.* 51°7N 0°0 **13** F8
East Hartford *U.S.A.* 41°46N 72°39W **83** E12
East Haydon *Australia* 18°0S 141°30E **62** B3
East Helena *U.S.A.* 46°35N 111°56W **76** C8
East Indies *Asia* 0°0 120°0E **26** J14
East Kilbride *U.K.* 55°47N 4°11W **11** F4
East Lamma Channel
   China 22°14N 114°9E **33** G11
East Lansing *U.S.A.* 42°44N 84°29W **81** D11
East Liverpool *U.S.A.* 40°37N 80°35W **82** F4
East London *S. Africa* 33°0S 27°55E **57** E4
East Lothian □ *U.K.* 55°58N 2°44W **11** F6
East Main = Eastmain
   Canada 52°10N 78°30W **72** B4
East Mariana Basin
   Pac. Oc. 12°0N 153°0E **64** F7
East Northport *U.S.A.* 40°53N 73°20W **83** F11
East Orange *U.S.A.* 40°46N 74°12W **83** F10
East Pacific Rise *Pac. Oc.* 15°0S 110°0W **65** J17
East Palestine *U.S.A.* 40°50N 80°33W **82** F4
East Pine *Canada* 55°48N 120°12W **70** B4
East Point *U.S.A.* 33°41N 84°25W **85** E12
East Providence *U.S.A.* 41°49N 71°23W **83** E13
East Pt. *Br. Virgin Is.* 18°40N 64°18W **89** e
East Pt. *Canada* 46°27N 61°58W **73** C7
East Renfrewshire □
   U.K. 55°46N 4°21W **11** F4
East Retford = Retford
   U.K. 53°19N 0°56W **12** D7
East Riding of Yorkshire □
   U.K. 53°55N 0°30W **12** D7
East Rochester *U.S.A.* 43°7N 77°29W **82** C7
East St. Louis *U.S.A.* 38°37N 90°9W **80** F8
East Schelde = Oosterschelde →
   Neths. 51°33N 4°0E **15** C4
East Sea = Japan, Sea of
   Asia 40°0N 135°0E **30** E7
East Siberian Sea *Russia* 73°0N 160°0E **29** B17
East Stroudsburg *U.S.A.* 41°1N 75°11W **83** E9
East Sussex □ *U.K.* 50°56N 0°19E **13** G8
East Tasman Plateau
   Pac. Oc. 43°30S 152°0E **64** M7
East Tawas *U.S.A.* 44°17N 83°29W **81** C12
East Timor ■ *Asia* 8°50S 126°0E **37** F7
East Toorale *Australia* 30°27S 145°28E **63** E4
East Walker → *U.S.A.* 38°52N 119°10W **78** G7
East Windsor *U.S.A.* 40°17N 74°34W **83** F10
Eastbourne *N.Z.* 41°19S 174°55E **59** D5
Eastbourne *U.K.* 50°46N 0°18E **13** G8
Eastend *Canada* 49°32N 108°50W **71** D7
Easter Fracture Zone
   Pac. Oc. 25°0S 115°0W **65** K16
Easter I. = Pascua, I. de
   Chile 27°7S 109°23W **65** K17
Eastern □ *Kenya* 0°0 38°30E **54** C4
Eastern Cape □ *S. Africa* 32°0S 26°0E **56** E4
Eastern Cr. → *Australia* 20°40S 141°35E **62** C3
Eastern Desert = Es Sahrâ' Esh
   Sharqîya *Egypt* 27°30N 32°30E **51** C12
Eastern Ghats *India* 14°0N 78°50E **40** N11
Eastern Group = Lau Group
   Fiji 17°0S 178°30W **59** a

Eastern Group *Australia* 33°30S 124°30E **61 F3**
Eastern Guruma ✧
  Australia 22°0S 117°30E **60 D2**
Eastern Transvaal =
  Mpumalanga □
  S. Africa 26°0S 30°0E **57 D5**
Easterville *Canada* 53°8N 99°49W **71 C9**
Easthampton *U.S.A.* 42°16N 72°40W **83 D12**
Eastlake *U.S.A.* 41°40N 81°26W **82 E3**
Eastland *U.S.A.* 32°24N 98°49W **84 E5**
Eastleigh *U.K.* 50°58N 1°21W **13 G6**
Eastmain *Canada* 52°10N 78°30W **72 B4**
Eastmain → *Canada* 52°27N 78°26W **72 B4**
Eastman *Canada* 45°18N 72°19W **83 A12**
Eastman *U.S.A.* 32°12N 83°11W **85 E13**
Easton *Md., U.S.A.* 38°47N 76°5W **81 F15**
Easton *Pa., U.S.A.* 40°41N 75°13W **83 F9**
Easton *Wash., U.S.A.* 47°14N 121°11W **78 C5**
Eastport *U.S.A.* 44°56N 67°0W **81 C20**
Eastsound *U.S.A.* 48°42N 122°55W **78 B4**
Eaton *U.S.A.* 40°32N 104°42W **76 F11**
Eatonia *Canada* 51°13N 109°25W **71 C7**
Eatonton *U.S.A.* 33°20N 83°23W **85 E13**
Eatontown *U.S.A.* 40°19N 74°4W **83 F10**
Eatonville *U.S.A.* 46°52N 122°16W **78 D4**
Eau Claire *U.S.A.* 44°49N 91°30W **80 C8**
Eau Claire, L. à l' *Canada* 56°10N 74°25W **72 A5**
Eauripik Rise *Pac. Oc.* 2°0N 142°0E **64 G6**
Ebano *Mexico* 22°13N 98°24W **87 C5**
Ebbw Vale *U.K.* 51°46N 3°12W **13 F4**
Ebeltoft *Denmark* 56°12N 10°41E **9 H14**
Ebensburg *U.S.A.* 40°29N 78°44W **82 F6**
Eberswalde-Finow
  Germany 52°50N 13°49E **16 B7**
Ebetsu *Japan* 43°7N 141°34E **30 C10**
Ebey's Landing ○
  U.S.A. 48°12N 122°41W **78 B4**
Ebinur Hu *China* 44°55N 82°55E **32 B3**
Ebolowa *Cameroon* 2°55N 11°10E **52 D2**
Ebonda
  Dem. Rep. of the Congo 2°12N 22°21E **52 D4**
Ebre = Ebro → *Spain* 40°43N 0°54E **21 B6**
Ebro → *Spain* 40°43N 0°54E **21 B6**
Ecatepec de Morelos
  Mexico 19°36N 99°3W **87 D5**
Ecbatana = Hamadān
  Iran 34°52N 48°32E **45 C6**
Eceabat *Turkey* 40°11N 26°21E **23 D12**
Ech Chéliff *Algeria* 36°10N 1°20E **50 A6**
Echigo-Sammyaku
  Japan 36°50N 139°50E **31 F9**
Echizen-Misaki *Japan* 35°59N 135°57E **31 G7**
Echo Bay *N.W.T., Canada* 66°5N 117°55W **68 D8**
Echo Bay *Ont., Canada* 46°29N 84°4W **72 C3**
Echoing → *Canada* 55°51N 92°5W **72 B1**
Echternach *Lux.* 49°49N 6°25E **15 E6**
Echuca *Australia* 36°10S 144°45E **63 F3**
Écija *Spain* 37°30N 5°10W **21 D3**
Eclipse I. *Australia* 35°5S 117°58E **61 G2**
Eclipse Is. *Australia* 13°54S 126°19E **60 B4**
Eclipse Sd. *Canada* 72°38N 79°0W **69 C16**
Ecuador ■ *S. Amer.* 2°0S 78°0W **92 D3**
Ed Da'ein *Sudan* 11°26N 26°9E **51 F10**
Ed Damazin *Sudan* 11°46N 34°21E **51 F12**
Ed Dâmer *Sudan* 17°27N 34°0E **51 E12**
Ed Dar el Beida = Casablanca
  Morocco 33°36N 7°36W **50 B4**
Ed Debba *Sudan* 18°0N 30°51E **51 E12**
Ed Déffa *Egypt* 30°40N 26°30E **51 B11**
Ed Dueim *Sudan* 14°0N 32°10E **51 F12**
Edam *Canada* 53°11N 108°46W **71 C7**
Edam *Neths.* 52°31N 5°3E **15 B5**
Eday *U.K.* 59°11N 2°47W **11 B6**
Eddrachillis B. *U.K.* 58°17N 5°14W **11 C3**
Eddystone *U.K.* 50°11N 4°16W **13 G3**
Eddystone Pt. *Australia* 40°59S 148°20E **63 G4**
Ede *Neths.* 52°4N 5°40E **15 B5**
Edehon L. *Canada* 60°25N 97°15W **71 A9**
Eden *Australia* 37°3S 149°55E **63 F4**
Eden *N.C., U.S.A.* 36°29N 79°53W **85 C15**
Eden *N.Y., U.S.A.* 42°39N 78°55W **82 D6**
Eden *Tex., U.S.A.* 31°13N 99°51W **84 F5**
Eden → *U.K.* 54°57N 3°1W **12 C4**
Edenburg *S. Africa* 29°43S 25°58E **56 D4**
Edendale *S. Africa* 29°39S 30°18E **57 D5**
Edenderry *Ireland* 53°21N 7°4W **10 C4**
Edenton *U.S.A.* 36°4N 76°39W **85 C16**
Edenville *S. Africa* 27°37S 27°34E **57 D4**
Eder → *Germany* 51°12N 9°28E **16 C5**
Edessa *Greece* 40°48N 22°5E **23 D10**
Edfu = Idfû *Egypt* 24°55N 32°49E **51 D12**
Edgar *U.S.A.* 40°22N 97°58W **80 E5**
Edgartown *U.S.A.* 41°23N 70°31W **83 E14**
Edge Hill *U.K.* 52°8N 1°26W **13 E6**
Edgefield *U.S.A.* 33°47N 81°56W **85 E14**
Edgeley *U.S.A.* 46°22N 98°43W **80 B4**
Edgemont *U.S.A.* 43°18N 103°50W **80 D2**
Edgeøya *Svalbard* 77°45N 22°30E **4 B9**
Édhessa = Edessa *Greece* 40°48N 22°5E **23 D10**
Edievale *N.Z.* 45°49S 169°22E **59 F2**
Edina *U.S.A.* 40°10N 92°11W **80 E7**
Edinboro *U.S.A.* 41°52N 80°8W **82 E4**
Edinburg *U.S.A.* 26°18N 98°10W **84 H5**
Edinburgh *U.K.* 55°57N 3°13W **11 F5**
Edinburgh ✈ (EDI) *U.K.* 55°54N 3°22W **11 F5**
Edinburgh, City of □
  U.K. 55°57N 3°17W **11 F5**
Edineţ *Moldova* 48°9N 27°18E **17 D14**
Edirne *Turkey* 41°40N 26°34E **23 D12**
Edison *U.S.A.* 48°33N 122°27W **78 B4**
Edithburg *Australia* 35°5S 137°43E **63 F2**
Edmeston *U.S.A.* 42°42N 75°15W **83 D9**
Edmond *U.S.A.* 35°39N 97°29W **84 D6**
Edmonds *U.S.A.* 47°48N 122°22W **78 C4**
Edmonton *Australia* 17°2S 145°46E **62 B4**
Edmonton *Canada* 53°30N 113°30W **70 C6**
Edmund L. *Canada* 54°45N 93°17W **72 B1**
Edmundston *Canada* 47°23N 68°20W **73 C6**
Edna *U.S.A.* 28°59N 96°39W **84 G6**

Edremit *Turkey* 39°34N 27°0E **23 E12**
Edremit Körfezi *Turkey* 39°30N 26°45E **23 E12**
Edson *Canada* 53°35N 116°28W **70 C5**
Eduardo Castex
  Argentina 35°50S 64°18W **94 D3**
Edward → *Australia* 35°5S 143°30E **63 F3**
Edward, L. *Africa* 0°25S 29°40E **54 C2**
Edward VII Land
  Antarctica 80°0S 150°0W **5 E13**
Edwards *Calif., U.S.A.* 34°50N 117°40W **79 L9**
Edwards *N.Y., U.S.A.* 44°20N 75°15W **83 B9**
Edwards Plateau
  U.S.A. 30°45N 101°20W **84 F4**
Edwardsville *U.S.A.* 41°15N 75°56W **83 E9**
Edzná *Mexico* 19°39N 90°19W **87 D6**
Edzo *Canada* 62°49N 116°4W **70 A5**
Eeklo *Belgium* 51°11N 3°33E **15 C3**
Effie *U.S.A.* 47°51N 93°38W **80 B7**
Effigy Mounds △ *U.S.A.* 43°5N 91°11W **80 D8**
Effingham *U.S.A.* 39°7N 88°33W **80 F9**
Égadi, Ísole *Italy* 37°55N 12°16E **22 F5**
Eganville *Canada* 45°32N 77°5W **82 A7**
Eger = Cheb *Czech Rep.* 50°9N 12°28E **16 C7**
Eger *Hungary* 47°53N 20°27E **17 E11**
Egersund *Norway* 58°26N 6°1E **9 G12**
Egg L. *Canada* 55°5N 105°30W **71 B7**
Éghezée *Belgium* 50°35N 4°55E **15 D4**
Egio *Greece* 38°15N 22°5E **23 E10**
Eglinton I. *Canada* 75°48N 118°30W **69 B8**
Egmont *Canada* 49°45N 123°56W **70 D4**
Egmont, C. *N.Z.* 39°16S 173°45E **59 C4**
Egmont, Mt. = Taranaki, Mt.
  N.Z. 39°17S 174°5E **59 C5**
Egmont △ *N.Z.* 39°17S 174°4E **59 C5**
Egra *India* 21°54N 87°32E **43 J12**
Eğridir *Turkey* 37°52N 30°51E **19 G5**
Eğridir Gölü *Turkey* 37°53N 30°50E **44 B1**
Egvekinot *Russia* 66°19N 179°50W **29 C19**
Egypt ■ *Africa* 28°0N 31°0E **51 C12**
Ehime □ *Japan* 33°30N 132°40E **31 H6**
Ehrenberg *U.S.A.* 33°36N 114°31W **79 M12**
Eibar *Spain* 43°11N 2°28W **21 A4**
Eidsvold *Australia* 25°25S 151°12E **63 D5**
Eidsvoll *Norway* 60°19N 11°14E **9 F14**
Eielson *U.S.A.* 64°40N 147°4W **74 C10**
Eifel *Germany* 50°15N 6°50E **16 C4**
Eiffel Flats *Zimbabwe* 18°20S 30°0E **55 F3**
Eigg *U.K.* 56°54N 6°10W **11 E2**
Eighty Mile Beach
  Australia 19°30S 120°40E **60 C3**
Eil, L. *U.K.* 56°51N 5°16W **11 E3**
Eildon, L. *Australia* 37°10S 146°0E **63 F4**
Eilean Sar = Western Isles □
  U.K. 57°30N 7°10W **11 D1**
Einasleigh *Australia* 18°32S 144°5E **62 B3**
Einasleigh → *Australia* 17°30S 142°17E **62 B3**
Eindhoven *Neths.* 51°26N 5°28E **15 C5**
Eire = Ireland ■ *Europe* 53°50N 7°52W **10 C4**
Eiríksjökull *Iceland* 64°46N 20°24W **8 D3**
Eirunepé *Brazil* 6°35S 69°53W **92 E5**
Eiseb → *Namibia* 20°33S 20°59E **56 C2**
Eisenach *Germany* 50°58N 10°19E **16 C6**
Eisenerz *Austria* 47°32N 14°54E **16 E8**
Eivissa *Spain* 38°54N 1°26E **24 C7**
Ejeda *Madag.* 24°20S 44°31E **57 C7**
Ejutla *Mexico* 16°34N 96°44W **87 D5**
Ekalaka *U.S.A.* 45°53N 104°33W **76 D11**
Ekaterinburg = Yekaterinburg
  Russia 56°50N 60°30E **28 D7**
Ekenäs = Tammisaari
  Finland 60°0N 23°26E **9 G20**
Eketahuna *N.Z.* 40°38S 175°43E **59 D5**
Ekibastuz *Kazakhstan* 51°50N 75°10E **28 D8**
Ekoli *Dem. Rep. of the Congo* 0°23S 24°13E **54 C1**
Eksjö *Sweden* 57°40N 14°58E **9 H16**
Ekuma → *Namibia* 18°40S 16°2E **56 B2**
Ekwan → *Canada* 53°12N 82°15W **72 B3**
Ekwan Pt. *Canada* 53°16N 82°7W **72 B3**
El Aaiún *W. Sahara* 27°9N 13°12W **50 C3**
El Abanico *Chile* 37°20S 71°31W **94 D1**
El 'Agrûd *Egypt* 30°14N 34°24E **46 E3**
El Alamein *Egypt* 30°48N 28°58E **51 B11**
El 'Aqaba, W. → *Egypt* 30°7N 33°54E **46 E2**
El Arîḥā *West Bank* 31°52N 35°27E **46 D4**
El 'Arîsh *Egypt* 31°8N 33°50E **46 D2**
El 'Arîsh, W. → *Egypt* 31°8N 33°47E **46 D2**
El Asnam = Ech Chéliff
  Algeria 36°10N 1°20E **50 A6**
El Bayadh *Algeria* 33°40N 1°1E **50 B6**
El Bluff *Nic.* 11°59N 83°40W **88 D3**
El Cajon *U.S.A.* 32°48N 116°58W **79 N10**
El Calafate *Argentina* 50°19S 72°15W **96 G2**
El Campo *U.S.A.* 29°12N 96°16W **84 G6**
El Capitan *U.S.A.* 37°44N 119°38E **78 H7**
El Carbón *Honduras* 15°25N 85°32W **88 C2**
El Carmen *Colombia* 9°43N 75°8W **92 B3**
El Centro *U.S.A.* 32°48N 115°34W **79 N11**
El Cerro *Bolivia* 17°30S 61°40W **92 G6**
El Compadre *Mexico* 32°20N 116°14W **79 N10**
El Cuy *Argentina* 39°55S 68°25W **96 D3**
El Cuyo *Mexico* 21°31N 87°41W **87 C7**
El Daheir *Egypt* 31°13N 34°10E **46 D3**
El Descanso *Mexico* 32°12N 116°58W **79 N10**
El Desemboque *Mexico* 30°33N 113°1W **86 A2**
El Diviso *Colombia* 1°22N 78°14W **92 C3**
El Djouf *Mauritania* 20°0N 9°0W **50 D4**
El Dorado *Mexico* 24°17N 107°21W **86 C3**
El Dorado *Ark., U.S.A.* 33°12N 92°40W **84 E8**
El Dorado *Kans., U.S.A.* 37°49N 96°52W **80 D6**
El Dorado *Venezuela* 6°55N 61°37W **92 B6**
El Dorado Springs *U.S.A.* 37°52N 94°1W **80 G6**
El Escorial *Spain* 40°35N 4°7W **21 B3**
El Faiyûm *Egypt* 29°19N 30°50E **51 C12**
El Fâsher *Sudan* 13°33N 25°26E **51 F11**
El Ferrol = Ferrol *Spain* 43°29N 8°15W **21 A1**
El Fuerte *Mexico* 26°25N 108°39W **86 B3**
El Geneina = Al Junaynah
  Sudan 13°27N 22°45E **51 F10**

El Gezira □ *Sudan* 15°0N 33°0E **51 F12**
El Gogorrón △ *Mexico* 21°49N 100°57W **86 C4**
El Gîza *Egypt* 30°0N 31°12E **51 C12**
El Goléa *Algeria* 30°30N 2°50E **50 B6**
El Golfo de Santa Clara
  Mexico 31°42N 114°30W **86 A2**
El Guácharo △ *Venezuela* 10°8N 63°21W **89 D7**
El Guache △ *Venezuela* 9°45N 69°30W **89 E6**
El Iskandarîya *Egypt* 31°13N 29°58E **51 B11**
El Istiwa'iya *Sudan* 5°0N 28°0E **51 G11**
El Jadida *Morocco* 33°11N 8°17W **50 B4**
El Jardal *Honduras* 14°54N 88°50W **88 D2**
El Kef □ *Tunisia* 36°0N 9°0E **51 A7**
El Khârga *Egypt* 25°30N 30°33E **51 C12**
El Khartûm *Sudan* 15°31N 32°35E **51 E12**
El Khartûm Bahrî
  Sudan 15°40N 32°31E **51 E12**
El Kuntilla *Egypt* 30°1N 34°45E **46 E3**
El Leoncito △ *Argentina* 31°58S 69°10W **94 C2**
El Lucero *Mexico* 30°37N 106°31W **86 A3**
El Maestrazgo *Spain* 40°30N 0°25W **21 B5**
El Mahalla el Kubra
  Egypt 31°0N 31°0E **51 B12**
El Malpais △ *U.S.A.* 34°53N 108°0W **77 J10**
El Mansûra *Egypt* 31°0N 31°19E **51 B12**
El Medano *Canary Is.* 28°3N 16°32W **24 F3**
El Ménia = El Goléa
  Algeria 30°30N 2°50E **50 B6**
El Milagro *Argentina* 30°59S 65°59W **94 C2**
El Minyâ *Egypt* 28°7N 30°33E **51 C12**
El Monte *U.S.A.* 34°4N 118°1W **79 L8**
El Obeid *Sudan* 13°8N 30°10E **51 F12**
El Odaiya *Sudan* 12°8N 28°12E **51 F11**
El Oro *Mexico* 19°51N 100°7W **87 D4**
El Oued *Algeria* 33°20N 6°58E **50 B7**
El Palmar △ *Argentina* 32°10S 58°31W **94 C4**
El Palmito, Presa
  Mexico 25°40N 105°30W **86 B3**
El Paso *U.S.A.* 31°45N 106°29W **84 F1**
El Pinacate y Gran Desierto de
  Altar = Gran Desierto del
  Pinacate △ *Mexico* 31°51N 113°32W **86 A2**
El Portal *U.S.A.* 37°41N 119°47W **78 H7**
El Porvenir *Mexico* 31°15N 105°51W **86 A3**
El Prat de Llobregat *Spain* 41°19N 2°5E **21 B7**
El Progreso *Honduras* 15°26N 87°51W **88 C2**
El Pueblito *Mexico* 29°6N 105°7W **86 B3**
El Pueblo *Canary Is.* 28°36N 17°47W **24 F2**
El Puerto de Santa María
  Spain 36°36N 6°13W **21 D2**
El Qâhira *Egypt* 30°2N 31°13E **51 B12**
El Qantara *Egypt* 30°51N 32°20E **46 E1**
El Quseima *Egypt* 30°40N 34°15E **46 E3**
El Real de Santa María
  Panama 8°0N 77°40W **92 B3**
El Reno *U.S.A.* 35°32N 97°57W **75 H20**
El Rey △ *Argentina* 24°40S 64°34W **94 A3**
El Rio *U.S.A.* 34°14N 119°10W **79 L7**
El Roque, Pta. *Canary Is.* 28°10N 15°25W **24 F4**
El Rosarito *Mexico* 28°38N 114°4W **86 B2**
El Salto *Mexico* 23°47N 105°22W **86 C3**
El Salvador ■ *Cent. Amer.* 13°50N 89°0W **88 D2**
El Sauce *Nic.* 13°0N 86°40W **88 D2**
El Sueco *Mexico* 29°54N 106°24W **86 B3**
El Suweis *Egypt* 29°58N 32°31E **51 C12**
El Tamarâni, W. → *Egypt* 30°7N 34°43E **46 E3**
El Thamad *Egypt* 29°40N 34°28E **46 F3**
El Tigre *Venezuela* 8°44N 64°15W **92 B6**
El Tîh, *Egypt* 29°40N 33°50E **46 F2**
El Tofo *Chile* 29°22S 71°18W **94 B1**
El Tránsito *Chile* 28°52S 70°17W **94 B1**
El Tûr *Egypt* 28°14N 33°36E **44 D2**
El Turbio *Argentina* 51°45S 72°5W **96 G2**
El Uqsur *Egypt* 25°41N 32°38E **51 C12**
El Vergel *Mexico* 26°28N 106°22W **86 B3**
El Vigía *Venezuela* 8°38N 71°39W **92 B4**
El Wabeira *Egypt* 29°34N 33°6E **46 F2**
El Wuz *Sudan* 15°5N 30°7E **51 E12**
Elat *Israel* 29°30N 34°56E **46 F3**
Elâzığ *Turkey* 38°37N 39°14E **44 B3**
Elba *Italy* 42°46N 10°17E **22 C4**
Elba *U.S.A.* 31°25N 86°4W **85 F11**
Elbasan *Albania* 41°9N 20°9E **23 D9**
Elbe → *U.S.A.* 46°45N 122°10W **78 D4**
Elbe → *Europe* 53°50N 9°0E **16 B5**
Elbert, Mt. *U.S.A.* 39°7N 106°27W **76 G10**
Elberton *U.S.A.* 34°7N 82°52W **85 D13**
Elbeuf *France* 49°17N 1°2E **20 B4**
Elbing = Elbląg *Poland* 54°10N 19°25E **17 A10**
Elbistan *Turkey* 38°13N 37°12E **44 B3**
Elbląg *Poland* 54°10N 19°25E **17 A10**
Elbow *Canada* 51°7N 106°35W **71 C7**
Elbrus *Russia* 43°21N 42°30E **19 F7**
Elburz Mts. = Alborz, Reshteh-ye
  Kūhhā-ye *Iran* 36°0N 52°0E **45 C7**
Elche *Spain* 38°15N 0°42W **21 C5**
Elcho I. *Australia* 11°55S 135°45E **62 A2**
Elda *Spain* 38°29N 0°47W **21 C5**
Eldama Ravine *Kenya* 0°3N 35°43E **54 B4**
Elde → *Germany* 53°7N 11°15E **16 B6**
Eldon *Mo., U.S.A.* 38°21N 92°35W **80 F7**
Eldon *Wash., U.S.A.* 47°33N 123°3W **78 C3**
Eldora *U.S.A.* 42°22N 93°5W **80 D7**
Eldorado *Argentina* 26°28S 54°43W **95 B5**
Eldorado *Canada* 44°35N 77°31W **82 B7**
Eldorado *Ill., U.S.A.* 37°49N 88°26W **80 G9**
Eldorado *Mexico* 24°20N 107°22W **86 C3**
Eldorado *Tex., U.S.A.* 30°52N 100°36W **84 F4**
Eldoret *Kenya* 0°30N 35°17E **54 B4**
Eldred *U.S.A.* 41°58N 78°23W **82 E6**
Elea, C. *Cyprus* 35°19N 34°4E **25 D13**
Eleanora, Pk. *Australia* 32°57S 121°9E **61 F3**
Elefantes → *Africa* 24°10S 32°40E **57 C5**
Elektrostal *Russia* 55°41N 38°32E **18 C6**
Elemi Triangle *Africa* 5°0N 35°20E **54 B4**
Elephant Butte Res.
  U.S.A. 33°9N 107°11W **77 K10**
Elephant I. *Antarctica* 61°0S 55°0W **5 C18**
Eleuthera *Bahamas* 25°0N 76°20W **88 B4**
Elgin *Canada* 44°36N 76°13W **83 B8**

Elgin *U.K.* 57°39N 3°19W **11 D5**
Elgin *Ill., U.S.A.* 42°2N 88°17W **80 D9**
Elgin *N. Dak., U.S.A.* 46°24N 101°51W **80 B3**
Elgin *Oreg., U.S.A.* 45°34N 117°55W **76 D5**
Elgin *Tex., U.S.A.* 30°21N 97°22W **84 F6**
Elgon, Mt. *Africa* 1°10N 34°30E **54 B3**
Eliase *Indonesia* 8°21S 130°48E **37 F8**
Elim *Namibia* 17°48S 15°31E **56 B2**
Elim *S. Africa* 34°35S 19°45E **56 E2**
Elista *Russia* 46°16N 44°14E **19 E7**
Elizabeth *Australia* 34°42S 138°41E **63 E2**
Elizabeth *U.S.A.* 40°39N 74°12W **83 F10**
Elizabeth City *U.S.A.* 36°18N 76°14W **85 C16**
Elizabethton *U.S.A.* 36°21N 82°13W **85 C13**
Elizabethtown *Ky.,
  U.S.A.* 37°42N 85°52W **81 G11**
Elizabethtown *N.Y.,
  U.S.A.* 44°13N 73°36W **83 B11**
Elizabethtown *Pa., U.S.A.* 40°9N 76°36W **83 F8**
Elk *Poland* 53°50N 22°21E **17 B12**
Elk → *U.S.A.* 34°46N 87°16W **85 D11**
Elk City *U.S.A.* 35°25N 99°25W **84 D5**
Elk Creek *U.S.A.* 39°36N 122°32W **78 F4**
Elk Grove *U.S.A.* 38°25N 121°22W **78 G5**
Elk Island △ *Canada* 53°35N 112°59W **70 C6**
Elk Lake *Canada* 47°40N 80°25W **72 C3**
Elk Point *Canada* 53°54N 110°55W **71 C6**
Elk River *Idaho, U.S.A.* 46°47N 116°11W **76 C5**
Elk River *Minn., U.S.A.* 45°18N 93°35W **80 C7**
Elkedra → *Australia* 21°8S 136°22E **62 C2**
Elkhart *Ind., U.S.A.* 41°41N 85°58W **81 E11**
Elkhart *Kans., U.S.A.* 37°0N 101°54W **80 G3**
Elkhorn *Canada* 49°59N 101°14W **71 D8**
Elkhorn → *U.S.A.* 41°8N 96°19W **80 E5**
Elkhovo *Bulgaria* 42°10N 26°35E **23 C12**
Elkin *U.S.A.* 36°15N 80°51W **85 C14**
Elkins *U.S.A.* 38°55N 79°51W **81 F14**
Elkland *U.S.A.* 41°59N 77°19W **82 E7**
Elko *Canada* 49°20N 115°10W **70 D5**
Elko *U.S.A.* 40°50N 115°46W **76 F6**
Elkton *U.S.A.* 43°49N 83°11W **82 C1**
Ellas = Greece ■ *Europe* 40°0N 23°0E **23 E9**
Ellef Ringnes I. *Canada* 78°30N 102°2W **69 B11**
Ellen, Mt. *U.S.A.* 44°9N 72°56W **83 B12**
Ellenburg *U.S.A.* 44°54N 73°48W **83 B11**
Ellendale *U.S.A.* 46°0N 98°32W **80 B4**
Ellensburg *U.S.A.* 46°59N 120°34W **76 C3**
Ellenville *U.S.A.* 41°43N 74°24W **83 E10**
Ellerton *Barbados* 13°7N 59°33W **89 g**
Ellery, Mt. *Australia* 37°28S 148°47E **63 F4**
Ellesmere, L. *N.Z.* 43°47S 172°28E **59 G4**
Ellesmere I. *Australia* 31°36S 138°14E **63 E2**
Ellesmere Island = Quttinirpaaq △
  Canada 82°13N 72°13W **69 A17**
Ellesmere Port *U.K.* 53°17N 2°54W **12 D5**
Ellice Is. = Tuvalu ■
  Pac. Oc. 8°0S 178°0E **58 B10**
Ellicottville *U.S.A.* 42°17N 78°40W **82 D6**
Ellington *U.S.A.* 42°13N 79°6W **82 D5**
Elliot *Australia* 17°33S 133°32E **62 B1**
Elliot *S. Africa* 31°22S 27°48E **57 E4**
Elliot Lake *Canada* 46°25N 82°35W **72 C3**
Elliotdale = Xhora
  S. Africa 31°55S 28°38E **57 E4**
Ellis *U.S.A.* 38°56N 99°34W **80 F4**
Elliston *Australia* 33°39S 134°53E **63 E1**
Ellisville *U.S.A.* 31°36N 89°12W **85 F10**
Ellon *U.K.* 57°22N 2°4W **11 D6**
Ellore = Eluru *India* 16°48N 81°8E **41 L12**
Ellsworth *Kans., U.S.A.* 38°44N 98°14W **80 F4**
Ellsworth *Maine, U.S.A.* 44°33N 68°25W **81 C19**
Ellsworth Land *Antarctica* 76°0S 89°0W **5 D16**
Ellsworth Mts. *Antarctica* 78°30S 85°0W **5 D16**
Ellwood City *U.S.A.* 40°52N 80°17W **82 F4**
Elma *Canada* 49°52N 95°55W **71 D9**
Elma *U.S.A.* 47°0N 123°25W **78 D3**
Elmalı *Turkey* 36°44N 29°56E **19 G4**
Elmhurst *U.S.A.* 41°53N 87°56W **80 E10**
Elmira *Canada* 43°36N 80°33W **82 C4**
Elmira *U.S.A.* 42°6N 76°48W **82 D8**
Elmira Heights *U.S.A.* 42°8N 76°50W **82 D8**
Elmore *Australia* 36°30S 144°37E **63 F3**
Elmshorn *Germany* 53°43N 9°40E **16 B5**
Elmvale *Canada* 44°35N 79°52W **82 B5**
Elora *Canada* 43°41N 80°26W **82 C4**
Elounda *Greece* 35°16N 25°42E **25 D7**
Eloy *U.S.A.* 32°45N 111°33W **77 K8**
Elphin *Canada* 44°55N 76°37W **83 B8**
Elrose *Canada* 51°12N 108°0W **71 C7**
Elsdy △ *Australia* 14°55S 133°10E **60 B5**
Elsie *U.S.A.* 45°52N 123°36W **78 E3**
Elsinore = Helsingør
  Denmark 56°2N 12°35E **9 H15**
Eltanin Fracture Zone System
  S. Ocean 54°0S 130°0W **5 B14**
Eltham *N.Z.* 39°26S 174°19E **59 C5**
Eluru *India* 16°48N 81°8E **41 L12**
Elvas *Portugal* 38°50N 7°10W **21 C2**
Elverum *Norway* 60°53N 11°34E **8 F14**
Elvire, Mt. *Australia* 17°51S 128°11E **60 C4**
Elvire → *Australia* 17°19S 129°36E **61 E2**
Elwell, L. = Tiber Res.
  U.S.A. 48°19N 111°6W **76 B8**
Elwood *Ind., U.S.A.* 40°17N 85°50W **81 E11**
Elwood *Nebr., U.S.A.* 40°36N 99°52W **80 E4**
Elx = Elche *Spain* 38°15N 0°42W **21 C5**
Ely *U.K.* 52°24N 0°16E **13 E8**
Ely *Minn., U.S.A.* 47°55N 91°51W **80 B8**
Ely *Nev., U.S.A.* 39°15N 114°54W **76 G6**
Elyria *U.S.A.* 41°22N 82°7W **82 E2**
eMalahleni *S. Africa* 25°51S 29°14E **57 D4**
eMalahleni *S. Africa* 31°28S 27°32E **57 E4**
Emāmrūd *Iran* 36°30N 55°0E **45 B7**
Embarcación *Argentina* 23°10S 64°0W **94 A3**
Embetsu *Japan* 44°44N 141°47E **30 B10**
Embi *Kazakhstan* 48°50N 58°8E **28 E6**
Embi → *Kazakhstan* 46°55N 53°28E **19 E9**
Embonas *Greece* 36°13N 27°51E **25 C9**
Embro *Canada* 43°9N 80°54W **82 C4**

Embrun *France* 44°34N 6°30E **20 D7**
Embu *Kenya* 0°32S 37°38E **54 C4**
Emden *Germany* 53°21N 7°12E **16 B4**
Emerald *Australia* 23°32S 148°10E **62 C4**
Emerald I. *Canada* 76°48N 114°10W **69 B9**
Emerson *Canada* 49°0N 97°10W **71 D9**
Emet *Turkey* 39°20N 29°15E **23 E13**
Emi Koussi *Chad* 19°45N 18°55E **51 E9**
Eminabad *Pakistan* 32°2N 74°8E **42 C6**
Emine, Nos *Bulgaria* 42°40N 27°56E **23 C12**
Emissi, Tarso *Chad* 21°27N 18°36E **51 D9**
Emlenton *U.S.A.* 41°11N 79°43W **82 E5**
Emmaus *S. Africa* 29°2S 25°15E **56 D4**
Emmaus *U.S.A.* 40°32N 75°30W **83 F9**
Emmeloord *Neths.* 52°44N 5°46E **15 B5**
Emmen *Neths.* 52°48N 6°57E **15 B6**
Emmet *Australia* 24°45S 144°30E **62 C3**
Emmetsburg *U.S.A.* 43°7N 94°41W **80 D6**
Emmett *Idaho, U.S.A.* 43°52N 116°30W **76 E5**
Emmett *Mich., U.S.A.* 42°59N 82°46W **82 D2**
Emmonak *U.S.A.* 62°47N 164°31W **74 C7**
Emo *Canada* 48°38N 93°50W **71 D10**
Empalme *Mexico* 27°58N 110°51W **86 B2**
Empangeni *S. Africa* 28°50S 31°52E **57 D5**
Empedrado *Argentina* 28°0S 58°46W **94 B4**
Emperor Seamount Chain
  Pac. Oc. 40°0N 170°0E **64 D9**
Emperor Trough *Pac. Oc.* 43°0N 175°30E **64 C9**
Emporia *Kans., U.S.A.* 38°25N 96°11W **80 F5**
Emporia *Va., U.S.A.* 36°42N 77°32W **81 G15**
Emporium *U.S.A.* 41°31N 78°14W **82 E6**
Empress *Canada* 50°57N 110°0W **71 C7**
Empty Quarter = Rub' al Khālī
  Si. Arabia 19°0N 48°0E **47 D4**
Ems → *Germany* 53°20N 7°12E **16 B4**
Emsdale *Canada* 45°32N 79°19W **82 A5**
Emu *China* 43°40N 128°6E **35 C15**
Emu Park *Australia* 23°13S 150°50E **62 C5**
eMuziwezinto *S. Africa* 30°15S 30°45E **57 E5**
'En 'Avrona *Israel* 29°43N 35°0E **46 F4**
'En Boqeq *Israel* 31°12N 35°21E **45 D4**
'En Gedi *Israel* 31°28N 35°25E **45 D4**
En Nahud *Sudan* 12°45N 28°25E **51 F11**
Ena *Japan* 35°25N 137°25E **31 G8**
Enana *Namibia* 17°30S 16°23E **56 B2**
Enard B. *U.K.* 58°5N 5°20W **11 C3**
Enare = Inarijärvi *Finland* 69°0N 28°0E **8 B23**
Enarotali *Indonesia* 3°55S 136°21E **37 E9**
Encampment *U.S.A.* 41°12N 106°47W **76 F10**
Encantadas, Serra *Brazil* 30°40S 53°0W **95 C5**
Encarnación *Paraguay* 27°15S 55°50W **95 B4**
Encarnación de Díaz
  Mexico 21°31N 102°14W **86 C4**
Encinitas *U.S.A.* 33°3N 117°17W **79 M9**
Encino *U.S.A.* 34°39N 105°28W **77 J11**
Encounter B. *Australia* 35°45S 138°45E **63 F2**
Endako *Canada* 54°6N 125°2W **70 C3**
Endau *Kenya* 1°18S 38°31E **54 C4**
Endau Rompin △
  Malaysia 2°27N 103°45E **39 L4**
Ende *Indonesia* 8°45S 121°40E **37 F6**
Endeavour Str. *Australia* 10°45S 142°0E **62 A3**
Enderbury I. *Kiribati* 3°8S 171°5W **64 H10**
Enderby *Canada* 50°35N 119°10W **70 C5**
Enderby Abyssal Plain
  S. Ocean 60°0S 40°0E **5 C5**
Enderby I. *Australia* 20°35S 116°30E **60 D2**
Enderby Land *Antarctica* 66°0S 53°0E **5 C5**
Enderlin *U.S.A.* 46°38N 97°36W **80 B5**
Enderrocat, C. *Spain* 39°28N 2°43E **24 B9**
Endicott *U.S.A.* 42°6N 76°4W **83 D8**
Endicott Mts. *U.S.A.* 68°0N 152°0W **74 B9**
Endwell *U.S.A.* 42°6N 76°2W **83 D8**
Endyalgout I. *Australia* 11°40S 132°35E **60 B5**
Eneabba *Australia* 29°49S 115°16E **61 E2**
Enewetak Atoll
  Marshall Is. 11°30N 162°15E **64 F8**
Enez *Turkey* 40°45N 26°5E **23 D12**
Enfer, Pte. d' *Martinique* 14°22N 60°54W **88 c**
Enfield *Canada* 44°56N 63°32W **73 D7**
Enfield *Conn., U.S.A.* 41°58N 72°36W **83 E12**
Enfield *N.C., U.S.A.* 36°11N 77°41W **85 C16**
Enfield *N.H., U.S.A.* 43°39N 72°9W **83 C12**
Engadin *Switz.* 46°45N 10°10E **20 C9**
Engaño, C. *Dom. Rep.* 18°30N 68°20W **89 C6**
Engaño, C. *Phil.* 18°35N 122°23E **37 A6**
Engaru *Japan* 44°3N 143°31E **30 B11**
Engcobo = Ngcobo
  S. Africa 31°37S 28°0E **57 E4**
Engels *Russia* 51°28N 46°6E **19 D8**
Engemann L. *Canada* 58°0N 106°55W **71 B7**
Enggano *Indonesia* 5°20S 102°40E **36 F2**
England → *Canada* 54°33N 91°58W **84 D9**
England □ *U.K.* 53°0N 2°0W **13 E5**
Englee *Canada* 50°45N 56°5W **73 B8**
Englehart *Canada* 47°49N 79°52W **72 C4**
Englewood *U.S.A.* 39°38N 104°59W **76 G11**
English → *Canada* 49°12N 91°5W **71 C10**
English Bazar = Ingraj Bazar
  India 24°58N 88°10E **43 G13**
English Channel *Europe* 50°0N 2°0W **13 G6**
English Company's Is., The
  Australia 11°50S 136°32E **62 A2**
English River *Canada* 49°14N 91°0W **72 C1**
Enid *U.S.A.* 36°24N 97°53W **84 C6**
Enkhuizen *Neths.* 52°42N 5°17E **15 B5**
Enna *Italy* 37°34N 14°16E **22 F6**
Ennadai L. *Canada* 60°58N 101°20W **71 A8**
Ennedi *Chad* 17°15N 22°0E **51 E10**
Engonia *Australia* 29°21S 145°50E **63 D4**
Ennis *Ireland* 52°51N 8°59W **10 D3**
Ennis *Mont., U.S.A.* 45°21N 111°44W **76 D8**
Ennis *Tex., U.S.A.* 32°20N 96°38W **84 E6**
Enniscorthy *Ireland* 52°30N 6°34W **10 D5**
Enniskillen *U.K.* 54°21N 7°39W **10 B4**
Ennistimon *Ireland* 52°57N 9°17W **10 D2**
Enns → *Austria* 48°14N 14°32E **16 D8**
Eno *Finland* 62°47N 30°10E **8 E24**
Enontekiö *Finland* 68°23N 23°37E **8 B20**

Enosburg Falls U.S.A. 44°55N 72°48W 83 B12
Enriquillo, L. Dom. Rep. 18°20N 72°5W 89 C5
Enschede Neths. 52°13N 6°53E 15 B6
Ensenada Argentina 34°55S 57°55W 94 C4
Ensenada Mexico 31°52N 116°37W 86 A1
Ensenada de los Muertos Mexico 23°59N 109°51W 86 C2
Ensiola, Pta. de n' Spain 39°7N 2°55E 24 B9
Entebbe Uganda 0°4N 32°28E 54 B3
Enterprise Canada 60°47N 115°45W 70 A5
Enterprise Ala., U.S.A. 31°19N 85°51W 85 F12
Enterprise Oreg., U.S.A. 45°25N 117°17W 76 D5
Entre Ríos Bolivia 21°30S 64°25W 94 A3
Entre Ríos □ Argentina 30°30S 58°30W 94 C4
Entroncamento Portugal 39°28N 8°28W 21 C1
Enugu Nigeria 6°30N 7°30E 50 G7
Enumclaw U.S.A. 47°12N 121°59W 78 C5
Eochail = Youghal Ireland 51°56N 7°52W 10 E4
Eólie, Ís. Italy 38°30N 14°57E 22 E6
Epe Neths. 52°21N 5°59E 15 B5
Épernay France 49°3N 3°56E 20 B5
Ephesus Turkey 37°55N 27°22E 23 F12
Ephraim U.S.A. 39°22N 111°35W 76 G8
Ephrata Pa., U.S.A. 40°11N 76°11W 83 F8
Ephrata Wash., U.S.A. 47°19N 119°33W 76 C4
Épinal France 48°10N 6°27E 20 B7
Episkopi Cyprus 34°40N 32°54E 25 E11
Episkopi Greece 35°20N 24°20E 25 D6
Episkopi Bay Cyprus 34°35N 32°50E 25 E11
Epsom U.K. 51°19N 0°16W 13 F7
Epukiro Namibia 21°40S 19°9E 56 C2
Equatoria = El Istiwa'iya Sudan 5°0N 28°0E 51 G11
Equatorial Guinea ■ Africa 2°0N 8°0E 52 D1
Er Hai China 25°48N 100°11E 41 G22
Er Rachidia Morocco 31°58N 4°20W 50 B5
Er Rahad Sudan 12°45N 30°32E 51 F12
Er Rif Morocco 35°1N 4°1W 50 A5
Erāwadī Myit = Irrawaddy → Burma 15°50N 95°6E 41 M19
Erāwadī Myitwanya = Irrawaddy, Mouths of the Burma 15°30N 95°0E 41 M19
Erawan △ Thailand 14°25N 98°58E 38 E2
Erbil = Arbīl Iraq 36°15N 44°5E 44 B5
Erçek Turkey 38°39N 43°36E 44 B4
Erciyaş Dağı Turkey 38°30N 35°30E 44 B2
Érd Hungary 47°22N 18°56E 17 E10
Erdao Jiang → China 42°37N 128°0E 35 C14
Erdek Turkey 40°23N 27°47E 23 D12
Erdene = Ulaan-Uul Mongolia 44°13N 111°10E 34 B6
Erdenet Mongolia 49°2N 104°5E 32 B5
Erdenetsogt Mongolia 42°55N 106°5E 34 C4
Erebus, Mt. Antarctica 77°35S 167°0E 5 D11
Erechim Brazil 27°35S 52°15W 95 B5
Ereğli Konya, Turkey 37°31N 34°4E 44 B2
Ereğli Zonguldak, Turkey 41°15N 31°24E 19 F5
Erenhot China 43°48N 112°2E 34 C7
Eresma → Spain 41°26N 4°45W 21 B3
Erfenisdam S. Africa 28°30S 26°50E 56 D4
Erfurt Germany 50°58N 11°2E 16 C6
Ergani Turkey 38°17N 39°49E 44 B3
Ergel Mongolia 43°8N 109°5E 34 C5
Ergeni Vozvyshennost Russia 47°0N 44°0E 19 E7
Ērgli Latvia 56°54N 25°38E 9 H21
Eriboll, L. U.K. 58°30N 4°42W 11 C4
Érice Italy 38°2N 12°35E 22 E5
Erie U.S.A. 42°8N 80°5W 82 D4
Erie, L. N. Amer. 42°15N 81°0W 82 D4
Erie Canal U.S.A. 43°5N 78°43W 82 C7
Erieau Canada 42°16N 81°57W 82 D3
Erigavo = Ceerigaabo Somali Rep. 10°35N 47°20E 47 E4
Erikoussa Greece 39°53N 19°34E 25 A3
Eriksdale Canada 50°52N 98°7W 71 C9
Erimanthos Greece 37°57N 21°50E 23 F9
Erimo-misaki Japan 41°50N 143°15E 30 D11
Erin Canada 43°45N 80°7W 82 C4
Erin Pt. Trin. & Tob. 10°3N 61°39W 93 K15
Erinpura India 25°9N 73°3E 42 G5
Eriskay U.K. 57°4N 7°18W 11 D1
Eritrea ■ Africa 14°0N 38°30E 47 D2
Erlangen Germany 49°36N 11°0E 16 D6
Erldunda Australia 25°14S 133°12E 62 D1
Ermelo Neths. 52°18N 5°35E 15 B5
Ermelo S. Africa 26°31S 29°59E 57 D4
Ermenek Turkey 36°38N 33°0E 44 B2
Ermones Greece 39°37N 19°46E 25 A3
Ermoupoli Greece 37°28N 24°57E 23 F11
Ernakulam India 9°59N 76°22E 40 Q10
Erne → Ireland 54°30N 8°16W 10 B3
Erne, Lower L. U.K. 54°28N 7°47W 10 B4
Erne, Upper L. U.K. 54°14N 7°32W 10 B4
Ernest Giles Ra. Australia 27°0S 123°45E 61 E3
Erode India 11°24N 77°45E 40 P10
Eromanga Australia 26°40S 143°11E 63 D3
Erongo Namibia 21°39S 15°58E 56 C2
Erramala Hills India 15°30N 78°15E 40 M11
Errentería Spain 43°19N 1°54W 21 A5
Erri-Nundra △ Australia 37°28S 148°5E 63 F4
Errigal Ireland 55°2N 8°6W 10 A3
Erris Hd. Ireland 54°19N 10°0W 10 B1
Erskine U.S.A. 47°40N 96°0W 80 B6
Ertis = Irtysh → Russia 61°4N 68°52E 28 C7
Erwin U.S.A. 36°9N 82°25W 85 C13
Erzgebirge Germany 50°27N 12°55E 16 C7
Erzin Russia 50°15N 95°10E 29 D10
Erzincan Turkey 39°46N 39°30E 44 B3
Erzurum Turkey 39°57N 41°15E 44 B4
Es Caló Spain 38°40N 1°30E 24 C8
Es Canar Spain 39°2N 1°36E 24 B8
Es Mercadal Spain 39°59N 4°5E 24 B11
Es Migjorn Gran Spain 39°57N 4°3E 24 B11
Es Sahrâ' Esh Sharqîya Egypt 27°30N 32°30E 51 C12
Es Sînâ' Egypt 29°0N 34°0E 46 F3
Es Vedrà Spain 38°52N 1°12E 24 C7
Esambo Dem. Rep. of the Congo 3°48S 23°30E 54 C1
Esan-Misaki Japan 41°40N 141°10E 30 D10
Esashi Hokkaidō, Japan 44°56N 142°35E 30 B11
Esashi Hokkaidō, Japan 41°52N 140°7E 30 D10
Esbjerg Denmark 55°29N 8°29E 9 J13
Esbo = Espoo Finland 60°12N 24°40E 9 F21
Escalante U.S.A. 37°47N 111°36W 77 H8
Escalante → U.S.A. 37°24N 110°57W 77 H8
Escalón Mexico 26°45N 104°20W 86 B4
Escambia → U.S.A. 30°32N 87°11W 85 F11
Escanaba U.S.A. 45°45N 87°4W 80 C10
Esch-sur-Alzette Lux. 49°32N 6°0E 15 E6
Escondido U.S.A. 33°7N 117°5W 79 M9
Escuinapa de Hidalgo Mexico 22°50N 105°50W 86 C3
Escuintla Guatemala 14°20N 90°48W 88 D1
Esenguly Turkmenistan 37°37N 53°59E 28 F6
Eşfahān Iran 32°39N 51°43E 45 C6
Eşfahān □ Iran 32°50N 51°50E 45 C6
Esfarāyen Iran 37°4N 57°30E 45 B8
Esfideh Iran 33°39N 59°46E 45 C8
Esh Sham = Dimashq Syria 33°30N 36°18E 46 B5
Esha Ness U.K. 60°29N 1°38W 11 A7
Esher U.K. 51°21N 0°20W 13 F7
Eshkol △ Israel 31°20N 34°30E 46 D3
Eshowe S. Africa 28°50S 31°30E 57 D5
Esigodini Zimbabwe 20°18S 28°56E 57 C4
Esil = Ishim → Russia 57°45N 71°10E 28 D8
Esira Madag. 24°20S 46°42E 57 C8
Esk → Dumf. & Gall., U.K. 54°58N 3°2W 11 G5
Esk → N. Yorks., U.K. 54°30N 0°37W 12 C7
Eskān Iran 26°48N 63°9E 45 E9
Esker Siding Canada 53°53N 66°25W 73 B6
Eskifjörður Iceland 65°3N 13°55W 8 D7
Eskilstuna Sweden 59°22N 16°32E 9 G17
Eskimo Point = Arviat Canada 61°6N 93°59W 71 A10
Eskişehir Turkey 39°50N 30°30E 19 G5
Esla → Spain 41°29N 6°3W 21 B2
Eslāmābād-e Gharb Iran 34°10N 46°30E 44 C5
Eslāmshahr Iran 35°40N 51°10E 45 C6
Eşme Turkey 38°23N 28°58E 23 E13
Esmeraldas Ecuador 1°0N 79°40W 92 C3
Esna = Isna Egypt 25°17N 32°30E 51 C12
Esnagi L. Canada 48°36N 84°33W 72 C3
España = Spain ■ Europe 39°0N 4°0W 21 B4
Española Canada 46°15N 81°46W 72 C3
Espanola U.S.A. 35°59N 106°5W 77 J10
Esparza Costa Rica 9°59N 84°40W 88 E3
Esperance Australia 33°45S 121°55E 61 F3
Esperance B. Australia 33°48S 121°55E 61 F3
Esperance Harbour St. Lucia 14°4N 60°55W 89 f
Esperanza Antarctica 65°0S 55°0W 5 C18
Esperanza Argentina 31°29S 61°3W 94 C3
Esperanza Puerto Rico 18°6N 65°28W 89 d
Espichel, C. Portugal 38°22N 9°16W 21 C1
Espigão, Serra do Brazil 26°35S 50°30W 95 B5
Espinazo, Sierra del = Espinhaço, Serra do Brazil 17°30S 43°30W 93 G10
Espinhaço, Serra do Brazil 17°30S 43°30W 93 G10
Espinilho, Serra do Brazil 28°30S 55°0W 95 B5
Espírito Santo □ Brazil 20°0S 40°45W 93 H10
Espírito Santo do Pinhal Brazil 22°10S 46°46W 95 A6
Espíritu Santo Vanuatu 15°15S 166°50E 58 C9
Espíritu Santo, B. del Mexico 19°20N 87°35W 87 D7
Espíritu Santo, I. Mexico 24°30N 110°22W 86 C2
Espita Mexico 21°1N 88°19W 87 C7
Espoo Finland 60°12N 24°40E 9 F21
Espungabera Mozam. 20°29S 32°45E 57 C5
Esquel Argentina 42°55S 71°20W 96 E2
Esquimalt Canada 48°26N 123°25W 78 B3
Esquina Argentina 30°0S 59°30W 94 C4
Essaouira Morocco 31°32N 9°42W 50 B4
Essebie Dem. Rep. of the Congo 2°58N 30°40E 54 B3
Essen Belgium 51°28N 4°28E 15 C4
Essen Germany 51°28N 7°2E 16 C4
Essendon, Mt. Australia 25°0S 120°29E 61 E3
Essequibo → Guyana 6°50N 58°30W 92 B7
Essex Canada 42°10N 82°49W 82 D2
Essex Calif., U.S.A. 34°44N 115°15W 79 L11
Essex N.Y., U.S.A. 44°19N 73°21W 83 B11
Essex □ U.K. 51°54N 0°27E 13 F8
Essex Junction U.S.A. 44°29N 73°7W 83 B11
Esslingen Germany 48°44N 9°18E 16 D5
Estación Camacho Mexico 24°25N 102°18W 86 C4
Estación Simón Mexico 24°42N 102°35W 86 C4
Estados, I. de Los Argentina 54°40S 64°30W 96 G4
Eşţahbānāt Iran 29°8N 54°4E 45 D7
Estância Brazil 11°16S 37°26W 93 F11
Estancia U.S.A. 34°46N 106°4W 77 J10
Estārm Iran 28°21N 58°21E 45 D8
Estcourt S. Africa 29°0S 29°53E 57 D4
Este △ Dom. Rep. 18°14N 68°42W 89 C6
Estelí Nic. 13°9N 86°22W 88 D2
Estellencs Spain 39°39N 2°29E 24 B9
Esterhazy Canada 50°37N 102°5W 71 C8
Estevan Canada 49°10N 102°59W 71 D8
Estevan Group Canada 53°3N 129°38W 70 C3
Estherville U.S.A. 43°24N 94°50W 80 D6
Eston Canada 51°8N 108°40W 71 C7
Estonia ■ Europe 58°30N 25°30E 9 G21
Estreito Brazil 6°32S 47°25W 93 E9
Estrela, Serra da Portugal 40°10N 7°45W 21 B2
Estremoz Portugal 38°51N 7°39W 21 C2
Estrondo, Serra do Brazil 7°20S 48°0W 93 E9
Esztergom Hungary 47°47N 18°44E 17 E10
Et Tîdra Mauritania 19°45N 16°20W 50 E2
Etah India 27°35N 78°40E 43 F8
Étampes France 48°26N 2°10E 20 B5
Etanga Namibia 17°55S 13°0E 56 B1
Etawah India 26°48N 79°6E 43 F8
Etawney L. Canada 57°50N 96°50W 71 B9
Etchojoa Mexico 26°55N 109°38W 86 B3
eThekwini = Durban S. Africa 29°49S 31°1E 57 D5
Ethel U.S.A. 46°32N 122°46W 78 D4
Ethelbert Canada 51°32N 100°25W 71 C8
Ethiopia ■ Africa 8°0N 40°0E 47 F3
Ethiopian Highlands Ethiopia 10°0N 37°0E 47 F2
Etive, L. U.K. 56°29N 5°10W 11 E3
Etna Italy 37°50N 14°55E 22 F6
Etoile Dem. Rep. of the Congo 11°33S 27°30E 55 E2
Etolin Strait U.S.A. 60°20N 165°15W 74 C6
Etosha △ Namibia 19°0S 16°0E 56 B2
Etosha Pan Namibia 18°40S 16°30E 56 B2
Etowah U.S.A. 35°20N 84°32W 85 D12
Etrek Turkmenistan 37°36N 54°46E 45 B7
Ettelbruck Lux. 49°51N 6°5E 15 E6
Ettrick Water → U.K. 55°31N 2°55W 11 F6
Etuku Dem. Rep. of the Congo 3°42S 25°45E 54 C2
Etzná-Tixmucuy = Edzná Mexico 19°39N 90°19W 87 D6
Eua Tonga 21°22S 174°56W 59 c
Euboea = Evia Greece 38°30N 24°0E 23 E11
Eucla Australia 31°41S 128°52E 61 F4
Euclid U.S.A. 41°34N 81°32W 82 E3
Eucumbene, L. Australia 36°2S 148°40E 63 F4
Eudora U.S.A. 33°7N 91°16W 84 E9
Eufaula Ala., U.S.A. 31°54N 85°9W 85 F12
Eufaula Okla., U.S.A. 35°17N 95°35W 84 D7
Eufaula L. U.S.A. 35°18N 95°21W 84 D7
Eugene U.S.A. 44°5N 123°4W 76 D2
Eugowra Australia 33°22S 148°24E 63 E4
Eulo Australia 28°10S 145°3E 63 D4
Eungella △ Australia 20°57S 148°40E 62 b
Eunice La., U.S.A. 30°30N 92°25W 84 F8
Eunice N. Mex., U.S.A. 32°26N 103°10W 77 K12
Eupen Belgium 50°37N 6°3E 15 D6
Euphrates = Furāt, Nahr al → Asia 31°0N 47°25E 44 D5
Eureka Canada 80°0N 85°56W 69 B14
Eureka Calif., U.S.A. 40°47N 124°9W 76 F1
Eureka Kans., U.S.A. 37°49N 96°17W 80 G5
Eureka Mont., U.S.A. 48°53N 115°3W 76 B6
Eureka Nev., U.S.A. 39°31N 115°58W 76 G6
Eureka S. Dak., U.S.A. 45°46N 99°38W 80 C4
Eureka, Mt. Australia 26°35S 121°35E 61 E3
Eureka Sd. Canada 79°0N 85°0W 69 B15
Euroa Australia 36°44S 145°35E 63 F4
Europa, Île Ind. Oc. 22°20S 40°22E 53 J8
Europa, Picos de Spain 43°10N 4°49W 21 A3
Europa, Pt. Gib. 36°3N 5°21W 21 D3
Europe 50°0N 20°0E 6 E10
Europoort Neths. 51°57N 4°10E 15 C4
Eustis U.S.A. 28°51N 81°41W 85 G14
Eutsuk L. Canada 53°20N 126°45W 70 C3
Evale Angola 16°33S 15°44E 56 B2
Evans U.S.A. 40°23N 104°41W 76 F11
Evans, L. Canada 50°50N 77°0W 72 B4
Evans City U.S.A. 40°46N 80°4W 82 F4
Evans Head Australia 29°7S 153°27E 63 D5
Evansburg Canada 53°36N 114°59W 70 C5
Evanston Ill., U.S.A. 42°3N 87°40W 80 D10
Evanston Wyo., U.S.A. 41°16N 110°58W 76 F8
Evansville U.S.A. 37°58N 87°35W 80 G10
Evaz Iran 27°46N 53°59E 45 E7
Eveleth U.S.A. 47°28N 92°32W 80 B7
Evensk Russia 62°12N 159°30E 29 C16
Everard, L. Australia 31°30S 135°0E 63 E2
Everard Ranges Australia 27°5S 132°28E 61 E5
Everest, Mt. Nepal 28°5N 86°58E 43 E12
Everett Pa., U.S.A. 40°1N 78°23W 82 F6
Everett Wash., U.S.A. 47°59N 122°12W 78 C4
Everglades, The U.S.A. 25°50N 81°0W 85 J14
Everglades △ U.S.A. 25°30N 81°0W 85 J14
Everglades City U.S.A. 25°52N 81°23W 85 J14
Evergreen Ala., U.S.A. 31°26N 86°57W 85 F11
Evergreen Mont., U.S.A. 48°14N 114°17W 76 B6
Evesham U.K. 52°6N 1°56W 13 E6
Evia Greece 38°30N 24°0E 23 E11
Evje Norway 58°36N 7°51E 9 G12
Évora Portugal 38°33N 7°57W 21 C2
Evowghlī Iran 38°43N 45°13E 44 B5
Évreux France 49°3N 1°8E 20 B4
Evros → Greece 41°40N 26°34E 23 D12
Évry France 48°38N 2°27E 20 B5
Évvoia = Evia Greece 38°30N 24°0E 23 E11
Ewe, L. U.K. 57°49N 5°38W 11 D3
Ewing U.S.A. 42°16N 98°21W 80 D4
Ewo Congo 0°48S 14°45E 52 E2
Exaltación Bolivia 13°10S 65°20W 92 F5
Excelsior Springs U.S.A. 39°20N 94°13W 80 F6
Exe → U.K. 50°41N 3°29W 13 G4
Exeter Canada 43°21N 81°29W 82 C3
Exeter U.K. 50°43N 3°31W 13 G4
Exeter Calif., U.S.A. 36°18N 119°9W 78 J7
Exeter N.H., U.S.A. 42°59N 70°57W 83 D14
Exmoor U.K. 51°12N 3°45W 13 F4
Exmoor △ U.K. 51°8N 3°42W 13 F4
Exmouth Australia 21°54S 114°10E 60 D1
Exmouth U.K. 50°37N 3°25W 13 G4
Exmouth G. Australia 22°15S 114°15E 60 D1
Exmouth Plateau Ind. Oc. 19°0S 114°0E 64 J3
Expedition △ Australia 25°41S 149°7E 63 D4
Expedition Ra. Australia 24°30S 149°12E 62 C4
Extremadura □ Spain 39°30N 6°5W 21 C2
Exuma Sound Bahamas 24°30N 76°20W 88 B4
Eyasi, L. Tanzania 3°30S 35°0E 54 C4
Eye Pen. U.K. 58°13N 6°10W 11 C2
Eyemouth U.K. 55°52N 2°5W 11 F6
Eyjafjörður Iceland 66°15N 18°30W 8 C4
Eyl Somali Rep. 8°0N 49°50E 47 F4
Eyre (North), L. Australia 28°30S 137°20E 63 D2
Eyre (South), L. Australia 29°18S 137°25E 63 D2
Eyre, L. Australia 29°30S 137°26E 58 D6
Eyre Mts. N.Z. 45°25S 168°25E 59 F2
Eyre Pen. Australia 33°30S 136°17E 63 E2
Eysturoy Færoe Is. 62°13N 6°54W 8 E9
Eyvān = Jūy Zar Iran 33°50N 46°18E 44 C5
Eyvānkī Iran 35°24N 51°56E 45 C6
Ezine Turkey 39°48N 26°20E 23 E12
Ezouza → Cyprus 34°44N 32°27E 25 E11

F

F.Y.R.O.M. = Macedonia ■ Europe 41°53N 21°40E 23 D9
Faaa Tahiti 17°34S 149°35W 59 d
Faaone Tahiti 17°40S 149°21W 59 d
Fabala Guinea 9°44N 9°5W 50 G4
Fabens U.S.A. 31°30N 106°10W 84 F1
Fabius U.S.A. 42°50N 75°59W 83 D9
Fabriano Italy 43°20N 12°54E 22 C5
Fachi Niger 18°6N 11°34E 51 E8
Fada Chad 17°13N 21°34E 51 E10
Fada-n-Gourma Burkina Faso 12°10N 0°30E 50 F6
Faddeyevskiy, Ostrov Russia 76°0N 144°0E 29 B15
Fadghāmī Syria 35°53N 40°52E 44 C4
Faenza Italy 44°17N 11°53E 22 B4
Færoe Is. = Føroyar ⧄ Atl. Oc. 62°0N 7°0W 8 F9
Făgăras Romania 45°48N 24°58E 17 F13
Fagersta Sweden 60°1N 15°46E 9 F16
Fagnano, L. Argentina 54°30S 68°0W 96 G3
Fahliān Iran 30°11N 51°28E 45 D6
Fahraj Kermān, Iran 29°0N 59°0E 45 D8
Fahraj Yazd, Iran 31°46N 54°36E 45 D7
Faial Azores 38°34N 28°42W 50 a
Faial Madeira 32°47N 16°53W 24 D3
Faichan Kangri India 35°48N 76°34E 43 B7
Fair Haven N.Y., U.S.A. 43°18N 76°42W 83 C8
Fair Haven Vt., U.S.A. 43°36N 73°16W 81 D17
Fair Hd. U.K. 55°14N 6°9W 10 A5
Fair Isle U.K. 59°32N 1°38W 14 B6
Fair Oaks U.S.A. 38°39N 121°16W 78 G5
Fairbanks U.S.A. 64°51N 147°43W 68 E2
Fairbury U.S.A. 40°8N 97°11W 80 E5
Fairfax U.S.A. 44°40N 73°1W 83 B11
Fairfield Ala., U.S.A. 33°29N 86°55W 85 E11
Fairfield Calif., U.S.A. 38°15N 122°3W 78 G4
Fairfield Conn., U.S.A. 41°9N 73°16W 83 E11
Fairfield Idaho, U.S.A. 43°21N 114°44W 76 E6
Fairfield Ill., U.S.A. 38°23N 88°22W 80 F9
Fairfield Iowa, U.S.A. 40°56N 91°57W 80 E8
Fairfield Tex., U.S.A. 31°44N 96°10W 84 F6
Fairford Canada 51°37N 98°38W 71 C9
Fairhope U.S.A. 30°31N 87°54W 85 F11
Fairlie N.Z. 44°5S 170°49E 59 F3
Fairmead U.S.A. 37°5N 120°10W 78 H6
Fairmont Minn., U.S.A. 43°39N 94°28W 80 D6
Fairmont W. Va., U.S.A. 39°29N 80°9W 81 F13
Fairmount Calif., U.S.A. 34°45N 118°26W 79 L8
Fairmount N.Y., U.S.A. 43°5N 76°12W 83 C8
Fairplay U.S.A. 39°15N 106°2W 76 G10
Fairport U.S.A. 43°6N 77°27W 82 C7
Fairport Harbor U.S.A. 41°45N 81°17W 82 E3
Fairview Canada 56°5N 118°25W 70 B5
Fairview Mont., U.S.A. 47°51N 104°3W 76 C11
Fairview Okla., U.S.A. 36°16N 98°29W 84 C5
Fairweather, Mt. U.S.A. 58°55N 137°32W 70 B1
Faisalabad Pakistan 31°30N 73°5E 42 D5
Faith U.S.A. 45°2N 102°2W 80 C2
Faizabad India 26°45N 82°10E 43 F10
Fajardo Puerto Rico 18°20N 65°39W 89 d
Fajr, W. → Si. Arabia 29°10N 38°10E 44 D3
Fakenham U.K. 52°51N 0°51E 12 E8
Fakfak Indonesia 2°55S 132°18E 37 E8
Faku China 42°32N 123°21E 35 C12
Falaise France 48°54N 0°12W 20 B3
Falaise, Mui Vietnam 19°6N 105°45E 38 C5
Falam Burma 23°0N 93°45E 41 H18
Falcó, C. des Spain 38°50N 1°23E 24 C7
Falcón, Presa Mexico 26°35N 99°10W 87 B5
Falcon Lake Canada 49°42N 95°15W 71 D9
Falcon Res. U.S.A. 26°34N 99°10W 84 H5
Falconara Marittima Italy 43°37N 13°24E 22 C5
Falcone, C. del Italy 40°58N 8°12E 22 D3
Falconer U.S.A. 42°7N 79°12W 82 D5
Faleafa Samoa 13°54S 171°31W 59 b
Falelatai Samoa 13°55S 171°59W 59 b
Falelima Samoa 13°32S 172°41W 59 b
Faleshty = Fălești Moldova 47°32N 27°44E 17 E14
Fălești Moldova 47°32N 27°44E 17 E14
Falfurrias U.S.A. 27°14N 98°9W 84 H5
Falher Canada 55°44N 117°15W 70 B5
Faliraki Greece 36°22N 28°12E 25 C10
Falkenberg Sweden 56°54N 12°30E 9 H15
Falkirk U.K. 56°0N 3°47W 11 F5
Falkirk □ U.K. 55°58N 3°49W 11 F5
Falkland U.K. 56°16N 3°12W 11 E5
Falkland Is. ⧄ Atl. Oc. 51°30S 59°0W 96 G5
Falkland Sd. Falk. Is. 52°0S 60°0W 96 G5
Fall River U.S.A. 41°43N 71°10W 83 E13
Fallbrook U.S.A. 33°23N 117°15W 79 M9
Fallon U.S.A. 39°28N 118°47W 76 G4
Falls City U.S.A. 40°3N 95°36W 80 E6
Falls Creek U.S.A. 41°9N 78°48W 82 E6
Falmouth Jamaica 18°30N 77°40W 88 a
Falmouth U.K. 50°9N 5°5W 13 G2
Falmouth U.S.A. 41°33N 70°37W 83 E14
Falsa, Pta. Mexico 27°51N 115°3W 86 B1
False B. S. Africa 34°15S 18°40E 56 E2
Falso, C. Honduras 15°12N 83°21W 88 C3
Falster Denmark 54°45N 11°55E 9 J14
Falsterbo Sweden 55°23N 12°50E 9 J15
Fălticeni Romania 47°21N 26°20E 17 E14
Falun Sweden 60°37N 15°37E 8 F16
Famagusta Cyprus 35°8N 33°55E 25 D12
Famagusta Bay Cyprus 35°15N 34°0E 25 D13
Famatina, Sierra de Argentina 27°30S 68°0W 94 B2
Family L. Canada 51°54N 95°27W 71 C9
Famoso U.S.A. 35°37N 119°12W 79 K7
Fan Xian China 35°55N 115°38E 34 G8
Fanad Hd. Ireland 55°17N 7°38W 10 A4
Fandriana Madag. 20°14S 47°21E 57 C8
Fang Thailand 19°55N 99°13E 38 C2
Fangcheng China 33°18N 112°59E 34 H7
Fangshan China 38°3N 111°25E 34 E6
Fangzi China 36°33N 119°10E 35 F10
Fanjakana Madag. 21°10S 46°53E 57 C8
Fanjiatun China 43°40N 125°15E 35 C13
Fanling China 22°30N 114°8E 33 F11
Fannich, L. U.K. 57°38N 4°59W 11 D4
Fannūj Iran 26°35N 59°38E 45 E8
Fanø Denmark 55°25N 8°25E 9 J13
Fano Italy 43°50N 13°1E 22 C5
Fanshi China 39°12N 113°20E 34 E7
Fao = Al Fāw Iraq 30°0N 48°30E 45 D6
Faqirwali Pakistan 29°27N 73°0E 42 E5
Far East = Dalnevostochnyy □ Russia 67°0N 140°0E 29 C14
Far East Asia 40°0N 130°0E 26 E14
Faradje Dem. Rep. of the Congo 3°50N 29°45E 54 B2
Farafangana Madag. 22°49S 47°50E 57 C8
Farāh Afghan. 32°20N 62°7E 40 C3
Farāh □ Afghan. 32°25N 62°10E 40 C3
Farahalana Madag. 14°26S 50°10E 57 A9
Faranah Guinea 10°3N 10°45W 50 F3
Farasān, Jazā'ir Si. Arabia 16°45N 41°55E 47 D3
Farasan Is. = Farasān, Jazā'ir Si. Arabia 16°45N 41°55E 47 D3
Faratsiho Madag. 19°24S 46°57E 57 B8
Fareham U.K. 50°51N 1°11W 13 G6
Farewell, C. N.Z. 40°29S 172°43E 59 D4
Farewell C. = Nunap Isua Greenland 59°48N 43°55W 66 D15
Farghona Uzbekistan 40°23N 71°19E 28 E8
Fargo U.S.A. 46°53N 96°48W 80 B5
Fār'iah, W. al → West Bank 32°12N 35°27E 46 C4
Faribault U.S.A. 44°18N 93°16W 80 C7
Faridabad India 28°26N 77°19E 42 E6
Faridkot India 30°44N 74°45E 42 D6
Faridpur Bangla. 23°15N 89°55E 43 H13
Faridpur India 28°13N 79°33E 43 E8
Farīmān Iran 35°40N 59°49E 45 C8
Fariones, Pta. Canary Is. 29°13N 13°28W 24 E6
Farleigh Australia 21°4S 149°8E 62 b
Farmerville U.S.A. 32°47N 92°24W 84 E8
Farmingdale U.S.A. 40°12N 74°10W 83 F10
Farmington Canada 55°54N 120°30W 70 B4
Farmington Calif., U.S.A. 37°55N 120°59W 78 H6
Farmington Maine, U.S.A. 44°40N 70°9W 81 C18
Farmington Mo., U.S.A. 37°47N 90°25W 80 G8
Farmington N.H., U.S.A. 43°24N 71°4W 83 C13
Farmington N. Mex., U.S.A. 36°44N 108°12W 77 H9
Farmington Utah, U.S.A. 40°59N 111°53W 76 F8
Farmington → U.S.A. 41°51N 72°38W 83 E12
Farmville U.S.A. 37°18N 78°24W 81 G14
Farne Is. U.K. 55°38N 1°37W 12 B6
Farnham Canada 45°17N 72°59W 83 A12
Farnham, Mt. Canada 50°29N 116°30W 70 C5
Faro Brazil 2°10S 56°39W 93 D7
Faro Canada 62°11N 133°22W 68 E5
Faro Portugal 37°2N 7°55W 21 D2
Fårö Sweden 57°55N 19°5E 9 H18
Farquhar, C. Australia 23°50S 113°36E 61 D1
Farrars Cr. → Australia 25°35S 140°43E 62 D3
Farrāshband Iran 28°57N 52°5E 45 D7
Farrell U.S.A. 41°13N 80°30W 82 E4
Farrokhī Iran 33°50N 59°31E 45 C8
Farruch, C. = Ferrutx, C. de Spain 39°47N 3°21E 24 B10
Farrukhabad India 27°24N 79°34E 43 F8
Fārs □ Iran 29°30N 55°0E 45 D7
Farsala Greece 39°17N 22°23E 23 E10
Fārsī Iran 27°58N 50°11E 45 E6
Farson U.S.A. 42°7N 109°26W 76 E9
Farsund Norway 58°5N 6°55E 9 G12
Fartak, Râs Si. Arabia 28°5N 34°34E 44 D2
Fartak, Ra's Yemen 15°38N 52°15E 47 D5
Fartura, Serra da Brazil 26°21S 52°52W 95 B5
Fārūj Iran 37°14N 58°14E 45 B8
Farvel, Kap = Nunap Isua Greenland 59°48N 43°55W 66 D15
Farwell U.S.A. 34°23N 103°2W 84 D3
Fāryāb □ Afghan. 36°0N 65°0E 40 B4
Fasā Iran 29°0N 53°39E 45 D7
Fasano Italy 40°50N 17°22E 22 D7
Fastiv Ukraine 50°7N 29°57E 17 C15
Fastnet Rock Ireland 51°22N 9°37W 10 E2
Fastov = Fastiv Ukraine 50°7N 29°57E 17 C15
Fatagar, Tanjung Indonesia 2°46S 131°57E 37 E8
Fatehabad Haryana, India 29°31N 75°27E 42 E6
Fatehabad Ut. P., India 27°1N 78°19E 42 F8
Fatehgarh India 27°25N 79°35E 43 F8
Fatehpur Bihar, India 24°38N 85°14E 43 G11
Fatehpur Raj., India 28°0N 74°40E 42 F6
Fatehpur Ut. P., India 25°56N 81°13E 43 G9
Fatehpur Ut. P., India 27°10N 81°13E 43 F9
Fatehpur Sikri India 27°6N 77°40E 42 F6
Fathom Five ⌂ Canada 45°17N 81°40W 82 A3
Fatima Canada 47°24N 61°53W 73 C7
Faulkton U.S.A. 45°2N 99°8W 80 C4
Faure I. Australia 25°52S 113°50E 61 E1
Fauresmith S. Africa 29°44S 25°17E 56 D4

Fauske Norway 67°17N 15°25E 8 C16
Favara Italy 37°19N 13°39E 22 F5
Faváritx, C. de Spain 40°0N 4°15E 24 B11
Favignana Italy 37°56N 12°20E 22 F5
Fawcett, Pt. Australia 11°46S 130°2E 60 B5
Fawn → Canada 55°20N 87°35W 72 A2
Fawnskin U.S.A. 34°16N 116°56W 79 L10
Faxaflói Iceland 64°29N 23°0W 8 D2
Faya-Largeau Chad 17°58N 19°6E 51 E9
Fayd Si. Arabia 27°1N 42°52E 44 E4
Fayette Ala., U.S.A. 33°41N 87°50W 85 E11
Fayette Mo., U.S.A. 39°9N 92°41W 80 F7
Fayette N.Y., U.S.A. 42°48N 76°48W 83 D8
Fayetteville Ark., U.S.A. 36°4N 94°10W 84 C7
Fayetteville N.C., U.S.A. 35°3N 78°53W 85 D15
Fayetteville N.Y., U.S.A. 43°1N 76°0W 83 D9
Fayetteville Tenn., U.S.A. 35°9N 86°34W 85 D11
Faylakah Kuwait 29°27N 48°20E 45 D6
Fazilka India 30°27N 74°2E 42 D6
Fazilpur Pakistan 29°18N 70°29E 42 E4
Fdérik Mauritania 22°40N 12°45W 50 D3
Feakle Ireland 52°56N 8°40W 10 D3
Feale → Ireland 52°27N 9°37W 10 D2
Fear, C. U.S.A. 33°50N 77°58W 85 E16
Feather → U.S.A. 38°47N 121°36W 76 G3
Feather Falls U.S.A. 39°36N 121°16W 78 F5
Featherston N.Z. 41°6S 175°20E 59 D5
Featherstone Zimbabwe 18°42S 30°55E 55 F3
Fécamp France 49°45N 0°22E 20 B4
Fedala = Mohammedia
Morocco 33°44N 7°21W 50 B4
Federación Argentina 31°0S 57°55W 94 C4
Féderal Argentina 30°57S 58°48W 96 C5
Federal Way U.S.A. 47°18N 122°19W 78 C4
Fedeshkūh Iran 28°49N 53°50E 45 D7
Fehmarn Germany 54°27N 11°7E 16 A6
Fehmarn Bælt Europe 54°35N 11°20E 9 J14
Fehmarn Belt = Fehmarn Bælt
Europe 54°35N 11°20E 9 J14
Fei Xian China 35°18N 117°59E 35 G9
Feijó Brazil 8°9S 70°21W 92 E4
Feilding N.Z. 40°13S 175°35E 59 D5
Feira de Santana Brazil 12°15S 38°57W 93 F11
Feixiang China 36°30N 114°45E 34 F8
Felanitx Spain 39°28N 3°9E 24 B10
Feldkirch Austria 47°15N 9°37E 16 E5
Félicité Seychelles 4°19S 55°52E 53 b
Felipe Carrillo Puerto
Mexico 19°38N 88°3W 87 D7
Felixburg Zimbabwe 19°29S 30°51E 57 B5
Felixstowe U.K. 51°58N 1°23E 13 F9
Felton U.S.A. 37°3N 122°4W 78 H4
Femer Bælt = Fehmarn Bælt
Europe 54°35N 11°20E 9 J14
Femunden Norway 62°10N 11°53E 8 E14
Fen He → China 35°36N 110°42E 34 G6
Fenelon Falls Canada 44°32N 78°45W 82 B6
Feng Xian Jiangsu, China 34°43N 116°35E 34 G9
Feng Xian Shaanxi,.
China 33°54N 106°40E 34 H4
Fengcheng China 40°28N 124°5E 35 D13
Fengfeng China 36°28N 114°8E 34 F8
Fengning China 41°10N 116°33E 34 D9
Fengqiu China 35°2N 114°25E 34 G8
Fengtai China 39°49N 116°14E 34 E9
Fengxiang China 34°29N 107°25E 34 G4
Fengyang China 32°51N 117°29E 35 H9
Fengzhen China 40°25N 113°2E 34 D7
Fenoarivo Fianarantsoa,
Madag. 21°43S 46°24E 57 C8
Fenoarivo Fianarantsoa,
Madag. 20°52S 46°53E 57 C8
Fenoarivo Afovoany
Madag. 18°26S 46°34E 57 B8
Fenoarivo Atsinanana
Madag. 17°22S 49°25E 57 B8
Fens, The U.K. 52°38N 0°2W 12 E7
Fenton U.S.A. 42°48N 83°42W 81 D12
Fenxi China 36°40N 111°31E 34 F6
Fenyang China 37°18N 111°48E 34 F6
Feodosiya Ukraine 45°2N 35°16E 19 E6
Ferbane Ireland 53°16N 7°50W 10 C4
Ferdows Iran 33°58N 58°2E 45 C8
Ferfer Somali Rep. 5°4N 45°9E 47 F4
Fergana = Farghona
Uzbekistan 40°23N 71°19E 28 E8
Fergus Canada 43°43N 80°24W 82 C4
Fergus Falls U.S.A. 46°17N 96°4W 80 B5
Ferkéssédougou Ivory C. 9°35N 5°6W 50 G4
Ferland Canada 50°19N 88°27W 72 B2
Ferlo, Vallée du Senegal 15°15N 14°15W 50 E3
Fermanagh □ U.K. 54°21N 7°40W 10 B4
Fermo Italy 43°9N 13°43E 22 C5
Fermont Canada 52°47N 67°5W 73 B6
Fermoy Ireland 52°9N 8°16W 10 D3
Fernández Argentina 27°55S 63°50W 94 B3
Fernandina Beach
U.S.A. 30°40N 81°27W 85 F14
Fernando de Noronha
Brazil 4°0S 33°10W 93 D12
Fernando Póo = Bioko
Eq. Guin. 3°30N 8°40E 52 D1
Ferndale Canada 44°58N 81°17W 82 B3
Ferndale U.S.A. 48°51N 122°36W 78 B4
Fernie Canada 49°30N 115°5W 70 D5
Fernlees Australia 23°51S 148°7E 62 C4
Fernley U.S.A. 39°36N 119°15W 76 G4
Fernwood U.S.A. 43°16N 73°38W 83 C11
Ferozepore = Firozpur
India 30°55N 74°40E 42 D6
Ferrara Italy 44°50N 11°35E 22 B4
Ferreñafe Peru 6°42S 79°50W 92 E3
Ferrerías Spain 39°59N 4°1E 24 B11
Ferret, C. France 44°38N 1°15W 20 D3
Ferriday U.S.A. 31°38N 91°33W 84 F9
Ferrol Spain 43°29N 8°15W 21 A1
Ferron U.S.A. 39°5N 111°8W 76 G8
Ferrutx, C. de Spain 39°47N 3°21E 24 B10

Ferryland Canada 47°2N 52°53W 73 C9
Fertile U.S.A. 47°32N 96°17W 80 B5
Fès Morocco 34°0N 5°0W 50 B5
Fessenden U.S.A. 47°39N 99°38W 80 B4
Festus U.S.A. 38°13N 90°24W 80 F8
Fetești Romania 44°22N 27°51E 17 F14
Fethiye Turkey 36°36N 29°6E 19 G4
Fetlar U.K. 60°36N 0°52W 11 A8
Feuilles → Canada 58°47N 70°4W 69 F17
Fez = Fès Morocco 34°0N 5°0W 50 B5
Fezzan Libya 27°0N 13°0E 51 C8
Fiambalá Argentina 27°45S 67°37W 94 B2
Fianarantsoa Madag. 21°26S 47°5E 57 C8
Fianarantsoa □ Madag. 19°30S 47°0E 57 B8
Ficksburg S. Africa 28°51S 27°53E 57 D4
Field → Australia 23°48S 138°0E 62 C2
Field I. Australia 12°5S 132°23E 60 B5
Fier Albania 40°43N 19°33E 23 D8
Fife □ U.K. 56°16N 3°1W 11 E5
Fife → U.K. 56°15N 3°15W 11 E5
Fife Ness U.K. 56°17N 2°35W 11 E6
Fifth Cataract Sudan 18°22N 33°50E 51 E12
Figeac France 44°37N 2°2E 20 D5
Figtree Zimbabwe 20°22S 28°20E 55 G2
Figueira da Foz Portugal 40°7N 8°54W 21 B1
Figueres Spain 42°18N 2°58E 21 A7
Figuig Morocco 32°5N 1°11W 50 B5
Fihaonana Madag. 18°36S 47°12E 57 B8
Fiherenana Madag. 18°29S 48°24E 57 B8
Fiherenana → Madag. 23°19S 43°37E 57 C7
Fiji ■ Pac. Oc. 17°20S 179°0E 59 a
Filabusi Zimbabwe 20°34S 29°20E 57 C4
Filadelfia Paraguay 22°21S 60°2W 94 A3
Filchner Ice Shelf Antarctica 79°0S 40°0W 5 D1
Filey U.K. 54°12N 0°18W 12 C7
Filey B. U.K. 54°12N 0°15W 12 C7
Filfla Malta 35°47N 14°24E 25 D1
Filiatra Greece 37°9N 21°35E 23 F9
Filingué Niger 14°21N 3°22E 50 F6
Filipstad Sweden 59°43N 14°9E 9 G16
Fillmore Calif., U.S.A. 34°24N 118°55W 79 L8
Fillmore Utah, U.S.A. 38°58N 112°20W 76 G7
Fimbul Ice Shelf S. Ocean 69°30S 1°0W 5 C2
Finch Canada 45°11N 75°7W 83 A9
Finch Hatton Australia 20°25S 148°39E 62 b
Findhorn → U.K. 57°38N 3°38W 11 D5
Findlay U.S.A. 41°2N 83°39W 81 E12
Fine U.S.A. 44°14N 75°8W 83 B9
Finger → Canada 53°33N 93°30W 72 B1
Finger Lakes U.S.A. 42°40N 76°30W 83 D8
Fíngoè Mozam. 14°55S 31°50E 55 E3
Finisterre, C. = Fisterra, C.
Spain 42°50N 9°19W 21 A1
Finke Australia 25°34S 134°35E 62 D1
Finke Gorge △ Australia 24°8S 132°49E 60 D5
Finland ■ Europe 63°0N 27°0E 8 E22
Finland, G. of Europe 60°0N 26°0E 9 G22
Finlay → Canada 57°0N 125°10W 70 B3
Finley Australia 35°38S 145°35E 63 F4
Finley U.S.A. 47°31N 97°50W 80 B5
Finn → Ireland 54°51N 7°28W 10 B4
Finnigan, Mt. Australia 15°49S 145°17E 62 B4
Finniss, C. Australia 33°8S 134°51E 63 E1
Finnmark Norway 69°37N 23°57E 8 B20
Finnsnes Norway 69°14N 18°0E 8 B18
Finspång Sweden 58°43N 15°47E 9 G16
Fiora → Italy 42°20N 11°34E 22 C4
Fiordland △ N.Z. 45°46S 167°0E 59 F1
Fiq Syria 32°46N 35°41E 46 C4
Firat = Furāt, Nahr al →
Asia 31°0N 47°25E 44 D5
Fire Island △ U.S.A. 40°38N 73°8W 83 F11
Firebag → Canada 57°45N 111°21W 71 B6
Firebaugh U.S.A. 36°52N 120°27W 78 J6
Firedrake L. Canada 61°25N 104°30W 71 A8
Firenze Italy 43°46N 11°15E 22 C4
Firk, Sha'ib → Iraq 30°59N 44°34E 44 D5
Firozabad India 27°10N 78°25E 43 F8
Firozpur India 30°55N 74°40E 42 D6
Firozpur-Jhirka India 27°48N 76°57E 42 F7
Fīrūzābād Iran 28°52N 52°35E 45 D7
Fīrūzkūh Iran 35°50N 52°50E 45 C7
Firvale Canada 52°27N 126°13W 70 C3
Fish → Namibia 28°7S 17°10E 56 D2
Fish → S. Africa 31°30S 20°16E 56 E3
Fish River Canyon
Namibia 27°40S 17°35E 56 D2
Fisher B. Canada 51°35N 97°13W 71 C9
Fishers I. U.S.A. 41°15N 72°0W 83 E13
Fishguard U.K. 52°0N 4°58W 13 E3
Fishing L. Canada 52°10N 95°24W 71 C9
Fishkill U.S.A. 41°32N 73°54W 83 E11
Fisterra, C. Spain 42°50N 9°19W 21 A1
Fitchburg Mass., U.S.A. 42°35N 71°48W 83 D13
Fitchburg Wis., U.S.A. 42°58N 89°28W 80 D9
Fitz Roy Argentina 47°0S 67°0W 96 F3
Fitz Roy, Cerro Argentina 49°17S 73°5W 96 F2
Fitzgerald Canada 59°51N 111°36W 70 B6
Fitzgerald U.S.A. 31°43N 83°15W 85 F13
Fitzgerald River △
Australia 33°53S 119°55E 61 F3
Fitzmaurice → Australia 14°45S 130°5E 60 B5
Fitzroy □ Queens.,
Australia 23°32S 150°52E 62 C5
Fitzroy → W. Austral.,
Australia 17°31S 123°35E 60 C3
Fitzroy Crossing
Australia 18°9S 125°38E 60 C4
Fitzwilliam I. Canada 45°30N 81°45W 82 A3
Fiume = Rijeka Croatia 45°20N 14°21E 16 F8
Five Points U.S.A. 36°26N 120°6W 78 J6
Fizi Dem. Rep. of the Congo 4°17S 28°55E 54 C2
Flagstaff U.S.A. 35°12N 111°39W 77 J8
Flagstaff L. U.S.A. 45°12N 70°18W 83 A14
Flaherty I. Canada 56°15N 79°15W 72 A4
Flåm Norway 60°50N 7°7E 8 F12
Flambeau → U.S.A. 45°18N 91°14W 80 C8
Flamborough Hd. U.K. 54°7N 0°5W 12 C7
Flaming Gorge →
U.S.A. 41°10N 109°25W 76 F9

Flaming Gorge Res.
U.S.A. 41°10N 109°25W 76 F9
Flamingo, Teluk Indonesia 5°30S 138°0E 37 F9
Flanders = Flandre
Europe 50°50N 2°30E 15 B9
Flandre Europe 50°50N 2°30E 15 B9
Flandre-Occidentale = West-
Vlaanderen □ Belgium 51°0N 3°0E 15 D2
Flandre-Orientale = Oost-
Vlaanderen □ Belgium 51°5N 3°50E 15 C3
Flandreau U.S.A. 44°3N 96°36W 80 C5
Flanigan U.S.A. 40°10N 119°53W 78 E7
Flannan Is. U.K. 58°9N 7°52W 11 C1
Flåsjön Sweden 64°5N 15°40E 8 D16
Flat → U.S.A. 61°33N 125°18W 70 A3
Flat I. Mauritius 19°53S 57°35E 53 d
Flathead L. U.S.A. 47°51N 114°8W 76 C6
Flattery, C. Australia 14°58S 145°21E 62 A4
Flattery, C. U.S.A. 48°23N 124°29W 78 B2
Flatwoods U.S.A. 38°31N 82°43W 81 F12
Fleetwood U.K. 53°55N 3°1W 12 D4
Fleetwood U.S.A. 40°27N 75°49W 83 F9
Flekkefjord Norway 58°18N 6°39E 9 G12
Flemington U.S.A. 41°7N 77°28W 82 E7
Flensburg Germany 54°47N 9°27E 16 A5
Flers France 48°47N 0°33W 20 B3
Flesherton Canada 44°16N 80°33W 82 B4
Flesko, Tanjung
Indonesia 0°29N 124°30E 37 D6
Fleurieu Pen. Australia 35°40S 138°5E 63 F2
Flevoland □ Neths. 52°30N 5°30E 15 B5
Flin Flon Canada 54°46N 101°53W 71 C8
Flinders → Australia 17°36S 140°36E 62 B3
Flinders B. Australia 34°19S 115°19E 61 F2
Flinders Group Australia 14°11S 144°15E 62 A3
Flinders I. S. Austral.,
Australia 33°44S 134°41E 63 E1
Flinders I. Tas., Australia 40°0S 148°0E 63 G4
Flinders Ranges
Australia 31°30S 138°30E 63 E2
Flinders Reefs Australia 17°37S 148°31E 62 B4
Flint U.K. 53°15N 3°8W 12 D4
Flint U.S.A. 43°1N 83°41W 81 D12
Flint → U.S.A. 30°57N 84°34W 85 F12
Flint I. Kiribati 11°26S 151°48W 65 J12
Flintshire □ U.K. 53°17N 3°17W 12 D4
Flodden U.K. 55°37N 2°8W 12 B5
Floodwood U.S.A. 46°56N 92°55W 80 B7
Flora U.S.A. 38°40N 88°29W 80 F9
Florala U.S.A. 31°0N 86°20W 85 F11
Florence = Firenze Italy 43°46N 11°15E 22 C4
Florence Ala., U.S.A. 34°48N 87°41W 85 D11
Florence Ariz., U.S.A. 33°2N 111°23W 77 K8
Florence Colo., U.S.A. 38°23N 105°8W 76 G11
Florence Oreg., U.S.A. 43°58N 124°7W 76 D1
Florence S.C., U.S.A. 34°12N 79°46W 85 D15
Florence, L. Australia 28°53S 138°9E 63 D2
Florencia Colombia 1°36N 75°36W 92 C3
Florennes Belgium 50°15N 4°35E 15 D4
Florenville Belgium 49°40N 5°19E 15 E5
Flores Azores 39°26N 31°13W 50 a
Flores Guatemala 16°59N 89°50W 88 C2
Flores Indonesia 8°35S 121°0E 37 F6
Flores I. Canada 49°20N 126°10W 70 D3
Flores Sea Indonesia 6°30S 120°0E 37 F6
Floreşti Moldova 47°53N 28°17E 17 E15
Floresville U.S.A. 29°8N 98°10W 84 G5
Floriano Brazil 6°50S 43°0W 93 E10
Florianópolis Brazil 27°30S 48°30W 95 B6
Florida Cuba 21°32N 78°14W 88 B4
Florida Uruguay 34°7S 56°10W 95 C4
Florida □ U.S.A. 28°0N 82°0W 85 G14
Florida, Straits of U.S.A. 25°0N 80°0W 88 B4
Florida B. U.S.A. 25°0N 80°45W 88 B3
Florida Keys U.S.A. 24°40N 81°0W 85 J14
Florin U.S.A. 38°30N 121°24W 78 G5
Florina Greece 40°48N 21°26E 23 D9
Florissant U.S.A. 38°47N 90°19W 80 F8
Florø Norway 61°35N 5°1E 8 F11
Flower Station Canada 45°10N 76°41W 83 A8
Flowerpot I. Canada 45°18N 81°38W 82 A3
Floydada U.S.A. 33°59N 101°20W 84 B4
Fluk Indonesia 1°42S 127°44E 37 E7
Flushing = Vlissingen
Neths. 51°26N 3°34E 15 C3
Fly → Papua N. G. 8°25S 143°0E 58 B7
Flying Fish, C. Antarctica 72°6S 102°29W 5 D15
Foa Tonga 19°45S 174°18W 59 c
Foam Lake Canada 51°40N 103°32W 71 C8
Foça Turkey 38°39N 26°46E 23 E12
Fochabers U.K. 57°37N 3°6W 11 D5
Focşani Romania 45°41N 27°15E 17 F14
Fóggia Italy 41°27N 15°34E 22 D6
Fogo Canada 49°43N 54°17W 73 C9
Fogo C. Verde Is. 15°5N 24°20W 50 b
Fogo I. Canada 49°40N 54°5W 73 C9
Föhr Germany 54°43N 8°30E 16 A5
Foix France 42°58N 1°38E 20 E4
Folda Nord-Trøndelag,
Norway 64°32N 10°30E 8 D14
Folda Nordland, Norway 67°38N 14°50E 8 C16
Foley Botswana 21°34S 27°21E 56 C4
Foley U.S.A. 30°24N 87°41W 85 F11
Foleyet Canada 48°15N 82°25W 72 C3
Folgefonna Norway 60°3N 6°23E 8 F12
Foligno Italy 42°57N 12°42E 22 C5
Folkestone U.K. 51°5N 1°12E 13 F9
Folkston U.S.A. 30°50N 82°0W 85 F13
Follansbee U.S.A. 40°19N 80°35W 82 F4
Folsom L. U.S.A. 38°42N 121°9W 78 G5
Fomboni Comoros Is. 12°18S 43°46E 53 a
Fond du Lac Canada 59°19N 107°12W 71 B7
Fond du Lac U.S.A. 43°47N 88°27W 80 D9
Fond-du-Lac → Canada 59°17N 106°0W 71 B7
Fonda U.S.A. 42°57N 74°23W 83 D10
Fondi Italy 41°21N 13°25E 22 D5
Fongafale Tuvalu 8°31S 179°13E 58 B10
Fonsagrada = A Fonsagrada
Spain 43°8N 7°4W 21 A2

Fonseca, G. de
Cent. Amer. 13°10N 87°40W 88 D2
Fontainebleau France 48°24N 2°40E 20 B5
Fontana U.S.A. 34°6N 117°26W 79 L9
Fontas → Canada 58°14N 121°48W 70 B4
Fonte Boa Brazil 2°33S 66°0W 92 D5
Fontenay-le-Comte
France 46°28N 0°48W 20 C3
Fontenelle Res. U.S.A. 42°1N 110°3W 76 E8
Fontur Iceland 66°23N 14°32W 8 C6
Fonuafo'ou Tonga 20°19S 175°25W 59 c
Fonualei Tonga 18°1S 174°19W 59 c
Foochow = Fuzhou
China 26°5N 119°16E 33 D6
Foping China 33°41N 108°0E 34 H5
Foraker, Mt. U.S.A. 62°58N 151°24W 74 C9
Forbes Australia 33°22S 148°5E 63 E4
Forbesganj India 26°17N 87°18E 43 F12
Ford City Calif., U.S.A. 35°9N 119°27W 79 K7
Ford City Pa., U.S.A. 40°46N 79°32W 82 F5
Førde Norway 61°27N 5°53E 8 F11
Fords Bridge Australia 29°41S 145°29E 63 D4
Fordyce U.S.A. 33°49N 92°25W 84 E8
Forel, Mt. Greenland 66°52N 36°55W 66 C16
Foremost Canada 49°26N 111°34W 70 D6
Forest Canada 43°6N 82°0W 82 C3
Forest U.S.A. 32°22N 89°29W 85 E10
Forest City Iowa, U.S.A. 43°16N 93°39W 80 D7
Forest City N.C., U.S.A. 35°20N 81°52W 85 D14
Forest City Pa., U.S.A. 41°39N 75°28W 83 E9
Forest Grove U.S.A. 45°31N 123°7W 78 E3
Forestburg Canada 52°35N 112°1W 70 C6
Foresthill U.S.A. 39°1N 120°49W 78 F6
Forestier Pen. Australia 43°0S 148°0E 63 G4
Forestville Canada 48°48N 69°2W 73 C6
Forestville Calif., U.S.A. 38°28N 122°54W 78 G4
Forestville N.Y., U.S.A. 42°28N 79°10W 82 D5
Forfar U.K. 56°39N 2°53W 11 E6
Forillon △ Canada 48°46N 64°12W 73 C7
Forks U.S.A. 47°57N 124°23W 78 C2
Forksville U.S.A. 41°29N 76°35W 83 E8
Forlì Italy 44°13N 12°3E 22 B5
Forman U.S.A. 46°7N 97°38W 80 B5
Formby Pt. U.K. 53°33N 3°6W 12 D4
Formentera Spain 38°43N 1°27E 24 C7
Formentor, C. de Spain 39°58N 3°13E 24 B10
Formentor, Pen. de
Spain 39°56N 3°11E 24 B10
Former Yugoslav Republic of
Macedonia = Macedonia ■
Europe 41°53N 21°40E 23 D9
Fórmia Italy 41°15N 13°37E 22 D5
Formosa = Taiwan ■
Asia 23°30N 121°0E 33 D7
Formosa Argentina 26°15S 58°10W 94 B4
Formosa Brazil 15°32S 47°20W 93 G9
Formosa □ Argentina 25°0S 60°0W 94 B4
Formosa B. = Ungwana B.
Kenya 2°45S 40°20E 54 C5
Fornells Spain 40°3N 4°7E 24 A11
Føroyar ☑ Atl. Oc. 62°0N 7°0W 8 F9
Forres U.K. 57°37N 3°37W 11 D5
Forrest Australia 30°51S 128°6E 61 F4
Forrest, Mt. Australia 24°48S 127°45E 61 D4
Forrest City U.S.A. 35°1N 90°47W 85 D9
Forsayth Australia 18°33S 143°34E 62 B3
Forssa Finland 60°49N 23°38E 8 F20
Forst Germany 51°45N 14°37E 16 C8
Forster Australia 32°12S 152°31E 63 E5
Forsyth U.S.A. 46°16N 106°41W 76 C10
Fort Abbas Pakistan 29°12N 72°52E 42 E5
Fort Albany Canada 52°15N 81°35W 72 B3
Fort Assiniboine
Canada 54°20N 114°45W 70 C6
Fort Augustus U.K. 57°9N 4°42W 11 D4
Fort Beaufort S. Africa 32°46S 26°40E 56 E4
Fort Benton U.S.A. 47°49N 110°40W 76 C8
Fort Bragg U.S.A. 39°26N 123°48W 76 G2
Fort Bridger U.S.A. 41°19N 110°23W 76 F8
Fort Chipewyan Canada 58°42N 111°8W 71 B6
Fort Clatsop = Lewis and Clark △
U.S.A. 46°8N 123°53W 78 D3
Fort Collins U.S.A. 40°35N 105°5W 76 F11
Fort-Coulonge Canada 45°50N 76°45W 72 C4
Fort Covington U.S.A. 44°59N 74°29W 83 B10
Fort Dauphin = Taolanaro
Madag. 25°2S 47°0E 57 D8
Fort Davis U.S.A. 30°35N 103°54W 84 F3
Fort Defiance U.S.A. 35°45N 109°5W 77 J9
Fort Dodge U.S.A. 42°30N 94°11W 80 D6
Fort Edward U.S.A. 43°16N 73°35W 83 C11
Fort Erie Canada 42°54N 78°56W 82 D6
Fort Fairfield U.S.A. 46°46N 67°50W 81 B20
Fort Frances Canada 48°36N 93°24W 71 D10
Fort Franklin = Déline
Canada 65°11N 123°25W 68 D7
Fort Garland U.S.A. 37°26N 105°26W 77 H11
Fort George = Chisasibi
Canada 53°50N 79°0W 72 B4
Fort Good Hope Canada 66°14N 128°40W 68 D6
Fort Hancock U.S.A. 31°18N 105°51W 84 F2
Fort Hope = Eabametoong
Canada 51°30N 88°0W 72 B2
Fort Irwin U.S.A. 35°16N 116°41W 79 K10
Fort Kent U.S.A. 47°15N 68°36W 81 B19
Fort Klamath U.S.A. 42°42N 122°0W 76 E3
Fort Laramie U.S.A. 42°13N 104°31W 76 E11
Fort Lauderdale U.S.A. 26°7N 80°8W 85 H14
Fort Liard Canada 60°14N 123°30W 70 A4
Fort Liberté Haiti 19°42N 71°51W 89 C5
Fort Lupton U.S.A. 40°5N 104°49W 76 F11
Fort MacKay Canada 57°12N 111°41W 70 B6
Fort Macleod Canada 49°45N 113°30W 70 D6
Fort McMurray Canada 56°44N 111°7W 70 B6
Fort McPherson
Canada 67°30N 134°55W 68 D5
Fort Madison U.S.A. 40°38N 91°27W 80 E8

Fort Meade U.S.A. 27°45N 81°48W 85 H14
Fort Morgan U.S.A. 40°15N 103°48W 76 F12
Fort Myers U.S.A. 26°39N 81°52W 85 H14
Fort Nelson Canada 58°50N 122°44W 70 B4
Fort Nelson → Canada 59°32N 124°0W 70 B4
Fort Norman = Tulita
Canada 64°57N 125°30W 68 E6
Fort Payne U.S.A. 34°26N 85°43W 85 D12
Fort Peck U.S.A. 48°1N 106°27W 76 B10
Fort Peck Dam U.S.A. 48°0N 106°26W 76 C10
Fort Peck L. U.S.A. 48°0N 106°26W 76 C10
Fort Pierce U.S.A. 27°27N 80°20W 85 H14
Fort Pierre U.S.A. 44°21N 100°22W 80 C3
Fort Plain U.S.A. 42°56N 74°37W 83 D10
Fort Portal Uganda 0°40N 30°20E 54 B3
Fort Providence Canada 61°3N 117°40W 70 A5
Fort Qu'Appelle
Canada 50°45N 103°50W 71 C8
Fort Resolution Canada 61°10N 113°40W 70 A6
Fort Rixon Zimbabwe 20°2S 29°17E 55 G2
Fort Ross U.S.A. 38°32N 123°13E 73 G3
Fort Rupert = Waskaganish
Canada 51°30N 78°40W 72 B4
Fort St. James Canada 54°30N 124°10W 70 C4
Fort St. John Canada 56°15N 120°50W 70 B4
Fort Saskatchewan
Canada 53°40N 113°15W 70 C6
Fort Scott U.S.A. 37°50N 94°42W 80 G6
Fort Severn Canada 56°0N 87°40W 72 A2
Fort Shevchenko
Kazakhstan 44°35N 50°23E 19 F9
Fort Simpson Canada 61°45N 121°15W 70 A4
Fort Smith Canada 60°0N 111°51W 70 B6
Fort Smith U.S.A. 35°23N 94°25W 84 D7
Fort Stockton U.S.A. 30°53N 102°53W 84 F3
Fort Sumner U.S.A. 34°28N 104°15W 77 J11
Fort Thompson U.S.A. 44°3N 99°26W 80 C4
Fort Union △ U.S.A. 35°54N 105°1W 77 J11
Fort Valley U.S.A. 32°33N 83°53W 85 E13
Fort Vermilion Canada 58°24N 116°0W 70 B5
Fort Walton Beach
U.S.A. 30°25N 86°36W 85 F11
Fort Ware Canada 57°26N 125°41W 70 B3
Fort Wayne U.S.A. 41°4N 85°9W 81 E11
Fort William U.K. 56°49N 5°7W 11 E3
Fort Worth U.S.A. 32°43N 97°19W 84 E6
Fort Yates U.S.A. 46°5N 100°38W 80 B3
Fort Yukon U.S.A. 66°34N 145°16W 68 D2
Fortaleza Brazil 3°45S 38°35W 93 D11
Forteau Canada 51°28N 56°58W 73 B8
Fortescue → Australia 21°0S 116°4E 60 D2
Fortescue River Roadhouse
Australia 21°17S 116°8E 60 D2
Forth → U.K. 56°9N 3°50W 11 E5
Forth, Firth of U.K. 56°5N 2°55W 11 E6
Fortrose U.K. 57°35N 4°9W 11 D4
Fortuna Calif., U.S.A. 40°36N 124°9W 76 F1
Fortuna N. Dak., U.S.A. 48°55N 103°47W 80 A2
Fortune Canada 47°4N 55°50W 73 C8
Fortune B. Canada 47°30N 55°22W 73 C8
Forūr Iran 26°17N 54°32E 45 E7
Fosen Norway 63°50N 10°20E 8 E14
Foshan China 23°6N 113°9E 33 D6
Fosnavåg Norway 62°22N 5°38E 8 E11
Fossano Italy 44°33N 7°43E 20 D7
Fossil U.S.A. 45°0N 120°9W 78 D5
Fossil Butte △ U.S.A. 41°50N 110°27W 76 F8
Foster Canada 45°17N 72°30W 83 A12
Foster → Canada 55°47N 105°49W 71 B7
Fosters Ra. Australia 21°35S 133°48E 62 C1
Fostoria U.S.A. 41°10N 83°25W 81 E12
Fotadrevo Madag. 24°3S 45°1E 57 C8
Fougères France 48°21N 1°14W 20 B3
Foul Pt. Sri Lanka 8°35N 81°18E 40 Q12
Foula U.K. 60°10N 2°5W 11 A6
Foulness I. U.K. 51°36N 0°55E 13 F8
Foulpointe Madag. 17°41S 49°31E 57 B8
Foumban Cameroon 5°45N 10°50E 52 C2
Foumbouni Comoros Is. 11°51S 43°29E 53 a
Fountain U.S.A. 38°41N 104°42W 76 G11
Fountain Hills U.S.A. 33°37N 111°43W 77 K8
Fountain Springs
U.S.A. 35°54N 118°51W 79 K8
Four Mountains, Is. of
U.S.A. 53°0N 170°0W 74 C2
Fouriesburg S. Africa 28°38S 28°14E 56 D4
Fourni Greece 37°36N 26°32E 23 F12
Fourth Cataract Sudan 18°47N 32°3E 51 E12
Fouta Djallon Guinea 11°20N 12°10W 50 F3
Foux, Cap-à- Haiti 19°43N 73°27W 89 C5
Foveaux Str. N.Z. 46°42S 168°10E 59 G2
Fowey U.K. 50°20N 4°39W 13 G3
Fowler Calif., U.S.A. 36°38N 119°41W 78 J7
Fowler Colo., U.S.A. 38°8N 104°2W 76 G11
Fowler, Pt. Australia 32°2S 132°3E 61 F5
Fowlers B. Australia 31°59S 132°34E 61 F5
Fowman Iran 37°13N 49°19E 45 B6
Fox → Canada 56°3N 93°18W 71 B10
Fox Creek Canada 54°24N 116°48W 70 C5
Fox Is. U.S.A. 53°0N 168°0W 74 E6
Fox Lake Canada 58°28N 114°31W 70 B6
Fox Valley Canada 50°30N 109°25W 71 C7
Foxboro U.S.A. 42°4N 71°16W 83 D13
Foxdale Australia 20°22S 148°35E 62 b
Foxe Basin Canada 66°0N 77°0W 69 D16
Foxe Chan. Canada 65°0N 80°0W 69 D15
Foxe Pen. Canada 65°0N 76°0W 69 D16
Foxford Ireland 53°59N 9°7W 10 C2
Foxton N.Z. 40°29S 175°18E 59 D5
Foyle, Lough U.K. 55°7N 7°4W 10 A4
Foynes Ireland 52°37N 9°7W 10 D2
Foz do Cunene Angola 17°15S 11°48E 56 B1
Foz do Iguaçu Brazil 25°30S 54°30W 95 B5
Frackville U.S.A. 40°47N 76°14W 83 F8
Fraile Muerto Uruguay 32°31S 54°32W 95 C5
Framingham U.S.A. 42°18N 71°24W 83 D13
Franca Brazil 20°33S 47°30W 93 H9
Francavilla Fontana
Italy 40°32N 17°35E 23 D7

France ■ *Europe* 47°N 3°0E **20 C5**
Frances *Australia* 36°41S 140°55E **63 F3**
Frances → *Canada* 60°16N 129°30W **70 A3**
Franceville *Gabon* 1°40S 13°32E **52 E2**
Franche-Comté □ *France* 46°50N 5°55E **20 C6**
Francis Case, L. *U.S.A.* 43°4N 98°34W **80 D4**
Francisco Beltrão *Brazil* 26°5S 53°4W **95 B5**
Francisco Ignacio Madero
  Coahuila, Mexico 25°48N 103°18W **86 B4**
Francisco Ignacio Madero *Durango,*
  Mexico 24°26N 104°18W **86 C4**
Francisco Ignacio Madero, Presa
  Mexico 28°10N 105°37W **86 B3**
Francistown *Botswana* 21°7S 27°33E **57 C4**
François *Canada* 47°35N 56°45W **73 C8**
François L. *Canada* 54°0N 125°30W **70 C3**
Francois Peron △
  Australia 25°42S 113°33E **61 E1**
Francs Pk. *U.S.A.* 43°58N 109°20W **76 E9**
Franeker *Neths.* 53°12N 5°33E **15 A5**
Frank Hann △ *Australia* 32°52S 120°19E **61 F3**
Frankford *Canada* 44°12N 77°36W **82 B7**
Frankfort *S. Africa* 27°17S 28°30E **57 D4**
Frankfort *Ind., U.S.A.* 40°17N 86°31W **80 E10**
Frankfort *Kans., U.S.A.* 39°42N 96°25W **80 F5**
Frankfort *Ky., U.S.A.* 38°12N 84°52W **81 F11**
Frankfort *N.Y., U.S.A.* 43°2N 75°4W **83 C9**
Frankfurt *Brandenburg,*
  Germany 52°20N 14°32E **16 B8**
Frankfurt *Hessen, Germany* 50°7N 8°41E **16 C5**
Fränkische Alb *Germany* 49°10N 11°23E **16 D6**
Frankland → *Australia* 35°0S 116°48E **61 G2**
Franklin *Ky., U.S.A.* 36°43N 86°35W **80 G10**
Franklin *La., U.S.A.* 29°48N 91°30W **84 G9**
Franklin *Mass., U.S.A.* 42°5N 71°24W **83 D13**
Franklin *N.H., U.S.A.* 43°27N 71°39W **83 C13**
Franklin *N.Y., U.S.A.* 42°20N 75°9W **83 D9**
Franklin *Nebr., U.S.A.* 40°6N 98°57W **80 E4**
Franklin *Pa., U.S.A.* 41°24N 79°50W **82 E5**
Franklin *Va., U.S.A.* 36°41N 76°56W **81 G15**
Franklin *W. Va., U.S.A.* 38°39N 79°20W **81 F14**
Franklin B. *Canada* 69°45N 126°0W **68 D6**
Franklin D. Roosevelt L.
  U.S.A. 48°18N 118°9W **76 B4**
Franklin-Gordon Wild Rivers △
  Australia 42°19S 145°51E **63 G4**
Franklin I. *Antarctica* 76°10S 168°30E **5 D11**
Franklin I. *Canada* 45°24N 80°20W **82 A4**
Franklin L. *U.S.A.* 40°25N 115°22W **76 F6**
Franklin Mts. *Canada* 65°0N 125°0W **68 C6**
Franklin Str. *Canada* 72°0N 96°0W **68 C12**
Franklinton *U.S.A.* 30°51N 90°9W **85 F9**
Franklinville *U.S.A.* 42°20N 78°27W **82 D6**
Frankston *Australia* 38°8S 145°8E **63 F4**
Fransfontein *Namibia* 20°12S 15°1E **56 C2**
Frantsa Iosifa, Zemlya
  Russia 82°0N 55°0E **28 A6**
Franz *Canada* 48°25N 84°30W **72 C3**
Franz Josef Land = Frantsa Iosifa,
  Zemlya *Russia* 82°0N 55°0E **28 A6**
Fraser → *Australia* 42°32N 82°57W **82 D2**
Fraser → *B.C., Canada* 49°7N 123°11W **78 A3**
Fraser → *Nfld. & L.,*
  Canada 56°39N 62°10W **73 A7**
Fraser, Mt. *Australia* 25°35S 118°20E **61 E2**
Fraser I. *Australia* 25°15S 153°10E **63 D5**
Fraser Lake *Canada* 54°0N 124°50W **70 C4**
Fraserburg *S. Africa* 31°55S 21°30E **56 E3**
Fraserburgh *U.K.* 57°42N 2°1W **11 D6**
Fraserdale *Canada* 49°55N 81°37W **72 C3**
Fray Bentos *Uruguay* 33°10S 58°15W **94 C4**
Fray Jorge △ *Chile* 30°42S 71°40W **94 C1**
Frazier Downs △
  Australia 18°48S 121°42E **60 C3**
Fredericia *Denmark* 55°34N 9°45E **9 J13**
Frederick *Md., U.S.A.* 39°25N 77°25W **81 F15**
Frederick *Okla., U.S.A.* 34°23N 99°1W **84 D5**
Frederick *S. Dak., U.S.A.* 45°50N 98°31W **80 C4**
Fredericksburg *Pa.,*
  U.S.A. 40°27N 76°26W **83 F8**
Fredericksburg *Tex.,*
  U.S.A. 30°16N 98°52W **84 F5**
Fredericksburg *Va.,*
  U.S.A. 38°18N 77°28W **81 F15**
Fredericktown *Mo.,*
  U.S.A. 37°34N 90°18W **80 G8**
Fredericktown *Ohio,*
  U.S.A. 40°29N 82°33W **82 F2**
Frederico Westphalen
  Brazil 27°22S 53°24W **95 B5**
Fredericton *Canada* 45°57N 66°40W **73 C6**
Fredericton Junction
  Canada 45°41N 66°40W **73 C6**
Frederlkshåb = Paamlut
  Greenland 62°0N 49°43W **4 C5**
Frederikshamn = Hamina
  Finland 60°34N 27°12E **8 F22**
Frederikshavn *Denmark* 57°28N 10°31E **9 H14**
Frederiksted
  U.S. Virgin Is. 17°43N 64°53W **89 C7**
Fredonia *Ariz., U.S.A.* 36°57N 112°32W **77 H7**
Fredonia *Kans., U.S.A.* 37°32N 95°49W **80 G6**
Fredonia *N.Y., U.S.A.* 42°26N 79°20W **82 D5**
Fredrikstad *Norway* 59°13N 10°57E **9 G14**
Free State □ *S. Africa* 28°30S 27°0E **56 D4**
Freehold *U.S.A.* 40°16N 74°17W **83 F10**
Freeland *U.S.A.* 41°1N 75°54W **83 E9**
Freels, C. *Nfld. & L.,*
  Canada 49°15N 53°30W **73 C9**
Freels, C. *Nfld. & L.,*
  Canada 46°37N 53°32W **73 C9**
Freeman *Calif., U.S.A.* 35°35N 117°53W **79 K9**
Freeman *S. Dak., U.S.A.* 43°21N 97°26W **80 D5**
Freeport *Bahamas* 26°30N 78°47W **88 A4**
Freeport *Ill., U.S.A.* 42°17N 89°36W **80 D9**
Freeport *N.Y., U.S.A.* 40°39N 73°35W **83 F11**
Freeport *Ohio, U.S.A.* 40°12N 81°15W **82 F3**
Freeport *Pa., U.S.A.* 40°41N 79°41W **82 F5**

Freeport *Tex., U.S.A.* 28°57N 95°21W **84 G7**
Freetown *S. Leone* 8°30N 13°17W **50 G3**
Freeville *U.S.A.* 42°30N 76°20W **83 D8**
Frégate, L. de la *Canada* 53°15N 74°45W **72 B5**
Fregenal de la Sierra
  Spain 38°10N 6°39W **21 C2**
Fregon *Australia* 26°45S 132°1E **61 E5**
Freibourg = Fribourg
  Switz. 46°49N 7°9E **20 C7**
Freiburg *Germany* 47°59N 7°51E **16 E4**
Freire *Chile* 38°54S 72°38W **96 D2**
Freirina *Chile* 28°30S 71°10W **94 B1**
Freising *Germany* 48°24N 11°45E **16 D6**
Freistadt *Austria* 48°30N 14°30E **16 D8**
Fréjus *France* 43°25N 6°44E **20 E7**
Fremantle *Australia* 32°7S 115°47E **61 F2**
Fremont *Calif., U.S.A.* 37°32N 121°57W **78 H4**
Fremont *Mich., U.S.A.* 43°28N 85°57W **81 D11**
Fremont *Nebr., U.S.A.* 41°26N 96°30W **80 E6**
Fremont *Ohio, U.S.A.* 41°21N 83°7W **81 E12**
Fremont → *U.S.A.* 38°24N 110°42W **76 G8**
French Camp *U.S.A.* 37°53N 121°16W **78 H5**
French Cays = Plana Cays
  Bahamas 22°38N 73°30W **89 B5**
French Creek → *U.S.A.* 41°24N 79°50W **82 E5**
French Frigate Shoals
  U.S.A. 23°45N 166°10W **75 L6**
French Guiana ☑ *S. Amer.* 4°0N 53°0W **93 C8**
French Polynesia ☑
  Pac. Oc. 20°0S 145°0W **65 J13**
Frenchman Cr. →
  N. Amer. 48°31N 107°10W **76 B10**
Frenchman Cr. →
  U.S.A. 40°14N 100°50W **80 E3**
Fresco → *Brazil* 7°15S 51°30W **93 E8**
Freshfield, C. *Antarctica* 68°25S 151°10E **5 C10**
Fresnillo *Mexico* 23°10N 102°53W **86 C4**
Fresno *U.S.A.* 36°44N 119°47W **78 J7**
Fresno Res. *U.S.A.* 48°36N 109°57W **76 B9**
Frew → *Australia* 20°0S 135°38E **62 C2**
Frewsburg *U.S.A.* 42°3N 79°10W **82 D5**
Freycinet △ *Australia* 42°11S 148°19E **63 G4**
Freycinet Pen. *Australia* 42°10S 148°25E **63 G4**
Fria *Guinea* 10°27N 13°38W **50 F3**
Fria, C. *Namibia* 18°0S 12°0E **56 B1**
Friant *U.S.A.* 36°59N 119°43W **78 J7**
Frías *Argentina* 28°40S 65°5W **94 B2**
Fribourg *Switz.* 46°49N 7°9E **20 C7**
Friday Harbor *U.S.A.* 48°32N 123°1W **78 B3**
Friedens *U.S.A.* 40°3N 78°59W **82 F6**
Friedrichshafen *Germany* 47°39N 9°30E **16 E5**
Friendship *U.S.A.* 42°12N 78°8W **82 D6**
Friesland □ *Neths.* 53°5N 5°50E **15 A5**
Frigate *Seychelles* 4°35S 55°56E **53 b**
Frio → *U.S.A.* 28°26N 98°11W **84 G5**
Frio, C. *Brazil* 22°50S 41°50W **90 F6**
Friona *U.S.A.* 34°38N 102°43W **84 D3**
Fritch *U.S.A.* 35°38N 101°36W **84 D4**
Frobisher B. *Canada* 62°30N 66°0W **69 E18**
Frobisher Bay = Iqaluit
  Canada 63°44N 68°31W **69 E18**
Frobisher L. *Canada* 56°20N 108°15W **71 B7**
Frohavet *Norway* 64°0N 9°30E **8 E13**
Frome *U.K.* 51°14N 2°19W **13 F5**
Frome → *U.K.* 50°41N 2°6W **13 G5**
Frome, L. *Australia* 30°45S 139°45E **63 E2**
Front Range *U.S.A.* 40°25N 105°45W **75 G18**
Front Royal *U.S.A.* 38°55N 78°12W **81 F14**
Frontenac △ *Canada* 44°32N 76°30W **83 B8**
Frontera *Canary Is.* 27°47N 17°59W **24 G2**
Frontera *Mexico* 18°32N 92°38W **87 D6**
Fronteras *Mexico* 30°56N 109°31W **86 A3**
Frosinone *Italy* 41°38N 13°19E **22 D5**
Frostburg *U.S.A.* 39°39N 78°56W **81 F14**
Frostisen *Norway* 68°14N 17°10E **8 B17**
Frøya *Norway* 63°43N 8°40E **8 E13**
Frunze = Bishkek
  Kyrgyzstan 42°54N 74°46E **28 E8**
Frutal *Brazil* 20°0S 49°0W **93 H9**
Frýdek-Místek
  Czech Rep. 49°40N 18°20E **17 D10**
Fryeburg *U.S.A.* 44°1N 70°59W **83 B14**
Fu Xian = Wafangdian
  China 39°38N 121°58E **35 E11**
Fu Xian *China* 36°0N 109°20E **34 G5**
Fucheng *China* 37°50N 116°10E **34 F9**
Fuchou = Fuzhou *China* 26°5N 119°16E **33 D6**
Fuchū *Japan* 34°34N 133°14E **31 G6**
Fuencaliente *Canary Is.* 28°28N 17°50W **24 F2**
Fuencaliente *Spain* 38°25N 4°18W **21 C3**
Fuencaliente, Pta.
  Canary Is. 28°27N 17°51W **24 F2**
Fuengirola *Spain* 36°32N 4°41W **21 D3**
Fuentes de Oñoro *Spain* 40°33N 6°52W **21 B2**
Fuerte → *Mexico* 25°54N 109°22W **86 B3**
Fuerte Olimpo *Paraguay* 21°0S 57°51W **94 A4**
Fuerteventura *Canary Is.* 28°30N 14°0W **24 F6**
Fuerteventura ✈ (FUE)
  Canary Is. 28°24N 13°52W **24 F6**
Fufeng *China* 34°22N 108°0E **34 G5**
Fugou *China* 34°3N 114°25E **34 G8**
Fugu *China* 39°2N 111°3E **34 E6**
Fuhai *China* 47°2N 87°25E **32 B3**
Fuḥaymī *Iraq* 34°16N 42°10E **44 C4**
Fuji *Japan* 35°9N 138°39E **31 G9**
Fuji-Hakone-Izu △
  Japan 35°15N 138°45E **31 G9**
Fuji-San *Japan* 35°22N 138°44E **31 G9**
Fuji-Yoshida *Japan* 35°30N 138°46E **31 G9**
Fujian □ *China* 26°0N 118°0E **33 D6**
Fujinomiya *Japan* 35°10N 138°40E **31 G9**
Fujisawa *Japan* 35°22N 139°29E **31 G9**
Fujiyama, Mt. = Fuji-San
  Japan 35°22N 138°44E **31 G9**
Fukagawa *Japan* 43°43N 142°2E **30 C11**
Fukien = Fujian □ *China* 26°0N 118°0E **33 D6**
Fukuchiyama *Japan* 35°19N 135°9E **31 G7**
Fukue-Shima *Japan* 32°35N 128°48E **31 H4**
Fukui *Japan* 36°5N 136°10E **31 F8**
Fukui □ *Japan* 36°0N 136°12E **31 G8**

Fukuoka *Japan* 33°39N 130°21E **31 H5**
Fukuoka □ *Japan* 33°30N 131°0E **31 H5**
Fukushima *Japan* 37°44N 140°28E **30 F10**
Fukushima □ *Japan* 37°30N 140°15E **30 F10**
Fukuyama *Japan* 34°35N 133°20E **31 G6**
Fulaga *Fiji* 19°8S 178°33W **59 a**
Fulda *Germany* 50°32N 9°40E **16 C5**
Fulda → *Germany* 51°25N 9°39E **16 C5**
Fulford Harbour
  Canada 48°47N 123°27W **78 B3**
Fullerton *Calif., U.S.A.* 33°53N 117°56W **79 M9**
Fullerton *Nebr., U.S.A.* 41°22N 97°58W **80 E5**
Fulongquan *China* 44°20N 124°42E **35 B13**
Fulton *Mo., U.S.A.* 38°52N 91°57W **80 F8**
Fulton *N.Y., U.S.A.* 43°19N 76°25W **83 C8**
Funabashi *Japan* 35°45N 140°0E **31 G10**
Funafuti = Fongafale
  Tuvalu 0°31G 179°13C **50 D10**
Funchal *Madeira* 32°38N 16°54W **24 D3**
Funchal ✈ (FNC)
  Madeira 32°42N 16°45W **24 D3**
Fundación *Colombia* 10°31N 74°11W **92 A4**
Fundão *Portugal* 40°8N 7°30W **21 B2**
Fundy, B. of *Canada* 45°0N 66°0W **73 D6**
Fundy △ *Canada* 45°35N 65°10W **73 C6**
Funhalouro *Mozam.* 23°3S 34°25E **57 C5**
Funing *Hebei, China* 39°53N 119°12E **35 E10**
Funing *Jiangsu, China* 33°45N 119°50E **35 H10**
Funiu Shan *China* 33°30N 112°20E **34 H7**
Funtua *Nigeria* 11°30N 7°18E **50 F7**
Fuping *Hebei, China* 38°48N 114°12E **34 E8**
Fuping *Shaanxi, China* 34°42N 109°10E **34 G5**
Furano *Japan* 43°21N 142°23E **30 C11**
Furāt, Nahr al → *Asia* 31°0N 47°25E **44 D5**
Fürg *Iran* 28°18N 55°13E **45 D7**
Furnás *Spain* 39°3N 1°32E **24 B8**
Furnas, Represa de
  Brazil 20°50S 45°30W **95 A6**
Furneaux Group
  Australia 40°10S 147°50E **63 G4**
Furqlus *Syria* 34°36N 37°8E **46 A6**
Fürstenwalde *Germany* 52°22N 14°3E **16 B8**
Fürth *Germany* 49°28N 10°59E **16 D6**
Furukawa *Japan* 38°34N 140°58E **30 E10**
Fury and Hecla Str.
  Canada 69°56N 84°0W **69 D15**
Fusagasugá *Colombia* 4°21N 74°22W **92 C4**
Fushan *Shandong,*
  China 37°30N 121°15E **35 F11**
Fushan *Shanxi, China* 35°58N 111°51E **34 G6**
Fushun *China* 41°50N 123°56E **35 D12**
Fusong *China* 42°20N 127°15E **35 C14**
Fustic *Barbados* 13°16N 59°38W **89 g**
Futian *China* 22°32N 114°4E **33 F11**
Fuxin *China* 42°5N 121°48E **35 C11**
Fuyang *China* 33°0N 115°48E **34 H8**
Fuyang He → *China* 38°12N 117°0E **34 E9**
Fuyong *China* 22°40N 113°49E **33 F10**
Fuyu *Heilongjiang, China* 47°49N 124°27E **35 B13**
Fuyu *Jilin, China* 45°12N 124°43E **35 B13**
Fuyun *China* 47°0N 89°28E **32 B3**
Fuzhou *China* 26°5N 119°16E **33 D6**
Fylde *U.K.* 53°50N 2°58W **12 D5**
Fyn *Denmark* 55°20N 10°30E **9 J14**
Fyne, L. *U.K.* 55°59N 5°23W **11 F3**

G

Gaalkacyo *Somali Rep.* 6°30N 47°30E **47 F4**
Gabba *Australia* 9°45S 142°38E **62 a**
Gabela *Angola* 11°0S 14°24E **52 G2**
Gabès *Tunisia* 33°53N 10°2E **51 B8**
Gabès, G. de *Tunisia* 34°0N 10°30E **51 B8**
Gabon ■ *Africa* 0°10S 10°0E **52 E2**
Gaborone *Botswana* 24°45S 25°57E **56 C4**
Gabriels *U.S.A.* 44°26N 74°12W **83 B10**
Gábrïk *Iran* 25°44N 58°28E **45 E8**
Gabrovo *Bulgaria* 42°52N 25°19E **23 C11**
Gāch Sār *Iran* 36°7N 51°19E **45 B6**
Gachsārān *Iran* 30°15N 50°45E **45 D6**
Gadag *India* 15°30N 75°45E **40 M9**
Gadap *Pakistan* 25°5N 67°28E **42 G2**
Gadarwara *India* 22°50N 78°50E **43 H8**
Gadhada *India* 22°0N 71°35E **42 J4**
Gadra *Pakistan* 25°40N 70°38E **42 G4**
Gadsden *U.S.A.* 34°1N 86°1W **85 D11**
Gadwal *India* 16°10N 77°50E **40 L10**
Gaffney *U.S.A.* 35°5N 81°39W **85 D14**
Gafsa *Tunisia* 34°24N 8°43E **50 B7**
Gagaria *India* 25°43N 70°46E **42 G4**
Găgăuzia □ *Moldova* 46°10N 28°40E **17 E15**
Gagnoa *Ivory C.* 6°56N 5°16W **50 G4**
Gagnon *Canada* 51°50N 68°5W **73 B6**
Gagnon, L. *Canada* 62°3N 110°27W **71 A6**
Gahini *Rwanda* 1°50S 30°30E **54 C3**
Gahmar *India* 25°27N 83°49E **43 G10**
Gai Xian = Gaizhou
  China 40°22N 122°20E **35 D12**
Gaidouronisi *Greece* 34°53N 25°41E **25 E7**
Gail *U.S.A.* 32°46N 101°27W **84 E4**
Gaillimh = Galway *Ireland* 53°17N 9°3W **10 C2**
Gaines *U.S.A.* 41°46N 77°35W **82 E7**
Gainesville *Fla., U.S.A.* 29°40N 82°20W **85 G13**
Gainesville *Ga., U.S.A.* 34°18N 83°50W **85 D13**
Gainesville *Mo., U.S.A.* 36°36N 92°26W **80 G8**
Gainesville *Tex., U.S.A.* 33°38N 97°8W **84 E6**
Gainsborough *U.K.* 53°24N 0°46W **12 D7**
Gairdner, L. *Australia* 31°30S 136°0E **63 E2**
Gairloch *U.K.* 57°43N 5°41W **11 D3**
Gairloch, L. *U.K.* 57°43N 5°45W **11 D3**
Gaizhou *China* 40°22N 122°20E **35 D12**
Gaj → *Pakistan* 26°26N 67°21E **42 F2**
Gakuch *Pakistan* 36°7N 73°45E **43 A5**
Galán, Cerro *Argentina* 25°55S 66°52W **94 B2**
Galana → *Kenya* 3°9S 40°8E **54 C5**
Galápagos = Colón, Arch. de
  Ecuador 0°0 91°0W **90 D1**
Galapagos Fracture Zone
  Pac. Oc. 0°0N 110°0W **65 G17**

Galapagos Rise *Pac. Oc.* 15°0S 95°0W **65 J18**
Galashiels *U.K.* 55°37N 2°49W **11 F6**
Galateia *Cyprus* 35°25N 34°4E **25 D13**
Galați *Romania* 45°27N 28°2E **17 F15**
Galatina *Italy* 40°10N 18°10E **23 D8**
Galax *U.S.A.* 36°40N 80°56W **81 G13**
Galcaio = Gaalkacyo
  Somali Rep. 6°30N 47°30E **47 F4**
Galdhøpiggen *Norway* 61°38N 8°18E **8 F13**
Galeana *Chihuahua,*
  Mexico 30°7N 107°38W **86 A3**
Galeana *Nuevo León,*
  Mexico 24°50N 100°4W **86 A3**
Galela *Indonesia* 1°50N 127°49E **37 D7**
Galeota Pt. *Trin. & Tob.* 10°8N 60°59W **93 K16**
Galera Pt. *Trin. & Tob.* 10°49N 60°54W **93 K16**
Galesburg *U.S.A.* 40°57N 90°22W **80 E9**
Galestan △ *Iran* 37°30N 50°0E **45 B8**
Galeton *U.S.A.* 41°44N 77°39W **82 E7**
Galich *Russia* 58°22N 42°24E **18 C7**
Galicia □ *Spain* 42°43N 7°45W **21 A2**
Galilee = Hagalil *Israel* 32°53N 35°18E **46 C4**
Galilee, L. *Australia* 22°20S 145°50E **62 C4**
Galilee, Sea of = Yam Kinneret
  Israel 32°45N 35°35E **46 C4**
Galina Pt. *Jamaica* 18°24N 76°58W **88 a**
Galinoporni *Cyprus* 35°31N 34°18E **25 D13**
Galion *U.S.A.* 40°44N 82°47W **82 F2**
Galiuro Mts. *U.S.A.* 32°30N 110°20W **77 K8**
Galiwinku *Australia* 12°2S 135°34E **62 A2**
Gallan Hd. *U.K.* 58°15N 7°2W **11 C1**
Gallatin *U.S.A.* 36°24N 86°27W **85 C11**
Galle *Sri Lanka* 6°5N 80°10E **40 R12**
Gállego → *Spain* 41°39N 0°51W **21 B5**
Gallegos → *Argentina* 51°35S 69°0W **96 G3**
Galley Hd. *Ireland* 51°32N 8°55W **10 E3**
Gallinas, Pta. *Colombia* 12°28N 71°40W **92 A4**
Gallipoli = Gelibolu
  Turkey 40°28N 26°43E **23 D12**
Gallipoli *Italy* 40°3N 17°58E **23 D8**
Gallipolis *U.S.A.* 38°49N 82°12W **81 F12**
Gällivare *Sweden* 67°9N 20°40E **8 C19**
Galloo I. *U.S.A.* 43°55N 76°25W **83 C8**
Galloway *U.K.* 55°1N 4°29W **11 F4**
Galloway, Mull of *U.K.* 54°39N 4°52W **11 G4**
Galloway □ *U.K.* 55°3N 4°27W **11 F4**
Gallup *U.S.A.* 35°32N 108°45W **77 J9**
Galoya *Sri Lanka* 8°10N 80°55E **40 Q12**
Galt *U.S.A.* 38°15N 121°18W **78 G5**
Galty Mts. *Ireland* 52°22N 8°10W **10 D3**
Galtymore *Ireland* 52°21N 8°11W **10 D3**
Galugah *Iran* 36°43N 53°48E **45 B7**
Galva *U.S.A.* 41°10N 90°3W **80 E8**
Galveston *U.S.A.* 29°18N 94°48W **84 G7**
Galveston B. *U.S.A.* 29°36N 94°50W **84 G7**
Gálvez *Argentina* 32°0S 61°14W **94 C3**
Galway *Ireland* 53°17N 9°3W **10 C2**
Galway □ *Ireland* 53°22N 9°1W **10 C2**
Galway B. *Ireland* 53°13N 9°10W **10 C2**
Gam → *Vietnam* 21°55N 105°12E **38 B5**
Gamagōri *Japan* 34°50N 137°14E **31 G8**
Gambat *Pakistan* 27°17N 68°26E **42 F3**
Gambhir → *India* 26°58N 77°27E **42 F6**
Gambia ■ *W. Afr.* 13°25N 16°0W **50 F2**
Gambia → *W. Afr.* 13°28N 16°34W **50 F2**
Gambier, C. *Australia* 11°56S 130°57E **60 B5**
Gambier, Ís.
  French Polynesia 23°8S 134°58W **65 K14**
Gambier Is. *Australia* 35°3S 136°3E **63 F2**
Gambo *Canada* 48°47N 54°13W **73 C9**
Gamboli *Pakistan* 29°53N 68°24E **42 E3**
Gamboma *Congo* 1°55S 15°52E **52 E3**
Gamka → *S. Africa* 33°18S 21°39E **56 E3**
Gamkab → *Namibia* 28°4S 17°54E **56 D2**
Gamlakarleby = Kokkola
  Finland 63°50N 23°8E **8 E20**
Gammon → *Canada* 51°24N 95°44W **71 C9**
Gammon Ranges △
  Australia 30°38S 139°8E **63 E2**
Gamtoos → *S. Africa* 33°58S 25°1E **56 E4**
Gan Jiang → *China* 29°15N 116°0E **33 D6**
Ganado *U.S.A.* 35°43N 109°33W **77 J9**
Gananoque *Canada* 44°20N 76°10W **83 B8**
Ganāveh *Iran* 29°35N 50°35E **45 D6**
Gäncä *Azerbaijan* 40°45N 46°20E **19 F8**
Gancheng *China* 18°51N 108°37E **38 C7**
Gand = Gent *Belgium* 51°2N 3°42E **15 C3**
Ganda *Angola* 13°3S 14°35E **53 G2**
Gandajika
  Dem. Rep. of the Congo 6°46S 23°58E **52 F4**
Gandak → *India* 25°39N 85°13E **43 G11**
Gandava *Pakistan* 28°32N 67°32E **42 E2**
Gander *Canada* 48°58N 54°35W **73 C9**
Gander L. *Canada* 48°58N 54°35W **73 C9**
Ganderowe Falls
  Zimbabwe 17°20S 29°10E **55 F2**
Gandhi Sagar *India* 24°40N 75°40E **42 G6**
Gandhinagar *India* 23°15N 72°45E **42 H5**
Gandia *Spain* 38°58N 0°9W **21 C5**
Gando, Pta. *Canary Is.* 27°55N 15°22W **24 G4**
Ganedidalem = Gani
  Indonesia 0°48S 128°14E **37 E7**
Ganga → *India* 23°20N 90°30E **43 H14**
Ganga Sagar *India* 21°38N 88°5E **43 J13**
Gangan → *India* 28°38N 78°58E **43 E8**
Ganganagar *India* 29°56N 73°56E **42 E5**
Gangapur *India* 26°32N 76°49E **42 F7**
Gangaw *Burma* 22°5N 94°5E **41 H19**
Gangdisê Shan *China* 31°20N 81°0E **43 D9**
Ganges = Ganga →
  India 23°20N 90°30E **43 H14**
Ganges *Canada* 48°51N 123°31W **70 D4**
Ganges, Mouths of the
  India 21°30N 90°0E **43 J14**
Ganggyeong *S. Korea* 36°10N 127°0E **35 F14**
Ganghwa *S. Korea* 37°45N 126°30E **35 F14**
Gangneung *S. Korea* 37°45N 128°54E **35 F15**
Gangoh *India* 29°46N 77°18E **42 E7**

Gangotri *India* 30°50N 79°10E **43 D8**
Gangotri △ *India* 30°50N 79°10E **43 D8**
Gangseong *S. Korea* 38°24N 128°30F **35 F15**
Gangtok *India* 27°20N 88°37E **41 F16**
Gangu *China* 34°40N 105°15E **34 G3**
Gangyao *China* 44°12N 126°37E **35 B14**
Gani *Indonesia* 0°48S 128°14E **37 E7**
Ganj *India* 27°45N 78°57E **43 F8**
Gannett Peak *U.S.A.* 43°11N 109°39W **76 E9**
Ganquan *China* 36°20N 109°20E **34 F5**
Gansu □ *China* 36°0N 104°0E **34 G3**
Ganta *Liberia* 7°15N 8°59W **50 G4**
Gantheaume, C.
  Australia 36°4S 137°32E **63 F2**
Gantheaume B.
  Australia 27°40S 114°10E **61 E1**
Gantsevichi = Hantsavichy
  Belarus 52°49N 26°30E **17 B14**
Ganyem = Genyem
  Indonesia 2°46S 140°12E **37 E10**
Ganyu *China* 34°50N 119°8E **35 G10**
Ganzhou *China* 25°51N 114°56E **33 D6**
Gao *Mali* 16°15N 0°5W **50 E5**
Gaomi *China* 36°20N 119°42E **35 F10**
Gaoping *China* 35°45N 112°55E **34 G7**
Gaotang *China* 36°50N 116°15E **34 F9**
Gaoua *Burkina Faso* 10°20N 3°8W **50 F5**
Gaoual *Guinea* 11°45N 13°25W **50 F3**
Gaoxiong = Kaohsiung
  Taiwan 22°35N 120°16E **33 D7**
Gaoyang *China* 38°40N 115°45E **34 E8**
Gaoyou Hu *China* 32°45N 119°20E **35 H10**
Gaoyuan *China* 37°8N 117°58E **35 F9**
Gap *France* 44°33N 6°5E **20 D7**
Gapat → *India* 24°30N 82°28E **43 G10**
Gapuwiyak *Australia* 12°25S 135°43E **62 A2**
Gar *China* 32°10N 79°58E **32 C2**
Gara, L. *Ireland* 53°57N 8°26W **10 C3**
Garabogazköl Aylagy
  Turkmenistan 41°0N 53°30E **19 F9**
Garachico *Canary Is.* 28°22N 16°46W **24 F3**
Garachiné *Panama* 8°0N 78°12W **88 E4**
Garafia *Canary Is.* 28°48N 17°57W **24 F2**
Garagum *Turkmenistan* 39°30N 60°0E **45 B8**
Garah *Australia* 29°5S 149°38E **63 D4**
Garajonay *Canary Is.* 28°7N 17°14W **24 F2**
Garamba △
  Dem. Rep. of the Congo 4°10N 29°40E **54 B2**
Garanhuns *Brazil* 8°50S 36°30W **93 E11**
Garautha *India* 25°34N 79°18E **43 G8**
Garawa ☼ *Australia* 16°43S 136°51E **62 B2**
Garba Tula *Kenya* 0°30N 38°32E **54 B4**
Garberville *U.S.A.* 40°6N 123°48W **76 F2**
Garbiyang *India* 30°8N 80°54E **43 D9**
Gard → *France* 43°51N 4°37E **20 E6**
Garda, L. di *Italy* 45°40N 10°41E **22 B4**
Garde L. *Canada* 62°50N 106°13W **71 A7**
Garden City *Ga., U.S.A.* 32°6N 81°9W **85 E14**
Garden City *Kans.,*
  U.S.A. 37°58N 100°53W **80 G3**
Garden City *Tex.,*
  U.S.A. 31°52N 101°29W **84 F4**
Garden Grove *U.S.A.* 33°47N 117°55W **79 M9**
Gardēz *Afghan.* 33°37N 69°9E **42 C3**
Gardiner *Maine, U.S.A.* 44°14N 69°47W **81 C19**
Gardiner *Mont., U.S.A.* 45°2N 110°22W **76 D8**
Gardiners I. *U.S.A.* 41°6N 72°6W **83 E12**
Gardner *U.S.A.* 42°34N 71°59W **83 D13**
Gardner Canal *Canada* 53°27N 128°8W **70 C3**
Gardner Pinnacles
  U.S.A. 25°0N 167°55W **75 L6**
Gardnerville *U.S.A.* 38°56N 119°45W **78 G7**
Gardo = Qardho
  Somali Rep. 9°30N 49°6E **47 F4**
Garey *U.S.A.* 34°53N 120°19W **79 L6**
Garfield *U.S.A.* 47°1N 117°9W **76 C5**
Garforth *U.K.* 53°47N 1°24W **12 D6**
Gargantua, C. *Canada* 47°36N 85°2W **81 B11**
Gargett *Australia* 21°9S 148°46E **62 b**
Garibaldi △ *Canada* 49°50N 122°40W **70 D4**
Gariep, L. *S. Africa* 30°45S 25°40E **56 E4**
Garies *S. Africa* 30°32S 17°59E **56 E2**
Garig Gunak Barlu △
  Australia 11°26S 131°58E **60 B5**
Garigliano → *Italy* 41°13N 13°45E **22 D5**
Garissa *Kenya* 0°25S 39°40E **54 C4**
Garland *Tex., U.S.A.* 32°54N 96°38W **84 E6**
Garland *Utah, U.S.A.* 41°45N 112°10W **76 F7**
Garmāb *Iran* 35°25N 56°45E **45 C8**
Garmisch-Partenkirchen
  Germany 47°30N 11°6E **16 E6**
Garmsār *Iran* 35°20N 52°25E **45 C7**
Garner *U.S.A.* 43°6N 93°36W **80 D7**
Garnett *U.S.A.* 38°17N 95°14W **80 F6**
Garo Hills *India* 25°30N 90°30E **43 G14**
Garoe = Garoowe
  Somali Rep. 8°25N 48°33E **47 F4**
Garonne → *France* 45°2N 0°36W **20 D3**
Garoowe *Somali Rep.* 8°25N 48°33E **47 F4**
Garot *India* 24°19N 75°41E **42 G6**
Garoua *Cameroon* 9°19N 13°21E **51 G8**
Garrauli *India* 25°5N 79°22E **43 G8**
Garrison *Mont., U.S.A.* 46°31N 112°49W **76 C7**
Garrison *N. Dak., U.S.A.* 47°40N 101°25W **80 B3**
Garrison Res. = Sakakawea, L.
  U.S.A. 47°30N 101°25W **80 B3**
Garron Pt. *U.K.* 55°3N 5°59W **10 A6**
Garry → *U.K.* 56°44N 3°47W **11 E5**
Garry, L. *Canada* 65°58N 100°18W **68 D11**
Garrygala *Turkmenistan* 38°31N 56°29E **45 B8**
Garsen *Kenya* 2°20S 40°5E **54 C5**
Garson L. *Canada* 56°19N 110°2W **71 B6**
Garstang *U.K.* 53°55N 2°46W **12 D5**
Garu *India* 23°40N 84°14E **43 H11**
Garub *Namibia* 26°37S 16°0E **56 D2**
Garut *Indonesia* 7°14S 107°53E **37 G12**
Garvie Mts. *N.Z.* 45°30S 168°50E **59 F2**
Garwa = Garoua
  Cameroon 9°19N 13°21E **51 G8**

Garwa *India* 24°11N 83°47E **43** G10
Gary *U.S.A.* 41°36N 87°20W **80** E10
Garzê *China* 31°38N 100°1E **32** C5
Garzón *Colombia* 2°10N 75°40W **92** C3
Gas-San *Japan* 38°32N 140°1E **30** E10
Gasan Kuli = Esenguly
  Turkmenistan 37°37N 53°59E **28** F6
Gascogne *France* 43°45N 0°20E **20** E4
Gascogne, G. de *Europe* 44°0N 2°0W **20** D2
Gascony = Gascogne
  France 43°45N 0°20E **20** E4
Gascoyne → *Australia* 24°52S 113°37E **61** D1
Gascoyne Junction
  Australia 25°2S 115°17E **61** E2
Gashaka *Nigeria* 7°20N 11°29E **51** G8
Gasherbrum *Pakistan* 35°40N 76°40E **43** B7
Gashua *Nigeria* 12°54N 11°0E **51** F8
Gasparillo *Trin. & Tob.* 10°18N 61°26W **93** K15
Gaspé *Canada* 48°52N 64°30W **73** C7
Gaspé, C. de *Canada* 48°48N 64°7W **73** C7
Gaspé Pen. = Gaspésie, Pén. de la
  Canada 48°45N 65°40W **73** C6
Gaspésie, Pén. de la
  Canada 48°45N 65°40W **73** C6
Gaspésie △ *Canada* 48°55N 66°10W **73** C6
Gasteiz = Vitoria-Gasteiz
  Spain 42°50N 2°41W **21** A4
Gastonia *U.S.A.* 35°16N 81°11W **85** D14
Gastre *Argentina* 42°20S 69°15W **96** E3
Gata, C. *Cyprus* 34°34N 33°2E **25** E12
Gata, C. de *Spain* 36°41N 2°13W **21** D4
Gata, Sierra de *Spain* 40°20N 6°45W **21** B2
Gataga → *Canada* 58°35N 126°59W **70** B3
Gatchina *Russia* 59°35N 30°9E **9** G24
Gatehouse of Fleet *U.K.* 54°53N 4°12W **11** G4
Gates *U.S.A.* 43°9N 77°42W **82** C7
Gateshead *U.K.* 54°57N 1°35W **12** C6
Gateshead I. *Canada* 70°36N 100°26W **68** C11
Gatesville *U.S.A.* 31°26N 97°45W **84** F6
Gateway △ *U.S.A.* 40°38N 73°51W **83** F11
Gaths *Zimbabwe* 20°2S 30°32E **55** G3
Gatineau *Canada* 45°29N 75°39W **83** A9
Gatineau → *Canada* 45°27N 75°42W **72** C4
Gatineau △ *Canada* 45°40N 76°0W **72** C4
Gatton *Australia* 27°32S 152°17E **63** D5
Gatún, L. *Panama* 9°7N 79°56W **88** E4
Gatwick, London ✈ (LGW)
  U.K. 51°10N 0°11W **13** F7
Gatyana *S. Africa* 32°16S 28°31E **57** E4
Gau *Fiji* 18°2S 179°18E **59** a
Gauer L. *Canada* 57°0N 97°50W **71** B9
Gauhati = Guwahati
  India 26°10N 91°45E **41** F17
Gauja → *Latvia* 57°10N 24°16E **9** H21
Gaujas △ *Latvia* 57°10N 24°50E **9** H21
Gaula → *Norway* 63°21N 10°14E **8** E14
Gauri Phanta *India* 28°41N 80°36E **43** E9
Gaustatoppen *Norway* 59°48N 8°40E **9** G13
Gauteng □ *S. Africa* 26°0S 28°0E **57** D4
Gāv Koshī *Iran* 28°38N 57°12E **45** D8
Gävakān *Iran* 29°37N 53°10E **45** D7
Gavāter *Iran* 25°10N 61°31E **45** E9
Gāvbandī *Iran* 27°12N 53°4E **45** E7
Gavdopoula *Greece* 34°56N 24°0E **25** E6
Gavdos *Greece* 34°50N 24°5E **25** E6
Gaviota *U.S.A.* 34°29N 120°13W **79** L6
Gāvkhūnī, Bāṭlāq-e *Iran* 32°6N 52°52E **45** C7
Gävle *Sweden* 60°40N 17°9E **8** F17
Gawachab *Namibia* 27°4S 17°55E **56** D2
Gawilgarh Hills *India* 21°15N 76°45E **40** J10
Gawler *Australia* 34°30S 138°42E **63** E2
Gawler Ranges
  Australia 32°30S 135°45E **63** E2
Gaxun Nur *China* 42°22N 100°30E **32** B5
Gay *Russia* 51°27N 58°27E **18** D10
Gaya *India* 24°47N 85°4E **43** G11
Gaya *Niger* 11°52N 3°28E **50** F6
Gaylord *U.S.A.* 45°2N 84°41W **81** C11
Gayndah *Australia* 25°35S 151°32E **63** D5
Gaysin = Haysyn
  Ukraine 48°57N 29°25E **17** D15
Gayvoron = Hayvoron
  Ukraine 48°22N 29°52E **17** D15
Gaza *Gaza Strip* 31°30N 34°28E **46** D3
Gaza □ *Mozam.* 23°10S 32°45E **57** C5
Gaza Strip ■ *Asia* 31°29N 34°25E **46** D3
Gazanjyk = Bereket
  Turkmenistan 39°16N 55°32E **45** B7
Gāžbor *Iran* 28°5N 58°51E **45** D8
Gazi *Dem. Rep. of the Congo* 1°3N 24°30E **54** B1
Gaziantep *Turkey* 37°6N 37°23E **44** B3
Gazimağusa = Famagusta
  Cyprus 35°8N 33°55E **25** D12
Gbadolite
  Dem. Rep. of the Congo 4°17N 21°1E **52** D4
Gbarnga *Liberia* 7°19N 9°13W **50** G4
Gcoverega *Botswana* 19°8S 24°18E **56** B3
Gcuwa *S. Africa* 32°20S 28°11E **57** E4
Gdańsk *Poland* 54°22N 18°40E **17** A10
Gdańska, Zatoka
  Poland 54°30N 19°20E **17** A10
Gdov *Russia* 58°48N 27°55E **9** G22
Gdynia *Poland* 54°35N 18°33E **17** A10
Gebe *Indonesia* 0°5N 129°25E **37** D7
Gebze *Turkey* 40°47N 29°25E **23** D13
Gedaref *Sudan* 14°2N 35°28E **51** F13
Gediz → *Turkey* 38°35N 26°48E **23** E12
Gedser *Denmark* 54°35N 11°55E **9** J14
Gedung, Pulau *Malaysia* 5°17N 100°23E **39** c
Geegully Cr. →
  Australia 18°32S 123°41E **60** C3
Geel *Belgium* 51°10N 4°59E **15** C4
Geelong *Australia* 38°10S 144°22E **63** F3
Geelvink B. = Cenderwasih, Teluk
  Indonesia 3°0S 135°20E **37** E9
Geelvink Chan. *Australia* 28°30S 114°0E **61** E1
Geesthacht *Germany* 53°26N 10°22E **16** B6
Geidam *Nigeria* 12°57N 11°57E **51** F8
Geikie → *Canada* 57°45N 103°52W **71** B8

Geikie Gorge △ *Australia* 18°3S 125°41E **60** C4
Geistown *U.S.A.* 40°18N 78°52W **82** F6
Geita *Tanzania* 2°48S 32°12E **54** C3
Gejiu *China* 23°20N 103°10E **32** D5
Gel, Meydān-e *Iran* 29°4N 54°50E **45** D7
Gela *Italy* 37°4N 14°15E **22** F6
Gelang Patah *Malaysia* 1°27N 103°35E **39** d
Gelderland □ *Neths.* 52°5N 6°10E **15** B6
Geldrop *Neths.* 51°25N 5°32E **15** C5
Geleen *Neths.* 50°57N 5°49E **15** D5
Gelib = Jilib *Somali Rep.* 0°29N 42°46E **47** G3
Gelibolu *Turkey* 40°28N 26°43E **23** D12
Gelsenkirchen *Germany* 51°32N 7°6E **16** C4
Gelugur *Malaysia* 5°22N 100°18E **39** c
Gemas *Malaysia* 2°37N 102°36E **39** L4
Gembloux *Belgium* 50°34N 4°43E **15** D4
Gemena
  Dem. Rep. of the Congo 3°13N 19°48E **52** D3
Gemerek *Turkey* 39°15N 36°10E **44** B3
Gemlik *Turkey* 40°26N 29°9E **23** D13
Gemsbok △ *Botswana* 25°5S 21°1E **56** D3
Genadi *Greece* 36°2N 27°56E **25** C9
Genale → *Ethiopia* 6°2N 39°1E **47** F2
General Acha *Argentina* 37°20S 64°38W **94** D3
General Alvear *B. Aires,*
  Argentina 36°0S 60°0W **94** D4
General Alvear *Mendoza,*
  Argentina 35°0S 67°40W **94** D2
General Artigas
  Paraguay 26°52S 56°16W **94** B4
General Belgrano
  Argentina 36°35S 58°47W **94** D4
General Bernardo O'Higgins
  Antarctica 63°0S 58°3W **5** C18
General Cabrera
  Argentina 32°53S 63°52W **94** C3
General Cepeda *Mexico* 25°21N 101°22W **86** B4
General Guido *Argentina* 36°40S 57°50W **94** D4
General Juan Madariaga
  Argentina 37°0S 57°0W **94** D4
General La Madrid
  Argentina 37°17S 61°20W **94** D3
General MacArthur
  Phil. 11°18N 125°28E **37** B7
General Martín Miguel de Güemes
  Argentina 24°50S 65°0W **94** A3
General Pico *Argentina* 35°45S 63°50W **94** D3
General Pinedo
  Argentina 27°15S 61°20W **94** B3
General Pinto *Argentina* 34°45S 61°50W **94** C3
General Roca *Argentina* 39°2S 67°35W **96** D3
General Santos *Phil.* 6°5N 125°14E **37** C7
General Treviño *Mexico* 26°14N 99°29W **87** B5
General Trías *Mexico* 28°21N 106°22W **86** B3
General Viamonte
  Argentina 35°1S 61°3W **94** D3
General Villegas *Argentina* 35°5S 63°0W **94** D3
Genesee *Idaho, U.S.A.* 46°33N 116°56W **76** C5
Genesee *Pa., U.S.A.* 41°59N 77°54W **82** E7
Genesee → *U.S.A.* 43°16N 77°36W **82** C7
Geneseo *Ill., U.S.A.* 41°27N 90°9W **80** E8
Geneseo *N.Y., U.S.A.* 42°48N 77°49W **82** D7
Geneva = Genève *Switz.* 46°12N 6°9E **20** C7
Geneva *Ala., U.S.A.* 31°2N 85°52W **85** F12
Geneva *N.Y., U.S.A.* 42°52N 76°59W **82** D8
Geneva *Nebr., U.S.A.* 40°32N 97°36W **80** E5
Geneva *Ohio, U.S.A.* 41°48N 80°57W **82** E4
Geneva, L. = Léman, L.
  Europe 46°26N 6°30E **20** C7
Genève *Switz.* 46°12N 6°9E **20** C7
Genil → *Spain* 37°42N 5°19W **21** D3
Genk *Belgium* 50°58N 5°32E **15** D5
Gennargentu, Mti. del
  Italy 40°1N 9°19E **22** D3
Genoa = Génova *Italy* 44°25N 8°57E **20** D8
Genoa *Australia* 37°29S 149°35E **63** F4
Genoa *N.Y., U.S.A.* 42°40N 76°32W **83** D8
Genoa *Nebr., U.S.A.* 41°27N 97°44W **80** E5
Genoa *Nev., U.S.A.* 39°2N 119°50W **78** F7
Génova *Italy* 44°25N 8°57E **20** D8
Génova, G. di *Italy* 44°0N 9°0E **22** C3
Genriyetty, Ostrov
  Russia 77°6N 156°30E **29** B16
Gent *Belgium* 51°2N 3°42E **15** C3
Genteng *Bali, Indonesia* 8°22S 114°9E **37** J17
Genteng *Jawa Barat,*
  Indonesia 7°22S 106°24E **37** G12
Genyem *Indonesia* 2°46S 140°12E **37** E10
Geochang *S. Korea* 35°41N 127°55E **35** G14
Geographe B. *Australia* 33°30S 115°15E **61** F2
Geographe Chan.
  Australia 24°30S 113°0E **61** D1
Georga, Zemlya *Russia* 80°30N 49°0E **28** A5
George *S. Africa* 33°58S 22°29E **56** E3
George → *Canada* 58°49N 66°10W **73** A6
George, L. *N.S.W.,*
  Australia 35°10S 149°25E **63** F4
George, L. *S. Austral.,*
  Australia 37°25S 140°0E **63** F3
George, L. *W. Austral.,*
  Australia 22°45S 123°40E **60** D3
George, L. *Uganda* 0°5N 30°10E **54** B3
George, L. *Fla., U.S.A.* 29°17N 81°36W **85** G5
George, L. *N.Y., U.S.A.* 43°37N 73°33W **83** C11
George Gill Ra.
  Australia 24°22S 131°45E **60** D5
George Pt. *Australia* 20°6S 148°36E **62** b
George River = Kangiqsualujjuaq
  Canada 58°30N 65°59W **69** F18
George Sound *N.Z.* 44°52S 167°25E **59** F1
George Town *Bahamas* 23°33N 75°47W **88** B4
George Town *Cayman Is.* 19°20N 81°24W **88** C3
George Town *Malaysia* 5°25N 100°20E **39** c
George V Land *Antarctica* 69°0S 148°0E **5** C10
George VI Sound
  Antarctica 71°0S 68°0W **5** D17
George West *U.S.A.* 28°20N 98°7W **84** G5
Georgetown = Janjanbureh
  Gambia 13°30N 14°47W **50** F3

Georgetown *Australia* 18°17S 143°33E **62** B3
Georgetown *Ont.,*
  Canada 43°40N 79°56W **82** C5
Georgetown *P.E.I.,*
  Canada 46°13N 62°24W **73** C7
Georgetown *Guyana* 6°50N 58°12W **92** B7
Georgetown *Calif.,*
  U.S.A. 38°54N 120°50W **78** G6
Georgetown *Colo.,*
  U.S.A. 39°42N 105°42W **76** G11
Georgetown *Ky., U.S.A.* 38°13N 84°33W **81** F11
Georgetown *N.Y.,*
  U.S.A. 42°46N 75°44W **83** D9
Georgetown *Ohio,*
  U.S.A. 38°52N 83°54W **81** F12
Georgetown *S.C.,*
  U.S.A. 33°23N 79°17W **85** E15
Georgetown *Tex., U.S.A.* 30°38N 97°41W **84** F6
Georgia □ *U.S.A.* 32°50N 83°15W **85** E13
Georgia ■ *Asia* 42°0N 43°0E **19** F7
Georgia, Str. of *N. Amer.* 49°25N 124°0W **78** A3
Georgia Basin *S. Ocean* 50°45S 35°30W **5** B1
Georgian B. *Canada* 45°15N 81°0W **82** A4
Georgian Bay Islands △
  Canada 44°53N 79°52W **82** B5
Georgiyevka *Kazakhstan* 49°19N 84°34E **28** E9
Georgina → *Australia* 23°30S 139°47E **62** C2
Georgina I. *Canada* 44°22N 79°17W **82** B5
Georgioupoli *Greece* 35°20N 24°15E **25** D6
Georgiyevsk *Russia* 44°12N 43°28E **19** F7
Gera *Germany* 50°53N 12°4E **16** C7
Geraardsbergen *Belgium* 50°45N 3°53E **15** D3
Geral, Serra *Brazil* 26°25S 50°0W **95** B6
Geral de Goiás, Serra
  Brazil 12°0S 46°0W **93** F9
Geraldine *U.S.A.* 47°36N 110°16W **76** C8
Geraldton *Australia* 28°48S 114°32E **61** E1
Geraldton *Canada* 49°44N 86°59W **72** C2
Gerdine, Mt. *U.S.A.* 61°35N 152°27W **74** C9
Gereshk *Afghan.* 31°47N 64°35E **40** D4
Gerik *Malaysia* 5°50N 101°15E **39** K3
Gering *U.S.A.* 41°50N 103°40W **80** E2
Gerlach *U.S.A.* 40°39N 119°21W **76** F4
German Bight = Deutsche Bucht
  Germany 54°15N 8°0E **16** A5
Germansen Landing
  Canada 55°43N 124°40W **70** B4
Germantown *U.S.A.* 35°5N 89°49W **85** D10
Germí *Iran* 39°1N 48°3E **45** B6
Germiston *S. Africa* 26°13S 28°10E **57** D4
Gernika-Lumo *Spain* 43°19N 2°40W **21** A4
Gero *Japan* 35°48N 137°14E **31** G8
Gerokgak *Indonesia* 8°11S 114°27E **37** J17
Gerona = Girona *Spain* 41°58N 2°46E **21** B7
Geropotamos → *Greece* 35°3N 24°50E **25** D6
Gerrard *Canada* 50°30N 117°17W **70** C5
Gertak Sanggul *Malaysia* 5°17N 100°12E **39** c
Gertak Sanggul, Tanjung
  Malaysia 5°16N 100°11E **39** c
Gerung *Indonesia* 8°43S 116°7E **37** K19
Geser *Indonesia* 3°50S 130°54E **37** E8
Getafe *Spain* 40°18N 3°43W **21** B4
Gettysburg *Pa., U.S.A.* 39°50N 77°14W **81** F15
Gettysburg *S. Dak., U.S.A.* 45°1N 99°57W **80** C4
Getxo *Spain* 43°21N 2°59W **21** A4
Getz Ice Shelf *Antarctica* 75°0S 130°0W **5** D14
Geyser *U.S.A.* 47°16N 110°30W **76** C8
Geyserville *U.S.A.* 38°42N 122°54W **78** G4
Ghadāf, W. al → *Iraq* 32°56N 43°30E **44** C4
Ghadāmis *Libya* 30°11N 9°29E **51** B8
Ghaggar → *India* 29°30N 74°53E **42** E6
Ghaghara → *India* 25°45N 84°40E **43** G11
Ghaghat → *Bangla.* 25°19N 89°38E **43** G13
Ghagra *India* 23°17N 84°33E **43** H11
Ghagra → *India* 27°29N 81°9E **43** F9
Ghallamane *Mauritania* 23°15N 10°0W **50** D4
Ghana ■ *W. Afr.* 8°0N 1°0W **50** G5
Ghansor *India* 22°39N 80°1E **43** H9
Ghanzi *Botswana* 21°50S 21°34E **56** C3
Gharb Bahr el Ghazāl □
  Sudan 7°30N 27°30E **48** F6
Ghardaïa *Algeria* 32°20N 3°37E **50** B6
Gharm *Tajikistan* 39°0N 70°20E **28** F8
Gharyān *Libya* 32°10N 13°0E **51** B8
Ghāt *Libya* 24°59N 10°11E **51** D8
Ghatal *India* 22°40N 87°46E **43** H12
Ghatampur *India* 26°8N 80°13E **43** F9
Ghats, Eastern *India* 14°0N 78°50E **40** N11
Ghats, Western *India* 14°0N 75°0E **40** N9
Ghatsila *India* 22°36N 86°29E **43** H12
Ghaṭṭī *Si. Arabia* 31°16N 37°31E **44** D3
Ghawdex = Gozo *Malta* 36°3N 14°15E **25** C1
Ghazal, Bahr el → *Chad* 13°0N 15°47E **51** F9
Ghazāl, Bahr el →
  Sudan 9°31N 30°25E **51** G12
Ghaziabad *India* 28°42N 77°26E **42** E7
Ghazipur *India* 25°38N 83°35E **43** G10
Ghaznī *Afghan.* 33°30N 68°28E **42** C3
Ghaznī □ *Afghan.* 32°10N 68°20E **40** C6
Ghent = Gent *Belgium* 51°2N 3°42E **15** C3
Gheorghe Gheorghiu-Dej = Oneşti
  Romania 46°17N 26°47E **17** E14
Ghīnah, Wādī al →
  Si. Arabia 30°27N 38°14E **44** D3
Ghizar → *Pakistan* 36°15N 73°43E **43** A5
Ghotaru *India* 27°20N 70°1E **42** F4
Ghotki *Pakistan* 28°5N 69°21E **42** E3
Ghowr □ *Afghan.* 34°0N 64°20E **40** C4
Ghughri *India* 22°39N 80°41E **43** H9
Ghugus *India* 19°58N 79°12E **40** K11
Ghulam Mohammad Barrage
  Pakistan 25°30N 68°20E **42** G3
Ghūrīān *Afghan.* 34°17N 61°25E **40** B2
Gia Dinh *Vietnam* 10°49N 106°42E **39** G6
Gia Lai = Plei Ku
  Vietnam 13°57N 108°0E **38** F7
Gia Nghia *Vietnam* 11°58N 107°42E **39** G6
Gia Ngoc *Vietnam* 14°50N 108°58E **38** E7

Gia Vuc *Vietnam* 14°42N 108°34E **38** E7
Giamama = Jamaame
  Somali Rep. 0°4N 42°44E **47** G3
Gianitsa *Greece* 40°46N 22°24E **23** D10
Giant Forest *U.S.A.* 36°36N 118°43W **78** J8
Giant Sequoia △
  U.S.A. 36°10N 118°35W **78** K8
Giants Causeway *U.K.* 55°16N 6°29W **10** A5
Gianyar *Indonesia* 8°32S 115°20E **37** K18
Giarabub = Al Jaghbūb
  Libya 29°42N 24°38E **51** C10
Giarre *Italy* 37°43N 15°11E **22** F6
Gibara *Cuba* 21°9N 76°11W **88** B4
Gibbon *U.S.A.* 40°45N 98°51W **80** E4
Gibeon *Namibia* 25°9S 17°43E **56** D2
Gibraltar ☑ *Europe* 36°7N 5°22W **21** D3
Gibraltar, Str. of *Medit. S.* 35°55N 5°40W **21** E3
Gibraltar Range △
  Australia 29°31S 152°19E **63** D5
Gibson Desert *Australia* 24°0S 126°0E **60** D4
Gibsons *Canada* 49°24N 123°32W **70** D4
Gibsonville *U.S.A.* 39°46N 120°54W **78** F6
Giddings *U.S.A.* 30°11N 96°56W **84** F6
Giebnegáisi = Kebnekaise
  Sweden 67°53N 18°33E **8** C18
Giessen *Germany* 50°34N 8°41E **16** C5
Gīfān *Iran* 37°54N 57°28E **45** B8
Gift Lake *Canada* 55°53N 115°49W **70** B5
Gifu *Japan* 35°30N 136°45E **31** G8
Gifu □ *Japan* 35°40N 137°0E **31** G8
Giganta, Sa. de la
  Mexico 26°0N 111°39W **86** B2
Gíglio *Italy* 42°20N 10°52E **22** C4
Gijón *Spain* 43°32N 5°42W **21** A3
Gikongoro *Rwanda* 2°28S 29°34E **54** C2
Gil I. *Canada* 53°12N 129°15W **70** C3
Gila → *U.S.A.* 32°43N 114°33W **77** K6
Gila Bend *U.S.A.* 32°57N 112°43W **77** K7
Gila Bend Mts. *U.S.A.* 33°10N 113°0W **77** K7
Gila Cliff Dwellings △
  U.S.A. 33°12N 108°16W **77** K9
Gīlān □ *Iran* 37°0N 50°0E **45** B6
Gilbert → *Australia* 16°35S 141°15E **62** B3
Gilbert Is. *Kiribati* 1°0N 172°0E **58** A10
Gilbert River *Australia* 18°9S 142°52E **62** B3
Gilbert Seamounts
  Pac. Oc. 52°50N 150°10W **4** D18
Gilead *U.S.A.* 44°24N 70°59W **83** B14
Gilf el Kebîr, Hadabat el
  Egypt 23°50N 25°50E **51** D11
Gilford I. *Canada* 50°40N 126°30W **70** C3
Gilgandra *Australia* 31°43S 148°39E **63** E4
Gilgil *Kenya* 0°30S 36°20E **54** C4
Gilgit *India* 35°50N 74°15E **43** B6
Gilgit → *Pakistan* 35°44N 74°37E **43** B6
Gili □ *Mozam.* 16°39S 38°27E **55** F4
Gilimanuk *Indonesia* 8°10S 114°26E **37** J17
Gillam *Canada* 56°20N 94°40W **71** B10
Gilles, L. *Australia* 32°50S 136°45E **63** E2
Gillette *U.S.A.* 44°18N 105°30W **76** D11
Gilliat *Australia* 20°40S 141°28E **62** C3
Gillingham *U.K.* 51°23N 0°33E **13** F8
Gilmer *U.S.A.* 32°44N 94°57W **84** E7
Gilmore, L. *Australia* 32°29S 121°37E **61** F3
Gilmour *Canada* 44°48N 77°37W **82** B7
Gilroy *U.S.A.* 37°1N 121°34W **78** H5
Gimcheon *S. Korea* 36°11N 128°4E **35** F15
Gimhae *S. Korea* 35°14N 128°53E **35** G15
Gimhwa *S. Korea* 38°17N 127°28E **35** E14
Gimie, Mt. *St. Lucia* 13°54N 61°0W **89** f
Gimje *S. Korea* 35°48N 126°45E **35** G14
Gimli *Canada* 50°40N 97°0W **71** C9
Gin Gin *Australia* 25°0S 151°58E **63** D5
Gingin *Australia* 31°22S 115°54E **61** F2
Gingindlovu *S. Africa* 29°2S 31°30E **57** D5
Ginir *Ethiopia* 7°6N 40°40E **47** F3
Giofyros → *Greece* 35°20N 25°6E **25** D7
Gioia, Oros *Greece* 38°38N 22°14E **23** E10
Gir △ *India* 21°0N 71°0E **42** J4
Gir Hills *India* 21°0N 71°0E **42** J4
Girab *India* 26°2N 70°38E **42** F4
Girāfī, W. → *Egypt* 29°58N 34°39E **46** F3
Girard *St. Lucia* 13°59N 60°57W **89** D7
Girard *Kans., U.S.A.* 37°31N 94°51W **80** G6
Girard *Ohio, U.S.A.* 41°9N 80°42W **82** E4
Girard *Pa., U.S.A.* 42°0N 80°19W **82** E4
Girardville *Canada* 49°0N 54°58W **73** C9
Girdle Ness *U.K.* 57°9N 2°3W **11** D6
Giresun *Turkey* 40°55N 38°30E **19** F6
Girga *Egypt* 26°17N 31°55E **51** C12
Girga → *India* 30°28N 77°41E **42** D7
Giridih *India* 24°10N 86°21E **43** G12
Giriftu *Kenya* 1°59N 39°46E **54** B4
Giriyondo *S. Africa* 23°15S 31°40E **57** C5
Girne = Kyrenia *Cyprus* 35°20N 33°20E **25** D12
Giron = Kiruna *Sweden* 67°52N 20°15E **8** C19
Girona *Spain* 41°58N 2°46E **21** B7
Gironde → *France* 45°32N 1°7W **20** D3
Girraween △ *Australia* 28°46S 151°54E **63** D5
Giru *Australia* 19°30S 147°5E **62** B4
Girvan *U.K.* 55°14N 4°51W **11** F4
Gisborne *N.Z.* 38°39S 178°5E **59** C7
Gisenyi *Rwanda* 1°41S 29°15E **54** C2
Gislaved *Sweden* 57°19N 13°32E **9** H15
Gitarama *Rwanda* 2°4S 29°45E **54** C2
Gitega *Burundi* 3°26S 29°56E **54** C2
Githio *Greece* 36°46N 22°34E **23** F10
Giuba = Juba →
  Somali Rep. 1°30N 42°35E **47** G3
Giurgiu *Romania* 43°52N 25°57E **17** G13
Giza = El Giza *Egypt* 30°0N 31°12E **51** C12
Giza Pyramids *Egypt* 30°0N 31°10E **51** C12
Gizab *Afghan.* 33°22N 66°17E **42** C1
Gizhiga *Russia* 62°3N 160°30E **29** C17
Gizhiginskaya Guba
  Russia 61°0N 158°0E **29** C16

Giżycko *Poland* 54°2N 21°48E **17** A11
Gjirokastër *Albania* 40°7N 20°10E **23** D9
Gjoa Haven *Canada* 68°38N 95°53W **68** D12
Gjøvik *Norway* 60°47N 10°43E **8** F14
Glace Bay *Canada* 46°11N 59°58W **73** C8
Glacier △ *Canada* 51°15N 117°30W **70** C5
Glacier △ *U.S.A.* 48°42N 113°48E **76** B7
Glacier Bay *U.S.A.* 58°40N 136°0W **68** F4
Glacier Bay △ *U.S.A.* 58°45N 136°30W **70** B1
Glacier Peak *U.S.A.* 48°7N 121°7W **78** B5
Gladewater *U.S.A.* 32°33N 94°56W **84** E7
Gladstone *Queens.,*
  Australia 23°52S 151°16E **62** C5
Gladstone *S. Austral.,*
  Australia 33°15S 138°22E **63** E2
Gladstone *Canada* 50°13N 98°57W **71** C9
Gladstone *U.S.A.* 45°51N 87°1W **80** C10
Gladwin *U.S.A.* 43°59N 84°29W **81** D11
Glagah *Indonesia* 8°13S 114°18E **37** J17
Glåma = Glomma →
  Norway 59°12N 10°57E **9** G14
Gláma *Iceland* 65°48N 23°0W **8** D2
Glamis *U.S.A.* 32°55N 115°5W **79** N11
Glamorgan, Vale of □
  U.K. 51°28N 3°25W **13** F4
Glasco *Kans., U.S.A.* 39°22N 97°50W **80** F5
Glasco *N.Y., U.S.A.* 42°3N 73°57W **83** D11
Glasgow *U.K.* 55°51N 4°15W **11** F4
Glasgow *Ky., U.S.A.* 37°0N 85°55W **81** G11
Glasgow *Mont., U.S.A.* 48°12N 106°38W **76** B10
Glasgow, City of □ *U.K.* 55°51N 4°12W **11** F4
Glasgow Int. ✈ (GLA)
  U.K. 55°51N 4°21W **11** F4
Glaslyn *Canada* 53°22N 108°21E **71** C7
Glastonbury *U.K.* 51°9N 2°43W **13** F5
Glastonbury *U.S.A.* 41°43N 72°37W **83** E12
Glazov *Russia* 58°9N 52°40E **18** C9
Gleichen *Canada* 50°52N 113°3W **70** C6
Gleiwitz = Gliwice
  Poland 50°22N 18°41E **17** C10
Glen *U.S.A.* 44°7N 71°11W **83** B13
Glen Affric □ *U.K.* 57°17N 5°1W **11** D3
Glen Canyon *U.S.A.* 37°30N 110°40W **77** H8
Glen Canyon △ *U.S.A.* 37°15N 111°0W **77** H8
Glen Canyon Dam
  U.S.A. 36°57N 111°29W **77** H8
Glen Coe *U.K.* 56°40N 5°0E **11** E3
Glen Cove *U.S.A.* 40°51N 73°38W **83** F11
Glen Garry *U.K.* 57°3N 5°7W **11** D3
Glen Innes *Australia* 29°44S 151°44E **63** D5
Glen Lyon *U.S.A.* 41°10N 76°5W **83** E8
Glen Mor *U.K.* 57°9N 4°37W **11** D4
Glen More *U.K.* 57°8N 3°40W **11** D5
Glen Moriston *U.K.* 57°11N 4°52W **11** D4
Glen Robertson *Canada* 45°22N 74°30W **83** A10
Glen Spean *U.K.* 56°53N 4°40W **11** E4
Glen Ullin *U.S.A.* 46°49N 101°50W **80** B3
Glenariff △ *Ireland* 55°6N 6°10W **10** A5
Glenbeigh *Ireland* 52°3N 9°58W **10** D2
Glencoe *Canada* 42°45N 81°43W **82** D3
Glencoe *S. Africa* 28°11S 30°11E **57** D5
Glencoe *U.S.A.* 44°46N 94°9W **80** C6
Glencolumbkille *Ireland* 54°43N 8°42W **10** B3
Glendale *Ariz., U.S.A.* 33°32N 112°11W **77** K7
Glendale *Calif., U.S.A.* 34°9N 118°15W **79** L8
Glendale *Zimbabwe* 17°22S 31°5E **55** F3
Glendive *U.S.A.* 47°7N 104°43W **76** C11
Glendo *U.S.A.* 42°30N 105°2W **76** E11
Glenelg → *Australia* 38°4S 140°59E **63** F3
Glenfield *U.S.A.* 43°43N 75°24W **83** C9
Glengad Hd. *Ireland* 55°20N 7°10W **10** A4
Glengarriff *Ireland* 51°45N 9°34W **10** E2
Glenmont *U.S.A.* 40°31N 82°6W **82** F2
Glenmorgan *Australia* 27°14S 149°42E **63** D4
Glenn *U.S.A.* 39°31N 122°1W **78** F4
Glennallen *U.S.A.* 62°7N 145°33W **68** E2
Glennamaddy *Ireland* 53°37N 8°33W **10** C3
Glenns Ferry *U.S.A.* 42°57N 115°18W **76** E6
Glenora *Canada* 44°2N 77°3W **82** B7
Glenorchy *Australia* 42°49S 147°18E **63** G4
Glenore *Australia* 17°50S 141°12E **62** B3
Glenreagh *Australia* 30°2S 153°1E **63** E5
Glenrock *U.S.A.* 42°52N 105°52W **76** E11
Glenrothes *U.K.* 56°12N 3°10W **11** E5
Glens Falls *U.S.A.* 43°19N 73°39W **83** C11
Glenside *U.S.A.* 40°6N 75°9W **83** F9
Glenties *Ireland* 54°49N 8°16W **10** B3
Glenveagh △ *Ireland* 55°3N 8°1W **10** A3
Glenville *U.S.A.* 38°56N 80°50W **81** F13
Glenwood *Canada* 49°0N 54°58W **73** C9
Glenwood *Ark., U.S.A.* 34°20N 93°33W **84** D8
Glenwood *Iowa, U.S.A.* 41°3N 95°45W **80** E6
Glenwood *Minn., U.S.A.* 45°39N 95°23W **80** C6
Glenwood *Wash., U.S.A.* 46°1N 121°17W **78** D5
Glenwood Springs
  U.S.A. 39°33N 107°19W **76** G10
Glettinganes *Iceland* 65°30N 13°37W **8** D7
Glin *Ireland* 52°34N 9°17W **10** D2
Gliwice *Poland* 50°22N 18°41E **17** C10
Globe *U.S.A.* 33°24N 110°47W **77** K8
Głogów *Poland* 51°37N 16°5E **16** C9
Glomma → *Norway* 59°12N 10°57E **9** G14
Glorieuses, Îs. *Ind. Oc.* 11°30S 47°20E **57** A8
Glossop *U.K.* 53°27N 1°56W **12** D6
Gloucester *Australia* 32°0S 151°59E **63** E5
Gloucester *U.K.* 51°53N 2°15W **13** F5
Gloucester *U.S.A.* 42°37N 70°40W **83** D14
Gloucester I. *Australia* 20°0S 148°30E **62** b
Gloucester Island △
  Australia 20°2S 148°30E **62** b
Gloucester Point
  U.S.A. 37°15N 76°30W **81** G15
Gloucestershire □ *U.K.* 51°46N 2°15W **13** F5
Gloversville *U.S.A.* 43°3N 74°21W **83** C10
Glovertown *Canada* 48°40N 54°3W **73** C9
Glusk *Belarus* 52°53N 28°41E **17** B15
Gmünd *Austria* 48°45N 15°0E **16** D8
Gmunden *Austria* 47°55N 13°48E **16** E7
Gniezno *Poland* 52°30N 17°35E **17** B9

Gnowangerup *Australia* 33°58S 117°59E **61** F2
Go Cong *Vietnam* 10°22N 106°40E **39** G6
Gō-no-ura *Japan* 33°44N 129°40E **31** H4
Goa *India* 15°33N 73°59E **40** M8
Goa □ *India* 15°33N 73°59E **40** M8
Goalen Hd. *Australia* 36°33S 150°4E **63** F5
Goalpara *India* 26°10N 90°40E **41** F17
Goaltor *India* 22°43N 87°10E **43** H12
Goalundo Ghat *Bangla.* 23°50N 89°47E **43** H13
Goat Fell *U.K.* 55°38N 5°11W **11** F3
Goba *Ethiopia* 7°1N 39°59E **47** F2
Goba *Mozam.* 26°15S 32°13E **57** D5
Gobabis *Namibia* 22°30S 19°0E **56** C2
Gobi *Asia* 44°0N 110°0E **34** C6
Gobō *Japan* 33°53N 135°10E **31** H7
Gochas *Namibia* 24°59S 18°55E **56** C2
Godalming *U.K.* 51°11N 0°36W **13** F7
Godavari → *India* 16°25N 82°18E **41** L13
Godavari Pt. *India* 17°0N 82°20E **41** L13
Godbout *Canada* 49°20N 67°38W **73** C6
Godda *India* 24°50N 87°13E **43** G12
Goderich *Canada* 43°45N 81°41W **82** C3
Godfrey Ra. *Australia* 24°0S 117°0E **60** D2
Godhavn = Qeqertarsuaq
　Greenland 69°15N 53°38W **4** C5
Godhra *India* 22°49N 73°40E **42** H5
Godoy Cruz *Argentina* 32°56S 68°52W **94** C2
Gods → *Canada* 56°22N 92°51W **72** A1
Gods L. *Canada* 54°40N 94°15W **72** B1
Gods River *Canada* 54°50N 94°5W **71** C10
Godthåb = Nuuk
　Greenland 64°10N 51°35W **67** C14
Goeie Hoop, Kaap die = Good
　Hope, C. of *S. Africa* 34°24S 18°30E **56** E2
Goéland, L. au *Canada* 49°50N 76°48W **72** C4
Goélands, L. aux *Canada* 55°27N 64°17W **73** A7
Goeree *Neths.* 51°50N 4°0E **15** C3
Goes *Neths.* 51°30N 3°55E **15** C3
Goffstown *U.S.A.* 43°1N 71°36W **83** C13
Gogama *Canada* 47°35N 81°43W **72** C3
Gogebic, L. *U.S.A.* 46°30N 89°35W **80** B9
Gogra = Ghaghara →
　India 25°45N 84°40E **43** G11
Gogrial *Sudan* 8°30N 28°8E **51** G11
Gohana *India* 29°8N 76°42E **42** E7
Goharganj *India* 23°1N 77°41E **42** H7
Goi → *India* 22°4N 74°46E **42** H6
Goiânia *Brazil* 16°43S 49°20W **93** G9
Goiás *Brazil* 15°55S 50°10W **93** G8
Goiás □ *Brazil* 12°10S 48°0W **93** F9
Goio-Erê *Brazil* 24°12S 53°1W **95** A5
Gojō *Japan* 34°21N 135°42E **31** G7
Gojra *Pakistan* 31°10N 72°40E **42** D5
Gökçeada *Turkey* 40°10N 25°50E **23** D11
Gökova Körfezi *Turkey* 36°55N 27°50E **23** F12
Göksu → *Turkey* 36°19N 34°5E **44** B2
Gokteik *Burma* 22°26N 97°0E **41** H20
Gokurt *Pakistan* 29°40N 67°26E **42** E2
Gokwe *Zimbabwe* 18°7S 28°58E **57** B4
Gola *India* 28°3N 80°32E **43** E9
Golakganj *India* 26°8N 89°52E **43** F13
Golan Heights = Hagolan
　Syria 33°0N 35°45E **46** C4
Goläshkerd *Iran* 27°59N 57°16E **45** E8
Golchikha *Russia* 71°45N 83°30E **4** B12
Golconda *U.S.A.* 40°58N 117°30W **76** F5
Gold *U.S.A.* 41°52N 77°50W **82** E7
Gold Beach *U.S.A.* 42°25N 124°25W **76** E1
Gold Coast *W. Afr.* 4°0N 1°40W **50** H5
Gold Hill *U.S.A.* 42°26N 123°3W **76** E2
Gold River *Canada* 49°46N 126°3W **70** D3
Golden *Canada* 51°20N 116°59W **70** C5
Golden B. *N.Z.* 40°40S 172°50E **59** D4
Golden Gate *U.S.A.* 37°54N 122°29W **77** H2
Golden Gate Highlands △
　S. Africa 28°40S 28°40E **57** D4
Golden Hinde *Canada* 49°40N 125°44W **70** D3
Golden Lake *Canada* 45°34N 77°21W **82** A7
Golden Spike △ *U.S.A.* 41°37N 112°33W **76** F7
Golden Vale *Ireland* 52°33N 8°17W **10** D3
Goldendale *U.S.A.* 45°49N 120°50W **76** D3
Goldfield *U.S.A.* 37°42N 117°14W **77** H5
Goldsand L. *Canada* 57°2N 101°8W **71** B8
Goldsboro *U.S.A.* 35°23N 77°59W **85** D16
Goldsmith *U.S.A.* 31°59N 102°37W **84** F3
Goldthwaite *U.S.A.* 31°27N 98°34W **84** F5
Goleniów *Poland* 53°35N 14°50E **16** B8
Golestän □ *Iran* 37°20N 55°25E **45** B7
Golestänak *Iran* 30°36N 54°14E **45** D7
Goleta *U.S.A.* 34°27N 119°50W **79** L7
Golfito *Costa Rica* 8°41N 83°5W **88** E3
Golfo Aranci *Italy* 40°59N 9°38E **22** D3
Goliad *U.S.A.* 28°40N 97°23W **84** G6
Golpäyegän *Iran* 33°27N 50°18E **45** C6
Golra *Pakistan* 33°37N 72°56E **42** C5
Golspie *U.K.* 57°58N 3°59W **11** D5
Goma
　Dem. Rep. of the Congo 1°37S 29°10E **54** C2
Gomal Pass *Pakistan* 31°56N 69°20E **42** D3
Gomati → *India* 25°32N 83°11E **43** G10
Gombari
　Dem. Rep. of the Congo 2°45N 29°3E **54** B2
Gombe *Nigeria* 10°19N 11°2E **51** F8
Gombe → *Tanzania* 4°38S 31°40E **54** C3
Gombe Stream △
　Tanzania 4°42S 29°37E **54** C2
Gomel = Homyel *Belarus* 52°28N 31°0E **17** B16
Gomera *Canary Is.* 28°7N 17°14W **24** F2
Gómez Palacio *Mexico* 25°34N 103°30W **86** B4
Gomīshān *Iran* 37°4N 54°6E **45** B7
Gomogomo *Indonesia* 6°39S 134°43E **37** F8
Gomoh *India* 23°52N 86°10E **43** H12
Gompa = Ganta *Liberia* 7°15N 8°59W **50** G4
Gonābād *Iran* 34°15N 58°45E **45** C8
Gonaïves *Haiti* 19°20N 72°42W **89** C5
Gonâve, G. de la *Haiti* 19°29N 72°42W **89** C5
Gonâve, Île de la *Haiti* 18°51N 73°3W **89** C5
Gonbad-e Kāvūs *Iran* 37°20N 55°25E **45** B7

Gonda *India* 27°9N 81°58E **43** F9
Gondal *India* 21°58N 70°52E **42** J4
Gonder *Ethiopia* 12°39N 37°30E **47** E2
Gondia *India* 21°23N 80°10E **40** J12
Gondola *Mozam.* 19°10S 33°37E **55** F3
Gönen *Turkey* 40°6N 27°39E **23** D12
Gongbei *China* 22°12N 113°32E **33** G10
Gonghe *China* 36°18N 100°32E **32** C5
Gongju *S. Korea* 36°27N 127°7E **35** F14
Gongming *China* 22°47N 113°53E **33** F10
Gongolgon *Australia* 30°21S 146°54E **63** E4
Gongzhuling *China* 43°30N 124°40E **35** C13
Goniri *Nigeria* 11°30N 12°15E **51** F8
Gonzales *Calif., U.S.A.* 36°30N 121°26W **78** J5
Gonzales *Tex., U.S.A.* 29°30N 97°27W **84** G6
González *Mexico* 22°48N 98°25W **87** C5
Good Hope, C. of *S. Africa* 34°24S 18°30E **56** E2
Good Hope Lake
　Canada 59°16N 129°18W **70** B3
Gooderham *Canada* 44°54N 78°21W **82** B6
Goodhouse *S. Africa* 28°57S 18°13E **56** D2
Gooding *U.S.A.* 42°56N 114°43W **76** E6
Goodland *U.S.A.* 39°21N 101°43W **80** F3
Goodlands *Mauritius* 20°2S 57°39E **53** d
Goodlow *Canada* 56°20N 120°8W **70** B4
Goodooga *Australia* 29°3S 147°28E **63** D4
Goodsprings *U.S.A.* 35°49N 115°27W **79** K11
Goole *U.K.* 53°42N 0°53W **12** D7
Goolgowi *Australia* 33°58S 145°41E **63** E4
Goomalling *Australia* 31°15S 116°49E **61** F2
Goomeri *Australia* 26°12S 152°6E **63** D5
Goonda *Mozam.* 19°48S 33°57E **55** F3
Goondiwindi *Australia* 28°30S 150°21E **63** D5
Goongarrie, L. *Australia* 30°3S 121°9E **61** F3
Goongarrie △ *Australia* 30°7S 121°30E **61** F3
Goonyella *Australia* 21°47S 147°58E **62** C4
Goose → *Canada* 53°20N 60°35W **73** B7
Goose Creek *U.S.A.* 32°59N 80°2W **85** E14
Goose L. *U.S.A.* 41°56N 120°26W **76** F3
Gop *India* 22°5N 69°50E **42** H3
Gopalganj *India* 26°28N 84°30E **43** F11
Göppingen *Germany* 48°42N 9°39E **16** D5
Gorakhpur *India* 26°47N 83°23E **43** F10
Goražde *Bos.-H.* 43°38N 18°58E **23** C8
Gorda, Pta. *Canary Is.* 28°45N 18°0W **24** F2
Gorda, Pta. *Nic.* 14°20N 83°10W **88** D3
Gordan B. *Australia* 11°35S 130°10E **60** B5
Gordon *U.S.A.* 42°48N 102°12W **80** D2
Gordon → *Australia* 42°27S 145°30E **63** G4
Gordon Bay *Canada* 45°12N 79°47W **82** A5
Gordon L., Alta., Canada* 56°30N 110°25W **71** B6
Gordon L. *N.W.T.,*
　Canada 63°5N 113°11W **70** A6
Gordonvale *Australia* 17°5S 145°50E **62** B4
Goré *Chad* 7°59N 16°31E **51** G9
Gore *Ethiopia* 8°12N 35°32E **47** F2
Gore *N.Z.* 46°5S 168°58E **59** G2
Gore Bay *Canada* 45°57N 82°28W **72** C3
Gorey *Ireland* 52°41N 6°18W **10** D5
Gorg *Iran* 29°29N 59°43E **45** D8
Gorgān *Iran* 36°55N 54°30E **45** B7
Gorgona, I. *Colombia* 3°0N 78°10W **92** C3
Gorham *U.S.A.* 44°23N 71°10W **83** B13
Goriganga → *India* 29°45N 80°23E **43** E9
Gorinchem *Neths.* 51°50N 4°59E **15** C4
Goris *Armenia* 39°31N 46°22E **19** G8
Gorizia *Italy* 45°56N 13°37E **22** B5
Gorkiy = Nizhniy Novgorod
　Russia 56°20N 44°0E **18** C7
Gorkovskoye Vdkhr.
　Russia 57°2N 43°4E **18** C7
Gorleston *U.K.* 52°35N 1°44E **13** E9
Gorlovka = Horlivka
　Ukraine 48°19N 38°5E **19** E6
Gorman *U.S.A.* 34°47N 118°51W **79** L8
Gorna Dzhumayo = Blagoevgrad
　Bulgaria 42°2N 23°5E **23** C10
Gorna Oryakhovitsa
　Bulgaria 43°7N 25°40E **23** C11
Gorno-Altay □ *Russia* 51°0N 86°0E **28** D9
Gorno-Altaysk *Russia* 51°50N 86°5E **28** D9
Gornozavodsk *Russia* 46°33N 141°50E **29** E15
Gornyatski *Russia* 67°32N 64°3E **18** A11
Gornyy *Russia* 44°57N 133°59E **30** B6
Gorodenka = Horodenka
　Ukraine 48°41N 25°29E **17** D13
Gorodok = Horodok
　Ukraine 49°46N 23°32E **17** D12
Gorokhov = Horokhiv
　Ukraine 50°30N 24°45E **17** C13
Goromonzi *Zimbabwe* 17°52S 31°22E **55** F3
Gorong, Kepulauan
　Indonesia 3°59S 131°25E **37** E8
Gorongosa △ *Mozam.* 18°50S 34°29E **57** B5
Gorongose → *Mozam.* 20°30S 34°40E **57** C5
Gorongoza *Mozam.* 18°44S 34°2E **55** F3
Gorongoza, Sa. da *Mozam.* 18°27S 34°2E **55** F3
Gorontalo *Indonesia* 0°35N 123°5E **37** D6
Gorontalo □ *Indonesia* 0°50N 122°20E **37** D6
Gort *Ireland* 53°3N 8°49W **10** C3
Gortis *Greece* 35°4N 24°58E **25** D6
Goryeong *S. Korea* 35°44N 128°15E **35** G15
Gorzów Wielkopolski
　Poland 52°43N 15°15E **16** B8
Gosford *Australia* 33°23S 151°18E **63** E5
Goshen *Calif., U.S.A.* 36°21N 119°25W **78** J7
Goshen *Ind., U.S.A.* 41°35N 85°50W **81** E11
Goshen *N.Y., U.S.A.* 41°24N 74°20W **83** E10
Goshogawara *Japan* 40°48N 140°27E **30** D10
Goslar *Germany* 51°54N 10°25E **16** C6
Gospič *Croatia* 44°35N 15°23E **16** F8
Gosport *U.K.* 50°48N 1°9W **13** G6
Gosse → *Australia* 19°32S 134°37E **62** B1
Göta älv → *Sweden* 57°42N 11°54E **9** H14
Göta kanal *Sweden* 58°30N 15°58E **9** G16
Götaland *Sweden* 57°30N 14°30E **9** H16
Göteborg *Sweden* 57°43N 11°59E **9** H14
Gotha *Germany* 50°56N 10°42E **16** C6

Gothenburg = Göteborg
　Sweden 57°43N 11°59E **9** H14
Gothenburg *U.S.A.* 40°56N 100°10W **80** E3
Gotland *Sweden* 57°30N 18°33E **9** H18
Gotska Sandön *Sweden* 58°24N 19°15E **9** G18
Gōtsu *Japan* 35°0N 132°14E **31** G6
Göttingen *Germany* 51°31N 9°55E **16** C5
Gottwaldov = Zlín
　Czech Rep. 49°14N 17°40E **17** D9
Goubangzi *China* 41°20N 121°52E **35** D11
Gouda *Neths.* 52°1N 4°42E **15** B4
Goudouras, Akra *Greece* 34°59N 26°6E **25** E8
Gouin, Rés. *Canada* 48°35N 74°40W **72** C5
Goulburn *Australia* 34°44S 149°44E **63** E4
Goulburn Is. *Australia* 11°40S 133°20E **62** A1
Goulimine *Morocco* 28°56N 10°0W **50** C3
Goundam *Mali* 16°27N 3°40W **50** E5
Gourits → *S. Africa* 34°21S 21°52E **56** E3
Gournes *Greece* 35°19N 25°16E **25** D7
Gourock *U.K.* 55°57N 4°49W **11** F4
Gouverneur *U.S.A.* 44°20N 75°28W **83** B9
Gouvia *Greece* 39°39N 19°50E **25** A3
Gove Peninsula
　Australia 12°17S 136°49E **62** A2
Governador Valadares
　Brazil 18°15S 41°57W **93** G10
Governor's Harbour
　Bahamas 25°10N 76°14W **88** A4
Govindgarh *India* 24°23N 81°18E **43** G9
Gowan Ra. *Australia* 25°0S 145°0E **62** C4
Gowanda *U.S.A.* 42°28N 78°56W **82** D6
Gower *U.K.* 51°35N 4°10W **13** F3
Gowna, L. *Ireland* 53°51N 7°34W **10** C4
Goya *Argentina* 29°10S 59°10W **94** B4
Goyang *S. Korea* 37°39N 126°50E **33** C7
Goyder Lagoon *Australia* 27°3S 138°58E **63** D2
Goyllarisquizga *Peru* 10°31S 76°24W **92** F3
Goz Beïda *Chad* 12°10N 21°20E **51** F10
Gozo *Malta* 36°3N 14°15E **25** C1
Graaff-Reinet *S. Africa* 32°13S 24°32E **56** E3
Gračac *Croatia* 44°18N 15°57E **16** F8
Gracias a Dios, C.
　Honduras 15°0N 83°10W **88** D3
Graciosa *Azores* 39°4N 28°0W **50** a
Graciosa, I. *Canary Is.* 29°15N 13°32W **24** E6
Grado *Spain* 43°23N 6°4W **21** A2
Grady *U.S.A.* 34°49N 103°19W **77** J12
Grafham Water *U.K.* 52°19N 0°18W **13** E7
Grafton *Australia* 29°38S 152°58E **63** D5
Grafton *N. Dak., U.S.A.* 48°25N 97°25W **80** A5
Grafton *W. Va., U.S.A.* 39°21N 80°2W **81** F13
Graham *Canada* 49°20N 90°30W **72** C1
Graham *U.S.A.* 33°6N 98°35W **84** E5
Graham, Mt. *U.S.A.* 32°42N 109°52W **77** K9
Graham Bell, Ostrov = Greem-
　Bell, Ostrov *Russia* 81°0N 62°0E **28** A7
Graham I. *B.C., Canada* 53°40N 132°30W **70** C2
Graham I. *Nunavut,*
　Canada 77°25N 90°30W **69** B13
Graham Land *Antarctica* 65°0S 64°0W **5** C17
Grahamstown *S. Africa* 33°19S 26°31E **56** E4
Grahamsville *U.S.A.* 41°51N 74°33W **83** E10
Grain Coast *W. Afr.* 4°20N 10°0W **50** H3
Grajagan *Indonesia* 8°35S 114°13E **37** K17
Grajagan, Teluk
　Indonesia 8°40S 114°18E **37** K17
Grajaú *Brazil* 5°50S 46°4W **93** E9
Grajaú → *Brazil* 3°41S 44°48W **93** D10
Grampian *U.S.A.* 40°58N 78°37W **82** F6
Grampian Highlands = Grampian
　Mts. *U.K.* 56°50N 4°0W **11** E5
Grampian Mts. *U.K.* 56°50N 4°0W **11** E5
Grampians, The
　Australia 37°15S 142°20E **63** F3
Gran Canaria *Canary Is.* 27°55N 15°35W **24** G4
Gran Chaco *S. Amer.* 25°0S 61°0W **94** B3
Gran Desierto del Pinacate △
　Mexico 31°51N 113°32W **86** A2
Gran Paradiso *Italy* 45°33N 7°17E **20** D7
Gran Sasso d'Itália *Italy* 42°27N 13°42E **22** C5
Granada *Nic.* 11°58N 86°0W **88** D2
Granada *Spain* 37°10N 3°35W **21** D4
Granada *U.S.A.* 38°4N 102°19W **76** G12
Granadilla de Abona
　Canary Is. 28°7N 16°33W **24** F3
Granard *Ireland* 53°47N 7°30W **10** C4
Granbury *U.S.A.* 32°27N 97°47W **84** E6
Granby *Canada* 45°25N 72°45W **83** A12
Granby *U.S.A.* 40°5N 105°56W **76** F11
Grand → *Canada* 42°51N 79°34W **82** D5
Grand → *Mo., U.S.A.* 39°23N 93°7W **80** F7
Grand → *S. Dak.,*
　U.S.A. 45°40N 100°45W **80** C3
Grand Bahama I.
　Bahamas 26°40N 78°30W **88** A4
Grand Baie *Mauritius* 20°0S 57°35E **53** d
Grand Bank *Canada* 47°6N 55°48W **73** C8
Grand Bassam *Ivory C.* 5°10N 3°49W **50** H5
Grand Bend *Canada* 43°18N 81°45W **82** C3
Grand Bourg *Guadeloupe* 15°53N 61°19W **88** b
Grand Canal = Da Yunhe →
　China 39°10N 117°10E **35** E9
Grand Canyon *U.S.A.* 36°3N 112°9W **77** H7
Grand Canyon △
　U.S.A. 36°15N 112°30W **77** H7
Grand Canyon-Parashant △
　U.S.A. 36°30N 113°45W **77** H7
Grand Cayman
　Cayman Is. 19°20N 81°20W **88** C3
Grand Coulee *U.S.A.* 47°57N 119°0W **76** C4
Grand Coulee Dam
　U.S.A. 47°57N 118°59W **76** C4
Grand Erg de Bilma *Niger* 18°30N 14°0E **51** E8
Grand Falls *Canada* 47°3N 67°44W **73** C6
Grand Falls-Windsor
　Canada 48°56N 55°40W **73** C8
Grand Forks *Canada* 49°0N 118°30W **70** D5
Grand Forks *U.S.A.* 47°55N 97°3W **80** B5

Grand Gorge *U.S.A.* 42°21N 74°29W **83** D10
Grand Haven *U.S.A.* 43°4N 86°13W **80** D10
Grand I. *Mich., U.S.A.* 46°31N 86°40W **80** B10
Grand I. *N.Y., U.S.A.* 43°0N 78°58W **82** D6
Grand Island *U.S.A.* 40°55N 98°21W **80** E4
Grand Isle *La., U.S.A.* 29°14N 90°0W **85** G9
Grand Isle *Vt., U.S.A.* 44°43N 73°18W **83** B11
Grand Junction *U.S.A.* 39°4N 108°33W **76** G9
Grand L. *N.B., Canada* 45°57N 66°7W **73** C6
Grand L. *Nfld. & L.,*
　Canada 49°0N 57°30W **73** C8
Grand L. *Nfld. & L.,*
　Canada 53°40N 60°30W **73** B7
Grand L. *U.S.A.* 29°55N 92°47W **84** G8
Grand Lake *U.S.A.* 40°15N 105°49W **76** F11
Grand Manan I. *Canada* 44°45N 66°52W **73** D6
Grand Marais *Mich.,*
　U.S.A. 46°40N 85°59W **81** B11
Grand Marais *Minn.,*
　U.S.A. 47°45N 90°25W **72** C1
Grand-Mère *Canada* 46°36N 72°40W **72** C5
Grand Portage *U.S.A.* 47°58N 89°41W **80** B9
Grand Prairie *U.S.A.* 32°44N 96°59W **84** E6
Grand Rapids *Canada* 53°12N 99°19W **71** C9
Grand Rapids *Mich.,*
　U.S.A. 42°58N 85°40W **81** D11
Grand Rapids *Minn.,*
　U.S.A. 47°14N 93°31W **80** B7
Grand St-Bernard, Col du
　Europe 45°50N 7°10E **20** D7
Grand Staircase-Escalante △
　U.S.A. 37°25N 111°33W **77** H8
Grand Teton *U.S.A.* 43°54N 110°50W **76** E8
Grand Teton △ *U.S.A.* 43°50N 110°50W **76** E8
Grand Union Canal *U.K.* 52°7N 0°53W **13** E7
Grande → *Jujuy,*
　Argentina 24°20S 65°2W **94** A2
Grande → *Mendoza,*
　Argentina 36°52S 69°45W **94** D2
Grande → *Bolivia* 15°51S 64°39W **92** G6
Grande → *Bahia, Brazil* 11°30S 44°30W **93** F10
Grande → *Minas Gerais,*
　Brazil 20°6S 51°4W **93** H8
Grande, B. *Argentina* 50°30S 68°20W **96** G3
Grande, Rio → *N. Amer.* 25°58N 97°9W **84** J6
Grande Anse *Seychelles* 4°18S 55°45E **53** b
Grande Baleine →
　Canada 55°16N 77°47W **72** A4
Grande Cache *Canada* 53°53N 119°8W **70** C5
Grande Comore
　Comoros Is. 11°35S 43°20E **53** a
Grande-Entrée *Canada* 47°30N 61°40W **73** C7
Grande Prairie *Canada* 55°10N 118°50W **70** B5
Grande-Rivière *Canada* 48°26N 64°30W **73** C7
Grande-Terre *Guadeloupe* 16°20N 61°25W **88** b
Grande-Vallée *Canada* 49°14N 65°8W **73** C6
Grande Vigie, Pte. de la
　Guadeloupe 16°32N 61°27W **88** b
Grandfalls *U.S.A.* 31°20N 102°51W **84** F3
Grands-Jardins △
　Canada 47°41N 70°51W **73** C5
Grandview *Canada* 51°10N 100°42W **71** C8
Grandview *U.S.A.* 46°15N 119°54W **76** C4
Graneros *Chile* 34°5S 70°45W **94** C1
Grangemouth *U.K.* 56°1N 3°42W **11** E5
Granger *U.S.A.* 41°35N 109°58W **76** F9
Grangeville *U.S.A.* 45°56N 116°7W **76** D5
Granisle *Canada* 54°53N 126°13W **70** C3
Granite City *U.S.A.* 38°42N 90°8W **80** F8
Granite Falls *U.S.A.* 44°49N 95°33W **80** C6
Granite L. *Canada* 48°8N 57°5W **73** C8
Granite Mt. *U.S.A.* 33°5N 116°28W **79** M10
Granite Pk. *U.S.A.* 45°10N 109°48W **76** D9
Graniteville *U.S.A.* 44°8N 72°29W **83** B12
Granity *N.Z.* 41°39S 171°51E **59** D3
Granja *Brazil* 3°7S 40°50W **93** D10
Granollers *Spain* 41°39N 2°18E **21** B7
Grant *U.S.A.* 40°50N 101°43W **80** E3
Grant, Mt. *U.S.A.* 38°34N 118°48W **76** G4
Grant City *U.S.A.* 40°29N 94°25W **80** E6
Grant I. *Australia* 11°10S 132°52E **60** B5
Grant Range *U.S.A.* 38°30N 115°25W **76** G6
Grantham *U.K.* 52°55N 0°38W **12** E7
Grantown-on-Spey *U.K.* 57°20N 3°36W **11** D5
Grants *U.S.A.* 35°9N 107°52W **77** J10
Grants Pass *U.S.A.* 42°26N 123°19W **76** E2
Grantsville *U.S.A.* 40°36N 112°28W **76** F7
Granville *France* 48°50N 1°35W **20** B3
Granville *N. Dak.,*
　U.S.A. 48°16N 100°47W **80** A3
Granville *N.Y., U.S.A.* 43°24N 73°16W **83** C11
Granville *Ohio, U.S.A.* 40°4N 82°31W **82** F2
Granville L. *Canada* 56°18N 100°30W **71** B8
Graskop *S. Africa* 24°56S 30°49E **57** C5
Grass → *Canada* 56°3N 96°33W **71** B9
Grass Range *U.S.A.* 47°0N 108°48W **76** C9
Grass River △ *Canada* 54°40N 100°50W **71** C8
Grass Valley *Calif.,*
　U.S.A. 39°13N 121°4W **78** F6
Grass Valley *Oreg.,*
　U.S.A. 45°22N 120°47W **76** D3
Grasse *France* 43°38N 6°56E **20** E7
Grassflat *U.S.A.* 41°0N 78°6W **82** F6
Grasslands △ *Canada* 49°11N 107°38W **71** D7
Grassy *Australia* 40°3S 144°5E **63** G3
Graulhet *France* 43°45N 1°59E **20** E4
Gravelbourg *Canada* 49°50N 106°35W **71** D7
's-Gravenhage *Neths.* 52°7N 4°17E **15** B4
Gravenhurst *Canada* 44°52N 79°20W **82** B5
Gravesend *Australia* 29°35S 150°20E **63** D5
Gravesend *U.K.* 51°26N 0°22E **13** F8
Gravois, Pointe-à- *Haiti* 16°15N 73°56W **89** C5
Grayling *U.S.A.* 44°40N 84°43W **81** C11
Grays *U.K.* 51°28N 0°21E **13** F8
Grays Harbor *U.S.A.* 46°59N 124°1W **76** C1
Grays L. *U.S.A.* 43°4N 111°26W **76** E8
Grays River *U.S.A.* 46°21N 123°37W **78** D3
Graz *Austria* 47°4N 15°27E **16** E8
Greasy L. *Canada* 62°55N 122°12W **70** A4

Great Abaco I. = Abaco I.
　Bahamas 26°25N 77°10W **88** A4
Great Artesian Basin
　Australia 23°0S 144°0E **62** C3
Great Australian Bight
　Australia 33°30S 130°0E **61** F5
Great Bahama Bank
　Bahamas 23°15N 78°0W **88** B4
Great Barrier I. *N.Z.* 36°11S 175°25E **59** B5
Great Barrier Reef
　Australia 18°0S 146°50E **62** B4
Great Barrier Reef △
　Australia 20°0S 150°0E **62** B4
Great Barrington
　U.S.A. 42°12N 73°22W **83** D11
Great Basalt Wall △
　Australia 19°52S 145°43E **62** B4
Great Basin *U.S.A.* 40°0N 117°0W **76** G5
Great Basin △ *U.S.A.* 38°56N 114°15W **76** G6
Great Bear → *Canada* 65°0N 126°0W **68** C7
Great Bear L. *Canada* 65°30N 120°0W **68** C8
Great Belt = Store Bælt
　Denmark 55°20N 11°0E **9** J14
Great Bend *Kans., U.S.A.* 38°22N 98°46W **80** F4
Great Bend *Pa., U.S.A.* 41°58N 75°45W **83** E9
Great Blasket I. *Ireland* 52°6N 10°32W **10** D1
Great Britain *Europe* 54°0N 2°15W **6** E5
Great Camanoe
　Br. Virgin Is. 18°30N 64°35W **89** e
Great Coco I. = Koko Kyunzu
　Burma 14°7N 93°22E **41** M18
Great Codroy *Canada* 47°51N 59°16W **73** C8
Great Divide, The = Great
　Dividing Ra. *Australia* 23°0S 146°0E **62** C4
Great Divide Basin
　U.S.A. 42°0N 108°0W **76** E9
Great Dividing Ra.
　Australia 23°0S 146°0E **62** C4
Great Driffield = Driffield
　U.K. 54°0N 0°26W **12** C7
Great Exuma I. *Bahamas* 23°30N 75°50W **88** B4
Great Falls *U.S.A.* 47°30N 111°17W **76** C8
Great Fish = Groot-Vis →
　S. Africa 33°28S 27°5E **56** E4
Great Guana Cay
　Bahamas 24°0N 76°20W **88** B4
Great Himalayan △
　India 31°30N 77°30E **42** D7
Great Inagua I. *Bahamas* 21°0N 73°20W **89** B5
Great Indian Desert = Thar Desert
　India 28°0N 72°0E **42** F5
Great Karoo *S. Africa* 31°55S 21°0E **56** E3
Great Khingan Mts. = Da
　Hinggan Ling *China* 48°0N 121°0E **33** B7
Great Lake *Australia* 41°50S 146°40E **63** G4
Great Lakes *N. Amer.* 46°0N 84°0W **66** E11
Great Limpopo Transfrontier △
　Africa 23°0S 31°45E **57** C5
Great Malvern *U.K.* 52°7N 2°18W **13** E5
Great Miami → *U.S.A.* 39°7N 84°49W **81** F11
Great Ormes Head *U.K.* 53°20N 3°52W **12** D4
Great Ouse → *U.K.* 52°48N 0°21E **12** E8
Great Palm I. *Australia* 18°45S 146°40E **62** B4
Great Pedro Bluff *Jamaica* 17°51N 77°44W **88** a
Great Pee Dee →
　U.S.A. 33°21N 79°10W **85** E15
Great Plains *N. Amer.* 47°0N 105°0W **66** E9
Great Ruaha → *Tanzania* 7°56S 37°52E **54** D4
Great Sacandaga L.
　U.S.A. 43°6N 74°16W **83** C10
Great Saint Bernard Pass = Grand
　St-Bernard, Col du
　Europe 45°50N 7°10E **20** D7
Great Salt Desert = Kavīr, Dasht-e
　Iran 34°30N 55°0E **45** C7
Great Salt Desert = Lūt, Dasht-e
　Iran 31°30N 58°0E **45** D8
Great Salt L. *U.S.A.* 41°15N 112°40W **76** F7
Great Salt Lake Desert
　U.S.A. 40°50N 113°30W **76** F7
Great Salt Plains L.
　U.S.A. 36°45N 98°8W **84** C5
Great Sand Dunes △
　U.S.A. 37°48N 105°45W **77** H11
Great Sandy △ *Australia* 26°13S 153°2E **63** D5
Great Sandy Desert
　Australia 21°0S 124°0E **60** D3
Great Sangi = Sangihe, Pulau
　Indonesia 3°35N 125°30E **37** D7
Great Sea Reef *Fiji* 16°15S 179°0E **59** a
Great Sitkin I. *U.S.A.* 52°3N 176°6W **74** E4
Great Skellig *Ireland* 51°47N 10°33W **10** E1
Great Slave L. *Canada* 61°23N 115°38W **70** A5
Great Smoky Mts. △
　U.S.A. 35°40N 83°40W **85** D13
Great Stour = Stour →
　U.K. 51°18N 1°22E **13** F9
Great Victoria Desert
　Australia 29°30S 126°30E **61** E4
Great Wall *Antarctica* 62°30S 58°0W **5** C18
Great Wall *China* 38°30N 109°30E **34** E5
Great Whernside *U.K.* 54°10N 1°58W **12** C6
Great Yarmouth *U.K.* 52°37N 1°44E **13** E9
Great Zab = Zāb al Kabīr →
　Iraq 36°1N 43°24E **44** B4
Great Zimbabwe
　Zimbabwe 20°16S 30°54E **55** G3
Greater Antilles *W. Indies* 17°40N 74°0W **89** C5
Greater London □ *U.K.* 51°31N 0°6W **13** F7
Greater Manchester □
　U.K. 53°30N 2°15W **12** D5
Greater St. Lucia Wetlands △
　S. Africa 28°6S 32°27E **57** D5
Greater Sudbury = Sudbury
　Canada 46°30N 81°0W **72** C3
Greater Sunda Is. *Indonesia* 7°0S 112°0E **36** F4
Greco, C. *Cyprus* 34°57N 34°5E **25** E13
Gredos, Sierra de *Spain* 40°20N 5°0W **21** B3
Greece *U.S.A.* 43°13N 77°41W **82** C7

Greece ■ Europe 40°0N 23°0E **23 E9**
Greeley Colo., U.S.A. 40°25N 104°42W **76 F11**
Greeley Nebr., U.S.A. 41°33N 98°32W **80 E4**
Greely Fd. Canada 80°30N 85°0W **69 A15**
Greem-Bell, Ostrov Russia 81°0N 62°0E **28 A7**
Green → Ky., U.S.A. 37°54N 87°30W **80 G10**
Green → Utah, U.S.A. 38°11N 109°53W **76 G9**
Green B. Australia 36°0N 87°30W **80 C10**
Green Bay U.S.A. 44°31N 88°0W **80 C9**
Green C. Australia 37°13S 150°1E **63 F5**
Green Cove Springs U.S.A. 29°59N 81°42W **85 G14**
Green Lake Canada 54°17N 107°47W **71 C7**
Green Mts. U.S.A. 43°45N 72°45W **83 C12**
Green River Utah, U.S.A. 38°59N 110°10W **76 G8**
Green River Wyo., U.S.A. 41°32N 109°28W **76 F9**
Green Valley U.S.A. 31°52N 110°56W **77 L8**
Greenbank U.S.A. 48°6N 122°34W **78 B4**
Greenbush Mich., U.S.A. 44°35N 83°19W **82 B1**
Greenbush Minn., U.S.A. 48°42N 96°11W **80 A5**
Greencastle U.S.A. 39°38N 86°52W **81 F10**
Greene U.S.A. 42°20N 75°46W **83 D9**
Greeneville U.S.A. 36°10N 82°50W **85 C13**
Greenfield Calif., U.S.A. 36°19N 121°15W **78 J5**
Greenfield Calif., U.S.A. 35°15N 119°0W **79 K8**
Greenfield Ind., U.S.A. 39°47N 85°46W **81 F11**
Greenfield Iowa, U.S.A. 41°18N 94°28W **80 E6**
Greenfield Mass., U.S.A. 42°35N 72°36W **83 D12**
Greenfield Mo., U.S.A. 37°25N 93°51W **80 G7**
Greenfield Park Canada 45°29N 73°28W **83 A11**
Greenland ☑ N. Amer. 66°0N 45°0W **67 C5**
Greenland Sea Arctic 73°0N 10°0W **4 B7**
Greenock U.K. 55°57N 4°46W **11 F4**
Greenore Ireland 54°2N 6°8W **10 B5**
Greenore Pt. Ireland 52°14N 6°19W **10 D5**
Greenough Australia 28°58S 114°43E **61 E1**
Greenough → Australia 28°51S 114°38E **61 E1**
Greenough Pt. Canada 44°58N 81°26W **82 B3**
Greenport U.S.A. 41°6N 72°22W **83 E12**
Greensboro Ga., U.S.A. 33°35N 83°11W **85 E13**
Greensboro N.C., U.S.A. 36°4N 79°48W **85 C15**
Greensboro Vt., U.S.A. 44°36N 72°18W **83 B12**
Greensburg Ind., U.S.A. 39°20N 85°29W **81 F11**
Greensburg Kans., U.S.A. 37°36N 99°18W **80 G4**
Greensburg Pa., U.S.A. 40°18N 79°33W **82 F5**
Greenstone = Geraldton Canada 49°44N 87°10W **72 C2**
Greenvale Australia 18°59S 145°7E **62 B4**
Greenville Liberia 5°1N 9°6W **50 G4**
Greenville Ala., U.S.A. 31°50N 86°38W **85 F11**
Greenville Calif., U.S.A. 40°8N 120°57W **78 E6**
Greenville Maine, U.S.A. 45°28N 69°35W **81 C19**
Greenville Mich., U.S.A. 43°11N 85°15W **81 D11**
Greenville Miss., U.S.A. 33°24N 91°4W **85 E9**
Greenville Mo., U.S.A. 37°8N 90°27W **80 G8**
Greenville N.C., U.S.A. 35°37N 77°23W **85 D16**
Greenville N.H., U.S.A. 42°46N 71°49W **83 D13**
Greenville N.Y., U.S.A. 42°25N 74°1W **83 D10**
Greenville Ohio, U.S.A. 40°6N 84°38W **81 E11**
Greenville Pa., U.S.A. 41°24N 80°23W **82 E4**
Greenville S.C., U.S.A. 34°51N 82°24W **85 D13**
Greenville Tex., U.S.A. 33°8N 96°7W **84 E6**
Greenwater Lake ○ Canada 52°32N 103°30W **71 C8**
Greenwich Conn., U.S.A. 41°2N 73°38W **83 E11**
Greenwich N.Y., U.S.A. 43°5N 73°30W **83 C11**
Greenwich Ohio, U.S.A. 41°2N 82°31W **82 E2**
Greenwich ☐ U.K. 51°29N 0°1E **13 F8**
Greenwood Canada 49°10N 118°40W **70 D5**
Greenwood Ark., U.S.A. 35°13N 94°16W **84 D7**
Greenwood Ind., U.S.A. 39°37N 86°7W **80 F10**
Greenwood Miss., U.S.A. 33°31N 90°11W **85 E9**
Greenwood S.C., U.S.A. 34°12N 82°10W **85 D13**
Greenwood, Mt. Australia 13°48S 130°4E **60 B5**
Gregory U.S.A. 43°14N 99°26W **80 D4**
Gregory → Australia 17°53S 139°17E **62 B2**
Gregory, L. S. Austral., Australia 28°55S 139°0E **63 D2**
Gregory, L. W. Austral., Australia 20°0S 127°40E **60 D4**
Gregory, L. W. Austral., Australia 25°38S 119°58E **61 E2**
Gregory △ Australia 15°38S 131°15E **60 C5**
Gregory Downs Australia 18°35S 138°45E **62 B2**
Gregory Ra. Queens., Australia 19°30S 143°40E **62 B3**
Gregory Ra. W. Austral., Australia 21°20S 121°12E **60 D3**
Greifswald Germany 54°5N 13°23E **16 A7**
Greiz Germany 50°39N 12°10E **16 C7**
Gremikha Russia 67°59N 39°47E **18 A6**
Grenaa Denmark 56°25N 10°53E **9 H14**
Grenada U.S.A. 33°47N 89°49W **85 E10**
Grenada ■ W. Indies 12°10N 61°40W **89 D7**
Grenadier I. U.S.A. 44°3N 76°22W **83 B8**
Grenadines, The St. Vincent 12°40N 61°20W **89 D7**
Grenen Denmark 57°44N 10°40E **9 H14**
Grenfell Australia 33°52S 148°8E **63 E4**
Grenfell Canada 50°30N 102°56W **71 C8**
Grenoble France 45°12N 5°42E **20 D6**
Grenville, C. Australia 12°0S 143°13E **62 A3**
Gresham U.S.A. 45°30N 122°25W **78 E4**
Gresik Indonesia 7°13S 112°38E **37 G15**
Gretna U.K. 55°0N 3°3W **11 F5**
Gretna U.S.A. 29°54N 90°3W **85 G9**
Grevenmacher Lux. 49°41N 6°26E **15 E6**
Grey → Canada 47°34N 57°6W **73 C8**
Grey → N.Z. 42°27S 171°12E **59 E3**
Grey, C. Australia 13°0S 136°35E **62 A2**

Grey Is. Canada 50°50N 55°35W **69 G20**
Grey Ra. Australia 27°0S 143°30E **63 D3**
Greybull U.S.A. 44°30N 108°3W **76 D9**
Greymouth N.Z. 42°29S 171°13E **59 E3**
Greystones Ireland 53°9N 6°5W **10 C5**
Greytown N.Z. 41°5S 175°29E **59 D5**
Greytown S. Africa 29°1S 30°36E **57 D5**
Gribbell I. Canada 53°23N 129°0W **70 C3**
Gridley U.S.A. 39°22N 121°42W **78 F5**
Griekwastad S. Africa 28°49S 23°15E **56 D3**
Griffin U.S.A. 33°15N 84°16W **85 E12**
Griffith Australia 34°18S 146°2E **63 E4**
Griffith Canada 45°15N 77°10W **82 A7**
Griffith I. Canada 44°50N 80°55W **82 B4**
Grimaylov = Hrymayliv Ukraine 49°20N 26°5E **17 D14**
Grimes U.S.A. 39°4N 121°54W **78 F5**
Grimsay U.K. 57°29N 7°14W **11 D1**
Grimsby Canada 43°12N 79°34W **82 C5**
Grimsby U.K. 53°34N 0°5W **12 D7**
Grímsey Iceland 66°33N 17°58W **8 C5**
Grimshaw Canada 56°10N 117°40W **70 B5**
Grimstad Norway 58°20N 8°35E **9 G13**
Grinnell U.S.A. 41°45N 92°43W **80 E7**
Grinnell Pen. Canada 76°40N 95°0W **69 B13**
Gris-Nez, C. France 50°52N 1°35E **20 A4**
Grise Fiord Canada 76°25N 82°57W **69 B15**
Groais I. Canada 50°55N 55°35W **73 B8**
Groblersdal S. Africa 25°15S 29°25E **57 D4**
Grodno = Hrodna Belarus 53°42N 23°52E **17 B12**
Grodzyanka = Hrodzyanka Belarus 53°31N 28°42E **17 B15**
Groesbeck U.S.A. 31°31N 96°32W **84 F6**
Grójec Poland 51°50N 20°58E **17 C11**
Grong Norway 64°25N 12°8E **8 D15**
Groningen Neths. 53°15N 6°35E **15 A6**
Groningen ☐ Neths. 53°16N 6°40E **15 A6**
Groom U.S.A. 35°12N 101°6W **84 D4**
Groot → S. Africa 33°45S 24°36E **56 E3**
Groot-Berg → S. Africa 32°47S 18°8E **56 E2**
Groot-Brakrivier S. Africa 34°2S 22°18E **56 E3**
Groot Karasberge Namibia 27°20S 18°40E **56 D2**
Groot-Kei → S. Africa 32°41S 28°22E **57 E4**
Groot-Vis → S. Africa 33°28S 27°5E **56 E4**
Grootdrink S. Africa 28°33S 21°42E **56 D3**
Groote Eylandt Australia 14°0S 136°40E **62 A2**
Grootfontein Namibia 19°31S 18°6E **56 B2**
Grootlaagte → Africa 20°55S 21°27E **56 C3**
Grootvloer → S. Africa 30°0S 20°40E **56 E3**
Gros C. Canada 61°59N 113°32W **70 A6**
Gros Islet St. Lucia 14°5N 60°58W **89 f**
Gros Morne △ Canada 49°40N 57°50W **73 C8**
Gros Piton St. Lucia 13°49N 61°5W **89 f**
Gros Piton Pt. St. Lucia 13°49N 61°5W **89 f**
Grossa, Pta. Spain 39°6N 1°36E **24 B8**
Grosse Point U.S.A. 42°23N 82°54W **82 D2**
Grosser Arber Germany 49°6N 13°8E **16 D7**
Grosseto Italy 42°46N 11°8E **22 C4**
Grossglockner Austria 47°5N 12°40E **16 E7**
Groswater B. Canada 54°20N 57°40W **73 B8**
Groton Conn., U.S.A. 41°21N 72°5W **83 E12**
Groton N.Y., U.S.A. 42°36N 76°22W **83 D8**
Groton S. Dak., U.S.A. 45°27N 98°6W **80 C4**
Grouard Mission Canada 55°33N 116°9W **70 B5**
Groundhog → Canada 48°45N 82°58W **72 C3**
Grouw Neths. 53°5N 5°51E **15 A5**
Grove City U.S.A. 41°10N 80°5W **82 E4**
Grove Hill U.S.A. 31°42N 87°47W **85 F11**
Groveland U.S.A. 37°50N 120°14W **78 H6**
Grover Beach U.S.A. 35°7N 120°37W **79 K6**
Groves U.S.A. 29°57N 93°54W **84 G8**
Groveton U.S.A. 44°36N 71°31W **83 B13**
Groznyy Russia 43°20N 45°45E **19 F8**
Grudziądz Poland 53°30N 18°47E **17 B10**
Gruinard B. U.K. 57°56N 5°35W **11 D3**
Grundy Center U.S.A. 42°22N 92°47W **80 D7**
Gruver U.S.A. 36°16N 101°24W **84 C4**
Gryazi Russia 52°30N 39°58E **18 D6**
Gryazovets Russia 58°50N 40°10E **18 C7**
Grytviken S. Georgia 54°19S 36°33W **96 G9**
Gua India 22°18N 85°20E **43 H11**
Gua Musang Malaysia 4°53N 101°58E **39 K3**
Guacanayabo, G. de Cuba 20°40N 77°20W **88 B4**
Guachípas → Argentina 25°40S 65°30W **94 B2**
Guadalajara Mexico 20°40N 103°20W **86 C4**
Guadalajara Spain 40°37N 3°12W **21 B4**
Guadalcanal Solomon Is. 9°32S 160°12E **58 B9**
Guadales Argentina 34°30S 67°55W **94 C2**
Guadalete → Spain 36°35N 6°13W **21 D2**
Guadalquivir → Spain 36°47N 6°22W **21 D2**
Guadalupe = Guadeloupe ☑ W. Indies 16°20N 61°40W **88 b**
Guadalupe Mexico 22°45N 102°31W **86 C4**
Guadalupe U.S.A. 34°58N 120°34W **79 L6**
Guadalupe → U.S.A. 28°27N 96°47W **84 G6**
Guadalupe, Sierra de Spain 39°28N 5°30W **21 C3**
Guadalupe Bravos Mexico 31°20N 106°10W **86 A3**
Guadalupe I. Pac. Oc. 29°0N 118°50W **66 G8**
Guadalupe Mts. △ U.S.A. 31°40N 104°30W **84 F2**
Guadalupe Peak U.S.A. 31°50N 104°52W **84 F2**
Guadalupe y Calvo Mexico 26°6N 106°58W **86 B3**
Guadarrama, Sierra de Spain 41°0N 4°0W **21 B4**
Guadeloupe ☑ W. Indies 16°20N 61°40W **88 b**
Guadeloupe △ Guadeloupe 16°10N 61°40W **88 b**
Guadeloupe Passage W. Indies 16°50N 62°15W **89 C7**
Guadiana → Portugal 37°14N 7°22E **21 D2**
Guadix Spain 37°18N 3°11W **21 D4**
Guafo, Boca del Chile 43°35S 74°0W **96 E2**
Guaico Trin. & Tob. 10°35N 61°9W **93 K15**
Guainía → Colombia 2°1N 67°7W **92 C5**

Guaíra Brazil 24°5S 54°10W **95 A5**
Guaíra ☐ Paraguay 25°45S 56°30W **94 B4**
Guaire = Gorey Ireland 52°41N 6°18W **10 D5**
Guaitecas, Is. Chile 44°0S 74°30W **96 E2**
Guajará-Mirim Brazil 10°50S 65°20W **92 F5**
Guajira, Pen. de la Colombia 12°0N 72°0W **92 A4**
Gualán Guatemala 15°8N 89°22W **88 C2**
Gualeguay Argentina 33°10S 59°14W **94 C4**
Gualeguaychú Argentina 33°3S 59°31W **94 C4**
Gualequay → Argentina 33°19S 59°39W **94 C4**
Guam ☑ Pac. Oc. 13°27N 144°45E **64 F6**
Guamini Argentina 37°1S 62°28W **94 D3**
Guamúchil Mexico 25°28N 108°6W **86 B3**
Guana I. Br. Virgin Is. 18°30N 64°30W **89 e**
Guanabacoa Cuba 23°8N 82°18W **88 B3**
Guanacaste, Cordillera de Costa Rica 10°40N 85°4W **88 D2**
Guanacaste △ Costa Rica 10°57N 85°30W **88 D2**
Guanacevi Mexico 25°56N 105°57W **86 B3**
Guanahani = San Salvador I. Bahamas 24°0N 74°40W **89 B5**
Guanaja Honduras 16°30N 85°55W **88 C2**
Guanajay Cuba 22°56N 82°42W **88 B3**
Guanajuato Mexico 21°1N 101°15W **86 C4**
Guanajuato ☐ Mexico 21°0N 101°0W **86 C4**
Guandacol Argentina 29°30S 68°40W **94 B2**
Guane Cuba 22°10N 84°7W **88 B3**
Guangdong ☐ China 23°0N 113°0E **33 D6**
Guangling China 39°47N 114°22E **34 E8**
Guangrao China 37°5N 118°25E **35 F10**
Guangwu China 37°48N 105°57E **34 F3**
Guangxi Zhuangzu Zizhiqu ☐ China 24°0N 109°0E **33 D5**
Guangzhou China 23°6N 113°13E **33 D6**
Guanica Puerto Rico 17°58N 66°55W **89 d**
Guanipa → Venezuela 9°56N 62°26W **92 B6**
Guannan China 34°8N 119°21E **35 G10**
Guantánamo Cuba 20°10N 75°14W **89 B4**
Guantánamo B. Cuba 19°59N 75°10W **89 C4**
Guantao China 36°42N 115°25E **34 F8**
Guanyun China 34°20N 119°18E **35 G10**
Guapay = Grande → Bolivia 15°51S 64°39W **92 G6**
Guápiles Costa Rica 10°10N 83°46W **88 D3**
Guapo B. Trin. & Tob. 10°12N 61°41W **93 K15**
Guaporé Brazil 28°51S 51°54W **95 B5**
Guaporé → Brazil 11°55S 65°4W **92 F5**
Guaqui Bolivia 16°41S 68°54W **92 G5**
Guaramacal △ Venezuela 9°13N 70°12W **89 E5**
Guarapari Brazil 20°40S 40°30W **95 A7**
Guarapuava Brazil 25°20S 51°30W **95 B5**
Guaratinguetá Brazil 22°49S 45°9W **95 A6**
Guaratuba Brazil 25°53S 48°38W **95 B6**
Guarda Portugal 40°32N 7°20W **21 B2**
Guardafui, C. = Asir, Ras Somali Rep. 11°55N 51°10E **47 E5**
Guárico ☐ Venezuela 8°40N 66°35W **92 B5**
Guarujá Brazil 24°2S 46°25W **95 A6**
Guarulhos Brazil 23°29S 46°33W **95 A6**
Guasave Mexico 25°34N 108°27W **86 B3**
Guasdualito Venezuela 7°15N 70°44W **92 B4**
Guatemala Guatemala 14°40N 90°22W **88 D1**
Guatemala ■ Cent. Amer. 15°40N 90°30W **88 C1**
Guatemala Basin Pac. Oc. 11°0N 95°0W **65 F18**
Guatemala Trench Pac. Oc. 14°0N 95°0W **66 H10**
Guatopo △ Venezuela 10°5N 66°30W **89 D6**
Guatuaro Pt. Trin. & Tob. 10°19N 60°59W **93 K16**
Guaviare ☐ Colombia 4°3N 67°44W **92 C5**
Guaviare → Colombia 4°3N 67°44W **92 C5**
Guaxupé Brazil 21°10S 47°5W **95 A6**
Guayaguayare Trin. & Tob. 10°8N 61°2W **93 K15**
Guayama Puerto Rico 17°59N 66°7W **89 d**
Guayaquil Ecuador 2°15S 79°52W **92 D3**
Guayaquil Mexico 29°59N 115°4W **86 B1**
Guayaquil, G. de Ecuador 3°10S 81°0W **92 D2**
Guaymas Mexico 27°56N 110°54W **86 B2**
Guba Dem. Rep. of the Congo 10°38S 26°27E **55 E2**
Gubkin Russia 51°17N 37°32E **19 D6**
Gubkinskiy Russia 64°27N 76°36E **28 C8**
Gudbrandsdalen Norway 61°33N 10°10E **8 F14**
Guddu Barrage Pakistan 28°30N 69°50E **42 E3**
Gudur India 14°12N 79°55E **40 M11**
Guecho = Getxo Spain 43°21N 2°59W **21 A4**
Guékédou Guinea 8°40N 10°5W **50 G3**
Guelmine = Goulimine Morocco 28°56N 10°0W **50 C3**
Guelph Canada 43°35N 80°20W **82 C4**
Guerara Algeria 32°51N 4°22E **50 B6**
Guéret France 46°11N 1°51E **20 C4**
Guernéville U.S.A. 38°30N 123°0W **78 G4**
Guernica = Gernika-Lumo Spain 43°19N 2°40W **21 A4**
Guernsey U.K. 49°26N 2°35W **13 H5**
Guernsey U.S.A. 42°16N 104°45W **76 E11**
Guerrero ☐ Mexico 17°40N 100°0W **87 D5**
Gügher Iran 29°28N 56°27E **45 D8**
Guhakolak, Tanjung Indonesia 6°50S 105°14E **37 G11**
Guia Canary Is. 28°8N 15°38W **24 F4**
Guia de Isora Canary Is. 28°12N 16°46W **24 F3**
Guia Lopes da Laguna Brazil 21°26S 56°7W **95 A4**
Guiana Highlands S. Amer. 5°10N 60°40W **90 C4**
Guidónia-Montecélio Italy 42°1N 12°45E **22 C5**
Guijá Mozam. 24°27S 33°0E **57 C5**
Guildford U.K. 51°14N 0°34W **13 F7**
Guilford U.S.A. 41°17N 72°41W **83 E12**
Guilin China 25°18N 110°15E **33 D6**
Guillaume-Delisle, L. Canada 56°15N 76°17W **72 A4**
Güímar Canary Is. 28°18N 16°24W **24 F3**

Guimarães Portugal 41°28N 8°24W **21 B1**
Guimaras ☐ Phil. 10°35N 122°37E **37 B6**
Guinda U.S.A. 38°50N 122°12W **78 G4**
Guinea Africa 8°0N 8°0E **48 F4**
Guinea ■ W. Afr. 10°20N 11°30W **50 F3**
Guinea, Gulf of Atl. Oc. 3°0N 2°30E **49 F4**
Guinea-Bissau ■ Africa 12°0N 15°0W **50 F3**
Güines Cuba 22°50N 82°0W **88 B3**
Guingamp France 48°34N 3°10W **20 B2**
Güiria Venezuela 10°32N 62°18W **93 K14**
Guiuan Phil. 11°5N 125°55E **37 B7**
Guiyang China 26°32N 106°40E **32 D5**
Guizhou ☐ China 27°0N 107°0E **32 D5**
Gujar Khan Pakistan 33°16N 73°19E **42 C5**
Gujarat ☐ India 23°20N 71°0E **42 H4**
Gujranwala Pakistan 32°10N 74°12E **42 C6**
Gujrat Pakistan 32°40N 74°2E **42 C6**
Gulbarga India 17°20N 76°50E **40 L10**
Gulbene Latvia 57°8N 26°52E **9 H22**
Gulf, The = Persian Gulf Asia 27°0N 50°0E **45 E6**
Gulf Islands △ U.S.A. 30°10N 87°10W **85 F11**
Gulfport U.S.A. 30°22N 89°6W **85 F10**
Gulgong Australia 32°20S 149°49E **63 E4**
Gulistan Pakistan 30°30N 66°35E **42 D2**
Gulja = Yining China 43°58N 81°10E **32 B3**
Gull Lake Canada 50°10N 108°29W **71 C7**
Güllük Turkey 37°14N 27°35E **23 F12**
Gulmarg India 34°3N 74°25E **43 B6**
Gülshat Kazakhstan 46°38N 74°21E **28 C8**
Gulu Uganda 2°48N 32°17E **54 B3**
Gulwe Tanzania 6°30S 36°25E **54 D4**
Gumal → Pakistan 31°40N 71°50E **42 D4**
Gumbaz Pakistan 30°2N 69°0E **42 D3**
Gumel Nigeria 12°39N 9°22E **50 F7**
Gumi S. Korea 36°10N 128°12E **35 F15**
Gumla India 23°3N 84°33E **43 H11**
Gumlu Australia 19°53S 147°41E **62 B4**
Gumma ☐ Japan 36°30N 138°20E **31 F9**
Gumzai Indonesia 5°28S 134°42E **37 F8**
Guna India 24°40N 77°19E **42 G7**
Gunbalanya Australia 12°20S 133°4E **60 B5**
Gundabooka △ Australia 30°30S 145°30E **63 E4**
Gunisao → Canada 53°56N 97°53W **71 C9**
Gunisao L. Canada 53°33N 96°15W **71 C9**
Gunjyal Pakistan 32°20N 71°55E **42 C4**
Gunnedah Australia 30°59S 150°15E **63 E5**
Gunnewin Australia 25°59S 148°33E **63 D4**
Gunningbar Cr. → Australia 31°14S 147°6E **63 E4**
Gunnison Colo., U.S.A. 38°33N 106°56W **76 G10**
Gunnison Utah, U.S.A. 39°9N 111°49W **76 G8**
Gunnison → U.S.A. 39°4N 108°35W **76 G9**
Gunsan S. Korea 35°59N 126°45E **35 G14**
Guntakal India 15°11N 77°27E **40 M10**
Gunter Canada 44°52N 77°32W **82 B7**
Guntersville U.S.A. 34°21N 86°18W **85 D11**
Guntong Malaysia 4°36N 101°3E **39 K3**
Guntur India 16°23N 80°30E **41 L12**
Gunungapi Indonesia 6°45S 126°30E **37 F7**
Gunungsitoli Indonesia 1°15N 97°30E **36 D1**
Gunza Angola 10°50S 13°50E **52 G2**
Guo He → China 32°59N 117°10E **35 H9**
Guoyang China 33°32N 116°12E **34 H9**
Gupis Pakistan 36°15N 73°20E **43 A5**
Gurbantünggüt Shamo China 45°8N 87°20E **32 B3**
Gurdaspur India 32°5N 75°31E **42 C6**
Gurdon U.S.A. 33°55N 93°9W **84 E8**
Gurgaon India 28°27N 77°1E **42 E7**
Gurgueia → Brazil 6°50S 43°24W **93 E10**
Gurha India 25°12N 71°39E **42 G4**
Guri, Embalse de Venezuela 7°50N 62°52W **92 B6**
Gurkha Nepal 28°5N 84°40E **43 E11**
Gurla Mandhata = Naimona'nyi Feng Nepal 30°26N 81°18E **43 D9**
Gurley Australia 29°45S 149°48E **63 D4**
Gurnet Point U.S.A. 42°1N 70°34W **83 D14**
Guro Mozam. 17°26S 32°30E **55 F3**
Gurué Mozam. 15°25S 36°58E **55 F4**
Gurun Malaysia 5°49N 100°27E **39 K3**
Gürün Turkey 38°43N 37°15E **19 G6**
Gurupá Brazil 1°25S 51°35W **93 D8**
Gurupá, I. Grande de Brazil 1°25S 51°45W **93 D8**
Gurupi Brazil 11°43S 49°4W **93 F9**
Gurupi → Brazil 1°13S 46°6W **93 D9**
Guruwe Zimbabwe 16°40S 30°42E **57 B5**
Gurvan Sayhan Uul Mongolia 43°50N 104°0E **32 B5**
Guryev = Atyraū Kazakhstan 47°5N 52°0E **19 E9**
Gusau Nigeria 12°12N 6°40E **50 F7**
Gushan China 39°50N 123°35E **35 E12**
Gushgy = Serhetabat Turkmenistan 35°20N 62°18E **45 C9**
Gusinoozersk Russia 51°16N 106°27E **29 D11**
Gustavus U.S.A. 58°25N 135°44W **70 B1**
Gustine U.S.A. 37°16N 121°0W **78 H6**
Güstrow Germany 53°47N 12°10E **16 B7**
Gütersloh Germany 51°54N 8°24E **16 C5**
Gutha Australia 28°58S 115°55E **61 E2**
Guthalungra Australia 19°52S 147°50E **62 B4**
Guthrie Canada 44°28N 79°32W **82 B5**
Guthrie Okla., U.S.A. 35°53N 97°25W **84 H6**
Guthrie Tex., U.S.A. 33°37N 100°19W **84 F4**
Guttenberg U.S.A. 42°47N 91°6W **80 D8**
Gutu Zimbabwe 19°41S 31°9E **57 B5**
Guwahati India 26°10N 91°45E **41 F17**
Guy Fawkes River △ Australia 30°5S 152°20E **63 E5**
Guyana ■ S. Amer. 5°0N 59°0W **92 C7**
Guyane française = French Guiana ■ S. Amer. 4°0N 53°0W **93 C8**

Guyang China 41°0N 110°5E **34 D6**
Guyenne France 44°30N 0°40E **20 D4**
Guymon U.S.A. 36°41N 101°29W **84 C4**
Guyra Australia 30°15S 151°40E **63 E5**
Guyuan Hebei, China 41°37N 115°40E **34 D8**
Guyuan Ningxia Huizu, China 36°0N 106°20E **34 F4**
Güzelyurt = Morphou Cyprus 35°12N 32°59E **25 D11**
Guzhou China 33°22N 117°18E **35 H9**
Guzmán, L. de Mexico 31°20N 107°30W **86 A3**
Gwa Burma 17°36N 94°34E **41 L19**
Gwaai Zimbabwe 19°15S 27°45E **55 F2**
Gwaai → Zimbabwe 17°59S 26°52E **55 F2**
Gwabegar Australia 30°37S 148°59E **63 E4**
Gwādar Pakistan 25°10N 62°18E **40 G3**
Gwaii Haanas △ Canada 52°21N 131°26W **70 C2**
Gwalior India 26°12N 78°10E **42 F8**
Gwanda Zimbabwe 20°55S 29°0E **55 G2**
Gwane Dem. Rep. of the Congo 4°45N 25°48E **54 B2**
Gwangju S. Korea 35°9N 126°54E **35 G14**
Gwanju = Gwangju S. Korea 35°9N 126°54E **35 G14**
Gweebarra B. Ireland 54°51N 8°23W **10 B3**
Gweedore Ireland 55°3N 8°13W **10 A3**
Gweru Zimbabwe 19°28S 29°45E **55 F2**
Gwinn U.S.A. 46°19N 87°27W **80 B10**
Gwydir → Australia 29°27S 149°48E **63 D4**
Gwynedd ☐ U.K. 52°52N 4°10W **12 E3**
Gyandzha = Gäncä Azerbaijan 40°45N 46°20E **19 F8**
Gyaring Hu China 34°50N 97°40E **32 C4**
Gydanskiy Poluostrov Russia 70°0N 78°0E **28 C8**
Gyeongju S. Korea 35°51N 129°14E **35 G15**
Gympie Australia 26°11S 152°38E **63 D5**
Gyöngyös Hungary 47°48N 19°56E **17 E10**
Győr Hungary 47°41N 17°40E **17 E9**
Gypsum Pt. Canada 61°53N 114°35W **70 A6**
Gypsumville Canada 51°45N 98°40W **71 C9**
Gyula Hungary 46°38N 21°17E **17 E11**
Gyumri Armenia 40°47N 43°50E **19 F7**
Gyzylarbat = Serdar Turkmenistan 39°4N 56°23E **45 B8**
Gyzyletrek = Etrek Turkmenistan 37°36N 54°46E **45 B7**

H

Ha 'Arava → Israel 30°50N 35°20E **46 E4**
Ha Coi Vietnam 21°26N 107°46E **38 B6**
Ha Dong Vietnam 20°58N 105°46E **38 B5**
Ha Giang Vietnam 22°50N 104°59E **38 A5**
Ha Karmel △ Israel 32°45N 35°5E **46 C4**
Ha Long, Vinh Vietnam 20°56N 107°3E **38 B6**
Ha Tien Vietnam 10°23N 104°29E **39 G5**
Ha Tinh Vietnam 18°20N 105°54E **38 C5**
Ha Trung Vietnam 19°58N 105°50E **38 C5**
Haaksbergen Neths. 52°9N 6°45E **15 B6**
Ha'ano Tonga 19°41S 174°18W **59 c**
Ha'apai Group Tonga 19°47S 174°27W **59 c**
Haapiti Moorea 17°34S 149°52W **59 d**
Haapsalu Estonia 58°56N 23°30E **9 G20**
Haarlem Neths. 52°23N 4°39E **15 B4**
Haast → N.Z. 43°50S 169°2E **59 E2**
Haasts Bluff Australia 23°22S 132°0E **60 D5**
Haasts Bluff ○ Australia 23°39S 130°34E **60 D5**
Hab → Pakistan 24°53N 66°41E **42 G3**
Hab Nadi Chauki Pakistan 25°0N 66°50E **42 G2**
Habahe China 48°3N 86°23E **32 B3**
Habaswein Kenya 1°2N 39°30E **54 B4**
Habay Canada 58°50N 118°44W **70 B5**
Ḩabbānīyah Iraq 33°17N 43°29E **44 C4**
Haboro Japan 44°22N 141°42E **30 B10**
Hachijō-Jima Japan 33°5N 139°45E **31 H9**
Hachinohe Japan 40°30N 141°29E **30 D10**
Hachiōji Japan 35°40N 139°20E **31 G9**
Hackensack U.S.A. 40°53N 74°4W **83 F10**
Hackettstown U.S.A. 40°51N 74°50W **83 F10**
Hadali Pakistan 32°16N 72°11E **42 C5**
Hadarba, Ras Sudan 22°4N 36°51E **51 D13**
Hadarom ☐ Israel 31°0N 35°0E **46 E4**
Ḩadd, Ra's al Oman 22°35N 59°50E **47 C6**
Haddington U.K. 55°57N 2°47W **11 F6**
Hadejia Nigeria 12°30N 10°5E **50 F7**
Hadera Israel 32°27N 34°55E **46 C3**
Hadera, N. → Israel 32°28N 34°52E **46 C3**
Haderslev Denmark 55°15N 9°30E **9 J13**
Hadhramaut = Ḩaḑramawt Yemen 15°30N 49°30E **47 D4**
Haḑiboh Yemen 12°39N 54°2E **47 E5**
Hadley B. Canada 72°31N 108°12W **68 C12**
Hadong S. Korea 35°5N 127°44E **35 G14**
Ḩaḑramawt Yemen 15°30N 49°30E **47 D4**
Ḩadrānīyah Iraq 35°38N 43°14E **44 C4**
Hadrian's Wall U.K. 55°0N 2°30W **12 B5**
Hae, Ko Thailand 7°44N 98°22E **39 a**
Haeju N. Korea 38°3N 125°45E **35 E13**
Hä'ena U.S.A. 22°14N 159°34W **75 L8**
Haenam S. Korea 34°34N 126°35E **35 G14**
Haenertsburg S. Africa 24°0S 29°50E **57 C4**
Haerhpin = Harbin China 45°48N 126°40E **35 B14**
Hafar al Bāṭin Si. Arabia 28°32N 45°52E **44 D5**
Hafirat al 'Aydā Si. Arabia 26°26N 39°12E **44 E3**
Hafit Oman 23°59N 55°49E **45 F7**
Hafizabad Pakistan 32°5N 73°40E **42 C5**
Haflong India 25°10N 93°5E **41 G18**
Haft Gel Iran 31°30N 49°32E **45 D6**
Hagalil Israel 32°53N 35°18E **46 C4**
Hagemeister I. U.S.A. 58°39N 160°54W **74 D7**
Hagen Germany 51°21N 7°27E **16 C4**
Hagerman U.S.A. 33°7N 104°20W **77 K11**

Hagerman Fossil Beds △
  U.S.A. 42°48N 114°57W **76** E6
Hagerstown U.S.A. 39°39N 77°43W **81** F15
Hagersville Canada 42°58N 80°3W **82** D4
Hagfors Sweden 60°3N 13°45E **9** F15
Hagi Japan 34°30N 131°22E **31** G5
Hagolan Syria 33°0N 35°45E **46** C4
Hagondange France 49°16N 6°11E **20** B7
Hags Hd. Ireland 52°57N 9°28W **10** D2
Hague, C. de la France 49°44N 1°56W **20** B3
Hague, The = 's-Gravenhage
  Neths. 52°7N 4°17E **15** B4
Haguenau France 48°49N 7°47E **20** B7
Hai Duong Vietnam 20°56N 106°19E **38** B6
Haicheng China 40°50N 122°45E **35** D12
Haidar Khel Afghan. 33°58N 68°38E **42** C3
Haidarâbâd = Hyderabad
  India 17°22N 78°29E **40** L11
Haidargarh India 26°37N 81°22E **43** F9
Haifa = Ḥefa Israel 32°46N 35°0E **46** C4
Haikou China 20°1N 110°16E **38** B8
Ḥā'il □ Si. Arabia 26°40N 41°40E **44** E4
Hailar China 49°10N 119°38E **33** B6
Hailey U.S.A. 43°31N 114°19W **76** E6
Haileybury Canada 47°30N 79°38W **72** C4
Hailin China 44°37N 129°30E **35** B15
Hailuoto Finland 65°3N 24°45E **8** D21
Hainan □ China 19°0N 109°30E **38** C7
Hainan Dao China 19°0N 109°30E **38** C7
Hainan Str. = Qiongzhou Haixia
  China 20°10N 110°15E **38** B8
Hainaut □ Belgium 50°30N 4°0E **15** D4
Haines Alaska, U.S.A. 59°14N 135°26W **70** B1
Haines Oreg., U.S.A. 44°55N 117°56W **76** D5
Haines City U.S.A. 28°7N 81°38W **85** G14
Haines Junction
  Canada 60°45N 137°30W **70** A1
Haiphong Vietnam 20°47N 106°41E **38** B6
Haiti ■ W. Indies 19°0N 72°30W **89** C5
Haiya Sudan 18°20N 36°21E **51** E13
Haiyan China 36°53N 100°59E **32** C5
Haiyang China 36°47N 121°9E **35** F11
Haiyuan China 36°35N 105°52E **34** F3
Haizhou China 34°37N 119°7E **35** G10
Haizhou Wan China 35°0N 119°30E **35** G10
Haj Ali Qoli, Kavīr Iran 35°55N 54°50E **45** C7
Hajdúböszörmény
  Hungary 47°40N 21°30E **17** E11
Haji Ibrahim Iraq 36°40N 44°30E **44** B5
Hājjīābād Iran 33°37N 60°0E **45** C9
Hajipur India 25°45N 85°13E **43** G11
Ḥajjah Yemen 15°42N 43°36E **47** D3
Ḥājjīābād Iran 28°19N 55°55E **45** D7
Ḥājjīābād-e Zarrīn Iran 33°9N 54°51E **45** C7
Hajnówka Poland 52°47N 23°35E **17** B12
Hakansson, Mts.
  Dem. Rep. of the Congo 8°40S 25°45E **55** D2
Hakkâri Turkey 37°34N 43°44E **44** B4
Hakken-Zan Japan 34°10N 135°54E **31** G7
Hakodate Japan 41°45N 140°44E **30** D10
Hakos Namibia 23°13S 16°21E **56** C2
Haku-San Japan 36°9N 136°46E **31** F8
Haku-San △ Japan 36°15N 136°45E **31** F8
Hakui Japan 36°53N 136°47E **31** F8
Hala Pakistan 25°43N 68°20E **40** G6
Ḥalab Syria 36°10N 37°15E **44** B3
Ḥalabjah Iraq 35°10N 45°58E **44** C5
Halaib Sudan 22°12N 36°30E **51** D13
Halaib Triangle Africa 22°30N 35°20E **51** D13
Ḥālat 'Ammār Si. Arabia 29°10N 36°4E **44** D3
Halbā Lebanon 34°34N 36°6E **46** A5
Halberstadt Germany 51°54N 11°3E **16** C6
Halcombe N.Z. 40°8S 175°30E **59** D5
Halcon Phil. 13°0N 121°30E **37** B6
Halde Fjäll = Haltiatunturi
  Finland 69°1'N 21°18E **8** B19
Halden Norway 59°9N 11°23E **9** G14
Haldia Bangla. 22°1N 88°3E **43** H13
Haldwani India 29°31N 79°30E **43** E8
Hale → Australia 24°56S 135°53E **62** C2
Halesowen U.K. 52°27N 2°3W **13** E5
Halesworth U.K. 52°20N 1°31E **13** E9
Haleyville U.S.A. 34°14N 87°37W **85** D11
Half Dome U.S.A. 37°44N 119°32E **78** H7
Halfmoon Bay N.Z. 46°50S 168°5E **59** G2
Halfway → Canada 56°12N 121°32W **70** B4
Halia India 24°50N 82°19E **43** G10
Haliburton Canada 45°3N 78°30W **82** A6
Halifax U.K. 18°32S 146°22E **62** B4
Halifax Canada 44°38N 63°35W **73** D7
Halifax U.S.A. 53°43N 1°52W **12** D6
Halifax U.S.A. 40°25N 76°55W **82** F8
Halifax B. Australia 18°50S 147°0E **62** B4
Halifax I. Namibia 26°38S 15°4E **56** D2
Halīl → Iran 27°40N 58°30E **45** E8
Halkida Greece 38°27N 23°42E **23** E10
Halkirk U.K. 58°30N 3°29W **11** C5
Hall Beach Canada 68°46N 81°12W **69** D15
Hall Pen. Canada 63°30N 66°0W **69** E18
Hall Pt. Australia 15°40S 124°23E **60** C3
Halland Sweden 57°8N 12°47E **9** H15
Hallāniyat, Jazā'ir al
  Oman 17°30N 55°58E **47** D6
Hallasan S. Korea 33°22N 126°32E **35** H14
Halle Belgium 50°44N 4°13E **15** D4
Halle Germany 51°30N 11°56E **16** C6
Hällefors Sweden 59°47N 14°31E **9** G16
Hallett Australia 33°25S 138°55E **63** E2
Hallettsville U.S.A. 29°27N 96°57W **84** G6
Halley Antarctica 75°35S 26°39W **5** D1
Hallim S. Korea 33°24N 126°15E **35** H14
Hallingdalselva →
  Norway 60°23N 9°35E **8** F13
Hallock U.S.A. 48°47N 96°57W **80** A5
Halls Creek Australia 18°16S 127°38E **60** C4
Halls Gap Australia 37°8S 142°34E **63** F3
Halls Lake Canada 45°7N 78°45W **82** A6
Hallsberg Sweden 59°5N 15°7E **9** G16
Hallstead U.S.A. 41°58N 75°45W **83** E9

Halmahera Indonesia 0°40N 128°0E **37** D7
Halmstad Sweden 56°41N 12°52E **9** H15
Hälsingborg = Helsingborg
  Sweden 56°3N 12°42E **9** H15
Hälsingland Sweden 61°40N 16°5E **8** F17
Halstead U.K. 51°57N 0°40E **13** F8
Haltiatunturi Finland 69°17N 21°18E **8** B19
Halton □ U.K. 53°22N 2°45W **12** D5
Haltwhistle U.K. 54°58N 2°26W **12** C5
Ḥālūl Qatar 25°40N 52°40E **45** E7
Halvad India 23°1N 71°11E **42** H4
Ḥalvān Iran 33°57N 56°15E **45** C8
Ham Tan Vietnam 10°40N 107°45E **39** G6
Ham Yen Vietnam 22°4N 105°3E **38** A5
Hamab Namibia 28°7S 19°16E **56** D2
Hamada Japan 34°56N 132°4E **31** G6
Hamadān Iran 34°52N 48°32E **45** C6
Hamadān □ Iran 35°0N 49°0E **45** C6
Ḥamāh Syria 35°5N 36°40E **44** C3
Hamamatsu Japan 34°45N 137°45E **31** G8
Hamar Norway 60°48N 11°7E **8** F14
Hamâta, Gebel Egypt 24°17N 35°0E **44** E2
Hambantota Sri Lanka 6°10N 81°10E **40** R12
Hamber △ Canada 52°20N 118°0W **70** C5
Hamburg Germany 53°33N 9°59E **16** B5
Hamburg Ark., U.S.A. 33°14N 91°48W **84** E9
Hamburg N.Y., U.S.A. 42°43N 78°50W **82** D6
Hamburg Pa., U.S.A. 40°33N 75°59W **83** F9
Ḥamd, W. al →
  Si. Arabia 24°55N 36°20E **44** E3
Hamden U.S.A. 41°23N 72°54W **83** E12
Häme Finland 61°38N 25°10E **8** F21
Hämeenlinna Finland 61°0N 24°28E **8** F21
Hamelin Pool Australia 26°22S 114°20E **61** E1
Hameln Germany 52°6N 9°21E **16** B5
Hamerkaz □ Israel 32°15N 34°55E **46** C3
Hamersley Ra. Australia 22°0S 117°45E **60** D2
Hamhŭng N. Korea 39°54N 127°30E **35** E14
Hami China 42°55N 93°25E **32** B4
Hamilton Australia 37°45S 142°2E **63** F3
Hamilton Canada 43°15N 79°50W **82** C5
Hamilton N.Z. 37°47S 175°19E **59** B5
Hamilton U.K. 55°46N 4°2W **11** F4
Hamilton Ala., U.S.A. 34°9N 87°59W **85** D11
Hamilton Mont., U.S.A. 46°15N 114°10W **76** C6
Hamilton N.Y., U.S.A. 42°50N 75°33W **83** D9
Hamilton Ohio, U.S.A. 39°24N 84°34W **81** F11
Hamilton Tex., U.S.A. 31°42N 98°7W **84** F5
Hamilton → Queens.,
  Australia 23°30S 139°47E **62** C2
Hamilton → S. Austral.,
  Australia 26°40S 135°19E **63** D2
Hamilton City U.S.A. 39°45N 122°1W **78** F4
Hamilton I. Australia 20°21S 148°56E **62** b
Hamilton Inlet Canada 54°0N 57°30W **73** B8
Hamilton Mt. U.S.A. 43°25N 74°22W **83** C10
Hamina Finland 60°34N 27°12E **8** F22
Hamirpur H.P., India 31°41N 76°31E **42** D7
Hamirpur Ut. P., India 25°57N 80°9E **43** G9
Hamju N. Korea 39°51N 127°26E **35** E14
Hamlet U.S.A. 34°53N 79°42W **85** D15
Hamley Bridge Australia 34°17S 138°35E **63** E2
Hamlin = Hameln
  Germany 52°6N 9°21E **16** B5
Hamlin N.Y., U.S.A. 43°17N 77°55W **82** C7
Hamlin Tex., U.S.A. 32°53N 100°8W **84** E4
Hamm Germany 51°40N 7°50E **16** C4
Hammār, Hawr al Iraq 30°50N 47°10E **44** D5
Hammerfest Norway 70°39N 23°41E **8** A20
Hammond La., U.S.A. 30°30N 90°28W **85** F9
Hammond Ind., U.S.A. 41°38N 87°30W **80** E10
Hammondsport U.S.A. 42°25N 77°13W **82** D7
Hammonton U.S.A. 39°39N 74°48W **81** F16
Hampden N.Z. 45°18S 170°50E **59** F3
Hampshire □ U.K. 51°7N 1°23W **13** F6
Hampshire Downs U.K. 51°15N 1°10W **13** F6
Hampton N.B., Canada 45°32N 65°51W **73** C6
Hampton Ont., Canada 43°58N 78°45W **82** C6
Hampton Ark., U.S.A. 33°32N 92°28W **84** E8
Hampton Iowa, U.S.A. 42°45N 93°13W **80** D7
Hampton N.H., U.S.A. 42°57N 70°50W **83** D14
Hampton S.C., U.S.A. 32°52N 81°7W **85** E14
Hampton Va., U.S.A. 37°2N 76°21W **81** G15
Hampton Bays U.S.A. 40°53N 72°30W **83** F12
Hampton Tableland
  Australia 32°0S 127°0E **61** F4
Hamyang S. Korea 35°32N 127°42E **35** G14
Han Pijesak Bos.-H. 44°5N 18°57E **23** B8
Hanak Si. Arabia 25°32N 37°0E **44** E3
Hanamaki Japan 39°23N 141°7E **30** E10
Hanang Tanzania 4°30S 35°25E **54** C4
Hanau Germany 50°7N 8°56E **16** C5
Hanbogd = Ihbulag
  Mongolia 43°11N 107°10E **34** C4
Hancheng China 35°31N 110°25E **34** G6
Hancock Mich., U.S.A. 47°8N 88°35W **80** B9
Hancock N.Y., U.S.A. 41°57N 75°17W **83** E9
Hancock Vt., U.S.A. 43°55N 72°50W **83** C12
Handa Japan 34°53N 136°55E **31** G8
Handa I. U.K. 58°23N 5°11W **11** C3
Handan China 36°35N 114°28E **34** F8
Handeni Tanzania 5°25S 38°2E **54** D4
Handwara India 34°21N 74°20E **43** B6
Hanegev Israel 30°50N 35°0E **46** E4
Hanford U.S.A. 36°20N 119°39W **78** J7
Hanford Reach △
  U.S.A. 46°40N 119°30W **76** C4
Hang Chat Thailand 18°20N 99°21E **38** C2
Hang Dong Thailand 18°41N 98°55E **38** C2
Hangang → S. Korea 37°50N 126°30E **35** F14
Hangchou = Hangzhou
  China 30°18N 120°11E **33** C7
Hanggin Houqi China 40°58N 107°4E **34** D4
Hanggin Qi China 39°52N 108°50E **34** E5
Hangu China 39°18N 117°53E **35** E9
Hangzhou China 30°18N 120°11E **33** C7
Hangzhou Wan China 30°15N 120°45E **33** C7

Hanh Mongolia 51°32N 100°35E **32** A5
Hanhongor Mongolia 43°55N 104°28E **34** C3
Hania = Chania Greece 35°30N 24°4E **25** D6
Ḥanīdh Si. Arabia 26°35N 48°38E **45** E6
Ḥanīsh Yemen 13°45N 42°46E **47** E3
Hankinson U.S.A. 46°4N 96°54W **80** B5
Hankö Finland 59°50N 22°57E **9** G20
Hanksville U.S.A. 38°22N 110°43W **76** G8
Hanle India 32°42N 79°4E **43** C8
Hanmer Springs N.Z. 42°32N 172°50E **59** E4
Hann → Australia 17°26S 126°17E **60** C4
Hann, Mt. Australia 15°45S 126°0E **60** C4
Hanna Canada 51°40N 111°54W **70** C6
Hanna U.S.A. 41°52N 106°34W **76** F10
Hannah B. Canada 51°40N 80°0W **72** B4
Hannibal Mo., U.S.A. 39°42N 91°22W **80** F8
Hannibal N.Y., U.S.A. 43°19N 76°35W **83** C8
Hannover Germany 52°22N 9°46E **16** B5
Hanoi Vietnam 21°5N 105°55E **38** B5
Hanover = Hannover
  Germany 52°22N 9°46E **16** B5
Hanover Canada 44°9N 81°2W **82** B3
Hanover S. Africa 31°4S 24°29E **56** E3
Hanover N.H., U.S.A. 43°42N 72°17W **83** C12
Hanover Ohio, U.S.A. 40°4N 82°16W **82** F2
Hanover Pa., U.S.A. 39°48N 76°59W **81** F15
Hanover, I. Chile 51°0S 74°50W **96** G2
Hans Lollik I.
  U.S. Virgin Is. 18°24N 64°53W **89** e
Hansdiha India 24°36N 87°5E **43** G12
Hansi H.P., India 32°27N 77°50E **42** C7
Hansi Haryana, India 29°10N 75°57E **42** E6
Hanson, L. Australia 31°0S 136°15E **63** E2
Hantsavichy Belarus 52°49N 26°30E **17** B14
Hanumangarh India 29°35N 74°19E **42** E6
Haora India 22°34N 88°18E **43** H13
Haparanda Sweden 65°52N 24°8E **8** D21
Happy U.S.A. 34°45N 101°52W **84** D4
Happy Camp U.S.A. 41°48N 123°23W **76** F2
Happy Valley-Goose Bay
  Canada 53°15N 60°20W **73** B7
Hapsu N. Korea 41°13N 128°51E **35** D15
Hapur India 28°45N 77°45E **42** E7
Ḥaql Si. Arabia 29°10N 34°58E **46** F3
Har Indonesia 5°16S 133°14E **37** F8
Har-Ayrag Mongolia 45°47N 109°16E **34** B5
Har Hu China 38°20N 97°38E **32** C4
Har Us Nuur Mongolia 48°0N 92°0E **32** B4
Har Yehuda Israel 31°35N 34°57E **46** D3
Ḥaraḍ Si. Arabia 24°22N 49°0E **47** C4
Haramosh Pakistan 35°50N 74°54E **43** B6
Haranomachi Japan 37°38N 140°58E **30** F10
Harare Zimbabwe 17°43S 31°2E **55** F3
Harazé Chad 9°57N 20°48E **51** G10
Harbin China 45°48N 126°40E **35** B14
Harbor Beach U.S.A. 43°51N 82°39W **82** C2
Harborcreek U.S.A. 42°9N 79°57W **82** D5
Harbour Breton Canada 47°29N 55°50W **73** C8
Harbour Deep Canada 50°25N 56°32W **73** B8
Harda India 22°27N 77°5E **42** H7
Hardangerfjorden Norway 60°5N 6°0E **9** F12
Hardangervidda Norway 60°7N 7°20E **8** F12
Hardap △ Namibia 24°29S 17°45E **56** C2
Hardap Dam Namibia 24°32S 17°50E **56** C2
Hardenberg Neths. 52°34N 6°37E **15** B6
Harderwijk Neths. 52°21N 5°38E **15** B5
Hardey → Australia 22°45S 116°8E **60** D2
Hardin U.S.A. 45°44N 107°37W **76** D10
Harding S. Africa 30°35S 29°55E **57** E4
Harding Ra. Australia 16°17S 124°55E **60** C3
Hardisty Canada 52°40N 111°18W **70** C6
Hardoi India 27°26N 80°6E **43** F9
Hardwar = Haridwar
  India 29°58N 78°9E **42** E8
Hardwick U.S.A. 44°30N 72°22W **83** B12
Hardwood Lake Canada 45°12N 77°26W **82** A7
Hardy, Pen. Chile 55°30S 68°20W **96** H3
Hardy, Pte. St. Lucia 14°6N 60°56W **89** f
Hare B. Canada 51°15N 55°45W **73** B8
Hareid Norway 62°22N 6°1E **8** E12
Harer Ethiopia 9°20N 42°8E **47** F3
Hargeisa Somali Rep. 9°30N 44°2E **47** F3
Hari → Indonesia 1°16S 104°5E **36** E2
Haria Canary Is. 29°8N 13°32W **24** F6
Haridwar India 29°58N 78°9E **42** E8
Harim, Jabal al Oman 25°58N 56°14E **45** E8
Haringhata → Bangla. 22°0N 89°58E **41** J16
Harīr, W. al → Syria 32°44N 35°59E **46** C4
Harīrūd → Asia 37°24N 60°38E **45** B9
Härjedalen Sweden 62°22N 13°5E **8** E15
Harlan Iowa, U.S.A. 41°39N 95°19W **80** E6
Harlan Ky., U.S.A. 36°51N 83°19W **81** G12
Harlech U.K. 52°52N 4°6W **12** E3
Harlem U.S.A. 48°32N 108°47W **76** B9
Harlingen Neths. 53°11N 5°25E **15** A5
Harlingen U.S.A. 26°12N 97°42W **84** H6
Harlow U.K. 51°46N 0°8E **13** F8
Harlowton U.S.A. 46°26N 109°50W **76** C9
Harnai Pakistan 30°6N 67°56E **42** D2
Harney Basin U.S.A. 43°30N 119°0W **76** E4
Harney L. U.S.A. 43°14N 119°8W **76** E4
Harney Peak U.S.A. 43°52N 103°32W **80** D2
Härnösand Sweden 62°38N 17°55E **8** E17
Haroldswick U.K. 60°48N 0°50W **11** A8
Harp L. Canada 55°5N 61°50W **73** A7
Harper Liberia 4°25N 7°43W **50** H4
Harper, Mt. U.S.A. 64°14N 143°51W **74** C11
Harrai India 22°37N 79°13E **43** H8
Harrand Pakistan 29°28N 70°3E **42** E4
Harricana → Canada 50°56N 79°32W **72** B4
Harriman U.S.A. 35°56N 84°33W **85** D12
Harrington Harbour
  Canada 50°31N 59°30W **73** B8
Harris, L. Australia 31°10S 135°10E **63** E2
Harris, Sd. of U.K. 57°44N 7°6W **11** D1
Harris Pt. Canada 43°6N 82°9W **82** C2

Harrisburg Ill., U.S.A. 37°44N 88°32W **80** G9
Harrisburg Nebr.,
  U.S.A. 41°33N 103°44W **80** E2
Harrisburg Pa., U.S.A. 40°16N 76°53W **82** F8
Harrismith S. Africa 28°15S 29°8E **57** D4
Harrison Ark., U.S.A. 36°14N 93°7W **84** C8
Harrison Maine, U.S.A. 44°7N 70°39W **83** B14
Harrison Nebr., U.S.A. 42°41N 103°53W **80** D2
Harrison, C. Canada 54°55N 57°55W **73** B8
Harrison Bay U.S.A. 70°40N 151°0W **74** A9
Harrison L. Canada 49°33N 121°50W **70** D4
Harrisonburg U.S.A. 38°27N 78°52W **81** F14
Harrisonville U.S.A. 38°39N 94°21W **80** F6
Harriston Canada 43°57N 80°53W **82** C4
Harrisville Mich., U.S.A. 44°39N 83°17W **82** B1
Harrisville N.Y., U.S.A. 44°9N 75°19W **83** B9
Harrisville Pa., U.S.A. 41°8N 80°0W **82** E5
Harrodsburg U.S.A. 37°46N 84°51W **81** G11
Harrogate U.K. 54°0N 1°33W **12** C6
Harrow U.K. 42°2N 82°55W **82** D2
Harrow □ U.K. 51°35N 0°21W **13** F7
Harrowsmith Canada 44°24N 76°40W **83** B8
Harry S. Truman Res.
  U.S.A. 38°16N 93°24W **80** F7
Harsīn Iran 34°18N 47°33E **44** C5
Harstad Norway 68°48N 16°30E **8** B17
Harsud India 22°6N 76°44E **42** H7
Hart U.S.A. 43°42N 86°22W **80** D10
Hart, L. Australia 31°10S 136°25E **63** E2
Hartbees → S. Africa 28°45S 20°32E **56** D3
Hartford Conn., U.S.A. 41°46N 72°41W **83** E12
Hartford Ky., U.S.A. 37°27N 86°55W **80** G10
Hartford S. Dak., U.S.A. 43°38N 96°57W **80** D5
Hartford Vt., U.S.A. 43°40N 72°20W **83** C12
Hartford Wis., U.S.A. 43°19N 88°22W **80** D9
Hartford City U.S.A. 40°27N 85°22W **81** E11
Hartland Canada 46°20N 67°32W **73** C6
Hartland Pt. U.K. 51°1N 4°32W **13** F3
Hartlepool U.K. 54°42N 1°13W **12** C6
Hartlepool □ U.K. 54°42N 1°17W **12** C6
Hartley Bay Canada 53°25N 129°15W **70** C3
Hartmannberge Namibia 17°0S 13°0E **56** B1
Hartney Canada 49°30N 100°35W **71** D8
Harts → S. Africa 28°24S 24°17E **56** D3
Harts Range Australia 23°6S 134°55E **62** C1
Hartselle U.S.A. 34°27N 86°56W **85** D11
Hartshorne U.S.A. 34°51N 95°34W **84** D7
Hartstown U.S.A. 41°33N 80°23W **82** E4
Hartsville S. Africa 27°34S 24°43E **56** D3
Hartsville U.S.A. 34°23N 80°4W **85** D14
Hartswater S. Africa 27°34S 24°43E **56** D3
Hartwell U.S.A. 34°21N 82°56W **85** D13
Harunabad Pakistan 29°35N 73°8E **42** E5
Harvand Iran 28°25N 55°43E **45** D7
Harvey Australia 33°5S 115°54E **61** F2
Harvey Ill., U.S.A. 41°36N 87°50W **80** E10
Harvey N. Dak., U.S.A. 47°47N 99°56W **80** B4
Harwich U.K. 51°56N 1°17E **13** F9
Haryana □ India 29°0N 76°10E **42** E7
Haryn → Belarus 52°7N 27°17E **17** B14
Harz Germany 51°38N 10°44E **16** C6
Hasa Iran 25°50N 49°0E **45** E6
Ḥasā, W. al → Jordan 31°4N 35°29E **46** D4
Ḥasanābād Iran 32°8N 52°44E **45** C7
Ḥasb, W. → Iraq 31°45N 44°17E **44** D5
Hasdo → India 21°44N 82°44E **43** J10
Hashimoto Japan 34°19N 135°37E **31** G7
Hashtjerd Iran 35°52N 50°40E **45** C6
Hashtpur = Tālesh Iran 37°58N 48°58E **45** B6
Haskell U.S.A. 33°10N 99°44W **84** E5
Haskovo = Khaskovo
  Bulgaria 41°56N 25°30E **23** D11
Haslemere U.K. 51°5N 0°43W **13** F7
Hasselt Belgium 50°56N 5°21E **15** D5
Hassi Messaoud Algeria 31°51N 6°1E **50** B7
Hässleholm Sweden 56°10N 13°46E **9** H15
Hastings N.Z. 39°39S 176°52E **59** C6
Hastings U.K. 50°51N 0°35E **13** G8
Hastings Mich., U.S.A. 42°39N 85°17W **81** D11
Hastings Minn., U.S.A. 44°44N 92°51W **80** C7
Hastings Nebr., U.S.A. 40°35N 98°23W **80** E4
Hastings Ra. Australia 31°15S 152°14E **63** E5
Hat Yai Thailand 7°1N 100°27E **39** J3
Hatanbulag = Ergel
  Mongolia 43°8N 109°5E **34** C5
Hatay Turkey 36°14N 36°10E **44** B3
Hatch U.S.A. 32°40N 107°9W **77** K10
Hatchet L. Canada 58°36N 103°40W **71** B8
Hateruma-Shima Japan 24°3N 123°47E **31** M1
Hatfield Australia 33°54S 143°49E **63** E3
Hatgal Mongolia 50°26N 100°9E **32** A5
Hathras India 27°36N 78°6E **42** F8
Hatia Bangla. 22°30N 91°5E **41** H17
Hato Mayor Dom. Rep. 18°46N 69°15W **89** C6
Hatta India 24°7N 79°36E **43** G8
Hattah U.A.E. 24°45N 56°4E **45** E8
Hattah Kulkyne △
  Australia 34°16S 142°33E **63** E3
Hatteras, C. U.S.A. 35°14N 75°32W **85** D17
Hattiesburg U.S.A. 31°20N 89°17W **85** F10
Hatvan Hungary 47°40N 19°45E **17** E10
Hau Duc Vietnam 15°20N 108°13E **38** E7
Haugesund Norway 59°23N 5°13E **9** G11
Haukipudas Finland 65°12N 25°20E **8** D21
Haultain → Canada 55°51N 106°46W **71** B7
Hauraki G. N.Z. 36°35S 175°5E **59** B5
Haut Atlas Morocco 32°30N 5°0W **50** B4
Hauts Plateaux Algeria 35°0N 1°0E **50** B6
Hautes Fagnes = Hohes Venn
  Belgium 50°30N 6°5E **15** D6
Havana = La Habana
  Cuba 23°8N 82°22W **88** B3
Havana U.S.A. 40°18N 90°4W **80** E8
Havant U.K. 50°51N 0°58W **13** G7
Havasu, L. U.S.A. 34°18N 114°28W **79** L12
Havel → Germany 52°50N 12°3E **16** B7
Havelian Pakistan 34°2N 73°10E **42** B5
Havelock Canada 44°26N 77°53W **82** B7

Havelock N.Z. 41°17S 173°48E **59** D4
Havelock U.S.A. 34°53N 76°54W **85** D16
Haverfordwest U.K. 51°48N 4°58W **13** F3
Haverhill U.K. 52°5N 0°28E **13** E8
Haverhill U.S.A. 42°47N 71°5W **83** D13
Haverstraw U.S.A. 41°12N 73°58W **83** E11
Havirga Mongolia 45°41N 113°5E **34** B7
Havířov Czech Rep. 49°46N 18°20E **17** D10
Havlíčkův Brod
  Czech Rep. 49°36N 15°33E **16** D8
Havre U.S.A. 48°33N 109°41W **76** B9
Havre-Aubert Canada 47°12N 61°56W **73** C7
Havre-St.-Pierre Canada 50°18N 63°33W **73** B7
Haw → U.S.A. 35°36N 79°3W **85** D15
Hawai'i □ U.S.A. 19°30N 155°30W **75** M8
Hawai'i U.S.A. 19°30N 155°30W **75** M8
Hawaiian Is. Pac. Oc. 20°30N 156°0W **65** E12
Hawaiian Ridge Pac. Oc. 24°0N 165°0W **65** E11
Hawarden U.S.A. 43°0N 96°29W **80** D5
Hawea, L. N.Z. 44°28S 169°19E **59** F2
Hawera N.Z. 39°35S 174°19E **59** C5
Hawi U.S.A. 20°14N 155°50W **75** L8
Hawick U.K. 55°26N 2°47W **11** F6
Hawk Junction Canada 48°5N 84°38W **72** C3
Hawke B. N.Z. 39°25S 177°20E **59** C6
Hawker Australia 31°59S 138°22E **63** E2
Hawke's Bay Canada 50°36N 57°10W **73** B8
Hawke's Bay □ N.Z. 39°45S 176°35E **59** C6
Hawkesbury Canada 45°37N 74°37W **72** C5
Hawkesbury I. Canada 53°37N 129°3W **70** C3
Hawkesbury Pt.
  Australia 11°55S 134°5E **62** A1
Hawkinsville U.S.A. 32°17N 83°28W **85** E13
Hawley Minn., U.S.A. 46°53N 96°19W **80** B5
Hawley Pa., U.S.A. 41°28N 75°11W **83** E9
Haworth Australia 31°59S 138°22E **63** E2
Hawthorne U.S.A. 38°32N 118°38W **76** G4
Hay Australia 34°30S 144°51E **63** E3
Hay → Australia 24°50S 138°0E **62** C2
Hay → Canada 60°50N 116°26W **70** A5
Hay, C. Australia 14°5S 129°29E **60** B4
Hay L. Canada 58°50N 118°50W **70** B5
Hay-on-Wye U.K. 52°5N 3°8W **13** E4
Hay Point Australia 21°18S 149°17E **62** C4
Hay River Canada 60°51N 115°44W **70** A5
Hay Springs U.S.A. 42°41N 102°41W **80** D2
Haya = Tehoru Indonesia 3°23S 129°30E **37** E7
Hayachine-San Japan 39°34N 141°29E **30** E10
Hayastan = Armenia ■
  Asia 40°20N 45°0E **19** F7
Hayden U.S.A. 40°30N 107°16W **76** F10
Hayes U.S.A. 44°23N 101°1W **80** C3
Hayes → Canada 57°3N 92°12W **72** A1
Hayes, Mt. U.S.A. 63°37N 146°43W **74** C10
Hayle U.K. 50°11N 5°26E **13** G2
Hayling I. U.K. 50°48N 0°59W **13** G7
Hayman I. Australia 20°4S 148°53E **62** b
Hayrabolu Turkey 41°12N 27°5E **23** D12
Hays Canada 50°6N 111°48W **70** C6
Hays U.S.A. 38°53N 99°20W **80** F4
Hayvoron Ukraine 48°22N 29°52E **17** D15
Hayward Calif., U.S.A. 37°40N 122°4W **78** H4
Hayward Wis., U.S.A. 46°1N 91°29W **80** B8
Haywards Heath U.K. 51°0N 0°5W **13** G7
Hazafon □ Israel 32°40N 35°20E **46** C4
Hazar Turkmenistan 39°34N 53°16E **19** G9
Hazaribag India 23°58N 85°26E **43** H11
Hazaribag Road India 24°12N 85°57E **43** G11
Hazelton Canada 55°20N 127°42W **70** B3
Hazelton U.S.A. 46°29N 100°17W **80** B3
Hazen U.S.A. 47°18N 101°38W **80** B3
Hazen, L. Canada 81°47N 71°1W **69** A17
Hazlehurst Ga., U.S.A. 31°52N 82°36W **85** F13
Hazlehurst Miss., U.S.A. 31°52N 90°24W **85** F9
Hazlet U.S.A. 40°25N 74°12W **83** F10
Hazleton U.S.A. 40°57N 75°59W **83** F9
Hazlett, L. Australia 21°30S 128°48E **60** D4
Hazro Turkey 38°15N 40°47E **44** B4
Head of Bight Australia 31°30S 131°25E **61** F5
Headlands Zimbabwe 18°15S 32°2E **55** F3
Healdsburg U.S.A. 38°37N 122°52W **78** G4
Healdton U.S.A. 34°14N 97°29W **84** D6
Healesville Australia 37°35S 145°30E **63** F4
Healy U.S.A. 63°52N 148°58W **74** C10
Heany Junction Zimbabwe 20°6S 28°54E **57** C4
Heard I. Ind. Oc. 53°6S 72°36E **3** G13
Hearne U.S.A. 30°53N 96°36W **84** F6
Hearst Canada 49°40N 83°41W **72** C3
Heart → U.S.A. 46°46N 100°50W **80** B3
Heart's Content Canada 47°54N 53°27W **73** C9
Heath, Pte. Canada 49°8N 61°40W **73** C7
Heathrow, London ✈ (LHR)
  U.K. 51°28N 0°27W **13** F7
Heavener U.S.A. 34°53N 94°36W **84** D7
Hebbronville U.S.A. 27°18N 98°41W **84** H5
Hebei □ China 39°0N 116°0E **34** E9
Hebel Australia 28°58S 147°47E **63** D4
Heber U.S.A. 34°30N 110°35E **77** K9
Heber Springs U.S.A. 35°30N 92°2W **84** D8
Hebgen L. U.S.A. 44°52N 111°20W **76** D8
Hebi China 35°57N 114°7E **34** G8
Hebrides U.K. 57°30N 7°0W **6** D4
Hebrides, Sea of the U.K. 57°5N 7°0W **11** D2
Hebron = Al Khalīl
  West Bank 31°32N 35°6E **46** D4
Hebron Canada 58°5N 62°30W **69** F19
Hebron N. Dak., U.S.A. 46°54N 102°3W **80** B2
Hebron Nebr., U.S.A. 40°10N 97°35W **80** E5
Hecate Str. Canada 53°10N 130°30W **70** C2
Hechi China 24°40N 108°2E **32** D5
Hechuan China 30°2N 106°12E **32** C5
Hecla U.S.A. 45°53N 98°9W **80** C4

Hecla I. *Canada* 51°10N 96°43W **71** C9
Hede *Sweden* 62°23N 13°30E **8** E15
Hedemora *Sweden* 60°18N 15°58E **9** F16
Heerde *Neths.* 52°24N 6°2E **15** B6
Heerenveen *Neths.* 52°57N 5°55E **15** B5
Heerhugowaard *Neths.* 52°40N 4°51E **15** B4
Heerlen *Neths.* 50°55N 5°58E **15** D5
Ḥefa *Israel* 32°46N 35°0E **46** C4
Ḥefa □ *Israel* 32°40N 35°0E **46** C4
Hefei *China* 31°52N 117°18E **33** C6
Hegang *China* 47°20N 130°19E **33** B8
Hei Ling Chau *China* 22°15N 114°2E **33** G11
Heichengzhen *China* 36°24N 106°3E **34** F4
Heidelberg *Germany* 49°24N 8°42E **16** D5
Heidelberg *S. Africa* 34°6S 20°59E **56** E3
Heihe *China* 50°10N 127°30E **33** A7
Heilbron *S. Africa* 27°16S 27°59E **57** D4
Heilbronn *Germany* 49°9N 9°13E **16** D5
Heilongjiang □ *China* 48°0N 126°0E **33** B7
Heilunkiang = Heilongjiang □
  China 48°0N 126°0E **33** B7
Heimaey *Iceland* 63°26N 20°17W **8** E3
Heinola *Finland* 61°13N 26°2E **8** F22
Heinze Kyun *Burma* 14°25N 97°45E **38** E1
Heishan *China* 41°40N 122°5E **35** D12
Heishui *China* 42°8N 119°30E **35** C10
Hejaz = Ḥijāz *Si. Arabia* 24°0N 40°0E **44** E3
Hejian *China* 38°25N 116°5E **34** E9
Hejin *China* 35°35N 110°42E **34** G6
Hekımhan *Turkey* 38°50N 37°55E **44** B3
Hekla *Iceland* 63°56N 19°35W **8** E4
Hekou *China* 22°30N 103°59E **32** D5
Helan Shan *China* 38°30N 105°55E **34** E3
Helen Atoll *Pac. Oc.* 2°40N 132°0E **37** D8
Helena *Ark., U.S.A.* 34°32N 90°36W **85** D9
Helena *Mont., U.S.A.* 46°36N 112°2W **76** C7
Helendale *U.S.A.* 34°44N 117°19W **79** L9
Helensburgh *U.K.* 56°1N 4°43W **11** E4
Helensville *N.Z.* 36°41S 174°29E **59** B5
Helenvale *Australia* 15°43S 145°14E **62** B4
Helgeland *Norway* 66°7N 13°29E **8** C15
Helgoland *Germany* 54°10N 7°53E **16** A4
Heligoland = Helgoland
  Germany 54°10N 7°53E **16** A4
Heligoland B. = Deutsche Bucht
  Germany 54°15N 8°0E **16** A5
Hell Hole Gorge △
  Australia 25°31S 144°12E **62** D3
Hella *Iceland* 63°50N 20°24W **8** E3
Hellas = Greece ■ *Europe* 40°0N 23°0E **23** E9
Hellertown *U.S.A.* 40°35N 75°21W **83** F9
Hellespont = Çanakkale Boğazı
  Turkey 40°17N 26°32E **23** D12
Hellevoetsluis *Neths.* 51°50N 4°8E **15** C4
Hellín *Spain* 38°31N 1°40W **21** C5
Hells Canyon △ *U.S.A.* 45°30N 117°45W **76** D5
Hell's Gate △ *Kenya* 0°54S 36°19E **54** C4
Helmand □ *Afghan.* 31°20N 64°0E **40** D4
Helmand → *Afghan.* 31°12N 61°34E **40** D2
Helmeringhausen
  Namibia 25°54S 16°57E **56** D2
Helmond *Neths.* 51°29N 5°41E **15** C5
Helmsdale *U.K.* 58°7N 3°39W **11** C5
Helmsdale → *U.K.* 58°8N 3°43W **11** C5
Helong *China* 42°40N 129°0E **35** C15
Helper *U.S.A.* 39°41N 110°51W **76** G8
Helsingborg *Sweden* 56°3N 12°42E **9** H15
Helsingfors = Helsinki
  Finland 60°10N 24°55E **9** F21
Helsingør *Denmark* 56°2N 12°35E **9** H15
Helsinki *Finland* 60°10N 24°55E **9** F21
Helston *U.K.* 50°6N 5°17W **13** G2
Helvellyn *U.K.* 54°32N 3°1W **12** C4
Helwân *Egypt* 29°50N 31°20E **51** C12
Hemel Hempstead *U.K.* 51°44N 0°28W **13** F7
Hemet *U.S.A.* 33°45N 116°58W **79** M10
Hemingford *U.S.A.* 42°19N 103°4W **80** D2
Hemis △ *India* 34°10N 77°15E **42** B7
Hemmingford *Canada* 45°3N 73°35W **83** A11
Hempstead *N.Y., U.S.A.* 40°42N 73°37W **83** F11
Hempstead *Tex., U.S.A.* 30°6N 96°5W **84** F6
Hemse *Sweden* 57°15N 18°22E **9** H18
Henan □ *China* 34°0N 114°0E **34** H8
Henares → *Spain* 40°24N 3°30W **21** B4
Henashi-Misaki *Japan* 40°37N 139°51E **30** D9
Henderson *Argentina* 36°18S 61°43W **94** D3
Henderson *Ky., U.S.A.* 37°50N 87°35W **80** G10
Henderson *N.C., U.S.A.* 36°20N 78°25W **85** G15
Henderson *N.Y., U.S.A.* 43°56N 76°10W **83** C8
Henderson *Nev., U.S.A.* 36°2N 114°58W **79** J12
Henderson *Tenn.,*
  U.S.A. 35°26N 88°38W **85** D10
Henderson *Tex., U.S.A.* 32°9N 94°48W **84** E7
Henderson I. *Pac. Oc.* 24°22S 128°19W **65** K15
Hendersonville *N.C.,*
  U.S.A. 35°19N 82°28W **85** D13
Hendersonville *Tenn.,*
  U.S.A. 36°18N 86°37W **85** C11
Hendījān *Iran* 30°14N 49°43E **45** D6
Hendorābī *Iran* 26°40N 53°37E **45** E7
Hengcheng *China* 38°18N 106°28E **34** E4
Hengdaohezi *China* 44°52N 129°0E **35** B15
Hengduan Shan *China* 25°30N 99°0E **32** D4
Hengelo *Neths.* 52°16N 6°48E **15** B6
Henggang *China* 22°39N 114°12E **33** F11
Hengmen *China* 22°33N 113°35E **33** G10
Hengqin Dao *China* 22°7N 113°34E **33** G10
Hengshan *China* 37°58N 109°5E **34** F5
Hengshui *China* 37°41N 115°40E **34** F8
Hengyang *China* 26°59N 112°22E **33** D6
Henley-on-Thames *U.K.* 51°32N 0°54W **13** F7
Henlopen, C. *U.S.A.* 38°48N 75°6W **81** F16
Hennenman *S. Africa* 27°59S 27°1E **56** D4
Hennessey *U.S.A.* 36°6N 97°54W **84** C6
Henri Pittier △
  Venezuela 10°26N 67°37W **89** D6
Henrietta *N.Y., U.S.A.* 43°4N 77°37W **82** C7
Henrietta *Tex., U.S.A.* 33°49N 98°12W **84** E5
Henrietta, Ostrov = Genriyetty,
  Ostrov *Russia* 77°6N 156°30E **29** B16

Henrietta Maria, C.
  Canada 55°9N 82°20W **72** A3
Henry *U.S.A.* 41°7N 89°22W **80** E9
Henryetta *U.S.A.* 35°27N 95°59W **84** D7
Henryville *Canada* 45°8N 73°11W **83** A11
Hensall *Canada* 43°26N 81°30W **82** C3
Hentiesbaai *Namibia* 22°8S 14°18E **56** C1
Hentiyn Nuruu
  Mongolia 48°30N 108°30E **33** B5
Henty *Australia* 35°30S 147°3E **63** F4
Henzada *Burma* 17°38N 95°26E **41** L19
Heppner *U.S.A.* 45°21N 119°33W **76** D4
Hepworth *Canada* 44°37N 81°9W **82** B3
Hequ *China* 39°20N 111°15E **34** E6
Héradsflói *Iceland* 65°42N 14°12W **8** D6
Héraðsvötn → *Iceland* 65°45N 19°25W **8** D4
Heraklion = Iraklio
  Greece 35°20N 25°12E **25** D7
Herald Cays *Australia* 16°58S 149°9E **62** B4
Herät *Afghan.* 34°20N 62°7E **40** B3
Herät □ *Afghan.* 35°0N 62°0E **40** B3
Herbert *Canada* 50°30N 107°10W **71** C7
Herbert → *Australia* 18°31S 146°17E **62** B4
Herberton *Australia* 17°20S 145°25E **62** B4
Herbertsdale *S. Africa* 34°1S 21°46E **56** E3
Herceg-Novi *Montenegro* 42°30N 18°33E **23** C8
Herchmer *Canada* 57°22N 94°10W **71** B10
Herðubreið *Iceland* 65°11N 16°21W **8** D5
Hereford *U.K.* 52°4N 2°43W **13** E5
Hereford *U.S.A.* 34°49N 102°24W **84** D3
Herefordshire □ *U.K.* 52°8N 2°40W **13** E5
Herentals *Belgium* 51°12N 4°51E **15** C4
Herford *Germany* 52°7N 8°39E **16** B5
Herington *U.S.A.* 38°40N 96°57W **80** F5
Herkimer *U.S.A.* 43°2N 74°59W **83** D10
Herlong *U.S.A.* 40°8N 120°8W **78** E6
Herm *U.K.* 49°30N 2°28W **13** H5
Hermann *U.S.A.* 38°42N 91°27W **80** F8
Hermannsburg
  Australia 23°57S 132°45E **60** D5
Hermanus *S. Africa* 34°27S 19°12E **56** E2
Hermidale *Australia* 31°30S 146°42E **63** E4
Hermiston *U.S.A.* 45°51N 119°17W **76** D4
Hermon *Canada* 45°6N 77°37W **82** A7
Hermon *U.S.A.* 44°28N 75°14W **83** B9
Hermon, Mt. = Shaykh, J. ash
  Lebanon 33°25N 35°50E **46** B4
Hermosillo *Mexico* 29°10N 111°0W **86** B2
Hernád → *Hungary* 47°56N 21°8E **17** D11
Hernandarias *Paraguay* 25°20S 54°40W **95** B5
Hernandez *U.S.A.* 36°24N 120°46W **78** J6
Hernando *Argentina* 32°28S 63°40W **94** C3
Hernando *U.S.A.* 34°50N 90°0W **85** D9
Herndon *U.S.A.* 40°43N 76°51W **82** F8
Herne *Germany* 51°32N 7°14E **15** C7
Herne Bay *U.K.* 51°21N 1°8E **13** F9
Herning *Denmark* 56°8N 8°58E **9** H13
Heroica Caborca = Caborca
  Mexico 30°37N 112°6W **86** A2
Heroica Nogales = Nogales
  Mexico 31°19N 110°56W **86** A2
Heron Bay *Canada* 48°40N 86°25W **72** C2
Heron I. *Australia* 23°27S 151°55E **62** C5
Herradura, Pta. de la
  Canary Is. 28°26N 14°8W **24** F5
Herreid *U.S.A.* 45°50N 100°4W **80** C3
Herrin *U.S.A.* 37°48N 89°2W **80** G9
Herriot *Canada* 56°22N 101°16W **71** B8
Herschel I. *Canada* 69°35N 139°5W **4** C1
Hershey *U.S.A.* 40°17N 76°39W **83** F8
Herstal *Belgium* 50°40N 5°38E **15** D5
Hertford *U.K.* 51°48N 0°4W **13** F7
Hertfordshire □ *U.K.* 51°51N 0°5W **13** F7
's-Hertogenbosch *Neths.* 51°42N 5°17E **15** C5
Hertzogville *S. Africa* 28°9S 25°30E **56** D4
Hervey B. *Australia* 25°0S 152°52E **62** C5
Ḥerzliyya *Israel* 32°10N 34°50E **46** C3
Ḥeşār *Fārs, Iran* 29°52N 50°16E **45** D6
Ḥeşār *Markazī, Iran* 35°50N 49°12E **45** C6
Heshui *China* 35°48N 108°0E **34** G5
Heshun *China* 37°22N 113°32E **34** F7
Hesperia *U.S.A.* 34°25N 117°18W **79** L9
Hesse = Hessen □
  Germany 50°30N 9°0E **16** C5
Hessen □ *Germany* 50°30N 9°0E **16** C5
Hetauda *Nepal* 27°25N 85°2E **43** F11
Hetch Hetchy Aqueduct
  U.S.A. 37°29N 122°19W **78** H5
Hettinger *U.S.A.* 46°0N 102°42W **80** B2
Heuksando *S. Korea* 34°40N 125°30E **35** G13
Heunghae *S. Korea* 36°12N 129°21E **35** F15
Heuvelton *U.S.A.* 44°37N 75°25W **83** B9
Hewitt *U.S.A.* 31°28N 97°12W **84** F6
Hexham *U.K.* 54°58N 2°4W **12** C5
Hexigten Qi *China* 43°18N 117°30E **35** C9
Heysham *U.K.* 54°3N 2°53W **12** C5
Heywood *Australia* 38°8S 141°37E **63** F3
Heze *China* 35°14N 115°20E **34** G8
Hi Vista *U.S.A.* 34°45N 117°46W **79** L9
Hialeah *U.S.A.* 25°51N 80°16W **85** J14
Hiawatha *U.S.A.* 39°51N 95°32W **80** F6
Hibbing *U.S.A.* 47°25N 92°56W **80** B7
Hibernia Reef *Australia* 12°0S 123°23E **60** B3
Hickman *U.S.A.* 36°34N 89°11W **80** G10
Hickory *U.S.A.* 35°44N 81°21W **85** D14
Hicks, Pt. *Australia* 37°49S 149°17E **63** F4
Hicks L. *Canada* 61°25N 100°0W **71** A9
Hicksville *U.S.A.* 40°46N 73°32W **83** F11
Hida-Gawa → *Japan* 35°26N 137°3E **31** G8
Hida-Sammyaku *Japan* 36°30N 137°40E **31** F8
Hidaka-Sammyaku
  Japan 42°35N 142°45E **30** C11
Hidalgo □ *Mexico* 20°30N 99°0W **87** C5
Hidalgo, Presa M.
  Mexico 26°30N 108°35W **86** B3
Hidalgo del Parral
  Mexico 26°56N 105°40W **86** B3
Hierro *Canary Is.* 27°44N 18°0W **24** G1

Higashiajima-San
  Japan 37°40N 140°10E **30** F10
Higashiōsaka *Japan* 34°39N 135°37E **31** G7
Higgins *U.S.A.* 36°7N 100°2W **84** C4
Higgins Corner *U.S.A.* 39°2N 121°5W **78** F5
High Bridge *U.S.A.* 40°40N 74°54W **83** F10
High Desert *U.S.A.* 43°40N 120°20W **74** G15
High Island Res. *China* 22°22N 114°21E **33** G11
High Level *Canada* 58°31N 117°8W **70** B5
High Point *U.S.A.* 35°57N 80°0W **85** D15
High Prairie *Canada* 55°30N 116°30W **70** B5
High River *Canada* 50°30N 113°50W **70** C6
High Tatra = Tatry
  Slovak Rep. 49°20N 20°0E **17** D11
High Veld *Africa* 27°0S 27°0E **48** J6
High Wycombe *U.K.* 51°37N 0°45W **13** F7
Highland □ *U.K.* 57°17N 4°21W **11** D4
Highland Park *U.S.A.* 42°11N 87°48W **80** D10
Highmore *U.S.A.* 44°31N 99°27W **80** C4
Highrock L. *Canada* 55°45N 100°30W **71** B8
Higüey *Dom. Rep.* 18°37N 68°42W **89** C6
Hiiumaa *Estonia* 58°50N 22°45E **9** G20
Ḥijārah, Şaḥrā' al *Iraq* 30°25N 44°30E **44** D5
Ḥijāz *Si. Arabia* 24°0N 40°0E **44** E3
Hijo = Tagum *Phil.* 7°33N 125°53E **37** C7
Hikari *Japan* 33°58N 131°58E **31** H5
Hiko *U.S.A.* 37°32N 115°14W **78** H11
Hikone *Japan* 35°15N 136°10E **31** G8
Hikurangi *Gisborne, N.Z.* 37°55S 178°4E **59** C6
Hikurangi *Northland,*
  N.Z. 35°36S 174°17E **59** A5
Hildesheim *Germany* 52°9N 9°56E **16** B5
Hill → *Australia* 30°23S 115°3E **61** F2
Hill City *Idaho, U.S.A.* 43°18N 115°3W **76** E6
Hill City *Kans., U.S.A.* 39°22N 99°51W **80** F4
Hill City *Minn., U.S.A.* 46°59N 93°36W **80** B7
Hill City *S. Dak., U.S.A.* 43°56N 103°35W **80** D3
Hill Island L. *Canada* 60°30N 109°50W **71** A7
Hillaby, Mt. *Barbados* 13°12N 59°35W **89** g
Hillcrest *Barbados* 13°13N 59°31W **89** g
Hillcrest Center *U.S.A.* 35°23N 118°57W **79** K8
Hillegom *Neths.* 52°18N 4°35E **15** B4
Hillsboro *Kans., U.S.A.* 38°21N 97°12W **80** F5
Hillsboro *N. Dak., U.S.A.* 47°26N 97°3W **80** B5
Hillsboro *Ohio, U.S.A.* 39°12N 83°37W **81** F12
Hillsboro *Oreg., U.S.A.* 45°31N 122°59W **78** E4
Hillsboro *Tex., U.S.A.* 32°1N 97°8W **84** E6
Hillsborough *Grenada* 12°28N 61°28W **89** D7
Hillsborough *U.S.A.* 36°4N 79°6W **85** D15
Hillsborough Channel
  Australia 20°56S 149°15E **62** b
Hillsdale *Mich., U.S.A.* 41°56N 84°38W **81** E11
Hillsdale *N.Y., U.S.A.* 42°11N 73°32W **83** D11
Hillsport *Canada* 49°27N 85°34W **72** C2
Hillston *Australia* 33°30S 145°31E **63** E4
Hilo *U.S.A.* 19°44N 155°5W **75** M8
Hilton *U.S.A.* 43°17N 77°48W **82** C7
Hilton Head Island
  U.S.A. 32°13N 80°45W **85** E14
Hilversum *Neths.* 52°14N 5°10E **15** B5
Himachal Pradesh □
  India 31°30N 77°0E **42** D7
Himalaya *Asia* 29°0N 84°0E **43** E11
Himatnagar *India* 23°37N 72°57E **42** H5
Himeji *Japan* 34°50N 134°40E **31** G7
Himi *Japan* 36°50N 136°55E **31** F8
Ḥimş *Syria* 34°40N 36°45E **46** A5
Ḥimş □ *Syria* 34°30N 37°0E **46** A6
Hinche *Haiti* 19°9N 72°1W **89** C5
Hinchinbrook I.
  Australia 18°20S 146°15E **62** B4
Hinchinbrook Island △
  Australia 18°14S 146°6E **62** B4
Hinckley *U.K.* 52°33N 1°22W **13** E6
Hinckley *U.S.A.* 46°1N 92°56W **80** B7
Hindaun *India* 26°44N 77°5E **42** F7
Hindmarsh, L. *Australia* 36°5S 141°55E **63** F3
Hindu Bagh *Pakistan* 30°56N 67°50E **42** D2
Hindu Kush *Asia* 36°0N 71°0E **40** B7
Hindupur *India* 13°49N 77°32E **40** N10
Hines Creek *Canada* 56°20N 118°40W **70** B5
Hinesville *U.S.A.* 31°51N 81°36W **85** F14
Hinganghat *India* 20°30N 78°52E **40** J11
Hingir *India* 21°57N 83°41E **43** J10
Hingoli *India* 19°41N 77°15E **40** K10
Hinna = Imi *Ethiopia* 6°28N 42°10E **47** F3
Hinnøya *Norway* 68°35N 15°50E **8** B16
Hinojosa del Duque *Spain* 38°30N 5°9W **21** C3
Hinsdale *U.S.A.* 42°47N 72°29W **83** D12
Hinthada = Henzada
  Burma 17°38N 95°26E **41** L19
Hinton *Canada* 53°26N 117°34W **70** C5
Hinton *U.S.A.* 37°40N 80°54W **81** G13
Hios *Greece* 38°27N 26°9E **23** E12
Hirado *Japan* 33°22N 129°33E **31** H4
Hirakud Dam *India* 21°32N 83°45E **41** J13
Hiran → *India* 23°6N 79°21E **43** H8
Hirapur *India* 24°22N 79°13E **43** G8
Hirara *Japan* 24°48N 125°17E **31** M2
Hiratsuka *Japan* 35°19N 139°21E **31** G9
Hiroo *Japan* 42°17N 143°19E **30** C11
Hirosaki *Japan* 40°34N 140°28E **30** D10
Hiroshima *Japan* 34°24N 132°30E **31** G6
Hiroshima □ *Japan* 34°50N 133°0E **31** G6
Hisar *India* 29°12N 75°45E **42** E6
Hisb, Sha'ib → *W.*
  Iraq 31°45N 44°17E **44** D5
Ḥismá *Si. Arabia* 28°30N 36°0E **44** D3
Hispaniola *W. Indies* 19°0N 71°0W **89** C5
Hīt *Iraq* 33°38N 42°49E **44** C4
Hita *Japan* 33°20N 130°58E **31** H5
Hitachi *Japan* 36°36N 140°39E **31** F10
Hitchin *U.K.* 51°58N 0°16W **13** F7
Hitiaa *Tahiti* 17°36S 149°18W **59** d
Hitoyoshi *Japan* 32°13N 130°45E **31** H5
Hitra *Norway* 63°30N 8°45E **8** E13
Hiva Oa *French Polynesia* 9°45S 139°0W **65** H14

Hixon *Canada* 53°25N 122°35W **70** C4
Ḥiyyon, N. → *Israel* 30°25N 35°10E **46** E4
Hjalmar L. *Canada* 61°33N 109°25W **71** A7
Hjälmaren *Sweden* 59°18N 15°40E **9** G16
Hjørring *Denmark* 57°29N 9°59E **9** H13
Hjort Trench *S. Ocean* 58°0S 157°30E **5** B10
Hkakabo Razi *Burma* 28°25N 97°23E **41** E20
Hkamti = Singkaling Hkamti
  Burma 26°0N 95°39E **41** G19
Hlobane *S. Africa* 27°42S 31°0E **57** D5
Hluhluwe *S. Africa* 28°1S 32°15E **57** D5
Hluhluwe △ *S. Africa* 22°10S 32°5E **57** C5
Hlyboka *Ukraine* 48°5N 25°56E **17** D13
Ho *Ghana* 6°37N 0°27E **50** G6
Ho Chi Minh City = Thanh Pho
Ho Chi Minh *Vietnam* 10°58N 106°40E **39** G6
Ho Thuong *Vietnam* 19°32N 105°48E **38** C5
Hoa Binh *Vietnam* 20°50N 105°20E **38** B5
Hoa Da *Vietnam* 11°16N 108°40E **39** G7
Hoa Hiep *Vietnam* 11°34N 105°51E **39** G5
Hoai Nhon *Vietnam* 14°28N 109°1E **38** E7
Hoang Lien Son *Vietnam* 22°0N 104°0E **38** A4
Hoanib → *Namibia* 19°27S 12°46E **56** B2
Hoare B. *Canada* 65°17N 62°30W **69** D19
Hoarusib → *Namibia* 19°3S 12°36E **56** B2
Hobart *Australia* 42°50S 147°21E **63** G4
Hobart *U.S.A.* 35°1N 99°6W **84** D5
Hobbs *U.S.A.* 32°42N 103°8W **77** K12
Hobbs Coast *Antarctica* 74°50S 131°0W **5** D14
Hobe Sound *U.S.A.* 27°4N 80°8W **85** H14
Hoboken *U.S.A.* 40°44N 74°3W **83** F10
Hobro *Denmark* 56°39N 9°46E **9** H13
Hoburgen *Sweden* 56°55N 18°7E **9** H18
Hobyo *Somali Rep.* 5°25N 48°30E **47** F4
Hochfeld *Namibia* 21°28S 17°58E **56** C2
Hodaka-Dake *Japan* 36°17N 137°39E **31** F8
Hodeida = Al Ḥudaydah
  Yemen 14°50N 43°0E **47** E3
Hodgeville *Canada* 50°7N 106°58W **71** C7
Hodgson *Canada* 51°13N 97°36W **71** C9
Hódmezővásárhely
  Hungary 46°28N 20°22E **17** E11
Hodna, Chott el *Algeria* 35°26N 4°43E **50** A6
Hodonín *Czech Rep.* 48°50N 17°10E **17** D9
Hoek van Holland *Neths.* 52°0N 4°7E **15** C4
Hoengseong *S. Korea* 37°29N 127°59E **35** F14
Hoeryong *N. Korea* 42°30N 129°45E **35** C15
Hoeyang *N. Korea* 38°43N 127°36E **35** E14
Hof *Germany* 50°19N 11°55E **16** C6
Hofmeyr *S. Africa* 31°39S 25°50E **56** E4
Höfn *Iceland* 64°15N 15°13W **8** D6
Hofors *Sweden* 60°31N 16°15E **9** F17
Hofsjökull *Iceland* 64°49N 18°48W **8** D4
Hōfu *Japan* 34°3N 131°34E **31** G5
Hogan Group *Australia* 39°13S 147°1E **63** F4
Hogarth, Mt. *Australia* 21°48S 136°58E **62** C2
Hoge Kempen △ *Belgium* 51°6N 5°35E **15** C5
Hoggar = Ahaggar *Algeria* 23°0N 6°30E **50** D7
Hogsty Reef *Bahamas* 21°41N 73°48W **89** B5
Hoh → *U.S.A.* 47°45N 124°29W **78** C2
Hoh Xil Shan *China* 35°0N 89°0E **32** C3
Hohenwald *U.S.A.* 35°33N 87°33W **85** D11
Hoher Rhön = Rhön
  Germany 50°24N 9°58E **16** C5
Hohes Venn *Belgium* 50°30N 6°5E **15** D6
Hohhot *China* 40°52N 111°40E **34** D6
Hoi An *Vietnam* 15°30N 108°19E **38** E7
Hoi Xuan *Vietnam* 20°25N 105°9E **38** B5
Hoisington *U.S.A.* 38°31N 98°47W **80** F4
Hōjō *Japan* 33°58N 132°46E **31** H6
Hokianga Harbour
  N.Z. 35°31S 173°22E **59** A4
Hokitika *N.Z.* 42°42S 171°0E **59** E3
Hokkaidō □ *Japan* 43°30N 143°0E **30** C11
Hola *Kenya* 1°29S 40°2E **54** B4
Holakas *Greece* 35°57N 27°53E **25** D9
Holbrook *Australia* 35°42S 147°18E **63** F4
Holbrook *U.S.A.* 34°54N 110°10W **77** J8
Holcomb *U.S.A.* 42°54N 77°25W **82** D7
Holden *U.S.A.* 39°6N 112°16W **76** G7
Holdenville *U.S.A.* 35°5N 96°24W **84** D6
Holdrege *U.S.A.* 40°26N 99°23W **80** E4
Holetown *Barbados* 13°11N 59°38W **89** g
Holguín *Cuba* 20°50N 76°20W **88** B4
Hollams Bird I. *Namibia* 24°40S 14°30E **56** C1
Holland = Netherlands ■
  Europe 52°0N 5°30E **15** C5
Holland *Mich., U.S.A.* 42°47N 86°7W **80** D10
Holland *N.Y., U.S.A.* 42°38N 78°32W **82** D6
Holland Centre *Canada* 44°23N 80°47W **82** B4
Holland Patent *U.S.A.* 43°14N 75°15W **83** C9
Hollandale *U.S.A.* 33°10N 90°51W **85** E9
Holley *U.S.A.* 43°14N 78°2W **82** C6
Hollidaysburg *U.S.A.* 40°26N 78°24W **82** F6
Hollis *U.S.A.* 34°41N 99°55W **84** D5
Hollister *Calif., U.S.A.* 36°51N 121°24W **78** J5
Hollister *Idaho, U.S.A.* 42°21N 114°35W **76** E6
Holly Hill *U.S.A.* 29°16N 81°3W **85** G14
Holly Springs *U.S.A.* 34°46N 89°27W **85** D10
Hollywood *U.S.A.* 26°0N 80°8W **85** J14
Holman *Canada* 70°44N 117°44W **68** C8
Hólmavík *Iceland* 65°42N 21°40W **8** D3
Holmen *U.S.A.* 43°58N 91°15W **80** D8
Holmes Reefs *Australia* 16°27S 148°0E **62** B4
Holmsund *Sweden* 63°41N 20°20E **8** E19
Holroyd → *Australia* 14°10S 141°36E **62** A3
Holstebro *Denmark* 56°22N 8°37E **9** H13
Holsworthy *U.K.* 50°48N 4°22E **13** G3
Holton *Canada* 54°31N 57°12W **73** B8
Holton *U.S.A.* 39°28N 95°44W **80** F6
Holtville *U.S.A.* 32°49N 115°23W **79** N11
Holwerd *Neths.* 53°22N 5°54E **15** A5
Holy Cross *U.S.A.* 62°12N 159°46W **74** C8
Holy I. *Anglesey, U.K.* 53°17N 4°37W **12** D3
Holy I. *Northumberland,*
  U.K. 55°40N 1°47W **12** B6
Holyhead *U.K.* 53°18N 4°38W **12** D3
Holyoke *Colo., U.S.A.* 40°35N 102°18W **76** F12
Holyoke *Mass., U.S.A.* 42°12N 72°37W **83** D12

Holyrood *Canada* 47°27N 53°8W **73** C9
Homa Bay *Kenya* 0°36S 34°30E **54** C3
Homalin *Burma* 24°55N 95°0E **41** G19
Homand *Iran* 32°28N 59°37E **45** C8
Homathko → *Canada* 51°0N 124°56W **70** C4
Hombori *Mali* 15°20N 1°38W **50** E5
Home B. *Canada* 68°40N 67°10W **69** D18
Home Hill *Australia* 19°43S 147°25E **62** B4
Home Reef *Tonga* 18°59S 174°47W **59** c
Homedale *U.S.A.* 43°37N 116°56W **76** E5
Homer *Alaska, U.S.A.* 59°39N 151°33W **68** F1
Homer *La., U.S.A.* 32°48N 93°4W **84** E8
Homer *N.Y., U.S.A.* 42°38N 76°10W **83** D8
Homer City *U.S.A.* 40°32N 79°10W **82** F5
Homestead *Australia* 20°20S 145°40E **62** C4
Homestead *U.S.A.* 25°28N 80°29W **85** J14
Homestead △ *U.S.A.* 40°17N 96°50W **80** E5
Homoine *Mozam.* 23°55S 35°8E **57** C6
Homs = Ḥimş *Syria* 34°40N 36°45E **46** A5
Homyel *Belarus* 52°28N 31°0E **17** B16
Hon Chong *Vietnam* 10°25N 104°30E **39** G5
Hon Hai *Vietnam* 10°0N 109°0E **39** H7
Hon Me *Vietnam* 19°23N 105°56E **38** C5
Honan = Henan □ *China* 34°0N 114°0E **34** H8
Honbetsu *Japan* 43°7N 143°37E **30** C11
Honcut *U.S.A.* 39°20N 121°32W **78** F5
Hondeklipbaai *S. Africa* 30°19S 17°17E **56** E2
Hondo *Japan* 32°27N 130°12E **31** H5
Hondo *U.S.A.* 29°21N 99°9W **84** G5
Hondo, Río → *Belize* 18°25N 88°21W **87** D7
Honduras ■ *Cent. Amer.* 14°40N 86°30W **88** D2
Honduras, G. de
  Caribbean 16°50N 87°0W **88** C2
Hønefoss *Norway* 60°10N 10°18E **9** F14
Honesdale *U.S.A.* 41°34N 75°16W **83** E9
Honey Harbour *Canada* 44°52N 79°49W **82** B5
Honey L. *U.S.A.* 40°15N 120°19W **78** E6
Honfleur *France* 49°25N 0°13E **20** B4
Hong Gai *Vietnam* 20°57N 107°5E **38** B6
Hong He → *China* 32°25N 115°35E **34** H8
Hong Kong □ *China* 22°11N 114°14E **33** G11
Hong Kong *China* 22°16N 114°12E **33** G11
Hong Kong Int. ✈ (HKG)
  China 22°19N 113°57E **33** G10
Hongcheon *S. Korea* 37°44N 127°53E **35** F14
Hongjiang *China* 27°7N 109°59E **33** D5
Hongliu He → *China* 38°0N 109°50E **34** F5
Hongor *Mongolia* 45°45N 112°50E **34** B7
Hongsa *Laos* 19°43N 101°20E **38** C3
Hongshui He → *China* 23°48N 109°30E **33** D5
Hongtong *China* 36°16N 111°40E **34** F6
Honguedo, Détroit d'
  Canada 49°15N 64°0W **73** C7
Hongwon *N. Korea* 40°0N 127°56E **35** E14
Hongze Hu *China* 33°15N 118°35E **35** H10
Honiara *Solomon Is.* 9°27S 159°57E **58** B8
Honiton *U.K.* 50°47N 3°11W **13** G4
Honjō *Japan* 39°23N 140°3E **30** E10
Honningsvåg *Norway* 70°59N 25°59E **8** A21
Honolulu *U.S.A.* 21°19N 157°52W **75** L8
Honshū *Japan* 36°0N 138°0E **30** F9
Hood, Mt. *U.S.A.* 45°23N 121°42W **78** E5
Hood, Pt. *Australia* 34°23S 119°34E **61** F2
Hood River *U.S.A.* 45°43N 121°31W **78** E5
Hoodsport *U.S.A.* 47°24N 123°9W **78** C3
Hoogeveen *Neths.* 52°44N 6°28E **15** B6
Hoogezand-Sappemeer
  Neths. 53°9N 6°45E **15** A6
Hooghly = Hugli →
  India 21°56N 88°4E **43** J13
Hooghly-Chinsura = Chunchura
  India 22°53N 88°27E **43** H13
Hook Hd. *Ireland* 52°7N 6°56W **10** D5
Hook I. *Australia* 20°4S 148°57E **62** b
Hook of Holland = Hoek van
  Holland *Neths.* 52°0N 4°7E **15** C4
Hooker *U.S.A.* 36°52N 101°13W **84** C4
Hooker Creek = Lajamanu
  Australia 18°23S 130°38E **60** C5
Hooker Creek ⊙
  Australia 18°6S 130°23E **60** C5
Hoonah *U.S.A.* 58°7N 135°27W **70** B1
Hooper Bay *U.S.A.* 61°32N 166°6W **74** C6
Hoopeston *U.S.A.* 40°28N 87°40W **80** E10
Hoopstad *S. Africa* 27°50S 25°55E **56** D4
Hoorn *Neths.* 52°38N 5°4E **15** B5
Hoover *U.S.A.* 33°24N 86°49W **85** E11
Hoover Dam *U.S.A.* 36°1N 114°44W **79** K12
Hooversville *U.S.A.* 40°9N 78°55W **82** F6
Hop Bottom *U.S.A.* 41°42N 75°46W **83** E9
Hope *Canada* 49°25N 121°25W **70** D4
Hope *Ariz., U.S.A.* 33°43N 113°42W **79** M13
Hope *Ark., U.S.A.* 33°40N 93°36W **84** E8
Hope, L. *S. Austral.,*
  Australia 28°24S 139°18E **63** D2
Hope, L. *W. Austral.,*
  Australia 32°35S 120°15E **61** F3
Hope, Pt. *U.S.A.* 68°21N 166°47W **74** B6
Hope I. *Canada* 44°55N 80°11W **82** B4
Hope Town *Bahamas* 26°35N 76°57W **88** A4
Hope Vale *Australia* 15°16S 145°20E **62** B4
Hope Vale ⊙ *Australia* 15°8S 145°15E **62** B4
Hopedale *Canada* 55°28N 60°13W **73** A7
Hopedale *U.S.A.* 42°8N 71°33W **83** D13
Hopefield *S. Africa* 33°3S 18°22E **56** E2
Hopei = Hebei □ *China* 39°0N 116°0E **34** E9
Hopelchén *Mexico* 19°46N 89°51W **87** D7
Hopetoun *Vic., Australia* 35°42S 142°22E **63** F3
Hopetoun *W. Austral.,*
  Australia 33°57S 120°7E **61** F3
Hopetown *S. Africa* 29°34S 24°3E **56** D3
Hopewell *U.S.A.* 37°18N 77°17W **81** G15
Hopkins, L. *Australia* 24°15S 128°35E **60** D4
Hopkinsville *U.S.A.* 36°52N 87°29W **80** G10
Hopland *U.S.A.* 38°58N 123°7W **78** G3
Hoquiam *U.S.A.* 46°59N 123°53W **78** D3
Hordern Hills *Australia* 20°15S 130°0E **60** D5

Horinger *China* 40°28N 111°48E **34 D6**
Horizontina *Brazil* 27°37S 54°19W **95 B5**
Horlick Mts. *Antarctica* 84°0S 102°0W **5 E15**
Horlivka *Ukraine* 48°19N 38°5E **19 E6**
Hormak *Iran* 29°58N 60°51E **45 D9**
Hormoz *Iran* 27°35N 55°0E **45 E8**
Hormoz, Jaz.-ye *Iran* 27°8N 56°28E **45 E8**
Hormozgān □ *Iran* 27°30N 56°0E **45 E8**
Hormuz, Kūh-e *Iran* 27°27N 55°10E **45 E7**
Hormuz, Str. of *The Gulf* 26°30N 56°30E **45 E8**
Horn *Austria* 48°39N 15°40E **16 D8**
Horn → *Canada* 61°30N 118°1W **70 A5**
Horn, Cape = Hornos, C. de
  Chile 55°50S 67°30W **96 H3**
Horn Head *Ireland* 55°14N 8°0W **10 A3**
Horn I. *Australia* 10°37S 142°17E **62 A3**
Horn Plateau *Canada* 62°15N 119°15W **70 A5**
Hornbeck *U.S.A.* 31°20N 93°24W **84 F8**
Hornbrook *U.S.A.* 41°55N 122°33W **76 F2**
Horncastle *U.K.* 53°13N 0°7W **12 D7**
Hornell *U.S.A.* 42°20N 77°40W **82 D7**
Hornell L. *Canada* 62°20N 119°25W **70 A5**
Hornepayne *Canada* 49°14N 84°48W **72 C3**
Hornings Mills *Canada* 44°9N 80°12W **82 B4**
Hornitos *U.S.A.* 37°30N 120°14W **78 H6**
Hornos, C. de *Chile* 55°50S 67°30W **96 H3**
Hornsby *Australia* 33°42S 151°2E **63 B5**
Hornsea *U.K.* 53°55N 0°11W **12 D7**
Horobetsu = Noboribetsu
  Japan 42°24N 141°6E **30 C10**
Horodenka *Ukraine* 48°41N 25°29E **17 D13**
Horodok *Khmelnytskyy,*
  Ukraine 49°10N 26°34E **17 D14**
Horodok *Lviv, Ukraine* 49°46N 23°32E **17 D12**
Horokhiv *Ukraine* 50°30N 24°45E **17 C13**
Horqin Youyi Qianqi
  China 46°5N 122°3E **35 A12**
Horqueta *Paraguay* 23°15S 56°55W **94 A4**
Horse Cr. → *U.S.A.* 41°57N 103°58W **76 F12**
Horse I. *Canada* 53°20N 99°6W **71 C9**
Horse Is. *Canada* 50°15N 55°50W **73 B8**
Horsefly L. *Canada* 52°25N 121°0W **70 C4**
Horseheads *U.S.A.* 42°10N 76°49W **82 D7**
Horsens *Denmark* 55°52N 9°51E **9 J13**
Horseshoe Lake *Canada* 45°12N 79°51W **82 A5**
Horsham *Australia* 36°44S 142°13E **63 F3**
Horsham *U.K.* 51°4N 0°20W **13 F7**
Horta *Azores* 38°32N 28°38W **50 a**
Horten *Norway* 59°25N 10°32E **9 G14**
Horton *U.S.A.* 39°40N 95°32W **80 F6**
Horton → *Canada* 69°56N 126°52W **68 B7**
Horwood L. *Canada* 48°5N 82°20W **72 C3**
Hosapete = Hospet
  India 15°15N 76°20E **40 M10**
Ḩoseynābād *Khuzestān,*
  Iran 32°45N 48°20E **45 C6**
Ḩoseynābād *Kordestān,*
  Iran 35°33N 47°8E **44 C5**
Hoshangabad *India* 22°45N 77°45E **42 H7**
Hoshiarpur *India* 31°30N 75°58E **42 D6**
Hospet *India* 15°15N 76°20E **40 M10**
Hoste, I. *Chile* 55°0S 69°0W **96 H3**
Hot *Thailand* 18°8N 98°29E **38 C2**
Hot Creek Range
  U.S.A. 38°40N 116°20W **76 G5**
Hot Springs *Ark., U.S.A.* 34°31N 93°3W **84 D8**
Hot Springs *S. Dak.,*
  U.S.A. 43°26N 103°29W **80 D2**
Hot Springs △ *U.S.A.* 34°31N 93°3W **84 D8**
Hotagen *Sweden* 63°59N 14°12E **8 E16**
Hotan *China* 37°25N 79°55E **32 C2**
Hotan He → *China* 40°22N 80°56E **32 C3**
Hotazel *S. Africa* 27°17S 22°58E **56 D3**
Hotchkiss *U.S.A.* 38°48N 107°43W **76 G10**
Hotham, C. *Australia* 12°2S 131°18E **60 B5**
Hoting *Sweden* 64°8N 16°15E **8 D17**
Hotte, Massif de la *Haiti* 18°30N 73°45W **89 C5**
Hottentotsbaai *Namibia* 26°8S 14°59E **56 D1**
Hou Hai *China* 22°32N 113°56E **33 F10**
Houei Sai *Laos* 20°18N 100°26E **38 B3**
Houffalize *Belgium* 50°8N 5°48E **15 D5**
Houghton *Mich., U.S.A.* 47°7N 88°34W **80 B9**
Houghton *N.Y., U.S.A.* 42°25N 78°10W **82 D6**
Houghton L. *U.S.A.* 44°21N 84°44W **81 C11**
Houghton-le-Spring
  U.K. 54°51N 1°28W **12 C6**
Houhora Heads *N.Z.* 34°49S 173°9E **59 A4**
Houlton *U.S.A.* 46°8N 67°51W **81 B20**
Houma *China* 35°36N 90°43W **85 G9**
Housatonic → *U.S.A.* 41°10N 73°7W **83 E11**
Houston *Canada* 54°25N 126°39W **70 C3**
Houston *Mo., U.S.A.* 37°22N 91°58W **80 G8**
Houston *Tex., U.S.A.* 29°45N 95°21W **84 G7**
Hout = Mogwadi →
  S. Africa 23°4S 29°36E **57 C4**
Houtkraal *S. Africa* 30°23S 24°5E **56 E3**
Houtman Abrolhos
  Australia 28°43S 113°48E **61 E1**
Hovd □ *Mongolia* 48°2N 91°37E **32 B4**
Hove *U.K.* 50°50N 0°10W **13 G7**
Hovenweep △ *U.S.A.* 37°20N 109°0W **77 H9**
Hoveyzeh *Iran* 31°27N 48°4E **45 D6**
Hövsgöl *Mongolia* 43°37N 109°39E **34 C5**
Hövsgöl Nuur *Mongolia* 51°0N 100°30E **32 A5**
Howar, Wadi → *Sudan* 17°30N 27°8E **51 E11**
Howard *Australia* 25°16S 152°32E **63 D5**
Howard *Pa., U.S.A.* 41°1N 77°40W **82 F7**
Howard *S. Dak., U.S.A.* 44°1N 97°32W **80 C5**
Howe *U.S.A.* 43°48N 113°0W **76 E7**
Howe, C. *Australia* 37°30S 150°0E **63 F5**
Howe, West Cape
  Australia 35°8S 117°36E **61 G2**
Howe I. *Canada* 44°16N 76°17W **83 B8**
Howell *U.S.A.* 42°36N 83°56W **81 D12**
Howick *Canada* 45°11N 73°51W **83 A11**
Howick *S. Africa* 29°28S 30°14E **57 D5**
Howick Group *Australia* 14°20S 145°30E **62 A4**
Howitt, L. *Australia* 27°40S 138°40E **63 D2**

Howland I. *Pac. Oc.* 0°48N 176°38W **64 G10**
Howrah = Haora *India* 22°34N 88°18E **43 H13**
Howth *Ireland* 53°23N 6°6W **10 C5**
Howth Hd. *Ireland* 53°22N 6°4W **10 C5**
Höxter *Germany* 51°46N 9°22E **16 C5**
Hoy *U.K.* 58°50N 3°15W **11 C5**
Høyanger *Norway* 61°13N 6°4E **8 F12**
Hoyerswerda *Germany* 51°26N 14°14E **16 C8**
Hoylake *U.K.* 53°24N 3°10W **12 D4**
Hpa-an = Pa-an *Burma* 16°51N 97°40E **41 L20**
Hpunan Pass *Burma* 27°30N 96°55E **41 F20**
Hradec Králové
  Czech Rep. 50°15N 15°50E **16 C8**
Hrodna *Belarus* 53°42N 23°52E **17 B12**
Hrodzyanka *Belarus* 53°31N 28°42E **17 B15**
Hron → *Slovak Rep.* 47°49N 18°45E **17 E10**
Hrvatska = Croatia ■
  Europe 45°20N 16°0E **16 F9**
Hrymayliv *Ukraine* 49°20N 26°5E **17 D14**
Hsenwi *Burma* 23°22N 97°55E **41 H20**
Hsiamen = Xiamen
  China 24°25N 118°4E **33 D6**
Hsian = Xi'an *China* 34°15N 109°0E **34 G5**
Hsinchu *Taiwan* 24°48N 120°58E **33 D7**
Hsinhailien = Lianyungang
  China 34°40N 119°11E **35 G10**
Hsüchou = Xuzhou
  China 34°18N 117°10E **35 G9**
Hu Xian *China* 34°8N 108°42E **34 G5**
Hua Hin *Thailand* 12°34N 99°58E **38 F2**
Hua Xian *Henan, China* 35°30N 114°30E **34 G8**
Hua Xian *Shaanxi, China* 34°30N 109°48E **34 G5**
Huab → *Namibia* 20°52S 13°25E **56 B2**
Huahine, Î.
  French Polynesia 16°46S 150°58W **65 J12**
Huai Hat △ *Thailand* 16°52N 104°17E **38 D5**
Huai Nam Dang △
  Thailand 19°30N 98°30E **38 C2**
Huai Yot *Thailand* 7°45N 99°37E **39 J2**
Huai'an *Hebei, China* 40°30N 114°20E **34 D8**
Huai'an *Jiangsu, China* 33°30N 119°10E **35 H10**
Huaibei *China* 34°0N 116°48E **34 G9**
Huaide = Gongzhuling
  China 43°30N 124°40E **35 C13**
Huaidezhen *China* 43°48N 124°50E **35 C13**
Huainan *China* 32°38N 116°58E **33 C6**
Huairen *China* 39°48N 113°20E **34 E7**
Huairou *China* 40°20N 116°35E **34 D9**
Huaiyang *China* 33°40N 114°52E **34 H8**
Huaiyin *China* 33°30N 119°2E **35 H10**
Huaiyuan *China* 32°55N 117°10E **35 H9**
Huajuápan de León
  Mexico 17°48N 97°46W **87 D5**
Hualapai Peak *U.S.A.* 35°5N 113°54W **77 J7**
Huallaga → *Peru* 5°15S 75°30W **92 E3**
Huambo *Angola* 12°42S 15°54E **53 G3**
Huan Jiang → *China* 34°28N 109°0E **34 G5**
Huan Xian *China* 36°33N 107°7E **34 F4**
Huancabamba *Peru* 5°10S 79°15W **92 E3**
Huancane *Peru* 15°10S 69°44W **92 G5**
Huancavelica *Peru* 12°50S 75°5W **92 F3**
Huancayo *Peru* 12°5S 75°12W **92 F3**
Huanchaca *Bolivia* 20°15S 66°40W **92 H5**
Huang Hai = Yellow Sea
  China 35°0N 123°0E **35 G12**
Huang He → *China* 37°55N 118°50E **35 F10**
Huang Xian *China* 37°38N 120°30E **35 F11**
Huangling *China* 35°34N 109°15E **34 G5**
Huanglong *China* 35°30N 109°59E **34 G5**
Huangshan *China* 29°42N 118°25E **33 D6**
Huangshi *China* 30°10N 115°3E **33 C6**
Huangsongdian *China* 43°45N 127°25E **35 C14**
Huanren *China* 41°23N 125°20E **35 D13**
Huantai *China* 36°58N 117°56E **35 F9**
Huánuco *Peru* 9°55S 76°15W **92 E3**
Huaraz *Peru* 9°30S 77°32W **92 E3**
Huarmey *Peru* 10°5S 78°5W **92 F3**
Huascarán, Nevado *Peru* 9°7S 77°37W **92 E3**
Huasco *Chile* 28°30S 71°15W **94 B1**
Huasco → *Chile* 28°27S 71°13W **94 B1**
Huasna *U.S.A.* 35°6N 120°24W **79 K6**
Huatabampo *Mexico* 26°50N 109°38W **86 B3**
Huauchinango *Mexico* 20°12N 98°3W **87 C5**
Huautla de Jiménez
  Mexico 18°8N 96°51W **87 D5**
Huayin *China* 34°35N 110°5E **34 G6**
Hubballi = Hubli *India* 15°22N 75°15E **40 M9**
Hubbard *Ohio, U.S.A.* 41°9N 80°34W **82 E4**
Hubbard *Tex., U.S.A.* 31°51N 96°48W **84 F6**
Hubbard Glacier
  Canada 60°18N 139°22W **68 E4**
Hubbart Pt. *Canada* 59°21N 94°41W **71 B10**
Hubei □ *China* 31°0N 112°0E **33 C6**
Hubli *India* 15°22N 75°15E **40 M9**
Huch'ang *N. Korea* 41°25N 127°2E **35 D14**
Hucknall *U.K.* 53°3N 1°13W **12 D6**
Huddersfield *U.K.* 53°39N 1°47W **12 D6**
Hudiksvall *Sweden* 61°43N 17°10E **8 F17**
Hudson *Canada* 50°6N 92°9W **72 B1**
Hudson *Mass., U.S.A.* 42°23N 71°34W **83 D13**
Hudson *N.Y., U.S.A.* 42°15N 73°46W **83 D11**
Hudson *Wis., U.S.A.* 44°58N 92°45W **80 C7**
Hudson *Wyo., U.S.A.* 42°54N 108°35W **76 E9**
Hudson → *U.S.A.* 40°42N 74°2W **83 F10**
Hudson, C. *Antarctica* 68°21S 153°45E **5 C10**
Hudson Bay *Nunavut,*
  Canada 60°0N 86°0W **69 F14**
Hudson Bay *Sask.,*
  Canada 52°51N 102°23W **71 C8**
Hudson Falls *U.S.A.* 43°18N 73°35W **83 C11**
Hudson Mts. *Antarctica* 74°32S 99°20W **5 D16**
Hudson Str. *Canada* 62°0N 70°0W **69 E18**
Hudson's Hope *Canada* 56°0N 121°54W **70 B4**
Hue *Vietnam* 16°30N 107°35E **38 D6**

Huehuetenango
  Guatemala 15°20N 91°28W **88 C1**
Iluejúcar *Mexico* 22°21N 103°13W **86 C4**
Huelva *Spain* 37°18N 6°57W **21 D2**
Huentelauquén *Chile* 31°38S 71°33W **94 C1**
Huerta, Sa. de la
  Argentina 31°10S 67°30W **94 C2**
Huesca *Spain* 42°8N 0°25W **21 A5**
Huetamo *Mexico* 18°35N 100°53W **86 D4**
Hugh → *Australia* 25°1S 134°1E **62 D1**
Hughenden *Australia* 20°52S 144°10E **62 C3**
Hughesville *U.S.A.* 41°14N 76°44W **83 E8**
Hugli → *India* 21°56N 88°4E **43 J13**
Hugo *Colo., U.S.A.* 39°8N 103°28W **76 G12**
Hugo *Okla., U.S.A.* 34°1N 95°31W **84 D7**
Hugoton *U.S.A.* 37°11N 101°21W **80 G3**
Hui Xian = Huixian
  China 35°27N 113°12E **34 G7**
Hui Xian *China* 33°50N 106°4E **34 H4**
Hui'anbu *China* 37°28N 106°38E **34 F4**
Huichapan *Mexico* 20°23N 99°39W **87 C5**
Huichon *N. Korea* 40°10N 126°16E **35 D14**
Huifa He → *China* 43°0N 127°50E **35 C14**
Huila, Nevado del *Colombia* 3°0N 76°0W **92 C3**
Huimin *China* 37°27N 117°28E **35 F9**
Huinan *China* 42°40N 126°2E **35 C14**
Huinca Renancó
  Argentina 34°51S 64°22W **94 C3**
Huining *China* 35°38N 105°0E **34 G3**
Huinong *China* 39°5N 106°35E **34 E4**
Huiting *China* 34°5N 116°5E **34 G9**
Huixian *China* 35°27N 113°12E **34 G7**
Huixtla *Mexico* 15°9N 92°28W **87 D6**
Huize *China* 26°24N 103°15E **32 D5**
Hukawng Valley
  Burma 26°30N 96°30E **41 F20**
Hukuntsi *Botswana* 23°58S 21°45E **56 C3**
Ḩulayfā' *Si. Arabia* 25°58N 40°45E **44 E4**
Hulin He → *China* 45°0N 122°10E **35 B12**
Hull = Kingston upon Hull
  U.K. 53°45N 0°21W **12 D7**
Hull *Canada* 45°26N 75°43W **83 A9**
Hull → *U.K.* 53°44N 0°20W **12 D7**
Hulst *Neths.* 51°17N 4°2E **15 C4**
Hulun Nur *China* 49°0N 117°30E **33 B6**
Huma, Tanjung *Malaysia* 5°29N 100°16E **39 c**
Humacao *Puerto Rico* 18°9N 65°50W **89 d**
Humahuaca *Argentina* 23°10S 65°25W **94 A2**
Humaitá *Brazil* 7°35S 63°1W **92 E6**
Humaitá *Paraguay* 27°2S 58°31W **94 B4**
Humansdorp *S. Africa* 34°2S 24°46E **56 E3**
Humbe *Angola* 16°40S 14°55E **56 B1**
Humber → *U.K.* 53°42N 0°27W **12 D7**
Humboldt *Canada* 52°15N 105°9W **71 C7**
Humboldt *Iowa, U.S.A.* 42°44N 94°13W **80 D6**
Humboldt *Tenn., U.S.A.* 35°50N 88°55W **85 D10**
Humboldt → *U.S.A.* 39°59N 118°36W **76 G4**
Humboldt Gletscher =
  Sermersuaq *Greenland* 79°30N 62°0W **69 B19**
Hume *U.S.A.* 36°48N 118°54W **78 J8**
Hume, L. *Australia* 36°0S 147°5E **63 F4**
Humen *China* 22°50N 113°40E **33 F10**
Humenné *Slovak Rep.* 48°55N 21°50E **17 D11**
Humphreys, Mt.
  U.S.A. 37°17N 118°40W **78 H8**
Humphreys Peak
  U.S.A. 35°21N 111°41W **77 J8**
Humptulips *U.S.A.* 47°14N 123°57W **78 C3**
Ḩūn *Libya* 29°2N 16°0E **51 C9**
Hun Jiang → *China* 40°50N 125°38E **35 D13**
Húnaflói *Iceland* 65°50N 20°50W **8 D3**
Hunan □ *China* 27°30N 112°0E **33 D6**
Hunchun *China* 42°52N 130°28E **35 C16**
Hundewali *Pakistan* 31°55N 72°38E **42 D5**
Hundred Mile House
  Canada 51°38N 121°18W **70 C4**
Hunedoara *Romania* 45°40N 22°50E **17 F12**
Hung Yen *Vietnam* 20°39N 106°4E **38 B6**
Hunga Ha'apai *Tonga* 20°41S 175°7W **59 c**
Hungary ■ *Europe* 47°20N 19°20E **17 E10**
Hungary, Plain of *Europe* 47°0N 20°0E **6 F10**
Hungerford *Australia* 28°58S 144°24E **63 D3**
Hŭngnam *N. Korea* 39°49N 127°45E **35 E14**
Hunjiang *China* 41°54N 126°28E **35 D14**
Hunsberge *Namibia* 27°45S 17°12E **56 D2**
Hunsrück *Germany* 49°56N 7°27E **16 D4**
Hunstanton *U.K.* 52°56N 0°29E **12 E8**
Hunter *U.S.A.* 42°13N 74°13W **83 D10**
Hunter I. *Australia* 40°30S 144°45E **63 G3**
Hunter I. *Canada* 51°55N 128°0W **70 C3**
Hunter Ra. *Australia* 32°45S 150°15E **63 E5**
Hunters Road *Zimbabwe* 19°9S 29°49E **55 F2**
Hunterville *N.Z.* 39°56S 175°35E **59 C5**
Huntingburg *U.S.A.* 38°18N 86°57W **80 F10**
Huntingdon *U.K.* 52°20N 0°11W **13 E7**
Huntingdon *U.S.A.* 40°30N 78°1W **82 F6**
Huntington *Ind., U.S.A.* 40°53N 85°30W **81 E11**
Huntington *N.Y.,*
  U.S.A. 40°52N 73°26W **83 F11**
Huntington *Oreg.,*
  U.S.A. 44°21N 117°16W **76 D5**
Huntington *Utah,*
  U.S.A. 39°20N 110°58W **76 G8**
Huntington *W. Va.,*
  U.S.A. 38°25N 82°27W **81 F12**
Huntington Beach
  U.S.A. 33°40N 118°5W **79 M9**
Huntly *N.Z.* 37°34S 175°11E **59 B5**
Huntly *U.K.* 57°27N 2°47W **11 D6**
Huntsville *Canada* 45°20N 79°14W **82 A5**
Huntsville *Ala., U.S.A.* 34°44N 86°35W **85 H11**
Huntsville *Tex., U.S.A.* 30°43N 95°33W **84 F7**
Hunyani → *Zimbabwe* 15°57S 30°39E **55 F3**
Hunyuan *China* 39°42N 113°42E **34 E7**
Hunza → *India* 35°54N 74°20E **43 B6**
Huo Xian = Huozhou
  China 36°36N 111°42E **34 F6**
Huong Khe *Vietnam* 18°13N 105°41E **38 C5**
Huonville *Australia* 43°0S 147°5E **63 G4**

Huozhou *China* 36°36N 111°42E **34 F6**
Hupeh = Hubei □ *China* 31°0N 112°0E **33 C6**
Ḩūr *Iran* 30°50N 57°7E **45 D8**
Hurānd *Iran* 38°51N 47°22E **44 B5**
Hurghada *Egypt* 27°15N 33°50E **51 C12**
Hurley *N. Mex., U.S.A.* 32°42N 108°8W **77 K9**
Hurley *Wis., U.S.A.* 46°27N 90°11W **80 B8**
Huron *Calif., U.S.A.* 36°12N 120°6W **78 J6**
Huron *Ohio, U.S.A.* 41°24N 82°33W **82 E2**
Huron *S. Dak., U.S.A.* 44°22N 98°13W **80 C4**
Huron, L. *U.S.A.* 44°30N 82°40W **82 B2**
Huron East *Canada* 43°37N 81°18W **82 C3**
Hurricane *U.S.A.* 37°11N 113°17W **77 H7**
Hurungwe △ *Zimbabwe* 16°7S 29°5E **55 F2**
Hurunui → *N.Z.* 42°54S 173°18E **59 E4**
Húsavík *Iceland* 66°3N 17°21W **8 C5**
Huşi *Romania* 46°41N 28°7E **17 E15**
Hustadvika *Norway* 63°0N 7°0E **8 E12**
Hustontown *U.S.A.* 40°3N 78°2W **82 F6**
Hutchinson *Kans., U.S.A.* 38°5N 97°56W **80 F5**
Hutchinson *Minn.,*
  U.S.A. 44°54N 94°22W **80 C6**
Hutte Sauvage, L. de la
  Canada 56°15N 64°45W **73 A7**
Hutton, Mt. *Australia* 25°51S 148°20E **63 D4**
Huy *Belgium* 50°31N 5°15E **15 D5**
Huzhou *China* 30°51N 120°10E **33 C7**
Hvammstangi *Iceland* 65°24N 20°57W **8 D3**
Hvar *Croatia* 43°11N 16°28E **22 C7**
Hvítá → *Iceland* 64°30N 21°58W **8 D3**
Hwacheon-Cheosuji
  S. Korea 38°5N 127°50E **35 E14**
Hwang Ho = Huang He →
  China 37°55N 118°50E **35 F10**
Hwange *Zimbabwe* 18°18S 26°30E **55 F2**
Hwange △ *Zimbabwe* 19°0S 26°30E **56 B4**
Hyannis *Mass., U.S.A.* 41°39N 70°17W **81 E18**
Hyannis *Nebr., U.S.A.* 42°0N 101°46W **80 E3**
Hyargas Nuur *Mongolia* 49°0N 93°0E **32 B4**
Hydaburg *U.S.A.* 55°15N 132°50W **70 B2**
Hyde Park *U.S.A.* 41°47N 73°56W **83 E11**
Hyden *Australia* 32°24S 118°53E **61 F2**
Hyder *U.S.A.* 55°55N 130°5W **70 B2**
Hyderabad *India* 17°22N 78°29E **40 L11**
Hyderabad *Pakistan* 25°23N 68°24E **42 G3**
Hydra *Greece* 37°20N 23°28E **23 F10**
Hyères *France* 43°8N 6°9E **20 E7**
Hyères, Îs. d' *France* 43°0N 6°20E **20 E7**
Hyesan *N. Korea* 41°20N 128°10E **35 D15**
Hyland → *Canada* 59°52N 128°12W **70 B3**
Hymia *India* 33°40N 78°2E **43 C8**
Hyndman Peak *U.S.A.* 43°45N 114°8W **76 E6**
Hyōgo □ *Japan* 35°15N 134°50E **31 G7**
Hyrum *U.S.A.* 41°38N 111°51W **76 F8**
Hysham *U.S.A.* 46°18N 107°14W **76 C10**
Hythe *U.K.* 51°4N 1°5E **13 F9**
Hyūga *Japan* 32°25N 131°35E **31 H5**
Hyvinge = Hyvinkää
  Finland 60°38N 24°50E **8 F21**
Hyvinkää *Finland* 60°38N 24°50E **8 F21**

I

I-n-Gall *Niger* 16°51N 7°1E **50 E7**
Iaco → *Brazil* 9°3S 68°34W **92 E5**
Iakora *Madag.* 23°6S 46°40E **57 C8**
Ialissos *Greece* 36°24N 28°10E **25 C10**
Ialomiţa → *Romania* 44°42N 27°51E **17 F14**
Iaşi *Romania* 47°10N 27°40E **17 E14**
Ib → *India* 21°34N 83°48E **43 J10**
Iba *Phil.* 15°22N 120°0E **37 A6**
Ibadan *Nigeria* 7°22N 3°58E **50 G6**
Ibagué *Colombia* 4°20N 75°20W **92 C3**
Ibar → *Serbia* 43°43N 20°45E **23 C9**
Ibaraki □ *Japan* 36°10N 140°10E **31 F10**
Ibarra *Ecuador* 0°21N 78°7W **92 C3**
Ibb *Yemen* 14°2N 44°10E **47 E3**
Ibembo
  Dem. Rep. of the Congo 2°35N 23°35E **54 B1**
Ibenga → *Congo* 2°19N 18°9E **52 D3**
Ibera, L. *Argentina* 28°30S 57°9W **94 B4**
Iberian Peninsula *Europe* 40°0N 5°0W **6 H5**
Iberville *Canada* 45°19N 73°17W **83 A11**
Iberville, Mt. d' *Canada* 58°50N 63°50W **69 F19**
Ibiá *Brazil* 19°30S 46°30W **93 G9**
Ibiapaba, Sa. da *Brazil* 4°0S 41°30W **93 D10**
Ibicuí → *Brazil* 29°25S 56°47W **95 B4**
Ibicuy *Argentina* 33°55S 59°10W **94 C4**
Ibiza = Eivissa *Spain* 38°54N 1°26E **24 C7**
Ibo *Mozam.* 12°22S 40°40E **55 E5**
Ibonma *Indonesia* 3°29S 133°31E **37 E8**
Ibotirama *Brazil* 12°13S 43°12W **93 F10**
Ibrāhīm → *Lebanon* 34°4N 35°38E **46 A4**
'Ibrī *Oman* 23°14N 56°30E **45 C8**
Ibu *Indonesia* 1°35N 127°33E **37 D7**
Ibusuki *Japan* 31°12N 130°40E **31 J5**
Ica *Peru* 14°0S 75°48W **92 F3**
Içá → *Brazil* 2°55S 67°58W **92 D5**
Içana *Brazil* 0°21N 67°19W **92 C5**
Içana → *Brazil* 0°26N 67°19W **92 C5**
İçel *Turkey* 36°51N 34°36E **44 B2**
Iceland ■ *Europe* 64°45N 19°0W **8 D4**
Iceland Basin *Atl. Oc.* 61°0N 19°0W **4 C7**
Icelandic Plateau *Arctic* 64°0N 10°0W **4 C7**
Ich'ang = Yichang
  China 30°40N 111°20E **33 C6**
Ichchapuram *India* 19°10N 84°40E **41 K14**
Icheon *S. Korea* 37°17N 127°27E **35 F14**
Ichhawar *India* 23°1N 77°1E **42 H7**
Ichihara *Japan* 35°28N 140°5E **31 G10**
Ichikawa *Japan* 35°44N 139°55E **31 G9**
Ichilo → *Bolivia* 15°57S 64°50W **92 G6**
Ichinohe *Japan* 40°13N 141°17E **30 D10**
Ichinomiya *Japan* 35°18N 136°48E **31 G8**

Ichinoseki *Japan* 38°55N 141°8E **30 E10**
Icod *Canary Is.* 28°22N 16°43W **24 F3**
Icy C. *U.S.A.* 70°20N 161°52W **66 B3**
Ida Grove *U.S.A.* 42°21N 95°28W **80 D6**
Idabel *U.S.A.* 33°54N 94°50W **84 E7**
Idaho □ *U.S.A.* 45°0N 115°0W **76 D6**
Idaho City *U.S.A.* 43°50N 115°50W **76 E6**
Idaho Falls *U.S.A.* 43°30N 112°2W **76 E7**
Idalia △ *Australia* 24°49S 144°36E **62 C3**
Idar-Oberstein *Germany* 49°43N 7°16E **16 D4**
Idensalmi = Iisalmi
  Finland 63°32N 27°10E **8 E22**
Idfû *Egypt* 24°55N 32°49E **51 D12**
Ídhra = Hydra *Greece* 37°20N 23°28E **23 F10**
Idi *Indonesia* 5°2N 97°37E **36 C1**
Idi, Oros = Psiloritis, Oros
  Greece 35°15N 24°45E **25 D6**
Idiofa
  Dem. Rep. of the Congo 4°55S 19°42E **52 E3**
Idlib *Syria* 35°55N 36°36E **44 C3**
Idria *U.S.A.* 36°25N 120°41W **78 J6**
Idutywa = Dutywa
  S. Africa 32°8S 28°18E **57 E4**
Ieper *Belgium* 50°51N 2°53E **15 D2**
Ierapetra *Greece* 35°1N 25°44E **25 E7**
Iesi *Italy* 43°31N 13°14E **22 C5**
Ifakara *Tanzania* 8°8S 36°41E **54 D4**
'Ifāl, W. al → *Si. Arabia* 28°7N 35°3E **44 D2**
Ifanadiana *Madag.* 21°19S 47°39E **57 C8**
Ife *Nigeria* 7°30N 4°31E **50 G6**
Iffley *Australia* 18°53S 141°12E **62 B3**
Iforas, Adrar des *Africa* 19°40N 1°40E **50 E6**
Ifould, L. *Australia* 30°52S 132°6E **61 F5**
Iganga *Uganda* 0°37N 33°28E **54 B3**
Igarapava *Brazil* 20°3S 47°47W **93 H9**
Igarka *Russia* 67°30N 86°33E **28 C9**
Iggesund *Sweden* 61°39N 17°10E **8 F17**
Iglésias *Italy* 39°19N 8°32E **22 E3**
Igloolik = Iglulik
  Canada 69°20N 81°49W **69 D15**
Iglulik *Canada* 69°20N 81°49W **69 D15**
Ignace *Canada* 49°30N 91°40W **72 C1**
İğneada Burnu *Turkey* 41°53N 28°2E **23 D13**
Igoumenitsa *Greece* 39°32N 20°18E **23 E9**
Igrim *Russia* 63°12N 64°30E **28 C7**
Iguaçu → *Brazil* 25°36S 54°36W **95 B5**
Iguaçu, Cat. del *Brazil* 25°41S 54°26W **95 B5**
Iguaçu △ *Brazil* 25°30S 54°0W **95 B5**
Iguaçu Falls = Iguaçu, Cat. del
  Brazil 25°41S 54°26W **95 B5**
Iguala *Mexico* 18°21N 99°32W **87 D5**
Igualada *Spain* 41°37N 1°37E **21 B6**
Iguassu = Iguaçu →
  Brazil 25°36S 54°36W **95 B5**
Iguatu *Brazil* 6°20S 39°18W **93 E11**
Iguazú △ *Argentina* 25°42S 54°22W **95 B5**
Iguidi, Erg *Africa* 27°0N 7°0W **50 C4**
Iharana *Madag.* 13°25S 50°0E **57 A9**
Ihbulag *Mongolia* 43°11N 107°10E **34 C4**
Iheya-Shima *Japan* 27°4N 127°58E **31 L3**
Ihosy *Madag.* 22°24S 46°8E **57 C8**
Ihotry, Farihy *Madag.* 21°56S 43°41E **57 C7**
Ii *Finland* 65°19N 25°22E **8 D21**
Ii-Shima *Japan* 26°43N 127°47E **31 L3**
Iida *Japan* 35°35N 137°50E **31 G8**
Iijoki → *Finland* 65°20N 25°20E **8 D21**
Iisalmi *Finland* 63°32N 27°10E **8 E22**
Iiyama *Japan* 36°51N 138°22E **31 F9**
Iizuka *Japan* 33°38N 130°42E **31 H5**
Ijâfene *Mauritania* 20°40N 8°0W **50 D4**
Ijebu-Ode *Nigeria* 6°47N 3°58E **50 G6**
IJmuiden *Neths.* 52°28N 4°35E **15 B4**
Ijo älv = Iijoki →
  Finland 65°20N 25°20E **8 D21**
IJssel → *Neths.* 52°35N 5°50E **15 B5**
IJsselmeer *Neths.* 52°45N 5°20E **15 B5**
Ijuí *Brazil* 28°23S 53°55W **95 B5**
Ijuí → *Brazil* 27°58S 55°20W **95 B4**
Ikalamavony *Madag.* 21°9S 46°35E **57 C8**
Ikanga *Kenya* 1°42S 38°4E **54 C4**
Ikare *Nigeria* 7°32N 5°40E **50 G7**
Ikaria *Greece* 37°35N 26°10E **23 F12**
Ikeda *Japan* 34°1N 133°48E **31 G6**
Ikela *Dem. Rep. of the Congo* 1°6S 23°6E **52 E4**
Iki *Japan* 33°45N 129°42E **31 H4**
Ikimba L. *Tanzania* 1°30S 31°20E **54 C3**
Ikongo *Madag.* 21°52S 47°27E **57 C8**
Ikopa → *Madag.* 16°45S 46°40E **57 B8**
Ikorongo △ *Tanzania* 1°50S 34°53E **54 C3**
Ikparjuk = Arctic Bay
  Canada 73°1N 85°7W **69 C14**
Iksan *S. Korea* 35°59N 127°0E **35 G14**
Ikungu *Tanzania* 1°33S 33°42E **54 C3**
Ikuntji = Haasts Bluff
  Australia 23°22S 132°0E **60 D5**
Ilagan *Phil.* 17°7N 121°53E **37 A6**
Ilaka *Madag.* 19°33S 48°52E **57 B8**
Īlām *Iran* 33°36N 46°36E **44 C5**
Ilam *Nepal* 26°58N 87°58E **43 F12**
Īlām □ *Iran* 33°0N 47°0E **44 C5**
Ilanskiy *Russia* 56°14N 96°3E **29 D10**
Iława *Poland* 53°36N 19°34E **17 B10**
Ile → *Kazakhstan* 45°53N 77°10E **28 E8**
Île-à-la-Crosse *Canada* 55°27N 107°53W **71 B7**
Île-à-la-Crosse, Lac
  Canada 55°40N 107°45W **71 B7**
Île-de-France □ *France* 49°0N 2°20E **20 B5**
Ilebo *Dem. Rep. of the Congo* 4°17S 20°55E **52 E4**
Ilek *Russia* 51°30N 53°22E **28 D6**
Ilek → *Russia* 51°30N 53°22E **18 D10**
Ilesha *Nigeria* 7°37N 4°40E **50 G6**
Ilford *Canada* 56°4N 95°35W **71 B9**
Ilfracombe *Australia* 23°30S 144°30E **62 C3**
Ilfracombe *U.K.* 51°12N 4°8W **13 F3**
Ilha Grande, Represa
  Brazil 23°10S 53°5W **95 A5**
Ilha Grande △ *Brazil* 23°10S 53°20W **95 A5**

Ilhéus *Brazil* 14°49S 39°2W **93** F11
Ili = Ile ⇸ *Kazakhstan* 45°53N 77°10E **28** E8
Iliamna L. *U.S.A.* 59°30N 155°0W **74** D8
Ilias, Profitis *Greece* 36°17N 27°56E **25** C9
Iligan *Phil.* 8°12N 124°13E **37** C6
Ilion *U.S.A.* 43°1N 75°2W **83** D9
Ilkeston *U.K.* 52°58N 1°19W **12** E6
Ilkley *U.K.* 53°56N 1°48W **12** D6
Illampu = Ancohuma, Nevado
  Bolivia 16°0S 68°50W **92** G5
Illana B. *Phil.* 7°35N 123°45E **37** C6
Illapel *Chile* 32°0S 71°10W **94** C1
Iller ⇸ *Germany* 48°23N 9°58E **16** D6
Illetas *Spain* 39°32N 2°35E **24** B9
Illimani, Nevado *Bolivia* 16°30S 67°50W **92** G5
Illinois □ *U.S.A.* 40°15N 89°30W **80** E9
Illinois ⇸ *U.S.A.* 38°58N 90°28W **80** F8
Illizi *Algeria* 26°31N 8°32E **50** C7
Ilma, L. *Australia* 29°13S 127°46E **61** E4
Ilmajoki *Finland* 62°44N 22°34E **8** E20
Ilmen, Ozero *Russia* 58°15N 31°10E **18** C5
Ilo *Peru* 17°40S 71°20W **92** G4
Iloilo *Phil.* 10°45N 122°33E **37** B6
Ilomantsi *Finland* 62°38N 30°57E **8** E24
Ilorin *Nigeria* 8°30N 4°35E **50** G6
Ilwaco *U.S.A.* 46°19N 124°3W **78** D2
Ilwaki *Indonesia* 7°55S 126°30E **37** F7
Imabari *Japan* 34°4N 133°0E **31** G6
Imaloto ⇸ *Madag.* 23°27S 45°13E **57** C8
Imandra, Ozero *Russia* 67°30N 33°0E **8** C25
Imanombo *Madag.* 24°26S 45°49E **57** C8
Imari *Japan* 33°15N 129°52E **31** H4
Imatra *Finland* 61°12N 28°48E **8** F23
imeni 26 Bakinskikh Komissarov
  = Neftçala *Azerbaijan* 39°19N 49°12E **45** B6
imeni 26 Bakinskikh Komissarov
  Turkmenistan 39°22N 54°10E **45** B7
imeni Ismail Samani, Pik
  Tajikistan 39°0N 72°2E **28** F8
Imeri, Serra *Brazil* 0°50N 65°25W **92** C5
Imerimandroso *Madag.* 17°26S 48°35E **57** B8
Imfolozi ⇸ *S. Africa* 28°18S 31°50E **57** D5
Imi *Ethiopia* 6°28N 42°10E **47** F3
Imlay *U.S.A.* 40°40N 118°9W **76** F4
Imlay City *U.S.A.* 43°2N 83°5W **82** D1
Immingham *U.K.* 53°37N 0°13W **12** D7
Immokalee *U.S.A.* 26°25N 81°25W **85** H14
Imola *Italy* 44°20N 11°42E **22** B4
Imperatriz *Brazil* 5°30S 47°29W **93** E9
Impéria *Italy* 43°53N 8°3E **20** E8
Imperial *Canada* 51°21N 105°28W **71** C7
Imperial *Calif., U.S.A.* 32°51N 115°34W **79** N11
Imperial *Nebr., U.S.A.* 40°31N 101°39W **80** E3
Imperial Beach *U.S.A.* 32°35N 117°6W **79** N9
Imperial Dam *U.S.A.* 32°55N 114°25W **79** N12
Imperial Res. *U.S.A.* 32°53N 114°28W **79** N12
Imperial Valley *U.S.A.* 33°0N 115°30W **79** N11
Imperieuse Reef
  Australia 17°36S 118°50E **60** C2
Impfondo *Congo* 1°40N 18°0E **52** D3
Imphal *India* 24°48N 93°56E **41** G18
İmroz = Gökçeada
  Turkey 40°10N 25°50E **23** D11
Imuris *Mexico* 30°47N 110°52W **86** A2
Imuruan B. *Phil.* 10°40N 119°10E **37** B5
In Guezzam *Algeria* 19°37N 5°52E **50** E7
In Salah *Algeria* 27°10N 2°32E **50** C6
Ina *Japan* 35°50N 137°55E **31** G8
Inagua △ *Bahamas* 21°5N 73°24W **89** B5
Inangahua *N.Z.* 41°52S 171°59E **59** D3
Inanwatan *Indonesia* 2°8S 132°10E **37** E8
Iñapari *Peru* 11°0S 69°40W **92** F5
Inari *Finland* 68°54N 27°1E **8** B22
Inarijärvi *Finland* 69°0N 28°0E **8** B23
Inawashiro-Ko *Japan* 37°29N 140°6E **30** F10
Inca *Spain* 39°43N 2°54E **24** B9
Inca de Oro *Chile* 26°45S 69°54W **94** B2
Incahuasi *Argentina* 27°2S 68°18W **94** B2
Incahuasi *Chile* 29°12S 71°5W **94** B1
İnce Burun *Turkey* 42°7N 34°56E **19** F5
İncesu *Turkey* 38°38N 35°11E **44** B2
Incheon *S. Korea* 37°27N 126°40E **35** F14
İncirliova *Turkey* 37°50N 27°41E **23** F12
Incline Village *U.S.A.* 39°10N 119°58W **76** G4
Incomáti ⇸ *Mozam.* 25°46S 32°43E **57** D5
Indalsälven ⇸ *Sweden* 62°36N 17°30E **8** E17
Indaw *Burma* 24°15N 96°5E **41** G20
Independence *Calif.,
  U.S.A.* 36°48N 118°12W **78** J8
Independence *Iowa,
  U.S.A.* 42°28N 91°54W **80** D8
Independence *Kans.,
  U.S.A.* 37°14N 95°42W **80** G6
Independence *Ky.,
  U.S.A.* 38°57N 84°33W **81** F11
Independence *Mo., U.S.A.* 39°6N 94°25W **80** F6
Independence Fjord
  Greenland 82°10N 29°0W **4** A6
Independence Mts.
  U.S.A. 41°20N 116°0W **76** F5
Index *U.S.A.* 47°50N 121°33W **78** C5
India ■ *Asia* 20°0N 78°0E **40** K11
Indian ⇸ *U.S.A.* 27°59N 80°34W **85** H14
Indian Cabins *Canada* 59°52N 117°40W **70** B5
Indian Harbour *Canada* 54°27N 57°13W **73** B8
Indian Head *Canada* 50°30N 103°41W **71** C8
Indian L. *U.S.A.* 43°46N 74°16W **83** C10
Indian Lake *U.S.A.* 43°47N 74°16W **83** C10
Indian Springs *U.S.A.* 36°35N 115°40W **79** J11
Indiana *U.S.A.* 40°37N 79°9W **82** F5
Indiana □ *U.S.A.* 40°0N 86°0W **81** F11
Indianapolis *U.S.A.* 39°46N 86°9W **80** F10
Indianola *Iowa, U.S.A.* 41°22N 93°34W **80** E7
Indianola *Miss., U.S.A.* 33°27N 90°39W **85** E9
Indiga *Russia* 67°38N 49°9E **18** A8
Indigirka ⇸ *Russia* 70°48N 148°54E **29** B15
Indio *U.S.A.* 33°43N 116°13W **79** M10
Indira Gandhi Canal *India* 28°0N 72°0E **42** F5
Indira Sagar *India* 22°15N 76°40E **42** H7

Indo-China *Asia* 15°0N 102°0E **26** G12
Indonesia ■ *Asia* 5°0S 115°0E **36** F5
Indore *India* 22°42N 75°53E **42** H6
Indramayu *Indonesia* 6°20S 108°19E **37** G13
Indravati ⇸ *India* 19°20N 80°20E **41** K12
Indre ⇸ *France* 47°16N 0°11E **20** C4
Indulkana *Australia* 26°58S 133°5E **63** D1
Indus ⇸ *Pakistan* 24°20N 67°47E **42** G2
Indus, Mouths of the
  Pakistan 24°0N 68°0E **42** H3
İnebolu *Turkey* 41°55N 33°40E **19** F5
Infiernillo, Presa del
  Mexico 18°35N 101°50W **86** D4
Ingenio *Canary Is.* 27°55N 15°26W **24** G4
Ingenio Santa Ana
  Argentina 27°25S 65°40W **94** B2
Ingersoll *Canada* 43°4N 80°55W **82** C4
Ingham *Australia* 18°43S 146°10E **62** B4
Ingleborough *U.K.* 54°10N 2°22W **12** C5
Inglewood *Queens.,
  Australia* 28°25S 151°2E **63** D5
Inglewood *Vic., Australia* 36°29S 143°53E **63** F3
Inglewood *N.Z.* 39°9S 174°14E **59** C5
Inglewood *U.S.A.* 33°58N 118°21W **79** M8
Ingólfshöfói *Iceland* 63°48N 16°39W **8** E5
Ingolstadt *Germany* 48°46N 11°26E **16** D6
Ingomar *U.S.A.* 46°35N 107°23W **76** C10
Ingonish *Canada* 46°42N 60°18W **73** C7
Ingraj Bazar *India* 24°58N 88°10E **43** G13
Ingrid Christensen Coast
  Antarctica 69°30S 76°0E **5** C6
Ingulec = Inhulec
  Ukraine 47°42N 33°14E **19** E5
Ingushetia □ *Russia* 43°20N 44°50E **19** F8
Ingwavuma *S. Africa* 27°9S 31°59E **57** D5
Inhaca *Mozam.* 26°1S 32°57E **57** D5
Inhafenga *Mozam.* 20°36S 33°53E **57** C5
Inhambane *Mozam.* 23°54S 35°30E **57** C6
Inhambane □ *Mozam.* 22°30S 34°20E **57** C5
Inhaminga *Mozam.* 18°26S 35°0E **55** F4
Inharrime *Mozam.* 24°30S 35°0E **57** C6
Inharrime ⇸ *Mozam.* 24°30S 35°0E **57** C6
Inhulec *Ukraine* 47°42N 33°14E **19** E5
Ining = Yining *China* 43°58N 81°10E **32** B3
Inírida ⇸ *Colombia* 3°55N 67°52W **92** C5
Inis = Ennis *Ireland* 52°51N 8°59W **10** D3
Inis Córthaidh = Enniscorthy
  Ireland 52°30N 6°34W **10** D5
Inishbofin *Ireland* 53°37N 10°13W **10** C1
Inisheer *Ireland* 53°3N 9°32W **10** C2
Inishfree B. *Ireland* 55°4N 8°23W **10** A3
Inishkea North *Ireland* 54°9N 10°11W **10** B1
Inishkea South *Ireland* 54°7N 10°12W **10** B1
Inishmaan *Ireland* 53°5N 9°35W **10** C2
Inishmore *Ireland* 53°8N 9°45W **10** C2
Inishmurray I. *Ireland* 54°26N 8°39W **10** B3
Inishowen Pen. *Ireland* 55°14N 7°15W **10** A4
Inishshark *Ireland* 53°37N 10°16W **10** C1
Inishturk *Ireland* 53°42N 10°7W **10** C1
Inishvickillane *Ireland* 52°3N 10°37W **10** D1
Injinoo ◌ *Australia* 10°56S 142°15E **62** A3
Injune *Australia* 25°53S 148°32E **63** D4
Inklin ⇸ *N. Amer.* 58°50N 133°10W **70** B2
Inland Kaikoura Ra.
  N.Z. 41°59S 173°41E **59** D4
Inland Sea = Setonaikai
  Japan 34°20N 133°30E **31** G6
Inle L. *Burma* 20°30N 96°58E **41** J20
Inlet *U.S.A.* 43°45N 74°48W **83** C10
Inn ⇸ *Austria* 48°35N 13°28E **16** D7
Innamincka *Australia* 27°44S 140°46E **63** D3
Inner Hebrides *U.K.* 57°0N 6°30W **11** E2
Inner Mongolia = Nei Monggol
  Zizhiqu □ *China* 42°0N 112°0E **34** D7
Inner Sound *U.K.* 57°30N 5°55W **11** D3
Innerkip *Canada* 43°13N 80°42W **82** C4
Innetalling I. *Canada* 56°0N 79°0W **72** A4
Innisfail *Australia* 17°33S 146°5E **62** B4
Innisfail *Canada* 52°2N 113°57W **70** C6
In'noshima *Japan* 34°19N 133°10E **31** G6
Innsbruck *Austria* 47°16N 11°23E **16** E6
Inny ⇸ *Ireland* 53°30N 7°50W **10** C4
Inongo
  Dem. Rep. of the Congo 1°55S 18°30E **52** E3
Inoucdjouac = Inukjuak
  Canada 58°25N 78°15W **69** F16
Inowrocław *Poland* 52°50N 18°12E **17** B10
Inscription, C. *Australia* 25°29S 112°59E **61** E1
Insein *Burma* 16°50N 96°5E **41** L20
Inta *Russia* 66°5N 60°8E **18** A11
Intendente Alvear
  Argentina 35°12S 63°32W **94** D3
Interlaken *Switz.* 46°41N 7°50E **20** C7
Interlaken *U.S.A.* 42°37N 76°44W **83** D8
International Falls
  U.S.A. 48°36N 93°25W **80** A7
Intiyaco *Argentina* 28°43S 60°5W **94** B3
Inukjuak *Canada* 58°25N 78°15W **69** F16
Inútil, B. *Chile* 53°30S 70°15W **96** G2
Inuvik *Canada* 68°16N 133°40W **68** D5
Inveraray *U.K.* 56°14N 5°5W **11** E3
Inverbervie *U.K.* 56°51N 2°17W **11** E6
Invercargill *N.Z.* 46°24S 168°24E **59** G2
Inverclyde □ *U.K.* 55°55N 4°49W **11** F4
Inverell *Australia* 29°45S 151°8E **63** D5
Invergordon *U.K.* 57°41N 4°10W **11** D4
Inverloch *Australia* 38°38S 145°45E **63** F4
Invermere *Canada* 50°30N 116°2W **70** C5
Inverness *Canada* 46°15N 61°19W **73** C7
Inverness *U.K.* 57°29N 4°13W **11** D4
Inverness *U.S.A.* 28°50N 82°20W **85** G13
Inverurie *U.K.* 57°17N 2°23W **11** D6
Investigator Group
  Australia 34°45S 134°20E **63** E1
Investigator Str.
  Australia 35°30S 137°0E **63** F2
Inya *Russia* 50°28N 86°37E **28** D9
Inyanga *Zimbabwe* 18°12S 32°40E **55** F3
Inyangani *Zimbabwe* 18°5S 32°50E **55** F3

Inyantue *Zimbabwe* 18°33S 26°39E **56** B4
Inyo Mts. *U.S.A.* 36°40N 118°0W **78** J9
Inyokern *U.S.A.* 35°39N 117°49W **79** K9
Inza *Russia* 53°55N 46°25E **18** D8
Isachsen, C. *Canada* 79°20N 105°28W **69** B10
Iō-Jima *Japan* 30°48N 130°18E **31** J5
Ioannina *Greece* 39°42N 20°47E **23** E9
Iola *U.S.A.* 37°55N 95°24W **80** G6
Iona *U.K.* 56°20N 6°25W **11** E2
Iona *U.S.A.* 38°21N 120°56W **78** G6
Ionia *U.S.A.* 42°59N 85°4W **81** D11
Ionian Is. = Ionioi Nisoi
  Greece 38°40N 20°0E **23** E9
Ionian Sea *Medit. S.* 37°30N 17°30E **23** E7
Ionioi Nisoi *Greece* 38°40N 20°0E **23** E9
Ios *Greece* 36°41N 25°20E **23** F11
Iowa □ *U.S.A.* 42°18N 93°30W **80** D7
Iowa ⇸ *U.S.A.* 41°10N 91°1W **80** E8
Iowa City *U.S.A.* 41°40N 91°32W **80** E8
Iowa Falls *U.S.A.* 42°31N 93°16W **80** D7
Iowa Park *U.S.A.* 33°57N 98°40W **84** E5
Ipala *Tanzania* 4°30S 32°52E **54** C3
Ipameri *Brazil* 17°44S 48°9W **93** G9
Ipatinga *Brazil* 19°32S 42°30W **93** G10
Ipiales *Colombia* 0°50N 77°37W **92** C3
Ipin = Yibin *China* 28°45N 104°32E **32** D5
Ipixuna *Brazil* 7°0S 71°40W **92** E4
Ipoh *Malaysia* 4°35N 101°5E **39** K3
Ippy *C.A.R.* 6°5N 21°7E **52** C4
Ípsala *Turkey* 40°55N 26°23E **23** D12
Ipswich *Australia* 27°35S 152°40E **63** D5
Ipswich *U.K.* 52°4N 1°10E **13** E9
Ipswich *Mass., U.S.A.* 42°41N 70°50W **83** D14
Ipswich *S. Dak., U.S.A.* 45°27N 99°2W **80** C4
Ipu *Brazil* 4°23S 40°44W **93** D10
Iqaluit *Canada* 63°44N 68°31W **69** E18
Iqaluktuutiaq = Cambridge Bay
  Canada 69°10N 105°0W **68** D11
Iquique *Chile* 20°19S 70°5W **92** H4
Iquitos *Peru* 3°45S 73°10W **92** D4
Irabu-Jima *Japan* 24°50N 125°10E **31** M2
Iracoubo *Fr. Guiana* 5°30N 53°10W **93** B8
Iráfoss *Iran* 26°42N 61°56E **45** E9
Iráklio *Greece* 35°20N 25°12E **25** D7
Iráklio □ *Greece* 35°10N 25°10E **25** D7
Iráklion = Iráklio *Greece* 35°20N 25°12E **25** D7
Irákliou, Kolpos *Greece* 35°23N 25°8E **25** D7
Irala *Paraguay* 25°55S 54°35W **95** B5
Iran ■ *Asia* 33°0N 53°0E **45** C7
Iran, Pegunungan
  Malaysia 2°20N 114°50E **36** D4
Iran Ra. = Iran, Pegunungan
  Malaysia 2°20N 114°50E **36** D4
Īrānshahr *Iran* 27°15N 60°40E **45** E9
Irapuato *Mexico* 20°41N 101°28W **86** C4
Iraq ■ *Asia* 33°0N 44°0E **44** C5
Irati *Brazil* 25°25S 50°38W **95** B5
Irbid *Jordan* 32°35N 35°48E **46** C4
Irbid □ *Jordan* 32°30N 35°50E **46** C5
Irebu *Dem. Rep. of the Congo* 0°40S 17°46E **52** E3
Ireland ■ *Europe* 53°50N 7°52W **10** C4
Iri = Iksan *S. Korea* 35°59N 127°0E **35** G14
Irian Jaya = Papua □
  Indonesia 4°0S 137°0E **37** E9
Irian Jaya Barat □
  Indonesia 2°5S 132°50E **37** E8
Iringa *Tanzania* 7°48S 35°43E **54** D4
Iringa □ *Tanzania* 7°48S 35°43E **54** D4
Iriomote △ *Japan* 24°29N 123°53E **31** M1
Iriomote-Jima *Japan* 24°19N 123°48E **31** M1
Iriona *Honduras* 15°57N 85°11W **88** C2
Iriri ⇸ *Brazil* 3°52S 52°37W **93** D8
Irish Republic ■ *Europe* 53°50N 7°52W **10** C4
Irish Sea *Europe* 53°38N 4°48W **12** D3
Irkutsk *Russia* 52°18N 104°20E **29** D11
Irma *Canada* 52°55N 111°14W **71** C6
Irō-Zaki *Japan* 34°36N 138°51E **31** G9
Iron Baron *Australia* 32°58S 137°11E **63** E2
Iron Gate = Portile de Fier
  Europe 44°44N 22°30E **17** F12
Iron Knob *Australia* 32°46S 137°8E **63** E2
Iron Mountain *U.S.A.* 45°49N 88°4W **80** C9
Iron Range △ *Australia* 12°34S 143°18E **62** A3
Iron River *U.S.A.* 46°6N 88°39W **80** B9
Irondequoit *U.S.A.* 43°13N 77°35W **82** C7
Ironton *Mo., U.S.A.* 37°36N 90°38W **80** G9
Ironton *Ohio, U.S.A.* 38°32N 82°41W **81** F12
Ironwood *U.S.A.* 46°27N 90°9W **80** B8
Ironwood Forest △
  U.S.A. 32°32N 111°28W **77** K8
Iroquois *Canada* 44°51N 75°19W **83** B9
Iroquois Falls *Canada* 48°46N 80°41W **72** C3
Irpin *Ukraine* 50°30N 30°15E **17** C16
Irrara Cr. ⇸ *Australia* 29°35S 145°31E **63** D4
Irrawaddy □ *Burma* 17°0N 95°0E **41** L19
Irrawaddy ⇸ *Burma* 15°50N 95°6E **41** M19
Irrawaddy, Mouths of the
  Burma 15°30N 95°0E **41** M19
Irricana *Canada* 51°19N 113°37W **70** C6
Irrunytju *Australia* 26°3S 128°56E **61** E4
Irtysh ⇸ *Russia* 61°4N 68°52E **28** C7
Irumu
  Dem. Rep. of the Congo 1°32N 29°53E **54** B2
Irún *Spain* 43°20N 1°52W **21** A5
Irunea = Pamplona-Iruña
  Spain 42°48N 1°38W **21** A5
Irvine *Canada* 49°57N 110°16W **71** D6
Irvine *U.K.* 55°37N 4°41W **11** F4
Irvine *Calif., U.S.A.* 33°41N 117°46W **79** M9
Irvine *Ky., U.S.A.* 37°42N 83°58W **81** G12
Irvinestown *U.K.* 54°28N 7°39W **10** B4
Irving *U.S.A.* 32°49N 96°56W **84** E6
Irvona *U.S.A.* 40°46N 78°33W **82** F6
Irwin ⇸ *Australia* 29°15S 114°54E **61** E1
Irymple *Australia* 34°14S 142°8E **63** E3
Isa Khel *Pakistan* 32°41N 71°17E **42** C4
Isaac ⇸ *Australia* 22°55S 149°20E **62** C4
Isabel *U.S.A.* 45°24N 101°26W **80** C3
Isabel, I. *Mexico* 21°51N 105°55W **86** C3

Isabela *Phil.* 6°40N 121°59E **37** C6
Isabela *Puerto Rico* 18°30N 67°2W **89** d
Isabela, Cord. *Nic.* 13°30N 85°25W **88** D2
Isabella Ra. *Australia* 21°0S 121°4E **60** D3
Isafjarðardjúp *Iceland* 66°10N 23°0W **8** C2
Ísafjörður *Iceland* 66°5N 23°9W **8** C2
Isagarh *India* 24°48N 77°51E **42** G7
Isahaya *Japan* 32°52N 130°2E **31** H5
Isaka *Tanzania* 3°56S 32°59E **54** C3
Isalo △ *Madag.* 22°23S 45°16E **57** C8
Isan ⇸ *India* 26°51N 80°7E **43** F9
Isana = Içana ⇸ *Brazil* 0°26N 67°19W **92** C5
Isangano △ *Zambia* 11°8S 30°35E **55** E3
Isar ⇸ *Germany* 48°48N 12°57E **16** D7
Íschia *Italy* 40°44N 13°57E **22** D5
Isdell ⇸ *Australia* 16°27S 124°51E **60** C3
Ise *Japan* 34°25N 136°45E **31** G8
Ise-Shima △ *Japan* 34°25N 136°48E **31** G8
Ise-Wan *Japan* 34°43N 136°43E **31** G8
Iseramagazi *Tanzania* 4°37S 32°10E **54** C3
Isère ⇸ *France* 44°59N 4°51E **20** D6
Isérnia *Italy* 41°36N 14°14E **22** D6
Isfahan = Eşfahān *Iran* 32°39N 51°43E **45** C6
Ishigaki *Japan* 24°26N 124°10E **31** M2
Ishikari-Gawa ⇸
  Japan 43°15N 141°23E **30** C10
Ishikari-Sammyaku
  Japan 43°30N 143°0E **30** C11
Ishikari-Wan *Japan* 43°25N 141°1E **30** C10
Ishikawa *Japan* 26°25N 127°49E **31** L3
Ishikawa □ *Japan* 36°30N 136°30E **31** F8
Ishim *Russia* 56°10N 69°30E **28** D7
Ishim ⇸ *Russia* 57°45N 71°10E **28** D8
Ishinomaki *Japan* 38°32N 141°20E **30** E10
Ishioka *Japan* 36°11N 140°16E **31** F10
Ishkoman *Pakistan* 36°30N 73°50E **43** A5
Ishpeming *U.S.A.* 46°29N 87°40W **80** B10
Isil Kul *Russia* 54°55N 71°16E **28** D8
Isiolo *Kenya* 0°24N 37°33E **54** B4
Isiro *Dem. Rep. of the Congo* 2°53N 27°40E **54** B2
Isisford *Australia* 24°15S 144°21E **62** C3
İskenderun *Turkey* 36°32N 36°10E **44** B3
İskenderun Körfezi
  Turkey 36°40N 35°50E **19** G6
Iskŭr ⇸ *Bulgaria* 43°45N 24°25E **23** C11
Iskut ⇸ *Canada* 56°45N 131°49W **70** B2
Isla ⇸ *U.K.* 56°32N 3°20W **11** E5
Isla Coiba △ *Panama* 7°33N 81°36W **88** E3
Isla de Salamanca △
  Colombia 10°59N 74°40W **89** D5
Isla Gorge △ *Australia* 25°10S 149°57E **62** D4
Isla Isabel △ *Mexico* 21°54N 105°58W **86** C3
Isla Tiburón y San Esteban △
  Mexico 29°0N 112°27W **86** B2
Isla Vista *U.S.A.* 34°25N 119°53W **79** L7
Islam Headworks
  Pakistan 29°49N 72°33E **42** E5
Islamabad *Pakistan* 33°40N 73°10E **42** C5
Islamgarh *Pakistan* 27°51N 70°48E **42** F4
Islamkot *Pakistan* 24°42N 70°13E **42** G4
Islampur *Bihar, India* 25°9N 85°12E **43** G11
Islampur *W. Bengal,
  India* 26°16N 88°12E **43** F13
Island = Iceland ■ *Europe* 64°45N 19°0W **8** D4
Island L. *Canada* 53°47N 94°25W **71** C10
Island Lagoon *Australia* 31°30S 136°40E **63** E2
Island Pond *U.S.A.* 44°49N 71°53W **83** B13
Islands, B. of *Canada* 49°11N 58°15W **73** C8
Islands, B. of *N.Z.* 35°15S 174°6E **59** A5
Islay *U.K.* 55°46N 6°10W **11** F2
Isle ⇸ *France* 44°55N 0°15W **20** D3
Isle aux Morts *Canada* 47°35N 59°0W **73** C8
Isle of Wight □ *U.K.* 50°41N 1°17W **13** G6
Isle Royale △ *U.S.A.* 48°0N 88°55W **80** B9
Isleton *U.S.A.* 38°10N 121°37W **78** G5
Ismail = Izmayil
  Ukraine 45°22N 28°46E **17** F15
Ismâ'iliya *Egypt* 30°37N 32°18E **51** B12
Isna *Egypt* 25°17N 32°30E **51** C12
Isoanala *Madag.* 23°50S 45°44E **57** C8
Isparta *Turkey* 37°47N 30°30E **19** G5
Íspica *Italy* 36°47N 14°55E **22** F6
Israel ■ *Asia* 32°0N 34°50E **46** D3
Issoire *France* 45°32N 3°15E **20** D5
Issyk-Kul = Balykchy
  Kyrgyzstan 42°26N 76°12E **32** B2
Issyk-Kul, Ozero = Ysyk-Köl
  Kyrgyzstan 42°25N 77°15E **28** E8
İstanbul *Turkey* 41°0N 28°58E **23** D13
İstanbul Boğazı *Turkey* 41°5N 29°3E **23** D13
Istiea *Greece* 38°57N 23°9E **23** E10
Isto, Mt. *U.S.A.* 69°12N 143°48W **74** B11
Istokpoga, L. *U.S.A.* 27°23N 81°17W **85** H14
Istra *Croatia* 45°10N 14°0E **16** F7
Istres *France* 43°31N 4°59E **20** E6
Istria = Istra *Croatia* 45°10N 14°0E **16** F7
Itá *Paraguay* 25°29S 57°21W **94** B4
Itaberaba *Brazil* 12°32S 40°18W **93** F10
Itabira *Brazil* 19°37S 43°13W **93** G10
Itabirito *Brazil* 20°15S 43°48W **95** A7
Itabuna *Brazil* 14°48S 39°16W **93** F11
Itacaunas ⇸ *Brazil* 5°21S 49°8W **93** E9
Itacoatiara *Brazil* 3°8S 58°25W **92** D7
Itaipú, Represa de *Brazil* 25°30S 54°30W **95** B5
Itaituba *Brazil* 4°10S 55°50W **93** D7
Itajaí *Brazil* 27°50S 48°39W **95** B6
Itajubá *Brazil* 22°24S 45°30W **95** A6
Itaka *Tanzania* 8°50S 32°49E **55** D3
Itala △ *S. Africa* 27°30S 31°7E **57** D5
Itamaraju *Brazil* 17°5S 39°8W **93** G11
Itampolo *Madag.* 24°41S 43°57E **57** C7
Itandrano *Madag.* 21°47S 45°17E **57** C8
Itapecuru Mirim *Brazil* 3°24S 44°20W **93** D10
Itaperuna *Brazil* 21°10S 41°54W **95** A7
Itapetinga *Brazil* 15°15S 40°15W **93** G10
Itapetininga *Brazil* 23°36S 48°7W **95** A6
Itapeva *Brazil* 23°59S 48°59W **95** A6

Itapicuru ⇸ *Bahia,
  Brazil* 11°47S 37°32W **93** F11
Itapicuru ⇸ *Maranhão,
  Brazil* 2°52S 44°12W **93** D10
Itapipoca *Brazil* 3°30S 39°35W **93** D11
Itapuá □ *Paraguay* 26°40S 55°40W **95** B4
Itaquí *Brazil* 29°8S 56°30W **94** B4
Itararé *Brazil* 24°6S 49°23W **95** A6
Itarsi *India* 22°36N 77°51E **42** H7
Itatí *Argentina* 27°16S 58°15W **94** B4
Itatiaia △ *Brazil* 22°22S 44°48W **95** A7
Itchen ⇸ *U.K.* 50°55N 1°22W **13** G6
Itezhi Tezhi, L. *Zambia* 15°30S 25°30E **55** F2
Ithaca *Greece* 38°25N 20°40E **23** E9
Ithaca *U.S.A.* 42°27N 76°30W **83** D8
Itháki *Greece* 38°25N 20°40E **23** E9
Itiquira ⇸ *Brazil* 17°18S 56°44W **93** G7
Itiyuro ⇸ *Argentina* 22°40S 63°50W **94** A3
Itō *Japan* 34°58N 139°5E **31** G9
Itoigawa *Japan* 37°2N 137°51E **31** F8
Itonamas ⇸ *Bolivia* 12°28S 64°24W **92** F6
Ittoqqortoormiit *Greenland* 70°20N 23°0W **4** B6
Itu *Brazil* 23°17S 47°15W **95** A6
Itu Aba I. *S. China Sea* 10°23N 114°21E **36** B4
Ituiutaba *Brazil* 19°0S 49°25W **93** G9
Itumbiara *Brazil* 18°20S 49°10W **93** G9
Itúna ⇸ *Canada* 51°10N 103°24W **71** C8
Iturbe *Argentina* 23°0S 65°25W **94** A2
Ituri ⇸
  Dem. Rep. of the Congo 1°40N 27°1E **54** B2
Iturup, Ostrov *Russia* 45°0N 148°0E **29** E15
Ituxi ⇸ *Brazil* 7°18S 64°51W **92** E6
Itzehoe *Germany* 53°55N 9°31E **16** B5
Ivahona *Madag.* 23°27S 46°10E **57** C8
Ivaí ⇸ *Brazil* 23°18S 53°42W **95** A5
Ivalo *Finland* 68°38N 27°35E **8** B22
Ivalojoki ⇸ *Finland* 68°40N 27°40E **8** B22
Ivanava *Belarus* 52°7N 25°29E **17** B13
Ivanhoe *Australia* 32°56S 144°20E **63** E3
Ivanhoe *Canada* 44°23N 77°28W **82** B7
Ivanhoe *Calif., U.S.A.* 36°23N 119°13W **78** J7
Ivanhoe *Minn., U.S.A.* 44°28N 96°15W **80** C6
Ivano-Frankivsk
  Ukraine 48°40N 24°40E **17** D13
Ivanovo = Ivanava
  Belarus 52°7N 25°29E **17** B13
Ivanovo *Russia* 57°5N 41°0E **18** C7
Ivato *Madag.* 20°37S 47°10E **57** C8
Ivatsevichy *Belarus* 52°43N 25°21E **17** B13
Ivdel *Russia* 60°42N 60°24E **18** B11
Ivinheima ⇸ *Brazil* 23°14S 53°42W **95** A5
Ivinhema *Brazil* 22°10S 53°37W **95** A5
Ivohibe *Madag.* 22°31S 46°57E **57** C8
Ivory Coast *W. Afr.* 4°20N 5°0W **50** H4
Ivory Coast ■ *Africa* 7°30N 5°0W **50** G4
Ivrea *Italy* 45°28N 7°52E **20** D7
Ivujivik *Canada* 62°24N 77°55W **69** E16
Ivvavik △ *Canada* 69°6N 139°30W **68** D4
Ivybridge *U.K.* 50°23N 3°56W **13** G4
Iwaizumi *Japan* 39°50N 141°45E **30** E10
Iwaki *Japan* 37°3N 140°55E **31** F10
Iwakuni *Japan* 34°15N 132°8E **31** G6
Iwamizawa *Japan* 43°12N 141°46E **30** C10
Iwanai *Japan* 42°58N 140°30E **30** C10
Iwata *Japan* 34°42N 137°51E **31** G8
Iwate □ *Japan* 39°30N 141°30E **30** E10
Iwate-San *Japan* 39°51N 141°0E **30** E10
Iwo *Nigeria* 7°39N 4°9E **50** G6
Iwŏn *N. Korea* 40°19N 128°39E **35** D15
Ixiamas *Bolivia* 13°50S 68°5W **92** F5
Ixopo *S. Africa* 30°11S 30°5E **57** E5
Ixtepec *Mexico* 16°34N 95°6W **87** D5
Ixtlán del Río *Mexico* 21°2N 104°22W **86** C4
Iyo *Japan* 33°45N 132°45E **31** H6
Izabal, L. de *Guatemala* 15°30N 89°10W **88** C2
Izamal *Mexico* 20°56N 89°1W **87** C7
Izena-Shima *Japan* 26°56N 127°56E **31** L3
Izhevsk *Russia* 56°51N 53°14E **18** C9
Izhma ⇸ *Russia* 65°19N 52°54E **18** A9
Izmayil *Ukraine* 45°22N 28°46E **17** F15
İzmir *Turkey* 38°25N 27°8E **23** E12
İznik Gölü *Turkey* 40°27N 29°30E **23** D13
İzmit = Kocaeli *Turkey* 40°45N 29°50E **19** F4
Izra *Syria* 32°51N 36°15E **46** C5
Izu-Shotō *Japan* 34°30N 140°0E **31** G10
Izúcar de Matamoros
  Mexico 18°36N 98°28W **87** D5
Izumi-Sano *Japan* 34°23N 135°18E **31** G7
Izumo *Japan* 35°20N 132°46E **31** G6
Izyaslav *Ukraine* 50°5N 26°50E **17** C14

J

J.F.K. Int. ✈ (JFK)
  U.S.A. 40°38N 73°47W **83** F11
J. Strom Thurmond L.
  U.S.A. 33°40N 82°12W **85** E13
Jabalpur *India* 23°9N 79°58E **43** H8
Jabbūl *Syria* 36°4N 37°30E **44** B3
Jablah *Syria* 35°20N 36°0E **44** C3
Jablonec nad Nisou
  Czech Rep. 50°43N 15°10E **16** C8
Jaboatão *Brazil* 8°7S 35°1W **93** E11
Jaboticabal *Brazil* 21°15S 48°17W **95** A6
Jaca *Spain* 42°35N 0°33W **21** A5
Jacareí *Brazil* 23°20S 46°0W **95** A6
Jacarèzinho *Brazil* 23°5S 49°58W **95** A6
Jáchymov *Czech Rep.* 50°22N 12°55E **16** C7
Jackman *U.S.A.* 45°37N 70°15W **81** C18
Jack River △ *Australia* 14°58S 144°19E **62** A3
Jackman *U.S.A.* 45°37N 70°15W **81** C18
Jackson *Barbados* 13°7N 59°36W **89** g
Jackson *Ala., U.S.A.* 31°31N 87°53W **85** F11
Jackson *Calif., U.S.A.* 38°21N 120°46W **78** G6
Jackson *Ky., U.S.A.* 37°33N 83°23W **81** G12
Jackson *Mich., U.S.A.* 42°15N 84°24W **81** D11
Jackson *Minn., U.S.A.* 43°37N 95°1W **80** D6

Jackson *Miss., U.S.A.* 32°18N 90°12W **85** E9
Jackson *Mo., U.S.A.* 37°23N 89°40W **80** G9
Jackson *N.H., U.S.A.* 44°10N 71°11W **83** B13
Jackson *Ohio, U.S.A.* 39°3N 82°39W **81** F12
Jackson *Tenn., U.S.A.* 35°37N 88°49W **85** D10
Jackson *Wyo., U.S.A.* 43°29N 110°46W **76** E8
Jackson B. *N.Z.* 43°58S 168°42E **59** E2
Jackson L. *U.S.A.* 43°52N 110°36W **76** E8
Jacksons *N.Z.* 42°46S 171°32E **59** E3
Jackson's Arm *Canada* 49°52N 56°47W **73** C8
Jacksonville *Ala., U.S.A.* 33°49N 85°46W **85** E12
Jacksonville *Ark., U.S.A.* 34°52N 92°07W **84** D8
Jacksonville *Calif., U.S.A.* 37°52N 120°24W **78** H6
Jacksonville *Fla., U.S.A.* 30°20N 81°39W **85** F14
Jacksonville *Ill., U.S.A.* 39°44N 90°14W **80** F9
Jacksonville *N.C., U.S.A.* 34°45N 77°26W **85** D16
Jacksonville *Tex., U.S.A.* 31°58N 95°17W **84** F7
Jacksonville Beach *U.S.A.* 30°17N 81°24W **85** F14
Jacmel *Haiti* 18°14N 72°32W **89** C5
Jacob Lake *U.S.A.* 36°43N 112°13W **77** H7
Jacobabad *Pakistan* 28°20N 68°29E **42** E3
Jacobina *Brazil* 11°11S 40°30W **93** F10
Jacques-Cartier, Dét. de *Canada* 50°0N 63°30W **73** C7
Jacques-Cartier, Mt. *Canada* 48°57N 66°0W **73** C6
Jacques-Cartier △ *Canada* 47°15N 71°33W **73** C5
Jacuí → *Brazil* 30°2S 51°15W **95** C5
Jacumba *U.S.A.* 32°37N 116°11W **79** N10
Jacundá → *Brazil* 1°57S 50°26W **93** D8
Jade City *Canada* 59°15N 129°37W **70** B3
Jaén *Peru* 5°25S 78°40W **92** E3
Jaén *Spain* 37°44N 3°43W **21** D4
Jafarabad *India* 20°52N 71°22E **42** J4
Jaffa = Tel Aviv-Yafo *Israel* 32°4N 34°48E **46** C3
Jaffa, C. *Australia* 36°58S 139°40E **63** F2
Jaffna *Sri Lanka* 9°45N 80°2E **40** Q12
Jaffrey *U.S.A.* 42°49N 72°2W **83** D12
Jagadhri *India* 30°10N 77°20E **42** D7
Jagadishpur *India* 25°30N 84°21E **43** G11
Jagdalpur *India* 19°3N 82°0E **41** K13
Jagersfontein *S. Africa* 29°44S 25°27E **56** D4
Jaghīn → *Iran* 27°17N 57°13E **45** E8
Jagodina *Serbia* 44°5N 21°15E **23** C9
Jagraon *India* 30°50N 75°25E **42** D6
Jagtial *India* 18°50N 79°0E **40** K11
Jaguariaíva *Brazil* 24°10S 49°50W **95** A6
Jaguaribe → *Brazil* 4°25S 37°45W **93** D11
Jagüey Grande *Cuba* 22°35N 81°7W **88** B3
Jahanabad *India* 25°13N 84°59E **43** G11
Jahazpur *India* 25°37N 75°17E **42** G6
Jahrom *Iran* 28°30N 53°31E **45** D7
Jaijon *India* 31°21N 76°9E **42** D7
Jailolo *Indonesia* 1°5N 127°30E **37** D7
Jailolo, Selat *Indonesia* 0°5N 129°5E **37** D7
Jaipur *India* 27°0N 75°50E **42** F6
Jais *India* 26°15N 81°32E **43** F9
Jaisalmer *India* 26°55N 70°54E **42** F4
Jaisinghnagar *India* 23°38N 78°34E **43** H8
Jaitaran *India* 26°12N 73°56E **42** F5
Jaithari *India* 23°14N 78°37E **43** H8
Jājarm *Iran* 36°58N 56°27E **45** B8
Jakam → *India* 23°54N 74°13E **42** H6
Jakarta *Indonesia* 6°9S 106°52E **37** G12
Jakhal *India* 29°48N 75°50E **42** E6
Jakhau *India* 23°13N 68°43E **42** H3
Jakobstad = Pietarsaari *Finland* 63°40N 22°43E **8** E20
Jal *U.S.A.* 32°7N 103°12W **77** K12
Jalājil *Si. Arabia* 25°40N 45°27E **44** E5
Jalālābād *Afghan.* 34°30N 70°29E **42** B4
Jalalabad *India* 27°41N 79°42E **43** F8
Jalalpur Jattan *Pakistan* 32°38N 74°11E **42** C6
Jalama *U.S.A.* 34°29N 120°29W **79** L6
Jalandhar = Jullundur *India* 31°20N 75°40E **42** D6
Jalapa *Guatemala* 14°39N 89°59W **88** D2
Jalapa Enríquez = Xalapa *Mexico* 19°32N 96°55W **87** D5
Jalasjärvi *Finland* 62°29N 22°47E **8** E20
Jalaun *India* 26°8N 79°25E **43** F8
Jaldhaka → *Bangla.* 26°16N 89°16E **43** F13
Jalesar *India* 27°29N 78°19E **42** F8
Jaleswar *Nepal* 26°38N 85°48E **43** F11
Jalgaon *India* 21°0N 75°42E **40** J9
Jalībah *Iraq* 30°35N 46°32E **44** D5
Jalingo *Nigeria* 8°55N 11°25E **51** G8
Jalisco □ *Mexico* 20°20N 103°40W **86** D4
Jalkot *Pakistan* 35°14N 73°24E **43** B5
Jalna *India* 19°48N 75°38E **40** K9
Jalón → *Spain* 41°47N 1°4W **21** B6
Jalor *India* 25°21N 72°37E **42** G5
Jalpa *Mexico* 21°38N 102°58W **86** C4
Jalpaiguri *India* 26°32N 88°46E **43** F13
Jalpan *Mexico* 21°14N 99°29W **87** C5
Jaluit I. *Marshall Is.* 6°0N 169°30E **64** G8
Jalūlā *Iraq* 34°16N 45°10E **44** C5
Jamaame *Somali Rep.* 0°4N 42°44E **47** G3
Jamaica ■ *W. Indies* 18°10N 77°30W **88** a
Jamalpur *Bangla.* 24°52N 89°56E **41** G16
Jamalpur *India* 25°18N 86°28E **43** G12
Jamalpurganj *India* 23°2N 87°59E **43** H13
Jamanxim → *Brazil* 4°43S 56°18W **93** D7
Jambewangi *Indonesia* 8°17S 114°7E **37** J17
Jambi *Indonesia* 1°38S 103°30E **36** E2
Jambi □ *Indonesia* 1°30S 102°30E **36** E2
Jambongan, Pulau *Malaysia* 6°45N 117°20E **36** C5
Jambusar *India* 22°3N 72°51E **42** H5

James Ranges *Australia* 24°10S 132°30E **60** D5
James Ross I. *Antarctica* 63°58S 57°50W **5** C18
Jamesabad *Pakistan* 25°17N 69°15E **42** G3
Jamestown *Australia* 33°10S 138°32E **63** E2
Jamestown *S. Africa* 31°6S 26°45E **56** E4
Jamestown *N. Dak., U.S.A.* 46°54N 98°42W **80** B4
Jamestown *N.Y., U.S.A.* 42°6N 79°14W **82** D5
Jamestown *Pa., U.S.A.* 41°29N 80°27W **82** E4
Jamīlābād *Iran* 34°24N 48°28E **45** C6
Jamira → *India* 21°35N 88°28E **43** J13
Jamkhandi *India* 16°30N 75°15E **40** L9
Jammu *India* 32°43N 74°54E **42** C6
Jammu & Kashmir □ *India* 34°25N 77°0E **43** B7
Jamnagar *India* 22°30N 70°6E **42** H4
Jamni → *India* 25°13N 78°35E **43** G8
Jampur *Pakistan* 29°39N 70°40E **42** E4
Jamrud *Pakistan* 33°59N 71°24E **42** C4
Jämsä *Finland* 61°53N 25°10E **8** F21
Jamshedpur *India* 22°44N 86°12E **43** H12
Jamtara *India* 23°59N 86°49E **43** H12
Jämtland *Sweden* 63°31N 14°0E **8** E16
Jan L. *Canada* 54°56N 102°55W **71** C8
Jan Mayen *Arctic* 71°0N 9°0W **4** B7
Janakpur *India* 26°42N 85°55E **43** F11
Janaúba *Brazil* 15°48S 43°19W **93** G10
Jand *Pakistan* 33°30N 72°6E **42** C5
Jandanku ⊙ *Australia* 16°20S 135°45E **62** B2
Jandaq *Iran* 34°3N 54°22E **45** C7
Jandía *Canary Is.* 28°6N 14°21W **24** F5
Jandía, Pta. de *Canary Is.* 28°3N 14°31W **24** F5
Jandía □ *Canary Is.* 28°4N 14°19W **24** F5
Jandola *Pakistan* 32°20N 70°9E **42** C4
Jandowae *Australia* 26°45S 151°7E **63** D5
Janesville *U.S.A.* 42°41N 89°1W **80** D9
Jangamo *Mozam.* 24°6S 35°21E **57** C6
Janghai *India* 25°33N 82°19E **43** G10
Jangheung *S. Korea* 34°41N 126°52E **35** G14
Janjanbureh *Gambia* 13°30N 14°47W **50** F3
Janjgir *India* 22°1N 82°34E **43** J10
Janjina *Madag.* 20°30S 45°50E **57** C8
Janos *Mexico* 30°54N 108°10W **86** A3
Januária *Brazil* 15°25S 44°25W **93** G10
Janubio *Canary Is.* 28°56N 13°50W **24** F6
Jaora *India* 23°40N 75°10E **42** H6
Japan ■ *Asia* 36°0N 136°0E **31** G8
Japan, Sea of *Asia* 40°0N 135°0E **30** D4
Japan Trench *Pac. Oc.* 32°0N 142°0E **64** D6
Japen = Yapen *Indonesia* 1°50S 136°0E **37** E9
Japla *India* 24°33N 84°1E **43** G11
Japurá → *Brazil* 3°8S 65°46W **92** D5
Jaquarão *Brazil* 32°34S 53°23W **95** C5
Jaqué *Panama* 7°27N 78°8W **88** E4
Jarābulus *Syria* 36°49N 38°1E **44** B3
Jarama → *Spain* 40°24N 3°32W **21** B4
Jaranwala *Pakistan* 31°15N 73°26E **42** D5
Jarash *Jordan* 32°17N 35°54E **46** C4
Jarash □ *Jordan* 32°17N 35°54E **46** C4
Jardim *Brazil* 21°28S 56°2W **94** A4
Jardín América *Argentina* 27°3S 55°14W **95** B4
Jardine River △ *Australia* 11°9S 142°21E **62** A3
Jardines de la Reina, Arch. de los *Cuba* 20°50N 78°50W **88** B4
Jargalang *China* 43°5N 122°55E **35** C12
Jari → *Brazil* 1°9S 51°54W **93** D8
Jarīr, W. al → *Si. Arabia* 25°38N 42°30E **44** E4
Jarrahdale *Australia* 32°24S 116°5E **61** F2
Jarrahi → *Iran* 30°49N 48°48E **45** D6
Jarres, Plaine des *Laos* 19°27N 103°10E **38** C4
Jartai *China* 39°45N 105°48E **34** E3
Jarud Qi *China* 44°28N 120°50E **35** B11
Järvenpää *Finland* 60°29N 25°5E **8** F21
Jarvis *Canada* 42°53N 80°6W **82** D4
Jarvis I. *Pac. Oc.* 0°15S 160°5W **65** H12
Jarwa *India* 27°38N 82°30E **43** F10
Jasdan *India* 22°2N 71°12E **42** H4
Jashpurnagar *India* 22°54N 84°9E **43** H11
Jasidih *India* 24°31N 86°39E **43** G12
Jāsimīyah *Iraq* 33°45N 44°41E **44** C5
Jasin *Malaysia* 2°20N 102°26E **39** L4
Jāsk *Iran* 25°38N 57°45E **45** E8
Jasło *Poland* 49°45N 21°30E **17** D11
Jaso *India* 24°30N 80°29E **43** G9
Jasper *Alta., Canada* 52°55N 118°5W **70** C5
Jasper *Ont., Canada* 44°52N 75°57W **83** B9
Jasper *Ala., U.S.A.* 33°50N 87°17W **85** E11
Jasper *Fla., U.S.A.* 30°31N 82°57W **85** F13
Jasper *Ind., U.S.A.* 38°24N 86°56W **80** F10
Jasper *Tex., U.S.A.* 30°56N 94°1W **84** F7
Jasper △ *Canada* 52°50N 118°8W **70** C5
Jasrasar *India* 27°43N 73°49E **42** F5
Jászberény *Hungary* 47°30N 19°55E **17** E10
Jataí *Brazil* 17°58S 51°48W **93** G8
Jati *India* 24°20N 68°19E **42** G3
Jatibarang *Indonesia* 6°28S 108°18E **37** G13
Jatiluwlh *Indonesia* 8°23S 115°8E **37** J18
Jatinegara *Indonesia* 6°13S 106°52E **37** G12
Játiva = Xàtiva *Spain* 38°59N 0°32W **21** C5
Jaú *Brazil* 22°10S 48°30W **95** A6
Jauja *Peru* 11°45S 75°15W **92** F3
Jaunpur *India* 25°46N 82°44E **43** G10
Java = Jawa *Indonesia* 7°0S 110°0E **36** F3
Java Sea *Indonesia* 4°35S 107°15E **36** E3
Java Trench *Ind. Oc.* 9°0S 105°0E **36** F3
Jawa *Indonesia* 7°0S 110°0E **36** F3
Jawa Barat □ *Indonesia* 7°0S 107°0E **37** G12
Jawa Tengah □ *Indonesia* 7°0S 110°0E **37** G14
Jawa Timur □ *Indonesia* 8°0S 113°0E **37** G15
Jawad *India* 24°36N 74°51E **42** G6
Jawhar *Somali Rep.* 2°48N 45°30E **47** G4
Jawoyn ⊙ *Australia* 14°16S 132°28E **60** B5
Jay Peak *U.S.A.* 44°55N 72°32W **83** B12
Jaya, Puncak *Indonesia* 3°57S 137°17E **37** E9
Jayanti *India* 26°45N 89°40E **41** F16
Jayapura *Indonesia* 2°28S 140°38E **37** E10
Jayawijaya, Pegunungan *Indonesia* 5°0S 139°0E **37** F9

Jaynagar *India* 26°43N 86°9E **43** F12
Jaypur = Jeypore *India* 18°50N 82°38E **41** K13
Jayrūd *Syria* 33°49N 36°44E **44** C3
Jayton *U.S.A.* 33°15N 100°34W **84** E4
Jāz Mūrīān, Hāmūn-e *Iran* 27°20N 58°55E **45** E8
Jazīreh-ye Shīf *Iran* 29°4N 50°54E **45** D6
Ji-Paraná *Brazil* 10°52S 62°57W **92** F6
Ji Xian *Hebei, China* 37°35N 115°30E **34** F8
Ji Xian *Henan, China* 35°22N 114°5E **34** G8
Ji Xian *Shanxi, China* 36°7N 110°40E **34** F6
Jiامusi *China* 46°40N 130°26E **33** B8
Jiamusi *China* 46°40N 130°26E **33** B8
Ji'an *Jiangxi, China* 27°6N 114°59E **35** D10
Ji'an *Jilin, China* 41°5N 126°10E **35** D14
Jianchang *China* 40°55N 120°35E **35** D11
Jianchangying *China* 40°10N 118°50E **35** D10
Jiangcheng *China* 22°36N 101°52E **32** D5
Jiangmen *China* 22°32N 113°0E **35** F9
Jiangsu □ *China* 33°0N 120°0E **35** H11
Jiangxi □ *China* 27°30N 116°0E **35** D6
Jiao Xian = Jiaozhou *China* 36°18N 120°1E **35** F11
Jiaohe *Hebei, China* 38°2N 116°20E **34** E9
Jiaohe *Jilin, China* 43°40N 127°22E **35** C14
Jiaozhou *China* 36°18N 120°1E **35** F11
Jiaozhou Wan *China* 36°5N 120°10E **35** F11
Jiaozuo *China* 35°16N 113°12E **34** G7
Jiawang *China* 34°28N 117°26E **35** G9
Jiaxiang *China* 35°25N 116°20E **34** G9
Jiaxing *China* 30°49N 120°45E **33** C7
Jiayi = Chiai *Taiwan* 23°29N 120°25E **33** D7
Jibuti = Djibouti ■ *Africa* 12°0N 43°0E **47** E3
Jicarón, I. *Panama* 7°10N 81°50W **88** E3
Jiddah *Si. Arabia* 21°29N 39°10E **44** E2
Jido *India* 29°2N 94°58E **41** E19
Jieshou *China* 33°18N 115°22E **34** H8
Jiexiu *China* 37°2N 111°55E **34** F6
Jigalong *Australia* 23°21S 120°47E **60** D3
Jigalong ⊙ *Australia* 23°21S 120°47E **60** D3
Jigni *India* 25°45N 79°25E **43** G8
Jihlava *Czech Rep.* 49°28N 15°35E **16** D8
Jihlava → *Czech Rep.* 48°55N 16°36E **17** D9
Jijiga *Ethiopia* 9°20N 42°50E **47** F3
Jilib *Somali Rep.* 0°29N 42°46E **47** G3
Jilin *China* 43°44N 126°30E **35** C14
Jilin □ *China* 44°0N 127°0E **35** C14
Jilong = Chilung *Taiwan* 25°3N 121°45E **33** D7
Jima *Ethiopia* 7°40N 36°47E **47** F2
Jimbaran, Teluk *Indonesia* 8°46S 115°9E **37** K18
Jiménez *Mexico* 27°8N 104°54W **86** B4
Jimeta *Nigeria* 9°17N 12°28E **52** C2
Jimo *China* 36°23N 120°30E **35** F11
Jin Xian = Jinzhou *Hebei, China* 38°2N 115°2E **34** E8
Jin Xian = Jinzhou *Liaoning, China* 38°55N 121°42E **35** E11
Jinan *China* 36°38N 117°1E **34** F9
Jinchang *China* 38°30N 102°10E **32** C5
Jincheng *China* 35°29N 112°50E **34** G7
Jind *India* 29°19N 76°22E **42** E7
Jindabyne *Australia* 36°25S 148°35E **63** F4
Jinding *China* 22°22N 113°33E **33** G10
Jindo *S. Korea* 34°28N 126°15E **35** G14
Jindřichův Hradec *Czech Rep.* 49°10N 15°2E **16** D8
Jing He → *China* 34°27N 109°4E **34** G5
Jingbian *China* 37°20N 108°30E **34** F5
Jingchuan *China* 35°20N 107°20E **34** G4
Jingdezhen *China* 29°20N 117°11E **33** D6
Jinggu *China* 23°35N 100°41E **32** D5
Jinghai *China* 38°55N 116°55E **34** E9
Jingle *China* 38°20N 111°55E **34** E6
Jingning *China* 35°30N 105°43E **34** G3
Jingpo Hu *China* 43°55N 128°55E **35** C15
Jingtai *China* 37°10N 104°6E **34** F3
Jingxing *China* 38°2N 114°8E **34** E8
Jingyang *China* 34°30N 108°50E **34** G5
Jingyu *China* 42°25N 126°45E **35** C14
Jingyuan *China* 36°30N 104°40E **34** F3
Jingziguan *China* 33°15N 111°0E **34** H6
Jinhua *China* 29°8N 119°38E **33** D6
Jining *Nei Monggol Zizhiqu, China* 41°5N 113°0E **34** D7
Jining *Shandong, China* 35°22N 116°34E **34** G9
Jinja *Uganda* 0°25N 33°12E **54** B3
Jinjang *Malaysia* 3°13N 101°39E **39** L3
Jinji *China* 37°58N 106°8E **34** F4
Jinju *S. Korea* 35°12N 128°2E **35** G15
Jinnah Barrage *Pakistan* 32°58N 71°33E **42** C4
Jinotega *Nic.* 13°6N 85°59W **88** D2
Jinotepe *Nic.* 11°50N 86°10W **88** D2
Jinsha Jiang → *China* 28°50N 104°36E **32** D5
Jinxi *China* 40°52N 120°50E **35** D11
Jinxiang *China* 35°5N 116°22E **34** G9
Jinzhong *China* 37°42N 112°46E **34** F7
Jinzhou *Hebei, China* 38°2N 115°2E **34** E8
Jinzhou *Liaoning, China* 41°5N 121°3E **35** D11
Jiparaná → *Brazil* 8°3S 62°52W **92** E6
Jipijapa *Ecuador* 1°0S 80°40W **92** D2
Jiquilpan *Mexico* 19°59N 102°43W **86** D4
Jirisan *S. Korea* 35°20N 127°44E **35** G14
Jiroft *Iran* 28°45N 57°50E **45** D8
Jishan *China* 35°34N 110°58E **34** G6
Jisr ash Shughūr *Syria* 35°49N 36°18E **44** C3
Jitarning *Australia* 32°48S 117°57E **61** F2
Jitra *Malaysia* 6°16N 100°25E **39** J3
Jiu → *Romania* 43°47N 23°48E **17** G12
Jiudengkou *China* 39°56N 106°40E **34** E4
Jiujiang *China* 29°42N 115°58E **33** D6
Jiulong = Kowloon *China* 22°19N 114°11E **33** G11
Jiuquan *China* 39°50N 98°20E **32** C4
Jiutai *China* 44°10N 125°50E **35** B13
Jiuxincheng *China* 39°17N 115°59E **34** E8

Jiwani *Pakistan* 25°1N 61°44E **40** G2
Jixi *China* 45°20N 130°50E **35** B16
Jiyang *China* 37°0N 117°12E **35** F9
Jiyuan *China* 35°7N 112°57E **34** G7
Jīzān *Si. Arabia* 17°0N 42°0E **47** D3
Jize *China* 36°54N 114°56E **34** F8
Jizl, Wādī al → *Si. Arabia* 25°39N 38°25E **44** E3
Jizō-Zaki *Japan* 35°34N 133°20E **31** G6
Jizzax *Uzbekistan* 40°6N 67°50E **28** E7
Joaçaba *Brazil* 27°5S 51°31W **95** B5
João Pessoa *Brazil* 7°10S 34°52W **93** E12
Joaquín V. González *Argentina* 25°10S 64°0W **94** B3
Jobat *India* 22°25N 74°34E **42** H6
Jodhpur *India* 26°23N 73°8E **42** F5
Jodiya *India* 22°42N 70°18E **42** H4
Joensuu *Finland* 62°37N 29°49E **8** E23
Jõetsu *Japan* 37°12N 138°10E **31** F9
Jofane *Mozam.* 21°15S 34°18E **57** C5
Jogbani *India* 26°25N 87°15E **43** F12
Jõgeva *Estonia* 58°45N 26°24E **9** G22
Jogjakarta = Yogyakarta *Indonesia* 7°49S 110°22E **37** G14
Johannesburg *S. Africa* 26°11S 28°2E **57** D4
Johannesburg *U.S.A.* 35°22N 117°38W **79** K9
Johilla → *India* 23°37N 81°14E **43** H9
John Crow Mts. *Jamaica* 18°5N 76°25W **88** a
John Day *U.S.A.* 44°25N 118°57W **76** D4
John Day → *U.S.A.* 45°44N 120°39W **76** D3
John Day Fossil Beds △ *U.S.A.* 44°33N 119°38W **76** D4
John D'or Prairie *Canada* 58°30N 115°8W **70** B5
John H. Kerr Res. *U.S.A.* 36°36N 78°18W **85** C15
John o' Groats *U.K.* 58°38N 3°4W **11** C5
Johnnie *U.S.A.* 36°25N 116°5W **79** J10
Johnson *U.S.A.* 44°38N 72°41W **83** B12
Johnson City *Kans., U.S.A.* 37°34N 101°45W **80** G3
Johnson City *N.Y., U.S.A.* 42°7N 75°58W **83** D9
Johnson City *Tenn., U.S.A.* 36°19N 82°21W **85** C13
Johnson City *Tex., U.S.A.* 30°17N 98°25W **84** F5
Johnsonburg *U.S.A.* 41°29N 78°41W **82** E6
Johnsondale *U.S.A.* 35°58N 118°32W **79** K8
Johnsons Crossing *Canada* 60°29N 133°18W **70** A2
Johnston, L. *Australia* 32°25S 120°30E **61** F3
Johnston Falls = Mambilima Falls *Zambia* 10°31S 28°45E **55** E2
Johnston I. *Pac. Oc.* 17°10N 169°8W **65** F11
Johnstone Str. *Canada* 50°28N 126°0W **70** C3
Johnstown *Ireland* 52°45N 7°33W **10** D4
Johnstown *N.Y., U.S.A.* 43°0N 74°22W **83** C10
Johnstown *Ohio, U.S.A.* 40°9N 82°41W **82** F2
Johnstown *Pa., U.S.A.* 40°20N 78°55W **82** F6
Johor, Selat *Asia* 1°28N 103°47E **39** d
Johor Bahru *Malaysia* 1°28N 103°46E **39** d
Jõhvi *Estonia* 59°22N 27°27E **9** G22
Joinville *Brazil* 26°15S 48°55W **95** B6
Joinville I. *Antarctica* 65°0S 55°30W **5** C18
Jojutla *Mexico* 18°37N 99°11W **87** D5
Jokkmokk *Sweden* 66°35N 19°50E **8** C18
Jökulsá á Bru → *Iceland* 65°40N 14°16W **8** D6
Jökulsá á Fjöllum → *Iceland* 66°10N 16°30W **8** C5
Jolfa *Āzarbājān-e Sharqī, Iran* 38°57N 45°38E **44** B5
Jolfa *Eṣfahan, Iran* 32°58N 51°37E **45** C6
Joliet *U.S.A.* 41°32N 88°5W **80** E9
Joliette *Canada* 46°3N 73°24W **72** C5
Jolo *Phil.* 6°0N 121°0E **37** C6
Jolon *U.S.A.* 35°58N 121°9W **78** K5
Jombang *Indonesia* 7°33S 112°14E **37** G15
Jonava *Lithuania* 55°8N 24°12E **9** J21
Jones Sound *Canada* 76°0N 85°0W **69** B15
Jonesboro *Ark., U.S.A.* 35°50N 90°42W **85** D9
Jonesboro *La., U.S.A.* 32°15N 92°43W **84** E8
Joniškis *Lithuania* 56°13N 23°35E **9** H20
Jönköping *Sweden* 57°45N 14°8E **9** H16
Jonquière *Canada* 48°27N 71°14W **73** C5
Joplin *U.S.A.* 37°6N 94°31W **80** G6
Jora *India* 26°20N 77°49E **42** F6
Jordan *Mont., U.S.A.* 47°19N 106°55W **76** C10
Jordan *N.Y., U.S.A.* 43°4N 76°29W **83** C8
Jordan ■ *Asia* 31°0N 36°0E **46** E5
Jordan → *Asia* 31°48N 35°32E **46** D4
Jordan Valley *U.S.A.* 43°12N 117°3W **76** E5
Jorhat *India* 26°45N 94°12E **41** F19
Jörn *Sweden* 65°4N 20°1E **8** D19
Jorong *Indonesia* 3°58S 114°56E **36** E4
Jørpeland *Norway* 59°3N 6°1E **9** G12
Jorquera → *Chile* 28°3S 69°58W **94** B2
Jos *Nigeria* 9°53N 8°51E **50** G7
José Batlle y Ordóñez *Uruguay* 33°20S 55°10W **95** C4
Joseph, L. *Canada* 45°10N 79°44W **82** A5
Joseph Bonaparte G. *Australia* 14°35S 128°50E **60** B4
Joseph L. *Canada* 52°45N 65°18W **73** B6
Joshinath *India* 30°34N 79°34E **43** D8
Joshinetsu-Kōgen △ *Japan* 36°34N 138°32E **31** F9
Joshua Tree *U.S.A.* 34°8N 116°19W **79** L10
Joshua Tree △ *U.S.A.* 33°55N 116°0W **79** M10
Jost Van Dyke I. *Br. Virgin Is.* 18°29N 64°47W **89** e
Jostedalsbreen *Norway* 61°40N 6°59E **8** F12
Jotunheimen *Norway* 61°35N 8°25E **8** F13
Joubertberge *Namibia* 18°30S 14°0E **56** B1
Jourdanton *U.S.A.* 28°55N 98°33W **84** G5
Jovellanos *Cuba* 22°40N 81°10W **88** B3
Ju Xian *China* 36°35N 118°20E **35** F10
Juan Aldama *Mexico* 24°19N 103°21W **86** C4
Juan Bautista Alberdi *Argentina* 34°26S 61°48W **94** C3
Juan de Fuca, Str. of. *N. Amer.* 48°15N 124°0W **78** B3

130 Juán de Nova
INDEX TO WORLD MAPS

Juán de Nova Ind. Oc. 17°3S 43°45E 57 B7
Juan Fernández, Arch. de Pac. Oc. 33°50S 80°0W 90 G2
Juan José Castelli Argentina 25°27S 60°57W 94 B3
Juan L. Lacaze Uruguay 34°26S 57°25W 94 C4
Juankoski Finland 63°3N 28°19E 8 E23
Juárez Mexico 27°37N 100°44W 86 B4
Juárez, Sierra de Mexico 32°0N 116°0W 86 A1
Juàzeiro Brazil 9°30S 40°30W 93 E10
Juàzeiro do Norte Brazil 7°10S 39°18W 93 E11
Jûbâ Sudan 4°50N 31°35E 51 H12
Juba → Somali Rep. 1°30N 42°35E 47 G3
Jubany Antarctica 62°30S 58°0W 5 C18
Jubayl Lebanon 34°5N 35°39E 46 A4
Jubbah Si. Arabia 28°2N 40°56E 44 D4
Jubbal India 31°5N 77°40E 42 D7
Jubbulpore = Jabalpur India 23°9N 79°58E 43 H8
Jubilee L. Australia 29°0S 126°50E 61 E4
Juby, C. Morocco 28°0N 12°59W 50 C3
Júcar = Xúquer → Spain 39°5N 0°10W 21 C5
Júcaro Cuba 21°37N 78°51W 88 B4
Juchitán de Zaragoza Mexico 16°26N 95°1W 87 D5
Judea = Har Yehuda Israel 31°35N 34°57E 46 D3
Judith → U.S.A. 47°44N 109°39W 76 C9
Judith, Pt. U.S.A. 41°22N 71°29W 83 E13
Judith Gap U.S.A. 46°41N 109°45W 76 C9
Juigalpa Nic. 12°6N 85°26W 88 D2
Juiz de Fora Brazil 21°43S 43°19W 95 A7
Jujuy □ Argentina 23°20S 65°40W 94 A2
Julesburg U.S.A. 40°59N 102°16W 76 F12
Juli Peru 16°10S 69°25W 92 G5
Julia Cr. → Australia 20°0S 141°11E 62 C3
Julia Creek Australia 20°39S 141°44E 62 C3
Juliaca Peru 15°25S 70°10W 92 G4
Julian U.S.A. 33°4N 116°38W 79 M10
Julian, L. Canada 54°25N 77°57W 72 B4
Julianatop Suriname 3°40N 56°30W 93 C7
Julianehåb = Qaqortoq Greenland 60°43N 46°0W 4 C5
Julimes Mexico 28°25N 105°27W 86 B3
Jullundur India 31°20N 75°40E 42 D6
Julu China 37°15N 115°2E 34 F8
Jumbo Zimbabwe 17°30S 30°58E 55 F3
Jumbo Pk. U.S.A. 36°12N 114°11W 79 J12
Jumentos Cays Bahamas 23°0N 75°40W 88 B4
Jumilla Spain 38°28N 1°19W 21 C5
Jumla Nepal 29°15N 82°13E 43 E10
Jumna = Yamuna → India 25°30N 81°53E 43 G9
Jumunjin S. Korea 37°55N 128°54E 35 F15
Junagadh India 21°30N 70°30E 42 J4
Junction Tex., U.S.A. 30°29N 99°46W 84 F5
Junction Utah, U.S.A. 38°14N 112°13W 77 G7
Junction B. Australia 11°52S 133°55E 62 A1
Junction City Kans., U.S.A. 39°2N 96°50W 80 F5
Junction City Oreg., U.S.A. 44°13N 123°12W 76 D2
Junction Pt. Australia 11°45S 133°50E 62 A1
Jundah Australia 24°46S 143°2E 62 C3
Jundiaí Brazil 24°30S 47°0W 95 A6
Juneau U.S.A. 58°18N 134°25W 70 B2
Junee Australia 34°53S 147°35E 63 E4
Jungfrau Switz. 46°32N 7°58E 20 C7
Junggar Pendi China 44°30N 86°0E 32 B3
Jungshahi Pakistan 24°52N 67°44E 42 G2
Juniata → U.S.A. 40°24N 77°1W 82 F7
Junín Argentina 34°33S 60°57W 94 C3
Junín de los Andes Argentina 39°45S 71°0W 96 D2
Jūniyah Lebanon 33°59N 35°38E 46 B4
Juntas Chile 28°24S 69°58W 94 B2
Juntura U.S.A. 43°45N 118°5W 76 E4
Jur, Nahr el → Sudan 8°45N 29°15E 51 G11
Jura = Jura, Mts. du Europe 46°40N 6°5E 20 C7
Jura = Schwäbische Alb Germany 48°20N 9°30E 16 D5
Jura U.K. 56°0N 5°50W 11 F3
Jura, Mts. du Europe 46°40N 6°5E 20 C7
Jura, Sd. of U.K. 55°57N 5°45W 11 F3
Jurbarkas Lithuania 55°4N 22°46E 9 J20
Jurien Bay Australia 30°18S 115°2E 61 F2
Jūrmala Latvia 56°58N 23°34E 9 H20
Jurong Singapore 1°19N 103°42E 39 d
Juruá → Brazil 2°37S 65°44W 92 D5
Juruena Brazil 13°0S 58°10W 92 F7
Juruena → Brazil 7°20S 58°3W 92 E7
Juruti Brazil 2°9S 56°4W 93 D7
Justo Daract Argentina 33°52S 65°12W 94 C2
Jutaí → Brazil 2°43S 66°57W 92 D5
Juticalpa Honduras 14°40N 86°12W 88 D2
Jutland = Jylland Denmark 56°25N 9°30E 9 H13
Juuka Finland 63°13N 29°17E 8 E23
Juventud, I. de la Cuba 21°40N 82°40W 88 B3
Jūy Zar Iran 33°50N 46°18E 44 C5
Juye China 35°22N 116°5E 34 G9
Jwaneng Botswana 24°45S 24°50E 56 C3
Jylland Denmark 56°25N 9°30E 9 H13
Jyväskylä Finland 62°14N 25°50E 8 E21

K

K2 Pakistan 35°58N 76°32E 43 B7
Kaakha = Kaka Turkmenistan 37°21N 59°36E 45 B8
Kaap Plateau S. Africa 28°30S 24°0E 56 D3
Kaapkruis Namibia 21°55S 13°57E 56 C1
Kaapstad = Cape Town S. Africa 33°55S 18°22E 56 E2
Kabaena Indonesia 5°15S 122°0E 37 F6
Kabala S. Leone 9°38N 11°37W 50 G3
Kabale Uganda 1°15S 30°0E 54 C3
Kabalo Dem. Rep. of the Congo 6°0S 27°0E 54 D2
Kabambare Dem. Rep. of the Congo 4°41S 27°39E 54 C2
Kabango Dem. Rep. of the Congo 8°35S 28°30E 55 D2
Kabanjahe Indonesia 3°6N 98°30E 36 D1
Kabara Fiji 18°59S 178°56W 59 a
Kabardino-Balkaria □ Russia 43°30N 43°30E 19 F7
Kabarega Falls = Murchison Falls Uganda 2°15N 31°30E 54 B3
Kabarnet Kenya 0°30N 35°45E 54 B4
Kabasalan Phil. 7°47N 122°44E 37 C6
Kabat Indonesia 8°16S 114°19E 37 J17
Kabin Buri Thailand 13°57N 101°43E 38 F3
Kabinakagami L. Canada 48°54N 84°25W 72 C3
Kabinda Dem. Rep. of the Congo 6°19S 24°20E 52 F4
Kabompo Zambia 13°36S 24°14E 55 E1
Kabompo → Zambia 14°11S 23°11E 53 G4
Kabondo Dem. Rep. of the Congo 8°58S 25°40E 55 D2
Kabongo Dem. Rep. of the Congo 7°22S 25°33E 54 D2
Kabrît, G. el Egypt 29°42N 33°16E 46 F2
Kabūd Gonbad Iran 37°5N 59°45E 45 B8
Kābul Afghan. 34°28N 69°11E 42 B3
Kābul □ Afghan. 34°30N 69°0E 40 B6
Kābul → Pakistan 33°55N 72°14E 42 C5
Kabunga Dem. Rep. of the Congo 1°38S 28°3E 54 C2
Kaburuang Indonesia 3°50N 126°30E 37 D7
Kabwe Zambia 14°30S 28°29E 55 E2
Kachchh, Gulf of India 22°50N 69°15E 42 H3
Kachchh, Rann of India 24°0N 70°0E 42 H4
Kachchhidhana India 21°44N 78°46E 43 J8
Kachebera Zambia 13°50S 32°50E 55 E3
Kachikau Botswana 18°8S 24°26E 56 B3
Kachin □ Burma 26°0N 97°30E 41 G20
Kachira, L. Uganda 0°40S 31°7E 54 C3
Kachīry Kazakhstan 53°10N 75°50E 28 D8
Kachnara India 23°50N 75°6E 42 H6
Kachot Cambodia 11°30N 103°3E 39 G4
Kaçkar Turkey 40°45N 41°10E 19 F7
Kadam, Mt. Uganda 1°45N 34°45E 54 B3
Kadan Kyun Burma 12°30N 98°20E 38 F2
Kadanai → Afghan. 31°22N 65°45E 42 D1
Kadavu Fiji 19°0S 178°15E 59 a
Kadavu Passage Fiji 18°45S 178°0E 59 a
Kade Ghana 6°7N 0°56W 50 G5
Kadhimain = Al Kāzimīyah Iraq 33°22N 44°18E 44 C5
Kadi India 23°18N 72°23E 42 H5
Kadina Australia 33°55S 137°43E 63 E2
Kadipur India 26°10N 82°23E 43 F10
Kadirli Turkey 37°23N 36°5E 44 B3
Kadiyevka = Stakhanov Ukraine 48°35N 38°40E 19 E6
Kadoka U.S.A. 43°50N 101°31W 80 D3
Kadoma Zimbabwe 18°20S 29°52E 55 F2
Kâdugli Sudan 11°0N 29°45E 51 F11
Kaduna Nigeria 10°30N 7°21E 50 F7
Kaédi Mauritania 16°9N 13°28W 50 E3
Kaeng Khoï Thailand 14°35N 101°0E 38 E3
Kaeng Krachan △ Thailand 12°57N 99°23E 38 F2
Kaeng Tana △ Thailand 15°25N 105°32E 38 E5
Kaesŏng N. Korea 37°58N 126°35E 35 F14
Kāf Si. Arabia 31°25N 37°29E 44 D3
Kafan = Kapan Armenia 39°18N 46°27E 44 B5
Kafanchan Nigeria 9°40N 8°20E 50 G7
Kafinda Zambia 12°32S 30°20E 55 E3
Kafue Zambia 15°46S 28°9E 55 F2
Kafue → Zambia 15°30S 29°0E 53 H5
Kafue △ Zambia 15°12S 25°38E 55 F2
Kafue Flats Zambia 15°40S 27°25E 55 F2
Kafulwe Zambia 9°0S 29°1E 55 D2
Kaga Afghan. 34°14N 70°10E 42 B4
Kaga Bandoro C.A.R. 7°0N 19°10E 52 C3
Kagawa □ Japan 34°15N 134°0E 31 G7
Kagera □ Tanzania 2°0S 31°30E 54 C3
Kagera → Uganda 0°57S 31°47E 54 C3
Kağızman Turkey 40°5N 43°10E 44 B4
Kagoshima Japan 31°35N 130°33E 31 J5
Kagoshima □ Japan 31°30N 130°30E 31 J5
Kagul = Cahul Moldova 45°50N 28°15E 17 F15
Kahak Iran 36°6N 49°46E 45 B6
Kahama Tanzania 4°8S 32°30E 54 C3
Kahan Pakistan 29°18N 68°54E 42 E3
Kahang Malaysia 2°12N 103°32E 39 L4
Kahayan → Indonesia 3°40S 114°0E 36 E4
Kahe Tanzania 3°30S 37°25E 54 C4
Kahemba Dem. Rep. of the Congo 7°18S 18°55E 52 F3
Kahnūj Iran 27°55N 57°40E 45 E8
Kahoka U.S.A. 40°25N 91°44W 80 E8
Kaho'olawe U.S.A. 20°33N 156°37W 75 L8
Kahramanmaraş Turkey 37°37N 36°53E 44 B3
Kâhta Turkey 37°46N 38°36E 44 B3
Kahului U.S.A. 20°54N 156°28W 75 L8
Kahurangi △ N.Z. 41°10S 172°32E 59 D4
Kahuta Pakistan 33°35N 73°24E 42 C5
Kahuzi-Biega △ Dem. Rep. of the Congo 1°50S 27°55E 54 C2
Kai, Kepulauan Indonesia 5°55S 132°45E 37 F8
Kai Besar Indonesia 5°35S 133°0E 37 F8
Kai Is. = Kai, Kepulauan Indonesia 5°55S 132°45E 37 F8
Kai Kecil Indonesia 5°45S 132°40E 37 F8
Kaiapoi N.Z. 43°24S 172°40E 59 E4
Kaidu He → China 41°46N 86°31E 32 B3
Kaieteur Falls Guyana 5°1N 59°10W 92 B7
Kaifeng China 34°48N 114°21E 34 G8
Kaikohe N.Z. 35°25S 173°49E 59 A4
Kaikoura N.Z. 42°25S 173°43E 59 E4
Kailash = Kangrinboqe Feng China 31°0N 81°25E 43 D9
Kailu China 43°38N 121°18E 35 C11
Kailua Kona U.S.A. 19°39N 155°59W 75 M8
Kaimana Indonesia 3°39S 133°45E 37 E8
Kaimanawa Mts. N.Z. 39°15S 175°56E 59 C5
Kaimganj India 27°33N 79°24E 43 F8
Kaimur Hills India 24°30N 82°0E 43 G10
Kainab → Namibia 28°32S 19°34E 56 D2
Kainji Res. Nigeria 10°1N 4°40E 50 F6
Kainuu Finland 64°30N 29°7E 8 D23
Kaipara Harbour N.Z. 36°25S 174°14E 59 B5
Kaipokok B. Canada 54°54N 59°47W 73 B8
Kaira India 22°45N 72°50E 42 H5
Kairana India 29°24N 77°15E 42 E7
Kaironi Indonesia 0°47S 133°40E 37 E8
Kairouan Tunisia 35°45N 10°5E 51 A8
Kaiserslautern Germany 49°26N 7°45E 16 D4
Kaitaia N.Z. 35°8S 173°17E 59 A4
Kaitangata N.Z. 46°17S 169°51E 59 G2
Kaithal India 29°48N 76°26E 42 E7
Kaitu → Pakistan 33°10N 70°30E 42 C4
Kaiwi Channel U.S.A. 21°15N 157°30W 75 L8
Kaiyuan Liaoning, China 42°28N 124°1E 35 C13
Kaiyuan Yunnan, China 23°40N 103°12E 32 D5
Kaiyuh Mts. U.S.A. 64°30N 158°0W 74 C8
Kajaani Finland 64°17N 27°46E 8 D22
Kajabbi Australia 20°0S 140°1E 62 C3
Kajana = Kajaani Finland 64°17N 27°46E 8 D22
Kajang Malaysia 2°59N 101°48E 39 L3
Kajiado Kenya 1°53S 36°48E 54 C4
Kajo Kaji Sudan 3°58N 31°40E 51 H12
Kaka Turkmenistan 37°21N 59°36E 45 B8
Kakabeka Falls Canada 48°24N 89°37W 72 C2
Kakadu △ Australia 12°0S 132°3E 60 B5
Kakamas S. Africa 28°45S 20°33E 56 D3
Kakamega Kenya 0°20N 34°46E 54 B3
Kakanui Mts. N.Z. 45°10S 170°30E 59 F3
Kakdwip India 21°53N 88°11E 43 J13
Kake Japan 34°36N 132°19E 31 G6
Kake U.S.A. 56°59N 133°57W 70 B2
Kakegawa Japan 34°45N 138°1E 31 G9
Kakeroma-Jima Japan 28°8N 129°14E 31 K4
Kākhak Iran 34°9N 58°38E 45 C8
Kakhovka Ukraine 46°45N 33°30E 19 E5
Kakhovske Vdskh. Ukraine 47°5N 34°0E 19 E5
Kakinada India 16°57N 82°11E 41 L13
Kakisa Canada 60°56N 117°25W 70 A5
Kakisa → Canada 61°3N 118°10W 70 A5
Kakisa L. Canada 60°56N 117°43W 70 A5
Kakogawa Japan 34°46N 134°51E 31 G7
Kakuma Kenya 3°43N 34°52E 54 B3
Kakwa → Canada 54°37N 118°28W 70 C5
Kāl Gūsheh Iran 30°59N 58°12E 45 D8
Kal Sefīd Iran 34°52N 47°23E 44 C5
Kalaallit Nunaat = Greenland ☒ N. Amer. 66°0N 45°0W 67 C15
Kalabagh Pakistan 33°0N 71°28E 42 C4
Kalabahi Indonesia 8°13S 124°31E 37 F6
Kalach Russia 50°22N 41°0E 19 D7
Kaladan → Burma 20°20N 93°5E 41 J18
Kaladar Canada 44°37N 77°5W 82 B7
Kalahari Africa 24°0S 21°30E 56 C3
Kalahari Gemsbok △ S. Africa 25°30S 20°30E 56 D3
Kalajoki Finland 64°12N 24°10E 8 D21
Kalakamati Botswana 20°40S 27°25E 57 C4
Kalakan Russia 55°15N 116°45E 29 D12
K'alak'unlun Shank'ou = Karakoram Pass Asia 35°33N 77°50E 43 B7
Kalam Pakistan 35°34N 72°30E 43 B5
Kalama Dem. Rep. of the Congo 2°52S 28°35E 54 C2
Kalama U.S.A. 46°1N 122°51W 78 E4
Kalamata Greece 37°3N 22°10E 23 F10
Kalamazoo U.S.A. 42°17N 85°35W 81 D11
Kalamazoo → U.S.A. 42°40N 86°10W 80 D10
Kalambo Falls Tanzania 8°37S 31°35E 55 D3
Kalan Turkey 39°7N 39°32E 44 B3
Kalannie Australia 30°22S 117°5E 61 F2
Kalāntarī Iran 32°10N 54°8E 45 C7
Kalao Indonesia 7°21S 121°0E 37 F6
Kalaotoa Indonesia 7°20S 121°50E 37 F6
Kalasin Thailand 16°26N 103°30E 38 D4
Kālat Iran 25°29N 59°22E 45 E8
Kalat Pakistan 29°8N 66°31E 40 E5
Kalāteh Iran 36°33N 55°41E 45 B7
Kalāteh-ye Ganj Iran 27°31N 57°55E 45 E8
Kalbā U.A.E. 25°5N 56°22E 45 E8
Kalbarri Australia 27°40S 114°10E 61 E1
Kalbarri △ Australia 27°51S 114°30E 61 E1
Kalburgi = Gulbarga India 17°20N 76°50E 40 L10
Kalce Slovenia 45°54N 14°13E 16 F8
Kale Turkey 37°27N 28°49E 23 F13
Kalegauk Kyun Burma 15°33N 97°35E 38 E1
Kalehe Dem. Rep. of the Congo 2°6S 28°50E 54 C2
Kalema Tanzania 1°12S 31°55E 54 C3
Kalemie Dem. Rep. of the Congo 5°55S 29°9E 54 D2
Kalewa Burma 23°10N 94°15E 41 H19
Kaleybar Iran 38°47N 47°2E 44 B5
Kalgoorlie-Boulder Australia 30°40S 121°22E 61 F3
Kali → India 27°6N 79°55E 43 F8
Kali Sindh → India 25°32N 76°17E 42 G6
Kaliakra, Nos Bulgaria 43°21N 28°30E 23 C13
Kalianda Indonesia 5°50S 105°45E 36 F3
Kalibo Phil. 11°43N 122°22E 37 B6
Kalima Dem. Rep. of the Congo 2°33S 26°32E 54 C2
Kalimantan Indonesia 0°0 114°0E 36 E4
Kalimantan Barat □ Indonesia 0°0 110°30E 36 E4
Kalimantan Selatan □ Indonesia 2°30S 115°30E 36 E5
Kalimantan Tengah □ Indonesia 2°0S 113°30E 36 E4
Kalimantan Timur □ Indonesia 1°30N 116°30E 36 D5
Kálimnos Greece 37°0N 27°0E 23 F12
Kalimpong India 27°4N 88°35E 43 F13
Kaliningrad Russia 54°42N 20°32E 9 J19
Kalinkavichy Belarus 52°12N 29°20E 17 B15
Kalinkovichi = Kalinkavichy Belarus 52°12N 29°20E 17 B15
Kaliro Uganda 0°56N 33°30E 54 B3
Kalispell U.S.A. 48°12N 114°19W 76 B6
Kalisz Poland 51°45N 18°8E 17 C10
Kaliua Tanzania 5°5S 31°48E 54 D3
Kalix = Kalixälven → Sweden 65°50N 23°11E 8 D20
Kalix Sweden 65°53N 23°12E 8 D20
Kalixälven → Sweden 65°50N 23°11E 8 D20
Kalka India 30°46N 76°57E 42 D7
Kalkarindji Australia 17°30S 130°47E 60 C5
Kalkaska U.S.A. 44°44N 85°11W 81 C11
Kalkfeld Namibia 20°57S 16°14E 56 C2
Kalkfontein Botswana 22°4S 20°57E 56 C3
Kalkrand Namibia 24°1S 17°35E 56 C2
Kallavesi Finland 62°58N 27°30E 8 E22
Kallsjön Sweden 63°38N 13°0E 8 E15
Kalmar Sweden 56°40N 16°20E 9 H17
Kalmykia □ Russia 46°5N 46°1E 19 E8
Kalna India 23°13N 88°25E 43 H13
Kalnai India 22°46N 83°30E 43 H10
Kalocsa Hungary 46°32N 19°0E 17 E10
Kalokhorio Cyprus 34°51N 33°2E 25 E12
Kaloko Dem. Rep. of the Congo 6°47S 25°48E 54 D2
Kalol Gujarat, India 22°37N 73°31E 42 H5
Kalol Gujarat, India 23°15N 72°33E 42 H5
Kalomo Zambia 17°0S 26°30E 55 F2
Kalpi India 26°8N 79°47E 43 F8
Kaltag U.S.A. 64°20N 158°43W 74 C8
Kaltukatjara Australia 24°52S 129°5E 61 D4
Kalu Pakistan 25°5N 67°39E 42 G2
Kaluga Russia 54°35N 36°10E 18 D6
Kalulushi Zambia 12°50S 28°3E 55 E2
Kalumburu Australia 13°55S 126°35E 60 B4
Kalumburu ✪ Australia 14°17S 126°38E 60 B4
Kalush Ukraine 49°3N 24°23E 17 D13
Kalutara Sri Lanka 6°35N 80°0E 40 R12
Kalya Russia 60°15N 59°59E 18 B10
Kalyan India 19°15N 73°9E 40 K8
Kama Dem. Rep. of the Congo 3°30S 27°5E 54 C2
Kama → Russia 55°45N 52°0E 18 C9
Kamachumu Tanzania 1°37S 31°37E 54 C3
Kamaishi Japan 39°16N 141°53E 30 E10
Kamalia Pakistan 30°44N 72°42E 42 D5
Kaman India 27°39N 77°16E 42 F6
Kamanjab Namibia 19°35S 14°51E 56 B2
Kamapanda Zambia 12°5S 24°0E 55 E1
Kamarān Yemen 15°21N 42°35E 47 D3
Kamativi Zimbabwe 18°20S 27°6E 56 B4
Kambalda West Australia 31°10S 121°37E 61 F3
Kambar Pakistan 27°37N 68°1E 42 F3
Kambarka Russia 56°15N 54°11E 18 C9
Kambolé Zambia 8°47S 30°48E 55 D3
Kambos Cyprus 35°2N 32°44E 25 D11
Kambove Dem. Rep. of the Congo 10°51S 26°33E 55 E2
Kamchatka, Poluostrov Russia 57°0N 160°0E 29 D17
Kamchatka Pen. = Kamchatka, Poluostrov Russia 57°0N 160°0E 29 D17
Kamchiya → Bulgaria 43°4N 27°44E 23 C12
Kame Ruins Zimbabwe 20°7S 28°25E 55 G2
Kamen Russia 53°50N 81°30E 28 D9
Kamen-Rybolov Russia 44°46N 132°2E 30 B6
Kamenjak, Rt Croatia 44°47N 13°55E 16 F7
Kamenka Russia 65°58N 44°0E 18 A7
Kamenka Bugskaya = Kamyanka-Buzka Ukraine 50°8N 24°16E 17 C13
Kamensk Uralskiy Russia 56°25N 62°2E 28 D7
Kamenskoye Russia 62°45N 165°30E 29 C17
Kameoka Japan 35°0N 135°35E 31 G7
Kamet India 30°55N 79°35E 43 D8
Kamiah U.S.A. 46°14N 116°2W 76 C5
Kamieskroon S. Africa 30°9S 17°56E 56 E2
Kamilukuak L. Canada 62°22N 101°40W 71 A8
Kamin-Kashyrskyy Ukraine 51°39N 24°56E 17 C13
Kamina Dem. Rep. of the Congo 8°45S 25°0E 55 D2
Kaminak L. Canada 62°10N 95°0W 71 A10
Kaministiquia Canada 48°32N 89°35W 72 C1
Kaminoyama Japan 38°9N 140°17E 30 E10
Kamiros Greece 36°20N 27°56E 25 C9
Kamituga Dem. Rep. of the Congo 3°2S 28°10E 54 C2
Kamla → India 25°35N 86°36E 43 G12
Kamloops Canada 50°40N 120°20W 70 C4
Kamo Japan 37°39N 139°3E 30 F9
Kamoke Pakistan 32°4N 74°4E 42 C6
Kampala Uganda 0°20N 32°30E 54 B3
Kampar Malaysia 4°18N 101°9E 39 K3
Kampar → Indonesia 0°30N 103°8E 36 D2
Kampen Neths. 52°33N 5°53E 15 B5
Kampene Dem. Rep. of the Congo 3°36S 26°40E 52 E5
Kamphaeng Phet Thailand 16°28N 99°30E 38 D2
Kampolombo, L. Zambia 11°37S 29°42E 55 E2
Kampong Chhnang Cambodia 12°20N 104°35E 39 F5
Kampong Pengerang Malaysia 1°22N 104°7E 39 d
Kampong Punggai Malaysia 1°27N 104°18E 39 d
Kampong Saom Cambodia 10°38N 103°30E 39 G4
Kampong Saom, Chaak Cambodia 10°50N 103°32E 39 G4
Kampong Tanjong Langsat Malaysia 1°28N 104°1E 39 d
Kampong Telok Ramunia Malaysia 1°22N 104°15E 39 d
Kampot Cambodia 10°36N 104°10E 39 G5
Kampuchea = Cambodia ■ Asia 12°15N 105°0E 38 F5
Kampung Air Putih Malaysia 4°15N 103°10E 39 K4
Kampung Jerangau Malaysia 4°50N 103°10E 39 K4
Kampung Raja Malaysia 5°45N 102°35E 39 K4
Kampungbaru = Tolitoli Indonesia 1°5N 120°50E 37 D6
Kamrau, Teluk Indonesia 3°30S 133°36E 37 E8
Kamsack Canada 51°34N 101°54W 71 C8
Kamsar Guinea 10°40N 14°36W 50 F3
Kamskoye Vdkhr. Russia 58°41N 56°7E 18 C10
Kamuchawie L. Canada 56°18N 101°59W 71 B8
Kamui-Misaki Japan 43°20N 140°21E 30 C10
Kamyanets-Podilskyy Ukraine 48°45N 26°40E 17 D14
Kamyanka-Buzka Ukraine 50°8N 24°16E 17 C13
Kāmyārān Iran 34°47N 46°56E 44 C5
Kamyshin Russia 50°10N 45°24E 19 D8
Kanaaupscow → Canada 54°2N 76°30W 72 B4
Kanab U.S.A. 37°3N 112°32W 77 H7
Kanab Cr. → U.S.A. 36°24N 112°38W 77 H7
Kanacea Lau Group, Fiji 17°15S 179°6W 59 a
Kanacea Taveuni, Fiji 16°59S 179°56E 59 a
Kanaga I. U.S.A. 51°45N 177°22W 74 E4
Kanagi Japan 40°54N 140°27E 30 D10
Kanairiktok → Canada 55°2N 60°18W 73 A7
Kananga Dem. Rep. of the Congo 5°55S 22°18E 52 F4
Kanash Russia 55°30N 47°32E 18 C8
Kanaskat U.S.A. 47°19N 121°54W 78 C5
Kanastraíon, Ákra = Paliouri, Akra Greece 39°57N 23°45E 23 E10
Kanawha → U.S.A. 38°50N 82°9W 81 F12
Kanazawa Japan 36°30N 136°38E 31 F8
Kanchanaburi Thailand 14°2N 99°31E 38 E2
Kanchenjunga Nepal 27°50N 88°10E 43 F13
Kanchipuram India 12°52N 79°45E 40 N11
Kandaghat India 30°59N 77°7E 42 D7
Kandahār Afghan. 31°32N 65°43E 40 D4
Kandahār □ Afghan. 31°0N 65°0E 40 D4
Kandalaksha Russia 67°9N 32°30E 8 C25
Kandalakshskiy Zaliv Russia 66°0N 35°0E 18 A6
Kandangan Indonesia 2°50S 115°20E 36 E5
Kandanghaur Indonesia 6°21S 108°6E 37 G13
Kandanos Greece 35°19N 23°44E 25 D5
Kandavu = Kadavu Fiji 19°0S 178°15E 59 a
Kandavu Passage = Kadavu Passage Fiji 18°45S 178°0E 59 a
Kandhkot Pakistan 28°16N 69°8E 42 E3
Kandhla India 29°18N 77°19E 42 E7
Kandi Benin 11°7N 2°55E 50 F6
Kandi India 23°58N 88°5E 43 H13
Kandiaro Pakistan 27°4N 68°13E 42 F3
Kandla India 23°0N 70°10E 42 H4
Kandos Australia 32°45S 149°58E 63 E4
Kandreho Madag. 17°29S 46°6E 57 B8
Kandy Sri Lanka 7°18N 80°43E 40 R12
Kane U.S.A. 41°40N 78°49W 82 E6
Kane Basin Greenland 79°1N 70°0W 69 B18
Kang Botswana 23°41S 22°50E 56 C3
Kang Krung △ Thailand 9°30N 98°50E 39 H2
Kangān Fārs, Iran 27°50N 52°3E 45 E7
Kangān Hormozgān, Iran 25°48N 57°28E 45 E8
Kangar Malaysia 6°27N 100°12E 39 J3
Kangaroo I. Australia 35°45S 137°0E 63 F2
Kangaroo Mts. Australia 23°29S 141°51E 62 C3
Kangasala Finland 61°28N 24°4E 8 F21
Kangāvar Iran 34°40N 48°0E 45 C6
Kangdong N. Korea 39°9N 126°5E 35 E14
Kangean, Kepulauan Indonesia 6°55S 115°23E 36 F5
Kangean Is. = Kangean, Kepulauan Indonesia 6°55S 115°23E 36 F5
Kanggye N. Korea 41°0N 126°35E 35 D14
Kangikajik Greenland 70°7N 22°0W 4 B6
Kangiqliniq = Rankin Inlet Canada 62°30N 93°0W 68 E13
Kangiqsualujjuaq Canada 58°30N 65°59W 69 F18
Kangiqsujuaq Canada 61°30N 72°0W 69 E17
Kangiqtugaapik = Clyde River Canada 70°30N 68°30W 69 C18
Kangirsuk Canada 60°0N 70°0W 69 F18
Kangkar Chemaran Malaysia 1°34N 104°12E 39 d
Kangkar Sungai Tiram Malaysia 1°35N 103°55E 39 d
Kangkar Teberau Malaysia 1°32N 103°51E 39 d
Kangping China 42°43N 123°18E 35 C12
Kangra India 32°6N 76°16E 42 C7
Kangrinboqe Feng China 31°0N 81°25E 43 D9
Kangto China 27°50N 92°35E 41 F18
Kanha △ India 22°15N 80°40E 43 H9
Kanhar → India 24°28N 83°8E 43 G10
Kaniama Dem. Rep. of the Congo 7°30S 24°12E 54 D1
Kaniapiskau = Caniapiscau → Canada 56°40N 69°30W 73 A6
Kaniapiskau, L. = Caniapiscau, L. Canada 54°10N 69°55W 73 B6
Kanin, Poluostrov Russia 68°0N 45°0E 18 A8
Kanin Nos, Mys Russia 68°39N 43°32E 18 A7
Kanin Pen. = Kanin, Poluostrov Russia 68°0N 45°0E 18 A8
Kaniva Australia 36°22S 141°18E 63 F3
Kanjut Sar Pakistan 36°7N 75°25E 43 A6
Kankaanpää Finland 61°44N 22°50E 8 F20
Kankakee U.S.A. 41°7N 87°52W 80 E10
Kankakee → U.S.A. 41°23N 88°15W 80 E9
Kankan Guinea 10°23N 9°15W 50 F4

Kankendy = Xankändi
  Azerbaijan 39°52N 46°49E **44 B5**
Kanker *India* 20°10N 81°40E **41 J12**
Kankroli *India* 25°4N 73°53E **42 G5**
Kannapolis *U.S.A.* 35°30N 80°37W **85 D14**
Kannauj *India* 27°3N 79°56E **43 F8**
Kannod *India* 22°45N 76°40E **40 H10**
Kannur = Cannanore
  India 11°53N 75°27E **40 P9**
Kannyakumari *India* 8°3N 77°40E **40 Q10**
Kano *Nigeria* 12°2N 8°30E **50 F7**
Kan'onji *Japan* 34°7N 133°39E **31 G6**
Kanowit *Malaysia* 2°14N 112°20E **36 D4**
Kanoya *Japan* 31°25N 130°50E **31 J5**
Kanpetlet *Burma* 21°10N 93°59E **41 J18**
Kanpur *India* 26°28N 80°20E **43 F9**
Kansas □ *U.S.A.* 38°30N 99°0W **80 F4**
Kansas ➤ *U.S.A.* 39°7N 94°37W **80 F6**
Kansas City *Kans., U.S.A.* 39°7N 94°38W **80 F6**
Kansas City *Mo., U.S.A.* 39°6N 94°35W **80 F6**
Kansenia
  Dem. Rep. of the Congo 10°20S 26°0E **55 E2**
Kansk *Russia* 56°20N 95°37E **29 D10**
Kansu = Gansu □ *China* 36°0N 104°0E **34 C5**
Kantaphor *India* 22°35N 76°34E **42 H7**
Kantharalak *Thailand* 14°39N 104°39E **38 E5**
Kanthi = Contai *India* 21°54N 87°46E **43 J12**
Kantli ➤ *India* 28°20N 75°30E **42 E6**
Kantō □ *Japan* 36°15N 139°30E **31 F9**
Kantō-Sanchi *Japan* 35°59N 138°50E **31 G9**
Kanturk *Ireland* 52°11N 8°54W **10 D3**
Kanuma *Japan* 36°34N 139°42E **31 F9**
Kanus *Namibia* 27°50S 18°39E **56 D2**
Kanye *Botswana* 24°55S 25°28E **56 C4**
Kanzenze
  Dem. Rep. of the Congo 10°30S 25°12E **55 E2**
Kanzi, Ras *Tanzania* 7°1S 39°33E **54 D4**
Kao *Tonga* 19°40S 175°1W **59 c**
Kao Phara *Thailand* 8°3N 98°22E **39 a**
Kaohsiung *Taiwan* 22°35N 120°16E **33 D7**
Kaokoveld *Namibia* 19°15S 14°30E **56 B1**
Kaolack *Senegal* 14°5N 16°8W **50 F2**
Kaoshan *China* 44°38N 124°50E **35 B13**
Kapa'a *U.S.A.* 22°5N 159°19W **75 L8**
Kapadvanj *India* 23°5N 73°0E **42 H5**
Kapan *Armenia* 39°18N 46°27E **44 B5**
Kapanga
  Dem. Rep. of the Congo 8°30S 22°40E **52 F4**
Kapchagai = Qapshaghay
  Kazakhstan 43°51N 77°14E **28 E8**
Kapedo *Kenya* 1°10N 36°6E **54 B4**
Kapela = Velika Kapela
  Croatia 45°10N 15°5E **16 F8**
Kapema
  Dem. Rep. of the Congo 10°45S 28°22E **55 E2**
Kapenguria *Kenya* 1°14N 35°7E **54 B4**
Kapfenberg *Austria* 47°26N 15°18E **16 E8**
Kapiri Mposhi *Zambia* 13°59S 28°43E **55 E2**
Kāpīsā □ *Afghan.* 35°0N 69°20E **40 B6**
Kapiskau ➤ *Canada* 52°47N 81°55W **72 B3**
Kapit *Malaysia* 2°0N 112°55E **36 D4**
Kapiti I. *N.Z.* 40°50S 174°56E **59 D5**
Kaplan *U.S.A.* 30°0N 92°17W **84 F8**
Kapoe *Thailand* 9°34N 98°32E **39 H2**
Kapoeta *Sudan* 4°50N 33°35E **51 H12**
Kaposvár *Hungary* 46°25N 17°47E **17 E9**
Kapowsin *U.S.A.* 46°59N 122°13W **78 D4**
Kapps *Namibia* 22°32S 17°18E **56 C2**
Kapsabet *Kenya* 0°12N 35°6E **54 B4**
Kapsan *N. Korea* 41°4N 128°19E **35 D15**
Kapsukas = Marijampolė
  Lithuania 54°33N 23°19E **9 J20**
Kaptai L. *Bangla.* 22°40N 92°20E **41 H18**
Kapuas ➤ *Indonesia* 0°25S 109°20E **36 E3**
Kapuas Hulu, Pegunungan
  Malaysia 1°30N 113°30E **36 D4**
Kapuas Hulu Ra. = Kapuas Hulu,
  Pegunungan *Malaysia* 1°30N 113°30E **36 D4**
Kapulo
  Dem. Rep. of the Congo 8°18S 29°15E **55 D2**
Kapunda *Australia* 34°20S 138°56E **63 E2**
Kapuni *N.Z.* 39°29S 174°8E **59 C5**
Kapurthala *India* 31°23N 75°25E **42 D6**
Kapuskasing *Canada* 49°25N 82°30W **72 C3**
Kapuskasing ➤ *Canada* 49°49N 82°0W **72 C3**
Kaputar, Mt. *Australia* 30°15S 150°10E **63 E5**
Kaputir *Kenya* 2°5N 35°28E **54 B4**
Kara *Russia* 69°10N 65°0E **28 C7**
Kara Bogaz Gol, Zaliv =
  Garabogazköl Aylagy
  Turkmenistan 41°0N 53°30E **19 F9**
Kara-Kala = Garrygala
  Turkmenistan 38°31N 56°29E **45 B8**
Kara Kalpak Republic =
  Qoraqalpogʻiston □
  Uzbekistan 43°0N 58°0E **28 E6**
Kara Kum = Garagum
  Turkmenistan 39°30N 60°0E **45 B8**
Kara Sea *Russia* 75°0N 70°0E **28 B8**
Karabiğa *Turkey* 40°23N 27°17E **23 D12**
Karabük *Turkey* 41°12N 32°37E **19 F5**
Karaburun *Turkey* 38°41N 26°28E **23 E12**
Karabutak = Qarabutaq
  Kazakhstan 49°59N 60°14E **28 E7**
Karacabey *Turkey* 40°12N 28°21E **23 D13**
Karacasu *Turkey* 37°43N 28°35E **23 F13**
Karachey-Cherkessia □
  Russia 43°40N 41°30E **19 F7**
Karachi *Pakistan* 24°50N 67°0E **42 G2**
Karad *India* 17°15N 74°10E **40 L9**
Karaganda = Qaraghandy
  Kazakhstan 49°50N 73°10E **28 E8**
Karagayly = Qaraghayly
  Kazakhstan 49°26N 76°0E **28 E8**
Karaginskiy, Ostrov
  Russia 58°45N 164°0E **29 D17**
Karagiye, Vpadina
  Kazakhstan 43°27N 51°45E **19 F9**
Karagiye Depression = Karagiye,
  Vpadina *Kazakhstan* 43°27N 51°45E **19 F9**

Karagola Road *India* 25°29N 87°23E **43 G12**
Karaikal *India* 10°59N 79°50E **40 P11**
Karaikkudi *India* 10°5N 78°45E **40 P11**
Karaj *Iran* 35°48N 51°0E **45 C6**
Karajarri ⊚ *Australia* 19°0S 122°30E **60 C3**
Karak *Malaysia* 3°25N 102°2E **39 L4**
Karakalpakstan =
  Qoraqalpogʻiston □
  Uzbekistan 43°0N 58°0E **28 E6**
Karakelong *Indonesia* 4°35N 126°50E **37 D7**
Karakitang *Indonesia* 3°14N 125°28E **37 D7**
Karakol *Kyrgyzstan* 42°30N 78°20E **32 B2**
Karakoram Pass *Asia* 35°33N 77°50E **43 B7**
Karakoram Ra. *Pakistan* 35°30N 77°0E **43 B7**
Karakuwisa *Namibia* 18°56S 19°40E **56 B2**
Karalon *Russia* 57°5N 115°50E **29 D12**
Karama *Jordan* 31°57N 35°35E **46 D4**
Karaman *Turkey* 37°14N 33°13E **44 B2**
Karamay *China* 45°30N 84°58E **32 B3**
Karambu *Indonesia* 3°53S 116°6E **36 E5**
Karamea Bight *N.Z.* 41°22S 171°40E **59 D3**
Karamnasa ➤ *India* 25°31N 83°52E **43 G10**
Karān *Si. Arabia* 27°43N 49°49E **45 E6**
Karand *Iran* 34°16N 46°15E **44 C5**
Karanganyar *Indonesia* 7°38S 109°37E **37 G13**
Karangasem *Indonesia* 8°27S 115°37E **37 J18**
Karanjia *India* 21°47N 85°58E **43 J11**
Karasburg *Namibia* 28°0S 18°44E **56 D2**
Karasino *Russia* 66°50N 86°50E **28 C9**
Karasjok *Norway* 69°27N 25°30E **8 B21**
Karasuk *Russia* 53°44N 78°2E **28 D8**
Karasuyama *Japan* 36°39N 140°9E **31 F10**
Karatau, Khrebet =
  Qarataū
  Kazakhstan 43°30N 69°30E **28 E7**
Karatax Shan *China* 35°57N 81°0E **32 C3**
Karatsu *Japan* 33°26N 129°58E **31 H5**
Karaul *Russia* 70°6N 82°15E **28 B9**
Karauli *India* 26°30N 77°4E **42 F7**
Karavostasi *Cyprus* 35°8N 32°50E **25 D11**
Karawang *Indonesia* 6°30S 107°15E **37 G12**
Karawanken *Europe* 46°30N 14°40E **16 E8**
Karayaz *Turkey* 39°41N 42°9E **19 G7**
Karazhal = Qarazhal
  Kazakhstan 48°2N 70°49E **28 E8**
Karbalā' *Iraq* 32°36N 44°3E **44 C5**
Karcag *Hungary* 47°19N 20°57E **17 E11**
Karcha ➤ *Pakistan* 34°45N 76°10E **43 B7**
Karchana *India* 25°17N 81°56E **43 G9**
Karditsa *Greece* 39°23N 21°54E **23 E9**
Kärdla *Estonia* 59°0N 22°45E **9 G20**
Kareeberge *S. Africa* 30°59S 21°50E **56 E3**
Kareha ➤ *India* 25°44N 86°21E **43 G12**
Kareima *Sudan* 18°30N 31°49E **51 E12**
Karelia □ *Russia* 65°30N 32°30E **8 D25**
Karelian Republic = Karelia □
  Russia 65°30N 32°30E **8 D25**
Karera *India* 25°32N 78°9E **42 G8**
Kārevāndar *Iran* 27°53N 60°44E **45 E9**
Kargasok *Russia* 59°3N 80°53E **28 D9**
Kargat *Russia* 55°10N 80°15E **28 D9**
Kargi *Kenya* 2°31N 37°34E **54 B4**
Kargil *India* 34°32N 76°12E **43 B7**
Kargopol *Russia* 61°30N 38°58E **18 B6**
Karhal *India* 27°1N 78°57E **43 F8**
Kariān *Iran* 26°57N 57°14E **45 E8**
Karianga *Madag.* 22°25S 47°22E **57 C8**
Kariba *Zimbabwe* 16°28S 28°50E **55 F2**
Kariba, L. *Zimbabwe* 16°40S 28°25E **55 F2**
Kariba Dam *Zimbabwe* 16°30S 28°35E **55 F2**
Kariba Gorge *Zambia* 16°30S 28°50E **55 F2**
Karibib *Namibia* 22°0S 15°56E **56 C2**
Karijini △ *Australia* 23°8S 118°15E **60 D2**
Karimata, Kepulauan
  Indonesia 1°25S 109°0E **36 E3**
Karimata, Selat *Indonesia* 2°0S 108°40E **36 E3**
Karimata Is. = Karimata,
  Kepulauan *Indonesia* 1°25S 109°0E **36 E3**
Karimnagar *India* 18°26N 79°10E **40 K11**
Karimun Kecil, Pulau
  Indonesia 1°8N 103°22E **39 d**
Karimunjawa, Kepulauan
  Indonesia 5°50S 110°30E **36 F4**
Karin *Somali Rep.* 10°50N 45°52E **47 E4**
Karīt *Iran* 33°29N 56°55E **45 C8**
Kariya *Japan* 34°58N 137°1E **31 G8**
Kariyangwe *Zimbabwe* 18°0S 27°38E **57 B4**
Karjala *Finland* 62°0N 30°25E **8 F24**
Karkaralinsk = Qarqaraly
  Kazakhstan 49°26N 75°30E **28 E8**
Karkheh ➤ *Iran* 31°2N 47°29E **44 D5**
Karkinitska Zatoka
  Ukraine 45°56N 33°0E **19 E5**
Karkinitskiy Zaliv = Karkinitska
  Zatoka *Ukraine* 45°56N 33°0E **19 E5**
Karkuk = Kirkük *Iraq* 35°30N 44°21E **44 C5**
Karlantijpa North ⊚
  Australia 19°27S 133°33E **60 C5**
Karlantijpa South ⊚
  Australia 20°31S 133°9E **60 D5**
Karleby = Kokkola
  Finland 63°50N 23°8E **8 E20**
Karlovac *Croatia* 45°31N 15°36E **16 F8**
Karlovo *Bulgaria* 42°38N 24°47E **23 C11**
Karlovy Vary *Czech Rep.* 50°13N 12°51E **16 C7**
Karlsbad = Karlovy Vary
  Czech Rep. 50°13N 12°51E **16 C7**
Karlsena, Mys *Russia* 77°0N 67°42E **28 B7**
Karlshamn *Sweden* 56°10N 14°51E **9 H16**
Karlskoga *Sweden* 59°28N 14°33E **9 G16**
Karlskrona *Sweden* 56°10N 15°35E **9 H16**
Karlsruhe *Germany* 49°0N 8°23E **16 D5**
Karlstad *Sweden* 59°23N 13°30E **9 G15**
Karlstad *U.S.A.* 48°35N 96°31W **80 A5**
Karmi'el *Israel* 32°55N 35°18E **46 C4**
Karnak *Egypt* 25°43N 32°39E **51 C12**
Karnali ➤ *Nepal* 28°45N 81°16E **43 E9**
Karnaphuli Res. = Kaptai L.
  Bangla. 22°40N 92°20E **41 H18**

Karnaprayag *India* 30°16N 79°15E **43 D8**
Karnataka □ *India* 13°15N 77°0E **40 N10**
Karnes City *U.S.A.* 28°53N 97°54W **84 G6**
Karnische Alpen *Europe* 46°36N 13°0E **16 E7**
Karoi *Zimbabwe* 16°48S 29°45E **55 F2**
Karon, Ao *Thailand* 7°51N 98°17E **39 a**
Karonga *Malawi* 9°57S 33°55E **55 D3**
Karoo △ *S. Africa* 32°18S 22°27E **56 E3**
Karoonda *Australia* 35°1S 139°59E **63 F2**
Karor *Pakistan* 31°15N 70°59E **42 D4**
Karora *Sudan* 17°44N 38°15E **51 E13**
Karpasia *Cyprus* 35°32N 34°15E **25 D13**
Karpathos *Greece* 35°37N 27°10E **23 G12**
Karpinsk *Russia* 59°45N 60°1E **18 C11**
Karpogory *Russia* 64°0N 44°27E **18 B7**
Karpuz Burnu = Apostolos
  Andreas, C. *Cyprus* 35°42N 34°35E **25 D13**
Karratha *Australia* 20°44S 116°52E **60 D2**
Kars *Turkey* 40°40N 43°5E **19 F7**
Karsakpay *Kazakhstan* 47°55N 66°40E **28 E7**
Karshi = Qarshi
  Uzbekistan 38°53N 65°48E **28 F7**
Karsiyang *India* 26°56N 88°18E **43 F13**
Karsog *India* 31°23N 77°12E **42 D7**
Kartala *Comoros Is.* 11°45S 43°21E **53 a**
Kartaly *Russia* 53°3N 60°40E **28 D7**
Kartapur *India* 31°27N 75°32E **42 D6**
Karthaus *U.S.A.* 41°8N 78°9W **82 E6**
Karufa *Indonesia* 3°50S 133°20E **37 E8**
Karuma △ *Uganda* 2°5N 32°15E **54 B3**
Karumba *Australia* 17°31S 140°50E **62 B3**
Karumo *Tanzania* 2°25S 32°50E **54 C3**
Karumwa *Tanzania* 3°12S 32°38E **54 C3**
Kārūn ➤ *Iran* 30°26N 48°10E **45 D6**
Karungu *Kenya* 0°50S 34°10E **54 C3**
Karwan ➤ *India* 27°26N 78°4E **42 F8**
Karwar *India* 14°55N 74°13E **40 M9**
Karwi *India* 25°12N 80°57E **43 G9**
Karymskoye *Russia* 51°36N 114°21E **29 D12**
Kasache *Malawi* 13°25S 34°20E **55 E3**
Kasai ➤
  Dem. Rep. of the Congo 3°30S 16°10E **52 E3**
Kasai-Oriental □
  Dem. Rep. of the Congo 5°0S 24°30E **54 D1**
Kasaji
  Dem. Rep. of the Congo 10°25S 23°27E **55 E1**
Kasama *Zambia* 10°16S 31°9E **55 E3**
Kasan *N. Korea* 41°18N 126°55E **35 D14**
Kasandra Kolpos *Greece* 40°5N 23°30E **23 D10**
Kasane *Namibia* 17°34S 24°50E **56 B3**
Kasanga *Tanzania* 8°30S 31°10E **55 D3**
Kasanka △ *Zambia* 11°34S 30°15E **55 E3**
Kasaragod *India* 12°30N 74°58E **40 N9**
Kasba L. *Canada* 60°20N 102°10W **71 A8**
Kāseh Garān *Iran* 34°5N 46°2E **44 C5**
Kasempa *Zambia* 13°30S 25°44E **55 E2**
Kasenga
  Dem. Rep. of the Congo 10°20S 28°45E **55 E2**
Kasese *Uganda* 0°13N 30°3E **54 B3**
Kasewa *Zambia* 14°28S 28°53E **55 E2**
Kasganj *India* 27°48N 78°42E **43 F8**
Kashabowie *Canada* 48°40N 90°26W **72 C1**
Kashaf ➤ *Iran* 35°58N 61°7E **45 C9**
Kāshān *Iran* 34°5N 51°30E **45 C6**
Kashechewan *Canada* 52°18N 81°37W **72 B3**
Kashgar = Kashi *China* 39°30N 76°2E **32 C2**
Kashi *China* 39°30N 76°2E **32 C2**
Kashimbo
  Dem. Rep. of the Congo 11°12S 26°19E **55 E2**
Kashipur *India* 29°15N 79°0E **43 E8**
Kashiwazaki *Japan* 37°22N 138°33E **31 F9**
Kashk-e Kohneh
  Afghan. 34°55N 62°30E **40 B3**
Kashkūʻīyeh *Iran* 30°31N 55°40E **45 D7**
Kāshmar *Iran* 35°16N 58°26E **45 C8**
Kashmir *Asia* 34°0N 76°0E **43 C7**
Kashmor *Pakistan* 28°28N 69°32E **42 E3**
Kashun Noerh = Gaxun Nur
  China 42°22N 100°30E **32 B5**
Kasiari *India* 22°8N 87°14E **43 H12**
Kasimov *Russia* 54°55N 41°20E **18 D7**
Kasinge
  Dem. Rep. of the Congo 6°15S 26°58E **54 D2**
Kasiruta *Indonesia* 0°25S 127°12E **37 E7**
Kaskaskia ➤ *U.S.A.* 37°58N 89°57W **80 G9**
Kaskattama ➤ *Canada* 57°3N 90°4W **71 B10**
Kaskinen *Finland* 62°22N 21°15E **8 E19**
Kaskö = Kaskinen
  Finland 62°22N 21°15E **8 E19**
Kaslo *Canada* 49°55N 116°55W **70 D5**
Kasmere L. *Canada* 59°34N 101°10W **71 B8**
Kasongo
  Dem. Rep. of the Congo 4°30S 26°33E **54 C2**
Kasongo Lunda
  Dem. Rep. of the Congo 6°35S 16°49E **52 F3**
Kasos *Greece* 35°20N 26°55E **23 G12**
Kassalâ *Sudan* 15°30N 36°0E **51 E13**
Kassel *Germany* 51°18N 9°26E **16 C5**
Kassiopi *Greece* 39°48N 19°53E **25 A3**
Kasson *U.S.A.* 44°2N 92°45W **80 C7**
Kastamonu *Turkey* 41°25N 33°43E **19 F5**
Kastélli *Greece* 35°29N 23°38E **25 D5**
Kastélli *Greece* 35°12N 25°20E **25 D7**
Kasterlee *Belgium* 51°15N 4°59E **15 C4**
Kastoria *Greece* 40°30N 21°19E **23 D9**
Kasulu *Tanzania* 4°37S 30°5E **54 C3**
Kasumi *Japan* 35°38N 134°38E **31 G7**
Kasungu *Malawi* 13°0S 33°29E **55 E3**
Kasungu △ *Malawi* 12°52S 33°9E **55 E3**
Kasur *Pakistan* 31°5N 74°25E **42 D6**
Kata, Ao *Thailand* 7°48N 98°18E **39 J2**
Kata Archnes *Greece* 35°15N 25°10E **25 D7**
Kata Tjuta *Australia* 25°20S 130°50E **61 E5**
Kataba *Zambia* 16°5S 25°10E **55 F2**
Katako Kombe
  Dem. Rep. of the Congo 3°25S 24°20E **54 C1**

Katale *Tanzania* 4°52S 31°7E **54 C3**
Katanda *Katanga,*
  Dem. Rep. of the Congo 7°52S 24°13E **54 D1**
Katanda *Nord-Kivu,*
  Dem. Rep. of the Congo 0°55S 29°21E **54 C2**
Katanga □
  Dem. Rep. of the Congo 8°0S 25°0E **54 D2**
Katangi *India* 21°56N 79°50E **40 J11**
Katanning *Australia* 33°40S 117°33E **61 F2**
Katavi △ *Tanzania* 6°51S 31°3E **54 D3**
Katavi Swamp *Tanzania* 6°50S 31°10E **54 D3**
Katerini *Greece* 40°18N 22°37E **23 D10**
Katghora *India* 22°30N 82°33E **43 H10**
Katha *Burma* 24°10N 96°30E **41 G20**
Katherîna, Gebel *Egypt* 28°30N 33°57E **44 D2**
Katherine *Australia* 14°27S 132°20E **60 B5**
Katherine Gorge = Nitmiluk △
  Australia 14°6S 132°15E **60 B5**
Kathi *India* 21°47N 71°3E **42 J4**
Kathiawar *India* 22°20N 71°0E **42 H4**
Kathikas *Cyprus* 34°55N 32°25E **25 E11**
Kathmandu *Nepal* 27°45N 85°20E **43 F11**
Kathua *India* 32°23N 75°34E **42 C6**
Katihar *India* 25°34N 87°36E **43 G12**
Katima Mulilo *Namibia* 17°28S 24°13E **56 B3**
Katimbira *Malawi* 12°40S 34°0E **55 E3**
Katingan = Mendawai ➤
  Indonesia 3°30S 113°0E **36 E4**
Katiola *Ivory C.* 8°10N 5°10W **50 G4**
Katiti ⊚ *Australia* 25°1S 131°11E **61 E5**
Katmandu = Kathmandu
  Nepal 27°45N 85°20E **43 F11**
Kato Chorio *Greece* 35°3N 25°47E **25 D7**
Kato Korakiana *Greece* 39°42N 19°45E **25 A3**
Káto Pyrgos *Cyprus* 35°11N 32°41E **25 D11**
Katompe
  Dem. Rep. of the Congo 6°2S 26°23E **54 D2**
Katong *Singapore* 1°18N 103°53E **39 d**
Katonga ➤ *Uganda* 0°34N 31°50E **54 B3**
Katoomba *Australia* 33°41S 150°19E **63 E5**
Katowice *Poland* 50°17N 19°5E **17 C10**
Katrine, L. *U.K.* 56°15N 4°30W **11 E4**
Katrineholm *Sweden* 59°9N 16°12E **9 G17**
Katsepe *Madag.* 15°45S 46°15E **57 B8**
Katsina *Nigeria* 13°0N 7°32E **50 F7**
Katsumoto *Japan* 33°51N 129°42E **31 H4**
Katsuura *Japan* 35°10N 140°20E **31 G10**
Katsuyama *Japan* 36°3N 136°30E **31 F8**
Kattavia *Greece* 35°57N 27°46E **25 D9**
Kattegat *Denmark* 56°40N 11°20E **9 H14**
Katumba
  Dem. Rep. of the Congo 7°40S 25°17E **54 D2**
Katwa *India* 23°30N 88°5E **43 H13**
Katwijk *Neths.* 52°12N 4°24E **15 B4**
Kaua'i *U.S.A.* 22°3N 159°30W **75 L8**
Kaudom △ *Namibia* 18°45S 20°51E **56 B3**
Kaufman *U.S.A.* 32°35N 96°19W **84 E6**
Kauhajoki *Finland* 62°25N 22°10E **8 E20**
Kaukauna *U.S.A.* 44°17N 88°17W **80 C9**
Kaukauveld *Namibia* 20°0S 20°15E **56 B3**
Kaʻula I. *U.S.A.* 21°40N 160°33W **75 L7**
Kaunakakai *U.S.A.* 21°6N 157°1W **75 L7**
Kaunas *Lithuania* 54°54N 23°54E **9 J20**
Kaunia *Bangla.* 25°46N 89°26E **43 G13**
Kautokeino *Norway* 69°0N 23°4E **8 B20**
Kauwapur *India* 27°31N 82°18E **43 F10**
Kavacha *Russia* 60°16N 169°51E **29 C17**
Kavala *Greece* 40°57N 24°28E **23 D11**
Kavalerovo *Russia* 44°15N 135°4E **30 B7**
Kavali *India* 14°55N 80°1E **40 M12**
Kavār *Iran* 29°11N 52°44E **45 D7**
Kavi *India* 22°12N 72°38E **42 H5**
Kavimba *Botswana* 18°2S 24°38E **56 B3**
Kavīr, Dasht-e *Iran* 34°30N 55°0E **45 C7**
Kavir △ *Iran* 34°40N 52°0E **45 C7**
Kavos *Greece* 39°23N 20°3E **25 B4**
Kaw *Fr. Guiana* 4°30N 52°15W **93 C8**
Kawagama L. *Canada* 45°18N 78°45E **82 A6**
Kawagoe *Japan* 35°55N 139°29E **31 G9**
Kawaguchi *Japan* 35°52N 139°45E **31 G9**
Kawambwa *Zambia* 9°48S 29°3E **55 D2**
Kawanoe *Japan* 34°1N 133°34E **31 G6**
Kawardha *India* 22°0N 81°17E **43 J9**
Kawasaki *Japan* 35°31N 139°43E **31 G9**
Kawasi *Indonesia* 1°38S 127°28E **37 E7**
Kawawachikamach
  Canada 54°48N 66°50W **73 B6**
Kawerau *N.Z.* 38°7S 176°42E **59 C6**
Kawhia *N.Z.* 38°4S 174°49E **59 C5**
Kawhia Harbour *N.Z.* 38°5S 174°51E **59 C5**
Kawio, Kepulauan
  Indonesia 4°30N 125°30E **37 D7**
Kawthaung *Burma* 10°5N 98°36E **39 H2**
Kawthoolei = Kayin □
  Burma 18°0N 97°30E **41 L20**
Kawthule = Kayin □
  Burma 18°0N 97°30E **41 L20**
Kaya *Burkina Faso* 13°4N 1°10W **50 F5**
Kayah □ *Burma* 19°15N 97°15E **41 K20**
Kayak I. *U.S.A.* 59°56N 144°23W **74 D11**
Kayan ➤ *Indonesia* 2°55N 117°35E **36 D5**
Kaycee *U.S.A.* 43°43N 106°38W **76 E10**
Kayeli *Indonesia* 3°20S 127°10E **37 E7**
Kayenta *U.S.A.* 36°44N 110°15W **77 H8**
Kayes *Mali* 14°25N 11°30W **50 F3**
Kayin □ *Burma* 18°0N 97°30E **41 L20**
Kayoa *Indonesia* 0°1S 127°28E **37 E7**
Kayoomba *Zambia* 13°11S 24°2E **55 E1**
Kayseri *Turkey* 38°45N 35°30E **44 B2**
Kaysville *U.S.A.* 41°2N 111°56W **76 F8**
Kazachye *Russia* 70°52N 135°58E **29 B14**
Kazakhstan ■ *Asia* 50°0N 70°0E **28 E8**
Kazan *Russia* 55°50N 49°10E **18 C8**
Kazan ➤ *Canada* 64°2N 95°29W **71 A9**
Kazan-Rettō *Pac. Oc.* 25°0N 141°0E **64 E6**
Kazanlŭk *Bulgaria* 42°38N 25°20E **23 C11**
Kazatin = Kozyatyn
  Ukraine 49°45N 28°50E **17 D15**

Kāzerūn *Iran* 29°38N 51°40E **45 D6**
Kazi Magomed = Qazımämmäd
  Azerbaijan 40°3N 49°0E **45 A6**
Kazuma Pan △
  Zimbabwe 18°20S 25°48E **55 F2**
Kazuno *Japan* 40°10N 140°45E **30 D10**
Kazym ➤ *Russia* 63°54N 65°50E **28 C7**
Kea *Greece* 37°35N 24°22E **23 F11**
Keady *U.K.* 54°15N 6°42W **10 B5**
Kearney *U.S.A.* 40°42N 99°5W **80 E4**
Kearney ⊚ *Australia* 20°10S 128°4E **60 D4**
Kearny *U.S.A.* 33°3N 110°55W **77 K8**
Kearsarge, Mt. *U.S.A.* 43°22N 71°50W **83 C13**
Keban *Turkey* 38°50N 38°50E **19 G6**
Keban Baraji *Turkey* 38°41N 38°33E **44 B3**
Kebnekaise *Sweden* 67°53N 18°33E **8 C18**
Kebri Dehar *Ethiopia* 6°45N 44°17E **47 F3**
Kebumen *Indonesia* 7°42S 109°40E **37 G13**
Kechika ➤ *Canada* 59°41N 127°12W **70 B3**
Kecskemét *Hungary* 46°57N 19°42E **17 E10**
Kédainiai *Lithuania* 55°15N 24°2E **9 J21**
Kedarnath *India* 30°44N 79°4E **43 D8**
Kedgwick *Canada* 47°40N 67°20W **73 C6**
Kediri *Indonesia* 7°51S 112°1E **37 G15**
Kedros Oros *Greece* 35°11N 24°37E **25 D6**
Keeler *U.S.A.* 36°29N 117°52W **78 J9**
Keeley L. *Canada* 54°54N 108°8W **71 C7**
Keeling Is. = Cocos Is.
  Ind. Oc. 12°10S 96°55E **64 J1**
Keelung = Chilung
  Taiwan 25°3N 121°45E **33 D7**
Keene *Canada* 44°15N 78°10W **82 B6**
Keene *Calif., U.S.A.* 35°13N 118°33W **79 K8**
Keene *N.H., U.S.A.* 42°56N 72°17W **83 D12**
Keene *N.Y., U.S.A.* 44°16N 73°46W **83 B11**
Keep River △ *Australia* 15°49S 129°8E **60 C4**
Keeper Hill *Ireland* 52°45N 8°16W **10 D3**
Keerweer, C. *Australia* 14°0S 141°32E **62 A3**
Keeseville *U.S.A.* 44°29N 73°30W **83 B11**
Keetmanshoop *Namibia* 26°35S 18°8E **56 D2**
Keewatin *Canada* 49°46N 94°34W **71 D10**
Keewatin ➤ *Canada* 56°29N 100°46W **71 B8**
Kefalonia *Greece* 38°15N 20°30E **23 E9**
Kefamenanu *Indonesia* 9°28S 124°29E **37 F6**
Kefar Sava *Israel* 32°11N 34°54E **46 C3**
Keffi *Nigeria* 8°55N 7°43E **50 G7**
Keflavík *Iceland* 64°2N 22°35W **8 D2**
Keg River *Canada* 57°54N 117°55W **70 B5**
Kegaska *Canada* 50°9N 61°18W **73 B7**
Kehancha *Kenya* 1°11S 34°37E **54 C3**
Keighley *U.K.* 53°52N 1°54W **12 D6**
Keila *Estonia* 59°18N 24°25E **9 G21**
Keimoes *S. Africa* 28°41S 20°59E **56 D3**
Keitele *Finland* 63°10N 26°20E **8 E22**
Keith *Australia* 36°6S 140°20E **63 F3**
Keith *U.K.* 57°32N 2°57W **11 D6**
Keiyasi *Fiji* 17°53S 177°46E **59 a**
Keizer *U.S.A.* 44°57N 123°1W **76 D2**
Kejimkujik △ *Canada* 44°25N 65°25W **73 D6**
Kejserr Franz Joseph Fd.
  Greenland 73°30N 24°30W **4 B6**
Kekri *India* 26°0N 75°10E **42 G6**
Kelan *China* 38°43N 111°31E **34 E6**
Kelang = Klang *Malaysia* 3°2N 101°26E **39 L3**
Kelantan ➤ *Malaysia* 6°13N 102°14E **39 J4**
Kelkit ➤ *Turkey* 40°45N 36°32E **19 F6**
Kellerberrin *Australia* 31°36S 117°38E **61 F2**
Kellett, C. *Canada* 72°0N 126°0W **4 B1**
Kelleys I. *U.S.A.* 41°36N 82°42W **82 E2**
Kellogg *U.S.A.* 47°32N 116°7W **76 C5**
Kells = Ceanannus Mor
  Ireland 53°44N 6°53W **10 C5**
Kélo *Chad* 9°10N 15°45E **51 G9**
Kelokedhara *Cyprus* 34°48N 32°39E **25 E11**
Kelowna *Canada* 49°50N 119°25W **70 D5**
Kelsey Creek *Australia* 20°26S 148°31E **62 b**
Kelseyville *U.S.A.* 38°59N 122°50W **78 G4**
Kelso *N.Z.* 45°54S 169°15E **59 F2**
Kelso *U.K.* 55°36N 2°26W **11 F6**
Kelso *U.S.A.* 46°9N 122°54W **78 D4**
Keluang = Kluang
  Malaysia 2°3N 103°18E **39 L4**
Kelvington *Canada* 52°10N 103°30W **71 C8**
Kem *Russia* 65°0N 34°38E **18 B5**
Kem ➤ *Russia* 64°57N 34°41E **18 B5**
Kema *Indonesia* 1°22N 125°8E **37 D7**
Kemah *Turkey* 39°32N 39°5E **44 B3**
Kemaman *Malaysia* 4°12N 103°18E **39 K4**
Kemano *Canada* 53°35N 128°0W **70 C3**
Kemasik *Malaysia* 4°25N 103°27E **39 K4**
Kemerovo *Russia* 55°20N 86°5E **28 D9**
Kemi *Finland* 65°44N 24°34E **8 D21**
Kemi älv = Kemijoki ➤
  Finland 65°47N 24°32E **8 D21**
Kemi träsk = Kemijärvi
  Finland 66°43N 27°22E **8 C22**
Kemijärvi *Finland* 66°43N 27°22E **8 C22**
Kemijoki ➤ *Finland* 65°47N 24°32E **8 D21**
Kemmerer *U.S.A.* 41°48N 110°32W **76 F8**
Kemmuna = Comino
  Malta 36°1N 14°20E **25 C1**
Kemp, L. *U.S.A.* 33°46N 99°9W **84 E5**
Kemp Land *Antarctica* 69°0S 55°0E **5 C5**
Kempas *Malaysia* 1°33N 103°42E **39 d**
Kempsey *Australia* 31°1S 152°50E **63 E5**
Kempt, L. *Canada* 47°25N 74°22W **72 C5**
Kempten *Germany* 47°45N 10°17E **16 E6**
Kempton *Australia* 42°31S 147°12E **63 G4**
Kemptville *Canada* 45°0N 75°38W **83 B9**
Ken ➤ *India* 25°13N 80°27E **43 G9**
Kenai *U.S.A.* 60°33N 151°16W **68 C4**
Kenai Mts. *U.S.A.* 60°0N 150°0W **74 D9**
Kenamuke Swamp *Sudan* 5°55N 33°48E **54 A3**
Kendai *India* 22°45N 82°37E **43 H10**
Kendal *Indonesia* 6°56S 110°14E **37 G14**
Kendal *U.K.* 54°20N 2°44W **12 C5**
Kendall *Australia* 31°35S 152°44E **63 E5**
Kendall *U.S.A.* 25°40N 80°19W **85 J14**
Kendall ➤ *Australia* 14°4S 141°35E **62 A3**

Kendallville U.S.A. 41°27N 85°16W 81 E11
Kendari Indonesia 3°50S 122°30E 37 E6
Kendawangan Indonesia 2°32S 110°17E 36 E4
Kendi, Pulau Malaysia 5°13N 100°11E 39 c
Kendrapara India 20°35N 86°30E 41 J15
Kendrew S. Africa 32°32S 24°30E 56 E3
Kene Thao Laos 17°44N 101°10E 38 D3
Kenedy U.S.A. 28°49N 97°51W 84 G6
Kenema S. Leone 7°50N 11°14W 50 G3
Keng Kok Laos 16°26N 105°12E 38 D5
Keng Tawng Burma 20°45N 98°18E 41 J21
Keng Tung Burma 21°0N 99°30E 41 J21
Kengeja Tanzania 5°26S 39°45E 54 D4
Kenhardt S. Africa 29°19S 21°12E 56 D3
Kenitra Morocco 34°15N 6°40W 50 B4
Kenli China 37°30N 118°20E 35 F10
Kenmare Ireland 51°53N 9°36W 10 E2
Kenmare U.S.A. 48°41N 102°5W 80 A2
Kenmare River Ireland 51°48N 9°51W 10 E2
Kennebago Lake U.S.A. 45°4N 70°40W 83 A14
Kennebec U.S.A. 43°54N 99°52W 80 D4
Kennebec → U.S.A. 43°45N 69°46W 81 D19
Kennebunk U.S.A. 43°23N 70°33W 83 C14
Kennedy Zimbabwe 18°52S 27°10E 56 B4
Kennedy Channel Arctic 80°50N 66°0W 69 A18
Kennedy Ra. Australia 24°45S 115°10E 61 D2
Kennedy Range △ Australia 24°34S 115°2E 61 D2
Kenner U.S.A. 29°59N 90°14W 85 G9
Kennet → U.K. 51°27N 0°57W 13 F7
Kenneth Ra. Australia 23°50S 117°8E 61 D2
Kennett U.S.A. 36°14N 90°3W 80 G8
Kennewick U.S.A. 46°12N 119°7W 76 C4
Kennisis Lake Canada 45°13N 78°36W 82 A6
Kenogami → Canada 51°6N 84°28W 72 B3
Kenora Canada 49°47N 94°29W 71 D10
Kenosha U.S.A. 42°35N 87°49W 80 D10
Kensington Canada 46°28N 63°34W 73 C7
Kent Ohio, U.S.A. 41°9N 81°22W 82 E3
Kent Tex., U.S.A. 31°4N 104°13W 84 F2
Kent Wash., U.S.A. 47°22N 122°14W 78 C4
Kent □ U.K. 51°12N 0°40E 13 F8
Kent Group Australia 39°30S 147°20E 63 F4
Kent Pen. Canada 68°30N 107°0W 68 D10
Kentaū Kazakhstan 43°32N 68°36E 28 E7
Kentland U.S.A. 40°46N 87°27W 80 E10
Kenton U.S.A. 40°39N 83°37W 81 E12
Kentucky □ U.S.A. 37°0N 84°0W 81 G11
Kentucky → U.S.A. 38°41N 85°11W 81 F11
Kentucky L. U.S.A. 37°1N 88°16W 80 G9
Kentville Canada 45°6N 64°29W 73 C7
Kentwood U.S.A. 30°56N 90°31W 85 F9
Kenya ■ Africa 1°0N 38°0E 54 B4
Kenya, Mt. Kenya 0°10S 37°18E 54 C4
Kenyir, Tasik Malaysia 5°1N 102°54E 39 K4
Keo Neua, Deo Vietnam 18°23N 105°10E 38 C5
Keokuk U.S.A. 40°24N 91°24W 80 E8
Keoladeo △ India 27°0N 77°20E 42 F7
Keonjhargarh India 21°28N 85°35E 43 J11
Kep Cambodia 10°29N 104°19E 39 G5
Kep Vietnam 21°24N 106°16E 38 B6
Kepala Batas Malaysia 5°31N 100°26E 39 c
Kepi Indonesia 6°32S 139°19E 37 F9
Kerala □ India 11°0N 76°15E 40 P10
Kerama-Rettō Japan 26°5N 127°15E 31 L3
Keran Pakistan 34°35N 73°59E 43 B5
Kerang Australia 35°40S 143°55E 63 F3
Keraudren, C. Australia 19°58S 119°45E 60 C2
Kerch Ukraine 45°20N 36°20E 19 E6
Kerguelen Ind. Oc. 49°15S 69°10E 3 G13
Kericho Kenya 0°22S 35°15E 54 C4
Kerinci Indonesia 1°40S 101°15E 36 E2
Kerki = Atamyrat Turkmenistan 37°50N 65°12E 28 F7
Kerkrade Neths. 50°53N 6°4E 15 D6
Kerkyra Greece 39°38N 19°50E 25 A3
Kerkyras, Notio Steno Greece 39°34N 20°0E 25 A4
Kermadec Is. Pac. Oc. 30°0S 178°15W 58 E11
Kermadec Trench Pac. Oc. 30°30S 176°0W 64 L10
Kermān Iran 30°15N 57°1E 45 D8
Kerman U.S.A. 36°43N 120°4W 78 J6
Kermān □ Iran 30°0N 57°0E 45 D8
Kermān, Bīābān-e Iran 28°45N 59°45E 45 D8
Kermānshāh Iran 34°23N 47°0E 44 C5
Kermānshāh □ Iran 34°0N 46°30E 44 C5
Kermit U.S.A. 31°52N 103°6W 84 F3
Kern → U.S.A. 35°16N 119°18W 79 K7
Kernow = Cornwall □ U.K. 50°26N 4°40W 13 G3
Kernville U.S.A. 35°45N 118°26W 79 K8
Keroh Malaysia 5°43N 101°1E 39 K3
Kerrera U.K. 56°24N 5°33W 11 E3
Kerrobert Canada 51°56N 109°8W 71 C7
Kerrville U.S.A. 30°3N 99°8W 84 F5
Kerry □ Ireland 52°7N 9°35W 10 D2
Kerry Hd. Ireland 52°25N 9°56W 10 D2
Kerulen → Asia 48°48N 117°0E 33 B6
Kerzaz Algeria 29°29N 1°37W 50 C5
Kesagami → Canada 51°40N 79°45W 72 B4
Kesagami L. Canada 50°23N 80°15W 72 B3
Keşan Turkey 40°49N 26°38E 23 D12
Kesennuma Japan 38°54N 141°35E 30 E10
Keshit Iran 29°43N 58°17E 45 D8
Kestell S. Africa 28°17S 28°42E 57 D4
Kestenga Russia 65°50N 31°45E 8 D24
Keswick U.K. 54°36N 3°8W 12 C4
Ket → Russia 58°55N 81°32E 28 D9
Ketapang Bali, Indonesia 8°9S 114°23E 37 J17
Ketapang Kalimantan, Indonesia 1°55S 110°0E 36 E4
Ketchikan U.S.A. 55°21N 131°39W 70 B2
Ketchum U.S.A. 43°41N 114°22W 76 E6
Ketef, Khalîg Umm el Egypt 23°40N 35°35E 44 F2
Keti Bandar Pakistan 24°8N 67°27E 42 G2
Ketri India 28°1N 75°50E 42 E6
Kętrzyn Poland 54°7N 21°22E 17 A11
Kettering U.K. 52°24N 0°43W 13 E7
Kettering U.S.A. 39°41N 84°10W 81 F11
Kettle → Canada 56°40N 89°34W 71 B11
Kettle Falls U.S.A. 48°37N 118°3W 76 B4
Kettle Point Canada 43°10N 82°1W 82 C2
Kettle Pt. Canada 43°13N 82°1W 82 C2
Kettleman City U.S.A. 36°1N 119°58W 78 J7
Keuka L. U.S.A. 42°30N 77°9W 82 D7
Keuruu Finland 62°16N 24°41E 8 E21
Kewanee U.S.A. 41°14N 89°56W 80 E9
Kewaunee U.S.A. 44°27N 87°31W 80 C10
Keweenaw B. U.S.A. 47°0N 88°15W 80 B9
Keweenaw Pen. U.S.A. 47°15N 88°15W 80 B9
Keweenaw Pt. U.S.A. 47°25N 87°43W 80 B10
Key, L. Ireland 54°0N 8°15W 10 C3
Key Lake Mine Canada 57°5N 105°32W 71 B7
Key Largo U.S.A. 25°5N 80°27W 85 J14
Key West U.S.A. 24°33N 81°48W 88 B3
Keynsham U.K. 51°24N 2°29W 13 F5
Keyser U.S.A. 39°26N 78°59W 81 F14
Kezhma Russia 58°59N 101°9E 29 D11
Kezi Zimbabwe 20°58S 28°32E 57 C4
Kgalagadi Transfrontier ⌂ Africa 25°10S 21°0E 56 D3
Khabarovsk Russia 48°30N 135°5E 29 E14
Khabr Iran 28°51N 56°22E 45 D8
Khābūr → Syria 35°17N 40°35E 44 C4
Khachmas = Xaçmaz Azerbaijan 41°31N 48°42E 19 F8
Khachrod India 23°25N 75°20E 42 H6
Khadro Pakistan 26°11N 68°50E 42 F3
Khadzhilyangar = Dahongliutan China 35°45N 79°20E 43 B8
Khaga India 25°47N 81°7E 43 G9
Khagaria India 25°30N 86°32E 43 G12
Khaipur Pakistan 29°34N 72°17E 42 E5
Khair India 27°57N 77°46E 42 F7
Khairabad India 27°33N 80°47E 43 F9
Khairagarh India 21°27N 81°2E 43 J9
Khairpur Pakistan 27°32N 68°49E 42 F3
Khairpur Nathan Shah Pakistan 27°6N 67°44E 42 F2
Khairwara India 23°58N 73°38E 42 H5
Khaisor → Pakistan 31°17N 68°59E 42 D3
Khajuri Kach Pakistan 32°4N 69°51E 42 C3
Khakassia □ Russia 53°0N 90°0E 28 D9
Khakhea Botswana 24°48S 23°22E 56 C3
Khalafābād Iran 30°54N 49°24E 45 D6
Khalilabad India 26°48N 83°5E 43 F10
Khalīlī Iran 27°38N 53°17E 45 E7
Khalkhāl Iran 37°37N 48°32E 45 B6
Khalkís = Halkida Greece 38°27N 23°42E 23 E10
Khalmer Yu Russia 67°58N 65°1E 28 C7
Khalturin Russia 58°40N 48°50E 18 C8
Khalūf Oman 20°30N 58°13E 47 C6
Kham Keut Laos 18°15N 104°43E 38 C5
Khamaria India 23°5N 80°48E 43 H9
Khambhaliya India 22°14N 69°41E 42 H3
Khambhat India 22°23N 72°33E 42 H5
Khambhat, G. of India 20°45N 72°30E 40 J8
Khamīr Iran 26°57N 55°36E 45 E7
Khamir Yemen 16°2N 44°0E 47 D3
Khamīs Mushayṭ Si. Arabia 18°18N 42°44E 47 D3
Khamsa Egypt 30°27N 32°23E 46 E1
Khan → Namibia 22°37S 14°56E 56 C2
Khān Abū Shāmat Syria 33°39N 36°53E 46 B5
Khān Azād Iraq 33°7N 44°22E 44 C5
Khān Mujiddah Iraq 32°21N 43°48E 44 C4
Khān Shaykhūn Syria 35°26N 36°38E 44 C3
Khan Tengri, Pik Asia 42°12N 80°10E 32 B3
Khān Yūnis Gaza Strip 31°21N 34°18E 46 D3
Khanai Pakistan 30°30N 67°8E 42 D2
Khānaqīn Iraq 34°23N 45°25E 44 C5
Khānbāghī Iran 36°10N 55°25E 45 B7
Khandwa India 21°49N 76°22E 40 J10
Khandyga Russia 62°42N 135°35E 29 C14
Khanewal Pakistan 30°20N 71°55E 42 D4
Khangah Dogran Pakistan 31°50N 73°37E 42 D5
Khanh Duong Vietnam 12°44N 108°44E 38 F7
Khaniá = Chania Greece 35°30N 24°4E 25 D6
Khaniadhana India 25°1N 78°8E 42 G8
Khanka, L. Asia 45°0N 132°24E 30 B6
Khankendy = Xankändi Azerbaijan 39°52N 46°49E 44 B5
Khanna India 30°42N 76°16E 42 D7
Khanozai Pakistan 30°37N 67°19E 42 D2
Khanpur Pakistan 28°42N 70°35E 42 E4
Khanty-Mansiysk Russia 61°0N 69°0E 28 C7
Khao Laem △ Thailand 14°56N 98°31E 38 E2
Khao Laem Res. Thailand 14°50N 98°30E 38 E2
Khao Lak △ Malaysia 8°38N 98°18E 39 H2
Khao Luang △ Thailand 8°34N 99°42E 39 H2
Khao Phlu Thailand 9°29N 99°59E 39 b
Khao Pu-Khao Ya △ Thailand 7°26N 99°57E 39 J2
Khao Sam Roi Yot △ Thailand 12°13N 99°57E 39 F2
Khao Sok △ Thailand 8°55N 98°38E 39 H2
Khao Yai △ Thailand 14°21N 101°29E 38 E3
Khaoen Si Nakarin △ Thailand 14°47N 99°0E 38 E2
Khapalu Pakistan 35°10N 76°20E 43 B7
Khapcheranga Russia 49°42N 112°24E 29 E12
Khaptao △ Nepal 29°20N 81°10E 43 E9
Kharaghoda India 23°11N 71°46E 42 H4
Kharagpur India 22°20N 87°25E 43 H12
Kharan Kalat Pakistan 28°34N 65°21E 40 E4
Kharānaq Iran 32°20N 54°45E 45 C7
Kharda India 18°40N 75°34E 40 K9
Khardung La India 34°20N 77°43E 43 B7
Kharg = Khārk, Jazīreh-ye Iran 29°15N 50°28E 45 D6
Khârga, El Wâhât el Egypt 25°10N 30°35E 51 C12
Khargon India 21°45N 75°40E 40 J9
Khari → India 25°54N 74°31E 42 G6
Kharian Pakistan 32°49N 73°52E 42 C5
Khārk, Jazīreh-ye Iran 29°15N 50°28E 45 D6
Kharkiv Ukraine 49°58N 36°20E 19 E6
Kharkov = Kharkiv Ukraine 49°58N 36°20E 19 E6
Kharovsk Russia 59°56N 40°13E 18 C7
Kharsawangarh India 22°48N 85°50E 43 H11
Kharta Turkey 40°55N 29°7E 23 D13
Khartoum = El Khartûm Sudan 15°31N 32°35E 51 E12
Khartum Canada 45°15N 77°5W 82 A7
Khasan Russia 42°25N 130°40E 30 C5
Khāsh Iran 28°15N 61°15E 45 D9
Khashm el Girba Sudan 14°59N 35°58E 51 F13
Khaskovo Bulgaria 41°56N 25°30E 23 D11
Khatanga Russia 72°0N 102°20E 29 B11
Khatanga → Russia 72°55N 106°0E 29 B11
Khatauli India 29°17N 77°43E 42 E7
Khatra India 22°59N 86°51E 43 H12
Khātūnābād Iran 30°1N 55°25E 45 D7
Khatyrka Russia 62°3N 175°15E 29 C18
Khavda India 23°51N 69°43E 42 H3
Khawr Fakkān U.A.E. 25°21N 56°22E 45 E8
Khaybar, Ḥarrat Si. Arabia 25°45N 40°0E 44 E4
Khāzimiyah Iraq 34°46N 43°37E 44 C4
Khe Bo Vietnam 19°8N 104°41E 38 C5
Khe Long Vietnam 21°29N 104°46E 38 B5
Khe Sanh Vietnam 16°37N 106°45E 38 D6
Khed Brahma India 24°7N 73°5E 42 G5
Khekra India 28°52N 77°20E 42 E7
Khemarak Phouminville = Krong Kaoh Kong Cambodia 11°37N 102°59E 39 G4
Khemisset Morocco 33°50N 6°1W 50 B4
Khemmarat Thailand 16°10N 105°15E 38 D5
Khenāmān Iran 30°27N 56°29E 45 D8
Khenchela Algeria 35°28N 7°11E 50 A7
Khersān → Iran 31°33N 50°22E 45 D6
Kherson Ukraine 46°35N 32°35E 19 E5
Kheta → Russia 71°54N 102°6E 29 B11
Khewari Pakistan 26°36N 68°52E 42 F3
Khilchipur India 24°2N 76°34E 42 G7
Khilok Russia 51°30N 110°45E 29 D12
Khíos = Hios Greece 38°27N 26°9E 23 E12
Khirsadoh India 22°11N 78°47E 43 H8
Khiuma = Hiiumaa Estonia 58°50N 22°45E 9 G20
Khiva Uzbekistan 41°30N 60°18E 28 E7
Khlong Khlung Thailand 16°12N 99°43E 38 D2
Khmelnik Ukraine 49°33N 27°58E 17 D14
Khmelnytskyy Ukraine 49°23N 27°0E 17 D14
Khmer Rep. = Cambodia ■ Asia 12°15N 105°0E 38 F5
Khoai, Hon Vietnam 8°26N 104°50E 39 H5
Khodoriv Ukraine 49°24N 24°19E 17 D13
Khodzent = Khŭjand Tajikistan 40°17N 69°37E 28 E7
Khojak Pass Afghan. 30°51N 66°34E 42 D2
Khok Kloi Thailand 8°17N 98°19E 39 a
Khok Pho Thailand 6°43N 101°6E 39 J3
Khok Samrong Thailand 15°3N 100°43E 38 E3
Kholm Russia 57°10N 31°15E 18 C5
Kholmsk Russia 47°40N 142°5E 29 E15
Khomas Hochland Namibia 22°40S 16°0E 56 C2
Khomeyn Iran 33°40N 50°7E 45 C6
Khomeynī Shahr Iran 32°41N 51°31E 45 C6
Khomodino Botswana 22°46S 23°52E 56 C3
Khon Kaen Thailand 16°30N 102°47E 38 D4
Khong → Cambodia 13°32N 105°58E 38 F5
Khong Sedone Laos 15°34N 105°49E 38 E5
Khonuu Russia 66°30N 143°12E 29 C15
Khoper → Russia 49°30N 42°20E 19 D6
Khorāsān □ Iran 34°0N 58°0E 45 C8
Khorat = Nakhon Ratchasima Thailand 14°59N 102°12E 38 E4
Khorat, Cao Nguyen Thailand 15°30N 102°50E 38 E4
Khorixas Namibia 20°16S 14°59E 56 C1
Khorramābād Khorāsān, Iran 35°6N 57°57E 45 C8
Khorramābād Lorestān, Iran 33°30N 48°25E 45 C6
Khorrāmshahr Iran 30°29N 48°15E 45 D6
Khorugh Tajikistan 37°30N 71°36E 28 F8
Khosravī Iran 30°48N 51°28E 45 D6
Khosrowābād Khuzestān, Iran 30°10N 48°25E 45 D6
Khosrowābād Kordestān, Iran 35°31N 47°38E 44 C5
Khost Pakistan 30°13N 67°35E 42 D2
Khosūyeh Iran 28°32N 54°26E 45 D7
Khotyn Ukraine 48°31N 26°27E 17 D14
Khouribga Morocco 32°58N 6°57W 50 B4
Khowst Afghan. 33°22N 69°58E 42 C3
Khowst □ Afghan. 33°20N 70°0E 40 C6
Khoyniki Belarus 51°54N 29°55E 17 C15
Khrysokhou B. Cyprus 35°6N 32°25E 25 D11
Khu Khan Thailand 14°42N 104°12E 38 E5
Khuan Wa Thailand 7°53N 98°17E 39 a
Khudzhand = Khŭjand Tajikistan 40°17N 69°37E 28 E7
Khuff Si. Arabia 24°55N 44°53E 44 E5
Khūgīānī Afghan. 31°34N 66°32E 42 D2
Khuis Botswana 26°40S 21°49E 56 D3
Khuiyala India 27°9N 70°25E 42 F4
Khŭjand Tajikistan 40°17N 69°37E 28 E7
Khujner India 23°47N 76°36E 42 H7
Khulna Bangla. 22°45N 89°34E 41 H16
Khulna □ Bangla. 22°25N 89°35E 41 H16
Khumago Botswana 20°26S 24°32E 56 C3
Khunjerab △ Pakistan 36°40N 75°30E 43 A6
Khunjerab Pass = Kinjirap Daban Asia 36°40N 75°25E 40 A9
Khūnsorkh Iran 27°9N 56°7E 45 E8
Khunti India 23°5N 85°17E 43 H11
Khūr Iran 32°55N 58°18E 45 C8
Khurai India 24°3N 78°23E 42 G8
Khurayş Si. Arabia 25°6N 48°2E 45 E6
Khurja India 28°15N 77°58E 42 E7
Khūrmāl Iraq 35°18N 46°2E 44 C5
Khurr, Wādī al Iraq 32°3N 43°52E 44 C4
Khūsf Iran 32°46N 58°53E 45 C8
Khushab Pakistan 32°20N 72°20E 42 C5
Khust Ukraine 48°10N 23°18E 17 D12
Khutse ⌂ Botswana 23°31S 24°12E 56 C3
Khuzdar Pakistan 27°52N 66°30E 42 F2
Khūzestān □ Iran 31°0N 49°0E 45 D6
Khvāf Iran 34°33N 60°8E 45 C9
Khvājeh Iran 38°9N 46°35E 44 B5
Khvānsār Iran 29°56N 54°8E 45 D7
Khvor Iran 33°45N 55°0E 45 C7
Khvorgū Iran 27°34N 56°27E 45 E8
Khvormūj Iran 28°40N 51°30E 45 D6
Khvoy Iran 38°35N 45°0E 44 B5
Khyber Pass Afghan. 34°10N 71°8E 42 B4
Kia Fiji 16°16S 179°8E 59 a
Kiabukwa Dem. Rep. of the Congo 8°40S 24°48E 55 D1
Kiama Australia 34°40S 150°50E 63 E5
Kiamba Phil. 6°2N 124°46E 37 C6
Kiambi Dem. Rep. of the Congo 7°15S 28°0E 54 D2
Kiambu Kenya 1°8S 36°50E 54 C4
Kiangara Madag. 17°58S 47°2E 57 B8
Kiangsi = Jiangxi □ China 27°30N 116°0E 33 D6
Kiangsu = Jiangsu □ China 33°0N 120°0E 35 H11
Kibale △ Uganda 0°16N 30°18E 54 B3
Kibanga Port Uganda 0°10N 32°58E 54 B3
Kibara Tanzania 2°8S 33°30E 54 C3
Kibare, Mts. Dem. Rep. of the Congo 8°25S 27°10E 54 D2
Kibira △ Burundi 3°6S 30°24E 54 C3
Kiboga Uganda 0°58N 31°45E 54 B3
Kibombo Dem. Rep. of the Congo 3°57S 25°53E 54 C2
Kibondo Tanzania 3°35S 30°45E 54 C3
Kibre Mengist Ethiopia 5°54N 38°59E 47 F2
Kıbrıs = Cyprus ■ Asia 35°0N 33°0E 25 E12
Kibumbu Burundi 3°32S 29°45E 54 C2
Kibungo Rwanda 2°10S 30°32E 54 C3
Kibuye Burundi 3°39S 29°59E 54 C2
Kibuye Rwanda 2°3S 29°21E 54 C2
Kibwesa Tanzania 6°30S 29°58E 54 D2
Kibwezi Kenya 2°27S 37°57E 54 C4
Kichha India 28°53N 79°30E 43 E8
Kichha → India 28°41N 79°18E 43 E8
Kichmengskiy Gorodok Russia 59°59N 45°48E 18 B8
Kicking Horse Pass Canada 51°28N 116°16W 70 C5
Kidal Mali 18°26N 1°22E 50 E6
Kidderminster U.K. 52°24N 2°15W 13 E5
Kidepo Valley △ Uganda 3°52N 33°50E 54 B3
Kidete Tanzania 6°25S 37°17E 54 D4
Kidnappers, C. N.Z. 39°38S 177°5E 59 C6
Kidsgrove U.K. 53°5N 2°14W 12 D5
Kidston Australia 18°52S 144°8E 62 B3
Kidugallo Tanzania 6°49S 38°15E 54 D4
Kiel Germany 54°19N 10°8E 16 A6
Kiel Canal = Nord-Ostsee-Kanal Germany 54°12N 9°32E 16 A5
Kielce Poland 50°52N 20°42E 17 C11
Kielder Water U.K. 55°11N 2°31W 12 B5
Kieler Bucht Germany 54°35N 10°25E 16 A6
Kien Binh Vietnam 9°55N 105°19E 39 H5
Kien Tan Vietnam 10°7N 105°17E 39 G5
Kienge Dem. Rep. of the Congo 10°30S 27°30E 55 E2
Kiev = Kyyiv Ukraine 50°30N 30°28E 17 C16
Kiffa Mauritania 16°37N 11°24W 50 E3
Kifrī Iraq 34°45N 45°0E 44 C5
Kigali Rwanda 1°59S 30°4E 54 C3
Kigarama Tanzania 1°1S 31°50E 54 C3
Kigezi ⌂ Uganda 0°34S 29°55E 54 C2
Kigoma □ Tanzania 5°0S 30°0E 54 D3
Kigoma-Ujiji Tanzania 4°55S 29°36E 54 C2
Kigomasha, Ras Tanzania 4°58S 38°58E 54 C4
Kigosi ⌂ Tanzania 4°10S 31°45E 54 C3
Kığzı Turkey 38°18N 43°25E 44 B4
Kihnu Estonia 58°9N 24°1E 9 G21
Kii-Sanchi Japan 34°20N 136°0E 31 G8
Kii-Suidō Japan 33°40N 134°45E 31 H7
Kiira Dam Uganda 0°25N 33°0E 54 B3
Kikaiga-Shima Japan 28°19N 129°59E 31 K4
Kikiak = Rigolet Canada 54°10N 58°23W 73 B8
Kikinda Serbia 45°50N 20°30E 23 B9
Kikládhes = Cyclades Greece 37°0N 24°30E 23 F11
Kikwit Dem. Rep. of the Congo 5°0S 18°45E 52 F3
Kilar India 33°6N 76°25E 42 C7
Kilbeggan Ireland 53°22N 7°30W 10 C4
Kilbrannan Sd. U.K. 55°37N 5°26W 11 F3
Kilbuck Mts. U.S.A. 60°36N 159°53W 74 C8
Kilchu N. Korea 40°57N 129°25E 35 D15
Kilcoy Australia 26°59S 152°30E 63 D5
Kildare Ireland 53°9N 6°55W 10 C5
Kildare □ Ireland 53°10N 6°50W 10 C5
Kildinstroy Russia 68°48N 33°6E 8 B25
Kilfinnane Ireland 52°21N 8°28W 10 D3
Kilgarvan Ireland 51°54N 9°27W 10 E2
Kilgore U.S.A. 32°23N 94°53W 84 E7
Kilgoris Kenya 1°0S 34°53E 54 C3
Kilifi Kenya 3°40S 39°48E 54 C4
Kilimanjaro Tanzania 3°7S 37°20E 54 C4
Kilimanjaro □ Tanzania 4°0S 38°0E 54 C4
Kilimanjaro △ Tanzania 3°2S 37°19E 54 C4
Kilindini Kenya 4°4S 39°40E 54 C4
Kilis Turkey 36°42N 37°6E 44 B3
Kiliya Ukraine 45°28N 29°16E 17 F15
Kilkee Ireland 52°41N 9°39W 10 D2
Kilkeel U.K. 54°4N 6°0W 10 B5
Kilkenny Ireland 52°39N 7°15W 10 D4
Kilkenny □ Ireland 52°35N 7°15W 10 D4
Kilkieran B. Ireland 53°20N 9°41W 10 C2
Kilkis Greece 40°58N 22°57E 23 D10
Killala Ireland 54°13N 9°12W 10 B2
Killala B. Ireland 54°16N 9°8W 10 B2
Killaloe Canada 45°33N 77°25W 82 A7
Killaloe Ireland 52°48N 8°28W 10 D3
Killarney Australia 28°20S 152°18E 63 D5
Killarney Canada 49°10N 99°40W 71 D9
Killarney Ireland 52°4N 9°30W 10 D2
Killarney △ Ireland 52°0N 9°33W 10 D2
Killary Harbour Ireland 53°38N 9°52W 10 C2
Killdeer U.S.A. 47°22N 102°45W 80 B2
Killeen U.S.A. 31°7N 97°44W 84 F6
Killin U.K. 56°28N 4°19W 11 E4
Killiney Ireland 53°15N 6°7W 10 C5
Killington Pk. U.S.A. 43°36N 72°49W 83 C12
Killini Greece 37°54N 22°25E 23 F10
Killorglin Ireland 52°6N 9°47W 10 D2
Killybegs Ireland 54°38N 8°26W 10 B3
Kilmarnock U.K. 55°37N 4°29W 11 F4
Kilmore Australia 37°25S 144°53E 63 F3
Kilmore Quay Ireland 52°10N 6°36W 10 D5
Kilondo Tanzania 9°45S 34°20E 55 D3
Kilosa Tanzania 6°48S 37°0E 54 D4
Kilrush Ireland 52°38N 9°29W 10 D2
Kilwa Kisiwani Tanzania 8°58S 39°32E 55 D4
Kilwa Kivinje Tanzania 8°45S 39°25E 55 D4
Kilwa Masoko Tanzania 8°55S 39°30E 55 D4
Kilwinning U.K. 55°39N 4°43W 11 F4
Kim U.S.A. 37°15N 103°21W 77 H12
Kimaam Indonesia 7°58S 138°53E 37 F9
Kimamba Tanzania 6°45S 37°10E 54 D4
Kimba Australia 33°8S 136°23E 63 E2
Kimball Nebr., U.S.A. 41°14N 103°40W 80 E2
Kimball S. Dak., U.S.A. 43°45N 98°57W 80 D4
Kimberley Australia 16°20S 127°0E 60 C4
Kimberley B.C., Canada 49°40N 115°59W 70 D5
Kimberley Ont., Canada 44°23N 80°32W 82 B4
Kimberley S. Africa 28°43S 24°46E 56 D3
Kimberly U.S.A. 42°32N 114°22W 76 E6
Kimch'aek N. Korea 40°40N 129°10E 35 D15
Kimhae = Gimhae S. Korea 35°14N 128°53E 35 G15
Kimmirut Canada 62°50N 69°50W 69 E18
Kimpese Dem. Rep. of the Congo 5°35S 14°26E 52 F2
Kimry Russia 56°55N 37°15E 18 C6
Kinabalu, Gunung Malaysia 6°3N 116°14E 36 C5
Kinango Kenya 4°8S 39°19E 54 C4
Kinaskan L. Canada 57°38N 130°8W 70 B2
Kinbasket L. Canada 52°0N 118°10W 70 C5
Kincardine Canada 44°10N 81°40W 82 B3
Kincolith Canada 55°0N 129°57W 70 C3
Kinda Dem. Rep. of the Congo 9°18S 25°4E 55 D2
Kinde U.S.A. 43°56N 83°0W 82 C2
Kinder Scout U.K. 53°24N 1°52W 12 D6
Kindersley Canada 51°30N 109°10W 71 C7
Kindia Guinea 10°0N 12°52W 50 F3
Kindu Dem. Rep. of the Congo 2°55S 25°50E 54 C2
Kineshma Russia 57°30N 42°5E 18 C7
Kinesi Tanzania 1°25S 33°50E 54 C3
King, L. Australia 33°10S 119°35E 61 F2
King, Mt. Australia 25°10S 147°30E 62 D4
King Christian I. Canada 77°48N 101°40W 69 B11
King City U.S.A. 36°13N 121°8W 78 J5
King Cr. → Australia 24°35S 139°30E 62 C2
King Edward → Australia 14°14S 126°35E 60 B4
King Edward Point S. Georgia 54°17S 36°30W 96 G9
King Frederick VI Land = Kong Frederik VI Kyst Greenland 63°0N 43°0W 4 C5
King George B. Falk. Is. 51°30S 60°30W 96 G4
King George I. Antarctica 60°0S 60°0W 5 C18
King George Is. Canada 57°20N 80°30W 69 F15
King George Sd. Australia 35°5S 118°0E 61 G2
King I. = Kadan Kyun Burma 12°30N 98°20E 38 F2
King I. Australia 39°50S 144°0E 63 F3
King I. Canada 52°10N 127°40W 70 C3
King Khalid Military City = Madinat al Malik Khālid al Askarīyah Si. Arabia 27°54N 45°31E 44 E5
King Leopold Ranges Australia 17°30S 125°45E 60 C4
King of Prussia U.S.A. 40°5N 75°23W 83 F9
King Sd. Australia 16°50S 123°20E 60 C3
King Sejong Antarctica 62°30S 58°0W 5 C18
King William I. Canada 69°10N 97°25W 68 D12
King William's Town S. Africa 32°51S 27°22E 56 E4
Kingaok = Bathurst Inlet Canada 66°50N 108°1W 68 D10
Kingaroy Australia 26°32S 151°51E 63 D5
Kingfisher U.S.A. 35°52N 97°56W 84 D6
Kingirbān Iraq 34°40N 44°54E 44 C5
Kingisepp = Kuressaare Estonia 58°15N 22°30E 9 G20
Kingisepp Russia 59°25N 28°40E 9 G23
Kingman Ariz., U.S.A. 35°12N 114°4W 79 K12
Kingman Kans., U.S.A. 37°39N 98°7W 80 G4
Kingoonya Australia 30°55S 135°19E 63 E2
Kingri Pakistan 30°27N 69°49E 42 D3
Kings → U.S.A. 36°3N 119°50W 78 J7
Kings Canyon Australia 24°15S 131°34E 60 D5
Kings Canyon △ U.S.A. 36°50N 118°40W 78 J8
King's Lynn U.K. 52°45N 0°24E 12 E8
Kings Park U.S.A. 40°53N 73°16W 83 F11
Kings Peak U.S.A. 40°46N 110°23W 76 F8
Kingsbridge U.K. 50°17N 3°47W 13 G4
Kingsburg U.S.A. 36°31N 119°33W 78 J7
Kingscote Australia 35°40S 137°38E 63 F2
Kingscourt Ireland 53°55N 6°48W 10 C4
Kingsford U.S.A. 45°48N 88°4W 80 C9

Kingsland U.S.A. 30°48N 81°41W 85 F14
Kingsport U.S.A. 36°33N 82°33W 85 C13
Kingston Canada 44°14N 76°30W 82 C8
Kingston Jamaica 18°0N 76°50W 88 a
Kingston N.Z. 45°20S 168°43E 59 F2
Kingston N.H., U.S.A. 42°56N 71°3W 83 D13
Kingston N.Y., U.S.A. 41°56N 73°59W 83 E11
Kingston Pa., U.S.A. 41°16N 75°54W 83 E9
Kingston R.I., U.S.A. 41°29N 71°30W 83 E13
Kingston Pk. U.S.A. 35°44N 115°55W 79 K11
Kingston South East
　Australia 36°51S 139°55E 63 F2
Kingston upon Hull U.K. 53°45N 0°21W 12 D7
Kingston upon Hull □
　U.K. 53°45N 0°21W 12 D7
Kingston-upon-Thames □
　U.K. 51°24N 0°17W 13 F7
Kingstown St. Vincent 13°10N 61°10W 89 D7
Kingstree U.S.A. 33°40N 79°50W 85 E15
Kingsville Canada 42°2N 82°45W 82 D2
Kingsville U.S.A. 27°31N 97°52W 84 H6
Kingussie U.K. 57°6N 4°2W 11 D4
Kingwood U.S.A. 30°2N 95°16W 84 F7
Kınık Turkey 39°6N 27°24E 23 E12
Kinistino Canada 52°57N 105°2W 71 C7
Kinjirap Daban Asia 36°40N 75°25E 40 A9
Kinkala Congo 4°18S 14°49E 52 E2
Kinki □ Japan 33°45N 136°0E 31 H8
Kinleith N.Z. 38°20S 175°56E 59 C5
Kinlochleven U.K. 56°43N 5°0W 11 E4
Kinmount Canada 44°48N 78°45W 82 B6
Kinna Sweden 57°32N 12°42E 9 H15
Kinnairds Hd. U.K. 57°43N 2°1W 11 D6
Kinngait Canada 64°14N 76°32W 69 E16
Kino Nuevo Mexico 28°52N 112°3W 86 B2
Kinoje → Canada 52°8N 81°25W 72 B3
Kinomoto Japan 35°30N 136°13E 31 G8
Kinoni Uganda 0°41S 30°28E 54 C3
Kinoosao Canada 57°5N 102°1W 71 B8
Kinross U.K. 56°13N 3°25W 11 E5
Kinsale Ireland 51°42N 8°31W 10 E3
Kinsale, Old Hd. of
　Ireland 51°37N 8°33W 10 E3
Kinsha = Chang Jiang →
　China 31°48N 121°10E 33 C7
Kinshasa
　Dem. Rep. of the Congo 4°20S 15°15E 52 E3
Kinsley U.S.A. 37°55N 99°25W 80 G4
Kinsman U.S.A. 41°26N 80°35W 82 E4
Kinston U.S.A. 35°16N 77°35W 85 D16
Kintamani Indonesia 8°14S 115°19E 37 J18
Kintore U.K. 57°14N 2°20W 11 D6
Kintore Ra. Australia 23°15S 128°47E 60 D4
Kintyre U.K. 55°30N 5°35W 11 F3
Kintyre, Mull of U.K. 55°17N 5°47W 11 F3
Kinushseo → Canada 55°15N 83°45W 72 A3
Kinuso Canada 55°20N 115°25W 70 B5
Kinvarra Ireland 53°8N 8°56W 10 C3
Kinyangiri Tanzania 4°25S 34°37E 54 C3
Kinyeti Sudan 3°57N 32°54E 54 B3
Kinzua U.S.A. 41°52N 78°58W 82 E6
Kiosk Canada 46°6N 78°53W 72 C4
Kiowa Kans., U.S.A. 37°1N 98°29W 80 G4
Kiowa Okla., U.S.A. 34°43N 95°54W 84 D7
Kipahigan L. Canada 55°20N 101°55W 71 B8
Kipanga Tanzania 6°15S 35°20E 54 D4
Kiparissia Greece 37°15N 21°40E 23 F9
Kiparissiakos Kolpos
　Greece 37°25N 21°25E 23 F9
Kipawa, L. Canada 46°50N 79°0W 72 C4
Kipembawe Tanzania 7°38S 33°27E 54 D3
Kipengere Ra. Tanzania 9°12S 34°15E 55 D3
Kipili Tanzania 7°28S 30°32E 54 D3
Kipini Kenya 2°30S 40°32E 54 C5
Kipling Canada 50°6N 102°38W 71 C8
Kippure Ireland 53°11N 6°21W 10 C5
Kipushi
　Dem. Rep. of the Congo 11°48S 27°12E 55 E2
Kiranomena Madag. 18°17S 46°2E 57 B8
Kirensk Russia 57°50N 107°55E 29 D11
Kirghiz Range Asia 42°40N 73°40E 32 B2
Kirghizia = Kyrgyzstan ■
　Asia 42°0N 75°0E 28 E8
Kirgiziya Steppe Eurasia 50°0N 55°0E 19 E10
Kiribati ■ Pac. Oc. 3°0S 180°0E 58 B10
Kırıkkale Turkey 39°51N 33°32E 19 G5
Kirillov Russia 59°49N 38°24E 18 C6
Kirin = Jilin China 43°44N 126°30E 35 C14
Kirinyaga = Kenya, Mt.
　Kenya 0°10S 37°18E 54 C4
Kirirom △ Cambodia 11°18N 104°5E 39 G5
Kirishima Yaku △
　Japan 31°24N 130°50E 31 J5
Kiritimati Kiribati 1°58N 157°27W 65 G12
Kirkby U.K. 53°30N 2°54W 12 D5
Kirkby-in-Ashfield U.K. 53°6N 1°14W 12 D6
Kirkby Lonsdale U.K. 54°12N 2°36W 12 C5
Kirkby Stephen U.K. 54°29N 2°21W 12 C5
Kirkcaldy U.K. 56°7N 3°9W 11 E5
Kirkcudbright U.K. 54°50N 4°2W 11 G4
Kirkenes Norway 69°40N 30°5E 8 B24
Kirkfield Canada 44°34N 78°59W 82 B6
Kirkintilloch U.K. 55°56N 4°8W 11 F4
Kirkjubæjarklaustur
　Iceland 63°47N 18°4W 8 E4
Kirkkonummi Finland 60°8N 24°26E 9 F21
Kirkland U.S.A. 47°40N 122°12W 78 C4
Kirkland Lake Canada 48°9N 80°2W 72 C3
Kırklareli Turkey 41°44N 27°15E 23 D12
Kirksville U.S.A. 40°12N 92°35W 80 E7
Kirkūk Iraq 35°30N 44°21E 44 C5
Kirkwall U.K. 58°59N 2°58W 11 C6
Kirkwood S. Africa 33°22N 25°15E 56 D4
Kirov Russia 58°35N 49°40E 18 C8
Kirovabad = Gäncä
　Azerbaijan 40°45N 46°20E 19 F8
Kirovograd = Kirovohrad
　Ukraine 48°35N 32°20E 19 E5
Kirovohrad Ukraine 48°35N 32°20E 19 E5

Kirovsk Russia 67°32N 33°41E 18 A5
Kirovskiy Kamchatka,
　Russia 54°27N 155°42E 29 D16
Kirovskiy Primorsk,
　Russia 45°7N 133°30E 30 B6
Kirriemuir U.K. 56°41N 3°1W 11 E5
Kirsanov Russia 52°35N 42°40E 18 D7
Kırşehir Turkey 39°14N 34°5E 44 B2
Kirthar △ Pakistan 25°45N 67°30E 42 F2
Kirthar Range Pakistan 27°0N 67°0E 42 F2
Kirtland U.S.A. 36°44N 108°21W 77 H9
Kiruna Sweden 67°52N 20°15E 8 C19
Kirundu
　Dem. Rep. of the Congo 0°50S 25°35E 54 C2
Kiryū Japan 36°24N 139°20E 31 F9
Kisaga Tanzania 4°30S 34°23E 54 C3
Kisanga
　Dem. Rep. of the Congo 2°30N 26°35E 54 B2
Kisangani
　Dem. Rep. of the Congo 0°35N 25°15E 54 B2
Kisar Indonesia 8°5S 127°10E 37 F7
Kisarawe Tanzania 6°53S 39°0E 54 D4
Kisarazu Japan 35°23N 139°55E 31 G9
Kiselevsk Russia 54°0N 86°39E 28 D9
Kish = Qeys Iran 26°32N 53°58E 45 E7
Kishanganga →
　Pakistan 34°18N 73°28E 43 B5
Kishanganj India 26°3N 88°14E 43 F13
Kishangarh Raj., India 26°34N 74°52E 42 F6
Kishangarh Raj., India 27°50N 70°30E 42 F4
Kishinev = Chişinău
　Moldova 47°2N 28°50E 17 E15
Kishiwada Japan 34°28N 135°22E 31 G7
Kishtwar India 33°20N 75°48E 42 C6
Kisigo → Tanzania 6°27S 34°17E 54 D3
Kisii Kenya 0°40S 34°45E 54 C3
Kisiju Tanzania 7°23S 39°19E 54 D4
Kisizi Uganda 1°0S 29°58E 54 C2
Kiska I. U.S.A. 51°59N 177°30E 74 E3
Kiskőrös Hungary 46°37N 19°20E 17 E10
Kiskunfélegyháza
　Hungary 46°42N 19°53E 17 E10
Kiskunhalas Hungary 46°28N 19°37E 17 E10
Kislovodsk Russia 43°50N 42°45E 19 F7
Kismaayo Somali Rep. 0°22S 42°32E 47 H3
Kiso-Gawa → Japan 35°20N 136°45E 31 G8
Kiso-Sammyaku Japan 35°45N 137°45E 31 G8
Kisofukushima Japan 35°52N 137°43E 31 G8
Kisoro Uganda 1°17S 29°48E 54 C2
Kissamos = Kasteli
　Greece 35°29N 23°38E 25 D5
Kissamos, Kolpos Greece 35°30N 23°38E 25 D5
Kissidougou Guinea 9°5N 10°5W 50 G3
Kissimmee U.S.A. 28°18N 81°24W 85 G14
Kissimmee → U.S.A. 27°9N 80°52W 85 H14
Kississing L. Canada 55°10N 101°20W 71 B8
Kissónerga Cyprus 34°49N 32°24E 25 E11
Kisumu Kenya 0°3S 34°45E 54 C3
Kiswani Tanzania 4°5S 37°57E 54 C4
Kiswere Tanzania 9°27S 39°30E 55 D4
Kit Carson U.S.A. 38°46N 102°48W 76 G12
Kita Mali 13°5N 9°25W 50 F4
Kitaibaraki Japan 36°50N 140°45E 31 F10
Kitakami Japan 39°20N 141°10E 30 E10
Kitakami-Gawa →
　Japan 38°25N 141°19E 30 E10
Kitakami-Sammyaku
　Japan 39°30N 141°30E 30 E10
Kitakata Japan 37°39N 139°52E 30 F9
Kitakyūshū Japan 33°50N 130°50E 31 H5
Kitale Kenya 1°0N 35°0E 54 B4
Kitami Japan 43°48N 143°54E 30 C11
Kitami-Sammyaku
　Japan 44°22N 142°43E 30 B11
Kitangiri, L. Tanzania 4°5S 34°20E 54 C3
Kitaya Tanzania 10°38S 40°8E 55 E5
Kitchener Canada 43°27N 80°29W 82 C4
Kitee Finland 62°5N 30°8E 8 E24
Kitega = Gitega Burundi 3°26S 29°56E 54 C2
Kitengo
　Dem. Rep. of the Congo 7°26S 24°8E 54 D1
Kitgum Uganda 3°17N 32°52E 54 B3
Kíthira = Kythira Greece 36°8N 23°0E 23 F10
Kithnos Greece 37°26N 24°27E 23 F11
Kiti Cyprus 34°50N 33°34E 25 E12
Kiti, C. Cyprus 34°48N 33°36E 25 E12
Kitimat Canada 54°3N 128°38W 70 C3
Kitinen → Finland 67°14N 27°27E 8 C22
Kitsuki Japan 33°25N 131°37E 31 H5
Kittakittaooloo, L.
　Australia 28°3S 138°14E 63 D2
Kittanning U.S.A. 40°49N 79°31W 82 F5
Kittatinny Mt. U.S.A. 41°19N 74°39W 83 F10
Kittery U.S.A. 43°5N 70°45W 83 C14
Kittilä Finland 67°40N 24°51E 8 C21
Kitui Kenya 1°17S 38°0E 54 C4
Kitwanga Canada 55°6N 128°4W 70 B3
Kitwe Zambia 12°54S 28°13E 55 E2
Kiunga Marine △ Kenya 2°1S 41°14E 54 C5
Kivarli India 24°33N 72°46E 42 G5
Kivertsi Ukraine 50°50N 25°28E 17 C13
Kividhes Cyprus 34°46N 32°51E 25 E11
Kivu, L.
　Dem. Rep. of the Congo 1°48S 29°0E 54 C2
Kiwirrkurra Australia 22°49S 127°45E 60 D4
Kiwirrkurra ۞
　Australia 22°49S 127°45E 60 D4
Kiyev = Kyyiv Ukraine 50°30N 30°28E 17 C16
Kiyevskoye Vdkhr. = Kyyivske
　Vdskh. Ukraine 51°0N 30°25E 17 C16
Kizel Russia 59°3N 57°40E 18 C10
Kiziba-Baluba △ Congo 11°50S 28°0E 55 E2
Kiziguru Rwanda 1°46S 30°23E 54 C3
Kızıl Irmak → Turkey 41°44N 35°58E 19 F6
Kızıl Jilga China 35°26N 78°50E 43 B8
Kızıldağ △ Turkey 36°15N 31°20E 44 B1
Kızıltepe Turkey 37°12N 40°35E 44 B4
Kizimkazi Tanzania 6°28S 39°30E 54 D4
Kizlyar Russia 43°51N 46°40E 19 F8

Kizyl-Arvat = Serdar
　Turkmenistan 39°4N 56°23E 45 B8
Kjölur Iceland 64°50N 19°25W 8 D4
Kladno Czech Rep. 50°10N 14°7E 16 C8
Klaeng Thailand 12°47N 101°39E 38 F3
Klagenfurt Austria 46°38N 14°20E 16 E8
Klaipėda Lithuania 55°43N 21°10E 9 J19
Klaksvík Faroe Is. 62°14N 6°35W 8 E9
Klamath → U.S.A. 41°33N 124°5W 76 F1
Klamath Falls U.S.A. 42°13N 121°46W 76 E3
Klamath Mts. U.S.A. 41°20N 123°0W 76 F2
Klamono Indonesia 1°8S 131°30E 37 E8
Klappan → Canada 58°0N 129°43W 70 B3
Klarälven → Sweden 59°23N 13°32E 9 G15
Klatovy Czech Rep. 49°23N 13°18E 16 D7
Klawer S. Africa 31°44S 18°36E 56 E2
Klawock U.S.A. 55°33N 133°6W 70 B2
Klazienaveen Neths. 52°44N 7°0E 15 B6
Kleena Kleene Canada 52°0N 124°59W 70 C4
Klein-Karas Namibia 27°33S 18°7E 56 D2
Klerksdorp S. Africa 26°53S 26°38E 56 D4
Kletsk = Klyetsk Belarus 53°5N 26°45E 17 B14
Kletskiy Russia 49°16N 43°11E 19 E7
Klickitat U.S.A. 45°49N 121°9W 76 D3
Klickitat → U.S.A. 45°42N 121°17W 78 E5
Klidhes Cyprus 35°42N 34°36E 25 D13
Klinaklini → Canada 51°21N 125°40W 70 C3
Klip → S. Africa 27°3S 29°3E 57 D4
Klipdale S. Africa 34°19S 19°57E 56 E2
Klipplaat S. Africa 33°1S 24°22E 56 E3
Kłodzko Poland 50°28N 16°38E 17 C9
Klondike Canada 64°0N 139°26W 68 E4
Klong Wang Chao △
　Thailand 16°20N 99°9E 38 D2
Klouto Togo 6°57N 0°44E 50 G6
Kluane △ Canada 60°45N 139°30W 70 A1
Kluane L. Canada 61°15N 138°40W 68 E4
Kluang Malaysia 2°3N 103°18E 39 L4
Kluczbork Poland 50°58N 18°12E 17 C10
Klukwan U.S.A. 59°24N 135°54W 70 B1
Klungkung Indonesia 8°32S 115°24E 37 K18
Klyetsk Belarus 53°5N 26°45E 17 B14
Klyuchevskaya, Gora
　Russia 55°50N 160°30E 29 D17
Klyuchi Russia 56°18N 160°51E 29 D17
Knaresborough U.K. 54°1N 1°28W 12 C6
Knee L. Man., Canada 55°3N 94°45W 72 A1
Knee L. Sask., Canada 55°51N 107°0W 71 B7
Knight Inlet Canada 50°45N 125°40W 70 C3
Knighton U.K. 52°21N 3°3W 13 E4
Knights Ferry U.S.A. 37°50N 120°40W 78 H6
Knights Landing
　U.S.A. 38°48N 121°43W 78 G5
Knob, C. Australia 34°32S 119°16E 61 F2
Knock Ireland 53°48N 8°55W 10 C3
Knockmealdown Mts.
　Ireland 52°14N 7°56W 10 D4
Knokke-Heist Belgium 51°21N 3°17E 15 C3
Knossós Greece 35°16N 25°10E 25 D7
Knowlton Canada 45°13N 72°31W 83 A12
Knox U.S.A. 41°18N 86°37W 80 E10
Knox Coast Antarctica 66°30S 108°0E 5 C8
Knoxville Iowa, U.S.A. 41°19N 93°6W 80 E7
Knoxville Pa., U.S.A. 41°57N 77°27W 82 E7
Knoxville Tenn., U.S.A. 35°58N 83°55W 85 D13
Knud Rasmussen Land
　Greenland 78°0N 60°0W 69 B20
Knysna S. Africa 34°2S 23°2E 56 E3
Ko Kha Thailand 18°11N 99°24E 38 C2
Ko Tarutao △ Thailand 6°31N 99°26E 39 J2
Ko Yao Thailand 8°7N 98°35E 39 a
Koartac = Quaqtaq
　Canada 60°55N 69°40W 69 E18
Koba Indonesia 6°37S 134°37E 37 F8
Kobarid Slovenia 46°15N 13°30E 16 E7
Kobayashi Japan 31°56N 130°59E 31 J5
Kōbe Japan 34°41N 135°13E 31 G7
København Denmark 55°40N 12°26E 9 J15
Kōbi-Sho Japan 25°56N 123°41E 31 M1
Koblenz Germany 50°21N 7°36E 16 C4
Kobryn Belarus 52°15N 24°22E 17 B13
Kobuk → U.S.A. 66°54N 160°38W 74 B7
Kocaeli Turkey 40°45N 29°50E 19 F4
Kočani Macedonia 41°55N 22°25E 23 D10
Koch Bihar India 26°22N 89°29E 41 F16
Kochas India 25°15N 83°56E 43 G10
Kochi = Cochin India 9°58N 76°20E 40 Q10
Kōchi Japan 33°30N 133°35E 31 H6
Kōchi □ Japan 33°40N 133°30E 31 H6
Kochiu = Gejiu China 23°20N 103°10E 32 D5
Kodarma India 24°28N 85°36E 43 G11
Kodi Indonesia 9°33S 119°0E 37 F5
Kodiak U.S.A. 57°47N 152°24W 74 D9
Kodiak I. U.S.A. 57°30N 152°45W 74 D9
Kodinar India 20°46N 70°46E 42 J4
Kodinsk Russia 58°40N 99°10E 29 D10
Koedoesberge S. Africa 32°40S 20°11E 56 E3
Koes Namibia 26°0S 19°15E 56 D2
Koffiefontein S. Africa 29°30S 25°0E 56 D4
Kofiau Indonesia 1°11S 129°50E 37 E7
Koforidua Ghana 6°3N 0°17W 50 G5
Kōfu Japan 35°40N 138°30E 31 G9
Koga Japan 36°11N 139°43E 31 F9
Kogaluc → Canada 56°12N 61°44W 73 A7
Køge Denmark 55°27N 12°11E 9 J15
Kogon Uzbekistan 39°43N 64°33E 28 F7
Koh-i-Khurd Afghan. 33°30N 65°59E 42 C1
Koh-i-Maran Pakistan 29°18N 66°50E 42 E2
Kohat Pakistan 33°40N 71°29E 42 C4
Kohima India 25°35N 94°10E 41 G19
Kohkīlūyeh va Būyer Aḥmadī □
　Iran 31°30N 50°30E 45 D6
Kohler Ra. Antarctica 77°0S 110°0W 5 D15
Kohlu Pakistan 29°54N 69°15E 42 E3
Kohtla-Järve Estonia 59°20N 27°20E 9 G22
Koi Sanjaq Iraq 36°5N 44°38E 44 B5
Koillismaa Finland 65°44N 28°36E 8 D23
Koin N. Korea 40°28N 126°18E 35 D14
Kojŏ N. Korea 38°58N 127°58E 35 E14

Kojonup Australia 33°48S 117°10E 61 F2
Kojūr Iran 36°23N 51°43E 45 B6
Kokand = Qŭqon
　Uzbekistan 40°31N 70°56E 28 E8
Kokas Indonesia 2°42S 132°26E 37 E8
Kokchetav = Kökshetaū
　Kazakhstan 53°20N 69°25E 28 D7
Kokemäenjoki →
　Finland 61°32N 21°44E 8 F19
Kokkola Finland 63°50N 23°8E 8 E20
Koko Kyunzu Burma 14°10N 93°25E 41 M18
Kokomo U.S.A. 40°29N 86°8W 80 E10
Koksan N. Korea 38°46N 126°40E 35 E14
Kökshetaū Kazakhstan 53°20N 69°25E 28 D7
Koksoak → Canada 58°30N 68°10W 69 F18
Kokstad S. Africa 30°32S 29°29E 57 E4
Kokubu Japan 31°44N 130°46E 31 J5
Kola Indonesia 5°35S 134°30E 37 F8
Kola Russia 68°45N 33°8E 8 B25
Kola Pen. = Kolskiy Poluostrov
　Russia 67°30N 38°0E 18 A6
Kolachi → Pakistan 27°8N 67°2E 42 F2
Kolahoi India 34°12N 75°22E 43 B6
Kolaka Indonesia 4°3S 121°46E 37 E6
Kolar India 13°12N 78°15E 40 N11
Kolar Gold Fields India 12°58N 78°16E 40 N11
Kolaras India 25°14N 77°36E 42 G6
Kolari Finland 67°20N 23°48E 8 C20
Kolayat India 27°50N 72°50E 42 F5
Kolda Senegal 12°55N 14°57W 50 F3
Kolding Denmark 55°30N 9°29E 9 J13
Kolepom = Dolak, Pulau
　Indonesia 8°0S 138°30E 37 F9
Kolguyev, Ostrov Russia 69°20N 48°30E 18 A8
Kolhapur India 16°43N 74°15E 40 L9
Kolimbia Greece 36°15N 28°10E 25 C10
Kolín Czech Rep. 50°2N 15°9E 16 C8
Kolkas rags Latvia 57°46N 22°37E 9 H20
Kolkata India 22°34N 88°21E 43 H13
Kollam = Quilon India 8°50N 76°38E 40 Q10
Kollum Neths. 53°17N 6°10E 15 A6
Kolmanskop Namibia 26°45S 15°14E 56 D2
Köln Germany 50°56N 6°57E 16 C4
Koło Poland 52°14N 18°40E 17 B10
Kołobrzeg Poland 54°10N 15°35E 16 A8
Kolokani Mali 13°35N 7°45W 50 F4
Kolomna Russia 55°8N 38°45E 18 C6
Kolomyya Ukraine 48°31N 25°2E 17 D13
Kolonodale Indonesia 2°0S 121°19E 37 E6
Kolosib India 24°15N 92°45E 41 G18
Kolpashevo Russia 58°20N 83°5E 28 D9
Kolpino Russia 59°44N 30°39E 18 C5
Kolskiy Poluostrov
　Russia 67°30N 38°0E 18 A6
Kolskiy Zaliv Russia 69°23N 34°0E 8 B26
Kolwezi
　Dem. Rep. of the Congo 10°40S 25°25E 55 E2
Kolyma → Russia 69°30N 161°0E 29 C17
Kolymskoye Nagorye
　Russia 63°0N 157°0E 29 C16
Kôm Ombo Egypt 24°25N 32°52E 51 D12
Komandorskiye Is. =
　Komandorskiye Ostrova
　Russia 55°0N 167°0E 29 D17
Komandorskiye Ostrova
　Russia 55°0N 167°0E 29 D17
Komárno Slovak Rep. 47°49N 18°5E 17 E10
Komatipoort S. Africa 25°25S 31°55E 57 D5
Komatou Yialou Cyprus 35°25N 34°8E 25 D13
Komatsu Japan 36°25N 136°30E 31 F8
Komatsushima Japan 34°0N 134°35E 31 H7
Kome Channel Uganda 0°10S 32°55E 54 C3
Komi □ Russia 64°0N 55°0E 18 B10
Kommunarsk = Alchevsk
　Ukraine 48°30N 38°45E 19 E6
Kommunizma, Pik = imeni Ismail
　Samani, Pik Tajikistan 39°0N 72°2E 28 F8
Komodo Indonesia 8°37S 119°20E 37 F5
Komoran, Pulau
　Indonesia 8°18S 138°45E 37 F9
Komoro Japan 36°19N 138°26E 31 F9
Komotini Greece 41°9N 25°26E 23 D11
Kompasberg S. Africa 31°45S 24°32E 56 E3
Kompong Cham
　Cambodia 12°0N 105°30E 39 G5
Kompong Chhnang = Kampong
　Chhnang Cambodia 12°20N 104°35E 39 G5
Kompong Chikreng
　Cambodia 13°5N 104°18E 39 F5
Kompong Kleang
　Cambodia 13°6N 104°8E 38 F5
Kompong Luong
　Cambodia 11°49N 104°48E 39 G5
Kompong Pranak
　Cambodia 13°35N 104°55E 38 F5
Kompong Som = Kampong Saom
　Cambodia 10°38N 103°30E 39 G4
Kompong Som, Chhung = Kampong
　Saom, Chaak Cambodia 10°50N 103°32E 38 G4
Kompong Speu
　Cambodia 11°26N 104°32E 39 G5
Kompong Sralau
　Cambodia 14°5N 105°46E 38 E5
Kompong Thom
　Cambodia 12°35N 104°51E 38 F5
Kompong Trabeck
　Cambodia 13°6N 105°14E 38 F5
Kompong Trabek
　Cambodia 11°9N 105°28E 39 G5
Kompong Trach
　Cambodia 11°25N 105°48E 39 G5
Kompong Tralach
　Cambodia 11°54N 104°47E 39 G5
Komrat = Comrat
　Moldova 46°18N 28°40E 17 E15
Komsberg S. Africa 32°40S 20°45E 56 E3
Komsomolets, Ostrov
　Russia 80°30N 95°0E 29 A10

Komsomolsk-na-Amur
　Russia 50°30N 137°0E 33 A8
Kon Tum Vietnam 14°24N 108°0E 38 E7
Kon Tum, Plateau du
　Vietnam 14°30N 108°30E 38 E7
Konar □ Afghan. 34°30N 71°3E 40 B7
Konārī Iran 28°13N 51°36E 45 D6
Konde Tanzania 4°57S 39°45E 54 C4
Kondinin Australia 32°34S 118°8E 61 F2
Kondoa Tanzania 4°55S 35°50E 54 C4
Kondopoga Russia 62°12N 34°17E 18 B5
Kondratyevo Russia 57°22N 98°15E 29 D10
Köneürgench
　Turkmenistan 42°19N 59°10E 28 E6
Konevo Russia 62°8N 39°20E 18 B6
Kong = Khong →
　Cambodia 13°32N 105°58E 38 F5
Kong Ivory C. 8°54N 4°36W 50 G5
Kong, Koh Cambodia 11°20N 103°0E 39 G4
Kong Christian IX Land
　Greenland 68°0N 36°0W 4 C6
Kong Christian X Land
　Greenland 74°0N 29°0W 4 B6
Kong Frederik IX Land
　Greenland 67°0N 52°0W 4 C5
Kong Frederik VI Kyst
　Greenland 63°0N 43°0W 4 C5
Kong Frederik VIII Land
　Greenland 78°30N 26°0W 4 B6
Kong Oscar Fjord
　Greenland 72°20N 24°0W 4 B6
Konglu Burma 27°13N 97°57E 41 F20
Kongola Namibia 17°45S 23°20E 56 B3
Kongolo Kasai-Or.,
　Dem. Rep. of the Congo 5°26S 24°49E 54 D1
Kongolo Katanga,
　Dem. Rep. of the Congo 5°22S 27°0E 54 D2
Kongsberg Norway 59°39N 9°39E 9 G13
Kongsvinger Norway 60°12N 12°2E 9 F15
Kongur Shan China 38°34N 75°18E 32 C2
Kongwa Tanzania 6°11S 36°26E 54 D4
Koni
　Dem. Rep. of the Congo 10°40S 27°11E 55 E2
Koni, Mts.
　Dem. Rep. of the Congo 10°36S 27°10E 55 E2
Konin Poland 52°12N 18°15E 17 B10
Konjic Bos.-H. 43°42N 17°58E 23 C7
Konkiep Namibia 26°49S 17°15E 56 D2
Konosha Russia 61°0N 40°5E 18 B7
Kōnosu Japan 36°3N 139°31E 31 F9
Konotop Ukraine 51°12N 33°7E 19 D5
Konqi He → China 41°0N 86°0E 32 B3
Końskie Poland 51°15N 20°23E 17 C11
Konstanz Germany 47°40N 9°10E 16 E5
Kont Iran 26°55N 61°50E 45 E9
Kontagora Nigeria 10°23N 5°27E 50 F7
Kontiolahti Finland 62°46N 29°50E 8 E23
Kontokali Greece 39°38N 19°51E 25 A3
Konya Turkey 37°52N 32°35E 44 B2
Konza Kenya 1°45S 37°7E 54 C4
Koocanusa, L. Canada 49°20N 115°15W 76 B6
Kookynie Australia 29°17S 121°22E 61 E3
Koolyanobbing
　Australia 30°48S 119°36E 61 F2
Koonibba Australia 31°54S 133°25E 63 E1
Koorawatha Australia 34°2S 148°33E 63 E4
Koorda Australia 30°48S 117°35E 61 F2
Kooskia U.S.A. 46°9N 115°59W 76 C6
Kootenay → U.S.A. 49°19N 117°39W 70 D5
Kootenay △ Canada 51°0N 116°0W 70 C5
Kootenay L. Canada 49°45N 116°50W 76 B5
Kootjieskolk S. Africa 31°15S 20°21E 56 E3
Kopaonik Serbia 43°10N 20°50E 23 C9
Kópavogur Iceland 64°6N 21°55W 8 D3
Koper Slovenia 45°31N 13°44E 16 F7
Kopervik Norway 59°17N 5°17E 9 G11
Kopet Dagh Asia 38°0N 58°0E 45 B8
Kopi Australia 33°24S 135°40E 63 E2
Köping Sweden 59°31N 16°3E 9 G17
Koppeh Dāgh = Kopet Dagh
　Asia 38°0N 58°0E 45 B8
Koppies S. Africa 27°20S 27°30E 57 D4
Koprivnica Croatia 46°12N 16°45E 22 A7
Köprülü △ Turkey 37°30N 31°5E 44 B1
Kopychyntsi Ukraine 49°7N 25°58E 17 D13
Kora △ Kenya 1°4S 38°44E 54 C4
Korab Macedonia 41°44N 20°40E 23 D9
Koral India 21°50N 73°12E 42 J5
Korba India 22°20N 82°45E 43 H10
Korbu, G. Malaysia 4°41N 101°18E 39 K3
Korçë Albania 40°37N 20°50E 23 D9
Korčula Croatia 42°56N 16°57E 22 C7
Kord Kūy Iran 36°48N 54°7E 45 B7
Kord Sheykh Iran 28°31N 52°53E 45 D7
Kordestān □ Iran 36°0N 47°0E 44 C5
Kordofân Sudan 13°0N 29°0E 51 F11
Korea, North ■ Asia 40°0N 127°0E 35 E14
Korea, South ■ Asia 36°0N 128°0E 35 G15
Korea Bay Korea 39°0N 124°0E 35 E13
Korea Strait Asia 34°0N 129°30E 35 H15
Korets Ukraine 50°40N 27°5E 17 C14
Korhogo Ivory C. 9°29N 5°28W 50 G4
Korinthiakos Kolpos
　Greece 38°16N 22°30E 23 E10
Korinthos Greece 37°56N 22°55E 23 F10
Korissia, L. Greece 39°27N 19°53E 25 B3
Kōriyama Japan 37°24N 140°23E 30 F10
Korla China 41°45N 86°4E 32 B3
Kormakitis, C. Cyprus 35°23N 32°56E 25 D11
Kornešty = Cornești
　Moldova 47°21N 28°1E 17 E15
Koro Ivory C. 8°32N 7°30W 50 G4
Koro Fiji 17°19S 179°23E 59 a
Koro Sea Fiji 17°30S 179°45W 59 a
Korogwe Tanzania 5°5S 38°25E 54 D4
Korolevu Fiji 18°12S 177°46E 59 a
Koronadal Phil. 6°12N 125°1E 37 C6
Koror Palau 7°20N 134°28E 64 G5

Körös → *Hungary* 46°43N 20°12E **17** E11
Korosten *Ukraine* 50°54N 28°36E **17** C15
Korostyshev *Ukraine* 50°19N 29°4E **17** C15
Korovou *Fiji* 17°47S 178°32E **59** a
Koroyanitu △ *Fiji* 17°40S 177°35E **59** a
Korraraika, Helodranon' i
  Madag. 17°45S 43°57E **57** B7
Korsakov *Russia* 46°36N 142°42E **29** E15
Korshunovo *Russia* 58°37N 110°10E **29** D12
Korsør *Denmark* 55°20N 11°9E **9** J14
Kortrijk *Belgium* 50°50N 3°17E **15** D3
Korwai *India* 24°7N 78°5E **42** G8
Koryakskoye Nagorye
  Russia 61°0N 171°0E **29** C18
Kos *Greece* 36°50N 27°15E **23** F12
Kosan *N. Korea* 38°52N 127°25E **35** E14
Kościan *Poland* 52°5N 16°40E **17** B9
Kosciusko *U.S.A.* 33°4N 89°35W **85** E10
Kosciuszko, Mt.
  Australia 36°27S 148°16E **63** F4
Kosha *Sudan* 20°50N 30°30E **51** D12
K'oshih = Kashi *China* 39°30N 76°2E **32** C2
Koshiki-Rettō *Japan* 31°45N 129°49E **31** J4
Kosi *India* 27°48N 77°29E **42** F7
Kosi → *India* 28°41N 78°57E **43** E8
Košice *Slovak Rep.* 48°42N 21°15E **17** D11
Koskinou *Greece* 36°23N 28°13E **25** C10
Koslan *Russia* 63°34N 49°14E **18** B8
Kosŏng *N. Korea* 38°40N 128°22E **35** E15
Kosovo □ *Europe* 42°30N 21°0E **23** C9
Kosovska Mitrovica
  Kosovo 42°54N 20°52E **23** C9
Kossou, L. de *Ivory C.* 6°59N 5°31W **50** G4
Koster *S. Africa* 25°52S 26°54E **56** D4
Kôstî *Sudan* 13°8N 32°43E **51** F12
Kostopil *Ukraine* 50°51N 26°22E **17** C14
Kostroma *Russia* 57°50N 40°58E **18** C7
Kostrzyn *Poland* 52°35N 14°39E **16** B8
Koszalin *Poland* 54°11N 16°8E **16** A9
Kot Addu *Pakistan* 30°30N 71°0E **42** D4
Kot Kapura *India* 30°35N 74°50E **42** D6
Kot Moman *Pakistan* 32°13N 73°0E **42** C5
Kot Sultan *Pakistan* 30°46N 70°56E **42** D4
Kota *India* 25°14N 75°49E **42** G6
Kota Barrage *India* 25°6N 75°51E **42** G6
Kota Belud *Malaysia* 6°21N 116°26E **36** C5
Kota Bharu *Malaysia* 6°7N 102°14E **39** J4
Kota Kinabalu *Malaysia* 6°0N 116°4E **36** C5
Kota Tinggi *Malaysia* 1°44N 103°53E **39** M4
Kotaagung *Indonesia* 5°38S 104°29E **36** F2
Kotabaru *Indonesia* 3°20S 116°20E **36** E5
Kotabumi *Indonesia* 4°49S 104°54E **36** E2
Kotamobagu *Indonesia* 0°57N 124°31E **37** D6
Kotapinang *Indonesia* 1°53N 100°5E **39** M3
Kotcho L. *Canada* 59°7N 121°12W **70** B4
Kotdwara *India* 29°45N 78°32E **43** E8
Kotelnich *Russia* 58°22N 48°24E **18** C8
Kotelnikovo *Russia* 47°38N 43°8E **19** E7
Kotelnyy, Ostrov
  Russia 75°10N 139°0E **29** B14
Kothari → *India* 25°20N 75°4E **42** G6
Kothi *Chhattisgarh, India* 23°21N 82°3E **43** H10
Kothi *Mad. P., India* 24°45N 80°40E **43** G9
Kotiro *Pakistan* 26°17N 67°13E **42** F2
Kotka *Finland* 60°28N 26°58E **8** F22
Kotlas *Russia* 61°17N 46°43E **18** B8
Kotli *Pakistan* 33°30N 73°55E **42** C5
Kotlik *U.S.A.* 63°2N 163°33W **74** C7
Kotma *India* 23°12N 81°58E **43** H9
Kotor *Montenegro* 42°25N 18°47E **23** C8
Kotovsk *Ukraine* 47°45N 29°35E **17** E15
Kotputli *India* 27°43N 76°12E **42** F7
Kotri *Pakistan* 25°22N 68°22E **42** G3
Kotto → *C.A.R.* 4°14N 22°2E **52** D4
Kotturu *India* 14°45N 76°10E **40** M10
Kotu Group *Tonga* 20°0S 174°45W **59** c
Kotuy → *Russia* 71°54N 102°6E **29** B11
Kotzebue *U.S.A.* 66°53N 162°39W **74** B7
Kotzebue Sound *U.S.A.* 66°20N 163°0W **74** B7
Kouchibouguac △
  Canada 46°50N 65°0W **73** C6
Koudougou *Burkina Faso* 12°10N 2°20W **50** F5
Koufonisi *Greece* 34°56N 26°8E **25** E8
Kougaberge *S. Africa* 33°48S 23°50E **56** E3
Kouilou → *Congo* 4°10S 12°5E **52** E2
Koukdjuak → *Canada* 66°43N 73°0W **69** D17
Koula Moutou *Gabon* 1°15S 12°25E **52** E2
Koulen = Kulen
  Cambodia 13°50N 104°40E **38** F5
Kouloura *Greece* 39°42N 19°54E **25** A3
Koumala *Australia* 21°38S 149°15E **62** C4
Koumra *Chad* 8°50N 17°35E **51** G9
Kountze *U.S.A.* 30°22N 94°19W **84** F7
Kouris → *Cyprus* 34°38N 32°54E **25** E11
Kourou *Fr. Guiana* 5°9N 52°39W **93** B8
Kouroussa *Guinea* 10°45N 9°45W **50** F4
Kousseri *Cameroon* 12°0N 14°55E **51** F8
Koutiala *Mali* 12°25N 5°23W **50** F4
Kouvola *Finland* 60°52N 26°43E **8** F22
Kovdor *Russia* 67°34N 30°24E **8** C24
Kovel *Ukraine* 51°11N 24°38E **17** C13
Kovrov *Russia* 56°25N 41°25E **18** C7
Kowanyama *Australia* 15°29S 141°44E **62** B3
Kowanyama ○
  Australia 15°20S 141°47E **62** B3
Kowloon *China* 22°19N 114°11E **33** G11
Kowŏn *N. Korea* 39°26N 127°14E **35** E14
Koyampattur = Coimbatore
  India 11°2N 76°59E **40** P10
Köyceğiz *Turkey* 36°57N 28°40E **23** F13
Koyukuk → *U.S.A.* 64°55N 157°32W **74** C8
Koza = Okinawa *Japan* 26°19N 127°46E **31** L3
Kozan *Turkey* 37°26N 35°50E **44** B6
Kozani *Greece* 40°19N 21°47E **23** D9
Kozhikode = Calicut
  India 11°15N 75°43E **40** P9
Kozhva *Russia* 65°10N 57°0E **18** A10
Kozyatyn *Ukraine* 49°45N 28°50E **17** D15
Kozyrevsk *Russia* 56°3N 159°51E **29** D16

Kpalimé *Togo* 6°57N 0°44E **50** G6
Kra, Isthmus of = Kra, Kho Khot
  Thailand 10°15N 99°30E **39** G2
Kra, Kho Khot *Thailand* 10°15N 99°30E **39** G2
Kra Buri *Thailand* 10°22N 98°46E **39** G2
Kraai → *S. Africa* 30°40S 26°45E **56** E4
Kracheh *Cambodia* 12°32N 106°10E **38** F6
Kragan *Indonesia* 6°43S 111°38E **37** G14
Kragerø *Norway* 58°52N 9°25E **9** G13
Kragujevac *Serbia* 44°2N 20°56E **23** B9
Krakatau = Rakata, Pulau
  Indonesia 6°10S 105°20E **36** F3
Krakatoa = Rakata, Pulau
  Indonesia 6°10S 105°20E **36** F3
Krakor *Cambodia* 12°32N 104°12E **38** F5
Kralanh *Cambodia* 13°35N 103°25E **38** F4
Kraljevo *Serbia* 43°44N 20°41E **23** C9
Kramatorsk *Ukraine* 48°50N 37°30E **19** E6
Kramfors *Sweden* 62°55N 17°48E **8** E17
Kranj *Slovenia* 46°16N 14°22E **16** E8
Krankskop *S. Africa* 28°0S 30°47E **57** D5
Krasavino *Russia* 60°58N 46°29E **18** B8
Kraskino *Russia* 42°44N 130°48E **30** C5
Kraśnik *Poland* 50°55N 22°15E **17** C12
Krasnoarmeysk *Russia* 51°0N 45°42E **28** D5
Krasnodar *Russia* 45°5N 39°0E **19** E6
Krasnokamensk *Russia* 50°3N 118°0E **29** D12
Krasnokamsk *Russia* 58°4N 55°48E **18** C10
Krasnoperekopsk *Ukraine* 46°0N 33°54E **19** E5
Krasnorechenskiy
  Russia 44°41N 135°14E **30** B7
Krasnoselkup *Russia* 65°20N 82°10E **28** C9
Krasnoturinsk *Russia* 59°46N 60°12E **18** C11
Krasnoufimsk *Russia* 56°36N 57°38E **18** C10
Krasnouralsk *Russia* 58°21N 60°3E **18** C11
Krasnovishersk *Russia* 60°23N 57°3E **18** B10
Krasnoyarsk *Russia* 56°8N 93°0E **29** D10
Krasnyy Kut *Russia* 50°50N 47°0E **19** D8
Krasnyy Luch *Ukraine* 48°13N 39°0E **19** E6
Krasnyy Yar *Russia* 46°43N 48°23E **19** E8
Kratie = Kracheh
  Cambodia 12°32N 106°10E **38** F6
Krau *Indonesia* 3°19S 140°5E **37** E10
Kravanh, Chuor Phnum
  Cambodia 12°0N 103°32E **39** G4
Krefeld *Germany* 51°20N 6°33E **16** C4
Kremen *Croatia* 44°28N 15°53E **16** F8
Kremenchuk *Ukraine* 49°5N 33°25E **19** E5
Kremenchuksk Vdskh.
  Ukraine 49°20N 32°30E **19** E5
Kremenets *Ukraine* 50°8N 25°43E **17** C13
Kremmling *U.S.A.* 40°4N 106°24W **76** F10
Krems *Austria* 48°25N 15°36E **16** D8
Kretinga *Lithuania* 55°53N 21°15E **9** J19
Krichev = Krychaw
  Belarus 53°40N 31°41E **17** B16
Kril'on, Mys *Russia* 45°53N 142°5E **30** B11
Krios, Akra *Greece* 35°13N 23°34E **25** D5
Krishna → *India* 15°57N 80°59E **41** M12
Krishnanagar *India* 23°24N 88°33E **43** H13
Kristiansand *Norway* 58°8N 8°1E **9** G13
Kristianstad *Sweden* 56°2N 14°9E **9** H16
Kristiansund *Norway* 63°7N 7°45E **8** E12
Kristiinankaupunki
  Finland 62°16N 21°21E **8** E19
Kristinehamn *Sweden* 59°18N 14°7E **9** G16
Kristinestad =
  Kristiinankaupunki
  Finland 62°16N 21°21E **8** E19
Kriti *Greece* 35°15N 25°0E **25** D7
Kritsa *Greece* 35°10N 25°41E **25** D7
Krivoy Rog = Kryvyy Rih
  Ukraine 47°51N 33°20E **19** E5
Krk *Croatia* 45°8N 14°40E **16** F8
Krokodil = Umgwenya →
  Mozam. 25°14S 32°18E **57** D5
Krong Kaoh Kong
  Cambodia 11°37N 102°59E **39** G4
Kronprins Frederik Land
  Greenland 81°0N 45°0W **4** B5
Kronprins Olav Kyst
  Antarctica 69°0S 42°0E **5** C5
Kronprinsesse Märtha Kyst
  Antarctica 73°30S 10°0W **5** D2
Kronshtadt *Russia* 59°57N 29°51E **18** B4
Kroonstad *S. Africa* 27°43S 27°19E **56** D4
Kropotkin *Russia* 45°28N 40°28E **19** E7
Krosno *Poland* 49°42N 21°46E **17** D11
Krotoszyn *Poland* 51°42N 17°23E **17** C9
Krousonas *Greece* 35°13N 24°59E **25** D6
Kruger △ *S. Africa* 24°50S 26°10E **57** C5
Krugersdorp *S. Africa* 26°5S 27°46E **57** D4
Kruisfontein *S. Africa* 33°59S 24°43E **56** E3
Krung Thep = Bangkok
  Thailand 13°45N 100°35E **38** F3
Krupki *Belarus* 54°19N 29°8E **17** A15
Kruševac *Serbia* 43°35N 21°28E **23** C9
Krychaw *Belarus* 53°40N 31°41E **17** B16
Krymskiy Poluostrov = Krymskyy
  Pivostriv *Ukraine* 45°0N 34°0E **19** F5
Krymskyy Pivostriv
  Ukraine 45°0N 34°0E **19** F5
Kryvyy Rih *Ukraine* 47°51N 33°20E **19** E5
Ksar el Kebir *Morocco* 35°0N 6°0W **50** B4
Ksar es Souk = Er Rachidia
  Morocco 31°58N 4°20W **50** B5
Kuah *Malaysia* 6°19N 99°51E **39** J2
Kuala Belait *Malaysia* 4°35N 114°11E **36** D4
Kuala Berang *Malaysia* 5°5N 103°1E **39** K4
Kuala Dungun = Dungun
  Malaysia 4°45N 103°25E **39** K4
Kuala Kangsar *Malaysia* 4°46N 100°56E **39** K3
Kuala Kelawang *Malaysia* 2°56N 102°5E **39** L4
Kuala Kerai *Malaysia* 5°30N 102°12E **39** K4
Kuala Kerian *Malaysia* 5°10N 100°25E **39** c
Kuala Kubu Bharu
  Malaysia 3°34N 101°39E **39** L3

Kuala Lipis *Malaysia* 4°10N 102°3E **39** K4
Kuala Lumpur *Malaysia* 3°9N 101°41E **39** L3
Kuala Nerang *Malaysia* 6°16N 100°37E **39** J3
Kuala Pilah *Malaysia* 2°45N 102°15E **39** L4
Kuala Rompin *Malaysia* 2°49N 103°29E **39** L4
Kuala Selangor *Malaysia* 3°20N 101°15E **39** L3
Kuala Sepetang
  Malaysia 4°49N 100°28E **39** K3
Kuala Terengganu
  Malaysia 5°20N 103°8E **39** K4
Kualajelai *Indonesia* 2°58S 110°46E **36** E4
Kualakapuas *Indonesia* 2°55S 114°20E **36** E4
Kualakurun *Indonesia* 1°10S 113°50E **36** E4
Kualapembuang
  Indonesia 3°14S 112°38E **36** E4
Kualasimpang *Indonesia* 4°17N 98°3E **36** D1
Kuancheng *China* 40°37N 118°30E **35** D10
Kuandang *Indonesia* 0°56N 123°1E **37** D6
Kuandian *China* 40°45N 124°45E **35** D13
Kuangchou = Guangzhou
  China 23°6N 113°13E **33** D6
Kuantan *Malaysia* 3°49N 103°20E **39** L4
Kuba = Quba *Azerbaijan* 41°21N 48°32E **19** F8
Kuban → *Russia* 45°20N 37°30E **19** E6
Kubokawa *Japan* 33°12N 133°8E **31** H6
Kubu *Indonesia* 8°16S 115°35E **37** J18
Kubutambahan
  Indonesia 8°5S 115°10E **37** J18
Kucar, Tanjung
  Indonesia 8°39S 114°34E **37** K18
Kuchaman *India* 27°13N 74°47E **42** F6
Kuchinda *India* 21°44N 84°21E **43** J11
Kuching *Malaysia* 1°33N 110°25E **36** D4
Kuchino-eruba-Jima
  Japan 30°28N 130°12E **31** J5
Kuchino-Shima *Japan* 29°57N 129°55E **31** K4
Kuchinotsu *Japan* 32°36N 130°11E **31** H5
Kucing = Kuching
  Malaysia 1°33N 110°25E **36** D4
Kud → *Pakistan* 26°5N 66°20E **42** F2
Kuda *India* 23°10N 71°15E **42** H4
Kudat *Malaysia* 6°55N 116°55E **36** C5
Kudus *Indonesia* 6°48S 110°51E **37** G14
Kudymkar *Russia* 59°1N 54°39E **18** C9
Kueiyang = Guiyang
  China 26°32N 106°40E **32** D5
Kufra Oasis = Al Kufrah
  Libya 24°17N 23°15E **51** D10
Kufstein *Austria* 47°35N 12°11E **16** E7
Kugaaruk = Pelly Bay
  Canada 68°38N 89°50W **69** D14
Kugluktuk *Canada* 67°50N 115°5W **68** D8
Kugong I. *Canada* 56°18N 79°50W **72** A4
Kūh Dasht *Iran* 33°32N 47°36E **44** C5
Kūhak *Iran* 27°12N 63°10E **45** E9
Kuhan *Pakistan* 28°19N 67°14E **42** E2
Kūhbonān *Iran* 31°23N 56°19E **45** D8
Kühestak *Iran* 26°47N 57°2E **45** E8
Kuhin *Iran* 36°22N 49°40E **45** B6
Kūhīrī *Iran* 26°55N 61°2E **45** E9
Kuhmo *Finland* 64°7N 29°31E **8** D23
Kühpāyeh *Esfahan, Iran* 32°44N 52°20E **45** C7
Kühpāyeh *Kermān, Iran* 30°35N 57°15E **45** D8
Kührān, Kūh-e *Iran* 26°46N 58°12E **45** E8
Kui Buri *Thailand* 12°3N 99°52E **39** F2
Kuichong *China* 22°38N 114°25E **33** a
Kuiseb → *Namibia* 22°59S 14°31E **56** C1
Kuito *Angola* 12°22S 16°55E **53** G3
Kuiu I. *U.S.A.* 57°45N 134°10W **70** B2
Kujang *N. Korea* 39°57N 126°1E **35** E14
Kuji *Japan* 40°11N 141°46E **30** D10
Kujū-San *Japan* 33°5N 131°15E **31** H5
Kukës *Albania* 42°5N 20°27E **23** C9
Kukup *Malaysia* 1°20N 103°27E **39** d
Kukup, Pulau *Malaysia* 1°18N 103°25E **39** d
Kula *Turkey* 38°32N 28°40E **23** E13
Kula Shan *Bhutan* 28°14N 90°36E **32** C4
Kulachi *Pakistan* 31°56N 70°27E **42** D4
Kulai *Malaysia* 1°44N 103°35E **39** M4
Kulasekarappattinam
  India 8°20N 78°5E **40** Q11
Kuldīga *Latvia* 56°58N 21°59E **9** H19
Kulen *Cambodia* 13°50N 104°40E **38** F5
Kulgam *India* 33°36N 75°2E **43** C6
Kulgera *Australia* 25°50S 133°18E **62** D1
Kulim *Malaysia* 5°22N 100°34E **39** K3
Kulin *Australia* 32°40S 118°2E **61** F2
Kulkayu = Hartley Bay
  Canada 53°25N 129°15W **70** C3
Kullu *India* 31°58N 77°6E **42** D7
Kŭlob *Tajikistan* 37°55N 69°50E **28** F7
Kulsary = Qulsary
  Kazakhstan 46°59N 54°1E **19** E9
Kulti *India* 23°43N 86°50E **43** H12
Kulunda *Russia* 52°35N 78°57E **28** D8
Kulungar *Afghan.* 34°0N 69°2E **42** C3
Kŭlvand *Iran* 31°21N 54°35E **45** D7
Kulwin *Australia* 35°2S 142°42E **63** F3
Kulyab = Kŭlob
  Tajikistan 37°55N 69°50E **28** F7
Kuma → *Russia* 44°55N 47°0E **19** F8
Kumaganum *Nigeria* 13°8N 10°38E **51** F8
Kumagaya *Japan* 36°9N 139°22E **31** F9
Kumai *Indonesia* 2°44S 111°43E **36** E4
Kumamba, Kepulauan
  Indonesia 1°36S 138°45E **37** E9
Kumamoto *Japan* 32°45N 130°45E **31** H5
Kumamoto □ *Japan* 32°55N 130°55E **31** H5
Kumanovo *Macedonia* 42°9N 21°42E **23** C9
Kumara *N.Z.* 42°37S 171°12E **59** E3
Kumarina Roadhouse
  Australia 24°41S 119°32E **61** D2
Kumasi *Ghana* 6°41N 1°38W **50** G5
Kumba *Cameroon* 4°36N 9°24E **52** D1
Kumbakonam *India* 10°58N 79°25E **40** P11
Kumbarilla *Australia* 27°15S 150°55E **63** D5
Kumbia *Australia* 26°41S 151°39E **63** D5

Kuala Lipis ... (cont.)
Kuch'ŏn *N. Korea* 38°10N 126°29E **35** E14
Kumch'ŏn *N. Korea* 38°10N 126°29E **35** E14
Kumdok *India* 33°32N 78°10E **43** C8
Kume-Shima *Japan* 26°20N 126°47E **31** L3
Kumertau *Russia* 52°45N 55°57E **18** D10
Kumharsain *India* 31°19N 77°27E **42** D7
Kumi *Uganda* 1°30N 33°58E **54** B3
Kumo *Nigeria* 10°1N 11°12E **51** F8
Kumo älv = Kokemäenjoki →
  Finland 61°32N 21°44E **8** F19
Kumon Bum *Burma* 26°30N 97°15E **41** F20
Kumtag Shamo *China* 39°40N 92°0E **32** C4
Kunashir, Ostrov *Russia* 44°0N 146°0E **29** E15
Kunda *Estonia* 59°30N 26°34E **9** G22
Kunda *India* 25°43N 81°31E **43** G9
Kundar → *Pakistan* 31°56N 69°19E **42** D3
Kundelungu △
  Dem. Rep. of the Congo 10°30S 27°40E **55** E2
Kundelungu Ouest △
  Dem. Rep. of the Congo 9°55S 27°17E **55** D2
Kundian *Pakistan* 32°27N 71°28E **42** C4
Kundla *India* 21°21N 71°25E **42** J4
Kung, Ao *Thailand* 8°5N 98°24E **39** a
Kunga → *Bangla.* 21°46N 89°30E **43** J13
Kunghit I. *Canada* 52°6N 131°3W **70** C2
Kungrad = Qŭnghirot
  Uzbekistan 43°2N 58°50E **28** E6
Kungsbacka *Sweden* 57°30N 12°5E **9** H15
Kungur *Russia* 57°25N 56°57E **18** C10
Kungurri *Australia* 21°4S 148°45E **62** C4
Kunhar → *Pakistan* 34°20N 73°30E **43** B5
Kuningan *Indonesia* 6°59S 108°29E **37** G13
Kunlong *Burma* 23°20N 98°50E **41** H21
Kunlun Shan *Asia* 36°0N 86°30E **32** C3
Kunming *China* 25°1N 102°41E **32** D5
Kunmunya ○ *Australia* 15°26S 124°42E **60** C3
Kununurra *Australia* 15°40S 128°50E **60** C4
Kunwari → *India* 26°26N 79°11E **43** F8
Kunya-Urgench = Köneürgench
  Turkmenistan 42°19N 59°10E **28** E6
Kuopio *Finland* 62°53N 27°35E **8** E22
Kupa → *Croatia* 45°28N 16°24E **16** F9
Kupang *Indonesia* 10°19S 123°39E **37** F6
Kupreanof I. *U.S.A.* 56°50N 133°30W **70** B2
Kupyansk-Uzlovoi
  Ukraine 49°40N 37°43E **19** E6
Kuqa *China* 41°35N 82°30E **32** B3
Kür → *Azerbaijan* 39°29N 49°15E **19** G8
Kür Dili *Azerbaijan* 39°3N 49°13E **45** B6
Kura = Kür →
  Azerbaijan 39°29N 49°15E **19** G8
Kuranda *Australia* 16°48S 145°35E **62** B4
Kuranga *India* 22°4N 69°10E **42** H3
Kurashiki *Japan* 34°40N 133°50E **31** G6
Kurayn *Si. Arabia* 27°38N 49°50E **45** E6
Kurayoshi *Japan* 35°26N 133°50E **31** G6
Kürchatov *Kazakhstan* 50°45N 78°32E **28** D8
Kürdzhali *Bulgaria* 41°38N 25°21E **23** D11
Kure *Japan* 34°14N 132°32E **31** G6
Kure I. *U.S.A.* 28°25N 178°25W **75** K4
Kuressaare *Estonia* 58°15N 22°30E **9** G20
Kurgan *Russia* 55°26N 65°18E **28** D7
Kuri *India* 26°37N 70°43E **42** F4
Kuria Maria Is. = Hallāniyat,
  Jazā'ir al *Oman* 17°30N 55°58E **47** D6
Kuridala *Australia* 21°16S 140°29E **62** C3
Kurigram *Bangla.* 25°49N 89°39E **41** G16
Kurikka *Finland* 62°36N 22°24E **8** E20
Kuril Basin *Pac. Oc.* 47°0N 150°0E **4** E15
Kuril Is. = Kurilskiye Ostrova
  Russia 45°0N 150°0E **29** E16
Kuril-Kamchatka Trench
  Pac. Oc. 44°0N 153°0E **64** C7
Kurilsk *Russia* 45°14N 147°53E **29** E15
Kurilskiye Ostrova
  Russia 45°0N 150°0E **29** E16
Kurino *Japan* 31°57N 130°43E **31** J5
Kurinskaya Kosa = Kür Dili
  Azerbaijan 39°3N 49°13E **45** B6
Kurlkuta ○ *Australia* 24°0S 127°56E **60** D4
Kurnool *India* 15°45N 78°0E **40** M11
Kuro-Shima *Kagoshima,*
  Japan 30°50N 129°57E **31** J4
Kuro-Shima *Okinawa,*
  Japan 24°14N 124°1E **31** M2
Kurow *N.Z.* 44°44S 170°29E **59** F3
Kurram → *Pakistan* 32°36N 71°20E **42** C4
Kurri Kurri *Australia* 32°50S 151°28E **63** E5
Kurrimine *Australia* 17°47S 146°6E **62** B4
Kurseong = Karsiyang
  India 26°56N 88°18E **43** F13
Kurshskiy Zaliv *Russia* 55°9N 21°6E **9** J19
Kursk *Russia* 51°42N 36°11E **18** D6
Kuruçay *Turkey* 39°39N 38°29E **44** B3
Kurukshetra = Thanesar
  India 30°1N 76°52E **42** D7
Kuruktag *China* 41°0N 89°0E **32** B3
Kuruman *S. Africa* 27°28S 23°28E **56** D3
Kuruman → *S. Africa* 26°56S 20°39E **56** D3
Kurume *Japan* 33°15N 130°30E **31** H5
Kurunegala *Sri Lanka* 7°30N 80°23E **40** R12
Kurya *Russia* 61°42N 57°9E **18** B10
Kus Gölü *Turkey* 40°10N 27°55E **23** D12
Kuşadası *Turkey* 37°52N 27°15E **23** F12
Kusamba *Indonesia* 8°34S 115°27E **37** K18
Kusatsu *Japan* 35°3N 135°57E **31** G7
Kusawa L. *Canada* 60°20N 136°13W **70** A1
Kushalgarh *India* 23°10N 74°27E **42** H6
Kushikino *Japan* 31°44N 130°16E **31** J5
Kushima *Japan* 31°29N 131°14E **31** J5
Kushimoto *Japan* 33°28N 135°47E **31** H7
Kushiro *Japan* 43°0N 144°25E **30** C12
Kushiro-Gawa →
  Japan 42°59N 144°23E **30** C12
Kushiro Shitsugen △
  Japan 43°9N 144°26E **30** C12
Kūshk *Iran* 28°46N 56°51E **45** D8
Kushol *India* 33°40N 76°36E **43** C7

Kushtia *Bangla.* 23°55N 89°5E **41** H16
Kushva *Russia* 58°18N 59°45E **18** C10
Kuskokwim → *U.S.A.* 60°5N 162°25W **74** C7
Kuskokwim B. *U.S.A.* 59°45N 162°25W **74** D7
Kuskokwim Mts.
  U.S.A. 62°30N 156°0W **74** C8
Kusmi *India* 23°17N 83°55E **43** H10
Kusŏng *N. Korea* 39°59N 125°15E **35** E13
Kussharo-Ko *Japan* 43°38N 144°21E **30** C12
Kustanay = Qostanay
  Kazakhstan 53°10N 63°35E **28** D7
Kut, Ko *Thailand* 11°40N 102°35E **39** G4
Kuta *Indonesia* 8°43S 115°11E **37** K18
Kütahya *Turkey* 39°30N 30°2E **19** G5
Kutaisi *Georgia* 42°19N 42°40E **19** F7
Kutaraja = Banda Aceh
  Indonesia 5°35N 95°20E **36** C1
Kutch, Gulf of = Kachchh, Gulf of
  India 22°50N 69°15E **42** H3
Kutch, Rann of = Kachchh, Rann
  of *India* 24°0N 70°0E **42** H4
Kutiyana *India* 21°36N 70°2E **42** J4
Kutno *Poland* 52°15N 19°23E **17** B10
Kutse *Botswana* 21°7S 22°16E **56** C3
Kuttabul *Australia* 21°1S 148°54E **62** b
Kutu *Dem. Rep. of the Congo* 2°40S 18°11E **52** E3
Kutum *Sudan* 14°10N 24°40E **51** F10
Kuujjuaq *Canada* 58°6N 68°15W **69** F18
Kuujjuarapik *Canada* 55°20N 77°35W **72** A4
Kuusamo *Finland* 65°57N 29°8E **8** D23
Kuusankoski *Finland* 60°55N 26°38E **8** F22
Kuwait = Al Kuwayt
  Kuwait 29°30N 48°0E **44** D5
Kuwait ■ *Asia* 29°30N 47°30E **44** D5
Kuwana *Japan* 35°5N 136°43E **31** G8
Kuwana → *India* 26°25N 83°15E **43** F10
Kuybyshev = Samara
  Russia 53°8N 50°6E **18** D9
Kuybyshev *Russia* 55°27N 78°19E **28** D8
Kuybyshevskoye Vdkhr.
  Russia 55°2N 49°30E **18** C8
Kuye He → *China* 38°23N 110°46E **34** E6
Küyeh *Iran* 38°45N 47°57E **44** B5
Kuyto, Ozero *Russia* 65°6N 31°20E **8** D24
Kuyumba *Russia* 60°58N 96°59E **29** C10
Kuzey Anadolu Dağları
  Turkey 41°0N 36°45E **19** F6
Kuznetsk *Russia* 53°12N 46°40E **18** D8
Kuzomen *Russia* 66°22N 36°50E **18** A6
Kvænangen *Norway* 70°5N 21°15E **8** A19
Kvaløya *Norway* 69°40N 18°30E **8** B18
Kvarner *Croatia* 44°50N 14°10E **16** F8
Kvarnerič *Croatia* 44°43N 14°37E **16** F8
Kwabhaca *S. Africa* 30°51S 29°0E **57** E4
Kwajalein *Marshall Is.* 9°5N 167°20E **64** G8
Kwakhanai *Botswana* 21°39S 21°16E **56** C3
Kwakoegron *Suriname* 5°12N 55°25W **93** B7
Kwale *Kenya* 4°15S 39°31E **54** C4
KwaMashu *S. Africa* 29°45S 30°58E **57** D5
Kwando → *Africa* 18°27S 23°32E **56** B3
Kwangchow = Guangzhou
  China 23°6N 113°13E **33** D6
Kwango →
  Dem. Rep. of the Congo 3°14S 17°22E **52** E3
Kwangsi-Chuang = Guangxi
  Zhuangzu Zizhiqu □
  China 24°0N 109°0E **33** D5
Kwangtung = Guangdong □
  China 23°0N 113°0E **33** D6
Kwataboahegan →
  Canada 51°9N 80°50W **72** B3
Kwatisore *Indonesia* 3°18S 134°50E **37** E8
KwaZulu Natal □ *S. Africa* 29°0S 30°0E **57** D5
Kweichow = Guizhou □
  China 27°0N 107°0E **32** D5
Kwekwe *Zimbabwe* 18°58S 29°48E **55** F2
Kwidzyn *Poland* 53°44N 18°55E **17** B10
Kwilu →
  Dem. Rep. of the Congo 3°22S 17°22E **52** E3
Kwinana *Australia* 32°15S 115°47E **61** F2
Kwoka *Indonesia* 0°31S 132°27E **37** E8
Kwun Tong *China* 22°19N 114°13E **33** G11
Kyabra Cr. → *Australia* 25°36S 142°55E **63** D3
Kyabram *Australia* 36°19S 145°4E **63** F4
Kyaikto *Burma* 17°20N 97°3E **38** D1
Kyakhta *Russia* 50°30N 106°25E **29** D11
Kyambura △ *Uganda* 0°7S 30°9E **54** C3
Kyancutta *Australia* 33°8S 135°33E **63** E2
Kyaukpadaung *Burma* 20°52N 95°8E **41** J19
Kyaukpyu *Burma* 19°28N 93°30E **41** K18
Kyaukse *Burma* 21°36N 96°10E **41** J20
Kyburz *U.S.A.* 38°47N 120°18W **78** G6
Kyelang *India* 32°35N 77°2E **42** C7
Kyenjojo *Uganda* 0°40N 30°37E **54** B3
Kyle *Canada* 50°50N 108°2W **71** C7
Kyle Dam *Zimbabwe* 20°15S 31°0E **55** G3
Kyle of Lochalsh *U.K.* 57°17N 5°44W **11** D3
Kymijoki → *Finland* 60°30N 26°55E **8** F22
Kymmene älv = Kymijoki →
  Finland 60°30N 26°55E **8** F22
Kyneton *Australia* 37°10S 144°29E **63** F3
Kyō-ga-Saki *Japan* 35°45N 135°15E **31** G7
Kyoga, L. *Uganda* 1°35N 33°0E **54** B3
Kyogle *Australia* 28°40S 153°0E **63** D5
Kyŏngju = Gyeongju
  S. Korea 35°51N 129°14E **35** G15
Kyŏngpyaw *Burma* 17°12N 95°10E **41** L19
Kyŏngsŏng *N. Korea* 41°35N 129°36E **35** D15
Kyōto *Japan* 35°0N 135°45E **31** G7
Kyōto □ *Japan* 35°15N 135°45E **31** G7
Kyparissovouno *Cyprus* 35°19N 33°10E **25** D12
Kyperounda *Cyprus* 34°56N 32°58E **25** E11
Kypros = Cyprus ■ *Asia* 35°0N 33°0E **25** E12
Kyrenia *Cyprus* 35°20N 33°20E **25** D12
Kyrgyzstan ■ *Asia* 42°0N 75°0E **28** E8
Kyro älv = Kyrönjoki →
  Finland 63°14N 21°45E **8** E19
Kyrönjoki → *Finland* 63°14N 21°45E **8** E19

Kystatyam Russia 67°20N 123°10E 29 C13
Kythira Greece 36°8N 23°0E 23 F10
Kythréa Cyprus 35°15N 33°29E 25 D12
Kyunhla Burma 23°25N 95°15E 41 H19
Kyuquot Sound Canada 50°2N 127°22W 70 D3
Kyūshū Japan 33°0N 131°0E 31 H5
Kyūshū □ Japan 33°0N 131°0E 31 H5
Kyūshū-Palau Ridge
  Pac. Oc. 20°0N 136°0E 64 E5
Kyūshū-Sanchi Japan 32°35N 131°17E 31 H5
Kyustendil Bulgaria 42°16N 22°41E 23 C10
Kyusyur Russia 70°19N 127°30E 29 B13
Kyyiv Ukraine 50°30N 30°28E 17 C16
Kyyivske Vdskh.
  Ukraine 51°0N 30°25E 17 C16
Kyzyl Russia 51°50N 94°30E 32 A4
Kyzyl Kum Uzbekistan 42°30N 65°0E 28 E7
Kyzyl Kyya Kyrgyzstan 40°16N 72°8E 28 E8
Kyzyl Orda = Qyzylorda
  Kazakhstan 44°48N 65°28E 28 E7

L

La Alcarria Spain 40°31N 2°45W 21 B4
La Amistad △ Cent. Amer. 9°28N 83°18W 88 E3
La Asunción Venezuela 11°2N 63°53W 92 A6
La Baie Canada 48°19N 70°53W 73 C5
La Banda Argentina 27°45S 64°10W 94 B3
La Barca Mexico 20°17N 102°34W 86 C4
La Barge U.S.A. 42°16N 110°12W 76 E8
La Barra Nic. 12°54N 83°33W 88 D3
La Belle U.S.A. 26°46N 81°26W 85 H14
La Biche → Canada 59°57N 123°50W 70 B4
La Biche, L. Canada 54°50N 112°3W 70 C6
La Brea Trin. & Tob. 10°15N 61°37W 93 K15
La Calera Chile 32°50S 71°10W 94 C1
La Campana △ Chile 32°58S 71°14W 94 C1
La Canal = Sa Canal
  Spain 38°51N 1°23E 24 C7
La Carlota Argentina 33°30S 63°20W 94 C3
La Ceiba Honduras 15°40N 86°50W 88 C2
La Chaux-de-Fonds Switz. 47°7N 6°50E 20 C7
La Chorrera Panama 8°53N 79°47W 88 E4
La Cocha Argentina 27°50S 65°40W 94 B2
La Concepción Panama 8°31N 82°37W 88 E3
La Concordia Mexico 16°5N 92°38W 87 D6
La Coruña = A Coruña
  Spain 43°20N 8°25W 21 A1
La Crescent U.S.A. 43°50N 91°18W 80 D8
La Crete Canada 58°11N 116°24W 70 B5
La Crosse Kans., U.S.A. 38°32N 99°18W 80 F4
La Crosse Wis., U.S.A. 43°48N 91°15W 80 D8
La Cruz Costa Rica 11°4N 85°39W 88 D2
La Cruz Mexico 23°55N 106°54W 86 C3
La Désirade Guadeloupe 16°18N 61°3W 88 b
La Digue Seychelles 4°20S 55°51E 53 b
La Esperanza Cuba 22°46N 83°44W 88 B3
La Esperanza Honduras 14°15N 88°10W 88 D2
La Estrada = A Estrada
  Spain 42°43N 8°27W 21 A1
La Fayette U.S.A. 34°42N 85°17W 85 D12
La Fé Cuba 22°2N 84°15W 88 B3
La Follette U.S.A. 36°23N 84°7W 85 C12
La Grande U.S.A. 45°20N 118°5W 76 D4
La Grande → Canada 53°50N 79°0W 72 B5
La Grande 3, Rés.
  Canada 53°40N 75°10W 72 B4
La Grande 4, Rés. Canada 54°0N 73°15W 72 B5
La Grange Calif., U.S.A. 37°42N 120°27W 78 H6
La Grange Ga., U.S.A. 33°2N 85°2W 85 E12
La Grange Ky., U.S.A. 38°24N 85°23W 81 F11
La Grange Tex., U.S.A. 29°54N 96°52W 84 G6
La Guaira Venezuela 10°36N 66°56W 92 A5
La Habana Cuba 23°8N 82°22W 88 B3
La Independencia Mexico 16°15N 92°1W 87 D6
La Isabela Dom. Rep. 19°58N 71°2W 89 C5
La Junta U.S.A. 37°59N 103°33W 76 H12
La Laguna Canary Is. 28°28N 16°18W 24 F3
La Libertad = Puerto Libertad
  Mexico 29°55N 112°43W 86 B2
La Libertad Guatemala 16°47N 90°7W 88 C1
La Ligua Chile 32°30S 71°16W 94 C1
La Línea de la Concepción
  Spain 36°15N 5°23W 21 D3
La Loche Canada 56°29N 109°26W 71 B7
La Louvière Belgium 50°27N 4°10E 15 D4
La Lune Trin. & Tob. 10°3N 61°22W 93 K15
La Malbaie Canada 47°40N 70°10W 73 C5
La Malinche △ Mexico 19°15N 98°3W 87 D5
La Mancha Spain 39°10N 2°54W 21 C4
La Martre, L. Canada 63°15N 117°55W 70 A5
La Mesa Mexico 32°30N 116°57W 79 N10
La Mesa U.S.A. 32°46N 117°1W 79 N9
La Mesilla U.S.A. 32°16N 106°48W 77 K10
La Misión Mexico 32°6N 116°53W 86 A1
La Moure U.S.A. 46°21N 98°18W 80 B4
La Negra Chile 23°46N 70°18W 94 A1
La Oliva Canary Is. 28°36N 13°57W 24 F6
La Orotava Canary Is. 28°23N 16°31W 24 F3
La Oroya Peru 11°22S 75°54W 92 F3
La Palma Canary Is. 28°40N 17°50W 24 F2
La Palma Panama 8°15N 78°0W 88 E4
La Palma del Condado
  Spain 37°21N 6°38W 21 D2
La Paloma Chile 30°35S 71°0W 94 C1
La Pampa □ Argentina 36°50S 66°0W 94 D2
La Paragua Venezuela 6°50N 63°20W 92 B6
La Paz Entre Ríos,
  Argentina 30°50S 59°45W 94 C4
La Paz San Luis,
  Argentina 33°30S 67°20W 94 C2
La Paz Bolivia 16°20S 68°10W 92 G5
La Paz Honduras 14°20N 87°47W 88 D2
La Paz Mexico 24°10N 110°18W 86 C2
La Paz Centro Nic. 12°20N 86°41W 88 D2
La Pedrera Colombia 1°18S 69°43W 92 D5
La Pérade Canada 46°35N 72°12W 73 C5
La Perla Mexico 28°18N 104°32W 86 B4

La Perouse Str. Asia 45°40N 142°0E 30 B11
La Pesca Mexico 23°46N 97°47W 87 C5
La Piedad Mexico 20°21N 102°0W 86 C4
La Pine U.S.A. 43°40N 121°30W 76 E3
La Plata Argentina 35°0S 57°55W 94 C4
La Pocatière Canada 47°22N 70°2W 73 C5
La Porte U.S.A. 41°36N 86°43W 81 E9
La Purísima Mexico 26°10N 112°4W 86 B2
La Push U.S.A. 47°55N 124°38W 78 C2
La Quiaca Argentina 22°5S 65°35W 94 A2
La Restinga Canary Is. 27°38N 17°59W 24 G2
La Rioja Argentina 29°20S 67°0W 94 B2
La Rioja □ Argentina 29°30S 67°0W 94 B2
La Rioja □ Spain 42°20N 2°20W 21 A4
La Robla Spain 42°50N 5°41W 21 A3
La Roche-en-Ardenne
  Belgium 50°11N 5°35E 15 D5
La Roche-sur-Yon France 46°40N 1°25W 20 C3
La Rochelle France 46°10N 1°9W 20 C3
La Roda Spain 39°13N 2°15E 21 C4
La Romaine Canada 50°13N 60°40W 73 B7
La Romana Dom. Rep. 18°27N 68°57W 89 C6
La Ronge Canada 55°5N 105°20W 71 B7
La Rumorosa Mexico 32°34N 116°6W 79 N10
La Sabina = Sa Savina
  Spain 38°44N 1°25E 24 C7
La Salle U.S.A. 41°20N 89°6W 80 E9
La Santa Canary Is. 29°5N 13°40W 24 E6
La Sarre Canada 48°45N 79°15W 72 C4
La Scie Canada 49°57N 55°36W 73 C8
La Selva Beach U.S.A. 36°56N 121°51W 78 J5
La Serena Chile 29°55S 71°10W 94 B1
La Seu d'Urgell Spain 42°22N 1°23E 21 A6
La Seyne-sur-Mer France 43°7N 5°52E 20 E6
La Soufrière St. Vincent 13°20N 61°11W 89 D7
La Spézia Italy 44°7N 9°50E 20 D8
La Tagua Colombia 0°3N 74°40W 92 C4
La Tortuga Venezuela 11°0N 65°22W 89 D6
La Trinité Martinique 14°43N 60°58W 88 c
La Tuque Canada 47°30N 72°50W 72 C5
La Unión Chile 40°10S 73°0W 96 E2
La Unión El Salv. 13°20N 87°50W 88 D2
La Unión Mexico 17°58N 101°49W 86 D4
La Urbana Venezuela 7°8N 66°56W 92 B5
La Vache Pt.
  Trin. & Tob. 10°47N 61°28W 93 K15
La Vall d'Uixó Spain 39°49N 0°15W 21 C5
La Vega Dom. Rep. 19°20N 70°30W 89 C5
La Vela de Coro
  Venezuela 11°27N 69°34W 92 A5
La Venta Mexico 18°5N 94°3W 87 D6
La Vergne U.S.A. 36°1N 86°35W 85 C11
La Villa Joiosa = Villajoyosa
  Spain 38°30N 0°12W 21 C5
Laascaanood = Las Anod
  Somali Rep. 8°26N 47°19E 47 F4
Labasa Fiji 16°30S 179°27E 59 a
Labdah = Leptis Magna
  Libya 32°40N 14°12E 51 B8
Labe = Elbe → Europe 53°50N 9°0E 16 B5
Labé Guinea 11°24N 12°16W 50 F3
Laberge, L. Canada 61°11N 135°12W 70 A1
Labinsk Russia 44°40N 40°48E 19 F7
Labis Malaysia 2°22N 103°2E 39 L4
Laborie St. Lucia 13°45N 61°2W 89 f
Laboulaye Argentina 34°10S 63°30W 94 C3
Labrador Canada 53°20N 61°0W 73 B7
Labrador City Canada 52°57N 66°55W 73 B6
Labrador Sea Atl. Oc. 57°0N 54°0W 69 F21
Lábrea Brazil 7°15S 64°51W 92 E6
Labuan Malaysia 5°20N 115°14E 36 C5
Labuan, Pulau Malaysia 5°21N 115°13E 36 C5
Labuha Indonesia 0°30S 127°30E 37 E7
Labuhan Indonesia 6°22S 105°50E 37 G11
Labuhanbajo Indonesia 8°28S 119°54E 37 F6
Labuhanbilik Indonesia 2°31N 100°10E 39 L3
Labuk, Telok Malaysia 6°10N 117°50E 36 C5
Labyrinth, L. Australia 30°40S 135°11E 63 E2
Labytnangi Russia 66°39N 66°21E 18 A12
Lac-Bouchette Canada 48°16N 72°11W 73 C5
Lac Édouard Canada 47°40N 72°16W 72 C5
Lac La Biche Canada 54°45N 111°58W 70 C6
Lac la Martre = Wha Ti
  Canada 63°8N 117°16W 68 B8
Lac La Ronge △ Canada 55°9N 104°41W 71 B7
Lac-Mégantic Canada 45°35N 70°53W 73 C5
Lac Thien Vietnam 12°25N 108°11E 38 F7
Lacanau France 44°58N 1°5W 20 D3
Lacantún → Mexico 16°36N 90°39W 87 D6
Laccadive Is. = Lakshadweep Is.
  India 10°0N 72°30E 3 D13
Lacepede B. Australia 36°40S 139°40E 63 F2
Lacepede Is. Australia 16°55S 122°0E 60 C3
Lacerdónia Mozam. 18°3S 35°35E 55 F4
Lacey U.S.A. 47°7N 122°49W 78 C4
Lachania Greece 35°58N 27°54E 25 D9
Lachhmangarh India 27°50N 75°4E 42 F6
Lachi Pakistan 33°25N 71°20E 42 C4
Lachine Canada 45°26N 73°42W 72 C5
Lachlan → Australia 34°22S 143°55E 63 E3
Lachute Canada 45°39N 74°21W 72 C5
Lackagh Hills Ireland 54°16N 8°10W 10 B3
Lackawanna U.S.A. 42°50N 78°50W 82 D6
Lackawaxen U.S.A. 41°29N 74°59W 83 E10
Lacolle Canada 45°5N 73°22W 83 A11
Lacombe Canada 52°30N 113°44W 70 C6
Lacona U.S.A. 43°39N 76°10W 83 C8
Laconia U.S.A. 43°32N 71°28W 83 C13
Ladakh Ra. India 34°0N 78°0E 43 C8
Ladismith S. Africa 33°28S 21°15E 56 E3
Lādīz Iran 28°55N 61°15E 45 D9
Ladnun India 27°38N 74°25E 42 F6
Ladoga, L. = Ladozhskoye Ozero
  Russia 61°15N 30°30E 8 F24
Ladozhskoye Ozero
  Russia 61°15N 30°30E 8 F24
Lady Elliott I. Australia 24°7S 152°42E 62 C5
Lady Grey S. Africa 30°43S 27°13E 56 E4
Ladybrand S. Africa 29°9S 27°29E 56 D4

Ladysmith Canada 49°0N 123°49W 78 B3
Ladysmith S. Africa 28°32S 29°46E 57 D4
Ladysmith U.S.A. 45°28N 91°12W 80 C8
Lae Papua N. G. 6°40S 147°2E 58 B7
Laem Hin Khom Thailand 9°25N 99°56E 39 b
Laem Khat Thailand 8°6N 98°26E 39 a
Laem Nga Thailand 7°55N 98°27E 39 a
Laem Ngop Thailand 12°10N 102°26E 39 F4
Laem Phan Wa Thailand 7°47N 98°25E 39 a
Laem Pho Thailand 6°55N 101°19E 39 J3
Laem Phrom Thep Thailand 7°45N 98°19E 39 a
Laem Riang Thailand 8°7N 98°22E 39 a
Laem Sam Rong Thailand 9°35N 100°4E 39 b
Laem Son Thailand 7°59N 98°16E 39 a
Laem Yamu Thailand 7°59N 98°26E 39 a
Laerma Greece 36°9N 27°57E 25 C9
Læsø Denmark 57°15N 11°5E 9 H14
Lafayette Ind., U.S.A. 40°25N 86°54W 80 E10
Lafayette La., U.S.A. 30°14N 92°1W 84 F8
Lafayette Tenn., U.S.A. 36°31N 86°2W 85 C11
Laferte → Canada 61°53N 117°44W 70 A5
Lafia Nigeria 8°30N 8°34E 50 G7
Lafleche Canada 49°45N 106°40W 71 D7
Lagan → U.K. 54°36N 5°55W 10 B6
Lagarfljót → Iceland 65°40N 14°18W 8 D6
Lagdo, L. de Cameroon 8°40N 14°0E 51 G8
Lågen → Oppland, Norway 61°8N 10°25E 8 F14
Lågen → Vestfold, Norway 59°3N 10°3E 9 G14
Lages Brazil 27°48S 50°20W 95 B5
Laghouat Algeria 33°50N 2°59E 50 B6
Lagoa do Peixe △ Brazil 31°12S 50°55W 95 C5
Lagoa Vermelha Brazil 28°13S 51°32W 95 B5
Lagonoy G. Phil. 13°35N 123°50E 37 B6
Lagos Nigeria 6°25N 3°27E 50 G6
Lagos Portugal 37°5N 8°41W 21 D1
Lagos de Moreno
  Mexico 21°21N 101°55W 86 C4
Lagrange = Bidyadanga
  Australia 18°45S 121°43E 60 C3
Lagrange B. Australia 18°38S 121°42E 60 C3
Laguna Brazil 28°30S 48°50W 95 B6
Laguna U.S.A. 35°2N 107°25W 77 J10
Laguna, Sa. de la
  Mexico 23°35N 109°55W 86 C3
Laguna Beach U.S.A. 33°33N 117°47W 79 M9
Laguna de la Restinga △
  Venezuela 10°58N 64°0W 89 D6
Laguna de Lachuá △
  Guatemala 15°55N 90°40W 88 C1
Laguna del Laja △ Chile 37°25S 71°20W 94 D1
Laguna del Tigre △
  Guatemala 17°32N 90°56W 88 C1
Laguna Limpia
  Argentina 26°32S 59°45W 94 B4
Lagunas Chile 21°0S 69°45W 94 A2
Lagunas Peru 5°10S 75°35W 92 E3
Lagunas de Chacahua △
  Mexico 16°0N 97°43W 87 D5
Lagunas de Montebello △
  Mexico 16°4N 91°42W 87 D6
Lahad Datu Malaysia 5°0N 118°20E 37 D5
Lahad Datu, Telok
  Malaysia 4°50N 118°20E 37 D5
Lahan Sai Thailand 14°25N 102°52E 38 E4
Lahanam Laos 16°16N 105°16E 38 D5
Lahar India 26°12N 78°57E 43 F8
Laharpur India 27°43N 80°56E 43 F9
Lahat Indonesia 3°45S 103°30E 36 E2
Lahewa Indonesia 1°22N 97°12E 36 D1
Lāhījān Iran 37°10N 50°6E 45 B6
Lahn → Germany 50°19N 7°37E 16 C4
Laholm Sweden 56°30N 13°2E 9 H15
Lahore Pakistan 31°32N 74°22E 42 D6
Lahri Pakistan 29°11N 68°13E 42 E3
Lahrūd Iran 38°30N 47°52E 44 B5
Lahti Finland 60°58N 25°40E 8 F21
Lahtis = Lahti Finland 60°58N 25°40E 8 F21
Laï Chad 9°25N 16°18E 51 G9
Lai Chau Vietnam 22°5N 103°3E 38 A4
Laila = Layla Si. Arabia 22°10N 46°40E 47 C4
Laingsburg S. Africa 33°9S 20°52E 56 E3
Lainioälven → Sweden 67°35N 22°40E 8 C20
Lairg U.K. 58°2N 4°24W 11 C4
Laisamis Kenya 1°36N 37°48E 54 B4
Laishui China 39°23N 115°45E 34 E8
Laiwu China 36°15N 117°40E 35 F9
Laixi China 36°50N 120°31E 35 F11
Laiyang China 36°59N 120°45E 35 F11
Laiyuan China 39°20N 114°40E 34 E8
Laizhou China 37°8N 119°57E 35 F10
Laizhou Wan China 37°30N 119°30E 35 F10
Laja → Mexico 20°55N 100°46W 86 C4
Lajamanu Australia 18°23S 130°38E 60 C5
Lak Sao Laos 18°11N 104°59E 38 C5
Lakaband Pakistan 31°2N 69°15E 42 D3
Lake U.S.A. 44°33N 110°24W 76 D8
Lake Alpine U.S.A. 38°29N 120°0W 78 G7
Lake Andes U.S.A. 43°9N 98°32W 80 D4
Lake Bindegolly △
  Australia 28°0S 144°0E 63 D3
Lake Cargelligo
  Australia 33°15S 146°22E 63 E4
Lake Charles U.S.A. 30°14N 93°13W 84 F8
Lake City Colo., U.S.A. 38°2N 107°19W 76 G10
Lake City Fla., U.S.A. 30°11N 82°38W 85 F13
Lake City Mich., U.S.A. 44°20N 85°13W 81 C11
Lake City Minn., U.S.A. 44°27N 92°16W 80 C7
Lake City Pa., U.S.A. 42°2N 80°21W 82 D4
Lake City S.C., U.S.A. 33°52N 79°45W 85 E15
Lake Cowichan Canada 48°49N 124°3W 70 D4
Lake District △ U.K. 54°30N 3°21W 12 C4
Lake Elsinore U.S.A. 33°40N 117°21W 79 M9
Lake Eyre △ Australia 28°40S 137°31E 63 D2
Lake Gairdner △
  Australia 31°41S 135°51E 63 E2
Lake George U.S.A. 43°26N 73°43W 83 C11
Lake Grace Australia 33°7S 118°28E 61 F2
Lake Gregory ⊙
  Australia 20°12S 127°27E 60 D4

Lake Harbour = Kimmirut
  Canada 62°50N 69°50W 69 E18
Lake Havasu City
  U.S.A. 34°27N 114°22W 79 L12
Lake Hughes U.S.A. 34°41N 118°26W 79 L8
Lake Isabella U.S.A. 35°38N 118°28W 79 K8
Lake Jackson U.S.A. 29°3N 95°27W 84 G7
Lake King Australia 33°5S 119°45E 61 F2
Lake Lenore Canada 52°24N 104°59W 71 C8
Lake Louise Canada 51°30N 116°10W 70 C5
Lake Mackay ⊙
  Australia 21°48S 129°46E 60 D4
Lake Mburo △ Uganda 0°33S 30°56E 54 C3
Lake Mead △ U.S.A. 36°30N 114°22W 79 K12
Lake Meredith △
  U.S.A. 35°50N 101°50W 84 D4
Lake Mills U.S.A. 43°25N 93°32W 80 D7
Lake Nakuru △ Kenya 0°21S 36°8E 54 C4
Lake Placid U.S.A. 44°17N 73°59W 83 B11
Lake Pleasant U.S.A. 43°28N 74°25W 83 C10
Lake Providence U.S.A. 32°48N 91°10W 84 E9
Lake Roosevelt △
  U.S.A. 48°5N 118°14W 76 B4
Lake St. Peter Canada 45°18N 78°2W 82 A6
Lake Superior △ Canada 47°45N 84°45W 72 C3
Lake Torrens △
  Australia 30°55S 137°40E 63 E2
Lake Village U.S.A. 33°20N 91°17W 84 E9
Lake Wales U.S.A. 27°54N 81°35W 85 H14
Lake Worth U.S.A. 26°37N 80°3W 85 H14
Lakeba Fiji 18°13S 178°47W 59 a
Lakeba Passage Fiji 18°0S 178°45W 59 a
Lakefield Canada 44°25N 78°16W 82 B6
Lakefield △ Australia 15°24S 144°6E 62 B3
Lakehurst U.S.A. 40°1N 74°19W 83 F10
Lakeland Australia 15°49S 144°57E 62 B3
Lakeland U.S.A. 28°3N 81°57W 85 G14
Lakemba = Lakeba Fiji 18°13S 178°47W 59 a
Lakeport Calif., U.S.A. 39°3N 122°55W 78 F4
Lakeport Mich., U.S.A. 43°7N 82°30W 82 C2
Lakes Entrance Australia 37°50S 148°0E 63 F4
Lakeside Calif., U.S.A. 32°52N 116°55W 79 N10
Lakeside Nebr., U.S.A. 42°3N 102°26W 80 D2
Lakeview U.S.A. 42°11N 120°21W 76 E3
Lakeville U.S.A. 44°39N 93°14W 80 C7
Lakewood Colo., U.S.A. 39°42N 105°4W 76 G11
Lakewood N.J., U.S.A. 40°6N 74°13W 83 F10
Lakewood N.Y., U.S.A. 42°6N 79°19W 82 D5
Lakewood Ohio, U.S.A. 41°28N 81°47W 82 E3
Lakewood Wash.,
  U.S.A. 47°11N 122°32W 78 C4
Lakha India 26°9N 70°54E 42 F4
Lakhimpur India 27°57N 80°46E 43 F9
Lakhisarai India 25°11N 86°5E 43 G12
Lakhnadon India 22°36N 79°36E 43 H8
Lakhnau = Lucknow
  India 26°50N 81°0E 43 F9
Lakhonpheng Laos 15°54N 105°34E 38 E5
Lakhpat India 23°48N 68°47E 42 H3
Lakin U.S.A. 37°57N 101°15W 80 G3
Lakitusaki → Canada 54°21N 82°25W 72 B3
Lakki Greece 35°24N 23°57E 25 D5
Lakki Pakistan 32°36N 70°55E 42 C4
Lakonikos Kolpos
  Greece 36°40N 22°40E 23 F10
Lakor Indonesia 8°15S 128°17E 37 F7
Lakota Ivory C. 5°50N 5°30W 50 G4
Lakota U.S.A. 48°2N 98°21W 80 A4
Laksar India 29°46N 78°3E 42 E8
Laksefjorden Norway 70°45N 26°50E 8 A22
Lakselv Norway 70°2N 25°0E 8 A21
Lakshadweep Is. India 10°0N 72°30E 3 D13
Lakshmanpur India 22°58N 83°3E 43 H10
Lakshmikantapur India 22°5N 88°20E 43 H13
Lala Musa Pakistan 32°40N 73°57E 42 C5
Lalaghat India 24°30N 92°40E 41 E8
Lalago Tanzania 3°28S 33°58E 54 C3
Lalapanzi Zimbabwe 19°20S 30°15E 55 F3
L'Albufera Spain 39°20N 0°27W 21 C5
Lalganj India 25°52N 85°13E 43 G11
Lalgola India 24°25N 88°15E 43 G13
Lalin China 45°12N 127°0E 35 B14
Lalín Spain 42°40N 8°5W 21 A1
Lalin He → China 45°32N 125°40E 35 B13
Lalitapur Nepal 27°40N 85°20E 43 F11
Lalitpur India 24°42N 78°28E 43 G8
Lalkua India 29°5N 79°31E 43 E8
Lalsot India 26°34N 76°20E 42 F7
Lam Pao Res. Thailand 16°50N 103°15E 38 D4
Lama Kara Togo 9°30N 1°15E 50 G6
Lamae Thailand 9°55S 99°53E 39 H2
Lamaing Burma 15°25N 97°53E 38 E1
Lamar Colo., U.S.A. 38°5N 102°37W 76 G12
Lamar Mo., U.S.A. 37°30N 94°16W 80 G6
Lamas Peru 6°28S 76°31W 92 E3
Lamayuru India 34°25N 76°56E 43 B7
Lambaréné Gabon 0°41S 10°12E 52 E2
Lambasa = Labasa Fiji 16°30S 179°27E 59 a
Lambay I. Ireland 53°29N 6°1W 10 C6
Lambert's Bay S. Africa 32°5S 18°17E 56 E2
Lambi Kyun Burma 10°50N 98°20E 39 G2
Lambomakondro
  Madag. 22°41S 44°44E 57 C7
Lame Deer U.S.A. 45°37N 106°40W 76 D10
Lamego Portugal 41°5N 7°52W 21 B2
Lamèque Canada 47°45N 64°38W 73 C7
Lameroo Australia 35°19S 140°33E 63 F3
Lamesa U.S.A. 32°44N 101°58W 84 E4
Lamia Greece 38°55N 22°26E 23 E10
Lamington △ Australia 28°13S 153°12E 63 D5
Lamma I. China 22°12N 114°7E 33 G11
Lamoille → U.S.A. 44°38N 73°13W 83 B11
Lamon B. Phil. 14°30N 122°20E 37 B6
Lamont Canada 53°46N 112°50W 70 C6
Lamont Calif., U.S.A. 35°15N 118°55W 79 K8
Lamont Wyo., U.S.A. 42°13N 107°29W 76 E10

Lampa Peru 15°22S 70°22W 92 G4
Lampang Thailand 18°16N 99°32E 38 C2
Lampasas U.S.A. 31°4N 98°11W 84 F5
Lampazos de Naranjo
  Mexico 27°1N 100°31W 86 B4
Lampedusa Medit. S. 35°36N 12°40E 22 G5
Lampeter U.K. 52°7N 4°4W 13 E3
Lampione Medit. S. 35°33N 12°20E 22 G5
Lampman Canada 49°25N 102°50W 71 D8
Lampung □ Indonesia 5°30S 104°30E 36 F2
Lamta India 22°8N 80°7E 43 H9
Lamu Kenya 2°16S 40°55E 54 C5
Lamy U.S.A. 35°29N 105°53W 77 J11
Lan Xian China 38°15N 111°35E 34 E6
Lana'i U.S.A. 20°50N 156°55W 75 L8
Lāna'i China 34°27N 79°32E 43 B8
Lanak La China 34°27N 79°32E 43 B8
Lanak'o Shank'ou = Lanak La
  China 34°27N 79°32E 43 B8
Lanark Canada 45°1N 76°22W 83 A8
Lanark U.K. 54°3N 2°48W 12 C5
Lancashire □ U.K. 53°50N 2°48W 12 D5
Lancaster Canada 45°10N 74°30W 83 A10
Lancaster U.K. 54°3N 2°48W 12 C5
Lancaster Calif., U.S.A. 34°42N 118°8W 79 L8
Lancaster Ky., U.S.A. 37°37N 84°35W 81 G11
Lancaster N.H., U.S.A. 44°29N 71°34W 83 B13
Lancaster Ohio, U.S.A. 39°43N 82°36W 81 F12
Lancaster Pa., U.S.A. 40°2N 76°19W 83 F8
Lancaster S.C., U.S.A. 34°43N 80°46W 85 D14
Lancaster Wis., U.S.A. 42°51N 90°43W 80 D8
Lancaster Sd. Canada 74°13N 84°0W 69 C15
Lancelin Australia 31°0S 115°18E 61 F2
Lanchow = Lanzhou
  China 36°1N 103°52E 34 F2
Lanciano Italy 42°14N 14°23E 22 C6
Lancun China 36°25N 120°10E 35 F11
Land Between the Lakes △
  U.S.A. 36°25N 88°0W 85 C11
Landeck Austria 47°9N 10°34E 16 E6
Lander U.S.A. 42°50N 108°44W 76 E9
Lander → Australia 22°0S 132°0E 60 D5
Landes France 44°0N 1°0W 20 D3
Landi Kotal Pakistan 34°7N 71°6E 42 B4
Landisburg U.S.A. 40°21N 77°19W 83 F7
Land's End U.K. 50°4N 5°44W 13 G2
Landmannalaugar Iceland 63°59N 19°4W 8 E4
Landsborough Cr. →
  Australia 22°28S 144°35E 62 C3
Landshut Germany 48°34N 12°8E 16 D7
Lanesboro U.S.A. 41°57N 75°34W 83 E9
Lanett U.S.A. 32°52N 85°12W 85 E12
Lang Shan China 41°0N 106°30E 34 D4
Lang Son Vietnam 21°52N 106°42E 38 B6
Lang Suan Thailand 9°57N 99°4E 39 H2
La'nga Co China 30°45N 81°15E 43 D9
Langar Iran 35°23N 60°25E 45 C9
Langara I. Canada 54°14N 133°1W 70 C2
Langarūd Iran 37°11N 50°8E 45 B6
Langdon U.S.A. 48°45N 98°22W 80 A4
Langeberg S. Africa 33°55S 21°0E 56 E3
Langeberge S. Africa 28°15S 22°33E 56 D3
Langeland Denmark 54°56N 10°48E 9 J14
Langenburg Canada 50°51N 101°43W 71 C8
Langholm U.K. 55°9N 3°0W 11 F5
Langjökull Iceland 64°39N 20°12W 8 D3
Langkawi, Pulau
  Malaysia 6°25N 99°45E 39 J2
Langklip S. Africa 28°12S 20°20E 56 D3
Langkon Malaysia 6°30N 116°40E 36 C5
Langley Canada 49°7N 122°39W 78 A4
Langøya Norway 68°45N 14°50E 8 B16
Langreo Spain 43°18N 5°40W 21 A3
Langres France 47°52N 5°20E 20 C6
Langres, Plateau de France 47°45N 5°3E 20 C6
Langsa Indonesia 4°30N 97°57E 36 D1
Langtang △ Nepal 28°12N 85°30E 43 E11
Langtry U.S.A. 29°49N 101°34W 84 G4
Langu Thailand 6°53N 99°47E 39 J2
Languedoc France 43°58N 3°55E 20 E5
Langwang China 22°38N 113°27E 33 F9
Langxiangzhen China 39°43N 116°8E 34 E9
Lanigan Canada 51°51N 105°2W 71 C7
Lankao China 34°48N 114°50E 34 G8
Länkäran Azerbaijan 38°48N 48°52E 45 B6
Lannion France 48°46N 3°29W 20 B2
L'Annonciation Canada 46°25N 74°55W 72 C5
Lansdale U.S.A. 40°14N 75°17W 83 F9
Lansdowne Australia 31°48S 152°30E 63 E5
Lansdowne Canada 44°24N 76°1W 83 B8
Lansdowne India 29°50N 78°41E 43 E8
Lansdowne House = Neskantaga
  Canada 52°14N 87°53W 72 B2
L'Anse U.S.A. 46°45N 88°27W 80 B9
L'Anse au Loup Canada 51°32N 56°50W 73 B8
L'Anse aux Meadows
  Canada 51°36N 55°32W 73 B8
L'Anse la Raye St. Lucia 13°55N 61°3W 89 f
Lansford U.S.A. 40°50N 75°53W 83 F9
Lansing U.S.A. 42°44N 84°33W 81 D11
Lantau I. China 22°15N 113°56E 33 G10
Lantian China 34°11N 109°20E 34 G5
Lanús Argentina 34°42S 58°23W 94 C4
Lanusei Italy 39°52N 9°34E 22 E3
Lanzarote Canary Is. 29°0N 13°40W 24 F6
Lanzarote ✈ (ACE)
  Canary Is. 28°57N 13°40W 24 F6
Lanzhou China 36°1N 103°52E 34 F2
Lao Bao Laos 16°35N 106°30E 38 D6
Lao Cai Vietnam 22°30N 103°57E 38 A4
Lao He → China 43°25N 120°35E 35 C11
Laoag Phil. 18°7N 120°34E 37 A6
Laoang Phil. 12°32N 125°8E 37 B7
Laoha He → China 43°25N 120°35E 35 C11
Laois □ Ireland 52°57N 7°36W 10 D4
Laon France 49°33N 3°35E 20 B5
Laona U.S.A. 45°34N 88°40W 80 C9

Laos ■ Asia 17°45N 105°0E 38 D5
Lapa Brazil 25°46S 49°44W 95 B6
Lapeer U.S.A. 43°3N 83°19W 81 D12
Lapithos Cyprus 35°21N 33°11E 25 D12
Lapland = Lappland Europe 68°7N 24°0E 8 B21
LaPorte Ind., U.S.A. 41°36N 86°43W 80 E10
Laporte Pa., U.S.A. 41°25N 76°30W 83 E8
Lappeenranta Finland 61°3N 28°12E 8 F23
Lappland Europe 68°7N 24°0E 8 B21
Lappo = Lapua Finland 62°58N 23°0E 8 E20
Laprida Argentina 37°34S 60°45W 94 D3
Lâpseki Turkey 40°20N 26°41E 23 D12
Laptev Sea Russia 76°0N 125°0E 29 B13
Lapua Finland 62°58N 23°0E 8 E20
L'Àquila Italy 42°22N 13°22E 22 C5
Lār Iran 27°40N 54°14E 45 E7
Laramie U.S.A. 41°19N 105°35W 76 F11
Laramie Mts. U.S.A. 42°0N 105°30W 76 F11
Laranjeiras do Sul Brazil 25°23S 52°23W 95 B5
Larantuka Indonesia 8°21S 122°55E 37 F6
Larat Indonesia 7°0S 132°0E 37 F8
Larde Mozam. 16°28S 39°43E 55 F4
Larder Lake Canada 48°5N 79°40W 72 C4
Lardos Greece 36°6N 28°1E 25 C10
Lardos, Akra = Lindos, Akra Greece 36°4N 28°10E 25 C10
Lardos, Ormos Greece 36°4N 28°2E 25 C10
Lare Kenya 0°20N 37°56E 54 C4
Laredo U.S.A. 27°30N 99°30W 84 H5
Laredo Sd. Canada 52°30N 128°53W 70 C3
Largo U.S.A. 27°54N 82°47W 85 H13
Largs U.K. 55°47N 4°52W 11 F4
Lariang Indonesia 1°26S 119°17E 37 E5
Larimore U.S.A. 47°54N 97°38W 80 B5
Larisa Greece 39°36N 22°27E 23 E10
Larkana Pakistan 27°32N 68°18E 42 F3
Larnaca Cyprus 34°55N 33°38E 25 E12
Larnaca Bay Cyprus 34°53N 33°45E 25 E12
Larne U.K. 54°51N 5°51W 10 B6
Larned U.S.A. 38°11N 99°6W 80 F4
Larose U.S.A. 29°34N 90°23W 85 G9
Larrimah Australia 15°35S 133°12E 60 C5
Larsen Ice Shelf Antarctica 67°0S 62°0W 5 C17
Larvik Norway 59°4N 10°2E 9 G14
Las Animas U.S.A. 38°4N 103°13W 76 G12
Las Anod Somali Rep. 8°26N 47°19E 47 F4
Las Brenãs Argentina 27°5S 61°7W 94 B3
Las Cañadas del Teide △ Canary Is. 28°15N 16°37W 24 F3
Las Cejas Argentina 26°53S 64°44W 96 B4
Las Chimeneas Mexico 32°8N 116°5W 79 N10
Las Cruces U.S.A. 32°19N 106°47W 77 K10
Las Flores Argentina 36°10S 59°7W 94 D4
Las Heras Argentina 32°51S 68°49W 94 C2
Las Lajas Argentina 38°30S 70°25W 96 D2
Las Lomitas Argentina 24°43S 60°35W 94 A3
Las Palmas Argentina 27°8S 58°45W 94 B4
Las Palmas Canary Is. 28°7N 15°26W 24 F4
Las Palmas → Mexico 32°31N 116°58W 79 N10
Las Palmas ✕ (LPA) Canary Is. 27°55N 15°25W 24 G4
Las Piedras Uruguay 34°44S 56°14W 95 C4
Las Pipinas Argentina 35°30S 57°19W 94 D4
Las Plumas Argentina 43°40S 67°15W 96 E3
Las Rosas Argentina 32°30S 61°35W 94 C3
Las Tablas Panama 7°49N 80°14W 88 E3
Las Toscas Argentina 28°21S 59°18W 94 B4
Las Truchas Mexico 17°57N 102°13W 86 D4
Las Tunas Cuba 20°58N 76°59W 88 B4
Las Varillas Argentina 31°50S 62°50W 94 C3
Las Vegas N. Mex., U.S.A. 35°36N 105°13W 77 J11
Las Vegas Nev., U.S.A. 36°10N 115°8W 79 J11
Las Vegas McCarran Int. ✕ (LAS) U.S.A. 36°5N 115°9W 79 J11
Lascano Uruguay 33°35S 54°12W 95 C5
Lash-e Joveyn Afghan. 31°45N 61°30E 40 D2
Lashburn Canada 53°10N 109°40W 71 C7
Lashio Burma 22°56N 97°45E 41 H20
Lashkar India 26°10N 78°10E 42 F8
Lasithi Greece 35°11N 25°31E 25 D7
Lasithi □ Greece 35°5N 25°50E 25 D7
Lāsjerd Iran 35°24N 53°4E 45 C7
Lassen Pk. U.S.A. 40°29N 121°30W 76 F3
Lassen Volcanic △ U.S.A. 40°30N 121°20W 76 F3
Last Mountain L. Canada 51°5N 105°14W 71 C7
Lastchance Cr. → U.S.A. 40°2N 121°15W 78 E5
Lastoursville Gabon 0°55S 12°38E 52 E2
Lastovo Croatia 42°46N 16°55E 22 C7
Lat Yao Thailand 15°45N 99°48E 38 E2
Latacunga Ecuador 0°50S 78°35W 92 D3
Latakia = Al Lādhiqīyah Syria 35°30N 35°45E 44 C2
Latchford Canada 47°20N 79°50W 72 C4
Late Tonga 18°48S 174°39W 59 c
Latehar India 23°45N 84°30E 43 H11
Latham Australia 29°44S 116°20E 61 E2
Lathi India 27°43N 71°23E 42 F4
Lathrop Wells U.S.A. 36°39N 116°24W 79 J10
Latina Italy 41°28N 12°52E 22 D5
Latium = Lazio □ Italy 42°10N 12°30E 22 C5
Laton U.S.A. 36°26N 119°41W 78 J7
Latouche Treville, C. Australia 18°27S 121°49E 60 C3
Latrobe Australia 41°14S 146°30E 63 G4
Latrobe U.S.A. 40°19N 79°23W 82 F5
Latvia ■ Europe 56°50N 24°0E 9 H21
Lau Fau Shan China 22°28N 113°59E 33 G10
Lau Group Fiji 17°0S 178°30W 59 a
Lauchhammer Germany 51°29N 13°47E 16 C7
Lauge Koch Kyst Greenland 75°45N 57°45W 69 B20
Laughlin U.S.A. 35°10N 114°34W 77 J6
Laukaa Finland 62°24N 25°56E 8 E21
Launceston Australia 41°24S 147°8E 63 G4
Launceston U.K. 50°38N 4°22W 13 G3
Laune → Ireland 52°7N 9°47W 10 D2
Launglon Bok Burma 13°50N 97°54E 38 F1
Laura Australia 15°32S 144°32E 62 B3
Laurel Miss., U.S.A. 31°41N 89°8W 85 F10
Laurel Mont., U.S.A. 45°40N 108°46W 76 D9
Laurel Hill U.S.A. 40°14N 79°6W 82 F5
Laurencekirk U.K. 56°50N 2°28W 11 E6
Laurens U.S.A. 34°30N 82°1W 85 D13
Laurentian Plateau Canada 52°0N 70°0W 73 B6
Lauria Italy 40°2N 15°50E 22 E6
Laurie L. Canada 56°35N 101°57W 71 B8
Laurinburg U.S.A. 34°47N 79°28W 85 D15
Laurium U.S.A. 47°14N 88°27W 80 B9
Lausanne Switz. 46°32N 6°38E 20 C7
Laut Indonesia 4°45N 108°0E 36 D3
Laut, Pulau Indonesia 3°40S 116°10E 36 E5
Laut Kecil, Kepulauan Indonesia 4°45S 115°40E 36 E5
Lautoka Fiji 17°37S 177°27E 59 a
Lava Beds ⌂ U.S.A. 41°40N 121°30W 76 F3
Lavagh More Ireland 54°46N 8°6W 10 B3
Laval France 48°4N 0°48W 20 B3
Laval-des-Rapides Canada 45°33N 73°42W 72 C5
Lavalle Argentina 28°15S 65°15W 94 B2
Lāvān Iran 26°48N 53°22E 45 E7
Lavant Canada 45°3N 76°42W 83 A8
Lāvar Meydān Iran 30°20N 54°30E 45 D7
Laverton Australia 28°44S 122°29E 61 E3
Lavras Brazil 21°20S 45°0W 95 A7
Lavrio Greece 37°40N 24°4E 23 F11
Lavris Greece 35°25N 24°40E 25 D6
Lavumisa Swaziland 27°20S 31°55E 57 D5
Lavushi Manda △ Zambia 12°46S 31°0E 55 E3
Lawaki Fiji 17°40S 178°35E 59 a
Lawas Malaysia 4°55N 115°25E 36 D5
Lawele Indonesia 5°13S 122°57E 37 F6
Lawn Hill = Boodjamulla △ Australia 18°15S 138°6E 62 B2
Lawqah Si. Arabia 29°49N 42°45E 44 D4
Lawrence N.Z. 45°55S 169°41E 59 F2
Lawrence Ind., U.S.A. 39°50N 86°2W 80 F10
Lawrence Kans., U.S.A. 38°58N 95°14W 80 F6
Lawrence Mass., U.S.A. 42°43N 71°10W 83 D13
Lawrenceburg Ind., U.S.A. 39°6N 84°52W 81 F11
Lawrenceburg Tenn., U.S.A. 35°14N 87°20W 85 D11
Lawrenceville Ga., U.S.A. 33°57N 83°59W 85 E13
Lawrenceville Pa., U.S.A. 41°59N 77°8W 82 E7
Laws U.S.A. 37°24N 118°20W 78 H8
Lawton U.S.A. 34°37N 98°25W 84 D5
Lawu Indonesia 7°40S 111°13E 37 G14
Laxford, L. U.K. 58°24N 5°6W 11 C3
Layla Si. Arabia 22°10N 46°40E 47 C4
Laylān Iraq 35°18N 44°31E 44 C5
Laysan I. U.S.A. 25°50N 171°50W 75 K5
Layton U.S.A. 41°4N 111°58W 76 F8
Laytonville U.S.A. 39°41N 123°29W 76 G2
Lazarev Russia 52°13N 141°30E 29 D15
Lazarev Sea S. Ocean 67°30S 3°0W 5 C2
Lazarivo Madag. 23°54S 44°59E 57 C8
Lázaro Cárdenas Mexico 17°55N 102°11W 86 D4
Lazio □ Italy 42°10N 12°30E 22 C5
Lazo Russia 43°25N 133°55E 30 C6
Le Bic Canada 48°20N 68°41W 73 C6
Le Creusot France 46°48N 4°24E 20 C6
Le François Martinique 14°38N 60°57W 88 c
Le Gosier Guadeloupe 16°14N 61°29W 88 b
Le Gris Gris Mauritius 20°31S 57°32E 53 d
Le Havre France 49°30N 0°5E 20 B4
Le Lamentin Martinique 14°35N 61°2W 88 c
Le Mans France 48°0N 0°10E 20 C4
Le Marin Martinique 14°27N 60°55W 88 c
Le Mars U.S.A. 42°47N 96°10W 80 D5
Le Mont-St-Michel France 48°40N 1°30W 20 B3
Le Moule Guadeloupe 16°20N 61°22W 88 b
Le Moyne, L. Canada 56°45N 68°47W 73 A6
Le Port Réunion 20°56S 55°18E 53 c
Le Prêcheur Martinique 14°50N 61°12W 88 c
Le Puy-en-Velay France 45°3N 3°52E 20 D5
Le Raysville U.S.A. 41°50N 76°10W 83 E8
Le Robert Martinique 14°40N 60°56W 88 c
Le Roy U.S.A. 42°58N 77°59W 82 D7
Le St-Esprit Martinique 14°34N 60°56W 88 c
Le Sueur U.S.A. 44°28N 93°55W 80 C7
Le Tampon Réunion 21°16S 55°32E 53 c
Le Thuy Vietnam 17°14N 106°49E 38 D6
Le Touquet-Paris-Plage France 50°30N 1°36E 20 A4
Le Tréport France 50°3N 1°20E 20 A4
Le Verdon-sur-Mer France 45°33N 1°4W 20 D3
Lea → U.K. 51°31N 0°1E 13 F8
Leach Cambodia 12°21N 103°46E 39 F4
Lead U.S.A. 44°21N 103°46W 80 C2
Leader Canada 50°50N 109°30W 71 C7
Leadville U.S.A. 39°15N 106°18W 76 G10
Leaf → U.S.A. 30°59N 88°44W 85 F10
Leaf Rapids Canada 56°30N 99°59W 71 B9
Leamington Canada 42°3N 82°36W 82 D2
Leamington U.S.A. 39°32N 112°17W 76 G7
Leamington Spa = Royal Leamington Spa U.K. 52°18N 1°31W 13 E6
Leandro Norte Alem Argentina 27°34S 55°15W 95 B4
Leane, L. Ireland 52°2N 9°32W 10 D2
Learmonth Australia 22°13S 114°10E 60 D1
Leask Canada 53°5N 106°45W 71 C7
Leatherhead U.K. 51°18N 0°20W 13 F7
Leavenworth Kans., U.S.A. 39°19N 94°55W 80 F6
Leavenworth Wash., U.S.A. 47°36N 120°40W 76 C3
Leawood U.S.A. 38°58N 94°37W 80 F6
Lebak Phil. 6°32N 124°5E 37 C6
Lebam U.S.A. 46°34N 123°33W 78 D3
Lebanon Ind., U.S.A. 40°3N 86°28W 80 E10
Lebanon Kans., U.S.A. 39°49N 98°33W 80 F4
Lebanon Ky., U.S.A. 37°34N 85°15W 81 G11
Lebanon Mo., U.S.A. 37°41N 92°40W 80 G7
Lebanon N.H., U.S.A. 43°39N 72°15W 83 C12
Lebanon Oreg., U.S.A. 44°32N 122°55W 76 D2
Lebanon Pa., U.S.A. 40°20N 76°26W 83 F8
Lebanon Tenn., U.S.A. 36°12N 86°18W 85 C11
Lebanon ■ Asia 34°0N 36°0E 46 B5
Lebec U.S.A. 34°51N 118°52W 79 L8
Lebel-sur-Quévillon Canada 49°3N 76°59W 72 C4
Lebomboberge S. Africa 24°30S 32°0E 57 C5
Lębork Poland 54°33N 17°46E 17 A9
Lebrija Spain 36°53N 6°5W 21 D2
Lebu Chile 37°40S 73°47W 94 D1
Lecce Italy 40°23N 18°11E 23 D8
Lecco Italy 45°51N 9°23E 20 D8
Lech → Germany 48°43N 10°56E 16 D6
Lecontes Mills U.S.A. 41°5N 78°17W 82 E6
Łęczyca Poland 52°5N 19°15E 17 B10
Ledong China 18°41N 109°5E 38 C7
Leduc Canada 53°15N 113°30W 70 C6
Lee U.S.A. 42°19N 73°15W 83 D11
Lee → Ireland 51°53N 8°56W 10 E3
Lee Vining U.S.A. 37°58N 119°7W 78 H7
Leech L. U.S.A. 47°10N 94°24W 80 B6
Leechburg U.S.A. 40°37N 79°36W 82 F5
Leeds U.K. 53°48N 1°33W 12 D6
Leeds U.S.A. 33°33N 86°33W 85 E11
Leek Neths. 53°10N 6°24E 15 A6
Leek U.K. 53°7N 2°1W 12 D5
Leeman Australia 29°57S 114°58E 61 E1
Leeper U.S.A. 41°22N 79°18W 82 E5
Leer Germany 53°13N 7°26E 16 B4
Leesburg U.S.A. 28°49N 81°53W 85 G14
Leesville U.S.A. 31°8N 93°16W 84 F8
Leeton Australia 34°33S 146°23E 63 E4
Leetonia U.S.A. 40°53N 80°45W 82 F4
Leeu Gamka S. Africa 32°47S 21°59E 56 E3
Leeuwarden Neths. 53°15N 5°48E 15 A5
Leeuwin, C. Australia 34°20S 115°9E 61 F2
Leeuwin Naturaliste △ Australia 34°6S 115°3E 61 F2
Leeward Is. Atl. Oc. 16°30N 63°30W 89 C7
Lefka Cyprus 35°6N 32°51E 25 D11
Lefkada Greece 38°40N 20°43E 23 E9
Lefkimi Greece 39°25N 20°3E 25 B4
Lefkimis, Akra Greece 39°29N 20°4E 25 B4
Lefkoniko Cyprus 35°18N 33°44E 25 D12
Lefroy Canada 44°16N 79°34W 82 B5
Lefroy, L. Australia 31°21S 121°40E 61 F3
Leganés Spain 40°19N 3°45W 21 B4
Legazpi Phil. 13°10N 123°45E 37 B6
Legendre I. Australia 20°22S 116°55E 60 D2
Leghorn = Livorno Italy 43°33N 10°19E 22 C4
Legionowo Poland 52°25N 20°50E 17 B11
Legnago Italy 45°11N 11°18E 22 B4
Legnica Poland 51°12N 16°10E 16 C9
Leh India 34°9N 77°35E 43 B7
Lehigh Acres U.S.A. 26°36N 81°39W 85 H14
Lehighton U.S.A. 40°50N 75°43W 83 F9
Lehututu Botswana 23°54S 21°55E 56 C3
Leiah Pakistan 30°58N 70°58E 42 D4
Leicester U.K. 52°38N 1°8W 13 E6
Leicester City □ U.K. 52°38N 1°8W 13 E6
Leicestershire □ U.K. 52°41N 1°17W 13 E6
Leichhardt → Australia 17°35S 139°48E 62 B2
Leichhardt Ra. Australia 20°46S 147°40E 62 C4
Leiden Neths. 52°9N 4°30E 15 B4
Leie → Belgium 51°2N 3°45E 15 C3
Leimus Nic. 14°40N 84°3W 88 D3
Leine → Germany 52°43N 9°36E 16 B5
Leinster Australia 27°51S 120°36E 61 E3
Leinster □ Ireland 53°3N 7°8W 10 C4
Leinster, Mt. Ireland 52°37N 6°46W 10 D5
Leipzig Germany 51°18N 12°22E 16 C7
Leiria Portugal 39°46N 8°53W 21 C1
Leirvik Norway 59°47N 5°28E 9 G11
Leisler, Mt. Australia 23°23S 129°20E 60 D4
Leith U.K. 55°59N 3°11W 11 F5
Leith Hill U.K. 51°11N 0°22W 13 F7
Leitir Ceanainn = Letterkenny Ireland 54°57N 7°45W 10 B4
Leitrim Ireland 54°0N 8°5W 10 B3
Leitrim □ Ireland 54°8N 8°0W 10 B4
Leizhou Bandao China 21°0N 110°0E 33 D6
Lek → Neths. 51°54N 4°35E 15 C4
Leka Norway 65°5N 11°35E 8 D14
Leland Mich., U.S.A. 45°1N 85°45W 81 C11
Leland Miss., U.S.A. 33°24N 90°54W 85 E9
Leleque Argentina 42°28S 71°0W 96 E2
Lelystad Neths. 52°30N 5°25E 15 B5
Léman, L. Europe 46°26N 6°30E 20 C7
Lembar Indonesia 8°45S 116°4E 37 K19
Lembuak Indonesia 8°36S 116°11E 37 K19
Lemera Dem. Rep. of the Congo 3°0S 28°55E 54 C2
Lemhi Ra. U.S.A. 44°0N 113°0W 76 D7
Lemmer Neths. 52°51N 5°43E 15 B5
Lemmon U.S.A. 45°57N 102°10W 80 C2
Lemon Grove U.S.A. 32°44N 117°1W 79 N9
Lemoore U.S.A. 36°18N 119°46W 78 J7
Lemvig Denmark 56°33N 8°20E 9 H13
Lena → Russia 72°52N 126°40E 29 B13
Lenadoon Pt. Ireland 54°18N 9°3W 10 B2
Lenggong Malaysia 5°6N 100°58E 39 K3
Lengua de Vaca, Pta. Chile 30°14S 71°38W 94 C1
Lengwe △ Malawi 16°14S 34°45E 55 F3
Leninogorsk Kazakhstan 50°20N 83°30E 28 D9
Leninsk Russia 48°40N 45°15E 19 E8
Leninsk-Kuznetskiy Russia 54°44N 86°10E 28 D9
Lenkoran = Länkäran Azerbaijan 38°48N 48°52E 45 B6
Lenmalu Indonesia 1°45S 130°15E 37 E8
Lennox U.S.A. 43°21N 96°53W 80 D5
Lennoxville Canada 45°22N 71°51W 83 A13
Lenoir U.S.A. 35°55N 81°32W 85 D14
Lenoir City U.S.A. 35°48N 84°16W 85 D12
Lenore L. Canada 52°30N 104°59W 71 C8
Lenox U.S.A. 42°22N 73°17W 83 D11
Lens France 50°26N 2°50E 20 A5
Lensk Russia 60°48N 114°55E 29 C12
Lentas Greece 34°56N 24°56E 25 E6
Lentini Italy 37°17N 15°0E 22 F6
Lenwood U.S.A. 34°53N 117°7W 79 L9
Lenya Burma 11°33N 98°57E 39 G2
Leoben Austria 47°22N 15°5E 16 E8
Leodhas = Lewis U.K. 58°9N 6°40W 11 C2
Leola U.S.A. 45°43N 98°56W 80 C4
Leominster U.K. 52°14N 2°43W 13 E5
Leominster U.S.A. 42°32N 71°46W 83 D13
León Mexico 21°6N 101°41W 86 C4
León Nic. 12°20N 86°51W 88 D2
León Spain 42°38N 5°34W 21 A3
Leon U.S.A. 40°44N 93°45W 80 E7
Leon → U.S.A. 31°14N 97°28W 84 F6
León, Montes de Spain 42°30N 6°18W 21 A2
Leonardtown U.S.A. 38°17N 76°38W 81 F15
Leonardville Namibia 23°29S 18°49E 56 C2
Leone Amer. Samoa 14°23S 170°48W 59 b
Leongatha Australia 38°30S 145°58E 63 F4
Leonora Australia 28°49S 121°19E 61 E3
Leopoldina Brazil 21°28S 42°40W 95 A7
Leopoldsburg Belgium 51°7N 5°13E 15 C5
Leoti U.S.A. 38°29N 101°21W 80 F3
Leova Moldova 46°28N 28°15E 17 E15
Leoville Canada 53°39N 107°33W 71 C7
Lepel = Lyepyel Belarus 54°50N 28°40E 9 J23
Lépo, L. do Angola 17°0S 19°0E 56 B2
Leppävirta Finland 62°29N 27°46E 8 E22
Leptis Magna Libya 32°40N 14°12E 51 B8
Leribe Lesotho 28°51S 28°3E 57 D4
Lérida = Lleida Spain 41°37N 0°39E 21 B6
Lerwick U.K. 60°9N 1°9W 11 A7
Les Cayes Haiti 18°15N 73°46W 89 C5
Les Coteaux Canada 45°15N 74°13W 83 A10
Les Escoumins Canada 48°21N 69°24W 73 C6
Les Sables-d'Olonne France 46°30N 1°45W 20 C3
Lesbos Greece 39°10N 26°20E 23 E12
Leshan China 29°33N 103°41E 32 D5
Leshukonskoye Russia 64°54N 45°46E 18 B8
Leshwe ⌂ Dem. Rep. of the Congo 12°45S 29°30E 55 E2
Leskov I. Antarctica 56°0S 28°0W 5 B1
Leskovac Serbia 43°0N 21°58E 23 C9
Lesopilnoye Russia 46°44N 134°20E 30 A7
Lesotho ■ Africa 29°40S 28°0E 57 D4
Lesozavodsk Russia 45°30N 133°29E 30 B6
Lesse → Belgium 50°15N 4°54E 15 D4
Lesse et Lomme ⌂ Belgium 50°8N 5°9E 15 D5
Lesser Antilles W. Indies 15°0N 61°0W 89 D7
Lesser Slave L. Canada 55°30N 115°25W 70 B5
Lesser Sunda Is. Indonesia 8°0S 120°0E 37 F6
Lessines Belgium 50°42N 3°50E 15 D3
Lester B. Pearson Int., Toronto ✕ (YYZ) Canada 43°46N 79°35W 82 C5
Lestock Canada 51°19N 103°59W 71 C8
Lesuer I. Australia 13°50S 127°17E 60 B4
Lesueur △ Australia 30°11S 115°10E 61 F2
Lésvos = Lesbos Greece 39°10N 26°20E 23 E12
Leszno Poland 51°50N 16°30E 17 C9
Letaba S. Africa 23°59S 31°50E 57 C5
Letchworth U.K. 51°59N 0°13W 13 F7
Lethbridge Canada 49°45N 112°45W 70 D6
Lethem Guyana 3°20N 59°50W 92 C7
Leti, Kepulauan Indonesia 8°10S 128°0E 37 F7
Leti Is. = Leti, Kepulauan Indonesia 8°10S 128°0E 37 F7
Letiahau → Botswana 21°16S 24°0E 56 C3
Leticia Colombia 4°9S 70°0W 92 D5
Leting China 39°23N 118°55E 35 E10
Letjiesbos S. Africa 32°34S 22°16E 56 E3
Letlhakane Botswana 21°27S 25°30E 56 C4
Letlhakeng Botswana 24°0S 24°59E 56 C3
Letpadan Burma 17°45N 95°45E 41 L19
Letpan Burma 19°28N 94°10E 41 K19
Letsôk-aw Kyun Burma 11°30N 98°25E 39 G2
Letterkenny Ireland 54°57N 7°45W 10 B4
Leucadia U.S.A. 33°4N 117°18W 79 M9
Leuchars U.K. 56°24N 2°53W 11 E6
Leuser, G. Indonesia 3°46N 97°12E 36 D1
Leuven Belgium 50°52N 4°42E 15 D4
Leuze-en-Hainaut Belgium 50°36N 3°37E 15 D3
Levanger Norway 63°45N 11°19E 8 E14
Levelland U.S.A. 33°35N 102°23W 84 E3
Leven U.K. 56°12N 3°0W 11 E6
Leven, L. U.K. 56°12N 3°22W 11 E5
Leven, Toraka Madag. 12°30S 47°45E 57 A8
Leveque C. Australia 16°20S 123°0E 60 C3
Levice Slovak Rep. 48°13N 18°35E 17 D10
Levin N.Z. 40°37S 175°18E 59 D5
Lévis Canada 46°48N 71°9W 73 C5
Levis, L. Canada 62°37N 117°58W 70 A5
Levittown N.Y., U.S.A. 40°44N 73°31W 83 F11
Levittown Pa., U.S.A. 40°9N 74°51W 83 F10
Levka Oros Greece 35°18N 24°3E 25 D6
Levkás = Lefkada Greece 38°40N 20°43E 23 E9
Levkôsia = Nicosia Cyprus 35°10N 33°25E 25 D12
Levskigrad = Karlovo Bulgaria 42°38N 24°47E 23 C11
Levuka Fiji 17°34S 179°0E 59 a
Lewes U.K. 50°52N 0°1E 13 G8
Lewes U.S.A. 38°46N 75°9W 81 F16
Lewis U.K. 58°9N 6°40W 11 C2
Lewis → U.S.A. 45°51N 122°48W 78 E4
Lewis, Butt of U.K. 58°31N 6°16W 11 C2
Lewis and Clark ⌂ U.S.A. 46°8N 123°53W 78 D3
Lewis Ra. Australia 20°3S 128°50E 60 D4
Lewis Range U.S.A. 48°5N 113°5W 76 B7
Lewis Run U.S.A. 41°52N 78°40W 82 E6
Lewisburg Pa., U.S.A. 40°58N 76°54W 82 F8
Lewisburg Tenn., U.S.A. 35°27N 86°48W 85 D11
Lewisburg W. Va., U.S.A. 37°48N 80°27W 81 G13
Lewisporte Canada 49°15N 55°3W 73 C8
Lewiston Idaho, U.S.A. 46°25N 117°1W 76 C5
Lewiston Maine, U.S.A. 44°6N 70°13W 81 C18
Lewiston N.Y., U.S.A. 43°11N 79°3W 82 C5
Lewistown Mont., U.S.A. 47°4N 109°26W 76 C9
Lewistown Pa., U.S.A. 40°36N 77°34W 82 F7
Lexington Ill., U.S.A. 40°39N 88°47W 80 E9
Lexington Ky., U.S.A. 38°3N 84°30W 81 F11
Lexington Mich., U.S.A. 43°16N 82°32W 82 C2
Lexington Mo., U.S.A. 39°11N 93°52W 80 F7
Lexington N.C., U.S.A. 35°49N 80°15W 85 D14
Lexington N.Y., U.S.A. 42°15N 74°22W 83 D10
Lexington Nebr., U.S.A. 40°47N 99°45W 80 E4
Lexington Ohio, U.S.A. 40°41N 82°35W 82 F2
Lexington Tenn., U.S.A. 35°39N 88°24W 85 D10
Lexington Va., U.S.A. 37°47N 79°27W 81 G14
Lexington Park U.S.A. 38°16N 76°27W 81 F15
Leyburn U.K. 54°19N 1°48W 12 C6
Leyland U.K. 53°42N 2°43W 12 D5
Leyte □ Phil. 11°0N 125°0E 37 B7
Lezhë Albania 41°47N 19°39E 23 D8
Lhasa China 29°25N 90°58E 32 D4
Lhazê China 29°5N 87°38E 32 D3
L'Hermite, I. Chile 55°50S 68°0W 96 H3
Lhokkruet Indonesia 4°55N 95°24E 36 D1
Lhokseumawe Indonesia 5°10N 97°10E 36 C1
L'Hospitalet de Llobregat Spain 41°21N 2°6E 21 B7
Li Thailand 17°48N 98°57E 38 D2
Li Xian Gansu, China 34°10N 105°5E 34 G3
Li Xian Hebei, China 38°30N 115°35E 34 E8
Liancourt Rocks = Tokdo Asia 37°15N 131°52E 31 F5
Lianga Phil. 8°38N 126°6E 37 C7
Liangcheng Nei Monggol Zizhiqu, China 40°28N 112°25E 34 D7
Liangcheng Shandong, China 35°32N 119°37E 35 G10
Liangdang China 33°56N 106°18E 34 H4
Liangpran Indonesia 1°4N 114°23E 36 D4
Lianshanguan China 40°53N 123°43E 35 D12
Lianshui China 33°42N 119°20E 35 H10
Lianyungang China 34°40N 119°11E 35 G10
Liao He → China 41°0N 121°50E 35 D11
Liaocheng China 36°28N 115°58E 34 F8
Liaodong Bandao China 40°0N 122°30E 35 E12
Liaodong Wan China 40°20N 121°10E 35 D11
Liaoning □ China 41°40N 122°30E 35 D12
Liaotung, G. of = Liaodong Wan China 40°20N 121°10E 35 D11
Liaoyang China 41°15N 122°58E 35 D12
Liaoyuan China 42°58N 125°2E 35 C13
Liaozhong China 41°23N 122°50E 35 D12
Liapades Greece 39°42N 19°40E 25 A3
Liard → Canada 61°51N 121°18W 70 A4
Liard River Canada 59°25N 126°5W 70 B3
Liari Pakistan 25°37N 66°30E 42 G2
Libau = Liepāja Latvia 56°30N 21°0E 9 H19
Libby U.S.A. 48°23N 115°33W 76 B6
Libenge Dem. Rep. of the Congo 3°40N 18°55E 52 D3
Liberal U.S.A. 37°3N 100°55W 80 G3
Liberec Czech Rep. 50°47N 15°7E 16 C8
Liberia Costa Rica 10°40N 85°30W 88 D2
Liberia ■ W. Afr. 6°30N 9°30W 50 G4
Libertador □ Chile 34°15S 70°45W 94 C1
Liberty Mo., U.S.A. 39°15N 94°25W 80 F6
Liberty N.Y., U.S.A. 41°48N 74°45W 83 E10
Liberty Pa., U.S.A. 41°34N 77°6W 82 E7
Liberty Tex., U.S.A. 30°3N 94°48W 84 F7
Liberty-Newark Int. ✕ (EWR) U.S.A. 40°42N 74°10W 83 F10
Lîbîya, Sahrâ' Africa 25°0N 25°0E 51 C10
Libobo, Tanjung Indonesia 0°54S 128°28E 37 E7
Libode S. Africa 31°33S 29°2E 57 E4
Libong, Ko Thailand 7°15N 99°23E 39 J2
Libourne France 44°55N 0°14W 20 D3
Libramont Belgium 49°55N 5°23E 15 E5
Libreville Gabon 0°25N 9°26E 52 D1
Libya ■ N. Afr. 27°0N 17°0E 51 C9
Libyan Desert = Lîbîya, Sahrâ' Africa 25°0N 25°0E 51 C10
Libyan Plateau = Ed Déffa Egypt 30°40N 26°30E 51 B11
Licantén Chile 35°55S 72°0W 94 D1
Licata Italy 37°6N 13°56E 22 F5
Licheng China 36°28N 113°20E 34 F7
Lichfield U.K. 52°41N 1°49W 13 E6
Lichinga Mozam. 13°13S 35°11E 55 E4
Lichtenburg S. Africa 26°8S 26°8E 56 D4
Licking → U.S.A. 39°6N 84°30W 81 F11
Licungo → Mozam. 17°40S 37°15E 55 F4
Lida Belarus 53°53N 25°15E 17 B13
Lidköping Sweden 58°31N 13°7E 9 G15
Liebig, Mt. Australia 23°18S 131°22E 60 D5
Liechtenstein ■ Europe 47°8N 9°35E 20 C8
Liège Belgium 50°38N 5°35E 15 D5
Liège □ Belgium 50°32N 5°35E 15 D5
Liegnitz = Legnica Poland 51°12N 16°10E 16 C9
Lieksa Finland 63°18N 30°2E 8 E24
Lienart Dem. Rep. of the Congo 3°3N 25°31E 54 B2
Lienyünchiangshih = Lianyungang China 34°40N 119°11E 35 G10
Lienz Austria 46°50N 12°46E 16 E7
Liepāja Latvia 56°30N 21°0E 9 H19
Lier Belgium 51°7N 4°34E 15 C4
Lietuva = Lithuania ■ Europe 55°30N 24°0E 9 J21
Lièvre → Canada 45°31N 75°26W 72 C4
Liffey → Ireland 53°21N 6°13W 10 C5
Lifford Ireland 54°51N 7°29W 10 B4

Lifudzin *Russia* 44°21N 134°58E **30** B7
Lightning Ridge
　Australia 29°22S 148°0E **63** D4
Ligonha ➤ *Mozam.* 16°54S 39°9E **55** F4
Ligonier *U.S.A.* 40°15N 79°14W **82** F5
L'Île-Rousse *France* 42°38N 8°57E **20** E8
Liguria □ *Italy* 44°30N 8°50E **20** D8
Ligurian Sea *Medit. S.* 43°20N 9°0E **22** C3
Lihou Reefs and Cays
　Australia 17°25S 151°40E **62** B5
Lihué Calel △ *Argentina* 38°0S 65°10W **94** D2
Lijiang *China* 26°55N 100°20E **32** D5
Likasi
　Dem. Rep. of the Congo 10°55S 26°48E **55** E2
Likoma I. *Malawi* 12°3S 34°45E **55** E3
Likumburu *Tanzania* 9°43S 35°8E **55** D4
Lille *France* 50°38N 3°3E **20** A5
Lille Bælt *Denmark* 55°20N 9°45E **9** J13
Lillehammer *Norway* 61°8N 10°30E **8** F14
Lillesand *Norway* 58°15N 8°23E **9** G13
Lillian Pt. *Australia* 27°40S 126°6E **61** E4
Lillooet *Canada* 50°44N 121°57W **70** C4
Lillooet ➤ *Canada* 49°15N 121°57W **70** D4
Lilongwe *Malawi* 14°0S 33°48E **55** E3
Liloy *Phil.* 8°4N 122°39E **37** C6
Lim ➤ *Europe* 43°45N 19°15E **23** C8
Lim Chu Kang *Singapore* 1°26N 103°43E **39** d
Lima *Indonesia* 3°39S 127°58E **37** E7
Lima *Peru* 12°3S 77°2W **92** F3
Lima *Mont., U.S.A.* 44°38N 112°36W **76** D7
Lima *N.Y., U.S.A.* 42°54N 77°36W **82** D7
Lima *Ohio, U.S.A.* 40°44N 84°6W **81** E11
Lima ➤ *Portugal* 41°41N 8°50W **21** B1
Liman *Indonesia* 7°48S 111°45E **37** G14
Limassol *Cyprus* 34°42N 33°1E **25** E12
Limavady *U.K.* 55°3N 6°56W **10** A5
Limay ➤ *Argentina* 39°0S 68°0W **96** D3
Limay Mahuida
　Argentina 37°10S 66°45W **94** D2
Limbang *Brunei* 4°42N 115°6E **36** D5
Limbaži *Latvia* 57°31N 24°42E **9** H21
Limbdi *India* 22°34N 71°51E **42** H4
Limbe *Cameroon* 4°1N 9°10E **52** D1
Limburg *Germany* 50°22N 8°4E **16** C5
Limburg □ *Belgium* 51°2N 5°25E **15** C5
Limburg □ *Neths.* 51°20N 5°55E **15** C5
Limeira *Brazil* 22°35S 47°28W **95** A6
Limerick *Ireland* 52°40N 8°37W **10** D3
Limerick *U.S.A.* 43°41N 70°48W **83** C14
Limerick □ *Ireland* 52°30N 8°50W **10** D3
Limestone *U.S.A.* 42°2N 78°38W **82** D6
Limestone ➤ *Canada* 56°31N 94°7W **71** B10
Limfjorden *Denmark* 56°55N 9°0E **9** H13
Limia = Lima ➤ *Portugal* 41°41N 8°50W **21** B1
Limingen *Norway* 64°48N 13°35E **8** D15
Limmen ◎ *Australia* 15°15S 135°30E **62** B2
Limmen Bight *Australia* 14°40S 135°35E **62** A2
Limmen Bight ➤
　Australia 15°7S 135°44E **62** B2
Limnos *Greece* 39°50N 25°5E **23** E11
Limoges *Canada* 45°20N 75°16W **83** A9
Limoges *France* 45°50N 1°15E **20** D4
Limón *Costa Rica* 10°0N 83°2W **88** E3
Limon *U.S.A.* 39°16N 103°41W **76** G12
Limousin □ *France* 45°30N 1°30E **20** D5
Limoux *France* 43°4N 2°12E **20** E5
Limpopo □ *S. Africa* 24°5S 29°0E **57** C4
Limpopo ➤ *Africa* 25°5S 33°30E **57** D5
Limuru *Kenya* 1°2S 36°35E **54** C4
Lin Xian *China* 37°57N 110°58E **34** F6
Linares *Chile* 35°50S 71°40W **94** D1
Linares *Mexico* 24°52N 99°34W **87** C5
Linares *Spain* 38°10N 3°40W **21** C4
Lincang *China* 23°58N 100°1E **32** D5
Lincheng *China* 37°25N 114°30E **34** F8
Lincoln – Beamsville
　Canada 43°12N 79°28W **82** C5
Lincoln *Argentina* 34°55S 61°30W **94** C3
Lincoln *N.Z.* 43°38S 172°30E **59** E4
Lincoln *U.K.* 53°14N 0°32W **12** D7
Lincoln *Calif., U.S.A.* 38°54N 121°17W **78** G5
Lincoln *Ill., U.S.A.* 40°9N 89°22W **80** E9
Lincoln *Kans., U.S.A.* 39°3N 98°9W **80** F4
Lincoln *Maine, U.S.A.* 45°22N 68°30W **81** C19
Lincoln *N.H., U.S.A.* 44°3N 71°40W **83** B13
Lincoln *N. Mex.,
　U.S.A.* 33°30N 105°23W **77** K11
Lincoln *Nebr., U.S.A.* 40°49N 96°41W **80** E5
Lincoln City *U.S.A.* 44°57N 124°1W **76** D1
Lincoln Hav = Lincoln Sea
　Arctic 84°0N 55°0W **69** A21
Lincoln Sea *Arctic* 84°0N 55°0W **69** A21
Lincolnshire □ *U.K.* 53°14N 0°32W **12** D7
Lincolnshire Wolds *U.K.* 53°26N 0°13W **12** D7
Lincolnton *U.S.A.* 35°29N 81°16W **85** D14
Lind *U.S.A.* 46°58N 118°37W **76** C4
Lindeman I. *Australia* 20°27S 149°3E **62** b
Lindeman Islands △
　Australia 20°28S 149°5E **62** b
Linden *Guyana* 6°0N 58°10W **92** B7
Linden *Ala., U.S.A.* 32°18N 87°48S **85** E11
Linden *Calif., U.S.A.* 38°1N 121°5W **78** G5
Linden *Tex., U.S.A.* 33°1N 94°22W **84** E7
Lindenhurst *U.S.A.* 40°41N 73°23W **83** F11
Lindesnes *Norway* 57°58N 7°3E **9** H12
Lindi *Tanzania* 9°58S 39°38E **55** D4
Lindi □ *Tanzania* 9°40S 38°30E **55** D4
Lindi ➤
　Dem. Rep. of the Congo 0°33N 25°5E **54** B2
Lindley *U.S.A.* 42°1N 77°8W **82** D7
Lindos *Greece* 36°6N 28°4E **25** C10
Lindos, Akra *Greece* 36°4N 28°10E **25** C10
Lindsay *Canada* 44°22N 78°43W **82** B6
Lindsay *Calif., U.S.A.* 36°12N 119°5W **78** J7
Lindsay *Okla., U.S.A.* 34°50N 97°38W **84** D6
Lindsborg *U.S.A.* 38°35N 97°40W **80** F5
Line Islands *Pac. Oc.* 7°0N 160°0W **65** H12
Linesville *U.S.A.* 41°39N 80°26W **82** E4

Linfen *China* 36°3N 111°30E **34** F6
Ling Xian *China* 37°22N 116°30E **34** F9
Lingao *China* 19°56N 109°42E **38** C7
Lingayen *Phil.* 16°1N 120°14E **37** A6
Lingayen G. *Phil.* 16°10N 120°15E **37** A6
Lingbi *China* 33°33N 117°33E **35** H9
Lingchuan *China* 35°45N 113°12E **34** G7
Lingding Yang *China* 22°25N 113°44E **33** G10
Lingen *Germany* 52°31N 7°19E **16** B4
Lingga *Indonesia* 0°12S 104°37E **36** E2
Lingga, Kepulauan
　Indonesia 0°10S 104°30E **36** E2
Lingga Arch. = Lingga,
　Kepulauan *Indonesia* 0°10S 104°30E **36** E2
Lingle *U.S.A.* 42°8N 104°21W **76** E11
Lingqiu *China* 39°28N 114°22E **34** E8
Lingshi *China* 36°48N 111°48E **34** F6
Lingshou *China* 38°20N 114°20E **34** E8
Lingshui *China* 18°27N 110°0E **38** C8
Lingtai *China* 35°0N 107°40E **34** G4
Linguère *Senegal* 15°25N 15°5W **50** E2
Lingwu *China* 38°6N 106°20E **34** E4
Lingyuan *China* 41°10N 119°15E **35** D10
Linhai *China* 28°50N 121°8E **33** D7
Linhares *Brazil* 19°25S 40°4W **93** G10
Linhe *China* 40°48N 107°20E **34** D4
Linjiang *China* 41°50N 127°0E **35** D14
Linköping *Sweden* 58°28N 15°36E **9** G16
Linkou *China* 45°15N 130°18E **35** B16
Linnhe, L. *U.K.* 56°36N 5°25W **11** E3
Linqi *China* 35°45N 113°52E **34** G7
Linqing *China* 36°50N 115°42E **34** F8
Linqu *China* 36°25N 118°30E **35** F10
Linru *China* 34°11N 112°52E **34** G7
Lins *Brazil* 21°40S 49°44W **95** A6
Linstead *Jamaica* 18°8N 77°2W **88** a
Linta ➤ *Madag.* 25°2S 44°5E **57** D7
Linton *Ind., U.S.A.* 39°2N 87°10W **80** F10
Linton *N. Dak., U.S.A.* 46°16N 100°14W **80** B3
Lintong *China* 34°20N 109°10E **34** G5
Linwood *Canada* 43°35N 80°43W **82** C4
Linxi *China* 43°36N 118°2E **35** C10
Linxia *China* 35°36N 103°10E **32** C5
Linyi *China* 35°5N 118°21E **35** G10
Linz *Austria* 48°18N 14°18E **16** D8
Linzhenzhen *China* 36°30N 109°59E **34** F5
Linzi *China* 36°50N 118°20E **35** F10
Lion, G. du *France* 43°10N 4°0E **20** E6
Lionárisso *Cyprus* 35°28N 34°8E **25** D13
Lions, G. of = Lion, G. du
　France 43°10N 4°0E **20** E6
Lion's Den *Zimbabwe* 17°15S 30°5E **55** F3
Lion's Head *Canada* 44°58N 81°15W **82** B3
Lipa *Phil.* 13°57N 121°10E **37** B6
Lipali *Mozam.* 15°50S 35°50E **55** F4
Lípari *Italy* 38°26N 14°58E **22** E6
Lípari, Is. = Eólie, Ís.
　Italy 38°30N 14°57E **22** E6
Lipcani *Moldova* 48°14N 26°48E **17** D14
Liperi *Finland* 62°31N 29°24E **8** E23
Lipetsk *Russia* 52°37N 39°35E **18** D6
Lipkany = Lipcani
　Moldova 48°14N 26°48E **17** D14
Lipkany *Ukraine* 49°12N 29°1E **17** D15
Lippe ➤ *Germany* 51°39N 6°36E **16** C4
Lipscomb *U.S.A.* 36°14N 100°16W **84** C4
Liptrap, C. *Australia* 38°50S 145°55E **63** F4
Lira *Uganda* 2°17N 32°57E **54** B3
Liria = Lliria *Spain* 39°37N 0°35W **21** C5
Lisala
　Dem. Rep. of the Congo 2°12N 21°38E **52** D4
Lisboa *Portugal* 38°42N 9°8W **21** C1
Lisbon = Lisboa *Portugal* 38°42N 9°8W **21** C1
Lisbon *N. Dak., U.S.A.* 46°27N 97°41W **80** B5
Lisbon *N.H., U.S.A.* 44°13N 71°55W **83** B13
Lisbon *N.Y., U.S.A.* 44°43N 75°19W **83** B9
Lisbon *Ohio, U.S.A.* 40°46N 80°46W **82** F4
Lisbon Falls *U.S.A.* 44°0N 70°4W **81** D18
Lisburn *U.K.* 54°31N 6°3W **10** B5
Lisburne, C. *U.S.A.* 68°53N 166°13W **74** B6
Liscannor B. *Ireland* 52°55N 9°24W **10** D2
Lisdoonvarna *Ireland* 53°2N 9°18W **10** C2
Lishi *China* 37°31N 111°8E **34** F6
Lishu *China* 43°20N 124°18E **35** C13
Lisianski I. *U.S.A.* 26°2N 174°0W **75** K5
Lisichansk = Lysychansk
　Ukraine 48°55N 38°30E **19** E6
Lisieux *France* 49°10N 0°12E **20** B4
Liski *Russia* 51°3N 39°30E **19** D6
Lismore *Australia* 28°44S 153°21E **63** D5
Lismore *Ireland* 52°8N 7°55W **10** D4
Lista *Norway* 58°7N 6°39E **9** G12
Lister, Mt. *Antarctica* 78°0S 162°0E **5** D11
Liston *Australia* 28°39S 152°6E **63** D5
Listowel *Canada* 43°44N 80°58W **82** C4
Listowel *Ireland* 52°27N 9°29W **10** D2
Litani ➤ *Lebanon* 33°20N 35°15E **46** B4
Litchfield *Conn., U.S.A.* 41°45N 73°11W **83** E11
Litchfield *Ill., U.S.A.* 39°11N 89°39W **80** F9
Litchfield △ *Australia* 13°14S 131°1E **60** B5
Lithgow *Australia* 33°25S 150°8E **63** E5
Líthino, Akra *Greece* 34°55N 24°44E **25** E6
Lithuania ■ *Europe* 55°30N 24°0E **9** J21
Lititz *U.S.A.* 40°9N 76°18W **83** F8
Litoměřice *Czech Rep.* 50°33N 14°10E **16** C8
Little Abaco *Bahamas* 26°50N 77°30W **88** A4
Little Barrier I. *N.Z.* 36°12S 175°8E **59** B5
Little Belt Mts. *U.S.A.* 46°40N 110°45W **76** C8
Little Bighorn Battlefield ◇
　U.S.A. 45°34N 107°25W **76** D10
Little Blue ➤ *U.S.A.* 39°42N 96°41W **80** F5
Little Buffalo ➤ *Canada* 61°0N 113°46W **70** A6
Little Cayman *Cayman Is.* 19°41N 80°3W **88** C3
Little Churchill ➤
　Canada 57°30N 95°22W **71** B9

Little Colorado ➤
　U.S.A. 36°12N 111°48W **77** H8
Little Current *Canada* 45°55N 82°0W **72** C3
Little Current ➤ *Canada* 50°57N 84°36W **72** B3
Little Diomede I.
　U.S.A. 65°45N 168°56W **74** B6
Little Falls *Minn., U.S.A.* 45°59N 94°22W **80** C6
Little Falls *N.Y., U.S.A.* 43°3N 74°51W **83** C10
Little Fork ➤ *U.S.A.* 48°31N 93°35W **80** A7
Little Grand Rapids
　Canada 52°0N 95°29W **71** C9
Little Humboldt ➤
　U.S.A. 41°1N 117°43W **76** F5
Little Inagua I. *Bahamas* 21°40N 73°50W **89** B5
Little Karoo *S. Africa* 33°45S 21°0E **56** E3
Little Khingan Mts. = Xiao
　Hinggan Ling *China* 49°0N 127°0E **33** B7
Little Lake *U.S.A.* 35°56N 117°55W **79** K9
Little Laut Is. = Laut Kecil,
　Kepulauan *Indonesia* 4°45S 115°40E **36** E5
Little Mecatina = Petit-
　Mécatina ➤ *Canada* 50°40N 59°30W **73** B8
Little Minch *U.K.* 57°35N 6°45W **11** D2
Little Missouri ➤
　U.S.A. 47°36N 102°25W **80** B2
Little Ouse ➤ *U.K.* 52°22N 1°12E **13** E9
Little Rann *India* 23°25N 71°25E **42** H4
Little Red ➤ *U.S.A.* 35°11N 91°27W **84** D9
Little River *N.Z.* 43°45S 172°49E **59** E4
Little Rock *U.S.A.* 34°45N 92°17W **84** D8
Little Ruaha ➤ *Tanzania* 7°57S 37°53E **54** D4
Little Sable Pt. *U.S.A.* 43°38N 86°33W **80** D10
Little Sioux ➤ *U.S.A.* 41°48N 96°4W **80** E6
Little Smoky ➤
　Canada 54°44N 117°11W **70** C5
Little Snake ➤ *U.S.A.* 40°27N 108°26W **76** F9
Little Tobago
　Trin. & Tob. 11°18N 60°30W **93** J16
Little Valley *U.S.A.* 42°15N 78°48W **82** D6
Little Wabash ➤ *U.S.A.* 37°55N 88°5W **80** G9
Little White ➤ *U.S.A.* 43°2N 100°40W **80** D3
Little Zab = Zāb aş Şaghīr ➤
　Iraq 35°17N 43°29E **44** C4
Littlefield *U.S.A.* 33°55N 102°20W **84** E3
Littlehampton *U.K.* 50°49N 0°32W **13** G7
Littleton *U.S.A.* 44°18N 71°46W **83** B13
Liu He ➤ *China* 40°55N 121°35E **35** D11
Liuba *China* 33°38N 106°55E **34** H4
Liugou *China* 40°57N 118°15E **35** D10
Liuhe *China* 42°17N 125°43E **35** C13
Liukang Tenggaja = Sabalana,
　Kepulauan *Indonesia* 6°45S 118°50E **37** F5
Liuli *Tanzania* 11°3S 34°38E **55** E3
Liupanshui *China* 26°38N 104°48E **32** D5
Liuwa Plain *Zambia* 14°20S 22°30E **53** G4
Liuzhou *China* 24°22N 109°22E **33** D5
Liuzhuang *China* 33°12N 120°18E **35** H11
Livadia *Cyprus* 34°57N 33°38E **25** E12
Livadia *Greece* 38°27N 22°54E **23** E10
Live Oak *Calif., U.S.A.* 39°17N 121°40W **78** F5
Live Oak *Fla., U.S.A.* 30°18N 82°59W **85** F13
Lively *Canada* 46°26N 81°9W **84** A4
Liveras *Cyprus* 35°23N 32°57E **25** D11
Livermore *U.S.A.* 37°41N 121°47W **78** H5
Livermore, Mt. *U.S.A.* 30°38N 104°11W **84** F2
Livermore Falls *U.S.A.* 44°29N 70°11W **81** C18
Liverpool *Australia* 33°54S 150°58E **63** B5
Liverpool *Canada* 44°5N 64°41W **73** D7
Liverpool *U.K.* 53°25N 3°0W **12** D4
Liverpool *U.S.A.* 43°6N 76°13W **83** C8
Liverpool Bay *U.K.* 53°30N 3°20W **12** D4
Liverpool Ra. *Australia* 31°50S 150°30E **63** E5
Livingston *Guatemala* 15°50N 88°50W **88** C2
Livingston *U.K.* 55°54N 3°30W **11** F5
Livingston *Ala., U.S.A.* 32°35N 88°11W **85** E10
Livingston *Calif., U.S.A.* 37°23N 120°43W **78** H6
Livingston *Mont.,
　U.S.A.* 45°40N 110°34W **76** D8
Livingston *S.C., U.S.A.* 33°38N 81°7W **85** E14
Livingston *Tenn.,
　U.S.A.* 36°23N 85°19W **85** C12
Livingston *Tex., U.S.A.* 30°43N 94°56W **84** F7
Livingston, L. *U.S.A.* 30°50N 95°10W **84** F7
Livingston Manor
　U.S.A. 41°54N 74°50W **83** E10
Livingstone *Zambia* 17°46S 25°52E **55** F2
Livingstone Mts. *Tanzania* 9°40S 34°20E **55** D3
Livingstonia *Malawi* 10°38S 34°5E **55** E3
Livny *Russia* 52°30N 37°30E **18** D6
Livonia *Mich., U.S.A.* 42°23N 83°23W **81** D12
Livonia *N.Y., U.S.A.* 42°49N 77°40W **82** D7
Livorno *Italy* 43°33N 10°19E **22** C4
Livramento *Brazil* 30°55S 55°30W **95** C4
Liwale *Tanzania* 9°48S 37°58E **55** D4
Liwonde *Malawi* 15°4S 35°13E **55** F4
Liwonde △ *Malawi* 14°48S 35°20E **55** E4
Lizard I. *Australia* 14°42S 145°30E **62** A4
Lizard Pt. *U.K.* 49°57N 5°13W **13** H2
Ljubljana *Slovenia* 46°4N 14°33E **16** E8
Ljungan ➤ *Sweden* 62°18N 17°23E **8** E17
Ljungby *Sweden* 56°49N 13°55E **9** H15
Ljusdal *Sweden* 61°46N 16°3E **8** F17
Ljusnan ➤ *Sweden* 61°12N 17°8E **8** F17
Ljusne *Sweden* 61°13N 17°7E **8** F17
Llancanelo, Salina
　Argentina 35°40S 69°8W **94** D2
Llandeilo *U.K.* 51°53N 3°59W **13** F4
Llandovery *U.K.* 51°59N 3°48W **13** F4
Llandrindod Wells *U.K.* 52°14N 3°22W **13** E4
Llandudno *U.K.* 53°19N 3°50W **12** D4
Llanelli *U.K.* 51°41N 4°10W **13** F3
Llanes *Spain* 43°25N 4°50W **21** A3
Llangollen *U.K.* 52°58N 3°11W **12** E4
Llanidloes *U.K.* 52°27N 3°31W **13** E4
Llano *U.S.A.* 30°45N 98°41W **84** F5
Llano ➤ *U.S.A.* 30°39N 98°26W **84** F5
Llano Estacado *U.S.A.* 33°30N 103°0W **84** E3
Llanos *S. Amer.* 5°0N 71°35W **92** C4
Llanos de Challe △ *Chile* 28°8S 71°1W **94** B1

Llanquihue, L. *Chile* 41°10S 72°50W **96** E1
Llanwrtyd Wells *U.K.* 52°7N 3°38W **13** E4
Llebeig, C. des *Spain* 39°33N 2°18E **24** B9
Lleida *Spain* 41°37N 0°39E **21** B6
Llera de Canales *Mexico* 23°19N 99°1W **87** C5
Lleyn Peninsula *U.K.* 52°51N 4°36W **12** E3
Llico *Chile* 34°46S 72°5W **94** C1
Lliria *Spain* 39°37N 0°35W **21** C5
Llobregat ➤ *Spain* 41°19N 2°5E **21** B7
Lloret de Mar *Spain* 41°41N 2°53E **21** B7
Lloseta *Spain* 39°43N 2°52E **24** B9
Lloyd B. *Australia* 12°45S 143°27E **62** A3
Lloyd L. *Canada* 57°22N 108°57W **71** B7
Lloydminster *Canada* 53°17N 110°0W **71** C7
Llubí *Spain* 39°42N 3°0E **24** B10
Llucmajor *Spain* 39°29N 2°53E **24** B9
Llullaillaco, Volcán
　S. Amer. 24°43S 68°30W **94** A2
Llullaillaco △ *Chile* 24°50S 68°51W **94** A2
Lo ➤ *Vietnam* 21°18N 105°25E **38** B5
Loa *U.S.A.* 38°24N 111°39W **76** G8
Loa ➤ *Chile* 21°26S 70°41W **94** A1
Loaita I. *S. China Sea* 10°41N 114°25E **36** B4
Loange ➤
　Dem. Rep. of the Congo 4°17S 20°2E **52** E4
Lobatse *Botswana* 25°12S 25°40E **56** D4
Lobería *Argentina* 38°10S 58°40W **94** D4
Lobito *Angola* 12°18S 13°35E **53** G2
Lobos *Argentina* 35°10S 59°0W **94** D4
Lobos, I. *Mexico* 27°20N 110°36W **86** B2
Lobos, I. de *Canary Is.* 28°45N 13°50W **24** F6
Loc Binh *Vietnam* 21°46N 106°54E **38** B6
Loc Ninh *Vietnam* 11°50N 106°34E **39** G6
Locarno *Switz.* 46°10N 8°47E **20** C8
Loch Baghasdail = Lochboisdale
　U.K. 57°9N 7°20W **11** D1
Loch Garman = Wexford
　Ireland 52°20N 6°28W **10** D5
Loch Lomond and the
　Trossachs △ *U.K.* 56°10N 4°40W **11** E4
Loch Nam Madadh = Lochmaddy
　U.K. 57°36N 7°10W **11** D1
Lochaber *U.K.* 56°59N 5°1W **11** E3
Locharbriggs *U.K.* 55°7N 3°35W **11** F5
Lochboisdale *U.K.* 57°9N 7°20W **11** D1
Loche, L. La *Canada* 56°30N 109°30W **71** B7
Lochem *Neths.* 52°9N 6°26E **15** B6
Loches *France* 47°7N 1°0E **20** C4
Lochgilphead *U.K.* 56°2N 5°26W **11** E3
Lochinvar △ *Zambia* 15°55S 27°15E **55** F2
Lochinver *U.K.* 58°9N 5°14W **11** C3
Lochmaddy *U.K.* 57°36N 7°10W **11** D1
Lochnagar *Australia* 23°33S 145°38E **62** C4
Lochnagar *U.K.* 56°57N 3°15W **11** E5
Lochy, L. *U.K.* 57°0N 4°53W **11** E4
Lock *Australia* 33°34S 135°46E **63** E2
Lock Haven *U.S.A.* 41°8N 77°28W **82** E7
Lockeford *U.S.A.* 38°10N 121°9W **78** G5
Lockeport *Canada* 43°47N 65°4W **73** D6
Lockerbie *U.K.* 55°7N 3°21W **11** F5
Lockhart *U.S.A.* 29°53N 97°40W **84** G6
Lockhart, L. *Australia* 33°15S 119°3E **61** F2
Lockhart River
　Australia 12°47S 143°20E **62** A3
Lockhart River ◎
　Australia 12°45S 143°20E **62** A3
Lockney *U.S.A.* 34°7N 101°27W **84** D4
Lockport *U.S.A.* 43°10N 78°42W **82** C6
Lod *Israel* 31°57N 34°54E **46** D3
Lodeinoye Pole *Russia* 60°44N 33°33E **18** B5
Lodge Bay *Canada* 52°14N 55°51W **73** B8
Lodge Grass *U.S.A.* 45°19N 107°22W **76** D10
Lodhran *Pakistan* 29°32N 71°30E **42** E4
Lodi *Italy* 45°19N 9°30E **20** D8
Lodi *Calif., U.S.A.* 38°8N 121°16W **78** G5
Lodi *Ohio, U.S.A.* 41°2N 82°1W **82** E3
Lodja
　Dem. Rep. of the Congo 3°30S 23°23E **54** C1
Lodwar *Kenya* 3°7N 35°36E **54** B4
Łódź *Poland* 51°45N 19°27E **17** C10
Loei *Thailand* 17°29N 101°35E **38** D3
Loengo
　Dem. Rep. of the Congo 4°48S 26°30E **54** D2
Loeriesfontein *S. Africa* 31°0S 19°26E **56** E2
Lofoten *Norway* 68°30N 13°59E **8** B16
Logan *Iowa, U.S.A.* 41°39N 95°47W **80** E6
Logan *Ohio, U.S.A.* 39°32N 82°25W **81** F12
Logan *Utah, U.S.A.* 41°44N 111°50W **76** F8
Logan *W. Va., U.S.A.* 37°51N 81°59W **81** G13
Logandale *U.S.A.* 36°36N 114°29W **79** J12
Logan, Mt. *Canada* 60°34N 140°23W **68** E3
Logansport *Ind., U.S.A.* 40°45N 86°22W **80** E10
Logansport *La., U.S.A.* 31°58N 94°0W **84** F8
Logone ➤ *Chad* 12°6N 15°2E **51** F8
Logroño *Spain* 42°28N 2°27W **21** A4
Lohardaga *India* 23°27N 84°45E **43** H11
Loharu *India* 28°27N 75°49E **42** E6
Lohri Wah ➤ *Pakistan* 27°27N 67°37E **42** F2
Loi-kaw *Burma* 19°40N 97°17E **41** K20
Loimaa *Finland* 60°50N 23°5E **8** F20
Loir ➤ *France* 47°33N 0°32W **20** C3
Loire ➤ *France* 47°16N 2°10W **20** C2
Loja *Ecuador* 3°59S 79°16W **92** D3
Loja *Spain* 37°10N 4°10W **21** D3
Loji = Kawasi *Indonesia* 1°38S 127°28E **37** E7
Lokandu
　Dem. Rep. of the Congo 2°30S 25°45E **54** C2
Lokeren *Belgium* 51°6N 3°59E **15** C3
Lokgwabe *Botswana* 24°10S 21°50E **56** C3
Lokichar *Kenya* 2°23N 35°39E **54** B4
Lokichokio *Kenya* 4°19N 34°13E **54** B3
Lokitaung *Kenya* 4°12N 35°48E **54** B4
Lokkan tekojärvi
　Finland 67°55N 27°35E **8** C22
Lokoja *Nigeria* 7°47N 6°45E **50** G7
Lokolo ➤
　Dem. Rep. of the Congo 1°43S 18°23E **52** E3

Lola, Mt. *U.S.A.* 39°26N 120°22W **78** F6
Lolgorien *Kenya* 1°14S 34°48E **54** C3
Loliondo *Tanzania* 2°2S 35°39E **54** C4
Lolland *Denmark* 54°45N 11°33E **9** J14
Lolo *U.S.A.* 46°45N 114°5W **76** C6
Loma *U.S.A.* 43°48N 23°12E **23** C10
Lom Kao *Thailand* 16°53N 101°14E **38** D3
Lom Sak *Thailand* 16°47N 101°15E **38** D3
Loma *U.S.A.* 47°56N 110°30W **76** C8
Loma Linda *U.S.A.* 34°3N 117°16W **79** L9
Lomaloma *Fiji* 17°17S 178°59W **59** a
Lomami ➤
　Dem. Rep. of the Congo 0°46N 24°16E **54** B1
Lomas de Zamora
　Argentina 34°45S 58°24W **94** C4
Lombadina *Australia* 16°31S 122°54E **60** C3
Lombárdia □ *Italy* 45°40N 9°30E **20** D8
Lombardy = Lombárdia □
　Italy 45°40N 9°30E **20** D8
Lomblen *Indonesia* 8°30S 123°32E **37** F6
Lombok *Indonesia* 8°45S 116°30E **37** K18
Lombok, Selat *Indonesia* 8°30S 115°50E **37** K18
Lomé *Togo* 6°9N 1°20E **50** G6
Lomela
　Dem. Rep. of the Congo 2°19S 23°15E **52** E4
Lomela ➤
　Dem. Rep. of the Congo 0°15S 20°40E **52** E4
Lommel *Belgium* 51°14N 5°19E **15** C5
Lomond *Canada* 50°24N 112°36W **70** C6
Lomond, L. *U.K.* 56°8N 4°38W **11** E4
Lomonosov Ridge *Arctic* 88°0N 140°0E **4** A
Lomphat *Cambodia* 13°30N 106°59E **38** F6
Lompobatang *Indonesia* 5°24S 119°56E **37** F5
Lompoc *U.S.A.* 34°38N 120°28W **79** L6
Łomża *Poland* 53°10N 22°2E **17** B12
Lon, Ko *Thailand* 7°47N 98°23E **39** a
Loncoche *Chile* 39°20S 72°50W **96** D2
Londa *India* 15°30N 74°30E **40** M9
Londiani *Kenya* 0°10S 35°33E **54** C4
London *Canada* 42°59N 81°15W **82** D3
London *U.K.* 51°30N 0°3W **13** F7
London *Ky., U.S.A.* 37°8N 84°5W **81** G11
London *Ohio, U.S.A.* 39°53N 83°27W **81** F12
London, Greater □ *U.K.* 51°36N 0°5W **13** F7
London Gatwick ✈ (LGW)
　U.K. 51°10N 0°11W **13** F7
London Heathrow ✈ (LHR)
　U.K. 51°28N 0°27W **13** F7
London Stansted ✈ (STN)
　U.K. 51°54N 0°14E **13** F8
Londonderry *U.K.* 55°0N 7°20W **10** B4
Londonderry □ *U.K.* 55°0N 7°20W **10** B4
Londonderry, C.
　Australia 13°45S 126°55E **60** B4
Londonderry, I. *Chile* 55°0S 71°0W **96** H2
Londres *Argentina* 27°43S 67°7W **96** B3
Londrina *Brazil* 23°18S 51°10W **95** A5
Lone Pine *U.S.A.* 36°36N 118°4W **78** J8
Lonely Mine *Zimbabwe* 19°30S 28°49E **57** B4
Long B. *U.S.A.* 33°35N 78°45W **85** E15
Long Beach *Calif.,
　U.S.A.* 33°46N 118°11W **79** M8
Long Beach *N.Y.,
　U.S.A.* 40°35N 73°39W **83** F11
Long Beach *Wash.,
　U.S.A.* 46°21N 124°3W **78** D2
Long Branch *U.S.A.* 40°18N 74°0W **83** F11
Long Creek *U.S.A.* 44°43N 119°6W **76** D4
Long Eaton *U.K.* 52°53N 1°15W **12** E6
Long I. *Australia* 20°22S 148°51E **62** b
Long I. *Bahamas* 23°20N 75°10W **89** B4
Long I. *Canada* 54°50N 79°20W **72** B4
Long I. *Ireland* 51°30N 9°34W **10** E2
Long I. *U.S.A.* 40°45N 73°30W **83** F11
Long Island Sd. *U.S.A.* 41°10N 73°0W **83** E11
Long L. *Canada* 49°30N 86°50W **72** C2
Long L. *U.S.A.* 44°0N 74°23W **83** C10
Long Lake *U.S.A.* 43°58N 74°25W **83** C10
Long Point *Canada* 42°34N 80°20W **82** D4
Long Point B. *Canada* 42°40N 80°10W **82** D4
Long Prairie *U.S.A.* 45°59N 94°52W **80** C6
Long Prairie ➤ *U.S.A.* 46°40N 94°36W **80** B6
Long Pt. *Ont., Canada* 42°35N 80°2W **82** D4
Long Pt. *Ont., Canada* 43°56N 76°53W **83** C8
Long Range Mts.
　Canada 49°30N 57°30W **73** C8
Long Reef *Australia* 14°1S 125°48E **60** B4
Long Sault *Canada* 45°2N 74°53W **83** A10
Long Str. = Longa, Proliv
　Russia 70°0N 175°0E **29** C18
Long Thanh *Vietnam* 10°47N 106°57E **39** G6
Long Xian *China* 34°55N 106°55E **34** G4
Long Xuyen *Vietnam* 10°19N 105°28E **39** G5
Longa, Proliv *Russia* 70°0N 175°0E **29** C18
Longbenton *U.K.* 55°1N 1°31W **12** B6
Longboat Key *U.S.A.* 27°23N 82°39W **85** H13
Longde *China* 35°30N 106°20E **34** G4
Longford *Australia* 41°32S 147°3E **63** G4
Longford *Ireland* 53°43N 7°49W **10** C4
Longford □ *Ireland* 53°42N 7°45W **10** C4
Longhua *Guangdong,
　China* 22°39N 114°0E **33** F11
Longhua *Hebei, China* 41°18N 117°45E **35** D9
Longido *Tanzania* 2°43S 36°42E **54** C4
Longiram *Indonesia* 0°5S 115°45E **36** E5
Longkou *China* 37°40N 120°18E **35** F11
Longlac *Canada* 49°45N 86°25W **72** C2
Longmeadow *U.S.A.* 42°3N 72°34W **83** D12
Longmont *U.S.A.* 40°10N 105°6W **76** F11
Longnawan *Indonesia* 1°51N 114°55E **36** D4
Longreach *Australia* 23°28S 144°14E **62** C3
Longueuil *Canada* 45°31N 73°29W **83** A11
Longview *Tex., U.S.A.* 32°30N 94°44W **84** E7
Longview *Wash., U.S.A.* 46°8N 122°57W **78** D4
Longxi *China* 34°53N 104°40E **34** G3
Longxue Dao *China* 22°41N 113°38E **33** F10
Longyearbyen *Svalbard* 78°13N 15°40E **4** B8
Lonoke *U.S.A.* 34°47N 91°54W **84** D9
Lonquimay *Chile* 38°26S 71°14W **96** D2

Lons-le-Saunier *France* 46°40N 5°31E **20 C6**
Looe *U.K.* 50°22N 4°28W **13 G3**
Lookout, C. *Canada* 55°18N 83°56W **72 A3**
Lookout, C. *U.S.A.* 34°35N 76°32W **85 D16**
Loolmalasin *Tanzania* 3°0S 35°53E **54 C4**
Loon → *Alta., Canada* 57°8N 115°3W **70 B5**
Loon → *Man., Canada* 55°53N 101°59W **71 B8**
Loon Lake *Canada* 54°2N 109°10W **71 C7**
Loongana *Australia* 30°52S 127°5E **61 F4**
Loop Hd. *Ireland* 52°34N 9°56W **10 D2**
Lop *China* 37°3N 80°11E **32 C3**
Lop Buri *Thailand* 14°48N 100°37E **38 E3**
Lop Nor = Lop Nur
  China 40°20N 90°10E **32 B4**
Lop Nur *China* 40°20N 90°10E **32 B4**
Lopatina, Gora *Russia* 50°47N 143°10E **29 D15**
Lopatka, Mys *Russia* 50°52N 156°40E **29 D16**
Lopez *U.S.A.* 41°27N 76°20W **83 E8**
Lopez, C. *Gabon* 0°47S 8°40E **52 E1**
Lopphavet *Norway* 70°27N 21°15E **8 A19**
Lora → *Afghan.* 31°35N 66°32E **40 D4**
Lora, Hāmūn-i- *Pakistan* 29°38N 64°58E **40 E4**
Lora Cr. → *Australia* 28°10S 135°22E **63 D2**
Lora del Río *Spain* 37°39N 5°33E **21 D3**
Lorain *U.S.A.* 41°28N 82°11W **82 E2**
Loralai *Pakistan* 30°20N 68°41E **42 D3**
Lorca *Spain* 37°41N 1°42W **21 D5**
Lord Howe I. *Pac. Oc.* 31°33S 159°6E **58 E8**
Lord Howe Rise *Pac. Oc.* 30°0S 162°30E **64 L8**
Lordsburg *U.S.A.* 32°21N 108°43W **77 K9**
Lorestān □ *Iran* 33°30N 48°40E **45 C6**
Loreto *Brazil* 7°5S 45°10W **93 E9**
Loreto *Mexico* 26°0N 111°21W **86 B2**
Lorient *France* 47°45N 3°23W **20 C2**
Lormi *India* 22°17N 81°41E **43 H9**
Lorn *U.K.* 56°26N 5°10W **11 E3**
Lorn, Firth of *U.K.* 56°20N 5°40W **11 E3**
Lorne *Australia* 38°33S 143°59E **63 F3**
Lorovouno *Cyprus* 35°8N 32°36E **25 D11**
Lorraine □ *France* 48°53N 6°0E **20 B7**
Los Alamos *Calif.,*
  U.S.A. 34°44N 120°17W **79 L6**
Los Alamos *N. Mex.,*
  U.S.A. 35°53N 106°19W **77 J10**
Los Altos *U.S.A.* 37°23N 122°7W **78 H4**
Los Andes *Chile* 32°50S 70°40W **94 C1**
Los Angeles *Chile* 37°28S 72°23W **94 D1**
Los Angeles *U.S.A.* 34°4N 118°15W **79 M8**
Los Angeles, Bahia de
  Mexico 28°56N 113°34W **86 B2**
Los Angeles Aqueduct
  U.S.A. 35°22N 118°5W **79 K9**
Los Angeles Int. ✈ (LAX)
  U.S.A. 33°57N 118°25W **79 M8**
Los Banos *U.S.A.* 37°4N 120°51W **78 H6**
Los Blancos *Argentina* 23°40S 62°30W **94 A3**
Los Cardones △ *Argentina* 25°8S 65°55W **94 B2**
Los Chiles *Costa Rica* 11°2N 84°43W **88 D3**
Los Cristianos *Canary Is.* 28°3N 16°42W **24 F3**
Los Gatos *U.S.A.* 37°14N 121°59W **78 H5**
Los Haïtises △ *Dom. Rep.* 19°4N 69°36W **89 C6**
Los Hermanos Is.
  Venezuela 11°45N 64°25W **89 D7**
Los Islotes *Canary Is.* 29°4N 13°44W **24 E6**
Los Llanos de Aridane
  Canary Is. 28°38N 17°54W **24 F2**
Los Loros *Chile* 27°50S 70°6W **94 B1**
Los Lunas *U.S.A.* 34°48N 106°44W **77 J10**
Los Mochis *Mexico* 25°45N 108°57W **86 B3**
Los Olivos *U.S.A.* 34°40N 120°7W **79 L6**
Los Palacios *Cuba* 22°35N 83°15W **88 B3**
Los Queñes *Chile* 35°1S 70°48W **94 D1**
Los Reyes de Salgado
  Mexico 19°35N 102°29W **86 D4**
Los Roques Is. *Venezuela* 11°50N 66°45W **89 D6**
Los Teques *Venezuela* 10°21N 67°2W **92 A5**
Los Testigos, Is. *Venezuela* 11°23N 63°6W **92 A6**
Los Vilos *Chile* 32°10S 71°30W **94 C1**
Loşinj *Croatia* 44°30N 14°30E **16 F8**
Loskop Dam *S. Africa* 25°23S 29°20E **57 D4**
Lossiemouth *U.K.* 57°42N 3°17W **11 D5**
Lostwithiel *U.K.* 50°24N 4°41W **13 G3**
Lot → *France* 44°18N 0°20E **20 D4**
Lota *Chile* 37°5S 73°10W **94 D1**
Lotfābād *Iran* 37°32N 59°20E **45 B8**
Lothair *S. Africa* 26°22S 30°27E **57 D5**
Lotta → *Europe* 68°42N 31°6E **8 B24**
Loubomo *Congo* 4°9S 12°47E **52 E2**
Loudonville *U.S.A.* 40°38N 82°14W **82 F2**
Louga *Senegal* 15°45N 16°5W **50 E2**
Loughborough *U.K.* 52°47N 1°11W **12 E6**
Lougheed I. *Canada* 77°26N 105°6W **69 B10**
Loughrea *Ireland* 53°12N 8°33W **10 C3**
Loughros More B. *Ireland* 54°48N 8°32W **10 B3**
Louis Tichardt *S. Africa* 23°1S 29°43E **57 C4**
Louis XIV, Pte. *Canada* 54°37N 79°45W **72 B4**
Louisa *U.S.A.* 38°7N 82°36W **81 F12**
Louisbourg *Canada* 45°55N 60°0W **73 C8**
Louisburgh *Ireland* 53°46N 9°49W **10 C2**
Louise I. *Canada* 52°55N 131°50W **70 C2**
Louiseville *Canada* 46°20N 72°56W **72 C5**
Louisiade Arch.
  Papua N. G. 11°10S 153°0E **58 C8**
Louisiana *U.S.A.* 39°27N 91°3W **80 F8**
Louisiana □ *U.S.A.* 30°50N 92°0W **84 F9**
Louisville *Ky., U.S.A.* 38°15N 85°46W **81 F11**
Louisville *Miss., U.S.A.* 33°7N 89°3W **85 E10**
Louisville *Ohio, U.S.A.* 40°50N 81°16W **82 F3**
Louisville Ridge
  Pac. Oc. 31°0S 172°30W **64 L10**
Loulé *Portugal* 37°9N 8°0W **21 D1**
Loup City *U.S.A.* 41°17N 98°58W **80 E4**
Loups Marins, Lacs des
  Canada 56°30N 73°45W **72 A5**
Lourdes *France* 43°6N 0°3W **20 E3**
Lourdes-de-Blanc-Sablon
  Canada 51°24N 57°12W **73 B8**
Louroujina *Cyprus* 35°0N 33°28E **25 E12**
Louth *Australia* 30°30S 145°8E **63 E4**

Louth *Ireland* 53°58N 6°32W **10 C5**
Louth *U.K.* 53°22N 0°1W **12 D7**
Louth □ *Ireland* 53°56N 6°34W **10 C5**
Louvain = Leuven
  Belgium 50°52N 4°42E **15 D4**
Louwsburg *S. Africa* 27°37S 31°7E **57 D5**
Lovech *Bulgaria* 43°8N 24°42E **23 C11**
Loveland *U.S.A.* 40°24N 105°5W **76 E2**
Lovell *U.S.A.* 44°50N 108°24W **76 D9**
Lovelock *U.S.A.* 40°11N 118°28W **76 F4**
Loviisa *Finland* 60°28N 26°12E **8 F22**
Loving *U.S.A.* 32°17N 104°6W **77 K11**
Lovington *U.S.A.* 32°57N 103°21W **77 K12**
Lovisa = Loviisa *Finland* 60°28N 26°12E **8 F22**
Low, L. *Canada* 52°29N 76°17W **72 B4**
Low Pt. *Australia* 32°25S 127°25E **61 F4**
Low Tatra = Nízké Tatry
  Slovak Rep. 48°55N 19°30E **17 D10**
Lowa
  Dem. Rep. of the Congo 1°25S 25°47E **54 C2**
Lowa →
  Dem. Rep. of the Congo 1°24S 25°51E **54 C2**
Lowell *U.S.A.* 42°38N 71°19W **83 D13**
Lowellville *U.S.A.* 41°2N 80°32W **82 E4**
Löwen → *Namibia* 26°51S 18°17E **56 D2**
Lower Alkali L. *U.S.A.* 41°16N 120°2W **76 F3**
Lower Arrow L. *Canada* 49°40N 118°5W **70 D5**
Lower California = Baja California
  Mexico 31°10N 115°12W **86 A1**
Lower Hutt *N.Z.* 41°10S 174°55E **59 D5**
Lower Lake *U.S.A.* 38°55N 122°37W **78 G4**
Lower Manitou L.
  Canada 49°15N 93°0W **71 D10**
Lower Post *Canada* 59°58N 128°30W **70 B3**
Lower Red L. *U.S.A.* 47°58N 95°0W **80 B6**
Lower Saxony = Niedersachsen □
  Germany 52°50N 9°0E **16 B5**
Lower Tunguska = Tunguska,
  Nizhnyaya → *Russia* 65°48N 88°4E **29 C9**
Lower Zambezi △ *Zambia* 15°25S 29°40E **55 F2**
Lowestoft *U.K.* 52°29N 1°45E **13 E9**
Lowgar □ *Afghan.* 34°0N 69°0E **40 B6**
Łowicz *Poland* 52°6N 19°55E **17 B10**
Lowther I. *Canada* 74°33N 97°30W **69 C12**
Lowville *U.S.A.* 43°47N 75°29W **83 C9**
Loxton *Australia* 34°28S 140°31E **63 E3**
Loxton *S. Africa* 31°30S 22°22E **56 E3**
Loyalton *U.S.A.* 39°41N 120°14W **78 F6**
Loyalty Is. = Loyauté, Îs.
  N. Cal. 20°50S 166°30E **58 D9**
Loyang = Luoyang
  China 34°40N 112°26E **34 G7**
Loyauté, Îs. *N. Cal.* 20°50S 166°30E **58 D9**
Loyev = Loyew *Belarus* 51°56N 30°46E **17 C16**
Loyew *Belarus* 51°56N 30°46E **17 C16**
Loyoro *Uganda* 3°22N 34°14E **54 B3**
Ltalaltuma ☉ *Australia* 23°57S 132°25E **60 D5**
Lu Wo *China* 22°33N 114°6E **33 F11**
Luachimo *Angola* 7°23S 20°48E **52 F4**
Luajan → *India* 24°44N 85°1E **43 G11**
Lualaba →
  Dem. Rep. of the Congo 0°26N 25°20E **54 B2**
Luambe △ *Zambia* 12°30S 32°15E **55 E3**
Luampa *Zambia* 15°4S 24°20E **55 F1**
Luan Chau *Vietnam* 21°38N 103°24E **38 B4**
Luan He → *China* 39°20N 119°5E **35 E10**
Luan Xian *China* 39°40N 118°40E **35 E10**
Luancheng *China* 37°53N 114°40E **34 F8**
Luanda *Angola* 8°50S 13°15E **52 F2**
Luang, Thale *Thailand* 7°30N 100°15E **39 J3**
Luang Prabang *Laos* 19°52N 102°10E **38 C4**
Luangwa *Zambia* 15°35S 30°16E **55 F3**
Luangwa → *Zambia* 14°25S 30°25E **55 E3**
Luangwa Valley *Zambia* 13°30S 31°30E **55 E3**
Luangwe = Loange →
  Dem. Rep. of the Congo 4°17S 20°2E **52 E4**
Luanne *China* 40°55N 117°40E **35 D9**
Luanping *China* 40°53N 117°23E **35 D9**
Luanshya *Zambia* 13°3S 28°28E **55 E2**
Luapula □ *Zambia* 11°0S 29°0E **55 E2**
Luapula → *Africa* 9°26S 28°33E **55 D2**
Luarca *Spain* 43°32N 6°32W **21 A2**
Luashi
  Dem. Rep. of the Congo 10°50S 23°36E **55 E1**
Luau *Angola* 10°40S 22°10E **52 G4**
Lubana, Ozero = Lubānas Ezers
  Latvia 56°45N 27°0E **9 H22**
Lubānas Ezers *Latvia* 56°45N 27°0E **9 H22**
Lubang Is. *Phil.* 13°50N 120°12E **37 B6**
Lubango *Angola* 14°55S 13°30E **53 G2**
Lubao
  Dem. Rep. of the Congo 5°17S 25°42E **54 D2**
Lubbock *U.S.A.* 33°35N 101°51W **84 E4**
Lübeck *Germany* 53°52N 10°40E **16 B6**
Lubefu
  Dem. Rep. of the Congo 4°47S 24°27E **54 C1**
Lubefu →
  Dem. Rep. of the Congo 4°10S 23°0E **54 C1**
Lubero = Luofu
  Dem. Rep. of the Congo 0°10S 29°15E **54 C2**
Lubicon L. *Canada* 56°23N 115°56W **70 B5**
Lubilash →
  Dem. Rep. of the Congo 6°2S 23°45E **52 F4**
Lublin *Poland* 51°12N 22°38E **17 C12**
Lubnān = Lebanon ■ *Asia* 34°0N 36°0E **46 B5**
Lubnān, Jabal *Lebanon* 33°45N 35°40E **46 B4**
Lubny *Ukraine* 50°3N 32°58E **28 D4**
Lubongola
  Dem. Rep. of the Congo 2°35S 27°0E **54 C2**
Lubudi
  Dem. Rep. of the Congo 9°57S 25°58E **52 F5**
Lubudi →
  Dem. Rep. of the Congo 9°0S 25°35E **55 D2**
Lubuklinggau *Indonesia* 3°15S 102°55E **36 E2**
Lubuksikaping *Indonesia* 0°10N 100°15E **36 D2**
Lubumbashi
  Dem. Rep. of the Congo 11°40S 27°28E **55 E2**

Lubunda
  Dem. Rep. of the Congo 5°12S 26°41E **54 D2**
Lubungu *Zambia* 14°35S 26°24E **55 E2**
Lubutu
  Dem. Rep. of the Congo 0°45S 26°30E **54 C2**
Luc An Chau *Vietnam* 22°6N 104°43E **38 A5**
Lucan *Canada* 43°11N 81°24W **82 C3**
Lucania, Mt. *Canada* 61°1N 140°27W **68 E3**
Lucas Channel = Main Channel
  Canada 45°21N 81°45W **82 A3**
Lucca *Italy* 43°50N 10°29E **22 C4**
Luce Bay *U.K.* 54°45N 4°48W **11 G4**
Lucea *Jamaica* 18°27N 78°10W **88 a**
Lucedale *U.S.A.* 30°56N 88°35W **85 F10**
Lucena *Phil.* 13°56N 121°37E **37 B6**
Lucena *Spain* 37°27N 4°31W **21 D3**
Lučenec *Slovak Rep.* 48°18N 19°42E **17 D10**
Lucerne = Luzern *Switz.* 47°3N 8°18E **20 C8**
Lucerne *U.S.A.* 39°6N 122°48W **78 F4**
Lucerne Valley *U.S.A.* 34°27N 116°57W **79 L10**
Lucero *Mexico* 30°49N 106°30W **86 A3**
Lucheng *China* 36°20N 113°11E **34 F7**
Lucheringo → *Mozam.* 11°43S 36°17E **55 E4**
Lucia *U.S.A.* 36°2N 121°33W **78 J5**
Lucinda *Australia* 18°32S 146°20E **62 B4**
Luckenwalde *Germany* 52°5N 13°10E **16 B7**
Luckhoff *S. Africa* 29°44S 24°43E **56 D3**
Lucknow *Canada* 43°57N 81°31W **82 C3**
Lucknow *India* 26°50N 81°0E **43 F9**
Lüda = Dalian *China* 38°50N 121°40E **35 E11**
Lüderitz *Namibia* 26°41S 15°8E **56 D2**
Lüderitzbaai *Namibia* 26°36S 15°8E **56 D2**
Ludhiana *India* 30°57N 75°56E **42 D6**
Ludington *U.S.A.* 43°57N 86°27W **80 D10**
Ludlow *U.K.* 52°22N 2°42W **13 E5**
Ludlow *Calif., U.S.A.* 34°43N 116°10W **79 L10**
Ludlow *Pa., U.S.A.* 41°43N 78°56W **82 E6**
Ludlow *Vt., U.S.A.* 43°24N 72°42W **83 C12**
Ludvika *Sweden* 60°8N 15°14E **9 F16**
Ludwigsburg *Germany* 48°53N 9°11E **16 D5**
Ludwigshafen *Germany* 49°29N 8°26E **16 D5**
Lueki
  Dem. Rep. of the Congo 3°20S 25°48E **54 C2**
Luena
  Dem. Rep. of the Congo 9°28S 25°43E **55 D2**
Luena *Zambia* 10°40S 30°25E **55 E3**
Luena Flats *Zambia* 14°47S 23°17E **53 G4**
Luenha = Ruenya →
  Africa 16°24S 33°48E **55 F3**
Lüeyang *China* 33°22N 106°10E **34 H4**
Lufira →
  Dem. Rep. of the Congo 9°30S 27°0E **55 D2**
Lufkin *U.S.A.* 31°21N 94°44W **84 F7**
Lufupa
  Dem. Rep. of the Congo 10°37S 24°56E **55 E1**
Luga *Russia* 58°40N 29°55E **9 G23**
Lugano *Switz.* 46°1N 8°57E **20 C8**
Lugansk = Luhansk
  Ukraine 48°38N 39°15E **19 E6**
Lugard's Falls *Kenya* 3°6S 38°41E **54 C4**
Lugela *Mozam.* 16°25S 36°43E **55 F4**
Lugenda → *Mozam.* 11°25S 38°33E **55 E4**
Lugh Ganana = Luuq
  Somali Rep. 3°48N 42°34E **47 G3**
Lugnaquillia *Ireland* 52°58N 6°28W **10 D5**
Lugo *Italy* 44°25N 11°54E **22 B4**
Lugo *Spain* 43°2N 7°35W **21 A2**
Lugoj *Romania* 45°42N 21°57E **17 F11**
Lugovoy = Qulan
  Kazakhstan 42°55N 72°43E **28 E8**
Luhansk *Ukraine* 48°38N 39°15E **19 E6**
Lui → *Angola* 8°21S 17°33E **52 F3**
Luiana *Angola* 17°25S 22°59E **56 B3**
Luiana → *Angola* 17°24S 23°3E **53 H4**
Luichow Pen. = Leizhou Bandao
  China 21°0N 110°0E **33 D6**
Luimneach = Limerick
  Ireland 52°40N 8°37W **10 D3**
Luing *U.K.* 56°14N 5°39W **11 E3**
Luís Correia *Brazil* 3°0S 41°35W **93 D10**
Luitpold Coast *Antarctica* 78°30S 32°0W **5 D1**
Luiza *Dem. Rep. of the Congo* 7°40S 22°30E **52 F4**
Luizi *Dem. Rep. of the Congo* 6°0S 27°25E **54 D2**
Luján *Argentina* 34°45S 59°5W **94 C4**
Lukanga Swamp *Zambia* 14°30S 27°40E **55 E2**
Lukenie →
  Dem. Rep. of the Congo 3°0S 18°50E **52 E3**
Lukolela
  Dem. Rep. of the Congo 5°23S 24°32E **54 D1**
Lukosi *Zimbabwe* 18°30S 26°30E **55 F2**
Luków *Poland* 51°55N 22°23E **17 C12**
Lukusuzi △ *Zambia* 12°43S 32°36E **55 E3**
Luleå *Sweden* 65°35N 22°10E **8 D20**
Luleälven → *Sweden* 65°35N 22°10E **8 D20**
Lüleburgaz *Turkey* 41°23N 27°22E **23 D12**
Lulima
  Dem. Rep. of the Congo 4°12S 25°36E **54 C2**
Luling *U.S.A.* 29°41N 97°39W **84 G6**
Lulong *China* 39°53N 118°51E **35 E10**
Lulonga →
  Dem. Rep. of the Congo 1°0N 18°10E **52 D3**
Lulua →
  Dem. Rep. of the Congo 4°30S 20°30E **52 E4**
Luma *Amer. Samoa* 14°16S 169°33W **59 b**
Lumajang *Indonesia* 8°8S 113°13E **37 H15**
Lumbala N'guimbo
  Angola 14°18S 21°18E **53 G4**
Lumberton *U.S.A.* 34°37N 79°0W **85 D15**
Lumsden *Canada* 50°39N 104°52W **71 C8**
Lumsden *N.Z.* 45°44S 168°27E **59 F2**
Lumut *Malaysia* 4°13N 100°37E **39 K3**
Lumut, Tanjung
  Indonesia 3°50S 105°58E **36 E3**
Luna *India* 23°43N 69°16E **42 H3**
Lunavada *India* 23°8N 73°37E **42 H5**
Lund *Sweden* 55°44N 13°12E **9 J15**
Lundazi *Zambia* 12°20S 33°7E **55 E3**
Lundi → *Zimbabwe* 21°43S 32°34E **55 G3**
Lundu *Malaysia* 1°40N 109°50E **36 D3**

Lundy *U.K.* 51°10N 4°41W **13 F3**
Lune → *U.K.* 54°0N 2°51W **12 C5**
Lüneburg *Germany* 53°15N 10°24E **16 B6**
Lüneburg Heath = Lüneburger
  Heide *Germany* 53°10N 10°12E **16 B6**
Lüneburger Heide
  Germany 53°10N 10°12E **16 B6**
Lunenburg *Canada* 44°22N 64°18W **73 D7**
Lunéville *France* 48°36N 6°30E **20 B7**
Lunga → *Zambia* 14°34S 26°25E **55 E2**
Lunga Lunga *Kenya* 4°33S 39°7E **54 C4**
Lunglei *India* 22°55N 92°45E **41 H18**
Luni *India* 26°0N 73°6E **42 G5**
Luni → *India* 24°41N 71°14E **42 G4**
Luninets = Luninyets
  Belarus 52°15N 26°50E **17 B14**
Luning *U.S.A.* 38°30N 118°11W **76 G4**
Luninyets *Belarus* 52°15N 26°50E **17 B14**
Lunkaransar *India* 28°29N 73°44E **42 E5**
Lunsemfwa → *Zambia* 14°54S 30°12E **55 E3**
Lunsemfwa Falls *Zambia* 14°30S 29°6E **55 E2**
Luo He → *China* 34°35N 110°20E **34 G6**
Luochuan *China* 35°45N 109°26E **34 G5**
Luofu
  Dem. Rep. of the Congo 0°10S 29°15E **54 C2**
Luohe *China* 33°32N 114°2E **34 H8**
Luonan *China* 34°5N 110°10E **34 G6**
Luoning *China* 34°35N 111°40E **34 G6**
Luoyang *China* 34°40N 112°26E **34 G7**
Luozigou *China* 43°42N 130°18E **35 C16**
Lupilichi *Mozam.* 11°47S 35°13E **55 E4**
Luque *Paraguay* 25°19S 57°25W **94 B4**
Luquillo, Sierra de
  Puerto Rico 18°20N 65°47W **89 d**
Luray *U.S.A.* 38°40N 78°28W **81 F14**
Lurgan *U.K.* 54°28N 6°19W **10 B5**
Lúrio *Mozam.* 13°32S 40°30E **55 E5**
Lusaka *Zambia* 15°28S 28°16E **55 F2**
Lusaka □ *Zambia* 15°30S 29°0E **55 F2**
Lusambo
  Dem. Rep. of the Congo 4°58S 23°28E **54 C1**
Lusangaye
  Dem. Rep. of the Congo 4°54S 26°0E **54 C2**
Luseland *Canada* 52°5N 109°24W **71 C7**
Lusenga Plain △ *Zambia* 9°22S 29°14E **55 D2**
Lushan *China* 33°45N 112°55E **34 H7**
Lushi *China* 34°3N 111°3E **34 G6**
Lushnjë *Albania* 40°55N 19°41E **23 D8**
Lushoto *Tanzania* 4°47S 38°20E **54 C4**
Lüshun *China* 38°45N 121°15E **35 E11**
Lusk *U.S.A.* 42°46N 104°27W **76 E11**
Lūt, Dasht-e *Iran* 31°30N 58°0E **45 D8**
Luta = Dalian *China* 38°50N 121°40E **35 E11**
Lutherstadt Wittenberg
  Germany 51°53N 12°39E **16 C7**
Luton *U.K.* 51°53N 0°24W **13 F7**
Luton □ *U.K.* 51°53N 0°24W **13 F7**
Lutsel K'e *Canada* 62°24N 110°44W **71 A6**
Lutsk *Ukraine* 50°50N 25°15E **17 C13**
Lutto = Lotta → *Europe* 68°42N 31°6E **8 B24**
Lützow Holmbukta
  Antarctica 69°10S 37°30E **5 C4**
Lutzputs *S. Africa* 28°3S 20°40E **56 D3**
Luverne *Ala., U.S.A.* 31°43N 86°16W **85 F11**
Luverne *Minn., U.S.A.* 43°39N 96°13W **80 D5**
Luvua
  Dem. Rep. of the Congo 8°48S 25°17E **55 D2**
Luvua →
  Dem. Rep. of the Congo 6°50S 27°30E **54 D2**
Luvuvhu → *S. Africa* 22°25S 31°18E **57 C5**
Luwegu → *Tanzania* 8°31S 37°23E **54 D4**
Luwero *Uganda* 0°50N 32°28E **54 B3**
Luwuk *Indonesia* 0°56S 122°47E **37 E6**
Luxembourg *Lux.* 49°37N 6°9E **15 E6**
Luxembourg □ *Belgium* 49°58N 5°30E **15 E5**
Luxembourg ■ *Europe* 49°45N 6°0E **15 E5**
Luxembourg ✈ (LUX)
  Lux. 49°37N 6°10E **15 E6**
Luxi *China* 24°27N 98°36E **32 D4**
Luxor = El Uqsur *Egypt* 25°41N 32°38E **51 C12**
Luyi *China* 33°50N 115°35E **34 H8**
Luza *Russia* 60°39N 47°10E **18 B8**
Luzern *Switz.* 47°3N 8°18E **20 C8**
Luziânia *Brazil* 16°20S 48°0W **93 G9**
Luzon *Phil.* 16°0N 121°0E **37 A6**
Lviv *Ukraine* 49°50N 24°0E **17 D13**
Lvov = Lviv *Ukraine* 49°50N 24°0E **17 D13**
Lyakhavichy *Belarus* 53°2N 26°32E **17 B14**
Lyakhovskiye, Ostrova
  Russia 73°40N 141°0E **29 B15**
Lyal I. *Canada* 44°57N 81°24W **82 B3**
Lyallpur = Faisalabad
  Pakistan 31°30N 73°5E **42 D5**
Lybster *U.K.* 58°18N 3°15W **11 C5**
Lycksele *Sweden* 64°38N 18°40E **8 D18**
Lydda = Lod *Israel* 31°57N 34°54E **46 D3**
Lydenburg *S. Africa* 25°10S 30°29E **57 D5**
Lydia *Turkey* 38°48N 28°19E **23 E13**
Lyell *N.Z.* 41°48S 172°4E **59 D4**
Lyell I. *Canada* 52°40N 131°35W **70 C2**
Lyepyel *Belarus* 54°50N 28°20E **9 J23**
Lykens *U.S.A.* 40°34N 76°42W **83 F8**
Lyman *U.S.A.* 41°20N 110°18W **76 F8**
Lyme B. *U.K.* 50°42N 2°53W **13 G5**
Lyme Regis *U.K.* 50°43N 2°57W **13 G5**
Lymington *U.K.* 50°45N 1°32W **13 G6**
Łyna → *Poland* 54°37N 21°14E **17 A11**
Lynd → *Australia* 16°28S 143°18E **62 B3**
Lynd Ra. *Australia* 25°30S 149°20E **63 D4**
Lynden *Canada* 43°14N 80°9W **82 C4**
Lynden *U.S.A.* 48°57N 122°27W **78 B4**
Lyndhurst *Australia* 30°15S 138°18E **63 E2**
Lyndon → *Australia* 23°29S 114°6E **61 D1**
Lyndonville *N.Y., U.S.A.* 43°20N 78°23W **82 C6**
Lyndonville *Vt., U.S.A.* 44°31N 72°1W **83 B12**
Lyngen *Norway* 69°45N 20°30E **8 B19**
Lynher Reef *Australia* 15°27S 121°55E **60 C3**

Lynn *U.S.A.* 42°28N 70°57W **83 D14**
Lynn Canal *U.S.A.* 58°50N 135°15W **74 D12**
Lynn Haven *U.S.A.* 30°15N 85°39W **85 F12**
Lynn Lake *Canada* 56°51N 101°3W **71 B8**
Lynnwood *U.S.A.* 47°49N 122°18W **78 C4**
Lynton *U.K.* 51°13N 3°50W **13 F4**
Lyntupy *Belarus* 55°4N 26°23E **9 J22**
Lynx L. *Canada* 62°25N 106°15W **71 A7**
Lyon *France* 45°46N 4°50E **20 D6**
Lyonnais *France* 45°45N 4°15E **20 D6**
Lyons = Lyon *France* 45°46N 4°50E **20 D6**
Lyons *Ga., U.S.A.* 32°12N 82°19W **85 E13**
Lyons *Kans., U.S.A.* 38°21N 98°12W **80 F4**
Lyons *N.Y., U.S.A.* 43°5N 77°0W **82 C8**
Lyons → *Australia* 25°2S 115°9E **61 E2**
Lyons Falls *U.S.A.* 43°37N 75°22W **83 C9**
Lys = Leie → *Belgium* 51°2N 3°45E **15 C3**
Lysí *Cyprus* 35°6N 33°41E **25 D12**
Lysva *Russia* 58°7N 57°49E **18 C10**
Lysychansk *Ukraine* 48°55N 38°30E **19 E6**
Lytham St. Anne's *U.K.* 53°45N 3°0W **12 D4**
Lyttelton *N.Z.* 43°35S 172°44E **59 E4**
Lytton *Canada* 50°13N 121°31W **70 C4**
Lyubertsy *Russia* 55°40N 37°51E **18 C6**
Lyuboml *Ukraine* 51°11N 24°4E **17 C13**

M

Ma → *Vietnam* 19°47N 105°56E **38 C5**
Ma'adaba *Jordan* 30°43N 35°47E **46 E4**
Maamba *Zambia* 17°17S 26°28E **56 B4**
Ma'ān *Jordan* 30°12N 35°44E **46 E4**
Ma'ān □ *Jordan* 30°0N 36°0E **46 E5**
Maanselkä *Finland* 63°52N 28°32E **8 E23**
Ma'anshan *China* 31°44N 118°29E **33 C6**
Maarianhamina = Mariehamn
  Finland 60°5N 19°55E **9 F18**
Ma'arrat an Nu'mān
  Syria 35°43N 36°43E **44 C3**
Maas → *Neths.* 51°45N 4°32E **15 C4**
Maaseik *Belgium* 51°6N 5°45E **15 C5**
Maasin *Phil.* 10°8N 124°58E **37 B6**
Maastricht *Neths.* 50°50N 5°40E **15 D5**
Maave *Mozam.* 21°4S 34°47E **57 C5**
Mababe Depression
  Botswana 18°50S 24°15E **56 B3**
Mabalane *Mozam.* 23°37S 32°31E **57 C5**
Mabel L. *Canada* 50°35N 118°43W **70 C5**
Mabenge
  Dem. Rep. of the Congo 4°15N 24°12E **54 B1**
Maberly *Canada* 44°50N 76°32W **83 B8**
Mablethorpe *U.K.* 53°20N 0°15E **12 D8**
Maboma
  Dem. Rep. of the Congo 2°30N 28°10E **54 B2**
Mabuasehube △
  Botswana 25°5S 21°10E **56 D3**
Mabuiag *Australia* 9°57S 142°11E **62 a**
Mac Bac *Vietnam* 9°46N 106°7E **39 H6**
Macachín *Argentina* 37°10S 63°43W **94 D3**
Macaé *Brazil* 22°20S 41°43W **95 A7**
McAlester *U.S.A.* 34°56N 95°46W **84 D7**
McAllen *U.S.A.* 26°12N 98°14W **84 H5**
MacAlpine L. *Canada* 66°32N 102°45W **68 C10**
Macamic *Canada* 48°45N 79°0W **72 C4**
Macao = Macau *China* 22°12N 113°33E **33 G10**
Macapá *Brazil* 0°5N 51°4W **93 C8**
Macarao △ *Venezuela* 10°22N 67°7W **89 D6**
McArthur → *Australia* 15°54S 136°40E **62 B2**
McArthur, Port *Australia* 16°4S 136°23E **62 B2**
Macau *Brazil* 5°15S 36°40W **93 E11**
Macau *China* 22°12N 113°33E **33 G10**
McBride *Canada* 53°20N 120°19W **70 C4**
McCall *U.S.A.* 44°55N 116°6W **76 D5**
McCamey *U.S.A.* 31°8N 102°14W **84 F3**
McCammon *U.S.A.* 42°39N 112°12W **76 E7**
McCarran Int., Las Vegas ✈ (LAS)
  U.S.A. 36°5N 115°9W **79 J11**
McCauley I. *Canada* 53°40N 130°15W **70 C2**
McCleary *U.S.A.* 47°3N 123°16W **78 C3**
Macclenny *U.S.A.* 30°17N 82°7W **85 F13**
Macclesfield *U.K.* 53°15N 2°8W **12 D5**
M'Clintock Chan.
  Canada 72°0N 102°0W **68 C11**
M'Clintock Ra.
  Australia 18°44S 127°38E **60 C4**
McCloud *U.S.A.* 41°15N 122°8W **76 F2**
McClure *U.S.A.* 40°42N 77°19W **82 F7**
McClure, L. *U.S.A.* 37°35N 120°16W **78 H6**
M'Clure Str. *Canada* 75°0N 119°0W **69 C8**
McClusky *U.S.A.* 47°29N 100°27W **80 B3**
McComb *U.S.A.* 31°15N 90°27W **85 F9**
McCook *U.S.A.* 40°12N 100°38W **80 E3**
McCreary *Canada* 50°47N 99°29W **71 C9**
McCullough Mt.
  U.S.A. 35°35N 115°13W **79 K11**
McCusker → *Canada* 55°32N 108°39W **71 B7**
McDermitt *U.S.A.* 41°59N 117°43W **76 F5**
McDonald *U.S.A.* 40°22N 80°14W **82 F4**
Macdonald, L. *Australia* 23°30S 129°0E **60 D4**
McDonald Is. *Ind. Oc.* 53°0S 73°0E **3 G13**
MacDonnell Ranges
  Australia 23°40S 133°0E **60 D5**
MacDowell L. *Canada* 52°15N 92°45E **72 B1**
Macdowell *U.K.* 57°40N 2°31W **11 D6**
Macedonia *U.S.A.* 41°19N 81°31W **82 E3**
Macedonia □ *Greece* 40°39N 22°0E **23 D10**
Macedonia ■ *Europe* 41°53N 21°40E **23 D9**
Maceió *Brazil* 9°40S 35°41W **93 E11**
Macerata *Italy* 43°18N 13°22E **22 C5**
McFarland *U.S.A.* 35°41N 119°14W **79 K7**
McFarlane → *Canada* 59°12N 107°58W **71 B7**
Macfarlane, L. *Australia* 32°0S 136°40E **63 E2**
McGehee *U.S.A.* 33°38N 91°24W **84 E9**
McGill *U.S.A.* 39°23N 114°47W **76 G6**
Macgillycuddy's Reeks
  Ireland 51°58N 9°45W **10 E2**
McGraw *U.S.A.* 42°36N 76°8W **83 D8**

McGregor U.S.A. 43°1N 91°11W 80 D8
McGregor Ra. Australia 27°0S 142°45E 63 D3
McGuire, Mt. Australia 27°43S 63°1E 62 b
Mach Pakistan 29°50N 67°20E 42 E2
Mãch Kowr Iran 25°48N 61°28E 45 E9
Machado → Jiparaná →
  Brazil 8°3S 62°52W 92 E6
Machagai Argentina 26°56S 60°2W 94 B3
Machakos Kenya 1°30S 37°15E 54 C4
Machala Ecuador 3°20S 79°57W 92 D3
Machanga Mozam. 20°59S 35°0E 57 C6
Machattie, L. Australia 24°50S 139°48E 62 C2
Machava Mozam. 25°54S 32°28E 57 D5
Machece Mozam. 19°15S 35°32E 57 C7
Macheke Zimbabwe 18°5S 31°51E 57 B5
Machhu → India 23°6N 70°46E 42 H4
Machiara △ Pakistan 34°40N 73°30E 42 B5
Machias Maine, U.S.A. 44°43N 67°28W 81 C20
Machias N.Y., U.S.A. 42°25N 78°29W 82 D6
Machichi → Canada 57°3N 92°6W 71 B10
Machico Madeira 32°43N 16°44W 24 D3
Machilipatnam India 16°12N 81°8E 41 L12
Machiques Venezuela 10°4N 72°34W 92 A4
Machu Picchu Peru 13°8S 72°30W 92 F4
Machynlleth U.K. 52°35N 3°50W 13 E4
Macia Mozam. 25°2S 33°8E 57 D5
McIlwraith Ra.
  Australia 13°50S 143°20E 62 A3
McInnes L. Canada 52°13N 93°45W 71 C10
McIntosh U.S.A. 45°55N 101°21W 80 C3
McIntosh L. Canada 55°45N 105°0W 71 B8
Macintosh Ra. Australia 27°39S 125°32E 61 E4
Macintyre → Australia 28°37S 150°47E 63 D5
Mackay Australia 21°8S 149°11E 62 K7
Mackay U.S.A. 43°55N 113°37W 76 E7
MacKay → Canada 57°10N 111°38W 70 B6
Mackay, L. Australia 22°30S 129°0E 60 D4
McKay Ra. Australia 23°0S 122°30E 60 D3
McKeesport U.S.A. 40°20N 79°51W 82 F5
McKellar Canada 45°30N 79°55W 82 A5
McKenna U.S.A. 46°56N 122°33W 78 D4
McKenzie U.S.A. 36°8N 88°31W 85 G10
Mackenzie → Australia 23°38S 149°46E 62 C4
Mackenzie → Canada 69°10N 134°20W 68 D5
McKenzie → U.S.A. 44°7N 123°6W 76 D2
Mackenzie Bay Canada 69°0N 137°30W 66 C6
Mackenzie City = Linden
  Guyana 6°0N 58°10W 92 B7
Mackenzie King I.
  Canada 77°45N 111°0W 69 B9
Mackenzie Mts. Canada 64°0N 130°0W 68 E6
Mackinac, Straits of
  U.S.A. 45°50N 84°40W 75 F23
Mackinaw City U.S.A. 45°47N 84°44W 81 C11
McKinlay Australia 21°16S 141°18E 62 C3
McKinlay → Australia 20°50S 141°28E 62 C3
McKinley, Mt. U.S.A. 63°4N 151°0W 68 E1
McKinley Sea Arctic 82°0N 0°0 4 A7
McKinney U.S.A. 33°12N 96°37W 84 E6
Mackinnon Road Kenya 3°40S 39°1E 54 C4
McKittrick U.S.A. 35°18N 119°37W 79 K7
Macklin Canada 52°20N 109°56W 71 C7
Macksville Australia 30°40S 152°56E 63 E5
McLaughlin U.S.A. 45°49N 100°49W 80 C3
Maclean Australia 29°26S 153°16E 63 D5
McLean U.S.A. 35°14N 100°36W 84 D4
McLeansboro U.S.A. 38°6N 88°32W 80 F9
Maclear S. Africa 31°2S 28°23E 57 E4
Maclear, C. Malawi 13°58S 34°49E 55 E3
Macleay → Australia 30°56S 153°0E 63 E5
McLennan Canada 55°42N 116°50W 70 B5
McLeod → Canada 54°9N 115°44W 70 C5
MacLeod, L. Australia 24°9S 113°47E 61 D1
McLeod B. Canada 62°53N 110°0W 71 A7
MacLeod Lake Canada 54°58N 123°0W 70 C4
McLoughlin, Mt.
  U.S.A. 42°27N 122°19W 76 E2
McMechen U.S.A. 39°57N 80°44W 82 G4
McMinnville Oreg.,
  U.S.A. 45°13N 123°12W 76 D2
McMinnville Tenn.,
  U.S.A. 35°41N 85°46W 85 D12
McMurdo Antarctica 77°0S 140°0E 5 D11
McMurdo Sd. Antarctica 77°0S 170°0E 5 D11
McMurray = Fort McMurray
  Canada 56°44N 111°7W 70 B6
McMurray U.S.A. 48°19N 122°14W 78 B4
Maçobere Mozam. 21°13S 32°47E 55 G3
Macodoene Mozam. 23°32S 35°5E 57 C6
Macomb U.S.A. 40°27N 90°40W 80 E8
Mâcon France 46°19N 4°50E 20 C6
Macon Ga., U.S.A. 32°51N 83°38W 85 E13
Macon Miss., U.S.A. 33°7N 88°34W 85 E10
Macon Mo., U.S.A. 39°44N 92°28W 80 F7
Macossa Mozam. 17°55S 33°56E 55 F3
Macoun L. Canada 56°32N 103°40W 71 B8
Macovane Mozam. 21°30S 35°2E 57 C6
McPherson U.S.A. 38°22N 97°40W 80 F5
McPherson Pk. U.S.A. 34°53N 119°53W 79 L7
McPherson Ra.
  Australia 28°15S 153°15E 63 D5
Macquarie → Australia 30°7S 147°24E 63 E4
Macquarie Harbour
  Australia 42°15S 145°23E 63 G4
Macquarie Is. Pac. Oc. 54°36S 158°55E 64 N7
Macquarie Ridge S. Ocean 57°0S 159°0E 5 B10
MacRobertson Land
  Antarctica 71°0S 64°0E 5 D6
Macroom Ireland 51°54N 8°57W 10 E3
MacTier Canada 45°8N 79°47W 82 A5
Macubela Mozam. 16°53S 37°49E 55 F4
Macuira △ Colombia 12°9N 71°21W 89 D5
Macuiza Mozam. 18°7S 34°29E 55 F3
Macumba → Australia 27°52S 137°12E 63 D2
Macusani Peru 14°4S 70°29W 92 F4
Macuse Mozam. 17°45S 37°10E 55 F4
Macuspana Mexico 17°46N 92°36W 87 D6

Macusse Angola 17°48S 20°23E 56 B3
Ma'dabā □ Jordan 31°43N 35°47E 46 D4
Madadeni S. Africa 27°43S 30°3E 57 D5
Madagascar ■ Africa 20°0S 47°0E 57 C8
Madama Niger 22°0N 13°40E 51 D8
Madame, I. Canada 45°30N 60°58W 73 C7
Madang Papua N. G. 5°12S 145°49E 58 B7
Madaripur Bangla. 23°19N 90°15E 41 H17
Madauk Burma 17°56N 96°52E 41 L20
Madawaska Canada 45°30N 78°0W 82 A7
Madawaska → Canada 45°27N 76°21W 82 A7
Madaya Burma 22°12N 96°10E 41 H20
Maddalena Italy 41°16N 9°23E 22 D3
Maddalena, La → Italy 52°7N 11°38E 16 B6
Madeira Atl. Oc. 32°50N 17°0W 24 D3
Madeira → Brazil 3°22S 58°45W 92 D7
Madeleine, Îs. de la
  Canada 47°30N 61°40W 73 C7
Madera Mexico 29°12N 108°7W 86 B3
Madera Calif., U.S.A. 36°57N 120°3W 78 J6
Madera Pa., U.S.A. 40°49N 78°26W 82 F6
Madha India 18°0N 75°30E 40 L9
Madhavpur India 21°15N 69°58E 42 J3
Madhepura India 26°11N 86°23E 43 F12
Madhubani India 26°21N 86°7E 43 F12
Madhupur India 24°16N 86°39E 43 G12
Madhya Pradesh □ India 22°50N 78°0E 42 H8
Madikeri India 12°30N 75°45E 40 N9
Madikwe △ S. Africa 27°38S 32°15E 57 D5
Madill U.S.A. 34°6N 96°46W 84 D6
Madimba
  Dem. Rep. of the Congo 4°58S 15°5E 52 E3
Ma'din Syria 35°45N 39°36E 44 C3
Madinat al Malik Khālid al
  Askarīyah Si. Arabia 27°54N 45°31E 44 E5
Madingou Congo 4°10S 13°33E 52 E2
Madirovalo Madag. 16°26S 46°32E 57 B8
Madison Calif., U.S.A. 38°41N 121°59W 78 G5
Madison Fla., U.S.A. 30°28N 83°25W 85 F13
Madison Ind., U.S.A. 38°44N 85°23W 81 F11
Madison Nebr., U.S.A. 41°50N 97°27W 80 E5
Madison Ohio, U.S.A. 41°46N 81°3W 82 E3
Madison S. Dak., U.S.A. 44°0N 97°7W 80 C5
Madison Wis., U.S.A. 43°4N 89°24W 80 D9
Madison → U.S.A. 45°56N 111°31W 76 D8
Madison Heights U.S.A. 37°25N 79°8W 81 G14
Madisonville Ky.,
  U.S.A. 37°20N 87°30W 80 G10
Madisonville Tex.,
  U.S.A. 30°57N 95°55W 84 F7
Madista Botswana 21°15S 25°6E 56 C4
Madiun Indonesia 7°38S 111°32E 37 G14
Mado Gashi Kenya 0°44N 39°10E 54 B4
Madoc Canada 44°30N 77°28W 82 B7
Madona Latvia 56°53N 26°5E 9 H22
Madrakah, Ra's al Oman 19°0N 57°50E 47 D6
Madras = Chennai India 13°8N 80°19E 40 N12
Madras = Tamil Nadu □
  India 11°0N 77°0E 40 P10
Madras U.S.A. 44°38N 121°8W 76 D3
Madre, L. U.S.A. 25°15N 97°30W 84 J6
Madre, Sierra Phil. 17°0N 122°0E 37 A6
Madre de Dios → Bolivia 10°59S 66°8W 92 F5
Madre de Dios, I. Chile 50°20S 75°10W 96 G1
Madre del Sur, Sierra
  Mexico 17°30N 100°0W 87 D5
Madre Occidental, Sierra
  Mexico 27°0N 107°0W 86 B3
Madre Oriental, Sierra
  Mexico 25°0N 100°0W 86 C5
Madri India 24°16N 73°32E 42 G5
Madrid Spain 40°24N 3°42W 21 B4
Madrid U.S.A. 44°45N 75°8W 83 B9
Madula
  Dem. Rep. of the Congo 0°27N 25°22E 54 B2
Madura Australia 31°55S 127°0E 61 F4
Madura Indonesia 7°30S 114°0E 37 G15
Madura, Selat Indonesia 7°30S 113°20E 37 G15
Madurai India 9°55N 78°10E 40 Q11
Madurantakam India 12°30N 79°50E 40 N11
Mae Chan Thailand 20°9N 99°52E 38 B2
Mae Hong Son Thailand 19°16N 97°56E 38 C2
Mae Khlong → Thailand 13°24N 100°0E 38 F3
Mae Phrik Thailand 17°27N 99°7E 38 D2
Mae Ping △ Thailand 17°37N 98°51E 38 D2
Mae Ramat Thailand 16°58N 98°31E 38 D2
Mae Rim Thailand 18°54N 98°57E 38 C2
Mae Sai Thailand 20°20N 99°55E 38 B2
Mae Sot Thailand 16°43N 98°34E 38 D2
Mae Suai Thailand 19°39N 99°33E 38 C2
Mae Tha Thailand 18°28N 99°8E 38 C2
Mae Wong △ Thailand 15°54N 99°12E 38 E2
Mae Yom △ Thailand 18°43N 100°15E 38 C3
Maebashi Japan 36°24N 139°4E 31 F9
Maelpaeg L. Canada 48°20N 56°30W 73 C8
Maesteg U.K. 51°36N 3°40W 13 F4
Maestra, Sierra Cuba 20°15N 77°0W 88 B4
Maevatanana Madag. 16°56S 46°49E 57 B8
Mafeking = Mafikeng
  S. Africa 25°50S 25°38E 56 D4
Mafeking Canada 52°40N 101°10W 71 C8
Mafeteng Lesotho 29°51S 27°15E 56 D4
Maffra Australia 37°53S 146°58E 63 F4
Mafia I. Tanzania 7°45S 39°50E 54 D4
Mafikeng S. Africa 25°50S 25°38E 56 D4
Mafra Brazil 26°10S 49°55W 95 B6
Mafra Portugal 38°55N 9°20W 21 C1
Mafungabusi Plateau
  Zimbabwe 18°30S 29°8E 55 F2
Magadan Russia 59°38N 150°50E 29 D16
Magadi Kenya 1°54S 36°19E 54 C4
Magadi, L. Kenya 1°54S 36°19E 54 C4
Magaliesburg S. Africa 26°0S 27°32E 57 D4
Magallanes, Estrecho de
  Chile 52°30S 75°0W 96 G2
Magangué Colombia 9°14N 74°45W 92 B4
Magdagachi Russia 53°27N 125°48E 29 D13

Magdalen Is. = Madeleine, Îs. de la
  Canada 47°30N 61°40W 73 C7
Magdalena Argentina 35°5S 57°30W 94 D4
Magdalena Bolivia 13°13S 63°57W 92 F6
Magdalena U.S.A. 34°7N 107°15W 77 J10
Magdalena → Colombia 11°6N 74°51W 92 A4
Magdalena, B. Mexico 24°35N 112°0W 86 C2
Magdalena, I. Mexico 24°40N 112°15W 86 C2
Magdalena, Llano de
  Mexico 25°0N 111°25W 86 C2
Magdeburg Germany 52°7N 11°38E 16 B6
Magdelaine Cays
  Australia 16°33S 150°18E 62 B5
Magee U.S.A. 31°52N 89°44W 85 F10
Magelang Indonesia 7°29S 110°13E 37 G14
Magellan's Str. = Magallanes,
  Estrecho de Chile 52°30S 75°0W 96 G2
Magenta, L. Australia 33°30S 119°2E 61 F2
Mageroya Norway 71°3N 25°40E 8 A21
Maggiore, Lago Italy 45°57N 8°39E 20 D8
Maggotty Jamaica 18°9N 77°46W 88 a
Maghâgha Egypt 28°38N 30°50E 51 C12
Magherafelt U.K. 54°45N 6°37W 10 B5
Maghreb N. Afr. 32°0N 4°0W 50 B5
Magistralnyy Russia 56°16N 107°36E 29 D11
Magnetic Pole (North)
  Canada 82°42N 114°24W 4 A2
Magnetic Pole (South)
  Antarctica 64°8S 138°8E 5 C9
Magnitogorsk Russia 53°27N 59°4E 18 D10
Magnolia Ark., U.S.A. 33°16N 93°14W 84 E8
Magnolia Miss., U.S.A. 31°9N 90°28W 85 F9
Mago Fiji 17°26S 179°8W 59 a
Magog Canada 45°18N 72°9W 83 A12
Magoro Uganda 1°45N 34°12E 54 B3
Magoša = Famagusta
  Cyprus 35°8N 33°55E 25 D12
Magoulades Greece 39°45N 19°42E 25 A3
Magoye Zambia 16°1S 27°30E 55 F2
Magpie, L. Canada 51°0N 64°41W 73 B7
Magrath Canada 49°25N 112°50W 70 D6
Magu Tanzania 2°30S 33°30E 54 C3
Maguarinho, C. Brazil 0°15S 48°30W 93 D9
Magude Mozam. 25°2S 32°40E 57 D5
Magura = Famagusta
  Cyprus 35°8N 33°55E 25 D12
Maguse L. Canada 61°37N 95°10W 71 A9
Maguse Pt. Canada 61°20N 93°50W 71 A10
Magvana India 23°13N 69°22E 42 H3
Magwe Burma 20°10N 95°0E 41 J19
Magyarorszag = Hungary ■
  Europe 47°20N 19°20E 17 E10
Maha Sarakham
  Thailand 16°12N 103°16E 38 D4
Mahābād Iran 36°50N 45°45E 44 B5
Mahabharat Lekh Nepal 28°30N 82°0E 43 F10
Mahabo Madag. 20°23S 44°40E 57 C7
Mahadeo Hills India 22°20N 78°30E 43 H8
Mahaffey U.S.A. 40°53N 78°44W 82 F6
Mahagi
  Dem. Rep. of the Congo 2°20N 31°0E 54 B3
Mahajamba → Madag. 15°33S 47°8E 57 B8
Mahajamba, Helodranon' i
  Madag. 15°24S 47°5E 57 B8
Mahajan India 28°48N 73°56E 42 E5
Mahajanga Madag. 15°40S 46°25E 57 B8
Mahajanga □ Madag. 17°0S 47°0E 57 B8
Mahajilo → Madag. 19°42S 45°22E 57 B8
Mahakam → Indonesia 0°35S 117°17E 36 E5
Mahalapye Botswana 23°1S 26°51E 56 C4
Mahale Mts. Tanzania 6°20S 30°0E 54 D3
Mahale Mts. △ Tanzania 6°10S 29°50E 54 D2
Mahallāt Iran 33°55N 50°30E 45 C6
Māhān Iran 30°5N 57°18E 45 D8
Mahan → India 23°30N 82°50E 43 H10
Mahanadi → India 20°20N 86°25E 41 J15
Mahananda → India 25°12N 87°52E 43 G12
Mahanoro Madag. 19°54S 48°48E 57 B8
Mahanoy City U.S.A. 40°49N 76°9W 83 F8
Maharashtra □ India 20°30N 75°30E 40 J9
Mahasham, W. →
  Egypt 30°15N 34°10E 46 E3
Mahasoa Madag. 22°12S 46°6E 57 C8
Mahasolo Madag. 19°7S 46°22E 57 B8
Mahattat ash Shīdīyah
  Jordan 29°55N 35°55E 46 F4
Mahattat 'Unayzah
  Jordan 30°30N 35°47E 46 E4
Mahavavy → Madag. 15°57S 45°54E 57 B8
Mahaxay Laos 17°22N 105°12E 38 D5
Mahbubnagar India 16°45N 77°59E 40 L10
Mahda U.A.E. 25°20N 56°15E 45 E7
Mahdah Oman 24°24N 55°59E 45 E7
Mahdia Tunisia 35°28N 11°0E 51 A8
Mahe India 11°42N 75°32E 43 C8
Mahé Seychelles 5°0S 55°30E 53 b
Mahé ✕ (SEZ) Seychelles 4°40S 55°31E 53 b
Mahébourg Mauritius 20°24S 57°42E 53 d
Mahendragarh India 28°17S 76°14E 42 E7
Mahendranagar Nepal 28°55N 80°20E 43 E9
Mahenge Tanzania 8°45S 36°41E 55 D4
Maheno N.Z. 45°10S 170°50E 59 F3
Mahesana India 23°39N 72°26E 42 H5
Maheshwar India 22°11N 75°35E 42 H6
Mahgawan India 26°29N 78°37E 43 F8
Mahi → India 22°15N 72°55E 42 H5
Mahia Pen. N.Z. 39°9S 177°55E 59 C6
Mahilyow Belarus 53°55N 30°18E 17 B16
Mahina Tahiti 17°30S 149°27W 59 d
Mahinerangi, L. N.Z. 45°50S 169°56E 59 F2
Mahmud Kot Pakistan 30°16N 71°0E 42 D4
Mahnomen U.S.A. 47°19N 95°58W 80 B6
Mahoba India 25°15N 79°55E 43 G8
Mahón = Maó Spain 39°53N 4°16E 24 B11
Mahone Bay Canada 44°27N 64°23W 73 D7
Mahopac U.S.A. 41°22N 73°45W 83 E11

Mahuva India 21°5N 71°48E 42 J4
Mai-Ndombe, L.
  Dem. Rep. of the Congo 2°0S 18°20E 52 E3
Mai Thon, Ko Thailand 7°40N 98°28E 39 a
Maicuru → Brazil 2°14S 54°17W 93 D8
Maidan Khula Afghan. 33°36N 69°50E 42 C3
Maidenhead U.K. 51°31N 0°42W 13 F7
Maidstone Canada 53°5N 109°20W 71 C7
Maidstone U.K. 51°16N 0°32E 13 F8
Maiduguri Nigeria 12°0N 13°20E 51 F8
Maigh Nuad = Maynooth
  Ireland 53°23N 6°34W 10 C5
Maihar India 24°16N 80°45E 43 G9
Maikala Ra. India 22°0N 81°0E 41 J12
Maiko △
  Dem. Rep. of the Congo 0°30S 27°50E 54 C2
Maili U.S.A. 21°25N 158°9W 75 L8
Mailani India 28°17N 80°21E 43 E9
Mailsi Pakistan 29°48N 72°15E 42 E5
Main → Germany 50°0N 8°18E 16 C5
Main → U.K. 54°48N 6°18W 10 B5
Main Channel Canada 45°21N 81°45W 82 A3
Main Range △
  Australia 28°11S 152°27E 63 D5
Main Ridge Trin. & Tob. 11°16N 60°40W 93 J16
Maine France 48°20N 0°15W 20 C3
Maine □ U.S.A. 45°20N 69°0W 81 C19
Maine → Ireland 52°9N 9°45W 10 D2
Maine, G. of U.S.A. 43°0N 68°30W 81 D19
Maingkwan Burma 26°15N 96°37E 41 F20
Mainit, L. Phil. 9°31N 125°30E 37 C7
Mainland Orkney, U.K. 58°59N 3°8W 11 C5
Mainland Shet., U.K. 60°15N 1°22W 11 A7
Mainpuri India 27°18N 79°4E 43 F8
Mainz Germany 50°1N 8°14E 16 C5
Maio C. Verde Is. 15°10N 23°10W 50 b
Maipú Argentina 36°52S 57°50W 94 D4
Maiquetía Venezuela 10°36N 66°57W 92 A5
Mairabari India 26°30N 92°22E 41 F18
Maisí Cuba 20°17N 74°9W 89 B5
Maisí, Pta. de Cuba 20°10N 74°10W 89 B5
Maitland N.S.W.,
  Australia 32°33S 151°36E 63 E5
Maitland S. Austral.,
  Australia 34°23S 137°40E 63 E2
Maitland → Canada 43°45N 81°43W 82 C3
Maitri Antarctica 70°0S 3°0W 5 D3
Maíz, Is. del Nic. 12°15N 83°4W 88 D3
Maizuru Japan 35°25N 135°22E 31 G7
Majalengka Indonesia 6°50S 108°13E 37 G13
Majene Indonesia 3°38S 118°57E 37 E5
Majete △ Malawi 15°54S 34°34E 55 F3
Majorca = Mallorca
  Spain 39°30N 3°0E 24 B10
Majuro Marshall Is. 7°9N 171°12E 64 G9
Maka Senegal 13°40N 14°10W 50 F3
Makaha Zimbabwe 17°20S 32°39E 57 B5
Makalamabedi Botswana 20°19S 23°51E 56 C3
Makale Indonesia 3°6S 119°51E 37 E5
Makalu-Barun △ Nepal 27°45N 87°10E 43 F12
Makamba Burundi 4°8S 29°49E 54 C2
Makarikari = Makgadikgadi Salt
  Pans Botswana 20°45S 25°45E 56 C4
Makarov Basin Arctic 87°0N 150°0W 4 A
Makarovo Russia 57°40N 107°45E 29 D11
Makasar = Ujung Pandang
  Indonesia 5°10S 119°20E 37 F5
Makasar, Selat Indonesia 1°0S 118°20E 37 E5
Makasar, Str. of = Makasar, Selat
  Indonesia 1°0S 118°20E 37 E5
Makat = Maqat
  Kazakhstan 47°39N 53°19E 19 E9
Makedonija = Macedonia ■
  Europe 41°53N 21°40E 23 D9
Makeni S. Leone 8°55N 12°5W 50 G3
Makeyevka = Makiyivka
  Ukraine 48°0N 38°0E 19 E6
Makgadikgadi △
  Botswana 20°27S 24°47E 56 C3
Makgadikgadi Salt Pans
  Botswana 20°40S 25°45E 56 C4
Makhachkala Russia 43°0N 47°30E 19 F8
Makhado = Louis Trichardt
  S. Africa 23°1S 29°43E 57 C4
Makham, Ao Thailand 7°51N 98°25E 39 a
Makhfar al Buşayyah
  Iraq 30°0N 46°10E 44 D5
Makhmūr Iraq 35°46N 43°35E 44 C4
Makian Indonesia 0°20N 127°20E 37 D7
Makindu Kenya 2°18S 37°50E 54 C4
Makinsk Kazakhstan 52°37N 70°26E 28 D8
Makira = San Cristóbal
  Solomon Is. 10°30S 161°0E 58 C9
Makiyivka Ukraine 48°0N 38°0E 19 E6
Makkah Si. Arabia 21°30N 39°54E 47 C2
Makkovik Canada 55°10N 59°10W 73 A8
Makó Hungary 46°14N 20°33E 17 E11
Makogai Fiji 17°28S 179°0E 59 a
Makokou Gabon 0°40N 12°50E 52 D2
Makongo
  Dem. Rep. of the Congo 3°25N 26°17E 54 B2
Makoro
  Dem. Rep. of the Congo 3°10N 29°59E 54 B2
Makrai India 22°2N 77°0E 42 H7
Makran Coast Range
  Pakistan 25°40N 64°0E 40 G4
Makrana India 27°2N 74°46E 42 F6
Makrigialos Greece 35°2N 25°59E 25 D7
Mākū Iran 39°15N 44°31E 44 B5
Makunda Botswana 22°30S 20°7E 56 C3
Makurazaki Japan 31°15N 130°20E 31 J5
Makurdi Nigeria 7°43N 8°35E 50 G7
Makushin Volcano
  U.S.A. 53°53N 166°55W 74 E6
Makūyeh Iran 28°7N 53°9E 45 D7
Makwassie S. Africa 27°17S 26°0E 56 D4

Makwiro Zimbabwe 17°58S 30°25E 57 B5
Mal B. Ireland 52°50N 9°30W 10 D2
Mala = Mallow Ireland 52°8N 8°39W 10 D3
Mala ✕ Australia 21°39S 130°45E 60 D5
Mala, Pta. Panama 7°28N 80°2W 88 E3
Malabar Coast India 11°0N 75°0E 40 P9
Malacca, Straits of
  Indonesia 3°0N 101°0E 39 L3
Malad City U.S.A. 42°12N 112°15W 76 E7
Maladzyechna Belarus 54°20N 26°50E 17 A14
Málaga Spain 36°43N 4°23W 21 D3
Málaga U.S.A. 32°14N 104°4W 77 K11
Malagarasi Tanzania 5°5S 30°50E 54 D3
Malagarasi → Tanzania 5°12S 29°47E 54 D2
Malagasy Rep. = Madagascar ■
  Africa 20°0S 47°0E 57 C8
Malahide Ireland 53°26N 6°9W 10 C5
Malaimbandy Madag. 20°20S 45°36E 57 C8
Malakâl Sudan 9°33N 31°40E 51 G12
Malakand Pakistan 34°40N 71°55E 42 B4
Malakula Vanuatu 16°15S 167°30E 58 C9
Malakwal Pakistan 32°34N 73°13E 42 C5
Malamala Indonesia 3°21S 120°55E 37 E6
Malanda Australia 17°22S 145°35E 62 B4
Malang Indonesia 7°59S 112°45E 37 G15
Malanga Mozam. 13°28S 36°7E 55 E4
Malanje Angola 9°36S 16°17E 52 F3
Mälaren Sweden 59°30N 17°10E 9 G17
Malargüe Argentina 35°32S 69°30W 94 D2
Malartic Canada 48°9N 78°9W 72 C4
Malaryta Belarus 51°50N 24°3E 17 C13
Malaspina Glacier
  U.S.A. 59°50N 140°30W 74 D11
Malatya Turkey 38°25N 38°20E 44 B3
Malawi ■ Africa 11°55S 34°0E 55 E3
Malawi, L. Africa 12°30S 34°30E 55 E3
Malay Pen. Asia 7°25N 100°0E 39 J3
Malaya Vishera Russia 58°55N 32°25E 18 C5
Malaybalay Phil. 8°5N 125°7E 37 C7
Malāyer Iran 34°19N 48°51E 45 C6
Malaysia ■ Asia 5°0N 110°0E 39 K4
Malazgirt Turkey 39°10N 42°33E 44 B4
Malbon Australia 21°5S 140°17E 62 C3
Malbooma Australia 30°41S 134°11E 63 E1
Malbork Poland 54°3N 19°1E 17 B10
Malcolm Australia 28°51S 121°25E 61 E3
Malcolm, Pt. Australia 33°48S 123°45E 61 F3
Maldah India 25°2N 88°9E 43 G13
Maldegem Belgium 51°14N 3°26E 15 C3
Malden Mass., U.S.A. 42°26N 71°3W 83 D13
Malden Mo., U.S.A. 36°34N 89°57W 80 G9
Malden I. Kiribati 4°3S 155°1W 65 H12
Maldives ■ Ind. Oc. 5°0N 73°0E 26 H9
Maldon U.K. 51°44N 0°42E 13 F8
Maldonado Uruguay 34°59S 55°0W 95 C5
Maldonado, Pta. Mexico 16°20N 98°33W 87 D5
Malé Karpaty Slovak Rep. 48°30N 17°20E 17 D9
Maleas, Akra Greece 36°28N 23°7E 23 F10
Malegaon India 20°30N 74°38E 40 J9
Malei Mozam. 17°12S 36°58E 55 F4
Malek Kandi Iran 37°9N 46°6E 44 B5
Malela
  Dem. Rep. of the Congo 4°22S 26°8E 54 C2
Malema Mozam. 14°57S 37°20E 55 E4
Maleme Greece 35°31N 23°49E 25 D5
Malerkotla India 30°32N 75°58E 42 D6
Males Greece 35°6N 25°35E 25 D7
Malgomaj Sweden 64°40N 16°30E 8 D17
Malha Sudan 15°8N 25°10E 51 E11
Malhargarh India 24°17N 74°59E 42 G6
Malheur → U.S.A. 44°4N 116°59W 76 D5
Malheur L. U.S.A. 43°20N 118°48W 76 E4
Mali ■ Africa 17°0N 3°0W 50 E5
Mali → Burma 25°42N 97°30E 41 G20
Mali Kyun Burma 13°0N 98°20E 38 F2
Malia Greece 35°17N 25°32E 25 D7
Malia, Kolpos Greece 35°19N 25°27E 25 D7
Malibu U.S.A. 34°2N 118°41W 79 L8
Maliku Indonesia 0°39S 123°16E 37 E6
Malili Indonesia 2°42S 121°6E 37 E6
Malimba, Mts.
  Dem. Rep. of the Congo 7°30S 29°30E 54 D2
Malin Hd. Ireland 55°23N 7°23W 10 A4
Malin Pen. Ireland 55°20N 7°17W 10 A4
Malindi Kenya 3°12S 40°5E 54 C5
Malindi Marine △ Kenya 3°15S 40°7E 54 C5
Malines = Mechelen
  Belgium 51°2N 4°29E 15 C4
Malino Indonesia 1°0N 121°0E 37 D6
Malinyi Tanzania 8°56S 36°0E 55 D4
Malita Phil. 6°19N 125°39E 37 C7
Maliwun Burma 10°17N 98°40E 39 G2
Maliya India 23°5N 70°46E 42 H4
Malka Mari △ Kenya 4°11N 40°46E 54 B5
Malkara Turkey 40°53N 26°53E 23 D12
Mallacoota Inlet
  Australia 37°34S 149°40E 63 F4
Mallaig U.K. 57°0N 5°50W 11 D3
Mallawan India 27°4N 80°12E 43 F9
Mallawi Egypt 27°44N 30°44E 51 C12
Mallicolo = Malakula
  Vanuatu 16°15S 167°30E 58 C9
Mallorca Spain 39°30N 3°0E 24 B10
Mallorytown Canada 44°29N 75°53W 83 B9
Mallow Ireland 52°8N 8°39W 10 D3
Malmberget Sweden 67°11N 20°40E 8 C19
Malmédy Belgium 50°25N 6°2E 15 D6
Malmesbury S. Africa 33°28S 18°41E 56 E2
Malmivaara = Malmberget
  Sweden 67°11N 20°40E 8 C19
Malmö Sweden 55°36N 12°59E 9 J15
Malolo Fiji 17°45S 177°11E 59 a
Malolos Phil. 14°50N 120°49E 37 B6
Malolotja △ Swaziland 26°4S 31°6E 57 D5
Malombe L. Malawi 14°40S 35°15E 55 E4
Malone U.S.A. 44°51N 74°18W 83 B10
Måløy Norway 61°57N 5°6E 8 F11

Malpaso Canary Is. 27°43N 18°3W 24 G1
Malpaso, Presa = Netzahualcóyotl, Presa
  Mexico 17°8N 93°35W 87 D6
Malpelo, I. de Colombia 4°3N 81°35W 92 C2
Malpur India 23°21N 73°27E 42 H5
Malpura India 26°17N 75°23E 42 F6
Malta Idaho, U.S.A. 42°18N 113°22W 76 E7
Malta Mont., U.S.A. 48°21N 107°52W 76 B10
Malta ■ Europe 35°55N 14°26E 25 D2
Maltahöhe Namibia 24°55S 17°0E 56 C2
Malton Canada 43°42N 79°38W 82 C5
Malton U.K. 54°8N 0°49W 12 C7
Maluku Indonesia 1°0S 127°0E 37 E7
Maluku □ Indonesia 3°0S 128°0E 37 E7
Maluku Sea = Molucca Sea
  Indonesia 0°0 125°0E 37 E6
Malvan India 16°2N 73°30E 40 L8
Malvern U.S.A. 34°22N 92°49W 84 D8
Malvern Hills U.K. 52°0N 2°19W 13 E5
Malvinas, Is. = Falkland Is. ☑
  Atl. Oc. 51°30S 59°0W 96 G5
Malya Tanzania 3°5S 33°38E 54 C3
Malyn Ukraine 50°46N 29°3E 17 C15
Malyy Lyakhovskiy, Ostrov
  Russia 74°7N 140°36E 29 B15
Malyy Taymyr, Ostrov
  Russia 78°6N 107°15E 29 B11
Mama Russia 58°18N 112°54E 29 D12
Mamanguape Brazil 6°50S 35°4W 93 E11
Mamanuca Group Fiji 17°35S 177°5E 59 a
Mamarr Mitlâ Egypt 30°2N 32°54E 46 E1
Mamasa Indonesia 2°55S 119°20E 37 E5
Mambasa
  Dem. Rep. of the Congo 1°22N 29°3E 54 B2
Mamberamo → Indonesia 2°0S 137°50E 37 E9
Mambilima Falls Zambia 10°31S 28°45E 55 E2
Mambirima
  Dem. Rep. of the Congo 11°25S 27°33E 55 E2
Mambo Tanzania 4°52S 38°22E 54 C4
Mambrui Kenya 3°5S 40°5E 54 C5
Mamburao Phil. 13°13N 120°39E 37 B6
Mameigwess L. Canada 52°35N 87°50W 72 B2
Mammoth U.S.A. 32°43N 110°39W 77 K8
Mammoth Cave △
  U.S.A. 37°8N 86°13W 80 G10
Mamoré → Bolivia 10°23S 65°53W 92 F5
Mamou Guinea 10°15N 12°0W 50 F3
Mamoudzou Mayotte 12°48S 45°14E 53 a
Mamuju Indonesia 2°41S 118°50E 37 E5
Mamuno Botswana 22°16S 20°1E 56 C3
Man Ivory C. 7°30N 7°40W 50 G4
Man, I. of U.K. 54°15N 4°30W 12 C3
Man-Bazar India 23°4N 86°39E 43 H12
Man Na Burma 23°27N 97°19E 41 H20
Mänä U.S.A. 22°2N 159°47W 75 L8
Mana → Fr. Guiana 5°45N 53°55W 93 B8
Mana Pools △ Zimbabwe 15°56S 29°25E 55 F2
Manaar, G. of = Mannar, G. of
  Asia 8°30N 79°0E 40 Q11
Manacapuru Brazil 3°16S 60°37W 92 D6
Manacor Spain 39°34N 3°13E 24 B10
Manado Indonesia 1°29N 124°51E 37 D6
Managua Nic. 12°6N 86°20W 88 D2
Managua, L. de Nic. 12°20N 86°30W 88 D2
Manakara Madag. 22°8S 48°1E 57 C8
Manali India 32°16N 77°10E 42 C7
Manama = Al Manāmah
  Bahrain 26°10N 50°30E 45 E6
Manambao → Madag. 17°35S 44°0E 57 B7
Manambato Madag. 13°43S 49°7E 57 A8
Manambolo → Madag. 19°18S 44°22E 57 B7
Manambolosy Madag. 16°2S 49°40E 57 B8
Mananara Madag. 16°10S 49°46E 57 B8
Mananara Madag. 23°21S 47°42E 57 C8
Mananara △ Madag. 16°14S 49°45E 57 B8
Mananjary Madag. 21°13S 48°20E 57 C8
Manantenina Madag. 24°17S 47°19E 57 C8
Manaos = Manaus Brazil 3°0S 60°0W 92 D7
Manapire → Venezuela 7°42N 66°7W 92 B5
Manapouri N.Z. 45°34S 167°39E 59 F1
Manapouri, L. N.Z. 45°32S 167°32E 59 F1
Manār, Jabal Yemen 14°2N 44°17E 47 E3
Manaravolo Madag. 23°59S 45°19E 57 C8
Manas China 44°17N 86°10E 32 B3
Manas → India 26°12N 90°40E 41 F17
Manas He → China 45°38N 85°12E 32 B3
Manaslu Nepal 28°33N 84°33E 43 E11
Manasquan U.S.A. 40°8N 74°3W 83 F10
Manassa U.S.A. 37°11N 105°56W 77 H11
Manatí Puerto Rico 18°26N 66°29W 89 d
Manaung Burma 18°45N 93°40E 41 K18
Manaus Brazil 3°0S 60°0W 92 D7
Manawan L. Canada 55°24N 103°14W 71 B8
Manbij Syria 36°31N 37°57E 44 B3
Manchegorsk Russia 67°54N 32°58E 28 C4
Manchester U.K. 53°29N 2°12W 12 D5
Manchester Calif.,
  U.S.A. 38°58N 123°41W 78 G3
Manchester Conn.,
  U.S.A. 41°47N 72°31W 83 E12
Manchester Ga., U.S.A. 32°51N 84°37W 85 E12
Manchester Iowa, U.S.A. 42°29N 91°27W 80 D8
Manchester Ky., U.S.A. 37°9N 83°46W 81 G12
Manchester N.H.,
  U.S.A. 42°59N 71°28W 83 D13
Manchester N.Y., U.S.A. 42°56N 77°16W 82 D7
Manchester Tenn.,
  U.S.A. 35°29N 86°5W 85 D11
Manchester Vt., U.S.A. 43°10N 73°5W 83 C11
Manchester Int. ✈ (MAN)
  U.K. 53°21N 2°17W 12 D5
Manchester L. Canada 61°28N 107°29W 71 A7
Manchhar L. Pakistan 26°25N 67°39E 42 F2
Manchuria = Dongbei
  China 45°0N 125°0E 30 A5
Manchurian Plain China 47°0N 124°0E 26 D14

Mand → India 21°42N 83°15E 43 J10
Mand → Iran 28°20N 52°30E 45 D7
Manda Ludewe, Tanzania 10°30S 34°40E 55 E3
Manda Mbeya, Tanzania 7°58S 32°29E 54 D3
Manda Mbeya, Tanzania 8°30S 32°49E 55 D3
Mandabé Madag. 21°0S 44°55E 57 C7
Mandaguari Brazil 23°32S 51°42W 95 A5
Mandah = Töhöm
  Mongolia 44°27N 108°2E 34 B5
Mandal Norway 58°2N 7°25E 9 G12
Mandala, Puncak
  Indonesia 4°44S 140°20E 37 E10
Mandalay Burma 22°0N 96°4E 41 J20
Mandale = Mandalay
  Burma 22°0N 96°4E 41 J20
Mandalgarh India 25°12N 75°6E 42 G6
Mandalgovĭ Mongolia 45°45N 106°10E 34 B4
Mandan U.S.A. 46°50N 100°54W 80 B3
Mandar, Teluk Indonesia 3°35S 119°15E 37 E5
Mandaue Phil. 10°20N 123°56E 37 B6
Mandera Kenya 3°55N 41°53E 54 B5
Mandeville Jamaica 18°2N 77°31W 88 a
Mandi India 31°39N 76°58E 42 D7
Mandi Burewala Pakistan 30°9N 72°41E 42 D5
Mandi Dabwali India 29°58N 74°42E 42 E6
Mandimba Mozam. 14°20S 35°40E 55 E4
Mandioli Indonesia 0°40S 127°20E 37 E7
Mandla India 22°39N 80°30E 43 H9
Mandorah Australia 12°32S 130°42E 60 B5
Mandoto Madag. 19°34S 46°17E 57 B8
Mandra Pakistan 33°23N 73°12E 42 C5
Mandrare → Madag. 25°10S 46°30E 57 D8
Mandritsara Madag. 15°50S 48°49E 57 B8
Mandronarivo Madag. 21°7S 45°38E 57 C8
Mandsaur India 24°3N 75°8E 42 G6
Mandurah Australia 32°36S 115°48E 61 F2
Mandvi India 22°51N 69°22E 42 H3
Mandya India 12°30N 77°0E 40 N10
Mandzai Pakistan 30°55N 67°6E 42 D2
Maneh Iran 37°39N 57°7E 45 B8
Manera Madag. 22°55S 44°20E 57 C7
Maneroo Cr. →
  Australia 23°21S 143°53E 62 C3
Manfalût Egypt 27°20N 30°52E 51 C12
Manfredónia Italy 41°38N 15°55E 22 D6
Mangabeiras, Chapada das
  Brazil 10°0S 46°30W 93 F9
Mangaia Cook Is. 21°55S 157°55W 65 K12
Mangalia Romania 43°50N 28°35E 17 G15
Mangalore India 12°55N 74°47E 40 N9
Mangaluru = Mangalore
  India 12°55N 74°47E 40 N9
Mangan India 27°31N 88°32E 43 F13
Mangawan India 24°41N 81°33E 43 G9
Mangaweka N.Z. 39°48S 175°47E 59 C5
Manggar Indonesia 2°50S 108°10E 36 E3
Manggawitu Indonesia 4°8S 133°32E 37 E8
Mangghystaŭ Tübegi
  Kazakhstan 44°30N 52°30E 28 E6
Manggis Indonesia 8°29S 115°31E 37 J18
Mangindrano Madag. 14°17S 48°58E 57 A8
Mangkalihat, Tanjung
  Indonesia 1°2N 118°59E 37 D5
Mangkururrpa ○
  Australia 20°35S 129°43E 60 D4
Mangla Pakistan 33°7N 73°39E 42 C5
Mangla Dam Pakistan 33°9N 73°44E 43 C5
Manglaur India 29°44N 77°49E 42 E7
Mangnai China 37°52N 91°43E 32 C4
Mangnai Zhen China 38°24N 90°14E 32 C4
Mango Togo 10°20N 0°30E 50 F6
Mango Tonga 20°17S 174°29W 59 c
Mangoche Malawi 14°25S 35°16E 55 E4
Mangoky → Madag. 21°29S 43°41E 57 C7
Mangole Indonesia 1°50S 125°55E 37 E6
Mangombe
  Dem. Rep. of the Congo 1°20S 26°48E 54 C2
Mangonui N.Z. 35°1S 173°32E 59 A4
Mangoro → Madag. 20°0S 48°45E 57 B8
Mangrol Mad. P., India 21°7N 70°7E 42 J4
Mangrol Raj., India 25°20N 76°31E 42 G6
Mangueira, L. da Brazil 33°0S 52°50W 95 C5
Mangum U.S.A. 34°53N 99°30W 84 H5
Manguri Australia 28°58S 134°22E 63 A1
Mangyshlak, Poluostrov = Mangghystaŭ Tübegi
  Kazakhstan 44°30N 52°30E 28 E6
Manhattan U.S.A. 39°11N 96°35W 80 F5
Manhiça Mozam. 25°23S 32°49E 57 D5
Mania → Madag. 19°42S 45°22E 57 B8
Manica Mozam. 18°58S 32°59E 57 B5
Manica □ Mozam. 19°10S 33°45E 57 B5
Manicaland □ Zimbabwe 19°0S 32°30E 55 F3
Manicoré Brazil 5°48S 61°16W 92 E6
Manicouagan →
  Canada 49°30N 68°30W 73 C6
Manicouagan, Rés.
  Canada 51°5N 68°40W 73 B6
Maniema □
  Dem. Rep. of the Congo 3°0S 26°0E 54 C2
Maniftah Si. Arabia 27°44N 49°0E 45 E6
Manifold, C. Australia 22°41S 150°50E 62 C5
Manigotagan Canada 51°6N 96°18W 71 C9
Manigotagan → Canada 51°7N 96°20W 71 C9
Manihari India 25°21N 87°38E 43 G12
Manihiki Cook Is. 10°24S 161°1W 65 J11
Manihki Plateau
  Pac. Oc. 11°0S 164°0W 65 J11
Manika, Plateau de la
  Dem. Rep. of the Congo 10°0S 25°5E 55 E2
Manikpur India 25°4N 81°7E 43 G9
Manila Phil. 14°35N 120°58E 37 B6
Manila U.S.A. 40°59N 109°43W 76 F9
Manila B. Phil. 14°40N 120°35E 37 B6
Manilla Australia 30°45S 150°43E 63 E5
Maningrida Australia 12°3S 134°13E 62 A1
Manipur □ India 25°0N 94°0E 41 G19
Manipur → Burma 23°45N 94°20E 41 H19

Manisa Turkey 38°38N 27°30E 23 E12
Manistee U.S.A. 44°15N 86°19W 80 C10
Manistee → U.S.A. 44°15N 86°21W 80 C10
Manistique U.S.A. 45°57N 86°15W 80 C10
Manitoba □ Canada 53°30N 97°0W 71 B9
Manitoba, L. Canada 51°0N 98°45W 71 C9
Manitou Canada 49°15N 98°32W 71 D9
Manitou, L. Canada 50°55N 65°17W 73 B6
Manitou Is. U.S.A. 45°8N 86°0W 80 C10
Manitou L. Canada 52°43N 109°43W 71 C7
Manitou Springs
  U.S.A. 38°52N 104°55W 76 G11
Manitoulin I. Canada 45°40N 82°30W 72 C3
Manitouwadge Canada 49°8N 85°48W 72 C2
Manitowoc U.S.A. 44°5N 87°40W 80 C10
Manizales Colombia 5°5N 75°32W 92 B3
Manja Madag. 21°26S 44°20E 57 C7
Manjacaze Mozam. 24°45S 34°0E 57 C5
Manjakandriana Madag. 18°55S 47°47E 57 B8
Manjhand Pakistan 25°50N 68°10E 42 G3
Manjimup Australia 34°15S 116°6E 61 F2
Manjra → India 18°49N 77°52E 40 K10
Mankato Kans., U.S.A. 39°47N 98°13W 80 F4
Mankato Minn., U.S.A. 44°10N 94°0W 80 C6
Mankayane Swaziland 26°40S 31°4E 57 D5
Mankera Pakistan 31°23N 71°26E 42 D4
Mankota Canada 49°25N 107°5W 71 D7
Manlay = Üydzin
  Mongolia 44°9N 107°0E 34 B4
Manmad India 20°18N 74°28E 40 J9
Mann Ranges Australia 26°6S 130°5E 61 E5
Manna Indonesia 4°25S 102°55E 36 E2
Mannahill Australia 32°25S 140°0E 63 E3
Mannar Sri Lanka 9°1N 79°54E 40 Q11
Mannar, G. of Asia 8°30N 79°0E 40 Q11
Mannar I. Sri Lanka 9°5N 79°45E 40 Q11
Mannheim Germany 49°29N 8°26E 16 D5
Manning Canada 56°53N 117°39W 70 B5
Manning Oreg., U.S.A. 45°45N 123°13W 78 E3
Manning S.C., U.S.A. 33°42N 80°13W 85 E14
Mannum Australia 34°50S 139°20E 63 E2
Manoharpur India 22°23N 85°12E 43 H11
Manokwari Indonesia 0°54S 134°0E 37 E8
Manombo Madag. 22°57S 43°28E 57 C7
Manono
  Dem. Rep. of the Congo 7°15S 27°25E 54 D2
Manono Samoa 13°50S 172°5W 59 b
Manorhamilton Ireland 54°18N 8°10W 10 B3
Manosque France 43°49N 5°47E 20 E6
Manotick Canada 45°13N 75°41W 83 A9
Manouane → Canada 49°30N 71°10W 73 C5
Manouane, L. Canada 50°45N 70°45W 73 B5
Manp'o N. Korea 41°6N 126°24E 35 D14
Manpojin = Manp'o
  N. Korea 41°6N 126°24E 35 D14
Manpur Chhattisgarh,
  India 23°17N 83°35E 43 H10
Manpur Mad. P., India 22°26N 75°37E 42 H6
Manresa Spain 41°48N 1°50E 21 B6
Mansa Gujarat, India 23°27N 72°45E 42 H5
Mansa Punjab, India 30°0N 75°27E 42 E6
Mansa Zambia 11°13S 28°55E 55 E2
Mansehra Pakistan 34°20N 73°15E 42 B5
Mansel I. Canada 62°0N 80°0W 69 E15
Mansfield Australia 37°4S 146°6E 63 F4
Mansfield U.K. 53°9N 1°11W 12 D6
Mansfield La., U.S.A. 32°2N 93°43W 84 E8
Mansfield Mass., U.S.A. 42°2N 71°13W 83 D13
Mansfield Ohio, U.S.A. 40°45N 82°31W 82 F2
Mansfield Pa., U.S.A. 41°48N 77°5W 82 E7
Mansfield Tex., U.S.A. 32°33N 97°8W 84 E6
Mansfield, Mt. U.S.A. 44°33N 72°49W 83 B12
Manson Creek Canada 55°37N 124°32W 70 B4
Manta Ecuador 1°0S 80°40W 92 D2
Mantadia △ Madag. 18°54S 48°21E 57 B8
Mantalingajan, Mt.
  Phil. 8°55N 117°45E 36 C5
Mantare Tanzania 2°42S 33°13E 54 C3
Manteca U.S.A. 37°48N 121°13W 78 H5
Manteo U.S.A. 35°55N 75°40W 85 D17
Mantes-la-Jolie France 48°58N 1°41E 20 B4
Manthani India 18°40N 79°31E 40 K11
Manti U.S.A. 39°16N 111°38W 76 G8
Mantiqueira, Serra da
  Brazil 22°0S 44°0W 95 A7
Manton U.S.A. 44°25N 85°24W 81 C11
Mántova Italy 45°9N 10°48E 22 B4
Mänttä Finland 62°3N 24°40E 8 E21
Mantua = Mántova Italy 45°9N 10°48E 22 B4
Manú Peru 12°10S 70°51W 92 F4
Manú → Peru 12°16S 70°55W 92 F4
Manu'a Is. Amer. Samoa 14°13S 169°35W 59 b
Manuel Alves → Brazil 11°19S 48°28W 93 F9
Manui Indonesia 3°35S 123°5E 37 E6
Manukau N.Z. 37°0S 174°52E 59 B5
Manuripi → Bolivia 11°6S 67°36W 92 F5
Many U.S.A. 31°34N 93°29W 84 F8
Manyallaluk ○
  Australia 14°16S 132°49E 60 B5
Manyara □ Kenya 3°5S 35°50E 54 C4
Manyara, L. Tanzania 3°40S 35°50E 54 C4
Manych-Gudilo, Ozero
  Russia 46°24N 42°38E 19 E7
Manyoni Tanzania 5°45S 34°55E 54 D3
Manzai Pakistan 32°12N 70°15E 42 C4
Manzanares Spain 39°2N 3°22W 21 C4
Manzanillo Cuba 20°20N 77°31W 88 B4
Manzanillo Mexico 19°3N 104°20W 86 D4
Manzanillo, Pta. Panama 9°30N 79°40W 88 E4
Manzariyeh Iran 34°53N 50°50E 45 C6
Manzhouli China 49°35N 117°25E 33 B6
Manzur Vadisi → Turkey 39°10N 39°30E 44 B3
Mao Chad 14°4N 15°19E 51 F9
Maó Spain 39°53N 4°16E 24 B11

Maoke, Pegunungan
  Indonesia 3°40S 137°30E 37 E9
Maolin China 43°58N 123°30E 35 C12
Maoming China 21°50N 110°54E 33 D6
Maoxing China 45°28N 124°40E 35 B13
Mapam Yumco China 30°45N 81°28E 43 D9
Mapastepec Mexico 15°26N 92°54W 87 D6
Mapia, Kepulauan
  Indonesia 0°50N 134°20E 37 D8
Mapimí Mexico 25°49N 103°51W 86 B4
Mapimí, Bolsón de
  Mexico 27°0N 104°15W 86 B4
Mapinga Tanzania 6°40S 39°12E 54 D4
Mapinhane Mozam. 22°20S 35°0E 57 C6
Maple Creek Canada 49°55N 109°29W 71 D7
Maple Valley U.S.A. 47°25N 122°3W 78 C4
Mapleton U.S.A. 44°2N 123°52W 76 D2
Mapon ○ Australia 11°44S 142°8E 62 A3
Mapuera → Brazil 1°5S 57°2W 92 D7
Mapulanguene Mozam. 24°29S 32°6E 57 C5
Mapungubwe △
  S. Africa 22°12S 29°22E 55 G2
Maputo Mozam. 25°58S 32°32E 57 D5
Maputo □ Mozam. 26°0S 32°25E 57 D5
Maputo, B. de Mozam. 25°50S 32°45E 57 D5
Maputo → Mozam. 25°58S 32°48E 57 D5
Maqat Kazakhstan 47°39N 53°19E 19 E9
Maqên China 34°24N 100°6E 32 C5
Maqiaohe China 44°40N 130°30E 35 B16
Maqnā Si. Arabia 28°25N 34°50E 44 D2
Maqteïr Mauritania 21°50N 11°40W 50 D3
Maquan He = Brahmaputra →
  Asia 23°40N 90°35E 43 H13
Maquela do Zombo Angola 6°0S 15°15E 52 F3
Maquinchao Argentina 41°15S 68°50W 96 E3
Maquoketa U.S.A. 42°4N 90°40W 80 D8
Mar Canada 44°49N 81°12W 82 B3
Mar, Serra do Brazil 25°30S 49°0W 95 B6
Mar Chiquita, L.
  Argentina 30°40S 62°50W 94 C3
Mar del Plata Argentina 38°0S 57°30W 94 D4
Mar Menor Spain 37°40N 0°45W 21 D5
Mara Tanzania 1°30S 34°32E 54 C3
Mara □ Tanzania 1°45S 34°20E 54 C3
Maraã Brazil 1°52S 65°25W 92 D5
Maraa Tahiti 17°46S 149°34W 59 d
Marabá Brazil 5°20S 49°5W 93 E9
Maraboon, L. Australia 23°41S 148°0E 62 C4
Maracá, I. de Brazil 2°10N 50°30W 93 C8
Maracaibo Venezuela 10°40N 71°37W 92 A4
Maracaibo, L. de
  Venezuela 9°40N 71°30W 92 B4
Maracaju Brazil 21°38S 55°9W 95 A4
Maracas Bay Village
  Trin. & Tob. 10°46N 61°28W 93 K15
Maracay Venezuela 10°15N 67°28W 92 A5
Marādah Libya 29°15N 19°15E 51 C9
Maradi Niger 13°29N 7°20E 50 F7
Marāgheh Iran 37°30N 46°12E 44 B5
Marāh Si. Arabia 25°0N 45°35E 44 E5
Marajó, I. de Brazil 1°0S 49°30W 93 D9
Marākand Iran 38°51N 45°16E 44 B5
Marakele △ S. Africa 32°14S 25°27E 57 E4
Maralal Kenya 1°0N 36°38E 54 B4
Maralinga Australia 30°13S 131°32E 61 F5
Maralinga Tjarutja ○
  Australia 29°30S 131°0E 61 E5
Marambio Antarctica 64°0S 56°0W 5 C18
Maran Malaysia 3°35N 102°45E 39 L4
Marana U.S.A. 32°27N 111°13W 77 K8
Maranboy Australia 14°40S 132°39E 60 B5
Marand Iran 38°30N 45°45E 44 B5
Marang Malaysia 5°12N 103°13E 39 K4
Maranguape Brazil 3°55S 38°50W 93 D11
Maranhão = São Luís
  Brazil 2°39S 44°15W 93 D10
Maranhão □ Brazil 5°0S 46°0W 93 E9
Maranoa → Australia 27°50S 148°37E 63 D4
Marañón → Peru 4°30S 73°35W 92 D4
Maraş = Kahramanmaraş
  Turkey 37°37N 36°53E 44 B3
Marathasa Cyprus 34°59N 32°51E 25 E11
Marathon Australia 20°51S 143°32E 62 C3
Marathon Canada 48°44N 86°23W 72 C2
Marathon N.Y., U.S.A. 42°27N 76°2W 83 D8
Marathon Tex., U.S.A. 30°12N 103°15W 84 F3
Marathóvouno Cyprus 35°13N 33°37E 25 D12
Maratua Indonesia 2°10N 118°35E 37 D5
Maraval Trin. & Tob. 10°40N 61°31W 93 K15
Maravatío Mexico 19°54N 100°27W 86 D4
Marāwih U.A.E. 24°18N 53°18E 45 E7
Marbella Spain 36°30N 4°57W 21 D3
Marble Bar Australia 21°9S 119°44E 60 D2
Marble Falls U.S.A. 30°35N 98°16W 84 F5
Marblehead Mass.,
  U.S.A. 42°29N 70°51W 83 D14
Marblehead Ohio, U.S.A. 41°32N 82°44W 82 E2
Marburg Germany 50°47N 8°46E 16 C5
Marca, Pta. do Angola 16°31S 11°43E 53 H2
March U.K. 52°33N 0°5E 13 E8
Marche France 46°5N 1°20E 20 C4
Marche-en-Famenne
  Belgium 50°14N 5°19E 15 D5
Marchena Spain 37°18N 5°23W 21 D3
Marco Island U.S.A. 25°58N 81°44W 85 J14
Marcos Juárez Argentina 32°42S 62°5W 94 C3
Marcus Baker, Mt.
  U.S.A. 61°26N 147°45W 74 C10
Marcus I. = Minami-Tori-Shima
  Pac. Oc. 24°20N 153°58E 64 E7
Marcy, Mt. U.S.A. 44°7N 73°56W 83 B11
Mardan Pakistan 34°20N 72°0E 42 B5
Mardie Australia 21°12S 115°59E 60 D2
Mardin Turkey 37°20N 40°43E 44 B4
Maree, L. U.K. 57°40N 5°26W 11 D3
Mareeba Australia 16°59S 145°28E 62 B4
Mareetsane S. Africa 26°9S 25°25E 56 D4

Marek = Stanke Dimitrov
  Bulgaria 42°17N 23°9E 23 C10
Marengo U.S.A. 41°48N 92°4W 80 E7
Marerano Madag. 21°23S 44°52E 57 C7
Marfa U.S.A. 30°19N 104°1W 84 F2
Marfa Pt. Malta 35°59N 14°19E 25 D1
Margaret → Australia 18°9S 125°41E 60 C4
Margaret Bay Canada 51°20N 127°35W 70 C3
Margaret L. Canada 58°56N 115°25W 70 B5
Margaret River Australia 33°57S 115°4E 61 F2
Margarita, I. de Venezuela 11°0N 64°0W 92 A6
Margaritovo Russia 43°25N 134°45E 30 C7
Margate S. Africa 30°50S 30°20E 57 E5
Margate U.K. 51°23N 1°23E 13 F9
Margherita Pk. Uganda 0°22N 29°51E 54 B3
Marghilon Uzbekistan 40°27N 71°42E 28 E8
Mārgow, Dasht-e
  Afghan. 30°40S 62°30E 40 D3
Marguerite Canada 52°30N 122°25W 70 C4
Mari El □ Russia 56°30N 48°0E 18 C8
Mari Indus Pakistan 32°57N 71°34E 42 C4
Mari Republic = Mari El □
  Russia 56°30N 48°0E 18 C8
María de la Salut Spain 39°40N 3°5E 24 B10
María Elena Chile 22°18S 69°40W 94 A2
María Grande Argentina 31°45S 59°55W 94 C4
María I. N. Terr.,
  Australia 14°52S 135°45E 62 A2
Maria I. Tas., Australia 42°35S 148°0E 63 G4
Maria Island △ Australia 42°38S 148°5E 63 G4
Maria van Diemen, C.
  N.Z. 34°29S 172°40E 59 A4
Mariakani Kenya 3°50S 39°27E 54 C4
Mariala △ Australia 25°57S 145°2E 63 D4
Marian Australia 21°9S 148°57E 62 b
Marian L. Canada 63°0N 116°15W 70 A5
Mariana Trench Pac. Oc. 13°0N 145°0E 64 F6
Marianna Ark., U.S.A. 34°46N 90°46W 85 D9
Marianna Fla., U.S.A. 30°46N 85°14W 85 F12
Maricourt = Kangiqsujuaq
  Canada 61°30N 72°0W 69 E17
Mariánské Lázně
  Czech Rep. 49°48N 12°41E 16 D7
Marias → U.S.A. 47°56N 110°30W 76 C8
Mariato, Punta Panama 7°12N 80°52W 88 E3
Maribor Slovenia 46°36N 15°40E 16 E8
Marico → Africa 23°35S 26°57E 56 C4
Maricopa Ariz., U.S.A. 33°4N 112°3W 77 K7
Maricopa Calif., U.S.A. 35°4N 119°24W 79 K7
Marié → Brazil 0°27S 66°26W 92 D5
Marie Byrd Land
  Antarctica 79°30S 125°0W 5 D14
Marie-Galante
  Guadeloupe 15°56N 61°16W 88 b
Mariecourt = Kangiqsujuaq
  Canada 61°30N 72°0W 69 E17
Mariehamn Finland 60°5N 19°55E 9 F18
Mariembourg Belgium 50°6N 4°31E 15 D4
Mariental Namibia 24°36S 18°0E 56 C2
Marienville U.S.A. 41°28N 79°8W 82 E5
Mariestad Sweden 58°43N 13°50E 9 G15
Marietta Ga., U.S.A. 33°57N 84°33W 85 E12
Marietta Ohio, U.S.A. 39°25N 81°27W 81 F13
Marieville Canada 45°26N 73°10W 83 A11
Mariinsk Russia 56°10N 87°20E 28 D9
Marijampolė Lithuania 54°33N 23°19E 9 J20
Marília Brazil 22°13S 50°0W 95 A6
Marín Spain 42°23N 8°42W 21 A1
Marina U.S.A. 36°41N 121°48W 78 J5
Marinduque Phil. 13°25N 122°0E 37 B6
Marine City U.S.A. 42°43N 82°30W 82 D2
Marinette U.S.A. 45°6N 87°38W 80 C10
Maringá Brazil 23°26S 52°2W 95 A5
Marion Ala., U.S.A. 32°38N 87°19W 85 E11
Marion Ill., U.S.A. 37°44N 88°56W 80 G9
Marion Ind., U.S.A. 40°32N 85°40W 81 E11
Marion Iowa, U.S.A. 42°2N 91°36W 80 D8
Marion Kans., U.S.A. 38°21N 97°1W 80 F5
Marion N.C., U.S.A. 35°41N 82°1W 85 D13
Marion Ohio, U.S.A. 40°35N 83°8W 81 E12
Marion S.C., U.S.A. 34°11N 79°24W 85 D15
Marion Va., U.S.A. 36°50N 81°31W 81 G13
Marion, L. U.S.A. 33°28N 80°10W 85 E14
Mariposa U.S.A. 37°29N 119°58W 78 H7
Mariscal Estigarribia
  Paraguay 22°3S 60°40W 94 A3
Maritime Alps = Maritimes, Alpes
  Europe 44°10N 7°10E 20 D7
Maritimes, Alpes Europe 44°10N 7°10E 20 D7
Maritsa = Evros →
  Greece 41°40N 26°34E 23 D12
Maritsa Greece 36°22N 28°8E 25 C10
Mariupol Ukraine 47°5N 37°31E 19 E6
Mariusa △ Venezuela 9°24N 61°27W 89 E7
Marīvān Iran 35°30N 46°25E 44 C5
Marj 'Uyūn Lebanon 33°21N 35°34E 46 B4
Marka Somali Rep. 1°48N 44°50E 47 G3
Markam China 29°42N 98°38E 41 E21
Marked Tree U.S.A. 35°32N 90°25W 85 D9
Markdale Canada 44°19N 80°39W 82 B4
Market Drayton U.K. 52°54N 2°29W 12 E5
Market Harborough
  U.K. 52°29N 0°55W 13 E7
Market Rasen U.K. 53°24N 0°20W 12 D7
Markham Canada 43°52N 79°16W 82 C5
Markham, Mt. Antarctica 83°0S 164°0E 5 E11
Markleeville U.S.A. 38°42N 119°47W 78 G7
Markovo Russia 64°40N 170°24E 29 C18
Marks Russia 51°45N 46°50E 18 D8
Marksville U.S.A. 31°8N 92°4W 84 F8
Marla Australia 27°19S 133°33E 63 D1
Marlbank Canada 44°26N 77°6W 82 B7
Marlboro U.S.A. 41°36N 73°59W 83 E11
Marlborough Australia 22°46S 149°52E 62 C4
Marlborough U.K. 51°25N 1°43W 13 F6
Marlborough Downs
  U.K. 51°27N 1°53W 13 F6
Marlin U.S.A. 31°18N 96°54W 84 F6
Marlow U.K. 51°34N 0°46W 13 F7
Marlow U.S.A. 34°39N 97°58W 84 H6
Marmagao India 15°25N 73°56E 40 M8

INDEX TO WORLD MAPS
Medvezhyegorsk 141

Marmara Turkey 40°35N 27°34E 23 D12
Marmara, Sea of = Marmara Denizi Turkey 40°45N 28°15E 23 D13
Marmara Denizi Turkey 40°45N 28°15E 23 D13
Marmaris Turkey 36°50N 28°14E 23 F13
Marmion, Mt. Australia 29°16S 119°50E 61 E2
Marmion L. Canada 48°55N 91°20W 72 C1
Marmolada, Mte. Italy 46°26N 11°51E 22 A4
Marmora Canada 44°28N 77°41W 82 B7
Marmugao = Marmagao India 15°25N 73°56E 40 M8
Marne → France 48°47N 2°29E 20 B5
Maro Reef U.S.A. 25°25N 170°35W 75 K5
Maroala Madag. 15°23S 47°59E 57 B8
Maroantsetra Madag. 15°26S 49°44E 57 B8
Maroelaboom Namibia 19°15S 18°53E 56 B2
Marofandilia Madag. 20°7S 44°34E 57 C7
Marojejy △ Madag. 14°26S 49°21E 57 A8
Marolambo Madag. 20°2S 48°7E 57 C8
Maromandia Madag. 14°13S 48°5E 57 A8
Maromokotro Madag. 14°0S 49°0E 57 A8
Marondera Zimbabwe 18°5S 31°42E 55 F3
Maroni → Fr. Guiana 5°30N 54°0W 93 B8
Maroochydore Australia 26°29S 153°5E 63 D5
Maroona Australia 37°27S 142°54E 63 F3
Marosakoa Madag. 15°26S 46°38E 57 B8
Maroseranana Madag. 18°32S 48°51E 57 B8
Marotandrano Madag. 16°10S 48°50E 57 B8
Marotaolano Madag. 12°47S 49°15E 57 A8
Maroua Cameroon 10°40N 14°20E 51 F8
Marovato Madag. 15°48S 48°5E 57 B8
Marovoay Madag. 16°6S 46°39E 57 B8
Marquard S. Africa 28°40S 27°28E 56 D4
Marquesas Fracture Zone Pac. Oc. 9°0S 125°0W 65 H15
Marquesas Is. = Marquises, Îs. French Polynesia 9°30S 140°0W 65 H14
Marquette U.S.A. 46°33N 87°24W 80 B10
Marquis St. Lucia 14°2N 60°54W 89 f
Marquises, Îs. French Polynesia 9°30S 140°0W 65 H14
Marra, Djebel Sudan 13°10N 24°22E 51 F10
Marracuene Mozam. 25°45S 32°35E 57 D5
Marrakech Morocco 31°9N 8°0W 50 B4
Marrawah Australia 40°55S 144°42E 63 G3
Marree Australia 29°39S 138°1E 63 D2
Marrero U.S.A. 29°53N 90°6W 85 G9
Marrimane Mozam. 22°58S 33°34E 57 C5
Marromeu Mozam. 18°15S 36°25E 57 B6
Marromeu △ Mozam. 19°0S 36°0E 57 B6
Marrowie Cr. → Australia 33°23S 145°40E 63 E4
Marrubane Mozam. 18°0S 37°0E 55 F4
Marrupa Mozam. 13°8S 37°30E 55 E4
Mars Hill U.S.A. 46°31N 67°52W 81 B20
Marsá 'Alam Egypt 25°5N 34°54E 47 B1
Marsá Matrûh Egypt 31°19N 27°9E 51 B11
Marsabit Kenya 2°18N 38°0E 54 B4
Marsabit △ Kenya 2°23N 37°56E 54 B4
Marsala Italy 37°48N 12°26E 22 F5
Marsalforn Malta 36°4N 14°16E 25 C1
Marsden Australia 33°47S 147°32E 63 E4
Marseille France 43°18N 5°23E 20 E6
Marseilles = Marseille France 43°18N 5°23E 20 E6
Marsh I. U.S.A. 29°34N 91°53W 84 G9
Marshall Ark., U.S.A. 35°55N 92°38W 84 D8
Marshall Mich., U.S.A. 42°16N 84°58W 81 D11
Marshall Minn., U.S.A. 44°27N 95°47W 80 C6
Marshall Mo., U.S.A. 39°7N 93°12W 80 F7
Marshall Tex., U.S.A. 32°33N 94°23W 84 E7
Marshall → Australia 22°59S 136°59E 62 C2
Marshall Is. ■ Pac. Oc. 9°0N 171°0E 58 A10
Marshalltown U.S.A. 42°3N 92°55W 80 D7
Marshbrook Zimbabwe 18°33S 31°9E 57 B5
Marshfield Mo., U.S.A. 37°15N 92°54W 80 G7
Marshfield Vt., U.S.A. 44°20N 72°20W 83 B12
Marshfield Wis., U.S.A. 44°40N 90°10W 80 C8
Marshūn Iran 36°19N 49°23E 45 B6
Märsta Sweden 59°37N 17°52E 9 G17
Mart U.S.A. 31°33N 96°50W 84 F6
Martaban Burma 16°30N 97°35E 41 L20
Martaban, G. of Burma 16°5N 96°30E 41 L20
Martapura Kalimantan, Indonesia 3°22S 114°47E 36 E4
Martapura Sumatera, Indonesia 4°19S 104°22E 36 E2
Marte R. Gómez, Presa Mexico 26°10N 99°0W 87 B5
Martelange Belgium 49°49N 5°43E 15 E5
Martha's Vineyard U.S.A. 41°25N 70°38W 83 E14
Martigny Switz. 46°6N 7°3E 20 C7
Martigues France 43°24N 5°4E 20 E6
Martin Slovak Rep. 49°6N 18°58E 17 D10
Martin S. Dak., U.S.A. 43°11N 101°44W 80 D3
Martin Tenn., U.S.A. 36°21N 88°51W 85 C10
Martin L. U.S.A. 32°41N 85°55W 85 E12
Martina Franca Italy 40°42N 17°20E 22 D7
Martinborough N.Z. 41°14S 175°29E 59 D5
Martinez Calif., U.S.A. 38°1N 122°8W 78 G4
Martinez Ga., U.S.A. 33°31N 82°5W 85 E13
Martinique ⧄ W. Indies 14°40N 61°0W 88 c
Martinique Passage W. Indies 15°15N 61°0W 89 C7
Martinópolis Brazil 22°11S 51°12W 95 A5
Martin's Bay Barbados 13°12N 59°29W 89 g
Martins Ferry U.S.A. 40°6N 80°44W 82 F4
Martinsburg Pa., U.S.A. 40°19N 78°20W 82 F6
Martinsburg W. Va., U.S.A. 39°27N 77°58W 81 F15
Martinsville Ind., U.S.A. 39°26N 86°25W 80 F10
Martinsville Va., U.S.A. 36°41N 79°52W 81 G14
Marton N.Z. 40°4S 175°23E 59 D5
Martos Spain 37°44N 3°58W 21 D4
Martu ✪ Australia 22°30S 122°30E 60 D3
Marudi Malaysia 4°11N 114°19E 36 D4
Maruf Afghan. 31°30N 67°6E 40 D5
Marugame Japan 34°15N 133°40E 31 G6
Marunga Angola 17°28S 20°2E 56 B3
Marungu, Mts. Dem. Rep. of the Congo 7°30S 30°0E 54 D3
Maruwa ✪ Australia 22°30S 127°30E 60 D4
Marv Dasht Iran 29°50N 52°40E 45 D7
Marvast Iran 30°30N 54°15E 45 D7
Marvel Loch Australia 31°28S 119°29E 61 F2
Marwar India 25°43N 73°45E 42 G5
Mary Turkmenistan 37°40N 61°50E 45 B9
Maryborough = Port Laoise Ireland 53°2N 7°18W 10 C4
Maryborough Queens., Australia 25°31S 152°37E 63 D5
Maryborough Vic., Australia 37°3S 143°44E 63 F3
Maryfield Canada 49°50N 101°35W 71 D8
Maryland □ U.S.A. 39°0N 76°30W 81 F15
Maryland Junction Zimbabwe 17°45S 30°31E 55 F3
Maryport U.K. 54°44N 3°28W 12 C4
Mary's Harbour Canada 52°18N 55°51W 73 B8
Marystown Canada 47°10N 55°10W 73 C8
Marysville Calif., U.S.A. 39°9N 121°35W 78 F5
Marysville Kans., U.S.A. 39°51N 96°39W 80 F5
Marysville Mich., U.S.A. 42°54N 82°29W 82 D2
Marysville Ohio, U.S.A. 40°14N 83°22W 81 E12
Marysville Wash., U.S.A. 48°3N 122°11W 78 B4
Maryville Mo., U.S.A. 40°21N 94°52W 80 E6
Maryville Tenn., U.S.A. 35°46N 83°58W 85 D13
Marzūq Libya 25°53N 13°57E 51 C8
Marzūq, Idehān Libya 24°50N 13°51E 51 D8
Masada Israel 31°15N 35°20E 46 D4
Masahunga Tanzania 2°6S 33°18E 54 C3
Masai Malaysia 1°29N 103°55E 39 d
Masai Mara △ Kenya 1°25S 35°5E 54 C4
Masai Steppe Tanzania 4°30S 36°30E 54 C4
Masaka Uganda 0°21S 31°45E 54 C3
Masalembo, Kepulauan Indonesia 5°35S 114°30E 36 F4
Masalima, Kepulauan Indonesia 5°4S 117°5E 36 F5
Masamba Indonesia 2°30S 120°15E 37 E6
Masan S. Korea 35°11N 128°32E 35 G15
Masandam, Ra's Oman 26°30N 56°30E 45 E8
Masasi Tanzania 10°45S 38°52E 55 E4
Masaya Nic. 12°0N 86°7W 88 D2
Masbate Phil. 12°21N 123°36E 37 B6
Mascara Algeria 35°26N 0°6E 50 A6
Mascota Mexico 20°32N 104°49W 86 C4
Masela Indonesia 8°9S 129°51E 37 F7
Maseru Lesotho 29°18S 27°30E 56 D4
Mashaba Zimbabwe 20°2S 30°29E 55 G3
Mashābih Si. Arabia 25°35N 36°30E 44 E3
Mashatu △ Botswana 22°45S 29°5E 57 C4
Masherbrum Pakistan 35°38N 76°18E 43 B7
Mashhad Iran 36°20N 59°35E 45 B8
Mashīz Iran 29°56N 56°37E 45 D8
Māshkel, Hāmūn-i- Pakistan 28°20N 62°56E 45 D9
Mashki Chāh Pakistan 29°5N 62°30E 40 E3
Mashonaland Zimbabwe 16°30S 31°0E 53 H6
Mashonaland Central □ Zimbabwe 17°30S 31°0E 57 B5
Mashonaland East □ Zimbabwe 18°0S 32°0E 57 B5
Mashonaland West □ Zimbabwe 17°30S 29°30E 57 B4
Mashrakh India 26°7N 84°48E 43 F11
Masi Manimba Dem. Rep. of the Congo 4°40S 17°54E 52 E3
Masig Australia 9°45S 143°24E 62 a
Masindi Uganda 1°40N 31°43E 54 B3
Masindi Port Uganda 1°43N 32°2E 54 B3
Masinga Res. Kenya 0°58S 37°38E 54 C4
Maşīrah, Jazīrat Oman 21°0N 58°50E 47 C6
Maşīrah, Khalīj Oman 20°10N 58°10E 47 C6
Masisi Dem. Rep. of the Congo 1°23S 28°49E 54 C2
Masjed Soleyman Iran 31°55N 49°18E 45 D6
Mask, L. Ireland 53°36N 9°22W 10 C2
Maskin Oman 23°44N 56°52E 45 F8
Masoala, Tanjon' i Madag. 15°59S 50°13E 57 B9
Masoala △ Madag. 15°30S 50°12E 57 B9
Masoarivo Madag. 19°3S 44°19E 57 B7
Masohi = Amahai Indonesia 3°20S 128°55E 37 E7
Masomeloka Madag. 20°17S 48°37E 57 C8
Mason Nev., U.S.A. 38°56N 119°8W 78 G7
Mason Tex., U.S.A. 30°45N 99°14W 84 F5
Mason City U.S.A. 43°9N 93°12W 80 D7
Maspalomas Canary Is. 27°46N 15°35W 24 G4
Maspalomas, Pta. Canary Is. 27°43N 15°36W 24 G4
Masqat Oman 23°37N 58°36E 47 C6
Massa Italy 44°1N 10°9E 20 D9
Massachusetts □ U.S.A. 42°30N 72°0W 83 D13
Massachusetts B. U.S.A. 42°25N 70°50W 83 D14
Massakory Chad 13°0N 15°49E 51 F9
Massamba Mozam. 15°58S 33°31E 55 F3
Massanella Spain 39°48N 2°51E 24 B9
Massangena Mozam. 21°34S 33°0E 57 C5
Massango Angola 8°2S 16°21E 52 F3
Massawa = Mitsiwa Eritrea 15°35N 39°25E 47 D2
Massena U.S.A. 44°56N 74°54W 83 B10
Massenya Chad 11°21N 16°9E 51 F9
Masset Canada 54°2N 132°10W 70 C2
Massiah Street Barbados 13°9N 59°29W 89 g
Massif Central France 44°55N 3°0E 20 D5
Massillon U.S.A. 40°48N 81°32W 82 F3
Massinga Mozam. 23°15S 35°22E 57 C6
Massingir Mozam. 23°51S 32°4E 57 C5
Masson-Angers Canada 45°32N 75°25W 83 A9
Masson I. Antarctica 66°10S 93°20E 5 C7
Mastanli = Momchilgrad Bulgaria 41°33N 25°23E 23 D11
Masterton N.Z. 40°56S 175°39E 59 D5
Mastic U.S.A. 40°47N 72°54W 83 F12
Mastuj Pakistan 36°20N 72°36E 43 A5
Mastung Pakistan 29°50N 66°56E 40 E5
Masty Belarus 53°27N 24°38E 17 B13
Masuda Japan 34°40N 131°51E 31 G5
Masuku = Franceville Gabon 1°40S 13°32E 52 E2
Masurian Lakes = Mazurski, Pojezierze Poland 53°50N 21°0E 17 B11
Masvingo Zimbabwe 20°8S 30°49E 55 G3
Masvingo □ Zimbabwe 21°0S 31°30E 55 G3
Maswa △ Tanzania 2°58S 34°19E 54 C3
Maşyāf Syria 35°4N 36°20E 44 C3
Mata-au = Clutha → N.Z. 46°20S 169°49E 59 G2
Matabeleland Zimbabwe 18°0S 27°0E 53 H5
Matabeleland North □ Zimbabwe 19°0S 28°0E 55 F2
Matabeleland South □ Zimbabwe 21°0S 29°0E 55 G2
Matachewan Canada 47°56N 80°39W 72 C3
Matadi Dem. Rep. of the Congo 5°52S 13°31E 52 F2
Matagalpa Nic. 13°0N 85°58W 88 D2
Matagami Canada 49°45N 77°34W 72 C4
Matagami, L. Canada 49°50N 77°40W 72 C4
Matagorda B. U.S.A. 28°40N 96°12W 84 G6
Matagorda I. U.S.A. 28°15N 96°30W 84 G6
Mataiea Tahiti 17°46S 149°25W 59 d
Matak Indonesia 3°18N 106°16E 36 D3
Matala Greece 34°59N 24°45E 25 E6
Matam Senegal 15°34N 13°17W 50 E3
Matamoros Campeche, Mexico 18°50N 90°50W 87 D6
Matamoros Coahuila, Mexico 25°32N 103°15W 86 B4
Matamoros Tamaulipas, Mexico 25°53N 97°30W 87 B5
Ma'ţan as Sarra Libya 21°45N 22°0E 51 D10
Matandu → Tanzania 8°45S 34°19E 55 D3
Matane Canada 48°50N 67°33W 73 C6
Matanomadh India 23°33N 68°57E 42 H3
Matanzas Cuba 23°0N 81°40W 88 B3
Matapa Botswana 23°11S 24°39E 56 C3
Matapan, C. = Tenaro, Akra Greece 36°22N 22°27E 23 F10
Matapédia Canada 48°0N 66°59W 73 C6
Matapo △ Zimbabwe 20°30S 29°40E 55 G2
Matara Sri Lanka 5°58N 80°30E 40 S12
Mataram Indonesia 8°35S 116°7E 37 K19
Matarani Peru 17°0S 72°10W 92 G4
Mataranka Australia 14°55S 133°4E 60 B5
Matarma, Râs Egypt 30°27N 32°44E 46 E1
Mataró Spain 41°32N 2°29E 21 B7
Matatiele S. Africa 30°20S 28°49E 57 E4
Mataura N.Z. 46°11S 168°51E 59 G2
Matavai, B. de Tahiti 17°30S 149°23W 59 d
Matehuala Mexico 23°39N 100°39W 86 C4
Mateke Hills Zimbabwe 21°48S 31°0E 55 G3
Matelot Trin. & Tob. 10°50N 61°7W 93 K15
Matera Italy 40°40N 16°36E 22 D7
Matetsi Zimbabwe 18°12S 26°0E 55 F2
Matheniko △ Uganda 2°49N 34°27E 54 B3
Mathis U.S.A. 28°6N 97°50W 84 G6
Mathraki Greece 39°48N 19°31E 25 A3
Mathura India 27°30N 77°40E 42 F7
Mati Phil. 6°55N 126°15E 37 C7
Matiali India 26°56N 88°49E 43 F13
Matías Romero Mexico 16°53N 95°2W 87 D5
Matibane Mozam. 14°49S 40°45E 55 E5
Matiri Ra. N.Z. 41°38S 172°20E 59 D4
Matjiesfontein S. Africa 33°14S 20°35E 56 E3
Matla → India 21°40N 88°40E 43 J13
Matlamanyane Botswana 19°33S 25°57E 56 B4
Matli Pakistan 25°2N 68°39E 42 G3
Matlock U.K. 53°9N 1°33W 12 D6
Mato Grosso □ Brazil 14°0S 55°0W 93 F8
Mato Grosso, Planalto do Brazil 15°0S 55°0W 93 G8
Mato Grosso do Sul □ Brazil 18°0S 55°0W 93 G8
Matobo = Matapo △ Zimbabwe 20°30S 29°40E 55 G2
Matochkin Shar, Proliv Russia 73°23N 55°12E 28 B6
Matopo Hills Zimbabwe 20°36S 28°20E 55 G2
Matopos Zimbabwe 20°20S 28°29E 55 G2
Matosinhos Portugal 41°11N 8°42W 21 B1
Matroosberg S. Africa 33°23S 19°40E 56 E2
Maţruḩ Oman 23°37N 58°30E 47 C6
Matsue Japan 35°25N 133°10E 31 G6
Matsum, Ko Thailand 9°22N 99°59E 39 b
Matsumae Japan 41°26N 140°7E 30 D10
Matsumoto Japan 36°15N 138°0E 31 F9
Matsusaka Japan 34°34N 136°32E 31 G8
Matsuura Japan 33°20N 129°49E 31 H4
Matsuyama Japan 33°45N 132°45E 31 H6
Mattagami → Canada 50°43N 81°29W 72 B3
Mattancheri India 9°50N 76°15E 40 Q10
Mattawa Canada 46°20N 78°45W 72 C4
Matterhorn Switz. 45°58N 7°39E 20 D7
Matthew Town Bahamas 20°57N 73°40W 89 B5
Matthews Ridge Guyana 7°37N 60°10W 92 B6
Mattice Canada 49°40N 83°20W 72 C3
Mattituck U.S.A. 40°59N 72°32W 83 F12
Mattō Japan 36°31N 136°34E 31 F8
Mattoon U.S.A. 39°29N 88°23W 80 F9
Matuba Mozam. 24°28S 32°49E 57 C5
Matucana Peru 11°55S 76°25W 92 F3
Matuku Fiji 19°10S 179°44E 59 a
Matūn = Khowst Afghan. 33°22N 69°58E 42 C3
Matura B. Trin. & Tob. 10°39N 61°1W 93 K15
Maturín Venezuela 9°45N 63°11W 92 B6
Matusadona △ Zimbabwe 16°58S 28°42E 55 F2
Mau Mad. P., India 26°17N 78°41E 43 F8
Mau Ut. P., India 25°56N 83°33E 43 G10
Mau Ut. P., India 25°17N 81°23E 43 G9
Mau Escarpment Kenya 0°40S 36°0E 54 C4
Mau Ranipur India 25°16N 79°8E 43 G8
Maua Kenya 0°14N 37°56E 54 C4
Maua Mozam. 13°53S 37°10E 55 E4
Maubeuge France 50°17N 3°57E 20 A6
Maubin Burma 16°44N 95°39E 41 L19
Maud, Pt. Australia 23°6S 113°45E 60 D1
Maud Rise S. Ocean 66°0S 3°0E 5 C3
Maude Australia 34°29S 144°18E 63 E3
Maudin Sun Burma 16°0N 94°30E 41 M19
Maués Brazil 3°20S 57°45W 92 D7
Mauganj India 24°50N 81°55E 43 G9
Maughold Hd. I. of Man 54°18N 4°18W 12 C3
Maui U.S.A. 20°48N 156°20W 75 L8
Maulamyaing = Moulmein Burma 16°30N 97°40E 41 L20
Maule □ Chile 36°5S 72°30W 94 D1
Maumee U.S.A. 41°34N 83°39W 81 E12
Maumee → U.S.A. 41°42N 83°28W 81 E12
Maumere Indonesia 8°38S 122°13E 37 F6
Maun Botswana 20°0S 23°26E 56 C3
Mauna Kea U.S.A. 19°50N 155°28W 75 M8
Mauna Loa U.S.A. 19°30N 155°35W 75 M8
Maunath Bhanjan = Mau India 25°56N 83°33E 43 G10
Maungmagan Kyunzu Burma 14°0N 97°48E 38 E1
Maungu Kenya 3°33S 38°45E 54 C4
Maupin U.S.A. 45°11N 121°5W 76 D3
Maurepas, L. U.S.A. 30°15N 90°30W 85 F9
Maurice, L. Australia 29°30S 131°0E 61 E5
Mauricie △ Canada 46°45N 73°0W 72 C5
Mauritania ■ Africa 20°50N 10°0W 50 E3
Mauritius ■ Ind. Oc. 20°0S 57°0E 53 d
Mauston U.S.A. 43°48N 90°5W 80 D8
Mavli India 24°45N 73°55E 42 G5
Mavuradonha Mts. Zimbabwe 16°30S 31°30E 55 F3
Mawa Dem. Rep. of the Congo 2°45N 26°40E 54 B2
Mawai India 22°30N 81°4E 43 H9
Mawana India 29°6N 77°58E 42 E7
Mawand Pakistan 29°33N 68°38E 42 E3
Mawjib, W. al → Jordan 31°28N 35°36E 46 D4
Mawk Mai Burma 20°14N 97°37E 41 J20
Mawlaik Burma 23°40N 94°26E 41 H19
Mawlamyine = Moulmein Burma 16°30N 97°40E 41 L20
Mawqaq Si. Arabia 27°25N 41°8E 44 E4
Mawson Base Antarctica 67°30S 62°53E 5 C6
Mawson Coast Antarctica 68°30S 63°0E 5 C6
Max U.S.A. 47°49N 101°18W 80 B3
Maxcanú Mexico 20°35N 90°0W 87 C6
Maxesibeni S. Africa 30°49S 29°23E 57 E4
Maxhamish L. Canada 59°50N 123°17W 70 B4
Maxixe Mozam. 23°54S 35°17E 57 C6
Maxville Canada 45°17N 74°51W 83 A10
Maxwell U.S.A. 39°17N 122°11W 78 F4
Maxwelton Australia 20°43S 142°41E 62 C3
May, C. U.S.A. 38°56N 74°58W 81 F16
May Pen Jamaica 17°58N 77°15W 88 a
Maya → Russia 60°28N 134°28E 29 D14
Maya Mts. Belize 16°30N 89°0W 87 D7
Mayaguana Bahamas 22°30N 72°44W 89 B5
Mayagüez Puerto Rico 18°12N 67°9W 89 d
Mayāmey Iran 36°24N 55°42E 45 B7
Mayanup Australia 33°57S 116°27E 61 F2
Mayapán Mexico 20°29N 89°11W 87 C7
Mayarí Cuba 20°40N 75°41W 89 B4
Mayaro B. Trin. & Tob. 10°14N 60°59W 93 K16
Maybell U.S.A. 40°31N 108°5W 76 F9
Maybole U.K. 55°21N 4°42W 11 F4
Maydān Iraq 34°55N 45°37E 44 C5
Mayenne → France 47°30N 0°32W 20 C3
Mayer U.S.A. 34°24N 112°14W 77 J7
Mayerthorpe Canada 53°57N 115°8W 70 C5
Mayfield Ky., U.S.A. 36°44N 88°38W 80 G9
Mayfield N.Y., U.S.A. 43°6N 74°16W 83 C10
Mayhill U.S.A. 32°53N 105°29W 77 K11
Maykop Russia 44°35N 40°10E 19 F7
Maymyo Burma 22°2N 96°28E 38 A1
Maynard Mass., U.S.A. 42°26N 71°27W 83 D13
Maynard Wash., U.S.A. 47°59N 122°55W 78 C4
Maynard Hills Australia 28°28S 119°49E 61 E2
Mayne → Australia 23°40S 141°55E 62 C3
Maynooth Canada 45°13N 77°56W 82 A7
Maynooth Ireland 53°23N 6°34W 10 C5
Mayo Canada 63°38N 135°57W 68 E4
Mayo □ Ireland 53°53N 9°3W 10 C2
Mayon Volcano Phil. 13°15N 123°41E 37 B6
Mayor I. N.Z. 37°16S 176°17E 59 B6
Mayotte ⧄ Ind. Oc. 12°50S 45°10E 53 a
Maysān □ Iraq 31°55N 47°15E 44 D5
Maysville U.S.A. 38°39N 83°46W 81 F12
Mayu Indonesia 1°30N 126°30E 37 D7
Mayville N. Dak., U.S.A. 47°30N 97°20W 80 B5
Mayville N.Y., U.S.A. 42°15N 79°30W 82 D5
Mazabuka Zambia 15°52S 27°44E 55 F2
Mazagán = El Jadida Morocco 33°11N 8°17W 50 B4
Mazagão Brazil 0°7S 51°16W 93 D8
Mazán Peru 3°30S 73°0W 92 D4
Māzandarān □ Iran 36°30N 52°0E 45 B7
Mazapil Mexico 24°39N 101°34W 86 C4
Mazar China 36°32N 77°1E 32 C2
Mazara del Vallo Italy 37°39N 12°35E 22 F5
Mazarrón Spain 37°38N 1°19W 21 D5
Mazaruni → Guyana 6°25N 58°35W 92 B7
Mazatán Mexico 29°0N 110°8W 86 B2
Mazatenango Guatemala 14°35N 91°30W 88 D1
Mazatlán Mexico 23°13N 106°25W 86 C3
Mažeikiai Lithuania 56°20N 22°20E 9 H20
Māzhān Iran 32°30N 59°0E 45 C8
Mazīnān Iran 36°19N 56°56E 45 B8
Mazoe Mozam. 16°42S 33°7E 55 F3
Mazoe → Mozam. 16°20S 33°30E 55 F3
Mazowe Zimbabwe 17°28S 30°58E 55 F3
Mazurski, Pojezierze Poland 53°50N 21°0E 17 B11
Mazyr Belarus 51°59N 29°15E 17 B15
Mba Fiji 17°33S 177°41E 59 a
Mbabane Swaziland 26°18S 31°6E 57 D5
Mbaïki C.A.R. 3°53N 18°1E 52 D3
Mbala Zambia 8°46S 31°24E 55 D3
Mbalabala Zimbabwe 20°27S 29°3E 57 C4
Mbale Uganda 1°8N 34°12E 54 B3
Mbalmayo Cameroon 3°33N 11°33E 52 D2
Mbamba Bay Tanzania 11°13S 34°49E 55 E3
Mbandaka Dem. Rep. of the Congo 0°1N 18°18E 52 D3
Mbanza Congo Angola 6°18S 14°16E 52 F2
Mbanza Ngungu Dem. Rep. of the Congo 5°12S 14°53E 52 F2
Mbarangandu Tanzania 10°11S 36°48E 55 D4
Mbarara Uganda 0°35S 30°40E 54 C3
Mbengga = Beqa Fiji 18°23S 178°8E 59 a
Mbenkuru → Tanzania 9°25S 39°50E 55 D4
Mberengwa Zimbabwe 20°29S 29°57E 55 G2
Mberengwa, Mt. Zimbabwe 20°37S 29°55E 55 G2
Mbesuma Zambia 10°0S 32°2E 55 E3
Mbeya Tanzania 8°54S 33°29E 55 D3
Mbeya □ Tanzania 8°15S 33°30E 54 D3
Mbhashe → S. Africa 32°15S 28°54E 57 E4
Mbinga Tanzania 10°50S 35°0E 55 E4
Mbini = Río Muni □ Eq. Guin. 1°30N 10°0E 52 D2
Mbizi Zimbabwe 21°23S 31°1E 55 G3
Mbouda Cameroon 5°38N 10°15E 50 G8
M'boukou, L. de Cameroon 6°23N 12°50E 52 C2
Mbour Senegal 14°22N 16°54W 50 F2
Mbuji-Mayi Dem. Rep. of the Congo 6°9S 23°40E 54 D1
Mbulu Tanzania 3°45S 35°30E 54 C4
Mburucuyá Argentina 28°1S 58°14W 94 B4
Mburucuyá △ Argentina 28°1S 58°12W 94 B4
Mchinja Tanzania 9°44S 39°45E 55 D4
Mchinji Malawi 13°47S 32°58E 55 E3
Mdantsane S. Africa 32°56S 27°46E 57 E4
Mead, L. U.S.A. 36°0N 114°44W 79 J12
Meade U.S.A. 37°17N 100°20W 80 G3
Meade River = Atqasuk U.S.A. 70°28N 157°24W 74 A8
Meadow Lake Canada 54°10N 108°26W 71 C7
Meadow Lake △ Canada 54°27N 109°0W 71 C7
Meadow Valley Wash → U.S.A. 36°40N 114°34W 79 J12
Meadville U.S.A. 41°39N 80°9W 82 E4
Meaford Canada 44°36N 80°35W 82 B4
Mealy Mts. Canada 53°10N 58°0W 73 B8
Meander River Canada 59°2N 117°42W 70 B5
Meares, C. U.S.A. 45°37N 124°0W 76 D1
Mearim → Brazil 3°4S 44°35W 93 D10
Meath □ Ireland 53°40N 6°57W 10 C5
Meath Park Canada 53°27N 105°22W 71 C7
Meaux France 48°58N 2°50E 20 B5
Mebechi-Gawa → Japan 40°31N 141°31E 30 D10
Mebulu, Tanjung Indonesia 8°50S 115°5E 37 K18
Mecanhelas Mozam. 15°12S 35°54E 55 F4
Mecca = Makkah Si. Arabia 21°30N 39°54E 47 C2
Mecca U.S.A. 33°34N 116°5W 79 M10
Mechanicsburg U.S.A. 40°13N 77°1W 82 F8
Mechanicville U.S.A. 42°54N 73°41W 83 D11
Mechelen Belgium 51°2N 4°29E 15 C4
Mecheria Algeria 33°35N 0°18W 50 B5
Mecklenburg Germany 53°33N 11°40E 16 B7
Mecklenburger Bucht Germany 54°20N 11°40E 16 A6
Meconta Mozam. 14°59S 39°50E 55 E4
Mecubúri Mozam. 14°39S 38°54E 55 E4
Mecubúri → Mozam. 14°10S 40°30E 55 E5
Mecúfi Mozam. 13°20S 40°32E 55 E5
Medan Indonesia 3°40N 98°38E 36 D1
Médanos de Coro △ Venezuela 11°35N 69°44W 89 D6
Medanosa, Pta. Argentina 48°8S 66°0W 96 F3
Médéa Algeria 36°12N 2°50E 50 A6
Medellín Colombia 6°15N 75°35W 92 B3
Medelpad Sweden 62°33N 16°30E 8 E17
Medemblik Neths. 52°46N 5°8E 15 B5
Medford Mass., U.S.A. 42°25N 71°7W 83 D13
Medford Oreg., U.S.A. 42°19N 122°52W 76 E2
Medford Wis., U.S.A. 45°9N 90°20W 80 C8
Medgidia Romania 44°15N 28°19E 17 F15
Media Agua Argentina 31°58S 68°25W 94 C2
Media Luna Argentina 34°45S 66°44W 94 C2
Medianeira Brazil 25°17S 54°5W 95 B5
Mediaş Romania 46°9N 24°22E 17 E13
Medicine Bow U.S.A. 41°54N 106°12W 76 F10
Medicine Bow Mts. U.S.A. 40°40N 106°0W 76 F10
Medicine Bow Pk. U.S.A. 41°21N 106°19W 76 F10
Medicine Hat Canada 50°0N 110°45W 71 D8
Medicine Lake U.S.A. 48°30N 104°30W 76 B11
Medicine Lodge U.S.A. 37°17N 98°35W 80 G4
Medina = Al Madīnah Si. Arabia 24°35N 39°52E 44 E3
Medina N. Dak., U.S.A. 46°54N 99°18W 80 B4
Medina N.Y., U.S.A. 43°13N 78°23W 82 C6
Medina Ohio, U.S.A. 41°8N 81°52W 82 E3
Medina → U.S.A. 29°16N 98°29W 84 G5
Medina del Campo Spain 41°18N 4°55W 21 B3
Medina L. U.S.A. 29°32N 98°56W 84 G5
Medina Sidonia Spain 36°28N 5°57W 21 D3
Medinipur India 22°25N 87°21E 43 H12
Mediterranean Sea Europe 35°0N 15°0E 6 H7
Médoc France 45°10N 0°50W 20 D3
Medveditsa → Russia 49°35N 42°41E 19 E7
Medvezhi, Ostrava Russia 71°0N 161°0E 29 B17
Medvezhyegorsk Russia 63°0N 34°25E 18 B5

Medway □ *U.K.* 51°25N 0°32E **13** F8
Medway ➤ *U.K.* 51°27N 0°46E **13** F8
Meekatharra *Australia* 26°32S 118°29E **61** E2
Meeker *U.S.A.* 40°2N 107°55W **76** F10
Meerut *India* 29°1N 77°42E **42** E7
Meeteetse *U.S.A.* 44°9N 108°52W **76** D9
Mega *Ethiopia* 3°57N 38°19E **47** G2
Megara *Greece* 37°58N 23°22E **23** F10
Megasini *India* 21°38N 86°21E **43** J12
Meghalaya □ *India* 25°50N 91°0E **41** G17
Meghna ➤ *Bangla.* 22°50N 90°50E **41** H17
Megion *Russia* 61°3N 76°6E **28** C8
Mégiscane, L. *Canada* 48°35N 75°55W **72** C4
Meharry, Mt. *Australia* 22°59S 118°35E **60** D2
Mehlville *U.S.A.* 38°31N 90°19W **80** F8
Mehndawal *India* 26°58N 83°5E **43** F10
Mehr Jān *Iran* 33°50N 55°6E **45** C7
Mehrābād *Iran* 36°53N 47°55E **44** B5
Mehrān *Iran* 33°7N 46°10E **44** C5
Mehrān ➤ *Iran* 26°45N 55°26E **45** E7
Mehrgarh *Pakistan* 29°30N 67°30E **42** E2
Mehrīz *Iran* 31°35N 54°28E **45** D7
Mei Xian *China* 34°18N 107°55E **34** G4
Meighen I. *Canada* 80°0N 99°30W **69** B12
Meihekou *China* 42°32N 125°40E **35** C13
Meiktila *Burma* 20°53N 95°54E **41** J19
Meissen *Germany* 51°9N 13°29E **16** C7
Meizhou *China* 24°16N 116°6E **33** D6
Meja *India* 25°9N 82°7E **43** G10
Mejillones *Chile* 23°10S 70°30W **94** A1
Mekele *Ethiopia* 13°33N 39°30E **47** E2
Mekerghene, Sebkra
  Algeria 26°21N 1°30E **50** C6
Mekhtar *Pakistan* 30°30N 69°15E **40** D6
Meknès *Morocco* 33°57N 5°33W **50** B4
Mekong ➤ *Asia* 9°30N 106°15E **39** H6
Mekongga *Indonesia* 3°39S 121°15E **37** E6
Mekvari = Kür ➤
  Azerbaijan 39°29N 49°15E **19** G8
Melagiri Hills *India* 12°20N 77°30E **40** N10
Melaka *Malaysia* 2°15N 102°15E **39** L4
Melalap *Malaysia* 5°10N 116°5E **36** C5
Melambes *Greece* 35°8N 24°40E **25** D6
Melanesia *Pac. Oc.* 4°0S 155°0E **64** H7
Melanesian Basin *Pac. Oc.* 0°5N 160°35E **64** G8
Melaya *Indonesia* 8°17S 114°30E **37** J17
Melbourne *Australia* 37°48S 144°58E **63** F4
Melbourne *U.S.A.* 28°5N 80°37W **85** G14
Melchor Múzquiz
  Mexico 27°53N 101°31W **86** B4
Melchor Ocampo
  Mexico 24°51N 101°39W **86** C4
Mélèzes ➤ *Canada* 57°40N 69°29W **72** A5
Melfort *Canada* 52°50N 104°37W **71** C8
Melfort *Zimbabwe* 18°0S 31°25E **55** F3
Melhus *Norway* 63°17N 10°18E **8** E14
Melilla *N. Afr.* 35°21N 2°57W **21** E4
Melipilla *Chile* 33°42S 71°15W **94** C1
Melissa *Canada* 45°24N 79°14W **82** A5
Melissa, Akra *Greece* 35°6N 24°33E **25** D6
Melita *Canada* 49°15N 101°0W **71** D8
Melitopol *Ukraine* 46°50N 35°22E **19** E6
Melk *Austria* 48°13N 15°20E **16** D8
Mellansel *Sweden* 63°26N 18°19E **8** E18
Mellen *U.S.A.* 46°20N 90°40W **80** B8
Mellerud *Sweden* 58°41N 12°28E **9** G15
Mellette *U.S.A.* 45°9N 98°30W **80** C4
Mellieha *Malta* 35°57N 14°22E **25** D1
Melo *Uruguay* 32°20S 54°10W **95** C5
Melolo *Indonesia* 9°53S 120°40E **37** F6
Melouprey *Cambodia* 13°48N 105°16E **38** F5
Melrhir, Chott *Algeria* 34°13N 6°30E **50** B7
Melrose *Australia* 32°42S 146°57E **63** E4
Melrose *U.K.* 55°36N 2°43W **11** F6
Melrose *Minn., U.S.A.* 45°40N 94°49W **80** C6
Melrose *N. Mex.,*
  U.S.A. 34°26N 103°38W **77** J12
Melstone *U.S.A.* 46°36N 107°52W **76** C10
Melton Mowbray *U.K.* 52°47N 0°54W **12** E7
Melun *France* 48°32N 2°39E **20** B5
Melville *Canada* 50°55N 102°50W **71** C8
Melville, C. *Australia* 14°11S 144°30E **62** A3
Melville, L. *Canada* 53°30N 60°0W **73** B8
Melville B. *Australia* 12°0S 136°45E **62** A2
Melville B. *Greenland* 75°30N 63°0W **69** B19
Melville I. *Australia* 11°30S 131°0E **60** B5
Melville I. *Canada* 75°30N 112°0W **69** B9
Melville Pen. *Canada* 68°0N 84°0W **69** D15
Melvin, Lough *Ireland* 54°26N 8°10W **10** B3
Memba *Mozam.* 14°11S 40°30E **55** E5
Memboro *Indonesia* 9°30S 119°30E **60** A2
Memel = Klaipėda
  Lithuania 55°43N 21°10E **9** J19
Memel *S. Africa* 27°38S 29°36E **57** D4
Memmingen *Germany* 47°58N 10°10E **16** E6
Mempawah *Indonesia* 0°30N 109°5E **36** D3
Memphis *Mich., U.S.A.* 42°54N 82°46W **82** D2
Memphis *Tenn., U.S.A.* 35°8N 90°2W **85** D9
Memphis *Tex., U.S.A.* 34°44N 100°33W **84** D4
Memphrémagog, L.
  N. Amer. 45°8N 72°17W **83** B12
Mena *U.S.A.* 34°35N 94°15W **84** D7
Menai Strait *U.K.* 53°11N 4°13W **12** D3
Ménaka *Mali* 15°59N 2°18E **50** E6
Menan = Chao Phraya ➤
  Thailand 13°40N 100°31E **38** F3
Menarandra ➤ *Madag.* 25°17S 44°30E **57** D7
Menard *U.S.A.* 30°55N 99°47W **84** F5
Menard Fracture Zone
  Pac. Oc. 43°0S 97°0W **65** M18
Mendaña Fracture Zone
  Pac. Oc. 16°0S 91°0W **65** J18
Mendawai ➤ *Indonesia* 3°30S 113°0E **36** E4
Mende *France* 44°31N 3°30E **20** D5
Mendhar *India* 33°35N 74°10E **43** C6
Mendip Hills *U.K.* 51°17N 2°40W **13** F5
Mendocino *U.S.A.* 39°19N 123°48W **76** G2
Mendocino, C. *U.S.A.* 40°26N 124°25W **76** F1

Mendocino Fracture Zone
  Pac. Oc. 40°0N 142°0W **65** D13
Mendota *Calif., U.S.A.* 36°45N 120°23W **78** J6
Mendota *Ill., U.S.A.* 41°33N 89°7W **80** E9
Mendoyo *Indonesia* 8°23S 114°42E **37** J17
Mendoza *Argentina* 32°50S 68°52W **94** C2
Mendoza □ *Argentina* 33°0S 69°0W **94** C2
Mene Grande *Venezuela* 9°49N 70°56W **92** B4
Menemen *Turkey* 38°34N 27°3E **23** E12
Menen *Belgium* 50°47N 3°7E **15** D3
Menggala *Indonesia* 4°30S 105°15E **36** E3
Mengjin *China* 34°55N 112°45E **34** G7
Mengyin *China* 35°40N 117°58E **35** G9
Mengzi *China* 23°20N 103°22E **32** D5
Menihek *Canada* 54°28N 56°36W **73** B6
Menihek L. *Canada* 54°0N 67°0W **73** B6
Menin = Menen *Belgium* 50°47N 3°7E **15** D3
Menindee *Australia* 32°20S 142°25E **63** E3
Menindee L. *Australia* 32°20S 142°25E **63** E3
Meningie *Australia* 35°50S 139°18E **63** F2
Menjangan, Pulau
  Indonesia 8°7S 114°31E **37** J17
Menlo Park *U.S.A.* 37°27N 122°12W **78** H4
Menngen ⊙ *Australia* 15°21S 131°16E **60** C5
Menominee *U.S.A.* 45°6N 87°37W **80** C10
Menominee ➤ *U.S.A.* 45°6N 87°35W **80** C10
Menomonie *U.S.A.* 44°53N 91°55W **80** C8
Menongue *Angola* 14°48S 17°52E **53** G3
Menorca *Spain* 40°0N 4°0E **24** B11
Mentakab *Malaysia* 3°29N 102°21E **39** L4
Mentawai, Kepulauan
  Indonesia 2°0S 99°0E **36** E1
Menton *France* 43°50N 7°29E **20** E7
Mentor *U.S.A.* 41°40N 81°21W **82** E3
Menzelinsk *Russia* 55°47N 53°11E **18** C9
Menzies *Australia* 29°40S 121°2E **61** E3
Meob B. *Namibia* 24°25S 14°34E **56** C1
Me'ona *Israel* 33°1N 35°15E **46** B4
Meoqui *Mexico* 28°17N 105°29W **86** B3
Mepaco *Mozam.* 15°57S 30°48E **55** F3
Meppel *Neths.* 52°42N 6°12E **15** B6
Merak *Indonesia* 6°10N 106°26E **37** F12
Meramangye, L.
  Australia 28°25S 132°13E **61** E5
Meran = Merano *Italy* 46°40N 11°9E **22** A4
Merano *Italy* 46°40N 11°9E **22** A4
Merauke *Indonesia* 8°29S 140°24E **37** F10
Merbein *Australia* 34°10S 142°2E **63** E3
Merbuk, Gunung
  Indonesia 8°13S 114°39E **37** J17
Merca = Marka
  Somali Rep. 1°48N 44°50E **47** G3
Merced *U.S.A.* 37°18N 120°29W **78** H6
Merced ➤ *U.S.A.* 37°21N 120°59W **78** H6
Merced Pk. *U.S.A.* 37°36N 119°24W **78** H7
Mercedes *B. Aires,*
  Argentina 34°40S 59°30W **94** C4
Mercedes *Corrientes,*
  Argentina 29°10S 58°5W **94** B4
Mercedes *San Luis,*
  Argentina 33°40S 65°21W **94** C2
Mercedes *Uruguay* 33°12S 58°0W **94** C4
Merceditas *Chile* 28°20S 70°35W **94** B1
Mercer *N.Z.* 37°16S 175°5E **59** B5
Mercer *U.S.A.* 41°14N 80°15W **82** E4
Mercer Island *U.S.A.* 47°34N 122°13W **78** C4
Mercury *U.S.A.* 36°40N 115°59W **79** J11
Mercy, C. *Canada* 65°0N 63°30W **69** E19
Mere *U.K.* 51°6N 2°16W **13** F5
Meredith, C. *Falk. Is.* 52°15S 60°40W **96** G4
Meredith, L. *U.S.A.* 35°43N 101°33W **84** D4
Mergui *Burma* 12°26N 98°34E **38** F2
Mergui Arch. = Myeik Kyunzu
  Burma 11°30N 97°30E **39** G1
Mérida *Mexico* 20°58N 89°37W **87** C7
Mérida *Spain* 38°55N 6°25W **21** C2
Mérida *Venezuela* 8°24N 71°8W **92** B4
Mérida, Cord. de *Venezuela* 9°0N 71°0W **92** B4
Meriden *U.K.* 52°26N 1°38W **13** E6
Meriden *U.S.A.* 41°32N 72°48W **83** E12
Meridian *Calif., U.S.A.* 39°9N 121°55W **78** F5
Meridian *Idaho, U.S.A.* 43°37N 116°24W **76** E5
Meridian *Miss., U.S.A.* 32°22N 88°42W **85** E10
Merinda *Australia* 20°2S 148°11E **62** C4
Merir *Pac. Oc.* 4°10N 132°30E **37** D8
Meriruma *Brazil* 1°15N 54°50W **93** C8
Merkel *U.S.A.* 32°28N 100°1W **84** E4
Merksem *Belgium* 51°16N 4°25E **15** C4
Mermaid Reef *Australia* 17°6S 119°36E **60** C1
Merredin *Australia* 31°28S 118°18E **61** F2
Merrick *U.K.* 55°8N 4°28W **11** F4
Merrickville *Canada* 44°55N 75°50W **83** B9
Merrill *Oreg., U.S.A.* 42°1N 121°36W **76** E3
Merrill *Wis., U.S.A.* 45°11N 89°41W **80** C9
Merrimack ➤ *U.S.A.* 42°49N 70°49W **83** D14
Merriman *U.S.A.* 42°55N 101°42W **80** D3
Merritt *Canada* 50°10N 120°45W **70** C4
Merritt Island *U.S.A.* 28°21N 80°42W **85** G14
Merriwa *Australia* 32°6S 150°22E **63** E5
Merry I. *Canada* 55°29N 77°31W **72** A4
Merryville *U.S.A.* 30°45N 93°33W **84** F8
Mersch *Lux.* 49°44N 6°7E **15** E6
Mersea I. *U.K.* 51°47N 0°58E **13** F8
Merseburg *Germany* 51°22N 11°59E **16** C6
Mersey ➤ *U.K.* 53°25N 3°1W **12** D4
Merseyside □ *U.K.* 53°31N 3°2W **12** D4
Mersin = İçel *Turkey* 36°51N 34°36E **44** B2
Mersing *Malaysia* 2°25N 103°50E **39** L4
Merta *India* 26°39N 74°4E **42** F6
Merta Road *India* 26°43N 73°55E **42** F5
Merthyr Tydfil *U.K.* 51°45N 3°22W **13** F4
Merthyr Tydfil □ *U.K.* 51°46N 3°21W **13** F4
Merti *Kenya* 1°4N 38°40E **54** B4
Mértola *Portugal* 37°40N 7°40E **21** D2
Mertzon *U.S.A.* 31°16N 100°49W **84** F4
Meru *Kenya* 0°3N 37°40E **54** B4
Meru *Tanzania* 3°15S 36°46E **54** C4
Meru △ *Kenya* 0°5N 38°10E **54** B4

Mesanagros *Greece* 36°1N 27°49E **25** C9
Mesaoría *Cyprus* 35°12N 33°14E **25** D12
Mesgouez, L. *Canada* 51°20N 75°0W **72** B5
Meshed = Mashhad *Iran* 36°20N 59°35E **45** B8
Meshgīn Shahr *Iran* 38°30N 47°45E **44** B5
Meshoppen *U.S.A.* 41°36N 76°3W **83** E8
Mesilinka ➤ *Canada* 56°6N 124°30W **70** B4
Mesologi *Greece* 38°21N 21°28E **23** E9
Mesongi *Greece* 39°29N 19°56E **25** B3
Mesopotamia = Al Jazirah
  Iraq 33°30N 44°0E **44** C5
Mesopotamia *U.S.A.* 41°27N 80°57W **82** E4
Mesquite *U.S.A.* 36°48N 114°4W **77** H6
Messaad *Algeria* 34°8N 3°30E **50** B6
Messalo ➤ *Mozam.* 12°25S 39°15E **55** E4
Messara, Kolpos *Greece* 35°6N 24°47E **25** D6
Messina = Musina
  S. Africa 22°20S 30°5E **57** C5
Messina *Italy* 38°11N 15°34E **22** E6
Messina, Str. di *Italy* 38°15N 15°35E **22** F6
Messini *Greece* 37°4N 22°1E **23** F10
Messiniakos Kolpos
  Greece 36°45N 22°5E **23** F10
Mesta = Nestos ➤
  Europe 40°54N 24°49E **23** D11
Meta ➤ *S. Amer.* 6°12N 67°28W **92** B5
Meta Incognita Pen.
  Canada 62°45N 68°30W **69** E18
Metabetchouan *Canada* 48°26N 71°52W **73** C5
Metairie *U.S.A.* 29°59N 90°9W **85** G9
Metaline Falls *U.S.A.* 48°52N 117°22W **76** B5
Metán *Argentina* 25°30S 65°0W **94** B3
Metangula *Mozam.* 12°40S 34°50E **55** E3
Metcalfe *Canada* 45°14N 75°28W **83** A9
Metema *Ethiopia* 12°58N 36°12E **47** E2
Metengobalame *Mozam.* 14°49S 34°30E **55** E3
Methven *N.Z.* 43°38S 171°40E **59** E3
Metil *Mozam.* 16°24S 39°0E **55** F4
Metlakatla *U.S.A.* 55°8N 131°35W **68** F5
Metropolis *U.S.A.* 37°9N 88°44W **80** G9
Metropolitana □ *Chile* 33°30S 70°50W **94** C1
Metu *Ethiopia* 8°18N 35°35E **47** F2
Metz *France* 49°8N 6°10E **20** B7
Meulaboh *Indonesia* 4°11N 96°3E **36** D1
Meureudu *Indonesia* 5°19N 96°10E **36** C1
Meuse ➤ *Europe* 50°45N 5°41E **15** D5
Mexia *U.S.A.* 31°41N 96°29W **84** F6
Mexiana, I. *Brazil* 0°0 49°30W **93** D9
Mexicali *Mexico* 32°40N 115°30W **79** N11
Mexican Plateau *Mexico* 25°0N 104°0W **66** G9
Mexican Water *U.S.A.* 36°57N 109°32W **77** H9
Mexico *Maine, U.S.A.* 44°34N 70°33W **83** B14
Mexico *Mo., U.S.A.* 39°10N 91°53W **80** F8
Mexico *N.Y., U.S.A.* 43°28N 76°14W **83** C8
México □ *Mexico* 19°20N 99°30W **87** D5
Mexico ■ *Cent. Amer.* 25°0N 105°0W **86** C4
México, Ciudad de
  Mexico 19°24N 99°9W **87** D5
Mexico, G. of *Cent. Amer.* 25°0N 90°0W **87** C7
Mexico B. *U.S.A.* 43°35N 76°20W **83** C8
Meydān, Ra's-e *Iran* 31°56N 49°18E **45** D6
Meydani, Ra's-e *Iran* 25°24N 59°6E **45** E8
Meyers Chuck *U.S.A.* 55°45N 132°15W **70** B2
Meymaneh *Afghan.* 35°53N 64°38E **40** B4
Mezen *Russia* 65°50N 44°20E **18** A7
Mezen ➤ *Russia* 65°44N 44°22E **18** A7
Mézenc, Mt. *France* 44°54N 4°11E **20** D6
Mezhdurechensk *Russia* 53°41N 88°3E **28** D9
Mezhdurechenskiy
  Russia 59°36N 65°56E **28** D7
Mezőkövesd *Hungary* 47°49N 20°35E **17** E11
Mezőtúr *Hungary* 47°1N 20°41E **17** E11
Mezquital *Mexico* 23°29N 104°23W **86** C4
Mfolozi ➤ *S. Africa* 28°25S 32°26E **57** D5
Mgeta *Tanzania* 8°22S 36°6E **55** D4
Mhlaba Hills *Zimbabwe* 18°30S 30°30E **55** F3
Mhow *India* 22°33N 75°50E **42** H6
Miahuatlán *Mexico* 16°20N 96°36W **87** D5
Miami *Fla., U.S.A.* 25°46N 80°11W **85** J14
Miami *Okla., U.S.A.* 36°53N 94°53W **84** C7
Miami *Tex., U.S.A.* 35°42N 100°38W **84** D4
Miami Beach *U.S.A.* 25°47N 80°7W **85** J14
Mian Xian *China* 33°10N 106°32E **34** H4
Mianchi *China* 34°48N 111°48E **34** G6
Miāndarreh *Iran* 35°37N 53°39E **45** C7
Miāndowāb *Iran* 37°0N 46°5E **44** B5
Miandrivazo *Madag.* 19°31S 45°29E **57** B8
Miāneh *Iran* 37°30N 47°40E **44** B5
Mianwali *Pakistan* 32°38N 71°28E **42** C4
Mianyang *China* 31°22N 104°47E **32** C5
Miarinarivo *Antananarivo,*
  Madag. 18°57S 46°55E **57** B8
Miarinarivo *Toamasina,*
  Madag. 16°38S 48°15E **57** B8
Miariravaratra *Madag.* 20°13S 47°31E **57** C8
Miass *Russia* 54°59N 60°6E **18** D11
Mica *S. Africa* 24°10S 30°48E **57** C5
Michalovce *Slovak Rep.* 48°47N 21°58E **17** D11
Michigan □ *U.S.A.* 44°0N 85°0W **81** C11
Michigan, L. *U.S.A.* 44°0N 87°0W **80** D10
Michigan City *U.S.A.* 41°43N 86°54W **80** E10
Michipicoten I. *Canada* 47°40N 85°40W **72** C2
Michoacán □ *Mexico* 19°10N 101°50W **86** D4
Michurin *Bulgaria* 42°9N 27°51E **23** C12
Michurinsk *Russia* 52°58N 40°27E **18** D7
Micoud *St. Lucia* 13°49N 60°54W **89** f
Micronesia *Pac. Oc.* 11°0N 160°0E **64** G7
Micronesia, Federated States of ■
  Pac. Oc. 9°0N 150°0E **58** A8
Mid-Pacific Seamounts
  Pac. Oc. 18°0N 177°0W **64** F10
Midai *Indonesia* 3°0N 107°47E **36** D3
Midale *Canada* 49°25N 103°20W **71** D8
Middelburg *Neths.* 51°30N 3°36E **15** C3
Middelburg *Eastern Cape,*
  S. Africa 31°30S 25°0E **56** E4
Middelburg *Mpumalanga,*
  S. Africa 25°49S 29°28E **57** D4

Middelpos *S. Africa* 31°55S 20°13E **56** E3
Middelwit *S. Africa* 24°51S 27°3E **56** C4
Middle Alkali L. *U.S.A.* 41°27N 120°5W **76** F3
Middle America Trench =
  Guatemala Trench
  Pac. Oc. 14°0N 95°0W **66** H10
Middle Bass I. *U.S.A.* 41°41N 82°48W **82** E2
Middle East *Asia* 35°0N 40°0E **26** E5
Middle Fork Feather ➤
  U.S.A. 38°33N 121°30W **78** F5
Middle I. *Australia* 34°6S 123°11E **61** F3
Middle Loup ➤ *U.S.A.* 41°17N 98°24W **80** E4
Middleboro *U.S.A.* 41°54N 70°55W **83** E14
Middleburg *Fla., U.S.A.* 30°4N 81°52W **85** F14
Middleburg *Pa., U.S.A.* 40°47N 77°3W **82** F7
Middleburgh *U.S.A.* 42°36N 74°20W **83** D10
Middlebury *U.S.A.* 44°1N 73°10W **83** B11
Middlefield *U.S.A.* 41°27N 81°4W **82** E3
Middlemount *Australia* 22°50S 148°40E **62** C4
Middleport *N.Y., U.S.A.* 43°13N 78°29W **82** C6
Middleport *Ohio, U.S.A.* 39°0N 82°3W **81** F12
Middlesboro *U.S.A.* 36°36N 83°43W **81** G12
Middlesbrough *U.K.* 54°35N 1°13W **12** C6
Middlesbrough □ *U.K.* 54°28N 1°13W **12** C6
Middlesex *Belize* 17°2N 88°31W **88** C2
Middlesex *N.J., U.S.A.* 40°36N 74°30W **83** F10
Middlesex *N.Y., U.S.A.* 42°42N 77°16W **82** D7
Middleton *Australia* 22°22S 141°32E **62** C3
Middleton *Canada* 44°57N 65°4W **73** D6
Middleton Cr. ➤
  Australia 22°35S 141°51E **62** C3
Middleton I. *U.S.A.* 59°26N 146°20W **74** D10
Middletown *U.K.* 54°17N 6°51W **10** B5
Middletown *Calif.,*
  U.S.A. 38°45N 122°37W **78** G4
Middletown *Conn.,*
  U.S.A. 41°34N 72°39W **83** E12
Middletown *N.Y.,*
  U.S.A. 41°27N 74°25W **83** E10
Middletown *Ohio,*
  U.S.A. 39°31N 84°24W **81** F11
Middletown *Pa., U.S.A.* 40°12N 76°44W **83** F8
Midge Point *Australia* 20°39S 148°43E **62** b
Midhurst *Canada* 44°26N 79°43W **82** B5
Midhurst *U.K.* 50°59N 0°44W **13** G7
Midi, Canal du ➤ *France* 43°45N 1°21E **20** E4
Midland *Australia* 31°54S 116°1E **61** F2
Midland *Canada* 44°45N 79°50W **82** B5
Midland *Calif., U.S.A.* 33°52N 114°48W **79** M12
Midland *Mich., U.S.A.* 43°37N 84°14W **81** D11
Midland *Pa., U.S.A.* 40°39N 80°27W **82** F4
Midland *Tex., U.S.A.* 32°0N 102°3W **84** F3
Midlands □ *Zimbabwe* 19°40S 29°0E **55** F2
Midleton *Ireland* 51°55N 8°10W **10** E3
Midlothian *U.S.A.* 32°30N 97°0W **84** E6
Midlothian □ *U.K.* 55°51N 3°5W **11** F5
Midnapore = Medinipur
  India 22°25N 87°21E **43** H12
Midongy, Tangorombohitr' i
  Madag. 23°30S 47°0E **57** C8
Midongy Atsimo *Madag.* 23°35S 47°1E **57** C8
Midway Is. *Pac. Oc.* 28°13N 177°22W **75** K4
Midway Wells *U.S.A.* 32°41N 115°7W **79** N11
Midwest *U.S.A.* 42°0N 90°0W **75** G22
Midwest *Wyo., U.S.A.* 43°25N 106°16W **76** E10
Midwest City *U.S.A.* 35°27N 97°24W **84** D6
Midyat *Turkey* 37°25N 41°23E **44** B4
Midžor *Bulgaria* 43°24N 22°40E **23** C10
Mie □ *Japan* 34°30N 136°10E **31** G8
Międzychód *Poland* 52°35N 15°53E **16** B8
Międzyrzec Podlaski
  Poland 51°58N 22°45E **17** C12
Mielec *Poland* 50°15N 21°25E **17** C11
Mienga *Angola* 17°12S 19°48E **56** B2
Miercurea-Ciuc
  Romania 46°21N 25°48E **17** E13
Mieres *Spain* 43°18N 5°48W **21** A3
Mifflintown *U.S.A.* 40°34N 77°24W **82** F7
Mifraz Ḥefa *Israel* 32°52N 35°0E **46** C4
Migori *Kenya* 1°4S 34°28E **54** C3
Miguel Alemán, Presa
  Mexico 18°15N 96°32W **87** D5
Mihara *Japan* 34°24N 133°5E **31** G6
Mikese *Tanzania* 6°48S 37°55E **54** D4
Mikha-Tskhakaya = Senaki
  Georgia [see below]
Mikhaylovgrad = Montana
  Bulgaria 43°27N 23°16E **23** C10
Mikhaylovka *Russia* 50°3N 43°5E **19** D7
Mikines *Greece* 37°43N 22°46E **23** F10
Mikkeli *Finland* 61°43N 27°15E **8** F22
Mikkwa ➤ *Canada* 58°25N 114°46W **70** B6
Míkonos = Mykonos
  Greece 37°30N 25°25E **23** F11
Mikumi *Tanzania* 7°26S 37°0E **54** D4
Mikumi △ *Tanzania* 7°35S 37°15E **54** D4
Mikun *Russia* 62°20N 50°0E **18** B9
Milaca *U.S.A.* 45°45N 93°39W **80** C7
Milagro *Ecuador* 2°11S 79°36W **92** D3
Milan = Milano *Italy* 45°28N 9°10E **20** D8
Milan *Mo., U.S.A.* 40°12N 93°7W **80** E7
Milan *Tenn., U.S.A.* 35°55N 88°46W **85** D10
Milange *Mozam.* 16°3S 35°45E **55** F4
Milano *Italy* 45°28N 9°10E **20** D8
Milanoa *Madag.* 13°35S 49°47E **57** A8
Milâs *Turkey* 37°20N 27°50E **23** F12
Milatos *Greece* 35°18N 25°34E **25** D7
Milazzo *Italy* 38°13N 15°15E **22** E6
Milbank *U.S.A.* 45°13N 96°38W **80** C5
Milbanke Sd. *Canada* 52°19N 128°33W **70** C3
Milden *Canada* 51°29N 107°32W **71** C7
Mildenhall *U.K.* 52°21N 0°32E **13** E8
Mildmay *Canada* 44°3N 81°7W **82** B3
Mildura *Australia* 34°13S 142°9E **63** E3
Miles *Australia* 26°40S 150°9E **63** D5
Miles City *U.S.A.* 46°25N 105°51W **76** C11
Milestone *Canada* 49°59N 104°31W **71** D8
Miletus *Turkey* 37°30N 27°18E **23** F12
Milford *Calif., U.S.A.* 40°10N 120°22W **78** E6
Milford *Conn., U.S.A.* 41°14N 73°3W **83** E11
Milford *Del., U.S.A.* 38°55N 75°26W **81** F16
Milford *Mass., U.S.A.* 42°8N 71°31W **83** D13

Milford *N.H., U.S.A.* 42°50N 71°39W **83** D13
Milford *N.Y., U.S.A.* 42°35N 74°56W **83** D10
Milford *Pa., U.S.A.* 41°19N 74°48W **83** E10
Milford *Utah, U.S.A.* 38°24N 113°1W **76** G7
Milford Haven *U.K.* 51°42N 5°7W **13** F2
Milford Sd. *N.Z.* 44°41S 167°47E **59** F1
Milford Sound *N.Z.* 44°41S 167°55E **59** F1
Milh, Baḥr al = Razāzah,
  Buḥayrat ar *Iraq* 32°40N 43°35E **44** C4
Milikapiti *Australia* 11°26S 130°40E **60** B5
Miling *Australia* 30°30S 116°17E **61** F2
Milk River *Canada* 49°10N 112°5W **70** D6
Mill I. *Antarctica* 66°0S 101°30E **5** C8
Mill I. *Canada* 63°58N 77°47W **69** E16
Mill Valley *U.S.A.* 37°54N 122°32W **78** H4
Millau *France* 44°8N 3°4E **20** D5
Millbridge *Canada* 44°41N 77°36W **82** B7
Millbrook *Canada* 44°10N 78°29W **82** B6
Millbrook *Ala., U.S.A.* 32°29N 86°22W **85** E11
Mille Lacs, L. des *Canada* 48°45N 90°35W **72** C1
Mille Lacs L. *U.S.A.* 46°15N 93°39W **80** B7
Milledgeville *U.S.A.* 33°5N 83°14W **85** E13
Millen *U.S.A.* 32°48N 81°57W **85** E14
Millennium I. = Caroline I.
  Kiribati 9°58S 150°13W **65** H12
Miller *U.S.A.* 44°31N 98°59W **80** C4
Miller Lake *Canada* 45°6N 81°26W **82** A3
Millersburg *Ohio, U.S.A.* 40°33N 81°55W **82** F3
Millersburg *Pa., U.S.A.* 40°32N 76°58W **82** F8
Millerton *U.S.A.* 41°57N 73°31W **83** E11
Millerton L. *U.S.A.* 37°1N 119°41W **78** J7
Millet *St. Lucia* 13°55N 60°59W **89** f
Millheim *U.S.A.* 40°54N 77°29W **82** F7
Millicent *Australia* 37°34S 140°21E **63** F3
Millington *U.S.A.* 35°20N 89°53W **85** D10
Millinocket *U.S.A.* 45°39N 68°43W **81** C19
Millmerran *Australia* 27°53S 151°16E **63** D5
Millom *U.K.* 54°13N 3°16W **12** C4
Mills L. *Canada* 61°30N 118°20W **70** A5
Millsboro *U.S.A.* 40°0N 80°0W **82** G5
Millstream Chichester △
  Australia 21°35S 117°6E **60** D2
Millstreet *Ireland* 52°4N 9°4W **10** D2
Milltown Malbay *Ireland* 52°52N 9°24W **10** D2
Millville *N.J., U.S.A.* 39°24N 75°2W **81** F16
Millville *Pa., U.S.A.* 41°7N 76°32W **83** E8
Millwood L. *U.S.A.* 33°42N 93°58W **84** E8
Milne ➤ *Australia* 21°10S 137°33E **62** C2
Milo ➤ *U.S.A.* 45°15N 68°59W **81** C19
Milon, Akra *Greece* 36°15N 28°11E **25** C10
Milos *Greece* 36°44N 24°25E **23** F11
Milparinka *Australia* 29°46S 141°57E **63** D3
Milpitas *U.S.A.* 37°26N 121°55W **78** H5
Milton *N.S., Canada* 44°4N 64°45W **73** D7
Milton *Ont., Canada* 43°31N 79°53W **82** C5
Milton *N.Z.* 46°7S 169°59E **59** G2
Milton *Calif., U.S.A.* 38°3N 120°51W **78** G6
Milton *Fla., U.S.A.* 30°38N 87°3W **85** F11
Milton *Pa., U.S.A.* 41°1N 76°51W **82** F8
Milton *Vt., U.S.A.* 44°38N 73°7W **83** B11
Milton-Freewater
  U.S.A. 45°56N 118°23W **76** D4
Milton Keynes *U.K.* 52°1N 0°44W **13** E7
Milton Keynes □ *U.K.* 52°1N 0°44W **13** E7
Milverton *Canada* 43°34N 80°55W **82** C4
Milwaukee *U.S.A.* 43°2N 87°54W **80** D10
Milwaukee Deep *Atl. Oc.* 19°50N 68°0W **89** C6
Milwaukie *U.S.A.* 45°26N 122°38W **78** E4
Mimili *Australia* 27°0S 132°42E **61** E5
Min Jiang ➤ *Fujian,*
  China 26°0N 119°35E **33** D6
Min Jiang ➤ *Sichuan,*
  China 28°45N 104°40E **32** D5
Min Xian *China* 34°25N 104°5E **34** G3
Mina' Jabal 'Alī *U.A.E.* 25°2N 55°8E **45** E7
Mina Pirquitas
  Argentina 22°40S 66°30W **94** A2
Mīnā Su'ud *Si. Arabia* 28°45N 48°28E **45** D6
Mīnā'al Aḥmadī *Kuwait* 29°5N 48°10E **45** D6
Minago ➤ *Canada* 54°33N 98°59W **71** C9
Minaki *Canada* 49°59N 94°40W **71** D10
Minamata *Japan* 32°10N 130°30E **31** H5
Minami-Arapusa △
  Japan 35°30N 138°9E **31** G9
Minami-Tori-Shima
  Pac. Oc. 24°20N 153°58E **64** E7
Minas *Uruguay* 34°20S 55°10W **95** C4
Minas, Sierra de las
  Guatemala 15°9N 89°31W **88** C2
Minas Basin *Canada* 45°20N 64°12W **73** C7
Minas Gerais □ *Brazil* 18°50S 46°0W **93** G9
Minatitlán *Mexico* 17°59N 94°31W **87** D6
Minbu *Burma* 20°10N 94°52E **41** J19
Minchinabad *Pakistan* 30°10N 73°34E **42** D5
Mindanao *Phil.* 8°0N 125°0E **37** C7
Mindanao Sea = Bohol Sea
  Phil. 9°0N 124°0E **37** C6
Mindanao Trench
  Pac. Oc. 12°0N 126°6E **37** B7
Mindelo *C. Verde Is.* 16°44N 25°0W **52** b
Minden *Canada* 44°55N 78°43W **82** B6
Minden *Germany* 52°17N 8°55E **16** B5
Minden *La., U.S.A.* 32°37N 93°17W **84** E8
Minden *Nev., U.S.A.* 38°57N 119°46W **78** G7
Mindiptana *Indonesia* 5°55S 140°22E **37** F10
Mindoro *Phil.* 13°0N 121°0E **37** B6
Mindoro Str. *Phil.* 12°30N 120°30E **37** B6
Mine *Japan* 34°12N 131°7E **31** G5
Minehead *U.K.* 51°12N 3°29W **13** F4
Mineola *N.Y., U.S.A.* 40°44N 73°38W **83** F11
Mineola *Tex., U.S.A.* 32°40N 95°29W **84** E7
Mineral King *U.S.A.* 36°27N 118°36W **78** J8
Mineral Wells *U.S.A.* 32°48N 98°7W **84** E5
Miners Bay *Canada* 44°49N 78°46W **82** B6
Minersville *U.S.A.* 40°41N 76°16W **83** F8

Minerva *N.Y., U.S.A.* 43°47N 73°59W **83** C11
Minerva *Ohio, U.S.A.* 40°44N 81°6W **82** F3
Minetto *U.S.A.* 43°24N 76°28W **83** C8
Minfeng *China* 37°4N 82°46E **32** C3
Mingäçevir Su Anbarı
  Azerbaijan 40°57N 46°50E **19** F8
Mingan *Canada* 50°20N 64°0W **73** B7
Mingechaurskoye Vdkhr. =
  Mingäçevir Su Anbarı
  Azerbaijan 40°57N 46°50E **19** F8
Mingela *Australia* 19°52S 146°38E **62** B4
Mingenew *Australia* 29°12S 115°21E **61** E2
Mingera Cr. →
  Australia 20°38S 137°45E **62** C2
Mingin *Burma* 22°50N 94°30E **41** H19
Mingo Junction *U.S.A.* 40°19N 80°37W **82** F4
Mingora *Pakistan* 34°48N 72°22E **43** B5
Mingteke Daban = Mintaka Pass
  Pakistan 37°0N 74°58E **43** A6
Mingyuegue *China* 43°2N 128°50E **35** C15
Minho = Miño → *Spain* 41°52N 8°40W **21** A2
Minho *Portugal* 41°25N 8°20W **21** B1
Minidoka *U.S.A.* 42°45N 113°29W **76** E7
Minigwal, L. *Australia* 29°31S 123°14E **61** E3
Minilya → *Australia* 23°45S 114°0E **61** D1
Minilya Roadhouse
  Australia 23°55S 114°0E **61** D1
Minipi L. *Canada* 52°25N 60°45W **73** B7
Minjilang *Australia* 11°8S 132°33E **60** B5
Mink L. *Canada* 61°54N 117°40W **70** A5
Minna *Nigeria* 9°37N 6°30E **50** G7
Minneapolis *Kans., U.S.A.* 39°8N 97°42W **80** F5
Minneapolis *Minn.,*
  U.S.A. 44°57N 93°16W **80** C7
Minnedosa *Canada* 50°14N 99°50W **71** C9
Minnesota □ *U.S.A.* 46°0N 94°15W **80** B6
Minnesota → *U.S.A.* 44°54N 93°9W **80** C7
Minnewaukan *U.S.A.* 48°4N 99°15W **80** A4
Minnipa *Australia* 32°51S 135°9E **63** E2
Minnitaki L. *Canada* 49°57N 92°10W **72** C1
Mino *Japan* 35°32N 136°55E **31** G8
Miño → *Spain* 41°52N 8°40W **21** A2
Minorca = Menorca *Spain* 40°0N 4°0E **24** B11
Minot *U.S.A.* 48°14N 101°18W **80** A3
Minqin *China* 38°38N 103°20E **34** E2
Minsk *Belarus* 53°52N 27°30E **17** B14
Mińsk Mazowiecki
  Poland 52°10N 21°33E **17** B11
Mintabie *Australia* 27°15S 133°7E **63** D1
Mintaka Pass *Pakistan* 37°0N 74°58E **43** A6
Minto *Canada* 46°5N 66°5W **73** C6
Minto, L. *Canada* 57°13N 75°0W **72** A5
Minton *Canada* 49°10N 104°35W **71** D8
Minturn *U.S.A.* 39°35N 106°26W **76** G10
Minudasht *Iran* 37°17N 56°7E **45** B8
Minusinsk *Russia* 53°43N 91°20E **29** D10
Minutang *India* 28°15N 96°30E **41** E20
Minvoul *Gabon* 2°9N 12°8E **52** D2
Minzhong *China* 22°37N 113°30E **33** F10
Miquelon *Canada* 49°25N 76°27W **72** C4
Miquelon *St-P. & M.* 47°8N 56°22W **73** C8
Mīr Kūh *Iran* 26°22N 58°55E **45** E8
Mīr Shahdād *Iran* 26°15N 58°29E **45** E8
Mira *Italy* 45°26N 12°8E **22** B5
Mira por vos Cay
  Bahamas 22°9N 74°30W **89** B5
Mirabello, Kolpos *Greece* 35°10N 25°50E **25** D7
Mirador-Río Azul △
  Guatemala 17°45N 89°50W **88** C2
Miraj *India* 16°50N 74°45E **40** L9
Miram Shah *Pakistan* 33°0N 70°2E **42** C4
Miramar *Argentina* 38°15S 57°50W **94** D4
Miramar *Mozam.* 23°50S 35°35E **57** C6
Miramichi *Canada* 47°2N 65°28W **73** C6
Miramichi B. *Canada* 47°15N 65°0W **73** C7
Miranda *Brazil* 20°10S 56°15W **93** H7
Miranda → *Brazil* 19°25S 57°20W **93** G7
Miranda de Ebro *Spain* 42°41N 2°57W **21** A4
Miranda do Douro
  Portugal 41°30N 6°16W **21** B2
Mirandópolis *Brazil* 21°9S 51°6W **95** A5
Mirango *Malawi* 13°32S 34°58E **55** E3
Mirani *Australia* 21°8S 148°53E **62** b
Mirassol *Brazil* 20°46S 49°28W **95** A6
Mirbāṭ *Oman* 17°0N 54°45E **47** D5
Mires *Greece* 35°4N 24°56E **25** D6
Miri *Malaysia* 4°23N 113°59E **36** D4
Miriam Vale *Australia* 24°20S 151°33E **62** C5
Mirim, L. *S. Amer.* 32°45S 52°50W **95** C5
Miriuwung Gajerrong ◇
  Australia 15°0S 128°45E **60** C4
Mīrjāveh *Iran* 29°1N 61°30E **45** D9
Mirnyy *Antarctica* 66°50S 92°30E **5** C14
Mirnyy *Russia* 62°33N 113°53E **29** C12
Mirokhan *Pakistan* 27°46N 68°6E **42** F3
Mirond L. *Canada* 55°6N 102°47W **71** B8
Mirpur *Pakistan* 33°32N 73°56E **43** C5
Mirpur Batoro *Pakistan* 24°44N 68°13E **42** G3
Mirpur Bibiwari *Pakistan* 28°33N 67°44E **42** E2
Mirpur Khas *Pakistan* 25°30N 69°0E **42** G3
Mirpur Sakro *Pakistan* 24°33N 67°41E **42** G2
Mirs Bay = Tai Pang Wan
  China 22°33N 114°24E **33** F11
Mirtağ *Turkey* 38°23N 41°56E **46** C5
Mirtoo Sea *Greece* 37°0N 23°20E **23** F10
Miryang *S. Korea* 35°31N 128°44E **35** G15
Mirzapur *India* 25°10N 82°34E **43** G10
Mirzapur-cum-Vindhyachal =
  Mirzapur *India* 25°10N 82°34E **43** G10
Misantla *Mexico* 19°56N 96°50W **87** D5
Misawa *Japan* 40°41N 141°24E **30** D10
Miscou I. *Canada* 47°57N 64°31W **73** C7
Mish'āb, Ra's al
  Si. Arabia 28°15N 48°43E **45** D6
Mishamo *Tanzania* 5°1S 30°41E **54** D3
Mishan *China* 45°37N 131°48E **30** B5
Mishima *Japan* 35°10N 138°52E **31** G9
Misión *Mexico* 32°6N 116°53W **79** N10

Misiones □ *Argentina* 27°0S 55°0W **95** B5
Misiones □ *Paraguay* 27°0S 56°0W **94** B4
Miskah *Si. Arabia* 24°40N 42°56E **44** E4
Miskitos, Cayos *Nic.* 14°26N 82°50W **88** D3
Miskolc *Hungary* 48°7N 20°50E **17** D11
Misoke
  Dem. Rep. of the Congo 0°42S 28°2E **54** C2
Misool *Indonesia* 1°52S 130°10E **37** E8
Miṣr = Egypt ■ *Africa* 28°0N 31°0E **51** C12
Miṣrātah *Libya* 32°24N 15°3E **51** B9
Missanabie *Canada* 48°20N 84°6W **72** C3
Missinaibi → *Canada* 50°43N 81°29W **72** B3
Missinaibi L. *Canada* 48°23N 83°40W **72** C3
Mission *Canada* 49°10N 122°15W **70** D4
Mission *S. Dak., U.S.A.* 43°18N 100°39W **80** D3
Mission *Tex., U.S.A.* 26°13N 98°20W **84** H5
Mission Beach *Australia* 17°53S 146°6E **62** B4
Mission Viejo *U.S.A.* 33°36N 117°40W **79** M9
Missisa L. *Canada* 52°20N 85°7W **72** B2
Missisicabi → *Canada* 51°14N 79°31W **72** B4
Mississagi → *Canada* 46°15N 83°9W **72** C3
Mississauga *Canada* 43°32N 79°35W **82** C5
Mississippi □ *U.S.A.* 33°0N 90°0W **85** E10
Mississippi → *U.S.A.* 29°9N 89°15W **85** G10
Mississippi L. *Canada* 45°5N 76°10W **83** A8
Mississippi River Delta
  U.S.A. 29°10N 89°15W **85** G10
Mississippi Sd. *U.S.A.* 30°20N 89°0W **85** G10
Missoula *U.S.A.* 46°52N 114°1W **76** C6
Missouri □ *U.S.A.* 38°25N 92°30W **80** F7
Missouri → *U.S.A.* 38°49N 90°7W **80** F9
Missouri City *U.S.A.* 29°37N 95°32W **84** G7
Missouri Valley *U.S.A.* 41°34N 95°53W **80** E6
Mist *U.S.A.* 45°59N 123°15W **78** E3
Mistassibi → *Canada* 48°53N 72°13W **73** B5
Mistassini *Canada* 48°53N 72°12W **73** C5
Mistassini → *Canada* 48°42N 72°20W **73** C5
Mistassini, L. *Canada* 51°0N 73°30W **72** B5
Mistastin L. *Canada* 55°57N 63°20W **73** A7
Mistinibi, L. *Canada* 55°56N 64°17W **73** A7
Mistissini *Canada* 50°42N 73°30W **72** B5
Misty L. *Canada* 58°53N 101°40W **71** B8
Misurata = Miṣrātah
  Libya 32°24N 15°3E **51** B9
Mitande *Mozam.* 14°6S 35°58E **55** E4
Mitchell *Australia* 26°29S 147°58E **63** D4
Mitchell *Canada* 43°28N 81°12W **82** C3
Mitchell *Nebr., U.S.A.* 41°57N 103°49W **80** E2
Mitchell *Oreg., U.S.A.* 44°34N 120°9W **76** D3
Mitchell *S. Dak., U.S.A.* 43°43N 98°2W **80** D4
Mitchell → *Australia* 15°12S 141°35E **62** B3
Mitchell, Mt. *U.S.A.* 35°46N 82°16W **85** D13
Mitchell-Alice Rivers △
  Australia 15°28S 142°5E **62** B3
Mitchell Ra. *Australia* 12°49S 135°36E **62** A2
Mitchelstown *Ireland* 52°15N 8°16W **10** D3
Mitha Tiwana *Pakistan* 32°13N 72°6E **42** C5
Mithi *Pakistan* 24°44N 69°48E **42** G3
Mithrao *Pakistan* 27°28N 69°40E **42** F3
Mitilíni *Greece* 39°6N 26°35E **23** E12
Mitla Pass = Mamarr Mitlā
  Egypt 30°2N 32°54E **46** E1
Mito *Japan* 36°20N 140°30E **31** F10
Mitrovica = Kosovska Mitrovica
  Kosovo 42°54N 20°52E **23** C9
Mitsamiouli *Comoros Is.* 11°20S 43°16E **53** a
Mitsinjo *Madag.* 16°1S 45°52E **57** B8
Mitsiwa *Eritrea* 15°35N 39°25E **47** D2
Mitsukaidō *Japan* 36°1N 139°59E **31** F9
Mittagong *Australia* 34°28S 150°29E **63** E5
Mittimatalik = Pond Inlet
  Canada 72°40N 77°0W **69** C16
Mitú *Colombia* 1°15N 70°13W **92** C4
Mitumba *Tanzania* 7°8S 31°2E **54** D3
Mitumba, Mts.
  Dem. Rep. of the Congo 7°0S 27°30E **54** D2
Mitwaba
  Dem. Rep. of the Congo 8°2S 27°17E **55** D2
Mityana *Uganda* 0°23N 32°2E **54** B3
Mixteco → *Mexico* 18°11N 98°30W **87** D5
Miyagi □ *Japan* 38°15N 140°45E **30** E10
Miyāh, W. el → *Syria* 34°44N 39°57E **44** C3
Miyake-Jima *Japan* 34°5N 139°30E **31** G9
Miyako *Japan* 39°40N 141°59E **30** E10
Miyako-Jima *Japan* 24°45N 125°20E **31** M2
Miyako-Rettō *Japan* 24°24N 125°0E **31** M2
Miyakonojō *Japan* 31°40N 131°5E **31** J5
Miyani *India* 21°50N 69°26E **42** J3
Miyanoura-Dake *Japan* 30°20N 130°31E **31** J5
Miyazaki *Japan* 31°56N 131°30E **31** J5
Miyazaki □ *Japan* 32°30N 131°30E **31** H5
Miyazu *Japan* 35°35N 135°10E **31** G7
Miyet, Bahr el = Dead Sea
  Asia 31°30N 35°30E **46** D4
Miyoshi *Japan* 34°48N 132°51E **31** G6
Miyun *China* 40°28N 116°50E **34** D9
Miyun Shuiku *China* 40°30N 117°0E **35** D9
Mizdah *Libya* 31°30N 13°0E **51** B8
Mizen Hd. *Cork, Ireland* 51°27N 9°50W **10** E2
Mizen Hd. *Wicklow, Ireland* 52°51N 6°4W **10** D5
Mizhi *China* 37°47N 110°12E **34** F6
Mizoram □ *India* 23°30N 92°40E **41** H18
Mizpe Ramon *Israel* 30°34N 34°49E **46** E3
Mizuho *Antarctica* 70°30S 41°0E **5** D5
Mizusawa *Japan* 39°8N 141°8E **30** E10
Mjölby *Sweden* 58°20N 15°10E **9** G16
Mjøsa *Norway* 60°40N 11°0E **8** F14
Mkata *Tanzania* 5°45S 38°20E **54** D4
Mkhaya △ *Swaziland* 26°34S 31°45E **57** D5
Mkhuze △ *S. Africa* 27°25S 32°0E **57** D5
Mkokotoni *Tanzania* 5°55S 39°15E **54** D4
Mkomazi *Tanzania* 4°40S 38°7E **54** C4
Mkomazi → *S. Africa* 30°12S 30°50E **57** E5
Mkomazi △ *Tanzania* 4°4S 30°0E **54** C4
Mkulwe *Tanzania* 8°37S 32°20E **55** D3
Mkumbi, Ras *Tanzania* 7°38S 39°55E **54** D4
Mkushi *Zambia* 14°25S 29°15E **55** E2
Mkushi River *Zambia* 13°32S 29°45E **55** E2
Mkuze *S. Africa* 27°10S 32°0E **57** D5

Mladá Boleslav
  Czech Rep. 50°27N 14°53E **16** C8
Mlala Hills *Tanzania* 6°50S 31°40E **54** D3
Mlange = Mulanje, Mt.
  Malawi 16°2S 35°33E **55** F4
Mlawa *Poland* 53°9N 20°25E **17** B11
Mlawula △ *Swaziland* 26°15N 34°30E **41** F19
Mljet *Croatia* 42°43N 17°30E **22** C7
Mmabatho *S. Africa* 25°49S 25°30E **56** D4
Mo i Rana *Norway* 66°20N 14°7E **8** C16
Moa *Australia* 10°11S 142°16E **62** a
Moa *Cuba* 20°40N 74°56W **89** B4
Moa *Indonesia* 8°0S 128°0E **37** F7
Moa → *S. Leone* 6°59N 11°36W **50** G3
Moab *U.S.A.* 38°35N 109°33W **76** G9
Moala *Fiji* 18°36S 179°53E **59** a
Moama *Australia* 36°7S 144°46E **63** F3
Moamba *Mozam.* 25°36S 32°15E **57** D5
Moapa *U.S.A.* 36°40N 114°37W **79** J12
Moate *Ireland* 53°24N 7°44W **10** C4
Moba *Dem. Rep. of the Congo* 7°0S 29°48E **54** D2
Mobārakābād *Iran* 28°24N 53°20E **45** D7
Mobaye *C.A.R.* 4°25N 21°5E **52** D4
Moberly *U.S.A.* 39°25N 92°26W **80** F7
Moberly Lake *Canada* 55°50N 121°44W **70** B4
Mobile *U.S.A.* 30°41N 88°3W **85** F10
Mobile B. *U.S.A.* 30°30N 88°0W **85** F11
Mobridge *U.S.A.* 45°32N 100°26W **80** C3
Moc Chau *Vietnam* 20°50N 104°38E **38** B5
Moc Hoa *Vietnam* 10°46N 105°56E **39** G5
Mocabe Kasari
  Dem. Rep. of the Congo 9°58S 26°12E **55** D2
Moçambique = Mozambique ■
  Africa 19°0S 35°0E **55** F4
Moçambique *Mozam.* 15°3S 40°42E **55** F5
Mocanaqua *U.S.A.* 41°9N 76°8W **83** E8
Moce *Fiji* 18°40S 178°29W **59** a
Mochima △ *Venezuela* 10°30N 64°5W **89** D7
Mochos *Greece* 35°16N 25°27E **25** D7
Mochudi *Botswana* 24°27S 26°7E **56** C4
Mocimboa da Praia
  Mozam. 11°25S 40°20E **55** E5
Moclips *U.S.A.* 47°14N 124°13W **78** C2
Mocoa *Colombia* 1°7N 76°35W **92** C3
Mococa *Brazil* 21°28S 47°0W **95** A6
Moctezuma *Mexico* 29°48N 109°42W **86** B3
Moctezuma → *Mexico* 21°59N 98°34W **87** C5
Mocuba *Mozam.* 16°54S 36°57E **55** F4
Modane *France* 45°12N 6°40E **20** D7
Modasa *India* 23°30N 73°21E **42** H5
Modder → *S. Africa* 29°2S 24°37E **56** D3
Modderrivier *S. Africa* 29°2S 24°38E **56** D3
Módena *Italy* 44°40N 10°55E **22** B4
Modena *U.S.A.* 37°48N 113°56W **77** H7
Modesto *U.S.A.* 37°39N 121°0W **78** H6
Módica *Italy* 36°52N 14°46E **22** F6
Modimolle *S. Africa* 24°42S 28°22E **57** C4
Modjadjiskloof *S. Africa* 23°42S 30°10E **57** C5
Moe *Australia* 38°12S 146°19E **63** F4
Moebase *Mozam.* 17°3S 38°41E **55** F4
Moengo *Suriname* 5°45N 54°20W **93** B8
Moffat *U.K.* 55°21N 3°27W **11** F5
Moga *India* 30°48N 75°8E **42** D6
Mogadishu = Muqdisho
  Somali Rep. 2°2N 45°25E **47** G4
Mogador = Essaouira
  Morocco 31°32N 9°42W **50** B4
Mogalakwena →
  S. Africa 22°38S 28°40E **57** C4
Mogami-Gawa →
  Japan 38°45N 140°0E **30** E10
Mogán *Canary Is.* 27°53N 15°43W **24** G4
Mogaung *Burma* 25°20N 97°0E **41** G20
Mogi das Cruzes *Brazil* 23°31S 46°11W **95** A6
Mogi-Guaçu → *Brazil* 20°53S 48°10W **95** A6
Mogi-Mirim *Brazil* 22°29S 47°0W **93** H9
Mogilev = Mahilyow
  Belarus 53°55N 30°18E **17** B16
Mogilev-Podolskiy = Mohyliv-
  Podilskyy *Ukraine* 48°26N 27°48E **17** D14
Mogincual *Mozam.* 15°35S 40°25E **55** F5
Mogocha *Russia* 53°40N 119°50E **29** D12
Mogok *Burma* 23°0N 96°40E **41** H20
Mogollon Rim *U.S.A.* 34°10N 110°50W **77** J8
Mogumber *Australia* 31°2S 116°3E **61** F2
Mogwadi → *S. Africa* 23°4S 29°36E **57** C4
Mohács *Hungary* 45°58N 18°41E **17** F10
Mohales Hoek *Lesotho* 30°7S 27°26E **57** E4
Mohall *U.S.A.* 48°46N 101°31W **80** A3
Moḥammadābād *Iran* 37°52N 59°5E **45** B8
Mohammedia *Morocco* 33°44N 7°21W **50** B4
Mohana → *India* 24°43N 85°0E **43** G11
Mohanlalganj *India* 26°41N 80°58E **43** F9
Mohave, L. *U.S.A.* 35°12N 114°34W **79** K12
Moher, Cliffs of *Ireland* 52°58N 9°27W **10** D2
Mohicanville Res. *U.S.A.* 40°45N 82°9W **82** F2
Mohns Ridge *Arctic* 72°30N 5°0W **4** D7
Mohoro *Tanzania* 8°6S 39°8E **54** D4
Mohsenābād *Iran* 36°40N 59°35E **45** B8
Mohyliv-Podilskyy
  Ukraine 48°26N 27°48E **17** D14
Moidart, L. *U.K.* 56°47N 5°52E **11** E3
Moira → *Canada* 44°21N 77°24W **82** B7
Moisaküla *Estonia* 58°3N 25°12E **9** G21
Moisie *Canada* 50°12N 66°1W **73** B6
Moisie → *Canada* 50°14N 66°5W **73** B6
Mojave *U.S.A.* 35°3N 118°10W **79** K8
Mojave → *U.S.A.* 35°7N 116°30W **79** L10
Mojave Desert *U.S.A.* 35°0N 116°30W **79** L10
Mojo *Bolivia* 21°48S 65°33W **94** A2
Mojokerto *Indonesia* 7°28S 112°26E **37** G15
Mokai *N.Z.* 38°32S 175°56W **59** C5
Mokameh *India* 25°24N 85°55E **43** G11

Mokau *N.Z.* 38°42S 174°39E **59** C5
Mokelumne → *U.S.A.* 38°13N 121°28W **78** G5
Mokelumne Hill
  U.S.A. 38°18N 120°43W **78** G6
Mokhotlong *Lesotho* 29°22S 29°2E **57** D4
Mokoan, L. *Australia* 36°27S 146°5E **63** C4
Mokokchung *India* 26°15N 94°30E **41** F19
Mokolo → *S. Africa* 23°14S 27°43E **57** C4
Mokopane *S. Africa* 24°10S 28°55E **57** C4
Mokpo *S. Korea* 34°50N 126°25E **35** G14
Mokra Gora *Europe* 42°50N 20°30E **23** C9
Mol *Belgium* 51°11N 5°5E **15** C5
Molchanovo *Russia* 57°40N 83°50E **28** D9
Mold *U.K.* 53°9N 3°8W **12** D4
Moldavia = Moldova ■
  Europe 47°0N 28°0E **17** E15
Moldavia *Romania* 46°30N 27°0E **17** E14
Molde *Norway* 62°45N 7°9E **8** E12
Moldova ■ *Europe* 47°0N 28°0E **17** E15
Moldoveanu, Vf.
  Romania 45°36N 24°45E **17** F13
Mole → *U.K.* 51°24N 0°21W **13** F7
Molepolole *Botswana* 24°28S 25°28E **56** C4
Molfetta *Italy* 41°12N 16°36E **22** D7
Moline *U.S.A.* 41°30N 90°31W **80** E8
Molinos *Argentina* 25°28S 66°15W **94** B2
Moliro
  Dem. Rep. of the Congo 8°12S 30°30E **54** D3
Mollendo *Peru* 17°0S 72°0W **92** G4
Mollerin, L. *Australia* 30°30S 117°35E **61** F2
Molo *Kenya* 0°15S 35°44E **54** C4
Molodechno = Maladzyechna
  Belarus 54°20N 26°50E **17** A14
Molodezhnaya *Antarctica* 67°40S 45°51E **5** C9
Moloka'i *U.S.A.* 21°8N 157°0W **75** L8
Molokai Fracture Zone
  Pac. Oc. 28°0N 125°0W **65** E15
Molong *Australia* 33°5S 148°54E **63** E4
Molopo → *Africa* 28°30S 20°12E **56** D3
Molson L. *Canada* 54°22N 96°40W **71** C9
Molteno *S. Africa* 31°22S 26°22E **56** E4
Molu *Indonesia* 6°45S 131°40E **37** F8
Molucca Sea *Indonesia* 0°0 125°0E **37** E6
Moluccas = Maluku
  Indonesia 1°0S 127°0E **37** E7
Moma
  Dem. Rep. of the Congo 1°35S 23°52E **54** C1
Moma *Mozam.* 16°47S 39°4E **55** F4
Mombasa *Kenya* 4°3S 39°40E **54** C4
Mombetsu *Japan* 44°21N 143°22E **30** B11
Momchilgrad *Bulgaria* 41°33N 25°23E **23** D11
Momi *Dem. Rep. of the Congo* 1°42S 27°0E **54** C2
Mompós *Colombia* 9°14N 74°26W **92** B4
Møn *Denmark* 54°57N 12°20E **9** J15
Mon □ *Burma* 16°0N 97°30E **41** L20
Mona, Canal de la = Mona
  Passage *W. Indies* 18°30N 67°45W **89** C6
Mona, Isla *Puerto Rico* 18°5N 67°54W **89** C6
Mona, Pta. *Costa Rica* 9°37N 82°36W **88** E3
Mona Passage *W. Indies* 18°30N 67°45W **89** C6
Monaca *U.S.A.* 40°41N 80°17W **82** F4
Monaco ■ *Europe* 43°46N 7°23E **20** E7
Monadhliath Mts. *U.K.* 57°10N 4°4W **11** D4
Monadnock, Mt. *U.S.A.* 42°52N 72°7W **83** D12
Monaghan *Ireland* 54°15N 6°57W **10** B5
Monaghan □ *Ireland* 54°11N 6°56W **10** B5
Monahans *U.S.A.* 31°36N 102°54W **84** F3
Monapo *Mozam.* 14°56S 40°19E **55** E5
Monar, L. *U.K.* 57°26N 5°8W **11** D3
Monarch Mt. *Canada* 51°55N 125°57W **70** C3
Monashee Mts. *Canada* 51°0N 118°43W **70** C5
Monasterevin *Ireland* 53°8N 7°4W **10** C4
Monastir = Bitola
  Macedonia 41°1N 21°20E **23** D9
Monastir *Tunisia* 35°50N 10°49E **51** A8
Moncayo, Sierra del
  Spain 41°48N 1°50W **21** B5
Monchegorsk *Russia* 67°54N 32°58E **8** C25
Mönchengladbach
  Germany 51°11N 6°27E **16** C4
Monchique *Portugal* 37°19N 8°38W **21** D1
Moncks Corner *U.S.A.* 33°12N 80°1W **85** E14
Monclova *Mexico* 26°54N 101°25W **86** B4
Moncton *Canada* 46°7N 64°51W **73** C7
Mondego → *Portugal* 40°9N 8°52W **21** B1
Mondeodo *Indonesia* 3°34S 122°9E **37** E6
Mondovì *Italy* 44°23N 7°49E **20** D7
Mondrain I. *Australia* 34°9S 122°14E **61** F3
Moneague *Jamaica* 18°16N 77°7W **88** a
Moneron, Ostrov
  Russia 46°15N 141°16E **30** A10
Monessen *U.S.A.* 40°9N 79°54W **82** F5
Monett *U.S.A.* 36°55N 93°55W **80** G7
Moneymore *U.K.* 54°41N 6°40W **10** B5
Monforte de Lemos *Spain* 42°31N 7°33W **21** A2
Mong Cai *Vietnam* 21°27N 107°54E **38** B6
Mong Hsu *Burma* 21°54N 98°30E **41** J21
Mong Kung *Burma* 21°35N 97°35E **41** J20
Mong Nai *Burma* 20°32N 97°46E **41** J20
Mong Pawk *Burma* 22°4N 99°16E **41** H21
Mong Ton *Burma* 20°17N 98°45E **41** J21
Mong Wa *Burma* 21°26N 100°27E **41** J22
Mong Yai *Burma* 22°21N 98°3E **41** H21
Mongalla *Sudan* 5°8N 31°42E **51** G12
Mongers, L. *Australia* 29°25S 117°5E **61** E2
Monghyr = Munger
  India 25°23N 86°30E **43** G12
Mongibello = Etna *Italy* 37°50N 14°55E **22** F6
Mongo *Chad* 12°14N 18°43E **51** F9
Mongolia ■ *Asia* 47°0N 103°0E **32** B5
Mongolia, Plateau of
  Asia 45°0N 105°0E **26** D12
Mongu *Zambia* 15°16S 23°12E **53** H4
Môngua *Angola* 16°43S 15°20E **56** B2
Monifieth *U.K.* 56°30N 2°48W **11** E6
Monkey Bay *Malawi* 14°7S 35°1E **55** E4
Monkey Mia *Australia* 25°48S 113°43E **61** E1
Monkey River *Belize* 16°22N 88°29W **87** D7
Monkland *Canada* 45°11N 74°52W **83** A10

Monkoto
  Dem. Rep. of the Congo 1°38S 20°35E **52** E4
Monkton *Canada* 43°35N 81°5W **82** C3
Monmouth *U.K.* 51°48N 2°42W **13** F5
Monmouth *Ill., U.S.A.* 40°55N 90°39W **80** E8
Monmouth *Oreg.,*
  U.S.A. 44°51N 123°14W **76** D2
Monmouthshire □ *U.K.* 51°48N 2°54W **13** F5
Mono, Pta. *Nic.* 12°0N 83°30W **88** D3
Mono L. *U.S.A.* 38°1N 119°1W **78** H7
Monolith *U.S.A.* 35°7N 118°22W **79** K8
Monolithos *Greece* 36°7N 27°45E **25** C9
Monongahela *U.S.A.* 40°12N 79°56W **82** F5
Monópoli *Italy* 40°57N 17°18E **22** D7
Monos I. *Trin. & Tob.* 10°42N 61°44W **93** K15
Monroe *Ga., U.S.A.* 33°47N 83°43W **85** E13
Monroe *La., U.S.A.* 32°30N 92°7W **84** E8
Monroe *Mich., U.S.A.* 41°55N 83°24W **81** E12
Monroe *N.C., U.S.A.* 34°59N 80°33W **85** D14
Monroe *N.Y., U.S.A.* 41°20N 74°11W **83** E10
Monroe *Utah, U.S.A.* 38°38N 112°7W **76** G7
Monroe *Wash., U.S.A.* 47°51N 121°58W **78** C5
Monroe *Wis., U.S.A.* 42°36N 89°38W **80** D9
Monroe City *U.S.A.* 39°39N 91°44W **80** F8
Monroeton *U.S.A.* 41°43N 76°29W **83** E8
Monroeville *Ala.,*
  U.S.A. 31°31N 87°20W **85** F11
Monroeville *Pa., U.S.A.* 40°26N 79°45W **82** F5
Monrovia *Liberia* 6°18N 10°47W **50** G3
Mons *Belgium* 50°27N 3°58E **15** D3
Monse *Indonesia* 4°7S 123°15E **37** E6
Mont-de-Marsan *France* 43°54N 0°31W **20** E3
Mont-Joli *Canada* 48°37N 68°10W **73** C6
Mont-Laurier *Canada* 46°35N 75°30W **72** C4
Mont-Louis *Canada* 49°15N 65°44W **73** C6
Mont-St-Michel, Le
  France 48°40N 1°30W **20** B3
Mont-Tremblant △
  Canada 46°30N 74°30W **72** C5
Montagne d'Ambre △
  Madag. 12°37S 49°8E **57** A8
Montagu *S. Africa* 33°45S 20°8E **56** E3
Montagu I. *Antarctica* 58°25S 26°20W **5** B1
Montague *Canada* 46°10N 62°39W **73** C7
Montague, I. *Mexico* 31°45N 114°48W **86** A2
Montague I. *U.S.A.* 60°0N 147°30W **74** D10
Montague Ra. *Australia* 27°15S 119°30E **61** E2
Montague Sd. *Australia* 14°28S 125°20E **60** B4
Montalbán *Spain* 40°50N 0°45W **21** B5
Montalvo *U.S.A.* 34°15N 119°12W **79** L7
Montana *Bulgaria* 43°27N 23°16E **23** C10
Montaña *Peru* 6°0S 73°0W **92** E4
Montana □ *U.S.A.* 47°0N 110°0W **76** C9
Montaña Clara, I.
  Canary Is. 29°17N 13°33W **24** E6
Montargis *France* 47°59N 2°43E **20** C5
Montauban *France* 44°2N 1°21E **20** D4
Montauk *U.S.A.* 41°3N 71°57W **83** E13
Montauk Pt. *U.S.A.* 41°4N 71°51W **83** E13
Montbéliard *France* 47°31N 6°48E **20** C7
Montceau-les-Mines
  France 46°40N 4°23E **20** C6
Montclair *U.S.A.* 40°49N 74°12W **83** F10
Monte Albán *Mexico* 17°2N 96°46W **87** D5
Monte Alegre *Brazil* 2°0S 54°0W **93** D8
Monte Azul *Brazil* 15°9S 42°53W **93** G10
Monte-Carlo *Monaco* 43°44N 7°25E **20** E7
Monte Caseros
  Argentina 30°10S 57°50W **94** C4
Monte Comán *Argentina* 34°40S 67°53W **94** C2
Monte Cristi *Dom. Rep.* 19°52N 71°39W **89** C5
Monte Lindo →
  Paraguay 23°56S 57°12W **94** A4
Monte Patria *Chile* 30°42S 70°58W **94** C1
Monte Quemado
  Argentina 25°53S 62°41W **94** B3
Monte Rio *U.S.A.* 38°28N 123°0W **78** G4
Monte Santu, C. di *Italy* 40°5N 9°44E **22** D3
Monte Vista *U.S.A.* 37°35N 106°9W **77** H10
Montealegre *Argentina* 27°14S 54°8W **95** B5
Montebello *Canada* 45°40N 74°55W **72** C5
Montebello Is. *Australia* 20°30S 115°45E **60** D2
Montecarlo *Argentina* 26°34S 54°47W **95** B5
Montecito *U.S.A.* 34°26N 119°40W **79** L7
Montecristo *Italy* 42°20N 10°19E **22** C4
Montego Bay *Jamaica* 18°28N 77°55W **88** a
Montélimar *France* 44°33N 4°45E **20** D6
Montemorelos *Mexico* 25°12N 99°49W **87** B5
Montenegro *Brazil* 29°39S 51°29W **95** B5
Montenegro ■ *Europe* 42°40N 19°20E **23** C8
Montepuez *Mozam.* 13°8S 38°59E **55** E4
Montepuez → *Mozam.* 12°32S 40°27E **55** E5
Monterey *U.S.A.* 36°37N 121°55W **78** J5
Monterey B. *U.S.A.* 36°45N 122°0W **78** J5
Montería *Colombia* 8°46N 75°53W **92** B3
Monteros *Argentina* 27°11S 65°30W **94** B2
Monterrey *Mexico* 25°40N 100°19W **86** B4
Montes Azules △ *Mexico* 16°20N 91°0W **87** D6
Montes Claros *Brazil* 16°30S 43°50W **93** G10
Montesilvano *Italy* 42°29N 14°8E **22** C6
Montevideo *Uruguay* 34°50S 56°11W **95** C4
Montevideo *U.S.A.* 44°57N 95°43W **80** C6
Montezuma *U.S.A.* 41°35N 92°32W **80** E7
Montezuma Castle △
  U.S.A. 34°39N 111°45W **77** J8
Montgomery *U.K.* 52°34N 3°8W **13** E4
Montgomery *Ala.,*
  U.S.A. 32°23N 86°19W **85** E11
Montgomery *Pa., U.S.A.* 41°10N 76°53W **82** E8
Montgomery *W. Va.,*
  U.S.A. 38°11N 81°19W **81** F13
Montgomery City
  U.S.A. 38°59N 91°30W **80** F8
Monticello *Ark., U.S.A.* 33°38N 91°47W **84** E9
Monticello *Fla., U.S.A.* 30°33N 83°52W **85** F13
Monticello *Ind., U.S.A.* 40°45N 86°46W **81** E9
Monticello *Iowa, U.S.A.* 42°15N 91°12W **80** D8

Monticello Ky., U.S.A. 36°50N 84°51W **81** G11
Monticello Minn., U.S.A. 45°18N 93°48W **80** C7
Monticello Miss., U.S.A. 31°33N 90°7W **85** F9
Monticello N.Y., U.S.A. 41°39N 74°42W **83** E10
Monticello Utah, U.S.A. 37°52N 109°21W **77** H9
Montijo Portugal 38°41N 8°54W **21** C1
Montilla Spain 37°36N 4°40W **21** D3
Montluçon France 46°22N 2°36E **20** C5
Montmagny Canada 46°58N 70°34W **73** C5
Montmartre Canada 50°14N 103°27W **71** C8
Montmorillon France 46°26N 0°50E **20** C4
Monto Australia 24°52S 151°6E **62** C5
Montongbuwoh Indonesia 8°33S 116°4E **37** K19
Montoro Spain 38°1N 4°27W **21** C3
Montour Falls U.S.A. 42°21N 76°51W **82** D8
Montoursville U.S.A. 41°15N 76°55W **82** E8
Montpelier Idaho, U.S.A. 42°19N 111°18W **76** E8
Montpelier Vt., U.S.A. 44°16N 72°35W **83** B12
Montpellier France 43°37N 3°52E **20** E5
Montréal Canada 45°30N 73°33W **83** A11
Montreal → Canada 47°14N 84°39W **72** C3
Montréal L. Canada 54°20N 105°45W **71** C7
Montreal Lake Canada 54°3N 105°46W **71** C7
Montreux Switz. 46°26N 6°55E **20** C7
Montrose U.K. 56°44N 2°27W **11** E6
Montrose Colo., U.S.A. 38°29N 107°53W **76** G10
Montrose Pa., U.S.A. 41°50N 75°53W **83** E9
Monts, Pte. des Canada 49°20N 67°12W **73** C6
Montserrat ☑ W. Indies 16°40N 62°10W **89** C7
Montuiri Spain 39°34N 2°59E **24** B9
Monywa Burma 22°7N 95°11E **41** H19
Monza Italy 45°35N 9°16E **20** D8
Monze Zambia 16°17S 27°29E **55** F2
Monze, C. Pakistan 24°47N 66°37E **42** G2
Monzón Spain 41°52N 0°10E **21** B6
Mooers U.S.A. 44°58N 73°35W **83** B11
Mooi → S. Africa 28°45S 30°34E **57** D5
Mooi River S. Africa 29°13S 29°50E **57** D4
Moomba Australia 28°6S 140°12E **63** A3
Moonah → Australia 22°3S 138°33E **62** C2
Moonda, L. Australia 25°52S 140°25E **62** D3
Moonie Australia 27°46S 150°20E **63** D5
Moonie → Australia 29°19S 148°43E **63** D4
Moonta Australia 34°6S 137°32E **63** E2
Moora Australia 30°37S 115°58E **61** F2
Moorcroft U.S.A. 44°16N 104°57W **76** D11
Moore → Australia 31°22S 115°30E **61** F2
Moore, L. Australia 29°50S 117°35E **61** E2
Moore Falls Canada 44°48N 78°48W **82** B6
Moore Res. U.S.A. 44°20N 71°53W **83** B13
Moore River △ Australia 31°7S 115°39E **61** F2
Moorea French Polynesia 17°30S 149°50W **59** d
Moorefield U.S.A. 39°4N 78°58W **81** F14
Moorfoot Hills U.K. 55°44N 3°8W **11** F5
Moorhead U.S.A. 46°53N 96°45W **80** B5
Moorpark U.S.A. 34°17N 118°53W **79** L8
Moorreesburg S. Africa 33°6S 18°38E **56** E2
Moorrinya △ Australia 21°42S 144°42E **62** C3
Moose → Canada 51°20N 80°25W **72** B3
Moose → U.S.A. 43°38N 75°24W **83** C9
Moose Creek Canada 45°15N 74°58W **83** A10
Moose Factory Canada 51°16N 80°32W **72** B3
Moose Jaw Canada 50°24N 105°30W **71** C7
Moose Jaw → Canada 50°34N 105°18W **71** C7
Moose Lake Canada 53°46N 100°8W **71** C8
Moose Lake U.S.A. 46°27N 92°46W **80** B7
Moose Mountain △ Canada 49°48N 102°25W **71** D8
Moosehead L. U.S.A. 45°38N 69°40W **81** C19
Mooselookmeguntic L. U.S.A. 44°55N 70°49W **83** B14
Moosilauke, Mt. U.S.A. 44°3N 71°40W **83** B13
Moosomin Canada 50°9N 101°40W **71** C8
Moosonee Canada 51°17N 80°39W **72** B3
Moosup U.S.A. 41°43N 71°53W **83** E13
Mopane S. Africa 22°37S 29°52E **57** C4
Mopeia Velha Mozam. 17°30S 35°40E **55** F4
Mopipi Botswana 21°6S 24°55E **56** C3
Mopoi C.A.R. 5°6N 26°54E **54** G2
Mopti Mali 14°30N 4°0W **50** F5
Moqor Afghan. 32°50N 67°42E **42** C2
Moquegua Peru 17°15S 70°46W **92** G4
Mora Sweden 61°2N 14°38E **8** F16
Mora Minn., U.S.A. 45°53N 93°18W **80** C7
Mora N. Mex., U.S.A. 35°58N 105°20W **77** J11
Moradabad India 28°50N 78°50E **43** E8
Morafenobe Madag. 17°50S 44°53E **57** B7
Moramanga Madag. 18°56S 48°12E **57** B8
Moran Kans., U.S.A. 37°55N 95°10W **80** G6
Moran Wyo., U.S.A. 43°50N 110°31W **76** E8
Moranbah Australia 22°1S 148°6E **62** C4
Morang = Biratnagar Nepal 26°27N 87°17E **43** F12
Morant Bay Jamaica 17°53N 76°25W **88** a
Morant Cays Jamaica 17°22N 76°0W **88** C4
Morant Pt. Jamaica 17°55N 76°12W **88** a
Morar India 26°14N 78°14E **42** F8
Morar, L. U.K. 56°57N 5°40W **11** E3
Moratuwa Sri Lanka 6°45N 79°55E **40** R11
Morava → Serbia 44°36N 21°4E **23** B9
Morava → Slovak Rep. 48°10N 16°59E **17** D9
Moravia U.S.A. 42°43N 76°25W **83** D8
Moravian Hts. = Českomoravská Vrchovina Czech Rep. 49°30N 15°40E **16** D8
Morawa Australia 29°13S 116°0E **61** E2
Morawhanna Guyana 8°30N 59°40W **92** B7
Moray □ U.K. 57°31N 3°18W **11** D5
Moray Firth U.K. 57°40N 3°52W **11** D5
Morbi India 22°42N 70°37E **42** H4
Morden Canada 49°15N 98°10W **71** D9
Mordovian Republic = Mordvinia □ Russia 54°20N 44°30E **18** D7
Mordvinia □ Russia 54°20N 44°30E **18** D7
Moreau → U.S.A. 45°18N 100°43W **80** C3
Morebeng S. Africa 23°30S 29°55E **57** C4
Morecambe U.K. 54°5N 2°52W **12** C5

Morecambe B. U.K. 54°7N 3°0W **12** C5
Moree Australia 29°28S 149°54E **63** D4
Morehead U.S.A. 38°11N 83°26W **81** F12
Morehead City U.S.A. 34°43N 76°43W **85** D16
Morel → India 26°13N 76°36E **42** F7
Morelia Mexico 19°42N 101°7W **86** D4
Morella Australia 23°0S 143°52E **62** C3
Morella Spain 40°35N 0°5W **21** B5
Morelos Mexico 26°42N 107°40W **86** B3
Morelos □ Mexico 18°45N 99°0W **87** D5
Moremi △ Botswana 19°18S 23°10E **56** B3
Morena India 26°30N 78°4E **42** F8
Morena, Sierra Spain 38°20N 4°0W **21** C3
Moreno Valley U.S.A. 33°56N 117°14W **79** M10
Moresby I. Canada 52°30N 131°40W **70** C2
Moreton I. Australia 27°10S 153°25E **63** D5
Moreton Island △ Australia 27°2S 153°24E **63** D5
Morgan U.S.A. 41°2N 111°41W **76** F8
Morgan City U.S.A. 29°42N 91°12W **84** G9
Morgan Hill U.S.A. 37°8N 121°39W **78** H5
Morganfield U.S.A. 37°41N 87°55W **80** G10
Morganton U.S.A. 35°45N 81°41W **85** D14
Morgantown U.S.A. 39°38N 79°57W **81** F14
Morgenzon S. Africa 26°45S 29°36E **57** D4
Morghak Iran 29°7N 57°54E **45** D8
Morhar → India 25°29N 85°11E **43** G11
Mori Japan 42°6N 140°35E **30** C10
Moriarty U.S.A. 34°59N 106°3W **77** J10
Morice L. Canada 53°50N 127°40W **70** C3
Morinville Canada 53°49N 113°41W **70** C6
Morioka Japan 39°45N 141°8E **30** E10
Moris Mexico 28°10N 108°32W **86** B3
Morlaix France 48°36N 3°52W **20** B2
Mornington Australia 38°15S 145°5E **63** F4
Mornington, I. Chile 49°50S 75°30W **96** F1
Mornington I. Australia 16°30S 139°30E **62** B2
Moro Pakistan 26°40N 68°0E **42** F2
Moro → Pakistan 29°42N 67°22E **42** E2
Moro G. Phil. 6°30N 123°0E **37** C6
Morocco ■ N. Afr. 32°0N 5°50W **50** B4
Morogoro Tanzania 6°50S 37°40E **54** D4
Morogoro □ Tanzania 8°0S 37°0E **54** D4
Moroleón Mexico 20°8N 101°12W **86** C4
Morombe Madag. 21°45S 43°22E **57** C7
Moron Argentina 34°39S 58°37W **94** C4
Morón Cuba 22°8N 78°39W **88** B4
Mörön Mongolia 49°38N 100°9E **32** B4
Morón de la Frontera Spain 37°6N 5°28W **21** D3
Morona → Peru 4°40S 77°10W **92** D3
Morondava Madag. 20°17S 44°17E **57** C7
Morongo Valley U.S.A. 34°3N 116°37W **79** L10
Moroni Comoros Is. 11°40S 43°16E **53** a
Moroni U.S.A. 39°32N 111°35W **76** G8
Morotai Indonesia 2°10N 128°30E **37** D7
Moroto Uganda 2°28N 34°42E **54** B3
Moroto, Mt. Uganda 2°30N 34°43E **54** B3
Morpeth Canada 42°23N 81°50W **82** D3
Morpeth U.K. 55°10N 1°41W **12** B6
Morphou Cyprus 35°12N 32°59E **25** D11
Morphou Bay Cyprus 35°15N 32°50E **25** D11
Morrilton U.S.A. 35°9N 92°44W **84** D8
Morrinhos Brazil 17°45S 49°10W **93** G9
Morrinsville N.Z. 37°40S 175°32E **59** B5
Morris Canada 49°25N 97°22W **71** D9
Morris Ill., U.S.A. 41°22N 88°26W **80** E9
Morris Minn., U.S.A. 45°35N 95°55W **80** C6
Morris N.Y., U.S.A. 42°33N 75°15W **83** D9
Morris Pa., U.S.A. 41°35N 77°17W **82** E7
Morris, Mt. Australia 26°9S 131°4E **61** E5
Morris Jesup, Kap Greenland 83°40N 34°0W **66** A16
Morrisburg Canada 44°55N 75°7W **83** B9
Morristown Ariz., U.S.A. 33°51N 112°37W **77** K7
Morristown N.J., U.S.A. 40°48N 74°29W **83** F10
Morristown N.Y., U.S.A. 44°35N 75°39W **83** B9
Morristown Tenn., U.S.A. 36°13N 83°18W **85** C13
Morrisville N.Y., U.S.A. 42°53N 75°35W **83** D9
Morrisville Pa., U.S.A. 40°13N 74°47W **83** F10
Morrisville Vt., U.S.A. 44°34N 72°36W **83** B12
Morro, Pta. Chile 27°6S 71°0W **94** B1
Morro Bay U.S.A. 35°22N 120°51W **78** K6
Morro del Jable Canary Is. 28°3N 14°23W **24** F5
Morro Jable, Pta. de Canary Is. 28°2N 14°20W **24** F5
Morrocoy △ Venezuela 10°48N 68°13W **89** D6
Morrosquillo, G. de Colombia 9°35N 75°40W **88** E4
Morrumbene Mozam. 23°31S 35°16E **57** C6
Morshansk Russia 53°28N 41°50E **18** D7
Morteros Argentina 30°50S 62°0W **94** C3
Mortlach Canada 50°27N 106°4W **71** C7
Mortlake Australia 38°5S 142°50E **63** F3
Morton Tex., U.S.A. 33°44N 102°46W **84** E3
Morton Wash., U.S.A. 46°34N 122°17W **78** D4
Moruga Trin. & Tob. 10°4N 61°16W **93** K15
Morundah Australia 34°57S 146°19E **63** E4
Moruya Australia 35°58S 150°3E **63** F5
Morvan France 47°5N 4°3E **20** C6
Morven Australia 26°22S 147°5E **63** D4
Morvern U.K. 56°38N 5°44W **11** E3
Morwell Australia 38°10S 146°22E **63** F4
Morzhovets, Ostrov Russia 66°44N 42°35E **18** A7
Mosakahiken = Moose Lake Canada 53°46N 100°8W **71** C8
Moscos Is. Burma 14°0N 97°30E **38** F1
Moscow = Moskva Russia 55°45N 37°37E **18** C6
Moscow Idaho, U.S.A. 46°44N 117°0W **76** C5
Moscow Pa., U.S.A. 41°20N 75°31W **83** E9
Mosel → Europe 50°22N 7°36E **20** A7
Moselle = Mosel → Europe 50°22N 7°36E **20** A7

Moshaweng → S. Africa 26°35S 22°50E **56** D3
Moshchnyy, Ostrov Russia 60°1N 27°50E **9** F22
Moshi Tanzania 3°22S 37°18E **54** C4
Moshupa Botswana 24°46S 25°29E **56** C4
Mosjøen Norway 65°51N 13°12E **8** D15
Moskenesøya Norway 67°58N 13°0E **8** C15
Moskenstraumen Norway 67°47N 12°45E **8** C15
Moskva Russia 55°45N 37°37E **18** C6
Mosomane Botswana 24°2S 26°19E **56** C4
Mosonmagyaróvár Hungary 47°52N 17°18E **17** E9
Mosquera Colombia 2°35N 78°24W **92** C3
Mosquero U.S.A. 35°47N 103°58W **77** J12
Mosquitia Honduras 15°20N 84°10W **88** C3
Mosquito Coast = Mosquitia Honduras 15°20N 84°10W **88** C3
Mosquito Creek L. U.S.A. 41°18N 80°46W **82** E4
Mosquito L. Canada 62°35N 103°20W **71** A8
Mosquitos, G. de los Panama 9°15N 81°10W **88** E3
Moss Norway 59°27N 10°40E **9** G14
Moss Vale Australia 34°32S 150°25E **63** E5
Mossaka Congo 1°15S 16°45E **52** E3
Mossbank Canada 49°56N 105°56W **71** D7
Mossburn N.Z. 45°41S 168°15E **59** F2
Mosselbaai S. Africa 34°11S 22°8E **56** E3
Mossendjo Congo 2°55S 12°42E **52** E2
Mossgiel Australia 33°15S 144°5E **63** E3
Mossman Australia 16°21S 145°15E **62** B4
Mossoró Brazil 5°10S 37°15W **93** E11
Mossuril Mozam. 14°58S 40°42E **55** E5
Most Czech Rep. 50°31N 13°38E **16** C7
Mosta Malta 35°55N 14°26E **25** D1
Mostaganem Algeria 35°54N 0°5E **50** A6
Mostar Bos.-H. 43°22N 17°50E **23** C7
Mostardas Brazil 31°2S 50°51W **95** C5
Mostiska = Mostyska Ukraine 49°48N 23°4E **17** D12
Mosty = Masty Belarus 53°27N 24°38E **17** B13
Mostyska Ukraine 49°48N 23°4E **17** D12
Mosul = Al Mawşil Iraq 36°15N 43°5E **44** B4
Motagua → Guatemala 15°44N 88°14W **88** C2
Motala Sweden 58°32N 15°1E **9** G16
Motaze Mozam. 24°48S 32°52E **57** C5
Moth India 25°43N 78°57E **43** G8
Motihari India 26°30N 84°55E **43** F11
Motozintla de Mendoza Mexico 15°22N 92°14W **87** D6
Motril Spain 36°31N 3°37W **21** D4
Mott U.S.A. 46°23N 102°20W **80** B2
Motueka N.Z. 41°7S 173°1E **59** D4
Motueka → N.Z. 41°5S 173°1E **59** D4
Motul Mexico 21°6N 89°17W **87** C7
Mouchalagane → Canada 50°56N 68°41W **73** B6
Moudros Greece 39°50N 25°18E **23** E11
Mouhoun = Black Volta → Africa 8°41N 1°33W **50** G5
Mouila Gabon 1°50S 11°0E **52** E2
Moulamein Australia 35°3S 144°1E **63** F3
Moule à Chique, C. St. Lucia 13°43N 60°57W **89** f
Mouliana Greece 35°10N 25°59E **25** D7
Moulins France 46°35N 3°19E **20** C5
Moulmein Burma 16°30N 97°40E **41** L20
Moulouya, O. → Morocco 35°5N 2°25W **50** B5
Moultrie U.S.A. 31°11N 83°47W **85** F13
Moultrie, L. U.S.A. 33°20N 80°5W **85** E14
Mound City Mo., U.S.A. 40°7N 95°14W **80** E6
Mound City S. Dak., U.S.A. 45°44N 100°4W **80** C3
Moundou Chad 8°40N 16°10E **51** G9
Moundsville U.S.A. 39°55N 80°44W **82** G4
Moung Cambodia 12°46N 103°27E **38** F4
Mount Airy U.S.A. 36°31N 80°37W **85** C14
Mount Albert Canada 44°8N 79°19W **82** B5
Mount Aspiring △ N.Z. 44°19S 168°47E **59** F2
Mount Barker S. Austral., Australia 35°5S 138°52E **63** F2
Mount Barker W. Austral., Australia 34°38S 117°40E **61** F2
Mount Barnett Roadhouse Australia 16°39S 125°57E **60** C4
Mount Bellew Bridge Ireland 53°28N 8°31W **10** C3
Mount Brydges Canada 42°54N 81°29W **82** D3
Mount Burr Australia 37°34S 140°26E **63** F3
Mount Carmel = Ha Karmel Israel 32°45N 35°5E **46** C4
Mount Carmel Ill., U.S.A. 38°25N 87°46W **80** F10
Mount Carmel Pa., U.S.A. 40°47N 76°26W **83** F8
Mount Clemens U.S.A. 42°35N 82°53W **82** D2
Mount Coolon Australia 21°25S 147°25E **62** C4
Mount Darwin Zimbabwe 16°47S 31°38E **55** F3
Mount Desert I. U.S.A. 44°21N 68°20W **81** C19
Mount Dora U.S.A. 28°48N 81°38W **85** G14
Mount Ebenezer Australia 25°6S 132°34E **61** E5
Mount Edziza △ Canada 57°30N 130°45W **70** B2
Mount Elgon △ E. Afr. 1°4N 34°42E **54** B3
Mount Field △ S. Africa 42°39S 146°35E **63** G4
Mount Fletcher S. Africa 30°40S 28°30E **57** E4
Mount Forest Canada 43°59N 80°43W **82** C4
Mount Frankland △ Australia 31°47S 116°37E **61** F2
Mount Frederick ○ Australia 19°39S 129°18E **60** C4
Mount Gambier Australia 37°50S 140°46E **63** F3
Mount Garnet Australia 17°37S 145°6E **62** B4
Mount Holly U.S.A. 39°59N 74°47W **83** G10

Mount Holly Springs U.S.A. 40°7N 77°12W **82** F7
Moshchnyy, Ostrov
Mount Hope N.S.W., Australia 32°51S 145°51E **63** E4
Mount Hope S. Austral., Australia 34°7S 135°23E **63** E2
Mount Isa Australia 20°42S 139°26E **62** C2
Mount James ○ Australia 24°51S 116°54E **61** D2
Mount Jewett U.S.A. 41°44N 78°39W **82** E6
Mount Kaputar △ Australia 30°16S 150°10E **63** E5
Mount Kenya △ Kenya 0°7S 37°21E **54** C4
Mount Kisco U.S.A. 41°12N 73°44W **83** E11
Mount Laguna U.S.A. 32°52N 116°25W **79** N10
Mount Larcom Australia 23°48S 150°59E **62** C5
Mount Lofty Ranges Australia 34°35S 139°5E **63** E2
Mount Magnet Australia 28°2S 117°47E **61** E2
Mount Maunganui N.Z. 37°40S 176°14E **59** B6
Mount Molloy Australia 16°42S 145°20E **62** B4
Mount Morgan Australia 23°40S 150°25E **62** C5
Mount Morris U.S.A. 42°44N 77°52W **82** D7
Mount Pearl Canada 47°31N 52°47W **73** C9
Mount Penn U.S.A. 40°20N 75°54W **83** F9
Mount Perry Australia 25°13S 151°42E **63** D5
Mount Pleasant Iowa, U.S.A. 40°58N 91°33W **80** E8
Mount Pleasant Mich., U.S.A. 43°36N 84°46W **81** D11
Mount Pleasant Pa., U.S.A. 40°9N 79°33W **82** F5
Mount Pleasant S.C., U.S.A. 32°47N 79°52W **85** E15
Mount Pleasant Tenn., U.S.A. 35°32N 87°12W **85** D11
Mount Pleasant Tex., U.S.A. 33°9N 94°58W **84** E7
Mount Pleasant Utah, U.S.A. 39°33N 111°27W **76** G8
Mount Pocono U.S.A. 41°7N 75°22W **83** E9
Mount Rainier △ U.S.A. 46°55N 121°50W **78** D5
Mount Revelstoke △ Canada 51°5N 118°30W **70** C5
Mount Robson △ Canada 53°0N 119°0W **70** C5
Mount St. Helens △ U.S.A. 46°14N 122°11W **78** D4
Mount Selinda Zimbabwe 20°24S 32°43E **57** C5
Mount Shasta U.S.A. 41°19N 122°19W **76** F2
Mount Signal U.S.A. 32°39N 115°37W **79** N11
Mount Sterling Ill., U.S.A. 39°59N 90°45W **80** F8
Mount Sterling Ky., U.S.A. 38°4N 83°56W **81** F12
Mount Surprise Australia 18°10S 144°17E **62** B3
Mount Union U.S.A. 40°23N 77°53W **82** F7
Mount Upton U.S.A. 42°26N 75°23W **83** D9
Mount Vernon Ill., U.S.A. 38°19N 88°55W **80** F9
Mount Vernon Ind., U.S.A. 37°56N 87°54W **80** G10
Mount Vernon N.Y., U.S.A. 40°54N 73°49W **83** F11
Mount Vernon Ohio, U.S.A. 40°23N 82°29W **82** F2
Mount Vernon Wash., U.S.A. 48°25N 122°20W **78** B4
Mount William △ Australia 40°56S 148°14E **63** G4
Mountain Ash U.K. 51°40N 3°23W **13** F4
Mountain Center U.S.A. 33°42N 116°44W **79** M10
Mountain City Nev., U.S.A. 41°50N 115°58W **76** F6
Mountain City Tenn., U.S.A. 36°29N 81°48W **85** C14
Mountain Dale U.S.A. 41°41N 74°32W **83** E10
Mountain Grove U.S.A. 37°8N 92°16W **80** G7
Mountain Home Ark., U.S.A. 36°20N 92°23W **84** C8
Mountain Home Idaho, U.S.A. 43°8N 115°41W **76** E6
Mountain Iron U.S.A. 47°32N 92°37W **80** B7
Mountain Pass U.S.A. 35°29N 115°35W **79** K11
Mountain View Ark., U.S.A. 35°52N 92°7W **84** D8
Mountain View Calif., U.S.A. 37°23N 122°5W **78** H4
Mountain Zebra △ S. Africa 32°14S 25°27E **56** E4
Mountainair U.S.A. 34°31N 106°15W **77** J10
Mountlake Terrace U.S.A. 47°47N 122°18W **78** C4
Mountmellick Ireland 53°7N 7°20W **10** C4
Mountrath Ireland 53°0N 7°28W **10** C4
Moura Australia 24°35S 149°58E **62** C4
Moura Brazil 1°32S 61°38W **92** D6
Moura Portugal 38°7N 7°30W **21** C2
Mourdi, Dépression du Chad 18°10N 23°0E **51** E10
Mourilyan Australia 17°35S 146°3E **62** B4
Mourne → U.K. 54°52N 7°26W **10** B4
Mourne Mts. U.K. 54°10N 6°0W **10** B5
Mournies Greece 35°29N 24°1E **25** D6
Mouscron Belgium 50°45N 3°12E **15** D3
Moussoro Chad 13°41N 16°35E **51** F9
Moutong Indonesia 0°28N 121°13E **37** D6
Movas Mexico 28°10N 109°25W **86** B3
Moville Ireland 55°11N 7°3W **10** A4
Mowandjum Australia 17°22S 123°40E **60** C3
Moy → Ireland 54°8N 9°8W **10** B2
Moya Comoros Is. 12°18S 44°15E **53** a
Moyale Ethiopia 3°34N 39°5E **54** B4
Moyale Kenya 3°30N 39°4E **54** B4

Moyen Atlas Morocco 33°0N 5°0W **50** B4
Moyo Indonesia 8°10S 117°40E **36** F5
Moyobamba Peru 6°0S 77°0W **92** E3
Moyowosi → Tanzania 3°50S 31°0E **54** C3
Moyyero → Russia 68°44N 103°42E **29** C11
Moyynqum Kazakhstan 44°12N 71°0E **32** B2
Moyynty Kazakhstan 47°10N 73°18E **28** E8
Mozambique = Moçambique Mozam. 15°3S 40°42E **55** F5
Mozambique ■ Africa 19°0S 35°0E **55** F4
Mozambique Chan. Africa 17°30S 42°30E **57** B7
Mozdok Russia 43°45N 44°48E **19** F7
Mozdūrān Iran 36°9N 60°35E **45** B9
Mozhnābād Iran 34°7N 60°6E **45** C9
Mozyr = Mazyr Belarus 51°59N 29°15E **17** B15
Mpanda Tanzania 6°23S 31°1E **54** D3
Mphoeng Zimbabwe 21°10S 27°51E **55** G2
Mpika Zambia 11°51S 31°25E **55** E3
Mpulungu Zambia 8°51S 31°5E **55** D3
Mpumalanga S. Africa 29°50S 30°33E **57** D5
Mpumalanga □ S. Africa 26°0S 30°0E **57** D5
Mpwapwa Tanzania 6°23S 36°30E **54** D4
Mqanduli S. Africa 31°49S 28°45E **57** E4
Msaken Tunisia 35°49N 10°33E **51** A8
Msambansovu Zimbabwe 15°50S 30°3E **55** F3
M'sila → Algeria 35°30N 4°29E **50** A6
Msoro Zambia 13°35S 31°50E **55** E3
Mstislavl = Mstsislaw Belarus 54°0N 31°50E **17** A16
Mstsislaw Belarus 54°0N 31°50E **17** A16
Mtama Tanzania 10°17S 39°21E **55** E4
Mtamvuna = Mthamvuna → S. Africa 31°6S 30°12E **57** E5
Mthamvuna → S. Africa 31°6S 30°12E **57** E5
Mthatha S. Africa 31°36S 28°49E **57** E4
Mtilikwe → Zimbabwe 21°9S 31°30E **55** G3
Mtito Andei Kenya 2°41S 38°10E **54** C4
Mtubatuba S. Africa 28°30S 32°8E **57** D5
Mtwalume S. Africa 30°30S 30°38E **57** E5
Mtwara-Mikindani Tanzania 10°20S 40°20E **55** E5
Mu Gia, Deo Vietnam 17°40N 105°47E **38** D5
Mu Ko Chang △ Thailand 11°59N 102°22E **39** G4
Mu Us Shamo China 39°0N 109°0E **34** E5
Muang Chiang Rai = Chiang Rai Thailand 19°52N 99°50E **38** C2
Muang Khong Laos 14°7N 105°51E **38** E5
Muang Lamphun Thailand 18°40N 99°2E **38** C2
Muang Mai Thailand 8°5N 98°21E **39** a
Muang Pak Beng Laos 19°54N 101°8E **38** C3
Muar Malaysia 2°3N 102°34E **39** L4
Muarabungo Indonesia 1°28S 102°52E **36** E2
Muaraenim Indonesia 3°40S 103°50E **36** E2
Muarajuloi Indonesia 0°12S 114°3E **36** E4
Muarakaman Indonesia 0°2S 116°45E **36** E5
Muaratebo Indonesia 1°30S 102°26E **36** E2
Muaratembesi Indonesia 1°42S 103°8E **36** E2
Muaratewe Indonesia 0°58S 114°52E **36** E4
Mubarakpur India 26°6N 83°18E **43** F10
Mubarraz = Al Mubarraz Si. Arabia 25°30N 49°40E **45** E6
Mubende Uganda 0°33N 31°22E **54** B3
Mubi Nigeria 10°18N 13°16E **51** F8
Mucajaí → Brazil 2°25N 60°52W **92** C6
Muchachos, Roque de los Canary Is. 28°44N 17°52W **24** F2
Muchinga Mts. Zambia 11°30S 31°30E **55** E3
Muck U.K. 56°50N 6°15W **11** E2
Muckadilla Australia 26°35S 148°23E **63** D4
Muckle Flugga U.K. 60°51N 0°54W **11** A8
Mucuri Brazil 18°0S 39°36W **93** G11
Mucusso Angola 18°1S 21°25E **56** B3
Muda Canary Is. 28°34N 13°57W **24** F6
Mudanjiang China 44°38N 129°30E **35** B15
Mudanya Turkey 40°25N 28°50E **23** D13
Muddy Cr. → U.S.A. 38°24N 110°42W **76** G8
Mudgee Australia 32°32S 149°31E **63** E4
Mudjatik → Canada 56°1N 107°36W **71** B7
Muecate Mozam. 14°55S 39°40E **55** E4
Mueda Mozam. 11°36S 39°28E **55** E4
Mueller Ranges Australia 18°18S 126°46E **60** C4
Muende Mozam. 14°28S 33°0E **55** E3
Muerto, Mar Mexico 16°10N 94°10W **87** D6
Mufulira Zambia 12°32S 28°15E **55** E2
Mufumbiro Range Africa 1°25S 29°30E **54** C2
Mughal Sarai India 25°18N 83°7E **43** G10
Mughayrā' Si. Arabia 29°17N 37°41E **44** D3
Mugi Japan 33°40N 134°25E **31** H7
Mugila, Mts. Dem. Rep. of the Congo 7°0S 28°50E **54** D2
Muğla Turkey 37°15N 28°22E **23** F13
Mugu Nepal 29°45N 82°30E **43** E10
Muhala Congo 4°43S 28°50E **54** D2
Muhammad, Râs Egypt 27°44N 34°16E **44** E2
Muhammad Qol Sudan 20°53N 37°9E **51** D13
Muhammadabad India 26°4N 83°25E **43** F10
Muhesi → Tanzania 7°0S 35°20E **54** D4
Mühlhausen Germany 51°12N 10°27E **16** C6
Mühlig Hofmann fjell Antarctica 72°30S 5°0E **5** D3
Muhos Finland 64°47N 25°59E **8** D21
Muhu Estonia 58°36N 23°11E **9** G20
Muhutwe Tanzania 1°35S 31°45E **54** C3
Mui Wo China 22°16N 113°59E **33** G10
Muine Bheag Ireland 52°42N 6°58W **10** D5
Muineachán = Monaghan Ireland 54°15N 6°57W **10** B5
Muir, L. Australia 34°30S 116°40E **61** F2
Muir of Ord U.K. 57°32N 4°28W **11** D4
Mujeres, I. Mexico 21°13N 86°43W **88** B2
Mujnak = Muynak Uzbekistan 43°44N 59°10E **28** E6
Muka, Tanjung Malaysia 5°28N 100°11E **39** c
Mukacheve Ukraine 48°27N 22°45E **17** D12

Mukachevo = Mukacheve
  Ukraine   48°27N 22°45E **17** D12
Mukah Malaysia   2°55N 112°5E **36** D4
Mukandwara India   24°49N 75°59E **42** G6
Mukawwa, Gezîret
  Egypt   23°55N 35°53E **44** F2
Mukdahan Thailand   16°32N 104°43E **38** D5
Mukden = Shenyang
  China   41°48N 123°27E **35** D12
Mukerian India   31°57N 75°37E **42** D6
Mukinbudin Australia 30°55S 118°5E **61** F2
Mukishi
  Dem. Rep. of the Congo 8°30S 24°44E **55** D1
Mukomuko Indonesia   2°30S 101°10E **36** E2
Mukomwenze
  Dem. Rep. of the Congo 6°49S 27°15E **54** D2
Mukono Uganda   0°21N 32°45E **54** B3
Muktsar India   30°30N 74°30E **42** D6
Mukur = Moqor Afghan. 32°50N 67°42E **42** C2
Mukutuwa → Canada   53°10N 97°24W **71** C9
Mukwela Zambia   17°0S 26°40E **55** F2
Mula Spain   38°3N 1°33W **21** C5
Mula → Pakistan   27°57N 67°36E **42** F2
Mulange
  Dem. Rep. of the Congo 3°40S 27°10E **54** C2
Mulanje, Mt. Malawi 16°0S 35°33E **55** F4
Mulchatna → U.S.A.   59°40N 157°7W **74** D8
Mulchén Chile   37°45S 72°20W **94** D1
Mulde → Germany   51°53N 12°15E **16** C7
Mule Creek Junction
  U.S.A.   43°23N 104°13W **76** E11
Muleba Tanzania   1°50S 31°37E **54** C3
Mulegé Mexico   26°53N 111°59W **86** B2
Muleshoe U.S.A.   34°13N 102°43W **84** D3
Mulgrave Canada   45°38N 61°31W **73** C7
Mulgrave I. = Badu
  Australia   10°7S 142°11E **62** a
Mulhacén Spain   37°4N 3°20W **21** D4
Mulhouse France   47°40N 7°20E **20** C7
Mulifanua Samoa   13°50S 171°59W **59** b
Muling China   44°35N 130°10E **35** B16
Mull U.K.   56°25N 5°56W **11** E3
Mull, Sound of U.K. 56°30N 5°50W **11** E3
Mullach Íde = Malahide
  Ireland   53°26N 6°9W **10** C5
Mullaittivu Sri Lanka 9°15N 80°49E **40** Q12
Mullen U.S.A.   42°3N 101°1W **80** D3
Mullengudgery
  Australia   31°43S 147°23E **63** B4
Mullens U.S.A.   37°35N 81°23W **81** G13
Muller, Pegunungan
  Indonesia   0°30N 113°30E **36** D4
Mullet Pen. Ireland 54°13N 10°2W **10** B1
Mullewa Australia   28°29S 115°30E **61** E2
Mulligan → Australia 25°0S 139°0E **62** D2
Mullingar Ireland   53°31N 7°21W **10** C4
Mullins U.S.A.   34°12N 79°15W **85** D15
Mullumbimby Australia 28°30S 153°30E **63** D5
Mulobezi Zambia   16°45S 25°7E **55** F2
Mulonga Plain Zambia 16°20S 22°40E **53** H4
Mulroy B. Ireland   55°15N 7°46W **10** A4
Multan Pakistan   30°15N 71°36E **42** D4
Mulumbe, Mts.
  Dem. Rep. of the Congo 8°40S 27°30E **55** D2
Mulungushi Dam
  Zambia   14°48S 28°48E **55** E2
Mulvane U.S.A.   37°29N 97°15W **80** G5
Mulwala, L. Australia 35°59S 146°1E **63** C4
Mumbai India   18°56N 72°50E **40** K8
Mumbwa Zambia   15°0S 27°0E **55** F2
Mumias Kenya   0°20N 34°29E **54** C4
Mun → Thailand   15°19N 105°30E **38** E5
Muna Indonesia   5°0S 122°30E **37** F6
Munabao India   25°45N 70°17E **42** G4
Munamagi Estonia   57°43N 27°4E **9** H22
Muncan Indonesia   8°34S 115°11E **37** K18
München Germany   48°8N 11°34E **16** D6
Munchen-Gladbach =
  Mönchengladbach
  Germany   51°11N 6°27E **16** C4
Muncho Lake Canada   59°0N 125°50W **70** B3
Munch'ŏn N. Korea   39°14N 127°19E **35** E14
Muncie U.S.A.   40°12N 85°23W **81** E11
Muncoonie L. West
  Australia   25°12S 138°40E **62** D2
Mundabbera Australia 25°36S 151°18E **63** D5
Munday U.S.A.   33°27N 99°38W **84** E5
Münden Germany   51°25N 9°38E **16** C5
Mundiwindi Australia 23°47S 120°9E **60** D3
Mundo Novo Brazil   11°50S 40°29W **93** F10
Mundra India   22°54N 69°48E **42** H3
Mundrabilla Australia 31°52S 127°51E **61** F4
Mungallala Australia 26°28S 147°34E **63** D4
Mungallala Cr. →
  Australia   28°53S 147°5E **63** D4
Mungana Australia   17°8S 144°27E **62** B3
Mungaoli India   24°24N 78°7E **42** G8
Mungari Mozam.   17°12S 33°30E **55** F3
Mungbere
  Dem. Rep. of the Congo 2°36N 28°28E **54** B2
Mungeli India   22°4N 81°41E **43** H9
Munger India   25°23N 86°30E **43** G12
Mungerannie Australia 28°1S 138°39E **63** A2
Mungilli ○ Australia 25°14S 124°17E **61** E3
Mungkan Kandju △
  Australia   13°35S 142°52E **62** A3
Mungkarta ○ Australia 20°22S 134°2E **62** C1
Munich = München
  Germany   48°8N 11°34E **16** D6
Munising U.S.A.   46°25N 86°40W **80** B10
Munku-Sardyk Russia 51°45N 100°20E **29** D11
Munnsville U.S.A.   42°58N 75°35W **83** D9
Muñoz Gamero, Pen.
  Chile   52°30S 73°5W **96** G2
Munroe L. Canada   59°13N 98°35W **71** B9
Munsan S. Korea   37°51N 126°48E **35** F14
Münster Germany   51°58N 7°37E **16** C4
Munster □ Ireland   52°18N 8°44W **10** D3

Muntadgin Australia 31°45S 118°33E **61** F2
Muntok Indonesia   2°5S 105°10E **36** E3
Muong Beng Laos   20°23N 101°46E **38** B3
Muong Boum Vietnam   22°24N 102°49E **38** A4
Muong Et Laos   20°49N 104°1E **38** B5
Muong Hai Laos   21°3N 101°49E **38** B3
Muong Hiem Laos   20°5N 103°22E **38** B4
Muong Houn Laos   20°8N 101°23E **38** B3
Muong Hung Vietnam   20°56N 103°53E **38** B4
Muong Kau Laos   15°6N 105°47E **38** E5
Muong Khao Laos   19°38N 103°32E **38** C4
Muong Khoua Laos   21°5N 102°31E **38** B4
Muong Liep Laos   18°29N 101°40E **38** C3
Muong May Laos   14°49N 106°56E **38** E6
Muong Ngeun Laos   20°36N 101°3E **38** B3
Muong Ngoi Laos   20°43N 102°41E **38** B4
Muong Nhie Vietnam   22°12N 102°28E **38** A4
Muong Nong Laos   16°22N 106°30E **38** D6
Muong Ou Tay Laos   22°7N 101°48E **38** A3
Muong Oua Laos   18°18N 101°20E **38** C3
Muong Peun Laos   20°13N 103°52E **38** B4
Muong Phalane Laos   16°39N 105°34E **38** D5
Muong Phieng Laos   19°6N 101°32E **38** C3
Muong Phine Laos   16°32N 106°2E **38** D6
Muong Sai Laos   20°42N 101°59E **38** B3
Muong Saiapoun Laos 18°24N 101°31E **38** C3
Muong Sen Vietnam   19°24N 104°8E **38** C5
Muong Sing Laos   21°11N 101°9E **38** B3
Muong Son Laos   20°27N 103°19E **38** B4
Muong Soui Laos   19°33N 102°52E **38** C4
Muong Va Laos   21°53N 102°19E **38** B4
Muong Xia Vietnam   20°19N 104°50E **38** B5
Muonio Finland   67°57N 23°40E **8** C20
Muonio älv = Muonionjoki →
  Finland   67°11N 23°34E **8** C20
Muonioälven = Muonionjoki →
  Finland   67°11N 23°34E **8** C20
Muonionjoki → Finland 67°11N 23°34E **8** C20
Mupa → Mozam.   18°58S 35°54E **55** F4
Muping China   37°22N 121°36E **35** F11
Muqdisho Somali Rep. 2°2N 45°25E **47** G4
Muqur Afghan.   32°50N 67°42E **42** C2
Mur → Austria   46°18N 16°52E **17** E9
Murakami Japan   38°14N 139°29E **30** E9
Muralag = Prince of Wales I.
  Australia   10°40S 142°10E **62** A3
Murallón, Cerro Chile 49°48S 73°30W **96** F2
Muranda Rwanda   1°52S 29°20E **54** C2
Murang'a Kenya   0°45S 37°9E **54** C4
Murashi Russia   59°30N 49°0E **18** C8
Murat → Turkey   38°46N 40°0E **19** G7
Muratlı Turkey   41°10N 27°29E **23** D12
Murayama Japan   38°30N 140°25E **30** E10
Murchison → Australia 27°45S 114°0E **61** E1
Murchison, Mt.
  Antarctica   73°25S 166°20E **5** D11
Murchison Falls Uganda 2°15N 31°30E **54** B3
Murchison Falls △
  Uganda   2°17N 31°48E **54** B3
Murchison Ra. Australia 20°0S 134°10E **62** C1
Murchison Rapids
  Malawi   15°55S 34°35E **55** F3
Murchison Roadhouse
  Australia   27°39S 114°14E **61** E1
Murcia Spain   38°5N 1°10W **21** D5
Murcia □ Spain   37°50N 1°30W **21** D5
Murdo U.S.A.   43°53N 100°43W **80** D3
Murdoch Pt. Australia 14°37S 144°55E **62** A3
Mureș → Romania   46°15N 20°13E **17** E11
Mureșul = Mureș →
  Romania   46°15N 20°13E **17** E11
Murewa Zimbabwe   17°39S 31°47E **57** B5
Murfreesboro N.C.,
  U.S.A.   36°27N 77°6W **85** C16
Murfreesboro Tenn.,
  U.S.A.   35°51N 86°24W **85** D11
Murgab = Murghob
  Tajikistan   38°10N 74°2E **28** F8
Murgap = Murghob Turkmenistan 38°18N 61°12E **45** B9
Murgenella Australia 11°34S 132°56E **60** B5
Murgha Kibzai Pakistan 30°44N 69°25E **42** D3
Murghob Tajikistan   38°10N 74°2E **28** F8
Murgon Australia   26°15S 151°54E **63** D5
Muri India   23°22N 85°52E **43** H11
Muria Indonesia   6°36S 110°53E **37** G14
Muriaé Brazil   21°8S 42°23W **95** A7
Muriel Mine Zimbabwe 17°14S 30°40E **57** B5
Müritz Germany   53°25N 12°42E **16** B7
Murliganj India   25°54N 86°59E **43** G12
Murmansk Russia   68°57N 33°10E **8** B25
Murmashi Russia   68°47N 32°42E **8** B25
Muro Spain   39°44N 3°3E **24** B10
Murom Russia   55°35N 42°3E **18** C7
Muroran Japan   42°25N 141°0E **30** C10
Muroto Japan   33°18N 134°9E **31** H7
Muroto-Misaki Japan 33°15N 134°10E **31** H7
Murphy U.S.A.   43°13N 116°33W **76** E5
Murphys U.S.A.   38°8N 120°28W **78** G6
Murray → Australia   9°5G 144°2E **62** a
Murray Ky., U.S.A.   36°37N 88°19W **80** G9
Murray Utah, U.S.A. 40°40N 111°53W **76** F8
Murray, L. U.S.A.   34°3N 81°13W **85** D14
Murray Bridge Australia 35°6S 139°14E **63** F2
Murray Fracture Zone
  Pac. Oc.   35°0N 130°0W **65** D14
Murray Harbour Canada 46°0N 62°28W **73** C7
Murray River △
  Australia   34°23S 140°32E **63** E3
Murraysburg S. Africa 31°58S 23°47E **56** E3
Murree Pakistan   33°56N 73°28E **42** C5
Murrieta U.S.A.   33°33N 117°13W **79** M9
Murrumbidgee →
  Australia   34°43S 143°12E **63** E3
Murrumburrah
  Australia   34°32S 148°22E **63** E4
Murrurundi Australia 31°42S 150°51E **63** E5
Murshidabad India   24°11N 88°19E **43** G13
Murtle L. Canada   52°8N 119°38W **70** C5
Murtoa Australia   36°35S 142°28E **63** F3

Murungu Tanzania   4°12S 31°10E **54** C3
Mururoa
  French Polynesia   21°52S 138°55W **65** K14
Murwara India   23°46N 80°28E **43** H9
Murwillumbah
  Australia   28°18S 153°27E **63** D5
Mürzzuschlag Austria 47°36N 15°41E **16** E8
Muş Turkey   38°45N 41°30E **44** B4
Mûsa, Gebel Egypt   28°33N 33°59E **44** D2
Musa Khel Pakistan   30°59N 69°52E **42** D3
Mûsa Qal'eh Afghan. 32°20N 64°50E **40** C4
Musafirkhana India   26°22N 81°48E **43** F9
Musala Bulgaria   42°13N 23°37E **23** C10
Musala Indonesia   1°41N 98°28E **36** D1
Musan N. Korea   42°12N 129°12E **35** C15
Musangu
  Dem. Rep. of the Congo 10°28S 23°55E **55** E1
Musasa Tanzania   3°25S 31°30E **54** C3
Musay'id Qatar   25°0N 51°33E **45** E6
Muscat = Masqaṭ Oman 23°37N 58°36E **47** C6
Muscatine U.S.A.   41°25N 91°3W **80** E8
Muscle Shoals U.S.A. 34°45N 87°40W **85** D11
Musengezi = Unsengedsi →
  Zimbabwe   15°43S 31°14E **55** F3
Musgrave Harbour
  Canada   49°27N 53°58W **73** C9
Musgrave Ranges
  Australia   26°0S 132°0E **61** E5
Mushie
  Dem. Rep. of the Congo 2°56S 16°55E **52** E3
Musi → Indonesia   2°20S 104°56E **36** E2
Musina S. Africa   22°20S 30°5E **57** C5
Muskeg → Canada   60°20N 123°20W **70** A4
Muskegon U.S.A.   43°14N 86°16W **80** D10
Muskegon → U.S.A.   43°14N 86°21W **80** D10
Muskegon Heights
  U.S.A.   43°12N 86°16W **80** D10
Muskoka, L. Canada   45°0N 79°25W **82** B5
Muskoka Falls Canada 44°59N 79°17W **82** B5
Muskwa → Canada   58°47N 122°48W **70** B4
Muskogee U.S.A.   35°45N 95°22W **84** D7
Muslīmiyah Syria   36°19N 37°12E **44** B3
Musofu Zambia   13°30S 29°0E **55** E2
Musoma Tanzania   1°30S 33°48E **54** C3
Musquaro, L. Canada 50°38N 61°5W **73** B7
Musquodoboit Harbour
  Canada   44°50N 63°9W **73** D7
Musselburgh U.K.   55°57N 3°2W **11** F5
Musselshell → U.S.A. 47°21N 107°57W **76** C10
Mussende Angola   10°32S 16°5E **52** G3
Mussoorie India   30°27N 78°6E **42** D8
Mussuco Angola   17°2S 19°3E **56** B2
Mustafakemalpaşa
  Turkey   40°2N 28°24E **23** D13
Mustang Nepal   29°10N 83°55E **43** E10
Musters, L. Argentina 45°20S 69°25W **96** F3
Musudan N. Korea   40°50N 129°43E **35** D15
Muswellbrook Australia 32°16S 150°56E **63** E5
Mût Egypt   25°28N 28°58E **51** C11
Mut Turkey   36°40N 33°28E **44** B2
Mutanda Mozam.   21°0S 33°34E **57** C5
Mutanda Zambia   12°24S 26°13E **55** E2
Mutare Zimbabwe   18°58S 32°38E **55** F3
Mutawintji △ Australia 31°10S 142°30E **63** E3
Mutha Kenya   1°48S 38°26E **54** C4
Muting Indonesia   7°23S 140°20E **37** F10
Mutki = Mirtağ Turkey 38°23N 41°56E **44** B4
Mutoko Zimbabwe   17°24S 32°1E **57** B5
Mutomo Kenya   1°51S 38°12E **54** C4
Mutoray Russia   61°0N 101°0E **29** C11
Mutsamudu Comoros Is. 12°10S 44°25E **53** a
Mutshatsha
  Dem. Rep. of the Congo 10°35S 24°20E **55** E1
Mutsu Japan   41°5N 140°55E **30** D10
Mutsu-Wan Japan   41°5N 140°55E **30** D10
Muttaburra Australia 22°38S 144°29E **62** C3
Mutton I. Ireland   52°49N 9°32W **10** D2
Mutuáli Mozam.   14°55S 37°0E **55** E4
Mutumba Burundi   3°25S 29°21E **54** C2
Muweilih Egypt   30°42N 34°19E **46** E3
Muy Muy Nic.   12°39N 85°36W **88** D2
Muyinga Burundi   3°14S 30°33E **54** C3
Muynak Uzbekistan   43°44N 59°10E **28** E6
Muyunkum, Peski = Moyynqum
  Kazakhstan   44°12N 71°0E **32** B2
Muz Tag China   36°25N 87°25E **32** D3
Muzaffarabad Pakistan 34°25N 73°30E **43** B5
Muzaffargarh Pakistan 30°5N 71°14E **42** D4
Muzaffarnagar India 29°26N 77°40E **42** E7
Muzaffarpur India   26°7N 85°23E **43** F11
Muzafirpur Pakistan 30°58N 69°9E **42** D3
Muzhi Russia   65°25N 64°40E **18** A11
Múztagh-Ata China   38°17N 75°7E **32** C2
Mvuma Zimbabwe   19°16S 30°30E **55** F3
Mvurwi Zimbabwe   17°0S 30°57E **55** F3
Mwabvi △ Malawi   16°42S 35°0E **55** F3
Mwadui Tanzania   3°26S 33°32E **54** C3
Mwali = Mohéli
  Comoros Is.   12°20S 43°40E **53** a
Mwambo Tanzania   10°30S 40°22E **55** E5
Mwandi Zambia   17°0S 24°51E **55** F1
Mwanza
  Dem. Rep. of the Congo 7°55S 26°43E **54** D2
Mwanza Tanzania   2°30S 32°58E **54** C3
Mwanza Zambia   16°58S 24°28E **55** F1
Mwanza □ Tanzania   2°0S 33°0E **54** C3
Mwaya Tanzania   9°32S 33°55E **55** D3
Mweelrea Ireland   53°39N 9°49W **10** C2
Mweka
  Dem. Rep. of the Congo 4°50S 21°34E **52** E4
Mwene-Ditu
  Dem. Rep. of the Congo 6°35S 22°27E **52** F4
Mwenezi Zimbabwe   21°15S 30°48E **55** G3
Mwenezi → Mozam.   22°40S 31°50E **55** G3
Mwenga
  Dem. Rep. of the Congo 3°1S 28°28E **54** C2
Mweru, L. Zambia   9°0S 28°40E **55** D2
Mweru Wantipa △
  Zambia   8°39S 29°25E **55** D2

Mweza Range Zimbabwe 21°0S 30°0E **55** G3
Mwilambwe
  Dem. Rep. of the Congo 0°7S 25°5E **54** D2
Mwimbi Tanzania   8°38S 31°39E **55** D3
Mwingi Kenya   0°56S 38°4E **54** C4
Mwinilunga Zambia   11°43S 24°25E **55** E1
My Tho Vietnam   10°29N 106°23E **39** G6
Myajlar India   26°15N 70°20E **42** F4
Myanaung Burma   18°18N 95°22E **41** K19
Myanmar = Burma ■
  Asia   21°0N 96°30E **41** J20
Myaungmya Burma   16°30N 94°40E **41** L19
Mycenæ = Mikines
  Greece   37°43N 22°46E **23** F10
Myeik Kyunzu Burma   11°30N 97°30E **39** G1
Myerstown U.S.A.   40°22N 76°19W **83** F8
Myingyan Burma   21°30N 95°20E **41** J19
Myitkyina Burma   25°24N 97°26E **41** G20
Mykines Greece   62°7N 7°35E **8** F9
Mykolayiv Ukraine   46°58N 32°0E **19** E5
Mykonos Greece   37°30N 25°25E **23** F11
Mymensingh Bangla.   24°45N 90°24E **41** G17
Mynydd Du U.K.   51°52N 3°50W **13** F4
Mýrdalsjökull Iceland 63°40N 19°6E **8** E4
Myrtle Beach U.S.A. 33°42N 78°53W **85** E15
Myrtle Creek U.S.A. 43°1N 123°17W **76** E2
Myrtle Point U.S.A. 43°4N 124°8W **76** E1
Myrtou Cyprus   35°18N 33°4E **25** D12
Mysia Turkey   39°50N 27°0E **23** E12
Mysore = Karnataka □
  India   13°15N 77°0E **40** N10
Mysore India   12°17N 76°41E **40** N10
Mystic U.S.A.   41°21N 71°58W **83** E13
Mysuru = Mysore India 12°17N 76°41E **40** N10
Myszków Poland   50°45N 19°22E **17** C10
Mytishchi Russia   55°50N 37°50E **18** C6
Mývatn Iceland   65°36N 17°0W **8** D5
Mzimba Malawi   11°55S 33°39E **55** E3
Mzimkulu → S. Africa 30°44S 30°28E **57** E5
Mzimvubu → S. Africa 31°38S 29°33E **57** E4
Mzuzu Malawi   11°30S 33°55E **55** E3

N

Na Clocha Liatha = Greystones
  Ireland   53°9N 6°5W **10** C5
Na Hearadh = Harris
  U.K.   57°50N 6°55W **11** D2
Na Noi Thailand   18°19N 100°43E **38** C3
Na Phao Laos   17°35N 105°44E **38** D5
Na Sam Vietnam   22°3N 106°37E **38** A6
Na San Vietnam   21°12N 104°2E **38** B5
Na Thon Thailand   9°32N 99°56E **39** b
Naab → Germany   49°1N 12°2E **16** D6
Naantali Finland   60°29N 22°2E **9** F20
Naas Ireland   53°12N 6°40W **10** C5
Nabadwip = Navadwip
  India   23°34N 88°20E **43** H13
Nabawa S. Africa   28°30S 114°48E **61** E1
Nabberu, L. Australia 25°50S 120°30E **61** E3
Naberezhnyye Chelny
  Russia   55°42N 52°19E **18** C9
Nabeul Tunisia   36°30N 10°44E **51** A8
Nabha India   30°26N 76°14E **42** D7
Nabīd Iran   29°40N 57°38E **45** D8
Nabire Indonesia   3°15S 135°26E **37** E9
Nabisar Pakistan   25°8N 69°40E **42** G3
Nabisipi → Canada   50°14N 62°13W **73** B7
Nabiswera Uganda   1°27N 32°15E **54** B3
Nablus = Nābulus
  West Bank   32°14N 35°15E **46** C4
Naboomspruit S. Africa 24°32S 28°40E **57** C4
Nabouwalu Fiji   17°0S 178°45E **59** a
Nābulus West Bank   32°14N 35°15E **46** C4
Nacala Mozam.   14°32S 40°34E **55** E5
Nacaome Honduras   13°31N 87°30W **88** D2
Nacaroa Mozam.   14°22S 39°56E **55** E4
Naches U.S.A.   46°44N 120°42W **76** C3
Naches → U.S.A.   46°38N 120°31W **76** D6
Nachicapau, L. Canada 56°40N 68°5W **73** A6
Nachingwea Tanzania 10°23S 38°49E **55** E4
Nachna India   27°34N 71°41E **42** F4
Nacimiento, L. U.S.A. 35°46N 120°53W **78** K6
Naco Mexico   31°19N 109°56W **86** A3
Nacogdoches U.S.A.   31°36N 94°39W **84** F7
Nácori Chico Mexico 29°40N 108°57W **86** B3
Nacozari de García
  Mexico   30°25N 109°38W **86** A3
Nacula Fiji   16°54S 177°27E **59** a
Nådendal = Naantali
  Finland   60°29N 22°2E **9** F20
Nadi Fiji   17°42S 177°20E **59** a
Nadiad India   22°41N 72°56E **42** H5
Nador Morocco   35°14N 2°58W **50** B5
Nadur Malta   36°2N 14°18E **25** C1
Nadūshan Iran   32°2N 53°35E **45** C7
Nadvirna Ukraine   48°37N 24°30E **17** D13
Nadvoitsy Russia   63°52N 34°14E **18** B5
Nadvornaya = Nadvirna
  Ukraine   48°37N 24°30E **17** D13
Nadym Russia   65°35N 72°42E **28** C8
Nadym → Russia   66°12N 72°0E **28** C8
Nærbø Norway   58°40N 5°39E **9** G11
Næstved Denmark   55°13N 11°44E **9** J14
Nafarroa □ = Navarra □ Spain 42°40N 1°40W **21** A5
Nafpaktos Greece   38°24N 21°50E **23** E9
Nafplio Greece   37°33N 22°50E **23** F10
Naft-e Safid Iran   31°40N 49°17E **45** D6
Naftshahr Iran   34°0N 45°30E **44** C5
Nafud Desert = An Nafūd
  Si. Arabia   28°15N 41°0E **44** D4
Naga Phil.   13°38N 123°15E **37** B6
Nagagami → Canada   50°23N 84°20W **72** B3
Nagahama Japan   35°23N 136°16E **31** G8
Nagai Japan   38°6N 140°2E **30** E10
Nagaland □ India   26°0N 94°30E **41** G19
Nagano Japan   36°40N 138°10E **31** F9
Nagano □ Japan   36°15N 138°0E **31** F9

Nagaoka Japan   37°27N 138°51E **31** F9
Nagaon = Nowgong
  India   26°20N 92°50E **41** F18
Nagappattinam India 10°46N 79°51E **40** P11
Nagar → Bangla.   24°27N 89°12E **43** G13
Nagar Parkar Pakistan 24°28N 70°46E **42** G4
Nagasaki Japan   32°47N 129°50E **31** H4
Nagasaki □ Japan   32°50N 129°40E **31** H4
Nagato Japan   34°19N 131°5E **31** G5
Nagaur India   27°15N 73°45E **42** F5
Nagda India   23°27N 75°25E **42** H6
Nagercoil India   8°12N 77°26E **40** Q10
Nagina India   29°30N 78°30E **43** E8
Nagîneh Iran   34°20N 57°15E **45** C8
Nagir Pakistan   36°12N 74°42E **43** A6
Nagles Mts. Ireland 52°8N 8°30W **10** D3
Nagod India   24°34N 80°36E **43** G9
Nagoorin Australia   24°17S 151°15E **62** C5
Nagorno-Karabakh □
  Azerbaijan   39°55N 46°45E **44** B5
Nagornyy Russia   55°58N 124°57E **29** D13
Nagoya Japan   35°10N 136°50E **31** G8
Nagpur India   21°8N 79°10E **40** J11
Nagua Dom. Rep.   19°23N 69°50W **89** C6
Naguabo Puerto Rico 18°13N 65°44W **89** d
Nagurunguru ○
  Australia   16°45S 129°45E **60** C4
Nagykanizsa Hungary 46°28N 17°0E **17** E9
Nagykőrös Hungary   47°5N 19°48E **17** E10
Naha Japan   26°13N 127°42E **31** L3
Nahan India   30°33N 77°18E **42** D7
Nahanni △ Canada   61°36N 125°41W **70** A4
Nahanni Butte Canada 61°2N 123°31W **70** A4
Nahargarh Mad. P., India 24°10N 75°14E **42** G6
Nahargarh Raj., India 24°55N 76°50E **42** G7
Nahariyya Israel   33°1N 35°5E **44** C2
Nahāvand Iran   34°10N 48°22E **45** C6
Nahuel Huapi, L.
  Argentina   41°0S 71°32W **96** E2
Nahuelbuta △ Chile   37°44S 72°57W **94** D1
Nai Yong Thailand   8°14N 98°22E **39** a
Naicá Mexico   27°53N 105°31W **86** B3
Naicam Canada   52°30N 104°30W **71** C8
Naikoon △ Canada   53°55N 131°55W **70** C2
Naimisharanya India 27°21N 80°30E **43** F9
Naimona'nyi Feng Nepal 30°26N 81°18E **43** D9
Nain Canada   56°34N 61°40W **73** A7
Na'in Iran   32°54N 53°0E **45** C7
Naini Tal India   29°30N 79°30E **43** E8
Nainpur India   22°30N 80°10E **43** H9
Nainwa India   25°46N 75°51E **42** G6
Nairai Fiji   17°49S 179°15E **59** a
Nairn U.K.   57°35N 3°53W **11** D5
Nairobi Kenya   1°17S 36°48E **54** C4
Nairobi △ Kenya   1°22S 36°50E **54** C4
Naissaar Estonia   59°34N 24°29E **9** G21
Naitaba Fiji   17°0S 179°16W **59** a
Naivasha Kenya   0°40S 36°30E **54** C4
Naivasha, L. Kenya   0°48S 36°20E **54** C4
Najaf = An Najaf Iraq 32°3N 44°15E **44** C5
Najafābād Iran   32°40N 51°15E **45** C6
Najd Si. Arabia   26°30N 42°0E **47** B3
Najibabad India   29°40N 78°20E **42** E8
Najin N. Korea   42°12N 130°15E **35** C16
Najmah Si. Arabia   26°42N 50°6E **45** E6
Najrān Si. Arabia   17°34N 44°18E **47** D3
Naju S. Korea   35°3N 126°43E **35** G14
Nakadōri-Shima Japan 32°57N 129°4E **31** H4
Nakalagba
  Dem. Rep. of the Congo 2°50N 27°58E **54** B2
Nakaminato Japan   36°21N 140°36E **31** F10
Nakamura Japan   32°59N 132°56E **31** H6
Nakano Japan   36°45N 138°22E **31** F9
Nakano-Shima Japan   29°51N 129°52E **31** K4
Nakashibetsu Japan   43°33N 144°59E **30** C12
Nakfa Eritrea   16°40N 38°32E **47** D2
Nakha Yai, Ko Thailand 8°3N 98°28E **39** a
Nakhichevan = Naxçıvan
  Azerbaijan   39°12N 45°15E **44** B5
Nakhichevan Rep. = Naxçıvan □
  Azerbaijan   39°25N 45°26E **44** B5
Nakhl Egypt   29°55N 33°43E **46** F2
Nakhl-e Taqī Iran   27°28N 52°36E **45** E7
Nakhodka Russia   42°53N 132°54E **30** C6
Nakhon Nayok
  Thailand   14°12N 101°13E **38** E3
Nakhon Pathom
  Thailand   13°49N 100°3E **38** F3
Nakhon Phanom
  Thailand   17°23N 104°43E **38** D5
Nakhon Ratchasima
  Thailand   14°59N 102°12E **38** E4
Nakhon Sawan
  Thailand   15°35N 100°10E **38** E3
Nakhon Si Thammarat
  Thailand   8°29N 100°0E **39** b
Nakhon Thai Thailand 17°5N 100°44E **38** D3
Nakhtarana India   23°20N 69°15E **42** H3
Nakina Canada   50°10N 86°40W **72** B2
Nakodar India   31°8N 75°31E **42** D6
Naktong → S. Korea   35°7N 128°57E **35** G15
Nakuru Kenya   0°15S 36°4E **54** C4
Nakuru, L. Kenya   0°23S 36°5E **54** C4
Nakusp Canada   50°20N 117°45W **70** C5
Nal Pakistan   25°20N 65°30E **42** G1
Nalázi Mozam.   24°3S 33°20E **57** C5
Nalchik Russia   43°30N 43°33E **19** F7
Nalgonda India   17°6N 79°15E **40** L11
Nalhati India   24°17N 87°52E **43** G12
Naliya India   23°16N 68°50E **42** H3
Nallamalai Hills India 15°30N 78°50E **40** M11
Nalubaale Dam Uganda 0°30N 33°5E **54** B3
Nam Can Vietnam   8°46N 104°59E **39** H5
Nam-ch'on N. Korea   38°15N 126°26E **35** E14
Nam Co China   32°0N 90°45E **32** D4
Nam Dinh Vietnam   20°25N 106°5E **38** B6
Nam Du, Hon Vietnam 9°41N 104°21E **39** H5
Nam Nao △ Thailand   16°44N 101°32E **38** D3

Nam Ngum Res. *Laos* 18°35N 102°34E 38 C4
Nam-Phan *Vietnam* 10°30N 106°0E 39 G6
Nam Phong *Thailand* 16°42N 102°52E 38 D4
Nam Tha *Laos* 20°58N 101°30E 38 B3
Nam Tok *Thailand* 14°21N 99°4E 38 E2
Namacunde *Angola* 17°18S 15°50E 56 B2
Namacurra *Mozam.* 17°30S 36°50E 57 B6
Namak, Daryācheh-ye *Iran* 34°30N 52°0E 45 C7
Namak, Kavir-e *Iran* 34°30N 57°30E 45 C8
Namakzār, Daryācheh-ye *Iran* 34°0N 60°30E 45 C9
Namaland *Namibia* 26°0S 17°0E 56 C2
Namanga *Kenya* 2°33S 36°47E 54 C4
Namangan *Uzbekistan* 41°0N 71°40E 28 E8
Namapa *Mozam.* 13°43S 39°50E 55 E4
Namaqualand *S. Africa* 30°0S 17°25E 56 E2
Namasagali *Uganda* 1°2N 33°0E 54 B3
Namber *Indonesia* 1°2S 134°49E 37 E8
Nambour *Australia* 26°32S 152°58E 63 D5
Nambouwalu = Nabouwalu *Fiji* 17°0S 178°45E 59 a
Nambucca Heads *Australia* 30°37S 153°0E 63 E5
Nambung △ *Australia* 30°30S 115°5E 61 F2
Namcha Barwa *China* 29°40N 95°10E 32 D4
Namche Bazar *Nepal* 27°51N 86°47E 43 F12
Namchonjŏm = Nam-ch'on *N. Korea* 38°15N 126°26E 35 E14
Namecunda *Mozam.* 14°54S 37°37E 55 E4
Namenalala *Fiji* 17°8S 179°9E 59 a
Nameponda *Mozam.* 15°50S 39°50E 55 F4
Nametil *Mozam.* 15°40S 39°21E 55 F4
Namew L. *Canada* 54°14N 101°56W 71 C8
Namgia *India* 31°48N 78°40E 43 D8
Namialo *Mozam.* 14°55S 39°59E 55 E4
Namib Desert *Namibia* 22°30S 15°0E 56 C2
Namib-Naukluft ⌂ *Namibia* 24°40S 15°16E 56 C2
Namibe *Angola* 15°7S 12°11E 53 H2
Namibe □ *Angola* 16°35S 12°30E 56 B1
Namibia ■ *Africa* 22°0S 18°9E 56 C2
Namibwoestyn = Namib Desert *Namibia* 22°30S 15°0E 56 C2
Namlea *Indonesia* 3°18S 127°5E 37 E7
Namoi → *Australia* 30°12S 149°30E 63 E4
Nampa *U.S.A.* 43°34N 116°34W 76 E5
Namp'o *N. Korea* 38°52N 125°10E 35 E13
Nampō-Shotō *Japan* 32°0N 140°0E 31 J10
Nampula *Mozam.* 15°6S 39°15E 55 F4
Namrole *Indonesia* 3°46S 126°46E 37 E7
Namse Shankou *China* 30°0N 82°25E 43 E10
Namsen → *Norway* 64°28N 11°37E 8 D14
Namsos *Norway* 64°29N 11°30E 8 D14
Namtok Chat Trakan △ *Thailand* 17°17N 100°40E 38 D3
Namtok Mae Surin △ *Thailand* 18°55N 98°2E 38 C2
Namtsy *Russia* 62°43N 129°37E 29 C13
Namtu *Burma* 23°5N 97°28E 41 H20
Namtumbo *Tanzania* 10°30S 36°4E 55 E4
Namu *Canada* 51°52N 127°50W 70 C3
Namuka-i-Lau *Fiji* 18°53S 178°37W 59 a
Namur *Belgium* 50°27N 4°52E 15 D4
Namur □ *Belgium* 50°17N 5°0E 15 D4
Namuruputh *Kenya* 4°34N 35°57E 54 B4
Namutoni *Namibia* 18°49S 16°55E 56 B2
Namwala *Zambia* 15°44S 26°30E 55 F2
Namwon *S. Korea* 35°23N 127°23E 35 G14
Namyang *N. Korea* 42°57N 129°52E 35 C15
Nan *Thailand* 18°48N 100°46E 38 C3
Nan → *Thailand* 15°42N 100°9E 38 E3
Nan-ch'ang = Nanchang *China* 28°42N 115°55E 33 D6
Nanaimo *Canada* 49°10N 124°0W 70 D4
Nānākuli *U.S.A.* 21°24N 158°9W 75 L8
Nanam *N. Korea* 41°44N 129°40E 35 D15
Nanango *Australia* 26°40S 152°0E 63 D5
Nanao *Japan* 37°0N 137°0E 31 F8
Nanchang *China* 28°42N 115°55E 33 D6
Nanching = Nanjing *China* 32°2N 118°47E 33 C6
Nanchong *China* 30°43N 106°2E 32 C5
Nancy *France* 48°42N 6°12E 20 B7
Nanda Devi *India* 30°23N 79°59E 43 D8
Nanda Devi △ *India* 30°30N 79°50E 43 D8
Nanda Kot *India* 30°17N 80°5E 43 D9
Nandan *Japan* 34°10N 134°42E 31 G7
Nanded *India* 19°10N 77°20E 40 K10
Nandewar Ra. *Australia* 30°15S 150°35E 63 E5
Nandi = Nadi *Fiji* 17°42S 177°20E 59 a
Nandi *Zimbabwe* 20°58S 31°44E 55 G3
Nandigram *India* 22°1N 87°58E 43 H12
Nandurbar *India* 21°20N 74°15E 40 J9
Nandyal *India* 15°30N 78°30E 40 M11
Nang Rong *Thailand* 14°38N 102°48E 38 E4
Nanga-Eboko *Cameroon* 4°41N 12°22E 52 D2
Nanga Parbat *Pakistan* 35°10N 74°35E 43 B6
Nangade *Mozam.* 11°5S 39°36E 55 E4
Nangapinoh *Indonesia* 0°20S 111°44E 36 E4
Nangarhār □ *Afghan.* 34°20N 70°0E 40 B7
Nangatayap *Indonesia* 1°32S 110°34E 36 E4
Nangeya Mts. *Uganda* 3°30N 33°30E 54 B3
Nangong *China* 37°23N 115°22E 34 F8
Nanhuang *China* 36°58N 121°48E 35 F11
Nanisivik *Canada* 73°2N 84°33W 69 C15
Nanjeko *Zambia* 15°31S 23°30E 55 F1
Nanjing *China* 32°2N 118°47E 33 C6
Nanjirinji *Tanzania* 9°41S 39°5E 55 D4
Nankana Sahib *Pakistan* 31°27N 73°38E 42 D5
Nanking = Nanjing *China* 32°2N 118°47E 33 C6
Nankoku *Japan* 33°39N 133°44E 31 H6
Nanlang *China* 22°30N 113°32E 33 G10
Nanning *China* 22°48N 108°20E 32 D5
Nannup *Australia* 33°59S 115°48E 61 F2
Nanpara *India* 27°52N 81°33E 43 F9
Nanpi *China* 38°2N 116°45E 34 E9
Nanping *China* 26°38N 118°10E 33 D6
Nanripe *Mozam.* 13°52S 38°52E 55 E4
Nansei-Shotō = Ryūkyū-rettō *Japan* 26°0N 126°0E 31 M3
Nansen Basin *Arctic* 84°0N 50°0E 4 A10
Nansen Sd. *Canada* 81°0N 91°0W 69 A13
Nansha *China* 22°45N 113°34E 33 F10
Nanshan I. *S. China Sea* 10°45N 115°49E 36 B5
Nansio *Tanzania* 2°3S 33°4E 54 C3
Nantawarrinna ✪ *Australia* 30°49S 138°58E 63 B2
Nantes *France* 47°12N 1°33W 20 C3
Nanticoke *U.S.A.* 41°12N 76°0W 83 E8
Nanton *Canada* 50°21N 113°46W 70 C6
Nantong *China* 32°1N 120°52E 33 C7
Nantou *China* 22°32N 113°55E 33 F10
Nantucket *U.S.A.* 41°17N 70°6W 81 E18
Nantucket I. *U.S.A.* 41°16N 70°5W 81 E18
Nantulo *Mozam.* 12°32S 38°45E 55 E4
Nantwich *U.K.* 53°4N 2°31W 12 D5
Nanty Glo *U.S.A.* 40°28N 78°50W 82 F6
Nanuku Passage *Fiji* 16°45S 179°15W 59 a
Nanuque *Brazil* 17°50S 40°21W 93 G10
Nanusa, Kepulauan *Indonesia* 4°45N 127°1E 37 D7
Nanutarra Roadhouse *Australia* 22°32S 115°30E 60 D2
Nanyang *China* 33°11N 112°30E 34 H7
Nanyuki *Kenya* 0°2N 37°4E 54 B4
Nao, C. de la *Spain* 38°44N 0°14E 21 C6
Naococane, L. *Canada* 52°50N 70°45W 73 B5
Napa *U.S.A.* 38°18N 122°17W 78 G4
Napa → *U.S.A.* 38°10N 122°19W 78 G4
Napanee *Canada* 44°15N 77°0W 82 B8
Napanoch *U.S.A.* 41°44N 74°22W 83 E10
Nape *Laos* 18°18N 105°6E 38 C5
Nape Pass = Keo Neua, Deo *Vietnam* 18°23N 105°10E 38 C5
Napier *N.Z.* 39°30S 176°56E 59 C6
Napier Broome B. *Australia* 14°2S 126°37E 60 B4
Napier Pen. *Australia* 12°4S 135°43E 62 A2
Napierville *Canada* 45°11N 73°25W 83 A11
Naples = Nápoli *Italy* 40°50N 14°15E 22 D6
Naples *U.S.A.* 26°8N 81°48W 85 H14
Napo → *Peru* 3°20S 72°40W 92 D4
Napoleon *N. Dak., U.S.A.* 46°30N 99°46W 80 B4
Napoleon *Ohio, U.S.A.* 41°23N 84°8W 81 E11
Nápoli *Italy* 40°50N 14°15E 22 D6
Napopo *Dem. Rep. of the Congo* 4°15N 28°0E 54 B2
Naqadeh *Iran* 36°57N 45°23E 44 B5
Naqb, Ra's an *Jordan* 29°48N 35°44E 46 F4
Naqqāsh *Iran* 35°40N 49°6E 45 C6
Nara *Japan* 34°40N 135°49E 31 G7
Nara *Mali* 15°10N 7°20W 50 E4
Nara □ *Japan* 34°30N 136°0E 31 G8
Nara Canal *Pakistan* 24°30N 69°20E 42 G3
Nara Visa *U.S.A.* 35°37N 103°6W 77 J12
Naracoorte *Australia* 36°58S 140°45E 63 F3
Naradhan *Australia* 33°34S 146°17E 63 E4
Naraini *India* 25°11N 80°29E 43 G9
Naranjos *Mexico* 21°21N 97°41W 87 C5
Narasapur *India* 16°26N 81°40E 41 L12
Narathiwat *Thailand* 6°30N 101°48E 39 J3
Narayangadh = Bharatpur *Nepal* 27°34N 84°10E 43 F11
Narayanganj *Bangla.* 23°40N 90°33E 41 H17
Narayanpet *India* 16°45N 77°30E 40 L10
Narberth *U.K.* 51°47N 4°44W 13 F3
Narbonne *France* 43°11N 3°0E 20 E5
Nardīn *Iran* 37°3N 55°59E 45 B7
Nardò *Italy* 40°11N 18°2E 23 D8
Narembeen *Australia* 32°7S 118°24E 61 F2
Narendranagar *India* 30°10N 78°18E 42 D8
Nares Str. *Arctic* 80°0N 70°0W 69 B18
Naretha *Australia* 31°0S 124°45E 61 F3
Narew → *Poland* 52°26N 20°41E 17 B11
Nari → *Pakistan* 28°0N 67°40E 42 F2
Narin *Afghan.* 36°5N 69°0E 40 A6
Narindra, Helodranon' i *Madag.* 14°55S 47°30E 57 A8
Narita *Japan* 35°47N 140°19E 31 G10
Nariva Swamp *Trin. & Tob.* 10°26N 61°4W 93 K15
Narmada → *India* 21°38N 72°36E 42 J5
Narnaul *India* 28°5N 76°11E 42 E7
Narodnaya *Russia* 65°5N 59°58E 18 A10
Narok *Kenya* 1°55S 35°52E 54 C4
Narooma *Australia* 36°14S 150°4E 63 F5
Narowal *Pakistan* 32°6N 74°52E 42 C6
Narrabri *Australia* 30°19S 149°46E 63 E4
Narran → *Australia* 28°37S 148°12E 63 D4
Narrandera *Australia* 34°42S 146°31E 63 E4
Narrogin *Australia* 32°58S 117°14E 61 F2
Narromine *Australia* 32°12S 148°12E 63 E4
Narrow Hills ⌂ *Canada* 54°0N 104°37W 71 C8
Narsimhapur *India* 22°54N 79°14E 43 H8
Narsinghgarh *India* 23°45N 76°40E 42 H7
Naruto *Japan* 34°11N 134°37E 31 G7
Narva *Estonia* 59°23N 28°12E 18 C4
Narva → *Russia* 59°27N 28°2E 9 G23
Narva Bay = Narva Laht *Estonia* 59°35N 27°35E 9 G22
Narva Laht *Estonia* 59°35N 27°35E 9 G22
Narvik *Norway* 68°28N 17°26E 8 B17
Narwana *India* 29°39N 76°6E 42 E7
Narwinbi ✪ *Australia* 16°7S 136°17E 62 B2
Naryan-Mar *Russia* 67°42N 53°12E 18 A9
Narym *Russia* 59°0N 81°30E 28 D9
Naryn *Kyrgyzstan* 41°26N 75°58E 28 E8
Naryn Qum *Kazakhstan* 47°30N 49°0E 28 E5
Nasa *Norway* 66°29N 15°23E 8 C16
Nasau *Fiji* 17°19S 179°27E 59 a
Nasca = Nazca *Peru* 14°50S 74°57W 92 F4
Naseby *N.Z.* 45°1S 170°10E 59 F3
Naselle *U.S.A.* 46°22N 123°49W 78 D3
Naser, Buheirat en *Egypt* 23°0N 32°30E 51 D12
Nashik = Nasik *India* 19°58N 73°50E 40 K8
Nashua *Mont., U.S.A.* 48°8N 106°22W 76 B10
Nashua *N.H., U.S.A.* 42°45N 71°28W 83 D13
Nashville *Ark., U.S.A.* 33°57N 93°51W 84 E8
Nashville *Ga., U.S.A.* 31°12N 83°15W 85 F13
Nashville *Tenn., U.S.A.* 36°10N 86°47W 85 C11
Nasik *India* 19°58N 73°50E 40 K8
Nasirabad *India* 26°15N 74°45E 42 F6
Nasirabad *Pakistan* 28°23N 68°24E 42 E3
Nasiri = Ahvāz *Iran* 31°20N 48°40E 45 D6
Nasiriyah = An Nāşirīyah *Iraq* 31°0N 46°15E 44 D5
Naskaupi → *Canada* 53°47N 60°51W 73 B7
Naşrābād *Iran* 34°8N 51°26E 45 C6
Naşriān-e Pā'īn *Iran* 32°52N 46°52E 44 C5
Nass → *Canada* 55°0N 129°40W 70 C3
Nassau *Bahamas* 25°5N 77°20W 88 A4
Nassau *U.S.A.* 42°31N 73°37W 83 D11
Nassau, B. *Chile* 55°20S 68°0W 96 H3
Nasser, L. = Naser, Buheirat en *Egypt* 23°0N 32°30E 51 D12
Nässjö *Sweden* 57°39N 14°42E 9 H16
Nastapoka → *Canada* 56°55N 76°33W 72 A4
Nastapoka, Is. *Canada* 56°55N 76°50W 72 A4
Nata *Botswana* 20°12S 26°12E 56 C4
Nata → *Botswana* 20°14S 26°10E 56 C4
Natal *Brazil* 5°47S 35°13W 93 E11
Natal *Indonesia* 0°35N 99°7E 36 D1
Natal Drakensberg ⌂ *S. Africa* 29°27S 29°30E 57 D4
Naţanz *Iran* 33°30N 51°55E 45 C6
Natashquan *Canada* 50°14N 61°46W 73 B7
Natashquan → *Canada* 50°7N 61°50W 73 B7
Natchez *U.S.A.* 31°34N 91°24W 84 F9
Natchitoches *U.S.A.* 31°46N 93°5W 84 F8
Natewa B. *Fiji* 16°35S 179°40E 59 a
Nathalia *Australia* 36°1S 145°13E 63 F4
Nathdwara *India* 24°55N 73°50E 42 G5
Nati, Pta. *Spain* 40°3N 3°50E 24 A10
Natimuk *Australia* 36°42S 142°0E 63 F3
Nation → *Canada* 55°30N 123°32W 70 B4
National City *U.S.A.* 32°40N 117°5W 79 N9
Natitingou *Benin* 10°20N 1°26E 50 F6
Natividad, I. *Mexico* 27°52N 115°11W 86 B1
Natkyizin *Burma* 14°57N 97°59E 38 E1
Natron, L. *Tanzania* 2°20S 36°0E 54 C4
Natrona Heights *U.S.A.* 40°37N 79°44W 82 F5
Natukanaoka Pan *Namibia* 18°40S 15°45E 56 B2
Natuna Besar, Kepulauan *Indonesia* 4°0N 108°15E 36 D3
Natuna Is. = Natuna Besar, Kepulauan *Indonesia* 4°0N 108°15E 36 D3
Natuna Selatan, Kepulauan *Indonesia* 2°45N 109°0E 36 D3
Natural Bridge *U.S.A.* 44°5N 75°30W 83 B9
Natural Bridges ⌂ *U.S.A.* 37°36N 110°0W 77 H9
Naturaliste, C. *Tas., Australia* 40°50S 148°15E 63 G4
Naturaliste, C. *W. Austral., Australia* 33°32S 115°0E 61 F2
Naturaliste Plateau *Ind. Oc.* 34°0S 112°0E 64 L3
Nau Qala *Afghan.* 34°5N 68°5E 42 B3
Naugatuck *U.S.A.* 41°30N 73°3W 83 E11
Naujaat = Repulse Bay *Canada* 66°30N 86°30W 69 D14
Naumburg *Germany* 51°9N 11°47E 16 C6
Nauru ■ *Pac. Oc.* 1°0S 166°0E 58 B9
Naushahra = Nowshera *Pakistan* 34°0N 72°0E 40 C8
Naushahro *Pakistan* 26°50N 68°7E 42 F3
Naushon I. *U.S.A.* 41°29N 70°45W 83 E14
Nausori *Fiji* 18°2S 178°32E 59 a
Nauta *Peru* 4°31S 73°35W 92 D4
Nautanwa *India* 27°20N 83°25E 43 F10
Naute ⌂ *Namibia* 26°55S 17°57E 56 D2
Nautla *Mexico* 20°13N 96°47W 87 C5
Nava *Mexico* 28°25N 100°45W 86 B4
Navadwip *India* 23°34N 88°20E 43 H13
Navahrudak *Belarus* 53°40N 25°50E 17 B13
Navajo Res. *U.S.A.* 36°48N 107°36W 77 H10
Navalmoral de la Mata *Spain* 39°52N 5°33W 21 C3
Navan = An Uaimh *Ireland* 53°39N 6°41W 10 C5
Navarin, Mys *Russia* 62°15N 179°5E 29 C18
Navarino, I. *Chile* 55°0S 67°40W 96 H3
Navarra □ *Spain* 42°40N 1°40W 21 A5
Navarre *U.S.A.* 40°43N 81°31W 82 F3
Navarro → *U.S.A.* 39°11N 123°45W 78 F3
Navasota *U.S.A.* 30°23N 96°5W 84 F6
Navassa I. *W. Indies* 18°30N 75°0W 89 C5
Naver → *U.K.* 58°32N 4°14W 11 C4
Navibandar *India* 21°26N 69°48E 42 J3
Navidad *Chile* 33°57S 71°50W 94 C1
Naviraí *Brazil* 23°8S 54°13W 95 A5
Naviti *Fiji* 17°7S 177°15E 59 a
Navlakhi *India* 22°58N 70°28E 42 H4
Năvodari *Romania* 44°19N 28°36E 17 F15
Navoiy *Uzbekistan* 40°9N 65°22E 28 E7
Navojoa *Mexico* 27°6N 109°26W 86 B3
Navolato *Mexico* 24°47N 107°42W 86 C3
Navsari *India* 20°57N 72°59E 40 J8
Navua *Fiji* 18°12S 178°11E 59 a
Nawa Kot *Pakistan* 28°21N 71°24E 42 E4
Nawab Khan *Pakistan* 30°17N 69°12E 42 D3
Nawabganj *Ut. P., India* 26°56N 81°14E 43 F9
Nawabganj *Ut. P., India* 28°32N 79°40E 43 E8
Nawabshah *Pakistan* 26°15N 68°25E 42 F3
Nawada *India* 24°50N 85°33E 43 G11
Nawakot *Nepal* 27°55N 85°10E 43 F11
Nawalgarh *India* 27°50N 75°15E 42 F6
Nawanshahr *India* 32°33N 74°48E 43 C6
Nawar, Dasht-i- *Afghan.* 33°52N 68°0E 42 C3
Nawoiy = Navoiy *Uzbekistan* 40°9N 65°22E 28 E7
Naxçıvan *Azerbaijan* 39°12N 45°15E 44 B5
Naxçıvan □ *Azerbaijan* 39°25N 45°26E 44 B5
Naxos *Greece* 37°8N 25°25E 23 F11
Nay, Mui = Varella, Mui *Vietnam* 12°54N 109°26E 38 F7
Nāy Band *Būshehr, Iran* 27°20N 52°40E 45 E7
Nāy Band *Khorāsān, Iran* 32°20N 57°34E 45 C8
Nayakhan *Russia* 61°56N 159°0E 29 C16
Nayarit □ *Mexico* 22°0N 105°0W 86 C4
Nayau *Fiji* 18°6S 178°10E 59 a
Nayoro *Japan* 44°21N 142°28E 30 B11
Naypyidaw *Burma* 19°44N 96°12E 38 C1
Nayyāl, W. → *Si. Arabia* 28°35N 39°4E 44 D3
Nazaré *Brazil* 13°2S 39°0W 93 F11
Nazareth = Nazerat *Israel* 32°42N 35°17E 46 C4
Nazareth *U.S.A.* 40°44N 75°19W 83 F9
Nazarovo *Russia* 57°2N 90°40E 29 D10
Nazas *Mexico* 25°14N 104°8W 86 B4
Nazas → *Mexico* 25°12N 104°12W 86 B4
Nazca *Peru* 14°50S 74°57W 92 F4
Nazca Ridge *Pac. Oc.* 20°0S 80°0W 65 K19
Naze *Japan* 28°22N 129°27E 31 K4
Naze, The *U.K.* 51°53N 1°18E 13 F9
Nazerat *Israel* 32°42N 35°17E 46 C4
Nāzīk *Iran* 39°1N 45°4E 44 B5
Nazilli *Turkey* 37°55N 28°15E 23 F13
Nazko *Canada* 53°1N 123°37W 70 C4
Nazko → *Canada* 53°7N 123°34W 70 C4
Nazret *Ethiopia* 8°32N 39°22E 47 F2
Nchanga *Zambia* 12°30S 27°49E 55 E2
Ncheu *Malawi* 14°50S 34°47E 55 E3
Ndala *Tanzania* 4°45S 33°15E 54 C3
Ndalatando *Angola* 9°12S 14°48E 52 F2
Ndareda *Tanzania* 4°12S 35°30E 54 C4
Ndélé *C.A.R.* 8°25N 20°36E 52 C4
Ndjamena *Chad* 12°10N 14°59E 51 F8
Ndola *Zambia* 13°0S 28°34E 55 E2
Ndomo ⌂ *S. Africa* 26°52S 32°15E 57 D5
Ndoto Mts. *Kenya* 2°0N 37°0E 54 B4
Nduguti *Tanzania* 4°18S 34°41E 54 C3
Neagh, Lough *U.K.* 54°37N 6°25W 10 B5
Neah Bay *U.S.A.* 48°22N 124°37W 78 B2
Neale, L. *Australia* 24°15S 130°0E 60 D5
Neales → *Australia* 28°8S 136°47E 63 D2
Neapoli *Greece* 35°15N 25°37E 25 D7
Near Is. *U.S.A.* 52°30N 174°0E 74 E2
Neath *U.K.* 51°39N 3°48W 13 F4
Neath Port Talbot □ *U.K.* 51°42N 3°45W 13 F4
Nebbi *Uganda* 2°28N 31°6E 54 B3
Nebine Cr. → *Australia* 29°27S 146°56E 63 D4
Nebitdag = Balkanabat *Turkmenistan* 39°30N 54°22E 45 B7
Nebo *Australia* 21°42S 148°42E 62 C4
Nebraska □ *U.S.A.* 41°30N 99°30W 80 E4
Nebraska City *U.S.A.* 40°41N 95°52W 80 E6
Nébrodi, Monti *Italy* 37°54N 14°35E 22 F6
Necedah *U.S.A.* 44°2N 90°4W 80 C8
Nechako → *Canada* 53°55N 122°42W 70 C4
Neches → *U.S.A.* 29°58N 93°51W 84 G8
Neckar → *Germany* 49°27N 8°29E 16 D5
Necker I. *U.S.A.* 23°35N 164°42W 75 L7
Necochea *Argentina* 38°30S 58°50W 94 D4
Nederland = Netherlands ■ *Europe* 52°0N 5°30E 15 C5
Needles *Canada* 49°53N 118°7W 70 D5
Needles *U.S.A.* 34°51N 114°37W 79 L12
Needles, The *U.K.* 50°39N 1°35W 13 G6
Neembucú □ *Paraguay* 27°0S 58°0W 94 B4
Neemuch = Nimach *India* 24°30N 74°56E 42 G6
Neenah *U.S.A.* 44°11N 88°28W 80 C9
Neepawa *Canada* 50°15N 99°30W 71 C9
Neftçala *Azerbaijan* 39°19N 49°12E 45 B6
Neftegorsk *Russia* 53°1N 142°58E 29 D15
Neftekumsk *Russia* 44°46N 44°50E 19 F7
Nefteyugansk *Russia* 61°5N 72°42E 28 C8
Nefyn *U.K.* 52°56N 4°31W 12 E3
Negapatam = Nagappattinam *India* 10°46N 79°51E 40 P11
Negara *Indonesia* 8°22S 114°37E 37 J17
Negaunee *U.S.A.* 46°30N 87°36W 80 B10
Negele *Ethiopia* 5°20N 39°36E 47 F2
Negev Desert = Hanegev *Israel* 30°50N 35°0E 46 E4
Negombo *Sri Lanka* 7°12N 79°50E 40 R11
Negotin *Serbia* 44°16N 22°37E 23 B10
Negra, Pta. *Mauritania* 22°54N 16°18W 50 D2
Negra, Pta. *Peru* 6°6S 81°10W 92 E2
Negrais, C. = Maudin Sun *Burma* 16°0N 94°30E 41 M19
Negril *Jamaica* 18°22N 78°20W 88 a
Negro → *Argentina* 41°2S 62°47W 96 E4
Negro → *Brazil* 3°0S 60°0W 92 D7
Negro → *Uruguay* 33°24S 58°22W 94 C4
Negros *Phil.* 9°30N 122°40E 37 C6
Neguac *Canada* 47°15N 65°5W 73 C6
Nehalem → *U.S.A.* 45°40N 123°56W 78 E3
Nehāvand *Iran* 35°56N 49°31E 45 C6
Nehbandān *Iran* 31°35N 60°5E 45 D9
Nei Monggol Zizhiqu □ *China* 42°0N 112°0E 34 D7
Neiafu *Tonga* 18°39S 173°59W 59 c
Neiges, Piton des *Réunion* 21°5S 55°29E 53 c
Neijiang *China* 29°35N 104°55E 32 D5
Neilingding Dao *China* 22°25N 113°48E 33 G10
Neillsville *U.S.A.* 44°34N 90°36W 80 C8
Neilton *U.S.A.* 47°25N 123°53W 76 C2
Neiqiu *China* 37°15N 114°30E 34 F8
Neiva *Colombia* 2°56N 75°18W 92 C3
Neixiang *China* 33°10N 111°52E 34 H6
Nejanilini L. *Canada* 59°33N 97°48W 71 B9
Nejd = Najd *Si. Arabia* 26°30N 42°0E 47 B3
Nekā *Iran* 36°39N 53°19E 45 B7
Nekemte *Ethiopia* 9°4N 36°30E 47 F2
Neksø *Denmark* 55°4N 15°8E 9 J16
Nelia *Australia* 20°39S 142°12E 62 C3
Neligh *U.S.A.* 42°8N 98°2W 80 D4
Nelkan *Russia* 57°40N 136°4E 29 D14
Nellore *India* 14°27N 79°59E 40 M11
Nelson *Canada* 49°30N 117°20W 70 D5
Nelson *N.Z.* 41°18S 173°16E 59 D4
Nelson *U.K.* 53°50N 2°13W 12 D5
Nelson *Ariz., U.S.A.* 35°31N 113°19W 77 J7
Nelson *Nev., U.S.A.* 35°42N 114°49W 79 K12
Nelson → *Canada* 54°33N 98°2W 71 C9
Nelson, C. *Australia* 38°26S 141°32E 63 F3
Nelson, Estrecho *Chile* 51°30S 75°0W 96 G2
Nelson Forks *Canada* 59°30N 124°0W 70 B4
Nelson House *Canada* 55°47N 98°51W 71 B9
Nelson L. *Canada* 55°48N 100°7W 71 B8
Nelson Lakes △ *N.Z.* 41°55S 172°44E 59 D4
Nelspoort *S. Africa* 32°7S 23°0E 56 E3
Nelspruit *S. Africa* 25°29S 30°59E 57 D5
Néma *Mauritania* 16°40N 7°15W 50 E4
Neman = Nemunas → *Lithuania* 55°25N 21°10E 9 J19
Nembrala *Indonesia* 10°53S 122°50E 60 B3
Nemeiben L. *Canada* 55°20N 105°20W 71 B7
Nemiscau *Canada* 51°18N 76°54W 72 B4
Nemiscau, L. *Canada* 51°25N 76°40W 72 B4
Nemunas → *Lithuania* 55°25N 21°10E 9 J19
Nemuro *Japan* 43°20N 145°35E 30 C12
Nemuro-Kaikyō *Japan* 43°30N 145°30E 30 C12
Nen Jiang → *China* 45°28N 124°30E 35 B13
Nenagh *Ireland* 52°52N 8°11W 10 D3
Nenana *U.S.A.* 64°34N 149°5W 74 C10
Nenasi *Malaysia* 3°9N 103°23E 39 L4
Nene → *U.K.* 52°49N 0°11E 13 E8
Nenjiang *China* 49°10N 125°10E 33 B7
Neno *Malawi* 15°25S 34°40E 55 F3
Neodesha *U.S.A.* 37°25N 95°41W 80 G6
Neora Valley △ *India* 27°0N 88°45E 43 F13
Neosho *U.S.A.* 36°52N 94°22W 80 G6
Neosho → *U.S.A.* 36°48N 95°18W 84 C7
Nepal ■ *Asia* 28°0N 84°30E 43 F11
Nepalganj *Nepal* 28°5N 81°40E 43 E9
Nepalganj Road *India* 28°1N 81°41E 43 E9
Nephi *U.S.A.* 39°43N 111°50W 76 G8
Nephin *Ireland* 54°1N 9°22W 10 B2
Nephin Beg Range *Ireland* 54°0N 9°40W 10 C2
Neptune *U.S.A.* 40°13N 74°2W 83 F10
Neqāb *Iran* 36°42N 57°25E 45 B8
Nerang *Australia* 27°58S 153°20E 63 D5
Nerastro, Sarīr *Libya* 24°20N 20°37E 51 D10
Nerchinsk *Russia* 52°0N 116°39E 29 D12
Néret, L. *Canada* 54°45N 70°44W 73 B5
Neretva → *Croatia* 43°1N 17°27E 23 C7
Neringa *Lithuania* 55°20N 21°5E 9 J19
Neris → *Lithuania* 55°8N 24°16E 9 J21
Neryungri *Russia* 57°38N 124°28E 29 D13
Nescopeck *U.S.A.* 41°3N 76°12W 83 E8
Neskantaga *Canada* 52°14N 87°53W 72 B2
Ness, L. *U.K.* 57°15N 4°32W 11 D4
Ness City *U.S.A.* 38°27N 99°54W 80 F4
Nesterov *Ukraine* 50°4N 23°58E 17 C12
Nestos → *Europe* 40°54N 24°49E 23 D11
Nesvizh = Nyasvizh *Belarus* 53°14N 26°38E 17 B14
Netanya *Israel* 32°20N 34°51E 46 C3
Netarhat *India* 23°29N 84°16E 43 H11
Nete → *Belgium* 51°7N 4°14E 15 C4
Netherdale *Australia* 21°10S 148°33E 62 b
Netherlands ■ *Europe* 52°0N 5°30E 15 C5
Netherlands Antilles ⊠ *W. Indies* 12°15N 69°0W 92 A5
Netrang *India* 21°39N 73°21E 42 J5
Nettilling L. *Canada* 66°30N 71°0W 69 D17
Netzahualcóyotl, Presa *Mexico* 17°8N 93°35W 87 D6
Neubrandenburg *Germany* 53°33N 13°15E 16 B7
Neuchâtel *Switz.* 47°0N 6°55E 20 C7
Neuchâtel, Lac de *Switz.* 46°53N 6°50E 20 C7
Neufchâteau *Belgium* 49°50N 5°25E 15 E5
Neumayer *Antarctica* 71°0S 68°30W 5 D17
Neumünster *Germany* 54°4N 9°58E 16 A5
Neunkirchen *Germany* 49°20N 7°9E 16 D4
Neuquén *Argentina* 38°55S 68°0W 96 D3
Neuquén □ *Argentina* 38°0S 69°50W 94 D2
Neuruppin *Germany* 52°55N 12°48E 16 B7
Neuse → *U.S.A.* 35°6N 76°29W 85 D16
Neusiedler See *Austria* 47°50N 16°47E 17 E9
Neustrelitz *Germany* 53°21N 13°4E 16 B7
Neva → *Russia* 59°56N 30°20E 18 C5
Nevada *Iowa, U.S.A.* 42°1N 93°27W 80 D7
Nevada *Mo., U.S.A.* 37°51N 94°22W 80 G6
Nevada □ *U.S.A.* 39°0N 117°0W 76 G5
Nevada City *U.S.A.* 39°16N 121°1W 78 F6
Nevado, Cerro *Argentina* 35°30S 68°32W 94 D2
Nevado de Colima = Volcán de Colima △ *Mexico* 19°30N 103°40W 86 D4
Nevado de Tres Cruces △ *Chile* 27°13S 69°5W 94 B2
Nevel *Russia* 56°0N 29°55E 18 C4
Nevelsk *Russia* 46°40N 141°51E 29 E15
Nevers *France* 47°0N 3°9E 20 C5
Nevertire *Australia* 31°50S 147°44E 63 E4
Neville *Canada* 49°58N 107°39W 71 D7
Nevinnomyssk *Russia* 44°40N 42°0E 19 F7
Nevis *St. Kitts & Nevis* 17°0N 62°30W 89 C7
Nevşehir *Turkey* 38°33N 34°40E 44 B2
Nevyansk *Russia* 57°30N 60°13E 18 C11
New → *U.S.A.* 38°10N 81°12W 81 F13
New Aiyansh *Canada* 55°12N 129°4W 70 B3
New Albany *Ind., U.S.A.* 38°18N 85°49W 81 F11
New Albany *Miss., U.S.A.* 34°29N 89°0W 85 D10
New Albany *Pa., U.S.A.* 41°36N 76°27W 83 E8
New Amsterdam *Guyana* 6°15N 57°36W 92 B7
New Baltimore *U.S.A.* 42°41N 82°44W 82 D2
New Bedford *U.S.A.* 41°38N 70°56W 83 E14
New Berlin *N.Y., U.S.A.* 42°37N 75°20W 83 D9
New Berlin *Pa., U.S.A.* 40°50N 76°57W 82 F8
New Bern *U.S.A.* 35°7N 77°3W 85 D16
New Bethlehem *U.S.A.* 41°0N 79°20W 82 F5
New Bight *Bahamas* 24°19N 75°24W 89 B4
New Bloomfield *U.S.A.* 40°25N 77°11W 82 F7

New Boston *U.S.A.* 33°28N 94°25W **84** E7
New Braunfels *U.S.A.* 29°42N 98°8W **84** G5
New Brighton *N.Z.* 43°29S 172°43E **59** C4
New Brighton *U.S.A.* 40°42N 80°19W **82** F4
New Britain *Papua N. G.* 5°50S 150°20E **58** B8
New Britain *U.S.A.* 41°40N 72°47W **83** E12
New Brunswick *U.S.A.* 40°30N 74°27W **83** F10
New Brunswick □
   Canada 46°50N 66°30W **73** C6
New Caledonia ☑ *Pac. Oc.* 21°0S 165°0E **58** D9
New Caledonia Trough
   Pac. Oc. 30°0S 165°0E **64** L8
New Castile = Castilla-La
   Mancha □ *Spain* 39°30N 3°30W **21** C4
New Castle *Ind., U.S.A.* 39°55N 85°22W **81** F11
New Castle *Pa., U.S.A.* 41°0N 80°21W **82** F4
New City *U.S.A.* 41°9N 73°59W **83** E11
New Concord *U.S.A.* 39°59N 81°54W **82** G3
New Cumberland
   U.S.A. 40°30N 80°36W **82** F4
New Cuyama *U.S.A.* 34°57N 119°38W **79** L7
New Delhi *India* 28°36N 77°11E **42** E7
New Denver *Canada* 50°0N 117°25W **70** D5
New Don Pedro Res.
   U.S.A. 37°43N 120°24W **78** H6
New England *U.S.A.* 43°0N 71°0W **75** G25
New England *N. Dak.,*
   U.S.A. 46°32N 102°52W **80** B2
New England Ra.
   Australia 30°20S 151°45E **63** E5
New Forest △ *U.K.* 50°53N 1°34W **13** G6
New Galloway *U.K.* 55°5N 4°9W **11** F4
New Glasgow *Canada* 45°35N 62°36W **73** C7
New Guinea *Oceania* 4°0S 136°0E **58** B6
New Hamburg *Canada* 43°23N 80°42W **82** C4
New Hampshire □
   U.S.A. 44°0N 71°30W **83** C13
New Hampton *U.S.A.* 43°3N 92°19W **80** D7
New Hanover *S. Africa* 29°22S 30°31E **57** D5
New Hartford *U.S.A.* 43°4N 75°18W **83** C9
New Haven *Conn.,*
   U.S.A. 41°18N 72°55W **83** E12
New Haven *Mich.,*
   U.S.A. 42°44N 82°48W **82** D2
New Haven *N.Y., U.S.A.* 43°28N 76°18W **83** C8
New Hazelton *Canada* 55°20N 127°30W **70** B3
New Hebrides = Vanuatu ■
   Pac. Oc. 15°0S 168°0E **58** G9
New Holland *U.S.A.* 40°6N 76°5W **83** F8
New Iberia *U.S.A.* 30°1N 91°49W **84** F9
New Ireland *Papua N. G.* 3°20S 151°50E **58** B8
New Jersey □ *U.S.A.* 40°0N 74°30W **81** F16
New Kensington *U.S.A.* 40°34N 79°46W **82** F5
New Lexington *U.S.A.* 39°43N 82°13W **81** F12
New Liskeard *Canada* 47°31N 79°41W **72** C4
New London *Conn.,*
   U.S.A. 41°22N 72°6W **83** E12
New London *Ohio, U.S.A.* 41°5N 82°24W **82** E2
New London *Wis.,*
   U.S.A. 44°23N 88°45W **80** C9
New Madrid *U.S.A.* 36°36N 89°32W **80** G9
New Martinsville
   U.S.A. 39°39N 80°52W **81** F13
New Meadows *U.S.A.* 44°58N 116°18W **76** D5
New Melones L. *U.S.A.* 37°57N 120°31W **78** H6
New Mexico □ *U.S.A.* 34°30N 106°0W **77** J11
New Milford *Conn.,*
   U.S.A. 41°35N 73°25W **83** E11
New Milford *Pa., U.S.A.* 41°52N 75°44W **83** E9
New Moore I. *Ind. Oc.* 21°37N 89°10E **43** J13
New Norcia *Australia* 30°57S 116°13E **61** F2
New Norfolk *Australia* 42°46S 147°2E **63** G4
New Orleans *U.S.A.* 29°57N 90°4W **85** G9
New Philadelphia
   U.S.A. 40°30N 81°27W **82** F3
New Plymouth *N.Z.* 39°4S 174°5E **59** C5
New Plymouth *U.S.A.* 43°58N 116°49W **76** E5
New Port Richey
   U.S.A. 28°16N 82°43W **85** G13
New Providence
   Bahamas 25°25N 78°35W **88** A4
New Quay *U.K.* 52°13N 4°21W **13** E3
New Radnor *U.K.* 52°15N 3°9W **13** E4
New Richmond *Canada* 48°15N 65°45W **73** C6
New Richmond *U.S.A.* 45°7N 92°32W **80** C7
New River Gorge △
   U.S.A. 37°53N 81°5W **81** G13
New Roads *U.S.A.* 30°42N 91°26W **84** F9
New Rochelle *U.S.A.* 40°55N 73°46W **83** F11
New Rockford *U.S.A.* 47°41N 99°8W **80** B4
New Romney *U.K.* 50°59N 0°57E **13** G8
New Ross *Ireland* 52°23N 6°57W **10** D5
New Salem *U.S.A.* 46°51N 101°25W **80** B3
New Scone = Scone *U.K.* 56°25N 3°24W **11** E5
New Siberian I. = Novaya Sibir,
   Ostrov Russia 75°10N 150°0E **29** B16
New Siberian Is. = Novosibirskiye
   Ostrova Russia 75°0N 142°0E **29** B15
New Smyrna Beach
   U.S.A. 29°1N 80°56W **85** G14
New South Wales □
   Australia 33°0S 146°0E **63** E4
New Tecumseth = Alliston
   Canada 44°9N 79°52W **82** B5
New Town *U.S.A.* 47°59N 102°30W **80** B2
New Tredegar *U.K.* 51°44N 3°16W **13** F4
New Ulm *U.S.A.* 44°19N 94°28W **80** C6
New Waterford *Canada* 46°13N 60°4W **73** C7
New Westminster
   Canada 49°13N 122°55W **78** A4
New York *U.S.A.* 40°43N 74°0W **83** F11
New York □ *U.S.A.* 43°0N 75°0W **83** D9
New York J.F. Kennedy Int. ✈
   (JFK) U.S.A. 40°38N 73°47W **83** F11
New Zealand ■ *Oceania* 40°0S 176°0E **59** D6
Newaj → *India* 24°24N 76°49E **42** G7
Newala *Tanzania* 10°58S 39°18E **55** E4
Newark *Del., U.S.A.* 39°41N 75°46W **81** F16
Newark *N.J., U.S.A.* 40°44N 74°10W **83** F10

Newark *N.Y., U.S.A.* 43°3N 77°6W **82** C7
Newark *Ohio, U.S.A.* 40°3N 82°24W **82** F2
Newark Liberty Int. ✈ (EWR)
   U.S.A. 40°42N 74°10W **83** F10
Newark-on-Trent *U.K.* 53°5N 0°48W **12** D7
Newark Valley *U.S.A.* 42°14N 76°11W **83** D8
Newberg *U.S.A.* 45°18N 122°58W **76** D2
Newberry *Mich., U.S.A.* 46°21N 85°30W **81** B11
Newberry *S.C., U.S.A.* 34°17N 81°37W **85** D14
Newberry Springs
   U.S.A. 34°50N 116°41W **79** L10
Newboro L. *Canada* 44°38N 76°20W **83** B8
Newbridge = Droichead Nua
   Ireland 53°11N 6°48W **10** C5
Newburgh *Canada* 44°19N 76°52W **82** B8
Newburgh *U.S.A.* 41°30N 74°1W **83** E10
Newbury *U.K.* 51°24N 1°20W **13** F6
Newbury *N.H., U.S.A.* 43°19N 72°3W **83** B12
Newbury *Vt., U.S.A.* 44°5N 72°4W **83** B12
Newburyport *U.S.A.* 42°49N 70°53W **83** D14
Newcastle *Australia* 33°0S 151°46E **63** E5
Newcastle *N.B., Canada* 47°1N 65°38W **73** C6
Newcastle *Ont., Canada* 43°55N 78°35W **72** D4
Newcastle *S. Africa* 27°45S 29°58E **57** D4
Newcastle *U.K.* 54°13N 5°54W **10** B6
Newcastle *Calif., U.S.A.* 38°53N 121°8W **78** G5
Newcastle *Wyo.,*
   U.S.A. 43°50N 104°11W **76** E11
Newcastle Emlyn *U.K.* 52°2N 4°28E **13** E3
Newcastle Ra. *Australia* 15°45S 130°15E **60** C5
Newcastle-under-Lyme
   U.K. 53°1N 2°14W **12** D5
Newcastle-upon-Tyne
   U.K. 54°58N 1°36W **12** C6
Newcastle Waters
   Australia 17°30S 133°28E **62** B1
Newcastle West *Ireland* 52°27N 9°3W **10** D2
Newcomb *U.S.A.* 43°58N 74°10W **83** C10
Newcomerstown *U.S.A.* 40°16N 81°36W **82** F3
Newdegate *Australia* 33°6S 119°0E **61** F2
Newell *Australia* 16°20S 145°16E **62** B4
Newell *U.S.A.* 44°43N 103°25W **80** C3
Newenham, C. *U.S.A.* 58°39N 162°11W **74** D7
Newfane *U.S.A.* 43°17N 78°43W **82** C6
Newfield *U.S.A.* 42°18N 76°33W **83** D8
Newfound L. *U.S.A.* 43°40N 71°47W **83** C13
Newfoundland *Canada* 49°0N 55°0W **73** C8
Newfoundland *U.S.A.* 41°18N 75°19W **83** E9
Newfoundland & Labrador □
   Canada 53°0N 58°0W **73** B8
Newhaven *U.K.* 50°47N 0°3E **13** G8
Newkirk *U.S.A.* 36°53N 97°3W **84** C6
Newlyn *U.K.* 50°6N 5°34W **13** G2
Newman *Australia* 23°18S 119°45E **60** D2
Newman *U.S.A.* 37°19N 121°1W **78** H5
Newmarket *Canada* 44°3N 79°28W **82** B5
Newmarket *Ireland* 52°13N 9°0W **10** D2
Newmarket *U.K.* 52°15N 0°25E **13** E8
Newmarket *U.S.A.* 43°5N 70°56W **83** C14
Newnan *U.S.A.* 33°23N 84°48W **85** E12
Newport *Ireland* 53°53N 9°33W **10** C2
Newport *I. of W., U.K.* 50°42N 1°17W **13** G6
Newport *Newport, U.K.* 51°35N 3°0W **13** F5
Newport *Ark., U.S.A.* 35°37N 91°16W **84** D9
Newport *Ky., U.S.A.* 39°5N 84°29W **81** F11
Newport *N.H., U.S.A.* 43°22N 72°10W **83** C12
Newport *N.Y., U.S.A.* 43°11N 75°1W **83** C9
Newport *Oreg., U.S.A.* 44°39N 124°3W **76** D1
Newport *Pa., U.S.A.* 40°29N 77°8W **82** F7
Newport *R.I., U.S.A.* 41°29N 71°19W **83** E13
Newport *Tenn., U.S.A.* 35°58N 83°11W **85** D13
Newport *Vt., U.S.A.* 44°56N 72°13W **83** B12
Newport *Wash., U.S.A.* 48°11N 117°3W **76** B5
Newport □ *U.K.* 51°33N 3°1W **13** F4
Newport Beach *U.S.A.* 33°37N 117°56W **79** M9
Newport News *U.S.A.* 36°59N 76°25W **81** G15
Newport Pagnell *U.K.* 52°5N 0°43W **13** E7
Newquay *U.K.* 50°25N 5°6W **13** G2
Newry *U.K.* 54°11N 6°21W **10** B5
Newry Islands △
   Australia 20°51S 148°56E **62** b
Newton *Ill., U.S.A.* 38°59N 88°10W **80** F9
Newton *Iowa, U.S.A.* 41°42N 93°3W **80** E7
Newton *Kans., U.S.A.* 38°3N 97°21W **80** F5
Newton *Mass., U.S.A.* 42°21N 71°12W **83** D13
Newton *Miss., U.S.A.* 32°19N 89°10W **85** E10
Newton *N.C., U.S.A.* 35°40N 81°13W **85** D14
Newton *N.J., U.S.A.* 41°3N 74°45W **83** E10
Newton *Tex., U.S.A.* 30°51N 93°46W **84** F8
Newton Abbot *U.K.* 50°32N 3°37W **13** G4
Newton Aycliffe *U.K.* 54°37N 1°34W **12** C6
Newton Falls *N.Y.,*
   U.S.A. 44°12N 74°59W **83** B10
Newton Falls *Ohio,*
   U.S.A. 41°11N 80°59W **82** E4
Newton Stewart *U.K.* 54°57N 4°30W **11** G4
Newtonmore *U.K.* 57°4N 4°0W **11** D4
Newtown *U.K.* 52°31N 3°19W **13** E4
Newtownabbey *U.K.* 54°40N 5°56W **10** B6
Newtownards *U.K.* 54°36N 5°42W **10** B6
Newtownbarry = Bunclody
   Ireland 52°39N 6°40W **10** D5
Newtownstewart *U.K.* 54°43N 7°23W **10** B4
Newville *U.S.A.* 40°10N 77°24W **82** F7
Neya *Russia* 58°21N 43°49E **18** C7
Neyrīz *Iran* 29°15N 54°19E **45** D7
Neyshābūr *Iran* 36°10N 58°50E **45** B8
Nezhin = Nizhyn *Ukraine* 51°5N 31°55E **19** D5
Nezperce *U.S.A.* 46°14N 116°14W **76** C5
Ngaanyatjarra ◇
   Australia 22°40S 127°0E **60** D4
Ngabang *Indonesia* 0°23N 109°55E **36** D3
Ngabordamlu, Tanjung
   Indonesia 6°56S 134°11E **37** F8
N'Gage *Angola* 7°46S 15°15E **52** F3
Ngalurrtju ◇ *Australia* 22°44S 132°5E **60** D5

Ngami Depression
   Botswana 20°30S 22°46E **56** C3
Ngamo *Zimbabwe* 19°3S 27°32E **55** F2
Nganglong Kangri *China* 33°0N 81°0E **43** C9
Ngao *Thailand* 18°46N 99°59E **38** C2
Ngaoundéré *Cameroon* 7°15N 13°35E **52** C2
Ngapara *N.Z.* 44°57S 170°46E **59** F3
Ngara *Tanzania* 2°29S 30°40E **54** C3
Ngawi *Indonesia* 7°24S 111°26E **37** G14
Ngcobo *S. Africa* 31°37S 28°0E **57** E4
Ngeru *Uganda* 0°27N 33°10E **54** B3
Nghia Lo *Vietnam* 21°33N 104°28E **38** B5
Ngoma *Malawi* 13°8S 33°45E **55** E3
Ngomahura *Zimbabwe* 20°26S 30°43E **55** G3
Ngomba *Tanzania* 8°20S 32°53E **55** D3
Ngomeni, Ras *Kenya* 2°59S 40°14E **54** C5
Ngong *Kenya* 1°36S 36°39E **54** C4
Ngoring Hu *China* 34°55N 97°5E **32** C4
Ngorongoro *Tanzania* 3°11S 35°32E **54** C4
Ngorongoro ◇ *Tanzania* 2°40S 35°30E **54** C4
Ngozi *Burundi* 2°54S 29°50E **54** C2
Ngudu *Tanzania* 2°58S 33°25E **54** C3
Nguigmi *Niger* 14°20N 13°20E **51** F8
Nguiu *Australia* 11°46S 130°38E **60** B5
Ngukurr *Australia* 14°44S 134°44E **62** A1
Ngundu *Zimbabwe* 18°11S 31°15E **55** F3
Ngunga *Tanzania* 3°37S 33°37E **54** C3
Nguru *Nigeria* 12°56N 10°29E **51** F8
Nguru Mts. *Tanzania* 6°0S 37°30E **54** D4
Ngusi *Malawi* 14°0S 34°50E **55** E3
Nguyen Binh *Vietnam* 22°39N 105°56E **38** A5
Nha Trang *Vietnam* 12°16N 109°10E **39** F7
Nhacoongo *Mozam.* 24°18S 35°14E **57** C6
Nhamaabué *Mozam.* 17°25S 35°5E **55** F4
Nhamundá *Brazil* 2°12S 56°41W **93** D7
Nhangulaze, L. *Mozam.* 24°0S 34°30E **57** C5
Nharnuwangga, Wajarri and
   Ngarlawangga ◇
   Australia 24°50S 118°0E **61** D2
Nhill *Australia* 36°18S 141°40E **63** F3
Nho Quan *Vietnam* 20°18N 105°45E **38** B5
Nhulunbuy *Australia* 12°10S 137°20E **62** A2
Nia-nia
   Dem. Rep. of the Congo 1°30N 27°40E **54** B2
Niafounké *Mali* 16°0N 4°5W **50** E5
Niagara Falls *Canada* 43°7N 79°5W **82** C5
Niagara Falls *U.S.A.* 43°5N 79°4W **82** C6
Niagara-on-the-Lake
   Canada 43°15N 79°4W **82** C5
Niah *Malaysia* 3°58N 113°46E **36** D4
Niamey *Niger* 13°27N 2°6E **50** F6
Niangara
   Dem. Rep. of the Congo 3°42N 27°50E **54** B2
Niantic *U.S.A.* 41°20N 72°11W **83** E12
Nias *Indonesia* 1°0N 97°30E **36** D1
Niassa □ *Mozam.* 13°30S 36°0E **55** E4
Niassa □ *Mozam.* 12°4S 36°57E **55** E4
Nibāk *Si. Arabia* 24°25N 50°50E **45** E7
Nicaragua ■
   Cent. Amer. 11°40N 85°30W **88** D2
Nicaragua, L. de *Nic.* 12°0N 85°30W **88** D2
Nicastro *Italy* 38°59N 16°19E **22** E7
Nice *France* 43°42N 7°14E **20** E7
Niceville *U.S.A.* 30°31N 86°30W **85** F11
Nichicun, L. *Canada* 53°5N 71°0W **73** B5
Nichinan *Japan* 31°38N 131°23E **31** J5
Nicholás, Canal *W. Indies* 23°30N 80°5W **88** B3
Nicholasville *U.S.A.* 37°53N 84°34W **81** G11
Nichols *U.S.A.* 42°1N 76°22W **83** D8
Nicholson *Australia* 18°2S 128°54E **60** C4
Nicholson *U.S.A.* 41°37N 75°47W **83** E9
Nicholson → *Australia* 17°31S 139°36E **62** B2
Nicholson L. *Canada* 62°40N 102°40W **71** A8
Nicholson Ra. *Australia* 27°15S 116°45E **61** E2
Nicholville *U.S.A.* 44°41N 74°39W **83** B10
Nicobar Is. *Ind. Oc.* 8°0N 93°30E **27** H11
Nicola *Canada* 50°12N 120°40W **70** C4
Nicolls Town *Bahamas* 25°8N 78°0W **88** A4
Nicosia *Cyprus* 35°10N 33°25E **25** D12
Nicoya *Costa Rica* 10°9N 85°27W **88** D2
Nicoya, G. de *Costa Rica* 10°0N 85°0W **88** E3
Nicoya, Pen. de
   Costa Rica 9°45N 85°40W **88** E2
Nidd → *U.K.* 53°59N 1°23W **12** D6
Niedersachsen □ *Germany* 52°50N 9°0E **16** B5
Niekerkshoop *S. Africa* 29°19S 22°51E **56** D3
Niemba
   Dem. Rep. of the Congo 5°58S 28°24E **54** D2
Niemen = Nemunas →
   Lithuania 55°25N 21°10E **9** J19
Nienburg *Germany* 52°39N 9°13E **16** B5
Nieu Bethesda *S. Africa* 31°51S 24°34E **56** E3
Nieuw Amsterdam
   Suriname 5°53N 55°5W **93** B7
Nieuw Nickerie *Suriname* 6°0N 56°59W **93** B7
Nieuwoudtville *S. Africa* 31°23S 19°7E **56** E2
Nieuwpoort *Belgium* 51°8N 2°45E **15** C2
Nieves, Pico de las
   Canary Is. 27°57N 15°35W **24** G4
Niğde *Turkey* 37°58N 34°40E **44** B2
Nigel *S. Africa* 26°27S 28°25E **57** D4
Niger ■ *W. Afr.* 17°30N 10°0E **50** E7
Niger → *W. Afr.* 5°33N 6°33E **50** G7
Nigeria ■ *W. Afr.* 8°30N 8°0E **50** G7
Nighasin *India* 28°14N 80°52E **43** E9
Nightcaps *N.Z.* 45°57S 168°2E **59** F2
Nihon = Japan ■ *Asia* 36°0N 136°0E **31** G8
Nihon → *Japan* ■ *Asia* 36°0N 136°0E **31** G8
Nii-Jima *Japan* 34°20N 139°15E **31** G9
Niigata *Japan* 37°58N 139°0E **30** F9
Niigata □ *Japan* 37°15N 138°45E **30** F9
Niihama *Japan* 33°55N 133°16E **31** H6
Ni'ihau *U.S.A.* 21°54N 160°9W **75** L7
Niimi *Japan* 34°59N 133°28E **31** G6
Niitsu *Japan* 37°48N 139°7E **30** F9
Nijil *Jordan* 30°32N 35°33E **46** E4
Nijkerk *Neths.* 52°13N 5°30E **15** B5
Nijmegen *Neths.* 51°50N 5°52E **15** C5

Nijverdal *Neths.* 52°22N 6°28E **15** B6
Nīk Pey *Iran* 36°50N 48°10E **45** B6
Nikel *Russia* 69°24N 30°13E **8** B24
Nikiniki *Indonesia* 9°49S 124°30E **60** A3
Nikkō *Japan* 36°45N 139°35E **31** F9
Nikkō △ *Japan* 36°56N 139°37E **31** F9
Nikolayev = Mykolayiv
   Ukraine 46°58N 32°0E **19** E5
Nikolayevsk *Russia* 50°0N 45°35E **19** E8
Nikolayevsk-na-Amur
   Russia 53°8N 140°44E **29** D15
Nikolskoye *Russia* 55°12N 166°0E **29** D17
Nikopol *Ukraine* 47°35N 34°25E **19** E5
Nīkshahr *Iran* 26°15N 60°10E **45** E9
Nikšić *Montenegro* 42°50N 18°57E **23** C8
Nîl, Nahr en → *Africa* 30°10N 31°6E **51** B12
Nîl el Abyad → *Sudan* 15°38N 32°31E **51** E12
Nîl el Azraq → *Sudan* 15°38N 32°31E **51** E12
Nila *Indonesia* 6°44S 129°31E **37** F7
Niland *U.S.A.* 33°14N 115°31W **79** M11
Nile = Nîl, Nahr en →
   Africa 30°10N 31°6E **51** B12
Niles *Mich., U.S.A.* 41°50N 86°15W **81** E11
Niles *Ohio, U.S.A.* 41°11N 80°46W **82** E4
Nim Ka Thana *India* 27°44N 75°48E **42** F6
Nimach *India* 24°30N 74°56E **42** G6
Nimbahera *India* 24°37N 74°45E **42** G6
Nîmes *France* 43°50N 4°23E **20** E6
Nimfaíon → Ákra = Pines, Akra
   Greece 40°5N 24°20E **23** D11
Nimmitabel *Australia* 36°29S 149°15E **63** F4
Nīnawá *Iraq* 36°25N 43°10E **44** B4
Nīnawá □ *Iraq* 36°15N 43°0E **44** B4
Nindigully *Australia* 28°21S 148°50E **63** D4
Ninepin Group *China* 22°16N 114°21E **33** G11
Nineveh = Nīnawá *Iraq* 36°25N 43°10E **44** B4
Ning Xian *China* 35°30N 107°58E **34** G4
Ningaloo Marine △
   Australia 22°23S 113°32E **60** D1
Ningbo *China* 29°51N 121°28E **33** D7
Ningcheng *China* 41°32N 119°53E **35** D10
Ningjin *China* 37°35N 114°57E **34** F8
Ningjing Shan *China* 30°0N 98°20E **41** E21
Ningling *China* 34°25N 115°22E **34** G8
Ningpo = Ningbo *China* 29°51N 121°28E **33** D7
Ningqiang *China* 32°47N 106°15E **34** H4
Ningshan *China* 33°21N 108°21E **34** H5
Ningsia Hui A.R. = Ningxia Huizu
   Zizhiqu □ *China* 38°0N 106°0E **34** E4
Ningwu *China* 39°0N 112°18E **34** E7
Ningxia Huizu Zizhiqu □
   China 38°0N 106°0E **34** E4
Ningyang *China* 35°47N 116°45E **34** G9
Ninh Binh *Vietnam* 20°15N 105°55E **38** B5
Ninh Giang *Vietnam* 20°44N 106°24E **38** B6
Ninh Hoa *Vietnam* 12°30N 109°7E **38** F7
Ninh Ma *Vietnam* 12°48N 109°21E **38** F7
Ninove *Belgium* 50°51N 4°2E **15** D4
Nioaque *Brazil* 21°5S 55°50W **95** A4
Niobrara *U.S.A.* 42°45N 98°2W **80** D4
Niobrara → *U.S.A.* 42°46N 98°3W **80** D4
Nioro du Sahel *Mali* 15°15N 9°30W **50** E4
Niort *France* 46°19N 0°29W **20** C3
Nipawin *Canada* 53°20N 104°0W **71** C8
Nipigon *Canada* 49°0N 88°17W **72** C2
Nipigon, L. *Canada* 49°50N 88°30W **72** C2
Nipishish L. *Canada* 54°12N 60°45W **73** B7
Nipissing, L. *Canada* 46°20N 80°0W **72** C4
Nipomo *U.S.A.* 35°3N 120°29W **79** K6
Nippon = Japan ■ *Asia* 36°0N 136°0E **31** G8
Nipton *U.S.A.* 35°28N 115°16W **79** K11
Niquelândia *Brazil* 14°33S 48°23W **93** F9
Nīr *Iran* 38°2N 47°59E **44** B5
Nirasaki *Japan* 35°42N 138°27E **31** G9
Nirmal *India* 19°3N 78°20E **40** K11
Nirmali *India* 26°20N 86°35E **43** F12
Niš *Serbia* 43°19N 21°58E **23** C9
Nişāb *Si. Arabia* 29°11N 44°43E **44** D5
Nişāb *Yemen* 14°25N 46°29E **47** E4
Nishinomiya *Japan* 34°45N 135°20E **31** G7
Nishino'omote *Japan* 30°43N 130°59E **31** J5
Nishiwaki *Japan* 34°59N 134°58E **31** G7
Niskibi → *Canada* 56°29N 88°9W **72** A2
Nisqually → *U.S.A.* 47°7N 122°42W **78** C4
Nissaki *Greece* 39°43N 19°52E **25** A3
Nissum Bredning
   Denmark 56°40N 8°20E **9** H13
Nistru = Dnister →
   Europe 46°18N 30°17E **17** E16
Nisutlin → *Canada* 60°14N 132°34W **70** A2
Nitchequon *Canada* 53°10N 70°58W **73** B5
Niterói *Brazil* 22°53S 43°7W **95** A7
Nith → *Canada* 43°12N 80°23W **82** C4
Nith → *U.K.* 55°14N 3°33W **11** F5
Nitmiluk △ *Australia* 14°6S 132°15E **60** B5
Nitra *Slovak Rep.* 48°19N 18°4E **17** D10
Nitra → *Slovak Rep.* 47°46N 18°10E **17** E10
Niue *Pac. Oc.* 19°2S 169°54W **65** J11
Niut *Indonesia* 0°55N 110°6E **36** D4
Niuzhuang *China* 40°58N 122°28E **35** D12
Nivala *Finland* 63°56N 24°57E **8** E21
Nivelles *Belgium* 50°35N 4°20E **15** D4
Nivernais *France* 47°15N 3°30E **20** C5
Niverville *Canada* 49°36N 97°3W **71** D9
Niwas *India* 23°3N 80°26E **43** H9
Nixa *U.S.A.* 37°3N 93°18W **80** G7
Nixon *U.S.A.* 29°16N 97°46W **84** G6
Nizamabad *India* 18°45N 78°7E **40** K11
Nizamghat *India* 28°20N 95°45E **41** E19
Nizhne Kolymsk
   Russia 68°34N 160°55E **29** C17
Nizhnekamsk *Russia* 55°38N 51°49E **18** C9
Nizhneudinsk *Russia* 54°54N 99°3E **29** D10
Nizhnevartovsk *Russia* 60°56N 76°38E **28** C8
Nizhniy Bestyakh
   Russia 61°57N 129°54E **29** C13
Nizhniy Novgorod *Russia* 56°20N 44°0E **18** C7
Nizhniy Tagil *Russia* 57°55N 59°57E **18** C10

Nizhyn *Ukraine* 51°5N 31°55E **19** D5
Nizip *Turkey* 37°5N 37°50E **44** B3
Nízke Tatry *Slovak Rep.* 48°55N 19°30E **17** D10
Nizwá *Oman* 22°56N 57°32E **47** C6
Njakwa *Malawi* 11°1S 33°56E **55** E3
Njanji *Zambia* 14°25S 31°46E **55** E3
Njazidja = Grande Comore
   Comoros Is. 11°35S 43°20E **53** a
Njinjo *Tanzania* 8°48S 38°54E **55** D4
Njombe *Tanzania* 9°20S 34°50E **55** D3
Njombe → *Tanzania* 6°56S 35°6E **54** D4
Nkana *Zambia* 12°50S 28°8E **55** E2
Nkandla *S. Africa* 28°37S 31°5E **57** D5
Nkawkaw *Ghana* 6°36N 0°49W **50** G5
Nkayi *Zimbabwe* 19°41S 29°20E **55** F2
Nkhotakota *Malawi* 12°56S 34°15E **55** E3
Nkhotakota △ *Malawi* 12°50S 34°0E **55** E3
Nkondwe *Tanzania* 5°51S 30°51E **54** D3
Nkongsamba *Cameroon* 4°55N 9°55E **52** D1
Nkurenkuru *Namibia* 17°42S 18°32E **56** B2
Nmai → *Burma* 25°30N 97°25E **41** G20
Noakhali *Bangla.* 22°48N 91°10E **41** H17
Nobel *Canada* 45°25N 80°6W **82** A4
Nobeoka *Japan* 32°36N 131°41E **31** H5
Noblesville *U.S.A.* 40°3N 86°1W **81** E10
Noboribetsu *Japan* 42°24N 141°6E **30** C10
Noccundra *Australia* 27°50S 142°36E **63** D3
Nocera Inferiore *Italy* 40°44N 14°38E **22** D6
Nocona *U.S.A.* 33°47N 97°44W **84** E6
Noda *Japan* 35°56N 139°52E **31** G9
Nogales *Mexico* 31°20N 110°56W **86** A2
Nogales *U.S.A.* 31°21N 110°56W **77** L8
Nōgata *Japan* 33°48N 130°44E **31** H5
Noggerup *Australia* 33°32S 116°5E **61** F2
Noginsk *Russia* 64°30N 90°50E **29** C10
Nogliki *Russia* 51°50N 143°10E **29** D15
Nogoa → *Australia* 23°40S 147°55E **62** C4
Nogoyá *Argentina* 32°24S 59°48W **94** C4
Nohar *India* 29°11N 74°49E **42** E6
Nohta *India* 23°40N 79°34E **43** H8
Noires, Mts. *France* 48°11N 3°40W **20** B2
Noirmoutier, Î. de *France* 46°58N 2°10W **20** C2
Nojane *Botswana* 23°15S 20°14E **56** C3
Nojima-Zaki *Japan* 34°54N 139°53E **31** G9
Nok Kundi *Pakistan* 28°50N 62°45E **40** E3
Nok Ta Phao, Ko *Thailand* 9°23N 99°40E **39** b
Nokaneng *Botswana* 19°40S 22°17E **56** B3
Nokomis *Canada* 51°35N 105°0W **71** C8
Nokomis L. *Canada* 57°0N 103°0W **71** B8
Nola *C.A.R.* 3°35N 16°4E **52** D3
Noma Omuramba →
   Namibia 18°52S 20°53E **56** B3
Nombre de Dios *Panama* 9°34N 79°28W **88** E4
Nome *U.S.A.* 64°30N 165°25W **74** C6
Nomo-Zaki *Japan* 32°35N 129°44E **31** H4
Nomuka *Tonga* 20°17S 174°48W **59** c
Nomuka Group *Tonga* 20°20S 174°48W **59** c
Nonacho L. *Canada* 61°42N 109°40W **71** A7
Nonda *Australia* 20°40S 142°28E **62** C3
Nong Chang *Thailand* 15°23N 99°51E **38** E2
Nong Het *Laos* 19°29N 103°59E **38** C4
Nong Khai *Thailand* 17°50N 102°46E **38** D4
Nong'an *China* 44°25N 125°5E **35** B13
Nongoma *S. Africa* 27°58S 31°35E **57** D5
Nongsa *Indonesia* 1°11N 104°8E **39** d
Nonoava *Mexico* 27°28N 106°44W **86** B3
Nonsan *S. Korea* 36°12N 127°5E **35** F14
Nonthaburi *Thailand* 13°50N 100°29E **38** F3
Noonamah *Australia* 12°40S 131°4E **60** B5
Noondie, L. *Australia* 28°30S 119°30E **61** E2
Noonkanbah ◇
   Australia 18°30S 124°50E **60** C3
Noord Brabant □ *Neths.* 51°40N 5°0E **15** C5
Noord Holland □ *Neths.* 52°30N 4°45E **15** B4
Noordbeveland *Neths.* 51°35N 3°50E **15** C3
Noordoostpolder *Neths.* 52°45N 5°45E **15** B5
Noordwijk *Neths.* 52°14N 4°26E **15** B4
Noosa Heads *Australia* 26°25S 153°6E **63** D5
Nootka I. *Canada* 49°32N 126°42W **70** D3
Nopiming △ *Canada* 50°30N 95°37W **71** C9
Noralee *Canada* 53°59N 126°26W **70** C3
Noranda = Rouyn-Noranda
   Canada 48°20N 79°0W **72** C4
Norco *U.S.A.* 33°56N 117°33W **79** M9
Nord-Kivu □
   Dem. Rep. of the Congo 1°0S 29°0E **54** C2
Nord-Ostsee-Kanal →
   Germany 54°12N 9°32E **16** A5
Nordaustlandet *Svalbard* 79°14N 23°0E **4** B9
Norddeich *Germany* 53°35N 7°10E **16** B4
Norden *Germany* 53°35N 7°12E **16** B4
Norderney *Germany* 53°42N 7°9E **16** B4
Norderstedt *Germany* 53°42N 10°1E **16** B5
Nordfjord *Norway* 61°55N 5°30E **8** F11
Nordfriesische Inseln
   Germany 54°40N 8°20E **16** A5
Nordhausen *Germany* 51°30N 10°47E **16** C6
Norðoyar *Færoe Is.* 62°17N 6°35W **8** E9
Nordkapp *Norway* 71°10N 25°50E **8** A21
Nordkapp *Svalbard* 80°31N 20°0E **4** A9
Nordkinnhalvøya
   Norway 70°55N 27°40E **8** A22
Nordrhein-Westfalen □
   Germany 51°45N 7°30E **16** C4
Nordvik *Russia* 74°2N 111°32E **29** B12
Nore → *Ireland* 52°25N 6°58W **10** D4
Norefjell *Norway* 60°17N 9°29E **9** F13
Norfolk *N.Y., U.S.A.* 44°48N 74°59W **83** B10
Norfolk *Nebr., U.S.A.* 42°2N 97°25W **80** D5
Norfolk *Va., U.S.A.* 36°50N 76°17W **81** G15
Norfolk □ *U.K.* 52°39N 0°54E **13** E8
Norfolk Broads △ *U.K.* 52°45N 1°30E **13** E9
Norfolk I. *Pac. Oc.* 28°58S 168°3E **58** K8
Norfolk Ridge *Pac. Oc.* 29°0S 168°0E **64** L8
Norfork L. *U.S.A.* 36°15N 92°14W **84** C8
Norge = Norway ■ *Europe* 63°0N 11°0E **8** E14
Norilsk *Russia* 69°20N 88°6E **29** C9

Norma, Mt. Australia 20°55S 140°42E 62 C3
Normal U.S.A. 40°31N 88°59W 80 E9
Norman U.S.A. 35°13N 97°26W 84 D6
Norman ~ Australia 19°18S 141°51E 62 B3
Norman Wells Canada 65°17N 126°51W 68 D6
Normandy ~ Australia 14°23S 144°10E 62 A3
Normandie France 48°45N 0°10E 20 B4
Normandin Canada 48°49N 72°31W 72 C5
Normandy = Normandie
France 48°45N 0°10E 20 B4
Normanhurst, Mt.
Australia 25°4S 122°30E 61 E3
Normanton Australia 17°40S 141°10E 62 B3
Normétal Canada 49°0N 79°22W 72 C4
Norquay Canada 51°53N 102°5W 71 C8
Norquinco Argentina 41°51S 70°55W 96 E2
Norrbottens län ☐
Sweden 66°50N 20°0E 8 C19
Norris Point Canada 49°31N 57°53W 73 C8
Norristown U.S.A. 40°7N 75°21W 83 F9
Norrköping Sweden 58°37N 16°11E 9 G17
Norrland Sweden 62°15N 15°45E 8 E16
Norrtälje Sweden 59°46N 18°42E 9 G18
Norseman Australia 32°8S 121°43E 61 F3
Norsk Russia 52°30N 130°5E 29 D14
Norte, Pta. del Canary Is. 27°51N 17°57W 24 G2
Norte, Serra do Brazil 11°20S 59°0W 92 F7
North, C. Canada 47°2N 60°20W 73 C7
North Adams U.S.A. 42°42N 73°7W 83 D11
North America 40°0N 100°0W 66 F10
North Arm Canada 62°0N 114°30W 70 A5
North Augusta U.S.A. 33°30N 81°59W 85 E14
North Australian Basin
Ind. Oc. 14°30S 116°30E 60 B2
North Ayrshire ☐ U.K. 55°45N 4°44W 11 F4
North Bass I. U.S.A. 41°40N 82°56W 82 E2
North Battleford
Canada 52°50N 108°17W 71 C7
North Bay Canada 46°20N 79°30W 72 C4
North Belcher Is. Canada 56°50N 79°50W 72 A4
North Bend Oreg.,
U.S.A. 43°24N 124°14W 76 E1
North Bend Pa., U.S.A. 41°20N 77°42W 82 E7
North Bend Wash.,
U.S.A. 47°30N 121°47W 78 C5
North Bennington
U.S.A. 42°56N 73°15W 83 D11
North Berwick U.K. 56°4N 2°42W 11 E6
North Berwick U.S.A. 43°18N 70°44W 83 C14
North Bruce Canada 44°22N 81°26W 82 B3
North C. U.S.A. 47°5N 64°0W 73 C7
North C. N.Z. 34°23S 173°4E 59 A4
North Canadian ~
U.S.A. 35°22N 95°37W 84 D7
North Canton U.S.A. 40°53N 81°24W 82 F3
North Cape = Nordkapp
Norway 71°10N 25°50E 8 A21
North Caribou L.
Canada 52°50N 90°40W 72 B1
North Carolina ☐
U.S.A. 35°30N 80°0W 85 D15
North Cascades △
U.S.A. 48°45N 121°10W 76 B3
North Channel Canada 46°0N 83°0W 72 C3
North Channel U.K. 55°13N 5°52W 11 F3
North Charleston
U.S.A. 32°53N 79°58W 85 E15
North Chicago U.S.A. 42°19N 87°51W 80 D10
North Collins U.S.A. 42°35N 78°56W 82 D6
North Creek U.S.A. 43°42N 73°59W 83 C11
North Dakota ☐
U.S.A. 47°30N 100°15W 80 B3
North Downs U.K. 51°19N 0°21E 13 F8
North East U.S.A. 42°13N 79°50W 82 D5
North East Frontier Agency =
Arunachal Pradesh ☐
India 28°0N 95°0E 41 F19
North East Lincolnshire ☐
U.K. 53°34N 0°2W 12 D7
North Eastern ☐ Kenya 1°30N 40°0E 54 B5
North Esk ~ U.K. 56°46N 2°24W 11 E6
North European Plain
Europe 55°0N 25°0E 6 E10
North Foreland U.K. 51°22N 1°28E 13 F9
North Fork ~ U.S.A. 37°14N 119°21W 78 H7
North Fork American ~
U.S.A. 38°57N 120°59W 78 G5
North Fork Feather ~
U.S.A. 38°33N 121°30W 78 F5
North Fork Grand ~
U.S.A. 45°47N 102°16W 80 C2
North Fork Red ~
U.S.A. 34°24N 99°14W 84 D5
North Frisian Is. = Nordfriesische
Inseln Germany 54°40N 8°20E 16 A5
North Gower Canada 45°8N 75°43W 83 A9
North Hd. Australia 30°14S 114°59E 61 F1
North Henik L. Canada 61°45N 97°40W 71 A9
North Highlands
U.S.A. 38°40N 121°23W 78 G5
North Horr Kenya 3°20N 37°8E 54 B4
North I. Kenya 4°5N 36°5E 54 B4
North I. N.Z. 38°0S 175°0E 59 C5
North I. Seychelles 4°25S 55°13E 53 b
North Kingsville U.S.A. 41°54N 80°42W 82 E4
North Kitui △ Kenya 0°15S 38°29E 54 C4
North Knife ~ Canada 58°53N 94°45W 71 B10
North Koel ~ India 24°45N 83°50E 43 G10
North Korea ■ Asia 40°0N 127°0E 35 E14
North Lakhimpur India 27°14N 94°7E 41 F19
North Lanarkshire ☐
U.K. 55°52N 3°56W 11 F5
North Las Vegas
U.S.A. 36°11N 115°7W 79 J11
North Lincolnshire ☐
U.K. 53°36N 0°30W 12 D7
North Little Rock
U.S.A. 34°45N 92°16W 84 D8
North Loup ~ U.S.A. 41°17N 98°24W 80 E4
North Luangwa △ Zambia 11°49S 32°9E 55 E3

North Magnetic Pole
Canada 82°42N 114°24W 4 A2
North Mankato U.S.A. 44°10N 94°2W 80 C6
North Minch U.K. 58°5N 5°55W 11 C3
North Moose L. Canada 54°4N 100°12W 71 C8
North Myrtle Beach
U.S.A. 33°48N 78°42W 85 E15
North Nahanni ~
Canada 62°15N 123°20W 70 A4
North Olmsted U.S.A. 41°25N 81°56W 82 E3
North Ossetia ☐ Russia 43°30N 44°30E 19 F7
North Pagai, I. = Pagai Utara,
Pulau Indonesia 2°35S 100°0E 36 E2
North Palisade U.S.A. 37°6N 118°31W 78 H8
North Platte U.S.A. 41°8N 100°46W 80 E3
North Platte ~ U.S.A. 41°7N 100°42W 80 E3
North Pole Arctic 90°0N 0°0 4 A
North Portal Canada 49°0N 102°33W 71 D8
North Powder U.S.A. 45°2N 117°55W 76 D5
North Pt. Barbados 13°20N 59°37W 89 g
North Pt. Trin. & Tob. 11°21N 60°31W 93 J16
North Pt. U.S.A. 45°2N 83°16W 82 A1
North Rhine Westphalia =
Nordrhein-Westfalen ☐
Germany 51°45N 7°30E 16 C4
North River Canada 53°49N 57°6W 73 B8
North Ronaldsay U.K. 59°22N 2°26N 11 B6
North Saskatchewan ~
Canada 53°15N 105°5W 71 C7
North Sea Europe 56°0N 4°0E 6 D6
North Seal ~ Canada 58°50N 98°7W 71 B9
North Slope ☆ U.S.A. 69°15N 152°0W 74 B9
North Somerset ☐ U.K. 51°24N 2°45W 13 F5
North Sydney Canada 46°12N 60°15W 73 C7
North Syracuse U.S.A. 43°8N 76°7W 83 C8
North Taranaki Bight
N.Z. 38°50S 174°15E 59 C5
North Thompson ~
Canada 50°40N 120°20W 70 C4
North Tonawanda
U.S.A. 43°2N 78°53W 82 C6
North Troy U.S.A. 45°0N 72°24W 83 B12
North Twin I. Canada 53°20N 80°0W 72 B4
North Tyne ~ U.K. 55°0N 2°8W 12 B5
North Uist U.K. 57°40N 7°15W 11 D1
North Vancouver
Canada 49°19N 123°4W 78 A3
North Vernon U.S.A. 39°0N 85°38W 81 F11
North Wabasca L.
Canada 56°0N 113°55W 70 B6
North Walsham U.K. 52°50N 1°22E 12 E9
North West = Severo-Zapadnyy ☐
Russia 65°0N 40°0E 28 C4
North-West ☐ S. Africa 27°0S 25°0E 56 D4
North West C. Australia 21°45S 114°9E 60 D1
North West Frontier ☐
Pakistan 34°0N 72°0E 42 C4
North West Highlands
U.K. 57°33N 4°58W 11 D4
North West River
Canada 53°30N 60°10W 73 B7
North Western ☐ Zambia 13°30S 25°30E 55 E2
North Wildwood U.S.A. 39°0N 74°48W 81 F16
North York Moors U.K. 54°23N 0°53W 12 C7
North York Moors △
U.K. 54°27N 0°51W 12 C7
North Yorkshire ☐ U.K. 54°15N 1°25W 12 C6
Northallerton U.K. 54°20N 1°26W 12 C6
Northam Australia 31°35S 116°42E 61 F2
Northam S. Africa 24°56S 27°18E 56 C4
Northampton Australia 28°27S 114°33E 61 E1
Northampton U.K. 52°15N 0°53W 13 E7
Northampton Mass.,
U.S.A. 42°19N 72°38W 83 D12
Northampton Pa.,
U.S.A. 40°41N 75°30W 83 F9
Northamptonshire ☐
U.K. 52°16N 0°55W 13 E7
Northbridge U.S.A. 42°9N 71°39W 83 D13
Northbrook Canada 44°44N 77°9W 82 B7
Northcliffe Australia 34°39S 116°7E 61 F2
Northeast Pacific Basin
Pac. Oc. 32°0N 145°0W 65 D13
Northeast Providence Chan.
W. Indies 26°0N 76°0W 88 A4
Northern = Limpopo ☐
S. Africa 24°5S 29°0E 57 C4
Northern ☐ Malawi 11°0S 34°0E 55 E3
Northern ☐ Zambia 10°30S 31°0E 55 E3
Northern Areas ☐
Pakistan 36°30N 73°0E 43 A5
Northern Cape ☐ S. Africa 30°0S 20°0E 56 D3
Northern Circars India 17°30N 82°30E 41 L13
Northern Indian L.
Canada 57°20N 97°20W 71 B9
Northern Ireland ☐ U.K. 54°45N 7°0W 10 B5
Northern Lau Group
Fiji 17°30S 178°59W 59 a
Northern Light L.
Canada 48°15N 90°39W 72 C1
Northern Marianas ☐
Pac. Oc. 17°0N 145°0E 64 F6
Northern Province ☐
S. Africa 24°0S 29°0E 57 C4
Northern Range
Trin. & Tob. 10°46N 61°15W 93 K15
Northern Sporades
Greece 39°15N 23°30E 23 E10
Northern Territory ☐
Australia 20°0S 133°0E 60 D5
Northfield Minn., U.S.A. 44°27N 93°9W 80 C7
Northfield Vt., U.S.A. 44°9N 72°40W 83 B12
Northgate Canada 49°0N 102°16W 71 D8
Northland ☐ N.Z. 35°30S 173°30E 59 A4
Northome U.S.A. 47°52N 94°17W 80 B6
Northport Ala., U.S.A. 33°14N 87°35W 85 E11
Northport Wash.,
U.S.A. 48°55N 117°48W 76 B5
Northumberland ☐ U.K. 55°12N 2°0W 12 B6

Northumberland, C.
Australia 38°5S 140°40E 63 F3
Northumberland Is.
Australia 21°30S 149°50E 62 C4
Northumberland Str.
Canada 46°20N 64°0W 73 C7
Northville Canada 43°10N 81°56W 82 C3
Northville U.S.A. 43°13N 74°11W 83 C10
Northwest Pacific Basin
Pac. Oc. 32°0N 165°0E 64 D8
Northwest Providence Channel
W. Indies 26°0N 78°0W 88 A4
Northwest Territories ☐
Canada 63°0N 118°0W 68 E8
Northwich U.K. 53°15N 2°31W 12 D5
Northwood Iowa, U.S.A. 43°27N 93°13W 80 D7
Northwood N. Dak.
U.S.A. 47°44N 97°34W 80 B5
Norton U.S.A. 39°50N 99°53W 80 F4
Norton Zimbabwe 17°52S 30°40E 55 F3
Norton Sd. U.S.A. 63°50N 164°0W 74 C7
Norwalk Calif., U.S.A. 33°54N 118°4W 79 M8
Norwalk Conn., U.S.A. 41°7N 73°22W 83 E11
Norwalk Iowa, U.S.A. 41°29N 93°41W 80 E7
Norwalk Ohio, U.S.A. 41°15N 82°37W 82 E2
Norway Maine, U.S.A. 44°13N 70°32W 83 C14
Norway Mich., U.S.A. 45°47N 87°55W 80 C10
Norway ■ Europe 63°0N 11°0E 8 E14
Norway House Canada 53°59N 97°50W 71 C9
Norwegian B. Canada 77°30N 90°0W 69 B14
Norwegian Basin Atl. Oc. 68°0N 2°0W 4 C7
Norwegian Sea Atl. Oc. 66°0N 1°0E 6 B6
Norwich Canada 42°59N 80°36W 82 D4
Norwich U.K. 52°38N 1°18E 13 E9
Norwich Conn., U.S.A. 41°31N 72°5W 83 E12
Norwich N.Y., U.S.A. 42°32N 75°32W 83 D9
Norwood Canada 44°23N 77°59W 82 B7
Norwood U.S.A. 44°45N 75°0W 83 B10
Nosappu-Misaki Japan 45°26N 141°39E 30 C12
Noshiro Japan 40°12N 140°0E 30 D10
Nosratābād Iran 29°55N 60°0E 45 D8
Noss Hd. U.K. 58°28N 3°3W 11 C5
Nossob ~ S. Africa 26°55S 20°45E 56 D3
Nosy Barren Madag. 18°25S 43°40E 53 H8
Nosy Bé Madag. 13°25S 48°15E 53 G9
Nosy Boraha Madag. 16°50S 49°55E 57 B8
Nosy Lava Madag. 14°33S 47°36E 57 A8
Nosy Varika Madag. 20°35S 48°32E 57 C8
Noteć ~ Poland 52°44N 15°26E 16 B8
Notikewin ~ Canada 57°2N 117°38W 70 B5
Notodden Norway 59°35N 9°17E 9 G13
Notre Dame B. Canada 49°45N 55°30W 73 C8
Notre-Dame-de-Koartac =
Quaqtaq Canada 60°55N 69°40W 69 E18
Notre-Dame-des-Bois
Canada 45°24N 71°4W 83 A13
Notre-Dame-d'Ivugivic = Ivujivik
Canada 62°24N 77°55W 69 E16
Notre-Dame-du-Nord
Canada 47°36N 79°30W 72 C4
Nottawasaga B. Canada 44°35N 80°15W 82 B4
Nottaway ~ Canada 51°22N 78°55W 72 B4
Nottingham U.K. 52°58N 1°10W 12 E6
Nottingham, City of ☐
U.K. 52°58N 1°10W 12 E6
Nottingham I. Canada 63°20N 77°55W 69 E16
Nottinghamshire ☐ U.K. 53°10N 1°3W 12 D6
Nottoway ~ U.S.A. 36°33N 76°55W 81 G15
Notwane ~ Botswana 23°35S 26°58E 56 C4
Nouâdhibou Mauritania 20°54N 17°0W 50 D2
Nouâdhibou, Râs
Mauritania 20°50N 17°0W 50 D2
Nouakchott Mauritania 18°9N 15°58W 50 E2
Nouméa N. Cal. 22°17S 166°30E 58 D9
Noupoort S. Africa 31°10S 24°57E 56 E3
Nouveau Comptoir = Wemindji
Canada 53°0N 78°49W 72 B4
Nouvelle Amsterdam, Î.
Ind. Oc. 38°30S 77°30E 3 F13
Nouvelle-Calédonie = New
Caledonia ■ Pac. Oc. 21°0S 165°0E 58 D9
Nova Esperança Brazil 23°8S 52°24W 95 A5
Nova Friburgo Brazil 22°16S 42°30W 95 A7
Nova Iguaçu Brazil 22°45S 43°28W 95 A7
Nova Iorque Brazil 7°0S 44°5W 93 E10
Nova Lamego
Guinea-Biss. 12°19N 14°11W 50 F3
Nova Lusitânia Mozam. 19°50S 34°34E 55 F3
Nova Mambone Mozam. 21°0S 35°3E 57 C6
Nova Scotia ☐ Canada 45°10N 63°0W 73 C7
Nova Sofala Mozam. 20°7S 34°42E 57 C5
Nova Venécia Brazil 18°45S 40°24W 93 G10
Nova Zagora Bulgaria 42°32N 26°1E 23 C11
Novar Canada 45°27N 79°15W 82 A5
Novara Italy 45°28N 8°38E 20 B8
Novato U.S.A. 38°6N 122°35W 78 G4
Novaya Ladoga Russia 60°7N 32°16E 18 B5
Novaya Lyalya Russia 59°4N 60°45E 18 C11
Novaya Sibir, Ostrov
Russia 75°10N 150°0E 29 B16
Novaya Zemlya Russia 75°0N 56°0E 28 B6
Nové Zámky Slovak Rep. 47°59N 18°11E 17 D10
Novgorod Russia 58°30N 31°25E 18 C5
Novgorod-Severskiy = Novhorod-
Siverskyy Ukraine 52°2N 33°10E 18 D5
Novhorod-Siverskyy
Ukraine 52°2N 33°10E 18 D5
Novi Lígure Italy 44°46N 8°47E 20 D8
Novi Pazar Serbia 43°12N 20°28E 23 C9
Novi Sad Serbia 45°18N 19°52E 23 B8
Novo Hamburgo Brazil 29°37S 51°7W 95 B5
Novo Mesto Slovenia 45°47N 15°12E 22 B6
Novo Remanso Brazil 9°41S 42°4W 93 E10
Novocherkassk Russia 47°27N 40°15E 19 E7
Novodvinsk Russia 64°25N 40°42E 18 B7
Novogrudok = Navahrudak
Belarus 53°40N 25°50E 17 B13
Novohrad-Volynskyy
Ukraine 50°34N 27°35E 17 C14

Novokachalinsk Russia 45°5N 132°0E 30 B5
Novokuybyshevsk Russia 53°7N 49°58E 18 D8
Novokuznetsk Russia 53°45N 87°10E 28 D9
Novolazarevskaya
Antarctica 71°0S 12°0E 5 D3
Novomoskovsk Russia 54°5N 38°15E 18 D6
Novorossiysk Russia 44°43N 37°46E 19 F6
Novoryobnoye Russia 72°50N 105°50E 29 B11
Novoselytsya Ukraine 48°14N 26°15E 17 D14
Novoshakhtinsk Russia 47°46N 39°58E 19 E6
Novosibirsk Russia 55°0N 83°5E 28 D9
Novosibirskiye Ostrova
Russia 75°0N 142°0E 29 B15
Novotroitsk Russia 51°10N 58°15E 18 D10
Novouzensk Russia 50°32N 48°17E 19 D8
Novovolynsk Ukraine 50°45N 24°4E 17 C13
Novska Croatia 45°19N 17°0E 22 B7
Novyy Bor Russia 66°43N 52°19E 18 A9
Novyy Port Russia 67°40N 72°30E 28 C8
Novyy Urengoy Russia 65°48N 76°52E 28 C8
Nowa Sól Poland 51°48N 15°44E 16 C8
Nowata U.S.A. 36°42N 95°38W 84 C7
Nowbarān Iran 35°8N 49°42E 45 C6
Nowghāb Iran 33°53N 59°4E 45 C8
Nowgong Assam, India 26°20N 92°50E 41 F18
Nowgong Mad. P., India 25°4N 79°27E 43 G8
Nowra Australia 34°53S 150°35E 63 E5
Nowshera Pakistan 34°0N 72°0E 40 C8
Nowy Sącz Poland 49°40N 20°41E 17 D11
Nowy Targ Poland 49°29N 20°2E 17 D11
Nowy Tomyśl Poland 52°19N 16°10E 16 B9
Noxen U.S.A. 41°25N 76°4W 83 E8
Noyabr'sk Russia 64°34N 76°21E 28 C8
Noyon France 49°34N 2°59E 20 B5
Noyon Mongolia 43°2N 102°4E 34 C2
Nqutu S. Africa 28°13S 30°32E 57 D5
Nsanje Malawi 16°55S 35°12E 55 F4
Nsawam Ghana 5°50N 0°24W 50 G5
Nseluka Zambia 9°58S 31°16E 55 D3
Nsomba Zambia 10°45S 29°51E 55 E2
Ntaria ☐ Australia 24°0S 132°41E 60 D5
Ntungamo Uganda 0°56S 30°17E 54 C3
Nu Jiang ~ China 29°58N 97°25E 32 D4
Nu Shan China 26°0N 99°20E 41 G21
Nuba Mts. = Nubah, Jibalan
Sudan 12°0N 31°0E 51 F12
Nubah, Jibalan Sudan 12°0N 31°0E 51 F12
Nubia Africa 21°0N 32°0E 48 D7
Nubian Desert = Nûbîya, Es Sahrâ
en Sudan 21°30N 33°30E 51 D12
Nûbîya, Es Sahrâ en
Sudan 21°30N 33°30E 51 D12
Nuboai Indonesia 2°10S 136°30E 37 E9
Nubra ~ India 34°35N 77°35E 43 B7
Nueces ~ U.S.A. 27°51N 97°30W 84 H6
Nueltin L. Canada 60°30N 99°30W 71 A9
Nuestra Señora del Rosario de
Caá-Catí Argentina 27°45S 57°36W 94 B4
Nueva Ciudad Guerrero
Mexico 26°34N 99°12W 87 B5
Nueva Gerona Cuba 21°53N 82°49W 88 B3
Nueva Palmira Uruguay 33°52S 58°20W 94 C4
Nueva Rosita Mexico 27°57N 101°13W 86 B4
Nueva San Salvador
El Salv. 13°40N 89°18W 88 D2
Nuéve de Julio Argentina 35°30S 61°0W 94 D3
Nuevitas Cuba 21°30N 77°20W 88 B4
Nuevo, G. Argentina 43°0S 64°30W 96 E4
Nuevo Casas Grandes
Mexico 30°25N 107°55W 86 A3
Nuevo Laredo Mexico 27°30N 99°31W 87 B5
Nuevo León ☐ Mexico 25°20N 100°0W 86 C5
Nuevo Rocafuerte
Ecuador 0°55S 75°27W 92 D3
Nugget Pt. N.Z. 46°27S 169°50E 59 G2
Nuhaka N.Z. 39°3S 177°45E 59 C6
Nukey Bluff Australia 32°26S 135°29E 63 E2
Nukhayb Iraq 32°4N 42°3E 44 C4
Nuku Hiva
French Polynesia 8°54S 140°6W 65 H13
Nuku'alofa Tonga 21°10S 175°12W 59 c
Nukus Uzbekistan 42°27N 59°41E 28 E6
Nulato U.S.A. 64°43N 158°6W 74 C8
Nullagine ~ Australia 21°53S 120°7E 60 D3
Nullagine Australia 21°20S 120°20E 60 D3
Nullarbor Australia 31°28S 130°55E 61 F5
Nullarbor △ Australia 32°35S 130°0E 61 F5
Nullarbor Plain Australia 31°10S 129°0E 61 F4
Numalla, L. Australia 28°43S 144°20E 63 D3
Numan Nigeria 9°29N 12°3E 51 G8
Numata Japan 36°45N 139°4E 31 F9
Numazu Japan 35°7N 138°51E 31 G9
Numbulwar Australia 14°15S 135°45E 62 A2
Numfoor Indonesia 1°0S 134°50E 37 E8
Numurkah Australia 36°5S 145°26E 63 F4
Nunaksaluk I. Canada 55°49N 60°20W 73 A7
Nunap Isua Greenland 59°48N 43°55W 66 D15
Nunavik Greenland 71°50N 54°25W 66 C17
Nunavut ☐ Canada 66°0N 85°0W 69 C11
Nunda U.S.A. 42°35N 77°56W 82 D7
Nuneaton U.K. 52°32N 1°27W 13 E6
Nungarin Australia 31°12S 118°6E 61 F2
Nungo Mozam. 13°23S 37°43E 55 E4
Nungwe Tanzania 2°48S 32°2E 54 C3
Nunivak I. U.S.A. 60°10N 166°30W 74 C6
Nunkun India 33°57N 76°2E 43 C7
Núoro Italy 40°20N 9°20E 22 D3
Nūr Iran 36°33N 52°1E 45 B7
Nūrābād Hormozgan, Iran 27°47N 57°12E 45 E8
Nūrābād Lorestān, Iran 34°4N 47°58E 44 C5
Nuremberg = Nürnberg
Germany 49°27N 11°3E 16 D6
Nuri Mexico 28°5N 109°22W 86 B3
Nuriootpa Australia 34°27S 139°0E 63 E2
Nuristān ☐ Afghan. 35°20N 71°0E 40 B7
Nurmes Finland 63°37N 29°10E 8 E23
Nürnberg Germany 49°27N 11°3E 16 D6

Nurpur Pakistan 31°53N 71°54E 42 D4
Nurran, L. = Terewah, L.
Australia 29°52S 147°35E 63 D4
Nurrari Lakes Australia 29°1S 130°5E 61 E5
Nusa Barung Indonesia 8°30S 113°30E 37 H15
Nusa Dua Indonesia 8°48S 115°14E 37 K18
Nusa Kambangan
Indonesia 7°40S 108°10E 37 G13
Nusa Tenggara Barat ☐
Indonesia 8°50S 117°30E 36 F5
Nusa Tenggara Timur ☐
Indonesia 9°30S 122°0E 37 F6
Nusaybin Turkey 37°3N 41°10E 19 G7
Nushki Pakistan 29°35N 66°0E 42 E2
Nuuk Greenland 64°10N 51°35W 67 C14
Nuupere, Pte. Moorea 17°36S 149°47W 59 d
Nuwakot Nepal 28°10N 83°55E 43 E10
Nuwayb'i, W. an ~
Si. Arabia 29°18N 34°57E 46 F3
Nuweiba' Egypt 28°59N 34°39E 44 D2
Nuwerus S. Africa 31°8S 18°24E 56 E2
Nuweveldberge S. Africa 32°10S 21°45E 56 E3
Nuyts, Pt. Australia 35°4S 116°38E 61 G2
Nuyts Arch. Australia 32°35S 133°20E 63 E1
Nxai Pan △ Botswana 19°50S 24°46E 56 B3
Nxaunxau Botswana 18°57S 21°4E 56 B3
Nyabing Australia 33°33S 118°9E 61 F2
Nyack U.S.A. 41°5N 73°55W 83 E11
Nyagan Russia 62°30N 65°38E 28 C7
Nyahanga Tanzania 2°20S 33°37E 54 C3
Nyahua Tanzania 5°25S 33°23E 54 D3
Nyahururu Kenya 0°2N 36°27E 54 B4
Nyainqêntanglha Shan
China 30°0N 90°0E 32 D3
Nyakanazi Tanzania 3°2S 31°10E 54 C3
Nyâlâ Sudan 12°2N 24°58E 51 F10
Nyamandhlovu
Zimbabwe 19°55S 28°16E 55 F2
Nyambiti Tanzania 2°48S 33°27E 54 C3
Nyamira Kenya 0°36S 34°52E 54 B4
Nyamwaga Tanzania 1°27S 34°33E 54 C3
Nyandekwa Tanzania 3°57S 32°32E 54 C3
Nyandoma Russia 61°40N 40°12E 18 B7
Nyanga ~ Zimbabwe 18°17S 32°46E 55 F3
Nyangana Namibia 18°0S 20°40E 56 B3
Nyanguge Tanzania 2°30S 33°12E 54 C3
Nyanza Rwanda 2°20S 29°42E 54 C2
Nyanza ☐ Kenya 0°10S 34°15E 54 C3
Nyanza-Lac Burundi 4°21S 29°36E 54 C2
Nyasa, L. = Malawi, L.
Africa 12°0S 34°30E 55 E3
Nyasvizh Belarus 53°14N 26°38E 17 B14
Nyazepetrovsk Russia 56°3N 59°36E 18 C10
Nyazwidzi ~ Zimbabwe 20°0S 31°17E 55 G3
Nybro Sweden 56°44N 15°55E 9 H16
Nyda Russia 66°40N 72°58E 28 C8
Nyeboe Land Greenland 82°0N 57°0W 69 A20
Nyeri Kenya 0°23S 36°56E 54 C4
Nyika △ Malawi 10°30S 33°53E 55 E3
Nyimba Zambia 14°33S 30°50E 55 E3
Nyíregyháza Hungary 47°58N 21°47E 17 E11
Nyiru, Mt. Kenya 2°8N 36°50E 54 B4
Nykarleby = Uusikaarlepyy
Finland 63°32N 22°31E 8 E20
Nykøbing Nordjylland,
Denmark 56°48N 8°51E 9 H13
Nykøbing Sjælland,
Denmark 54°56N 11°52E 9 J14
Nykøbing Sjælland,
Denmark 55°55N 11°40E 9 J14
Nyköping Sweden 58°45N 17°1E 9 G17
Nylstroom = Modimolle
S. Africa 24°42S 28°22E 57 C4
Nymagee Australia 32°7S 146°20E 63 E4
Nymboida △ Australia 29°38S 152°26E 63 D5
Nynäshamn Sweden 58°54N 17°57E 9 G17
Nyngan Australia 31°30S 147°8E 63 E4
Nyoma Rap India 33°10N 78°40E 43 C8
Nyoman = Nemunas ~
Lithuania 55°25N 21°10E 9 J19
Nysa Poland 50°30N 17°22E 17 C9
Nysa ~ Europe 52°4N 14°46E 16 B8
Nyslott = Savonlinna
Finland 61°52N 28°53E 8 F23
Nyssa U.S.A. 43°53N 117°0W 76 E5
Nystad = Uusikaupunki
Finland 60°47N 21°25E 8 F19
Nyunzu
Dem. Rep. of the Congo 5°57S 27°58E 54 D2
Nyurba Russia 63°17N 118°28E 29 C12
Nzega Tanzania 4°10S 33°12E 54 C3
Nzérékoré Guinea 7°49N 8°48W 50 G4
Nzeto Angola 7°10S 12°52E 52 F2
Nzilo, Chutes de
Dem. Rep. of the Congo 10°18S 25°27E 55 E2
Nzubuka Tanzania 4°45S 32°50E 54 C3
Nzwani = Anjouan
Comoros Is. 12°15S 44°20E 53 a

O

O Le Pupū Pu'e △
Samoa 13°59S 171°43W 59 b
Ō-Shima Hokkaidō,
Japan 41°30N 139°22E 30 D9
Ō-Shima Shizuoka, Japan 34°44N 139°24E 31 G9
Oa, Mull of U.K. 55°35N 6°20W 11 F2
Oacoma U.S.A. 43°48N 99°24W 80 D4
Oahe, L. U.S.A. 44°27N 100°24W 80 C3
O'ahu U.S.A. 21°28N 157°58W 75 L8
Oak Harbor U.S.A. 48°18N 122°39W 78 B4
Oak Hill U.S.A. 37°59N 81°9W 81 G13
Oak Island U.S.A. 33°55N 78°10W 85 E15
Oak Ridge U.S.A. 36°1N 84°16W 85 C12
Oak View U.S.A. 34°24N 119°18W 79 L7
Oakan-Dake Japan 43°27N 144°10E 30 C12

Oakdale *Calif., U.S.A.* 37°46N 120°51W **78** H6
Oakdale *La., U.S.A.* 30°49N 92°40W **84** F8
Oakes *U.S.A.* 46°8N 99°0W **80** B4
Oakesdale *U.S.A.* 47°8N 117°15W **76** D5
Oakey *Australia* 27°25S 151°43E **63** D5
Oakfield *U.S.A.* 43°4N 78°16W **82** C6
Oakham *U.K.* 52°40N 0°43W **13** E7
Oakhurst *U.S.A.* 37°19N 119°40W **78** H7
Oakland *Calif., U.S.A.* 37°48N 122°18W **78** H4
Oakland *Pa., U.S.A.* 41°57N 75°36W **83** E9
Oakley *Kans., U.S.A.* 39°8N 100°51W **80** F4
Oakley *Idaho, U.S.A.* 42°15N 113°53W **76** E7
Oakover → *Australia* 21°0S 120°40E **60** D3
Oakridge *U.S.A.* 43°45N 122°28W **76** E2
Oakville *Canada* 43°27N 79°41W **82** C5
Oakville *U.S.A.* 46°51N 123°14W **78** D3
Oamaru *N.Z.* 45°5S 170°59E **59** F3
Oasis *Calif., U.S.A.* 37°29N 117°55W **78** H9
Oasis *Calif., U.S.A.* 33°28N 116°6W **79** M10
Oates Land *Antarctica* 69°0S 160°0E **5** C11
Oatman *U.S.A.* 35°1N 114°19W **79** K12
Oaxaca *Mexico* 17°3N 96°43W **87** D5
Oaxaca □ *Mexico* 17°0N 96°30W **87** D5
Ob → *Russia* 66°45N 69°30E **28** C7
Oba *Canada* 49°4N 84°7W **72** C3
Obama *Japan* 35°30N 135°45E **31** G7
Oban *U.K.* 56°25N 5°29W **11** E3
Obbia = Hobyo
Somali Rep. 5°25N 48°30E **47** F4
Oberá *Argentina* 27°21S 55°2W **95** B4
Oberhausen *Germany* 51°28N 6°51E **16** C4
Oberlin *Kans., U.S.A.* 39°49N 100°32W **80** F4
Oberlin *La., U.S.A.* 30°37N 92°46W **84** F8
Oberlin *Ohio, U.S.A.* 41°18N 82°13W **82** E2
Oberon *Australia* 33°45S 149°52E **63** E4
Obi, Kepulauan *Indonesia* 1°23S 127°45E **37** E7
Óbidos *Brazil* 1°50S 55°30W **93** D7
Obihiro *Japan* 42°56N 143°12E **30** C11
Obilatu *Indonesia* 1°25S 127°20E **37** E7
Obluchye *Russia* 49°1N 131°4E **29** E14
Obo *C.A.R.* 5°20N 26°32E **54** A2
Oboyan *Russia* 51°15N 36°21E **28** D4
Obozerskaya = Obozerskiy
Russia 63°34N 40°21E **18** B7
Obozerskiy *Russia* 63°34N 40°21E **18** B7
Observatory Inlet
Canada 55°10N 129°54W **70** B3
Obshchi Syrt *Russia* 52°0N 53°0E **6** F16
Obskaya Guba *Russia* 69°0N 73°0E **28** C8
Obuasi *Ghana* 6°17N 1°40W **50** G5
Ocala *U.S.A.* 29°11N 82°8W **85** G13
Ocampo *Chihuahua,*
Mexico 28°11N 108°23W **86** B3
Ocampo *Tamaulipas,*
Mexico 22°50N 99°20W **87** C5
Ocaña *Spain* 39°55N 3°30W **21** C4
Occidental, Cordillera
Colombia 5°0N 76°0W **92** C3
Occidental, Grand Erg
Algeria 30°20N 1°0E **50** B6
Ocean City *Md., U.S.A.* 38°20N 75°5W **81** F16
Ocean City *N.J., U.S.A.* 39°17N 74°35W **81** F16
Ocean City *Wash.,*
U.S.A. 47°4N 124°10W **78** C2
Ocean Falls *Canada* 52°18N 127°48W **70** C3
Ocean I. = Banaba
Kiribati 0°45S 169°50E **64** H8
Ocean Park *U.S.A.* 46°30N 124°3W **78** D2
Oceano *U.S.A.* 35°6N 120°37W **79** K6
Oceanport *U.S.A.* 40°19N 74°3W **83** F10
Oceanside *U.S.A.* 33°12N 117°23W **79** M9
Ochil Hills *U.K.* 56°14N 3°40W **11** E5
Ocho Rios *Jamaica* 18°24N 77°6W **88** a
Ocilla *U.S.A.* 31°36N 83°15W **85** F13
Ocmulgee → *U.S.A.* 31°58N 82°33W **85** F13
Ocniţa *Moldova* 48°25N 27°30E **17** D14
Oconee → *U.S.A.* 31°58N 82°33W **85** F13
Oconomowoc *U.S.A.* 43°7N 88°30W **80** D9
Oconto *U.S.A.* 44°53N 87°52W **80** C10
Oconto Falls *U.S.A.* 44°52N 88°9W **80** C9
Ocosingo *Mexico* 16°53N 92°6W **87** D6
Ocotal *Nic.* 13°41N 86°31W **88** D2
Ocotlán *Jalisco, Mexico* 20°21N 102°46W **86** C4
Ocotlán *Oaxaca, Mexico* 16°48N 96°40W **87** D5
Ōda *Japan* 35°11N 132°30E **31** G6
Ódáðahraun *Iceland* 65°5N 17°0W **8** D5
Ōdaejin *N. Korea* 41°34N 129°40E **30** D10
Odate *Japan* 40°16N 140°34E **30** D10
Odawara *Japan* 35°20N 139°6E **31** G9
Odda *Norway* 60°3N 6°35E **9** F12
Odei → *Canada* 56°6N 96°54W **71** B9
Ödemiş *Turkey* 38°15N 28°0E **23** E13
Odendaalsrus *S. Africa* 27°48S 26°45E **56** D4
Odense *Denmark* 55°22N 10°23E **9** J14
Oder → *Europe* 53°33N 14°38E **16** B8
Odesa *Ukraine* 46°30N 30°45E **19** E5
Odessa = Odesa *Ukraine* 46°30N 30°45E **19** E5
Odessa *Canada* 44°17N 76°43W **83** B8
Odessa *Tex., U.S.A.* 31°52N 102°23W **84** F3
Odessa *Wash., U.S.A.* 47°20N 118°41W **76** C4
Odiakwe *Botswana* 20°12S 25°17E **56** C4
Odienné *Ivory C.* 9°30N 7°34W **50** G4
Odintsovo *Russia* 55°40N 37°16E **18** C6
O'Donnell *U.S.A.* 32°58N 101°50W **84** E4
O'Donnell Pt. *Canada* 45°5N 80°5W **82** A4
Odorheiu Secuiesc
Romania 46°21N 25°21E **17** E13
Odra = Oder → *Europe* 53°33N 14°38E **16** B8
Odzi *Zimbabwe* 19°0S 32°20E **57** B5
Odzi → *Zimbabwe* 19°45S 32°23E **57** B5
Oeiras *Brazil* 7°0S 42°8W **93** E10
Oelrichs *U.S.A.* 43°11N 103°14W **80** D2
Oelwein *U.S.A.* 42°41N 91°55W **80** D8
Oeno I. *Pac. Oc.* 24°0S 131°0W **65** K14
Oenpelli = Gunbalanya
Australia 12°20S 133°4E **60** B5
Offa *Italy* 41°22N 16°13E **22** D7
Offa *Nigeria* 8°13N 4°42E **50** G6
Offaly □ *Ireland* 53°15N 7°30W **10** C4

Offenbach *Germany* 50°6N 8°44E **16** C5
Offenburg *Germany* 48°28N 7°56E **16** D4
Officer Cr. → *Australia* 27°46S 132°30E **61** E5
Ofolanga *Tonga* 19°38S 174°27W **59** c
Ofotfjorden *Norway* 68°27N 17°0E **8** B17
Ōfunato *Japan* 39°4N 141°43E **30** E10
Oga *Japan* 39°55N 139°50E **30** E9
Oga-Hantō *Japan* 39°58N 139°47E **30** E9
Ogaden *Ethiopia* 7°30N 45°30E **47** F3
Ōgaki *Japan* 35°21N 136°37E **31** G8
Ogallala *U.S.A.* 41°8N 101°43W **80** E3
Ogasawara Gunto
Pac. Oc. 27°0N 142°0E **27** F16
Ogbomosho *Nigeria* 8°1N 4°11E **50** G6
Ogden *U.S.A.* 41°13N 111°58W **76** F8
Ogea Driki *Fiji* 19°12S 178°27W **59** c
Ogea Levu *Fiji* 19°8S 178°24W **59** a
Ogeechee → *U.S.A.* 31°50N 81°3W **85** F14
Ogilby *U.S.A.* 32°49N 114°50W **79** N12
Óglio → *Italy* 45°2N 10°39E **22** B4
Ogmore *Australia* 22°37S 149°35E **62** C4
Ogoki *Canada* 51°38N 85°58W **72** B2
Ogoki → *Canada* 51°38N 85°57W **72** B2
Ogoki L. *Canada* 50°50N 87°10W **72** B2
Ogoki Res. *Canada* 50°45N 88°15W **72** B2
Ogooué = Ogoué → *Gabon* 1°0S 9°0E **52** E1
Ogowe = Ogooué → *Gabon* 1°0S 9°0E **52** E1
Ogre *Latvia* 56°49N 24°36E **9** H21
Ogurchinskiy, Ostrov
Turkmenistan 38°55N 53°2E **45** B7
Ohai *N.Z.* 45°55S 168°0E **59** F2
Ohakune *N.Z.* 39°24S 175°24E **59** F5
Ohata *Japan* 41°24N 141°10E **30** D10
Ohio □ *U.S.A.* 40°15N 82°45W **82** F2
Ohio → *U.S.A.* 36°59N 89°8W **80** G9
Ohře → *Czech Rep.* 50°30N 14°10E **16** C8
Ohrid *Macedonia* 41°8N 20°52E **23** D9
Ohridsko Jezero
Macedonia 41°8N 20°52E **23** D9
Ohrigstad *S. Africa* 24°39S 30°36E **57** C5
Oikou *China* 38°35N 117°42E **35** E9
Oil City *U.S.A.* 41°26N 79°42W **82** E5
Oil Springs *Canada* 42°47N 82°7W **82** D2
Oildale *U.S.A.* 35°25N 119°1W **79** K7
Oise → *France* 49°0N 2°4E **20** B5
Oistins *Barbados* 13°4N 59°33W **89** g
Oistins B. *Barbados* 13°4N 59°33W **89** g
Ōita *Japan* 33°14N 131°36E **31** H5
Ōita □ *Japan* 33°15N 131°30E **31** H5
Oiticica *Brazil* 5°3S 41°5W **93** E10
Ojai *U.S.A.* 34°27N 119°15W **79** L7
Ojinaga *Mexico* 29°34N 104°25W **86** B4
Ojiya *Japan* 37°18N 138°48E **31** F9
Ojo Caliente *Mexico* 21°53N 102°15W **86** C4
Ojo de Liebre, L.
Mexico 27°45N 114°15W **86** B2
Ojos del Salado, Cerro
Argentina 27°0S 68°40W **94** B2
Oka → *Russia* 56°20N 43°59E **18** C7
Okaba *Indonesia* 8°6S 139°42E **37** F9
Okahandja *Namibia* 22°0S 16°59E **56** C2
Okandja *Gabon* 0°35S 13°45E **52** E2
Okanogan *U.S.A.* 48°22N 119°35W **76** B4
Okanogan → *U.S.A.* 48°6N 119°44W **76** B4
Okanogan Range
N. Amer. 49°0N 119°55W **70** D5
Okapi △
Dem. Rep. of the Congo 2°30N 27°20E **54** B2
Okaputa *Namibia* 20°5S 17°0E **56** C2
Okara *Pakistan* 30°50N 73°31E **42** D5
Okaukuejo *Namibia* 19°10S 16°0E **56** B2
Okavango Delta
Botswana 18°45S 22°45E **56** B3
Okavango Swamp = Okavango
Delta Botswana 18°45S 22°45E **56** B3
Okaya *Japan* 36°5N 138°10E **31** F9
Okayama *Japan* 34°40N 133°54E **31** G6
Okayama □ *Japan* 35°0N 133°50E **31** G6
Okazaki *Japan* 34°57N 137°10E **31** G8
Okeechobee *U.S.A.* 27°15N 80°50W **85** H14
Okeechobee, L. *U.S.A.* 27°0N 80°50W **85** H14
Okefenokee △ *U.S.A.* 30°45N 82°18W **85** F13
Okefenokee Swamp
U.S.A. 30°40N 82°20W **85** F13
Okehampton *U.K.* 50°44N 4°0W **13** G4
Okha *India* 22°27N 69°4E **42** H3
Okha *Russia* 53°40N 143°0E **29** D15
Okhotsk *Russia* 59°20N 143°10E **29** D15
Okhotsk, Sea of *Asia* 55°0N 145°0E **29** D15
Okhotskiy Perevoz
Russia 61°52N 135°35E **29** C14
Okhtyrka *Ukraine* 50°25N 35°0E **19** D5
Oki-Shotō *Japan* 36°5N 133°15E **31** F6
Okiep *S. Africa* 29°39S 17°53E **56** D2
Okinawa □ *Japan* 26°40N 128°0E **31** L4
Okinawa-Guntō *Japan* 26°40N 128°0E **31** L4
Okinawa-Jima *Japan* 26°32N 128°0E **31** L4
Okino-erabu-Shima
Japan 27°21N 128°33E **31** L4
Oklahoma □ *U.S.A.* 35°20N 97°30W **84** D6
Oklahoma City *U.S.A.* 35°30N 97°30W **84** D6
Okmulgee *U.S.A.* 35°37N 95°58W **84** D7
Oknitsa = Ocniţa
Moldova 48°25N 27°30E **17** D14
Okolo *Uganda* 2°37N 31°8E **54** B3
Okolona *U.S.A.* 34°0N 88°45W **85** E10
Okombahe *Namibia* 21°23S 15°22E **56** C2
Okotoks *Canada* 50°43N 113°58W **70** C6
Oksibil *Indonesia* 4°59S 140°35E **37** E10
Oksovskiy *Russia* 62°33N 39°57E **18** B6
Oktyabrsk = Qandyaghash
Kazakhstan 49°28N 57°25E **19** E10

Oktyabrskiy = Aktsyabrski
Belarus 52°38N 28°53E **17** B15
Oktyabrskiy *Bashkortostan,*
Russia 54°28N 53°28E **18** D9
Oktyabrskiy *Kamchatka,*
Russia 52°39N 156°14E **29** D16
Oktyabrskoy Revolyutsii, Ostrov
Russia 79°30N 97°0E **29** B10
Okuru *N.Z.* 43°55S 168°55E **59** E2
Okushiri-Tō *Japan* 42°15N 139°30E **30** C9
Okwa → *Botswana* 22°30S 23°0E **56** C3
Ola *Russia* 59°35N 151°17E **29** D16
Ola *U.S.A.* 35°2N 93°13W **84** D8
Ólafsfjörður *Iceland* 66°4N 18°39W **8** C4
Ólafsvík *Iceland* 64°53N 23°43E **8** D2
Olancha *U.S.A.* 36°17N 118°1W **79** J8
Olancha Pk. *U.S.A.* 36°16N 118°7W **79** J8
Olanchito *Honduras* 15°30N 86°30W **88** C2
Öland *Sweden* 56°45N 16°38E **9** H17
Olary *Australia* 32°18S 140°19E **63** E3
Olascoaga *Argentina* 35°15S 60°39W **94** D3
Olathe *U.S.A.* 38°53N 94°49W **80** F6
Olavarría *Argentina* 36°55S 60°20W **94** D3
Oława *Poland* 50°57N 17°20E **17** C9
Ólbia *Italy* 40°55N 9°31E **22** D3
Olcott *U.S.A.* 43°20N 78°42W **82** C6
Old Bahama Chan. = Bahama,
Canal Viejo de
W. Indies 22°10N 77°30W **88** B4
Old Baldy Pk. = San Antonio, Mt.
U.S.A. 34°17N 117°38W **79** L9
Old Bridge *U.S.A.* 40°25N 74°22W **83** F10
Old Castile = Castilla y Leon □
Spain 42°0N 5°0W **21** B3
Old Crow *Canada* 67°30N 139°55W **68** D4
Old Dale *U.S.A.* 34°8N 115°47W **79** L11
Old Forge *N.Y., U.S.A.* 43°43N 74°58W **83** C10
Old Forge *Pa., U.S.A.* 41°22N 75°45W **83** E9
Old Mapoon ◊ *Australia* 11°5S 142°22E **62** A3
Old Perlican *Canada* 48°5N 53°1W **73** C9
Old Shinyanga *Tanzania* 3°33S 33°27E **54** C3
Old Speck Mt. *U.S.A.* 44°34N 70°57W **83** B14
Old Town *U.S.A.* 44°56N 68°39W **81** C19
Old Washington *U.S.A.* 40°2N 81°27W **82** F3
Old Wives L. *Canada* 50°5N 106°0W **71** C7
Oldbury *U.K.* 51°38N 2°33W **13** F5
Oldcastle *Ireland* 53°46N 7°10W **10** C4
Oldeani *Tanzania* 3°22S 35°35E **54** C4
Oldenburg *Germany* 53°9N 8°13E **16** B5
Oldenzaal *Neths.* 52°19N 6°53E **15** B6
Oldham *U.K.* 53°33N 2°7W **12** D5
Oldman → *Canada* 49°57N 111°42W **70** D6
Oldmeldrum *U.K.* 57°20N 2°19W **11** D6
Olds *Canada* 51°50N 114°10W **70** C6
Olduvai Gorge *Tanzania* 2°57S 35°23E **54** C4
Oldziyt *Mongolia* 44°40N 109°1E **34** B5
Olean *U.S.A.* 42°5N 78°26W **82** D6
Olekma → *Russia* 60°22N 120°42E **29** C13
Olekminsk *Russia* 60°25N 120°30E **29** C13
Oleksandriya *Ukraine* 50°37N 26°19E **17** C14
Olema *U.S.A.* 38°3N 122°47W **78** G4
Olenegorsk *Russia* 68°9N 33°18E **8** B25
Olenek *Russia* 68°28N 112°18E **29** C12
Olenek → *Russia* 73°0N 120°10E **29** B13
Oléron, Î. d' *France* 45°55N 1°15W **20** D3
Oleśnica *Poland* 51°13N 17°22E **17** C9
Olevsk *Ukraine* 51°12N 27°39E **17** C14
Olga, L. *Canada* 49°47N 77°15W **72** C4
Olgas, The = Kata Tjuta
Australia 25°20S 130°50E **61** E5
Ölgiy *Mongolia* 48°56N 89°57E **32** B3
Olhão *Portugal* 37°3N 7°48W **21** D2
Olifants = Elefantes →
Africa 24°10S 32°40E **57** C5
Olifants → *Namibia* 25°30S 19°30E **56** C2
Olifantshoek *S. Africa* 27°57S 22°42E **56** D3
Ólimbos, Óros = Olympos Oros
Greece 40°6N 22°23E **23** D10
Olímpia *Brazil* 20°44S 48°54W **95** A6
Olinda *Brazil* 8°1S 34°51W **93** E12
Oliva *Argentina* 32°0S 63°38W **94** C3
Olivares, Cerro los
Argentina 30°18S 69°55W **94** C2
Olive Branch *U.S.A.* 34°57N 89°49W **85** D10
Olivehurst *U.S.A.* 39°6N 121°34W **78** F5
Olivenza *Spain* 38°41N 7°9W **21** C2
Oliver *Canada* 49°13N 119°37W **70** D5
Oliver L. *Canada* 56°56N 103°22W **71** B8
Ollagüe *Chile* 21°15S 68°10W **94** A2
Olmaliq *Uzbekistan* 40°50N 69°35E **28** E7
Olney *Ill., U.S.A.* 38°44N 88°5W **80** F9
Olney *Tex., U.S.A.* 33°22N 98°45W **84** E5
Oloitokitok *Kenya* 2°56S 37°39E **54** C4
Olomane → *Canada* 50°14N 60°37W **73** B7
Olomouc *Czech Rep.* 49°38N 17°12E **17** D9
Olonets *Russia* 61°0N 32°54E **18** B5
Olongapo *Phil.* 14°50N 120°18E **37** B6
Olosega *Amer. Samoa* 14°10S 169°37W **59** b
Olosenga = Swains I.
Amer. Samoa 11°11S 171°4W **65** J11
Olot *Spain* 42°11N 2°58E **21** A7
Olovyannaya *Russia* 50°58N 115°35E **29** D12
Oloy → *Russia* 66°29N 159°29E **29** C16
Olsztyn *Poland* 53°48N 20°29E **17** B11
Olt → *Romania* 43°43N 24°51E **17** G13
Olteniţa *Romania* 44°7N 26°42E **17** F14
Olton *U.S.A.* 34°11N 102°8W **84** D3
Olymbos *Cyprus* 35°21N 33°45E **25** D12
Olymbos Oros *Greece* 40°6N 22°23E **23** D10
Olympia *Greece* 37°39N 21°39E **23** F9
Olympia *U.S.A.* 47°3N 122°53W **78** D4
Olympic △ *U.S.A.* 47°45N 123°43W **78** C3
Olympic Dam *Australia* 30°30S 136°55E **63** E2
Olympic Mts. *U.S.A.* 47°55N 123°45W **78** C3
Olympus *Cyprus* 34°56N 32°52E **25** E11
Olympus, Mt. = Olymbos Oros
Greece 40°6N 22°23E **23** D10
Olympus, Mt. = Uludağ
Turkey 40°4N 29°13E **23** D13

Olympus, Mt. *U.S.A.* 47°48N 123°43W **78** C3
Olyphant *U.S.A.* 41°27N 75°36W **83** E9
Om → *Russia* 54°59N 73°22E **28** D8
Om Koi *Thailand* 17°48N 98°22E **38** D2
Ōma *Japan* 41°45N 141°5E **30** D10
Ōmachi *Japan* 36°30N 137°50E **31** F8
Omae-Zaki *Japan* 34°36N 138°14E **31** G9
Ōmagari *Japan* 39°27N 140°29E **30** E10
Omagh *U.K.* 54°36N 7°19W **10** B4
Omagh □ *U.K.* 54°35N 7°15W **10** B4
Omaha *U.S.A.* 41°17N 95°58W **80** E7
Omak *U.S.A.* 48°25N 119°31W **76** B4
Omalos *Greece* 35°19N 23°55E **25** D5
Oman ■ *Asia* 23°0N 58°0E **47** C6
Oman, G. of *Asia* 24°30N 58°30E **45** E8
Omaruru *Namibia* 21°26S 16°0E **56** C2
Omaruru → *Namibia* 22°7S 14°15E **56** C1
Omate *Peru* 16°45S 71°0W **92** G4
Ombai, Selat *Indonesia* 8°30S 124°50E **37** F6
Omboué *Gabon* 1°35S 9°15E **52** E1
Ombrone → *Italy* 42°42N 11°5E **22** C4
Omdurmân *Sudan* 15°40N 32°28E **51** E12
Omemee *Canada* 44°18N 78°33W **82** B6
Omeonga
Dem. Rep. of the Congo 3°40S 24°22E **54** C1
Ometepe, I. de *Nic.* 11°32N 85°35W **88** D2
Ometepec *Mexico* 16°41N 98°25W **87** D5
Ominato *Japan* 41°17N 141°10E **30** D10
Omineca → *Canada* 56°3N 124°16W **70** B4
Omineca Mts. *Canada* 56°30N 125°30W **70** B3
Omitara *Namibia* 22°16S 18°2E **56** C2
Ōmiya = Saitama *Japan* 35°54N 139°38E **31** G9
Ommen *Neths.* 52°31N 6°26E **15** B6
Ömnögovĭ □ *Mongolia* 43°15N 104°0E **34** C3
Omo → *Ethiopia* 6°25N 36°10E **47** F2
Omodhos *Cyprus* 34°51N 32°48E **25** E11
Omolon → *Russia* 68°42N 158°36E **29** C16
Omono-Gawa → *Japan* 39°46N 140°3E **30** E10
Ompha *Canada* 45°0N 76°50W **83** B8
Omsk *Russia* 55°0N 73°12E **28** D8
Omsukchan *Russia* 62°32N 155°48E **29** C16
Ōmu *Japan* 44°34N 142°58E **30** B11
Omul, Vf. *Romania* 45°27N 25°29E **17** F13
Ōmura *Japan* 32°56N 129°57E **31** H4
Omuramba Omatako →
Namibia 17°45S 20°25E **56** B2
Omuramba Ovambo →
Namibia 18°45S 16°59E **56** B2
Ōmuta *Japan* 33°5N 130°26E **31** H5
Onaga *U.S.A.* 39°29N 96°10W **80** F5
Onalaska *U.S.A.* 43°53N 91°14W **80** D8
Onancock *U.S.A.* 37°43N 75°45W **81** G16
Onang *Indonesia* 3°2S 118°49E **37** E5
Onangue, L. *Gabon* 0°57S 10°4E **52** E2
Onaping L. *Canada* 47°3N 81°30W **72** C3
Onavas *Mexico* 28°31N 109°35W **86** B3
Onawa *U.S.A.* 42°2N 96°6W **80** D5
Oncócua *Angola* 16°30S 13°25E **56** B1
Onda *Spain* 39°55N 0°17W **21** C5
Ondangwa *Namibia* 17°57S 16°4E **56** B2
Ondjiva *Angola* 16°48S 15°50E **56** B2
Öndörhaan *Mongolia* 47°19N 110°39E **33** B6
Öndörshil *Mongolia* 45°13N 108°5E **34** B5
Öndverðarnes *Iceland* 64°52N 24°0W **8** D2
One Arm Point *Australia* 16°26S 123°3E **60** C3
One Arm Point ◊
Australia 16°31S 122°53E **60** C3
One Tree *Australia* 34°11S 144°43E **63** E3
Oneata *Fiji* 18°26S 178°25W **59** a
Onega → *Russia* 64°0N 38°10E **18** B6
Onega, G. of = Onezhskaya Guba
Russia 64°24N 36°38E **18** B6
Onega, L. = Onezhskoye Ozero
Russia 61°44N 35°22E **18** B6
Oneida *U.S.A.* 43°6N 75°39W **83** C9
Oneida L. *U.S.A.* 43°12N 75°54W **83** C9
O'Neill *U.S.A.* 42°27N 98°39W **80** D4
Onekotan, Ostrov
Russia 49°25N 154°45E **29** E16
Onema
Dem. Rep. of the Congo 4°35S 24°30E **54** C1
Oneonta *U.S.A.* 42°27N 75°4W **83** D9
Oneşti *Romania* 46°17N 26°47E **17** E14
Onezhskaya Guba
Russia 64°24N 36°38E **18** B6
Onezhskoye Ozero
Russia 61°44N 35°22E **18** B6
Ongarue *N.Z.* 38°42S 175°19E **59** C5
Ongea Levu = Ogea Levu
Fiji 19°8S 178°24W **59** a
Ongers → *S. Africa* 31°4S 23°13E **56** E3
Ongerup *Australia* 33°58S 118°28E **61** F2
Ongjin *N. Korea* 37°56N 125°21E **35** F13
Ongkharak *Thailand* 14°8N 101°1E **38** E3
Ongoluk Ol *China* 43°0N 118°38E **35** C10
Ongole *India* 15°33N 80°2E **40** M12
Ongon = Havirga
Mongolia 45°41N 113°5E **34** B7
Onida *U.S.A.* 44°42N 100°4W **80** C3
Onilahy → *Madag.* 23°34S 43°45E **57** C7
Onitsha *Nigeria* 6°6N 6°42E **50** G7
Ono *Fiji* 18°55S 178°29E **59** a
Onoda *Japan* 33°59N 131°11E **31** G5
Onslow *Australia* 21°40S 115°12E **60** D2
Onslow B. *U.S.A.* 34°20N 77°15W **85** D16
Ontake-San *Japan* 35°53N 137°29E **31** G8
Ontario *Calif., U.S.A.* 34°4N 117°39W **79** L9
Ontario *Oreg., U.S.A.* 44°2N 116°58W **76** D5
Ontario □ *Canada* 48°0N 83°0W **72** B2
Ontario, L. *N. Amer.* 43°20N 78°0W **82** C7
Ontonagon *U.S.A.* 46°52N 89°19W **80** B9
Onyx *U.S.A.* 35°41N 118°14W **79** K8
Oodnadatta *Australia* 27°33S 135°30E **63** D2
Ooldea *Australia* 30°27S 131°50E **61** F5

Oombulgurri *Australia* 15°15S 127°45E **60** C4
Oombulgurri ◊
Australia 15°10S 127°50E **60** C4
Oorindi *Australia* 20°40S 141°1E **62** C3
Oost-Vlaanderen □
Belgium 51°5N 3°50E **15** C3
Oostende *Belgium* 51°15N 2°54E **15** C2
Oosterhout *Neths.* 51°39N 4°47E **15** C4
Oosterschelde → *Neths.* 51°33N 4°0E **15** C4
Oosterwolde *Neths.* 53°0N 6°17E **15** B6
Ootacamund = Udagamandalam
India 11°30N 76°44E **40** P10
Ootsa L. *Canada* 53°50N 126°2W **70** C3
Ooty = Udagamandalam
India 11°30N 76°44E **40** P10
Op Luang △ *Thailand* 18°12N 98°32E **38** C2
Opala
Dem. Rep. of the Congo 0°40S 24°20E **54** C1
Opanake *Sri Lanka* 6°35N 80°40E **40** R12
Opasatika *Canada* 49°30N 82°50W **72** C3
Opasquia *Canada* 53°33N 93°5W **72** B1
Opava *Czech Rep.* 49°57N 17°58E **17** D9
Opelika *U.S.A.* 32°39N 85°23W **85** E12
Opelousas *U.S.A.* 30°32N 92°5W **84** F8
Opémisca, L. *Canada* 49°56N 74°52W **72** C5
Opheim *U.S.A.* 48°51N 106°24W **76** B10
Ophthalmia Ra.
Australia 23°15S 119°30E **60** D2
Opinaca → *Canada* 52°15N 78°2W **72** B4
Opinaca, Rés. *Canada* 52°39N 76°20W **72** B4
Opinnagau → *Canada* 54°12N 82°25W **72** B3
Opiscotéo, L. *Canada* 53°10N 68°10W **73** B6
Opobo *Nigeria* 4°35N 7°34E **50** H7
Opole *Poland* 50°42N 17°58E **17** C9
Oponono L. *Namibia* 18°8S 15°45E **56** B2
Oporto = Porto *Portugal* 41°8N 8°40W **21** B1
Opotiki *N.Z.* 38°1S 177°19E **59** C6
Opp *U.S.A.* 31°17N 86°16W **85** F11
Oppdal *Norway* 62°35N 9°41E **8** E13
Opportunity *U.S.A.* 47°39N 117°15W **76** C5
Opua *N.Z.* 35°19S 174°9E **59** A5
Opunake *N.Z.* 39°26S 173°52E **59** C4
Opuwo *Namibia* 18°3S 13°45E **56** B1
Ora *Cyprus* 34°51N 33°12E **25** E12
Oracle *U.S.A.* 32°37N 110°46W **77** K8
Oradea *Romania* 47°2N 21°58E **17** E11
Öræfajökull *Iceland* 64°2N 16°39W **8** D5
Orai *India* 25°58N 79°30E **43** G8
Oral = Zhayyq →
Kazakhstan 47°0N 51°48E **19** E9
Oral *Kazakhstan* 51°20N 51°20E **19** D9
Oran *Algeria* 35°45N 0°39W **50** A5
Orange *Australia* 33°15S 149°7E **63** E4
Orange *France* 44°8N 4°47E **20** D6
Orange *Calif., U.S.A.* 33°47N 117°51W **79** M9
Orange *Mass., U.S.A.* 42°35N 72°19W **83** D12
Orange *Tex., U.S.A.* 30°6N 93°44W **84** F8
Orange *Va., U.S.A.* 38°15N 78°7W **81** F14
Orange → *S. Africa* 28°41S 16°28E **56** D2
Orange, C. *Brazil* 4°20N 51°30W **93** C8
Orange Cove *U.S.A.* 36°38N 119°19W **78** J7
Orange Free State = Free State □
S. Africa 28°30S 27°0E **56** D4
Orange Grove *U.S.A.* 27°58N 97°56W **84** H6
Orange Walk *Belize* 18°6N 88°33W **87** D7
Orangeburg *U.S.A.* 33°30N 80°52W **85** E14
Orangeville *Canada* 43°55N 80°5W **82** C4
Orango *Guinea-Biss.* 11°5N 16°0W **50** F2
Oranienburg *Germany* 52°45N 13°14E **16** B7
Oranje = Orange →
S. Africa 28°41S 16°28E **56** D2
Oranjemund *Namibia* 28°38S 16°29E **56** D2
Oranjerivier *S. Africa* 29°40S 24°12E **56** D3
Oranjestad *Aruba* 12°32N 70°2W **89** D5
Orapa *Botswana* 21°15S 25°30E **53** J5
Oras *Phil.* 12°9N 125°28E **37** B7
Orbetello *Italy* 42°27N 11°13E **22** C4
Orbisonia *U.S.A.* 40°15N 77°54W **82** F7
Orbost *Australia* 37°40S 148°29E **63** F4
Orcadas *Antarctica* 60°44S 44°37W **5** C18
Orcas I. *U.S.A.* 48°42N 122°56W **78** B4
Orchard City *U.S.A.* 38°50N 107°58W **76** G10
Orchard Homes *U.S.A.* 46°55N 114°4W **76** C6
Orchila, I. *Venezuela* 11°48N 66°10W **89** D6
Orchilla, Pta. *Canary Is.* 27°42N 18°10W **24** G1
Orcutt *U.S.A.* 34°52N 120°27W **79** L6
Ord → *Australia* 15°33N 128°15E **60** C4
Ord, Mt. *Australia* 17°20S 125°34E **60** C4
Ord Mts. *U.S.A.* 34°39N 116°45W **79** L10
Orderville *U.S.A.* 37°17N 112°38W **77** H7
Ordos = Mu Us Shamo
China 39°0N 109°0E **34** E5
Ordu *Turkey* 40°55N 37°53E **19** F6
Ordway *U.S.A.* 38°13N 103°46W **76** G12
Ore *Dem. Rep. of the Congo* 3°17N 29°30E **54** B2
Ore Mts. = Erzgebirge
Germany 50°27N 12°55E **16** C7
Örebro *Sweden* 59°20N 15°18E **9** G16
Oregon *U.S.A.* 42°1N 89°20W **80** D9
Oregon □ *U.S.A.* 44°0N 121°0W **76** E3
Oregon City *U.S.A.* 45°21N 122°36W **78** E4
Oregon Dunes △
U.S.A. 43°40N 124°10W **76** E1
Orekhovo-Zuyevo
Russia 55°50N 38°55E **18** C6
Orel *Russia* 52°57N 36°3E **18** D6
Orem *U.S.A.* 40°19N 111°42W **76** F8
Ören *Turkey* 37°3N 27°57E **23** F12
Orenburg *Russia* 51°45N 55°6E **18** D10
Orense = Ourense *Spain* 42°19N 7°55W **21** A2
Orepuki *N.Z.* 46°19S 167°46E **59** G1
Orestes Pereyra *Mexico* 26°30N 105°39W **86** B3
Orestiada *Greece* 41°30N 26°33E **23** D12
Orfanos Kolpos *Greece* 40°33N 24°0E **23** D11
Orford Ness *U.K.* 52°5N 1°35E **13** E9
Organ Pipe Cactus △
U.S.A. 32°0N 112°52W **77** K7

Organos, Pta. de los
  Canary Is. 28°12N 17°17W 24 F2
Orgaz Spain 39°39N 3°53W 21 C4
Orgeyev = Orhei
  Moldova 47°24N 28°50E 17 E15
Orhaneli Turkey 39°54N 28°59E 23 E13
Orhangazi Turkey 40°29N 29°18E 23 D13
Orhei Moldova 47°24N 28°50E 17 E15
Orhon Gol → Mongolia 50°21N 106°0E 32 A5
Oriental, Cordillera
  Colombia 6°0N 73°0W 92 B4
Oriental, Grand Erg Algeria 30°0N 6°30E 50 B7
Orientale □
  Dem. Rep. of the Congo 2°20N 26°0E 54 B2
Oriente Argentina 38°44S 60°37W 94 D3
Orihuela Spain 38°7N 0°55W 21 C5
Orillia Canada 44°40N 79°24W 82 B5
Orinoco → Venezuela 9°15N 61°30W 92 B6
Orion U.S.A. 49°27N 97°18W 71 D6
Oriskany U.S.A. 43°10N 75°20W 83 C9
Orissa □ India 20°0N 84°0E 41 K14
Orissaare Estonia 58°34N 23°5E 9 G20
Oristano Italy 39°54N 8°36E 22 E3
Oristano, G. di Italy 39°50N 8°29E 22 E3
Orizaba Mexico 18°51N 97°6W 87 D5
Orizaba, Pico de Mexico 18°58N 97°15W 87 D5
Orkanger Norway 63°18N 9°52E 8 E13
Orkla → Norway 63°18N 9°51E 8 E13
Orkney S. Africa 26°58S 26°40E 56 D4
Orkney □ U.K. 59°2N 3°13W 11 B5
Orkney Is. U.K. 59°0N 3°0W 11 B6
Orland U.S.A. 39°45N 122°12W 78 F4
Orlando U.S.A. 28°32N 81°22W 85 G14
Orléanais France 48°0N 2°0E 20 C5
Orléans France 47°54N 1°52E 20 C4
Orleans U.S.A. 44°49N 72°12W 83 B12
Orléans, Î. d' Canada 46°54N 70°58W 73 C5
Ormara Pakistan 25°16N 64°33E 40 G4
Ormoc Phil. 11°0N 124°37E 37 B6
Ormond N.Z. 38°33S 177°56E 59 C6
Ormond Beach U.S.A. 29°17N 81°3W 85 G14
Ormskirk U.K. 53°35N 2°54W 12 D5
Ormstown Canada 45°8N 74°0W 83 A11
Örnsköldsvik Sweden 63°17N 18°40E 8 E18
Oro N. Korea 40°1N 127°27E 35 D14
Oro → Mexico 25°35N 105°2W 86 B3
Oro Grande U.S.A. 34°36N 117°20W 79 L9
Oro Valley U.S.A. 32°26N 110°58W 77 K8
Orocué Colombia 4°48N 71°20W 92 C4
Orofino U.S.A. 46°29N 116°15W 76 C5
Orohena, Mt. Tahiti 17°37S 149°28W 59 d
Orol Dengizi = Aral Sea
  Asia 44°30N 60°0E 28 E7
Oromocto Canada 45°54N 66°29W 73 C6
Orono Canada 43°59N 78°37W 82 C6
Orono U.S.A. 44°53N 68°40W 81 C19
Oronsay U.K. 56°1N 6°15W 11 E2
Oroqen Zizhiqi China 50°34N 123°43E 33 A7
Oroquieta Phil. 8°32N 123°44E 37 C6
Orosei Italy 40°23N 9°42E 22 D3
Orosháza Hungary 46°32N 20°42E 17 E11
Orotukan Russia 62°16N 151°42E 29 C16
Oroville Calif., U.S.A. 39°31N 121°33W 78 F5
Oroville Wash., U.S.A. 48°56N 119°26W 76 B4
Oroville, L. U.S.A. 39°33N 121°29W 78 F5
Ororoco Australia 32°43S 138°38E 63 E2
Orrville U.S.A. 40°50N 81°46W 82 F3
Orsha Belarus 54°30N 30°25E 18 D5
Orsk Russia 51°12N 58°34E 28 D6
Orşova Romania 44°41N 22°25E 17 F12
Ortaca Turkey 36°49N 28°45E 23 F13
Ortegal, C. Spain 43°43N 7°52W 21 A2
Orthez France 43°29N 0°48W 20 E3
Ortigueira Spain 43°40N 7°50W 21 A2
Orting U.S.A. 47°6N 122°12W 78 C4
Ortles Italy 46°31N 10°33E 20 C9
Ortón → Bolivia 10°50S 67°0W 92 F5
Ortonville U.S.A. 45°19N 96°27W 80 C5
Orūmīyeh Iran 37°40N 45°0E 44 B5
Orūmīyeh, Daryācheh-ye
  Iran 37°50N 45°30E 44 B5
Oruro Bolivia 18°0S 67°9W 92 G5
Orust Sweden 58°10N 11°40E 9 G14
Orvieto Italy 42°43N 12°7E 22 C5
Orwell N.Y., U.S.A. 43°35N 75°50W 83 C9
Orwell Ohio, U.S.A. 41°32N 80°52W 82 E4
Orwell → U.K. 51°59N 1°18E 13 F9
Orwigsburg U.S.A. 40°38N 76°6W 83 F8
Oryakhovo Bulgaria 43°40N 23°57E 23 C10
Oryol = Orel Russia 52°57N 36°3E 18 D6
Osa Russia 57°17N 55°26E 18 C10
Osa, Pen. de Costa Rica 8°0N 83°30W 88 E3
Osage U.S.A. 43°17N 92°49W 80 D7
Osage → U.S.A. 38°35N 91°57W 80 F8
Osage City U.S.A. 38°38N 95°50W 80 F6
Ōsaka Japan 34°42N 135°30E 31 G7
Osan S. Korea 37°11N 127°4E 35 F14
Osawatomie U.S.A. 38°31N 94°57W 80 F6
Osborne U.S.A. 39°26N 98°42W 80 F4
Osceola Ark., U.S.A. 35°42N 89°58W 85 D10
Osceola Iowa, U.S.A. 41°2N 93°46W 80 E7
Oscoda U.S.A. 44°26N 83°20W 82 B1
Ösel = Saaremaa Estonia 58°30N 22°30E 9 G20
Osgoode Canada 45°8N 75°36W 83 A9
Osh Kyrgyzstan 40°37N 72°49E 32 D2
Oshakati Namibia 17°45S 15°40E 53 H3
Oshawa Canada 43°50N 78°50W 82 C6
Oshigambo Namibia 17°45S 16°5E 56 B2
Oshkosh Nebr., U.S.A. 41°24N 102°21W 80 E2
Oshkosh Wis., U.S.A. 44°1N 88°33W 80 D9
Oshmyany = Ashmyany
  Belarus 54°26N 25°52E 17 A13
Oshnovīyeh Iran 37°2N 45°6E 44 B5
Oshogbo Nigeria 7°48N 4°37E 50 G6
Oshtorīnān Iran 34°1N 48°38E 45 C6
Oshwe
  Dem. Rep. of the Congo 3°25S 19°28E 52 E3

Osijek Croatia 45°34N 18°41E 23 B8
Osipovichi = Asipovichy
  Belarus 53°19N 28°33E 17 B15
Osiyan India 26°43N 72°55E 42 F5
Osizweni S. Africa 27°49S 30°7E 57 D5
Oskaloosa U.S.A. 41°18N 92°39W 80 E7
Oskarshamn Sweden 57°15N 16°27E 9 H17
Oskélanéo Canada 48°5N 75°15W 72 C4
Öskemen Kazakhstan 50°0N 82°36E 28 E9
Oslo Norway 59°54N 10°43E 9 G14
Oslofjorden Norway 59°20N 10°35E 9 G14
Osmanabad India 18°5N 76°10E 40 K10
Osmaniye Turkey 37°5N 36°10E 44 B3
Osnabrück Germany 52°17N 8°3E 16 B5
Osório Brazil 29°53S 50°17W 95 B5
Osorno Chile 40°25S 73°0W 96 E2
Osorno, Vol. Chile 41°0S 72°30W 96 D2
Osoyoos Canada 49°0N 119°30W 70 D5
Osøyro Norway 60°9N 5°30E 8 F11
Ospika → Canada 56°20N 124°0W 70 B4
Osprey Reef Australia 13°52S 146°36E 62 A4
Oss Neths. 51°46N 5°32E 15 C5
Ossa, Mt. Australia 41°52S 146°3E 63 G4
Ossa, Oros Greece 39°47N 22°42E 23 E10
Ossabaw I. U.S.A. 31°50N 81°5W 85 F14
Ossining U.S.A. 41°10N 73°55W 83 E11
Ossipee U.S.A. 43°41N 71°7W 83 C13
Ossokmanuan L. Canada 53°25N 65°0W 73 B7
Ossora Russia 59°20N 163°13E 29 D17
Ostend = Oostende
  Belgium 51°15N 2°54E 15 C2
Oster Ukraine 50°57N 30°53E 17 C16
Österbotten = Pohjanmaa
  Finland 62°58N 22°50E 8 E20
Osterburg U.S.A. 40°16N 78°31W 82 F6
Österdalälven Sweden 61°30N 13°45E 8 F15
Østerdalen Norway 61°40N 10°50E 8 F14
Östermyra = Seinäjoki
  Finland 62°40N 22°51E 8 E20
Österreich = Austria ■
  Europe 47°0N 14°0E 16 E8
Östersund Sweden 63°10N 14°38E 8 E16
Ostfriesische Inseln
  Germany 53°42N 7°0E 16 B4
Ostrava Czech Rep. 49°51N 18°18E 17 D10
Ostróda Poland 53°42N 19°58E 17 B10
Ostroh Ukraine 50°20N 26°30E 17 C14
Ostrołęka Poland 53°4N 21°32E 17 B11
Ostrów Mazowiecka
  Poland 52°50N 21°51E 17 B11
Ostrów Wielkopolski
  Poland 51°36N 17°44E 17 C9
Ostrowiec-Świętokrzyski
  Poland 50°55N 21°22E 17 C11
Ostuni Italy 40°44N 17°35E 23 D7
Ōsumi-Kaikyō Japan 30°55N 131°0E 31 J5
Ōsumi-Shotō Japan 30°30N 130°0E 31 J5
Osuna Spain 37°14N 5°8W 21 D3
Oswegatchie → U.S.A. 44°42N 75°30W 83 B9
Oswego U.S.A. 43°27N 76°31W 83 C8
Oswego → U.S.A. 43°27N 76°30W 83 C8
Oswestry U.K. 52°52N 3°3W 12 E4
Oświęcim Poland 50°2N 19°11E 17 C10
Otago □ N.Z. 45°15S 170°0E 59 F2
Otago Harbour N.Z. 45°47S 170°42E 59 F3
Otaheite B. Trin. & Tob. 10°15N 61°30W 93 K15
Ōtake Japan 34°12N 132°13E 31 G6
Ōtaki N.Z. 40°45S 175°10E 59 D5
Otaru Japan 43°10N 141°0E 30 C10
Otaru-Wan = Ishikari-Wan
  Japan 43°25N 141°1E 30 C10
Otavalo Ecuador 0°13N 78°20W 92 C3
Otavi Namibia 19°40S 17°24E 56 B2
Otchinjau Angola 16°30S 13°56E 56 B1
Otego U.S.A. 42°23N 75°10W 83 D9
Otelnuk, L. Canada 56°9N 68°12W 73 A6
Othello U.S.A. 46°50N 119°10W 76 C4
Otish, Mts. Canada 52°22N 70°30W 73 B5
Otjiwarongo Namibia 20°30S 16°33E 56 C2
Oto Tolu Group Tonga 20°21S 174°32W 59 c
Otoineppu Japan 44°44N 142°16E 30 B11
Otorohanga N.Z. 38°12S 175°14E 59 C5
Otoskwin → Canada 52°13N 88°6W 72 B2
Otra → Norway 58°9N 8°1E 9 G13
Otranto Italy 40°9N 18°28E 23 D8
Otranto, C. d' Italy 40°7N 18°30E 23 D8
Otranto, Str. of Italy 40°15N 18°40E 23 D8
Otse S. Africa 25°2S 25°45E 56 D4
Otsego L. U.S.A. 42°45N 74°53W 83 D10
Ōtsu Japan 35°0N 135°50E 31 G7
Ōtsuki Japan 35°36N 138°57E 31 G9
Ottawa = Outaouais →
  Canada 45°27N 74°8W 72 C5
Ottawa Canada 45°26N 75°42W 83 A9
Ottawa Ill., U.S.A. 41°21N 88°51W 80 E9
Ottawa Kans., U.S.A. 38°37N 95°16W 80 F6
Ottawa Is. Canada 59°35N 80°10W 69 F15
Otter Cr. → U.S.A. 44°13N 73°17W 83 B11
Otter Lake Canada 45°17N 79°56W 82 A5
Otterville Canada 42°55N 80°36W 82 D4
Ottery St. Mary U.K. 50°44N 3°17W 13 G4
Otto Beit Bridge
  Zimbabwe 15°59S 28°56E 57 F2
Ottosdal S. Africa 26°46S 25°59E 56 D4
Ottumwa U.S.A. 41°1N 92°25W 80 E7
Oturkpo Nigeria 7°16N 8°8E 50 G7
Otway, B. Chile 53°30S 74°0W 96 G2
Otway, C. Australia 38°52S 143°30E 63 F3
Otwock Poland 52°5N 21°20E 17 B11
Ou → Laos 20°4N 102°13E 38 B4
Ou Neua Laos 22°18N 101°48E 38 A3
Ou-Sammyaku Japan 39°20N 140°35E 30 E10
Ouachita → U.S.A. 31°38N 91°49W 84 F9
Ouachita, L. U.S.A. 34°34N 93°12W 84 D8
Ouachita Mts. U.S.A. 34°30N 94°30W 84 D7
Ouagadougou
  Burkina Faso 12°25N 1°30W 50 F5
Ouahigouya Burkina Faso 13°31N 2°25W 50 F5

Ouahran = Oran Algeria 35°45N 0°39W 50 A5
Ouallene Algeria 24°41N 1°11E 50 D6
Ouarâne Mauritania 21°0N 10°30W 50 D3
Ouargla Algeria 31°59N 5°16E 50 B7
Ouarra → C.A.R. 5°5N 24°26E 52 C4
Ouarzazate Morocco 30°55N 6°50W 50 B4
Oubangi →
  Dem. Rep. of the Congo 0°30S 17°50E 52 E3
Ouddorp Neths. 51°50N 3°57E 15 C3
Oude Rijn → Neths. 52°12N 4°24E 15 B4
Oudenaarde Belgium 50°50N 3°37E 15 D3
Oudtshoorn S. Africa 33°35S 22°14E 56 E3
Ouessa = Ouessant, Î. d' France 48°28N 5°6W 20 B1
Ouesso Congo 1°37N 16°5E 52 D3
Ouest, Pte. de l' Canada 49°52N 64°40W 73 C7
Ouezzane Morocco 34°51N 5°35W 50 B4
Oughter, L. Ireland 54°1N 7°28W 10 B4
Oughterard Ireland 53°26N 9°18W 10 C2
Ouidah Benin 6°25N 2°0E 50 G6
Oujda Morocco 34°41N 1°55W 50 B5
Oulainen Finland 64°17N 24°47E 8 D21
Oulu Finland 65°1N 25°29E 8 D21
Oulujärvi Finland 64°25N 27°15E 8 D22
Oulujoki → Finland 65°1N 25°30E 8 D21
Oum Chalouba Chad 15°48N 20°46E 51 E10
Oum Hadjer Chad 13°18N 19°41E 51 F9
Ounasjoki → Finland 66°31N 25°40E 8 C21
Ounguati Namibia 22°0S 15°46E 56 C2
Ounianga Kébir Chad 19°4N 20°29E 51 E10
Our → Lux. 49°55N 6°5E 15 E6
Ouray U.S.A. 38°1N 107°40W 77 G10
Ourense Spain 42°19N 7°55W 21 A2
Ouricuri Brazil 7°53S 40°5W 93 E10
Ourinhos Brazil 23°0S 49°54W 95 A6
Ouro Fino Brazil 22°16S 46°25W 95 A6
Ouro Prêto Brazil 20°20S 43°30W 95 A7
Ourthe → Belgium 50°29N 5°35E 15 D5
Ouse → E. Sussex, U.K. 50°47N 0°4E 13 G8
Ouse → N. Yorks., U.K. 53°44N 0°55W 12 D7
Outaouais → Canada 45°27N 74°8W 72 C5
Outardes → Canada 49°24N 69°30W 73 C6
Outer Hebrides U.K. 57°30N 7°40W 11 D1
Outjo Namibia 20°5S 16°7E 56 C2
Outlook Canada 51°30N 107°0W 71 C7
Outokumpu Finland 62°43N 29°1E 8 E23
Ouyen Australia 35°1S 142°22E 63 F3
Ovalau Fiji 17°40S 178°48E 59 a
Ovalle Chile 30°33S 71°18W 94 C1
Ovamboland Namibia 18°30S 16°0E 56 B2
Overflakkee Neths. 51°44N 4°10E 15 C4
Overijssel □ Neths. 52°25N 6°35E 15 B6
Overland Park U.S.A. 38°58N 94°40W 80 F6
Overlander Roadhouse
  Australia 26°19S 114°28E 61 E1
Overton U.S.A. 36°33N 114°27W 79 J12
Övertorneå Sweden 66°23N 23°38E 8 C20
Ovid U.S.A. 42°41N 76°49W 83 D8
Oviedo Spain 43°25N 5°50W 21 A3
Ovišrags Latvia 57°33N 21°44E 9 H19
Övoot Mongolia 45°21N 113°45E 34 B7
Övör Hangay □
  Mongolia 45°0N 102°30E 34 B2
Øvre Årdal Norway 61°19N 7°48E 8 F12
Ovruch Ukraine 51°25N 28°45E 17 C15
Owaka N.Z. 46°27S 169°40E 59 G2
Owambo = Ovamboland
  Namibia 18°30S 16°0E 56 B2
Owasco L. U.S.A. 42°50N 76°31W 83 D8
Owase Japan 34°7N 136°12E 31 G8
Owatonna U.S.A. 44°5N 93°14W 80 C7
Owbeh Afghan. 34°28N 63°10E 40 B3
Owego U.S.A. 42°6N 76°16W 83 D8
Owen Falls Dam = Nalubaale
  Dam Uganda 0°30N 33°5E 54 B3
Owen Sound Canada 44°35N 80°55W 82 B4
Owen Stanley Ra.
  Papua N. G. 8°30S 147°0E 58 B7
Oweniny → Ireland 54°8N 9°34W 10 B2
Owens → U.S.A. 36°32N 117°59W 78 J9
Owens L. U.S.A. 36°26N 117°57W 79 J9
Owensboro U.S.A. 37°46N 87°7W 80 G10
Owl → Canada 57°51N 92°44W 71 B10
Owo Nigeria 7°10N 5°39E 50 G7
Owosso U.S.A. 43°0N 84°10W 81 D11
Owyhee U.S.A. 41°57N 116°6W 76 F5
Owyhee → U.S.A. 43°49N 117°2W 76 E5
Owyhee, L. U.S.A. 43°38N 117°14W 76 E5
Ox Mts. = Slieve Gamph
  Ireland 54°6N 9°0W 10 B3
Öxarfjörður Iceland 66°15N 16°45W 8 C5
Oxbow Canada 49°14N 102°10W 71 D8
Oxelösund Sweden 58°43N 17°5E 9 G17
Oxford N.Z. 43°18S 172°11E 59 E4
Oxford U.K. 51°46N 1°15W 13 F6
Oxford Mass., U.S.A. 42°7N 71°52W 83 D13
Oxford Miss., U.S.A. 34°22N 89°31W 85 D10
Oxford N.C., U.S.A. 36°19N 78°35W 85 G15
Oxford N.Y., U.S.A. 42°27N 75°36W 83 D9
Oxford Ohio, U.S.A. 39°31N 84°45W 81 F11
Oxford L. Canada 54°51N 95°37W 71 C9
Oxfordshire □ U.K. 51°48N 1°16W 13 F6
Oxnard U.S.A. 34°12N 119°11W 79 L7
Oxus = Amudarya →
  Uzbekistan 43°58N 59°34E 28 E6
Oya Malaysia 2°55N 111°55E 36 D4
Oyama Japan 36°18N 139°48E 31 F9
Oyem Gabon 1°34N 11°31E 52 D2
Oyen Canada 51°22N 110°28W 71 C6
Oykel → U.K. 57°56N 4°26W 11 D4
Oymyakon Russia 63°25N 142°44E 29 C15
Oyo Nigeria 7°46N 3°56E 50 G6
Oyster Bay U.S.A. 40°52N 73°32W 83 F11
Ōyūbari Japan 43°1N 142°5E 30 C11
Ozamiz Phil. 8°15N 123°50E 37 C6
Ozark Ala., U.S.A. 31°28N 85°39W 85 F12
Ozark Ark., U.S.A. 35°29N 93°50W 84 D8
Ozark Mo., U.S.A. 37°1N 93°12W 80 G7
Ozark Plateau U.S.A. 37°20N 91°40W 80 G8

Ozarks, L. of the U.S.A. 38°12N 92°38W 80 F7
Özd Hungary 48°14N 20°15E 17 D11
Ozernovskiy Russia 51°30N 156°31E 29 D16
Ozette, L. U.S.A. 48°6N 124°38W 78 B2
Ozieri Italy 40°35N 9°0E 22 D3
Ozona U.S.A. 30°43N 101°12W 84 F4
Ozuluama Mexico 21°40N 97°51W 87 C5

P

Pa-an Burma 16°51N 97°40E 41 L20
Pa Mong Dam Thailand 18°0N 102°22E 38 D4
Pa Sak → Thailand 15°30N 101°0E 38 E3
Paamiut Greenland 62°0N 49°43W 4 C5
Paarl S. Africa 33°45S 18°56E 56 E2
Pab Hills Pakistan 26°30N 66°45E 42 F2
Pabbay U.K. 57°46N 7°14W 11 D1
Pabianice Poland 51°40N 19°20E 17 C10
Pabna Bangla. 24°1N 89°18E 41 G16
Pabo Uganda 3°1N 32°10E 54 B3
Pacaja → Brazil 1°56S 50°50W 93 D8
Pacaraima, Sa. S. Amer. 4°0N 62°30W 92 C6
Pacasmayo Peru 7°20S 79°35W 92 E3
Pachitea → Peru 8°46S 74°33W 92 E4
Pachmarhi India 22°28N 78°26E 43 H8
Pachnes Greece 35°16N 24°4E 25 D6
Pachpadra India 25°58N 72°10E 42 G5
Pachuca Mexico 20°7N 98°44W 87 C5
Pacific Antarctic Ridge
  Pac. Oc. 43°0S 115°0W 5 B13
Pacific Grove U.S.A. 36°38N 121°56W 78 J5
Pacific Ocean 10°0N 140°0W 65 G14
Pacific Rim △ Canada 48°40N 124°45W 78 B2
Pacifica U.S.A. 37°37N 122°27W 78 H4
Pacitan Indonesia 8°12S 111°7E 37 H14
Packwood U.S.A. 46°36N 121°40W 78 D5
Padaido, Kepulauan
  Indonesia 1°15S 136°30E 37 E9
Padang Riau, Indonesia 1°30N 102°30E 39 M4
Padang Sumatera Barat,
  Indonesia 1°0S 100°20E 36 E2
Padang Endau Malaysia 2°40N 103°38E 39 L4
Padangpanjang
  Indonesia 0°40S 100°20E 36 E2
Padangsidempuan
  Indonesia 1°30N 99°15E 36 D1
Paddle Prairie Canada 57°57N 117°29W 70 B5
Paderborn Germany 51°42N 8°45E 16 C5
Padma India 24°12N 85°22E 43 G11
Pádova Italy 45°25N 11°53E 22 B4
Padra India 22°15N 73°7E 42 H5
Padrauna India 26°54N 83°59E 43 F10
Padre I. U.S.A. 27°10N 97°25W 84 H6
Padre Island △ U.S.A. 27°0N 97°25W 84 H6
Padstow U.K. 50°33N 4°58W 13 G3
Padua = Pádova Italy 45°25N 11°53E 22 B4
Paducah Ky., U.S.A. 37°5N 88°37W 80 G9
Paducah Tex., U.S.A. 34°1N 100°18W 84 D4
Paea Tahiti 17°41S 149°35W 59 d
Paeroa N.Z. 37°23S 175°41E 59 B5
Pafúri Mozam. 22°28S 31°17E 57 C5
Pag Croatia 44°25N 15°3E 16 F8
Pagadian Phil. 7°55N 123°30E 37 C6
Pagai Selatan, Pulau
  Indonesia 3°0S 100°15E 36 E2
Pagai Utara, Pulau
  Indonesia 2°35S 100°0E 36 E2
Pagalu = Annobón Atl. Oc. 1°25S 5°36E 49 G4
Pagara India 24°22N 80°1E 43 G9
Pagastikos Kolpos
  Greece 39°15N 23°0E 23 E10
Pagatan Indonesia 3°33S 115°59E 36 E5
Page U.S.A. 36°57N 111°27W 77 H8
Paget, Mt. S. Georgia 54°26S 36°31W 96 G9
Pago Pago Amer. Samoa 14°16S 170°43W 59 b
Pagosa Springs U.S.A. 37°16N 107°1W 77 H10
Pagwa River Canada 50°2N 85°14W 72 B2
Pāhala U.S.A. 19°12N 155°29W 75 M8
Pahang → Malaysia 3°30N 103°9E 39 L4
Pahiatua N.Z. 40°27S 175°50E 59 D5
Pahokee U.S.A. 26°50N 80°40W 85 H14
Pahrump U.S.A. 36°12N 115°59W 79 J11
Pahute Mesa U.S.A. 37°20N 116°45W 78 H10
Pai Thailand 19°19N 98°27E 38 C2
Paicines U.S.A. 36°44N 121°17W 78 J5
Paide Estonia 58°53N 25°33E 9 G21
Paignton U.K. 50°26N 3°35W 13 G4
Päijänne Finland 61°30N 25°30E 8 F21
Pailani India 25°45N 80°26E 43 G9
Pailin Cambodia 12°46N 102°36E 38 F4
Painan Indonesia 1°21S 100°34E 36 E2
Painesville U.S.A. 41°43N 81°15W 82 E3
Paint Hills = Wemindji
  Canada 53°0N 78°49W 72 B4
Paint L. Canada 55°28N 97°57W 71 B9
Painted Desert U.S.A. 36°0N 111°0W 77 H8
Paintsville U.S.A. 37°49N 82°48W 81 G12
País Vasco □ Spain 42°50N 2°45W 21 A4
Paisley Canada 44°18N 81°16W 82 B3
Paisley U.K. 55°50N 4°25W 11 F4
Paisley U.S.A. 42°42N 120°32W 76 E3
Paita Peru 5°11S 81°9W 92 E2
Pajares, Puerto de Spain 43°0N 5°58W 21 A3
Pak Lay Laos 18°15N 101°27E 38 C3
Pak Phanang Thailand 8°21N 100°12E 39 H3
Pak Sane Laos 18°22N 103°39E 38 C4
Pak Song Laos 15°11N 106°14E 38 E6
Pak Suong Laos 19°58N 102°18E 38 C4
Pak Tam Chung China 22°24N 114°19E 33 G11
Pakaur India 24°38N 87°51E 43 G12
Pakch'ŏn N. Korea 39°44N 125°35E 35 E13
Pakenham Canada 45°18N 76°18W 83 A8
Pakhuis S. Africa 32°9S 19°5E 56 E2
Pakistan ■ Asia 30°0N 70°0E 42 E4
Pakkading Laos 18°19N 103°59E 38 C4
Pakokku Burma 21°20N 95°0E 41 J19
Pakowki L. Canada 49°20N 111°0W 71 D6
Pakpattan Pakistan 30°25N 73°27E 42 D5

Paktīā □ Afghan. 33°30N 69°15E 40 C6
Paktīkā □ Afghan. 32°30N 69°0E 40 C6
Pakwach Uganda 2°28N 31°27E 54 B3
Pakxe Laos 15°5N 105°52E 38 E5
Pal Lahara India 21°27N 85°11E 43 J11
Pala Chad 9°25N 15°5E 51 G9
Pala Dem. Rep. of the Congo 6°45S 29°30E 54 D2
Pala U.S.A. 33°22N 117°5W 79 M9
Palabek Uganda 3°22N 32°33E 54 B3
Palacios U.S.A. 28°42N 96°13W 84 G6
Palagruža Croatia 42°24N 16°15E 22 C7
Palakkad = Palghat
  India 10°46N 76°42E 40 P10
Palam India 19°0N 77°0E 40 K10
Palampur India 32°10N 76°30E 42 C7
Palana Australia 39°45S 147°55E 63 F4
Palana Russia 59°10N 159°59E 29 D16
Palanan Phil. 17°8N 122°29E 37 A6
Palanan Pt. Phil. 17°17N 122°30E 37 A6
Palandri Pakistan 33°42N 73°40E 43 C5
Palanga Lithuania 55°58N 21°3E 9 J19
Palangkaraya Indonesia 2°16S 113°56E 36 E4
Palani Hills India 10°14N 77°33E 40 P10
Palanpur India 24°10N 72°25E 42 G5
Palapye Botswana 22°30S 27°7E 56 C4
Palas India 35°4N 73°14E 43 B5
Palasponga India 21°47N 85°34E 43 J11
Palatka Russia 60°6N 150°54E 29 C16
Palatka U.S.A. 29°39N 81°38W 85 G14
Palau ■ Palau 7°30N 134°30E 58 A6
Palauk Burma 13°10N 98°40E 38 F2
Palawan Phil. 9°30N 118°30E 36 C5
Palayankottai India 8°45N 77°45E 40 Q10
Paldiski Estonia 59°23N 24°9E 9 G21
Palekastro Greece 35°12N 26°15E 25 D8
Paleleh Indonesia 1°10N 121°50E 37 D6
Palembang Indonesia 3°0S 104°50E 36 E2
Palencia Spain 42°1N 4°34W 21 A3
Palenque Mexico 17°29N 92°1W 87 D6
Paleochora Greece 35°16N 23°39E 25 D5
Paleokastritsa Greece 39°40N 19°41E 25 A3
Paleometokho Cyprus 35°7N 33°11E 25 D12
Palermo Italy 38°7N 13°22E 22 E5
Palermo U.S.A. 39°26N 121°33W 76 G3
Palestina Chile 23°50S 69°47W 96 A3
Palestine U.S.A. 31°46N 95°38W 84 F7
Paletwa Burma 21°10N 92°50E 41 J18
Palghat India 10°46N 76°42E 40 P10
Palgrave, Mt. Australia 23°22S 115°58E 60 D2
Pali India 25°50N 73°20E 42 G5
Palikir Micronesia 6°55N 158°9E 64 G7
Paliouri, Akra Greece 39°57N 23°45E 23 E10
Palisades Res. U.S.A. 43°20N 111°12W 76 E8
Paliseul Belgium 49°54N 5°8E 15 E5
Palitana India 21°32N 71°49E 42 J4
Palizada Mexico 18°15N 92°5W 87 D6
Palk Bay Asia 9°30N 79°15E 40 Q11
Palk Strait Asia 10°0N 79°45E 40 Q11
Palkānah Iraq 35°49N 44°26E 44 C5
Palkot India 22°53N 84°39E 43 H11
Pallanza = Verbánia Italy 45°56N 8°33E 20 D8
Pallarenda Australia 19°12S 146°46E 62 B4
Pallinup → Australia 34°27S 118°50E 61 F2
Pallisa Uganda 1°12N 33°43E 54 B3
Pallu India 28°59N 74°14E 42 E6
Palm Bay U.S.A. 28°2N 80°35W 85 G14
Palm Beach U.S.A. 26°43N 80°2W 85 H14
Palm Coast U.S.A. 29°35N 81°12W 85 G14
Palm Desert U.S.A. 33°43N 116°22W 79 M10
Palm-Grove △ Australia 24°57S 149°21E 62 C4
Palm Is. Australia 18°40S 146°35E 62 B4
Palm Springs U.S.A. 33°50N 116°33W 79 M10
Palma Mozam. 10°46S 40°29E 55 E5
Palma, B. de Spain 39°30N 2°39E 24 B9
Palma de Mallorca Spain 39°35N 2°39E 24 B9
Palma Nova = Palmanova
  Spain 39°32N 2°34E 24 B9
Palma Soriano Cuba 20°15N 76°0W 88 B4
Palmanova Spain 39°32N 2°34E 24 B9
Palmares Brazil 8°41S 35°28W 93 E11
Palmas Brazil 26°29S 52°0W 95 B5
Palmas, C. Liberia 4°27N 7°46W 50 H4
Pálmas, G. di Italy 39°0N 8°30E 22 E3
Palmdale U.S.A. 34°35N 118°7W 79 L8
Palmeira das Missões
  Brazil 27°55S 53°17W 95 B5
Palmeira dos Índios
  Brazil 9°25S 36°37W 93 E11
Palmer Antarctica 64°35S 65°0W 5 C17
Palmer → Australia 16°0S 142°26E 62 B3
Palmer Arch. Antarctica 64°35S 65°0W 5 C17
Palmer Lake U.S.A. 39°7N 104°55W 76 G11
Palmer Land Antarctica 73°0S 63°0W 5 D18
Palmerston Australia 12°31S 130°59E 60 B5
Palmerston Canada 43°50N 80°51W 82 C4
Palmerston N.Z. 45°29S 170°43E 59 F3
Palmerston North N.Z. 40°21S 175°39E 59 D5
Palmerton U.S.A. 40°48N 75°37W 83 F9
Palmetto U.S.A. 27°31N 82°34W 85 H13
Palmira Argentina 32°59S 68°34W 94 C2
Palmira Colombia 3°32N 76°16W 92 C3
Palmyra = Tudmur
  Syria 34°36N 38°15E 44 C3
Palmyra Mo., U.S.A. 39°48N 91°32W 80 F8
Palmyra N.J., U.S.A. 40°0N 75°1W 83 F9
Palmyra N.Y., U.S.A. 43°5N 77°18W 82 C7
Palmyra Pa., U.S.A. 40°18N 76°36W 83 F8
Palmyra Is. Pac. Oc. 5°52N 162°5W 65 G11
Palo Alto U.S.A. 37°27N 122°10W 78 H4
Palo Seco Trin. & Tob. 10°4N 61°36W 93 K15
Palo Verde U.S.A. 33°26N 114°44W 79 M12
Palo Verde △ Costa Rica 10°21N 85°21W 88 D2
Palomar Mt. U.S.A. 33°23N 116°50W 79 M10
Palopo Indonesia 3°0S 120°16E 37 E6
Palos, C. de Spain 37°38N 0°40W 21 D5

Palos Verdes, Pt.
  U.S.A.   33°46N 118°25W 79 M8
Palos Verdes Estates
  U.S.A.   33°48N 118°23W 79 M8
Palu Indonesia   1°0S 119°52E 37 E5
Palu Turkey   38°45N 40°0E 44 B3
Paluma Ra. Australia   19°9S 146°22E 62 B4
Palwal India   28°8N 77°19E 42 E7
Pamanukan Indonesia   6°16S 107°49E 37 G12
Pamekasan Indonesia   7°10S 113°28E 37 G15
Pamenang Indonesia   8°24S 116°6E 37 J19
Pamiers France   43°7N 1°39E 20 E4
Pamir Tajikistan   37°40N 73°0E 28 F8
Pamlico → U.S.A.   35°20N 76°28W 85 D16
Pamlico Sd. U.S.A.   35°20N 76°0W 85 D17
Pampa U.S.A.   35°32N 100°58W 84 D4
Pampa de las Salinas
  Argentina   32°1S 66°58W 94 C2
Pampanua Indonesia   4°16S 120°8E 37 E6
Pampas Argentina   35°0S 63°0W 94 D3
Pampas Peru   12°20S 74°50W 92 F4
Pamplona Colombia   7°23N 72°39W 92 B4
Pamplona-Iruña Spain   42°48N 1°38W 21 A5
Pampoenpoort S. Africa   31°3S 22°40E 56 E3
Pan de Azúcar Chile   24°5S 68°10W 94 A2
Pan de Azúcar △ Chile   26°0S 70°40W 94 B1
Pana U.S.A.   39°23N 89°5W 80 F9
Panaca U.S.A.   37°47N 114°23W 79 H6
Panaitan Indonesia   6°36S 105°12E 37 G11
Panaji India   15°25N 73°50E 40 M8
Panamá Panama   9°0N 79°25W 88 E4
Panama ■ Cent. Amer.   8°48N 79°55W 88 E4
Panamá, G. de Panama   8°4N 79°20W 88 E4
Panama, Isthmus of
  Cent. Amer.   9°0N 79°0W 66 J12
Panama Basin Pac. Oc.   5°0N 83°30W 65 C19
Panama Canal Panama   9°10N 79°37W 88 E4
Panama City U.S.A.   30°10N 85°40W 85 F12
Panamint Range
  U.S.A.   36°20N 117°20W 79 J9
Panamint Springs
  U.S.A.   36°20N 117°28W 79 J9
Panão Peru   9°55S 75°55W 92 E3
Panare Thailand   6°51N 101°30E 39 J3
Panay Phil.   11°10N 122°30E 37 B6
Panay G. Phil.   11°0N 122°30E 37 B6
Panayarvi → Russia   66°16N 30°10E 8 C5
Pančevo Serbia   44°52N 20°41E 23 B9
Panda Mozam.   24°2S 34°45E 57 C5
Pandan Malaysia   1°32N 103°46E 39 d
Pandan Phil.   11°45N 122°10E 37 B6
Pandan, Selat Singapore   1°15N 103°44E 39 d
Pandan Tampoi = Tampoi
  Malaysia   1°30N 103°39E 39 d
Pandegelang Indonesia   6°25S 106°5E 37 G12
Pandhana India   21°42N 76°13E 42 J7
Pandharpur India   17°41N 75°20E 40 L9
Pando Uruguay   34°44S 56°0W 95 C4
Pando, L. = Hope, L.
  Australia   28°24S 139°18E 63 D2
Pandokratoras Greece   39°45N 19°50E 25 A3
Pandora Costa Rica   9°43N 83°3W 88 E3
Panevėžys Lithuania   55°42N 24°25E 9 J21
Pang-Long Burma   23°11N 98°45E 41 H21
Pang Sida △ Thailand   14°5N 102°17E 38 E4
Pang-Yang Burma   22°7N 98°48E 41 H21
Panga
  Dem. Rep. of the Congo   1°52N 26°18E 54 B2
Pangalanes, Canal des =
  Ampangalana, Lakandranon'
  Madag.   22°48S 47°50E 57 C8
Pangani Tanzania   5°25S 38°58E 54 D4
Pangani → Tanzania   5°26S 38°58E 54 D4
Pangfou = Bengbu
  China   32°58N 117°20E 35 H9
Pangil
  Dem. Rep. of the Congo   3°10S 26°35E 54 C2
Pangkah, Tanjung
  Indonesia   6°51S 112°33E 37 G15
Pangkajene Indonesia   4°46S 119°34E 37 E5
Pangkalanbrandan
  Indonesia   4°1N 98°20E 36 D1
Pangkalanbuun
  Indonesia   2°41S 111°37E 36 E4
Pangkalpinang Indonesia   2°0S 106°0E 36 E3
Pangkor, P. Malaysia   4°13N 100°34E 39 K3
Pangniqtuuq = Pangnirtung
  Canada   66°8N 65°43W 69 D18
Pangnirtung Canada   66°8N 65°43W 69 D18
Pangody Russia   65°52N 74°27E 28 C8
Pangong Tso = Bangong Co
  China   35°0N 78°43E 43 C8
Panguitch U.S.A.   37°50N 112°26W 77 H7
Panguitaran Group Phil.   6°18N 120°34E 37 C6
Panhandle U.S.A.   35°21N 101°23W 84 D4
Pani Hills India   22°29N 73°4E 42 H5
Pania-Mutombo
  Dem. Rep. of the Congo   5°11S 23°51E 54 D1
Panikota I. India   20°46N 71°21E 42 J4
Panipat India   29°25N 77°2E 42 E7
Panjal Range = Pir Panjal Range
  India   32°30N 76°50E 42 C7
Panjgur Pakistan   26°58N 64°5E 40 F4
Panjim = Panaji India   15°25N 73°50E 40 M8
Panjin China   41°3N 122°2E 35 D12
Panjnad → Pakistan   28°57N 70°30E 42 E4
Panjnad Barrage
  Pakistan   29°22N 71°15E 42 E4
Panjwai Afghan.   31°26N 65°27E 42 D1
Panmunjŏm N. Korea   37°59N 126°38E 35 F14
Panna India   24°40N 80°15E 43 G9
Panna △ India   24°40N 80°0E 43 G8
Panna Hills India   24°40N 81°15E 43 G9
Pannawonica Australia   21°39S 116°19E 60 D2
Panngga, Tanjung
  Indonesia   8°4S 116°2E 37 K19
Pano Akil Pakistan   27°51N 69°7E 42 F3
Pano Lefkara Cyprus   34°53N 33°20E 25 E12

Pano Panayia Cyprus   34°55N 32°38E 25 E11
Panorama Brazil   21°21S 51°51W 95 A5
Panormos Greece   35°25N 24°41E 26 D6
Pansemal India   21°39N 74°42E 42 J6
Panshan = Panjin China   41°3N 122°2E 35 D12
Panshi China   42°58N 126°5E 35 C14
Pantanal Brazil   17°30S 57°40W 92 H7
Pantanos de Centla △
  Mexico   18°25N 92°25W 87 D6
Pantar Indonesia   8°28S 124°10E 37 F6
Pante Macassar E. Timor   9°30S 123°58E 37 F6
Pantelleria Italy   36°50N 11°57E 22 F4
Pánuco Mexico   22°3N 98°10W 87 C5
Panzhihua China   26°33N 101°44E 32 D5
Paola Malta   35°52N 14°30E 25 D2
Paola U.S.A.   38°35N 94°53W 80 F6
Paonia U.S.A.   38°52N 107°36W 76 G10
Paopao Moorea   17°30S 149°49W 59 d
Paoting = Baoding
  China   38°50N 115°28E 34 E8
Paot'ou = Baotou China   40°32N 110°2E 34 D6
Paoua C.A.R.   7°9N 16°20E 52 C3
Pápa Hungary   47°22N 17°30E 17 E9
Papa Stour U.K.   60°20N 1°42W 11 A7
Papa Westray U.K.   59°20N 2°55W 11 B6
Papagayo → Mexico   16°46N 99°43W 87 D5
Papagayo, G. de
  Costa Rica   10°30N 85°50W 88 D2
Papakura N.Z.   37°4S 174°59E 59 B5
Papantla Mexico   20°27N 97°19W 87 C5
Papar Malaysia   5°45N 116°0E 36 C5
Papara Tahiti   17°43S 149°31W 59 d
Paparoa △ N.Z.   42°7S 171°26E 59 E3
Papeete Tahiti   17°32S 149°34W 59 d
Papenoo Tahiti   17°30S 149°25W 59 d
Papenoo → Tahiti   17°30S 149°25W 59 d
Papetoai Moorea   17°29S 149°52W 59 d
Paphos Cyprus   34°46N 32°25E 25 E11
Paposo Chile   25°0S 70°30W 94 B1
Papoutsa Cyprus   34°54N 33°4E 25 E12
Papua □ Indonesia   4°0S 137°0E 37 E9
Papua, G. of Papua N. G.   9°0S 144°50E 58 B7
Papua New Guinea ■
  Oceania   8°0S 145°0E 58 B7
Papudo Chile   32°29S 71°27W 94 C1
Papun Burma   18°2N 97°30E 41 K20
Papunya Australia   23°15S 131°54E 60 D5
Pará = Belém Brazil   1°20S 48°30W 93 D9
Pará □ Brazil   3°20S 52°0W 93 D8
Paraburdoo Australia   23°14S 117°32E 60 D2
Paracatu Brazil   17°10S 46°50W 93 G9
Paracel Is. S. China Sea   15°50N 112°0E 36 A4
Parachilna Australia   31°10S 138°21E 63 E2
Parachinar Pakistan   33°55N 70°5E 42 C4
Paradip India   20°15N 86°35E 41 J15
Paradise Calif., U.S.A.   39°46N 121°37W 78 F5
Paradise Nev., U.S.A.   36°5N 115°8W 79 J11
Paradise → Canada   53°27N 57°19W 73 B8
Paradise Hill Canada   53°32N 109°28W 71 C7
Paradise River Canada   53°27N 57°17W 73 B8
Paradise Valley U.S.A.   41°30N 117°32W 76 F5
Paradisi Greece   36°18N 28°7E 25 C10
Parado Indonesia   8°42S 118°30E 37 F5
Paragould U.S.A.   36°3N 90°29W 85 C9
Paragua → Venezuela   6°55N 62°55W 92 B6
Paraguaçú → Brazil   12°45S 38°54W 93 F11
Paraguaçu Paulista
  Brazil   22°22S 50°35W 95 A5
Paraguaná, Pen. de
  Venezuela   12°0N 70°0W 92 A5
Paraguarí Paraguay   25°36S 57°0W 94 B4
Paraguarí □ Paraguay   26°0S 57°10W 94 B4
Paraguay ■ S. Amer.   23°0S 57°0W 94 A4
Paraguay → Paraguay   27°18S 58°38W 94 B4
Paraíba = João Pessoa
  Brazil   7°10S 34°52W 93 E12
Paraíba □ Brazil   7°0S 36°0W 93 E11
Paraíba do Sul → Brazil   21°37S 41°3W 95 A7
Parainen Finland   60°18N 22°18E 9 F20
Paraíso Mexico   18°24N 93°14W 87 D6
Parak Iran   27°38N 52°25E 45 E7
Parakou Benin   9°25N 2°40E 50 G6
Paralimni Cyprus   35°2N 33°58E 25 D12
Paramaribo Suriname   5°50N 55°10W 93 B7
Páramos del Batallón y La
  Negra △ Venezuela   8°2N 71°55W 89 E5
Paramushir, Ostrov
  Russia   50°24N 156°0E 29 D16
Paran → Israel   30°20N 35°10E 46 E4
Paraná Argentina   31°45S 60°30W 94 C3
Paraná □ Brazil   12°30S 47°48W 93 F9
Paraná □ Brazil   24°30S 51°0W 95 A5
Paraná → Argentina   33°43S 59°15W 94 C4
Paranaguá Brazil   25°30S 48°30W 95 B6
Paranaíba Brazil   19°40S 51°11W 93 G8
Paranaíba → Brazil   20°6S 51°4W 93 H8
Paranapanema → Brazil   22°40S 53°9W 95 A5
Paranapiacaba, Serra do
  Brazil   24°31S 48°35W 95 A6
Paranavaí Brazil   23°4S 52°56W 95 A5
Paranga Maguindanao,
  Phil.   7°23N 124°16E 37 C6
Parang Sulu, Phil.   5°55N 120°54E 37 C6
Parângul Mare, Vf.
  Romania   45°20N 23°37E 17 F12
Paraparaumu N.Z.   40°57S 175°3E 59 D5
Parbati → Mad. P., India   25°50N 76°30E 42 G7
Parbati → Raj., India   26°54N 77°53E 42 F7
Parbhani India   19°8N 76°52E 40 K10
Parchim Germany   53°26N 11°52E 16 B6
Pardes Hanna-Karkur
  Israel   32°28N 34°57E 46 C3
Pardo → Bahia, Brazil   15°40S 39°0W 93 G11
Pardo → Mato Grosso,
  Brazil   21°46S 52°9W 95 A5
Pardoo Roadhouse
  Australia   20°6S 119°3E 60 D2
Pardubice Czech Rep.   50°3N 15°45E 16 C8
Pare Indonesia   7°43S 112°12E 37 G15

Pare Mts. Tanzania   4°0S 37°45E 54 C4
Parecis, Serra dos Brazil   13°0S 60°0W 92 F7
Paren Russia   62°30N 163°15E 29 C17
Parent Canada   47°55N 74°35W 72 C5
Parent, L. Canada   48°31N 77°1W 72 C4
Parepare Indonesia   4°0S 119°40E 37 E5
Parga Greece   39°15N 20°29E 23 E9
Pargas = Parainen
  Finland   60°18N 22°18E 9 F20
Parham Canada   44°39N 76°43W 83 B8
Paria → Canada   36°52N 111°36W 77 H8
Paria, Pta. do Madeira   32°49N 17°17W 24 D2
Paria, G. de Venezuela   10°20N 62°0W 93 K14
Pariaguán Venezuela   8°51N 64°34W 92 B6
Paricutín, Cerro
  Mexico   19°28N 102°15W 86 D4
Parigi Indonesia   0°50S 120°5E 37 E6
Parika Guyana   6°50N 58°20W 92 B7
Parikkala Finland   61°33N 29°31E 8 F23
Parima, Serra Brazil   2°30N 64°0W 92 C6
Parinari Peru   4°35S 74°25W 92 D4
Pariñas, Pta. Peru   4°30S 82°0W 90 D2
Parintins Brazil   2°40S 56°50W 93 D7
Pariparit Kyun Burma   14°53N 93°41E 41 M18
Paris Canada   43°12N 80°25W 82 D4
Paris France   48°53N 2°20E 20 B5
Paris Idaho, U.S.A.   42°14N 111°24W 76 E8
Paris Ky., U.S.A.   38°13N 84°15W 81 F11
Paris Tenn., U.S.A.   36°18N 88°19W 85 C10
Paris Tex., U.S.A.   33°40N 95°33W 84 E7
Parish U.S.A.   43°25N 76°8W 83 C8
Parishville U.S.A.   44°38N 74°49W 83 B10
Pariti Indonesia   10°1S 123°45E 60 B3
Park U.S.A.   48°45N 122°18W 78 B4
Park City U.S.A.   37°48N 97°20W 80 G5
Park Falls U.S.A.   45°56N 90°27W 80 C8
Park Head Canada   44°36N 81°9W 82 B3
Park Hills U.S.A.   37°51N 90°51W 80 G9
Park Range U.S.A.   40°41N 106°41W 76 F10
Park Rapids U.S.A.   46°55N 95°4W 80 B7
Park River U.S.A.   48°24N 97°45W 80 A5
Park Rynie S. Africa   30°25S 30°45E 57 E5
Parkā Bandar Iran   25°55N 59°35E 45 E8
Parkano Finland   62°1N 23°0E 8 E20
Parker Ariz., U.S.A.   34°9N 114°17W 79 L12
Parker Pa., U.S.A.   41°5N 79°41W 82 E5
Parker Dam U.S.A.   34°18N 114°8W 79 L12
Parkersburg U.S.A.   39°16N 81°34W 81 F13
Parkes Australia   33°9S 148°11E 63 E4
Parkfield U.S.A.   35°54N 120°26W 78 K6
Parkhill Canada   43°15N 81°38W 82 C3
Parkland U.S.A.   47°9N 122°26W 78 C4
Parkston U.S.A.   43°24N 97°59W 80 D5
Parksville Canada   49°20N 124°21W 70 D4
Parkway U.S.A.   38°32N 121°26W 78 G5
Parla Spain   40°14N 3°46W 21 B4
Parma Italy   44°48N 10°20E 20 D9
Parma Idaho, U.S.A.   43°47N 116°57W 76 E5
Parma Ohio, U.S.A.   41°24N 81°43W 82 E3
Parnaguá Brazil   10°10S 44°38W 93 F10
Parnaíba Brazil   2°54S 41°47W 93 D10
Parnaíba → Brazil   3°0S 41°50W 93 D10
Parnassos Greece   38°35N 22°30E 23 E10
Pärnu Estonia   58°28N 24°33E 9 G21
Paro Dzong Bhutan   27°32N 89°53E 43 F13
Paroo → Australia   31°28S 143°32E 63 E3
Paros Greece   37°5N 25°12E 23 F11
Parowan U.S.A.   37°51N 112°50W 77 H7
Parral Chile   36°10S 71°52W 94 D1
Parramatta Australia   33°48S 151°1E 63 B5
Parras Mexico   25°25N 102°11W 86 B4
Parrett → U.K.   51°12N 3°1W 13 F4
Parris I. U.S.A.   32°20N 80°41W 85 E14
Parrsboro Canada   45°30N 64°25W 73 C7
Parry Channel Canada   74°15N 94°0W 69 C13
Parry I. Canada   45°18N 80°10W 82 A4
Parry Is. Canada   77°0N 110°0W 69 B10
Parry Sound Canada   45°20N 80°0W 82 A5
Parsaloi Kenya   1°16N 36°51E 54 B4
Parsnip → Canada   55°10N 123°2W 70 B4
Parsons U.S.A.   37°20N 95°16W 80 G6
Parsons Ra. Australia   13°30S 135°15E 62 A2
Partinico Italy   38°3N 13°7E 22 E5
Partizansk Russia   43°8N 133°9E 30 C6
Partridge I. Canada   55°59N 87°37W 72 A2
Partry Mts. Ireland   53°40N 9°28W 10 C2
Paru → Brazil   1°33S 52°38W 93 D8
Parvān □ Afghan.   35°0N 69°0E 40 B6
Parvatipuram India   18°50N 83°25E 41 K13
Parvatsar India   26°52N 74°49E 42 F6
Parys S. Africa   26°52N 27°29E 56 D4
Pas, Pta. des Spain   38°46N 1°26E 24 C7
Pas, The Canada   53°45N 101°15W 71 C8
Pasadena Canada   49°1N 57°36W 73 C8
Pasadena Calif., U.S.A.   34°9N 118°8W 79 L8
Pasadena Tex., U.S.A.   29°43N 95°13W 84 L7
Pasaje → Argentina   25°39S 63°56W 94 B3
Pasar Indonesia   0°273 114°54E 37 J17
Pascagoula U.S.A.   30°21N 88°33W 85 F10
Pascagoula → U.S.A.   30°23N 88°37W 85 F10
Paşcani Romania   47°14N 26°45E 17 E14
Pasco U.S.A.   46°14N 119°6W 76 C4
Pasco I. Australia   20°57S 115°20E 60 D2
Pascoag U.S.A.   41°57N 71°42W 83 E13
Pascua, I. de Chile   27°7S 109°23W 65 K17
Pasfield L. Canada   58°24N 105°20W 71 B7
Pasir Mas Malaysia   6°2N 102°8E 39 J4
Pasir Panjang Singapore   1°18N 103°46E 39 d
Pasir Putih Malaysia   5°50N 102°24E 39 K4
Pasirian Indonesia   8°13S 113°8E 37 H15
Pasirkuning Indonesia   0°30S 104°33E 36 E2
Paskūh Iran   27°34N 63°58E 45 E9
Pasley, C. Australia   33°52S 123°35E 61 F3
Pašman Croatia   43°58S 15°20E 16 G8
Pasni Pakistan   25°15N 63°27E 40 G3
Paso Bravo △ Paraguay   22°32S 57°5W 94 A4
Paso Cantinela
  Mexico   32°33N 115°47W 79 N11
Paso de Indios Argentina   43°55S 69°0W 96 E3

Paso de los Libres
  Argentina   29°44S 57°10W 94 B4
Paso de los Toros
  Uruguay   32°45S 56°30W 94 C4
Paso Robles U.S.A.   35°38N 120°41W 78 K6
Paspébiac Canada   48°3N 65°17W 73 C6
Pasrur Pakistan   32°16N 74°43E 42 C6
Passage East Ireland   52°14N 7°0W 10 D5
Passage West Ireland   51°52N 8°21W 10 E3
Passau Germany   48°34N 13°28E 16 D7
Passero, C. Italy   36°41N 15°10E 22 F6
Passo Fundo Brazil   28°10S 52°20W 95 B5
Passos Brazil   20°45S 46°37W 93 H9
Pastavy Belarus   55°4N 26°50E 9 J22
Pastaza → Peru   4°50S 76°52W 92 D3
Pasto Colombia   1°13N 77°17W 92 C3
Pasuruan Indonesia   7°40S 112°44E 37 G15
Patagonia Argentina   45°0S 69°0W 96 F3
Patagonia U.S.A.   31°33N 110°45W 77 L8
Patambar Iran   29°45N 60°17E 45 D9
Patan = Lalitapur Nepal   27°40N 85°20E 43 F11
Patan = Somnath India   20°53N 70°22E 42 J4
Patan India   23°54N 72°14E 42 H5
Patani Indonesia   0°20N 128°50E 37 D7
Pataudi India   28°18N 76°48E 42 E7
Patchewollock Australia   35°22S 142°12E 63 F3
Patchogue U.S.A.   40°46N 73°1W 83 F11
Pate Kenya   2°10S 41°0E 54 C5
Patensie S. Africa   33°46S 24°49E 56 E3
Paternò Italy   37°34N 14°54E 22 F6
Pateros U.S.A.   48°3N 119°54W 76 B4
Paterson U.S.A.   40°54N 74°9W 83 F10
Paterson Ra. Australia   21°45S 122°10E 60 D3
Pathankot India   32°18N 75°45E 42 C6
Pathein = Bassein
  Burma   16°45N 94°30E 41 L19
Pathfinder Res. U.S.A.   42°28N 106°51W 76 E10
Pathiu Thailand   10°42N 99°19E 39 G2
Pathum Thani Thailand   14°1N 100°32E 38 E3
Pati Indonesia   6°45S 111°1E 37 G14
Patía → Colombia   2°13N 78°40W 92 C2
Patiala Punjab, India   30°23N 76°26E 42 D7
Patiala Ut. P., India   27°43N 79°1E 43 F8
Patkai Bum India   27°0N 95°30E 41 F19
Patmos Greece   37°21N 26°36E 23 F12
Patna India   25°35N 85°12E 43 G11
Pato Branco Brazil   26°13S 52°40W 95 B5
Patong, Ao Thailand   7°54N 98°17E 39 a
Patonga Uganda   2°45N 33°15E 54 B3
Patos Brazil   6°55S 37°16W 93 E11
Patos, L. dos Brazil   31°20S 51°0W 95 C5
Patos, Río de los →
  Argentina   31°18S 69°25W 94 C2
Patos de Minas Brazil   18°35S 46°32W 93 G9
Patquía Argentina   30°2S 66°55W 94 C2
Patra Greece   38°14N 21°47E 23 E9
Patraikos Kolpos Greece   38°17N 21°30E 23 E9
Patras = Patra Greece   38°14N 21°47E 23 E9
Patriot Hills Antarctica   82°20S 81°25W 5 E16
Patrocínio Brazil   18°57S 47°0W 93 G9
Pattani Thailand   6°48N 101°15E 39 J3
Pattaya Thailand   12°52N 100°55E 38 F3
Patten U.S.A.   46°0N 68°38W 81 B19
Patterson Calif., U.S.A.   37°28N 121°8W 78 H5
Patterson La., U.S.A.   29°42N 91°18W 84 G9
Patterson, Mt. U.S.A.   38°29N 119°20W 78 G7
Patti Punjab, India   31°17N 74°54E 42 D6
Patti Ut. P., India   25°55N 82°12E 43 G10
Pattoki Pakistan   31°5N 73°52E 42 D5
Patuakhali Bangla.   22°20N 90°25E 41 H17
Patuanak Canada   55°55N 107°43W 71 B7
Patuca → Honduras   15°50N 84°18W 88 C3
Patuca, Punta Honduras   15°49N 84°14W 88 C3
Patvinsuo △ Finland   63°7N 30°45E 8 E24
Pátzcuaro Mexico   19°31N 101°38W 86 D4
Pau France   43°19N 0°25W 20 E3
Paudash Canada   44°59N 77°58W 82 B7
Pauk Burma   21°27N 94°30E 41 J19
Paul I. Canada   56°30N 61°20W 73 A7
Paul Smiths U.S.A.   44°26N 74°15W 83 B10
Paulatuk Canada   69°25N 124°0W 68 D7
Paulding Bay S. Ocean   66°0S 118°0E 5 C8
Paulistana Brazil   8°9S 41°9W 93 E10
Paulo Afonso Brazil   9°21S 38°15W 93 E11
Paulpietersburg S. Africa   27°23S 30°50E 57 D5
Pauls Valley U.S.A.   34°44N 97°13W 84 D6
Pauma Valley U.S.A.   33°16N 116°58W 79 M10
Pauri India   30°9N 78°47E 43 D8
Pāveh Iran   35°3N 46°22E 44 C5
Pavia Italy   45°7N 9°8E 20 D8
Pávilosta Latvia   56°53N 21°14E 9 H19
Pavlodar Kazakhstan   52°33N 77°0E 28 D8
Pavlohrad Ukraine   48°30N 35°52E 19 E6
Pavlovo Russia   55°58N 43°5E 18 C7
Pavlovsk Russia   50°26N 40°5E 19 D7
Pavlovskaya Russia   46°17N 39°47E 19 E6
Pawai, Pulau Singapore   1°11N 103°44E 39 d
Pawayan India   28°4N 80°6E 43 E9
Pawhuska U.S.A.   36°40N 96°20W 84 C6
Pawling U.S.A.   41°34N 73°36W 83 E11
Pawnee U.S.A.   36°20N 96°48W 84 C6
Pawnee City U.S.A.   40°7N 96°9W 80 E5
Pawtucket U.S.A.   41°53N 71°23W 83 E13
Paxi Greece   39°14N 20°12E 23 E9
Paximadia Greece   35°0N 24°35E 25 E6
Paxton U.S.A.   40°27N 88°6W 80 E9
Payakumbuh Indonesia   0°20S 100°35E 36 E2
Payette U.S.A.   44°5N 116°56W 76 D5
Payne Bay = Kangirsuk
  Canada   60°0N 70°0W 69 F18
Payne L. Canada   59°30N 74°30W 69 F17
Paynes Find Australia   29°15S 117°42E 61 E2

Paynesville U.S.A.   45°23N 94°43W 80 C6
Paysandú Uruguay   32°19S 58°8W 94 C4
Payson Ariz., U.S.A.   34°14N 111°20W 77 J8
Payson Utah, U.S.A.   40°3N 111°44W 76 F8
Paz → Guatemala   13°44N 90°10W 88 D1
Paz, B. de la Mexico   24°9N 110°25W 86 C2
Pāzanān Iran   30°35N 49°59E 45 D6
Pazardzhik Bulgaria   42°12N 24°20E 23 C11
Pe Ell U.S.A.   46°34N 123°18W 78 D3
Peabody U.S.A.   42°31N 70°56W 83 D14
Peace → Canada   59°0N 111°25W 70 B6
Peace Point Canada   59°7N 112°27W 70 B6
Peace River Canada   56°15N 117°18W 70 B5
Peach Springs U.S.A.   35°32N 113°25W 77 J7
Peachland Canada   49°47N 119°45W 70 D5
Peachtree City U.S.A.   33°25N 84°35W 85 E12
Peak, The = Kinder Scout
  U.K.   53°24N 1°52W 12 D6
Peak Charles △
  Australia   32°42S 121°10E 61 F3
Peak District △ U.K.   53°24N 1°46W 12 D6
Peak Hill Australia   32°47S 148°11E 63 E4
Peak Ra. Australia   22°50S 148°20E 62 C4
Peake Cr. → Australia   28°2S 136°7E 63 D2
Peale, Mt. U.S.A.   38°26N 109°14W 76 G9
Pearblossom U.S.A.   34°30N 117°55W 79 L9
Pearl → U.S.A.   30°11N 89°32W 85 F10
Pearl and Hermes Reef
  U.S.A.   27°55N 175°45W 75 K4
Pearl River U.S.A.   41°4N 74°2W 83 E10
Pearsall U.S.A.   28°54N 99°6W 84 G5
Peary Land Greenland   82°40N 33°0W 4 A6
Pease → U.S.A.   34°12N 99°2W 84 D5
Peawanuck Canada   55°15N 85°12W 72 A2
Pebane Mozam.   17°10S 38°8E 55 F4
Pebas Peru   3°10S 71°46W 92 D4
Pebble Beach U.S.A.   36°34N 121°57W 78 J5
Peć Kosovo   42°40N 20°17E 23 C9
Pechenga Russia   69°29N 31°4E 8 B24
Pechenizhyn Ukraine   48°30N 24°48E 17 D13
Pechiguera, Pta.
  Canary Is.   28°51N 13°53W 24 F6
Pechora Russia   65°10N 57°11E 18 A10
Pechora → Russia   68°13N 54°15E 18 A9
Pechorskaya Guba Russia   68°40N 54°0E 18 A9
Pechory Russia   57°48N 27°40E 9 H22
Pecos N. Mex., U.S.A.   35°35N 105°41W 77 J11
Pecos Tex., U.S.A.   31°26N 103°30W 84 F3
Pecos → U.S.A.   29°42N 101°22W 84 G4
Pécs Hungary   46°5N 18°15E 17 E10
Pedasí Panama   7°32N 80°3W 88 E3
Pedder, L. Australia   42°55S 146°10E 63 G4
Peddie S. Africa   33°14S 27°7E 57 E4
Pedernales Dom. Rep.   18°2N 71°44W 89 C5
Pedieos → Cyprus   35°10N 33°54E 25 D12
Pedirka Desert Australia   26°40S 134°11E 63 D1
Pedra Azul Brazil   16°2S 41°17W 93 G10
Pedra Lume C. Verde Is.   16°40N 22°52W 50 b
Pedreiras Brazil   4°32S 44°40W 93 D10
Pedro Afonso Brazil   9°0S 48°10W 93 E9
Pedro Cays Jamaica   17°5N 77°48W 88 C4
Pedro de Valdivia Chile   22°55S 69°38W 94 A2
Pedro Juan Caballero
  Paraguay   22°30S 55°40W 95 A4
Pee Dee = Great Pee Dee →
  U.S.A.   33°21N 79°10W 85 E15
Peebinga Australia   34°52S 140°57E 63 E3
Peebles U.K.   55°40N 3°11W 11 F5
Peekskill U.S.A.   41°17N 73°55W 83 E11
Peel I. of Man   54°13N 4°40W 12 C3
Peel → Australia   30°50S 150°29E 63 E5
Peel → Canada   67°0N 135°0W 68 D5
Peel Sd. Canada   73°0N 96°0W 68 C12
Peera Peera Poolanna L.
  Australia   26°30S 138°0E 63 D2
Peerless Lake Canada   56°37N 114°40W 70 B6
Peers Canada   53°40N 116°0W 70 C5
Pegasus Bay N.Z.   43°20S 173°10E 59 E4
Pegu Burma   17°20N 96°29E 41 L20
Pegu Yoma Burma   19°0N 96°0E 41 K20
Pehuajó Argentina   35°45S 62°0W 94 D3
Pei Xian = Pizhou
  China   34°44N 116°55E 34 G9
Peine Chile   23°45S 68°8W 94 A2
Peine Germany   52°19N 10°14E 16 B6
Peip'ing = Beijing China   39°53N 116°21E 34 E9
Peipus, L. = Chudskoye, Ozero
  Russia   58°13N 27°30E 9 G22
Peixe Brazil   12°0S 48°40W 93 F9
Peixe → Brazil   21°31S 51°58W 93 H8
Pekalongan Indonesia   6°53S 109°40E 37 G13
Pekan Malaysia   3°30N 103°25E 39 L4
Pekan Nenas Malaysia   1°31N 103°31E 39 d
Pekanbaru Indonesia   0°30N 101°15E 36 D2
Pekin U.S.A.   40°35N 89°40W 80 E9
Peking = Beijing China   39°53N 116°21E 34 E9
Pekutatan Indonesia   8°25S 114°49E 37 J17
Pelabuhan Klang
  Malaysia   3°0N 101°23E 39 L3
Pelabuhanratu, Teluk
  Indonesia   7°5S 106°30E 37 G12
Pelagie, Is. Italy   35°39N 12°33E 22 G5
Pelaihari Indonesia   3°55S 114°45E 36 E4
Peleaga, Vf. Romania   45°22N 22°55E 17 F12
Pelée, Mt. Martinique   14°48N 61°10W 88 d
Pelee, Pt. Canada   41°54N 82°31W 72 D3
Pelee I. Canada   41°47N 82°40W 72 E3
Pelekech Kenya   3°52N 35°8E 54 B4
Peleng Indonesia   1°20S 123°30E 37 E6
Pelentong Malaysia   1°32N 103°49E 39 d
Pelican U.S.A.   57°58N 136°14W 70 B1
Pelican L. Canada   52°28N 100°20W 71 C8
Pelican Narrows
  Canada   55°10N 102°56W 71 B8
Peljesac Croatia   42°55N 17°25E 22 C7
Pelkosenniemi Finland   67°6N 27°28E 8 C22

Pella *S. Africa* 29°1S 19°6E **56** D2
Pella *U.S.A.* 41°25N 92°55W **80** E7
Pello *Finland* 66°47N 23°59E **8** C20
Pelly → *Canada* 62°47N 137°19W **70** A1
Pelly Bay *Canada* 68°38N 89°50W **69** D14
Peloponnese □ *Greece* 37°10N 22°0E **23** F10
Pelorus Sd. *N.Z.* 40°59S 173°59E **59** D4
Pelotas *Brazil* 31°42S 52°23W **95** C5
Pelotas → *Brazil* 27°28S 51°55W **95** B5
Pelvoux, Massif du
France 44°52N 6°20E **20** D7
Pemalang *Indonesia* 6°53S 109°23E **37** G13
Pemanggil, Pulau
Malaysia 2°37N 104°21E **39** L5
Pematangsiantar *Indonesia* 2°57N 99°5E **36** D1
Pemba *Mozam.* 12°58S 40°30E **55** E5
Pemba *Zambia* 16°30S 27°28E **55** F2
Pemba Channel *Tanzania* 5°0S 39°37E **54** D4
Pemba I. *Tanzania* 5°0S 39°45E **54** D4
Pemberton *Australia* 34°30S 116°0E **61** F2
Pemberton *Canada* 50°25N 122°50W **70** C4
Pembina → *Canada* 54°45N 114°17W **70** C6
Pembroke *Canada* 45°50N 77°7W **72** C4
Pembroke *U.K.* 51°41N 4°55W **13** F3
Pembrokeshire □ *U.K.* 51°52N 4°56W **13** F3
Pembrokeshire Coast △
U.K. 51°50N 5°2W **13** F2
Pen-y-Ghent *U.K.* 54°10N 2°14W **12** C5
Penal *Trin. & Tob.* 10°9N 61°29W **93** K15
Penang = Pinang
Malaysia 5°25N 100°15E **39** c
Penápolis *Brazil* 21°30S 50°0W **95** A6
Peñarroya-Pueblonuevo
Spain 38°19N 5°16W **21** C3
Penarth *U.K.* 51°26N 3°11W **13** F4
Peñas, C. de *Spain* 43°42N 5°52W **21** A3
Peñas, G. de *Chile* 47°0S 75°0W **96** F2
Peñas del Chache
Canary Is. 29°6N 13°33W **24** E6
Pench △ *India* 21°45N 79°20E **43** J8
Penchʻi = Benxi *China* 41°20N 123°48E **35** D12
Pend Oreille → *U.S.A.* 49°4N 117°37W **76** B5
Pend Oreille, L. *U.S.A.* 48°10N 116°21W **76** B5
Pendembu *S. Leone* 9°7N 11°14W **50** G3
Pender B. *Australia* 16°45S 122°42E **60** C3
Pendleton *U.S.A.* 45°40N 118°47W **76** D4
Pendra *India* 22°46N 81°57E **43** H9
Penedo *Brazil* 10°15S 36°36W **93** F11
Penelokan *Indonesia* 8°17S 115°22E **37** J18
Penetanguishene
Canada 44°50N 79°55W **82** B5
Penfield *U.S.A.* 41°13N 78°35W **82** E6
Peng Chau *China* 22°17N 114°2E **33** G11
Pengalengan *Indonesia* 7°9S 107°30E **37** G12
Penge *Kasai-Or.,*
Dem. Rep. of the Congo 5°30S 24°33E **54** D1
Penge *Sud-Kivu,*
Dem. Rep. of the Congo 4°27S 28°25E **54** C2
Penglai *China* 37°48N 120°42E **35** F11
Penguin *Australia* 41°8S 146°6E **63** G4
Penhalonga *Zimbabwe* 18°52S 32°40E **55** F3
Peniche *Portugal* 39°19N 9°22W **21** C1
Penicuik *U.K.* 55°50N 3°13W **11** F5
Penida, Nusa *Indonesia* 8°45S 115°30E **37** K18
Peninsular Malaysia □
Malaysia 4°0N 102°0E **39** L4
Penitente, Serra do *Brazil* 8°45S 46°20W **93** E9
Penkridge *U.K.* 52°44N 2°6W **12** E5
Penmarch, Pte. de *France* 47°48N 4°22W **20** C1
Penn Hills *U.S.A.* 40°28N 79°52W **82** F5
Penn Yan *U.S.A.* 42°40N 77°3W **82** D7
Pennant *Canada* 50°32N 108°14W **71** C7
Penner → *India* 14°35N 80°10E **40** M12
Pennines *U.K.* 54°45N 2°27W **12** C5
Pennington *U.S.A.* 39°15N 121°47W **78** F5
Pennsburg *U.S.A.* 40°23N 75°29W **83** F9
Pennsylvania □ *U.S.A.* 40°45N 77°30W **81** E15
Penny *Canada* 53°51N 121°20W **70** C4
Penobscot → *U.S.A.* 44°30N 68°48W **81** C19
Penobscot B. *U.S.A.* 44°35N 68°50W **81** C19
Penola *Australia* 37°25S 140°48E **63** F3
Penong *Australia* 31°56S 133°1E **61** F5
Penonomé *Panama* 8°31N 80°21W **88** E3
Penrhyn *Cook Is.* 9°0S 158°0W **65** H12
Penrith *Australia* 33°43S 150°38E **63** E5
Penrith *U.K.* 54°40N 2°45W **12** C5
Penryn *U.K.* 50°9N 5°7W **13** G2
Pensacola *U.S.A.* 30°25N 87°13W **85** F11
Pensacola Mts. *Antarctica* 84°0S 40°0W **5** E1
Pense *Canada* 50°25N 104°59W **71** C8
Penshurst *Australia* 37°49S 142°20E **63** F3
Penticton *Canada* 49°30N 119°38W **70** D5
Pentland *Australia* 20°32S 145°25E **62** C4
Pentland Firth *U.K.* 58°43N 3°10W **11** C5
Pentland Hills *U.K.* 55°48N 3°25W **11** F5
Pentland Hills △ *U.K.* 55°49N 3°20W **11** F5
Penza *Russia* 53°15N 45°5E **18** D8
Penzance *U.K.* 50°7N 5°33W **13** G2
Penzhino *Russia* 63°30N 167°55E **29** C17
Penzhinskaya Guba
Russia 61°30N 163°0E **29** C17
Peoria *Ariz., U.S.A.* 33°43N 112°14W **77** K7
Peoria *Ill., U.S.A.* 40°42N 89°36W **80** E9
Pepacton Res. *U.S.A.* 42°5N 74°58W **83** D10
Pepani → *S. Africa* 25°49S 22°47E **56** D3
Pera Hd. *Australia* 12°55S 141°37E **62** A3
Perabumulih *Indonesia* 3°27S 104°15E **36** E2
Perak → *Malaysia* 4°0N 100°50E **39** K3
Perama *Kerkyra, Greece* 39°34N 19°54E **25** A3
Perama *Kriti, Greece* 35°20N 24°40E **25** D6
Perancak *Indonesia* 8°24S 114°37E **37** J17
Peräpohjola *Finland* 66°16N 26°10E **8** C22
Percé *Canada* 48°31N 64°13W **73** C7
Perche, Collines du
France 48°30N 0°40E **20** B4
Percival Lakes *Australia* 21°25S 125°0E **60** D4
Percy Is. *Australia* 21°39S 150°16E **62** C5
Perdido, Mte. *Spain* 42°40N 0°5E **21** A6

Perdu, Mt. = Perdido, Mte.
Spain 42°40N 0°5E **21** A6
Pereira *Colombia* 4°49N 75°43W **92** C3
Perenjori *Australia* 29°26S 116°16E **61** E2
Pereyaslav-Khmelnytskyy
Ukraine 50°3N 31°28E **19** D5
Pérez, I. *Mexico* 22°24N 89°42W **87** C7
Pergamino *Argentina* 33°52S 60°30W **94** C3
Pergau → *Malaysia* 5°23N 102°2E **39** K3
Perham *U.S.A.* 46°36N 95°34W **80** B6
Perhentian, Kepulauan
Malaysia 5°54N 102°42E **39** K4
Péribonka → *Canada* 48°45N 72°5W **73** C5
Péribonka, L. *Canada* 50°1N 71°10W **73** B5
Perico *Argentina* 24°20S 65°5W **94** A2
Pericos *Mexico* 25°3N 107°42W **86** B3
Périgueux *France* 45°10N 0°42E **20** D4
Perijá, Sierra de *Colombia* 9°30N 73°3W **92** B4
Perijá △ *Venezuela* 9°30N 72°55W **89** E5
Peristerona → *Cyprus* 35°8N 33°5E **25** D12
Perito Moreno *Argentina* 46°36S 70°56W **96** F2
Perkasie *U.S.A.* 40°22N 75°18W **83** F9
Perlas, Arch. de las
Panama 8°41N 79°7W **88** E4
Perlas, Punta de *Nic.* 12°30N 83°30W **88** D3
Perm *Russia* 58°0N 56°10E **18** C10
Pernambuco = Recife
Brazil 8°0S 35°0W **93** E12
Pernambuco □ *Brazil* 8°0S 37°0W **93** E11
Pernatty Lagoon
Australia 31°30S 137°12E **63** E2
Pernik *Bulgaria* 42°35N 23°2E **23** C10
Peron Is. *Australia* 13°9S 130°4E **60** B5
Peron Pen. *Australia* 26°0S 113°10E **61** E1
Perow *Canada* 54°35N 126°10W **70** C3
Perpignan *France* 42°42N 2°53E **20** E5
Perris *U.S.A.* 33°47N 117°14W **79** M9
Perry *Fla., U.S.A.* 30°7N 83°35W **85** F13
Perry *Ga., U.S.A.* 32°28N 83°44W **85** E13
Perry *Iowa, U.S.A.* 41°51N 94°6W **80** E6
Perry *N.Y., U.S.A.* 42°42N 78°0W **82** D7
Perry *Okla., U.S.A.* 36°17N 97°14W **84** C6
Perryton *U.S.A.* 36°24N 100°48W **84** C4
Perryville *U.S.A.* 37°43N 89°52W **80** G9
Persepolis *Iran* 29°55N 52°50E **45** D7
Pershotravensk *Ukraine* 50°13N 27°40E **17** C14
Persia = Iran ■ *Asia* 33°0N 53°0E **45** C7
Persian Gulf *Asia* 27°0N 50°0E **45** E6
Perth *Australia* 31°57S 115°52E **61** F2
Perth *Canada* 44°55N 76°15W **83** B8
Perth *U.K.* 56°24N 3°26W **11** E5
Perth & Kinross □ *U.K.* 56°45N 3°55W **11** E5
Perth Amboy *U.S.A.* 40°30N 74°16W **83** F10
Perth-Andover *Canada* 46°44N 67°42W **73** C6
Perth Basin *Ind. Oc.* 30°0S 108°0E **64** L2
Peru *Ind., U.S.A.* 40°45N 86°4W **80** E10
Peru *N.Y., U.S.A.* 44°35N 73°32W **83** B11
Peru ■ *S. Amer.* 4°0S 75°0W **92** D4
Peru Basin *Pac. Oc.* 20°0S 95°0W **65** J18
Peru-Chile Trench
Pac. Oc. 20°0S 72°0W **92** G3
Perúgia *Italy* 43°7N 12°23E **22** C5
Pervomaysk *Ukraine* 48°10N 30°46E **19** E5
Pervouralsk *Russia* 56°59N 59°59E **18** C10
Pésaro *Italy* 43°54N 12°55E **22** C5
Pescara *Italy* 42°28N 14°13E **22** C6
Peshawar *Pakistan* 34°2N 71°37E **42** B4
Peshkopi *Albania* 41°41N 20°25E **23** D9
Peshtigo *U.S.A.* 45°3N 87°45W **80** C10
Pesqueira *Brazil* 8°20S 36°42W **93** E11
Petah Tiqwa *Israel* 32°6N 34°53E **46** C3
Petaling Jaya *Malaysia* 3°4N 101°42E **39** L3
Petaloudes *Greece* 36°18N 28°5E **25** C10
Petaluma *U.S.A.* 38°14N 122°39W **78** G4
Pétange *Lux.* 49°33N 5°55E **15** E5
Petaro *Pakistan* 25°31N 68°18E **42** G3
Petatlán *Mexico* 17°31N 101°16W **86** D4
Petauke *Zambia* 14°14S 31°20E **55** E3
Petawawa *Canada* 45°54N 77°17W **72** C4
Petén Itzá, L. *Guatemala* 16°58N 89°50W **88** C2
Peter I. *Br. Virgin Is.* 18°22N 64°35W **89** e
Peter I. Øy *Antarctica* 69°0S 91°0W **5** C16
Peter Pond L. *Canada* 55°55N 108°44W **71** B7
Peterbell *Canada* 48°36N 83°21W **72** C3
Peterborough *Australia* 32°58S 138°51E **63** E2
Peterborough *Canada* 44°20N 78°20W **82** B6
Peterborough *U.K.* 52°35N 0°15W **13** E7
Peterborough *U.S.A.* 42°53N 71°57W **83** D13
Peterborough □ *U.K.* 52°35N 0°15W **13** E7
Peterculter *U.K.* 57°6N 2°16W **11** D6
Peterhead *U.K.* 57°31N 1°48W **11** D7
Peterlee *U.K.* 54°47N 1°20W **12** C6
Petermann ✸ *Australia* 24°58S 130°0E **61** E4
Petermann Gletscher
Greenland 80°30N 60°0W **69** A20
Petermann Ranges
Australia 26°0S 130°30E **61** E5
Petersburg *Alaska,*
U.S.A. 56°48N 132°58W **68** F5
Petersburg *Pa., U.S.A.* 40°34N 78°3W **82** F6
Petersburg *Va., U.S.A.* 37°14N 77°24W **81** G15
Petersburg *W. Va., U.S.A.* 39°1N 79°5W **81** F14
Petersfield *U.K.* 51°1N 0°56W **13** F7
Petit-Canal *Guadeloupe* 16°25N 61°31W **88** b
Petit Goâve *Haiti* 18°27N 72°51W **89** C5
Petit Lac Manicouagan
Canada 51°25N 67°40W **73** B6
Petit-Mécatina →
Canada 50°40N 59°30W **73** B8
Petit-Mécatina, Î. du
Canada 50°30N 59°25W **73** B8
Petit Piton *St. Lucia* 13°51N 61°5W **89** f
Petit-Saguenay *Canada* 48°15N 70°4W **73** C5
Petitcodiac *Canada* 45°57N 65°11W **73** C6
Petite Terre, Îles de la
Guadeloupe 16°13N 61°9W **88** b
Petitot → *Canada* 60°14N 123°29W **70** A4
Petitsikapau L. *Canada* 54°37N 66°25W **73** B6
Petlad *India* 22°30N 72°45E **42** H5

Peto *Mexico* 20°8N 88°55W **87** C7
Petone *N.Z.* 41°13S 174°53E **59** D5
Petorca *Chile* 32°15S 70°56W **94** C1
Petoskey *U.S.A.* 45°22N 84°57W **81** C11
Petra *Jordan* 30°20N 35°22E **46** E4
Petra *Spain* 39°37N 3°6E **24** B10
Petra, Ostrova *Russia* 76°15N 118°30E **29** B12
Petra Velikogo, Zaliv
Russia 42°40N 132°0E **30** C6
Petre, Pt. *Canada* 43°50N 77°9W **82** C7
Petrich *Bulgaria* 41°24N 23°13E **23** D10
Petrified Forest △ *U.S.A.* 35°0N 109°30W **77** J9
Petrikov = Pyetrikaw
Belarus 52°11N 28°29E **17** B15
Petrolândia *Brazil* 9°5S 38°20W **93** E11
Petrolia *Canada* 42°54N 82°9W **82** D2
Petrolina *Brazil* 9°24S 40°30W **93** E10
Petropavl *Kazakhstan* 54°53N 69°13E **28** D7
Petropavlovsk = Petropavl
Kazakhstan 54°53N 69°13E **28** D7
Petropavlovsk-Kamchatskiy
Russia 53°3N 158°43E **29** D16
Petrópolis *Brazil* 22°33S 43°9W **95** A7
Petroșani *Romania* 45°28N 23°20E **17** F12
Petrovaradin *Serbia* 45°16N 19°55E **23** B8
Petrovsk *Russia* 52°22N 45°19E **18** D8
Petrovsk-Zabaykalskiy
Russia 51°20N 108°55E **29** D11
Petrozavodsk *Russia* 61°41N 34°20E **18** B5
Petrus Steyn *S. Africa* 27°38S 28°8E **57** D4
Petrusburg *S. Africa* 29°4S 25°26E **56** D4
Peumo *Chile* 34°21S 71°12W **94** C1
Peureulak *Indonesia* 4°48N 97°45E **36** D1
Pevek *Russia* 69°41N 171°19E **29** C18
Pforzheim *Germany* 48°52N 8°41E **16** D5
Pha Taem △ *Thailand* 15°32N 105°30E **38** E5
Phaestos *Greece* 35°2N 24°50E **25** D6
Phagwara *India* 31°10N 75°40E **42** D6
Phala *Botswana* 23°45S 26°50E **56** C4
Phalera = Phulera *India* 26°52N 75°16E **42** F6
Phalodi *India* 27°12N 72°24E **42** F5
Phaluai, Ko *Thailand* 9°32N 99°41E **39** b
Phan *Thailand* 19°28N 99°43E **38** C2
Phan Rang *Vietnam* 11°34N 109°0E **39** G7
Phan Ri = Hoa Da
Vietnam 11°16N 108°40E **39** G7
Phan Si Pan *Vietnam* 22°18N 103°46E **38** A4
Phan Thiet *Vietnam* 11°1N 108°9E **39** G7
Phanat Nikhom
Thailand 13°27N 101°11E **38** F3
Phangan, Ko *Thailand* 9°45N 100°0E **39** H3
Phangnga *Thailand* 8°28N 98°30E **39** H2
Phangnga, Ao *Thailand* 8°16N 98°33E **39** a
Phanom Sarakham
Thailand 13°45N 101°21E **38** F3
Phaphund *India* 26°36N 79°28E **43** F8
Pharenda *India* 27°5N 83°17E **43** F10
Pharr *U.S.A.* 26°12N 98°11W **84** H5
Phatthalung *Thailand* 7°39N 100°6E **39** J3
Phayao *Thailand* 19°11N 99°55E **38** C2
Phelps *U.S.A.* 42°58N 77°3W **82** D7
Phelps L. *Canada* 59°15N 103°15W **71** B8
Phenix City *U.S.A.* 32°28N 85°0W **85** E12
Phet Buri *Thailand* 13°1N 99°55E **38** F2
Phetchabun *Thailand* 16°25N 101°8E **38** D3
Phetchabun, Thiu Khao
Thailand 16°0N 101°20E **38** E3
Phetchaburi = Phet Buri
Thailand 13°1N 99°55E **38** F2
Phi Phi, Ko *Thailand* 7°45N 98°46E **39** J2
Phiafay *Laos* 14°48N 106°0E **38** E6
Phibun Mangsahan
Thailand 15°14N 105°14E **38** E5
Phichai *Thailand* 17°22N 100°10E **38** D3
Phichit *Thailand* 16°26N 100°22E **38** D3
Philadelphia *Miss.,*
U.S.A. 32°46N 89°7W **85** E10
Philadelphia *N.Y., U.S.A.* 44°9N 75°43W **83** B9
Philadelphia *Pa., U.S.A.* 39°57N 75°9W **83** G9
Philip *U.S.A.* 44°2N 101°40W **80** C3
Philip Smith Mts. *U.S.A.* 68°0N 148°0W **74** B10
Philippeville *Belgium* 50°12N 4°33E **15** D4
Philippi *U.S.A.* 39°9N 80°3W **81** F13
Philippi L. *Australia* 24°20S 138°55E **62** C2
Philippine Basin *Pac. Oc.* 17°0N 132°0E **64** F5
Philippine Sea *Pac. Oc.* 18°0N 125°0E **64** F4
Philippine Trench = Mindanao
Trench *Pac. Oc.* 12°0N 126°6E **37** B7
Philippines ■ *Asia* 12°0N 123°0E **37** B6
Philippolis *S. Africa* 30°15S 25°16E **56** E4
Philippopolis = Plovdiv
Bulgaria 42°8N 24°44E **23** C11
Philipsburg *Canada* 45°2N 73°5W **83** A11
Philipsburg *Mont.,*
U.S.A. 46°20N 113°18W **76** C7
Philipsburg *Pa., U.S.A.* 40°54N 78°13W **82** F6
Philipstown = Daingean
Ireland 53°18N 7°17W **10** C4
Philipstown *S. Africa* 30°28S 24°30E **56** E3
Phillip I. *Australia* 38°30S 145°12E **63** F4
Phillips *U.S.A.* 45°42N 90°24W **80** C8
Phillipsburg *Kans.,*
U.S.A. 39°45N 99°19W **80** F4
Phillipsburg *N.J., U.S.A.* 40°42N 75°12W **83** F9
Philmont *U.S.A.* 42°15N 73°39W **83** D11
Philomath *U.S.A.* 44°32N 123°22W **76** D2
Phimai *Thailand* 15°13N 102°30E **38** E4
Phitsanulok *Thailand* 16°50N 100°12E **38** D3
Phnom Kulen △
Cambodia 13°38N 104°15E **38** F5
Phnom Penh *Cambodia* 11°33N 104°55E **39** G5
Phnum Penh = Phnom Penh
Cambodia 11°33N 104°55E **39** G5
Phoenicia *U.S.A.* 42°5N 74°14W **83** D10
Phoenix *Mauritius* 20°17S 57°30E **53** d
Phoenix *Ariz., U.S.A.* 33°26N 112°4W **77** K7
Phoenix *N.Y., U.S.A.* 43°14N 76°18W **83** C8
Phoenix Is. *Kiribati* 3°30S 172°0W **64** H10
Phoenixville *U.S.A.* 40°8N 75°31W **83** F9

Phon *Thailand* 15°49N 102°36E **38** E4
Phon Tiou *Laos* 17°53N 104°37E **38** D5
Phong → *Thailand* 16°23N 102°56E **38** D4
Phong Saly *Laos* 21°42N 102°9E **38** A4
Phong Tho *Vietnam* 22°32N 103°21E **38** A4
Phonhong *Laos* 18°30N 102°25E **38** C4
Phonum *Thailand* 8°49N 98°48E **39** H2
Phosphate Hill *Australia* 21°53S 139°58E **62** C2
Photharam *Thailand* 13°41N 99°51E **38** F2
Phra Nakhon Si Ayutthaya
Thailand 14°25N 100°30E **38** E3
Phra Pradaeng *Thailand* 13°39N 100°33E **38** F3
Phra Thong, Ko *Thailand* 9°5N 98°17E **39** H2
Phrae *Thailand* 18°7N 100°9E **38** C3
Phrom Phiram *Thailand* 17°2N 100°12E **38** D3
Phu Bia *Laos* 19°10N 103°0E **38** C4
Phu Chong-Na Yoi △
Thailand 14°25N 105°30E **38** E5
Phu Dien *Vietnam* 18°58N 105°31E **38** C5
Phu Hin Rang Kla △
Thailand 17°0N 100°59E **38** D3
Phu Kradung △ *Thailand* 17°2N 101°44E **38** D3
Phu Loi *Laos* 20°14N 103°14E **38** B4
Phu Luang △ *Thailand* 17°18N 101°29E **38** D3
Phu Ly *Vietnam* 20°35N 105°50E **38** B5
Phu Phan △ *Thailand* 17°0N 103°56E **38** D4
Phu Quoc, Dao *Vietnam* 10°20N 104°0E **39** G4
Phu Tho *Vietnam* 21°24N 105°13E **38** B5
Phu Wiang △ *Thailand* 16°39N 102°23E **38** D4
Phuc Yen *Vietnam* 21°16N 105°45E **38** B5
Phuket *Thailand* 7°53N 98°24E **39** a
Phuket, Ko *Thailand* 8°0N 98°22E **39** a
Phul *India* 30°19N 75°14E **42** D6
Phulad *India* 25°38N 73°49E **42** G5
Phulchari *Bangla.* 25°11N 89°37E **43** G13
Phulera *India* 26°52N 75°16E **42** F6
Phulpur *India* 25°31N 82°49E **43** G10
Phun Phin *Thailand* 9°7N 99°12E **39** H2
Phuntsholing *Bhutan* 26°51N 89°23E **43** F13
Pia ✸ *India* 27°7S 116°23E **61** E2
Piacenza *Italy* 45°1N 9°40E **20** D8
Piai, Tanjung *Malaysia* 1°17N 103°30E **39** d
Pian Cr. → *Australia* 30°2S 148°12E **63** E4
Pian-Upe △ *Uganda* 1°44N 34°20E **54** B3
Pianosa *Italy* 42°35N 10°5E **22** C4
Piapot *Canada* 49°59N 109°8W **71** D7
Piatra Neamț *Romania* 46°56N 26°21E **17** E14
Piauí □ *Brazil* 7°0S 43°0W **93** E10
Piauí → *Brazil* 6°38S 42°42W **93** E10
Piave → *Italy* 45°32N 12°44E **22** B5
Pibor Post *Sudan* 6°47N 33°3E **51** G12
Picardie □ *France* 49°50N 3°0E **20** B5
Picardy = Picardie □
France 49°50N 3°0E **20** B5
Picayune *U.S.A.* 30°32N 89°41W **85** F10
Pichhor *India* 25°58N 78°20E **43** G8
Pichilemu *Chile* 34°22S 72°0W **94** C1
Pichor *India* 25°11N 78°11E **42** G8
Pickerel L. *Canada* 48°40N 91°25W **72** C1
Pickering *U.K.* 54°15N 0°46W **12** C7
Pickering, Vale of *U.K.* 54°14N 0°45W **12** C7
Pickle Lake *Canada* 51°30N 90°12W **72** B1
Pickwick L. *U.S.A.* 35°4N 88°15W **85** D10
Pico *Azores* 38°28N 28°20W **50** a
Pico Bonito △ *Honduras* 15°34N 86°48W **88** C2
Pico Truncado *Argentina* 46°40S 68°0W **96** F3
Picos *Brazil* 7°5S 41°28W **93** E10
Picton *Canada* 44°1N 77°9W **82** B7
Picton *N.Z.* 41°18S 174°3E **59** D5
Pictou *Canada* 45°41N 62°42W **73** C7
Picture Butte *Canada* 49°55N 112°45W **70** D6
Pictured Rocks △
U.S.A. 46°30N 86°30W **80** B10
Picún Leufú *Argentina* 39°30S 69°5W **96** D3
Pidurutalagala *Sri Lanka* 7°10N 80°50E **40** R12
Piedmont = Piemonte □
Italy 45°0N 8°0E **20** D7
Piedmont *Ala., U.S.A.* 33°55N 85°37W **85** E12
Piedmont *S.C., U.S.A.* 34°42N 82°28W **66** F11
Piedras Negras *Mexico* 28°42N 100°31W **86** B4
Pieksämäki *Finland* 62°18N 27°10E **8** E22
Pielinen *Finland* 63°15N 29°40E **8** E23
Piemonte □ *Italy* 45°0N 8°0E **20** D7
Pienaarsrivier *S. Africa* 25°15S 28°18E **57** D4
Piercefield *U.S.A.* 44°13N 74°35W **83** B10
Pierceland *Canada* 54°20N 109°46W **71** C7
Pierpont *U.S.A.* 41°45N 80°34W **82** E4
Pierre *U.S.A.* 44°22N 100°21W **80** C3
Pierrefonds *Canada* 45°29N 73°51W **83** A11
Pierreville *Trin. & Tob.* 10°16N 61°0W **93** K16
Piet Retief *S. Africa* 27°1S 30°50E **57** D5
Pietarsaari *Finland* 63°40N 22°43E **8** E20
Pietermaritzburg
S. Africa 29°35S 30°25E **57** D5
Pietersburg = Polokwane
S. Africa 23°54S 29°25E **57** C4
Pietrosul, Vf. *Maramureș,*
Romania 47°35N 24°43E **17** E13
Pietrosul, Vf. *Suceava,*
Romania 47°12N 25°18E **17** E13
Pigeon L. *Canada* 44°27N 78°30W **82** B6
Piggott *U.S.A.* 36°23N 90°11W **85** C9
Pigüe *Argentina* 37°36S 62°25W **94** D3
Pihani *India* 27°36N 80°15E **43** F9
Pihlajavesi *Finland* 61°45N 28°45E **8** F23
Pijijiapan *Mexico* 15°42N 93°14W **87** D6
Pikangikum *Canada* 51°49N 94°0W **71** C10
Pikes Peak *U.S.A.* 38°50N 105°3W **76** G11
Piketberg *S. Africa* 32°55S 18°40E **56** E2
Pikeville *U.S.A.* 37°29N 82°31W **81** G12
Pikou *China* 39°18N 122°22E **35** E12
Pikwitonei *Canada* 55°35N 97°9W **71** B9
Piła *Poland* 53°10N 16°48E **17** B9
Pilanesberg △ *S. Africa* 25°15S 27°4E **56** D4
Pilani *India* 28°22N 75°33E **42** E6
Pilar *Paraguay* 26°50S 58°20W **94** B4
Pilaya → *Bolivia* 20°55S 64°4W **92** H6
Pilbara *Australia* 21°15S 118°16E **60** D2
Pilcomayo → *Paraguay* 25°21S 57°42W **94** B4

Pilgrim's Rest *S. Africa* 24°55S 30°44E **57** C5
Pilibhit *India* 28°40N 79°50E **43** E8
Pilica → *Poland* 51°52N 21°17E **17** C11
Pilipinas = Philippines ■
Asia 12°0N 123°0E **37** B6
Pilkhawa *India* 28°43N 77°42E **42** E7
Pilliga *Australia* 30°21S 148°54E **63** E4
Pilos *Greece* 36°55N 21°42E **23** F9
Pilot Mound *Canada* 49°15N 98°54W **71** D9
Pilot Point *U.S.A.* 33°24N 96°58W **84** E6
Pilot Rock *U.S.A.* 45°29N 118°50W **76** D4
Pima *U.S.A.* 32°54N 109°50W **77** K9
Pimba *Australia* 31°18S 136°46E **63** E2
Pimenta Bueno *Brazil* 11°35S 61°10W **92** F6
Pimentel *Peru* 6°45S 79°55W **92** E3
Pin Valley △ *India* 31°50N 77°56E **42** D7
Pinang *Malaysia* 5°25N 100°15E **39** c
Pinar, C. des *Spain* 39°53N 3°12E **24** B10
Pinar del Río *Cuba* 22°26N 83°40W **88** B3
Pınarhisar *Turkey* 41°37N 27°30E **23** D12
Pinatubo, Mt. *Phil.* 15°8N 120°21E **37** A6
Pinawa *Canada* 50°9N 95°50W **71** C9
Pincher Creek *Canada* 49°30N 113°57W **70** D6
Pinchi L. *Canada* 54°38N 124°30W **70** C4
Pinckneyville *U.S.A.* 38°5N 89°23W **80** F9
Pińczów *Poland* 50°32N 20°32E **17** C11
Pindar *Australia* 28°30S 115°47E **61** E2
Pindera Downs ✸
Australia 29°24S 142°37E **63** A3
Pindi Gheb *Pakistan* 33°14N 72°21E **42** C5
Pindos Oros *Greece* 40°0N 21°0E **23** E9
Pindus Mts. = Pindos Oros
Greece 40°0N 21°0E **23** E9
Pine → *B.C., Canada* 56°8N 120°43W **70** B4
Pine → *Sask., Canada* 58°50N 105°38W **71** B7
Pine Bluff *U.S.A.* 34°13N 92°1W **84** D8
Pine Bluffs *U.S.A.* 41°11N 104°4W **76** F11
Pine City *U.S.A.* 45°50N 92°59W **80** C7
Pine Cr. → *U.S.A.* 41°10N 77°16W **82** E7
Pine Creek *Australia* 13°50S 131°50E **60** B5
Pine Falls *Canada* 50°34N 96°11W **71** C9
Pine Flat L. *U.S.A.* 36°50N 119°20W **78** J7
Pine Grove *U.S.A.* 40°33N 76°23W **83** F8
Pine Hill *Australia* 23°38S 146°57E **62** C4
Pine Pass *Canada* 55°25N 122°42W **70** B4
Pine Point *Canada* 60°50N 114°28W **70** A6
Pine Ridge *U.S.A.* 43°2N 102°33W **80** D2
Pine River *Canada* 51°45N 100°30W **71** C8
Pine River *U.S.A.* 46°43N 94°24W **80** B6
Pine Valley *U.S.A.* 32°50N 116°32W **79** N10
Pinecrest *U.S.A.* 38°12N 120°1W **78** G6
Pinedale *Calif., U.S.A.* 36°50N 119°48W **78** J7
Pinedale *Wyo., U.S.A.* 42°52N 109°52W **76** E9
Pinega → *Russia* 64°30N 44°19E **18** B8
Pinehouse L. *Canada* 55°32N 106°35W **71** B7
Pineimuta → *Canada* 52°8N 88°33W **72** B1
Pinerolo *Italy* 44°53N 7°21E **20** D7
Pines, Akra *Greece* 40°5N 24°20E **23** D11
Pinetop-Lakeside *U.S.A.* 34°9N 109°58W **77** J9
Pinetown *S. Africa* 29°48S 30°54E **57** D5
Pineville *U.S.A.* 31°19N 92°26W **84** F8
Ping → *Thailand* 15°42N 100°9E **38** E3
Pingaring *Australia* 32°40S 118°32E **61** F2
Pingding *China* 37°47N 113°38E **34** F7
Pingdingshan *China* 33°43N 113°27E **34** H7
Pingdong *Taiwan* 22°39N 120°30E **33** D7
Pingdu *China* 36°42N 119°59E **35** F10
Pingelly *Australia* 32°32S 117°5E **61** F2
Pingliang *China* 35°35N 106°31E **34** G4
Pingluo *China* 39°31N 112°30E **34** E7
Pingluo *China* 38°52N 106°30E **34** E4
Pingquan *China* 41°1N 118°37E **35** D10
Pingrup *Australia* 33°32S 118°29E **61** F2
Pʻingtung *Taiwan* 22°38N 120°30E **33** D7
Pingwu *China* 32°25N 104°30E **34** H3
Pingxiang *China* 22°6N 106°46E **32** D5
Pingyao *China* 37°12N 112°10E **34** F7
Pingyi *China* 35°30N 117°35E **35** G9
Pingyin *China* 36°20N 116°25E **34** F9
Pingyuan *China* 37°10N 116°22E **34** F8
Pinheiro *Brazil* 2°31S 45°5W **93** D9
Pinheiro Machado
Brazil 31°34S 53°23W **95** C5
Pinhel *Portugal* 40°50N 7°1W **21** B2
Pini *Indonesia* 0°10N 98°40E **36** D1
Pinios → *Greece* 39°55N 22°41E **23** E10
Pinjarra *Australia* 32°37S 115°52E **61** F2
Pink Mountain *Canada* 57°3N 122°52W **70** B4
Pinnacles △ *U.S.A.* 36°25N 121°12W **78** J5
Pinnaroo *Australia* 35°17S 140°53E **63** F3
Pinon Hills *U.S.A.* 34°26N 117°39W **79** L9
Pinos *Mexico* 22°18N 101°34W **86** C4
Pinos, Mt. *U.S.A.* 34°49N 119°8W **79** L7
Pinos Pt. *U.S.A.* 36°38N 121°57W **78** J5
Pinrang *Indonesia* 3°46S 119°41E **37** E5
Pins, Pte. aux *Canada* 42°15N 81°51W **82** D3
Pinsk *Belarus* 52°10N 26°1E **17** B14
Pintados *Chile* 20°35S 69°40W **92** H5
Pinyug *Russia* 60°5N 48°0E **18** B8
Pioche *U.S.A.* 37°56N 114°27W **77** H6
Piombino *Italy* 42°55N 10°32E **22** C4
Pioner, Ostrov *Russia* 79°50N 92°0E **29** B10
Piopiotaki = Milford Sd.
N.Z. 44°41S 167°47E **59** F1
Piorini, L. *Brazil* 3°15S 62°35W **92** D6
Piotrków Trybunalski
Poland 51°23N 19°43E **17** C10
Pip *Iran* 26°45N 60°10E **45** E9
Pipar *India* 26°25N 73°31E **42** F5
Pipar Road *India* 26°25N 73°27E **42** F5
Piparia *Mad. P., India* 22°45N 78°23E **42** H8
Piparia *Mad. P., India* 21°49N 77°37E **42** J7
Pipestone *U.S.A.* 44°0N 96°19W **80** D6
Pipestone → *Canada* 52°53N 89°23W **72** B2
Pipestone Cr. →
Canada 49°38N 100°15W **71** D8
Piplan *Pakistan* 32°17N 71°21E **42** C4
Piploda *India* 23°37N 74°56E **42** H6
Pipmuacan, Rés. *Canada* 49°45N 70°30W **73** C5

Pippingarra *Australia*   20°27S 118°42E **60 D2**
Piqua *U.S.A.*   40°9N 84°15W **81 E11**
Piquiri → *Brazil*   24°3S 54°14W **95 A5**
Pir Panjal Range *India*   32°30N 76°50E **42 C7**
Pír Sohráb *Iran*   25°44N 60°54E **45 E9**
Piracicaba *Brazil*   22°45S 47°40W **95 A6**
Piracuruca *Brazil*   3°50S 41°50W **93 D10**
Pirae *Tahiti*   17°31S 149°32W **59 d**
Piræus = Pireas *Greece*   37°57N 23°42E **23 F10**
Piraiévs = Pireas *Greece*   37°57N 23°42E **23 F10**
Pirajuí *Brazil*   21°59S 49°29W **95 A6**
Piram I. *India*   21°36N 72°21E **42 J5**
Pirané *Argentina*   25°42S 59°6W **94 B4**
Pirapora *Brazil*   17°20S 44°56W **93 G10**
Pirawa *India*   24°10N 76°2E **42 G7**
Pireas *Greece*   37°57N 23°42E **23 F10**
Pírgos *Greece*   37°40N 21°27E **23 f9**
Piribebuy *Paraguay*   25°26S 57°2W **94 B4**
Pirimapun *Indonesia*   6°20S 138°24E **37 F9**
Pirin Planina *Bulgaria*   41°40N 23°30E **23 D10**
Pírineos = Pyrenees
  Europe   42°45N 0°18E **20 E4**
Piripiri *Brazil*   4°15S 41°46W **93 D10**
Pirlangimpi *Australia*   11°24S 130°26E **60 B5**
Pirmasens *Germany*   49°12N 7°36E **16 D4**
Pirot *Serbia*   43°9N 22°33E **23 C10**
Piru *Indonesia*   3°4S 128°12E **37 E7**
Piru *U.S.A.*   34°25N 118°48W **79 L8**
Pisa *Italy*   43°43N 10°23E **22 C4**
Pisagua *Chile*   19°40S 70°15W **92 G4**
Pisco *Peru*   13°50S 76°12W **92 F3**
Písek *Czech Rep.*   49°19N 14°10E **16 D8**
Pishan *China*   37°30N 78°33E **32 C2**
Pishín *Iran*   26°6N 61°47E **45 E9**
Pishin *Pakistan*   30°35N 67°0E **42 D2**
Pishin Lora → *Pakistan*   29°9N 64°5E **42 E1**
Pising *Indonesia*   5°8S 121°53E **37 F6**
Pismo Beach *U.S.A.*   35°9N 120°38W **79 K6**
Pissis, Cerro *Argentina*   27°45S 68°48W **94 B2**
Pissouri *Cyprus*   34°40N 32°42E **25 E11**
Pistóia *Italy*   43°55N 10°54E **22 C4**
Pistol B. *Canada*   62°25N 92°37W **71 A10**
Pisuerga → *Spain*   41°33N 4°52W **21 B3**
Pit → *U.S.A.*   40°47N 122°6W **76 F2**
Pitarpunga L. *Australia*   34°24S 143°30E **63 E3**
Pitcairn I. *Pac. Oc.*   25°5S 130°5W **65 K14**
Pitch L., *Trin. & Tob.*   10°12N 61°39W **93 K15**
Piteå *Sweden*   65°20N 21°25E **8 D19**
Piteälven → *Sweden*   65°20N 21°25E **8 D19**
Pitești *Romania*   44°52N 24°54E **17 F13**
Pithapuram *India*   17°10N 82°15E **41 L13**
Pithara *Australia*   30°20S 116°35E **61 F2**
Pithoragarh *India*   29°35N 80°13E **43 E9**
Pithoro *Pakistan*   25°31N 69°23E **42 G3**
Pitlochry *U.K.*   56°42N 3°44W **11 E5**
Pitsilia *Cyprus*   34°55N 33°0E **25 E12**
Pitt I. *Canada*   53°30N 129°50W **70 C3**
Pittsburg *Calif., U.S.A.*   38°2N 121°53W **78 G5**
Pittsburg *Kans., U.S.A.*   37°25N 94°42W **80 G6**
Pittsburg *Tex., U.S.A.*   33°0N 94°59W **84 E7**
Pittsburgh *U.S.A.*   40°26N 79°58W **82 F5**
Pittsfield *Ill., U.S.A.*   39°36N 90°49W **80 F8**
Pittsfield *Maine, U.S.A.*   44°47N 69°23W **81 C19**
Pittsfield *Mass., U.S.A.*   42°27N 73°15W **83 D11**
Pittsfield *N.H., U.S.A.*   43°18N 71°20W **83 C13**
Pittston *U.S.A.*   41°19N 75°47W **83 E9**
Pittsworth *Australia*   27°41S 151°37E **63 D5**
Pituri → *Australia*   22°35S 138°30E **62 C2**
Piura *Peru*   5°15S 80°38W **92 E2**
Pixley *U.S.A.*   35°58N 119°18W **78 K7**
Pizhou *China*   34°44N 116°55E **34 G9**
Placentia *Canada*   47°20N 54°0W **73 C9**
Placentia B. *Canada*   47°0N 54°40W **73 C9**
Placerville *U.S.A.*   38°44N 120°48W **78 G6**
Placetas *Cuba*   22°15S 79°44W **88 B4**
Plainfield *N.J., U.S.A.*   40°37N 74°25W **83 F10**
Plainfield *Ohio, U.S.A.*   40°13N 81°43W **82 F3**
Plainfield *Vt., U.S.A.*   44°17N 72°26W **83 B12**
Plains *Mont., U.S.A.*   47°28N 114°53W **76 C6**
Plains *Tex., U.S.A.*   33°11N 102°50W **84 E3**
Plainview *Nebr., U.S.A.*   42°21N 97°47W **80 D5**
Plainview *Tex., U.S.A.*   34°11N 101°43W **84 D4**
Plainwell *U.S.A.*   42°27N 85°38W **81 D11**
Plaistow *U.S.A.*   42°50N 71°6W **83 D13**
Plaka, Ákra *Greece*   35°11N 26°19E **25 D8**
Plana Cays *Bahamas*   22°38N 73°30W **89 B5**
Planada *U.S.A.*   37°16N 120°19W **78 H6**
Plano *U.S.A.*   33°1N 96°42W **84 E6**
Plant City *U.S.A.*   28°1N 82°7W **85 G13**
Plaquemine *U.S.A.*   30°17N 91°14W **84 F9**
Plasencia *Spain*   40°3N 6°8W **21 B2**
Plaster City *U.S.A.*   32°47N 115°51W **79 N11**
Plaster Rock *Canada*   46°53N 67°22W **73 C6**
Plastun *Russia*   44°45N 136°19E **30 B8**
Plata, Río de la →
  S. Amer.   34°45S 57°30W **94 C4**
Plátani → *Italy*   37°23N 13°16E **22 F5**
Plátanos *Greece*   35°28N 23°33E **25 D5**
Platte *U.S.A.*   43°23N 98°51W **80 D4**
Platte → *Mo., U.S.A.*   39°16N 94°50W **80 F6**
Platte → *Nebr., U.S.A.*   41°4N 95°53W **80 E7**
Platteville *U.S.A.*   42°44N 90°29W **80 D9**
Plattsburgh *U.S.A.*   44°42N 73°28W **83 B11**
Plattsmouth *U.S.A.*   41°1N 95°53W **80 E6**
Plauen *Germany*   50°30N 12°8E **16 C7**
Plavinas *Latvia*   56°35N 25°46E **9 H21**
Playa Blanca *Canary Is.*   28°55N 13°37W **24 F6**
Playa Blanca Sur
  Canary Is.   28°51N 13°50W **24 F6**
Playa de las Americas
  Canary Is.   28°5N 16°43W **24 F3**
Playa de Mogán
  Canary Is.   27°48N 15°47W **24 G4**
Playa del Carmen *Mexico*   20°37N 87°4W **87 C7**
Playa del Inglés
  Canary Is.   27°45N 15°33W **24 G4**
Playa Esmeralda
  Canary Is.   28°8N 14°16W **24 F5**

Playgreen L. *Canada*   54°0N 98°15W **71 C9**
Pleasant Bay *Canada*   46°51N 60°48W **73 C7**
Pleasant Hill *U.S.A.*   37°57N 122°4W **78 H4**
Pleasant Mount *U.S.A.*   41°44N 75°26W **83 E9**
Pleasanton *Calif.,*
  U.S.A.   37°39N 121°52W **78 H5**
Pleasanton *Tex., U.S.A.*   28°58N 98°29W **84 G5**
Pleasantville *N.J.,*
  U.S.A.   39°24N 74°32W **81 F10**
Pleasantville *Pa., U.S.A.*   41°35N 79°34W **82 E5**
Plei Ku *Vietnam*   13°57N 108°0E **38 F7**
Plenty → *Australia*   23°25S 136°31E **62 C2**
Plenty, B. of *N.Z.*   37°45S 177°0E **59 B6**
Plentywood *U.S.A.*   48°47N 104°34W **76 B11**
Plesetsk *Russia*   62°43N 40°20E **18 B7**
Plessisville *Canada*   46°14N 71°47W **73 C5**
Plétipi, L. *Canada*   51°44N 70°6W **73 B5**
Pleven *Bulgaria*   43°26N 24°37E **23 C11**
Plevlja *Montenegro*   43°21N 19°21E **23 C8**
Plevna *Bulgaria*   44°58N 76°59W **82 B8**
Plock *Poland*   52°32N 19°40E **17 B10**
Plöckenstein *Germany*   48°46N 13°51E **16 D7**
Ploiești *Romania*   44°57N 26°5E **17 F14**
Plonge, Lac la *Canada*   55°8N 107°20W **71 B7**
Plovdiv *Bulgaria*   42°8N 24°44E **23 C11**
Plover Cove Res. *China*   22°28N 114°15E **33 G11**
Plum *U.S.A.*   40°29N 79°47W **82 F5**
Plum I. *U.S.A.*   41°11N 72°12W **83 E12**
Plumas *U.S.A.*   39°45N 120°4W **78 F6**
Plummer *U.S.A.*   47°20N 116°53W **76 C5**
Plumridge Lakes
  Australia   29°26S 125°16E **61 E4**
Plumtree *Zimbabwe*   20°27S 27°55E **55 G2**
Plunge *Lithuania*   55°53N 21°59E **9 J19**
Plymouth *Trin. & Tob.*   11°14N 60°48W **93 J16**
Plymouth *U.K.*   50°22N 4°10W **13 G3**
Plymouth *Calif., U.S.A.*   38°29N 120°51W **78 G6**
Plymouth *Ind., U.S.A.*   41°21N 86°19W **80 E10**
Plymouth *Mass., U.S.A.*   41°57N 70°40W **83 E14**
Plymouth *N.C., U.S.A.*   35°52N 76°43W **85 D16**
Plymouth *N.H., U.S.A.*   43°46N 71°41W **83 C13**
Plymouth *Pa., U.S.A.*   41°14N 75°57W **83 E9**
Plymouth *Wis., U.S.A.*   43°45N 87°59W **80 D10**
Plympton-Wyoming = Wyoming
  Canada   42°57N 82°7W **82 D2**
Plynlimon = Pumlumon Fawr
  U.K.   52°28N 3°46W **13 E4**
Plyusa *Russia*   58°28N 29°27E **9 G23**
Plzeň *Czech Rep.*   49°45N 13°22E **16 D7**
Pmere Nyente ◎
  Australia   24°15S 136°10E **62 C2**
Po → *Italy*   44°57N 12°4E **22 B5**
Po Hai = Bo Hai *China*   39°0N 119°0E **35 E10**
Po Toi *China*   22°10N 114°16E **33 G11**
Pobeda *Russia*   65°12N 146°12E **29 C15**
Pobedy, Pik *Kyrgyzstan*   42°0N 79°58E **32 B2**
Pocahontas *Ark., U.S.A.*   36°16N 90°58W **85 C9**
Pocahontas *Iowa, U.S.A.*   42°44N 94°40W **80 D6**
Pocatello *U.S.A.*   42°52N 112°27W **76 E7**
Pocomoke City *U.S.A.*   38°5N 75°34W **81 F16**
Poços de Caldas *Brazil*   21°50S 46°33W **95 A6**
Podgorica *Montenegro*   42°30N 19°19E **23 C8**
Podlaska Vysochyna
  Ukraine   49°0N 28°0E **17 D14**
Podolsk *Russia*   55°25N 37°30E **18 C6**
Podporozhye *Russia*   60°55N 34°2E **18 B5**
Pofadder *S. Africa*   29°10S 19°22E **56 D2**
Pogranichnyy *Russia*   44°25N 131°24E **30 B5**
Poh *Indonesia*   0°46S 122°51E **37 E6**
Pohang *S. Korea*   36°1N 129°23E **35 F15**
Pohjanmaa *Finland*   62°58N 22°50E **8 E20**
Pohnpei *Micronesia*   6°55N 158°10E **64 G7**
Pohri *India*   25°32N 77°22E **42 G6**
Poinsett, C. *Antarctica*   65°42S 113°18E **5 C8**
Point Arena *U.S.A.*   38°55N 123°41W **78 G3**
Point Baker *U.S.A.*   56°21N 133°37W **70 B2**
Point Fortin
  Trin. & Tob.   10°10N 61°42W **93 K15**
Point Hope *U.S.A.*   68°21N 166°47W **74 B6**
Point L. *Canada*   65°15N 113°4W **68 D9**
Point Lisas *Trin. & Tob.*   10°24N 61°29W **93 K15**
Point Pedro *Sri Lanka*   9°50N 80°15E **40 Q12**
Point Pelee △ *Canada*   41°57N 82°31W **82 E2**
Point Pleasant *N.J.,*
  U.S.A.   40°5N 74°4W **83 F10**
Point Pleasant *W. Va.,*
  U.S.A.   38°51N 82°8W **81 F12**
Point Reyes △ *U.S.A.*   38°10N 122°55W **78 G2**
Pointe-à-Pitre *Guadeloupe*   16°10N 61°32W **88 b**
Pointe-au-Pic = La Malbaie
  Canada   47°40N 70°10W **73 C5**
Pointe-Claire *Canada*   45°26N 73°50W **83 A11**
Pointe-Gatineau *Canada*   45°28N 75°42W **83 A9**
Pointe-Noire *Congo*   4°48S 11°53E **52 E2**
Pointe-Noire *Guadeloupe*   16°14N 61°47W **88 b**
Poipet *Cambodia*   13°39N 102°33E **38 F4**
Poisonbush Ra.
  Australia   19°57S 119°10E **60 C2**
Poissonnier Pt.
  Australia   19°57S 119°10E **60 C2**
Poitiers *France*   46°35N 0°20E **20 C4**
Poitou *France*   46°40N 0°10W **20 C3**
Pojoaque *U.S.A.*   35°54N 106°1W **77 J11**
Pokaran *India*   27°0N 71°50E **42 F4**
Pokataroo *Australia*   29°30S 148°36E **63 D4**
Pokhara *Nepal*   28°14N 83°58E **43 E10**
Poko *Dem. Rep. of the Congo*   3°7N 26°52E **54 B2**
Pokrovsk *Russia*   61°29N 129°0E **29 C13**
Pola = Pula *Croatia*   44°54N 13°57E **16 F7**
Polacca *U.S.A.*   35°50N 110°23W **77 J8**
Polan *Iran*   25°30N 61°10E **45 E9**
Poland ■ *Europe*   52°0N 20°0E **17 C10**
Polar Bear △ *Canada*   54°30N 83°45W **72 A2**
Polatsk *Belarus*   55°30N 28°50E **9 J23**
Polcura *Chile*   37°17S 71°43W **94 D1**
Polesye = Pripet Marshes
  Europe   52°10N 28°10E **17 B15**
Polevskoy *Russia*   56°26N 60°11E **18 C11**

Police *Poland*   53°33N 14°33E **16 B8**
Police, Pte. *Seychelles*   4°51S 55°32E **53 b**
Poligiros *Greece*   40°23N 23°25E **23 D10**
Polillo Is. *Phil.*   14°56N 122°0E **37 B6**
Polis *Cyprus*   35°2N 32°26E **25 D11**
Polk *U.S.A.*   41°22N 79°56W **82 E5**
Pollachi *India*   10°35N 77°0E **40 P10**
Pollença *Spain*   39°54N 3°1E **24 B10**
Pollença, B. de *Spain*   39°53N 3°8E **24 B10**
Polnovat *Russia*   63°50N 65°54E **28 C7**
Polokwane *S. Africa*   23°54S 29°25E **57 C4**
Polokwane → *S. Africa*   22°25S 30°5E **57 C5**
Polonne *Ukraine*   50°6N 27°30E **17 C14**
Polonnoye = Polonne
  Ukraine   50°6N 27°30E **17 C14**
Polson *U.S.A.*   47°41N 114°9W **76 C6**
Poltava *Ukraine*   49°35N 34°35E **19 E5**
Põltsamaa *Estonia*   58°39N 25°58E **9 G21**
Polunochnoye *Russia*   60°52N 60°25E **28 C7**
Põlva *Estonia*   58°3N 27°3E **9 G22**
Polyarny *Russia*   69°8N 33°20E **8 B25**
Polyarnyye Zori *Russia*   67°22N 32°30E **8 C25**
Polynesia *Pac. Oc.*   10°0S 162°0W **65 F11**
Polynésie française = French
  Polynesia ☑ *Pac. Oc.*   20°0S 145°0W **65 F13**
Pombal *Portugal*   39°55N 8°40W **21 C1**
Pombia *Greece*   35°0N 24°51E **25 E6**
Pomene *Mozam.*   22°53S 35°33E **57 C6**
Pomeroy *Ohio, U.S.A.*   39°2N 82°2W **81 F12**
Pomeroy *Wash., U.S.A.*   46°28N 117°36W **76 C5**
Pomézia *Italy*   41°40N 12°30E **22 D5**
Pomona *Australia*   26°22S 152°52E **63 D5**
Pomona *U.S.A.*   34°4N 117°45W **79 L9**
Pomorskie, Pojezierze
  Poland   53°40N 16°37E **17 B9**
Pomos *Cyprus*   35°9N 32°33E **25 D11**
Pomos, C. *Cyprus*   35°10N 32°33E **25 D11**
Pompano Beach *U.S.A.*   26°14N 80°7W **85 H14**
Pompeys Pillar *U.S.A.*   45°59N 107°57W **76 D10**
Pompeys Pillar △
  U.S.A.   46°0N 108°0W **76 D10**
Pompton Lakes *U.S.A.*   41°0N 74°17W **83 F10**
Ponape = Pohnpei
  Micronesia   6°55N 158°10E **64 G7**
Ponask L. *Canada*   54°0N 92°41W **72 B1**
Ponca *U.S.A.*   42°34N 96°43W **80 D5**
Ponca City *U.S.A.*   36°42N 97°5W **84 C6**
Ponce *Puerto Rico*   18°1N 66°37W **89 d**
Ponchatoula *U.S.A.*   30°26N 90°26W **85 F9**
Poncheville, L. *Canada*   50°10N 76°55W **72 B4**
Pond *U.S.A.*   35°43N 119°20W **79 K7**
Pond Inlet *Canada*   72°40N 77°0W **69 C16**
Pondicherry = Puducherry
  India   11°59N 79°50E **40 P11**
Ponds, I. of *Canada*   53°27N 55°52W **73 B8**
Ponferrada *Spain*   42°32N 6°35W **21 A2**
Ponnani *India*   10°45N 75°59E **40 P9**
Ponoka *Canada*   52°42N 113°40W **70 C6**
Ponorogo *Indonesia*   7°52S 111°27E **37 G14**
Ponoy *Russia*   67°0N 41°13E **18 A7**
Ponoy → *Russia*   66°59N 41°17E **18 A7**
Ponta Delgada *Azores*   37°44N 25°40W **50 a**
Ponta do Sol *Madeira*   32°42N 17°7W **24 D2**
Ponta Grossa *Brazil*   25°7S 50°10W **95 B5**
Ponta Porã *Brazil*   22°20S 55°35W **95 A4**
Pontarlier *France*   46°54N 6°20E **20 C7**
Pontchartrain, L. *U.S.A.*   30°5N 90°5W **85 F9**
Ponte do Pungué
  Mozam.   19°30S 34°33E **55 F3**
Ponte Nova *Brazil*   20°25S 42°54W **95 A7**
Ponteix *Canada*   49°46N 107°29W **71 D7**
Pontevedra *Spain*   42°26N 8°40W **21 A1**
Pontiac *Ill., U.S.A.*   40°53N 88°38W **80 E9**
Pontiac *Mich., U.S.A.*   42°38N 83°18W **81 D12**
Pontian Kechil *Malaysia*   1°29N 103°23E **39 d**
Pontianak *Indonesia*   0°3S 109°15E **36 E3**
Pontine Is. = Ponziane, Ísole
  Italy   40°55N 12°57E **22 D5**
Pontine Mts. = Kuzey Anadolu
  Dağları *Turkey*   41°0N 36°45E **19 F6**
Pontivy *France*   48°5N 2°58W **20 B2**
Pontoise *France*   49°3N 2°5E **20 B5**
Ponton → *Canada*   58°27N 116°11W **70 B5**
Pontypool *Canada*   44°6N 78°38W **82 B6**
Pontypool *U.K.*   51°42N 3°2W **13 F4**
Ponziane, Ísole *Italy*   40°55N 12°57E **22 D5**
Poochera *Australia*   32°43S 134°51E **63 E1**
Poole *U.K.*   50°43N 1°59W **13 G6**
Poole □ *U.K.*   50°43N 1°59W **13 G6**
Poona = Pune *India*   18°29N 73°57E **40 K8**
Pooncarie *Australia*   33°22S 142°31E **63 E3**
Poopelloe L. *Australia*   31°40S 144°0E **63 E3**
Poopó, L. de *Bolivia*   18°30S 67°35W **92 G5**
Popayán *Colombia*   2°27N 76°36W **92 C3**
Poperinge *Belgium*   50°51N 2°42E **15 D2**
Popilta L. *Australia*   33°10S 141°42E **63 E3**
Popio L. *Australia*   33°10S 141°52E **63 E3**
Poplar *U.S.A.*   48°7N 105°12W **76 B11**
Poplar → *Canada*   53°0N 97°19W **71 C9**
Poplar Bluff *U.S.A.*   36°46N 90°24W **80 G9**
Poplarville *U.S.A.*   30°51N 89°32W **85 F10**
Popocatépetl, Volcán
  Mexico   19°2N 98°38W **87 D5**
Popokabaka
  Dem. Rep. of the Congo   5°41S 16°40E **52 F3**
Poprad *Slovak Rep.*   49°3N 20°18E **17 D11**
Porali → *Pakistan*   25°58N 66°26E **42 G2**
Porbandar *India*   21°44N 69°43E **42 J3**
Porcher I. *Canada*   53°50N 130°30W **70 C2**
Porcupine → *Canada*   59°11N 104°46W **71 B8**
Porcupine → *U.S.A.*   66°34N 145°19W **68 D2**
Porcupine Gorge △
  Australia   20°22S 144°26E **62 C3**
Pordenone *Italy*   45°57N 12°39E **22 B5**
Pori *Finland*   61°29N 21°48E **8 F19**
Porkhov *Russia*   57°45S 29°38E **9 H23**
Porlamar *Venezuela*   10°57N 63°51W **92 A6**
Pormpuraaw *Australia*   14°59S 141°26E **62 A3**

Pormpuraaw ◎
  Australia   14°55S 141°47E **62 A3**
Poronaysk *Russia*   49°13N 143°0E **29 E15**
Poroshiri-Dake *Japan*   42°41N 142°52E **30 C11**
Poroto Mts. *Tanzania*   9°0S 33°30E **55 D3**
Porpoise B. *Antarctica*   66°0S 127°0E **5 C9**
Porreres *Spain*   39°31N 3°2E **24 B10**
Porsangerfjorden
  Norway   70°40N 25°40E **8 A21**
Porsgrunn *Norway*   59°10N 9°40E **9 G13**
Port Alberni *Canada*   49°14N 124°50W **70 D4**
Port Alfred *S. Africa*   33°36S 26°55E **56 E4**
Port Alice *Canada*   50°20N 127°25W **70 C3**
Port Allegany *U.S.A.*   41°48N 78°17W **82 E6**
Port Allen *U.S.A.*   30°27N 91°12W **84 F9**
Port Alma *Australia*   23°38S 150°53E **62 C5**
Port Alma *Canada*   42°10N 82°14W **82 D2**
Port Angeles *U.S.A.*   48°7N 123°27W **78 B3**
Port Antonio *Jamaica*   18°10N 76°26W **88 a**
Port Aransas *U.S.A.*   27°50N 97°4W **84 H6**
Port Arthur *Australia*   43°7S 147°50E **63 G4**
Port Arthur *U.S.A.*   29°54N 93°56W **84 G8**
Port au Choix *Canada*   50°43N 57°22W **73 B8**
Port au Port B. *Canada*   48°40N 58°50W **73 C8**
Port-au-Prince *Haiti*   18°40N 72°20W **89 C5**
Port Augusta *Australia*   32°30S 137°50E **63 E2**
Port Austin *U.S.A.*   44°3N 83°1W **82 B2**
Port Bell *Uganda*   0°18N 32°35E **54 B3**
Port Bergé Vaovao
  Madag.   15°33S 47°40E **57 B8**
Port Blandford *Canada*   48°20N 54°10W **73 C9**
Port Bradshaw
  Australia   12°30S 136°42E **62 A2**
Port Broughton
  Australia   33°37S 137°56E **63 E2**
Port Bruce *Canada*   42°39N 81°0W **82 D3**
Port Burwell *Canada*   42°40N 80°48W **82 D4**
Port Canning *India*   22°23N 88°40E **43 H13**
Port Carling *Canada*   45°7N 79°35W **82 A5**
Port-Cartier *Canada*   50°2N 66°50W **73 B6**
Port Chalmers *N.Z.*   45°49S 170°30E **59 F3**
Port Charlotte *U.S.A.*   26°59N 82°6W **85 H13**
Port Chester *U.S.A.*   41°0N 73°40W **83 F11**
Port Clements *Canada*   53°40N 132°10W **70 C2**
Port Clinton *U.S.A.*   41°31N 82°56W **81 E12**
Port Colborne *Canada*   42°50N 79°10W **82 D5**
Port Coquitlam *Canada*   49°15N 122°45W **78 A4**
Port Credit *Canada*   43°33N 79°35W **82 C5**
Port Curtis *Australia*   23°57S 151°20E **62 C5**
Port d'Alcúdia *Spain*   39°50N 3°7E **24 B10**
Port Dalhousie *Canada*   43°13N 79°16W **82 C5**
Port d'Andratx *Spain*   39°32N 2°23E **24 B9**
Port Darwin *Canada*   12°24S 130°45E **60 B5**
Port Darwin *Falk. Is.*   51°50S 59°0W **96 G5**
Port Davey *Australia*   43°16S 145°55E **63 G4**
Port-de-Paix *Haiti*   19°50N 72°50W **89 C5**
Port de Pollença *Spain*   39°54N 3°4E **24 B10**
Port de Sóller *Spain*   39°48N 2°42E **24 B9**
Port Dickson *Malaysia*   2°30N 101°49E **39 L3**
Port Douglas *Australia*   16°30S 145°30E **62 B4**
Port Dover *Canada*   42°47N 80°12W **82 D4**
Port Edward *Canada*   54°12N 130°10W **70 C2**
Port Elgin *Canada*   44°25N 81°25W **82 B3**
Port Elizabeth *S. Africa*   33°58S 25°40E **56 E4**
Port Ellen *U.K.*   55°38N 6°11W **11 F2**
Port Erin *I. of Man*   54°5N 4°45W **12 C3**
Port Essington *Australia*   11°15S 132°10E **60 B5**
Port Ewen *U.S.A.*   41°54N 73°59W **83 E11**
Port Fairy *Australia*   38°22S 142°12E **63 F3**
Port Gamble *U.S.A.*   47°51N 122°34W **78 C4**
Port-Gentil *Gabon*   0°40S 8°50E **52 E1**
Port Germein *Australia*   33°1S 138°1E **63 E2**
Port Gibson *U.S.A.*   31°58N 90°59W **84 F9**
Port Glasgow *U.K.*   55°56N 4°41W **11 F4**
Port Harcourt *Nigeria*   4°40N 7°10E **50 H7**
Port Hardy *Canada*   50°41N 127°30W **70 C3**
Port Harrison = Inukjuak
  Canada   58°25N 78°15W **69 F16**
Port Hawkesbury
  Canada   45°36N 61°22W **73 C7**
Port Hedland *Australia*   20°25S 118°35E **60 D2**
Port Henry *U.S.A.*   44°3N 73°28W **83 B11**
Port Hood *Canada*   46°0N 61°32W **73 C7**
Port Hope *Canada*   43°56N 78°20W **82 C6**
Port Hope *U.S.A.*   43°57N 82°43W **82 C2**
Port Hope Simpson
  Canada   52°33N 56°18W **73 B8**
Port Hueneme *U.S.A.*   34°7N 119°12W **79 L7**
Port Huron *U.S.A.*   42°58N 82°26W **82 D2**
Port Jefferson *U.S.A.*   40°57N 73°3W **83 F11**
Port Jervis *U.S.A.*   41°22N 74°41W **83 E10**
Port Kelang = Pelabuhan Klang
  Malaysia   3°0N 101°23E **39 L3**
Port Kenny *Australia*   33°10S 134°41E **63 E1**
Port Lairge = Waterford
  Ireland   52°15N 7°8W **10 D4**
Port Laoise *Ireland*   53°2N 7°18W **10 C4**
Port Lavaca *U.S.A.*   28°37N 96°38W **84 G6**
Port Leyden *U.S.A.*   43°35N 75°21W **83 C9**
Port Lincoln *Australia*   34°42S 135°52E **63 E2**
Port Loko *S. Leone*   8°48N 12°46W **50 G3**
Port-Louis *Guadeloupe*   16°28N 61°32W **88 b**
Port Louis *Mauritius*   20°10S 57°30E **53 d**
Port MacDonnell
  Australia   38°5S 140°48E **63 F3**
Port McNeill *Canada*   50°35N 127°6W **70 C3**
Port Macquarie
  Australia   31°25S 152°25E **63 E5**
Port Maria *Jamaica*   18°22N 76°54W **88 a**
Port Matilda *U.S.A.*   40°48N 78°3W **82 F6**
Port McNicoll *Canada*   44°44N 79°48W **82 B5**
Port Mellon *Canada*   49°32N 123°31W **78 A3**
Port-Menier *Canada*   49°51N 64°15W **73 C7**
Port Moody *Canada*   49°17N 122°51W **78 A4**
Port Morant *Jamaica*   17°54N 76°19W **88 a**
Port Moresby *Papua N. G.*   9°24S 147°8E **58 B7**
Port Musgrave
  Australia   11°55S 141°50E **62 A3**

Port Neches *U.S.A.*   30°0N 93°59W **84 G8**
Port Nolloth *S. Africa*   29°17S 16°52E **56 D2**
Port Nouveau-Québec =
  Kangiqsualujjuaq
  Canada   58°30N 65°59W **69 F18**
Port of Climax *Canada*   49°10N 108°20W **71 D7**
Port of Coronach
  Canada   49°7N 105°31W **71 D7**
Port of Spain
  Trin. & Tob.   10°40N 61°31W **93 K15**
Port Orange *U.S.A.*   29°9N 80°59W **85 G14**
Port Orchard *U.S.A.*   47°32N 122°38W **78 C4**
Port Orford *U.S.A.*   42°45N 124°30W **76 E1**
Port Pegasus *N.Z.*   47°12S 167°41E **59 G1**
Port Perry *Canada*   44°6N 78°56W **82 B6**
Port Phillip B. *Australia*   38°10S 144°50E **63 F3**
Port Pirie *Australia*   33°10S 138°1E **63 E2**
Port Renfrew *Canada*   48°30N 124°20W **78 B2**
Port Roper *Australia*   14°45S 135°25E **62 A2**
Port Rowan *Canada*   42°40N 80°30W **82 D4**
Port Safaga = Bûr Safâga
  Egypt   26°43N 33°57E **44 E2**
Port Said = Bûr Sa'îd
  Egypt   31°16N 32°18E **51 B12**
Port St. Joe *U.S.A.*   29°49N 85°18W **85 G12**
Port St. Johns = Umzimvubu
  S. Africa   31°38S 29°33E **57 E4**
Port St. Lucie *U.S.A.*   27°18N 80°21W **85 H14**
Port Sanilac *U.S.A.*   43°26N 82°33W **82 C2**
Port Severn *Canada*   44°48N 79°43W **82 B5**
Port Shepstone *S. Africa*   30°44S 30°28E **57 E5**
Port Simpson *Canada*   54°30N 130°20W **70 C2**
Port Stanley = Stanley
  Falk. Is.   51°40S 59°51W **96 G5**
Port Stanley *Canada*   42°40N 81°10W **82 D3**
Port Sudan = Bûr Sûdân
  Sudan   19°32N 37°9E **51 E13**
Port Sulphur *U.S.A.*   29°29N 89°42W **85 G10**
Port Talbot *U.K.*   51°35N 3°47W **13 F4**
Port Townsend *U.S.A.*   48°7N 122°45W **78 B4**
Port-Vendres *France*   42°32N 3°8E **20 E5**
Port Vila *Vanuatu*   17°45S 168°18E **58 C9**
Port Vladimir *Russia*   69°25N 33°6E **8 B25**
Port Wakefield *Australia*   34°12S 138°10E **63 E2**
Port Washington
  U.S.A.   43°23N 87°53W **80 D10**
Porta Orientalis *Romania*   45°6N 22°18E **17 F12**
Portaclov *Ireland*   54°20N 9°46W **10 B2**
Portadown *U.K.*   54°25N 6°27W **10 B5**
Portaferry *U.K.*   54°23N 5°33W **10 B6**
Portage *Pa., U.S.A.*   40°23N 78°41W **82 F6**
Portage *Wis., U.S.A.*   43°33N 89°28W **80 D9**
Portage la Prairie
  Canada   49°58N 98°18W **71 D9**
Portageville *U.S.A.*   36°26N 89°42W **80 G9**
Portalegre *Portugal*   39°19N 7°25W **21 C2**
Portales *U.S.A.*   34°11N 103°20W **77 J12**
Portarlington *Ireland*   53°9N 7°14W **10 C4**
Portbou *Spain*   42°25N 3°9E **21 A7**
Porter L., *N.W.T., Canada*   61°41N 108°5W **71 A7**
Porter L., *Sask., Canada*   56°20N 107°20W **71 B7**
Porterville *S. Africa*   33°0S 19°0E **56 E2**
Porterville *U.S.A.*   36°4N 119°1W **78 J8**
Porthcawl *U.K.*   51°29N 3°42W **13 F4**
Porthill *U.S.A.*   48°59N 116°30W **76 B5**
Porthmadog *U.K.*   52°55N 4°8W **12 E3**
Portile de Fier *Europe*   44°44N 22°30E **17 F12**
Portimão *Portugal*   37°8N 8°32W **21 D1**
Portishead *U.K.*   51°29N 2°46W **13 F5**
Portknockie *U.K.*   57°42N 2°51W **11 D6**
Portland *N.S.W.,*
  Australia   33°20S 150°0E **63 E5**
Portland *Vic., Australia*   38°20S 141°35E **63 F3**
Portland *Canada*   44°42N 76°12W **83 B8**
Portland *Conn., U.S.A.*   41°34N 72°38W **83 E12**
Portland *Maine, U.S.A.*   43°39N 70°16W **81 D18**
Portland *Mich., U.S.A.*   42°52N 84°54W **81 D11**
Portland *Oreg., U.S.A.*   45°32N 122°37W **78 E4**
Portland *Pa., U.S.A.*   40°55N 75°6W **83 F9**
Portland *Tex., U.S.A.*   27°53N 97°20W **84 H6**
Portland, I. of *U.K.*   50°33N 2°26W **13 G5**
Portland B. *Australia*   38°15S 141°45E **63 F3**
Portland Bight *Jamaica*   17°52N 77°5W **88 a**
Portland Bill *U.K.*   50°31N 2°28W **13 G5**
Portland Canal *U.S.A.*   55°56N 130°0W **70 B2**
Portland Int. ✈ (PDX)
  U.S.A.   45°35N 122°36W **78 E4**
Portland Pt. *Jamaica*   17°42N 77°11W **88 a**
Portmadoc = Porthmadog
  U.K.   52°55N 4°8W **12 E3**
Portmore *Jamaica*   17°53N 76°53W **88 a**
Porto *France*   42°16N 8°42E **20 E8**
Porto *Portugal*   41°8N 8°40W **21 B1**
Pôrto Alegre *Brazil*   30°5S 51°10W **95 C5**
Porto Colom *Spain*   39°33N 3°15E **24 B10**
Porto Cristo *Spain*   39°33N 3°20E **24 B10**
Porto de Moz *Brazil*   1°41S 52°13W **93 D8**
Porto Empédocle *Italy*   37°17N 13°32E **22 F5**
Porto Esperança *Brazil*   19°37S 57°29W **92 G7**
Porto Franco *Brazil*   6°20S 47°24W **93 E9**
Porto Inglês *C. Verde Is.*   15°8N 23°10W **50 b**
Porto Mendes *Brazil*   24°30S 54°15W **95 A5**
Porto Moniz *Madeira*   32°52N 17°11W **24 D2**
Porto Murtinho *Brazil*   21°45S 57°55W **92 H7**
Porto Nacional *Brazil*   10°40S 48°30W **93 F9**
Porto-Novo *Benin*   6°23N 2°42E **50 G6**
Porto Primavera, Represa
  Brazil   22°10S 52°45W **95 A5**
Porto Santo, I. de
  Madeira   33°45N 16°25W **50 B2**
Pôrto São José *Brazil*   22°43S 53°10W **95 A5**
Porto Seguro *Brazil*   16°26S 39°5W **93 G11**
Pôrto Tôrres *Italy*   40°50N 8°24E **22 D3**
Porto União *Brazil*   26°10S 51°10W **95 B5**
Porto-Vecchio *France*   41°35N 9°16E **20 F8**
Pôrto Velho *Brazil*   8°46S 63°54W **92 E6**
Port Walter *U.S.A.*   8°15S 72°40W **92 A2**
Portobelo *Panama*   9°35N 79°42W **88 E4**
Portoferráio *Italy*   42°48N 10°20E **22 C4**

Portola *U.S.A.* 39°49N 120°28W 78 F6
Portopetro *Spain* 39°22N 3°13E 24 B10
Portoscuso *Italy* 39°12N 8°24E 22 E3
Portoviejo *Ecuador* 1°7S 80°28W 92 D2
Portpatrick *U.K.* 54°51N 5°7W 11 G3
Portree *U.K.* 57°25N 6°12W 11 D2
Portrush *U.K.* 55°12N 6°40W 10 A5
Portsmouth *Dominica* 15°34N 61°27W 89 C7
Portsmouth *U.K.* 50°48N 1°6W 13 G6
Portsmouth *N.H., U.S.A.* 43°5N 70°45W 83 C14
Portsmouth *Ohio, U.S.A.* 38°44N 82°57W 81 F12
Portsmouth *R.I., U.S.A.* 41°36N 71°15W 83 E13
Portsmouth *Va., U.S.A.* 36°58N 76°23W 81 G15
Portsmouth □ *U.K.* 50°48N 1°6W 13 G6
Portsoy *U.K.* 57°41N 2°41W 11 D6
Portstewart *U.K.* 55°11N 6°43W 10 A5
Porttipahdan tekojärvi *Finland* 68°5N 26°40E 8 B22
Portugal ■ *Europe* 40°0N 8°0W 21 C1
Portumna *Ireland* 53°6N 8°14W 10 C3
Portville *U.S.A.* 42°3N 78°20W 82 D6
Poruma *Australia* 10°2S 143°4E 62 a
Porvenir *Chile* 53°10S 70°16W 96 G2
Posadas *Argentina* 27°30S 55°50W 95 B4
Posht-e Badam *Iran* 33°2N 55°23E 45 C7
Poso *Indonesia* 1°20S 120°55E 37 E6
Posse *Brazil* 14°4S 46°18W 93 F9
Possession I. *Antarctica* 72°4S 172°0E 5 D11
Possum Kingdom L. *U.S.A.* 32°52N 98°26W 84 E5
Post *U.S.A.* 33°12N 101°23W 84 E4
Post Falls *U.S.A.* 47°43N 116°57W 76 C5
Postavy = Pastavy *Belarus* 55°4N 26°50E 9 J22
Poste-de-la-Baleine = Kuujjuarapik *Canada* 55°20N 77°35W 72 A4
Postmasburg *S. Africa* 28°18S 23°5E 56 D3
Postojna *Slovenia* 45°46N 14°12E 16 F8
Poston *U.S.A.* 34°0N 114°24W 79 M12
Postville *Canada* 54°54N 59°47W 73 B8
Posyet *Russia* 42°39N 130°48E 30 C5
Potchefstroom *S. Africa* 26°41S 27°7E 56 D4
Poteau *U.S.A.* 35°3N 94°37W 84 D7
Poteet *U.S.A.* 29°2N 98°35W 84 G5
Potenza *Italy* 40°38N 15°48E 22 D6
Poteriteri, L. *N.Z.* 46°5S 167°10E 59 G1
Potgietersrus = Mokopane *S. Africa* 24°10S 28°55E 57 C4
Poti *Georgia* 42°10N 41°38E 19 F7
Potiskum *Nigeria* 11°39N 11°2E 51 F8
Potomac → *U.S.A.* 38°0N 76°23W 81 F14
Potosí *Bolivia* 19°38S 65°50W 92 G5
Potosi Mt. *U.S.A.* 35°57N 115°29W 79 K11
Pototan *Phil.* 10°54N 122°38E 37 B6
Potrerillos *Chile* 26°30S 69°30W 94 B2
Potsdam *Germany* 52°23N 13°3E 16 B7
Potsdam *U.S.A.* 44°40N 74°59W 83 B10
Pottersville *U.S.A.* 43°43N 73°50W 83 C11
Pottstown *U.S.A.* 40°15N 75°39W 83 F9
Pottsville *U.S.A.* 40°41N 76°12W 83 F8
Pottuvil *Sri Lanka* 6°55N 81°50E 40 R12
Pouce Coupé *Canada* 55°40N 120°10W 70 B4
Poughkeepsie *U.S.A.* 41°42N 73°56W 83 E11
Poulaphouca Res. *Ireland* 53°8N 6°30W 10 C5
Poulsbo *U.S.A.* 47°44N 122°38W 78 C4
Poultney *U.S.A.* 43°31N 73°14W 83 C11
Poulton-le-Fylde *U.K.* 53°51N 2°58W 12 D5
Pouso Alegre *Brazil* 22°14S 45°57W 95 A6
Pouthisat *Cambodia* 12°34N 103°50E 38 F4
Považská Bystrica *Slovak Rep.* 49°8N 18°27E 17 D10
Povenets *Russia* 62°50N 34°50E 18 B5
Poverty B. *N.Z.* 38°43S 178°2E 59 C7
Póvoa de Varzim *Portugal* 41°25N 8°46W 21 B1
Povorotnyy, Mys *Russia* 42°40N 133°2E 30 C6
Povungnituk = Puvirnituq *Canada* 60°2N 77°10W 69 E16
Powassan *Canada* 46°5N 79°25W 72 C4
Poway *U.S.A.* 32°58N 117°2W 79 N9
Powder → *U.S.A.* 46°45N 105°26W 76 C11
Powder River *U.S.A.* 43°2N 106°59W 76 E10
Powell *U.S.A.* 44°45N 108°46W 76 D9
Powell, L. *U.S.A.* 36°57N 111°29W 77 H8
Powell River *Canada* 49°50N 124°35W 70 D4
Powers *U.S.A.* 45°41N 87°32W 80 C10
Pownal *U.S.A.* 42°45N 73°14W 83 D11
Powys □ *U.K.* 52°20N 3°20W 13 E4
Poyang Hu *China* 29°5N 116°20E 33 D6
Poyarkovo *Russia* 49°36N 128°41E 29 E13
Poza Rica *Mexico* 20°33N 97°27W 87 C5
Požarevac *Serbia* 44°35N 21°18E 23 B9
Poznań *Poland* 52°25N 16°55E 17 B9
Pozo *U.S.A.* 35°20N 120°24W 79 K6
Pozo Almonte *Chile* 20°10S 69°50W 92 H5
Pozo Colorado *Paraguay* 23°30S 58°45W 94 A4
Pozoblanco *Spain* 38°23N 4°51W 21 C3
Pozzuoli *Italy* 40°49N 14°7E 22 D6
Prachin Buri *Thailand* 14°0N 101°25E 38 F3
Prachuap Khiri Khan *Thailand* 11°49N 99°48E 39 G2
Prado *Brazil* 17°20S 39°13W 93 G11
Prague = Praha *Czech Rep.* 50°4N 14°25E 16 C8
Praha *Czech Rep.* 50°4N 14°25E 16 C8
Praia *C. Verde Is.* 15°2N 23°34W 50 b
Prainha *Brazil* 1°45S 53°30W 93 D8
Prainha Nova *Brazil* 7°10S 60°30W 92 E6
Prairie *Australia* 20°50S 144°35E 62 C3
Prairie City *U.S.A.* 44°28N 118°43W 76 D4
Prairie Dog Town Fork Red → *U.S.A.* 34°34N 99°58W 84 D5
Prairie du Chien *U.S.A.* 43°3N 91°9W 80 D8
Prairies, L. of the *Canada* 51°16N 101°32W 71 C8
Pran Buri *Thailand* 12°23N 99°55E 38 F2
Prapat *Indonesia* 2°41N 98°58E 36 D1
Praslin *Seychelles* 4°18S 55°45E 53 b
Prasonisi, Akra *Greece* 35°42N 27°46E 25 D9
Prata *Brazil* 19°25S 48°54W 93 G9
Pratabpur *India* 23°28N 83°15E 43 H10
Pratapgarh *Raj., India* 24°2N 74°40E 42 G6
Pratapgarh *Ut. P., India* 25°56N 81°59E 43 G9
Prato *Italy* 43°53N 11°6E 22 C4
Pratt *U.S.A.* 37°39N 98°44W 80 G4
Prattville *U.S.A.* 32°28N 86°29W 85 E11
Pravia *Spain* 43°30N 6°12W 21 A2
Praya *Indonesia* 8°39S 116°17E 36 F5
Prayag = Allahabad *India* 25°25N 81°58E 43 G9
Preble *U.S.A.* 42°44N 76°8W 83 D8
Precipice △ *Australia* 25°18S 150°5E 63 D5
Precordillera *Argentina* 30°0S 69°1W 94 C2
Preeceville *Canada* 51°57N 102°40W 71 C8
Preiļi *Latvia* 56°18N 26°43E 9 H22
Premont *U.S.A.* 27°22N 98°7W 84 H5
Prentice *U.S.A.* 45°33N 90°17W 80 C8
Preobrazheniye *Russia* 42°54N 133°54E 30 C6
Preparis I. = Pariparit Kyun *Burma* 14°52N 93°41E 41 M18
Preparis North Channel *Ind. Oc.* 15°27N 94°5E 41 M18
Preparis South Channel *Ind. Oc.* 14°33N 93°30E 41 M18
Přerov *Czech Rep.* 49°28N 17°27E 17 D9
Prescott *Canada* 44°45N 75°30W 83 B9
Prescott *Ariz., U.S.A.* 34°33N 112°28W 77 J7
Prescott *Ark., U.S.A.* 33°48N 93°23W 84 E8
Prescott Valley *U.S.A.* 34°40N 112°18W 77 J7
Preservation Inlet *N.Z.* 46°8S 166°35E 59 G1
Presho *U.S.A.* 43°54N 100°3W 80 D3
Presidencia de la Plaza *Argentina* 27°0S 59°50W 94 B4
Presidencia Roque Saenz Peña *Argentina* 26°45S 60°30W 94 B3
Presidente Epitácio *Brazil* 21°56S 52°6W 93 H8
Presidente Hayes □ *Paraguay* 24°0S 59°0W 94 A4
Presidente Prudente *Brazil* 22°5S 51°25W 95 A5
Presidio *Mexico* 29°29N 104°23W 86 B4
Presidio *U.S.A.* 29°34N 104°22W 84 G2
Prešov *Slovak Rep.* 49°0N 21°15E 17 D11
Prespa, L. = Prespansko Jezero *Macedonia* 40°55N 21°0E 23 D9
Prespansko Jezero *Macedonia* 40°55N 21°0E 23 D9
Presque I. *U.S.A.* 42°10N 80°6W 82 D4
Presque Isle *U.S.A.* 46°41N 68°1W 81 B19
Prestatyn *U.K.* 53°20N 3°24W 12 D4
Presteigne *U.K.* 52°17N 3°0W 13 E5
Preston *Canada* 43°23N 80°21W 82 C4
Preston *U.K.* 53°46N 2°42W 12 D5
Preston *Idaho, U.S.A.* 42°6N 111°53W 76 E8
Preston *Minn., U.S.A.* 43°40N 92°5W 80 D7
Preston, C. *Australia* 20°51S 116°12E 60 D2
Prestonsburg *U.S.A.* 37°40N 82°47W 81 G12
Prestwick *U.K.* 55°29N 4°37W 11 F4
Pretoria *S. Africa* 25°44S 28°12E 57 D4
Preveza *Greece* 38°57N 20°45E 23 E9
Prey Veng *Cambodia* 11°35N 105°29E 39 G5
Pribilof Is. *U.S.A.* 57°0N 170°0W 74 D6
Příbram *Czech Rep.* 49°41N 14°2E 16 D8
Price *U.S.A.* 39°36N 110°49W 76 G8
Price I. *Canada* 52°23N 128°41W 70 C3
Prichard *U.S.A.* 30°44N 88°5W 85 F10
Priekule *Latvia* 56°26N 21°35E 9 H19
Prienai *Lithuania* 54°38N 23°57E 9 J20
Prieska *S. Africa* 29°40S 22°42E 56 D3
Priest L. *U.S.A.* 48°35N 116°52W 76 B5
Priest River *U.S.A.* 48°11N 116°55W 76 B5
Priest Valley *U.S.A.* 36°10N 120°39W 78 J6
Prievidza *Slovak Rep.* 48°46N 18°36E 17 D10
Prikaspiyskaya Nizmennost = Caspian Depression *Eurasia* 47°0N 48°0E 19 E8
Prilep *Macedonia* 41°21N 21°32E 23 D9
Priluki = Pryluky *Ukraine* 50°30N 32°24E 19 D5
Prime Seal I. *Australia* 40°3S 147°43E 63 G4
Primo Tapia *Mexico* 32°16N 116°54W 79 N10
Primorskiy Kray □ *Russia* 45°0N 135°0E 30 B7
Primrose L. *Canada* 54°55N 109°45W 71 C7
Prince Albert *Canada* 53°15N 105°50W 71 C7
Prince Albert *S. Africa* 33°12S 22°2E 56 E3
Prince Albert △ *Canada* 54°0N 106°25W 71 C7
Prince Albert Mts. *Antarctica* 76°0S 161°30E 5 D11
Prince Albert Pen. *Canada* 72°30N 116°0W 68 C8
Prince Albert Sd. *Canada* 70°25N 115°0W 68 C9
Prince Alfred, C. *Canada* 74°20N 124°40W 4 B1
Prince Charles I. *Canada* 67°47N 76°12W 69 D16
Prince Charles Mts. *Antarctica* 72°0S 67°0E 5 D6
Prince Edward Fracture Zone *Ind. Oc.* 46°0S 35°0E 5 A4
Prince Edward I. □ *Canada* 46°20N 63°20W 73 C7
Prince Edward Is. *Ind. Oc.* 46°35S 38°0E 3 G11
Prince George *Canada* 53°55N 122°50W 70 C4
Prince of Wales, C. *U.S.A.* 65°36N 168°5W 74 B6
Prince of Wales I. *Australia* 10°40S 142°10E 62 A3
Prince of Wales I. *Canada* 73°0N 99°0W 68 C12
Prince of Wales I. *U.S.A.* 55°47N 132°50W 68 F5
Prince of Wales Icefield *Canada* 78°15N 79°0W 69 B16
Prince of Wales Str. *Canada* 73°0N 117°0W 68 C8
Prince Patrick I. *Canada* 77°0N 120°0W 69 B8
Prince Regent Inlet *Canada* 73°0N 90°0W 69 C14
Prince Rupert *Canada* 54°20N 130°20W 70 C2
Prince William Sd. *U.S.A.* 60°40N 147°0W 68 E2
Princes Town *Trin. & Tob.* 10°16N 61°23W 93 K15
Princess Charlotte B. *Australia* 14°25S 144°0E 62 A3
Princess Elizabeth Trough *S. Ocean* 64°10S 83°0E 5 C7
Princess May Ranges *Australia* 15°30S 125°30E 60 C4
Princess Royal I. *Canada* 53°0N 128°40W 70 C3
Princeton *Canada* 49°27N 120°30W 70 D4
Princeton *Calif., U.S.A.* 39°24N 122°1W 78 F4
Princeton *Ill., U.S.A.* 41°23N 89°28W 80 E9
Princeton *Ind., U.S.A.* 38°21N 87°34W 80 F10
Princeton *Ky., U.S.A.* 37°7N 87°53W 80 G10
Princeton *Mo., U.S.A.* 40°24N 93°35W 80 E7
Princeton *N.J., U.S.A.* 40°21N 74°39W 83 F10
Princeton *W. Va., U.S.A.* 37°22N 81°6W 81 G13
Príncipe *São Tomé & Príncipe* 1°37N 7°25E 48 F4
Principe da Beira *Brazil* 12°20S 64°30W 92 F6
Prineville *U.S.A.* 44°18N 120°51W 76 D3
Prins Harald Kyst *Antarctica* 70°0S 35°1E 5 D4
Prinsesse Astrid Kyst *Antarctica* 70°45S 12°30E 5 D3
Prinsesse Ragnhild Kyst *Antarctica* 70°15S 27°30E 5 D4
Prinzapolca *Nic.* 13°20N 83°35W 88 D3
Priozersk *Russia* 61°2N 30°7E 8 F24
Pripet = Prypyat → *Europe* 51°20N 30°15E 17 C16
Pripet Marshes *Europe* 52°10N 28°10E 17 B15
Pripyat Marshes = Pripet Marshes *Europe* 52°10N 28°10E 17 B15
Pripyats = Prypyat → *Europe* 51°20N 30°15E 17 C16
Priština *Kosovo* 42°40N 21°13E 23 C9
Privas *France* 44°45N 4°37E 20 D6
Privolzhskaya Vozvyshennost *Russia* 51°0N 46°0E 19 D8
Privolzhskiy □ *Russia* 56°0N 50°0E 28 D6
Prizren *Kosovo* 42°13N 20°45E 23 C9
Probolinggo *Indonesia* 7°46S 113°13E 37 G15
Proctor *U.S.A.* 43°40N 73°2W 83 C11
Proddatur *India* 14°45N 78°30E 40 M11
Prodhromos *Cyprus* 34°57N 32°50E 25 E11
Profilia *Greece* 36°5N 27°51E 25 C9
Profondeville *Belgium* 50°23N 4°52E 15 D4
Progreso *Coahuila, Mexico* 27°28N 100°59W 86 B4
Progreso *Yucatán, Mexico* 21°20N 89°40W 87 C7
Progress *Antarctica* 66°22S 76°22E 5 C12
Progress *Russia* 49°45N 129°37E 29 E13
Prokopyevsk *Russia* 54°0N 86°45E 28 D9
Prokuplje *Serbia* 43°16N 21°36E 23 C9
Prome *Burma* 18°49N 95°13E 41 K19
Prophet → *Canada* 58°48N 122°40W 70 B4
Prophet River *Canada* 58°6N 122°43W 70 B4
Propriá *Brazil* 10°13S 36°51W 93 F11
Propriano *France* 41°41N 8°52E 20 F8
Proserpine *Australia* 20°21S 148°36E 62 b
Prosna → *Poland* 52°6N 17°44E 17 B9
Prospect *U.S.A.* 43°18N 75°9W 83 C9
Prosser *U.S.A.* 46°12N 119°46W 76 C4
Prostějov *Czech Rep.* 49°30N 17°9E 17 D9
Proston *Australia* 26°8S 151°32E 63 D5
Provence *France* 43°40N 5°46E 20 E6
Providence *Ky., U.S.A.* 37°24N 87°46W 80 G10
Providence *R.I., U.S.A.* 41°49N 71°24W 83 E13
Providence Bay *Canada* 45°41N 82°15W 72 C3
Providence Mts. *U.S.A.* 35°10N 115°15W 79 K11
Providencia, I. de *Colombia* 13°25N 81°26W 88 D3
Provideniya *Russia* 64°23N 173°18W 29 C19
Provincetown *U.S.A.* 42°3N 70°11W 81 D18
Provins *France* 48°33N 3°15E 20 B5
Provo *U.S.A.* 40°14N 111°39W 76 F8
Provost *Canada* 52°25N 110°20W 71 C6
Prudhoe Bay *U.S.A.* 70°18N 148°22W 74 A10
Prudhoe I. *Australia* 21°19S 149°41E 62 C4
Prud'homme *Canada* 52°20N 105°54W 71 C7
Pruszków *Poland* 52°9N 20°49E 17 B11
Prut → *Romania* 45°28N 28°10E 17 F15
Pruzhany *Belarus* 52°33N 24°28E 17 B13
Prydz B. *Antarctica* 69°0S 74°0E 5 C6
Pryluky *Ukraine* 50°30N 32°24E 19 D5
Pryor *U.S.A.* 36°19N 95°19W 84 C7
Prypyat → *Europe* 51°20N 30°15E 17 C16
Przemyśl *Poland* 49°50N 22°45E 17 D12
Przhevalsk = Karakol *Kyrgyzstan* 42°30N 78°20E 32 B2
Psara *Greece* 38°37N 25°38E 23 E11
Psiloritis, Oros *Greece* 35°15N 24°45E 25 D6
Psira *Greece* 35°12N 25°52E 25 D7
Pskov *Russia* 57°50N 28°25E 9 H23
Ptich = Ptsich → *Belarus* 52°9N 28°52E 17 B15
Ptichia = Vidos *Greece* 39°38N 19°55E 25 A3
Ptolemaida *Greece* 40°30N 21°43E 23 D9
Ptsich → *Belarus* 52°9N 28°52E 17 B15
Pu Xian *China* 36°24N 111°6E 34 F6
Pua *Thailand* 19°11N 100°55E 38 C3
Puán *Argentina* 37°30S 62°45W 94 D3
Pu'apu'a *Samoa* 13°34S 172°9W 59 b
Pucallpa *Peru* 8°25S 74°30W 92 E4
Puch'on = Bucheon *S. Korea* 37°28N 126°45E 35 F14
Pudasjärvi *Finland* 65°23N 26°53E 8 D22
Pudozh *Russia* 61°48N 36°32E 18 B6
Puducherry *India* 11°59N 79°50E 40 P11
Pudukkottai *India* 10°28N 78°47E 40 P11
Puebla *Mexico* 19°3N 98°12W 87 D5
Puebla □ *Mexico* 18°50N 98°0W 87 D5
Pueblo *U.S.A.* 38°16N 104°37W 76 G11
Puelches *Argentina* 38°5S 65°51W 94 D2
Puelén *Argentina* 37°32S 67°38W 94 D2
Puente Alto *Chile* 33°32S 70°35W 94 C1
Puente-Genil *Spain* 37°22N 4°47W 21 D3
Puerca, Pta. *Puerto Rico* 18°13N 65°36W 89 d
Puerco → *U.S.A.* 34°22N 107°50W 77 J10
Puerto Aisén *Chile* 45°27S 73°0W 96 F2
Puerto Ángel *Mexico* 15°40N 96°29W 87 D5
Puerto Arista *Mexico* 15°56N 93°48W 87 D6
Puerto Armuelles *Panama* 8°20N 82°51W 88 E3
Puerto Ayacucho *Venezuela* 5°40N 67°35W 92 B5
Puerto Barrios *Guatemala* 15°40N 88°32W 88 C2
Puerto Bermejo *Argentina* 26°55S 58°34W 94 B4
Puerto Bermúdez *Peru* 10°20S 74°58W 92 F4
Puerto Bolívar *Ecuador* 3°19S 79°55W 92 D3
Puerto Cabello *Venezuela* 10°28N 68°1W 92 A5
Puerto Cabezas *Nic.* 14°0N 83°30W 88 D3
Puerto Cabo Gracias á Dios *Nic.* 15°0N 83°10W 88 D3
Puerto Carreño *Colombia* 6°12N 67°22W 92 B5
Puerto Castilla *Honduras* 16°0N 86°0W 88 C2
Puerto Chicama *Peru* 7°45S 79°20W 92 E3
Puerto Coig *Argentina* 50°54S 69°15W 96 G3
Puerto Cortés *Honduras* 15°51N 88°0W 88 C2
Puerto Cumarebo *Venezuela* 11°29N 69°30W 92 A5
Puerto de Alcudia = Port d'Alcúdia *Spain* 39°50N 3°7E 24 B10
Puerto de Cabrera *Spain* 39°8N 2°56E 24 B9
Puerto de Gran Tarajal *Canary Is.* 28°13N 14°1W 24 F5
Puerto de la Cruz *Canary Is.* 28°24N 16°32W 24 F3
Puerto de los Angeles ⌓ *Mexico* 23°39N 105°45W 86 C3
Puerto de Pozo Negro *Canary Is.* 28°19N 13°55W 24 F6
Puerto de Sóller = Port de Sóller *Spain* 39°48N 2°42E 24 B9
Puerto del Carmen *Canary Is.* 28°55N 13°38W 24 F6
Puerto del Rosario *Canary Is.* 28°30N 13°52W 24 F6
Puerto Deseado *Argentina* 47°55S 66°0W 96 F3
Puerto Escondido *Mexico* 15°50N 97°3W 87 D5
Puerto Heath *Bolivia* 12°34S 68°39W 92 F5
Puerto Inírida *Colombia* 3°53N 67°52W 92 C5
Puerto Juárez *Mexico* 21°11N 86°49W 87 C7
Puerto La Cruz *Venezuela* 10°13N 64°38W 92 A6
Puerto Leguízamo *Colombia* 0°12S 74°46W 92 D4
Puerto Lempira *Honduras* 15°16N 83°46W 88 C3
Puerto Libertad *Mexico* 29°55N 112°43W 86 B2
Puerto Limón *Colombia* 3°23N 73°30W 92 C4
Puerto Lobos *Argentina* 42°0S 65°3W 96 E3
Puerto Madryn *Argentina* 42°48S 65°4W 96 E3
Puerto Maldonado *Peru* 12°30S 69°10W 92 F5
Puerto Manatí *Cuba* 21°22N 76°50W 88 B4
Puerto Montt *Chile* 41°28S 73°0W 96 E2
Puerto Morazán *Nic.* 12°51N 87°11W 88 D2
Puerto Morelos *Mexico* 20°50N 86°52W 87 C7
Puerto Natales *Chile* 51°45S 72°15W 96 G2
Puerto Oscuro *Chile* 31°24S 71°35W 94 C1
Puerto Padre *Cuba* 21°13N 76°35W 88 B4
Puerto Páez *Venezuela* 6°13N 67°28W 92 B5
Puerto Peñasco *Mexico* 31°20N 113°33W 86 A2
Puerto Pinasco *Paraguay* 22°36S 57°50W 94 A4
Puerto Plata *Dom. Rep.* 19°48N 70°45W 89 C5
Puerto Pollensa = Port de Pollença *Spain* 39°54N 3°4E 24 B10
Puerto Princesa *Phil.* 9°46N 118°45E 37 C5
Puerto Quepos *Costa Rica* 9°29N 84°6W 88 E3
Puerto Rico *Canary Is.* 27°47N 15°42W 24 G4
Puerto Rico ☑ *W. Indies* 18°15N 66°45W 89 d
Puerto Rico Trench *Atl. Oc.* 19°50N 66°0W 89 C6
Puerto San Julián *Argentina* 49°18S 67°43W 96 F3
Puerto Santa Cruz *Argentina* 50°0S 68°32W 96 G3
Puerto Sastre *Paraguay* 22°2S 57°55W 94 A4
Puerto Suárez *Bolivia* 18°58S 57°52W 92 G7
Puerto Vallarta *Mexico* 20°37N 105°15W 86 C3
Puerto Varas *Chile* 41°19S 72°59W 96 E2
Puerto Wilches *Colombia* 7°21N 73°54W 92 B4
Puertollano *Spain* 38°43N 4°7W 21 C3
Pueu *Tahiti* 17°44S 149°13W 59 d
Pueyrredón, L. *Argentina* 47°20S 72°0W 96 F2
Puffin I. *Ireland* 51°50N 10°24W 10 E1
Pugachev *Russia* 52°0N 48°49E 18 D8
Pugal *India* 28°30N 72°48E 42 E5
Puge *Tanzania* 4°45S 33°11E 54 C3
Puget Sound *U.S.A.* 47°50N 122°30W 76 C2
Pugŏdong *N. Korea* 42°5N 130°0E 35 C16
Pugu *Tanzania* 6°55S 39°4E 54 D4
Pūgūnzī *Iran* 25°49N 59°10E 45 E8
Puig Major *Spain* 39°48N 2°47E 24 B9
Puigcerdà *Spain* 42°24N 1°50E 21 A6
Puigpunyent *Spain* 39°38N 2°32E 24 B9
Pujon-ho *N. Korea* 40°35N 127°35E 35 D14
Pukaki, L. *N.Z.* 44°4S 170°1E 59 F3
Pukapuka *Cook Is.* 10°53S 165°49W 65 J11
Pukaskwa △ *Canada* 48°20N 86°0W 72 C2
Pukatawagan *Canada* 55°45N 101°20W 71 B8
Pukchin *N. Korea* 40°12N 125°45E 35 D13
Pukch'ŏng *N. Korea* 40°14N 128°10E 35 D15
Pukekohe *N.Z.* 37°12S 174°55E 59 B5
Pukhrayan *India* 26°14N 79°51E 43 F8
Pula *Croatia* 44°54N 13°57E 16 F7
Pulacayo *Bolivia* 20°25S 66°41W 92 H5
Pulai *Malaysia* 1°20N 103°31E 39 d
Pulandian *China* 39°25N 121°58E 35 E11
Pulaski *N.Y., U.S.A.* 43°34N 76°8W 83 C8
Pulaski *Tenn., U.S.A.* 35°12N 87°2W 85 D11
Pulaski *Va., U.S.A.* 37°3N 80°47W 81 G13
Pulau → *Indonesia* 5°50S 138°15E 37 F9
Puławy *Poland* 51°23N 21°59E 17 C11
Pulga *U.S.A.* 39°48N 121°29W 78 F5
Pulicat L. *India* 13°40N 80°15E 40 N12
Pullman *U.S.A.* 46°44N 117°10W 76 C5
Pulog, Mt. *Phil.* 16°40N 120°50E 37 A6
Pułtusk *Poland* 52°43N 21°6E 17 B11
Pumlumon Fawr *U.K.* 52°28N 3°46W 13 E4
Puná, I. *Ecuador* 2°55S 80°5W 92 D2
Punaauia *Tahiti* 17°37S 149°34W 59 d
Punakaiki *N.Z.* 42°7S 171°20E 59 E3
Punakha Dzong *Bhutan* 27°42N 89°52E 41 F16
Punasar *India* 27°6N 73°6E 42 F5
Punata *Bolivia* 17°32S 65°50W 92 G5
Punch *India* 33°48N 74°4E 43 C6
Punch → *Pakistan* 33°12N 73°40E 42 C5
Punda Maria *S. Africa* 22°40S 31°5E 57 C5
Pune *India* 18°29N 73°57E 40 K8
P'ungsan *N. Korea* 40°50N 128°9E 35 D15
Pungue, Ponte de *Mozam.* 19°0S 34°0E 55 F3
Punjab □ *India* 31°0N 76°0E 42 D7
Punjab □ *Pakistan* 32°0N 72°30E 42 E6
Puno *Peru* 15°55S 70°3W 92 G4
Punpun → *India* 25°31N 85°18E 43 G11
Punta, Cerro de *Puerto Rico* 18°10N 66°37W 89 d
Punta Alta *Argentina* 38°53S 62°4W 96 D4
Punta Arenas *Chile* 53°10S 71°0W 96 G2
Punta del Díaz *Chile* 28°0S 70°45W 94 B1
Punta del Hidalgo *Canary Is.* 28°33N 16°19W 24 F3
Punta Gorda *Belize* 16°10N 88°45W 87 D7
Punta Gorda *U.S.A.* 26°56N 82°3W 85 H13
Punta Prieta *Mexico* 28°58N 114°17W 86 B2
Punta Prima *Spain* 39°48N 4°16E 24 B11
Puntarenas *Costa Rica* 10°0N 84°50W 88 E3
Puntland *Somali Rep.* 8°0N 49°0E 47 F4
Punto Fijo *Venezuela* 11°50N 70°13W 92 A4
Punxsutawney *U.S.A.* 40°57N 78°59W 82 F6
Pupuan *Indonesia* 8°19S 115°0E 37 J18
Puquio *Peru* 14°45S 74°10W 92 F4
Pur → *Russia* 67°31N 77°55E 28 C8
Puracé, Vol. *Colombia* 2°21N 76°23W 92 C3
Puralia = Puruliya *India* 23°17N 86°24E 43 H12
Puranpur *India* 28°31N 80°9E 43 E9
Purbeck, Isle of *U.K.* 50°39N 1°59W 13 G5
Purcell *U.S.A.* 35°1N 97°22W 84 D6
Purcell Mts. *Canada* 49°55N 116°15W 70 D5
Purdy *Canada* 45°19N 77°44W 82 A7
Puri *India* 19°50N 85°58E 41 K14
Purmerend *Neths.* 52°32N 4°58E 15 B4
Purnia *India* 25°45N 87°31E 43 G12
Purnululu △ *Australia* 17°20S 128°20E 60 C4
Pursat = Pouthisat *Cambodia* 12°34N 103°50E 38 F4
Purukcahu *Indonesia* 0°35S 114°35E 36 E4
Puruliya *India* 23°17N 86°24E 43 H12
Purus → *Brazil* 3°42S 61°28W 92 D6
Puruvesi *Finland* 61°50N 29°30E 8 F23
Purvis *U.S.A.* 31°9N 89°25W 85 F10
Purwa *India* 26°28N 80°47E 43 F9
Purwakarta *Indonesia* 6°35S 107°29E 37 G12
Purwo, Tanjung *Indonesia* 8°44S 114°21E 37 K18
Purwodadi *Indonesia* 7°7S 110°55E 37 G14
Purwokerto *Indonesia* 7°25S 109°14E 37 G13
Puryŏng *N. Korea* 42°5N 129°43E 35 C15
Pusa *India* 25°59N 85°41E 43 G11
Pusan = Busan *S. Korea* 35°5N 129°0E 35 G15
Pushkin *Russia* 59°45N 30°25E 9 G24
Pushkino *Russia* 51°16N 47°0E 19 D8
Put-in-Bay *U.S.A.* 41°39N 82°49W 82 E2
Putahow L. *Canada* 59°54N 100°40W 71 B8
Putao *Burma* 27°28N 97°30E 41 F20
Putaruru *N.Z.* 38°2S 175°50E 59 C5
Putignano *Italy* 40°51N 17°7E 22 D7
Puting, Tanjung *Indonesia* 3°31S 111°46E 36 E4
Putnam *U.S.A.* 41°55N 71°55W 83 E13
Putorana, Gory *Russia* 69°0N 95°0E 29 C10
Putrajaya *Malaysia* 2°55N 101°40E 39 L3
Puttalam *Sri Lanka* 8°1N 79°55E 40 Q11
Puttgarden *Germany* 54°30N 11°10E 16 A6
Putumayo → *S. Amer.* 3°7S 67°58W 92 D5
Putussibau *Indonesia* 0°50N 112°56E 36 D4
Puvirnituq *Canada* 60°2N 77°10W 69 E16
Puy-de-Dôme *France* 45°46N 2°57E 20 D5
Puyallup *U.S.A.* 47°12N 122°18W 78 C4
Puyang *China* 35°40N 115°1E 34 G8
Pūzeh Rīg *Iran* 27°20N 58°40E 45 E8
Pwani □ *Tanzania* 7°0S 39°0E 54 D4
Pweto *Dem. Rep. of the Congo* 8°25S 28°51E 55 D2
Pwllheli *U.K.* 52°53N 4°25W 12 E3
Pyaozero, Ozero *Russia* 66°5N 30°58E 8 C24
Pyapon *Burma* 16°20N 95°40E 41 L19
Pyasina → *Russia* 73°30N 87°0E 29 B9
Pyatigorsk *Russia* 44°2N 43°6E 19 F7
Pyè = Prome *Burma* 18°49N 95°13E 41 K19
Pyeongtaek *S. Korea* 37°1N 127°4E 35 F14
Pyetrikaw *Belarus* 52°11N 28°29E 17 B15
Pyhäjoki *Finland* 64°28N 24°14E 8 D21
Pyinmana *Burma* 19°45N 96°12E 41 K20
Pyla, C. *Cyprus* 34°56N 33°51E 25 E12
Pymatuning Res. *U.S.A.* 41°30N 80°28W 82 E4
Pyŏktong *N. Korea* 40°50N 125°50E 35 D13
Pyŏnggang *N. Korea* 38°24N 127°17E 35 E14
P'yŏngsong *N. Korea* 39°14N 125°52E 35 E13
P'yŏngyang *N. Korea* 39°0N 125°30E 35 E13
Pyote *U.S.A.* 31°32N 103°8W 84 F3
Pyramid L. *U.S.A.* 40°1N 119°35W 76 F4
Pyramid Pk. *U.S.A.* 36°25N 116°37W 79 J10
Pyramids *Egypt* 29°58N 31°9E 51 C12
Pyrénées *Europe* 42°45N 0°18E 20 E4
Pyu *Burma* 18°30N 96°28E 41 K20

Q

Qaanaaq *Greenland* 77°30N 69°10W **69** B18
Qachasnek *S. Africa* 30°6S 28°42E **57** E4
Qa'el Jafr *Jordan* 30°20N 36°25E **46** E5
Qa'emābād *Iran* 31°44N 60°2E **45** D9
Qā'emshahr *Iran* 36°30N 52°53E **45** B7
Qagan Nur *China* 43°30N 114°55E **34** C8
Qahar Youyi Zhongqi *China* 41°12N 112°40E **34** D7
Qahremānshahr = Kermānshāh *Iran* 34°23N 47°0E **44** C5
Qaidam Pendi *China* 37°0N 95°0E **32** C4
Qajarīyeh *Iran* 31°1N 48°22E **45** D6
Qala, Ras il *Malta* 36°2N 14°20E **25** C1
Qala-i-Jadid = Spīn Būldak *Afghan.* 31°1N 66°25E **42** D2
Qala Point = Qala, Ras il *Malta* 36°2N 14°20E **25** C1
Qala Viala *Pakistan* 30°49N 67°17E **42** D2
Qala Yangi *Afghan.* 34°20N 66°30E **42** B2
Qal'at al Akhḍar *Si. Arabia* 28°4N 37°9E **44** E3
Qal'at Dīzah *Iraq* 36°11N 45°7E **44** B5
Qal'at Ṣāliḥ *Iraq* 31°31N 47°16E **44** D5
Qal'at Sukkar *Iraq* 31°51N 46°5E **44** D5
Qamani'tuaq = Baker Lake *Canada* 64°20N 96°3W **68** E12
Qamdo *China* 31°15N 97°6E **32** C4
Qamea *Fiji* 16°45S 179°45W **59** a
Qamruddin Karez *Pakistan* 31°45N 68°20E **42** D3
Qandahār = Kandahār *Afghan.* 31°32N 65°43E **40** D4
Qandahār = Kandahār □ *Afghan.* 31°0N 65°0E **40** D4
Qandyaghash *Kazakhstan* 49°28N 57°25E **19** E10
Qapān *Iran* 37°40N 55°47E **45** B7
Qapshaghay *Kazakhstan* 43°51N 77°14E **28** E8
Qaqortoq *Greenland* 60°43N 46°0W **4** C5
Qara Qash → *China* 35°0N 78°30E **43** B8
Qarabutaq *Kazakhstan* 49°59N 60°14E **28** E7
Qaraghandy *Kazakhstan* 49°50N 73°10E **28** E8
Qaraghayly *Kazakhstan* 49°26N 76°0E **28** E8
Qārah *Si. Arabia* 29°55N 40°3E **44** D4
Qarataū *Ongtüstik Qazaqstan, Kazakhstan* [illegible] E7
Qarataū *Zhambyl, Kazakhstan* 43°10N 70°28E **28** E8
Qarazhal *Kazakhstan* 48°2N 70°49E **28** E8
Qardho *Somali Rep.* 9°30N 49°6E **47** F4
Qareh → *Iran* 39°25N 47°22E **44** B5
Qareh Tekān *Iran* 36°38N 49°29E **45** B6
Qarnein *U.A.E.* 24°56N 52°52E **45** E7
Qarqan He → *China* 39°30N 88°30E **32** C3
Qarqaraly *Kazakhstan* 49°26N 75°30E **28** E8
Qarshi *Uzbekistan* 38°53N 65°48E **28** F7
Qartabā *Lebanon* 34°4N 35°50E **46** A4
Qārūh *Kuwait* 28°49N 48°46E **45** D6
Qaryat al Gharab *Iraq* 31°27N 44°48E **44** D5
Qaryat al 'Ulyā *Si. Arabia* 27°33N 47°42E **44** E5
Qasr 'Amra *Jordan* 31°48N 36°35E **44** D3
Qaṣr-e Qand *Iran* 26°15N 60°45E **45** E9
Qaṣr-e Shīrīn *Iran* 34°31N 45°35E **44** C5
Qasr Farâfra *Egypt* 27°0N 28°1E **51** C11
Qasuittuq = Resolute *Canada* 74°42N 94°54W **69** C13
Qatanā *Syria* 33°26N 36°4E **46** B5
Qatar ■ *Asia* 25°30N 51°15E **45** E6
Qatlīsh *Iran* 37°50N 57°19E **45** B8
Qattâra, Munkhafed el *Egypt* 29°30N 27°30E **51** C11
Qattâra Depression = Qattâra, Munkhafed el *Egypt* 29°30N 27°30E **51** C11
Qawām al Ḥamzah = Al Ḥamzah *Iraq* 31°43N 44°58E **44** D5
Qāyen *Iran* 33°40N 59°10E **45** C8
Qazaqstan = Kazakhstan ■ *Asia* 50°0N 70°0E **28** E8
Qazımämmäd *Azerbaijan* 40°3N 49°0E **45** A6
Qazvīn *Iran* 36°15N 50°0E **45** B6
Qazvīn □ *Iran* 36°20N 50°0E **45** B6
Qena *Egypt* 26°10N 32°43E **51** C12
Qeqertarsuaq *Greenland* 69°15N 53°38W **4** C5
Qeqertarsuaq *Greenland* 69°45N 53°30W **66** C14
Qeshlāq *Iran* 34°55N 46°28E **44** C5
Qeshm *Iran* 26°55N 56°10E **45** E8
Qeys *Iran* 26°32N 53°58E **45** E7
Qezel Owzen → *Iran* 36°45N 49°22E **45** B6
Qezi'ot *Israel* 30°52N 34°26E **46** E3
Qi Xian *China* 34°40N 114°48E **34** G8
Qian Gorlos *China* 45°5N 124°42E **35** B13
Qian Hai *China* 22°32N 113°54E **33** F10
Qian Xian *China* 34°31N 108°15E **34** G5
Qianshan *China* 22°15N 113°31E **33** G10
Qianyang *China* 34°40N 107°8E **34** G4
Qi'ao *China* 22°25N 113°39E **33** G10
Qi'ao Dao *China* 22°25N 113°38E **33** G10
Qiemo *China* 38°8N 85°32E **32** C3
Qijiaojing *China* 43°28N 91°36E **32** B4
Qikiqtarjuaq *Canada* 67°33N 63°0W **69** D19
Qila Saifullāh *Pakistan* 30°45N 68°17E **42** D3
Qilian Shan *China* 38°30N 96°0E **32** C4
Qin He → *China* 35°1N 113°22E **34** G7
Qin Ling = Qinling Shandi *China* 33°50N 108°10E **34** H5
Qin'an *China* 34°48N 105°40E **34** G3
Qing Xian *China* 38°35N 116°45E **34** E9
Qingcheng *China* 37°15N 117°40E **35** F9
Qingdao *China* 36°5N 120°20E **35** F11
Qingfeng *China* 35°52N 115°8E **34** G8
Qinghai □ *China* 36°0N 98°0E **32** C4
Qinghai Hu *China* 36°40N 100°10E **32** C5
Qinghecheng *China* 41°28N 124°15E **35** D13
Qinghemen *China* 41°48N 121°25E **35** D11
Qingjian *China* 37°8N 110°8E **34** F6
Qingjiang = Huaiyin *China* 33°30N 119°2E **35** H10
Qingshui *China* 34°48N 106°8E **34** G4
Qingshuihe *China* 39°55N 111°35E **34** E6
Qingtongxia Shuiku *China* 37°50N 105°58E **34** F3
Qingxu *China* 37°34N 112°22E **34** F7
Qingyang *China* 36°2N 107°55E **34** F4
Qingyuan *China* 42°10N 124°55E **35** C13
Qingyun *China* 37°45N 117°20E **35** F9
Qinhuangdao *China* 39°56N 119°30E **35** E10
Qinling Shandi *China* 33°50N 108°10E **34** H5
Qinshui *China* 35°40N 112°8E **34** G7
Qinyang = Jiyuan *China* 35°7N 112°57E **34** G7
Qinyuan *China* 36°29N 112°20E **34** F7
Qinzhou *China* 21°58N 108°38E **32** D5
Qionghai *China* 19°15N 110°26E **38** C8
Qiongzhou Haixia *China* 20°10N 110°15E **38** B8
Qiqihar *China* 47°26N 124°0E **33** B7
Qira *China* 37°0N 80°48E **32** C3
Qiraîya, W. → *Egypt* 30°27N 34°0E **46** E3
Qiryat Ata *Israel* 32°47N 35°6E **46** C4
Qiryat Gat *Israel* 31°32N 34°46E **46** D3
Qiryat Mal'akhi *Israel* 31°44N 34°44E **46** D3
Qiryat Shemona *Israel* 33°13N 35°35E **46** B4
Qiryat Yam *Israel* 32°51N 35°4E **46** C4
Qishan *China* 34°25N 107°38E **34** G4
Qitai *China* 44°2N 89°35E **32** B3
Qitaihe *China* 45°48N 130°51E **30** B5
Qixia *China* 37°17N 120°52E **35** F11
Qızılağac Körfäzi *Azerbaijan* 39°9N 49°0E **45** B6
Qojūr *Iran* 36°12N 47°55E **44** B5
Qom *Iran* 34°40N 51°0E **45** C6
Qom □ *Iran* 34°40N 51°0E **45** C6
Qomolangma Feng = Everest, Mt. *Nepal* 28°5N 86°58E **43** E12
Qomsheh *Iran* 32°0N 51°55E **45** D6
Qoqek = Tacheng *China* 46°40N 82°58E **32** B3
Qoqon = Qŭqon *Uzbekistan* 40°31N 70°56E **28** E8
Qoraqalpoghistan □ *Uzbekistan* 43°0N 58°0E **28** E6
Qorveh *Iran* 35°10N 47°48E **44** C5
Qosshaghyl *Kazakhstan* 46°40N 54°0E **19** E9
Qostanay *Kazakhstan* 53°10N 63°35E **28** D7
Quabbin Res. *U.S.A.* 42°20N 72°20W **83** D12
Quairading *Australia* 32°0S 117°21E **61** F2
Quakertown *U.S.A.* 40°26N 75°21W **83** F9
Qualicum Beach *Canada* 49°22N 124°26W **70** D4
Quambatook *Australia* 35°49S 143°34E **63** F3
Quambone *Australia* 30°57S 147°53E **63** E4
Quamby *Australia* 20°22S 140°17E **62** C3
Quan Long = Ca Mau *Vietnam* 9°7N 105°8E **39** H5
Quanah *U.S.A.* 34°18N 99°44W **84** D5
Quang Ngai *Vietnam* 15°13N 108°58E **38** E7
Quang Tri *Vietnam* 16°45N 107°13E **38** D6
Quang Yen *Vietnam* 20°56N 106°52E **38** B6
Quantock Hills *U.K.* 51°8N 3°10W **13** F4
Quanzhou *China* 24°55N 118°34E **33** D6
Qu'Appelle → *Canada* 50°33N 103°53W **71** C8
Quaqtaq *Canada* 60°55N 69°40W **69** E18
Quaraí *Brazil* 30°15S 56°20W **94** C4
Quartu Sant'Élena *Italy* 39°15N 9°10E **22** E3
Quartzsite *U.S.A.* 33°40N 114°13W **79** M12
Quatre Bornes *Mauritius* 20°15S 57°28E **53** d
Quatsino Sd. *Canada* 50°25N 127°58W **70** C3
Quba *Azerbaijan* 41°21N 48°32E **19** F8
Qūchān *Iran* 37°10N 58°27E **45** B8
Queanbeyan *Australia* 35°17S 149°14E **63** F4
Québec *Canada* 46°52N 71°13W **73** C5
Québec □ *Canada* 48°0N 74°0W **73** C6
Quebrada del Condorito △ *Argentina* 31°49S 64°40W **94** C3
Queen Alexandra Ra. *Antarctica* 85°0S 170°0E **5** E11
Queen Charlotte City *Canada* 53°15N 132°2W **70** C2
Queen Charlotte Is. *Canada* 53°20N 132°10W **70** C2
Queen Charlotte Sd. *Canada* 51°0N 128°0W **70** C3
Queen Charlotte Strait *Canada* 50°45N 127°10W **70** C3
Queen Elizabeth △ *Uganda* 0°0 30°0E **54** C3
Queen Elizabeth ⌂ *U.K.* 56°7N 4°30W **11** E4
Queen Elizabeth Is. *Canada* 76°0N 95°0W **69** B13
Queen Mary Land *Antarctica* 70°0S 95°0E **5** D7
Queen Maud G. *Canada* 68°15N 102°30W **68** D11
Queen Maud Land = Dronning Maud Land *Antarctica* 72°30S 12°0E **5** D3
Queen Maud Mts. *Antarctica* 86°0S 160°0W **5** E13
Queens Channel *Australia* 15°0S 129°30E **60** C4
Queenscliff *Australia* 38°16S 144°39E **63** F3
Queensland □ *Australia* 22°0S 142°0E **62** C3
Queenstown *Australia* 42°4S 145°35E **63** G4
Queenstown *N.Z.* 45°1S 168°40E **59** F2
Queenstown *Singapore* 1°18N 103°48E **39** d
Queenstown *S. Africa* 31°52S 26°52E **56** E4
Queets *U.S.A.* 47°32N 124°19W **78** C2
Queguay Grande → *Uruguay* 32°9S 58°9W **94** C4
Queimadas *Brazil* 11°0S 39°38W **93** F11
Quelimane *Mozam.* 17°53S 36°58E **55** F4
Quellón *Chile* 43°7S 73°37W **96** E2
Quelpart = Jeju-do *S. Korea* 33°29N 126°34E **35** H14
Quemado *N. Mex., U.S.A.* 34°20N 108°30W **77** J9
Quemado *Tex., U.S.A.* 28°56N 100°37W **84** G4
Quemú-Quemú *Argentina* 36°3S 63°36W **94** D3
Quequén *Argentina* 38°30S 58°30W **94** D4
Querétaro *Mexico* 20°36N 100°23W **86** C4
Querétaro □ *Mexico* 21°0N 99°55W **86** C5
Queshan *China* 32°55N 114°2E **34** H8
Quesnel *Canada* 53°0N 122°30W **70** C4
Quesnel → *Canada* 52°58N 122°29W **70** C4
Quesnel L. *Canada* 52°30N 121°20W **70** C4
Questa *U.S.A.* 36°42N 105°36W **77** H11
Quetico ⌂ *Canada* 48°30N 91°45W **72** C1
Quetta *Pakistan* 30°15N 66°55E **42** D2
Quezaltenango *Guatemala* 14°50N 91°30W **88** D1
Quezon City *Phil.* 14°37N 121°2E **37** B6
Qufār *Si. Arabia* 27°26N 41°37E **44** E4
Qui Nhon *Vietnam* 13°40N 109°13E **38** F7
Quibala *Angola* 10°46S 14°59E **52** G2
Quibaxe *Angola* 8°24S 14°27E **52** F2
Quibdó *Colombia* 5°42N 76°40W **92** B3
Quiberon *France* 47°29N 3°9W **20** C2
Quiet L. *Canada* 61°5N 133°5W **70** A2
Quiindy *Paraguay* 25°58S 57°14W **94** B4
Quilá *Mexico* 24°23N 107°13W **86** C3
Quilán, C. *Chile* 43°15S 74°30W **96** E2
Quilcene *U.S.A.* 47°49N 122°53W **78** C4
Quilimarí *Chile* 32°5S 71°30W **94** C1
Quilino *Argentina* 30°14S 64°29W **94** C3
Quillabamba *Peru* 12°50S 72°50W **92** F4
Quillagua *Chile* 21°40S 69°40W **94** A2
Quillota *Chile* 32°54S 71°16W **94** C1
Quilmes *Argentina* 34°43S 58°15W **94** C4
Quilon *India* 8°50N 76°38E **40** Q10
Quilpie *Australia* 26°35S 144°11E **63** D3
Quilpué *Chile* 33°5S 71°33W **94** C1
Quilua *Mozam.* 16°17S 39°54E **55** F4
Quimilí *Argentina* 27°40S 62°30W **94** B3
Quimper *France* 48°0N 4°9W **20** B1
Quimperlé *France* 47°53N 3°33W **20** C2
Quinault → *U.S.A.* 47°21N 124°18W **78** C2
Quincy *Calif., U.S.A.* 39°56N 120°57W **78** F6
Quincy *Fla., U.S.A.* 30°35N 84°34W **85** F12
Quincy *Ill., U.S.A.* 39°56N 91°23W **80** F8
Quincy *Mass., U.S.A.* 42°14N 71°0W **83** D14
Quincy *Wash., U.S.A.* 47°14N 119°51W **76** C4
Quines *Argentina* 32°13S 65°48W **94** C2
Quinga *Mozam.* 15°49S 40°15E **55** F5
Quintana Roo □ *Mexico* 19°40N 88°30W **87** D7
Quintanar de la Orden *Spain* 39°36N 3°5W **21** C4
Quintero *Chile* 32°45S 71°30W **94** C1
Quirihue *Chile* 36°15S 72°35W **94** D1
Quirimbas △ *Mozam.* 12°30S 40°15E **55** E5
Quirindi *Australia* 31°28S 150°40E **63** E5
Quirinópolis *Brazil* 18°32S 50°30W **93** G8
Quissanga *Mozam.* 12°24S 40°28E **55** E5
Quissico *Mozam.* 24°42S 34°44E **57** C5
Quitilipi *Argentina* 26°50S 60°13W **94** B3
Quitman *U.S.A.* 30°47N 83°34W **85** F13
Quito *Ecuador* 0°15S 78°35W **92** D3
Quixadá *Brazil* 4°55S 39°0W **93** D11
Quixaxe *Mozam.* 15°17S 40°4E **55** F5
Qulan *Kazakhstan* 42°55N 72°43E **28** E8
Qul'ân, Jazâ'ir *Egypt* 24°22N 35°31E **44** E2
Qulsary *Kazakhstan* 46°59N 54°1E **19** E9
Qumbu *S. Africa* 31°10S 28°48E **57** E4
Quneitra *Syria* 33°7N 35°48E **46** B4
Qŭnghirot *Uzbekistan* 43°2N 58°50E **28** E6
Quoin I. *Australia* 14°54S 129°32E **60** B4
Quoin Pt. *S. Africa* 34°46S 19°37E **56** E2
Quorn *Australia* 32°25S 138°5E **63** E2
Qŭqon *Uzbekistan* 40°31N 70°56E **28** E8
Qurimbas *Mozam.* 12°20S 40°10E **55** E5
Qurnat as Sawdā' *Lebanon* 34°18N 36°6E **46** A5
Quṣaybā' *Si. Arabia* 26°53N 43°35E **44** E4
Qusaybah *Iraq* 34°24N 40°59E **44** C4
Quseir *Egypt* 26°7N 34°16E **44** E2
Qūshchī *Iran* 37°59N 45°3E **44** B5
Quthing *Lesotho* 30°25S 27°36E **57** E4
Qūṭīābād *Iran* 35°47N 48°30E **45** C6
Quttinirpaaq △ *Canada* 82°13N 72°13W **69** A17
Quwo *China* 35°38N 111°25E **34** G6
Quyang *China* 38°35N 114°40E **34** E8
Quynh Nhai *Vietnam* 21°49N 103°33E **38** B4
Quyon *Canada* 45°31N 76°14W **83** A8
Quzhou *China* 28°57N 118°54E **33** D6
Quzi *China* 36°20N 107°20E **34** F4
Qyzylorda *Kazakhstan* 44°48N 65°28E **28** E7

R

Ra, Ko *Thailand* 9°13N 98°16E **39** H2
Raahe *Finland* 64°40N 24°28E **8** D21
Raalte *Neths.* 52°23N 6°16E **15** B6
Raasay *U.K.* 57°25N 6°4W **11** D2
Raasay, Sd. of *U.K.* 57°30N 6°8W **11** D2
Raba *Indonesia* 8°36S 118°55E **37** F5
Rába → *Hungary* 47°38N 17°38E **17** E9
Rabai *Kenya* 3°50S 39°31E **54** C4
Rabat = Victoria *Malta* 36°3N 14°14E **25** C1
Rabat *Malta* 35°53N 14°24E **25** D1
Rabat *Morocco* 34°2N 6°48W **50** B4
Rabaul *Papua N. G.* 4°24S 152°18E **58** B8
Rabbit Flat *Australia* 20°11S 130°1E **60** D5
Rabbit Lake Mine *Canada* 58°4N 104°5W **71** B8
Rabi *Fiji* 16°30S 179°59W **59** a
Rābigh *Si. Arabia* 22°50N 39°5E **47** C2
Râbniţa *Moldova* 47°45N 29°0E **17** E15
Rābor *Iran* 29°17N 56°55E **45** D8
Rabwah = Chenab Nagar *Pakistan* 31°45N 72°55E **42** D5
Race, C. *Canada* 46°40N 53°5W **73** C9
Rach Gia *Vietnam* 10°5N 105°5E **39** G5
Rachid *Mauritania* 18°45N 11°35W **50** E3
Racibórz *Poland* 50°7N 18°18E **17** C10
Racine *U.S.A.* 42°44N 87°47W **80** D10
Rackerby *U.S.A.* 39°26N 121°22W **78** F5
Radama, Nosy *Madag.* 14°0S 47°47E **57** A8
Radama, Saikanosy *Madag.* 14°16S 47°53E **57** A8
Rădăuţi *Romania* 47°50N 25°59E **17** E13
Radcliff *U.S.A.* 37°51N 85°57W **81** G11
Radekhiv *Ukraine* 50°25N 24°32E **17** C13
Radekhov = Radekhiv *Ukraine* 50°25N 24°32E **17** C13
Radford *U.S.A.* 37°8N 80°34W **81** G13
Radhanpur *India* 23°50N 71°38E **42** H4
Radhwa, Jabal *Si. Arabia* 24°34N 38°18E **44** E3
Radisson *Qué., Canada* 53°47N 77°37W **72** B4
Radisson *Sask., Canada* 52°30N 107°20W **71** C7
Radium Hot Springs *Canada* 50°35N 116°2W **70** C5
Radnor Forest *U.K.* 52°17N 3°10W **13** E4
Radom *Poland* 51°23N 21°12E **17** C11
Radomsko *Poland* 51°5N 19°28E **17** C10
Radomyshl *Ukraine* 50°30N 29°12E **17** C15
Radstock, C. *Australia* 33°12S 134°20E **63** E1
Raduzhnyy *Russia* 62°5N 77°28E **28** C8
Radviliškis *Lithuania* 55°49N 23°33E **9** J20
Radville *Canada* 49°30N 104°15W **71** D8
Rae *Canada* 62°50N 116°3W **70** A5
Rae Bareli *India* 26°18N 81°20E **43** F9
Rae Isthmus *Canada* 66°40N 87°30W **69** D14
Raeren *Belgium* 50°41N 6°7E **15** D6
Raeside, L. *Australia* 29°20S 122°0E **61** E3
Raetihi *N.Z.* 39°25S 175°17E **59** C5
Rafaela *Argentina* 31°10S 61°30W **94** C3
Rafah *Gaza Strip* 31°18N 34°14E **46** D3
Rafai *C.A.R.* 4°59N 23°58E **54** B1
Rafḥā *Si. Arabia* 29°35N 43°35E **44** D4
Rafsanjān *Iran* 30°30N 56°5E **45** D8
Raft Pt. *Australia* 16°4S 124°26E **60** C3
Râgâ *Sudan* 8°28N 25°41E **51** G11
Ragachow *Belarus* 53°8N 30°5E **17** B16
Ragama *Sri Lanka* 7°0N 79°50E **40** R11
Ragged, Mt. *Australia* 33°27S 123°25E **61** F3
Ragged Pt. *Barbados* 13°10N 59°26W **89** g
Raghunathpalli *India* 22°14N 84°48E **43** H11
Raghunathpur *India* 23°33N 86°40E **43** H12
Raglan *N.Z.* 37°55S 174°55E **59** B5
Ragusa *Italy* 36°55N 14°44E **22** F6
Raha *Indonesia* 4°55S 123°0E **37** E6
Rahaeng = Tak *Thailand* 16°52N 99°8E **38** D2
Rahatgarh *India* 23°47N 78°22E **43** H8
Rahimyar Khan *Pakistan* 28°30N 70°25E **42** E4
Rāhjerd *Iran* 34°22N 50°22E **45** C6
Rahole ⌂ *Kenya* 0°5N 38°57E **54** B4
Rahon *India* 31°3N 76°7E **42** D7
Raiatéa, Î. *French Polynesia* 16°50S 151°25W **65** J12
Raichur *India* 16°10N 77°20E **40** L10
Raiganj *India* 25°37N 88°10E **43** G13
Raigarh *India* 21°56N 83°25E **41** J13
Raijua *Indonesia* 10°37S 121°36E **37** F6
Raikot *India* 30°41N 75°42E **42** D6
Railton *Australia* 41°25S 146°28E **63** G4
Rainbow Bridge ⌂ *U.S.A.* 37°5N 110°58W **77** H8
Rainbow Lake *Canada* 58°30N 119°23W **70** B5
Rainier *U.S.A.* 46°53N 122°41W **78** D4
Rainier, Mt. *U.S.A.* 46°52N 121°46W **78** D5
Rainy L. *Canada* 48°42N 93°10W **71** D10
Rainy River *Canada* 48°43N 94°29W **71** D10
Raippaluoto *Finland* 63°13N 21°14E **8** E19
Raipur *India* 21°17N 81°45E **41** J12
Raisen *India* 23°20N 77°48E **42** H8
Raisio *Finland* 60°28N 22°11E **9** F20
Raj Nandgaon *India* 21°5N 81°5E **41** J12
Raj Nilgiri *India* 21°28N 86°46E **43** J12
Raja, Ujung *Indonesia* 3°40N 96°25E **36** D1
Raja Ampat, Kepulauan *Indonesia* 0°30S 130°0E **37** E8
Rajahmundry *India* 17°1N 81°48E **41** L12
Rajaji △ *India* 30°10N 78°20E **42** D8
Rajang → *Malaysia* 2°30N 112°0E **36** D4
Rajanpur *Pakistan* 29°6N 70°19E **42** E4
Rajapalaiyam *India* 9°25N 77°35E **40** Q10
Rajasthan □ *India* 26°45N 73°30E **42** F5
Rajasthan Canal = Indira Gandhi Canal *India* 28°0N 72°0E **42** F5
Rajauri *India* 33°25N 74°21E **43** C6
Rajgarh *Mad. P., India* 24°2N 76°45E **42** G7
Rajgarh *Raj., India* 27°14N 76°38E **42** F7
Rajgarh *Raj., India* 28°40N 75°25E **42** E6
Rajgir *India* 25°2N 85°25E **43** G11
Rajkot *India* 22°15N 70°56E **42** H4
Rajmahal Hills *India* 24°30N 87°30E **43** G12
Rajpipla *India* 21°50N 73°30E **40** J8
Rajpur *India* 22°18N 74°21E **42** H6
Rajpura *India* 30°25N 76°32E **42** D7
Rajsamand = Kankroli *India* 25°4N 73°53E **42** G5
Rajshahi *Bangla.* 24°22N 88°39E **41** G16
Rajshahi □ *Bangla.* 25°0N 89°0E **43** G13
Rajula *India* 21°3N 71°26E **42** J4
Rakaia *N.Z.* 43°45S 172°1E **59** E4
Rakaia → *N.Z.* 43°36S 172°15E **59** E4
Rakan, Ra's *Qatar* 26°10N 51°20E **45** E6
Rakaposhi *Pakistan* 36°10N 74°25E **43** A6
Rakata, Pulau *Indonesia* 6°10S 105°20E **36** F3
Rakhiv *Ukraine* 48°3N 24°12E **17** D13
Rakhni *Pakistan* 30°4N 69°56E **42** D3
Rakhni → *Pakistan* 29°31N 69°36E **42** E3
Rakiraki *Fiji* 17°22S 178°11E **59** a
Rakitnoye *Russia* 45°36N 134°17E **30** B7
Rakiura = Stewart I. *N.Z.* 46°58S 167°54E **59** G1
Rakiura △ *N.Z.* 47°0S 167°50E **59** G1
Rakops *Botswana* 21°1S 24°28E **56** C3
Rakvere *Estonia* 59°20N 26°25E **9** G22
Raleigh *U.S.A.* 35°47N 78°39W **85** D15
Ralik Chain *Pac. Oc.* 8°0N 168°0E **64** G8
Ralls *U.S.A.* 33°41N 101°24W **84** E4
Ralston *U.S.A.* 41°30N 76°57W **82** E8
Ram → *Canada* 62°1N 123°41W **70** A4
Rām Allāh *West Bank* 31°55N 35°10E **46** D4
Rama *Nic.* 12°9N 84°15W **88** D3
Ramakona *India* 21°43N 78°50E **43** J8
Rāmallāh = Rām Allāh *West Bank* 31°55N 35°10E **46** D4
Raman *Thailand* 6°29N 101°18E **39** J3
Ramanathapuram *India* 9°25N 78°55E **40** Q11
Ramanetaka, B. de *Madag.* 14°13S 47°52E **57** A8
Ramanujganj *India* 23°48N 83°42E **43** H10
Ramat Gan *Israel* 32°4N 34°48E **46** C3
Ramatlhabama *S. Africa* 25°37S 25°33E **56** D4
Ramban *India* 33°14N 75°12E **43** C6
Rambi = Rabi *Fiji* 16°30S 179°59W **59** a
Rambipuji *Indonesia* 8°12S 113°37E **37** H15
Rame Hd. *Australia* 37°47S 149°30E **63** F4
Ramechhap *Nepal* 27°25N 86°10E **43** F12
Ramganga → *India* 27°5N 79°58E **43** F8
Ramgarh *Jharkhand, India* 23°40N 85°35E **43** H11
Ramgarh *Raj., India* 27°16N 75°14E **42** F6
Ramgarh *Raj., India* 27°30N 70°36E **42** F4
Rāmhormoz *Iran* 31°15N 49°35E **45** D6
Ramīān *Iran* 37°3N 55°16E **45** B7
Ramingining *Australia* 12°19S 135°3E **62** A2
Ramla *Israel* 31°55N 34°52E **46** D3
Ramm = Rum *Jordan* 29°39N 35°26E **46** F4
Ramm, Jabal *Jordan* 29°35N 35°24E **46** F4
Ramnad = Ramanathapuram *India* 9°25N 78°55E **40** Q11
Ramnagar *Jammu & Kashmir, India* 32°47N 75°18E **43** C6
Ramnagar *Uttarakhand, India* 29°24N 79°7E **43** E8
Râmnicu Sărat *Romania* 45°26N 27°3E **17** F14
Râmnicu Vâlcea *Romania* 45°9N 24°21E **17** F13
Ramona *U.S.A.* 33°2N 116°52W **79** M10
Ramore *Canada* 48°30N 80°25W **72** C3
Ramotswa *Botswana* 24°50S 25°52E **56** C4
Rampur *H.P., India* 31°26N 77°43E **42** D7
Rampur *Mad. P., India* 23°25N 73°53E **42** H5
Rampur *Ut. P., India* 28°50N 79°5E **43** E8
Rampur Hat *India* 24°10N 87°50E **43** G12
Rampura *India* 24°30N 75°27E **42** G6
Ramrama Tola *India* 21°52N 79°55E **43** J8
Ramree I. *Burma* 19°0N 93°40E **41** K19
Rāmsar *Iran* 36°53N 50°41E **45** B6
Ramsey *I. of Man* 54°20N 4°22W **12** C3
Ramsey *U.S.A.* 41°4N 74°9W **83** E10
Ramsey L. *Canada* 47°13N 82°15W **72** C3
Ramsgate *U.K.* 51°20N 1°25E **13** F9
Ramtek *India* 21°20N 79°15E **40** J11
Ramu *Kenya* 3°55N 41°10E **54** B5
Rana Pratap Sagar Dam *India* 24°58N 75°38E **42** G6
Ranaghat *India* 23°15N 88°35E **43** H13
Ranahu *Pakistan* 25°55N 69°45E **42** G3
Ranau *Malaysia* 6°2N 116°40E **36** C5
Rancagua *Chile* 34°10S 70°50W **94** C1
Rancheria → *Canada* 60°13N 129°7W **70** A3
Ranchester *U.S.A.* 44°54N 107°10W **76** D10
Ranchi *India* 23°19N 85°27E **43** H11
Rancho Cordova *U.S.A.* 38°36N 121°18W **78** G5
Rancho Cucamonga *U.S.A.* 34°10N 117°30W **79** L9
Randalstown *U.K.* 54°45N 6°19W **10** B5
Randers *Denmark* 56°29N 10°1E **9** H14
Randfontein *S. Africa* 26°8S 27°45E **57** D4
Randle *U.S.A.* 46°32N 121°57W **78** D5
Randolph *Mass., U.S.A.* 42°10N 71°2W **83** D13
Randolph *N.Y., U.S.A.* 42°10N 78°59W **82** D6
Randolph *Utah, U.S.A.* 41°40N 111°11W **76** F8
Randolph *Vt., U.S.A.* 43°55N 72°40W **83** C12
Randsburg *U.S.A.* 35°22N 117°39W **79** K9
Råneälven → *Sweden* 65°50N 22°20E **8** D20
Rangae *Thailand* 6°19N 101°44E **39** J3
Rangaunu B. *N.Z.* 34°51S 173°15E **59** A4
Range, The *Zimbabwe* 19°2S 31°2E **55** F3
Rangeley *U.S.A.* 44°58N 70°39W **83** B14
Rangeley L. *U.S.A.* 44°55N 70°43W **83** B14
Rangely *U.S.A.* 40°5N 108°48W **76** F9
Ranger *U.S.A.* 32°28N 98°41W **84** E5
Rangia *India* 26°28N 91°38E **41** F17
Rangiora *N.Z.* 43°19S 172°36E **59** E4
Rangitaiki → *N.Z.* 37°54S 176°49E **59** B6
Rangitata → *N.Z.* 43°45S 171°15E **59** E3
Rangitoto ke te tonga = D'Urville I. *N.Z.* 40°50S 173°55E **59** D4
Rangkasbitung *Indonesia* 6°21S 106°15E **37** G12
Rangon → *Burma* 16°28N 96°40E **41** L20
Rangoon *Burma* 16°45N 96°20E **41** L20
Rangpur *Bangla.* 25°42N 89°22E **41** G16
Rangsang *Indonesia* 1°20N 103°30E **39** M4
Rangsit *Thailand* 13°59N 100°37E **38** F3
Ranibennur *India* 14°35N 75°30E **40** M9
Raniganj *Ut. P., India* 27°3N 82°13E **43** F9
Raniganj *W. Bengal, India* 23°40N 87°5E **41** H15
Ranikhet *India* 29°39N 79°25E **43** E8
Raniwara *India* 24°50N 72°10E **42** G5
Rāniyah *Iraq* 36°15N 44°53E **44** B5
Ranka *India* 23°59N 83°47E **43** H10
Ranken → *Australia* 20°31S 137°36E **62** C2
Rankin *U.S.A.* 31°13N 101°56W **84** F4
Rankin Inlet *Canada* 62°30N 93°0W **68** E13
Rankins Springs *Australia* 33°49S 146°14E **63** E4
Rannoch, L. *U.K.* 56°41N 4°20W **11** E4
Rannoch Moor *U.K.* 56°38N 4°48W **11** E4
Ranobe, Helodranon' i *Madag.* 23°3S 43°33E **57** C7
Ranohira *Madag.* 22°29S 45°24E **57** C8
Ranomafana *Toamasina, Madag.* 18°57S 48°50E **57** B8
Ranomafana *Toliara, Madag.* 24°34S 47°0E **57** C8
Ranomafana △ *Madag.* 21°16S 47°25E **57** C8
Ranomena *Madag.* 23°25S 47°17E **57** C8

Ranong Thailand 9°56N 98°40E 39 H2
Ranotsara Nord Madag. 22°48S 46°36E 57 C8
Rānsa Iran 33°39N 48°18E 45 C6
Ransiki Indonesia 1°30S 134°10E 37 E8
Rantabe Madag. 15°42S 49°39E 57 B8
Rantauprapat Indonesia 2°15N 99°50E 36 D1
Rantemario Indonesia 3°15S 119°57E 37 E5
Ranthambore △ India 26°10N 76°30E 42 F7
Rantoul U.S.A. 40°19N 88°9W 80 E9
Raohe China 46°47N 134°0E 30 A7
Raoyang China 38°15N 115°45E 34 E8
Rap, Ko Thailand 9°19N 99°58E 39 b
Rapa French Polynesia 27°35S 144°20W 65 K13
Rapa Nui = Pascua, I. de Chile 27°7S 109°23W 65 K17
Rapallo Italy 44°21N 9°14E 20 D8
Rapar India 23°34N 70°38E 42 H4
Rāpch Iran 25°40N 59°15E 45 E8
Rapel, Lago Chile 34°20S 71°14W 94 C1
Raper, C. Canada 69°44N 67°6W 69 D18
Rapid City U.S.A. 44°5N 103°14W 80 C2
Rapid River U.S.A. 45°55N 86°58W 80 C10
Rapla Estonia 59°1N 24°52E 9 G21
Rapti → India 26°18N 83°41E 43 F10
Raquette → U.S.A. 45°0N 74°42W 83 B10
Raquette Lake U.S.A. 43°49N 74°40W 83 C10
Rara △ Nepal 29°30N 82°10E 43 E10
Rarotonga Cook Is. 21°30S 160°0W 65 K12
Ra's al 'Ayn Syria 36°45N 40°12E 44 B4
Ra's al Khaymah U.A.E. 25°50N 55°59E 45 E7
Ra's aṭ Tīb Tunisia 37°1N 11°2E 22 F4
Rasa, Pta. Argentina 36°20S 56°41W 94 D4
Rasca, Pta. de la Canary Is. 27°59N 16°41W 24 G3
Raseiniai Lithuania 55°25N 23°5E 9 J20
Rashmi India 25°4N 74°22E 42 G6
Rasht Iran 37°20N 49°40E 45 B6
Rasi Salai Thailand 15°20N 104°9E 38 E5
Rason L. Australia 28°45S 124°25E 61 E3
Rasra India 25°50N 83°50E 43 G10
Rasul Pakistan 32°42N 73°34E 42 C5
Rat → Canada 49°35N 97°10W 71 D9
Rat Buri Thailand 13°30N 99°54E 38 F2
Rat Islands U.S.A. 52°0N 178°0E 74 E3
Rat L. Canada 56°10N 99°40W 71 B9
Ratak Chain Pac. Oc. 1°0N 170°0E 64 G8
Ratangarh India 28°5N 74°35E 42 E6
Raṭāwī Iraq 30°38N 47°13E 44 D5
Rath India 25°36N 79°37E 43 G8
Rath Luirc Ireland 52°21N 8°40W 10 D3
Rathangan Ireland 53°13N 7°1W 10 C4
Rathdrum Ireland 52°56N 6°14W 10 D5
Rathenow Germany 52°37N 12°19E 16 B7
Rathkeale Ireland 52°32N 8°56W 10 D3
Rathlin I. U.K. 55°18N 6°14W 10 A5
Rathmelton Ireland 55°2N 7°38W 10 A4
Ratibor = Racibórz Poland 50°7N 18°18E 17 C10
Ratlam India 23°20N 75°0E 42 H6
Ratmanova Ostrov Russia 65°46N 169°6W 74 B6
Ratnagiri India 16°57N 73°18E 40 L8
Ratodero Pakistan 27°48N 68°18E 42 F3
Raton U.S.A. 36°54N 104°24W 77 H11
Rattaphum Thailand 7°8N 100°16E 39 J3
Rattray Hd. U.K. 57°38N 1°50W 11 D7
Ratz, Mt. Canada 57°23N 132°12W 70 B2
Raub Malaysia 3°47N 101°52E 39 L3
Rauch Argentina 36°45S 59°5W 94 D4
Raudales Mexico 17°27N 93°39W 87 D6
Raufarhöfn Iceland 66°27N 15°57W 8 C6
Raufoss Norway 60°44N 10°37E 8 F14
Raukumara Ra. N.Z. 38°5S 177°55E 59 C6
Rauma Finland 61°10N 21°30E 8 F19
Raumo = Rauma Finland 61°10N 21°30E 8 F19
Raung, Gunung Indonesia 8°8S 114°3E 37 J17
Raurkela India 22°14N 84°50E 43 H11
Rausu-Dake Japan 44°4N 145°7E 30 B12
Rava-Ruska Ukraine 50°15N 23°42E 17 C12
Rava Russkaya = Rava-Ruska Ukraine 50°15N 23°42E 17 C12
Ravalli U.S.A. 47°17N 114°11W 76 C6
Ravānsar Iran 34°43N 46°40E 44 C5
Rāvar Iran 31°20N 56°51E 45 D8
Ravena U.S.A. 42°28N 73°49W 83 D11
Ravenna Italy 44°25N 12°12E 22 B5
Ravenna Nebr., U.S.A. 41°1N 98°55W 80 E4
Ravenna Ohio, U.S.A. 41°9N 81°15W 82 E3
Ravensburg Germany 47°46N 9°36E 16 E5
Ravenshoe Australia 17°37S 145°29E 62 B4
Ravensthorpe Australia 33°35S 120°2E 61 F3
Ravenswood Australia 20°6S 146°54E 62 C4
Ravenswood U.S.A. 38°57N 81°46W 81 F13
Ravi → Pakistan 30°35N 71°49E 42 D4
Rawalpindi Pakistan 33°38N 73°8E 42 C5
Rawang Malaysia 3°20N 101°35E 39 L3
Rawene N.Z. 35°25S 173°32E 59 A4
Rawlinna Australia 30°58S 125°28E 61 F4
Rawlins U.S.A. 41°47N 107°14W 76 F10
Rawlinson Ra. Australia 24°40S 128°30E 61 D4
Rawson Argentina 43°15S 65°5W 96 E3
Raxaul India 26°59N 84°51E 43 F11
Ray U.S.A. 48°21N 103°10W 80 A2
Ray, C. Canada 47°33N 59°15W 73 C8
Ray Mts. U.S.A. 66°0N 152°0W 74 B9
Raya Ring, Ko Thailand 8°18N 98°29E 39 a
Rayadurg India 14°40N 76°50E 40 M10
Rayagada India 19°15N 83°20E 41 K13
Raychikhinsk Russia 49°46N 129°25E 29 E13
Rāyen Iran 29°34N 57°26E 45 D8
Rayleigh U.K. 51°36N 0°37E 13 F8
Raymond Canada 49°30N 112°35W 70 D6
Raymond Calif., U.S.A. 37°13N 119°54W 78 H7
Raymond N.H., U.S.A. 43°2N 71°11W 83 C13
Raymond Wash., U.S.A. 46°41N 123°44W 78 D3
Raymondville U.S.A. 26°29N 97°47W 84 H6
Raymore Canada 51°25N 104°31W 71 C8
Rayón Mexico 29°43N 110°35W 86 B2
Rayong Thailand 12°40N 101°20E 38 F3
Raystown L. U.S.A. 40°25N 78°5W 82 F6
Rayville U.S.A. 32°29N 91°46W 84 E9
Raz, Pte. du France 48°2N 4°47W 20 C1
Razan Iran 35°23N 49°2E 45 C6
Razāzah, Buḩayrat ar Iraq 32°40N 43°35E 44 C4
Razazah, L. = Razāzah, Buḩayrat ar Iraq 32°40N 43°35E 44 C4
Razdel'naya = Rozdilna Ukraine 46°50N 30°2E 17 E16
Razdolnoye Russia 43°30N 131°52E 30 C5
Razeh Iran 32°47N 48°9E 45 C6
Razgrad Bulgaria 43°33N 26°34E 23 C12
Razim, Lacul Romania 44°50N 29°0E 17 F15
Razmak Pakistan 32°45N 69°50E 42 C3
Re, Cu Lao Vietnam 15°22N 109°8E 38 E7
Ré, Î. de France 46°12N 1°30W 20 C3
Reading U.K. 51°27N 0°58W 13 F7
Reading U.S.A. 40°20N 75°56W 83 F9
Reading □ U.K. 51°27N 0°58W 13 F7
Realicó Argentina 35°0S 64°15W 94 D3
Ream Cambodia 10°34N 103°39E 39 G4
Ream △ Cambodia 10°30N 103°45E 39 G4
Reay Forest U.K. 58°22N 4°55W 11 C4
Rebecca, L. Australia 30°0S 122°15E 61 F3
Rebi Indonesia 6°23S 134°7E 37 F8
Rebiana Libya 24°12N 22°10E 51 D10
Rebiana, Sahrâ' Libya 24°30N 21°0E 51 D10
Reboly Russia 63°49N 30°47E 8 E24
Rebun-Tō Japan 45°23N 141°2E 30 B10
Recherche, Arch. of the Australia 34°15S 122°50E 61 F3
Rechna Doab Pakistan 31°35N 73°30E 42 D5
Rechytsa Belarus 52°21N 30°24E 17 B16
Recife Brazil 8°0S 35°0W 93 E12
Recife Seychelles 4°36S 55°42E 53 b
Recklinghausen Germany 51°37N 7°12E 15 C7
Reconquista Argentina 29°10S 59°45W 94 B4
Recreo Argentina 29°25S 65°10W 94 B2
Red → U.S.A. 31°1N 91°45W 84 F9
Red Bank U.S.A. 40°21N 74°5W 83 F10
Red Bay Canada 51°44N 56°25W 73 B8
Red Bluff U.S.A. 40°11N 122°15W 76 F2
Red Bluff Res. U.S.A. 31°54N 103°55W 77 L12
Red Cliffs Australia 34°19S 142°11E 63 E3
Red Cloud U.S.A. 40°5N 98°32W 80 E4
Red Creek U.S.A. 43°14N 76°45W 83 C8
Red Deer Canada 52°20N 113°50W 70 C6
Red Deer → Alta., Canada 50°58N 110°0W 71 C7
Red Deer → Man., Canada 52°53N 101°1W 71 C8
Red Deer L. Canada 52°55N 101°20W 71 C8
Red Hook U.S.A. 41°55N 73°53W 83 E11
Red Indian L. Canada 48°35N 57°0W 73 C8
Red L. Canada 51°3N 93°49W 71 C10
Red Lake Canada 51°3N 93°49W 71 C10
Red Lake Falls U.S.A. 47°53N 96°16W 80 B5
Red Lake Road Canada 49°59N 93°25W 71 C10
Red Lodge U.S.A. 45°11N 109°15W 76 D9
Red Mountain U.S.A. 35°37N 117°38W 79 K9
Red Oak U.S.A. 41°1N 95°14W 80 E6
Red River of the North → N. Amer. 49°0N 97°15W 80 A5
Red Rock Canada 48°55N 88°15W 72 C2
Red Rock, L. U.S.A. 41°22N 92°59W 80 E7
Red Rocks Pt. Australia 32°13S 127°32E 61 F4
Red Sea Asia 25°0N 36°0E 47 C2
Red Slate Mt. U.S.A. 37°31N 118°52W 78 H8
Red Sucker L. Canada 54°9N 93°40W 72 B1
Red Tower Pass = Turnu Roşu, P. Romania 45°33N 24°17E 17 F13
Red Wing U.S.A. 44°34N 92°31W 80 C7
Redang Malaysia 5°49N 103°2E 39 K4
Redange Lux. 49°46N 5°52E 15 E5
Redcar U.K. 54°37N 1°4W 12 C6
Redcar & Cleveland □ U.K. 54°29N 1°0W 12 C7
Redcliff Canada 50°10N 110°50W 76 A8
Redcliffe Australia 27°12S 153°6E 63 D5
Redcliffe, Mt. Australia 28°30S 121°30E 61 E3
Reddersburg S. Africa 29°41S 26°10E 56 D4
Redding U.S.A. 40°35N 122°24W 76 F2
Redditch U.K. 52°18N 1°55W 13 E6
Redfield U.S.A. 44°53N 98°31W 80 C4
Redford U.S.A. 44°38N 73°48W 83 B11
Redhead Trin. & Tob. 10°44N 60°58W 93 K16
Redlands U.S.A. 34°4N 117°11W 79 M9
Redmond Oreg., U.S.A. 44°17N 121°11W 76 D3
Redmond Wash., U.S.A. 47°40N 122°7W 78 C4
Redon France 47°40N 2°6W 20 C2
Redonda Antigua & B. 16°58N 62°19W 89 C7
Redondela Spain 42°15N 8°38W 21 A1
Redondo Beach U.S.A. 33°50N 118°23W 79 M8
Redoubt Volcano U.S.A. 60°29N 152°45W 74 C9
Redruth U.K. 50°14N 5°14W 13 G2
Redvers Canada 49°35N 101°40W 71 D8
Redwater Canada 53°55N 113°6W 70 C6
Redwood U.S.A. 44°18N 75°48W 83 B9
Redwood △ U.S.A. 41°40N 124°5W 76 F1
Redwood City U.S.A. 37°30N 122°15W 78 H4
Redwood Falls U.S.A. 44°32N 95°7W 80 C6
Ree, L. Ireland 53°35N 8°0W 10 C3
Reed City U.S.A. 43°53N 85°31W 81 D11
Reed L. Canada 54°38N 100°30W 71 C8
Reedley U.S.A. 36°36N 119°27W 78 J7
Reedsburg U.S.A. 43°32N 90°0W 80 D8
Reedsport U.S.A. 43°42N 124°6W 76 E1
Reedsville U.S.A. 40°39N 77°35W 82 F7
Reefton N.Z. 42°6S 171°51E 59 E3
Reese → U.S.A. 40°48N 117°4W 76 F5
Refugio U.S.A. 28°18N 97°17W 84 G6
Regana, C. de Spain 39°25N 2°43E 24 B9
Regensburg Germany 49°1N 12°6E 16 D7
Reggâne = Zaouiet Reggâne Algeria 26°32N 0°3E 50 C6
Réggio di Calábria Italy 38°6N 15°39E 22 E6
Réggio nell'Emília Italy 44°43N 10°36E 22 B4
Reghin Romania 46°46N 24°42E 17 E13
Regina Canada 50°27N 104°35W 71 C8
Regina Beach Canada 50°47N 105°0W 71 C8
Registro Brazil 24°29S 47°49W 95 A6
Rehar → India 23°55N 82°40E 43 H10
Rehli India 23°38N 79°5E 43 H8
Rehoboth Namibia 23°15S 17°4E 56 C2
Rehovot Israel 31°54N 34°48E 46 D3
Reichenbach Germany 50°37N 12°17E 16 C7
Reid Australia 30°49S 128°26E 61 F4
Reidsville U.S.A. 36°21N 79°40W 85 C15
Reigate U.K. 51°14N 0°12W 13 F7
Reims France 49°15N 4°1E 20 B6
Reina Adelaida, Arch. Chile 52°20S 74°0W 96 G2
Reina Sofia, Tenerife ✕ (TFS) Canary Is. 28°3N 16°33W 24 F3
Reindeer → Canada 55°36N 103°11W 71 B8
Reindeer I. Canada 52°30N 98°0W 71 C9
Reindeer L. Canada 57°15N 102°15W 71 B8
Reinga, C. N.Z. 34°25S 172°43E 59 A4
Reinosa Spain 43°2N 4°15W 21 A3
Reitz S. Africa 27°48S 28°29E 57 D4
Reivilo S. Africa 27°36S 24°8E 56 D3
Reliance Canada 63°0N 109°20W 71 A7
Remanso Brazil 9°41S 42°4W 93 E10
Remarkable, Mt. Australia 32°48S 138°10E 63 E2
Rembang Indonesia 6°42S 111°21E 37 G14
Remedios Panama 8°15N 81°50W 88 E3
Remeshk Iran 26°55N 58°50E 45 E8
Remich Lux. 49°32N 6°22E 15 E6
Remscheid Germany 51°11N 7°12E 15 C7
Ren Xian China 37°8N 114°40E 34 F8
Rendang Indonesia 8°26S 115°25E 37 J18
Rendsburg Germany 54°17N 9°39E 16 A5
Renfrew Canada 45°30N 76°40W 83 A8
Renfrewshire □ U.K. 55°49N 4°38W 11 F4
Rengat Indonesia 0°30S 102°45E 36 E2
Rengo Chile 34°24S 70°50W 94 C1
Reni = Taranagar India 28°43N 74°50E 42 E6
Reni Ukraine 45°28N 28°15E 17 F15
Renmark Australia 34°11S 140°43E 63 E3
Rennell Sd. Canada 53°23N 132°35W 70 C2
Renner Springs Australia 18°20S 133°47E 62 B1
Rennes France 48°7N 1°41W 20 B3
Rennick Glacier Antarctica 70°30S 161°45E 5 D21
Rennie L. Canada 61°32N 105°35W 71 A7
Reno U.S.A. 39°31N 119°48W 78 F7
Reno → Italy 44°38N 12°16E 22 B5
Renovo U.S.A. 41°20N 77°45W 82 E7
Renqiu China 38°43N 116°5E 34 E9
Rensselaer Ind., U.S.A. 40°57N 87°9W 80 E10
Rensselaer N.Y., U.S.A. 42°38N 73°45W 83 D11
Renton U.S.A. 47°28N 122°12W 78 C4
Renukoot India 24°12N 83°2E 43 G10
Reotipur India 25°33N 83°45E 43 G10
Republic Mo., U.S.A. 37°7N 93°29W 80 G7
Republic Wash., U.S.A. 48°39N 118°44W 76 B4
Republican → U.S.A. 39°4N 96°48W 80 F5
Repulse B. Australia 20°35S 148°46E 62 b
Repulse Bay Canada 66°30N 86°30W 69 D14
Requena Peru 5°5S 73°52W 92 E4
Requena Spain 39°30N 1°4W 21 C5
Reserve U.S.A. 33°43N 108°45W 77 K9
Resht = Rasht Iran 37°20N 49°40E 45 B6
Resistencia Argentina 27°30S 59°0W 94 B4
Reşiţa Romania 45°18N 21°53E 17 F11
Reso = Raisio Finland 60°28N 22°11E 9 F20
Resolute Canada 74°42N 94°54W 69 C13
Resolution I. Canada 61°30N 65°0W 69 E19
Resolution I. N.Z. 45°40S 166°40E 59 F1
Ressano Garcia Mozam. 25°25S 32°0E 57 D5
Reston Canada 49°33N 101°6W 71 D8
Retalhuleu Guatemala 14°33N 91°46W 88 D1
Retenue, L. de Dem. Rep. of the Congo 11°0S 27°0E 55 E2
Retford U.K. 53°19N 0°56W 12 D7
Rethimno Greece 35°18N 24°30E 25 D6
Rethimno □ Greece 35°23N 24°28E 25 D6
Reti Pakistan 28°5N 69°48E 42 E3
Réunion ☒ Ind. Oc. 21°0S 56°0E 53 c
Reus Spain 41°10N 1°5E 21 B6
Reutlingen Germany 48°29N 9°12E 16 D5
Reval = Tallinn Estonia 59°22N 24°48E 9 G21
Revda Russia 56°48N 59°57E 18 C10
Revelganj India 25°50N 84°40E 43 G11
Revelstoke Canada 51°0N 118°10W 70 C5
Reventazón Peru 6°10S 80°58W 92 E2
Revillagigedo, Is. de Pac. Oc. 18°40N 112°0W 86 D2
Revuè → Mozam. 19°50S 34°0E 55 F3
Rewa India 24°33N 81°25E 43 G9
Rewari India 28°15N 76°40E 42 E7
Rexburg U.S.A. 43°49N 111°47W 76 E8
Rey Iran 35°35N 51°25E 45 C6
Rey, I. del Panama 8°20N 78°30W 88 E4
Rey, L. del Mexico 27°1N 103°26W 86 B4
Rey Malabo Eq. Guin. 3°45N 8°50E 52 D1
Reyðarfjörður Iceland 65°2N 14°13W 8 D6
Reyes, Pt. U.S.A. 38°0N 123°0W 78 H3
Reykjahlið Iceland 65°40N 16°55W 8 D5
Reykjanes Iceland 63°48N 22°40W 8 E2
Reykjavík Iceland 64°10N 21°57W 8 D3
Reynolds Ra. Australia 22°30S 133°0E 60 D5
Reynoldsville U.S.A. 41°6N 78°53W 82 E6
Reynosa Mexico 26°7N 98°18W 87 B5
Rēzekne Latvia 56°30N 27°17E 9 H22
Rezvān Iran 27°34N 56°6E 45 E8
Rhayader U.K. 52°18N 3°29W 13 E4
Rhein → Europe 51°52N 6°2E 15 C6
Rhein-Main-Donau-Kanal Germany 49°1N 11°27E 16 D6
Rheine Germany 52°17N 7°26E 16 B4
Rheinland-Pfalz □ Germany 50°0N 7°0E 16 C4
Rhin = Rhein → Europe 51°52N 6°2E 15 C6
Rhine = Rhein → Europe 51°52N 6°2E 15 C6
Rhinebeck U.S.A. 41°56N 73°55W 83 E11
Rhineland-Palatinate = Rheinland-Pfalz □ Germany 50°0N 7°0E 16 C4
Rhinelander U.S.A. 45°38N 89°25W 80 C9
Rhinns Pt. U.K. 55°40N 6°29W 11 F2
Rhino Camp Uganda 3°0N 31°22E 54 B3
Rhir, Cap Morocco 30°38N 9°54W 50 B4
Rhode Island □ U.S.A. 41°40N 71°30W 83 E13
Rhodes Greece 36°15N 28°10E 25 C10
Rhodope Mts. = Rhodopi Planina Bulgaria 41°40N 24°20E 23 D11
Rhodopi Planina Bulgaria 41°40N 24°20E 23 D11
Rhön Germany 50°24N 9°58E 16 C5
Rhondda U.K. 51°39N 3°31W 13 F4
Rhondda Cynon Taff □ U.K. 51°42N 3°27W 13 F4
Rhône → France 43°28N 4°42E 20 E6
Rhum U.K. 57°0N 6°20W 11 E2
Rhyl U.K. 53°20N 3°29W 12 D4
Riachão Brazil 7°20S 46°37W 93 E9
Riasi India 33°10N 74°50E 43 C6
Riau □ Indonesia 0°0 102°35E 36 E2
Riau, Kepulauan Indonesia 0°30N 104°20E 36 D2
Riau Arch. = Riau, Kepulauan Indonesia 0°30N 104°20E 36 D2
Ribadeo Spain 43°35N 7°5W 21 A2
Ribas do Rio Pardo Brazil 20°27S 53°46W 93 H8
Ribauè Mozam. 14°57S 38°17E 55 E4
Ribble → U.K. 53°52N 2°25W 12 D5
Ribe Denmark 55°19N 8°44E 9 J13
Ribeira Brava Madeira 32°41N 17°4W 24 D2
Ribeira Grande C. Verde Is. 17°0N 25°4W 50 b
Ribeirão Prêto Brazil 21°10S 47°50W 95 A6
Riberalta Bolivia 11°0S 66°0W 92 F5
Riccarton N.Z. 43°32S 172°37E 59 E4
Rice U.S.A. 34°5N 114°51W 79 L12
Rice L. Canada 44°12N 78°10W 82 B6
Rice Lake U.S.A. 45°30N 91°44W 80 C8
Rich, C. Canada 44°43N 80°38W 82 B4
Richards Bay S. Africa 28°48S 32°6E 57 D5
Richardson → Canada 58°25N 111°14W 71 B6
Richardson Lakes U.S.A. 44°46N 70°58W 81 C18
Richardson Springs U.S.A. 39°51N 121°46W 78 F5
Riche, C. Australia 34°36S 118°47E 61 F2
Richey U.S.A. 47°39N 105°4W 76 C11
Richfield U.S.A. 38°46N 112°5W 76 G7
Richfield Springs U.S.A. 42°51N 74°59W 83 D10
Richford U.S.A. 45°0N 72°40W 83 B12
Richibucto Canada 46°42N 64°54W 73 C7
Richland Ga., U.S.A. 32°5N 84°40W 85 E12
Richland Wash., U.S.A. 46°17N 119°18W 76 C4
Richland Center U.S.A. 43°21N 90°23W 80 D8
Richlands U.S.A. 37°6N 81°48W 81 G13
Richmond Australia 20°43S 143°8E 62 C3
Richmond N.Z. 41°20S 173°12E 59 D4
Richmond U.K. 54°25N 1°43W 12 C6
Richmond Calif., U.S.A. 37°56N 122°21W 78 H4
Richmond Ind., U.S.A. 39°50N 84°53W 81 F11
Richmond Ky., U.S.A. 37°45N 84°18W 81 G11
Richmond Mich., U.S.A. 42°49N 82°45W 82 D2
Richmond Mo., U.S.A. 39°17N 93°58W 80 F7
Richmond Tex., U.S.A. 29°35N 95°46W 84 G7
Richmond Utah, U.S.A. 41°56N 111°48W 76 F8
Richmond Va., U.S.A. 37°33N 77°27W 81 G15
Richmond Vt., U.S.A. 44°24N 72°59W 83 B12
Richmond Hill Canada 43°52N 79°27W 82 C5
Richmond Ra. Australia 29°0S 152°45E 63 D5
Richmondville U.S.A. 42°38N 74°33W 83 D10
Richtersveld △ S. Africa 28°15S 17°10E 56 D2
Richville U.S.A. 44°25N 75°23W 83 B9
Richwood U.S.A. 38°14N 80°32W 81 F13
Ridder = Leninogorsk Kazakhstan 50°20N 83°30E 28 D9
Riddlesburg U.S.A. 40°9N 78°15W 82 F6
Ridgecrest U.S.A. 35°38N 117°40W 79 K9
Ridgefield Conn., U.S.A. 41°17N 73°30W 83 E11
Ridgefield Wash., U.S.A. 45°49N 122°45W 78 E4
Ridgeland Miss., U.S.A. 32°26N 90°8W 85 E9
Ridgeland S.C., U.S.A. 32°29N 80°59W 85 E14
Ridgetown Canada 42°26N 81°52W 82 D3
Ridgewood U.S.A. 40°59N 74°7W 83 F10
Ridgway U.S.A. 41°25N 78°44W 82 E6
Riding Mountain △ Canada 50°50N 100°0W 71 C9
Ridley, Mt. Australia 33°12S 122°7E 61 F3
Riebeek-Oos S. Africa 33°10S 26°10E 56 E4
Ried Austria 48°14N 13°30E 16 D7
Riesa Germany 51°17N 13°17E 16 C7
Riet → S. Africa 29°0S 23°54E 56 D3
Rietbron S. Africa 32°54S 23°10E 56 E3
Rietfontein Namibia 21°58S 20°58E 56 C3
Rieti Italy 42°24N 12°51E 22 C5
Rif = Er Rif Morocco 35°1N 4°1W 50 A5
Riffe L. U.S.A. 46°32N 122°26W 78 D4
Rifle U.S.A. 39°32N 107°47W 76 G10
Rift Valley Africa 7°0N 30°0E 48 G7
Rift Valley □ Kenya 0°20N 36°0E 54 B4
Rīga Latvia 56°53N 24°8E 9 H21
Riga, G. of Latvia 57°40N 23°45E 9 H20
Rīgān Iran 28°37N 58°58E 45 D8
Rīgas Jūras Līcis = Riga, G. of Latvia 57°40N 23°45E 9 H20
Rigaud Canada 45°29N 74°18W 83 A10
Rigby U.S.A. 43°40N 111°55W 76 E8
Rīgestān Afghan. 30°15N 65°0E 40 D4
Riggins U.S.A. 45°25N 116°19W 76 D5
Rigolet Canada 54°10N 58°23W 73 B8
Rihand Dam India 24°9N 83°2E 43 G10
Riihimäki Finland 60°45N 24°48E 8 F21
Riiser-Larsen-halvøya Antarctica 68°0S 35°0E 5 C4
Riiser-Larsen Ice Shelf S. Ocean 74°0S 19°0W 5 D2
Riiser-Larsen Sea S. Ocean 67°30S 22°0E 5 C4
Rijeka Croatia 45°20N 14°21E 16 F8
Rijssen Neths. 52°19N 6°31E 15 B6
Rikuchū-Kaigan △ Japan 39°20N 142°0E 30 E11
Rikuzentakada Japan 39°0N 141°40E 30 E10
Riley U.S.A. 43°32N 119°28W 76 E4
Rima → Nigeria 13°4N 5°10E 50 F7
Rimah, Wadi ar → Si. Arabia 26°5N 41°30E 44 E4
Rimau, Pulau Malaysia 5°15N 100°16E 39 c
Rimbey Canada 52°35N 114°15W 70 C6
Rimersburg U.S.A. 41°3N 79°30W 82 E5
Rímini Italy 44°3N 12°33E 22 B5
Rimouski Canada 48°27N 68°30W 73 C6
Rimrock U.S.A. 46°40N 121°7W 78 D5
Rinca Indonesia 8°45S 119°35E 37 F5
Rincón de Romos Mexico 22°14N 102°18W 86 C4
Rinconada Argentina 22°26S 66°10W 94 A2
Rind → India 25°53N 80°33E 43 G9
Ringas India 27°21N 75°34E 42 F6
Ringgold Is. Fiji 16°15S 179°25W 59 a
Ringkøbing Denmark 56°5N 8°15E 9 H13
Ringvassøya Norway 69°56N 19°15E 8 B18
Ringwood U.S.A. 41°7N 74°15W 83 E10
Rinjani Indonesia 8°24S 116°28E 36 F5
Rio Branco Brazil 9°58S 67°49W 92 E5
Río Branco Uruguay 32°40S 53°40W 95 C5
Río Bravo Mexico 25°59N 98°6W 87 B5
Río Bravo ⌓ N. Amer. 29°2N 102°45W 86 B4
Río Bravo del Norte → Mexico 25°57N 97°9W 87 B5
Rio Brilhante Brazil 21°48S 54°33W 95 A5
Rio Claro Brazil 22°19S 47°35W 95 A6
Rio Claro Trin. & Tob. 10°20N 61°25W 93 K15
Río Colorado Argentina 39°0S 64°0W 96 D4
Río Cuarto Argentina 33°10S 64°25W 94 C3
Rio das Pedras Mozam. 23°8S 35°28E 57 C6
Rio de Janeiro Brazil 22°54S 43°12W 95 A7
Rio de Janeiro □ Brazil 22°50S 43°0W 95 A7
Rio do Sul Brazil 27°13S 49°37W 95 B6
Río Dulce △ Guatemala 15°43N 88°50W 88 C2
Río Gallegos Argentina 51°35S 69°15W 96 G3
Río Grande Argentina 53°50S 67°45W 96 G3
Rio Grande Brazil 32°0S 52°20W 95 C5
Río Grande Mexico 23°50N 103°2W 86 C4
Río Grande Puerto Rico 18°23N 65°50W 89 d
Rio Grande → N. Amer. 25°58N 97°9W 84 J6
Rio Grande City U.S.A. 26°23N 98°49W 84 H5
Río Grande de Santiago → Mexico 21°36N 105°26W 86 C3
Rio Grande do Norte □ Brazil 5°40S 36°0W 93 E11
Rio Grande do Sul □ Brazil 30°0S 53°0W 95 C5
Río Hato Panama 8°22N 80°10W 88 E3
Río Lagartos Mexico 21°36N 88°10W 87 C7
Rio Largo Brazil 9°28S 35°50W 93 E11
Río Mulatos Bolivia 19°40S 66°50W 92 G5
Río Muni □ Eq. Guin. 1°30N 10°0E 52 D2
Rio Negro Brazil 26°0S 49°55W 95 B6
Rio Pardo Brazil 30°0S 52°30W 95 C5
Río Pilcomayo △ Argentina 25°5S 58°5W 94 B4
Río Platano ⌓ Honduras 15°45N 85°0W 88 C3
Rio Rancho U.S.A. 35°14N 106°41W 77 J10
Río Segundo Argentina 31°40S 63°59W 94 C3
Río Tercero Argentina 32°15S 64°8W 94 C3
Rio Verde Brazil 17°50S 51°0W 93 G8
Río Verde Mexico 21°56N 99°59W 87 C5
Rio Vista U.S.A. 38°10N 121°42W 78 G5
Ríobamba Ecuador 1°50S 78°45W 92 D3
Ríohacha Colombia 11°33N 72°55W 92 A4
Ríosucio Colombia 7°27N 77°7W 92 B3
Riou L. Canada 59°7N 106°25W 71 B7
Ripley Canada 44°4N 81°35W 82 B3
Ripley Calif., U.S.A. 33°32N 114°39W 79 M12
Ripley N.Y., U.S.A. 42°16N 79°43W 82 D5
Ripley Tenn., U.S.A. 35°45N 89°32W 85 D10
Ripley W. Va., U.S.A. 38°49N 81°43W 81 F13
Ripon U.K. 54°9N 1°31W 12 C6
Ripon Calif., U.S.A. 37°44N 121°7W 78 H5
Ripon Wis., U.S.A. 43°51N 88°50W 80 D9
Rishā', W. ar → Si. Arabia 25°33N 44°5E 44 E5
Rishiri-Rebun-Sarobetsu △ Japan 45°26N 141°30E 30 B10
Rishiri-Tō Japan 45°11N 141°15E 30 B10
Rishon le Ẕiyyon Israel 31°58N 34°48E 46 D3
Rison U.S.A. 33°58N 92°11W 84 E8
Risør Norway 58°43N 9°13E 9 G13
Rita Blanca Cr. → U.S.A. 35°40N 102°29W 84 D3
Ritter, Mt. U.S.A. 37°41N 119°12W 78 H7
Rittman U.S.A. 40°58N 81°47W 82 F3
Ritzville U.S.A. 47°8N 118°23W 76 C4
Riva del Garda Italy 45°53N 10°50E 22 B4
Rivadavia B. Aires, Argentina 35°29S 62°59W 94 D3
Rivadavia Mendoza, Argentina 33°13S 68°30W 94 C2
Rivadavia Salta, Argentina 24°5S 62°54W 94 A3
Rivadavia Chile 29°57S 70°35W 94 B1
Rivas Nic. 11°30N 85°50W 88 D2
Rivash Iran 35°28N 58°26E 45 C8
River Cess Liberia 5°30N 9°32W 50 G4
River Jordan Canada 48°26N 124°3W 78 B2
Rivera Argentina 37°12S 63°14W 94 D3
Rivera Uruguay 31°0S 55°50W 95 C4
Riverbank U.S.A. 37°44N 120°56W 78 H6
Riverdale U.S.A. 36°26N 119°52W 78 J7
Riverhead U.S.A. 40°55N 72°40W 83 F12
Riverhurst Canada 50°55N 106°50W 71 C7
Rivers Canada 50°2N 100°14W 71 C8
Rivers Inlet Canada 51°42N 127°15W 70 C3

Riversdale *Canada* 44°5N 81°20W **82** B3
Riversdale *S. Africa* 34°7S 21°15E **56** E3
Riverside *U.S.A.* 33°59N 117°22W **79** M9
Riverton *Australia* 34°10S 138°46E **63** E2
Riverton *Canada* 51°1N 97°0W **71** C9
Riverton *N.Z.* 46°21S 168°0E **59** G2
Riverton *U.S.A.* 43°2N 108°23W **76** E9
Riviera *U.S.A.* 35°4N 114°35W **79** K12
Riviera di Levante *Italy* 44°15N 9°30E **20** D8
Riviera di Ponente *Italy* 44°10N 8°20E **20** D8
Rivière-au-Renard
    Canada 48°59N 64°23W **73** C7
Rivière-du-Loup *Canada* 47°50N 69°30W **73** C6
Rivière-Pentecôte *Canada* 49°57N 67°1W **73** C6
Rivière-Pilote *Martinique* 14°26N 60°53W **88** c
Rivière-Salée *Martinique* 14°31N 61°0W **88** c
Rivne *Ukraine* 50°40N 26°10E **17** C14
Rívoli *Italy* 45°3N 7°31E **20** D7
Rivoli B. *Australia* 37°32S 140°3E **63** F3
Riyadh = Ar Riyāḍ
    Si. Arabia 24°41N 46°42E **44** E5
Riyadh al Khabrā'
    Si. Arabia 26°2N 43°33E **44** E4
Rize *Turkey* 41°0N 40°30E **19** F7
Rizhao *China* 35°25N 119°30E **35** G10
Rizokarpaso *Cyprus* 35°36N 34°23E **25** D13
Rizzuto, C. *Italy* 38°53N 17°5E **22** E7
Rjukan *Norway* 59°54N 8°33E **9** G13
Road Town *Br. Virgin Is.* 18°27N 64°37W **89** e
Roan Plateau *U.S.A.* 39°20N 109°20W **76** G9
Roanne *France* 46°3N 4°4E **20** C6
Roanoke *Ala., U.S.A.* 33°9N 85°22W **85** E12
Roanoke *Va., U.S.A.* 37°16N 79°56W **81** G14
Roanoke → *U.S.A.* 35°57N 76°42W **85** D16
Roanoke I. *U.S.A.* 35°53N 75°39W **85** D17
Roanoke Rapids *U.S.A.* 36°28N 77°40W **85** C16
Roatán *Honduras* 16°18N 86°35W **88** C2
Robāt Sang *Iran* 35°35N 59°10E **45** C8
Robāṭkarīm *Iran* 35°25N 50°59E **45** C6
Robbins I. *Australia* 40°42S 145°0E **63** G4
Robe → *Australia* 21°42S 116°15E **60** D2
Robe → *Australia* 33°59N 8°33E Robert Bourassa, Rés.
    Canada 53°40N 76°55W **72** B4
Robert Lee *U.S.A.* 31°54N 100°29W **84** F4
Robertsganj *India* 24°44N 83°4E **43** G10
Robertson *S. Africa* 33°46S 19°50E **56** E2
Robertson I. *Antarctica* 65°15S 59°30W **5** C18
Robertson Ra. *Australia* 23°15S 121°0E **60** D3
Robertstown *Australia* 33°58S 139°5E **63** E2
Roberval *Canada* 48°32N 72°15W **73** C5
Robeson Chan. *N. Amer.* 82°0N 61°30W **69** A19
Robesonia *U.S.A.* 40°21N 76°8W **83** F8
Robinson *U.S.A.* 39°0N 87°44W **80** F10
Robinson → *Australia* 16°3S 137°16E **62** B2
Robinson Crusoe I.
    Pac. Oc. 33°38S 78°52W **90** F2
Robinson Ra. *Australia* 25°40S 119°0E **61** E2
Robinvale *Australia* 34°40S 142°45E **63** E3
Roblin *Canada* 51°14N 101°21W **71** C8
Roboré *Bolivia* 18°10S 59°45W **92** G7
Robson, Mt. *Canada* 53°10N 119°10W **70** C5
Robstown *U.S.A.* 27°47N 97°40W **84** H6
Roca, C. da *Portugal* 38°40N 9°31W **21** C1
Roca Partida, I. *Mexico* 19°1N 112°2W **86** D2
Rocas, I. *Brazil* 4°0S 34°1W **93** D12
Rocha *Uruguay* 34°30S 54°25W **95** C5
Rochdale *U.K.* 53°38N 2°9W **12** D5
Rochefort *Belgium* 50°9N 5°12E **15** D5
Rochefort *France* 45°56N 0°57W **20** D3
Rochelle *U.S.A.* 41°56N 89°4W **80** E9
Rocher River *Canada* 61°23N 112°44W **70** A6
Rochester *U.K.* 51°23N 0°31E **13** F8
Rochester *Ind., U.S.A.* 41°4N 86°13W **80** E10
Rochester *Minn., U.S.A.* 44°1N 92°28W **80** C7
Rochester *N.H., U.S.A.* 43°18N 70°59W **83** C14
Rochester *N.Y., U.S.A.* 43°10N 77°37W **82** C7
Rock → *U.S.A.* 60°7N 127°7W **70** A3
Rock, The *Australia* 35°15S 147°2E **63** F4
Rock Creek *U.S.A.* 41°40N 80°52W **82** E4
Rock Falls *U.S.A.* 41°47N 89°41W **80** E9
Rock Hill *U.S.A.* 34°56N 81°1W **85** D14
Rock Island *U.S.A.* 41°30N 90°34W **80** E8
Rock Port *U.S.A.* 40°25N 95°31W **80** E6
Rock Rapids *U.S.A.* 43°26N 96°10W **80** D5
Rock Sound *Bahamas* 24°54N 76°12W **88** B4
Rock Springs *Mont.,
    U.S.A.* 46°49N 106°15W **76** C10
Rock Springs *Wyo.,
    U.S.A.* 41°35N 109°14W **76** F9
Rock Valley *U.S.A.* 43°12N 96°18W **80** D5
Rockall *Atl. Oc.* 57°37N 13°42W **6** D3
Rockdale *Tex., U.S.A.* 30°39N 97°0W **84** F6
Rockdale *Wash., U.S.A.* 47°22N 121°28W **78** C5
Rockeby = Mungkan Kandju △
    Australia 13°35S 142°52E **62** A3
Rockefeller Plateau
    Antarctica 76°0S 130°0W **5** E14
Rockford *U.S.A.* 42°16N 89°6W **80** D9
Rockglen *Canada* 49°11N 105°57W **71** D7
Rockhampton *Australia* 23°22S 150°32E **62** C5
Rockingham *Australia* 32°15S 115°38E **61** F2
Rockingham *N.C.,
    U.S.A.* 34°57N 79°46W **85** D15
Rockingham *Vt.,
    U.S.A.* 43°11N 72°29W **83** C12
Rockingham B. *Australia* 18°5S 146°10E **62** B4
Rocklake *U.S.A.* 48°47N 99°15W **80** A4
Rockland *Canada* 45°33N 75°17W **83** A9
Rockland *Idaho, U.S.A.* 42°34N 112°53W **76** E7
Rockland *Maine, U.S.A.* 44°6N 69°7W **81** C19
Rockland *Mich., U.S.A.* 46°44N 89°11W **80** B9
Rocklin *U.S.A.* 38°48N 121°14W **78** G5
Rockly B. *Trin. & Tob.* 11°9N 60°46W **93** J16
Rockmart *U.S.A.* 34°0N 85°3W **85** D12
Rockport *Mass., U.S.A.* 42°39N 70°37W **83** D14
Rockport *Tex., U.S.A.* 28°2N 97°3W **84** G6
Rocksprings *U.S.A.* 30°1N 100°13W **84** F4

Rockville *Conn., U.S.A.* 41°52N 72°28W **83** E12
Rockville *Md., U.S.A.* 39°5N 77°9W **81** F15
Rockwall *U.S.A.* 32°56N 96°28W **84** E6
Rockwell City *U.S.A.* 42°24N 94°38W **80** D6
Rockwood *Canada* 43°37N 80°8W **82** C4
Rockwood *Maine,
    U.S.A.* 45°41N 69°45W **81** C19
Rockwood *Tenn.,
    U.S.A.* 35°52N 84°41W **85** D12
Rocky Ford *U.S.A.* 38°3N 103°43W **76** G12
Rocky Gully *Australia* 34°30S 116°57E **61** F2
Rocky Harbour *Canada* 49°36N 57°55W **73** C8
Rocky Island L. *Canada* 46°55N 83°0W **72** C3
Rocky Lane *Canada* 58°31N 116°22W **70** B5
Rocky Mount *U.S.A.* 35°57N 77°48W **85** D16
Rocky Mountain △
    U.S.A. 40°25N 105°45W **76** F11
Rocky Mountain House
    Canada 52°22N 114°55W **70** C6
Rocky Mts. *N. Amer.* 49°0N 115°0W **76** B6
Rocky Point *Namibia* 19°3S 12°30E **56** B1
Rod *Pakistan* 28°10N 63°5E **40** E3
Roda *Greece* 39°48N 19°46E **25** A3
Rødbyhavn *Denmark* 54°39N 11°22E **9** J14
Roddickton *Canada* 50°51N 56°8W **73** B8
Rodez *France* 44°21N 2°33E **20** D5
Ródhos = Rhodes
    Greece 36°15N 28°10E **25** C10
Rodia *Greece* 35°22N 25°1E **25** D7
Rodna △ *Australia* 23°45S 132°4E **60** D5
Rodney *Canada* 42°34N 81°41W **82** D3
Rodney, C. *N.Z.* 36°17S 174°50E **59** B5
Rodopos *Greece* 35°34N 23°45E **25** D5
Rodrigues *Ind. Oc.* 19°45S 63°20E **3** E13
Roe → *U.K.* 55°6N 6°59W **10** A5
Roebling *U.S.A.* 40°7N 74°47W **83** F10
Roebourne *Australia* 20°44S 117°9E **60** D2
Roebuck B. *Australia* 18°5S 122°20E **60** C3
Roebuck Roadhouse
    Australia 17°59S 122°36E **60** C3
Roermond *Neths.* 51°12N 6°0E **15** C6
Roes Welcome Sd.
    Canada 65°0N 87°0W **69** E14
Roeselare *Belgium* 50°57N 3°7E **15** D3
Rogachev = Ragachow
    Belarus 53°8N 30°5E **17** B16
Rogagua, L. *Bolivia* 13°43S 66°50W **92** F5
Rogatyn *Ukraine* 49°24N 24°36E **17** D13
Rogers *U.S.A.* 36°20N 94°7W **84** C7
Rogers City *U.S.A.* 45°25N 83°49W **81** C12
Rogersville *Canada* 46°44N 65°26W **73** C6
Roggan → *Canada* 54°24N 79°25W **72** B4
Roggan L. *Canada* 54°8N 77°50W **72** B4
Roggeveen Basin
    Pac. Oc. 31°30S 95°30W **65** L18
Roggeveldberge *S. Africa* 32°10S 20°10E **56** E3
Rogoaguado, L. *Bolivia* 13°0S 65°30W **92** F5
Rogojampi *Indonesia* 8°19S 114°17E **37** J17
Rogue → *U.S.A.* 42°26N 124°26W **76** E1
Rohnert Park *U.S.A.* 38°16N 122°40W **78** G4
Rohri *Pakistan* 27°45N 68°51E **42** F3
Rohri Canal *Pakistan* 26°15N 68°27E **42** F3
Rohtak *India* 28°55N 76°43E **42** E7
Roi Et *Thailand* 16°4N 103°40E **38** D4
Roja *Latvia* 57°29N 22°43E **9** H20
Rojas *Argentina* 34°10S 60°45W **94** C3
Rojo, C. *Mexico* 21°33N 97°20W **87** C5
Rokan → *Indonesia* 2°0N 100°50E **36** D2
Rokiškis *Lithuania* 55°55N 25°35E **9** J21
Rolândia *Brazil* 23°18S 51°23W **95** A5
Rolla *Mo., U.S.A.* 37°57N 91°46W **80** G8
Rolla *N. Dak., U.S.A.* 48°52N 99°37W **80** A4
Rolleston *Australia* 24°28S 148°35E **62** C4
Rollingstone *Australia* 19°2S 146°24E **62** B4
Roma *Australia* 26°32S 148°49E **63** D4
Roma *Italy* 41°54N 12°28E **22** D5
Roma *Sweden* 57°32N 18°26E **9** H18
Roma-Los Saenz *U.S.A.* 26°24N 99°1W **84** H5
Romain, C. *U.S.A.* 33°0N 79°22W **85** E15
Romaine → *Canada* 50°18N 63°47W **73** B7
Roman *Romania* 46°57N 26°55E **17** E14
Romang *Indonesia* 7°30S 127°20E **37** F7
Români *Egypt* 30°59N 32°38E **46** E1
Romania ■ *Europe* 46°0N 25°0E **17** F12
Romano, Cayo *Cuba* 22°0N 77°30W **88** B4
Romans-sur-Isère *France* 45°3N 5°3E **20** D6
Romanzof C. *U.S.A.* 61°49N 166°6W **74** C6
Romblon *Phil.* 12°33S 122°17E **37** B6
Rome = Roma *Italy* 41°54N 12°28E **22** D5
Rome *Ga., U.S.A.* 34°15N 85°10W **85** D12
Rome *N.Y., U.S.A.* 43°13N 75°27W **83** C9
Rome *Pa., U.S.A.* 41°51N 76°21W **83** E8
Romney *U.S.A.* 39°21N 78°45W **81** F14
Romney Marsh *U.K.* 51°2N 0°54E **13** F8
Rømø *Denmark* 55°10N 8°30E **9** J13
Romorantin-Lanthenay
    France 47°21N 1°45E **20** C4
Romsdalen *Norway* 62°25N 7°52E **8** E12
Romsey *U.K.* 51°0N 1°29W **13** G6
Ron *Vietnam* 17°53N 106°27E **38** D6
Rona *U.K.* 57°34N 5°59W **11** D3
Ronan *U.S.A.* 47°32N 114°6W **76** C6
Roncador, Cayos
    Colombia 13°32N 80°4W **88** D3
Roncador, Serra do
    Brazil 12°30S 52°30W **93** F8
Ronda *Spain* 36°46N 5°12W **21** D3
Rondane *Norway* 61°57N 9°50E **8** F13
Rondônia □ *Brazil* 11°0S 63°0W **92** F6
Rondonópolis *Brazil* 16°28S 54°38W **93** G8
Rondu *Pakistan* 35°32N 75°10E **43** B6
Rong, Koh *Cambodia* 10°45N 103°15E **39** G4
Ronge, L. la *Canada* 55°6N 105°17W **71** B7
Rønne *Denmark* 55°6N 14°43E **9** J16
Ronne Ice Shelf
    Antarctica 77°30S 60°0W **5** D18
Ronsard, C. *Australia* 24°46S 113°10E **61** D1
Ronse *Belgium* 50°45N 3°35E **15** D3
Roodepoort *S. Africa* 26°11S 27°54E **57** D4

Roof Butte *U.S.A.* 36°28N 109°5W **77** H9
Rooiboklaagte →
    Namibia 20°50S 21°0E **56** C3
Rooniu, Mt. *Tahiti* 17°49S 149°12W **59** d
Roorkee *India* 29°52N 77°59E **42** E7
Roosendaal *Neths.* 51°32N 4°29E **15** C4
Roosevelt *U.S.A.* 40°18N 109°59W **76** F9
Roosevelt → *Brazil* 7°35S 60°20W **92** E6
Roosevelt, Mt. *Canada* 58°26N 125°20W **70** B3
Roosevelt I. *Antarctica* 79°30S 162°0W **5** D12
Roper → *Australia* 14°43S 135°27E **62** A2
Roper Bar *Australia* 14°44S 134°44E **62** A1
Roper River = St. Vidgeon's ◇
    Australia 14°47S 134°53E **62** A1
Roque Pérez *Argentina* 35°25S 59°24W **94** D4
Roquetas de Mar *Spain* 36°46N 2°36W **21** D4
Roraima □ *Brazil* 2°0N 61°30W **92** C6
Roraima, Mt. *Venezuela* 5°10N 60°40W **92** B6
Røros *Norway* 62°35N 11°23E **8** E14
Ros Comáin = Roscommon
    Ireland 53°38N 8°11W **10** C3
Rosa *Zambia* 9°33S 31°15E **55** D3
Rosa, Monte *Europe* 45°57N 7°53E **20** D7
Rosalia *U.S.A.* 47°14N 117°22W **76** C5
Rosamond *U.S.A.* 34°52N 118°10W **79** L8
Rosário *Argentina* 33°0S 60°40W **94** C3
Rosário *Brazil* 3°0S 44°15W **93** D10
Rosario *Baja Calif.,
    Mexico* 30°0N 115°50W **86** B1
Rosario *Sinaloa, Mexico* 22°58N 105°53W **86** C3
Rosario *Paraguay* 24°30S 57°35W **94** A4
Rosario de la Frontera
    Argentina 25°50S 65°0W **94** B3
Rosario de Lerma
    Argentina 24°59S 65°35W **94** A2
Rosario del Tala
    Argentina 32°20S 59°10W **94** C4
Rosário do Sul *Brazil* 30°15S 54°55W **95** C5
Rosarito *Mexico* 32°20N 117°2W **79** N9
Roscoe *U.S.A.* 41°56N 74°55W **83** E10
Roscommon *Ireland* 53°38N 8°11W **10** C3
Roscommon □ *Ireland* 53°49N 8°23W **10** C3
Roscrea *Ireland* 52°57N 7°49W **10** D4
Rose → *Australia* 14°16S 135°45E **62** A2
Rose, L. *Bahamas* 21°0N 73°30W **89** B5
Rose Belle *Mauritius* 20°24S 57°36E **53** d
Rose Blanche *Canada* 47°38N 58°45W **73** C8
Rose Hill *Mauritius* 20°14S 57°27F **53** d
Rose Pt. *Canada* 54°11N 131°39W **70** C2
Rose Valley *Canada* 52°19N 103°49W **71** C8
Roseau *Dominica* 15°17N 61°24W **89** C7
Roseau *U.S.A.* 48°51N 95°46W **80** A6
Rosebery *Australia* 41°46S 145°33E **63** G4
Rosebud *S. Dak., U.S.A.* 43°14N 100°51W **80** D3
Rosebud *Tex., U.S.A.* 31°4N 96°59W **84** F6
Roseburg *U.S.A.* 43°13N 123°20W **76** E2
Rosedale *U.S.A.* 33°51N 91°2W **85** E9
Rosehearty *U.K.* 57°42N 2°7W **11** D6
Roseires Res. *Sudan* 11°51N 34°23E **51** F12
Roseland *U.S.A.* 38°25N 122°43W **78** G4
Rosemary *Canada* 50°46N 112°5W **70** C6
Rosenberg *U.S.A.* 29°34N 95°49W **84** G7
Rosenheim *Germany* 47°51N 12°7E **16** E7
Roses, G. de *Spain* 42°10N 3°15E **21** A7
Rosetown *Canada* 51°35N 107°59W **71** C7
Roseville *Calif., U.S.A.* 38°45N 121°17W **78** G5
Roseville *Mich., U.S.A.* 42°30N 82°56W **82** D2
Roseville *Pa., U.S.A.* 41°51N 76°57W **83** E8
Rosewood *Australia* 27°38S 152°36E **63** D5
Roshkhvār *Iran* 34°58N 59°37E **45** C8
Rosignano Maríttimo
    Italy 43°24N 10°28E **22** C4
Rosignol *Guyana* 6°15N 57°30W **92** B7
Roșiori de Vede *Romania* 44°9N 25°0E **17** F13
Roskilde *Denmark* 55°38N 12°3E **9** J15
Roslavl *Russia* 53°57N 32°55E **18** D5
Rosmead *S. Africa* 31°29S 25°8E **56** E4
Ross *Australia* 42°2S 147°30E **63** G4
Ross *N.Z.* 42°53S 170°49E **59** E3
Ross Dependency
    Antarctica 76°0S 170°0W **5** D12
Ross I. *Antarctica* 77°30S 168°0E **5** D11
Ross Ice Shelf *Antarctica* 80°0S 180°0E **5** E12
Ross L. *U.S.A.* 48°44N 121°4W **76** B3
Ross Mhic Thriúin = New Ross
    Ireland 52°23N 6°57W **10** D5
Ross-on-Wye *U.K.* 51°54N 2°34W **13** F5
Ross River *Australia* 23°44S 134°30E **62** C1
Ross River *Canada* 62°30N 131°30W **70** A2
Ross Sea *Antarctica* 74°0S 178°0E **5** D11
Rossall Pt. *U.K.* 53°55N 3°3W **12** D4
Rossano *Italy* 39°36N 16°39E **22** E7
Rossburn *Canada* 50°40N 100°49W **71** C8
Rosseau *Canada* 45°16N 79°39W **82** A5
Rosseau, L. *Canada* 45°10N 79°35W **82** A5
Rosses, The *Ireland* 55°2N 8°20W **10** A3
Rossignol, L. *Canada* 52°43N 73°40W **72** B5
Rossignol L. *Canada* 44°12N 65°10W **73** D6
Rossland *Canada* 49°6N 117°50W **70** D5
Rosslare *Ireland* 52°17N 6°24W **10** D5
Rosslare Harbour *Ireland* 52°15N 6°20W **10** D5
Rossmore *Canada* 44°8N 77°23W **82** B7
Rosso *Mauritania* 16°40N 15°45W **50** E2
Rossosh *Russia* 50°15N 39°28E **19** D6
Røssvatnet *Norway* 65°45N 14°5E **8** D16
Røst *Norway* 67°32N 12°0E **8** C15
Rosthern *Canada* 52°40N 106°20W **71** C7
Rostock *Germany* 54°5N 12°8E **16** A7
Rostov *Don, Russia* 47°15N 39°45E **19** E6
Rostov *Yaroslavl, Russia* 57°14N 39°25E **18** C6
Roswell *Ga., U.S.A.* 34°2N 84°22W **85** D12
Roswell *N. Mex.,
    U.S.A.* 33°24N 104°32W **77** K11
Rotan *U.S.A.* 32°51N 100°28W **84** E4
Rother → *U.K.* 50°59N 0°45E **13** G8
Rothera *Antarctica* 67°34S 68°8W **5** C17

Rotherham *U.K.* 53°26N 1°20W **12** D6
Rothes *U.K.* 57°32N 3°13W **11** D5
Rothesay *Canada* 45°23N 66°0W **73** C6
Rothesay *U.K.* 55°50N 5°3W **11** F3
Roti *Indonesia* 10°50S 123°0E **37** F6
Roto *Australia* 33°0S 145°30E **63** E4
Rotondo, Mte. *France* 42°14N 9°8E **20** E8
Rotoroa, L. *N.Z.* 41°55S 172°39E **59** D4
Rotorua *N.Z.* 38°9S 176°16E **59** C6
Rotorua, L. *N.Z.* 38°5S 176°18E **59** C6
Rotterdam *Neths.* 51°55N 4°30E **15** C4
Rotterdam *U.S.A.* 42°48N 74°1W **83** D10
Rottnest I. *Australia* 32°0S 115°27E **61** F2
Rottumeroog *Neths.* 53°33N 6°34E **15** A6
Rottweil *Germany* 48°9N 8°37E **16** D5
Rotuma *Fiji* 12°25S 177°5E **58** C10
Roubaix *France* 50°40N 3°10E **20** A5
Rouen *France* 49°27N 1°4E **20** B4
Rouleau *Canada* 50°10N 104°56W **71** C8
Roulpmaulpma ◇
    Australia 23°52S 133°0E **60** D5
Round I. *Mauritius* 19°51S 57°45E **53** d
Round Mountain
    U.S.A. 38°43N 117°4W **76** G5
Round Mt. *Australia* 30°26S 152°16E **63** E5
Round Rock *U.S.A.* 30°31N 97°41W **84** F6
Roundup *U.S.A.* 46°27N 108°33W **76** C9
Rousay *U.K.* 59°10N 3°2W **11** B5
Rouses Point *U.S.A.* 44°59N 73°22W **83** B11
Rouseville *U.S.A.* 41°28N 79°42W **82** E5
Rousse = Ruse *Bulgaria* 43°48N 25°59E **23** C12
Roussillon *France* 42°30N 2°35E **20** E5
Rouxville *S. Africa* 30°25S 26°50E **56** E4
Rouyn-Noranda *Canada* 48°20N 79°0W **72** C4
Rovaniemi *Finland* 66°29N 25°41E **8** C21
Rovereto *Italy* 45°53N 11°3E **22** B4
Rovigo *Italy* 45°4N 11°47E **22** B4
Rovinj *Croatia* 45°5N 13°40E **16** F7
Rovno = Rivne *Ukraine* 50°40N 26°10E **17** C14
Rovuma = Ruvuma →
    Tanzania 10°29S 40°28E **55** E5
Row'ān *Iran* 35°8N 48°51E **45** C6
Rowena *Australia* 29°48S 148°55E **63** D4
Rowley → *Canada* 69°6N 77°52W **69** D16
Rowley Shoals *Australia* 17°30S 119°0E **60** C2
Roxas *Phil.* 11°36N 122°49E **37** B6
Roxboro *U.S.A.* 36°24N 78°59W **85** C15
Roxborough
    Trin. & Tob. 11°15N 60°35W **93** J16
Roxburgh *N.Z.* 45°33S 169°19E **59** F2
Roxbury *N.Y., U.S.A.* 42°17N 74°33W **83** D10
Roxbury *Pa., U.S.A.* 40°6N 77°39W **82** F7
Roxby Downs *Australia* 30°43S 136°46E **63** E2
Roy *Mont., U.S.A.* 47°20N 108°58W **76** C9
Roy *N. Mex., U.S.A.* 35°57N 104°12W **77** J11
Roy *Utah, U.S.A.* 41°10N 112°2W **76** F7
Royal Bardia △ *Nepal* 28°20N 81°20E **43** E9
Royal Canal *Ireland* 53°30N 7°13W **10** C4
Royal Chitawan △
    Nepal 26°30N 84°30E **43** F11
Royal Geographical Society Is.
    Canada 68°56N 100°15W **68** D11
Royal Leamington Spa
    U.K. 52°18N 1°31W **13** E6
Royal Natal △ *S. Africa* 28°43S 28°51E **57** D4
Royal Tunbridge Wells
    U.K. 51°7N 0°16E **13** F8
Royale, Isle *U.S.A.* 48°0N 88°54W **80** B9
Royan *France* 45°37N 1°2W **20** D3
Royston *U.K.* 52°3N 0°0 **13** E7
Rozdilna *Ukraine* 46°50N 30°2E **17** E16
Rozhyshche *Ukraine* 50°54N 25°15E **17** C13
Rtishchevo *Russia* 52°18N 43°46E **18** D7
Ruacaná *Namibia* 17°20S 14°12E **56** B1
Ruaha △ *Tanzania* 7°41S 34°30E **54** D3
Ruahine Ra. *N.Z.* 39°55S 176°2E **59** C6
Ruapehu *N.Z.* 39°17S 175°35E **59** C5
Ruapuke I. *N.Z.* 46°46S 168°31E **59** G2
Ruâq, W. → *Egypt* 30°0N 33°49E **46** F2
Rub' al Khālī *Si. Arabia* 19°0N 48°0E **47** D4
Rubeho Mts. *Tanzania* 6°50S 36°25E **54** D4
Rubh a' Mhail *U.K.* 55°56N 6°8W **11** F2
Rubha Hunish *U.K.* 57°42N 6°20W **11** D2
Rubha Robhanais = Lewis, Butt of
    U.K. 58°31N 6°16W **11** C2
Rubicon → *U.S.A.* 38°53N 121°4W **78** G5
Rubio *Venezuela* 7°43N 72°22W **92** B4
Rubondo △ *Tanzania* 2°18S 31°58E **54** C3
Rubtsovsk *Russia* 51°30N 81°10E **28** D9
Ruby L. *U.S.A.* 40°10N 115°28W **76** F6
Ruby Mts. *U.S.A.* 40°30N 115°20W **76** F6
Rubyvale *Australia* 23°25S 147°42E **62** C4
Rüd Sar *Iran* 37°8N 50°18E **45** B6
Rudall *Australia* 33°43S 136°17E **63** E2
Rudall → *Australia* 22°34S 122°13E **60** D3
Rudall River △
    Australia 22°38S 122°30E **60** D3
Rudbar *Iran* 30°0N 62°30E **45** D9
Rudewa *Tanzania* 10°7S 34°40E **55** E3
Rudnik *Ostrov* Russia 21°30N ??
Rudnyy *Kazakhstan* 52°57N 63°7E **28** D7
Rudolfa, Ostrov *Russia* 81°45N 58°30E **28** A6
Rudyard *U.S.A.* 46°14N 84°36W **81** B11
Ruenya → *Africa* 16°24S 33°48E **55** F3
Ruffling Pt. *Br. Virgin Is.* 18°44N 64°27W **89** e
Rufiji → *Tanzania* 7°50S 39°15E **54** D4
Rufino *Argentina* 34°20S 62°50W **94** C3
Rufunsa *Zambia* 15°4S 29°34E **55** F2
Rugby *U.K.* 52°23N 1°16W **13** E6
Rugby *U.S.A.* 48°22N 100°0W **80** A4
Rügen *Germany* 54°22N 13°24E **16** A7
Ruhengeri *Rwanda* 1°30S 29°36E **54** C2
Ruhnu *Estonia* 57°48N 23°15E **9** H20
Ruhr → *Germany* 51°27N 6°43E **16** C4
Ruhuhu → *Tanzania* 10°31S 34°56E **55** E3
Ruidoso *U.S.A.* 33°20N 105°41W **77** K11
Ruivo, Pico *Madeira* 32°45N 16°56W **24** D3
Rujm Tal'at al Jamā'ah
    Jordan 30°24N 35°30E **46** E4
Ruk *Pakistan* 27°50N 68°42E **42** F3

Rukhla *Pakistan* 32°27N 71°57E **42** C4
Ruki →
    Dem. Rep. of the Congo 0°5N 18°17E **52** E3
Rukwa □ *Tanzania* 7°0S 31°30E **54** D3
Rukwa, L. *Tanzania* 8°0S 32°20E **54** D3
Rulenge *Burundi* 2°43S 30°37E **54** C3
Rulhieres, C. *Australia* 13°56S 127°22E **60** B4
Rum = Rhum *U.K.* 57°0N 6°20W **11** E2
Rum *Jordan* 29°39N 35°26E **46** F4
Rum Cay *Bahamas* 23°40N 74°58W **89** B5
Rum Jungle *Australia* 13°0S 130°59E **60** B5
Ruma □ *Kenya* 0°39S 34°18E **54** C3
Rumāḥ *Si. Arabia* 25°29N 47°10E **44** E5
Rumania = Romania ■
    Europe 46°0N 25°0E **17** F12
Rumaylah *Iraq* 30°47N 47°37E **44** D5
Rumbêk *Sudan* 6°54N 29°37E **51** G11
Rumford *U.S.A.* 44°33N 70°33W **83** B14
Rumia *Poland* 54°37N 18°25E **17** A10
Rumoi *Japan* 43°56N 141°39E **30** C10
Rumonge *Burundi* 3°59S 29°26E **54** C2
Rumphi *Malawi* 11°1S 33°52E **55** E3
Rumson *U.S.A.* 40°23N 74°0W **83** F11
Runan *China* 33°0N 114°30E **34** H8
Runanga *N.Z.* 42°25S 171°15E **59** E3
Runaway, C. *N.Z.* 37°32S 177°59E **59** B6
Runaway Bay *Jamaica* 18°27N 77°20W **88** a
Runcorn *U.K.* 53°21N 2°44W **12** D5
Rundu *Namibia* 17°52S 19°43E **56** B2
Rungwa *Tanzania* 6°55S 33°32E **54** D3
Rungwa → *Tanzania* 7°36S 31°50E **54** D3
Rungwa △ *Tanzania* 6°53S 34°2E **54** D3
Rungwe *Tanzania* 9°11S 33°32E **55** D3
Rungwe, Mt. *Tanzania* 9°8S 33°40E **52** F6
Runton Ra. *Australia* 23°31S 123°6E **60** D3
Ruo Shui → *China* 41°0N 100°16E **32** B5
Ruokolahti *Finland* 61°17N 28°50E **8** F23
Ruoqiang *China* 38°55N 88°10E **32** C3
Rupa *India* 27°15N 92°21E **41** F18
Rupar *India* 31°2N 76°38E **42** D7
Rupat *Indonesia* 1°45N 101°40E **36** D2
Rupen → *India* 23°28N 71°31E **42** H4
Rupert *U.S.A.* 42°37N 113°41W **76** E7
Rupert → *Canada* 51°29N 78°45W **72** B4
Rupert B. *Canada* 51°35N 79°0W **72** B4
Rupert House = Waskaganish
    Canada 51°30N 78°40W **72** B4
Rupsa *India* 21°37N 87°1E **43** J12
Rurrenabaque *Bolivia* 14°30S 67°32W **92** F5
Rusambo *Zimbabwe* 16°30S 32°4E **55** F3
Rusape *Zimbabwe* 18°35S 32°8E **55** F3
Ruschuk = Ruse
    Bulgaria 43°48N 25°59E **23** C12
Ruse *Bulgaria* 43°48N 25°59E **23** C12
Rush *Ireland* 53°31N 6°6W **10** C5
Rushan *China* 36°56N 121°30E **35** F11
Rushden *U.K.* 52°18N 0°35E **13** E7
Rushmore, Mt. *U.S.A.* 43°53N 103°28W **80** D2
Rushville *Ill., U.S.A.* 40°7N 90°34W **80** E8
Rushville *Ind., U.S.A.* 39°37N 85°27W **81** F11
Rushville *Nebr., U.S.A.* 42°43N 102°28W **80** D2
Russas *Brazil* 4°55S 37°50W **93** D11
Russell *Canada* 50°50N 101°20W **71** C8
Russell *Kans., U.S.A.* 38°54N 98°52W **80** F4
Russell *N.Y., U.S.A.* 44°27N 75°9W **83** B9
Russell *Pa., U.S.A.* 41°56N 79°8W **82** E5
Russell Cave △ *U.S.A.* 34°59N 85°49W **85** D12
Russell L. *Man., Canada* 56°15N 101°30W **71** B8
Russell L. *N.W.T.,
    Canada* 63°5N 115°44W **70** A5
Russellkonda *India* 19°57N 84°42E **41** K14
Russellville *Ala., U.S.A.* 34°30N 87°44W **85** D11
Russellville *Ark., U.S.A.* 35°17N 93°8W **84** D8
Russellville *Ky., U.S.A.* 36°51N 86°53W **80** G10
Russia ■ *Eurasia* 62°0N 105°0E **29** C11
Russian → *U.S.A.* 38°27N 123°8W **78** G3
Rustam Shahr *Pakistan* 26°58N 66°6E **42** F2
Rustavi *Georgia* 41°30N 45°0E **19** F8
Rustenburg *S. Africa* 25°41S 27°14E **56** D4
Ruston *U.S.A.* 32°32N 92°38W **84** E8
Rutana *Burundi* 3°55S 30°0E **54** C3
Ruteng *Indonesia* 8°35S 120°30E **37** F6
Rutenga *Zimbabwe* 21°15S 30°44E **55** G3
Ruth *U.S.A.* 43°42N 82°45W **82** C2
Rutherford *U.S.A.* 38°26N 122°24W **78** G4
Rutland *U.S.A.* 43°37N 72°58W **83** C12
Rutland □ *U.K.* 52°38N 0°40W **13** E7
Rutland Water *U.K.* 52°39N 0°38W **13** E7
Rutledge → *Canada* 61°4N 112°0W **71** A6
Rutledge L. *Canada* 61°33N 110°47W **71** A6
Rutog *China* 33°27N 79°42E **32** C2
Rutshuru
    Dem. Rep. of the Congo 1°13S 29°25E **54** C2
Ruvu *Tanzania* 6°49S 38°43E **54** D4
Ruvu → *Tanzania* 6°23S 38°52E **54** D4
Ruvuba △ *Burundi* 3°3S 29°33E **54** C2
Ruvuma □ *Tanzania* 10°20S 36°0E **55** E4
Ruvuma → *Tanzania* 10°29S 40°28E **55** E5
Ruwais *U.A.E.* 24°5N 52°50E **45** E7
Ruwenzori □ *Africa* 0°30N 29°55E **54** B2
Ruwenzori △ *Uganda* 0°20N 30°0E **54** B2
Ruyigi *Burundi* 3°29S 30°15E **54** C3
Ružomberok *Slovak Rep.* 49°3N 19°17E **17** D10
Rwanda ■ *Africa* 2°0S 30°0E **54** C3
Ryan, L. *U.K.* 55°0N 5°2W **11** G3
Ryazan *Russia* 54°40N 39°40E **18** D6
Ryazhsk *Russia* 53°45N 40°3E **18** D7
Rybachiy Poluostrov
    Russia 69°43N 32°0E **8** B25
Rybachye = Balykchy
    Kyrgyzstan 42°26N 76°12E **32** B2
Rybinsk *Russia* 58°5N 38°50E **18** C6
Rybinskoye Vdkhr.
    Russia 58°30N 38°25E **18** C6
Rybnitsa = Rîbniţa
    Moldova 47°45N 29°0E **17** E15
Rycroft *Canada* 55°45N 118°40W **70** B5

Ryde U.K. 50°43N 1°9W 13 G6
Ryderwood U.S.A. 46°23N 123°3W 78 D3
Rye U.K. 50°57N 0°45E 13 G8
Rye → U.K. 54°11N 0°44W 12 C7
Rye Bay U.K. 50°52N 0°49E 13 G8
Rye Patch Res. U.S.A. 40°28N 118°19W 76 F4
Ryegate U.S.A. 46°18N 109°15W 76 C9
Ryley Canada 53°17N 112°26W 70 C6
Rylstone Australia 32°46S 149°58E 63 E4
Ryn Peski = Naryn Qum Kazakhstan 47°30N 49°0E 28 E5
Ryōtsu Japan 38°5N 138°26E 30 E9
Rypin Poland 53°3N 19°25E 17 B10
Ryūgasaki Japan 35°54N 140°11E 31 G10
Ryukyu Is. = Ryūkyū-rettō Japan 26°0N 126°0E 31 M3
Ryūkyū-rettō Japan 26°0N 126°0E 31 M3
Rzeszów Poland 50°5N 21°58E 17 C11
Rzhev Russia 56°20N 34°20E 18 C5

S

Sa Thailand 18°34N 100°45E 38 C3
Sa Cabaneta Spain 39°37N 2°45E 24 B9
Sa Canal Spain 38°51N 1°23E 24 C7
Sa Conillera Spain 38°59N 1°13E 24 C7
Sa Dec Vietnam 10°20N 105°46E 39 G5
Sa Dragonera Spain 39°35N 2°19E 24 B9
Sa Kaeo Thailand 13°49N 102°4E 38 F4
Sa Mesquida Spain 39°55N 4°16E 24 B11
Sa Pa Vietnam 22°20N 103°47E 38 A4
Sa Savina Spain 38°44N 1°25E 24 C7
Sa'ādatābād Fārs, Iran 30°10N 53°5E 45 D7
Sa'ādatābād Hormozgān, Iran 28°3N 55°53E 45 D7
Sa'ādatābād Kermān, Iran 29°40N 55°51E 45 D7
Saale → Germany 51°56N 11°54E 16 C6
Saalfeld Germany 50°38N 11°21E 16 C6
Saanich Canada 48°29N 123°26W 78 B3
Saar → Europe 49°41N 6°32E 15 E6
Saarbrücken Germany 49°14N 6°59E 16 D4
Saaremaa Estonia 58°30N 22°30E 9 G20
Saarijärvi Finland 62°43N 25°16E 8 E21
Saariselkä Finland 68°16N 28°15E 8 B23
Sab 'Ābar Syria 33°46N 37°41E 44 C3
Saba W. Indies 17°38N 63°14W 89 C7
Šabac Serbia 44°48N 19°42E 23 B8
Sabadell Spain 41°28N 2°7E 21 B7
Sabah □ Malaysia 6°0N 117°0E 36 C5
Sabak Malaysia 3°46N 100°58E 39 L3
Sabalān, Kūhhā-ye Iran 38°15N 47°45E 44 B5
Sabalana, Kepulauan Indonesia 6°45S 118°50E 37 F5
Sábana de la Mar Dom. Rep. 19°7N 69°24W 89 C6
Sábanalarga Colombia 10°38N 74°55W 92 A4
Sabang Indonesia 5°50N 95°15E 36 C1
Sabarmati → India 22°18N 72°22E 42 H5
Sabattis U.S.A. 44°6N 74°40W 83 B10
Saberania Indonesia 2°5S 138°18E 37 E9
Sabhā Libya 27°9N 14°29E 51 C8
Sabi → India 28°29N 76°44E 42 E7
Sabie S. Africa 25°10S 30°48E 57 D5
Sabinal Mexico 30°57N 107°30W 86 A3
Sabinal U.S.A. 29°19N 99°28W 84 G5
Sabinas Mexico 27°51N 101°7W 86 B4
Sabinas → Mexico 27°37N 100°42W 86 B4
Sabinas Hidalgo Mexico 26°30N 100°10W 86 B4
Sabine → U.S.A. 29°59N 93°47W 84 G8
Sabine L. U.S.A. 29°53N 93°51W 84 G8
Sabine Pass U.S.A. 29°44N 93°54W 84 G8
Sablayan Phil. 12°50N 120°50E 37 B6
Sable Canada 55°30N 68°21W 73 A6
Sable, C. Canada 43°29N 65°38W 73 D6
Sable, C. U.S.A. 25°9N 81°8W 88 A3
Sable I. Canada 44°0N 60°0W 73 D8
Sabrina Coast Antarctica 68°0S 120°0E 5 C9
Sabulubbek Indonesia 1°36S 98°40E 36 E1
Sabzevār Iran 36°15N 57°40E 45 B8
Sabzvārān = Jiroft Iran 28°45N 57°50E 45 D8
Sac City U.S.A. 42°25N 95°0W 80 D6
Săcele Romania 45°37N 25°41E 17 F13
Sacheon S. Korea 35°0N 128°6E 35 G15
Sachigo → Canada 55°6N 88°58W 72 A2
Sachigo, L. Canada 53°50N 92°12W 72 B1
Sachimbo Angola 9°14S 20°16E 52 F4
Sachsen □ Germany 50°55N 13°10E 16 C7
Sachsen-Anhalt □ Germany 52°0N 12°0E 16 C7
Sackets Harbor U.S.A. 43°57N 76°7W 83 C8
Sackville Canada 45°54N 64°22W 73 C7
Saco Maine, U.S.A. 43°30N 70°27W 83 C14
Saco Mont., U.S.A. 48°28N 107°21W 76 B10
Sacramento U.S.A. 38°35N 121°29W 78 G5
Sacramento → U.S.A. 38°3N 121°56W 78 G5
Sacramento Mts. U.S.A. 32°30N 105°30W 77 K11
Sacramento Valley U.S.A. 39°30N 122°0W 78 G5
Sada-Misaki Japan 33°20N 132°5E 31 H6
Sadabad India 27°27N 78°3E 42 F8
Sadani Tanzania 5°58S 38°35E 54 D4
Sadani ⌂ Tanzania 6°3S 38°47E 54 D4
Sadao Thailand 6°38N 100°26E 39 J3
Sadd el Aali Egypt 23°54N 32°54E 51 D12
Saddle Mt. U.S.A. 45°58N 123°41W 78 E3
Sadimi Dem. Rep. of the Congo 9°25S 23°32E 55 D1
Sado Japan 38°0N 138°25E 30 F9
Sadra India 23°21N 72°43E 42 H5
Sadri India 25°11N 73°26E 42 G5
Sæby Denmark 57°21N 10°30E 9 H14
Saegertown U.S.A. 41°43N 80°9W 82 E4
Şafājah Si. Arabia 26°25N 39°0E 44 E3
Safata B. Samoa 14°0S 171°50W 59 b
Säffle Sweden 59°8N 12°55E 9 G15
Safford U.S.A. 32°50N 109°43W 77 K9
Saffron Walden U.K. 52°1N 0°16E 13 E8
Safi Morocco 32°18N 9°20W 50 B4
Şafīābād Iran 36°45N 57°58E 45 B8
Safīd Dasht Iran 33°27N 48°11E 45 C6
Safīd Kūh Afghan. 34°45N 63°0E 40 B3
Safīd Rūd → Iran 37°23N 50°11E 45 B6
Safipur India 26°44N 80°21E 43 F9
Şāfītā Syria 34°48N 36°7E 44 C3
Safune Samoa 13°25S 172°21W 59 b
Şafwān Iraq 30°7N 47°43E 44 D5
Sag Harbor U.S.A. 41°0N 72°18W 83 F12
Saga Japan 33°15N 130°16E 31 H5
Saga □ Japan 33°15N 130°20E 31 H5
Sagae Japan 38°22N 140°17E 30 E10
Sagaing Burma 21°52N 95°59E 41 J19
Sagamore U.S.A. 40°46N 79°14W 82 F5
Saganaga L. Canada 48°14N 90°52W 80 A8
Sagar Karnataka, India 14°14N 75°6E 40 M9
Sagar Mad. P., India 23°50N 78°44E 43 H8
Sagara, L. Tanzania 5°20S 31°0E 54 D3
Sagarmatha = Everest, Mt. Nepal 28°5N 86°58E 43 E12
Sagarmatha △ Nepal 27°55N 86°45E 43 F12
Saginaw U.S.A. 43°26N 83°56W 81 D12
Saginaw B. U.S.A. 43°50N 83°40W 81 D12
Saglouc = Salluit Canada 62°14N 75°38W 69 E16
Sagone France 42°7N 8°42E 20 E8
Sagua la Grande Cuba 22°50N 80°10W 88 B3
Saguache U.S.A. 38°5N 106°8W 76 G10
Saguaro △ U.S.A. 32°12N 110°38W 77 K8
Saguenay → Canada 48°22N 71°0W 73 C5
Sagunt Spain 39°42N 0°18W 21 C5
Sagunto = Sagunt Spain 39°42N 0°18W 21 C5
Sagwara India 23°41N 74°1E 42 H6
Sahagún Spain 42°18N 5°2W 21 A3
Saḩam al Jawlān Syria 32°45N 35°55E 46 C4
Sahamandrevo Madag. 23°15S 45°35E 57 C8
Sahand, Kūh-e Iran 37°44N 46°27E 44 B5
Sahara Africa 23°0N 5°0E 50 D6
Saharan Atlas = Saharien, Atlas Algeria 33°30N 1°0E 50 B6
Saharanpur India 29°58N 77°33E 42 E7
Saharien, Atlas Algeria 33°30N 1°0E 50 B6
Saharsa India 25°53N 86°36E 43 G12
Sahasinaka Madag. 21°49S 47°49E 57 C8
Sahaswan India 28°5N 78°45E 43 E8
Saheira, W. el → Egypt 30°5N 33°25E 46 E2
Sahel Africa 16°0N 5°0E 50 E5
Sahibganj India 25°12N 87°40E 43 G12
Sāḩilīyah Iraq 33°43N 42°42E 44 C4
Sahiwal Pakistan 30°45N 73°8E 42 D5
Şahneh Iran 34°29N 47°41E 44 C5
Sahrawi = Western Sahara ■ Africa 25°0N 13°0W 50 D3
Sahuaripa Mexico 29°3N 109°14W 86 B3
Sahuarita U.S.A. 31°57N 110°58W 77 L8
Sahuayo de Díaz Mexico 20°4N 102°43W 86 C4
Sai → India 25°39N 82°47E 43 G10
Sai Buri Thailand 6°43N 101°45E 39 J3
Sai Kung China 22°23N 114°16E 33 G11
Sai Twong △ Thailand 15°56N 101°10E 38 E3
Sai Yok △ Thailand 14°25N 98°40E 38 E2
Saibai I. Australia 9°25S 142°40E 62 a
Sa'id Bundâs Sudan 8°24N 24°48E 51 G10
Sa'īdābād = Sīrjān Iran 29°30N 55°45E 45 D7
Sa'īdābād Iran 36°8N 54°11E 45 B7
Sa'īdīyeh Iran 36°20N 48°55E 45 B6
Saidpur Bangla. 25°48N 89°0E 41 G16
Saidpur India 25°33N 83°11E 43 G10
Saidu Sharif Pakistan 34°43N 72°24E 43 B5
Saigō Japan 36°12N 133°20E 31 F6
Saigon = Thanh Pho Ho Chi Minh Vietnam 10°58N 106°40E 39 G6
Saijō Japan 33°55N 133°11E 31 H6
Saikai △ Japan 33°12N 129°36E 31 H4
Saikanosy Masoala Madag. 15°45S 50°10E 57 B9
Saikhoa Ghat India 27°50N 95°40E 41 F19
Saiki Japan 32°58N 131°51E 31 H5
Şā'īl Si. Arabia 27°28N 41°45E 44 E4
Sailana India 23°28N 74°55E 42 H6
Sailolof Indonesia 1°15S 130°46E 37 E8
Saimaa Finland 61°15N 28°15E 8 F23
Saimen = Saimaa Finland 61°15N 28°15E 8 F23
Şa'in Dezh Iran 36°40N 46°25E 44 B5
St. Abb's Head U.K. 55°55N 2°8W 11 F6
St. Alban's Canada 47°51N 55°50W 73 C8
St. Albans U.K. 51°45N 0°19W 13 F7
St. Albans Vt., U.S.A. 44°49N 73°5W 83 B11
St. Albans W. Va., U.S.A. 38°23N 81°50W 81 F13
St. Alban's Head U.K. 50°34N 2°4W 13 G5
St. Albert Canada 53°37N 113°32W 70 C6
St-André Réunion 20°57S 55°39E 53 c
St. Andrew's Canada 47°45N 59°15W 73 C8
St. Andrews U.K. 56°20N 2°47W 11 E6
St-Anicet Canada 45°8N 74°22W 83 A10
St. Annes Canada 49°40N 96°39W 71 D9
St. Anns B. Canada 46°22N 60°25W 73 C7
St. Ann's Bay Jamaica 18°26N 77°12W 88 a
St. Anthony Canada 51°22N 55°35W 73 B8
St. Anthony U.S.A. 43°58N 111°41W 76 E8
St-Antoine Canada 46°22N 64°45W 73 C7
St. Arnaud Australia 36°40S 143°16E 63 F3
St-Augustin Canada 51°13N 58°38W 73 B8
St-Augustin → Canada 51°16N 58°40W 73 B8
St. Augustine U.S.A. 29°54N 81°19W 85 G14
St. Austell U.K. 50°20N 4°47W 13 G3
St. Barbe Canada 51°12N 56°46W 73 B8
St-Barthélemy W. Indies 17°50N 62°50W 89 C7
St. Bees Hd. U.K. 54°31N 3°38W 12 C4
St. Bees I. Australia 20°56S 149°26E 62 b
St-Benoît Réunion 21°2S 55°43E 53 c
St. Bride's Canada 46°56N 54°10W 73 C9
St. Brides B. U.K. 51°49N 5°9W 13 F2
St-Brieuc France 48°30N 2°46W 20 B2
St. Catharines Canada 43°10N 79°15W 82 C5
St. Catherines I. U.S.A. 31°40N 81°10W 85 F14
St. Catherine's Pt. U.K. 50°34N 1°18W 13 G6
St-Chamond France 45°28N 4°31E 20 D6
St. Charles Ill., U.S.A. 41°54N 88°19W 80 E9
St. Charles Md., U.S.A. 38°36N 76°56W 81 F15
St. Charles Mo., U.S.A. 38°47N 90°29W 80 F8
St. Charles Va., U.S.A. 36°48N 83°4W 81 G12
St. Christopher-Nevis = St. Kitts & Nevis ■ W. Indies 17°20N 62°40W 89 C7
St. Clair Mich., U.S.A. 42°50N 82°30W 82 D2
St. Clair Pa., U.S.A. 40°43N 76°12W 83 F8
St. Clair → U.S.A. 42°38N 82°31W 82 D2
St. Clair, L. N. Amer. 42°27N 82°39W 82 D2
St. Clairsville U.S.A. 40°5N 80°54W 82 F4
St. Claude Canada 49°40N 98°20W 71 D9
St. Clears U.K. 51°49N 4°31W 13 F3
St-Clet Canada 45°21N 74°13W 83 A10
St. Cloud Fla., U.S.A. 28°15N 81°17W 85 G14
St. Cloud Minn., U.S.A. 45°34N 94°10W 80 C6
St. Cricq, C. Australia 25°17S 113°6E 61 E1
St. Croix U.S. Virgin Is. 17°45N 64°45W 89 C7
St. Croix → U.S.A. 44°45N 92°48W 80 C7
St. Croix Falls U.S.A. 45°24N 92°38W 80 C7
St. David's Canada 48°12N 58°52W 73 C8
St. David's U.K. 51°53N 5°16W 13 F2
St. David's Head U.K. 51°54N 5°19W 13 F2
St-Denis France 48°56N 2°20E 20 B5
St-Denis Réunion 20°52S 55°27E 53 c
St-Denis ✈ (RUN) Réunion 20°53S 55°32E 53 c
St-Dizier France 48°38N 4°56E 20 B6
St. Elias, Mt. U.S.A. 60°18N 140°56W 68 E3
St. Elias Mts. N. Amer. 60°33N 139°28W 70 A1
St-Étienne France 45°27N 4°22E 20 D6
St. Eugène Canada 45°30N 74°28W 83 A10
St. Eustatius W. Indies 17°20N 63°0W 89 C7
St-Félicien Canada 48°40N 72°25W 72 C5
St-Flour France 45°2N 3°6E 20 D5
St. Francis U.S.A. 39°47N 101°48W 80 F3
St. Francis → U.S.A. 34°38N 90°36W 85 D9
St. Francis, C. S. Africa 34°14S 24°49E 56 E3
St. Francisville U.S.A. 30°47N 91°23W 84 F9
St-François, L. Canada 45°10N 74°22W 83 A10
St-Gabriel Canada 46°17N 73°24W 72 C5
St. Gallen = Sankt Gallen Switz. 47°26N 9°22E 20 C8
St-Gaudens France 43°6N 0°44E 20 E4
St. George Australia 28°1S 148°30E 63 D4
St. George N.B., Canada 45°11N 66°50W 73 C6
St. George Ont., Canada 43°15N 80°15W 82 C4
St. George S.C., U.S.A. 33°11N 80°35W 85 E14
St. George Utah, U.S.A. 37°6N 113°35W 77 H7
St. George, C. Canada 48°30N 59°16W 73 C8
St. George, C. U.S.A. 29°40N 85°5W 85 G12
St. George I. U.S.A. 56°35N 169°35W 74 D6
St. George Ra. Australia 18°40S 125°0E 60 C4
St. George's Canada 48°26N 58°31W 73 C8
St-Georges Canada 46°8N 70°40W 73 C5
St. George's Grenada 12°5N 61°43W 89 D7
St. George's B. Canada 48°24N 58°53W 73 C8
St. Georges Basin N.S.W., Australia 35°7S 150°36E 63 F5
St. Georges Basin W. Austral., Australia 15°23S 125°2E 60 C4
St. George's Channel Europe 52°0N 6°0W 10 E6
St. Georges Hd. Australia 35°12S 150°42E 63 F5
St. Gotthard P. = San Gottardo, P. del Switz. 46°33N 8°33E 20 C8
St. Helena Atl. Oc. 15°58S 5°42W 48 H3
St. Helena U.S.A. 38°30N 122°28W 76 G2
St. Helena, Mt. U.S.A. 38°40N 122°36W 78 G4
St. Helena B. S. Africa 32°40S 18°10E 56 E2
St. Helens Australia 41°20S 148°15E 63 G4
St. Helens U.K. 53°27N 2°44W 12 D5
St. Helens U.S.A. 45°52N 122°48W 78 E4
St. Helens, Mt. U.S.A. 46°12N 122°12W 78 D4
St. Helier U.K. 49°10N 2°7W 13 H5
St-Hubert Belgium 50°2N 5°23E 15 D5
St-Hubert Canada 45°29N 73°25W 83 A11
St-Hyacinthe Canada 45°40N 72°58W 72 C5
St. Ignace U.S.A. 45°52N 84°44W 81 C11
St. Ignace I. Canada 48°45N 88°0W 72 C2
St. Ignatius U.S.A. 47°19N 114°6W 76 C6
St. Ives Cambs., U.K. 52°20N 0°4W 13 E7
St. Ives Corn., U.K. 50°12N 5°30W 13 G2
St. James U.S.A. 43°59N 94°38W 80 D6
St-Jean → Canada 50°17N 64°20W 73 B7
St-Jean, L. Canada 48°40N 72°0W 73 C5
St-Jean-Port-Joli Canada 47°15N 70°13W 73 C5
St-Jean-sur-Richelieu Canada 45°20N 73°20W 83 A11
St-Jérôme Canada 45°47N 74°0W 72 C5
St. John Canada 45°20N 66°8W 73 C6
St. John U.S.A. 38°0N 98°46W 80 F4
St. John → N. Amer. 45°12N 66°5W 81 C20
St. John, C. Canada 50°0N 55°32W 73 C8
St. John I. U.S. Virgin Is. 18°20N 64°42W 89 e
St. John's Antigua & B. 17°6N 61°51W 89 C7
St. John's Canada 47°35N 52°40W 73 C9
St. Johns Ariz., U.S.A. 34°30N 109°22W 77 J9
St. Johns Mich., U.S.A. 43°0N 84°33W 81 D11
St. Johns → U.S.A. 30°24N 81°24W 85 F14
St. John's Pt. Ireland 54°34N 8°27W 10 B3
St. Johnsbury U.S.A. 44°25N 72°1W 83 B12
St. Johnsville U.S.A. 43°0N 74°43W 83 C10
St. Joseph Canada 43°24N 81°42W 82 C3
St-Joseph Martinique 14°39N 61°4W 88 c
St-Joseph Réunion 21°22S 55°37E 53 c
St. Joseph La., U.S.A. 31°55N 91°14W 84 F9
St. Joseph Mo., U.S.A. 39°46N 94°50W 80 F6
St. Joseph → U.S.A. 42°7N 86°29W 80 D10
St. Joseph, I. Canada 46°12N 83°58W 72 C3
St. Joseph, L. Canada 51°10N 90°35W 72 B1
St-Jovite Canada 46°8N 74°38W 72 C5
St. Kilda U.K. 57°49N 8°34W 14 C2
St. Kitts & Nevis ■ W. Indies 17°20N 62°40W 89 C7
St. Laurent Canada 50°25N 97°58W 71 C9
St. Lawrence Australia 22°16S 149°31E 62 C4
St. Lawrence Canada 46°54N 55°23W 73 C8
St. Lawrence → Canada 49°30N 66°0W 73 C6
St. Lawrence, Gulf of Canada 48°25N 62°0W 73 C7
St. Lawrence I. U.S.A. 63°30N 170°30W 74 C5
St. Lawrence Islands △ Canada 44°27N 75°52W 83 B9
St. Léonard Canada 47°12N 67°58W 73 C6
St-Leu Réunion 21°9S 55°18E 53 c
St. Lewis → Canada 52°26N 56°11W 73 B8
St-Lô France 49°7N 1°5W 20 B3
St-Louis Guadeloupe 15°56N 61°19W 88 b
St-Louis Réunion 21°16S 55°25E 53 c
St. Louis Senegal 16°8N 16°27W 50 E2
St. Louis U.S.A. 38°37N 90°11W 80 F8
St. Louis → U.S.A. 46°44N 92°9W 80 B7
St-Luc Canada 45°22N 73°18W 83 A11
St. Lucia ■ W. Indies 14°0N 60°57W 89 f
St. Lucia, L. S. Africa 28°5S 32°30E 57 D5
St. Lucia Channel W. Indies 14°15N 61°0W 89 D7
St. Maarten ☒ W. Indies 18°0N 63°5W 89 C7
St. Magnus B. U.K. 60°25N 1°35W 11 A7
St-Malo France 48°39N 2°1W 20 B2
St-Marc Haiti 19°10N 72°41W 89 C5
St. Maries U.S.A. 47°19N 116°35W 76 C5
St-Martin ☒ W. Indies 18°0N 63°0W 89 C7
St-Martin, C. Martinique 14°52N 61°14W 88 c
St. Martin, L. Canada 51°40N 98°30W 71 C9
St. Martins Barbados 13°5N 59°28W 89 g
St. Mary Pk. Australia 31°32S 138°34E 63 E2
St. Marys Australia 41°35S 148°11E 63 G4
St. Marys Canada 43°20N 81°10W 82 C3
St. Mary's Corn., U.K. 49°55N 6°18W 13 H1
St. Mary's Orkney, U.K. 58°54N 2°54W 11 C6
St. Marys Ga., U.S.A. 30°44N 81°33W 85 F14
St. Marys Pa., U.S.A. 41°26N 78°34W 82 E6
St. Mary's, C. Canada 46°50N 54°12W 73 C9
St. Mary's B. Canada 46°50N 53°50W 73 C9
St. Mary's Bay Canada 44°25N 66°10W 73 D6
St-Mathieu, Pte. France 48°20N 4°45W 20 B1
St. Matthew I. U.S.A. 60°24N 172°42W 74 C5
St-Maurice → Canada 46°21N 72°31W 72 C5
St. Mawes U.K. 50°10N 5°2W 13 G2
St-Nazaire France 47°17N 2°12W 20 C2
St. Neots U.K. 52°14N 0°15W 13 E7
St-Niklaas Belgium 51°10N 4°8E 15 C4
St-Omer France 50°45N 2°15E 20 A5
St-Pamphile Canada 46°58N 69°48W 73 C6
St-Pascal Canada 47°32N 69°48W 73 C6
St. Paul Canada 54°0N 111°17W 70 C6
St-Paul Réunion 20°59S 55°17E 53 c
St. Paul Minn., U.S.A. 44°56N 93°5W 80 C7
St. Paul Nebr., U.S.A. 41°13N 98°27W 80 E4
St-Paul → Canada 51°27N 57°42W 73 B8
St. Paul, I. Ind. Oc. 38°55S 77°34E 3 F13
St. Paul I. Canada 47°12N 60°9W 73 C7
St. Paul I. U.S.A. 57°10N 170°15W 74 D5
St. Peter U.S.A. 44°20N 93°57W 80 C7
St. Peter Port U.K. 49°26N 2°33W 13 H5
St. Peters N.S., Canada 45°40N 60°53W 73 C7
St. Peters P.E.I., Canada 46°25N 62°35W 73 C7
St. Petersburg = Sankt-Peterburg Russia 59°55N 30°20E 9 G24
St. Petersburg U.S.A. 27°46N 82°40W 85 H13
St-Philippe Réunion 21°21S 55°44E 53 c
St-Pie Canada 45°30N 72°54W 83 A12
St-Pierre Martinique 14°45N 61°10W 88 c
St-Pierre Réunion 21°19S 55°28E 53 c
St-Pierre St-P. & M. 46°46N 56°12W 73 C8
St-Pierre, L. Canada 46°12N 72°52W 72 C5
St-Pierre-et-Miquelon ☒ N. Amer. 46°55N 56°10W 73 C8
St-Quentin Canada 47°30N 67°23W 73 C6
St-Quentin France 49°50N 3°16E 20 B5
St. Regis U.S.A. 47°18N 115°6W 76 C6
St. Regis Falls U.S.A. 44°40N 74°32W 83 B10
St. Sebastien, Tanjon' i Madag. 12°26S 48°44E 57 A8
St-Siméon Canada 47°51N 69°54W 73 C6
St. Simons I. U.S.A. 31°12N 81°15W 85 F14
St. Simons Island U.S.A. 31°9N 81°22W 85 F14
St. Stephen Canada 45°16N 67°17W 73 C6
St. Thomas Canada 42°45N 81°10W 82 D3
St. Thomas I. U.S. Virgin Is. 18°20N 64°55W 89 e
St-Tite Canada 46°45N 72°34W 72 C5
St-Tropez France 43°17N 6°38E 20 E7
St-Troud = St. Truiden Belgium 50°48N 5°10E 15 D5
St. Truiden Belgium 50°48N 5°10E 15 D5
St. Vidgeon's ✪ Australia 14°47S 134°53E 62 A1
St. Vincent = São Vicente C. Verde Is. 17°0N 25°0W 50 b
St. Vincent, G. Australia 35°0S 138°0E 63 F2
St. Vincent & the Grenadines ■ W. Indies 13°0N 61°10W 89 D7
St. Vincent Passage W. Indies 13°30N 61°0W 89 D7
St-Vith Belgium 50°17N 6°9E 15 D6
St. Walburg Canada 53°39N 109°12W 71 C7
Ste-Agathe-des-Monts Canada 46°3N 74°17W 72 C5
Ste-Anne Guadeloupe 16°13N 61°24W 88 b
Ste-Anne Seychelles 4°36S 55°31E 53 b
Ste-Anne, L. Canada 50°0N 67°42W 73 B6
Ste-Anne-des-Monts Canada 49°8N 66°30W 73 C6
Ste. Genevieve U.S.A. 37°59N 90°2W 80 G8
Ste-Marguerite → Canada 50°9N 66°36W 73 B6
Ste-Marie Canada 46°26N 71°0W 73 C5
Ste-Marie Martinique 14°48N 61°1W 88 c
Ste-Marie Réunion 20°53S 55°33E 53 c
Ste-Marie, Ile = Nosy Boraha Madag. 16°50S 49°55E 57 B8
Ste-Rose Guadeloupe 16°20N 61°45W 88 b
Ste-Rose Réunion 21°8S 55°45E 53 c
Ste. Rose du Lac Canada 51°4N 99°30W 71 C9
Saintes France 45°45N 0°37W 20 D3
Saintes, Îs. des Guadeloupe 15°50N 61°35W 88 b
Saintfield U.K. 54°28N 5°49W 10 B6
Saintonge France 45°40N 0°50W 20 D3
Saipan N. Marianas 15°12N 145°45E 64 F6
Sairang India 23°50N 92°45E 41 H18
Sairecábur, Cerro Bolivia 22°43S 67°54W 94 A2
Saitama Japan 35°54N 139°38E 31 G9
Saitama □ Japan 36°25N 139°30E 31 F9
Saiyid Pakistan 33°7N 73°2E 42 C5
Sajama Bolivia 18°7S 69°0W 92 G5
Sajószentpéter Hungary 48°12N 20°44E 17 D11
Sajum India 33°20N 79°0E 43 C8
Sak → S. Africa 30°52S 20°25E 56 E3
Saka Kenya 0°9S 39°20E 54 B4
Sakai Japan 34°34N 135°27E 31 G7
Sakaide Japan 34°19N 133°50E 31 G6
Sakaiminato Japan 35°38N 133°11E 31 G6
Sakākah Si. Arabia 30°0N 40°8E 44 D4
Sakakawea, L. U.S.A. 47°30N 101°25W 80 B3
Sakami → Canada 53°40N 76°40W 72 B4
Sakami, L. Canada 53°15N 77°0W 72 B4
Sakania Dem. Rep. of the Congo 12°43S 28°30E 55 E2
Sakaraha Madag. 22°55S 44°32E 57 C7
Sakartvelo = Georgia ■ Asia 42°0N 43°0E 19 F7
Sakarya Turkey 40°48N 30°25E 19 F5
Sakashima-Guntō Japan 24°46N 124°0E 31 M2
Sakata Japan 38°55N 139°50E 30 E9
Sakchu N. Korea 40°23N 125°2E 35 D13
Sakeny → Madag. 20°0S 45°25E 57 C8
Sakha □ Russia 66°0N 130°0E 29 C14
Sakhalin Russia 51°0N 143°0E 29 D15
Sakhalinskiy Zaliv Russia 54°0N 141°0E 29 D15
Šakiai Lithuania 54°59N 23°2E 9 J20
Sakon Nakhon Thailand 17°10N 104°9E 38 D5
Sakrand Pakistan 26°10N 68°15E 42 F3
Sakri India 26°13N 86°5E 43 F12
Sakrivier S. Africa 30°54S 20°28E 56 E3
Sakti India 22°2N 82°58E 43 H10
Sakuma Japan 35°3N 137°49E 31 G8
Sakurai Japan 34°30N 135°51E 31 G7
Sal C. Verde Is. 16°45N 22°55W 50 b
Sal Rei C. Verde Is. 16°11N 22°53W 50 b
Sala Sweden 59°58N 16°35E 9 G17
Sala Consilina Italy 40°23N 15°36E 22 D6
Sala-y-Gómez Pac. Oc. 26°28S 105°28W 65 K17
Sala y Gómez Ridge Pac. Oc. 25°0S 98°0W 65 K18
Salaberry-de-Valleyfield Canada 45°15N 74°8W 83 A10
Salada, L. Mexico 32°20N 115°40W 77 K6
Saladas Argentina 28°15S 58°40W 94 B4
Saladillo Argentina 35°40S 59°55W 94 D4
Salado → B. Aires, Argentina 35°44S 57°22W 94 D4
Salado → La Pampa, Argentina 37°30S 67°0W 96 D3
Salado → Santa Fe, Argentina 31°40S 60°41W 94 C3
Salado → Mexico 26°52N 99°19W 84 H5
Salaga Ghana 8°31N 0°31W 50 G5
Salāh Syria 32°40N 36°45E 46 C5
Şalāḩ ad Dīn □ Iraq 34°35N 43°35E 44 C4
Salakos Greece 36°17N 27°57E 25 C9
Salālah Oman 16°56N 53°59E 47 D5
Salamanca Chile 31°46S 70°59W 94 C1
Salamanca Spain 40°58N 5°39W 21 B3
Salamanca U.S.A. 42°10N 78°43W 82 D6
Salāmatābād Iran 35°39N 47°50E 44 C5
Salamina Greece 37°56N 23°30E 23 F10
Salamis Cyprus 35°11N 33°54E 25 D12
Salar de Atacama Chile 23°30S 68°25W 94 A2
Salar de Uyuni Bolivia 20°30S 67°45W 92 H5
Salatiga Indonesia 7°19S 110°30E 37 G14
Salavat Russia 53°21N 55°55E 18 D10
Salaverry Peru 8°15S 79°0W 92 E3
Salawati Indonesia 1°7S 130°52E 37 E8
Salaya India 22°19N 69°35E 42 H3
Salayar Indonesia 6°7S 120°30E 37 F6
S'Albufera Spain 39°47N 3°7E 24 B10
Salcombe U.K. 50°14N 3°47W 13 G4
Saldanha S. Africa 33°0S 17°58E 56 E2
Saldanha B. S. Africa 33°6S 18°0E 56 E2
Saldus Latvia 56°38N 22°30E 9 H20
Sale Australia 38°6S 147°6E 63 F4
Salé Morocco 34°3N 6°48W 50 B4
Sale U.K. 53°26N 2°19W 12 D5
Salekhard Russia 66°30N 66°35E 28 C7
Salelologa Samoa 13°41S 172°11W 59 b
Salem India 11°40N 78°11E 40 P11
Salem Ill., U.S.A. 38°38N 88°57W 80 F9
Salem Ind., U.S.A. 38°36N 86°6W 80 F10
Salem Mass., U.S.A. 42°31N 70°53W 83 D14
Salem Mo., U.S.A. 37°39N 91°32W 80 G8
Salem N.H., U.S.A. 42°45N 71°12W 83 D13
Salem N.J., U.S.A. 39°34N 75°28W 81 F16
Salem N.Y., U.S.A. 43°10N 73°20W 83 C11
Salem Ohio, U.S.A. 40°54N 80°52W 82 F4
Salem Oreg., U.S.A. 44°56N 123°2W 76 D2
Salem S. Dak., U.S.A. 43°44N 97°23W 80 D5
Salem Va., U.S.A. 37°18N 80°3W 81 G13
Salerno Italy 40°41N 14°47E 22 D6
Salford U.K. 53°30N 2°18W 12 D5
Salgótarján Hungary 48°5N 19°47E 17 D10
Salgueiro Brazil 8°4S 39°6W 93 E11
Salibabu Indonesia 3°51N 126°40E 37 D7
Salibea = Salybia Trin. & Tob. 10°43N 61°2W 93 K15
Salida U.S.A. 38°32N 106°0W 75 H18
Salihli Turkey 38°28N 28°8E 23 E13
Salihorsk Belarus 52°51N 27°27E 17 B14
Salima Malawi 13°47S 34°28E 53 G6

Salina *Italy* 38°34N 14°50E **22 E6**
Salina *Kans., U.S.A.* 38°50N 97°33W **80 F5**
Salina *Utah, U.S.A.* 38°58N 111°51W **76 G8**
Salina Cruz *Mexico* 16°10N 95°12W **87 D5**
Salinas *Brazil* 16°10S 42°10W **93 G10**
Salinas *Ecuador* 2°10S 80°58W **92 D2**
Salinas *U.S.A.* 36°40N 121°39W **78 J5**
Salinas → *Guatemala* 16°28N 90°31W **87 D6**
Salinas → *U.S.A.* 36°45N 121°48W **78 J5**
Salinas, B. de *Nic.* 11°4N 85°45W **88 D2**
Salinas, Pampa de las
Argentina 31°58S 66°42W **94 C2**
Salinas Ambargasta
Argentina 29°0S 65°0W **94 B3**
Salinas de Hidalgo
Mexico 22°38N 101°43W **86 C4**
Salinas Grandes *Argentina* 30°0S 65°0W **94 C3**
Salinas Pueblo Missions △
U.S.A. 34°6N 106°4W **77 J10**
Salinas Valley *U.S.A.* 36°15N 121°15W **78 J5**
Saline → *Ark., U.S.A.* 33°10N 92°8W **84 E8**
Saline → *Kans., U.S.A.* 38°52N 97°30W **80 F5**
Salines, C. de ses *Spain* 39°16N 3°4E **24 B10**
Salinópolis *Brazil* 0°40S 47°20W **93 D9**
Salisbury *Australia* 34°46S 138°38E **63 E2**
Salisbury *U.K.* 51°4N 1°47W **13 F6**
Salisbury *Md., U.S.A.* 38°22N 75°36W **81 F16**
Salisbury *N.C., U.S.A.* 35°40N 80°29W **85 D14**
Salisbury I. *Canada* 63°30N 77°0W **69 E16**
Salisbury Plain *U.K.* 51°14N 1°55W **13 F6**
Şalkhad *Syria* 32°29N 36°43E **46 C5**
Salla *Finland* 66°50N 28°49E **8 C23**
Salliq = Coral Harbour
Canada 64°8N 83°10W **69 E15**
Sallisaw *U.S.A.* 35°28N 94°47W **84 D7**
Salluit *Canada* 62°14N 75°38W **69 E16**
Salmãs *Iran* 38°11N 44°47E **44 B5**
Salmon *U.S.A.* 45°11N 113°54W **76 D7**
Salmon → *Canada* 54°3N 122°40W **70 C4**
Salmon → *U.S.A.* 45°51N 116°47W **76 D5**
Salmon Arm *Canada* 50°40N 119°15W **70 C5**
Salmon Gums *Australia* 32°59S 121°38E **61 F3**
Salmon Pt. *Canada* 43°52N 77°15W **82 C7**
Salmon River Mts.
U.S.A. 44°50N 115°30W **76 D6**
Salmon River Res.
U.S.A. 43°32N 75°55W **83 C9**
Salo *Finland* 60°22N 23°10E **9 F20**
Salome *U.S.A.* 33°47N 113°37W **79 M13**
Salon *India* 26°2N 81°27E **43 F9**
Salon-de-Provence *France* 43°39N 5°6E **20 E6**
Salonica = Thessaloniki
Greece 40°38N 22°58E **23 D10**
Salonta *Romania* 46°49N 21°42E **17 E11**
Salpausselkä *Finland* 61°3N 26°15E **8 F22**
Salsacate *Argentina* 31°20S 65°5W **94 C2**
Salsk *Russia* 46°28N 41°30E **19 E7**
Salso → *Italy* 37°6N 13°57E **22 F5**
Salt → *Canada* 60°0N 112°25W **70 B6**
Salt → *U.S.A.* 33°23N 112°19W **77 K7**
Salt Fork Red → *U.S.A.* 34°27N 99°21W **84 D5**
Salt L. *Australia* 30°6S 142°8E **63 E3**
Salt Lake City *U.S.A.* 40°45N 111°53W **76 F8**
Salt Range *Pakistan* 32°30N 72°25E **42 C5**
Salta *Argentina* 24°57S 65°25W **94 A2**
Salta □ *Argentina* 24°48S 65°30W **94 A2**
Saltash *U.K.* 50°24N 4°14W **13 G3**
Saltburn by the Sea *U.K.* 54°35N 0°58W **12 C7**
Saltcoats *U.K.* 55°38N 4°47W **11 F4**
Saltee Is. *Ireland* 52°7N 6°37W **10 D5**
Saltfjellet *Norway* 66°40N 15°15E **8 C16**
Saltfjorden *Norway* 67°15N 14°10E **8 C16**
Saltillo *Mexico* 25°25N 101°0W **86 B4**
Salto *Argentina* 34°20S 60°15W **94 C3**
Salto *Uruguay* 31°27S 57°50W **94 C4**
Salto → *Italy* 42°26N 12°25E **22 C5**
Salto del Guairá *Paraguay* 24°3S 54°17W **95 A5**
Salton City *U.S.A.* 33°18N 115°57W **79 M11**
Salton Sea *U.S.A.* 33°15N 115°45W **79 M11**
Saluda → *U.S.A.* 34°1N 81°4W **85 D14**
Salûm *Egypt* 31°31N 25°7E **51 B11**
Salur *India* 18°27N 83°18E **41 K13**
Salvador *Brazil* 13°0S 38°30W **93 F11**
Salvador *Canada* 52°10N 109°32W **71 C7**
Salvador, El ■
Cent. Amer. 13°50N 89°0W **88 D2**
Salvador, L. *U.S.A.* 29°43N 90°15W **85 G9**
Salween → *Burma* 16°31N 97°37E **41 L20**
Salyan *Azerbaijan* 39°33N 48°59E **45 B6**
Salybia *Trin. & Tob.* 10°43N 61°2W **93 K15**
Salzach → *Austria* 48°12N 12°56E **16 D7**
Salzburg *Austria* 47°48N 13°2E **16 E7**
Salzgitter *Germany* 52°9N 10°19E **16 B6**
Salzwedel *Germany* 52°52N 11°10E **16 B6**
Sam *India* 26°50N 70°31E **42 F4**
Sam Neua *Laos* 20°29N 104°5E **38 B5**
Sam Ngao *Thailand* 17°18N 99°0E **38 D2**
Sam Rayburn Res. *U.S.A.* 31°4N 94°5W **84 F7**
Sam Son *Vietnam* 19°44N 105°54E **38 C5**
Sam Teu *Laos* 19°59N 104°38E **38 C5**
Sama de Langreo = Langreo
Spain 43°18N 5°40W **21 A3**
Samagaltay *Russia* 50°36N 95°3E **29 D10**
Samales Group *Phil.* 6°0N 122°0E **37 C6**
Samana *India* 30°10N 76°13E **42 D7**
Samana Cay *Bahamas* 23°3N 73°45W **89 B5**
Samanga *Tanzania* 8°20S 39°13S **54 D4**
Samangân □ *Afghan.* 36°15N 68°3E **40 B5**
Samangwa
Dem. Rep. of the Congo 4°23S 24°10E **54 C1**
Samani *Japan* 42°7N 142°56E **30 C11**
Samar *Phil.* 12°0N 125°0E **37 B7**
Samara *Russia* 53°8N 50°6E **18 D9**
Samaria = Shōmrōn
West Bank 32°15N 35°13E **46 C4**
Samaria △ *Greece* 35°17N 23°58E **25 D5**
Samarinda *Indonesia* 0°30S 117°9E **36 E5**

Samarkand = Samarqand
Uzbekistan 39°40N 66°55E **28 F7**
Samarqand *Uzbekistan* 39°40N 66°55E **28 F7**
Sāmarrā' *Iraq* 34°12N 43°52E **44 C4**
Samastipur *India* 25°50N 85°50E **43 G11**
Samba
Dem. Rep. of the Congo 4°38S 26°22E **54 C2**
Samba *India* 32°32N 75°10E **43 C6**
Sambalpur *India* 21°28N 84°4E **41 J14**
Sambar, Tanjung
Indonesia 2°59S 110°19E **36 E4**
Sambas *Indonesia* 1°20N 109°20E **36 D3**
Sambava *Madag.* 14°16S 50°10E **57 A9**
Sambawizi *Zimbabwe* 18°24S 26°13E **55 F2**
Sambhajinagar = Aurangabad
India 19°50N 75°23E **40 K9**
Sambhal *India* 28°35N 78°37E **43 E8**
Sambhar *India* 26°52N 75°6E **42 F6**
Sambhar L. *India* 26°55N 75°12E **42 F6**
Sambiase *Italy* 38°58N 16°17E **22 E7**
Sambir *Ukraine* 49°30N 23°10E **17 D12**
Sambor *Cambodia* 12°46N 106°0E **38 F6**
Samborombón, B.
Argentina 36°5S 57°20W **94 D4**
Samburu △ *Kenya* 0°37N 37°31E **54 B4**
Samcheok *S. Korea* 37°30N 129°10E **35 F15**
Samfya *Zambia* 11°22S 29°31E **55 E2**
Samnah *Si. Arabia* 25°10N 37°15E **44 E3**
Samo Alto *Chile* 30°22S 71°0W **94 C1**
Samoa ■ *Pac. Oc.* 14°0S 172°0W **59 b**
Samokov *Bulgaria* 42°18N 23°35E **23 C10**
Samos *Greece* 37°45N 26°50E **23 F12**
Samothráki = Mathráki
Greece 39°48N 19°31E **25 A3**
Samothráki *Greece* 40°28N 25°28E **23 D11**
Sampacho *Argentina* 33°20S 64°50W **94 C3**
Sampalan *Indonesia* 8°41S 115°34E **37 K18**
Sampang *Indonesia* 7°11S 113°13E **37 G15**
Sampit *Indonesia* 2°34S 113°0E **36 E4**
Sampit, Teluk *Indonesia* 3°5S 113°3E **36 E4**
Samrong *Cambodia* 14°15N 103°30E **38 E4**
Samrong *Thailand* 15°10N 100°40E **38 E3**
Samsø *Denmark* 55°50N 10°35E **9 J14**
Samsun *Turkey* 41°15N 36°22E **19 F6**
Samui, Ko *Thailand* 9°30N 100°0E **39 b**
Samusole
Dem. Rep. of the Congo 10°2S 24°0E **55 E1**
Samut Prakan *Thailand* 13°40N 100°36E **38 F3**
Samut Songkhram
Thailand 13°24N 100°1E **38 F3**
Samwari *Pakistan* 28°30N 66°46E **42 E2**
San *Mali* 13°15N 4°57W **50 F5**
San → *Cambodia* 13°32N 105°57E **38 F5**
San → *Poland* 50°45N 21°51E **17 C11**
San Agustín, C. *Phil.* 6°20N 126°13E **37 C7**
San Agustín de Valle Fértil
Argentina 30°35S 67°30W **94 C2**
San Ambrosio *Pac. Oc.* 26°28S 79°53W **90 F3**
San Andreas *U.S.A.* 38°12N 120°41W **78 G6**
San Andrés, I. de
Caribbean 12°42N 81°46W **88 D3**
San Andres Mts.
U.S.A. 33°0N 106°30W **77 K10**
San Andrés Tuxtla
Mexico 18°27N 95°13W **87 D5**
San Angelo *U.S.A.* 31°28N 100°26W **84 F4**
San Anselmo *U.S.A.* 37°59N 122°34W **78 H4**
San Antonio *Belize* 16°15N 89°2W **87 D7**
San Antonio *Chile* 33°40S 71°40W **94 C1**
San Antonio *N. Mex.,*
U.S.A. 33°55N 106°52W **77 K10**
San Antonio *Tex.,*
U.S.A. 29°25N 98°29W **84 G5**
San Antonio → *U.S.A.* 28°30N 96°54W **84 G6**
San Antonio, C.
Argentina 36°15S 56°40W **94 D4**
San Antonio, C. de *Cuba* 21°50N 84°57W **88 B3**
San Antonio, Mt.
U.S.A. 34°17N 117°38W **79 L9**
San Antonio de los Baños
Cuba 22°54N 82°31W **88 B3**
San Antonio de los Cobres
Argentina 24°10S 66°17W **94 A2**
San Antonio Oeste
Argentina 40°40S 65°0W **96 E4**
San Ardo *U.S.A.* 36°1N 120°54W **78 J6**
San Agustín *Canary Is.* 27°47N 15°32W **24 G4**
San Augustine *U.S.A.* 31°32N 94°7W **84 F7**
San Bartolomé
Canary Is. 28°59N 13°37W **24 F6**
San Bartolomé de Tirajana
Canary Is. 27°54N 15°34W **24 G4**
San Benedetto del Tronto
Italy 42°57N 13°53E **22 C5**
San Benedicto, I.
Mexico 19°18N 110°49W **86 D2**
San Benito *U.S.A.* 26°8N 97°38W **84 H6**
San Benito → *U.S.A.* 36°53N 121°34W **78 J5**
San Benito Mt. *U.S.A.* 36°22N 120°37W **78 J6**
San Bernardino *U.S.A.* 34°7N 117°19W **79 L0**
San Bernardino Mts.
U.S.A. 34°10N 116°45W **79 L10**
San Bernardino Str. *Phil.* 13°0N 125°0E **37 B7**
San Bernardo *Chile* 33°40S 70°50W **94 C1**
San Bernardo, I. de
Colombia 9°45N 75°50W **92 B3**
San Blas *Mexico* 26°5N 108°46W **86 B3**
San Blas, Arch. de
Panama 9°50N 78°31W **88 E4**
San Blas, C. *U.S.A.* 29°40N 85°21W **85 G12**
San Borja *Bolivia* 14°50S 66°52W **92 F5**
San Buenaventura = Ventura
U.S.A. 34°17N 119°18W **79 L7**
San Buenaventura
Mexico 27°5N 101°32W **86 B4**
San Carlos = Sant Carles
Spain 39°3N 1°34E **24 B8**
San Carlos *Argentina* 33°50S 69°0W **94 C2**

San Carlos *Chile* 36°10S 72°0W **94 D1**
San Carlos *Baja Calif. S.,*
Mexico 24°47N 112°7W **86 C2**
San Carlos *Coahuila,*
Mexico 29°1N 100°51W **86 B4**
San Carlos *Nic.* 11°12N 84°50W **88 D3**
San Carlos *Phil.* 10°29N 123°25E **37 B6**
San Carlos *Uruguay* 34°46S 54°58W **95 C5**
San Carlos *U.S.A.* 33°21N 110°27W **77 K8**
San Carlos *Venezuela* 9°40N 68°36W **92 B5**
San Carlos de Bariloche
Argentina 41°10S 71°25W **96 E2**
San Carlos de Bolívar
Argentina 36°15S 61°6W **94 D3**
San Carlos del Zulia
Venezuela 9°1N 71°55W **92 B4**
San Carlos L. *U.S.A.* 33°11N 110°32W **77 K8**
San Clemente *Chile* 35°30S 71°29W **94 C1**
San Clemente *U.S.A.* 33°26N 117°37W **79 M9**
San Clemente I. *U.S.A.* 32°53N 118°29W **79 N8**
San Cristóbal = Es Migjorn Gran
Spain 39°57N 4°3E **24 B11**
San Cristóbal *Argentina* 30°20S 61°10W **94 C3**
San Cristóbal *Dom. Rep.* 18°25N 70°6W **89 C5**
San Cristóbal *Solomon Is.* 10°30S 161°0E **58 D9**
San Cristóbal *Venezuela* 7°46N 72°14W **92 B4**
San Cristóbal de las Casas
Mexico 16°45N 92°38W **87 D6**
San Diego *Calif., U.S.A.* 32°42N 117°9W **79 N9**
San Diego *Tex., U.S.A.* 27°46N 98°14W **84 H5**
San Diego → *Argentina* 54°40S 65°10W **96 G3**
San Diego de la Unión
Mexico 21°28N 100°52W **86 C4**
San Diego Int. ✈ **(SAN)**
U.S.A. 32°44N 117°11W **79 N9**
San Dimitri, Ras *Malta* 36°4N 14°11E **25 C1**
San Dimitri Point = San Dimitri,
Ras *Malta* 36°4N 14°11E **25 C1**
San Estanislao *Paraguay* 24°39S 56°26W **94 A4**
San Felipe *Chile* 32°43S 70°42W **94 C1**
San Felipe *Mexico* 31°1N 114°52W **86 A2**
San Felipe *Venezuela* 10°20N 68°44W **92 A5**
San Felipe → *U.S.A.* 33°10N 115°49W **79 M11**
San Félix *Chile* 28°56S 70°28W **94 B1**
San Félix *Pac. Oc.* 26°23S 80°0W **90 F2**
San Fernando = Sant Ferran
Spain 38°42N 1°28E **24 C7**
San Fernando *Chile* 34°30S 71°0W **94 C1**
San Fernando *Mexico* 24°51N 98°10W **87 C5**
San Fernando *La Union,*
Phil. 16°40N 120°23E **37 A6**
San Fernando *Pampanga,*
Phil. 15°5N 120°37E **37 A6**
San Fernando *Spain* 36°28N 6°17W **21 D2**
San Fernando
Trin. & Tob. 10°16N 61°28W **93 K15**
San Fernando *U.S.A.* 34°17N 118°26W **79 L8**
San Fernando de Apure
Venezuela 7°54N 67°15W **92 B5**
San Fernando de Atabapo
Venezuela 4°3N 67°42W **92 C5**
San Francisco *Argentina* 31°30S 62°5W **94 C3**
San Francisco *U.S.A.* 37°46N 122°23W **78 H4**
San Francisco →
U.S.A. 32°59N 109°22W **77 K9**
San Francisco, C. de
Colombia 6°18N 77°29W **90 C3**
San Francisco, Paso de
S. Amer. 27°0S 68°0W **94 B2**
San Francisco de Macorís
Dom. Rep. 19°19N 70°15W **89 C5**
San Francisco del Monte de Oro
Argentina 32°36S 66°8W **94 C2**
San Francisco del Oro
Mexico 26°52N 105°51W **86 B3**
San Francisco Int. ✈ **(SFO)**
U.S.A. 37°37N 122°22W **78 H4**
San Francesc Javier = Sant
Francesc de Formentera
Spain 38°42N 1°26E **24 C7**
San Gabriel *Chile* 33°47S 70°15W **94 C1**
San Gabriel Chilac
Mexico 18°19N 97°21W **87 D5**
San Gabriel Mts.
U.S.A. 34°17N 117°38W **79 L9**
San Gavino Monreale
Italy 39°33N 8°47E **22 E3**
San German *Puerto Rico* 18°4N 67°4W **89 d**
San Gorgonio Mt.
U.S.A. 34°6N 116°50W **79 L10**
San Gottardo, P. del
Switz. 46°33N 8°33E **20 C8**
San Gregorio *Uruguay* 32°37S 55°40W **95 C4**
San Gregorio *U.S.A.* 37°20N 122°23W **78 H4**
San Guillermo △
Argentina 27°50S 69°45W **94 B2**
San Ignacio *Belize* 17°10N 89°5W **87 D7**
San Ignacio *Bolivia* 16°20S 60°55W **92 G6**
San Ignacio *Mexico* 27°27N 112°51W **86 B2**
San Ignacio *Paraguay* 26°52S 57°3W **94 B4**
San Ildefonso, C. *Phil.* 16°0N 122°1E **37 A6**
San Isidro *Argentina* 34°29S 58°31W **94 C4**
San Jacinto *U.S.A.* 33°47N 116°57W **79 M10**
San Jaime = Sant Jaume
Spain 39°54N 4°4E **24 B11**
San Javier *Misiones,*
Argentina 27°55S 55°5W **95 B4**
San Javier *Santa Fe,*
Argentina 30°40S 59°55W **94 C4**
San Javier *Bolivia* 16°18S 62°30W **92 G6**
San Javier *Chile* 35°40S 71°45W **94 D1**
San Jerónimo Taviche
Mexico 16°44N 96°35W **87 D5**
San Joaquin *Bolivia* 13°8S 63°43W **92 F6**
San Joaquín *U.S.A.* 36°36N 120°11W **78 J6**
San Joaquin → *U.S.A.* 38°4N 121°51W **78 G5**
San Joaquin Valley
U.S.A. 37°20N 121°0W **78 J6**
San Jon *U.S.A.* 35°6N 103°20W **77 J12**

San Jordi = Sant Jordi
Spain 39°33N 2°46E **24 B9**
San Jorge *Argentina* 31°54S 61°50W **94 C3**
San Jorge, B. *Mexico* 31°20N 113°20W **86 A2**
San Jorge, G. *Argentina* 46°0S 66°0W **96 F3**
San José = San Josep
Spain 38°55N 1°18E **24 C7**
San José *Argentina* 32°12S 58°15W **94 C4**
San José *Costa Rica* 9°55N 84°2W **88 E3**
San José *Guatemala* 14°0N 90°50W **88 D1**
San Jose *Mind. Occ., Phil.* 12°27N 121°4E **37 B6**
San Jose *Nueva Ecija,*
Phil. 15°45N 120°55E **37 A6**
San Jose *U.S.A.* 37°20N 121°53W **78 H5**
San Jose → *U.S.A.* 34°25N 106°45W **77 J10**
San José, I. *Mexico* 25°0N 110°38W **86 C2**
San Jose de Buenavista
Phil. 10°45N 121°56E **37 B6**
San José de Chiquitos
Bolivia 17°53S 60°50W **92 G6**
San José de Feliciano
Argentina 30°26S 58°46W **94 C4**
San José de Jáchal
Argentina 30°15S 68°46W **94 C2**
San José de Mayo
Uruguay 34°27S 56°40W **94 C4**
San José del Cabo
Mexico 23°3N 109°41W **86 C3**
San José del Guaviare
Colombia 2°35N 72°38W **92 C4**
San Josep *Spain* 38°55N 1°18E **24 C7**
San Juan *Argentina* 31°30S 68°30W **94 C2**
San Juan □ *Argentina* 31°9S 69°0W **94 C2**
San Juan → *Argentina* 32°20S 67°25W **94 C2**
San Juan → *Nic.* 10°56N 83°42W **88 D3**
San Juan → *U.S.A.* 37°16N 110°26W **77 H8**
San Juan Bautista = Sant Joan de
Labritja *Spain* 39°5N 1°31E **24 B8**
San Juan Bautista
Paraguay 26°37S 57°6W **94 B4**
San Juan Bautista
U.S.A. 36°51N 121°32W **78 J5**
San Juan Capistrano
U.S.A. 33°30N 117°40W **79 M9**
San Juan Cr. → *U.S.A.* 35°40N 120°22W **78 J5**
San Juan de Guadalupe
Mexico 24°38N 102°44W **86 C4**
San Juan de la Costa
Mexico 24°20N 110°41W **86 C2**
San Juan de los Lagos
Mexico 21°15N 102°18W **86 C4**
San Juan de los Morros
Venezuela 9°55N 67°21W **92 B5**
San Juan del Norte *Nic.* 10°58N 83°40W **88 D3**
San Juan del Norte, B. de
Nic. 11°0N 83°40W **88 D3**
San Juan del Río *Mexico* 20°23N 100°0W **87 C5**
San Juan del Sur *Nic.* 11°20N 85°51W **88 D2**
San Juan I. *U.S.A.* 48°32N 123°5W **78 B3**
San Juan Island △
U.S.A. 48°35N 123°8W **78 B3**
San Juan Mts. *U.S.A.* 37°30N 107°0W **77 H10**
San Justo *Argentina* 30°47S 60°30W **94 C3**
San Kamphaeng *Thailand* 18°45N 99°8E **38 C2**
San Lázaro, C. *Mexico* 24°50N 112°18W **86 C2**
San Leandro *U.S.A.* 37°42N 122°9W **78 H4**
San Lorenzo = Sant Llorenç des
Cardassar *Spain* 39°37N 3°17E **24 B10**
San Lorenzo *Argentina* 32°45S 60°45W **94 C3**
San Lorenzo *Ecuador* 1°15N 78°50W **92 C3**
San Lorenzo *Paraguay* 25°20S 57°32W **94 B4**
San Lorenzo → *Mexico* 24°15N 107°24W **86 C3**
San Lorenzo, I. *Mexico* 28°38N 112°51W **86 B2**
San Lorenzo, Mte.
Argentina 47°40S 72°20W **96 F2**
San Lucas = Cabo San Lucas
Mexico 22°53N 109°54W **86 C3**
San Lucas *Bolivia* 20°5S 65°7W **92 H5**
San Lucas *Mexico* 27°10N 112°14W **86 B2**
San Lucas, C. *Mexico* 22°52N 109°53W **86 C3**
San Luis *Argentina* 33°20S 66°20W **94 C2**
San Luis *Cuba* 22°17N 83°46W **88 B3**
San Luis *Guatemala* 16°14N 89°27W **88 C2**
San Luis *Ariz., U.S.A.* 32°29N 114°47W **77 K6**
San Luis *Colo., U.S.A.* 37°12N 105°25W **77 H11**
San Luis □ *Argentina* 34°0S 66°0W **94 C2**
San Luis, I. *Mexico* 29°58N 114°26W **86 B2**
San Luis, Sierra de
Argentina 32°30S 66°10W **94 C2**
San Luis de la Paz
Mexico 21°18N 100°31W **86 C4**
San Luis Obispo *U.S.A.* 35°17N 120°40W **79 K6**
San Luis Potosí *Mexico* 22°9N 100°59W **86 C4**
San Luis Potosí □ *Mexico* 23°0N 101°0W **86 C4**
San Luis Río Colorado
Mexico 32°29N 114°58W **86 A2**
San Manuel *U.S.A.* 32°36N 110°38W **77 K8**
San Marcos *Guatemala* 14°59N 91°52W **88 D1**
San Marcos *Calif.,*
U.S.A. 33°9N 117°10W **79 M9**
San Marcos *Tex., U.S.A.* 29°53N 97°56W **84 G6**
San Marcos, I. *Mexico* 27°13N 112°6W **86 B2**
San Marino *San Marino* 43°55N 12°30E **16 G7**
San Marino ■ *Europe* 43°56N 12°25E **22 C5**
San Martín *Antarctica* 68°11S 67°0W **5 C17**
San Martín → *Bolivia* 13°8S 63°43W **92 F6**
San Martín, L. *Argentina* 48°50S 72°50W **96 F2**
San Martín de los Andes
Argentina 40°10S 71°20W **96 E2**
San Mateo = Sant Mateu
Spain 39°3N 1°23E **24 B7**
San Mateo *U.S.A.* 37°34N 122°19W **78 H4**
San Matías *Bolivia* 16°25S 58°20W **92 G7**
San Matías, G. *Argentina* 41°30S 64°0W **96 E4**

San Miguel = Sant Miquel
Spain 39°3N 1°26E **24 B7**
San Miguel *El Salv.* 13°30N 88°12W **88 D2**
San Miguel *Panama* 8°27N 78°55W **88 E4**
San Miguel *U.S.A.* 35°45N 120°42W **78 K6**
San Miguel → *Bolivia* 13°52S 63°56W **92 F6**
San Miguel de Tucumán
Argentina 26°50S 65°20W **94 B2**
San Miguel del Monte
Argentina 35°23S 58°50W **94 D4**
San Miguel I. *U.S.A.* 34°2N 120°23W **79 L6**
San Nicolás *Canary Is.* 27°58N 15°47W **24 G4**
San Nicolás de los Arroyos
Argentina 33°25S 60°10W **94 C3**
San Nicolas I. *U.S.A.* 33°15N 119°30W **79 M7**
San Onofre *U.S.A.* 33°22N 117°34W **79 M9**
San Pablo *Bolivia* 21°43S 66°38W **94 A2**
San Pablo *U.S.A.* 37°58N 122°21W **78 H4**
San Pedro *B. Aires,*
Argentina 33°40S 59°40W **94 C4**
San Pedro *Misiones,*
Argentina 26°30S 54°10W **95 B5**
San Pedro *Chile* 33°54S 71°28W **94 C1**
San Pedro *Ivory C.* 4°50N 6°33W **50 H4**
San Pedro *Mexico* 23°55N 110°17W **86 C2**
San Pedro □ *Paraguay* 24°0S 57°0W **94 A4**
San Pedro → *Chihuahua,*
Mexico 28°20N 106°10W **86 B3**
San Pedro → *Nayarit,*
Mexico 21°45N 105°30W **86 C3**
San Pedro → *U.S.A.* 32°59N 110°47W **77 K8**
San Pedro, Pta. *Chile* 25°30S 70°38W **94 B1**
San Pedro Channel
U.S.A. 33°30N 118°25W **79 M8**
San Pedro de Atacama
Chile 22°55S 68°15W **94 A2**
San Pedro de Jujuy
Argentina 24°12S 64°55W **94 A3**
San Pedro de las Colonias
Mexico 25°45N 102°59W **86 B4**
San Pedro de Macorís
Dom. Rep. 18°30N 69°18W **89 C6**
San Pedro del Norte *Nic.* 13°4N 84°33W **88 D3**
San Pedro del Paraná
Paraguay 26°43S 56°13W **94 B4**
San Pedro Mártir, Sierra
Mexico 31°0N 115°30W **86 A1**
San Pedro Mártir △
Mexico 31°0N 115°21W **86 A1**
San Pedro Ocampo = Melchor
Ocampo *Mexico* 24°51N 101°39W **86 C4**
San Pedro Pochutla
Mexico 15°44N 96°28W **87 D5**
San Pedro Sula *Honduras* 15°30N 88°0W **88 C2**
San Pedro Tututepec
Mexico 16°9N 97°38W **87 D5**
San Pietro *Italy* 39°8N 8°17E **22 E3**
San Rafael *Argentina* 34°40S 68°21W **94 C2**
San Rafael *Calif., U.S.A.* 37°58N 122°32W **78 H4**
San Rafael *N. Mex.,*
U.S.A. 35°7N 107°53W **77 J10**
San Rafael Mt. *U.S.A.* 34°41N 119°52W **79 L7**
San Rafael Mts. *U.S.A.* 34°40N 119°50W **79 L7**
San Ramón de la Nueva Orán
Argentina 23°10S 64°20W **94 A3**
San Remo *Italy* 43°49N 7°46E **20 E7**
San Roque *Argentina* 28°25S 58°45W **94 B4**
San Roque *Spain* 36°17N 5°21W **21 D3**
San Rosendo *Chile* 37°16S 72°43W **94 D1**
San Saba *U.S.A.* 31°12N 98°43W **84 F5**
San Salvador *El Salv.* 13°40N 89°10W **88 D2**
San Salvador de Jujuy
Argentina 24°10S 64°48W **94 A3**
San Salvador I. *Bahamas* 24°0N 74°40W **89 B5**
San Sebastián = Donostia-San
Sebastián *Spain* 43°17N 1°58W **21 A5**
San Sebastián *Argentina* 53°10S 68°30W **96 G3**
San Sebastián de la Gomera
Canary Is. 28°5N 17°7W **24 F2**
San Serra = Son Serra
Spain 39°43N 3°13E **24 B10**
San Severo *Italy* 41°41N 15°23E **22 C6**
San Simeon *U.S.A.* 35°39N 121°11W **78 K5**
San Simon *U.S.A.* 32°16N 109°14W **77 K9**
San Telmo = Sant Elm
Spain 39°35N 2°21E **24 B9**
San Telmo *Mexico* 30°58N 116°6W **86 A1**
San Tiburcio *Mexico* 24°8N 101°32W **86 C4**
San Valentin, Mte. *Chile* 46°30S 73°30W **96 F2**
San Vicente de Cañete
Peru 13°8S 76°30W **92 F3**
San Vicente de la Barquera
Spain 43°23N 4°29W **21 A3**
San Vito *Costa Rica* 8°50N 82°58W **88 E3**
Sana' *Yemen* 15°27N 44°12E **47 D3**
Sanae IV *Antarctica* 70°20S 9°0W **5 D2**
Sanaga → *Cameroon* 3°35N 9°38E **52 D1**
Sanak I. *U.S.A.* 54°25N 162°40W **74 E7**
Sanandaj *Iran* 35°18N 47°1E **44 C5**
Sanandita *Bolivia* 21°40S 63°45W **94 A3**
Sanawad *India* 22°11N 76°5E **42 H7**
Sancellas = Sencelles
Spain 39°39N 2°54F **24 B9**
Sanchahe *China* 44°50N 126°2E **35 B14**
Sánchez *Dom. Rep.* 19°15N 69°36W **89 C6**
Sanchor *India* 24°45N 71°55E **42 G4**
Sancti Spíritus *Cuba* 21°52N 79°33W **88 B4**
Sancy, Puy de *France* 45°32N 2°50E **20 D5**
Sand → *Polokwane →*
S. Africa 22°25S 30°5E **57 C5**
Sand Hills *U.S.A.* 42°10N 101°30W **80 D3**
Sand Lakes △ *Canada* 57°51N 98°32W **71 B9**
Sand Springs *U.S.A.* 36°9N 96°7W **84 C6**
Sanda *Japan* 34°53N 135°14E **31 G7**

Sandakan Malaysia 5°53N 118°4E 36 C5
Sandan = Sambor
  Cambodia 12°46N 106°0E 38 F6
Sandanski Bulgaria 41°35N 23°16E 23 D10
Sanday U.K. 59°16N 2°31W 11 B6
Sandefjord Norway 59°10N 10°15E 9 G14
Sanders U.S.A. 35°13N 109°20W 77 J9
Sanderson U.S.A. 30°9N 102°24W 84 F3
Sandersville U.S.A. 32°59N 82°48W 85 E13
Sandfire Roadhouse
  Australia 19°45S 121°15E 60 C3
Sandfly L. Canada 55°43N 106°6W 71 B7
Sandfontein Namibia 23°48S 19°1E 56 C2
Sandheads, The India 21°10N 88°20E 43 J13
Sandía Peru 14°10S 69°30W 92 F5
Sandila India 27°5N 80°31E 43 F9
Sandnes Norway 58°50N 5°45E 9 G11
Sandnessjøen Norway 66°2N 12°38E 8 C15
Sandoa
  Dem. Rep. of the Congo 9°41S 23°0E 52 F4
Sandomierz Poland 50°40N 21°43E 17 C11
Sandover → Australia 21°43S 136°32E 62 C2
Sandoway = Thandwe
  Burma 18°20N 94°30E 41 K19
Sandoy Færoe Is. 61°52N 6°46W 8 F9
Sandpoint U.S.A. 48°17N 116°33W 76 B5
Sandray U.K. 56°53N 7°31W 11 E1
Sandringham U.K. 52°51N 0°31E 12 E8
Sandstone Australia 27°59S 119°16E 61 E2
Sandusky Mich., U.S.A. 43°25N 82°50W 82 C2
Sandusky Ohio, U.S.A. 41°27N 82°42W 82 E2
Sandveld Namibia 21°25S 20°0E 56 C3
Sandviken Sweden 60°38N 16°46E 8 F17
Sandwich, C. Australia 18°14S 146°18E 62 B4
Sandwich B. Canada 53°40N 57°15W 73 B8
Sandwich B. Namibia 23°25S 14°20E 56 C1
Sandy Oreg., U.S.A. 45°24N 122°16W 78 E4
Sandy Pa., U.S.A. 41°6N 78°46W 82 E6
Sandy Utah, U.S.A. 40°32N 111°50W 76 F8
Sandy Bay Canada 55°31N 102°19W 71 B8
Sandy Bight Australia 33°50S 123°20E 61 F3
Sandy C. Queens.,
  Australia 24°42S 153°15E 62 C5
Sandy C. Tas., Australia 41°25S 144°45E 63 G3
Sandy Cay Bahamas 23°13N 75°18W 89 B4
Sandy Cr. → Australia 31°54S 145°18E 63 E4
Sandy Cr. → U.S.A. 41°51N 109°47W 76 F9
Sandy Creek U.S.A. 43°38N 76°5W 83 C8
Sandy L. Canada 53°2N 93°0W 72 B1
Sandy Lake Canada 53°0N 93°15W 72 B1
Sandy Valley U.S.A. 35°49N 115°38W 79 K11
Sanford Fla., U.S.A. 28°48N 81°16W 85 G14
Sanford Maine, U.S.A. 43°27N 70°47W 83 C14
Sanford N.C., U.S.A. 35°29N 79°10W 85 D15
Sanford → Australia 27°22S 115°53E 61 E2
Sanford, Mt. U.S.A. 62°13N 144°8W 68 E3
Sang-i-Masha Afghan. 33°8N 67°27E 42 C2
Sanga Mozam. 12°22S 35°21E 55 E4
Sanga → Congo 1°5S 17°0E 52 E3
Sangamner India 19°37N 74°15E 40 K9
Sangān Iran 34°23N 60°15E 45 C9
Sangar Afghan. 32°56N 65°30E 42 C1
Sangar Russia 64°2N 127°31E 29 C13
Sangar Sarai Afghan. 34°27N 70°35E 42 B4
Sangarh → Pakistan 30°43N 70°44E 42 D4
Sangay Ecuador 2°0S 78°20W 92 D3
Sange
  Dem. Rep. of the Congo 6°58S 28°21E 54 D2
Sangeang Indonesia 8°12S 119°6E 37 F5
Sanger U.S.A. 36°42N 119°33W 78 J7
Sangerhausen Germany 51°28N 11°18E 16 C6
Sanggan He → China 38°12N 117°15E 34 E9
Sanggau Indonesia 0°5N 110°30E 36 D4
Sanghar Pakistan 26°2N 68°57E 42 F3
Sangihe, Kepulauan
  Indonesia 3°0N 125°30E 37 D7
Sangihe, Pulau Indonesia 3°35N 125°30E 37 D7
Sangju S. Korea 36°25N 128°10E 35 F15
Sangkapura Indonesia 5°52S 112°40E 36 F4
Sangkhla Buri Thailand 14°57N 98°28E 38 E2
Sangkulirang Indonesia 0°59N 117°58E 36 D5
Sangla Pakistan 31°43N 73°23E 42 D5
Sangli India 16°55N 74°33E 40 L9
Sangmélima Cameroon 2°57N 12°1E 52 D2
Sango Zimbabwe 18°44S 31°44E 55 F3
Sangod India 24°55N 76°17E 42 G7
Sangre de Cristo Mts.
  U.S.A. 37°30N 105°20W 77 H11
Sangre Grande
  Trin. & Tob. 10°35N 61°8W 93 K15
Sangrur India 30°14N 75°50E 42 D6
Sangudo Canada 53°50N 114°54W 70 C6
Sangue → Brazil 11°1S 58°39W 92 F7
Sanibel U.S.A. 26°27N 82°1W 85 H13
Sanikluaq Canada 56°32N 79°14W 72 A4
Sanin-Kaigan △ Japan 35°39N 134°37E 31 G7
Sanirajak = Hall Beach
  Canada 68°46N 81°12W 69 D15
Sanjawi Pakistan 30°17N 68°21E 42 D3
Sanje Uganda 0°49S 31°30E 54 C3
Sanjo Japan 37°37N 138°57E 30 F9
Sankh → India 22°15N 84°48E 43 H11
Sankt Gallen Switz. 47°26N 9°22E 20 C8
Sankt Michel = Mikkeli
  Finland 61°43N 27°15E 8 F22
Sankt Moritz Switz. 46°30N 9°51E 20 C8
Sankt-Peterburg Russia 59°55N 30°20E 9 G24
Sankt Pölten Austria 48°12N 15°38E 16 D8
Sankuru →
  Dem. Rep. of the Congo 4°17S 20°25E 52 E4
Sanliurfa Turkey 37°12N 38°50E 44 B3
Sanlúcar de Barrameda
  Spain 36°46N 6°21W 21 D2
Sanmenxia China 34°47N 111°12E 34 G6
Sanming China 26°15N 117°40E 33 D6
Sannicandro Gargánico
  Italy 41°50N 15°34E 22 D6
Sânnicolau Mare
  Romania 46°5N 20°39E 17 E11

Sannieshof S. Africa 26°30S 25°47E 56 D4
Sannin, J. Lebanon 33°57N 35°52E 46 B4
Sanniquellie Liberia 7°19N 8°38W 50 G4
Sanok Poland 49°35N 22°10E 17 D12
Sanquhar U.K. 55°22N 3°54W 11 F5
Sans Souci Trin. & Tob. 10°50N 61°0W 93 K16
Sant Antoni de Portmany
  Spain 38°59N 1°19E 24 C7
Sant Carles Spain 39°3N 1°34E 24 B8
Sant Elm Spain 39°35N 2°21E 24 B9
Sant Feliu de Guíxols Spain 41°45N 3°1E 21 B7
Sant Ferran Spain 38°42N 1°28E 24 C7
Sant Francesc de Formentera
  Spain 38°42N 1°26E 24 C7
Sant Jaume Spain 39°54N 4°4E 24 B11
Sant Joan Spain 39°36N 3°4E 24 B10
Sant Joan de Labritja Spain 39°5N 1°31E 24 B8
Sant Jordi Ibiza, Spain 38°53N 1°24E 24 C7
Sant Jordi Mallorca, Spain 39°33N 2°46E 24 B9
Sant Jordi, G. de Spain 40°53N 1°2E 21 B6
Sant Llorenç des Cardassar
  Spain 39°37N 3°17E 24 B10
Sant Mateu Spain 39°3N 1°23E 24 B7
Sant Miquel Spain 39°3N 1°26E 24 B7
Sant Salvador Spain 39°27N 3°11E 24 B10
Santa Agnés Spain 39°3N 1°21E 24 B7
Santa Ana Bolivia 13°50S 65°40W 92 F5
Santa Ana El Salv. 14°0N 89°31W 88 D2
Santa Ana Mexico 30°33N 111°7W 86 A2
Sant' Antíoco Italy 39°4N 8°27E 22 E3
Santa Bárbara Chile 37°40S 72°1W 94 D1
Santa Bárbara Honduras 14°53N 88°14W 88 D2
Santa Bárbara Mexico 26°48N 105°49W 86 B3
Santa Barbara U.S.A. 34°25N 119°42W 79 L7
Santa Barbara Channel
  U.S.A. 34°15N 120°0W 79 L7
Santa Barbara I. U.S.A. 33°29N 119°2W 79 M7
Santa Catalina, Gulf of
  U.S.A. 33°10N 117°50W 79 N9
Santa Catalina, I.
  Mexico 25°40N 110°47W 86 B2
Santa Catalina I.
  U.S.A. 33°23N 118°25W 79 M8
Santa Catarina □ Brazil 27°25S 48°30W 95 B6
Santa Catarina, I. de
  Brazil 27°30S 48°40W 95 B6
Santa Cecília Brazil 26°56S 50°18W 95 B5
Santa Clara Cuba 22°20N 80°0W 88 B4
Santa Clara Calif.,
  U.S.A. 37°21N 121°57W 78 H5
Santa Clara N.Y.,
  U.S.A. 44°38N 74°27W 83 B10
Santa Clara Utah, U.S.A. 37°8N 113°39W 77 H7
Santa Clara de Olimar
  Uruguay 32°50S 54°54W 95 C5
Santa Clara Valley
  U.S.A. 36°50N 121°30W 78 J5
Santa Clarita U.S.A. 34°24N 118°33W 79 L8
Santa Clotilde Peru 2°33S 73°45W 92 D4
Santa Coloma de Gramenet
  Spain 41°27N 2°13E 21 B7
Santa Cruz Bolivia 17°43S 63°10W 92 G6
Santa Cruz Chile 34°38S 71°27W 94 C1
Santa Cruz Costa Rica 10°15N 85°35W 88 D2
Santa Cruz Madeira 32°42N 16°46W 24 D3
Santa Cruz Phil. 14°20N 121°24E 37 B6
Santa Cruz U.S.A. 36°58N 122°1W 78 J4
Santa Cruz → Argentina 50°10S 68°20W 96 G3
Santa Cruz de la Palma
  Canary Is. 28°41N 17°46W 24 F2
Santa Cruz de la Palma ✈ (SPC)
  Canary Is. 28°38N 17°45W 24 F2
Santa Cruz de Tenerife
  Canary Is. 28°28N 16°15W 24 F3
Santa Cruz del Norte
  Cuba 23°9N 81°55W 88 B3
Santa Cruz del Sur Cuba 20°44N 78°0W 88 B4
Santa Cruz do Rio Pardo
  Brazil 22°54S 49°37W 95 A6
Santa Cruz do Sul Brazil 29°42S 52°25W 95 B5
Santa Cruz I. U.S.A. 34°1N 119°43W 79 M7
Santa Cruz Is. Solomon Is. 10°30S 166°0E 58 C9
Santa Cruz Mts. Jamaica 17°58N 77°43W 88 a
Santa Domingo, Cay
  Bahamas 21°25N 75°15W 88 B4
Santa Elena Argentina 30°58S 59°47W 94 C4
Santa Elena, C.
  Costa Rica 10°54N 85°56W 88 D2
Santa Eulària des Riu
  Spain 38°59N 1°32E 24 C8
Santa Fé Argentina 31°35S 60°41W 94 C3
Santa Fe U.S.A. 35°41N 105°57W 77 J11
Santa Fé do Sul Brazil 20°13S 50°56W 93 H8
Santa Filomena Brazil 9°6S 45°50W 93 E9
Santa Gertrudis Spain 39°0N 1°26E 24 C7
Santa Inês Brazil 13°17S 39°48W 93 F11
Santa Inés, I. Chile 54°0S 73°0W 96 G2
Santa Isabel Argentina 36°10S 66°54W 94 D2
Santa Isabel do Morro
  Brazil 11°34S 50°40W 93 F8
Santa Lucía Corrientes,
  Argentina 28°58S 59°5W 94 B4
Santa Lucía San Juan,
  Argentina 31°30S 68°30W 94 C2
Santa Lucía Uruguay 34°27S 56°24W 94 C4
Santa Lucia Range
  U.S.A. 36°0N 121°20W 78 K5
Santa Luzia C. Verde Is. 16°50N 24°35W 50 b
Santa Margalida Spain 39°42N 3°6E 24 B10
Santa Margarita
  Argentina 38°28S 61°35W 94 D3
Santa Margarita
  U.S.A. 35°9N 120°37W 78 K6
Santa Margarita →
  U.S.A. 33°13N 117°23W 79 M9
Santa Margarita, I.
  Mexico 24°27N 111°50W 86 C2

Santa María Argentina 26°40S 66°0W 94 B2
Santa Maria Azores 36°58N 25°6W 50 a
Santa Maria Brazil 29°40S 53°48W 95 B5
Santa Maria C. Verde Is. 16°31N 22°53W 50 b
Santa Maria U.S.A. 34°57N 120°26W 79 L6
Santa María → Mexico 31°0N 107°14W 86 A3
Santa María, B. de
  Mexico 25°4N 108°6W 86 B3
Santa Maria da Vitória
  Brazil 13°24S 44°12W 93 F10
Santa María del Camí
  Spain 39°38N 2°47E 24 B9
Santa Maria di Léuca, C.
  Italy 39°47N 18°22E 23 E8
Santa Marta Colombia 11°15N 74°13W 92 A4
Santa Marta, Sierra Nevada de
  Colombia 10°55N 73°50W 92 A4
Santa Marta Grande, C.
  Brazil 28°43S 48°50W 95 B6
Santa Maura = Lefkada
  Greece 38°40N 20°43E 23 E9
Santa Monica U.S.A. 34°1N 118°29W 79 M8
Santa Monica Mts. △
  U.S.A. 34°4N 118°44W 79 L8
Santa Paula U.S.A. 34°21N 119°4W 79 L7
Santa Ponça Spain 39°30N 2°28E 24 B9
Santa Rosa La Pampa,
  Argentina 36°40S 64°17W 94 D3
Santa Rosa San Luis,
  Argentina 32°21S 65°10W 94 C2
Santa Rosa Brazil 27°52S 54°29W 95 B5
Santa Rosa Calif.,
  U.S.A. 38°26N 122°43W 78 G4
Santa Rosa N. Mex.,
  U.S.A. 34°57N 104°41W 77 J11
Santa Rosa and San Jacinto
  Mts. △ U.S.A. 33°28N 116°20W 79 M10
Santa Rosa de Copán
  Honduras 14°47N 88°46W 88 D2
Santa Rosa de Río Primero
  Argentina 31°8S 63°20W 94 C3
Santa Rosa del Sara
  Bolivia 17°7S 63°35W 92 G6
Santa Rosa I. Calif.,
  U.S.A. 33°58N 120°6W 79 M6
Santa Rosa I. Fla.,
  U.S.A. 30°20N 86°50W 85 F11
Santa Rosa Range
  U.S.A. 41°45N 117°40W 76 F5
Santa Rosalía Mexico 27°19N 112°17W 86 B2
Santa Sylvina Argentina 27°50S 61°10W 94 B3
Santa Tecla = Nueva San
  Salvador El Salv. 13°40N 89°18W 88 D2
Santa Teresa Argentina 33°25S 60°47W 94 C3
Santa Teresa Australia 24°8S 134°22E 62 C1
Santa Teresa Mexico 25°17N 97°51W 87 B5
Santa Teresa △ Uruguay 33°57S 53°31W 95 C5
Santa Teresita Argentina 36°32S 56°41W 94 D4
Santa Vitória do Palmar
  Brazil 33°32S 53°25W 95 C5
Santa Ynez → U.S.A. 34°41N 120°36W 79 L6
Santa Ynez Mts. U.S.A. 34°30N 120°0W 79 L6
Santa Ysabel U.S.A. 33°7N 116°40W 79 M10
Santai China 31°5N 104°58E 32 C5
Santana Madeira 32°48N 16°52W 24 D3
Santana, Coxilha de
  Brazil 30°50S 55°35W 95 C4
Santana do Livramento
  Brazil 30°55S 55°30W 95 C4
Santander Spain 43°27N 3°51W 21 A4
Santander Jiménez
  Mexico 24°13N 98°28W 87 C5
Santanilla, Is. Honduras 17°22N 83°57W 88 C3
Santanyí Spain 39°20N 3°5E 24 B10
Santaquin U.S.A. 39°59N 111°47W 76 G8
Santarém Brazil 2°25S 54°42W 93 D8
Santarém Portugal 39°12N 8°42W 21 C1
Santaren Channel
  W. Indies 24°0N 79°30W 88 B4
Santee U.S.A. 32°50N 116°58W 79 N10
Santee → U.S.A. 33°7N 79°17W 85 E15
Santiago = Río Grande de
  Santiago → Mexico 21°36N 105°26W 86 C3
Santiago = São Tiago
  C. Verde Is. 15°0N 23°40W 50 b
Santiago Brazil 29°11S 54°52W 95 B5
Santiago Canary Is. 28°2N 17°12W 24 F2
Santiago Chile 33°26S 70°40W 94 C1
Santiago Panama 8°0N 81°0W 88 E3
Santiago Peru 4°27S 77°38W 92 D3
Santiago de Compostela
  Spain 42°52N 8°37W 21 A1
Santiago de Cuba Cuba 20°0N 75°49W 88 C4
Santiago de los Caballeros
  Dom. Rep. 19°30N 70°40W 89 C5
Santiago del Estero
  Argentina 27°50S 64°15W 94 B3
Santiago del Estero □
  Argentina 27°40S 63°15W 94 B3
Santiago del Teide
  Canary Is. 28°17N 16°48W 24 F3
Santiago Ixcuintla
  Mexico 21°49N 105°13W 86 C3
Santiago Jamiltepec
  Mexico 16°17N 97°49W 87 D5
Santiago Papasquiaro
  Mexico 25°0N 105°20W 86 C3
Santiago Pinotepa Nacional
  Mexico 16°19N 98°1W 87 D5
Santiaguillo, L. de
  Mexico 24°48N 104°48W 86 C4
Santo Amaro Brazil 12°30S 38°43W 93 F11
Santo Anastácio Brazil 21°58S 51°39W 95 A5
Santo André Brazil 23°39S 46°29W 95 A6
Santo Ângelo Brazil 28°15S 54°15W 95 B5
Santo Antão C. Verde Is. 16°52N 25°10W 50 b
Santo Antônio do Içá
  Brazil 3°5S 67°57W 92 D5
Santo Antônio do Leverger
  Brazil 15°52S 56°5W 93 G7

Santo Antônio do Leverger
  Brazil 15°52S 56°5W 93 G7
Santo Domingo
  Dom. Rep. 18°30N 69°59W 89 C6
Santo Domingo Baja Calif.,
  Mexico 30°43N 116°2W 86 A1
Santo Domingo Baja Calif. S.,
  Mexico 25°29N 111°55W 86 B2
Santo Domingo Nic. 12°14N 84°59W 88 D3
Santo Domingo de los Colorados
  Ecuador 0°15S 79°9W 92 D3
Santo Domingo Pueblo
  U.S.A. 35°31N 106°22W 77 J10
Santo Tomás Mexico 31°33N 116°24W 86 A1
Santo Tomás Peru 14°26S 72°8W 92 F4
Santo Tomé Argentina 28°40S 56°5W 95 B4
Santo Tomé de Guayana = Ciudad
  Guayana Venezuela 8°0N 62°30W 92 B6
Santoña Spain 43°29N 3°27W 21 A4
Santorini Greece 36°23N 25°27E 23 F11
Santos Brazil 24°0S 46°20W 95 A6
Santos Dumont Brazil 22°55S 43°10W 95 A7
Sanur Indonesia 8°41S 115°15E 37 K18
Sanwer India 22°59N 75°50E 42 H6
Sanxia Shuiku China 30°10N 108°0E 33 C5
Sanxiang China 22°21N 113°25E 33 G9
Sanya China 18°14N 109°29E 38 C7
Sanyuan China 34°35N 108°58E 34 G5
São Bernardo do Campo
  Brazil 23°45S 46°34W 95 A6
São Borja Brazil 28°39S 56°0W 95 B4
São Carlos Brazil 22°0S 47°50W 95 A6
São Cristóvão Brazil 11°1S 37°15W 93 F11
São Domingos Brazil 13°25S 46°19W 93 F9
São Filipe C. Verde Is. 15°2N 24°30W 50 b
São Francisco Brazil 16°0S 44°50W 93 G10
São Francisco →
  Brazil 10°30S 36°24W 93 F11
São Francisco do Sul
  Brazil 26°15S 48°36W 95 B6
São Gabriel Brazil 30°20S 54°20W 95 C5
São Gonçalo Brazil 22°48S 43°5W 95 A7
Sao Hill Tanzania 8°20S 35°12E 55 D4
São João da Boa Vista
  Brazil 22°0S 46°52W 95 A6
São João da Madeira
  Portugal 40°54N 8°30W 21 B1
São João del Rei Brazil 21°8S 44°15W 95 A7
São João do Araguaia
  Brazil 5°23S 48°46W 93 E9
São João do Piauí Brazil 8°21S 42°15W 93 E10
São Joaquim Brazil 28°18S 49°56W 95 B6
São Joaquim △ Brazil 28°12S 49°37W 95 B6
São Jorge Azores 38°38N 28°3W 50 a
São Jorge, Pta. de
  Madeira 32°50N 16°53W 24 D3
São José Brazil 27°38S 48°39W 95 B5
São José do Norte Brazil 32°1S 52°3W 95 C5
São José do Rio Preto
  Brazil 20°50S 49°20W 95 A6
São José dos Campos
  Brazil 23°7S 45°52W 95 A6
São Leopoldo Brazil 29°50S 51°10W 95 B5
São Lourenço Brazil 22°7S 45°3W 95 A6
São Lourenço →
  Brazil 17°53S 57°27W 93 G7
São Lourenço, Pta. de
  Madeira 32°44N 16°39W 24 D3
São Lourenço do Sul
  Brazil 31°22S 51°58W 95 C5
São Luís Brazil 2°39S 44°15W 93 D10
São Luís Gonzaga Brazil 28°25S 55°0W 95 B5
São Marcos → Brazil 18°15S 47°37W 93 G9
São Marcos, B. de Brazil 2°0S 44°0W 93 D10
São Mateus Brazil 18°44S 39°50W 93 G11
São Mateus do Sul
  Brazil 25°52S 50°23W 95 B5
São Miguel Azores 37°47N 25°30W 50 a
São Miguel do Oeste
  Brazil 26°45S 53°34W 95 B5
São Nicolau C. Verde Is. 16°20N 24°20W 50 b
São Paulo Brazil 23°32S 46°38W 95 A6
São Paulo □ Brazil 22°0S 49°0W 95 A6
São Paulo de Olivença
  Brazil 3°27S 68°48W 92 D5
São Roque Madeira 32°46N 16°48W 24 D3
São Roque, C. de Brazil 5°30S 35°16W 93 E11
São Sebastião, I. de
  Brazil 23°50S 45°18W 95 A6
São Sebastião do Paraíso
  Brazil 20°54S 46°59W 95 A6
São Tiago C. Verde Is. 15°0N 23°40W 50 b
São Tomé
  São Tomé & Príncipe 0°10N 6°39E 48 F4
São Tomé, C. de Brazil 22°0S 40°59W 95 A7
São Tomé & Príncipe ■
  Africa 0°12N 6°39E 49 F4
São Vicente Brazil 23°57S 46°23W 95 A6
São Vicente C. Verde Is. 17°0N 25°0W 50 b
São Vicente Madeira 32°48N 17°3W 24 D2
São Vicente, C. de Portugal 37°0N 9°0W 21 D1
Saona, I. Dom. Rep. 18°10N 68°40W 89 C6
Saône → France 45°44N 4°50E 20 D6
Saonek Indonesia 0°22S 130°55E 37 E8
Sapam, Ao Thailand 8°0N 98°26E 39 a
Saparua Indonesia 3°33S 128°40E 37 E7
Sapele Nigeria 5°50N 5°40E 50 G7
Sapelo I. U.S.A. 31°25N 81°12W 85 F14
Sapi △ Zimbabwe 15°48S 29°52E 55 F2
Saposoa Peru 6°55S 76°45W 92 E3
Sapphire Australia 23°28S 147°43E 62 C4
Sappho U.S.A. 48°4N 124°16W 78 B2
Sapporo Japan 43°0N 141°21E 30 C10
Sapulpa U.S.A. 35°59N 96°5W 84 D6
Saqqez Iran 36°15N 46°20E 44 B5
Sar Dasht Āzarbāyjān-e Gharbī,
  Iran 36°9N 45°28E 44 B5
Sar Dasht Khuzestan, Iran 32°32N 48°52E 45 C6

Sar-e Pol □ Afghan. 36°20N 65°50E 40 B4
Sar Gachīneh = Yāsūj
  Iran 30°31N 51°31E 45 D6
Sar Planina Macedonia 42°0N 21°0E 23 C9
Sara Buri = Saraburi
  Thailand 14°30N 100°55E 38 E3
Sarāb Iran 37°55N 47°40E 44 B5
Sarābādī Iraq 33°1N 44°48E 44 C5
Saraburi Thailand 14°30N 100°55E 38 E3
Saradiya India 21°34N 70°2E 42 J4
Saragossa = Zaragoza
  Spain 41°39N 0°53W 21 B5
Saraguro Ecuador 3°35S 79°16W 92 D3
Sarahs Turkmenistan 36°32N 61°13E 45 B9
Sarai Naurang Pakistan 32°50N 70°47E 42 C4
Saraikela India 22°42N 85°56E 43 H11
Sarajevo Bos.-H. 43°52N 18°26E 23 C8
Sarakhs = Sarahs
  Turkmenistan 36°32N 61°13E 45 B9
Saran, Gunung Indonesia 0°30S 111°25E 36 E4
Saranac Lake U.S.A. 44°20N 74°8W 83 B10
Saranac Lakes U.S.A. 44°20N 74°28W 83 B10
Saranda Tanzania 5°45S 34°59E 54 D3
Sarandí del Yí Uruguay 33°18S 55°38W 95 C4
Sarandí Grande
  Uruguay 33°44S 56°20W 94 C4
Sarangani B. Phil. 6°0N 125°13E 37 C7
Sarangani Is. Phil. 5°25N 125°25E 37 C7
Sarangarh India 21°30N 83°5E 41 J13
Saransk Russia 54°10N 45°10E 18 D8
Sarapul Russia 56°28N 53°48E 18 C9
Sarasota U.S.A. 27°20N 82°32W 85 H13
Saratoga Calif., U.S.A. 37°16N 122°2W 78 H4
Saratoga Wyo., U.S.A. 41°27N 106°49W 76 F10
Saratoga □ U.S.A. 43°0N 73°38W 83 D11
Saratoga L. U.S.A. 43°1N 73°44W 83 C11
Saratoga Springs U.S.A. 43°5N 73°47W 83 C11
Saratok Malaysia 1°55N 111°17E 36 D4
Saratov Russia 51°30N 46°2E 19 D8
Saravane Laos 15°43N 106°25E 38 E6
Sarawak □ Malaysia 2°0N 113°0E 36 D4
Saray Turkey 41°26N 27°55E 23 D12
Saraykoy Turkey 37°55N 28°54E 23 F13
Sarbāz Iran 26°38N 61°19E 45 E9
Sarbīsheh Iran 32°30N 59°40E 45 C8
Sarda → India 27°21N 81°23E 43 F9
Sardarshahr India 28°30N 74°29E 42 E6
Sardegna □ Italy 40°0N 9°0E 22 D3
Sardhana India 29°9N 77°39E 42 E7
Sardina, Pta. Canary Is. 28°9N 15°44W 24 F4
Sardinia = Sardegna □
  Italy 40°0N 9°0E 22 D3
Sardis Turkey 38°28N 27°58E 23 E12
Sārdūīyeh = Dar Mazār
  Iran 29°14N 57°20E 45 D8
Saren Indonesia 8°26S 115°34E 37 J18
S'Arenal Spain 39°30N 2°45E 24 B9
Sarera, G. of Indonesia 2°0S 135°0E 58 B6
Sargasso Sea Atl. Oc. 27°0N 72°0W 66 G13
Sargodha Pakistan 32°10N 72°40E 42 C5
Sarh Chad 9°5N 18°23E 51 G9
Sārī Iran 36°30N 53°4E 45 B7
Saria India 21°38N 83°22E 43 J10
Sariab Pakistan 30°6N 66°59E 42 D2
Sarigöl Turkey 38°14N 28°41E 23 E13
Sarikei Malaysia 2°8N 111°30E 36 D4
Sarila India 25°46N 79°41E 43 G8
Sarina Australia 21°22S 149°13E 62 C4
Sarita U.S.A. 27°13N 97°47W 84 H6
Sariwŏn N. Korea 38°31N 125°46E 35 E13
Sarju → India 27°21N 81°23E 43 F9
Sark U.K. 49°25N 2°22W 13 H5
Sarkari Tala India 27°39N 70°52E 42 F4
Şarköy Turkey 40°36N 27°6E 23 D12
Sarlat-la-Canéda France 44°54N 1°13E 20 D4
Sarmi Indonesia 1°49S 138°44E 37 E9
Sarmiento Argentina 45°35S 69°5W 96 F3
Särna Sweden 61°41N 13°8E 8 F15
Sarnia Canada 42°58N 82°23W 82 D2
Sarolangun Indonesia 2°19S 102°42E 36 E2
Saronikos Kolpos
  Greece 37°45N 23°45E 23 F10
Saros Körfezi Turkey 40°30N 26°15E 23 D12
Sarpsborg Norway 59°16N 11°7E 9 G14
Sarqan Kazakhstan 45°24N 79°55E 32 B2
Sarre = Saar → Europe 49°41N 6°32E 15 E6
Sarreguemines France 49°5N 7°4E 20 B7
Sarthe → France 47°33N 0°31W 20 C3
Saruna → Pakistan 26°31N 67°7E 42 F2
Sarvar India 26°4N 75°0E 42 F6
Sarvestān Iran 29°20N 53°10E 45 D7
Sary-Tash Kyrgyzstan 39°44N 73°15E 28 F8
Saryshagan Kazakhstan 46°12N 73°38E 28 E8
Sasan Gir India 21°10N 70°36E 42 J4
Sasaram India 24°57N 84°5E 43 G11
Sasebo Japan 33°10N 129°43E 31 H4
Saser Kangri India 34°50N 77°50E 43 B7
Saskatchewan □
  Canada 54°40N 106°0W 71 C7
Saskatchewan →
  Canada 53°37N 100°40W 71 C8
Saskatoon Canada 52°10N 106°38W 71 C7
Saskylakh Russia 71°55N 114°1E 29 B12
Saslaya △ Nic. 13°45N 85°4W 88 D2
Sasolburg S. Africa 26°46S 27°49E 57 D4
Sasovo Russia 54°25N 41°55E 18 D7
Sassandra Ivory C. 4°55N 6°8W 50 H4
Sassandra → Ivory C. 4°58N 6°5W 50 H4
Sássari Italy 40°43N 8°34E 22 D3
Sassie Australia 10°2S 142°51E 62 a
Sassnitz Germany 54°29N 13°39E 16 A7
Sassuolo Italy 44°33N 10°47E 22 B4
Sasyk, Ozero Ukraine 45°45N 29°20E 17 F15
Sata-Misaki Japan 31°0N 130°40E 31 J5
Satadougou Mali 12°25N 11°25W 50 F3
Satakunda = Satakunta
  Finland 61°45N 23°0E 8 F20
Satakunta Finland 61°45N 23°0E 8 F20

Satara *India* 17°44N 73°58E **40 L8**
Satara *S. Africa* 24°29S 31°47E **57 C5**
Satbarwa *India* 23°55N 84°16E **43 H11**
Satevó *Mexico* 27°57N 106°7W **86 B3**
Satilla ► *U.S.A.* 30°59N 81°29W **85 F14**
Satka *Russia* 55°3N 59°1E **18 C10**
Satmala Hills *Andhra Pradesh, India* 19°45N 78°45E **40 K11**
Satmala Hills *Maharashtra, India* 20°15N 74°40E **40 J9**
Satna *India* 24°35N 80°50E **43 G9**
Sátoraljaújhely *Hungary* 48°25N 21°41E **17 D11**
Satpura △ *India* 22°40N 78°15E **42 H8**
Satpura Ra. *India* 21°25N 76°10E **40 J10**
Satsuna-Shotō *Japan* 30°0N 130°0E **31 K5**
Sattahip *Thailand* 12°41N 100°54E **38 F3**
Satui *Indonesia* 3°50S 115°27E **36 E5**
Satun *Thailand* 6°43N 100°2E **39 J3**
Satupa'itea *Samoa* 13°45S 172°18W **59 b**
Saturnina ► *Brazil* 12°15S 58°10W **92 F7**
Sauce *Argentina* 30°5S 58°46W **94 C4**
Sauceda *Mexico* 25°46N 101°19W **86 B4**
Saucillo *Mexico* 28°1N 105°17W **86 B3**
Sauda *Norway* 59°40N 6°20E **9 G12**
Sauðarkrókur *Iceland* 65°45N 19°40W **8 D4**
Saudi Arabia ■ *Asia* 26°0N 44°0E **44 B3**
Sauerland *Germany* 51°12N 7°59E **16 C4**
Saugeen ► *Canada* 44°30N 81°22W **82 B3**
Saugerties *U.S.A.* 42°5N 73°57W **83 D11**
Saugus *U.S.A.* 34°25N 118°32W **79 L8**
Sauk Centre *U.S.A.* 45°44N 94°57W **80 C6**
Sauk Rapids *U.S.A.* 45°35N 94°10W **80 C6**
Sault Ste. Marie *Canada* 46°30N 84°20W **72 C3**
Sault Ste. Marie *U.S.A.* 46°30N 84°21W **81 B11**
Saumlaki *Indonesia* 7°55S 131°20E **37 F8**
Saumur *France* 47°15N 0°5W **20 C3**
Saunders, C. *N.Z.* 45°53S 170°45E **59 F3**
Saunders I. *Antarctica* 57°48S 26°28W **5 B1**
Saunders Pt. *Australia* 27°52S 125°38E **61 E4**
Saurimo *Angola* 9°40S 20°12E **52 F4**
Sausalito *U.S.A.* 37°51N 122°29W **78 H4**
Savá *Honduras* 15°32N 86°15W **88 C2**
Sava ► *Serbia* 44°50N 20°26E **23 B9**
Savage *U.S.A.* 47°27N 104°21W **76 C11**
Savage I. = Niue *Pac. Oc.* 19°2S 169°54W **65 J11**
Savage River *Australia* 41°35S 145°14E **63 G4**
Savai'i *Samoa* 13°28S 172°24W **59 b**
Savalou *Benin* 7°57N 1°58E **50 G6**
Savane *Mozam.* 19°37S 35°8E **55 F4**
Savanna *U.S.A.* 42°5N 90°8W **80 D8**
Savanna-la-Mar *Jamaica* 18°10N 78°10W **88 a**
Savannah *Ga., U.S.A.* 32°5N 81°6W **85 E14**
Savannah *Mo., U.S.A.* 39°56N 94°50W **80 F6**
Savannah *Tenn., U.S.A.* 35°14N 88°15W **85 D10**
Savannah ► *U.S.A.* 32°2N 80°53W **85 E14**
Savannakhet *Laos* 16°30N 104°49E **38 D5**
Savant L. *Canada* 50°16N 90°44W **72 B1**
Savant Lake *Canada* 50°14N 90°40W **72 B1**
Savarkundla = Kundla *India* 21°21N 71°25E **42 J4**
Save ► *Mozam.* 21°16S 34°0E **57 C5**
Sāveh *Iran* 35°2N 50°20E **45 C6**
Savelugu *Ghana* 9°38N 0°54W **50 G5**
Savo *Finland* 62°45N 27°30E **8 E22**
Savoie □ *France* 45°26N 6°25E **20 D7**
Savolax = Savo *Finland* 62°45N 27°30E **8 E22**
Savona *Italy* 44°17N 8°30E **20 D8**
Savona *U.S.A.* 42°17N 77°13W **82 D7**
Savonlinna *Finland* 61°52N 28°53E **8 F23**
Savoy = Savoie □ *France* 45°26N 6°25E **20 D7**
Savur *Turkey* 37°34N 40°53E **44 B4**
Savusavu *Fiji* 16°34S 179°15E **59 a**
Savusavu B. *Fiji* 16°45S 179°15E **59 a**
Sawahlunto *Indonesia* 0°40S 100°52E **36 E2**
Sawai *Indonesia* 3°0S 129°5E **37 E7**
Sawai Madhopur *India* 26°0N 76°25E **42 G7**
Sawaleke *Fiji* 17°59S 179°18E **59 a**
Sawang Daen Din *Thailand* 17°28N 103°28E **38 D4**
Sawankhalok *Thailand* 17°19N 99°50E **38 D2**
Sawara *Japan* 35°55N 140°30E **31 G10**
Sawatch Range *U.S.A.* 39°0N 106°30W **76 G10**
Sawel Mt. *U.K.* 54°50N 7°2W **10 B4**
Sawi *Thailand* 10°14N 99°5E **39 G2**
Sawmills *Zimbabwe* 19°30S 28°2E **55 F2**
Sawtooth △ *U.S.A.* 44°0N 114°50W **76 D6**
Sawtooth Range *U.S.A.* 44°3N 114°58W **76 D6**
Sawu *Indonesia* 10°35S 121°50E **37 F6**
Sawu Sea *Indonesia* 9°30S 121°50E **37 F6**
Saxby ► *Australia* 18°25S 140°53E **62 B3**
Saxmundham *U.K.* 52°13N 1°30E **13 E9**
Saxony = Sachsen □ *Germany* 50°55N 13°10E **16 C7**
Saxony, Lower = Niedersachsen □ *Germany* 52°50N 9°0E **16 B5**
Saxton *U.S.A.* 40°13N 78°15W **82 F6**
Sayabec *Canada* 48°35N 67°41W **73 C6**
Sayaboury *Laos* 19°15N 101°45E **38 C3**
Sayán *Peru* 11°8S 77°12W **92 F3**
Sayan, Vostochnyy *Russia* 54°0N 96°0E **29 D10**
Sayan, Zapadnyy *Russia* 52°30N 94°0E **32 A4**
Sayanogorsk *Russia* 53°5N 91°23E **29 D10**
Saydā *Lebanon* 33°35N 35°25E **46 B4**
Sayhandulaan = Oldziyt *Mongolia* 44°40N 109°1E **34 B5**
Sayḩūt *Yemen* 15°12N 51°10E **47 D5**
Saynshand = Buyant-Uhaa *Mongolia* 44°55N 110°11E **33 B6**
Sayre *Okla., U.S.A.* 35°18N 99°38W **84 D5**
Sayre *Pa., U.S.A.* 41°59N 76°32W **83 E8**
Sayreville *U.S.A.* 40°28N 74°22W **83 F10**
Sayula *Mexico* 19°52N 103°36W **86 D4**
Sayward *Canada* 50°21N 125°55W **70 C3**

Sazanit *Albania* 40°30N 19°20E **23 D8**
Sázava ► *Czech Rep.* 49°53N 14°24E **16 D8**
Sazin *Pakistan* 35°35N 73°30E **43 B5**
Scafell Pike *U.K.* 54°27N 3°14W **12 C4**
Scalloway *U.K.* 60°9N 1°17W **11 A7**
Scalpay *U.K.* 57°18N 6°0W **11 D3**
Scandia *Canada* 50°20N 112°2W **70 C6**
Scandicci *Italy* 43°45N 11°11E **22 C4**
Scandinavia *Europe* 64°0N 12°0E **8 E15**
Scapa Flow *U.K.* 58°53N 3°3W **11 C5**
Scappoose *U.S.A.* 45°45N 122°53W **78 E4**
Scarba *U.K.* 56°11N 5°43W **11 E3**
Scarborough *Trin. & Tob.* 11°11N 60°42W **93 J16**
Scarborough *U.K.* 54°17N 0°24W **12 C7**
Scariff I. *Ireland* 51°44N 10°15W **10 E1**
Scarp *U.K.* 58°1N 7°8W **11 C1**
Scebeli = Shabeelle ► *Somali Rep.* 2°0N 44°0E **47 G3**
Schaffhausen *Switz.* 47°42N 8°39E **20 C8**
Schagen *Neths.* 52°49N 4°48E **15 B4**
Schaghticoke *U.S.A.* 42°54N 73°35W **83 D11**
Schefferville *Canada* 54°48N 66°50W **73 B6**
Schelde ► *Belgium* 51°15N 4°16E **15 C4**
Schell Creek Ra. *U.S.A.* 39°25N 114°40W **76 G6**
Schellsburg *U.S.A.* 40°3N 78°39W **82 F6**
Schenectady *U.S.A.* 42°49N 73°57W **83 D11**
Schenevus *U.S.A.* 42°33N 74°50W **83 D10**
Schiedam *Neths.* 51°55N 4°25E **15 C4**
Schiermonnikoog *Neths.* 53°30N 6°15E **15 A6**
Schio *Italy* 45°43N 11°21E **22 B4**
Schiphol, Amsterdam ✈ (AMS) *Neths.* 52°18N 4°45E **15 B4**
Schleswig *Germany* 54°31N 9°34E **16 A5**
Schleswig-Holstein □ *Germany* 54°30N 9°30E **16 A5**
Schœlcher *Martinique* 14°36N 61°7W **88 c**
Schoharie *U.S.A.* 42°40N 74°19W **83 D10**
Schoharie Cr. ► *U.S.A.* 42°57N 74°18W **83 D10**
Scholls *U.S.A.* 45°24N 122°56W **78 E4**
Schouten I. *Australia* 42°20S 148°20E **63 G4**
Schouten Is. = Supiori *Indonesia* 1°0S 136°0E **37 E9**
Schouwen *Neths.* 51°43N 3°45E **15 C3**
Schreiber *Canada* 48°45N 87°20W **72 C2**
Schroffenstein *Namibia* 27°11S 18°42E **56 D2**
Schroon Lake *U.S.A.* 43°50N 73°46W **83 C11**
Schuler *Canada* 50°20N 110°6W **71 C6**
Schumacher *Canada* 48°30N 81°16W **72 C3**
Schurz *U.S.A.* 38°57N 118°49W **76 G4**
Schuyler *U.S.A.* 41°27N 97°4W **80 E5**
Schuylerville *U.S.A.* 43°6N 73°35W **83 C11**
Schuylkill ► *U.S.A.* 39°53N 75°12W **83 G9**
Schuylkill Haven *U.S.A.* 40°37N 76°11W **83 F8**
Schwäbische Alb *Germany* 48°20N 9°30E **16 D5**
Schwaner, Pegunungan *Indonesia* 1°0S 112°30E **36 E4**
Schwarzrand *Namibia* 25°37S 16°50E **56 D2**
Schwarzwald *Germany* 48°30N 8°20E **16 D5**
Schwatka Mts. *U.S.A.* 67°20N 156°30W **74 B8**
Schwedt *Germany* 53°3N 14°16E **16 B8**
Schweinfurt *Germany* 50°3N 10°14E **16 C6**
Schweiz = Switzerland ■ *Europe* 46°30N 8°0E **20 C8**
Schweizer-Reneke *S. Africa* 27°11S 25°18E **56 D4**
Schwenningen = Villingen-Schwenningen *Germany* 48°3N 8°26E **16 D5**
Schwerin *Germany* 53°36N 11°22E **16 B6**
Schwyz *Switz.* 47°2N 8°39E **20 C8**
Sciacca *Italy* 37°31N 13°3E **22 F5**
Scilla *Italy* 38°15N 15°43E **22 E6**
Scilly, Isles of *U.K.* 49°56N 6°22W **13 H1**
Scioto ► *U.S.A.* 38°44N 83°1W **81 F12**
Scituate *U.S.A.* 42°12N 70°44W **83 D14**
Scobey *U.S.A.* 48°47N 105°25W **76 B11**
Scone *Australia* 32°5S 150°52E **63 E5**
Scone *U.K.* 56°25N 3°24W **11 E5**
Scoresbysund = Ittoqqortoormiit *Greenland* 70°20N 23°0W **4 B6**
Scotia *Calif., U.S.A.* 40°29N 124°6W **76 F1**
Scotia *N.Y., U.S.A.* 42°50N 73°58W **83 D11**
Scotia Sea *Antarctica* 56°5S 56°0W **5 B18**
Scotland *Canada* 43°1N 80°22W **82 C4**
Scotland *U.K.* 57°0N 4°0W **11 E5**
Scotland *Canada* 77°0S 165°0E **5 D11**
Scott, C. *Australia* 13°30S 129°49E **60 B4**
Scott City *U.S.A.* 38°29N 100°54W **80 F4**
Scott Glacier *Antarctica* 66°15S 100°5E **5 C8**
Scott I. *Antarctica* 67°0S 179°0E **5 C11**
Scott Is. *Canada* 50°48N 128°40W **70 C3**
Scott L. *Canada* 59°55N 106°18W **71 B7**
Scott Reef *Australia* 14°0S 121°50E **60 B3**
Scottburgh *S. Africa* 30°15S 30°47E **57 E5**
Scottdale *U.S.A.* 40°6N 79°35W **82 F5**
Scottish Borders □ *U.K.* 55°35N 2°50W **11 F6**
Scotts Valley *U.S.A.* 37°3N 122°1W **78 H4**
Scottsbluff *U.S.A.* 41°52N 103°40W **80 E2**
Scottsboro *U.S.A.* 34°40N 86°2W **85 D11**
Scottsburg *U.S.A.* 38°41N 85°47W **81 F11**
Scottsdale *Australia* 41°9S 147°31E **63 G4**
Scottsdale *U.S.A.* 33°40N 111°53W **77 K8**
Scottsville *Ky., U.S.A.* 36°45N 86°11W **80 G10**
Scottsville *N.Y., U.S.A.* 43°2N 77°47W **82 C7**
Scottville *U.S.A.* 43°58N 86°17W **80 D10**
Scranton *U.S.A.* 41°25N 75°40W **83 E9**
Scugog, L. *Canada* 44°10N 78°55W **82 B6**
Scunthorpe *U.K.* 53°36N 0°39W **12 D7**
Scutari = Shkodër *Albania* 42°4N 19°32E **23 C8**
Sea Is. *U.S.A.* 31°30N 81°7W **85 F14**
Seabrook, L. *Australia* 30°55S 119°40E **61 F2**
Seaford *U.K.* 50°47N 0°7E **13 G8**
Seaford *U.S.A.* 38°39N 75°37W **81 F16**
Seaforth *Australia* 20°55S 148°57E **62 b**
Seaforth *Canada* 43°35N 81°25W **82 C3**
Seaforth, L. *U.K.* 57°52N 6°36W **11 D2**

Seagraves *U.S.A.* 32°57N 102°34W **84 E3**
Seaham *U.K.* 54°50N 1°20W **12 C6**
Seal ► *Canada* 59°4N 94°48W **71 B10**
Seal L. *Canada* 54°20N 61°30W **73 B7**
Sealy *U.S.A.* 29°47N 96°9W **84 G6**
Searchlight *U.S.A.* 35°28N 114°55W **79 K12**
Searcy *U.S.A.* 35°15N 91°44W **84 D9**
Searles L. *U.S.A.* 35°44N 117°21W **79 K9**
Seascale *U.K.* 54°24N 3°29W **12 C4**
Seaside *Calif., U.S.A.* 36°37N 121°50W **78 J5**
Seaside *Oreg., U.S.A.* 46°0N 123°56W **78 E3**
Seaspray *Australia* 38°25S 147°15E **63 F4**
Seattle *U.S.A.* 47°36N 122°19W **78 C4**
Seattle-Tacoma Int. ✈ (SEA) *U.S.A.* 47°27N 122°18W **78 C4**
Seba *Indonesia* 10°29S 121°50E **60 B3**
Sebago L. *U.S.A.* 43°52N 70°34W **83 C14**
Sebago Lake *U.S.A.* 43°51N 70°34W **83 C14**
Sebastián Vizcaíno, B. *Mexico* 28°0N 114°30W **86 B2**
Sebastopol = Sevastopol *Ukraine* 44°35N 33°30E **19 F5**
Sebastopol *U.S.A.* 38°24N 122°49W **78 G4**
Sebewaing *U.S.A.* 43°44N 83°27W **81 D12**
Sebha = Sabḩā *Libya* 27°9N 14°29E **51 C8**
Şebinkarahisar *Turkey* 40°22N 38°28E **19 F6**
Sebring *Fla., U.S.A.* 27°30N 81°27W **85 H14**
Sebring *Ohio, U.S.A.* 40°55N 81°2W **82 F3**
Sebringville *Canada* 43°24N 81°4W **82 C3**
Sebta = Ceuta *N. Afr.* 35°52N 5°18W **21 E3**
Sebuku *Indonesia* 3°30S 116°25E **36 E5**
Sebuku, Teluk *Malaysia* 4°0N 118°10E **36 D5**
Sechelt *Canada* 49°25N 123°42W **70 D4**
Sechura, Desierto de *Peru* 6°0S 80°30W **92 E2**
Secretary I. *N.Z.* 45°15S 166°56E **59 F1**
Secunderabad *India* 17°28N 78°30E **40 L11**
Security *U.S.A.* 38°45N 104°45W **76 G11**
Sedalia *U.S.A.* 38°42N 93°14W **80 F8**
Sedan *France* 49°43N 4°57E **20 B6**
Sedan *U.S.A.* 37°8N 96°11W **80 G5**
Sedbergh *U.K.* 54°20N 2°31W **12 C5**
Seddon *N.Z.* 41°40S 174°7E **59 D5**
Seddonville *N.Z.* 41°33S 172°1E **59 D4**
Sedé Boqér *Israel* 30°52N 34°47E **46 E3**
Sedeh *Fārs, Iran* 30°45N 52°11E **45 D7**
Sedeh *Khorāsān, Iran* 33°20N 59°14E **45 C8**
Sederot *Israel* 31°32N 34°37E **46 D3**
Sédhiou *Senegal* 12°44N 15°30W **50 F2**
Sedley *Canada* 50°10N 104°0W **71 C8**
Sedona *U.S.A.* 34°52N 111°46W **77 J8**
Sedova, Pik *Russia* 73°29N 54°58E **28 B6**
Sedro-Woolley *U.S.A.* 48°30N 122°14W **78 B4**
Seeheim *Namibia* 26°50S 17°45E **56 D2**
Seeis *Namibia* 22°29S 17°39E **56 C2**
Seekoei ► *S. Africa* 30°18S 25°1E **56 E4**
Seeley's Bay *Canada* 44°29N 76°14W **83 B8**
Seferihisar *Turkey* 38°10N 26°50E **23 E12**
Sefophe *Botswana* 22°11S 27°58E **55 G2**
Seg-ozero *Russia* 63°20N 33°46E **18 B5**
Segamat *Malaysia* 2°30N 102°50E **39 L4**
Segesta *Italy* 37°56N 12°50E **22 F5**
Seget *Indonesia* 1°24S 130°58E **37 E8**
Segezha *Russia* 63°44N 34°19E **18 B5**
Ségou *Mali* 13°30N 6°16W **50 F4**
Segovia = Coco ► *Cent. Amer.* 15°0N 83°8W **88 D3**
Segovia *Spain* 40°57N 4°10W **21 B3**
Segre ► *Spain* 41°40N 0°43E **21 B6**
Seguam I. *U.S.A.* 52°19N 172°30W **74 E5**
Séguéla *Ivory C.* 7°55N 6°40W **50 G4**
Seguin *U.S.A.* 29°34N 97°58W **84 G6**
Segundo ► *Argentina* 30°53S 62°44W **94 C3**
Segura ► *Spain* 38°3N 0°44E **21 C5**
Seh Konj, Kūh-e *Iran* 30°6N 57°30E **45 D8**
Seh Qal'eh *Iran* 33°40N 58°24E **45 C8**
Sehitwa *Botswana* 20°30S 22°30E **56 C3**
Sehlabathebe △ *Lesotho* 29°53S 29°7E **57 D4**
Sehore *India* 23°10N 77°5E **42 H7**
Sehwan *Pakistan* 26°28N 67°53E **42 F2**
Seikan Tunnel *Japan* 41°28N 140°10E **30 D10**
Seil *U.K.* 56°18N 5°38W **11 E3**
Seiland *Norway* 70°25N 23°15E **8 A20**
Seiling *U.S.A.* 36°9N 98°56W **84 C5**
Seinäjoki *Finland* 62°40N 22°51E **8 E20**
Seine ► *France* 49°26N 0°26E **20 B4**
Seistan = Sīstān *Asia* 30°50N 61°0E **45 D9**
Seistan, Daryācheh-ye = Sīstān, Daryācheh-ye *Iran* 31°0N 61°0E **45 D9**
Sekayu *Indonesia* 2°51S 103°51E **36 E2**
Seke *Tanzania* 3°20S 33°31E **54 C3**
Sekenke *Tanzania* 4°18S 34°11E **54 C3**
Sekondi-Takoradi *Ghana* 4°58N 1°45W **50 H5**
Sekudai *Malaysia* 1°32N 103°39E **39 d**
Sekuma *Botswana* 24°36S 23°50E **56 C3**
Selah *U.S.A.* 46°39N 120°32W **76 C3**
Selama *Malaysia* 5°12N 100°42E **39 K3**
Selaru *Indonesia* 8°9S 131°0E **37 F8**
Selat, Selat *Malaysia* 5°15N 100°20E **39 c**
Selawik L. *U.S.A.* 66°30N 160°45W **74 B7**
Selby *U.K.* 53°47N 1°5W **12 D6**
Selby *U.S.A.* 45°31N 100°2W **80 C3**
Selçuk *Turkey* 37°56N 27°22E **23 F12**
Selden *U.S.A.* 39°33N 100°34W **80 F4**
Sele ► *Italy* 40°29N 14°56E **22 D6**
Selebi-Phikwe *Botswana* 21°58S 27°48E **57 C4**
Selemdzha ► *Russia* 51°42N 128°53E **29 D13**
Selenga = Selenge Mörön ► *Asia* 52°16N 106°16E **32 A5**
Selenge Mörön ► *Asia* 52°16N 106°16E **32 A5**
Seletan, Tanjung *Indonesia* 4°10S 114°40E **36 E4**
Sélibabi *Mauritania* 15°10N 12°15W **50 E3**
Seligman *U.S.A.* 35°20N 112°53W **77 J7**
Selîma *Sudan* 21°22N 29°19E **51 D11**
Selinda Spillway *Botswana* 18°35S 23°10E **56 B3**
Selinsgrove *U.S.A.* 40°48N 76°52W **82 F8**
Selkirk *Man., Canada* 50°10N 96°55W **71 C9**
Selkirk *Ont., Canada* 42°49N 79°56W **82 D5**

Selkirk *U.K.* 55°33N 2°50W **11 F6**
Selkirk I. = Horse I. *Canada* 53°20N 99°6W **71 C9**
Selkirk Mts. *Canada* 51°15N 117°40W **68 G8**
Sellafield *U.K.* 54°25N 3°29W **12 C4**
Sellia *Greece* 35°12N 24°23E **25 D6**
Sells *U.S.A.* 31°55N 111°53W **77 L8**
Selma *Ala., U.S.A.* 32°25N 87°1W **85 E11**
Selma *Calif., U.S.A.* 36°34N 119°37W **78 J7**
Selma *N.C., U.S.A.* 35°32N 78°17W **85 D15**
Selmer *U.S.A.* 35°10N 88°36W **85 D10**
Selous △ *Tanzania* 8°37S 37°42E **55 D4**
Selowandoma Falls *Zimbabwe* 21°15S 31°50E **55 G3**
Selpele *Indonesia* 0°1S 130°5E **37 E8**
Selsey Bill *U.K.* 50°43N 0°47W **13 G7**
Seltso *Russia* 53°22N 34°4E **18 D5**
Selu *Indonesia* 7°32S 130°55E **37 F8**
Selva *Argentina* 29°50S 62°0W **94 B3**
Selva *Spain* 39°46N 2°54E **24 B9**
Selva Lancandona = Montes Azules △ *Mexico* 16°21N 91°3W **87 D6**
Selvagens, Ilhas *Madeira* 30°5N 15°55W **50 B2**
Selvas *Brazil* 6°30S 67°0W **92 E5**
Selwyn L. *Canada* 60°0N 104°30W **71 B8**
Selwyn Mts. *Canada* 63°0N 130°0W **68 E5**
Selwyn Ra. *Australia* 21°10S 140°0E **62 C3**
Seman ► *Albania* 40°47N 19°30E **23 D8**
Semarang *Indonesia* 7°0S 110°26E **37 G14**
Sembabule *Uganda* 0°4S 31°25E **54 C3**
Sembawang *Singapore* 1°27N 103°50E **39 d**
Sembung *Indonesia* 8°28S 115°11E **37 J18**
Semenanjung Blambangan *Indonesia* 8°42S 114°29E **37 K17**
Semeru *Indonesia* 8°4S 112°55E **37 H15**
Semey *Kazakhstan* 50°30N 80°10E **28 D9**
Seminoe Res. *U.S.A.* 42°9N 106°55W **76 E10**
Seminole *Okla., U.S.A.* 35°14N 96°41W **84 D6**
Seminole *Tex., U.S.A.* 32°43N 102°39W **84 E3**
Seminole Draw ► *U.S.A.* 32°27N 102°20W **84 E3**
Semipalatinsk = Semey *Kazakhstan* 50°30N 80°10E **28 D9**
Semirara Is. *Phil.* 12°0N 121°20E **37 B6**
Semisopochnoi I. *U.S.A.* 51°55N 179°36E **74 E3**
Semitau *Indonesia* 0°29N 111°57E **36 D4**
Semmering P. *Austria* 47°41N 15°45E **16 E8**
Semnān *Iran* 35°40N 53°23E **45 C7**
Semnān □ *Iran* 36°0N 54°0E **45 C7**
Semporna *Malaysia* 4°30N 118°33E **37 D5**
Semuda *Indonesia* 2°51S 112°58E **36 E4**
Sen ► *Cambodia* 12°32N 104°28E **38 F5**
Senā *Iran* 28°27N 51°36E **45 D6**
Sena *Mozam.* 17°25S 35°0E **55 F4**
Sena Madureira *Brazil* 9°5S 68°45W **92 E5**
Senador Pompeu *Brazil* 5°40S 39°20W **93 E11**
Senang, Pulau *Singapore* 1°11N 103°52E **39 d**
Senanga *Zambia* 16°7S 23°16E **53 H4**
Senatobia *U.S.A.* 34°37N 89°58W **85 D10**
Sencelles *Spain* 39°39N 2°54E **24 B9**
Sendai *Kagoshima, Japan* 31°50N 130°20E **31 J5**
Sendai *Miyagi, Japan* 38°15N 140°53E **30 E10**
Sendai-Wan *Japan* 38°15N 141°0E **30 E10**
Sendhwa *India* 21°41N 75°6E **42 J6**
Seneca *U.S.A.* 34°41N 82°57W **85 D13**
Seneca Falls *U.S.A.* 42°55N 76°48W **83 D8**
Seneca L. *U.S.A.* 42°40N 76°54W **82 D8**
Senecaville L. *U.S.A.* 39°55N 81°25W **82 G3**
Senegal ■ *W. Afr.* 14°30N 14°30W **50 F3**
Sénégal ► *W. Afr.* 15°48N 16°32W **50 E2**
Senegambia *Africa* 12°45N 12°0W **48 E2**
Senekal *S. Africa* 28°20S 27°36E **57 D4**
Senga Hill *Zambia* 9°19S 31°11E **55 D3**
Senge Khambab = Indus ► *Pakistan* 24°20N 67°47E **42 G2**
Sengerema *Tanzania* 2°43S 32°35E **54 C3**
Sengua ► *Zimbabwe* 17°7S 28°5E **55 F2**
Senhor-do-Bonfim *Brazil* 10°30S 40°10W **93 F10**
Senigállia *Italy* 43°43N 13°13E **22 C5**
Senj *Croatia* 45°0N 14°58E **16 F8**
Senja *Norway* 69°25N 17°30E **8 B17**
Senkaku-Shotō *E. China Sea* 25°45N 123°30E **31 M1**
Senkuang *Indonesia* 1°11N 104°2E **39 d**
Senlis *France* 49°13N 2°35E **20 B5**
Senmonorom *Cambodia* 12°27N 107°12E **38 F6**
Senneterre *Canada* 48°25N 77°15W **72 C4**
Seno *Laos* 16°35N 104°50E **38 D5**
Senqu = Orange ► *S. Africa* 28°41S 16°28E **56 D2**
Sens *France* 48°11N 3°15E **20 B5**
Senta *Serbia* 45°55N 20°3E **23 B9**
Sentani *Indonesia* 2°36S 140°37E **37 E10**
Sentery = Lubao *Dem. Rep. of the Congo* 5°17S 25°42E **54 D2**
Sentinel *U.S.A.* 32°52N 113°13W **77 K7**
Sentosa *Singapore* 1°15N 103°50E **39 d**
Seo de Urgel = La Seu d'Urgell *Spain* 42°22N 1°23E **21 A6**
Seogwipo *S. Korea* 33°13N 126°34E **35 H14**
Seohara *India* 29°15N 78°33E **43 E8**
Seonath ► *India* 21°44N 82°28E **43 J10**
Seondha *India* 26°9N 78°48E **43 F8**
Seongnam *S. Korea* 37°26N 127°9E **35 F14**
Seoni *India* 22°5N 79°30E **43 H8**
Seoni Malwa *India* 22°27N 77°28E **42 H8**
Seonsan *S. Korea* 36°14N 128°17E **35 F15**
Seosan *S. Korea* 36°47N 126°27E **35 F14**
Seoul *S. Korea* 37°31N 126°58E **35 F14**
Sepīdān *Iran* 30°20N 52°5E **45 D7**
Sep'o *N. Korea* 38°57N 127°25E **35 E14**
Sepone *Laos* 16°45N 106°13E **38 D6**
Sept-Îles *Canada* 50°13N 66°22E **73 B6**
Sequim *U.S.A.* 48°5N 123°6W **78 B3**
Sequoia △ *U.S.A.* 36°30N 118°30W **78 J8**
Seraing *Belgium* 50°35N 5°32E **15 D5**

Serakhis ► *Cyprus* 35°13N 32°55E **25 D11**
Seram *Indonesia* 3°10S 129°0E **37 E7**
Seram Sea = Indonesia 2°30S 128°30E **37 E7**
Serampore = Shrirampur *India* 22°44N 88°21E **43 H13**
Serang *Indonesia* 6°8S 106°10E **37 G12**
Serangoon *Singapore* 1°23N 103°54E **39 d**
Serasan *Indonesia* 2°29N 109°4E **36 D3**
Serbia ■ *Europe* 43°20N 20°0E **23 B9**
Serdar *Turkmenistan* 39°4N 56°23E **45 B8**
Serdobsk *Russia* 52°28N 44°10E **18 D7**
Seremban *Malaysia* 2°43N 101°53E **39 L3**
Serengeti △ *Tanzania* 2°11S 35°0E **54 C3**
Serengeti Plain *Tanzania* 2°40S 35°0E **54 C4**
Serenje *Zambia* 13°14S 30°15E **55 E3**
Sereth = Siret ► *Romania* 45°24N 28°1E **17 F14**
Sergeya Kirova, Ostrova *Russia* 77°30N 90°0E **29 B10**
Sergino *Russia* 62°25N 65°12E **28 C7**
Sergipe □ *Brazil* 10°30S 37°30W **93 F11**
Sergiyev Posad *Russia* 56°20N 38°10E **18 C6**
Serhetabat *Turkmenistan* 35°20N 62°18E **45 C9**
Seria *Brunei* 4°37N 114°23E **36 D4**
Serian *Malaysia* 1°10N 110°31E **36 D4**
Seribu, Kepulauan *Indonesia* 5°36S 106°33E **36 F3**
Sericho *Kenya* 1°5N 39°5E **54 B4**
Serifos *Greece* 37°9N 24°30E **23 F11**
Sérigny ► *Canada* 56°47N 66°0W **73 A6**
Seringapatam Reef *Australia* 13°38S 122°5E **60 B3**
Seririt *Indonesia* 8°12S 114°56E **37 J17**
Serkout *Algeria* 23°56N 6°47E **50 D7**
Sermata *Indonesia* 8°15S 128°50E **37 F7**
Sermersuaq *Greenland* 79°30N 62°0W **69 B19**
Serov *Russia* 59°29N 60°35E **18 C11**
Serowe *Botswana* 22°25S 26°43E **56 C4**
Serpentine Lakes *Australia* 28°30S 129°10E **61 E4**
Serpent's Mouth = Sierpe, Bocas de la *Venezuela* 10°0N 61°30W **93 L15**
Serpukhov *Russia* 54°55N 37°28E **18 D6**
Serra do Navio *Brazil* 0°59N 52°3W **93 C8**
Serranía San Luís △ *Paraguay* 22°35S 57°22W **94 A4**
Serranía San Rafael △ *Paraguay* 26°30S 56°0W **95 B4**
Serres *Greece* 41°5N 23°31E **23 D10**
Serrezuela *Argentina* 30°40S 65°20W **94 C2**
Serrinha *Brazil* 11°39S 39°0W **93 F11**
Sertanópolis *Brazil* 23°4S 51°2W **95 A5**
Serua *Indonesia* 6°18S 130°1E **37 F8**
Serui *Indonesia* 1°53S 136°10E **37 E9**
Serule *Botswana* 21°57S 27°20E **56 C4**
Ses Salines *Spain* 39°21N 3°3E **24 B10**
Sese Is. *Uganda* 0°20S 32°20E **54 C3**
Sesepe *Indonesia* 1°30S 127°59E **37 E7**
Sesfontein *Namibia* 19°7S 13°39E **56 B1**
Sesheke *Zambia* 17°29S 24°13E **56 B3**
S'Espalmador *Spain* 38°47N 1°26E **24 C7**
S'Espardell *Spain* 38°48N 1°29E **24 C7**
S'Estanyol *Spain* 39°22N 2°54E **24 B9**
Setana *Japan* 42°26N 139°51E **30 C9**
Sète *France* 43°25N 3°42E **20 E5**
Sete Lagoas *Brazil* 19°27S 44°16W **93 G10**
Sétif *Algeria* 36°9N 5°26E **50 A7**
Seto *Japan* 35°14N 137°6E **31 G8**
Setonaikai *Japan* 34°20N 133°30E **31 G6**
Setonaikai △ *Japan* 34°15N 133°15E **31 G6**
Settat *Morocco* 33°0N 7°40W **50 B4**
Setting L. *Canada* 55°0N 98°38W **71 C9**
Settle *U.K.* 54°5N 2°16W **12 C5**
Settlement, The *Br. Virgin Is.* 18°43N 64°22W **89 e**
Settlers *S. Africa* 25°2S 28°30E **57 C4**
Setúbal *Portugal* 38°30N 8°58W **21 C1**
Setúbal, B. de *Portugal* 38°40N 8°56W **21 C1**
Seul, Lac *Canada* 50°20N 92°30W **72 B1**
Sevan, Ozero = Sevana Lich *Armenia* 40°30N 45°20E **44 A5**
Sevana Lich *Armenia* 40°30N 45°20E **44 A5**
Sevastopol *Ukraine* 44°35N 33°30E **19 F5**
Seven Sisters *Canada* 54°56N 128°10W **70 C3**
Severn ► *Canada* 56°2N 87°36W **72 A2**
Severn ► *U.K.* 51°35N 2°40W **13 F5**
Severnaya Zemlya *Russia* 79°0N 100°0E **29 B11**
Severnyye Uvaly *Russia* 60°0N 50°0E **18 C8**
Severo-Kurilsk *Russia* 50°40N 156°8E **29 D16**
Severo-Yeniseyskiy *Russia* 60°22N 93°1E **29 C10**
Severo-Zapadnyy □ *Russia* 65°0N 40°0E **28 C4**
Severobaykalsk *Russia* 55°39N 109°19E **29 D11**
Severodvinsk *Russia* 64°27N 39°58E **18 B6**
Severomorsk *Russia* 69°5N 33°27E **8 B25**
Severouralsk *Russia* 60°9N 59°57E **18 B10**
Seversk *Russia* 56°36N 84°49E **28 D9**
Sevier ► *U.S.A.* 39°4N 113°6W **76 G7**
Sevier Desert *U.S.A.* 39°40N 112°45W **76 G7**
Sevier L. *U.S.A.* 38°54N 113°9W **76 G7**
Sevilla *Spain* 37°23N 5°58W **21 D2**
Seville = Sevilla *Spain* 37°23N 5°58W **21 D2**
Sevlievo *Bulgaria* 43°2N 25°6E **23 C11**
Sewani *India* 28°58N 75°39E **42 E6**
Seward *Alaska, U.S.A.* 60°7N 149°27W **68 B5**
Seward *Nebr., U.S.A.* 40°55N 97°6W **80 E5**
Seward *Pa., U.S.A.* 40°25N 79°1W **82 F5**
Seward Peninsula *U.S.A.* 65°30N 166°0W **74 B6**
Sewell *Chile* 34°10S 70°23W **94 C1**
Sewer *Indonesia* 5°53S 134°40E **37 F8**
Sewickley *U.S.A.* 40°32N 80°12W **82 F4**
Sexsmith *Canada* 55°21N 118°47W **70 B5**
Seychelles ■ *Ind. Oc.* 5°0S 56°0E **53 b**
Seyðisfjörður *Iceland* 65°16N 13°57W **8 D7**
Seydişehir *Turkey* 37°25N 31°51E **19 G5**

Seydván Iran 38°34N 45°2E 44 B5
Seyhan Turkey 36°43N 34°53E 44 B2
Seym → Ukraine 51°27N 32°34E 19 D5
Seymour Australia 37°2S 145°10E 63 F4
Seymour S. Africa 32°33S 26°46E 57 E4
Seymour Conn., U.S.A. 41°24N 73°4W 83 E11
Seymour Ind., U.S.A. 38°58N 85°53W 81 F11
Seymour Tex., U.S.A. 33°35N 99°16W 84 E5
Sfântu Gheorghe Romania 45°52N 25°48E 17 F13
Sfax Tunisia 34°49N 10°48E 51 B8
Sha Tau Kok China 22°33N 114°13E 33 F11
Sha Tin China 22°23N 114°12E 33 G11
Shaanxi □ China 35°0N 109°0E 34 G5
Shaba = Katanga □
Dem. Rep. of the Congo 8°0S 25°0E 54 D2
Shaba △ Kenya 0°38N 37°48E 54 B4
Shabeelle → Somali Rep. 2°0N 44°0E 47 G3
Shabogamo L. Canada 53°15N 66°30W 73 B6
Shabunda
Dem. Rep. of the Congo 2°40S 27°16E 54 C2
Shache China 38°20N 77°10E 32 C2
Shackleton Fracture Zone
S. Ocean 60°0S 60°0W 5 B18
Shackleton Ice Shelf
Antarctica 66°0S 100°0E 5 C8
Shackleton Inlet
Antarctica 83°0S 160°0E 5 E11
Shādegān Iran 30°40N 48°38E 45 D6
Shadi India 33°24N 77°14E 43 C7
Shadrinsk Russia 56°5N 63°32E 28 D7
Shadyside U.S.A. 39°58N 80°45W 82 G4
Shafter U.S.A. 35°30N 119°16W 79 K7
Shaftesbury U.K. 51°0N 2°11W 13 F5
Shaftsbury U.S.A. 43°0N 73°11W 83 D11
Shagram Pakistan 36°24N 72°20E 43 A5
Shah Alam Malaysia 3°5N 101°32E 39 L3
Shah Alizai Pakistan 29°25N 66°33E 42 E2
Shah Bunder Pakistan 24°13N 67°56E 42 G2
Shahabad Punjab, India 30°10N 76°55E 42 D7
Shahabad Raj., India 25°15N 77°11E 42 G7
Shahabad Ut. P., India 27°36N 79°56E 43 F8
Shahadpur Pakistan 25°55N 68°35E 42 G3
Shahbā' Syria 32°52N 36°38E 46 C5
Shahdād Iran 30°30N 57°40E 45 D8
Shahdād, Namakzār-e
Iran 30°20N 58°20E 45 D8
Shahdadkot Pakistan 27°50N 67°55E 42 F2
Shahdol India 23°19N 81°26E 43 H9
Shahe China 37°0N 114°32E 34 F8
Shahganj India 26°3N 82°44E 43 F10
Shahgarh India 27°15N 69°50E 42 F3
Shahjahanpur India 27°54N 79°57E 43 F8
Shahpur = Salmās Iran 38°11N 44°47E 44 B5
Shahpur India 22°12N 77°58E 42 H7
Shahpur Baluchistan,
Pakistan 28°46N 68°27E 42 E3
Shahpur Punjab, Pakistan 32°17N 72°26E 42 C5
Shahpur Chakar Pakistan 26°9N 68°39E 42 F3
Shahpura Mad. P., India 23°10N 80°45E 43 H9
Shahpura Raj., India 25°38N 74°56E 42 G6
Shahr-e Bābak Iran 30°7N 55°9E 45 D7
Shahr-e Kord Iran 32°15N 50°55E 45 C6
Shāhrakht Iran 33°38N 60°16E 45 C9
Shahrezā = Qomsheh
Iran 32°0N 51°55E 45 D6
Shahrig Pakistan 30°15N 67°40E 42 D2
Shāhrud = Emāmrūd
Iran 36°30N 55°0E 45 B7
Shahukou China 40°20N 112°18E 34 D7
Shaikhabad Afghan. 34°2N 68°45E 42 B3
Shajapur India 23°27N 76°21E 42 H7
Shajing China 22°44N 113°48E 33 F10
Shakargarh Pakistan 32°17N 75°10E 42 C6
Shakawe Botswana 18°28S 21°49E 56 B3
Shaker Heights U.S.A. 41°28N 81°32W 82 E3
Shakhtersk Russia 49°10N 142°8E 29 E15
Shakhty Russia 47°40N 40°16E 19 E7
Shakhunya Russia 57°40N 46°46E 18 C8
Shaki Nigeria 8°41N 3°21E 50 G6
Shaksam Valley Asia 36°0N 76°20E 43 A7
Shallow Lake Canada 44°36N 81°5W 82 B3
Shalqar Kazakhstan 47°48N 59°39E 28 E6
Shaluli Shan China 30°40N 99°55E 41 D21
Shām Iran 26°39N 57°21E 45 E8
Shām, Bādiyat ash Asia 32°0N 40°0E 44 C3
Shamal Sīnī □ Egypt 30°30N 33°30E 46 E2
Shamattawa Canada 55°51N 92°5W 72 A1
Shamattawa → Canada 55°1N 85°23W 72 A2
Shamil Iran 27°30N 56°55E 45 E8
Shāmkūh Iran 35°47N 57°50E 45 C8
Shamli India 29°32N 77°18E 42 E7
Shammar, Jabal Si. Arabia 27°40N 41°0E 44 E4
Shamo = Gobi Asia 44°0N 110°0E 34 C6
Shamo, L. Ethiopia 5°45N 37°30E 47 F2
Shamokin U.S.A. 40°47N 76°34W 83 F8
Shamrock Canada 45°23N 76°50W 83 A8
Shamrock U.S.A. 35°13N 100°15W 84 D4
Shamva Zimbabwe 17°20S 31°32E 55 F3
Shan □ Burma 21°30N 98°30E 41 J21
Shan Xian China 34°50N 116°5E 34 G9
Shanchengzhen China 42°20N 125°20E 35 C13
Shāndak Iran 28°28N 60°27E 45 D9
Shandon U.S.A. 35°39N 120°23W 78 K6
Shandong □ China 36°0N 118°0E 35 G10
Shandong Bandao China 37°0N 121°0E 35 F11
Shandur Pass Pakistan 36°4N 72°31E 43 A5
Shang Xian = Shangzhou
China 33°50N 109°58E 34 H5
Shangalowe
Dem. Rep. of the Congo 10°50S 26°30E 55 E2
Shangani Zimbabwe 19°41S 29°20E 57 B4
Shangani → Zimbabwe 18°41S 27°10E 55 F2
Shangbancheng China 40°50N 118°1E 35 D10
Shangdu China 41°30N 113°30E 34 D7
Shanghai China 31°15N 121°26E 33 C7
Shanghe China 37°20N 117°10E 35 F9
Shangnan China 33°32N 110°50E 34 H6
Shangqiu China 34°26N 115°36E 34 G8

Shangrao China 28°25N 117°59E 33 D6
Shangri-La = Zhongdian
China 27°48N 99°42E 32 D4
Shangshui China 33°42N 114°35E 33 C6
Shangzhi China 45°22N 127°56E 35 B14
Shangzhou China 33°50N 109°58E 34 H5
Shanhetun China 44°33N 127°15E 35 B14
Shanklin U.K. 50°38N 1°11W 13 G6
Shannon N.Z. 40°33S 175°25E 59 D5
Shannon → Ireland 52°35N 9°30W 10 D2
Shannon ✈ (SNN)
Ireland 52°42N 8°57W 10 D3
Shannon, Mouth of the
Ireland 52°30N 9°55W 10 D2
Shannon △ Australia 34°35S 116°25E 61 F2
Shannonbridge Ireland 53°17N 8°3W 10 C3
Shansi = Shanxi □ China 37°0N 112°0E 34 F7
Shantar, Ostrov Bolshoy
Russia 55°9N 137°40E 29 D14
Shantipur India 23°17N 88°25E 43 H13
Shantou China 23°18N 116°40E 33 D6
Shantung = Shandong □
China 36°0N 118°0E 35 G10
Shanxi □ China 37°0N 112°0E 34 F7
Shanyang China 33°31N 109°55E 34 H5
Shanyin China 39°25N 112°56E 34 E7
Shaoguan China 24°48N 113°35E 33 D6
Shaoxing China 30°0N 120°35E 33 D7
Shaoyang China 27°14N 111°25E 33 D6
Shap U.K. 54°32N 2°40W 12 C5
Shapinsay U.K. 59°3N 2°51W 11 B6
Shaqra' Si. Arabia 25°15N 45°16E 44 E5
Shaqra' Yemen 13°22N 45°44E 47 E4
Sharafkhāneh Iran 38°11N 45°29E 44 B5
Sharbot Lake Canada 44°46N 76°41W 83 B8
Shari Japan 43°55N 144°40E 30 C12
Sharjah = Ash Shāriqah
U.A.E. 25°23N 55°26E 45 E7
Shark B. Australia 25°30S 113°32E 61 E1
Shark Bay △ Australia 25°30S 113°30E 61 E1
Sharm el Sheikh Egypt 27°53N 34°18E 51 C12
Sharon Canada 44°6N 79°26W 82 B5
Sharon Mass., U.S.A. 42°7N 71°11W 83 D13
Sharon Pa., U.S.A. 41°14N 80°31W 82 E4
Sharon Springs Kans.,
U.S.A. 38°54N 101°45W 80 F3
Sharon Springs N.Y.,
U.S.A. 42°48N 74°37W 83 D10
Sharp Pt. Australia 10°58S 142°43E 62 A3
Sharpe L. Canada 54°24N 93°40W 72 B1
Sharpsville U.S.A. 41°15N 80°29W 82 E4
Sharqi, Al Jabal ash
Lebanon 33°40N 36°10E 46 B5
Sharya Russia 58°22N 45°20E 18 C8
Shashemene Ethiopia 7°13N 38°33E 47 F2
Shashi Botswana 21°15S 27°27E 57 C4
Shashi China 30°25N 112°14E 33 C6
Shashi → Africa 21°14S 29°20E 55 G2
Shasta, Mt. U.S.A. 41°25N 122°12W 76 F2
Shasta L. U.S.A. 40°43N 122°25W 76 F2
Shatsky Rise Pac. Oc. 34°0N 157°0E 64 D7
Shatt al Arab Asia 29°57N 48°34E 45 D6
Shaunavon Canada 49°35N 108°25W 71 D7
Shaver L. U.S.A. 37°9N 119°18W 78 H7
Shaw → Australia 20°21S 119°17E 60 D2
Shaw I. Australia 20°30S 149°2E 62 b
Shawanaga Canada 45°31N 80°17W 82 A4
Shawangunk Mts.
U.S.A. 41°35N 74°30W 83 E10
Shawano U.S.A. 44°47N 88°36W 80 C9
Shawinigan Canada 46°35N 72°50W 72 C5
Shawmari, J. ash Jordan 30°35N 36°35E 46 E5
Shawnee U.S.A. 35°20N 96°55W 84 D6
Shay Gap Australia 20°30S 120°10E 60 D3
Shaybārā Si. Arabia 25°26N 36°47E 44 E3
Shaykh, J. ash Lebanon 33°25N 35°50E 46 B4
Shaykh Miskīn Syria 32°49N 36°9E 46 C5
Shaykh Sa'd Iraq 32°34N 46°17E 44 C5
Shāzand Iran 33°56N 49°24E 45 C6
She Xian China 36°30N 113°40E 34 F7
Shebele = Shabeelle →
Somali Rep. 2°0N 44°0E 47 G3
Sheboygan U.S.A. 43°46N 87°45W 80 D10
Shediac Canada 46°14N 64°32W 73 C7
Sheelin, L. Ireland 53°48N 7°20W 10 C4
Sheenjek → U.S.A. 66°45N 144°33W 74 B11
Sheep Haven Ireland 55°11N 7°52W 10 A4
Sheep Range U.S.A. 36°35N 115°15W 79 J11
Sheerness U.K. 51°26N 0°47E 13 F8
Sheet Harbour Canada 44°56N 62°31W 73 D7
Sheffield U.K. 53°23N 1°28W 12 D6
Sheffield Ala., U.S.A. 34°46N 87°41W 85 D11
Sheffield Mass., U.S.A. 42°5N 73°21W 83 D11
Sheffield Pa., U.S.A. 41°42N 79°3W 82 E5
Sheikhpura India 25°9N 85°53E 43 G11
Shekhupura Pakistan 31°42N 73°58E 42 D5
Shekou China 22°30N 113°55E 33 G10
Shelburne N.S., Canada 43°47N 65°20W 73 D6
Shelburne Ont., Canada 44°4N 80°15W 82 B4
Shelburne U.S.A. 44°23N 73°14W 83 B11
Shelburne B. Australia 11°50S 142°50E 62 A3
Shelburne Falls U.S.A. 42°36N 72°45W 83 D12
Shelby Mich., U.S.A. 43°37N 86°22W 80 D10
Shelby Miss., U.S.A. 33°57N 90°46W 85 E9
Shelby Mont., U.S.A. 48°30N 111°51W 76 B8
Shelby N.C., U.S.A. 35°17N 81°32W 85 D14
Shelby Ohio, U.S.A. 40°53N 82°40W 82 F2
Shelbyville Ill., U.S.A. 39°24N 88°48W 80 F10
Shelbyville Ind., U.S.A. 39°31N 85°47W 81 F11
Shelbyville Ky., U.S.A. 38°13N 85°14W 81 F11
Shelbyville Tenn.,
U.S.A. 35°29N 86°28W 85 D11
Sheldon U.S.A. 43°11N 95°51W 80 D6
Shelikhova, Zaliv
Russia 59°30N 157°0E 29 D16
Shelikof Strait U.S.A. 57°30N 155°0W 74 D9
Shell Lakes Australia 29°20S 127°30E 61 E4

Shellbrook Canada 53°13N 106°24W 71 C7
Shellharbour Australia 34°31S 150°51E 63 E5
Shelter I. U.S.A. 41°4N 72°20W 83 E12
Shelton Conn., U.S.A. 41°19N 73°5W 83 E11
Shelton Wash., U.S.A. 47°13N 123°6W 78 C3
Shen Xian China 36°15N 115°40E 34 F8
Shenandoah Iowa,
U.S.A. 40°46N 95°22W 80 E6
Shenandoah Pa., U.S.A. 40°49N 76°12W 83 F8
Shenandoah Va.,
U.S.A. 38°29N 78°37W 81 F14
Shenandoah → U.S.A. 39°19N 77°44W 81 F15
Shenandoah △ U.S.A. 38°35N 78°22W 81 F14
Shenchi China 39°8N 112°10E 34 E7
Shendam Nigeria 8°49N 9°30E 50 G7
Shendi Sudan 16°46N 33°22E 51 E12
Shengfang China 39°3N 116°42E 34 E9
Shenjingzi China 44°40N 124°30E 35 B13
Shenmu China 38°50N 110°29E 34 E6
Shenqiu China 33°25N 115°5E 34 H8
Shensi = Shaanxi □
China 35°0N 109°0E 34 G5
Shenyang China 41°48N 123°27E 35 D12
Shenzhen China 22°32N 114°5E 33 F10
Shenzhen ✈ (SZX)
China 22°41N 113°49E 33 F10
Shenzhen Shuiku China 22°34N 114°8E 33 F11
Shenzhen Wan China 22°27N 113°55E 33 G10
Sheo India 26°11N 71°15E 42 F4
Sheopur Kalan India 25°40N 76°40E 42 G7
Shepparton Australia 36°23S 145°26E 63 F4
Sheppey, I. of U.K. 51°25N 0°48E 13 F8
Shepton Mallet U.K. 51°11N 2°33W 13 F5
Sheqi China 33°12N 112°57E 34 H7
Sher Qila Pakistan 36°7N 74°2E 43 A6
Sherborne U.K. 50°57N 2°31W 13 G5
Sherbro I. S. Leone 7°30N 12°40W 50 G3
Sherbrooke N.S., Canada 45°8N 61°59W 73 C7
Sherbrooke Qué.,
Canada 45°28N 71°57W 83 A13
Sherburne U.S.A. 42°41N 75°30W 83 D9
Shergarh India 26°20N 72°18E 42 F5
Sherghati India 24°34N 84°47E 43 G11
Sheridan Ark., U.S.A. 34°19N 92°24W 84 D8
Sheridan Wyo., U.S.A. 44°48N 106°58W 76 D10
Sheringham U.K. 52°56N 1°13E 12 E9
Sherkin I. Ireland 51°28N 9°26W 10 E2
Sherkot India 29°22N 78°35E 43 E8
Sherlovaya Gora
Russia 50°34N 116°15E 29 D12
Sherman N.Y., U.S.A. 42°9N 79°35W 82 D5
Sherman Tex., U.S.A. 33°38N 96°36W 84 E6
Sherpur India 25°34N 83°47E 43 G10
Sherridon Canada 55°8N 101°5W 71 B8
Sherwood Forest U.K. 53°6N 1°7W 12 D6
Sherwood Park Canada 53°31N 113°19W 70 C6
Sheslay → Canada 58°48N 132°5W 70 B2
Shethanei L. Canada 58°48N 97°50W 71 B9
Shetland □ U.K. 60°30N 1°30W 11 A7
Shetland Is. U.K. 60°30N 1°30W 11 A7
Shetrunji → India 21°19N 72°7E 42 J5
Sheung Shui China 22°31N 114°7E 33 F11
Shey-Phoksundo △
Nepal 29°30N 82°45E 43 E10
Sheyenne → U.S.A. 47°2N 96°50W 80 B5
Shiashkotan, Ostrov
Russia 48°49N 154°6E 29 E16
Shibām Yemen 15°59N 48°36E 47 D4
Shibata Japan 37°57N 139°20E 30 F9
Shibecha Japan 43°17N 144°36E 30 C12
Shibetsu Japan 44°10N 142°23E 30 B11
Shibogama L. Canada 53°35N 88°15W 72 B2
Shibushi Japan 31°25N 131°8E 31 J5
Shickshinny U.S.A. 41°9N 76°9W 83 E8
Shickshock Mts. = Chic-Chocs,
Mts. Canada 48°55N 66°0W 73 C6
Shidao China 36°50N 122°25E 35 F12
Shido Japan 34°19N 134°10E 31 G7
Shiel, L. U.K. 56°48N 5°34W 11 E3
Shield, C. Australia 13°20S 136°20E 62 A2
Shīeli Kazakhstan 44°20N 66°15E 28 E7
Shiga □ Japan 35°20N 136°0E 31 G8
Shiguaigou China 40°52N 110°15E 34 D6
Shihchiachuangi = Shijiazhuang
China 38°2N 114°28E 34 E8
Shihezi China 44°15N 86°2E 32 B3
Shijiazhuang China 38°2N 114°28E 34 E8
Shikarpur India 28°17N 78°7E 42 E8
Shikarpur Pakistan 27°57N 68°39E 42 F3
Shikohabad India 27°6N 78°36E 43 F8
Shikoku □ Japan 33°30N 133°30E 31 H6
Shikoku-Sanchi Japan 33°30N 133°30E 31 H6
Shikotan, Ostrov Asia 43°47N 146°44E 29 E15
Shikotsu-Ko Japan 42°45N 141°25E 30 C10
Shikotsu-Tōya △ Japan 42°44N 145°9E 30 C10
Shiliguri India 26°45N 88°25E 41 F16
Shiliu = Changjiang
China 19°20N 108°55E 38 C7
Shilka Russia 52°0N 115°55E 29 D12
Shilka → Russia 53°20N 121°26E 29 D13
Shillelagh Ireland 52°45N 6°32W 10 D5
Shillington U.S.A. 40°18N 75°58W 83 F9
Shillong India 25°35N 91°53E 41 G17
Shilo West Bank 32°4N 35°18E 46 C4
Shilou China 37°0N 110°48E 34 F6
Shimabara Japan 32°48N 130°20E 31 H5
Shimada Japan 34°49N 138°10E 31 G9
Shimane □ Japan 35°0N 132°30E 31 G6
Shimanovsk Russia 52°15N 127°30E 29 D13
Shimba Hills △ Kenya 4°14S 39°25E 54 C4
Shimbiris Somali Rep. 10°44N 47°14E 47 E4
Shimizu Japan 35°0N 138°30E 31 G9
Shimla India 31°2N 77°9E 42 D7
Shimodate Japan 36°20N 139°55E 31 F9
Shimoga = Shimoga
India 13°57N 75°32E 40 N9
Shimoni Kenya 4°38S 39°20E 54 C4
Shimonoseki Japan 33°58N 130°55E 31 H5

Shimpuru Rapids
Namibia 17°45S 19°55E 56 B2
Shin, L. U.K. 58°5N 4°30W 11 C4
Shinano-Gawa →
Japan 36°50N 138°30E 31 F9
Shināş Oman 24°46N 56°28E 45 E8
Shindand Afghan. 33°12N 62°8E 40 C3
Shinglehouse U.S.A. 41°58N 78°12W 82 E6
Shingū Japan 33°40N 135°55E 31 H7
Shingwidzi S. Africa 23°5S 31°25E 57 C5
Shinjō Japan 38°46N 140°18E 30 E10
Shinkolobwe
Dem. Rep. of the Congo 11°10S 26°40E 52 G5
Shinshār Syria 34°36N 36°43E 46 A5
Shinyanga Tanzania 3°45S 33°27E 54 C3
Shinyanga □ Tanzania 3°50S 34°0E 54 C3
Shio-no-Misaki Japan 33°25N 135°45E 31 H7
Shiogama Japan 38°19N 141°1E 30 E10
Shiojiri Japan 36°6N 137°58E 31 F8
Shipchenski Prokhod
Bulgaria 42°45N 25°15E 23 C11
Shiping China 23°45N 102°23E 32 D5
Shippagan Canada 47°45N 64°45W 73 C7
Shippensburg U.S.A. 40°3N 77°31W 82 F7
Shippenville U.S.A. 41°15N 79°28W 82 E5
Shiprock U.S.A. 36°47N 108°41W 77 H9
Shiqma, N. → Israel 31°37N 34°30E 46 D3
Shiquan China 33°5N 108°15E 34 H5
Shiquan He = Indus →
Pakistan 24°20N 67°47E 42 G2
Shīr Kūh Iran 31°39N 54°3E 45 D7
Shiragami-Misaki
Japan 41°24N 140°12E 30 D10
Shirakawa Fukushima,
Japan 37°7N 140°13E 31 F10
Shirakawa Gifu, Japan 36°17N 136°56E 31 F8
Shirane-San Gumma,
Japan 36°48N 139°22E 31 F9
Shirane-San Yamanashi,
Japan 35°42N 138°9E 31 G9
Shiraoi Japan 42°33N 141°21E 30 C10
Shīrāz Iran 29°42N 52°30E 45 D7
Shire → Africa 17°42S 35°19E 55 F4
Shiretoko-Misaki
Japan 44°21N 145°20E 30 B12
Shirinab → Pakistan 30°15N 66°28E 42 D2
Shiriya-Zaki Japan 41°25N 141°30E 30 D10
Shiroishi Japan 38°0N 140°37E 30 F10
Shirshov Ridge Pac. Oc. 58°0N 170°0E 64 B8
Shīrvān Iran 37°30N 57°50E 45 B8
Shirwa, L. = Chilwa, L.
Malawi 15°15S 35°40E 55 F4
Shishaldin Volcano
U.S.A. 54°45N 163°58W 74 E7
Shivamogga = Shimoga
India 13°57N 75°32E 40 N9
Shivpuri India 25°26N 77°42E 42 G7
Shixian China 43°5N 129°50E 35 C15
Shiyan China 22°42N 113°54E 33 F10
Shiyan Shuiku China 22°42N 113°54E 33 F10
Shizuishan China 39°15N 106°50E 34 E4
Shizuoka Japan 34°57N 138°24E 31 G9
Shizuoka □ Japan 35°15N 138°40E 31 G9
Shklov = Shklow
Belarus 54°16N 30°15E 17 A16
Shklow Belarus 54°16N 30°15E 17 A16
Shkumbini → Albania 41°2N 19°31E 23 D8
Shmidta, Ostrov Russia 81°0N 91°0E 29 A10
Shō-Gawa → Japan 36°47N 137°4E 31 F8
Shoal L. Canada 49°33N 95°1W 71 D9
Shoal Lake Canada 50°30N 100°35W 71 C8
Shōdo-Shima Japan 34°30N 134°15E 31 G7
Sholapur = Solapur
India 17°43N 75°56E 40 L9
Shōmrōn West Bank 32°15N 35°13E 46 C4
Shoreham by Sea U.K. 50°50N 0°16W 13 G7
Shori → Pakistan 28°29N 69°44E 42 E3
Shorkot Pakistan 30°50N 72°0E 42 D4
Shorkot Road Pakistan 30°47N 72°15E 42 D5
Shoshone Calif.,
U.S.A. 35°58N 116°16W 79 K10
Shoshone Idaho, U.S.A. 42°56N 114°25W 76 E6
Shoshone L. U.S.A. 44°22N 110°43W 76 D8
Shoshone Mts. U.S.A. 39°20N 117°25W 76 G5
Shoshong Botswana 22°56S 26°31E 56 C4
Shoshoni U.S.A. 43°14N 108°7W 76 E9
Shouguang China 37°52N 118°45E 35 F10
Shouyang China 37°54N 113°8E 34 F7
Show Low U.S.A. 34°15N 110°2W 77 J8
Shreveport U.S.A. 32°31N 93°45W 84 E8
Shrewsbury U.K. 52°43N 2°45W 13 E5
Shri Mohangarh India 27°17N 71°18E 42 F4
Shrirampur India 22°44N 88°21E 43 H13
Shropshire □ U.K. 52°36N 2°45W 13 E5
Shū Kazakhstan 43°36N 73°42E 28 E8
Shuangcheng China 45°20N 126°15E 35 B14
Shuanggou China 34°2N 117°30E 35 G9
Shuangliao China 43°29N 123°30E 35 C12
Shuangshanzi China 40°20N 119°8E 35 D10
Shuangyang China 43°28N 125°40E 35 C13
Shuangyashan China 46°28N 131°5E 33 B8
Shuguri Falls Tanzania 8°33S 37°22E 54 D4
Shuiye China 36°7N 114°8E 34 F8
Shujalpur India 23°18N 76°46E 42 H7
Shukpa Kunzang India 34°22N 78°22E 43 B8
Shulan China 44°28N 127°0E 35 B14
Shule China 39°25N 76°3E 32 C2
Shule He → China 40°20N 92°50E 32 B7
Shumagin Is. U.S.A. 55°7N 160°30W 74 D7
Shumen Bulgaria 43°18N 26°55E 23 C12
Shumikha Russia 55°10N 63°15E 28 D7
Shungnak U.S.A. 66°52N 157°9W 74 B7
Shuo Xian = Shuozhou
China 39°20N 112°33E 34 E7

Shūr → Fārs, Iran 28°30N 55°0E 45 D7
Shūr → Kermān, Iran 30°52N 57°37E 45 D8
Shūr → Yazd, Iran 31°45N 55°15E 45 D7
Shūr Āb Iran 34°23N 51°11E 45 C6
Shūr Gaz Iran 29°10N 59°20E 45 D8
Shūrāb Iran 33°43N 56°29E 45 C8
Shūrjestān Iran 31°24N 52°25E 45 D7
Shurugwi Zimbabwe 19°40S 30°0E 55 F3
Shūsf Iran 31°50N 60°5E 45 D9
Shūshtar Iran 32°0N 48°50E 45 D6
Shuswap L. Canada 50°55N 119°3W 70 C5
Shuyang China 34°10N 118°42E 35 G10
Shūzū Iran 29°52N 54°30E 45 D7
Shwebo Burma 22°30N 95°45E 41 H19
Shwegu Burma 24°15N 96°26E 41 G20
Shweli → Burma 23°45N 96°45E 41 H20
Shymkent Kazakhstan 42°18N 69°36E 28 E7
Shyok India 34°13N 78°12E 43 B8
Shyok → Pakistan 35°13N 75°53E 43 B6
Si Kiang = Xi Jiang →
China 22°5N 113°20E 33 D6
Si Lanna △ Thailand 19°17N 99°12E 38 C2
Si Nakarin Res. Thailand 14°35N 99°0E 38 E2
Si-ngan = Xi'an China 34°15N 109°0E 34 G5
Si Prachan Thailand 14°37N 100°9E 38 E3
Si Racha Thailand 13°10N 100°48E 38 F3
Si Xian China 33°30N 117°50E 35 H9
Siachen Glacier Asia 35°20N 77°30E 43 B7
Siahaf → Pakistan 29°3N 68°57E 42 E3
Siahan Range Pakistan 27°30N 64°40E 40 F4
Siaksriindrapura
Indonesia 0°51N 102°0E 36 D2
Sialkot Pakistan 32°32N 74°30E 42 C6
Siam = Thailand ■ Asia 16°0N 102°0E 38 E4
Sian = Xi'an China 34°15N 109°0E 34 G5
Sian Ka'an △ Mexico 19°35N 87°40W 87 D7
Siantan Indonesia 3°10N 106°15E 36 D3
Siargao I. Phil. 9°52N 126°3E 37 C7
Siari Pakistan 34°55N 76°40E 43 B7
Siasi Phil. 5°34N 120°50E 37 C6
Siau Indonesia 2°50N 125°25E 37 D7
Šiauliai Lithuania 55°56N 23°15E 9 J20
Sibâi, Gebel el Egypt 25°45N 34°10E 44 E2
Sibang Indonesia 8°34S 115°13E 37 K18
Sibay Russia 52°42N 58°39E 18 D10
Sibayi, L. S. Africa 27°20S 32°45E 57 D5
Šibenik Croatia 43°48N 15°54E 22 C6
Siberia = Sibirskiy □
Russia 58°0N 90°0E 29 D10
Siberia Russia 60°0N 100°0E 4 D13
Siberut Indonesia 1°30S 99°0E 36 E1
Sibi Pakistan 29°30N 67°54E 42 E2
Sibil = Oksibil Indonesia 4°59S 140°35E 37 E10
Sibiloi △ Kenya 4°0N 36°20E 54 B4
Sibiti Congo 3°38S 13°19E 52 E2
Sibiu Romania 45°45N 24°9E 17 F13
Sibley U.S.A. 43°24N 95°45W 80 D6
Sibolga Indonesia 1°42N 98°45E 36 D1
Siborongborong Indonesia 2°13N 98°59E 39 L2
Sibsagar India 27°0N 94°36E 41 F19
Sibu Malaysia 2°18N 111°49E 36 D4
Sibuco Phil. 7°20N 122°10E 37 C6
Sibuguey B. Phil. 7°50N 122°45E 37 C6
Sibut C.A.R. 5°46N 19°10E 52 C3
Sibutu Phil. 4°45N 119°30E 37 D5
Sibutu Passage E. Indies 4°50N 120°0E 37 D5
Sibuyan I. Phil. 12°25N 122°40E 37 B6
Sibuyan Sea Phil. 12°30N 122°20E 37 B6
Sicamous Canada 50°49N 119°0W 70 C5
Siccus → Australia 31°55S 139°17E 63 E2
Sichon Thailand 9°0N 99°54E 39 H2
Sichuan □ China 30°30N 103°0E 32 C5
Sicilia Italy 37°30N 14°30E 22 F6
Sicily = Sicilia Italy 37°30N 14°30E 22 F6
Sicily, Str. of Medit. S. 37°35N 11°56E 22 F4
Sico → Honduras 15°58N 84°58W 88 C3
Sicuani Peru 14°21S 71°10W 92 F4
Sidári Greece 39°47N 19°41E 25 A3
Siddhapur India 23°56N 72°25E 42 H5
Siddipet India 18°5N 78°51E 40 K11
Sideros, Akra Greece 35°19N 26°19E 25 D8
Sidhauli India 27°17N 80°50E 43 F9
Sidhi India 24°25N 81°53E 43 G9
Sidi-bel-Abbès Algeria 35°13N 0°39W 50 A5
Sidi Ifni Morocco 29°29N 10°12W 50 C3
Sidikalang Indonesia 2°45N 98°19E 39 L2
Sidlaw Hills U.K. 56°32N 3°2W 11 E5
Sidley, Mt. Antarctica 77°2S 126°2W 5 D14
Sidmouth U.K. 50°40N 3°15W 13 G4
Sidmouth, C. Australia 13°25S 143°36E 62 A3
Sidney Canada 48°39N 123°24W 78 B3
Sidney Mont., U.S.A. 47°43N 104°9W 76 C11
Sidney N.Y., U.S.A. 42°19N 75°24W 83 D9
Sidney Nebr., U.S.A. 41°8N 102°59W 80 E2
Sidney Ohio, U.S.A. 40°17N 84°9W 81 E11
Sidney Lanier, L. U.S.A. 34°10N 84°4W 85 D12
Sidoarjo Indonesia 7°27S 112°43E 37 G15
Sidon = Saydā Lebanon 33°35N 35°25E 46 B4
Sidra, G. of = Surt, Khalīj
Libya 31°40N 18°30E 51 B9
Siedlce Poland 52°10N 22°20E 17 B12
Sieg → Germany 50°46N 7°6E 16 C4
Siegen Germany 50°51N 8°0E 16 C5
Siem Pang Cambodia 14°7N 106°23E 38 E6
Siem Reap = Siemreab
Cambodia 13°20N 103°52E 38 F4
Siemreab Cambodia 13°20N 103°52E 38 F4
Siena Italy 43°19N 11°21E 22 C4
Sieradz Poland 51°37N 18°41E 17 C10
Sierpe, Bocas de la
Venezuela 10°0N 61°30W 93 L15
Sierra Blanca U.S.A. 31°11N 105°22W 84 F2
Sierra Blanca Peak
U.S.A. 33°23N 105°49W 77 K11

Sierra City *U.S.A.* 39°34N 120°38W **78** F6
Sierra Colorada
  Argentina 40°35S 67°50W **96** E3
Sierra de Agalta △
  Honduras 15°1N 85°48W **88** C2
Sierra de Bahoruco △
  Dom. Rep. 18°10N 71°25W **89** C5
Sierra de La Culata △
  Venezuela 8°45N 71°10W **89** E5
Sierra de Lancandón △
  Guatemala 16°59N 90°23W **88** C1
Sierra de las Quijadas △
  Argentina 32°29S 67°5W **94** C2
Sierra de San Luis △
  Venezuela 11°20N 69°43W **89** D6
Sierra de San Pedro Mártir △
  Mexico 31°10N 115°30W **86** A1
Sierra Gorda *Chile* 22°50S 69°15W **94** A2
Sierra Leone ■ *W. Afr.* 9°0N 12°0W **50** G3
Sierra Madre *Mexico* 16°0N 93°0W **87** D6
Sierra Madre Occidental
  Mexico 27°0N 107°0W **86** B3
Sierra Madre Oriental
  Mexico 25°0N 100°0W **86** C5
Sierra Mojada *Mexico* 27°18N 103°41W **86** B4
Sierra Nevada *Spain* 37°3N 3°15W **21** D4
Sierra Nevada *U.S.A.* 39°0N 120°30W **78** H8
Sierra Nevada △
  Venezuela 8°35N 70°45W **89** E5
Sierra Nevada de Santa Marta △
  Colombia 10°56N 73°36W **89** D5
Sierra Vista *U.S.A.* 31°33N 110°18W **77** L8
Sierraville *U.S.A.* 39°36N 120°22W **78** F6
Sifnos *Greece* 37°0N 24°45E **23** F11
Sifton *Canada* 51°21N 100°8W **71** C8
Sifton Pass *Canada* 57°52N 126°15W **70** B3
Sig *Algeria* 35°32N 0°12W **50** A5
Sigatoka *Fiji* 18°8S 177°32E **59** a
Sighetu-Marmaţiei
  Romania 47°57N 23°52E **17** E12
Sighişoara *Romania* 46°12N 24°50E **17** E13
Sigli *Indonesia* 5°25N 96°0E **36** C1
Siglufjörður *Iceland* 66°12N 18°55W **8** C4
Signal de Botrang *Belgium* 50°29N 6°4E **15** D6
Signal Pk. *U.S.A.* 33°20N 114°2W **79** M12
Signy I. *Antarctica* 60°43S 45°36W **5** C18
Sigsig *Ecuador* 3°0S 78°50W **92** D3
Sigüenza *Spain* 41°3N 2°40W **21** B4
Sigulda *Latvia* 57°10N 24°55E **9** H21
Sihora *India* 23°29N 80°6E **43** H9
Siikajoki → *Finland* 64°50N 24°43E **8** D21
Siilinjärvi *Finland* 63°4N 27°39E **8** E22
Sijarira Ra. = Chizarira
  Zimbabwe 17°36S 27°45E **55** F2
Sika *India* 22°26N 69°47E **42** H3
Sikanni Chief →
  Canada 57°47N 122°15W **70** B4
Sikao *Thailand* 7°34N 99°21E **39** J2
Sikar *India* 27°33N 75°10E **42** F6
Sikasso *Mali* 11°18N 5°35W **50** F4
Sikeston *U.S.A.* 36°53N 89°35W **80** G9
Sikhote Alin, Khrebet
  Russia 45°0N 136°0E **30** B8
Sikhote Alin Ra. = Sikhote Alin,
  Khrebet *Russia* 45°0N 136°0E **30** B8
Sikinos *Greece* 36°40N 25°8E **23** F11
Sikkim □ *India* 27°50N 88°30E **41** F16
Sil → *Spain* 42°27N 7°43W **21** A2
Silacayoapan *Mexico* 17°30N 98°9W **87** D5
Silawad *India* 21°54N 74°54E **42** J6
Silchar *India* 24°49N 92°48E **41** G18
Siler City *U.S.A.* 35°44N 79°28W **85** D15
Silesia = Śląsk *Poland* 51°0N 16°30E **16** C9
Silgarhi Doti *Nepal* 29°15N 81°0E **43** E9
Silghat *India* 26°35N 93°0E **41** F18
Silhouette *Seychelles* 4°29S 55°12E **53** b
Silifke *Turkey* 36°22N 33°58E **44** B2
Siliguri = Shiliguri *India* 26°45N 88°25E **41** F16
Siling Co *China* 31°50N 89°20E **32** C3
Silistra *Bulgaria* 44°6N 27°19E **23** B12
Silivri *Turkey* 41°4N 28°14E **23** D13
Siljan *Sweden* 60°55N 14°45E **8** F16
Silkeborg *Denmark* 56°10N 9°32E **9** H13
Silkwood *Australia* 17°45S 146°2E **62** B4
Sillajhuay, Cordillera
  Chile 19°46S 68°40W **92** G5
Sillamäe *Estonia* 59°24N 27°45E **9** G22
Silloth *U.K.* 54°52N 3°23W **12** C4
Siloam Springs *U.S.A.* 36°11N 94°32W **84** C7
Silopi *Turkey* 37°15N 42°27E **44** B4
Silsbee *U.S.A.* 30°21N 94°11W **84** F7
Šilutė *Lithuania* 55°21N 21°33E **9** J19
Silvan *Turkey* 38°7N 41°2E **44** B4
Silvani *India* 23°18N 78°25E **43** H8
Silver City *U.S.A.* 32°46N 108°17W **77** K9
Silver Cr. → *U.S.A.* 43°16N 119°13W **76** E4
Silver Creek *U.S.A.* 42°33N 79°10W **82** D5
Silver L. *U.S.A.* 38°39N 120°6W **78** G6
Silver Lake *Calif.,*
  U.S.A. 35°21N 116°7W **79** K10
Silver Lake *Oreg., U.S.A.* 43°8N 121°3W **76** E3
Silvermine Mts. *Ireland* 52°47N 8°15W **10** D3
Silverton *Colo., U.S.A.* 37°49N 107°40W **77** H10
Silverton *Tex., U.S.A.* 34°28N 101°19W **84** D4
Silvies → *U.S.A.* 43°34N 119°2W **76** E4
Simaltala *India* 24°43N 86°33E **43** G12
Simanggang = Sri Aman
  Malaysia 1°15N 111°32E **36** D4
Simard, L. *Canada* 47°40N 78°40W **72** C4
Simav *Turkey* 39°4N 28°58E **23** E13
Simba *Tanzania* 2°10S 37°36E **54** C4
Simbirsk = Ulyanovsk
  Russia 54°20N 48°25E **18** D8
Simcoe *Canada* 42°50N 80°20W **82** D4
Simcoe, L. *Canada* 44°25N 79°20W **82** B5
Simdega *India* 22°37N 84°31E **43** H11
Simeria *Romania* 45°51N 23°1E **17** F12

Simeulue *Indonesia* 2°45N 95°45E **36** D1
Simferopol *Ukraine* 44°55N 34°3E **19** F5
Sími *Greece* 36°35N 27°50E **23** F12
Simi Valley *U.S.A.* 34°16N 118°47W **79** L8
Simikot *Nepal* 30°0N 81°50E **43** E9
Simla = Shimla *India* 31°2N 77°9E **42** D7
Simlipal △ *India* 21°45N 86°30E **43** J12
Simmie *Canada* 49°56N 108°6W **71** D7
Simmler *U.S.A.* 35°21N 119°59W **79** K7
Simo älv = Simojoki →
  Finland 65°35N 25°1E **8** D21
Simojoki → *Finland* 65°35N 25°1E **8** D21
Simojovel *Mexico* 17°12N 92°38W **87** D6
Simonette → *Canada* 55°9N 118°15W **70** B5
Simonstown *S. Africa* 34°14S 18°26E **56** E2
Simpang Empat *Malaysia* 5°27N 100°29E **39** c
Simplonpass *Switz.* 46°15N 8°3E **20** C8
Simpson Desert *Australia* 25°0S 137°0E **62** D2
Simpson Desert △
  Australia 24°59S 138°21E **62** C2
Simpson Pen. *Canada* 68°34N 88°45W **69** D14
Simrishamn *Sweden* 55°33N 14°22E **9** J16
Simsbury *U.S.A.* 41°53N 72°48W **83** E12
Simushir, Ostrov
  Russia 46°50N 152°30E **29** E16
Sin Cowe I. *S. China Sea* 9°53N 114°19E **36** C4
Sina Dhago *Somali Rep.* 5°50N 47°0E **47** F4
Sinabang *Indonesia* 2°30N 96°24E **36** D1
Sinai = Es Sînâ' *Egypt* 29°0N 34°0E **46** F3
Sinai, Mt. = Mûsa, Gebel
  Egypt 28°33N 33°59E **44** D2
Sinaloa □ *Mexico* 25°0N 107°30W **86** C3
Sinaloa de Leyva
  Mexico 25°50N 108°14W **86** B3
Sinarades *Greece* 39°34N 19°51E **25** A3
Sincelejo *Colombia* 9°18N 75°24W **92** B3
Sinch'ang *N. Korea* 40°7N 128°28E **35** D15
Sinch'ŏn *N. Korea* 38°17N 125°21E **35** E13
Sinclair *U.S.A.* 41°47N 107°7W **76** F10
Sinclair Mills *Canada* 54°5N 121°40W **70** C4
Sinclairville *U.S.A.* 42°16N 79°16W **82** D5
Sincorá, Serra do *Brazil* 13°30S 41°0W **93** F10
Sind = Sindh □ *Pakistan* 26°0N 69°0E **42** G3
Sind → *Jammu & Kashmir,*
  India 34°18N 74°45E **43** B6
Sind → *Mad. P., India* 26°26N 79°13E **43** F8
Sind Sagar Doab *Pakistan* 32°0N 71°30E **42** D4
Sindangan *Phil.* 8°10N 123°5E **37** C6
Sindangbarang *Indonesia* 7°27S 107°1E **37** G12
Sinde *Zambia* 17°28S 25°51E **55** F2
Sindh □ *Pakistan* 26°0N 69°0E **42** G3
Sindri *India* 23°45N 86°42E **43** H12
Sines *Portugal* 37°56N 8°51W **21** D1
Sines, C. de *Portugal* 37°58N 8°53W **21** D1
Sineu *Spain* 39°38N 3°1E **24** B10
Sing Buri *Thailand* 14°53N 100°25E **38** E3
Singa *Sudan* 13°10N 33°57E **51** F12
Singalila △ *India* 27°10N 88°5E **43** F13
Singapore ■ *Asia* 1°17N 103°51E **39** d
Singapore, Straits of *Asia* 1°15N 104°0E **39** d
Singapore Changi ✈ (SIN)
  Singapore 1°23N 103°59E **39** M4
Singaraja *Indonesia* 8°7S 115°6E **37** J18
Singatoka = Sigatoka *Fiji* 18°8S 177°32E **59** a
Singida *Tanzania* 4°49S 34°48E **54** C3
Singida □ *Tanzania* 6°0S 34°30E **54** D3
Singkaling Hkamti
  Burma 26°0N 95°39E **41** G19
Singkang *Indonesia* 4°8S 120°1E **37** E6
Singkawang *Indonesia* 1°0N 108°57E **36** D3
Singkep *Indonesia* 0°30S 104°25E **36** E2
Singkil *Indonesia* 2°17N 97°49E **36** D1
Singleton *Australia* 32°33S 151°0E **63** E5
Singleton, Mt. *N. Terr.,*
  Australia 22°0S 130°46E **60** D5
Singleton, Mt. *W. Austral.,*
  Australia 29°27S 117°15E **61** E2
Singoli *India* 25°0N 75°22E **42** G6
Singora = Songkhla
  Thailand 7°13N 100°37E **39** J3
Sinhung *N. Korea* 40°11N 127°34E **35** D14
Siniscóla *Italy* 40°34N 9°41E **22** D3
Sinjai *Indonesia* 5°7S 120°20E **37** F6
Sinjär *Iraq* 36°19N 41°52E **44** B4
Sinkat *Sudan* 18°55N 36°49E **51** E13
Sinkiang = Xinjiang Uygur
  Zizhiqu □ *China* 42°0N 86°0E **32** C3
Sinmak *N. Korea* 38°25N 126°14E **35** E14
Sinmi-do *N. Korea* 39°33N 124°53E **35** E13
Sinnamary *Fr. Guiana* 5°25N 53°0W **93** B8
Sinni → *Italy* 40°8N 16°41E **22** D7
Sinop *Turkey* 42°1N 35°11E **19** F6
Sinor *India* 21°55N 73°20E **42** J5
Sinp'o *N. Korea* 40°0N 128°13E **35** E15
Sinsk *Russia* 61°8N 126°48E **29** C13
Sintang *Indonesia* 0°5N 111°35E **36** D4
Sinton *U.S.A.* 28°2N 97°31W **84** G6
Sintra *Portugal* 38°47N 9°25W **21** C1
Sinŭiju *N. Korea* 40°5N 124°24E **35** D13
Siocon *Phil.* 7°40N 122°10E **37** C6
Siófok *Hungary* 46°54N 18°3E **17** E10
Sion *Switz.* 46°14N 7°20E **20** C7
Sion Mills *U.K.* 54°48N 7°29W **10** B4
Sionainn = Shannon →
  Ireland 52°35N 9°30W **10** D2
Sioux Center *U.S.A.* 43°5N 96°11W **80** D5
Sioux City *U.S.A.* 42°30N 96°24W **80** D5
Sioux Falls *U.S.A.* 43°33N 96°44W **80** D5
Sioux Lookout *Canada* 50°10N 91°50W **72** B1
Sioux Narrows *Canada* 49°25N 94°10W **71** D10
Sipadan *Malaysia* 4°6N 118°38E **37** D5
Siparia *Trin. & Tob.* 10°8N 61°31W **93** K15
Siping *China* 43°8N 124°21E **35** C13
Sipiwesk L. *Canada* 55°5N 97°35W **71** B9
Siple *Antarctica* 75°0S 74°0W **5** D7
Sipra → *India* 23°55N 75°28E **42** H6

Sipura *Indonesia* 2°18S 99°40E **36** E1
Siquia → *Nic.* 12°10N 84°20W **88** D3
Siquijor *Phil.* 9°12N 123°35E **37** C6
Siquirres *Costa Rica* 10°6N 83°30W **88** D3
Şīr Abu Nu'ayr *U.A.E.* 25°20N 54°20E **45** E7
Şīr Banī Yās *U.A.E.* 24°19N 52°37E **45** E7
Sir Edward Pellew Group
  Australia 15°40S 137°10E **62** B2
Sir Graham Moore Is.
  Australia 13°53S 126°34E **60** B4
Sir James MacBrien, Mt.
  Canada 62°7N 127°41W **68** E6
Sira → *Norway* 58°23N 6°34E **9** G12
Siracusa *Italy* 37°4N 15°17E **22** F6
Sirajganj *Bangla.* 24°25N 89°47E **43** G13
Sirathu *India* 25°39N 81°19E **43** G9
Şīrdān *Iran* 36°39N 49°12E **45** B6
Siren *U.S.A.* 45°47N 92°24W **80** C7
Sirer *Spain* 38°56N 1°22E **24** C7
Siret → *Romania* 45°24N 28°1E **17** F14
Sirghāyā *Syria* 33°51N 36°8E **46** B5
Sirinat △ *Thailand* 8°6N 98°17E **39** a
Şīrjān *Iran* 29°30N 55°45E **45** D7
Sirmaur *India* 24°51N 81°23E **43** G9
Sirmilik △ *Canada* 72°50N 80°35W **69** C15
Sirohi *India* 24°52N 72°53E **42** G5
Sironj *India* 24°5N 77°39E **42** G7
Síros = Ermoupoli
  Greece 37°28N 24°57E **23** F11
Sirr, Nafud as *Si. Arabia* 25°33N 44°35E **44** E5
Sirretta Pk. *U.S.A.* 35°56N 118°19W **79** K8
Sirrī *Iran* 25°55N 54°32E **45** E7
Sirsa *India* 29°33N 75°4E **42** E6
Sirsa → *India* 26°51N 79°4E **43** F8
Sisak *Croatia* 45°30N 16°21E **16** F9
Sisaket *Thailand* 15°8N 104°23E **38** E5
Sishen *S. Africa* 27°47S 22°59E **56** D3
Sishui *Henan, China* 34°48N 113°15E **34** G7
Sishui *Shandong, China* 35°42N 117°18E **35** G9
Sisipuk L. *Canada* 55°45N 101°50W **71** B8
Sisophon *Cambodia* 13°38N 102°59E **38** F4
Sisseton *U.S.A.* 45°40N 97°3W **80** C5
Sīstān *Asia* 30°50N 61°0E **45** D9
Sīstān, Daryācheh-ye *Iran* 31°0N 61°0E **45** D9
Sīstān va Balūchestān □
  Iran 27°0N 62°0E **45** E9
Sisters *U.S.A.* 44°18N 121°33W **76** D3
Sisters, The *Seychelles* 4°16S 55°52E **53** b
Siswa Bazar *India* 27°9N 83°46E **43** F10
Sitamarhi *India* 26°37N 85°30E **43** F11
Sitampiky *Madag.* 16°41S 46°6E **57** B8
Sitapur *India* 27°38N 80°45E **43** F9
Siteki *Swaziland* 26°32S 31°58E **57** D5
Sitges *Spain* 41°17N 1°47E **21** B6
Sitia *Greece* 35°13N 26°6E **25** D8
Sitito-Ozima Ridge
  Pac. Oc. 23°0N 143°0E **64** E6
Sitka *U.S.A.* 57°3N 135°20W **70** B1
Sitoti *Botswana* 23°15S 23°40E **56** C3
Sittang Myit → *Burma* 17°20N 96°45E **41** L20
Sittard *Neths.* 51°0N 5°52E **15** C5
Sittingbourne *U.K.* 51°21N 0°45E **13** F8
Sittoung = Sittang Myit →
  Burma 17°20N 96°45E **41** L20
Sittwe *Burma* 20°18N 92°45E **41** J18
Situbondo *Indonesia* 7°42S 114°0E **37** G16
Si'umu *Samoa* 14°1S 171°48W **59** b
Siuna *Nic.* 13°37N 84°45W **88** D3
Siuri *India* 23°50N 87°34E **43** H12
Sivand *Iran* 30°5N 52°55E **45** D7
Sivas *Turkey* 39°43N 36°58E **44** B3
Siverek *Turkey* 37°50N 39°19E **44** B3
Sivomaskinskiy *Russia* 66°40N 62°35E **18** A11
Sivrihisar *Turkey* 39°30N 31°35E **19** G5
Sîwa *Egypt* 29°11N 25°31E **51** C11
Siwa, El Wâhât es *Egypt* 29°10N 25°30E **48** D6
Siwa Oasis = Sîwa, El Wâhât es
  Egypt 29°10N 25°30E **48** D6
Siwalik Range *Nepal* 28°0N 83°0E **43** F10
Siwan *India* 26°13N 84°21E **43** F11
Siwana *India* 25°38N 72°25E **42** G5
Six Cross Roads *Barbados* 13°7N 59°28W **89** g
Sixmilebridge *Ireland* 52°44N 8°46W **10** D3
Sixth Cataract *Sudan* 16°20N 32°42E **51** E12
Siyah Kuh, Kavīr-e *Iran* 32°55N 53°55E **45** C7
Siziwang Qi *China* 41°25N 111°40E **34** D6
Sjælland *Denmark* 55°30N 11°30E **9** J14
Sjumen = Shumen
  Bulgaria 43°18N 26°55E **23** C12
Skadarsko Jezero *Europe* 42°10N 19°20E **23** C8
Skaftafell △ *Iceland* 64°1N 17°0W **8** D5
Skaftafell △ *Iceland* 64°9N 16°50W **8** D5
Skagafjörður *Iceland* 65°54N 19°35W **8** D4
Skagastølstindane
  Norway 61°28N 7°52E **8** F12
Skagaströnd *Iceland* 65°50N 20°19W **8** D3
Skagen *Denmark* 57°43N 10°35E **9** H14
Skagerrak *Denmark* 57°30N 9°0E **9** H13
Skagit → *U.S.A.* 48°23N 122°22W **78** B4
Skagway *U.S.A.* 59°28N 135°19W **68** F4
Skala-Podilska *Ukraine* 48°50N 26°15E **17** D14
Skalat *Ukraine* 49°23N 25°55E **17** D13
Skåne *Sweden* 55°59N 13°30E **9** J15
Skaneateles *U.S.A.* 42°57N 76°26W **83** D8
Skaneateles L. *U.S.A.* 42°51N 76°22W **83** D8
Skardu *Pakistan* 35°20N 75°44E **43** B6
Skarżysko-Kamienna
  Poland 51°7N 20°52E **17** C11
Skeena → *Canada* 54°9N 130°5W **70** C2
Skeena Mts. *Canada* 56°40N 128°30W **70** B3
Skegness *U.K.* 53°9N 0°20E **12** D8
Skeldon = Corriverton
  Guyana 5°55N 57°20W **92** B7
Skeleton Coast *Namibia* 20°0S 13°0E **53** J2
Skeleton Coast △ *Namibia* 20°0S 13°20E **56** B1
Skellefteå *Sweden* 64°45N 20°50E **8** D19
Skellefteälven →
  Sweden 64°45N 21°10E **8** D19
Skelleftehamn *Sweden* 64°40N 21°9E **8** D19

Skerries, The *U.K.* 53°25N 4°36W **12** D3
Ski *Norway* 59°43N 10°52E **9** G14
Skiathos *Greece* 39°12N 23°30E **23** E10
Skiddaw *U.K.* 54°39N 3°9W **12** C4
Skidegate *Canada* 53°15N 132°1W **70** C2
Skien *Norway* 59°12N 9°35E **9** G13
Skierniewice *Poland* 51°58N 20°10E **17** C11
Skikda *Algeria* 36°50N 6°58E **50** A7
Skilloura *Cyprus* 35°14N 33°10E **25** D12
Skipton *U.K.* 53°58N 2°3W **12** D5
Skirmish Pt. *Australia* 11°59S 134°17E **62** A1
Skiros *Greece* 38°55N 24°34E **23** E11
Skive *Denmark* 56°33N 9°2E **9** H13
Skjálfandafljót → *Iceland* 65°59N 17°25W **8** D5
Skjálfandi *Iceland* 66°5N 17°30W **8** C5
Skole *Ukraine* 49°3N 23°30E **17** D12
Skopelos *Greece* 39°9N 23°47E **23** E10
Skopi *Greece* 35°11N 26°2E **25** D8
Skopje *Macedonia* 42°1N 21°26E **23** C9
Skövde *Sweden* 58°24N 13°50E **9** G15
Skovorodino *Russia* 54°0N 123°46E **29** D13
Skowhegan *U.S.A.* 44°46N 69°43W **81** C19
Skull *Ireland* 51°32N 9°34W **10** E2
Skunk → *U.S.A.* 40°42N 91°7W **80** E8
Skuodas *Lithuania* 56°16N 21°33E **9** H19
Skvyra *Ukraine* 49°44N 29°40E **17** D15
Skye *U.K.* 57°15N 6°10W **11** D2
Skykomish *U.S.A.* 47°42N 121°22W **78** C5
Skyros = Skiros *Greece* 38°55N 24°34E **23** E11
Slade Point *Australia* 21°4S 149°13E **62** b
Slade Pt. *Australia* 21°5S 149°13E **62** b
Slættaratindur *Faroe Is.* 62°18N 7°1W **8** E9
Slagelse *Denmark* 55°23N 11°19E **9** J14
Slamet *Indonesia* 7°16S 109°8E **37** G13
Slane *Ireland* 53°42N 6°33W **10** C5
Slaney → *Ireland* 52°26N 6°33W **10** D5
Slangberge *S. Africa* 31°32S 20°48E **56** E3
Śląsk *Poland* 51°0N 16°30E **16** C9
Slate Is. *Canada* 48°40N 87°0W **72** C2
Slatina *Romania* 44°28N 24°22E **17** F13
Slatington *U.S.A.* 40°45N 75°37W **83** F9
Slaton *U.S.A.* 33°26N 101°39W **84** E4
Slave → *Canada* 61°18N 113°39W **70** A6
Slave Coast *W. Afr.* 6°0N 2°30E **50** G6
Slave Lake *Canada* 55°17N 114°43W **70** B6
Slavgorod *Russia* 53°1N 78°37E **28** D8
Slavonski Brod *Croatia* 45°11N 18°1E **23** B8
Slavuta *Ukraine* 50°15N 27°2E **17** C14
Slavyanka *Russia* 42°53N 131°21E **30** C5
Slavyansk = Slovyansk
  Ukraine 48°55N 37°36E **19** E6
Slawharad *Belarus* 53°27N 31°0E **17** B16
Sleaford *U.K.* 53°0N 0°24E **12** D7
Sleaford B. *Australia* 34°55S 135°45E **63** E2
Sleat, Sd. of *U.K.* 57°5N 5°47W **11** D3
Sleeper Is. *Canada* 58°30N 81°0W **69** F15
Sleeping Bear Dunes ○
  U.S.A. 44°50N 86°5W **80** C10
Sleepy Eye *U.S.A.* 44°18N 94°43W **80** C6
Slemon L. *Canada* 63°13N 116°4W **70** A5
Slide Mt. *U.S.A.* 42°0N 74°25W **83** E10
Slidell *U.S.A.* 30°17N 89°47W **85** F10
Sliema *Malta* 35°55N 14°30E **25** D2
Slieve Aughty *Ireland* 53°4N 8°30W **10** C3
Slieve Bloom *Ireland* 53°4N 7°40W **10** C4
Slieve Donard *U.K.* 54°11N 5°55W **10** B6
Slieve Gamph *Ireland* 54°6N 9°0W **10** B3
Slieve Gullion *U.K.* 54°7N 6°26W **10** B5
Slieve League *Ireland* 54°40N 8°42W **10** B3
Slieve Mish *Ireland* 52°12N 9°50W **10** D2
Slievenamon *Ireland* 52°25N 7°34W **10** D4
Sligeach = Sligo *Ireland* 54°16N 8°28W **10** B3
Sligo *Ireland* 54°16N 8°28W **10** B3
Sligo *U.S.A.* 41°6N 79°29W **82** E5
Sligo □ *Ireland* 54°8N 8°42W **10** B3
Sligo B. *Ireland* 54°18N 8°40W **10** B3
Slippery Rock *U.S.A.* 41°3N 80°3W **82** E4
Slite *Sweden* 57°42N 18°48E **9** H18
Sliven *Bulgaria* 42°42N 26°19E **23** C12
Sloan *U.S.A.* 35°57N 115°13W **79** K11
Sloansville *U.S.A.* 42°45N 74°22W **83** D10
Slobodskoy *Russia* 58°40N 50°6E **18** C9
Slobozia *Romania* 44°34N 27°23E **17** F14
Slocan *Canada* 49°48N 117°28W **70** D5
Slonim *Belarus* 53°4N 25°19E **17** B13
Slough *U.K.* 51°30N 0°36W **13** F7
Slough □ *U.K.* 51°30N 0°36W **13** F7
Sloughhouse *U.S.A.* 38°26N 121°12W **78** G5
Slovak Rep. ■ *Europe* 48°30N 20°0E **17** D10
Slovakia = Slovak Rep. ■
  Europe 48°30N 20°0E **17** D10
Slovakian Ore Mts. = Slovenské
  Rudohorie *Slovak Rep.* 48°45N 20°0E **17** D10
Slovenia ■ *Europe* 45°58N 14°30E **16** F8
Slovenija = Slovenia ■
  Europe 45°58N 14°30E **16** F8
Slovenská = Slovak Rep. ■
  Europe 48°30N 20°0E **17** D10
Slovenské Rudohorie
  Slovak Rep. 48°45N 20°0E **17** D10
Slovyansk *Ukraine* 48°55N 37°36E **19** E6
Sluch → *Ukraine* 51°37N 26°38E **17** C14
Sluis *Neths.* 51°18N 3°23E **15** C3
Słupsk *Poland* 54°30N 17°3E **17** A9
Slurry *S. Africa* 25°49S 25°42E **56** D4
Slutsk *Belarus* 53°2N 27°31E **17** B14
Slyne Hd. *Ireland* 53°25N 10°10W **10** C1
Slyudyanka *Russia* 51°40N 103°40E **29** D11
Småland *Sweden* 57°15N 15°25E **9** H16
Smalltree L. *Canada* 61°0N 105°0W **71** A8
Smallwood Res. *Canada* 54°5N 64°30W **73** B7
Smarhon *Belarus* 54°20N 26°24E **17** A14
Smartt Syndicate Dam
  S. Africa 30°45S 23°10E **56** E3
Smartville *U.S.A.* 39°13N 121°18W **78** F5
Smeaton *Canada* 53°30N 104°49W **71** C8

Smederevo *Serbia* 44°40N 20°57E **23** B9
Smerwick Harbour
  Ireland 52°12N 10°23W **10** D1
Smethport *U.S.A.* 41°49N 78°27W **82** E6
Smidovich *Russia* 48°36N 133°49E **29** E14
Smith *Canada* 55°10N 114°0W **70** B6
Smith Center *U.S.A.* 39°47N 98°47W **80** F4
Smith I. *Canada* 60°45N 78°25W **69** E16
Smith Islands △ *Australia* 20°40S 149°9E **62** b
Smith River △ *Canada* 41°55N 124°0W **76** F1
Smithburne → *Australia* 17°3S 140°57E **62** B3
Smithers *Canada* 54°45N 127°10W **70** C3
Smithfield *S. Africa* 30°9S 26°30E **57** E4
Smithfield *N.C., U.S.A.* 35°31N 78°21W **85** D15
Smithfield *Utah, U.S.A.* 41°50N 111°50W **76** F8
Smiths Falls *Canada* 44°55N 76°0W **83** B9
Smithton *Australia* 40°53S 145°6E **63** G4
Smithton *U.S.A.* 43°6N 79°33W **82** C5
Smithville *Canada* 43°6N 79°33W **82** C5
Smithville *U.S.A.* 30°1N 97°10W **84** F6
Smoke Creek Desert
  U.S.A. 40°30N 119°40W **76** F4
Smoky → *Canada* 56°10N 117°21W **70** B5
Smoky Bay *Australia* 32°22S 134°13E **63** E1
Smoky Hill → *U.S.A.* 39°4N 96°48W **80** F5
Smoky Hills *U.S.A.* 39°15N 99°30W **80** F4
Smoky Lake *Canada* 54°10N 112°30W **70** C6
Smøla *Norway* 63°23N 8°3E **8** E13
Smolensk *Russia* 54°45N 32°5E **18** D5
Smolikas, Oros *Greece* 40°9N 20°58E **23** D9
Smolyan *Bulgaria* 41°36N 24°38E **23** D11
Smooth Rock Falls
  Canada 49°17N 81°37W **72** C3
Smoothstone L. *Canada* 54°40N 106°50W **71** C7
Smorgon = Smarhon
  Belarus 54°20N 26°24E **17** A14
Smyrna = İzmir *Turkey* 38°25N 27°8E **23** E12
Smyrna *U.S.A.* 39°18N 75°36W **81** F16
Snæfell *Iceland* 64°48N 15°34W **8** D6
Snaefell *I. of Man* 54°16N 4°27W **12** C3
Snæfellsjökull *Iceland* 64°49N 23°46W **8** D2
Snake → *U.S.A.* 46°12N 119°2W **76** C4
Snake I. *Australia* 38°47S 146°33E **63** F4
Snake Range *U.S.A.* 39°0N 114°20W **76** G6
Snake River Plain
  U.S.A. 42°50N 114°0W **76** E7
Snåsavatnet *Norway* 64°12N 12°0E **8** D15
Sneek *Neths.* 53°2N 5°40E **15** A5
Sneem *Ireland* 51°50N 9°54W **10** E2
Sneeuberge *S. Africa* 31°46S 24°20E **56** E3
Snelling *U.S.A.* 37°31N 120°26W **78** H6
Snežka *Europe* 50°41N 15°50E **16** C8
Snizort, L. *U.K.* 57°33N 6°28W **11** D2
Snøhetta *Norway* 62°19N 9°16E **8** E13
Snohomish *U.S.A.* 47°55N 122°6W **78** C4
Snoqualmie Pass
  U.S.A. 47°25N 121°25W **78** C5
Snoul *Cambodia* 12°4N 106°26E **39** F6
Snover *U.S.A.* 43°27N 82°58W **82** C2
Snow Hill *U.S.A.* 38°11N 75°24W **81** F16
Snow Lake *Canada* 54°52N 100°3W **71** C8
Snow Mt. *Calif., U.S.A.* 39°23N 122°58W **78** F4
Snow Mt. *Maine, U.S.A.* 45°18N 70°48W **83** A14
Snow Shoe *U.S.A.* 41°2N 77°57W **82** E7
Snowbird L. *Canada* 60°45S 103°0W **71** A8
Snowdon *U.K.* 53°4N 4°5W **12** D3
Snowdonia △ *U.K.* 53°7N 3°59W **12** D4
Snowdrift = Lutsel K'e
  Canada 62°24N 110°44W **71** A6
Snowdrift → *Canada* 62°24N 110°44W **71** A6
Snowflake *U.S.A.* 34°30N 110°5W **77** J8
Snowshoe Pk. *U.S.A.* 48°13N 115°41W **76** B6
Snowtown *Australia* 33°46S 138°14E **63** E2
Snowville *U.S.A.* 41°58N 112°43W **76** F7
Snowy → *Australia* 37°46S 148°30E **63** F4
Snowy Mt. *U.S.A.* 43°42N 74°23W **83** C10
Snowy Mts. *Australia* 36°30S 148°20E **63** F4
Snug Corner *Bahamas* 22°33N 73°52W **89** B5
Snug Harbour *Canada* 45°22N 80°17W **82** A4
Snyatyn *Ukraine* 48°27N 25°38E **17** D13
Snyder *Okla., U.S.A.* 34°40N 98°57W **84** D5
Snyder *Tex., U.S.A.* 32°44N 100°55W **84** E4
Soahanina *Madag.* 18°42S 44°13E **57** B7
Soalala *Madag.* 16°6S 45°20E **57** B8
Soaloka *Madag.* 18°32S 45°15E **57** B8
Soamanonga *Madag.* 23°52S 44°47E **57** C7
Soan → *Pakistan* 33°1N 71°44E **42** C4
Soanierana-Ivongo
  Madag. 16°55S 49°35E **57** B8
Soanindraniny *Madag.* 19°54S 47°14E **57** B8
Soavina *Madag.* 20°23S 46°56E **57** C8
Soavinandriana *Madag.* 19°9S 46°45E **57** B8
Sobat, Nahr → *Sudan* 9°22N 31°33E **51** G12
Sobhapur *India* 22°47N 78°17E **42** H8
Sobradinho, Represa de
  Brazil 9°30S 42°0W **93** E10
Sobral *Brazil* 3°50S 40°20W **93** D10
Soc Giang *Vietnam* 22°54N 106°1E **38** A6
Soc Trang *Vietnam* 9°37N 105°50E **39** H5
Socastee *U.S.A.* 33°41N 78°59W **85** D15
Soch'e = Shache *China* 38°20N 77°10E **32** C2
Sochi *Russia* 43°35N 39°40E **19** F6
Société, Îs. de la
  French Polynesia 17°0S 151°0W **65** J12
Society Is. = Société, Îs. de la
  French Polynesia 17°0S 151°0W **65** J12
Socompa, Portezuelo de
  Chile 24°27S 68°18W **94** A2
Socorro *N. Mex., U.S.A.* 34°4N 106°54W **77** J10
Socorro *Tex., U.S.A.* 31°39N 106°18W **84** F1
Socorro, I. *Mexico* 18°45N 110°58W **86** D2
Socotra *Yemen* 12°30N 54°0E **47** E5
Soda L. *U.S.A.* 35°10N 116°4W **79** J5
Soda Plains *India* 35°30N 79°0E **43** B8
Soda Springs *U.S.A.* 42°39N 111°36W **76** E8
Sodankylä *Finland* 67°29N 26°40E **8** C22
Soddy-Daisy *U.S.A.* 35°17N 85°10W **85** D12
Söderhamn *Sweden* 61°18N 17°10E **8** F17
Söderköping *Sweden* 58°31N 16°20E **9** G17
Södermanland *Sweden* 58°56N 16°55E **9** G17

Södertälje *Sweden* 59°12N 17°39E **9** G17
Sodiri *Sudan* 14°27N 29°0E **51** F11
Sodus *U.S.A.* 43°14N 77°4W **82** C7
Sodwana Bay △ *S. Africa* 27°35S 32°43E **57** D5
Soe *Indonesia* 9°52S 124°17E **60** A3
Soekmekaar = Morebeng
　S. Africa 23°30S 29°55E **57** C4
Soest *Neths.* 52°9N 5°19E **15** B5
Sofala △ *Mozam.* 19°30S 34°30E **57** B5
Sofia = Sofiya *Bulgaria* 42°45N 23°20E **23** C10
Sofia → *Madag.* 15°27S 47°23E **57** B8
Sofiya *Bulgaria* 42°45N 23°20E **23** C10
Sōfu-Gan *Japan* 29°49N 140°21E **31** K10
Sogamoso *Colombia* 5°43N 72°56W **92** B4
Sogār *Iran* 25°53N 58°6E **45** E8
Sogndalsfjøra *Norway* 61°14N 7°5E **8** F12
Søgne *Norway* 58°5N 7°48E **9** G12
Sognefjorden *Norway* 61°10N 5°50E **8** F11
Soh *Iran* 33°26N 51°27E **45** C6
Sohâg *Egypt* 26°33N 31°43E **51** C12
Sohagpur *India* 22°42N 78°12E **42** H8
Soignies *Belgium* 50°35N 4°5E **15** D4
Soissons *France* 49°25N 3°19E **20** B5
Sōja *Japan* 34°40N 133°45E **31** G6
Sojat *India* 25°55N 73°45E **42** G5
Sokal *Ukraine* 50°31N 24°15E **17** C13
Sokcho *S. Korea* 38°12N 128°36E **35** E15
Söke *Turkey* 37°48N 27°28E **23** F12
Sokelo
　Dem. Rep. of the Congo 9°55S 24°36E **55** D1
Sokhumi *Georgia* 43°0N 41°0E **19** F7
Soko Is. *China* 22°10N 113°54E **33** G10
Sokodé *Togo* 9°0N 1°11E **50** G6
Sokol *Russia* 59°30N 40°5E **18** C7
Sokółka *Poland* 53°25N 23°30E **17** B12
Sokołów Podlaski
　Poland 52°25N 22°15E **17** B12
Sokoto *Nigeria* 13°2N 5°16E **50** F7
Sol Iletsk *Russia* 51°10N 55°0E **18** D10
Solai *Kenya* 0°2N 36°12E **54** B4
Solan *India* 30°55N 77°7E **42** D7
Solana Beach *U.S.A.* 32°58N 117°16W **79** N9
Solander I. *N.Z.* 46°34S 166°54E **59** G1
Solano *Phil.* 16°31N 121°15E **37** A6
Solapur *India* 17°43N 75°56E **40** L9
Soldotna *U.S.A.* 60°29N 151°3W **68** G1
Soléa *Cyprus* 35°5N 33°4E **25** D12
Soledad *Colombia* 10°55N 74°46W **92** A4
Soledad *U.S.A.* 36°26N 121°20W **78** J5
Soledad *Venezuela* 8°10N 63°34W **92** B6
Solent, The *U.K.* 50°45N 1°25W **13** G6
Solfonntaggen *Norway* 60°2N 6°57E **9** F12
Solhan *Turkey* 38°57N 41°3E **44** B4
Soligalich *Russia* 59°5N 42°10E **18** C7
Soligorsk = Salihorsk
　Belarus 52°51N 27°27E **17** B14
Solihull *U.K.* 52°26N 1°47W **13** E6
Solikamsk *Russia* 59°38N 56°50E **18** C10
Solila *Madag.* 21°25S 46°37E **57** C8
Solimões = Amazonas →
　S. Amer. 0°5S 50°0W **93** D8
Solingen *Germany* 51°10N 7°5E **16** C4
Sollefteå *Sweden* 63°12N 17°20E **8** E17
Sóller *Spain* 39°46N 2°43E **24** B9
Solo → *Indonesia* 6°47S 112°22E **37** G15
Sologne *France* 47°40N 1°45E **20** C4
Solok *Indonesia* 0°45S 100°40E **36** E2
Sololá *Guatemala* 14°49N 91°10W **88** D1
Sololo *Kenya* 3°33N 38°39E **54** B4
Solomon, N. Fork →
　U.S.A. 39°29N 98°26W **80** F4
Solomon, S. Fork →
　U.S.A. 39°25N 99°12W **80** F4
Solomon Is. ■ *Pac. Oc.* 6°0S 155°0E **58** B8
Solomon Rise *Pac. Oc.* 1°0N 157°0E **64** G7
Solon *China* 46°32N 121°10E **33** B7
Solon Springs *U.S.A.* 46°22N 91°49W **80** B8
Solor *Indonesia* 8°27S 123°0E **37** F6
Solothurn *Switz.* 47°13N 7°32E **20** C7
Šolta *Croatia* 43°24N 16°15E **22** C7
Solţānābād *Khorāsān,
　Iran* 34°13N 59°58E **45** C8
Solţānābād *Khorāsān, Iran* 36°29N 58°5E **45** B8
Solunska Glava
　Macedonia 41°44N 21°31E **23** D9
Solvang *U.S.A.* 34°36N 120°8W **79** L6
Solvay *U.S.A.* 43°3N 76°13W **83** C8
Sölvesborg *Sweden* 56°5N 14°35E **9** H16
Solvychegodsk *Russia* 61°21N 46°56E **18** B8
Solway Firth *U.K.* 54°49N 3°35W **12** C4
Solwezi *Zambia* 12°11S 26°21E **55** E2
Sōma *Japan* 37°40N 140°50E **30** F10
Soma *Turkey* 39°10N 27°35E **23** E12
Somabhula *Zimbabwe* 19°42S 29°40E **57** B4
Somali Pen. *Africa* 7°0N 46°0E **48** F8
Somali Rep. ■ *Africa* 7°0N 47°0E **47** F4
Somalia = Somali Rep. ■
　Africa 7°0N 47°0E **47** F4
Somaliland □ *Somali Rep.* 9°0N 46°0E **47** F4
Sombor *Serbia* 45°46N 19°9E **23** B8
Sombra *Canada* 42°43N 82°29W **82** D2
Sombrerete *Mexico* 23°38N 103°39W **86** C4
Sombrero *Anguilla* 18°37N 63°30W **89** C7
Somdari *India* 25°47N 72°38E **42** G5
Somers *U.S.A.* 48°5N 114°13W **76** B6
Somerset *Ky., U.S.A.* 37°5N 84°36W **81** G11
Somerset *Mass., U.S.A.* 41°47N 71°8W **83** E13
Somerset *Pa., U.S.A.* 40°1N 79°5W **82** F5
Somerset □ *U.K.* 51°9N 3°0W **13** F5
Somerset East *S. Africa* 32°42S 25°35E **56** E4
Somerset I. *Canada* 73°30N 93°0W **68** C13
Somerset West *S. Africa* 34°8S 18°50E **56** E2
Somersworth *U.S.A.* 43°16N 70°52W **83** C14
Somerton *U.S.A.* 32°36N 114°43W **77** K6
Somerville *U.S.A.* 40°35N 74°38W **83** F10
Someş → *Romania* 47°49N 22°43E **17** D12
Somme → *France* 50°11N 1°38E **20** A4
Somnath *India* 20°53N 70°22E **42** J4

Somosierra, Puerto de
　Spain 41°4N 3°35W **21** B4
Somosomo *Fiji* 16°47S 179°58W **59** a
Somosomo Str. *Fiji* 16°0S 180°0E **59** a
Somoto *Nic.* 13°28N 86°37W **88** D2
Somport, Tunnel de
　Spain 42°48N 0°31W **20** E3
Son → *India* 25°42N 84°52E **43** G11
Son Ha *Vietnam* 15°3N 108°34E **38** E7
Son Hoa *Vietnam* 13°2N 108°58E **38** F7
Son La *Vietnam* 21°20N 103°50E **38** B4
Son Morrell *Spain* 39°44N 3°20E **24** B10
Son Rapinya *Spain* 39°35N 2°37E **24** B9
Son Sardina *Spain* 39°37N 2°40E **24** B9
Son Serra *Spain* 39°43N 3°13E **24** B10
Son Tay *Vietnam* 21°8N 105°30E **38** B5
Soná *Panama* 8°0N 81°20W **88** E3
Sonamarg *India* 34°18N 75°21E **43** B6
Sonamukhi *India* 23°18N 87°27E **43** H12
Sonar → *India* 24°24N 79°56E **43** G8
Sŏnch'ŏn *N. Korea* 39°48N 124°55E **35** E13
Sondags → *S. Africa* 33°44S 25°51E **56** E4
Sondar *India* 33°28N 75°56E **43** C6
Sønderborg *Denmark* 54°55N 9°49E **9** J13
Sóndrio *Italy* 46°10N 9°52E **20** C8
Sone *Mozam.* 17°23S 34°55E **55** F3
Sonepur *India* 20°55N 83°50E **41** J13
Song *Thailand* 18°28N 100°11E **38** C3
Song Cau *Vietnam* 13°27N 109°18E **38** F7
Song Hong → *Vietnam* 22°0N 104°0E **32** D5
Song Xian *China* 34°12N 112°8E **34** G7
Songan *Indonesia* 8°13S 115°24E **37** J18
Songea *Tanzania* 10°40S 35°40E **55** E4
Songgang *China* 22°46N 113°50E **33** F10
Songhua Hu *China* 43°35N 126°50E **35** C14
Songhua Jiang →
　China 47°45N 132°30E **33** B8
Songimvelo △ *S. Africa* 25°50S 31°2E **57** D5
Sŏngjin = Kimch'aek
　N. Korea 40°40N 129°10E **35** D15
Songkhla *Thailand* 7°13N 100°37E **39** J3
Songnim *N. Korea* 38°45N 125°39E **35** E13
Songo *Mozam.* 15°34S 32°38E **55** F3
Songo *Sudan* 9°47N 24°21E **51** G10
Songpan *China* 32°40N 103°30E **32** C5
Songwe
　Dem. Rep. of the Congo 3°20S 26°16E **54** C2
Songwe → *Africa* 9°44S 33°58E **55** D3
Sonhat *India* 23°29N 82°31E **43** H10
Sonid Youqi *China* 42°45N 112°48E **34** C7
Sonipat *India* 29°0N 77°5E **42** E7
Sonkach *India* 22°59N 76°21E **42** H7
Sonmiani *Pakistan* 25°25N 66°40E **42** G2
Sonmiani B. *Pakistan* 25°15N 66°30E **42** G2
Sono → *Brazil* 9°58S 48°11W **93** E9
Sonoma *U.S.A.* 38°18N 122°28W **78** G4
Sonora *Calif., U.S.A.* 37°59N 120°23W **78** H6
Sonora *Tex., U.S.A.* 30°34N 100°39W **84** F4
Sonora □ *Mexico* 29°20N 110°40W **86** B2
Sonora → *Mexico* 29°5N 110°55W **86** B2
Sonoran Desert
　U.S.A. 33°40N 113°30W **79** L12
Sonoyta *Mexico* 31°51N 112°50W **86** A2
Sonsonate *El Salv.* 13°43N 89°44W **88** D2
Soochow = Suzhou
　China 31°19N 120°38E **33** C7
Sooke *Canada* 48°13N 123°43W **78** B3
Soomaaliya = Somali Rep. ■
　Africa 7°0N 47°0E **47** F4
Sop Hao *Laos* 20°33N 104°27E **38** B5
Sop Prap *Thailand* 17°53N 99°20E **38** D2
Sopi *Indonesia* 2°34N 128°28E **37** D7
Sopot *Poland* 54°27N 18°31E **17** A10
Sopron *Hungary* 47°45N 16°32E **17** E9
Sopur *India* 34°18N 74°27E **43** B6
Sør-Rondane *Antarctica* 72°0S 25°0E **5** D4
Sorah *Pakistan* 27°13N 68°56E **42** F3
Soraon *India* 25°37N 81°51E **43** G9
Sord = Swords *Ireland* 53°28N 6°13W **10** C5
Sorel-Tracy *Canada* 46°0N 73°10W **72** C5
Sórgono *Italy* 40°1N 9°6E **22** D3
Soria *Spain* 41°43N 2°32W **21** B4
Soriano *Uruguay* 33°24S 58°19W **94** C4
Sorkh, Kuh-e *Iran* 35°40N 58°30E **45** C8
Soroca *Moldova* 48°8N 28°12E **17** D15
Sorocaba *Brazil* 23°31S 47°27W **95** A6
Sorochinsk *Russia* 52°26N 53°10E **18** D9
Soroki = Soroca *Moldova* 48°8N 28°12E **17** D15
Sorong *Indonesia* 0°55S 131°15E **37** E8
Soroni *Greece* 36°21N 28°1E **25** C10
Soroti *Uganda* 1°43N 33°35E **54** B3
Sørøya *Norway* 70°40N 22°30E **8** A20
Sørøysundet *Norway* 70°25N 23°0E **8** A20
Sorrell *Australia* 42°47S 147°34E **63** G4
Sorrento *Italy* 40°37N 14°22E **22** D6
Sorsele *Sweden* 65°31N 17°30E **8** D17
Sorsogon *Phil.* 13°0N 124°0E **37** B6
Sortavala *Russia* 61°42N 30°41E **8** F24
Sortland *Norway* 68°42N 15°25E **8** B16
Soscumica, L. *Canada* 50°15N 77°27W **72** B4
Sosnogorsk *Russia* 63°37N 53°51E **18** B9
Sosnowiec *Poland* 50°20N 19°10E **17** C10
Sossus Vlei *Namibia* 24°40S 15°23E **56** C2
Sŏsura *N. Korea* 42°16N 130°36E **35** C16
Sot → *India* 27°27N 79°37E **43** F8
Sotatvento *C. Verde Is.* 15°0N 25°0W **50** b
Sotik *Kenya* 0°41S 35°7E **54** C4
Sotkamo *Finland* 64°8N 28°23E **8** D23
Soto la Marina *Mexico* 23°46N 98°13W **87** C5
Soto la Marina →
　Mexico 23°45N 97°45W **87** C5
Sotuta *Mexico* 20°36N 89°1W **87** C7
Souanké *Congo* 2°10N 14°3E **52** D2
Souda *Greece* 35°29N 24°4E **25** D6
Soudas, Ormos *Greece* 35°25N 24°10E **25** D6
Souderton *U.S.A.* 40°19N 75°19W **83** F9
Soufrière *Guadeloupe* 16°5N 61°40W **88** b
Soufrière *St. Lucia* 13°51N 61°3W **89** f
Soufrière Bay *Dominica* 15°13N 61°22W **89** f

Soukhouma *Laos* 14°38N 105°48E **38** E5
Sŏul = Seoul *S. Korea* 37°31N 126°58E **35** F14
Sound, The *U.K.* 21°37N 89°10E **43** J13
Sources, Mt. aux *Lesotho* 28°45S 28°50E **57** D4
Soure *Brazil* 0°35S 48°30W **93** D9
Souris *Man., Canada* 49°40N 100°20W **71** D8
Souris *P.E.I., Canada* 46°21N 62°15W **73** C7
Souris → *N. Amer.* 49°40N 99°34W **80** A4
Sousa *Brazil* 6°45S 38°10W **93** E11
Sousse *Tunisia* 35°50N 10°38E **51** A8
Sout → *S. Africa* 31°35S 18°24E **56** E2
South Africa ■ *Africa* 32°0S 23°0E **56** E3
South America 10°0S 60°0W **90** E5
South Aulatsivik I.
　Canada 56°45N 61°30W **73** A7
South Australia □
　Australia 32°0S 139°0E **63** E2
South Australian Basin
　Ind. Oc. 38°0S 126°0E **64** L4
South Ayrshire □ *U.K.* 55°18N 4°41W **11** F4
South Baldy Pk. *U.S.A.* 34°6N 107°11W **77** J10
South Bass I. *U.S.A.* 41°39N 82°49W **82** E2
South Bend *Ind., U.S.A.* 41°41N 86°15W **80** E10
South Bend *Wash.,
　U.S.A.* 46°40N 123°48W **78** D3
South Boston *U.S.A.* 36°42N 78°54W **81** G14
South Branch *Canada* 47°55N 59°2W **73** C8
South Brook *Canada* 49°26N 56°5W **73** C8
South Bruny I. *Australia* 43°20S 147°15E **63** G4
South Carolina □ *U.S.A.* 34°0N 81°0W **85** E14
South Charleston
　U.S.A. 38°22N 81°44W **81** F13
South China Sea *Asia* 10°0N 113°0E **36** C4
South Cumberland Is. △
　Australia 20°42S 149°11E **62** b
South Dakota □ *U.S.A.* 44°15N 100°0W **80** C4
South Dayton *U.S.A.* 42°21N 79°3W **82** D5
South Deerfield *U.S.A.* 42°29N 72°37W **83** D12
South Downs *U.K.* 50°52N 0°25W **13** G7
South East C. *Australia* 43°40S 146°50E **63** G4
South East Is. *Australia* 34°17S 123°30E **61** F3
South Esk → *U.K.* 56°43N 2°31W **11** E6
South Fiji Basin *Pac. Oc.* 26°0S 174°0E **64** K9
South Foreland *U.K.* 51°8N 1°24E **13** F9
South Fork American →
　U.S.A. 38°57N 120°59W **78** G5
South Fork Feather →
　U.S.A. 39°17N 121°36W **78** F5
South Fork Grand →
　U.S.A. 45°43N 102°17W **80** C2
South Fork Milk →
　U.S.A. 48°4N 106°19W **76** B10
South Fork Republican →
　U.S.A. 40°3N 101°31W **80** E3
South Georgia *Antarctica* 54°30S 37°0W **96** G9
South Gloucestershire □
　U.K. 51°32N 2°28W **13** F5
South Hadley *U.S.A.* 42°16N 72°35W **83** D12
South Haven *U.S.A.* 42°24N 86°16W **80** D10
South Henik L. *Canada* 61°30N 97°20W **71** A9
South Horr *Kenya* 2°12N 36°56E **54** B4
South I. *Kenya* 2°35N 36°35E **54** B4
South I. *N.Z.* 44°0S 170°0E **59** F3
South Indian Lake
　Canada 56°47N 98°56W **71** B9
South Invercargill *N.Z.* 46°26S 168°23E **59** G2
South Island △ *Kenya* 2°39N 36°35E **54** B4
South Kitui △ *Kenya* 1°48S 38°46E **54** C4
South Knife → *Canada* 58°55N 94°37W **71** B10
South Koel → *India* 22°32N 85°14E **43** H11
South Korea ■ *Asia* 36°0N 128°0E **35** G15
South Lake Tahoe
　U.S.A. 38°57N 119°59W **78** G6
South Lanarkshire □
　U.K. 55°37N 3°53W **11** F5
South Loup → *U.S.A.* 41°4N 98°39W **80** E4
South Luangwa △ *Zambia* 13°0S 31°20E **55** E3
South Magnetic Pole
　Antarctica 64°8S 138°8E **5** C9
South Milwaukee
　U.S.A. 42°55N 87°52W **80** D10
South Molton *U.K.* 51°1N 3°51W **13** F4
South Moose L. *Canada* 53°49N 100°1W **71** C8
South Nahanni →
　Canada 61°3N 123°21W **70** A4
South Nation → *Canada* 45°34N 75°6W **83** A9
South Natuna Is. = Natuna
　Selatan, Kepulauan
　Indonesia 2°45N 109°0E **36** D3
South Negril Pt. *Jamaica* 18°16N 78°22W **88** a
South Orkney Is.
　Antarctica 63°0S 45°0W **5** C18
South Ossetia □ *Georgia* 42°21N 44°2E **19** F7
South Otselic *U.S.A.* 42°38N 75°46W **83** D9
South Pagai, I. = Pagai Selatan,
　Pulau *Indonesia* 3°0S 100°15E **36** E2
South Paris *U.S.A.* 44°14N 70°31W **83** B14
South Pittsburg *U.S.A.* 35°1N 85°42W **85** D12
South Platte → *U.S.A.* 41°7N 100°42W **80** E3
South Pole *Antarctica* 90°0S 0°0 E **5** E
South Porcupine *Canada* 48°30N 81°12W **72** C3
South Portland *U.S.A.* 43°38N 70°15W **83** D14
South Pt. *Barbados* 13°2N 59°32W **89** g
South Pt. *U.S.A.* 44°52N 83°19W **82** B1
South River *Canada* 45°52N 79°23W **72** C4
South River *U.S.A.* 40°27N 74°23W **83** F10
South Ronaldsay *U.K.* 58°48N 2°58W **11** C6
South Rukuru → *Malawi* 10°44S 34°14E **55** E3
South Sandwich Is.
　Antarctica 57°0S 27°0W **5** B1
South Sandwich Trench
　Atl. Oc. 56°0S 24°0W **5** B1
South Saskatchewan →
　Canada 53°15N 105°5W **71** C7
South Seal → *Canada* 58°48N 98°8W **71** B9
South Shetland Is.
　Antarctica 62°0S 59°0W **5** C18
South Shields *U.K.* 55°0N 1°25W **12** C6
South Sioux City *U.S.A.* 42°28N 96°24W **80** D5

South Sister *U.S.A.* 44°4N 121°51W **76** D3
South Talpatti = New Moore I.
　Ind. Oc. 21°37N 89°10E **43** J13
South Taranaki Bight
　N.Z. 39°40S 174°5E **59** C5
South Tasman Rise
　S. Ocean 48°0S 146°0E **5** A10
South Thompson →
　Canada 50°40N 120°20W **70** C4
South Twin I. *Canada* 53°7N 79°52W **72** B4
South Tyne → *U.K.* 54°59N 2°8W **12** C5
South Uist *U.K.* 57°20N 7°15W **11** D1
South Valley *U.S.A.* 35°1N 106°41W **77** J10
South Wellesley Is.
　Australia 16°58S 139°17E **62** B2
South West C. *Australia* 43°34S 146°3E **63** G4
South West C. *N.Z.* 47°17S 167°28E **59** G1
South Williamsport
　U.S.A. 41°13N 77°0W **82** E8
South Yorkshire □ *U.K.* 53°27N 1°36W **12** D6
Southampton *Canada* 44°30N 81°25W **82** B3
Southampton *U.K.* 50°54N 1°23W **13** G6
Southampton *U.S.A.* 40°53N 72°23W **83** F12
Southampton □ *U.K.* 50°54N 1°23W **13** G6
Southampton I. *Canada* 64°30N 84°0W **69** E15
Southaven *U.S.A.* 34°59N 90°0W **85** D9
Southbank *Canada* 54°2N 125°46W **70** C3
Southbridge *N.Z.* 43°48S 172°16E **59** E4
Southbridge *U.S.A.* 42°5N 72°2W **83** D12
Southend *Canada* 56°19N 103°22W **71** B8
Southend-on-Sea *U.K.* 51°32N 0°44E **13** F8
Southend-on-Sea □ *U.K.* 51°32N 0°44E **13** F8
Southern □ *Malawi* 15°0S 35°0E **55** F4
Southern □ *Zambia* 16°20S 26°20E **55** F2
Southern Alps *N.Z.* 43°41S 170°11E **59** E3
Southern Cross
　Australia 31°12S 119°15E **61** F2
Southern Indian L.
　Canada 57°10N 98°30W **71** B9
Southern Lau Group
　Fiji 18°40S 178°40W **59** a
Southern Ocean *Antarctica* 62°0S 60°0E **5** C6
Southern Pines *U.S.A.* 35°11N 79°24W **85** D15
Southern Uplands *U.K.* 55°28N 3°52W **11** F5
Southington *U.S.A.* 41°36N 72°53W **83** E12
Southland □ *N.Z.* 45°30S 168°0E **59** F1
Southold *U.S.A.* 41°4N 72°26W **83** E12
Southport *Australia* 27°58S 153°25E **63** D5
Southport *U.K.* 53°39N 3°0W **12** D4
Southport *U.S.A.* 42°3N 76°49W **82** D8
Southwest △ *Australia* 43°8S 146°5E **63** G4
Southwest Pacific Basin
　Pac. Oc. 40°0S 140°0W **5** A12
Southwold *U.K.* 52°20N 1°41E **13** E9
Southwood △ *Australia* 27°48S 150°8E **63** D5
Soutpansberg *S. Africa* 23°0S 29°30E **57** C4
Sovetsk *Kaliningrad, Russia* 55°6N 21°50E **9** J19
Sovetsk *Kirov, Russia* 57°38N 48°53E **18** C8
Sovetskaya Gavan
　Russia 48°58N 140°18E **29** E15
Soweto *S. Africa* 26°14S 27°52E **57** D4
Sowma'eh Sarā *Iran* 37°17N 49°18E **45** B6
Sōya-Kaikyō = La Perouse Str.
　Asia 45°40N 142°0E **30** B11
Sōya-Misaki *Japan* 45°30N 141°55E **30** B10
Soyo *Angola* 6°13S 12°20E **52** F2
Sozh → *Belarus* 51°57N 30°48E **17** B16
Spa *Belgium* 50°29N 5°53E **15** D5
Spain ■ *Europe* 39°0N 4°0W **21** B4
Spalding *Australia* 33°30S 138°37E **63** E2
Spalding *U.K.* 52°48N 0°9W **12** E7
Spanaway *U.S.A.* 47°6N 122°26W **78** C4
Spangler *U.S.A.* 40°39N 78°48W **82** F6
Spanish *Canada* 46°12N 82°20W **72** C3
Spanish Fork *U.S.A.* 40°7N 111°39W **76** F8
Spanish Town
　Br. Virgin Is. 17°43N 64°26W **89** e
Spanish Town *Jamaica* 18°0N 76°57W **88** a
Sparks *U.S.A.* 39°32N 119°45W **78** F7
Sparta = Sparti *Greece* 37°5N 22°25E **23** F10
Sparta *Mich., U.S.A.* 43°10N 85°42W **81** D11
Sparta *N.J., U.S.A.* 41°2N 74°38W **83** E10
Sparta *Wis., U.S.A.* 43°56N 90°49W **80** D8
Spartanburg *U.S.A.* 34°56N 81°57W **85** D14
Sparti *Greece* 37°5N 22°25E **23** F10
Spartivento, C. *Calabria,
　Italy* 37°55N 16°4E **22** F7
Spartivento, C. *Sard., Italy* 38°53N 8°50E **22** E3
Sparwood *Canada* 49°44N 114°53W **70** D6
Spassk Dalniy *Russia* 44°40N 132°48E **30** B6
Spatha, Akra *Greece* 35°42N 23°43E **25** D5
Spatsizi → *Canada* 57°42N 128°7W **70** B3
Spatsizi Plateau Wilderness △
　Canada 57°40N 128°0W **70** B3
Spean → *U.K.* 56°55N 4°59W **11** E4
Spearfish *U.S.A.* 44°30N 103°52W **80** C2
Spearman *U.S.A.* 36°12N 101°12W **84** C4
Speculator *U.S.A.* 43°30N 74°22W **83** C10
Speightstown *Barbados* 13°15N 59°39W **89** g
Speke Gulf *Tanzania* 2°20S 32°50E **54** C3
Spence Bay = Taloyoak
　Canada 69°32N 93°32W **68** D13
Spencer *Idaho, U.S.A.* 44°22N 112°11W **76** D7
Spencer *Iowa, U.S.A.* 43°9N 95°9W **80** D6
Spencer *N.Y., U.S.A.* 42°13N 76°30W **83** D8
Spencer, C. *Australia* 35°20S 136°53E **63** F2
Spencer B. *Namibia* 25°30S 14°47E **56** D1
Spencer G. *Australia* 34°0S 137°20E **63** E2
Spencerville *Canada* 44°51N 75°33W **83** B9
Spences Bridge *Canada* 50°25N 121°20W **70** C4
Spennymoor *U.K.* 54°42N 1°36W **12** C6
Spenser Mts. *N.Z.* 42°15S 172°45E **59** E4
Sperrin Mts. *U.K.* 54°50N 7°0W **10** B5
Spey → *U.K.* 57°40N 3°6W **11** D5
Speyer *Germany* 49°29N 8°25E **16** D5
Spezand *Pakistan* 29°59N 67°0E **42** E2

Spiddle *Ireland* 53°15N 9°18W **10** C2
Spili *Greece* 35°13N 24°31E **25** D6
Spīn Būldak *Afghan.* 31°1N 66°25E **42** D2
Spinalonga *Greece* 35°18N 25°44E **25** D7
Spinifex ✪ *Australia* 28°30S 128°30E **61** E4
Spirit Lake *U.S.A.* 46°15N 122°9W **78** D4
Spirit River *Canada* 55°45N 118°50W **70** B5
Spiritwood *Canada* 53°24N 107°33W **71** C7
Spithead *U.K.* 50°45N 1°10W **13** G6
Spitzbergen = Svalbard
　Arctic 78°0N 17°0E **4** B8
Spjelkavik *Norway* 62°28N 6°22E **8** E12
Split *Croatia* 43°31N 16°26E **22** C7
Split L. *Canada* 56°8N 96°15W **71** B9
Split Lake *Canada* 56°8N 96°15W **71** B9
Spofford *U.S.A.* 29°10N 100°25W **84** G4
Spokane *U.S.A.* 47°40N 117°24W **76** C5
Spoleto *Italy* 42°44N 12°44E **22** C5
Spooner *U.S.A.* 45°50N 91°53W **80** C8
Sporry Navolok, Mys
　Russia 75°50N 68°40E **28** B7
Sprague *U.S.A.* 47°18N 117°59W **76** C5
Spratly I. *S. China Sea* 8°38N 111°55E **36** C4
Spratly Is. *S. China Sea* 8°20N 112°0E **36** C4
Spray *U.S.A.* 44°50N 119°48W **76** D4
Spree → *Germany* 52°32N 13°12E **16** B7
Sprengisandur *Iceland* 64°52N 18°7W **8** D4
Spring City *U.S.A.* 40°11N 75°33W **83** F9
Spring Creek *U.S.A.* 40°44N 115°35W **76** F6
Spring Garden *U.S.A.* 39°52N 120°47W **78** F6
Spring Hall *Barbados* 13°18N 59°36W **89** g
Spring Hill *U.S.A.* 28°27N 82°41E **85** G13
Spring Mts. *U.S.A.* 36°0N 115°45W **79** J11
Spring Valley *Calif.,
　U.S.A.* 32°44N 116°59W **79** N10
Spring Valley *Nev.,
　U.S.A.* 36°6N 115°14W **79** J11
Springbok *S. Africa* 29°42S 17°54E **56** D2
Springboro *U.S.A.* 41°48N 80°22W **82** E4
Springdale *Canada* 49°30N 56°6W **73** C8
Springdale *U.S.A.* 36°11N 94°8W **84** C7
Springer *U.S.A.* 36°22N 104°36W **77** H11
Springerville *U.S.A.* 34°8N 109°17W **77** J9
Springfield *Canada* 42°50N 80°56W **82** D3
Springfield *N.Z.* 43°19S 171°56E **59** E3
Springfield *Colo.,
　U.S.A.* 37°24N 102°37W **77** H12
Springfield *Ill., U.S.A.* 39°48N 89°39W **80** F9
Springfield *Mass., U.S.A.* 42°6N 72°35W **83** D12
Springfield *Mo., U.S.A.* 37°13N 93°17W **80** G7
Springfield *Ohio, U.S.A.* 39°55N 83°49W **81** F12
Springfield *Oreg., U.S.A.* 44°3N 123°1W **76** D2
Springfield *Tenn.,
　U.S.A.* 36°31N 86°53W **85** C11
Springfield *Vt., U.S.A.* 43°18N 72°29W **83** C12
Springfontein *S. Africa* 30°15S 25°42E **56** E4
Springhill *Canada* 45°40N 64°4W **73** C7
Springhill *U.S.A.* 33°0N 93°28W **84** E8
Springhouse *Canada* 51°56N 122°7W **70** C4
Springs *S. Africa* 26°13S 28°25E **57** D4
Springsure *Australia* 24°8S 148°6E **62** C4
Springvale *U.S.A.* 43°28N 70°48W **83** C14
Springville *Calif., U.S.A.* 36°8N 118°49W **78** J8
Springville *N.Y., U.S.A.* 42°31N 78°40W **82** D6
Springville *Utah, U.S.A.* 40°10N 111°37W **76** F8
Springwater *U.S.A.* 42°38N 77°35W **82** D7
Spruce-Creek *U.S.A.* 40°36N 78°9W **82** F6
Spruce Knob-Seneca Rocks △
　U.S.A. 38°50N 79°30W **81** F14
Spruce Mt. *U.S.A.* 44°12N 72°19W **83** B12
Sprucedale *Canada* 45°29N 79°28W **82** A5
Spur *U.S.A.* 33°28N 100°52W **84** E4
Spurn Hd. *U.K.* 53°35N 0°8E **12** D8
Spuzzum *Canada* 49°37N 121°23W **70** D4
Squam L. *U.S.A.* 43°45N 71°32W **83** C13
Squamish *Canada* 49°45N 123°10W **70** D4
Square Islands *Canada* 52°47N 55°47W **73** B8
Squires, Mt. *Australia* 26°14S 127°28E **61** E4
Srbija = Serbia ■ *Europe* 43°20N 20°0E **23** B9
Sre Ambel *Cambodia* 11°8N 103°46E **39** G4
Sre Khtum *Cambodia* 12°10N 106°52E **39** F6
Sre Umbell = Sre Ambel
　Cambodia 11°8N 103°46E **39** G4
Srebrenica *Bos.-H.* 44°6N 19°18E **23** B8
Sredinny Ra. = Sredinnyy Khrebet
　Russia 57°0N 160°0E **29** D17
Sredinnyy Khrebet
　Russia 57°0N 160°0E **29** D17
Srednekolymsk *Russia* 67°27N 153°40E **29** C16
Śrem *Poland* 52°6N 17°2E **17** B9
Sremska Mitrovica
　Serbia 44°59N 19°38E **23** B8
Srepok → *Cambodia* 13°33N 106°16E **38** F6
Sretensk *Russia* 52°10N 117°40E **29** D12
Sri Aman *Malaysia* 1°15N 111°32E **36** D4
Sri Lanka ■ *Asia* 7°30N 80°50E **40** R12
Srikakulam *India* 18°14N 83°58E **41** K13
Srinagar *India* 34°5N 74°50E **43** B6
Srono *Indonesia* 8°24S 114°16E **37** J17
Staaten → *Australia* 16°24S 141°17E **62** B3
Staaten River △
　Australia 16°15S 142°40E **62** B3
Stade *Germany* 53°35N 9°29E **16** B5
Stadskanaal *Neths.* 53°4N 6°55E **15** A6
Staffa *U.K.* 56°27N 6°21W **11** E2
Stafford *U.K.* 52°49N 2°7W **12** E5
Stafford *U.S.A.* 37°58N 98°36W **80** G4
Stafford Springs *U.S.A.* 41°57N 72°18W **83** E12
Staffordshire □ *U.K.* 52°53N 2°10W **12** E5
Staines *U.K.* 51°26N 0°29W **13** F7
Stakhanov *Ukraine* 48°35N 38°40E **19** E6
Stalida *Greece* 35°17N 25°25E **25** D7
Stalowa Wola *Poland* 50°34N 22°3E **17** C12
Stalybridge *U.K.* 53°28N 2°3W **12** D5
Stamford *Australia* 21°15S 143°46E **62** C3
Stamford *U.K.* 52°39N 0°29W **13** E7
Stamford *Conn., U.S.A.* 41°3N 73°32W **83** E11
Stamford *N.Y., U.S.A.* 42°25N 74°38W **83** D10

Stamford *Tex., U.S.A.* 32°57N 99°48W **84** E5
Stampriet *Namibia* 24°20S 18°28E **56** C2
Stamps *U.S.A.* 33°22N 93°30W **84** E8
Standerton *S. Africa* 26°55S 29°7E **57** D4
Standish *U.S.A.* 43°59N 83°57W **81** D12
Stanford *S. Africa* 34°26S 19°29E **56** E2
Stanford *U.S.A.* 47°9N 110°13W **76** C8
Stanger *S. Africa* 29°27S 31°14E **57** D5
Stängselåsen = Salpausselkä
  Finland 61°3N 26°15E **8** F22
Stanislaus → *U.S.A.* 37°40N 121°14W **78** H5
Stanke Dimitrov
  Bulgaria 42°17N 23°9E **23** C10
Stanley *Australia* 40°46S 145°19E **63** G4
Stanley *China* 22°13N 114°12E **33** G11
Stanley *Falk. Is.* 51°40S 59°51W **96** G5
Stanley *U.K.* 54°53N 1°41W **12** C6
Stanley *Idaho, U.S.A.* 44°13N 114°56W **76** D6
Stanley *N. Dak., U.S.A.* 48°19N 102°23W **80** A2
Stanley *N.Y., U.S.A.* 42°48N 77°6W **82** D7
Stanley Mission
  Canada 55°25N 104°33W **71** B8
Stannards *U.S.A.* 42°5N 77°55W **82** D7
Stanovoy Khrebet
  Russia 55°0N 130°0E **29** D14
Stanovoy Ra. = Stanovoy Khrebet
  Russia 55°0N 130°0E **29** D14
Stansmore Ra. *Australia* 21°23S 128°33E **60** D4
Stansted, London ✈ (STN)
  U.K. 51°54N 0°14E **13** F8
Stanthorpe *Australia* 28°36S 151°59E **63** D5
Stanton *U.S.A.* 32°8N 101°48W **84** E4
Stanwood *U.S.A.* 48°15N 122°23W **78** B4
Staples *Canada* 42°10N 82°35W **82** D2
Staples *U.S.A.* 46°21N 94°48W **80** B6
Stapleton *U.S.A.* 41°29N 100°31W **80** E3
Star City *Canada* 52°50N 104°20W **71** C8
Star Lake *U.S.A.* 44°10N 75°2W **83** B9
Stara Planina *Bulgaria* 43°15N 23°0E **23** C10
Stara Zagora *Bulgaria* 42°26N 25°39E **23** C11
Starachowice *Poland* 51°3N 21°2E **17** C11
Staraya Russa *Russia* 57°58N 31°23E **18** C5
Starbuck I. *Kiribati* 5°37S 155°55W **65** H12
Starcke △ *Australia* 14°56S 145°2E **62** A4
Stargard Szczeciński
  Poland 53°20N 15°0E **16** B8
Staritsa *Russia* 56°33N 34°55E **18** C5
Starke *U.S.A.* 29°57N 82°7W **85** G13
Starkville *U.S.A.* 33°28N 88°49W **85** E10
Starogard Gdański
  Poland 53°59N 18°30E **17** B10
Starokonstantinov =
  Starokonstyantyniv
  Ukraine 49°48N 27°10E **17** D14
Starokonstyantyniv
  Ukraine 49°48N 27°10E **17** D14
Start Pt. *U.K.* 50°13N 3°39W **13** G4
Staryy Chartoriysk
  Ukraine 51°15N 25°54E **17** C13
Staryy Oskol *Russia* 51°19N 37°55E **19** D6
State College *U.S.A.* 40°48N 77°52W **82** F7
Stateline *U.S.A.* 38°57N 119°56W **78** G7
Staten, I. = Estados, I. de Los
  Argentina 54°40S 64°30W **96** G4
Staten I. *U.S.A.* 40°35N 74°9W **83** F10
Statesboro *U.S.A.* 32°27N 81°47W **85** E14
Statesville *U.S.A.* 35°47N 80°53W **85** D14
Statia = St. Eustatius
  W. Indies 17°20N 63°0W **89** C7
Stauffer *U.S.A.* 34°45N 119°3W **79** L7
Staunton *Ill., U.S.A.* 39°1N 89°47W **80** F9
Staunton *Va., U.S.A.* 38°9N 79°4W **81** F14
Stavanger *Norway* 58°57N 5°40E **9** G11
Staveley *N.Z.* 43°40S 171°32E **59** E3
Stavelot *Belgium* 50°23N 5°55E **15** D5
Stavern *Norway* 59°0N 10°1E **9** G14
Stavoren *Neths.* 52°53N 5°22E **15** B5
Stavropol *Russia* 45°5N 42°0E **19** E7
Stavros *Cyprus* 35°1N 32°38E **25** D11
Stavros *Greece* 35°12N 24°45E **25** D6
Stavros, Ákra *Greece* 35°26N 24°58E **25** D6
Stawell *Australia* 37°5S 142°47E **63** F3
Stawell → *Australia* 20°20S 142°55E **62** C3
Stayner *Canada* 44°25N 80°5W **82** B4
Stayton *U.S.A.* 44°48N 122°48W **76** D2
Steamboat Springs
  U.S.A. 40°29N 106°50W **76** F10
Steele *U.S.A.* 46°51N 99°55W **80** B4
Steelton *U.S.A.* 40°14N 76°50W **82** F8
Steen River *Canada* 59°40N 117°12W **70** B5
Steens Mt. *U.S.A.* 42°35N 118°40W **76** E4
Steenwijk *Neths.* 52°47N 6°7E **15** B6
Steep Pt. *Australia* 26°8S 113°8E **61** E1
Steep Rock *Canada* 51°30N 98°48W **71** C9
Stefanie L. = Chew Bahir
  Ethiopia 4°40N 36°50E **47** G2
Stefansson Bay *Antarctica* 67°20S 59°8E **5** C5
Stefansson I. *Canada* 73°20N 105°45W **69** C10
Steiermark □ *Austria* 47°26N 15°0E **16** E8
Steilacoom *U.S.A.* 47°10N 122°36W **78** C4
Steinberger = Namibia* 17°43S 13°20E **56** B1
Steinbach *Canada* 49°32N 96°40W **71** D9
Steinhausen *Namibia* 21°49S 18°20E **56** C2
Steinkjer *Norway* 64°1N 11°31E **8** D14
Steinkopf *S. Africa* 29°18S 17°43E **56** D2
Stellarton *Canada* 45°32N 62°30W **73** C7
Stellenbosch *S. Africa* 33°58S 18°50E **56** E2
Stendal *Germany* 52°36N 11°53E **16** B6
Steornabhaigh = Stornoway
  U.K. 58°13N 6°23W **11** C2
Stepanakert = Xankändi
  Azerbaijan 39°52N 46°49E **44** B5
Stephens Creek
  Australia 31°50S 141°30E **63** E3
Stephens I. *Canada* 54°10N 130°45W **70** C2
Stephens L. *Canada* 56°32N 95°0W **71** B9
Stephenville *Canada* 48°31N 58°35W **73** C8
Stephenville *U.S.A.* 32°13N 98°12W **84** E5
Steppe *Asia* 50°0N 50°0E **26** C7

Sterkstroom *S. Africa* 31°32S 26°32E **56** E4
Sterling *Colo., U.S.A.* 40°37N 103°13W **76** F12
Sterling *Ill., U.S.A.* 41°48N 89°42W **80** E9
Sterling *Kans., U.S.A.* 38°13N 98°12W **80** F4
Sterling City *U.S.A.* 31°51N 101°0W **84** F4
Sterling Heights *U.S.A.* 42°35N 83°2W **81** D12
Sterling Run *U.S.A.* 41°25N 78°12W **82** E6
Sterlitamak *Russia* 53°40N 56°0E **18** D10
Sternes *Greece* 35°30N 24°9E **25** D6
Stettin = Szczecin *Poland* 53°27N 14°27E **16** B8
Stettiner Haff *Germany* 53°47N 14°15E **16** B8
Stettler *Canada* 52°19N 112°40W **70** C6
Steubenville *U.S.A.* 40°22N 80°37W **82** F4
Stevenage *U.K.* 51°55N 0°13W **13** F7
Stevens Point *U.S.A.* 44°31N 89°34W **80** C9
Stevenson *U.S.A.* 45°42N 121°53W **78** E5
Stevenson → *Australia* 27°6S 135°33E **63** D2
Stevenson L. *Canada* 53°55N 96°0W **71** C9
Stevensville *U.S.A.* 46°30N 114°5W **76** C6
Stewart *Canada* 55°56N 129°57W **70** B3
Stewart *U.S.A.* 39°5N 119°46W **78** F7
Stewart → *Canada* 63°19N 139°26W **68** E4
Stewart, C. *Australia* 11°57S 134°56E **62** A1
Stewart, I. *Chile* 54°50S 71°15W **96** G2
Stewart I. *N.Z.* 46°58S 167°54E **59** G1
Stewarts Point *U.S.A.* 38°39N 123°24W **78** G3
Stewartville *U.S.A.* 43°51N 92°29W **80** D7
Stewiacke *Canada* 45°9N 63°22W **73** C7
Steynsburg *S. Africa* 31°15S 25°49E **56** E4
Steyr *Austria* 48°3N 14°25E **16** D8
Steytlerville *S. Africa* 33°17S 24°19E **56** E3
Stigler *U.S.A.* 35°15N 95°8W **84** D7
Stikine → *Canada* 56°40N 132°30W **70** B2
Stilfontein *S. Africa* 26°51S 26°50E **56** D4
Stillwater *N.Z.* 42°27S 171°20E **59** E3
Stillwater *N.Y., U.S.A.* 42°55N 73°41W **83** D11
Stillwater *Okla., U.S.A.* 36°7N 97°4W **84** C6
Stillwater Range *U.S.A.* 39°50N 118°5W **76** G4
Stillwater Res. *U.S.A.* 43°54N 75°3W **83** C9
Stilwell *U.S.A.* 35°49N 94°38W **84** D7
Stînga Nistrului □
  Moldova 47°20N 29°15E **17** E15
Știp *Macedonia* 41°42N 22°10E **23** D10
Stirling *Canada* 44°18N 77°33W **82** B7
Stirling *U.K.* 56°8N 3°57W **11** E5
Stirling □ *U.K.* 56°12N 4°18W **11** E4
Stirling Ra. *Australia* 34°23S 118°0E **61** F2
Stirling Range △
  Australia 34°26S 118°20E **61** F2
Stittsville *Canada* 45°15N 75°55W **83** A9
Stjernøya *Norway* 70°20N 22°40E **8** A20
Stockerau *Austria* 48°24N 16°12E **16** D9
Stockholm *Sweden* 59°19N 18°4E **9** G18
Stockport *U.K.* 53°25N 2°9W **12** D5
Stocksbridge *U.K.* 53°29N 1°35W **12** D6
Stockton *Calif., U.S.A.* 37°58N 121°17W **78** H5
Stockton *Kans., U.S.A.* 39°26N 99°16W **80** F4
Stockton *Mo., U.S.A.* 37°42N 93°48W **80** G7
Stockton-on-Tees *U.K.* 54°35N 1°19W **12** C6
Stockton-on-Tees □
  U.K. 54°35N 1°19W **12** C6
Stockton Plateau
  U.S.A. 30°30N 102°30W **84** F3
Stoeng Treng *Cambodia* 13°31N 105°58E **38** F5
Stoer, Pt. of *U.K.* 58°16N 5°23W **11** C3
Stoke-on-Trent *U.K.* 53°1N 2°11W **12** D5
Stoke-on-Trent □ *U.K.* 53°1N 2°11W **12** D5
Stokes △ *Australia* 33°45S 121°11E **61** F3
Stokes Bay *Canada* 45°0N 81°28W **82** B3
Stokes Pt. *Australia* 40°10S 143°56E **63** G3
Stokes Ra. *Australia* 15°50S 130°50E **60** C5
Stokksnes *Iceland* 64°14N 14°58W **8** D6
Stokmarknes *Norway* 68°34N 14°54E **8** B16
Stolac *Bos.-H.* 43°5N 17°59E **23** C7
Stolbovoy, Ostrov
  Russia 74°44N 135°14E **29** B14
Stolbtsy = Stowbtsy
  Belarus 53°30N 26°43E **17** B14
Stolin *Belarus* 51°53N 26°50E **17** C14
Stomio *Greece* 35°21N 23°32E **25** D5
Stone *U.K.* 52°55N 2°9W **12** E5
Stoneboro *U.S.A.* 41°20N 80°7W **82** E4
Stonehaven *U.K.* 56°59N 2°12W **11** E6
Stonehenge *Australia* 24°22S 143°17E **62** C3
Stonehenge *U.K.* 51°9N 1°45W **13** F6
Stonewall *Canada* 50°10N 97°19W **71** C9
Stony L. *Man., U.S.A.* 43°53N 76°19W **83** C8
Stony L. *Man., Canada* 58°51N 98°40W **71** B9
Stony L. *Ont., Canada* 44°30N 78°5W **82** B6
Stony Point *U.S.A.* 41°14N 73°59W **83** E11
Stony Pt. *U.S.A.* 43°50N 76°18W **83** C8
Stony Rapids *Canada* 59°16N 105°50W **71** B7
Stony Tunguska = Tunguska,
  Podkamennaya →
  Russia 61°50N 90°13E **29** C10
Stonyford *U.S.A.* 39°23N 122°33W **78** F4
Stora Lulevatten *Sweden* 67°10N 19°30E **8** C18
Storavan *Sweden* 65°45N 18°10E **8** D18
Stord *Norway* 59°52N 5°23E **9** G11
Støre Bælt *Denmark* 55°20N 11°0E **9** J14
Storkerson Pen.
  Canada 72°30N 106°30W **68** C10
Storm B. *Australia* 43°10S 147°30E **63** G4
Storm Lake *U.S.A.* 42°39N 95°13W **80** D6
Stormberge *S. Africa* 31°16S 26°17E **56** E4
Stormsrivier *S. Africa* 33°59S 23°52E **56** E3
Stornoway *U.K.* 58°13N 6°23W **11** C2
Storozhinets = Storozhynets
  Ukraine 48°14N 25°45E **17** D13
Storozhynets *Ukraine* 48°14N 25°45E **17** D13
Storrs *U.S.A.* 41°49N 72°15W **83** E12
Storsjön *Sweden* 63°9N 14°30E **8** E16
Storuman *Sweden* 65°5N 17°10E **8** D17
Storuman, L. *Sweden* 65°13N 16°50E **8** D17
Stouffville *Canada* 43°58N 79°15W **82** C5
Stoughton *Canada* 49°40N 103°0W **71** D8
Stour → *Dorset, U.K.* 50°43N 1°47W **13** G6
Stour → *Kent, U.K.* 51°18N 1°22E **13** F9

Stour → *Suffolk, U.K.* 51°57N 1°4E **13** F9
Stourbridge *U.K.* 52°28N 2°8W **13** E5
Stout L. *Canada* 52°0N 94°40W **71** C10
Stove Pipe Wells Village
  U.S.A. 36°35N 117°11W **79** J9
Stow *U.S.A.* 41°10N 81°27W **82** E3
Stowbtsy *Belarus* 53°30N 26°43E **17** B14
Stowmarket *U.K.* 52°12N 1°0E **13** E9
Strabane *U.K.* 54°50N 7°27W **10** B4
Strahan *Australia* 42°9S 145°20E **63** G4
Stralsund *Germany* 54°18N 13°4E **16** A7
Strand *S. Africa* 34°9S 18°48E **56** E2
Stranda *Møre og Romsdal,*
  Norway 62°19N 6°58E **8** E12
Stranda *Nord-Trøndelag,*
  Norway 63°33N 10°14E **8** E14
Strangford L. *U.K.* 54°30N 5°37W **10** B6
Stranorlar *Ireland* 54°48N 7°46W **10** B4
Stranraer *U.K.* 54°54N 5°1W **11** G3
Strasbourg *Canada* 51°4N 104°55W **71** C8
Strasbourg *France* 48°35N 7°42E **20** B7
Stratford *Canada* 43°23N 81°0W **82** C4
Stratford *N.Z.* 39°20S 174°19E **59** C5
Stratford *Calif., U.S.A.* 36°11N 119°49W **78** J7
Stratford *Conn., U.S.A.* 41°12N 73°8W **83** E11
Stratford *Tex., U.S.A.* 36°20N 102°4W **84** C3
Stratford-upon-Avon
  U.K. 52°12N 1°42W **13** E6
Strath Spey *U.K.* 57°9N 3°49W **11** D5
Strathalbyn *Australia* 35°13S 138°53E **63** F2
Strathaven *U.K.* 55°40N 4°5W **11** F4
Strathcona △ *Canada* 49°38N 125°40W **70** D3
Strathmore *Canada* 51°5N 113°18W **70** C6
Strathmore *U.K.* 56°37N 3°7W **11** E5
Strathmore *U.S.A.* 36°9N 119°4W **78** J7
Strathnaver *Canada* 53°20N 122°33W **70** C4
Strathpeffer *U.K.* 57°35N 4°32W **11** D4
Strathroy *Canada* 42°58N 81°38W **82** D3
Strathy Pt. *U.K.* 58°36N 4°1W **11** C4
Strattanville *U.S.A.* 41°12N 79°19W **82** E5
Stratton *U.S.A.* 45°8N 70°26W **83** A14
Stratton Mt. *U.S.A.* 43°4N 72°55W **83** C12
Straubing *Germany* 48°52N 12°34E **16** D7
Straumnes *Iceland* 66°26N 23°8W **8** C2
Strawberry → *U.S.A.* 40°10N 110°24W **76** F8
Streaky B. *Australia* 32°48S 134°13E **63** E1
Streaky Bay *Australia* 32°51S 134°18E **63** E1
Streator *U.S.A.* 41°8N 88°50W **80** E9
Streetsboro *U.S.A.* 41°14N 81°21W **82** E3
Streetsville *Canada* 43°35N 79°42W **82** C5
Streng → *Cambodia* 13°12N 103°37E **38** F4
Strezhevoy *Russia* 60°42N 77°34E **28** C8
Strimonas → *Greece* 40°46N 23°51E **23** D10
Strokestown *Ireland* 53°46N 8°7W **10** C3
Stroma *U.K.* 58°41N 3°7W **11** C5
Strómboli *Italy* 38°47N 15°13E **22** E6
Stromeferry *U.K.* 57°21N 5°33W **11** D3
Stromness *U.K.* 58°58N 3°17W **11** C5
Stromsburg *U.S.A.* 41°7N 97°36W **80** E5
Strömstad *Sweden* 58°56N 11°10E **9** G14
Strömsund *Sweden* 63°51N 15°33E **8** E16
Strongsville *U.S.A.* 41°19N 81°50W **82** E3
Stronsay *U.K.* 59°7N 2°35W **11** B6
Stroud *U.K.* 51°45N 2°13W **13** F5
Stroud Road *Australia* 32°18S 151°57E **63** E5
Stroudsburg *U.S.A.* 40°59N 75°12W **83** F9
Stroumbi *Cyprus* 34°53N 32°29E **25** E11
Struer *Denmark* 56°30N 8°35E **9** H13
Strugi Krasnyye *Russia* 58°21N 29°1E **9** G23
Struma → *Bulgaria* 40°46N 23°51E **23** D10
Strumica *Macedonia* 41°28N 22°41E **23** D10
Struthers *U.S.A.* 41°4N 80°39W **82** E4
Stryker *U.S.A.* 48°41N 114°46W **76** B6
Stryy *Ukraine* 49°16N 23°48E **17** D12
Strzelecki Cr. →
  Australia 29°37S 139°59E **63** D2
Strzelecki Desert
  Australia 29°30S 140°0E **63** D3
Stuart *Fla., U.S.A.* 27°12N 80°15W **85** H14
Stuart *Nebr., U.S.A.* 42°36N 99°8W **80** D4
Stuart → *Canada* 54°0N 123°35W **70** C4
Stuart Bluff Ra.
  Australia 22°50S 131°52E **60** D5
Stuart I. *U.S.A.* 63°35N 162°30W **74** C7
Stuart L. *Canada* 54°30N 124°30W **70** C4
Stuart Ra. *Australia* 29°10S 134°56E **63** D1
Stull L. *Canada* 54°24N 92°34W **72** B1
Stung Treng = Stoeng Treng
  Cambodia 13°31N 105°58E **38** F5
Stupart → *Canada* 56°0N 93°25W **72** A1
Sturge I. *Antarctica* 67°26S 164°47E **5** C11
Sturgeon B. *Canada* 52°0N 97°50W **71** C9
Sturgeon Bay *U.S.A.* 44°50N 87°23W **80** C10
Sturgeon Falls *Canada* 46°25N 79°57W **72** C4
Sturgeon L. *Alta., Canada* 55°6N 117°32W **70** B5
Sturgeon L. *Ont., Canada* 50°0N 90°45W **72** C1
Sturgeon L. *Ont., Canada* 44°28N 78°43W **82** B6
Sturgis *Canada* 51°56N 102°36W **71** C8
Sturgis *Mich., U.S.A.* 41°48N 85°25W **81** E11
Sturgis *S. Dak., U.S.A.* 44°25N 103°31W **80** C2
Sturt Cr. → *Australia* 20°8S 127°24E **60** C4
Sturt Stony Desert
  Australia 28°30S 141°0E **63** D3
Stutterheim *S. Africa* 32°33S 27°28E **56** E4
Stuttgart *Germany* 48°48N 9°11E **16** D5
Stuttgart *U.S.A.* 34°30N 91°33W **84** D9
Stuyvesant *U.S.A.* 42°23N 73°45W **83** D11
Stykkishólmur *Iceland* 65°2N 22°40W **8** D2
Styria = Steiermark □
  Austria 47°26N 15°0E **16** E8
Su Xian = Suzhou
  China 33°41N 116°59E **34** H9
Suakin *Sudan* 19°8N 37°20E **51** E13
Suan *N. Korea* 38°42N 126°22E **35** E14
Suar *India* 29°2N 79°3E **43** E8
Şubā *Si. Arabia* 27°10N 35°40E **44** E2
Subang *Indonesia* 6°34S 107°45E **37** G12
Subansiri → *India* 26°48N 93°50E **41** F18

Subarnarekha → *India* 22°34N 87°24E **43** H12
Subayhah *Si. Arabia* 30°2N 38°50E **44** D3
Subi *Indonesia* 2°58N 108°50E **36** D3
Subotica *Serbia* 46°6N 19°39E **23** A8
Suceava *Romania* 47°38N 26°16E **17** E14
Suchan = Partizansk
  Russia 43°8N 133°9E **30** C6
Suchil *Mexico* 23°39N 103°54W **86** C4
Suchou = Suzhou
  China 31°19N 120°38E **33** C7
Süchow = Xuzhou
  China 34°18N 117°10E **35** G9
Suck → *Ireland* 53°17N 8°3W **10** C3
Sucre *Bolivia* 19°0S 65°15W **92** G5
Sucuriú → *Brazil* 20°47S 51°38W **93** H8
Sud, Pte. du *Canada* 49°3N 62°14W **73** C7
Sud-Kivu □
  Dem. Rep. of the Congo 3°0S 28°30E **54** C2
Sud-Ouest, Pte. *Canada* 49°23N 63°36W **73** C7
Sud Ouest, Pte. *Mauritius* 20°28S 57°18E **53** d
Sudan ■ *Africa* 15°0N 30°0E **51** E11
Sudbury *Canada* 46°30N 81°0W **72** C3
Sudbury *U.K.* 52°2N 0°45E **13** E8
Sûdd *Sudan* 8°20N 30°0E **51** G12
Sudeten Mts. = Sudety
  Europe 50°20N 16°45E **17** C9
Sudety *Europe* 50°20N 16°45E **17** C9
Suðuroy *Føroe Is.* 61°32N 6°50W **8** F9
Sudi *Tanzania* 10°11S 39°57E **55** E4
Sudirman, Pegunungan
  Indonesia 4°30S 137°0E **37** E9
Sudong, Pulau *Singapore* 1°13N 103°44E **39** d
Sueca *Spain* 39°12N 0°21W **21** C5
Suemez I. *U.S.A.* 55°15N 133°20W **70** B2
Suez = El Suweis *Egypt* 29°58N 32°31E **51** C12
Suez, G. of = Suweis, Khalig el
  Egypt 28°40N 33°0E **51** C12
Suez Canal = Suweis, Qanâ es
  Egypt 31°0N 32°20E **51** B12
Suffield *Canada* 50°12N 111°10W **70** C6
Suffolk *U.S.A.* 36°44N 76°35W **81** G15
Suffolk □ *U.K.* 52°16N 1°0E **13** E9
Sugar Grove *U.S.A.* 41°59N 79°20W **82** E5
Sugarcreek *U.S.A.* 41°25N 79°52W **82** E5
Sugarive → *India* 26°16N 86°24E **43** F12
Sugluk = Salluit
  Canada 62°14N 75°38W **69** E16
Şuḩār *Oman* 24°20N 56°40E **45** E8
Sühbaatar *Mongolia* 50°17N 106°10E **32** A5
Sühbaatar □ *Mongolia* 45°30N 114°0E **34** B8
Suhl *Germany* 50°36N 10°42E **16** C6
Sui *Pakistan* 28°37N 69°19E **42** E3
Sui Xian *China* 34°25N 115°2E **34** G8
Suide *China* 37°30N 110°12E **34** F6
Suifenhe *China* 44°25N 131°10E **35** B16
Suihua *China* 46°32N 126°55E **33** B7
Suining *Jiangsu, China* 33°56N 117°58E **35** H9
Suining *Sichuan, China* 30°26N 105°35E **32** C5
Suiping *China* 33°10N 113°59E **34** H7
Suir → *Ireland* 52°16N 7°9W **10** D4
Suisse = Switzerland ■
  Europe 46°30N 8°0E **20** C8
Suisun City *U.S.A.* 38°15N 122°2W **78** G4
Suiyang *China* 44°30N 130°56E **35** B16
Suizhong *China* 40°21N 120°20E **35** D11
Sujangarh *India* 27°42N 74°31E **42** F6
Sukabumi *Indonesia* 6°56S 106°50E **37** G12
Sukadana *Indonesia* 1°10S 110°0E **36** E4
Sukagawa *Japan* 37°17N 140°23E **31** F10
Sukaraja *Indonesia* 2°28S 110°25E **36** E4
Sukawati *Indonesia* 8°35S 115°17E **37** K18
Sukch'ŏn *N. Korea* 39°22N 125°35E **35** E13
Sukhona → *Russia* 61°15N 46°39E **18** C6
Sukhothai *Thailand* 17°1N 99°49E **38** D2
Sukhumi = Sokhumi
  Georgia 43°0N 41°0E **19** F7
Sukkur *Pakistan* 27°42N 68°54E **42** F3
Sukkur Barrage *Pakistan* 27°40N 68°50E **42** F3
Sukri → *India* 25°4N 71°43E **42** G4
Sukumo *Japan* 32°56N 132°44E **31** H6
Sukunka → *Canada* 55°45N 121°15W **70** B4
Sula, Kepulauan *Indonesia* 1°45S 125°0E **37** E7
Sulaco → *Honduras* 15°2N 87°44W **88** C2
Sulaiman Range
  Pakistan 30°30N 69°50E **42** D3
Sülär *Iran* 31°53N 51°54E **45** D6
Sulawesi □ *Indonesia* 2°0S 120°0E **37** E6
Sulawesi Barat □ *Indonesia* 3°0S 119°0E **37** E5
Sulawesi Sea = Celebes Sea
  Indonesia 3°0N 123°0E **37** D6
Sulawesi Selatan □
  Indonesia 2°30S 120°0E **37** E6
Sulawesi Tengah □
  Indonesia 1°30S 121°0E **37** E6
Sulawesi Tenggara □
  Indonesia 3°50S 122°0E **37** E6
Sulawesi Utara □ *Indonesia* 1°0N 124°0E **37** D6
Sulima *S. Leone* 6°58N 11°32W **50** G3
Sulina *Romania* 45°10N 29°40E **17** F15
Sulitjelma *Norway* 67°9N 16°3E **8** C17
Sullana *Peru* 4°52S 80°39W **92** D2
Sullivan *Ill., U.S.A.* 39°36N 88°37W **80** F9
Sullivan *Mo., U.S.A.* 38°13N 91°10W **80** F8
Sullivan Bay *Canada* 50°55N 126°50W **70** C3
Sullivan I. = Lanbi Kyun
  Burma 10°50N 98°20E **39** G2
Sullom Voe *U.K.* 60°27N 1°20W **11** A7
Sulphur *La., U.S.A.* 30°14N 93°23W **84** F8
Sulphur *Okla., U.S.A.* 34°31N 96°58W **84** D6
Sulphur Pt. *Canada* 60°56N 114°48W **70** A6
Sulphur Springs *U.S.A.* 33°8N 95°36W **84** E7
Sultan *Canada* 47°36N 82°47W **72** C3
Sultan *U.S.A.* 47°52N 121°49W **78** C5
Sultan Hamud *Kenya* 2°1S 37°22E **54** C4
Sultanabad = Arāk *Iran* 34°0N 49°40E **45** C6
Sultanpur *Mad. P., India* 23°9N 77°56E **42** H8
Sultanpur *Punjab, India* 31°13N 75°11E **42** D6

Sultanpur *Ut. P., India* 26°18N 82°4E **43** F10
Sulu Arch. *Phil.* 6°0N 121°0E **37** C6
Sulu Sea *E. Indies* 8°0N 120°0E **37** C6
Sulūq *Libya* 31°44N 20°14E **51** B10
Sulzberger Ice Shelf
  Antarctica 78°0S 150°0W **5** E13
Sumalata *Indonesia* 1°0N 122°31E **37** D6
Sumampa *Argentina* 29°25S 63°29W **94** B3
Sumatera *Indonesia* 0°40N 100°20E **36** D2
Sumatera Barat □
  Indonesia 1°0S 101°0E **36** E2
Sumatera Utara □
  Indonesia 2°30N 98°0E **36** D1
Sumatra = Sumatera
  Indonesia 0°40N 100°20E **36** D2
Sumba *Indonesia* 9°45S 119°35E **37** F5
Sumba, Selat *Indonesia* 9°0S 118°40E **37** F5
Sumbawa *Indonesia* 8°26S 117°30E **36** F5
Sumbawa Besar
  Indonesia 8°30S 117°26E **36** F5
Sumbawanga □ *Tanzania* 8°0S 31°30E **52** F6
Sumbe *Angola* 11°10S 13°48E **52** G2
Sumbu □ *Zambia* 8°43S 30°22E **55** D3
Sumburgh Hd. *U.K.* 59°52N 1°17W **11** B7
Sumdeo *India* 31°26N 78°44E **43** D8
Sumdo *India* 35°6N 78°41E **43** B8
Sumedang *Indonesia* 6°52S 107°55E **37** G12
Šumen = Shumen
  Bulgaria 43°18N 26°55E **23** C12
Sumenep *Indonesia* 7°1S 113°52E **37** G15
Sumgait = Sumqayıt
  Azerbaijan 40°34N 49°38E **19** F8
Summer L. *U.S.A.* 42°50N 120°45W **76** E3
Summerland *Canada* 49°32N 119°41W **70** D5
Summerside *Canada* 46°24N 63°47W **73** C7
Summersville *U.S.A.* 38°17N 80°51W **81** F13
Summerville *Ga.,*
  U.S.A. 34°29N 85°21W **85** D12
Summerville *S.C., U.S.A.* 33°1N 80°11W **85** E14
Summit Lake *Canada* 54°20N 122°40W **70** C4
Summit Peak *U.S.A.* 37°21N 106°42W **77** H10
Sumner *Iowa, U.S.A.* 42°51N 92°6W **80** D7
Sumner *Wash., U.S.A.* 47°12N 122°14W **78** C4
Sumoto *Japan* 34°21N 134°54E **31** G7
Šumperk *Czech Rep.* 49°59N 16°59E **17** D9
Sumqayıt *Azerbaijan* 40°34N 49°38E **19** F8
Sumter *U.S.A.* 33°55N 80°21W **85** E14
Sun City *S. Africa* 25°17S 27°3E **56** D4
Sun City *Ariz., U.S.A.* 33°35N 112°16W **77** K7
Sun City *Calif., U.S.A.* 33°42N 117°11W **79** M9
Sun City Center *U.S.A.* 27°43N 82°21W **85** H13
Sun Valley *U.S.A.* 43°42N 114°21W **76** E6
Sunagawa *Japan* 43°29N 141°55E **30** C10
Sunan *N. Korea* 39°15N 125°40E **35** E13
Sunart, L. *U.K.* 56°42N 5°43W **11** E3
Sunburst *U.S.A.* 48°53N 111°55W **76** B8
Sunbury *Australia* 37°35S 144°44E **63** F3
Sunbury *U.S.A.* 40°52N 76°48W **83** F8
Sunchales *Argentina* 30°58S 61°35W **94** C3
Suncheon *S. Korea* 34°52N 127°31E **35** G14
Suncho Corral *Argentina* 27°55S 63°27W **94** B3
Suncook *U.S.A.* 43°8N 71°27W **83** C13
Sunda, Selat *Indonesia* 6°20S 105°30E **36** F3
Sunda Is. *Indonesia* 5°0S 105°0E **64** H2
Sunda Str. = Sunda, Selat
  Indonesia 6°20S 105°30E **36** F3
Sunda Trench = Java Trench
  Ind. Oc. 9°0S 105°0E **36** F3
Sundance *Canada* 56°32N 94°4W **71** B10
Sundance *U.S.A.* 44°24N 104°23W **76** D11
Sundar Nagar *India* 31°32N 76°53E **42** D7
Sundarbans *Asia* 22°0N 89°0E **41** J16
Sundargarh *India* 22°4N 84°5E **41** H14
Sundays = Sondags →
  S. Africa 33°44S 25°51E **56** E4
Sunderland *Canada* 44°16N 79°4W **82** B5
Sunderland *U.K.* 54°55N 1°23W **12** C6
Sundown △ *Australia* 28°49S 151°38E **63** D5
Sundre *Canada* 51°49N 114°38W **70** C6
Sung Hei *Vietnam* 10°20N 106°2E **39** G6
Sungai Acheh *Malaysia* 5°8N 100°30E **39** c
Sungai Kolok *Thailand* 6°2N 101°58E **39** J3
Sungai Lembing *Malaysia* 3°55N 103°3E **39** L4
Sungai Petani *Malaysia* 5°37N 100°30E **39** K3
Sungaigerong *Indonesia* 2°59S 104°52E **36** E2
Sungailiat *Indonesia* 1°51S 106°8E **36** E3
Sungaipenuh *Indonesia* 2°1S 101°20E **36** E2
Sungari = Songhua Jiang →
  China 47°45N 132°30E **33** B8
Sunghua Chiang = Songhua
  Jiang → *China* 47°45N 132°30E **33** B8
Sunland Park *U.S.A.* 31°50N 106°40W **77** L10
Sunndalsøra *Norway* 62°40N 8°33E **8** E13
Sunnyside *U.S.A.* 46°20N 120°0W **76** C4
Sunnyvale *U.S.A.* 37°23N 122°2W **78** H4
Sunrise Manor *U.S.A.* 36°12N 115°4W **79** J12
Suntar *Russia* 62°15N 117°30E **29** C12
Suomenselkä *Finland* 62°52N 24°0E **8** E21
Suomi = Finland ■ *Europe* 63°0N 27°0E **8** E22
Suomussalmi *Finland* 64°54N 29°10E **8** D23
Suoyarvi *Russia* 62°3N 32°20E **18** B5
Supaul *India* 26°10N 86°40E **43** F12
Superior *Ariz., U.S.A.* 33°18N 111°6W **77** K8
Superior *Mont., U.S.A.* 47°12N 114°53W **76** C6
Superior *Nebr., U.S.A.* 40°1N 98°4W **80** E4
Superior *Wis., U.S.A.* 46°44N 92°6W **80** B6
Superior, L. *N. Amer.* 47°0N 87°0W **72** C2
Suphan Buri *Thailand* 14°14N 100°10E **38** E3
Suphan Dağı *Turkey* 38°54N 42°48E **44** B4
Supiori *Indonesia* 1°0S 136°0E **37** E9
Suppung Shuiku *China* 40°35N 124°50E **35** D13
Suqian *China* 33°54N 118°8E **35** H10
Sūq ash Shuyūkh *Iraq* 30°53N 46°28E **44** D5
Sūq Suwayq *Si. Arabia* 24°23N 38°27E **44** E3

Suqian *China* 33°54N 118°8E **35 H10**
Suquṭra = Socotra *Yemen* 12°30N 54°0E **47 E5**
Şūr *Lebanon* 33°19N 35°16E **46 B4**
Şūr *Oman* 22°34N 59°32E **47 C6**
Sur, Pt. *U.S.A.* 36°18N 121°54W **78 J5**
Sura → *Russia* 56°6N 46°0E **18 C8**
Surab *Pakistan* 28°25N 66°15E **42 E2**
Surabaja = Surabaya
  Indonesia 7°17S 112°45E **37 G15**
Surabaya *Indonesia* 7°17S 112°45E **37 G15**
Surakarta *Indonesia* 7°35S 110°48E **37 G14**
Surat *Australia* 27°10S 149°6E **63 D4**
Surat *India* 21°12N 72°55E **40 J8**
Surat Thani *Thailand* 9°6N 99°20E **39 H2**
Suratgarh *India* 29°18N 73°55E **42 E5**
Şuraymilā *Si. Arabia* 25°7N 46°7E **44 E5**
Surendranagar *India* 22°45N 71°40E **42 H4**
Surf *U.S.A.* 34°41N 120°36W **79 L6**
Surfers Paradise
  Australia 28°0S 153°25E **63 D5**
Surgut *Russia* 61°14N 73°20E **28 C8**
Suriapet *India* 17°10N 79°40E **40 L11**
Surigao *Phil.* 9°47N 125°29E **37 C7**
Surin *Thailand* 14°50N 103°34E **38 E4**
Surin Nua, Ko *Thailand* 9°30N 97°55E **39 H1**
Surinam = Suriname ■
  S. Amer. 4°0N 56°0W **93 C7**
Suriname ■ *S. Amer.* 4°0N 56°0W **93 C7**
Suriname → *Suriname* 5°50N 55°15W **93 B7**
Sūrmaq *Iran* 31°3N 52°48E **45 D7**
Surrey *Canada* 49°7N 122°45W **78 A4**
Surrey □ *U.K.* 51°15N 0°31W **13 F7**
Sursand *India* 26°39N 85°43E **43 F11**
Sursar → *India* 26°14N 87°3E **43 F12**
Surt *Libya* 31°11N 16°39E **51 B9**
Surt, Khalīj *Libya* 31°40N 18°30E **51 B9**
Surtanaha *Pakistan* 26°22N 70°0E **42 F4**
Surtsey *Iceland* 63°20N 20°30W **8 E3**
Suruga-Wan *Japan* 34°45N 138°30E **31 G9**
Sūsah *Libya* 32°52N 21°59E **51 B10**
Susaki *Japan* 33°22N 133°17E **31 H6**
Süsangerd *Iran* 31°35N 48°6E **45 D6**
Susanville *U.S.A.* 40°25N 120°39W **76 F3**
Susner *India* 23°57N 76°5E **42 H7**
Susquehanna *U.S.A.* 41°57N 75°36W **83 E9**
Susquehanna → *U.S.A.* 39°33N 76°5W **83 G8**
Susques *Argentina* 23°35S 66°25W **94 A2**
Sussex *Canada* 45°45N 65°37W **73 C6**
Sussex *U.S.A.* 41°13N 74°37W **83 E10**
Sussex, E. □ *U.K.* 51°0N 0°20E **13 G8**
Sussex, W. □ *U.K.* 51°0N 0°30E **13 G7**
Sustut → *Canada* 56°20N 127°30W **70 B3**
Susuman *Russia* 62°47N 148°10E **29 C15**
Susunu *Indonesia* 3°7S 133°39E **37 E8**
Susurluk *Turkey* 39°54N 28°8E **23 E13**
Sutay Uul *Asia* 46°35N 93°38E **32 B4**
Sutherland *S. Africa* 32°24S 20°40E **56 E3**
Sutherland *U.K.* 58°12N 4°50N **11 C4**
Sutherland *U.S.A.* 41°10N 101°8W **80 E3**
Sutherland Falls *N.Z.* 44°48S 167°46E **59 F1**
Sutherlin *U.S.A.* 43°23N 123°19W **76 E2**
Suthri *India* 23°3N 68°55E **42 H3**
Sutlej → *Pakistan* 29°23N 71°3E **42 E4**
Sutter *U.S.A.* 39°10N 121°45W **78 F5**
Sutter Buttes *U.S.A.* 39°12N 121°49W **78 F5**
Sutter Creek *U.S.A.* 38°24N 120°48W **78 G6**
Sutton *Canada* 45°6N 72°37W **83 A12**
Sutton *Nebr., U.S.A.* 40°36N 97°52W **80 E5**
Sutton *W. Va., U.S.A.* 38°40N 80°43W **81 F13**
Sutton → *Canada* 55°15N 83°45W **72 A3**
Sutton Coldfield *U.K.* 52°35N 1°49W **13 E6**
Sutton in Ashfield *U.K.* 53°8N 1°16W **12 D6**
Sutton L. *Canada* 54°15N 84°42W **72 B3**
Suttor → *Australia* 21°36S 147°2E **62 C4**
Suttsu *Japan* 42°48N 140°14E **30 C10**
Sutwik I. *U.S.A.* 56°34N 157°12W **74 D8**
Suva *Fiji* 18°6S 178°30E **59 a**
Suva Planina *Serbia* 43°10N 22°5E **23 C10**
Suvorov Is. = Suwarrow Is.
  Cook Is. 13°15S 163°5W **65 J11**
Suwałki *Poland* 54°8N 22°59E **17 A12**
Suwana *Indonesia* 8°44S 115°36E **37 K18**
Suwannaphum
  Thailand 15°33N 103°47E **38 E4**
Suwannee → *U.S.A.* 29°17N 83°10W **85 G13**
Suwanose-Jima *Japan* 29°38N 129°43E **31 K4**
Suwarrow Is. *Cook Is.* 13°15S 163°5W **65 J11**
Suweis, Khalīg el *Egypt* 28°40N 33°0E **51 C12**
Suweis, Qanâ es *Egypt* 31°0N 32°20E **51 B12**
Suwon *S. Korea* 37°17N 127°1E **35 F14**
Suzdal *Russia* 56°29N 40°26E **18 C7**
Suzhou *Anhui, China* 33°41N 116°59E **34 H9**
Suzhou *Jiangsu, China* 31°19N 120°38E **33 C7**
Suzu *Japan* 37°25N 137°17E **31 F8**
Suzu-Misaki *Japan* 37°31N 137°21E **31 F8**
Suzuka *Japan* 34°55N 136°36E **31 G8**
Svalbard *Arctic* 78°0N 17°0E **4 B8**
Svalbard Radio = Longyearbyen
  Svalbard 78°13N 15°40E **4 B8**
Svappavaara *Sweden* 67°40N 21°3E **8 C19**
Svartisen *Norway* 66°40N 13°59E **8 C16**
Svay Chek *Cambodia* 13°48N 102°58E **38 F4**
Svay Rieng *Cambodia* 11°9N 105°45E **39 G5**
Svealand □ *Sweden* 60°20N 15°0E **9 G16**
Sveg *Sweden* 62°2N 14°21E **8 E16**
Svendborg *Denmark* 55°4N 10°35E **9 J14**
Sverdrup Chan. *Canada* 79°56N 96°25W **69 B12**
Sverdrup Is. *Canada* 79°0N 97°0W **66 B10**
Sverige = Sweden ■
  Europe 57°0N 15°0E **9 H16**
Svetlaya *Russia* 46°33N 138°18E **30 A9**
Svetlogorsk = Svyetlahorsk
  Belarus 52°38N 29°46E **17 B15**
Svir → *Russia* 60°30N 32°48E **18 B6**
Svishtov *Bulgaria* 43°36N 25°23E **23 C11**
Svislach *Belarus* 53°3N 24°2E **17 B13**
Svizzera = Switzerland ■
  Europe 46°30N 8°0E **20 C8**
Svobodnyy *Russia* 51°20N 128°0E **29 D13**

Svolvær *Norway* 68°15N 14°34E **8 B16**
Svyetlahorsk *Belarus* 52°38N 29°46E **17 B15**
Swabian Alps = Schwäbische Alb
  Germany 48°20N 9°30E **16 D5**
Swaffham *U.K.* 52°39N 0°42E **13 E8**
Swains I. *Amer. Samoa* 11°11S 171°4W **65 J11**
Swainsboro *U.S.A.* 32°36N 82°20W **85 E13**
Swakop → *Namibia* 22°38S 14°36E **56 C2**
Swakopmund *Namibia* 22°37S 14°30E **56 C1**
Swale → *U.K.* 54°5N 1°20W **12 C6**
Swan → *Australia* 32°3S 115°45E **61 F2**
Swan → *Canada* 52°30N 100°45W **71 C8**
Swan Hill *Australia* 35°20S 143°33E **63 F3**
Swan Hills *Canada* 54°43N 115°24W **70 C5**
Swan Is. = Santanilla, Is.
  Honduras 17°22N 83°57W **88 C3**
Swan L. *Man., Canada* 52°30N 100°40W **71 C8**
Swan L. *Ont., Canada* 54°16N 91°11W **72 B1**
Swan Ra. *U.S.A.* 48°0N 113°45W **76 C7**
Swan River *Canada* 52°10N 101°16W **71 C8**
Swanage *U.K.* 50°36N 1°58W **13 G6**
Swansea *Australia* 42°8S 148°4E **63 G4**
Swansea *Canada* 43°38N 79°28W **82 C5**
Swansea *U.K.* 51°37N 3°57W **13 F4**
Swansea □ *U.K.* 51°38N 4°3W **13 F3**
Swartberge *S. Africa* 33°20S 22°0E **56 E3**
Swartmodder *S. Africa* 28°1S 20°32E **56 D3**
Swartnossob → *Namibia* 23°8S 18°42E **56 C2**
Swartruggens *S. Africa* 25°39S 26°42E **56 D4**
Swastika *Canada* 48°7N 80°6W **72 C3**
Swat → *Pakistan* 34°40N 72°5E **43 B5**
Swatow = Shantou
  China 23°18N 116°40E **33 D6**
Swaziland ■ *Africa* 26°30S 31°30E **57 D5**
Sweden ■ *Europe* 57°0N 15°0E **9 H16**
Sweet Grass *U.S.A.* 48°59N 111°58W **76 B8**
Sweet Home *U.S.A.* 44°24N 122°44W **76 D2**
Sweetwater *Nev., U.S.A.* 38°27N 119°9W **78 G7**
Sweetwater *Tenn., U.S.A.* 35°36N 84°28W **85 D12**
Sweetwater *Tex., U.S.A.* 32°28N 100°25W **84 E4**
Sweetwater → *U.S.A.* 42°31N 107°2W **76 E10**
Swellendam *S. Africa* 34°1S 20°26E **56 E3**
Świdnica *Poland* 50°50N 16°30E **17 C9**
Świdnik *Poland* 51°13N 22°39E **17 C12**
Świebodzin *Poland* 52°15N 15°31E **16 B8**
Świecie *Poland* 53°25N 18°30E **17 B10**
Swift Current *Canada* 50°20N 107°45W **71 C7**
Swift Current →
  Canada 50°38N 107°44W **71 C7**
Swilly, L. *Ireland* 55°12N 7°33W **10 A4**
Swindon *U.K.* 51°34N 1°46W **13 F6**
Swindon □ *U.K.* 51°34N 1°46W **13 F6**
Swinemünde = Świnoujście
  Poland 53°54N 14°16E **16 B8**
Swinford *Ireland* 53°57N 8°58W **10 C3**
Świnoujście *Poland* 53°54N 14°16E **16 B8**
Switzerland ■ *Europe* 46°30N 8°0E **20 C8**
Swords *Ireland* 53°28N 6°13W **10 C5**
Swoyerville *U.S.A.* 41°18N 75°53W **83 E9**
Sydenham → *Canada* 42°33N 82°25W **82 D2**
Sydney *Australia* 33°52S 151°12E **63 E5**
Sydney *Canada* 46°7N 60°7W **73 C7**
Sydney L. *Canada* 50°41N 94°25W **71 C10**
Sydney Mines *Canada* 46°18N 60°15W **73 C7**
Sydprøven = Alluitsup Paa
  Greenland 60°30N 45°35W **4 C5**
Sydra, G. of = Surt, Khalīj
  Libya 31°40N 18°30E **51 B9**
Sykesville *U.S.A.* 41°3N 78°50W **82 E6**
Syktyvkar *Russia* 61°45N 50°40E **18 B10**
Sylacauga *U.S.A.* 33°10N 86°15W **85 E11**
Sylarna *Sweden* 63°2N 12°13E **8 E15**
Sylhet *Bangla.* 24°54N 91°52E **41 G17**
Sylhet □ *Bangla.* 24°50N 91°50E **41 G17**
Sylt *Germany* 54°54N 8°22E **16 A5**
Sylvan Beach *U.S.A.* 43°12N 75°44W **83 C9**
Sylvan Lake *Canada* 52°20N 114°3W **70 C6**
Sylvania *Ga., U.S.A.* 32°45N 81°38W **85 E14**
Sylvania *Ohio, U.S.A.* 41°43N 83°42W **81 E12**
Sylvester *U.S.A.* 31°32N 83°50W **85 F13**
Sym *Russia* 60°20N 88°18E **28 C9**
Synnot Ra. *Australia* 16°30S 125°20E **60 C4**
Syowa *Antarctica* 68°50S 12°0E **5 C5**
Syracuse *Kans., U.S.A.* 37°59N 101°45W **80 G3**
Syracuse *N.Y., U.S.A.* 43°3N 76°9W **83 C8**
Syracuse *Nebr., U.S.A.* 40°39N 96°11W **80 E5**
Syrdarya → *Kazakhstan* 46°3N 61°0E **28 E7**
Syria ■ *Asia* 35°0N 38°0E **44 C3**
Syrian Desert = Shām, Bādiyat
  ash *Asia* 32°0N 40°0E **44 C3**
Syros = Ermoupoli
  Greece 37°28N 24°57E **23 F11**
Syzran *Russia* 53°12N 48°30E **18 D8**
Szczecin *Poland* 53°27N 14°27E **16 B8**
Szczecinek *Poland* 53°43N 16°41E **17 B9**
Szczeciński, Zalew = Stettiner Haff
  Germany 53°47N 14°15E **16 B8**
Szczytno *Poland* 53°33N 21°0E **17 B11**
Szechwan = Sichuan □
  China 30°30N 103°0E **32 C5**
Szeged *Hungary* 46°16N 20°10E **17 E11**
Székesfehérvár *Hungary* 47°15N 18°25E **17 E10**
Szekszárd *Hungary* 46°22N 18°42E **17 E10**
Szentes *Hungary* 46°39N 20°21E **17 E11**
Szolnok *Hungary* 47°10N 20°15E **17 E11**
Szombathely *Hungary* 47°14N 16°38E **17 E9**

T

Ta Khli *Thailand* 15°15N 100°21E **38 E3**
Ta Khli Khok *Thailand* 15°18N 100°20E **38 E3**
Ta Lai *Vietnam* 11°24N 107°23E **39 G6**
Tabacal *Argentina* 23°15S 64°15W **94 A3**
Tabaco *Phil.* 13°22N 123°44E **37 B6**
Tābah *Si. Arabia* 26°55N 42°38E **44 E4**
Tabanan *Indonesia* 8°32S 115°8E **37 K18**

Ţabas *Khorāsān, Iran* 32°48N 60°12E **45 C9**
Ţabas *Yazd, Iran* 33°35N 56°55E **45 C8**
Tabasará, Serranía de
  Panama 8°35N 81°40W **88 E3**
Tabasco □ *Mexico* 18°0N 92°40W **87 D6**
Tabāsīn *Iran* 31°12N 57°54E **45 D8**
Tabatinga, Serra da
  Brazil 10°30S 44°0W **93 F10**
Taber *Canada* 49°47N 112°8W **70 D6**
Tablas *Phil.* 12°25N 122°2E **37 B6**
Table, Pte. de la *Réunion* 21°14S 55°48E **53 c**
Table B. *Canada* 53°40N 56°25W **73 B8**
Table B. *S. Africa* 33°35S 18°25E **56 E2**
Table Mountain △
  S. Africa 34°2S 18°28E **56 E2**
Table Mt. *S. Africa* 33°58S 18°26E **56 E2**
Table Rock L. *U.S.A.* 36°36N 93°19W **80 G7**
Tabletop, Mt. *Australia* 23°24S 147°11E **62 C4**
Tábor *Czech Rep.* 49°25N 14°39E **16 D8**
Tabora *Tanzania* 5°2S 32°50E **54 D3**
Tabora □ *Tanzania* 5°0S 33°0E **54 D3**
Tabou *Ivory C.* 4°30N 7°20W **50 H4**
Tabrīz *Iran* 38°7N 46°20E **44 B5**
Tabuaeran *Kiribati* 3°51N 159°22W **65 G12**
Tabūk *Si. Arabia* 28°23N 36°36E **44 D3**
Tabūk □ *Si. Arabia* 27°40N 36°50E **44 E3**
Tacámbaro de Codallos
  Mexico 19°14N 101°28W **86 D4**
Tacheng *China* 46°40N 82°58E **32 B3**
Tach'ing Shan = Daqing Shan
  China 40°40N 111°0E **34 D6**
Tacloban *Phil.* 11°15N 124°58E **37 B6**
Tacna *Peru* 18°0S 70°20W **92 G4**
Tacoma *U.S.A.* 47°14N 122°26W **78 C4**
Tacuarembó *Uruguay* 31°45S 56°0W **95 C4**
Tademaït, Plateau du
  Algeria 28°30N 2°30E **50 C6**
Tadjoura *Djibouti* 11°50N 42°55E **47 E3**
Tadmor *N.Z.* 41°27S 172°45E **59 D4**
Tadoule L. *Canada* 58°36N 98°20W **71 B9**
Tadoussac *Canada* 48°11N 69°42W **73 C6**
Tadzhikistan = Tajikistan ■
  Asia 38°30N 70°0E **28 F8**
Taegu = Daegu
  S. Korea 35°50N 128°37E **35 G15**
Taegwan *N. Korea* 40°13N 125°12E **35 D13**
Taejŏn = Daejeon
  S. Korea 36°20N 127°28E **35 F14**
Taen, Ko *Thailand* 9°22N 99°57E **39 b**
Tafalla *Spain* 42°30N 1°41W **21 A5**
Tafelbaai = Table B.
  S. Africa 33°35S 18°25E **56 E2**
Tafermaar *Indonesia* 6°47S 134°10E **37 F8**
Tafi Viejo *Argentina* 26°43S 65°17W **94 B2**
Tafīhān *Iran* 29°25N 52°39E **45 D7**
Tafresh *Iran* 34°45N 49°57E **45 C6**
Taft *Iran* 31°45N 54°14E **45 D7**
Taft *Phil.* 11°57N 125°30E **37 B7**
Taft *U.S.A.* 35°8N 119°28W **79 K7**
Taftan *Pakistan* 29°0N 61°30E **40 E2**
Taftān, Kūh-e *Iran* 28°40N 61°0E **45 D9**
Taga *Samoa* 13°46S 172°28W **59 b**
Taga Dzong *Bhutan* 27°5N 89°55E **41 F16**
Taganrog *Russia* 47°12N 38°50E **19 E6**
Tagbilaran *Phil.* 9°39N 123°51E **37 C6**
Tagish *Canada* 60°19N 134°16W **70 A2**
Tagish L. *Canada* 60°10N 134°20W **70 A2**
Tagliamento → *Italy* 45°38N 13°6E **22 B5**
Tagomago *Spain* 39°2N 1°39E **24 B8**
Taguatinga *Brazil* 12°27S 46°22W **93 F10**
Tagum *Phil.* 7°33N 125°53E **37 C7**
Tagus = Tejo → *Europe* 38°40N 9°24W **21 C1**
Tahakopa *N.Z.* 46°30S 169°23E **59 G2**
Tahan, Gunung
  Malaysia 4°34N 102°17E **39 K4**
Tahat *Algeria* 23°18N 5°33E **50 D7**
Tāherī *Iran* 27°43N 52°20E **45 E7**
Tahiti *French Polynesia* 17°37S 149°27W **59 d**
Tahiti, I. *Tahiti* 17°37S 149°27W **59 d**
Tahlequah *U.S.A.* 35°55N 94°58W **84 D7**
Tahoe, L. *U.S.A.* 39°6N 120°2W **78 G6**
Tahoe City *U.S.A.* 39°10N 120°9W **78 F6**
Tahoka *U.S.A.* 33°10N 101°48W **84 E4**
Taholah *U.S.A.* 47°21N 124°17W **78 C2**
Tahoua *Niger* 14°57N 5°16E **50 F7**
Tahrūd *Iran* 29°26N 57°49E **45 D8**
Tahsis *Canada* 49°55N 126°40W **70 D3**
Tahta *Egypt* 26°44N 31°32E **51 C12**
Tahulandang *Indonesia* 2°27N 125°23E **37 D7**
Tahuna *Indonesia* 3°38N 125°30E **37 D7**
Tai Au Mun *China* 22°18N 114°17E **33 G11**
Tai Mo Shan *China* 22°25N 114°7E **33 G11**
Tai O *China* 22°15N 113°52E **33 G10**
Tai Pang Wan *China* 22°33N 114°24E **33 F11**
Tai Po *China* 22°27N 114°10E **33 G11**
Tai Rom Yen △ *Thailand* 8°45N 99°30E **39 H2**
Tai Shan *China* 36°25N 117°20E **35 F9**
Tai Yue Shan = Lantau I.
  China 22°15N 113°56E **33 G10**
Tai'an *China* 36°12N 117°8E **35 F9**
Taiarapu, Presqu'ile de
  Tahiti 17°47S 149°14W **59 d**
Taibei = T'aipei *Taiwan* 25°4N 121°29E **33 D7**
Taibique *Canary Is.* 27°42N 17°58W **24 G2**
Taibus Qi *China* 41°54N 115°22E **34 D8**
T'aichung *Taiwan* 24°12N 120°35E **33 D7**
Taieri → *N.Z.* 46°3S 170°12E **59 G3**
Taigu *China* 37°28N 112°30E **34 F7**
Taihang Shan *China* 36°0N 113°30E **34 G7**
Taihape *N.Z.* 39°41S 175°48E **59 C5**
Taihe *China* 33°20N 115°42E **34 H8**
Tailem Bend *Australia* 35°12S 139°29E **63 F2**
Taimyr Peninsula = Taymyr,
  Poluostrov *Russia* 75°0N 100°0E **29 B11**
Tain *U.K.* 57°49N 4°4W **11 D4**
T'ainan *Taiwan* 23°0N 120°10E **33 D7**
Taipa *China* 22°10N 113°35E **33 G10**
T'aipei *Taiwan* 25°4N 121°29E **33 D7**

Taiping *Malaysia* 4°51N 100°44E **39 K3**
Taipingzhen *China* 33°35N 111°42E **34 H6**
Tairbeart = Tarbert *U.K.* 57°54N 6°49W **11 D2**
Taita Hills *Kenya* 3°25S 38°15E **54 C4**
Taitao, Pen. de *Chile* 46°30S 75°0W **96 F2**
T'aitung *Taiwan* 22°43N 121°4E **33 D7**
Taivalkoski *Finland* 65°33N 28°12E **8 D23**
Taiwan ■ *Asia* 23°30N 121°0E **33 D7**
Taiyiba *Israel* 32°36N 35°27E **46 C4**
Taiyuan *China* 37°52N 112°33E **34 F7**
Taizhong = T'aichung
  Taiwan 24°9N 120°37E **33 D7**
Ta'izz *Yemen* 13°35N 44°2E **47 E3**
Tājābād *Iran* 30°2N 54°24E **45 D7**
Tajikistan ■ *Asia* 38°30N 70°0E **28 F8**
Tajima *Japan* 37°12N 139°46E **31 F9**
Tajo = Tejo → *Europe* 38°40N 9°24W **21 C1**
Tajrīsh *Iran* 35°48N 51°25E **45 C6**
Tak *Thailand* 16°52N 99°8E **38 D2**
Takāb *Iran* 36°24N 47°7E **44 B5**
Takachiho *Japan* 32°42N 131°18E **31 H5**
Takada *Japan* 37°7N 138°15E **31 F9**
Takahagi *Japan* 36°43N 140°45E **31 F10**
Takaka *N.Z.* 40°51S 172°50E **59 D4**
Takamaka *Seychelles* 4°50S 55°30E **53 b**
Takamatsu *Japan* 34°20N 134°5E **31 G7**
Takaoka *Japan* 36°47N 137°0E **31 F8**
Takapuna *N.Z.* 36°47S 174°47E **59 B5**
Takasaki *Japan* 36°20N 139°0E **31 F9**
Takatsuki *Japan* 34°51N 135°37E **31 G7**
Takaungu *Kenya* 3°38S 39°52E **54 C4**
Takayama *Japan* 36°18N 137°11E **31 F8**
Take-Shima *Japan* 30°49N 130°26E **31 J5**
Takefu *Japan* 35°50N 136°10E **31 G8**
Takengon *Indonesia* 4°45N 96°50E **36 D1**
Takeo *Japan* 33°12N 130°1E **31 H5**
Takeshima = Tokdo
  Asia 37°15N 131°52E **31 F5**
Taketa *Japan* 32°58N 131°24E **31 H5**
Takev *Cambodia* 10°59N 104°47E **39 G5**
Takh *India* 33°6N 77°32E **43 C7**
Takhmau *Cambodia* 11°29N 104°57E **39 G5**
Takht-Sulaiman
  Pakistan 31°40N 69°58E **42 D3**
Takikawa *Japan* 43°33N 141°54E **30 C10**
Takla L. *Canada* 55°15N 125°45W **70 B3**
Takla Landing *Canada* 55°30N 125°50W **70 B3**
Takla Makan = Taklamakan Shamo *China* 38°0N 83°0E **32 C3**
Taklamakan Shamo = Takla
  Makan *China* 38°0N 83°0E **32 C3**
Taksimo *Russia* 56°20N 114°52E **29 D12**
Taku → *Canada* 58°30N 133°50W **70 B2**
Takua Pa *Thailand* 8°52N 98°21E **39 H2**
Takua Thung *Thailand* 8°24N 98°27E **39 a**
Tal Halāl *Iran* 28°54N 55°1E **45 D7**
Tala *Uruguay* 34°21S 55°46W **95 C4**
Talagang *Pakistan* 32°55N 72°25E **42 C5**
Talagante *Chile* 33°40S 70°50W **94 C1**
Talamanca, Cordillera de
  Cent. Amer. 9°20N 83°20W **88 E3**
Talampaya △ *Argentina* 29°43S 67°42W **94 B2**
Talara *Peru* 4°38S 81°18W **92 D2**
Talas *Kyrgyzstan* 42°30N 72°13E **28 E8**
Talâta *Egypt* 30°36N 32°20E **46 E1**
Talaud, Kepulauan
  Indonesia 4°30N 126°50E **37 D7**
Talaud Is. = Talaud, Kepulauan
  Indonesia 4°30N 126°50E **37 D7**
Talavera de la Reina
  Spain 39°55N 4°46W **21 C3**
Talayan *Phil.* 6°52N 124°24E **37 C6**
Talbandh *India* 22°3N 86°20E **43 H12**
Talbot, C. *Australia* 13°48S 126°43E **60 B4**
Talbragar → *Australia* 32°12S 148°37E **63 E4**
Talca *Chile* 35°28S 71°40W **94 D1**
Talcahuano *Chile* 36°40S 73°10W **94 D1**
Talcher *India* 21°0N 85°18E **41 J14**
Taldy Kurgan = Taldyqorghan
  Kazakhstan 45°10N 78°45E **28 E8**
Taldyqorghan
  Kazakhstan 45°10N 78°45E **28 E8**
Tälesh *Iran* 37°58N 48°58E **45 B6**
Tālesh, Kūhhā-ye *Iran* 37°42N 48°55E **45 B6**
Tali Post *Sudan* 5°55N 30°44E **51 G12**
Taliabu *Indonesia* 1°50S 125°0E **37 E6**
Talibon *Phil.* 10°9N 124°20E **37 B6**
Talihina *U.S.A.* 34°45N 95°3W **84 D7**
Taliwang *Indonesia* 8°50S 116°55E **36 F5**
Tall 'Afar *Iraq* 36°22N 42°27E **44 B4**
Tall Kalakh *Syria* 34°41N 36°15E **46 A5**
Talladega *U.S.A.* 33°26N 86°6W **85 E11**
Tallahassee *U.S.A.* 30°27N 84°17W **85 F12**
Tallangatta *Australia* 36°15S 147°19E **63 F4**
Tallering Pk. *Australia* 28°6S 115°37E **61 E2**
Talli *Pakistan* 29°32N 68°8E **42 E3**
Tallinn *Estonia* 59°22N 24°48E **9 G21**
Tallmadge *U.S.A.* 41°6N 81°27W **82 E3**
Tallulah *U.S.A.* 32°25N 91°11W **84 E9**
Talnakh *Russia* 69°29N 88°22E **29 C9**
Taloyoak *Canada* 69°32N 93°32W **68 D13**
Talpa de Allende
  Mexico 20°23N 104°51W **86 C4**
Talparo *Trin. & Tob.* 10°30N 61°17W **93 K15**
Talsi *Latvia* 57°10N 22°30E **9 H20**
Taltal *Chile* 25°23S 70°33W **94 B1**
Taltson → *Canada* 61°24N 112°46W **70 A6**
Talwood *Australia* 28°29S 149°29E **63 D4**
Talyawalka Cr. →
  Australia 32°28S 142°22E **63 E3**
Tam Ky *Vietnam* 15°34N 108°12E **38 E7**
Tam Quan *Vietnam* 14°35N 109°3E **38 E7**
Tama *U.S.A.* 41°58N 92°35W **80 E7**
Tama Abu, Banjaran
  Malaysia 3°10N 115°5E **36 D5**
Tamale *Ghana* 9°22N 0°50W **50 G5**
Taman Negara △
  Malaysia 4°38N 102°26E **39 K4**

Tamano *Japan* 34°29N 133°59E **31 G6**
Tamanrasset *Algeria* 22°50N 5°30E **50 D7**
Tamaqua *U.S.A.* 40°48N 75°58W **83 F9**
Tamar → *U.K.* 50°27N 4°15W **13 G3**
Tamarin *Mauritius* 20°19S 57°20E **53 d**
Tamarinda *Spain* 39°55N 3°49E **24 B10**
Tamashima *Japan* 34°32N 133°40E **31 G6**
Tamatave = Toamasina
  Madag. 18°10S 49°25E **57 B8**
Tamaulipas □ *Mexico* 24°0N 98°45W **87 C5**
Tamaulipas, Sierra de
  Mexico 23°30N 98°20W **87 C5**
Tamazula *Mexico* 24°57N 106°57W **86 C3**
Tamazunchale *Mexico* 21°16N 98°47W **87 C5**
Tambach *Kenya* 0°36N 35°31E **54 B4**
Tambacounda *Senegal* 13°45N 13°40W **50 F3**
Tambelan, Kepulauan
  Indonesia 1°0N 107°30E **36 D3**
Tambellup *Australia* 34°4S 117°37E **61 F2**
Tambo *Australia* 24°54S 146°14E **62 C4**
Tambo de Mora *Peru* 13°30S 76°8W **92 F3**
Tambohorano *Madag.* 17°30S 43°58E **57 B7**
Tambora *Indonesia* 8°12S 118°5E **36 F5**
Tamboura *C.A.R.* 5°10N 25°12E **54 A2**
Tambov *Russia* 52°45N 41°28E **18 D7**
Tambuku *Indonesia* 7°8S 113°40E **37 G15**
Tâmega → *Portugal* 41°5N 8°21W **21 B1**
Tamenglong *India* 25°0N 93°35E **41 G18**
Tamiahua, L. de *Mexico* 21°35N 97°35W **87 C5**
Tamil Nadu □ *India* 11°0N 77°0E **40 P10**
Tamluk *India* 22°18N 87°58E **43 H12**
Tammerfors = Tampere
  Finland 61°30N 23°50E **8 F20**
Tammisaari *Finland* 60°0N 23°26E **9 G20**
Tampa *U.S.A.* 27°56N 82°27W **85 H13**
Tampa, Tanjung
  Indonesia 8°55S 116°12E **37 K19**
Tampa B. *U.S.A.* 27°50N 82°30W **85 H13**
Tampere *Finland* 61°30N 23°50E **8 F20**
Tampico *Mexico* 22°13N 97°51W **87 C5**
Tampin *Malaysia* 2°28N 102°13E **39 L4**
Tampoi *Malaysia* 1°30N 103°39E **39 d**
Tamu *Burma* 24°13N 94°12E **41 G19**
Tamworth *Australia* 31°7S 150°58E **63 E5**
Tamworth *Canada* 44°29N 77°0W **82 B8**
Tamworth *U.K.* 52°39N 1°41W **13 E6**
Tan An *Vietnam* 10°32N 106°25E **39 G6**
Tan Chau *Vietnam* 10°48N 105°12E **39 G5**
Tan-Tan *Morocco* 28°29N 11°1W **50 C3**
Tana → *Kenya* 2°32S 40°31E **54 C5**
Tana → *Norway* 70°30N 28°14E **8 A23**
Tana, L. *Ethiopia* 13°5N 37°30E **47 E2**
Tana River Primate △
  Kenya 1°55S 40°7E **54 C5**
Tanabe *Japan* 33°44N 135°22E **31 H7**
Tanafjorden *Norway* 70°45N 28°25E **8 A23**
Tanaga I. *U.S.A.* 51°48N 177°53W **74 E4**
Tanahbala *Indonesia* 0°30S 98°30E **36 E1**
Tanahgrogot *Indonesia* 1°55S 116°15E **36 E5**
Tanahjampea *Indonesia* 7°10S 120°35E **37 F6**
Tanahmasa *Indonesia* 0°12S 98°39E **36 E1**
Tanahmerah *Indonesia* 6°5S 140°16E **37 F10**
Tanakpur *India* 29°5N 80°7E **43 E9**
Tanakura *Japan* 37°10N 140°20E **31 F10**
Tanami Desert *Australia* 18°50S 132°0E **60 C5**
Tanana *U.S.A.* 65°10N 152°4W **74 B9**
Tanana → *U.S.A.* 65°10N 151°58W **68 C1**
Tananarive = Antananarivo
  Madag. 18°55S 47°31E **57 B8**
Tánaro → *Italy* 44°55N 8°40E **20 D8**
Tancheng *China* 34°25N 118°20E **35 G10**
Tanch'ŏn *N. Korea* 40°27N 128°54E **35 D15**
Tanda *Ut. P., India* 26°33N 82°35E **43 F10**
Tanda *Ut. P., India* 28°57N 78°56E **43 E8**
Tandag *Phil.* 9°4N 126°9E **37 C7**
Tandaia *Tanzania* 9°25S 34°15E **55 D3**
Tandaué *Angola* 16°58S 18°5E **56 B2**
Tandil *Argentina* 37°15S 59°6W **94 D4**
Tandil, Sa. del *Argentina* 37°30S 59°0W **94 D4**
Tandlianwala *Pakistan* 31°3N 73°9E **42 D5**
Tando Adam *Pakistan* 25°45N 68°40E **42 G3**
Tando Allahyar *Pakistan* 25°28N 68°43E **42 G3**
Tando Bago *Pakistan* 24°47N 68°58E **42 G3**
Tando Mohommed Khan
  Pakistan 25°8N 68°32E **42 G3**
Tandou L. *Australia* 32°40S 142°5E **63 E3**
Tandoureh △ *Iran* 37°50N 59°0E **45 B8**
Tandragee *U.K.* 54°21N 6°24W **10 B5**
Tane-ga-Shima *Japan* 30°30N 131°0E **31 J5**
Taneatua *N.Z.* 38°4S 177°1E **59 C6**
Tanen Tong Dan = Dawna Ra.
  Burma 16°30N 98°30E **38 D2**
Tanezrouft *Algeria* 23°9N 0°11E **50 D6**
Tang, Koh *Cambodia* 10°16N 103°7E **39 G4**
Tang, Ra's-e *Iran* 25°21N 59°52E **45 E8**
Tang Krasang *Cambodia* 12°34N 105°3E **38 F5**
Tanga *Tanzania* 5°5S 39°2E **54 D4**
Tanga □ *Tanzania* 5°20S 38°0E **54 D4**
Tanganyika, L. *Africa* 6°40S 30°0E **54 D3**
Tanger *Morocco* 35°50N 5°49W **50 A4**
Tangerang *Indonesia* 6°11S 106°37E **37 G12**
Tanggu *China* 39°2N 117°40E **35 E9**
Tanggula Shan *China* 32°40N 92°10E **32 C4**
Tanggula Shankou
  China 32°42N 92°27E **32 C4**
Tanghe *China* 32°47N 112°50E **34 H7**
Tanghla Range = Tanggula Shan
  China 32°40N 92°10E **32 C4**
Tangier = Tanger
  Morocco 35°50N 5°49W **50 A4**
Tangjia *China* 22°21N 113°35E **33 G10**
Tangjia Wan *China* 22°21N 113°36E **33 G10**
Tangorin *Australia* 21°47S 144°12E **62 C3**
Tangorombohitr'i Makay
  Madag. 21°0S 45°15E **57 C8**
Tangra Yumco *China* 31°0N 86°38E **32 C3**
Tangshan *China* 39°38N 118°10E **35 E10**
Tangtou *China* 35°28N 118°30E **35 G10**

Tanimbar, Kepulauan
  Indonesia 7°30S 131°30E **37** F8
Tanimbar Is. = Tanimbar,
  Kepulauan Indonesia 7°30S 131°30E **37** F8
Taninthari = Tenasserim
  Burma 12°6N 99°3E **39** F2
Tanjay Phil. 9°30N 123°5E **37** C6
Tanjong Malim Malaysia 3°42N 101°31E **39** L3
Tanjong Pelepas Malaysia 1°21N 103°33E **39** d
Tanjore = Thanjavur
  India 10°48N 79°12E **40** P11
Tanjung Bali, Indonesia 8°21S 116°9E **37** J19
Tanjung Kalimantan,
  Indonesia 2°10S 115°25E **36** E5
Tanjung Tokong Malaysia 5°28N 100°18E **39** c
Tanjungbalai Indonesia 2°55N 99°44E **36** D1
Tanjungbatu Indonesia 2°23N 118°3E **36** D5
Tanjungkarang Telukbetung =
  Bandar Lampung
  Indonesia 5°20S 105°10E **36** F3
Tanjungpandan
  Indonesia 2°43S 107°38E **36** E3
Tanjungpinang Indonesia 1°5N 104°30E **36** D2
Tanjungredeb Indonesia 2°9N 117°29E **36** D5
Tanjungselor Indonesia 2°55N 117°25E **36** D5
Tank Pakistan 32°14N 70°25E **42** C4
Tankhala India 21°58N 73°47E **42** J5
Tankwa-Karoo △
  S. Africa 32°14S 19°50E **56** E2
Tannersville U.S.A. 41°3N 75°18W **83** E9
Tannu Ola Asia 51°0N 94°0E **29** D10
Tannum Sands
  Australia 23°57S 151°22E **62** C5
Tanout Niger 14°50N 8°55E **50** F7
Tanta Egypt 30°45N 30°57E **51** B12
Tantoyuca Mexico 21°21N 98°14W **87** C5
Tantung = Dandong
  China 40°10N 124°20E **35** D13
Tanunda Australia 34°30S 139°0E **63** E2
Tanzania ■ Africa 6°0S 34°0E **54** D3
Tanzhou China 22°16N 113°28E **33** G9
Tanzilla → Canada 58°8N 130°43W **70** B2
Tao, Ko Thailand 10°5N 99°52E **39** G2
Tao'an = Taonan
  China 45°22N 122°40E **35** B12
Tao'er He → China 45°45N 124°5E **35** B13
Taolanaro Madag. 25°2S 47°0E **57** D8
Taole China 38°48N 106°40E **34** E4
Taonan China 45°22N 122°40E **35** B12
Taos U.S.A. 36°24N 105°35W **77** H11
Taoudenni Mali 22°40N 3°55W **50** D5
Tapa Estonia 59°15N 25°50E **9** G21
Tapa Shan = Daba Shan
  China 32°0N 109°0E **33** C5
Tapachula Mexico 14°54N 92°17W **87** E6
Tapah Malaysia 4°12N 101°15E **39** K3
Tapaktuan Indonesia 3°15N 97°10E **36** D1
Tapajós → Brazil 2°24S 54°41W **93** D8
Tapanahoni → Suriname 4°20N 54°25W **93** C8
Tapanui N.Z. 45°56S 169°18E **59** F2
Tapauá → Brazil 5°40S 64°21W **92** E6
Tapes Brazil 30°40S 51°23W **95** C5
Tapeta Liberia 6°29N 8°52W **50** G4
Taphan Hin Thailand 16°13N 100°26E **38** D3
Tapirapecó, Serra
  Venezuela 1°10N 65°0W **92** C6
Tapo-Capara △ Venezuela 7°55N 71°15W **89** E5
Tapti → India 21°8N 72°41E **40** J8
Tapuae-o-Uenuku N.Z. 42°0S 173°39E **59** E4
Tapul Group Phil. 5°35N 120°50E **37** C6
Tapurucuará Brazil 0°24S 65°2W **92** D5
Taqtaq Iraq 35°53N 44°35E **44** C5
Taquara Brazil 29°36S 50°46W **95** B5
Taquari → Brazil 19°15S 57°17W **92** G7
Tara Australia 27°17S 150°31E **63** D5
Tara Canada 44°28N 81°9W **82** B3
Tara Russia 56°55N 74°24E **28** D8
Tara Zambia 16°58S 26°45E **55** F2
Tara → Montenegro 43°21N 18°51E **23** C8
Tarābulus Lebanon 34°31N 35°50E **46** A4
Tarābulus Libya 32°49N 13°7E **51** B8
Tarābulus N. Afr. 31°0N 13°0E **51** B8
Taradehi India 23°18N 79°21E **43** H8
Tarajalejo Canary Is. 28°12N 14°7W **24** F5
Tarakan Indonesia 3°20N 117°35E **36** D5
Tarakit, Mt. Kenya 2°2N 35°10E **54** B4
Tarama-Jima Japan 24°39N 124°42E **31** M2
Taran, Mys Russia 54°56N 19°59E **9** J18
Taranaki □ N.Z. 39°25S 174°30E **59** C5
Taranaki, Mt. N.Z. 39°17S 174°5E **59** C5
Tarancón Spain 40°1N 3°1W **21** B4
Tarangire △ Tanzania 4°21S 36°7E **54** C4
Taransay U.K. 57°54N 7°0W **11** D1
Táranto Italy 40°28N 17°14E **22** D7
Táranto, G. di Italy 40°8N 17°20E **22** D7
Tarapacá Colombia 2°56S 69°46W **92** D5
Tarapacá □ Chile 20°45S 69°30W **94** A2
Tarapoto Peru 6°30S 76°20W **92** E3
Tararua Ra. N.Z. 40°45S 175°25E **59** D5
Tarashcha Ukraine 49°30N 30°31E **17** D10
Tarauacá Brazil 8°6S 70°48W **92** E4
Tarauacá → Brazil 6°42S 69°48W **92** E5
Taravao Tahiti 17°43S 149°19W **59** d
Taravao, Isthme de
  Tahiti 17°43S 149°19W **59** d
Tarawa Kiribati 1°30N 173°0E **64** G9
Tarawera N.Z. 39°2S 176°36E **59** C6
Tarawera, L. N.Z. 38°13S 176°27E **59** C6
Taraz Kazakhstan 42°54N 71°22E **28** E8
Tarazona Spain 41°55N 1°43W **21** B5
Tarbagatay, Khrebet
  Kazakhstan 48°0N 83°0E **28** E9
Tarbat Ness U.K. 57°52N 3°47W **11** D5
Tarbela Dam Pakistan 34°8N 72°52E **42** B5
Tarbert Ireland 52°34N 9°22W **10** D2
Tarbert Argyll & Bute,
  U.K. 55°52N 5°25W **11** F3
Tarbert W. Isles, U.K. 57°54N 6°49W **11** D2

Tarbes France 43°15N 0°3E **20** E4
Tarboro U.S.A. 35°54N 77°32W **85** D16
Tarcoola Australia 30°44S 134°36E **63** E1
Tarcoon Australia 30°15S 146°43E **63** E4
Taree Australia 31°50S 152°30E **63** E5
Tarfaya Morocco 27°55N 12°55W **50** C3
Târgovişte Romania 44°55N 25°27E **17** F13
Târgu Jiu Romania 45°5N 23°19E **17** F12
Târgu Mureş Romania 46°31N 24°38E **17** E13
Tarif U.A.E. 24°3N 53°46E **45** E7
Tarifa Spain 36°1N 5°36W **21** D3
Tarija Bolivia 21°30S 64°40W **94** A3
Tarija □ Bolivia 21°30S 63°30W **94** A3
Tariku → Indonesia 2°55S 138°26E **37** E9
Tarim Basin = Tarim Pendi
  China 40°0N 84°0E **32** B3
Tarim He → China 39°30N 88°30E **32** C3
Tarim Pendi China 40°0N 84°0E **32** B3
Taritatu → Indonesia 2°54S 138°27E **37** E9
Tarka → S. Africa 32°10S 26°0E **56** E4
Tarka La Bhutan 27°12N 89°44E **43** F13
Tarkastad S. Africa 32°0S 26°16E **56** E4
Tarkhankut, Mys
  Ukraine 45°25N 32°30E **19** E5
Tarko Sale Russia 64°55N 77°50E **28** C8
Tarkwa Ghana 5°20N 2°0W **50** G5
Tarlac Phil. 15°29N 120°35E **37** A6
Tarma Peru 11°25S 75°45W **92** F3
Tarn → France 44°5N 1°6E **20** E4
Târnăveni Romania 46°19N 24°13E **17** E13
Tarnobrzeg Poland 50°35N 21°41E **17** C11
Tarnów Poland 50°3N 21°0E **17** C11
Tarnowskie Góry
  Poland 50°27N 18°54E **17** C10
Tărom Iran 28°11N 55°46E **45** D7
Taroom Australia 25°36S 149°48E **63** D4
Taroudannt Morocco 30°30N 8°52W **50** B4
Tarpon Springs U.S.A. 28°9N 82°45W **85** G13
Tarrafal C. Verde Is. 15°18N 23°39W **50** b
Tarragona Spain 41°5N 1°17E **21** B6
Tarraleah Australia 42°17S 146°26E **63** G4
Tarrasa = Terrassa Spain 41°34N 2°1E **21** B7
Tarrytown U.S.A. 41°4N 73°52W **83** E11
Tarshiha = Me'ona Israel 33°1N 35°15E **46** B4
Tarsus Turkey 36°58N 34°55E **44** B5
Tartagal Argentina 22°30S 63°50W **94** A3
Tartu Estonia 58°20N 26°44E **9** G22
Tartūs Syria 34°55N 35°55E **44** C2
Tarumizu Japan 31°29N 130°42E **31** J5
Tarutao = Ko Tarutao △
  Thailand 6°31N 99°26E **39** J2
Tarutao, Ko Thailand 6°33N 99°40E **39** J2
Tarutung Indonesia 2°0N 98°54E **36** D1
Taseko → Canada 52°8N 123°45W **70** C4
Tash-Kömür Kyrgyzstan 41°40N 72°10E **28** E8
Tash-Kumyr = Tash-Kömür
  Kyrgyzstan 41°40N 72°10E **28** E8
Tashauz = Dashoguz
  Turkmenistan 41°49N 59°58E **28** E6
Tashi Chho Dzong = Thimphu
  Bhutan 27°31N 89°45E **41** F16
Tashk, Daryācheh-ye
  Iran 29°45N 53°35E **45** D7
Tashkent = Toshkent
  Uzbekistan 41°20N 69°10E **28** E7
Tashtagol Russia 52°47N 87°53E **28** D9
Tasiilaq Greenland 65°40N 37°20W **4** C6
Tasik Kenyir Malaysia 5°5N 102°45E **39** K4
Tasikmalaya Indonesia 7°18S 108°12E **37** G13
Tåsjön Sweden 64°15N 15°40E **8** D16
Taskan Russia 62°59N 150°20E **29** C16
Tasman B. N.Z. 40°59S 173°25E **59** D4
Tasman Basin Pac. Oc. 46°0S 158°0E **64** M7
Tasman Mts. N.Z. 41°3S 172°25E **59** D4
Tasman Pen. Australia 43°10S 148°0E **63** G4
Tasman Sea Pac. Oc. 36°0S 160°0E **58** E9
Tasmania □ Australia 42°0S 146°30E **63** G4
Tasmanian Wilderness World
  Heritage Area △
  Australia 42°0S 146°0E **63** G4
Tassili n'Ajjer Algeria 25°47N 8°1E **50** C7
Tassili-Oua-n-Ahaggar
  Algeria 20°41N 5°30E **50** D7
Tat Ton △ Thailand 15°57N 102°2E **38** E4
Tata Morocco 29°46N 7°56W **50** C4
Tatabánya Hungary 47°32N 18°25E **17** E10
Tatahouine Tunisia 32°56N 10°27E **51** B8
Tataouine Tunisia 32°57N 10°29E **51** B8
Tatar Republic = Tatarstan □
  Russia 55°30N 51°30E **18** C9
Tatarbunary Ukraine 45°50N 29°39E **17** F15
Tatarsk Russia 55°14N 76°0E **28** D8
Tatarskiy Proliv Russia 50°0N 141°0E **29** E15
Tatarstan □ Russia 55°30N 51°30E **18** C9
Tatatua, Pte. Tahiti 17°44S 149°8W **59** d
Tateyama Japan 35°0N 139°50E **31** G9
Tathlina L. Canada 60°33N 117°39W **70** A5
Tathra Australia 36°44S 149°59E **63** F4
Tatinnai L. Canada 60°55N 97°40W **71** A9
Tatla Lake Canada 52°0N 124°20W **70** C4
Tatnam, C. Canada 57°16N 91°0W **71** B10
Tatra = Tatry Slovak Rep. 49°20N 20°0E **17** D11
Tatry Slovak Rep. 49°20N 20°0E **17** D11
Tatshenshini →
  Canada 59°28N 137°45W **70** B1
Tatsuno Japan 34°52N 134°33E **31** G7
Tatta Pakistan 24°42N 67°55E **42** G2
Tatuī Brazil 23°25S 47°53W **95** A6
Tatum U.S.A. 33°16N 103°19W **77** K12
Tat'ung = Datong China 40°6N 113°18E **34** D7
Tatvan Turkey 38°31N 42°15E **44** B4
Ta'ū Amer. Samoa 14°15S 169°23W **59** b
Taubaté Brazil 23°0S 45°36W **95** A6
Tauern Austria 47°15N 12°40E **16** E7
Taumarunui N.Z. 38°53S 175°15E **59** C5
Taumaturgo Brazil 8°54S 72°51W **92** E4
Taung S. Africa 27°33S 24°47E **56** D3
Taungdwingyi Burma 20°1N 95°40E **41** J19
Taunggyi Burma 20°50N 97°0E **41** J20

Taungup Burma 18°51N 94°14E **41** K19
Taunsa Pakistan 30°42N 70°39E **42** D4
Taunsa Barrage Pakistan 30°42N 70°50E **42** D4
Taunton U.K. 51°1N 3°5W **13** F4
Taunton U.S.A. 41°54N 71°6W **83** E13
Taunus Germany 50°13N 8°34E **16** C5
Taupo N.Z. 38°41S 176°7E **59** C6
Taupo, L. N.Z. 38°46S 175°55E **59** C5
Tauragė Lithuania 55°14N 22°16E **9** J20
Tauranga N.Z. 37°42S 176°11E **59** B6
Tauranga Harb. N.Z. 37°30S 176°5E **59** B6
Taureau, Rés. Canada 46°46N 73°50W **72** C5
Taurianova Italy 38°21N 16°1E **22** E7
Taurus Mts. = Toros Dağları
  Turkey 37°0N 32°30E **44** B2
Tautira Tahiti 17°44S 149°9W **59** d
Tauyskaya Guba
  Russia 59°20N 150°20E **29** D16
Tavan Bogd Uul
  Mongolia 49°10N 87°49E **32** B3
Tavastehus = Hämeenlinna
  Finland 61°0N 24°28E **8** F21
Tavda Russia 58°7N 65°8E **28** D7
Tavda → Russia 57°47N 67°18E **28** D7
Taverner B. Canada 67°12N 72°25W **69** D17
Taveta Kenya 3°23S 37°37E **54** C4
Taveuni Fiji 16°51S 179°58W **59** a
Tavira Portugal 37°8N 7°40W **21** D2
Tavistock Canada 43°19N 80°50W **82** C4
Tavistock U.K. 50°33N 4°9W **13** G3
Tavoy Burma 14°2N 98°12E **38** E2
Tavrichanka Russia 43°18N 131°59E **30** C5
Tavua Fiji 17°37S 177°5E **59** a
Tavuki Fiji 19°7S 178°8E **59** a
Taw → U.K. 51°4N 4°4W **13** F3
Tawa → India 22°48N 77°48E **42** H8
Tawas City U.S.A. 44°16N 83°31W **81** C12
Tawau Malaysia 4°20N 117°55E **36** D5
Tawi-Tawi Phil. 5°10N 120°15E **37** C6
Taxco Mexico 18°33N 99°36W **87** D5
Taxila Pakistan 33°42N 72°52E **42** C5
Taxkorgan Tajik Zizhixian
  China 37°49N 75°14E **32** C2
Tay → U.K. 56°37N 3°38W **11** E5
Tay, Firth of U.K. 56°25N 3°8W **11** E5
Tay, L. Australia 32°55S 120°48E **61** F3
Tay, L. U.K. 56°32N 4°8W **11** E4
Tayabamba Peru 8°15S 77°16W **92** E3
Tayabamba Peru 8°15S 77°16W **92** E3
Taygetos Oros Greece 37°0N 22°23E **23** F10
Taylakova Russia 59°13N 74°0E **28** D8
Taylor Canada 56°13N 120°40W **70** B4
Taylor Nebr., U.S.A. 41°46N 99°23W **80** E4
Taylor Pa., U.S.A. 41°23N 75°43W **83** E9
Taylor Tex., U.S.A. 30°34N 97°25W **84** F6
Taylor, Mt. U.S.A. 35°14N 107°37W **77** J10
Taylorville U.S.A. 39°33N 89°18W **80** F9
Taymā Si. Arabia 27°35N 38°45E **44** E3
Taymyr, Oz. Russia 74°20N 102°0E **29** B11
Taymyr, Poluostrov
  Russia 75°0N 100°0E **29** B11
Taypaq Kazakhstan 49°0N 51°47E **19** E9
Tayport U.K. 56°27N 2°52W **11** E6
Tayshet Russia 55°58N 98°1E **29** D10
Taytay Phil. 10°45N 119°30E **37** B5
Taytay Phil. 10°45N 119°30E **37** B5
Tāyyebād Iran 34°45N 60°45E **45** C9
Tāyyebād □ Iran 34°44N 60°44E **45** C9
Taz → Russia 67°32N 78°40E **28** C8
Taza Morocco 34°16N 4°6W **50** B5
Tāza Khurmātū Iraq 35°18N 44°20E **44** C5
Tazawa-Ko Japan 39°43N 140°40E **30** E10
Tazin → Canada 59°48N 109°55W **71** B7
Tazin L. Canada 59°44N 108°42W **71** B7
Tazovskiy Russia 67°30N 78°44E **28** C8
Tbilisi Georgia 41°43N 44°50E **19** F7
Tchad = Chad ■ Africa 15°0N 17°15E **51** F8
Tchad, L. Chad 13°30N 14°30E **51** F8
Tch'eng-tou = Chengdu
  China 30°38N 104°2E **32** C5
Tchentlo L. Canada 55°15N 125°0W **70** B4
Tchibanga Gabon 2°45S 11°0E **52** E2
Tch'ong-k'ing = Chongqing
  China 29°35N 106°25E **32** D5
Tczew Poland 54°8N 18°50E **17** A10
Te Anau, L. N.Z. 45°15S 167°45E **59** F1
Te Aroha N.Z. 37°32S 175°44E **59** B5
Te Awamutu N.Z. 38°1S 175°20E **59** C5
Te Ika a Maui = North I.
  N.Z. 38°0S 175°0E **59** C5
Te Kuiti N.Z. 38°20S 175°11E **59** C5
Te Puke N.Z. 37°46S 176°22E **59** B6
Te Waewae B. N.Z. 46°13S 167°33E **59** G1
Te Wai Pounamu = South I.
  N.Z. 44°0S 170°0E **59** F2
Teague U.S.A. 31°38N 96°17W **84** F6
Teahupoo Tahiti 17°50S 149°16W **59** d
Teapa Mexico 17°33N 92°57W **87** D6
Tebakang Malaysia 1°6N 110°30E **36** D4
Teberu Malaysia 1°30N 103°42E **39** d
Tébessa Algeria 35°22N 8°8E **50** A7
Tebicuary → Paraguay 26°36S 58°16W **94** B4
Tebingtinggi Riau,
  Indonesia 1°0N 102°45E **36** E2
Tebingtinggi Sumatera Utara,
  Indonesia 3°20N 99°9E **36** D1
Tecate Mexico 32°34N 116°38W **79** N10
Tecka Argentina 43°29S 70°48W **96** E2
Tecomán Mexico 18°55N 103°53W **86** D4
Tecopa U.S.A. 35°51N 116°13W **79** K10
Tecoripa Mexico 28°37N 109°57W **86** B3
Tecuala Mexico 22°23N 105°27W **86** C3
Tecuci Romania 45°51N 27°27E **17** F14
Tecumseh Mich., U.S.A. 42°0N 83°57W **81** D12
Tecumseh Okla., U.S.A. 35°15N 96°56W **84** D6

Tedzhen = Tejen
  Turkmenistan 37°23N 60°31E **28** F7
Tees → U.K. 54°37N 1°10W **12** C6
Tees B. U.K. 54°40N 1°9W **12** C6
Teeswater Canada 43°59N 81°17W **82** C3
Tefé Brazil 3°25S 64°50W **92** D6
Tegal Indonesia 6°52S 109°8E **37** G13
Tegallalang Indonesia 8°27S 115°17E **37** J18
Tegalsari Indonesia 8°25S 114°8E **37** J17
Tegid, L. = Bala, L. U.K. 52°53N 3°37E **12** E4
Tegucigalpa Honduras 14°5N 87°14W **88** D2
Tehachapi U.S.A. 35°8N 118°27W **79** K8
Tehachapi Mts. U.S.A. 35°0N 118°30W **79** L8
Teheran = Tehrān Iran 35°41N 51°25E **45** C6
Tehoru Indonesia 3°23S 129°30E **37** E7
Tehrān Iran 35°41N 51°25E **45** C6
Tehrān □ Iran 35°30N 51°30E **45** C6
Tehri India 30°23N 78°29E **43** D8
Tehuacán Mexico 18°27N 97°23W **87** D5
Tehuantepec Mexico 16°21N 95°13W **87** D5
Tehuantepec, G. de
  Mexico 15°50N 95°12W **87** D5
Tehuantepec, Istmo de
  Mexico 17°15N 94°30W **87** D6
Teide, Pico de Canary Is. 28°15N 16°38W **24** F3
Teifi → U.K. 52°5N 4°41W **13** E3
Teign → U.K. 50°32N 3°32W **13** G4
Teignmouth U.K. 50°33N 3°31W **13** G4
Tejam India 29°57N 80°11E **43** E9
Tejen Turkmenistan 37°23N 60°31E **28** F7
Tejen → Turkmenistan 37°24N 60°38E **45** B9
Tejo → Europe 38°40N 9°24W **21** C1
Tejon Pass U.S.A. 34°49N 118°53W **79** L8
Tekamah U.S.A. 41°47N 96°13W **80** E5
Tekapo, L. N.Z. 43°53S 170°33E **59** E3
Tekax Mexico 20°12N 89°17W **87** C7
Tekeli Kazakhstan 44°50N 79°0E **28** E8
Tekirdağ Turkey 40°58N 27°30E **23** D12
Tekkali India 18°37N 84°15E **41** K14
Tekoa U.S.A. 47°14N 117°4W **76** C5
Tekong Besar, Pulau
  Singapore 1°25N 104°3E **39** d
Tel Aviv ✈ (TLV) Israel 32°5N 34°49E **46** C3
Tel Aviv-Yafo Israel 32°4N 34°48E **46** C3
Tel Lakhish Israel 31°34N 34°51E **46** D3
Tel Megiddo Israel 32°35N 35°11E **46** C4
Tela Honduras 15°40N 87°28W **88** C2
Telanaipura = Jambi
  Indonesia 1°38S 103°30E **36** E2
Telavi Georgia 42°0N 45°30E **19** F8
Telde Canary Is. 27°59N 15°25W **24** G4
Telegraph Creek Canada 58°0N 131°10W **70** B2
Telekhany = Tsyelyakhany
  Belarus 52°30N 25°46E **17** B13
Telemark Norway 59°15N 7°40E **9** G12
Telén Argentina 36°15S 65°31W **94** D2
Teleng Iran 25°47N 61°3E **45** E9
Teles Pires → Brazil 7°21S 58°3W **92** E7
Telescope Pk. U.S.A. 36°10N 117°5W **79** J9
Telford U.K. 52°40N 2°27W **13** E5
Telford and Wrekin □
  U.K. 52°45N 2°27W **12** E5
Telkwa Canada 54°41N 127°5W **70** C3
Tell City U.S.A. 37°57N 86°46W **80** G10
Teller U.S.A. 65°16N 166°22W **74** B6
Tellicherry India 11°45N 75°30E **40** P9
Telluride U.S.A. 37°56N 107°49W **77** H10
Teloloapán Mexico 18°21N 99°51E **87** D5
Telpos Iz Russia 63°16N 59°13E **18** B10
Telsen Argentina 42°30S 66°50W **96** E3
Telšiai Lithuania 55°59N 22°14E **9** J20
Teluk Anson = Teluk Intan
  Malaysia 4°3N 101°0E **39** K3
Teluk Bahang Malaysia 5°28N 100°13E **39** c
Teluk Betung = Bandar Lampung
  Indonesia 5°20S 105°10E **36** F3
Teluk Intan Malaysia 4°3N 101°0E **39** K3
Teluk Kumbar Malaysia 5°18N 100°14E **39** c
Telukbutun Indonesia 4°13N 108°12E **36** D3
Telukdalam Indonesia 0°33N 97°30E **36** D1
Tema Ghana 5°41N 0°0 **50** G5
Temagami, L. Canada 47°0N 80°10W **72** C3
Temax Mexico 21°9N 88°56W **87** C7
Temba S. Africa 25°20S 28°17E **57** D4
Tembagapura Indonesia 4°20S 137°0E **37** E9
Tembe
  Dem. Rep. of the Congo 0°16S 28°14E **54** C2
Tembe ≏ S. Africa 26°51S 32°24E **57** D5
Temblor Range U.S.A. 35°20N 119°50W **79** K7
Teme → U.K. 52°11N 2°13W **13** E5
Temecula U.S.A. 33°30N 117°9W **79** M9
Temengor, Tasik
  Malaysia 5°24N 101°18E **39** K3
Temerloh Malaysia 3°27N 102°25E **39** L4
Teminabuan Indonesia 1°26S 132°1E **37** E8
Temir Kazakhstan 49°1N 57°14E **19** E10
Temirtau Kazakhstan 50°5N 72°56E **32** A1
Temirtau Russia 53°10N 87°30E **28** D9
Témiscamie → Canada 50°59N 73°5W **73** B5
Témiscamingue →
  Canada 46°44N 79°5W **72** C4
Témiscamingue, L.
  Canada 47°10N 79°25W **72** C4
Temosachic Mexico 28°57N 107°51W **86** B3
Tempe U.S.A. 33°24N 111°54W **77** K8
Tempiute U.S.A. 37°39N 115°38W **78** H11
Temple U.S.A. 31°6N 97°21W **84** F6
Temple B. Australia 12°15S 143°3E **62** A3
Templemore Ireland 52°47N 7°51W **10** D4
Templeton U.S.A. 35°33N 120°42W **78** K6
Templeton → Australia 21°0S 138°40E **62** C2
Tempoal de Sánchez
  Mexico 21°31N 98°23W **87** C5
Temuco Chile 38°45S 72°40W **96** D2
Temuka N.Z. 44°14S 171°17E **59** F3
Tenabo Mexico 20°3N 90°14W **87** C6
Tenaha U.S.A. 31°57N 94°15W **84** F7
Tenakee Springs
  U.S.A. 57°47N 135°13W **70** B1

Tenali India 16°15N 80°35E **41** L12
Tenancingo de Degollado
  Mexico 18°58N 99°36W **87** D5
Tenango del Valle
  Mexico 19°7N 99°33W **87** D5
Tenaro, Akra Greece 36°22N 22°27E **23** F10
Tenasserim Burma 12°6N 99°3E **39** F2
Tenasserim □ Burma 14°0N 98°30E **38** F2
Tenby U.K. 51°40N 4°42W **13** F3
Tenda, Colle di France 44°7N 7°36E **20** D7
Tendaho Ethiopia 11°48N 40°54E **47** E3
Tendukhera India 23°24N 79°33E **43** H8
Teneguía, Volcanes de
  Canary Is. 28°28N 17°51W **24** F2
Ténéré, Erg du Niger 17°35N 10°55E **51** E8
Tenerife Canary Is. 28°15N 16°35W **24** F3
Tenerife, Pico Canary Is. 27°43N 18°1W **24** G1
Tenerife Norte ✈ (TFN)
  Canary Is. 28°16N 16°17W **24** F3
Tenerife Sur ✈ (TFS)
  Canary Is. 28°3N 16°33W **24** F3
Teng Xian China 35°5N 117°10E **35** G9
Tengah, Kepulauan
  Indonesia 7°5S 118°15E **36** F5
Tengchong China 25°0N 98°28E **32** D4
Tengchowfu = Penglai
  China 37°48N 120°42E **35** F11
Tenggarong Indonesia 0°24S 116°58E **36** E5
Tengger Shamo China 38°0N 104°0E **34** E3
Tenggol, Pulau Malaysia 4°48N 103°41E **39** K4
Tengiz Köli Kazakhstan 50°30N 69°0E **32** A1
Teniente Enciso △
  Paraguay 21°5S 61°8W **94** A3
Teniente Rodolfo Marsh
  Antarctica 62°30S 58°0W **5** C18
Tenino U.S.A. 46°51N 122°51W **78** D4
Tenkasi India 8°55N 77°20E **40** Q10
Tenke Katanga,
  Dem. Rep. of the Congo 11°22S 26°40E **55** E2
Tenke Katanga,
  Dem. Rep. of the Congo 10°32S 26°7E **55** E2
Tennant Creek
  Australia 19°30S 134°15E **62** B1
Tennessee □ U.S.A. 36°0N 86°30W **85** D11
Tennessee → U.S.A. 37°4N 88°34W **80** G9
Teno, Pta. de Canary Is. 28°21N 16°55W **24** F3
Tenom Malaysia 5°4N 115°57E **36** C5
Tenosique Mexico 17°30N 91°24W **87** D6
Tenryū-Gawa → Japan 35°39N 137°48E **31** G8
Tenterden U.K. 51°4N 0°42E **13** F8
Tenterfield Australia 29°0S 152°0E **63** D5
Teófilo Otoni Brazil 17°50S 41°30W **93** G10
Tepa Indonesia 7°52S 129°31E **37** F7
Tepalcatepec →
  Mexico 18°35N 101°59W **86** D4
Tepehuanes Mexico 25°21N 105°44W **86** B3
Tepetongo Mexico 22°28N 103°9W **86** C4
Tepic Mexico 21°30N 104°54W **86** C4
Teplice Czech Rep. 50°40N 13°48E **16** C7
Tepoca, C. Mexico 30°20N 112°25W **86** A2
Tequila Mexico 20°54N 103°47W **86** C4
Ter → Spain 42°2N 3°12E **21** A7
Ter Apel Neths. 52°53N 7°5E **15** B7
Téra Niger 14°0N 0°45E **50** F6
Teraina Kiribati 4°43N 160°25W **65** G12
Téramo Italy 42°39N 13°42E **22** C5
Terang Australia 38°15S 142°55E **63** F3
Terceira Azores 38°43N 27°13W **50** a
Terceiro → Argentina 32°58S 61°47W **94** C3
Terebovlya Ukraine 49°18N 25°44E **17** D13
Terek → Russia 44°0N 47°30E **19** F8
Terepaima △ Venezuela 9°58N 69°17W **89** E6
Teresina Brazil 5°9S 42°45W **93** E10
Terewah, L. Australia 29°52S 147°35E **63** D4
Teridgerie Cr. →
  Australia 30°25S 148°50E **63** E4
Termas de Río Hondo
  Argentina 27°29S 64°52W **94** B3
Termez = Termiz
  Uzbekistan 37°15N 67°15E **28** F7
Términi Imerese Italy 37°59N 13°42E **22** F5
Términos, L. de Mexico 18°37N 91°33W **87** D6
Termiz Uzbekistan 37°15N 67°15E **28** F7
Térmoli Italy 42°0N 15°0E **22** C6
Ternate Indonesia 0°45N 127°25E **37** D7
Terneuzen Neths. 51°20N 3°50E **15** C3
Terney Russia 45°3N 136°37E **30** B8
Terni Italy 42°34N 12°37E **22** C5
Ternopil Ukraine 49°30N 25°40E **17** D13
Ternopol = Ternopil
  Ukraine 49°30N 25°40E **17** D13
Terowie Australia 33°8S 138°55E **63** E2
Terra Bella U.S.A. 35°58N 119°3W **79** K7
Terra Nova △ Canada 48°33N 53°55W **73** C9
Terrace Canada 54°30N 128°35W **70** C3
Terrace Bay Canada 48°47N 87°5W **72** C2
Terracina Italy 41°17N 13°15E **22** D5
Terralba Italy 39°43N 8°39E **22** E3
Terrassa Spain 41°34N 2°1E **21** B7
Terre Haute U.S.A. 39°28N 87°25W **80** F10
Terrebonne B. U.S.A. 29°5N 90°35W **85** G9
Terrell U.S.A. 32°44N 96°17W **84** E6
Terrenceville Canada 47°40N 54°44W **73** C9
Terry U.S.A. 46°47N 105°19W **76** C11
Terschelling Neths. 53°25N 5°20E **15** A5
Teruel Spain 40°22N 1°8W **21** B5
Tervola Finland 66°6N 24°49E **8** C21
Teryaweynya L.
  Australia 32°18S 143°22E **63** E3
Teshio Japan 44°53N 141°44E **30** B10
Teshio-Gawa → Japan 44°53N 141°45E **30** B10
Tesiyn Gol → Mongolia 50°40N 93°20E **32** A4
Teslin Canada 60°10N 132°43W **70** A2
Teslin → Canada 61°34N 134°35W **70** A2
Teslin L. Canada 60°15N 132°57W **70** A2
Tessalit Mali 20°12N 1°0E **50** D6
Tessaoua Niger 13°47N 7°56E **50** F7

Test → U.K. 50°56N 1°29W 13 G6
Testigos, Is. Los Venezuela 11°23N 63°7W 89 D7
Tetachuck L. Canada 53°18N 125°55W 70 C3
Tetas, Pta. Chile 23°31S 70°38W 94 A1
Tete Mozam. 16°13S 33°33E 55 F3
Tete □ Mozam. 15°15S 32°40E 55 F3
Teterev → Ukraine 51°1N 30°5E 17 C16
Teteven Bulgaria 42°58N 24°17E 23 C11
Tethul → Canada 60°35N 112°12W 70 A6
Tetiyev Ukraine 49°22N 29°38E 17 D15
Tetlit Zheh = Fort McPherson
  Canada 67°30N 134°55W 68 D5
Teton → U.S.A. 47°56N 110°31W 76 C8
Tétouan Morocco 35°35N 5°21W 50 A4
Tetovo Macedonia 42°1N 20°59E 23 C9
Tetufera, Mt. Tahiti 17°40S 149°26W 59 d
Teuco → Argentina 25°35S 60°11W 94 B3
Teulon Canada 50°23N 97°16W 71 C9
Teun Indonesia 6°59S 129°8E 37 F7
Teuri-Tō Japan 44°26N 141°19E 30 B10
Teutoburger Wald
  Germany 52°5N 8°22E 16 B5
Tevere → Italy 41°44N 12°14E 22 D5
Teverya Israel 32°47N 35°32E 46 C4
Teviot → U.K. 55°29N 2°38W 11 F6
Tewantin Australia 26°27S 153°3E 63 D5
Tewkesbury U.K. 51°59N 2°9W 13 F5
Texada I. Canada 49°40N 124°25W 70 D4
Texarkana Ark., U.S.A. 33°26N 94°2W 84 E7
Texarkana Tex., U.S.A. 33°26N 94°3W 84 E7
Texas Australia 28°49S 151°9E 63 D5
Texas □ U.S.A. 31°40N 98°30W 84 F5
Texas City U.S.A. 29°24N 94°54W 84 G7
Texel Neths. 53°5N 4°50E 15 A4
Texline U.S.A. 36°23N 103°2W 84 C3
Texoma, L. U.S.A. 33°50N 96°34W 84 E6
Teyateyaneng Lesotho 29°7S 27°34E 53 K5
Tezin Afghan. 34°24N 69°30E 42 B3
Teziutlán Mexico 19°49N 97°21W 87 D5
Tezpur India 26°40N 92°45E 41 F18
Tezzeron L. Canada 54°43N 124°30W 70 C4
Tha-anne → Canada 60°31N 94°37W 71 A10
Tha Deua Laos 17°57N 102°53E 38 D4
Tha Deua Laos 19°26N 101°50E 38 C3
Tha Li Thailand 17°37N 101°25E 38 D3
Tha Pla Thailand 17°48N 100°32E 38 D3
Tha Rua Thailand 14°34N 100°44E 38 E3
Tha Sala Thailand 8°40N 99°56E 39 H2
Tha Song Yang Thailand 17°34N 97°55E 38 D1
Thaba Putsoa Lesotho 29°45S 28°0E 57 D4
Thabana Ntlenyana
  Lesotho 29°30S 29°16E 57 D4
Thabazimbi S. Africa 24°40S 27°21E 57 C4
Thādiq Si. Arabia 25°18N 45°52E 44 E5
Thai Binh Vietnam 20°35N 106°1E 38 B6
Thai Muang Thailand 8°24N 98°16E 39 H2
Thai Nguyen Vietnam 21°35N 105°55E 38 B5
Thailand ■ Asia 16°0N 102°0E 38 E4
Thailand, G. of Asia 11°30N 101°0E 39 G3
Thakhek Laos 17°25N 104°45E 38 D5
Thal Pakistan 33°28N 70°33E 42 C4
Thal Desert Pakistan 31°10N 71°30E 42 D4
Thala La = Hkakabo Razi
  Burma 28°25N 97°23E 41 E20
Thalabarivat Cambodia 13°33N 105°57E 38 F5
Thalassery = Tellicherry
  India 11°45N 75°30E 40 P9
Thallon Australia 28°39S 148°49E 63 D4
Thalu, Ko Thailand 9°26N 99°54E 39 b
Thames N.Z. 37°7S 175°34E 59 B5
Thames → Canada 42°20N 82°25W 82 D2
Thames → U.K. 51°29N 0°34E 13 F8
Thames → U.S.A. 41°18N 72°5W 83 E12
Thames Estuary U.K. 51°29N 0°52E 13 F8
Thamesford Canada 43°4N 81°0W 82 C4
Thamesville Canada 42°33N 81°59W 82 D3
Than India 22°34N 71°11E 42 H4
Than Uyen Vietnam 22°0N 103°54E 38 B4
Thana Gazi India 27°25N 76°19E 42 F7
Thandla India 23°0N 74°34E 42 H6
Thandwe Burma 18°20N 94°30E 41 K19
Thane India 19°12N 72°59E 40 K8
Thanesar India 30°1N 76°52E 42 D7
Thanet, I. of U.K. 51°21N 1°20E 13 F9
Thangool Australia 24°38S 150°42E 62 C5
Thanh Hoa Vietnam 19°48N 105°46E 38 C5
Thanh Hung Vietnam 9°55N 105°43E 39 H5
Thanh Pho Ho Chi Minh
  Vietnam 10°58N 106°40E 39 G6
Thanh Thuy Vietnam 22°55N 104°51E 38 A5
Thanjavur India 10°48N 79°12E 40 P11
Thanlwin = Salween →
  Burma 16°31N 97°37E 41 L20
Thano Bula Khan
  Pakistan 25°22N 67°50E 42 G2
Thaolintoa L. Canada 61°30N 96°25W 71 A9
Thap Lan △ Thailand 14°15N 102°16E 38 E4
Thap Sakae Thailand 11°30N 99°37E 39 G2
Thap Than Thailand 15°27N 99°54E 38 E2
Thar Desert India 28°0N 72°0E 42 F5
Tharad India 24°30N 71°44E 42 G4
Thargomindah
  Australia 27°58S 143°46E 63 D3
Tharp Fracture Zone
  S. Ocean 54°0S 135°0W 5 B14
Tharrawaddy Burma 17°38N 95°48E 41 L19
Tharthar, Buhayrat ath
  Iraq 34°0N 43°15E 44 C4
Tharthar, L. = Tharthār,
  Buḩayrat ath Iraq 34°0N 43°15E 44 C4
Tharthār, W. ath → Iraq 34°32N 43°4E 44 C4
Thasos Greece 40°40N 24°40E 23 D11
That Khe Vietnam 22°16N 106°28E 38 A6
Thatcher Ariz., U.S.A. 32°51N 109°46W 77 K9
Thatcher Colo., U.S.A. 37°33N 104°7W 77 H11
Thaton Burma 16°55N 97°22E 41 L20
Thaungdut Burma 24°30N 94°40E 41 G19
Thayer U.S.A. 36°31N 91°33W 80 G8
Thayetmyo Burma 19°20N 95°10E 41 K19

Thazi Burma 21°0N 96°5E 41 J20
Thbeng Meanchey
  Cambodia 13°49N 104°58E 38 F5
The Broads U.K. 52°45N 1°30E 12 E9
The Everglades U.S.A. 25°50N 81°0W 85 J14
The Gulf = Persian Gulf
  Asia 27°0N 50°0E 45 E6
The Hague = 's-Gravenhage
  Neths. 52°7N 4°17E 15 B4
The Pas Canada 53°45N 101°15W 71 C8
The Wash U.K. 52°58N 0°20E 12 E8
The Weald U.K. 51°4N 0°20E 13 F8
Thebes = Thiva Greece 38°19N 23°19E 23 E10
Thebes Egypt 25°40N 32°35E 51 C12
Thedford U.S.A. 41°59N 100°35W 80 E3
Theebine Australia 25°57S 152°34E 63 D5
Thekulthili L. Canada 61°3N 110°0W 71 A7
Thelon → Canada 64°16N 96°4W 71 A8
Theodore Australia 24°55S 150°3E 62 C5
Theodore Canada 51°26N 102°55W 71 C8
Theodore U.S.A. 30°33N 88°10W 85 F10
Theodore Roosevelt △
  U.S.A. 47°0N 103°25W 80 B2
Theodore Roosevelt L.
  U.S.A. 33°40N 111°10W 77 K8
Thepha Thailand 6°52N 100°58E 39 J3
Theresa U.S.A. 44°13N 75°48W 83 B9
Thermopolis U.S.A. 43°39N 108°13W 76 D9
Thermopylae Greece 38°48N 22°35E 23 E10
Thessalon Canada 46°20N 83°30W 72 C3
Thessalonica, Gulf of =
  Thessaloniki Kolpos
  Greece 40°15N 22°45E 23 D10
Thessaloniki Greece 40°38N 22°58E 23 D10
Thessaloniki Kolpos
  Greece 40°15N 22°45E 23 D10
Thetford U.K. 52°25N 0°45E 13 E8
Thetford Mines Canada 46°8N 71°18W 73 C5
Theun → Laos 18°19N 104°0E 38 C5
Theunissen S. Africa 28°26S 26°43E 56 D4
Thevenard Australia 32°9S 133°38E 63 E1
Thibodaux U.S.A. 29°48N 90°49W 85 G9
Thicket Portage Canada 55°19N 97°42W 71 B9
Thief River Falls U.S.A. 48°7N 96°10W 80 A5
Thiel Mts. Antarctica 85°15S 91°0W 5 E16
Thiers France 45°52N 3°33E 20 D5
Thiès Senegal 14°50N 16°51W 50 F2
Thika Kenya 1°1S 37°5E 54 C4
Thimphu Bhutan 27°31N 89°45E 41 F16
Thina → S. Africa 31°18S 29°13E 57 E4
Þingvallavatn Iceland 64°11N 21°9W 8 D3
Thionville France 49°20N 6°10E 20 B7
Thira = Santorini
  Greece 36°23N 25°27E 23 F11
Third Cataract Sudan 19°42N 30°20E 51 E12
Thirsk U.K. 54°14N 1°19W 12 C6
Thiruvananthapuram =
  Trivandrum India 8°41N 77°0E 40 Q10
Thisted Denmark 56°58N 8°40E 9 H13
Thistle I. Australia 35°0S 136°8E 63 F2
Thithia = Cicia Fiji 17°45S 179°18W 59 a
Thiva Greece 38°19N 23°19E 23 E10
Þjórsá → Iceland 63°47N 20°48W 8 E3
Thlewiaza → Canada 60°29N 94°40W 71 A10
Thmar Puok Cambodia 13°57N 103°4E 38 F4
Tho Vinh Vietnam 19°16N 105°42E 38 C5
Thoa → Canada 60°31N 109°47W 71 A7
Thoen Thailand 17°43N 99°12E 38 D2
Thoeng Thailand 19°41N 100°12E 38 C3
Thohoyandou S. Africa 22°58S 30°29E 53 J6
Tholdi Pakistan 35°5N 76°6E 43 B7
Thomas U.S.A. 35°45N 98°45W 84 D5
Thomas, L. Australia 26°4S 137°58E 63 D2
Thomas Hubbard, C.
  Canada 82°0N 94°25W 69 A13
Thomaston U.S.A. 32°53N 84°20W 85 E12
Thomasville Ala.,
  U.S.A. 31°55N 87°44W 85 F11
Thomasville Ga., U.S.A. 30°50N 83°59W 85 F13
Thomasville N.C., U.S.A. 35°53N 80°5W 85 D15
Thompson → Canada 50°15N 121°24W 70 C4
Thompson → U.S.A. 39°46N 93°37W 80 F7
Thompson Falls U.S.A. 47°36N 115°21W 76 C6
Thompson Pk. U.S.A. 41°0N 123°2W 76 F2
Thompson Springs
  U.S.A. 38°58N 109°43W 76 G9
Thompsontown U.S.A. 40°33N 77°14W 82 F7
Thomson U.S.A. 33°28N 82°30W 85 E13
Thomson → Australia 25°11S 142°53E 62 C3
Thong Yang Thailand 9°28N 99°56E 39 b
Thoothukudi = Tuticorin
  India 8°50N 78°12E 40 Q11
Þórisvatn Iceland 64°20N 18°55W 8 D4
Thornaby on Tees U.K. 54°33N 1°18W 12 C6
Thornbury Canada 44°34N 80°26W 82 B4
Thorne U.K. 53°37N 0°57W 12 D7
Thornton Canada 44°16N 79°43W 82 B5
Thornton U.S.A. 39°52N 104°58W 76 G11
Thorold Canada 43°7N 79°12W 82 C5
Þórshöfn Iceland 66°12N 15°20W 8 C6
Thouin, C. Australia 20°20S 118°10E 60 D2
Thousand Islands U.S.A. 44°20N 76°0W 83 B9
Thousand Oaks U.S.A. 34°10N 118°50W 79 L8
Thrace Turkey 41°0N 27°0E 23 D12
Three Forks U.S.A. 45°54N 111°33W 76 D8
Three Gorges Res. = Sanxia
  Shuiku China 30°10N 108°0E 33 C5
Three Hills Canada 51°43N 113°15W 70 C6
Three Hummock I.
  Australia 40°25S 144°55E 63 G3
Three Pagodas Pass Asia 15°20N 98°30E 38 E2
Three Points, C. Ghana 4°42N 2°6W 50 H5
Three Rivers Calif.,
  U.S.A. 36°26N 118°54W 78 J8
Three Rivers Tex.,
  U.S.A. 28°28N 98°11W 84 G5
Three Springs Australia 29°32S 115°45E 61 E2

Thrissur = Trichur
  India 10°30N 76°18E 40 P10
Throssell, L. Australia 27°33S 124°10E 61 E3
Throssell Ra. Australia 22°3S 121°43E 60 D3
Thrushton △ Australia 27°47S 147°40E 63 D4
Thua → Kenya 1°31S 39°30E 54 C4
Thuan Hoa Vietnam 8°58N 105°30E 39 H5
Thubun Lakes Canada 61°30N 112°0W 71 A6
Thuin Belgium 50°20N 4°17E 15 D4
Thule = Qaanaaq
  Greenland 77°30N 69°10W 69 B18
Thule Air Base = Uummannaq
  Greenland 77°33N 68°52W 69 B18
Thun Switz. 46°45N 7°38E 20 C7
Thunder B. U.S.A. 45°0N 83°20W 82 B1
Thunder Bay Canada 48°20N 89°15W 72 C2
Thung Salaeng Luang △
  Thailand 16°43N 100°50E 38 D3
Thung Song Thailand 8°10N 99°40E 39 H2
Thunkar Bhutan 27°55N 91°0E 41 F17
Thuong Tra Vietnam 16°2N 107°42E 38 D6
Thüringer Wald Germany 50°35N 11°0E 16 C6
Thuringowa △
  Australia 19°18S 146°43E 62 B4
Thurles Ireland 52°41N 7°49W 10 D4
Thurrock □ U.K. 51°31N 0°23E 13 F8
Thursday I. Australia 10°30S 142°3E 62 A3
Thurso Canada 45°36N 75°15W 72 C4
Thurso U.K. 58°36N 3°32W 11 C5
Thurso → U.K. 58°36N 3°32W 11 C5
Thurston I. Antarctica 72°0S 100°0W 5 D16
Thutade L. Canada 57°0N 126°55W 70 B3
Thyolo Malawi 16°7S 35°5E 55 F4
Ti-Tree Australia 22°5S 133°22E 62 C1
Tian Shan Asia 40°30N 76°0E 32 B3
Tianjin China 39°7N 117°12E 35 E9
Tianshifu China 41°17N 124°22E 35 D13
Tianshui China 34°32N 105°40E 34 G3
Tianyar Indonesia 8°12S 115°30E 37 J18
Tianzhen China 40°24N 114°5E 34 D8
Tianzhuangtai China 40°43N 122°5E 35 D12
Tiarei Tahiti 17°32S 149°20W 59 d
Tiaret Algeria 35°20N 1°21E 50 A6
Tibagi Brazil 24°30S 50°24W 95 A5
Tibagi → Brazil 22°47S 51°1W 95 A5
Tibati Cameroon 6°22N 12°30E 52 C2
Tiber = Tevere → Italy 41°44N 12°14E 22 D5
Tiber Res. U.S.A. 48°19N 111°6W 76 B8
Tiberias = Teverya Israel 32°47N 35°32E 46 C4
Tiberias, L. = Yam Kinneret
  Israel 32°45N 35°35E 46 C4
Tibesti Chad 21°0N 17°30E 51 D9
Tibet = Xizang Zizhiqu □
  China 32°0N 88°0E 32 C3
Tibet, Plateau of Asia 32°0N 86°0E 26 E10
Tibnī Syria 35°36N 39°50E 44 C3
Tibooburra Australia 29°26S 142°1E 63 D3
Tiburón, I. Mexico 29°0N 112°25W 86 B2
Ticino → Italy 45°9N 9°14E 20 D8
Ticonderoga U.S.A. 43°51N 73°26W 83 C11
Ticul Mexico 20°24N 89°32W 87 C7
Tidaholm Sweden 58°12N 13°58E 9 G15
Tiddim Burma 23°28N 93°45E 41 H18
Tidioute U.S.A. 41°41N 79°24W 82 E5
Tidjikja Mauritania 18°29N 11°35W 50 E3
Tidore Indonesia 0°40N 127°25E 37 D7
Tiefa China 42°28N 123°26E 35 C12
Tiegang Shuiku China 22°37N 113°53E 33 F10
Tiel Neths. 51°53N 5°26E 15 C5
Tieling China 42°20N 123°55E 35 C12
Tielt Belgium 51°0N 3°20E 15 C3
Tien Shan = Tian Shan
  Asia 40°30N 76°0E 32 B3
Tien-tsin = Tianjin
  China 39°7N 117°12E 35 E9
Tien Yen Vietnam 21°20N 107°24E 38 B6
T'ienching = Tianjin
  China 39°7N 117°12E 35 E9
Tienen Belgium 50°48N 4°57E 15 D4
Tientsin = Tianjin China 39°7N 117°12E 35 E9
Tieri Australia 23°2S 148°21E 62 C4
Tierra Amarilla Chile 27°28S 70°18W 94 B1
Tierra Amarilla
  U.S.A. 36°42N 106°33W 77 H10
Tierra Colorada Mexico 17°11N 99°32W 87 D5
Tierra de Campos Spain 42°10N 4°50W 21 A3
Tierra del Fuego, I. Grande de
  Argentina 54°0S 69°0W 96 G3
Tiétar → Spain 39°50N 6°1W 21 C3
Tietê → Brazil 20°40S 51°35W 95 A5
Tiffin U.S.A. 41°7N 83°11W 81 E12
Tifton U.S.A. 31°27N 83°31W 85 F13
Tifu Indonesia 3°39S 126°24E 37 E7
Tighina Moldova 46°50N 29°30E 17 E15
Tigil Russia 57°49N 158°40E 29 D16
Tignish Canada 46°58N 64°2W 73 C7
Tigre → Peru 4°30S 74°10W 92 D4
Tigre → Venezuela 9°20N 62°30W 92 B6
Tigris = Dijlah, Nahr →
  Asia 31°0N 47°25E 44 D5
Tigyaing Burma 23°45N 96°10E 41 H20
Tihāmah Asia 15°3N 41°55E 47 D3
Tijara India 27°56N 76°31E 42 F7
Tijuana Mexico 32°32N 117°1W 79 N9
Tikal Guatemala 17°13N 89°24W 88 C2
Tikal △ Guatemala 17°23N 89°34W 88 C2
Tikamgarh India 24°44N 78°50E 43 G8
Tikchik Lakes U.S.A. 60°0N 159°0W 74 D8
Tikhoretsk Russia 45°56N 40°5E 19 E7
Tikhvin Russia 59°35N 33°30E 18 C5
Tikirarjuaq = Whale Cove
  Canada 62°10N 92°34W 71 A10
Tikrīt Iraq 34°35N 43°37E 44 C4
Tiksi Russia 71°40N 128°45E 29 B13
Tilamuta Indonesia 0°32N 122°23E 37 D6
Tilburg Neths. 51°31N 5°6E 15 C5
Tilbury Canada 42°17N 82°23W 82 D2
Tilbury U.K. 51°27N 0°22E 13 F8

Tilcara Argentina 23°36S 65°23W 94 A2
Tilden U.S.A. 42°3N 97°50W 80 D5
Tilhar India 28°0N 79°45E 43 F8
Tilichiki Russia 60°27N 166°5E 29 C17
Tilissos Greece 35°20N 25°1E 25 D7
Till → U.K. 55°41N 2°13W 12 B5
Tillamook U.S.A. 45°27N 123°51W 76 D2
Tillsonburg Canada 42°53N 80°44W 82 D4
Tillyeria Cyprus 35°6N 32°40E 25 D11
Tilos Greece 36°27N 27°27E 23 F12
Tilpa Australia 30°57S 144°24E 63 E3
Tilt → U.K. 56°46N 3°51W 11 E5
Tilton U.S.A. 43°27N 71°36W 83 C13
Tiltonsville U.S.A. 40°10N 80°41W 82 F4
Timanfaya △ Canary Is. 29°0N 13°46W 24 F6
Timanskiy Kryazh Russia 65°58N 50°5E 18 A9
Timaru N.Z. 44°23S 171°14E 59 F3
Timau Kenya 0°4N 37°15E 54 B4
Timbaki Greece 35°4N 24°45E 25 D6
Timber Creek Australia 15°40S 130°29E 60 C5
Timber Lake U.S.A. 45°26N 101°5W 80 C3
Timber Mt. U.S.A. 37°6N 116°28W 78 H10
Timbué, Ponta Mozam. 18°47S 36°22E 55 F4
Timbuktu = Tombouctou
  Mali 16°50N 3°0W 50 E5
Timi Cyprus 34°44N 32°31E 25 E11
Timimoun Algeria 29°14N 0°16E 50 C6
Timiris, Râs Mauritania 19°21N 16°30W 50 E2
Timiskaming, L. =
  Témiscamingue, L.
  Canada 47°10N 79°25W 72 C4
Timișoara Romania 45°43N 21°15E 17 F11
Timmins Canada 48°28N 81°25W 72 C3
Timok → Serbia 44°10N 22°40E 23 B10
Timoleague Ireland 51°39N 8°46W 10 E3
Timor Asia 9°0S 125°0E 37 F7
Timor Leste = East Timor ■
  Asia 8°50S 126°0E 37 F7
Timor Sea Ind. Oc. 12°0S 127°0E 60 B4
Timor Timur = East Timor ■
  Asia 8°50S 126°0E 37 F7
Tin Can Bay Australia 25°56S 153°0E 63 D5
Tin Mt. U.S.A. 36°50N 117°10W 78 J9
Tina → Thina → S. Africa 31°18S 29°13E 57 E4
Tina, Khalîg el Egypt 31°10N 32°40E 46 D1
Tinaca Pt. Phil. 5°30N 125°25E 37 C7
Tinajo Canary Is. 29°4N 13°42W 24 E6
Tindal Australia 14°31S 132°22E 60 B5
Tindouf Algeria 27°42N 8°10W 50 C4
Tinfunque △ Paraguay 23°55S 60°17W 94 A3
Tinggi, Pulau Malaysia 2°18N 104°7E 39 L5
Tingo María Peru 9°10S 75°54W 92 E3
Tingrela Ivory C. 10°27N 6°25W 50 F4
Tinh Bien Vietnam 10°36N 104°57E 39 G5
Tinian N. Marianas 15°0N 145°38E 64 F6
Tinnevelly = Tirunelveli
  India 8°45N 77°45E 40 Q10
Tinogasta Argentina 28°5S 67°32W 94 B2
Tinos Greece 37°33N 25°8E 23 F11
Tinpahar India 24°59N 87°44E 43 G12
Tintina Argentina 27°2S 62°45W 94 B3
Tintinara Australia 35°48S 140°2E 63 F3
Tioga N. Dak., U.S.A. 48°24N 102°56W 80 A2
Tioga Pa., U.S.A. 41°55N 77°8W 82 E7
Tioman, Pulau Malaysia 2°50N 104°10E 39 L5
Tionesta U.S.A. 41°30N 79°28W 82 E5
Tipperary Ireland 52°28N 8°10W 10 D3
Tipperary □ Ireland 52°37N 7°55W 10 D4
Tipton Calif., U.S.A. 36°4N 119°19W 78 J7
Tipton Iowa, U.S.A. 41°46N 91°8W 80 E8
Tipton Mt. U.S.A. 35°32N 114°12W 79 K12
Tiptonville U.S.A. 36°23N 89°29W 85 C10
Tīrān Iran 32°45N 51°8E 45 C6
Tiranë Albania 41°18N 19°49E 23 D8
Tirari Desert Australia 28°22S 138°7E 63 D2
Tiraspol Moldova 46°55N 29°35E 17 E15
Tire Turkey 38°5N 27°45E 23 E12
Tirebolu Turkey 40°58N 38°45E 19 F6
Tiree U.K. 56°31N 6°55W 11 E2
Tiree, Passage of U.K. 56°30N 6°30W 11 E2
Tîrgoviște = Târgoviște
  Romania 44°55N 25°27E 17 F13
Tîrgu Jiu = Târgu Jiu
  Romania 45°5N 23°19E 17 F12
Tîrgu Mureș = Târgu Mureș
  Romania 46°31N 24°38E 17 E13
Tirich Mir Pakistan 36°15N 71°55E 40 A7
Tiritiri o te Moana = Southern
  Alps N.Z. 43°41S 170°11E 59 E3
Tirnavos Greece 39°45N 22°18E 23 E10
Tirodi India 21°40N 79°44E 40 J11
Tirol □ Austria 47°3N 10°43E 16 E6
Tirso → Italy 39°53N 8°32E 22 E3
Tiruchchirappalli India 10°45N 78°45E 40 P11
Tirunelveli India 8°45N 77°45E 40 Q10
Tirupati India 13°39N 79°25E 40 N11
Tiruppur India 11°5N 77°22E 40 P10
Tiruvannamalai India 12°15N 79°5E 40 N11
Tisa India 32°50N 76°9E 42 C7
Tisa → Serbia 45°15N 20°17E 23 B9
Tisdale Canada 52°50N 104°0W 71 C8
Tishomingo U.S.A. 34°14N 96°41W 84 D6
Tisza = Tisa → Serbia 45°15N 20°17E 23 B9
Tit-Ary Russia 71°55N 127°2E 29 B13
Tithwal Pakistan 34°21N 73°50E 43 B5
Titicaca, L. S. Amer. 15°30S 69°30W 92 G5
Titiwa Nigeria 12°14N 12°53E 51 F8
Titule
  Dem. Rep. of the Congo 3°15N 25°31E 54 B2
Titusville Fla., U.S.A. 28°37N 80°49W 85 G14
Titusville Pa., U.S.A. 41°38N 79°41W 82 E5
Tivaouane Senegal 14°56N 16°45W 50 F2
Tiverton Canada 44°16N 81°32W 82 B3
Tiverton U.K. 50°54N 3°29W 13 G4
Tívoli Italy 41°58N 12°45E 22 D5
Tiwi ⊙ Australia 11°33S 130°42E 60 B5
Tizi-Ouzou Algeria 36°42N 4°3E 50 A6
Tizimín Mexico 21°9N 88°9W 87 C7
Tiznit Morocco 29°48N 9°45W 50 C4

Tjeggelvas Sweden 66°37N 17°45E 8 C17
Tjieggelvas = Tjeggelvas
  Sweden 66°37N 17°45E 8 C17
Tjirebon = Cirebon
  Indonesia 6°45S 108°32E 37 G13
Tjirrkarli ⊙ Australia 26°0S 125°28E 61 E4
Tjluring Indonesia 8°25S 114°13E 37 J17
Tjörn Sweden 58°0N 11°35E 9 H14
Tjukayirla Roadhouse
  Australia 27°9S 124°34E 61 E3
Tjurabalan ⊙ Australia 19°50S 128°0E 60 C4
Tlacotalpan Mexico 18°37N 95°40W 87 D5
Tlahualilo de Zaragoza
  Mexico 26°7N 103°27W 86 B4
Tlaquepaque Mexico 20°39N 103°19W 86 C4
Tlaxcala Mexico 19°19N 98°14W 87 D5
Tlaxcala □ Mexico 19°25N 98°10W 87 D5
Tlaxiaco Mexico 17°25N 97°35W 87 D5
Tlemcen Algeria 34°52N 1°21W 50 B5
To Bong Vietnam 12°45N 109°16E 38 F7
Toa Payoh Singapore 1°20N 103°51E 39 d
Toad → Canada 59°25N 124°57W 70 B4
Toad River Canada 58°51N 125°14W 70 B3
Toamasina Madag. 18°10S 49°25E 57 B8
Toamasina □ Madag. 18°0S 49°0E 57 B8
Toay Argentina 36°43S 64°38W 94 D3
Toba Japan 34°30N 136°51E 31 G8
Toba, Danau Indonesia 2°30N 97°30E 36 D1
Toba Kakar Pakistan 31°30N 69°0E 42 D3
Toba Tek Singh Pakistan 30°55N 72°25E 42 D5
Tobago Trin. & Tob. 11°10N 60°30W 93 J16
Tobelo Indonesia 1°45N 127°56E 37 D7
Tobermory Canada 45°12N 81°40W 82 A3
Tobermory U.K. 56°38N 6°5W 11 E2
Tobi Pac. Oc. 2°40N 131°10E 37 D8
Tobi-Shima Japan 41°12N 139°34E 30 D9
Tobin, L. Australia 21°45S 125°49E 60 D4
Tobin L. Canada 53°35N 103°30W 71 C8
Toboali Indonesia 3°0S 106°25E 36 E3
Tobol → Russia 58°10N 68°12E 28 D7
Tobolsk Russia 58°15N 68°10E 28 D7
Tobruk = Tubruq Libya 32°7N 23°55E 51 B10
Tobyhanna U.S.A. 41°11N 75°25W 83 E9
Tobyl = Tobol → Russia 58°10N 68°12E 28 D7
Tocantinópolis Brazil 6°20S 47°25W 93 E9
Tocantins □ Brazil 10°0S 48°0W 93 F9
Tocantins → Brazil 1°45S 49°10W 93 D9
Toccoa U.S.A. 34°35N 83°19W 85 D13
Tochi → Pakistan 32°49N 70°41E 42 C4
Tochigi Japan 36°25N 139°45E 31 F9
Tochigi □ Japan 36°45N 139°45E 31 F9
Toco Trin. & Tob. 10°49N 60°57W 93 K16
Toconao Chile 23°11S 68°1W 94 A2
Tocopilla Chile 22°5S 70°10W 94 A1
Tocumwal Australia 35°51S 145°31E 63 F4
Tocuyo → Venezuela 11°3N 68°23W 92 A5
Todd → Australia 24°52S 135°48E 62 C2
Todeli Indonesia 1°40S 124°29E 37 E6
Todenyang Kenya 4°35N 35°56E 54 B4
Todgarh India 25°42N 73°58E 42 G5
Todos os Santos, B. de
  Brazil 12°48S 38°38W 93 F11
Todos Santos Mexico 23°26N 110°13W 86 C2
Toe Hd. U.K. 57°50N 7°8W 11 D1
Tofield Canada 53°25N 112°40W 70 C6
Tofino Canada 49°11N 125°55W 70 D3
Tofua Tonga 19°45S 175°5W 59 c
Tōgane Japan 35°33N 140°22E 31 G10
Togian, Kepulauan
  Indonesia 0°20S 121°50E 37 E6
Togliatti Russia 53°32N 49°24E 18 D8
Togo ■ W. Afr. 8°30N 1°35E 50 G6
Togtoh China 40°15N 111°10E 34 D6
Tohiea, Mt. Moorea 17°33S 149°49W 59 d
Tōhoku □ Japan 39°50N 141°45E 30 E10
Tōhōm Mongolia 44°27N 108°2E 34 B5
Toinya Sudan 6°17N 29°46E 51 G11
Toiyabe Range U.S.A. 39°30N 117°0W 76 G5
Tojikiston = Tajikistan ■
  Asia 38°30N 70°0E 28 F8
Tojo Indonesia 1°20S 121°15E 37 E6
Tōjō Japan 34°53N 133°16E 31 G6
Tok U.S.A. 63°20N 142°59W 68 E3
Tokachi-Dake Japan 43°17N 142°5E 30 C11
Tokachi-Gawa →
  Japan 42°44N 143°42E 30 C11
Tokala Indonesia 1°30S 121°40E 37 E6
Tōkamachi Japan 37°8N 138°43E 31 F9
Tokanui N.Z. 46°34S 168°56E 59 G2
Tokara-Rettō Japan 29°37N 129°43E 31 K4
Tokarahi N.Z. 44°56S 170°39E 59 F3
Tokashiki-Shima Japan 26°11N 127°21E 31 L3
Tokat Turkey 40°22N 36°35E 19 F6
Tōkch'ŏn N. Korea 39°45N 126°18E 35 E14
Tokdo Asia 37°15N 131°52E 31 F5
Tokeland U.S.A. 46°42N 123°59W 78 D3
Tokelau Is. Pac. Oc. 9°0S 171°45W 64 H10
Tokmak Kyrgyzstan 42°49N 75°15E 28 E8
Toko Ra. Australia 23°5S 138°20E 62 C2
Tokoro-Gawa → Japan 44°7N 144°5E 30 B12
Toku Tonga 18°10S 174°11W 59 c
Tokuno-Shima Japan 27°56N 128°55E 31 L4
Tokushima Japan 34°4N 134°34E 31 G7
Tokushima □ Japan 33°55N 134°0E 31 H7
Tokuyama Japan 34°3N 131°50E 31 G5
Tōkyō Japan 35°43N 139°45E 31 G9
Tolaga Bay N.Z. 38°21S 178°20E 59 C7
Tolbukhin = Dobrich
  Bulgaria 43°37N 27°49E 23 C12
Toledo Brazil 24°44S 53°45W 95 A5
Toledo Spain 39°50N 4°2W 21 C3
Toledo Ohio, U.S.A. 41°39N 83°33W 81 E12
Toledo Oreg., U.S.A. 44°37N 123°56W 76 D2
Toledo Wash., U.S.A. 46°26N 122°51W 78 D4
Toledo, Montes de Spain 39°33N 4°20W 21 C3
Toledo Bend Res. U.S.A. 31°11N 93°34W 84 F8
Tolga Australia 17°15S 145°29E 62 B4
Toliara Madag. 23°21S 43°40E 57 C7

Toliara □ Madag. 21°0S 45°0E 57 C8
Tolima Colombia 4°40N 75°19W 92 C3
Tolitoli Indonesia 1°5N 120°50E 37 D6
Tollhouse U.S.A. 37°1N 119°24W 78 H7
Tolmachevo Russia 58°56N 29°51E 9 G23
Tolo, Teluk Indonesia 2°20S 122°10E 37 E6
Tolo Harbour China 22°27N 114°12E 33 G11
Toluca Mexico 19°17N 99°40W 87 D5
Tolyatti = Togliatti
  Russia 53°32N 49°24E 18 D8
Tom Burke S. Africa 23°5S 28°0E 57 C4
Tom Price Australia 22°40S 117°48E 60 D2
Tomah U.S.A. 43°59N 90°30W 80 D8
Tomahawk U.S.A. 45°28N 89°44W 80 C9
Tomakomai Japan 42°38N 141°36E 30 C10
Tomales U.S.A. 38°15N 122°53W 78 G4
Tomales B. U.S.A. 38°15N 123°58W 78 G3
Tomanivi Fiji 17°37S 178°1E 59 a
Tomar Portugal 39°36N 8°25W 21 C1
Tomaszów Mazowiecki
  Poland 51°30N 20°2E 17 C10
Tomatlán Mexico 19°56N 105°15W 86 D3
Tombador, Serra do Brazil 12°0S 58°0W 92 F7
Tombigbee → U.S.A. 31°8N 87°57W 85 F11
Tombouctou Mali 16°50N 3°0W 50 E5
Tombstone U.S.A. 31°43N 110°4W 77 L8
Tombua Angola 15°55S 11°55E 56 B1
Tomé Chile 36°36S 72°57W 94 D1
Tomelloso Spain 39°10N 3°2W 21 C4
Tomini Indonesia 0°30N 120°30E 37 D6
Tomini, Teluk Indonesia 0°10S 121°0E 37 E6
Tomintoul U.K. 57°15N 3°23W 11 D5
Tomkinson Ranges
  Australia 26°11S 129°5E 61 E4
Tommot Russia 59°4N 126°20E 29 D13
Tomnop Ta Suos
  Cambodia 11°20N 104°15E 39 G5
Tomo → Colombia 5°20N 67°48W 92 B5
Toms Place U.S.A. 37°34N 118°41W 78 H8
Toms River U.S.A. 39°58N 74°12W 83 G10
Tomsk Russia 56°30N 85°5E 28 D9
Tonalá Chiapas, Mexico 16°4N 93°45W 87 D6
Tonalá Jalisco, Mexico 20°37N 103°14W 86 C4
Tonantins Brazil 2°45S 67°45W 92 D5
Tonasket U.S.A. 48°42N 119°26W 76 B4
Tonawanda U.S.A. 43°1N 78°53W 82 D6
Tonb Iran 26°15N 55°15E 45 E7
Tonbridge U.K. 51°11N 0°17E 13 F8
Tondano Indonesia 1°35N 124°54E 37 D6
Tondoro Namibia 17°45S 18°50E 56 B2
Tone → Australia 34°25S 116°25E 61 F2
Tone-Gawa → Japan 35°44N 140°51E 31 F9
Tonekābon Iran 36°45N 51°12E 45 B6
Tong Xian China 39°55N 116°35E 34 E9
Tong-Yeong S. Korea 34°50N 128°20E 35 G15
Tonga ■ Pac. Oc. 19°50S 174°30W 59 c
Tonga Trench Pac. Oc. 18°0S 173°0W 64 J10
Tongaat S. Africa 29°33S 31°9E 57 D5
Tongareva = Penrhyn
  Cook Is. 9°0S 158°0W 65 H12
Tongariro △ N.Z. 39°8S 175°33E 59 C5
Tongatapu Tonga 21°10S 175°0W 59 c
Tongatapu Group Tonga 21°0S 175°0W 59 c
Tongchuan China 35°6N 109°3E 34 G5
Tongeren Belgium 50°47N 5°28E 15 D5
Tonggu Jiao China 22°22N 113°37E 33 G10
Tongguan China 34°40N 110°25E 34 G6
Tonghua China 41°42N 125°58E 35 D13
Tongjosŏn Man
  N. Korea 39°30N 128°0E 35 E14
Tongking, G. of = Tonkin, G. of
  Asia 20°0N 108°0E 38 C7
Tongliao China 43°38N 122°18E 35 C12
Tongling China 30°55N 117°48E 33 C6
Tongobory Madag. 23°32S 44°20E 57 C7
Tongoy Chile 30°16S 71°31W 94 C1
Tongres = Tongeren
  Belgium 50°47N 5°28E 15 D5
Tongsa Dzong Bhutan 27°31N 90°31E 41 F17
Tongshi China 18°30N 109°20E 38 C7
Tongue U.K. 58°29N 4°25W 11 C4
Tongue → U.S.A. 46°25N 105°52W 76 C11
Tongwei China 35°0N 105°5E 34 G3
Tongxin China 36°59N 105°58E 34 F3
Tongyang N. Korea 39°9N 126°53E 35 E14
Tongyu China 44°45N 123°4E 35 B12
Tonj Sudan 7°20N 28°44E 51 G11
Tonk India 26°6N 75°54E 42 F6
Tonkawa U.S.A. 36°41N 97°18W 84 C6
Tonkin = Bac Phan
  Vietnam 22°0N 105°0E 38 B5
Tonkin, G. of Asia 20°0N 108°0E 38 C7
Tonle Sap Cambodia 13°0N 104°0E 38 F5
Tono Japan 39°19N 141°32E 30 E10
Tonopah U.S.A. 38°4N 117°14W 77 G5
Tonosí Panama 7°20N 80°20W 88 E3
Tons → Haryana, India 30°30N 77°39E 42 D7
Tons → Ut. P., India 26°1N 83°33E 43 F10
Tønsberg Norway 59°19N 10°25E 9 G14
Tonto △ U.S.A. 33°39N 111°7W 77 K8
Tonumea Tonga 20°30S 174°30W 59 c
Toobanna Australia 18°42S 146°9E 62 B4
Toodyay Australia 31°34S 116°28E 61 F2
Tooele U.S.A. 40°32N 112°18W 76 F7
Toompine Australia 27°15S 144°19E 63 D3
Toora Australia 38°39S 146°23E 63 F4
Toora-Khem Russia 52°28N 96°17E 29 D10
Toowoomba Australia 27°32S 151°56E 63 D5
Top Springs Australia 16°37S 131°51E 60 C5
Topaz U.S.A. 38°41N 119°30W 78 G7
Topeka U.S.A. 39°3N 95°40W 80 F7
Topley Canada 54°49N 126°18W 70 C3
Topocalma, Pta. Chile 34°10S 72°2W 94 C1
Topock U.S.A. 34°46N 114°29W 79 L12
Topol'čany Slovak Rep. 48°35N 18°12E 17 D10
Topolobampo Mexico 25°36N 109°3W 86 B3
Topozero, Ozero Russia 65°35N 32°0E 8 D25
Toppenish U.S.A. 46°23N 120°19W 76 C3
Toraka Vestale Madag. 16°20S 43°58E 57 B7

Torata Peru 17°23S 70°1W 92 G4
Torbalı Turkey 38°10N 27°21E 23 E12
Torbat-e Heydārīyeh
  Iran 35°15N 59°12E 45 C8
Torbat-e Jām Iran 35°16N 60°35E 45 C9
Torbay Canada 47°40N 52°42W 73 C9
Torbay □ U.K. 50°26N 3°31W 13 G4
Tordesillas Spain 41°30N 5°0W 21 B3
Torfaen □ U.K. 51°43N 3°3W 13 F4
Torgau Germany 51°34N 13°0E 16 C7
Torhout Belgium 51°5N 3°7E 15 C3
Tori-Shima Japan 30°29N 140°19E 31 J10
Torilla Pen. Australia 22°29S 150°5E 62 C5
Torino Italy 45°3N 7°40E 20 D7
Torit Sudan 4°27N 32°31E 51 H12
Torkamān Iran 37°35N 47°23E 44 B5
Tormes → Spain 41°18N 6°29W 21 B2
Tornado Mt. Canada 49°55N 114°40W 70 D6
Torneå = Tornio Finland 65°50N 24°12E 8 D21
Torneälven → Europe 65°50N 24°12E 8 D21
Torneträsk Sweden 68°24N 19°15E 8 B18
Torngat Mts. Canada 59°0N 63°40W 69 F19
Tornio Finland 65°50N 24°12E 8 D21
Tornionjoki = Torneälven →
  Europe 65°50N 24°12E 8 D21
Tornquist Argentina 38°8S 62°15W 94 D3
Toro Spain 39°59N 4°8E 24 B11
Toro, Cerro del Chile 29°10S 69°50W 94 B2
Toro → Uganda 1°5N 30°22E 54 C3
Toro Pk. U.S.A. 33°34N 116°24W 79 M10
Toronto Canada 43°39N 79°20W 82 C5
Toronto U.S.A. 40°28N 80°36W 82 F4
Toronto Lester B. Pearson Int. ✈
  (YYZ) Canada 43°46N 79°35W 82 C5
Toropets Russia 56°30N 31°40E 18 C5
Tororo Uganda 0°45N 34°12E 54 B3
Toros Dağları Turkey 37°0N 32°30E 44 B2
Torpa India 22°57N 85°6E 43 H11
Torquay U.K. 50°27N 3°32W 13 G4
Torrance U.S.A. 33°50N 118°20W 79 M8
Torre de Moncorvo
  Portugal 41°12N 7°8W 21 B2
Torre del Greco Italy 40°47N 14°22E 22 D6
Torrejón de Ardoz Spain 40°27N 3°29W 21 B4
Torrelavega Spain 43°20N 4°5W 21 A3
Torremolinos Spain 36°38N 4°30W 21 D3
Torrens, L. Australia 31°0S 137°50E 63 E2
Torrens Cr. → Australia 22°23S 145°9E 62 C4
Torrens Creek Australia 20°48S 145°3E 62 C4
Torrent Spain 39°27N 0°28W 21 C5
Torreón Mexico 25°33N 103°26W 86 B4
Torres Brazil 29°21S 49°44W 95 B5
Torres Mexico 28°46N 110°47W 86 B2
Torres Strait Australia 9°50S 142°20E 62 a
Torres Vedras Portugal 39°5N 9°15W 21 C1
Torrevieja Spain 37°59N 0°42W 21 D5
Torrey U.S.A. 38°18N 111°25W 76 G8
Torridge → U.K. 51°0N 4°13W 13 G3
Torridon, L. U.K. 57°35N 5°50W 11 D3
Torrington Conn., U.S.A. 41°48N 73°7W 83 E11
Torrington Wyo.,
  U.S.A. 42°4N 104°11W 76 E11
Tórshavn Færoe Is. 62°5N 6°56W 8 E9
Tortola Br. Virgin Is. 18°19N 64°45W 89 e
Tortosa Spain 40°49N 0°31E 21 B6
Tortosa, C. Spain 40°41N 0°52E 21 B6
Tortue, Î. de la Haiti 20°5N 72°57W 89 B5
Tortuguero △ Costa Rica 10°31N 83°29W 88 D3
Toruń Iran 35°25N 55°5E 45 C7
Toruń Poland 53°2N 18°39E 17 B10
Tory Hill Canada 44°58N 78°16W 82 B6
Tory I. Ireland 55°16N 8°14W 10 A3
Tosa Japan 33°24N 133°23E 31 H6
Tosa-Shimizu Japan 32°52N 132°58E 31 H6
Tosa-Wan Japan 33°15N 133°30E 31 H6
Toscana □ Italy 43°25N 11°0E 22 C4
Toshka, Buheirat en
  Egypt 22°50N 31°0E 51 D12
Toshka Lakes = Toshka, Buheirat
  en Egypt 22°50N 31°0E 51 D12
Toshkent Uzbekistan 41°20N 69°10E 28 E7
Tostado Argentina 29°15S 61°50W 94 B3
Tostón, Pta. de Canary Is. 28°42N 14°2W 24 F5
Tosu Japan 33°22N 130°31E 31 H5
Totak Norway 59°40N 7°45E 9 G12
Toteng Botswana 20°22S 22°58E 56 C3
Totma Russia 60°0N 42°40E 18 C7
Totnes U.K. 50°26N 3°42W 13 G4
Totness Suriname 5°53N 56°19W 93 B7
Totonicapán Guatemala 14°58N 91°12W 88 D1
Totoya, I. Fiji 18°57S 179°50W 59 a
Totten Glacier Antarctica 66°45S 116°10E 5 C8
Tottenham Australia 32°14S 147°21E 63 E4
Tottenham Canada 44°1N 79°49W 82 B5
Tottori Japan 35°30N 134°15E 31 G7
Tottori □ Japan 35°30N 134°12E 31 G7
Toubkal, Djebel Morocco 31°0N 8°0W 50 B4
Tougan Burkina Faso 13°11N 2°58W 50 F5
Touggourt Algeria 33°6N 6°4E 50 B7
Toul France 48°40N 5°53E 20 B6
Toulon France 43°10N 5°55E 20 E6
Toulouse France 43°37N 1°27E 20 E4
Toummo Niger 22°45N 14°8E 51 D8
Toungoo Burma 19°0N 96°30E 41 K20
Touraine France 47°20N 0°30E 20 C4
Tourcoing France 50°42N 3°10E 20 A5
Touriñán, C. Spain 43°3N 9°18W 21 A1
Tournai Belgium 50°35N 3°25E 15 D3
Tournon-sur-Rhône
  France 45°4N 4°50E 20 D6
Tours France 47°22N 0°40E 20 C4
Toussoro, Mt. C.A.R. 9°7N 23°14E 52 C4
Touws → S. Africa 33°45S 21°11E 56 E3
Touwsrivier S. Africa 33°20S 20°2E 56 E3
Towada Japan 40°37N 141°13E 30 D10
Towada-Hachimantai △
  Japan 40°20N 140°55E 30 D10
Towada-Ko Japan 40°28N 140°55E 30 D10
Towanda U.S.A. 41°46N 76°27W 83 E8
Tower U.S.A. 47°48N 92°17W 80 B7

Towerhill Cr. →
  Australia 22°28S 144°35E 62 C3
Towner U.S.A. 48°21N 100°25W 80 A3
Townsend U.S.A. 46°19N 111°31W 76 C8
Townshend I. Australia 22°10S 150°31E 62 C5
Townsville Australia 19°15S 146°45E 62 B4
Towot Sudan 6°12N 34°25E 54 A3
Towraghondī Afghan. 35°13N 62°16E 40 B3
Towson U.S.A. 39°24N 76°36W 81 F15
Towuti, Danau Indonesia 2°45S 121°32E 37 E6
Toya-Ko Japan 42°35N 140°51E 30 C10
Toyama Japan 36°40N 137°15E 31 F8
Toyama □ Japan 36°45N 137°30E 31 F8
Toyama-Wan Japan 37°0N 137°30E 31 F8
Toyapakeh Indonesia 8°41S 115°29E 37 K18
Toyohashi Japan 34°45N 137°25E 31 G8
Toyokawa Japan 34°48N 137°27E 31 G8
Toyonaka Japan 34°46N 135°28E 31 G7
Toyooka Japan 35°35N 134°48E 31 G7
Toyota Japan 35°3N 137°7E 31 G8
Tozeur Tunisia 33°56N 8°0E 51 B7
Trá Lí = Tralee Ireland 52°16N 9°42W 10 D2
Trá Mhór = Tramore
  Ireland 52°10N 7°10W 10 D4
Tra On Vietnam 9°58N 105°55E 39 H5
Trabzon Turkey 41°0N 39°45E 19 F6
Tracadie Canada 47°30N 64°55W 73 C7
Tracy Canada 46°1N 73°9W 72 C5
Tracy Calif., U.S.A. 37°44N 121°26W 78 H5
Tracy Minn., U.S.A. 44°14N 95°37W 80 C6
Trafalgar, C. Spain 36°10N 6°2W 21 D2
Trail Canada 49°5N 117°40W 70 D5
Trainor L. Canada 60°24N 120°17W 70 A4
Trakai □ Lithuania 54°30N 25°10E 9 J21
Trákhonas Cyprus 35°12N 33°21E 25 D12
Tralee Ireland 52°16N 9°42W 10 D2
Tralee B. Ireland 52°17N 9°55W 10 D2
Tramore Ireland 52°10N 7°10W 10 D4
Tramore B. Ireland 52°9N 7°10W 10 D4
Tramuntana, Serra de
  Spain 39°48N 2°54E 24 B9
Tran Ninh, Cao Nguyen
  Laos 19°30N 103°10E 38 C4
Tranås Sweden 58°3N 14°59E 9 G16
Trancas Argentina 26°11S 65°20W 94 B2
Trang Thailand 7°33N 99°38E 39 J2
Trangahy Madag. 19°7S 44°31E 57 B7
Trangan Indonesia 6°40S 134°20E 37 F8
Trangie Australia 32°4S 148°0E 63 E4
Trani Italy 41°17N 16°25E 22 D7
Tranoroa Madag. 24°42S 45°4E 57 C8
Tranqueras Uruguay 31°13S 55°45W 95 C4
Transantarctic Mts.
  Antarctica 85°0S 170°0W 5 E12
Transilvania Romania 46°30N 24°0E 17 E12
Transilvanian Alps = Carpații
  Meridionali Romania 45°30N 25°0E 17 F13
Transnistria = Stînga Nistrului □
  Moldova 47°20N 29°15E 17 E15
Transylvania = Transilvania
  Romania 46°30N 24°0E 17 E12
Trápani Italy 38°1N 12°29E 22 E5
Trapper Pk. U.S.A. 45°54N 114°18W 76 D6
Traralgon Australia 38°12S 146°34E 63 F4
Trasimeno, L. Italy 43°8N 12°6E 22 C5
Trat Thailand 12°14N 102°33E 39 F4
Tratani → Pakistan 29°19N 68°20E 42 E3
Traun Austria 48°14N 14°15E 16 D8
Travellers L. Australia 33°20S 142°0E 63 E3
Travemünde Germany 53°57N 10°52E 16 B6
Travers, Mt. N.Z. 42°1S 172°45E 59 E4
Traverse City U.S.A. 44°46N 85°38W 81 C11
Travis, L. U.S.A. 30°24N 97°55W 84 F6
Travnik Bos.-H. 44°17N 17°39E 23 B7
Trawbreaga B. Ireland 55°20N 7°25W 10 A4
Trébbia → Italy 45°4N 9°41E 20 D8
Trebič Czech Rep. 49°14N 15°55E 16 D8
Trebinje Bos.-H. 42°44N 18°22E 23 C8
Trebonne Australia 18°37S 146°5E 62 B4
Tregaron U.K. 52°14N 3°56W 13 E4
Tregrosse Is. Australia 17°41S 150°43E 62 B5
Treherne Canada 49°38N 98°42W 71 D9
Treinta y Tres Uruguay 33°16S 54°17W 95 C5
Trelawney Zimbabwe 17°30S 30°30E 57 B5
Trelew Argentina 43°10S 65°20W 96 E3
Trelleborg Sweden 55°20N 13°10E 9 J15
Tremadog Bay U.K. 52°51N 4°18W 12 E3
Tremonton U.S.A. 41°43N 112°10W 76 F7
Tremp Spain 42°10N 0°52E 21 A6
Trenche → Canada 47°46N 72°53W 72 C5
Trenčín Slovak Rep. 48°52N 18°4E 17 D10
Trenggalek Indonesia 8°3S 111°43E 37 H14
Trenque Lauquen
  Argentina 36°5S 62°45W 94 D3
Trent → Canada 44°6N 77°34W 82 B7
Trent → U.K. 53°41N 0°42W 12 D7
Trento Italy 46°4N 11°8E 22 A4
Trenton Canada 44°10N 77°34W 82 B7
Trenton Mo., U.S.A. 40°5N 93°37W 80 E7
Trenton N.J., U.S.A. 40°14N 74°46W 83 F10
Trenton Nebr., U.S.A. 40°11N 101°1W 80 E3
Trepassey Canada 46°43N 53°25W 73 C9
Tres Arroyos Argentina 38°26S 60°20W 94 D3
Três Corações Brazil 21°44S 45°15W 95 A6
Três Lagoas Brazil 20°50S 51°43W 93 H8
Tres Lomas Argentina 36°27S 62°51W 94 D3
Tres Montes, C. Chile 46°50S 75°30W 96 F1
Tres Pinos U.S.A. 36°48N 121°19W 78 J5
Três Pontas Brazil 21°23S 45°29W 95 A6
Tres Puentes Chile 27°50S 70°15W 94 B1
Tres Puntas, C. Argentina 47°0S 66°0W 96 F3
Três Rios Brazil 22°6S 43°15W 95 A7
Tres Valles Mexico 18°15N 96°8W 87 D5
Tresco U.K. 49°57N 6°20W 13 H1
Treviso Italy 45°40N 12°15E 22 B5
Triabunna Australia 42°30S 147°55E 63 G4
Trianda Greece 36°25N 28°10E 25 C10
Triangle Zimbabwe 21°2S 31°28E 57 C5
Tribal Areas □ Pakistan 33°0N 70°0E 42 C4

Tribulation, C. Australia 16°5S 145°29E 62 B4
Tribune U.S.A. 38°28N 101°45W 80 F3
Trichinopoly = Tiruchchirappalli
  India 10°45N 78°45E 40 P11
Trichur India 10°30N 76°18E 40 P10
Trichy = Tiruchchirappalli
  India 10°45N 78°45E 40 P11
Trida Australia 33°1S 145°1E 63 E4
Trier Germany 49°45N 6°38E 16 D4
Trieste Italy 45°40N 13°46E 22 B5
Triglav Slovenia 46°21N 13°50E 16 E7
Trikala Greece 39°34N 21°47E 23 E9
Trikomo Cyprus 35°17N 33°52E 25 D12
Trikora, Puncak
  Indonesia 4°15S 138°45E 37 E9
Trim Ireland 53°33N 6°48W 10 C5
Trimmu Dam Pakistan 31°10N 72°8E 42 D5
Trincomalee Sri Lanka 8°38N 81°15E 40 Q12
Trindade Brazil 16°40S 49°30W 93 G9
Trindade, I. Atl. Oc. 20°20S 29°50W 2 F8
Trinidad Bolivia 14°46S 64°50W 92 F6
Trinidad Cuba 21°48N 80°0W 88 B4
Trinidad Trin. & Tob. 10°30N 61°15W 93 K15
Trinidad Uruguay 33°30S 56°50W 94 C4
Trinidad U.S.A. 37°10N 104°31W 77 H11
Trinidad → Mexico 17°49N 95°9W 87 D5
Trinidad & Tobago ■
  W. Indies 10°30N 61°20W 89 D7
Trinity Canada 48°59N 53°55W 73 C9
Trinity U.S.A. 30°57N 95°22W 84 F7
Trinity → Calif., U.S.A. 41°11N 123°42W 76 F2
Trinity → Tex., U.S.A. 29°45N 94°43W 84 G7
Trinity B. Canada 48°20N 53°10W 73 C9
Trinity Hills Trin. & Tob. 10°7N 61°7W 93 K15
Trinity Is. U.S.A. 56°33N 154°25W 74 D9
Trinity Range U.S.A. 40°10N 118°40W 76 F4
Trinkitat Sudan 18°45N 37°51E 51 E13
Trinway U.S.A. 40°9N 82°1W 82 F2
Triolet Mauritius 20°4S 57°32E 53 d
Tripoli = Tarābulus
  Lebanon 34°31N 35°50E 46 A4
Tripoli = Tarābulus Libya 32°49N 13°7E 51 B8
Tripoli Greece 37°31N 22°25E 23 F10
Tripolitania = Tarābulus
  N. Afr. 31°0N 13°0E 51 B8
Tripura □ India 24°0N 92°0E 41 H18
Tripylos Cyprus 34°59N 32°41E 25 E11
Tristan da Cunha Atl. Oc. 37°6S 12°20W 49 K2
Trisul India 30°19N 79°47E 43 D8
Trivandrum India 8°41N 77°0E 40 Q10
Trnava Slovak Rep. 48°23N 17°35E 17 D9
Trochu Canada 51°50N 113°13W 70 C6
Trodely I. Canada 52°15N 79°26W 72 B4
Troglav Croatia 43°56N 16°36E 22 C7
Troilus, L. Canada 50°50N 74°35W 72 B5
Trois-Pistoles Canada 48°5N 69°10W 73 C6
Trois-Rivières Canada 46°25N 72°34W 72 C5
Trois-Rivières Guadeloupe 15°57N 61°40W 88 b
Troitsk Russia 54°10N 61°35E 28 D7
Troitsko Pechorsk
  Russia 62°40N 56°10E 18 B10
Trölladyngja Iceland 64°54N 17°16W 8 D5
Trollhättan Sweden 58°17N 12°20E 9 G15
Trollheimen Norway 62°46N 9°1E 8 E13
Trombetas → Brazil 1°55S 55°35W 93 D7
Tromsø Norway 69°40N 18°56E 8 B18
Tron Thailand 17°28N 100°7E 38 D3
Trona U.S.A. 35°46N 117°23W 79 K9
Tronador, Mte.
  Argentina 41°10S 71°50W 96 E2
Trøndelag Norway 64°17N 11°50E 8 D14
Trondheim Norway 63°36N 10°25E 8 E14
Trondheimsfjorden
  Norway 63°35N 10°30E 8 E14
Troodos Cyprus 34°55N 32°52E 25 E11
Troon U.K. 55°33N 4°39W 11 F4
Tropic U.S.A. 37°37N 112°5W 77 H7
Trostan U.K. 55°3N 6°10W 10 A5
Trou Gras Pt. St. Lucia 13°51N 60°53W 89 f
Trout → Canada 61°19N 119°51W 70 A5
Trout L. N.W.T., Canada 60°40N 121°14W 70 A4
Trout L. Ont., Canada 51°20N 93°15W 71 C10
Trout Lake Canada 56°30N 114°32W 70 B6
Trout Lake U.S.A. 46°0N 121°32W 78 E5
Trout River Canada 49°29N 58°8W 73 C8
Trout Run U.S.A. 41°23N 77°3W 82 E7
Trouville-sur-Mer France 49°21N 0°5E 20 B4
Trowbridge U.K. 51°18N 2°12W 13 F5
Troy Turkey 39°57N 26°12E 23 E12
Troy Ala., U.S.A. 31°48N 85°58W 85 F12
Troy Kans., U.S.A. 39°47N 95°5W 80 F6
Troy Mo., U.S.A. 38°59N 90°59W 80 F8
Troy Mont., U.S.A. 48°28N 115°53W 76 B6
Troy N.Y., U.S.A. 42°44N 73°41W 83 D11
Troy Ohio, U.S.A. 40°2N 84°12W 81 E11
Troy Pa., U.S.A. 41°47N 76°47W 83 E8
Troyes France 48°19N 4°3E 20 B6
Truchas Pk. U.S.A. 35°58N 105°39W 77 J11
Trucial States = United Arab
  Emirates ■ Asia 23°50N 54°0E 45 F7
Truckee U.S.A. 39°20N 120°11W 78 F6
Trudovoye Russia 43°17N 132°5E 30 C6
Trujillo Honduras 16°0N 86°0W 88 C2
Trujillo Peru 8°6S 79°0W 92 E3
Trujillo Spain 39°28N 5°55W 21 C3
Trujillo U.S.A. 35°32N 104°42W 77 J11
Trujillo Venezuela 9°22N 70°38W 92 B4
Truk Micronesia 7°25N 151°46E 64 G7
Trumann U.S.A. 35°41N 90°31W 85 D9
Trumansburg U.S.A. 42°33N 76°40W 83 D8
Trumbull, Mt. U.S.A. 36°25N 113°19W 77 H7
Trundle Australia 32°53S 147°35E 63 E4
Trung-Phan = Annam
  Vietnam 16°30N 107°30E 38 D7
Truro Canada 45°21N 63°14W 73 C7
Truro U.K. 50°16N 5°4W 13 G2
Truskavets Ukraine 49°17N 23°30E 17 D12
Trutch Canada 57°44N 122°57W 70 B4

Truth or Consequences
  U.S.A. 33°8N 107°15W 77 K10
Trutnov Czech Rep. 50°37N 15°54E 16 C8
Tryonville U.S.A. 41°42N 79°48W 82 E5
Tsandi Namibia 17°42S 14°50E 56 B1
Tsaratanana Madag. 16°47S 47°39E 57 B8
Tsaratanana, Mt. de =
  Maromokotro Madag. 14°0S 49°0E 57 A8
Tsaratanana △ Madag. 13°57S 48°52E 57 A8
Tsau Botswana 20°8S 22°22E 56 C3
Tsavo Kenya 2°59S 38°28E 54 C4
Tsavo East △ Kenya 2°44S 38°47E 54 C4
Tsavo West △ Kenya 3°19S 37°57E 54 C4
Tsentralnyy □ Russia 52°0N 40°0E 28 D4
Tses Namibia 25°58S 18°8E 56 D2
Tsetserleg Mongolia 47°36N 101°32E 32 B5
Tsévié Togo 6°25N 1°20E 50 G6
Tshabong Botswana 26°2S 22°29E 56 D3
Tshane Botswana 24°5S 21°54E 56 C3
Tshela
  Dem. Rep. of the Congo 4°57S 13°4E 52 F2
Tshesebe Botswana 21°51S 27°32E 57 C4
Tshibeke
  Dem. Rep. of the Congo 2°40S 28°35E 54 C2
Tshibinda
  Dem. Rep. of the Congo 2°23S 28°43E 54 C2
Tshikapa
  Dem. Rep. of the Congo 6°28S 20°48E 52 F4
Tshilenge
  Dem. Rep. of the Congo 6°17S 23°48E 54 D1
Tshinsenda
  Dem. Rep. of the Congo 12°20S 28°0E 55 E2
Tshofa
  Dem. Rep. of the Congo 5°13S 25°16E 54 D2
Tshwane = Pretoria
  S. Africa 25°44S 28°12E 57 D4
Tshwane Botswana 22°24S 22°1E 56 C3
Tsigara Botswana 20°22S 25°54E 56 C4
Tsihombe Madag. 25°10S 45°41E 57 D8
Tsiigehtchic Canada 67°15N 134°0W 68 D5
Ts'il-os △ Canada 51°9N 123°59W 70 C4
Tsimlyansk Res. = Tsimlyanskoye
  Vdkhr. Russia 48°0N 43°0E 19 E7
Tsimlyanskoye Vdkhr.
  Russia 48°0N 43°0E 19 E7
Tsinan = Jinan China 36°38N 117°1E 34 F9
Tsineng S. Africa 27°5S 23°5E 56 D3
Tsing Yi China 22°21N 114°6E 33 G11
Tsinghai = Qinghai □
  China 36°0N 98°0E 32 C4
Tsingtao = Qingdao
  China 36°5N 120°20E 35 F11
Tsingy de Bemaraha △
  Madag. 18°35S 45°25E 57 B8
Tsingy de Namoroka △
  Madag. 16°29S 45°25E 57 B8
Tsinjoarivo Madag. 19°37S 47°40E 57 B8
Tsinjomitondraka Madag. 15°40S 47°8E 57 B8
Tsirigo = Kythira Greece 36°8N 23°0E 23 F10
Tsiroanomandidy Madag. 18°46S 46°2E 57 B8
Tsitondroina Madag. 21°19S 46°0E 57 C8
Tsitsikamma △ S. Africa 34°3S 23°40E 56 E3
Tsivory Madag. 24°4S 46°5E 57 C8
Tskhinvali Georgia 42°14N 44°1E 19 F7
Tsna → Russia 54°55N 41°58E 18 D7
Tso Moriri, L. India 32°50N 78°20E 43 C8
Tsobis Namibia 19°27S 17°30E 56 B2
Tsodilo Hill Botswana 18°49S 21°43E 56 B3
Tsogttsetsiy = Baruunsuu
  Mongolia 43°43N 105°35E 34 C3
Tsolo S. Africa 31°18S 28°37E 57 E4
Tsomo S. Africa 32°0S 27°42E 57 E4
Tsu Japan 34°45N 136°25E 31 G8
Tsu L. Canada 60°40N 111°52W 70 A6
Tsuchiura Japan 36°5N 140°15E 31 F10
Tsuen Wan China 22°22N 114°6E 33 G11
Tsugaru-Kaikyō Japan 41°35N 141°0E 30 D10
Tsumeb Namibia 19°9S 17°44E 56 B2
Tsumis Namibia 23°39S 17°29E 56 C2
Tsuruga Japan 35°45N 136°2E 31 G8
Tsurugi-San Japan 33°51N 134°6E 31 H7
Tsuruoka Japan 38°44N 139°50E 30 E9
Tsushima Gifu, Japan 35°10N 136°43E 31 G8
Tsushima Nagasaki,
  Japan 34°20N 129°20E 31 G4
Tsuyama Japan 35°3N 134°0E 31 G7
Tsyelyakhany Belarus 52°30N 25°46E 17 B13
Tuaim = Tuam Ireland 53°31N 8°51W 10 C3
Tual Indonesia 5°38S 132°44E 37 F8
Tualatin U.S.A. 45°23N 122°45W 78 E4
Tuam Ireland 53°31N 8°51W 10 C3
Tuamotu, Ís.
  French Polynesia 17°0S 144°0W 65 J13
Tuamotu Arch. = Tuamotu, Ís.
  French Polynesia 17°0S 144°0W 65 J13
Tuamotu Ridge Pac. Oc. 20°0S 138°0W 65 K14
Tuan Giao Vietnam 21°35N 103°25E 38 B4
Tuao Phil. 17°55N 121°22E 37 A6
Tuapse Russia 44°5N 39°10E 19 F6
Tuas Singapore 1°19N 103°39E 39 d
Tuatapere N.Z. 46°8S 167°41E 59 G1
Tuba City U.S.A. 36°8N 111°14W 77 H8
Tuban Indonesia 6°54S 112°3E 37 G15
Tubani Botswana 24°46S 24°18E 56 C3
Tubarão Brazil 28°30S 49°0W 95 B6
Tūbās West Bank 32°20N 35°22E 46 C4
Tubas → Namibia 22°54S 14°35E 56 C1
Tübingen Germany 48°31N 9°4E 16 D5
Tubou Fiji 18°13S 178°48W 59 a
Tubuaï, Ís.
  French Polynesia 25°0S 150°0W 65 K13
Tuc Trung Vietnam 11°1N 107°12E 39 G6
Tucacas Venezuela 10°48N 68°19W 92 A5
Tuchitua Canada 60°55N 129°13W 70 A3
Tuchodi → Canada 58°17N 123°42W 70 B4
Tucson U.S.A. 32°13N 110°58W 77 K8
Tucumán □ Argentina 26°48S 66°2W 94 B2

Tucumcari *U.S.A.* 35°10N 103°44W **77** J12
Tucupita *Venezuela* 9°2N 62°3W **92** B6
Tucuruí *Brazil* 3°42S 49°44W **93** D9
Tucuruí, Represa de
Brazil 4°0S 49°30W **93** D9
Tudela *Spain* 42°4N 1°39W **21** A5
Tudmur *Syria* 34°36N 38°15E **44** C3
Tudor, L. *Canada* 55°50N 65°25W **73** A6
Tuen Mun *China* 22°24N 113°59E **33** G10
Tugela → *S. Africa* 29°14S 31°30E **57** D5
Tuguegarao *Phil.* 17°35N 121°42E **37** A6
Tugur *Russia* 53°44N 136°45E **29** D14
Tui *Spain* 42°3N 8°39W **21** A1
Tuineje *Canary Is.* 28°19N 14°3W **24** F5
Tukangbesi, Kepulauan
Indonesia 6°0S 124°0E **37** F6
Tukarak I. *Canada* 56°15N 78°45W **72** A4
Tukayyid *Iraq* 29°47N 45°36E **44** D5
Tuktoyaktuk *Canada* 69°27N 133°2W **68** D5
Tuktut Nogait △
Canada 69°15N 122°0W **68** D7
Tukums *Latvia* 56°58N 23°10E **9** H20
Tukuyu *Tanzania* 9°17S 33°35E **55** D3
Tula *Hidalgo, Mexico* 20°3N 99°21W **87** C5
Tula *Tamaulipas, Mexico* 23°0N 99°43W **87** C5
Tula *Russia* 54°13N 37°38E **18** D6
Tulach Mhór = Tullamore
Ireland 53°16N 7°31W **10** C4
Tulancingo *Mexico* 20°5N 98°22W **87** C5
Tulare *U.S.A.* 36°13N 119°21W **78** J7
Tulare Lake Bed *U.S.A.* 36°0N 119°48W **78** K7
Tularosa *U.S.A.* 33°5N 106°1W **77** K10
Tulbagh *S. Africa* 33°16S 19°6E **56** E2
Tulcán *Ecuador* 0°48N 77°43W **92** C3
Tulcea *Romania* 45°13N 28°46E **17** F15
Tulchyn *Ukraine* 48°41N 28°49E **17** D15
Tūleh *Iran* 34°35N 52°33E **45** C7
Tulemalu L. *Canada* 62°58N 99°25W **71** A9
Tuli *Zimbabwe* 21°58S 29°13E **55** G2
Tulia *U.S.A.* 34°32N 101°46W **84** D4
Tulita *Canada* 64°57N 125°30W **68** E6
Tūlkarm *West Bank* 32°19N 35°2E **46** C4
Tulla *Ireland* 52°53N 8°46W **10** D3
Tullahoma *U.S.A.* 35°22N 86°13W **85** D11
Tullamore *Australia* 32°39S 147°36E **63** E4
Tullamore *Ireland* 53°16N 7°31W **10** C4
Tulle *France* 45°16N 1°46E **20** D4
Tullow *Ireland* 52°49N 6°45W **10** D5
Tully *Australia* 17°56S 145°55E **62** B4
Tully *U.S.A.* 42°48N 76°7W **83** D8
Tulsa *U.S.A.* 36°10N 95°55W **84** C7
Tulsequah *Canada* 58°39N 133°35W **70** B2
Tuluá *Colombia* 4°6N 76°11W **92** C3
Tulun *Russia* 54°32N 100°35E **29** D11
Tulungagung *Indonesia* 8°5S 111°54E **37** H14
Tuma → *Nic.* 13°6N 84°35W **88** D3
Tumacacori △ *U.S.A.* 31°35N 111°6W **77** L8
Tumaco *Colombia* 1°50N 78°45W **92** C3
Tumakuru = Tumkur
India 13°18N 77°6E **40** N10
Tumatumari *Guyana* 5°20N 58°55W **92** B7
Tumba *Sweden* 59°12N 17°48E **9** G17
Tumba, L.
Dem. Rep. of the Congo 0°50S 18°0E **52** E3
Tumbarumba *Australia* 35°44S 148°0E **63** F4
Tumbaya *Argentina* 23°50S 65°26W **94** A2
Tumbes *Peru* 3°37S 80°27W **92** D2
Tumbler Ridge *Canada* 55°8N 121°0W **70** B4
Tumbwe
Dem. Rep. of the Congo 11°25S 27°15E **55** E2
Tumby Bay *Australia* 34°21S 136°8E **63** E2
Tumd Youqi *China* 40°30N 110°30E **34** D6
Tumen *China* 43°0N 129°50E **30** C4
Tumen Jiang → *China* 42°20N 130°35E **35** C16
Tumeremo *Venezuela* 7°18N 61°30W **92** B6
Tumkur *India* 13°18N 77°6E **40** N10
Tump *Pakistan* 26°7N 62°16E **40** F3
Tumpat *Malaysia* 6°11N 102°10E **39** J4
Tumu *Ghana* 10°56N 1°56W **50** F5
Tumucumaque, Serra
Brazil 2°0N 55°0W **93** C8
Tumut *Australia* 35°16S 148°13E **63** F4
Tumwater *U.S.A.* 47°1N 122°54W **78** C4
Tuna *India* 22°59N 70°5E **42** H4
Tunapuna *Trin. & Tob.* 10°38N 61°24W **93** K15
Tunas de Zaza *Cuba* 21°39N 79°34W **88** B4
Tunbridge Wells = Royal
Tunbridge Wells *U.K.* 51°7N 0°16E **13** F8
Tuncurry *Australia* 32°17S 152°29E **63** E5
Tundla *India* 27°12N 78°17E **42** F8
Tunduru *Tanzania* 11°8S 37°25E **55** E4
Tundzha → *Bulgaria* 41°40N 26°35E **23** C11
Tung Chung *China* 22°17N 113°57E **33** G10
Tung Lung Chau
China 22°15N 114°17E **33** G11
Tungabhadra → *India* 15°57N 78°15E **40** M11
Tungla *Nic.* 13°24N 84°21W **88** D3
Tungsten *Canada* 61°57N 128°16W **70** A3
Tunguska, Nizhnyaya →
Russia 65°48N 88°4E **29** C9
Tunguska, Podkamennaya →
Russia 61°50N 90°13E **29** C10
Tunica *U.S.A.* 34°41N 90°23W **85** D9
Tunis *Tunisia* 36°50N 10°11E **50** A7
Tunisia ■ *Africa* 33°30N 9°10E **51** A7
Tunja *Colombia* 5°33N 73°25W **92** B4
Tunkhannock *U.S.A.* 41°32N 75°57W **83** E9
Tunliu *China* 36°13N 112°52E **34** F7
Tunnel Creek △
Australia 17°41S 125°18E **60** C4
Tunnsjøen *Norway* 64°45N 13°25E **8** D15
Tunungayualok I. *Canada* 56°0N 61°0W **73** A7
Tunuyán *Argentina* 33°35S 69°0W **94** C2
Tunuyán → *Argentina* 33°33S 67°30W **94** C2
Tuolumne *U.S.A.* 37°58N 120°15W **78** H6
Tuolumne → *U.S.A.* 37°36N 121°13W **78** H5
Tūp Āghāj *Iran* 36°3N 47°50E **44** B5
Tupã *Brazil* 21°57S 50°28W **95** A5
Tupelo *U.S.A.* 34°16N 88°43W **85** D10

Tupinambarana, I. *Brazil* 3°0S 58°0W **92** D7
Tupiza *Bolivia* 21°30S 65°40W **94** A2
Tupman *U.S.A.* 35°18N 119°21W **79** K7
Tupper *Canada* 55°32N 120°1W **70** B4
Tupper L. *U.S.A.* 44°10N 74°32W **83** B10
Tupper Lake *U.S.A.* 44°14N 74°28W **83** B10
Tupungato, Cerro
S. Amer. 33°15S 69°50W **94** C2
Tuquan *China* 45°18N 121°38E **35** B11
Túquerres *Colombia* 1°5N 77°37W **92** C3
Tura *Russia* 64°20N 100°17E **29** C11
Turabah *Si. Arabia* 28°20N 43°15E **44** D4
Tūrān *Iran* 35°39N 56°42E **45** C8
Turan *Russia* 51°55N 94°0E **29** D10
Turayf *Si. Arabia* 31°41N 38°39W **44** D3
Turda *Romania* 46°34N 23°47E **17** E12
Turek *Poland* 52°3N 18°30E **17** B10
Turén *Venezuela* 9°17N 69°6W **92** B5
Turfan = Turpan *China* 43°58N 89°10E **32** B3
Turfan Basin = Turpan Pendi
China 42°40N 89°25E **32** B3
Turfan Depression = Turpan
Pendi *China* 42°40N 89°25E **32** B3
Turgeon → *Canada* 50°0N 78°56W **72** C4
Türgovishte *Bulgaria* 43°17N 26°38E **23** C12
Turgutlu *Turkey* 38°30N 27°43E **23** E12
Turgwe → *Zimbabwe* 21°31S 32°15E **57** C5
Turia → *Spain* 39°27N 0°19W **21** C5
Turiaçu *Brazil* 1°40S 45°19W **93** D9
Turiaçu → *Brazil* 1°36S 45°19W **93** D9
Turin = Torino *Italy* 45°3N 7°40E **20** D7
Turkana, L. *Africa* 3°30N 36°5E **54** B4
Turkestan = Türkistan
Kazakhstan 43°17N 68°16E **28** E7
Turkey ■ *Eurasia* 39°0N 36°0E **19** G6
Turkey Creek = Warmun
Australia 17°2S 128°12E **60** C4
Türkistan *Kazakhstan* 43°17N 68°16E **28** E7
Türkmenabat
Turkmenistan 39°6N 63°34E **45** B9
Türkmenbashi
Turkmenistan 40°5N 53°5E **45** A7
Turkmenistan ■ *Asia* 39°0N 59°0E **28** F6
Turks & Caicos Is. ☑
W. Indies 21°20N 71°20W **89** B5
Turks Island Passage
W. Indies 21°30N 71°30W **89** B5
Turku *Finland* 60°30N 22°19E **9** F20
Turkwel → *Kenya* 3°6N 36°6E **54** B4
Turlock *U.S.A.* 37°30N 120°51W **78** H6
Turnagain *Australia* 9°34S 142°17E **62** a
Turnagain → *Canada* 59°12N 127°35W **70** B3
Turnagain, C. *N.Z.* 40°28S 176°38E **59** D6
Turneffe Is. *Belize* 17°20N 87°50W **87** D7
Turner *U.S.A.* 48°51N 108°24W **76** B9
Turner Pt. *Australia* 11°47S 133°32E **62** A1
Turner Valley *Canada* 50°40N 114°17W **70** C6
Turners Falls *U.S.A.* 42°36N 72°33W **83** D12
Turnhout *Belgium* 51°19N 4°57E **15** C4
Turnor L. *Canada* 56°35N 108°35W **71** B7
Türnovo = Veliko Tŭrnovo
Bulgaria 43°5N 25°41E **23** C11
Turnu Măgurele
Romania 43°46N 24°56E **17** G13
Turnu Roşu, P.
Romania 45°33N 24°17E **17** F13
Turpan *China* 43°58N 89°10E **32** B3
Turpan Pendi *China* 42°40N 89°25E **32** B3
Turriff *U.K.* 57°32N 2°27W **11** D6
Tursāq *Iraq* 33°27N 45°47E **44** C5
Turtle Head I. *Australia* 10°56S 142°37E **62** A3
Turtle L. *Canada* 53°36N 108°38W **71** C7
Turtle Lake *U.S.A.* 47°31N 100°53W **80** B3
Turtleford *Canada* 53°23N 108°57W **71** C7
Turuépano △ *Venezuela* 10°34N 62°43W **89** D7
Turukhansk *Russia* 65°21N 88°5E **29** C9
Tuscaloosa *U.S.A.* 33°12N 87°34W **85** E11
Tuscany = Toscana □
Italy 43°25N 11°0E **22** C4
Tuscarawas → *U.S.A.* 40°24N 81°25W **82** F3
Tuscarora Mt. *U.S.A.* 40°55N 77°55W **82** F7
Tuscola *Ill., U.S.A.* 39°48N 88°17W **80** F9
Tuscola *Tex., U.S.A.* 32°12N 99°48W **84** E5
Tuscumbia *U.S.A.* 34°44N 87°42W **85** D11
Tuskegee *U.S.A.* 32°25N 85°42W **85** E12
Tuticorin *India* 8°50N 78°12E **40** Q11
Tutóia *Brazil* 2°45S 42°20W **93** D10
Tutong *Brunei* 4°47N 114°40E **36** D4
Tutrakan *Bulgaria* 44°2N 26°40E **23** B12
Tuttle Creek L. *U.S.A.* 39°15N 96°36W **80** F5
Tuttlingen *Germany* 47°58N 8°48E **16** E5
Tutuala *E. Timor* 8°25S 127°15E **37** F7
Tutuila *Amer. Samoa* 14°19S 170°50W **59** b
Tutume *Botswana* 20°30S 27°5E **53** J5
Tuul Gol → *Mongolia* 48°30N 104°25E **32** B5
Tuva □ *Russia* 51°30N 95°0E **29** D10
Tuvalu ■ *Pac. Oc.* 8°0S 178°0E **58** B10
Tuvuca *Fiji* 17°40S 178°48W **59** a
Tuxpan *Mexico* 20°57N 97°24W **87** C5
Tuxtla Gutiérrez *Mexico* 16°45N 93°7W **87** D6
Tuy = Tui *Spain* 42°3N 8°39W **21** A1
Tuy An *Vietnam* 13°17N 109°16E **38** F7
Tuy Duc *Vietnam* 12°15N 107°27E **39** F6
Tuy Hoa *Vietnam* 13°5N 109°10E **38** F7
Tuy Phong *Vietnam* 11°14N 108°43E **39** G7
Tuya L. *Canada* 59°7N 130°35W **70** B2
Tuyen Hoa *Vietnam* 17°50N 106°10E **38** D6
Tuyen Quang *Vietnam* 21°50N 105°10E **38** B5
Tüysarkän *Iran* 34°33N 48°27E **45** C6
Tuz Gölü *Turkey* 38°42N 33°18E **19** G5
Tūz Khurmātū *Iraq* 34°56N 44°38E **44** C5
Tuzigoot △ *U.S.A.* 34°46N 112°2W **77** J7
Tuzla *Bos.-H.* 44°34N 18°41E **23** B8
Tver *Russia* 56°55N 35°55E **18** C6
Twain *U.S.A.* 40°1N 121°3W **78** E5
Twain Harte *U.S.A.* 38°2N 120°14W **78** G6
Tweed *Canada* 44°29N 77°19W **82** B7
Tweed → *U.K.* 55°45N 2°0W **11** F6
Tweed Heads *Australia* 28°10S 153°31E **63** D5

Tweedsmuir △ *Canada* 53°0N 126°20W **70** C3
Twentynine Palms
U.S.A. 34°8N 116°3W **79** L10
Twillingate *Canada* 49°42N 54°45W **73** C9
Twin Bridges *U.S.A.* 45°33N 112°20W **76** D7
Twin Falls *Canada* 53°30N 64°32W **73** B7
Twin Falls *U.S.A.* 42°34N 114°28W **76** E6
Twin Valley *U.S.A.* 47°16N 96°16W **80** B5
Twinsburg *U.S.A.* 41°19N 81°26W **82** E3
Twitchell Res. *U.S.A.* 34°59N 120°19W **79** L6
Two Harbors *U.S.A.* 47°2N 91°40W **80** B8
Two Hills *Canada* 53°43N 111°52W **70** C6
Two Rivers *U.S.A.* 44°9N 87°34W **80** C10
Two Rocks *Australia* 31°30S 115°35E **61** F2
Twofold B. *Australia* 37°8S 149°59E **63** F4
Tyachiv *Ukraine* 48°1N 23°35E **17** D12
Tychy *Poland* 50°9N 18°59E **17** C10
Tyler *Minn., U.S.A.* 44°17N 96°8W **80** C5
Tyler *Tex., U.S.A.* 32°21N 95°18W **84** E7
Tynda *Russia* 55°10N 124°43E **29** D13
Tyndall *U.S.A.* 43°0N 97°50W **80** D5
Tyne → *U.K.* 54°59N 1°32W **12** C6
Tyne & Wear □ *U.K.* 55°6N 1°17W **12** B6
Tynemouth *U.K.* 55°1N 1°26W **12** B6
Tyre = Sūr *Lebanon* 33°19N 35°16E **46** B4
Tyrifjorden *Norway* 60°2N 10°8E **9** F14
Tyrol = Tirol □ *Austria* 47°3N 10°43E **16** E6
Tyrone *U.S.A.* 40°40N 78°14W **82** F6
Tyrone □ *U.K.* 54°38N 7°11W **10** B4
Tyrrell → *Australia* 35°26S 142°51E **63** F3
Tyrrell, L. *Australia* 35°20S 142°50E **63** F3
Tyrrell L. *Canada* 63°7N 105°27W **71** A7
Tyrrhenian Sea *Medit. S.* 40°0N 12°30E **22** E5
Tysfjorden *Norway* 68°7N 16°25E **8** B17
Tyulgan *Russia* 52°22N 56°12E **18** D10
Tyumen *Russia* 57°11N 65°29E **28** D7
Tywi → *U.K.* 51°48N 4°21W **13** F3
Tywyn *U.K.* 52°35N 4°5W **13** E3
Tzaneen *S. Africa* 23°47S 30°9E **57** C5
Tzermiado *Greece* 35°12N 25°29E **25** D7
Tzukong = Zigong
China 29°15N 104°48E **32** D5

U

U.S.A. = United States of
America ■ *N. Amer.* 37°0N 96°0W **75** H20
U.S. Virgin Is. ☑ *W. Indies* 18°20N 65°0W **89** e
Uanle Uen = Wanlaweyne
Somali Rep. 2°37N 44°54E **47** G3
Uatumã → *Brazil* 2°26S 57°37W **92** D7
Uaupés *Brazil* 0°8S 67°5W **92** D5
Uaupés → *Brazil* 0°2N 67°16W **92** C5
Uaxactún *Guatemala* 17°25N 89°29W **88** C2
Ubá *Brazil* 21°8S 43°0W **95** A7
Ubaitaba *Brazil* 14°18S 39°20W **93** F11
Ubangi = Oubangi →
Dem. Rep. of the Congo 0°30S 17°50E **52** E3
Ubauro *Pakistan* 28°15N 69°45E **42** E3
Ubayyiḍ, W. al → *Iraq* 32°34N 43°48E **44** C4
Ube *Japan* 33°56N 131°15E **31** H5
Úbeda *Spain* 38°3N 3°23W **21** C4
Uberaba *Brazil* 19°50S 47°55W **93** G9
Uberlândia *Brazil* 19°0S 48°20W **93** G9
Ubin, Pulau *Singapore* 1°24N 103°57E **39** d
Ubly *U.S.A.* 43°42N 82°55W **82** C2
Ubolratna Res. *Thailand* 16°45N 102°30E **38** D4
Ubombo *S. Africa* 27°31S 32°4E **57** D5
Ubon Ratchathani
Thailand 15°15N 104°50E **38** E5
Ubondo
Dem. Rep. of the Congo 0°55S 25°42E **54** C2
Ubort → *Belarus* 52°6N 28°30E **17** B15
Ubud *Indonesia* 8°30S 115°16E **37** J18
Ubundu
Dem. Rep. of the Congo 0°22S 25°30E **54** C2
Ucayali → *Peru* 4°30S 73°30W **92** D4
Uchab *Namibia* 19°47S 17°42E **56** B2
Uchiura-Wan *Japan* 42°25N 140°40E **30** C10
Uchquduq *Uzbekistan* 41°50N 62°50E **28** E7
Uchur → *Russia* 58°48N 130°35E **29** D14
Ucluelet *Canada* 48°57N 125°32W **70** D3
Uda → *Russia* 54°42N 135°14E **29** D14
Udachnyy *Russia* 66°25N 112°24E **29** C12
Udagamandalam *India* 11°30N 76°44E **40** P10
Udainagar *India* 22°33N 76°13E **42** H7
Udaipur *India* 24°36N 73°44E **42** G5
Udaipur Garhi *Nepal* 27°0N 86°35E **43** F12
Udala *India* 21°35N 86°34E **43** J12
Uddevalla *Sweden* 58°21N 11°55E **9** G14
Uddjaure *Sweden* 65°56N 17°49E **8** D17
Uden *Neths.* 51°40N 5°37E **15** C5
Udgir *India* 18°25N 77°5E **40** K10
Udhampur *India* 33°0N 75°5E **43** C6
Údine *Italy* 46°3N 13°14E **22** A5
Udintsev Fracture Zone
S. Ocean 57°0S 145°0W **5** B13
Udmurtia □ *Russia* 57°30N 52°30E **18** C9
Udon Thani *Thailand* 17°29N 102°46E **38** D4
Udong *Cambodia* 11°48N 104°45E **39** G5
Udskaya Guba *Russia* 54°50N 135°45E **29** D14
Udu Pt. *Fiji* 16°9S 179°57W **59** a
Udupi *India* 13°25N 74°42E **40** N9
Udzungwa △ *Tanzania* 7°52S 36°35E **54** D4
Udzungwa Range
Tanzania 9°30S 35°10E **55** D4
Ueda *Japan* 36°24N 138°16E **31** F9
Uedineniya, Os. *Russia* 78°0N 85°0E **4** B12
Uele →
Dem. Rep. of the Congo 3°45N 24°45E **52** D4
Uelen *Russia* 66°10N 170°0W **29** C19
Uelzen *Germany* 52°57N 10°32E **16** B6
Ufa *Russia* 54°45N 55°55E **18** D10
Ufa → *Russia* 54°40N 56°0E **18** D10
Umm ad Daraj, J. *Jordan* 32°18N 35°48E **46** C4
Umm al Qaywayn
U.A.E. 25°30N 55°35E **45** E7
Umm al Qittayn *Jordan* 32°18N 36°40E **46** C5
Umm Bāb *Qatar* 25°12N 50°48E **45** E6

Ugie *S. Africa* 31°10S 28°13E **57** E4
Uglegorsk *Russia* 49°5N 142°2E **29** E15
Ugljan *Croatia* 44°12N 15°10E **16** F8
Ugolnye Kopi *Russia* 64°44N 177°42E **29** C18
Uhlenhorst *Namibia* 23°45S 17°55E **56** C2
Uhrichsville *U.S.A.* 40°24N 81°21W **82** F3
Uibhist a Deas = South Uist
U.K. 57°20N 7°15W **11** D1
Uibhist a Tuath = North Uist
U.K. 57°40N 7°15W **11** D1
Uig *U.K.* 57°35N 6°21W **11** D2
Uíge *Angola* 7°30S 14°40E **52** F2
Uiha *Tonga* 19°54S 174°25W **59** c
Uijeongbu *S. Korea* 37°44N 127°2E **35** F14
Ŭiju *N. Korea* 40°15N 124°35E **35** D13
Uinta Mts. *U.S.A.* 40°45N 110°30W **76** F8
Uis *Namibia* 21°8S 14°49E **56** C1
Uiseong *S. Korea* 36°21N 128°45E **35** F15
Uitenhage *S. Africa* 33°40S 25°28E **56** E4
Uithuizen *Neths.* 53°24N 6°41E **15** A6
Ujh → *India* 32°10N 75°18E **42** C6
Ujhani *India* 28°0N 79°6E **43** F8
Uji-guntō *Japan* 31°15N 129°25E **31** J4
Ujjain *India* 23°9N 75°43E **42** H6
Ujung Pandang *Indonesia* 5°10S 119°20E **37** F5
Uka *Russia* 57°50N 162°0E **29** D17
Ukara I. *Tanzania* 1°50S 33°0E **54** C3
Uke-Shima *Japan* 28°2N 129°14E **31** K4
Ukerewe I. *Tanzania* 2°0S 33°0E **54** C3
Ukhrul *India* 25°10N 94°25E **41** G19
Ukhta *Russia* 63°34N 53°41E **18** B9
Ukiah *U.S.A.* 39°9N 123°13W **78** F3
Ukmergė *Lithuania* 55°15N 24°45E **9** J21
Ukraine ■ *Europe* 49°0N 32°0E **19** E5
Ukwi *Botswana* 23°29S 20°30E **56** C3
Ulaan-Uul *Mongolia* 44°13N 111°10E **34** B6
Ulaanbaatar *Mongolia* 47°55N 106°53E **32** B5
Ulaangom *Mongolia* 50°5N 92°10E **32** A4
Ulaanjirem *Mongolia* 45°5N 105°30E **34** B3
Ulak I. *U.S.A.* 51°22N 178°57W **74** E4
Ulamba
Dem. Rep. of the Congo 9°3S 23°38E **55** D1
Ulan Bator = Ulaanbaatar
Mongolia 47°55N 106°53E **32** B5
Ulan Ude *Russia* 51°45N 107°40E **29** D11
Ulanhad = Chifeng
China 42°18N 118°58E **35** C10
Ulaya *Morogoro, Tanzania* 7°3S 36°55E **54** D4
Ulaya *Tabora, Tanzania* 4°25S 33°30E **54** C3
Ulcinj *Montenegro* 41°58N 19°10E **23** D8
Ulco *S. Africa* 28°21S 24°15E **56** D3
Ule älv = Oulujoki →
Finland 65°1N 25°30E **8** D21
Ule träsk = Oulujärvi
Finland 64°25N 27°15E **8** D22
Uleåborg = Oulu *Finland* 65°1N 25°29E **8** D21
Ulefoss *Norway* 59°17N 9°16E **9** G13
Ulhasnagar *India* 19°15N 73°10E **40** K8
Uliastay *Mongolia* 47°56N 97°28E **32** B4
Uljin *S. Korea* 36°59N 129°24E **35** F15
Ulladulla *Australia* 35°21S 150°29E **63** F5
Ullapool *U.K.* 57°54N 5°9W **11** D3
Ulleungdo *S. Korea* 37°30N 130°30E **31** F5
Ullswater *Canada* 45°12N 79°29W **82** A5
Ullswater *U.K.* 54°34N 2°52W **12** C5
Ulm *Germany* 48°23N 9°58E **16** D5
Ulmarra *Australia* 29°37S 153°4E **63** D5
Ulonguè *Mozam.* 14°37S 34°19E **55** E3
Ulricehamn *Sweden* 57°46N 13°26E **9** H15
Ulsan *S. Korea* 35°20N 129°15E **35** G15
Ulsta *U.K.* 60°30N 1°9W **11** A7
Ulster □ *U.K.* 54°35N 6°30W **10** B5
Ulubat Gölü *Turkey* 40°9N 28°35E **23** D13
Uludağ *Turkey* 40°4N 29°13E **23** D13
Uluguru Mts. *Tanzania* 7°15S 37°40E **54** D4
Ulungur He → *China* 47°1N 87°24E **32** B3
Ulungur Hu *China* 47°20N 87°10E **32** B3
Uluru *Australia* 25°23S 131°5E **61** E5
Uluru-Kata Tjuta △
Australia 25°19S 131°1E **61** E5
Ulutau *Kazakhstan* 48°39N 67°1E **28** E7
Uluwatu *Indonesia* 8°50S 115°5E **37** K18
Ulva *U.K.* 56°29N 6°13W **11** E2
Ulverston *U.K.* 54°13N 3°5W **12** C4
Ulverstone *Australia* 41°11S 146°11E **63** G4
Ulya *Russia* 59°10N 142°0E **29** D15
Ulyanovsk *Russia* 54°20N 48°25E **18** D8
Ulyasutay = Uliastay
Mongolia 47°56N 97°28E **32** B4
Ulysses *Kans., U.S.A.* 37°35N 101°22W **80** G3
Ulysses *Pa., U.S.A.* 41°54N 77°46W **82** E7
Ulysses, Mt. *Canada* 57°20N 124°5W **70** B4
Umala *Bolivia* 17°25S 68°5W **92** G5
'Umān = Oman ■ *Asia* 23°0N 58°0E **47** C6
Uman *Ukraine* 48°40N 30°12E **17** D16
Umaria *India* 23°35N 80°50E **43** H9
Umarkot *Pakistan* 25°15N 69°40E **42** G3
Umarpada *India* 21°27N 73°30E **42** J5
Umatilla *U.S.A.* 45°55N 119°21W **76** D4
Umba *Russia* 66°42N 34°11E **18** A5
Umbagog L. *U.S.A.* 44°46N 71°3W **83** B13
Umbakumba *Australia* 13°47S 136°50E **62** A2
Umbrella Mts. *N.Z.* 45°35S 169°5E **59** F2
Umeå *Sweden* 63°45N 20°20E **8** E19
Umeälven → *Sweden* 63°45N 20°20E **8** E19
Umera *Indonesia* 0°12S 129°37E **37** E7
Umfuli → *Zimbabwe* 17°30S 29°23E **55** F2
Umfurudzi △ *Zimbabwe* 17°6S 31°40E **55** F3
Umgusa *Zimbabwe* 19°29S 27°52E **55** F2
Umgwenya → *Mozam.* 25°14S 32°18E **57** D5
Umiujaq *Canada* 56°33N 76°33W **72** A4
Umkomaas *S. Africa* 30°13S 30°48E **57** E5
Umlazi *S. Africa* 29°59S 30°54E **57** E5
Umm ad Daraj, J. *Jordan* 32°18N 35°48E **46** C4
Umm al Qaywayn
U.A.E. 25°30N 55°35E **45** E7
Umm al Qittayn *Jordan* 32°18N 36°40E **46** C5
Umm Bāb *Qatar* 25°12N 50°48E **45** E6

Umm Durman = Omdurmân
Sudan 15°40N 32°28E **51** E12
Umm el Fahm *Israel* 32°31N 35°9E **46** C4
Umm Keddada *Sudan* 13°33N 26°35E **51** F11
Umm Lajj *Si. Arabia* 25°0N 37°23E **44** E3
Umm Qasr *Iraq* 30°1N 47°58E **44** D5
Umm Ruwaba *Sudan* 12°50N 31°20E **51** F12
Umnak I. *U.S.A.* 53°15N 168°20W **74** E6
Umniati → *Zimbabwe* 16°49S 28°45E **55** F2
Umpqua → *U.S.A.* 43°40N 124°12W **76** E1
Umreth *India* 22°41N 73°4E **42** H5
Umtata = Mthatha
S. Africa 31°36S 28°49E **57** E4
Umuarama *Brazil* 23°45S 53°20W **95** A5
Umvukwe Ra. *Zimbabwe* 16°45S 30°45E **55** F3
Umzimvubu *S. Africa* 31°38S 29°33E **57** E4
Umzingwane →
Zimbabwe 22°12S 29°56E **55** G2
Umzinto = eMuziwezinto
S. Africa 30°15S 30°45E **57** E5
Una *India* 20°46N 71°8E **42** J4
Una → *Bos.-H.* 45°0N 16°20E **16** F9
Unadilla *U.S.A.* 42°20N 75°19W **83** D9
Unalakleet *U.S.A.* 63°52N 160°47W **74** C7
Unalaska *U.S.A.* 53°53N 166°32W **74** E6
Unalaska I. *U.S.A.* 53°35N 166°50W **74** E6
'Unayzah *Si. Arabia* 26°6N 43°58E **44** E4
'Unayzah, J. *Asia* 32°12N 39°18E **44** C3
Uncía *Bolivia* 18°25S 66°40W **92** G5
Uncompahgre Peak
U.S.A. 38°4N 107°28W **76** G10
Uncompahgre Plateau
U.S.A. 38°20N 108°15W **76** G9
Undara Volcanic △
Australia 18°14S 144°41E **62** B3
Underbool *Australia* 35°10S 141°51E **63** F3
Underwood *Canada* 44°18N 81°29W **82** B3
Ungarie *Australia* 33°38S 146°56E **63** E4
Ungarra *Australia* 34°12S 136°2E **63** E2
Ungava, Pén. d' *Canada* 60°0N 74°0W **69** F17
Ungava B. *Canada* 59°30N 67°30W **69** F18
Ungeny = Ungheni
Moldova 47°11N 27°51E **17** E14
Unggi *N. Korea* 42°16N 130°28E **35** C16
Ungheni *Moldova* 47°11N 27°51E **17** E14
Ungwana B. *Kenya* 2°45S 40°20E **54** C5
União da Vitória *Brazil* 26°13S 51°5W **95** B5
Unimak I. *U.S.A.* 54°45N 164°0W **74** E7
Unimak Pass. *U.S.A.* 54°15N 164°30W **74** E7
Union *Miss., U.S.A.* 32°34N 89°7W **85** E10
Union *Mo., U.S.A.* 38°27N 91°0W **80** F8
Union *S.C., U.S.A.* 34°43N 81°37W **85** D14
Union City *Calif., U.S.A.* 37°36N 122°1W **78** H4
Union City *N.J., U.S.A.* 40°45N 74°2W **83** F10
Union City *Pa., U.S.A.* 41°54N 79°51W **82** E5
Union City *Tenn., U.S.A.* 36°26N 89°3W **85** C10
Union Dale *U.S.A.* 41°43N 75°29W **83** E9
Union Gap *U.S.A.* 46°33N 120°28W **76** C3
Union Springs *Ala.,*
U.S.A. 32°9N 85°43W **85** E12
Union Springs *N.Y.,*
U.S.A. 42°50N 76°41W **83** D8
Uniondale *S. Africa* 33°39S 23°7E **56** E3
Uniontown *U.S.A.* 39°54N 79°44W **81** F14
Unionville *U.S.A.* 40°29N 93°1W **80** E7
United Arab Emirates ■
Asia 23°50N 54°0E **45** F7
United Kingdom ■ *Europe* 53°0N 2°0W **14** E6
United States of America ■
N. Amer. 37°0N 96°0W **75** H20
Unity *Canada* 52°30N 109°5W **71** C7
University Park
U.S.A. 32°17N 106°45W **77** K10
University Place *U.S.A.* 47°14N 122°33W **78** C4
Unjha *India* 23°46N 72°24E **42** H5
Unnao *India* 26°35N 80°30E **43** F9
Unsengedsi → *Zimbabwe* 15°43S 31°14E **55** F3
Unst *U.K.* 60°44N 0°53W **11** A8
Unuk → *Canada* 56°5N 131°3W **70** B2
Unzen-Amakusa △
Japan 32°15N 130°10E **31** H5
Uozu *Japan* 36°48N 137°24E **31** F8
Upata *Venezuela* 8°1N 62°24W **92** B6
Upemba, L.
Dem. Rep. of the Congo 8°30S 26°20E **55** D2
Upemba △
Dem. Rep. of the Congo 9°0S 26°35E **55** D2
Upernavik *Greenland* 72°49N 56°20W **4** B5
Upington *S. Africa* 28°25S 21°15E **56** D3
Upleta *India* 21°46N 70°16E **42** J4
'Upolu *Samoa* 13°58S 172°0W **59** b
Upper Alkali L. *U.S.A.* 41°47N 120°8W **76** F3
Upper Arrow L. *Canada* 50°30N 117°50W **70** C5
Upper Daly △ *Australia* 14°26S 131°3E **60** B5
Upper Darby *U.S.A.* 39°55N 75°16W **81** F16
Upper Foster L. *Canada* 56°47N 105°20W **71** B7
Upper Hutt *N.Z.* 41°8S 175°5E **59** D5
Upper Klamath L.
U.S.A. 42°25N 121°55W **76** E3
Upper Lake *U.S.A.* 39°10N 122°54W **78** F4
Upper Liard *Canada* 60°3N 128°54W **70** A3
Upper Manzanilla
Trin. & Tob. 10°31N 61°4W **93** K15
Upper Missouri Breaks △
U.S.A. 47°50N 109°55W **76** C9
Upper Musquodoboit
Canada 45°10N 62°58W **73** C7
Upper Red L. *U.S.A.* 48°8N 94°45W **80** A6
Upper Sandusky
U.S.A. 40°50N 83°17W **81** E12
Upper Volta = Burkina Faso ■
Africa 12°0N 1°0W **50** F5
Uppland *Sweden* 59°59N 17°48E **9** G17
Uppsala *Sweden* 59°53N 17°38E **9** G17
Upshi *India* 33°48N 77°52E **43** C7
Upton *U.S.A.* 44°6N 104°38W **76** D11
Uqsuqtuuq = Gjoa Haven
Canada 68°38N 95°53W **68** D12
Ur *Iraq* 30°55N 46°25E **44** D5

Urad Qianqi *China* 40°40N 108°30E **34** D5
Urakawa *Japan* 42°9N 142°47E **30** C11
Ural = Uralskiy □ *Russia* 64°0N 70°0E **28** C7
Ural = Zhayyq ➜
  Kazakhstan 47°0N 51°48E **19** E9
Ural *Australia* 33°21S 146°12E **63** E4
Ural Mts. = Uralskie Gory
  Eurasia 60°0N 59°0E **18** C10
Uralla *Australia* 30°37S 151°29E **63** E5
Uralsk = Oral *Kazakhstan* 51°20N 51°20E **19** D9
Uralskie Gory *Eurasia* 60°0N 59°0E **18** C10
Uralskiy □ *Russia* 64°0N 70°0E **28** C7
Urambo *Tanzania* 5°4S 32°0E **54** D3
Urandangi *Australia* 21°32S 138°14E **62** C2
Uranium City *Canada* 59°34N 108°37W **71** B7
Urapuntja = Utopia
  Australia 22°14S 134°33E **62** C1
Uraricoera ➜ *Brazil* 3°2N 60°30W **92** C6
Urasoe *Japan* 26°15N 127°43E **31** L3
Urawa = Saitama *Japan* 35°54N 139°38E **31** G9
Uray *Russia* 60°5N 65°15E **28** C7
'Uray'irah *Si. Arabia* 25°57N 48°53E **45** E6
Urbana *Ill., U.S.A.* 40°7N 88°12W **80** E9
Urbana *Ohio, U.S.A.* 40°7N 83°45W **81** E12
Urbandale *U.S.A.* 41°38N 93°43W **80** E7
Urbino *Italy* 43°43N 12°38E **22** C5
Urbión, Picos de *Spain* 42°1N 2°52W **21** A4
Urcos *Peru* 13°40S 71°38W **92** F4
Urdinarrain *Argentina* 32°37S 58°52W **94** C4
Ure ➜ *U.K.* 54°5N 1°20W **12** C6
Urengoy *Russia* 65°58N 78°22E **28** C8
Ures *Mexico* 29°26N 110°24W **86** B2
Urewera △ *N.Z.* 38°29S 177°7E **59** C6
Urfa = Şanlıurfa *Turkey* 37°12N 38°50E **44** B3
Urganch *Uzbekistan* 41°40N 60°41E **28** E7
Urgench = Urganch
  Uzbekistan 41°40N 60°41E **28** E7
Ürgün *Turkey* 38°38N 34°56E **44** B2
Uri *India* 34°8N 74°2E **43** B6
Uribia *Colombia* 11°43N 72°16W **92** A4
Uriondo *Bolivia* 21°41S 64°41W **94** A3
Urique *Mexico* 27°13N 107°55W **86** B3
Urique ➜ *Mexico* 26°29N 107°58W **86** B3
Urk *Neths.* 52°39N 5°36E **15** B5
Urla *Turkey* 38°20N 26°47E **23** E12
Urmia = Orūmīyeh *Iran* 37°40N 45°0E **44** B5
Uroševac *Kosovo* 42°23N 21°10E **23** C9
Uroyan, Montanas de
  Puerto Rico 18°12N 67°0W **89** d
Urrampinyi Iltjiltarri ☉
  Australia 24°20S 132°10E **60** D5
Uruaçu *Brazil* 14°30S 49°10W **93** F9
Uruapan *Mexico* 19°24N 102°3W **86** D4
Urubamba ➜ *Peru* 10°43S 73°48W **92** F4
Urucará *Brazil* 2°32S 57°45W **92** D7
Uruçuí *Brazil* 7°20S 44°28W **93** E10
Uruguai ➜ *Brazil* 26°0S 53°30W **95** B5
Uruguaiana *Brazil* 29°50S 57°0W **94** B4
Uruguay ■ *S. Amer.* 32°30S 56°30W **94** C4
Uruguay ➜ *S. Amer.* 34°12S 58°18W **94** C4
Urumchi = Ürümqi
  China 43°45N 87°45E **32** B3
Ürümqi *China* 43°45N 87°45E **32** B3
Uruna □ *Australia* 24°3S 133°1E **60** D5
Urup, Ostrov *Russia* 46°0N 151°0E **29** E16
Ürzhar *Kazakhstan* 47°5N 81°38E **28** E9
Usa ➜ *Russia* 66°16N 59°49E **18** A10
Uşak *Turkey* 38°43N 29°28E **19** G4
Usakos *Namibia* 21°54S 15°31E **56** C2
Usedom *Germany* 53°55N 14°2E **16** B8
Useless Loop *Australia* 26°8S 113°23E **61** E1
Ushakova, Ostrov *Russia* 82°0N 80°0E **29** A8
Ushant = Ouessant, Î. d'
  France 48°28N 5°6W **20** B1
Ushashi *Tanzania* 1°59S 33°57E **54** C3
'Ushayrah *Si. Arabia* 25°35N 45°47E **44** E5
Ushibuka *Japan* 32°11N 130°1E **31** H5
Ūshtōbe *Kazakhstan* 45°16N 78°0E **28** E8
Ushuaia *Argentina* 54°50S 68°23W **96** G3
Ushumun *Russia* 52°47N 126°32E **29** D13
Usinsk *Russia* 65°57N 57°27E **18** A10
Usk *Canada* 54°38N 128°26W **70** C3
Usk ➜ *U.K.* 51°33N 2°58W **13** F5
Uska *India* 27°12N 83°7E **43** F10
Usman *Russia* 52°5N 39°48E **18** D6
Usoke *Tanzania* 5°8S 32°24E **54** D3
Usolye-Sibirskoye
  Russia 52°48N 103°40E **29** D11
Uspallata, P. de
  Argentina 32°37S 69°22W **94** C2
Ussuriysk *Russia* 43°48N 131°59E **30** C5
Ussurka *Russia* 45°12N 133°31E **30** B6
Ust-Chaun *Russia* 68°47N 170°30E **29** C18
Ust-Ilimsk *Russia* 58°3N 102°39E **29** D11
Ust-Ishim *Russia* 57°45N 71°10E **28** D8
Ust-Kamchatsk *Russia* 56°10N 162°28E **29** D17
Ust-Kamenogorsk = Öskemen
  Kazakhstan 50°0N 82°36E **28** E9
Ust-Khayryuzovo
  Russia 57°15N 156°45E **29** D16
Ust-Kut *Russia* 56°50N 105°42E **29** D11
Ust-Kuyga *Russia* 70°1N 135°43E **29** B14
Ust-Maya *Russia* 60°30N 134°28E **29** C14
Ust-Mil *Russia* 59°40N 133°11E **29** D14
Ust-Nera *Russia* 64°35N 143°15E **29** C15
Ust-Nyukzha *Russia* 56°34N 121°37E **29** D13
Ust-Olenek *Russia* 73°0N 120°5E **29** B12
Ust-Omchug *Russia* 61°9N 149°38E **29** C15
Ust-Port *Russia* 69°40N 84°26E **28** C9
Ust-Tsilma *Russia* 65°28N 52°11E **18** A9
Ust-Urt = Ustyurt Plateau
  Asia 44°0N 55°0E **28** E6
Ust-Usa *Russia* 66°2N 56°57E **18** A10
Ust-Vorkuta *Russia* 67°24N 64°0E **18** A11
Ustí nad Labem *Czech Rep.* 50°41N 14°3E **16** C8
Ústica *Italy* 38°42N 13°11E **22** E5
Ustinov = Izhevsk
  Russia 56°51N 53°14E **18** C9
Ustyurt Plateau *Asia* 44°0N 55°0E **28** E6

Usu *China* 44°27N 84°40E **32** B3
Usuki *Japan* 33°8N 131°49E **31** H5
Usulután *El Salv.* 13°25N 88°28W **88** D2
Usumacinta ➜ *Mexico* 18°24N 92°38W **87** D6
Usumbura = Bujumbura
  Burundi 3°16S 29°18E **54** C2
Usure *Tanzania* 4°40S 34°22E **54** C3
Usutuo ➜ *Mozam.* 26°48S 32°7E **57** D5
Uta *Indonesia* 4°33S 136°0E **37** E9
Utah □ *U.S.A.* 39°20N 111°30W **76** G8
Utah, L. *U.S.A.* 40°12N 111°48W **76** F8
Utara, Selat *Malaysia* 5°28N 100°20E **39** c
Utarni *India* 26°5N 71°58E **42** F4
Utatlan *Guatemala* 15°2N 91°11W **88** C1
Ute Creek ➜ *U.S.A.* 35°21N 103°50W **77** J12
Utena *Lithuania* 55°27N 25°40E **9** J21
Utete *Tanzania* 8°0S 38°45E **54** D4
Uthai Thani *Thailand* 15°22N 100°3E **38** E3
Uthal *Pakistan* 25°44N 66°40E **42** G2
Utiariti *Brazil* 13°0S 58°10W **92** F7
Utica *N.Y., U.S.A.* 43°6N 75°14W **83** D9
Utica *Ohio, U.S.A.* 40°14N 82°27W **82** F2
Utikuma L. *Canada* 55°50N 115°30W **70** B5
Utila *Honduras* 16°6N 86°56W **88** C2
Utopia *Australia* 22°14S 134°33E **62** C1
Utraula *India* 27°19N 82°25E **43** F10
Utrecht *Neths.* 52°5N 5°8E **15** B5
Utrecht *S. Africa* 27°38S 30°20E **57** D5
Utrecht □ *Neths.* 52°6N 5°7E **15** B5
Utrera *Spain* 37°12N 5°48W **21** D3
Utsjoki ➜ *Finland* 69°51N 26°59E **8** B22
Utsunomiya *Japan* 36°30N 139°50E **31** F9
Uttar Pradesh □ *India* 27°0N 80°0E **43** F9
Uttaradit *Thailand* 17°36N 100°5E **38** D3
Uttarakhand □ *India* 30°0N 79°30E **43** D8
Utterson *Canada* 45°12N 79°19W **82** A5
Uttoxeter *U.K.* 52°54N 1°52W **12** E6
Utuado *Puerto Rico* 18°16N 66°42W **89** d
Uummannaq *Avannaarsua,*
  Greenland 77°33N 68°52W **69** B18
Uummannaq *Kitaa,*
  Greenland 70°58N 52°17W **4** B5
Uummannarsuaq = Nunap Isua
  Greenland 59°48N 43°55W **66** D15
Uusikaarlepyy *Finland* 63°32N 22°31E **8** E20
Uusikaupunki *Finland* 60°47N 21°25E **8** F19
Uva *Russia* 56°59N 52°13E **18** C9
Uvalde *U.S.A.* 29°13N 99°47W **84** G5
Uvat *Russia* 59°5N 68°50E **28** D7
Uvinza *Tanzania* 5°5S 30°24E **54** D3
Uvira *Dem. Rep. of the Congo* 3°22S 29°3E **54** C2
Uvs Nuur *Mongolia* 50°20N 92°30E **32** A4
'Uwairidh, Ḥarrat al
  Si. Arabia 26°50N 38°0E **44** E3
Uwajima *Japan* 33°10N 132°35E **31** H6
Uwanda △ *Tanzania* 7°46S 32°0E **54** D3
Uweinat, Jebel *Sudan* 21°54N 24°58E **51** D10
Uxbridge *Canada* 44°6N 79°7W **82** B5
Uxin Qi *China* 38°50N 109°5E **34** E5
Uxmal *Mexico* 20°22N 89°46W **87** C7
Üydzin *Mongolia* 44°9N 107°0E **34** B4
Uyo *Nigeria* 5°1N 7°53E **50** G7
Uyûn Mûsa *Egypt* 29°53N 32°40E **46** F1
Uyuni *Bolivia* 20°28S 66°47W **92** H5
Uzbekistan ■ *Asia* 41°30N 65°0E **28** E7
Uzboy ➜ *Turkmenistan* 39°30N 55°0E **45** B7
Uzen, Bolshoi = Uzen, Mal ➜
  Kazakhstan 49°4N 49°44E **19** E8
Uzen, Mal ➜ *Kazakhstan* 49°4N 49°44E **19** E8
Uzerche *France* 45°25N 1°34E **20** D4
Uzh ➜ *Ukraine* 51°15N 30°12E **17** C16
Uzhgorod = Uzhhorod
  Ukraine 48°36N 22°18E **17** D12
Uzhhorod *Ukraine* 48°36N 22°18E **17** D12
Užice *Serbia* 43°55N 19°50E **23** C8
Uzunköprü *Turkey* 41°16N 26°43E **23** D12

V

Vaal ➜ *S. Africa* 29°4S 23°38E **56** D3
Vaal Dam *S. Africa* 27°0S 28°14E **57** D4
Vaalbos △ *S. Africa* 28°22S 24°20E **56** D3
Vaalwater *S. Africa* 24°15S 28°8E **57** C4
Vaasa *Finland* 63°6N 21°38E **8** E19
Vác *Hungary* 47°49N 19°10E **17** E10
Vacaria *Brazil* 28°31S 50°52W **95** B5
Vacata *Fiji* 17°15S 179°31W **59** a
Vacaville *U.S.A.* 38°21N 121°59W **78** G5
Vach = Vakh ➜ *Russia* 60°45N 76°45E **28** C8
Vache, Î. à *Haiti* 18°2N 73°35W **89** C5
Vacoas *Mauritius* 20°18S 57°29E **53** d
Vadakara = Badagara
  India 11°35N 75°40E **40** P9
Vadnagar *India* 23°47N 72°40E **42** H5
Vadodara *India* 22°20N 73°10E **42** H5
Vadsø *Norway* 70°3N 29°50E **8** A23
Vaduz *Liech.* 47°8N 9°31E **20** C8
Værøy *Norway* 67°40N 12°40E **8** C15
Vágar *Færoe Is.* 62°5N 7°15W **8** E9
Vagla, Akra *Greece* 36°15N 28°11E **25** C10
Vågsfjorden *Norway* 68°50N 16°50E **8** B17
Váh ➜ *Slovak Rep.* 47°43N 18°7E **17** D9
Vahsel B. *Antarctica* 75°0S 35°0W **5** D1
Váhtjer = Gällivare
  Sweden 67°9N 20°40E **8** C19
Vaï *Greece* 35°15N 26°18E **25** D8
Vaihiria, L. *Tahiti* 17°40S 149°25W **59** d
Vail *U.S.A.* 39°40N 106°20W **75** H18
Vairao *Tahiti* 17°47S 149°17W **59** d
Vaisali ➜ *India* 26°28N 78°53E **43** F8
Vaitogi *Amer. Samoa* 14°24S 170°44W **59** b
Vakh ➜ *Russia* 60°45N 76°45E **28** C8
Val-d'Or *Canada* 48°7N 77°47W **72** C4
Val Marie *Canada* 49°15N 107°45W **71** D7
Valaam *Russia* 61°22N 30°57E **8** B5
Valahia *Romania* 44°35N 25°0E **17** F13
Valandovo *Macedonia* 41°19N 22°34E **23** D10
Valatie *U.S.A.* 42°24N 73°40W **83** D11

Valcheta *Argentina* 40°40S 66°8W **96** E3
Valdai Hills = Valdayskaya
  Vozvyshennost *Russia* 57°0N 33°30E **18** C5
Valdayskaya Vozvyshennost
  Russia 57°0N 33°30E **18** C5
Valdepeñas *Spain* 38°43N 3°25W **21** C4
Valdés, Pen. *Argentina* 42°30S 63°45W **96** E4
Valdez *U.S.A.* 61°7N 146°16W **68** B5
Valdivia *Chile* 39°50S 73°14W **96** D2
Valdivia Abyssal Plain
  S. Ocean 62°30S 70°0E **5** C6
Valdosta *U.S.A.* 30°50N 83°17W **85** F13
Valdres *Norway* 61°5N 9°5E **8** F13
Vale *U.S.A.* 43°59N 117°15W **76** E5
Vale of Glamorgan □
  U.K. 51°28N 3°25W **13** F4
Valemount *Canada* 52°50N 119°15W **70** C5
Valença *Brazil* 13°20S 39°5W **93** F11
Valença do Piauí *Brazil* 6°20S 41°45W **93** E10
Valence *France* 44°57N 4°54E **20** D6
Valencia *Spain* 39°27N 0°23W **21** C5
Valencia *Trin. & Tob.* 10°39N 61°11W **93** K15
Valencia *U.S.A.* 34°48N 106°43W **77** J10
Valencia *Venezuela* 10°11N 68°0W **92** A5
Valencia □ *Spain* 39°20N 0°40W **21** C5
Valencia, G. de *Spain* 39°30N 0°20E **21** C6
Valencia de Alcántara
  Spain 39°25N 7°14W **21** C2
Valencia I. *Ireland* 51°54N 10°22W **10** E1
Valenciennes *France* 50°20N 3°34E **20** A5
Valentim, Sa. do *Brazil* 6°0S 43°30W **93** E10
Valentin *Russia* 43°8N 134°17E **30** C7
Valentine *Nebr., U.S.A.* 42°52N 100°33W **80** D3
Valentine *Tex., U.S.A.* 30°35N 104°30W **84** F2
Valera *Venezuela* 9°19N 70°37W **92** B4
Valga *Estonia* 57°47N 26°2E **9** H22
Valier *U.S.A.* 48°18N 112°16W **76** B7
Valjevo *Serbia* 44°18N 19°53E **23** B8
Valka *Latvia* 57°46N 26°3E **9** H22
Valkeakoski *Finland* 61°16N 24°2E **8** F21
Valkenswaard *Neths.* 51°21N 5°29E **15** C5
Vall de Uxó = La Vall d'Uixó
  Spain 39°49N 0°15W **21** C5
Valladolid *Mexico* 20°41N 88°12W **87** C7
Valladolid *Spain* 41°38N 4°43W **21** B3
Valldemossa *Spain* 39°43N 2°37E **24** B9
Valle de la Pascua
  Venezuela 9°13N 66°0W **92** B5
Valle de las Palmas
  Mexico 32°20N 116°43W **79** N10
Valle de Santiago
  Mexico 20°23N 101°12W **86** C4
Valle de Zaragoza
  Mexico 27°25N 105°50W **86** B3
Valle Fértil, Sierra del
  Argentina 30°20S 68°0W **94** C2
Valle Gran Rey *Canary Is.* 28°5N 17°20W **24** F2
Valle Hermoso *Mexico* 25°35N 97°40W **87** B5
Valle Nacional *Mexico* 17°47N 96°18W **87** D5
Valledupar *Colombia* 10°29N 73°15W **92** A4
Vallehermoso *Canary Is.* 28°10N 17°15W **24** F2
Vallejo *U.S.A.* 38°7N 122°14W **78** G4
Vallenar *Chile* 28°30S 70°50W **94** B1
Valletta *Malta* 35°54N 14°31E **25** D2
Valley Center *U.S.A.* 33°13N 117°2W **79** M9
Valley City *U.S.A.* 46°55N 98°0W **80** B5
Valley Falls *Oreg.,*
  U.S.A. 42°29N 120°17W **76** E3
Valley Falls *R.I., U.S.A.* 41°54N 71°24W **83** E13
Valley of Flowers △
  India 30°50N 79°40E **43** D8
Valley Springs *U.S.A.* 38°12N 120°50W **78** G6
Valley View *U.S.A.* 40°39N 76°33W **83** F8
Valley Wells *U.S.A.* 35°27N 115°46W **79** K11
Valleyview *Canada* 55°5N 117°17W **70** B5
Vallimanca, Arroyo
  Argentina 35°40S 59°10W **94** D4
Valls *Spain* 41°18N 1°15E **21** B6
Valmiera *Latvia* 57°37N 25°29E **9** H21
Valognes *France* 49°30N 1°28W **20** B3
Valona = Vlorë *Albania* 40°32N 19°28E **23** D8
Valozhyn *Belarus* 54°3N 26°30E **17** A14
Valparaíso *Chile* 33°2S 71°40W **94** C1
Valparaíso *Mexico* 22°46N 103°34W **86** C4
Valparaiso *U.S.A.* 41°28N 87°4W **80** E10
Valparaíso □ *Chile* 33°2S 71°40W **94** C1
Vals ➜ *S. Africa* 27°23S 26°30E **56** D4
Vals, Tanjung *Indonesia* 8°26S 137°25E **37** F9
Valsad *India* 20°40N 72°58E **40** J8
Valverde *Canary Is.* 27°48N 17°55W **24** G2
Valverde del Camino
  Spain 37°35N 6°47W **21** D2
Vamizi, I. *Mozam.* 11°2S 40°40E **55** E5
Vammala *Finland* 61°20N 22°54E **8** F20
Vamos *Greece* 35°24N 24°13E **25** D6
Van *Turkey* 38°30N 43°20E **44** B4
Van, L. = Van Gölü
  Turkey 38°30N 43°0E **44** B4
Van Alstyne *U.S.A.* 33°25N 96°35W **84** E6
Van Blommestein Meer
  Suriname 4°45N 55°5W **93** C7
Van Buren *Canada* 47°10N 67°55W **73** C6
Van Buren *Ark., U.S.A.* 35°26N 94°21W **84** D7
Van Buren *Maine,*
  U.S.A. 47°10N 67°58W **81** B20
Van Buren *Mo., U.S.A.* 37°0N 91°1W **80** G8
Van Canh *Vietnam* 13°37N 109°0E **38** F7
Van Diemen, C. *N. Terr.,*
  Australia 11°9S 130°24E **60** B5
Van Diemen, C. *Queens.,*
  Australia 16°30S 139°46E **62** B2
Van Diemen G. *Australia* 11°45S 132°0E **60** B5
Van Gölü *Turkey* 38°30N 43°0E **44** B4
Van Horn *U.S.A.* 31°3N 104°50W **84** F2
Van Ninh *Vietnam* 12°42N 109°14E **38** F7
Van Rees, Pegunungan
  Indonesia 2°35S 138°15E **37** E9
Van Wert *U.S.A.* 40°52N 84°35W **81** E11
Van Yen *Vietnam* 21°4N 104°42E **38** B5

Van Zylsrus *S. Africa* 26°52S 22°4E **56** D3
Vanadzor *Armenia* 40°48N 44°30E **19** F7
Vanavara *Russia* 60°22N 102°16E **29** C11
Vancouver *Canada* 49°15N 123°7W **78** A3
Vancouver *U.S.A.* 45°38N 122°40W **78** E4
Vancouver, C. *Australia* 35°2S 118°11E **61** G2
Vancouver I. *Canada* 49°50N 126°0W **78** B2
Vancouver Int. ✈ (YVR)
  Canada 49°10N 123°10W **78** A3
Vanda = Vantaa *Finland* 60°18N 24°56E **9** F21
Vandalia *Ill., U.S.A.* 38°58N 89°6W **80** F9
Vandalia *Mo., U.S.A.* 39°19N 91°29W **80** F8
Vandenberg Village
  U.S.A. 34°43N 120°28W **79** L6
Vandergrift *U.S.A.* 40°36N 79°34W **82** F5
Vanderhoof *Canada* 54°0N 124°0W **70** C4
Vanderkloof Dam
  S. Africa 30°4S 24°40E **56** E3
Vanderlin I. *Australia* 15°44S 137°2E **62** B2
Vänern *Sweden* 58°47N 13°30E **9** G15
Vänersborg *Sweden* 58°26N 12°19E **9** G15
Vang Vieng *Laos* 18°58N 102°32E **38** C4
Vanga *Kenya* 4°35S 39°12E **54** C4
Vangaindrano *Madag.* 23°21S 47°36E **57** C8
Vanguard *Canada* 49°55N 107°20W **71** D7
Vanino *Russia* 48°50N 140°5E **29** E15
Vankleek Hill *Canada* 45°32N 74°40E **83** A10
Vännäs *Sweden* 63°58N 19°48E **8** E18
Vannes *France* 47°40N 2°47W **20** C2
Vannøya *Norway* 70°6N 19°50E **8** A18
Vanrhynsdorp *S. Africa* 31°36S 18°44E **56** E2
Vansbro *Sweden* 60°32N 14°15E **9** F16
Vansittart B. *Australia* 14°3S 126°17E **60** B4
Vansittart I. *Canada* 65°50N 84°0W **69** D15
Vantaa *Finland* 60°18N 24°56E **9** F21
Vanua Balavu *Fiji* 17°12S 178°55W **59** a
Vanua Levu *Fiji* 16°33S 179°15E **59** a
Vanua Vatu *Fiji* 19°0S 178°0E **59** a
Vanuatu ■ *Pac. Oc.* 15°0S 168°0E **58** C9
Vanwyksvlei *S. Africa* 30°18S 21°49E **56** E3
Vapnyarka *Ukraine* 48°32N 28°45E **17** D15
Var ➜ *France* 43°39N 7°12E **20** E7
Varāmīn *Iran* 35°20N 51°39E **45** C6
Varāmīn *Iran* 35°18N 51°35E **45** B6
Varanasi *India* 25°22N 83°0E **43** G10
Varangerfjorden *Norway* 70°3N 29°25E **8** A23
Varangerhalvøya
  Norway 70°25N 29°30E **8** A23
Varaždin *Croatia* 46°20N 16°20E **16** E9
Varberg *Sweden* 57°6N 12°20E **9** H15
Vardak □ *Afghan.* 34°0N 68°0E **40** B6
Vardar = Axios ➜
  Greece 40°57N 22°35E **23** D10
Varde *Denmark* 55°38N 8°29E **9** J13
Vardø *Norway* 70°23N 31°5E **8** A24
Varella, Mui *Vietnam* 12°54N 109°26E **38** F7
Varėna *Lithuania* 54°12N 24°30E **9** J21
Varese *Italy* 45°48N 8°50E **20** D8
Varginha *Brazil* 21°33S 45°25W **95** A6
Varillas *Chile* 24°0S 70°10W **94** A1
Varkaus *Finland* 62°19N 27°50E **8** E22
Varna *Bulgaria* 43°13N 27°56E **23** C12
Värnamo *Sweden* 57°10N 14°3E **9** H16
Vars *Canada* 45°21N 75°21W **83** A9
Varysburg *U.S.A.* 42°46N 78°19W **82** D6
Varzaneh *Iran* 32°25N 52°40E **45** C7
Vasa = Vaasa *Finland* 63°6N 21°38E **8** E19
Vasa Barris ➜ *Brazil* 11°10S 37°10W **93** F11
Vascongadas = País Vasco □
  Spain 42°50N 2°45W **21** A4
Vasht = Khāsh *Iran* 28°15N 61°15E **45** D9
Vasilevichi *Belarus* 52°15N 29°50E **17** B15
Vasilkov = Vasylkiv
  Ukraine 50°7N 30°15E **17** C16
Vaslui *Romania* 46°38N 27°42E **17** E14
Vassar *Canada* 49°10N 95°55W **71** D9
Vassar *U.S.A.* 43°22N 83°35W **81** D12
Västeräs *Sweden* 59°37N 16°38E **9** G17
Västerbotten *Sweden* 64°36N 20°4E **8** D19
Västerdalälven ➜ *Sweden* 60°30N 14°7E **8** F16
Västervik *Sweden* 57°43N 16°33E **9** H17
Västmanland *Sweden* 59°45N 16°20E **9** G17
Vasto *Italy* 42°8N 14°40E **22** C6
Vasylkiv *Ukraine* 50°7N 30°15E **17** C16
Vatersay *U.K.* 56°55N 7°32W **11** E1
Vati *Greece* 36°3N 27°53E **25** D9
Vatican City ■ *Europe* 41°54N 12°27E **22** D5
Vatili *Cyprus* 35°6N 33°40E **25** D12
Vatiu = Atiu *Cook Is.* 20°0S 158°10W **65** J12
Vatnajökull *Iceland* 64°30N 16°48W **8** D5
Vatoa *Fiji* 19°50S 178°13W **59** a
Vatolakkos *Greece* 35°27N 23°53E **25** D5
Vatoloha *Madag.* 17°52S 47°48E **57** B8
Vatomandry *Madag.* 19°20S 48°59E **57** B8
Vatra-Dornei *Romania* 47°22N 25°22E **17** E13
Vatrak ➜ *India* 23°9N 73°2E **42** H5
Vättern *Sweden* 58°25N 14°30E **9** G16
Vatu Vara *Fiji* 17°19S 179°12W **59** a
Vatulele *Fiji* 18°33S 177°37E **59** a
Vaudreuil-Dorion
  Canada 45°23N 74°3W **83** A11
Vaughn *Mont., U.S.A.* 47°33N 111°33W **76** C8
Vaughn *N. Mex.,*
  U.S.A. 34°36N 105°13W **77** J11
Vaujours L. *Canada* 55°27N 74°15W **72** A5
Vaupés = Uaupés ➜
  Brazil 0°2N 67°16W **92** C5
Vaupés □ *Colombia* 1°0N 71°0W **92** C4
Vauxhall *Canada* 50°5N 112°9W **70** C6
Vav *India* 24°22N 71°31E **42** G4
Vavatenina *Madag.* 17°28S 49°12E **57** B8
Vava'u *Tonga* 18°36S 174°0W **59** c
Vava'u Group *Tonga* 18°40S 174°0W **59** c
Vawkavysk *Belarus* 53°9N 24°30E **17** B13
Växjö *Sweden* 56°52N 14°50E **9** H16
Vaygach, Ostrov *Russia* 70°0N 60°0E **28** C7
Veaikevárri = Svappavaara
  Sweden 67°40N 21°3E **8** C19
Vechte ➜ *Neths.* 52°34N 6°6E **15** B6
Vedea ➜ *Romania* 43°42N 25°41E **17** G13

Vedia *Argentina* 34°30S 61°31W **94** C3
Veendam *Neths.* 53°5N 6°52E **15** A6
Veenendaal *Neths.* 52°2N 5°34E **15** B5
Vefsna ➜ *Norway* 65°48N 13°10E **8** D15
Vega *Norway* 65°40N 11°55E **8** D14
Vega *U.S.A.* 35°15N 102°26W **84** D3
Vega Baja *Puerto Rico* 18°27N 66°23W **89** d
Vegreville *Canada* 53°30N 112°5W **70** C6
Vejer de la Frontera
  Spain 36°15N 5°59W **21** D3
Vejle *Denmark* 55°43N 9°30E **9** J13
Velas, C. *Costa Rica* 10°21N 85°52W **88** D2
Velasco, Sierra de
  Argentina 29°20S 67°10W **94** B2
Velddrif *S. Africa* 32°42S 18°11E **56** E2
Velebit Planina *Croatia* 44°50N 15°20E **16** F8
Veles *Macedonia* 41°46N 21°47E **23** D9
Vélez-Málaga *Spain* 36°48N 4°5W **21** D3
Vélez Rubio *Spain* 37°41N 2°5W **21** D4
Velhas ➜ *Brazil* 17°13S 44°49W **93** G10
Velika Kapela *Croatia* 45°10N 15°5E **16** F8
Velika ➜ *Russia* 57°48N 28°10E **18** C4
Velikaya Kema *Russia* 45°30N 137°12E **30** B8
Veliki Ustyug *Russia* 60°47N 46°20E **18** B8
Velikiye Luki *Russia* 56°25N 30°32E **18** C5
Veliko Tŭrnovo *Bulgaria* 43°5N 25°41E **23** C11
Velikonda Range *India* 14°45N 79°10E **40** M11
Velletri *Italy* 41°41N 12°47E **22** D5
Vellore *India* 12°57N 79°10E **40** N11
Velsk *Russia* 61°10N 42°5E **18** B7
Veluwezoom △ *Neths.* 52°5N 6°0E **15** B6
Velva *U.S.A.* 48°4N 100°56W **80** A3
Venado *Mexico* 22°56N 101°6W **86** C4
Venado Tuerto *Argentina* 33°50S 62°0W **94** C3
Vendée □ *France* 46°50N 1°35W **20** C3
Vendôme *France* 47°47N 1°3E **20** C4
Venézia *Italy* 45°27N 12°21E **22** B5
Venézia, G. di *Italy* 45°15N 13°0E **22** B5
Venezuela ■ *S. Amer.* 8°0N 66°0W **92** B5
Venezuela, G. de
  Venezuela 11°30N 71°0W **92** A4
Vengurla *India* 15°53N 73°45E **40** M8
Venice = Venézia *Italy* 45°27N 12°21E **22** B5
Venice *U.S.A.* 27°6N 82°27W **85** H13
Venkatapuram *India* 18°20N 80°30E **41** K12
Venlo *Neths.* 51°22N 6°11E **15** C6
Vennachar Junction
  Canada 45°5N 77°14W **82** A7
Vennesla *Norway* 58°15N 7°59E **9** G12
Venray *Neths.* 51°31N 6°0E **15** C6
Ventana, Punta de la
  Mexico 24°4N 109°48W **86** C3
Ventana, Sa. de la
  Argentina 38°0S 62°30W **94** D3
Ventersburg *S. Africa* 28°7S 27°9E **56** D4
Venterstad *S. Africa* 30°47S 25°48E **56** E4
Ventnor *U.K.* 50°36N 1°12W **13** G6
Ventoténe *Italy* 40°47N 13°25E **22** D5
Ventoux, Mt. *France* 44°10N 5°17E **20** D6
Ventspils *Latvia* 57°25N 21°32E **9** H19
Ventuarí ➜ *Venezuela* 3°58N 67°2W **92** C5
Ventucopa *U.S.A.* 34°50N 119°29W **79** L7
Ventura *U.S.A.* 34°17N 119°18W **79** L7
Vénus, Pte. *Tahiti* 17°29S 149°29W **59** d
Venus B. *Australia* 38°40S 145°42E **63** F4
Venustiano Carranza
  Mexico 30°25N 115°53W **86** A1
Vera *Argentina* 29°30S 60°20W **94** B3
Vera *Spain* 37°15N 1°51W **21** D5
Veracruz *Mexico* 19°11N 96°8W **87** D5
Veracruz □ *Mexico* 19°0N 96°15W **87** D5
Veraval *India* 20°53N 70°27E **42** J4
Verbánia *Italy* 45°56N 8°33E **20** D8
Vercelli *Italy* 45°19N 8°25E **20** D8
Verdalsøra *Norway* 63°48N 11°30E **8** E14
Verde ➜ *Argentina* 41°56N 65°5W **96** E3
Verde ➜ *Goiás, Brazil* 18°1S 50°14W **93** G8
Verde ➜ *Mato Grosso do Sul,*
  Brazil 21°25S 52°20W **93** H8
Verde ➜ *Chihuahua,*
  Mexico 26°29N 107°58W **86** B3
Verde ➜ *Oaxaca, Mexico* 15°59N 97°50W **87** D5
Verde ➜ *Veracruz,*
  Mexico 21°10N 102°50W **86** C4
Verde ➜ *Paraguay* 23°9S 57°37W **94** A4
Verde, Cay *Bahamas* 23°0N 75°5W **88** B4
Verden *Germany* 52°55N 9°14E **16** B5
Verdi *U.S.A.* 39°31N 119°59W **78** F7
Verdun *France* 49°9N 5°24E **20** B6
Vereeniging *S. Africa* 26°38S 27°57E **57** D4
Verga, C. *Guinea* 10°30N 14°10W **50** F3
Vergara *Uruguay* 32°56S 53°57W **95** C5
Vergemont Cr. ➜
  Australia 24°16S 143°16E **62** C3
Vergennes *U.S.A.* 44°10N 73°15W **83** B11
Vería *Greece* 40°34N 22°12E **23** D10
Verín *Spain* 41°57N 7°27W **21** B2
Verkhnetulomskoye Vdkhr.
  Russia 68°36N 31°12E **8** B24
Verkhnevilyuysk
  Russia 63°27N 120°18E **29** C13
Verkhniy Baskunchak
  Russia 48°14N 46°44E **19** E8
Verkhoyansk *Russia* 67°35N 133°25E **29** C14
Verkhoyansk Ra. =
  Verkhoyanskiy Khrebet
  Russia 66°0N 129°0E **29** C13
Verkhoyanskiy Khrebet
  Russia 66°0N 129°0E **29** C13
Vermilion *Canada* 53°20N 110°50W **71** C6
Vermilion *U.S.A.* 41°25N 82°22W **82** E2
Vermilion ➜ *Canada* 53°22N 110°51W **71** C6
Vermilion B. *Canada* 29°42N 92°0W **84** G9
Vermilion Bay *Canada* 49°51N 93°34W **71** D10
Vermilion L. *U.S.A.* 47°53N 92°26W **80** B7
Vermillion □ *Canada* 47°38N 72°56W **72** C5
Vermont □ *U.S.A.* 44°0N 73°0W **83** C12

Vernadsky Antarctica 65°S 64°W 5 C17
Vernal U.S.A. 40°27N 109°32W 76 F9
Vernalis U.S.A. 37°36N 121°17W 78 H5
Verner Canada 46°25N 80°8W 72 C3
Verneukpan S. Africa 30°S 21°0E 56 E3
Vernon Canada 50°20N 119°15W 70 C5
Vernon U.S.A. 34°9N 99°17W 84 D5
Vernonia U.S.A. 45°52N 123°11W 78 E3
Vero Beach U.S.A. 27°38N 80°24W 85 H14
Véroia = Veria Greece 40°34N 22°12E 23 D10
Verona Canada 44°29N 76°42W 83 B8
Verona Italy 45°27N 10°59E 22 B4
Versailles France 48°48N 2°7E 20 B5
Vert, C. Senegal 14°45N 17°30W 50 F2
Verulam S. Africa 29°38S 31°2E 57 D5
Verviers Belgium 50°37N 5°52E 15 D5
Veselovskoye Vdkhr. Russia 46°58N 41°25E 19 E7
Vesoul France 47°40N 6°11E 20 C7
Vesterålen Norway 68°45N 15°0E 8 B16
Vestfjorden Norway 67°55N 14°0E 8 C16
Vestmannaeyjar Iceland 63°27N 20°15W 8 E3
Vestspitsbergen Svalbard 78°40N 17°0E 4 B8
Vestvågøya Norway 68°18N 13°50E 8 B15
Vesuvio Italy 40°49N 14°26E 22 D6
Vesuvius, Mt. = Vesuvio Italy 40°49N 14°26E 22 D6
Veszprém Hungary 47°8N 17°57E 17 E9
Vetlanda Sweden 57°24N 15°3E 9 H16
Vetlugu → Russia 56°36N 46°4E 18 C8
Vettore, Mte. Italy 42°49N 13°16E 22 C5
Veurne Belgium 51°5N 2°40E 15 C2
Veys Iran 31°30N 49°0E 45 D6
Vezhen Bulgaria 42°50N 24°20E 23 C11
Vi Thanh Vietnam 9°42N 105°26E 39 H5
Viacha Bolivia 16°39S 68°18W 92 G5
Viamão Brazil 30°5S 51°0W 95 C5
Viana Brazil 3°13S 44°55W 93 D10
Viana do Alentejo Portugal 38°17N 7°59W 21 C2
Viana do Castelo Portugal 41°42N 8°50W 21 B1
Vianden Lux. 49°56N 6°12E 15 E6
Viangchan = Vientiane Laos 17°58N 102°36E 38 D4
Vianópolis Brazil 16°40S 48°35W 93 G9
Vianos Greece 35°2N 25°21E 25 D7
Viaréggio Italy 43°52N 10°14E 22 C4
Vibo Valéntia Italy 38°40N 16°6E 22 E7
Viborg Denmark 56°27N 9°23E 9 H13
Vic Spain 41°58N 2°19E 21 B7
Vicenza Italy 45°33N 11°33E 22 B4
Vich = Vic Spain 41°58N 2°19E 21 B7
Vichada → Colombia 4°55N 67°50W 92 C5
Vichy France 46°9N 3°26E 20 C5
Vicksburg Ariz., U.S.A. 33°45N 113°45W 79 M13
Vicksburg Miss., U.S.A. 32°21N 90°53W 85 E9
Victor India 21°0N 71°30E 42 J4
Victor Harbor Australia 35°30S 138°37E 63 F2
Victoria Argentina 32°40S 60°10W 94 C3
Victoria Canada 48°30N 123°25W 78 B3
Victoria Chile 38°13S 72°20W 96 D2
Victoria China 22°17N 114°9E 33 G1
Victoria Malta 36°3N 14°14E 25 C1
Victoria Seychelles 4°38S 55°28E 53 b
Victoria Kans., U.S.A. 38°52N 99°9W 80 F4
Victoria Tex., U.S.A. 28°48N 97°0W 84 G6
Victoria □ Australia 37°0S 144°0E 63 F3
Victoria → Australia 15°10S 129°40E 60 C4
Victoria, Grand L. Canada 47°31N 77°30W 72 C4
Victoria, L. Africa 1°0S 33°0E 54 C3
Victoria, L. Australia 33°57S 141°15E 63 E3
Victoria, Mt. Burma 21°14N 93°55E 41 J18
Victoria Beach Canada 50°40N 96°35W 71 C9
Victoria de Durango = Durango Mexico 24°3N 104°39W 86 C4
Victoria de las Tunas = Las Tunas Cuba 20°58N 76°59W 88 B4
Victoria Falls Zimbabwe 17°58S 25°52E 55 F2
Victoria Harbour Canada 44°45N 79°45W 82 B5
Victoria I. Canada 71°0N 111°0W 68 B8
Victoria L. Canada 48°20N 57°27W 73 C8
Victoria Ld. Antarctica 75°0S 160°0E 5 D11
Victoria Nile → Uganda 2°14N 31°26E 54 B3
Victoria Pk. Belize 16°48N 88°37W 87 D7
Victoria River Australia 16°25S 131°0E 60 C5
Victoria Str. Canada 69°31N 100°30W 68 D11
Victoria West S. Africa 31°25S 23°4E 56 E3
Victoriaville Canada 46°4N 71°56W 73 C5
Victorica Argentina 36°20S 65°30W 94 D2
Victorville U.S.A. 34°32N 117°18W 79 L9
Vicuña Chile 30°0S 70°50W 94 C1
Vicuña Mackenna Argentina 33°53S 64°25W 94 C3
Vidal U.S.A. 34°7N 114°31W 79 L12
Vidalia U.S.A. 32°13N 82°25W 85 E13
Vidin Bulgaria 43°59N 22°50E 23 C10
Vidisha India 23°28N 77°53E 42 H7
Vidos Greece 39°38N 19°55E 25 A3
Vidzy Belarus 55°23N 26°37E 9 J22
Viedma Argentina 40°50S 63°0W 96 E4
Viedma, L. Argentina 49°30S 72°30W 96 F2
Vielsalm Belgium 50°17N 5°54E 15 D5
Vieng Pou Kha Laos 20°41N 101°4E 38 B3
Vienna = Wien Austria 48°12N 16°22E 16 D9
Vienna Canada 42°41N 80°48W 82 D4
Vienna Ill., U.S.A. 37°25N 88°54W 80 G9
Vienna Mo., U.S.A. 38°11N 91°57W 80 F8
Vienne France 45°31N 4°53E 20 D6
Vienne → France 47°13N 0°5E 20 C4
Vientiane Laos 17°58N 102°36E 38 D4
Vientos, Paso de los Caribbean 20°0N 74°0W 89 C5
Vieques Puerto Rico 18°8N 65°25W 89 d
Vierge Pt. St. Lucia 13°49N 60°53W 89 f
Vierzon France 47°13N 2°5E 20 C5
Viet Tri Vietnam 21°18N 105°25E 38 B5

Vietnam ■ Asia 19°0N 106°0E 38 C6
Vieux Fort St. Lucia 13°46N 60°58W 89 f
Vigan Phil. 17°35N 120°28E 37 A6
Vigévano Italy 45°19N 8°51E 20 D8
Vigia Brazil 0°50S 48°5W 93 D9
Viglas, Akra Greece 35°54N 27°51E 25 D9
Vigo Spain 42°12N 8°41W 21 A1
Vihowa Pakistan 31°8N 70°30E 42 D4
Vihowa → Pakistan 31°8N 70°41E 42 D4
Vijayawada India 16°31N 80°39E 41 L12
Vijosë → Albania 40°37N 19°24E 23 D8
Vík Iceland 63°25N 19°1W 8 E4
Vikeke = Viqueque E. Timor 8°52S 126°23E 37 F7
Viking Canada 53°7N 111°50W 70 C6
Vikna Norway 64°55N 10°58E 8 D14
Vila da Maganja Mozam. 17°18S 37°30E 55 F4
Vila da Ribeira Brava C. Verde Is. 16°32N 24°25W 50 b
Vila do Bispo Portugal 37°5N 8°53W 21 D1
Vila Franca de Xira Portugal 38°57N 8°59W 21 C1
Vila Gamito Mozam. 14°12S 33°0E 55 E3
Vila Gomes da Costa Mozam. 24°20S 33°37E 57 C5
Vila Machado Mozam. 19°15S 34°14E 55 F3
Vila Mouzinho Mozam. 14°48S 34°25E 55 E3
Vila Nova de Gaia Portugal 41°8N 8°37W 21 B1
Vila Real Portugal 41°17N 7°48W 21 B2
Vila-Real Spain 39°55N 0°3W 21 C5
Vila Real de Santo António Portugal 37°10N 7°28W 21 D2
Vila Vasco da Gama Mozam. 14°54S 32°14E 55 E3
Vila Velha Brazil 20°20S 40°17W 95 A7
Vilagarcía de Arousa Spain 42°34N 8°46W 21 A1
Vilaine → France 47°30N 2°27W 20 C2
Vilanandro, Tanjona Madag. 16°11S 44°27E 57 B7
Vilanculos Mozam. 22°1S 35°17E 57 C6
Vilanova i la Geltrú Spain 41°13N 1°40E 21 B6
Vilcheka, Ostrov Russia 80°0N 58°31E 28 B6
Vilcheka, Zemlya Russia 80°30N 60°30E 4 A11
Vileyka Belarus 54°30N 26°53E 17 A14
Vilhelmina Sweden 64°35N 16°39E 8 D17
Vilhena Brazil 12°40S 60°5W 92 F6
Viliya = Neris → Lithuania 55°8N 24°16E 9 J21
Viljandi Estonia 58°28N 25°30E 9 G21
Vilkitskogo, Proliv Russia 78°0N 103°0E 29 B11
Vilkovo = Vylkove Ukraine 45°28N 29°32E 17 F15
Villa Abecia Bolivia 21°0S 68°18W 94 A2
Villa Ana Argentina 28°28S 59°40W 94 B4
Villa Angela Argentina 27°34S 60°45W 94 B3
Villa Bella Bolivia 10°25S 65°22W 92 F5
Villa Cañás Argentina 34°0S 61°35W 94 C3
Villa Constitución Argentina 33°15S 60°20W 94 C3
Villa de Arriaga Mexico 21°56N 101°20W 86 C4
Villa de María Argentina 29°55S 63°43W 94 B3
Villa de Méndez Mexico 25°7N 98°34W 87 B5
Villa Dolores Argentina 31°58S 65°15W 94 C2
Villa Frontera Mexico 26°56N 101°27W 86 B4
Villa Gesell Argentina 37°15S 56°55W 94 D4
Villa Guillermina Argentina 28°15S 59°29W 94 B4
Villa Hayes Paraguay 25°5S 57°20W 94 B4
Villa Hidalgo Mexico 24°15N 99°26W 87 C5
Villa Iris Argentina 38°12S 63°12W 94 D3
Villa María Argentina 32°20S 63°10W 94 C3
Villa Mazán Argentina 28°40S 66°30W 94 B2
Villa Montes Bolivia 21°10S 63°30W 94 A3
Villa Ocampo Argentina 28°30S 59°20W 94 B4
Villa Ocampo Mexico 26°27N 105°31W 86 B3
Villa Ojo de Agua Argentina 29°30S 63°44W 94 B3
Villa San Martín Argentina 28°15S 64°9W 94 B3
Villa Unión Mexico 23°12N 106°14W 86 C3
Villacarlos Spain 39°53N 4°17E 24 B11
Villacarrillo Spain 38°7N 3°3W 21 C4
Villach Austria 46°37N 13°51E 16 E7
Villafranca de Bonany Spain 39°34N 3°5E 24 B10
Villagrán Mexico 24°29N 99°29W 87 C5
Villaguay Argentina 32°0S 59°0W 94 C4
Villahermosa Mexico 17°59N 92°55W 87 D6
Villajoyosa Spain 38°30N 0°12W 21 C5
Villalba Spain 43°26N 7°40W 21 A2
Villanueva U.S.A. 35°16N 105°22W 77 J11
Villanueva de la Serena Spain 38°59N 5°50W 21 C3
Villanueva y Geltrú = Vilanova i la Geltrú Spain 41°13N 1°40E 21 B6
Villarreal = Vila-Real Spain 39°55N 0°3W 21 C5
Villarrica Chile 39°15S 72°15W 96 D2
Villarrica Paraguay 25°40S 56°30W 94 B4
Villarrobledo Spain 39°18N 2°36W 21 C4
Villavicencio Argentina 32°28S 69°0W 94 C2
Villavicencio Colombia 4°9N 73°37W 92 C4
Villaviciosa Spain 43°32N 5°27W 21 A3
Villazón Bolivia 22°0S 65°35W 94 A2
Ville-Marie Canada 47°20N 79°30W 72 C4
Ville Platte U.S.A. 30°41N 92°17W 84 F8
Villena Spain 38°39N 0°52W 21 C5
Villeneuve-d'Ascq France 50°38N 3°9E 20 A5
Villeneuve-sur-Lot France 44°24N 0°42E 20 D4
Villiers S. Africa 27°2S 28°36E 57 D4
Villingen-Schwenningen Germany 48°3N 8°26E 16 D5
Villmanstrand = Lappeenranta Finland 61°3N 28°12E 8 F23
Vilna Canada 54°7N 111°55W 70 C6
Vilnius Lithuania 54°38N 25°19E 9 J21
Vilvoorde Belgium 50°56N 4°26E 15 D4

Vilyuchinsk Russia 52°55N 158°24E 29 D16
Vilyuy → Russia 64°24N 126°26E 29 C13
Vilyuysk Russia 63°40N 121°35E 29 C13
Viña del Mar Chile 33°0S 71°30W 94 C1
Vinarós Spain 40°30N 0°27E 21 B6
Vincennes U.S.A. 38°41N 87°32W 80 F10
Vincennes Bay S. Ocean 66°0S 109°0E 5 C8
Vincent U.S.A. 34°33N 118°11W 79 L8
Vinchina Argentina 28°45S 68°15W 94 B2
Vindelälven → Sweden 63°55N 19°50E 8 E18
Vindeln Sweden 64°12N 19°43E 8 D18
Vindhya Ra. India 22°50N 77°0E 42 H7
Vineland U.S.A. 39°29N 75°2W 81 F16
Vinh Vietnam 18°45N 105°38E 38 C5
Vinh Linh Vietnam 17°4N 107°2E 38 D6
Vinh Long Vietnam 10°16N 105°57E 39 G5
Vinh Yen Vietnam 21°21N 105°35E 38 B5
Vinita U.S.A. 36°39N 95°9W 84 C7
Vinkovci Croatia 45°19N 18°48E 23 B8
Vinnitsa = Vinnytsya Ukraine 49°15N 28°30E 17 D15
Vinnytsya Ukraine 49°15N 28°30E 17 D15
Vinson Massif Antarctica 78°35S 85°25W 5 D16
Vinton Calif., U.S.A. 39°48N 120°10W 78 F6
Vinton Iowa, U.S.A. 42°10N 92°1W 80 D7
Vinton La., U.S.A. 30°11N 93°35W 84 F8
Violet Valley ○ Australia 17°10S 127°55E 60 C4
Viqueque E. Timor 8°52S 126°23E 37 F7
Virac Phil. 13°30N 124°20E 37 B6
Virachey Cambodia 13°59N 106°49E 38 F6
Virachey △ Cambodia 14°14N 106°55E 38 E6
Virago Sd. Canada 54°0N 132°30W 70 C2
Viramgam India 23°5N 72°0E 42 H5
Viranşehir Turkey 37°13N 39°45E 44 B3
Virawah Pakistan 24°31N 70°46E 42 G4
Virden Canada 49°50N 100°56W 71 D8
Vire France 48°50N 0°53W 20 B3
Vírgenes, C. Argentina 52°19S 68°21W 96 G3
Virgin → U.S.A. 36°28N 114°21W 77 H6
Virgin Gorda Br. Virgin Is. 18°30N 64°26W 89 e
Virgin Is. (British) ☑ W. Indies 18°30N 64°30W 89 e
Virgin Is. (U.S.) ☑ W. Indies 18°20N 65°0W 89 e
Virgin Islands △ U.S. Virgin Is. 18°21N 64°43W 89 C7
Virginia S. Africa 28°8S 26°55E 56 D4
Virginia U.S.A. 47°31N 92°32W 80 B7
Virginia □ U.S.A. 37°30N 78°45W 81 G14
Virginia Beach U.S.A. 36°49N 76°9W 81 F16
Virginia City Mont., U.S.A. 45°18N 111°56W 76 D8
Virginia City Nev., U.S.A. 39°19N 119°39W 78 F7
Virginia Falls Canada 61°38N 125°42W 70 A3
Virginiatown Canada 48°9N 79°36W 72 C4
Viroqua U.S.A. 43°34N 90°53W 80 D8
Virovitica Croatia 45°51N 17°21E 22 B7
Virpur India 21°51N 70°42E 42 J4
Virton Belgium 49°35N 5°32E 15 E5
Virudunagar India 9°30N 77°58E 40 Q10
Virunga △ Dem. Rep. of the Congo 0°5N 29°38E 54 B2
Vis Croatia 43°4N 16°10E 22 C7
Visalia U.S.A. 36°20N 119°18W 78 J7
Visayan Sea Phil. 11°30N 123°30E 37 B6
Visby Sweden 57°37N 18°18E 9 H18
Viscount Melville Sd. Canada 74°10N 108°0W 69 C10
Visé Belgium 50°44N 5°41E 15 D5
Vise, Ostrov Russia 79°33N 76°50E 28 B8
Višegrad Bos.-H. 43°47N 19°17E 23 C8
Viseu Brazil 1°10S 46°5W 93 D9
Viseu Portugal 40°40N 7°55W 21 B2
Vishakhapatnam India 17°45N 83°20E 41 L13
Visnagar India 23°45N 72°32E 42 H5
Viso, Mte. Italy 44°38N 7°5E 20 D7
Visokoi I. Antarctica 56°43S 27°15W 5 B1
Vista U.S.A. 33°12N 117°14W 79 M9
Vistula = Wisła → Poland 54°22N 18°55E 17 A10
Vitebsk = Vitsyebsk Belarus 55°10N 30°15E 18 C5
Viterbo Italy 42°25N 12°6E 22 C5
Viti Levu Fiji 17°30S 177°30E 59 a
Vitigudino Spain 41°1N 6°26W 21 B2
Vitim Russia 59°28N 112°35E 29 D12
Vitim → Russia 59°26N 112°34E 29 D12
Vitória Brazil 20°20S 40°22W 93 H10
Vitória da Conquista Brazil 14°51S 40°51W 93 F10
Vitória de Santo Antão Brazil 8°10S 35°20W 93 E11
Vitoria-Gasteiz Spain 42°50N 2°41W 21 A4
Vitsyebsk Belarus 55°10N 30°15E 18 C5
Vittória Italy 36°57N 14°32E 22 F6
Vittório Véneto Italy 45°59N 12°18E 22 B5
Viveiro Spain 43°39N 7°38W 21 A2
Vivian U.S.A. 32°53N 93°59W 84 E8
Viwa Fiji 17°10S 177°58E 59 a
Vizcaíno, Desierto de Mexico 27°30N 113°45W 86 B2
Vizcaíno, Sierra Mexico 27°30N 114°0W 86 B2
Vize Turkey 41°34N 27°45E 23 D12
Vizianagaram India 18°6N 83°30E 41 K13
Vlaardingen Neths. 51°55N 4°21E 15 C4
Vladikavkaz Russia 43°0N 44°35E 19 F7
Vladimir Russia 56°15N 40°30E 18 C7
Vladimir Volynskiy = Volodymyr-Volynskyy Ukraine 50°50N 24°18E 17 C13
Vladivostok Russia 43°10N 131°53E 30 C5
Vlieland Neths. 53°16N 4°55E 15 A4
Vlissingen Neths. 51°26N 3°34E 15 C3
Vlorë Albania 40°32N 19°28E 23 D8
Vltava → Czech Rep. 50°21N 14°30E 16 C8
Vo Dat Vietnam 11°9N 107°31E 39 G6
Voe U.K. 60°21N 1°16W 11 A7

Vogelkop = Doberai, Jazirah Indonesia 1°25S 133°0E 37 E8
Vogelsberg Germany 50°31N 9°12E 16 C5
Voghera Italy 44°59N 9°1E 20 D8
Vohibinany Madag. 18°49S 49°4E 57 B8
Vohilava Madag. 21°4S 48°0E 57 C8
Vohimarina = Iharana Madag. 13°25S 50°0E 57 A9
Vohimena, Tanjon' i Madag. 25°36S 45°8E 57 D8
Vohipeno Madag. 22°22S 47°51E 57 C8
Voi Kenya 3°25S 38°32E 54 C4
Voiron France 45°22N 5°35E 20 D6
Voisey B. Canada 56°15N 61°50W 73 A7
Vojmsjön Sweden 65°0N 16°24E 8 D17
Vojvodina □ Serbia 45°20N 20°0E 23 B9
Volborg U.S.A. 45°51N 105°41W 76 D11
Volcán de Colima △ Mexico 19°30N 103°40W 86 D4
Volcano Is. = Kazan-Rettō Pac. Oc. 25°0N 141°0E 64 E6
Volcans △ Rwanda 1°30S 29°26E 54 C2
Volda Norway 62°9N 6°5E 8 E12
Volga = Privolzhskiy □ Russia 56°0N 50°0E 28 D8
Volga → Russia 46°0N 48°30E 19 E8
Volga Hts. = Privolzhskaya Vozvyshennost Russia 51°0N 46°0E 19 D8
Volgodonsk Russia 47°33N 42°5E 19 E7
Volgograd Russia 48°40N 44°25E 19 E7
Volgogradskoye Vdkhr. Russia 50°0N 45°20E 19 D8
Volkhov → Russia 60°8N 32°20E 18 B5
Volkovysk = Vawkavysk Belarus 53°9N 24°30E 17 B13
Volksrust S. Africa 27°24S 29°53E 57 D4
Volochanka Russia 71°0N 94°28E 29 B10
Volodymyr-Volynskyy Ukraine 50°50N 24°18E 17 C13
Vologda Russia 59°10N 39°45E 18 C6
Volos Greece 39°24N 22°59E 23 E10
Volosovo Russia 59°27N 29°32E 9 G23
Volovets Ukraine 48°43N 23°11E 17 D12
Volozhin = Valozhyn Belarus 54°3N 26°30E 17 A14
Volsk Russia 52°5N 47°22E 18 D8
Volta → Ghana 5°46N 0°41E 48 F4
Volta, L. Ghana 7°30N 0°0 50 G6
Volta Redonda Brazil 22°31S 44°5W 95 A7
Voltaire, C. Australia 14°16S 125°35E 60 B4
Volterra Italy 43°24N 10°51E 22 C4
Volturno → Italy 41°1N 13°55E 22 D5
Volzhskiy Russia 48°56N 44°46E 19 E7
Vomo Fiji 17°30S 177°15E 59 a
Vondrozo Madag. 22°49S 47°20E 57 C8
Vopnafjörður Iceland 65°45N 14°50W 8 D6
Vorkuta Russia 67°48N 64°20E 18 A11
Vormsi Estonia 59°1N 23°13E 9 G20
Voronezh Russia 51°40N 39°10E 18 D6
Võrts Järv Estonia 58°16N 26°3E 9 G22
Võru Estonia 57°48N 26°54E 9 H22
Vosges France 48°20N 7°10E 20 B7
Voss Norway 60°38N 6°26E 8 F12
Vostok Antarctica 78°30S 106°50E 5 D8
Vostok I. Kiribati 10°5S 152°23W 65 J12
Votkinsk Russia 57°0N 53°55E 18 C9
Votkinskoye Vdkhr. Russia 57°22N 55°12E 18 C10
Votsuri-Shima Japan 25°45N 123°29E 31 M1
Vouga → Portugal 40°41N 8°40W 21 B1
Vouxa, Akra Greece 35°37N 23°32E 25 D5
Voyageurs △ U.S.A. 48°32N 93°0W 80 A7
Voynitsa Russia 65°10N 30°20E 8 D24
Voyvozh Russia 62°56N 54°56E 18 B10
Vozhe, Ozero Russia 60°45N 39°0E 18 B6
Voznesensk Ukraine 47°35N 31°21E 19 E5
Voznesenye Russia 61°0N 35°28E 18 B6
Vrangel Russia 42°43N 133°5E 30 C6
Vrangelya, Ostrov Russia 71°0N 180°0E 29 B18
Vranje Serbia 42°34N 21°54E 23 C9
Vratsa Bulgaria 43°15N 23°30E 23 C10
Vrbas → Bos.-H. 45°8N 17°29E 22 B7
Vrede S. Africa 27°24S 29°6E 57 D4
Vredefort S. Africa 27°0S 27°22E 56 D4
Vredenburg S. Africa 32°56S 18°0E 56 E2
Vredendal S. Africa 31°41S 18°35E 56 E2
Vrindavan India 27°37N 77°40E 42 F7
Vrisses Greece 35°23N 24°13E 25 D6
Vršac Serbia 45°8N 21°20E 23 B9
Vryburg S. Africa 26°55S 24°45E 56 D3
Vryheid S. Africa 27°45S 30°47E 57 D5
Vu Liet Vietnam 18°43N 105°23E 38 C5
Vukovar Croatia 45°21N 18°59E 23 B8
Vuktyl Russia 63°52N 57°20E 28 C6
Vulcan Canada 50°25N 113°15W 70 C6
Vulcan Romania 45°23N 23°17E 17 F12
Vulcaneşti Moldova 45°41N 28°18E 17 F15
Vulcano Italy 38°24N 14°58E 22 E6
Vulkaneshty = Vulcaneşti Moldova 45°41N 28°18E 17 F15
Vunduzi → Mozam. 18°56S 34°1E 55 F3
Vung Tau Vietnam 10°21N 107°4E 39 G6
Vunidawa Fiji 17°50S 178°21E 59 a
Vunisea Fiji 19°3S 178°10E 59 a
Vwaza ○ Malawi 10°58S 33°25E 55 E3
Vyartsilya Russia 62°8N 30°45E 8 E24
Vyatka = Kirov Russia 58°35N 49°40E 18 C8
Vyatka → Russia 56°30N 51°16E 18 C9
Vyatskiye Polyany Russia 56°14N 51°5E 18 C9
Vyazemskiy Russia 47°32N 134°45E 29 E14
Vyazma Russia 55°10N 34°15E 18 C5
Vyazniki Russia 56°10N 42°10E 18 C7
Vyborg Russia 60°43N 28°47E 8 F23
Vychegda → Russia 61°18N 46°36E 18 B8
Vychodné Beskydy Europe 49°20N 22°0E 17 D11
Vyg-ozero Russia 63°47N 34°29E 18 B5
Vylkove Ukraine 45°28N 29°32E 17 F15
Vynohradiv Ukraine 48°9N 23°2E 17 D12

Vyrnwy, L. U.K. 52°48N 3°31W 12 E4
Vyshniy Volochek Russia 57°30N 34°30E 18 C5
Vyshzha = imeni 26 Bakinskikh Komissarov Turkmenistan 39°22N 54°10E 45 B7
Vyškov Czech Rep. 49°17N 17°0E 17 D9
Vytegra Russia 61°0N 36°27E 18 B6

W

W.A.C. Bennett Dam Canada 56°2N 122°6W 70 B4
Wa Ghana 10°7N 2°25W 50 F5
Waal → Neths. 51°37N 5°0E 15 C5
Waalwijk Neths. 51°42N 5°4E 15 C5
Waanyi-Garawa ○ Australia 18°2S 137°33E 62 B2
Wabakimi △ Canada 50°43N 89°29W 72 B2
Wabana Canada 47°40N 53°0W 73 C9
Wabasca → Canada 58°22N 115°20W 70 B5
Wabasca-Desmarais Canada 55°57N 113°56W 70 B6
Wabash U.S.A. 40°48N 85°49W 81 E11
Wabash → U.S.A. 37°48N 88°2W 80 G9
Wabigoon L. Canada 49°44N 92°44W 71 D10
Wabowden Canada 54°55N 98°38W 71 C9
Wabuk Pt. Canada 55°20N 85°5W 72 A2
Wabush Canada 52°55N 66°52W 73 B6
Waco U.S.A. 31°33N 97°9W 84 F6
Waconichi, L. Canada 50°8N 74°0W 72 B5
Wad Hamid Sudan 16°30N 32°45E 51 E12
Wad Medanî Sudan 14°28N 33°30E 51 F12
Wad Thana Pakistan 27°22N 66°23E 42 F2
Wadai Africa 12°0N 19°0E 48 E5
Wadayama Japan 35°19N 134°52E 31 G7
Waddeneilanden Neths. 53°25N 5°10E 15 A5
Waddenzee Neths. 53°6N 5°10E 15 A5
Waddington U.S.A. 44°52N 75°12W 83 B9
Waddington, Mt. Canada 51°23N 125°15W 70 C3
Waddy Pt. Australia 24°58S 153°21E 63 C5
Wadebridge U.K. 50°31N 4°51W 13 G3
Wadena Canada 51°57N 103°47W 71 C8
Wadena U.S.A. 46°26N 95°8W 80 B7
Wadeye Australia 14°28S 129°52E 60 B4
Wadhams Canada 51°30N 127°30W 70 C3
Wadhwan India 22°42N 71°41E 42 H4
Wâdî as Sîr Jordan 31°56N 35°49E 46 D4
Wadi Halfa Sudan 21°53N 31°19E 51 D12
Wadi Rum △ Jordan 29°30N 35°20E 46 F4
Wadsworth Nev., U.S.A. 39°38N 119°17W 76 G4
Wadsworth Ohio, U.S.A. 41°2N 81°44W 82 E3
Waegwan S. Korea 35°59N 128°23E 35 G15
Wafangdian China 39°38N 121°58E 35 E11
Wafrah Kuwait 28°33N 47°56E 44 D5
Wageningen Neths. 51°58N 5°40E 15 C5
Wager B. Canada 65°26N 88°40W 69 D14
Wagga Wagga Australia 35°7S 147°24E 63 F4
Waghete Indonesia 4°10S 135°50E 37 E9
Wagin Australia 33°17S 117°25E 61 F2
Wagner U.S.A. 43°5N 98°18W 80 D4
Wagon Mound U.S.A. 36°1N 104°42W 77 H11
Wagoner U.S.A. 35°58N 95°22W 84 D7
Wah Pakistan 33°45N 72°40E 42 C5
Wahai Indonesia 2°48S 129°35E 37 E7
Wahoo U.S.A. 41°13N 96°37W 80 E5
Wahpeton U.S.A. 46°16N 96°36W 80 B5
Waialua U.S.A. 21°34N 158°8W 75 L8
Waiau → N.Z. 42°47S 173°22E 59 E4
Waibeem Indonesia 0°30S 132°59E 37 E8
Waigeo Indonesia 0°20S 130°40E 37 E8
Waihi N.Z. 37°23S 175°52E 59 B5
Waihou → N.Z. 37°15S 175°40E 59 B5
Waikabubak Indonesia 9°45S 119°25E 37 F5
Waikaremoana, L. N.Z. 38°49S 177°9E 59 C6
Waikari N.Z. 42°58S 172°41E 59 E4
Waikato → N.Z. 37°23S 174°43E 59 B5
Waikelo Indonesia 9°24S 119°19E 60 A2
Waikokopu N.Z. 39°3S 177°52E 59 C6
Waikouaiti N.Z. 45°36S 170°41E 59 F3
Wailingding Dao China 22°6N 114°2E 33 G11
Waimakariri → N.Z. 43°24S 172°42E 59 E4
Waimate N.Z. 44°45S 171°3E 59 F3
Wainganga → India 18°50N 79°55E 40 K11
Waingapu Indonesia 9°35S 120°11E 37 F6
Waini → Guyana 8°20N 59°50W 92 B7
Wainwright Canada 52°50N 110°50W 71 C6
Wainwright U.S.A. 70°38N 160°2W 74 A7
Waiouru N.Z. 39°28S 175°41E 59 C5
Waipara N.Z. 43°3S 172°46E 59 E4
Waipawa N.Z. 39°56S 176°38E 59 C6
Waipiro N.Z. 38°2S 178°22E 59 C7
Waipoua Forest N.Z. 35°39S 173°33E 59 A4
Waipu N.Z. 35°59S 174°29E 59 A5
Waipukurau N.Z. 40°1S 176°33E 59 D6
Wairakei N.Z. 38°37S 176°6E 59 C6
Wairarapa, L. N.Z. 41°14S 175°15E 59 D5
Wairoa N.Z. 39°3S 177°25E 59 C6
Waitaki → N.Z. 44°56S 171°7E 59 F3
Waitangi N.Z. 35°16S 174°5E 59 A5
Waitara N.Z. 38°59S 174°15E 59 C5
Waitomo Caves N.Z. 38°16S 175°7E 59 C5
Waitsburg U.S.A. 46°16N 118°9W 76 C4
Waiuku N.Z. 37°15S 174°45E 59 B5
Wajima Japan 37°30N 137°0E 31 F8
Wajir Kenya 1°42N 40°5E 54 B5
Wakasa Japan 35°20N 134°24E 31 G7
Wakasa-Wan Japan 35°40N 135°30E 31 G7
Wakatipu, L. N.Z. 45°5S 168°33E 59 F2
Wakaw Canada 52°39N 105°44W 71 C7

Wakaya *Fiji* 17°37S 179°0E **59** a
Wakayama *Japan* 34°15N 135°15E **31** G7
Wakayama □ *Japan* 33°50N 135°30E **31** H7
Wake Forest *U.S.A.* 35°59N 78°30W **85** D15
Wake I. *Pac. Oc.* 19°18N 166°36E **64** F8
WaKeeney *U.S.A.* 39°1N 99°53W **80** F4
Wakefield *Jamaica* 18°26N 77°42W **88** a
Wakefield *N.Z.* 41°24S 173°5E **59** D4
Wakefield *U.K.* 53°41N 1°29W **12** D6
Wakefield *Mass., U.S.A.* 42°30N 71°5W **83** D13
Wakefield *Mich., U.S.A.* 46°29N 89°56W **80** B9
Wakkanai *Japan* 45°28N 141°35E **30** B10
Wakkerstroom *S. Africa* 27°24S 30°10E **57** D5
Wakool *Australia* 35°28S 144°23E **63** F3
Wakool → *Australia* 35°5S 143°33E **63** F3
Wakre *Indonesia* 0°19S 131°5E **37** E8
Wakuach, L. *Canada* 55°34N 67°32W **73** A6
Walagunya ◇ *Australia* 23°10S 120°50E **60** D3
Walamba *Zambia* 13°30S 28°42E **55** E2
Wałbrzych *Poland* 50°45N 16°18E **16** C9
Walbury Hill *U.K.* 51°21N 1°28W **13** F6
Walcha *Australia* 30°55S 151°31E **63** E5
Walcheren *Neths.* 51°30N 3°35E **15** C3
Walcott *U.S.A.* 41°46N 106°51W **76** F10
Wałcz *Poland* 53°17N 16°27E **16** B9
Waldburg Ra. *Australia* 24°40S 117°35E **61** D2
Walden *Colo., U.S.A.* 40°44N 106°17W **76** F10
Walden *N.Y., U.S.A.* 41°34N 74°11W **83** E10
Waldport *U.S.A.* 44°26N 124°4W **76** D1
Waldron *U.S.A.* 34°54N 94°5W **84** D7
Walebing *Australia* 30°41S 116°13E **61** F2
Wales □ *U.K.* 52°19N 4°43W **13** E3
Wales I. *Canada* 68°1N 86°40W **69** D14
Walgett *Australia* 30°0S 148°5E **63** E4
Walgreen Coast
   Antarctica 75°15S 105°0W **5** D15
Walker *U.S.A.* 47°6N 94°35W **80** B6
Walker, L. *Canada* 50°20N 67°11W **73** B6
Walker L. *Canada* 54°42N 95°57W **71** C9
Walker L. *U.S.A.* 38°42N 118°43W **76** G4
Walkerston *Australia* 21°11S 149°8E **62** b
Walkerton *Canada* 44°10N 81°10W **82** B3
Wall *U.S.A.* 44°0N 102°8W **80** C2
Walla Walla *U.S.A.* 46°4N 118°20W **76** C4
Wallace *Idaho, U.S.A.* 47°28N 115°56W **76** C6
Wallace *N.C., U.S.A.* 34°44N 77°59W **85** D16
Wallaceburg *Canada* 42°34N 82°23W **82** D2
Wallachia = Valahia
   Romania 44°35N 25°0E **17** F13
Wallal *Australia* 26°32S 146°7E **63** D4
Wallam Cr. →
   Australia 28°40S 147°20E **63** D4
Wallambin, L. *Australia* 30°57S 117°35E **61** F2
Wallangarra *Australia* 28°56S 151°58E **63** D5
Wallaroo *Australia* 33°56S 137°39E **63** E2
Wallenpaupack, L.
   U.S.A. 41°25N 75°15W **83** E9
Wallingford *Conn.,*
   U.S.A. 41°27N 72°50W **83** E12
Wallingford *Vt., U.S.A.* 43°28N 72°58W **83** C12
Wallis & Futuna, Is.
   Pac. Oc. 13°18S 176°10W **58** C11
Wallowa *U.S.A.* 45°34N 117°32W **76** D5
Wallowa Mts. *U.S.A.* 45°20N 117°30W **76** D5
Walls *U.K.* 60°14N 1°33W **11** A7
Walls of Jerusalem △
   Australia 41°56S 146°15E **63** G4
Wallula *U.S.A.* 46°5N 118°54W **76** C4
Wallumbilla *Australia* 26°33S 149°9E **63** D4
Walmsley, L. *Canada* 63°25N 108°36W **71** A7
Walney, I. of *U.K.* 54°6N 3°15W **12** C4
Walnut Canyon △
   U.S.A. 35°15N 111°20W **77** J8
Walnut Creek *U.S.A.* 37°54N 122°4W **78** H4
Walnut Ridge *U.S.A.* 36°4N 90°57W **85** C9
Walpole *Australia* 34°58S 116°44E **61** F2
Walpole *U.S.A.* 42°9N 71°15W **83** D13
Walpole-Nornalup △
   Australia 35°0S 116°45E **61** G2
Walsall *U.K.* 52°35N 1°58W **13** E6
Walsenburg *U.S.A.* 37°38N 104°47W **77** H11
Walsh *U.S.A.* 37°23N 102°17W **77** H12
Walsh → *Australia* 16°31S 143°42E **62** B3
Walsingham *Canada* 42°40N 80°31W **82** D4
Walter F. George Res.
   U.S.A. 31°38N 85°4W **85** F12
Walterboro *U.S.A.* 32°55N 80°40W **85** E14
Walters *U.S.A.* 34°22N 98°19W **84** D5
Waltham *U.S.A.* 42°23N 71°14W **83** D13
Waltman *U.S.A.* 43°4N 107°12W **76** E10
Walton *U.S.A.* 42°10N 75°8W **83** D9
Walton-on-the-Naze *U.K.* 51°51N 1°17E **13** F9
Walvis Bay *Namibia* 23°0S 14°28E **56** C1
Walvisbaai = Walvis Bay
   Namibia 23°0S 14°28E **56** C1
Wamba
   Dem. Rep. of the Congo 2°10N 27°57E **54** B2
Wamba *Kenya* 0°58N 37°19E **54** D4
Wambardi ◇ *Australia* 16°2S 130°55E **60** C5
Wamego *U.S.A.* 39°12N 96°18W **80** F6
Wamena *Indonesia* 4°4S 138°57E **37** E9
Wampana Karlantijpa
   Australia 17°45S 132°10E **60** C5
Wampaya ◇ *Australia* 17°20S 135°0E **62** B2
Wampsville *U.S.A.* 43°4N 75°42W **83** C9
Wamsutter *U.S.A.* 41°40N 107°58W **76** F10
Wamulan *Indonesia* 3°27S 126°7E **37** E7
Wan Xian *China* 38°47N 115°7E **34** E8
Wana *Pakistan* 32°20N 69°32E **42** C3
Wanaaring *Australia* 29°38S 144°9E **63** D3
Wanaka *N.Z.* 44°42S 169°9E **59** F2
Wanaka, L. *N.Z.* 44°33S 169°7E **59** F2
Wanapitei L. *Canada* 46°45N 80°40W **72** C3
Wandel Sea = McKinley Sea
   Arctic 82°0N 0°0 **4** A7
Wanderer *Zimbabwe* 19°36S 30°1E **55** F3
Wandhari *Pakistan* 27°42N 66°48E **42** F2
Wandoan *Australia* 26°5S 149°55E **63** D4
Wanfu *China* 40°8N 122°38E **35** D12

Wang → *Thailand* 17°8N 99°2E **38** D2
Wang Noi *Thailand* 14°13N 100°44E **38** E3
Wang Saphung
   Thailand 17°18N 101°46E **38** D3
Wang Thong *Thailand* 16°50N 100°26E **38** D3
Wanga
   Dem. Rep. of the Congo 2°58N 29°12E **54** B2
Wangal *Indonesia* 6°8S 134°9E **37** F8
Wanganella *Australia* 35°6S 144°49E **63** F3
Wanganui *N.Z.* 39°56S 175°3E **59** C5
Wangaratta *Australia* 36°21S 146°19E **63** F4
Wangary *Australia* 34°35S 135°29E **63** E2
Wangdu *China* 38°40N 115°7E **34** E8
Wangerooge *Germany* 53°47N 7°54E **16** B4
Wangiwangi *Indonesia* 5°22S 123°37E **37** F6
Wangqing *China* 43°12N 129°42E **35** C15
Wanimiyn ◇ *Australia* 15°55S 130°49E **60** C5
Wanjina Wunggurr Wilinggin ◇
   Australia 16°0S 127°0E **60** C4
Wankaner *India* 22°35N 71°0E **42** H4
Wanless *Canada* 54°11N 101°21W **71** C8
Wanleweyne *Somali Rep.* 2°37N 44°54E **47** G3
Wanneroo *Australia* 31°42S 115°46E **61** F2
Wanning *China* 18°48N 110°22E **38** C8
Wannoo Billabong Roadhouse
   Australia 27°25S 115°49E **61** E2
Wanon Niwat *Thailand* 17°38N 103°46E **38** D4
Wanqinsha *China* 22°43N 113°33E **33** F10
Wanquan *China* 40°50N 114°40E **34** D8
Wanrong *China* 35°25N 110°50E **34** G6
Wanshan Qundao
   China 21°57N 113°45E **33** G10
Wantage *U.K.* 51°35N 1°25W **13** F6
Wanxian *China* 30°42N 108°20E **32** C5
Wanzai *China* 22°12N 113°31E **33** G10
Wapakoneta *U.S.A.* 40°34N 84°12W **81** E11
Wapato *U.S.A.* 46°27N 120°25W **76** C3
Wapawekka L. *Canada* 54°55N 104°40W **71** C8
Wapikopa L. *Canada* 52°56N 87°53W **72** B2
Wapiti → *Canada* 55°5N 118°18W **70** B5
Wappingers Falls
   U.S.A. 41°36N 73°55W **83** E11
Wapsipinicon → *U.S.A.* 41°44N 90°19W **80** E8
Wapusk △ *Canada* 57°46N 93°22W **71** B10
Warakurna *Australia* 24°55S 128°17E **61** D4
Warangal *India* 17°58N 79°35E **40** L11
Waratah *Australia* 41°30S 145°30E **63** G4
Waratah B. *Australia* 38°54S 146°5E **63** F4
Warburton *Vic.,*
   Australia 37°47S 145°42E **63** F4
Warburton *W. Austral.,*
   Australia 26°8S 126°35E **61** E4
Warburton ◇ *Australia* 26°7S 126°34E **61** E4
Warburton → *Australia* 28°4S 137°28E **63** D2
Warburton Groove
   Australia 28°18S 137°8E **63** A2
Warburton Ra.
   Australia 25°55S 126°28E **61** E4
Ward *N.Z.* 41°49S 174°11E **59** D5
Ward → *Australia* 26°28S 146°6E **63** D4
Ward Mt. *U.S.A.* 37°12N 118°54W **78** H8
Warden *S. Africa* 27°50S 29°0E **57** D4
Wardha *India* 20°45N 78°39E **40** J11
Wardha → *India* 19°57N 79°11E **40** K11
Wardsville *Canada* 42°39N 81°45W **82** D3
Ware *U.K.* 51°49N 0°0 **13** F8
Ware *U.S.A.* 42°16N 72°14W **83** D12
Waregem *Belgium* 50°53N 3°27E **15** D3
Wareham *U.S.A.* 41°46N 70°43W **83** E14
Waremme *Belgium* 50°43N 5°15E **15** D5
Warialda *Australia* 29°29S 150°33E **63** D5
Wariap *Indonesia* 1°30S 134°5E **37** E8
Warin Chamrap
   Thailand 15°12N 104°53E **38** E5
Warkopi *Indonesia* 1°12S 134°9E **37** E8
Warm Springs *U.S.A.* 38°10N 116°20W **77** G5
Warman *Canada* 52°19N 106°30W **71** C7
Warmbad = Bela Bela
   S. Africa 24°51S 28°19E **57** C4
Warmbad *Namibia* 28°25S 18°42E **56** D2
Warminster *U.K.* 51°12N 2°10W **13** F5
Warminster *U.S.A.* 40°12N 75°6W **83** F9
Warmun *Australia* 17°2S 128°12E **60** C4
Warner Mts. *U.S.A.* 41°40N 120°15W **76** F3
Warner Robins *U.S.A.* 32°37N 83°36W **85** E13
Waroona *Australia* 32°50S 115°58E **61** F2
Warrabri ◇ *Australia* 21°1S 134°19E **62** C1
Warracknabeal *Australia* 36°9S 142°26E **63** F3
Warragul *Australia* 38°10S 145°58E **63** F4
Warrego → *Australia* 30°24S 145°21E **63** E4
Warrego Ra. *Australia* 24°58S 146°0E **62** C4
Warren *Australia* 31°42S 147°51E **63** E4
Warren *Ark., U.S.A.* 33°37N 92°4W **84** E8
Warren *Mich., U.S.A.* 42°28N 83°1W **81** D12
Warren *Minn., U.S.A.* 48°12N 96°46W **80** A5
Warren *Ohio, U.S.A.* 41°14N 80°49W **82** E4
Warren *Pa., U.S.A.* 41°51N 79°9W **82** E5
Warrenpoint *U.K.* 54°6N 6°15W **10** B5
Warrensburg *Mo.,*
   U.S.A. 38°46N 93°44W **80** F7
Warrensburg *N.Y.,*
   U.S.A. 43°29N 73°46W **83** C11
Warrenton *S. Africa* 28°9S 24°47E **56** D3
Warrenton *U.S.A.* 46°10N 123°56W **78** D3
Warri *Nigeria* 5°30N 5°41E **50** G7
Warrington *U.K.* 53°24N 2°35W **12** D5
Warrington *U.S.A.* 30°23N 87°17W **85** F11
Warrington □ *U.K.* 53°24N 2°35W **12** D5
Warrnambool *Australia* 38°25S 142°30E **63** F3
Warroad *U.S.A.* 48°54N 95°19W **80** A6
Warruwi *Australia* 11°36S 133°20E **62** A1
Warsa *Indonesia* 0°47S 135°55E **37** E9
Warsak Dam *Pakistan* 34°11N 71°19E **42** B4
Warsaw = Warszawa
   Poland 52°14N 21°0E **17** B11
Warsaw *Ind., U.S.A.* 41°14N 85°51W **81** E11
Warsaw *N.Y., U.S.A.* 42°45N 78°8W **82** D6
Warsaw *Ohio, U.S.A.* 40°20N 82°0W **82** F3

Warszawa *Poland* 52°14N 21°0E **17** B11
Warta → *Poland* 52°35N 14°39E **16** B8
Warthe = Warta →
   Poland 52°35N 14°39E **16** B8
Waru *Indonesia* 3°30S 130°36E **37** E8
Warumungu ◇
   Australia 19°15S 134°44E **62** B1
Warwick *Australia* 28°10S 152°1E **63** D5
Warwick *U.K.* 52°18N 1°35W **13** E6
Warwick *N.Y., U.S.A.* 41°16N 74°22W **83** E10
Warwick *R.I., U.S.A.* 41°42N 71°28W **83** E13
Warwickshire □ *U.K.* 52°14N 1°38W **13** E6
Wasaga Beach *Canada* 44°31N 80°1W **82** B4
Wasagaming *Canada* 50°39N 99°58W **71** C9
Wasatch Ra. *U.S.A.* 40°0N 111°30W **76** F8
Wasbank *S. Africa* 28°15S 30°9E **57** D5
Wasco *Calif., U.S.A.* 35°36N 119°20W **79** K7
Wasco *Oreg., U.S.A.* 45°36N 120°42W **76** D3
Waseca *U.S.A.* 44°5N 93°30W **80** C7
Wasekamio L. *Canada* 56°45N 108°45W **71** B7
Wash, The *U.K.* 52°58N 0°20E **12** E8
Washago *Canada* 44°45N 79°20W **82** B5
Washburn *N. Dak.,*
   U.S.A. 47°17N 101°2W **80** B3
Washburn *Wis., U.S.A.* 46°40N 90°54W **80** B8
Washim *India* 20°3N 77°0E **40** J10
Washington *U.K.* 54°55N 1°30W **12** C6
Washington *D.C., U.S.A.* 38°53N 77°2W **81** F15
Washington *Ga.,*
   U.S.A. 33°44N 82°44W **85** E13
Washington *Ind.,*
   U.S.A. 38°40N 87°10W **80** F10
Washington *Iowa,*
   U.S.A. 41°18N 91°42W **80** E8
Washington *Mo., U.S.A.* 38°33N 91°1W **80** F8
Washington *N.C.,*
   U.S.A. 35°33N 77°3W **85** D16
Washington *N.J.,*
   U.S.A. 40°46N 74°59W **83** F10
Washington *Pa., U.S.A.* 40°10N 80°15W **82** F4
Washington *Utah,*
   U.S.A. 37°8N 113°31W **77** H7
Washington □ *U.S.A.* 47°30N 120°30W **76** C3
Washington, Mt.
   U.S.A. 44°16N 71°18W **83** B13
Washington Court House
   U.S.A. 39°32N 83°26W **81** F12
Washington I. *U.S.A.* 45°23N 86°54W **80** C2
Washougal *U.S.A.* 45°35N 122°21W **78** E4
Washpool △ *Australia* 29°22S 152°20E **63** D5
Wasian *Indonesia* 1°47S 133°19E **37** E8
Wasilla *U.S.A.* 61°35N 149°26W **68** B5
Wasini Marine ○ *Kenya* 4°33S 39°14E **54** C4
Wasior *Indonesia* 2°43S 134°37E **37** E8
Wasit □ *Iraq* 32°50N 45°50E **44** C5
Waskaganish *Canada* 51°30N 78°40W **72** B4
Waskaiowaka L.
   Canada 56°33N 96°23W **71** B9
Waskesiu Lake *Canada* 53°55N 106°5W **71** C7
Wasserkuppe *Germany* 50°29N 9°56E **16** C5
Waswanipi *Canada* 49°40N 76°29W **72** C4
Waswanipi, L. *Canada* 49°35N 76°40W **72** C4
Watampone *Indonesia* 4°29S 120°25E **37** E6
Watamu *Kenya* 3°23S 40°0E **54** C5
Watarrka △ *Australia* 24°20S 131°30E **60** D5
Water Park Pt.
   Australia 22°56S 150°47E **62** C5
Water Valley *U.S.A.* 34°10N 89°38W **85** D10
Waterberg Plateau △
   Namibia 20°25S 17°18E **56** C2
Waterberge *S. Africa* 24°10S 28°0E **57** C4
Waterbury *Conn., U.S.A.* 41°33N 73°3W **83** E11
Waterbury *Vt., U.S.A.* 44°20N 72°46W **83** C12
Waterbury L. *Canada* 58°10N 104°22W **71** B8
Waterdown *Canada* 43°20N 79°53W **82** C5
Waterford *Canada* 42°56N 80°17W **82** D4
Waterford *Ireland* 52°15N 7°8W **10** D4
Waterford *Calif., U.S.A.* 37°38N 120°46W **78** H6
Waterford *Pa., U.S.A.* 41°57N 79°59W **82** E5
Waterford □ *Ireland* 52°10N 7°40W **10** D4
Waterford Harbour
   Ireland 52°8N 6°58W **10** D5
Waterhen L. *Canada* 52°10N 99°40W **71** C9
Waterloo *Belgium* 50°43N 4°25E **15** D4
Waterloo *Ont., Canada* 43°30N 80°32W **82** C4
Waterloo *Qué., Canada* 45°22N 72°32W **83** A12
Waterloo *Ill., U.S.A.* 38°20N 90°9W **80** F8
Waterloo *Iowa, U.S.A.* 42°30N 92°21W **80** D7
Waterloo *N.Y., U.S.A.* 42°54N 76°52W **82** D8
Watersmeet *U.S.A.* 46°16N 89°11W **80** B9
Waterton Lakes △
   Canada 48°45N 115°0W **70** D6
Watertown *Conn.,*
   U.S.A. 41°36N 73°7W **83** E11
Watertown *N.Y., U.S.A.* 43°59N 75°55W **83** C9
Watertown *S. Dak.,*
   U.S.A. 44°54N 97°7W **80** C5
Watertown *Wis., U.S.A.* 43°12N 88°43W **80** D9
Waterval-Boven *S. Africa* 25°40S 30°18E **57** D5
Waterville *Maine,*
   U.S.A. 44°33N 69°38W **81** C19
Waterville *N.Y., U.S.A.* 42°56N 75°23W **83** D9
Waterville *Pa., U.S.A.* 41°19N 77°21W **82** E7
Waterville *Wash., U.S.A.* 47°39N 120°4W **76** C3
Watervliet *U.S.A.* 42°44N 73°42W **83** D11
Wates *Indonesia* 7°51S 110°10E **37** G14
Watford *Canada* 42°57N 81°53W **82** D3
Watford *U.K.* 51°40N 0°24W **13** F7
Watford City *U.S.A.* 47°48N 103°17W **80** B2
Wathaman → *Canada* 57°16N 102°59W **71** B8
Wathaman L. *Canada* 56°58N 103°44W **71** B8
Watheroo *Australia* 30°15S 116°0E **61** F2
Watheroo △ *Australia* 30°19S 115°48E **61** F2
Wating *China* 35°40N 106°38E **34** G4
Watkins Glen *U.S.A.* 42°23N 76°52W **82** D8
Watling I. = San Salvador I.
   Bahamas 24°0N 74°40W **89** B5
Watonga *U.S.A.* 35°51N 98°25W **84** D5

Watrous *Canada* 51°40N 105°25W **71** C7
Watrous *U.S.A.* 35°48N 104°59W **77** J11
Watsa
   Dem. Rep. of the Congo 3°4N 29°30E **54** B2
Watseka *U.S.A.* 40°47N 87°44W **80** E10
Watson *Canada* 52°10N 104°30W **71** C8
Watson Lake *Canada* 60°6N 128°49W **70** A3
Watsontown *U.S.A.* 41°5N 76°52W **82** E8
Watsonville *U.S.A.* 36°55N 121°45W **78** J5
Wattiwarriganna Cr. →
   Australia 28°57S 136°10E **63** D2
Watuata = Batuata
   Indonesia 6°12S 122°42E **37** F6
Watubela, Kepulauan
   Indonesia 4°28S 131°35E **37** E8
Watubela Is. = Watubela,
   Kepulauan *Indonesia* 4°28S 131°35E **37** E8
Wau = Wâw *Sudan* 7°45N 28°1E **51** G11
Waubamik *Canada* 45°27N 80°1W **82** A4
Waubay *U.S.A.* 45°20N 97°18W **80** C5
Wauchope *N.S.W.,*
   Australia 31°28S 152°45E **63** E5
Wauchope *N. Terr.,*
   Australia 20°36S 134°15E **62** C1
Wauchula *U.S.A.* 27°33N 81°49W **85** H14
Waukarlycarly, L.
   Australia 21°18S 121°56E **60** D3
Waukegan *U.S.A.* 42°22N 87°50W **80** D10
Waukesha *U.S.A.* 43°1N 88°14W **80** D9
Waukon *U.S.A.* 43°16N 91°29W **80** D8
Waupaca *U.S.A.* 44°21N 89°5W **80** C9
Waupun *U.S.A.* 43°38N 88°44W **80** D9
Waurika *U.S.A.* 34°10N 98°0W **84** D6
Wausau *U.S.A.* 44°58N 89°38W **80** C9
Wautoma *U.S.A.* 44°4N 89°18W **80** C9
Wauwatosa *U.S.A.* 43°2N 88°0W **80** D9
Wave Hill = Kalkarindji
   Australia 17°30S 130°47E **60** C5
Wave Rock △ *Australia* 32°26S 118°53E **61** F2
Waveney → *U.K.* 52°35N 1°39E **13** E9
Waverley *N.Z.* 39°46S 174°37E **59** C5
Waverly *Iowa, U.S.A.* 42°44N 92°29W **80** D7
Waverly *N.Y., U.S.A.* 42°1N 76°32W **83** E8
Wavre *Belgium* 50°43N 4°38E **15** D4
Wâw *Sudan* 7°45N 28°1E **51** G11
Wâw al Kabīr *Libya* 25°20N 16°43E **51** C9
Wawa *Canada* 47°59N 84°47W **72** C3
Wawona *U.S.A.* 37°32N 119°39W **78** H7
Waxahachie *U.S.A.* 32°24N 96°51W **84** E6
Way, L. *Australia* 26°45S 120°16E **61** E3
Waya *Fiji* 17°19S 177°10E **59** a
Waycross *U.S.A.* 31°13N 82°21W **85** F13
Wayland *U.S.A.* 42°34N 77°35W **82** D7
Wayne *Nebr., U.S.A.* 42°14N 97°1W **80** D5
Wayne *W. Va., U.S.A.* 38°13N 82°27W **81** F12
Waynesboro *Ga., U.S.A.* 33°6N 82°1W **85** E13
Waynesboro *Miss.,*
   U.S.A. 31°40N 88°39W **85** F10
Waynesboro *Pa.,*
   U.S.A. 39°45N 77°35W **81** F15
Waynesboro *Va., U.S.A.* 38°4N 78°53W **81** F14
Waynesburg *U.S.A.* 39°54N 80°11W **81** F13
Waynesville *U.S.A.* 35°28N 82°58W **85** D13
Waynoka *U.S.A.* 36°35N 98°53W **84** C5
Wazirabad *Pakistan* 32°30N 74°8E **42** C6
Waziristan *Pakistan* 33°0N 70°0E **42** C4
We *Indonesia* 5°51N 95°18E **36** C1
Weald, The *U.K.* 51°4N 0°20E **13** F8
Wear → *U.K.* 54°55N 1°23W **12** C6
Weatherford *Okla.,*
   U.S.A. 35°32N 98°43W **84** D5
Weatherford *Tex., U.S.A.* 32°46N 97°48W **84** E6
Weaverville *U.S.A.* 40°44N 122°56W **76** F2
Webb City *U.S.A.* 37°9N 94°28W **80** G6
Webequie *Canada* 52°59N 87°21W **72** B2
Webster *Mass., U.S.A.* 42°3N 71°53W **83** D13
Webster *N.Y., U.S.A.* 43°13N 77°26W **82** C7
Webster *S. Dak., U.S.A.* 45°20N 97°31W **80** C5
Webster City *U.S.A.* 42°28N 93°49W **80** D7
Webster Springs *U.S.A.* 38°29N 80°25W **81** F13
Webuye *Kenya* 0°37N 34°46E **54** B3
Weda *Indonesia* 0°21N 127°50E **37** D7
Weda, Teluk *Indonesia* 0°20N 128°0E **37** D7
Weddell Abyssal Plain
   S. Ocean 65°0S 20°0W **5** C2
Weddell I. *Falk. Is.* 51°50S 61°0W **96** G4
Weddell Sea *Antarctica* 72°30S 40°0W **5** D1
Wedderburn *Australia* 36°26S 143°33E **63** F3
Wedgeport *Canada* 43°44N 65°59W **73** D6
Wedza *Zimbabwe* 18°40S 31°33E **55** F3
Wee Waa *Australia* 30°11S 149°26E **63** E4
Weed *U.S.A.* 41°25N 122°23W **76** F2
Weed Heights *U.S.A.* 38°59N 119°13W **78** G7
Weedsport *U.S.A.* 43°2N 76°33W **83** C8
Weedville *U.S.A.* 41°17N 78°30W **82** E6
Weenen *S. Africa* 28°48S 30°7E **57** D5
Weert *Neths.* 51°15N 5°43E **15** C5
Wei He → *Hebei, China* 36°10N 115°45E **34** F8
Wei He → *Shaanxi,*
   China 34°38N 110°15E **34** G6
Weichang *China* 41°58N 117°49E **35** D9
Weichuan *China* 34°20N 113°59E **34** G7
Weiden *Germany* 49°41N 12°10E **16** D7
Weifang *China* 36°44N 119°7E **35** F10
Weihai *China* 37°30N 122°6E **35** F12
Weimar *Germany* 50°58N 11°19E **16** C6
Weinan *China* 34°31N 109°29E **34** G5
Weipa *Australia* 12°40S 141°50E **62** A3
Weir → *Australia* 28°20S 149°50E **63** D4
Weir → *Canada* 56°54N 93°21W **71** B10
Weir River *Canada* 56°49N 94°6W **71** B10
Weirton *U.S.A.* 40°24N 80°35W **82** F4
Weiser *U.S.A.* 44°15N 116°58W **76** D5
Weishan *China* 34°47N 117°5E **35** G9
Weiyuan *China* 35°7N 104°10E **34** G3
Weizhou *China* 37°56N 106°50E **34** F4
Wejherowo *Poland* 54°35N 18°12E **17** A10
Wekusko L. *Canada* 54°40N 99°50W **71** C9
Welch *U.S.A.* 37°26N 81°35W **81** G13

Welford △ *Australia* 25°5S 143°16E **62** D3
Welkom *S. Africa* 28°0S 26°46E **56** D4
Welland *Canada* 43°0N 79°15W **82** D5
Welland → *U.K.* 52°51N 0°5W **13** E7
Wellesley Is. *Australia* 16°42S 139°30E **62** B2
Wellesley Islands ◇
   Australia 16°32S 139°23E **62** B2
Wellingborough *U.K.* 52°19N 0°41W **13** E7
Wellington *Australia* 32°35S 148°59E **63** E4
Wellington *Canada* 43°57N 77°20W **82** C7
Wellington *N.Z.* 41°19S 174°46E **59** D5
Wellington *S. Africa* 33°38S 19°1E **56** E2
Wellington *Somst., U.K.* 50°58N 3°13W **13** G4
Wellington *Telford & Wrekin,*
   U.K. 52°42N 2°30W **13** E5
Wellington *Colo.,*
   U.S.A. 40°42N 105°0W **76** F11
Wellington *Kans., U.S.A.* 37°16N 97°24W **80** G5
Wellington *Nev., U.S.A.* 38°45N 119°23W **78** G7
Wellington *Ohio, U.S.A.* 41°10N 82°13W **82** E2
Wellington *Tex., U.S.A.* 34°51N 100°13W **84** D4
Wellington, I. *Chile* 49°30S 75°0W **96** F2
Wellington, L. *Australia* 38°6S 147°20E **63** F4
Wellington Chan. *Canada* 75°0N 93°0W **69** C13
Wells *U.K.* 51°13N 2°39W **13** F5
Wells *Maine, U.S.A.* 43°20N 70°35W **83** C14
Wells *N.Y., U.S.A.* 43°24N 74°17W **83** C10
Wells *Nev., U.S.A.* 41°7N 114°58W **76** F6
Wells, L. *Australia* 26°44S 123°15E **61** E3
Wells, Mt. *Australia* 17°25S 127°8E **60** C4
Wells Gray △ *Canada* 52°30N 120°15W **70** C4
Wells-next-the-Sea *U.K.* 52°57N 0°51E **12** E8
Wells River *U.S.A.* 44°9N 72°4W **83** B12
Wellsboro *U.S.A.* 41°45N 77°18W **82** E7
Wellsburg *U.S.A.* 40°16N 80°37W **82** F4
Wellsville *N.Y., U.S.A.* 42°7N 77°57W **82** D7
Wellsville *Ohio, U.S.A.* 40°36N 80°39W **82** F4
Wellsville *Utah, U.S.A.* 41°38N 111°56W **76** F8
Wellton *U.S.A.* 32°40N 114°8W **77** K6
Wels *Austria* 48°9N 14°1E **16** D8
Welshpool *U.K.* 52°39N 3°8E **13** E4
Welwyn Garden City
   U.K. 51°48N 0°12W **13** F7
Wem *U.K.* 52°52N 2°44W **12** E5
Wembere → *Tanzania* 4°10S 34°15E **54** C3
Wemindji *Canada* 53°0N 78°49W **72** B4
Wemyss *Canada* 44°52N 76°23W **83** B8
Wen Xian *China* 04°06N 110°0E **34** G7
Wenatchee *U.S.A.* 47°25N 120°19W **76** C3
Wenchang *China* 19°38N 110°42E **38** C8
Wenchi *Ghana* 7°46N 2°8W **50** G5
Wenchow = Wenzhou
   China 28°0N 120°38E **33** D7
Wenden *U.S.A.* 33°49N 113°33W **79** M13
Wendeng *China* 37°15N 122°5E **35** F12
Wendesi *Indonesia* 2°30S 134°17E **37** E8
Wendover *U.S.A.* 40°44N 114°2W **76** F6
Wenlock → *Australia* 12°2S 141°55E **62** A3
Wenshan *China* 23°20N 104°18E **32** D5
Wenshang *China* 35°45N 116°30E **34** G9
Wenshui *China* 37°26N 112°1E **34** F7
Wensleydale *U.K.* 54°17N 2°0W **12** C6
Wensu *China* 41°15N 80°10E **32** B3
Wensum → *U.K.* 52°40N 1°15E **12** E8
Wentworth *Australia* 34°2S 141°54E **63** E3
Wentzel L. *Canada* 59°2N 114°28W **70** B6
Wenut *Indonesia* 3°11S 133°19E **37** E8
Wenxi *China* 35°20N 111°10E **34** G6
Wenxian *China* 32°43N 104°36E **34** H3
Wenzhou *China* 28°0N 120°38E **33** D7
Weott *U.S.A.* 40°20N 123°55W **78** F2
Wepener *S. Africa* 29°42S 27°3E **56** D4
Werda *Botswana* 25°24S 23°15E **56** D3
Weri *Indonesia* 3°10S 132°38E **37** E8
Werra → *Germany* 51°24N 9°39E **16** C5
Werrimull *Australia* 34°25S 141°38E **63** E3
Werris Creek *Australia* 31°18S 150°38E **63** E5
Weser → *Germany* 53°36N 8°28E **16** B5
Wesiri *Indonesia* 7°30S 126°30E **37** F7
Weslaco *U.S.A.* 26°10N 97°58W **84** M6
Weslemkoon L. *Canada* 45°2N 77°25W **82** A7
Wesleyville *Canada* 49°9N 53°33W **73** C9
Wesleyville *U.S.A.* 42°9N 80°1W **82** D4
Wessel, C. *Australia* 10°59S 136°46E **62** A2
Wessel Is. *Australia* 11°10S 136°45E **62** A2
Wessington Springs
   U.S.A. 44°5N 98°34W **80** C4
West *U.S.A.* 31°48N 97°6W **84** F6
West → *U.S.A.* 42°52N 72°33W **83** D12
West Allis *U.S.A.* 43°1N 88°0W **80** D9
West Antarctica
   Antarctica 80°0S 90°0W **5** D15
West Baines →
   Australia 15°38S 129°59E **60** C4
West Bank ■ *Asia* 32°6N 35°13E **46** C4
West Bend *U.S.A.* 43°25N 88°11W **80** D9
West Bengal □ *India* 23°0N 88°0E **43** H13
West Berkshire □ *U.K.* 51°25N 1°17W **13** F6
West Beskids = Západné Beskydy
   Europe 49°30N 19°0E **17** D10
West Branch *U.S.A.* 44°17N 84°14W **81** C11
West Branch Susquehanna
   → *U.S.A.* 40°53N 76°48W **83** F8
West Bromwich *U.K.* 52°32N 1°59W **13** E6
West Burra *U.K.* 60°5N 1°21W **11** A7
West Canada Cr. →
   U.S.A. 43°1N 74°58W **83** C10
West Caroline Basin
   Pac. Oc. 4°0N 138°0E **64** G5
West Chazy *U.S.A.* 44°49N 73°28W **83** B11
West Chester *U.S.A.* 39°58N 75°36W **83** G9
West Coast △ *Namibia* 21°53S 14°14E **56** C1
West Coast □ *S. Africa* 33°13S 18°0E **56** E2
West Columbia *U.S.A.* 29°9N 95°39W **84** G7
West Covina *U.S.A.* 34°4N 117°54W **79** L9
West Des Moines *U.S.A.* 41°35N 93°43W **80** E7
West Dunbartonshire □
   U.K. 55°59N 4°30W **11** F4
West End *Bahamas* 26°41N 78°58W **88** A4

174 West Falkland
INDEX TO WORLD MAPS

West Falkland Falk. Is. 51°40S 60°0W 96 G4
West Fargo U.S.A. 46°52N 96°54W 80 B5
West Fiji Basin Pac. Oc. 17°0S 173°0E 64 J9
West Fjord = Vestfjorden Norway 67°55N 14°0E 8 C16
West Fork Trinity → U.S.A. 32°48N 96°54W 84 E6
West Frankfort U.S.A. 37°54N 88°55W 80 G9
West Grand L. U.S.A. 45°14N 67°51W 81 C20
West Hartford U.S.A. 41°45N 72°44W 83 E12
West Haven U.S.A. 41°17N 72°57W 83 E12
West Hazleton U.S.A. 40°58N 76°0W 83 F9
West Helena U.S.A. 34°33N 90°38W 85 D9
West Hurley U.S.A. 41°59N 74°7W 83 E10
West Ice Shelf Antarctica 67°0S 85°0E 5 C7
West Indies Cent. Amer. 15°0N 65°0W 89 D7
West Jordan U.S.A. 40°36N 111°56W 76 F8
West Lamma Channel China 22°14N 114°4E 33 G11
West Linn U.S.A. 45°21N 122°36W 78 E4
West Lorne Canada 42°36N 81°36W 82 D3
West Lothian □ U.K. 55°54N 3°36W 11 F5
West Lunga → Zambia 13°6S 24°39E 55 E1
West MacDonnell △ Australia 23°38S 132°59E 60 D5
West Mariana Basin Pac. Oc. 15°0N 137°0E 64 F5
West Memphis U.S.A. 35°8N 90°10W 85 D9
West Midlands □ U.K. 52°26N 2°0W 13 E6
West Mifflin U.S.A. 40°21N 79°52W 82 F5
West Milford U.S.A. 41°8N 74°22W 83 E10
West Milton U.S.A. 41°1N 76°50W 82 E8
West Monroe U.S.A. 32°31N 92°9W 84 E8
West Newton U.S.A. 40°14N 79°46W 82 F5
West Nicholson Zimbabwe 21°2S 29°20E 55 G2
West Odessa U.S.A. 31°50N 102°30W 84 F3
West Palm Beach U.S.A. 26°43N 80°3W 85 H14
West Plains U.S.A. 36°44N 91°51W 80 G8
West Point Miss., U.S.A. 33°36N 88°39W 85 E10
West Point N.Y., U.S.A. 41°24N 73°58W 83 E11
West Point Nebr., U.S.A. 41°51N 96°43W 80 E5
West Point Va., U.S.A. 37°32N 76°48W 81 G15
West Point L. U.S.A. 33°8N 85°0W 85 E12
West Pt. = Ouest, Pte. de l' Canada 49°52N 64°40W 73 C7
West Pt. Australia 35°1S 135°56E 63 F2
West Road → Canada 53°18N 122°53W 70 C4
West Rutland U.S.A. 43°38N 73°5W 83 C11
West Schelde = Westerschelde → Neths. 51°25N 3°25E 15 C3
West Seneca U.S.A. 42°51N 78°48W 82 D6
West Siberian Plain Russia 62°0N 75°0E 26 B9
West Sussex □ U.K. 50°55N 0°30W 13 G7
West-Terschelling Neths. 53°22N 5°13E 15 A5
West Valley City U.S.A. 40°42N 111°58W 76 F8
West Virginia □ U.S.A. 38°45N 80°30W 81 F13
West-Vlaanderen □ Belgium 51°0N 3°0E 15 D2
West Walker → U.S.A. 38°54N 119°9W 78 G7
West Wyalong Australia 33°56S 147°10E 63 E4
West Yellowstone U.S.A. 44°40N 111°6W 76 D8
West Yorkshire □ U.K. 53°45N 1°40W 12 D6
Westall, Pt. Australia 32°55S 134°4E 63 E1
Westbrook U.S.A. 43°41N 70°22W 81 D18
Westbury Australia 41°30S 146°51E 63 G4
Westby U.S.A. 48°52N 104°3W 76 B11
Westend U.S.A. 35°42N 117°24W 79 K9
Westerland Germany 54°54N 8°17E 16 A5
Westerly U.S.A. 41°22N 71°50W 83 E13
Western □ Kenya 0°30N 34°30E 54 B3
Western □ Zambia 15°0S 24°4E 55 F1
Western Australia □ Australia 25°0S 118°0E 61 E2
Western Cape □ S. Africa 34°0S 20°0E 56 E3
Western Dvina = Daugava → Latvia 57°4N 24°3E 9 H21
Western Ghats India 14°0N 75°0E 40 N9
Western Isles □ U.K. 57°30N 7°10W 11 D1
Western Sahara ■ Africa 25°0N 13°0W 50 D3
Western Samoa = Samoa ■ Pac. Oc. 14°0S 172°0W 59 b
Western Sierra Madre = Madre Occidental, Sierra Mexico 27°0N 107°0W 86 B3
Westernport U.S.A. 39°29N 79°3W 81 F14
Westerschelde → Neths. 51°25N 3°25E 15 C3
Westerwald Germany 50°38N 7°56E 16 C4
Westfield Mass., U.S.A. 42°7N 72°45W 83 D12
Westfield N.Y., U.S.A. 42°20N 79°35W 82 D5
Westfield Pa., U.S.A. 41°55N 77°32W 82 E7
Westhill U.K. 57°9N 2°19W 11 D6
Westhope U.S.A. 48°55N 101°1W 80 A3
Westland △ N.Z. 43°16S 170°16E 59 E2
Westland Bight N.Z. 42°55S 170°5E 59 E3
Westlock Canada 54°9N 113°55W 70 C6
Westmar Australia 27°55S 149°44E 63 D4
Westmeath □ Ireland 53°33N 7°34W 10 C4
Westminster Calif., U.S.A. 33°45N 118°0W 79 M8
Westminster Colo., U.S.A. 39°50N 105°2W 76 G11
Westminster Md., U.S.A. 39°34N 76°59W 81 F15
Westmont U.S.A. 40°19N 78°58W 82 F6
Westmoreland Barbados 13°13N 59°37W 89 g
Westmorland U.S.A. 33°2N 115°37W 79 M11
Weston Oreg., U.S.A. 45°49N 118°26W 76 D4
Weston W. Va., U.S.A. 39°2N 80°28W 81 F13
Weston I. Canada 52°33N 79°36W 72 B4
Weston-super-Mare U.K. 51°21N 2°58W 13 F5
Westover U.S.A. 40°45N 78°40W 82 F6
Westport Canada 44°40N 76°25W 83 B8
Westport Ireland 53°48N 9°31W 10 C2
Westport N.Z. 41°46S 171°37E 59 D3
Westport N.Y., U.S.A. 44°11N 73°26W 83 B11
Westport Oreg., U.S.A. 46°8N 123°23W 78 D3
Westport Wash., U.S.A. 46°53N 124°6W 78 D2
Westray Canada 53°36N 101°24W 71 C8
Westray U.K. 59°18N 3°0W 11 B5
Westree Canada 47°26N 81°34W 72 C3
Westville U.S.A. 39°8N 120°42W 78 F6
Westwood U.S.A. 40°18N 121°0W 76 F3
Wetar Indonesia 7°48S 126°30E 37 F7
Wetaskiwin Canada 52°55N 113°24W 70 C6
Wete Tanzania 5°4S 39°43E 52 F7
Wetherby U.K. 53°56N 1°23W 12 D6
Wethersfield U.S.A. 41°42N 72°40W 83 E12
Wetteren Belgium 51°0N 3°53E 15 D3
Wetzlar Germany 50°32N 8°31E 16 C5
Wewoka U.S.A. 35°9N 96°30W 84 D6
Wexford Ireland 52°20N 6°28W 10 D5
Wexford □ Ireland 52°20N 6°25W 10 D5
Wexford Harbour Ireland 52°20N 6°25W 10 D5
Weyburn Canada 49°40N 103°50W 71 D8
Weymouth Canada 44°30N 66°1W 73 D6
Weymouth U.K. 50°37N 2°28W 13 G5
Weymouth U.S.A. 42°13N 70°58W 83 D14
Weymouth, C. Australia 12°37S 143°27E 62 A3
Wha Ti Canada 63°8N 117°16W 68 E8
Whakaari N.Z. 37°30S 177°13E 59 B6
Whakatane N.Z. 37°57S 177°1E 59 B6
Whale = Baleine → Canada 58°15N 67°40W 73 A6
Whale Cove Canada 62°10N 92°34W 71 A10
Whales, B. of Antarctica 78°0S 160°0W 5 D12
Whalsay U.K. 60°22N 0°59W 11 A8
Whangamata N.Z. 37°12S 175°53E 59 B5
Whangamomona N.Z. 39°8S 174°44E 59 C5
Whanganui △ N.Z. 39°17S 174°53E 59 C5
Whangarei N.Z. 35°43S 174°21E 59 A5
Whangarei Harb. N.Z. 35°45S 174°28E 59 A5
Wharekauri = Chatham Is. Pac. Oc. 44°0S 176°40W 64 M10
Wharfe → U.K. 53°51N 1°9W 12 D6
Wharfedale U.K. 54°6N 2°1W 12 C5
Wharton N.J., U.S.A. 40°54N 74°35W 83 F10
Wharton Pa., U.S.A. 41°31N 78°1W 82 E6
Wharton Tex., U.S.A. 29°19N 96°6W 84 G6
Wharton Basin Ind. Oc. 22°0S 92°0E 64 K1
Wheatland Calif., U.S.A. 39°1N 121°25W 78 F5
Wheatland Wyo., U.S.A. 42°3N 104°58W 76 E11
Wheatley Canada 42°6N 82°27W 82 D2
Wheaton Md., U.S.A. 39°3N 77°3W 81 F15
Wheaton Minn., U.S.A. 45°48N 96°30W 80 C5
Wheelbarrow Pk. U.S.A. 37°26N 116°5W 78 H10
Wheeler Oreg., U.S.A. 45°41N 123°53W 76 D2
Wheeler Tex., U.S.A. 35°27N 100°16W 84 D4
Wheeler → Canada 57°2N 67°13W 73 A6
Wheeler L. U.S.A. 34°48N 87°23W 85 D11
Wheeler Pk. N. Mex., U.S.A. 36°34N 105°25W 77 H11
Wheeler Pk. Nev., U.S.A. 38°57N 114°15W 76 G6
Wheeler Ridge U.S.A. 35°0N 118°57W 79 L8
Wheelersburg U.S.A. 38°44N 82°51W 81 F12
Wheeling U.S.A. 40°4N 80°43W 82 F4
Whernside U.K. 54°14N 2°24W 12 C5
Whiddy I. Ireland 51°41N 9°31W 10 E2
Whim Creek Australia 20°50S 117°49E 60 D2
Whiskey Jack L. Canada 58°23N 101°55W 71 B8
Whiskeytown-Shasta-Trinity ⌂ U.S.A. 40°45N 122°15W 76 F2
Whistleduck Cr. → Australia 20°15S 135°18E 62 C2
Whistler Canada 50°7N 122°58W 70 C4
Whitby Canada 43°52N 78°56W 82 C6
Whitby U.K. 54°29N 0°37W 12 C7
White → Ark., U.S.A. 33°57N 91°5W 84 E9
White → Ind., U.S.A. 38°25N 87°45W 80 F10
White → S. Dak., U.S.A. 43°42N 99°27W 80 D4
White → Tex., U.S.A. 33°14N 100°56W 84 E4
White → Utah, U.S.A. 40°4N 109°41W 76 F9
White → Vt., U.S.A. 43°37N 72°20W 83 C12
White → Wash., U.S.A. 47°12N 122°15W 78 C4
White, L. Australia 21°9S 128°56E 60 D4
White B. Canada 50°0N 56°35W 73 C8
White Bird U.S.A. 45°46N 116°18W 76 D5
White Butte U.S.A. 46°23N 103°18W 80 B2
White City U.S.A. 42°26N 122°51W 76 E2
White Cliffs Australia 30°50S 143°10E 63 E3
White Hall U.S.A. 39°26N 90°24W 80 F8
White Haven U.S.A. 41°4N 75°47W 83 E9
White Horse, Vale of U.K. 51°37N 1°30W 13 F6
White I. = Whakaari N.Z. 37°30S 177°13E 59 B6
White L. Canada 45°18N 76°31W 83 A8
White L. U.S.A. 29°44N 92°30W 84 G8
White Lake Canada 45°21N 76°29W 83 A8
White Mountain Peak U.S.A. 37°38N 118°15W 77 H4
White Mts. Calif., U.S.A. 37°30N 118°15W 78 H8
White Mts. N.H., U.S.A. 44°15N 71°15W 83 B13
White Mts. △ Australia 20°43S 145°12E 62 C4
White Nile = Nîl el Abyad → Sudan 15°38N 32°31E 51 E12
White Otter L. Canada 49°5N 91°55W 72 C1
White Pass U.S.A. 46°38N 121°24W 78 D5
White Plains U.S.A. 41°2N 73°46W 83 E11
White River Canada 48°35N 85°20W 72 C2
White River U.S.A. 43°34N 100°45W 80 D3
White Rock Canada 49°2N 122°48W 78 A4
White Rock U.S.A. 35°50N 106°12W 77 J10
White Russia = Belarus ■ Europe 53°30N 27°0E 17 B14
White Sands ⌂ U.S.A. 32°46N 106°20W 77 K10
White Sea = Beloye More Russia 66°30N 38°0E 8 C25
White Sulphur Springs Mont., U.S.A. 46°33N 110°54W 76 C8
White Sulphur Springs W. Va., U.S.A. 37°48N 80°18W 81 G13
White Swan U.S.A. 46°23N 120°44W 78 D6
Whitecliffs N.Z. 43°26S 171°55E 59 E3
Whitecourt Canada 54°10N 115°45W 70 C5
Whiteface Mt. U.S.A. 44°22N 73°54W 83 B11
Whitefield U.S.A. 44°23N 71°37W 83 B13
Whitefish U.S.A. 48°25N 114°20W 76 B6
Whitefish B. U.S.A. 46°40N 84°55W 72 C3
Whitefish L. Canada 62°41N 106°48W 71 A7
Whitefish Pt. U.S.A. 46°45N 84°59W 81 B11
Whitegull, L. = Goélands, L. aux Canada 55°27N 64°17W 73 A7
Whitehall Mich., U.S.A. 43°24N 86°21W 80 D10
Whitehall Mont., U.S.A. 45°52N 112°6W 76 D7
Whitehall N.Y., U.S.A. 43°33N 73°24W 83 C11
Whitehall Wis., U.S.A. 44°22N 91°19W 80 C8
Whitehaven U.K. 54°33N 3°35W 12 C4
Whitehorse Canada 60°43N 135°3W 70 A1
Whitemark Australia 40°7S 148°3E 63 G4
Whiteriver U.S.A. 33°50N 109°58W 77 K9
Whitesand → Canada 60°9N 115°45W 70 A5
Whitesands S. Africa 34°23S 20°50E 56 E3
Whitesboro N.Y., U.S.A. 43°7N 75°18W 83 C9
Whitesboro Tex., U.S.A. 33°39N 96°54W 84 E6
Whiteshell ⌂ Canada 50°0N 95°40W 71 D9
Whiteville U.S.A. 34°20N 78°42W 85 D15
Whitewater U.S.A. 42°50N 88°44W 80 D9
Whitewater Baldy U.S.A. 33°20N 108°39W 77 K9
Whitewater L. Canada 50°50N 89°10W 72 B2
Whitewood Australia 21°28S 143°30E 62 C3
Whitewood Canada 50°20N 102°20W 71 C8
Whithorn U.K. 54°44N 4°26W 11 G4
Whitianga N.Z. 36°47S 175°41E 59 B5
Whitman U.S.A. 42°5N 70°56W 83 D14
Whitney Canada 45°31N 78°14W 82 A6
Whitney, Mt. U.S.A. 36°35N 118°18W 78 J8
Whitney Point U.S.A. 42°20N 75°58W 83 D9
Whitstable U.K. 51°21N 1°3E 13 F9
Whitsunday I. Australia 20°15S 149°4E 62 b
Whitsunday Islands △ Australia 20°15S 149°0E 62 b
Whittier Alaska, U.S.A. 60°47N 148°41W 74 C10
Whittier Calif., U.S.A. 33°58N 118°2W 79 M8
Whittlesea Australia 37°27S 145°9E 63 F4
Wholdaia L. Canada 60°43N 104°20W 71 A8
Whyalla Australia 33°2S 137°30E 63 E2
Wiang Kosai △ Thailand 17°54N 99°29E 38 D2
Wiang Sa Thailand 18°34N 100°45E 38 C3
Wiarton Canada 44°40N 81°10W 82 B3
Wiay U.K. 57°24N 7°13W 11 D1
Wibaux U.S.A. 46°59N 104°11W 76 C11
Wichian Buri Thailand 15°39N 101°7E 38 E3
Wichita U.S.A. 37°42N 97°20W 80 G5
Wichita Falls U.S.A. 33°54N 98°30W 84 E5
Wick U.K. 58°26N 3°5W 11 C5
Wickenburg U.S.A. 33°58N 112°44W 77 K7
Wickepin Australia 32°50S 117°30E 61 F2
Wickham Australia 20°42S 117°11E 60 D2
Wickham, C. Australia 39°35S 143°57E 63 F3
Wickliffe U.S.A. 41°36N 81°28W 82 E3
Wicklow Ireland 52°59N 6°3W 10 D5
Wicklow □ Ireland 52°57N 6°25W 10 D5
Wicklow Hd. Ireland 52°58N 6°0W 10 D6
Wicklow Mts. Ireland 52°58N 6°26W 10 C5
Wicklow Mts. △ Ireland 53°6N 6°21W 10 C5
Widgeegoara Cr. → Australia 28°51S 146°34E 63 D4
Widgiemooltha Australia 31°30S 121°34E 61 F3
Widnes U.K. 53°23N 2°45W 12 D5
Wieluń Poland 51°15N 18°34E 17 C10
Wien Austria 48°12N 16°22E 16 D9
Wiener Neustadt Austria 47°49N 16°16E 16 E9
Wiesbaden Germany 50°4N 8°14E 16 C5
Wigan U.K. 53°33N 2°38W 12 D5
Wiggins Colo., U.S.A. 40°14N 104°4W 76 F11
Wiggins Miss., U.S.A. 30°51N 89°8W 85 F10
Wight, I. of U.K. 50°41N 1°17W 13 G6
Wigston U.K. 52°35N 1°6W 13 E6
Wigton U.K. 54°50N 3°10W 12 C4
Wigtown U.K. 54°53N 4°27W 11 G4
Wigtown B. U.K. 54°46N 4°15W 11 G4
Wik and Wikway People ✪ Australia 13°55S 142°28E 62 A3
Wilber U.S.A. 40°29N 96°58W 80 E5
Wilberforce Canada 45°2N 78°13W 82 A6
Wilberforce, C. Australia 11°54S 136°35E 62 A2
Wilburton U.S.A. 34°55N 95°19W 84 D7
Wilcannia Australia 31°30S 143°26E 63 E3
Wilcox U.S.A. 41°35N 78°41W 82 E6
Wildrose U.S.A. 36°14N 117°11W 79 J9
Wildspitze Austria 46°53N 10°53E 16 E6
Wilge → S. Africa 27°3S 28°20E 57 D4
Wilhelm II Coast Antarctica 68°0S 90°0E 5 C7
Wilhelmshaven Germany 53°31N 8°7E 16 B5
Wilhelmstal Namibia 21°58S 16°21E 56 C2
Wilkes-Barre U.S.A. 41°15N 75°53W 83 E9
Wilkes Land Antarctica 69°0S 120°0E 5 D9
Wilkie Canada 52°27N 108°42W 71 C7
Wilkinsburg U.S.A. 40°26N 79°52W 82 F5
Wilkinson Lakes Australia 29°40S 132°39E 61 E5
Willandra Creek → Australia 33°22S 145°52E 63 E4
Willapa B. U.S.A. 46°40N 124°0W 76 C1
Willapa Hills U.S.A. 46°35N 123°25W 78 D3
Willard U.S.A. 41°3N 82°44W 82 E2
Willare Bridge Roadhouse Australia 17°43S 123°38E 60 C3
Willcox U.S.A. 32°15N 109°50W 77 K9
Willemstad Neth. Ant. 12°5N 68°55W 89 D6
William → Canada 59°8N 109°19W 71 B7
William 'Bill' Dannelly Res. U.S.A. 32°6N 87°24W 85 E11
William Creek Australia 28°58S 136°22E 63 D2
Williams Australia 33°2S 116°52E 61 F2
Williams Ariz., U.S.A. 35°15N 112°11W 77 J7
Williams Calif., U.S.A. 39°9N 122°9W 78 F4
Williams Harbour Canada 52°33N 55°47W 73 B8
Williams Lake Canada 52°10N 122°10W 70 C4
Williamsburg Ky., U.S.A. 36°44N 84°10W 81 G11
Williamsburg Pa., U.S.A. 40°28N 78°12W 82 F6
Williamsburg Va., U.S.A. 37°16N 76°43W 81 G15
Williamson N.Y., U.S.A. 43°14N 77°11W 82 C7
Williamson W. Va., U.S.A. 37°41N 82°17W 81 G12
Williamsport U.S.A. 41°15N 77°1W 82 E7
Williamston U.S.A. 35°51N 77°4W 85 D16
Williamstown Australia 37°51S 144°52E 63 F3
Williamstown Ky., U.S.A. 38°38N 84°34W 81 F11
Williamstown Mass., U.S.A. 42°43N 73°12W 83 D11
Williamstown N.Y., U.S.A. 43°26N 75°53W 83 C9
Willimantic U.S.A. 41°43N 72°13W 83 E12
Willingboro U.S.A. 40°3N 74°54W 81 E16
Williston S. Africa 31°20S 20°53E 56 E3
Williston Fla., U.S.A. 29°23N 82°27W 85 G13
Williston N. Dak., U.S.A. 48°9N 103°37W 80 A2
Williston L. Canada 56°0N 124°0W 70 B4
Willits U.S.A. 39°25N 123°21W 76 G2
Willmar U.S.A. 45°7N 95°3W 80 C6
Willmore Wilderness ⌂ Canada 53°45N 119°30W 70 C5
Willoughby U.S.A. 41°39N 81°24W 82 E3
Willow Bunch Canada 49°20N 105°35W 71 D7
Willow L. Canada 62°10N 119°8W 70 A5
Willow Wall, The China 42°10N 122°0E 35 C12
Willowick U.S.A. 41°38N 81°28W 82 E3
Willowlake → Canada 62°42N 123°8W 70 A4
Willowmore S. Africa 33°15S 23°30E 56 E3
Willows U.S.A. 39°31N 122°12W 78 F4
Willowvale = Gatyana S. Africa 32°16S 28°31E 57 E4
Wills, L. Australia 21°25S 128°51E 60 D4
Wills Cr. → Australia 22°43S 140°2E 62 C3
Willsboro U.S.A. 44°21N 73°24W 83 B11
Willunga Australia 35°15S 138°30E 63 F2
Wilmette U.S.A. 42°4N 87°42W 80 D10
Wilmington Australia 32°39S 138°7E 63 E2
Wilmington Del., U.S.A. 39°45N 75°33W 81 F16
Wilmington N.C., U.S.A. 34°14N 77°55W 85 D16
Wilmington Ohio, U.S.A. 39°27N 83°50W 81 F12
Wilmington Vt., U.S.A. 42°52N 72°52W 83 D12
Wilmslow U.K. 53°19N 2°13W 12 D5
Wilpena Cr. → Australia 31°25S 139°29E 63 E2
Wilsall U.S.A. 45°59N 110°38W 76 D8
Wilson N.C., U.S.A. 35°44N 77°55W 85 D16
Wilson N.Y., U.S.A. 43°19N 78°50W 82 C6
Wilson Pa., U.S.A. 40°41N 75°15W 83 F9
Wilson → Australia 16°48S 128°16E 60 C4
Wilson Bluff Australia 31°41S 129°0E 61 F4
Wilson Inlet Australia 35°0S 117°22E 61 G2
Wilsons Promontory Australia 38°59S 146°23E 63 F4
Wilton U.S.A. 47°10N 100°47W 80 B3
Wilton → Australia 14°45S 134°33E 62 A1
Wiltshire □ U.K. 51°18N 1°53W 13 F6
Wiltz Lux. 49°57N 5°55E 15 E5
Wiluna Australia 26°36S 120°14E 61 E3
Wimborne Minster U.K. 50°48N 1°59W 13 G6
Wimmera → Australia 36°8S 141°56E 63 F3
Winam G. Kenya 0°20S 34°15E 54 C3
Winburg S. Africa 28°30S 27°2E 56 D4
Winchendon U.S.A. 42°41N 72°3W 83 D12
Winchester U.K. 51°4N 1°18W 13 F6
Winchester Conn., U.S.A. 41°53N 73°9W 83 E11
Winchester Idaho, U.S.A. 46°14N 116°38W 76 C5
Winchester Ind., U.S.A. 40°10N 84°59W 81 E11
Winchester Ky., U.S.A. 37°59N 84°11W 81 G11
Winchester N.H., U.S.A. 42°46N 72°23W 83 D12
Winchester Nev., U.S.A. 36°7N 115°7W 79 J11
Winchester Tenn., U.S.A. 35°11N 86°7W 85 D11
Winchester Va., U.S.A. 39°11N 78°10W 81 F14
Wind → U.S.A. 43°12N 108°12W 76 E9
Wind Cave △ U.S.A. 43°32N 103°17W 80 D2
Wind River Range U.S.A. 43°0N 109°30W 76 E9
Windamere, L. Australia 32°48S 149°51E 63 B4
Windau = Ventspils Latvia 57°25N 21°32E 9 H19
Windber U.S.A. 40°14N 78°50W 82 F6
Winder U.S.A. 34°0N 83°45W 85 D13
Windermere U.K. 54°23N 2°55W 12 C5
Windhoek Namibia 22°35S 17°4E 56 C2
Windidda ✪ Australia 26°23S 122°12E 61 E3
Windjana Gorge △ Australia 17°51S 125°0E 60 C3
Windom U.S.A. 43°52N 95°7W 80 D6
Windorah Australia 25°24S 142°36E 62 D3
Window Rock U.S.A. 35°41N 109°3W 77 J9
Windrush → U.K. 51°43N 1°24W 13 F6
Windsor Australia 33°37S 150°50E 63 E5
Windsor N.S., Canada 44°59N 64°5W 73 D7
Windsor Ont., Canada 42°18N 83°0W 82 D2
Windsor U.K. 51°29N 0°36W 13 F7
Windsor Calif., U.S.A. 38°33N 122°49W 76 G2
Windsor Colo., U.S.A. 40°29N 104°54W 76 F11
Windsor Conn., U.S.A. 41°50N 72°39W 83 E12
Windsor Mo., U.S.A. 38°32N 93°31W 80 F7
Windsor N.Y., U.S.A. 42°5N 75°37W 83 D9
Windsor Vt., U.S.A. 43°29N 72°24W 83 C12
Windsor & Maidenhead □ U.K. 51°29N 0°40W 13 F7
Windsorton S. Africa 28°16S 24°44E 56 D3
Windward Is. W. Indies 13°0N 61°0W 89 D7
Windward Passage = Vientos, Paso de los Caribbean 20°0N 74°0W 89 C5
Winefred L. Canada 55°30N 110°30W 71 B6
Winfield U.S.A. 37°15N 96°59W 80 G5
Wingate Mts. Australia 14°25S 130°40E 60 B5
Wingellina = Irrunytju Australia 26°3S 128°56E 61 E4
Wingham Australia 31°48S 152°22E 63 E5
Wingham Canada 43°55N 81°20W 82 C3
Winisk → Canada 55°17N 85°5W 72 A2
Winisk L. Canada 52°55N 87°22W 72 B2
Wink U.S.A. 31°45N 103°9W 84 F3
Winkler Canada 49°10N 97°56W 71 D9
Winlock U.S.A. 46°30N 122°56W 78 D4
Winneba Ghana 5°25N 0°36W 50 G5
Winnebago, L. U.S.A. 44°0N 88°26W 80 D9
Winnecke Cr. → Australia 18°35S 131°34E 60 C5
Winnemucca U.S.A. 40°58N 117°44W 76 F5
Winnemucca L. U.S.A. 40°7N 119°21W 76 F4
Winner U.S.A. 43°22N 99°52W 80 D4
Winnett U.S.A. 47°0N 108°21W 76 C9
Winnfield U.S.A. 31°56N 92°38W 84 F8
Winnibigoshish, L. U.S.A. 47°27N 94°13W 80 B6
Winnipeg Canada 49°54N 97°9W 71 D9
Winnipeg → Canada 50°38N 96°19W 71 C9
Winnipeg, L. Canada 52°0N 97°0W 71 C9
Winnipeg Beach Canada 50°30N 96°58W 71 C9
Winnipegosis Canada 51°39N 99°55W 71 C9
Winnipegosis L. Canada 52°30N 100°0W 71 C9
Winnipesaukee, L. U.S.A. 43°38N 71°21W 83 C13
Winnisquam L. U.S.A. 43°33N 71°31W 83 C13
Winnsboro La., U.S.A. 32°10N 91°43W 84 E9
Winnsboro S.C., U.S.A. 34°23N 81°5W 85 D14
Winnsboro Tex., U.S.A. 32°58N 95°17W 84 E7
Winokapau, L. Canada 53°15N 62°50W 73 B7
Winona Minn., U.S.A. 44°3N 91°39W 80 C8
Winona Miss., U.S.A. 33°29N 89°44W 85 E10
Winooski U.S.A. 44°29N 73°11W 83 B11
Winooski → U.S.A. 44°32N 73°17W 83 B11
Winschoten Neths. 53°9N 7°3E 15 A7
Winsford U.K. 53°12N 2°31W 12 D5
Winslow = Bainbridge Island U.S.A. 47°38N 122°32W 78 C4
Winslow U.S.A. 35°2N 110°42W 77 J8
Winsted U.S.A. 41°55N 73°4W 83 E11
Winston-Salem U.S.A. 36°6N 80°15W 85 C14
Winter Garden U.S.A. 28°34N 81°35W 85 G14
Winter Haven U.S.A. 28°1N 81°44W 85 G14
Winter Park U.S.A. 28°36N 81°20W 85 G14
Winterhaven U.S.A. 32°44N 114°38W 79 N12
Winters U.S.A. 38°32N 121°58W 78 G5
Winterset U.S.A. 41°20N 94°1W 80 E6
Wintersville U.S.A. 40°23N 80°42W 82 F4
Winterswijk Neths. 51°58N 6°43E 15 C6
Winterthur Switz. 47°30N 8°44E 20 C8
Winthrop U.S.A. 48°28N 120°10W 76 B3
Winton Australia 22°24S 143°3E 62 C3
Winton N.Z. 46°8S 168°20E 59 G2
Wirlyajarrayi ✪ Australia 21°45S 132°35E 60 D5
Wirrulla Australia 32°24S 134°31E 63 E1
Wisbech U.K. 52°41N 0°9E 13 E8
Wisconsin □ U.S.A. 44°45N 89°30W 80 C9
Wisconsin → U.S.A. 43°0N 91°15W 80 D8
Wisconsin Rapids U.S.A. 44°23N 89°49W 80 C9
Wisdom U.S.A. 45°37N 113°27W 76 D7
Wiseman U.S.A. 67°25N 150°6W 74 B9
Wishaw U.K. 55°46N 3°54W 11 F5
Wishek U.S.A. 46°16N 99°33W 80 B4
Wisła → Poland 54°22N 18°55E 17 A10
Wismar Germany 53°54N 11°29E 16 B6
Wisner U.S.A. 41°59N 96°55W 80 E5
Witbank = eMalahleni S. Africa 25°51S 29°14E 57 D4
Witdraai S. Africa 26°58S 20°48E 56 D3
Witham U.K. 51°48N 0°40E 13 F8
Witham → U.K. 52°59N 0°2W 12 E7
Withernsea U.K. 53°44N 0°1E 12 D8
Witjira △ Australia 26°22S 135°37E 63 D2
Witless Bay Canada 47°17N 52°50W 73 C9
Witney U.K. 51°48N 1°28W 13 F6
Witnossob → Namibia 23°55S 18°45E 56 D3
Witrivier S. Africa 25°20S 31°0E 57 D5
Wittenberge Germany 53°0N 11°45E 16 B6
Wittenoom Australia 22°15S 118°20E 60 D2
Witu Kenya 2°23S 40°26E 54 C5
Witvlei Namibia 22°23S 18°32E 56 C2
Wiwon N. Korea 40°54N 126°3E 35 D14
Wkra → Poland 52°27N 20°44E 17 B11
Wlingi Indonesia 8°5S 112°25E 37 H15
Włocławek Poland 52°40N 19°3E 17 B10
Włodawa Poland 51°33N 23°31E 17 C12
Woburn U.S.A. 42°29N 71°9W 83 D13
Wodian China 32°50N 112°35E 34 H7
Wodonga Australia 36°5S 146°50E 63 F4
Wokam Indonesia 5°45S 134°28E 37 F8
Woking U.K. 51°19N 0°34W 13 F7
Wokingham U.K. 51°24N 0°49W 13 F7
Wokingham □ U.K. 51°25N 0°51W 13 F7
Wolf → Canada 60°17N 132°33W 70 A2
Wolf Creek U.S.A. 47°0N 112°4W 76 C7
Wolf L. Canada 60°24N 131°40W 70 A2
Wolf Point U.S.A. 48°5N 105°39W 76 B11
Wolfe Creek Crater △ Australia 19°10S 127°47E 60 C4
Wolfe I. Canada 44°7N 76°20W 83 B8
Wolfeboro U.S.A. 43°35N 71°13W 83 C13
Wolfsberg Austria 46°50N 14°52E 16 E8
Wolfsburg Germany 52°25N 10°48E 16 B6
Wolin Poland 53°50N 14°37E 16 B8
Wollaston, Is. Chile 55°40S 67°30W 96 H3

Wollaston L. Canada 58°7N 103°10W 71 B8
Wollaston Lake Canada 58°3N 103°33W 71 B8
Wollaston Pen. Canada 69°30N 115°0W 68 D9
Wollongong Australia 34°25S 150°54E 63 E5
Wolmaransstad S. Africa 27°12S 25°59E 56 D4
Wolseley S. Africa 33°26S 19°7E 56 E2
Wolsey U.S.A. 44°25N 98°28W 80 C4
Wolstenholme, C.
Canada 62°35N 77°30W 66 C12
Wolvega Neths. 52°52N 6°0E 15 B6
Wolverhampton U.K. 52°35N 2°7W 13 E5
Wondai Australia 26°20S 151°49E 63 D5
Wongalarroo L. Australia 31°32S 144°0E 63 E3
Wongan Hills Australia 30°51S 116°37E 61 F2
Wonju S. Korea 37°22N 127°58E 35 F14
Wonosari Indonesia 7°58S 110°36E 37 G14
Wonosobo Indonesia 7°22S 109°54E 37 G13
Wonowon Canada 56°44N 121°48W 70 B4
Wŏnsan N. Korea 39°11N 127°27E 35 E14
Wonthaggi Australia 38°37S 145°37E 63 F4
Wood Buffalo △ Canada 59°0N 113°41W 70 B6
Wood Is. Australia 16°24S 123°19F 60 C3
Wood L. Canada 55°17N 103°17W 71 B8
Woodah, I. Australia 13°27S 136°10E 62 A2
Woodbourne U.S.A. 41°46N 74°36W 83 E10
Woodbridge Canada 43°47N 79°36W 82 C5
Woodbridge U.K. 52°6N 1°20E 13 E9
Woodburn Australia 29°6S 153°23E 63 A5
Woodburn U.S.A. 45°9N 122°51W 76 D2
Woodenbong Australia 28°24S 152°39E 63 D5
Woodend Australia 37°20S 144°33E 63 F3
Woodford Australia 26°58S 152°47E 63 D5
Woodfords U.S.A. 38°47N 119°50W 78 G7
Woodlake U.S.A. 36°25N 119°6W 78 J7
Woodland Calif., U.S.A. 38°41N 121°46W 78 G5
Woodland Maine, U.S.A. 45°9N 67°25W 81 C20
Woodland Pa., U.S.A. 41°0N 78°21W 82 F6
Woodland Wash.,
U.S.A. 45°54N 122°45W 78 E4
Woodland Caribou △
Canada 51°0N 94°45W 71 C10
Woodlands Singapore 1°26N 103°46E 39 d
Woodlands, The U.S.A. 30°9N 95°29W 84 F7
Woodonga Australia 36°10S 146°50E 63 F4
Woodridge Canada 49°20N 96°9W 71 D9
Woodroffe, Mt.
Australia 26°20S 131°45E 61 E5
Woods, L. Australia 17°50S 133°30E 62 B1
Woods, L. of the
N. Amer. 49°15N 94°45W 71 D10
Woodstock Australia 19°35S 146°50E 62 B4
Woodstock N.B., Canada 46°11N 67°37W 73 C6
Woodstock Ont., Canada 43°10N 80°45W 82 D4
Woodstock U.K. 51°51N 1°20W 13 F6
Woodstock Ill., U.S.A. 42°19N 88°27W 80 D9
Woodstock N.Y., U.S.A. 42°2N 74°7W 83 D10
Woodstock Vt., U.S.A. 43°37N 72°31W 83 C12
Woodsville U.S.A. 44°9N 72°2W 83 B13
Woodview Canada 44°35N 78°8W 82 B6
Woodville N.Z. 40°20S 175°53E 59 D5
Woodville Miss., U.S.A. 31°6N 91°18W 84 F9
Woodville Tex., U.S.A. 30°47N 94°25W 84 F7
Woodward U.S.A. 36°26N 99°24W 84 C5
Woody U.S.A. 35°42N 118°50W 79 K8
Woody → Canada 52°31N 100°51W 71 C8
Woolacombe U.K. 51°10N 4°13W 13 F3
Woolamai, C. Australia 38°30S 145°23E 63 F4
Wooler U.K. 55°33N 2°1W 12 B5
Woolgoolga Australia 30°6S 153°11E 63 E5
Woomera Australia 31°5S 136°50E 63 E2
Woonsocket R.I., U.S.A. 42°0N 71°31W 83 E13
Woonsocket S. Dak.,
U.S.A. 44°3N 98°17W 80 C4
Wooramel → Australia 25°47S 114°10E 61 E1
Wooramel Roadhouse
Australia 25°45S 114°17E 61 E1
Wooroonooran △
Australia 16°25S 146°1E 62 B4
Wooster U.S.A. 40°48N 81°56W 82 F3
Worcester S. Africa 33°39S 19°27E 56 E2
Worcester U.K. 52°11N 2°12W 13 E5
Worcester Mass.,
U.S.A. 42°16N 71°48W 83 D13
Worcester N.Y., U.S.A. 42°36N 74°45W 83 D10
Worcestershire □ U.K. 52°13N 2°10W 13 E5
Workington U.K. 54°39N 3°33W 12 C4
Worksop U.K. 53°18N 1°7W 12 D6
Workum Neths. 52°59N 5°26E 15 B5
Worland U.S.A. 44°1N 107°57W 76 D10
Worms Germany 49°37N 8°21E 16 D5
Worsley Canada 56°31N 119°8W 70 B5
Wortham U.S.A. 31°47N 96°28W 84 F6
Worthing Barbados 13°5S 59°35W 89 g
Worthing U.K. 50°49N 0°21W 13 G7
Worthington Minn.,
U.S.A. 43°37N 95°36W 80 D6
Worthington Pa., U.S.A. 40°50N 79°38W 82 F5
Wosi Indonesia 0°15S 128°0E 37 E7
Wote Kenya 1°47S 37°38E 54 C4
Wotjalum ✪ Australia 16°30S 123°45E 60 C3
Wotjobaluk △ Australia 37°0S 142°0E 63 F3
Wou-han = Wuhan
China 30°31N 114°18E 33 C6
Wousi = Wuxi China 31°33N 120°18E 33 C7
Wowoni Indonesia 4°5S 123°5E 37 E6
Wrangel I. = Vrangelya, Ostrov
Russia 71°0N 180°0E 29 B18
Wrangell U.S.A. 56°28N 132°23W 70 B2
Wrangell Mts. U.S.A. 61°30N 142°0W 68 C5
Wrath, C. U.K. 58°38N 5°1W 11 C3
Wray U.S.A. 40°5N 102°13W 76 F12
Wrekin, The U.K. 52°41N 2°32W 13 E5
Wrens U.S.A. 33°12N 82°23W 85 E13
Wrexham U.K. 53°3N 3°0W 12 D5
Wrexham □ U.K. 53°1N 2°58W 12 D5
Wright Fla., U.S.A. 30°27N 86°38W 85 F11
Wright Wyo., U.S.A. 43°45N 105°28W 76 E11
Wright Pt. Canada 43°48N 81°44W 82 C3

Wrightson, Mt. U.S.A. 31°42N 110°51W 77 L8
Wrightwood U.S.A. 34°22N 117°38W 79 L9
Wrigley Canada 63°16N 123°37W 68 E7
Wrocław Poland 51°5N 17°5E 17 C9
Września Poland 52°21N 17°36E 17 B9
Wu Jiang → China 29°40N 107°20E 32 D5
Wu Kau Tang China 22°30N 114°14E 33 F11
Wu'an China 36°40N 114°15E 34 F8
Wubalawun ✪ Australia 15°28S 133°1E 60 C5
Wubin Australia 30°6S 116°37E 61 F2
Wubu China 37°28N 110°42E 34 F6
Wuchang China 44°55N 127°5E 35 B14
Wucheng China 37°12N 116°20E 34 F9
Wuchuan China 41°5N 111°28E 34 D6
Wudi China 37°40N 117°35E 35 F9
Wuding He → China 37°2N 110°23E 34 F6
Wudinna Australia 33°0S 135°22E 63 E2
Wudu China 33°22N 104°54E 34 H3
Wuguishan China 22°25N 113°25E 33 G9
Wugullar = Beswick
Australia 14°34S 132°53E 60 B5
Wuhai China 39°47N 106°52E 32 C5
Wuhan China 30°31N 114°18E 33 C6
Wuhe China 33°10N 117°50E 35 H9
Wuhsi = Wuxi China 31°33N 120°18E 33 C7
Wuhu China 31°22N 118°21E 33 C6
Wukari Nigeria 7°51N 9°42E 50 G7
Wulajie China 44°6N 126°33E 35 B14
Wulanbulang China 41°5N 110°55E 34 D6
Wular L. India 34°20N 74°30E 43 B6
Wuliaru Indonesia 7°27S 131°0E 37 F8
Wulumuchi = Ürümqi
China 43°45N 87°45E 32 B3
Wundanyi Kenya 3°25S 38°22E 54 C4
Wunnummin L. Canada 52°55N 89°10W 72 B2
Wuntho Burma 23°55N 95°45E 41 H19
Wupatki △ U.S.A. 35°35N 111°20W 77 J8
Wuppertal Germany 51°16N 7°12E 16 C4
Wuppertal S. Africa 32°13S 19°12E 56 E2
Wuqing China 39°23N 117°4E 35 E9
Wurralibi ✪ Australia 15°43S 137°1E 62 B2
Wurtsboro U.S.A. 41°35N 74°29W 83 E10
Würzburg Germany 49°46N 9°55E 16 D5
Wushan China 34°43N 104°53E 34 G3
Wushi China 41°9N 79°13E 32 B2
Wutai China 38°40N 113°12E 34 E7
Wuting = Huimin
China 37°27N 117°28E 35 F9
Wutonghaolai China 42°50N 120°5E 35 C11
Wutongqiao China 29°22N 103°50E 32 D5
Wuwei China 37°57N 102°34E 32 C5
Wuxi China 31°33N 120°18E 33 C7
Wuxiang China 36°49N 112°50E 34 F7
Wuyang China 33°25N 113°35E 34 H7
Wuyi China 37°46N 115°56E 34 F8
Wuyi Shan China 27°0N 117°0E 33 D6
Wuyuan China 41°2N 108°20E 34 D5
Wuzhai China 38°54N 111°48E 34 E6
Wuzhi Shan China 18°45N 109°45E 38 C7
Wuzhong China 38°2N 106°12E 34 E4
Wuzhou China 23°30N 111°18E 33 D6
Wyaaba Cr. →
Australia 16°27S 141°35E 62 B3
Wyalkatchem Australia 31°8S 117°22E 61 F2
Wyalusing U.S.A. 41°40N 76°16W 83 E8
Wyandotte U.S.A. 42°12N 83°9W 81 D12
Wyandra Australia 27°12S 145°56E 63 D4
Wyangala, L. Australia 33°54S 149°0E 63 E4
Wyara, L. Australia 28°42S 144°14E 63 D3
Wycheproof Australia 36°5S 143°17E 63 F3
Wycliffe Well Australia 20°48S 134°14E 62 C1
Wye → U.K. 51°38N 2°40W 13 F5
Wyemandoo Australia 28°28S 118°29E 61 E2
Wymondham U.K. 52°35N 1°7E 13 E9
Wymore U.S.A. 40°7N 96°40W 80 E5
Wyndham Australia 15°33S 128°3E 60 C4
Wyndham N.Z. 46°20S 168°51E 59 G2
Wynne U.S.A. 35°14N 90°47W 85 D9
Wynyard Australia 41°5S 145°44E 63 G4
Wynyard Canada 51°45N 104°10W 71 C8
Wyola L. Australia 29°8S 130°17E 61 E5
Wyoming Canada 42°57N 82°7W 82 D2
Wyoming □ U.S.A. 43°0N 107°30W 76 E10
Wyomissing U.S.A. 40°20N 75°59W 83 F9
Wyong Australia 33°14S 151°24E 63 E5
Wytheville U.S.A. 36°57N 81°5W 81 G13

X

Xaafuun Somali Rep. 10°25N 51°16E 47 E5
Xaafuun, Ras Somali Rep. 10°27N 51°24E 47 E5
Xaçmaz Azerbaijan 41°31N 48°42E 19 F8
Xai-Xai Mozam. 25°6S 33°31E 57 D5
Xalapa Mexico 19°32N 96°55W 87 D5
Xangongo Angola 16°45S 15°5E 56 B2
Xankändi Azerbaijan 39°52N 46°49E 44 B5
Xanthi Greece 41°10N 24°58E 23 D11
Xanxerê Brazil 26°53S 52°23W 95 B5
Xapuri Brazil 10°35S 68°35W 92 F5
Xar Moron He →
China 43°25N 120°35E 35 C11
Xátiva Spain 38°59N 0°32W 21 C5
Xau, L. Botswana 21°15S 24°44E 56 C3
Xavantina Brazil 21°15S 52°48W 95 A5
Xenia U.S.A. 39°41N 83°56W 81 F12
Xeropotamos →
Cyprus 34°42N 32°33E 25 E11
Xhora S. Africa 31°55S 28°38E 57 E4
Xhumo Botswana 21°7S 24°35E 56 C3
Xi Jiang → China 22°5N 113°20E 33 D6
Xi Xian China 36°41N 110°58E 34 F6
Xia Xian China 35°8N 111°12E 34 G6
Xiachengzi China 44°40N 130°18E 35 B16
Xiaguan China 25°32N 100°16E 32 D5
Xiajin China 36°56N 116°0E 34 F9
Xiamen China 24°25N 118°4E 33 D6

Xi'an China 34°15N 109°0E 34 G5
Xi Xian China 38°12N 116°6E 34 E9
Xiang Jiang → China 28°55N 112°50E 33 D6
Xiangcheng Henan,
China 33°29N 114°52E 34 H8
Xiangcheng Henan,
China 33°50N 113°27E 34 H7
Xiangfan China 32°2N 112°8E 33 C6
Xianggang = Hong Kong □
China 22°11N 114°14E 33 G11
Xianghuang Qi China 42°2N 113°50E 34 C7
Xiangning China 35°58N 110°50E 34 G6
Xiangquan China 36°30N 113°1E 34 F7
Xiangquan He = Sutlej →
Pakistan 29°23N 71°3E 42 E4
Xiangshui China 34°12N 119°33E 35 G10
Xiangtan China 27°51N 112°54E 33 D6
Xianyang China 34°20N 108°40E 34 G5
Xiao Hinggan Ling China 49°0N 127°0E 33 B7
Xiao Xian China 34°15N 116°55E 34 G9
Xiaoyi China 37°8N 111°48E 34 F6
Xiawa China 42°35N 120°38E 35 C11
Xiayi China 34°15N 116°10E 34 G9
Xichang China 27°51N 102°19E 32 D5
Xichuan China 33°0N 111°30E 34 H6
Xieng Khouang Laos 19°17N 103°25E 38 C4
Xifei He → China 32°45N 116°40E 34 H9
Xifeng Gansu, China 35°40N 107°40E 34 G4
Xifeng Liaoning, China 42°42N 124°45E 35 C13
Xifengzhen = Xifeng
China 35°40N 107°40E 34 G4
Xigazê China 29°5N 88°45E 32 D3
Xihe China 34°2N 105°20E 34 G3
Xihua China 33°45N 114°30E 34 H8
Xili Shuiku China 22°36N 113°57E 33 F10
Xiliao He → China 43°32N 123°35E 35 C12
Xilinhot China 43°52N 116°2E 34 C9
Ximana Mozam. 19°24S 33°58E 55 F3
Xin Xian = Xinzhou
China 38°22N 112°46E 34 E7
Xinavane Mozam. 25°2S 32°47E 57 D5
Xinbin China 41°40N 125°2E 35 D13
Xincun China 38°15N 117°45E 34 E9
Xing Xian China 38°27N 111°7E 34 E6
Xing'an China 25°38N 110°40E 33 D6
Xingcheng China 40°40N 120°45E 35 D11
Xinghe China 40°55N 113°55E 34 D7
Xinglong China 33°58N 110°49E 34 H6
Xingning China 24°3N 115°42E 33 D6
Xingping China 34°20N 108°28E 34 G5
Xingtai China 37°3N 114°32E 34 F8
Xingu → Brazil 1°30S 51°53W 93 D8
Xingyang China 34°45N 112°52E 34 G7
Xingyi China 25°3N 104°59E 32 D5
Xinhe China 37°30N 115°4E 34 F8
Xining China 36°34N 101°40E 32 C5
Xinjiang China 35°34N 111°11E 34 G6
Xinjiang Uygur Zizhiqu □
China 42°0N 86°0E 32 C3
Xinjin = Pulandian
China 39°25N 121°58E 35 E11
Xinkai He → China 43°32N 123°35E 35 C12
Xinken China 22°39N 113°36E 33 F10
Xinle China 38°25N 114°40E 34 E8
Xinlitun China 42°0N 122°8E 35 D12
Xinmin China 41°59N 122°50E 35 D12
Xintai China 35°55N 117°45E 35 G9
Xinwan China 22°47N 113°40E 33 F10
Xinxiang China 35°18N 113°50E 34 G7
Xinzhan China 43°50N 127°18E 35 C14
Xinzheng China 34°20N 113°45E 34 G7
Xinzhou Hainan, China 19°43N 109°17E 38 C7
Xinzhou Shanxi, China 38°22N 112°46E 34 E7
Xiongyuecheng China 40°12N 122°5E 35 D12
Xiping Henan, China 33°22N 114°5E 34 H8
Xiping Henan, China 33°25N 111°8E 34 H6
Xique-Xique Brazil 10°50S 42°40W 93 F10
Xisha Qundao = Paracel Is.
S. China Sea 15°50N 112°0E 36 A4
Xiuyan China 40°18N 123°11E 35 D12
Xixabangma Feng
China 28°20N 85°40E 43 E11
Xixia China 33°25N 111°29E 34 H6
Xixiang China 33°0N 107°44E 34 H4
Xtxón = Gijón Spain 43°32N 5°42W 21 A3
Xiyang China 37°38N 113°38E 34 F7
Xizang Zizhiqu □ China 32°0N 88°0E 32 C3
Xlendi Malta 36°1N 14°12E 25 C1
Xochob Mexico 19°21N 89°48W 87 D7
Xuan Loc Vietnam 10°56N 107°14E 39 G6
Xuanhua China 40°40N 115°2E 34 D8
Xuchang China 34°2N 113°48E 34 G7
Xun Xian China 35°42N 114°33E 34 G8
Xunyang China 32°48N 109°22E 34 H5
Xunyi China 35°8N 108°20E 34 G5
Xuyen Moc Vietnam 10°34N 107°25E 39 G6
Xuzhou China 34°18N 117°10E 35 G9
Xylophagou Cyprus 34°54N 33°51E 25 E12

Y

Ya Xian = Sanya China 18°14N 109°29E 38 C7
Yaamba Australia 23°8S 150°22E 62 C5
Yaapeet Australia 35°45S 142°3E 63 F3
Yablonovyy Khrebet
Russia 53°0N 114°0E 29 D12
Yablonovyy Ra. = Yablonovyy
Khrebet Russia 53°0N 114°0E 29 D12
Yabrai Shan China 39°40N 103°0E 34 E2
Yabrūd Syria 33°58N 36°39E 46 B5
Yabucoa Puerto Rico 18°3N 65°53W 89 d
Yacambú △ Venezuela 9°42N 69°27W 89 E6
Yacheng China 18°22N 109°6E 38 C7
Yacuiba Bolivia 22°0S 63°43W 94 A3
Yacuma → Bolivia 13°38S 65°23W 92 F5
Yadgir India 16°45N 77°5E 40 L10

Yadkin → U.S.A. 35°23N 80°4W 85 D14
Yadua Fiji 16°49S 178°18E 59 a
Yaeyama-Rettō Japan 24°30N 123°40E 31 M1
Yagasa Cluster Fiji 18°57S 178°28W 59 a
Yagodnoye Russia 62°33N 149°40E 29 C15
Yahila
Dem. Rep. of the Congo 0°13N 24°28E 54 B1
Yahk Canada 49°6N 116°10W 70 D5
Yahuma
Dem. Rep. of the Congo 1°0N 23°10E 52 D4
Yaita Japan 36°48N 139°56E 31 F9
Yaiza Canary Is. 28°57N 13°46W 24 F6
Yakima U.S.A. 46°36N 120°31W 76 C3
Yakima → U.S.A. 46°15N 119°14W 76 C4
Yakishiri-Jima Japan 44°26N 141°25E 30 B10
Yakobi I. U.S.A. 58°0N 136°30W 70 B1
Yakovlevka Russia 44°26N 133°28E 30 B6
Yaku-Shima Japan 30°20N 130°30E 31 J5
Yakumo Japan 42°15N 140°16E 30 C10
Yakutat U.S.A. 59°33N 139°44W 68 F4
Yakutat B. U.S.A. 59°45N 140°45W 74 D11
Yakutia = Sakha □
Russia 66°0N 130°0E 29 C14
Yakutsk Russia 62°5N 129°50E 29 C13
Yala Thailand 6°33N 101°18E 39 J3
Yalata Australia 31°59S 132°6E 61 F5
Yalata ✪ Australia 31°35S 132°7E 61 F5
Yalboroo Australia 20°50S 148°40E 62 b
Yale U.S.A. 43°8N 82°48W 82 C2
Yalgorup △ Australia 32°39S 115°38E 61 F2
Yalinga C.A.R. 6°33N 23°10E 52 C4
Yalkabul, Pta. Mexico 21°32N 88°37W 87 C7
Yalleroi Australia 24°3S 145°42E 62 C4
Yalobusha → U.S.A. 33°33N 90°10W 85 E9
Yalong Jiang → China 26°40N 101°55E 32 D5
Yalova Turkey 40°41N 29°15E 23 D13
Yalpirakinu ✪ Australia 22°24S 132°15E 60 D5
Yalta Ukraine 44°30N 34°10E 19 F5
Yalu Jiang → China 39°55N 124°19E 35 E13
Yam Australia 9°54S 142°46E 62 a
Yam Ha Melah = Dead Sea
Asia 31°30N 35°30E 46 D4
Yam Kinneret Israel 32°45N 35°35E 46 C4
Yamada Japan 33°33N 130°49E 31 H5
Yamagata Japan 38°15N 140°15E 30 E10
Yamagata □ Japan 38°30N 140°0E 30 E10
Yamaguchi Japan 34°10N 131°32E 31 G5
Yamaguchi □ Japan 34°20N 131°40E 31 G5
Yamal, Poluostrov Russia 71°0N 70°0E 28 B8
Yamal Pen. = Yamal, Poluostrov
Russia 71°0N 70°0E 28 B8
Yamanashi □ Japan 35°40N 138°40E 31 G9
Yamantau, Gora Russia 54°15N 58°6E 18 D10
Yamato Ridge
Sea of Japan 39°20N 135°0E 30 E7
Yamba Australia 29°26S 153°23E 63 D5
Yambarran Ra.
Australia 15°10S 130°25E 60 C5
Yambio Sudan 4°35N 28°16E 51 H11
Yambol Bulgaria 42°30N 26°30E 23 C12
Yamburg Russia 68°21N 77°8E 28 C8
Yamdena Indonesia 7°45S 131°20E 37 F8
Yame Japan 33°13N 130°35E 31 H5
Yamethin Burma 20°29N 96°18E 41 J20
Yamma Yamma, L.
Australia 26°16S 141°20E 63 D3
Yamoussoukro Ivory C. 6°49N 5°17W 50 G4
Yampa → U.S.A. 40°32N 108°59W 76 F9
Yampi Sd. Australia 16°8S 123°38E 60 C3
Yampil Moldova 48°15N 28°15E 17 D15
Yampol = Yampil
Moldova 48°15N 28°15E 17 D15
Yamuna → India 25°30N 81°53E 43 G9
Yamunanagar India 30°7N 77°17E 42 D7
Yamzho Yumco China 28°48N 90°35E 32 D4
Yana → Russia 71°30N 136°0E 29 B14
Yanagawa Japan 33°10N 130°24E 31 H5
Yanai Japan 33°58N 132°7E 31 H6
Yan'an China 36°35N 109°26E 34 F5
Yanaul Russia 56°25N 55°0E 18 C10
Yanbu 'al Baḥr Si. Arabia 24°0N 38°5E 44 F3
Yanchang China 36°43N 110°1E 34 F6
Yancheng Henan, China 33°35N 114°0E 34 H8
Yancheng Jiangsu, China 33°23N 120°8E 35 H11
Yanchep Australia 31°33S 115°37E 61 F2
Yanchi China 37°48N 107°20E 34 F4
Yanchuan China 36°51N 110°10E 34 F6
Yanco Cr. → Australia 35°14S 145°35E 63 F4
Yandeyarra ✪ Australia 21°17S 118°24E 60 D2
Yandicoogina Australia 22°45S 119°12E 60 D2
Yandoon Burma 17°0N 95°40E 41 L19
Yang Xian China 33°15N 107°30E 34 H4
Yang-yang S. Korea 38°4N 128°38E 35 E15
Yangambi
Dem. Rep. of the Congo 0°47N 24°24E 54 B1
Yangcheng China 35°28N 112°22E 34 G7
Yangch'ü = Taiyuan
China 37°52N 112°33E 34 F7
Yanggao China 40°21N 113°55E 34 D7
Yanggu China 36°8N 115°43E 34 F8
Yangliuqing China 39°2N 117°5E 35 E9
Yangon = Rangoon
Burma 16°45N 96°20E 41 L20
Yangpingguan China 32°58N 106°5E 34 H4
Yangquan China 37°58N 113°31E 34 F7
Yangtse = Chang Jiang →
China 31°48N 121°10E 33 C7
Yangtze Kiang = Chang Jiang →
China 31°48N 121°10E 33 C7
Yangyuan China 40°1N 114°10E 34 D8
Yangzhou China 32°21N 119°26E 33 C6
Yanji China 42°59N 129°30E 35 C15
Yankton U.S.A. 42°53N 97°23W 80 D5
Yankunytjatjara-Antakirinja ✪
Australia 27°20S 134°30E 63 A1
Yanonge
Dem. Rep. of the Congo 0°35N 24°38E 54 B1
Yanqi China 42°5N 86°35E 32 B3
Yanqing China 40°30N 115°58E 34 D8

Yanshan China 38°4N 117°22E 35 E9
Yantabulla Australia 29°21S 145°0E 63 D4
Yantai China 37°34N 121°22E 35 F11
Yantian China 22°35N 114°16E 33 F11
Yanuca Fiji 18°24S 178°0E 59 a
Yanzhou China 35°35N 116°49E 34 G9
Yao Noi, Ko Thailand 8°7N 98°37E 39 a
Yao Xian China 34°55N 108°59E 34 G5
Yao Yai, Ko Thailand 8°0N 98°35E 39 a
Yaoundé Cameroon 3°50N 11°35E 52 D2
Yaowan China 34°15N 118°3E 35 G10
Yap Pac. Oc. 9°30N 138°10E 64 G5
Yapen Indonesia 1°50S 136°0E 37 E9
Yapen, Selat Indonesia 1°20S 136°10E 37 E9
Yapero Indonesia 4°59S 137°11E 37 E9
Yappar → Australia 18°22S 141°16E 62 B3
Yapuparra ✪ Australia 27°15S 126°20E 61 E4
Yaqaga Fiji 16°35S 178°36E 59 a
Yaqui → Mexico 27°37N 110°39W 86 B2
Yar-Sale Russia 66°50N 70°50E 28 C8
Yaraka Australia 24°53S 144°3E 62 C3
Yaransk Russia 57°22N 47°49E 18 C8
Yare → U.K. 52°35N 1°38E 13 E9
Yaremcha Ukraine 48°27N 24°33E 17 D13
Yarensk Russia 62°11N 49°15E 18 B8
Yarí → Colombia 0°20S 72°20W 92 D4
Yarkand = Shache
China 38°20N 77°10E 32 C2
Yarkant He → China 40°26N 80°59E 32 B3
Yarker Canada 44°23N 76°46W 83 B8
Yarkhun → Pakistan 36°17N 72°30E 43 A5
Yarlung Ziangbo Jiang = Brahmaputra →
Asia 23°40N 90°35E 43 H13
Yarmouth Canada 43°50N 66°7W 73 D6
Yarmūk → Syria 32°42N 35°40E 46 C4
Yaroslavl Russia 57°35N 39°55E 18 C6
Yarra Yarra Lakes
Australia 29°40S 115°45E 61 E1
Yarram Australia 38°29S 146°39E 63 F4
Yarraman Australia 26°50S 152°0E 63 D5
Yarras Australia 31°25S 152°20E 63 E5
Yarrie Australia 20°40S 120°12E 60 D3
Yartsevo Russia 60°20N 90°0E 29 C10
Yarumal Colombia 6°58N 75°24W 92 B3
Yasawa Group Fiji 17°0S 177°23E 59 a
Yaselda Belarus 52°7N 26°28E 17 B14
Yasin Pakistan 36°24N 73°23E 43 A5
Yasinski, L. Canada 53°16N 77°35W 72 B4
Yasinya Ukraine 48°16N 24°21E 17 D13
Yasothon Thailand 15°50N 104°10E 38 E5
Yass Australia 34°49S 148°54E 63 E4
Yāsūj Iran 30°31N 51°31E 45 D6
Yatağan Turkey 37°20N 28°10E 23 F13
Yates Center U.S.A. 37°53N 95°44W 80 G7
Yathkyed L. Canada 62°40N 98°0W 71 A9
Yatsushiro Japan 32°30N 130°40E 31 H5
Yatta Plateau Kenya 2°0S 38°0E 54 C4
Yauco Puerto Rico 18°2N 66°51W 89 d
Yavari → Peru 4°21S 70°2W 92 D4
Yávaros Mexico 26°42N 109°31W 86 B3
Yavatmal India 20°20N 78°15E 40 J11
Yavne Israel 31°52N 34°45E 46 D3
Yavoriv Ukraine 49°55N 23°20E 17 D12
Yavorov = Yavoriv
Ukraine 49°55N 23°20E 17 D12
Yawatahama Japan 33°27N 132°24E 31 H6
Yawri B. S. Leone 8°22N 13°0W 50 G3
Yaxian = Sanya China 18°14N 109°29E 38 C7
Yazd Iran 31°55N 54°27E 45 D7
Yazd □ Iran 32°0N 55°0E 45 D7
Yazd-e Khvāst Iran 31°31N 52°7E 45 D7
Yazman Pakistan 29°8N 71°45E 42 E4
Yazoo → U.S.A. 32°22N 90°54W 85 E9
Yazoo City U.S.A. 32°51N 90°25W 85 E9
Ybycuí △ Paraguay 26°5S 56°46W 94 B4
Ybytyruzú △ Paraguay 25°51S 56°11W 95 B4
Ye Burma 15°15N 97°15E 38 E1
Ye Xian China 33°35N 113°25E 34 H7
Yebyu Burma 14°15N 98°13E 38 E2
Yecheng China 37°54N 77°26E 32 C2
Yecheon S. Korea 36°39N 128°27E 35 F15
Yecla Spain 38°35N 1°5W 21 C5
Yécora Mexico 28°20N 108°58W 86 B3
Yedintsy = Edineţ
Moldova 48°9N 27°18E 17 D14
Yegros Paraguay 26°20S 56°25W 94 B4
Yehbuah Indonesia 8°23S 114°45E 37 J17
Yehuda, Midbar Israel 31°35N 35°15E 46 D4
Yei Sudan 4°9N 30°40E 51 H12
Yekaterinburg Russia 56°50N 60°30E 28 D7
Yelarbon Australia 28°33S 150°38E 63 D5
Yelets Russia 52°40N 38°30E 18 D6
Yelizavetgrad = Kirovohrad
Ukraine 48°35N 32°20E 19 E5
Yelizovo Russia 53°11N 158°23E 29 D16
Yell U.K. 60°35N 1°5W 11 A7
Yell Sd. U.K. 60°33N 1°15W 11 A7
Yellow = Huang He →
China 37°55N 118°50E 35 F10
Yellow Sea China 35°0N 123°0E 35 G12
Yellowhead Pass
Canada 52°53N 118°25W 70 C5
Yellowknife Canada 62°27N 114°29W 70 A6
Yellowknife → Canada 62°31N 114°19W 70 A6
Yellowstone →
U.S.A. 47°59N 103°59W 76 C12
Yellowstone △ U.S.A. 44°40N 110°30W 76 D8
Yellowstone L. U.S.A. 44°27N 110°22W 76 D8
Yelsk Belarus 51°50N 29°10E 17 C15
Yemen ■ Asia 15°0N 44°0E 47 E3
Yen Bai Vietnam 21°42N 104°52E 38 B5
Yenangyaung Burma 20°30N 95°0E 41 J19
Yenbo = Yanbu 'al Baḥr
Si. Arabia 24°0N 38°5E 44 F3
Yenda Australia 34°13S 146°14E 63 E4

Yeni Erenköy = Yialousa
  Cyprus 35°32N 34°10E **25** D13
Yenice Turkey 39°55N 27°17E **23** E12
Yenisey → Russia 71°50N 82°40E **28** B9
Yeniseysk Russia 58°27N 92°13E **29** D10
Yenyuka Russia 57°57N 121°15E **29** D13
Yeo → U.K. 51°2N 2°49W **13** G5
Yeo, L. Australia 28°0S 124°30E **61** E3
Yeo I. Canada 45°24N 81°48W **82** A3
Yeoju S. Korea 37°20N 127°35E **35** F14
Yeola India 20°2N 74°30E **40** J9
Yeong-wol S. Korea 37°11N 128°28E **35** F15
Yeongcheon S. Korea 35°58N 128°56E **35** G15
Yeongdeok S. Korea 36°24N 129°22E **35** F15
Yeongdeungpo
  S. Korea 37°31N 126°54E **35** F14
Yeongdong S. Korea 36°10N 127°46E **35** F14
Yeongju S. Korea 36°50N 128°40E **35** F15
Yeosu S. Korea 34°47N 127°45E **35** G14
Yeotmal = Yavatmal
  India 20°20N 78°15E **40** J11
Yeovil U.K. 50°57N 2°38W **13** G5
Yeppoon Australia 23°5S 150°47E **62** C5
Yerbent Turkmenistan 39°30N 58°50E **28** F6
Yerbogachen Russia 61°16N 108°0E **29** C11
Yerevan Armenia 40°10N 44°31E **44** A5
Yerington U.S.A. 38°59N 119°10W **76** G4
Yermak Kazakhstan 52°2N 76°55E **28** D8
Yermo U.S.A. 34°54N 116°50W **79** L10
Yerólakkos Cyprus 35°11N 33°15E **25** D12
Yeropol Russia 65°15N 168°40E **29** C17
Yeroskipos Cyprus 34°46N 32°28E **25** E11
Yershov Russia 51°23N 48°27E **19** D8
Yerushalayim = Jerusalem
  Israel/West Bank 31°47N 35°10E **46** D4
Yes Tor U.K. 50°41N 4°0W **13** G4
Yesan S. Korea 36°41N 126°51E **35** F14
Yeso U.S.A. 34°26N 104°37W **77** J11
Yessey Russia 68°29N 102°10E **29** C11
Yetman Australia 28°56S 150°48E **63** D5
Yeu, Î. d' France 46°42N 2°20W **20** C2
Yevpatoriya Ukraine 45°15N 33°20E **19** E5
Yeysk Russia 46°40N 38°12E **19** E6
Yezd = Yazd Iran 31°55N 54°27E **45** D7
Ygatimi Paraguay 24°5S 55°40W **95** A4
Yhati Paraguay 25°45S 56°35W **94** B4
Yhú Paraguay 25°0S 56°0W **95** B4
Yí → Uruguay 33°7S 57°8W **94** C4
Yi 'Allaq, G. Egypt 30°21N 33°31E **46** E2
Yi He → China 34°10N 118°8E **35** G10
Yi Xian Hebei, China 39°20N 115°30E **34** E8
Yi Xian Liaoning, China 41°30N 121°22E **35** D11
Yialiás → Cyprus 35°9N 33°44E **25** D12
Yialousa Cyprus 35°32N 34°10E **25** D13
Yibin China 28°45N 104°32E **32** D5
Yichang China 30°40N 111°20E **33** C6
Yicheng China 35°42N 111°40E **34** G6
Yichuan China 36°2N 110°10E **34** F6
Yichun China 47°44N 128°52E **33** B7
Yidu China 36°43N 118°28E **35** F10
Yijun China 35°28N 109°8E **34** G5
Yıldız Dağları Turkey 41°48N 27°36E **23** D12
Yilehuli Shan China 51°20N 124°20E **33** A7
Yimianpo China 45°7N 128°2E **35** B15
Yinchuan China 38°30N 106°15E **34** E4
Yindarlgooda, L.
  Australia 30°40S 121°52E **61** F3
Yindjibarndi ○ Australia 22°0S 118°35E **60** D2
Ying He → China 32°30N 116°30E **34** H9
Ying Xian China 39°32N 113°10E **34** E7
Yingkou China 40°37N 122°18E **35** D12
Yingualyalya ○
  Australia 18°49S 129°12E **60** C4
Yining China 43°58N 81°10E **32** B3
Yiningarra ○ Australia 20°53S 129°27E **60** D4
Yinmabin Burma 22°10N 94°55E **41** H19
Yirga Alem Ethiopia 6°48N 38°22E **47** F2
Yirrkala Australia 12°14S 136°56E **62** A2
Yishan China 24°28N 108°38E **32** D5
Yishui China 35°47N 118°30E **35** G10
Yishun Singapore 1°26N 103°51E **39** d
Yitong China 43°13N 125°20E **35** C13
Yixing China 31°21N 119°48E **33** C6
Yiyang Henan, China 34°27N 112°10E **34** G7
Yiyang Hunan, China 28°35N 112°18E **33** D6
Yli-Kitka Finland 66°8N 28°30E **8** C23
Ylitornio Finland 66°19N 23°39E **8** C20
Ylivieska Finland 64°4N 24°28E **8** D21
Yoakum U.S.A. 29°17N 97°9W **84** G6
Yog Pt. Phil. 14°6N 124°12E **37** B6
Yogyakarta Indonesia 7°49S 110°22E **37** G14
Yogyakarta □ Indonesia 7°48S 110°22E **37** G14
Yoho △ Canada 51°25N 116°30W **70** C5
Yojoa, L. de Honduras 14°53N 88°0W **88** D2
Yok Don △ Vietnam 12°50N 107°40E **38** F6
Yokadouma Cameroon 3°26N 14°55E **52** D2
Yokkaichi Japan 34°55N 136°38E **31** G8
Yoko Cameroon 5°32N 12°20E **52** C2
Yokohama Japan 35°27N 139°28E **31** G9
Yokosuka Japan 35°20N 139°40E **31** G9
Yokote Japan 39°20N 140°30E **30** E10
Yola Nigeria 9°10N 12°29E **51** G8
Yolaina, Cordillera de
  Nic. 11°30N 84°0W **88** D3
Yŏlöten Turkmenistan 37°18N 62°21E **45** B9
Yom → Thailand 15°35N 100°1E **38** E3
Yonago Japan 35°25N 133°19E **31** G6
Yonaguni-Jima Japan 24°27N 123°0E **31** M1
Yŏnan N. Korea 37°55N 126°11E **35** F14
Yonezawa Japan 37°57N 140°4E **30** F10
Yong Peng Malaysia 2°0N 103°3E **39** M4
Yong Sata Thailand 7°8N 99°41E **39** J2
Yongamp'o N. Korea 39°56N 124°23E **35** E13
Yongcheng China 33°55N 116°20E **34** H9
Yongdeng China 36°38N 103°25E **34** F2
Yonghe China 36°46N 110°38E **34** F6
Yŏnghŭng N. Korea 39°31N 127°18E **35** E14
Yongji China 34°52N 110°28E **34** G6

Yongnian China 36°47N 114°29E **34** F8
Yongning China 38°15N 106°14E **34** E4
Yongqing China 39°25N 116°28E **34** E9
Yonibana S. Leone 8°30N 12°19W **50** G3
Yonkers U.S.A. 40°56N 73°52W **83** F11
Yonne → France 48°23N 2°58E **20** B5
York Australia 31°52S 116°47E **61** F2
York U.K. 53°58N 1°6W **12** D6
York Ala., U.S.A. 32°29N 88°18W **85** E10
York Nebr., U.S.A. 40°52N 97°36W **80** E5
York Pa., U.S.A. 39°58N 76°44W **81** F15
York, C. Australia 10°42S 142°31E **62** A3
York, City of □ U.K. 53°58N 1°6W **12** D6
York, Kap Greenland 75°55N 66°25W **69** B18
York, Vale of U.K. 54°15N 1°25W **12** C6
York Sd. Australia 15°0S 125°5E **60** C4
Yorke Pen. Australia 34°50S 137°40E **63** E2
Yorkshire Dales △ U.K. 54°12N 2°10W **12** C5
Yorkshire Wolds U.K. 54°8N 0°31W **12** C7
Yorkton Canada 51°11N 102°28W **71** C8
Yorkville U.S.A. 38°52N 123°13W **78** G3
Yoro Honduras 15°9N 87°7W **88** C2
Yoron-Jima Japan 27°2N 128°26E **31** L4
Yos Sudarso, Pulau = Dolak,
  Pulau Indonesia 8°0S 138°30E **37** F9
Yosemite △ U.S.A. 37°45N 119°40W **78** H7
Yosemite Village
  U.S.A. 37°45N 119°35W **78** H7
Yoshino-Kumano △
  Japan 34°12N 135°55E **31** H8
Yoshkar Ola Russia 56°38N 47°55E **18** C8
Yotvata Israel 29°55N 35°2E **46** F4
Youbou Canada 48°53N 124°13W **78** B2
Youghal Ireland 51°56N 7°52W **10** E4
Youghal B. Ireland 51°55N 7°49W **10** E4
Young Australia 34°19S 148°18E **63** E4
Young Canada 51°47N 105°45W **71** C7
Young Uruguay 32°44S 57°36W **94** C4
YoungI. Antarctica 66°25S 162°24E **5** C11
Younghusband, L.
  Australia 30°50S 136°5E **63** E2
Younghusband Pen.
  Australia 36°0S 139°25E **63** F2
Youngstown Canada 51°35N 111°10W **71** C6
Youngstown N.Y., U.S.A. 43°15N 79°3W **82** C5
Youngstown Ohio, U.S.A. 41°6N 80°39W **82** E4
Youngsville U.S.A. 41°51N 79°19W **82** E5
Youngwood U.S.A. 40°14N 79°34W **82** F5
Youyu China 40°10N 112°20E **34** D7
Yozgat Turkey 39°51N 34°47E **19** G5
Ypacaraí △ Paraguay 25°18S 57°19W **94** B4
Ypané → Paraguay 23°29S 57°19W **94** A4
Ypres = Ieper Belgium 50°51N 2°53E **15** D2
Yreka U.S.A. 41°44N 122°38W **76** F2
Ystad Sweden 55°26N 13°50E **9** J15
Ysyk-Köl = Balykchy
  Kyrgyzstan 42°26N 76°12E **32** B2
Ysyk-Köl Kyrgyzstan 42°25N 77°15E **28** E8
Ythan → U.K. 57°19N 1°59W **11** D7
Ytyk-Kyuyel Russia 62°30N 133°45E **29** C14
Yu Jiang → China 23°22N 110°3E **33** D6
Yu Xian = Yuzhou
  China 34°10N 113°28E **34** G7
Yu Xian Hebei, China 39°50N 114°35E **34** E8
Yu Xian Shanxi, China 38°5N 113°20E **34** E7
Yuan Jiang → China 28°55N 111°50E **33** D6
Yuanqu China 35°18N 111°40E **34** G6
Yuanyang China 35°3N 113°58E **34** G7
Yuba → U.S.A. 39°8N 121°36W **78** F5
Yuba City U.S.A. 39°8N 121°37W **78** F5
Yūbari Japan 43°4N 141°59E **30** C10
Yūbetsu Japan 44°13N 143°50E **30** B11
Yucatán □ Mexico 20°50N 89°0W **87** C7
Yucatán, Canal de
  Caribbean 22°0N 86°30W **88** B2
Yucatán, Península de
  Mexico 19°30N 89°0W **66** H11
Yucatan Basin Cent. Amer. 19°0N 86°0W **87** D7
Yucatan Channel = Yucatán,
  Canal de Caribbean 22°0N 86°30W **88** B2
Yucca U.S.A. 34°52N 114°9W **79** L12
Yucca Valley U.S.A. 34°8N 116°27W **79** L10
Yucheng China 36°55N 116°32E **34** F9
Yuci = Jinzhong China 37°42N 112°46E **34** F7
Yuen Long China 22°26N 114°2E **33** G11
Yuendumu Australia 22°16S 131°49E **60** D5
Yuendumu ○ Australia 22°21S 131°40E **60** D5
Yugorenok Russia 59°47N 137°40E **29** D14
Yukon U.S.A. 35°31N 97°45W **84** D6
Yukon → U.S.A. 62°32N 163°54W **74** C7
Yukon Flats U.S.A. 66°40N 145°45W **74** B10
Yukon Territory □
  Canada 63°0N 135°0W **68** E5
Yukta Russia 63°26N 105°42E **29** C11
Yukuhashi Japan 33°44N 130°59E **31** H5
Yulara Australia 25°10S 130°55E **61** E5
Yule → Australia 20°41S 118°17E **60** D2
Yuleba Australia 26°37S 149°24E **63** D4
Yulin Hainan, China 18°10N 109°31E **38** C7
Yulin Shaanxi, China 38°20N 109°30E **34** E5
Yuma Ariz., U.S.A. 32°43N 114°37W **79** N12
Yuma Colo., U.S.A. 40°8N 102°43W **76** F12
Yuma, B. de Dom. Rep. 18°20N 68°35W **89** C6
Yumbe Uganda 3°28N 31°15E **54** B3
Yumbi
  Dem. Rep. of the Congo 1°12S 26°15E **54** C2
Yumen China 39°50N 97°30E **32** C4
Yuna Australia 28°20S 115°0E **61** E2
Yuncheng Henan, China 35°15N 115°57E **34** G8
Yuncheng Shanxi, China 35°2N 111°0E **34** G6
Yungas Bolivia 17°0S 66°0W **92** G5
Yungay Chile 37°10S 72°5W **94** D1
Yunkanjini ○ Australia 22°33S 131°6E **60** D5
Yunnan □ China 25°0N 102°0E **32** D5
Yunta Australia 32°34S 139°36E **63** E2
Yunxi China 33°0N 110°22E **34** H6

Yurimaguas Peru 5°55S 76°7W **92** E3
Yurubí △ Venezuela 10°26N 68°42W **89** D6
Yuscarán Honduras 13°58N 86°45W **88** D2
Yushe China 37°4N 112°58E **34** F7
Yushu Jilin, China 44°43N 126°38E **35** B14
Yushu Qinghai, China 33°5N 96°55E **32** C4
Yutai China 35°0N 116°45E **34** G9
Yutian Hebei, China 39°53N 117°45E **35** E9
Yutian Sinkiang-Uigur,
  China 36°52N 81°42E **32** C3
Yuxan Qarabağ =
  Nagorno-Karabakh □
  Azerbaijan 39°55N 46°45E **44** B5
Yuxi China 24°30N 102°35E **32** D5
Yuzawa Japan 39°10N 140°30E **30** E10
Yuzhno-Kurilsk Russia 44°1N 145°51E **29** E15
Yuzhno-Sakhalinsk
  Russia 46°58N 142°45E **29** E15
Yuzhnyy □ Russia 44°0N 40°0E **28** E5
Yuzhou China 34°10N 113°28E **34** G7
Yvetot France 49°37N 0°44E **20** B4

Z

Zaanstad Neths. 52°27N 4°50E **15** B4
Zāb al Kabīr → Iraq 36°1N 43°24E **44** B4
Zāb aş Şaghīr → Iraq 35°17N 43°29E **44** C4
Zabaykalsk Russia 49°40N 117°25E **29** E12
Zabol Iran 31°0N 61°32E **45** D9
Zābol □ Afghan. 32°0N 67°0E **40** D5
Zābolī Iran 27°10N 61°35E **45** E9
Zabrze Poland 50°18N 18°50E **17** C10
Zacapa Guatemala 14°59N 89°31W **88** D2
Zacapu Mexico 19°50N 101°43W **86** D4
Zacatecas Mexico 22°47N 102°35W **86** C4
Zacatecas □ Mexico 23°0N 103°0W **86** C4
Zacatecoluca El Salv. 13°29N 88°51W **88** D2
Zachary U.S.A. 30°39N 91°9W **84** F9
Zacoalco de Torres
  Mexico 20°14N 103°35W **86** C4
Zacualtipán Mexico 20°39N 98°36W **87** C5
Zadar Croatia 44°8N 15°14E **16** F8
Zadetkyi Kyun Burma 10°0N 98°25E **39** G2
Zafarqand Iran 33°11N 52°29E **45** C7
Zafra Spain 38°26N 6°30W **21** C2
Żagań Poland 51°39N 15°22E **16** C8
Zagaoua Chad 15°30N 22°24E **51** E10
Zagazig Egypt 30°40N 31°30E **51** B12
Zāgheh Iran 33°30N 48°42E **45** C6
Zagreb Croatia 45°50N 15°58E **16** F9
Zāgros, Kūhhā-ye Iran 33°45N 48°5E **45** C6
Zagros Mts. = Zāgros, Kūhhā-ye
  Iran 33°45N 48°5E **45** C6
Zāhamena △ Madag. 17°37S 48°49E **57** B8
Zāhedān Fārs, Iran 28°46N 53°52E **45** D7
Zāhedān Sīstān va Balūchestān,
  Iran 29°30N 60°50E **45** D9
Zahlah Lebanon 33°52N 35°50E **46** B4
Zaïre = Congo → Africa 6°4S 12°24E **52** F2
Zaječar Serbia 43°53N 22°18E **23** C10
Zaka Zimbabwe 20°20S 31°29E **57** C5
Zakamensk Russia 50°23N 103°17E **29** D11
Zakhodnaya Dzvina =
  Daugava → Latvia 57°4N 24°3E **9** H21
Zākhū Iraq 37°10N 42°50E **44** B4
Zakinthos = Zakynthos
  Greece 37°47N 20°54E **23** F9
Zakopane Poland 49°18N 19°57E **17** D10
Zakros Greece 35°6N 26°10E **25** D8
Zakynthos Greece 37°47N 20°54E **23** F9
Zalaegerszeg Hungary 46°53N 16°47E **17** E9
Zalari Russia 53°33N 102°30E **29** D11
Zalău Romania 47°12N 23°3E **17** E12
Zaleshchiki = Zalishchyky
  Ukraine 48°45N 25°45E **17** D13
Zalew Wiślany Poland 54°20N 19°50E **17** A10
Zalishchyky Ukraine 48°45N 25°45E **17** D13
Zama L. Canada 58°45N 119°5W **70** B5
Zambeke
  Dem. Rep. of the Congo 2°8N 25°17E **54** B2
Zambeze → Africa 18°35S 36°20E **55** F4
Zambezi = Zambeze →
  Africa 18°35S 36°20E **55** F4
Zambezi Zambia 13°30S 23°15E **53** G4
Zambezi △ Zimbabwe 17°54S 25°41E **55** F2
Zambezia □ Mozam. 16°15S 37°30E **55** F4
Zambia ■ Africa 15°0S 28°0E **55** F2
Zamboanga Phil. 6°59N 122°3E **37** C6
Zamora Mexico 19°59N 102°16W **86** D4
Zamora Spain 41°30N 5°45W **21** B3
Zamość Poland 50°43N 23°15E **17** C12
Zanda China 31°32N 79°50E **32** C2
Zandvoort Neths. 52°22N 4°32E **15** B4
Zanesville U.S.A. 39°56N 82°1W **82** G2
Zangābād Iran 38°26N 46°44E **44** B5
Zangue → Mozam. 17°50S 35°21E **55** F4
Zanjān Iran 36°40N 48°35E **45** B6
Zanjān □ Iran 37°20N 49°30E **45** B6
Zanjān → Iran 37°8N 47°47E **45** B6
Zante = Zakynthos
  Greece 37°47N 20°54E **23** F9
Zanthus Australia 31°2S 123°34E **61** F3
Zanzibar Tanzania 6°12S 39°12E **54** D4
Zaouiet El-Kala = Bordj Omar
  Driss Algeria 28°10N 6°40E **50** C7
Zaouiet Reggâne Algeria 26°32N 0°3E **50** C6
Zaozhuang China 34°50N 117°35E **35** G9
Zap Suyu = Zāb al Kabīr →
  Iraq 36°1N 43°24E **44** B4
Zapadnaya Dvina = Daugava →
  Latvia 57°4N 24°3E **9** H21
Západné Beskydy Europe 49°30N 19°0E **17** D10
Zapala Argentina 39°0S 70°5W **96** D2
Zapaleri, Cerro Bolivia 22°49S 67°11W **94** A2
Zapata U.S.A. 26°55N 99°16W **84** H5
Zapolyarnyy Russia 69°26N 30°51E **8** B24
Zapopán Mexico 20°43N 103°24W **86** C4

Zhidan China 36°48N 108°48E **34** F5
Zhigansk Russia 66°48N 123°27E **29** C13
Zhilinda Russia 70°0N 114°20E **29** C12
Zhitomir = Zhytomyr
  Ukraine 50°20N 28°40E **17** C15
Zhlobin Belarus 52°55N 30°0E **17** B16
Zhmerynka Ukraine 49°2N 28°2E **17** D15
Zhob Pakistan 31°20N 69°31E **42** D3
Zhob → Pakistan 32°4N 69°50E **42** C3
Zhodzina Belarus 54°5N 28°17E **17** A15
Zhokhova, Ostrov
  Russia 76°4N 152°40E **29** B16
Zhongdian China 27°48N 99°42E **32** D4
Zhongning China 37°29N 105°40E **34** F3
Zhongshan Antarctica 69°0S 39°50E **5** C6
Zhongshan China 22°26N 113°20E **33** G10
Zhongshankong China 22°35N 113°29E **33** G10
Zhongtiao Shan China 35°0N 111°10E **34** G6
Zhongwei China 37°30N 105°12E **34** F3
Zhongyang China 37°20N 111°11E **34** F6
Zhosaly Kazakhstan 45°29N 64°4E **28** E7
Zhoucun China 36°47N 117°48E **35** F9
Zhouzhi China 34°10N 108°12E **34** G5
Zhuanghe China 39°40N 123°0E **35** E12
Zhucheng China 36°0N 119°27E **35** G10
Zhugqu China 33°40N 104°30E **34** H3
Zhuhai China 22°17N 113°34E **33** G10
Zhujiang Kou China 22°20N 113°45E **33** G10
Zhumadian China 32°59N 114°2E **34** H8
Zhuo Xian = Zhuozhou
  China 39°28N 115°58E **34** E8
Zhuolu China 40°20N 115°12E **34** D8
Zhuozhou China 39°28N 115°58E **34** E8
Zhuozi China 41°0N 112°25E **34** D7
Zhuzhou China 27°49N 113°12E **33** D6
Zhytomyr Ukraine 50°20N 28°40E **17** C15
Ziarat Pakistan 30°25N 67°49E **42** D2
Zibo China 36°47N 118°3E **35** F10
Zichang China 37°18N 109°40E **34** F5
Zidi = Wandhari
  Pakistan 27°42N 66°48E **42** F2
Zielona Góra Poland 51°57N 15°31E **16** C8
Zierikzee Neths. 51°40N 3°55E **15** C3
Zigong China 29°15N 104°48E **32** D5
Ziguéy Chad 14°43N 15°50E **51** F9
Ziguinchor Senegal 12°35N 16°20W **50** F2
Zihuatanejo Mexico 17°39N 101°33W **86** D4
Žilina Slovak Rep. 49°12N 18°42E **17** D10
Zillah Libya 28°30N 17°33E **51** C9
Zima Russia 54°0N 102°5E **29** D11
Zimapán Mexico 20°45N 99°21W **87** C5
Zimba Zambia 17°20S 26°11E **55** F2
Zimbabwe Zimbabwe 20°16S 30°54E **55** G3
Zimbabwe ■ Africa 19°0S 30°0E **55** F3
Zimnicea Romania 43°40N 25°22E **17** G13
Zinave △ Mozam. 21°35S 33°40E **57** C5
Zinder Niger 13°48N 9°0E **50** F7
Zinga Tanzania 9°16S 38°49E **55** D4
Zion △ U.S.A. 37°15N 113°5W **77** H7
Ziros Greece 35°5N 26°8E **25** D8
Zirreh, Gowd-e Afghan. 29°45N 62°0E **40** E3
Zitácuaro Mexico 19°24N 100°22W **86** D4
Zitundo Mozam. 26°48S 32°47E **57** D5
Ziwa Maghariba = Kagera □
  Tanzania 2°0S 31°30E **54** C3
Ziway, L. Ethiopia 8°0N 38°50E **47** F2
Ziyang China 32°32N 108°31E **34** H5
Zlatograd Bulgaria 41°22N 25°7E **23** D11
Zlatoust Russia 55°10N 59°40E **18** C10
Zlín Czech Rep. 49°14N 17°40E **17** D9
Zmeinogorsk Kazakhstan 51°10N 82°13E **28** D9
Znojmo Czech Rep. 48°50N 16°2E **16** D9
Zobeyrī Iran 34°10N 46°40E **44** C5
Zobia Dem. Rep. of the Congo 3°0N 25°59E **54** B2
Zoetermeer Neths. 52°3N 4°30E **15** B4
Zohreh → Iran 30°16N 51°15E **45** D6
Zolochiv Ukraine 49°45N 24°51E **17** D13
Zomba Malawi 15°22S 35°19E **55** F4
Zongo
  Dem. Rep. of the Congo 4°20N 18°35E **52** D3
Zonguldak Turkey 41°28N 31°50E **19** F5
Zonqor Pt. Malta 35°52N 14°34E **25** D2
Zorritos Peru 3°43S 80°40W **92** D2
Zou Xiang China 35°30N 116°58E **34** G9
Zouar Chad 20°30N 16°32E **51** D9
Zouérate = Zouîrât
  Mauritania 22°44N 12°21W **50** D3
Zouîrât Mauritania 22°44N 12°21W **50** D3
Zoutkamp Neths. 53°20N 6°18E **15** A6
Zrenjanin Serbia 45°22N 20°23E **23** B9
Zufar Oman 17°40N 54°0E **47** D5
Zug Switz. 47°10N 8°31E **20** C8
Zugspitze Germany 47°25N 10°59E **16** E6
Zuid-Holland □ Neths. 52°0N 4°35E **15** C4
Zuidbeveland Neths. 51°30N 3°50E **15** C3
Zuidhorn Neths. 53°15N 6°23E **15** A6
Zula Eritrea 15°17N 39°40E **47** D2
Zumbo Mozam. 15°35S 30°26E **55** F3
Zumpango Mexico 19°48N 99°6W **87** D5
Zunhua China 40°18N 117°58E **35** D9
Zuni Pueblo U.S.A. 35°4N 108°51W **77** J9
Zunyi China 27°42N 106°53E **32** D5
Zurbātīyah Iraq 33°9N 46°3E **44** C5
Zürich Switz. 47°22N 8°32E **20** C8
Zutphen Neths. 52°9N 6°12E **15** B6
Zuurberg △ S. Africa 33°12S 25°32E **56** E4
Zuwārah Libya 32°58N 12°1E **51** B8
Zūzan Iran 34°22N 59°53E **45** C8
Zvishavane Zimbabwe 20°17S 30°2E **55** G3
Zvolen Slovak Rep. 48°33N 19°10E **17** D10
Zwettl Austria 48°35N 15°9E **16** D8
Zwickau Germany 50°44N 12°30E **16** C7
Zwolle Neths. 52°31N 6°6E **15** B6
Zwolle U.S.A. 31°38N 93°39W **84** F8
Żyrardów Poland 52°3N 20°28E **17** B11
Zyryan Kazakhstan 49°43N 84°20E **28** E9
Zyryanka Russia 65°45N 150°51E **29** C16
Zyryanovsk = Zyryan
  Kazakhstan 49°43N 84°20E **28** E9
Żywiec Poland 49°42N 19°10E **17** D10